lonely planet

Western Europe

Janet Austin
Carolyn Bain
Neal Bedford
Lou Callan
Geert Cole
Fionn Davenport
Paul Dawson
Susan Forsyth
Jeremy Gray
Anthony Haywood

Paul Hellander
Mark Honan
John King
Leanne Logan
Sarah Mathers
John Noble
Tim Nollen
Oda O'Carol
Nick Ray
Daniel Robinson

Miles Roddis
Andrea
  Schulte-Peevers
Tom Smallman
Bryn Thomas
Rebecca Turner
Julia Wilkinson
David Willett
Nicola Williams
Ryan Ver Berkmoes

LONELY PLANET PUBLICATIONS
Melbourne • Oakland • London • Paris

WESTERN EUROPE

ATLANTIC OCEAN

NORWAY

Bergen
Stavanger
Kristiansand

DENMARK
Aalborg
Århus
Odense
Lübeck
Hamburg
Bremen
Hanover

Shetland Islands
Orkney Islands
Outer Hebrides

Inverness
Oban
Scotland
Aberdeen
Glasgow
Dundee
Edinburgh

Nthn Ireland
Derry
Belfast
Isle of Man
Newcastle-upon-Tyne
Middlesborough

Galway
IRELAND
Irish Sea
Liverpool
York
Manchester

Dublin
BRITAIN
Birmingham

Killarney
Cork
Rosslare
St George's Channel
Wales
Swansea
England
Cambridge
Cardiff
Bristol
Oxford
Bath
London
The Hague
Amsterdam
NETHERLANDS

Plymouth
Portsmouth
Channel Islands
English Channel
Str of Dover
Bruges
Antwerp
Brussels
Liège
BELGIUM

NORTH SEA
Frisian Islands

GERM
Düsseldorf
Cologne
Bonn
Weimar
Erfurt
Frankfurt/Main

Brest
St Malo
Caen
Le Havre
Rouen
Rheims
Lille
LUXEMBOURG
Luxembourg

Quimper
Rennes
Paris
Nancy
Nuremberg
Heidelberg
Stuttgart
Baden-Baden
Freiburg

St Nazaire
Nantes
Blois
Tours
Dijon
Strasbourg
Basel
Liechtenstein

La Rochelle
FRANCE
Limoges
Lausanne
Bern
Zürich
SWITZERLAND
Innsbruck

La Coruña
Gijón
Santander
Bordeaux
Clermont-Ferrand
Lyon
Annecy
Geneva
Grenoble
Turin
Milan
Verona

Vigo
Santiago de Compostela
León
Bilbao
San Sebastián
Bayonne
PYRENEES
Toulouse
Nîmes
Avignon
Monaco
Nice
La Spezia
Genoa
Bologna
San Marino

Porto
Burgos
Valladolid
Pamplona
Andorra la Vella
ANDORRA
Marseille
Golfe du Lion
Ligurian Sea
Florence
Pisa
Perugia
See The Alps Inset

Coimbra
PORTUGAL
Salamanca
Zaragoza
Barcelona
Tarragona
Corsica
Elba
Rome

Lisbon
Badajoz
Toledo
Madrid
SPAIN
Ajaccio

Évora
Valencia
Majorca
Palma
Sardinia
Sassari

Faro
Córdoba
Seville
Granada
Murcia
Alicante
Balearic Islands

Cádiz
Málaga
Almería
Cartagena
Tyrrhenian
Cagliari

Str of Gibraltar
Tangier
Gibraltar Br
Ceuta Sp
Melilla Sp
Oran
MEDITERRANEAN SEA
Algiers
Annaba
Bizerte
Tunis

Rabat
Fès
Meknès
Oujda
Constantine
Sousse
Pantelleria Italy Isole Pelagie

Casablanca
MOROCCO
ALGERIA
TUNISIA

250   500 km
150   300 mi

THE ALPS

Lillehammer

Gulf of Bothnia

16°E Tampere 24°E 32°E 40°E

Oslo SWEDEN FINLAND Besançon Basel Zürich Vaduz Innsbruck AUSTRIA Lienz
Turku Helsinki Neuchâtel Lucerne Chur LIECHTENSTEIN Bolzano
Uppsala Lake Neuchâtel Lausanne Bern SWITZERLAND DOLOMITES Trento 46°N
Örebro Stockholm Åland Gulf of Finland Geneva Sion Lugano Brescia Verona Venice
Norrköping Tallinn Chamonix Annecy Mt Blanc Aosta Milan Padova Adriatic
Linköping ESTONIA Grenoble 4807m Turin ITALY Piacenza Ferrara Bologna Sea
Jönköping Saaremaa Gulf of Riga FRANCE Parma Modena Ravenna 44°N
Gothenborg Gotland Riga Genoa La Spezia Rimini SAN MARINO
Helsingborg LATVIA Aix-en-Provence Nice San Remo Pisa Florence Perugia
Malmö Öland Liepāja LITHUANIA Marseille Cannes Monte Carlo 0 100 km Livorno Siena 12°E
Copenhagen Klaipėda Kaunas Toulon Côte d'Azur 0 60 mi
Bornholm Kaliningrad RUSSIA Vilnius 8°E

Strasslund Gdańsk RUSSIA
Schwerin Szczecin Białystok Hrodna
Berlin POLAND BELARUS GREEK ISLANDS
Magdeburg Poznań Vistula Brest Limnos 0 100 km
GERMANY Łódź SPORADES 60 mi
Halle Dresden Wrocław Lublin Skyros Lesvos Mytilini
Leipzig Oder Katowice UKRAINE Evia Chios İzmir
Plzeň Prague Kraków Lviv GREECE Aegean Sea TURKEY
Munich CZECH REPUBLIC Ostrava Brno Dniester Athens Andros Samos Kuşadası 38°N
Linz SLOVAKIA Košice Chernivtsi Piraeus Tinos Ikaria
Salzburg Vienna Bratislava Debrecen Kythnos Mykonos Leros Bodrum
AUSTRIA Győr Budapest Cluj-Napoca Hydra Serifos Paros Naxos ISLANDS Kos
Lienz Graz HUNGARY Pécs Szeged Mirtoön Sifnos CYCLADES Amorgos Tilos Symni
SLOVENIA Ljubljana Zagreb Novi Sad Timișoara ROMANIA Sea Milos Ios Astypalea Rhodes
Trieste CROATIA Santorini Anafi Karpathos DODECANESE Rhodes
Venice Rijeka BOSNIA-HERCEGOVINA Bucharest (Thira) Kassos
Udine Zadar Danube Craiova 36°N Sea of Crete
Ancona Sarajevo Belgrade Hania Rethymno Iraklio Karpathos
Split YUGOSLAVIA Sofia Gaydos 24°E Ierapetra CRETE 28°E
Pescara Dubrovnik Podgorica Plovdiv BULGARIA Burgas BLACK SEA 42°N
Naples Foggia Bari Skopje MACEDONIA Xanthi İstanbul Samsun
Salerno Tirana Thessaloniki Bursa Ankara Sivas
Taranto ALBANIA Ioannina Larisa İzmir Kayseri
Golfo di Taranto Corfu GREECE Lesvos Aegean Sea TURKEY
Palermo Ionian Sea Evia Adana
Messina Reggio di Calabria Ionian Islands Patras Athens Antalya SYRIA
Sicily Catania Kalamata Piraeus Rhodes CYPRUS Lefkosia (Nicosia) LEBANON
Valletta MEDITERRANEAN SEA Cyclades Islands Sea of Crete Dodecanese Islands Lemessos Beirut
MALTA 16°E Hania Iraklio Crete See Greek Islands Inset 24°E 32°E 34°E

Western Europe
5th edition   January 2001
First published   January 1993

Published by
Lonely Planet Publications Pty Ltd ABN 36 005 607 983
90 Maribyrnong St, Footscray, Victoria 3011, Australia

Lonely Planet Offices
Australia Locked Bag 1, Footscray, Victoria 3011
USA 150 Linden St, Oakland, CA 94607
UK 10a Spring Place, London NW5 3BH
France 1 rue du Dahomey, 75011 Paris

Photographs
Many of the images in this guide are available for licensing from
Lonely Planet Images.
email: lpi@lonelyplanet.com.au

Front cover photograph
Cyclist in snowscape, Chamonix, Haute-Savoie, France
(Jess Stock, Stone)

D
967
·W4
2001

ISBN 1 86450 163 4

Printed by The Bookmaker International Ltd
Printed in China

Contents – Text

GERMANY 461

GREECE 627

Contents – Maps

7

8 Contents – Maps

The Authors

Janet Austin

Janet worked on the Italy chapter. Her taste for travel was fostered at an early age with two childhood ocean voyages from Australia to the UK. She was lured back in her teenage years by a love for all things European and the London punk rock explosion, remaining for over 10 years. Janet edits Lonely Planet's travel literature series, Journeys, which allows her to vicariously clock up some kilometres while sitting in front of a computer screen. She is married and lives in Melbourne with two grey cats.

Carolyn Bain

Carolyn worked on the Greece chapter. She was born in Melbourne, Australia (the third-largest Greek city in the world) and first visited Greece as a teenager (on a package tour from Scandinavia, no less). She was therefore eminently qualified to ferry-hop around two dozen Greek islands in search of the perfect beach, best calamari and any unattached shipping magnates. Due to an unfortunate shortage of shipping magnates, she returned to her job as an editor at Lonely Planet's Melbourne office.

Neal Bedford

Neal worked on the Spain and Britain chapters. Born in Papakura, New Zealand, Neal gave up an exciting career in accounting after university to experience the mundane life of a traveller. With the urge to move, travel led him through a number of countries and jobs, ranging from an au pair in Vienna, lifeguard in the USA, fruit picker in Israel and lettuce washer at rock concerts. Deciding to give his life some direction, he well and truly got his foot stuck in the door by landing the lucrative job of packing books in Lonely Planet's London office. One thing led to another and he managed to cross over to the mystic world of authoring. Neal currently resides in London, but the need to move will probably soon kick in and force him to try his luck somewhere else.

Lou Callan

Lou worked on the Britain chapter. After four years at LP as an editor, she packed up and followed her husband to the red dunes of the United Arab Emirates for a very long, hot 2½ years. Here she wrote LP's *Dubai* city guide and, with Gordon Robison, *Oman & UAE* as well as an update for *Middle East* (3rd edition). Lou is now very nicely wedged between beaches and wineries on the Mornington Peninsula in Victoria with Tony the husband and Ziggy the cat.

Fionn Davenport

Fionn worked on the Britain and Italy chapters. He was born in and spent most of his youth in Dublin – that is, when his family wasn't moving him to Buenos Aires or Geneva or New York (all thanks to his Dad, whose job took him far and wide). Infected with the travel disease, he became a nomad in his own right after graduating from Trinity College, moving first to Paris and then to New York, where he spent five years as a travel editor and some-time writer. The call of home was too much to resist, however, so armed with his portable computer, his record collection and an empty wallet he returned to Dublin where he decided to contin-ue where he left off in New York. Only it was quieter, wetter and a hell of a lot smaller. When he's not DJing in pubs and clubs throughout the city he's writing and updating travel guides. He has worked on Lonely Planet guides to *Spain*, *Dublin*, *Ireland*, *Sicily*, *England* and *Britain*.

Paul Dawson

Paul worked on the Ireland chapter. He was born in Melbourne, and after a lengthy degree in architecture he studied literature, travelled, then ended up drawing maps and laying out pages for Lonely Planet's European guidebooks.

Jeremy Gray

Jeremy worked on the France chapter. A Louisiana native, he studied literature and business in the wilds of Texas before moving to Germany on a scholarship in 1984. Infatuated with Europe, he chucked his MBA plans and stayed on to teach English, translate and best of all, file plumbing orders for the US Air Force. In the meantime he grew to appreciate many things French, such as the wonderful way the *pâtisseries* wrap takeaway cakes like baby gifts.

A master's degree in international relations from Canterbury led Jeremy back to Germany, where he spent the 1990s chasing politicians and CEOs for news agencies, newspapers and televi-sion. While freelancing for the *Financial Times* he discovered Lonely Planet, and since 1998 has contributed to or written *Germany, The Netherlands* and city guides for *Munich* and *Mon-treal*. He lives in Amsterdam, a mere three-hour drive from the French border.

Anthony Haywood

Anthony worked on the Germany chapter. Born in the port town of Fremantle, Australia, Anthony first pulled anchor at 18 to spend two years travelling through Europe and the USA. He studied lit-erature and then Russian language at university, and worked as a technical writer, editor and trainer in Melbourne before taking up residence in Germany in 1992. Since then he has worked on a

number of Lonely Planet guidebooks, including *Germany* and *Russia, Ukraine & Belarus,* while also contributing to Lonely Planet's travel literature and restaurant guides series. He is based in Frankfurt am Main, where he works as a journalist, author and translator.

Paul Hellander

Paul worked on the France chapter. He has never really stopped travelling since he first looked at a map in his native England. He graduated from Birmingham University with a degree in Greek before heading for Australia. He taught Modern Greek and trained interpreters and translators for thirteen years before throwing it all away for a life as a travel writer. Paul has contributed to over 20 LP titles including guides to *Greece, Cyprus, Israel, Eastern Europe, Singapore* and *Central America*. When not travelling with his PC and Nikon, he lives in Adelaide, South Australia. He was last spotted heading once more for Greece to write a guide to *Rhodes & the Dodecanese*.

Mark Honan

Mark worked on the Austria, Liechtenstein, Switzerland and Getting Around chapters. After a university degree in philosophy opened up a glittering career as an office clerk, Mark decided that there was more to life than data entry. He set off on a two-year trip round the world, armed with a backpack and an intent to sell travel stories and pictures upon his return. Astonishingly, this barely-formed plan succeeded and Mark has since contributed regularly to magazine travel pages.

He started writing for Lonely Planet in 1991 and has worked on guides to *Vienna, Austria, Switzerland, India, Mexico, Central America* and *Solomon Islands* – next up are *Vienna* and *Austria* again.

Leanne Logan & Geert Cole

Leanne and Geert worked on the Belgium, Luxembourg and Netherlands chapters. Leanne has long been lured by travel. Bitten by the bug before even reaching her teens, she has spent much of the past 10 years travelling and writing for Lonely Planet. A journalist by trade, Leanne was conducting research into Belgium's multitude of beers when she met local connoisseur, Geert Cole, in 1991. The pair have been a team ever since.

Born in Antwerp in Belgium, Geert swapped university and art studies in the 1970s to discover broader horizons and other cultures.

Each trip resulted in an extra diary being put on the shelf and another job experience being added to life's list. A spark of destiny saw this artist, traveller, writer, cook and landscaper linked to partner/colleague, Leanne, with whom he lives in Australia on the fertile slopes of an extinct volcano.

John Noble & Susan Forsyth

John and Susan worked on the Spain chapter. John comes from the Ribblesdale, England, Susan from Melbourne, Australia. After studies, John worked in Fleet Street journalism and Susan taught secondary and adult students. But travel distracted them both and one year they found themselves simultaneously in Sri Lanka _ Susan working as a volunteer teacher and John carrying out his first commission for Lonely Planet. They married three years later and have since been kept extremely busy rearing two children, Isabella and Jack, as well as coauthoring heaps of Lonely Planet titles such as *Mexico*, *Spain*, *Andalucía*, *Indonesia*, *Russia*, *Ukraine & Belarus* and *Baltic States*. Current home base is an Andalucian hill village.

Oda O'Carol

Oda worked on the Britain chapter – her first assignment with Lonely Planet. Born in Roscommon, in the windy mid-west of Ireland, she packed her knapsack for the big smoke of Dublin where she studied communications until 1990. Since graduating she has worked as a television researcher and writer for the independent sector in Ireland. Oda also spent some time donkey-working on film sets and made her own short film in 1998. She has travelled extensively in Europe and last summer, chugged between America's coasts, with friends, in a clapped-out 1967 Cadillac (without air-con) and hopes to return soon for the northern route. She still lives happily in Dublin with her husband Eoin.

Nick Ray

Nick worked on the Britain chapter. A Londoner of sorts, he comes from Watford, the sort of town that makes you want to travel. For once he didn't have to travel too far, darting about the green fields of England, not to mention a few pubs along the way. Usually, he is to be found in the more obscure parts of Africa or Asia, Cambodia in particular, a country he thinks of as a second home. If you are heading that way, you might well run into him in Phnom Penh or Siem Reap.

Daniel Robinson

Daniel worked on the France chapter. He was raised in the USA (the San Francisco Bay Area and Glen Ellyn, Illinois) and Israel. His passion for shoestring travel was kindled at age 17 with a trip to Cyprus, and since then he has spent several years on the road exploring some of the more remote parts of Asia, the Middle East and Europe.

Daniel's work for Lonely Planet has included the 1st editions of the award-winning *Vietnam* and (with Tony Wheeler) *Cambodia*, and all four editions of *France*. Daniel has a BA in Near Eastern Studies from Princeton University and is currently finishing up an MA in Israeli history at Tel Aviv University.

Miles Roddis

Miles worked on the Andorra, France and Spain chapters. Miles and his partner Ingrid live in a shoe-box sized apartment in the Barrio del Carmen, the oldest and most vibrant quarter of Valencia, Spain.

His involvement with France began when, 15 and spotty, he noisily threw up the night's red wine in a Paris cafe. Undeterred, he mainlined in French at university, became seriously hooked and later bought an equally tiny place in a hamlet in the Jura that will never feature in any guidebook.

Miles has contributed to Lonely Planet's *Africa on a Shoestring, West Africa, Read This First: Africa, Lonely Planet Unpacked, France, Spain, Walking in Britain, Walking in France* and *Walking in Spain*.

Andrea Schulte-Peevers

Andrea worked on the Spain chapter. She is a Los Angeles-based writer, editor and translator who caught the travel bug early and had been to all continents but Antarctica by the age of 18. After finishing high school in Germany, she decided the world was too big to stay in one place and moved first to London, then to Los Angeles. Armed with a degree from UCLA, she managed to turn her wanderlust into a professional career as a travel writer and may still chase penguins around the South Pole one of these days.

Since joining the LP team in 1995 Andrea has updated and/or authored the guides to *Los Angeles, Berlin, Germany, California & Nevada* and *Spain*.

Tom Smallman

Tom worked on the Britain chapter. He lives in Melbourne, Australia, and had a number of jobs before joining Lonely Planet as an editor. He now works full time as an author and has worked on Lonely Planet guides to *Britain, Scotland, Edinburgh, Australia, New South Wales, Sydney, Canada, Ireland, Dublin* and *Pennsylvania*.

Bryn Thomas

Bryn worked on the Britain, Facts for the Visitor and Getting There & Away chapters. Born in Zimbabwe, where he grew up on a farm, Bryn contracted an incurable case of wanderlust during camping holidays by the Indian Ocean in Mozambique. An anthropology degree at Durham University in England earned him a job polishing the leaves of pot plants in London. He also has been a ski-lift operator, encyclopedia seller, and an English teacher in Cairo, Singapore and Tokyo. Travel on six continents has included a 2500km Andean cycling trip. Bryn's first guide, the *Trans-Siberia Handbook*, was shortlisted for the Thomas Cook Guidebook of the Year awards. He is also coauthor of Lonely Planet's *Britain*, *India* and *Goa*, and has contributed to *Walking in Britain*.

Rebecca Turner

Rebecca worked on the Germany chapter and found that years of torturing the German language finally paid off during her research trip there, her first authoring job for LP. Rebecca grew up in Perth, Western Australia. After her studies, a journalism cadetship in lovely south-west WA (where she excelled in giant vegetable stories) and some overseas travel, poverty drove her into the Australian desert to write for the *Kalgoorlie Miner*. Later she moved to Melbourne to work for Lonely Planet as an editor and senior editor, and now lives in Sydney.

Julia Wilkinson & John King

Julia and John worked on the Portugal chapter. After leaving university, Julia set off from England for a jaunt round the world and immediately got sidetracked in Hong Kong, where she stayed for some 20 years, exploring Asia as a freelance travel writer and photographer. A frequent PATA award winner, she has contributed to numerous international publications. She is also author of Lonely Planet's *Lisbon* guide and coauthor, with her husband John King, of LP's *Portugal* and *South-West France*. John grew up in the USA, and in earlier incarnations has been a physics teacher and an environmental consultant. In 1984 he headed off to China and ended up living there for half a year. He and Julia met in Lhasa. John took up travel writing with the 1st edition of LP's *Karakoram Highway*. He has also coauthored LP's *Pakistan*; *Central Asia*; *Russia, Ukraine & Belarus*; *Czech & Slovak Republics*; and the *Prague* city guide.

David Willett

David worked on the Greece chapter. He is a freelance journalist based near Bellingen on the north coast of New South Wales, Australia. He grew up in Hampshire, England, and wound up in Australia in 1980 after stints working on newspapers in Iran (1975-78) and Bahrain. He spent two years working as a sub-editor on the Melbourne *Sun* before trading a steady job for a warmer climate. Between jobs, David has travelled extensively in Europe, the Middle East and Asia. He is also the author of Lonely Planet's guide to *Tunisia* and coordinating author of *Greece*. He has contributed to various other guides, including *Africa*, *Australia*, *New South Wales*, *Indonesia* and *South-East Asia*.

Nicola Williams

Nicola worked on the France chapter. Since her first trip to Romania in 1991 with 10 Welsh policemen as part of an international aid convoy, her work as a journalist has taken her to most corners of Eastern Europe. Following 12 months in Latvia as features editor of the *Baltic Times* newspaper, she moved to Lithuania to bus it around the Baltics as editor-in-chief of the *In Your Pocket* city-guide series. In 1996 she traded in Lithuanian *cepelinai* for Lyonnais *andouillette*. Nicola has authored or updated several Lonely Planet titles, including *Romania & Moldova*, *Estonia, Latvia & Lithuania* and *Russia, Ukraine & Belarus*.

Ryan Ver Berkmoes

Ryan worked on the Britain chapter. He grew up in Santa Cruz, California and has held a number of jobs in journalism that have taken him far from the fog-drenched land of his youth. Among his work for Lonely Planet, he is the author of *Chicago* and *Moscow*, co-wrote *Texas* and *Canada* and co-ordinated *Russia, Ukraine & Belarus*, *Great Lakes*, *Out to Eat London*, *Netherlands*, *Britain* and *England*. In the future, Ryan hopes to add more warm weather destinations to the list above. He and his journalist wife Sara Marley reside in London near the point of inspiration for noted musician Nigel Tufnel.

This Book

This Book

Many people have helped to create this 5th edition. Among the major contributors to past editions were Mark Armstrong, Mark Balla, Stefano Cavedoni, Rob van Driesum, Richard Everist, Steve Fallon, Helen Gillman, Rosemary Hall, Clem Lindenmayer, Frances Linzee Gordon, Scott McNeely, David Peevers, Sean Sheehan, Corinne Simcock, Damien Simonis, David Stanley, Robert Strauss, Dorinda Talbot, Greg Videon, Gary Walsh, Tony Wheeler, Neil Wilson and Pat Yale.

Western Europe is part of Lonely Planet's Europe series, which includes *Eastern Europe*, *Mediterranean Europe*, *Central Europe*, *Scandinavian & Baltic Europe* and *Europe on a Shoestring*. Lonely Planet also publishes phrasebooks to these regions.

FROM THE PUBLISHER

The editing of this edition of *Western Europe* was coordinated by Craig MacKenzie and the cartography by Lisa Borg. They were assisted by Yvonne Bischofberger, Simon Bracken, Yvonne Byron, Csanád Csutoros, Hunor Csutoros, Tony Davidson, Paul Dawson, Janine Eberle, Tony Fankhauser, Susannah Farfor, Liz Filleul, Quentin Frayne, Cris Gibcus, Rachel Imeson, Ann Jeffree, Birgit Jordan, Russell Kerr, Joelene Kowalski, Sarah Mathers, Fiona Meiers, Sally Morgan, Shelley Muir, Tim Nollen, Darren O'Connell, Brett Pascoe, Adrian Persoglia, Agustín Poó y Balbontin, Jacqui Saunders, Chris Thomas, Ray Thompson, Tim Uden, Natasha Velleley, Celia Wood and Chris Wyness.

THANKS
Many thanks to the travellers who used the last edition and wrote to us with helpful hints, advice and interesting anecdotes. Your names appear in the back of this book.

Foreword

ABOUT LONELY PLANET GUIDEBOOKS

The story begins with a classic travel adventure: Tony and Maureen Wheeler's 1972 journey across Europe and Asia to Australia. Useful information about the overland trail did not exist at that time, so Tony and Maureen published the first Lonely Planet guidebook to meet a growing need.

From a kitchen table, then from a tiny office in Melbourne (Australia), Lonely Planet has become the largest independent travel publisher in the world, an international company with offices in Melbourne, Oakland (USA), London (UK) and Paris (France).

Today Lonely Planet guidebooks cover the globe. There is an ever-growing list of books and there's information in a variety of forms and media. Some things haven't changed. The main aim is still to help make it possible for adventurous travellers to get out there – to explore and better understand the world.

At Lonely Planet we believe travellers can make a positive contribution to the countries they visit – if they respect their host communities and spend their money wisely. Since 1986 a percentage of the income from each book has been donated to aid projects and human rights campaigns.

Updates Lonely Planet thoroughly updates each guidebook as often as possible. This usually means there are around two years between editions, although for more unusual or more stable destinations the gap can be longer. Check the imprint page (following the colour map at the beginning of the book) for publication dates.

Between editions up-to-date information is available in two free newsletters – the paper *Planet Talk* and email *Comet* (to subscribe, contact any Lonely Planet office) – and on our Web site at www.lonelyplanet.com. The *Upgrades* section of the Web site covers a number of important and volatile destinations and is regularly updated by Lonely Planet authors. *Scoop* covers news and current affairs relevant to travellers. And, lastly, the *Thorn Tree* bulletin board and *Postcards* section of the site carry unverified, but fascinating, reports from travellers.

Correspondence The process of creating new editions begins with the letters, postcards and emails received from travellers. This correspondence often includes suggestions, criticisms and comments about the current editions. Interesting excerpts are immediately passed on via newsletters and the Web site, and everything goes to our authors to be verified when they're researching on the road. We're keen to get more feedback from organisations or individuals who represent communities visited by travellers.

Lonely Planet gathers information for everyone who's curious about the planet – and especially for those who explore it first-hand. Through guidebooks, phrasebooks, activity guides, maps, literature, newsletters, image library, TV series and Web site we act as an information exchange for a worldwide community of travellers.

Research Authors aim to gather sufficient practical information to enable travellers to make informed choices and to make the mechanics of a journey run smoothly. They also research historical and cultural background to help enrich the travel experience and allow travellers to understand and respond appropriately to cultural and environmental issues.

Authors don't stay in every hotel because that would mean spending a couple of months in each medium-sized city and, no, they don't eat at every restaurant because that would mean stretching belts beyond capacity. They do visit hotels and restaurants to check standards and prices, but feedback based on readers' direct experiences can be very helpful.

Many of our authors work undercover, others aren't so secretive. None of them accept freebies in exchange for positive write-ups. And none of our guidebooks contain any advertising.

Production Authors submit their raw manuscripts and maps to offices in Australia, USA, UK or France. Editors and cartographers – all experienced travellers themselves – then begin the process of assembling the pieces. When the book finally hits the shops, some things are already out of date, we start getting feedback from readers and the process begins again …

WARNING & REQUEST

Things change – prices go up, schedules change, good places go bad and bad places go bankrupt – nothing stays the same. So, if you find things better or worse, recently opened or long since closed, please tell us and help make the next edition even more accurate and useful. We genuinely value all the feedback we receive. Julie Young coordinates a well travelled team that reads and acknowledges every letter, postcard and email and ensures that every morsel of information finds its way to the appropriate authors, editors and cartographers for verification.

Everyone who writes to us will find their name in the next edition of the appropriate guidebook. They will also receive the latest issue of *Planet Talk*, our quarterly printed newsletter, or *Comet*, our monthly email newsletter. Subscriptions to both newsletters are free. The very best contributions will be rewarded with a free guidebook.

Excerpts from your correspondence may appear in new editions of Lonely Planet guidebooks, the Lonely Planet Web site, *Planet Talk* or *Comet*, so please let us know if you *don't* want your letter published or your name acknowledged.

Send all correspondence to the Lonely Planet office closest to you:

Australia: Locked Bag 1, Footscray, Victoria 3011
USA: 150 Linden St, Oakland, CA 94607
UK: 10A Spring Place, London NW5 3BH
France: 1 rue du Dahomey, 75011 Paris

Or email us at: talk2us@lonelyplanet.com.au

For news, views and updates see our Web site: www.lonelyplanet.com

---

HOW TO USE A LONELY PLANET GUIDEBOOK

The best way to use a Lonely Planet guidebook is any way you choose. At Lonely Planet we believe the most memorable travel experiences are often those that are unexpected, and the finest discoveries are those you make yourself. Guidebooks are not intended to be used as if they provide a detailed set of infallible instructions!

Contents All Lonely Planet guidebooks follow roughly the same format. The Facts about the Destination chapters or sections give background information ranging from history to weather. Facts for the Visitor gives practical information on issues like visas and health. Getting There & Away gives a brief starting point for researching travel to and from the destination. Getting Around gives an overview of the transport options when you arrive.

The peculiar demands of each destination determine how subsequent chapters are broken up, but some things remain constant. We always start with background, then proceed to sights, places to stay, places to eat, entertainment, getting there and away, and getting around information – in that order.

Heading Hierarchy Lonely Planet headings are used in a strict hierarchical structure that can be visualised as a set of Russian dolls. Each heading (and its following text) is encompassed by any preceding heading that is higher on the hierarchical ladder.

Entry Points We do not assume guidebooks will be read from beginning to end, but that people will dip into them. The traditional entry points are the list of contents and the index. In addition, however, some books have a complete list of maps and an index map illustrating map coverage.

There may also be a colour map that shows highlights. These highlights are dealt with in greater detail in the Facts for the Visitor chapter, along with planning questions and suggested itineraries. Each chapter covering a geographical region usually begins with a locator map and another list of highlights. Once you find something of interest in a list of highlights, turn to the index.

Maps Maps play a crucial role in Lonely Planet guidebooks and include a huge amount of information. A legend is printed on the back page. We seek to have complete consistency between maps and text, and to have every important place in the text captured on a map. Map key numbers usually start in the top left corner.

Although inclusion in a guidebook usually implies a recommendation we cannot list every good place. Exclusion does not necessarily imply criticism. In fact there are a number of reasons why we might exclude a place – sometimes it is simply inappropriate to encourage an influx of travellers.

Introduction

Western Europe is many things to many people. Some marvel at the diversity of cultures and languages crammed into such a small area, the wealth of the region's museums, theatre and architecture, and the seemingly endless shopping, restaurants and nightlife on offer in the bustling cities. Others are attracted to Western Europe's varied scenery, from its sun-drenched beaches and dense forests to its snowcapped peaks. Many citizens of the Americas and Australasia see Western Europe as the birthplace of much of their culture and civilisation, while almost all visitors are delighted by the minimal amount of bureaucracy, and the well-developed tourist facilities and efficient transport that make it possible to explore the region with little fuss.

Western Europe is often looked upon as the hub of the developed world – at least historically. Though its growth rate is not what it was in the heady days of the 1950s and '60s, Western Europe remains an economic powerhouse and a leader in art, literature and music. For the visitor to the region, the biggest problem is simply choosing where to go, and what to see and do. There are magnificent museums and galleries such as the British Museum in London, the Louvre in Paris and the Prado in Madrid. There are architectural treasures like the Parthenon in Athens, Gaudí's fantastic church in Barcelona and fairy-tale castles in Germany. And there are superb natural features: the soaring Swiss Alps, the magnificent stretches of rugged coastline in western Ireland and

the tranquil, sunny islands of Greece. For the energetic, there are walking trails ranging from the high-altitude circuit of Mt Blanc in France to the Cotswolds Way in England, ski runs from Andorra to Zermatt in Switzerland and sailing, windsurfing and swimming all along the Atlantic, Baltic and Mediterranean coasts. And there are places where it's simply just fun to be, whether it's clubbing in Berlin, pub-crawling through Dublin or watching the world go by from a sidewalk cafe in Paris or Rome.

Western Europe provides an insight into the history, people and culture of this diverse collection of countries and offers practical information to help you make the most of your time and money.

There's information on how to get to Western Europe and how to get around once you're there. There are extensive details on what to see, when to see it and how much it all costs. The thousands of recommendations about places to stay range from French camping grounds and German hostels to Spanish pensions and Irish B&Bs. Cafes, restaurants and bars are covered in equally exhaustive detail, with suggestions ranging from the cheapest of cheap eats to the ideal place for that big splurge. There are even recommendations on what to buy and where to buy it.

Western Europe is a wonderful region to visit and there is a whole lot out there waiting to be enjoyed. This newly updated edition of *Western Europe* will guide you – all you have to do is go.

Facts for the Visitor

HIGHLIGHTS
The Top 10
There is so much to see in Western Europe that compiling a top 10 is next to impossible. But we asked the authors of this book to list their personal highlights. The results are as follows:

1. Paris
2. London
3. Rome
4. Berlin
5. Amsterdam
6. The Alps
7. Venice
8. Scotland's highlands and islands
9. Florence and Tuscany
10. Greek island-hopping

Other nominations included Barcelona, Munich, the Algarve, western Ireland, Hamburg, the North Frisian Islands, Umbria, Provence, Corsica, the Pyrenees, the wine cellars of Oporto, Bruges, the Yorkshire Dales, Languedoc-Roussillon and Edinburgh.

The Bottom 10
The writers were also asked to list the 10 worst 'attractions' of the region and offered the following:

1. Spanish coastal resorts
2. Paris
3. Dog turds on the streets of Amsterdam and Paris
4. Traffic jams in Paris, London and Rome
5. The *Sound of Music* tour in Salzburg
6. France's far northern coast
7. Munich *Bierfest*
8. Monte Carlo casino
9. British coastal resorts
10. Bullfights in Spain

Other nominations included rising racism, Britain's weather, Madame Tussaud's in London, the Scottish east coast – and the litter on the beaches, Milan, Rotterdam and Palma de Mallorca. A visit to any of these places could leave you feeling that you've wasted your time. Note that Paris is almost as good at repelling our authors as attracting them.

PLANNING
There are those who say that Europe, especially Western Europe, is so well developed and organised that you don't have to plan a thing before your trip; anything can be arranged on the spot. As any experienced traveller knows, the problems you thought about at home often turn out to be irrelevant or sort themselves out once you're on the move.

This is fine if you've decided to blow the massive inheritance in your bank account, but if your financial status is somewhat more modest, a bit of prior knowledge and careful planning can make your travel budget stretch further than you ever thought it would. You'll also want to make sure that the things you plan to see and do will be possible at the particular time of year when you'll be travelling.

Lonely Planet's *Read This First – Europe* is a worthwhile addition to your library.

When to Go
Any time can be the best time to visit Western Europe, depending on what you want to see and do. Summer lasts roughly from June to September and offers the best weather for outdoor pursuits in the northern half of Europe. In the southern half (Mediterranean coast, Iberian Peninsula, southern Italy and Greece), where the summers tend to be hotter, you can extend that period by one or even two months either way, when temperatures may also be more agreeable.

You won't be the only tourist in Western Europe during the summer months – all of France and Italy, for instance, goes on holiday in August. Prices can be high, accommodation fully booked and the sights packed. You'll find much better deals – and far fewer crowds – in the shoulder seasons on either side of summer; in April and May, for instance, flowers are in bloom and the weather can be surprisingly mild, and Indian summers are common in September and October.

On the other hand, if you're keen on winter sports, resorts in the Alps and the Pyrenees begin operating in late November and move into full swing after the New Year, closing down when the snows begin to melt in March or even April.

The Climate and When to Go sections in individual country chapters explain what to expect and when to expect it, and the Climate Charts in Appendix I in the back of the book will help you compare the weather in different destinations. As a rule, spring and autumn tend to be wetter and windier than summer and winter. The temperate maritime climate along the Atlantic is relatively wet all year, with moderate extremes in temperature. The Mediterranean coast is hotter and drier, with most rainfall occurring during the mild winter. The continental climate in eastern Germany and the Alps tends to show much stronger extremes in weather between summer and winter.

What Kind of Trip

Travelling Companions If you decide to travel with others, keep in mind that travel can put relationships to the test like few other experiences can. Many a long-term friendship has collapsed under the strain of constant negotiations about where to stay and eat, what to see and where to go next. But many friendships have also become closer than ever before. You won't find out until you try, but make sure you agree on itineraries and routines beforehand, and try to remain flexible about everything – even in the heat of an August afternoon in Paris or Berlin. Travelling with someone else also has financial benefits as single rooms are more expensive per person than a double in most countries.

If travel is a good way of testing established friendships, it's also a great way of making new ones. Hostels and camping grounds are good places to meet fellow travellers, so even if you're travelling alone you need never be lonely.

The Getting Around chapter has information on organised tours.

Move or Stay? 'If this is Tuesday, it must be Brussels.' Though often ridiculed, the mad dash that crams six countries into a month does have its merits. If you've never visited Western Europe before, you won't know which areas you'll like, and a quick 'scouting' tour will give an overview of the options. A rail pass that offers unlimited travel within a set period of time is the best way to do this.

But if you know where you want to go or find a place you like, the best advice is to stay put for a while, discover some of the lesser known sights, make a few local friends and settle in. It's also cheaper in the long run.

For information on working in Western Europe, see the Work section later in this chapter.

Maps

Good maps are easy to come by once you're in Europe, but you might want to buy a few beforehand to plan and track your route. The maps in this book will help you get an idea of where you might want to go and will be a useful first reference when you arrive in a city. Proper road maps are essential if you're driving or cycling.

For some European cities (eg, Amsterdam, Berlin, London, Paris, Rome and Brussels) Lonely Planet now has detailed city maps. Michelin maps are also good and, because of their soft covers, they fold up easily so you can stick them in your pocket. Some people prefer the maps meticulously produced by Freytag & Berndt, Kümmerly + Frey and Hallwag. As a rule, maps published by European automobile associations (the AA in Britain, the ADAC and AvD in Germany etc) are excellent and sometimes free if membership of your local association gives you reciprocal rights. Some of the best city maps are produced by Falk; RV Verlag's EuroCity series is another good bet. Tourist offices are often another good source for (usually free and fairly basic) maps.

What to Bring

It's very easy to find almost anything you need in Western Europe and, since you'll probably buy things as you go along, it's better to start with too little rather than too much.

A backpack is still the most popular method of carrying gear as it is convenient, especially for walking. On the down side, a backpack doesn't offer too much protection for your valuables, the straps tend to get caught on things and some airlines may refuse to accept responsibility if the pack is damaged or tampered with.

Travelpacks, a combination backpack/shoulder bag, are very popular. The backpack straps zip away inside the pack when they are not needed, so you almost have the best of both worlds. Some packs have sophisticated shoulder-strap adjustment systems and can be used comfortably even on long hikes.

World Heritage List

Unesco's list of 'cultural and natural treasures of the world's heritage' includes the following places in Western Europe:

AUSTRIA

Graz's historic centre
Hallstatt-Dachstein (Salzkammergut) cultural landscape

Palaces and gardens of Schönbrunn near Vienna
Semmering railway

Salzburg's historic city centre

BELGIUM

The Four Lifts on the Canal du Centre and their environs

La Louviere and Le Roeulx (Hainault)

Grand Place, Brussels
Belfries of Flanders and Wallonia

FRANCE

Amiens Cathedral
Arc-et-Senans' Royal Saltworks
Arles' Roman and Romanesque monuments
Avignon's historic centre
Bourges Cathedral
Carcassonne
Canal du Midi
Chambord's chateau and estate
Chartres Cathedral
Corsica's Cape Girolata, Cape Porto, Les Calanche and Scandola Natural Reserve

Fontainebleau Palace and Park
Fontenay's Cistercian abbey
Lascaux and other caves in the Vézère Valley
Lyon's historic centre
Mont Saint Michel and its bay
Place Stanislas, Place de la Carrière and Place d'Alliance in Nancy
Pont du Gard Roman aqueduct near Nîmes
Roman theatre and triumphal arch at Orange

Notre Dame and the banks of the Seine in Paris
Abbey of St Rémi and Tau Palace at Reims
St Émilion
Church of Saint Savin sur Gartempe
Grande Île section of Strasbourg
Chateau of Versailles and gardens
Vézelay's basilica

GERMANY

Aachen Cathedral
Bamberg
Berlin's Museuminsel (Museum Island)
Augustusburg Castle at Brühl
Cologne Cathedral
Luther memorials in Eisleben and Wittenberg
Goslar and mines of Rammelsberg
Cathedral and St Michael's

Church at Hildesheim
Abbey and Altenmünster of Lorsch
Lübeck
Maulbronn Monastery complex
Messel fossil site
The palaces and parks of Potsdam
Quedlinburg's Collegiate Church, castle and old town
Speyer Cathedral

Trier's Roman monuments, cathedral and Liebfrauen Church
Völkling ironworks
Wartburg Castle
The Bauhaus sites in Weimar and Dessau
Wies' pilgrimage church
Würzburg's Residence and Court Gardens

GREECE

The Acropolis in Athens
Mount Athos
Temple of Apollo Epicurius at Bassae
Monasteries of Daphni, Hossios, Luckas and Nea Moni at Chios
Delos
Delphi archaeological site

Epidaurus archaeological site
Meteora
Mycenae and Tyrins' archaeological sites
Mystras
Olympia's archaeological site
Hora, the Monastery of Saint John and the Monastery of the

Apocalypse on Patmos
Medieval city of Rhodes
Pythagorio and Hereon at Samos
Thessaloniki's Early Christian and Byzantine monuments
Vergina's archaeological site

IRELAND

Boyne Valley archaeological sites
Skellig Michael

ITALY

Agrigento archaeological area
Alberobello's *trulli*
Aquileia archaeological area and the patriarchal Basilica
Caserta's Royal Palace with the park, aqueduct of Vanvitelli and the San Leucio complex
Castel del Monte
Cilento and Vallo di Diano National Park with the archaeological sites of Paestum and Velia, and the Certosa di Padula
Cinque Terre, Portvenere and islands
Costiera Amalfitana
Crespi d'Adda

The Renaissance city of Ferrara
The historic centre of Florence
The *sassi* (traditional stone houses) of Matera
Milan's Church of Santa Maria delle Grazie and convent including *The Last Supper* by Leonardo da Vinci
Modena's cathedral, Torre Civica and Piazza Grande
The historic centre of Naples
Padua's botanical garden
Pienza's historic centre
Pisa's Piazza del Duomo
Archaeological areas of Pompei and Herculaneum
Ravenna's Early Christian

monuments and mosaics
Rome's historic centre
The historic centre of San Gimignano
Residences of the royal house of Savoy
Siena's historic centre
Su Nuraxi fortress at Barumini
Urbino's historic centre
Valle Camonica's rock carvings
Vatican City
Venice and its lagoon
Villa Adriana (Tivoli)
Villa Romana del Casale
Vincenza and its Palladian villas

LUXEMBOURG

Old quarter and fortifications of Luxembourg City

NETHERLANDS

Amsterdam's Defence Line
Droogmakerij de Beemster (Beemster Polder)

Kinderdijk-Elshout's mill network
Schokland and surroundings
Willemstad's historic area

DF Wouda steam pumping station

PORTUGAL

Monastery of Alcobaça
The central zone of Angra do Heroism in the Azores
Batalha Monastery
Côa Valley's prehistoric rock-art sites

Évora's historic centre
Lisbon's Monastery of the Hieronymites and Tower of Belém
Madeira's Laurisilva
Oporto's historic centre

The cultural landscape of Sintra
Convent of Christ in Tomar

SPAIN

Alcalá de Henares university and historic area
Altamira Cave
Churches of the kingdom of Asturias
The old town section of Ávila
Güell park and palace, Casa Mila, Palace of the Música Catalana and Sant Pau hospital, Barcelona
Burgos Cathedral
The old town section of Cáceres
Historic centre of Córdoba
Cuenca's walled city

Doñana National Park
Garajonay National Park
Rock art on the Iberian Peninsula
La Alhambra, El Generalife summer palace and Albaicín Moorish quarter of Granada
Biodiversity and culture of Ibiza
El Escorial near Madrid
Las Médulas
Archaeological ensemble of Mérida
Poblet Monastery
Salamanca's old town

Royal Monastery of Santa María de Guadelupe
San Cristóbal de la Laguna
Santiago de Compostela's old town and route
The old town and aqueduct of Segovia
Sevilla's cathedral, Alcázar Archivo de Indias
Mudejar architecture of Teruel
Toledo's historic centre
Valencia's La Lonja de la Seda (silk exchange)

World Heritage List

SWITZERLAND

The old city section of Bern	Müstair's Convent of St John	St Gall Convent

UK

Bath	Gough Island Wildlife Reserve	St Kilda
Blenheim Palace	Greenwich	Stonehenge and Avebury
Canterbury Cathedral, St	Gwynedd's castles and town	Studley Royal Park and ruins of
Augustine's Abbey and St	walls	Fountains Abbey
Martin's Church	Hadrian's Wall	Westminster Abbey, Westminster Palace and St Margaret's
Durham Castle and Cathedral	Henderson Island	Church
Edinburgh (old and new towns)	Ironbridge Gorge	
Giant's Causeway and Causeway Coast	Tower of London	
	Neolithic Orkney	

Backpacks or travelpacks are always much easier to carry than a bag, and can be made reasonably theft-proof with small padlocks. Another alternative is a large, soft zip bag with a wide shoulder strap so it can be carried with relative ease. Forget suitcases unless you're travelling in style, but if you do take one, make sure it has wheels to allow you to drag it along behind you.

As for clothing, the climate will have a bearing on what you take along, but be prepared for rain at any time of year. Remember that insulation works on the principle of trapped air, so several layers of thin clothing are warmer than a single thick one (and will be easier to dry). You'll also be much more flexible if the weather suddenly turns warm. Bearing in mind that you can buy virtually anything on the spot, a minimum packing list could include:

- underwear, socks and swimming gear
- a pair of jeans and maybe a pair of shorts or skirt
- a few T-shirts and shirts
- a warm sweater
- a solid pair of walking shoes
- sandals or thongs for showers
- a coat or jacket
- a raincoat, waterproof jacket or umbrella
- a medical kit and sewing kit
- a padlock
- a Swiss Army knife
- soap and towel
- toothpaste, toothbrush and other toiletries

A padlock is useful to lock your bag to a luggage rack in a bus or train; it may also be needed to secure your hostel locker. A Swiss Army knife comes in handy for all sorts of things. *Any* pocketknife is fine, but make sure it includes such essentials as a bottle opener and strong corkscrew! Soap, toothpaste and toilet paper are readily obtainable almost anywhere, but you'll need your own supply of paper in many public toilets and at those in camping grounds. Tampons are available at pharmacies and supermarkets in all but the remotest places. Condoms are widely available in Western Europe.

A tent and sleeping bag are vital if you want to save money by camping. Even if you're not camping, a sleeping bag is still very useful. Get one that can be used as a quilt. A sleeping sheet with pillow cover (case) is necessary if you plan to stay in hostels – you may have to hire or purchase one if you don't bring your own. In any case, a sheet that fits into your sleeping bag is easier to wash than the bag itself. Make one yourself out of old sheets (include a built-in pillow cover) or buy one from your hostel association.

Other optional items include a compass, a torch (flashlight), a pocket calculator for currency conversions, an alarm clock, an adapter plug for electrical appliances (such as a cup or immersion water heater to save on expensive tea and coffee), a universal bath/sink plug (a film canister sometimes works), portable short-wave radio, sunglasses, a few clothes pegs and premoistened towelettes or a large cotton handkerchief that you can soak in fountains and use to cool off while touring cities in the hot summer months. During city sightseeing, a small daypack is better than a shoulder bag for deterring thieves (see Theft in the Dangers & Annoyances section of this chapter).

Also, consider using plastic carry bags or bin liners inside your backpack to keep things separate but also dry if the pack gets soaked.

RESPONSIBLE TOURISM

As a visitor, you have a responsibility to the local people and to the environment. For guidelines on how to avoid offending the people you meet, read the following Appearances & Conduct section. When it comes to the environment, the key rules are to preserve natural resources and to leave the countryside as you find it. Those Alpine flowers look much better on the mountainside than squashed in your pocket (many species are protected anyway).

Wherever you are, littering is irresponsible and offensive. Mountain areas have fragile ecosystems, so stick to prepared paths whenever possible, and always carry your rubbish away with you. Don't use detergents or toothpaste in or near watercourses, even if they are biodegradable. If you just gotta go when you're out in the wilderness somewhere, bury human waste in holes at least 15cm deep and at least 100m from any watercourse.

Recycling is an important issue, especially in Austria, Germany and Switzerland, and you will be encouraged to follow suit. Traffic congestion on the roads is a major problem, and visitors will do themselves and residents a favour if they forgo driving and use public transport.

Appearances & Conduct

Although dress standards are fairly informal in northern Europe, your clothes may well have some bearing on how you're treated in southern Europe. Dress casually, but keep your clothes clean, and ensure sufficient body cover (trousers or a knee-length dress) if your sightseeing includes churches, monasteries, synagogues or mosques. Wearing shorts away from the beach or camping ground is not very common among men in Europe. Some nightclubs and fancy restaurants may refuse entry to people wearing jeans, a tracksuit or sneakers (trainers); men might consider packing a tie as well, just in case.

While nude bathing is usually restricted to certain beaches, topless bathing is very common in many parts of Europe. Nevertheless, women should be wary of taking their tops off as a matter of course. The basic rule is that if nobody else seems to be doing it, you shouldn't either.

You'll soon notice that Europeans are heavily into shaking hands and even kissing when they greet one another. Don't worry about the latter with those you don't know well, but get into the habit of shaking hands with virtually everyone you meet. In many parts of Europe, it's also customary to greet the proprietor when entering a shop, cafe or quiet bar, and to say goodbye when you leave.

VISAS & DOCUMENTS
Passport

Your most important travel document is your passport, which should remain valid until well after you return home. If it's just about to expire, renew it before you go. This may not be easy to do overseas, and some countries insist that your passport remains valid for a specified period (usually three months beyond the date of your departure from that country).

Applying for or renewing a passport can take anything from an hour to several months, so don't leave it till the last minute. Bureaucratic wheels usually turn faster if you do everything in person rather than relying on the post or agents, but check first what you need to take with you: photos of a certain size, birth certificate, population register extract, signed statements, exact payment in cash etc.

Australian citizens can apply at a post office or the passport office in their state capital; Britons can pick up application forms from major post offices, and the passport is issued by the regional passport office; Canadians can apply at regional passport offices; New Zealanders can apply at any district office of the Department of Internal Affairs; US citizens must apply in person (but may usually renew by mail) at a US Passport Agency office or at some courthouses and post offices.

Once you start travelling, carry your passport at all times and guard it carefully. Camping grounds and hotels sometimes insist that you hand over your passport for the duration of your stay, which is very inconvenient, but a driving licence or Camping Card International usually solves the problem.

Citizens of the European Union (EU) and those from certain other European countries (eg, Switzerland) don't need a valid passport to travel to another EU country or even some non-EU countries; a national identity card is sufficient. If you want to exercise this option, check with your travel agent or the embassies of the countries you plan to visit.

Visas

A visa is a stamp in your passport or on a separate piece of paper permitting you to enter the country in question and stay for a specified period of time. Often you can get the visa at the border or at the airport on arrival, but not always – check first with the embassies or consulates of the countries you plan to visit – and seldom on trains.

There's a wide variety of visas, including tourist, transit and business ones. Transit visas are usually cheaper than tourist or business visas, but they only allow a very short stay (one or two days) and can be difficult to extend. Most readers of this book, however, will have very little to do with visas. With a valid passport they'll be able to visit most European countries for up to three (sometimes even six) months, provided they have some sort of onward or return ticket and/or 'sufficient means of support' (money).

In line with the Schengen Agreement there are no passport controls at the borders between Germany, France, Spain, Portugal, the Benelux countries (Belgium, Netherlands and Luxembourg), Italy and Austria; an identity card should suffice, but it's always safest to carry your passport. The other EU countries (Britain, Denmark, Finland, Greece, Ireland and Sweden) are not yet full members of Schengen and still maintain low-key border controls over traffic from other EU countries.

Border procedures between EU and non-EU countries can still be fairly thorough, though citizens of Australia, Canada, Israel, Japan, New Zealand, Norway, Switzerland and the USA do not need visas for tourist visits to any Schengen country.

All non-EU citizens visiting a Schengen country and intending to stay for longer than three days or to visit another Schengen country are supposed to obtain an official entry stamp in their passport either at the point of entry or from the local police within 72 hours. This is very loosely enforced, however, and in general registering at a hotel will be sufficient.

For those who do require visas, it's important to remember that these will have a 'use-by' date, and you'll be refused entry after that period has elapsed. It may not be checked when entering these countries overland, but major problems can arise if it is requested during your stay or on departure and you can't produce it.

Visa requirements can change, and you should always check with the individual embassies or a reputable travel agent before travelling. It's generally easier to get your visas as you go along, rather than arranging them all beforehand. Carry spare passport photos (you may need from one to four every time you apply for a visa).

Travel Insurance

A travel insurance policy to cover theft, loss and medical problems is a good idea. The policies handled by STA Travel and other student travel organisations are usually good value. Some policies offer lower and higher medical expense options; the higher ones are chiefly for countries such as the USA that have extremely high medical costs. There is a wide variety of policies available so check the small print.

Some policies specifically exclude 'dangerous activities', which can include scuba diving, motorcycling and even trekking. A locally acquired motorcycle licence is not valid under some policies.

You may prefer a policy that pays doctors or hospitals directly rather than you having to pay on the spot and claim later. If you have to claim later, make sure you keep all documentation. Some policies ask you to call back (reverse charges) to a centre in your home country where an immediate assessment of your problem is made.

Check that the policy covers ambulances or an emergency flight home.

Driving Licence & Permits

Many non-European driving licences are valid in Europe, but it's still a good idea to bring along an International Driving Permit

(IDP), which can make life much simpler, especially when hiring cars and motorcycles. Basically a multilingual translation of the vehicle class and personal details noted on your local driving licence, an IDP is not valid unless accompanied by your original licence. An IDP can be obtained for a small fee from your local automobile association – bring along a passport photo and a valid licence.

Camping Card International

The Camping Card International (CCI; formerly the Camping Carnet) is a camping ground ID that can be used instead of a passport when checking into a camp site and includes third party insurance. As a result, many camping grounds offer a small discount if you sign in with one. CCIs are issued by automobile associations, camping federations and, sometimes, on the spot at camping grounds. In the UK, the AA issues them to its members for UK£4.50.

Hostel Cards

A hostelling card is useful – if not always mandatory – for those staying at hostels. Some hostels in Western Europe don't require that you be a hostelling association member, but they often charge less if you have a card. Many hostels will issue one on the spot or after a few stays, though this might cost a bit more than getting it in your home country. See Hostels in the Accommodation section later in this chapter.

Student & Youth Cards

The most useful of these is the International Student Identity Card (ISIC), a plastic ID-style card with your photograph, which provides discounts on many forms of transport (including airlines and local public transport), cheap or free admission to museums and sights, and inexpensive meals in some student cafeterias and restaurants. If you're aged under 26 but not a student, you can apply for a GO25 card issued by the Federation of International Youth Travel Organisations (FIYTO) or the Euro<26 card. Both go under different names in various countries and give much the same discounts and benefits as an ISIC. All these cards are issued by student unions, hostelling organisations or youth-oriented travel agencies.

Seniors Cards

Museums and other sights, public swimming pools and spas, and transport companies frequently offer discounts to retired people/old age pensioners/those over 60 (slightly younger for women). Make sure you bring proof of age; that suave *signore* in Italy or that polite Parisian *mademoiselle* is not going to believe you're a day over 39.

European nationals aged 60 and over can get a Railplus (formerly Rail Europe Senior) Card. For more information see Cheap Tickets under Train in the Getting Around chapter.

International Health Certificate

You'll need this yellow booklet only if you're coming to the region from certain parts of Asia, Africa and South America, where diseases such as yellow fever are prevalent. See Predeparture Planning in the Health section for more information on jabs.

Copies

All important documents (passport data page and visa page, credit cards, travel insurance policy, air/bus/train tickets, driving licence etc) should be photocopied before you leave home. Leave one copy with someone at home and keep the other with you.

While you're on the road add the serial numbers of your travellers cheques (cross them off as you cash them) to these photocopies and keep all this emergency material separate from your passport, cheques and cash. Add some emergency money (eg, US$50 to US$100 in cash) to this separate stash as well. If you do lose your passport, notify the police immediately to get a statement, and contact your nearest consulate.

It's also a good idea to store details of your vital travel documents in Lonely Planet's free online Travel Vault in case you lose the photocopies or can't be bothered with them. Your password-protected Travel Vault is accessible online anywhere in the world – create it at www.ekno.lonelyplanet.com.

EMBASSIES & CONSULATES

See individual country chapters for the addresses of embassies and consulates.

Getting Help from Your Embassy

As a tourist, it's important to realise what your own embassy – the embassy of the country of which you are a citizen – can and cannot do.

Generally speaking, it won't be much help in emergencies if the trouble you're in is remotely your fault. Remember that you are bound by the laws of the country you are in. Your embassy will not be sympathetic if you end up in jail after committing a crime locally, even if such actions are legal in your own country.

In genuine emergencies you might get some assistance, but only if other channels have been exhausted. For example, if you need to get home urgently, a free ticket home is exceedingly unlikely as the embassy would expect you to have insurance. If you have all your money and documents stolen, it might assist with getting a new passport, but a loan for onward travel is almost always out of the question.

Embassies used to keep letters for travellers or have a small reading room with home newspapers, but these days mail holding services have been stopped and newspapers tend to be out of date.

CUSTOMS

Duty-free goods are no longer sold to those travelling from one EU country to another. For goods purchased at airports or on ferries *outside* the EU, the usual allowances apply for tobacco (200 cigarettes, 50 cigars or 250g of loose tobacco), alcohol (1L of spirits or 2L of liquor with less than 22% alcohol by volume; 2L of wine) and perfume (50g of perfume and 0.25L of toilet water).

Do not confuse these with *duty-paid* items (including alcohol and tobacco) bought at normal shops and supermarkets in another EU country, where certain goods might be more expensive. (Cigarettes in France, for example, are half the price they are in the UK.) Then the allowances are more than generous: 800 cigarettes, 200 cigars or 1kg of loose tobacco; 10L of spirits (more than 22% alcohol by volume), 20L of fortified wine or aperitif, 90L of wine or 110L of beer; unlimited quantities of perfume.

MONEY
Exchanging Money

By the year 2002, the EU will have a single currency called the euro (see boxed text 'The Euro'). Until then francs, marks and pesetas remain in place or share equal status with the euro.

In general, US dollars, Deutschmarks, pounds sterling, and French and Swiss francs are the most easily exchanged currencies in Europe, followed by Italian lire and Dutch guilders, but you may well decide that other currencies suit your purposes better. You lose out through commissions and customer exchange rates every time you change money, so if you only visit Portugal, for example, you may be better off buying escudos straight away if your bank at home can provide them.

All Western European currencies are fully convertible, but you may have trouble exchanging some of the lesser known ones at small banks, while currencies of countries with high inflation face unfavourable exchange rates. Try not to have too many leftover Portuguese escudos, Spanish pesetas, Belgian or Luxembourg francs, or Austrian Schillings. Get rid of Scottish and Northern Irish pounds before leaving the UK; nobody outside Britain will touch them.

Most airports, central train stations, big hotels and many border posts have banking facilities outside normal office hours, sometimes on a 24-hour basis. You'll often find automatic exchange machines outside banks or tourist offices that accept the currencies of up to two dozen countries. Post offices in Europe often perform banking tasks and outnumber banks in remote places; they also tend to be open longer hours. Be aware, though, that while they always exchange cash, they might baulk at handling travellers cheques unless they're denominated in the local currency.

The best exchange rates are usually at banks. *Bureaux de change* usually – but not always by any means – offer worse rates or charge higher commissions. Hotels are almost always the worst places to change money. American Express and Thomas Cook offices usually do not charge commission for changing their own cheques, but may offer a less favourable exchange rate than banks.

Cash Nothing beats cash for convenience, or risk. If you lose it, it's gone forever and very few travel insurers will come to your rescue. Those that will, limit the amount to somewhere around US$300. For tips on carrying your money safely, see Theft in the Dangers & Annoyances section later in this chapter.

The Euro

Don't be surprised if you come across two sets of prices for goods and services in Western Europe. Since 1 January 1999 Europe's new currency – the euro – has been legal tender here along with the local monetary unit.

While Britain, Denmark, Sweden and Greece have not yet joined, the other 11 EU countries (Austria, Belgium, Finland, France, Germany, Ireland, Italy, Luxembourg, Netherlands, Portugal, Spain) are all counting down the days when venerable currencies like the franc and escudo will be no longer be legal tender – 1 July 2002, to be precise. Between now and that date the countries in Euroland operate two currencies – running their old currencies alongside the euro.

No actual coins or banknotes will be issued until 1 January 2002; until then, the euro is, in effect, 'paperless'. Prices are quoted in euros, but there aren't actually any euros in circulation. Companies use the new currency for their accounting, banks offer euro accounts and travellers cheques in euros, credit-card companies bill in euros. Essentially, the euro is used any time it is not necessary to hand over hard cash.

This can lead to confusion – a restaurant might list prices in both francs and euros or escudos and euros. Check your bill carefully – the total might have the amount in francs or escudos, your credit card may bill you in the euro equivalent. In practice, however, the total is usually listed in both currencies. Things could be more complicated during the first half of 2002 when countries can use both their old currencies and the newly issued euro notes and coins.

The euro has the same value in all member countries of the EU; the E5 note in France is the same E5 note you will use in Italy and Portugal. The official exchange rates were set on 1 January 1999.

Coins and notes have already been designed. There are seven euro notes (five, 10, 20, 50, 100, 200 and 500 euros), and eight euro coins (one and two euros, then one, two, five, 10, 20 and 50 cents). Each country is permitted to design coins with one side standard for all euro coins and the other bearing a national emblem.

Rates of exchange of the euro and foreign currencies against local currencies are given in the country chapters.

country	unit		euro	country	unit		euro
Australia	A$1	=	€0.64	Canada	C$1	=	€0.75
France	1FF	=	€0.15	Germany	DM1	=	€0.51
Ireland	IR£1	=	€1.26	Italy	L1000	=	€0.52
Japan	¥100	=	€1.02	Netherlands	f1	=	€0.45
New Zealand	NZ$1	=	€0.50	Spain	100 ptas	=	€0.60
South Africa	R1	=	€0.16	UK	UK£1	=	€1.66
USA	US$1	=	€1.11				

It's still a good idea, though, to bring some local currency in cash, if only to tide you over until you get to an exchange facility or find an automatic teller machine (ATM). The equivalent of, say, US$50 or US$100 should usually be enough. Some extra cash in an easily exchanged currency (eg, US dollars or Deutschmarks) is also a good idea.

Travellers Cheques The main idea of carrying travellers cheques rather than cash is the protection they offer from theft, though they are losing their popularity as more travellers – including those on tight budgets – deposit their money in their bank at home and withdraw it as they go along through ATMs.

American Express, Visa and Thomas Cook travellers cheques are widely accepted and have efficient replacement policies. If you're going to remote places, it's worth sticking to American Express since small local banks may not always accept other brands.

When you change cheques, don't look at just the exchange rate; ask about fees and commissions as well. There may be a service fee per cheque, a flat transaction fee or a percentage of the total amount irrespective of the number of cheques. Some banks charge fees (often exorbitant) to cash cheques and not cash; others do the reverse.

Plastic Cards & ATMs If you're not familiar with the options, ask your bank to explain the workings and relative merits of credit, credit/debit, debit, charge and cash cards.

A major advantage of credit cards is that they allow you to pay for expensive items (eg, airline tickets) without your having to carry great wads of cash around. They also allow you to withdraw cash at selected banks or from the many ATMs that are linked up internationally. However, if an ATM in Europe swallows a card that was issued outside Europe, it can be a major headache. Also, some credit cards aren't linked to ATM networks unless you ask your bank to do this.

Cash cards, which you use at home to withdraw money directly from your bank account or savings account, can be used throughout Europe at ATMs linked to international networks like Cirrus and Maestro.

Credit and credit/debit cards like Visa and MasterCard are widely accepted. MasterCard is linked to Europe's extensive Eurocard system, and Visa (sometimes called Carte Bleue) is particularly strong in France and Spain. However, these cards often have a credit limit that is too low to cover major expenses like long-term car rental or airline tickets and can be difficult to replace if lost abroad. Also, when you get a cash advance against your Visa or MasterCard credit card account, your issuer charges a transaction fee and/or finance charge. With some issuers, the fees can reach as high as US$10 *plus* interest per transaction so it's best to check with your card issuer before leaving home and compare rates.

Charge cards like American Express and Diners Club have offices in the major cities of most countries that will replace a lost card within 24 hours. However, charge cards are not widely accepted off the beaten track.

Another option is Visa TravelMoney, a prepaid travel card that gives 24-hour access to your funds in local currency via Visa ATMs. The card is PIN-protected and its value is stored on the system, not on the card. So if you lose the card, your money's safe.

Visa TravelMoney can be purchased in any amount from Citicorp and Thomas Cook/Interpayment. For more details go to www.visa.com/pd/trav/main.html.

The best advice is not to put all your eggs in one basket. If you want to rely heavily on bits of plastic, go for two different cards – an American Express or Diners Club, for instance, along with a Visa or MasterCard. Better still is a combination of credit or cash card and travellers cheques so you have something to fall back on if an ATM swallows your card or the banks in the area are closed.

A word of warning – fraudulent shopkeepers have been known to quickly make several charge slip imprints with your credit card when you're not looking, and then simply copy your signature from the one that you authorise. Try not to let your card out of sight, and always check your statements upon your return.

International Transfers Telegraphic transfers are not very expensive but, despite their name, can be quite slow. Be sure to specify the name of the bank and the name and address of the branch where you'd like to pick it up.

It's quicker and easier to have money wired via an American Express office (US$60 for US$1000). Western Union's Money Transfer system (available at post offices in some countries) and Thomas Cook's MoneyGram service are also popular.

Guaranteed Cheques Guaranteed personal cheques are another way of carrying money or obtaining cash. Eurocheques, available if you have a European bank account, are guaranteed up to a certain limit. When cashing them (eg, at post offices), you will be asked to show your Eurocheque card bearing your signature and registration number, and perhaps a passport or ID card. Your Eurocheque card should be kept separately from the cheques. Many hotels and merchants refuse to accept Eurocheques because of the relatively large commissions.

Costs

The secret to budget travel in Western Europe is cheap accommodation. Europe has a highly developed network of camping grounds and hostels, some of them quite luxurious, and they're great places to meet people.

Other money-saving strategies include preparing your own meals and avoiding alcohol; using a student card (see Visas & Documents earlier in this chapter) and buying any of the various rail and public transport passes (see the Getting Around chapter). Also remember that the more time you spend in any one place, the lower your daily expenses are likely to be as you get to know your way around.

Including transport, but not private motorised transport, your daily expenses could work out to around US$35 to US$40 a day if you're operating on a rock-bottom budget. This means camping or staying in hostels, eating economically and using a transport pass.

Travelling on a moderate budget, you should be able to manage on US$60 to US$80 a day. This would allow you to stay at cheap hotels, guesthouses or B&Bs. You could afford meals in economical restaurants and even a few beers! But planning on US$100 is probably more realistic. Greece and Portugal would be somewhat cheaper, while Switzerland and the UK would be pricier.

A general warning about the prices we list in this book – they're likely to change, usually moving upward, but if last season was particularly slow they may remain the same or even come down a bit. Nevertheless, relative price levels should stay fairly constant – if hotel A costs twice as much as hotel B, it's likely to stay that way.

Tipping

In many European countries it's common (and the law in France) for a service charge to be added to restaurant bills, in which case no tipping is necessary. In others, simply rounding up the bill is sufficient. See the individual country chapters for more details.

Taxes & Refunds

A kind of sales tax called value-added tax (VAT) applies to most goods and services throughout Western Europe; it's 21% in Ireland, 19.6% in France, 18% in Greece, 17.5% in the UK, 16% in Germany and 7.5% in Switzerland. In most countries, visitors can claim back the VAT on purchases that are being taken out of the country. Those actually *residing* in one EU country are not entitled to a refund on VAT paid on goods bought in another EU country. Thus an American citizen living in London is not entitled to a VAT rebate on items bought in Paris, while an EU passport holder residing in New York is.

The procedure for making the claim is fairly straightforward, though it may vary somewhat from country to country and there are minimum-purchase amounts imposed (eg, in France you must be over 15, spend less than six months in the country and purchase goods worth at least 1200FF). First of all make sure the shop offers duty-free sales (often identified with a sign reading 'Tax-Free for Tourists'). When making your purchase, ask the shop attendant for a VAT refund voucher (sometimes called a Tax-Free Shopping Cheque) filled in with the correct amount and the date. This can either be refunded directly at international airports on departure or stamped at ferry ports or border crossings and mailed back for refund.

POST & COMMUNICATIONS
Post

From major European centres, airmail typically takes about five days to North America and a week to Australasian destinations, though mail from the UK can be much faster and from Greece much slower. Postage costs vary from country to country, as does post office efficiency – the Italian post office is notoriously unreliable.

You can collect mail from poste restante sections at major post offices. Ask people writing to you to print your name clearly and underline your surname. When collecting mail, your passport may be required for identification and you may have to pay a small fee. If an expected letter is not awaiting you, ask to check under your given name; letters commonly get misfiled. Post offices usually hold mail for about a month, but sometimes less (in Germany, for instance, they only keep mail for two weeks). Unless the sender specifies otherwise, mail will always be sent to the city's main post office (or GPO in the UK and Ireland).

You can also have mail (but not parcels) sent to you at American Express offices so long as you have an American Express card or are carrying American Express travellers cheques. When you buy the cheques, ask for a booklet listing all the American Express offices worldwide.

Telephone

You can ring abroad from almost any phone box in Europe. Public telephones accepting stored-value phonecards (available from post offices, telephone centres, newsstands or retail outlets) are virtually the norm now; in some countries (eg, France) coin-operated phones are almost impossible to find.

There's a wide range of local and international phonecards. Lonely Planet's eKno global communication service provides low cost international calls, a range of innovative messaging services, an online travel vault where you can securely store all your important documents, free email and travel information, all in one easy service. You can join online at www.ekno.lonelyplanet.com, where you can also find the best local access numbers to connect to the 24-hour customer service centre to join or find out more. Once you have joined always check the eKno Web site for the latest access numbers for each country and updates on new features.

For local calls you're usually better off with a local phonecard.

Without a phonecard, you can ring from a booth inside a post office or telephone centre and settle your bill at the counter. Reverse-charge (collect) calls are often possible, but not always. From many countries, however, the Country Direct system lets you phone home by billing the long-distance carrier you use at home. The numbers can often be dialled from public phones without even inserting a phone card.

Area codes for individual cities are provided in the country chapters. For country codes, see Appendix II – Telephones at the end of the book.

Fax

You can send faxes and telexes from most main post offices in Western Europe.

Email & Internet Access

Travelling with a portable computer is a great way to stay in touch with life back home but, unless you know what you're doing, it's fraught with potential problems. A good investment is a universal AC adapter for your appliance, so you can plug it in anywhere without frying the innards if the power supply voltage varies. You'll also need a plug adapter for each country you visit, often easiest bought before you leave home.

Secondly, your PC-card modem may or may not work once you leave your home country – and you won't know for sure until you try. The safest option is to buy a reputable 'global' or 'world' modem before you leave home, or buy a local PC-card modem if you're spending an extended time in any one country. Keep in mind that the telephone socket in each country you visit will probably be different from that at home, so ensure that you have at least a US RJ-11 telephone adapter that works with your modem. You can almost always find an adapter that will convert from RJ-11 to the local variety. For more information on travelling with a portable computer, see www.teleadapt.com or www.warrior.com.

Major Internet service providers (ISPs) such as AOL (www.aol.com), CompuServe (www.compuserve.com) and IBM Net (www.ibm.net) have dial-in nodes throughout Europe; it's best to download a list of the dial-in numbers before you leave home. If you access your Internet email account at home through a smaller ISP or your office or school network, your best option is either to open an account with a global ISP, like those mentioned above, or to rely on cybercafes and other public access points to collect your mail.

If you do intend to rely on cybercafes, you'll need to carry three pieces of information with you so you can access your Internet mail account: your incoming (POP or IMAP) mail server name, your account name, and your password. Your ISP or network supervisor will give you these. Armed with this information, you should be able to access your Internet mail account from any Internet-connected machine in the world, provided it runs some kind of email software (remember that Netscape and Internet Explorer both have mail modules). It pays to become familiar with the process for doing this before you leave home. A final option to collect mail through cybercafes is to open a free eKno Web-based email account on-line at www.ekno.lonelyplanet.com. You can then access your mail from anywhere in the world from any Internet-connected machine running a standard Web browser.

You'll find cybercafes throughout Europe – check the country chapters in this book, and see www.netcafeguide.com for an up-to-date list. You may also find public Internet access in post offices, libraries, hostels, hotels, universities and so on.

INTERNET RESOURCES

The World Wide Web is a rich resource for travellers. You can research your trip, hunt down bargain air fares, book hotels, check weather conditions or chat with locals and other travellers about the best places to visit.

Lonely Planet There's no better place to start your Web explorations than the Lonely Planet Web site. Here you'll find succinct summaries on travelling to most places on earth, postcards from other travellers and the Thorn Tree bulletin board, where you can ask questions before you go or dispense advice when you get back. You can also find travel news and updates to many of our most popular guidebooks, and the subWWWay section links you to the most useful travel resources elsewhere on the Web.
www.lonelyplanet.com

Tourist Offices Lists tourist offices at home and around the world for most countries.
www.mbnet.mb.ca/lucas/travel

Rail Information Train fares and schedules on the most popular routes in Europe, including information on rail and youth passes.
www.raileurope.com

Airline Information What airlines fly where, when and for how much.
www.travelocity.com

Airline Tickets Name the price you're willing to pay for an airline seat and if an airline has an empty seat for which it would rather get something than nothing, US-based Priceline lets you know.
www.priceline.com

Currency Conversions Exchange rates of hundreds of currencies worldwide.
www.xe.net/ucc

NEWSPAPERS & MAGAZINES

Keeping up with the news in English is obviously no problem in the UK or Ireland. In larger towns in the rest of Western Europe you can buy the excellent *International Herald Tribune* on the day of publication, as well as the colourful but superficial *USA Today*. Among other English-language newspapers widely available are the *Guardian*, the *Financial Times* and *The Times*. The *European* weekly newspaper is also readily available, as are *Newsweek*, *Time* and the *Economist*.

RADIO & TV

Radio

Close to the Channel, you can pick up British radio stations, particularly BBC's Radio 4. There are also numerous English-language broadcasts – or even BBC World Service and Voice of America (VOA) re-broadcasts on local AM and FM radio stations. Otherwise, you can pick up a mixture of the BBC World Service and BBC for Europe on medium wave at 648kHz AM and on short wave at 6195kHz, 9410kHz, 11955kHz, 12095kHz (a good daytime frequency) and 15575kHz, depending on the time of day. BBC Radio 4 broadcasts on long wave at 198kHz. VOA can usually be found at various times of the day on 7170kHz, 9535kHz, 9680kHz, 9760kHz, 9770kHz, 11805kHz, 15135kHz, 15205kHz, 15255kHz, 15410kHz and 15580kHz.

TV

Cable and satellite TV have spread across Europe with much more gusto than radio. Sky TV can be found in many upmarket hotels throughout Western Europe, as can CNN, BBC Prime and other networks. You can also pick up many cross-border TV stations, including British stations close to the Channel.

VIDEO SYSTEMS

If you want to record or buy video tapes to play back home, you won't get a picture if the image registration systems are different. Europe generally uses PAL (SECAM in France), which is incompatible with the North American and Japanese NTSC system. Australia also uses PAL.

PHOTOGRAPHY & VIDEO

Both your destination and the weather will dictate what film to take or buy locally. In places like Ireland and Britain, where the sky is often overcast, photographers should bring higher-speed film (eg, 200 ASA). For southern Europe (or northern Europe under a blanket of snow and sunny skies) slower film (100 ASA and lower) is the answer.

Read Lonely Planet's *Travel Photography: a Guide to Taking Better Pictures*.

Film and camera equipment are available everywhere in Western Europe, but obviously shops in larger cities and towns have a wider selection.

Avoid buying film at tourist sites in Europe (eg, at kiosks below the Eiffel Tower in Paris or at the Tower of London). It may have been stored badly or reached its sell-by date. It will certainly be expensive.

Properly used, a video camera can give a fascinating record of your holiday. Unlike still photography, video 'flows' so, for example, you can shoot scenes of countryside rolling past the train window. Make sure you keep the batteries charged and have the necessary charger, plugs and transformer for the country you are visiting. In most countries, it is possible to obtain video cartridges easily in large towns and cities, but make sure you buy the correct format. It is usually worth buying at least a few cartridges duty-free at the start of your trip.

TIME

Most of the countries covered in this book are on Central European Time (GMT/UTC plus one hour), the same time used from Spain to Poland. Britain and Ireland are on GMT/UTC for half of the year and Greece is on East European Time (GMT plus two hours).

Clocks are advanced for daylight-saving time on the last Sunday in March and set back one hour on the last Sunday in October. During daylight-saving time Britain and Ireland are GMT/UTC plus one hour, Central European Time is GMT/UTC plus two hours and Greece is GMT/UTC plus three hours.

ELECTRICITY
Voltages & Cycles

Most of Europe runs on 220V, 50Hz AC. The exceptions are the UK, which has 240V, and Spain, which usually has 220V but sometimes still the old 125V, depending on the network (some houses can have both). Some old buildings and hotels in Italy (including Rome) might also have 125V. All EU countries were supposed to have been standardised at 230V by now, but like everything else in the EU, this is taking longer than anticipated.

Check the voltage and cycle (usually 50Hz) used in your home country. Most appliances that are set up for 220V will handle 240V without modifications (and vice versa); the same goes for 110V and 125V combinations. It's always preferable to adjust your appliance

to the exact voltage if you can (some modern battery chargers and radios will do this automatically). Just don't mix 110/125V with 220/240V without a transformer (which will be built into an adjustable appliance).

Several countries outside Europe (such as the USA and Canada) have 60Hz AC, which will affect the speed of electric motors even after the voltage has been adjusted to European values. CD and tape players (where motor speed is all-important) will be useless, but things like electric razors, hair dryers, irons and radios will be fine.

Plugs & Sockets

The UK and Ireland use a design with three flat pins – two for current and one for earth/grounding. Most of Continental Europe uses the 'europlug' with two round pins. Many europlugs and some sockets don't have provision for earth since most local home appliances are double-insulated; when provided, earth usually consists of two contact points along the edge, although Italy, Greece and Switzerland use a third round pin in such a way that the standard two-pin plug still fits the sockets (though not always in Italy and Switzerland).

If your plugs are of a different design, you'll need an adapter. Get one before you leave, since the adapters available in Europe usually go the other way. If you find yourself without one, however, a specialist electrical-supply shop should be able to help.

HEALTH

Travel health depends on your predeparture preparations, your daily health care while travelling and how you handle any medical problem that does develop.

Predeparture Planning

Immunisations Jabs are not really necessary for Western Europe, but they may be an entry requirement if you're coming from an infected area – yellow fever is the most likely requirement. If you're going to Europe with stopovers in Asia, Africa or South America, check with your travel agent or with the embassies of the countries you plan to visit.

There are, however, a few routine vaccinations that are recommended whether you're travelling or not, and this Health section assumes that you've had them: polio (usually administered during childhood), tetanus and diphtheria (usually administered together during childhood, with a booster shot every 10 years) and measles. See your physician or nearest health agency about these. You might also consider having an immunoglobulin or hepatitis A (Havrix) vaccine before extensive travels in southern Europe; a tetanus booster; an immunisation against hepatitis B before travelling to Malta; or a rabies (pre-exposure) vaccination.

All vaccinations should be recorded on an International Health Certificate (see that entry under Visas & Documents earlier in this chapter). Don't leave this till the last minute, as the vaccinations may have to be staggered over a period of time.

Health Insurance Make sure that you have adequate health insurance. See Travel Insurance under Visas & Documents earlier in this chapter for details.

Other Preparations Make sure you're healthy before you start travelling. If you are going on a long trip make sure your teeth are OK. If you wear glasses take a spare pair and your prescription.

If you require a particular medication take an adequate supply, as it may not be available locally. Take part of the packaging showing the generic name, rather than the brand, which will make getting replacements easier. To avoid any problems, it's a good idea to have a legible prescription or letter from your doctor to show that you legally use the medication.

Basic Rules
Food Salads and fruit should be safe throughout Europe. Ice cream is usually OK, but beware if it has melted and been refrozen. Take great care with fish or shellfish (cooked mussels that haven't opened properly can be dangerous, for instance), and avoid undercooked meat.

If a place looks clean and well run, and if the vendor also looks clean and healthy, then the food is probably safe. In general, places that are packed with travellers or locals will be fine. Be careful with food that has been cooked and left to go cold.

Picking mushrooms is a favourite pastime in some parts of Europe as autumn approaches, but make sure you don't eat any

Medical Kit Check List

Following is a list of items you should consider including in your medical kit – consult your pharmacist for brands available in your country.

☐ **Aspirin or paracetamol (acetaminophen in the USA)** – for pain or fever
☐ **Antihistamine** – for allergies, eg, hay fever; to ease the itch from insect bites or stings; and to prevent motion sickness
☐ **Cold and flu tablets, throat lozenges and nasal decongestant**
☐ **Multivitamins** – consider for long trips, when dietary vitamin intake may be inadequate
☐ **Antibiotics** – consider including these if you're travelling well off the beaten track; see your doctor, as they must be prescribed, and carry the prescription with you
☐ **Loperamide or diphenoxylate** –'blockers' for diarrhoea
☐ **Prochlorperazine or metaclopramide** – for nausea and vomiting
☐ **Rehydration mixture** – to prevent dehydration, which may occur, for example, during bouts of diarrhoea; particularly important when travelling with children
☐ **Insect repellent, sunscreen, lip balm and eye drops**
☐ **Calamine lotion, sting relief spray or aloe vera** – to ease irritation from sunburn and insect bites or stings
☐ **Antifungal cream or powder** – for fungal skin infections and thrush
☐ **Antiseptic (such as povidone-iodine)** – for cuts and grazes
☐ **Bandages, Band-Aids (plasters) and other wound dressings**
☐ **Water purification tablets or iodine**
☐ **Scissors, tweezers and a thermometer** – note that mercury thermometers are prohibited by airlines

that haven't been positively identified as safe. Many cities and towns set up inspection tables at markets or at entrances to national parks to separate the good from the deadly.

Water Tap water is almost always safe to drink in Europe, but be wary of natural water unless you can be sure that there are no people or cattle upstream; run-off from fertilised fields is also a concern. If you are planning extended hikes where you have to rely on natural water, it may be useful to know about water purification.

The simplest way of purifying water is to boil it thoroughly. Vigorous boiling should be satisfactory; however, at high altitude water boils at a lower temperature, so germs are less likely to be killed. Boil it for longer in these environments.

Simple filtering will not remove all dangerous organisms, so if you cannot boil water it should be treated chemically. Chlorine tablets will kill many pathogens, but not some parasites like giardia and amoebic cysts. Iodine is more effective in purifying water and is available in tablet form. Follow the directions carefully and remember that too much iodine can be harmful.

Medical Problems & Treatment

Local pharmacies or neighbourhood medical centres are good places to visit if you have a small medical problem and can explain what the problem is. Hospital casualty wards will help if it's more serious. Major hospitals and emergency numbers are mentioned in the various country chapters of this book and sometimes indicated on the maps. Tourist offices and hotels can put you on to a doctor or dentist, and your embassy or consulate will probably know one who speaks your language.

Environmental Hazards

Altitude Sickness Lack of oxygen at high altitudes (over 2500m) affects most people to some extent. The effect may be mild or severe and occurs because less oxygen reaches the muscles and the brain, requiring the heart and lungs to compensate by working harder. Symptoms of Acute Mountain Sickness (AMS) usually develop during the first 24 hours at high altitude but may be delayed up to three weeks. Mild symptoms include headache, lethargy, dizziness, difficulty sleeping and loss of appetite. AMS may become more severe without warning and can be fatal. Severe symptoms include breathlessness, a dry, irritating cough (which may progress to the production of pink, frothy sputum), severe headache, lack of coordination and balance, confusion, irrational behaviour, vomiting, drowsiness and unconsciousness. There is no

hard-and-fast rule as to what is too high; AMS has been fatal at 3000m, although 3500m to 4500m is the usual range.

Treat mild symptoms by resting at the same altitude until recovery, usually a day or two. Paracetamol or aspirin can be taken for headaches. If symptoms persist or become worse, however, immediate descent is necessary; even 500m can help. Drug treatments should never be used to avoid descent or to enable further ascent.

Heat Exhaustion Dehydration and salt deficiency can cause heat exhaustion. Take time to acclimatise to high temperatures, drink sufficient liquids and do not do anything too physically demanding.

Salt deficiency is characterised by fatigue, lethargy, headaches, giddiness and muscle cramps; salt tablets may help, but adding extra salt to your food is better.

Heatstroke This serious and occasionally fatal condition can occur if the body's heat-regulating mechanism breaks down and the body temperature rises to dangerous levels. Long, continuous periods of exposure to high temperatures and insufficient fluids can leave you vulnerable to heatstroke.

The symptoms are feeling unwell, not sweating very much (or at all) and a high body temperature (39° to 41°C or 102° to 106°F). Where sweating has ceased, the skin becomes flushed and red. Severe, throbbing headaches and lack of coordination will also occur, and the sufferer may be confused or aggressive. Eventually the victim will become delirious or convulse. Hospitalisation is essential, but in the interim get victims out of the sun, remove their clothing, cover them with a wet sheet or towel and then fan continually. Give fluids if they are conscious.

Hypothermia Too much cold can be just as dangerous as too much heat. Be prepared for cold, wet or windy conditions even if you're just out walking or hitching.

Hypothermia occurs when the body loses heat faster than it can produce it and the core temperature of the body falls. It is surprisingly easy to progress from very cold to dangerously cold due to a combination of wind, wet clothing, fatigue and hunger, even if the air temperature is above freezing. It is best to dress in layers; silk, wool and some of the new artificial fibres are all good insulating materials. A hat is important, as a lot of heat is lost through the head. A strong, waterproof outer layer (and a 'space' blanket for emergencies) is essential. Carry basic supplies, including food containing simple sugars to generate heat quickly and fluid to drink.

Symptoms of hypothermia are exhaustion, numb skin (particularly toes and fingers), shivering, slurred speech, irrational or violent behaviour, lethargy, stumbling, dizzy spells, muscle cramps and violent bursts of energy. Irrationality may take the form of sufferers claiming they are warm and trying to take off their clothes.

To treat mild hypothermia, first get the person out of the wind and/or rain, remove their clothing if it's wet and replace it with dry, warm clothing. Give them hot liquids – not alcohol – and some high-kilojoule, easily digestible food. Do not rub victims; instead, allow them to slowly warm themselves. This should be enough to treat the early stages of hypothermia. The early recognition and treatment of mild hypothermia is the only way to prevent severe hypothermia, which is a critical condition.

Jet Lag Jet lag is experienced when a person travels by air across more than three time zones (each time zone usually represents a one-hour time difference). It occurs because many of the functions of the human body (such as temperature, pulse rate and emptying of the bladder and bowels) are regulated by internal 24-hour cycles. When we travel long distances rapidly, our bodies take time to adjust to the 'new time' of our destination, and we may experience fatigue, disorientation, insomnia, anxiety, impaired concentration and loss of appetite. These effects will usually be gone within three days of arrival, but to minimise the impact of jet lag:

- Rest for a couple of days prior to departure.
- Try to select flight schedules that minimise sleep deprivation; arriving late in the day means you can go to sleep soon after you arrive. For very long flights, try to organise a stopover.
- Avoid excessive eating (which bloats the stomach) and alcohol (which causes dehydration) during the flight. Instead, drink plenty of noncarbonated, nonalcoholic drinks such as fruit juice or water.

- Avoid smoking.
- Make yourself comfortable by wearing loose-fitting clothes and perhaps bringing an eye mask and ear plugs to help you sleep.
- Try to sleep at the appropriate time for the time zone you are travelling to.

Motion Sickness Eating lightly before and during a trip will reduce the chances of motion sickness. If you are prone to motion sickness try to find a place that minimises movement – near the wing on aircraft, close to midships on boats, near the centre on buses. Fresh air usually helps; reading and cigarette smoke don't. Commercial motion-sickness preparations, which can cause drowsiness, have to be taken before the trip commences. Ginger (available in capsule form) and peppermint (including mint-flavoured sweets) are natural preventatives.

Prickly Heat Prickly heat is an itchy rash caused by excessive perspiration trapped under the skin. It usually strikes people who have just arrived in a hot climate. Keeping cool, bathing often, drying the skin and using a mild talcum or prickly heat powder or resorting to air-conditioning may help.

Sunburn In the tropics, the desert or at high altitude you can get sunburnt surprisingly quickly, even through cloud. Use a sunscreen, a hat, and a barrier cream for your nose and lips. Calamine lotion or a commercial after-sun preparation are good for mild sunburn. Protect your eyes with good quality sunglasses, particularly if you will be near water, sand or snow.

Infectious Diseases

Diarrhoea Simple things like a change of water, food or climate can all cause a mild bout of diarrhoea, but a few rushed toilet trips with no other symptoms is not indicative of a major problem.

Dehydration is the main danger with any diarrhoea, particularly in children or the elderly as dehydration can occur quite quickly. Under all circumstances, fluid replacement is the most important thing to remember. Weak black tea with a little sugar, soda water, or soft drinks allowed to go flat and diluted 50% with clean water are all good. With severe diarrhoea a rehydrating solution is preferable to replace minerals and salts lost. Commercially available oral rehydration salts (ORS) are very useful; add them to boiled or bottled water. In an emergency you can make up a solution of six teaspoons of sugar and half a teaspoon of salt to a litre of boiled or bottled water. You need to drink at least the same volume of fluid that you are losing in bowel movements and vomiting. Urine is the best guide to the adequacy of replacement – if you have small amounts of concentrated urine, you need to drink more. Keep drinking small amounts often. Stick to a bland diet as you recover.

Lomotil or Imodium can be used to bring relief from the symptoms, but they do not actually cure the problem. Only use these drugs if you do not have access to toilets (eg, if you *must* travel). For children under 12 years Lomotil and Imodium are not recommended. Do not use these drugs if the person has a high fever or is severely dehydrated.

Viral Gastroenteritis This is caused not by bacteria but, as the name suggests, by a virus. It is characterised by stomach cramps, diarrhoea and sometimes by vomiting and/or a slight fever. All you can do is rest and drink lots of fluids.

Fungal Infections Fungal infections occur more commonly in hot weather and are usually found on the scalp, between the toes (athlete's foot) or fingers, in the groin and on the body (ringworm). You get ringworm (which is a fungal infection, not a worm) from infected animals or other people. Moisture encourages these infections.

To prevent fungal infections wear loose, comfortable clothes, avoid artificial fibres, wash frequently and dry yourself carefully. If you do get an infection, wash the infected area at least daily with a disinfectant or medicated soap and water, and rinse and dry well. Apply an antifungal cream or powder like tolnaftate. Try to expose the infected area to air or sunlight as much as possible and wash all towels and underwear in hot water, change them often and let them dry in the sun.

Hepatitis Hepatitis is a general term for inflammation of the liver. It is a common disease worldwide. The symptoms are fever, chills, headache, fatigue, feelings of weakness, and aches and pains, followed by loss of appetite, nausea, vomiting, abdominal pain, dark urine, light-coloured faeces, jaundiced (yellow) skin and the whites of the eyes may turn yellow. **Hepatitis A** is transmitted by contaminated food and drinking water. You should seek medical advice, but there is not much you can do apart from resting, drinking lots of fluids, eating lightly and avoiding fatty foods. People who have had hepatitis should avoid alcohol for some time after the illness, as the liver needs time to recover.

There are almost 300 million chronic carriers of **hepatitis B** in the world. It is spread through contact with infected blood, blood products or body fluids, for example through sexual contact, unsterilised needles and blood transfusions, or contact with blood via small breaks in the skin. Other risk situations include having a shave, getting a tattoo or having your body pierced with contaminated equipment. The symptoms of type B may be more severe and may lead to long-term problems. Hepatitis C and D are spread in the same way as hepatitis B and can also lead to long-term complications.

HIV & AIDS Infection with the human immunodeficiency virus (HIV) may lead to acquired immune deficiency syndrome (AIDS), which is a fatal disease. Any exposure to blood, blood products or body fluids may put the individual at risk. The disease is often transmitted through sexual contact or dirty needles – vaccinations, acupuncture, tattooing and body piercing can be potentially as dangerous as intravenous drug use. HIV/AIDS can also be spread through infected blood transfusions; some developing countries cannot afford to screen blood used for transfusions.

Sexually Transmitted Diseases HIV/AIDS and hepatitis B can be transmitted through sexual contact – see the relevant sections earlier for more details. Other STDs include gonorrhoea, herpes and syphilis; sores, blisters or rashes around the genitals and discharges or pain when urinating are common symptoms. In some STDs, such as wart virus or chlamydia, symptoms may be less marked or not observed at all, especially in women. Chlamydia infection can cause infertility in men and women before any symptoms have been noticed. Syphilis symptoms eventually disappear completely but the disease continues and can cause severe problems in later years. While abstinence from sexual contact is the only 100% effective prevention, using condoms is also effective. The treatment of gonorrhoea and syphilis is with antibiotics. The different sexually transmitted diseases each require specific antibiotics.

Cuts, Bites & Stings

Cuts & Scratches Wash well and treat any cut with an antiseptic, eg, povidone-iodine. Where possible avoid bandages and Band-Aids, which can keep wounds wet.

Bedbugs & Lice Bedbugs live in various places, but particularly in dirty mattresses and bedding, evidenced by spots of blood on bedclothes or on the wall. Bedbugs leave itchy bites in neat rows. Calamine lotion or a sting relief spray may help.

All lice cause itching and discomfort. They make themselves at home in your hair (head lice), your clothing (body lice) or in your pubic hair (crabs). You catch lice through direct contact with infected people or by sharing combs, clothing and the like. Powder or shampoo treatment will kill the lice and infected clothing should then be washed in very hot, soapy water and left in the sun to dry.

Bites & Stings Bee and wasp stings are usually painful rather than dangerous. However, in people who are allergic to them severe breathing difficulties may occur and require urgent medical care. Calamine lotion or a sting relief spray will give relief and ice packs will reduce the pain and swelling.

Mosquitoes can be a nuisance in southern Europe, but can almost drive you insane during the summer months in northern Europe, particularly around lakes and rivers. They also cause sleepless nights in a swampy country like the Netherlands or on the Camargue delta in southern France. Fortunately, mosquito-borne diseases like malaria are for the most part unknown in Western Europe. Most people get used to mosquito bites after a few days as their bodies adjust, and the itching and swelling will become less severe. An antihistamine cream may help alleviate the symptoms. For some people, a daily dose of vitamin B will keep mosquitoes at bay.

Midges – small, blood-sucking flies related to mosquitoes – are a major problem in some parts of Europe (eg, Scotland and parts of England) during summer.

Ticks You should always check all over your body if you have been walking through a potentially tick-infested area as ticks can cause skin infections and other more serious diseases. If a tick is found attached, press down around the tick's head with tweezers, grab the head and gently pull upwards. Avoid pulling the rear of the body as this may squeeze the tick's gut contents through the attached mouth parts into the skin, increasing the risk of infection and disease. Smearing chemicals on the tick will not make it let go and is not recommended.

Lyme disease is a tick-transmitted infection that may be acquired in parts of southern Europe. The illness usually begins with a spreading rash at the site of the tick bite and is accompanied by fever, headache, extreme fatigue, aching joints and muscles, and mild neck stiffness. If untreated, these symptoms usually resolve over several weeks but over subsequent weeks or months disorders of the nervous system, heart and joints may develop. Treatment works best early in the illness. Medical help should be sought.

Another tick that can bring on more than just an itch is the forest tick, which burrows under the skin, causing inflammation and even encephalitis. It has become a common problem in parts of Central and Eastern Europe, especially eastern Austria, Germany, Hungary and the Czech Republic. You might also consider getting an FSME (meningoencephalitis) vaccination if you plan to do extensive hiking and camping between May and September.

Rabies Rabies is a fatal viral infection but is rare in most countries in Western Europe. Rabies is nonexistent in the UK, Ireland, Portugal, Monaco and Malta. Many animals can be infected (such as dogs, cats, foxes and bats) and it is their saliva which is infectious. Any bite, scratch or even lick from a warm-blooded, furry animal should be cleaned immediately and thoroughly. Scrub with soap and running water, and then apply alcohol or iodine solution. Medical help should be sought promptly to receive a course of injections to prevent the onset of symptoms and death.

Snakes To minimise your chances of being bitten always wear boots, socks and long trousers when walking through undergrowth where snakes may be present. Don't put your hands into holes and crevices, and be careful when collecting firewood.

Snake bites do not cause instantaneous death, and antivenenes are usually available. Immediately wrap the bitten limb tightly, as you would for a sprained ankle, and then attach a splint to immobilise it. Keep the victim still and seek medical help, if possible with the dead snake for identification. Don't attempt to catch the snake if there is a possibility of being bitten again. Tourniquets and sucking out the poison are now comprehensively discredited.

Women's Health

Gynaecological Problems Antibiotic use, synthetic underwear, sweating and contraceptive pills can lead to fungal vaginal infections, especially when travelling in hot climates. Fungal infections are characterised by a rash, itch and discharge and can be treated with a vinegar or lemon-juice douche, or with yogurt. Nystatin, miconazole or clotrimazole pessaries or vaginal cream are the usual treatment. Maintaining good personal hygiene and wearing loose-fitting clothes and cotton underwear may help prevent these infections.

Sexually transmitted diseases are a major cause of vaginal problems. Symptoms include a smelly discharge, painful intercourse and sometimes a burning sensation when urinating. Medical attention should be sought and male sexual partners must also be treated. For more details see the section on Sexually Transmitted Diseases earlier. Besides abstinence, the best thing is to practise safer sex using condoms.

WOMEN TRAVELLERS

Women are more likely to attract unwanted attention in rural Spain and southern Italy, particularly in Sicily, where many men still think that staring suavely at or calling out to a passing woman is to pay her a flattering compliment. This behaviour is not confined to these areas, however, and the potential is, sadly, everywhere. Slightly conservative dress can help to deter lascivious gazes and wolf whistles, and dark sunglasses may prevent unwanted eye contact. Marriage is highly respected in southern Europe, and a wedding ring (on the left ring finger) sometimes helps, along with talk about 'my husband'. Hitchhiking alone in these southern areas is asking for trouble.

GAY & LESBIAN TRAVELLERS

This book lists contact addresses and gay and lesbian venues in the individual country chapters; look in the Facts for the Visitor and Entertainment sections.

The *Spartacus International Gay Guide* (Bruno Gmünder, US$39.95) is a good male-only international directory of gay entertainment venues in Europe and elsewhere. It's best when used in conjunction with listings in local gay papers, usually distributed for free at gay bars and clubs. For lesbians, *Women's Travel in Your Pocket* (Ferrari Publications, UK£8.99) is a good international guide.

DISABLED TRAVELLERS

If you have a physical disability, get in touch with your national support organisation (preferably the 'travel officer' if there is one) and ask about the countries you plan to visit. They often have complete libraries devoted to travel, and they can put you in touch with travel agents who specialise in tours for the disabled.

The British-based Royal Association for Disability & Rehabilitation (RADAR) publishes a useful guide entitled *European Holidays & Travel Abroad: A Guide for Disabled People* (published in even-numbered years; UK£5), which gives a good overview of facilities available to disabled travellers in Western Europe, and one to places farther afield called *Long-Haul Holidays* (in odd-numbered years). *Holidays in the British Isles: A Guide for Disabled Travellers* (£7.50) also includes Ireland. Contact RADAR (☎ 020-7250 3222, fax 7250 0212) at 12 City Forum, 250 City Rd, London EC1V 8AF.

SENIOR TRAVELLERS

Senior citizens are entitled to many discounts in Europe on things like public transport, museum admission fees etc, provided they show proof of their age. In some cases they might need a special pass. The minimum qualifying age is generally 60 or 65 for men and slightly younger for women.

In your home country, a lower age may already entitle you to all sorts of interesting travel packages and discounts (on car hire, for instance) through organisations and travel agents that cater for senior travellers. Start hunting at your local senior citizens advice bureau. European residents over 60 are eligible for the Railplus Card; see Cheap Tickets under Train in the Getting Around chapter for details.

TRAVEL WITH CHILDREN

Successful travel with young children requires planning and effort. Don't try to overdo things; even for adults, packing too much into the time available can cause problems. And make sure the activities include the kids as well – balance that day at the Louvre with a day at Disneyland Paris. Include children in the trip planning; if they've helped to work out where you will be going, they will be much more interested when they get there. Lonely Planet's *Travel with Children* by Maureen Wheeler is a good source of information.

Most car-rental firms in Europe have children's safety seats for hire at a nominal cost, but it's essential that you book them in advance. The same goes for highchairs and cots (cribs); they're standard in most restaurants and hotels, but numbers are limited. The choice of baby food, formulas, soy and cow's milk, disposable nappies (diapers) and the like is as great in the supermarkets of most Western European countries as it is at home, but the opening hours might be different. Run out of nappies on Saturday afternoon and you're in for a messy weekend.

DANGERS & ANNOYANCES

On the whole, you should experience few problems travelling in Western Europe – even alone – as the region is well developed and relatively safe. But do exercise common sense. Whatever you do, don't leave friends and relatives back home worrying about how to get in touch with you in case of emergency. Work out a list of places where they can contact you or, best of all, phone home now and then or email.

Theft

Theft is definitely a problem in Europe, and nowadays you also have to be wary of other travellers. The most important things to guard are your passport, papers, tickets and money – in that order. It's always best to carry these next to your skin or in a sturdy leather pouch on your belt. Train station lockers or luggage storage counters are useful places to store your bags (but *never* valuables) while you get your bearings in a new town. Be very suspicious about people who offer to help you operate your locker. Carry your own padlock for hostel lockers.

You can lessen the risks further by being careful of snatch thieves. Cameras or shoulder bags are an open invitation for these people, who sometimes operate from motorcycles or scooters and expertly slash the strap before you have a chance to react. A small daypack is better, but watch your rear. Be very careful at cafes and bars; loop the strap around your leg while seated.

Pickpockets are most active in dense crowds, especially in busy train stations and on public transport during peak hours. A common ploy is for one person to distract you while another zips through your pockets. Beware of gangs of kids – dishevelled-looking *and* well dressed – waving newspapers and demanding attention. In the blink of an eye, a wallet or camera can go missing.

Be careful even in hotels; don't leave valuables lying around in your room. Parked cars containing luggage and other bags are prime targets for petty criminals in most cities.

Drugs

Always treat drugs with a great deal of caution. There are a lot of drugs available in Western Europe, sometimes quite openly (eg, in the Netherlands), but that doesn't mean they're legal. Even a little harmless hashish can cause a great deal of trouble in some places.

Don't even think about bringing drugs home with you either. With what they may consider 'suspect' stamps in your passport (eg, Amsterdam's Schiphol airport), energetic customs officials could well decide to take a closer look.

ACTIVITIES

Europe offers countless opportunities to indulge in more active pursuits than sightseeing. The varied geography and climate supports the full range of outdoor pursuits: windsurfing, skiing, fishing, trekking, cycling and mountaineering. For more local information, see the individual country chapters.

Cycling

Along with hiking, cycling is the best way to really get close to the scenery and the people, keeping yourself fit in the process. It's also a good way to get around many cities and towns.

Much of Western Europe is ideally suited to cycling. In the north-west, the flat terrain ensures that bicycles are a popular form of everyday transport, though rampant headwinds often spoil the fun. In the rest of the region, hills and mountains can make for heavy going, but this is offset by the dense concentration of things to see. Cycling is a great way to explore many of the Mediterranean islands, though the heat can get to you after a while (make sure you drink enough fluids).

Some popular cycling areas among holiday-makers include the Belgian Ardennes, the west of Ireland, the upper reaches of the Danube in southern Germany, the coasts of Sardinia and Apulia, anywhere in the Alps (for those fit enough) and the south of France.

If you are arriving from outside Europe, you can often bring your own bicycle along on the plane (see Bicycle in the Getting Around chapter). Alternatively, this book lists many places where you can hire one (make sure it has plenty of gears if you plan anything serious), though apart from in Ireland they might take a dim view of rentals lasting more than a week.

See the introductory Getting Around chapter for more information on bicycle touring, and the Getting Around sections in individual country chapters for rental agencies and tips on places to go to.

Skiing

In winter, Europeans flock to the hundreds of resorts located in the Alps and Pyrenees for downhill skiing and snowboarding, though cross-country is very popular in some areas.

A skiing holiday can be an expensive one due to the costs of ski lifts, accommodation and the inevitable après-ski drinking sessions. Equipment hire (or even purchase), on the other hand, can be relatively cheap if you follow the tips in this book, and the hassle of bringing your own skis may not be worth it. As a rule, a skiing holiday in Europe will work out twice as expensive as a summer holiday of the same length. Cross-country skiing costs less than downhill since you don't rely as much on ski lifts.

The skiing season generally lasts from early December to late March, though at higher altitudes it may extend an extra month either way. Snow conditions can vary greatly from one year to the next and from region to region, but January and February tend to be the best (and busiest) months.

Ski resorts in the French and Swiss Alps offer great skiing and facilities, but are also the most expensive. Expect high prices, too, in the German Alps, though Germany has cheaper (but far less spectacular) options in the Black Forest and Harz Mountains. Austria is generally slightly cheaper than France and Switzerland (especially in Carinthia). Prices in the Italian Alps are similar to Austria (with some upmarket exceptions like Cortina d'Ampezzo), and can be relatively cheap, given the right package. Cheaper still is the skiing in Slovenia's Julian Alps, just over the border from Austria and Italy, which offer some attractive deals.

Possibly the cheapest skiing in Western Europe is to be found in the Pyrenees in Spain and Andorra, and in the Sierra Nevada range in the south of Spain. Greece and Scotland also boast growing ski industries – good value in Greece but disappointing in Scotland. See the individual country chapters for more information.

Hiking

Keen hikers can spend a lifetime exploring Europe's many exciting trails. Probably the most spectacular are to be found in the Alps and Italian Dolomites, which are criss-crossed with well-marked trails; food and accommodation are available along the way in season. The equally sensational Pyrenees are less developed, which can add to the experience as you often rely on remote mountain villages for rest and sustenance. Hiking areas that are less well known but nothing short of stunning are Corsica, Sardinia and northern Portugal. The Picos de Europa range in Spain is also rewarding.

The Ramblers' Association (☎ 020-7339 8500) is a London charity that promotes long-distance walking in the UK and can help with maps and information. The British-based Ramblers Holidays (☎ 01707-331133) in Hertfordshire offers hiking-oriented trips in Europe and elsewhere.

Every country in Europe has national parks and other interesting areas that may qualify as a trekker's paradise, depending on your preferences. Guided treks are often available for those who aren't sure about their physical abilities or who simply don't know what to look for. Read the Hiking information in the individual country chapters in this book and take your pick.

Windsurfing & Surfing

After swimming and fishing, windsurfing could well be the most popular of the many water sports on offer in Europe. It's easy to rent sailboards in many tourist centres, and courses are usually available for beginners.

Believe it or not, you can also go surfing in Europe. Forget the shallow North Sea and Mediterranean, and the calm Baltic, but there can be excellent surf, and an accompanying surfer scene, in south-west England and west Scotland (wetsuit advisable!), along Ireland's west coast, the Atlantic coast of France and Portugal, and along the north and south-west coasts of Spain.

Boating

Europe's many lakes, rivers and diverse coastlines offer a variety of boating options unmatched anywhere in the world. You can canoe in Finland, raft down rapids in Slovenia, charter a yacht in the Aegean, hire a catamaran in the Netherlands, row on a peaceful Alpine lake, join a Danube River cruise from Amsterdam to Vienna (see the Getting Around chapter), rent a sailing boat on the Côte d'Azur or dream away on a canal boat along Britain's (or Ireland's or France's) extraordinary canal network – the possibilities are endless. The country chapters have more details.

COURSES

If your interests are more cerebral, you can enrol in courses in Western Europe on anything from language to alternative medicine. Language courses are available to foreigners through universities or private schools, and are justifiably popular since the best way to learn a language is in the country where it's spoken. But you can also take courses in art, literature, architecture, drama, music, cooking, alternative energy, photography and organic farming, among other subjects.

The individual country chapters in this book give pointers on where to start looking. In general, the best sources of information are the cultural institutes maintained by many European countries around the world; failing that, try their national tourist offices or embassies. Student exchange organisations, student travel agencies and organisations such as the YMCA/YWCA and Hostelling International (HI) can also put you on the right track. Ask about special holiday packages that include a course.

WORK

European countries aren't keen on handing out jobs to foreigners when unemployment rates are what they are in some areas. Officially, an EU citizen is allowed to work in any other EU country, but the paperwork isn't always straightforward for long-term employment. Other country/nationality combinations require special work permits that can be almost impossible to arrange, especially for temporary work. That doesn't prevent enterprising travellers from topping up their funds occasionally by working in the hotel or restaurant trades at beach or ski resorts or teaching a little English, and they don't always have to do this illegally either.

The UK, for example, issues special 'working holiday' visas to Commonwealth citizens aged between 17 and 27, valid for two years. Your national student exchange organisation may be able to arrange temporary work permits to several countries through special programs. For more details on working as a foreigner, see Work in the Facts for the Visitor sections of the individual country chapters.

If you have a parent or grandparent who was born in an EU country, you may have certain rights you never knew about. Get in touch with that country's embassy and ask about dual citizenship and work permits – if you go for citizenship, also ask about any obligations, such as military service and residency. Ireland is particularly easy-going about granting citizenship to people with an Irish parent or grandparent, and with an Irish passport, the EU is your oyster. Be aware that your home country may not recognise dual citizenship.

If you do find a temporary job, the pay may be less than that offered to local people. The one big exception is teaching English, but these jobs are hard to come by – at least officially. Other typical tourist jobs (picking grapes in France, washing dishes in Alpine resorts) often come with board and lodging, and the pay is little more than pocket money, but you'll have a good time partying with other travellers.

Work Your Way Around the World by Susan Griffith gives good, practical advice on a wide range of issues. Its publisher, Vacation Work, has many other useful titles, including *Summer Jobs Abroad*, edited by David Woodworth. Check the Web site at www .vacationwork.co.uk. *Working Holidays*, published by the Central Bureau for Educational Visits & Exchanges in London, is another good source.

If you play an instrument or have other artistic talents, you could try working the streets. As every Peruvian pipe player (and his fifth cousin) knows, busking is fairly common in major Western European cities like Amsterdam and Paris, but is illegal in some parts of Switzerland and Austria. In Belgium and Germany it has been more or less tolerated in the past but crackdowns are not unknown. Most other countries require municipal permits that can be hard to obtain. Talk to other street artists before you start.

Selling goods on the street is generally frowned upon and can be tantamount to vagrancy, apart from at flea markets. It's also a hard way to make money if you're not selling something special. Most countries require permits for this sort of thing. It's fairly common, though officially illegal, in the UK, Germany and Spain.

ACCOMMODATION

The cheapest places to stay in Europe are camping grounds, followed by hostels and accommodation in student dormitories. Cheap hotels are virtually unknown in the northern half of Europe, but guesthouses, pensions, private rooms and B&Bs often offer good value. Self-catering flats and cottages are worth considering with a group, especially if you plan to stay somewhere for a while.

See the Facts for the Visitor sections in the individual country chapters for an overview of the local accommodation options. During peak holiday periods accommodation can be hard to find, and unless you're camping it's advisable to book ahead. Even camping grounds can fill up, especially in or around big cities.

Reservations

Cheap hotels in popular destinations (eg, Paris, London, Rome) – especially the well-run ones smack in the middle of desirable or central neighbourhoods – fill up quickly. It's a good idea to make reservations as many weeks ahead as possible, at least for the first night or two. A three-minute international phone call to reserve a room (followed, if necessary, by written confirmation and/or deposit) is a lot cheaper and less frustrating than wasting your first day in a city looking for a place to stay.

If you arrive in a country by air and without a reservation, there is often an airport accommodation booking desk, although it rarely covers the lower strata of hotels. Tourist offices often have extensive accommodation lists, and the more helpful ones will go out of their way to find you something suitable. In most countries the fee for this service is very low and, if accommodation is tight, it can save you a lot of running around. This is also an easy way to get around any language problems. Agencies offering private rooms can be good value. Staying with a local family doesn't always mean that you'll lack privacy, but you'll probably have less freedom than in a hotel.

Sometimes people will come up to you on the street offering a private room or a hostel bed. This can be good or bad, there's no hard-and-fast rule – just make sure it's not way out in a dingy suburb somewhere and that you negotiate a clear price. As always, be careful when someone offers to carry your luggage; they might carry it away altogether.

Camping

Camping is immensely popular in Western Europe (especially among Germans and the Dutch) and provides the cheapest accommodation. There's usually a charge per tent or site, per person and per vehicle. National tourist offices should have booklets or brochures listing camping grounds all over their country. See Visas & Documents earlier in this chapter for information on the Camping Card International.

In large cities, most camp sites will be some distance from the centre. For this reason, camping is most popular with people who have their own transport. If you're on foot, the money you save by camping can quickly be eaten up by the cost of commuting to/from a town centre. You may also need a tent, sleeping bag and cooking equipment, though not always: many camping grounds hire bungalows or cottages accommodating from two to eight people.

Camping other than at designated camping grounds is difficult because the population density of Western Europe makes it hard to find a suitable spot to pitch a tent away from prying eyes. It is also illegal without permission from the local authorities (the police or local council office) or from the owner of the land (don't be shy about asking – you may be pleasantly surprised by the response).

In some countries, such as Austria, the UK, France and Germany, free camping is illegal on all but private land, and in Greece it's illegal altogether. This doesn't prevent hikers from occasionally pitching their tent for the night, and they'll usually get away with it if they have only a small tent, are discreet, stay only one or two nights, take the tent down during the day and do not light a campfire or leave rubbish. At worst, they'll be woken up by the police and asked to move on.

Hostels

Hostels offer the cheapest (secure) roof over your head in Europe, and you don't have to be a youngster to use them. Most hostels are part of the national youth hostel association (YHA), which is affiliated with what was formerly called the IYHF (International Youth Hostel Federation) and has been renamed Hostelling International (HI) in order to attract a wider clientele and move away from the emphasis on 'youth'. The situation remains slightly confused, however. Some countries, such as the USA and Canada, immediately adopted the new name, but many European countries will take a few years to change their logos. In practice it makes no difference; IYHF and HI are the same thing and the domestic YHA almost always belongs to the parent group.

There are also some privately run hostels, although it's only in Britain and Ireland (and less so in Germany) that private backpacker hostels have really taken off.

Technically, you're supposed to be a YHA or HI member to use affiliated hostels, but you can often stay by paying an extra charge and this will usually be set against future membership. Stay enough nights as a nonmember and you're automatically a member.

Bavaria, in Germany, is one of the few places with a strict age limit (27 years old) for hostelling members.

To join the HI, you can ask at any hostel or contact your local or national hostelling office. There's a very useful Web site at www.iyhf .org/index.html with links to most HI sites. The offices for English-speaking countries appear below. Otherwise, check the individual country chapters for addresses.

Australia Australian Youth Hostels Association (☎ 02-9565 1699, fax 9565 1325, @ yha@yha.org.au), Level 3, 10 Mallett St, Camperdown, NSW 2050

Canada Hostelling International Canada (☎ 613-237 7884, fax 237 7868, @ info@hostellingintl.ca), 205 Catherine St, Suite 400, Ottawa, Ont K2P 1C3

England & Wales Youth Hostels Association (☎ 01727-855215, fax 844126, @ customerservices@yha.org.uk), Trevelyan House, 8 St Stephen's Hill, St Albans, Herts AL1 2DY

Ireland An Óige (Irish Youth Hostel Association; ☎ 01-830 4555, fax 830 5808, @ mailbox@anoige.ie), 61 Mountjoy St, Dublin 7

New Zealand Youth Hostels Association of New Zealand (☎ 03-379 9970, fax 365 4476, @ info@yha.org.nz), PO Box 436, Union House, 193 Cashel St, 3rd floor, Union House, Christchurch

Northern Ireland Hostelling International Northern Ireland (☎ 0128-9031 5435, fax 9043 9699, @ info@hini.org.uk), 22-32 Donegall Rd, Belfast BT12 5JN

Scotland Scottish Youth Hostels Association (☎ 01786-891400, fax 891333, @ info@syha.org.uk), 7 Glebe Crescent, Stirling FK8 2JA

South Africa Hostelling International South Africa (☎ 021-424 2511, fax 424 4119, @ info@hisa.org.za), PO Box 4402, St George's House, 73 St George's Mall, Cape Town 8001

USA Hostelling International/American Youth Hostels (☎ 202-783 6161, fax 783 6171, @ hiayhserv@hiayh.org), 733 15th St NW, Suite 840, Washington DC 20005

At a hostel, you get a bed for the night plus use of communal facilities, which often include a kitchen where you can prepare your own meals. You are usually required to have a sleeping sheet and simply using your sleeping bag is not permitted. If you don't have your own approved sleeping sheet, you can usually hire or buy one. Hostels vary widely in character, but the growing number of travellers and the increased competition from other forms of accommodation, particularly private 'backpacker hostels', have prompted many hostels to improve their facilities and cut back on rules and regulations. Increasingly, hostels are open all day, curfews are disappearing and 'wardens' with sergeant-major mentalities are an endangered species. In some places you'll even find hostels with single and double rooms. Everywhere the trend has been towards smaller dormitories with just four to six beds.

There are many hostel guides with listings available, including HI's *Europe* (£7.50) and the England & Wales YHA's *YHA Accommodation Guide* (£2.99), as well as a couple of co-operatively produced guides to the Irish backpacker hostels. Many hostels accept reservations by phone or fax, but usually not during peak periods; they'll often book the next hostel you're heading to for a small fee. You can also book hostels through national hostel offices. Popular hostels can be heavily booked in summer and limits may even be placed on how many nights you can stay.

University Accommodation

Some university towns rent out student accommodation during holiday periods. This is very popular in France and the UK (see those chapters for more details) as universities become more accountable financially.

Accommodation will sometimes be in single rooms (more commonly in doubles or triples) and may have cooking facilities. Inquire at the college or university, at student information services or at local tourist offices.

B&Bs, Guesthouses & Hotels

There's a huge range of accommodation above the hostel level. In the UK and Ireland myriad B&Bs are the real bargains in this field, where you get a room (a bed) and breakfast in a private home. In some areas every other house will have a B&B sign out the front. In other countries similar private

accommodation – though often without breakfast – may go under the name of pension, guesthouse, *Gasthaus, Zimmer frei, chambre d'hôte* and so on. Although the majority of guesthouses are simple affairs, there are more expensive ones where you'll find en suite bathrooms and other luxuries.

Above this level are hotels, which at the bottom of the bracket may be no more expensive than B&Bs or guesthouses, while at the other extreme extend to luxury five-star properties with price tags to match. Although categorisation depends on the country, the hotels recommended in this book will generally range from no stars to one or two stars. You'll often find inexpensive hotels clustered around the bus and train station areas, which are always good places to start hunting.

Check your hotel room and the bathroom before you agree to take it, and make sure you know what it's going to cost – discounts are often available for groups or for longer stays. Ask about breakfast; sometimes it's included, but other times it may be obligatory and you'll have to pay extra for it. If the sheets don't look clean, ask to have them changed right away. Check where the fire exits are.

If you think a hotel room is too expensive, ask if there's anything cheaper; often, hotel owners may have tried to steer you into more expensive rooms. In southern Europe in particular, hotel owners may be open to a little bargaining if times are slack. In France and the UK it is common practice for business hotels (usually more than two stars) to slash their rates by up to 40% on Friday and Saturday nights when business is dead. Save your big hotel splurge for the weekend.

FOOD

Few regions in the world offer such a variety of cuisines in such a small area as Western Europe. The Facts for the Visitor sections in the individual country chapters contain details of local cuisines, and the Places to Eat sections list many suggestions.

Restaurant prices vary enormously. The cheapest places for a decent meal are often the self-service restaurants in department stores. University restaurants are dirt cheap, but the food tends to be bland and you may not be allowed in if you're not a local student. Kiosks often sell cheap snacks that can be as much a part of the national cuisine as the fancy dishes.

Self-catering – buying your ingredients at a shop or market and preparing them yourself – can be a cheap and wholesome way of eating. Even if you don't cook, a lunch on a park bench with half a loaf of fresh bread, some local cheese, salami and a tomato or two, washed down with a bottle of local wine, can be one of the recurring highlights of your trip. It also makes a nice change from restaurant food.

If you have dietary restrictions – you're a vegetarian or you keep kosher, for example – tourist organisations may be able to advise you or provide lists of suitable restaurants. We list some vegetarian and kosher restaurants in this book.

In general, vegetarians needn't worry about going hungry in Western Europe; many restaurants have one or two vegetarian options, and southern European menus in particular tend to contain many vegetable dishes and salads.

Getting There & Away

Step one of your trip is actually getting to Western Europe, and in these days of severe competition among airlines there are plenty of opportunities to find cheap tickets to a variety of gateway cities.

Forget shipping – only a handful of ships still carry passengers across the Atlantic; they don't sail often and are very expensive, even compared with full-fare air tickets. Some travellers still arrive or leave overland – the options being Africa, the Middle East and Asia via Russia on the Trans-Siberian Railway from China.

AIR

Always remember to reconfirm your onward or return bookings by the specified time – at least 72 hours before departure on international flights. Otherwise there's a real risk that you'll turn up at the airport only to find that you've missed your flight because it was rescheduled, or that you've been reclassified as a 'no show' and 'bumped' (see the Air Travel Glossary in this chapter).

Buying Tickets

An air ticket alone can gouge a great slice out of anyone's budget, but you can reduce the cost by finding discounted fares. Stiff competition has resulted in widespread discounting – good news for travellers! The only people likely to be paying full fare these days are travellers flying in 1st or business class. Passengers flying in economy can usually manage some sort of discount. But unless you buy carefully and flexibly, it is still possible to end up paying exorbitant amounts for a journey.

For long-term travel there are plenty of discount tickets which are valid for 12 months, allowing multiple stopovers with open dates. For short-term travel cheaper fares are available by travelling mid-week, staying away at least one Saturday night or taking advantage of short-lived promotional offers.

When you're looking for bargain air fares, go to a travel agent rather than directly to the airline. From time to time, airlines do have promotional fares and special offers, but generally they only sell fares at the official listed price. One exception to this rule is the ex-

Warning
The information in this chapter is particularly vulnerable to change: Prices for international travel are volatile, routes are introduced and cancelled, schedules change, special deals come and go, and rules and visa requirements are amended. Airlines and governments seem to take a perverse pleasure in making price structures and regulations as complicated as possible. You should check directly with the airline or a travel agent to make sure you understand how a fare (and ticket you may buy) works. In addition, the travel industry is highly competitive and there are many lurks and perks.

The upshot of this is that you should get opinions, quotes and advice from as many airlines and travel agents as possible before you part with your hard-earned cash. The details given in this chapter should be regarded as pointers and are not a substitute for your own careful, up-to-date research.

panding number of 'no-frills' carriers operating in the USA and north-west Europe, which mostly sell direct to travellers. Unlike the 'full service' airlines, no-frills carriers often make one-way tickets available at around half the return fare, meaning that it is easy to put together a return ticket when you fly to one place but leave from another.

The other exception is booking on the Internet. Many airlines, full-service and no-frills, offer some excellent fares to Web surfers. They may sell seats by auction or simply cut prices to reflect the reduced cost of electronic selling. Many travel agents around the world have Web sites, which can make the Internet a quick and easy way to compare prices, a good start for when you're ready to start negotiating with your favourite travel agency. Online ticket sales work well if you are doing a simple one-way or return trip on specified dates. However, online superfast fare generators are no substitute for a travel agent who knows all about special deals, has strategies for avoiding stopovers and can offer advice on everything from which airline has the best vegetarian food to the best travel insurance to bundle with your ticket.

The days when some travel agents would routinely fleece travellers by running off with their money are, happily, almost over. Paying by credit card generally offers protection, as most card issuers provide refunds if you can prove you didn't get what you paid for. Similar protection can be obtained by buying a ticket from a bonded agent, such as one covered by the Air Transport Operators Licence (ATOL) scheme in the UK. Agents who only accept cash should hand over the tickets straight away and not tell you to 'come back tomorrow'. After you've made a booking or paid your deposit, call the airline and confirm that the booking was made. It's generally not advisable to send money (even cheques) through the post unless the agent is very well established – some travellers have reported being ripped off by fly-by-night mail-order ticket agents.

You may decide to pay more than the rock-bottom fare by opting for the safety of a better known travel agent. Firms such as STA Travel, which has offices worldwide, Council Travel in the USA and usit CAMPUS (formerly Campus Travel) in the UK are not going to disappear overnight and they do offer good prices to most destinations.

If you purchase a ticket and later want to make changes to your route or get a refund, you need to contact the original travel agent. Airlines only issue refunds to the purchaser of a ticket – usually the travel agent who bought the ticket on your behalf. Many travellers change their routes halfway through their trips, so think carefully before you buy a ticket which is not easily refunded.

Student & Youth Fares Full-time students and people under 26 have access to better deals than other travellers. The better deals may not always be cheaper fares but can include more flexibility to change flights and/or routes. You have to show a document proving your date of birth or a valid International Student Identity Card (ISIC) when buying your ticket and boarding the plane. There are plenty of places around the world where nonstudents can get fake student cards, but if you get caught using a fake card you could have your ticket confiscated.

Frequent Flyers Most airlines offer frequent flyer deals that can earn you a free air ticket or other goodies. To qualify, you have to accumulate sufficient mileage with the same airline or airline alliance. Many airlines have 'blackout periods', or times when you cannot fly for free on your frequent flyer points (Christmas and Chinese New Year, for example). The worst thing about frequent flyer programs is that they tend to lock you into one airline, and that airline may not always have the cheapest fares or most convenient flight schedule.

Courier Flights Courier flights are a great bargain if you're lucky enough to find one. Air-freight companies expedite delivery of urgent items by sending them with you as your baggage allowance. You are permitted to bring along a carry-on bag, but that's all. In return, you get a steeply discounted ticket.

There are other restrictions: courier tickets are sold for a fixed date and schedule changes can be difficult to make. If you buy a return ticket, your schedule will be even more rigid. You need to clarify before you fly what restrictions apply to your ticket, and don't expect a refund once you've paid.

Booking a courier ticket takes some effort. They are not readily available and arrangements have to be made a month or more in advance. You won't find courier flights on all routes either – just on the major air routes.

Courier flights are occasionally advertised in the newspapers, or you could contact air-freight companies listed in the phone book. You may even have to go to the air-freight company to get an answer – the companies aren't always keen to give out information over the phone. Travel Unlimited (PO Box 1058, Allston, MA 02134, USA) is a monthly travel newsletter based in the USA that publishes many courier flight deals from destinations worldwide. A 12-month subscription to the newsletter costs US$25, or US$35 for readers outside the USA. Another possibility (at least for US residents) is to join the International Association of Air Travel Couriers (IAATC). The membership fee of $45 gets members a bimonthly update of air-courier offerings, access to a fax-on-demand service with daily updates of last minute specials and the bimonthly newsletter *The Shoestring Traveler*. For more information, contact

Air Travel Glossary

Cancellation Penalties If you have to cancel or change a discounted ticket, there are often heavy penalties involved; insurance can sometimes be taken out against these penalties. Some airlines impose penalties on regular tickets as well, particularly against 'no-show' passengers.

Courier Fares Businesses often need to send urgent documents or freight securely and quickly. Courier companies hire people to accompany the package through customs and, in return, offer a discount ticket which is sometimes a phenomenal bargain. However, you may have to surrender all your baggage allowance and take only carry-on luggage.

Full Fares Airlines traditionally offer 1st class (coded F), business class (coded J) and economy class (coded Y) tickets. These days there are so many promotional and discounted fares available that few passengers pay full economy fare.

Lost Tickets If you lose your airline ticket an airline will usually treat it like a travellers cheque and, after inquiries, issue you with another one. Legally, however, an airline is entitled to treat it like cash and if you lose it then it's gone forever. Take good care of your tickets.

Onward Tickets An entry requirement for many countries is that you have a ticket out of the country. If you're unsure of your next move, the easiest solution is to buy the cheapest onward ticket to a neighbouring country or a ticket from a reliable airline which can later be refunded if you do not use it.

Open-Jaw Tickets These are return tickets where you fly out to one place but return from another. If available, this can save you backtracking to your arrival point.

Overbooking Since every flight has some passengers who fail to show up, airlines often book more passengers than they have seats. Usually excess passengers make up for the no-shows, but occasionally somebody gets 'bumped' onto the next available flight. Guess who it is most likely to be? The passengers who check in late.

Promotional Fares These are officially discounted fares, available from travel agencies or direct from the airline.

Reconfirmation If you don't reconfirm your flight at least 72 hours prior to departure, the airline may delete your name from the passenger list. Ring to find out if your airline requires reconfirmation.

Restrictions Discounted tickets often have various restrictions on them – such as needing to be paid for in advance and incurring a penalty to be altered. Others are restrictions on the minimum and maximum period you must be away.

Round-the-World Tickets RTW tickets give you a limited period (usually a year) in which to circumnavigate the globe. You can go anywhere the carrying airlines go, as long as you don't backtrack. The number of stopovers or total number of separate flights is decided before you set off and they usually cost a bit more than a basic return flight.

Transferred Tickets Airline tickets cannot be transferred from one person to another. Travellers sometimes try to sell the return half of their ticket, but officials can ask you to prove that you are the person named on the ticket. On an international flight tickets are compared with passports.

Travel Periods Ticket prices vary with the time of year. There is a low (off-peak) season and a high (peak) season, and often a low-shoulder season and a high-shoulder season as well. Usually the fare depends on your outward flight – if you depart in the high season and return in the low season, you pay the high-season fare.

IAATC (☎ 561-582-8320) or visit its Web site, www.courier.org. However, be aware that joining this organisation does not guarantee that you'll get a courier flight.

Second-Hand Tickets You'll occasionally see advertisements on youth hostel bulletin boards and newspapers for 'second-hand tickets'. That is, somebody purchased a return ticket or a ticket with multiple stopovers and now wants to sell the unused portion of the ticket. Unfortunately, these tickets, if used for international travel, are usually worthless, as the name on the ticket must match the name on the passport of the person checking in. Some people reason that the seller of the ticket can check you in with his or her passport, and then give you the boarding pass – wrong again! Usually the immigration people want to see your boarding pass, and if it doesn't match the name in your passport, then you won't be able to board your flight.

Travellers with Special Needs
Most international airlines can cater to people with special needs – travellers with disabilities, people with young children and even children travelling alone.

Travellers with special dietary preferences (vegetarian, kosher etc) can request appropriate meals with advance notice. If you are travelling in a wheelchair, most international airports can provide an escort from check-in desk to plane where needed, and ramps, lifts, toilets and phones are generally available.

Airlines usually allow babies up to two years of age to fly for 10% of the adult fare, although a few may allow them free of charge. Reputable international airlines usually provide nappies (diapers), tissues, talcum and all the other paraphernalia needed to keep babies clean, dry and half-happy. For children between the ages of two and 12, the fare on international flights is usually 50% of the regular fare or 67% of a discounted fare.

The USA
Discount travel agents in the USA are known as consolidators. San Francisco is the ticket consolidator capital of America, although some good deals can be found in Los Angeles, New York and other big cities. Consolidators can be found through the Yellow Pages or the major daily newspapers. Ticket Planet

is a leading ticket consolidator and is recommended. Visit its Web site at www.ticket planet.com.

The *New York Times*, *LA Times*, *Chicago Tribune* and *San Francisco Chronicle* all have weekly travel sections in which you'll find any number of travel agents' ads. Council Travel, America's largest student travel organisation, has around 60 offices in the USA; its head office (☎ 800-226-8624) is at 205 E 42 St, New York, NY 10017. Call it for the office nearest you or visit its Web site at www.ciee.org. STA Travel (☎ 800-777-0112) has offices in major cities. Call for office locations or visit its Web site at www .statravel.com.

You should be able to fly from New York to London or Paris and back for US$400 to US$500 in the low season and US$550 to US$800 in the high season. Equivalent fares from the west coast are US$100 to US$300 higher.

On a stand-by basis, one-way fares can work out to be remarkably cheap. New York-based Airhitch (☎ 212-864 2000) can get you to/from Europe for US$185/235/265/215 each way from the east coast/midwest/west coast/south-east. Visit its Web site at www .airhitch.org.

Another option is a courier flight. A New York-London return ticket can be had for as little as US$210 in the low season. See Courier Flights under Buying Tickets earlier in this chapter or try As You Like It Travel (☎ 212-216 0644) or Now Voyager Travel (☎ 212-431 1616) and their Web sites at www.asulikeit.com and www.nowvoyagertr avel.com respectively.

Canada
Canadian discount air ticket sellers are also known as consolidators and their air fares tend to be about 10% higher than those sold in the USA. The *Globe & Mail*, *Toronto Star*, *Montreal Gazette* and *Vancouver Sun* carry travel agents' ads and are a good place to look for cheap fares.

Travel CUTS (☎ 800-667-2887) is Canada's national student travel agency and has offices in all major cities. Its Web address is www.travelcuts.com.

Airhitch (see the USA section) has stand-by fares to/from Toronto, Montreal and Vancouver.

Australia

Cheap flights from Australia to Europe generally go via South-East Asian capitals, involving stopovers at Kuala Lumpur, Bangkok or Singapore. If a long stopover between connections is necessary, transit accommodation is sometimes included in the price of the ticket. If it's at your own expense, it may be worth considering a more expensive ticket.

Quite a few travel offices specialise in discount air tickets. Some travel agents, particularly smaller ones, advertise cheap air fares in the travel sections of weekend newspapers, such as the *Age* in Melbourne and the *Sydney Morning Herald*.

Two well-known agents for cheap fares are STA Travel and Flight Centre. STA Travel (☎ 03-9349 2411) has its main office at 224 Faraday St, Carlton, VIC 3053, and offices in all major cities and on many university campuses. Call ☎ 131 776 Australia-wide for the location of your nearest branch or visit its Web site at www.statravel.com.au. Flight Centre (☎ 131 600 Australia-wide) has a central office at 82 Elizabeth St, Sydney, and there are dozens of offices throughout Australia. Its Web address is www.flightcentre.com.au. The usit CAMPUS representative in Australia is Student Uni Travel (☎ 02-9232 8444, ✉ sydney@backpackers.net).

Thai, Malaysian, Qantas and Singapore airlines cost from about A$1700 (low season) up to A$2500. All have frequent promotional fares so it pays to check daily newspapers. Flights to/from Perth are a couple of hundred dollars cheaper.

Another option for travellers wanting to go to Britain between November and February is to hook up with a charter flight returning to Britain. These low-season, one-way fares do have restrictions, but may work out to be considerably cheaper. Ask your travel agent for details.

New Zealand

As in Australia, STA and Flight Centres International are popular travel agents in New Zealand. The usit CAMPUS representative is usit BEYOND (☎ 09-379 4224) with a useful Web site at www.usitbeyond.co.nz. The cheapest fares to Europe are routed through Asia. A discounted return flight to London from Auckland costs around NZ$2100. An RTW ticket with Air New Zealand or Lufthansa via the USA is around NZ$2400 in the low season.

Africa

Nairobi and Johannesburg are probably the best places in Africa to buy tickets to Europe, thanks to the many bucket shops and the lively competition between them. Student Travel Centre (☎ 011-716 3945) in Johannesburg and the Africa Travel Centre (☎ 021-235 555) in Cape Town are worth trying for cheap tickets.

Several West African countries such as Senegal and The Gambia offer cheap charter flights to France and London. Charter fares to Morocco and Tunisia can be quite cheap if you're lucky enough to find a seat.

Asia

Singapore and Bangkok are the discount airfare capitals of Asia. Shop around and ask the advice of other travellers before handing over any money. STA has branches in Hong Kong, Tokyo, Singapore, Bangkok, Jakarta and Kuala Lumpur.

In India, tickets may be slightly cheaper from the bucket shops around Delhi's Connaught Place. Check with other travellers about their current trustworthiness.

The UK

Discount air travel is big business in London. Advertisements for many travel agents appear in the travel pages of the weekend broadsheets, such as the *Independent on Saturday* and the *Sunday Times*. Look out for free magazines, such as *TNT*, which are widely available in London – start by looking outside the main train and underground stations.

For students or travellers under 26, popular travel agencies in the UK include STA Travel (☎ 020-7361 6144), which has an office at 86 Old Brompton Rd, London SW7 3LQ, and other offices in London and Manchester. Visit its Web site at www.statravel.co.uk. Usit CAMPUS (☎ 0870-240 1010), 52 Grosvenor Gardens, London SW1WOAG, has branches throughout the UK. The Web address is www.usitcampus.co.uk. Both of these agencies sell tickets to all travellers but cater especially to young people and students. Charter flights can work out as a cheaper alternative to scheduled flights, especially if you do not qualify for the under-26 and student discounts.

Other recommended travel agencies include Trailfinders (☎ 020-7938 3939), 194 Kensington High St, London W8 7RG; Bridge the World (☎ 020-7734 7447), 4 Regent Place, London W1R 5FB; and Flightbookers (☎ 020-7757 2000) which is at 177-178 Tottenham Court Rd, London W1P 9LF.

Continental Europe

Though London is the travel discount capital of Europe, there are several other cities in which you will find a range of good deals. Generally, there is not much variation in air fare prices for departures from the main European cities. All the major airlines are usually offering some sort of deal, and travel agents generally have a number of deals on offer, so shop around.

Across Europe many travel agencies have ties with STA Travel, where cheap tickets can be purchased and STA-issued tickets can be altered (usually for a US$25 fee). Outlets in major cities include: Voyages Wasteels (☎ 08 03 88 70 04; this number can only be dialled from within France), 11 rue Dupuytren, 75006 Paris; STA Travel (☎ 030-311 0950), Goethestrasse 73, 10625 Berlin; Passaggi (☎ 06-474 0923), Stazione Termini FS, Galleria Di Tesla, Rome; and ISYTS (☎ 01-322 1267), 11 Nikis St, Upper Floor, Syntagma Square, Athens.

France has a network of student travel agencies which can supply discount tickets to travellers of all ages. OTU Voyages (☎ 01 44 41 38 50) has a central Paris office at 39 Ave Georges Bernanos (5e) and another 42 offices around the country. The Web address is www.otu.fr. Acceuil des Jeunes en France (☎ 01 42 77 87 80), 119 rue Saint Martin (4e), is another popular discount travel agency. General travel agencies in Paris which offer some of the best services and deals include Nouvelles Frontières (☎ 08 03 33 33 33), 5 Ave de l'Opéra (1er), Web address www.nouvelles-frontieres.com; and Voyageurs du Monde (☎ 01 42 86 16 00) at 55 rue Sainte Anne (2e).

Belgium, Switzerland, the Netherlands and Greece are also good places for buying discount air tickets. In Belgium, Acotra Student Travel Agency (☎ 02-512 86 07) at Rue de la Madeleine, Brussels, and WATS Reizen (☎ 03-226 16 26) at de Keyserlei 44, Antwerp, are both well-known agencies. In Switzerland, SSR Voyages (☎ 01-297 11 11) specialises in student, youth and budget fares. In Zurich, there is a branch at Leonhardstrasse 10 and there are others in most major Swiss cities. The Web address is www.ssr.ch.

In the Netherlands, NBBS Reizen is the official student travel agency. You can find it in Amsterdam (☎ 020-624 09 89) at Rokin 66 and there are several other agencies around the city. Another recommended travel agent in Amsterdam is Malibu Travel (☎ 020-626 32 30) at Prinsengracht 230.

In Athens, check the many travel agencies in the backstreets between Syntagma and Omonia Squares. For student and full fares, try Magic Bus (☎ 01-323 7471).

LAND
Train

Morocco and most of Turkey lie outside Europe, but the rail systems of both countries are still covered by Inter-Rail (Zone F and Zone G respectively). The price of a cheap return train ticket from London to Morocco compares favourably with equivalent bus fares. (See Train in the Getting Around chapter.)

It *is* possible to get to Western Europe by rail from Central and eastern Asia, though count on spending at least eight days doing it. You can choose from four different routes to Moscow: the Trans-Siberian (9297km from Vladivostok), the Trans-Mongolian (7860km from Beijing) and the Trans-Manchurian (9001km from Beijing), which all use the same tracks across Siberia but have different routes east of Lake Baikal; and the Trans-Kazakhstan, which runs between Moscow and Urumqi in north-western China. Prices vary enormously, depending on where you buy the ticket and what is included – advertised 2nd-class fares cost around US$330 from Beijing to Moscow. Web sites worth consulting for trans-Siberian packages include: www.finnsov.fi, www.monkeyshrine.com, www.regent-holidays.co.uk and www.trans-siberian.co.uk.

There are countless travel options between Moscow and the rest of Europe. Most people will opt for the train, usually to/from Berlin, Helsinki, Munich, Budapest or Vienna. The *Trans-Siberian Handbook* (Trailblazer) by Bryn Thomas is a comprehensive guide to the route, as is the *Trans-Siberian Rail Guide* (Compass Star) by Robert Strauss & Tamsin Turnbull. Lonely Planet's *Russia, Ukraine &*

Belarus has a separate chapter on trans-Siberian travel.

Overland Trails

In the early 1980s, the overland trail to/from Asia lost much of its popularity as the Islamic regime in Iran made life difficult for most independent travellers, and the war in Afghanistan closed that country off to all but the foolhardy. Now that Iran seems to be rediscovering the merits of tourism, the Asia route has begun to pick up again, though unsettled conditions in Afghanistan, southern Pakistan and north-west India could prevent the trickle of travellers turning into a flood for the time being.

Discounting the complicated Middle East route via Egypt, Jordan, Syria, Turkey and Eastern Europe, going to/from Africa involves a Mediterranean ferry crossing (see the following Sea section). Due to unrest in Africa, the most feasible overland routes through the continent have all but closed down.

Travelling by private transport beyond Europe requires plenty of paperwork and other preparations. A detailed description is beyond the scope of this book, but the following Getting Around chapter tells you what's required within Europe.

SEA
Mediterranean Ferries

There are many ferries across the Mediterranean between Africa and Europe. The ferry you take will depend on your travels in Africa, but options include: Spain-Morocco, Italy-Tunisia, and France-Morocco and France-Tunisia. There are also ferries between Greece and Israel via Cyprus.

Ferries are often filled to capacity in summer, especially to/from Tunisia, so it's advisable to book well in advance if you're taking a vehicle across. See the relevant country chapters.

Passenger Ships & Freighters

Regular, long-distance passenger ships disappeared with the advent of cheap air travel and were replaced by a small number of luxury cruise ships. Cunard's *Queen Elizabeth 2* sails between New York and Southampton 20 times a year; the trip takes six nights each way and costs around UK£1500 for the return trip, though there are also one-way and 'fly one-way' deals. The bible for passenger ships and sea travel is the *OAG Cruise & Ferry Guide* published by the UK-based Reed Travel Group (☎ 01582-600 111), but it costs UK£50 per issue so you may want to consult it at your library.

A more adventurous alternative is as a paying passenger on a freighter. Freighters are far more numerous than cruise ships and there are many more routes from which to choose. The previously mentioned *OAG Cruise & Ferry Guide* is the most comprehensive source of information, though *Travel by Cargo Ship* (Cadogan) is also a good source. Passenger freighters typically carry six to 12 passengers (more than 12 would require a doctor on board), and though less luxurious than dedicated cruise ships, give you a real taste of life at sea. Schedules tend to be flexible and costs vary, but seem to hover around US$100 a day; vehicles can often be included for an additional fee.

DEPARTURE TAX

Some countries charge you a fee for the privilege of leaving from their airports. Some also charge port fees when departing by ship. Such fees are *usually* included in the price of your ticket, but it pays to check this when purchasing it. If not, you'll have to have the fee ready when leaving. Details of departure taxes are given at the end of the Getting There & Away sections of individual country chapters.

Getting Around

Travel within most of the EU, whether by air, rail or car, has been made easier following the Schengen Agreement. This abolished border controls between signed-up states. Britain and Ireland are the only EU countries currently outside the agreement.

AIR

Air travel is best viewed as a means to get you to the starting point of your itinerary rather than as your main means of travel, since it lacks the flexibility of ground transport. Using air travel for short hops can be extremely expensive, though for longer trips the air option might be cheaper than going by bus or train.

Since 1997 air travel within the EU has been deregulated. This 'open skies' policy allows greater flexibility in routing, wider competition and lower prices. Air travel is still dominated by the large state-run and private carriers, but these have been joined by several no-frills small airlines which sell budget tickets directly to the customer. They operate routes from the UK to most countries in Western Europe, though note they sometimes use smaller, less convenient airports.

Refer to the Air Travel Glossary in the previous Getting There & Away chapter for information on types of air tickets. London is a good centre for picking up cheap, restricted-validity tickets through bucket shops. Amsterdam and Athens are other good places for bucket-shop tickets in Europe. For more information, see the individual country chapters. Some airlines, such as the UK-based easyJet (Web site: www.easyJet.com), give discounts for tickets purchased via the Internet.

So-called open-jaw returns, by which you can travel into one city and exit from another, are worth considering, though they sometimes work out more expensive than simple returns. In the UK, Trailfinders (☎ 020-7937 5400) and STA Travel (☎ 020-7361 6161) can give you tailor-made versions of these tickets. Your chosen cities don't necessarily have to be in the same country. STA sells Young Europe Special (YES) flights, which allow travel around Europe using Lufthansa German Airlines at UK£39, UK£59 or UK£79 per flight (minimum four flights, maximum 10). Britain is the starting point, and the offer is open to students under 31 years of age and anybody under 26.

If you are travelling alone, courier flights are a possibility. You get cheap passage in return for accompanying packages or documents through customs and delivering them to a representative at the destination airport. EU integration and electronic communications mean there's increasingly less call for couriers, but you might find something. British Airways, for example, offers courier flights through the Travel Shop (☎ 0870-606 1133). London to Budapest return starts at UK£60.

Getting between airports and city centres is rarely a problem in Europe thanks to good public transport networks, though it can be rather time-consuming in large cities like Paris.

BUS
International Buses

International bus travel tends to take second place to going by train. The bus has the edge in terms of cost, sometimes quite substantially, but is generally slower and less comfortable. Europe's biggest network of international buses is provided by a group of bus companies operating under the name Eurolines. Web site: www.eurolines.com.

Eurolines' representatives include:

Deutsche-Touring (☎ 069-790 30), Am Römerhof 17, Frankfurt
Eurolines Austria (☎ 01-712 04 53), Autobusbahnhof Wien-Mitte, Landstrasser Hauptstrasse, 1030 Vienna
Eurolines Belgium (☎ 02-203 07 07), Coach Station, CCN North Station, Brussels
Eurolines France (☎ 08-36 69 52 52), Gare Routière Internationale, 28 Ave du Général de Gaulle, 75020 Paris
Eurolines Italy (☎ Florence: 055-35 71 10), Ciconvallazione Nonentana 574, Lato Stazione Tiburtina, Rome
Eurolines Nederland (☎ 020-560 87 87), Rokin 10, 1012 KR Amsterdam
Eurolines UK (☎ 0870-514 3219), 52 Grosvenor Gardens, London SW1, Britain

These may also be able to advise you on other bus companies and deals.

Eurolines UK has nine circular explorer routes, always starting and ending in London (no youth/senior reductions). The popular London-Amsterdam-Brussels-Paris route is UK£59, so too with London-Dublin-Galway-Killarney-Cork-London. The London-Vienna-Budapest-Prague-London route is UK£116.

Eurolines also offers passes. Compared to rail passes, they're cheaper but not as extensive or as flexible. They cover 48 European cities as far afield as Dublin, Glasgow, Stockholm, Tallinn, Bucharest, Rome and Madrid. All trips must be international (ie, you can't get on at Paris and get off at Lyon, even though both cities are included in the pass). The cost is UK£245 for 30 days (UK£195 for youths and senior citizens) or UK£283 for 60 days (UK£227). The passes are cheaper off-season.

On ordinary return trips, youths under 26 and seniors over 60 pay less; eg, a London-Munich return ticket costs UK£91 for adults or UK£85 for youths/seniors. Explorer or return tickets are valid for six months.

Busabout (☎ 020-7950 1661), 258 Vauxhall Bridge Rd, Victoria, London SW1, England, operates buses that complete set circuits round Europe, stopping at major cities. You get unlimited travel per sector, and can 'hop-on, hop-off' at any scheduled stop, then resume with a later bus. Buses are often oversubscribed, so prebook each sector to avoid being stranded. Departures are every two days from April to October, or May to September for Spain and Portugal. The circuits cover all countries in continental Western Europe, and you can pay to 'add on' Greece, Scandinavia and/or a London-Paris link. See the Web site www.busabout.com.

Busabout's Consecutive Pass allows unlimited travel within the given time period. For 15/21 days the cost is UK£155/219 for adults or UK£139/199 for students and those under 26. Passes are also available for one, two or three months, or for the whole season (UK£659 for adults, UK£589 for students/youths). The Flexipass allows you to select travel days within the given time period. Ten or 15 days in two months costs UK£235 or UK£335; 21 days in three months costs UK£445 and 30 days in four months is UK£609. Student/youth prices are about 10% lower than these adult prices.

See the individual country chapters for more information about long-distance buses.

National Buses

Domestic buses provide a viable alternative to the rail network in most countries. Again, compared to trains they are usually slightly cheaper and somewhat slower. Buses tend to be best for shorter hops such as getting around cities and reaching remote villages. They are often the only option in mountainous regions. Advance reservations are rarely necessary. On many city buses you usually buy your ticket in advance from a kiosk or machine and validate it on entering.

See the individual country chapters and city sections for more details on local buses.

TRAIN

Trains are a popular way of getting around: they are comfortable, frequent, and generally on time. The Channel Tunnel makes it possible to get from Britain to continental Europe using the Eurostar service (see the France and Britain Getting There & Away sections). In some countries, such as Spain, Portugal and (to some extent) Italy, fares are reasonably low; in others, European rail passes make travel more affordable. Supplements and reservation costs are not covered by passes, and pass holders must always carry their passport for identification purposes.

If you plan to travel extensively by train, it might be worth getting hold of the *Thomas Cook European Timetable*, which gives a complete listing of train schedules and indicates where supplements apply or where reservations are necessary. It is updated monthly and is available from Thomas Cook outlets in the UK, and in the USA from Forsyth Travel Library (☎ 800-367 7984). Check the Web sites www.thomascook.com and www.forsyth.com. In Australia, contact Mercury Travel Books (☎ 02-9344 8877).

If you intend to do a lot of train travel in one or a handful of countries – Benelux, say – it might be worthwhile getting hold of the national timetable(s) published by the state railroad(s). The *European Planning & Rail Guide* is an informative annual magazine, primarily geared towards North American travellers. To get a copy, call the toll-free USA number ☎ 877-441 2387, or visit the

Web site www.budgeteuropetravel.com. It's free within the USA; send US$3 if you want it posted anywhere else.

Paris, Amsterdam, Munich, Milan and Vienna are important hubs for international rail connections. See the relevant city sections for details and budget ticket agents.

Note that European trains sometimes split en route in order to service two destinations, so even if you know you're on the right train, make sure you're in the correct carriage too.

Express Trains

Fast trains or those that make few stops are identified by the symbols EC (EuroCity) or IC (InterCity). The French TGV, Spanish AVE and German ICE trains are even faster. Supplements can apply on fast trains, and it is a good idea (sometimes obligatory) to make seat reservations at peak times and on certain lines.

Overnight Trains

Overnight trains will usually offer a choice of couchette or sleeper if you don't fancy sleeping in your seat with somebody else's elbow in your ear. Again, reservations are advisable as sleeping options are allocated on a first-come, first-served basis.

Couchette bunks are comfortable enough, if lacking a bit in privacy. There are four per compartment in 1st class or six in 2nd class. A bunk costs a fixed price of around US$28 for most international trains, irrespective of the length of the journey.

Sleepers are the most comfortable option, offering beds for one or two passengers in 1st class, and two or three passengers in 2nd class. Charges vary depending upon the journey, but they are significantly more expensive than couchettes. Most long-distance trains have a dining (buffet) car or an attendant who wheels a snack trolley through carriages. Prices tend to be steep.

Security

Stories occasionally surface about train passengers being gassed or drugged and then robbed, though bag-snatching is more of a worry. Sensible security measures include not letting your bags out of your sight (especially when stopping at stations), chaining them to the luggage rack, and locking compartment doors overnight.

Rail Passes

Shop around, as pass prices can vary between different outlets. Once purchased, take care of your pass, as it cannot be replaced or refunded if lost or stolen. European passes get reductions on Eurostar through the Channel Tunnel and on ferries on certain routes (eg, between France and Ireland). In the USA, Rail Europe (☎ 800-438 7245) sells all sorts of rail passes. See the Web site www.raileurope.com.

Eurail These passes can only be bought by residents of non-European countries, and are supposed to be purchased before arriving in Europe. However, Eurail passes *can* be purchased within Europe, so long as your passport proves you've been there for less than six months, but the outlets where you can do this are limited, and the passes will be more expensive than getting them outside Europe. Rail Europe in London (see later under Cheap Tickets) is one such outlet, as is Drifters Travel Centre (☎ 020-7402 9171), 22 Craven Terrace, London, which may have lower prices. If you've lived in Europe for more than six months, you are eligible for an Inter-Rail pass, which is a better buy.

Eurail passes are valid for unlimited travel on national railways and some private lines in Austria, Belgium, Denmark, Finland, France (including Monaco), Germany, Greece, Hungary, Ireland, Italy, Luxembourg, the Netherlands, Norway, Portugal, Spain, Sweden and Switzerland (including Liechtenstein). The UK is not covered.

Eurail is also valid on some ferries between Italy and Greece, and between Sweden and Finland. Reductions are given on some other ferry routes and on river/lake steamer services in various countries.

Eurail passes offer reasonable value to those aged under 26. A Youthpass gives unlimited 2nd-class travel within a choice of five validity periods: 15/21 days (US$388/499) or one/two/three months (US$623/882/1089). The Youth Flexipass, also for 2nd class, is valid for freely chosen days within a two-month period: 10 days for US$458 or 15 days for US$599. Overnight journeys commencing after 7 pm count as the following day's travel. The traveller must fill out in ink the relevant box in the calendar before starting a day's travel.

For those aged over 26, the equivalent passes provide 1st-class travel. The standard Eurail pass costs US$554/718 for 15/21 days or US$890/1260/1558 for one/two/three months. The Flexipass costs US$654/862 for 10/15 days within two months. Two people travelling together can get a 'saver' version of either pass, saving about 15%. Eurail passes for children are also available.

Europass Also for non-Europeans, Europass gives unlimited travel on freely chosen days within a two-month period. Youth (aged under 26) and adult (solo, or two sharing) versions are available, and purchasing requirements and sales outlets are as for Eurail passes. They are cheaper than Eurail passes as they cover only France, Germany, Italy, Spain and Switzerland. The youth/adult price is US$296/348 for a minimum five travel days, or US$620/728 for a maximum 15 days. 'Associate countries' can be added on to the basic pass. The charge to add any one/two countries is US$52/86 for youths or US$60/100 for adults. These associate countries are Austria (including Hungary), Belgium (including Luxembourg and the Netherlands), Greece (including ferries from Italy) and Portugal.

Inter-Rail Inter-Rail passes are available to European residents of more than six months standing (passport identification is required). Terms and conditions vary slightly from country to country, but in the country of origin there is only a discount of around 50% on normal fares.

The Inter-Rail pass is split into zones. Zone A is Ireland and Britain (though if you buy your Zone A pass in Britain, you get only 30% off, or no discount at all with the 26+ version); B is Sweden, Norway and Finland; C is Denmark, Germany, Switzerland and Austria; D is the Czech Republic, Slovakia, Poland, Hungary and Croatia; E is France, Belgium, the Netherlands and Luxembourg; F is Spain, Portugal and Morocco; G is Italy, Greece, Turkey, Slovenia and Italy-Greece ferries; and H is Bulgaria, Romania, Yugoslavia and Macedonia.

The normal Inter-Rail pass is for people under 26, though travellers over 26 can get the Inter-Rail 26+ version. The price for any one zone is UK£129 (UK£179 for 26+) for 22 days. Multizone passes are valid for one month: two zones cost UK£169 (UK£235), three zones UK£195 (UK£269) and the all-zone global pass is UK£219 (UK£309).

Euro Domino There is a Euro Domino pass for each of the countries covered in the Inter-Rail pass, and they're worth considering if you're homing in on a particular region. They're sold in Europe to European residents. Adults (travelling 1st or 2nd class) and youths under 26 can opt for three to eight days valid travel within one month. Examples of adult/youth prices for eight days in 2nd class are UK£79/£60 for the Netherlands and UK£165/£122 for Germany.

National Rail Passes If you intend to travel extensively within one country, check which national rail passes are available. These can sometimes save you a lot of money; details can be found in the Getting Around sections in the individual country chapters. You need to plan ahead if you intend to take this option, as some passes can only be purchased prior to arrival in the country concerned. Some national flexi passes, near-equivalents to the Domino passes mentioned above, are only available to non-Europeans.

Cheap Tickets

European rail passes are only worth buying if you plan to do a reasonable amount of inter-country travelling within a short space of time. Some people tend to overdo it and spend every night they can on the train, ending up too tired to enjoy sightseeing the next day.

When weighing up options, consider the cost of other cheap ticket deals, including advance purchase reductions, one-off promotions or special circular-route tickets. Normal international tickets are valid for two months, and you can make as many stops as you like en route; make your intentions known when purchasing, and inform the train conductor how far you're going before they punch your ticket.

Travellers aged under 26 can pick up Billet International de Jeunesse (BIJ) tickets which cut fares by up to about 30%. Unfortunately, you can't always bank on a substantial reduction. Paris-Madrid return is UK£142 instead of UK£178, whereas there's no saving on the Paris-Munich return fare of UK£142. Various agents issue BIJ tickets in Europe, eg, Voyages Wasteels (☎ 01 43 43 46 10), 2 rue Michel Chasles, Paris. There are over 60 branches of Wasteels throughout France. Web site: www.voyages-wasteels.fr. Rail Europe (☎ 08705-848 848), 179 Piccadilly, London, sells BIJ tickets, Eurail and Inter-Rail. Web site: www.raileurope.co.uk.

For a small fee, European residents can buy a Railplus Card, entitling the holder to a 25% discount on international train journeys. In most countries (eg, in the UK) it is sold only to people over 60 as a replacement for the Rail Europe Senior Card, which is being phased out. However, some national rail networks may make the Railplus Card available also to young people or other travellers.

CAR & MOTORCYCLE

Travelling with your own vehicle is the best way to get to remote places and it gives you the most flexibility. Unfortunately, the independence you enjoy does tend to isolate you from the local people. Also, cars are usually inconvenient in city centres, where it is generally worth ditching your vehicle and relying on public transport. Various car-carrying trains (motorail) can help you avoid long, tiring drives. Eurotunnel through the Channel Tunnel transports cars; see the Britain and France Getting There & Away sections.

Paperwork & Preparations

Proof of ownership of a private vehicle should always be carried (Vehicle Registration Document for British-registered cars) when touring Europe. An EU driving licence is acceptable for driving throughout Europe. However, old-style green UK licences are no good for Spain or Italy and should be backed up by a German translation in Austria. If you have any other type of licence it is advisable or necessary to obtain an International Driving Permit (IDP) from your motoring organisation (see Visas & Documents in the earlier Facts for the Visitor chapter). An IDP is recommended for Turkey even if you have a European licence.

Third party motor insurance is a minimum requirement in Europe. Most UK motor insurance policies automatically provide this for EU countries. Get your insurer to issue a Green Card (which may cost extra), an internationally recognised proof of insurance, and check that it lists all the countries you intend to visit. You'll need this in the event of an accident outside the country where the vehicle is insured. Also ask your insurer for a European Accident Statement form, which can simplify things if the worst happens. Never sign statements you can't read or understand – insist on a translation and sign that only if it's acceptable.

If you want to insure a vehicle you've just purchased (see the following Purchase section) and have a good insurance record, you might be eligible for considerable discounts if you can show a letter to this effect from your insurance company back home.

Taking out a European motoring assistance policy is a good investment, such as the AA Five Star Service or the RAC European Motoring Assistance. Expect to pay about UK£54 for 14 days cover with a small discount for association members. Non-Europeans might find it cheaper to arrange international coverage with their national motoring organisation before leaving home. Ask your motoring organisation for details about free services offered by affiliated organisations around Europe.

Every vehicle travelling across an international border should display a sticker showing its country of registration (see the International Country Abbreviations appendix). A warning triangle, to be used in the event of breakdown, is compulsory almost everywhere. Recommended accessories are a first-aid kit (compulsory in Greece and several Central European countries), a spare bulb kit (compulsory in Croatia and Spain) and a fire extinguisher (compulsory in Greece and Turkey). Bail bonds are no longer required for Spain. In the UK, contact the RAC (☎ 0800-550055) or the AA (☎ 08705-500 600) for more information.

Road Rules

Motoring organisations can supply members with country-by-country information about motoring regulations, or they may produce motoring guidebooks for general sale. Find useful motoring information on the RAC Web site (www.rac.co.uk).

With the exception of Britain and Ireland, driving is on the right. Vehicles brought over from either of these countries should have their headlights adjusted to avoid blinding oncoming traffic at night (a simple solution on older headlight lenses is to cover up a triangular section of the lens with tape). Priority is usually given to traffic approaching from the right in countries that drive on the right-hand side.

Take care with speed limits, as they vary from country to country. You may be surprised at the apparent disregard of traffic regulations in some places (particularly in Italy and Greece), but as a visitor it is always best to be cautious. Many driving infringements are subject to an on-the-spot fine in all countries except Britain and Ireland. Always ask for a receipt.

European drink-driving laws are particularly strict. The blood-alcohol concentration (BAC) limit when driving is between 0.05% and 0.08%, but in certain areas – Gibraltar and some Eastern European countries – it can be *zero* per cent. See the introductory Getting Around sections in the country chapters for more details on traffic laws.

Roads

Conditions and types of roads vary across Europe, but it is possible to make some generalisations. The fastest routes are four or six-lane dual carriageways/highways, ie, two or three lanes either side (motorway, *Autobahn*, *autoroute*, *autostrada* etc). These tend to skirt cities and plough through the countryside in straight lines, often avoiding the most scenic bits. Some of these roads incur tolls, often quite hefty (eg, in Italy, France and Spain), or have a general tax for usage (Switzerland and Austria), but there will always be an alternative route you can take. Motorways and other primary routes are almost always in good condition.

Road surfaces on minor routes are not perfect in some countries (eg, Greece and Ireland), although normally they will be more than adequate. These roads are narrower and progress is generally much slower. To compensate, you can expect much better scenery and plenty of interesting villages along the way.

Rental

The big international firms will give you reliable service and a good standard of vehicle.

Usually you will have the option of returning the car to a different outlet at the end of the rental period. Prebook for the lowest rates – if you walk into an office and ask for a car on the spot, you will pay over the odds, even allowing for special weekend deals. Fly-drive combinations and other programs are worth looking into. You should be able to make advance reservations online. Check the Web sites:

Hertz: www.hertz.com
Avis: www.avis.com
Budget: www.budget.com
Europcar: www.europcar.com

Brokers can cut hire costs. Holiday Autos (UK ☎ 0870-400 4477) has low rates and offices or representatives in over 20 countries. Visit its Web site at www.holidayautos.com. In the USA call Kemwel Holiday Autos (☎ 800-576 1590). In the UK, a competitor with even lower prices is Autos Abroad (☎ 020-7287 6000). Web site: www.autosabroad.co.uk.

If you want to rent a car and haven't prebooked, look for national or local firms, which can often undercut the big companies by up to 40%. Nevertheless, you need to be wary of dodgy deals where they take your money and point you towards some clapped-out wreck, or where the rental agreement is bad news if you have an accident or the car is stolen – a cause for concern if you can't even read what you sign.

No matter where you rent, make sure you understand what is included in the price (unlimited or paid kilometres, tax, injury insurance, collision damage waiver etc) and what your liabilities are. We recommend taking the collision damage waiver, though you can probably skip the injury insurance if you and your passengers have decent travel insurance. Ask in advance if you can drive a rented car across borders, such as from Germany (where hire prices are low) to Austria (where they're high).

The minimum rental age is usually 21 or even 23, and you'll probably need a credit card. Note that prices at airport rental offices are usually higher than at branches in the city centre.

Motorcycle and moped rental is common in some countries, such as Italy, Spain, Greece and the south of France. Sadly, it's also common to see inexperienced riders leap on rented bikes and very quickly fall off them again, leaving a layer or two of skin on the road in the process.

Purchase

The purchase of vehicles in some European countries is illegal for non-nationals or non-EU residents. Britain is probably the best place to buy: second-hand prices are good and, whether buying privately or from a dealer, the absence of language difficulties will help you establish exactly what you are getting and what guarantees you can expect in the event of a breakdown. See the Britain Getting Around section for information on purchase paperwork and European insurance.

Bear in mind that you will be getting a car with the steering wheel on the right in Britain. If you want left-hand drive and can afford to buy new, prices are usually reasonable in Greece, France, Germany, Belgium, Luxembourg and the Netherlands. Paperwork can be tricky wherever you buy, and many countries have compulsory roadworthiness checks on older vehicles.

Leasing

Leasing a vehicle has none of the hassles of purchasing and can work out considerably cheaper than hiring over longer periods. The Renault Eurodrive scheme provides new cars for non-EU residents for a period of between 17 and 170 days. Under this arrangement, a Renault Clio 1.2 for 30 days, for example, would cost 4710FF (if picked up/dropped off in France), including insurance and roadside assistance. Other companies with comparable leasing programs include Peugeot and Citroen. Check out the options before leaving home. In the US, Kemwel Holiday Autos (see under Rental earlier) arranges European leasing deals.

Camper Van

A popular way to tour Europe is for three or four people to band together to buy or rent a camper van. London is the usual embarkation point. Look at the advertisements in London's free magazine *TNT* if you wish to form or join a group. *TNT* is also a good source for purchasing a van, as is the *Loot* newspaper and the Van Market in Market Rd, London N7 (near the Caledonian Rd tube station), where private vendors congregate on a daily basis.

Some second-hand dealers offer a 'buyback' scheme for when you return from the Continent, but we've received warnings that some dealers don't fully honour their refund commitments. Anyway, buying and re-selling privately should be more advantageous if you have the time. A reader recommended Down Under Insurance (☎ 020-7402 9211) for European cover. Check the Web site at www.downu nderinsurance.co.uk.

Camper vans usually feature a fixed high-top or elevating roof and two to five bunk beds. Apart from the essential camping gas cooker, professional conversions may include a sink, fridge and built-in cupboards. You will need to spend at least UK£2000 (US$3200) for something reliable enough to get you around Europe for any length of time. Getting a mechanical check (from UK£30) is a good idea before you buy. Once on the road you should be able to keep budgets lower than backpackers using trains, but don't forget to set some money aside for emergency repairs.

The main advantage of going by camper van is flexibility: with transport, eating and sleeping requirements all taken care of in one unit, you are tied to nobody's timetable but your own. It's also easier to set up at night than if you rely on a car and tent.

A disadvantage of camper vans is that you are in a confined space for much of the time. Four adults in a small van can soon get on each other's nerves, particularly if the group has been formed at short notice. You might also become too self-contained, and miss out on experiences in the world outside your van.

Other negatives are that vans are not very manoeuvrable around town, and you'll often have to leave your gear unattended inside (many people bolt extra locks onto the van). They're also expensive to buy in spring and hard to sell in autumn.

Motorcycle Touring

Europe is made for motorcycle touring, with good-quality winding roads, stunning scenery and an active motorcycling scene. Just make sure your wet-weather gear is up to scratch.

The wearing of helmets for rider and passenger is compulsory everywhere in Western Europe. Austria, Belgium, France, Germany,

Luxembourg, Portugal and Spain also require that motorcyclists use headlights during the day; in other countries it is recommended.

On ferries, motorcyclists rarely have to book ahead as they can generally be squeezed in. Take note of local custom about parking motorcycles on pavements (sidewalks). Though this is illegal in some countries, the police usually turn a blind eye so long as the vehicle doesn't obstruct pedestrians. Don't try this in Britain, however.

Fuel

Fuel prices can vary enormously from country to country (though it's always more expensive than in North America or Australia) and may bear little relation to the general cost of living. Refuelling in Luxembourg saves at least 30% compared to prices in neighbouring countries. Britain has Europe's most expensive petrol, followed by Scandinavia and the Netherlands; Andorra, Luxembourg, Spain and Greece are by far the cheapest in Western Europe. Switzerland is also reasonably cheap. Motoring organisations such as the RAC can supply more details.

Unleaded petrol is widely available throughout Europe and is usually slightly cheaper than super (premium grade, the only 'leaded' choice in some countries). Diesel is usually significantly cheaper, though the difference is only marginal in Britain, Ireland and Switzerland.

TAXI

Taxis in Europe are metered and rates are high. There might also be supplements (depending on the country) for things like luggage, the time of day, the location from which you boarded and for extra passengers. Good bus, rail and underground (subway/metro) railway networks make the taking of taxis all but unnecessary, but if you need one in a hurry they can usually be found idling near train stations or outside big hotels. Lower fares make taxis more viable in some countries, such as Spain, Greece and Portugal.

BICYCLE

A tour of Europe by bike may seem a daunting prospect, but one organisation that can help in the UK is the Cyclists' Touring Club (CTC; ☎ 01483-417 217, @ cycling@ctc.org.uk), Cotterell House, 69 Meadrow, Godalming,

Surrey GU7 3HS. It can supply information to members on cycling conditions in Europe as well as detailed routes, itineraries and maps. Membership includes specialised insurance and costs UK£25 per annum, or UK£12.50 for people aged under 27 or over 65. Web site: www.ctc.org.uk.

A primary consideration on a cycling tour is to travel light, but you should take a few tools and spare parts, including a puncture repair kit and an extra inner tube. Panniers are essential to balance your possessions on either side of the bike frame. A bike helmet is also a very good idea. Take a good lock and always use it when you leave your bike unattended.

Michelin maps indicate scenic routes, which can help you construct good cycling itineraries. Seasoned cyclists can average 80km a day, but there's no point in overdoing it. The slower you travel, the more local people you are likely to meet. If you get tired of pedalling or simply want to skip a boring transport section, you can put your feet up on the train. See the following Transporting a Bicycle section.

For more information on cycling, see Activities in the earlier Facts for the Visitor chapter and in the individual country chapters.

Rental

It is easy to hire bikes throughout most of Western Europe on an hourly, half-day, daily or weekly basis. Many train stations have bike-rental counters; see the country chapters for more details. Often it is possible to return the machine at a different outlet (as in Ireland) so you don't have to retrace your route.

Purchase

For major cycling tours, it's best to have a bike you're familiar with, so consider bringing your own (see the following section) rather than buying on arrival. There are plenty of places to buy in Europe (shops sell new and second-hand bicycles or you can check local papers for private vendors) but you'll need a specialist bicycle shop for a machine capable of withstanding European touring. CTC can provide members with a leaflet on purchasing. Cycling is very popular in the Netherlands and Germany, and they are good places to pick up a well-equipped touring bicycle. European prices are quite high (certainly higher than in

North America), but non-Europeans should be able to claim back VAT on the purchase.

Transporting a Bicycle

If you want to bring your own bicycle to Europe, you should be able to take it along with you on the plane relatively easily. You can either take it apart and pack everything in a bike bag or box, or simply wheel it to the check-in desk, where it should be treated as a piece of luggage. You may have to remove the pedals and turn the handlebars sideways so that it takes up less space in the aircraft's hold; check all this with the airline well in advance, preferably before you pay for your ticket. If your bicycle and other luggage exceed your weight allowance, ask about alternatives or you may suddenly find yourself being charged a fortune for excess baggage.

Within Europe, bikes can usually be transported as luggage on slower trains, subject to a small supplementary fee.

Fast trains can rarely accommodate bikes: they might need to be sent as registered luggage and may end up on a different train from the one you take. This is often the case in France and Spain. British train companies are not part of the European luggage registration scheme, but Eurostar is: it charges UK£20 to send a bike as registered luggage on its routes. You can transport your bicycle with you on Eurotunnel through the Channel Tunnel. With a bit of tinkering and dismantling (eg removing wheels), you might be able to get your bike into a bag or sack and take it on a train as hand luggage.

The European Bike Express is a coach service where cyclists can travel with their bicycles. It runs in the summer from north-east England to France, Italy and Spain, with pick-up/drop-off points en route. The maximum return fare is UK£169 (£10 off for CTC members); phone ☎ 01642-251 440 in the UK. Web site: www.bike-express.co.uk.

HITCHING

Hitching is never entirely safe in any country in the world, and we don't recommend it. Travellers who decide to hitch should understand that they are taking a small but potentially serious risk. People who do choose to hitch will be safer if they travel in pairs and let someone know where they plan to go.

Hitching can be the most rewarding and frustrating way of getting around. Rewarding, because you get to meet and interact with local people and are forced into unplanned detours that may yield unexpected highlights off the beaten track. Frustrating, because you may get stuck on the side of the road to nowhere with nowhere (or nowhere cheap) to stay. Then it begins to rain...

That said, hitchers can end up making good time, but obviously your plans need to be flexible in case a trick of the light makes you appear invisible to passing motorists. A man and woman travelling together is probably the best combination. Two or more men must expect some delays; two women together will make good time and should be relatively safe. A woman hitching on her own is taking a big risk, particularly in parts of southern Europe.

Don't try to hitch from city centres: take public transport to suburban exit routes. Hitching is usually illegal on motorways (freeways) – stand on the slip roads, or approach drivers at petrol stations and truck stops. Look presentable and cheerful, and make a cardboard sign indicating your intended destination in the local language. Never hitch where drivers can't stop in good time or without causing an obstruction. At dusk, give up and think about finding somewhere to stay. If your itinerary includes a ferry crossing (for instance, across the Channel), it might be worth trying to score a ride before the ferry rather than after, since vehicle tickets sometimes include all passengers free of charge. This also applies to Eurotunnel via the Channel Tunnel.

It is sometimes possible to arrange a lift in advance: scan student notice boards in colleges, or contact car-sharing agencies. Such agencies are particularly popular in France (Allostop Provoya, Auto-Partage) and Germany (Mitfahrzentralen); see the relevant country chapters.

BOAT
Ferry

Several ferry companies compete on all the main ferry routes, and the resulting service is comprehensive but complicated. The same ferry company can have a host of different prices for the same route, depending upon the time of day or year, the validity of the ticket or the length of your vehicle. It is worth planning (and booking) ahead where possible as there may be special reductions on off-peak crossings and advance purchase tickets. Most ferry companies adjust prices according to the level of demand (so-called 'fluid' or 'dynamic' pricing) so it may pay to offer alternative travel dates. Vehicle tickets usually include the driver and a full complement of passengers.

P&O Stena Line is one of the largest ferry companies in the world. It serves British, Irish and some Scandinavian routes. P&O Portsmouth and Brittany Ferries sail direct between England and northern Spain, taking 24 to 35 hours. The shortest cross-Channel routes (Dover to Calais, or Folkestone to Boulogne) are also the busiest, though there is now great competition from the Channel Tunnel. You can book ferry tickets online (often at a discount) on the following Web sites: www.Brittany-ferries.com; www.posl .com; www.poportsmouth.com; www.seafr ance.com. Hoverspeed (☎ 0870-240 8070) is quicker – Folkestone-Boulogne takes only 50 minutes – yet competitively priced; check the Web site at www.hoverspeed.co.uk.

Italy (Brindisi or Bari) to Greece (Corfu, Igoumenitsa and Patras) is also a popular route. Greek islands are connected to the mainland and each other by a spider's web of routings; Lonely Planet's *Greek Islands* gives details.

Rail-pass holders are entitled to discounts or free travel on some lines (see the earlier Train section), and most ferry companies give discounts to disabled drivers. Food on ferries is often expensive (and lousy), so it is worth bringing your own when possible. It is also worth knowing that if you take your vehicle on board, you are usually denied access to it during the voyage.

Steamer

Europe's main lakes and rivers are served by steamers, and as you'd expect, schedules are more extensive in the summer months. Railpass holders are entitled to some discounts (see the earlier Train section). Extended boat trips should be considered as relaxing and scenic excursions; viewed merely as a functional means of transport, they can be very expensive.

Long cruises are possible in the Mediterranean and along Europe's rivers, but you'll need a boatload of cash. Since the early 1990s

the Danube has been connected to the Rhine by the Main-Danube canal in Germany. The MS *River Queen* does 13-day cruises along this route, from Amsterdam to Vienna, between May and September. It departs monthly in each direction. In Britain, bookings can be made through Noble Caledonia (☎ 020-7409 0376); deck prices start at UK£1995. In the USA, you can book through Uniworld (☎ 800-733 7820). Check the Web sites at www.noble-caledonia.co.uk and www.cruise uniworld.com.

ORGANISED TOURS

Tailor-made tours abound; see your travel agent or look in the small ads in newspaper travel pages. Specialists include Ramblers Holidays (☎ 01707-331 133) in Britain for hiking trips and CBT Tours (☎ 800-736-2453) in the USA for bicycle trips. Web sites: www.cbttours.com. and www.ram blersholidays.co.uk.

Young revellers can party on Europewide bus tours. Contiki and Top Deck offer camping or hotel-based bus tours for the 18 to 35 age group. The duration of Contiki's tours are 10 to 46 days, and prices start at around UK£25 per day including 'food fund'. Contiki (☎ 020-7290 6422) and Top Deck (☎ 020-7370 4555) have London offices, as well as offices or representatives in Europe, North America, Australasia and South Africa. Check the Web sites www.contiki.com and www.topdecktravel.co.uk.

For people aged over 50, Saga Holidays (☎ 0800-300 500), Saga Building, Middelburg Square, Folkestone, Kent CT20 1AZ, England, offers holidays ranging from cheap coach tours to luxury cruises (and has cheap travel insurance). In the USA, Saga Holidays (☎ 800-343 0273) is at 222 Berkeley St, Boston, MA 02116.

National tourist offices in most countries offer organised trips to points of interest. These may range from one-hour city tours to several-day circular excursions. They often work out more expensive than going it alone, but are sometimes worth it if you are pressed for time.

A short city tour will give you a quick overview of the place and can be a good way to begin your visit.

Andorra

The principality of Andorra, nestled in the Pyrenees mountains between France and Spain, covers an area of just 464 sq km. Although tiny, this political anomaly is at the heart of some of Europe's most dramatic scenery. It's also a budget skiing venue and duty-free shopping haven. These activities, together with great summer walking, attract over eight million visitors a year and bring not only wealth but some unsightly development around the capital of Andorra la Vella.

From the middle ages until as recently as 1993, Andorra's sovereignty was invested in two 'princes': the Catholic bishop of the Spanish town of La Seu d'Urgell and the French president (who inherited the job from France's pre-Revolutionary kings). Nowadays, democratic Andorra is a 'parliamentary co-princedom', the bishop and president remaining joint but largely nominal heads of state. Andorra is a member of the United Nations and the Council of Europe, but not a full member of the EU.

Andorrans form only about a quarter of the total population of 66,000, and are outnumbered by Spaniards. The official language is Catalan, which is related to both Spanish and French. Most people speak a couple of these languages and sometimes all three, while younger people, especially in the capital and ski resorts, manage more than a smattering of English also.

AT A GLANCE

Capital	Andorra la Vella
Population	66,000
Official Language	Catalan
Currency	1 French franc (FF) = 100 centimes
	1 peseta (pta) = 100 centimos
Time	GMT/UTC+0100
Country Phone Code	☎ 376

❶ Andorra la Vella pp70-1

Facts for the Visitor

VISAS & DOCUMENTS
Visas aren't necessary; the authorities figure that if Spain or France let you in, that's good enough for them – but bring your passport or national ID card with you.

EMBASSIES & CONSULATES
Andorra has embassies in France and Spain, both of whom have reciprocal diplomatic missions in Andorra.

MONEY
Andorra uses the Spanish peseta (ptas) and the French franc (FF) and, like both countries, will use the euro from 2002. It's best to use pesetas – the exchange rate for francs in shops and restaurants is seldom in your favour. See the France and Spain chapters for exchange rates.

POST & COMMUNICATIONS
Post
Andorra has no postal system of its own; France and Spain each operate separate systems with their own Andorran stamps, which

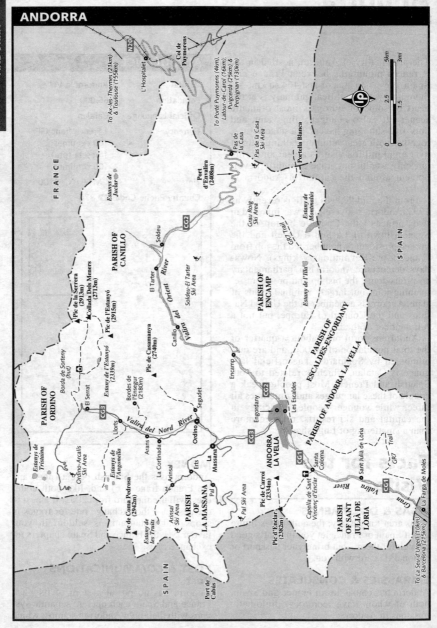

ANDORRA

To Ax-les-Thermes (21km)
& Toulouse (155km)

N20

L'Hospitalet

Col de
Puymorens

To Porté Puymorens (4km),
Latour-de-Carol (16km),
Puigcerdà (25km) &
Perpignan (130km)

Pas de la Casa

Pas de la Casa
Ski Area

Portella Blanca

Port
d'Envalira
(2408m)

Estany de
Juclar

Estany de
Montmalús

FRANCE

Grau Roig
Ski Area

GR7 Trail

CG2

Soldeu

PARISH OF
CANILLO

El Tarter

Soldeu-El Tarter
Ski Area

SPAIN

Pic de la Serrera
(2913m)
Collada Dels Meners
(2713m)

Pic de l'Estanyó
(2915m)

Estany de l'Estanyó
(2339m)

Borda de Sorteny
(hut)

Pic de Casamanya
(2740m)

Canillo

Valira del Orient River

PARISH OF
ENCAMP

Estany de l'Illa

El Serrat

Bordes de
l'Ensegur
(2180m)

CG3

PARISH OF
ORDINO

Llorts

Valira del Nord River

Segudet

Encamp

CG2

PARISH OF
ESCALDES-ENGORDANY

Arans

La Cortinada

Ordino

Les Escaldes

CG3

Estanys de
Tristaina

Ordino-Arcalis
Ski Area

Estanys de
l'Angonella

La Massana

Engordany

PARISH OF ANDORRA LA VELLA

Pic de Coma Pedrosa
(2942m)

Arinsal

Erts

La
Massana

Pic de Carroi
(2334m)

ANDORRA
LA VELLA

Santa
Coloma

Sant Julià de Lòria

Estany de
les Truits

Arinsal
Ski Area

Pal

Pal Ski Area

PARISH
OF
LA MASSANA

Capella de Sant
Vicenç d'Enclar

GR7
Trail

CG1

Pic d'Enclar
(2382m)

PARISH OF SANT
JULIÀ DE
LÒRIA

Gran Valira River

CG1

Port de
Cabús

SPAIN

To La Seu d'Urgell (10km)
& Barcelona (215km)

La Farga de Moles

5km
3ml
2.5
1.5
0
0

are needed only for international mail, ie, letters within the country are delivered free. Regular French and Spanish stamps cannot be used in Andorra.

It's usually swifter to route international mail (except letters to Spain) through the French postal system.

Telephone

Andorra's country code is ☎ 376. The cheapest way to make an international call is to buy a *teletarja* (phonecard, sold for 500 ptas, 900 ptas and 1350 ptas at tourist offices and kiosks) and ring off-peak (9 pm to 7 am plus all day Sunday). At these times a three-minute call to Europe costs 210 ptas (306 ptas to the US or Australia). You can't make a reverse-charge (collect) call from Andorra.

Email & Internet Access

Log on at Punt Internet on the 5th floor of Carrer Bonaventura 39, very near the bus station (1000 ptas per hour). It is open 10 am to 1 pm and 3.30 to 9 pm weekdays, and 4 to 8 pm Saturday in August and September.

TIME

Andorra is one hour ahead of GMT/UTC in winter (two hours ahead from the last Sunday in March to the last Sunday in September).

BUSINESS HOURS

Shops in Andorra la Vella are generally open 9.30 am to 1 pm and 3.30 to 8 pm daily, except (usually) Sunday afternoon.

ACTIVITIES

Above the main valleys, you'll find attractive lake-dotted mountain country, good for skiing in winter and walking in summer. The largest and best ski resorts are Soldeu-El Tarter and Pas de la Casa/Grau Roig. The others – Ordino-Arcalís, Arinsal and Pal – are a bit cheaper but often colder and windier. Ski passes cost 2800 ptas to 4200 ptas a day, depending on location and season; downhill ski-gear is 1200 ptas to 1600 ptas a day, and snowboards are 2500 ptas to 3000 ptas a day.

Tourist offices have a useful English-language booklet, *Sport Activities*, describing numerous hiking and mountain-bike routes. In summer, mountain bikes can be rented in some resorts for around 2800 ptas a day.

ACCOMMODATION

Tourist offices stock a comprehensive free brochure, *Hotels, Restaurants, Apartaments i Cámpings*. Be warned, however, that the prices it quotes are merely indicative.

There are no youth hostels and, outside Andorra la Vella, few budget options for independent travellers. In compensation, there are plenty of camping grounds, many beautifully situated. In high season (December to March and July/August), some hotels put prices up substantially and others don't take in independent travellers.

For walkers, Andorra has 26 off-the-beaten-track *refugis* (mountain refuges), all except one unstaffed and free. If you're trekking, invest 200 ptas in the *Mapa de Refugis i Grans Recorreguts*, which pinpoints and describes them all.

Getting There & Away

The only way to reach Andorra, unless you trek across the mountains, is by road.

FRANCE

Autocars Nadal (☎ 821138) has two buses a day (2750 ptas, four hours) on Monday, Wednesday, Friday and Sunday, linking Toulouse's Gare Routière (bus station) and Andorra la Vella.

By rail, take a train from Toulouse to either L'Hospitalet (2¼ to 2¾ hours, four daily) or Latour-de-Carol (2½ to 3¼ hours). Two daily connecting buses link Andorra la Vella with both L'Hospitalet (960 ptas) and Latour-de-Carol (1125 ptas). On Saturdays, up to five buses run from L'Hospitalet to Pas de la Casa, just inside Andorra.

SPAIN

Alsina Graells (☎ 827379) runs up to seven buses daily between Barcelona's Estació del Nord and Andorra la Vella's bus station (2435 ptas to 2715 ptas, four hours). Eurolines (☎ 860010) has four services daily (2800 ptas)

ANDORRA

between Andorra (departing from the car park of Hotel Diplomàtic) and Barcelona's Sants bus station.

Samar/Andor-Inter (☎ 826289) operates three times weekly between Andorra and Madrid (4700 ptas, nine hours) via Zaragoza (2300 ptas).

La Hispano Andorrana (☎ 821372) has five to eight buses daily between La Seu d'Urgell, across the border, and Carrer Doctor Nequi in Andorra la Vella (345 ptas, 30 minutes).

Getting Around

BUS
Ask at a tourist office for a timetable of the eight bus routes, run by Cooperativa Interurbana (☎ 820412), which follow Andorra's three main highways.

Destinations from the Avinguda Príncep Benlloch stop in Andorra la Vella include Ordino (130 ptas, every half-hour), Arinsal (185 ptas, three daily), Soldeu (375 ptas,

hourly) and Pas de la Casa (620 ptas, daily at 9 am).

CAR & MOTORCYCLE
The speed limit is 40km/h in populated areas and 90km/h elsewhere. Two problems are the recklessness of local drivers on the tight, winding roads and Andorra la Vella's horrendous traffic jams. Bypass the worst of the latter by taking the ring road around the south side of town.

Petrol in Andorra is about 25% cheaper than in Spain or France.

Andorra la Vella

pop 23,300
Andorra la Vella (elevation 1029m) is squeezed into the Riu Gran Valira Valley and is mainly engaged in retailing electronic and luxury-goods. With the constant din of jackhammers and shopping-mall architecture, you might be in Hong Kong – but for the

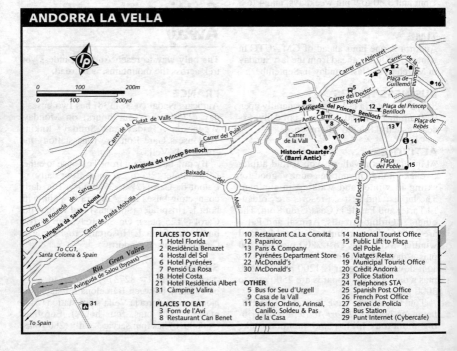

ANDORRA LA VELLA

PLACES TO STAY
1 Hotel Florida
2 Residència Benazet
4 Hostal del Sol
6 Hotel Pyrénées
7 Pensió La Rosa
18 Hotel Costa
21 Hotel Residència Albert
31 Càmping Valira

PLACES TO EAT
3 Forn de l'Avi
8 Restaurant Can Benet

10 Restaurant Ca La Conxita
12 Papanico
13 Pans & Company
17 Pyrénées Department Store
22 McDonald's
30 McDonald's

OTHER
5 Bus for Seu d'Urgell
9 Casa de la Vall
11 Bus for Ordino, Arinsal, Canillo, Soldeu & Pas de la Casa

14 National Tourist Office
15 Public Lift to Plaça del Poble
16 Viatges Relax
19 Municipal Tourist Office
20 Crèdit Andorrà
23 Police Station
24 Telephones STA
25 Spanish Post Office
26 French Post Office
27 Servei de Policía
28 Bus Station
29 Punt Internet (Cybercafe)

snowcapped peaks and an absence of noodle shops!

Orientation

Andorra la Vella is strung out along the main drag, whose name changes from Avinguda del Príncep Benlloch to Avinguda de Meritxell to Avinguda de Carlemany. The tiny historic quarter (Barri Antic) is split by this heavily trafficked artery. The town merges with the once-separate villages of Escaldes and Engordany to the east and Santa Coloma to the south-west.

Information

Tourist Offices The helpful municipal tourist office (☎ 827117) at Plaça de la Rotonda is open 9 am to 1 pm and 4 to 8 pm daily (to 7 pm on Sunday, continuously to 9 pm in July and August). It sells stamps and telephone cards.

The national tourist office (☎ 820214) is just off Plaça de Rebés. It's open 10 am (9 am from July to September) to 1 pm and 3

to 7 pm Monday to Saturday, plus Sunday morning.

Money Crèdit Andorrà, Avinguda Meritxell 80, has a 24-hour banknote exchange machine that accepts 15 currencies.

Banks, open 9 am to 1 pm and 3 to 5 pm weekdays and to noon Saturday, abound.

American Express is represented by Viatges Relax (☎ 822044), Carrer de Mossén Tremosa 2.

Post & Communications La Poste, the French post office, Carrer de Pere d'Urg 1, takes only French francs. Conversely, the Spanish post office, Correus i Telègrafs, Carrer de Joan Maragall 10, accepts only pesetas. Both are open 8.30 am to 2.30 pm weekdays and 9 am to noon Saturday.

You can make international calls from pay phones or from the Servei de Telecomunicacions d'Andorra (STA), Avinguda Meritxell 110, which also has a fax service. It's open 9 am to 9 pm daily.

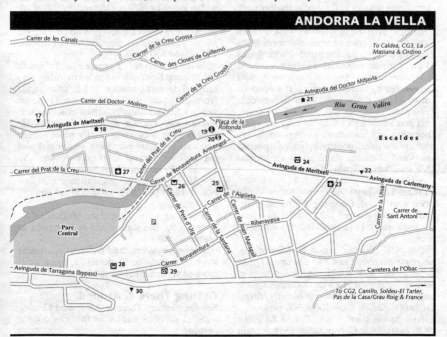

ANDORRA LA VELLA

ANDORRA

Things to See & Do

The small **Barri Antic** (old quarter) was the heart of Andorra la Vella when the principality's capital was little more than a village. The narrow cobblestone streets around the **Casa de la Vall** are flanked by attractive stone houses.

Built in 1580 as a private home, the Casa de la Vall has served as Andorra's parliament building since 1702. Downstairs is **El Tribunal de Corts**, the country's only courtroom. Free guided tours (available in English) are given 9.30 am to 1 pm and 3 to 7 pm, Monday to Saturday (daily in August). In summer, book at least a week ahead (☎ 829129) to ensure a place – though individuals can often be squeezed in at the last minute.

The **Plaça del Poble**, a large public square just south of Plaça de Rebés occupies the roof of a modern government office building. Giving good views, it's a popular local gathering place, especially in the evening. The free public lift in the southeast corner whisks you away to the car park below.

Pamper yourself at **Caldea** (☎ 800995) in Escaldes, a 10-minute walk upstream from Plaça de la Rotonda. Enclosed in what looks like a futuristic cathedral is Europe's largest spa complex of lagoons, hot tubs and saunas, fed by thermal springs. It's open 10 am to 11 pm daily; three-hour tickets cost 2950 ptas.

If you've enough left in the kitty for some **shopping**, you can make savings on things like sports gear, photographic equipment, shoes and clothing, where prices are around 25% less than in Spain or France.

Places to Stay

Open year-round, *Camping Valira* on Avinguda de Salou charges 1575 ptas for two people and a tent. It has a small indoor swimming pool.

For 1400 ptas per person *Residència Benazet* (☎ 820698, *Carrer la Llacuna 21*) has large rooms with washbasin for up to four people. Nearby on Plaça de Guillemó, spruce singles/doubles with shower at friendly *Hostal del Sol* (☎ 823701) cost 2000/3900 ptas.

Also in the Barri Antic, *Pensió La Rosa* (☎ 821810, *Antic Carrer Major 18*) has plain

singles/doubles for 2000/3500 ptas, plus triples, quads and a veritable dormitory sleeping six for 1500 ptas per person.

Hotel Costa (☎ 821439, *3rd floor, Avinguda de Meritxell 44*) has basic but clean rooms for 1700/3000 ptas. *Hotel Residència Albert* (☎ 820156, *Avinguda del Doctor Mitjavila 16*) has recently had a face lift. Good value singles/doubles/triples, the majority with bathroom, cost 2700/4500/6000 ptas.

More upmarket, the delightful *Hotel Florida* (☎ 82 01 05, fax 86 19 25, ✉ aran@solucions.ad), one block from Plaça de Guillemó, has well-equipped singles/doubles for 5425/7850 ptas (6750/9500 ptas on weekends), including breakfast. At *Hotel Pyrénées* (☎ 86 00 06, fax 82 02 65, ✉ ph@mypic.ad), singles/doubles cost 5000/8250 ptas; you're required to take half-board in the high season.

Places to Eat

Pans & Company at Plaça de Rebés 2 and Avinguda de Meritxell 91 is good for baguettes with a range of fillings (350 ptas to 500 ptas). Just off Plaça de Guillemó, *Forn de l'Aví* has an excellent *menú* for 850 ptas and does good *platos combinados* (plentiful mixed dishes; 725 ptas to 850 ptas).

In the Barri Antic, *Papanico* on Avinguda del Príncep Benlloch is fun for morning coffee to late-night snacks. It has tasty *tapas* from 250 ptas each and does a range of sandwiches and hunky platos combinados. *Restaurant Ca La Conxita (Placeta de Monjó 3)* is a bustling family place where you can see staff preparing your meal and eat well for around 2500 ptas. Around the corner is *Restaurant Can Benet (Antic Carrer Major 9)* where main dishes cost between 1600 ptas and 2300 ptas, is equally delightful.

There are a couple of clone McDonald's – opposite the bus station and at Avinguda de Meritxell 105.

For self-caterers, the *Pyrénées* department store, Avinguda de Meritxell 21, has a well-stocked supermarket on the 2nd floor.

Getting There & Around

See the Getting There & Away and Getting Around sections earlier in this chapter for options.

Around Andorra la Vella

CANILLO & SOLDEU

Canillo, 11km east of Andorra la Vella, and Soldeu, a further 7km up the valley along the CG2, are as complementary as summer and winter.

In summer, Canillo offers canyon clambering, a *vía ferrata* climbing gully and climbing wall, the year-round Palau de Gel with ice rink and swimming pool, guided walks and endless possibilities for hiking (including an easy, signposted nature walk which follows the valley downstream from Soldeu). The helpful tourist office (☎ 851002) is on the main road at the east end of the village.

Particularly in winter, Soldeu and its smaller neighbour **El Tarter** bring into their own as 23 lifts (including a cabin lift up from Canillo) connect 86km of runs with a vertical drop of 850m. The slopes, wooded in their lower reaches, are often warmer than Andorra's other more exposed ski areas and offer the Pyrenees' finest skiing and snowboarding. Lift passes for one/three days cost 3650/8580 ptas (low season) and 4200/10,050 ptas (high season).

Places to Stay

Year round, accommodation in Canillo is markedly less expensive than in Andorra La Vella. Of its five camping grounds, *Camping Santa Creu* (☎ 851462) is the greenest and quietest. *Hotel Casa Nostra* (☎ 851023) has simple rooms for 2500 ptas (3250 ptas with shower, 3750 ptas with full bathroom). *Hotel Pellissé* (☎ 851205, fax 85 18 75), just east of town, has quite decent singles/doubles for 2750/4400 ptas, while the *Hotel Canigó* (☎ 851024, fax 851824) provides comfortable singles/doubles at 3000/5000 ptas.

Places to Eat

On Soldeu's main drag, the cheerful *Hotel Bruxelles* restaurant does well-filled sandwiches (450 ptas to 575 ptas), whopping burgers and a tasty *menú* at 1175 ptas.

Entertainment

The music pounds on winter nights in Soldeu. *Pussy Cat* and its neighbour, *Fat Albert*, both one block from the main drag, rock until far too late for impressive skiing next day. *Capital Discoteca* has free entry on Tuesday, Wednesday and weekends and is a busy dance hang-out.

Getting There & Around

Buses run from Andorra la Vella to El Tarter and Soldeu (375 ptas, 40 minutes, hourly) between 9 am to 8 pm. In winter there are free shuttle buses (just flash your ski pass) between Canillo and the two upper villages. These run approximately hourly (with a break from noon to 3 pm) until 11 pm.

All three villages are also on the bus route between Andorra la Vella and the French railheads of Latour-de-Carol and L'Hospitalet (see the main Getting There & Away section earlier in this chapter).

ORDINO & AROUND

Despite recent development, Ordino (population 1000), on highway CG3 8km north of Andorra la Vella, retains its Andorran character, with most building still in local stone. At 1000m it's a good starting point for summer activity holidays. The tourist office (☎ 737080), beside the CG3, is open 9 am to 1 pm and 3 to 7 pm daily (closed Sunday afternoon).

Things to See & Do

The **Museu d'Areny i Plandolit** (☎ 836908) is a 17th-century manor house with a richly furnished interior. Within the same grounds, is the far from nerdy **Museo Postal de Andorra**. It has an interesting 15-minute audiovisual program (available in English) and stamps by the thousand, issued by France and Spain specifically for Andorra (see Post & Communications earlier in this chapter). Admission to each museum costs 300 ptas. Both are open 9.30 am to 1.30 pm and 3 to 6.30 pm Tuesday to Saturday plus Sunday morning.

There are some excellent walking trails around Ordino. From the hamlet of **Segudet**, 500m east of Ordino, a path goes up through fir woods to the **Coll d'Ordino** (1980m), reached in about 1½ hours. **Pic de Casamanya** (2740m), with knock-me-down views is some two hours north of the col.

Other trails lead off from the tiny settlements beside the CG3 north of Ordino. A track (three hours one way) heads west from Llorts (1413m) up the Riu de l'Angonella Valley to a group of lakes, the Estanys de l'Angonella at about 2300m.

Just north of El Serrat (1600m), a secondary road leads 4km east to the Borda de Sorteny mountain refuge (1969m), from where trails lead into the high mountain area.

From Arans (1385m), a trail goes northeastwards to Bordes de l'Ensegur (2180m), where there's an old shepherd's hut.

Places to Stay & Eat

The cheapest option in the village is the cavernous *Hotel Casamanya* (☎ 835011), with singles/doubles for 4000/7000 ptas. *Bar Restaurant Quim* on the Plaça Major has a basic *menú* for 1350 ptas. Next door, *Restaurant Armengol* offers a *menú* for 1500 ptas and a good range of meat dishes.

Up the valley and some 200m north of Llorts, *Camping Els Pardassos* (☎ 850022) is one of Andorra's most beautiful camp sites. Open mid-June to mid-September, it charges 975 ptas for two people and a tent. Bring your own provisions. *Hotel Vilaró* (☎ 850225) 200m south of the village has rooms for 2200/2400 ptas.

Getting There & Away

Buses between Andorra la Vella and Ordino (130 ptas) run about every half-hour from 7 am to 9 pm daily. Buses to El Serrat (240 ptas) via Ordino leave Andorra la Vella at 1 and 8.30 pm. The valley is also served by four buses daily (10 in the ski season) linking Ordino and Arcalís.

ARINSAL

In winter, Arinsal, 10km north-west of Andorra la Vella, has good skiing and snowboarding and a lively après-ski scene. There are 13 lifts (including a smart new cabin lift to hurtle you up from the village), 28km of pistes and a vertical drop of 1010m.

In summer, Arinsal is a good departure point for medium mountain walks. From Aparthotel Crest at Arinsal's northern extremity, a trail leads north-west then west to Estany de les Truites (2260m), a natural lake. The steepish walk up takes around 1½ hours. From

here, it's about a further 1½ to two hours to bag Pic de la Coma Pedrosa (2964m), Andorra's highest point.

Places to Stay

Just above Estany de les Truites, *Refugi de Coma Pedrosa* (☎ 327955) is open June to late September, and charges 1100 ptas overnight. It does snacks and meals (dinner 1800 ptas).

The large, well equipped *Camping Xixerella* between Arinsal and Pal is open all year and has an outdoor swimming pool. Charges are 500 ptas to 600 ptas each per adult, tent and car.

In Arinsal, the recently renovated *Hostal Pobladó* (☎ 835122, fax 838 79, ✉ hospobl ado@andornet.ad) beside the new cabin lift is friendliness itself. With a lively bar (which offers Internet access on the side), its rooms cost 4400 ptas (6100 ptas with bathroom), including breakfast.

Places to Eat

As a change from the plentiful snack and sandwich joints, try *Refugi de la Fondue*, which does cheese or meat *fondue* dishes. *Restaurant el Moli* bills itself as Italian – and indeed offers the usual staple pastas and pizzas (both 900 ptas to 1200 ptas) – but also has more exotic fare such as pork stir fry (1575 ptas) and Thai green coconut chicken curry (1650 ptas). *Rocky Mountain* has a gringo menu with dishes such as T-bone steak and 'New York style cheesecake'.

Entertainment

In winter, Arinsal fairly throbs after sunset. In summer, it can be almost mournful. When the snow's around, call by *Surf* near the base of the cabin lift. A pub, dance venue and restaurant, it specialises in juicy Argentinian meat dishes (1250 ptas to 2200 ptas). *Quo Vadis* occasionally has live music.

Getting There & Away

Buses leave Andorra la Vella for Arinsal (185 ptas) via La Massana at 9.30 am, 1 and 6.15 pm. There are also more than 10 buses daily between La Massana and Arinsal. In winter, Skibus (325 ptas) runs five times daily between La Massana and Arinsal.

Austria

Austria (Österreich) is situated at the cross-roads of Europe. In the heady days of the Habsburgs, its empire encompassed both east and west, though nowadays it enjoys a more modest role in European affairs.

The country thrives on tourism, and is one of the most popular destinations in Europe. Its rich cultural heritage, historic cities, winter sports and stunning scenery are hard to beat. Its capital, Vienna, is one of the world's great cities; Salzburg is a living baroque museum; and Innsbruck is dramatically situated in a perfect panorama of peaks. And everywhere you go, the country moves to the rhythm of its unrivalled musical tradition.

Facts about Austria

HISTORY

In its early years, the land that became Austria was invaded by a succession of tribes and armies using the Danube Valley as a conduit – the Celts, Romans, Vandals, Visigoths, Huns, Avars and Slavs all came and went. Charlemagne established a territory in the Danube Valley known as the Ostmark in 803, and the area became Christianised and predominantly Germanic. The Ostmark was undermined by invading Magyars but was re-established by Otto I in 955. In 962, Pope John XII crowned Otto as Holy Roman Emperor of the German princes.

A period of growth and prosperity followed under the reign of the Babenbergs, and the territory acquired the status of a duchy in 1156. Influence in what is now Lower Austria expanded and the duchy of Styria came under central control in 1192. The last Babenberg died in battle in 1246 without an heir. The future of the duchy was uncertain until, in 1278, it fell into the hands of the Habsburgs, who ruled Austria until WWI.

The Habsburg Dynasty

Austrian territory gradually expanded under the rule of the Habsburgs. Carinthia (Kärnten) and Carniola were annexed in 1335, followed by Tirol in 1363. However, the Habsburgs

Capital	Vienna
Population	8.1 million
Official Language	German
Currency	1 Austrian Schilling = 100 Groschen
Time	GMT/UTC+0100
Country Phone Code	☎ 43

preferred to extend their territory without force. Much of Vorarlberg, for example, was purchased from bankrupt lords and significant gains were achieved by politically motivated marriages. Intermarriage was extremely effective, although it did have a genetic side-effect – a distended lower jaw became an increasingly visible family trait, albeit discreetly ignored in official portraits.

In 1477, Maximilian gained control of Burgundy and the Netherlands by marriage to Maria of Burgundy. His eldest son, Philip, was married to the Infanta of Spain in 1496. In 1516, Philip's son became Charles I of Spain, a title which granted control of vast overseas territories. Three years later, he also became Charles V of the Holy Roman Empire.

These acquisitions were too diverse for one person to rule effectively, so Charles handed over the Austrian territories to his younger brother Ferdinand in 1521. Ferdinand, the first Habsburg to live in Vienna, also ruled Hungary and Bohemia after the death of his brother-in-law King Lewis II in 1526. In 1556, Charles abdicated as emperor and Ferdinand I was crowned in his place. Charles' remaining territory was inherited by his son, Philip II, thereby splitting the Habsburg dynasty into two distinct lines – the Spanish and Austrian.

In 1571, when the emperor granted religious freedom, the vast majority of Austrians turned to Protestantism. Then, in 1576, the new emperor, Rudolf II, embraced the Counter-Reformation and much of the country reverted to Catholicism – not always without coercion. The attempt to impose Catholicism on Protestant areas of Europe led to the Thirty Years' War, which started in 1618 and devastated much of Central Europe. Peace was finally achieved in 1648 with the Treaty of Westphalia, which signalled the end of the push for a Catholic empire over Europe. Austria was preoccupied for much of the rest of the century with halting the advance of the Turks into Europe.

In 1740, Maria Theresa ascended the throne, despite the fact that as a woman she was ineligible to do so. A war followed to ensure that she stayed there. Her rule lasted 40 years, and is generally acknowledged as the era in which Austria developed as a modern state. She centralised control, established a civil service, reformed the army and the economy, and introduced a public education system. Progress was halted when Napoleon defeated Austria at Austerlitz in 1805 and forced the abolition of the title of Holy Roman Emperor. European conflict dragged on until the settlement at the Congress of Vienna in 1814-15, which was dominated by the Austrian foreign minister, Klemens von Metternich. Austria was left with control of the German Confederation but suffered internal upheaval during the 1848 revolutions and eventual defeat in the 1866 Austro-Prussian War.

Defeat led to the formation of the dual monarchy of Austria-Hungary in 1867 under Emperor Franz Josef, and exclusion from the new German empire unified by Bismarck. The dual monarchy established a common defence, foreign and economic policy, but retained two separate parliaments.

Another period of prosperity followed and Vienna, in particular, flourished. The situation changed in 1914 when the emperor's nephew, Archduke Franz Ferdinand, was assassinated in Sarajevo on 28 June. A month later, Austria-Hungary declared war on Serbia and WWI began.

Post Habsburgs

Franz Josef died in 1916. His successor abdicated at the conclusion of the war in 1918 and the Republic of Austria was created on 12 November. In 1919 the new, shrunken state was forced to recognise the independent states of Czechoslovakia, Poland, Hungary and Yugoslavia which, along with Transylvania (now in Romania), had previously been largely under the control of the Habsburgs. Losing so much land caused severe economic difficulties and political and social unrest.

More problems were created by the rise of Germany's Nazis, who tried to start a civil war in Austria and succeeded in killing Chancellor Dolfuss. Hitler manipulated the new chancellor to increase the power of the National Socialists in Austria, and was so successful that German troops met little resistance when they invaded Austria in 1938 and incorporated it into the German Reich. A national referendum in April of that year supported the *Anschluss* (annexation).

Austria was bombed heavily in WWII, and in 1945 the victorious Allies restored Austria to its 1937 frontiers. Allied troops from the USA, UK, Soviet Union and France remained in the country and divided it into four zones. Vienna, in the Soviet zone, was also divided into four zones. Fortunately, there was free movement between zones, which allowed Vienna to escape the fate that eventually befell Berlin, though the period of occupation was generally a tough time for Austrians. The ratification of the Austrian State Treaty and the withdrawal of the occupying powers was not completed until 1955, when Austria proclaimed its neutrality and agreed not to confederate with Germany.

Since WWII, Austria has worked hard to overcome economic difficulties. It established

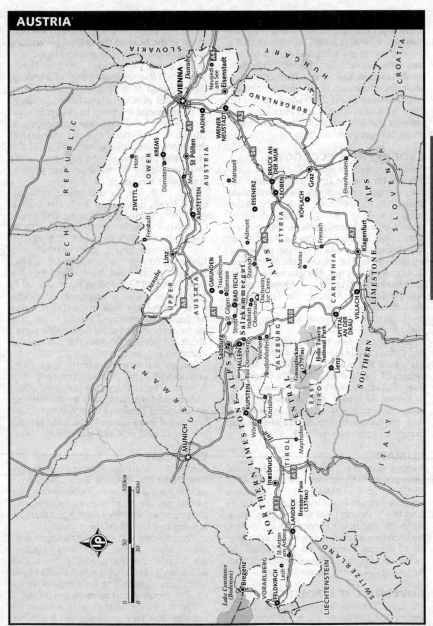

euro currency converter 1AS = €0.07

a free-trade treaty with the EU (then known as the EC) in 1972, and full membership was applied for in 1989. In a 1994 referendum 66.4% voted in favour of joining, and Austria became part of the EU on 1 January 1995. Since then, most Austrians have been rather ambivalent about the advantages of EU membership. EU relations worsened in 2000 when Austria became politically isolated after a coalition government was formed that contained members of the far-right Freedom Party.

GEOGRAPHY & ECOLOGY

Austria occupies an area of 83,855 sq km, extending for 560km from west to east, and 280km from north to south. Two-thirds of the country is mountainous, with three chains running west to east. The Northern Limestone Alps reach nearly 3000m. They are separated from the High or Central Alps, which form the highest peaks in Austria, by the valley of the River Inn. Many of the ridges in the Central Alps are topped by glaciers and most of the mountains are above 3000m, making north-south travel difficult. The Grossglockner is the highest peak at 3797m. The Southern Limestone Alps form a natural barrier along the border with Italy.

The most fertile land is in the Danube Valley. Cultivation is intensive and 90% of Austria's food is home-grown. North of Linz is an area of forested hills; the only other relatively flat area is south-east of Graz.

Austria is highly environmentally conscious. Recycling is enforced by law, and flora and fauna are protected in Hohe Tauern, Europe's largest national park.

CLIMATE

Average rainfall is 71cm per year. Maximum temperatures in Vienna are January 1°C, April 15°C, July 25°C and October 14°C. Minimum temperatures are lower by about 10°C (summer) to 4°C (winter). Salzburg and Innsbruck match the maximum temperature of Vienna, but average minimum temperatures are a couple of degrees lower. Some people find the Föhn, a hot, dry wind that sweeps down from the mountains, rather uncomfortable.

GOVERNMENT & POLITICS

The head of state is the president, who is chosen by the electorate for a six-year term. Thomas Klestil has been president since 1998. The chancellor, appointed by the president, is the head of the federal government and the most influential political figure.

The country is divided into nine federal provinces (Bundesländer), each of which has its own head of government (Landeshauptmann) and provincial assembly (Landtag). Each provincial assembly has a degree of autonomy over local issues and elects representatives to the Federal Council (Bundesrat), the upper house of the national legislative body. The lower house, the National Council (Nationalrat), is elected every four years by voters over the age of 18.

The 1970s saw the dominance of the Socialist Party, now called the Social Democrats (SPÖ). During the 1990s the SPÖ formed successive coalition governments with the right-wing People's Party (ÖVP). Following the 1999 election, a new coalition was formed in 2000 by the second and third-place parties, the ÖVP and the far-right Freedom Party (FPÖ). The Freedom Party was led by Jörg Haider, who is notorious for making several pro-Nazi statements. International condemnation prompted Haider to resign as leader of the FPÖ, but he remains the party's dominant personality and the governor of Carinthia province.

Haider's rise to popularity hints that a groundswell of pro-Nazi sentiment persists in Austria. The country had previously been embarrassed internationally by the 1986 appointment of President Kurt Waldheim, who had served in a German Wehrmacht unit that was implicated in WWII war crimes.

ECONOMY

Austria has a strong economy (unemployment under 6%, inflation under 2%), yet it is poor in natural resources. Deposits of oil and natural gas are supplemented by hydroelectric power and imported coal. Agriculture and forestry employ 5% of the population.

The economy is bolstered by a large contingent of foreign labour, particularly from Eastern Europe. Austria generally has a trade deficit in visible earnings, which is offset by income from tourism. The main exports are machinery, metallurgical products and textiles.

The country's wide-ranging welfare services include free education and health care (for locals), good pensions and a generous housing policy. A continuing privatisation program has bitten into Austria's large nationalised sector.

POPULATION & PEOPLE

Austria has a population of about 8.1 million; Vienna has the highest city population with 1.6 million people, followed by Graz (242,000), Linz (190,000), Salzburg (145,000), and Innsbruck (111,000).

On average, there are 96 inhabitants per sq km. Native Austrians are mostly of Germanic origin.

ARTS

Austria is renowned for its musical heritage. Composers throughout Europe were drawn to Austria in the 18th and 19th centuries by the willingness of the Habsburgs to patronise music. The various forms of classical music – symphony, concerto, sonata, opera and operetta – were developed and explored in Austria by the most eminent exponents of the day. The waltz originated in Vienna in the 19th century and was perfected as a musical genre by Johann Strauss senior and junior. The musical tradition continued in the 20th century with the innovative work of Arnold Schönberg. Today, Austrian orchestras have a worldwide reputation, and important annual musical festivals are held in Vienna, Salzburg and Graz.

Architecture is another important part of Austria's cultural heritage. The Gothic style was popular in the 14th, 15th and 16th centuries. The next major stylistic influence was baroque. Learning from the Italian model, Fischer von Erlach developed a national style called Austrian baroque; examples in Vienna are the National Library and the Church of St Charles.

SOCIETY & CONDUCT

Traditional costumes are still worn in rural areas of Tirol, but you're more likely to see local costumes during celebrations and processions. Traditional attire for men is shorts with wide braces, and jackets without collars or lapels. The best-known form of dress for women is the Dirndl: pleated skirt, apron, and white, pleated corsage with full sleeves.

Many festivals act out ancient traditions, such as welcoming the spring with painted masks and the ringing of bells. The departure of herders and cattle to high alpine pastures in early summer and their return in autumn are the cause of much jollity in village life.

It is customary to greet people, even shop assistants, with the salute *Grüss Gott*, and to say *Auf Wiedersehen* before leaving. Upon being introduced to someone, shake hands.

RELIGION

Roman Catholicism is embraced by 80% of the population; most of the remainder are Protestants, who are concentrated in Burgenland and Carinthia, or nondenominational. Religion plays an important part in the lives of many Austrians. It is not unusual to see small, roadside shrines decorated with fresh flowers.

LANGUAGE

Austrians speak German, although in the eastern province of Burgenland about 25,000 people speak Croatian, and in the southern province of Carinthia about 20,000 people speak Slovene.

English is widely understood in the main cities and tourist resorts. In smaller towns, hotel and railway staff usually know some English, but don't bank on it.

Knowledge of some German phrases is an asset appreciated by locals. See the Language chapter at the back of the book for pronunciation guidelines and useful words and phrases.

Facts for the Visitor

HIGHLIGHTS

Vienna is the Habsburgs' legacy to the world, offering awe-inspiring public buildings, art treasures culled from the old empire, and music, music and more music – don't miss a trip to the opera. Salzburg is another shrine to music, and its baroque skyline is a breathtaking sight. A cruise on the not-quite-blue Danube is a must. Visits to the distinctive provincial capitals of Innsbruck and Graz will be rewarded with interesting sights. Away from the cities, there are endless mountain views and hikes to enjoy. For skiing and glitz, head for Kitzbühel or Lech; for a less elitist ambience, try St Anton am Arlberg.

AUSTRIA

SUGGESTED ITINERARIES

Depending on the length of your stay, you might want to see and do the following:

Two days
  Vienna – see the central sights, visit the Opera, sample a few *Heurigen* (wine taverns).
One week
  Spend four days in Vienna, including a Danube cruise; two days in Salzburg; and one day visiting the Salzkammergut lakes.
Two weeks
  Spend five days in Vienna, three days in Salzburg (with a day trip to the Werfen ice caves and fortress), two days at the Salzkammergut lakes, two days in Innsbruck and two days at an alpine resort.
One month
  Visit the same places as the two-week scenario at a more leisurely pace, and add a tour of the south, taking in Graz, Klagenfurt and Lienz.

PLANNING
When to Go

Summer sightseeing and winter sports make Austria a year-round destination, though alpine resorts are pretty dead between seasons, ie, May, June and November. The summer high season is July and August. Christmas to late February is the winter high season in the ski resorts, though Christmas and New Year are also peak times elsewhere.

Maps

Freytag & Berndt of Vienna publishes good maps in varying scales. Its 1:100,000 series and 1:50,000 blue series are popular with hikers. Extremely detailed maps are produced by the Austrian Alpine Club. Bikeline maps are good for cyclists.

What to Bring

Pack warm clothing for nights at high altitude. Sheets are usually included in hostel prices; occasionally, you can save the 'sheet charge' if you bring your own.

TOURIST OFFICES
Local Tourist Offices

Local tourist offices (usually called *Kurverein* or *Verkehrsamt*) are very efficient and helpful, and can be found in all towns and villages of touristic interest. At least one of the staff will speak English. Most offices have a room-finding service, often without commission. Maps are always available and usually free. Each region has a provincial tourist board.

Tourist Offices Abroad

Austrian National Tourist Office (ANTO) branches abroad include:

Australia (☎ 02-9299 3621, fax 9299 3808, ✉ oewsyd@world.net) 1st floor, 36 Carrington St, Sydney, NSW 2000
UK (☎ 020-7629 0461, fax 7499 6038, ✉ info@anto.co.uk) 14 Cork St, London W1A 2QB
USA (☎ 212-944 6880, fax 730 4568, ✉ info@oewnyc.com) PO Box 1142, New York, NY 10108-1142

Some offices aren't open to personal callers, so phone first. There are also tourist offices in Tokyo, Milan, Munich, Paris, and Zürich. New Zealanders can get information from the Austrian consulate in Wellington (see Embassies & Consulates later in this section).

VISAS & DOCUMENTS

Visas are not required for EU, US, Canadian, Australian or New Zealand citizens. Visitors may stay a maximum of three months (six months for Japanese). There are no time limits for EU and Swiss nationals, but they should register with the police before taking up residency. Some developing world and Arab nationals require a visa.

EMBASSIES & CONSULATES
Austrian Embassies & Consulates

Diplomatic representation abroad includes:

Australia (☎ 02-6295 1533, fax 6239 6751) 12 Talbot St, Forrest, Canberra, ACT 2603
Canada (☎ 613-789 1444, fax 789 3431) 445 Wilbrod St, Ottawa, Ont KIN 6M7
New Zealand (☎ 04-499 6393, fax 499 6392) Austrian Consulate, Level 2, Willbank House, 587 Willis St, Wellington – does not issue visas or passports; contact the Australian office for these services
UK (☎ 020-7235 3731, fax 7235 8025) 18 Belgrave Mews West, London SW1X 8HU
USA (☎ 202-895 6700, fax 895 6750) 3524 International Court NW, Washington, DC 20008

Embassies & Consulates in Austria

The following foreign embassies are in Vienna. All these nations have a consulate in Vienna too, but not necessarily at the same address. Check the telephone book for more embassies *(Botschaften)* or consulates *(Konsulate)*.

Australia (☎ 01-512 85 80-0) 04, Mattiellistrasse 2-4
Canada (☎ 01-531 38-3000) 01, Laurenzerberg 2
Czech Republic (☎ 01-894 37 41) 14, Penzingerstrasse 11-13
Germany (☎ 01-711 54-0) 03, Metternichgasse 3
Hungary (☎ 01-533 26 31) 01, Bankgasse 4-6
Italy (☎ 01-712 51 21-0) 03, Rennweg 27
New Zealand The embassy (☎ 030-20 62 10) is in Berlin, Germany; Vienna has only an honorary consul (☎ 01-318 85 05)
Slovakia (☎ 01-318 60 16) 19, Armbrustergasse 24
Switzerland (☎ 01-795 05-0) 03, Prinz Eugen Strasse 7
UK (☎ 01-716 13-0) 03, Jaurèsgasse 12
USA (☎ 01-313 39) 09, Boltzmanngasse 16

Foreign consulates in other cities include:

Germany (☎ 0662-84 15 91) Bürgerspitalplatz 1-II, Salzburg;
(☎ 0512-596 65-0), Adamgasse 5, Innsbruck
Italy (☎ 0512-58 13 33) Conradstrasse 9, Innsbruck
Switzerland (☎ 0662-62 25 30), Alpenstrasse 85, Salzburg
UK (☎ 0662-84 81 33) Alter Markt 4, Salzburg (☎ 0512-58 83 20) Matthias Schmid Strasse 12/I, Innsbruck
USA (☎ 0662-84 87 76), Alter Markt 1/2, Salzburg

CUSTOMS

Duty-free shopping has been abolished within the EU, so there are no set limits on goods purchased for personal use. People aged 17 or over from non-EU countries can bring in 200 cigarettes (or 50 cigars or 250g of tobacco), 2L of wine and 1L of spirits.

MONEY
Currency

The Austrian Schilling (AS, or ÖS in German) is divided into 100 Groschen. There are coins to the value of one, five, 10, 25, 50, 100 and 500 Schillings, and for two, five, 10 and 50 Groschen. Banknotes come in denominations of AS20, AS50, AS100, AS500, AS1000 and AS5000. Austria is part of EU monetary union, and dual pricing (in Schillings and euros) is the norm. Visa and MasterCard credit cards are more widely accepted than American Express (AmEx) and Diners Club, though some places accept no cards at all.

Exchange rates and commission charges can vary between banks, so it pays to shop around. Changing cash usually attracts lower commission rates, but always check first. Some private exchange offices charge a shocking 10% commission on transactions. AmEx offices have so-so rates but low commission charges (for Austria) – from about AS15 for cash and AS50 to AS80 for travellers cheques; no commission applies on AmEx's own travellers cheques. The post office charges AS30 minimum for cash but doesn't change cheques. Train stations charge about AS40 for cash and AS64 minimum for cheques. Banks typically charge AS100 or more. Avoid changing a lot of low-value cheques because commission costs will be higher.

An efficient way to manage your money in Austria is to get cash advances with a Visa card, Eurocard or MasterCard; there are numerous Bankomat machines (ATMs) offering this service, even in small villages. However, getting cash advances with Australian-issued cards is sometimes a problem. Using debit cards is another possibility.

Sending funds electronically is fast and inexpensive using Western Union (offices at many train stations) or AmEx – there's no fee at the receiving end.

Exchange Rates

country	unit		Austrian Schilling
Australia	A$1	=	AS8.83
Canada	C$1	=	AS10.27
euro	€1	=	AS13.76
France	1FF	=	AS2.10
Germany	DM1	=	AS7.04
Japan	¥100	=	AS14.02
New Zealand	NZ$1	=	AS6.85
UK	UK£1	=	AS22.90
USA	US$1	=	AS15.23

Costs

Expenses are average for Western Europe, and prices are highest in big cities and ski resorts. Budget travellers can get by on AS450 a day,

AUSTRIA

after rail-card costs; double this if you want to avoid self-catering or staying in hostels. The *minimum* you can expect to pay per person is AS140/250 for a hostel/hotel and AS60/100 for a lunch/dinner, excluding drinks.

Tipping & Bargaining

It is customary to tip an extra 5% in restaurants (pay the server direct, don't leave it on the table); taxi drivers will expect tips of 10%. Prices are fixed, so bargaining for goods is not generally an option.

Taxes & Refunds

For most goods and services, value-added tax, or VAT *(Mehrwertsteuer; MWST)*, is charged at 20%. Prices are always displayed inclusive of all taxes.

For purchases over AS1000, non-EU residents can reclaim the MWST (though one-third will be absorbed in charges), either upon leaving the EU or afterwards. First ensure the shop has the relevant forms, as they must be filled out at the time of purchase. Present the documentation to customs on departure for checking and stamping. The airports at Vienna, Salzburg, Innsbruck, Linz and Graz have counters for instant refunds, as do some land crossings, but you can only claim your refunds at these points if you're *not* going to another EU country. You can also reclaim by post.

POST & COMMUNICATIONS
Post

Post office hours vary: typical hours are 8 am to noon and 2 to 6 pm Monday to Friday (money exchange to 5 pm), and 8 to 11 am Saturday, but a few main post offices in big cities are open daily till late, or even 24 hours. Stamps are also available in tobacco *(Tabak)* shops.

Postcards and letters within Austria cost AS6.50 and AS7 respectively. Letters (up to 20g) cost AS6.50/7 nonpriority/priority to Europe and AS7.50/13 elsewhere.

Poste restante is *Postlagernde Briefe* in German. Mail can be sent care of any post office and is held for a month (address it to 'Postamt', followed by the postcode); a passport must be shown to collect mail. AmEx will also hold mail for 30 days for customers who have its card or cheques.

Telephone & Fax

Telekom Austria has two zones for national calls – Regional-Zone (up to 50km) and Österreich-Zone (over 50km), which is about 300% more expensive. The minimum tariff in phone boxes is AS2. International direct dialling is nearly always possible; otherwise, dial ☎ 09 for the operator. A three-minute call to the USA costs AS24, normal rate. The national and international cheap rate is from 6 pm to 8 am, and on weekends; rates drop greatly for national calls, but only marginally for international calls. Look out for cut-price telephone call centres in cities.

Post offices usually have telephones outside. Be wary of using telephones in hotels because they can cost several times as much as public pay phones. Some call boxes now take only phonecards *(Telefon-Wertkarte)*. For AS50 you get AS50 worth of calls, though for AS95 and AS190 you get AS100 and AS200 worth of calls respectively. To send a fax via the post office costs AS18 plus the call charge.

INTERNET RESOURCES

There is public Internet access in most big towns – see in the city sections. Most Austrian businesses have email addresses and Web sites.

The Austrian National Tourist Office Web site (www.austria-tourism.at) has plenty of useful information, while the Austrian Press

Phone Quirks

A peculiar complication of Austrian phone numbers is that telephone extensions *(DW)* are often tacked onto the main telephone number, and it's necessary to dial these to get through. Often this extension will be for a fax number. In this chapter, any telephone extensions are separated from the main number by a hyphen, and fax extensions are shown by a hyphen and the extension number (ie, you'd have to dial the main number first to reach it). Sometimes the fax number is a completely different number, but still with an extension, in which case the whole number is shown.

& Information Service (www.austria.org) offers weekly news and visa details.

BOOKS

Lonely Planet has published guides to *Austria* and *Vienna*, and Western/Central Europe phrasebooks. *The Xenophobe's Guide to the Austrians* by Louis James is informative and amusing. Graham Greene's famous spy story *The Third Man* and John Irving's *Setting Free the Bears* are both set in Austria.

NEWSPAPERS & MAGAZINES

English-language newspapers and magazines (*The Times, International Herald Tribune, Newsweek*) are available for AS25 to AS50.

RADIO & TV

FM4 is a news and music station, mostly in English, with news on the hour till 7 pm. It's found at 103.8FM in Vienna. Austria has only two (terrestrial) national TV channels, and a national cable channel (ATV). Many hotels have multilingual cable TV.

PHOTOGRAPHY & VIDEO

The Niedermeyer chain is one of the cheapest stores for buying film; a twin-pack of 36-exposure rolls costs AS69.80 for Kodak Gold 100 and AS119.80 for Ektachrome. Note that slide film usually *excludes* mounting, and sometimes processing too. Austria uses the PAL video system.

TIME

Austrian time is GMT/UTC plus one hour. Clocks go forward one hour on the last Saturday night in March and back again on the last Saturday night in October.

LAUNDRY

Look out for a *Wäscherei* for self-service or service washes. Expect to pay around AS100 to wash and dry a load. Many hostels have cheaper laundry facilities.

TOILETS

There's no shortage of public toilets, though cubicles may have a charge of about AS5.

WOMEN TRAVELLERS

Women should experience no special problems. Physical violations and verbal harassment are less common than in many other countries. Vienna has a Rape Crisis Hotline: ☎ 01-717 19.

GAY & LESBIAN TRAVELLERS

Public attitudes to homosexuality are less tolerant than in most other Western European countries, except perhaps in Vienna. A good information centre in Vienna is Rosa Lila (☎ 01-586 8150), 06, Linke Wienziele 102. The age of consent for gay men is 18; for everyone else it's 14. Vienna has a Pride march, the Rainbow Parade, on the last Saturday in June. A German-language Web site with lots of useful links is www.hosi.at.

DISABLED TRAVELLERS

Many sights and venues have wheelchair ramps. Local tourist offices usually have good information for the disabled; the Vienna office, for example, has a free 90-page booklet. Car drivers have free, unlimited parking in blue zones with the international disabled sticker.

DANGERS & ANNOYANCES

You always have to beware of theft, even in a relatively orderly country like Austria. Dial ☎ 133 for the police, ☎ 144 for an ambulance or ☎ 122 in the event of fire. Take care in the mountains; helicopter rescue is expensive unless you are covered by insurance (that's assuming they find you in the first place).

BUSINESS HOURS

Shops are usually open at 8 am (except Sunday), and close between 6 and 7.30 pm on weekdays, and 1 to 5 pm on Saturday. They generally close for up to two hours at noon, except in big cities. Some shops in train stations have extended hours. Banking hours can vary but are commonly 9 am to 12.30 pm and 1.30 to 3 pm Monday to Friday, with late closing on Thursday.

PUBLIC HOLIDAYS & SPECIAL EVENTS

Public holidays are 1 and 6 January, Easter Monday, 1 May, Ascension Day, Whit Monday, Corpus Christi, 15 August, 26 October, 1 November, and 8, 25 and 26 December.

Numerous events take place at a local level throughout the year, so it's worth checking

AUSTRIA

with the tourist office. ANTO compiles an updated list of annual and one-off events. Vienna and Salzburg have almost continuous music festivals (see their Special Events heading). Linz has the Bruckner Festival in September.

There are trade fairs in Vienna, Innsbruck and Graz in September. Religious holidays provide an opportunity to stage colourful processions. Look out for Fasching (Shrovetide carnival) in early February, maypoles on 1 May, midsummer night's celebrations on 21 June, the autumn cattle roundup at the end of October, much flag-waving on national day on 26 October and St Nicholas Day parades on 5 and 6 December.

ACTIVITIES
Skiing
Austria has world-renowned skiing areas, particularly in Vorarlberg and Tirol. There's also skiing in Salzburg province, Upper Austria and Carinthia, where prices can be lower. Equipment can always be hired at resorts.

Ski coupons for ski lifts can sometimes be bought, but usually there are general passes available for complete or partial days. For one day, count on spending AS240 to AS470 for a ski pass, AS250 for downhill rental and AS150 for cross-country rental; rates drop for multiple days. The skiing season starts in December and lasts well into April at higher altitude resorts. Year-round skiing is possible at the Stubai Glacier near Innsbruck.

Hiking & Mountaineering
Walking and climbing are popular with visitors and Austrians alike. Mountain paths are marked with direction indicators, and most tourist offices have maps of hiking routes. There are 10 long-distance national hiking routes, and three European routes pass through Austria. Options include the northern alpine route from Lake Constance to Vienna, via Dachstein, or the central route from Feldkirch to Hainburger Pforte, via Hohe Tauern.

Mountaineering should not be undertaken without proper equipment and some previous experience. Tirol province has many mountain guides and mountaineering schools; these are listed in the *Walking Guide Tirol*, free from the tourist office. The Austrian Alpine Club (Österreichischer Alpenverein, ÖAV; ☎ 0512-58 78 28, fax 58 88 42), Wilhelm

Greil Strasse 15, A-6010 Innsbruck, has touring programs, and also maintains alpine huts. These are situated between 900 and 2700m in hill-walking regions; they're inexpensive and often have meals or cooking facilities. Members of the club take priority but anyone can stay. Web site: www.alpenverein-ibk.at.

Spa Resorts
There are spa resorts throughout the country. They are identifiable by the prefix *Bad* (Bath), eg, Bad Ischl. Long, leisurely walks and much wallowing in hot springs are typical ingredients of these salubrious locations.

WORK
EU nationals can work in Austria without a permit. Everyone else must obtain in advance a work permit and (except for seasonal work) a residency permit. In ski resorts there are often vacancies for jobs with unsociable hours. Likely opportunities are in snow clearing, chalet cleaning, restaurants and ski-equipment shops. Employers face big fines if they're caught employing workers illegally.

ACCOMMODATION
Reservations are recommended in July and August and at the peak times of Christmas and Easter. Reservations are binding on either side and compensation may be claimed if you do not take a reserved room or if a reserved room is unavailable.

A cheap and widely available option is to take a room in a private house (AS160 to AS280 per person). Look out for *Zimmer frei* (room(s) available) signs. See Hiking & Mountaineering under Activities earlier in this chapter for information on alpine huts. Tourist offices can supply listings of all types of accommodation, and often make reservations. Accommodation sometimes costs more for a single night's stay. Prices are lower out of season. Assume breakfast is included in places listed in this chapter, unless otherwise stated.

In many resorts (rarely in towns) a guest card is issued to people who stay overnight; it offers useful discounts and is well worth having. Check with the tourist office if you're not offered one at your resort accommodation. Guest cards are funded by a resort tax of around AS10 to AS20 per night, paid to the accommodation. Prices quoted in accommodation lists generally include this tax.

Camping

There are over 400 camping grounds, but most close in the winter. They charge around AS40 to AS70 per person, plus about AS40 for a tent and AS40 for a car. Free camping in camper vans is OK (in tents it's illegal), except in urban and protected rural areas, as long as you don't set up camping equipment outside the van. The Austrian Camping Club (Österreichischer Camping Club; ☎ 01-711 99-1272) is at Schubertring 1-3, A-1010 Vienna.

Hostels

In Austria there is an excellent network of HI-affiliated hostels (Jugendherbergen). Membership cards are always required, except in a few private hostels. Nonmembers pay a surcharge of AS40 per night for a guest card; after six nights, the guest card counts as a full membership card. Some hostels will accept reservations by telephone, and some are part of the worldwide computer reservations system. Hostel prices are around AS140 to AS240. Austria has two hostel associations but either can give information on hostels. Contact the Österreichischer Jugendherbergswerk (☎ 01-533 18 33, ✉ oejhw@oejhw.or.at), 01, Helferstorferstrasse 4, Vienna. Web site: www.oejhw.or.at.

Hotels & Pensions

With very few exceptions, rooms are clean and adequately appointed. Expect to pay from AS280/500 for a single/double. In low-budget accommodation, a room with a private shower may mean a room with a shower cubicle rather than a proper en suite bathroom. Prices in major cities (particularly Vienna) are significantly higher than in the untouristed rural areas. A small country inn (Gasthaus or Gasthof) or a guesthouse (Pension) tends to be more intimate than a hotel. Self-catering chalets or apartments are common in ski resorts.

FOOD

The main meal is taken at midday. Most restaurants have a set meal or menu of the day (Tagesteller or Tagesmenu), which gives the best value for money. The cheapest deal around is in university restaurants (mensas); these are only mentioned in the text if they are open to all. Wine taverns are fairly cheap places to eat, and some food shops have tables for customers to eat on the premises. For a stand-up snack, head for a sausage stall (Würstel Stand). Chinese restaurants and pizzerias are numerous and good value.

Soups are good, often with dumplings (Knödel) and pasta added. Wiener Schnitzel is a veal or pork cutlet coated in breadcrumbs. Chicken (Huhn) is also popular. Paprika is used to flavour several dishes, including Gulasch (beef stew). Look out for regional dishes such as Tiroler Bauernschmaus, a selection of meats served with sauerkraut, potatoes and dumplings. Austrians eat a lot of meat; vegetarians will have a fairly tough time finding suitable or varied dishes.

Famous desserts include the Strudel (baked dough filled with a variety of fruits) and Salzburger Nockerl (an egg, flour and sugar pudding). Pancakes are also popular.

DRINKS

Eastern Austria specialises in producing white wines. Heuriger wine is the year's new vintage. It's avidly consumed, even (in autumn) when still semi-fermented (called Sturm). Austria is famous for its lager beer; some well-known brands include Gösser, Schwechater, Stiegl and Zipfer. Also try Weizenbier (wheat beer). Beer is usually served by the 0.5L or 0.3L; in eastern Austria, these are respectively called a Krügerl and a Seidel.

Tea and coffee are expensive, but bottled water isn't and tap water is fine to drink anyway. Coffee houses are an established part of Austrian life, particularly in Vienna. Strong Turkish coffee is popular. Linger over a cup (from AS22) and read the free newspapers. Coffee houses basically fall into two types, though the distinction is rather blurred nowadays. A Kaffeehaus, traditionally preferred by men, offers games such as chess and billiards and serves wine, beer, spirits and light meals. The Café Konditorei attracts more women and typically has a salon look, with rococo mouldings and painted glass. A wide variety of cakes and pastries is usually on offer.

ENTERTAINMENT

Late opening is common in the cities, and in Vienna you can party all night long. It isn't

AUSTRIA

hard to find bars or taverns featuring traditional or rock music.

In cinemas (cheaper on Monday) some films are dubbed, but look for *OF*, meaning *Original Fassung* (original-language production), or *OmU*, meaning *Original mit Untertiteln* (original language with subtitles).

The main season for opera, theatre and concerts is September to June. Cheap, standing-room tickets are often available shortly before performances begin and they represent excellent value.

Gamblers can indulge at a dozen casinos around the country, including in Vienna, Graz, Linz and Salzburg. Admission is free. To gamble, you will pay AS260 for an initial AS300-worth of chips. Smart dress is required; opening hours are typically 3 pm to midnight or later.

SHOPPING

Local crafts such as textiles, pottery, painted glassware, woodcarving and wrought-iron work make popular souvenirs.

Getting There & Away

AIR

The airports at Vienna, Linz, Graz, Salzburg, Innsbruck and Klagenfurt all receive international flights. Vienna is the busiest airport, with several daily, nonstop flights to major transport hubs such as Amsterdam, Berlin, Frankfurt, London, Paris and Zürich.

LAND
Bus

Buses depart from London's Victoria Station five days a week (daily in summer), arriving in Vienna 22 hours later (UK£72/111 one way/return). See the Vienna Getting There & Away section for services to Eastern Europe. The Web site for Eurolines in Austria is www.eurolines.at.

Train

Austria has excellent rail connections to all important destinations. Vienna is the main hub (see its Getting There & Away section for details). Salzburg has at least hourly trains

to Munich (AS298, two hours) with onward connections north. Express services to Italy go via Innsbruck or Villach; trains to Slovenia are routed through Graz.

Generally, reserving 2nd-class train seats in Austria costs AS40; in 1st class it's free. Supplements sometimes apply on international trains.

Car & Motorcycle

There are numerous entry points from the Czech Republic, Hungary, Slovakia, Slovenia, and Switzerland; main border crossings are open 24 hours. There are no border controls to/from Germany and Italy. Austria charges an annual fee for using its motorways, though tourists can opt to buy a weekly pass (AS70, valid Friday to two Sundays hence) or two-month pass (AS150 for cars, AS80 for motorcycles). These can be purchased at borders, on freeways or from service stations. Without one you will be fined.

BOAT

Steamers and hydrofoils operate along the Danube in the summer. See the Vienna and Danube Valley sections for details.

DEPARTURE TAX

There is no departure tax to pay at the airport, as all taxes are automatically included in the ticket price.

Getting Around

AIR

There are several flights a day from Vienna to Graz, Klagenfurt, Innsbruck, Salzburg and Linz. The main national carrier is Austrian Airlines; its subsidiary, Tyrolean Airlines, has nonstop flights between most domestic airports. Schedules change half-yearly.

BUS

Yellow or orange/red buses are run by the post office or Austrian Railways. Either way, they're called *Bundesbus*, which is the term used throughout this chapter. Some rail routes are duplicated by buses, but buses generally operate in the more inaccessible mountainous regions. They're clean, efficient and on time. Advance reservations are possible, but sometimes you can only buy tickets from the drivers. Fares are comparable to train fares. For national Bundesbus information, call ☎ 01-711 01.

TRAIN

Trains are efficient and frequent. The state network covers the whole country, and is supplemented by a few private lines. Eurail and Inter-Rail passes are valid on the former; inquire before embarking on the latter. Many stations have information centres where the staff speak English. Tickets can be purchased on the train, but they cost AS30 extra. In this chapter, fares quoted are for 2nd class.

Trains are expensive (eg, AS178 for 100km, AS300 for 200km), and Austria has withdrawn most of its railpasses. You could consider buying a Domino Pass (see the Getting Around chapter) – the Austrian version costs UK£68/108 for three/eight days. The VORTEILScard (AS1290, valid one year) reduces fares by 50% – fine if you stay a while, but of no value for short stays. Two or more people travelling together can get fare reductions on journeys over 100km (1 Plus-Ticket).

Stations are called *Bahnhof* (train station) or *Hauptbahnhof* (main train station). Ordinary single/return tickets (over 100km) are valid for three days/one month and you can break your journey, but tell the conductor first. Some provinces have zonal day passes, (valid for trains and buses), which may save money compared with buying ordinary tickets. Reduced fares are sometimes available for those aged under 26; wave your passport and ask. Nationwide train information can be obtained by dialling ☎ 05-1717 (local rate).

CAR & MOTORCYCLE

Austrians drive on the right (it's best if you do likewise). Roads are generally good, but take it carefully on difficult mountain routes. In addition to the motorway tax (see Car & Motorcycle in the Getting There & Away section earlier in this chapter), there are hefty toll charges for some mountain tunnels. The tourist office has details of the few roads and passes which are closed in winter.

Give priority to vehicles coming from the right. On mountain roads, Bundesbuses always have priority; otherwise, priority lies with uphill traffic. Drive in low gear on steep downhill stretches. Penalties for drink-driving (over 0.05% BAC) are a steep on-the-spot fine and confiscation of your driving licence. Normal speed limits are 50km/h in towns, 130km/h on motorways and 100km/h on other roads. Snow chains are highly recommended in winter. Many city streets have restricted parking (called blue zones); parking is free and unrestricted outside the specified times, which normally correspond to shopping hours. Parking is unrestricted on unmarked streets.

Cars can be transported by train; Vienna is linked by a daily motorail service to Feldkirch, Innsbruck, Salzburg and Villach. Motorcycles must have their headlights on during the day. The Austrian Automobile Club (Österreichischer Automobil, Motorrad und Touring Club, ÖAMTC; ☎ 01-711 99-0) is at Schubertring 1-3, A-1010 Vienna. Dial ☎ 120 for emergency assistance.

Rental

Hertz, Avis, Budget and Europcar all have offices in main cities. The 'Lokal-Tarif' rate is normally the best deal, and you can get cheaper rates for weekend rental. Europcar usually has the best unlimited-kilometre rates of the multinationals, from AS599 per day. Local rental agencies often have cheaper prices; the local tourist office will be able to supply details.

BICYCLE

Bicycles can be hired from most train stations from April to October. The rate is AS180 per day, or AS120 with a train ticket valid for that day or for after 3 pm the previous day. There's a surcharge of AS90 to return bikes to a different station. Cycling is popular even though minor roads can be steep and have sharp bends. You can take your bike on slow trains (AS40/90 for a day/week ticket); on fast trains you may have to send your bike as registered luggage (AS90/140 national/international).

HITCHING

Hitching is patchy, but not too bad – though we don't recommend it. Trucks are often the best bet, and can be enticed to stop at border posts, truck stops or truck parking stops (signposted as *Autohof*). Always display a sign showing your destination. It is illegal for

AUSTRIA

minors under 16 to hitch in Burgenland, Upper Austria, Styria and Vorarlberg. Austria has only one *Mitfahrzentrale* hitching agency – see Hitching under Getting There & Away in the Vienna section for details.

BOAT

Services along the Danube are slow, expensive, scenic excursions rather than functional transport. Nevertheless, a boat ride is definitely worth it if you like lounging on deck and having the scenery come to you rather than the other way round. The larger Salzkammergut lakes have ferry services.

LOCAL TRANSPORT

Buses, trams and underground railways are efficient and reliable. Most towns have an integrated system and offer good-value daily or 24-hour tickets (AS25 to AS60), which are available in advance from dispensers or Tabak shops. Even single tickets can sometimes only be purchased prior to boarding buses/trams. On-the-spot fines apply to those caught travelling without tickets, though some locals are prepared to take the risk.

Taxis are metered, although all but unnecessary given the good public transport. If you need one, look around train stations and large hotels.

For a rundown on mountain transport, see the introductory Getting Around section in the Switzerland chapter.

ORGANISED TOURS

These vary from two-hour walks in city centres to all-inclusive packages at ski resorts. Inquire at tourist offices.

Vienna

☎ 01 • pop 1.6 million

The character of modern Vienna (Wien) owes much to its colourful political and cultural past. It proffers impressive architecture, world-renowned museums and an enviable musical tradition alongside characteristic Viennese institutions such as coffee houses and wine taverns. Vienna is not as staid as some would make out – you can party all night if you want to. The city that gave the waltz to the world also pursued radical socialist policies through much of the last century.

The Habsburgs settled in Vienna in 1278 and made it the capital of the Austrian empire. The city flourished under their strong leadership, despite being dragged into various European conflicts and withstanding attacks by the Turks in 1529 and 1683. Vienna's 'golden years' as the cultural centre of Europe were the 18th and 19th centuries. Musically, there was only one place to be during this period. Haydn, Mozart, Beethoven, Brahms, Strauss, and Schubert are some of the great composers who made Vienna their home. Anybody with an interest in the arts will love this city.

Orientation

Many of the historic sights are in the old city, the *Innere Stadt*. This is encircled by the Danube Canal to the north-east and a series of broad boulevards known as the Ring or Ringstrasse. St Stephen's Cathedral is in the heart of the city and is the principal landmark. Most attractions in the centre are within walking distance of each other.

Take care when reading addresses. The number of a building within a street *follows* the street name. Any number *before* the street name denotes the district, of which there are 23. District 1 (the Innere Stadt) is the central region, mostly within the Ring. Generally speaking, the higher the district number, the further it is from the city centre. The middle two digits of postcodes always refer to the district, hence places with a postcode 1010 are in district 1, and 1230 means district 23.

The main train stations are Franz Josefs Bahnhof to the north, Westbahnhof to the west and Südbahnhof to the south; transferring between them is easy. The majority of hotels and pensions are in the centre and to the west.

Information

Tourist Offices The main tourist office is at 01, Am Albertinaplatz, and has extensive free literature including an excellent city map. The *10 good reasons for Vienna*, clearly aimed at youths with its overly hip style, contains lots of useful information for everyone. The office is open 9 am to 7 pm daily. There is a tourist office in the arrival hall of the airport, open 8.30 am to 9 pm daily.

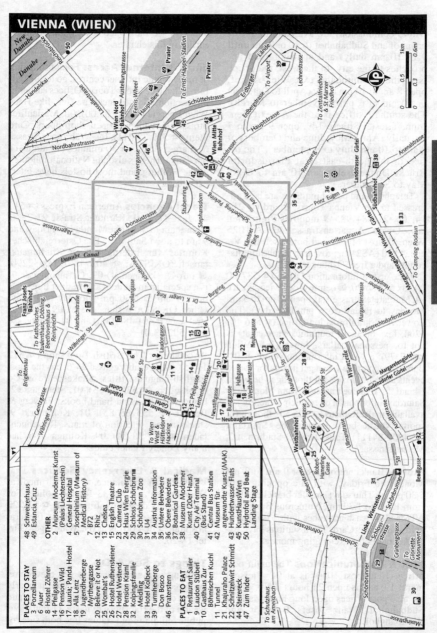

VIENNA (WIEN)

AUSTRIA

PLACES TO STAY
3 Porzellaneum
6 Auer
8 Hostel Zöhrer
14 Pfeilgasse
16 Pension Wild
17 Lauria; Panda Hostel
18 Alla Lenz
19 Jugendherberge Myrthengasse
20 Believe it or Not
25 Wombat's
26 Hostel Ruthensteiner
27 Hotel Westend
28 Pension Kraml
32 Kolpingsfamilie Meidling
33 Hotel Kölbeck
39 Turmherberge Don Bosco
46 Praterstern

PLACES TO EAT
1 Restaurant Sailer
10 Laudon Stüberl
Gasthaus Zur Böhmischen Kuchl
11 Tunnel
21 Khajuraho Palace
22 Schnitzelwirt Schmidt
44 Steirereck
47 Zum Inder

48 Schweizerhaus
49 Estancia Cruz

OTHER
2 Museum Moderner Kunst (Palais Liechtenstein)
4 General Hospital
5 Josephinium (Museum of Medical History)
7 B72
12 Rhiz
13 Chelsea
15 English Theatre
23 Camera Club
24 Haus Wien Energie
29 Schloss Schönbrunn
30 Schönbrunn Zoo
31 U4
34 Austria Information
35 Untere Belvedere
36 Obere Belvedere
37 Botanical Gardens
38 Museum Moderner Kunst (20er Haus)
40 City Air Terminal (Bus Stand)
41 Central Bus Station
42 Museum für angewandte Kunst (MAK)
43 Hundertwasser Flats
45 KunstHausWien
50 Hydrofoil and Boat Landing Stage

Information and room reservations (AS40 commission) are available in Westbahnhof and Südbahnhof (6.30 or 7 am until 9 or 10 pm daily) and at major road approaches to the city. In the west, the office is at the A1 autobahn exit Wien-Auhof, open 8 am to 10 pm daily (April to October) or 10 am to 6 pm (November to March). The southern office is at the A2 exit Zentrum, Triester Strasse 149, open 9 am to 7 pm daily (April, May, June and October) or 8 am to 10 pm (July to September). The office in the north-east is at Floridsdorfer Brücke/Donauinsel, open 10 am to 6 pm May to September.

Telephone and postal inquiries are best addressed to the Vienna Tourist Board (☎ 211 14, fax 216 84 92, ✉ inquiries@info.wien .at), Obere Augartenstrasse 40, A-1025 Wien. Tourist offices and hotels sell the Vienna Card (AS210), providing admission discounts and a free 72-hour travel pass.

The Austria Information Office (☎ 587 20 00, fax 588 66-20, ✉ oeinfo@oewwien.via.at), 04, Margaretenstrasse 1, is open 10 am to 5 pm Monday to Friday (to 6 pm Thursday). The Lower Austria Information Office (☎ 536 10-6200, fax -6060, ✉ tourismus@noe.co.at) is not for personal callers. Jugend-Info Wien (☎ 17 79), a youth information centre at 01, Babenbergerstrasse 1, can get tickets for varied events at reduced rates for those aged between 14 and 26. It is open noon to 7 pm Monday to Saturday. Information on municipal facilities is available in the Rathaus (☎ 525 50), though for sports you'd best contact the Sportamt (☎ 4000-84111), Ernst-Happel-Stadion, 02, Meiereistrasse 7.

Money Banks are open 8 or 9 am to 3 pm Monday to Friday, with late opening until 5.30 pm on Thursday; smaller branches close from 12.30 to 1.30 pm. Numerous Bankomat ATMs allow cash advances with Visa, Eurocard and MasterCard. Train stations have extended hours for exchanging money.

Post & Communications The main post office (Hauptpost 1010) is at 01, Fleischmarkt 19, and is open 24 hours daily. There are also post offices open long hours daily at Südbahnhof, Franz Josefs Bahnhof and Westbahnhof.

For information on hyphenated phone numbers see the boxed text 'Phone Quirks' earlier in this chapter.

Email & Internet Access For a full listing of many public Internet centres, go to Jugend-Info Wien (see under Tourist Offices earlier in this section). Some places are free, like Haus Wien Energie (☎ 581 05 00), 06, Mariahilfer Strasse 63, which is open shop hours. Café Stein (☎ 319 72 411), 09, Währinger Strasse 6, charges AS65 for 30 minutes (10 am to 11 pm daily). There's also the Nationalbibliothek in the Hofburg, and most hostels have Internet access.

Travel Agencies American Express (☎ 515 40, fax -777), 01, Kärntner Strasse 21-23, is open 9 am to 5.30 pm Monday to Friday and 9 am to noon Saturday. The Österreichisches Komitee für Internationalen Studienaustausch (ÖKISTA; ☎ 401 48-0, fax -2290, ✉ info@oekista.co.at) 09, Garnisongasse 7, is a specialist in student and budget fares. It's open 9 am to 5.30 pm Monday to Friday. Other ÖKISTA offices are at 09, Türkenstrasse 6 (☎ 401 48-7000) and 04, Karlsgasse 3 (☎ 502 43-0).

Bookshops The British Bookshop (☎ 512 19 45), 01, Weihburggasse 24-6, has the most English-language titles. Shakespeare & Co Booksellers (☎ 535 50 53), 01, Sterngasse 2, has new and second-hand books. Freytag & Berndt (☎ 533 85 85), 01, Kohlmarkt 9, stocks a vast selection of maps. Reisebuchladen (☎ 317 33 84), 09, Kolingasse 6, has many Lonely Planet guides.

Medical & Emergency Services Dial ☎ 144 for an ambulance, ☎ 141 for medical emergencies and ☎ 133 for the police. For out-of-hours dental treatment call ☎ 512 20 78. The Allgemeines Krankenhaus (general hospital; ☎ 404 00) is at 09, Währinger Gürtel 18-20.

Things to See & Do
Walking is the best way to see the centre. Architectural riches confront you at nearly every corner, testimony to the power and wealth of the Habsburg dynasty. Ostentatious public buildings and statues line both sides of

the Ring, and a tour of this boulevard by foot (or tram, or bicycle) is strongly recommended. The buildings that stand out include the neo-Gothic *Rathaus* (city hall), the Greek Revival-style Parlament (in particular the Athena statue), the 19th-century Burgtheater and the baroque Karlskirche (St Charles' Church). Carefully tended gardens and parks break up the brickwork.

Walk north up the pedestrian-only Kärntner Strasse, a walkway of plush shops, trees, cafe tables and street entertainers. It leads directly to Stephansplatz and the prime landmark of **Stephansdom** (St Stephen's Cathedral).

The latticework spire of this 13th-century Gothic masterpiece rises high above the city. Interior walls and pillars are decorated with fine statues; the stone pulpit is particularly striking. Take the lift up the north tower (AS40) or the stairs up the higher south tower (AS30) for an impressive view.

The internal organs of the Habsburgs reside in the *Katakomben* (catacombs), open daily; entry is AS40. One of the privileges of being a Habsburg was to be dismembered and dispersed after death: their hearts are in the Augustinerkirche, 01, Augustinerstrasse 3; the rest of their bits are in the Kaisergruft in the Kapuzinerkirche, 01, Neuer Markt.

From Stephansplatz, turn west down Graben, which is dominated by the knobbly outline of the Plague Column. Turn left into Kohlmarkt, which leads to the St Michael's Gateway of the **Hofburg** (Imperial Palace).

The Hofburg has been periodically enlarged since the 13th century, resulting in the current mixture of architectural styles. The Spanish Riding School office is to the left within the entrance dome (see under Entertainment later in this chapter). Opposite are the **Kaiserappartements**, which cost AS80 to visit (students aged under 26 pay AS60; open daily). The rooms in Schönbrunn (see the following section) are more impressive. Walk into the large courtyard, and take a left into the small Swiss Courtyard. Here you'll find the **Burgkapelle** (Royal Chapel; entry AS20), and the **Schatzkammer** (Imperial Treasury), which contains treasures and relics spanning 1000 years, including the crown jewels. Allow up to one hour to get round (entry AS80, students under 30 AS50; closed Tuesday).

Schloss Schönbrunn This sumptuous 1440-room palace is open daily and can be reached by U-Bahn No 4. Self-guided tours of 22/40 rooms are AS95/125 (students under 26 AS80/105), including a personal audio guide in English. The interior is suitably majestic, with frescoed ceilings, crystal chandeliers and gilded ornaments. The pinnacle of finery is reached in the Great Gallery. Mozart played his first royal concert in the Mirror Room at the ripe age of six in the presence of Maria Theresa and her family. Extensive formal gardens are enlivened by several fountains, and a Maze (AS30). You can enjoy excellent views from the **Gloriette monument** on the hill (AS30). Gloriette and the maze are open April to October, and are included in a AS160 combination ticket with the palace. The attractive zoo *(Tiergarten)* is also worth a look (entry AS120).

Schloss Belvedere This baroque palace is within walking distance of the Ring and has good views of the city. It houses the **Österreichische Galerie** (Austrian Gallery), located in the two main buildings which flank the spacious gardens. Untere (Lower) Belvedere (entrance Rennweg 6A) contains some elaborate baroque pieces, but the more important art collection is in Obere (Upper) Belvedere, and includes instantly recognisable works by Gustav Klimt, Egon Schiele and other Austrian artists from the 19th and 20th centuries (entrance Prinz Eugen Strasse 27). It's open 10 am to 5 pm Tuesday to Sunday; combined entry AS90 (students AS60).

Kunsthistorisches Museum This must-see museum, known as the Museum of Fine Arts, houses a vast collection of 16th and 17th-century paintings, ornaments and glassware, and Greek, Roman and Egyptian antiquities.

The huge extent of the Habsburg empire led to many important works of art being funnelled back to Vienna. Rubens was appointed to the service of a Habsburg governor in Brussels, so it's not surprising that the Kunsthistorisches has one of the world's best collections of his works. There is also an unrivalled collection of paintings by Peter Brueghel the Elder. Look out for Vermeer's *Allegory of Painting*, Cellini's stunning saltcellar, and the unbelievably lavish

AUSTRIA

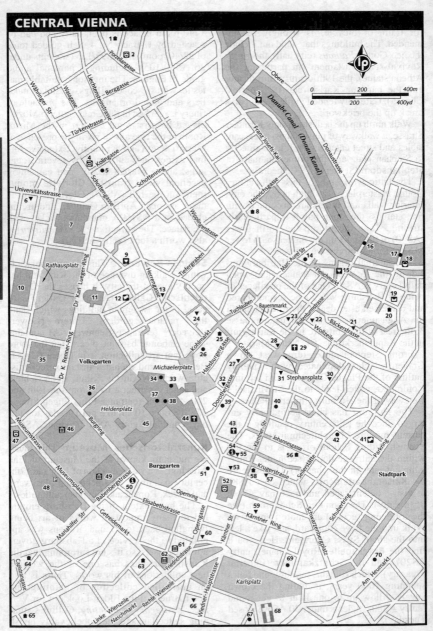

CENTRAL VIENNA

Porzellangasse
Liechtensteinstrasse
Berggasse
Wähinger Str
Wasagasse
Türkenstrasse
Obere
Danube Canal (Donau Kanal)
Franz Josefs-Kai
Donaustrasse
Kolingasse
Schottengasse
Schottenring
Universitätsstrasse
Heinrichsgasse
Rathausplatz
Dr Karl Lueger-Ring
Herrengasse
Wipplingerstrasse
Tiefergraben
Marc-Aurel Str
Fleischmarkt
Volksgarten
Tuchlauben
Bauernmarkt
Rotenturmstrasse
Wollzeile
Bäckerstrasse
Dr K Renner-Ring
Kohlmarkt
Habsburgergasse
Graben
Michaelerplatz
Stephansplatz
Heldenplatz
Dorotheegasse
Burgring
Kärntner Str
Johannesgasse
Seilerstätte
Stadtpark
Museumstrasse
Burggarten
Krugerstrasse
Schwarzenbergplatz
Schubertring
Babenbergstrasse
Opernring
Museumsplatz
Mariahilfer Str
Getreidemarkt
Elisabethstrasse
Opernngasse
Kärntner Str
Kärntner Ring
Linke Wienzeile
Naschmarkt
Rechte Wienzeile
Wiedner-Hauptstrasse
Friedrichstrasse
Capistrangasse
Karlsplatz

0   200   400m
0   200   400yd

AUSTRIA

CENTRAL VIENNA

PLACES TO STAY
1 Pension Falstaff
8 Schweizer Pension Solderer
20 Hotel Post
25 Pension Nossek
56 Music Academy Hotel & Mensa
58 Pension Am Operneck
63 Hotel-Pension Schneider
64 Quisisana
65 Kolping-Gästehaus

PLACES TO EAT
6 University Mensa
13 Café Central
21 Alt Wien
22 Pizza Bizi
23 Wrenkh
24 Esterházykeller
27 Café Hawelka
28 DO & CO Restaurant
30 La Crêperie
31 Akakiko
32 Café Bräunerhof
53 Hotel Sacher Café
55 Rosenberger Markt Restaurant
57 Restaurant Siam

59 Restaurant Marché Movenpick
60 Café Museum
66 Technical University Mensa

OTHER
2 International Theatre
3 Flex
4 Café Stein
5 Reisebuchladen (Bookshop & Tourguide)
7 University
9 Molly Darcy's Irish Pub
10 Rathaus (City Hall)
11 Burgtheater (National Theatre)
12 Hungarian Embassy
14 Shakespeare & Co Booksellers
15 Krah Krah
16 Marienbrücke
17 Schwedenbrücke
18 Danube Canal Tour Landing Stage
19 Main Post Office
26 Freytag & Berndt
29 Stephansdom (St Stephen's Cathedral)
33 Spanish Riding School

34 Kaiserappartements
35 Parlament
36 Volksgarten
37 Burgkapelle
38 Schatzkammer
39 Dorotheum
40 American Express
41 US Consulate
42 British Bookshop
43 Kaisergruft
44 Augustinerkirche
45 Hofburg
46 Naturhistorisches Museum
47 Volkstheater
48 Museumsquartier
49 Kunsthistorisches Museum (Museum of Fine Arts)
50 Jugend-Info Wien
51 State Ticket Office
52 Staatsoper (State Opera)
54 Main Tourist Office
61 Akademiehof (Albertina)
62 Secession Building
67 ÖKISTA
68 Karlskirche
69 Musikverein
70 Konzerthaus

AUSTRIA

clocks from the 16th and 17th centuries. The composite paintings by Archimboldo in room No 29 predate modern surrealism by nearly 400 years.

The museum is open 10 am to 6 pm Tuesday to Sunday, with the picture gallery closing at 9 pm on Thursday. Entry is AS100 (students AS70).

Secession Building This Art Nouveau 'temple of art', built at 01, Friedrichstrasse 12 in 1898, bears a delicate golden dome that deserves a better sobriquet than the description 'golden cabbage' accorded it by some Viennese. The 1902 exhibition here featured the famous 34m-long *Beethoven Frieze* by Klimt, which has been restored and can be seen in the basement. The rest of the building is primarily devoted to contemporary art. 'Sometimes people just walk past the art; they think they're in empty rooms', the ticket-seller told us. You have been warned! It's open 10 am to 6 pm Tuesday to Sunday (to 8 pm Thursday); entry costs AS60 (students AS40).

KunstHausWien This extraordinary gallery at 03, Untere Weissgerberstrasse 13 looks like something out of a toyshop. Designed by Friedensreich Hundertwasser to house his own works of art, it features coloured ceramics, uneven floors, irregular corners and grass on the roof. His vivid paintings are equally distinctive and there are some interesting models of other building projects. It is open 10 am to 7 pm daily and entry costs AS95 (concessions AS70), or AS160 (AS120) including temporary exhibitions. Monday is half-price. When you're in the area, walk down the road to see a block of residential flats built by Hundertwasser on the corner of Löwengasse and Kegelgasse. It is now one of Vienna's most prestigious addresses.

Other Museums The **Naturhistorisches Museum**, 01, Maria Theresien Platz, is the architectural mirror image of the Kunsthistorisches Museum. It holds temporary exhibitions and houses a collection of minerals, meteorites and an assortment of animal remains in jars. The museum is open daily except Tuesday; entry costs AS30 (students AS15). If you're going to Salzburg, the equivalent museum there is superior. For a bizarre take on anatomy, visit the **Josephinium** at 09, Währinger Strasse 25 (AS20, students AS10; closed weekends).

You can certainly overdose on art in Vienna. During long-term renovations to its usual premises, temporary exhibitions from the **Albertina** graphic arts collection are sited at the Akademiehof, 01, Markatgasse 3 (AS70; closed Monday). The **Museum für angewandte Kunst** (MAK) is an impressive collection of applied arts at 01, Stubenring 5. Entry is AS90 (concessions AS45) and it's closed Monday. The **Museum Moderner Kunst** displays modern art in two locations: Palais Liechtenstein, 09, Fürstengasse 1 and 20er Haus, 03, Arsenalstrasse 1 (combined ticket available; closed Monday). The former homes of the great composers are also open to the public; these are municipal museums, which are free on Friday morning.

Cemeteries Beethoven, Schubert, Brahms and Schönberg have memorial tombs in the **Zentralfriedhof** (Central Cemetery), 11, Simmeringer Hauptstrasse 232-244. Mozart also has a monument here, but he was actually buried in an unmarked grave in the **St Marxer Friedhof** (Cemetery of St Mark), 03, Leberstrasse 6-8. It was only many years after the true location had been forgotten that grave diggers cobbled together a poignant memorial from a broken pillar and a discarded stone angel.

Naschmarkt The Naschmarkt is along 06, Linke Wienzeile, and is open 6 am to 6 pm Monday to Saturday. It consists mainly of fruit, vegetable and meat stalls, but there are a few stalls selling clothing and curios as well. There is also an atmospheric flea market on Saturday, which is well worth a visit. Snack bars provide cheap, hot food, especially kebabs.

Prater This large amusement park is dominated by the giant Ferris Wheel, built in 1897, which featured prominently in *The Third Man* movie. Rides in the park cost AS15 to AS55, but it is also a great place to just have a wander. On Rondeau and Calafatti Platz

there are colourful metal sculptures depicting humans caught up in strange hallucinogenic happenings. The park adjoins a complex of sports grounds and a large forested area ideal for rambling.

Activities

Hiking To the west of the city, the rolling hills and marked trails of the Vienna Woods are perfect for walkers; the *Wander bares Wien* leaflet available from the Sportamt outlines hiking routes and explains how to get there. The Lower Austria Information office has a free map of routes further from the city.

Watersports In the north-east of the city, the Old Danube and the New Danube provide opportunities for swimming, sailing, boating and windsurfing. There are stretches with free swimming access, or bathing complexes like **Gänsehäufel** (open May to September) have swimming pools and charge AS70 for a full day, including a locker (AS50 after noon).

Organised Tours

Several companies offer tours of the city and surrounding areas, either by coach, foot (try the Third Man Tour, which visits spots featured in the famous film, including the underground sewers) or bicycle (contact Pedal Power on ☎ 729 72 34). Reisebuchladen (☎ 317 33 84) 09, Kolingasse 6, gives an interesting tour of 'alternative' Vienna (around AS380). Boat operators conduct tours of the Danube Canal; the tourist office has details. See also The Danube Valley section later in this chapter.

Special Events

The cycle of musical events is unceasing, and although Mozart features heavily, all varieties of music are represented. The Vienna Festival, from mid-May to mid-June, has a wide-ranging program of the arts. Contact Wiener Festwochen (☎ 589 22-22, fax -49), Lehárgasse 11, A-1060 Vienna, for details. Web site: www.festwochen.or.at.

Vienna's Summer of Music runs from mid-July to mid-September; contact Klang-Boden (☎ 4000-8410), 01, Stadiongasse 9. Reduced student tickets go on sale at the venue 10 minutes before the performance.

At the end of June, look out for free rock, jazz and folk concerts in the Donauinselfest.

The free open-air Opera Film Festival on Rathausplatz runs throughout July and August.

Vienna's traditional Christmas market (*Christkindlmarkt*) takes place in front of the city hall between mid-November and 24 December. Other seasonal events include New Year concerts and gala balls (January and February), the Vienna Spring Marathon (April/May), and the Schubert Festival (November). The tourist office does not sell tickets, but has full details.

Places to Stay – Budget

Vienna can be a nightmare for backpackers. Budget places are often full, especially in summer. Reserve ahead or at least use the telephone before you trek around everywhere. Tourist offices have lists of private rooms, as well as the useful *Camping* pamphlet which details hostels and camping grounds. See Tourist Offices under Information earlier in this section for room-booking services.

Camping *Wien West* (☎ 914 23 14; 14, Hüttelbergstrasse 80) is open all year except February. It costs AS68/40 per adult/tent, or AS75/45 in July and August. Two or four-person bungalows are AS300/440. To get there, take U4 or the S-Bahn to Hütteldorf, then bus No 148 or 152. *Camping Rodaun* (☎ 888 41 54; 23, An der Au 2) is open from late March to mid-November and charges AS73/60 per adult/tent. Take S1 or S2 to Liesing then bus No 60A.

Hostels No hostels invade the imperial elegance of the Innere Stadt. The nearest is HI *Jugendherberge Myrthengasse* (☎ 523 63 16, fax 523 58 49, ❷ hostel@chello.at; 07, Myrthengasse 7). Based in two buildings, it's efficiently run and has daytime check-in. All rooms have a private shower and bedside lights. Beds are AS170 in six or four-bed dorms or AS200 in double rooms. Lunch or dinner is AS65 and laundry is AS50 per load. Curfew is at 1 am. Telephone reservations are accepted and strongly advised.

Believe it or Not (☎ 526 46 58; 07, Apartment 14, Myrthengasse 10) is a small private hostel. There are no signs outside, except on the doorbell. It has a friendly atmosphere, but one room has triple-level bunks and can get hot in summer. There's no breakfast; use the kitchen facilities instead. Beds are AS160 in summer or AS110 from November to Easter, and you get your own key so there's no curfew.

Panda Hostel (☎ 522 53 53; 07, 3rd floor, Kaiserstrasse 77) also charges AS160 for hostel beds. There's a TV in every room, no breakfast but use of a kitchen. It's linked to *Lauria* which is listed under Hotels & Pensions.

Hostel Zöhrer (☎ 406 07 30, fax 408 04 09, ❷ zoehrer@compuserve.com; 08, Skodagasse 26) is a private hostel close to the Ring, and is reasonable value. Six to eight-bed dorms are AS170 and doubles (bunk beds) are AS460, all with private shower. There's a kitchen, courtyard and own-key entry; reception is open 7.30 am to 10 pm. *Turmherberge Don Bosco* (☎ 713 14 94; 03, Lechnerstrasse 12), southeast of the Ring, is unrenovated but has a kitchen and the cheapest beds in town – AS80 without breakfast. Sheets are AS25. Reception is closed between noon and 5 pm, and the hostel is open from 1 March to 31 November.

Two hostels, both open 24 hours, are near Westbahnhof. *Hostel Ruthensteiner* (☎ 893 42 02, fax 893 27 96, ❷ hostel.ruthensteiner@telecom.at; 15, Robert Hamerling Gasse 24) is one block south of Mariahilfer Strasse. Large dorms are AS130 or AS145 (without sheets). Sheets are provided in the smaller dorms (AS169) and in the basic singles/doubles which go for AS245/470. Breakfast costs AS29; there's a kitchen and shady rear courtyard. *Wombat's* (☎ 897 23 36, fax 897 25 77, ❷ wombats@chello.at; 15, Grangasse 6) is a new non-HI hostel, with a pub. Dorms/doubles are AS175/490 and breakfast is AS35.

Kolpingsfamilie Meidling (☎ 813 54 87, fax 812 21 30, ❷ office@wien12.kolping.at; 12, Bendlgasse 10-12) is near the Niederhofstrasse U6 stop, south of Westbahnhof. Beds are AS130 to AS180 in different-sized dorms. Non-HI members pay AS40 extra but don't get the guest stamp. Breakfast/dinner costs AS45/65. Curfew is at midnight, though reception is open 24 hours.

There are two large HI hostels out in the suburbs. *Brigittenau* (☎ 332 82 94, fax 330 83 79, ❷ jgh1200@chello.at; 20, Friedrich Engels Platz 24), to the north (tram N, 31 or 33), has 24-hour reception. Dorms/doubles are AS170/400. *Hütteldorf-Hacking* (☎ 877 02 63, fax -2, ❷ jgh@wigast.com; 13, Schlossberggasse 8) has 307 beds and charges

AS158/376. The doors are locked from 9.30 am to 3 pm; take the U4 west.

Student Residences These are available to tourists from 1 July to 30 September while students are on holiday. The cheapest is *Porzellaneum* (☎ 317 72 82, fax -30; 09, *Porzellangasse 30*), with singles/doubles for AS190/308, without breakfast. Some other *Studentenheime* to try, in ascending price order, are: *Katholisches Studenthaus* (☎ 369 55 85-0; 19, *Peter Jordan Strasse 29*); *Döbling* (☎ 369 54 90-0; 19, *Gymnasiumstrasse 85*); *Pfeilgasse* (☎ 401 74, fax 401 76-20; 08, *Pfeilgasse 4-6*); and *Music Academy* (☎ 514 84 48; 01, *Johannesgasse 8*).

Hotels & Pensions *Lauria* (☎ 522 25 55, @ *lauria.apartments@chello.at; 07, 3rd floor, Kaiserstrasse 77*) is in a residential building, close to transport and shops. It has friendly staff, own-key entry, kitchen facilities (no breakfast), TVs, and thoughtful, homy touches. Doubles are AS530 (AS480 with bunk beds), or AS700 with private shower. Triples (AS600 or AS750), quads (AS880) and large apartments (from AS1400 for four) are also available. There may be a two-day minimum stay for reservations.

Pension Wild (☎ 406 51 74, fax 402 21 68; 08, *Langegasse 10*) is a central, gay-friendly, everyone-friendly place. 'Wild' is the family name, not a description. Singles/doubles are AS490/590 and singles/doubles/triples with private shower are AS590/790/1050. There are kitchens and reception is open 24 hours.

Kolping-Gästehaus (☎ 587 56 31-0, fax 586 36 30, @ *reservierung@wien-zentral .kolping.at; 06, Gumpendorfer Strasse 39*), has singles/doubles with shower, toilet and TV for AS720/980, and a few singles without for AS300. This is partially a student residence and feels like it. Book well ahead.

Auer (☎ 406 21 21, fax -4; 09, *Lazarettgasse 3*) is friendly, pleasant and more Viennese in style. Singles/doubles start at AS370/560; doubles with private shower are AS630.

Hotel Westend (☎ 597 67 29-0, fax -27; 06, *Fügergasse 3*) is close to Westbahnhof and has reasonable singles/doubles for AS355/625, or AS405/745 with shower. Reception is open 24 hours.

Pension Kraml (☎ 587 85 88, fax 586 75 73) is nearby at 06, Brauergasse 5. Small, friendly, and family-run, it offers singles/doubles for AS340/640 and large doubles with private shower for AS700.

Quisisana (☎ 587 33 41, fax -33; 06, *Windmühlgasse 6*) is convenient, with variable but good-value rooms for AS390/640 with shower, AS330/540 without.

Pension Falstaff (☎ 317 91 86, fax -4; 09, *Müllnergasse 5*) has singles/doubles for AS420/660 (with an irksome AS30 fee to use the hall shower) or AS500/760 with private shower. Prices are around AS100 lower in winter. The rooms are long but some lack width; fittings are ageing but adequate. It's convenient for tram D to the Ring and Nussdorf.

Praterstern (☎ 214 01 23, fax 214 78 80, @ *hotelpraterstern@aon.at; 02, Mayergasse 6*), east of the Ring, has a garden. Singles/doubles are AS330/585, or AS395/740 with shower.

Ten minutes walk from Südbahnhof is *Hotel Kolbeck* (☎ 604 17 73, fax 602 94 86, @ *hotelkolbeck@chello.at; 10, Laxenburger Strasse 19*). Singles/doubles with hall shower are AS450/800; those with private shower, WC and cable TV are AS700/1100. Reception is open 24 hours.

Places to Stay – Mid-Range
In the Innere Stadt, you inevitably pay more for the convenience of a central location. *Pension Nossek* (☎ 533 70 41, fax 535 36 46; 01, *Graben 17*) has baroque-style singles (AS650 to AS850) and doubles (AS1250 to AS1560), priced depending on the size, view and private facilities.

Schweizer Pension Solderer (☎ 533 81 56, fax 535 64 69, @ *schweizer.pension@gmx.at; 01, Heinrichsgasse 2*) provides clean singles/doubles from AS480/780 with hall shower, AS700/900 including private shower and AS800/1050 with shower and WC. *Pension Am Operneck* (☎ 512 93 10; 01, *Kärntner Strasse 47*) has a few singles/doubles for AS620/900 with private shower and WC. Reserve well in advance.

Rooms in the following places have private shower, WC, TV and telephone. *Hotel Post* (☎ 515 83-0, fax -808; 01, *Fleischmarkt 24*) is renovated in bright colours. Singles/doubles are AS880/1260, or AS490/840 without shower.

Alla Lenz (☎ *523 69 89-0, fax -55,* 📧 *alla-lenz@magnet.at; 07, Halbgasse 3-5)* has a swimming pool and good doubles from AS1180. Singles are a bit pokey and pricey (AS800).

Hotel-Pension Schneider (☎ *588 38-0, fax -212,* 📧 *hotel-schneider@netway.at; 06, Getreidemarkt 5)* is close to the Theater an der Wien, and has signed photos in the lobby of the actors and opera stars who have stayed here. Singles are AS980 to AS1400, doubles are AS1720, and there are outstanding self-contained two-person apartments for AS2200. Prices are slightly lower in the winter.

Places to Eat

You can stock up on groceries outside normal shopping hours at the train stations; prices are considerably higher except in the *Billa* supermarket at Franz Josefs Bahnhof (open 7 am to 7.30 pm daily). Westbahnhof has a large shop in the main hall, which is open 5.30 am to 11 pm daily; and Südbahnhof has a few tiny kiosks open daily till late. The *Billa* supermarket in the airport is open 7.30 am to 10 pm daily.

Würstel stands are scattered around the city and provide a quick snack of sausage and bread for around AS30.

Vienna's best known dish, the Wiener Schnitzel, is available everywhere; goulash is also common. Vienna is renowned for its excellent pastries and desserts, which are very effective at transferring the bulk from your moneybelt to your waistline.

Restaurants – Budget

The best deal is in the various student cafeterias (mensas). They're usually only open for weekday lunches between 11 am and 2 pm. Meals are AS35 to AS60, often with AS4 reduction for students. *University Mensa (01, Universitätsstrasse 7)* has an adjoining cafe open 8 am to 6 pm weekdays. *Technical University Mensa (04, Resselgasse 7-9)* is also convenient. *Music Academy Mensa (01, Johannesgasse 8)* is the only one inside the Ring.

Tunnel (☎ *405 34 65; 08, Florianigasse 39)* is another student haunt, open 9 am to 2 am daily. The food is satisfying and easy on the pocket – breakfast is AS29, lunch specials

AS45, spaghetti from AS38, big pizzas from AS60 and salads from AS20. Bottled beer costs from AS25 for 0.5L. There is a cellar bar which has live music nightly from 9 pm; entry costs from AS30, though on Sunday there's generally free jazz.

Nearby is *Laudon Stüberl (08, Laudongasse 16)*, open 9 am to early evening on weekdays. Daily *menus* with soup are AS50 or AS55. Along the road is *Gasthaus Zur Böhmischen Kuchl (08, Schlösselgasse 18)*, an atmospheric place for Czech and Slovak food from AS62 (closed weekends).

Rosenberger Markt Restaurant (01, Maysedergasse 2) has a buffet downstairs with a fine array of meats, drinks and desserts. If you really want to save Schillings, concentrate on the salad or vegetable buffet (from AS32). Don't be ashamed to pile a Stephansdom-like spire of food on your plate – everyone else does. It's open 11 am to 11 pm daily. *Restaurant Marché Movenpick (Ringstrassen Galerien, 01, Kärntner Ring 5-7)* is similar, with small plates from AS22. Another good feature is the pizza for AS65, where you can help yourself to a variety of toppings. It's open till 8 pm daily (7 pm Sunday).

Chinese restaurants are numerous, and many offer weekday lunches from around AS60. *Restaurant Siam (01, Krugerstrasse 6)* has Chinese lunches from AS59, and an all-you-can-eat lunch buffet for AS78. On the ground floor is a 'running sushi' buffet (from AS118), where dishes are delivered by conveyer belt. Also for inexpensive Japanese meals, try *Akakiko (01, Singerstrasse 4)*.

There are a few Indian restaurants about; *Zum Inder (02, Praterstrasse 57)* and *Khajuraho Palace (07, Burggasse 64)* have cheap lunch buffets.

Pizza Bizi (01, Rotenturmstrasse 4) is a convenient self-service place with hot food from 11 am to 11.30 pm daily. Pasta with a choice of sauces is AS65, and pizzas are AS60 to AS75.

Schnitzelwirt Schmidt (07, Neubaugasse 52) is good for a range of schnitzels (from AS65, plus garnishes). Service is sloppy but portions are ridiculously large. It's closed Sunday.

Wrenkh (☎ *533 15 26; 01, Bauernmarkt 10)* is a fairly upmarket specialist vegetarian

AUSTRIA

restaurant. Meticulously prepared dishes are AS95 to AS130 and it's open till midnight daily.

For a complete contrast, head down to **Schweizerhaus** *(02, Strasse des Ersten Mai 116)* in the Prater. It's famous for its roasted pork hocks *(Hintere Schweinsstelze)*. A meal consists of a massive chunk of meat on the bone (about 750g minimum at AS186 per kg), with mustard and grated horseradish (AS15). Chomping your way through vast slabs of pig smacks of medieval banqueting, but it's very tasty when washed down with draught Czech Budweiser. Schweizerhaus is open 10 am to 11 pm daily (March to October only) and has many outside tables. Nearby, **Estancia Cruz** on Hauptallee has sizable Latin American dishes from about AS80. It's open 11 am to 11 pm daily (opening at 4 pm weekdays in low season).

Schutzhaus am Ameisbach *(14, Braillegasse 1)* is worth the trek to the western suburbs (take bus No 51A from Hietzing to Braillegasse). There's a big garden and excellent spare ribs (the AS80 half-portion will feed one). It's closed Tuesday (and Monday in winter).

Restaurants – Mid-Range & Top-End

La Crêperie *(☎ 512 56 87; 01, Grünangergasse 10)* has different rooms with varied and creative decor. Meat and fish dishes are above AS145. Savoury crepes (AS82 to AS225) are tasty, if not overly large. It's closed weekday lunchtimes.

Restaurant Sailer *(☎ 479 21 21-0; 18, Gersthofer Strasse 14)* serves traditional Viennese dishes for around AS200, but with refined touches. The quality and service are exceptional for the price. There's also a garden.

The busy **DO & CO** *(☎ 535 39 69; 01, Haas Haus, Stephansplatz 12)* has good food to match the view. Superb international and oriental dishes are around AS250; book well ahead. It is open noon to 3 pm and 6 pm to midnight daily, and there's an adjoining cafe/bar (9 am to 2 am).

The classy **Steirereck** *(☎ 713 31 68; 08, Rasumofskygasse 2)* is one of the best restaurants in Austria. Different rooms have a different ambience, but it's pretty formal throughout. Tempting main courses all top AS300, but you get to choose from lobster,

rabbit, pigeon and venison. It's open Monday to Friday; book at least a week in advance.

Coffee Houses The coffee house is an integral part of Viennese life. The tradition supposedly began after retreating Turkish invaders left behind their supplies of coffee beans in the 17th century. Today, Vienna has hundreds of coffee houses. They're great places for observing the locals in repose and for recovering after a hard day's sightseeing. Small/big coffees cost about AS24/38 and the custom is to take your time. Most places have lots of newspapers to read, including expensive British titles, which make a coffee an excellent investment.

Café Museum *(01, Friedrichstrasse 6)* is open 8 am to midnight daily and has chess, many newspapers and outside tables. **Café Bräunerhof** *(01, Stallburggasse 2)* offers free classical music from 3 to 6 pm on weekends and holidays, and British newspapers. It's open to 8.30 pm weekdays and to 6 pm weekends. **Alt Wien** *(01, Bäckerstrasse 9)* is a rather dark coffee house by day and a good drinking venue by night. It's open 9 am to 2 am daily and is famed for its goulash (AS90 large, AS60 small).

Café Central *(01, Herrengasse 14)* has a fine ceiling and pillars, and piano music from 4 to 7 pm. Trotsky came here to play chess. Opening hours are 8 am to 8 pm (10 am to 6 pm on Sunday).

The **Hotel Sacher Café** *(01, Philharmonikerstrasse 4)* behind the State Opera is a picture of opulence, complete with chandeliers, battalions of waiters and rich, red walls and carpets. It's famous for its chocolate apricot cake, Sacher Torte (AS55 a slice; coffee from AS32). More arty and down to earth is **Café Hawelka** *(01, Dorotheergasse 6)*. It's closed Tuesday.

Heurigen Heurigen wine taverns only sell 'new' wine produced on the premises, a concession granted by Joseph II. They can be identified by a green wreath or branch hanging over the door. Outside tables are common and you can bring your own food or make a selection from inexpensive hot and cold buffet counters.

Heurigen usually have a relaxed atmosphere, which gets more and more lively as the customers get drunk on mugs of wine. Many feature traditional live music; these can be a bit touristy but great fun nonetheless. Native Viennese tend to prefer a music-free environment. Opening times are approximately 4 to 11 pm, and wine costs around AS28 a *Viertel* (0.25L).

Heurigen are concentrated in the wine-growing suburbs to the north, south and west of the city. Taverns are so close together that it is best to pick a region and just explore.

The Heurigen areas of Nussdorf and Heiligenstadt are near each other at the terminus of tram D. In 1817, Beethoven lived in the *Beethovenhaus (19, Pfarrplatz 3, Heiligenstadt).* Down the road (bus No 38A from Heiligenstadt or tram 38 from the Ring) is Grinzing, a large, lively area favoured by tour groups (count the tour buses lined up outside in the evening). There are several good Heurigen in a row where Cobenzlgasse and Sandgasse meet. *Reinprecht (19, Cobenzlgasse 22)* has mobile musicians and a real sing-along environment.

Stammersdorf (tram No 31) and Strebersdorf (tram No 32) are cheaper, quieter regions. *Esterházykeller (01, Haarhof 1),* off Naglergasse in the city centre, has cheap wine (from AS24 a Viertel), meals and snacks; it's open 11 am (4 pm weekends and holidays) to 10 pm daily.

Entertainment

The tourist office has copies of *Vienna Scene* and produces a monthly listing of events. Weekly magazines with extensive listings include *Wienside* (free), *City* (AS10) and *Falter* (AS28).

Cheap standing-room *(Stehplatz)* tickets are sold in the *Staatsoper*, *Volksoper*, *Burgtheater* and *Akademietheater*. You'll need to start queuing up to three hours before the start to get tickets for major productions; minor works require only minimal queuing. Also at these four venues, students aged under 27 queue to buy unsold tickets at the same price as the cheapest seats (from AS50; home university ID necessary, plus ISIC card). Both types of ticket are sold about an hour before the start of the performance. Buying cheap, restricted-view seats doesn't involve queuing. The state ticket office, Bundestheaterverkassen (☎ 514 44-7880) 01, Goethegasse 1, does not charge a commission for these venues. For other places, try Wien Ticket (☎ 588 85) in the hut by the Oper; it charges little or no commission for cash sales.

Cinema & Theatre Check local papers for listings. All cinema seats are cheaper (AS70 or AS80) on Monday. There are performances in English at the *English Theatre (☎ 402 82 84; 08, Josefsgasse 12)* and the *International Theatre (☎ 319 62 72; 09, Porzellangasse 8).*

Classical Music Classical music is so much a part of Vienna that you really should make an effort to sample some. In fact, it's difficult to avoid because so many of the buskers playing along Kärntner Strasse and Graben are classical musicians. Check with the tourist office for free events around town, eg, free concerts at the Rathaus or in churches.

Numerous be-wigged Mozart lookalikes sell concert tickets, but a couple of readers have warned against buying tickets from such people – stick to productions in the *Staatsoper* (State Opera) instead. These are lavish affairs. Seats cost anything from AS70 (restricted view) to AS2450. AS50 *Stehparterre* standing-room tickets give a good position at the back of the stalls; AS30 tickets are closer to the roof than the stage. The Viennese take their opera very seriously and dress up accordingly (you'd better leave your clown costume at home). Wander around the foyer and the refreshment rooms in the interval to fully appreciate the gold and crystal interior. There are no performances in July and August. The Vienna Philharmonic Orchestra performs in the *Musikverein*.

Vienna Boy's Choir The Wiener Sängerknaben sings at Mass every Sunday (except during July and August) at 9.15 am in the Burgkapelle in the Hofburg. Seats are AS70 to AS380, but standing room is free. Queue by 8.30 am to find a place inside the open doors, but you can get a flavour of what's going on from the TV in the foyer. Also interesting is the scrum afterwards when everybody struggles to photograph and be photographed with the serenely patient choirboys. The choir regularly sings a mixed program of music in the *Konzerthaus*.

AUSTRIA

Nightclubs & Bars Vienna has no shortage of good spots for a night out. The best-known area is around Ruprechtsplatz, Seitenstettengasse and Rabensteig in the Innere Stadt, dubbed the 'Bermuda Triangle' because drinkers can disappear into the numerous pubs and clubs and apparently be lost to the outside world. Most places there are lively and inexpensive; some have live music. *Krah Krah (01, Rabensteig 8)* has 50 different brands of beer (from AS39 a 0.5L bottle) and is open 11 am until late, daily.

Volksgarten (01, Burgring 1) is three linked venues: a cafe with DJs and a garden, a disco with theme evenings, and a more formal 'Walzer Dancing' place. *Flex*, by Schottenring and Donau Kanal, is another good late night bar and disco. Irish bars are popular – try *Molly Darcy's Irish Pub (01, Teinfaltstrasse 6)*.

Late-night bars are by no means limited to the Innere Stadt. *Chelsea (08, Lechenfelder Gürtel 29-31)* has DJs, occasional indie bands, and English football via satellite. Bars within the same U-Bahn arches, heading north, are *Rhiz (No 37-38)*, favouring modern electronic music, and *B72 (No 72)*, featuring varied bands and DJs. *Camera Club*, 07, on Neubaugasse by Mariahilfer Strasse, is a mellow bar and disco, frequented by dope smokers; it's open 10 pm to 4 am (modest cover charge).

One of the best-known discos in Vienna is *U4 (☎ 815 83 07; 12, Schönbrunner Strasse 222)*, open 10 or 11 pm to 4 or 5 am daily. Drink prices are reasonable (small beers from AS38). Each night has a different theme. Sunday is 1960s and 1970s music (cover charge AS60); Thursday is gay night.

Spanish Riding School The famous Lipizzaner stallions strut their stuff in the Spanish Riding School behind the Hofburg. Performances are sold out months in advance, so write to the Spanische Reitschule, Michaelerplatz 1, A-1010 Wien or ask in the office about cancellations (unclaimed tickets are sold 45 minutes before performances). Deal directly with the school to avoid the hefty 20% to 30% commission charged by travel agents.

You need to be pretty keen on horses to be happy about paying AS250 to AS900 for seats or AS200 for standing room, although a few of the tricks, such as seeing a stallion bounding along on only its hind legs like a demented kangaroo, do tend to stick in the mind. Tickets to watch them train can be bought the same day (AS100). Training is from 10 am to noon, Tuesday to Friday and some Saturdays, from mid-February to mid-December except in July and August when the stallions go on their summer holidays. These sessions are only intermittently interesting. Queues are very long early in the day, but if you try around 11 am you can usually get in fairly quickly.

Shopping
Local specialities include porcelain, ceramics, handmade dolls, wrought-iron and leather goods. Selling works of art is big business; check the art auctions at the partially state-owned Dorotheum (☎ 515 60-0), 01, Dorotheergasse 17. Lots can be inspected in advance with their opening prices marked. Some prices include VAT, which can be claimed back (see Consumer Taxes under Money in the Facts for the Visitor section earlier in this chapter).

Getting There & Away
Air Regular scheduled flights link Vienna to Linz, Salzburg, Innsbruck, Klagenfurt and Graz. There are daily nonstop flights to all major European destinations. Austrian Airlines (☎ 1789) has a city office at 01, Kärntner Ring 18.

Bus Departures to many destinations go from the central bus station at Wien Mitte. These include several daily buses to Budapest, starting at 7 am (AS350, 3½ hours). Buses to Prague depart daily at 7 am (2 pm on Friday and Sunday) from 01, Rathausplatz 5 (AS325, five hours). Get tickets for all buses from the Eurolines counter (☎ 712 04 53) at Wien Mitte, open noon to 9 pm daily.

Train Train schedules are subject to change, and not all destinations are exclusively serviced by one station, so check with train information centres in stations or call ☎ 1717.

Westbahnhof has trains to Western and northern Europe and western Austria. Approximately hourly services head to Salzburg; some continue to Munich and terminate in Paris (14½ hours total). To Zürich, there are two day trains (AS1122, nine hours) and one night train that departs at 9.15 pm (AS1102, plus charge for fold-down seat/couchette). A direct overnight train goes to Bucharest at 8.05 pm (18 hours). Eight trains a day go to Budapest (AS440, 3½ hours).

Südbahnhof has trains to Italy (eg, Rome, via Venice and Florence), Slovakia, the Czech Republic, Hungary and Poland, and southern Austria. Five trains a day go to Bratislava (AS204, 1½ hours), four go to Prague (AS536, five hours), with two continuing to Berlin (10 hours total).

Franz Josefs Bahnhof and Wien-Mitte Bahnhof handle local trains only.

Car & Motorcycle

The Gürtel is an outer ring road which joins up with the A22 on the north bank of the Danube and the A23 southeast of town. All the main road routes intersect with this system, including the A1 from Linz and Salzburg, and the A2 from Graz.

Hitching

Mitfahrzentrale Josefstadt (☎ 408 22 10), 08, Daungasse 1a, links hitchhikers and drivers. It's only open 7 to 8 pm daily, but telephone to check availability before going to the office. There are usually many cars going into Germany. Examples of fares are Salzburg AS250, Innsbruck AS370, Frankfurt AS500 and Munich AS350.

Boat

Fast hydrofoils travel eastwards in the summer to Bratislava and Budapest, once per day. To Bratislava (Wednesday to Sunday, 1½ hours) costs AS240/370 one way/return. To Budapest (5½ hours) costs AS780/1100. Bookings can be made through G Glaser (☎ 726 08 201), 02, Handelskai 265, or DDSG Blue Danube (☎ 588 80-0, fax -440), 01, Friedrichstrasse 7.

Heading west, a series of boats ply the Danube between Krems and Passau, on the German border, though services originating in Vienna are very infrequent. For details of more operators see the Danube Valley section later in this chapter.

Getting Around

To/From the Airport

Wien Schwechat airport (☎ 7007-2233) is 19km from the city centre. There are buses every 20 or 30 minutes, 24 hours day, between the airport and the city

air terminal at the Hotel Hilton. Buses also run every 30 or 60 minutes from Westbahnhof and Südbahnhof (AS70; not from midnight to 5.30 am). It's cheaper to take the S-Bahn (S7 line, two an hour) from Wien Mitte. The fare is AS38, or AS19 additional to a city pass. A taxi should cost about AS430.

Public Transport

Vienna has a comprehensive and unified public transport network. Flat-fare tickets are valid for trains, trams, buses, the underground (U-Bahn) and suburban (S-Bahn) trains. All advance-purchase tickets must be validated in the machines before use. Routes are outlined in the free tourist office map; for a more detailed listing, buy a map from a Vienna Transit window (AS20). Single tickets cost AS22 via machines on buses/trams. Otherwise they cost AS19 each from ticket machines in U-Bahn stations; it's the same rate in multiples of four/five from ticket offices, machines or Tabak shops. You may change lines on the same trip. Children under six always travel free; those under 16 go free on Sunday, public holidays and during Vienna school holidays (photo ID necessary).

Daily passes (Stunden-Netzkarte) are a better deal at AS60 (valid 24 hours from first use) or AS150 (valid 72 hours). Validate the ticket in the machine at the beginning of your first journey. An eight-day multiple-user pass (8-Tage-Karte) costs AS300; validate the ticket once per day per person. Weekly tickets, valid Monday to Sunday, cost AS155. Ticket inspections are not very frequent, but fare dodgers who are caught pay an on-the-spot fine of AS560, plus the fare. Austrian and European rail passes are valid on the S-Bahn only. Public transport finishes around midnight, but there's also a comprehensive night bus service. They run every 30 minutes nightly, around the Ring and to the suburbs, and tickets are AS15 (day tickets/passes not valid).

Car & Motorcycle

Parking is a problem in the city centre and the Viennese are impatient drivers. Using public transport is therefore preferable while sightseeing. Blue parking zones allow a maximum stop of 1½ or two hours from 9 am to 8 pm (to 7 pm in the Innere Stadt) on weekdays. Parking vouchers (AS6 per 30 minutes) for these times can be purchased in Tabak shops. The cheapest parking garage in the centre is at Museumsplatz (AS25 per hour, AS150 for 24 hours).

Taxi Taxis are metered for city journeys: AS26 or AS27 flag fall, plus AS13 or AS14 per kilometre – the higher rate is on Sunday and at night. There is a AS26 surcharge for phoning a radio taxi.

Bicycle Bikes can be hired daily from the main train stations, though they may be offered free of charge by the city authorities – inquire at the information office in the Rathaus. *Tips für Radfahrer* is available from the tourist office and shows circular bike tours.

Fiacres The pony traps lined up at the Stephansdom are strictly for the well-heeled tourist. Commanding AS500 for a 20-minute trot, these ponies must be among Vienna's richest inhabitants.

The Danube Valley

The strategic importance of the Danube (Donau) Valley as an east-west corridor meant that control of the area was hotly contested. As a result, there are hundreds of castles and fortified abbeys in the region. But all is idyllic and peaceful now – the only invaders are tourists. The Wachau section of the Danube, between Krems and Melk, is the river's most picturesque stretch, with wine-growing villages, forested slopes, vineyards and imposing fortresses at nearly every bend.

Several companies run boats along the Danube. DDSG Blue Danube (see Boat under Getting There & Away in the Vienna section earlier in this chapter) offers various Wachau trips. A short one way/return trip costs AS100/150; the full trip from Melk to Krems (1¼ hours) or from Krems to Melk (2¾ hours) costs AS200, or AS270 return. Boats sail from early April to late October, with three departures daily (one only in April and October). DDSG carries bicycles free of charge.

Ardagger (☎ 07479-64 64-0) connects Linz and Krems three times a week in each direction in summer. Donauschiffahrt Wurm + Köck (☎ 0732-78 36 07) offers package trips

between Linz and the German town of Passau (six hours); Web site: www.donauschiffahrt .com. G Glaser (see Boat under Getting There & Away in the Vienna section earlier in this chapter) does all the above trips, and its prices for Wachau tours slightly undercut DDSG's rates – Krems-Melk is AS190/260 one way/return.

The route by road is also scenic. Highway 3 links Vienna and Linz and stays close to the north bank of the Danube for much of the way. There is a cycle track along the south bank from Vienna to Krems, and along both sides of the river from Krems to Linz.

St Pölten is the state capital of Lower Austria, but refer to the Lower Austria Information Office mentioned in the Vienna section for region-wide information. If you stay in the Wachau, be sure to get the Wachau guest card – among the benefits is free entry to Melk's open-air swimming pool in summer.

KREMS
☎ 02732 • pop 23,000
The historic town of Krems reclines on the north bank of the Danube, surrounded by terraced vineyards. Krems stetches 2km westwards into Stein, and the walk between the two is a fine way to spend a couple of hours. Wander round the cobbled streets of Landstrasse in Krems and Steiner Landstrasse in Stein, noting the adjoining courtyards and ancient city walls. If you have time, there are several churches worth a look, such as the **Dominikanerkirche**, which contains a collection of religious and modern art and wine-making artefacts. By the Kremser Tor (gate) is the **Kunsthalle** arts centre.

Midway between Krems and Stein you'll pass the tourist office (☎ 826 76, @ austropa .krems@netway.at) at Undstrasse 6, in the Kloster Und.

Places to Stay & Eat
Budget options include *Camping Donau* (☎ 844 55, *Wiedengasse 7*), near the boat station, and the HI *Jugendherberge* (☎ 834 52, *Ringstrasse 77*), which has excellent facilities for cyclists. Both are open around April to October.

Other accommodation is also affordable. In Stein, try *Gästehaus Einzinger* (☎ 823 16,

Steiner Landstrasser 82). Attractive singles/doubles round a courtyard are AS350/700 with shower, WC and TV.

In Krems, you'll find a range of places to eat along Obere and Untere Landstrasse, including a supermarket. Ask the tourist office for the opening schedules of the local Heurigen (wine taverns).

Getting There & Away

The boat station *(Schiffsstation)* is a 20-minute walk west from the train station along Donaulände. Infrequent buses to Melk (AS74, 65 minutes) leave from outside the train station. Trains to Vienna (AS133, one hour) arrive at Franz Josefs Bahnhof.

DÜRNSTEIN
☎ 02711 • pop 1000

West of Krems, reached by boat or rail, lies picturesque Dürnstein. Ascend to the Kuenringerburg ruins for a sweeping view of the river. This castle is where Richard the Lionheart of England was imprisoned in 1192. In the village, visit the parish church, a baroque structure that has been meticulously restored. Dürnstein offers cheap accommodation, quaint restaurants and enjoyable wine taverns. Find out more from the tourist office (☎ 200) or the Rathaus (☎ 219).

MELK
☎ 02752 • pop 6500

Lying in the lee of its imposing monastery-fortress, Melk is an essential stop on the Wachau stretch.

Orientation & Information

The train station is 300m from the town centre. Walk straight ahead down Bahnhofstrasse to get to the post office (Postamt 3390), where money exchange is available to 5 pm on weekdays and 10 am on Saturday. Turn right for the HI hostel or carry straight on, taking the Bahngasse path, for the central Rathausplatz.

Turn right for the tourist office (☎ 23 07-32, ✆ melk@smaragd.at) at Babenbergerstrasse 1. It's closed from November to March; otherwise it's open 9 am to noon and 2 to 6 pm weekdays, 10 am to 2 pm Saturday. In summer, hours are 9 am to 7 pm Monday to Saturday, 10 am to 2 pm Sunday.

Things to See & Do

Stift Melk, the Benedictine Abbey, dominates the town from the hill and offers excellent views. Regular guided tours explain its historical importance and are well worth taking.

The huge monastery church is baroque gone mad, with endless prancing angels and gold twirls but it's very impressive nonetheless. The fine library and the mirror room both have an extra tier painted on the ceiling to give the illusion of greater height. The ceilings are slightly curved to aid the effect.

It is open 9 am to 5 pm from the Saturday before Palm Sunday to All Saints' Day, except between May and September when it closes at 6 pm. Entry costs AS70 (students aged up to 27 years AS35), and the guided tour is AS20 extra (phone ahead to make sure of a tour in English). During winter, the monastery can only be visited by guided tour (☎ 555-232 for information).

There are other interesting sights around town – the free tourist office map highlights historic buildings. **Schloss Schallaburg**, 5km south of Melk (AS30 by infrequent bus), is a 16th-century Renaissance palace which has marvellous terracotta arches and hosts prestigious exhibitions. It's open from late April to late October and costs AS90 (students AS40; combination ticket with Stift Melk available).

Places to Stay & Eat

Camping Melk is on the west bank of the canal that joins the Danube. It's open from March to October and charges AS45 per adult, AS35 per tent and AS25 for a car. Reception is in the restaurant *Melker Fährhaus* (☎ 532 91, *Kolomaniau 3*), which is open 8 am to midnight Wednesday to Sunday (daily in summer). When it's closed, just camp and pay later. The restaurant has decent lunchtime fare from AS75.

The HI *Jugendherberge* (☎ 526 81, fax 542 57, *Abt Karl Strasse 42*) has good showers and four-bed dorms. Beds are AS144 (AS119 for those aged under 19), plus a AS25 surcharge for single night stays. The reception is closed from 10 am to 5 pm, but during the day you can reserve a bed and leave your bags. The hostel is closed from 1 November to mid-March.

Gasthof Weisses Lamm (☎ 540 85, *Linzer Strasse 7*) has a few singles/doubles

AUSTRIA

for AS350/550. On the premises is *Pizzeria Venezia* (open daily), with many tasty pizzas starting at AS65. *Gasthof Goldener Stern* (☎ 522 14, fax -4, Sterngasse 17) provides slightly cheaper accommodation, and has a restaurant serving affordable Austrian food. It's closed Friday and Saturday in winter, or Tuesday evening and Wednesday in summer.

There is a *Spar* supermarket at Rathausplatz 9.

Getting There & Away

Boats leave from the canal by Pionierstrasse, 400m to the rear of the monastery. Bicycle hire is available in the train station. Trains to Vienna Westbahnhof (AS150, 60 to 70 minutes) are direct or via St Pölten.

LINZ
☎ 0732 • pop 190,000

Despite the heavy industry based in Linz, the provincial capital of Upper Austria retains a picturesque old-town centre. It's just a pity about the belching smokestacks on the outskirts that smudge your view of the distant Alps.

Orientation & Information

Most of the town is on the south bank of the Danube. The tourist office (☎ 7070-1777), Hauptplatz 1, is on the main square and has a free room-finding service and an interesting walking tour pamphlet. It is open to 7 pm daily (to 6 pm from 1 November to 30 April). To get there from the train station, walk right, then turn left at the far side of the park and continue along Landstrasse for 10 minutes; alternatively, catch tram No 3.

In the train station there's restaurants, bike rental (daily till 9.30 pm), and the Sparda Bank, with a free telephone to the tourist office.

The large post office (Postamt 4020), opposite the station and to the left, is open daily: to 8 pm weekdays and 5.30 pm weekends.

American Express (☎ 66 90 13) is at Bürgerstrasse 14. The provincial tourist office (☎ 77 12 64, fax 60 02 20, ✉ info@uppperaustria.or.at), Schillerstrasse 50, with information on Salzkammergut, is open 9 am to noon and 1 to 4.30 pm weekdays (closed Friday afternoon).

Things to See & Do

The large, baroque **Hauptplatz** has the Pillar of the Holy Trinity at its centre. The pillar was sculpted in Salzburg marble in 1723. From Hauptplatz, turn onto Hofgasse and climb the hill to **Schloss Linz**. The castle has been periodically rebuilt since AD 799 and provides a good view of the many church spires in the centre. It also houses the **Schlossmuseum**, open daily except Monday (entry AS50; temporary exhibitions cost extra).

The neo-Gothic **Neuer Dom** (New Cathedral), built in 1855, features a graceless exterior and exceptional stained-glass windows, including one depicting the history of the town. At the north side of the Nibelungenbrücke (bridge) is the **Ars Electronica Center**. It reveals interactive computer wizardry and gives free Internet access. It's open 10 am to 7 pm Wednesday to Sunday (AS80, students AS40). The **Neue Galerie**, Blütenstrasse 15, also on the north bank, exhibits modern German and Austrian art. Depending on exhibitions, entry costs from AS60 (students AS30; closed Sunday). On the summit of nearby **Pöstlingberg** are a twin-spired church and a children's grotto railway. The **Posthof** (☎ 77 05 48-0), Posthofstrasse 43, is a centre for contemporary music, dance and theatre.

Places to Stay

Camping is south-east of town at *Pichlinger See* (☎ 30 53 14, Wiener Bundesstrasse 937), or at *Pleschinger See* (☎ 24 78 70), a protected area (no motor vehicles) on the north bank.

There are three HI hostels in Linz, all offering rooms with private shower and WC. The *Jugendgästehaus* (☎ 66 44 34, fax -75, Stanglhofweg 3) near Linz Stadium, has singles/doubles for AS343/486, and four-bed dorms for AS173 per person. Morning check-in is possible on weekdays; otherwise it's from 6 pm.

The *Landesjugendherberge* (☎ 73 70 78, fax -15, Blütenstrasse 19-23), on the north bank, has two to five-bed rooms and charges AS130 per person, plus AS25 for breakfast. Take the lift within the multistorey car park. There's daytime check-in on weekdays. The *Jugendherberge* (☎ 77 87 77, fax 78 17 28 94, Kapuzinerstrasse 14) is small, near the centre, and more personal. Beds are AS190/160 for people over/under 19. Check-in is from 5 to 8 pm; it's closed from around November to 1 March.

Goldenes Dachl (☎ 77 58 97, *Hafnerstrasse 27*), one block away from the Neuer Dom, has basic singles/doubles for AS260/460, without breakfast and using hall showers. Doubles with shower are AS520. Reception is closed till 5 pm Saturday, all day Sunday and from 2 to 5 pm weekdays. *Wienerwald* (☎ 77 78 81, fax -30, *Freinbergstrasse 18*) is 1.5km from the town centre (take bus No 26 to Freinberg – last one at 7.46 pm!). It has a restaurant and decent rooms for AS350/580 (those for AS290/490 have no access to a shower).

Goldener Anker (☎ 77 10 88, *Hofgasse 5*), off Hauptplatz, has more convenient rooms from AS305/590. Breakfast is AS75 per person.

Places to Eat

A *Mondo* supermarket is at Blumauerplatz, by the start of Landstrasse. Leading north are plenty of Würstel stands. One of the cheapest places to sit down and eat is *Schnitzel Express* on Hauptstrasse, just north of Nibelungenbrücke. Schnitzels start at only AS49 and it's open daily to 10 pm.

Mangolds (Hauptplatz 3) is a self-service vegetarian restaurant, open 11 am to 8 pm (to 5 pm Saturday; closed Sunday). *Josef Stadtbräu (Landestrasse 49)* occupies several rooms and has a big beer garden. There are all-you-can-eat weekday brunches for AS88 and other meals for under AS100. They make their own beer, too. Along the road at No 13 is *Verona*, where pizzas start at AS59. Next door is *Lotos*, one of many Chinese restaurants scattered around town.

Café Ex-Blatt (Waltherstrasse 15) is a drinking joint favoured by students (beer for AS42 per 0.5L), though it also has pizza for AS84. It's open daily to at least 1 am (closed weekends till 6 pm).

Getting There & Around

Linz is on the main rail and road route between Vienna and Salzburg. Buy city transport tickets before boarding: AS18 per journey or AS36 for a day card. Some bus services stop early evening.

The South

The two principal states in the south, Styria (Steiermark) and Carinthia (Kärnten), are often neglected by visitors, yet they offer mountains, lakes, varied cities and interesting influences from the neighbouring countries of Italy, Slovenia and Hungary.

GRAZ

☎ 0316 • pop 242,000

Graz is the capital of Styria, a province characterised by mountains and dense forests. In former times, Graz was an important bulwark against invading Turks; today, it is fast becoming an essential stop on the tourist trail.

Orientation

Graz is dominated by the Schlossberg, the castle hill which rises over the medieval town centre. The River Mur cuts a north-south path west of the hill, dividing the old centre from the main train station. Tram Nos 3, 6 and 14 run from the station to Hauptplatz in the centre. A number of streets radiate from the square, including Sporgasse, an important shopping street, and Herrengasse, the main pedestrian thoroughfare. Herrengasse leads to Jakominiplatz, a major transport hub.

Information

There is a tourist information office, in the train station, open 9 am to 6 pm Monday to Friday from March to December, and till 6 pm Saturday in July and August. The station also has bike rental, a money exchange office and a Bankomat (for credit card cash advances).

The main tourist office (☎ 80 75-0, fax -55, ✉ info@graztourismus.at), Herrengasse 16, is open until 6 pm weekdays and 3 pm weekends, except from June to September when it closes 7 pm weekdays, 6 pm Saturday and 3 pm Sunday. The main post office is at Neutorgasse 46 (Hauptpostamt 8010), and is open until 9 pm weekdays and until 2 pm Saturday.

Café Zentral, Andreas Hofer Platz, has Internet access (AS60 for 60 minutes), as does the Jugendgästehaus (AS1 for two minutes).

Things to See & Do

The tourist office organises guided walks of the city (AS75), daily in summer and on Saturday

AUSTRIA

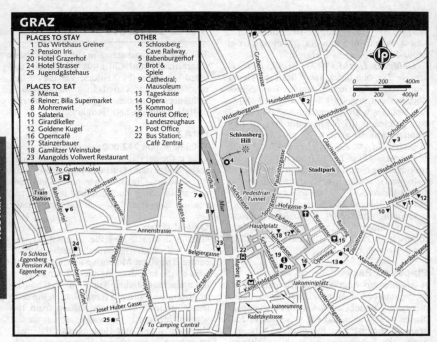

GRAZ

PLACES TO STAY
1 Das Wirtshaus Greiner
2 Pension Iris
20 Hotel Grazerhof
24 Hotel Strasser
25 Jugendgästehaus

PLACES TO EAT
3 Mensa
6 Reiner; Billa Supermarket
8 Mohrenwirt
10 Salateria
11 Girardikeller
12 Goldene Kugel
16 Operncafé
17 Stainzerbauer
18 Gamlitzer Weinstube
23 Mangolds Vollwert Restaurant

OTHER
4 Schlossberg
  Cave Railway
5 Babenburgerhof
7 Brot &
  Spiele
9 Cathedral;
  Mausoleum
13 Tageskasse
14 Opera
15 Kommod
19 Tourist Office;
  Landeszeughaus
21 Post Office
22 Bus Station;
  Café Zentral

in winter. Paths wind up the **Schlossberg** from all sides. The climb up takes less than 30 minutes and repays the effort with excellent views. At the top are an open-air theatre, a small military museum and the bell tower which dates from 1588. Unusually, the larger hand on the clock face shows the hours. The townsfolk paid the French not to destroy it during the Napoleonic Wars.

The nearby **Stadtpark** (City Park) is a relaxing place to sit or wander. The **cathedral**, on the corner of Hofgasse and Bürgergasse, is worth a look. The impressive baroque **Mausoleum** next door is the resting place of Ferdinand II and several other Habsburgs. It is open 11 am to noon and 2 to 3 pm June to September, 11 am to noon the rest of the year; it's closed Sunday. Admission costs AS10 (students AS5).

Visit the **Landeszeughaus** (Armoury), Herrengasse 16, which houses an incredible array of gleaming armour and weapons, enough to equip about 30,000 soldiers. Most of it dates from the 17th century, when the

original Armoury was built. Some of the armour is beautifully engraved; other exhibits are crude and intimidating. The view from the 4th floor to the Landhaus courtyard and the Schlossberg is perfect. The Armoury is open 9 am to 5 pm from March to October and 10 am to 3 pm November and December. It's closed Monday and entry costs AS80 (students/seniors AS60).

The **Schlossberg Cave Railway** is fun for children. It's the longest grotto railway in Europe, and winds its way for 2km around scenes from fairy tales. It's open daily and costs AS35 for one (adult or child), AS65 for two, AS85 for three etc. The entrance is on Schlossbergplatz, next to a pedestrian tunnel through the hill that passes WWII shelters (free entry).

Schloss Eggenberg, Eggenbergen Allee 90, is 4km west of the centre (take tram No 1). The **Prunkräume** (state rooms) of this opulent 17th-century residence, complete with astrological motifs, can be visited by guided tour (closed Monday and from 1 November to 31 March); the admission for AS80 (students AS60) includes two museums. Its extensive parklands are open daily all year and cost AS2 to enter.

Places to Stay

Camping Central (☎ 28 18 31, Martinhofstrasse 3) is open from 1 April to 31 October, and costs AS295 for a two-person site, including swimming pool entry. It's about 6km south-west of the city centre; take bus No 32 from Jakominiplatz.

The HI *Jugendgästehaus (☎ 71 48 76, fax -88, Idlhofgasse 74)* has four-bed dorms for AS230, and singles/doubles for AS325/550. These all have private shower and WC, but the larger dorms in the basement (AS155) don't. Add AS20 first night's surcharge if you're only staying one/two nights. Reception is open 7 am to 10 pm (closed 10 am to 5 pm on weekends and holidays), and there's always daytime access. Laundry costs from AS40 to wash and dry. There are extensive lawns, parking, and self-service weekday lunches for AS69 (available to nonguests).

Five minutes from the station is *Hotel Strasser (☎ 71 39 77, fax 71 68 56, ✆ hotel .strasser@noten.com, Eggenberger Gürtel 11)*. It has pleasant singles/doubles for AS480/690 with private shower, or AS380/590 without.

Gasthof Kokol (☎/fax 68 43 20, Thalstrasse 3) is north-west of the centre, easily reached by bus No 40 from Jakominiplatz or No 85 from the train station. Rooms cost AS390/640 with shower and toilet, or AS240/480 without (reservations advised). On weekends, reception closes from 1 to 6 pm.

Das Wirtshaus Greiner (☎ 68 50 90, fax -4, ✆ das.wirtshaus.greiner@eunet.at, Grabenstrasse 64), north of Schlossberg, has renovated rooms with shower, toilet and TV. Singles/doubles are AS440/590 or more, depending upon size and situation. Phone ahead for weekends as the restaurant/reception is closed.

Pension Iris (☎ 32 20 81, fax -5, Bergmanngasse 10) has comfortable rooms with shower and WC for about AS550/800. Double-glazing eliminates traffic noise. *Pension Alt Eggenberg (☎/fax 58 66 15, Baiernstrasse 3)* has good-value singles/doubles with private shower and WC for AS400/600.

It's out of the centre, but easily reached by tram No 1 (the stop after Schloss Eggenberg).

Hotel Grazerhof (☎ 82 43 58, fax 81 96 33-40, Stubenberggasse 10) has smallish, innocuous rooms for AS440/780, or from AS600/1090 with private shower. Prices are relatively high for a three-star hotel, but that's because it is the only one in the old centre. The hotel borders two pedestrian streets, but the receptionist can tell you where to park.

Places to Eat

The Annenpassage shopping centre opposite the train station has a *Billa* supermarket and the cheap *Reiner* self-service restaurant. Also look out for cheap weekday lunches in Chinese restaurants.

A good deal is at the *University Mensa (Schubertstrasse 2-4)*. Main meals (including a vegetarian choice) cost AS39 to AS61 (AS4 discount with ISIC Card). It's open 8.30 am to 2.30 pm Monday to Friday, and has breakfasts for AS29. Explore the university vicinity for other restaurants and bars.

Girardikeller (Leonhardstrasse 28) is a cellar bar with cheap food – the weekday special is just AS50, and pizzas with seven toppings are AS65. It's open daily from 5 pm (6 pm on weekends) till 2 am. Vegetarians can eat for a similarly low price at both *Salateria (Leonhardstrasse 18)*, which closes at 7 pm (5 pm Friday) and on the weekend, and at *Mangolds Vollwert Restaurant (Griesgasse 11)*, which closes at 8 pm weekdays, 4 pm on Saturday, and all day Sunday.

Mohrenwirt (Mariahilfer Strasse 16) is a typical small Gasthof with snacks and meals from AS20 to AS90. Ask the server about daily specials as they're not written down (open Saturday to Wednesday). A little more expensive but also with authentic Styrian cooking is *Gamlitzer Weinstube (Mehlplatz 4)*; try the tasty Steirerpfand'l (AS80; closed weekends). To sample numerous varieties of beer and affordable Austrian food (under AS100), go to *Goldene Kugel (Leonhardstrasse 32)*. It's closed Saturday.

For a splurge, head to the traditional *Stainzerbauer (☎ 82 11 06, Bürgergasse 4)*. Wooden archways, numerous photographs and background classical music add to the atmosphere. Styrian and Austrian specialities are mostly AS100 to AS235, though the weekday two-course lunch is a mere AS80 (closed Sunday).

Graz has several coffee houses, including *Operncafé (Opernring 22)*, which is open 7.30 am (9 am Sunday) to midnight daily.

Entertainment
In the centre of town, many bars and clubs are around Mehlplatz and Prokopigasse. *Kommod (Burggasse 15)* is a bright and busy bar, often packed with students, which serves affordable pizza and pasta (closed till 5 pm on weekends). *Brot & Spiele (Mariahilfer Strasse 17)* offers beer, inexpensive food, chess and pool tables. *Babenburgerhof (Babenburgerstrasse 39)* is a friendly bar with free live jazz on Wednesday (closed weekends).

Graz is an important cultural centre and hosts musical events throughout the year. The Tageskasse (☎ 8000), Kaiser Josef Platz 10, sells tickets without commission for the *Schauspielhaus* (theatre) and *Opernhaus* (opera). Students aged under 27 pay half-price. An hour before performances, students can buy leftover tickets for AS80 at the door, and anybody can buy standing room tickets for AS40 or AS45.

Getting There & Away
Direct IC trains to Vienna's Südbahnhof depart every two hours (AS320, 2¾ hours). Trains depart every two hours to Salzburg (AS430, 4¼ hours), either direct or changing at Bischofshofen. Two daily direct trains depart for Zagreb (AS364, four hours). Getting to Budapest via Szentgotthard and Szombathely is slightly quicker and cheaper (AS598, 6½ hours) than going via Vienna. Trains to Klagenfurt (AS340, three hours) go via Bruck an der Mur. The bus station is at Andreas Hofer Platz. The A2 autobahn from Vienna to Klagenfurt passes a few kilometres south of the city.

Getting Around
Public transport tickets cover the Schlossberg-bahn (castle-hill railway) that runs from Sack-strasse up the Schlossberg. Tickets cost AS20 each or AS160 for a block of 10. The 24-hour and weekly passes cost AS42 and AS100 respectively, and are valid from first use. Blue parking zones allow a three-hour stop (AS8 for 30 minutes) during specified times.

AROUND GRAZ
The stud farm of the Lipizzaner stallions, those famous performers in Vienna, is about 40km west of Graz at **Piber**. The farm can be visited from Easter to the end of October (AS100, students AS40). Get more details from the Graz tourist office or the Köflach tourist office (☎ 03144-25 19-750), which is 3km from the farm. Köflach can be reached by train or bus from Graz. The fare is AS72 each way (reduction with Graz city pass). One stop nearer Graz on the train line is **Bärnbach**, where there's a remarkable parish church created by Hundertwasser and other artists.

KLAGENFURT
☎ 0463 • pop 87,000
The capital of Carinthia (Kärnten) since 1518, Klagenfurt merits a brief visit en route between Graz and Lienz.

Orientation & Information
Neuer Platz, the heart of the city, is 1km north of the main train station; walk straight down Bahnhofstrasse and turn left at Paradieser Gasse. Here you will find the tourist office (☎ 537 223, fax 537 295, @ tourismus@klagenfurt.at) in the Rathaus. Opening hours are 8 am to 8 pm weekdays, 10 am to 5 pm weekends and holidays; from 1 October to 30 April, it closes at 6.30 pm on weekdays and 3 pm on weekends. There's bike rental at the tourist office and at the train station. The main post office is on Dr Hermann Gasse (Postamt 9010), one block west of Neuer Platz.

Things to See & Do
The **Neuer Platz** (New Square) is dominated by the town emblem, the Dragon Fountain. **Alter Platz** (Old Square) is the oldest part of the city, and an interesting area to explore. Adjoining it is the 16th-century **Landhaus**, worth visiting for the Hall of Arms (Wappensaal), open between 1 April and 31 September, weekdays only (AS15, students AS10). The walls are covered in paintings of 655 coats of arms, and the ceiling sports an effective mural of an illusory extra tier.

The **Wörther See**, 4km west of the city centre, is one of the warmer lakes in the region thanks to subterranean thermal springs. You can swim or go boating in summer at the lakeside **Strandbad**. Nearby is the boat station, from where steamers embark on circular tours in summer; get details from STW (☎ 211 55). The adjoining Europa Park has various attractions, including the touristy **Minimundus**, which displays over 150 models of famous international buildings on a 1:25 scale; it is open daily from mid-April to late October (AS120, students AS90, children AS40).

Places to Stay

Camping Strandbad (☎ 211 69) in Europa Park provides lakeside camping in summer.

The HI *Jugendherberge (☎ 23 00 20, fax -20, Neckheimgasse 6)*, near Europa Park, has four-bed dorms with own shower and WC for AS210. Single/double occupancy costs AS310/520.

Hotel Liebetegger (☎ 569 35, fax -6, Völkermarkter Strasse 8) is stylish, central and affordable. It charges AS400/700 with shower, WC and TV or AS250/500 without; breakfast is AS80. *Schlosshotel Wörthersee (☎ 211 58, fax -8, ✆ office@schlosshotel-woethersee.at, Villacher Strasse 338)* is by the lake. It has well-presented rooms, some with balcony, all with cable TV and bath or shower. Singles/doubles start at AS590/980. Both hotels have parking, but no lift.

Places to Eat

The *University Mensa (Universitätsstrasse 90)*, by Europa Park, is open to all for cut-price meals, from 11 am to 2.30 pm Monday to Friday. Eating cheaply in the centre isn't too hard either; try the tiny shops in the Benediktinerplatz market where you can have a hot meal for only about AS50. *Zur Chinesischen Mauer (Lidmanskygasse 19)* offers good weekday Chinese lunches for around AS73. *Gasthaus Pirker* on the corner of Adlergasse and Lidmanskygasse has a decent selection of Austrian food (AS70 to AS150), beer and wine. It's open 8 am to midnight Monday to Friday.

Getting There & Around

Trains to Graz depart every one to two hours (AS340, three hours). Trains to west Austria, Italy and Germany go via Villach, which is 40 minutes away by rail.

Bus drivers sell single tickets (AS22) or 24-hour passes (AS55), but buy 24-hour passes in advance for AS44 from ticket machines or the ticket office on Heiligengeistplatz in the centre. For the Europa Park vicinity, take bus No 10, 11, 12, 20, 21, or 22 from Heiligengeistplatz.

Salzburg

☎ 0662 • 145,000

The city that delivered Mozart to the world has much to recommend it, despite the fact that in more recent years the nearby hills have been alive to *The Sound of Music*. The influence of Mozart is everywhere. There is Mozartplatz, the Mozarteum, Mozart's Birthplace and Mozart's Residence. He even has chocolate bars and liqueurs named after him.

But even Wolfgang Amadeus Mozart must take second place to the powerful bishopprinces who shaped the skyline and the destiny of the city after AD 798. The old town, impossibly quaint and picturesque, is deservedly a Unesco World Heritage site.

Orientation

The centre of the city is split by the River Salzach. The old part of town (mostly pedestrian-only) is on the left (south) bank, with the unmistakable Hohensalzburg Fortress dominant on the hill above. Most of the attractions are on this side of the river. The new town, the centre of business activity, is on the right (north) bank, along with most of the cheaper hotels.

Information

Tourist Offices There are several tourist offices (☎ 889 87-0, ✆ tourist@salzburginfo.at). Dial ☎ 889 87-314 (fax -32) for hotel reservations at AS30 commission. The central office is at Mozartplatz 5. It's open 9 am to 7 pm daily from April to October (to 8 pm in July and August); it closes at 6 pm and on Sunday from November to March. The provincial information section (☎ 66 88 0) in the same building is open 9 am to 6 pm (to 5.30 pm in winter) on weekdays, and to 3.30 pm Saturday.

Information offices open throughout the year are also in the train station on platform 2a; in the airport; at Mitte, Münchner Bundesstrasse 1; and in the south at Park & Ride Parkplatz, Alpensiedlung Süd, Alpenstrasse.

AUSTRIA

AUSTRIA

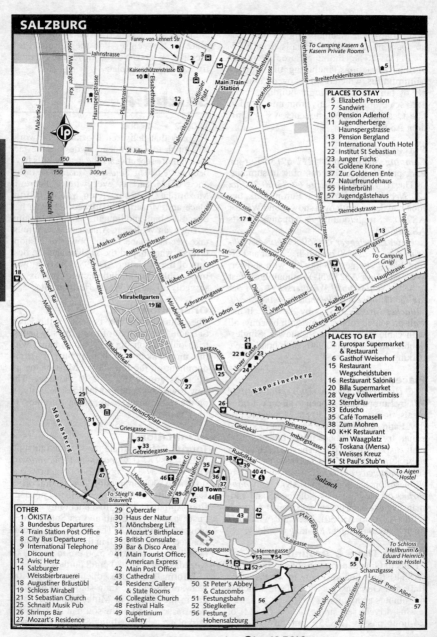

SALZBURG

PLACES TO STAY
5 Elizabeth Pension
7 Sandwirt
10 Pension Adlerhof
11 Jugendherberge Haunspergstrasse
13 Pension Bergland
17 International Youth Hotel
22 Institut St Sebastian
23 Junger Fuchs
24 Goldene Krone
37 Zur Goldenen Ente
47 Naturfreundehaus
55 Hinterbrühl
57 Jugendgästehaus

PLACES TO EAT
2 Eurospar Supermarket & Restaurant
6 Gasthof Weiserhof
15 Restaurant Wegscheidstuben
16 Restaurant Saloniki
20 Billa Supermarket
28 Vegy Vollwertimbiss
32 Sternbräu
33 Eduscho
35 Café Tomaselli
38 Zum Mohren
40 K+K Restaurant am Waagplatz
45 Toskana (Mensa)
53 Weisses Kreuz
54 St Paul's Stub'n

OTHER
1 ÖKISTA
3 Bundesbus Departures
4 Train Station Post Office
8 City Bus Departures
9 International Telephone Discount
12 Avis; Hertz
14 Salzburger Weissbierbrauerei
18 Augustiner Bräustübl
19 Schloss Mirabell
21 St Sebastian Church
25 Schnaitl Musik Pub
26 Shrimps Bar
27 Mozart's Residence
29 Cybercafe
30 Haus der Natur
31 Mönchsberg Lift
34 Mozart's Birthplace
36 British Consulate
39 Bar & Disco Area
41 Main Tourist Office; American Express
42 Main Post Office
43 Cathedral
44 Residenz Gallery & State Rooms
46 Collegiate Church
48 Festival Halls
49 Rupertinium Gallery
50 St Peter's Abbey & Catacombs
51 Festungsbahn
52 Stieglkeller
56 Festung Hohensalzburg

The office in the north, at Autobahnstation Kasern, is open from June to September. Tourist offices and hotels sell the Salzburg Card. This provides free museum entry and free public transport, and gives various reductions. The price is AS225/300/390 for 24/48/72 hours. Salzburg Plus is a prepaid card including meals and accommodation.

Money Banks are open 8 am to noon and 2 to 4.30 pm Monday to Friday. Currency exchange at the train station counters is available to at least 8.30 pm daily. At the airport, money can be exchanged between 8 am and 8 pm daily. There are plenty of exchange offices in the centre, but beware of high commission rates.

Post & Communications The post office at the train station (Bahnhofspostamt 5020) is open daily, including for money exchange, 6 am to 9.30 pm weekdays and 8 or 9 am to 8 pm weekends. In the town centre, the main post office (Hauptpostamt 5010), Residenzplatz 9, is open 7 am to 7 pm weekdays, 8 to 10 am Saturday.

Email & Internet Access Cybercafe (☎ 84 26 16-22), Gstättengasse 27, is open 2 to 11 pm or later. Surfing costs AS40 for 30 minutes. International Telephone Discount, Kaiserschützenstrasse 8, is AS1.70 per minute, but does have cheap international telephone calls (9 am to midnight daily).

Travel Agencies American Express (☎ 80 80) is next to the tourist office at Mozartplatz 5. It is open 9 am to 5.30 pm Monday to Friday, to noon Saturday. ÖKISTA (☎ 45 87 33), Fanny-von-Lehnert Strasse 1, is closed weekends. Young Austrla (☎ 62 57 58-0) at Alpenstrasse 108a is another budget travel agency.

Medical & Emergency Services The Landeskrankenhaus hospital, St Johanns-Spital (☎ 44 82-0), is at Müllner Hauptstrasse 48, just north of the Mönchsberg. Dial ☎ 141 for an ambulance.

Things to See & Do
The old town is a baroque masterpiece set amid the Kapuzinerberg and Mönchsberg

mountains, both of which have a good network of footpaths. Take time to wander around the many plazas, courtyards, fountains and churches.

Start at the vast **Dom** (cathedral) on Domplatz, which has three bronze doors symbolising faith, hope and charity. Head west along Franziskanergasse, and turn left into a courtyard for **St Peter's Abbey**, dating from AD 847. The interesting graveyard contains the catacombs, which can be perused till 5 pm in summer, 3.30 pm in winter (AS12; students AS8). The western end of Franziskanergasse opens out into Max Reinhardt Platz, where you'll see the back of Fisher von Erlach's **Collegiate Church** on Universitätsplatz. This is considered an outstanding example of baroque architecture, although the cherubs and clouds above the altar are a bit ridiculous.

Festung Hohensalzburg In many ways this fortress is the high point of a visit to Salzburg. It's a 15-minute walk up the hill to the castle, or you can take the Festungsbahn (AS24 up, AS34 return) from Festungsgasse 4. Admission is AS42. Note the many turnip reliefs – this was the symbol of Archbishop Leonhard von Keutschach, who greatly extended the fortress. It's worth paying for the audio guided tour (AS40) which allows entrance to the torture chambers, state rooms, the tower and two museums. The view from the castle over the city is stupendous. The view on the south side includes an isolated house amid a big field. According to tourguide mythology it was the home of the shunned official executioner, but more veracious sources indicate it actually belonged to the archbishop's groundskeeper.

Schloss Mirabell This palace was built by the worldly prince-archbishop Wolf Dietrich for his mistress in 1606. Its attractive gardens featured in *The Sound of Music*, and they're a great place to spend some time. 'Musical Spring' concerts (among others) are held in the palace. Take a look inside at the marble staircase, which is adorned with baroque sculptures.

Mausoleum of Wolf Dietrich Located in the graveyard of the 16th-century St Sebastian Church on Linzer Gasse, this restored

AUSTRIA

mausoleum has some interesting epitaphs. In a wonderful piece of arrogance, the archbishop commands the faithful to 'piously commemorate the founder of this chapel' (ie, himself) and 'his close relations', or expect 'God Almighty to be an avenging judge'. Mozart's father and widow are buried in the graveyard.

Museums The **Haus der Natur** (Museum of Natural History) is at Museumsplatz 5. You could spend hours wandering round its diverse exhibits. In addition to the usual flora, fauna and mineral displays, it has exhibits on physics and astronomy (pity about the lack of English signs), plus bizarre oddities such as the stomach-churning display of deformed animals on the 4th floor. There are also many tropical fish and an excellent reptile house with lizards, snakes and alligators. It even has an inexpensive terrace cafe with a lunch *menu*. The museum is open 9 am to 5 pm daily, and admission costs AS55 (students under 27 AS30).

The other museums don't take too long to get around. In the **Residenz**, Residenzplatz 1, you can visit the baroque state rooms of the archbishop's palace (by audio guided tour only, AS70) and the gallery which houses some good 16th and 17th-century Dutch and Flemish paintings (AS50). Combined tickets are AS91 (students AS70). The **Rupertinium**, Wiener Philharmoniker Gasse 9, has 20th-century works of art and temporary exhibitions. Entry costs AS40 (students AS20).

Mozart's **Geburtshaus** (Birthplace) at Getreidegasse 9 and **Wohnhaus** (Residence) at Makartplatz 8 are popular but cover similar ground. Entry costs AS70/AS65 respectively, or AS110 (students/seniors AS85) for a combined ticket. They both contain musical instruments, sheet music and other memorabilia of the great man. The Wohnhaus is perhaps the better of the two, and it also houses the Mozart Sound and Film Museum (free entry).

If beer's more your thing, visit **Stiegl's Brauwelt** (☎ 8387-1492), Brauhausstrasse 9, for a tour and a couple of free beers (entry AS125, Wednesday to Sunday).

Organised Tours
One-hour walking tours (AS100) of the old city leave from the main tourist office. Other tours of Salzburg mostly leave from Mirabellplatz, including *The Sound of Music* tour (see the Jugendgästehaus under Places to Stay for the lowest price).

The Sound of Music tour is enduringly popular with English-speaking visitors, despite its many detractors. Tours last three to four hours, cost around AS350, take in major city sights featured in the movie and include a visit to Salzkammergut. Some find the tour quite dull, but if you go with a group with the right mix of tongue-in-cheek enthusiasm, it can be brilliant fun – we have fond memories of manic Julie Andrews impersonators flouncing in the fields, screeching 'the hills are alive' in voices to wake the dead, and of loutish youths skipping in the summer house (gazebo), chanting 'I am 16 going on 17'. However, a reader wrote to report:

> The gazebo is now locked. No tourists can leap from bench to bench as a result of an 85-year-old fan imitating Liesel and falling – breaking a hip.
>
> J Smethurst

Special Events
The Salzburg International Festival takes place from late July to the end of August, and includes music ranging from Mozart (of course!) to contemporary. Several events take place each day in different locations. Prices vary from AS50 to a trifling AS4600. The cheapest prices are for standing-room tickets, which can usually be prebooked. Most things sell out months in advance. Write for information as early as October to: Kartenbüro der Salzburger Festspiele, Postfach 140, A-5010 Salzburg. Try checking closer to the event for cancellations – inquire at the ticket office (☎ 84 45 760), Herbert von Karajan Platz 11, behind the horse fountain. Opening hours during the festival are 9.30 am to 6.30 pm daily. Web site: www.salzburgfestival.at. Other important music festivals are at Easter and Whit Sunday.

Places to Stay – Budget
Ask for the tourist office's hotel map which gives prices for hotels, pensions, six hostels and five camping grounds. Accommodation is at a premium during festivals.

Camping Just north of the A1 Nord exit, *Camping Kasern* (☎/fax 45 05 76, Carl Zuckmayer Strasse 4) costs AS65 per adult and AS35 each for a car and tent (open 1 April to 31 October). *Camping Gnigl* (☎ 64 30 60, Parscher Strasse 4), east of Kapuzinerberg, costs less (open mid-May to mid-September).

Private Rooms The tourist office's list of private rooms (from AS220) and apartments does not list the Kasern area, as this is just north of the city limits. But Kasern, up the hill from Salzburg-Maria Plain train station (AS20 from Salzburg Hauptbahnhof), has the best bargains, with prices from AS180 per person. Look for 'Zimmer frei' signs, or try *Haus Christine* (☎ 45 67 73, Panoramaweg 3) or the next-door *Haus Lindner* (☎ 45 66 81).

Hostels If you're travelling to party, head for the sociable *International Youth Hotel* or YoHo (☎ 87 96 49, fax 87 88 10, ✉ office@ yoho.at, Paracelsusstrasse 9). There's a bar with loud music and cheap beer (AS30 for 0.5L), and discounts offered on town sights. The staff are almost exclusively young, native English-speakers. This popular place accepts phone reservations no earlier than one day in advance. Beds per person are AS150 (eight-bed dorm), AS170 (four-bed dorm, own key) and AS200 (double room, own key). There's a 1 am curfew and it's open all day. Showers/lockers cost AS10 for each use (an annoying charge, especially for the lockers), and sheets if required cost AS20 (one-off fee). Breakfasts are AS15 to AS45, dinners AS60 to AS75. The hotel also organises outings and shows *The Sound of Music* daily.

The HI *Jugendgästehaus* (☎ 84 26 70-0, fax 84 11 01, Josef Preis Allee 18), is large, modern and busy, and probably the most comfortable hostel. Eight-bed dorms are AS162, four-bed rooms are AS212 and two-bed rooms are AS262; all prices are per person and include a AS10 surcharge for the first night's stay. Telephone reservations are accepted. Check-in is from 11 am, though reception is closed for intermittent periods during the day. It has good showers, free lockers, a bar, small kitchen, and bike rental for AS90 per day. Daily *Sound of Music* tours are the cheapest in town at AS300 for anybody

who shows up by 8.45 am or 1.30 pm. The film is also shown daily.

The HI *Jugendherberge* (☎ 87 50 30, fax 88 34 77, Haunspergstrasse 27) near the train station is only open around July and August, and costs AS170. *Institut St Sebastian* (☎ 87 13 86, fax -85, Linzer Gasse 41) has a roof terrace and kitchens, and dorms for AS190 plus AS30 for sheets. Singles/doubles are AS400/700 with shower and WC or AS360/600 without. The sound of church bells is loud in some rooms.

The *Naturfreundehaus* (☎ 84 17 29, Mönchsberg 19), also called Gasthaus Bürgerwehr, is clearly visible high on the hill between the fortress and Café Winkler. Take the footpath up from near Max Reinhardt Platz, or the Mönchsberg lift (AS16 up, AS27 return) from A Neumayr Platz. It offers dorm beds for AS120 (showers AS10) and marvellous views. It's open all day, but with a 1 am curfew. The restaurant provides breakfast from AS30 and hot meals from AS65 to AS110. It's open for meals from April to October, but rooms are only from about May to September, depending on the weather (phone ahead).

If everywhere is full in town, try two *HI hostels* in the south: at Aignerstrasse 34, Aigen (☎ 62 32 48), and at Eduard Heinrich Strasse 2 (☎ 62 59 76); beds in both are AS186.

Hotels & Pensions *Sandwirt* (☎/fax 87 43 51, Lastenstrasse 6a) is near the rail tracks. Singles/doubles are AS300/480 using hall shower; doubles/triples/quads are AS508/720/880 with private shower and TV. The rooms are clean, reasonably large and quiet, and staff are helpful.

Elizabeth Pension (☎/fax 87 16 64, Vogelweiderstrasse 5) has smaller rooms but they have been nicely renovated. It's close to the Breitenfelderstrasse stop of bus No 15, which heads for the town centre every 15 minutes. Singles/doubles are AS300/480 using hall shower, or AS350/540 with shower cubicle in the room. Singles are not available in summer.

Junger Fuchs (☎ 87 54 96, Linzer Gasse 54) has singles/doubles/triples for AS280/380/480, without breakfast and with a AS15 charge for using the shower in summer. The rooms are better than the cramped corridors would suggest and it's in a convenient location.

AUSTRIA

Everywhere in the old town is pricey, though **Hinterbrühl** (☎ *84 67 98, fax 84 18 59, Schanzlgasse 12*) is affordable. Here singles/doubles cost from AS420/520 using hall shower, and breakfast is AS50. Reception, in the restaurant downstairs, is open 8 am to 11 pm daily.

Places to Stay – Mid-Range

Pension Adlerhof (☎ *87 52 36, fax 87 36 636, Elisabethstrasse 25*), near the train station, offers a choice of modern or rustic-style rooms, and there's a baroque breakfast room. Singles/doubles are from AS590/790 with private shower and toilet.

Goldene Krone (☎ *87 23 00, fax -66, Linzer Gasse 48*) has singles/doubles with private shower and WC for AS570/970; some of the rooms have church-like groined ceilings which add a bit of character.

Good value, but 10 minutes walk east, is **Pension Bergland** (☎ *87 23 18, fax -8,* ✉ *pku hn@berglandhotel.at, Rupertgasse 15*) which charges AS620/1020 for pristine rooms with bathroom and TV.

If you're prepared to pay more to be in the old town, try **Zur Goldenen Ente** (☎ *84 56 22, fax -9,* ✉ *ente@eunet.at, Goldgasse 10*). Rooms in this old house are variable, but all have private bath/shower and TV and cost AS820/1280 per single/double. The atmospheric restaurant (usually closed weekends) offers quality meals.

Places to Eat – Budget

There's a *fruit and vegetable market* at Mirabellplatz on Thursday morning. On Universitätsplatz and Kapitelplatz there are *market stalls* and *fast-food stands*. A *Billa* supermarket is on Schallmooser Hauptstrasse. The large *Eurospar* supermarket by the train station has a self-service restaurant; meals are around AS60, or half-price after 6 pm (closes 7 pm, 5 pm Saturday). Between sightseeing, nip into *Eduscho* (*Getreidegasse 34*) for a small, strong cup of coffee for AS12; you'll have to stand.

The best budget deals are in the university mensas. Lunches are served from 11.30 am to 2 pm on weekdays, and cost from AS40 for ISIC-card holders and from AS45 for others. The most convenient is *Toskana* (*Sigmund Haffner Gasse 11*).

One of the few vegetarian places in town is **Vegy Vollwertimbiss** (*Schwarzstrasse 21*). This shop and restaurant has a salad buffet from AS38, and a lunch *menu* for AS89, including soup and dessert. It is open 11 am to 5 pm Monday to Friday.

Gasthof Weiserhof (*Weiserhofstrasse 4*) is a friendly, typical Austrian tavern, with two-course *menus* lunch and evening from just AS70. **Restaurant Wegscheidstuben** (*Lasserstrasse 1*) is similar, albeit a little more expensive. Both places are closed Sunday evening and on Saturday. Opposite Wegscheidstuben is **Restaurant Saloniki**, for affordable Greek food (closed Monday).

St Paul's Stub'n (*Herrengasse 16*), on the 1st floor, has a low-key entrance and terrace tables. Pasta and tasty pizzas from AS72 are served until late (open from 6 pm; closed Sunday). Long tables make it easy to meet the students who drink here.

Weisses Kreuz (*Bierjodlgasse 6*) has Austrian food above AS100, but a better choice is its Balkan specialities. Djuvec (rice, succulent pork and paprika) for AS82 is excellent. It's closed on Tuesday except in summer. Worth visiting for the view, though the food is good value too, is the **Naturfreundehaus** restaurant, up on Mönchsberg.

Places to Eat – Mid-Range

Sternbräu, set in a courtyard between Getreidegasse 36 and Griegasse 23, is a bit touristy, but it has a nice garden and many different rooms. It serves good Austrian food and fish specials from AS85 to AS225. Opening hours are 10 am to 11 pm daily. The adjoining courtyard has a self-service summer buffet and a pizzeria.

Zum Mohren (☎ *484 23 87, Judengasse 9*) is a cellar restaurant with distinctive decor. Most main courses are above AS160, though salads and vegie dishes are cheaper. It's usually closed Sunday.

K+K Restaurant am Waagplatz (☎ *84 21 56, Waagplatz 2*) has affordable food served in the casual ground-floor Stüberl, or at outside tables. Upstairs, the restaurant is more formal and restrained, with quality Austrian fare for around AS140 to AS260 (open daily).

Coffee houses are a well-established tradition in Salzburg. **Café Tomaselli** and **Café Konditorei Fürst** face each other in an ideal central position overlooking Alter Markt. Both have newspapers, lots of cakes and outside tables.

Entertainment

The atmospheric *Augustiner Bräustübl (Augustinergasse 4-6)* proves that monks can make beer as well as anybody. The quaffing clerics have been supplying the lubrication for this huge beer hall for years. Beer is served in litre (AS60) or half-litre (AS30) mugs. Buy sandwich ingredients or hot meals in the deli shops in the foyer, then eat inside or in the large, shady beer garden. It's open 3 pm (2.30 pm weekends) to 11 pm daily.

Stieglkeller (Festungsgasse 10) is another beer hall, open from around April to October only. Ignore the touristy *Sound of Music* show here and head for the garden overlooking the town. Food is around AS90 to AS180, and there's cheaper self-service beer upstairs. Opening hours are 10 am to 10 pm daily.

For wheat beer made on the premises, try *Salzburger Weissbierbrauerei*, on the corner of Rupertgasse and Virgilgasse.

The *Schnaitl Musik Pub (Bergstrasse 5)* has occasional live 'underground' music. It's open 7 pm to 2 am Monday to Saturday.

The liveliest area for bars, clubs and discos is the area near the Radisson Hotel on Rudolfskai. There's a range of (often packed) places, including a couple of *Irish pubs* with live music. There are also a few decent places on Steingasse, including the *Shrimps Bar* at No 5, where the food is worth a taste.

Shopping

Not many people leave without sampling some Mozart confectionery. Chocolate-coated combinations of nougat and marzipan cost around AS6 per piece (cheaper in supermarkets), available individually or in souvenir presentation packs. Getreidegasse is the main shopping street.

Getting There & Away

Air The airport (☎ 85 80) handles regular scheduled flights to Amsterdam, Brussels, Frankfurt, London, Paris and Zürich. British Airways (☎ 84 21 08) has an office at Griesgasse 29. For Austrian Airlines or Swissair, call ☎ 85 45 11-0.

Bus Bundesbuses depart from Südtiroler Platz (where there's a timetable board), across from the train station post office. There's also a bus information office in the train station; alternatively, call ☎ 4660-333 for information. There are at least three departures a day to Kitzbühel (2¼ hours), changing at Lofer. Numerous buses leave for the Salzkammergut region between 6.30 am and 8 pm; destinations include Bad Ischl (AS100, 1¾ hours), Mondsee (AS60, 50 minutes), St Gilgen (AS60, 50 minutes) and St Wolfgang (AS90, 1½ hours).

Train Fast trains leave for Vienna (3¼ hours) via Linz every hour. The express service to Klagenfurt (three hours) goes via Villach. The quickest way to Innsbruck (two hours) is by the 'corridor' train through Germany via Kufstein; trains depart at least every two hours and the fare is AS360. There are trains every 30 to 60 minutes to Munich (AS298, about two hours), some of which continue to Karlsruhe via Stuttgart.

Car & Motorcycle Three autobahns converge on Salzburg and form a loop round the city: the A1 from Linz, Vienna and the east; the A8/E52 from Munich and the west; and the A10/E55 from Villach and the south. Heading south to Carinthia on the A10, there are two tunnels through the mountains; the combined toll is AS140 (AS100 for motorcycles).

Getting Around

To/From the Airport Salzburg airport is 4km west of the city centre. Bus No 77 goes there from the main train station.

Public Transport Bus drivers sell single bus tickets for AS20. Other tickets must be bought from Tabak shops or tourist offices: day passes are AS40; single tickets (AS15 each) and 24-hour passes (AS32 each) are both sold in units of five. Prices are 50% less for children aged six to 15 years; those aged under six travel free.

Car & Motorcycle Driving in the city centre is hardly worth the effort. Parking places are limited and much of the old town is pedestrian access only. The largest car park near the centre is the Altstadt Garage under

AUSTRIA

the Mönchsberg. Attended car parks cost around AS25 per hour. On streets with automatic ticket machines (blue zones), a three-hour maximum applies (AS42, or AS7 for 30 minutes) during specified times – usually shopping hours.

Other Transport Taxis cost AS33 (AS43 at night), plus about AS14 per kilometre inside the city or AS22 per kilometre outside the city. To book a radio taxi, call ☎ 87 44 00. Bike rental in the main train station is open 24 hours; bikes for rent in Residenzplatz are more expensive. Rates for a pony-and-trap (*fiacre*) for up to four passengers are AS420 for 25 minutes and AS820 for 50 minutes.

AROUND SALZBURG
Hellbrunn
Four kilometres south of Salzburg's old-town centre is the popular **Schloss Hellbrunn**, built in the 17th century by bishop Marcus Sitticus, Wolf Dietrich's nephew. The main attraction is the ingenious trick fountains and water-powered figures installed by the bishop and activated today by the tour guides. Expect to get wet! This section of the gardens is open daily from April to October, with the last tour at 4.30 pm (5.30 pm in summer). Tickets cost AS80 (students AS60). You can also visit the baroque palace (AS40, students AS30) and the small Folklore Museum on the hill (AS20, students AS10). There is no charge to stroll round the attractive palace gardens, which are open year-round till dusk.

The **Hellbrunn Zoo** is as naturalistic and as open-plan as possible: the more docile animals are barely confined. It is open 8.30 am to between 4 pm (winter) and 7 pm (summer) daily. Admission costs AS80 (students AS55).

Getting There & Away City bus No 55 runs to the palace every half-hour from Salzburg Hauptbahnhof, via Rudolfskai in the old town (Salzburg tickets are valid).

Hallein
☎ 06245 • pop 20,000
Hallein is primarily visited for the **salt mine** (Salzbergwerk) at Bad Dürrnberg, on the hill above the town. Much of Salzburg's past prosperity was dependent upon salt mines, and this one is the closest and easiest to visit

from the city. The mine stopped production in 1989 to concentrate on guided tours. Some people rave about the experience, others find the one-hour tour disappointing and over-priced (AS200, students AS180). Careering down the wooden slides in the caves is fun, and you get to take a brief raft trip on the salt lake, but there's little else to see. It is open 9 am to 5 pm daily (11 am to 3 pm in winter). Overalls are supplied for the tour. Note that salt-mine tours in the Salzkammergut are cheaper – see the Salzkammergut section later in this chapter.

The tourist office in Hallein (☎ 853 94, ⓔ info-tg@eunet.at), Mauttorpromenade, is on the narrow island adjoining the Stadtbrücke. It is open 9 am to 6.30 pm Monday to Friday. In summer its hours are from 9 am (from 10 am Saturday, 4 pm Sunday) to 9 pm daily.

Getting There & Away Hallein is 30 minutes or less from Salzburg by bus or train (AS40). There are several ways to reach Bad Dürrnberg. The easiest option is to take the cable car, which is a signposted 10-minute walk from the train station. The AS270 (students AS240) return fare includes entry to the mines. A cheaper option is the hourly 11-minute bus ride (AS19) from outside the station, but departures are infrequent on weekends. You could also hike to the mine, though it's a steep 40-minute climb – at the church with the bare concrete tower, turn left along Ferchl Strasse, and follow the sign pointing to the right after the yellow Volksschule building.

Werfen
☎ 06468 • pop 3000
Werfen is a rewarding day trip from Salzburg. The **Hohenwerfen Fortress** stands on the hill above the village. Originally built in 1077, the present building dates from the 16th century and can be visited daily from April to November. Entry costs AS110 (students AS100) and includes an exhibition, a guided tour of the interior and a dramatic falconry show, where birds of prey swoop low over the heads of the crowd. The walk up from the village takes 20 minutes.

The **Eisriesenwelt Höhle** in the mountains are the largest accessible ice caves in the world. The ice formations inside are vast, elaborate and beautiful, yet completely naturally formed. The 70-minute tour costs AS100, and the caves are open from 1 May to 26 October. Some elderly visitors find the going too arduous. Take warm clothes because it can get cold inside.

Both attractions can be fitted into the same day if you start early (visit the caves first, and be at the castle by 3 pm for the falconry show). The tourist office (☎ 5388, @ info@werfen.at), Markt 24, in the village main street is open 9 am to 5 pm weekdays; mid-July to mid-August it's open till 7 pm on weekdays and 5 to 7 pm on Saturday.

Getting There & Around Werfen (and Hallein) can be reached from Salzburg by Highway 10. By train (AS80) it takes 50 minutes. The village is a five-minute walk from Werfen station. Getting to the caves is more complicated, though it yields fantastic views. A minibus service (AS70 return) from the station operates along the steep, 6km road to the car park, which is as far as cars can go. A 15-minute walk brings you to the cable car (AS120 return) from which it is a further 15-minute walk to the caves. Allow four hours return from the station, or three hours from the car park (peak-season queues may add an hour). The whole route can be hiked, but it's a very hard four-hour ascent, rising 1100m above the village.

Salzkammergut

Salzkammergut, named after its salt mines, is a holiday region of mountains and lakes to the east of Salzburg. It's an area where you can simply relax and take in the scenery, or get involved in the numerous sports and activities on offer. The main season is summer, when hiking and water sports are the preferred pursuits. In winter, some hiking paths stay open and there's downhill or cross-country skiing. The Salzkammergut-Tennengau ski region includes 80 cable cars and lifts, serving 145km of ski runs; the general ski pass costs AS625 for a minimum two days. You can also get one-day passes for specific resorts.

Orientation & Information

Bad Ischl is the geographical centre of Salzkammergut. The largest lake is Attersee

to the north. Most of the lakes south of Bad Ischl are much smaller, the largest being Hallstätter See. West of Bad Ischl is the Wolfgangsee.

The provincial tourist office in Salzburg has information on the area, including transport schedules and a list of camping grounds. Most of Salzkammergut is in Upper Austria, so the Linz provincial tourist office is perhaps a better source of information. Styria stretches up to claim the area around Bad Aussee and the relevant brochures are dispensed by the Graz tourist offices. Once within the Salzkammergut, the best place to head for region-wide information is the Salzkammergut Info-Center (☎ 06132-240 00-0, @ office@salzkammergut.co.at) at Götzstrasse 12, Bad Ischl. It's open 9 am to 8 pm daily (to 10 pm in summer). The staff are helpful, but as it's a private agency they might try to sell you holiday packages.

The area is dotted with hostels and affordable hotels, but often the best deal is a room in a private home or farmhouse, despite the prevalence of single-night surcharges (about AS30). Tourist offices can supply lists of private rooms, and will sometimes make free hotel bookings. Some pensions and private rooms close in winter. Resorts have a holiday/guest card (*Gästekarte*) which offers a variety of discounts in the whole region. Make sure you ask for a card if it is not offered spontaneously. It must be stamped at the place where you're staying (even camping grounds) to be valid.

If you plan to spend a while here, pick up the Salzkammergut Card for AS65. It is valid between May and October for the duration of your stay, and earns a 25% discount on sights, ferries, cable cars and some Bundesbuses.

Getting Around

The main rail routes pass either side of Salzkammergut, but the area can be crossed by regional trains on a north-south route. You can get on this route from Attnang Puchheim on the Salzburg-Linz line. The track from here connects Gmunden, Traunkirchen, Ebensee, Bad Ischl, Hallstatt and Obertraun. At small unstaffed stations (*unbesetzter Bahnhof*), you'll need to buy your ticket on the train (surcharge not applicable). After Obertraun, the railway continues east via Bad Aussee before

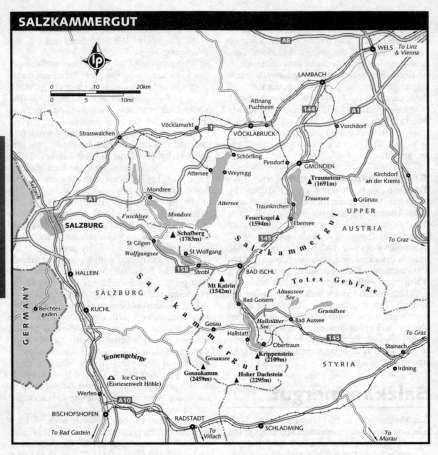

SALZKAMMERGUT

connecting with the main Bischofshofen-Graz line at Stainach Irdning. Attersee can also be reached from the Salzburg-Linz line prior to the Attnang Puchheim stop.

Regular Bundesbuses connect all towns and villages in the area, though less frequently on weekends. Timetables are displayed at stops, and tickets can be bought from the driver.

Passenger boats ply the waters of the Attersee, Traunsee, Mondsee, Hallstätter See and Wolfgangsee.

To reach Salzkammergut from Salzburg by car or motorcycle, take the A1 or Highway 158.

BAD ISCHL
☎ 06132 • pop 13,000

This spa town's reputation soared after Princess Sophie took a treatment to cure her infertility in 1828. Within two years she had given birth to Franz Josef (the penultimate Habsburg emperor); two other sons followed.

Orientation & Information

The centre of town is compactly contained within a bend of the River Traun.

The tourist office or *Kurdirektion* (☎ 277 57-0, fax -77, @ office@kd-badischl.or.at) is close to the train station (straight ahead and bear left) at Bahnhofstrasse 6. It is open 8 am to 6 pm weekdays, 9 am to 4 pm Saturday and 9 to 11.30 am Sunday. From 1 October to 31 June it closes at 5 pm (noon on Saturday) and all day Sunday. The post office (Postamt 4820), along the road at Aübockplatz, changes money (cash only), as does the train station. The station rents bikes daily until 6 pm. Cyberplace, Grazerstrasse 12, has Internet access.

Things to See & Do

Salzkammergut became popular in the mid-19th century when Emperor Franz Josef began spending his summers in Bad Ischl in the **Kaiservilla**. Not only did he sign the declaration of war here that started WWI, he also had a habit of getting up every day at 3.30 am for his bath. Somebody should have told him that holidays are meant for relaxation. The villa was his hunting lodge and contains an obscene number of hunting trophies. It can be visited only by guided tour (in German but with written English translations). The 40-minute tour runs from Easter to mid-October, costs AS130, and includes entry to the Kaiserpark grounds (which costs AS35 on its own). The small **Photomuseum** in the park nearby has some interesting old photographs and cameras (entry AS15, students AS10).

Free **Kurkonzerte** (spa concerts) are performed once or twice a day (except Tuesday) during summer; ask the tourist office for venues and times. An operetta festival is held in July and August; for advance details and reservations, call ☎ 238 39.

Bad Ischl has downhill skiing from **Mt Katrin** (a winter day-pass costs AS240) and a variety of cross-country skiing routes. In summer, the Mt Katrin cable car costs AS160 return (AS140 with the guest card). The **salt mine** (Salzberwerk) is to the south of town; tours cost AS140 and are conducted daily from 1 May to late September.

The tourist office has information on health treatments available in the resort.

Places to Stay & Eat

The HI **Jugendgästehaus** (☎ 265 77, fax -75, Am Rechensteg 5) is in the town centre behind Kreuzplatz. Dorms are AS155 (plus tax), singles/doubles are AS255/370 and dinner is AS65. Reception is open 8 am to 1 pm and 5 to 7 pm.

The best deal is **Haus Rothauer** (☎ 236 28, Kaltenbachstrasse 12). It has singles from AS180 (hall shower) and doubles with shower for AS200. **Haus Unterreiter** (☎ 244 71, Stiegengasse 1) has four singles and two doubles for around AS200 per person, using a hall shower. TVs are in most rooms, though there's no breakfast (closed in winter). Nearby is **Haus Stadt Prag** (☎/fax 236 16, Eglmoosgasse 9) which has large, old-style singles/doubles for AS370/700 with shower and WC or AS320/600 without.

China Restaurant Happy Dragon, by the Schröpferplatz bridge, overlooks the river and has lunch menus from AS64. It's open daily, as is **Pizzeria Don Camillo** (Wiesingerstrasse 5), where decent pizza and pasta costs from AS55. **Blauen Enzian** (Wirerstrasse 2) is back from the main street. This informal place offers a varied menu (AS90 to AS185 per dish) covering pasta, salads, and regional and national food (closed Sunday in the low season).

There's a **Konsum** supermarket behind the Trinkhalle.

Getting There & Away

Bundesbuses leave from outside the station. There are hourly buses to Salzburg (AS100) via St Gilgen between 5.05 am and 8.10 pm. To St Wolfgang (AS40), you often have to change at Strobl (the bus will be waiting, and the same ticket is valid). Buses run to Hallstatt every couple of hours (AS50, 50 minutes), with some services continuing to Obertraun.

Trains depart hourly. It costs AS38 to Hallstatt but, unlike the bus, you must add the cost of the boat (see the Hallstatt Getting There & Away section). The fare to Salzburg (two hours) by train, via Attnang Puchheim, is AS208.

HALLSTATT

☎ 06134 • pop 1150

Hallstatt has a history stretching back 4500 years. In AD 50, the Romans were attracted by the rich salt deposits. Today, this Unesco World Heritage site is prized mainly for its picturesque location. In summer it is invaded by crowds of day-trippers; fortunately, they only stay a few hours and then the village returns to its natural calm.

Orientation & Information

Seestrasse is the main street. Turn left from the ferry to reach the tourist office (☎ 8208, fax 8352, ✉ hallstatt-info@eunet.at), Seestrasse 169. It is open 9 am to 5 pm Monday to Friday and 10 am to 2 pm weekends; from 1 September to 30 June it is closed on weekends and for one hour at noon. The post office (Postamt 4830) is around the corner, and changes money.

Things to See & Do

Hallstatt resides in idyllic, picture-postcard scenery, wedged in a narrow space between steep mountains and the placid lake. The setting alone is enough to justify a visit.

Above the village are the **Salzbergwerk** (saltworks), open late April to 26 October, from 9.30 am daily. During the shoulder seasons the last tour is at 3 pm; in summer it's at 4.30 pm. Admission costs AS140 (reduction with guest card). The funicular to the top costs AS105 return, but there are two scenic hiking trails you can take instead. Near the mine, 2000 flat graves were discovered, dating from 1000 to 500 BC. Don't miss the macabre **Beinhaus** (Bone House) near the village parish church; it contains rows of decorated skulls (AS10). Around the lake at Obertraun are the **Dachstein Rieseneishöhle** (Giant Ice Caves), open early May to mid-October. Entry costs AS90, or AS150 in combination with the nearby Mammoth cave. A cable car provides easy access.

Places to Stay & Eat

Some private rooms in the village are only available during the busiest months of July and August; others require a minimum three-night stay. Your best bet is to ask at the tourist office, which will willingly telephone around for you without charge. *Campingplatz Höll* (☎ 8329, Lahnstrasse 6) costs AS55 per adult (plus tax), AS45 per tent and AS35 per car. It's open from 15 April to 15 October.

The HI *Jugendherberge* (☎ 8212, Salzbergstrasse 50), is open from around 1 May to 30 September, though July and August is reserved for groups only. Beds cost AS112 excluding breakfast (AS35) and sheets (AS45). Check-in is from 5 pm, but phone ahead as hours are irregular. *TVN Naturfreunde Herberge* (☎/fax 8318, Kirchenweg 36)

is just below the road tunnel, by the waterfall. It has dorm beds for AS115, plus AS40 each for sheets and breakfast (if required). Dorms vary in size in both places – some are cramped. TVN is part of and is run by the *Zur Mühle Gasthaus*, which has pizza and pasta from AS68, and Austrian dishes from AS75. It's often closed on Wednesday, when there's also no TVN check-in.

Go to *Bräu Gasthof* (☎ 8221, fax -4, Seestrasse 120) if you want typical Austrian food in an old-fashioned atmosphere. Meals cost from AS60 to AS150. The restaurant is open daily, but only from 1 May to 26 October. Double rooms with private WC and shower are available all year for AS920.

Nearby Obertraun is also a possible base: there's a *youth hostel* (☎ 06131-360, Winkl 26) and a couple of restaurants with affordable rooms. Inquire at the local tourist office (☎ 06131-351, ✉ tourismus@obertraun.or.at).

Getting There & Away

There are around six buses a day to/from Obertraun and Bad Ischl. Get off the Bundesbus at Hallstatt's 'Parkterrasse' stop for the centre and the tourist office, or at 'Lahn' (at the southern end of the road tunnel) for the hostel. Beware – services finish very early and the last guaranteed departure from Bad Ischl is 4.05 pm. The train station is across the lake. The boat service from there to the village (AS23) coincides with train arrivals (at least nine a day from Bad Ischl; total trip 45 minutes). Though trains run later, the last ferry connection leaves Hallstatt train station at 6.46 pm. Parking in the village is free if you have a guest card, though car access is restricted in the summer.

WOLFGANGSEE

This lake can become crowded in summer because of its proximity to Salzburg, but its scenery and lakeside villages make it well worth a visit.

Orientation & Information

The lake is dominated by the Schafberg (1783m) on the northern shore. Next to it is the resort of St Wolfgang. The tourist office (☎ 06138-2239, ✉ info@stwolfgang.gv.at) is on the main street by the entrance to the road tunnel, open till 5 or 6 pm weekdays and Saturday till noon. St Gilgen, on the western shore, provides easy access to Salzburg, 29km away. Its tourist office (☎ 06227-2348, ✉ info@stgilgen.co.at), Mozartplatz 1, in the Rathaus, is open Monday to Friday, or daily in July and August.

Things to See & Do

The major sight in St Wolfgang is the **Pilgrimage Church**, built in the 14th and 15th centuries. This incredible church is virtually a gallery of religious art. The best piece is the winged high altar made by Michael Pacher between 1471 and 1481, which has astonishing detail on the carved figures and Gothic designs. The church wardens used to be so protective that the wings were kept closed except for important festivals. Now they are always open, except for eight weeks before Easter. The baroque double altar by Thomas Schwanthaler is also excellent. The church is open 9 am to 6 pm daily. The **White Horse Inn** in the village centre was the setting for a famous operetta.

Ascend the **Schafberg** for good hikes and views. The Schafberg cog-wheel railway runs from 1 May to 26 October, approximately hourly during the day and reaches 1734m. The cost is AS150 up and AS260 return; holders of European rail passes get a 15% reduction. **St Gilgen** has good views of the lake and some pleasant swimming spots. The birthplace of Mozart's mother is now a tiny museum (little to see), plus there's a musical instruments museum.

Places to Stay & Eat

Camping Appesbach (☎ 06138-2206, *Au 99*) is on the lakefront, 1km from St Wolfgang in the direction of Strobl. It's open from Easter to October and costs AS63 per adult, and from AS65 for a tent and car.

St Gilgen has a good HI *Jugendgästehaus* (☎ 06227-2365, *Mondseestrasse 7*). Prices are AS135 to AS285 per person, in anything from singles to 10-bed dorms, with or without WC and lake view but always with shower and a fine buffet breakfast. Check-in is from 5 to 7 pm.

Both St Wolfgang and St Gilgen have a good selection of pensions, private rooms and holiday apartments, all starting at about AS180 per person. The respective tourist offices can supply lists, or they will phone around for you without charging. The chalet-style *Gästehaus Raudaschl* (☎ 06138-2329, *Pilgerstrasse 4*) in the centre of St Wolfgang has homy singles/doubles for AS370/700 with shower and toilet; doubles using hall shower are AS440. In St Gilgen, *Gasthof Zur Post* (☎ 2157, fax -600, *Mozartplatz 8*) is a rustic-style chalet with rooms for around AS450 per person with shower, WC and cable TV. Its restaurant serves regional food for about AS85 to AS190 (closed Monday in the off-season). Both places are convenient and decent value, though there are cheaper choices.

There are lots of places to eat in the centre of St Wolfgang, ranging from cheap snack joints to quaint touristy restaurants. Just follow your nose.

Getting There & Away

A ferry service operates from Strobl to St Gilgen, stopping at various points en route, including St Wolfgang. Services are from late April to 26 October, but are more frequent during the high season from early July to early September. The journey from St Wolfgang to St Gilgen takes 40 minutes (AS54), with boats sailing in high season approximately twice an hour between 8 am and 8 pm. Holders of European rail passes get a 15% reduction.

Buses from St Wolfgang to St Gilgen and Salzburg go via Strobl on the east side of the lake. St Gilgen is 50 minutes from Salzburg by bus, with hourly departures till at least 8.30 pm. The fare is AS60.

NORTHERN SALZKAMMERGUT

West of Attersee is Mondsee, a picturesque warm water lake which is a favoured swimming spot. The village of Mondsee has an attractive church that was used in the wedding scenes of *The Sound of Music*.

To the east of Attersee is Traunsee and its three main resorts: Gmunden, Traunkirchen and Ebensee. Gmunden is famous for its twin castles linked by a causeway on the lake, and the manufacturing of ceramics. Buses go east from Gmunden to Grünau (or take the train from Wels). This out-of-the-way place has a good backpacker hostel, *The Tree House* (☎ 0761-8499, ✉ treehouse hotel@hotmail.com, Schindlbachstrasse 525). Dorms/doubles are AS180/220, and activities are organised.

AUSTRIA

Tirol

The province of Tirol (sometimes spelled Tyrol) has some of the best mountain scenery in Austria. It's an ideal playground for skiers, hikers, mountaineers and anglers, and the tourist offices release plenty of glossy material to promote these pursuits. The province is divided into two parts: East Tirol has been isolated from the main part of the state ever since prosperous South Tirol was ceded to Italy at the end of WWI.

Train and bus journeys within Tirol are cheaper using VVT tickets, which can only be bought within Tirol (from train stations etc). These tickets can be combined with city passes. The system is quite complicated; the IVB Kundenbüro (☎ 0512-53 07-103), Stainerstrasse 2, Innsbruck, can give information.

INNSBRUCK
☎ 0512 • pop 111,000

Innsbruck has been an important trading post since the 12th century, thanks in part to the Brenner Pass, the gateway to the south. It wasn't long before the city found favour with the Habsburgs, particularly Emperor Maximilian and Maria Theresa, who built many of the important buildings that still survive in the well-preserved old town centre. More recently, the capital of Tirol has become an important winter sports centre, and staged the Winter Olympics in 1964 and 1976.

Orientation

Innsbruck lies in the valley of the River Inn, scenically squeezed between the northern chain of the Alps and the Tuxer mountain range to the south. Extensive mountain transport facilities surround the city and provide ample hiking and skiing opportunities. The centre of town is very compact, with the main train station (Hauptbahnhof) only a 10-minute walk from the pedestrian-only, old town centre (Altstadt). The main street in the Altstadt is Herzog Friedrich Strasse.

Information

Tourist Offices The main tourist office (☎ 598 50, fax -7, ✉ info@innsbruck.tvb .co.at), Burggraben 3, books hotel rooms (AS40 commission) and sells ski passes and public transport tickets. Office opening hours are 8 am to 7 pm Monday to Saturday, 9 am to 6 pm Sunday and holidays. Instead of buying their map for AS10 you can ask for the free tear-off map sheet.

There are hotel reservation centres in the main train station (open 9 am to 9 pm daily, to 10 pm in summer) and at motorway exits near the city. The youth waiting room (*Jugendwarteraum*) in the train station also offers useful information; it's closed mid-July to mid-September.

The Tirol Information office (☎ 72 72, fax -7, ✉ tirol.info@tirolwerbung.at), Maria Theresien Strasse 55, is open 8 am to 6 pm weekdays.

Ask at your hotel for 'Club Innsbruck' membership – it is free and provides various discounts and benefits, such as free, guided mountain hikes between the months of June to September. The Innsbruck Card, available at the main tourist office, gives free entry to museums and free use of public transport. It costs AS230/300/370 for 24/48/72 hours.

Money The train station has exchange facilities (compare rates and commission between the ticket counters and the office) and a Bankomat. The tourist office also exchanges money.

Post & Communications The main post office is at Maximilianstrasse 2 (Hauptpostamt 6010) and is open 7 am to 11 pm weekdays and 8 am to 9 pm weekends. The train station post office is at Brunecker Strasse 1-3 and is open 7 am to 7 pm weekdays.

Email & Internet Access Free Internet access is available in the bar at Utopia (see Entertainment later in this section), though you won't have to queue at International Telephone Discount, Brunecker Strasse 12 (AS1.70 per minute).

Travel Agencies American Express (☎ 58 24 91), Brixnerstrasse 3, is open 9 am to 5.30 pm Monday to Friday, to noon Saturday. ÖKISTA (☎ 58 89 97), Wilhelm Greil Strasse 17, is open 9 am to 5.30 pm weekdays.

Medical Services The University Clinic (☎ 504-0), also called the Landeskrankenhaus, is at Anichstrasse 35.

AUSTRIA

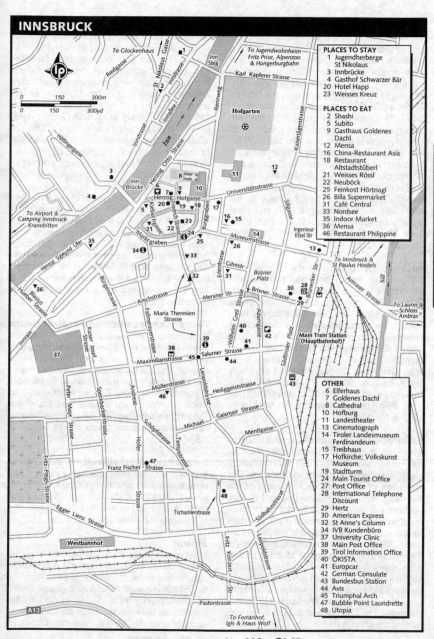

INNSBRUCK

PLACES TO STAY
1 Jugendherberge St Nikolaus
3 Innbrücke
4 Gasthof Schwarzer Bär
20 Hotel Happ
23 Weisses Kreuz

PLACES TO EAT
2 Shashi
5 Subito
9 Gasthaus Goldenes Dachl
12 Mensa
16 China-Restaurant Asia
18 Restaurant Altstadtstüberl
21 Weisses Rössl
22 Neuböck
25 Feinkost Hörtnagl
31 Billa Supermarket
33 Nordsee
35 Indoor Market
36 Mensa
46 Restaurant Philippine

OTHER
6 Elferhaus
7 Goldenes Dachl
8 Cathedral
10 Hofburg
11 Landestheater
13 Cinematograph
14 Tiroler Landesmuseum Ferdinandeum
15 Treibhaus
17 Hofkirche; Volkskunst Museum
19 Stadtturm
24 Main Tourist Office
27 Post Office
28 International Telephone Discount
29 Hertz
30 American Express
32 St Anne's Column
34 IVB Kundenbüro
37 University Clinic
38 Main Post Office
39 Tirol Information Office
40 ÖKISTA
41 Europcar
42 German Consulate
43 Bundesbus Station
44 Avis
45 Triumphal Arch
47 Bubble Point Laundrette
48 Utopia

AUSTRIA

Things to See & Do

For an overview of the city, climb the 14th-century **Stadtturm** (City Tower) in Herzog Friedrich Strasse. It's open 10 am to 5 pm daily except in summer when it closes at 6 pm. Entry costs AS27 (students and children AS15). Across the square is the famous **Goldenes Dachl** (Golden Roof); it comprises 2657 gilded copper tiles dating from the 16th century. Emperor Maximilian used to observe street performers from the balcony. Inside the building, appropriately enough, there's a museum devoted to Maximilian (AS50, students AS20). Behind the Golden Roof is the **cathedral** – its interior is typically over-the-top baroque. Turning back to the south, take note of the elegant 15th and 16th-century buildings on all sides, and stroll down Maria Theresien Strasse to the 1767 **Triumphal Arch**.

Hofburg The Imperial Palace dates from 1397, but has been rebuilt and restyled several times since, particularly by Maria Theresa. It's worth seeing, but if you're going to Vienna, save your money for Schönbrunn instead. The grand rooms are decorated with numerous paintings of Maria Theresa and family; the faces of her 16 children all look identical. The baroque Giant's Hall is a highlight. The palace is open 9 am to 5 pm every day. Admission costs AS70 (students AS45). There are guided tours in German (AS25), or for a do-it-yourself tour buy the booklet in English for AS25.

Hofkirche The Hofkirche (Imperial Church) is opposite the palace. It contains the massive but empty sarcophagus of Maximilian I, which is decorated with scenes of his life. The twin rows of 28 giant bronze figures of the Habsburgs are memorable. The dull bronze has been polished in parts by the sheer number of hands that have touched them; a certain private part of Kaiser Rudolf is very shiny indeed! The church is open 9 am to 5 pm (to 5.30 pm in July and August) Monday to Saturday, when it costs AS30 (students under 27 AS20) to get in. Combined tickets (AS75, students AS55) are available which include the adjoining **Volkskunst Museum** (Folk Art Museum). On Sunday and holidays you can get into the church free.

Schloss Ambras Located east of the centre (take tram No 3 or 6, or bus K), this medieval castle was greatly extended by Archduke Ferdinand II in the 16th century. It features the Renaissance Spanish Hall, fine gardens, exhaustive portraits of Habsburgs and other dignitaries, and collections of weapons, armour and oddities. Opening hours are 10 am to 5 pm Wednesday to Monday, from 1 April to 31 October; admission costs AS60 for adults (students, seniors and children AS30). From 1 December to 31 March, interior visits are by guided tour at 2 pm only, costing an extra AS25.

Alpine Zoo The zoo, north of the River Inn on Weiherburggasse, features a comprehensive collection of alpine animals, including amorous bears and combative ibexes. It is open 9 am to 6 pm (to 5 pm in winter) daily. Admission costs AS70 for adults (students and children AS35). Walk up the hill to get there or take the Hungerburgbahn, which is free if you buy your zoo ticket at the Hungerburgbahn station.

Tiroler Landesmuseum Ferdinandeum

This museum at Museumstrasse 15 houses a good collection of art and artefacts, including Gothic statues and altarpieces. There's a relief map of Tirol in the basement. Opening hours are 10 am to 5 pm daily May to September (Thursday also from 7 to 9 pm); October to April, they're 10 am to noon and 2 to 5 pm Tuesday to Saturday, 10 am to 1 pm Sunday and holidays. Entry costs AS60 (students AS30).

Swarovski Kristallwelten The Crystal Worlds, Kristallweltenstrasse 1, is a well-presented series of caverns featuring the famous Swarovski crystals (open 9 am to 6 pm daily; AS75). It's in Wattens, 20 minutes east of Innsbruck by Bundesbus or train.

Skiing

Most of the ski runs around Innsbruck are intermediate or easy, but there are a few difficult ones as well. Many areas, such as Seefeld, were used in Olympic competitions. A one-day ski pass is AS240 to AS330, depending on the area, and there are several versions of multiday tickets available. Downhill equipment rental starts at AS200. With 'Club Innsbruck', ski buses are free.

You can ski all year at the **Stubai Glacier**, which is a popular excursion. A one-day pass costs AS420. The journey there takes 80 minutes by the white IVB Stubaltalbahn bus, departing hourly from the bus station (buy tickets from the driver; AS163 return). The last bus back is usually at 5.30 pm. Several places offer complete packages to the glacier, which compare favourably with going it alone. The tourist office package for AS599 (AS540 in winter) includes transport, passes and equipment rental.

Places to Stay

Camping *Camping Innsbruck Kranebitten* (*☎/fax 28 41 80, Kranebitter Allee 214*) is west of the town centre and open year-round. Prices are AS75 per adult and AS40 for a tent. There is a restaurant on site.

Private Rooms The tourist office has lists of private rooms in Innsbruck and Igls ranging from AS180 to AS280 per person. Igls is south of town; get there by tram No 6 or bus J. Further afield is *Haus Wolf* (*☎ 54 86 73, Dorfstrasse 48, Mutters*). Rooms with one to three beds cost AS190 per person, including a big breakfast. Take the Stubaitalbahn tram from in front of the train station (AS26, 30 minutes; stop: Birchfeld), which departs every 50 minutes till 10.30 pm.

Hostels A convenient backpacker hostel is *Jugendherberge St Nikolaus* (*☎ 28 65 15, fax -14, @ yhnikolaus@tirol.com, Innstrasse 95*). There's a cellar bar which can be noisy, and Internet access. Dorm beds are AS180 for the first night and AS165 for additional nights, including sheets. Singles/doubles without shower are AS265/430. Check-in is from 5 to 10 pm, though you can usually leave bags during the day. Get a key for late nights out. This place gets very mixed reports from travellers, some highly critical of the staff. The attached restaurant has inexpensive Austrian food and is a good place for socialising.

Two HI hostels down Reichenauerstrasse are accessible by bus O from Museumstrasse. *Innsbruck* (*☎ 34 61 79, fax -12*) at No 147 is reportedly not the most friendly place either. It costs from AS155 the first night, AS125

thereafter (AS7 less if you're aged under 18). Curfew is at 11 pm, and the place is closed from 10 am to 5 pm (to 3 pm in summer). It has a kitchen, double rooms (from AS440) and slow washing machines (AS45). *St Paulus* (*☎ 34 42 91*) at No 72 has large dorms for AS125 and sheets for AS20. Breakfast costs AS30, although kitchen facilities are available. The hostel is only open from mid-June to early September, and the doors are locked till 5 pm.

Another hostel to try in summer is *Jugendwohnheim Fritz Prior* (*☎ 58 58 14, fax -4, Rennweg 17b*), where beds cost AS125, breakfast is AS45 and sheets are AS20 (open July, August and New Year).

Hotels & Pensions The *Glockenhaus* pension, up the hill at Weiherburggasse 3, has fairly secluded singles/doubles for AS345/470 with private shower and WC. Reception, check-in and breakfast are at the Jugendherberge St Nikolaus.

Ferrarihof (*☎/fax 57 88 98, Brennerstrasse 8*) is south of town, just off the main road, and is under new ownership. Ageing (but soon to be renovated) singles/doubles are AS250/500 with either private or hall shower. Reception is in the bar downstairs, open 10 am to midnight, and breakfast is extra. There is plenty of parking and it's 500m from tram No 1.

Laurin (*☎ 34 11 04, Gumppstrasse 19*) is behind the station, near tram No 3. Singles/doubles are AS350/520, or AS430/680 with private shower, and there's a lift and parking spaces.

The *Innbrücke* (*☎ 28 19 34, fax 27 84 10, @ innbrueke@magnet.at, Innstrasse 1*) is nearer the Altstadt. Simple, sometimes noisy rooms are AS450/800 with shower and WC or AS350/600 without. Along the road, *Gasthof Schwarzer Bär* (*☎ 29 49 00, fax -4, Mariahilfstrasse 16*) is an old house but has big, modern doubles with shower, toilet and TV for AS840.

The pick of the hotels in the Altstadt is *Weisses Kreuz* (*☎ 594 79, fax -90, @ hotel .weisses.kreuz@eunet.at, Herzog Friedrich Strasse 31*), which has singles for AS460 with hall shower, and singles/doubles for AS790/1180 with private shower and WC. The 'superior' doubles for AS1340 are worth

AUSTRIA

the extra cost. This 500-year-old inn played host to Mozart when he was 13, and all the rooms are spacious, well presented and comfortable. Prices drop slightly in winter. If it's full, try *Hotel Happ* (☎ 58 29 80, fax -11) across the street at No 14. It's almost as atmospheric, and rooms with shower, WC and TV are AS700/1200.

Places to Eat
There are various Würstel stands and Imbiss shops for fast, cheap snacks around the city. *Feinkost Hörtnagl* on Burggasse is a supermarket with both a cafe and a self-service section for hot meals. *Subito (Kiebachgasse 2)* has cheap pizza-slice deals and Italian ice cream; it's open 11 am to 1 am daily. Other places with inexpensive food, open normal shop hours, are *Neuböck (Herzog Friedrich Strasse 30)* for Austrian fare and *Nordsee (Maria Theresian Strasse 11)* for fish meals.

A large indoor food market awaits by the river in *Markthalle*, Herzog Siegmund Ufer (closed Sunday). *University Mensa (Herzog Siegmund Ufer 15)* on the 1st floor serves good lunches between 11 am and 1.30 pm Monday to Thursday, 11 am to 2 pm Friday and Saturday. For less than AS75 you can get a main dish, soup and salad (closed summer/Christmas holidays). Another *Mensa* is at Universitätsstrasse 15.

Restaurant Philippine (☎ 58 91 57, Müllerstrasse 9) is a specialist vegetarian restaurant, decked out in light colours. It has a range of main dishes for AS88 to AS140, and a fine salad buffet for AS32/98 for a small/big plate. It is open 10 am to 11 pm Monday to Saturday.

China-Restaurant Asia (Angerzellgasse 10) offers good three-course weekday lunch specials and you get a *lot* of food for AS69. *Shashi (Innstrasse 81)* has big pizzas from AS60; excellent Indian meals for around AS95 include rice, poppadoms and bread (closed Monday).

Café Central (Gilmstrasse 5) is a typical Austrian coffee house. It has English newspapers, daily specials from around AS95, and piano music from 8 to 10 pm on Sunday. It opens 7.30 am to 11 pm daily.

Most places in the Altstadt are a little pricey, and generally serve a combination of Tirolean, Austrian and international food.

Gasthaus Goldenes Dachl (Hofgasse 1) provides a civilised environment for tasting Tirolean specialities such as *Bauerngröstl*, a pork, bacon, potato and egg concoction served with salad (AS124). It is open 7.30 am to midnight daily.

Weisses Rössl (☎ 58 30 57, Kiebachgasse 8) is good for regional food for around AS90 to AS180. For more upmarket eating, *Restaurant Altstadtstüberl* (☎ 58 23 47, Riesengasse 13) is one of the best places to try typical Tirolean food, with dishes in the range of AS115 to AS245. Both places are closed on Sunday and holidays.

Entertainment
The tourist office sells tickets for 'Tirolean evenings' (AS220 gets alpine music, folk dancing, yodelling and one drink), classical concerts, and performances in the *Landestheater*. Commission is usually charged.

Utopia (☎ 58 85 87, Tschamlerstrasse 3) stages theatre, art, parties and live music in the cellar downstairs, around four nights a week; entry is free or up to AS200. There's also a cafe/bar, open 6 pm to 1 am Monday to Saturday. Web site: www.utopia.or.at.

Treibhaus (☎ 58 68 74, Angerzellgasse 8) has live music most nights (in a circus-style tent in summer). Entry costs AS100 to AS250. There's also a play area for kids, as well as pizzas and other food. It's closed Sunday, except for the once-monthly Tango night (free).

Cinemas around town are cheaper on Monday, when seats are AS70 or AS80. *Cinematograph* (☎ 57 85 00, Museumstrasse 31) shows independent films in their original language. Nearby is Ingenieur Etzel Strasse, where there are lively bars within the railway arches. Or, try *Elferhaus (Herzog Friedrich Strasse 11)* for a huge choice of beers.

Getting There & Away
Air Tyrolean Airways flies daily to Amsterdam, Frankfurt, Paris, Vienna and Zürich.

Bus Bundesbuses leave from by the main train station. The bus ticket office is near the youth waiting room in the smaller of the station's two halls.

Train Fast trains depart every two hours for Bregenz (3¾ hours) and Salzburg (two

AUSTRIA

hours). Regular express trains head north to Munich (via Kufstein; two hours) and south to Verona (3½ hours). Connections are hourly to Kitzbühel (AS142, 1¼ hours). Four daily trains (three on Sunday) go to Lienz, passing through Italy (3½ hours). The 1.53 pm train is an international train; it costs AS290, and if you're travelling on an Austrian Domino pass, you must pay for the Italian section (AS132). The other trains (AS165) are Austrian 'corridor' trains, and you can disembark in Italy. For train information, call ☎ 05-1717.

Car & Motorcycle The A12 and the parallel Highway 171 are the main roads to the west and east. Highway 177, to the west of Innsbruck, heads north to Germany and Munich. The A13 motorway is a toll road (AS55) southwards through the Brenner Pass to Italy; it includes the impressive Europabrücke (Europe Bridge) several kilometres south of the city. Toll-free Highway 182 follows the same route, passing under the bridge.

Getting Around
To/From the Airport The airport is 4km to the west of the centre. To get there, take bus F, which leaves every 20 minutes from Maria Theresien Strasse (AS21).

Tickets bought on buses and trams cost AS21. In advance, you can buy a block of four for AS61, or a 24-hour pass for AS35. These are not valid for the Hungerburgbahn. A weekly pass costs AS123 and is valid from the day you select.

It's hardly worth using private transport in the compact city centre. Most central streets are blue zones with maximum parking of 1½ hours; the charge is AS5/10/20 for 30/60/90 minutes (tickets from pavement dispensers). Parking garages (eg, under the Altstadt) are around AS200 per day.

Taxis cost AS52 for the first 1.3km, then AS2 per 111m. Bike rental in the main train station is open daily till 6 or 6.30 pm.

KITZBÜHEL
☎ 05356 • 8200
Kitzbühel is a fashionable and prosperous winter resort, offering excellent skiing and a variety of other sports.

Orientation & Information
From the main train station to the town centre is 1km: turn left from Bahnhofstrasse onto Josef Pirchl Strasse; take the right fork (no entry for cars), which is still Josef Pirchl Strasse, and continue past the post office (Postamt 6370).

The tourist office (☎ 62155-0, fax 62307, ✉ info@kitzbuehel.com), Hinterstadt 18, is in the centre, open daily (closed Saturday afternoon and Sunday in the low season). Ask about the guest card, which offers various discounts.

Activities
Skiing In winter, there is good intermediate skiing on Kitzbüheler Horn to the north and Hahnenkamm to the south. A one-day general ski pass costs AS420, though some pensions/hotels can offer 'Ski Hit' reductions before mid-December or after mid-March. The cost of a day's ski rental is around AS180/120 for downhill/cross-country. The professional Hahnenkamm downhill ski race takes place in late January.

Hiking Dozens of summer hiking trails surround the town and provide a good opportunity to take in the scenery; the tourist office gives free maps and free guided hikes. Get a head start to the heights with the three-day cable-car pass for AS450. There is an alpine flower garden (free) on the slopes of the Kitzbüheler Horn (toll-road for drivers). The scenic Schwarzsee lake is a fine location for summer swimming.

Places to Stay & Eat
Rates often rise by AS20 to AS40 for stays of one or two nights. Prices are higher at Christmas and in February, July and August – peaking in the winter high season, which are the prices quoted here. Many private rooms and apartments are available. *Campingplatz Schwarzsee* (☎ 628 06), by the Schwarzsee lake, is open year-round.

Despite its three stars, *Hotel Kaiser* (☎ 647 08, fax 662 13, Bahnhofstrasse 2) courts youth groups and backpackers, charging AS260 to AS320 per person in four-bed rooms (with bunks, shower and WC). Singles/doubles in summer are about AS420/640 (phone ahead). It's closed between seasons,

AUSTRIA

but would-be resort workers should ask about cheap deals in November.

Round the corner, **Pension Hörl** (*☎/fax 631 44, Josef Pirchl Strasse 60*) has simple but pleasant rooms for AS270/500, or AS300/560 with shower. **Pension Schmidinger** (*☎ 631 34, Ehrenbachgasse 13*) has rooms for AS300 per person with shower and WC, or AS250 without. Prices can be fairly fluid – young people would probably get a discount. It's usually open in the off season.

On Bichlstrasse there's a **Spar** supermarket and **Prima**, a cheap self-service restaurant (open every day in season). **Huberbräu Stüberl** (*Vorderstadt 18*) offers good Austrian food and an AS85 *menu*. After the kitchens close at 10 pm it stays busy with drinkers (beer AS34 for 0.5L). It's open daily until midnight. **La Fonda** (*Hinterstadt 13*) is a Tex-Mex place with a bar, a good atmosphere, and cheap but average food. **Adria**, next to the post office, serves Italian food from AS72 and is open daily all year.

Gasthof Eggerwirt (*☎ 624 55, fax 624 37-22, Untere Gänsbachgasse 12*), down the steps from the three churches, provides quality regional cuisine for AS100 to AS220. It also has mid-priced rooms.

Getting There & Away
There are trains approximately hourly from Kitzbühel to Innsbruck (AS142, 1¼ hours) and Salzburg (AS260, 2½ hours). Slower trains stop at Kitzbühel-Hahnenkamm, which is closer to the centre than the main Kitzbühel stop.

Getting to Lienz is awkward and slow by train. The bus is much easier, albeit infrequent (AS153, two hours). There's only one on Sunday at 7.20 pm; otherwise, there are three per day. Heading south to Lienz, you pass through some marvellous scenery. Highway 108 (the Felber Tauern Tunnel) and Highway 107 (the Grossglockner mountain road, closed in winter) both have toll sections.

KUFSTEIN
☎ 05372 • pop 15,000
A 13th-century **fortress** dominates Kufstein town centre. It's closed off-season, and entry is a pricey AS130. Inside is a wide-ranging but not over-large **Heimat Museum**, and a massive 'Heroes Organ' (recital at noon, and

in summer also at 5 pm, which can be heard all over town). There is a lift to the fortress (AS30 return), but the 15-minute walk uphill is not demanding. After 5 pm the castle grounds are free.

The **lakes** around Kufstein are an ideal destination for cyclists; you can rent bikes in the train station. Buses visit some of the lakes; they leave from outside the train station. A free city bus goes to the Hechtsee lake in summer.

Information
The tourist office (☎ 62207, ✉ kufstein@ netway.at), Unterer Stadtplatz 8, is in the centre of town, across the River Inn and three minutes walk from the train station. It's open weekdays year-round, Saturday morning in summer, and makes room reservations without charge.

Places to Stay & Eat
If you decide to stay overnight, ask for the guest card. There is a **camping ground** by the river (*☎ 622 29-55, Salurner Strasse 36*). A few blocks south-east of the castle is **Pension Striede** (*☎ 623 16, fax -33, Mitterndorfer Strasse 20*), with hospital-like rooms with shower and WC for AS320 per person. There are several affordable places to eat on Stadtplatz, and a **supermarket**.

Getting There & Away
Kufstein is on the main Innsbruck-Salzburg 'corridor' train route. To reach Kitzbühel (AS96, one hour), change at Wörgl; the easiest road route is also via Wörgl.

LIENZ
☎ 04852 • pop 13,000
The capital of East Tirol combines winter sports and summer hiking with a relaxed, small-town ambience. The jagged Dolomite mountain range crowds the southern skyline.

Orientation & Information
The town centre is within the junction of the Rivers Isel and Drau. The pivotal Hauptplatz is by the train station, beyond the post office (Postamt 9900). The tourist office (☎ 652 65, fax -2, ✉ lienz@netway.at) is at Europaplatz 1, open 8 am to at least 6 pm Monday to Friday and 9 am to noon Saturday. It also opens

on Sunday in the summer and winter high seasons. Staff will find rooms free of charge, or you can use the hotel board (free telephone) outside.

Things to See & Do

Overlooking the town, **Schloss Bruck** contains folklore displays and the work of local artist Albin Egger (1868-1926), who created powerful if dour images. It's open 10 am to 5 pm (to 6 pm in summer), Tuesday to Sunday but only from Palm Sunday to 1 November. Admission costs AS70 (students AS45).

Most of the downhill skiing takes place on the **Zettersfeld** peak north of town (mostly medium to easy runs), and there are several cross-country trails in the valley. **Hochstein** is another skiing area. A one-day ski pass for both peaks is AS325. In summer, hiking is good in the mountains. The cable cars are closed during the off season (April, May, October and November).

Places to Stay

Camping Falken (☎ 640 22, *Eichholz 7*) is south of the town, and closed from November to mid-December. Private rooms in and around the town are great value and a single night's stay is often possible. This is the case at *Haus Egger* (☎ 720 98, *Alleestrasse 3*), which costs AS200 per person.

Haus Wille (☎ 629 25) is an excellent deal at only AS140 per person, though there's a three-night minimum stay. Next door, *Gästehaus Masnata* (☎ 655 36, *Drahtzuggasse 4*) has good doubles and three-person apartments for around AS530. *Gästehaus Gretl* (☎ 621 06, *Schweizergasse 32*) has courtyard parking and is closed between seasons. There are big singles/doubles with own shower and WC for AS280/520.

The atmospheric, spacious *Altstadthotel Eck* (☎ 647 85, fax -3, ❸ altstadthotel.eck@ utanet.at, *Hauptplatz 20*) has large rooms with high ceilings, shower, WC, TV, sofa and comfy chairs, all from AS420/840.

Places to Eat

There's a *Spar* supermarket on Tiroler Strasse. *Imbissstube* (*Albin Egger Strasse 5*) has mouth-watering rotisserie chicken sprinkled with spices. They're so popular, that's usually all it sells. The smell of the chickens sizzling on the spit outside is enough to make vegetarians join Meat Eaters Anonymous. It's open daily from 11 am to 9 pm; a half chicken *(Hendl)* with a roll is just AS32.

China-Restaurant Sehcuan (*Beda Weber Gasse 13*) has various weekday lunches for AS55. *Pick Nick Ossi* (*Europaplatz 2*) is open 11 am to 2 am Monday to Saturday. There's a range of food for less than AS100, including pizzas, schnitzels and snacks.

There are lots of places to try regional dishes, such as *Adlerstüberl Restaurant* (*Andrä Kranz Gasse 5*). Most meals are above AS100, though daily specials are cheaper. *Goldener Fisch* (*Kärntner Strasse 9*) is also good; meals start at AS70. Both places are open daily.

Entertainment

The *Flair Musikpub* in the Creativ Center off Zwergergasse is a rather smoky bar. Once a week there's live music (anything from rock to country; no techno), when entry costs AS70 to AS120. It is open 5 pm to 1 am nightly. A meeting place for young locals is *Pick Nick Ossi* (see Places to Eat), especially in the cellar where there's pool tables and other games.

Getting There & Away

Except for the 'corridor' route to Innsbruck (see the Innsbruck Getting There & Away section earlier in this chapter), trains to the rest of Austria connect via Spittal Millstättersee to the east. Trains to Salzburg (AS320) take at least three hours. Villach, between Spittal and Klagenfurt, is a main junction for rail routes to the south. To head south by car, you must first divert west or east along Highway 100.

HOHE TAUERN NATIONAL PARK

Flora and fauna are protected in this 1786 sq km hiking paradise that straddles Tirol, Salzburg and Carinthia.

It contains **Grossglockner** (3797m), Austria's highest mountain, which towers over the 10km-long Pasterze Glacier. The best viewing point is **Franz Josefs Höhe**, reached from Lienz by Bundesbus; it runs from mid-June to late September and costs AS103/206 single/return (including a AS40 toll for the park). If you plan to return the same day, get a zonal day pass for Carinthia (available in Lienz; AS130 plus toll). However, the route

AUSTRIA

(Highway 107, the Grossglockner Hochalpenstrasse) is so scenic that you should consider continuing north instead of backtracking. For longer stays, ask about the seven-day Bundesbus pass for the park (AS290).

Along the way you pass Heiligenblut (buses year-round from Lienz), where there's a HI *Jugendherberge* (☎ 04824-2259, Hof 36). However, it's closed from mid-October to mid-December. By car, you can reach Franz Josefs Höhe from May to November, but the daily toll for using the road is AS350 for cars and AS230 for motorcycles. An eight-day pass is AS460 and AS310 respectively. There are places to stay overnight. Cyclists and hikers pay nothing to enter the park.

Farther west, Felbertaurenstrasse also goes north-south through the park. For the tunnel section, there's a toll of AS140 for cars (AS130 in winter) and AS110 for motorcycles. At the northern end of the park, turn west along Highway 165 to reach **Krimml Falls**. These triple-level falls make a great spectacle. It takes 1½ hours to walk to the top, where there's an equally good view looking back down the valley.

Vorarlberg

The small state of Vorarlberg encompasses plains by Lake Constance (Bodensee) and mighty alpine ranges. It provides skiing, dramatic landscapes and access to Liechtenstein, Switzerland and Germany. To get around the province you can buy VVV tickets, which work like VVT tickets (see the Tirol introduction earlier in this chapter).

BREGENZ
☎ 05574 • pop 27,500
Bregenz, the provincial capital of Vorarlberg, offers lake excursions, mountain views and an important annual music festival.

Orientation & Information
The town is on the eastern shore of Lake Constance. From the train station, walk left along Bahnhofstrasse to reach the town centre (10 minutes). The tourist office (☎ 4959-0, fax -59, @ tourismus@bregenz.at), Bahnhofstrasse 14, is open 9 am to noon and 1 to 5 pm Monday to Friday, to noon Saturday. During

the Bregenz Festival it's open daily to 7 pm. Upstairs is Vorarlberg Tourismus (☎ 425 25-0, fax -5, @ info@vbgtour.at).

The post office is on Seestrasse (Postamt 6900), open until 7 pm weekdays, and to 2 pm Saturday. Send emails at S'Logo, Kirchstrasse 47, from 5 pm daily. The train station has bike rental daily till 9.40 pm; Bundesbuses leave from outside.

Things to See & Do
The old town merits a stroll. Its centrepiece is the bulbous, baroque **St Martin's Tower**, built in 1599.

The **Pfänder** mountain offers an impressive panorama over the lake and beyond. A cable car to the top operates from 9 am to 6 pm (7 pm in summer). Fares are AS70 each way, AS125 return.

The **Bregenz Festival** takes place from late July to late August. Operas and classical works are performed from a vast floating stage on the edge of the lake. Contact the Kartenbüro (☎ 407-6, fax -400), Postfach 311, A-6901, about nine months prior to the festival for tickets and information. Web site: www.bregenzerfestspiele.com.

Places to Stay & Eat
The cheapest of several sites is *Camping Lamm* (☎ 717 01, Mehrerauerstrasse 51), 1.5km west of the station. It's open from May to mid-October, and prices are AS50 adults, AS35 tents and AS35 cars.

The HI *Jugendgästehaus* (☎ 7083-0, fax-88, Mehrerauerstrasse 3-5), across from the swimming pool, is always open. There's a cafe, lift, and dorms from AS180 (AS230 in summer).

Private rooms (from AS220 per person) and apartments are good value; inquire at the tourist office, which also has a room-booking service (AS30). A surcharge normally applies for a single night's stay.

Pension Gunz (☎/fax 436 57, Anton Schneider Strasse 38) has simple singles/doubles for around AS380/680 with shower, AS340/600 without. Reception is in the cafe downstairs (closed Tuesday). *Pension Sonne* (☎ 425 72, fax -4, @ g.diem@bbn.at, Kaiserstrasse 8) is convenient, family-run and closed in winter. It costs AS550/1000 with shower and toilet and AS470/840 without.

China-Restaurant Da-Li (*Anton Schnei-der Strasse 34*) has weekday lunch *menus* from AS65 (open daily).

Gösserbräu (*Anton Schneider Strasse 1*) offers a beery *Bräustuble* or a calmer restaurant. There's Austrian and vegetarian dishes from AS85 to AS205 (open daily).

Goldener Hirschen (*Kirchstrasse 8*) has good Austrian food for AS75 to AS215, served in an old-style, wood-panelled room (closed Tuesday).

There's a *Spar* supermarket with a cheap self-service restaurant downstairs in the GWL shopping centre on Römerstrasse.

Getting There & Away

Trains to Munich (AS474, 2½ hours) go via Lindau; trains to Constance (AS172, 1½ hours) go via the Swiss shore of the lake. There are also regular departures to St Gallen and Zürich. Trains to Innsbruck (2¾ hours) depart every one to two hours. Feldkirch is on the same rail route (AS58, 30 minutes).

Boat services operate from late May to late October, with a reduced schedule from early March. For information, call ☎ 428 68. Bregenz to Constance by boat (via Lindau) takes about 3½ hours and there are up to six departures per day. Inquire about special boat passes giving free or half-price travel.

FELDKIRCH

☎ 05522 • pop 29,000

Feldkirch, the gateway to Liechtenstein, was granted its town charter in 1218, and retains some medieval buildings. There are good views from the 12th-century **Schattenburg** castle, which houses a museum (AS25, students AS10; closed Monday and November). There's a free **animal park** (*Wildpark*), with 200 species, 1km from the centre. Feldkirch hosts the important **Schubertiade** music festival in late June; inquire well in advance (☎ 05576-720 91, fax 754 50). The Web site is www.schubertiade.at.

Information

Feldkirch tourist office (☎ 734 67, fax 798 67, ✉ tourismus@wtg.feldkirch.com), Herrengasse 12, is open 9 am to 6 pm Monday to Friday (closed for lunch in winter), and 9 am to noon Saturday. It reserves rooms free of charge.

Places to Stay & Eat

The HI *Jugendherberge* (☎ 731 81, fax 793 99, *Reichsstrasse 111*) is 1.5km north of the train station in a historic but modernised building (closed for two weeks in early December). Beds are AS142 (dorms) or AS193 (rooms) and dinners are AS82. Add AS25 heating surcharge in winter, subtract AS20 if you don't need sheets. Reception is open 7 am to 10 pm.

Gasthof Engel (☎/fax 720 56, *Liechtensteiner Strasse, Tisis*), on the bus route to Liechtenstein, has elderly rooms with painted wardrobes for AS340/520 using hall shower. The restaurant and reception are closed Monday. *Interspar* (*St Leonhards Platz*) has a supermarket and cheap restaurant, open until 7 pm Monday to Thursday, to 7.30 pm Friday and to 5 pm Saturday. *Oriental Grill* (*Schmied Gasse 4*) has weekday Japanese lunches for AS85, or for Austrian food, try *Johanniterhof* (*Marktgasse 1*).

Getting There & Away

Two buses an hour (one on weekends) depart for Liechtenstein from in front of the train station. To Liechtenstein's capital, Vaduz (AS32, 40 minutes), buses are either direct or require a change in Schaans. Trains to Buchs on the Swiss border pass through Schaans, but only a few stop there. Buchs has connections to major destinations in Switzerland, including Zürich and Chur.

ARLBERG REGION

The Arlberg region, shared by Vorarlberg and neighbouring Tirol, is considered to have some of the best skiing in Austria. Summer is less busy, and many of the bars are closed then.

St Anton am Arlberg is the largest resort, enjoying an easy-going atmosphere and vigorous nightlife. There's always a large contingent of Australasian skiers. It has good medium-to-advanced runs, as well as nursery slopes on Gampen and Kapall. Get information from the tourist office (☎ 05446-226 90, ✉ st.anton@netway.at) on the main street.

Lech, a more upmarket resort, is a favourite with royalty and film stars. Runs are predominantly medium to advanced. For details, contact the Lech tourist office (☎ 05583-2161-0, ✉ lech-info@lech.at).

AUSTRIA

A ski pass valid for 85 ski lifts in Lech, Zürs, Stuben, St Anton and St Christoph costs AS475 for one day and AS2670 for one week (reductions for children and senior citizens). Rental starts at AS190 for skis and poles, and AS90 for boots.

Places to Stay & Eat

Accommodation is mainly in small B&Bs – there are nearly 200 in St Anton alone. Tourist office brochures have full listings, or try the accommodation boards with free telephones outside the tourist offices. Budget prices start at around AS350 per person in winter high season, reducing by about 30% to 50% in low season and summer.

Try **Tiroler Frieden** (☎ 05446-2247, ✉ tiroler.frieden@ski-arlberg.com) on St Anton's main street (phone ahead), or the cheaper **Franz Schuler** (☎ 05446-3108) in nearby St Jakob. Back in St Anton, there are good pizzas at **Pomodoro**, or try the take-away stands that are scattered around town. Supermarkets include **Spar**, which has hot lunches before noon. Good après-ski bars include **Krazy Kanguruh** on the slopes, and **Piccadilly** in the village.

Despite its sophisticated profile, Lech has a **Jugendherberge** (☎ 05583-2419, Stubenbach 244), 2km from the main resort. It is closed between seasons.

Getting There & Away

St Anton is on the main railway route between Bregenz and Innsbruck, less than 1½ hours from either place. St Anton is close to the eastern entrance of the Arlberg Tunnel, the toll road connecting Vorarlberg and Tirol. The tunnel toll is AS130/100 for cars/motorcycles. You can avoid the toll by taking the B197, but no vehicles with trailers are allowed on this winding road. There is a choice of about 3/12 buses a day in summer/winter to Lech (AS46, 40 minutes) from St Anton.

euro currency converter €1 = 13.76AS

Belgium

Think of Belgium (België in Flemish, Belgique in French) and it's 'Bruges, beer and chocolate' that generally spring to mind. Surprisingly little else is commonly known about this much-embattled country which spawned Western Europe's first great towns, and whose early artists are credited with inventing oil painting.

Perhaps it's a lack of fervent nationalism – the result of many dominant cultures integrating here over the centuries – which has kept Belgium's spotlight dim on the European stage. Rarely boastful, the country has in fact plenty to fascinate the visitor – from historically rich towns to the serenity of the hilly Ardennes, and everywhere wonderful bars and cafes where Belgians feel at home.

Facts about Belgium

HISTORY

Belgium's position between France, Germany and, across the North Sea, England has long made it one of Europe's main battlegrounds. Prosperous throughout the 13th and 14th centuries, the Flemish towns of Ypres, Bruges and Ghent were the first major cities, booming on the manufacturing and trading of cloth. Their craftspeople established powerful guilds (organisations to stringently control arts and crafts) whose elaborate guildhalls you'll see in many cities. Alas, the Flemish weavers were ruined by competition from England and, due largely to Bruges' refusal to handle the foreign cloth as well as the silting of its river, the towns faded. Trade moved east to Antwerp, which soon became the greatest port in Europe.

When Protestantism swept Europe in the 16th century, the Low Countries (present-day Belgium, the Netherlands and Luxembourg, often referred to as the Benelux) embraced it, much to the chagrin of their ruler, the fanatically Catholic Philip II of Spain. He sent the cruel Inquisition to enforce Catholicism, thus inflaming the smouldering religious tensions. The eruption came with the Iconoclastic Fury,

in which Protestants ran riot, ransacking the churches. Philip retaliated with a force of 10,000 soldiers, and thousands of citizens were imprisoned or executed before war broke out in 1568. The Revolt of the Netherlands lasted 80 years, and in the end roughly laid the region's present-day borders – Holland and its allied provinces victoriously expelling the Spaniards while Belgium and Luxembourg stayed under their rule.

For the next 200 years Belgium remained a battlefield for successive foreign powers. After the Spaniards, the Austrians came and

BELGIUM

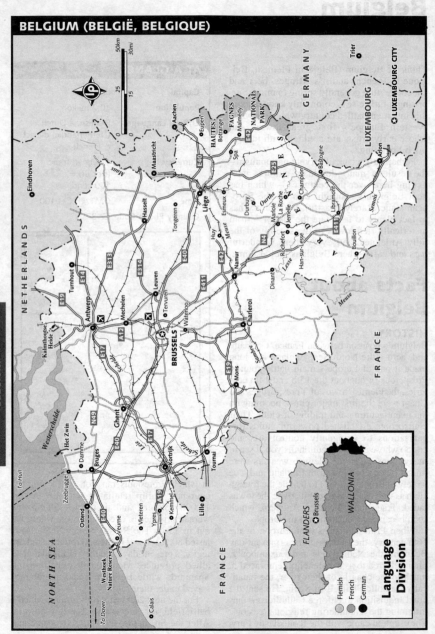

BELGIUM (BELGIË, BELGIQUE)

Language Division

Flemish
French
German

in turn the French. The largely unpopular French occupation ended in 1814 with the creation of the United Kingdom of the Netherlands, which incorporated Belgium and Luxembourg. Napoleon was finally trounced the following year at the Battle of Waterloo near Brussels. In 1830, the Catholic Belgians revolted, winning independence from the Netherlands and forming their own kingdom.

The ensuing years saw the start of Flemish nationalism, with tension growing between Flemish (Dutch) and French speakers which would eventually lead to a language partition that divided the country (see Population & People later in this chapter).

In 1885 the then king, Léopold II, personally acquired the Congo in Africa. He was later disgraced over the continuing slave trade there. In the early 1900s the Congo was made a Belgian colony; much-disputed independence was granted in 1960.

Despite Belgium's neutral policy, the Germans invaded in 1914. Used as a bloody battleground throughout WWI, the town of Ypres was wiped off the map. In WWII the whole country was taken over within three weeks of a surprise German attack in May 1940. Controversy over the questionable early capitulation by the then king, Léopold III, led to his abdication in 1950 in favour of his son, King Baudouin, whose popular reign ended with his death (at age 62) in 1993. Childless, Baudouin was succeeded by his brother, the present King Albert II.

Postwar Belgium was characterised by an economic boom, later accentuated by Brussels' appointment as the headquarters of the EU and the North Atlantic Treaty Organisation (NATO).

GEOGRAPHY

Occupying 30,510 sq km, Belgium is one of Europe's smallest nations, sandwiched between the Netherlands, Germany, Luxembourg and France. The north is flat, the south dominated by the hilly, forested Ardennes, and the 66km North Sea coastline monopolised by resorts, save for a few patches of windswept dunes.

CLIMATE

The country has a generally mild, maritime climate. July and August are the warmest months. They are also the wettest, although precipitation is spread pretty evenly over the year. The Ardennes is often a few degrees colder than the rest of the country, with snow from November to March.

ECOLOGY & ENVIRONMENT

Water and noise pollution, urbanisation and waste management are the most pressing environmental issues. Public concern over these issues has led to growing support for the Green parties, which are a part of the present coalition government.

Belgium's largest nature reserve is the Hautes Fagnes National Park, a region of swampy heath and woods in the Ardennes. Other important reserves include the Kalmthoutse Heide (heather and dunes) north of Antwerp, as well as Het Zwin (polders and mudflats) and the Westhoek (dunes), which sit at either end of Belgium's coastal strip. By anyone's standards these reserves are small, and the country's flora and fauna is under enormous pressure.

GOVERNMENT & POLITICS

Belgium is a constitutional hereditary monarchy, led by King Albert II and a parliament. In 1993 the government was decentralised through the creation of three regional governments which represented the Flemish and French-speaking communities (Flanders and Wallonia respectively) as well as the Brussels-Capital region.

The overall political scene has long been dominated by the (Catholic) Christian Democrats, Socialists and Liberals, though support for the Green parties as well as the ultra-right-wing Vlaams Blok (Flemish Block) is on the increase.

In recent years, political and judicial scandals have left Belgium with the nickname of the 'Italy of the north'. The most famous incident was the Dutroux affair, in which police and judicial incompetence was held partly to blame for the crimes of suspected murderer and paedophile, Marc Dutroux.

In 1999, the mishandling of a crisis over dioxin-contaminated chicken led to the trouncing of the government at the June election. The Liberals headed by current prime minister, Guy Verhofstadt, now lead the coalition government.

BELGIUM

ECONOMY

Over the centuries, Belgium's economic prosperity has swung between one language community and the other, starting with Flanders' medieval textile wealth, which was later supplanted by Wallonia's mining and steel industries. The latter's decline means Flanders is again the country's industrial backbone. The economy as a whole, however, is struggling with a huge public debt and high unemployment (12%). In 1998, the GDP was US$236 billion. The main industries are chemicals, car manufacturing, textiles, iron and steel. Agriculture (cereals), horticulture and stock breeding are also important.

POPULATION & PEOPLE

While spread over 10 provinces, Belgium's population is basically split in two: the Flemish and the Walloons. Language is the dividing factor, made official in 1962 when an invisible line – or Linguistic Divide as it's called – was drawn across the country, cutting it almost equally in half. To the north lies Flanders, whose Flemish speakers make up 60% of Belgium's population of 10.2 million. To the south lies Wallonia, where French-speaking Walloons make up most of the remainder. To further complicate matters, Brussels is officially bilingual but predominantly French speaking, and lies within the Flemish region but is governed separately. There's also a tiny German-speaking enclave in the far east.

The language issue stems from discrimination against the Flemish when the Belgian constitution was drawn up – French was official, Flemish banned – and over the years has caused many political and social conflicts.

ARTS

Belgium has produced many influential painters of world renown. The master of early Flemish painting is undoubtedly Jan van Eyck (ca. 1390-1441), who perfected the technique of oil painting and founded the Flemish school. He worked in both Bruges and The Hague in the Netherlands. The 16th-century painter and draughtsman Pieter Brueghel the Elder (1525-69) regained fame in the 20th century for his landscapes and religious paintings. Pieter Paul Rubens (1577-1640) was the dominant influence on Flemish painting in the 17th century. He founded a studio which consolidated his reputation as the most important exponent of Baroque painting in Europe. The famous portrait painter Anthony (Antoon) van Dyck (1599-1641) and his contemporary Jacob Jordaens (1593-1678) were natives of Antwerp and graduated from the Rubens studio.

The start of the 20th century saw the beginnings of sinuous Art Nouveau architecture in Brussels. The movement was led by Henri van de Velde and by Victor Horta, who was famed for interiors that displayed few straight lines – ceilings simply became curved continuations of walls. Stained glass and wrought iron fashioned in stylised natural forms were also used. The painter René Magritte (1898-1967) lived most of his life in Brussels, but his disturbing surreal images have earned him an enduring international reputation.

Belgians who became famous in the music world include Adolphe Sax (1814-94), who invented the saxophone; Jean 'Toots' Thielemans, whose harmonica playing earnt him fame in the USA; and the raspy-voiced Jacques Brel, who rose to stardom in Paris in the 1950s for his songs about Belgium that still are popular today.

The country's most prestigious classical music event is the Concours Musical International Reine Élisabeth de Belgique (Queen Elisabeth International Musical Competition), which attracts young talent from around the world.

Very little local literature has been translated into English. One book you may want to get hold of is *The Sorrow of Belgium* by Hugo Claus, which describes wartime Belgium through the eyes of a Flemish adolescent. Marguerite Yourcenar is arguably the country's most famous female poet and writer. Liège detective novelist Georges Simenon is famed for his detective character, Inspector Maigret.

Comic strips are a Belgian forte. Hergé, the creator of Tintin, is the best internationally known cartoonist.

SOCIETY & CONDUCT

With their history of foreign domination, Belgians are used to visitors and their different habits, and there are few social taboos that travellers are likely to break. It is customary to greet shopkeepers and cafe/pub owners when entering their premises.

BELGIUM

RELIGION

Long a Catholic stronghold, Belgium has experienced a decrease in church attendances but religious traditions continue, influencing many aspects of daily life, including politics and education.

LANGUAGE

See the History and Population & People sections for information on the language issue. For a rundown of the Flemish (Dutch), French and German languages, see the Language chapter at the back of this book. English is widely spoken, although less frequently in Wallonia and the Ardennes.

For travellers, the Linguistic Divide will cause few problems. The most confusing part will be on the road, when the sign you're following to Bergen (as it's known in Flemish) disappears and the town of Mons (the French name) appears. A list of alternative place names is also included at the back of this book.

Facts for the Visitor

HIGHLIGHTS

The following are some of Belgium's highlights:

Museums & Sights
Grand Place, Musée Horta and Musées Royaux des Beaux-Arts, Brussels; Begijnhof and canal cruise, Bruges; Onze Lieve Vrouwkathedraal and Rubenshuis, Antwerp; In Flanders Fields Museum, Ypres

Pubs
Falstaff and Le Greenwich, Brussels; 't Brugs Beertje, Bruges; Oud Arsenaal, Antwerp

Beers
Duvel, Westmalle Triple, Castillon Gueuze, Hoegaarden, Rochefort 10, Oerbier, Delirium Tremens

Hiking
La Roche, Rochefort or the Hautes Fagnes areas of the Ardennes

SUGGESTED ITINERARIES

Depending on the length of your stay, you might want to see and do the following:

Two days
Spend one day each in Brussels and Bruges.

One week
Spend two days each in Brussels and the Ardennes, and one day each in Antwerp, Bruges and Ypres.

Two weeks
Spend three days in and around Brussels, two days each in Antwerp and the Ardennes, two days in Bruges and Ypres, two days in coastal resorts, and one day each in Ghent, Namur and Liège.

One month
This should give you plenty of time to explore the above-mentioned places and discover a few new places of your own.

PLANNING
When to Go

Spring is the best time to go, as there's less chance of rain, many flowers (including daffodils and tulips) are in bloom and tourist crowds are minimal.

Maps

The best road maps of Belgium are those produced by Michelin – map No 909 (scale: 1:350,000) covers both Belgium and Luxembourg. The Institut Géographique National (IGN) publishes topographical maps (scale: 1:25,000), and tourist offices have decent city maps.

TOURIST OFFICES
Local Tourist Offices

The Flemish and Walloon tourist authorities (Toerisme Vlaanderen and Office de Promotion du Tourisme, respectively) have their head office (☎ 02-504 03 90, fax 02-504 02 70) at Rue du Marché aux Herbes 63, B-1000 Brussels. Much of the tourist literature is free.

Tourist Offices Abroad

Belgian tourist offices abroad include:

Canada
(☎ 514-484 3594, fax 489 8965) PO Box 760, Succursale NDG, Montreal, Que H4A 3S2

France
(☎ 01 47 42 41 18, fax 01 47 42 71 83) blvd des Capucines 21, 75002 Paris

Germany
(☎ 0211-86 48 40, fax 13 42 85) Berliner Allee 47, 40212 Düsseldorf

The Netherlands
(☎ 023-534 44 34, fax 531 32 93) Kennemerplein 3, 2011 MH Haarlem

BELGIUM

UK
(☎ 020-7458 0044, fax 7458 0045, ✉ office@flanders-tourism.org) 31 Pepper St, London E14 9FW
(☎ 020-7531 0390, fax 7531 0393, ✉ info@belgium-tourism.org) 225 Marsh Wall, London E14 9FW

USA
(☎ 212-758 8130, fax 355 7675, ✉ info@visitbelgium.com) 780 Third Ave, Suite 1501, New York, NY 10017

VISAS & DOCUMENTS

Visitors from many countries need only a valid passport for three-month visits. Regulations are basically the same as for entering the Netherlands (for more details, see the Facts for the Visitor section in that chapter).

EMBASSIES & CONSULATES
Belgian Embassies

Belgian embassies abroad include:

Australia (☎ 02-6273 2501, fax 6273 3392) 19 Arkana St, Yarralumla, Canberra, ACT 2600
Canada (☎ 613-236 7267/69, fax 236 7882) 80 Elgin St, 4th floor, Ottawa, Ont K1P 1B7
New Zealand (☎ 04-472 9558/59, fax 471 2764) 1-3 Willeston St, Wellington
UK (☎ 020-7470 3700, fax 7259 6213) 103-105 Eaton Square, London SW1 9AB
USA (☎ 202-333 6900, fax 333 3079) 3330 Garfield St NW, Washington DC 20008

Embassies in Belgium

All the following embassies are in Brussels:

Australia (☎ 02-231 05 00, fax 02-230 68 02) Rue Guimard 6, B-1040
Canada (☎ 02-741 06 11, fax 02-741 96 43) Ave de Tervueren 2, B-1040
France (☎ 02-548 87 11, fax 02-513 68 71) Rue Ducale 65, B-1000
Germany (☎ 02-774 19 11, fax 02-772 36 92) Ave de Tervueren 190, B-1150
Ireland (☎ 02-230 53 37, fax 02-230 53 12) Rue Froissart 89, B-1040
Luxembourg (☎ 02-737 57 00, fax 02-737 57 10) Ave de Cortenbergh 75, B-1000
The Netherlands (☎ 02-679 17 11, fax 02-679 17 75) Ave Herrmann-Debroux 48, B-1160
New Zealand (☎ 02-512 10 40, fax 02-513 48 56) Square de Meeus 1, 7th floor, B-1000
UK (☎ 02-287 62 11, fax 02-287 63 55) Rue d'Arlon 85, B-1040
USA (☎ 02-508 21 11, fax 02-511 27 25) Blvd du Régent 27, B-1000

CUSTOMS

In Belgium, the usual allowances apply to duty-free goods if you are coming from a non-EU country and to duty-paid goods if you're arriving from within the EU.

MONEY

Belgium is participating in the euro, the European single currency (see the boxed text 'The Euro' in the introductory Facts for the Visitor chapter).

Currency

The money unit is the Belgian franc, usually written as f or BF. There are f1, f5, f20 and f50 coins, and notes in denominations of f100, f200, f500, f1000, f2000 and f10,000. Belgian francs are equal to Luxembourg francs and are widely used there, but the reverse does not apply.

Exchange Rates

country	unit		Belgian franc
Australia	A$1	=	f25.87
Canada	C$1	=	f30.10
euro	€1	=	f40.34
France	1FF	=	f6.15
Germany	DM1	=	f20.63
Japan	¥100	=	f41.10
New Zealand	NZ$1	=	f20.09
UK	UK£1	=	f67.13
USA	US$1	=	f44.65

Exchanging Money

Banks are the best place to change money, charging about 1.25% commission on cash for EU currencies, f50 on other currencies, and f225 on travellers cheques. Out of hours there are exchange bureaus which mostly have lower rates. All the major credit cards are widely accepted. You'll find ATMs in major cities and at Zaventem (Brussels) airport.

Costs

If you stay at hostels and eat at cafes you can get by on about f900 to f1000 a day. Because of the country's size, getting around is not a major outlay. Most museums offer a concession price for students and seniors – these prices are indicated throughout this chapter.

Tipping & Bargaining

Tipping is not obligatory and bargaining not customary.

Taxes & Refunds

Value-added tax, or VAT (BTW in Flemish, TVA in French), is calculated at 6% (food, hotels, camping) and either 17% or the more common 21% for everything else. To get a rebate, you must get your purchase invoice stamped by customs as you leave. You then send it back to the shop and it'll forward the refund. Alternatively, buy from shops affiliated with the Tax Cheque Refund Service (see the Money section in the Netherlands chapter for details).

POST & COMMUNICATIONS
Post

Post offices are generally open 8 or 9 am to 5 or 6 pm weekdays and on Saturday mornings. Letters (under 20g) cost f17 within Belgium, f21 in the EU, f23 in the rest of Europe or f34 elsewhere. They average seven to nine days to reach places outside Europe and two to three days inside. Poste restante can attract a f14 fee (often waived).

Telephone

Belgium's international country code is ☎ 32. To telephone abroad, the international access code is ☎ 00 (see the Telephones Appendix).

Telephone numbers in Belgium have recently changed. Under the new system, you must dial the full area code when phoning anywhere in the country, including within the city you're in. For example, if you're in Brussels and phoning a Brussels number, you must use the '02' area code.

Local phone calls are metered and cost a minimum of f10. Most telephone numbers prefixed with 0900 or 070 are pay-per-minute numbers – the usual charge is f18 per minute. Numbers prefixed with 0800 are free calls, and those prefixed with 075, 0476 to 0479, 0486 and 0496 are mobile numbers.

Call boxes take f5 and f10 coins as well as f200, f500 and f1000 Telecards (Belgacom phonecards), available from post offices and newsagents. International calls can be made using phonecards such as XL-Call and The Phonecard. A three-minute phone call to the USA from a phone box costs f120.

For travellers with mobile phones, Belgium uses GSM 900/1800, which is compatible with the rest of Europe and Australia but not with the North American GSM 1900 or the system used in Japan.

Fax

Faxes can be sent and received from Belgacom shops (known as *teleboetieks/téléboutiques*) and cost f85 for the first page to the UK and the USA, and f350 to Australia, plus f75 and f150 respectively for each additional consecutive page. Receiving a fax costs f10 per page.

Email & Internet Access

Internet cafes are plentiful; expect to pay f200 to f250 per hour.

INTERNET RESOURCES

Excellent Web sites offering heaps of information on transport, accommodation and tourism, plus links to other Belgium-related sites, are www.visitbelgium.com and www.trabel.com. For an overview of Brussels, go to www.bruxelles.irisnet.be on the Web.

BOOKS

Lonely Planet's *Brussels, Bruges & Antwerp* city guide gives you the country's top three cities in the palm of your hand. For an affectionate look at Belgium's many idiosyncrasies, pick up *A Tall Man in a Low Land*. Written by Englishman Harry Pearson it's full of witty insight and observations.

Brussels and Antwerp both have stores specialising in English-language books; alternatively, head to a chain store like FNAC or Standaard Boekhandel.

FILMS

The most recently acclaimed Belgian film is *Rosetta* by the Dardenne brothers – it won the Palme D'Or at Cannes in 1999. Other noted films include *The Eighth Day* and *Toto le Héros*, both by Jaco Van Dormael; *The Sexual Life of the Belgians* by Jan Bucquoy; and *Daens* by Stijn Coninckx.

NEWSPAPERS & MAGAZINES

American and English newspapers and magazines are widely available. *Le Soir* (French) and *De Standaard* (Flemish) are the best national daily newspapers.

The English-language *Bulletin* magazine (f90) comes out on Thursday and has national news and a good entertainment guide.

BELGIUM

RADIO & TV

The BBC's World Service can be picked up on 648kHz medium wave. Two popular Belgian radio stations are Radio 1 (Flemish) and Radio 21 (French). The main Belgian TV channels are TV1 and VTM (Flemish), and RT1 and ARTE (French). Most homes have cable TV and can access about 35 stations, including the BBC and CNN.

TIME

Belgium runs on Central European Time. At noon it's 11 am in London, 6 am in New York, 3 am in San Francisco, 6 am in Toronto, 9 pm in Sydney and 11 pm in Auckland. Daylight-saving time comes into effect at 2 am on the last Sunday in March, when clocks are moved an hour forward; they're moved an hour back again at 2 am on the last Sunday in October. The 24-hour clock is commonly used.

LAUNDRY

Self-service laundries (wassalon/laverie) on average charge f120 for a 5kg wash and f20 per dryer cycle. Take plenty of f5 and f20 coins.

TOILETS

Public toilets tend to be few and far between, which is why most people avail themselves of the toilets in pubs and cafes. A f10 fee is commonly charged in public toilets or toilets in popular cafes.

WOMEN TRAVELLERS

Women should encounter few problems travelling around Belgium. However, in the event of rape or attack, contact SOS Viol (☎ 02-534 36 36) or Helpline (☎ 02-648 40 14).

GAY & LESBIAN TRAVELLERS

Attitudes to homosexuality are becoming less conservative and same-sex marriages are now legal. The age of consent is 16.

Flanders' biggest gay/lesbian organisation is Federatie Werkgroepen Homoseksualiteit (FWH; ☎ 09-223 69 29, fax 09-223 58 21, ✉ info@fwh.be), Kammerstraat 22, 9000 Ghent. It has an information/help hotline called Holebifoon (☎ 09-238 26 26).

The main French-speaking gay/lesbian group is Tels Quels (☎ 02-512 45 87, fax 02-511 31 48, ✉ telsquels@skynet.be), Rue du Marché au Charbon 81 in Brussels.

Artemys (☎ 02-512 03 47), Galerie Bortier, Rue St Jean, 1000 Brussels, is a women's bookshop and lesbian information centre.

The Belgian Pride is held on the first weekend of May.

DISABLED TRAVELLERS

Belgium is not terribly user-friendly for travellers with a mobility problem. Some government buildings, museums, hotels and restaurants have lifts and/or ramps, but not the majority. Wheelchair users will be up against rough, uneven pavements, and will need to give an hour's notice when travelling by train.

For more information, contact Mobility International (☎ 02-201 56 08, fax 02-201 57 63, ✉ mobint@acradis.be), 18 Blvd Baudouin, 1000 Brussels.

SENIOR TRAVELLERS

Most museums and other attractions offer reductions to those aged over 65. Travellers aged over 60 can buy a Golden Railpass which gives six one-way train trips in one year. It costs f1260/1940 in 2nd/1st class.

On the whole, getting around should pose few major problems, although at some train stations, platforms are low-set, making it difficult to climb into carriages.

TRAVEL WITH CHILDREN

Belgians generally have a positive attitude towards children and there's plenty to keep youngsters occupied. Kids usually enjoy canal rides in Bruges, the Atomium in Brussels, the caves at Han-sur-Lesse in the Ardennes and a bike ride in the countryside. Indulging in waffles, chocolates and frites (chips) is sure to be a winner.

DANGERS & ANNOYANCES

The only danger you're likely to encounter is a big night out on Belgian beer. The national emergency numbers are police ☎ 101 and fire/ambulance ☎ 100.

LEGAL MATTERS

Police usually treat tourists with respect. Under Belgian law, you must carry either a passport or national identity card at all times. Should you be arrested, you have the right to ask for your consul to be immediately notified.

BUSINESS HOURS

Shops are open 8.30 or 9 am to 6 pm weekdays – often closing for lunch – with similar hours on Saturday. Shops in some cities also open on Sunday. Banks are open 9 am to noon or 1 pm, and 2 to 4 or 5 pm weekdays, and Saturday mornings; in large cities, they often don't close for lunch.

PUBLIC HOLIDAYS & SPECIAL EVENTS

Public holidays include New Year's Day, Easter Monday, Labour Day (1 May), Ascension Day, Whit Monday, National Day (21 July), Assumption (15 August), All Saints' Day (1 November), Armistice Day (11 November) and Christmas Day.

The religious festival of Carnival is celebrated throughout Belgium, but is at its most colourful in the villages of Binche and Stavelot. There's a swarm of local and national, artistic or religious festivals – pick up the tourist office's free brochure.

ACTIVITIES

The Ardennes is Belgium's outdoor playground. Here you can (sometimes) ski in winter and, in summer, kayak or go hiking or mountain biking (using a *vélo tout terrain* or VTT – a mountain bike) along a good network of forest tracks.

WORK

For non-EU nationals it's officially illegal, but it may be possible to pick up work in hostels and in resorts along the coast.

ACCOMMODATION

In summer, all forms of accommodation are heavily booked. The national tourist office will reserve accommodation for free and has camping and hotel leaflets, as well as booklets on guesthouses (*chambres d'hôtes* in French; *gastenkamers* in Flemish) and rural houses available for weekly rental. You can also book hotels via Belgian Tourist Reservations (☎ 02-513 74 84, fax 02-513 92 77), Blvd Anspach 111 bte 4, B-1000 Brussels.

Camping rates vary widely, but on average you'll be looking at between f260 to f500 for two adults, a tent and vehicle.

There are private hostels in some cities. Otherwise, Belgium has two HI hostelling groups. Les Auberges de Jeunesse (☎ 02-219 56 76, fax 02-219 14 51, ✉ info@laj.be), Rue de la Sablonnière 28, 1000 Brussels, runs hostels in Wallonia; its Flemish counterpart is the Vlaamse Jeugdherbergcentrale (☎ 03-232 72 18, fax 03-231 81 26, ✉ info@vjh.be), Van Stralenstraat 40, 2060 Antwerp. Rates range from f420 to f475 per night in a dorm, including breakfast. Some hostels have single/double rooms for f800/1170. Most charge f125 extra for sheets.

B&Bs/guesthouses are rapidly gaining ground in Belgium – prices range from f800 to f1200 for singles, f1200 to f1800 for doubles and f1500 to f2700 for triples.

The cheapest hotels charge about f1000/1500 for singles/doubles without bathroom facilities but with breakfast. The starting price for a mid-range hotel is about f2500/3000. Some mid-range and top-end hotels in Brussels drop their rates dramatically on weekends, when the EU quarter is dead and all the businesspeople have gone home. Great deals can be had.

FOOD

Belgian cuisine is highly regarded throughout Europe – some say it's second only to French, while in others' eyes it's equal. Combining French style with German portions, you'll rarely have reason to complain. Meat and seafood are abundantly consumed, and then of course there are frites – chips or fries – which the Belgians swear they invented and which, judging by availability, is a claim few would contest.

Snacks

The popularity of frites cannot be understated. Every village has at least one *frituur/friture* where frites are served up in a paper cone or dish, smothered until almost unrecognisable with large blobs of thick mayonnaise and eaten with a small wooden fork in a mostly futile attempt to keep your fingers clean. Another favourite snack is a *belegd broodje/sandwich garni* – half a baguette filled with an array of garnishes.

On the sweet side, waffles (*wafels/gaufres*) are eaten piping hot from market stalls. Then there are filled chocolates (*pralines*), whose fame rivals Belgian beer. One of the most exclusive chocolate shops is Godiva, where you'll pay for the white gloves staff wear to

BELGIUM

hand-pick each piece. The poor person's delicious equivalent, the elephant-emblazoned Côte d'Or, can be found in supermarkets.

Main Dishes

Meat, poultry and hearty vegetable soups figure prominently on menus, but it's *mosselen/moules* (mussels) cooked in white wine and served with a mountain of frites that's regarded as the national dish. Cultivated mainly in the Delta region in the Netherlands, the rule of thumb for mussels is: eat them during the months that include an 'r', and don't touch the ones that haven't opened properly when cooked.

Game, including pheasant and boar, is an autumn speciality from the Ardennes, which is also famed for its hams. Horse, rabbit and guinea fowl are also typical offerings. In spring, asparagus from Mechelen is a firm favourite. When dining out, the *dagschotel/plat du jour* (dish of the day) is often the cheapest option. Vegetarians will find many cafes and brasseries have at least one suitable option.

DRINKS

Beer rules – and deservedly so. The quality is excellent and the variety incomparable – somewhere upwards of 400 types, from standard lagers to specialist brews. The most noted are the abbey-brewed Trappist beers, dark in colour, grainy in taste and dangerously strong (from 6% to 11.5% alcohol by volume). Then there's *lambiek/lambic*, a spontaneously fermented beer which comes sweet or sour depending on what's added during fermentation – *gueuze*, a sour variety, is the most famous. Beer prices match quality, with a 250mL lager costing f40 to f50, and a 330mL Trappist f75 to f130. For recommendations, see the Highlights section at the start of this section.

ENTERTAINMENT

Nightlife almost uniformly centres around the ubiquitous bars and cafes. Cinemas in Flanders usually screen films in their original language with Flemish subtitles, while those in Wallonia tend to dub them into French. Screenings are sometimes cheaper on Monday.

SHOPPING

Chocolate, lace and beer are the specialities, but the first two don't come cheap. Pralines cost f500 to f1000 per kilo, and a lace handkerchief will set you back somewhere between f200 and f1000.

Getting There & Away

AIR

Belgium's national airline is Sabena and the main international airport is Zaventem (also known as Brussels National), 14km northeast of Brussels. A much smaller airport, Deurne, is close to Antwerp and has less frequent flights to Amsterdam and London.

Airline passengers departing from Zaventem pay a f550 departure tax, and f300 from Deurne (this tax is commonly included in airline tickets).

LAND
Bus

Eurolines operates international bus services to and from Belgium. Tickets can be bought from its offices in Antwerp, Brussels or Liège, or from travel agencies. Reduced fares for people aged under 26 are offered. In July and August, some fares – such as those to London – are subject to a peak season supplement.

Eurolines has regular buses to many Western, Eastern, Mediterranean and Central European destinations, as well as Scandinavia and North Africa. Depending on the destination and the time of year, its buses stop in Brussels, Antwerp, Bruges, Ghent and Liège. To most major destinations there's just one price whether you depart from Brussels or, for example, Antwerp. Given Belgium's small size, there's also not much difference in journey times – Brussels-Paris takes 3¾ hours, or 4¾ hours from Antwerp. As an indication, services from Brussels include Amsterdam (f600, four hours, eight per day), Cologne (f700, four hours, two per day), London (f1690, 8½ hours, seven per day) and Paris (f790, 3¾ hours, eight per day).

Train

Belgium built continental Europe's first railway line (Brussels-Mechelen) in the 1830s. The national network is run by the Belgische Spoorwegen/Société National des Chemins de Fer Belges, whose logo is a 'B' in an oval. Major train stations have information offices, usually open until about 7 pm (later in Brussels). For all international inquiries – including Eurostar and Thalys trains – call ☎ 0900-10366 (f18 per minute).

Brussels is the international hub and has three main train stations – Gare du Nord, Gare du Midi, and Gare Centrale. Gare du Midi is the main station for international connections: the Eurostar and Thalys fast trains stop here only.

All other international trains stop at Gare du Nord and Gare du Midi.

Eurostar trains between Brussels and London (2¾ hours, 10 trains per day) operate through the Channel Tunnel. Standard 2nd-class fares are f6500/13,000 one-way/return, but cheaper weekend and mid-week fares are available (conditions apply). For more, check www.eurostar.com on the Web.

Thalys fast trains connect Brussels with Paris (f2180, 1½ hours, hourly), Cologne (f1230, 2½ hours, seven trains per day) and Amsterdam (f1310, 2¾ hours, five per day). However, as these trains are still using old tracks through Belgium, Germany and the Netherlands, there is as yet little difference in journey time between the Thalys and ordinary trains on these legs.

In general, Thalys prices are reduced on weekends and those aged under 26 get a 50% discount. For more details see www.thalys.com.

Examples of one-way, 2nd-class adult fares and journey times with ordinary trains from Brussels to some neighbouring countries include Amsterdam (f1150, three hours, hourly trains), Cologne (f1150, three hours, every two hours), and Luxembourg City (f920, 2¾ hours, hourly). To London's Charing Cross station (five hours), there's a train-boat-train combo which costs f1440/2160 one-way/return. On weekends, all return fares are reduced by 40%.

Car & Motorcycle

The main motorways into Belgium are the E19 from the Netherlands, the E40 from Germany, the E411 from Luxembourg and the E17 and E19 from France. For details on car ferries between Belgium and the UK, see the following section.

SEA

Hoverspeed's high-speed Seacat sails from Ostend to Dover (England) in two hours (two to five services per day). One-way fares for cars plus one adult range from f4792 to f9274, depending on the season. Passengers are charged f1642.

P&O/North Sea Ferries sails overnight from Zeebrugge to Hull (14 hours) and charges f3700/7660 for a car in the low/high season and f2300/4900 for adult passengers. Cabins start at f888 per person.

There's no departure tax when leaving by sea.

Getting Around

BUS

Buses connect towns and villages in more remote areas, particularly throughout the Ardennes. Local tourist offices will generally have details, or contact the regional bus information office in Namur (see the Namur Getting There & Away section later in this chapter for details).

TRAIN

Belgium's transport system is dominated by its efficient rail network. There are four levels of service: InterCity (IC) trains (which are the fastest), InterRegional (IR), local (L) and peak-hour (P) commuter trains. Depending on the line, there will be an IC and an IR train every half-hour or hour. Most train stations have either luggage lockers (f60/100 for small/large lockers for 24 hours) or luggage rooms, which are generally open 5 am until midnight and charge f60 per article per day. For all national train information, call ☎ 02-555 25 55.

Costs

First-class fares are 50% more than 2nd class. On weekends, return tickets within Belgium are reduced by 40% for the first passenger and 60% for the rest of the group (to a maximum of six people). Discount excursion tickets, known as B-Excursions, to a huge number of destinations around the country are also available.

Several rail passes are available. The Benelux Tourrail, which gives five days travel in one month in Belgium, the Netherlands and

BELGIUM

Luxembourg, costs f6600/4400 in 1st/2nd class for adults and f3400 (2nd class only) for those aged under 26. This pass can no longer be bought in the Netherlands, but passes bought in either Belgium or Luxembourg are valid for all three countries.

The Belgian Tourrail pass gives five days travel in one month within Belgium for f3230/2100 in 1st/2nd class. A Fixed Price Reduction Card (f650) gives up to 50% off all train tickets for a month. The Go Pass (f1490; under 26 only) gives 10 one-way journeys anywhere in Belgium and is valid for six months.

CAR & MOTORCYCLE

Drive on the right and give way to the right. The speed limit is 50km/h in towns, 90km/h outside and 120km/h on motorways. The blood alcohol limit is 0.05%. Fuel prices per litre are f44 for super, f42 for lead-free and f30 for diesel. More motoring information can be obtained from the Touring Club de Belgique (☎ 02-233 22 11), Rue de la Loi 44, 1040 Brussels.

BICYCLE

Bicycles are popular in the flat north, and many roads have separate cycle lanes. Normal/mountain bikes can be hired from some train stations for f365/680 per day (plus a f500/1500 deposit). They must be returned to the same station. Bikes can be taken on trains (only from stations in cities and major towns) for f150.

HITCHING

Its illegal on motorways and you'll find few Belgians hitching these days. TaxiStop agencies (see Travel Agencies in the Brussels Information section) match drivers with travellers on the road for a reasonable fee.

LOCAL TRANSPORT

Buses and trams (and small metro systems in Brussels and Antwerp) are efficient and reliable. Single tickets cost f40 to f50 but often you can buy a multistrip ticket – 10 strips for f300 to f350 – or a one-day card for about f115. Services generally run until about 11 pm or midnight.

Taxis are metered and expensive. You'll find them outside train stations.

ORGANISED TOURS

From Brussels, it's possible to take day trips by bus to Ghent, Bruges and Antwerp, or even to the Ardennes and Luxembourg City, Paris or Cologne. The main operator is De Boeck (☎ 02-513 77 44), Rue de la Colline 8, 1000 Brussels.

Brussels

☎ 02 • pop 977,868

Brussels (Brussel in Flemish, Bruxelles in French) is an unpretentious mix of grand edifices and modern skyscrapers. Its character largely follows that of the nation it governs: modest, confident, but rarely striving to overtly impress. Having grown from a 6th-century marshy village on the banks of the Senne River (filled in long ago for sanitary reasons), this bilingual city is now headquarters of the EU and NATO, and home to Europe's most impressive central square.

Orientation

The Grand Place, Brussels' imposing 15th-century market square, sits dead centre in the Petit Ring, a pentagon of boulevards enclosing central Brussels. Many of the main sights are within the Ring, but there's also plenty to see outside. Gare Centrale, Brussels' most central train station, is about five minutes' walk from the Grand Place; Gare du Midi, where most international trains arrive, is 2.5km from the famous square.

Almost everything in Brussels – from the names of streets to train stations – is written in both French and Flemish. We have used the French versions here.

Information

Tourist Offices There are two offices: one for Brussels, the other for national information.

Tourist Information Brussels (TIB; ☎ 02-513 89 40, fax 02-514 45 38, ✉ tourism.brus sels@tib.be), in the city hall on the Grand Place, is open 9 am to 6 pm daily (10 am to 2 pm Sunday from October to December). It sells two discount passes – the Must of Brussels (f600), which gives access to most of the top attractions, and the Brussels Passport (f300), a booklet containing discounts to museums/restaurants and two public transport one-day cards.

The national office (☎ 02-504 03 90, fax 02-504 02 70), Rue du Marché aux Herbes 63, is open 9 am to 6 pm daily (until 1 pm Sunday from November to April).

Money Outside banking hours, there are exchange bureaus at the airport, at Gare Centrale and Gare du Nord (both open until 9 pm) and at Gare du Midi (until 10 pm). ATMs are at the airport and at Citibank, Carrefour de l'Europe 13, immediately opposite Gare Centrale. A good central exchange agency (cash only) is Basle, Rue au Beurre 23. Thomas Cook (☎ 02-513 28 45) is at Grand Place 4.

Post & Communications The main post office is in the Centre Monnaie (1st floor) on Blvd Anspach near Place de Brouckère, and is open 8 am to 6 pm weekdays and 9.30 am to 3 pm Saturday.

The Belgacom Téléboutique (fax 02-540 67 85) on Blvd de l'Impératrice is open 9 am to 6 pm Monday to Saturday.

Email & Internet Access The city's premier cybercafe is CyberTheatre (☎ 02-500 78 78, @ info@cybertheatre.net), Ave de la Toison d'Or 4. It charges f250 per hour, and is open 10 am to 11 pm Monday to Saturday. More central is Point Net Surf (☎ 02-513 14 15, @ info@pointnet.be), Petite Rue des Bouchers 16, which charges f140 per half-hour, or f200 per hour.

Travel Agencies AirStop/TaxiStop (☎ 070-23 31 88 for AirStop; ☎ 02-223 23 10 for TaxiStop), Rue du Fossé aux Loups 28, offer cheap charter flights and paid rides (f1.3 per kilometre) in cars going to other European cities. A good general travel agency is usit/CONNECTIONS (☎ 02-550 01 30), Rue du Midi 19.

Bookshops Waterstones (☎ 02-219 27 08), Blvd Adolphe Max 71, and Sterling Books (☎ 02-223 62 23), Rue du Fossé aux Loups 38, are specialist English-language bookshops.

Laundry Lavoir Friza, Rue Haute, and Wash Club, Place St Géry 25, are self-service laundries.

Medical & Emergency Services For 24-hour medical emergencies including ambulance services, dial ☎ 100. Helpline (☎ 02-648 40 14) is a Brussels-based, 24-hour English-speaking crisis line and information service.

Things to See & Do

The **Grand Place** is the obvious start for exploring within the Petit Ring. It was formerly home to the craft guilds, whose rich guildhalls – topped by golden figures which glisten by day and are illuminated by night – line the square.

Off the Grand Place to the south on Rue Charles Buls is one of the earliest works of the city's once-famous Art Nouveau cult – an 1899 **gilded plaque** dedicated to the city by its appreciative artists. It's beside a reclining **statue of Everard 't Serclaes**, a 14th-century hero whose gleaming torso passers-by rub for good luck.

Manneken Pis, the famous statue of a small boy weeing, is a couple of blocks to the south-west on the corner of Rue du Chêne and Rue de l'Étuve.

One block north-east of the Grand Place is the **Galeries St Hubert**, Europe's oldest glass-covered shopping arcade (and home to Neuhaus, one of the city's finest chocolate shops) and, farther north, the impressive **Centre Belge de la Bande Dessinée** (see the Museum section). Alternatively, head east up the hill past the Gare Centrale to Rue Royale and the refinement of the upper town. Here, near the **Palais Royal** and Paul Saintenoy's Art Nouveau showpiece, the **Old England Building**, you'll find the **Musées Royaux des Beaux-Arts** (see the Museum section for details). From here it's a short walk to the **Sablon**, an exclusive area known for its many antique shops.

Museums The Grand Place is home to several museums, the most interesting of which is the **Musée de la Ville de Bruxelles** in the Maison du Roi. It gives a historical rundown on the city and exhibits every piece of clothing ever worn by Manneken Pis. It's open 10 am to 12.30 pm and 1.30 to 4 or 5 pm Monday to Thursday, and 10 am to 1 pm weekends; entry costs f100 (concession f80).

BELGIUM

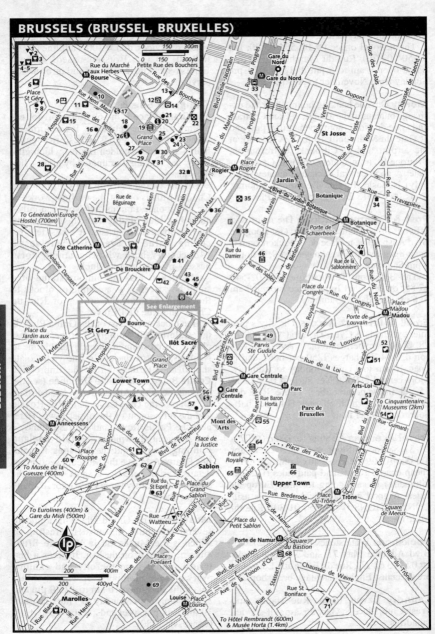

BRUSSELS (BRUSSEL, BRUXELLES)

BRUSSELS (BRUSSEL, BRUXELLES)

	PLACES TO STAY				
30	Hôtel Saint Michel	15	Ancienne Belgique	35	City 2 Shopping Centre
32	Hôtel Le Dixseptième	28	Tels Quels	36	Waterstones (Bookshop)
34	Centre Vincent van Gogh	39	Le Wings	40	Eurolines
37	Hôtel Noga	48	À la Mort Subite	42	Main Post Office
38	Sleep Well Hostel	61	La Fleur en Papier Doré	43	AirStop/TaxiStop
41	Hôtel Métropole	70	La Démence	44	Théâtre Royal de la Monnaie
47	Jacques Brel Hostel			45	Sterling Books
59	Hôtel à la Grande Cloche		OTHER	46	Centre Belge de la Bande
62	Bruegel Hostel	7	Wash Club		Dessinée
		9	Kladaradatch! Palace	49	Saints Michel & Gudule
	PLACES TO EAT	10	Bourse (Stock Exchange)		Cathedral
1	Kasbash	12	Point Net Surf	50	Belgacom Téléboutique
2	Le Pain Quotidien	14	Théâtre Royal de Toone	51	French Embassy
4	Fin de Siècle	16	usit/CONNECTIONS	52	NZ Embassy
8	Sushi Factory	17	Basle	53	USA Embassy
13	Aux Armes de Bruxelles	18	Thomas Cook	54	Australian Embassy
23	Panos	19	Musée de la Ville de Bruxelles	55	Palais des Beaux-Arts
31	Frites/Pitta Places	20	National Tourist Office	56	Citibank
60	Comme Chez Soi	21	De Biertempel	57	Artemys Bookshop
67	Le Perroquet	22	Galeries St Hubert	58	Manneken Pis
71	L'Ultime Atome	24	De Boeck	63	Lavoir Friza
		25	Godiva	64	Musée des Instruments de
	PLACES TO DRINK	26	Tourist Information Brussels		Musique
3	L'Archiduc		(TIB)	65	Musées Royaux des
5	Le Greenwich	27	Hôtel de Ville (City Hall)		Beaux-Arts
6	Mappa Mundo	29	Art-Nouveau Gilded Plaque	66	Palais Royal
11	Falstaff	33	Eurolines Bus Station/Main	67	CyberTheatre
			Office	69	Palais de Justice

BELGIUM

The **Musées Royaux des Beaux-Arts**, Rue de la Régence 3, houses Belgium's premier collections of ancient and modern art. The Flemish Primitives, Brueghel and Rubens are all well represented. It's open 10 am to 5 pm Tuesday to Sunday; admission is f150 (concession f100). Visit the Web site at www.fine-arts-museum.be.

The nearby **Musée des Instruments de Musique**, Place Royale, boasts the world's biggest collection of musical instruments. What's more, it has just relocated to the stunning Old England building – check with the TIB for new opening times and prices.

Tintin fans must not miss the **Centre Belge de la Bande Dessinée**, Rue des Sables 20. It has the nation's best ensemble of comic-strip art, and occupies an airy Art Nouveau building designed by Horta. It's open 10 am to 6 pm Tuesday to Sunday; admission is f200.

There are several museums to draw you out of the Petit Ring. The **Musée Horta**, Rue Américaine 25 in St Gilles, was Horta's house

and is an excellent introduction to his architectural movement – open 2 to 5.30 pm daily except Monday; admission is f150/200 on weekdays/weekends (tram: No 92).

To the east, **Cinquantenaire** is a large museum conglomerate – art, history, military and motor vehicles sit together in a huge complex (metro: Mérode).

About 500m north-west of Gare du Midi is the **Musée Bruxellois de la Gueuze**, Rue Gheude 56 in Anderlecht – a working brewery still using traditional methods, and where you can sample Brussels' unique gueuze beer. It's open 8.30 am to 5 pm weekdays and 10 am to 5 pm Saturday; entry is f100 and includes a drink.

Other Attractions The Atomium, Blvd du Centenaire in the northern suburb of Laeken, is the space-age leftover from the 1958 World Fair. It's open 9 am to 8 pm daily (10 am to 6 pm from 1 September to 31 March); entry is f200 (concession f150). Take tram No 81 to Heysel.

The biggest **market** is Sunday morning's food and general goods market around Gare du Midi.

Organised Tours

Three-hour bus tours of Brussels are run by De Boeck (☎ 02-513 77 44), Rue de la Colline 8 (just off the Grand Place).

From 1 June to 15 September, Chatterbus (☎ 02-673 18 35), Rue des Thuyas 12, has three-hour walking/minibus tours led by Brusselians; phone for details.

For specialised tours – Horta and Art Nouveau, or Brussels in the Art Deco era, for example – contact ARAU (☎ 02-219 33 45), Blvd Adolphe Max 55.

Both Chatterbus and ARAU tours can be booked at the TIB.

Special Events

The most prestigious annual event is Ommegang, a 16th-century-style procession staged within the illuminated Grand Place in early July. Just as popular is the biennial flower carpet that colours the square in mid-August every second year (even-numbered years).

Places to Stay

Visitors can find good accommodation deals on weekends – Friday to Sunday – when many hotels cut prices to compensate for the absence of businesspeople.

Camping Heading south, *Beersel* (☎ 02-331 05 61, fax 02-378 19 77, *Steenweg op Ukkel 75)* is a small ground which charges f100/80 for an adult/child and f80/50 per tent/car, and is open all year. Tram No 55 (direction: Uccle) stops 3km away, from where you take bus UB to Beersel.

Hostels Three HI-affiliated hostels are dotted around Brussels, all with the same prices – singles/doubles for f800/1170 and dorms from f420 to f495 per person. The most central is *Bruegel* (☎ 02-511 04 36, ✉ *jeugdherberg.bruegel@ping.be, Rue du St Esprit 2)*. About 15 minutes' walk from the centre is *Jacques Brel* (☎ 02-218 01 87, fax 02-219 14 51, ✉ *brussels.brel@laj.be, Rue de la Sablonnière 30)* and there's *Génération Europe* (☎ 02-410 38 58, fax 02-410 39 05, ✉ *gener .europe@infonie.be, Rue de l'Éléphant 4)*, a 20-minute walk north-west of the Grand Place.

Central, modern and very popular is *Sleep Well* (☎ 02-218 50 50, fax 02-218 13 13, ✉ *info@sleepwell.be, Rue du Damier 23)*. Single/double rooms go for f695/1140, and there are six/eight-bed dorms for f410/350 per person.

Centre Vincent van Gogh (☎ 02-217 01 58, fax 02-219 79 95, ✉ *chab@ping.be, Rue Traversière 8)* is more laid-back but just as likable. Rooms cost f700/1160, four/six-bed dorms go for f480/410 and eight to 10-bed dorms are f340. It's 1.25km north, uphill from Gare Centrale or take the metro to Botanique.

Guesthouses For B&B accommodation, contact Bed & Brussels (☎ 02-646 07 37, fax 02-644 01 14), Rue Gustave Biot 2, 1050 Brussels, or visit www.BnB-Brussels.be. Prices start at f1200/2000 for a single/double room, and rise to f1800/3000 (there's a 30% surcharge for bookings of just one night).

Hotels The *Hôtel à la Grande Cloche* (☎ 02-512 61 40, fax 02-512 65 91, ✉ *info@ hotelgrandecloche.com, Place Rouppe 10)* has well-kept doubles without private bathroom for f1750, or f2350 with. Just off Ave Louise is the homy *Hôtel Rembrandt* (☎ 02-512 71 39, fax 02-511 71 36, Rue de la Concorde 42)*. Immaculate single/double rooms with classical furnishings go for f1400/2300, or f1900/2600 with private facilities.

The city's best mid-range choice is *Hôtel Noga* (☎ 02-218 67 63, fax 02-218 16 03, ✉ *info@nogahotel.com, Rue du Béguinage 38)*. This charming hotel is well positioned in the Ste Catherine quarter, 10 minutes' walk from the Grand Place, and has rooms from f2950/3300 (discounted to f2600 on weekends). If you'd prefer to be dead centre, *Hôtel Saint Michel* (☎ 02-511 09 56, fax 02-511 46 00, Grand Place 11)* is the place. Predictably, it's overpriced – rooms from f4250/5100 – but that's to be expected with such a unique location.

Top-end hotels are abundant. The most charming is *Hôtel Le Dixseptième* (☎ 02-502 57 44, fax 02-502 64 24, ✉ *ledixseptieme@ net7.be, Rue de la Madeleine 25)*, which has

BELGIUM

rooms from f6300/7100 (or f5400/6400 on weekends). For *belle époque* luxury, head to *Hôtel Métropole* (☎ 02-217 23 00, fax 02-218 02 20, ✉ info@metropolehotel.be, Place de Brouckère 31) where rooms start at f10,500/12,500. On weekends, these drop to f4500 (email bookings only), or f6500/8500 for other bookings.

Places to Eat
Restaurants Brussels' dining heart is Rue des Bouchers (Butcher's Street), near the Grand Place. Here you'll find lobster, crab, mussels and fish awaiting conspicuous consumption in one terrace restaurant after another. Most are tourist traps – *Aux Armes de Bruxelles* (☎ 02-511 55 98, Rue des Bouchers 13) is a notable exception. Expect efficient service, Belgian classics and main courses for about f500.

Fin de Siècle (☎ 513 51 23, Rue des Chartreux 9) is a popular bistro with a blackboard menu and meals in the f350 to f450 bracket.

Kasbash (☎ 02-502 40 26, Rue Antoine Dansaert 20) is a lovely, lantern-lit restaurant on one of the city's trendiest streets. Moroccan dishes – couscous (f400 to f500) and *tajines* (meat-based stews) – are the order of the day.

Ask any Bruxellois to name the city's finest restaurant and the answer is always *Comme Chez Soi* (☎ 02-512 29 21, Place Rouppe 23). The cuisine is French, mains start at f1000 and reservations are essential.

Cafes For wholesome savoury pies and filled sandwiches in a pleasant nonsmoking environment, head to *Le Pain Quotidien* (☎ 02-502 23 61, Rue Antoine Dansaert 16), a country-style bakery-cum-tearoom. In the Sablon, *Le Perroquet* (☎ 02-512 99 22, Rue Watteeu 31) is a lovely Art Nouveau cafe with a great range of salads (f175 to f375), exotic stuffed pitta bread (from f170) and vegetarian fare. *L'Ultime Atome* (☎ 02-513 48 84, Rue St Boniface 14) is a bit off the beaten track but the ambience is invigorating, the food eclectic, and the kitchen is open until midnight.

Fast Food Rue Marché aux Fromages near the Grand Place is stacked with *frites/pitta-bread places*. For a half-baguette sandwich, head to *Panos* (Rue du Marché aux Herbes

85). Japanese snacks are available from the *Sushi Factory* (Place St Géry 28).

Self-Catering There's a *GB supermarket* in the basement of the City 2 shopping centre on Rue Neuve, open until 8 pm Monday to Saturday.

Entertainment
The *Bulletin's* 'What's On' guide lists live contemporary and classical music, opera and the cinema scene. Otherwise, there are enough bars and cafes to keep you on a very long pub crawl. *Falstaff* (Rue Henri Maus 17) is an Art Nouveau showpiece popular with tourists. *Mappa Mundo* (Rue du Pont de la Carpe 2) is where the young and trendy flock. Those into Art Deco and live jazz shouldn't go past the *L'Archiduc* (Rue Antoine Dansaert 6). *Le Greenwich* (Rue des Chartreux 7), *À la Mort Subite* (Rue Mont aux Herbes Potagères 7) and *La Fleur en Papier Doré* (Rue des Alexiens 53) are three wonderful ancient cafes each with a unique ambience.

The biggest gay rave is *La Démence* (Rue Blaes 208) held one Sunday per month at the Fuse, a techno/house club. *Le Wings* (Rue du Cyprès 3) is a lesbian disco (Saturday only).

For local and international bands, check out the line-up at the *Ancienne Belgique* (☎ 02-548 24 24, Blvd Anspach 110). The main performing arts venues are the *Palais des Beaux-Arts* (☎ 02-507 82 00, Rue Ravenstein 23) and the *Théâtre Royal de la Monnaie* (☎ 070-233 939, Place de la Monnaie). A good central cinema is *Kladaradatch! Palace* (☎ 02-501 67 76, Blvd Anspach 85).

For something a bit different, head to *Théâtre Royal de Toone* (Petite Rue des Bouchers), a popular marionette theatre where the cast speak the local Brussels dialect.

Shopping
Head to the Sablon area for antiques. Neuhaus, in the Galeries St Hubert, and Godiva at Grand Place 37, are just two of the many exclusive chocolate shops. De Biertempel, Rue du Marché aux Herbes 56, stocks some 250 sorts of Belgian beers. Rue Antoine Dansaert is good for avant-garde fashion.

BELGIUM

Getting There & Away

Air Airline offices in Brussels include British Airways (☎ 02-548 21 33), Rue du Trône 98; KLM (☎ 02-717 20 70), Rue Maurice Charlent 53; and Sabena (☎ 02-723 23 23) at Zaventem airport.

Bus Eurolines has three offices in Brussels. The main office (☎ 02-274 13 50), Rue du Progrès 80, is next to Gare du Nord. Most of its buses depart from here. A more central office (☎ 02-217 00 25) is at Place de Brouckère 50; the third office (☎ 02-538 20 49) is at Ave Fonsny 9 near Gare du Midi. For details on fares and schedules, see the main Getting There & Away section earlier in this chapter.

Train There are train information offices, open until 9 or 10 pm, at all three stations. For all national inquiries, call ☎ 02-555 25 55.

For prices and journey times from Brussels to other Belgian cities and towns, check the Getting There & Away sections for those places. For international services, see the Getting There & Away section at the beginning of this chapter.

Getting Around

Brussels' transport network consists of buses, trams and a metro. Transport maps are handed out from the tourist offices or metro information kiosks.

To/From the Airport The national airport, Zaventem, is connected to all three central stations by four trains per hour (f90, 20 minutes). Taxis generally charge about f1000.

Public Transport Brussels' efficient bus, tram and metro network is operated by the Société des Transports Intercommunaux de Bruxelles (STIB in French, MIVB in Flemish). Single-journey tickets cost f50, five/10-journey cards f240/350 and a one-day card f140. Valid on all transport, tickets can be bought from metro stations or bus drivers; the one-day card is also available from the TIB. Public transport runs until about midnight.

Car Car rental (including insurance, VAT and unlimited kilometres) starts at about f2300 a day or f8000 a week. Rental firms include Avis (☎ 02-537 12 80) Rue Américaine 145; Budget (☎ 02-646 51 30) Ave Louise 327b; Hertz (☎ 02-513 28 86) Blvd Maurice Lemonnier 8; and National/Alamo (☎ 02-753 20 60) at Zaventem airport.

Taxi There are plenty of ranks, or phone Taxis Bleus (☎ 02-268 00 00) or Taxis Verts (☎ 02-349 49 49).

AROUND BRUSSELS

A huge stone lion and nearly a million visitors a year look out over the plains where Napoleon was defeated and European history changed course at the Battle of **Waterloo**, south of Brussels. At the base of the **Butte du Lion** is a **Visitor's Centre** (☎ 02-385 19 12) at Route du Lion 254 – take bus W from Place Rouppe in Brussels. Those interested in the British version of events should head to the **Musée Wellington**, Chaussée de Bruxelles 147, 5km away in the village of Waterloo – bus W also passes here. To the south-east of Brussels is the **Forêt de Soignes**, a beech and oak forest covering some 43 sq km and an ideal spot for walking.

The **Musée Royal de l'Afrique Centrale**, Leuvensesteenweg 13 at Tervuren, is 14km to the east. It contains fascinating artefacts from the Democratic Republic of Congo (formerly Zaïre), collected during the scandalous reign of Léopold II. Admission is f80 (concession f40). It's closed Monday; take the metro to Montgomery, then tram No 44.

About 25km east of Brussels, **Leuven** (Louvain in French) is a lively student town and home to Belgium's oldest university (dating from 1425). The town's main sight is the 15th-century town hall, a flamboyant structure with terraced turrets and wrought stonework. From Brussels, there are two trains an hour (f140, 30 minutes).

Antwerp

☎ 03 • pop 456,706

Second in size to the capital and often more likable, Antwerp (Antwerpen in Flemish, Anvers in French) is perhaps Belgium's most underrated tourist city. It's compact and beautifully endowed with baroque buildings, and was once home to 17th-century artist Pieter Paul Rubens.

With a prime spot on the Schelde River, Antwerp came to the fore as Western Europe's greatest economic centre in the early 16th century. But the times of prosperity were relatively short-lived. When Protestants smashed up the city's cathedral in 1566 as part of the Iconoclastic Fury, the Spanish ruler Philip II sent troops to take control. Ten years later the unpaid garrison mutinied, ransacking the city – in three nights they massacred 8000 people in the Spanish Fury. The final blow came in 1648, when the Dutch closed the Schelde to all non-Dutch ships, blocking Antwerp's vital link to the sea. It wasn't until Napoleon arrived and the French rebuilt the docks that Antwerp got back on its feet.

Today it's brimming with self-confidence. As a world port, its air is international, though at times seedy, while behind the discreet facades of the Jewish quarter the world's largest diamond-cutting industry is run.

Orientation

Antwerp is bordered by the Schelde and the Ring, a highway built on a moat which once encircled the city. Many of the sights are concentrated between the impressive Centraal Station and the old centre – a 20-minute walk away, based around the Grote Markt. Other sights are spread around Het Zuid, the city's trendiest area (about 1.25km south of the Grote Markt).

Information

Tourist Office The tourist office (☎ 03-232 01 03, fax 03-231 19 37, ✉ toerisme@ antwerpen.be), Grote Markt 15, is open 9 am to 6 pm daily (until 5 pm Sunday).

Money Good exchange rates (cash only) are offered by Leo Stevens exchange bureau, De Keyserlei 64 near Centraal Station; it's open 9 am to 5 pm weekdays, until 1 pm Saturday. There's a Kredietbank at Eiermarkt 20, in the base of the Torengebouw (Europe's first skyscraper). Thomas Cook (☎ 03-226 29 53), Koningin Astridplein 33, is open until 9 pm daily.

Post & Communications The main post office is at Groenplaats 43; there's also a branch office opposite Centraal Station and another on Jezusstraat. There's a Belgacom

Teleboetiek at Jezusstraat 1. For Internet access, head to the cybercafe 2Zones (☎ 03-232 24 00), Wolstraat 15.

Bookshops De Slegte (☎ 03-231 66 27), Wapper 5, has a good range of second-hand English novels; more can be found at Jenny Hannivers, a tiny bookshop at Melkmarkt 30. For travel guides and maps, there's the VTB Reisboekhandel (☎ 03-220 33 66), St Jacobsmarkt 45, or FNAC (☎ 03-231 20 56), Groenplaats 31.

Laundry There's a Wassalon located at Nationalestraat 18.

Things to See & Do

The city's skyline is best viewed from the raised **promenades**, known as *wandelterrassen*, leading off from Steenplein, or from the river's west bank, accessible by the **St Annatunnel**, a pedestrian tunnel under the Schelde at St Jansvliet.

Museums The major museums mostly charge f100 (concession f50), or you can buy a three-museum discount ticket for f200. All those listed here are, unless stated otherwise, open 10 am to 4.45 pm Tuesday to Saturday.

The **Rubenshuis** (Rubens' House), Wapper 9, tops most visitors' lists although the artist's most noted works are in the Onze Lieve Vrouwkathedraal. Admission costs f100. Another fine 17th-century home is the **Rockoxhuis**, Keizerstraat 10; admission is free. For more Rubens, as well as Flemish Primitives and contemporary works, there's the **Koninklijk Museum voor Schone Kunsten** (Royal Museum of Fine Arts), Leopold de Waelplaats 1-9 in Het Zuid. Admission is f150.

The 16th-century home and workshop of a prosperous printing family, the **Museum Plantin-Moretus**, Vrijdagmarkt 22, displays antique presses and splendid old globes; admission costs f100. The **Steen**, the city's medieval riverside castle at Steenplein, houses a maritime museum; entry is f100. The **Diamantmuseum**, Lange Herentalsestraat 31, traces aspects of the city's diamond industry, and is open 10 am to 5 pm daily (admission free).

To get a glimpse of the amount of diamonds and gold being traded in Antwerp, just

BELGIUM

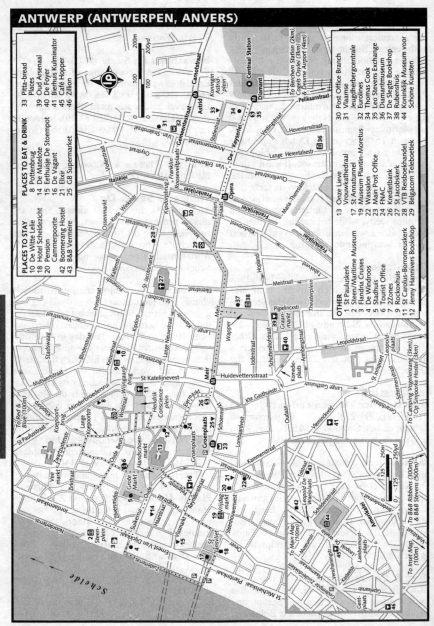

ANTWERP (ANTWERPEN, ANVERS)

PLACES TO STAY
10 De Witte Lelie
18 Hotel Scheldezicht
20 Pension
     Cammerpoorte
42 Boomerang Hostel
43 B&B Vermire

PLACES TO EAT & DRINK
8 Pottenbrug
14 De Matelote
15 Eethuisje De Stoempot
16 De Vagant
21 Elixr
25 GB Supermarket
33 Pitta-bread
     Places
39 Oud Arsenaal
40 De Foyer
41 Bierhuis Kulminator
45 Café Hopper
46 Zillion

OTHER
1 St Pauluskerk
2 Steen/Maritime Museum
3 Flandria Cruises
4 De Windroos
5 Stadhuis
6 Tourist Office
7 2Zones
9 Rockoxhuis
11 St Carolus-Borromeuskerk
12 Jenny Hanivers Bookshop
13 Onze Lieve
     Vrouwkathedraal
17 St Annatunnel
19 Museum Plantin-Moretus
22 Wassalon
23 Main Post Office
24 FNAC
26 Kredietbank
27 St Jacobskerk
28 VTB Reisboekhandel
29 Belg.com Teleboetiek
30 Post Office Branch
31 Vlaamse
     Jeugdherbergcentrale
32 Eurolines
34 Thomas Cook
35 Leo Stevens Exchange
36 Diamantmuseum
37 De Slegte Bookshop
38 Rubenshuis
44 Koninklijk Museum voor
     Schone Kunsten

BELGIUM

wander along Pelikaanstraat or Vestingstraat near Centraal Station any time during the day (except Saturday when Shabbat, the Jewish holy day, closes everything down).

Onze Lieve Vrouwkathedraal With its 120m spire, the splendid Cathedral of Our Lady is Belgium's largest Gothic cathedral and home to Rubens' *Descent from the Cross*. Entry is from Handschoenmarkt; it's open 10 am to 5 pm weekdays, to 3 pm Saturday, 1 to 4 pm Sunday, and costs f70 (concession f40).

Cogels-Osylei This is a street of radical *fin-de-siècle* houses built in eclectic styles from Art Nouveau to classical or neo-Renaissance. It's a little way from the centre but well worth a wander – tram No 11 runs along it.

Boat Trips Flandria (☎ 03-231 31 00) on Steenplein offers cruises on the Schelde (f260, 50 minutes) or around the port (f450, 2½ hours).

Markets On Friday mornings, the Vrijdagmarkt has second-hand goods. On Saturday the Vogelmarkt (Bird Market), held on Theaterplein, is a lively food market; on Sunday it has general stuff. Hoogstraat and Kloosterstraat are good hunting grounds for bric-a-brac.

Places to Stay
In summer, it's wise to reserve B&Bs and hotels in advance.

Camping There are two camping grounds, both open from April to September and charging f70 for a person, plus f35 for a tent, caravan or a car. *De Molen* (☎ 03-219 81 79, St Annastrand) is on the west bank of the Schelde (bus No 81 or 82). *Vogelzang* (☎ 03-238 57 17, Vogelzanglaan) is near the Bouwcentrum (tram No 2, direction 'Hoboken').

Hostels The HI-affiliated hostel, *Op Sinjoorke* (☎ 03-238 02 73, fax 03-248 19 32, Eric Sasselaan 2) is about 10 minutes by tram No 2 (direction: Hoboken) or bus No 27 (direction: Zuid, ie, south) from Centraal Station – get off at Bouwcentrum and follow the signs.

The laid-back *Boomerang* (☎ 03-238 47 82, fax 03-288 66 67, Volkstraat 49) has

dorms for f360 – get bus No 23 (direction: Zuid) from Centraal Station.

Guesthouses The number of B&Bs in Antwerp grows each year; ask the tourist office for its current list. Particularly nice is *B&B Stevens* (☎ 03-259 15 90, fax 03-259 15 99, ✉ fdj.greta@wol.be, Molenstraat 35), which has single/double rooms from f1250/1900 (more on weekends). *B&B Ribbens* (☎ 03-248 15 39, Justitiestraat 43) is wonderfully spacious and charges f1250/1700. For a peak inside a local artist's home, head to *B&B Vermeire* (☎ 03-237 07 13, fax 03-248 44 06, ✉ vascobel@glo.be, Tolstraat 26). Rooms cost f1600/1850 and have shared bathroom facilities.

Hotels The *Hotel Scheldezicht* (☎ 03-231 66 02, fax 03-231 90 02, St Jansvliet 2) is a new hotel in a great location near the river. Rooms are spacious and well priced at f1250/1850. A sage mid-range choice is *Pension Cammerpoorte* (☎ 03-231 28 36, fax 03-226 28 43, ✉ jactoe@net4all.be, Steenhouwersvest 55). Tucked away on a quiet street in the heart of town, it has 16 bright rooms for f1950/2450. *De Witte Lelie* (☎ 03-266 19 66, fax 03-234 00 19, Keizerstraat 16) is the top address in Antwerp. It sports just 10 luxurious rooms furnished in a winning mix of modern and antique. Rates start at f6500/8500.

Places to Eat
For authentic Flemish *stoemp* (mashed potatoes), go no further than *Eethuisje De Stoempot* (☎ 03-231 36 86, Vlasmarkt 12). This down-to-earth eatery offers meals the way mum made them, at prices to match.

Vegetarians should try *Elixir* (☎ 03-231 73 21, Steenhouwersvest 57), a 1st-floor restaurant with a good dagschotel for f345. It's open mainly for lunch, but also 6 to 8 pm on Saturday.

Pottenbrug (☎ 03-231 51 47, Minderbroedersrui 38) is a wonderful old bistro with mains for f520 to f650.

For excellent seafood there's one port of call – *De Matelote* (☎ 03-231 32 07, Haarstraat 9). This exclusive little restaurant does sumptuous main dishes from f850.

Pitta-bread places reign in the streets in front of Centraal Station. Self-caterers will

BELGIUM

find a *GB supermarket* in the basement of the Grand Bazaar shopping centre at Groenplaats.

Entertainment

Antwerp is fast establishing itself as a party city. With some 4000 bars and cafes, you'll be hard-pressed to find a better place to pub crawl.

For terrace cafes, head to Groenplaats or the more intimate Handschoenmarkt. The *Oud Arsenaal (Pijpelincxstraat 4)* is a popular local haunt (and the beers are among the cheapest in town). *De Vagant (Reyndersstraat 21)* serves more than 200 *jenevers* (Belgian gins). *Bierhuis Kulminator (Vleminckveld 32)* is the place to sink a host of Belgian brews – there's more than 600 on the menu. *De Foyer (Komedieplaats 18)* is a highly civilised cafe/bistro on the 1st floor of the neoclassical Bourlaschouwburg theatre.

The big name on the club scene is *Zillion (Jan Van Gentstraat 4)* in Het Zuid. *Red & Blue (Lange Schipperskapelstraat 11)* bills itself as the biggest gay disco in the country. For live jazz, head to *Café Hopper (Leopold De Waelstraat 2)* in Het Zuid.

Getting There & Away

Air Deurne airport, 5km south-east of Antwerp, is connected by bus No 16 from Centraal Station. Taxis cost about f350. For Sabena reservations and information, call ☎ 03-231 68 25.

Bus Eurolines (☎ 03-233 86 62) has an office at Van Stralenstraat 8 – all buses depart from here. For information on fares and routes, see the Getting There & Away section at the start of this chapter.

Train Antwerp has two main train stations – Centraal Station, about 1.5km from the old city centre, and Berchem station, some 2km south-east of Centraal Station. The magnificent Centraal Station is currently undergoing extensive underground expansion. This work is not expected to be finished until 2005, which means you may find train services into Centraal Station disrupted. National connections from Antwerp include IC trains to Brussels (f200, 35 minutes), Bruges (f405,70 minutes) and Ghent (f260, 45 minutes). There are also frequent Thalys trains to Amsterdam (f1110, two hours).

Getting Around

A good network of buses, trams and a premetro (a tram that runs underground for part of its journey) is run by De Lijn. Public transport information kiosks are at premetro station Diamant (in front of Centraal Station) and Groenplaats. The main bus hubs are Koningin Astridplein next to Centraal Station and Franklin Rooseveltplaats a few blocks west. Bikes (f75/hour, f300/day) can be hired from De Windroos (☎ 03-480 93 88), Steenplein 1a.

Ghent

☎ 09 • pop 229,168

Medieval Europe's largest city outside Paris is Ghent (known as Gent in Flemish, Gand in French). Its glory lies in its industrious and rebellious past. Sitting on the junction of the Leie and Schelde Rivers, by the mid-14th century it had become Europe's largest cloth producer, importing wool from England and employing thousands of people. The townsfolk were well known for their armed battles: for civil liberties, and against the heavy taxes imposed on them. Today home to many students, it's not picturesque like Bruges, but ultimately more realistic.

Orientation

Unlike many Belgian cities, Ghent does not have one central square. Instead, the medieval core is a row of open areas separated by two imposing churches and a belfry – their line of towers has long been the trademark of Ghent's skyline. The Korenmarkt is the westernmost square, and is technically the city's centre – it's a 25-minute walk from the main train station, St Pietersstation, but is regularly connected with it by tram Nos 1, 10 and 11. Halfway between the two is the university quarter, based along St Pietersnieuwstraat.

Information

The tourist office (☎ 09-266 52 32, fax 09-225 62 88, ✉ voorlichting@gent.be), Botermarkt 17, is open 9 am to 8 pm daily from April to early November, and 9.30 am to 6 pm the rest of the year.

The Europabank inside St Pietersstation and the Goffin Change at Mageleinstraat 36 are both open daily. The post office is at Lange

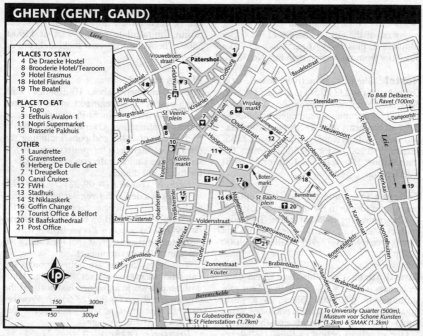

GHENT (GENT, GAND)

PLACES TO STAY
4 De Draecke Hostel
8 Brooderie Hotel/Tearoom
9 Hotel Erasmus
18 Hotel Flandria
19 The Boatel

PLACE TO EAT
2 Togo
3 Eethuis Avalon 1
11 Nopri Supermarket
15 Brasserie Pakhuis

OTHER
1 Laundrette
5 Gravensteen
6 Herberg De Dulle Griet
7 't Dreupelkot
10 Canal Cruises
12 FWH
13 Stadhuis
14 St Niklaaskerk
16 Goffin Change
17 Tourist Office & Belfort
20 St Baafskathedraal
21 Post Office

Kruisstraat 55. Internet users should head to Globetrotter (☎ 09-269 08 60), Kortrijkse Poortstraat 180. There's a laundrette located at Oudburg 25.

Things to See

Ghent's most noted sight is the van Eyck brothers' *Adoration of the Mystic Lamb* housed in the **St Baafskathedraal**. This 15th-century painting is a lavish representation of medieval religious thinking and one of the earliest known oil paintings. The entrance to the cathedral is on St Baafsplein; it's open 8.30 am to 6 pm daily. The crypt with the Mystic Lamb is open 9.30 am to 5 pm Monday to Saturday and 1 to 5 pm Sunday; in winter it's open 10.30 am to noon and 2.30 to 4 pm daily, and 2 to 5 pm Sunday. Entry to the cathedral is free but it costs f100 to see the Mystic Lamb.

Rising from the old Cloth Hall, the 14th-century **belfort** (belfry) on Botermarkt affords spectacular views of the city. Entry costs f100 (concession f60).

With moat, turrets and arrow slits, the fearsome 12th-century **Gravensteen**, St Veerleplein, is the quintessential castle. It was built to protect the townsfolk as well as to intimidate them into law-abiding submission. It's open 9 am to 5 or 6 pm daily and costs f200 (concession f50).

The **Museum voor Schone Kunsten** in Citadelpark is home to some Flemish Primitives and a couple of typically nightmarish works by Hieronymus Bosch. Across the road is **SMAK**, the city's new contemporary art museum. Both museums are open 10 am to 5 or 6 pm (closed Monday), and admission to each is f100 (concession f50).

Organised Tours

City canal cruises (f170, 35 minutes) depart from the Graslei and Korenlei.

Places to Stay

Ghent's dearth of budget accommodation has been eased by the recent proliferation of guesthouses.

Camping The *Camping Blaarmeersen* (☎ *09-221 53 99, Zuiderlaan 12*) is a long way west of the city. It charges f130/60 per adult/child, plus f140/70 per tent/car. Take bus No 9 from the station then bus No 38.

Hostel Ghent's attractive hostel, *De Draecke* (☎ *09-233 70 50, fax 09-233 80 01,* ✉ *youthhostel.gent@skynet.be, St Wido-straat 11*), occupies a renovated warehouse close to the heart of town. A bunk in a six-bed room, with private facilities, costs f385; singles/doubles go for f625/950. From the train station, take tram No 1, 10 or 11 to St Veerleplein.

Colleges From mid-July to late September, single rooms in the university colleges can be rented for f600 per night. To book, contact Mevr van den Branden (☎ *09-264 71 00, fax 09-264 72 96), Stalhof 6, 9000 Ghent.

Guesthouses The Gilde der Gentse Gastenkamers (GGG; ☎ *09-233 30 99), Tentoonstellingslaan 69, 9000 Ghent, is a guild organising the city's B&Bs. It publishes a free booklet (in English) detailing guesthouses.

One excellent option is *B&B Delbaere-Ravet* (☎*/fax 09-233 43 52,* ✉ *sderavet@worldonline.be, Hagelandkaai 38*), which is run by a young couple and has three fantastically spacious rooms for f1000/1600, or f2100/2600 for three/four people. Take bus No 70 from St Pietersstation.

Hotels *Hotel Flandria* (☎ *09-223 06 26, fax 09-233 77 89,* ✉ *gent@flandria-centrum.be, Barrestraat 3*) is a warren of cheap but decent rooms – the rates are f1300/1400 for singles/doubles. Much more atmospheric is *Brooderie* (☎ *09-225 06 23, Jan Breydelstraat 8*). This place is principally a bakery-cum-tearoom but it also has four lovely rooms upstairs. Each has a sink but shared bathroom; the rooms cost f1500/2300.

Hotel Erasmus (☎ *09-224 21 95, fax 09-233 42 41, Poel 25*) is a renovated 16th-century house with 12 rooms, some with stained-glass windows and oak beam ceilings. Prices start at f2500/3650.

The Boatel (☎ *09-267 10 30, fax 09-267 10 39,* ✉ *info@theboatel.com, Voorhoutkaai 29a*) is a renovated canal boat that has recently been turned into a hotel. Its seven bright, immaculate rooms start at f2900/3800. Check it out at www.theboatel.com on the Web.

Places to Eat
The student ghetto, about 10 minutes' walk south-east of the Korenmarkt, is the best area for cheap eats. Here on St Pietersnieuwstraat and its continuation, Overpoortstraat, you'll find plenty of cafes and pubs including the *Overpoort mensa* (*Overpoortstraat 49*), a self-service student cafeteria open weekdays for lunch and dinner.

Eethuis Avalon 1 (☎ *09-224 37 24, Geldmunt 32*) is a delightful vegetarian restaurant with a small outdoor terrace. It's open for lunch only and closed on Sunday. *Brooderie* (☎ *09-225 06 23, Jan Breydelstraat 8*) is a rustic tearoom and a great spot for a snack (in a nonsmoking environment).

Trendy restaurants are dotted around the Patershol quarter, a thicket of cobbled lanes with an old-world ambience just north of the city centre. *Togo* (☎ *09-223 65 51, Vrouwebroerstraat 21*) is a wise choice and specialises in African cuisine.

Brasserie Pakhuis (☎ *09-223 55 55, Schuurkenstraat 4*) is arguably Ghent's hottest dining address. This huge new brasserie-cum-restaurant occupies a beautifully restored textile warehouse on a quiet backstreet and draws young and old alike. The cuisine is eclectic and mains range from f600 to f950.

Self-caterers can find a *Nopri supermarket* at Hoogpoort 42.

Entertainment
The free *Week Up* agenda has cinema, live music and theatre listings – pick it up from cafes or the tourist office.

Herberg De Dulle Griet (*Vrijdagmarkt 50*) is one of the city's best known beer pubs, while *'t Dreupelkot* (*Groentenmarkt 12*) specialises in jenevers and has a pleasant waterfront terrace.

Vooruit (☎ *09-267 28 28, St Pietersnieuwstraat 23*) is *the* venue for dance and performances by visiting theatre companies. Opera is most commonly performed at *De Vlaamse Opera* (☎ *09-225 24 25, Schouwburgstraat 3*).

BELGIUM

Getting There & Away

The Eurolines office (☎ 09-220 90 24), Koningin Elisabethlaan 73, is 100m from the train station. Buses leave from this office.

The train station information office (☎ 09-241 44 44) is open from 7 am to 9 pm daily. There are IC trains to Antwerp (f250, 45 minutes), Bruges (f175, 20 minutes), Brussels (f235, 45 minutes) and Ypres (f315, one hour).

Getting Around

The public transport information kiosk outside the station sells tickets and has free tram/bus maps.

Bruges

☎ 050 • pop 119,239

Known as the 'perfect' tourist attraction, Bruges (Brugge in Flemish) is one of Europe's best-preserved medieval cities and Belgium's most visited town. Its richly ornate 13th-century centre has changed little in the five centuries since the silting of the Zwin River. At that time, Bruges was a prosperous cloth manufacturing town and the centre of Flemish Primitive art. When the river silted Bruges died, its wealthy merchants abandoning it for Antwerp, leaving unoccupied homes and deserted canals.

Today, particularly in summer, this 'living museum' is smothered with people. Go out of season or stay around late on summer evenings, when the carillon chimes seep through the cobbled streets and local boys (illegally) cast their fishing rods into willow-lined canals, and Bruges will show its age-old beauty.

Orientation

Neatly encased by an oval-shaped series of canals, Bruges is an amblers' ultimate dream, its sights sprinkled within leisurely walking distance of its compact centre. There are two central squares, the Markt and the Burg. Many local buses stop at the former, while the more impressive latter is home to the tourist office. The train station is 1.5km south of the Markt – buses shuttle regularly between the two.

Information

Tourist Offices The main tourist office (☎ 050-44 86 86, fax 050-44 86 00, ✆ toer isme@brugge.be), Burg 11, is open 9.30 am

to 6.30 pm weekdays, and 10 am to noon and 2 to 6.30 pm weekends from 1 April to 30 September. From October to March, it's open 9.30 am to 5 pm weekdays, and 9.30 am to 1 pm and 2 to 5.30 pm Saturday. In the foyer is a handful of luggage lockers.

The tiny office (☎ 050-38 80 83) at the train station is open 10.30 am to 1 pm and 2 to 6.30 pm weekdays, and 9.30 am to 1 pm and 2 to 5.30 pm weekends.

Money There's a BBL Bank at Markt 19. Alternatively, you can change cash, albeit usually at lower rates, at the train station ticket counters from 5 am to 10.30 pm daily. Weghsteen & Driege Exchange (☎ 050-33 33 61), Oude Burg 6, has good rates (cash only); it's open weekdays. The exchange bureau at the tourist office is open daily from 1 April to 30 November; the rest of the year it's open weekends only.

Post & Communications The post office is at Markt 5. Faxes can be sent and received at Varicopy (☎ 050-33 59 43, fax 050-34 61 92), Oude Burg 22a. For Internet access, head to The Coffee Link (☎ 050-34 93 52, ✆ info@thecoffeelink.com), Mariastraat 38 in St Janshospitaal (a former hospital).

Laundry The Ipsomat, Langestraat 151, and the Wassalon, Ezelstraat 51, are self-service laundries.

Things to See & Do

There are many sights but also a wealth of things to do, from climbing the belfry to cruising the canals.

You can also start a walking tour at the **Markt**, the city's medieval core, from which rises the mighty **belfort** (see later in this section). The nearby **Burg**, connected to the Markt by an alley lined with lace shops, features Belgium's oldest **Stadhuis** (town hall), as well as the **Heilig Bloed Basiliek** (Basilica of the Holy Blood), where a few coagulated drops of Christ's blood are said to be kept. From the Burg, go through the archway marking Blinde Ezelstraat (Blind Donkey St) to the **Vismarkt** (fish market). From here, Steenhouwersdijk leads into **Groenerei**, a short but delightful promenade along a pretty part of the canal.

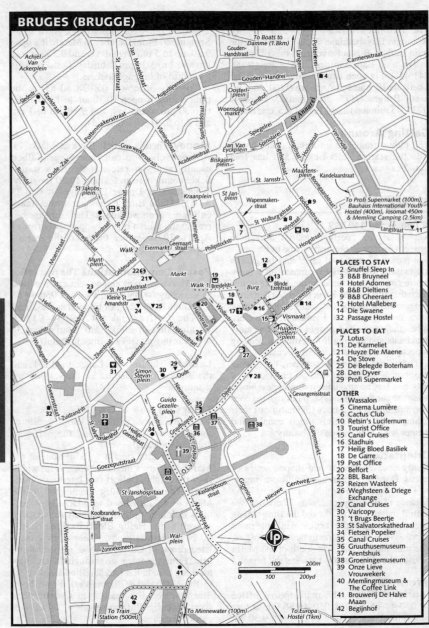

BRUGES (BRUGGE)

PLACES TO STAY
2 Snuffel Sleep In
3 B&B Bruyneel
4 Hotel Adornes
8 B&B Dieltiens
9 B&B Gheeraert
12 Hotel Malleberg
14 Die Swaene
32 Passage Hostel

PLACES TO EAT
7 Lotus
11 De Karmeliet
21 Huyze Die Maene
24 De Stove
25 De Belegde Boterham
28 Den Dyver
29 Profi Supermarket

OTHER
1 Wassalon
5 Cinema Lumière
6 Cactus Club
10 Retsin's Lucifernum
13 Tourist Office
15 Canal Cruises
16 Stadhuis
17 Heilig Bloed Basiliek
18 De Garre
19 Post Office
20 Belfort
22 BBL Bank
23 Reizen Wasteels
26 Weghsteen & Driege Exchange
27 Canal Cruises
30 Varicopy
31 't Brugs Beertje
33 St Salvatorskathedraal
34 Fietsen Popelier
35 Canal Cruises
36 Gruuthusemuseum
37 Arentshuis
38 Groeningemuseum
39 Onze Lieve Vrouwekerk
40 Memlingmuseum & The Coffee Link
41 Brouwerij De Halve Maan
42 Begijnhof

Immediately west of Vismarkt is **Huiden-vettersplein**, a charming little square lined with popular restaurants. This is the start of the **Dijver**, along which you'll find departure points for **canal cruises**, as well as the town's premier museums. Nearby is the **Onze Lieve Vrouwekerk**, which houses Michelangelo's *Madonna and Child*, a delicate statue and his only sculpture to leave Italy in his lifetime. Across from the church, in the old St Janshospitaal complex on Mariastraat, is the prestigious **Memlingmuseum**. Farther south along Mariastraat, signs lead to the **Begijnhof** (see later in this section), from where you can easily cross to the **Minnewater** (Lake of Love), once an inner-city port. The waterway is edged by a tranquil park.

Museums There's a f400 discount ticket (representing a saving of f110) available if you're visiting the Groeninge, Memling, Gruuthuse and Arentshuis museums. These museums are open 9.30 am to 5 pm daily from 1 April to 30 September, and 9.30 am to 12.30 pm and 2 to 5 pm the rest of the year (closed Tuesday).

The **Groeningemuseum**, Dijver 12, is home to the city's prized collection of art from the 14th to 20th centuries. Most notable is the impressive section on Flemish Primitives.

The **Arentshuis**, Dijver 16, contains two collections: lace, and the artwork of Frank Brangwyn, a Bruges-born artist of British parentage. An excellent collection of applied and decorative arts is displayed in the rambling **Gruuthusemuseum**, Dijver 17. The **Memlingmuseum**, Mariastraat 38, houses works by Hans Memling, one of the early Flemish Primitives.

Belfort Some 366 steps lead to the top of this 83m-high belfry. It's open 9.30 am to 5 pm daily (closed 12.30 to 1.30 pm October to March) and costs f100 (concession f80/50 students/children).

Begijnhof The Begijnhof was home to a 13th-century religious community of unmarried or widowed women who were known as *begijnen* (Beguines). It's enclosed by modest, whitewashed houses which these days are inhabited by single women of all ages. The large convent at the rear of the square is home to Benedictine nuns. The Begijnhof is about 10 minutes' walk south of the Markt.

Brouwerij De Halve Maan The Half Moon Brewery, Walplein 26, will show you the workings of one of Belgium's many little breweries. Tours (f140) run hourly from 11 am to 5 pm daily (less frequent in winter).

Organised Tours

Bruges by boat, bike, bus, foot or horse-drawn carriage – name it and you can tour by it. The tourist office has copious details.

One company that's highly recommended is Quasimodo (☎ 050-37 04 70, fax 050-37 49 60, ✉ info@quasimodo.be), Leenhoofweg 7. The young couple who run this outfit organise mountain-bike and minibus tours. Their 'back-road bike tours' through the villages around Bruges are run daily from Easter to September. The cost is f650/550 for those aged over/under 26. The minibus tours go either to Ypres and around the WWI battlefields of Flanders or on a 'Triple Treat' experience to indulge in waffles, beer and chocolate. Prices are f1400/1100 for those over/under 26 years, and include a picnic lunch.

Places to Stay

Bruges' attractiveness has resulted in a mass of accommodation – all heavily booked in summer.

Camping The nicest camping ground is *Memling (☎ 050-35 58 45, Veltemweg 109)*. It's open all year and charges f110/100/130 per adult/tent/car. Get bus No 11 from the station.

Hostels Several hostels compete for Bruges' backpacker market.

Passage (☎ 050-34 02 32, fax 050-34 01 40, Dweersstraat 26-28) has modern dorms as well as a hotel section next door. A bed in a six/four-bed room costs f380/480 per person (breakfast f100 extra), or there are doubles including breakfast for f1400/1600 without/with private bathroom. Take bus No 16 from the train station.

Snuffel Sleep In (☎ 050-33 31 33, fax 050-33 32 50, ✉ snuffel@freegates.be, Ezelstraat 47-49) has dorms ranging from f350 to f490. There's a kitchen at the disposal of guests;

BELGIUM

alternatively, breakfast costs f80. To get there from the train station take bus No 3 or 13.

Bauhaus International Youth Hotel (☎ 050-34 10 93, fax 050-33 41 80, ✉ bauhaus@bauhaus.be, Langestraat 135) is big, bustling and constantly expanding. It charges from f380 to f450 for dorms and f550/1050 for single/double rooms; there's a popular restaurant and bar. Breakfast is f60. Get bus No 6 or 16 from the train station.

The HI-affiliated hostel, **Europa** (☎ 050-35 26 79, fax 050-35 37 32, Baron Ruzettelaan 143), is 500m south of the city walls.

Guesthouses There's a swarm of B&Bs and many represent excellent value.

The three lofty rooms at **B&B Gheeraert** (☎ 050-33 56 27, fax 050-34 52 01, ✉ paul.gheeraert@skynet.be, Riddersstraat 9) are simply gorgeous. Singles/doubles/triples cost f1700/1900/2400.

B&B Dieltiens (☎ 050-33 42 94, fax 050-33 52 30, ✉ koen.dieltiens@skynet.be, St Walburgastraat 14) has been welcoming visitors for over a decade, and the hospitality still shines. Prices start at f1300/1600.

One of the town's most original B&Bs is **Bruyneel** (☎/fax 050-33 35 90, ✉ dbrynee@be.packardbell.org, Ezelstraat 24). Rooms choc full with art and bric-a-brac cost f2600.

Hotels The **Hotel Malleberg** (☎ 050-34 41 11, fax 050-34 67 69, Hoogstraat 7) is an immaculate little two-star hotel with eight lovely rooms. Prices are f2100/2900, or f3500/4100 for three/four people.

Hotel Adornes (☎ 050-34 13 36, fax 050-34 20 85, ✉ hotel.adornes@proximedia.be, St Annarei 26) is a charming hotel in the often overlooked St Anna quarter. It occupies three old gabled houses and has rooms from f2700/2900.

For a room with an unbeatable view of the Markt head to **Huyze Die Maene** (☎ 050-33 39 59, fax 050-33 44 60, ✉ huyzediemaene@pandora.be, Markt 17). This place is predominantly a brasserie but it has three fabulous upstairs rooms for between f3950 and f5940.

One of Bruges' most opulent choices is **Die Swaene** (☎ 050-34 27 98, fax 050-33 66 74, ✉ info@dieswaene-hotel, Steenhouwersdijk 1). The 24 lavish rooms are individually styled and cost from f5200/6250.

Places to Eat

For a sandwich or snack, try the rustic little **De Belegde Boterham** (☎ 050-34 91 31, Kleine St Amandsstraat 5). The pleasant **Lotus** (☎ 050-33 10 78, Wapenmakerstraat 5) is a vegetarian restaurant open mainly for lunch (closed Sunday), and also open Friday evening.

Huyze Die Maene (☎ 050-33 39 59, Markt 17) is a proficient brasserie that attracts a mixed local/tourist clientele. The speciality Vlaamse hutsepot (f525), a meat-based stew, is very good.

Den Dyver (☎ 050-33 60 69, Dijver 5) is a large restaurant which uses the nation's many beers to spice up traditional-style cuisine. The f1400 three-course menu (including drinks) is great value.

For something more charming there's **De Stove** (☎ 050-33 78 35, Kleine St Amandsstraat 4). This refined little place (just eight tables) does excellent fish specialities, with mains from f600 to f750.

Three-star Michelin greatness has made **De Karmeliet** (☎ 050-33 82 59, Langestraat 19) the talk of the town. Serving French haute cuisine, set menus here range from f2600 to f4200.

Self-caterers will find **Profi supermarkets** at Oude Burg 22 and Langestraat 55.

Entertainment

Retsin's Lucifernum (Twijnstraat 8) must rate as one of Belgium's weirdest places to drink. A huge mansion strewn with moody paintings, it's frequented by those who love a shot of hot rum (that's about all you can order) and modern art. It's open Friday, Saturday and Monday evenings.

If you're fanging for a beer, or better still, 300 different types of them, go directly to **'t Brugs Beertje** (Kemelstraat 5). Another great bar is **De Garre** (Garre 1).

The main venue for live contemporary and world music is the **Cactus Club** (☎ 050-33 20 14, St Jakobsstraat 33).

Cinema Lumière (☎ 050-33 48 57, St Jakobsstraat 36a) screens foreign and mainstream films.

Getting There & Away

Bus From mid-July to mid-September, one of the Eurolines buses to London picks up passengers at the train station in Bruges.

Telling time in Tirol, Austria

Street cafe scenes in Innsbruck, Austria

Edelweiss, the national flower of Austria

Prost! Partially fermented wines are called Sturm, Naschtmarkt, Vienna

The grave of Mary of Burgundy, Bruges, Belgium

Begijnhof, once a home for single women and widows, now a convent for Benedictine nuns, Belgium

The sun sets on another day, Houses of Parliament, London, England

Tickets can be bought from Reizen Wasteels (☎ 050-33 65 31), Geldmuntstraat 30a. For more information, see the Getting There & Away section at the start of this chapter.

Train The station information office (☎ 050-38 23 82) is open 7 am to 8.30 pm daily. There are IC trains to Brussels (f390, one hour), Antwerp (f405, 70 minutes), Ghent (f175, 20 minutes) and Kortrijk (f205, 40 minutes), from where there are hourly connections to Ypres and Tournai.

Getting Around
There's a small network of buses, most leaving from the Markt, and many pass by the train station. The boards at the tourist office list the routes and timetables, or you can ring ☎ 059-56 53 53.

Fietsen Popelier (☎ 050-34 32 62), Mariastraat 26, rents 40cc mopeds for f500/1000/1500 for one/three/five hours, petrol included. No special driving licence is required. This shop also rents bicycles for f110 per hour, or f250/325 per half-day/day.

AROUND BRUGES
The famous, poppy-filled **battlefields of Flanders** draw many people south for a day or longer (see the Ypres section). In the opposite direction, the former fishing village of **Damme** is just 5km away, connected by the Napoleon Canal, and popular for day trips.

Ypres

☎ 057 • pop 35,282

Stories have long been told about the WWI battlefields of Flanders. There were the tall red poppies that rose over the flat, flat fields; the soldiers who disappeared forever in the quagmire of battle; and the little town of Ypres (Ieper in Flemish), which was wiped off the map.

Sitting in the country's south-west corner, Ypres and its surrounding land were the last bastion of Belgian territory unoccupied by the Germans in WWI. As such, the region was a barrier to a German advance towards the French coastal ports around Calais. More than 300,000 Allied soldiers were killed here during four years of fighting that left the me-

dieval town flattened. Convincingly rebuilt, its outlying farmlands are today dotted with cemeteries, and in early summer, the poppies still flower.

Orientation & Information
The town's hub is the Grote Markt. It's a leisurely 10 minutes' walk from the train station – head straight up Stationsstraat and, at the end, turn left onto Tempelstraat and then right onto Boterstraat. Three blocks on, at the beginning of the Markt, is the Renaissance-style Lakenhalle (cloth hall) with its 70m-high belfry.

The Ieper Visitors Centre (☎ 057-22 85 84, fax 057-22 85 89) is in the Lakenhalle on the Grote Markt. It's open 9 am to 5 or 6 pm daily.

Things to See
Ypres ranked alongside Bruges and Ghent as an important cloth town in medieval times, and its postwar reconstruction holds true to its former prosperity.

The excellent **In Flanders Fields Museum** (☎ 057-22 85 84), Grote Markt 34, opened in 1998 on the 1st floor of the Lakenhalle. It is devoted to the promotion of peace as much as the remembrance of war, and is a moving testament to the wartime horrors experienced by ordinary people. It's open 10 am to 5 or 6 pm daily (closed Monday from October to March). Admission costs f250 (children's concession f125). It's at www.inflandersfields.be on the Web.

One of the saddest reminders of the Great War is Ypres' **Meensepoort** (Menin Gate), inscribed with the names of 55,000 British and Commonwealth troops who were lost in the quagmire of the trenches and who have no graves. A bugler sounds the last post here at 8 pm every evening. It's about 300m from the tourist office.

Around Ypres, in outlying fields and hamlets, are 170 **cemeteries** and now upon row of crosses. The tourist office sells maps of car and bike routes that wind through the old battlefields. However, if you've limited time, it's best to go with an organised tour.

Organised Tours
Salient Tours (☎ 057-91 02 23) organises very good tours of the cemeteries and important battle sites. Short/standard tours of 2½/four

BELGIUM

hours cost f650/950. You should book ahead. Alternatively, join Quasimodo's tour (see the Organised Tours section in Bruges for details).

Places to Stay & Eat

For camping, there's *Jeugdstadion* (☎ 057-21 72 82, *Leopold III laan 16*), 900m southeast of the town centre. The closest private hostel is *De Iep* (☎/fax 057-20 88 11, *Poperingseweg 34*), 2km west of town.

B&B Brouwers (☎ 057-20 27 23, *Adjudant Masscheleinlaan 18*), 500m north of the Grote Markt, is one of few B&Bs in town. It's homy and fastidiously clean, with rooms for f800/1500.

An affordable central hotel is the newly renovated *Gasthof 't Zweerd* (☎ 057-20 04 75, *fax 057-21 78 96, Grote Markt 2*) with rooms for f2000/2500.

Hotel Regina (☎ 057-21 88 88, *fax 057-21 90 20*, @ *info@hotelregina.be, Grote Markt 45*) has two types of rooms – old and very ordinary for f3000, or new and beautifully rustic for f4000.

Cafes and restaurants line the Grote Markt – a good choice is *In het Klein Stadhuis*, a cosy brasserie right next to the town hall. *Pita Farao* (☎ 057-20 65 72, *Tempelstraat 7*), halfway to the train station, serves excellent stuffed pitta breads. An excellent restaurant is *Eethuis De Ecurie* (☎ 057-21 73 78), Rijselsestraat 49. The cuisine is innovative and the atmosphere (it was once a horse stable) is enticing.

For picnic supplies, there's a *Spar* supermarket on Rijselstraat.

Getting There & Around

There are direct hourly trains to Kortrijk (f145, 30 minutes), Ghent (f315, one hour,) and Brussels (f480). For Antwerp and Bruges, you have to change in Kortrijk.

Regional buses leave from a stop to the left outside the train station.

Bicycles can be rented from the luggage room at the station or from Hotel Sultan (☎ 057-21 90 30), Grote Markt 33.

Tournai

☎ 069 • pop 68,365

Tournai (Doornik in Flemish) is, together with Tongeren, the oldest city in Belgium.

Just 10km from the French border and 80km south-west of Brussels, its skyline is dominated by the five towers of its austere 12th-century cathedral and the more ornate 13th-century belfry.

Orientation & Information

The train station is a 10-minute walk from the centre of town – head straight up Rue Royale until you reach the cathedral. To the left up the hill is the tourist office (☎ 069-22 20 45, fax 069-21 62 21, @ tourisme@tournai.be), Vieux Marché aux Poteries 14, near the base of the belfry. It's open 9 am to 6 or 7 pm weekdays, 10 am to 1 pm and 3 to 6 pm Saturday, and 10 am to noon and 2 to 6 pm Sunday.

Things to See

Besides the belfry and the cathedral (which is undergoing massive repairs after being damaged in a tornado in 1999), Tournai has several interesting museums. The most prestigious is the **Musée des Beaux-Arts**, Enclos St Martin, in a building designed by Victor Horta. The **Musée de la Tapisserie et des Arts du Tissu** (Museum of Tapestry and Cloth Arts), Place Reine Astrid, is testament to the revival of the city's historically important tapestry industry. Both museums are open 10 am to noon and 2 to 5.30 pm daily (closed Tuesday).

Places to Stay & Eat

The *Camping de l'Orient* (☎ 069-22 26 35, *Vieux Chemin de Mons*) is 4km south-east of town near the Aqua Tournai (an indoor swimming complex). Take bus W from the station. The HI-affiliated *Auberge de Jeunesse* (☎ 069-21 61 36, *fax 069-21 61 40, Rue St Martin 64*) is a 20-minute walk from the station – take bus No 4 (direction: Baisieux).

As for hotels, if price is a problem head to *Tour Saint-Georges* (☎ 069-22 53 00, *Rue St Georges 2*). Rooms start at f765/1050 – it's passable if you don't expect much. The four-star *Hôtel d'Alcantara* (☎ 069-21 26 48, *fax 069-21 28 24, Rue des Bouchers St Jacques 2*) is a charmingly discreet hotel with well-priced, modern rooms from f2700/3100.

The *Pita Pyramide* (☎ 069-84 35 83, *Rue Tête d'Or 7*) has large stuffed pitta breads for f210. Picnic supplies can be had from the *GB* supermarket across the road. There are two good restaurants options here: *L'Écurie*

BELGIUM

d'Ennetières (☎ *069-21 56 89, Ruelle d'Ennetières*) is a lovely mid-range French restaurant, or consider the excellent and more expensive *Le Pressior* (☎ *069-22 35 13, Vieux Marché aux Poteries 2*).

Getting There & Away
There are regular trains to Kortrijk (f145, 40 minutes), Brussels (f250, one hour) and Ypres via Kortrijk (f250, one hour).

Liège

☎ 04 • pop 189,903

Liège (Luik in Flemish) is one of those cities people tend to love or loath. Sprawled along the Meuse River in the eastern part of Wallonia, it's busy and gritty and is the sort of place that takes time to know. If you're passing en route to the Ardennes, it's well worth a stop, particularly for the rich showcase of local and religious art in its many museums.

Orientation
The central district is strewn along the western bank of the Meuse River, which splits in two here creating the island of Outremeuse. The main train station, Gare Guillemins, is 2km south of Place St Lambert, the city's nominal heart.

Information
The main Office du Tourisme (☎ 04-221 92 21, fax 04-221 92 22), Féronstrée 92, is open 9 am to 5 or 6 pm weekdays and 10 am to 4 pm weekends (to 2 pm on Sunday).

For regional information, head to the provincial tourist office (Fédération du Tourisme de la Province de Liège; ☎ 04-232 65 10), Blvd de la Sauvenière 77.

At Gare Guillemins there's a small bureau dispensing both city and provincial information.

Things to See & Do
Excellent views of the city can be had from the top of the **Montagne de Bueren** – an impressive flight of 373 stairs which lead up from Hors Château. On Sunday mornings there's **La Batte**, a street market which stretches along 1.5km of riverfront quays.

The area around the tourist office is old and quite picturesque and also home to the city's best museums. The **Musée d'Art Religieux et d'Art Mosan** (Museum of Religious Art and Art from the Meuse Valley), Rue Mère Dieu, is open 11 am to 6 pm Tuesday to Saturday and until 4 pm Sunday; admission is f100. The nearby **Musée de la Vie Wallonne** (Walloon Life Museum), Cour des Mineurs, is open 10 am to 5 pm Tuesday to Saturday and until 4 pm Sunday; it costs f80. Life as it was for some in the 18th century is depicted in the **Musée d'Ansembourg**, Féronstrée 114, a Regency-style mansion open 1 to 6 pm Tuesday to Sunday; entry is f50.

Places to Stay
One of the closest camping grounds is *Les Murets* (☎ *04-380 19 87, Chemin d'Enonck 57*) in Esneux, about 20km to the south.

The big HI-affiliated *Auberge de Jeunesse* (☎ *04-344 56 89, fax 04-344 56 87,* @ *ajlie ge@gate71.be, Rue Georges Simenon 2*) in Outremeuse, charges f495 in a dorm and has singles/doubles for f800/1170 – take bus No 4 from Gare Guillemins.

The *Hôtel Le Berger* (☎ *04-223 00 80, fax 04-221 19 48, Rue des Urbanistes 10*) is simple but well kept and charges f1000/1400 for rooms (breakfast is f200). Bus No 1 or 4 stops a block away.

With extra francs head to Outremeuse and the *Hôtel Simenon* (☎ *04-342 86 90, fax 04-344 26 69, Blvd de l'Est 16*). Occupying a 1908 Art Nouveau house, the gaily decorated rooms reflect the writings of local author Georges Simenon, and cost from f2000 (breakfast is f200). The city's best hotel is the *Bedford* (☎ *04-228 81 11, fax 04-227 45 75, Quai St Léonard 36*). It's right on the riverfront and has rooms from f8450/9450 (discounted to f3400/3850 on weekends).

Places to Eat
For serene surroundings, cross the river to Outremeuse, where there's an old cobbled street, En Roture, lined with little restaurants. In the city centre, Rue St-Jean-en-Isle is also filled with restaurants and brasseries. Nearby, *La Feuille de Vigne* (☎ *04-222 20 10, Rue Sœurs de Hasque 12*) is a vegetarian restaurant open noon to 3 pm weekdays. One

BELGIUM

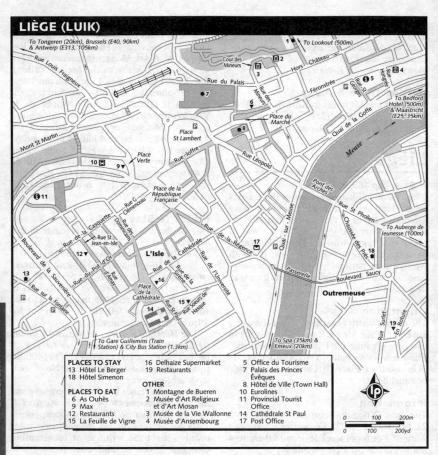

LIÈGE (LUIK)

To Tongeren (20km), Brussels (E40, 90km)
& Antwerp (E313, 105km)

To Lookout (500m)

Rue Louis Fraigneux

Cour des
Mineurs

Hors Château

Rue du Palais

Féronstrée

Rue St-
Georges

To Bedford
Hotel (500m)
& Maastricht
(E25, 35km)

Place du
Marché

Quai de la Goffe

Meuse

Mont St Martin

Place
St Lambert

Place
Verte

Rue Joffre

Rue Léopold

Pont des
Arches

Place de la
République
Française

Rue G.
Clemenceau

Rue de la Régence

Quai sur Meuse

Rue St Pholien

Chaussée des Prés

To Auberge de
Jeunesse (100m)

Boulevard de la Sauvenière

Rue de la Casquette

Rue des
Dominicains

Rue St
Jean-en-Isle

L'Isle

Rue de la Cathédrale

Rue de la
Sirène

Rue de l'Université

Passerelle

Boulevard Saucy

Outremeuse

Rue du Pot d'Or

Rue
d'Amay

Place
de la
Cathédrale

Rue St-Paul

Rue Sœurs de
Hasque

En Roture

Rue Surlet

To Gare Guillemins (Train
Station) & City Bus Station (1.3km)

To Spa (35km) &
Emeux (20km)

PLACES TO STAY
13 Hôtel Le Berger
18 Hôtel Simenon

PLACES TO EAT
6   As Ouhès
9   Max
12 Restaurants
15 La Feuille de Vigne

16 Delhaize Supermarket
19 Restaurants

OTHER
1   Montagne de Bueren
2   Musée d'Art Religieux
    et d'Art Mosan
3   Musée de la Vie Wallonne
4   Musée d'Ansembourg

5   Office du Tourisme
7   Palais des Princes
    Évêques
8   Hôtel de Ville (Town Hall)
10 Eurolines
11 Provincial Tourist
    Office
14 Cathédrale St Paul
17 Post Office

0   100   200m
0   100   200yd

---

of the trendiest restaurants in town is *As Ouhès* (☎ *04-223 32 25, Place du Marché 21*). This place specialises in rich Wallonian cuisine – the servings are extra generous and the prices are reasonable. For superb seafood, the answer is *Max* (☎ *04-222 08 59, Place Verte 2*).

Self-caterers will find a *Delhaize* supermarket on Place de la Cathédrale.

Getting There & Away
Bus Eurolines (☎ 04-222 36 18) has an office at Blvd de la Sauvenière 26, from where buses depart.

Train The principal hub, Gare Guillemins, is 2km from Place St Lambert but connected by bus No 1 or 4. The train information office (☎ 0900-10177) is open 7 am to 8 pm daily.

The Thalys fast train connects Liège with Cologne (f840, 1½ hours, seven trains per day) but the cheaper, normal trains (f740, eight per day) take the same time. Other regular connections include Brussels (f405, 1¼ hours, two trains per hour), Maastricht (f270, 30 minutes, hourly trains) and Luxembourg City (f900, 2½ hours, seven per day). Locally, there are hourly trains to Namur (f245, 50 minutes), Spa (f145, 50 minutes) and Tongeren (f125, 30 minutes).

BELGIUM

Getting Around

Inner-city buses leave from the right as you leave Gare Guillemins. Bus No 1 or 4 plies between here and the centre.

AROUND LIÈGE

Tongeren

☎ 012 • pop 29,920

About 20km north of Liège, Tongeren has the honour (together with Tournai) of being Belgium's oldest town. The original locals put up considerable resistance under the leadership of Ambiorix when the area was conquered by Roman troops in 15 BC. The impressive Gallo-Roman Museum in the heart of town houses many findings from early times. Tongeren is also well known for its Sunday antique market, which draws buyers from near and far.

For more information, the tourist office (☎ 012-39 02 55, fax 012-39 11 43), Stadhuisplein 9, is open daily.

Overnighters will find a pleasant HI hostel, *Begijnhof* (☎ 012-39 13 70, fax 012-39 13 48, *St Ursulastraat 1*) or the mid-range *Hotel Lido* (☎ 012-23 19 48, fax 012-39 27 27, *Grote Markt 19*).

Spa

☎ 087 • pop 10,813

Spa was for centuries the luxurious retreat for royalty and the wealthy who came to drink, bathe and cure themselves in the mineral-rich waters which bubble forth here. Today it is a rather run-down reminder of what was, but is nevertheless pleasant enough for a day or overnight. The surrounding hills offer enjoyable walks along well-marked paths.

The town is about 35km south-east of Liège, connected by regular trains (see the Liège Getting There & Away section). The local Office du Tourisme (☎ 087-79 53 53, fax 087-79 53 54), Place Royale 41, is open 9 or 10 am to 5 or 6 pm daily.

Hautes Fagnes National Park

Bordering the Eifel Hills in Germany, with which it forms one geographical entity, the Hautes Fagnes park is a region of swampy heath and woods. Within the park is the Botrange Centre Nature (☎ 080-44 03 00, fax 080-44 44 29, ✆ botrange.centrenature@ skynet.be), close to the highest point in

Belgium – the Signal de Botrange (694m). This area is a popular base for serious hikers, cyclists and cross-country skiers. Those wanting just a short walk (1½ hours) through this bleak but interesting landscape should head to the boardwalk at Fagne de Polleur, nearby at Mt Rigi.

The Botrange Centre Nature is about 50km east of Liège. It takes about 1¼ hours to get to on public transport from Liège – take the train to Verviers and then bus No 390 in the direction of Rocherath.

The Ardennes

Home to deep river valleys and high forests, Belgium's south-eastern corner is often overlooked by travellers hopping between the old art towns and the capital. But here, in the provinces of Namur, Liège and Luxembourg, you'll find tranquil villages nestled into the grooves of the Meuse, Lesse and Ourthe Valleys or sitting atop the verdant hills. Historically, this is where the Battle of the Bulge once raged.

The town of Namur is the best base for exploration – it's well positioned on the railway line to Luxembourg and has rail and bus connections to some of the region's less accessible spots. Without your own transport, getting around can take time.

NAMUR

☎ 081 • pop 105,123

Just 50km south-east of Brussels, Namur (Namen in Flemish) is the capital of Wallonia. The town is relatively small and picturesque, and is dominated by its 15th-century citadel.

The tourist office (☎ 081-24 64 49), Square Léopold, is 200m to the left of the station, as you leave. It's open 9.30 am to 6 pm daily. There's also a small tourist kiosk at Place du Grognon at the base of the citadel.

Things to See & Do

Perched dramatically above the town, the **citadel** can be reached either on foot, by car along the Route Merveilleuse, or by a shuttle bus (f40) which departs half-hourly from the tourist office. Admission to the citadel is free; guided visits cost f210/100 for adults/ children.

Of the handful of museums, the two most intriguing are the **Félicien Rops**, Rue Fumal 12, which has works by the 19th-century Namur-born artist who fondly illustrated erotic lifestyles, and the tiny **Musée du Prieuré d'Oignies**, Rue Julie Billiart 17, a one-roomed hoard of exquisite Gothic treasures in a modern convent.

Places to Stay & Eat
Campers can head to *Camping Les 4 Fils Aymon* (☎ 081-58 02 94, *Chaussée de Liège*) about 8km east – get bus No 12 from the bus station.

The riverfront *Auberge de Jeunesse* (☎ 081-22 36 88, fax 081-22 44 12, @ *ajna mur@skynet.be, Ave F Rops 8*) is 3km from the train station, or jump on bus No 3 or 4.

Grand Hôtel de Flandre (☎ 081-23 18 68, fax 081-22 80 60, *Place de la Gare 14*) has no-nonsense rooms starting at f1700/2100. For considerably more charm try *Hôtel Les Tanneurs* (☎ 081-24 00 24, fax 081-24 00 25, @ *info@tanneurs.com, Rue des Tanneries 13*). Every room in this unique hotel is different – prices (and luxury) range from f1250 to f8000 for a single, and f2000 to f8500 for a double.

Tea Time Café (☎ 081-23 10 75, *35 Rue St Jean*) is a stylish tearoom which does excellent filled multigrain baguettes (f120), as well as crepes and waffles. A delicious range of international meals is served at *Brasserie Henry* (☎ 081-22 02 04, *3 Place St Aubain*).

Getting There & Away
Namur's train station (☎ 081-25 22 22) is undergoing massive renovation (expected to be completed in 2001). The temporary information and ticket office is out the back near the train lines. There are trains to Brussels (f245, one hour, half-hourly), Luxembourg City (f820, 1¼ hours, hourly) and Liège (f245, 50 minutes, hourly). For information on regional trains, see Getting There & Away sections for each of the following towns: Dinant, Han-sur-Lesse, Rochefort, La Roche-en-Ardenne and Bastogne.

Local and regional buses are operated by TEC (☎ 081-25 35 55) which has an office (open 7 am to 7 pm daily) opposite the train station. Regional buses leave from the bus station near the C&A department store (to the left of the train station as you leave).

DINANT
☎ 082 ● pop 12,615
This heavy, distinctive town, 28km south of Namur, is one of the Ardennes' real touristy hot spots. Its bulbous cathedral competes for attention with the cliff-front citadel, while below, a hive of boat operators competes for the Meuse River day-trippers or the Lesse Valley kayakers. The tourist office (☎ 082-22 28 70, fax 082-22 77 88), Rue Grande 37, is open 9.30 am to 6 pm daily.

Things to See & Do
The citadel is open all year and accessible by cable car – a combined ticket costs f195/145 for adults/children.

For **kayaking**, several companies have trips leaving in the morning upriver from Houyet, ending at Anseremme next to Dinant several hours later. Try Kayaks Ansiaux (☎ 082-22 23 25), Rue du Vélodrome 15 in Anseremme. This same company also hires mountain bikes (f850 per day).

More sedate are the **boat cruises** down the Meuse. Companies include Bayard (☎ 082-22 30 42), Quai de Meuse 1, which has a range of voyages including a 45-minute trip to Anseremme (f180/140 for adults/children) and a nine-hour haul to Givet over the French border and back (f520/400).

Places to Stay
Hotels are not plentiful and there's no hostel to turn to. One of the cheapest options is *Le Rouge et Noir* (☎ 082-22 69 44, fax 082-64 64 01, *Rue Grande 26*) which has rudimentary rooms without/with private bathroom for f1500/2000. Much nicer is *Hôtel de la Couronne* (☎ 082-22 24 41, fax 082-22 70 31, *Rue Sax 1*) where pleasant single/double rooms cost f2200/2300.

Getting There & Away
There are hourly trains from Namur to Dinant (f135, 30 minutes). Bus No 433 (50 minutes, one every two hours) also connects the two.

HAN-SUR-LESSE & ROCHEFORT
☎ 084
The millennia-old limestone grottoes are the drawing card of these two villages, which sit just 8km apart on the Lesse and Lomme Rivers respectively. The impressive Han caves

BELGIUM

are a little way out of town – a tram takes you to the entrance and a boat brings you back. Open 10 am to noon and 1 to 4.30 pm from April to October (from 11.30 am the rest of the year and closed January), they cost f360/240 for adults/children. Rochefort's cave, known as the Grotte de Lorette, is much smaller. It's open April to mid-November; hour-long tours start at 10 am and cost f220/145.

There are tourist offices in both towns: in Han (☎ 084-37 75 96, fax 084-37 75 76) at Place Théo Lannoy, and in Rochefort (☎ 084-21 25 37, fax 084-22 13 74) at Rue de Behogne 5.

Places to Stay

In Han, *Camping de la Lesse* (☎ *084-37 72 90, Rue du Grand Hy*) is open all year; so too is the *Gîte d'Étape* hostel (☎*/fax 084-37 74 41, Rue du Gîte d'Étape 10*) which charges f385/485 for those under/over 26 years. Alternatively, *Hôtel le Central* (☎ *084-37 72 61, Rue des Grottes 20*) has basic singles/doubles for f1250/2500.

Rochefort has a better range of accommodation. The *Gîte d'Étape* hostel (☎*/fax 084-21 46 04, Rue du Hableau 25*) charges f385/485 for guests under/over 26. Just up the same road is *Camping Communal* (☎ *084-21 19 00*), open from Easter to 31 October.

Hotel La Fayette (☎ *084-21 42 73, fax 084-22 11 63, Rue Jacquet 87*) has bright, attractive rooms starting at f1220/1520. More pleasant still is *Le Vieux Logis* (☎ *084-21 10 24, fax 084-22 12 30, Rue Jacquet 71*) with singles/doubles for f1800/2100 or the slightly more expensive *Hôtel La Malle Poste* (☎ *084-21 09 86, fax 084-22 11 13, Rue de Behogne 46*). The latter was the town's original stagecoach stop, and has rooms for f2150/2650.

Getting There & Away

Take the Namur-Luxembourg train to Jemelle (40 minutes, hourly) and transfer to the hourly bus No 29 (seven minutes to Rochefort, 14 minutes to Han).

LA ROCHE-EN-ARDENNE
☎ 084 • pop 4100

Hugging a bend in the Ourthe River, La Roche is a vibrant little town, hidden in a deep valley, crowned by a ruined castle and surrounded by verdant hills much enjoyed by hikers. The tourist office (☎ 084-41 13 42, fax 084-41 23 43) is at Place du Marché 15.

Places to Stay

Camping Le Vieux Moulin (☎ *084-41 13 80, Petite Strument 62*) is beautifully positioned. It charges f95 per adult and f295 per tent site, and is open Easter to 31 October. *Hôtel les Olivettes* (☎ *084-41 16 52, fax 084-41 21 69,* **◎** *olivettes@ping.be, Chemin de Soeret 12*) is popular with horse-riding enthusiasts. In addition to hotel rooms from f1100/2200 for singles/doubles, it has a separate *auberge* with dormitory-style accommodation (four to eight beds) for f500 per person (excluding breakfast). For a quaint B&B, head to *Le Vieux La Roche* (☎ *084-41 25 86,* **◎** *levieuxlaroche@online.be, Rue du Chalet 45*). The five homy rooms cost f1400. The charming *Moulin de la Strument* (☎ *084-41 15 07, fax 084-41 10 80, Petite Strument 62*) is a hotel/restaurant with eight rooms for f2350/2550.

Places to Eat

Les Clos René (☎ *084-41 26 17, Rue Chamont 30*) is a good, modern little creperie in the heart of town. Prices are reasonable (f120 to f235). For classic French cuisine and ultra-attentive service, head to *La Clairefontaine* (☎ *084-41 24 70, Route de Hotton 64*). This hotel/restaurant has three-course *menus* from f720 to f950; it's 1.5km from town.

Getting There & Away

From Namur, take a Luxembourg-bound train to Marloie, then bus No 15 (four per day) to La Roche (35 minutes).

BASTOGNE
☎ 061

It was here, north of Arlon and close to the Luxembourg border, that thousands of soldiers and civilians died during the Battle of the Bulge in the winter of 1944-45. Testament to these events is a huge, star-shaped **American memorial**, on a hill 2km from Bastogne, and the neighbouring **Bastogne Historical Centre**, open 10 am to 4 pm daily from 1 March to 31 October (8.30 am to 5 pm July and August). The tourist office (☎ 061-21 27 11) is at Place McAuliffe.

BELGIUM

Places to Stay

Camping de Renval (☎ 061-21 29 85, *Rue du Marché 148)* is 1km from the tourist office and open all year. *Hôtel du Sud* (☎ 061-21 11 14, *fax 061-21 79 08,* ✉ *hotel.du.sud@ping.be, Rue du Marché 39)* has basic rooms starting at f1635/1960. More upmarket is the new *Hôtel Collin* (☎ 061-21 43 58, fax 061-21 80 83, *Place McAuliffe 8)* which has lovely modern rooms from f2500/3000.

Getting There & Away

From Namur, take a Luxembourg-bound train to the rail junction of Libramont, from where bus No 163b departs every two hours for Bastogne's defunct train station (35 minutes).

Britain

The first stop on many people's European tour, Britain can easily occupy a trip of it's own. London is booming and has a definite buzz and vibrancy. The cultural money raised by the national lottery has rained down not just on the capital, but throughout the nation. Exciting new galleries and attractions abound.

At one stage of its history this small island ruled half the world's population and had a major impact on many of the rest. For those whose countries once lay in the shadow of its great empire a visit may almost be a cliche, but it's also essential – a peculiar mixture of homecoming and confrontation.

To the surprise of many, Britain remains one of the most beautiful islands in the world. All the words, paintings and pictures that have been produced are not just romantic, patriotic exaggerations.

In terms of area, Britain is small, but the more you explore the bigger it seems to become. Visitors from the New World are often fooled by this magical expansion and try to do too much too quickly. JB Priestley observed of England, 'She is just pretending to be small'. Covering it all in one trip is impossible – and that's before you start thinking of Scotland and Wales.

The United Kingdom comprises Britain (England, Wales and Scotland) and Northern Ireland. Its full name is the United Kingdom of Great Britain and Northern Ireland. This chapter confines itself to the island of Britain, the largest of the British Isles, the Isle of Man, the Channel Islands and Scotland's outlying islands – the Hebrides in the west and Orkney and Shetland in the northeast. For reasons of geographical and practical coherence, Northern Ireland is dealt with alongside the Irish Republic in the Ireland chapter.

Sometimes in summer it can feel as if the whole world has come to Britain. But it's certainly possible to avoid the rush. Don't spend all your time in the big, tourist-ridden towns; rather, pick a small area and spend at least a week or so wandering around the country lanes and villages.

AT A GLANCE

Capital	London
Population	56.7 million
Official Language	English, Welsh, Scottish Gaelic
Currency	1 British pound (£) = 100 pence
Time	GMT/UTC+0000
Country Phone Code	☎ 44

Scotland p281
Glasgow p296 Central Edinburgh p290
York p264
IRELAND
Wales p312
Oxford p250 Cambridge p258
Bath p243 Central London pp200-1
Central West London pp206-7
Brighton pp230-1
BELGIUM
FRANCE

Facts about Britain

HISTORY
Celts & Romans

England had long been settled by small bands of hunters when, around 4000 BC, a new group of immigrants arrived from Europe. The new arrivals used stone tools, and they were the first to leave enduring marks on the island. They farmed the chalk hills radiating from Salisbury Plain, and began the construction of stone tombs and, around 3000 BC, the great ceremonial complexes at Avebury and Stonehenge.

BRITAIN

To Shetland Islands
(see inset)

SHETLAND ISLANDS

Foula   Lerwick

ORKNEY ISLANDS

Stromness

Thurso   Wick

Thurso   Wick

OUTER HEBRIDES

Lewis

St Kilda

North Uist

Harris

South Uist

North Minch

Ullapool

North West Highlands

Kyle of Lochalsh

Skye

INNER HEBRIDES

Rhum

Coll

Tiree

Mull

Oban

Colonsay

Jura

Islay

Loch Awe

Loch Lomond

Fort William

Loch Ness

Aviemore

Spey

Elgin

Inverness

Moray Firth

Peterhead

Grampians

Braemar

Dee

Aberdeen

S C O T L A N D

Dundee

Arbroath

Montrose

Perth

St Andrews

Kirkaldy

Firth of Forth

Stirling

GLASGOW

Motherwell

EDINBURGH

Dunbar

Lammermuir Hills

Berwick-upon-Tweed

Galashiels

Tweed

Southern Uplands

Jedburgh

Cheviot Hills

Ashington

Nith

Kilmarnock

Arran

Ayr

Sanquhar

Dumfries

Firth of Clyde

North Channel

NORTH SEA

ATLANTIC OCEAN

Derry

NORTHERN IRELAND

Larne

BELFAST

Stranraer

Solway Firth

Carlisle

Pennines

Tyne

NEWCASTLE UPON TYNE

Sunderland

Durham

Hartlepool

Darlington

Middlesbrough

Lake District

Workington

Cumbrian Mtns

Windermere

North York Moors

Scarborough

I R E L A N D

Douglas

Isle of Man

Barrow-in-Furness

Lancaster

Ure

Ouse

York

Yorkshire Wolds

Bridlington

DUBLIN

Dun Laoghaire

IRISH SEA

Blackpool

Blackburn

Bradford

LEEDS

KINGSTON-UPON-HULL

Southport

Bolton

MANCHESTER

Humber

Grimsby

Cleethorpes

NORTH SEA

Holyhead

Anglesey

Colwyn Bay

Rhyl

Birkenhead

Chester

LIVERPOOL

Peaks District

SHEFFIELD

Lincolnshire Wolds

Lincoln

Bangor

Wrexham

Stoke-on-Trent

Derby

Boston

The Wash

King's Lynn

Great Yarmouth

Ffestiniog

Cambrian Mtns

Shrewsbury

Stafford

Nottingham

Leicester

Peterborough

Norwich

Lowestoft

Cardigan Bay

Aberystwyth

Newtown

BIRMINGHAM

Coventry

Rugby

Northampton

Bedford

The Fens

Ely

Cambridge

Bury St Edmunds

Ipswich

W A L E S

Wye

Worcester

Stratford-upon-Avon

E N G L A N D

Colchester

Felixstowe

Harwich

Wexford

Rosslare

Fishguard

Llandovery

Hereford

Cheltenham

Gloucester

Oxford

Chiltern Hills

Luton

Harlow

Brecon Beacons

Merthyr Tydfil

Cotswold Hills

Swindon

Windsor

LONDON

Southend-on-Sea

Margate

St Georges Channel

Pembroke

Llanelli

Swansea

Newport

CARDIFF

White Horse Hills

Reading

Basingstoke

North Downs

Ramsgate

Canterbury

CELTIC SEA

Bristol Channel

Bristol

Bath

Guildford

Crawley

South Downs

Royal Tunbridge Wells

Folkestone

Channel Tunnel

Calais

CHANNEL ISLANDS

Alderney

Cherbourg

FRANCE

St Peter Port

Guernsey

Sark

Jersey

St Helier

Exmoor

Barnstaple

Taunton

Salisbury

Winchester

Chichester

Brighton

Hastings

Eastbourne

Boulogne

Bude

North Dorset Downs

Southampton

Bournemouth

Portsmouth

Exe

Exeter

Exmouth

Weymouth

Isle of Wight

Strait of Dover

Newquay

Tamar

Dartmoor

Torquay

ENGLISH CHANNEL

Penzance

Truro

Plymouth

Land's End

Isles of Scilly

See Channel Islands Inset

Cherbourg

Alderney

FRANCE

F R A N C E

Dieppe

0   50   100km
0   30   60mi

BRITAIN

The next great influx of people were the Celts, a people from central Europe who had mastered the smelting of bronze and later of iron. They brought two forms of the Celtic language: Gaelic, which is still spoken in parts of Ireland and Scotland, and Brythonic, which was spoken in England and is still spoken in parts of Wales.

In AD 43, the Romans arrived in force and, despite fierce resistance, established themselves in England. The mountains of Wales and Scotland remained Celtic strongholds, but England was a part of the Roman Empire for 350 years. Paved roads radiated from London to important regional centres: Ermine St ran north to Lincoln, York and Hadrian's Wall, and Watling St ran north-west to Chester. Christianity arrived in the 3rd century.

English

By the 4th century the empire was in retreat, and in 410 the last Roman troops withdrew. The British were left to the tender mercies of the heathen Angles, Jutes and Saxons – Teutonic tribes originating from north of the Rhine. During the 5th century they advanced across what had been Roman England and by the 7th century they had come to think of themselves collectively as English. The Celts, particularly in Ireland, kept Latin and Roman Christian culture alive.

Vikings & Normans

The English were ill-prepared to meet the challenge posed by the next wave of invaders. The Norwegian Vikings conquered northern Scotland, Cumbria and Lancashire, and the Danes conquered eastern England, making York their capital. Eastern England (north of the Romans' Watling St) was called the Danelaw. They were finally stopped by Alfred the Great, and he and his successors created a tenuously unified country. Danish raids continued, however, and in 1016 the crown was taken by Canute the Great, who was also King of Norway and Denmark.

After a brief period of Danish rule, Edward the Confessor was made king. He had been brought up in Normandy – a Viking duchy in France – alongside his cousin Duke William, the future Conqueror. Edward's death left two contenders for the crown: Harold Godwin, his English brother-in-law, and William,

his Norman cousin. In 1066 William landed with 12,000 men and defeated Harold at the Battle of Hastings.

The conquest of England by the Normans was completed rapidly: English aristocrats were replaced by French-speaking Normans, dominating castles were built and the feudal system was imposed.

Middle Ages

In the 12th century, after a disastrous civil war fought over the succession to the crown, Henry II, Count of Anjou, was made king. He had inherited more than half of modern France and clearly surpassed the King of France in the extent of his power.

The struggle to retain this empire was a dominant concern of the Plantagenet and Lancastrian kings leading to the Hundred Years' War, and finally to English defeat. In order to finance these adventures, the Plantagenet kings conceded a considerable amount of power to Parliament, which jealously protected its traditional right to control taxation.

Further disputes over the royal succession allowed Parliament to consolidate its power. The Wars of the Roses, a dynastic struggle between the houses of York and Lancaster, lasted for 30 years. The final victor in 1485 was Henry VII, the first Tudor king.

Tudors & Stuarts

Under Henry VIII, the long struggle of the English kings against the power of the pope came to a head. Parliament made Henry the head of the Church of England, and the Bible was translated into English. In 1536 the monasteries were dissolved – a largely popular move because the wealthy and often corrupt religious orders were widely resented.

The 16th century was a golden age. Greek learning was rediscovered, the European powers explored the world, trade boomed, Shakespeare wrote his plays, and Francis Bacon laid the foundations for modern science.

An age of religious intolerance was beginning, however, and after Elizabeth I the relationship between Parliament and the autocratic Stuart kings deteriorated. In 1642 the conflict became a civil war. Catholics, traditionalist members of the Church of England and the old gentry supported Charles I, whose power base was the north and west. The

BRITAIN

Protestant Puritans and the new rising merchant class, based in London and the towns of the south-east, supported Parliament.

Parliament found a brilliant leader in Oliver Cromwell; the royalists were defeated and then in 1649 Charles I was executed. Cromwell assumed dictatorial powers, but he also laid the foundation for the British Empire by modernising the army and navy. Two years after his death in 1658, a reconstituted Parliament recalled Charles II from exile.

The Restoration was a period of expansion – colonies stretched down the American coast and the East India Company established its headquarters in Bombay.

Empire & Industry

In the 18th century, the Hanoverian kings increasingly relied on Parliament to govern the kingdom, and Sir Robert Walpole became the first prime minister in all but name.

By 1770 France had ceded all of Canada and surrendered all but two of its trading stations in India, while Captain Cook claimed Australia for Britain in 1778. The empire's first major reverse came when the American colonies won their independence in 1783.

Also in the 1780s were the first developments that would lead to the Industrial Revolution and Britain was its crucible. Canals, trains, coal, water and steam power transformed the means of production and transport, and the rapidly growing towns of the Midlands became the first industrial cities.

By the time Queen Victoria took the throne in 1837, Britain was the greatest power in the world. Its fleets dominated the seas linking an enormous empire, and its factories dominated world trade.

Under prime ministers Disraeli and Gladstone, the worst excesses of the Industrial Revolution were addressed, education became universal and the right to vote was extended to most men (women did not get equal voting rights until 1928).

The 20th Century

Victoria died at the very beginning of the new century and the old order was shattered by the Great War (WWI). By the war's end in 1918 a million British men had died and 15% of the country's accumulated capital had been spent.

The euphoria of victory didn't last long. In the late 1920s the world economy slumped, ushering in more than a decade of misery and political upheaval. The Labour Party first came to power in 1924, but lasted less than a year.

On 1 September 1939, Hitler provoked a new war by invading Poland. By mid-1940, most of Europe was either ruled by or under the direct influence of the Nazis, Stalin had negotiated a peace, the USA was neutral, and Britain, under the extraordinary leadership of Winston Churchill, was virtually isolated. Between July and October 1940 the Royal Air Force fought and won the Battle of Britain and Hitler's invasion plans were blocked (43,000 Britons died in the bombing raids of 1940-41).

The postwar years have been challenging. The last of the empire has gained independence (India in 1947, Malaya in 1957, Kenya in 1963), many traditional industries have collapsed and the nation has had to accept a new role as a partner in the EU. Britain is still a wealthy and influential country, but it's no longer a superpower and no longer able to maintain that it is anything more than an island just off the mainland of Europe.

GEOGRAPHY & ECOLOGY

Britain has an area of 240,000 sq km, about the same size as New Zealand or half the size of France. It is less than 600 miles from south to north and under 300 miles at its widest point.

There are no great mountains in terms of height, but this does not prevent a number of ranges from being spectacular. The mountains of Snowdonia in north-west Wales, the Cumbrian mountains in north-west England, and the Glenkens in south-west Scotland all reach around 1000m. The Grampians form the mountainous barrier between the Scottish Lowlands and Highlands, and include Ben Nevis, at 1343m the highest mountain on the island.

The seas surrounding the British Isles are shallow, and relatively warm because of the influence of the warm North Atlantic Current, also known as the Gulf Stream. This creates a temperate, changeable, maritime climate with few extremes of temperature but few cloudless sunny days!

With almost 57 million people living on a relatively small island, environmental issues, especially in relation to pollution from the ever-growing number of cars, are forcing their way on to the agenda. Britain has several high-profile environmental pressure groups. For more information try Greenpeace (☎ 020-7354 5100), Cannonbury Villas, London N1 2PN.

CLIMATE

Anyone who spends an extended period in Britain will soon sympathise with the locals' conversational obsession with the weather. Although in relative terms the climate is mild (London can go through winter without snowfall) and the annual rainfall not spectacular (912mm, or 35 inches), grey skies can make for an utterly depressing atmosphere. Settled periods of sunny weather are rare.

Even in midsummer you can go for days without seeing the sun, and showers (or worse) should be expected. To enjoy Britain you have to convince yourself that you *like* the rain – after all, that's what makes it so incredibly green! The average July temperature in London is 17.6°C (64°F), and the average January temperature is 4°C (39°F), and generally cooler the farther north you go.

GOVERNMENT & POLITICS

As yet the United Kingdom doesn't have a written constitution. Instead it operates under a mixture of parliamentary statutes, common law (a body of legal principles based on precedents that go back to Anglo-Saxon customs) and convention.

The monarch is the head of state, but real power has been whittled away to the point where the current Queen is a figurehead who acts almost entirely on the advice of 'her' ministers and Parliament.

Parliament has three separate elements: the Queen, the House of Commons and the House of Lords. In practice, the supreme body is the House of Commons, which is directly elected every five years. Voting is not compulsory, and candidates are elected if they win a simple majority in their constituencies. There are 659 constituencies (seats) – 529 for England, 40 for Wales, 72 for Scotland and 18 for Northern Ireland.

The House of Lords consists of the Lords Spiritual (26 senior bishops of the Church of England), the Lords Temporal (all hereditary and life peers), and the Lords of Appeal (or 'law lords'). None are elected by the general population, and the Labour government has pledged to remove the hereditary peers within the next few years.

If the Lords refuses to pass a bill, but it is passed twice by the Commons, it is sent to the Queen for her automatic assent.

The Queen appoints the leader of the majority party in the House of Commons as prime minister; all other ministers are appointed on the recommendation of the prime minister, most from the House of Commons. Ministers are responsible for government departments. The senior ministers make up the Cabinet, which, although answerable to Parliament, meets confidentially and in effect manages the government and its policies.

For the last 150 years a predominantly two-party system has operated. Since 1945 either the Conservative Party or the Labour Party has held power, the Conservatives largely drawing their support from suburbia and the countryside, and Labour from urban industrialised areas.

Put crudely, the Conservatives are right-wing, free-enterprise supporters, and Labour is left-wing in the social-democratic tradition. In recent years, however, the Labour Party has shed most of its socialist credo, and the Conservatives have softened their hard-right approach. In the 1997 elections, Tony Blair led the Labour Party to a landslide victory. Since then Scotland and Wales have been given their own elected parliaments and London has voted for its first elected mayor, the mercurial Ken Livingstone. However, promises to replace the first-past-the-post electoral system that has exaggerated the see-saw politics of the past half-century, with an alternative vote or proportional representation system, have not materialised. Still, the Labour Party looks set for a few more years in power, so time is likely on its side.

ECONOMY

Until the 18th century the economy was based on agriculture and the manufacture of woollen cloth. In the late 18th century the empire and the Industrial Revolution allowed Britain to become the first industrialised trading nation, and the population of South Wales, the Midlands, Yorkshire and the Scottish Lowlands

BRITAIN

expanded rapidly. Conditions for workers were appalling, but 19th-century Britain dominated world trade.

In the 20th century, a considerable proportion of industry was nationalised (railways, utilities, coal mines, steel, shipbuilding, even the motor industry), a process that was reversed under Margaret Thatcher.

Today free enterprise rules the roost, and although manufacturing continues to play an important role (particularly in the Midlands), service industries like banking and finance have grown rapidly (particularly in London and the south-east). Most of the traditional mining, engineering and cotton industries (especially in the Midlands and north) have disappeared.

The last 20 years have seen a battle against unemployment and inflation. By 2000, the economy had emerged from the doldrums. Unemployment is still high in areas like Liverpool, but inflation had shrunk to around 1%.

POPULATION & PEOPLE

Britain has a population of almost 57 million, an average 236 inhabitants per sq km, making the island one of the most crowded on the planet. The majority are concentrated in and around London, Birmingham, Manchester, Liverpool, Sheffield and Nottingham.

Since the war there has been significant immigration from the ex-colonies, especially the West Indies, Bangladesh, Pakistan and India. The 1990s also saw an influx of refugees from troubled areas of the world like Somalia and eastern Turkey. Outside London and big northern cities, however, the population is overwhelmingly white (although even small towns have Chinese and Indian restaurants).

ARTS

The greatest artistic contributions of the British have been in theatre, literature and architecture. Although there are notable individual exceptions, there is not an equivalent tradition of great painters, sculptors or composers.

Literature

For anyone who has studied 'English' literature, travelling in the footsteps of the great English, Scottish and Welsh writers and their characters can be one of the highlights of a visit. Hundreds of famous books capture specific moments in time, favourite landscapes, or particular groups of people. This guide can only suggest where to start.

In the beginning was Chaucer and his *Canterbury Tales*. This book may be responsible for more boring lectures than any other, but in its natural environment it comes to life, providing a vivid insight into medieval society, in particular into the lives of pilgrims on their way to Canterbury. Neville Coghill has written a good modern translation.

The next great figure to blight schoolchildren's lives was Shakespeare. Despite this, many will be tempted to follow in his footsteps to Stratford-upon-Avon where he lived and to the new Globe Theatre in London, built close to the site where he acted and where many of his plays were originally staged.

The most vivid insight into 17th-century London life comes courtesy of Samuel Pepys' *Diary*. In particular, he gives the most complete account of the Plague and the Great Fire of London.

The popular English novel, as we know it, only really appeared in the 18th century. If you plan to spend time in the Midlands, read Elizabeth Gaskell's *Mary Barton*, which paints a sympathetic picture of the plight of workers during the Industrial Revolution. This was also the milieu about which Charles Dickens wrote most powerfully. *Hard Times*, set in fictional Coketown, paints a brutal picture of the capitalists who prospered in it.

Jane Austen wrote about a very different, prosperous, provincial middle class. The intrigues and passions boiling away under the stilted constraints of 'propriety' are beautifully portrayed in *Emma* and *Pride and Prejudice*.

If you visit the Lake District you'll find countless references to William Wordsworth, the romantic poet who lived there for the first half of the 19th century. Modern readers may find him difficult, but at his best he has an exhilarating appreciation of the natural world.

More than most writers, Thomas Hardy was dependent on a sense of place and on the relationship between place and people. This makes his best work an evocative picture of Wessex, the region of England centred on Dorchester (Dorset) where he lived. *Tess of the D'Urbervilles* is one of his greatest novels.

Moving into the 20th century, DH Lawrence chronicled life in coal-mining Nottinghamshire in the brilliant *Sons and Lovers*. Written in the Depression of the 1930s, George Orwell's *Down and Out in Paris and London* describes his grim existence as a temporary vagrant. About the same time, Graham Greene wrote of the seedy side of Brighton in *Brighton Rock*.

One of the funniest and most vicious portrayals of late 20th-century Britain is Martin Amis' *London Fields*, while Hanef Kureishi writes of growing up in London's Pakistani community in *The Buddha of Suburbia* and Caryl Phillips writes of the Caribbean immigrants' experience in *The Final Passage*. Irvine Welsh's *Trainspotting*, which explores the world of Scottish heroin addiction, was made into a successful film.

Of the straightforward modern travelogues, the most successful has been Bill Bryson's highly entertaining and perceptive *Notes from a Small Island*. *The Kingdom by the Sea* by Paul Theroux, and Jonathan Raban's *Coasting* are both a little dated, but nonetheless readable. Nick Danziger's *Danziger's Britain* strips the gloss and the jokes aside to reveal the darker side of 'Cool Britannia'.

Architecture

Wherever you travel in Britain you'll not be far from a beautiful medieval church or cathedral. Perhaps the most distinctive architectural phenomenon in the country, however, is the huge number of extraordinary country houses that dot the landscape. The 18th and 19th-century aristocrats knew quality when they saw it and surrounded themselves with treasures in the most beautiful houses and gardens of Europe.

Although their successors have often inherited the arrogance of their ancestors, it is fortunate that inheritance taxes have forced many of them to open their houses and priceless art collections to the public. Even on a short visit you should try and visit Hatfield House, Blenheim Palace, Castle Howard or one of the other great stately homes.

Much of Britain's modern architecture is, however, regarded as a failure. Exceptions are works by Richard Rogers and Norman Foster, whose multifarious buildings dot the capital. Foster designed Stansted airport,

while Rogers was responsible for the Lloyd's Building. He's also the brains behind the controversial Millennium Dome in Greenwich.

Some of the most interesting architectural developments of recent years have not been new buildings so much as adaptations of existing buildings for new uses. Fine examples are London's Oxo Tower, which has been converted into a mixture of flats and eateries, and the Bankside power station, which now is the awesome Tate Modern gallery.

SOCIETY & CONDUCT

It is difficult to generalise about the British, but there's no doubt they are a creative, energetic and aggressive people whose impact on the world has been disproportionate to their numbers. They're also a diverse bunch, as one would expect given the variety of peoples who have made this island their home – from the original inhabitants, to the Celts, Romans, Angles, Jutes, Saxons, Vikings, Normans, Huguenots and Jews, and to the relatively recent arrivals from Asia, Africa and the Middle East.

Many people have strong preconceptions about the British but, if you're one of them, you'd be wise to abandon them. The most common stereotype is of a reserved, anally-retentive politeness and conservatism. Remember, however, that this is one of the planet's most crowded islands and some of these characteristics have developed as a method of coping with the constant crush of people. Regional and class differences may have shrunk, but accents and behaviour still vary widely depending on where you are and with which class you are mingling.

The extraordinary scenes following the death of Diana, Princess of Wales, probably laid to rest the cliches about the British 'stiff upper lip'. And the phrases 'cold' and 'inhibited' don't generally leap to mind when you're mixing with the working classes, the northern English, the Welsh or the Scots. Visit a nightclub in one of the big cities, a football match, a good local pub, or a country B&B and you might more readily describe the Brits as uninhibited, exhibitionist, passionate, aggressive, humorous, sentimental and hospitable.

It's certainly true that no other country in the world has more obsessive hobbyists – train *and* bus spotters, twitchers (bird-watchers), sports supporters, fashion victims, royalists, model-makers and collectors of every description, heritage preservationists, ramblers, pet owners, gardeners...

Britain is a country of sceptical individualists who resent any intrusion on their privacy or freedom, so it's hardly surprising that their flirtation with socialism was brief. Change happens slowly, and only after proceeding through endless consultations, committees, departments and layers of government. As a result, most things (including the cities) have developed organically and chaotically. This is a country where streets are rarely straight and trains rarely run on time.

Despite the cynics who proclaim that Britain is in a state of terminal decline, the major cities remain cultural powerhouses. You can only wonder what will appear next. A new tribe on the cutting edge of popular culture – like the mods, hippies, new romantics, punks and goths? Or a new political or economic movement – like industrialisation, imperialist capitalism, parliamentary democracy, socialism and Thatcherism?

RELIGION

The Church of England (C of E), a Christian church that became independent from Rome in the 16th century, is the largest, wealthiest and most influential in Britain. Along with the Church of Scotland, it's an 'established' church, meaning it's the official national church, with a close relationship to the state; the Queen appoints archbishops and bishops on the advice of the prime minister. The traditionally conservative C of E has shown some signs of recognising the need for change. In 1994, after many years of debate, the first women were ordained as priests. The debate has now moved on to the acceptability of gay clergy.

Although in a similar position as a national church, the Church of Scotland is quite different from the C of E – it is not subject to any outside authority and is much more a child of the Reformation. Other significant Protestant churches, or 'free' churches with no connection to the state, include Methodist, Baptist and United Reformed churches and the Salvation Army. Women have been priests in all these churches for some years.

Since the 16th century, Roman Catholics have experienced several periods of terrible persecution; one modern legacy is the ongoing problem of Northern Ireland. They did not gain political rights until 1829 or a formal structure until 1850, but today about one in 10 Britons considers themselves Catholic.

Recent estimates suggest there are now over one million Muslims and significant numbers of Sikhs and Hindus in Britain. But although attendances at Sunday church services continue to fall, the majority of the British population probably still regard themselves as Christians.

LANGUAGE

English may be one of the world's most widely spoken languages, but the language as it's spoken in some parts of Britain is sometimes incomprehensible to overseas visitors – even to those who think they've spoken it all their lives.

Facts for the Visitor

HIGHLIGHTS

Of Britain's many attractions, the most outstanding are listed here:

Islands
  Orkney, Skye, Lewis and Harris (Scotland)
Coastline
  Beachy Head (East Sussex), Land's End to St Ives (Cornwall), Tintagel (Cornwall), Ilfracombe to Lynton/Lynmouth (Devon), St David's to Cardigan (Wales), Scarborough to Saltburn (North Yorkshire), the Scottish coastline (particularly the west coast)
Museums & Galleries
  British Museum, Victoria & Albert Museum, Science Museum, Natural History Museum, National Gallery, Tate Galleries (London); HMS Victory (Portsmouth); Ironbridge Gorge (near Shrewsbury); Castle Museum (York); Burrell Collection (Glasgow)
Historic Towns
  Salisbury, Winchester, Bath, Oxford, Cambridge, Shrewsbury, St David's, York, Whitby, Durham, Edinburgh, St Andrews
Houses
  Hampton Court Palace, Hatfield House (London), Knole House (Kent), Blenheim Palace (Oxfordshire), Chatsworth (Derbyshire), Castle Howard (North Yorkshire)

Castles
Tower of London, Windsor, Dover, Leeds (near Canterbury), Conwy, Alnwick, Edinburgh
Cathedrals
Canterbury, Salisbury, Winchester, Wells, York, Durham
Regions
Exmoor National Park, the Cotswolds, Brecon Beacons National Park, Pembrokeshire Coast National Park, Peak District National Park, Lake District National Park, Scottish Highlands (especially the west coast)
Other Highlights
Avebury prehistoric complex, Hadrian's Wall

SUGGESTED ITINERARIES

Depending on the length of your stay, you might want to see and do the following:

Two days
Visit London.
One week
Visit London, Oxford, the Cotswolds, Bath and Bristol.
Two weeks
Visit London, Salisbury, Avebury, Bath, Bristol, Wells, Oxford, York and Edinburgh.
One month
Visit London, Cambridge, York, Edinburgh, Inverness, Isle of Skye, Fort William, Oban, Glasgow, the Lake District, Snowdonia (North Wales), Shrewsbury, the Cotswolds, Wells, Bath, Avebury and Oxford, before returning to London.
Two months
As for one month, but stay in one or two places for a week, and do a week-long walk.

PLANNING
When to Go

July and August are the busiest months, and should be avoided if possible. The crowds in London and popular cities like Oxford, York and Edinburgh have to be seen to be believed. You are just as likely to get good weather in spring and autumn, so May/June and September/October are the best times to visit, although October is getting too late for the Scottish Highlands.

Maps

The best introductory map to Britain is published by the British Tourist Authority (BTA), and is widely available.

Drivers will find there is a range of excellent road atlases. If you plan to go off the beaten track you will need 3 miles to the inch or better.

The Ordnance Survey caters to walkers, with a wide variety of maps at different scales. Its Landranger maps at 1:50,000 or about 1¼ inches to the mile are ideal. Look out for Harveys hiking maps, which can sometimes be more user-friendly and up to date than Ordnance Survey maps.

What to Bring

Since anything you think of can be bought in major towns and cities (including Vegemite), pack light and pick up extras as you go along.

TOURIST OFFICES

The British Tourist Authority (BTA) has a remarkably extensive collection of information, quite a lot of it free and relevant to budget travellers. Make sure you contact the BTA before you leave home, because some of the material and discounts are only available outside Britain. Overseas, it represents the regional tourist boards.

Tourist Information Centres (TICs) can be found even in small towns. They can give invaluable advice on accommodation and cheap ways of seeing the area, often including excellent guided walking tours.

Tourist Offices Abroad

The addresses of some overseas offices are as follows:

Australia
(☎ 02-9377 4400, fax 9377 4499) Level 16, The Gateway, 1 Macquarie Place, Circular Quay, Sydney, NSW 2000
Canada
(☎ 416-925 6326, fax 961 2175) Suite 450, 111 Avenue Rd, Toronto, Ont M5R 3JD
New Zealand
(☎ 09-303 1446, fax 776 965) 3rd floor, Dilworth Bldg, corner Queen and Customs Sts, Auckland 1
South Africa
(☎ 011-325 0343) Lancaster Gate, Hyde Lane, Hyde Park, Sandton 2196
USA
Chicago: (personal callers only) 625 N Michigan Avenue, Suite 1510, Chicago IL 60611
New York: (☎ 1 800 GO 2 BRITAIN) 551 Fifth Avenue, Suite 701, New York, NY 10176-0799

BRITAIN

There are more than 40 BTA offices worldwide. Addresses are listed on its Web site (www.bta.org.uk).

VISAS & DOCUMENTS
Visas

Visa regulations are always subject to change, so it's essential to check with your local embassy, high commission or consulate before leaving home.

Currently, you don't need a visa if you are a citizen of Australia, Canada, New Zealand, South Africa or the USA. Tourists are generally permitted to stay for up to six months, but are prohibited from working. Citizens of the EU can live and work in Britain free of immigration control – they don't need a visa to enter the country.

The immigration authorities have always been tough, and this is unlikely to change; dress neatly when entering the country, and carry some evidence that you have sufficient funds to support yourself. A credit card and/or an onward ticket will help. People have been refused entry because they happened to be carrying documents (perhaps work references) that suggested they intended to work.

Work Permits

EU nationals don't need a work permit, but all other nationalities must have one to work legally. If the *main* purpose of your visit is to work, you basically have to be sponsored by a British company.

However, if you're a citizen of a Commonwealth country, and aged between 17 and 26 inclusive, you may apply for a Working Holiday Entry Certificate that allows you to spend up to two years in the UK, and to take work that is 'incidental to a holiday'.

You must apply to your nearest UK mission overseas, prior to your arrival. It is not possible to switch from being a visitor to a working holiday-maker, nor is it possible to claim back any time spent out of the UK during the two-year period.

If you're a Commonwealth citizen and have a parent born in the UK, you may be eligible for a Certificate of Entitlement to the Right of Abode, which means you can live and work in Britain free of immigration control.

If you are a Commonwealth citizen and have a grandparent born in the UK, or if the grandparent was born before 31 March 1922 in what is now the Republic of Ireland, you may qualify for a UK Ancestry-Employment Certificate, which means you can work full time for up to four years in the UK.

Visiting students from the USA can get a work permit allowing them to work for six months; you have to be at least 18 years old and a full-time student at a college or university. The permit is available through the Council on International Educational Exchange (☎ 212-822 2600), 205 East 42nd St, New York, NY 10017; Web site www.ciee .org. Contact the council for current details and fees.

If you have queries once you are in the UK, contact the Home Office, Immigration & Nationality Department (☎ 020-8686 0688), Lunar House, Wellesley Rd, Croydon CR9 2BY (East Croydon train station).

Driving Licence

Your normal driving licence is legal for 12 months from the date you last entered the country; for stays longer than a year you should apply for a British licence at a post office.

See the introductory Facts for the Visitor chapter for information on international student identity and discount cards.

EMBASSIES & CONSULATES
UK Embassies Abroad

UK embassies in Western Europe are listed in the relevant country chapters in this book. Other UK embassies abroad include:

Australia – British High Commission
(☎ 02-6270 6666) Commonwealth Ave, Yarralumla, Canberra, ACT 2600

Canada – British High Commission
(☎ 613-237 1530) 80 Elgin St, Ottawa, Ont K1P 5K7

Japan – British Embassy
(☎ 03-3265 5511) 1 Ichiban-cho, Chiyoda-ku, Tokyo

New Zealand – British High Commission
(☎ 04-472 6049) 44 Hill St, Wellington 1

South Africa – British High Commission
(☎ 21-461 7220) 91 Parliament St, Cape Town 8001

USA – British Embassy
(☎ 202-462 1340) 3100 Massachusetts Ave NW, Washington DC 20008

Foreign Embassies in the UK

Countries with diplomatic representation in the UK include the following:

Australian High Commission
(☎ 020-7379 4334) Australia House, The Strand, London WC2; tube: Temple

Canadian High Commission
(☎ 020-7258 6600) 1 Grosvenor Square, London W1; tube: Bond St

French Consulate General
(☎ 0891-887733) 6A Cromwell Place, London SW7; tube: South Kensington

German Embassy
(☎ 020-7824 1300) 23 Belgrave Square, London SW1; tube: Hyde Park Corner

Irish Embassy
(☎ 020-7235 2171) 17 Grosvenor Place, London SW1; tube: Hyde Park Corner

Japanese Embassy
(☎ 020-7465 6500) 101-04 Piccadilly, London W1; tube: Green Park

New Zealand High Commission
(☎ 020-7930 8422) New Zealand House, 80 Haymarket, London SW1; tube: Piccadilly Circus

Royal Netherlands Embassy
(☎ 020-7590 3200) 38 Hyde Park Gate, London SW7; tube: Gloucester Rd

South African High Commission
(☎ 020-7930 4488) South Africa House, Trafalgar Square, London WC2; tube: Trafalgar Square

Spanish Consulate General
(☎ 020-7235 5555) 20 Draycott Place, London SW3; tube: Sloane Square

US Embassy
(☎ 020-7499 9000) 24 Grosvenor Square, London W1; tube: Bond St

CUSTOMS

For imported goods there's a two-tier system: the first for goods bought duty-free, the second for goods bought in an EU country where tax and duty have been paid. Duty-free purchases within the EU have been phased out.

The second tier is relevant because a number of products (eg, alcohol and tobacco) are much cheaper on the Continent. Under the single-market rules, however, as long as tax and duty have been paid somewhere in the EU, there is no prohibition on importing them within the EU, so long as the goods are for individual consumption. Consequently, a thriving business has developed with Britons making day trips to France to load their cars up with cheap beer, wine and cigarettes – the savings can more than pay for the trip.

Duty Free

If coming from a non-EU country, you can import 200 cigarettes or 250g of tobacco, 2L of still wine plus 1L of spirits or another 2L of wine (sparkling or otherwise), 60cc of perfume, 250cc of *eau de Cologne*, and other duty-free goods to the value of £145.

Tax & Duty Paid

If you buy from a normal retail outlet, customs uses the following guidelines to distinguish personal imports from those on a commercial scale: 800 cigarettes or 1kg of tobacco, 10L of spirits, 20L of fortified wine, 90L of wine (not more than 60 sparkling) and 110L of beer!

MONEY
Currency

No euros here...yet! The currency is the pound sterling (£), and there are 100 pence (p) in a pound. One and 2p coins are copper; 5p, 10p, 20p and 50p coins are silver; the bulky £1 coin is gold-coloured; and the £2 coin is coloured gold and silver. The word pence is rarely used in common language; like its written counterpart it is abbreviated and pronounced pee.

Notes (bills) come in £5, £10, £20 and £50 denominations and vary in colour and size. You may also come across notes issued by several Scottish banks, including a £1 note; they are legal tender on both sides of the border, though shopkeepers in England and Wales may be reluctant to accept them in which case ask a bank to swap them for you.

Exchange Rates

country	unit		pound sterling
Australia	A$1	=	£0.39
Canada	C$1	=	£0.45
euro	€1	=	£0.60
France	1FF	=	£0.09
Germany	DM1	=	£0.31
Ireland	IR£1	=	£0.76
Japan	¥100	=	£0.61
New Zealand	NZ$1	=	£0.30
USA	US$1	=	£0.67

BRITAIN

Costs

Britain is extremely expensive and London is horrendous. While you are in London you will need to budget around £25 to £30 a day just for bare survival. Any sightseeing, restaurant meals or nightlife will be on top of that. There's not much point visiting if you can't participate in some of the city's life, so if possible add another £15. Costs will obviously be even higher if you choose to stay in a central hotel and eat restaurant meals.

Once you start moving around the country, particularly if you have a transport pass of some description, or you're walking or hitching, the costs can drop. Fresh food is roughly the same price as in Australia and the US. However, without including long-distance transport, and assuming you stay in hostels, you'll still need £15 to £20 per day.

If you hire a car or use a transport pass, stay in B&Bs, eat one sit-down meal a day, and don't stint on entry fees, you'll need £40 to £60 per day (not including long-distance transport costs). If you're travelling by car you'll probably average a further £9 a day on petrol and parking; if you travel by some sort of pass you will probably need to average a couple of pounds a day on local transport or for hiring a bike.

Bureaux de Change & Banks

Be careful using *bureaux de change*; they may offer good exchange rates, but they frequently levy outrageous commissions and fees. Make sure you establish the rate, the percentage commission and any fees in advance.

The bureaus at international airports are exceptions to the rule. They charge less than most high-street banks (ie, major or city-centre banks) and cash sterling travellers cheques for free.

Bank hours vary, but you'll be safe if you visit between 9.30 am and 3.30 pm, Monday to Friday. Some banks are open on Saturday, generally from 9.30 am till noon. Once again, the total cost of foreign exchange can vary quite widely; in particular, watch for the minimum charge.

It's difficult to open a bank account, although if you're planning to work, it may be essential. Building societies tend to be more welcoming and often have better interest rates. You'll need a (semi) permanent address, and

you'll smooth the way considerably if you have a reference or introductory letter from your bank manager at home, *plus* bank statements for the previous year. Owning credit/charge cards also helps. Look for a bank or building society current account that pays interest, gives you a cheque book and guarantee card, and has access to ATMs (called cashpoints in Britain).

Cheques & Credit Cards

Travellers cheques are rarely accepted outside banks or used for everyday transactions so you need to cash them in advance.

Your cheques should ideally be in pounds. Use American Express or Thomas Cook – they are widely recognised, well represented and don't charge for cashing their own cheques. Thomas Cook has an office in every decent-sized town, and American Express has representation in most cities.

Visa, MasterCard, Access, American Express and Diners Club cards are widely used, although most B&Bs require cash. If your bank has an agreement with an international money system such as Cirrus, Maestro or Plus, you can often withdraw money direct from your home account using ATMs in Britain.

Tipping & Bargaining

Taxi drivers and waiters all expect 10% tips. Some restaurants include a service charge (tip) of 10% to 15% on the bill, but this should be clearly advertised. Prices are almost always fixed. Bargaining is only really expected if you're buying second-hand gear, especially vehicles. Always check whether there are discounts for students, young/old people or hostel members.

Consumer Taxes

Value-added tax (VAT) is a 17.5% sales tax levied on virtually all goods and services, but not on food and books. Restaurant menu prices must by law include VAT.

In some cases it's possible to claim a refund of VAT paid on goods – a considerable saving. If you have spent fewer than 365 days living in Britain out of the two years prior to making the purchase, and if you are leaving the EU within three months of making the purchase, you are eligible.

There are a number of companies that offer a centralised refunding service to shops. Participating shops carry a sign in their window. You can avoid bank charges usually encountered when cashing pound travellers cheques by using a credit card for purchases and requesting that your VAT refund be credited to your card account. In some cases, cash refunds are now available at the major airports.

POST & COMMUNICATIONS
Post
Post office hours can vary, but most are open 9 am to 5 pm Monday to Friday, and to noon on Saturday. Within the UK, first-class mail is quicker and more expensive (27p per letter) than 2nd-class mail (19p).

Airmail letters to Europe are 31p, to the Americas and Australasia 43p (up to 10g) and 63p (up to 20g). An airmail letter to the USA or Canada will generally take less than a week; to Australia or New Zealand, around a week.

Telephone
Since British Telecom (BT) was privatised, several companies have started competing for its business. However, most public phone booths are still operated by BT.

The famous red phone booth survives in conservation areas. More usually you'll see glass cubicles of two types: one takes cash, while the other uses prepaid, plastic debit cards and, increasingly, credit cards.

All phones come with reasonably clear instructions. If you're likely to make some calls (especially international) and don't want to be caught out, make sure you buy a phonecard. There are numerous cheap phonecards around which massively undercut BT rates on international calls.

Most BT services are expensive; make your directory assistance calls (☎ 192) from a public telephone – they're free that way.

Local & National Calls Dial ☎ 100 for a BT operator. Local calls are charged by time, and national calls (including Scotland, Wales and Northern Ireland) are charged by time and distance. Standard rates apply 8 am to 6 pm Monday to Friday; the cheap rate is 6 pm to 8 am, Monday to Friday; and the weekend rate is midnight Friday to midnight Sunday.

Note that any number that begins with the code 0870- is charged at the national rate; a number that begins with the code 0845- is charged at the (cheaper) local rate.

International Calls Dial ☎ 155 to get the international operator. Direct dialling is cheaper, but some budget travellers prefer operator-connected reverse-charge (collect) calls.

To get an international line (for international direct dialling) dial ☎ 00, then the country code, area code (drop the first zero if there is one) and number.

Purchase the discount phonecards advertised on newsagent windows in major towns and cities or look for the independently operated telecom centres. International rates offered at these places are generally the lowest available.

Fax & Email
Most hotels now have faxes. Some shops also offer fax services, advertised by a sign in the window. To collect your email visit one of the growing number of cybercafes and pubs.

INTERNET RESOURCES
Most Internet Service Providers (ISPs) no longer charge for access time. Just pick up a free CD from Dixons to join Freeserve. Other companies such as BT offer cheap tie-ins with call time included for less than £10 a month.

Britain is second only to the USA in its number of Web sites, and there are many that are of interest to cyber travellers. The Lonely Planet site (www.lonelyplanet.com.au) offers a speedy link to numerous sites for travellers. Also see the UK Travel Guide (www. uktravel.com).

BOOKS
There are countless guidebooks covering every nook and cranny in the British Isles. When you arrive, one of your first stops should be at a good book/map shop – see the London Bookshops section.

Guidebooks
For greater detail on the country, look for Lonely Planet's *Britain* and *Scotland* guidebooks as well as the *London* and *Edinburgh* city guides.

For in-depth information on history, art and architecture, the *Blue Guide* series is excellent. The separate guides to *England* (£14.99), *Scotland* (£15.99), and *Wales* (£12.99) have a wealth of scholarly information on all the important sites.

Numerous books list B&Bs, restaurants, hotels, country houses, camping and caravan parks, self-catering cottages etc. The objectivity of most of these books is questionable as the places they cover have to pay for the privilege of being included; however, they can still be useful. Those published by the tourist authorities are reliable (although not comprehensive) and are widely available in information centres, usually for around £5.

Hikers should check Lonely Planet's guide to *Walking in Britain*. Individual long-distance trails are all covered by the *Countryside Commission National Trail Guide* series published by Aurum Press, usually costing around £10.99. For shorter day walks the *Bartholomew Map & Guide* series (£5.99) is recommended. They are spiral-bound books with good maps and descriptions; most walks they describe take around two to three hours.

NEWSPAPERS & MAGAZINES

There are few countries in the world where you can wake up to such a range of newspapers. The quality daily papers are the *Independent*, the *Guardian*, the *Telegraph* and the *Times*. At the other extreme, outrageous tabloids like the *Sun*, and on Sunday the *News of the World*, continue to plumb new depths. Curiously, media magnate Rupert Murdoch owns both the *Times* and the *Sun*. There's an equally diverse range of magazines.

RADIO & TV

There are five regular TV channels – BBC1, ITV and Channel 5 are quite mainstream, while BBC2 and Channel 4 are rather more serious – plus Murdoch's satellite Sky TV and numerous cable channels. Radio also has a mix of BBC and commercial stations. Try BBC Radio 4 for news and drama; BBC Radio 5 for sport; GLR, Heart, Virgin or Capital Radio (London) for pop/rock; Kiss FM for soul; and Classic FM for classical music.

PHOTOGRAPHY & VIDEO

Print film is widely available, but slide film can be harder to find except in specialist photographic retailers (Boots usually stocks it). Dull, overcast conditions are common, so high-speed films (ISO 200 or 400, around £5 for 36 exposures) are useful.

Most videos sold in Britain are for VHS format, incompatible with NTSC and SECAM.

TIME

Wherever you are in the world, the time on your watch is measured in relation to the time in London's Greenwich Mean Time (GMT).

Daylight-saving time (also known as British summer time) confuses the issue, but to give you an idea, New York is five hours behind GMT, San Francisco is eight hours behind, and Sydney is 10 hours ahead of GMT. Phone the international operator on ☎ 155 to find out the exact difference.

LAUNDRY

You'll find a laundrette on every high street. The average cost for a single load is £1.20 for washing, and around £1 for drying.

TOILETS

Public toilets are well signposted. There may be a charge of 10p to 20p for their use.

WOMEN TRAVELLERS

Women will find Britain a reasonably enlightened country. Lone travellers should have no problems, although common-sense caution should be observed in big cities, especially when walking alone at night. Hitch-hiking, while possible, is extremely risky. Some pubs still retain a heavy masculine atmosphere but on the whole they're becoming increasingly family-friendly.

The London Rape Crisis Centre (☎ 020-7837 1600) is run by women and gives confidential advice and support to women who have been sexually assaulted.

GAY & LESBIAN TRAVELLERS

London, Manchester and Brighton are Britain's main gay and lesbian centres. You'll also find gay and lesbian information centres in most other cities and large towns. Check the listings in *Gay Times*, available from newsagents for details of major events such as London Pride in early July. The age of consent is 16.

DISABLED TRAVELLERS

The Royal Association for Disability and Rehabilitation (RADAR) publishes a useful guide, *Holidays and Travel Abroad: A Guide for Disabled People*, which gives a good overview of facilities available. For disabled travellers in the capital, it also stocks *Access in London* (£7.95). Contact RADAR (☎ 020-7250 3222) at 12 City Forum, 250 City Rd, London EC1V 8AF.

SENIOR TRAVELLERS

All senior citizens (over 60s) are entitled to discounts on public transport, museum admission fees etc, provided they show proof of their age. Sometimes a pass must be purchased to qualify for discounts. Rail companies offer a Senior Citizens' Railcard (£18 for one year) giving a third off fares. Bus companies have similar cards.

USEFUL ORGANISATIONS

Membership of the Youth Hostels Association (YHA) is a must (£10 over-18, £5 under-18). There are more than 300 hostels in Britain and members are also eligible for an impressive list of discounts. See this book's introductory Facts for the Visitor chapter for information on the various ISIC and FIYTO cards.

Membership of English Heritage and the National Trust is worth considering, especially if you are going to be in Britain for an extended period and are interested in fine historical buildings. Both are nonprofit organisations dedicated to environmental preservation and care for many spectacular sites.

Australasian Clubs
The London Walkabout Club (☎ 020-7938 3001), 7 Abingdon Rd W8; Deckers London Club (☎ 020-7244 8641), 35 Earl's Court Rd SW5; and Drifters (☎ 020-7402 9171), 22A Craven Terrace W2, all offer back-up services like mail holding, local information, discounts on film processing, freight forwarding and equipment purchase, and cheap tours. They're mainly aimed at Aussies and Kiwis, but anyone is welcome. Membership is around £15.
English Heritage (EH)
Most EH (☎ 020-7973 3000) properties cost nonmembers around £2.30 to enter. Adult membership is £28 and gives free entry to all EH properties, half-price entry to Historic Scotland and Cadw (Welsh) properties, and an excellent guidebook and map. You can join at most major sites.
Great British Heritage Pass
This pass gives you access to National Trust and English Heritage properties and some of the expensive private properties. A seven-day pass costs £32, 15 days is £45, one month is £60. It's available overseas (ask your travel agent or contact the nearest Thomas Cook office) or at the British Travel Centre in London.
National Trust (NT)
Most NT (☎ 020-7222 9251) properties cost nonmembers from £1 to £6 to enter. Adult membership is £30, under 26 is £15. It gives free entry to all English, Welsh, Scottish and Northern Irish properties, and an excellent guidebook and map. You can join at most major sites. There are reciprocal arrangements with the National Trust organisations in Scotland, Australia, New Zealand, Canada and the USA (the Royal Oak Foundation) all of which are cheaper to join.

DANGERS & ANNOYANCES

Britain is remarkably safe considering its size and the disparities in wealth. However, city crime is certainly not unknown, so caution, especially at night, is necessary. Pickpockets and bag snatchers operate in crowded public places.

When travelling by tube at night in London, choose a carriage with other people and avoid some of the deserted tube stations in the suburbs; a bus can be a better choice. Avoid large groups of young lads after the pubs shut down (11 pm), as violence is worryingly commonplace in town centres across Britain.

Drugs of every description are widely available, especially in the clubs where Ecstasy (not all of it pure) is at the heart of the rave scene. Nonetheless, all the usual dangers associated with black-market drugs apply.

Cannabis is still illegal, although possession of small quantities usually attracts only a caution.

Hotel/hostel touts descend on backpackers at London underground stations like Earl's Court, Liverpool St and Victoria. Treat their claims with scepticism and don't accept offers of free lifts (you could end up miles away). Be careful of unauthorised taxi drivers approaching you at these same stations; play safe and stick with the regulated black cabs.

BRITAIN

The big cities have many beggars; if you must give don't wave a full wallet around and carry some change in a separate pocket. It is preferable, however, to donate to a recognised charity. Shelter (☎ 020-7253 0202), 88 Old St, London EC1, is a voluntary organisation that helps the homeless; or consider buying the *Big Issue*, an interesting weekly magazine available from street vendors who benefit directly from sales.

Britain is not without racial problems, particularly in some of the deprived suburbs of big cities, but in general tolerance prevails. Few visitors have problems associated with their skin colour.

Traditionally the British have preferred baths to showers. In many B&Bs and private houses you may find just a bath or a highly complicated contraption that produces a thin trickle of scalding hot or freezing cold water. Get the homeowner to explain exactly how it works if you want a half-decent shower.

BUSINESS HOURS

Offices are open 9 am to 5 pm Monday to Friday. Shops may be open for longer hours, and all shops are open 9 am to 5 pm Saturday. Except in rural areas, some shops also open 10 am to 4 pm Sunday. Late-night shopping is usually possible on Thursday or Friday.

PUBLIC HOLIDAYS & SPECIAL EVENTS

Most banks, businesses and a number of museums and other places of interest are closed on public holidays (also known as Bank Holidays): New Year's Day; 2 January (Bank Holiday in Scotland); Good Friday; Easter Monday (not in Scotland); May Day Bank Holiday (first Monday in May); Spring Bank Holiday (last Monday in May); Summer Bank Holiday (first Monday in August in Scotland, last Monday in August outside Scotland); Christmas Day; and Boxing Day.

There are countless, diverse special events held around the country all year. Even small villages have weekly markets, and many still enact traditional customs and ceremonies, some of which are believed to date back thousands of years.

New Year
Hogmanay Huge street parties in Edinburgh

March
Edinburgh Folk Festival Held in the last week of the month
Oxford/Cambridge University Boat Race Traditional rowing race; River Thames, Putney to Mortlake, London

April
Grand National Famous horse-racing meeting held on the first Saturday of the month; Aintree, Liverpool

May
English FA Cup Final Deciding match in football tournament; Wembley, London
Glasgow Mayfest High-quality arts festival running for three weeks
Bath International Festival Arts festival; runs for two weeks in late May
Chelsea Flower Show Premier flower show held in the last week of the month; Royal Hospital, London

June
Beating Retreat Military bands and marching held in the first week of the month; Whitehall, London
Derby Week Horse racing and people-watching in the first week of the month; Epsom, Surrey
Trooping the Colour The Queen's birthday parade in mid-June with spectacular pageantry; Whitehall, London
Royal Ascot More horses and hats in mid-June; Ascot, Berkshire
Lawn Tennis Championships Runs for two weeks in late June; Wimbledon, London
Henley Royal Regatta Premier rowing and social event in late June; Henley-on-Thames, Oxfordshire
Glastonbury Festival Enormous, open-air music festival and hippy happening in late June; Pilton, Somerset

July
Cowes Week Yachting extravaganza in late July; Isle of Wight

August
Edinburgh Military Tattoo Pageantry and military displays, starting early in the month, running for three weeks
Edinburgh International & Fringe Festivals Premier international arts festivals, starting mid-August, running for three weeks

August (August Bank Holiday)
Notting Hill Carnival Enormous Caribbean
carnival held late in the month; London
Reading Festival Three days of outdoor rock
and roll late in the month; Reading, Berkshire

September
Royal Braemar Gathering (Highland Games)
Kilts, cabers and other Highland paraphernalia, held in early September; Braemar, Aberdeenshire

November
Guy Fawkes Day Held on 5 November in
memory of an unsuccessful Catholic coup;
bonfires and fireworks around the country

ACTIVITIES
Hiking
Travellers on a budget are inevitably going to
do plenty of walking, but this is also the best
way to see Britain. With the exception of
Scotland, you are rarely going to be far away
from civilisation, so it's easy to put together
walks that connect with public transport and
take you from hostel to hostel, village to village. A tent and cooking equipment aren't always essential but warm waterproof clothing,
sturdy footwear and a map and compass are.

The countryside is crisscrossed by a network of rights of way, or public footpaths,
most of them crossing private land. They
have existed for centuries and are marked on
the excellent Ordnance Survey maps.

Every small town and village is surrounded by walks; look for local guidebooks
in TICs, newsagents and bookshops. Consider spending a week based in one spot and
doing a series of circular walks in the surrounding countryside.

For long-distance walks, the best areas include the Cotswolds, the Exmoor National
Park, the North York Moors National Park,
the Yorkshire Dales National Park, the Lake
District, the Pembrokeshire Coast National
Park, and the Scottish islands. There are
many superb long-distance walks in Scotland
but, day walks aside, these tend to require
more preparation.

The national parks were set up to protect
the finest landscapes, but much of the land remains privately owned. It's almost always
necessary to get permission from a landowner
before pitching a tent.

There are 10 national long-distance trails
in England and Wales, and three in Scotland,
created and administered by the relevant
countryside commissions (which, along with
Aurum Press, publish excellent guides). A
number of these are mentioned in this chapter. There are also a growing number of regional routes created by county councils,
some of which are well organised and excellent. Finally, there are unofficial long-distance
routes, often devised by individuals or groups
like the Ramblers' Association. Bear in mind
that some walks, particularly along the coast
and in the Yorkshire Dales and Lake District,
can be very crowded on weekends and in
July/August.

The British countryside looks deceptively
gentle. Especially in the hills or on the open
moors, however, the weather can close in and
turn nasty very quickly at any time of the
year. It is vital if you're walking in upland
areas to carry good maps and a compass (and
know how to use them), plus, of course,
warm and waterproof clothing.

Those intent on a serious walking holiday
should contact the Ramblers' Association
(☎ 020-7339 8500), 1 Wandsworth Rd, London SW8 2XX; the group's *Yearbook* (£4.99)
is widely available and itemises the information available for each walk, the appropriate
maps, and nearby accommodation (hostels,
B&Bs and bunkhouses). Ramblers Web site
is at www.ramblers.org.uk.

Boating
Even budget travellers should consider the
possibility of hiring a canal boat and cruising
part of the extraordinary 2000-mile network
of canals that has survived the railway era.

Especially if you go outside the high season, prices are quite reasonable, ranging from
about £300 per week in April to £650 in August for a boat that sleeps four. Try
Alvechurch Boat Centres (☎ 0121-445 2909)
or Hoseason's Holidays (☎ 01502-501501).

The Inland Waterways Association (☎ 020-7586 2556), 114 Regent's Park Rd, London
NW1 8UQ, publishes an annual *Directory* and
can provide mail-order maps and guides.

Cycling
The scenery changes swiftly, you're never
far away from food and accommodation, and

there is a great network of backroads and lanes that are comparatively traffic-free. It's also cheap, and you see more from a bike than from any other form of transport.

There are numerous places where you can hire them. Prices vary, but you should be able to get a three-speed bike for around £20 per week, or a mountain bike for £60. Book ahead if you want a bike in July or August. Hiring is easiest if you have a credit card; a signed slip is used in lieu of a large deposit. You will also need ID (a passport will do).

Bicycles can be taken on most rail services, but the regulations are complex and inconsistent so it is essential to check in advance. In some cases it is also necessary to make a reservation. The major coach operators (National Express, Citylink etc) don't carry bikes, but most local bus lines do.

The Cyclists' Touring Club (☎ 01483-417217), Cotterell House, 69 Meadrow, Godalming, Surrey GU7 3HS, is a national cycling association that can provide a great deal of helpful information for visiting cyclists, including detailed information on a range of routes. Call or write for a list of its publications; Web site www.ctc.org.uk. For more ideas on where to tour check Lonely Planet's *Cycling in Britain*.

ACCOMMODATION

This will almost certainly be your single largest expense. Even camping can be expensive at official sites. For budget travellers, there are really only three options: hostels, B&Bs and some hotels. Outside London, there are more and more independent backpackers hostels, particularly in the south-west, Scotland and some of the popular hiking regions.

Camping

Free camping is rarely possible, except in Scotland. Camping grounds vary widely in quality but most have reasonable facilities, although they're often ugly and usually inaccessible unless you have a car or bike. For an extensive listing, buy *Camping & Caravanning in Britain* published by the Automobile Association (£7.99); local TICs also have lists.

YHA/HI Hostels

Hostelling International/Youth Hostel Association (YHA) membership gives you access to a huge network of hostels throughout England, Wales, Scotland and Ireland.

There are separate, local associations for England/Wales, Scotland, Northern Ireland and Ireland, and each publishes individual accommodation guides. If you're travelling extensively it's essential to get hold of these. Most importantly, they include the (often complicated) days and hours during which the hostels are open, as well as information on price, facilities and how to reach each place.

Accommodation guides and association membership (£5 for under 18s, £10 for adults) are available at the YHA Adventure Shop (☎ 020-7836 1036), 14 Southampton St, London WC2 (tube: Covent Garden).

All hostels have facilities for self-catering and some have cheap meals. Advance booking is advisable, especially on weekends, Bank Holidays and at any time over the summer months. Booking policies vary: most hostels accept phone bookings and payment with Visa or MasterCard; some will accept same-day bookings, although they will usually only hold a bed until 6 pm; some work on a first come, first served basis. Bear in mind that some hostels have curfews at night and are locked during the day.

Overnight prices are in two tiers: under 18, with prices from £5 to £19, but mostly around £7; and adult, with prices from £6 to £23, but mostly around £11. Bear in mind that when you add £3 for breakfast, you can get very close to cheap B&B prices. Bed linen is free at hostels in England and Wales but costs 60p in Scotland.

Independent Hostels

The growing network of independent hostels offers the opportunity to escape curfews and lockouts for a price of around £10 per night in a basic bunkroom. Like youth hostels these are great places to meet other travellers, and they tend to be in town centres rather than out in the sticks. *The Independent Hostel Guide* (£3.95) covers England, Scotland, Wales and the whole of Ireland, but new places are opening fast so it's always worth asking at the TIC.

Universities

Many British universities offer their student accommodation to visitors during the Christmas, Easter and summer holidays. Bed and breakfast will normally cost from £18 to £25 per person.

For more information contact the British Universities Accommodation Consortium (BUAC; ☎ 0115-950 4571, fax 942 2505), Box No 967, University Park, Nottingham NG7 2RD.

B&Bs, Guesthouses & Pubs

B&Bs are a great British institution and the cheapest private accommodation you can find. At the bottom end (£13 to £18 per person) you get a bedroom in a normal house, a shared bathroom and an enormous cooked breakfast. Small B&Bs may only have one room to let, and you can really feel like a guest of the family. More upmarket B&Bs have *en suite* bathrooms and TVs in each room. Single rooms are in short supply and many B&B owners would rather not let a room at all than let a single person have it for less than the price of both beds.

Guesthouses, which are often just large converted houses with half a dozen rooms, are an extension of the idea. They range from £15 to £50 a night, depending on the quality of the food and accommodation. In general, they tend to be less personal than B&Bs, and more like small budget hotels. Local pubs and inns also often have cheap rooms; they can be good fun since they place you at the hub of the community.

All these options are promoted and organised by local TICs, which can provide you with a list of possibilities in the area.

Booking The TICs can make bookings. These services are particularly handy for big cities and over weekends and during the summer high season. Bookings can be free, but are usually £2.75 (£5 in the case of London). In addition you often pay a 10% deposit, which is subtracted from the price.

Classification & Grading The national tourist boards operate a classification and grading system; participating hotels, guesthouses and B&Bs have a plaque at the front door. If you want to be reasonably confident that your accommodation reaches basic standards of safety and cleanliness, the first classification is 'listed', denoting clean and comfortable accommodation. Better places

are indicated by one to five crowns – the more crowns, the more facilities and, generally, the more expensive the room.

In addition to the classifications there are gradings which are perhaps more significant. 'Approved', 'commended' and 'highly commended' gradings reflect a subjective judgment of quality.

In practice, actually seeing the place, even from the outside, will give you a better idea of what to expect. Don't be afraid to ask to have a look at your room before you sign up.

Bear in mind that some accommodation providers prefer not to pay the TIC to promote them, so there are always more places available than appear in the lists. Unlisted places are often as good as those that are listed, but in big towns it's wise to stick with registered places since some B&Bs now earn their living from accommodating homeless people...not necessarily the atmosphere you'd expect for a holiday.

Rental

There has been a big increase in the number of houses and cottages available for short-term rent. Staying in one place – preferably an attractive village – gives you an unmatched opportunity to get a real feel for a region and a community. Cottages for four can be as little as £100 per week; some even let for three days.

It's often possible to book through TICs, but there are also a number of excellent agencies that can supply you with glossy brochures to help the decision-making process. Outside weekends and July/August, it's not essential to book a long way ahead. Most organisations have agents in North America and Australasia. Among them, Country Holidays (☎ 01282-445095), Spring Mill, Earby, Colne, Lancashire BB8 6RN, has been recommended. English Country Cottages (☎ 01328-864041), Grove Farm Barns, Fakenham, Norfolk NR21 9NB, is one of the largest agencies.

FOOD

British cuisine used to crop up more often in comedy sketches than on the restaurant review pages but fortunately those days are long gone. Nowadays you don't have to try hard to find a decent restaurant even in some of the most out-of-the-way places.

BRITAIN

In the main towns and cities a cosmopolitan range of cuisines is available. Particularly if you like pizza, pasta and curry, you should be able to get a reasonable meal for under £10 pretty well anywhere.

Vegetarians should buy a copy of *The Vegetarian Travel Guide*, published annually by the UK Vegetarian Society and covering hundreds of places to eat and stay. Most restaurants have at least a token vegetarian dish, although, as anywhere, vegans will find the going tough. Indian restaurants offer welcome salvation.

Takeaways, Cafes & Pubs

Britain has a full complement of takeaway chains, from McDonald's, Burger King and Pizza Hut to the home-grown and aptly named Wimpy.

The days of the 'greasy spoon' cafe which used to dispense cheap breakfasts (eggs, bacon and sausages) and English tea (strong, sweet and milky) on every high street look numbered, their place taken by the ubiquitous cafe-bars which prefer pasta and pesto to beans and burgers. The Pret A Manger readymade sandwich chain is also spreading its tentacles out of London, although you'll probably find cheaper sarnies (surprisingly) at Boots the Chemist!

If you're on a tight budget pubs will often be one of your best sources of cheap nutrition. At the bottom end they're not much different from cafes, while at the expensive end they're closer to restaurants. Chilli con carne or lasagne are often the cheapest offerings on the menu. A filling 'ploughman's lunch' of bread, cheese and pickle costs around £3.50.

Self-Catering

The cheapest way to eat in Britain is to cook for yourself. Hopefully, however, you won't be forced to the extremes of an Australian backpacker who was arrested and jailed for attempting to cook a Canada goose in Hyde Park.

DRINKS

British pubs generally serve an impressive range of beers – lagers, bitters, ales and stouts. The drink most people from the New World know as beer is actually lager and, much to the distress of local connoisseurs, lagers (including Foster's and Budweiser) now take a huge proportion of the market. Fortunately, the traditional English bitter has made something of a comeback, thanks to the Campaign for Real Ale (CAMRA) organisation. Look for its endorsement sticker on pub windows.

If you've been raised on lager, a traditional bitter or ale is something of a shock – not as cold or as effervescent. Ale is similar to bitter – it's more a regional difference in name than anything else. Stout is a dark, rich, foamy drink; Guinness is the most famous brand.

Don't think of any of these drinks as beers, but as something completely new; if you do, you'll discover subtle flavours that a cold and chemical lager cannot match.

Beers are usually served in pints (from £1.50 to £3), but you can also ask for a 'half' (a half-pint). The stronger brews are usually 'specials' or 'extras'. Beware – potency can vary from around 2% to more than 10%!

Pubs are allowed to open 11 am to 11 pm daily, but beware – the bell for last drinks rings out at about 10.45 pm. In bigger cities, many pubs and bars have late licences until 2 am. Takeaway alcoholic drinks are sold from 'off-licence' shops, but rarely from pubs. Every neighbourhood has one.

Good wines are widely available and very reasonably priced (except in pubs). Check the supermarkets; an ordinary but drinkable *vin de pays* will cost around £3.

Unfortunately, most restaurants are licensed and their alcoholic drinks, particularly good wines, are always expensive. There are very few BYO restaurants (where you can Bring Your Own bottles for free), although there are a small number in London. Most places charge an extortionate amount of money for 'corkage' – opening your own bottle for you.

ENTERTAINMENT

For many Brits, the local (pub) is still the main focus for a good night out. For the visitor, the country offers some of the world's best drama, dance and music. A visit to a London theatre is a real must. TICs have lists of nightclubs and discos.

SPECTATOR SPORTS

The British are responsible for either inventing or codifying many of the world's most popular spectator sports such as tennis, football (soccer), rugby and golf. To this list add billiards and snooker, lawn bowls, boxing, darts, hockey, squash and table tennis.

The country also hosts premier events for a number of sports, Wimbledon (tennis) and the English FA Cup Final (football) among them. See Public Holidays & Special Events earlier in this section.

SHOPPING

Napoleon once dismissively described the British as a nation of shopkeepers; today, as chains take over the high streets, it would be truer to say they are a nation of shoppers. Shopping is the most popular recreational activity in the country.

Multinational capitalism being what it is, there are very few things you can buy that are unique to Britain. On the other hand, if you can't find it for sale in London, it probably doesn't exist.

Although few things are cheap, books and clothing can be good value. Shopping at one of London's street markets, especially on Sunday morning, can be a highlight of your trip. Similarly, trawling the nation's charity shops (second-hand shops where the profit goes to a charity) can be very rewarding.

Check *TNT Magazine* for the names of shipping companies when you realise you've exceeded your baggage limit. Choose an established company rather than just opting for the cheapest quote if you want to see your stuff again.

Getting There & Away

London is one of the most important transport hubs in the world. As a result, there's an enormous number of travel agents, some of dubious reliability. All the main 'student' travel services have offices in London; they understand budget travellers and are competitive and reliable. You don't have to be a student to use their services. See the London section later in this chapter for details.

Buses are the cheapest, most exhausting method of transport, although discount rail tickets are competitive, and budget flights

(especially last-minute offers) can be good value. Shop around. A small saving on the fare may not adequately compensate you for an agonising two days on a bus that leaves you completely exhausted for another two days. When making an assessment don't forget the hidden expenses: getting to/from airports, airport departure taxes and food and drink consumed en route.

See the Getting There & Away chapter at the beginning of this book for information on long-haul flights from Australia, Canada, New Zealand and the USA; the Getting Around chapter for details on Eurail, Inter-Rail, Billet International de Jeunesse (international youth) tickets, and other European travel passes; and the Ireland chapter for details of transport to/from Ireland.

AIR

There are international air links with London, Manchester, Newcastle, Edinburgh and Glasgow, but budget travellers will find that cheap flights all wind up in one of the five London airports: Heathrow is the largest, followed by Gatwick, Stansted, Luton and London City.

London is an excellent centre for cheap tickets; the best resource is *TNT Magazine*, but Sunday papers also carry travel ads. If you're prepared to shop around and don't mind flying at short notice, you can pick up some bargains, particularly with discount carriers such as Easyjet, Ryanair and Go.

Excellent discount charter flights are often available to full-time students aged under 30 and all young travellers aged under 26 (you need an ISIC or youth card), and are available through the large student travel agencies. See Information under London later in this chapter.

Low season one-way/return flights from London bucket shops start at: Amsterdam £45/65, Athens £69/99, Frankfurt £55/75, Istanbul £79/129, Madrid £79/99, Paris £40/59 and Rome £69/89. Official tickets with carriers like British Airways can cost a lot more.

LAND

The Channel Tunnel gives Britain a land link with Europe (albeit rail only), but even without using the tunnel, you can still get to Europe by bus or train – there's just a short ferry ride thrown in as part of the deal. The ferries carry cars and motorcycles.

Bus

Eurolines (☎ 0870-514 3219), 52 Grosvenor Gardens, Victoria, London SW1, a division of National Express (the largest UK bus line), has an enormous network of European destinations, including Ireland and Eastern Europe.

You can book through any National Express office, including Victoria coach station in London (which is where Eurolines' buses depart and arrive), and at many travel agents. It also has agents in Europe, including Paris (☎ 01 49 72 51 51), Amsterdam (☎ 020-560 8787), Frankfurt (☎ 069-790 32 40), Madrid (☎ 91 530 7600), Rome (☎ 06-884 08 40), Warsaw (☎ 22-652 05 03) and Istanbul (☎ 1-547 7022).

The following single/return prices and journey times are representative: Amsterdam £33/39 (12 hours), Frankfurt £42/69 (18½ hours), Madrid £77/89 (27 hours), Paris £31/33 (10 hours) and Rome £69/79 (36 hours).

Eurolines also has some good value Explorer tickets that are valid for up to six months and allow travel between a number of major cities. For example, you can visit Amsterdam, Brussels and Paris and return to London for £59.

Train

Trains that connect with European ferries leave from London's Victoria or Liverpool St stations. The prices given here are for adults; youth tickets and passes are considerably lower. For inquiries concerning European trains contact the following: International Rail Centre (☎ 020-7834 2345) and Wasteels (☎ 020-7834 7066), both at Platform 2, Victoria station, London SW1; and Rail Europe (☎ 0870-584 8848), 179 Piccadilly, London W1.

Nontunnel rail options depend on whether you cross the Channel on catamaran or ferry, or from Folkestone, Harwich or Newhaven. For example, to Paris in 2nd class via Newhaven and the Sealink ferry costs adult single/return £39/65 and the journey takes nine hours; you can book onward rail connections to anywhere in Europe. London to Amsterdam via Harwich and the Stena high speed catamaran costs £49/75; journey time is about 8¾ hours.

Travellers aged under 26 can pick up Billet International de Jeunesse (BIJ) tickets which cut fares by up to 50%. Various agents issue BIJ tickets in London, including usit CAMPUS (☎ 0870-240 1010), 52 Grosvenor Gardens, London SW1 (tube: Victoria), which sells Eurotrain (BIJ) tickets. Eurotrain options include circular Explorer tickets, allowing a different route for the return trip: London to Madrid, for instance, takes in Barcelona, Paris and numerous other cities. The International Rail Centre and Wasteels also sell BIJ tickets. For an extensive trip around Europe, however, the Eurail or Inter-Rail tickets are still better value.

Channel Tunnel Two services operate through the tunnel: Eurotunnel operates a rail shuttle service for motorcycles, cars, buses and freight vehicles, using specially designed railway carriages, between terminals at Folkestone in the UK and Calais in France; and the railway companies of Britain, France and Belgium operate a high-speed passenger service, known as Eurostar, between London, Paris and Brussels.

Eurotunnel Trains run 24 hours a day, departing up to four times an hour in each direction between 6 am and 10 pm, and every hour between 10 pm and 6 am. British and French customs and immigration formalities are carried out before you drive on to Le Shuttle. A car and all passengers cost £220. You can make advance reservations (☎ 0870-535 3535) or pay by cash or credit card at a toll booth.

Eurostar Eurostar (☎ 0870-530 0003) runs up to 20 trains a day between London and Paris, up to 12 between London and Brussels. There are direct Eurostar services from Glasgow and Manchester to both Paris and Brussels, and from Birmingham to Paris.

In England, trains arrive at and depart from the international terminal at Waterloo station. Some trains stop at Ashford international station in Kent, and at Frethun (near Calais) or Lille. Immigration formalities are completed on the train, but British customs are at Waterloo.

London to Paris takes three hours, Brussels two hours 40 minutes. Get tickets from travel agents and major train stations. Singles are between £45 and £120.

SEA

There is a bewildering array of alternatives between Britain and mainland Europe. It's impossible to list all the services because of space limitations. See the Ireland chapter for details on links between Britain and Ireland.

Prices vary widely depending on the time of year that you travel. Return tickets may be much cheaper than two one-way fares; on some routes a standard five-day return costs the same as a one-way ticket; and vehicle tickets may also cover a driver and passenger. Unless otherwise noted, the prices quoted for cars don't include passengers.

France

On a clear day, you can see across the Channel. A true budget traveller would obviously swim – it's only seven hours and 40 minutes if you match the record. However, those prepared to compromise their budget traveller principles have numerous options.

Dover & Folkestone The shortest ferry link to Europe is from Dover and Folkestone to Calais and Boulogne. Dover is the most convenient port for those who plan onward travel (in Britain) by bus or train. Between Dover and Calais, P&O Stena Line (☎ 0870-598 0980) operates every one to two hours.

On its 75-minute ferry service it charges one-way foot passengers £24; car plus driver and up to nine passengers £129 to £255; motorcycles and riders £75 to £132. Special offers make a big difference.

Hoverspeed's catamarans only take 35 minutes to cross the Channel. It charges £24 for a one-way passenger, £58 for a five-day return.

Portsmouth P&O (☎ 0870-598 0555) operates three to four ferries a day to/from Cherbourg and Le Havre. The day ferries take five to six hours and the night ferries take seven to eight hours. One-way foot passenger fare is £9 to £30, and a car costs from a bargain £21 to a steep £138. Brittany Ferries (☎ 0870-536 0360) has at least one sailing a day to/from Caen and St Malo.

Spain

From Plymouth, Brittany Ferries (☎ 0870-536 0360) operates at least one ferry a week to Santander on Spain's north coast (£47 to £98 single, £112 to £317 for a vehicle, 24 hours). Brittany also operates a service between Santander and Portsmouth that takes 30 hours. P&O (☎ 0870-598 0555) operates a service between Portsmouth and Bilbao at similar rates.

Scandinavia

Until you see the ferry possibilities, it's easy to forget how close Scandinavia and Britain are.

Aberdeen & Shetland One of the most interesting possibilities is the summer-only link between Shetland, Norway, the Faroe Islands and Iceland. The operator is Smyril Line but the agent is P&O (☎ 01224-572615). First you have to get to Shetland from Orkney, or from Aberdeen, Scotland. P&O has daily sailings from Aberdeen to Lerwick (Shetland) from Monday to Friday, seats from £58.

The Smyril Line operates from late May to early September. Depending on the season, one-way couchette fares (a couchette is a sleeping berth) through from Aberdeen to Norway are from £111, to the Faroes £111, to Denmark £192, and to Iceland £193.

Newcastle Norway's Color Line (☎ 0191-296 1313) operates ferries all year to Stavanger, Haugesund and Bergen in Norway. These are overnight trips. The high-season fare for a reclining chair is £80; a car and five people costs £315. Bicycles are free.

Scandinavian Seaways (☎ 0870-533 3000) operates ferries to Gothenburg, Sweden (£187 and up, 22 hours) on Friday from early June to mid-August.

Harwich Scandinavian Seaways (☎ 0870-533 3000) has ferries to Esbjerg in Denmark (£134 and up, 20 hours) and Gothenburg in Sweden (£187 and up, 24 hours).

Belgium, the Netherlands & Germany

There are two direct links with Germany; many people prefer to drive to/from the Dutch ferry ports.

Harwich Scandinavian Seaways (☎ 0870-533 3000) has ferries to Hamburg (Germany) every two days for most of the year (£135 to £225 return in a four-berth couchette, 19 hours).

Stena Line (☎ 0870-570 7070) has two ferries a day to the Hook of Holland in the Netherlands (£22 one way, 7½ to 9½ hours).

Newcastle Scandinavian Seaways (☎ 0870-533 3000) has a twice-weekly ferry to Hamburg from late May to early September, taking 20 hours. The fare is the same as from Harwich.

LEAVING BRITAIN

People taking flights from Britain need to pay an Air Passenger Duty: those flying to countries in the EU will pay £10; those flying beyond it, £20. There's no departure tax if you leave by sea or tunnel.

See Money in the Facts for the Visitor section earlier in this chapter for details about reclaiming VAT when you depart.

Getting Around

Although public transport is generally of a high standard, most budget travellers are going to want to get to the national parks and small villages where transport is worst. If time is limited, a car becomes a serious temptation, although with a mix of local buses, the occasional taxi, plenty of time, walking and occasionally hiring a bike, you can get almost anywhere.

Buses are nearly always the cheapest way to get around. Unfortunately, they're also the slowest (sometimes by a considerable margin) and on main routes they are confined to major roads, which screen you from the small towns and landscapes that make travel worthwhile in the first place. With discount passes and tickets (especially Apex), trains can be competitive; they're quicker and often take you through beautiful countryside.

Ticket types and prices vary considerably, advance purchase often saving you as much as 50% of the full price fare.

The BTA distributes an excellent brochure, *Getting About Britain for the Independent Traveller*, which gives details of bus, train,

plane and ferry transport around Britain and into mainland Europe.

AIR

Most regional centres and islands are linked to London. However, unless you're going to the outer reaches of Britain, in particular northern Scotland, planes (including the time it takes to get to and from airports) are only marginally quicker than trains. Prices are generally higher than 1st-class rail, but see the Scotland Getting There & Away section later in this chapter for details of no-frills flights from London to Scotland. Note that there is now a £10 tax (Air Passenger Duty) added to the quoted price of tickets.

BUS

Road transport in Britain is almost entirely privately owned and run. National Express (☎ 0870-580 8080) runs the largest national network – it completely dominates the market and is a sister company to Eurolines – but there are often smaller competitors on the main routes. Check the Web site at www.gobycoach.com.

In Britain, long-distance express buses are usually referred to as coaches, and in many towns there are separate terminals for coaches and local buses. Over short distances, coaches are more expensive (though quicker) than buses.

A number of counties operate telephone inquiry lines which try to explain the fast-changing and often chaotic situation with timetables; wherever possible, these numbers have been given. Before commencing a journey off the main routes it is wise to phone for the latest information.

Unless otherwise stated, prices quoted in this chapter are for economy single (one-way) tickets.

Passes & Discounts

The National Express Discount Coach Card allows 30% off standard adult fares. It is available to full-time students, and those aged from 16 to 25 and 50 or over. The cards are available from all National Express agents. They cost £8 and require a passport photo – ISIC cards are accepted as proof of student status and passports for date of birth.

Guarding Buckingham Palace

King's College Chapel, Cambridge

Big Ben, a renowned London landmark

Lochness and Castle Urquhart, Scotland

Piper, Edinburgh, Scotland

BETHUNE CARMICHAEL

Castle Campbell, Dollar, Central Scotland

JEAN-BERNARD CARILLET

The blue waters surrounding Corsica, France

DAVID ELSE

Froggatt Edge, Derbyshire, England

DIANA MAYFIELD

Poppy fields near Veneuvre, Normandy, France

On the Buses

For all National Express bus information regarding departure times and ticket prices, call ☎ 08705-808080. For National Express bus information and ticket booking over the Internet, visit www.GoByCoach.com.

The National Express Explorer Pass allows unlimited coach travel within a specified period. It's available to all overseas visitors but it must be bought outside Britain. You will be given a travel voucher which can be exchanged for the pass at Heathrow or Gatwick airports, or at any of the larger National Express agencies around the country. For adults/concessions they cost £59/45 for three days travel within five consecutive days, £110/80 for seven days in a 21-day period and £170/130 for 14 days in a 30-day period.

National Express Tourist Trail Passes are available to UK and overseas citizens. They provide unlimited travel on all services for two days travel within three consecutive days (£49/39 for an adult/discount card-holder), any five days travel within 10 consecutive days (£85/69), any seven days travel within 21 consecutive days (£120/94) and any 14 days travel within 30 consecutive days (£187/143). The passes can be bought overseas, or at any National Express agent in the UK.

Hop-On Hop-Off Buses

Stray Travel Network (Slowcoach; ☎ 020-7373 7737) is an excellent bus service designed especially for those staying in hostels, but useful for all budget travellers. Buses run on a regular circuit between London, Windsor, Bath, Manchester, Howarth, the Lake District, Glasgow, Stirling, Edinburgh, York, Nottingham, Cambridge and London, calling at hostels. You can get on and off the bus where you like, and the £119 ticket is valid for the whole circuit for six months. Buses leave London three times a week throughout the year; the price includes some activities and visits en route. Tickets are available from branches of STA; look in the *Yellow Pages* for the nearest branch.

Postbus

Many small places can only be reached by postbuses – minibuses that follow postal delivery routes (which are circuitous through many of the most beautiful areas of England, Wales and Scotland). For the free *Postbus Guide to England & Wales* contact Postbus Services (☎ 020-7490 2888), Post Office HQ, 130 Old St, London EC1V 9PQ; for the Scottish version contact Postbus Services (☎ 01463-256723), Royal Mail, 7 Strothers Lane, Inverness IV1 1AA.

TRAIN

Despite the cutbacks of the last decade and the privatisation program, Britain still has an impressive rail service – if you're using it as a tourist rather than a commuter, that is. There are several particularly recommended trips on beautiful lines through sparsely populated country, the most famous being in Wales and Scotland.

Unfortunately, Eurail passes are not recognised in Britain. There are local equivalents, but they aren't recognised in Europe.

Rail Privatisation

British Rail is no more. Services are provided by 25 train operating companies (TOCs). A separate company, Railtrack, owns and maintains the track and the stations. For the sake of convenience the British Rail logo and name are still used on direction signs.

The main railcards (which give holders a reduction on fares – see Railcards later in this section) are accepted by all the companies, and travellers are still able to buy a ticket to any destination from any rail station or from authorised travel agents, though travel agents are not able to sell the full range of tickets.

Passengers can travel only on services provided by the company who issued their ticket and each company is able to set whatever fare it chooses. Thus on routes served by more than one operator, passengers can choose to buy a cheaper ticket with a company offering a less frequent/direct service or pay more for a faster (usually Virgin) service. In some cases competing companies use the same route. The era of competition also means that companies often have special offers such as 'two for the price of one', or special reductions for tickets bought in advance.

The main routes are served by excellent intercity trains that travel at speeds of up to

On the Rails

For all train information regarding departure times and ticket prices, call ☎ 0845-7484950. For train information and ticket booking over the Internet, visit www.thetrainline.com.

140mph and whisk you from London to Edinburgh in just over four hours.

If you don't have one of the passes listed in the following entries, the cheapest tickets must be bought at least one week in advance. Phone the general inquiry line (☎ 0845-748 4950) for timetables, fares and the numbers to ring for credit-card bookings. For short journeys, it's not really necessary to purchase tickets or make seat reservations in advance. Just buy them at the station before you go.

Unless otherwise stated, the prices quoted in this chapter are for adult single tickets.

BritRail Passes

BritRail passes are the most interesting possibility for visitors, but they are *not available in Britain* and must be bought in your country of origin. Contact the BTA in your country for details.

A BritRail pass, which allows unlimited travel, can be bought for eight, 15, 22 or 30 days. An eight-day pass for an adult/youth is (in US$) $259/205, a 15-day pass is $395/318, a 22-day pass is $510/410 and a 30-day pass is $590/475.

A BritRail plus Ireland pass costs $359 for five days in a month or $511 for 10 days in a month and includes unlimited rail travel in both countries and the ferry trip from one to the other and back.

An even more useful deal is the Flexipass, which allows four days unlimited travel in a month ($219/175), eight days in one month ($315/253), 15 days in one month for adults ($480) and 15 days in two months for young people ($385).

Holders of BritRail, Eurail and Euro passes are entitled to discounted fares on Eurostar trains (eg, London to Paris/Brussels for $79/69).

BritRail/Drive

BritRail/Drive combines a Flexipass (see previous entry) with the use of a Hertz rental

car for side trips, and the car-rental price is competitive. The package is available in various combinations – a three-day Flexipass plus two days car hire in one month costs $264 (this price assumes you use a small car). Contact the BTA in your country for details.

Rail Rovers

The domestic versions of these passes are called BritRail Rovers: a seven-day All Line Rover is £300/198 for adults/youths, and 14 days is £440/198. There are also regional Rovers and some Flexi Rovers to Wales, north and mid-Wales, the North Country, the north-west coast and Peaks, the south-west, and Scotland. Details have been given in the appropriate sections.

Railcards

Various railcards, available from major stations, give a third off most tickets and are valid for a year.

The Young Person's Railcard (£18) is for people aged from 16 to 25, or for those studying full time. You'll need two passport photos and proof of age (birth certificate or passport) or student status. There are also railcards for seniors (over 60s), disabled people and families.

If you're planning to do a lot of rail travel in the south of England, a Network card may be worth considering. This is valid for the region previously known as Network SouthEast London and the entire south-east of England, from Dover to Weymouth, Cambridge to Oxford. It costs £20. Discounts apply to up to four adults travelling together providing a member of the party is a card-holder. Children pay a flat fare of £1. Travel is permitted only after 10 am Monday to Friday and at any time on the weekend. A couple of journeys can pay for the card.

Tickets

If the various train passes aren't complicated enough, try making sense of the different tickets:

Single ticket – Valid for a single one-way journey at any time on the day specified; expensive
Day Return ticket – Valid for a return journey at any time on the day specified; relatively expensive

Cheap Day Return ticket – Valid for a return journey on the day specified on the ticket, but there are time restrictions and it is usually only available for short journeys; often about the same price as a single

Apex – One of the cheapest fares, rivalling National Express prices; for distances of more than 100 miles; you must book at least seven days in advance, but seats are limited so book early

SuperApex – The cheapest fare for the most direct route between London and Edinburgh/Glasgow; you must book at least 14 days in advance, but seats are limited and not available on all trains so book early

SuperSaver – The cheapest ticket where advance purchase is not necessary but there are many restrictions not available in south-eastern England; cannot be used on Friday after 2.30 pm, Saturday in July and August or on Bank Holidays, or on days after these before 2.30 pm, nor in London at peak times; return journey must be within one calendar month

SuperAdvance – Similarly priced to the SuperSaver but fewer time/day restrictions; however tickets must be bought before 2 pm on the day before travel and both the outward and return journey times must be specified; limited availability so book as early as possible

Saver – Higher priced than the SuperSaver, but can be used any day and there are fewer time restrictions

AwayBreak ticket – For off-peak travel in south-eastern England. Valid for four nights (five days) for journeys over 30 miles or 40 miles from London

StayAway ticket – As above but valid for one month

CAR & MOTORCYCLE

There are five grades of road. Motorways are dual or triple carriageway and deliver you quickly from one end of the country to the other. In general, they are not a particularly pleasant experience. You miss the most interesting countryside, and the driving can be very aggressive. Avoid them whenever possible, and be very careful if you use them in foggy or wet conditions when their usually good safety record plummets. Unfortunately, the primary routes (main A roads) are often very similar.

Minor A roads are single carriageway and are likely to be clogged with slow-moving trucks, but life on the road starts to look up once you join the B roads and minor roads.

Fenced by hedgerows, these wind through the countryside from village to village. You can't travel fast, but you won't want to.

Americans and Australians will find petrol expensive (around 85p per litre, or £3.20 for a US gallon), but distances aren't great.

Road Rules

Anyone using the roads should get hold of the *Highway Code* (99p), which is often available in TICs. If you're bringing a car from Europe make sure you're adequately insured.

Briefly, vehicles drive on the left-hand side of the road; front seat belts are compulsory and belts must be worn if they are fitted in the back; the speed limit is 30mph in built-up areas, 60mph on single carriageways and 70mph on dual carriageways and motorways; you give way to your right at roundabouts (that is, traffic already on the roundabout has the right of way); and motorcyclists must wear helmets.

A yellow line painted along the edge of the road indicates there are parking restrictions. The only way to establish the exact restrictions is to find the nearby sign that spells them out. A single line means no parking for at least an eight-hour period between 7 am and 7 pm, five days a week; a double line means no parking for at least an eight-hour period between 7 am and 7 pm more than five days a week; and a broken line means there are some restrictions.

Rental

Rates are expensive in the UK; often you will be best off making arrangements in your home country for some sort of package deal. See this book's introductory Getting Around chapter for more details. The large international rental companies charge from around £160 per week for a small car (Ford Fiesta, Peugeot 106).

Holiday Autos (☎ 0870-530 0400) operates through a number of rental companies and can generally offer excellent deals. A week's all-inclusive hire starts at around £150. EasyRentacar.com is a cheap online rental service from as little as £9 per day for a Mercedes A Class, but *watch out* for the hidden extras. For other cheap operators check the ads in *TNT Magazine*. TICs have lists of local car-hire companies, and these are often much cheaper than the major operators.

If you're travelling as a couple or a group, a camper van is worth considering. Sunseeker Rentals (☎ 020-8960 5747) has four-berth and two-berth vans from £250 per week.

Purchase

In Britain all cars require the following: a Ministry of Transport (MOT) safety certificate (the certificate itself is usually referred to simply as an MOT) valid for one year and issued by licensed garages; full third party insurance – shop around but expect to pay at least £300; registration – a standard form signed by the buyer and seller, with a section to be sent to the Ministry of Transport; and tax – from main post offices on presentation of a valid MOT certificate, insurance and registration documents. Note that cars that are 25 or more years old are tax exempt.

You are strongly recommended to buy a vehicle with valid MOT and tax. MOT and tax remain with the car through a change of ownership; third-party insurance goes with the driver rather than the car, so you will still have to arrange this (and beware of letting others drive the car). For further information about registering, licensing, insuring and testing your vehicle, contact a post office or Vehicle Registration Office for leaflet V100.

See the introductory Getting Around and Facts for the Visitor chapters at the beginning of this book for general information on private transport and the paperwork involved.

BICYCLE

See the Activities section earlier in this chapter.

HITCHING

If you're not worried about the safety implications, hitching is reasonably easy, except around the big cities and built-up areas, where you'll need to use public transport. It's against the law to hitch on motorways or their immediate slip roads; make a sign and use approach roads, nearby roundabouts, or the service stations.

BOAT

See the appropriate sections later in this chapter for ferry information and the Activities section earlier in this chapter for canal boating.

LOCAL TRANSPORT

See the London Getting Around section for information on the famous London taxis and their minicab competitors. In taxis outside London, you could expect to pay around £1.40 per mile, which means they are definitely worth considering to get to an out-of-the-way hostel or sight, or the beginning of a walk. If there are three or four people to share the cost, a taxi over a short distance will often be competitive with the cost of a local bus.

ORGANISED TOURS

Since travel is so easy to organise in Britain, there is very little need to consider a tour. Still, if your time is limited and you prefer to travel in a group there are some interesting possibilities; the BTA has information.

Outback UK (☎ 01327-704115, fax 703883), The Cottage, Church Green, Badby, Northants, NN11 3AS, offers two to 14-day tours around Britain with departures every Saturday (March to November) from London, though it's possible to join at any point. Costs are approximately £35 per day (includes two meals and accommodation in youth hostels) or £20 (travel only). Also see Hop-on Hop-off Buses earlier in this section.

England

Mistake this part of Britain with Scotland or Wales at your peril. The largest part of the island is also the part most linked in people's minds with all things 'British'. For centuries, the English have buried their identity in that of greater Britain, but as Scotland and Wales devolve, the English are rediscovering themselves. The George Cross, the white flag with the red cross, can increasingly be found on display.

London is the heart of England. Other significant English sites include the Cotswolds, Bath, Oxford, the historic south-east, Cambridge, York and the Lake District.

LONDON
☎ 020

Once the capital of the greatest empire the world has ever known, London is still Europe's largest city and is embedded in the culture, vocabulary and dreams of English speakers worldwide. At times it will be more grand, evocative, beautiful and stimulating than you could have imagined; at others it will be colder, greyer, dirtier and more expensive than you believed possible.

It's a cosmopolitan mixture of the developed and developing worlds, of chauffeurs and beggars, of the establishment and the avant-garde, with seven to 12 million inhabitants (depending on where you stop counting), and 26 million visitors a year. London has been a major recipient of the vast sums of culture money raised by the National Lottery. Projects such as the huge new Tate Modern gallery opened in 2000 and the number of visitors to the city seems likely to grow ever more.

For the budget traveller, London is a challenge. Money has a way of mysteriously evaporating every time you move. With limited funds it's necessary to plan, book ahead and prioritise. There's little point in putting up with the crowds, the underground and the pollution if you can't take advantage of at least some of the theatres, exhibitions, shops, pubs and clubs, cafes and restaurants. On a moderate budget, you can find reasonable value. And some of the very best – including most of the major museums – remains free or very cheap.

History

Although a Celtic community established itself around a ford across the River Thames, it was the Romans who first developed the square mile now known as the City of London. They built a bridge and an impressive city wall, and made the city an important port and the hub of their road system.

The Romans left, but trade went on. Few traces of Dark Age London can now be found, but the city survived the incursions of the Saxons and Vikings. Fifty years before the Normans arrived, Edward the Confessor built his abbey and palace at Westminster.

William the Conqueror found a city that was the richest and largest in the kingdom. He raised the White Tower (part of the Tower of London) and confirmed the city's independence and right to self-government.

During the reign of Elizabeth I the capital began to expand rapidly. Unfortunately, medieval Tudor and Jacobean London was virtually destroyed by the Great Fire of 1666.

The fire gave Christopher Wren the opportunity to build his famous churches, but did nothing to halt or discipline the city's growth.

By 1720 there were 750,000 inhabitants and London, as the seat of Parliament and focal point for a growing empire, was becoming ever richer and more important. Georgian architects replaced the last of medieval London with their imposing symmetrical architecture and residential squares.

As a result of the Industrial Revolution and rapidly expanding commerce, the population jumped from 2.7 million in 1851 to 6.6 million in 1901 and a vast expanse of suburbs developed to accommodate the newcomers.

Georgian and Victorian London was devastated by the Luftwaffe in WWII – huge swathes of the centre and the East End were totally flattened. After the war, ugly housing and low-cost developments were thrown up on the bomb sites. The docks never recovered – shipping moved to Tilbury, and the Docklands declined to the point of dereliction, until rediscovery by developers in the 1980s.

Riding on a wave of Thatcherite confidence and deregulation, London boomed in the 1980s. The downturn of the early 1990s proved short-lived and by the end of the century, the town was booming again. In 2000, London elected its first city-wide mayor, Ken Livingstone. A populist with deeply liberal roots, Livingstone quickly set about tweaking the noses of the establishment, including Tony Blair.

Orientation

London's main geographical feature is the Thames, a tidal river that enabled an easily defended port to be established far from the dangers of the English Channel. Flowing around wide bends from west to east, it divides the city into northern and southern halves.

London sprawls over an enormous area. Fortunately, the underground railway system (the 'tube') makes most of it easily accessible, and the ubiquitous (though geographically misleading) underground map is easy to use. Any train heading from left to right on the map is designated as eastbound, any train heading from top to bottom is southbound. Each line has its own colour.

Most important sights, theatres, restaurants and even some cheap places to stay lie within a reasonably compact rectangle formed by the tube's Circle line, just to the north of the river. All the international airports lie some distance from the city centre but transport to and from them is easy (see Getting Around later in this London section for details).

London blankets mostly imperceptible hills, but there are good views from Primrose Hill (adjoining Regent's Park), Hampstead Heath (north of Camden), and Greenwich Park (downriver east of central London).

Throughout this chapter, the nearest tube or main-line station has been given with addresses; the Central London map shows the location of tube stations and the areas covered by the detailed district maps.

Maps A decent map is vital. Ideally, get a single-sheet map so you can see all of central London at a glance; the Lonely Planet *London City Map* has three separate maps at different scales as well as an inset map of Theatreland and an index. The bound *Mini London A-Z Street Atlas & Index* provides comprehensive coverage of London in a discreet size.

Terminology 'London' is an imprecise term used loosely to describe the over 2000 sq km of Greater London enclosed by the M25 ring road. It's difficult to see outlying towns like Luton, Reading and Guildford (each around 30 miles from the city centre) as anything more than suburbs.

London is not administered as a single unit, but divided into widely differing boroughs governed by local governments with significant autonomy.

Boroughs are further subdivided into districts (or suburbs, or precincts if you prefer), which mainly tally with the first group of letters and numbers of the postal code. The letters correspond to compass directions from the centre of London, which according to the post office must lie somewhere not too far from St Paul's Cathedral: EC means East Central, WC means West Central, W means West, NW means North-West, and so on. The numbering system after the letters is less helpful: 1 is the centre of the zone, further numbers relate to the alphabetical order of the postal-district names, which are not always in common use.

Districts and postal codes are often given on street signs, which is obviously vital when names are duplicated (there are 47 Station Rds), or cross through a number of districts. To further confuse visitors, many streets change name. Holland Park Ave becomes Notting Hill Gate, which becomes Bayswater Rd, which becomes Oxford St – sometimes they duck and weave like the country lanes they once were. Street numbering can also bewilder: on big streets the numbers on opposite sides can be way out of kilter (315 might be opposite 520); or, for variation, they can go up one side and down the other.

To add to the confusion, some London suburbs – well within the M25 – don't give London as a part of their addresses, and don't use London postal codes. Instead they're considered part of a county, even one like Middlesex which no longer exists!

The City & the East The City refers to the area that was once the Roman and medieval walled city, before the inexorable colonisation of the surrounding towns and villages began. Although it lies in the south-eastern corner of the Circle tube line, the City is regarded as the centre of London. As you may have guessed, the West End (much more the tourist centre) lies to the west of the City.

The City is one of the world's most important financial centres; full of bankers and dealers during the working week, deserted outside work hours. The same is not true of its most famous sights: the Tower of London, St Paul's Cathedral and Petticoat Lane market.

To the east, beyond the Circle line, is the East End, once the exclusive habitat of the cockney, now a cultural melting pot. The East End incorporates districts like now-trendy Shoreditch and Bethnal Green, with some lively corners and relatively cheap rents. Much of the East End was flattened during WWII and it still shows.

Farther east again lie the Docklands. Once part of the busiest port in the world, these thousands of acres of prime real estate fell into disuse after WWII, mirroring the decline of the empire. In the early 1980s, the property developers moved in and they're still hard at work. It's well worth visiting, especially as part of a visit to Greenwich across the river.

The West West of the City, but before the West End proper, are Holborn and Blooms-bury. Holborn (pronounced hoeburn) is Britain's sedate legal heartland, the home of Rumpole and common law. Bloomsbury is still synonymous with the literary and publishing worlds. Besides dozens of specialist shops, this is where you'll find the incomparable British Museum, stuffed to the hilt with loot from every corner of the globe.

The West End proper lies west of Tottenham Court Rd and Covent Garden, which is tourist-ridden but fun, and south of Oxford St, an endless succession of department stores. It includes such magnets as Trafalgar Square, the restaurants and clubs of lively and infamous Soho, the West End cinemas and theatres around Piccadilly Circus and Leicester Square, and the elegant shops of Regent and Bond Sts – not forgetting Mayfair, the most valuable property on the British Monopoly board.

St James's and Westminster lie to the south-west. This is where you'll find White-hall, No 10 Downing St, the Houses of Parliament, Big Ben, Westminster Abbey and Buckingham Palace.

To the south of Victoria station lies Pimlico, not a particularly attractive district but with a good supply of cheapish, decentish hotels to top up the lure of the Tate Britain Gallery.

Earl's Court, South Kensington and Chelsea are in the south-west corner formed by the Circle line. Earl's Court, once infamous as Kangaroo Valley and home to countless expatriate Australians, now feels more Middle Eastern but still boasts the drawcards of some cheap hotels, several backpackers hostels and a couple of Australian pubs, plus cheap restaurants and travel agents.

South Kensington is much more chic and trendy, with a clutch of world-famous museums (the Victoria & Albert, Science and Natural History). It is also home to scores of expats, including hordes of Americans. Chelsea is expensively chic and King's Rd is an interesting place to hunt out the latest fashion.

Farther west you come to some very comfortable residential districts like Richmond and Chiswick. Sites worth trekking out west for include Hampton Court Palace, Kew Gardens and Syon House.

The North Notting Hill is a lively, interesting district, with a large West Indian population and lots of yuppies. It gets trendier by the day, but the Portobello Rd market is still fun and there are pubs, lively bars and interesting shops.

North of Kensington Gardens and Hyde Park, Bayswater and Paddington are virtual tourist ghettos, but there are plenty of hostels, cheap and mid-range hotels and interesting restaurants (particularly along Queensway and Westbourne Grove).

From west to east, the band of districts to the north of the Central tube line include Kilburn, Hampstead, Camden Town, Highgate, Highbury and Islington. Kilburn is London's Irish capital amid bedsit land. Hampstead, with its great views and the marvellous heath, is quiet, civilised and extremely expensive, while Camden Town, although well on its way to gentrification, still nurtures a gaggle of over-populated but enjoyable weekend markets.

Islington went from gritty to trendy in the mid-1990s. In Upper St it also boasts one of London's most densely packed collections of eating places.

The South Cross the Thames from central London and you encounter one of London's hottest areas. The British Airways London Eye observation wheel across from Parliament and the huge new Tate Modern gallery on the Thames in Southwark are the most notable of scores of developments that are transforming this once gritty area. The troubled Millennium Bridge near the Tate Modern, the all-new pedestrian areas on the Hungerford Bridge and the new extension to the Jubilee tube line all greatly improve access from north of the river. Further away from the water is working-class London, which seems a long way from the elegant, antiseptic streets of Westminster.

Even short-term visitors are likely to want to take in cultural oases like the Tate Modern, the South Bank Centre (a venue for interesting exhibitions and concerts) and Wimbledon with its tennis courts. Beautiful Greenwich is also home to the *Cutty Sark*, and contains superb architecture, open space and the Prime Meridian. It was also home to the Dome, centre of controversy and poor attendance figures during 2000.

BRITAIN

CENTRAL LONDON

PLACES TO STAY

1 Ashlee House
3 St Pancras International Hostel
6 International Students House
8 John Adams Hall
9 Euro Hotel
12 The Generator
13 Cambria House
15 Arran House Hotel
16 Ridgemount Hotel
17 Academy Hotel
24 Central Club YMCA
29 Oxford St Hostel
38 Hazlitt's
50 Fielding Hotel
55 The Savoy
57 St Martins Lane
62 Regent Palace Hotel
91 Rubens at the Palace
96 Luna-Simone Hotel
99 Winchester Hotel
100 Brindle House Hotel
101 Windermere Hotel

PLACES TO EAT

4 Diwana
5 Chutneys
11 North Sea Fish Restaurant
19 Mandeer
20 Museum St Café
21 Coffee Gallery
23 Wagamama
25 Sevilla Mia
26 Costa Dorada
27 Rasa Samudra
30 Star Café
33 Rock & Sole Plaice
34 Food for Thought
35 Franx Snack Bar
39 Mildred's
41 Pollo
44 Pâtisserie Valerie
46 Soup
47 Melati
48 The Ivy
49 Café Pacifico
51 Café des Amis du Vin
52 Joe Allen
54 Simpson's-in-the-Strand
58 Poons
59 Chuen Cheng Ku
63 L'Odéon
65 The Criterion
67 Tibetan Restaurant

CENTRAL LONDON

94	The Footstool
97	Mekong
98	UNo 1

OTHER

2	British Library
7	London University
10	Red & White Laundrette
14	Dillons the Bookstore
18	The Queen's Larder
22	British Museum
28	Council Travel
31	Astoria
32	Bikepark
36	Velvet Room
37	Borderline
40	Foyle's Bookshop
42	Coach & Horses
43	Ronnie Scott's
45	Berwick St Market
53	Courtauld Institute Gallery
56	Stanfords Bookshop
60	Bar Rhumba
61	Scruffy Murphy's
64	Tower Records
66	Half-Price Ticket Booth
68	Trafalgar Square Post Office
69	EasyEverything
70	National Portrait Gallery
71	National Gallery
72	American Express
73	British Travel Centre
74	Waterstones Bookshop
75	St James's Piccadilly
76	Thomas Cook
77	ICA (Institute for Contemporary Arts)
78	Royal Festival Hall
79	Queen Elizabeth Hall
80	National Film Theatre
81	National Theatre
82	Hayward Gallery
83	British Airways London Eye
84	Banqueting House
85	Horse Guards
86	No 10 Downing St
87	Cabinet War Rooms
88	Westminster Pier
89	Houses of Parliament
90	Westminster Abbey
92	EasyEverything
93	Westminster Cathedral
95	Tate Britain Gallery
102	Victoria Coach Station

Notorious for racial problems in the early 1980s, Brixton is London at its most multicultural. Gentrification mixes with the downscale and whatever edge is left from two decades ago has only added to the excitement of its many restaurants and clubs.

Information

Lonely Planet has several publications with more detailed coverage of London. For comprehensive coverage, see *London*. For colourful coverage in a handy pocket size, try *London Condensed*, while *Out to Eat – London* describes an enormous selection of London's best eateries.

Time Out magazine (issued every Tuesday) is a complete listing of everything happening and is recommended for every visitor.

Free magazines are available from pavement bins, especially in Earl's Court, Notting Hill and Bayswater. *TNT Magazine*, *Southern Cross* and *SA Times* cover Australian, New Zealand and South African news and sports results, but are mostly invaluable for their entertainment listings, excellent travel sections and useful classifieds covering jobs, cheap tickets, shipping services and accommodation.

Loot is a daily paper made up of classified ads placed free by sellers. It's the best place to look for flats and house-share ads.

Tourist Offices London is a major travel centre, so aside from information on London there are also offices that deal specifically with England, Scotland, Wales, Ireland and most countries round the world.

British Travel Centre

(☎ 8846 9000) 1 Regent St, Piccadilly Circus SW1Y 4PQ. Two minutes walk from Piccadilly Circus, this is a chaotic and comprehensive information and booking service under one roof. It offers tours; a *bureau de change*; theatre tickets; train, air and car travel; accommodation; map and guidebook shop; and the Scotland, Wales and Ireland tourist boards. It's very busy and open daily: 9 am to 6.30 pm weekdays, 10 am to 4.30 pm weekends.

London Tourist Information Centres

There are TICs in Heathrow Terminals 1, 2 and 3, in the Arrivals Hall at Waterloo International Terminal and Liverpool St underground station. The centre in Victoria station offers accommodation booking services for various fees. It can be extremely busy. There are also information

desks at Gatwick, Stansted and Luton airports. Like the Britain Visitor Centre, the main TICs handle walk-ins only. The offices are all open at least from 9.30 am to 6 pm daily and often much longer in summer. Written inquiries should be sent to the London Tourist Board & Convention Bureau, Glen House, Stag Place, London SW1E 5LT (or fax 7932 0222). You can also make use of its Visitorcall system. You simply dial ☎ 09064 123 and then add another three digits, depending on what information you're looking for. These are premium-rate calls costing 60p a minute and can only be dialled within the UK.

The City of London Corporation

The City of London maintains an information centre (☎ 7332 1456) in St Paul's Churchyard, opposite St Paul's Cathedral. It's open 9.30 am to 5 pm daily from April to September, closing Saturday afternoon and Sunday for the rest of the year. It doesn't handle accommodation inquiries.

Money Banks and ATMs abound across central London. If you must use *bureaux de change* to change your money, at least check their commission rates carefully first.

There are 24-hour bureaus in Heathrow Terminals 1, 3 and 4. Terminal 2's bureau is open 6 am to 11 pm daily. Thomas Cook has branches at Terminals 1, 3 and 4. There are 24-hour bureaus in Gatwick's South and North Terminals and one at Stansted. Luton and London City airports have desks open during their operating hours. The airport bureaus are actually good value; they don't charge commission on sterling travellers cheques, and on other currencies it's 1.5% with a £3 minimum.

The main American Express office (☎ 7930 4411), 6 Haymarket (tube: Piccadilly Circus), is open for currency exchange 9 am to 5.30 pm Monday to Friday, 9 am to 4 pm Saturday and Sunday. There are slightly longer hours June to September.

The main Thomas Cook office (☎ 7853 6400), 30 St James's St (tube: Green Park), is open 9 am (10 am Wednesday) to 5.30 pm weekdays and until 4 pm Saturday. The office at Victoria train station is open 8 am to 8 pm daily (until 6 pm Sunday). There are many other branches scattered around central London.

Discounts If you plan to do a lot of sightseeing, the London GoSee card (£10/16/26 for one/three/seven days) can be purchased and is valid for entry to 17 museums and galleries. Family cards, offering free admission for up to two adults and four children, cost £30/50 for three/seven days.

The participating museums are Apsley House (Wellington Museum), Barbican Art Gallery, BBC Experience, BFI London IMAX Cinema, Design Museum, Hayward Gallery, Imperial War Museum, London Transport Museum, Museum of London, National Maritime Museum, Natural History Museum, Royal Academy of Arts, Science Museum, Shakespeare's Globe, Theatre Museum, Tower Bridge Experience and Victoria & Albert Museum.

Post & Communications It's convenient to have your mail sent to Poste Restante, Trafalgar Square Branch Office, London WC2N 4DL. The physical address is 24-28 William IV St (tube: Charing Cross). Mail will be held for four weeks; ID is required.

CallShop etc has lower charges than British Telecom (BT) for international calls, and faxes may also be sent or received. It has shops at 181a Earls Court Rd (tube: Earl's Court) and 189 Edgeware Rd (tube: Edgeware Road).

Email & Internet Access EasyEverything, a division of no-frills airline easyJet, is opening numerous huge cybercafes around London that are open 24 hours. Charges vary by how busy the location is: £1 buys you from 40 minutes to six hours of access. Locations include Trafalger Square (☎ 7930 4094), 457-459 The Strand WC2 (tube: Charing Cross), and Victoria (☎ 7233 8456), 9-13 Wilton Road SW1 (tube: Victoria).

Travel Agencies London has always been a centre for cheap travel. Refer to the Sunday papers (especially the *Sunday Times*), *TNT Magazine* and *Time Out* for listings of cheap flights, but beware of sharks.

Long-standing and reliable firms include:

usit CAMPUS
(☎ 7938 2188) YHA Adventure Shop, 174 Kensington High St W8 (tube: High St Kensington)
Council Travel
(☎ 7287 3337) 28 Poland St, London W1 (tube: Oxford Circus)
STA Travel
(☎ 7361 6262) 86 Old Brompton Rd SW7 (tube: South Kensington)
Trailfinders
(☎ 7938 3939) 194 Kensington High St W8 (tube: High St Kensington)

Bookshops All the major chains are good, but Waterstones, Books etc and Borders have particularly strong travel sections. Waterstones has a branch (☎ 7851 2400) that is Europe's largest bookshop at 203-206 Piccadilly W1 (tube: Piccadilly Circus). Several specialist bookshops are tourist attractions in their own right:

Daunt Books
(☎ 7224 2295) 83 Marylebone High St W1; tube: Baker St – a wide selection of travel guides in a beautiful old shop
Dillons the Bookstore
(☎ 7636 1577) 82 Gower St WC1; tube: Euston Square – an enormous bookshop with particularly strong academic sections
Foyles
(☎ 7437 5660) 119 Charing Cross Rd WC2; tube: Leicester Square – the biggest, most disorganised bookshop in the world
Stanfords
(☎ 7836 1321) 12 Long Acre WC2; tube: Covent Garden – the largest and best selection of maps and guides in the world
Travel Bookshop
(☎ 7229 5260) 13 Blenheim Crescent W11; tube: Ladbroke Grove – claims to be the inspiration for the bookshop in *Notting Hill*, with all the new guides, plus a selection of out-of-print and antiquarian gems

Cultural Centres These oases of information often provide free entertainment, while doubling up as a civilised way of escaping the weather.

Institute for Contemporary Arts (ICA)
(☎ 7930 3647) Nash House, The Mall SW1; tube: Piccadilly Circus. An innovative complex incorporating a small bookshop, an art gallery, cinema, bar, cafe and theatre. There's always something worthwhile to see, the bar and restaurant are good value, and there's a young and relaxed crowd.
Riverside Studios complex
(☎ 7420 0100) Crisp Rd W6; tube: Hammersmith. Originally a TV studio, this is another innovative centre with an excellent gallery, a cafe and restaurant, a bar, two performance spaces

(often showing dance or theatre), an art gallery and a bookshop.

South Bank Centre
Belvedere Rd, Waterloo SE1; tube: Waterloo. London's centre for classical music, South Bank includes the Royal Festival Hall, Queen Elizabeth Hall, Hayward Gallery (☎ 7928 3144), the National Film Theatre, the National Theatre and a range of restaurants and cafes. There are free foyer events at the National Theatre and Festival Hall daily.

Laundry There's bound to be a laundry within walking distance of your accommodation; a wash and dry is likely to cost £2.50 to £3. Otherwise, try Red & White Laundrette, 78 Marchmont St WC1 in Bloomsbury; Bubbles, 113 Earl's Court Rd SW5 in Earl's Court; or Laundrette Centre, 5 Porchester Rd W2 in Bayswater.

Left Luggage See the London Getting Around section later in this chapter for left-luggage facilities at Heathrow and Gatwick airports. The main train stations and Victoria coach station also have left-luggage facilities, but these can be very expensive.

Medical & Emergency Services Dial ☎ 999 for fire, police or ambulance.

The following hospitals have 24-hour accident and emergency (A&E) departments:

Guy's Hospital
(☎ 7955 5000) St Thomas St SE1; tube: London Bridge
University College Hospital
(☎ 7387 9300) Grafton Way WC1; tube: Euston Square
Charing Cross Hospital
(☎ 8846 1234) Fulham Palace Rd W6; tube: Hammersmith
Royal Free Hospital
(☎ 7794 0500) Pond St NW3; tube: Belsize Park

To find an emergency dentist phone the Dental Emergency Care Service (☎ 7955 2186) or Eastman Dental Hospital (☎ 7915 1000), 256 Gray's Inn Rd WC1 (tube: Chancery Lane).

Pharmacies display the address of the nearest late-night pharmacy in their windows. Drop-in doctor services have opened in several main-line railway terminals but their charges can be high.

Visas & Immunisations Several of the companies offering visa and immunisation services advertise in *TNT Magazine*. Charges can differ widely. Trailfinders (☎ 7938 3999), 194 Kensington High St W8 (tube: High St Kensington), has both a visa service and an immunisation centre. The International Medical Centre (☎ 7486 3063) has a branch at Top Deck Travel, 131 Earl's Court Rd SW5 (tube: Earl's Court). Top Deck also hosts the Rapid Visa Service (☎ 7373 3026). Nomad (☎ 8889 7014), 3 Turnpike Lane N8 (tube: Turnpike Lane), sells travel equipment and medical kits, and gives immunisations on certain days.

Dangers & Annoyances Although city crime is certainly not unknown, most tourists spend their two weeks in the capital without anything worse happening than being overcharged for a beer. Considering its size and the disparities in wealth, London is fairly safe. That said, you should take the usual precautionary measures against pickpockets who operate in crowded public places like the Tube. Also, keep an eye on your belongings at all times, especially in pubs, theatres, restaurants and museums.

Women should be careful about travelling alone after pub closing hours, particularly in areas off the main tourist tracks.

Things to See & Do
The centre of London can easily be explored on foot. The following tour could be covered in a day but doesn't allow time to explore the individual sights in detail; it will, however, introduce you to the West End, the South Bank and Westminster.

Start at **St Paul's Cathedral**, Christopher Wren's masterpiece completed in 1710 (tube: St Paul's). Entry costs £5, which gains you access to the cathedral plus the dome and crypt.

From the Cathedral, walk down to the Thames. Here you should be able to cross on the new **Millennium Bridge** directly to the **Tate Modern**. Housed in the huge old Bankside Power Station, this is the new home for the Tate's collection of modern art.

Walk west along the river past the many attractions of the **South Bank Centre** and stop when you reach the **British Airways London Eye**. At 135m it is the world's tallest observation wheel and on a rare clear day you can see 40 miles. It's very popular whatever the weather and you best book your ride in advance (☎ 0870-500 0600). Tickets cost £7.45 and some are held back for same-day sale, but beware of the crowds.

Cross the **Hungerford Bridge**, which is getting new walkways, cut through Charing Cross Station and walk east along the Strand to Southhampton St and head north to **Covent Garden piazza**. Once London's fruit and vegetable market, it has been turned into a bustling tourist attraction. It's one of the few places in London where pedestrians rule, and you can watch the buskers for a few coins and the tourists for free.

Leave the piazza walking west on Long Acre (look for Stanfords bookshop on your left). Continue across Charing Cross Rd to **Leicester Square** with its cinemas and franchise food. Note the Leicester Square Half-Price Ticket Booth, which sells half-price theatre tickets on the day of performance.

Continue along Coventry St to **Piccadilly Circus**, with Tower Records, arguably London's best music shop. On the north-eastern corner a cluster of cheap kebab/pizza counters heralds the junction with Shaftesbury Ave. This theatre-lined street runs back into **Soho**, with its myriad restaurants. Regent St curves out of the north-western corner.

Continue west along Piccadilly to the **Royal Academy of Arts**, which often has special shows and Wren's **St James's Piccadilly**. Detour into the timeless **Burlington Arcade**, just after the academy, and see the many smart shops.

Return to Piccadilly and continue until you get to St James's St on your left. This runs down to **St James's Palace**, the royal home from 1660 to 1837 until it was judged insufficiently impressive. It's now the home of Prince Charles. Skirt around its eastern side and you come to the Mall.

Trafalgar Square is to the east, **Buckingham Palace** (☎ 7799 2331) to the west. The palace is open 9.30 am to 4.15 pm daily from early August to early October. Admission costs £10.50. Don't be surprised if the palace reminds you of a series of ornate hotel lobbies.

From mid-April to late July the changing of the guard happens outside Buckingham Palace daily at 11.30 am; the rest of the year it is at 11.30 am on alternate days. The best place to be is by the gates of Buckingham House, but the crowds are awesome.

Cross back into St James's Park, the most beautiful in London, and follow the lake to its eastern end. Turn right onto Horse Guards Rd. This takes you past the **Cabinet War Rooms** (£4.80), which give an extraordinary insight into the dark days of WWII. They're open 10 am to 6 pm daily.

Continue along Horse Guards Rd and then turn left onto Great George St, which takes you through to beautiful Westminster Abbey, the Houses of Parliament and Westminster Bridge. **Westminster Abbey** is so rich in history you need a few hours to do it justice. The coronation chair, where all but two monarchs since 1066 have been crowned, is behind the altar, and many greats – from Darwin to Chaucer – have been buried here. Unfortunately the crowds are now so dense that an admission fee of £5 is charged to go into any part of the cathedral. The best way to soak in the atmosphere is to attend evensong, which takes place at 5 pm weekdays and 3 pm weekends.

The **Houses of Parliament** and the clock tower (actually its bell), **Big Ben**, were built in the 19th century in neo-Gothic style. The best way to get into the building is to attend the Commons or Lords visitors galleries during a Parliamentary debate. Phone ☎ 7219 4272 for information.

Walking away from Westminster Bridge, turn right onto Parliament St, which becomes Whitehall. On your left, the hard-to-see but ordinary-looking house at **No 10 Downing St** offers accommodation to prime ministers. Farther along on the right is the Inigo Jones-designed **Banqueting House** (entry £3.60), outside which Charles I was beheaded. Continue past the **Horse Guards**, where you can see a less crowded changing of the guard at 11 am Monday to Saturday, 10 am on Sunday.

Finally, you reach **Trafalgar Square** and Nelson's Column. The National Gallery and National Portrait Gallery, both free, are on the northern side.

River Tour If walking doesn't seem such a great idea, consider catching a boat (☎ 7930 4097) from Westminster Pier (beside Westminster Bridge) down the river to Greenwich (single/return £6.30/7.60, every half-hour

CENTRAL WEST LONDON

Regent's Park
Boating
Lake

Gloucester Pl

Marylebone

Park

Road

MARYLEBONE

Rossmore

Grove

Lodge Road

Lisson

Penfold

Church St

Broadley

Edgware

Street

Hall

Pl

Bell

St

Marylebone Road

Old Marylebone Rd

Crawford St

Seymore Place

George St

Edgware

Street

Seymour Road

Connaught St

Bayswater Road

North Carriage Dr

To the West End

Hyde Park

The Ring

The Long

φ 1

φ 7

Chapel

Street

Road

φ 13

Praed Street

φ 15

φ 14

Sussex Gardens

φ 16

Sussex Pl

Paddington

φ 12

Eastbourne Terrace

Westbourne Terrace

Gloucester Terrace

Craven

Terrace

Craven Hill

Lancaster Gate

Craven Terrace

φ 17

Leinster Gardens

Leinster Terrace

BAYSWATER

Bishop's Bridge

Road

Porchester Terrace

Gloucester Terrace

Cleveland

Queensborough Terrace

φ 18

φ 19

Bayswater

φ 20

φ 21

φ 22

Inverness
Terrace

Gardens

Queensway

Porchester

φ 2

Road

φ 11

Garway Rd

Moscow Rd

Palace Ct

Kensington

φ 10

Hereford Rd

Chepstow

Place

Pembridge

Square

Kensington Gate

Chepstow Road

Westbourne Grove

Pembridge Villas

Dawson Pl

Pembridge Place

Pembridge Gdns

φ 25

φ 26

Pembridge Rd

φ 24

φ 23

Notting Hill

Chepstow Road

Talbot Road

Ledbury Road

Westbourne Park Road

NOTTING HILL

Portobello Road

Kensington Park Road

Pembridge

Villas

φ 9

Hamilton Ter

Maida Vale

Randolph Avenue

St John's Wood

Edgware Road

Blomfield Road

Little Venice

Howley Pl

PADDINGTON

A40(M)

Warwick Avenue

Clifton Gdns

Clifton Road

Lauderdale Road

Castellain

Delaware Road

Shirland Road

Sutherland Avenue

Harrow Road

Westway

Westbourne

Park Road

Avenue

Elgin

Widley Rd

Essendine Rd

Malvern Rd

Chippenham Road

Walterton Road

Fernhead Road

Shirland Road

Ashmore Road

Portnall Road

Bravington Road

Harrow Road

Elgin Avenue

Great Western Road

All Saints Rd

Tavistock Road

φ 3

φ 4

φ 5

φ 6

φ 8

Elkstone Rd

Portobello Rd

Elgin Ct

Colville

Terrace

Golborne Rd

Ladbroke Grove

Ladbroke Road

Ladbroke Square

Ladbroke Gate

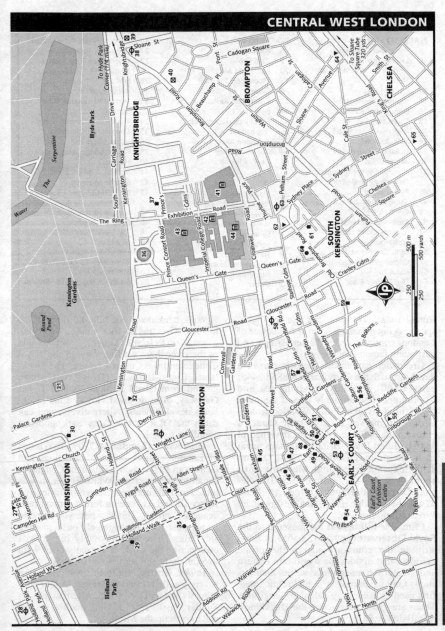

BRITAIN

CENTRAL WEST LONDON

PLACES TO STAY		PLACES TO EAT		17	Lancaster Gate Tube Station
9	Portobello Gold Hotel	5	Bali Sugar	21	Bayswater Tube Station
10	Leinster Inn	7	Café Grove	22	Queensway Tube Station
13	Norfolk Court & St David's	20	Kalamaras Micro	25	Notting Hill Tube Station
	Hotel	23	Modhubon Tandoori	28	Holland Park Tube Station
14	Cardiff Hotel	26	Geales	31	Kensington Palace
15	Balmoral House Hotel	27	Costas Fish Restaurant	33	High St Kensington Tube
16	Europa House Hotel	32	Bellini's		Station
18	Quest Hotel	39	Fifth Floor Harvey Nichols	34	Trailfinders; Campus Travel
19	Inverness Court Hotel	55	Troubadour	35	Commonwealth Institute
24	Hillgate Hotel	62	Rotisserie Jules	36	Royal Albert Hall
29	Holland House Hostel	64	Chelsea Kitchen	38	Knightsbridge Tube Station
30	Abbey Court	65	Henry J Bean's	40	Harrods
37	Imperial College of Science,			41	Victoria & Albert Museum
	Technology & Medicine	**OTHER**		42	Science Museum
45	Amber Hotel	ML - (Main-Line)		43	Imperial College of Science &
47	Barmy Badger Backpackers	1	Edgeware Rd Tube Station		Technology
49	Court Hotel	2	Royal Oak Tube Station	44	Natural History Museum
51	Merlyn Court Hotel	3	Westbourne Park Tube Station	46	Bubbles Laundrette
52	Regency Court Hotel	4	Subterania	48	Top Deck Travel
54	York House Hotel	6	Portobello Rd Market	50	Callshop
56	Earl's Court Hostel	8	Travel bookshop	53	Earl's Court Tube Station
57	Curzon House Hotel	11	Laundrette Centre	58	Gloucester Rd Tube Station
59	Hotel 167	12	Paddington ML & Tube	60	STA Travel
61	Five Sumner Place		Station	63	South Kensington Tube Station

from 10 am). You pass the site of Shakespeare's Globe Theatre, stop at the Tower of London, continue under Tower Bridge and past many famous docks.

Greenwich can absorb the best part of a day. Start with the *Cutty Sark* (☎ 8858 3445; entry £3.50), the only surviving tea and wool clipper and arguably one of the most beautiful ships ever built. Wander around Greenwich market, then visit the **Queen's House**, a Palladian masterpiece designed in 1616 by Inigo Jones. Britain's famous naval traditions are covered in fascinating fashion at the expanded **National Maritime Museum** (☎ 8858 4422; entry £7.50). The elegant **Old Royal Naval College** (☎ 8269 4744), beside the river, was designed by Wren. Admission is £5.

Climb the hill behind the museum to the **Royal Observatory** (☎ 8312 6565). A brass strip in the courtyard marks the prime meridian that divides the world into eastern and western hemispheres while displays show famous timepieces, including those first used to accurately calculate longitude. There are great views over the Docklands. Admission is £6.

Walk back down the hill and through the historic Greenwich foot tunnel (near the *Cutty Sark*) to Island Gardens. From this side of the river there's a fine view of the Naval College and the Queen's House. The Docklands Light Railway (DLR) runs above ground from Island Gardens back to Tower Gateway, offering good views of the Docklands developments. Alternatively, you can catch the DLR at the Cutty Sark stop and avoid the tunnel.

The **Tower of London** (☎ 7709 0765) is one of London's most popular attractions and dates from 1078, when William the Conqueror began to construct the White Tower. It was turned into an enormous concentric fortress by Henry III and has been a fortress, royal residence and prison. This is where you come to whisk past the crown jewels on a moving sidewalk. There are inevitably big crowds even during the week. It's usually open 9 am to 5 pm daily and admission is £10.50.

Tower Bridge, built in 1894, is often wrongly called 'London Bridge'. A tour covering its history costs £6.25. Alternatively, on Sunday, visit Petticoat Lane market, a short walk north up the Minories.

Museums The greatest of them all is the British Museum with its unparalleled Egyptian, Mesopotamian, Greek and Roman collections. London's main museum precinct, however, is in Kensington, just north of the South Kensington tube station; the sprawling Victoria & Albert Museum (decorative arts) and the rejuvenated Science and Natural History museums (animated dinosaurs and interactive displays) are all highly recommended.

The **British Museum** (☎ 7636 1555), Great Russell St WC1 (tube: Russell Square or Tottenham Court Rd), is emerging from a grand make-over. It has the world's greatest collection of antiquities and is open 10 am to 5 pm daily (noon to 6 pm Sunday). Admission is free.

The **Victoria & Albert Museum** (☎ 7938 8500), Cromwell Rd SW7 (tube: South Kensington), has the world's greatest collection of decorative arts, including clothes. It's open 10 am to 5.45 pm daily and costs £5. The V&A has the best of the Kensington museum cafes.

The kid-friendly **Science Museum** (☎ 7942 4454), Exhibition Rd SW7 (tube: South Kensington) has a huge new wing that covers the latest science and technological developments. It's open 10 am to 6 pm daily. Admission costs £6.50.

The **Natural History Museum** (☎ 7942 5000), Cromwell Rd SW7 (tube: South Kensington) consists of the wonderful Life and Earth Galleries, looking at natural history and geology respectively. It's open 10 am to 5.50 pm daily (Sunday from 11 am); admission is £6.50.

The **Museum of London** (☎ 7600 3699), 150 London Wall EC2 (tube: St Paul's), showcases London's history, from the Romans to the Dome. It's open 10 am to 5.50 pm daily (from noon Sunday) and costs £5.

The **Imperial War Museum** (☎ 7416 5320), Lambeth Rd SE1 (tube: Lambeth North), houses many thoughtful exhibits (the new Holocaust Museum is especially recommended). It's open 10 am to 6 pm daily and costs £5.20.

Galleries Visits to the National and Tate Modern galleries are musts, but there are also likely to be interesting exhibitions at the Hayward Gallery (South Bank Centre), the ICA (see Cultural Centres) and the Royal Academy of Arts among many others. Check *Time Out* for current shows.

The **National Gallery** (☎ 7747 2885), Trafalgar Square WC2 (tube: Charing Cross) has masterpieces from all the leading European schools from the 13th to 20th centuries. It's open 10 am to 6 pm daily (until 9 pm Wednesday) and is free.

Around the corner, the **National Portrait Gallery** (☎ 7306 0055), 2 St Martin's Place WC2 (tube: Charing Cross), has received a major make-over that opens up the fascinating galleries of images from British political life and popular culture. It's open 10 am to 6 pm daily (from noon Sunday) and is free.

The **Courtauld Institute Gallery** (☎ 7848 2526), Somerset House, the Strand WC2 (tube: Temple), has a mind-blowing collection of postimpressionists (Cézanne, Gauguin, van Gogh). Its amazing building has reopened after a long restoration. It's open 10 am to 6 pm daily (from noon Sunday) and costs £4.

The **Tate Modern** (☎ 7887 8000), 25 Sumner St SE1 (tube: Southwark), is the new big deal on the London cultural scene. Housed in a huge old power station on the Thames, it has a huge collection of modern art dating from 1900 to the present. It's open 10 am to 6 pm daily (until 10 pm Friday to Sunday) and is free.

The **Tate Britain** (☎ 7887 8000), Millbank SW11 (tube: Pimlico), majors in the history of British art, especially Turner. It's open 10 am to 5.50 pm daily and is free.

Markets Bustling, interesting and full of character(s), the markets are where you see London life at its best. Most are in full swing by 9 am and fold up by mid-afternoon.

Soho's **Berwick St** (tube: Piccadilly) is one of the last strongholds of real life in the West End. The stallholders are as theatrical as you can find, and the fruit and vegetables are some of London's best and cheapest (stock up for a picnic). There are also some good record shops.

Camden (tube: Camden Town) attracts huge crowds all weekend. It's a lot of fun but the litter and clutter can make it feel pretty tacky. The Electric Ballroom on High St sells second-hand clothes on Sunday, but all you need do is start at Camden Lock and follow the crowds.

BRITAIN

Supposed home of the cockney barrow-boy, **Petticoat Lane**, Middlesex St (tube: Aldgate), is open Sunday and sells a wide variety of clothing (particularly leather) and odds and ends.

Brick Lane (tube: Aldgate East), open Sunday, is cheap, chaotic and dominated by Bengalis, but there are still some fresh bagels to be found (at the north end, away from Whitechapel).

Portobello Rd (tube: Ladbroke Grove) has fruit and vegetables Monday to Saturday except Thursday afternoon, and general goods on Friday and Saturday. There are reasonable second-hand stalls at the Westway end, expensive antiques at the Notting Hill end.

Brixton (tube: Brixton) is open Monday to Saturday except Wednesday afternoon. Barrows are piled high with Caribbean fruit and vegetables, and there are lively arcades that cry out to be explored.

Other Attractions All visitors, but especially travellers on a tight budget, should make the most of London's glorious parks. A long walk starting at St James's and continuing through Green, Hyde, Kensington and Holland parks will banish any urban blues.

Hyde Park is central London's largest park. Row a boat on the Serpentine, listen to a military band (on summer Sundays), take a dip in the outdoor swimming pool or heckle the soapbox orators on Sunday at Speakers' Corner (Marble Arch corner).

Kensington Palace (☎ 7937 9561), Kensington Gardens W8 (tube: High St Kensington), was home to the late Princess Diana. The State Apartments are open 10 am to 4 pm daily and cost £9.50.

Kew Gardens (☎ 8332 5000), Richmond (tube: Kew Gardens), the Royal Botanic Gardens, are a haven of tranquillity amid the urban sprawl. Entry costs £5. As an alternative to the tube, ferries sail from Westminster Pier from 10.15 am to 2 pm (April to October). They take 1¾ hours and cost £7. While you're out here, cross Kew Bridge and walk to the right along the bank of the Thames to Strand-on-the-Green, where there are several delightful riverside pubs.

Hampton Court Palace (☎ 8781 9500) is Britain's grandest Tudor house. Built by Cardinal Wolsey in 1514 and 'adopted' by Henry VIII, it's a beautiful mix of architectural styles from Henry's splendid Great Hall to the State Apartments built by Wren for King William III and Queen Mary II. The superb palace grounds, near the Thames, include a deer park and a 300-year-old maze. It's open 9.30 am to 6 pm daily (to 4.30 pm in winter) and admission is £10.50; the grounds are free, the maze alone £2.50. There are trains every half-hour from Waterloo (£4.40 return), or you can catch a ferry from Westminster Pier. Ferries sail from April to late-September at 10.30 and 11.15 am, and noon; they take 3½ hours and cost £10.

Tourist Traps London's alternative attractions are long on commercialism and short on culture.

Madame Tussaud's (☎ 7935 6861), Marylebone Rd (tube: Baker St), is permanently crowded, proving that people really, really want to see wax versions of the rich and famous, especially if they can have their picture taken with them. The queues are horrendous, so get there at 9.30 am for the 10 am opening. Next door is the **Planetarium**, your chance to get to grips with the heavens. Admission to Madame Tussaud's is a hefty £10.50; £12.95 with the Planetarium.

Harrods (☎ 7730 1234), Knightsbridge SW1 (tube: Knightsbridge), is a once grand store that has become a parody of itself. Items bearing the store's logo predominate – beware of thug-like guards at the doors who yell at the hapless tourists toting day-packs.

Organised Tours

The **Original London Sightseeing Tour** (☎ 8877 1722), the **Big Bus Company** (☎ 7233 9533) and **London Pride Sightseeing** (☎ 7520 2050) offer tours of the main sights on double-decker buses which allow you either to go straight round without getting off or to hop on and off along the way. They're all expensive (around £12) and probably worth considering if you're only going to be in London for a day or two. Most companies can sell you advance tickets to the biggest attractions to save wasting time in queues.

Convenient starting points are in Trafalgar Square in front of the National Gallery, in front of the Trocadero on Coventry St between Leicester Square and Piccadilly Circus, and in Wilton Gardens opposite Victoria Station.

London Pride Sightseeing includes Docklands and Greenwich in one of its tours, while the Original London Sightseeing Tour has an express tour for those with limited time.

Places to Stay

However you look at it, accommodation in London is ridiculously expensive no matter what your budget. Expect less than you've received elsewhere and you won't be so disappointed.

It's always wise to book a night or two's accommodation in advance, especially in July and August. The official TICs at the airports and at Victoria station can arrange last-minute bookings. You can also phone the TIC bookings hotline (☎ 7932 2020), but it is only staffed weekdays and charges £5. There are several private services at Victoria which charge £5. Free B&B bookings can be made through Bed & Breakfast GB (☎ 01491-578803), PO Box 66, Henley-on-Thames RG9 1XS.

Camping Camping is not a realistic option in the centre of the capital but there are a few possibilities within striking distance.

Tent City Acton (☎ 8743 5708, fax 8749 9074, Old Oak Common Lane W3; tube: East Acton) in far west London is the cheapest option short of camping rough and is well situated within break-out distance of Wormwood Scrubs prison. One of 320 beds in dormitory-style tents costs £6. It's open from June to mid-September, and you should book. There are also about 200 pitches for tents only.

Tent City Hackney (☎ 8985 7656, Millfields Rd E5; Hackney Central station, then bus No 236 or 276) is a north-east London branch of the previous place. It has a hostel tent with 90 beds and 200 tent pitches for £5 per person. It's open June to August.

Lee Valley Leisure Centre (☎ 8345 6666, fax 8803 6900, Lee Valley Regional Park, Meridian Way N9; Northumberland Park station) is to the north-east and has more than 200 pitches for tents and caravans. It's open year-round and the nightly charge is £5.35/2.25 adults/children; electricity hookup is £2.30 extra.

YHA/HI Hostels There are seven hostels in central London which are affiliated to Hostelling International (HI), known as Youth Hostels Association (YHA) in Britain.

Central London's hostels get very crowded in summer. They all take advance bookings by phone (if you pay by Visa or MasterCard). They also hold some beds for those who wander in on the day, but come early and be prepared to queue. All but one offer 24-hour access and all have a *bureau de change*. Most have facilities for self-catering and some offer cheap meals.

City of London (☎ 7236 4965, fax 7236 7681, @ city@yha.org.uk, 36 Carter Lane EC4; tube: St Paul's) is an excellent hostel (193 beds) standing in the shadow of St Paul's Cathedral. Rooms have mainly two, three or four beds though there are a dozen rooms with five to eight beds. There's a licensed cafeteria but no kitchen. The rates per person start at £22.95 (£19.70 for children), depending on the room type. Remember, this part of town is pretty quiet outside working hours.

Earl's Court (☎ 7373 7083, fax 7835 2034, @ earlscourt@yha.org.uk, 38 Bolton Gardens SW5; tube: Earl's Court) hostel (154 beds) is a Victorian town house in a shabby, though lively, part of town. Rooms are mainly 10-bed dorms with communal showers. There's a cafe, a kitchen for self-catering and a small garden courtyard for summer barbecues. Rates for adults/children are £19.95/17.95.

Hampstead Heath (☎ 8458 9054, fax 8209 0546, @ hampstead@yha.org.uk, 4 Wellgarth Rd NW11; tube: Golders Green) hostel (190 beds) has a beautiful setting with a well-kept garden, although it's rather isolated. The dormitories are comfortable and each room has a washbasin. There's a licensed cafe and a kitchen. Rates are £19.70/17.30.

Holland House (☎ 7937 0748, fax 7376 0667, @ hollandhouse@yha.org.uk, Holland Walk, Kensington W8; tube: High Street Kensington) hostel (201 beds) is built into the Jacobean wing of Holland House in the middle of Holland Park. It's large, very busy and rather institutional, but the position can't be beaten. There's a cafe and kitchen. Rates are £19.95/17.95.

Oxford St (☎ 7734 1618, fax 7734 1657, 14 Noel St W1; tube: Oxford Circus or Tottenham Court Road). This most central of the hostels (75 beds) is basic but clean and welcoming. It

BRITAIN

has a large kitchen but no meals are served apart from breakfast (£2.30). Rates are £20.55/16.85 in rooms with three or four beds and £22.20 per person in twin rooms, which make up the majority.

Rotherhithe (☎ *7232 2114, fax 7237 2919,* ✉ *rotherhithe@yha.org.uk, 20 Salter Rd SE16; tube: Rotherhithe*), the YHA flagship hostel (320 beds) in London, was purpose-built in 1993. It's right by the River Thames and recommended, but the location is a bit remote and quiet. Most rooms have four or six beds, though there are also 22 doubles (four of them adapted for disabled visitors); all have an attached bathroom. There's a bar and restaurant as well as kitchen facilities and a laundry. B&B rates are £22.95/19.70.

St Pancras International (☎ *7388 9998, fax 7388 6766,* ✉ *stpancras@yha.org.uk, 79-81 Euston Rd N1; tube: King's Cross St Pancras*) is central and is London's newest YHA hostel. The area isn't great, but the hostel itself (153 beds) is up to date, with kitchen, restaurant, lockers, cycle shed and lounge. Rates are £22.95/19.70.

Independent Hostels London's independent hostels tend to be more relaxed and cheaper than the YHA ones though standards can be pretty low; some of the places are downright grotty. Expect to pay a minimum of £10 per night in a basic dormitory.

Most hostels have at least three or four bunk beds jammed into each small room, a kitchen and some kind of lounge. Some have budget restaurants and a bar attached. Be careful with your possessions and deposit your valuables in the office safe, safe-deposit box or secure locker if provided. Check that fire escapes and stairwells are accessible.

Ashlee House (☎ *7833 9400, fax 7833 9677,* ✉ *ashleehouse@tsnxt.co.uk, 261-265 Gray's Inn Rd WC1; tube: King's Cross St Pancras*) is clean and well maintained on three floors close to King's Cross station. Dorm rooms (most with bunks) can be very cramped, but there's double-glazing on the windows, a laundry and a decent-sized kitchen. Rooms with between four and 16 beds cost between £17 and £13 per person in the low season and between £19 and £15 in the high season. There are a few twins for £44 (£48 in high season).

Barmy Badger Backpackers (☎/fax *7370 5213,* ✉ *barmy–badger.b@virgin.net, 17 Longridge Rd SW5; tube: Earl's Court*) is a basic dormitory with dorm beds from £13 per person, including breakfast. Twins without/with facilities cost £28/31. There's a large kitchen and safe-deposit boxes.

Court Hotel (☎ *7373 0027, fax 7912 9500, 194-196 Earl's Court Rd SW5; tube: Earl's Court*) is under Australasian management and has well equipped kitchens and TVs in most rooms. Dorm beds cost £11 to £14, while singles/doubles are £26/35 a night (£160/210 a week).

Curzon House Hotel (☎ *7581 2116, fax 7835 1319, 58 Courtfield Gardens SW5; tube: Gloucester Road*) is a relaxed, friendly place in Earl's Court and is one of the better private hostels around. Dorm beds are £16 per person, singles/doubles with facilities £26/36. Rates include breakfast.

The Generator (☎ *7388 7666, fax 7388 7644,* ✉ *generator@lhdr.demon.co.uk, Compton Place, 37 Tavistock Place WC1; tube: Russell Square*) in Bloomsbury is one of the grooviest budget places in central London and the futuristic decor looks like an updated set of Terry Gilliam's film *Brazil.* Along with 207 rooms (830 beds), it has a bar open to 2 am, a large lounge for eating, watching TV or playing pool, a room with Internet kiosks, safe-deposit boxes and a large eating area, but no kitchen. Depending on the season, a place in a dorm with seven or eight beds costs from £18 to £19.50 and with three to six beds £19 to £21. Singles are £36, while twins are £46. All prices include breakfast.

International Students House (☎ *7631 8300, fax 7631 8315, 229 Great Portland St W1; tube: Great Portland Street*) feels more like a university residential college. The single and double rooms are ordinary but clean, and there are excellent facilities and a friendly, relaxed atmosphere. It's open year-round. Prices range from £10 for a place in an eight-bed dorm without breakfast to £29.50 for a single with washbasin and breakfast. *En suite* singles/doubles cost £30/47.

Leinster Inn (☎ *7229 9641, fax 7229 5255,* ✉ *astorhotels@msn.com, 7-12 Leinster Square W2; tube: Bayswater*) is in a large old house north-west of Bayswater tube station and close to Portobello Market. This is the largest of the Astor hostels (100 beds) and has a bar, cafe and laundry. Rates in dorms with up to 10 beds are £14, doubles are £28 to £42 per person.

Quest Hotel (☎ 7229 7782, fax 7727 8106, @ astorhotels@msn.com, 45 Queensborough Terrace W2; tube: Bayswater) is an Astor hostel one block to the east of Hyde Park. It gets pretty crowded, which may account for some bad-tempered staff. However, the monthly theme parties are popular and there's a kitchen for self-catering. Dorms with four to eight beds cost £15, doubles £18 per person, including breakfast.

Student Accommodation University halls of residence are let to nonstudents during the holidays, usually from the end of June to mid-September and sometimes over the Easter break. They're a bit more expensive than the hostels, but you usually get a single room (there are a few doubles) with shared facilities, plus breakfast.

University catering is usually reasonable and includes bars, self-service cafes, takeaway places and restaurants. Full-board, half-board, B&B and self-catering options are usually available.

The London School of Economics and Political Science (☎ 7955 7531), Room B508, Page Building, Houghton St, London WC2A 2AE, lets half a dozen of its halls in summer and sometimes during the Easter break. *Bankside Residence (☎ 7633 9877, 24 Sumner St SE1; tube: Blackfriars)* has an enviable location near the Globe Theatre and the new Tate Modern gallery at Bankside. It has beds in four-bed rooms for £20 to £35 and entire quads for £80, including breakfast. *High Holborn (☎ 7379 5589, fax 7379 5640, 178 High Holborn WC1; tube: Holborn)* has self-catering twins for £44 to £55 (£55 to £65 with bathrooms). *Passfield Hall (☎ 7387 3584, fax 7387 7743, 1-7 Endsleigh Place WC1; tube: Euston)* is composed of 10 late-Georgian houses in the heart of Bloomsbury. B&B costs from £25 to £27 for a single, £43 to £48 for a twin and £55 to £60 for a triple. *Goldsmid House (☎ 7493 8911, fax 7491 0586, 36 North Row W1; tube: Marble Arch)* is a centrally located hall with 10 singles (£16) and 120 twins (£22) available from mid-June to mid-September.

Imperial College of Science, Technology & Medicine (☎ 7594 9507, fax 7594 9504, @ reservations@ic.ac.uk, Watts Way, Prince's Gardens SW7; tube: South Kensington) is two minutes from some of London's greatest museums. It's open at Easter and in summer (July to late September), and B&B with shared bathroom costs £35/55 for a single/twin. The college also has rooms with private bathrooms in Pembridge Gardens, Notting Hill W2 (tube: Notting Hill Gate), for £38/54 in summer only.

John Adams Hall (☎ 7387 4086, fax 7383 0164, @ jah@ioe.ac.uk, 15-23 Endsleigh St WC1; tube: Euston) is quite a grand residence in a row of Georgian houses. It's open at Easter and from July to September. B&B costs from £23/39 for a single/double, depending on the time of year.

King's Campus Vacation Bureau (☎ 7928 3777, fax 928 5777, Riddell House, St Thomas's Campus, Lambeth Palace Rd SE1; tube: Waterloo) administers bookings for four central King's College halls of residence. There's one on Stamford St SE1 with apartments for £34 per person.

University of Westminster (☎ 7911 5000, fax 7911 5141, 35 Marylebone Rd NW1; tube: Baker Street) has beds in singles or doubles for £20/130 per night/week for people under 26, £25/165 for those over 26.

YMCAs YMCA England (☎ 8520 5599), 640 Forest Rd, London E17 3DZ, can supply you with a list of all its hostels in the Greater London area.

Barbican YMCA (☎ 7628 0697, fax 7638 2420, @ admin@barbican.ymca.org.uk, 2 Fann St EC2; tube: Barbican) has 240 beds with singles/doubles costing £23/41 with breakfast.

Central Club YMCA (☎ 7636 7512, fax 7636 5278, 16-22 Great Russell St WC1; tube: Tottenham Court Road) also has 240 beds. Singles/doubles cost £38/69.

London City YMCA (☎ 7628 8832, fax 7628 4080, 8 Errol St EC1; tube: Barbican) has 111 beds. B&B costs £25 per person.

B&Bs & Hotels This may come as a shock, but any figure below £30/50 for a single/double with shared facilities and below £40/60 with private bathroom is considered 'budget' in London. A mere £100 won't get you much and many business travellers grumble about the standards at places charging £200 a night or more.

B&Bs are among the cheapest private accommodation around. At the bottom end (hovering around £30 minimum) you get a bedroom in a private house, a shared bathroom and a cooked breakfast. In central London most cheaper accommodation is in guesthouses, often just large converted houses with half a dozen rooms, which tend to be less personal than B&Bs. Double rooms often have twin beds so you don't have to be intimate to share a room.

Don't be afraid to ask for the 'best' price or a discount if you're staying out of season or for more than a couple of nights, or if you don't want a cooked breakfast. In July, August and September prices can jump by 25% or more, and it's advisable to book ahead. Be warned – some of the cheaper places don't accept credit cards.

The following listings are arranged by neighbourhood and listed in order of price.

Pimlico & Victoria Victoria may not be the most attractive part of London, but you'll be very close to the action and the budget hotels are better value than those in Earl's Court. Pimlico is more residential though convenient for the Tate British gallery at Millbank.

Luna-Simone Hotel (☎ 7834 5897, fax 7828 2474, 47 Belgrave Rd SW1; tube: Victoria) is central, spotlessly clean and comfortable. Singles/doubles without bathroom start at £30/50; a double with facilities ranges from £55 to £70. A full English breakfast is included, and there are free storage facilities if you want to leave bags while travelling. If the Luna-Simone is full, there are a lot more B&Bs on Belgrave Rd.

Brindle House Hotel (☎ 7828 0057, fax 7931 8805, 1 Warwick Place North SW1; tube: Victoria) is a recently renovated place in an old building on a quiet street. The rooms are small but clean. Singles are £34 (shared facilities), doubles are £48/44 (with/without bathroom), triples are £69.

Windermere Hotel (☎ 7834 5163, fax 7630 8831, ✉ windermere@compuserve.com, 142-144 Warwick Way SW1; tube: Victoria) has 22 small but individually designed rooms in a sparkling white mid-Victorian town house.

The Windermere has singles/doubles with shared bathroom for £64/65; those with their own facilities start at £77/93.

Winchester Hotel (☎ 7828 2972, fax 7828 5191, 17 Belgrave Rd SW1; tube: Victoria). This clean, comfortable and welcoming place is also good value for the area; doubles and twins with private bathroom and TV cost £70.

Rubens at the Palace (☎ 7834 6600, fax 7233 6037, ✉ reservations@rubens.redcarn ationhotels.com, 39 Buckingham Palace Rd SW1; tube: Victoria) has a brilliant position overlooking the walls of the Royal Mews and Buckingham Palace. Singles/doubles start at £160/200 without breakfast. It's popular with groups.

The West End & Covent Garden Here you're in the centre of the action, but you pay for the convenience.

Regent Palace Hotel (☎ 7734 7000, fax 7734 6435; tube: Piccadilly) is ripe for a make-over but pretty cheap for its position right beside Piccadilly Circus. This enormous hotel has rooms – none with bathroom – for £64 Sunday to Thursday and £80 on weekends without breakfast.

Fielding Hotel (☎ 7836 8305, fax 7497 0064, 4 Broad Court, Bow St WC2; tube: Covent Garden) is on a pedestrianised street a block away from the Royal Opera House. It's remarkably good value, clean and well run. All rooms have private bathroom, TV and phone. Singles/doubles start at £74/98.

Hazlitt's (☎ 7434 1771, fax 7439 1524, 6 Frith St W1; tube: Tottenham Court Road) was built in 1718 and comprises three original Georgian houses. It is one of central London's finest hotels, with efficient personal service. All 23 rooms are named after former residents or visitors to the house and are individually decorated with antique furniture and prints. Singles/doubles start at £135/170. Booking is advisable.

St Martins Lane (☎ 7300 5500, 0800 634 5500, 45 St Martin's Lane; tube: Leicester Square) is a designer hotel that provides a 'slice of New York urban chic' just a stone's throw from Covent Garden. It's a good place for bumping into supermodels in the lift. Indulging in its late-90s minimalism costs from £225 for a double.

The Savoy (☎ 7836 4343, fax 7240 6040, @ info@the-savoy.co.uk, Strand WC2; tube: Charing Cross) stands on the site of the old Savoy Palace, which was burned down during the Peasants' Revolt of 1381. The 207 rooms are so comfortable and have such great views that some people have been known to take up permanent residence. Singles/doubles start at £265/290.

Bloomsbury Bloomsbury is very convenient, especially for the West End. There are lots of places on Gower and North Gower Sts.

Hotel Cavendish (☎ 7636 9079, fax 7580 3609, 75 Gower St WC1; tube: Goodge Street) is a clean and pleasant family-run place, with singles/doubles without bath for £32/47 and with *en suite* facilities for £42/62, including breakfast.

Cambria House (☎ 7837 1654, fax 7837 1229, 37 Hunter St WC1; tube: Russell Square) is run by the Salvation Army and is one of the best deals around. Singles/doubles with shared bathroom are £29/47 a night or £196/308 a week. *En suite* doubles are £57/378 a night/ week. Prices include breakfast.

Euro Hotel (☎ 7387 4321, fax 7383 5044, 53 Cartwright Gardens WC1; tube: Russell Square) has simple singles/doubles for £45/63. Those with shower and toilet cost £68/85. The Euro is recommended.

Ridgemount Hotel (☎ 7636 1141, fax 7636 2558, 65-67 Gower St WC1; tube: Goodge Street) has garnered favourable comments from readers. Basic singles/doubles are £31/46; with facilities they're £41/58 (including breakfast). It also has a laundry room.

Arran House Hotel (☎ 7636 2186, fax 7436 5328, 77 Gower St WC1; tube: Goodge Street) is a welcoming place with a lovely garden and laundry facilities. Singles range from £40 with no facilities to £50 with shower, doubles from £50 to £70, triples from £68 to £78. Prices include breakfast. The rooms all have TV and phone.

Academy Hotel (☎ 7631 4115, fax 6636 3442, 17-25 Gower St WC1; tube: Goodge Street) is in a rather busy street, although double-glazing keeps the noise down. Its 47 rooms are pale and pretty, and there's a pleasant back garden. Singles cost £100 to £115, doubles from £125 to £185.

Chelsea, South Kensington & Earl's Court Most people in these bustling areas seem to be in transit. Chelsea and South Kensington are close to museums and restaurants. Earl's Court is not really within walking distance of many places of interest, but the tube station is a busy interchange, so getting around is easy.

Regency Court Hotel (☎ 7244 6615, 14 Penywern Rd SW5; tube: Earl's Court) has undergone a much needed renovation. Its 20 bright rooms, all with *en suite* facilities, cost £30 to £35 for singles and £40 to £45 for doubles.

York House Hotel (☎ 7373 7519, fax 7370 6641, 27-28 Philbeach Gardens SW5; tube: Earl's Court) is good value for what and where it is – on a quiet crescent – and the welcome is warm. The rooms are basic, although some have showers. Singles/doubles without facilities are £34/55; with, they're £38/73.

Merlyn Court Hotel (☎ 7370 1640, fax 7370 4986, 2 Barkston Gardens SW5; tube: Earl's Court) is an unpretentious place with a nice atmosphere and a lovely location close to the tube. Small but clean singles/doubles with bathroom cost £53/60; without they're £35/50. Triples with/without bathroom are £70/65.

Annandale House Hotel (☎ 7730 5051, fax 7730 2727, 39 Sloane Gardens SW1; tube: Sloane Square) is a discreet, traditional hotel just south of Sloane Square. Rooms, all with facilities, phone and TV, cost £40 to £60 for singles and £80 to £95 for doubles.

Hotel 167 (☎ 7373 0672, fax 7373 3360, 167 Old Brompton Rd SW5; tube: Gloucester Road) is small, stylish and has an unusually uncluttered and attractive decor. All 19 rooms have private bathroom. Singles are from £72, doubles from £90 to £99.

Five Sumner Place (☎ 7584 7586, fax 7823 9962, @ no.5@dial.pipex.com, 5 Sumner Place SW7; tube: South Kensington) is on a quiet leafy road just off Old Brompton St. It has 13 comfortable and well equipped rooms (all with bathroom, TV, phone, drinks cabinet and more), and there's an attractive conservatory and courtyard garden. Singles/ doubles start at £90/120.

Amber Hotel (☎ 7373 8666, fax 7835 1194, 101 Lexham Gardens W8; tube: Earl's Court) is pretty good value for its location halfway between Kensington and Earl's

BRITAIN

Court. Fully equipped singles/doubles are £105/110.

Bayswater, Paddington & Notting Hill

Bayswater is extremely convenient, though some of the streets immediately to the west of Queensway, which has a decent selection of restaurants, are run-down and depressing. Paddington can be a bit seedy, especially right around the station, but there are lots of cheap hotels and it's a good transit location; you can reach Heathrow in 15 minutes from here. Notting Hill is the opposite – it's upbeat and fun.

Norfolk Court & St David's Hotel (☎ 7723 4963, fax 7402 9061, 16-20 Norfolk Square W2; tube: Paddington) is right in the centre of the action and is clean, comfortable and friendly with the usual out-of-control decor. Basic singles/doubles have washbasin, colour TV and phone and cost £36/45; doubles with shower and toilet are £60, including a huge breakfast.

Balmoral House Hotel (☎ 7723 7445, fax 7402 0118, 156-157 Sussex Gardens W2; tube: Paddington) is immaculate and very comfortable. It is one of the better places to stay along Sussex Gardens, a street lined with small hotels but unfortunately it's a major traffic artery. Singles without/with bathroom cost £38/48, doubles with facilities are £67 (breakfast included and all rooms have TVs).

Portobello Gold Hotel (☎ 7460 4910, fax 7460 4911, 95 Portobello Rd W11; tube: Notting Hill Gate) is a somewhat scruffy hotel with a pleasant restaurant and bar on the ground floor and an Internet cafe upstairs. Singles/doubles without facilities are £39/55; with shower and toilet they're £54/70.

Cardiff Hotel (☎ 7723 9068, fax 7402 2342, 5-9 Norfolk Square W2; tube: Paddington) is on the same lovely square, which is a green oasis in summer. The family-run Cardiff has singles/doubles from £40/55 to £50/72.

Europa House Hotel (☎ 7723 7343, fax 7224 9331, ✉ europahouse@enterprise.net, 151 Sussex Gardens; tube: Paddington) is another excellent choice, where you're always assured a warm welcome (something not as common as you'd think at small London hotels). Singles cost from £50, doubles £68 and all rooms have bathroom, TV and phone.

Inverness Court Hotel (☎ 7229 1444, fax 7706 4240, Inverness Terrace W2; tube:

Queensway) was commissioned by Edward VII for his 'confidante' (ie, mistress), the actress Lillie Langtry, and comes complete with a private theatre, now the cocktail bar. The panelled walls, stained glass and huge open fires of the public areas give it a Gothic feel but most of the 183 rooms – some of which overlook Hyde Park – are modern and pretty ordinary. Singles/doubles cost £82/102.

Hillgate Hotel (☎ 7221 3433, fax 7229 4808, ✉ hillgate@lth-hotels.com, 6-14 Pembridge Gardens W2; tube: Notting Hill Gate) is set on a quiet street off Notting Hill Gate. The 70 rooms are spread over five Victorian terrace houses. *En suite* singles/doubles are £81/109.

Abbey Court (☎ 7221 7518, fax 7792 0858, 20 Pembridge Gardens W2; tube: Notting Hill Gate) has individually decorated rooms, some with fine views over the rooftops. Its singles/doubles start at £95/130. The breakfast room with a garden courtyard view is particularly fine.

Rental Prices for rental accommodation are high and standards are low. At the bottom end of the market are bedsits – a single furnished room, usually with a shared bathroom and kitchen, although some have basic cooking facilities. Expect to pay £70 to £150 per week. The next step up is a studio, normally with a separate bathroom and kitchen for between £90 and £200. One-bedroom flats average between £120 and £250. Shared houses and flats are the best value, with a bedroom for between £60 and £90 plus bills. Most landlords demand a security deposit (normally one month's rent) plus a month's rent in advance.

For help in finding a flat visit the foyer of Capital Radio at 29/30 Leicester Square WC2 and pick up its flatshare list; new lists appear at 4 pm every Friday and the best places will go fast. Friday's *Guardian* contains a useful supplement, *Space*, which reproduces this list. Rooms and flats are also advertised in *TNT*, *Time Out*, the *Evening Standard* and *Loot*. When you inspect a flat it's wise to take someone else with you, both for safety reasons and for help in spotting any snags.

If you decide to use an agency, check that it doesn't charge fees to tenants; Jenny Jones

(☎ 7493 4381), 40 South Molton St W1 (tube: Bond Street) charges the landlord.

Places to Eat

With hundreds of ethnic groups in London, you can find just about anything to eat imaginable. There is the considerable population of immigrants from the former British Empire as well as refugees from every corner of the globe, so a wide variety of ethnic food is consumed by everyone – from the tandooris of the Indian subcontinent and Turkish and Cypriot kebabs to the chicken Kievs of Ukraine and the noodles and dim sum of Hong Kong and China. Pizza and pasta are the staples of every high street in London and curry remains the takeaway of choice.

British food often lives down to its dismal reputation, especially in touristy pubs. However, many places now do fine versions of local chow and overall standards are up from even 10 years ago. At any price range, you'll be surprised at just how fast things can add up, even in seemingly cheap places.

The listings here just scratch the surface. You'll find many other places to eat near the choices we've listed, so feel free to wander off and make your own selection. Supermarkets and grocery stores are common everywhere.

Westminster & Pimlico Heavy on government buildings, this part of town is light on restaurants.

The Footstool (☎ 7222 2779, *St John's, Smith Square SW1; tube: Westminster*) is housed in the crypt of an 18th-century church (now a concert hall). It offers a buffet with soups from £3.50 and a more formal restaurant for a la carte lunches (main courses from £9.95 to £11.25) and post-concert set dinners (£10.95 for two courses).

UNo 1 (☎ 7834 1001, *1 Denbigh St SW1; tube: Victoria*) has pastas costing from £5.50 to £8. The cheery dining room is decorated in reds and yellows.

Mekong (☎ 7630 9568, *46 Churton St SW1; tube: Victoria*) is a popular neighbourhood Vietnamese restaurant with set meals for £13 (minimum of two people).

The West End: Piccadilly, Soho & Chinatown These days Soho is London's gastronomic heart with numerous restaurants and cuisines to choose from. The liveliest streets tend to be Greek, Frith, Old Compton and Dean Sts. Gerrard and Lisle Sts are full of Chinese eateries of every description.

Franx Snack Bar (☎ 7836 7989, *192 Shaftesbury Ave WC2; tube: Tottenham Court Road*) is as authentic a London 'caff' as you'll find in these parts, with eggs and bacon and other one-plate specials for around £3.

Pâtisserie Valerie (☎ 7437 3466, *44 Old Compton St W1; tube: Leicester Square or Tottenham Court Road*) is a Soho institution for coffee or tea and something really sweet (calorie-crunching cakes around £2.50). It also does filled croissants and club sandwiches (from £4 to £5.50).

Stockpot (☎ 7287 1066, *18 Old Compton St W1; tube: Leicester Square*) does a long list of basic dishes (including some vegetarian options) like fish and chips (£4.50), spaghetti bolognese (£3) and chicken Provençale (£3.90).

Star Café (☎ 7437 8778, *22 Great Chapel St W1; tube: Tottenham Court Road*) is a reliable cheapie dating from the 1930s. It serves up bangers and mash, fried breakfasts and pastas for under £5. It's open 7 am to 6 pm weekdays only.

Soup (☎ 7287 9100, *1 Newburgh St W1; tube: Oxford Circus*) has a wide variety of choices – from pea and mushroom claret to Indonesian crab *laksa*. Prices start at £2.95 for a small cup.

Pollo (☎ 7734 5917, *20 Old Compton St W1; tube: Leicester Square*) attracts a student crowd with its pastas, risottos, pizzas and chicken dishes for under £4.

Chuen Cheng Ku (☎ 7437 1398, *17 Wardour St W1*) is ideal for the uninitiated because all the dishes (dumplings, noodles, paper-wrapped prawns etc) are trundled around on trolleys. Dishes are about £4 each.

Poons (☎ 7437 4549, *27 Lisle St WC2*) offers OK food at very good prices and specialises in dried duck and pork (£4.20 per plate). Be prepared to queue at busy times and to be hustled out again pretty quickly.

Wagamama (☎ 7292 0990, *10A Lexington St W1; tube: Piccadilly Circus*) is a brash and spartan place that does great Japanese food but is hardly the place for a quiet dinner. Main dishes range from £5 to £7.50 while Japanese-style set menus are from £8 to £9.50.

BRITAIN

There are a couple of decent Spanish eateries with tapas (£2 to £6.95) that tourists never get to on Hanway St (tube: Tottenham Court Road), a narrow street running north off Oxford St. These include *Costa Dorada* (☎ 7636 7139) at Nos 47 to 55 and its sister restaurant, the cheaper *Sevilla Mia* (☎ 7637 3756), a hole-in-the-wall basement eatery at No 22.

Melati (☎ 7437 2745, 21 Great Windmill St W1; tube: Piccadilly Circus) offers good Indonesian/Malaysian/Singaporean food and a respectable range of vegetarian options. Various noodle and rice dishes cost from £6 to £8 and the fish in chilli sauce (£7.25) is excellent.

Mildred's (☎ 7494 1634, 58 Greek St W1; tube: Tottenham Court Road) is so small (and popular) that you may have to share a table. The chaos is worth it, however, because the vegetarian food is both good and well priced (from £5 to £7 for a large main course).

L'Odéon (☎ 7287 1400, 65 Regent St W1; tube: Piccadilly Circus) is worth a visit just for the views of Regent St from its lofty windows. The food also gets good reports, especially if you go for the £15.50/19.50 two/three-course set lunch or dinner (from 5.30 to 7 pm only).

The Criterion (☎ 7930 0488, 224 Piccadilly W1; tube: Piccadilly Circus) has a spectacular interior. The menu offers fashionable modern French food (eg, sauteed goat's cheese and roasted peppers), but there are also some English classics like fish and chips. You won't see much change from £35 per person at dinner, but set two/three-course lunches (also available from 6 to 6.30 pm) cost just £14.95/17.95.

Rasa Samudra (☎ 7637 0222, 5 Charlotte St W1; tube: Goodge Street) has classy South Indian vegetarian cuisine and fine seafood. Expect to pay at least £15 each.

The Ivy (☎ 7836 4751, 1 West St WC2; tube: Leicester Square) has a liveried doorman and celebrity clientele and is a showbizzy event in itself. The English menu includes dishes like shepherd's pie (£9.75), steak tartare (£7.75), kedgeree (£9.95) and Cumberland sausages with onions and mash.

Covent Garden & The Strand
Right beside Soho and technically part of the West End, Covent Garden is also densely packed with places to eat. The following are all accessible from Covent Garden tube station unless indicated otherwise.

Rock & Sole Plaice (☎ 7836 3785, 47 Endell St WC2) has basic Formica tables and delicious cod or haddock in batter (£3.50, or £4.50 with chips). It's unlicensed but you can BYO (bring your own).

Food for Thought (☎ 7836 0239, 31 Neal St WC2) features dishes like West Indian curry for £3.80 and stir-fried vegetables with brown rice for £3.30.

Café Pacifico (☎ 7379 7728, 5 Langley St WC2) serves Mexican food in a cheerful dining room, with main courses for £6.25 to £8.95 and great margaritas.

Café des Amis du Vin (☎ 7379 3444, 11-14 Hanover Place WC2) is a French brasserie that's handy for pre or post-theatre meals. Starters are from £4.95 to £6.50, main courses from £9.85 to £13.50 and set lunches of two/three courses £9.95/12.50.

Tibetan Restaurant (☎ 7839 2090, 17 Irving St WC2; tube: Leicester Square) specialises in the esoteric cuisine hailing from the rooftop of the world (a bit like Chinese mixed with Indian, with a pat of yak butter thrown in for authenticity). A host of three-course set menus (including vegetarian ones) cost from £8.50 to £13.50.

Simpson's-in-the-Strand (☎ 7836 9112, 100 Strand WC2) has been dishing up hot meats in a fine panelled dining room since 1848 (when it was called Simpson's Divan and Tavern). Steak and kidney pudding will set you back £13.80, lamb and redcurrant jelly is £18.50 and duck and apple sauce £15.50.

Joe Allen (☎ 7836 0651, 13 Exeter St WC2) has high-end American food like steaks. There's a real buzz here and it gets crowded, so book. A three-course meal will be from £20 to £25, though there are cheap two/three-course lunch menus for £11/13 and pretheatre dinners for £12/14.

Bloomsbury
Though usually thought of as B&B land, Bloomsbury has a large number of restaurants, many of them reasonably priced.

Mandeer (☎ 7242 6202, 8 Bloomsbury Way WC1; tube: Tottenham Court Road) serves vegetarian Indian, with main dishes from £3.75 to £5.25 and thalis for £10.95.

North Sea Fish Restaurant (☎ 7387 5892, 7-8 Leigh St WC1; tube: Russell Square) sets out to cook fresh fish and potatoes – a somewhat limited ambition in which it succeeds admirably. Cod, haddock and plaice, deep-fried or grilled, and a huge serving of chips will set you back between £6.95 and £7.95.

Museum St Café (☎ 7405 3211, *47 Museum St WC1; tube: Tottenham Court Road*) is packed at lunchtime (it opens at 8 or 9 am and closes after tea) and is totally nonsmoking. Mediterranean-inspired main courses cost from £7.50. Set tea (served from 3 to 6 pm) costs £8.

Coffee Gallery (☎ 7436 0455, *23 Museum St WC1*) is a tremendously popular place. It serves pasta dishes and main courses like grilled sardines and salad (£7) in a bright, cheerful room with modern paintings on the walls.

The City The City can be an irritating place in which to try to find a decent, affordable restaurant that stays open after office hours. The following are the pick of the crop.

Dim Sum (☎ 7236 1114, *5-6 Deans Court EC4; tube: St Paul's*) is a budget traveller's delight and convenient to St Paul's and the City of London YHA hostel. It serves Peking and Szechuan dishes for £3 to £6, but the best deal is the £9.99 all-you-can-eat buffet (minimum four people) available weekdays from 6 to 10.30 pm.

Café Spice Namaste (☎ 7488 9242, *16 Prescot St E1; tube: Tower Hill*) is an excellent Indian restaurant. Try *frango piri-piri* (£7.75), a fiery hot chicken tikka marinated in red masala; or the *muglai maas* (£10.25), Kashmiri lamb in a nut-based sauce. There are plenty of vegetarian side and main dishes.

Sweeting's (☎ 7248 3062, *39 Queen Victoria St EC4; tube: Mansion House*) is an old-fashioned place, with a mosaic floor and waiters in white aprons standing behind narrow counters serving up all sorts of traditional fishy delights. Main courses run from £8 to £19. Oysters are sold in season and cost £11.25 a half-dozen.

Southwark Options in this part of town (tube: London Bridge) range from workers' caffs and pie shops to some higher-end choices.

Manze's (☎ 7407 2985, *87 Tower Bridge Rd SE1*) is the oldest pie shop still trading in London and is handy for Bermondsey Market. In its pleasantly tiled interior, jellied eels cost £1.80, pie and mash £2.05, and pie and liquor £1.40.

Borough Café (*11 Park St SE1*) is the quintessential London market caff, where you can eat a full meal for less than £4 from 4 am to 3 pm weekdays and to 11 am on Saturday.

Fish! (☎ 7836 3236, *Cathedral St SE1*) is situated in an all-glass Victorian pavilion overlooking Borough Market and Southwark Cathedral. It serves fresher-than-fresh fish and seafood. Expect to pay anything from £8.50 to £15.95 for a main course.

Chelsea, South Kensington & Earl's Court These three areas boast an incredible array of eateries to suit all budgets.

Chelsea Kitchen (☎ 7589 1330, *98 King's Rd SW3; tube: Sloane Square*) has some of the cheapest food in London, with a set meal costing under £5.

Troubadour (☎ 7370 1434, *265 Old Brompton Rd SW10; tube: Earl's Court*) boasts an illustrious past as a coffee shop and folk music venue. These days it still occasionally has bands, plus good-value food, with soups at £3.50, bangers and mash is £4, a full breakfast £4.25 and a set meal with a drink £4.50.

Henry J Bean's (☎ 7352 9255, *195 King's Rd SW3; tube: Sloane Square or South Kensington*) is a popular American bar and restaurant with a garden. Main dishes cost from £5 to £7.

Rôtisserie Jules (☎ 7584 0600, *6-8 Bute St SW3; tube: South Kensington*) is a simple French-style cafeteria with dishes from £4.95 to £9.75.

New Culture Revolution (☎ 7352 9281, *305 King's Rd SW3; tube: Sloane Square*) is a good-value dumpling and noodle bar with main dishes at around £6.

Oriel (☎ 7730 2804, *50-51 Sloane Square SW1; tube: Sloane Square*) is the perfect place to meet before going shopping on King's Rd or Sloane St. Main dishes cost from £5 to £10; lighter fare like pasta and salads is from £6 to £8.50.

Kensington & Knightsbridge The restaurants, cafes and bars in these posh 'villages' of west and south-west London cater for a very

BRITAIN

well-heeled clientele, but there's always something good (and affordable) off the high streets.

Bellini's (☎ 7937 5520, 47 Kensington Court W8; tube: High Street Kensington) is a stylish Italian place with a few pavement tables. Lunches average £7.

Fifth Floor (☎ 7235 5250, Harvey Nichols, 109-125 Knightsbridge SW1; tube: Knightsbridge) is the perfect place to drop after you've shopped at this trendy department store. It's expensive, averaging £30 per head at dinner, but there's a three-course set lunch for £23.50.

Notting Hill & Bayswater Notting Hill, so popular ever since that film, has all sorts of interesting places to eat, and there are literally dozens of places lining Queensway and Westbourne Grove, with everything from cheap takeaways to good quality restaurants.

Sausage & Mash Café (☎ 8968 8898, 268 Portobello Rd W10; tube: Ladbroke Grove) is just the ticket if you're looking for cheap English stodge (£5) in upbeat surroundings.

Café Grove (☎ 7243 1094, 253A Portobello Rd; tube: Ladbroke Grove) has gigantic and imaginative breakfasts as well as cheap and cheerful vegetarian food at around £5. The large balcony overlooking the market is great for watching all the action on a weekend morning.

Geales (☎ 7727 7969, 2 Farmer St W8; tube: Notting Hill Gate) is a popular fish restaurant which prices everything according to weight and season. Fish and chips costs about £8.50 and it's worth every penny.

Kalamaras Micro (☎ 7727 5082, 66 Inverness Mews W2; tube: Bayswater) is a small but fine Greek spot in a quiet mews off Queensway. Main courses average about £7.50 and you can BYO.

Costas Fish Restaurant (☎ 7229 3794, 12-14 Hillgate St W8; tube: Notting Hill Gate) is a reliable Greek fish restaurant. It has meze with dips from £1.50, souvlaki for under £5 and a huge array of fresher-than-fresh fish at market prices.

Modhubon Tandoori (☎ 7727 3399, 29 Pembridge Rd W11; tube: Notting Hill Gate) has been recommended for its inexpensive Indian food. Main dishes are under £5, set lunch is £3.95 and a Sunday buffet £7.50.

Bali Sugar (☎ 7221 4477, 33a All Saints Rd W11; tube: Westbourne Park) is lovely and has food described as 'fusion' that averages £27 per person.

Euston While 'Euston' and 'good food' do not usually a valid phrase make, a street a short distance south-west of the station is a mecca for vegies looking for a little bite in their legumes.

Drummond St (tube: Euston Square or Euston) has a number of good South Indian vegetarian restaurants. *Diwana* (☎ 7387 5556) at No 121, the first (and some reckon it's still the best) of its kind on the street, specialises in Bombay-style *bel poori* (a kind of 'party mix' snack) and *dosas* and has an all-you-can-eat lunch-time buffet for £3.95. Nearby at No 124, *Chutneys* (☎ 7388 0604) has a better lunch buffet (available all day on Sunday) for £4.95.

Camden Camden High Street is lined with good places to eat, although to watch the Sunday day-trippers snacking on takeaway sausages and chips you'd hardly believe it.

Café Delancey (☎ 7387 1985, 3 Delancey St NW1; tube: Camden Town) is the grand-daddy of French-style brasseries in London. It offers the chance of getting a decent cup of coffee with a snack or a full meal in relaxed European-style surroundings complete with newspapers. Main dishes are from £8 to £13.

El Parador (☎ 7387 2789, 245 Eversholt St NW1; tube: Mornington Crescent) is a quiet Spanish place where the selection of some 15 vegetarian dishes and tapas includes *empanadillas de espinacas y queso* (a spinach and cheese dish) for £3.80.

Wazobia (☎ 7284 1059, 257 Royal College St NW1; tube: Camden Town) is a charmingly laid-back West African place that serves Nigerian-style pepper soups (£3) and hearty stews (£7).

Lemon Grass (☎ 7284 1116, 243 Royal College St; tube: Camden Town) is one of the better Thai eateries in Camden with authentic food and charming decor and staff. Main dishes are around £6.

Lemonia (☎ 7586 7454, 89 Regent's Park Rd NW1; tube: Chalk Farm) is an upmarket and very popular Greek restaurant that offers good-value food and a lively atmosphere. Meze costs £12.25 per person and both the vegetarian and meat moussakas for £7.50 are particularly tasty.

Islington Islington is an excellent place for a night out. At the last count there were more than 60 cafes and restaurants between Angel and Highbury Corner, with most of the action on Upper St.

Le Sacré Coeur Bistro (☎ 7354 2618, 18 Theberton St N1; tube: Angel) is a cramped little restaurant with reliable French food. It has several fixed-price menus for under £7.

Upper St Fish Shop (☎ 7359 1401, 324 Upper St N1; tube: Highbury & Islington) doles out classy fish and chips for £7 to £7.50 and seafood like half a dozen Irish oysters for around £6.

Inter Mezzo (☎ 7607 4112, 207 Liverpool Rd N1; tube: Angel) is a Turkish restaurant that gets our vote as one of the best value and friendliest eateries in town. Set lunches are £5.90/6.90 for two/three courses, dinners £8.90/10.90.

East End From the Indian and Bangladeshi restaurants of Brick Lane to the trendy Modern British/European eateries of Hoxton and Shoreditch, the East End has finally made it onto the culinary map of London. The Docklands, however, remains in general the territory of expense accounts and quick lunches.

Brick Lane Beigel Bake (☎ 7729 0616, 159 Brick Lane E2; tube: Shoreditch) is a delicatessen and open 24 hours. You won't find fresher or cheaper bagels anywhere in London.

Brick Lane (tube: Shoreditch or Aldgate East) is lined wall-to-wall with cheap Indian and Bangladeshi restaurants – not all of them very good. *Aladin* (☎ 7247 8210) at No 132, a favourite of Prince Charles, and *Nazrul* (☎ 7247 2505) at No 130 are worth a try; both are unlicensed but you can BYO and should eat for around £8.

Mesón Los Barriles (☎ 7375 3136, 8a Lamb St E1; tube: Liverpool Street) is a tapas bar and restaurant inside Spitalfields Market that has an excellent selection of fish and seafood. Tapas range from £2 to £5. There are several other good spots within the market.

Viet Hoa (☎ 7729 8293, 70-72 Kingsland Rd E2; bus No 67 or 149) serves excellent and authentic Vietnamese dishes. A meal should cost you less than £10 and it's always full.

Great Eastern Dining Room (☎ 7729 0022, 93 Great Eastern St EC2; tube: Old Street) is a prime example of the new breed of eatery in London. It's a large, open-plan, simple restaurant serving starters like fish soup with *rouille* (garlic-mayonnaise sauce; £3.95) and main courses like roast cod fillet (£9.95).

Greenwich Beautiful Greenwich has both old-style eateries and trendy new restaurants from which to choose. And don't forget the market from Friday to Sunday. The new Cutty Sark DLR station is convenient for all the places here.

Greenwich Church St has a couple of decent and inexpensive cafes, including *Il Batello* (☎ 8858 5124) at No 39 and *Peter de Wit's* (☎ 8305 0048) at No 21 with cream teas for £3.80.

Hatomana (☎ 8293 5263, 10-11 Nelson Rd SE10) has cheap Japanese noodles and rice dishes (£2.80 to £4.50).

Beachcomber (☎ 8853 0055, 34 Greenwich Church St SE10) is an old stalwart festooned with flower baskets and potted plants that does set two/three/four-course lunches for £5.90/7.95/9.90 and full breakfasts for £4.

Entertainment

The essential events guide is *Time Out*, published every Tuesday. Though most pubs close at a puritanical 11 pm, there are plenty of late-night clubs (many charge a £5 to £10 cover). Note that the last underground trains leave between 11.30 pm and 12.30 am, after which you must figure out the night-bus system or take a taxi.

Pubs London is awash in pubs. Unfortunately many are uninspired boozers or charmless chain outlets. However there are many gems to be found, including those listed here.

Scruffy Murphy's (15 Denman St W1; tube: Piccadilly Circus) is the most authentic – snugs, brogues, Guinness and drunks – of the Irish pubs in Soho.

Coach & Horses (29 Greek St W1; tube: Leicester Square) is a small, busy pub with a regular clientele but is nonetheless hospitable to visitors.

The Queen's Larder (1 Queen Square WC1; tube: Russell Square) offers a handy retreat, with outside benches and pub grub.

Ye Olde Mitre (1 Ely Court EC1; tube: Chancery Lane) is one of London's oldest

BRITAIN

and most historic pubs, although the 18th-century-sized rooms can be a bit tight.

The Angel (*101 Bermondsey Wall East SE16*) is a riverside pub dating from the 15th century (though the present building is early 17th century). Captain Cook supposedly prepared for his trip to Australia from here.

George Inn (*Talbot Yard, 77 Borough High St SE1; tube: London Bridge or Borough*) is London's last surviving galleried coaching inn. It dates from 1676 and is mentioned in Charles Dickens' *Little Dorrit*. Here too is the site of the Tabard Inn (thus the Talbot Yard address), where the pilgrims gathered in Chaucer's *Canterbury Tales* before setting out.

King's Head & Eight Bells (*50 Cheyne Walk; tube: Sloane Square SW3*) is an attractive corner pub, pleasantly hung with flower baskets in summer. It has a wide range of beers and was a favourite of the painter Whistler.

Music & Clubs

Major venues for live contemporary music include the *Brixton Academy* (*☎ 7924 9999, 211 Stockwell Rd SW9; tube: Brixton*), the *Hackney Empire* (*☎ 8985 242, 291 Mare St E8; tube: Bethnal Green*), and the *Wembley Arena* (*☎ 8900 1234, Empire Way, Middlesex, tube: Wembley Park*).

Smaller places with a more club-like atmosphere that are worth checking for interesting bands include *Borderline* (*☎ 7734 2095, Orange Yard, off Manette St WC2; tube: Tottenham Court Rd*), *Barfly at the Falcon* (*☎ 7485 3834, 234 Royal College St NW1; tube: Camden Town*), *Subterania* (*☎ 8960 4590, 12 Acklam Rd W10; tube: Ladbroke Grove*), and *Garage* (*☎ 7607 1818, 20-22 Highbury Corner N5; tube: Highbury & Islington*). Ring ahead to find out what kind of band you'll get.

Venues that are usually reliable for club nights and recorded music include: *Fabric* (*☎ 7490 0444, 77a Charterhouse St EC1; tube: Farringdon*), which has three floors; *Astoria* (*☎ 7434 9592, 157-165 Charing Cross Rd WC2; tube: Tottenham Court Rd*), which is popular with gays; the multifaceted *Fridge* (*☎ 7326 5100, Town Hall Parade SW2; tube: Brixton*); the friendly *Velvet Room* (*☎ 7439 4655, 143 Charing Cross Rd WC2; tube: Tottenham Court Rd*); and the famous *Ministry of Sound* (*☎ 7378 6528, 103 Gaunt St SE1; tube: Elephant & Castle*).

If you're a jazz fan, keep your eye on *Ronnie Scott's* (*☎ 7439 0747, 47 Frith St W1; tube: Leicester Square*) and the *Jazz Café* (*☎ 7344 0044, 5 Parkway NW1; tube: Camden Town*).

Theatre & Cinema

London theatre and musicals are extraordinarily diverse, high quality (at their best) and reasonably priced by world standards. Even if you don't normally go to the theatre, you really should look at the reviews and organise cheap tickets for one of the best productions. The South Bank's *National Theatre* (*☎ 7452 3000*) is actually three theatres in one – the Olivier, Lyttleton and Cottesloe – and puts on consistently good performances, often with some of the best young actors and directors.

The Half Price Theatre Ticket Booth (tube: Leicester Square), on the southern side of Leicester Square, sells half-price tickets (plus £2 commission) on the day of performance. It opens noon to 6.30 pm daily, but the queues can be awesome.

Some theatres and concert halls sell stand-by tickets 90 minutes before performances. The National Theatre sells even cheaper student stand-bys but only 45 minutes before curtain up.

Don't miss a performance at *Shakespeare's Globe Theatre* (*☎ 7401 9919, 21 New Globe Walk; tube: London Bridge*), the replica of Shakespeare's 'wooden O' which now dominates Bankside. Although there are wooden bench seats in tiers around the stage, many people copy the 17th-century 'groundlings' who stood in front of the stage, moving around as the mood took them. With no roof, the Globe is open to the elements; you should wrap up warmly although no umbrellas are allowed. Performances are staged from May to September. Tickets cost from £10 to £25. The 500 standing spaces per performance cost £5 each and can be booked, although you may find a few unsold on the day.

The *National Film Theatre* (*☎ 7928 3232, South Bank Centre; tube Waterloo*) screens an impressive range of classic, unusual, experimental and foreign films.

Spectator Sports

Tickets for Premier League football matches start at around £15. Some of the big teams worth watching are Arsenal (☎ 7413 3366), Tottenham Hotspur (☎ 0870-012 0200), Chelsea (☎ 7386 7799) and West Ham (☎ 8548 2700). International fixtures at Wembley Stadium (☎ 8900 1234) will cost more once the famous venue recovers in a few years time from a multimillion pound make-over.

Tickets to rugby union internationals at Twickenham (☎ 8831 6666) cost around £30. The ground also boasts a Museum of Rugby (£5), which includes a tour of the stadium.

The two major venues for cricket are Lord's (☎ 7432 1066), St John Rd NW8; and Foster's Oval (☎ 7582 7764), Kennington Oval SE11.

Crystal Palace (☎ 8778 0131) is the venue for important athletics events and tickets start at £10. Expect to pay a lot more to watch tennis at Wimbledon (☎ 8946 2244).

Getting There & Away

As London is Britain's major gateway, Getting There & Away information has been given in the introductory transport sections of this chapter.

Bus Bus travellers will arrive at Victoria coach station, Buckingham Palace Rd, about 10 minutes walk south of Victoria station (or there's a shuttle bus if you're carrying loads of luggage).

Train London's eight major train stations are all connected by tube. For those with a combined rail/ferry ticket, Victoria is your station for getting to and from Dover and Folkestone, Liverpool St for getting to and from Harwich, and King's Cross for getting to and from Newcastle. The international terminal at Waterloo services Eurostar trains.

For national rail inquiries, fares and timetables, phone ☎ 0845-748 4950.

Getting Around

To/From the Airports Transport to and from London's five airports is as follows:

Heathrow The airport (☎ 0870-000 0123) is accessible by bus, underground (between 5 am and 11 pm) and main-line train.

The Heathrow Express rail link whisks passengers from Paddington station to Heathrow in just 15 minutes. Tickets cost an exorbitant £12 each way. Trains leave every 15 minutes from around 5 am to 10.30 pm. Many airlines have advance check-in desks at Paddington.

The underground station for Terminals 1, 2 and 3 is directly linked to the terminus buildings; there's a separate station for Terminal 4. Check which terminal your flight uses when you reconfirm. The adult single fare is £3.50, or you can use an All Zone travelcard (£4.70). The journey time from central London is about 50 minutes – allow an hour.

The Airbus (☎ 7222 1234) services are prone to traffic congestion. There are two routes: the A1, which runs along Cromwell Rd to Victoria; and the A2, which runs along Notting Hill Gate and Bayswater Rd to Russell Square. Buses run every half-hour and cost £7. A minicab to and from central London will cost from around £25; a metered black cab around £35.

All four terminals have left-luggage services run by private companies. Call the main Heathrow number for details.

Gatwick The Gatwick Express train (☎ 0870-530 1530) runs nonstop between the main terminal and Victoria station 24 hours daily. Singles are £10.20 and the journey takes about 30 minutes. The Connex SouthCentral service takes a little longer and costs £8.20. Jetlink 777 buses (☎ 8668 7261) from Victoria coach station cost £8 but take 90 minutes to get there.

Gatwick's north and south terminals (☎ 01293-535353) are linked by a monorail; check which terminal your flight uses. Some airlines have check-in desks at Victoria. A minicab to or from central London will cost around £35; a metered black cab around £50.

There are luggage storage facilities in both terminals.

London City The airport (☎ 7646 0000) is two minutes walk from the Silvertown & City Airport train station, which is linked by train to Stratford. A frequent shuttle bus also connects the airport with the Canning Town tube, DLR and train station. The Airbus connects the airport with Liverpool St station (£5, 30 minutes) and Canary Wharf (£2, 10 minutes).

Luton The airport (☎ 01582-405100) is connected by frequent shuttle bus to the Luton

Airport Parkway station. Several trains (☎ 0845-748 4950) an hour go to/from London through the Kings Cross Thameslink station. Fares cost £9 and the journey takes about 35 minutes.

Stansted The airport (☎ 01279-680500) is served by the Stansted Express (☎ 0845-748 4950) from Liverpool St station, which costs £11 and takes 45 minutes. The trains depart every 15 to 30 minutes.

Bus & Underground London Regional Transport is responsible for the buses and the tube. It has several information centres where you can get free maps, tickets and information on night buses. Among others, there are centres in each Heathrow terminal, and at Victoria, Piccadilly and King's Cross stations; or phone ☎ 7222 1234. It's well worth asking for one of the free bus maps.

Buses are much more interesting and pleasant to use than the tube, although they can be frustratingly slow. Prices depend on how many geographic zones your journey covers. Central London is covered by Zone 1. A ticket good for Zones 1 and 2 should suffice for most visitors. Single journeys on the bus cost 70p/£1 for Zone 1/Zones 1 and 2 and by tube £1.50/£1.80.

Travelcards are the easiest and cheapest option, and they can be used on all forms of transport (trains in London, buses and the tube) after 9.30 am. A Zones 1 and 2 card costs £3.90. Weekly travelcards are also available; they require an ID card with a passport photo (Zones 1 and 2 cost £18.20). A carnet of Zone 1 tube tickets good for 10 rides costs £11.

Times of the last tube trains vary from 11.30 pm to 12.30 am, depending on the station and line. A reasonably comprehensive network of night buses runs from or through Trafalgar Square. London Regional Transport has a free brochure listing all the services. One-day travelcards can't be used on night buses, but weekly travelcards can.

Train Most main lines interchange with the tube and you can use your travelcard for any parts of the journey within London. Trains are the primary means of transport to many London locations south of the river.

Taxi London's famous black cabs (☎ 7272 0272) are excellent, but not cheap. A cab is available for hire when the yellow sign is lit. Fares are metered and a 10% tip is expected. They can carry five people.

Minicabs are cheap, freelance competitors to the black cabs; anyone with a car can work, though they can supposedly only be hired by phone, but hawkers abound in bust places like Soho. Beware. Some have a very limited idea of how to get around efficiently (and safely). They don't have meters, so it's essential to get a quote before you start. They can carry four people. Women are advised to use black cabs.

Small minicab companies are based in particular areas – ask a local for the name of a reputable company, or phone one of the large 24-hour operations (☎ 7272 2612, 8340 2450 or 8567 1111). Women could phone Lady Cabs (☎ 7254 3501). Gays and lesbians can choose Freedom Cars (☎ 7734 1313).

Car & Motorcycle If you're blessed/cursed with private transport, avoid peak hours (7.30 to 9 am, 4.30 to 7 pm). Cars parked illegally will be clamped; a clamp is locked on a wheel and in order to have it removed you have to travel across town, pay an enormous fine, then wait most of the day for someone to come and release you.

Bicycle You can hire bikes at Bikepark (☎ 7430 0083), 11 Macklin St WC2 (tube: Holborn). The minimum rental charge is £10 for the first day, £5 the second day and £3 for subsequent days. A large deposit is required.

Boat There are all sorts of services on the river. See River Tour and Other Attractions under Things to See & Do earlier in this London section for two popular trips. The main starting points are at Westminster Bridge and Charing Cross. For information call ☎ 7222 1234.

AROUND LONDON

Because of the speed of the train system, you can visit a surprisingly large part of Britain on day trips – basically, all of England southeast of an arc drawn through Bournemouth to Bath, and round through Stratford-upon-Avon, Nottingham and Norwich.

Windsor & Eton
☎ 01753

Home to British royalty for over 900 years, **Windsor Castle** is one of the greatest surviving medieval castles. It was built in stages between 1165 and the 16th century on chalk bluffs overlooking the Thames.

The strategic value of Windsor has long since disappeared, but its symbolic importance has never waned. Today's royal family made this connection clear when George V, the current queen's grandfather, changed the family name from the too Germanic Saxe-Coburg-Gotha to Windsor.

Inside the castle, St George's Chapel is a masterpiece of Perpendicular Gothic architecture. You can also examine Queen Mary's Doll's House and the recently restored State Apartments. The castle is open from 10 am daily, but can be closed at short notice when members of the royal family are in residence; for opening arrangements, phone ☎ 831118. In summer, the changing of the guard takes place from Monday to Saturday, weather permitting, at 11 am. Entry to the castle is £10, except on Sunday when it drops to £8.50 because St George's Chapel is closed.

A short walk along Thames St and across the river brings you to another enduring symbol of Britain's class system, **Eton College**, a famous public (meaning private) school that has educated no fewer than 18 prime ministers. It's open to visitors from 2 to 4.30 pm during term, and from 10.30 am during Easter and summer holidays (admission £2.70). Several buildings date from the mid-15th century, when the school was founded by Henry VI.

Easily accessible from London, Windsor (population 31,000) crawls with tourists. If possible, avoid weekends. There are numerous trains direct from London's Waterloo to Windsor & Eton Riverside station for £5.90 return.

Hatfield House

Six miles from St Albans, north of London, Hatfield House (☎ 01707-262823, fax 275719) is England's most celebrated Jacobean house – a graceful red-brick and stone mansion full of treasures amid 42 acres of gardens. The house is open noon to 4 pm Tuesday, Wednesday and Thursday (for private tours only), and 1 to 5 pm Saturday and Sunday from March to September. The gardens are open 11 am to 6 pm daily (except Monday). Admission to both is £6.20. There are numerous trains from King's Cross Thameslink station.

South-East England

Due to their proximity to London, the counties of Kent, East and West Sussex and Hampshire are home to a large chunk of the capital's workforce. For this reason there are plenty of fast, regular rail and bus services, making it possible to see the main sights on day trips, though you are advised to avoid weekends and school holidays.

The south-east is a region exceptionally rich in beauty and history and it caters to those unshakeable traditional images of England – picturesque villages with welcoming old pubs, spectacular coastlines, impressive castles and magnificent cathedrals. There are also a number of excellent walks along the South and North Downs.

Be warned, though. Prices for accommodation and food are much higher here than in the northern parts of England.

Orientation & Information

The main roads and railway lines radiate from London like spokes in a wheel, linking the south-coast ports and resorts with the capital. Chalk country runs through the region along two hilly east-west ridges, or 'downs'.

The North Downs curve from Guildford towards Rochester, then to Dover where they become the famous white cliffs. The South Downs run from north of Portsmouth to end spectacularly at Beachy Head near Eastbourne. Lying between the two is the Weald, once an enormous stretch of forest, now orchards and market gardens.

Getting Around

For information on all public transport options in Kent, ring ☎ 0845-769 6996 or free call 0800-69699; for West Sussex, ring ☎ 01243-777556 or 0845-795 9099; for East Sussex, ring ☎ 01273-474747; for Hampshire, ring ☎ 01962-846992.

Bus Virtually all bus companies accept Explorer tickets, which give unlimited travel for one day and cost £6/4 for adults/children. Country Rover tickets (£5/2.50) can be used after 9 am Monday to Friday and all day on weekends, though they are accepted less frequently. They can be bought from bus drivers or bus stations, and are nearly always the best value option if you are travelling extensively.

Train For rail information call ☎ 0845-748 4950. It is possible to do an interesting rail loop from London via Canterbury East, Dover, Ashford, Rye, Hastings, Battle (via Hastings), Brighton, Arundel, Portsmouth and Winchester. If you are considering extensive rail travel, a Network SouthEast Card (£20 – allowing one-third off fares and kids to travel for £1) is essential. A BritRail SouthEast Pass allows unlimited rail travel for three or four days out of seven, or eight days out of 15, but they must be purchased outside the UK. See the main Getting Around section earlier in this chapter.

CANTERBURY
☎ 01227 • pop 36,000

Canterbury's greatest treasure is its magnificent cathedral, the successor to the church St Augustine built after he began converting the English to Christianity in AD 597. In 1170 Archbishop Thomas à Becket was murdered in the cathedral by four of Henry II's knights as a result of a dispute over the church's independence. An enormous cult grew up around the martyred Becket and Canterbury became the centre of one of the most important medieval pilgrimages in Europe, immortalised by Geoffrey Chaucer in the *Canterbury Tales*.

Canterbury was severely damaged during WWII, and parts have been rebuilt insensitively. However, there's still plenty to see and the bustling town centre has a good atmosphere. The place crawls with tourists and there's not much chance of escaping queues.

Orientation & Information
The centre of Canterbury is enclosed by a medieval city wall and a modern ring road. It's easily covered on foot. The two train stations are both a short walk from the centre. The bus station is just within the city walls at the eastern end of High St.

The TIC (☎ 766567, fax 459840, @ canterburyinformation@canterbury.gov.uk), 34 St Margaret's St, is open 9.30 am to 5 pm daily. It has a free booking service for B&Bs.

The Library on High St has free Internet access but you will need to book ahead on ☎ 463608. There's a laundrette at 36 St Peter's St.

Things to See & Do
The **Canterbury Cathedral** (☎ 762862) was built in two stages between 1070 and 1184, and 1391 and 1505. The cathedral complex can easily absorb half a day. It is a massive rabbit warren of a building, with treasures tucked away in corners and a trove of associated stories, so a tour is recommended. They take place at 10.30 am, noon and 2 pm for £3.50, or you can take a Walkman tour for £2.95 (30 minutes). Admission is £3/2. On weekdays and Saturday the cathedral is open 9 am to 7 pm (to 5 pm from October to Easter), with shorter hours on Sunday.

Also not to be missed is the **Roman Museum** (☎ 785575) – built underground around the remains of a Roman town house in Butchery Lane – where you get to visit the marketplace, smell the odours of a Roman kitchen and handle artefacts. Kids will love it. It's open 10 am to 5 pm Monday to Saturday, and 1.30 to 5 pm on Sunday from June to October; £2.40/1.60 adults/children.

Places to Stay
Head to London Rd or New Dover Rd for good value B&Bs. Otherwise try *Yew Tree Park* (☎ 700306, Stone St, Petham), 5 miles (8km) south of Canterbury off the B2068. It's £4 for one adult plus tent; £6 for two. A bus from Canterbury to Petham village (a half-mile walk to the camp site) leaves hourly.

The *Youth Hostel* (☎ 462911, 54 New Dover Rd) is about a mile east of the centre. The nightly charge is £9.75 and there is one twin room for £28.

Let's Stay (☎ 463628, 26 New Dover Rd) is homy and good value. It costs £10 per person with breakfast. Men and women are accommodated separately.

The University of Kent (☎ 828000, Tanglewood) is a 20-minute walk from the centre and is open in April and from July to September. B&B costs from £14.50 per person.

Charnwood Lodge B&B (☎/fax 451712, 64 New Dover Rd) – the sign out front just says 'B&B' – is the best value in town and we can highly recommend it. For £35 you get a clean, self-contained flat that can sleep up to three people. Breakfast is included and you are welcome to cook it yourself if you prefer.

Tudor House (☎ 765650, 6 Best Lane) is very good value for somewhere so central. This slightly eccentric 450-year-old building has rooms for £18/36. It also has canoes and boats for guests to hire at £10 per day.

Magnolia House (☎/fax 765121, 36 St Dunstan's Tce) off London Rd is very luxurious, but so is the price – it costs $38/78, and the room with a four-poster bed and a spa bath costs £110.

Places to Eat

The crowds of pilgrims and students ensure that there's a good range of reasonably priced eating places in Canterbury. There's a *Safeway* supermarket on the corner of New Dover Rd and Lower Chantry Rd, just south-east of the centre.

The Custard Tart (☎ 785178, 35a St Margaret's St) charges from £2.30 for delicious baguettes and sandwiches, and £1 for sausage rolls. Try to avoid the 1 pm lunch rush.

Three Tuns Hotel (☎ 456391, 24 Watling St) stands on the site of a Roman theatre and dates from the 16th century. It serves good-value pub meals for around £4.

You'll find a great variety of cuisines for various budgets along Castle St. *Canterbury Grill & Kebab* (☎ 765458, 66 Castle St) has chip butties for £1.30. Kebabs cost from £3 and burgers from £2.20.

Viêt Nam (☎ 760022, 72 Castle St) has a very modern menu. Prawns with french beans and garlic costs £5.95. The very tempting Vietnamese tapas menu features dishes costing £2.75 to £3.50.

Pinocchio's Trattoria (☎ 457538, 64 Castle St) is more expensive but it's cheerful, with a superb Italian wine selection and a terrace out the back. Pasta costs £5.60 to £8.95 and pizzas go for £4.70 to £7.30.

Entertainment

Get hold of a copy of *What & Where When* – a free leaflet to what's on in Canterbury, available from the TIC. *The Miller's Arms* (☎ 456057, Mill Lane) is a cosy student hangout and *Caseys* (☎ 463252, 5 Butchery Lane),

near the main gate to the cathedral, has a large selection of Irish ales and stouts.

Marlowe Theatre (☎ 787787, fax 479622, ✉ boxoffice@canterbury.gov.uk, The Friars) puts on a variety of plays and concerts. The box office is open 10 am to 8 pm Monday to Saturday.

Getting There & Away

Canterbury makes a good base for exploring the eastern and northern coastal areas of Kent, namely Herne Bay and Whitstable, Margate, Broadstairs and Sandwich.

Bus National Express buses to Canterbury leave every half-hour from London Victoria (£7 one way, £9 day return, two hours). Stagecoach East Kent's (☎ 472082) No 100 bus runs hourly (less on Sunday) from Canterbury to Dover, Deal, Sandwich, Ramsgate, Broadstairs, Margate, Herne Bay, Whitstable and back to Canterbury. Canterbury to Dover costs £2.50/3.50 one way/return and takes 30 minutes.

Train Canterbury East station (for the YHA hostel) is accessible from London's Victoria station, and Canterbury West is accessible from London's Charing Cross and Waterloo stations (£14.80 day return, £19.99 for two adults, 1½ hours). There are regular trains between Canterbury East and Dover Priory (£4.50, 45 minutes).

DOVER

☎ 01304 • pop 37,000

Dover may be England's 'Gateway to Europe' but the place has just two things going for it: the famous white cliffs and a spectacular medieval hill-top castle. The foreshore of Dover is basically an enormous, complicated (though well signposted) and unattractive vehicle ramp for the ferries. Everyone's in transit, few stay.

Orientation & Information

Dover is dominated by the looming profile of the castle to the east. The town itself runs back from the sea along a valley formed by the unimpressive River Dour.

Ferry departures are from the Eastern Docks (accessible by bus) below the castle. Dover Priory train station is off Folkestone

BRITAIN

Rd, a short walk to the west of the town centre. The bus station is on Pencester Rd.

The TIC (☎ 205108, fax 225498, ✉ tic@ doveruk.com) is on Townwall St near the seafront and is open 9 am to 6 pm daily. It has an accommodation and ferry-booking service. The Mangle laundrette is situated on Worthington St.

Things to See & Do
Dover's main attraction, **Dover Castle** (☎ 201628), is a well-preserved medieval fortress with spectacular views. The excellent tour of **Hellfire Corner** covers the castle's history during WWII, and takes you through the tunnels which burrow beneath the castle. It's open 10 am to 6 pm daily (to 4 pm from October to March); entry is £6.90/5.20/3.50 adult/concession/children, including Hellfire Corner.

The **Dover Museum** on Market Square is one of the best around and definitely should not be missed, while the **White Cliffs Experience** next door offers a diverting recreation of Dover's history – especially good for kids. They're open 10 am to 5.30 pm daily (last admission 5 pm); entry to both is £5.75/3.95, or £1.80/90p for the museum only.

Places to Stay
Book well ahead if you intend to be here in July and August.

Martin Mill Caravan Park (☎ 852658) is at Hawthorn Farm, 3 miles (4.8km) northeast of Dover, off the A258. It's open from March to November and costs £6 for one person plus tent (£7 for two).

Dover Central Youth Hostel (☎ 201314, 306 London Rd) is five minutes walk from Market Square and costs £10.50 per night.

The *YMCA* (☎ 225500, 4 Leyburne Rd) was closed for refurbishment at the time of writing but may be open now for overnight accommodation.

There are a few cheap B&Bs on Castle St and Maison Dieu Rd. *East Lee Guest House* (☎ 210176, 108 Maison Dieu Rd) is friendly and luxurious and rooms (no TV) cost from £24/48.

St Martin's Guesthouse (☎ 205938, fax 208229, 17 Castle Hill Rd) is highly recommended. The landlady is helpful and rooms

are spotless. It costs £45 for two (singles vary). From November to March this rate can drop to as low as £30.

Most of the B&Bs along Marine Parade are grotty and run-down, and they aren't even super cheap to make up for it. *Loddington House* (☎/fax 201947, 14 East Cliff, Marine Parade) is an exception and rooms cost £45/56.

Places to Eat
Dover is short on decent places to eat, so you'll need to look around a bit. *Jermain's* (☎ 205956, Beaconsfield Rd) is near the hostel and has a range of good value traditional lunches like roast beef for £5 and pudding for £1.

Curry Garden (☎ 206357, 24 High St) is a cheap Indian restaurant with plush decor where prawn korma costs £4.20 and dhal is £1.95.

Riveria Coffee House (☎ 201766, 9311 Worthington St) is very good value with cream teas for £1.80, or sandwiches and light meals from £1.20.

Topo Gigio (☎ 201048, 1-2 King St) is an Italian place with pasta from £3.45 and pizzas from £5.20.

The Cabin (☎ 206118, 91 High St) is one of the few offerings for gourmets. This intimate restaurant specialises in traditional English and game dishes but vegetarians are catered for too. Haunch of wild boar with red wine and fresh herbs costs £11.70, while haggis in whiskey sauce is £2.95.

Getting There & Away
See the Getting There & Away section at the beginning of this chapter for details on ferries to mainland Europe.

Bus National Express coaches leave hourly from London Victoria (£9 one way, £11 day return, two hours 20 minutes). Stagecoach East Kent has an office on Pencester Rd (☎ 240024). Canterbury to Dover (30 minutes) costs £2.50. There's an hourly bus to Brighton but you'll need to change at Eastbourne. Later in the evenings it's a direct service. An Explorer ticket for £6 is better value on this route.

Train There are over 40 trains a day from London Victoria and Charing Cross stations to Dover Priory via Ashford and Sevenoaks (£18.20 one way, 1½ hours).

Getting Around

The ferry companies run complimentary buses between the docks and train stations. There are infrequent town buses – a trip from one side of town to the other costs about £1.50. Central Taxis (☎ 240441) and Heritage (☎ 204420) have 24-hour services. A one-way trip to Folkestone or Deal costs about £8.

HEVER CASTLE

Idyllic Hever Castle (☎ 01732-861702) near Edenbridge, a few miles west of Tonbridge, was the childhood home of Anne Boleyn, mistress to Henry VIII and then his doomed queen. Walking through the main gate into the courtyard of Hever is like stepping onto the set of a period film. It's a truly fairy-tale place and one of the highlights of the area. Restored by the Astor family, it also has magnificent gardens.

It's open 11 am to 5 pm daily, March to late November. Admission to the castle and gardens is £7.80/6.60/4.20; gardens only are £6.10/5.20/4. The nearest train station is Hever, a mile from the castle itself.

KNOLE HOUSE

In a country that is full of extraordinary country houses, Knole (☎ 01732-450608) is outstanding. It seems as if *nothing* substantial has changed since early in the 17th century. Virginia Woolf based the novel *Orlando* on the history of the house and family.

Now a National Trust property, it is open noon to 4 pm Wednesday to Saturday and 11 am to 5 pm Sunday and Bank Holidays from April to October; admission is £5/2 adults/children or £12.50 for a family ticket.

Knole is 1½ miles to the south of Sevenoaks, which is on the rail line from London's Charing Cross to Tonbridge.

LEEDS CASTLE

Near Maidstone in Kent, Leeds Castle (☎ 01622-765400) is one of the world's most famous and most visited castles. It stands on two small islands in a lake, and is surrounded by a park housing an aviary, a maze and a grotto. Unfortunately, it's usually overrun by families and schoolgroups. Also, some of the rooms are closed from time to time for conferences and functions. If you want to be sure of getting your money's worth from the rather high admission price, call ahead.

It's open 10 am to 5 pm daily (to 3 pm November to February). Entry is £9.50/7.50 adults/concession. National Express has a bus from Victoria coach station, leaving at 9 am and returning at 3.50 pm (1¼ hours). It must be prebooked, and combined admission and travel is £12.50. Greenline Buses (☎ 020-8668 7261) have the same deal costing £13/7 (leave London Victoria at 9.35 am, return 4 pm).

BRIGHTON

☎ 01273 • pop 180,000

Brighton is deservedly Britain's number one seaside town – a fascinating mixture of seediness and sophistication. Just an hour away from London by train, it's the perfect choice for day-trippers looking for a drop of froth and ozone.

Londoners have been travelling to Brighton ever since the 1750s, when a shrewd doctor suggested that bathing in, and drinking, the local seawater was good for them. It's still fine to swim here, though a little on the cool side, and the pebble beach comes as a bit of a shock if you're used to fine sand. Drinking the seawater, however, is definitely not recommended.

Brighton has a reputation as the club and party capital of the south. Fat Boy Slim hails from these mean streets, and he DJs regularly around town. There's a vibrant population of students and travellers, excellent shopping, a terrific arts scene and countless restaurants, pubs and cafes.

In May, Brighton hosts the largest arts festival (☎ 292961) outside Edinburgh. Check the Web site at www.brighton-festival.org.uk. Though mostly mainstream, there are fringe events too.

Orientation & Information

Brighton train station is a 15-minute walk north of the beach. The bus station is tucked away in Poole Valley. The interesting part of Brighton is a series of streets north of North

BRITAIN

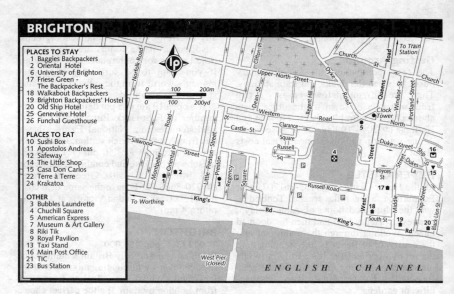

BRIGHTON

PLACES TO STAY
1 Baggies Backpackers
2 Oriental Hotel
6 University of Brighton
17 Friese Green –
   The Backpacker's Rest
18 Walkabout Backpackers
19 Brighton Backpackers' Hostel
20 Old Ship Hotel
25 Genevieve Hotel
26 Funchal Guesthouse

PLACES TO EAT
10 Sushi Box
11 Apostolos Andreas
12 Safeway
14 The Little Shop
15 Casa Don Carlos
22 Terre à Terre
24 Krakatoa

OTHER
3 Bubbles Laundrette
4 Chuchill Square
5 American Express
7 Museum & Art Gallery
8 Riki Tik
9 Royal Pavilion
13 Taxi Stand
16 Main Post Office
21 TIC
23 Bus Station

St, including Bond, Gardner, Kensington and Sydney Sts.

The TIC (☎ 292599, ✉ tourism@brighton .co.uk), 10 Bartholomew Square, has maps and copies of magazines such as the *Brighton Latest* (30p), *Brighton & Hove Scene* (25p) and *New Insight* (45p).

Bubbles Laundrette (☎ 738556) is at 75 Preston St. For Internet access go to Riki Tik (☎ 683844) at 18a Bond St.

Things to See & Do

The **Royal Pavilion** is an extraordinary fantasy: an Indian palace on the outside, a Chinese brothel on the inside, all built between 1815 and 1822 for George IV. The whole edifice is way over the top in every respect and is not to be missed. It's open 10 am to 6 pm daily (to 5 pm from October to May); £4.50/3.25 adult/concession.

The **Brighton Museum & Art Gallery** (☎ 290900) was closed for renovations at the time of writing, but it is sure to continue housing Art Deco and Art Nouveau furniture, archaeological finds and surrealist paintings (including Salvador Dali's sofa in the shape of lips). The nearby **Palace Pier** is the very image of Brighton with its fast food, flashing lights and rides. **The Lanes** is a maze of narrow alleyways crammed with antique and jewellery shops, restaurants and bars, just south of North St.

Places to Stay

There are loads of accommodation options in Brighton.

Baggies Backpackers (☎ 733740, *33 Oriental Place*) has beds for £10 (plus £5 deposit for a room key) and double rooms for £25. It's more friendly and homy here than at the other hostels.

Brighton Backpackers' Hostel (☎ 777717, *fax 887778,* ✉ *stay@brightonbackpackers .com, 75-6 Middle St*) seems to be trying very hard to cultivate a lackadaisical atmosphere. It too is £10 per night (or £11 in the seafront annexe). Weekly rates are £55/60.

Friese Green – The Backpacker's Rest (☎ 747551, *20 Middle St*) is comfortable and charges £9 for a bed and £30 for a double room.

Walkabout Backpackers (☎ 770232, *79-81 West St*) is not exclusively for Australians and New Zealanders but it might seem that way. Beds in bland rooms cost £10 (£12 in a double room). They don't take reservations.

The *University of Brighton* (☎ 643167, *fax 642610*) has flats for two to eight people

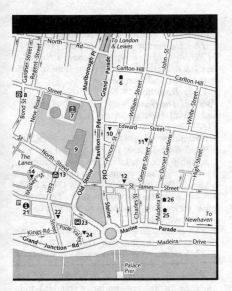

Apostolos Andreas (☎ 687935, George St) is a Greek coffee-house with English-style food. It's extremely good value and, if you can get a seat in this tiny place, you'll pay about 65p for a coffee, 95p to £1.45 for a sandwich and from £1.35 for a hot meal.

Sushi Box (☎ 818040, 181 Edward St) is close to the university and charges £3 to £4 for a takeaway lunch box of *sashimi* and/or california rolls.

The Little Shop (☎ 325594, 48a Market St, The Lanes) has delicious and chunky sandwiches from £2.25.

Krakatoa (☎ 719009, 7 Poole Valley), near the bus station, is a small, casual restaurant with a modern oriental fusion menu. It's for serious foodies.

Terre à Terre (☎ 729051, 71 East St) is an expensive vegetarian restaurant with a huge menu. Starters are around £5 and mains are about £9.50. Book ahead, especially on weekends.

Casa Don Carlos (☎ 327177 or 303274, 5 Union St, The Lanes) is an intimate Spanish tapas house and restaurant with a large selection of Spanish plonk. A big serve of paella costs £4.25 and a spanish omelette is £3.10.

Entertainment
Ever since the 1960s, Brighton has had a reputation as the club and party capital of the south. In the late 1970s this reputation was enshrined in the cult movie *Quadraphenia*. Pubs, bars and clubs are constantly opening, closing and changing their themes – check *The Brighton Latest*, *New Insight* and bar and cafe walls for places of the moment. There is a huge gay scene in Brighton and most of the gay bars and clubs can be found around St James' St and the Old Steine.

Getting There & Away
National Express coaches leave hourly from London Victoria (£7 one way, £5 off-peak). Stagecoach East Kent bus No 711 runs between Brighton and Dover via Hastings and Rye. There are twice hourly train services to Brighton from London Victoria and King's Cross stations (£13.70/14.60 one way/day return, 50 minutes). There are hourly trains to Portsmouth (£11.70 one way, one hour 20 minutes), and frequent services to Canterbury and Dover.

available from July to September. Prices start at £60 per person per week.

The main cluster of cheap B&Bs is to the east of the Palace Pier, off St James' St. *Funchal Guesthouse* (☎/fax 603975, 17 Madeira Place) tries very hard to please with cosy, clean rooms that are serviced daily. Prices begin at £20 per person but these rates may go up a few pounds from June to August.

Genevieve Hotel (☎ 681653, 18 Madeira Place) is clean and new. Rooms cost £20 to £25 per person.

Oriental Hotel (☎ 205050, fax 821096, ✉ info@orientalhotel.co.uk, 9 Oriental Place) is a real breath of fresh air among B&Bs. Decorated with bright colours, homemade furniture and cool decor, it's very funky. Doubles go for £54/70 during the week/weekends. There are no single occupancy rates.

Old Ship Hotel (☎ 329001, fax 820718) also on Kings Rd, is the doyen of Brighton's hotels. In the 1830s, Thackeray stayed there while writing *Vanity Fair*. It costs from £75/99.

Places to Eat
Brighton is packed with great eating places. Vegetarians and vegans are well catered for. There's a *Safeway* on St James St.

PORTSMOUTH
☎ 023 • pop 183,000

For much of British history, Portsmouth has been the home of the Royal Navy and it is littered with reminders that this was, for hundreds of years, a force that shaped the world. Portsmouth is still a busy naval base and the sleek, grey killing machines of the 20th century are also very much in evidence.

Unfortunately, Portsmouth is not a particularly attractive city, largely due to WWII bombing, so there is no persuasive reason to stay overnight.

Orientation & Information
The train and bus stations and ferry terminal for Isle of Wight are a stone's throw from the Naval Heritage Area and the TIC (☎ 9282 6722) on The Hard. It's worth having a wander round the atmospheric Old Portsmouth, just south of the Naval Heritage Area. Southsea, where the beaches are, as well as most of the cheap accommodation and restaurants, is about 2 miles (3.2km) south of Portsmouth Harbour.

There's Internet access at Southsea Backpackers Lodge (see Places to Stay later in this section).

Things to See & Do
Portsmouth's centrepiece is the **Naval Heritage Area**. Exploring HMS *Victory*, Lord Nelson's flagship at the Battle of Trafalgar, is about as close as you can get to time travel – a fascinating experience. After 437 years underwater, Henry VIII's favourite ship, the *Mary Rose*, and its time-capsule contents can now be seen. **The Royal Navy Museum** is really for naval buffs, and HMS *Warrior* does not have the same magic as the *Victory*. Entry is around £6 for each ship, or £11.90 for an All-Ships ticket which includes the Royal Navy Museum and the Mary Rose Museum.

Places to Stay
Most budget accommodation is in Southsea. One exception is the **Youth Hostel** (☎ *9237 5661, Old Wymering Lane, Cosham*), about 4 miles (6.5km) from the main sights. The nightly cost is £8.80/5.95 adults/children; bus Nos 12/12a operate to Cosham from the harbour bus station.

Southsea Backpackers Lodge (☎ *9283 2495, 4 Florence Rd, Southsea*) is far more convenient and charges £10 for a bed in a dorm and £15/25 for singles/doubles.

The University of Portsmouth (☎ *9284 3178, Nuffield Centre, St Michael's Rd*) offers B&B accommodation from June to August from £16.75 per person.

Lady Hamilton (☎ *9287 0505, fax 9283 7366, 21 The Hard*) is right by the bus station and Naval Heritage Area, and B&B costs £18/32 or £25/38 for *en suite*.

Sailmaker's Loft (☎ *9282 3045, fax 9229 5961, 5 Bath Square*) is very tasteful and we can highly recommend it. The place is run by a retired merchant seaman who can tell you a lot about Portsmouth. He charges £20/22 for a room with shared bath/*en suite*. There are great views across the harbour and one room has its own balcony.

The greatest range of cheaper B&Bs are in Southsea. **Gainsborough House** (☎ *9282 2322, 9 Malvern Rd*) is very good value at £17 per person (no *en suite*).

Kilbenny Guesthouse (☎ *9286 1347, 2 Malvern Rd*) is very similar in standard and costs £16/35 for clean, large rooms. *En suite* is a few pounds dearer.

Places to Eat
The **snack bar** near the bus station on The Hard has tasty, greasy morsels from 80p.

Twigs (☎ *9282 8316, 39 High St*) is a small coffeeshop with sandwiches, baguettes and baps (rolls) from £1.80 to £3.30.

Osborne Rd and Palmerston Rd are the main restaurant strips in Southsea. **Kashmir Restaurant** (☎ *9282 2013, 91 Palmerston Rd*) is relatively cheap and you can get a prawn vindaloo for £4.30, chicken tikka for £5.75 and chapati for 75p.

Mai Thai (☎ *9273 2322, 27A Burgoyne Rd*) is a good Thai restaurant, just off South Parade. A four-course meal is £11, chicken coconut curry costs £4.95.

Getting There & Away
Bus Some National Express buses from London go via Heathrow (£9 one way, £11 day return, 2½ hours). Stagecoach Coastline (☎ 01903-237661) bus No 700 runs between Brighton and Portsmouth every 30 minutes (£3.20 one way) and Stagecoach bus No 69 runs to/from Winchester hourly from Monday to Saturday.

Train There are over 40 trains a day from London Victoria and Waterloo stations (£17.80, 1½ hours). There are plenty of trains to/from Brighton (£11.70, 1½ hours) and Winchester (£6.70, one hour).

Boat Wightlink (☎ 0990-827744) operates a passenger ferry from The Hard to Ryde pier (15 minutes) and a car-and-passenger ferry (35 minutes) to Fishbourne every half-hour. The day-return fare is £7.40/3.70. Car fares start at £46.30 for a day return.

P&O Ferries (☎ 0870-242 4999) sails twice a week to Bilbao in Spain and daily to Cherbourg and Le Havre in France. Brittany Ferries (☎ 0870-901 2400) has overnight services to St Malo, Caen and Cherbourg in France. The Continental Ferryport is north of Flagship Portsmouth.

WINCHESTER
☎ 01962 • pop 37,000

Winchester is a beautiful cathedral city on the River Itchen, interspersed with water meadows. It has played an important role in the history of England, being both the capital of Saxon England and the seat of the powerful Bishops of Winchester from AD 670. Much of the present-day city dates from the 18th century, and its main attraction is the stunning cathedral. Despite its appeal, Winchester has escaped inundation by tourists, certainly by comparison to nearby Salisbury and to theme parks like Bath and Oxford.

Winchester makes a good base for exploring the south coast (ie, Portsmouth and New Forest) or the country farther west towards Salisbury.

Orientation & Information

The city centre is compact and easily negotiated on foot. The train station is a 10-minute walk to the west of the centre, and the bus and coach station is on Broadway, directly opposite the Guildhall and TIC.

The TIC (☎ 840500), the Guildhall, Broadway, is open daily from June to September. Regular guided walking tours (£3/50p) operate from April to October.

Things to See

One of the most beautiful cathedrals in the country is **Winchester Cathedral**, a mixture of Norman, Early English and Perpendicular styles. The north and south transepts are a magnificent example of pure Norman architecture. There are fascinating 20th-century paintings and sculptures dotted around the place. Cathedral tours are run by enthusiastic local volunteers. Suggested entry is £2.50.

Nearby is **Winchester College**, founded in 1382 and the model for the great public (meaning private) schools of England. The chapel and cloisters are open to visitors 10 am to 1 pm and 2 to 5 pm daily, except Sunday morning. Guided tours operate several times daily and cost £2.50.

In town it's also worth visiting the **Great Hall**, begun by William the Conqueror and the site of the trial of Sir Walter Raleigh in 1603. It houses **King Arthur's Round Table**, now known to be a fake at 'only' 600 years of age.

Places to Stay

B&Bs in Winchester tend not to hang signs out the front. You'll have to get a list from the TIC.

Morn Hill Caravan Club Site (☎ 869877, Morn Hill) is 3 miles (4.8km) east of the city centre off the A31. There are tent sites for £6.40 per person.

The **Youth Hostel** (☎ 853723, City Mill, 1 Water Lane) is in a beautiful 18th-century water mill. The nightly cost is £8.80/5.95 for adults/children.

There are plenty of small B&Bs, most with only one or two rooms. **Cathedral View** (☎ 863802, Magdalen Hill) is a friendly place with a lounge and a sunny conservatory. It costs £30/40 for rooms with shared bath and £40/50 en suite.

East View (☎ 862986, 16 Clifton Hill) is conveniently located and there are three small but comfortable en suite rooms from £35/45.

Places to Eat

You'll find a **Sainsbury's** supermarket on Middle Brook St. At **Granny Pastries** (☎ 878370, The Square) try a Thai Green Curry Chicken pie or a Stilton and celery pastie. Huge baguettes are around £2.

The Refectory, near the entrance to the cathedral, has sandwiches from £1.70 and a cream tea costs £3.45.

BRITAIN

There are tables outside in summer at *Harveys Restaurant & Wine Bar (☎ 843438, 31B The Square)* and the menu includes bar snacks (eg, baguettes £5) as well as more substantial meals from £8.50 to £15.

The Elizabethan Restaurant (☎ 853566, 18 Jewry St) is in a Tudor-style house dating from 1509. The menu is traditional English and French and a set three-course dinner costs £10.50.

Getting There & Away

National Express bus No 32 leaves every two hours from London Victoria via Heathrow (£7, one hour 55 minutes). Stagecoach Hampshire Bus (☎ 01256-464501) has a good network of services linking Salisbury, Southampton, Portsmouth and Brighton. Trains depart about every 15 minutes from London Waterloo (£17.30 one way, one hour), Southampton (£3.60, 18 minutes) and Portsmouth (£6.70, one hour).

CHANNEL ISLANDS

Across the Channel from Dorset and just off the coast of France lie the small islands of Jersey, Guernsey, Alderney, Sark and Herm. As well as being a tax haven, the Channel Islands are a popular summer holiday resort for the British. Although there are pleasant beaches, good walks and cycle rides on some islands, and there's the famous **Jersey Zoo** (☎ 01534-864666) started by Gerald Durrell, compared to mainland Britain or the Scottish islands there's really not a lot to see and do. Jersey is the biggest and busiest of the islands, Alderney the most peaceful. There are numerous camp sites and B&Bs from £15 per person. For more information contact Jersey Tourism (☎ 01534-500777, fax 500808, ✉ info@ jtourism.com) and, for all the other islands, Guernsey Tourism (☎ 01481-723552, fax 714951).

Getting There & Away

There are daily flights to the Channel Islands from nine UK airports on several airlines including British European (☎ 0870-567 6676) and Aurigny Air Services (☎ 01481-822886). Fares start at £60.

Condor (☎ 01305-761551) runs daily ferries between Portsmouth and Poole in Dorset and Jersey (from £70 return, four hours) via Guernsey.

South-West England

The counties of Wiltshire, Dorset, Somerset, Devon and Cornwall include some of the most beautiful countryside and spectacular coastline in Britain. They are also littered with the evidence of successive cultures and kingdoms that have been swept away by one invader after another.

The region can be divided between Devon and Cornwall out on a limb in the far west, and Dorset, Wiltshire and Somerset in the east, which are more readily accessible.

In the east, the story of English civilisation is signposted by some of its greatest monuments: the Stone Age left Stonehenge and spellbinding Avebury; the Iron Age Britons left Maiden Castle just outside Dorchester; between them, the Romans and the Georgians created Bath; the legendary King Arthur is said to be buried at Glastonbury; the Middle Ages left the great cathedrals at Exeter, Salisbury and Wells; and the landed gentry left great houses like Montacute and Wilton.

The east is densely packed with things to see, and the countryside, though varied, is a classic English patchwork of hedgerows, thatched cottages, stone churches, great estates and emerald-green fields.

Parts of Somerset and Wiltshire, particularly Bath and Salisbury, are major tourist attractions, but they are still, unquestionably, worth visiting. Dorset and North Devon are counties where you can happily wander without too many plans and without stumbling over too many people.

Devon and particularly Cornwall were once Britain's 'wild west', and smuggling was rife. Until the 18th century there were still Cornish speakers in Cornwall. The 'English Riviera' is almost too popular for its own good. It's wise to steer clear of the coastal towns in July and August, not least because the narrow streets are choked with traffic.

The weather is milder in the south-west all year and there are beaches with golden sand and surfable surf. And then there are the exquisite villages tucked into unexpected valleys or overlooking beautiful harbours, and lanes squeezed between high hedges.

Some people find Cornwall disappointing, however. Land's End – a veritable icon – has been reduced to an overly commercialised tourist trap, and inland much of the peninsula has been devastated by generations of tin and china-clay mining. However, many of the coastal villages retain their charm, especially if you visit out of season.

The South West Coast Path, a long-distance walking route, follows the coastline round the peninsula for 613 miles from Poole, near Bournemouth in Dorset, to Minehead in Somerset, giving spectacular access to the best and most untouched sections. Walkers can also head to the Dartmoor and Exmoor national parks.

Orientation & Information

The chalk downs centred on Salisbury Plain run across Wiltshire and down through the centre of Dorset to the coast. In the west, Exmoor and Dartmoor dominate the landscape. The railways converge on Exeter, the most important city in the west, then run round the coast to Truro and Penzance. Bristol and Salisbury are also important crossroads.

Among others, there are several YHA hostels in Dartmoor and Exmoor national parks, and at Salisbury, Bath, Bristol, Winchester, Exeter, Plymouth, Penzance, Land's End, Tintagel and Ilfracombe.

Activities

Hiking The south-west has plenty of beautiful countryside, but walks in Dartmoor and Exmoor national parks, and round the coastline, are the best known. The barren, open wilderness of Dartmoor can be an acquired taste, but Exmoor covers some of the most beautiful countryside in England, and the coastal stretch from Ilfracombe to Minehead is particularly spectacular. See the separate sections on Dartmoor and Exmoor national parks later in this chapter for more information.

The South West Coast Path is not a wilderness walk. Villages are generally within easy reach. It's the longest national trail and follows a truly magnificent coastline. Completing a section of the path is essential for any keen walker; if possible avoid busy summer weekends.

Another famous walk, the Ridgeway, starts near Avebury and runs north-east for 85

miles to Ivinghoe Beacon near Aylesbury. Much of it follows ancient roads over the high open ridge of the chalk downs, before descending to the Thames Valley and climbing into the Chilterns. The western section (to Streatley) can be used by mountain bikes, horses, farm vehicles and recreational 4WDs. For peace and quiet, walk during the week.

Surfing The capital of British surfing is Newquay on the west Cornish coast, and it's complete with surf shops, bleached hair and Kombi vans. The surfable coast runs from Porthleven (near Helston) in Cornwall, west around Land's End and north to Ilfracombe. The most famous reef breaks are at Porthleven, Lynmouth and Milbrook; though good, they are inconsistent.

Cycling Bikes can be hired in most major regional centres, and the infrequent bus connections make cycling more sensible than usual. There's no shortage of hills, but the mild weather and quiet back roads make this excellent cycling country.

Getting Around

Bus National Express buses (☎ 0870-580 8080) provide reasonable connections between the main towns, particularly in the east, but the farther west you go the more dire the situation becomes. Transport around Dartmoor and Exmoor is very difficult in summer, and nigh on impossible at any other time. This is territory that favours those with their own transport.

Phone numbers for regional timetables include Bristol and Bath ☎ 0117-955 5111, Somerset ☎ 01823-355455, Wiltshire ☎ 0845-709 0899, Dorset ☎ 01305-224535, Devon ☎ 01392-382800 and Cornwall ☎ 01872-322142.

Train Train services in the east are reasonably comprehensive, linking Bristol, Bath, Salisbury, Weymouth and Exeter. Beyond Exeter a single line follows the south coast as far as Penzance, with spurs to Barnstaple, Gunnislake, Looe, Falmouth, St Ives and Newquay. For rail information, phone ☎ 0845-748 4950.

Several regional rail passes are available, including the Freedom of the SouthWest

BRITAIN

Rover which, over 15 days, allows eight days of unlimited travel west of a line drawn through (and including) Salisbury, Bath, Bristol and Weymouth (£71.50 in summer, £61 in winter).

SALISBURY
☎ 01722 • pop 37,000

Salisbury is justly famous for the cathedral and its close, but its appeal also lies in the fact that it is still a bustling market town, not just a tourist trap. Markets have been held in the town centre every Tuesday and Saturday since 1361, and the jumble of stalls still draws a large, cheerful crowd.

The town's architecture is a blend of every style since the Middle Ages, including some beautiful, half-timbered black-and-white buildings. It's a good base for visiting the Wiltshire Downs, Stonehenge, Old Sarum, Wilton House and Avebury. Portsmouth and Winchester are also easy day trips if you're travelling by rail.

Orientation & Information

The town centre is a 10-minute walk from the train station, and it's another 15 minutes walk to the YHA hostel. Everything is within walking distance.

From the train station, walk down the hill and turn right at the T-junction onto Fisherton St. This leads directly into town (which is well signposted). The bus station is just north of the centre of town, along not-so Endless St.

The helpful TIC (☎ 334956), Fish Row, is behind the impressive 18th-century Guildhall, on the south-eastern corner of Market Square.

Things to See

Beautiful **St Mary's Cathedral** is built in a uniform style known as Early English (or Early Pointed). This period is characterised by the first pointed arches and flying buttresses, and has a rather austere feel. The cathedral owes its uniformity to the speed with which it was built. Between 1220 and 1266, over 70,000 tons of stone were piled up. The spire, at 123m, is the highest in Britain. A donation of £3 is requested.

The adjacent **chapter house** is one of the most perfect achievements of Gothic architecture. There is plenty more to see in the **cathedral close**, including two houses that

have been restored and two museums. The **Salisbury & South Wiltshire Museum** (£3) is also worth visiting.

Places to Stay & Eat

Salisbury Youth Hostel (☎ 327572, *Milford Hill*) is an attractive old building, an easy walk from the centre of Salisbury. From the TIC, turn left onto Fish Row, then immediately right onto Queen St, first left onto Milford St, straight for about 400m, under the overpass and the hostel is on the left.

Friendly *Matt & Tiggy's* (☎ 327443, *51 Salt Lane*), close to the bus station, is an independent hostel-like guesthouse with dorm rooms, but without a curfew. A bed costs £10.

The *Old Bakery* (☎ 320100, *35 Bedwin St*) is near the centre. Rooms are £18/38 for a single/double, some with attached bathroom.

Fisherton St, running from the centre to the train station, has Chinese, Thai, Indian and other restaurants. *Le Hérisson* on Crane St has tasty vegetarian meals and a deli. *Haunch of Venison* (*1 Minster St*) is a recommended pub that dates from the 16th century.

Getting There & Away

Bus National Express has one bus a day from Salisbury to Bath (£6.25) and Bristol, however, it's more expensive than the local bus lines. Badgerline/Wiltshire buses also run the hourly X4 to Bath (£3.90, two hours) via Wilton and Bradford-on-Avon. Three buses a day run from London via Heathrow to Salisbury (£12, three hours).

There are three unlimited travel tickets available in Wiltshire – Wiltshire Bus Lines (☎ 0845-709 0899) or Wilts & Dorset (☎ 336855) can tell you more. There are daily buses to Avebury, Stonehenge and Old Sarum. If you're going through to Bristol or Bath, via Somerset (Wells, Glastonbury) or Gloucestershire (Cotswolds), get the Badgerline Day Rambler.

Train Salisbury is linked by rail to London Waterloo station (£21.80, 1½ hours), Portsmouth (1¼ hours), Bath (£9.80, two hours) and Exeter (two hours).

Getting Around

Local buses are reasonably well organised and link Salisbury with Stonehenge, Old

Sarum and Wilton House; phone ☎ 336855 for details. Bikes can be hired for £9 per day from Hayball Cycle Shop (☎ 411378), Winchester St.

STONEHENGE

Stonehenge is the most famous prehistoric site in Europe – a ring of enormous stones (some of which were brought from Wales), built in stages beginning 5000 years ago. Reactions vary; some find that the car park, gift shop and crowds of tourists swamp the monument. Avebury, 18 miles to the north, is much more impressive in scale and recommended for those who would like to commune with the ley lines in relative peace.

Stonehenge is 2 miles west of Amesbury at the junction of the A303 and A344/A360, and 9 miles from Salisbury (the nearest station); entry is £4. Some feel that it's unnecessary to pay the entry fee, because you can get a good view from the road and even if you do enter you are kept at some distance from the stones. There are at least four buses a day from Salisbury. Consider a Wilts & Dorset Explorer ticket for £5. Phone ☎ 01722-336855 for details.

AVEBURY
☎ 01672

Avebury (between Calne and Marlborough, just off the A4) stands at the hub of a prehistoric complex of ceremonial sites, ancient avenues and burial chambers dating from 3500 BC. In scale the remains are more impressive than Stonehenge, and if you visit outside summer weekends it's quite possible to escape the crowds.

In addition to an enormous stone circle, there's Silbury Hill (the largest constructed mound in Europe), West Kennet Long Barrow (a burial chamber) and a pretty village with an ancient church.

Avebury TIC (☎ 539425) can help with accommodation. The *Old Vicarage* (☎ 539362) does B&B for £22 per person, or there's *The Red Lion* (☎ 539266), a pub with doubles for £30. The very popular *Stones Restaurant* serves great cafeteria-style food and cream teas.

Avebury can be easily reached by frequent buses from Salisbury (Wiltshire Bus No 5 or 6) or Swindon. To travel to and from Bath

you'll have to change buses at Devizes; check connections (☎ 0845-709 0899).

DORSET

The greater part of Dorset is designated as an area of outstanding natural beauty but, with the exceptions of Poole and Weymouth, it avoids inundation by tourists.

The coast varies from sandy beaches to shingle banks and towering cliffs. Lyme Regis is a particularly attractive spot, made famous as the setting for John Fowles' book *The French Lieutenant's Woman*, and the subsequent film.

For those who've read Thomas Hardy, however, Dorset is inextricably linked with his novels. You can visit his birthplace at Higher Bockhampton, or Dorchester (Casterbridge), the unspoilt market town where he lived. Maiden Castle, the largest Iron Age fort in England, is nearby.

Orientation & Information

Dorchester makes a good base for exploring the best of Dorset, but on the coast colourful Weymouth or quieter Bridport are good alternatives. One of the reasons for Dorset's backwater status is that no major transport routes cross it. A rail loop runs west from Southampton to Dorchester, then north to Yeovil.

There are good TICs in all the main towns.

Places to Stay

There is no YHA hostel in Dorchester or Weymouth but there are hostels in Swanage, Lulworth Cove and Litton Cheney, all convenient for walkers on the Dorset Coast Path. Dorchester and Lyme Regis have some B&Bs while Weymouth is positively packed with them.

Getting There & Away

Trains to Dorchester from London depart about every hour; they take about three hours, cost £32.40 and continue to Weymouth. Dorchester to Weymouth takes just 15 minutes by train and costs £2.50. Trains continue north to Bath and Bristol from Dorchester.

There are also buses on these routes but, although cheaper, they tend to be much slower. Axminster is also a reasonable transport hub.

BRITAIN

Getting Around

There are regular buses between Dorchester and Weymouth, Salisbury, Bournemouth and Bridport. Buses also operate regularly between Bridport/Lyme Regis and Axminster. Contact Southern National (☎ 01305-783645) or Wilts & Dorset (☎ 01722-336855) for more information.

EXETER

☎ 01392 • pop 102,000

Exeter is the heart of the West Country. It was devastated during WWII and, as a result, first impressions are not particularly inspiring; if you get over these, you'll find a lively university city with a thriving nightlife. It's a good starting point for Dartmoor and Cornwall.

The cathedral is one of the most attractive in England, with two huge Norman towers surviving from the 11th century. From AD 50, when the city was established by the Romans, until the 19th century, Exeter was a very important port, and the waterfront (including a large boat museum) is gradually being restored.

There are a number of highly recommended free tours, which cover both cathedral and town.

Orientation & Information

There are two train stations, but most intercity trains use St David's, which is a 20-minute walk west of the city centre and Central station. From St David's, cross the station forecourt and Bonhay Rd, climb some steps to St David's Hill then turn right up the hill for the centre. You'll pass a batch of reasonably priced B&Bs on your right; keep going for three-quarters of a mile, then turn left up High St. The centre of the city is well signposted.

The TIC (☎ 265700) in the Civic Centre, Paris St, is just across the road from the bus station, a short walk north-east of the cathedral; it's closed on Sunday.

Places to Stay & Eat

Exeter Youth Hostel (☎ 873329, 47 Countess Wear Rd) is 2 miles south-east of the city towards Topsham. It's open year-round except over the Christmas/New Year break. From High St, catch minibus J, K or T (10 minutes) and ask for the Countess Wear post office.

Globe Backpackers (☎ 215521, 71 Holloway St) is a thankful addition to the budget scene and has beds for £11, a good vibe and Internet access.

The best value accommodation in central Exeter is the university's *St Luke's Hall* (☎ 211500) from just £13.50 per person, including breakfast. The catch is that it's only available in college vacations.

There are several B&Bs on St David's Hill. The *Highbury* (☎ 434737, 89 St David's Hill) is good value with singles/doubles for £20/35. There's another batch on Blackall Rd (near the prison). *Rhona's Guest House* (☎ 277791, 15 Blackall Rd) offers singles/doubles for £15/29.

Coolings is a busy wine bar on medieval Gandy St, which is signposted off High St. The *Ship Inn*, down the alley between the cathedral and the High St, was where Sir Francis Drake used to drink. *Herbies*, on North St, is an excellent vegetarian restaurant. Carnivores should be satisfied by the steaks at *Mad Meg's* (☎ 221225) on Fore St.

Getting There & Away

Bus There are nine buses a day between London, Heathrow airport and Exeter (£16.50, four hours). There are three direct buses a day to Penzance (£16, 4½ hours). Phone ☎ 0870-580 8080 for National Express information, ☎ 01392-427711 for Stagecoach bus information.

Train For rail information, phone ☎ 0845-748 4950. Exeter is at the hub of lines running from Bristol (1½ hours), Salisbury (two hours) and Penzance (three hours). There are hourly trains from London's Waterloo and Paddington stations (three hours). The train to and from London is much quicker than the bus.

The 39-mile branch line to Barnstaple gives good views of traditional Devon countryside and Barnstaple is a useful starting point for North Devon.

PLYMOUTH

☎ 01752 • pop 240,000

Plymouth's renown as a maritime centre was established long before Sir Francis Drake's famous game of bowls on Plymouth Hoe in 1588. Devastated by WWII bombing raids, much of the city is modern but the old quarter by the harbour, from where the Pilgrim Fathers set sail for the New World in 1620, has been preserved.

Orientation & Information
The TIC (☎ 264849), Island House, the Barbican, is open daily. North of here are the bus station (half-mile) and train station (1 mile). To the west is Plymouth Hoe, a grassy park with wide views over the sea.

Places to Stay
Plymouth Youth Hostel (☎ 562189, Belmont Place, Stoke) is 1½ miles from the centre. It's open all year except over the Christmas/New Year period. B&Bs cluster round the northwestern corner of the Hoe and are generally good value, from £13. *Plymouth Backpackers International Hostel (☎ 225158, 172 Citadel Rd, The Hoe)* has dorm beds for £8.50 a night.

Getting There & Away
Stagecoach (☎ 01392-427711) has frequent buses to and from Exeter. National Express has direct connections to numerous cities, including London (£20.50, 4½ hours) and Bristol (£18, 2½ hours). Trains are faster to London (3½ hours) and Penzance (1½ hours) but more expensive.

DARTMOOR NATIONAL PARK
Although the park is only about 25 miles from north to south and east to west, it encloses some of the wildest, bleakest country in England – a suitable terrain for the hound of the Baskervilles (one of Sherlock Holmes' most notorious foes).

The park covers a granite plateau punctuated by distinctive tors, which can look uncannily like ruined castles, and cut by deep valleys known as coombs. The high moorland is covered by windswept gorse and heather (there are no trees, apart from some limited plantations), and is grazed by sheep and semiwild Dartmoor ponies.

There are several small market towns surrounding the tableland, but the only village of any size on the moor is Princetown, which is not a particularly attractive place.

The countryside in the south-east is more conventionally beautiful, with wooded valleys and thatched villages. This is hiking country par excellence.

Orientation & Information
Dartmoor is accessible from Exeter and Plymouth, and rare buses run from these regional centres to the surrounding market towns. There are only two roads across the moor and they meet near Princetown.

The National Park Authority (NPA) has eight information centres in and around the park, or visit the TICs at Exeter and Plymouth before setting off. The High Moorland Visitor Centre (☎ 01822-890414) in Princetown is open all year. The Ministry of Defence (☎ 01392-270164) has three live firing ranges in the north-western section.

Places to Stay
Most of Dartmoor is privately owned, but the owners of unenclosed moorland don't usually object to backpackers who keep to a simple code: don't camp on moorland enclosed by walls or within sight of roads or houses; don't stay on one site for more than two nights; and leave the site as you found it.

There are YHA hostels bang in the middle near Postbridge and at Steps Bridge, near Dunsford between Moretonhampstead and Exeter, as well as at Okehampton, Exeter, Plymouth and Dartington.

The *Bellever Youth Hostel (☎ 01822-880227)*, Postbridge, is very popular. It closes from November to mid-March and on Sunday, except in July and August. *Steps Bridge Youth Hostel (☎ 01647-252435)* is closed from October through March. *Plume of Feathers Inn Bunkhouse (☎ 01822-890240)* in Princetown has 42 beds for £3.50 to £5.50 a head, but three months advance booking is wise for summer weekends. Beds cost £6 at *Dartmoor Expedition Centre (☎ 01364-621249)* in Widecombe-in-the-Moor.

Phone ☎ 01271-324420 for information on the camping barn network from £3.50 a night.

The larger towns on the edge of the park (like Buckfastleigh, Moretonhampstead, Okehampton and Tavistock) all have plentiful supplies of B&Bs.

Getting There & Away
Exeter or Plymouth are the best starting points for the park, but Exeter has the better transport connections to the rest of England. Public transport in and around the park is

lousy, so consider hiring a bike (about £6 a day) from Flash Gordon (☎ 01392-213141) in Exeter.

From Exeter, DevonBus 359 follows a circular route through Steps Bridge, Moretonhampstead and Chagford (Monday to Saturday). The most important bus that actually crosses Dartmoor is DevonBus 82, the Transmoor Link (☎ 01752-222666), running between Exeter and Plymouth via Moretonhampstead and Princetown. Unfortunately, it only runs daily from late May to late September, and even then there are only three buses each way.

A one-day Rover ticket (£5) allows you to get on and off as often as you like. Outside summer, life becomes considerably more difficult, with infrequent services and changing schedules. Work out roughly what you want to do, then contact the Devon County Public Transport Help Line (☎ 01392-382800).

SOUTH CORNWALL COAST
Truro
☎ 01872 • pop 18,000

You may need to use Cornwall's uninspiring regional centre as a transport hub. For bus information, ring ☎ 01209-719988.

Penzance
☎ 01736 • pop 20,000

At the end of the line from London, Penzance is a busy little town that has not yet completely sold its soul to tourists. It makes a good base for walking the Coastal Path from Land's End to St Ives. This dramatic 25-mile section can be broken at the YHA hostel at St Just (near Land's End), and there are many cheap farm B&Bs along the way.

The TIC (☎ 362207) is just outside the train station.

Places to Stay *Penzance Youth Hostel* (*☎ 362666, Castle Horneck, Alverton*) is an 18th-century mansion on the outskirts of town. Walk west through town on the Land's End road (Market Jew St) until you get to a thatched cottage opposite the Pirate Inn, turn right and cross the A30 bypass road until you get to the signposted lane.

Closer to the centre, on Alexander Rd, is *Penzance Backpackers* (*☎ 363836*), charging £10.

Getting There & Away There are four buses a day from Penzance to Bristol via Truro and Plymouth; one direct bus a day to Exeter (five hours); and five buses a day from London and Heathrow (7½ hours).

The train is definitely the civilised, if expensive, way to get to Penzance from London's Paddington station (£54, five hours). There are frequent trains from Penzance to St Ives (£2.90, 20 minutes).

Land's End
☎ 01736

The coastal scenery on either side of Land's End is some of the finest in Britain, although the development at Land's End itself is shameful. However, the *Youth Hostel* (*☎ 788437*) at St Just, 8 miles from Penzance, is highly recommended. It's fully open from April to October. You can also stay at the independent *Whitesand's Lodge* (*☎ 871776*) backpackers hostel in Sennen village; dorm beds cost £10. Even cheaper is *Kelynack Bunkbarn* (*☎ 787633*), 1 mile south of St Just; a bunk bed costs £6, but book ahead.

The coastal hills between St Just and St Ives, with their dry stone walling, form one of the oldest, most fascinating agricultural landscapes in Britain, still following an Iron Age pattern. There are numerous prehistoric remains and the abandoned engine houses of old tin and copper mines.

WEST CORNWALL COAST
St Ives
☎ 01736 • pop 9500

St Ives is the ideal to which other seaside towns can only aspire. The omnipresent sea, the harbour, the beaches, the narrow alleyways, steep slopes and hidden corners are captivating but it gets mighty busy in summer. Artists have long been attracted to St Ives, and in 1993 a branch of London's **Tate Gallery** was opened here. It's easily accessible by train from Penzance and London via St Erth. There are numerous B&Bs in the £15 bracket.

The TIC (☎ 796297), the Guildhall, Streetan-Pol, a short walk from the train station, is open all year. There are several surf shops on the Wharf (the street edging the harbour) where it's possible to rent boards.

St Ives Backpackers (*☎ 799444, Lower Stennack*) is a converted chapel with beds from £12 a night. Nearby are many B&Bs. There are a number of cheap restaurants around the harbour and on Fore St behind.

Newquay
☎ 01637 • pop 14,000

Newquay, the original Costa del Cornwall, was drawing them in long before the British learned to say Torremolinos. There are numerous sandy beaches, several of them right in town (including Fistral Beach for board riders).

The TIC (☎ 871345) is near the bus station in the centre of town. There are several surf shops on Fore St and they all hire fibreglass boards and wetsuits, each around £6 per day. Compare prices; they're competitive.

Newquay has several independent hostels geared up for surfers. *Newquay Cornwall Backpackers* (☎ 874668) in an excellent central position overlooking Towan Beach in Beachfield Ave, has dorm beds from £7 per night. *Home Surf Lodge* (☎ 873387, 18 Tower Rd) has beds from £10 and free Internet access.

There are four trains a day between Par (on the main London to Penzance line) and Newquay, and numerous buses to Truro.

Tintagel
☎ 01840 • pop 1750

Even the summer crowds and the grossly commercialised village can't destroy the surf-battered grandeur of **Tintagel Head**. According to legend the scanty ruins mark the birthplace of King Arthur, hence the plethora of King Arthur tea shops etc. Entry to the ruins costs £2.90. It's also worth visiting the picturesque 14th-century **Old Post Office**; admission £2.20.

Tintagel Youth Hostel (☎ 770334) at Dunderhole Point is open April through September. Alternatively *Boscastle Youth Hostel* (☎ 250287) has a lovely situation overlooking the harbour. It's open daily from mid-May through September; phone for other opening hours. For information on the irregular bus services, phone ☎ 01872-322142.

NORTH DEVON

North Devon is one of the most beautiful regions in England, with a spectacular, largely unspoilt coastline and the superb Exmoor National Park, which protects the best of it.

Barnstaple
☎ 01270 • pop 25,000

Barnstaple is a large town and transport hub, a good starting point for North Devon. There are some handsome old buildings, but there's no reason to stay. Contact the TIC (☎ 375000) for B&Bs.

Barnstaple is at the western end of the Tarka Line from Exeter and connects with a number of bus services around the coast. Red Bus (☎ 345444) runs a service to Bideford with connections to Bude. Red Bus service No 310 runs direct to Lynton, but the most interesting option is the excellent No 300 scenic service (summer only) that crosses Exmoor from Barnstaple, through Lynton to Minehead (£5 for a one-day Explorer Pass).

Mountain bikes are available from Tarka Trail (☎ 324202) in the train station from £6.50 per day.

Exmoor National Park

Exmoor is a small national park (265 sq miles) enclosing a wide variety of beautiful landscapes. In the north and along the coast the scenery is particularly breathtaking, with dramatic humpbacked headlands giving superb views across the Bristol Channel.

A high plateau rises steeply behind the coast, but is cut by steep, fast-flowing streams. On the southern side the two main rivers, the Exe and Barle, wind their way south along the wooded coombs. Pony herds descended from ancient hill stock still roam the commons, as do England's last herds of wild red deer.

There are a number of particularly attractive villages: Lynton/Lynmouth, twin villages joined by a water-operated railway; Porlock, at the edge of the moor in a beautiful valley; Dunster, which is dominated by a castle, a survivor from the Middle Ages; and Selworthy, a National Trust village with many classic thatched cottages.

Arguably the best and easiest section of the South West Coast Path is between Minehead and Padstow (sometimes known as the Somerset & North Devon Coast Path).

Orientation & Information Exmoor is accessible from Barnstaple (train from Exeter) and Taunton.

The NPA has five information centres in and around the park, but it's also possible to get information from the TICs at Barnstaple, Ilfracombe, Lynton and Minehead. The NPA centres at Dunster (☎ 01643-821835) and Lynmouth (☎ 01598-752509) are open from the end of March to November. The main visitor centre (☎ 01398-323841), Fore St, Dulverton (between Bampton and Minehead), is open all year.

Places to Stay There are *YHA hostels* at Ilfracombe *(☎ 01271-865337)*, Minehead *(☎ 01643-702595)*, near Lynton *(☎ 01598-53237)* and Exford *(☎ 01643-831288)* in the centre of the park. All these hostels close over winter (Lynton only in January) and are only open daily in July and August. *Ocean Backpackers (☎ 867835, 29 St James Place)* is a fine, friendly hostel with beds for just £9.

The main swarm of *B&Bs* can be found around Lynton/Lynmouth, but they are scattered throughout the park. They aren't cheap – about £16 a head and up. Contact the Lynton TIC (☎ 01598-752225) for suggestions.

Getting There & Away From Exeter catch the Tarka Line to Barnstaple, from where buses run to Ilfracombe, Lynton and Minehead. See the Exeter and Barnstaple sections earlier in this chapter for more details.

Alternatively, there are buses from Taunton (one hour) to Minehead. Contact Southern National (☎ 01823-272033) for details. A timetable covering local public transport is available from TICs, or you can phone Devon County Council's bus inquiry line (☎ 01392-382800).

BATH
☎ 01225 • pop 85,000
For more than 2000 years Bath's fortune has been linked to its hot springs and tourism. The Romans developed a complex of baths and a temple to Sulis-Minerva. Today, however, Bath's Georgian architecture is an equally important attraction.

Throughout the 18th century, Bath was the most fashionable haunt of English society. Aristocrats flocked here to gossip, gamble and flirt. Fortunately, they had the good sense and fortune to employ a number of brilliant architects who designed the Palladian terrace that dominates the city.

Like Italy's Florence, Bath is an architectural jewel, with a much-photographed, shop-lined bridge. In high summer the town can seem little more than an exotic shopping mall for wealthy tourists. However, when sunlight brightens the honey-coloured stone, no one can deny Bath's exceptional beauty.

Orientation & Information
Bath sprawls more than you'd expect (as you'll discover if you stay at the hostel). Fortunately, the centre is compact and easy to get around, although the tangle of streets, arcades and squares can be confusing. The train and bus stations are both south of the TIC, by the river.

From mid-June to mid-September, the TIC (☎ 462831), Abbey Chambers, Abbey Churchyard, is open until 7 pm Monday to Saturday and until 6 pm on Sunday. For the rest of the year it closes at 5 pm (4 pm on Sunday). Advance booking of accommodation is essential over Easter, during the Bath International Festival (late May), over summer weekends and throughout July and August.

Things to See & Do
Bath was designed for wandering around and you need at least a full day. Don't miss the **covered market** next to the Guildhall, or the maze of passageways just north of the Abbey Churchyard. Free walking tours (recommended) leave from the Abbey Churchyard at 10.30 am (except Saturday).

Try to see a play at Bath's sumptuous **Theatre Royal** (☎ 448844), which often features shows on their pre-London run.

Bath's flea market (antiques and clothes) is a popular place for bargain hunters. It's held on Saturday and Sunday mornings on Walcot St, near the YMCA.

A convenient starting point for a walking tour is **Bath Abbey** (donation £2). Built between 1499 and 1616, it's more glass than stone.

On the southern side of the Abbey Churchyard (an open square), the **Pump Room** houses an opulent restaurant that exemplifies the elegant style that once drew the aristocrats.

Nearby, the **Roman Baths Museum** is a series of excavated passages and chambers beneath street level, taking in the sulphurous mineral springs (still flowing after all these years), the ancient central-heating system

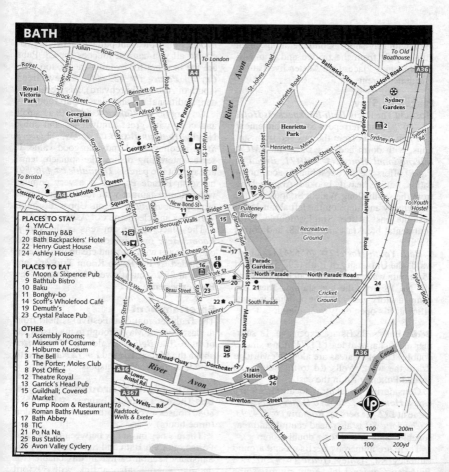

BATH

PLACES TO STAY
4 YMCA
7 Romany B&B
20 Bath Backpackers' Hotel
22 Henry Guest House
24 Ashley House

PLACES TO EAT
6 Moon & Sixpence Pub
9 Bathtub Bistro
10 Baku
11 Bonghy-bo
14 Scoff's Wholefood Café
19 Demuth's
23 Crystal Palace Pub

OTHER
1 Assembly Rooms;
   Museum of Costume
2 Holburne Museum
3 The Bell
5 The Porter; Moles Club
8 Post Office
12 Theatre Royal
13 Garrick's Head Pub
15 Guildhall; Covered
   Market
16 Pump Room & Restaurant;
   Roman Baths Museum
17 Bath Abbey
18 TIC
21 Po Na Na
25 Bus Station
26 Avon Valley Cyclery

and the bath itself, which retains its Roman paving and lead base. This is Bath's top attraction, open 9 am to 6 pm daily (5 pm in winter and on Sunday), and entry is £6.30, or £8.40 including the Museum of Costume in the Assembly Rooms, a 20-minute walk up the hill. It can get hopelessly overcrowded in summer.

From the Roman Baths, walk north until you come to the main shopping drag, Milsom St, and finally the **Assembly Rooms** and the **Museum of Costume**, which contains an enormous collection of clothing from 1590 to the present day.

Turn left on Bennet St and walk west to the **Circus**, an architectural masterpiece by John Wood the Elder, designed so that a true crescent faces each of its three approaches. Continue to **Royal Crescent**, designed by John Wood the Younger and even more highly regarded than his father's effort. No 1 has been superbly restored to its 1770 glory, down to the minutest detail (entry is certainly worth £4/3 for adults/students).

From Royal Crescent, wander back to the Abbey, then keep going east until you find yourself overlooking the formal **Parade Gardens** with their famous view up the Avon to

BRITAIN

Pulteney Bridge, built by Robert Adam and lined with tiny shops. Continue along Great Pulteney St from the bridge and you will reach Sydney Place. Jane Austen lived at No 4 with her parents.

Places to Stay

Hostels The lively *Bath Backpackers Hotel* (☎ 446787) on Pierrepont St is a convenient five-minute walk from the bus and train stations, with dorm beds for £12. The *YMCA International House* (☎ 460471, *Broad St Place*) offers the next best budget accommodation, but it's heavily booked. Approaching from the south along Walcot St, look out for an archway and steps on the left about 150m past the post office. Singles/doubles with continental breakfast are £15/28, and dorms are £11.

Bath Youth Hostel (☎ 465674) is out towards the University of Bath (£9.75), a good 25-minute walk, or you can catch Badgerline bus No 18 from the bus station. There are compensatory views and the building is magnificent. It's open daily year-round.

B&Bs Bath's B&Bs are expensive. In summer most charge at least £17/35 for a single/double. The main areas are along Newbridge Rd to the west, Wells Rd to the south and around Pulteney Rd in the east.

Considering its central location, *Henry Guest House* (☎ 424052, *6 Henry St*) is good value at £22 per person. *Romany* (☎ 424193, *9 Charlotte St*) is also dead central, and reasonable value at £30 for a double room.

There are numerous B&Bs on and around Pulteney Rd. *Ashley House* (☎ 425027, *8 Pulteney Gardens*) has eight rooms, some with attached shower, from £25 per person. In an idyllic location beside the River Avon, the *Old Boathouse* (☎ 466407), Forester Rd, is an Edwardian boating station within walking distance of the centre. Comfortable rooms with attached bathrooms are £55 a double (no singles).

Places to Eat

Scoff's Wholefood Café on Kingsmead Square has excellent filled rolls and light lunches (tandoori burgers, spinach pancakes etc) with up to 30% off if you don't eat in. There are several fast-food places in this area.

The *Moon & Sixpence* (☎ 460962, *6 Broad St*) is a pleasant pub which offers two-course all-you-can-eat lunches for £5. Pubs are the best bet for evening meals, too. The *Crystal Palace* (☎ 423944), Abbey Green (south of Abbey Churchyard), has a beer garden, traditional ale and classic pub food.

On Argyle St, *Baku* (☎ 444440) is small and cosy with great sandwiches and subs. Nearby, *Bathtub Bistro* (☎ 460593, *2 Grove St*) is recommended and also good value. It serves interesting dishes like spinach, lentil and apricot filo parcels. *Demuth's* (☎ 446059) in North Parade Passage is a very popular vegetarian restaurant with food to die for at around £5. *Bonghy-bo* on Upper Borough Walls has an eclectic mix of Asian dishes.

The place for cream teas is the *Pump Room*. Here one sips one's tea and heaps one's scones with jam and cream while being serenaded by the Pump Room Trio. It's not cheap at £5.75, but it's very much part of the Bath experience.

Entertainment

The Bath International Festival is held from the last week of May through to the first week of June. The *Bell* on Walcot St, *The Porter* above the *Moles* club and *Po Na Na* on North Parade are all cool nightspots.

Getting There & Around

Bus There are National Express (☎ 0870-580 8080) buses every two hours from London (three hours).

There's one bus a day between Bristol and Portsmouth via Bath and Salisbury – see the Salisbury section earlier in this chapter for details. There's also a link with Oxford (£9.75, two hours) and Stratford-upon-Avon via Bristol (£15.75, 2½ hours).

Some excellent map/timetables are available from the bus station (☎ 464446). The Badgerline Day Rambler (£5.30) gives you access to a good network of buses in Bristol, Somerset (Wells, Glastonbury), Gloucestershire (Gloucester via Bristol) and Wiltshire (Lacock, Bradford-on-Avon, Salisbury).

Train There are numerous trains from London's Paddington station (£30, 1½ hours). There are also plenty of trains through to Bristol for onward travel to Cardiff, Exeter or the

North. There are hourly trains between Portsmouth and Bristol via Salisbury and Bath. A single ticket from Bath to Salisbury is £10.

Bicycle The Bristol & Bath Cycle Walkway is an excellent footpath and cycleway that follows the route of the disused railway. Bikes are available from Avon Valley Cyclery (☎ 461880) from £9/14 per half-day/full day. It's just behind the train station.

AROUND BATH
Lacock
Three miles south of Chippenham, Lacock is a classic, dreamy Cotswolds village with an **abbey** dating back to the 13th century and a **museum of photography**. The abbey and museum are open 11 am to 5.30 pm daily (except Tuesday) April through October; entry £5.80. Badgerline bus No 234/7 (Chippenham to Trowbridge) serves Lacock.

Bradford-on-Avon
Eight miles east of Bath, this beautiful small town has somehow managed to avoid becoming a tourist trap. Its narrow streets tumble down a steep bluff overlooking the Avon. There are good bus connections with Bath, and hourly trains, so the town could easily be used as a base; Bradford's few B&Bs tend to be pricey. Contact the TIC (☎ 01225-865797) for more information.

WELLS
☎ 01749 • pop 9500
Wells is a small cathedral city that has kept much of its medieval character; many claim that the cathedral is England's most beautiful, and it is certainly one of the best surviving examples of a full cathedral complex.

Wells is 21 miles south-west of Bath on the edge of the Mendip Hills. The TIC (☎ 672552) is in the town hall on the picturesque Market Place. Bike City (☎ 343111, 91 Broad St) has bicycles for hire at £8 a day.

Things to See & Do
The **cathedral** was built in stages from 1180 to 1508 and incorporates several styles. The most famous features are the extraordinary west facade, an immense sculpture gallery with over 300 surviving figures; the interior scissor arches, a brilliant solution to the problem posed by the subsidence of the central tower; the delicate chapter house; and the ancient mechanical clock in the north transept. Try and join one of the free tours.

Beyond the cathedral is the moated **Bishop's Palace**, with its beautiful gardens (open Tuesday, Thursday and Sunday summer afternoons only; daily in August; £3), Market Place (markets Wednesday and Saturday) and the 14th-century Vicars' Close.

Places to Stay & Eat
The nearest YHA hostel is at Street near Glastonbury, but there are plenty of B&Bs with prices around £15.

Opposite St Cuthbert's church is *19 St Cuthbert St* (☎ 673166) with rooms from £16.50 per person. The *Old Poor House* (☎ 675052) is a comfortable 14th-century cottage just outside the cathedral precincts, with singles for £25 for the first night. The B&B at *9 Chamberlain St* (☎ 672270) is very central and charges £22/38 for singles/doubles.

The *City Arms* (☎ 673916, 69 High St) used to be the city jail but now serves good pub grub with main dishes from around £5. Near the bus station the *Good Earth Restaurant* produces excellent home-made pizzas and puddings.

Getting There & Away
Badgerline operates hourly buses from Bath and Bristol (1¼ hours). No 376 from Bristol continues through Wells to Glastonbury and Street. No 163 runs from Wells to Bridgwater (for connections to Exmoor) via Glastonbury and Street.

GLASTONBURY
☎ 01458 • pop 7000
Legend and history combine at Glastonbury to produce an irresistible attraction for romantics and eccentrics of every description. It's a small market town with the ruins of a 14th-century **abbey**, and a nearby **tor** with superb views.

According to various legends, Jesus travelled here with Joseph of Arimathea and the chalice from the Last Supper, it is the burial place of King Arthur and Queen Guinevere, and the tor is either the Isle of Avalon or a gateway to the underworld. Whatever you choose to believe, a climb to the top of the tor is well worthwhile. Turn right at the top of High St (the far end from the TIC) onto Chilkwell St and then left onto Dod Lane; there's a footpath to the tor from the end of the lane.

The Glastonbury Festival, a three-day festival of theatre, music, circus, mime, natural healing etc, is a massive affair with over 1000 acts. It takes place in late June at Pilton, 8 miles from Glastonbury; admission is by advance ticket only (around £90 for the whole festival). Phone ☎ 832020 for details.

The TIC (☎ 832954) can supply maps and accommodation information; there are plenty of B&Bs for around £15. At the *Glastonbury Backpackers Hostel* (☎ 833353, *Crown Hotel, 4 Market Place*) dorm beds are £10. Another possibility is *Street Youth Hostel* (☎ 442961), 4 miles south.

There are Badgerline buses from Bristol to Wells, Glastonbury and Street. Glastonbury is only 6 miles from Wells, so walking or hitching is feasible. Bus No 163 from Wells continues to Bridgwater, from where there are buses to Minehead (for Exmoor).

BRISTOL
☎ 0117 • pop 415,000

Bristol is by far and away the region's largest and coolest city, home to Massive Attack and Tricky. Approaching through the unlovely southern suburbs, you might wonder what the hell you're getting into, but the centre has some magnificent architecture, docks and warehouses that are being rescued from ruin, and a plethora of bars, pubs and restaurants.

Unlike its glamorous neighbour, the tourist honeypot of Bath, Bristol remains very much a working city where tourism is almost incidental. Consequently, many folk may prefer it. Bristol is most famous as a port, although it is 6 miles from the Severn estuary, and it grew rich on the 17th-century trade with the North American colonies and the West Indies (rum, slaves, sugar and tobacco).

It continues to prosper today (although it has had to switch some commodities) and it's an important transport hub, with connections north to the Cotswolds and the Midland cities, west to southern Wales, south-west to Devon and Cornwall, and south-east to Bath (an easy day trip).

Orientation & Information
The city centre lies north of the Floating Harbour – a system of locks, canals and docks fed by the tidal River Avon. The central area is compact and easy to get around on foot, if rather hilly.

The main train station is Bristol Temple Meads, about 1 mile to the south-east of the centre, although some trains use Bristol Parkway 5 miles to the north, which is accessible from the centre by bus and train. There are also some suburban train stations. The bus and coach station is to the north of the city centre.

Open daily, the TIC (☎ 926 0767) is impressively located in St Nicholas Church, St Nicholas St, with the magnificent 18th-century altarpiece by William Hogarth still in place.

Things to See & Do
The first thing on a visitor's agenda should be a wander around the twisting streets of the old city centre, followed by a ferry trip on the Floating Harbour (see Getting Around later in this section).

From the TIC, start by exploring **St Nicholas Market**, then continue westwards to medieval **St John's Church** and across busy Rupert St to the **Christmas Steps**. Walk south to College Green, flanked by the impressive council offices and imposing **Bristol Cathedral**.

Up the hill (Park St) there are numerous restaurants, the university and, 1½ miles beyond, the genteel suburb of Clifton, which is dominated by fine Georgian architecture. The spectacular **Clifton Suspension Bridge**, designed by Brunel to cross the equally spectacular Avon Gorge, is also here.

Back in the centre, you could visit the **Arnolfini Centre**, an important contemporary arts complex, or the **Watershed**, on opposite sides of St Augustine's Reach. Then walk down King St, with its old buildings, now used as restaurants and clubs, and the Llandoger Trow, a 17th-century pub reputed to be the Admiral Benbow in Robert Louis Stevenson's *Treasure Island*.

There are numerous other important sights: the beautiful **Church of St Mary Redcliffe**; the **Maritime Heritage Centre** (free) with Brunel's **SS *Great Britain*** (£6.25), the first ocean-going iron ship with a screw propeller; and the free **Industrial Museum**.

Places to Stay

Bristol Youth Hostel (☎ 922 1659, 14 Narrow Quay St) is an excellent place to stay. It occupies a converted warehouse five minutes from the centre of town. The dorms are small, mostly four-bed (£11.90), and most have shower rooms attached. *Bristol Backpackers* (☎ 925 7900, 17 St Stephen's St) is a new, central place in a charming house with beds for £12.50.

During holidays, the university lets out rooms at well located *The Hawthorns* (☎ 954 5900, Woodland Rd, Clifton) from £25/38 a single/double, including breakfast.

Most of the cheap B&Bs tend to be a fair distance from the centre, although there is a good town bus service. There are a number of places on Bath Rd (the A4) and Wells Rd (the A37).

Clifton, 1½ miles from the centre, is a very attractive suburb but most of the B&Bs here cost £25 per person. On Oakfield Rd (off Whiteladies Rd), the *Oakfield Hotel* (☎ 973 5556) has singles/doubles for £28.50/38.50.

Places to Eat

Bristol is well endowed with restaurants, and most are reasonably priced.

The cafes in the *Watershed* and *Arnolfini* art centres on either side of the Floating Harbour have some delicious dishes for under £5. Up the steep hill that is Park St the *Boston Tea Party* is an excellent place for a sandwich. *Arc* on Broad St is a trendy little cafe with tasty soups, bargain pizzas and Thai curries.

Recently the grand old bank buildings along Corn St have been given new life as pubs, cafe/bars and restaurants, including *All Bar One* and *San Carlo*. However, for something a whole lot more sophisticated try *Riverstation* or *severshed*, both designer restaurants on the dockside, but with prices that won't leave you gasping. Nearby *Aqua* has a mouth-watering menu, and *Belgo* provides the mussels to take on its Belgian beers.

Across the road from the TIC, *Las Iguanas* (☎ 927 6233, 10 St Nicholas St) does Mexican and South American dishes. Park St has several pizza places, but the best – if not necessarily the cheapest – is *Pizza Express* (☎ 926 0300, 31 Berkeley Square) near the University.

Entertainment

There's plenty going on at night, ranging from high culture to low. Get a copy of *Venue* (£1.90), the Bristol and Bath answer to *Time Out*.

There are several entertainment options on King St, ranging from the *Old Duke* (great jazz) to the *New Vic* (theatre) – check *Renato's Taverna dell Artista* next door for a spot of late night drinking. On St Nicholas St, there's often live music at *Las Iguanas* (see the preceding Places to Eat section) and at *St Nicholas House* on weekends. The *Queenshilling* on Unity St is Bristol's most popular gay bar.

Clubs come in and out, but those that seem to be in at the moment include *Lakota* on Upper York St, the *Silent Peach* on Unity St and *Thekla* at the Grove.

The legendary *Bierkeller* (☎ 926 8514), All Saints St, which has played host to luminaries like the Stone Roses and the Stranglers, is a good bet. Entry usually costs around £8, depending on the night of the week and who's playing.

Getting There & Away

Bus Bristol has excellent bus connections. There are hourly National Express (☎ 0870-580 8080) buses to London's Victoria coach station (2½ hours) and Heathrow and Gatwick airports, but Bakers Dolphin (☎ 961 4000) usually sells the cheapest tickets – £10/18 for a single/return.

National Express has frequent buses to Cardiff (1¼ hours). There are a couple of buses a day to Barnstaple (2¾ hours) and regular buses to Exeter (1¾ hours), Oxford (2½ hours) and Stratford-upon-Avon (2½ hours).

Badgerline has numerous services a day to and from Bath. There are also services to Salisbury and north to Gloucester. A Day Rambler ticket is £5.30. For city-wide information, phone ☎ 955 5111.

Train Bristol is an important rail hub, with regular connections to London's Paddington station (1½ hours). Most trains (except those to the south) use both Temple Meads and Parkway stations. Bath is only 20 minutes away by rail, so it makes an easy day trip. There are frequent links to Cardiff (45 minutes), Exeter (one hour), Fishguard (3½ hours), Oxford (1½ hours) and Birmingham

(1½ hours). Phone ☎ 0845-748 4950 for timetable information.

Getting Around

The nicest way to get around is on the ferry which, from April to September, plies the Floating Harbour. There are a number of stops including Bristol Bridge, the Industrial Museum, the SS *Great Britain* and Hotwells. The ferry (☎ 927 3416) runs every 20 minutes; a single fare is £1, a round trip £3.

There's a taxi rank in the city centre opposite the Hippodrome Theatre, but it's not a good idea to hang around here late at night. To call a cab free, ring 1A Premier Cabs on ☎ 0800-716777.

There's a good local bus system – phone ☎ 955 5111 for details. The suspension bridge is quite a walk from the centre of town so catch bus No 8 or 9 (Nos 508 and 509 on weekends) from bus stop 'Cu' on Colston Ave, or from Temple Meads station.

Central England

The heart of England covers a vast swathe of land that includes some of the highs and lows of England. Many of the areas around the M1 corridor can look pretty miserable on a wet and windy day, but some of the region's liveliest cities are here such as Nottingham, Leicester, Coventry and Birmingham. What it lacks in prettiness, it makes up for in personality, and there is a real feel to the East Midlands that isn't always found in the tourist meccas of the Cotswolds and the Peaks.

To the west, however, it's a different story. Oxford remains a very beautiful city that is a must for any visitor. The south-west sections of the Chilterns remain largely unspoilt and are accessible to walkers of the Ridgeway.

The Cotswolds, more than any other region, embody the popular image of English countryside. The prettiness can be forced, and the villages are certainly not strangers to mass tourism, but there are also moments when you will be transfixed by the beauty of the landscape. The combination of golden stone, flower-draped cottages, church spires, towering chestnuts and oaks, rolling hills and green, stone-walled fields can be too extraordinarily picturesque to seem quite real.

West again, you reach the Bristol Channel and the wide Severn Valley, a natural border to the counties of Herefordshire and Worcestershire and the region known as the Welsh Marches. Herefordshire and Worcestershire have rich agricultural countryside with orchards and market gardens. The Wye Valley is a famous spot of beauty, popularised by the first Romantic poets in the 18th century.

To the north, Shrewsbury is an attractive town that's well worth a visit, and the Peak District National Park is one of England's most beautiful regions.

Some of Britain's most popular tourist sites are in the southern part of the Midlands, among them Blenheim Palace, Warwick Castle, Stratford-upon-Avon and Oxford.

Orientation & Information

The southern section of this region is cut by two ranges of hills and two major rivers. From east to west, you first meet the chalk ridge of the Chilterns which runs north-east from Salisbury Plain to Hertfordshire, then come the Thames Valley, the limestone Cotswolds which run north from Bath, and finally the Severn Valley. The Peak District National Park lies in the far north of the Midlands.

Major northbound transport arteries (including the M1 and M40) cross the region, so it's highly likely you'll pass through it at some stage.

Hiking

The best hiking in the southern section of the Midlands is in the Cotswolds, although there are a number of other interesting paths in the region.

The Cotswolds Way, with easy accessibility to accommodation, is the best way to discover the Cotswolds. The path follows the western escarpment overlooking the Bristol Channel for 100 miles from Chipping Campden to Bath, but it is quite feasible to tackle a smaller section. Bath is obviously easily accessible, but you'll have to contact the Gloucestershire inquiry line (☎ 01452-425543) for information about the infrequent buses that run between Chipping Campden and Stratford or Moreton-in-Marsh.

Ordnance Survey/Aurum Press publishes a comprehensive guide to *The Cotswold Way*

(£10.99) by Anthony Burton, complete with maps and walking details.

The main walking area in the north of this region is the stunning Peak District National Park.

Getting Around

Bus transport around the region is fairly efficient, and particularly good in the Peak District.

There's also a good network of railway lines; you'll rarely need to resort to buses other than for financial reasons. See Shrewsbury later in this chapter for details on an interesting rail loop around northern Wales.

OXFORD

☎ 01865 • pop 115,000

It's impossible to pick up any tourist literature about Oxford without reading about its dreaming spires. Like all great clichés it's strikingly apt. Looking across the meadows or rooftops or Oxford's golden spires is certainly an experience to inspire purple prose.

These days, however, Oxford battles against a flood of tourists that can dilute the charm during summer. It is not just a university city, but the home of Morris cars (the plant is now owned by BMW), and it expanded rapidly in the 20th century. This has created a city with a bustling heart surrounded by sprawling industrial suburbs.

Oxford University is the oldest university in Britain, but no one can find an exact starting date. It evolved during the 11th century as an informal centre for scholars and students. The colleges began to appear from the mid-13th century onwards. There are now about 14,500 undergraduates and 36 colleges.

Orientation & Information

The city centre is surrounded by rivers and streams on the eastern, southern and western sides, and can easily be covered on foot. Carfax Tower at the intersection of Queen St and Cornmarket St/St Aldate's is a useful central marker. The tower is all that remains of St Martin's Church. There's a fine view from the top, which is good for orienting yourself. It's open daily and admission costs £1.20.

The train station is to the west of the city, with frequent buses to Carfax Tower. Alter-natively, turn left off the station concourse onto Park End St and it's a 15-minute walk.

The bus station is nearer the centre, on Gloucester Green (there's no green).

A visit to the hectic TIC (☎ 726871), also on Gloucester Green, is essential. It's open 9.30 am to 5 pm Monday to Saturday, and 10 am to 3.30 pm Sunday during summer. A hefty £2.75 charge (plus 10% deposit) is made for local B&B bookings.

You need more information than this guide can give if you're going to do the town justice. The *Welcome to Oxford* brochure (£1) has a walking tour with college opening times. The TIC has daily two-hour walking tours of the colleges (£4.50/2.50). Guide Friday (☎ 790522) runs a hop-on, hop-off city bus tour every 15 minutes from 9.30 am to 7 pm in summer. It leaves from the train station and tickets cost £8.50/2.50.

Things to See & Do

Colleges You need more than a day to 'do' Oxford, but, at a minimum, make sure you visit Christ Church (with Oxford Cathedral), Merton and Magdalen (pronounced maudlen) colleges and the Ashmolean Museum. The colleges remain open throughout the year (unlike Cambridge) but their hours vary; many are closed in the morning. Some never admit visitors.

Starting at the Carfax Tower, cross Cornmarket St and walk down the hill, along St Aldate's, to **Christ Church**, perhaps the most famous college in Oxford. The main entrance is beneath Tom Tower, which was built by Christopher Wren in 1680, but the usual visitors entrance is farther down the hill via the wrought-iron gates of the War Memorial Gardens and the Broad Walk facing out over Christ Church Meadow. There's a £3 admission charge. The college chapel is the smallest cathedral in England, but it is a beautiful example of late Norman (1140-80) architecture.

Return to the Broad Walk, follow the stone wall, then turn left up Merton Grove, through wrought-iron gates, then right onto Merton St. **Merton College** was founded in 1264 and its buildings are among the oldest in Oxford. The present buildings mostly date from the 15th to the 17th centuries. The entrance to the 14th-century Mob Quad, with its medieval library, is on your right.

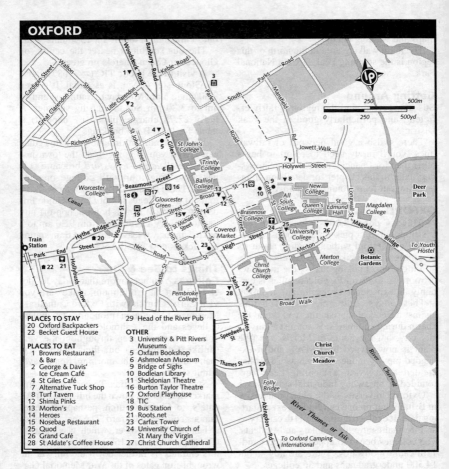

OXFORD

PLACES TO STAY
20 Oxford Backpackers
22 Becket Guest House

PLACES TO EAT
1 Browns Restaurant
   & Bar
2 George & Davis'
   Ice Cream Café
4 St Giles Café
7 Alternative Tuck Shop
8 Turf Tavern
12 Shimla Pinks
13 Morton's
14 Heroes
15 Nosebag Restaurant
25 Quod
26 Grand Café
28 St Aldate's Coffee House

29 Head of the River Pub

OTHER
3 University & Pitt Rivers
   Museums
5 Oxfam Bookshop
6 Ashmolean Museum
9 Bridge of Sighs
10 Bodleian Library
11 Sheldonian Theatre
16 Burton Taylor Theatre
17 Oxford Playhouse
18 TIC
19 Bus Station
21 Roots.net
23 Carfax Tower
24 University Church of
   St Mary the Virgin
27 Christ Church Cathedral

Turn left onto Merton St, then take the first right onto Magpie Lane, which will take you through to High St with its fascinating mix of architectural styles. Turn right down the hill until you come to **Magdalen** just before the river on your left. Magdalen is one of the richest Oxford colleges and has the most extensive and beautiful grounds, with a deer park, river walk, three quadrangles and superb lawns. This was CS Lewis' college and the setting for the film *Shadowlands*.

Walk back up High St until you come to the **University Church of St Mary the Virgin** on your right (there's a good view from

the tower), turn right up Cattle St to the distinctive, circular **Radcliffe Camera**, a reading room for the **Bodleian Library**. Continue up Cattle St passing the **Bridge of Sighs** on your right, then turn left onto Broad St. On your left you pass Wren's **Sheldonian Theatre**, and on your right **Trinity** and **Balliol** colleges. Turn left at Cornmarket St and you'll be back where you started.

Museums Established in 1683, the **Ashmolean** in Beaumont St is the country's oldest museum and houses extensive displays of European art (including works by Raphael and Michelangelo) and Middle Eastern antiquities. It's open 10 am to 5 pm Tuesday to Saturday, 2 to 5 pm Sunday, and Bank Holiday Mondays; £3 donation.

Housed in a superb Victorian Gothic building on Parks Rd, the **University Museum** is devoted to natural science. You reach the **Pitt Rivers Museum** through the University Museum. The glass cases here are crammed to overflowing with everything from a sailing boat to a gory collection of shrunken South American heads. Entry to the University Museum is free and a £3 donation is accepted at Pitt Rivers. Both museums are open Monday to Saturday, the University from noon to 5 pm, Pitt Rivers from 1 to 4.30 pm.

Punts From Easter to September, punts and boats can be hired at Folly Bridge and Magdalen Bridge (£9 per hour, £25 deposit). There's no better way of letting the atmosphere of Oxford seep in. The seepage can be dramatic – punting is not as easy as it looks. From Magdalen Bridge, go left for peace and quiet, and right for views back to the colleges across the Botanic Gardens and Christ Church Meadow.

Places to Stay

The most convenient hostel is *Oxford Backpackers* (☎ 721761, 9A Hythe Bridge St), less than five minutes walk from the train station. Beds in dorms cost £11 each. Although *Oxford Youth Hostel* (☎ 62997, 32 Jack Straw's Lane) is not centrally located, it does get booked up very quickly in summer. Beds cost £10.85. Bus Nos 13, 14 and 14A run from outside the St Aldate's post office to the hostel.

Oxford Camping International (☎ 246551, 426 Abingdon Rd) is conveniently located by the Park & Ride car park roughly 3 miles south of the centre. Charges are £5.30 for a tent and £4.30 per person.

B&Bs are expensive and suburban, the two main areas being Abingdon Rd and Cowley/Iffley Rds both on regular bus routes. You're looking at £18 per person, rising to over £20 in peak season.

Athena Guest House (☎ 243124, 253 Cowley Rd) is within walking distance of shops and restaurants and provides singles/doubles for £20/40. A bit farther out, *Earl-mont* (☎ 240236) at No 322 is a large and comfortable B&B with rooms for £30/50.

Sportsview Guest House (☎ 244268, 106 Abingdon Rd) is a two-star guesthouse for nonsmokers, with rooms from £30/52. *Becket Guest House* (☎ 724675, 5 Becket St) is convenient to the train station, with singles/doubles from £30/45.

Places to Eat

There are some excellent sandwich bars throughout the centre and many a student debate has centred on which is best. *Morton's*, on Broad St, can't be faulted for its tasty baguettes and attractive garden; nearby *Heroes* builds to order with a fine selection of fillings; and *St Aldate's Coffee House* is a favourite with students.

Pubs are also a good bet. There's excellent pub grub at *Turf Tavern*, Bath Place, a recommended watering hole hidden away down an alley. *Head of the River*, ideally situated by Folly Bridge, is very popular.

Self-caterers should visit the *covered market*, on the northern side of High St near Carfax Tower, for fruit and vegetables. *Alternative Tuck Shop*, Holywell St, is the place to go for filled rolls and sandwiches at lunchtime.

Nosebag Restaurant (☎ 721033, St Michael's St), has filling soups and a good range of vegetarian choices. *George & Davis' Ice Cream Café*, Little Clarendon St, serves light meals as well as delicious homemade ice cream. It's open until midnight. At *Convocation Coffee House*, attached to St Mary the Virgin church, soup and a roll is cheap.

A popular place for snacky meals is *St Giles Café* on St Giles with good greasy spoon fare. *Browns Restaurant & Bar* (☎ 511995, 5 Woodstock Rd) is a popular, stylish brasserie. Main dishes here are around £7.

The Grand Café on the High St is just that with divine salads and sandwiches for around £5. *Shimla Pinks* (16 Turl St) is an excellent Indian restaurant with lunchtime buffets for about £6. *Quod* is a classy new Italian restaurant on the High St and worth a splash.

Entertainment

Roots.net is a bar and club with a good range of world music, while *Po Na Na* is a late night bar then club.

BRITAIN

Oxford Playhouse (☎ 798600, *Beaumont St*) has a mixed bag of theatre, dance and music. *Burton Taylor Theatre* (☎ 798600, *Gloucester St*) has more offbeat productions.

Getting There & Away

Bus Oxford is easily and quickly reached from London, and there are a number of competitive bus lines on the route. The Oxford Tube (☎ 772250) starts at London's Victoria coach station but also stops at Marble Arch, Notting Hill Gate and Shepherd's Bush; a return ticket valid for two days costs £7.50. The journey takes around 1½ hours and the service operates 24 hours a day.

National Express (☎ 0870-580 8080) has numerous buses to London and Heathrow airport. There are two or three services a day to and from Bath (£9.75, two hours) and Bristol (£12.75, 2¼ hours), and two services to and from Gloucester (£8, 1½ hours) and Cheltenham (£7.75, one hour). From Bristol there are connections to Wales, Devon and Cornwall. Buses to Shrewsbury, North Wales, York and Durham go via Birmingham.

Oxford Citylink (☎ 711312) is another major operator, with frequent departures to London, Heathrow, Gatwick, Birmingham and Stratford. Stagecoach (☎ 772250) runs six buses a day to Cambridge.

Train There are very frequent trains from London's Paddington station (£13 single, 1½ hours). Network SouthEast cards apply.

There are regular trains north to Coventry and Birmingham, and north-west to Worcester and Hereford (for Moreton-in-Marsh, Gloucester and Cheltenham in the Cotswolds). Birmingham is the main hub for transport farther north.

To connect with trains to the south-west you have to change at Didcot Parkway (15 minutes). There are plenty of connections to Bath; with a bit of luck the whole trip won't take longer than 1½ hours. Change at Swindon for another line running into the Cotswolds (Kemble, Stroud and Gloucester). For train inquiries, phone ☎ 0845-748 4950.

Getting Around

Local buses and minibuses leave from the streets around Carfax Tower. For information on Stagecoach services phone ☎ 772250.

There are a number of places where you can hire bicycles – Warlands (☎ 241336, Botley Rd), near the station, rents bikes for £18 a day or £15 a week. In the centre, Bike Zone (☎ 728877, 6 Broad St) charges £10 a day or £20 a week.

Boat trips and punts are available at Folly Bridge and Magdalen Bridge. Salter Bros (☎ 243421) offers several interesting boat trips from Folly Bridge between May and September.

BLENHEIM PALACE

Blenheim Palace (☎ 01993-811325), one of the largest palaces in Europe, was a gift to John Churchill from Queen Anne and Parliament as a reward for his role in defeating Louis XIV. Curiously, the palace was the birthplace of Winston Churchill, who perhaps more than any other individual was responsible for checking Hitler.

Designed and built by Vanbrugh and Hawksmoor between 1704 and 1722 with gardens by Capability Brown, Blenheim is an enormous baroque fantasy, and is definitely worth visiting. The house is open 10.30 am to 5.30 pm from mid-March through October, and costs £9, or £6.50 with a student card; the park is open from 9 am daily, all year.

Blenheim is just south of the village of Woodstock. Catch a Thames Transit Minibus No 20A from Gloucester Green in Oxford to the palace's entrance.

STRATFORD-UPON-AVON
☎ 01789 • pop 22,000

Stratford is a pleasant Midlands market town that just happened to be William Shakespeare's birthplace. Due to shrewd management of the cult of Bill, it's now one of England's busiest tourist attractions. Fans can visit several buildings associated with his life, including Shakespeare's Birthplace, New Place, Nash's House, Hall's Croft, Anne Hathaway's Cottage and Mary Arden's House. A passport ticket to all the Shakespearian properties costs £12.

As it's just beyond the northern edge of the Cotswolds, Stratford makes a handy stopover en route to and from the north. The Royal Shakespeare Company has three theatres here, in addition to its London venues, and there's nearly always something on. Warwick, with its wonderful castle, is just to the north.

Orientation & Information

Stratford is easy to explore on foot. The main street changes names several times as it extends from the river to the train station.

The TIC (☎ 293127), Bridgefoot, has plenty of information about the numerous B&Bs. Seeing a production by the Royal Shakespeare Company (☎ 295623) is definitely worthwhile. Tickets are often available on the day of performance, but get in early; the box office opens at 9.30 am. Standby tickets are available to students immediately before performances (£13 or £16.50) and there are almost always standing room tickets (£5).

Places to Stay & Eat

Bad news for the YHA, *Backpackers Hostel* (☎ 263838, 33 Greenhill St) has centrally located beds for £11. It is on the road between the train station and the town centre. The *Youth Hostel* (☎ 297093, Hemmingford House, Alveston)* is 2.5km out of town – from the TIC, cross Clopton Bridge and follow the B4086, or take bus No 18 from Wood St near the TIC. Bed and breakfast costs £14.90.

Prices for B&Bs can lurch skywards in summer, but there are plenty of places at around £24 on Evesham Place, Grove Rd and Broad Walk, just west of the centre. Try the cheerful *Grosvenor Villa* (☎ 266192, 9 Evesham Place), the *Dylan* (☎ 204819) at No 10, or the good-value *Clomendy* (☎ 266957) at No 157. Alcester Rd, by the train station, also has several options.

Sheep St has a fine selection of dining possibilities, or try the stylish *Edward Moon's (9 Chapel St)*, where you'll pay around £8.50 for a meal. The *Dirty Duck* on Waterside is good for an ale.

Getting There & Away

National Express (☎ 0870-580 8080) buses link Birmingham, Stratford, Warwick, Oxford, Heathrow and London.

Phone ☎ 01788-535555 for local bus information. The X20 operates regularly to Birmingham (£3.05, one hour), the X16 to Warwick (£2.10, 20 minutes) and Coventry (£2.75, 1¼ hours), and the X50 to Oxford (£4.25, 1½ hours).

Direct train services to and from London's Paddington station cost £20. There are trains to Warwick (£2.50) and Birmingham (£3.50). For further information phone ☎ 0845-748 4950.

COTSWOLDS

The Cotswolds are a range of beautiful limestone hills rising gently from the Thames and its tributaries in the east but forming a steep escarpment overlooking the Bristol Channel in the west. The hills are characterised by honey-coloured stone villages and a gently rolling landscape. The villages were built on the wealth of the medieval wool trade.

Many of the villages are extremely popular with tourists; it's difficult to escape commercialism unless you have your own transport or are walking. The best advice is to take your time and wander off the beaten track in search of your own ideal Cotswold village.

Orientation & Information

The hills run north from Bath for 100 miles to Chipping Campden. The most attractive countryside is bounded in the west by the M5 and Chipping Sodbury, and in the east by Stow-on-the-Wold, Burford, Bibury, Cirencester and Chippenham.

There are train stations at Cheltenham, Kemble (serving Cirencester), Moreton-in-Marsh (serving Stow-on-the-Wold) and Stroud.

Bath, Cheltenham, Stratford-upon-Avon and Oxford are the best starting points for the Cotswolds. Cirencester likes to think of itself as the region's capital.

The TICs in surrounding towns all stock information on the Cotswolds, but the TICs dealing specifically with the region are at Market Place, Cirencester (☎ 01285-654180), and The Square, Stow-on-the-Wold (☎ 01451-831082).

Stow-on-the-Wold
☎ 01451 • pop 2000

Stow, as it is known, is one of the most impressive (and visited) towns in the Cotswolds. It's a terrific base if you don't have a vehicle, because several particularly beautiful villages, including the famous Upper and Lower Slaughters, are within a day's walk or cycle ride.

The *Youth Hostel* (☎ 830497), in a 16th-century building, is open Monday to Saturday from March through September and also on Sunday from April through August.

Stow can be reached by bus from Moreton-in-Marsh, which is on the main Cotswolds line between Worcester and Oxford. Regular buses leave from the town hall, a five-minute walk from the station. Contact Pulhams' Coaches (☎ 820369) for a timetable.

Cheltenham
☎ 01242 • pop 88,000
Cheltenham is a large and elegant spa town easily accessible by bus and train. The TIC (☎ 522878) is helpful. Cheltenham is on the main Bristol to Birmingham train line, and can be reached easily by train from South Wales, Bath and South-West England, and Oxford (changing at Didcot and Swindon).

Places to Stay
The Cotswolds area is not particularly well served by YHA hostels, but there are countless B&Bs. There are hostels at Slimbridge and Charlbury, but the most central and most interesting are at Stow-on-the-Wold (see the earlier Stow-on-the-Wold section) and Duntisbourne Abbots (no public transport here).

Getting Around
Getting around the Cotswolds by public transport isn't easy. If you're trying anything ambitious, contact the Gloucestershire inquiry line (☎ 01452-425543). Bikes can be hired in Bath, Oxford and Cheltenham. Compass Holidays (☎ 250642) has bicycles for hire for £11 per day at Cheltenham station.

BIRMINGHAM
☎ 0121 • pop 1.01 million
Birmingham is Britain's second largest city, culturally vibrant, socially dynamic but aesthetically challenged. Traditionally it's been thought of as a rather dreary city with no essential sights and not particularly accessible to the short-term visitor. Recently, however, things have looked up, with the restoration of the old canal network and the opening of innumerable restaurants and bars in the Brindleyplace area. The **Museum & Art Gallery** has a fine collection of Pre-Raphaelite paintings and overlooks **Victoria** and **Chamberlain Squares**, both of them full of interesting statuary. The old **Jewellery Quarter**, where, surprise, surprise, jewellery was made, is also

looking much smarter and houses a couple of interesting small museums.

It's unlikely that you'll want to stay long in Birmingham even now, and a dearth of cheap accommodation in the city centre hardly helps (there's no hostel). However, New St Station and Digbeth St Coach station are both major transport hubs. If you're passing through it might be worth stepping out to explore for a few hours. Try a balti restaurant for the Midlands' own version of Indian cooking.

The TIC (☎ 693 6300) on Victoria Square is open daily.

ALTHORP
With the late Diana, Princess of Wales, continuing to attract the public's attention from beyond the grave, the memorial and museum in the grounds of her ancestral home, Althorp Park, off the A428 north-west of Northampton, remain popular tourist attractions. But the park is only open in July and August and tickets cost a hefty £10/5 (profits go to her Memorial Fund). The limited number of tickets must be booked in advance (☎ 01604-592020), although availability should improve as public interest wanes. Incidentally, Althorp should be pronounced altrup!

SHREWSBURY
☎ 01743 • pop 60,000
Shrewsbury is the attractive regional capital of Shropshire, and is famous for its black-and-white, half-timbered buildings. Because there are no vitally important sights, Shrewsbury has been saved from inundation by tourists but it makes a good base for visiting Ironbridge, Stokesay Castle, Shropshire's wonderful walking country, and even Wales. Two famous small railways into Wales terminate here and it's possible to do a fascinating circuit of North Wales.

Orientation & Information
The station lies across the narrow land bridge formed by the loop of the Severn, a five-minute walk north of the centre of town. The bus station is central and the whole town is well signposted.

The TIC (☎ 350761) in The Square shares its premises with a cinema and cafe. There are daily walking tours of the town (£2/1) at 2.30 pm from May to October.

Things to See & Do

Strategically sited within a loop of the River Severn, the city provides the setting for the *Brother Cadfael Chronicles*. In case you've never heard of him, Brother Cadfael is a fictional medieval sleuth, the subject of the books by the late Ellis Peters. Across the street from the abbey, the **Shrewsbury Quest** (☎ 243324) plays on this theme with clues to find among the displays on 12th-century monastery life. Shrewsbury also boasts **medieval streets** (including Butcher's Row and Fish St), **Quarry Park** (with a famous flower show in August) and river walks.

Places to Stay & Eat

Shrewsbury Youth Hostel (☎ 360179), Abbey Foregate, is 1 mile from the train and bus stations, 10 minutes after crossing English Bridge. Walk down High St, cross the bridge and veer right when Abbey Foregate splits in two around the abbey. There are numerous cheap B&Bs in this area. *Prynce's Villa Guest House (☎ 356217, 15 Monkmoor Rd)* has B&B accommodation from £16 per person.

Dating from 1460, quaint *Tudor House (☎ 351735, 2 Fish St)* is centrally located on a quiet medieval street. Beds cost from around £21 per person.

Owen's Café-Bar (☎ 363633) on Butcher's Row has a wide range of wines and beers, and interesting dishes like mixed tapas for £5. *Good Life Wholefood Restaurant (☎ 350455)*, Barracks Passage, is a fantastic place for lunch with huge portions of righteous food, all at absurdly reasonable prices. *Peach Tree (21 Abbey Foregate)* is a great, if expensive, restaurant and bar.

Getting There & Away

Bus National Express (☎ 0870-580 8080) has three buses a day to and from London (five hours) via Telford and Birmingham. Change at Birmingham for both Oxford and Stratford-upon-Avon.

For information on transport in Shropshire, contact the county help line (☎ 0845-705 6785). Bus No X5 (☎ 01952-200005) runs between Shrewsbury and Telford via Ironbridge regularly. Bus No 420 connects Shrewsbury with Birmingham twice daily. Arriva (☎ 01453-466123) has regular buses to and from Ludlow (service No 435).

Train Two fascinating small railways terminate at Shrewsbury, in addition to plenty of main-line connections. It's possible to do a brilliant, highly recommended rail loop from Shrewsbury around North Wales. Timetabling is a challenge so phone ☎ 01743-364041 for information. The journey is possible in a day as long as you don't miss any of the connections, but it's much better to allow at least a couple of days as there are plenty of interesting places to visit along the way. The North & Mid-Wales Flexi Rover ticket is the most economical way of covering this route. It costs £26.30/17.35 and allows travel on three days out of seven.

From Shrewsbury you head due west across Wales to Dovey Junction (1¾ hours), where you connect with the famous Cambrian Coast Line, which hugs the beautiful coast on its way north to Porthmadog (1½ hours).

At Porthmadog you can pick up the Ffestiniog Railway, a restored narrow-gauge steam train that winds up into Snowdonia National Park to the slate-mining town of Blaenau Ffestiniog (1¼ hours). From Blaenau another small railway carves its way through the mountains and down the beautiful, tourist-infested Conwy Valley to Llandudno (1¼ hours) and Conwy. From there it's a short trip to Chester.

Another famous line, promoted as the Heart of Wales Line, runs south-west to Swansea (four hours), connecting with the main line from Cardiff to Fishguard (six hours).

There are numerous trains to and from London's Euston station (£17 Apex, three hours), and regular links to Chester (£5.80, one hour). There are also regular trains from Cardiff to Manchester via Bristol, Ludlow and Shrewsbury.

AROUND SHREWSBURY
Ironbridge Gorge
☎ 01952

The Silicon Valley of the 1700s, Ironbridge, on the southern edge of Telford, is a monument to the Industrial Revolution. This World Heritage site was the wonder of its age, developing iron smelting on a scale never seen before – easy transport on the Severn and rich deposits of iron and coal in the gorge itself made it all possible.

Ironbridge Gorge Museum (☎ 433522) is open daily and comprises seven main museums and several smaller sites strung along the gorge. There's Blists Hill Open Air Museum, which recreates an entire community, including shops, houses, forges and pub; the Coalport China Museum with more than you ever wanted to know about porcelain; the beautiful first iron bridge; the Museum of Iron; and the Museum of the River and Visitor Centre (the best starting point). A passport ticket allowing entrance to all the museums is £10/6 for adults/students.

Ironbridge Gorge has two **Youth Hostels**, one in Coalbrookdale, near the Museum of Iron, the other in Coalport, near the China Museum (☎ 588755 for both). They're open daily from February through October and beds cost £10.85.

Regular trains and buses run to Telford from Shrewsbury and some go on to the gorge. Otherwise, there are regular buses from Telford's town centre. You'll need a car or a bike to get around the sites – it's 3 miles from Blists Hill to the Museum of Iron.

PEAK DISTRICT

Squeezed between the industrial Midlands to the south, Manchester to the west and Sheffield to the east, the Peak District seems an unlikely site for one of England's most beautiful regions. Even the name is misleading being derived from the tribes who once lived here, not from the existence of any significant peaks (there are none!). Nonetheless, the 542 sq mile Peak District National Park is a delight, particularly for walkers and cyclists.

The Peak District divides into the green fields and steep-sided dales of the southern White Peak and the bleak, gloomy moors of the northern Dark Peak. Buxton, to the west, and Matlock, to the east, are good bases for exploring the park, or you can stay right in the centre at Bakewell or Castleton. In May and June the ancient custom of 'well dressing' can be seen at many villages. There are also prehistoric sites, limestone caves, the tragic plague village of Eyam and the fine stately homes of Chatsworth and Haddon Hall.

Castleton and nearby Edale are popular villages on the border between the White and Dark Peaks. From Edale, the Pennine Way starts its 250-mile meander northwards. From the town of Castleton, the 25-mile Limestone Way is a superb day walk covering the length

of the White Peak to Matlock. In addition, a number of disused railway lines in the White Peak have been redeveloped as walking and cycling routes, with strategically situated bicycle-rental outlets at old station sites.

There are information centres at Edale (☎ 01433-670207), Castleton (☎ 01433-620679) and Bakewell (☎ 01629-813227). The Peak District is packed with B&Bs, YHA hostels and a collection of camping barns (☎ 01629-825850), together with plenty of convivial pubs and good restaurants. Visitors to Bakewell should make sure to sample Bakewell pudding not tart.

The regular Transpeak bus service cuts right across the Peak District from Nottingham and Derby to Manchester via Matlock, Bakewell and Buxton.

East England

With the exception of the city of Cambridge, most of the eastern counties – Essex, Suffolk, Norfolk, Cambridgeshire and Lincolnshire – have been overlooked by tourists. East Anglia, as the region is often known, has always been distinct, historically separated from the rest of England by the fens and the Essex forests.

The fens were strange marshlands that stretched from Cambridge north to the Wash and beyond into Lincolnshire. They were home to people who led an isolated existence among a maze of waterways, fishing, hunting and farming scraps of arable land. In the 17th century, however, Dutch engineers were brought in to drain the fens, and the flat open plains with their rich, black soil were created. The region is the setting for Graham Swift's novel *Waterland*.

To the east of the fens, Norfolk and Suffolk have gentle, unspectacular scenery that can still be very beautiful. John Constable and Thomas Gainsborough painted in the area known as Dedham Vale, the valley of the River Stour. Villages like East Bergholt (Constable's birthplace), Thaxted and Cavendish are quintessentially English with their beautiful churches and thatched cottages.

The distinctive architectural character of the region has been determined by the lack of suitable building stone. Stone was occasionally imported for important buildings, but for humble churches and houses three local materials were used: flint, clay bricks and oak. The most unusual of the three, flint, can be chipped into usable shapes, but a single stone is rarely larger than a fist. Often the flint is used in combination with dressed stone or bricks to form decorative patterns.

More than any other part of England, East Anglia has close links with northern Europe. In the 6th and 7th centuries it was overrun by the Norsemen. From the late Middle Ages, Suffolk and Norfolk grew rich by trading wool and cloth with the Flemish; this wealth built scores of churches and helped subsidise the development of Cambridge. The windmills, the long straight drainage canals and even sometimes the architecture (especially in King's Lynn) call to mind the Low Countries.

Orientation & Information

East Anglia and Lincolnshire lie to the west of the main northbound transport arteries. The region's southern boundary is the Thames estuary, and its western boundary (now marked by the M1 and A1) was formed by that huge expanse of almost impenetrable marshland, the fens. Peterborough, Norwich and Lincoln are the most important cities. Harwich is the main port for ferries to Germany, Holland and Denmark.

There are YHA hostels at Cambridge, Colchester, Ely, King's Lynn, Norwich and Lincoln, among others. The East of England Tourist Board (☎ 01473-822922) can provide further information.

Activities

Hiking The 94-mile Peddars Way & Norfolk Coast Path runs across the middle of Norfolk from Knettishall Heath until it reaches the beautiful north Norfolk coast at Holme-next-the-Sea. It follows this coastline through a number of attractive, untouched villages, like Wells-next-the-Sea, to Cromer. The Peddars Way Association (☎ 01603-503207), Knights Cottage, The Old School, Honing, NR28 9TR, publishes a guide and accommodation list for £2.36 (including UK post and packaging).

Cycling This is ideal cycling country. Where there are hills, they're gentle. Bicycles can be hired cheaply in Cambridge, and the TIC there can suggest several interesting routes.

Boating The Norfolk Broads, a series of inland lakes (ancient flooded peat diggings) to the east of Norwich, are popular with boat people of every description. Contact Blake's Holidays (☎ 01603-782911) for information about hiring narrow boats, cruisers, yachts and houseboats.

Getting There & Away

Harwich, Norwich, King's Lynn and Cambridge are all easily accessible by train from London.

Stena Line (☎ 01255-243333) runs two ferries a day from Harwich to the Hook of Holland (the Netherlands); Scandinavian Seaways (☎ 01255-240240) runs at least three a week to Esbjerg (Denmark) and Hamburg (Germany), and at least two a week to Gothenburg (Sweden). See the introductory Getting There & Away section at the beginning of this chapter for more details.

Getting Around

Bus Bus transport around the region is slow and disorganised. For regional timetables and information phone Norfolk (☎ 01603-613613), Suffolk (☎ 01473-583000) or Lincolnshire (☎ 01522-553135). For transport information, Cambridgeshire operates an 0891 number; call ☎ 0891-910910 (calls are expensive).

Train From Norwich you can catch trains to the Norfolk coast and Sheringham, but there's an unfortunate gap between Sheringham and King's Lynn (bus or hitch?) which prevents a rail loop back to Cambridge. It may be worth considering Anglia Plus passes which offer three days travel out of seven for £18, one day for £8.50.

CAMBRIDGE
☎ 01223 • pop 100,000

Cambridge can hardly be spoken of without reference to Oxford – so much so that the term Oxbridge is used to cover them both. The two cities are not just ancient and beautiful university towns; they embody preconceptions and prejudices that are almost mythical in dimension.

An Oxbridge graduate is popularly characterised as male, private-school educated, intelligent and upper class, but the value

BRITAIN

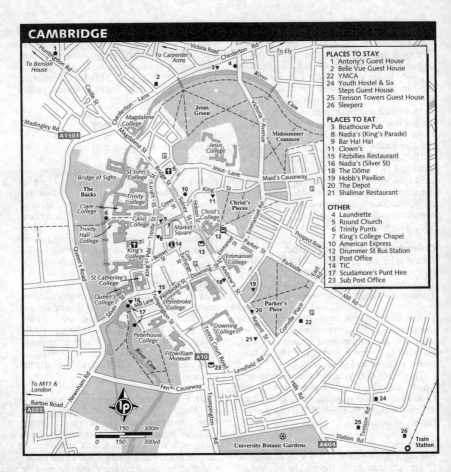

CAMBRIDGE

PLACES TO STAY
1 Antony's Guest House
2 Belle Vue Guest House
22 YMCA
24 Youth Hostel & Six
   Steps Guest House
25 Tenison Towers Guest House
26 Sleeperz

PLACES TO EAT
3 Boathouse Pub
9 Nadia's (King's Parade)
9 Bar Ha! Ha!
11 Clown's
15 Fitzbillies Restaurant
16 Nadia's (Silver St)
18 The Dôme
19 Hobb's Pavilion
20 The Depot
21 Shalimar Restaurant

OTHER
4 Laundrette
5 Round Church
6 Trinity Punts
7 King's College Chapel
10 American Express
12 Drummer St Bus Station
13 Post Office
14 TIC
17 Scudamore's Punt Hire
23 Sub Post Office

judgments attached to the term will very often depend on who is using it. It can be both abusive and admiring: for some it means academic excellence, for others it denotes an elitist club whose members unfairly dominate many aspects of British life.

Cambridge University is the newer of the two, probably beginning some time in the early 13th century, perhaps a century later than Oxford. There is a fierce rivalry between the two cities and the two universities, and a futile debate over which is best and most beautiful. If you have the time, visit both. Oxford draws many more tourists than Cambridge. Partly because of this, if you only have time for one and the colleges are open, choose Cambridge. Its trump card is the choir and chapel of King's College, which should not be missed by any visitor to Britain. If the colleges are closed (see the following section for opening dates), choose Oxford.

Orientation & Information

Cambridge is 54 miles north of London. The central area, which lies in a wide bend of the River Cam, is easy to get around on foot or bike.

The bus station is in the centre of town, but the train station is a 20-minute walk to the south-east. Sidney St is the main shopping street. The most important group of colleges (including King's) and the Backs (the meadows adjoining the Cam) are to the west of Sidney St, which changes its name many times. The bus station is on Drummer St; Sidney St is 50m to the west.

The TIC (☎ 322640, @ tourism@cambridge.gov.uk), Wheeler St, is open 10 am to 6 pm Monday to Saturday all year, and also on Sunday (11 am to 4 pm) from Easter to September. It organises walking tours at 1.30 pm daily, all year, with more during summer. Group sizes are limited, so buy your ticket in advance (£7 including King's college, £6 including St John's).

The university has three eight-week terms: Michaelmas (October to December), Lent (mid-January to mid-March) and Easter (mid-April to mid-June). Exams are held from mid-May to mid-June. There's general mayhem for the 168 hours following exams. the so-called May Week. Most colleges are closed to visitors for the Easter term, and all are closed for exams. Precise details of opening hours vary from college to college and year to year, so contact the TIC for up-to-date information.

Things to See & Do

Cambridge is an architectural treasure house. If you are seriously interested you will need considerably more information than this guide can give, and more than a day.

Starting at Magdalene Bridge, walk south down Bridge St until you reach the unmistakable **Round Church**, one of only four surviving medieval round churches, dating from the 12th century. Turn right down St John's St (immediately across the road) which is named in honour of **St John's College** (on the right). The gatehouse dates from 1510 and on the other side are three beautiful courts, the second and third dating from the 17th century. From the third court, the picturesque **Bridge of Sighs** (not open to the public) crosses the river.

Next door, **Trinity College** is one of the largest and most attractive colleges. It was established in 1546 by Henry VIII on the site of several earlier foundations. The Great Court, Cambridge's largest enclosed court,

incorporates buildings from the 15th century. Beyond Great Court is Nevile's Court with one of Cambridge's most important buildings on its western side – Sir Christopher Wren's library, built in the 1680s.

Next comes Caius (pronounced keys) College, and then **King's College** (☎ 331100), and its famous chapel, one of Europe's greatest buildings. The reason its late Gothic style is described as Perpendicular is immediately obvious. The chapel was begun in 1446 by Henry VI, but it was not completed until 1545. Majestic as this building is from the outside, it is its interior, with its breathtaking scale and intricate fan vaulting, that makes the greater impact. It comes alive when the choir sings; even the most pagan heavy-metal fan will find choral evensong an extraordinary experience. Entry costs £3.50/2.25.

There are services from mid-January to mid-March, mid-April to mid-June, mid-July to late July, early October to early December, and 24 and 25 December. Evensong is sung at 5.30 pm Tuesday to Saturday (men's voices only on Wednesday) and at 3.30 pm on Sunday.

Continue south on what is now King's Parade and turn right onto Silver St (St Catherine's College is on the corner) which takes you down to the Cam and the hiring point for punts.

Punting along the Backs is at best sublime, but it can also be a wet and hectic experience, especially on a busy weekend. Cheapest is Trinity Punts (£7 per hour) behind Trinity College; Scudamore's rents punts for £11 from the Silver St branch, or £9 from the Magdalene Bridge branch. Punting the 3 miles up the river to the idyllic village of Grantchester makes a great day out. Punts hold up to six people; deposits of £50 are required. If you do wimp out, the Backs are also perfect for a walk or a picnic – cross the bridge and walk along the river to the right.

Places to Stay

Cambridge Youth Hostel (☎ 354601, 97 Tenison Rd) has small dormitories and a restaurant near the train station. It's very popular – book ahead. Adult/junior rates are £11.70/8.50. *Carpenter's Arms* (☎ 351814) on Victoria Rd in the north of the city has two six-bed dorms and charges £9 per person.

There are numerous B&Bs at all times, even more during university vacation from late June to late September. Right outside the train station is **Sleeperz** (☎ 304050, © info@sleeperz.com, Station Rd), an attractively converted railway warehouse with single/twin rooms for £35/45 with a shower. Rooms with a double bed are larger and cost £55.

There are several B&Bs on Tenison Rd, including **Tenison Towers Guest House** (☎ 363924) at No 148, which charges from £22 to £27 per person. **Six Steps Guest House** (☎ 353968) at No 93 costs from £25 per person.

The **YMCA** (☎ 356998, Gonville Place) charges £22.65/37 and is good value for weekly stays (£127.50/224). Breakfast is included.

The other B&B area is in the north of the city around Chesterton Rd. **Antony's Guest House** (☎ 357444, 4 Huntingdon Rd) is spacious and comfortable, with four singles, four doubles and three triples at £15 to £22 per person. Similarly priced but a bit farther out, **Benson House** (☎ 311594, 24 Huntingdon Rd) has well-equipped doubles with showers.

Closer to the city centre, **Belle Vue Guest House** (☎ 351859, 33 Chesterton Rd) has comfortable doubles for £40. A pricier but much more elegant option is **Arundel House Hotel** (☎ 67701) at No 53 with rooms ranging from £53 to £72 for a single and £69 to £96 for a double.

Places to Eat

Cambridge may be a university town, but tourism is an enormous cash cow, a fact reflected in restaurant prices. There are, however, a number of reasonably priced restaurants, some of which give student discounts. **Nadia's** is a small chain of bakeries that are excellent value (eg, bacon sandwich and coffee for 95p before 10.30 am). A smoked ham and Emmental cheese baguette is £1.05. There are branches on King's Parade and Silver St.

Across the road from King's College is **Rainbow** (☎ 321551, 9 King's Parade), a good vegetarian restaurant.

Clowns (☎ 355711, 54 King St) is popular with students and serves light meals that are good value. **Hobb's Pavilion** (☎ 67480, Park Terrace) occupies the old cricket pavilion and specialises in filled pancakes. It's closed on Sunday and Monday.

There's a number of reasonably priced restaurants on Regent St. **The Depot** is stylish yet good value, offering an interesting international menu based around starters (about £4.50 each). **Shalimar Restaurant** (☎ 355378, 84 Regent St) is an Indian place offering discounts to students.

One of the most pleasant and central dining options is **The Dôme** (☎ 313818, 33-34 St Andrew's St), a French-style brasserie with friendly staff, a small garden at the back and a fabulous steak sandwich for £9. There are a few vegetarian options too. **Bar Ha! Ha!** (☎ 305089) is a trendy new cafe-bar with a good selection of salads and sandwiches between £3 and £6.

Fitzbillies (☎ 352500, 52 Trumpington St) is a brilliant bakery/restaurant. The Chelsea buns are an outrageous experience, and so is the chocolate cake beloved by generations of students, but there are many other temptations in addition to the usual sandwiches and pies – stock up before you go punting.

The **Boathouse** (14 Chesterton Rd) is a good riverside pub.

Getting There & Away

Cambridge can easily be visited as a day trip from London (although it is worth staying at least a night) or en route to the north. It's well served by trains, but not so well by buses.

Bus For more detailed bus information phone ☎ 317740. National Express (☎ 0870-580 8080) has hourly buses to London (£8.50, two hours). There are four buses a day to and from Bristol (two stop at Bath). Unfortunately, links to the north aren't very straightforward. To get to Lincoln or York you'll have to change at Peterborough or Nottingham respectively. King's Lynn is also only accessible via Peterborough.

Cambridge Coach Services (☎ 423900) runs the Inter-Varsity Link via London's Stansted airport to Oxford (£8/14 for a single/return, three hours, six per day). It also runs buses to Heathrow (£15.50) and Gatwick (£18.50) airports.

Train There are trains every half-hour from London's King's Cross and Liverpool St stations (one hour). If you catch the train at King's Cross you travel via Hatfield (see

Hatfield House in the Around London section earlier in this chapter) and Stevenage. There are also regular train connections to Bury St Edmunds (£5.30), Ely (£2.90) and King's Lynn (£6.70). There are connections at Peterborough with the main northbound trains to Lincoln, York and Edinburgh. If you want to head west to Oxford or Bath, you'll have to return to London first. For more information, phone ☎ 0845-748 4950.

Getting Around

There's a free gas-powered shuttle service round the town. Cambus (☎ 423554) runs numerous buses around town from Drummer St, including bus No 1 from the train station to the town centre. It's easy enough to get around Cambridge on foot, but if you're staying out of the centre, or plan to wander into the fens (fine flat country for the lazy cyclist), a bicycle can be hired from Geoff's Bike Hire (☎ 365629), 65 Devonshire Rd, near the youth hostel.

ELY
☎ 01353 • pop 9000

Ely is set on a low hill that was once an island deep in the watery world of the fens. It is dominated by the overwhelming bulk of Ely Cathedral, a superb example of the Norman Romanesque style, built between 1081 and 1200. Phone the TIC (☎ 662062) for places to stay.

There are regular trains from Cambridge (£2.90, 20 minutes).

LINCOLNSHIRE
Lincoln
☎ 01522 • pop 81,500

Since it's not on a main tourist route, many people bypass Lincoln, missing a magnificent 900-year-old cathedral (the third largest in Britain) and an interesting city with a compact medieval centre of narrow, winding streets. The suburbs are unattractive and depressing; however, perhaps because Lincoln escapes the hordes of visitors that places like York attract, the people are particularly friendly.

The TIC (☎ 529828), 9 Castle Hill, has information on cheap B&Bs; the *Youth Hostel* (☎ 522076, 77 South Park) is excellent with beds for £9.80.

Lincoln is 132 miles from London, with direct bus and rail services.

NORFOLK
Norwich
☎ 01603 • pop 170,000

This ancient capital was for many years larger than London, its prosperity based on trade with the Low Countries. Norwich's medieval centre has been retained along with its castle, cathedral and no fewer than 33 churches. There are numerous B&Bs – contact the TIC (☎ 666071), the Guildhall, Gaol Hill, for details. There's also a *Youth Hostel* (☎ 627647, 112 Turner Rd). There are direct rail and bus links with Cambridge and London.

King's Lynn
☎ 01553 • pop 37,500

King's Lynn is an interesting old port with some notable buildings, some of which were distinctly influenced by the trading links with Holland. Contact the TIC (☎ 763044), Saturday Market Place, for further information. The *Youth Hostel* (☎ 772461), College Lane, is fully open in July and August and haphazardly outside that time. There are regular trains from Cambridge (£6.90, one hour).

SUFFOLK
Harwich
☎ 01255 • pop 15,000

Contact the TIC (☎ 506139) if you need a B&B at this typically ugly shipping terminal.

There are numerous trains from Harwich (International Port) to London (Liverpool St station); on some services you will have to change trains at Manningtree or Colchester. Alternatively, you could go north to Norwich, or change for Bury St Edmunds and Cambridge at Ipswich. See the introductory Getting There & Away section at the beginning of this chapter for details on the ferries.

North-East England

North-East England is quite different from the rest of the country, although it's misleading to think of it as a single entity. The major sections are Yorkshire to the south, and Durham and Northumberland in the north, with the latter area bordering Scotland.

As a rule, the countryside is more rugged than in the south and it's as if the history reflects this, because every inch has been fought

BRITAIN

over. The central conflict was the long struggle between north and south, with the battle lines shifting over the centuries. The Romans were the first to attempt to delineate a border with Hadrian's Wall, but the struggle continued into the 18th century.

The Danes made York their capital and ruled the Danelaw – all of England north and east of a line between Chester and London. Later, their Norman cousins left a legacy of spectacular fortresses and the marvellous Durham Cathedral. The region prospered on the medieval wool trade, which sponsored the great cathedral at York and enormous monastic communities, the remains of which can be seen at Rievaulx and Fountains abbeys.

The countryside is a grand backdrop to this human drama, containing three of England's best national parks and some spectacular coastline. The Yorkshire Dales are the best known and arguably most beautiful of the parks, but the North York Moors have a great variety of landscapes and a superb coastline. Both parks can be very crowded in summer, and it's easier to escape the masses in the Moors.

Orientation & Information

The dominating geological feature is the Pennine Hills, which form a north-south spine dividing the region from Cumbria and Lancashire in the west and providing the source for major rivers.

The major transport routes both rail and road basically run east of this spine, northward from York to Newcastle upon Tyne and Edinburgh. Newcastle upon Tyne is an important ferry port for Scandinavia.

There are YHA hostels at York and Newcastle and, more importantly, dozens scattered about the national parks. Book ahead in summer.

Hiking

There are many great hikes in this region. The most famous is the Pennine Way, which stretches 250 miles from Edale in the Peak District to Kelso in Scotland. Unfortunately, its popularity means that long sections turn into unpleasant bogs.

An alternative like the Cleveland Way in the North York Moors National Park (see that section) is likely to be quieter and drier underfoot. The Dales Way, from Ilkley to Windermere, is one of many other interesting possibilities.

Getting There & Around

Bus Bus transport around the region can be difficult, particularly around the national parks. Fortunately there is now a central information phone line (☎ 0870-608 2608) that covers all of Yorkshire, County Durham and Northumberland.

There are several one-day Explorer tickets; always ask if one might be appropriate. The Explorer North East is useful, covering a vast area north of York to the Scottish Borders and west to Hawes (in the Yorkshire Dales) and Carlisle. There are numerous admission discounts for holders of Explorer tickets. You can purchase the tickets on the buses.

Train The main-line routes run north to Edinburgh via York, Durham and Newcastle upon Tyne and west to Carlisle roughly following Hadrian's Wall.

There are numerous special-price Rover tickets, for single-day travel and longer periods, so ask if one might be appropriate. For example, the North East Rover allows unlimited travel throughout the North (not including Northumberland). A version allowing travel for any four days out of eight costs £55.

YORK

☎ 01904 • pop 127,200

For nearly 2000 years York has been the capital of the north. It existed before the Romans, but entered the world stage under their rule. In AD 306, Constantine, the first Christian emperor and founder of Constantinople (now Istanbul), was probably proclaimed emperor on the site of the cathedral.

In Saxon times York became an important centre for Christianity and learning – the first church on the site of the current cathedral was built in 627. Danish invaders captured the city in 867, transforming it into an important trading centre and port, the River Ouse providing the link with the sea and the capital of the Danelaw.

York continued to prosper as a political and trading centre after William the Conqueror's initial 'pacification'. In the 15th and 16th centuries, however, it declined economically. Although it remained the social and cultural capital of the north, it was the arrival of the railway in 1839 that gave York a new lease of commercial life, allowing the expansion of Rowntree's and Terry's confectionery factories and the development of tourism.

The city walls were built during the 13th century and are among the most impressive surviving medieval fortifications in Europe. They enclose a thriving, fascinating centre with medieval streets, Georgian town houses and riverside pubs. The crowning glory is the Minster, the largest Gothic cathedral in England. York attracts millions of visitors, and the crowds can get you down, especially in July and August. But it's too old, too impressive, too real and too convinced of its own importance to be totally overwhelmed by mere tourists.

Orientation & Information

Although the centre is relatively small, York's streets are a confusing medieval tangle. Bear in mind that *gate* means street, and *bar* means gate.

There are five major landmarks: the walkable 2½-mile wall that encloses the city centre; the Minster at the northern corner; Clifford's Tower, a 13th-century castle and mound at the southern end; the River Ouse that cuts the centre in two; and the enormous train station just outside the western corner.

The main TIC (☎ 621756, fax 551801, ✆ tic@york-tourism.co.uk) is in De Grey Rooms, Exhibition Square, north of the river near Bootham Bar. It opens 9 am to 6 pm daily (10 am to 4 pm Sunday). There's also a small TIC at the train station.

Things to See & Do

There's a lot to see in York, and this guide just scratches the surface with an introductory ramble.

If you want to walk, start at the main TIC, Exhibition Square. Climb the city wall at **Bootham Bar** (on the site of a Roman gate) and walk north-east along the wall to Monk Bar, where there are beautiful views of the Minster.

York Minster (☎ 557216) took over 250 years to complete (from 1220 to 1480), so it incorporates a number of architectural styles. From the wall you can see the nave, which was built in the Decorated style between 1291 and 1350; the central or lantern tower in the

Perpendicular style, which was the last addition (there are brilliant views from the top); the north transept (Early English, 1241-60) and, extending from it, the octagonal chapter house, a Decorated masterpiece (1260-1300); and the choir (the eastern end), also in the Decorated style. The cathedral is most famous for its extensive medieval stained glass, particularly the enormous Great Eastern Window (1405-08) which depicts the beginning and end of the world.

By the 1960s the cathedral was in danger of collapse. If you go down to the foundations you can see how it was saved, as well as traces of earlier buildings on the site going back as far as the Roman garrison. Seeing everything could easily absorb the best part of a day. The cathedral is open 7 am to 6 pm daily. It is free, but a £2 donation is requested and areas such as the tower cost extra. There are worthwhile free guided tours.

Monk Bar is the best preserved medieval gate, with a working portcullis. Leave the walls here, walk along Goodramgate and take the first right onto Ogleforth, then left onto Chapter House St. The **Treasurer's House** (☎ 624247; open April to October; £3.50), on the right, has been restored by the National Trust. Turn left again onto College St (back towards Goodramgate) and pass a 15th-century, timber-framed building, **St William's College**.

Turn right onto Goodramgate again, passing the ancient Lady Row houses. Cross diagonally over King's Square and you'll reach the much-photographed and much-touristed **Shambles**, a medieval butcher's street. Walk down the Shambles, then turn left and immediately right onto Fossgate for the **Merchant Adventurers' Hall** (☎ 654818), which was built in the 14th century by a guild of merchants who controlled the cloth export trade; entry £2.

Continue down Walmgate (the continuation of Fossgate) to **Walmgate Bar**, the only city gate in England with an intact barbican – an extended gateway designed to make life difficult for uninvited guests. Follow the wall around to the right and across the River Foss to **Clifford's Tower** and the popular York Castle Museum.

The **York Castle Museum** (☎ 653611) contains displays of everyday life that will bring memories back for any Brit. There are complete streets, but the most fascinating

YORK

To York
Youth Hostel

Clifton

Deanery
Gardens

Museum
Gardens

River

War-
Memorial
Gardens

York
Train
Station

Ouse
Bridge

Ouse

PLACES TO STAY
10 Riverside Walk B&B
   & Abbey Guest House
16 Judges Lodging Hotel
23 York Backpackers
28 Rowntree Park Camping
29 Nunmill House

PLACES TO EAT & DRINK
11 Grand Assembly
   Rooms/Ask
12 La Piazza
13 Lime House
14 Betty's
17 Maltings
21 King's Arms
24 Blake Head Bookshop
   & Café

OTHER
1 Bootham Bar
2 Bootham Tower
3 Treasurer's House
4 Monk Bar
5 St William's College
   & Restaurant
6 York Minster
7 Main TIC
8 Yorkshire Museum
9 St Mary's Abbey

15 Main Post Office
18 Rougier St Bus Station
19 Merchant Adventurers'
   Hall
20 Jorvik Viking Centre
22 Ziggy's
25 Clifford's Tower
26 York Castle Museum
27 Walmgate Bar

Clementhorpe

Rowntree
Park

0   150   300m
0   150   300yd

reconstructions are of domestic interiors. The extraordinary collection of odds and ends, TVs, washing machines and vacuum cleaners is guaranteed to bring childhood memories flooding back. It's open 9.30 am to 5 pm daily and admission is £5.25.

One of York's most popular attractions is the smells-and-all **Jorvik Viking Centre** (☎ 643211), a re-creation of Viking York (£5.65). The **National Railway Museum** (☎ 621261), Leeman Rd behind the station, has numerous restored engines and carriages from the 1820s to the present day (£6.50). The **Yorkshire Museum** (☎ 629745) has the best collection of remnants from the Roman past (£3.95); the grounds are worth visiting for the ruins of **St Mary's Abbey** and the predominantly Roman tower.

Places to Stay

York gets very crowded. Fortunately, the TIC has an accommodation-booking service (£4).

Camping The *Rowntree Park Camping* (☎ 658997, *Terry Ave*) is a 20-minute walk from the station in the park by the river. It has a few sites for backpackers at £10 for two adults.

Hostels *York Youth Hostel* (☎ 653147, *fax 651230*, ☻ *york@yha.org.uk, Water End, Clifton*) is open all year. Seniors/children pay £15.05/11.25, including breakfast. It's a large but very busy YHA hostel, so book ahead. The hostel is about 1 mile north-west of the TIC; turn left onto Bootham, which becomes Clifton (the A19), then left onto Water End. Alternatively, there's a riverside footpath from the station.

York Youth Hotel (☎ 625904, *fax 612494*, ☻ *info@yorkyouthhotel.demon.co.uk, 11 Bishophill Senior*) is equally popular, particularly with school and student parties. There's a range of rooms, from 20-bed dorms (£11) to twin bunk rooms (£15 per person).

York Backpackers (☎ 627720, *fax 339350*, ☻ *yorkbackpackers@cwcom.net, 88-90 Micklegate*) is a friendly place in a 1752 Georgian building. Beds in the large dorms cost £11; doubles are £30.

B&Bs & Hotels With its central position next to the river, the Abbey Guest House

(☎ 627782, *fax 671743*, ☻ *abbey@rsummers.cix.co.uk, 14 Earlsborough Terrace*) is a standard B&B offering rooms from £20 per person.

The comfortable *Riverside Walk B&B* (☎ 620769, *fax 646249*, ☻ *julie@riversidewalkbb.demon.co.uk, 9 Earlsborough Terrace*) has rooms with bath from £24 a head.

Running along the railway line, both Bootham Terrace (south of Bootham) and Grosvenor Terrace (north of Bootham) are virtually lined with B&Bs. Bishopthorpe Rd is another road lined with B&Bs – *Nunmill House* (☎ 634047, *fax 655879*, ☻ *b&b@nunmill.co.uk*) at No 85 is a good place with rooms from £25 per person.

Judges Lodging Hotel (☎ 638733, *fax 679947, 9 Lendal*) is a classy place in a Georgian mansion. Well-equipped singles/doubles go for £75/100.

Places to Eat & Drink

There are several decent restaurants along Goodramgate from Monk Bar. *La Piazza* (☎ 642641) at No 51 has excellent Italian food, including pizzas from £5.30. *Lime House* (☎ 632734) at No 55 is busy, especially on weekends (closed Monday and Tuesday). The speciality is steaks (£12) and there are vegetarian dishes (£8.50).

Micklegate has many fine places. The best vegetarian eatery in York is *The Blake Head Bookshop & Café* (☎ 623767, *104 Micklegate*). The emphasis is on simple but imaginative cooking. It's open daily for lunch; soup costs £2.50 and a three-course meal is £7.50.

St William's Restaurant (☎ 634830) off College St is a great spot to relax after exploring the cathedral. It's open 10 am to 10 pm. Lunch includes soups for £3.25. Two-course dinners are £12.95. There is a beautiful cobbled courtyard.

The gorgeous Grand Assembly Rooms on Blake St are home to *Ask* (☎ 637254), a good moderately priced Italian place for lunch and dinner.

Betty's (☎ 659142, *St Helen's Square*) is a local institution for tea and it has a fine bakery.

King's Arms, King's Staith, is a pub with tables overlooking the river on the south-eastern side of the Ouse Bridge.

BRITAIN

Maltings (☎ 655387) on Tanners Moat below Lendal Bridge, has a great beer selection, a fine atmosphere and good lunch specials.

Ziggy's (☎ 620602, 53-55 Micklegate) is a relaxed club with theme nights ranging from Gothic to disco.

Getting There & Away

Bus The main bus terminal is on Rougier St (off Station Rd, inside the city walls on the western side of Lendal Bridge), but some local buses leave from the train station.

National Express (☎ 0870-580 8080) buses leave from Rougier St. There are at least three services a day to London (4½ hours), two a day to Birmingham (2½ hours) and one to Edinburgh (5½ hours).

For information on local buses (to Castle Howard, Helmsley, Scarborough, Whitby etc), contact the regional bus information number or in York call ☎ 551400. Yorkshire Coastliner has buses to Leeds, Malton and Scarborough.

Train There are numerous trains from London's King's Cross station (£59, two hours) and on to Edinburgh (£47, 2¾ hours).

North-south trains also connect with Peterborough (£33, 1½ hours) for Cambridge and East Anglia. There are good connections with South-West England including Oxford, via Birmingham (£25.50, 2¼ hours).

Local trains to/from Scarborough take 45 minutes (£9.10). For Whitby it's necessary to change at Middlesbrough.

Baggage check-in at the station has been farmed out by Railtrack to the Europcar office by track No 1.

Getting Around

You can hire a bike from the Europcar office (☎ 656161) in the train station for £7.50 per day.

If you're energetic you could do an interesting loop out to Castle Howard (15½ miles), Helmsley and Rievaulx Abbey (12½ miles) and Thirsk (another 12½ miles), where you could catch a train back to York. There's also a Trans-Pennine Trail cycle path section from Bishopthorpe in York to Selby (15 miles) along the old railway line. The TICs have maps.

AROUND YORK
Castle Howard

There are few buildings in the world that are so perfect their visual impact is almost a physical blow – Castle Howard (☎ 01653-648333), of *Brideshead Revisited* fame, is one. The house has a picturesque setting in the rolling Howardian Hills and is surrounded by 400 hectares of superb terraces and landscaped grounds dotted with monumental follies.

Castle Howard is 15 miles north of York off the A64 (4 miles). It's open at 10 am (last admission 4.30 pm) daily mid-March to early-October. Entry is £7.

The castle can be reached by several tours from York. Check with the York TIC for up-to-date schedules. Yorkshire Coastliner has a morning bus from York that links Castle Howard and Pickering.

NORTH YORK MOORS NATIONAL PARK

Only rivalled by Exmoor in the south and the Lake District, the North York Moors National Park (☎ 01439-770657) is less crowded than the Lake District and more expansive than Exmoor. The coast is superb, with high cliffs and long, sandy beaches backing onto beautiful countryside. From the ridge-top roads and open moors there are wonderful views, and the dales shelter abbeys, castles and small stone villages.

The Cleveland Way (108 miles), the long-distance path, curves around the edge of the park along the western hills from Helmsley to Saltburn-by-the-Sea, then down the coast to Scarborough. Maps and a booklet with information on accommodation is available from TICs. The North Yorkshire Moors Railway (NYMR), a privately owned steam train, runs up the beautiful wooded Newtondale from Pickering to Grosmont (with train connections to Whitby and Middlesbrough).

Orientation & Information

The park's western boundary is a steep escarpment formed by the Hambleton and Cleveland Hills; the moors run east-west and stretch along the coast between Scarborough and Staithes. Rainwater escapes from the moors down deep, parallel dales to the Rye and Derwent rivers in the south and the Esk in the north. After the open space of the moors, the dales form a gentler, greener landscape, sometimes wooded, and often with a beautiful stone village.

The coastline is as impressive as any in Britain, and considerably less spoilt than most; Scarborough and Whitby are both popular resorts, but Whitby retains its charm.

There's a useful tabloid park-visitors guide (50p), which is widely available in surrounding towns. The best visitors centre for the park is at Danby (☎ 01287-660654), but it's only open daily from April to October (weekends from November to March).

Getting Around

A must for public transport users is the excellent free brochure *Moors Connections*, available from TICs.

The Moorsbus (☎ 01439-770657) is a special service that runs daily from mid-July to early September that links a web of destinations in the Moors.

The North Yorkshire Moors Railway (☎ 01751-472508) cuts through the park from Pickering to Grosmont, which is on the Esk Valley line between Whitby and Middlesbrough. It operates April to October (£9.50, one hour). There are pleasant walks from most of the stations along the line; brochures are available from NYMR shops.

Bicycles are hired by Footloose (☎ 01439-770886) in Helmsley from £7.50 a day.

Pickering

☎ 01751 • pop 5315

Pickering is a terminus for the NYMR. The helpful TIC (☎ 473791) can suggest one of the numerous B&Bs. The nearest YHA hostel is the *Old School Youth Hostel* (☎/fax 460376), Lockton, about 4 miles north. It's another good walking base, and is open Monday to Saturday mid-April to late-September (daily in July and August).

Pickering can be reached from York and Whitby on Yorkshire Coastliner, Helmsley and Scarborough on Scarborough & District buses.

Helmsley & Around

☎ 01439

Helmsley is an attractive market town (Friday is market day) with excellent short walks in the beautiful surrounding countryside, including a short stretch of the Cumberland Way. There's the picturesque ruined Helmsley Castle on the edge of town, and, within easy walking distance, Rievaulx Abbey, Duncombe Park and Nunnington Hall. The TIC (☎ 770173) is open April to October.

Everything is grouped around the marketplace; it's worth checking the elegant little shops off Borogate, including the Footloose bicycle rental shop.

The remains of 13th-century **Rievaulx Abbey** (☎ 798228), a 3½-mile uphill walk from Helmsley along the Cleveland Way, are arguably the most beautiful monastic ruins in England. It's open from 10 am daily; admission is £2.90. The Moorsbus runs from Helmsley to the site.

There are several camping grounds in the area, the nearest being *Foxholme Caravan Park* (☎ 770416), Harome, 2 miles southeast of town. At the YHA *Helmsley Youth Hostel* (☎/fax 770433) the nightly rate is £9. Opening times vary so phone ahead. There's a number of B&Bs with prices around £18; a group of them is on Ashdale Rd. The TIC offers a booking service.

Stephenson's bus No 57 runs once daily between York and Helmsley (one hour). Scarborough & District has hourly buses Monday to Saturday, three on Sunday, between Helmsley and Scarborough via Pickering (1½ hours).

Whitby

☎ 01947 • pop 15,000

Somehow Whitby transcends the amusement arcades, coaches and fish and chip shops – the imposing ruins of the abbey loom over red-brick houses that spill down a headland to a beautiful harbour. Captain James Cook was apprenticed to a Whitby shipowner in 1746, and HMS *Endeavour* was built here, originally to carry coal.

The helpful TIC (☎ 602674) near the train station is open year-round and books rooms. The YHA *Whitby Youth Hostel* (☎ 602878, fax 825146), beside the abbey, has fantastic views. Alternatively, the well-designed *Harbour Grange Hostel* (☎ 600817, ✉ backpackers@harbourgrange.onyxnet.co.uk), Spital Bridge, on the eastern side of the harbour, opens all year.

BRITAIN

There are plenty of B&Bs. The *Langley Hotel* (*☎/fax 604250, 3-4 Crescent Place*) has good views, and rooms from £27 per person with breakfast.

The *Magpie Café* on the harbour has a reputation for the best fish and chips in England, perhaps the world!

Consider attempting the 5½-mile cliff-top walk south to Robin Hood's Bay, but don't plan on staying there as accommodation is limited and always prebooked; the last bus returns to Whitby around 4 pm. To the north, there are also some beautiful fishing villages, like Staithes.

There are buses to Whitby from Scarborough and York, or you can catch the Esk Valley train from Middlesbrough (£6.50, 1½ hours, four per day), which connects with the NYMR at Grosmont.

Scarborough
☎ 01723 • pop 40,000

Scarborough is a traditional seaside resort with a spectacular location. It's jam-packed with arcades, boarding houses and B&Bs. The coastline to the north, especially around Robin Hood's Bay, is beautiful. With its two bays and ruined castle looming over the harbour, Scarborough must once have been very beautiful itself. The town was also the setting for the film *Little Voice*.

If you need to stay, contact the TIC (☎ 373333). The YHA *White House Youth Hostel* (☎ 361176, fax 500054, ✆ scarborough@yha.org.uk), Burniston Rd, is 2 miles north of town. It has complex opening times, so ring ahead.

Scarborough is a good transport hub, connected by rail with York and Kingston-upon-Hull. There are reasonably frequent buses west along the A170 to Pickering and Helmsley. North East has regular buses to Whitby via Robin Hood's Bay.

DURHAM
☎ 0191 • pop 85,000

Durham is the most dramatic cathedral city in Britain; the massive Norman cathedral stands on a high, wooded promontory above a bend in the River Wear. Other cathedrals are more refined, but none has more impact.

Durham is also home to the third-oldest university in England (founded in 1832); the banks of the river and the old town are worth exploring.

Orientation & Information

The marketplace (and TIC), castle and cathedral are on the teardrop-shaped peninsula surrounded by the River Wear. The train station is above and north-west of the cathedral, on the other side of the river. The bus station is also on the western side. The TIC (☎ 384 3720), Market Place, is a short walk north of the castle and cathedral. Internet access is available at Reality X, west of Market Place on your way to the bus station.

Things to See & Do

The World Heritage-listed **Durham Cathedral** is the most complete Norman cathedral, with characteristic round arches, enormous columns and zigzagged chevron ornament. The vast interior is like a cave; don't miss the beautiful Galilee Chapel at the western end. There are tours (£3) at 10.30 am and 2.30 pm Monday to Saturday late May to September.

Durham Castle dates from 1093 and served as the home for Durham's prince-bishops. These bishops had powers and responsibilities normally more associated with a warrior king than a priest, however, this was wild frontier country. It's now a residential college for the university, and it's possible to stay here during summer holidays (see the following Places to Stay & Eat section). Late March to October there are guided tours (£3/2).

There are superb views back to the cathedral and castle from the outer bank of the river; walk around the bend between Elvet and Framwelgate bridges, or hire a boat at Elvet Bridge.

Places to Stay & Eat

Several colleges rent their rooms during the university vacations (particularly July to September); inquire at the TIC. The most exciting possibility is *University College* (☎ 374 3863), in the old Durham Castle, which has B&B at £20.50 per person.

The TIC makes local bookings free, which is useful since convenient B&Bs aren't numerous; the situation is particularly grim during graduation week in late June. There are a number of B&Bs for around £16 per person on Gilesgate – leave the market square from its northern end, over the freeway onto Claypath, which becomes Gilesgate. *Mrs Koltai* (☎ 386 2026) is at No 10, and *Mr Nimmins* (☎ 384 6485) is at No 14.

Most of the eating possibilities are within a short walk of the market square. *Emilio's Ristorante* (☎ 384 0096), just over the old Elvet Bridge, is good value and reputable with pizzas and pastas from £5.45. The *Almshouses* (☎ 386 1054, Palace Green) serves up an imaginative and satisfying selection including spinach pie (£4.60) and celery soup with roll (£2.75).

Getting There & Away

There are six National Express (☎ 0870-580 8080) buses a day to London (6½ hours), one to Edinburgh (4½ hours), and plenty to/from Newcastle (30 minutes). Primrose Coaches (☎ 232 5567) runs daily via Durham between Newcastle upon Tyne and Blackpool.

There are numerous trains to York (£13.90, one hour), a good number of which head on to London (£68, three hours) via Peterborough (for Cambridge). Frequent trains from London continue through to Edinburgh (two hours).

NEWCASTLE UPON TYNE
☎ 0191 • pop 210,000

Newcastle is the largest city in the north-east. It grew famous as a coal-exporting port and in the 19th century became an important industrial centre, before falling into decline after WWII. Newcastle's city centre retains some 19th-century grandeur, and has gained new impetus through the redevelopment of the Quayside area. Plan to stay at least one night; the exuberance with which Geordies let their hair down is well worth getting involved in.

Orientation & Information

The city centre is easy to get around on foot, and the metro (for the YHA hostel and B&Bs) is cheap and pleasant to use. The Central train station is just south of the city centre and the coach station is just east. There's a TIC at the train station (closed Sunday) and a main office (☎ 277 8000) on Grainger St. Both have a free map, guide and accommodation list. Surf the Net at McNulty's Internet Café on Market St, behind the main TIC.

Things to See & Do

The new **Life Interactive World** (☎ 243 8210) is a hands-on experience delving into all aspects of life. Both **St Nicholas Cathedral** and **Castle Garth Keep** are also worth visiting. There are river cruises in summer and in nearby Jarrow, **Bede's World** (☎ 489 2106) is a park with many reconstructed medieval buildings. **Segedunum** (☎ 295 5757), in Wallsend, is the newly reconstructed last outpost of Hadrian's Wall.

Places to Stay

Newcastle Youth Hostel (☎ 281 2570, 107 Jesmond Rd) opens February to November (and other times). Catch the metro to Jesmond station (55p), turn left from the station, cross Osborne Rd and continue for five minutes. A bed costs £10.85. Call in advance, as it can be busy.

North East YWCA (☎ 281 1233, Jesmond House, Clayton Rd) accepts male and female guests at £16 per person. Turn left on Osborne Rd from Jesmond station and take the second street on the right. There are quite a number of B&Bs within easy walking distance of West Jesmond station, mostly along Jesmond and Osborne Rds. The *Portland Guest House* (☎ 232 7868, 134 Sandyford Rd) is close to the town centre with singles/doubles starting at £18/36.

Places to Eat

For interesting restaurants and nightlife walk south down Grey St, which becomes Dean St and takes you down to Quayside and the River Tyne. On Grey St itself, *Marco Polo* (☎ 232 5533) at No 33 has pizzas and pastas for as little as £2.95. *Shikara* (☎ 233 0005, 52 St Andrew's St) serves excellent Indian food and is cheap for lunch, with mains in the evening costing £6 to £10. There are a number of interesting pubs at the bottom of the hill. *Flynns Bar* on Quayside has a beer garden and cheap food and drink. Also check *Bob Trollop* and *Red House*, which have pub meals for about £3.

Newcastle's nightlife is well worth checking, especially around Bigg Market and the Quayside. The *Cooperage* (☎ 232 8286, 32 The Close, Quayside) is a popular pub and dance club. Another popular club on the Quayside is *Tuxedo Royale* (☎ 477 8899,

BRITAIN

Hillgate Quay) on the *Tuxedo Princess* ship under the Tyne Bridge.

Getting There & Away

Bus There are numerous National Express (☎ 0870-580 8080) connections with virtually every major city in the country. For local buses around the north-east, don't forget the excellent value Explorer North East ticket, valid on most services (£5.25). Bus No 505 serves Berwick-upon-Tweed and No 685 Hadrian's Wall; see the appropriate sections.

Train There are numerous trains (☎ 0845-748 4950) to Edinburgh (1¾ hours), London (three hours) and York (one hour). Berwick-upon-Tweed and Alnmouth (for Alnwick) are also served. There is also an interesting, scenic line known as the Tyne Valley Line west to Carlisle (1½ hours), roughly every two hours.

Boat Regular ferries link Stavanger and Bergen (Norway) and in summer Gothenburg (Sweden) to Newcastle. See the introductory Getting There & Away section in this chapter for details.

Getting Around

There's an excellent metro (underground railway) with fares from 55p. The service also links up with Newcastle airport. For advice and information use the travel line (☎ 232 5325). Bus No 327 links the ferry (at Tyne Commission Quay) and Central train station. The fare is £3, and it leaves the station 2½ and 1¼ hours before ferry departure times.

NORTHUMBERLAND

Northumberland is one of the wildest, least spoilt of England's counties. There are probably more castles and battlefield sites here than anywhere else in England, testifying to the long, bloody struggle with the Scots.

The Romans were the first to attempt to draw a line separating north from south. Hadrian's Wall, which stretches for 73 miles from Newcastle to Bowness-on-Solway near Carlisle, was the northern frontier of the empire for almost 300 years. It was abandoned around AD 410, but enough remains to bring the past dramatically alive. After the arrival of the Normans, large numbers of castles and fortified houses (or *peles*) were built. Most have

now lapsed into peaceful ruin, but others, like Bamburgh and Alnwick, were converted into great houses which you can visit today.

Northumberland National Park lies north of Hadrian's Wall, incorporating the sparsely populated Cheviot Hills. The walks can be challenging, and cross some of the loneliest parts of England. There are information centres open mid-March to the end of October at Rothbury (☎ 01669-620887) and Once Brewed (☎ 01434-344396). There's another at Housesteads (☎ 01434-344525) on Hadrian's Wall. All the centres handle accommodation bookings.

Berwick-upon-Tweed & Around
☎ 01289

Berwick, beautifully sited at the mouth of the River Tweed, changed hands between the Scots and the English 13 times from the 12th to the 15th centuries. This merry-go-round ceased after the construction of massive ramparts that still enclose the town centre. The TIC (☎ 330733) should help you find a B&B for around £17; there's no hostel. There are two superb castles between Newcastle and Berwick: **Alnwick Castle** (☎ 01665-510777) is particularly fascinating (inside and out), while **Bamburgh Castle** (☎ 01668-214515) looks dramatic, but is not so interesting inside.

Getting There & Away Berwick is on the main London to Edinburgh line. Phone ☎ 0870-608 2608 for connecting bus services. Monday to Saturday, service No 501 runs to/from Alnwick via Bamburgh.

Berwick is a good starting point for exploring the Scottish Borders. There are buses on to Edinburgh around the coast via Dunbar and west to Coldstream, Kelso and Galashiels; the TIC can advise you.

Hadrian's Wall

Hadrian's Wall follows a naturally defensible line and peaks at the bleak and windy Winshields Crags. The most spectacular section of all is between Hexham and Brampton. It's possible to walk the entire length (allow at least five days), but the first section through Newcastle is pretty uninteresting (the TICs in Newcastle and Carlisle have information). There are many fascinating Roman sites, often set in beautiful countryside.

Chesters Roman Fort & Museum (☎ 01434-681379) is in a pleasant valley by the River Tyne (£2.80). There's an interesting museum, an extraordinary bathhouse and the remains of a massive bridge.

Housesteads Fort (☎ 01434-344363) is the most dramatic ruin. The well-preserved foundations include a famous latrine and are perched on a ridge overlooking the Northumbrian countryside (£2.80).

Vindolanda Fort & Museum (☎ 01434-344277), 2½ miles south, is an extensively excavated fort (excavations continue) and civil settlement with a museum that has some unusual artefacts, including shoes and evocative letters (£3.80).

Birdoswald Roman Fort (☎ 016977-47602) overlooks the picturesque Irthing Gorge, and is less inundated with visitors than some of the other sites (£2.50).

Places to Stay Corbridge, Hexham, Haltwhistle and Brampton are attractive small towns with plentiful B&Bs, although Carlisle is also a good base for exploring the wall. Starting in the east, the *Acomb Youth Hostel* (☎ *01434-602864*) is about 2½ miles north of Hexham and 2 miles south of the wall; dorms are £6.65. Hexham can be reached by bus or train.

Once Brewed Youth Hostel (☎ *01434-344360*) is central for both Housesteads Fort (3 miles) and Vindolanda (1 mile). Northumbria bus No 685 (from Hexham or Haltwhistle stations) will drop you at Henshaw, 2 miles south; bus Nos 682 and 890 will drop you at the front door. The nearest train station is at Bardon Mill, 2½ miles south-east.

Greenhead Youth Hostel (☎ *016977-47401*) is 3 miles west of Haltwhistle station, but is also served by the trusty bus No 685. Cheap, basic accommodation is available at *Bankshead Camping Barn* (☎ *01200-420102*), close to Banks East Turret. It's £3.60 per person. Bus No 682 drops you outside.

Getting There & Away Bus No 685 (☎ 0870-608 2608) runs hourly between Carlisle and Newcastle on the A69. The Newcastle to Carlisle railway line (☎ 0845-748 4950) has stations at Hexham, Haydon Bridge, Bardon Mill, Haltwhistle and Brampton, but not all trains stop at all stations.

From late May to September the special hail-and-ride Hadrian's Wall Bus (No 682) runs between Hexham and Haltwhistle train stations along the B6318, connecting with trains and calling at the main sites and Once Brewed Youth Hostel. This puts the youth hostels at Acomb and Greenhead within easy reach. For further information contact Hexham TIC (☎ 01434-605225).

Explorer tickets on all the bus services cost £5.

YORKSHIRE DALES

Austere stone villages with simple, functional architecture; streams and rivers cutting through the rolling hills; empty moors and endless stone walls snaking over the slopes – this is the region that was made famous by James Herriot and the TV series *All Creatures Great and Small*.

The landscape is completely different from that of the Lake District. The high tops of the limestone hills are exposed moorland, and the sheltered dales between them range from Swaledale, which is narrow and sinuous, Wensleydale and Wharfedale, which are broad and open, to Littondale and Ribblesdale, which are more rugged.

The Yorkshire Dales are very beautiful, but unfortunately in summer, like the Lake District, they are extremely crowded. Avoid weekends and the peak summer period, or try to get off the beaten track. The Pennine Way runs through the area and can be unbelievably busy, while other footpaths are deserted.

Orientation & Information

The Dales can be broken into northern and southern halves. In the north, the two main dales run parallel and east-west. Swaledale, the northernmost, is particularly beautiful. If you have transport, the B6270 from Kirkby Stephen to Richmond is highly recommended.

In the southern half, the north-to-south Ribblesdale is the route taken by the Leeds-Settle-Carlisle (LSC) railway line (see Trains under Carlisle's Getting There & Away section later in this chapter). Wharfedale is parallel to the east.

Skipton is the most important transport hub for the region, while Richmond is a beautiful town which is handy for the north. For visitors without transport, the best bet will be

BRITAIN

those places accessible on the LSC line such as Settle, which has many accommodation and hiking choices.

The main National Park Visitors Centre (☎/fax 01756-752774) in Grassington, 6 miles north of Skipton, opens daily from May to October. It publishes the useful *Visitor* newspaper.

Getting Around

Apart from the Leeds-Settle-Carlisle (LSC) railway line, public transport is grim. Bus users need a copy of the *Dales Connections* timetable available from TICs. Cycling is an excellent way to get around; there are some steep climbs, but mostly the roads and trails follow the bottom of the Dales.

Skipton

☎ 01756 • pop 13,000

Skipton is a popular gateway to the Dales, but there's little to hold you once you've raided the TIC (☎ 792809, fax 797528) and stormed the castle. The nearest youth hostel with access to the Dales is closer to Grassington. It is served by frequent trains from Leeds (30 minutes).

Grassington

☎ 01756

Grassington, one of the prettiest, most popular Dales villages, is home to a combined National Park Visitors Centre and TIC (☎/fax 752774) that's open year-round. It is a good base for walks in Wharfedale. *Linton Youth Hostel* (☎ 752400, fax 753159), just south of Grassington, can be reached by the Skipton to Grassington bus.

Pride of Dales runs several buses a day to/from Skipton.

Settle

☎ 01729

Settle is a charming village right on the LSC. The compact centre makes for a good pause and there are many walks in the area, including a popular and gorgeous one to Malham (6 miles). The TIC (☎ 825192, fax 824381), open year-round, can supply maps and find rooms. The YHA *Stainforth Youth Hostel* (☎ 823577, fax 825404, ℮ stainforth@yha .org.uk) is 2 miles north of town. Opening times are complex, so call first.

North-West England

The southern part of this region is often dismissed as England's industrial back yard. The dense network of motorways you see on maps gives forewarning of both the level of development and the continuing economic importance of the region, despite the decline of some traditional industries. On the other hand, there are still some beautiful corners, and the larger cities are important cultural centres with a legacy of brilliant Victorian architecture.

In a very real sense this is the working-class heartland of England. There's a big gap between these northern cities and those south of Birmingham. Since the Industrial Revolution created them, life for their inhabitants has often been an uncompromising struggle. The main industrial corridor runs from Merseyside (Liverpool) to the River Humber. The cities of Liverpool and Manchester sprawl into the countryside, burying it under motorways, grim suburbs, power lines, factories and mines. There are, nonetheless, some important exceptions – walled Chester, makes a good starting point for North Wales. To the north, however, it's a different story. The Lake District is the most beautiful corner of England and also one of the most popular.

MANCHESTER

☎ 0161 • pop 460,000

Probably best known for the football team Manchester United, the modern city that produced Oasis, The Smiths and New Order is also a monument to England's industrial history. The 1990s saw a gradual transformation of parts of the city centre, a process given added impetus by the IRA bomb blast of 1996 that devastated much of the area round the Arndale Shopping Centre. If every cloud has a silver lining, the bombing has allowed the city to create some wonderful public spaces and stunning modern architecture. There are still areas where empty warehouses and factories rub shoulders with stunning Victorian Gothic buildings, rusting train tracks and motorway overpasses with flashy bars and nightclubs – but things are improving as warehouses are given new life as upmarket apartment blocks. The longer you stay, the more you'll like Manchester. Not many cities in England can rival Manchester for its vibrancy and nightlife, its gay scene and fantastic sports facilities. And England's largest student population gives it that extra spark.

Orientation & Information

The centre of Manchester is easy to get around on foot and with the help of the excellent Metrolink tramway. The University of Manchester lies to the south of the city centre (on Oxford St/Rd). Continue south on Oxford St/Rd and you reach Rusholme, a thriving centre for cheap Indian restaurants. To the west of the university is Moss Side, a ghetto with high unemployment and a thriving drug trade – keep well clear. The TIC (☎ 234 3157) is in the town hall extension, off St Peter Square, with another branch at the airport. *City Life* is the local 'what's on' magazine – a compulsory purchase. Cybercafe Cyberia is at the north end of Oxford St.

Things to See & Do

Castlefield Urban Heritage Park has an extraordinary landscape littered with industrial relics that have been tumbled together like giant pieces of Lego. Unpromising as this may sound, the result is fascinating, and the region is now being imaginatively developed. It includes the excellent Museum of Science & Industry, a reconstruction of a Roman fort, as well as footpaths, boat trips, pubs, hotels and a YHA hostel.

Dominating Albert Square in the city centre is an enormous Victorian Gothic **Town Hall**, designed by Albert Waterhouse (of London's Natural History Museum fame) in 1876 and with a 280-foot-high tower.

The **City Art Gallery** on the corner of Princess and Mosley Sts was designed by Sir Charles Barry (architect for the Houses of Parliament) in 1824. Its impressive collection covers everything from early Italian, Dutch and Flemish painters to Gainsborough, Blake, Constable and the Pre-Raphaelites. It's currently undergoing redevelopment and is expected to reopen in late 2001; check with the TIC for opening times. Manchester's latest, **The Lowry**, is an eye-catching modern construction on Salford Quay. Two theatres and a number of galleries (one devoted to LS Lowry

himself) are encapsulated in the complex. The galleries are free to enter. Take the Metrolink to either Broadway or Harbour City.

Places to Stay

There's a reasonable range of places to stay, but most cheap options are some distance from the city centre. The TIC's free booking service is recommended.

The **Youth Hostel** (☎ 839 9960), across the road from the Museum of Science & Industry in the Castlefield area, has comfortable four-bed rooms for £17.40 per person. From mid-June to mid-September, the University of Manchester lets students rooms to visitors from around £12.25 per person. Contact *St Anselm Hall* (☎ 224 7327) or *Woolaton Hall* (☎ 224 7244).

Newly opened **Woodies Backpackers** (☎ 228 3456, 19 Blossom St), 10 minutes walk north-east of Piccadilly Gardens, is comfortable and offers Internet access; dorm beds are £12 per night.

The *Commercial Hotel* (☎ 834 3504, 125 Liverpool Rd, Castlefield) is a smartly renovated traditional pub close to the museum. Rooms are £25/40.

Places to Eat

The most distinctive restaurant zones are Chinatown in the city centre and Rusholme in the south. Chinatown is bounded by Charlotte, Portland, Oxford and Mosley Sts, and it has a number of restaurants, not all Chinese, and most not particularly cheap. The most acclaimed is *Little Yang Sing* (☎ 228 7722, 17 George St) which specialises in Cantonese cuisine. During the day it has a set menu for £8.95, but expect to pay twice that in the evening. *Dimitrl's* (☎ 839 3319) in Campfield Arcade, serves up a mixture of Greek, Italian and Spanish food with a good vegetarian selection. A quick lunch will set you back £3. Rusholme is to the south of the university on Wilmslow Rd, the extension of Oxford St/Rd, and has numerous popular, cheap and very good Indian/Pakistani places. *Darbar* (☎ 224 4392, 65-67 Wilmslow Rd) is not only cheap (student discounts) but exceptionally good; most mains are between £6.50 and £6.90. Bring your own booze.

Cafe-bars have taken off in a big way in Manchester. *Dry 201* (☎ 236 5920, 28 Oldham

St) and *Manto (☎ 236 2667, 46 Canal St)* are among the best. If you're shopping in the indoor market of Affleck's Palace, there are several good cafes there.

Entertainment

Manchester comes into its own at night, offering a remarkable range of high quality entertainment. One of the best venues for live music is *Band on the Wall (☎ 832 6625)*, Swan St, which has an eclectic variety of acts from jazz, blues and folk to pop. The *Lass O'Gowrie* on Charles St, off Oxford St, is a popular student hang-out, with an excellent small brewery on site. Two historic pubs are the *Old Wellington Inn* and *Sinclairs Oyster Bar* at the top of New Cathedral St.

There are several popular places to drink in Castlefield, including Mick Hucknall of Simply Red's *Bar Ça* in Catalan Square, with outdoor seating for sunny days; and *Dukes 92*, a popular canalside pub.

Canal St is the centre of Manchester's enormous gay nightlife scene. There are over 20 bars and clubs in the so-called 'Gay Village'. *Paradise Factory (☎ 273 5422, 112 Princess St)* is a cutting edge club, with gay nights on the weekend.

Getting There & Away

There are numerous coach links with the rest of the country. National Express (☎ 0870-580 8080) operates out of Chorlton St station in the city centre to pretty well anywhere you'll want to go.

Piccadilly is the main station for trains to and from the rest of the country, although Victoria serves Halifax and Bradford. The two stations are linked by Metrolink. For information phone ☎ 0845-748 4950.

Getting Around

For general inquiries about local transport, including night buses, phone ☎ 228 7811 (open 8 am to 8 pm daily). A Day Saver ticket for £6.50 covers travel throughout the Great Manchester area on buses, train and Metrolink. Manchester's Metrolink light-railway (tram) makes frequent connections between Victoria and Piccadilly train stations and G-Mex (for Castlefield). Buy tickets from machines on the platforms.

CHESTER

☎ 01244 • pop 80,000

Despite steady streams of tourists, Chester remains a beautiful town, ringed by an unbroken, red sandstone city wall which is the best in Britain and dates back to the Romans. Many of the city's medieval-looking buildings are actually only Victorian! The eyecatching two-level shopping streets may date back to the post-Roman period and certainly make convenient rainproof shopping arcades.

The 2-mile walk along the top of the wall is the best way to see the town – allow a couple of hours to include detours down to the river and a visit to the cathedral.

Orientation & Information

Built in a bow formed by the River Dee, the walled centre is now surrounded by suburbs. The train station is a 15-minute walk from the city centre – go up City Rd, then turn right onto Foregate at the large roundabout. From the bus station, turn left onto Northgate St.

The TIC (☎ 402111) is in the town hall opposite the cathedral. There's a second information centre just outside Newgate opposite the Roman amphitheatre, and another at the train station. There are excellent guided walks around the city at 10.30 and 10.45 am daily (£3). The Internet can be accessed at *i*-station in Rufus Court.

Things to See & Do

The present **Chester Cathedral** (☎ 324756) was built between 1250 and 1540. It retains its fine 12th-century cloister but there were later alterations and a lot of Victorian reconstruction. Visitors are asked to donate £2.

The **Dewa Roman Experience** (☎ 343407), Pierpoint Lane (off Bridge St), aims to show what life was like in Roman times. It's open 9 am to 5 pm daily; entry is £3.95/2.25.

Places to Stay & Eat

The *Youth Hostel (☎ 680056, 40 Hough Green)* is over a mile from the centre and on the opposite side from the train station. Leave by Grosvenor Rd past the castle on your left, cross the river and turn right at the roundabout. Beds cost £10.85.

There are numerous good-value B&Bs along Hoole Rd, the road into the city from the M53/M56. The *Bawn Park Hotel (☎ 324971)* at No 10 is typical. The **Aplas Guest House** (☎ *312401, 106 Brook St*) is very comfortable and only a five-minute walk from the train station. Both have rooms starting at £17. B&Bs can also be found inside the city walls.

Chester's pubs have good, basic food at reasonable prices. Try **Watergates** on Watergate or **Pied Bull** on Northgate. The fine Edwardian **Albion Inn** serves reliable English food without chips or fry-ups. The atmospheric **cathedral refectory** serves soup for £1.95, and another good place for a light lunch is **Katie's Tea Rooms** (☎ *400322*), spread over three floors of a historic building on Watergate St. **Francs** (☎ *317952, 14 Cuppin St*) turns out reasonably priced traditional French food. **Alexander's Jazz Theatre** (☎ *340005*), Rufus Court by Northgate, is a wine, coffee and tapas bar with great music.

Getting There & Away
Chester has excellent transport connections, especially to and from North Wales.

Bus National Express (☎ 0870-580 8080) has numerous connections with Chester, including Birmingham (£8.25, 2½ hours) and on to London (£15, 5½ hours), Manchester (£4.50, 1¼ hours), Glasgow (£22.50, six hours), Liverpool (£5, one hour) and Llandudno (£5.50, 1¾ hours). For many destinations in the south or east it's necessary to change at Birmingham; for the north, change at Manchester.

For information on local bus services ring Chester City Transport (☎ 602666). Local buses leave from Market Square behind the town hall.

Train Any bus from the station goes into the centre. There are numerous trains to Shrewsbury (£5.80, one hour), Manchester (£8.50, 1½ hours) and Liverpool (£3); Holyhead (£16.15, two hours), via the North Wales coast, for ferries to Ireland; and London's Euston station (£44, three hours). Phone ☎ 0845-748 4950 for details.

LIVERPOOL
☎ 0151 • pop 510,000
Of all northern England's cities, Liverpool has perhaps the strongest sense of its own identity, an identity which is closely tied up with the totems of the Beatles, the Liverpool and Ever-

ton football teams, and the Grand National steeplechase, run at Aintree since 1839.

The city has a dramatic site, rising on a series of steps above the broad Mersey estuary with its shifting light, its fogs, its gulls and its mournful emptiness. The contrast between grandeur and decay, between decrepit streets and boarded-up windows, massive cathedrals and imperious buildings, creates some of the most arresting sights in Britain.

Liverpool's economic collapse has been even more dramatic than Manchester's, which gives the whole city a sharp edge you'd do well not to explore. But on weekends the centre vibrates to music from countless pubs and clubs, a vivid testimony to the perverse exhilaration of the city's decline.

It's well worth stopping off to see the revitalised Albert Dock, the interesting Western Approaches Museum and the city's twin cathedrals.

Orientation & Information
Liverpool stretches north-south along the Mersey estuary for more than 13 miles. The main visitor attraction is Albert Dock (which is well signposted) to the south of the city centre. The centre, including the two cathedrals to the east, is quite compact – about 1½ by 1 mile.

Lime St, the main train station, is just to the east of the city centre. The National Express coach station is on the corner of Norton and Islington Sts in the north of the city. The bus station is in the centre on Paradise St. The main TIC (☎ 709 5111) in the Queen Square Centre is open 9 am to 5.30 pm Monday to Saturday and 10.30 am to 4.30 pm Sunday. There's also a branch at Albert Dock (☎ 708 8854). Both can book accommodation.

If you're staying a few days make sure to spend £3/1.50 on an NMGM Eight Pass, covering admission to six city centre attractions: Liverpool Museum, Walker Art Gallery, Merseyside Maritime Museum, HM Customs & Excise National Museum, Museum of Liverpool Life and the new Conservation Centre. It's valid for 12 months and is on sale at all the museums.

You're advised to be a bit cautious while in Liverpool. Although the main hazard is likely to be over-friendly drunks, it's best to avoid dark side streets even in the city centre.

BRITAIN

Things to See & Do

In the 1980s the derelict **Albert Dock** was restored. It has since become a deservedly popular tourist attraction housing several outstanding modern museums (the **Merseyside Maritime Museum**, the **Museum of Liverpool Life** and the **Tate Gallery Liverpool**) as well as shops and restaurants, a branch of the TIC and several tacky tourist attractions (the **Beatles Story** is disappointing).

The **Western Approaches Museum**, the secret command centre for the Battle of the Atlantic, was buried under yards of concrete beneath an undistinguished building behind the town hall in Rumford Square. At the end of the war the bunker was abandoned, with virtually everything left intact. It's now a museum (☎ 227 2008) and is open daily except Friday and Sunday for £4.75.

A visit to Liverpool wouldn't be complete without a **Beatles tour**. There are numerous sites around town associated with the Beatles, all of whom grew up here. Both TICs sell tickets to the Magical Mystery Tour, a 2¼-hour bus trip taking in homes, schools, venues, Penny Lane, Strawberry Fields and many other landmarks. It departs daily from inside the Albert Dock TIC at 2.20 pm and from the main TIC at 2.30 pm. Tickets are £10.95.

A re-creation of the original music venue where the Beatles made their name, the **Cavern Club** (☎ 236 1964) on Mathew St still attracts a big crowd. Phone for opening times.

Places to Stay

The new *Youth Hostel* (☎ 248 5647, 25 Tabley St) is right across the road from Albert Dock. Beds cost £17.40.

The excellent *Embassie Hostel* (☎ 707 1089, 1 Falkner Square) to the west of the Anglican Cathedral but still within walking distance of the centre, has dorm beds from £9.50, and facilities including a laundry.

The *University of Liverpool* (☎ 794 3298) has self-catering rooms at Mulberry Court, Oxford St, near the Metropolitan Cathedral, for £16 a head.

There are several well-positioned hotels on Mount Pleasant, between the city centre and the Metropolitan Cathedral. *Feathers Hotel* (☎ 709 9655), No 119, is a particularly good mid-range hotel where rooms start at £29/44. The award-winning *Aachen Hotel* (☎ 709

3477) at No 89 has well-equipped rooms, mostly with showers, for £34/40. The smaller and more basic *Belvedere* (☎ 709 2356), No 83, is cheaper, with beds from £18.50.

Places to Eat

There are lots of places to eat down Bold St in the city centre. At the eastern end of this street is *Cafe Tabac* (☎ 709 3735), No 124, a relaxed wine bar that attracts a young crowd.

Everyman Bistro (☎ 708 9545, 5 Hope St) underneath the famous Everyman Theatre, is highly recommended for its good cheap food and atmosphere (pizza slices under £2). The *refectory* at the Anglican Cathedral serves great value hot lunches for around £4. There are also excellent cafes in the Walker Art Gallery and the Conservation Centre.

Entertainment

The free entertainment guide *In Touch* makes good reading or just wander around Mathew St and south-west to Bold, Seel and Slater Sts and you'll stumble upon an amazing array of clubs and pubs catering to every style you can imagine. One of the best known of the clubs is *Cream* (☎ 709 1693), off Parr St, which rings the changes between jazz, samba and techno. On the corner of Hope and Hardman Sts, the *Philharmonic Dining Room*, built in 1900, is one of Britain's most extraordinary pubs. The interior is resplendent with etched glass, stained glass, wrought iron, mosaics and ceramic tiling. *The Baltic Fleet*, next to the YHA Hostel, pours a superb traditional ale.

Everyman Theatre (☎ 709 4776) is one of the best repertory theatres in the country.

Getting There & Away

There are National Express (☎ 0870-580 8080) services linking Liverpool to most major towns. Numerous intercity services run to Lime St station.

Getting Around

Public transport in the region is coordinated by Merseytravel (☎ 236 7676). There are various zone tickets, such as the £4.30 ticket for bus, train and ferry (except cruises). These are also sold at post offices.

Bus There are a number of bus companies. Smart Bus Nos 1 and 5 run from Albert Dock through the city centre to the university, and vice versa, every 20 minutes.

Ferry The ferry across the Mersey (£1.05), started 800 years ago by Benedictine monks but made famous by Gerry & the Pacemakers, still offers one of the best views of Liverpool. Boats depart from Pier Head ferry terminal, to the north of Albert Dock and next to the Liver Building. Special one-hour commentary cruises run year-round departing hourly from 10 am to 3 pm on weekdays and until 6 pm on weekends (£3.50). Phone ☎ 639 0609 for more information.

ISLE OF MAN
☎ 01624 • pop 70,000

Equidistant from Liverpool, Dublin and Belfast in the Irish Sea, the number one industry on this island is tax avoidance. The capital, Douglas, is a run-down relic of Victorian tourism, but the island also has beautiful countryside and a proud heritage as the site of the world's oldest continuous parliament. The annual TT races (May-June) draw 45,000 motorcycle fans.

Phone the Douglas TIC (☎ 686766) for B&Bs. The Isle of Man Steam Packet Company (☎ 0870-552 3523) has several sailings a week to Douglas from Liverpool (from £25 single, four hours), daily departures from Heysham (near Lancaster), and connections to Belfast and Dublin (see the Ireland chapter later in this book).

LAKE DISTRICT

The Lake District is arguably the most beautiful corner of England: a combination of green dales, so perfect they could almost be parks, rocky mountains that seem to heave themselves into the sky, and lakes that multiply the scenery with their reflections. The Cumbrian Mountains are not particularly high – none reach 1000m – but they're much more dramatic than their height would suggest.

This is Wordsworth country, and his houses at Grasmere (Dove Cottage, ☎ 015394-35544) and Rydal (☎ 015394-33002, between Ambleside and Grasmere) are literary shrines.

There are over 10 million visitors a year to the Lake District. The crowds can be so intense over summer that it's probably best to visit weekdays in May and June, or in September and October to experience the Lake District fully.

Orientation & Information

The two principal bases for the Lake District are Keswick in the north (particularly for walkers) and the tourist trap conurbation of Bowness/Windermere in the south. Kendal, Coniston, Ambleside, Grasmere and Cockermouth are less hectic alternatives. All these towns have hostels, numerous B&Bs and places to eat.

Ullswater, Grasmere, Windermere, Coniston Water and Derwent Water are usually considered the most beautiful lakes, but they also teem with boats. Wastwater, Crummock Water and Buttermere are equally spectacular and less crowded.

In general, the mob stays on the A roads, and the crowds thin out west of a line drawn from Keswick to Coniston.

TICs stock a frightening quantity of local guidebooks and brochures and both Windermere and Keswick have decent TICs with free booking services. If you're staying more than a day or so, buy a copy of *A Walk Round the Lakes* by Hunter Davies. Those interested in Wordsworth's life might also enjoy reading his sister Dorothy's *Grasmere Journals*. The classic walking guides are the seven volumes of Alfred Wainwright's *Pictorial Guide to the Lakeland Fells*. Handwritten and hand-drawn, they're still useful despite their age.

The numerous walking/climbing shops in the region, particularly in Ambleside and Keswick, are good sources of local information. The Climber's Shop (☎ 015394-32297), Compston Rd, Ambleside, and George Fisher (☎ 017687-72178), Lake Rd, Keswick, are both excellent shops for stocking up on equipment. George Fisher also has a pleasant cafe.

There are almost 30 YHA hostels in the region, many of which can be linked by foot. Look for *The Lake District Youth Hostellers' Walking Guide*.

Getting There & Away

National Express (☎ 0870-580 8080) buses run from Manchester via Preston (three hours) and on to Keswick and from London via Birmingham and on to Keswick (seven

BRITAIN

hours). There's a train service from Manchester airport to Windermere (two hours).

The free paper, *Explorer*, available from TICs, gives bus and boat timetable details for Cumbria and the lakes. Stagecoach Cumberland (☎ 0870-608 2608) has several important services, including bus No 555, which links Lancaster with Carlisle, via Kendal, Windermere, Ambleside, Grasmere and Keswick. Bus No 518 runs between Windermere and Barrow-in-Furness, via Ulverston on the Cumbrian Coast Line. No 505/506, runs from Bowness Pier to Coniston via the Steamboat Museum, Brockhole, Ambleside and Hawkshead. Ask about Day Ranger and Explorer tickets.

Windermere is at the end of a spur off the main railway line between London's Euston station and Glasgow. For Windermere, change at Oxenholme.

Getting Around

Walking or cycling are the best ways to get around, but bear in mind that conditions can be treacherous, and the going can be very, very steep. Country Lanes Cycle Centre (☎ 015394-44544), The Railway Station, in Windermere rents out bikes for £14 a day.

There are numerous boat trips and a number of steam railways; the TICs have countless brochures covering the alternatives in detail.

Bowness & Windermere
☎ 015394 • pop 8500

It's thanks to the railway that the Bowness/ Windermere conglomerate is the largest tourist town in the Lake District. At times it feels like a seaside resort. The town is quite strung out, with Windermere a 30-minute uphill walk from Bowness on the lakeside. The excellent TIC (☎ 46499), Victoria St, is conveniently located near the train station at the northern end of town.

Within spitting distance of the train station, *Lake District Backpackers Lodge* (☎ 46374) on the High St offers beds in small dormitories for £11. *Windermere Youth Hostel* (☎ 43543) at High Cross Bridge Lane, Troutbeck, is larger but 2 miles from the station. Numerous buses run past Troutbeck Bridge and in summer the hostel sends a minibus to meet trains.

Windermere is wall-to-wall B&Bs, most of them costing about £16 a night. Most of the restaurants are in Bowness near the lake. *Miller Howe Café* in the Lakeland Limited factory shop behind the train station, serves surprisingly nice cakes. *Millers* (☎ 43877, 31 Crescent Rd) offers a standard, cheapish tourist menu. *Gibby's*, a few doors down, is cheap and filling, with home-made chicken and mushroom pie for £4.60.

Keswick
☎ 017687 • pop 5000

Keswick is an important walking centre, and although the town centre lacks the green charm of Windermere, the lake is beautiful. The *Youth Hostel* (☎ 72484) is open most of the year (£10.85), a short walk down Station Rd from the TIC (☎ 72645). Wright's No 888 bus serves Penrith station and continues eastwards to Langwathby on the LSC Line, Hexham and Corbridge on Hadrian's Wall, and finally Newcastle.

Coniston
☎ 015394 • pop 1800

Though still a tourist town, Coniston is decidedly less busy than Keswick or Windermere, probably because it's slightly less accessible by public transport. The TIC (☎ 41533) is open in summer only.

There are two excellent YHA hostels near the town. *Holly How Youth Hostel* (☎ 41323), just north of Coniston on the Ambleside Rd, is open daily over Easter and from late June to mid-September; phone for other opening times. The marginally cheaper *Coppermines* (☎ 41261) is 1 mile along the minor road between the Black Bull Hotel and the Co-op, but is often closed on Sunday and Monday.

Kendal
☎ 01539

On the eastern outskirts of the Lake District National Park, Kendal is a lively town with several interesting museums. The TIC (☎ 725758) is in the Town Hall on Highgate.

To the south of town on the banks of the River Kent are the **Museum of Lakeland Life** and the **Abbot Hall Art Gallery**. The museum is a particular delight, with reconstructed period shops and rooms, a model of a local mine and lots of information on lost local industries. One room is devoted to local author Arthur Ransome, writer of the *Swallows & Amazons* books, and another to John Cunliffe, more recent creator of Postman Pat. Both are open 10.30 am to 5 pm daily. Entry to each is £3.

Kendal Youth Hostel (☎ 724066, 118 Highgate) is open daily from mid-April to August, closing on Sunday and Monday at other times. Beds are £12.80/9.65. Right next door is the *Brewery*, a wonderful arts complex with a theatre, cinema and bar-bistro. Soup of the day is £2.95 and dishes such as seared tuna with salsa verde go for £8.25.

Kendal is on the branch railway line from Windermere to Oxenholme, with connections north to Manchester and south to Lancaster and Barrow-in-Furness.

CARLISLE
☎ 01228 • pop 72,000

For 1600 years, Carlisle defended the north of England, or south of Scotland, depending on who was winning. In 1745 Bonnie Prince Charlie proclaimed his father king at the market cross.

Although the city's character was diminished by industrialisation in the 19th century, it's still an interesting place and makes a useful base for getting to or from Northumberland, Dumfries & Galloway and the Borders (the beautiful Scottish border counties), and the Lake District. It's also the hub for five excellent railway journeys.

Orientation & Information
The train station is south of the city centre, a five-minute walk to Greenmarket (the market square) and the TIC. The bus station is on Lowther St, just one block east of the square. The TIC in the old town hall (☎ 625600) offers a free accommodation booking service for Cumbria.

Things to See & Do
The 11th-century **Carlisle Castle** is to the north of the cathedral, overlooking the River Eden (£3). The excellent **Tullie House Museum** (☎ 534781) reveals the region's fascinating history, with much emphasis on the Border Reivers, bandits who rampaged around the border areas during the Middle Ages (entry £3.75).

Places to Stay
The University halls double as the *Carlisle Youth Hostel (☎ 597352)* from early July to

early September in the Old Brewery Residences on Bridge Lane. A bed costs £12.50.

There are plenty of comfortable and accessible B&Bs for around £16, especially along Warwick Rd; from the station, cross Butchergate, walk around the crescent and it's on your right. The small and friendly *Stratheden (☎ 520192)* at No 93 has pleasingly decorated rooms for £16 to £20 a head. *Cornerways Guest House (☎ 521733)* at No 107 is larger and does B&B from £16.

Getting There & Away
Bus Main National Express (☎ 0870-580 8080) bus connections run to/from London (£22, 6½ hours), Glasgow (£12.75, two hours) and Manchester (£16, three hours). A Rail Link coach service runs to Galashiels in the Scottish Borders – see the South-East Scotland section later in this chapter.

Train Carlisle is the terminus for five famous scenic railways; phone ☎ 0845-748 4950 for information. There are 15 trains a day to Carlisle from London's Euston station (from £26, four hours). Most of the following lines have Day Ranger tickets that allow you unlimited travel – ask for details.

Leeds-Settle-Carlisle Line (LSC)
  This famous line cuts south-east across the Yorkshire Dales through beautiful countryside and is one of the great engineering achievements of the Victorian railway age – the Ribblehead Viaduct is 32m high. Several stations make good starting points for walks in the Yorkshire Dales National Park.
Lake District Line
  This line branches off the main north-south line between Preston and Carlisle at Oxenholme, just outside Kendal, for Windermere. The landscape on the main line is beautiful, but you're whisked through pretty quickly. The Windermere branch is only about 10 miles long but takes nearly half an hour.
Tyne Valley Line
  This line follows Hadrian's Wall to and from Newcastle. There are fine views, and it's useful for visitors to the wall; see the Newcastle upon Tyne and Hadrian's Wall sections earlier in this chapter.
Cumbrian Coast Line
  This line follows the coast in a great arc around to Lancaster, with views over the Irish Sea and back to the Lake District. Change at Barrow for

BRITAIN

trains to Lancaster on the main line. Ulverston, on the line just past Barrow, is the starting point for the Cumbria Way, which traverses the lakes to Carlisle.

Glasgow to Carlisle Line
The main route north to Glasgow gives you a glimpse of the grand scale of Scottish landscapes.

Scotland

No visitor to Britain should miss the opportunity to visit Scotland. Despite its official union with England in 1707, it maintains an independent national identity that extends considerably further than the occasional kilt and bagpipes. Similarities and close links exist, but there are also considerable differences.

It's also very beautiful and suffers less than England from poor urban planning. The Highlands are extraordinary. It's hardly a secret, but for a region that has some of the world's most dramatic scenery, it's curiously under-appreciated, especially by the English, many of whom don't realise what an extraordinary neighbour they have.

Scottish urban culture is also quite different. Edinburgh is one of the world's most beautiful cities; energetic Glasgow is a vibrant cultural centre; St Andrews is a beautiful coastal university town; and prosperous Aberdeen surveys the North Sea with a proprietorial interest.

FACTS ABOUT SCOTLAND
History
Celts It's believed that the earliest settlement of Scotland was undertaken by hunters and fishers 6000 years ago. They were followed by the Celtic Picts, whose loose tribal organisation survived to the 18th century in the clan structure of the Highlands. They never bowed to the Romans, who retreated and built the Hadrian and Antonine walls, defining the north as a separate entity.

Another Celtic tribe, the Gaels (Scotti), arrived from northern Ireland (Scotia) in the 6th century AD. They finally united with the Picts in the 9th century in response to the threat posed by the Scandinavians who dominated the northern islands and west coast. By the time the Normans arrived, most of Scotland was Christian and loosely united under the Canmore dynasty.

Normans The Normans never conquered Scotland, although they wielded a major influence over several weak kings, and the Lowlands (with the most important arable land) were controlled by French-speaking aristocrats from northern England. The Highland clans remained staunchly Gaelic, the Islands remained closely linked to Norway, and neither paid much attention to central authority.

Despite almost continuous border warfare, it wasn't until a dispute over the Canmore succession that Edward I attempted the conquest of Scotland. Beginning with the siege of Berwick in 1296, fighting finally ended in 1328 with the Treaty of Northampton, which recognised Robert the Bruce as king of an independent country. Robert, more Norman than Scottish in his ancestry, cemented an alliance with France that would complicate the political map for almost 400 years.

Stuarts In 1371 the kingship passed to the Fitzalan family. The Fitzalans had served William the Conqueror and his descendants as High Stewards, and Stewart (changed to Stuart following Mary's accession) became the dynasty's name.

In 1503 James IV married the daughter of Henry VII of England, the first of the Tudor monarchs, thereby linking the two families. However, this didn't prevent the French from persuading James to go to war against his in-laws; he was killed at the disastrous battle of Flodden Hill (1513) along with 10,000 of his subjects.

By the 16th century, Scotland was a nationalistic society, with close links to Europe and a visceral hatred for the English. It had universities at St Andrews, Glasgow, Edinburgh and Aberdeen (there were only two in England) and a rigorous intellectual climate that was fertile ground for the ideas of the Reformation, a critique of the medieval Catholic church, and the rise of Protestantism.

Mary Queen of Scots In 1542 James V died, leaving his two-week-old daughter Mary to be proclaimed queen. Henry VIII of England decided she would make a suitable daughter-in-law, and his armies ravaged the Borders and sacked Edinburgh in a failed attempt to force agreement from the Scots (the 'Rough Wooing'). At 15, Mary married the

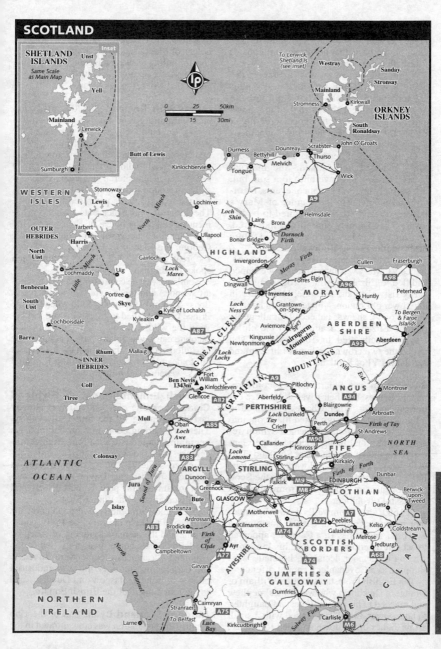

SCOTLAND

SHETLAND ISLANDS

Same Scale as Main Map

Inset

Unst

Yell

Mainland

Lerwick

Sumburgh

WESTERN ISLES

Butt of Lewis

Stornoway

Lewis

OUTER HEBRIDES

Tarbert

Harris

North Uist

Uig

Benbecula

South Uist

Portree

Skye

Lochboisdale

Barra

Rhum

INNER HEBRIDES

Coll

Tiree

Mull

Colonsay

ATLANTIC OCEAN

Jura

Islay

Kinlochbervie

Durness

Bettyhill

Tongue

Melvich

Dounreay

Scrabster

Thurso

John O'Groats

Westray

Mainland

Stromness

Kirkwall

ORKNEY ISLANDS

Sanday

Stronsay

South Ronaldsay

To Lerwick, Shetland Is (see inset)

Wick

Helmsdale

Brora

Lairg

Loch Shin

Lochinver

Ullapool

Bonar Bridge

Dornoch Firth

Gairloch

Loch Maree

HIGHLAND

Invergordon

Dingwall

Inverness

Moray Firth

Cullen

Fraserburgh

Forres

Elgin

A96

Peterhead

Huntly

A98

To Bergen & Faroe Islands

Kyle of Lochalsh

Kyleakin

Loch Ness

Grantown-on-Spey

MORAY

ABERDEEN SHIRE

Aberdeen

A93

Mallaig

GREAT GLEN

A87

Aviemore

Spey

Kingussie

Newtonmore

Cairngorm Mountains

Loch Lochy

Braemar

MOUNTAINS

Nth Esk

Ben Nevis 1343m

Fort William

Kinlochleven

Glencoe

A82

GRAMPIAN

A9

Pitlochry

ANGUS

A94

Montrose

Aberfeldy

PERTHSHIRE

Blairgowrie

Arbroath

Oban

Loch Awe

A85

Loch Tay

Dunkeld

Dundee

Perth

Firth of Tay

St Andrews

NORTH SEA

Inveraray

Crieff

Callander

Kinross

M90

FIFE

A83

Loch Lomond

Stirling

Kirkaldy

Firth of Forth

Dunbar

ARGYLL

STIRLING

Falkirk

M9

EDINBURGH

Dunoon

Greenock

M8

LOTHIAN

Berwick-upon-Tweed

Bute

GLASGOW

Motherwell

Duns

Lochranza

Ardrossan

Kilmarnock

Lanark

Peebles

A7

A72

Brodick

Arran

Firth of Clyde

Ayr

M74

Galashiels

Kelso

Coldstream

Campbeltown

AYRSHIRE

SCOTTISH BORDERS

Melrose

Jedburgh

Girvan

A77

A74

A68

North Channel

DUMFRIES & GALLOWAY

Dumfries

ENGLAND

NORTHERN IRELAND

Cairnryan

Stranraer

A75

To Belfast

Larne

Luce Bay

Kirkcudbright

Solway Firth

Carlisle

M6

North Minch

Lochmaddy

Little Minch

Sound of Jura

Loch Lochy

French dauphin and duly became Queen of France as well as Scotland; she claimed England, on the basis that her Protestant cousin, Elizabeth I, was illegitimate.

While Catholic Mary was in France, the Scottish Reformation was underway under the leadership of John Knox. In 1560 the Scottish Parliament abolished the Latin mass and the authority of the pope, creating a Protestant church that was independent of Rome and the monarchy.

On the death of her husband, 18-year-old Mary returned to Scotland. She married Henry Darnley and gave birth to a son, but, in a scarcely believable train of events, Darnley was involved in the murder of Mary's Italian secretary Rizzio (rumoured to be her lover). Then Darnley himself was murdered, presumably by Mary and her lover and future husband, the Earl of Bothwell.

Forced to abdicate in favour of her son, James VI, Mary was imprisoned, but escaped and fled to Elizabeth, who, recognising a security risk when she saw one, locked her in the Tower of London. Nineteen years later, at the age of 44, she was beheaded for allegedly plotting Elizabeth's death. When the childless Elizabeth died in 1603, Mary's son united the two crowns as James I of England and James VI of Scotland.

Revolution The Stuarts have become romantic figures, but their royal skills were extremely suspect. When Charles I meddled in religious matters, he provoked the Scots into organising a National Covenant which reaffirmed the total independence of the General Assembly of the Church of Scotland. This led to armed conflict. Civil war between Parliament and the king followed, with the Scottish Covenanters supporting Cromwell in his successful revolution.

In 1660, after Cromwell's death, the Stuart monarchy was restored, but the honeymoon was brief and James II, a Catholic, appeared to set out determinedly to lose his kingdom. Among other poor decisions, he made worshipping as a Covenanter a capital offence.

The English Protestants invited William of Orange, a Dutchman who was James' nephew and married to his oldest Protestant daughter, to take power. In 1689 he landed with a small army; James broke down and fled to France.

In 1692, people were horrified by the treacherous massacre, on English government orders, of MacDonalds by Campbells in Glencoe, for failing to swear allegiance to William. The massacre became Jacobite (Stuart) propaganda that still resonates today.

Union with England In 1707, after complex bargaining (and buying a few critical votes), England's government persuaded the Scottish Parliament to agree to the union of the two countries under a single parliament. The Scots received trading privileges and retained their independent church and legal system.

The decision was unpopular from the start, and the exiled Stuarts promised to repeal it. The situation was exacerbated when Parliament turned to the house of Hanover to find a Protestant successor to Queen Anne. George, the Elector of Hanover, was James I's great-grandson, but he was German and spoke no English.

Scotland was the centre for Jacobitism (Stuart support) and there were two major rebellions – first in 1715, then in 1745 when Bonnie Prince Charlie failed to extend his support beyond the wild, Catholic Highland clans. The Jacobite cause was finally buried at the Battle of Culloden (1746), after which the English set out to destroy the clans, prohibiting Highland dress, weapons and military service.

Scottish Enlightenment & Highland Clearances The old Scotland was already fast disappearing by the mid-18th century. There was strong economic growth and the beginning of industrialisation. Eighteenth-century Scotland was a sceptical and well-educated society. Among other figures, it produced philosopher David Hume, economist Adam Smith, poet Robert Burns and novelist and poet Sir Walter Scott.

In the mid-19th century, overpopulation, the collapse of the kelp industry, the 1840s potato famine and the increased grazing of sheep by the lairds (landowning aristocrats) led to the Highland Clearances. People were driven to the burgeoning slums of the new industrial cities – especially Glasgow and Dundee – and to the four corners of the British Empire.

Modern Scotland By the end of the 19th century the population was concentrated in the grim industrial towns and cities of the Lowlands. Working-class disillusionment led to the development of fierce left-wing politics. After WWI Scotland's ship, steel, coal, cotton and jute industries began to fail, and, though there was a recovery during WWII, since the 1960s they have been in terminal decline.

In the 1970s and 1980s, North Sea oil (Scottish oil, as many will tell you) gave the economy a boost. Despite the bonanza, Thatcherism failed to impress the Scots. From 1979 to 1997, Scotland was ruled by a Conservative government for which the majority of Scots didn't vote. Following the Labour Party's 1997 electoral victory, voters in a referendum chose overwhelmingly in favour of the creation of a Scottish Parliament, which began sitting in Edinburgh in 1999. The government, called the Scottish Executive, is a coalition of the Labour Party and Liberal-Democrats, while the Scottish National Party is the second largest in Parliament.

Climate

Scotland has a cool temperate climate, with winds from the Atlantic warmed by the Gulf Stream. The east coast tends to be cool and dry, the west coast milder and wetter. The weather changes quickly – a rainy day is often followed by a sunny one and there are wide variations over small distances. May and June are generally the driest months, but expect rain at any time.

Geography & Ecology

Scotland can be divided into three areas: Southern Uplands, with ranges of hills bordering England; the Central Lowlands, a triangular slice from Edinburgh and Dundee in the east to Glasgow in the west, containing the majority of the population; and the Highlands and Islands in the north.

The Lowlands is an imprecise term that's often used to describe everything south of a line from Aberdeen to Loch Lomond. It suggests that mountains and spectacular scenery are found only in the north, which is incorrect. Scotland's highest village, for example, is Wanlockhead in Dumfries in the south-west.

Edinburgh is the capital and financial centre, Glasgow the industrial centre, and Aberdeen and Dundee the two largest regional centres.

Some two-thirds of Scotland is mountain and moorland. Once it was almost entirely covered by the Caledonian forest, but now only 1% remains. In parts of the country no new trees have grown since the red deer population started to increase around 300 years ago, a continuing ecological problem. If you see a pollution incident, call the emergency number ☎ 0800-807060.

Population

Scotland has just over five million people, nearly 9% of the UK's total.

Language

There are three main languages. Gaelic is spoken by some 80,000 people, mainly in the Highlands and Islands, and is undergoing a revival. It's taught in many colleges and some schools, mainly in Gaelic-speaking areas, but there is now a Gaelic-only school in Glasgow. Lallans or Lowland Scots is spoken in the south. Then there's English, which the Scottish accent can make almost impenetrable to the *Sassenach* (the English or Lowland Scots) and other foreigners. Numerous Gaelic and Lallan words linger in everyday English speech. Ye ken? Some common terms you might encounter are:

aye	yes/always
bairn	child
bap	bread roll
ben	mountain
brae	hill
burn	creek
ceilidh	(pronounced kaylee) informal evening of entertainment and dance
croft	small farm
firth	estuary
glen	valley
haar	fog off the North Sea
Hogmanay	New Year's Eve
ken	know
kirk	church
Munro	mountain of 3000 feet (914m) or higher
wynd	lane

FACTS FOR THE VISITOR
Planning

When to Go The best time to visit is May to September. April and October are also acceptable weather risks, although many businesses close in October. In summer, daylight hours are long; the midsummer sun sets around 11 pm in the Shetland Islands and even in Edinburgh there are seemingly endless evenings.

Edinburgh becomes impossibly crowded during the festivals in August. Book a long way ahead if you plan to visit then.

In winter the weather's cold and daylight hours are short but Edinburgh and Glasgow are still worth visiting. Though travel in the Highlands can be difficult, roads are rarely closed and Scotland's ski resorts are popular then. Although many facilities close for the season, there's usually one TIC open for an area, and more B&Bs and hotels are staying open year-round. Travel in the islands can be a problem in winter because high winds easily disrupt ferries.

Tourist Offices
Outside Britain, contact the British Tourist Authority (BTA; see Tourist Offices under Facts for the Visitor earlier in this chapter). The Scottish Tourist Board (STB; ☎ 0131-332 2433, fax 315 4545) has its headquarters at 23 Ravelston Terrace (PO Box 705), Edinburgh EH4 3EU. In London, contact the STB (☎ 020-7930 8661), 19 Cockspur St, London SW1 5BL, off Trafalgar Square, for routes, detailed information and reservations. Its Web site is www.visitscotland.com.

Most towns have TICs that open 9 am to 5 pm weekdays, often opening on weekends in summer. In small places, particularly in the Highlands, TICs only open Easter to September.

Visas & Diplomatic Missions
No visas are required if you arrive from England, Wales or Northern Ireland. If you arrive from the Republic of Ireland or any other country, normal British regulations apply (see Facts for the Visitor earlier in this chapter). Edinburgh has numerous diplomatic missions (check the *Yellow Pages*).

Customs
If you arrive from the Republic of Ireland or any other country, normal British regulations apply (see Facts for the Visitor earlier in this chapter).

Money
Accommodation for backpackers is more readily available in Scotland than in England, so you can keep sleeping costs right down. Edinburgh and Glasgow are more expensive than most other mainland towns, but prices also rise steeply in remote parts of the Highlands and on the Islands where supplies depend on ferries.

The same currency is valid both sides of the border; however, the Clydesdale Bank, the Royal Bank of Scotland and the Bank of Scotland print their own pound notes. You won't have any trouble changing Scottish notes immediately south of the Scotland-England border, but elsewhere it's best to change them at banks.

You can use MasterCard and Visa in ATMs belonging to the Royal Bank of Scotland, Clydesdale Bank and Bank of Scotland; American Express card-holders can use the Bank of Scotland.

Useful Organisations
Historic Scotland (HS; ☎ 0131-668 8800), Longmore House, Salisbury Place, Edinburgh EH9 1SH, manages more than 330 historic sites, including top attractions like Edinburgh and Stirling castles. It offers short-term 'Explorer' membership – three/seven/14 days for £10/15/20. Visit it's Web site at www.historic-scotland.gov.uk.

The National Trust for Scotland (NTS; ☎ 0131-226 5922), 28 Charlotte Square, Edinburgh EH2 4ET, cares for over 100 properties and 185,000 acres of countryside. It's Web site is at www.nts.org.uk. YHA/SYHA members and student-card holders get half-price entry to its properties.

Dangers & Annoyances
Edinburgh and Glasgow are big cities with the usual problems, so normal caution is required.

Highland hikers should be properly equipped and cautious – the weather can become vicious at any time of the year. After rain, peaty soil can become boggy, so always wear stout shoes and carry a change of clothing.

The most infuriating and painful problem facing visitors to the west coast and Highlands, however, is midges. These tiny blood-sucking flies, related to mosquitoes, can be prolific. They're worse in the evenings or in cloudy or shady conditions; their season lasts from late May to mid-September, peaking mid-June to mid-August. There are several possible defences: cover up, particularly in the evening; wear light-coloured clothing (midges are attracted to dark colours); and, most importantly, buy a reliable insect repellent which includes either DEET or DMP.

Business Hours

Banking hours are normally 9.30 am to 4 pm weekdays, but in remote areas banks may only open two or three days. Post offices and shops open 9 am to 5.30 pm weekdays; post offices close at 1 pm Saturday. Shops in small towns sometimes have an early closing day midweek, while in cities there's often late-night shopping until 7 or 8 pm on Thursday or Friday.

Public Holidays & Special Events

Although Bank Holidays are also public holidays in England, in Scotland they only apply to banks and some other commercial offices. Bank Holidays occur at the start of January, Good Friday, the first and last weekend in May, the last weekend in August, St Andrew's Day (30 November) and Christmas Day and Boxing Day. New Year's Day and Good Friday are general holidays, and Scottish towns normally have a spring and autumn holiday. Dates vary.

The Edinburgh International Festival (the world's largest arts festival), the Edinburgh Fringe Festival and the Military Tattoo, take place during August each year.

Activities

Hiking Long-distance hiking routes in Scotland include the Southern Upland Way (see Stranraer later in this chapter), the West Highland Way (see Glasgow later in this chapter), the Fife Coastal Path and the Speyside Way. There's also a network of thousands of miles of paths and tracks. Scotland has a long tradition of relatively free access to open country. Numerous guidebooks are available, including Lonely Planet's *Walking in Britain*.

The southern Highlands are popular (but not crowded), particularly the Cairngorms west of Aberdeen and the Grampians east of Oban and Fort William. The walking and climbing is spectacular, but Scottish mountains can be killers. Caution is required – the

climate over 1000m is equivalent to that north of the Arctic Circle. Cold, wet conditions are common so you must be properly equipped and if necessary stay put until the weather improves. Thick mist can descend suddenly at any time so it's essential to be able to use a map and compass. It's also important to notify someone reliable of your plans.

Cycling Cycling is a popular way to see the lochs, forests, glens and hills of central and southern Scotland. Intrepid cyclists can visit the more remote, but majestic Highlands and mystical Islands.

Skiing Scotland has a flourishing skiing industry and the season runs between December and April. Although there's nothing to rival the European Alps, there are several resorts of international standard within a day's travel from London in the Cairngorms (near Aviemore and Braemar) and around Ben Nevis (Scotland's highest mountain, near Fort William). The STB has details.

Surfing The north coast of Scotland, especially around Thurso, offers some of the best (and coldest) surfing in Britain.

Accommodation

You can camp free on all public land (unless it's specifically protected). Commercial camping grounds are geared to caravans and vary widely in quality, but usually have tent sites for £5 to £10. The STB's *Scotland: Camping & Caravan Parks* (£3.99), available from TICs, lists many, but by no means all, camping grounds.

'Bothies' and camping barns are primitive shelters, often in remote places.

There are numerous hostels and B&Bs. The Scottish Youth Hostel Association (SYHA; ☎ 01786-891400, fax 891333, ✆ syha@ syha.org.uk), 7 Glebe Crescent, Stirling FK8 2JA, produces a handbook (£1.50) giving details on over 70 hostels, including transport links. Its hostels are generally cheaper and often better than its English counterparts. In big cities costs are £12.75/11.25 for adults/children; the rest range from £6.75/6 to £9.25/8. Its Web address is www.syha.org.uk.

These are supplemented by independent hostels and bunkhouses, most between £7 and £11. Look out for *Independent Hostel Guide Budget Accommodation*, which lists over 100 hostels in Scotland and is available from some TICs. Alternatively send a stamped, self-addressed envelope to Pete Thomas, Croft Bunkhouse & Bothies, 7 Portnalong, Isle of Skye IV47 8SL. Its Web site is www.hostel-scotland.uk.

B&Bs and small hotels are usually cheaper than their English counterparts and budget-conscious travellers rarely need pay more than £20 per person. The TICs have local booking services (usually £1 or £2) and a Book-a-Bed-Ahead scheme (£3). A 10% deposit is also required for most bookings. The service is worth using in July and August, but isn't necessary otherwise, unless you plan to arrive in a town after business hours (when the local TIC will be closed). If you arrive in the evening without prebooked accommodation, it may still be worth going to the TIC, since many leave a list in the window showing B&Bs that had rooms free when it closed.

Food

Scotland's chefs have an enviable range of fresh meat, seafood and vegetables at their disposal. Most restaurants are reasonably good and will cater for vegetarians. In small villages and hotels, alternatives are usually limited, although village bakeries have a good range of pies, cakes and snacks. Almost every town has at least one Chinese or Indian restaurant.

GETTING THERE & AWAY
Air

There are direct services from many European cities to Edinburgh, Glasgow, Dundee, Aberdeen and Inverness, and from North America to Glasgow. New York to Glasgow is around US$670. You can also connect with numerous flights from London to Scotland (including Inverness).

If you're coming from overseas, it's often more economical to buy a cheap fare to London, then take a train or internal flight to Scotland. Standard return flights from London to Glasgow or Edinburgh cost around £275, but discount return flights can be as low as £70 and there are often no-frills special deals from companies like Easyjet (☎ 0870-600 0000) and Go (☎ 0845-605 4321).

Land

Bus Long-distance buses (coaches) are usually the cheapest method of getting to Scotland. The main operator is Scottish Citylink (☎ 0870-550 5050), part of the National Express group, with numerous services from London and other points in England and Wales (see Getting There & Away under Edinburgh or Glasgow later in this chapter). Check the Web site at www.citylink.co.uk.

Fares on the main routes are competitive, with some operators undercutting National Express. Silver Choice (☎ 020-7730 3466) offers the cheapest deal at £19/24 for a single/return from London to Edinburgh or Glasgow. Cheap tickets sell out quickly so book in advance. See Getting Around at the beginning of this chapter for more information.

Train Intercity services (☎ 0845-748 4950) can take you from London's King's Cross to Edinburgh in as little as 4½ hours or from London's Euston or Paddington stations to Glasgow in 5½ hours (see the Getting There & Away sections for those cities).

There's a range of fares but you can make considerable savings by planning ahead, even though restrictions will apply to the cheaper ones (eg, travelling off peak). With Virgin Trains the cheapest adult return ticket between London and Edinburgh or Glasgow is the Virgin Value seven day advance ticket, which costs only £29. This compares with the standard open return fare of £175.

Car & Motorcycle Edinburgh is 373 miles from London and Glasgow is 392 miles away. Allow eight hours. The main roads are the M6, A74 and M74 to Glasgow, the A1 and A68 to Edinburgh.

Hitching It's easy enough though not necessarily wise to hitch to Scotland along the A68 to Edinburgh or the M6 to Glasgow. The coastal routes are scenic but slow.

Sea

For more details on the ferry services listed here, see Getting There & Away at the start of this chapter.

Northern Ireland P&O (☎ 0870-242 4666 for Irish services) has ferry links from

Cairnryan to Larne, near Belfast. SeaCat (☎ 0870-552 3523) operates a high-speed catamaran between Belfast, Stranraer and Troon. It's Web site is at www.seacat.co.uk.

Scandinavia From mid-May to early September, P&O/Smyril Line (☎ 01224-572615, www.smyril-line.fo) operates between Lerwick (Shetland), Bergen (Norway), Tórshavn (Faroes) and Seydisfjördur (Iceland), calling at Lerwick twice weekly. To make a fascinating northern sea route, you could link this ferry service with P&O services to Stromness (Orkney), Scrabster (near Thurso) and Aberdeen on the mainland.

See the Getting There & Away chapter at the start of this book for more details.

GETTING AROUND

If you're not a student, it's worth considering ScotRail's Freedom of Scotland Travelpass, which gives unlimited travel on ScotRail trains and most Caledonian MacBrayne (CalMac) ferries to the west-coast islands, as well as discounts on some other ferry services (see Train later in this section).

Another possibility is Haggis Backpackers or Go Blue Banana, bus companies which run a jump-on, jump-off circuit from hostel to hostel around the Highlands (see Bus later in this section).

Air

British Airways (☎ 0845-773 3377), with its partners Loganair and British Regional Airlines, and Gill Airways (☎ 0191-214 6666) connect the mainland towns, the Western Isles, Orkney and Shetland.

Bus

Since no single bus company provides full coverage of Scotland, you're likely to be using the services of different operators. Scotland's major player is Scottish Citylink (☎ 0870-550 5050), part of the National Express group. It's Web site is at www.citylink.co.uk. There are also smaller regional operators many of which form part of the Stagecoach or First networks. Royal Mail postbuses (☎ 01246-546329, 0845-774 0740) provide a stable, reliable service to remoter areas and can be particularly useful for walkers. Most buses don't carry bicycles.

Regional inquiry telephone numbers have been given throughout the text; you are advised to use them.

The National Express Tourist Trail Pass (see Getting Around at the beginning of this chapter) can be used on Scottish Citylink services. Citylink also honours Europe under-26 cards, and provides discounts all over Scotland and Europe.

If you don't have one of these cards, fulltime students and people aged under 26 can buy the so-called Smart Card, the equivalent to the National Express Discount Coach Card, which can be purchased when you're buying your ticket. On presentation of proof of age or student status (an NUS card or ISIC), a passport photo and a £5 fee, you get the Smart Card to add to your collection. It entitles you to a 30% discount, so chances are you'll be ahead after buying your first ticket.

June to September, Haggis Backpackers (☎ 0131-557 9393, ✉ haggis@radicaltravel.com), 60 High St, Edinburgh, operates a daily 'Highland Fling' circuit between hostels in Edinburgh, Pitlochry, Inverness, Loch Ness, Ullapool, Isle of Skye, Fort William, Oban, Loch Lomond and Glasgow, finishing back in Edinburgh. You can hop on and off the minibus wherever and whenever you like in a three-month period, booking up to 24 hours before departure. There's no compulsion to stay in hostels either. Fares start at £85.

Go Blue Banana (☎ 0131-220-6868), Suite 8, North Bridge House, 28 North Bridge, Edinburgh, also runs a jump-on, jump-off service on a similar circuit for the same price. Both also offer excellent-value, three-day Highlands tours for £79 from Edinburgh.

Train

ScotRail (☎ 0845-748 4950) operates Scotland's trains, which travel on some stunning routes, but they're limited and expensive, so you'll probably have to combine rail travel with other modes of transport. The West Highland line through Fort William to Mallaig and the routes from Stirling to Inverness, Inverness to Thurso and Inverness to Kyle of Lochalsh are some of the most scenic in the world. ScotRail's Web site is at www.scotrail.co.uk.

The BritRail pass, which includes travel in Scotland, must be bought outside Britain.

BRITAIN

ScotRail's Freedom of Scotland Travelpass and its regional rover tickets can be bought in Britain, from the British Travel Centre, Regent St, London and from most staffed train stations in Scotland. The pass gives unlimited travel on ScotRail trains, Caledonia Mac-Brayne (CalMac) ferries and Strathclyde Public Transport (SPT) ferries; 33% discount on postbuses and selected regional bus routes with Scottish Citylink, Fife Scottish and First Edinburgh; 33% discount on the P&O Orkney (Stromness) to Scrabster ferry; 20% discount on P&O Aberdeen to Shetland, Aberdeen to Orkney; and £1.50 off Guide Friday city tours of Edinburgh, Glasgow, Stirling, Perth and Inverness.

The Travelpass costs £79 for four days travel out of eight consecutive days, £109 for eight days out of 15, and £119 for 12 days out of 15.

Students get equivalent discounts anyway and could get a much cheaper rail rover ticket. The Highland Rover ticket covers the West Highlands, north-east coast and the Aberdeen-Inverness-Kyle line (£49 for four out of eight consecutive days). The Central Scotland Rover covers the central area (£29 for three out of seven consecutive days).

Reservations for bicycles (£3.50) are compulsory on many services.

Sometimes the cheap day-return fare is cheaper than the full one-way fare.

Hitching

Hitching is reasonably good in Scotland, with the average wait 30 to 40 minutes. Although the north-west is more difficult because there's less traffic, waits of over two hours are unusual (except on Sunday in 'Sabbath' areas). Public transport isn't scheduled to stop on the A9 (except in villages), though buses will usually stop and rescue you if they're not full.

Boat

Caledonian MacBrayne (CalMac; ☎ 0870-565 0000) is the most important ferry operator on the west coast, with services from Ullapool to the Outer Hebrides, and from Mallaig to Skye and on to the Outer Hebrides. Its main west-coast port, however, is Oban, with ferries to the Inner Hebridean islands of Coll, Tiree, Lismore, Mull and Colonsay and the Outer Hebridean islands of Barra and South Uist. CalMac's Web site is at www.calmac.co.uk.

A single passenger fare from Oban to Lochboisdale, South Uist (Hebrides), for example, is £18.25. CalMac's Island Hopscotch tickets are usually the best deal, which offer ferry combinations on 20 set routes. CalMac also has Island Rover tickets, offering unlimited travel for eight/15 days (£42/61).

P&O (☎ 01224-574411) has ferries from Aberdeen and Scrabster to Orkney and from Aberdeen to Shetland. June to August, the cheapest one-way tickets to Stromness (Orkney) cost £16 from Scrabster (near Thurso) and £42 from Aberdeen. Between Aberdeen and Lerwick (Shetland) fares start at £58. There's a 10% student discount. P&O's Web site is at www.poscottishferries.co.uk.

EDINBURGH
☎ 0131 • pop 409,000

Edinburgh has an incomparable location, studded with volcanic hills, on the southern edge of the Firth of Forth. Its superb architecture ranges from extraordinary 16th-century tenements to monumental Georgian and Victorian masterpieces. Sixteen thousand buildings are listed as architecturally or historically important, in a city that is a World Heritage Site.

In some ways, however, it's the least Scottish of Scotland's cities partly because of the impact of tourism, partly because of its closeness to England and the links between the two countries' upper classes, and partly because of its multicultural, sophisticated population.

The royal capital since the 11th century, all the great dramas of Scottish history played at least one act in Edinburgh. Even after the union of 1707 it remained the centre for government administration (now the Scottish Executive), the separate Scottish legal system and the Presbyterian Church of Scotland. With devolution and the location of the new Scottish Parliament in Edinburgh, the city once again wields real political power.

History

Castle Rock, a volcanic crag with three vertical sides, dominates the city centre. This natural defensive position was probably the feature that first attracted settlers; it has been fortified since at least AD 600 and there are even older traces of habitation.

The old, walled city grew on the east-west ridge (the Royal Mile, which runs from the Palace of Holyroodhouse to the castle) and south of the castle around Grassmarket. This restricted, defensible zone became a medieval Manhattan, forcing its densely packed inhabitants to build multistoreyed tenements. Even so, the city was sacked by the English seven times.

In the second half of the 18th century a new city was created across the ravine to the north of the old city. Before it was drained, this valley was a lake – now it's the Princes St Gardens, cut but not spoilt by the railway line.

The population was expanding, defence declined in importance, and the thinkers and architects of the Scottish Enlightenment planned to distance themselves from Edinburgh's Jacobite past. Built on a grid, the New Town owes its brilliance to the way that it opens onto the castle, the Old Town and the Firth of Forth, and to the genius of architects like Robert Adams whose gracious, disciplined buildings line the streets.

The population exploded in the 19th century – Edinburgh quadrupled in size to 400,000, not much less than it is today – and the Old Town's tenements were taken over by refugees from the Irish famines. A new ring of crescents and circuses was built south of the New Town, then grey Victorian terraces sprang up. In the 20th century the slums were emptied into new housing estates even farther out, which now foster severe social problems.

Edinburgh entered a new era following the 1997 referendum in favour of an independent Scottish Parliament, which began functioning in July 1999. The parliament is temporarily housed in the Church of Scotland Assembly Rooms in the Old Town while a modern Parliament building is being constructed at the eastern end of the Royal Mile.

Orientation

The most important landmark is Arthur's Seat, the 251m-high rocky peak south-east of the centre. The Old and New Towns are separated by Princes St Gardens and Waverley station, with the castle dominating them both.

Princes St, the main shopping street, runs along the northern side of the gardens.

Buildings are restricted to the northern side of Princes St, which has the usual high-street shops. At the eastern end, Calton Hill is crowned by several monuments including an incomplete war memorial modelled on the Parthenon, and a tower honouring Nelson. The Royal Mile (Lawnmarket, High St and Canongate) is the parallel equivalent in the Old Town.

Information

Tourist Offices The busy main TIC (☎ 557 1700), Waverley Market, 3 Princes St EH2 2QP, opens daily all year. In July and August it stays open to 8 pm. There's also a branch (☎ 338 2167) at Edinburgh airport. Both have Scotland-wide information, and sell the useful *Essential Guide to Edinburgh* (£1). They also have an accommodation service, but charge £3, so you should consider using the excellent free accommodation brochure. The TIC's Web site is at www.edinburgh.org.

Money The TIC *bureau de change* is open the same hours as the TIC. American Express (☎ 225 7881), 139 Princes St, opens 9 am to 5.30 pm Monday to Friday (from 9.30 on Thursday) and 9 am to 4 pm Saturday. Thomas Cook (☎ 465 7700), 26-28 Frederick St, opens 9 am to 5.30 pm Monday to Saturday (from 10 am Thursday).

Email & Internet Access Web 13 Internet Café (☎ 229 8883), 13 Bread St, offers online access for £5 per hour; check the Web site at www.web13.co.uk. It opens 9 am to 10 pm weekdays, to 6 pm Saturday, noon to 6 pm Sunday. Cyberia (☎ 220 4403), 88 Hanover St, charges £2.50 per half-hour and opens 10 am to 10 pm daily. Its Web site is at www.cybersurf.co.uk.

Emergency Dial ☎ 999 for police, fire or ambulance (free call).

Things to See & Do

The best place to start any tour of Edinburgh is **Edinburgh Castle** (☎ 225 9846), which has excellent views overlooking the city.

The castle is the headquarters for the British army's Scottish Division, and is a complex of buildings that were altered many times by war and the demands of the military.

BRITAIN

CENTRAL EDINBURGH

OTHER
1 St Andrew Square
   Bus & Coach Station
2 St James' Shopping Centre/
   Post Office
3 City Observatory
4 National Monument
5 Nelson Monument
7 Cyberia Internet Cafe
9 Georgian House
10 American Express
11 Thomas Cook
12 National Gallery
13 Sir Walter Scott Monument
14 Tour Bus Departure Point
15 TIC
16 Venue Night Club
17 New Scottish Parliament
   (Under Construction)
18 Dynamic Earth
19 John Knox House
22 The Writers' Museum
23 Church of Scotland General
   Assembly Hall/Temporary
   Scottish Parliament
24 Gladstone's Land
25 Museum of Childhood
27 The Vaults
28 Fringe Festival Box Office
29 St Giles Cathedral
30 Edinburgh Festival Office,
   The Hub
34 Parliament House
35 City Café
36 Bannerman's
37 Haggis Backpackers
39 Edinburgh University
41 Greyfriars Kirk
42 Web 13 Internet Café
45 The Peartree House

PLACES TO STAY
6 Princes St Backpackers
20 Royal Mile Backpackers
21 Edinburgh Backpackers Hostel
26 High St Hostel
48 Pollock Halls of Residence
49 Menzies Guest House; Villa Nina
51 Bruntsfield Youth Hostel

PLACES TO EAT
8 La P'tite Folie
31 Ristorante Gennaro
32 Mamma's
   Pizzas
33 Baracoa
38 Khushi's
40 Negociants
43 Kebab Mahal
44 Susie's Wholefood
   Diner
46 La Bonne Mer
47 Kalpna
50 Parrots

The small, 12th-century **St Margaret's Chapel** is the oldest building in Edinburgh. The castle was the seat of Scottish kings, and the royal apartments include the tiny room where Mary Queen of Scots gave birth to the boy who became James VI of Scotland and James I of England. You can also see the **Stone of Destiny**, returned to Scotland in 1996. It's open 9.30 am to 6 pm daily (5 pm from October to March); entry £7.

The castle is at the western end of the Royal Mile, which runs down to the Palace of Holyroodhouse. The streetscape is an extraordinary collage of 16th and 17th-century architecture, and an exploration of the closes and wynds that radiate from it evokes the crowded and vital city of these times.

On the left, **Gladstone's Land** (☎ 226 5856) and **The Writers' Museum** (Lady Stair's House; ☎ 529 4901) are restored townhouses that give fascinating insights into the urban life of the past. Gladstone's Land was completed in 1620 and has been skilfully restored; it's open April to October and costs £3.50. The Writers' Museum contains memorabilia belonging to Robert Burns, Sir Walter Scott and Robert Louis Stevenson.

Turn right onto the George IV Bridge, which crosses Cowgate (an ancient, narrow street). Grassmarket, below and to the right, has a number of pubs and restaurants. Continue until you reach the angled intersection with Candlemaker Row and **Greyfriars Kirk** (where the National Covenant was signed) with its beautiful old churchyard; there are views from here across the roofs to the castle.

Return to the Royal Mile and turn right past the much-restored 15th-century **St Giles Cathedral**. At the cathedral's rear is **Parliament House**, now the seat of the supreme law courts of Scotland. Immediately east of St Giles stands the **Mercat Cross**, where public proclamations were made.

Continue down the Royal Mile over North/South Bridge to the **Museum of Childhood** (☎ 529 4142) on your right and **John Knox House** (☎ 556 9579) on your left. The Museum of Childhood has a fascinating collection of toys (free entry). John Knox was the fiery leader of the Scottish Reformation (open Monday to Saturday; £2.25).

The **Palace of Holyroodhouse** at the eastern end of the Royal Mile is a Stuart palace mostly dating from a reconstruction by Charles II in 1671. Holyroodhouse is the official Scottish residence of the British royal family. Although you're carefully shepherded through a limited part of the palace, it has a certain fascination. It's open daily from April to October except when the Queen is in residence (usually around mid-May or mid-June); £6.

Close to Holyroodhouse, the new **Scottish Parliament** is under construction. Opposite is the engaging **Dynamic Earth** exhibition on the planet's geology and natural history; it's open daily from Easter to October, and Wednesday to Sunday the rest of the year; £6.95.

From the palace, turn right and climb Abbey Hill (under the railway overpass). Turn left onto Regent Rd, which takes you back to Princes St. On your right you pass **Calton Hill**, worth climbing for its superb views across to the castle.

Continue along Princes St until you get to the extravagant 200-foot spire of the **Sir Walter Scott Monument**. Turn right and walk up the slight hill to **St Andrew Square**, home to several financial institutions, including the Bank of Scotland. Turn left down **George St**, the main street of the New Town, which is lined with many fine buildings.

If you're a little thirsty at this stage, turn left and then right onto **Rose St**, which is famous for its large number of pubs. Then continue west until you come out onto **Charlotte Square**; the northern side is Robert Adam's masterpiece. No 7 is the **Georgian House** (☎ 225 2160), furnished by the NTS to bring it back to its full 18th-century glory. It's open daily April to October (closed Sunday morning); £5.

Special Events

The Edinburgh International Festival is the world's largest, most important arts festival and the world's premier companies play to packed audiences. The Fringe Festival grew up alongside it, presenting the would-be future stars. It now claims to be the largest such event in the world, with over 500 amateur and professional groups presenting every possible kind of avant-garde performance. Just to make sure that every bed within 40 miles is taken, the Edinburgh Military Tattoo is held at the same time.

BRITAIN

The festivals take place around mid-August, but the Tattoo finishes four or five days earlier, so the last week is less hectic. If you want to attend the International Festival, it's necessary to book; the program, published in April, is available from the Edinburgh Festival Office (☎ 473 2000), The Hub, Castlehill, Royal Mile, EH1 2NE. It's Web site is at www.eif.co.uk. The Fringe Festival is less formal, and many performances have empty seats the day before. Programs are available from June from the Festival Fringe Society (☎ 226 5257), 180 High St EH1 1QS. It's Web site is at www.edfringe.com. To book the Military Tattoo, contact the Tattoo Office (☎ 225 1188), 32 Market St EH1 1QS. It's Web site is at www.edintattoo.co.uk.

Book accommodation as far in advance as possible. Contact the Edinburgh & Lothian Tourist Board (☎ 473 3800, fax 473 3881, @ esic@eltb.org), 3 Princes St EH2 2QP, or for a reservation in a university college, Reservations Office (☎ 667 0662), Pollock Halls, 18 Holyrood Park Rd EH16 5AY.

Hogmanay, the Scottish celebration of the New Year, is another major fixture in Edinburgh's festival calendar. Edinburgh is *the* place to be in the New Year and you'll need to book well ahead if you want to be part of the fun.

Places to Stay

Edinburgh has numerous accommodation options, but fills quickly over New Year, at Easter and also between mid-May and mid-September, particularly August. Single rooms are always in short supply. Book in advance if possible, or use the accommodation services operated by the TIC or Thomas Cook.

Camping The *Mortonhall Caravan Park* (☎ 664 1533, 38 Mortonhall Gate) off Frogston Rd East, 5 miles south-east of the centre, opens March to October. Sites are £8.25 to £12.75.

Hostels & Colleges The most popular hostel accommodation is the friendly, central, independent *High St Hostel* (☎ 557 3984, 8 Blackfriars St)*. From Princes St, turn right onto North Bridge and walk up the hill until you get to the Royal Mile (High St at this point), turn left and Blackfriars St is the second on the right. Beds are £10.50. Nearby is *Royal Mile*

Backpackers (☎ 557 6120, 105 High St) with beds from £11.50. *Edinburgh Backpackers Hostel* (☎ 220 1717, 65 Cockburn St) is close to all the action and has a licensed cafe; dorm beds cost from £11.50.

Princes St Backpackers (☎ 556 6894, 5 West Register St) has an equally good location, behind Princes St and close to the bus station, although you do have to negotiate 77 exhausting steps to reach reception. It charges £9.50 in a dorm, or £24 for a double (Sunday night dinner is free!).

Belford Hostel (☎ 225 6209, 6 Douglas Gardens) in a converted church is well run and cheerful. Dorm beds cost from £11.50, and there are several doubles for £33.

Quiet *Palmerston Lodge* (☎ 220 5141, 25 Palmerston Place) on the corner of Chester St was once a boarding school. The rates, including continental breakfast, start at £12 for a dorm bed; singles/doubles with bathroom are £30/40.

There are two good SYHA hostels. *Eglinton Youth Hostel* (☎ 337 1120, 18 Eglinton Crescent) is about 1 mile west of the city near Haymarket train station; beds cost £12.75 /11.25 for seniors/children. Walk down Princes St and continue on Shandwick Place which becomes West Maitland St; veer right at Haymarket along Haymarket Terrace, then turn right onto Coates Gardens which runs into Eglinton Crescent.

Bruntsfield Youth Hostel (☎ 447 2994, 7 Bruntsfield Crescent) is trickier to get to but has an attractive location overlooking Bruntsfield Links about 2½ miles south-west of Waverley train station. Rates are £11.75/10.50. Catch bus No 11 or 16 from the garden side of Princes St and alight at Forbes Rd just after the gardens on the left.

During university vacations the *Pollock Halls of Residence* (☎ 667 0662, 18 Holyrood Park Rd) has modern singles/doubles for £25/48, including breakfast.

B&Bs The best budget bet will be one of numerous private houses; get the TIC's free accommodation guide and make some phone calls. Outside festival time you should have no trouble getting something for around £20, although it'll be a bus ride away in the suburbs.

Guesthouses are generally £2 or £3 more expensive, and to get a private bathroom you'll have to pay about £25 to £30. The main concentrations are around Pilrig St, Pilrig; Minto St (a southern continuation of North Bridge), Newington; and Gilmore Place and Leamington Terrace, Bruntsfield.

Ardenlee Guest House (☎ 556 2838, 9 *Eyre Place*) north of the New Town and 1 mile from the centre has rooms from £26 per person, while *Dene Guest House* (☎ 556 2700, 7 *Eyre Place*) has B&B from £19.50.

Pilrig St, left off Leith Walk (veer left at the eastern end of Princes St), is a happy hunting ground for guesthouses. *Balmoral Guest House* (☎ 554 1857), No 32, has easy access to the city and rooms from £20 to £30 per person. Similar is *Barrosa* (☎ 554 3700), No 21, with doubles for £22/32 without/with private bath. At No 94, attractive, two-crown *Balquhidder Guest House* (☎ 554 3377) has rooms with bathrooms from £20 to £40 a head.

There are numerous guesthouses on and around Minto St/Mayfield Gardens in Newington, south of the centre, accessed by plenty of buses. This is the main traffic artery from the south and carries traffic from the A7 and A68 (both routes are signposted). The best places are on the streets on either side of the main road.

Nonsmoking *Salisbury Guest House* (☎ 667 1264, 45 *Salisbury Rd*) east of Newington and 10 minutes from the centre by bus is quiet and comfortable. Singles/double with bathroom cost £25/48. *Casa Buzzo* (☎ 667 8998, 8 *Kilmaurs Rd*) east of Dalkeith Rd has doubles for £20 per person.

Using the same bus stop as for the Bruntsfield Youth Hostel, you can get to *Menzies Guest House* (☎ 229 7033, 33 *Leamington Terrace*) where singles/doubles cost from £20/28. *Villa Nina* (☎ 229 2644, 39 *Leamington Terrace*) only has doubles from £34 per room.

Places to Eat

For cheap eats, the best areas are around Grassmarket; near the university around Nicolson St, the extension of North/South Bridge; and in Bruntsfield.

Those staying at Bruntsfield can enjoy the quirky, popular *Parrots* (☎ 229 3252, 5 *Viewforth*) off Bruntsfield Place. It has an interesting, good-value menu with offerings such as chicken rigatoni for £4.95.

In the West End at the Haymarket end of Dalry Rd, there's *Verandah Restaurant* (☎ 337 5828), No 17, which serves tasty tandoori food and offers a three-course lunch for £5.95.

There are some lively pubs and reasonable restaurants on the northern side of Grassmarket, catering to a young crowd. Casual *Ristorante Gennaro* (☎ 226 3706), No 64, has standard Italian fare, with pizzas and pastas from £4.80 to £7. Nearby, *Mamma's Pizzas* (☎ 225 6464), No 30, is an informal pizzeria where excellent pizzas with imaginative toppings cost £3.95 to £9.95. The more exotic *Baracoa* (☎ 225 5846, 7 *Victoria St*) is a Cuban restaurant and bar, serving quite tasty, filling mains for under £10.

In the New Town *La P'tite Folie* (☎ 225 7893, 61 *Frederick St*) offers reasonably priced, good-quality French food. Most mains are under £10.

La Bonne Mer (☎ 622 9111, 113 *Buccleuch St*) specialises in seafood with a French twist. A three-course meal costs £17.95.

The university students budget favourites can be found between Nicolson St and Bristo Place at the end of the George IV Bridge. *Kebab Mahal* (☎ 667 5214, 7 *Nicolson Square*) is a legendary source of cheap sustenance with kebabs from £2.95, curries from £3.25.

Vegetarians should also look for *Susie's Wholefood Diner* (☎ 667 8729, 51 *West Nicolson St*), which has good, inexpensive, healthy mains from £3.75 to £4.95, and in the evenings live music and a belly dancer. *Negociants* (☎ 225 6313, 45-7 *Lothian St*) is a cool, comfortable, cafe and music venue. The food is good value with mains from £6.75. It opens 9 am till late daily.

Kalpna (☎ 667 9890, 2 *St Patrick's Square*), a reasonably priced Gujarati (Indian) vegetarian restaurant, offers lunch buffets for £5. *Khushi's* (☎ 556 8996, 16 *Drummond St*) is Edinburgh's original curry house. Lamb *bhuna* at £4.95 is said to be the local favourite, and you can BYO booze. It takes cash only and is closed Sunday.

Entertainment

The fortnightly magazine *List* (£1.95), giving full coverage of events in Edinburgh (and

Glasgow), is essential if you're staying for a few days.

There are several busy pubs on Grassmarket's northern side, often with live music. Turn up Cowgate, off Grassmarket's southeast, and you reach a couple of good pubs (with live music), including the relaxed *Bannerman's*. For the long summer evenings *The Peartree House (West Nicolson St)* has a large outdoor courtyard popular with students.

There are some interesting music/club venues in old vaults under the George IV and South bridges. *The Vaults (☎ 558 9052, 15 Niddry St)*, under South Bridge, has a variety of reliable club nights Thursday to Saturday.

City Café (☎ 220 0125, 19 Blair St) is a cool, 1950s US-style bar and diner. *Venue Night Club (☎ 557 3073, 17 Calton Rd)* has dance music on three floors and is worth checking.

Getting There & Away

Bus Fares from London are competitive and you may be able to get cheap promotional tickets. National Express (☎ 0870-580 8080) and Scottish Citylink (☎ 0870-550 5050) are the main operators. The journey time is 9½ to 11¼ hours depending on the route, and the cheapest fare with National Express is £22 one way (£19 with Silver Choice).

There are links to cities throughout England and Wales, including Newcastle (£8, 2¾ hours) and York (£21.75, 5½ hours). Scottish Citylink has buses to major towns in Scotland. Most west coast towns are reached via Glasgow to which there are buses every 15 to 20 minutes from Edinburgh (£5 return, 1¼ hours); there are also regular services to St Andrews, Aberdeen and Inverness.

The bus station is in the New Town, off the south-eastern corner of St Andrew Square, north of Princes St.

Train There are up to 20 trains daily from London's King's Cross station (4½ to 5½ hours); apart from Saver fares which must be booked in advance and can't be changed they're expensive (see also the introductory Getting There & Away section under Scotland).

ScotRail has two northern lines from Edinburgh: one cuts north across the Grampians to Inverness (3½ hours) and on to Thurso, the other follows the coast north around to Aberdeen (three hours) and on to Inverness.

There are trains every 15 minutes to Glasgow (£7.30 one way, 50 minutes).

For rail inquiries, phone ☎ 0845-748 4950.

Getting Around

To/From the Airport LRT's frequent Airlink buses run from Waverley Bridge near the train station to the airport, taking 35 minutes and costing £3.30/5 one way/return. A taxi costs around £15 one way.

Bus The two main companies, Lothian Regional Transport (LRT; ☎ 555 6363) and First Edinburgh (☎ 663 9233) provide frequent, cheap services. You can buy tickets when you board buses, but you must have the exact change. For short trips in the city, fares are 50p to £1. After midnight there are special night buses. The free *Edinburgh Travelmap* shows the most important services and is available from the TIC, or during weekdays contact Traveline (☎ 225 3858, 0800-232323), 2 Cockburn St.

Bicycle Edinburgh Cycle Hire (☎ 556 5560, ✆ info@cyclescotland.co.uk), 29 Blackfriars St, hires out mountain and hybrid bikes for £10 to £15 a day, or from £35 a week. It also hires out tents and touring equipment, arranges cycling tours of the city, organises tours of Scotland, and sells used bikes and buys them back.

GLASGOW
☎ 0141 • pop 611,500

Glasgow is one of Britain's largest, most interesting cities. It doesn't have the instantly inspiring beauty of Edinburgh, but it does have interesting Georgian and Victorian architecture and some distinguished suburbs of terraced squares and crescents. What makes it appealing is its vibrancy.

Although influenced by thousands of Irish immigrants, this is the most Scottish of cities, with a unique blend of friendliness, urban chaos, black humour and energy. There are some excellent art galleries and museums (most free), numerous good-value restaurants, countless pubs and bars and a lively arts scene.

Glasgow is also close to great scenery – Loch Lomond, the Trossachs and the Highlands to the north, the Hebrides to the west and the rolling hills of southern Scotland to the south.

History

Glasgow grew around the cathedral founded by St Mungo in the 6th century. In 1451 the University of Glasgow was founded – the fourth-oldest university in Britain. Unfortunately, with the exception of the cathedral, virtually nothing of the medieval city remains. It was swept away by the energetic people of a new age – the age of capitalism, the Industrial Revolution, and the British Empire.

In the 19th century, Glasgow – transformed by cotton, steel, coal, shipbuilding and trade – justifiably called itself the second city of the empire. Grand Victorian public buildings were built, but the working class lived in ghastly slums.

In the 20th century, Glasgow's port and its engineering industries went into terminal decline. By the early 1970s Glasgow looked doomed, but it has fought back by developing service industries and has rediscovered its rich cultural roots. Certainly there's renewed confidence in the city, but behind the optimism, the standard of living remains low for the UK and life continues to be tough for those affected by relatively high unemployment, inadequate housing and generally poor diet.

Orientation

The city centre is built on a grid system on the northern side of the River Clyde. The two train stations (Central and Queen St), Buchanan bus station and the TIC are all within a couple of blocks of George Square, the main city square. Running along a ridge in the northern part of the city, Sauchiehall St has a pedestrian mall with numerous high-street shops at its eastern end, and pubs and restaurants to the west. The University of Glasgow and SYHA hostel are north-west of the city centre around Kelvingrove Park. Motorways bore through the suburbs and the M8 slices through the western and northern edges of the centre. Glasgow airport lies 10 miles west.

Information

Tourist Offices The main TIC (☎ 204 4400) at 11 George Square provides a £2 accommodation-booking service. It's open 9 am to 6 pm Monday to Saturday; to 7 pm in June and September; and to 8 pm in July and August. It's also open 10 am to 6 pm Sunday, Easter to September. There's another branch (☎ 848 4440) at Glasgow airport. Check the Web site at www.seeglasgow.com.

Money American Express (☎ 221 4366), 115 Hope St, opens 8.30 am to 5.30 pm weekdays, and 9 am to noon Saturday. The TIC and the post office, on the corner of Buchanan and St Vincent Sts, both have currency exchange facilities.

Email & Internet Access You can access the Internet at the Internet Café (☎ 564 1052), 569 Sauchiehall St, for £3 for 30 minutes. For insomniacs there's the 24-hour Surfin' Internet Café (☎ 332 0404), 81 St George's Rd. The cheapest time is 5 am to noon – 3p a minute (minimum of 15 minutes) or £1 per hour.

Emergency The free emergency numbers are ☎ 999 or ☎ 112.

Things to See & Do

A good starting point is **George Square**, surrounded by imposing Victorian architecture, including the post office, the Bank of Scotland and, along its eastern side, the City Chambers (☎ 221 9600). The chambers were built in the 1880s at the high point of the city's wealth; their interior is even more extravagant than their exterior. There are free tours from the main entrance, Monday to Friday at 10.30 am and 2.30 pm.

The current **Glasgow Cathedral** (☎ 552 6891) is a direct descendant of St Mungo's simple church. It was begun in 1238 and is seen as a perfect example of pre-Reformation Gothic architecture. The lower church is reached by a stairway, and its forest of pillars creates a powerful atmosphere around St Mungo's tomb, the focus of a famous medieval pilgrimage that was believed to be as meritorious as a visit to Rome.

Beside the cathedral, the **St Mungo Museum of Religious Life & Art** (☎ 553 2557) is well worth visiting. In the main gallery, Dali's *Christ of St John of the Cross* hangs beside statues of the Buddha and Hindu deities. Outside you'll find Britain's only **Zen garden**. The museum opens 10 am to 5 pm Monday to Saturday (from 11 am Sunday); free.

There are some superb Art Nouveau buildings designed by famous Scottish architect and designer Charles Rennie Mackintosh. In

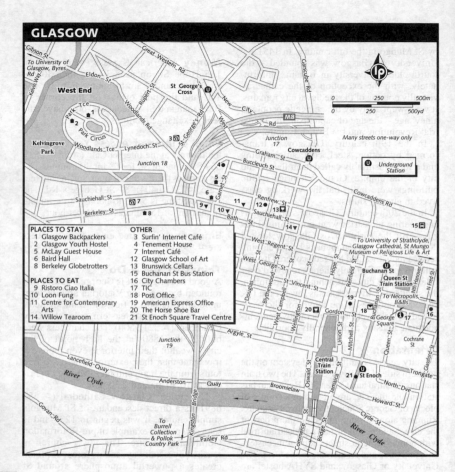

GLASGOW

West End

Kelvingrove Park

PLACES TO STAY
1 Glasgow Backpackers
2 Glasgow Youth Hostel
5 McLay Guest House
6 Baird Hall
8 Berkeley Globetrotters

PLACES TO EAT
9 Ristoro Ciao Italia
10 Loon Fung
11 Centre for Contemporary Arts
14 Willow Tearoom

OTHER
3 Surfin' Internet Café
4 Tenement House
7 Internet Café
12 Glasgow School of Art
13 Brunswick Cellars
15 Buchanan St Bus Station
16 City Chambers
17 TIC
18 Post Office
19 American Express Office
20 The Horse Shoe Bar
21 St Enoch Square Travel Centre

Many streets one-way only

U Underground Station

To University of Strathclyde, Glasgow Cathedral, St Mungo Museum of Religious Life & Art

To Necropolis, B&Bs

To Burrell Collection & Pollok Country Park

particular, check the **Glasgow School of Art** (☎ 353 4526), 167 Renfrew St, which has guided tours from Monday to Saturday (£5/3), and the **Willow Tearoom** (☎ 332 0521), 217 Sauchiehall St.

For an extraordinary time-capsule experience, visit the apartment in the **Tenement House** (☎ 333 0183), 145 Buccleuch St. It gives a vivid insight into middle-class life at the turn of the 20th century, and opens 2 to 5 pm daily, March to October (£3.50).

The **Burrell Collection** (☎ 649 7151), in a superb museum in Pollok Country Park, 3 miles south of the city centre, was amassed

by a wealthy local before it was given to the city. This idiosyncratic collection includes Chinese porcelain, medieval furniture and paintings by Renoir and Cézanne. It isn't so big as to be overwhelming, and the stamp of the individual collector seems to create an intriguing coherence. It's open 10 am to 5 pm Monday to Saturday, and 11 am to 5 pm Sunday. Catch a train from Central station to Pollokshaws West (second station on the light-blue line south, trains for East Kilbride and Kilmarnock; three per hour), then walk for 10 minutes through the pleasant park.

BRITAIN

Special Events
Like Edinburgh, Glasgow has developed several festivals of its own, starting with a two-week Celtic Connections (☎ 332 6633) music festival from mid-January. The West End Festival (☎ 341 0844) of music and the arts runs for two weeks in mid-June and is Glasgow's biggest festival. The excellent International Jazz Festival (☎ 400 5000) is held in early July.

Places to Stay
Finding a decent B&B in July and August can be difficult, so get into town reasonably early and use the TIC's booking service. Unfortunately, Glasgow's B&Bs are expensive by Scottish standards – you may have to pay up to £25.

Camping *Craigendmuir Caravan Park* *(☎ 779 4159, Campsie View)*, 4 miles northeast of the city in Stepps, is the nearest, but it's still a 15-minute walk from Stepps station. It takes vans and tents for £8.50 (two people).

Hostels & Colleges The excellent *Glasgow Youth Hostel (☎ 332 3004, 7 Park Terrace)* has mainly four-bed rooms, many with *en suite* facilities; book in summer. It's open all day and costs £13.25/11.75. From Central station take bus No 44 or 59 and ask for the first stop on Woodlands Rd.

Berkeley Globetrotters (☎ 221 7880, 63 Berkeley St) has beds from £8.50 to £10.50 in dorms, or £12.50 in twin rooms. Phone ahead for bookings; the reception is at No 56 opposite the hostel. Berkeley St is a western continuation of Bath St (one block south of Sauchiehall St). The hostel's just past Mitchell Library Theatre.

Near the SYHA hostel, the popular *Glasgow Backpackers Hostel (☎ 332 5412, Maclay Hall, 17 Park Terrace)* is one of the university's halls of residence, and only opens July to September. Beds cost £10 to £12.50.

Mid-March to mid-April and July to September, the *University of Glasgow (☎ 330 5385, 3 The Square)* has self-catering hostel accommodation from £13/81 a day/week and a range of B&Bs from £30 per room.

The *University of Strathclyde (☎ 553 4148, Cathedral St)* also opens its halls of residence to tourists mid-June to September. Its *Campus Village (☎ 552 0626, 24 hours)* opposite Glasgow Cathedral offers hostel accommodation on a weekly basis (£43 per week, sleeping bag required). Farther out of town, its cheapest B&B accommodation is at *Jordanhill Campus (76 Southbrae Drive)*. Comfortable singles/doubles are £20.50/30, and bus No 44 from Central station goes to the college gates. The university's impressive Art Deco *Baird Hall (460 Sauchiehall St)* offers some B&B accommodation year-round for £19/33, in a central location.

B&Bs Central Renfrew St north of Sauchiehall St has several places. *McLay Guest House (☎ 332 4796, 264 Renfrew St)* is labyrinthine, but considering the location, you can't quibble at £21/27 for a single room without/with bathroom, doubles are £38/46.

There's a batch of reasonable-value B&Bs east of the Necropolis. *Campsie Guest House (☎ 554 6797, 2 Onslow Drive)* has decent rooms from £18 per person. *Craigpark Guest House (☎ 554 4160, 33 Circus Drive)* has singles/doubles from £16/28.

Places to Eat
Glasgow has an excellent range of moderately priced restaurants. Along Sauchiehall St or around the city centre you'll find the ethnic cuisine of your choice. Set lunches offered by many restaurants are usually good value at £3 to £5.

Sauchiehall St has some interesting choices. The *Centre for Contemporary Arts (☎ 332 7521)*, No 346, is an interesting visual and performing-arts venue, which has a well-regarded cafe, but it was closed for renovations at the time of research.

Ristoro Ciao Italia (☎ 332 4565, 441 Sauchiehall St) is an efficient Italian restaurant where filling three-course lunches cost only £6.50. *Loon Fung (☎ 332 1240)*, No 417, is one of the best Cantonese places in town. A three-course lunch costs £6.30.

The *Willow Tearoom (☎ 332 0521, 217 Sauchiehall St)*, above a jewellery shop, was designed as a tearoom by Charles Rennie Mackintosh in 1904, and its menu is mostly Scottish. At lunch and tea the queues can be long: avoid them by arriving when it opens at 9.30 am (noon on Sunday) and splash out on a superior breakfast (served all day) for £5.30. It closes at 4.30 pm daily.

BRITAIN

In the Kelvingrove Park area there's a scattering of restaurants along Gibson St and on and around Great Western Rd. Vegetarian/vegan *Bay Tree Café (☎ 334 5898, 403 Great Western Rd)* is excellent value. Filling mains (mostly Middle Eastern) cost less than £5. *Back Alley (☎ 334 7165, 8 Ruthven Lane)*, off Byres Rd, has a wide-ranging menu from fajitas to fish and chips (£6 to £8) including vegetarian options.

Entertainment

Some of the best nightlife in Scotland is found in the pubs, bars and clubs of Glasgow. The *List* (£1.95) is Glasgow's (and Edinburgh's) comprehensive, invaluable fortnightly entertainment guide; there's also the monthly *Go* (£1.90).

There's no shortage of fun places. The centre is where the club action is focused; West Regent and Bath Sts have a plethora of small, subterranean hang-outs; and Merchant City is full of larger, hip joints. The West End offers a cool nightlife alternative.

In the centre *Brunswick Cellars (☎ 572 0016, 239 Sauchiehall St)* is a popular, smokey, candlelit, basement bar that's popular with a younger crowd. *The Horse Shoe Bar (☎ 229 5711, 17 Drury Lane)* has the longest continuous bar in the UK, but its main attraction is what's served over it – real ale and excellent-value food.

In the West End, there are numerous pubs on or around Byres Rd. *Curlers (☎ 334 1284)*, No 256, is popular with students who come for the bargain food. The *Halt Bar (☎ 564 1527, 160 Woodlands Rd)* is a popular university pub that hasn't been tarted up. There's a great atmosphere and free live music most nights.

Getting There & Away

Air Glasgow airport (☎ 887 1111), 8 miles west, handles domestic and international flights.

Bus Fares from London are competitive. Silver Choice (☎ 333 7133) offers the best deal at £19/24 a single/return. Departures are daily at 10 pm from both Victoria coach station, London, and Buchanan bus station in Glasgow; the run takes 8½ hours. The service is popular so you'll need to book.

National Express (☎ 0870-580 8080) also leaves from Victoria and Buchanan St and has up to four daily services for £20/30. Try to catch the 8.15 am bus from London so that you arrive in good time to organise accommodation. There are direct links with Heathrow and Gatwick airports.

There are numerous links with other English cities. National Express services include four daily buses from Birmingham (5½ hours), two from Cambridge (nine hours), numerous from Carlisle (two hours), two from Newcastle (four hours), and one from York (6½ hours).

Scottish Citylink (☎ 0870-550 5050) has buses to most major towns in Scotland. There are buses every 15 minutes to Edinburgh (£5 return, 1¼ hours); and frequent buses to Stirling (45 minutes), Inverness (from 3½ hours), Oban (three hours), Aberdeen (four hours), Fort William (three hours) and Skye (6¼ hours).

Stagecoach Western (☎ 01387-253496) runs hourly buses to Stranraer (£7.50, three hours) from where there are ferries to Larne in Northern Ireland.

Stagecoach Fife (☎ 01592-642394) operates services to St Andrews (2¼ hours, hourly) and Dundee (2½ hours, hourly) via Glenrothes. The return fare to both is £12.50.

First Edinburgh (☎ 01324-613777) runs hourly buses to Milngavie (£2.10 one way, 30 minutes), which is the start of the West Highland Way.

Train As a general rule, Central station serves southern Scotland, England and Wales, and Queen St serves the north and east. There are buses every 10 minutes between the two (50p, or free with a through train ticket). There are up to 10 direct trains daily from London's Euston station; they're not cheap, but they're much quicker (five to six hours) and more comfortable than the bus. There are also up to nine direct services from London's King's Cross.

ScotRail operates the West Highland line north to Oban and Fort William (see those sections later in this chapter) and direct links to Dundee, Aberdeen and Inverness. There are trains every 15 minutes to Edinburgh (£7.30 one way, 50 minutes). For rail inquiries call ☎ 0845-748 4950.

BRITAIN

Getting Around

At the St Enoch Square Travel Centre (☎ 226 4826), St Enoch Square, Strathclyde Passenger Transport (STP) provides information on transport in the Glasgow region. It's open 8.30 am to 5.30 pm Monday to Saturday. Here you can get a copy of the *Guide to Getting Around Glasgow* (free) which includes a map.

The Roundabout Glasgow ticket (£3.50/1.75) covers all public transport in the city for a day; it also entitles you to a £1.50 discount on city bus tours.

To/From the Airport There are buses every 15 to 30 minutes from the airport to Buchanan bus station (£2.70, 25 minutes). A taxi costs about £12 to £15.

Bus Bus services are frequent and cheap. You can buy tickets when you board buses, but on some you have to have the exact change. For short trips in the city, fares are 70p. After midnight there are limited night buses from George Square.

Train There's an extensive suburban network; tickets should be bought before travel if the station is staffed, or from the conductor if it isn't. The network connects with the Underground at Buchanan St station. The circular Underground serves 15 stations in the centre and west (north and south of the river) for 80p one way; a Discovery Pass (£2.50) gives unlimited travel for a day.

SOUTH-WEST SCOTLAND

The tourist board bills this region as Scotland's surprising south-west, but it's only surprising if you expect beautiful mountain and coastal scenery to be confined to the Highlands. What really is surprising is that you can escape the crowds that flock to the better known Western Highlands.

Ayrshire, immediately south-west of Glasgow, is the least spectacular part of the region, though it was the home of Scotland's national poet, Robert Burns. Dumfries & Galloway covers the southern half of this western elbow, and is where the coast and mountains approach the grandeur of the north. Warmed by the Gulf Stream, this is also the mildest corner of Scotland, and

there are some famous gardens. There are many notable historic and prehistoric attractions linked by the **Solway Coast Heritage Trail** (information from TICs). Spectacular Caerlaverock Castle and fascinating Whithorn Priory are just two of many. Kirkcudbright is a picturesque town that makes a good base.

This is excellent cycling and walking country, and it's crossed by the coast-to-coast **Southern Upland Way** (see the Stranraer & Cairnryan section later in this chapter) and a number of cycle trails (the TICs have brochures).

Orientation & Information

Southern Scotland is divided from east to west by the Southern Uplands. The western coast from Glasgow to Girvan is busy, but south of there, the crowds diminish. Stranraer (with nearby Cairnryan) is the ferry port to Larne in Northern Ireland; it's the shortest link from Britain to Ireland, taking less than 2½ hours. The area's SYHA hostels are at Ayr, Newton Stewart (Minnigaff), Kendoon and Wanlockhead.

Getting There & Around

Bus National Express (☎ 0870-580 8080) has coaches from London and Birmingham (via Manchester and Carlisle), and Glasgow/Edinburgh to Stranraer. These coaches service the main towns and villages along the A75 (including Ayr, Dumfries and Newton Stewart). Stagecoach Western (☎ 01387-253496) provides local bus services.

Train See Getting There & Away under Carlisle for information on the Carlisle to Glasgow rail link. There are regular services between Glasgow and Stranraer (£15.30, 2½ hours). For inquiries call ☎ 0845-748 4950.

Boat Frequent car and passenger ferries operate between Stranraer and Larne in Northern Ireland (Stena Line, ☎ 0870-570 7070) and between Cairnryan (5 miles south of Stranraer) and Larne (P&O, ☎ 0870-242 4666). The fastest option is the SeaCat (☎ 0870-552 3523) between Stranraer and Belfast. See Northern Ireland in the Ireland chapter for details.

Isle of Arran
☎ 01770 • pop 4800
Described as 'Scotland in miniature' because of its varied scenery, Arran is an hour's ferry ride from Ardrossan, conveniently accessible from Glasgow.

With 10 peaks over 600m, this is excellent walking country. A coastal road right around the island provides good cycling, except on weekends at the height of the tourist season when traffic can be bad. The TIC (☎ 302140), by the pier in **Brodick** (the main town), has details of accommodation on the island. There's little in Brodick, although **Brodick Castle** (☎ 302202), 2½ miles north, is worth visiting.

Head instead for the peaceful village of **Lochranza**, 14 miles north, where *Lochranza Youth Hostel* (☎ 830631) is a great place to stay; a bed is £9.25.

Stranraer & Cairnryan
☎ 01776 • pop 10,700
Stranraer is more pleasant than the average ferry port, but there's no reason to stay. Make for the south coast (maybe nearby Portpatrick), or Glasgow. The bus and train stations, accommodation and TIC are close to the Stena Sealink and SeaCat terminals. At the TIC (☎ 702595), 28 Harbour St, you can make National Express/Citylink bookings. Cairnryan is 5 miles north on the eastern side of Loch Ryan (accessed by bus from Stranraer).

The **Southern Upland Way** starts at Portpatrick about 9 miles south of Stranraer and runs for 212 miles to Cockburnspath near Berwick-upon-Tweed on the east coast. It offers varied walking country, but includes some long, demanding stretches – those tackling the whole route should be experienced. TICs stock guides and maps.

London to Stranraer by rail is nine hours.

Kirkcudbright
☎ 01557 • pop 3500
Kirkcudbright, with its dignified streets of 17th and 18th-century merchants houses and its lively harbour, is the ideal base if you wish to explore the beautiful southern coast. There's no SYHA hostel but the TIC (☎ 330494), Harbour Square, can provide information about local B&Bs.

SOUTH-EAST SCOTLAND
There's a tendency by some to think that the 'real' Scotland only begins north of Perth, but the castles, forests and glens of the Scottish Borders have a romance and beauty of their own. The region survived centuries of war and plunder and was romantically portrayed by Robert Burns and Sir Walter Scott.

Few people pause in their rush to get to Edinburgh, but if you do stop, you'll find the lovely valley of the River Tweed, rolling hills, castles, ruined abbeys and sheltered towns. The cycling and walking opportunities are excellent. Among many possibilities are the challenging 212-mile coast-to-coast **Southern Upland Way**' (see Stranraer & Cairnryan in the earlier South-West Scotland section) and the 62-mile **Tweed Cycleway**, a signposted route between Biggar (on the A702 west of Peebles) to Berwick-upon-Tweed.

Orientation & Information
The Scottish Borders region lies between the Cheviot Hills along the English border, and the Pentland, Moorfoot and Lammermuir hills, which form the border with Lothian and overlook the Firth of Forth. The most interesting country surrounds the River Tweed and its tributaries.

Getting There & Around
Bus There's a good network of local buses. For those coming from the south-west, McEwan's Coaches (☎ 01387-710357 in Dumfries) operates a Rail Link coach service between Carlisle in north-west Cumbria and Galashiels; up to eight a day, Monday to Saturday, three on Sunday (£5 one way, two hours).

First Edinburgh (☎ 01896-752237 in Galashiels) has numerous buses between Galashiels, Melrose and Edinburgh. Regular First Edinburgh buses run between Berwick-upon-Tweed and Galashiels via Coldstream, Melrose and Kelso. Another useful, frequent service links Jedburgh, Melrose and Galashiels. First Edinburgh's Waverley Wanderer ticket allows a day (£11.50) or week (£33.50) of unlimited travel around the Scottish Borders and to Edinburgh.

National Express (☎ 0870-580 8080) bus No 383 runs twice a day between Chester and Edinburgh via Manchester, Leeds, Newcastle, Jedburgh and Melrose.

Train The main line north from Carlisle skirts the region's west, and the line north from Newcastle/Berwick-upon-Tweed skirts the east along the coast. In between, buses are the only option.

Bicycle Scottish Border Trails (☎ 01721-720336), Glentress, delivers bikes in the Peebles area and organises cycling tours.

Jedburgh & Around
☎ 01835

The most complete of the ruined Border abbeys is **Jedburgh Abbey** (☎ 863925). After a famous ride to visit her lover, the Earl of Bothwell, at Hermitage Castle, Mary Queen of Scots was nursed back to health in a Jedburgh house (now a museum) that bears her name. The TIC (☎ 863435), Murray's Green, opens April to October.

Hermitage Castle (☎ 013873-76222), off the B6399 from Hawick, is only accessible if you have transport, but it's well worth a detour; its forbidding architecture bears testimony to the Scottish Borders' brutal history.

Melrose & Around
☎ 01896

Melrose is a small, attractive town 4 miles east of Galashiels, and is a popular base for exploring the Borders. This is the only Borders town with a convenient *Youth Hostel* (☎ 822521). Open Easter to September, it overlooks the ruined **Melrose Abbey**.

Sir Walter Scott's house, **Abbotsford** (☎ 752043), in a beautiful spot 2 miles west of Melrose on the banks of the Tweed, has an extraordinary collection of the great man's possessions.

Thirlestane Castle (☎ 01578-722430), 10 miles north, near Lauder off the A68, is one of Scotland's most fascinating castles and still a family home. The original keep, built in the 13th century, was refashioned and added to in the 16th century with fairytale turrets and towers. It opens 11 am to 4.15 pm, Sunday to Friday, from Easter to October.

STIRLING
☎ 01786 • pop 37,000

Twenty-six miles north of Glasgow and occupying the most strategically important location in Scotland, Stirling has witnessed many of the struggles of the Scots against the English. The cobbled streets of the attractive old town surround the castle. The TIC (☎ 475019), 41 Dumbarton Rd, is open all year.

The town is dominated by **Stirling Castle** (☎ 450000), perched dramatically on a rock. Mary Queen of Scots was crowned here and it was a favourite royal residence. Open daily, it's one of Scotland's most interesting castles.

Stirling Youth Hostel (☎ 473442, St John St) is central and an excellent place to stay. There are regular buses to Edinburgh, Glasgow and Aberdeen.

ST ANDREWS
☎ 01334 • pop 13,900

St Andrews is a beautiful, unusual seaside town – a concoction of medieval ruins, obsessed golfers, windy coastal scenery, tourist kitsch and a contradictory university where wealthy English undergraduates rub shoulders with Scottish theology students.

Although St Andrews was once the ecclesiastical capital of Scotland, both its cathedral and castle are now in ruins. For most people the town is the home of golf. It's the headquarters of the game's governing body, the Royal & Ancient Golf Club, and home of the world's most famous golf course, the 16th-century Old Course.

Orientation & Information

The most important parts of old St Andrews, lying east of the bus station, are easily explored on foot. The TIC (☎ 472021), 70 Market St, opens year-round. Pick up a copy of *Getting Around Fife*, a free guide to public transport.

Things to See

At the eastern end of North St, **St Andrews Cathedral** is the ruined west end of what was once the largest and one of the most magnificent cathedrals in Scotland. Many of the town's buildings are constructed from its stones. **St Andrews Castle**, not far from the cathedral, has a spectacular clifftop location. Near the Old Course is the **British Golf Museum** (☎ 478880), open daily April to mid-October (Thursday to Monday, mid-October to March).

Places to Stay

The cheapest accommodation in the area is 9 miles south of Stirling at the *Bunkhouse* (☎ *310768)* in West Pitkierie, near Anstruther. Beds cost £7.50; it's popular so phone ahead, especially in summer.

Back in St Andrews, two of the cheaper B&Bs are *Cairnsden* (☎ *476326, 2 King St)*, south of the centre, with singles/doubles from £20/36, and in the centre, *Fairnie House* (☎ *474094, 10 Abbey St)* for £15 to £30 per person.

Other central B&Bs and hotels line Murray Park and Murray Place, but are expensive; most charge from around £22 per person.

Places to Eat

If you're on a tight budget, *PM*, on the corner of Market and Union Sts, does breakfast, burgers and fish and chips from £1.95. For more upmarket snacks, try *Fisher & Donaldson*, which sells Selkirk bannocks (rich fruit bread) and a wonderful range of pastries.

Brambles (5 College St) has excellent soups, salads and vegetarian choices. *Ziggy's* (☎ *473686, 6 Murray Place)* is popular with students and has burgers from £3.95 and a good range of Mexican, vegetarian and seafood dishes. *Ogston's* (☎ *473473, 116 South St)* is a trendy but reasonably priced bar and bistro.

Getting There & Away

Stagecoach Fife (☎ 01592-642394) has a half-hourly bus service from Edinburgh's St Andrew Square, to St Andrews (£5.70, two hours) and on to Dundee (£2.40, 30 minutes).

The nearest train station is Leuchars (one hour from Edinburgh), 5 miles away on the Edinburgh, Dundee, Aberdeen, Inverness coastal line. Bus Nos X59 and X60 leave every half-hour Monday to Saturday to St Andrews, hourly on Sunday.

EASTERN HIGHLANDS

A great elbow of land juts into the North Sea between Perth and the Firth of Tay in the south, and Inverness and Moray Firth in the north. The Cairngorm Mountains are as bleak and demanding as any of the Scottish ranges, and the coastline, especially from Stonehaven to Buckie, is excellent. The valley of the River Dee – the Royal Dee thanks to the

Queen's residence at Balmoral – has sublime scenery.

Orientation & Information

The Grampian Mountains march from Oban in a great arc north-eastward, becoming the Cairngorm Mountains in this eastern region. Aberdeen is the main ferry port for Shetland, and Inverness is the centre for the northern Highlands. The division between the Eastern and Western Highlands reflects the transport realities – there are few coast-to-coast links between Perth and Inverness.

Getting Around

The main bus and train routes from Edinburgh to Inverness run directly north through Perth, or around the coast to Aberdeen and then north-west and inland back to Inverness.

Bus Scottish Citylink (☎ 0870-550 5050) links the main towns. Edinburgh to Inverness via Perth takes four hours (£12.50); to Aberdeen, changing at Dundee, takes four hours (£13.50). There are also regular buses from both cities to Glasgow for much the same price. Aberdeen to Inverness takes three hours for £10 and passes through Elgin.

For detailed information on local bus services, phone Perth & Kinross (☎ 0845-301 1130), Angus (☎ 01307-461775), Dundee (☎ 01382-433125) and Aberdeenshire & Moray (☎ 01224-664581).

Train The train journey from Perth to Inverness is one of the most spectacular in Scotland, with a beautiful climb through the Cairngorms from Dunkeld to Aviemore. There are up to 10 trains daily Monday to Saturday, and five on Sunday (2¼ hours). There are many trains from Edinburgh and Glasgow to Aberdeen (2½ hours from Edinburgh) and from Aberdeen to Inverness (2¼ hours).

Perthshire & Cairngorms

On the direct route from Edinburgh to Inverness, **Perth**, once the capital of Scotland, is an attractive town ringed by castles. Both **Dunkeld** and **Pitlochry** to the north are appealing but touristy villages. **Aviemore** is a very touristy town, best used just as a walking base, but popular in winter as a skiing base. *Aviemore Youth Hostel (☎ 01479-810345)* opens from late December to mid-November. Frequent buses and trains service this route.

Grampian Country Coast

Following the coastal route from Perth to Aberdeen and Inverness, you quickly reach **Dundee**, one of Scotland's largest cities. Despite its excellent location, it suffered from poor modern development and the loss of industries. It's now experiencing a revival and it's worth pausing here to visit Captain Scott's Antarctic ship *Discovery*, moored beside Discovery Point Visitor Centre.

The Grampian range meets the sea at **Stonehaven**, with its spectacular Dunnottar Castle. Continuing around the coast from Aberdeen there are long stretches of sand, and, on the north coast, some magical fishing villages like **Pennan**, where the film *Local Hero* was shot.

Old and new hippies should check the **Findhorn Foundation** (☎ 01309-673655), Forres IV36 0RD, east of Inverness. It's Web site is at www.findhorn.org. The foundation is an international spiritual community, founded in 1962. There are about 150 members and many more sympathetic souls who have moved into the vicinity. The community is dedicated to creating 'a deeper sense of the sacred in everyday life, and to dealing with work, relationships and our environment in new and more fulfilling ways'. In many ways it's very impressive. There are daily tours and residential programs from £240, including food and accommodation.

The community isn't particularly attractive itself; it started life in the *Findhorn Bay Caravan Park* (☎ 01309-690203) and still occupies one end of the site. It's possible to camp here from £6.50. More attractive are the nearby fishing village of **Findhorn** (1 mile) and the town of **Forres** (4 miles).

Buses and trains follow the coast to Aberdeen, then the train cuts inland to Inverness (via Forres). Bus transport around the northeast coast is reasonable.

Grampian Country Inland

The region between Braemar and Huntly and east to the coast is castle country, and includes the Queen's residence at Balmoral. There are more fanciful examples of Scottish baronial architecture, with its turret-capped towers, than anywhere else in the country. The TICs have information on a Castle Trail, but you really need private transport. **Balmoral Castle** (☎ 013397-42334) opens Easter to early August, and attracts large numbers of visitors; it can be reached by the Aberdeen to Braemar bus.

Braemar is an attractive small town surrounded by mountains. There's a helpful TIC (☎ 013397-41600) open all year, and the town makes a fine walking base. On the first Saturday in September the town is invaded by 20,000 people, led by the royal family, for the Braemar Gathering (Highland Games); bookings are essential. There are several B&Bs and two hostels, *Braemar Youth Hostel* (☎ *013397-41659*) and *Braemar Bunkhouse* (☎ *013397-41242*). The bunkhouse has dorm accommodation from £7 to £8.50.

It's a beautiful drive between Perth and Braemar, but public transport is limited. From Aberdeen to Braemar (2¼ hours) there are up to six buses a day operated by Stagecoach Bluebird (☎ 01224-212266), which travel along the beautiful valley of the River Dee.

The direct inland route from Aberdeen to Inverness, serviced by bus and train, traverses rolling agricultural country that, thanks to a mild climate, produces everything from grain to flower bulbs. The grain is turned into a magical liquid known as malt whisky. Aficionados might be tempted by the **Malt Whisky Trail** (information from TICs) which gives you an inside look and complimentary tastings at a number of famous distilleries (including Cardhu, Glenfiddich and Glenlivet).

Aberdeen

☎ 01224 • pop 217,260

Aberdeen is an extraordinary symphony in grey; almost everything is built of granite. In the sun, especially after a shower of rain, the stone turns silver and shines like a fairytale, but with low grey clouds and rain scudding in off the North Sea it can be a bit depressing.

Aberdeen was a prosperous North Sea trading and fishing port centuries before oil was considered a valuable commodity. Now it services one of the largest oilfields in the world. Start with over 200,000 Scots, add multinational oil workers and a large student population, the result – a thriving nightlife.

Orientation & Information Aberdeen is built on a ridge that runs east-west to the north of the train and bus stations (next to each other off Guild St) and the ferry quay. The TIC (☎ 632727), in St Nicholas House, Broad St, opens year-round.

Places to Stay The *Aberdeen Youth Hostel* (☎ 646988, 8 Queen's Rd), 1 mile west of the train station, opens all year. Walk east along Union St and take the right fork along Albyn Place until you reach a roundabout; Queen's Rd continues on the western side.

Clusters of B&Bs line Bon Accord St and Springbank Terrace (both close to the centre) and Great Western Rd (the A93, a 25-minute walk). They're more expensive than is usually the case in Scotland. *Crynoch Guest House* (☎ 582743, 164 Bon Accord St) has singles/doubles from £20/34. Around the corner at *Nicoll's Guest House* (☎ 572867, 63 Springbank Terrace) is a friendly place with rooms from £20/32. There are plenty of other alternatives.

Places to Eat The *Ashvale Fish Restaurant* (☎ 596981, 42 Great Western Rd) is a fish and chip shop well known outside the city, having won several awards. Mushy peas with haddock and chips (£6.25) tastes much better than it sounds.

Lemon Tree (☎ 621610, 5 West North St), an excellent cafe attached to the theatre of the same name, does great coffee, meals and cakes. It's open noon to 3 pm Wednesday to Sunday. The 1st-floor *Victoria Restaurant* (☎ 621381, 140 Union St) does good-quality snacks and sandwiches. For a classier ambience and delicious cakes, try *Wild Boar* (☎ 625357, 19 Belmont St) around the corner.

The *Prince of Wales* (7 St Nicholas Lane) is a good, traditional pub. There are many others along Union and Belmont Sts, some with live music.

Getting There & Away For transport around the region, see the Getting Around section under Eastern Highlands.

Bus & Train Scottish Citylink (☎ 0870-550 5050) has daily buses from London, but it's a tedious 12-hour trip. Stagecoach Bluebird (☎ 212266) is the major local bus operator.

There are numerous trains from London's King's Cross station taking an acceptable seven hours, although they're more expensive than buses.

Ferry The passenger terminal is a short walk east of the train and bus stations. P&O (☎ 572615) has daily evening departures Monday to Friday for Lerwick (Shetland). The trip takes 14 hours (20 hours via Orkney). A reclining seat costs £52/58 in the low/high season, one way. Mid-April to mid-December there are weekly Saturday (plus Tuesday from June to August) departures to Stromness (Orkney); £39/42, 10 hours.

WESTERN HIGHLANDS

This is the Highlands of the tour bus, but there are also some unspoilt peninsulas and serious mountains where you can be very isolated. The scenery is unquestionably dramatic; Ben Nevis (1343m) is Britain's highest mountain; brooding Glencoe still seems haunted by the massacre of the Mac-Donalds; the Cowal and Kintyre peninsulas have a magic of their own; and Loch Lomond may be a tourist cliche but is still beautiful.

This area provides challenges for the most experienced and well-equipped mountaineers, rock climbers and walkers, but there are also moderate walks that are quite safe if you're properly equipped and take the normal precautions. The 95-mile **West Highland Way** runs between Fort William and Glasgow.

Orientation & Information

Fort William, at the southern end of the Great Glen, is a major tourist centre, easily reached by bus and train and a good base for the mountains. Oban, on the west coast, is the most important ferry port for boats to the Inner Hebrides (Mull, Coll, Tiree, Colonsay, Jura and Islay) and the Outer Hebridean islands of South Uist and Barra. There's a reasonable scattering of SYHA hostels, including those at Glencoe village, Oban, Tobermory and Crianlarich. There are also independent bunkhouses at Glencoe, Inchree and Corpach (the Fort William TIC has details).

Getting There & Around

Although the road network is comprehensive and traffic sparse, travel around this region is still difficult – many of the roads are single-track, steep and have hairpin bends.

Bus From Glasgow, Scottish Citylink (☎ 0870-550 5050) and its subsidiary Skyeways Travel (☎ 01599-534328), are the main operators, with daily connections to Oban (£10, three hours), Fort William (£10.50, three hours) and Inverness (£12, from 3½ hours). Highland Country (☎ 01397-702373) also runs buses along these routes at similar prices.

Train The spectacular West Highland line runs from Glasgow north to Fort William and Mallaig, with a spur to Oban from Crianlarich. There are three trains daily Monday to Saturday from Glasgow to Oban (three hours) and two on Sunday. There are the same number of Glasgow to Fort William trains (3¼ hours). The Highland Rover ticket (£49) gives unlimited travel for four days in an eight-day period.

Fort William
☎ 01397 • pop 10,774
Fort William is an attractive little town and an excellent base for the mountains, but don't plan on hanging around.

The town meanders along the edge of Loch Linnhe for several miles. The centre, with its small selection of shops, takeaways and pubs, is easy to get around on foot unless you're staying at a far-flung B&B. The TIC (☎ 703781), Cameron Square, opens year-round.

Fort William is at the northern end of the **West Highland Way** which runs to Glasgow. This is an excellent walk through some of Scotland's finest scenery. Parts of the way can be tackled, or the whole 95 miles could easily be walked in a week. If you plan to walk the whole route, it's best to start in Glasgow and walk north. The best map/guide is Harveys *West Highland Way* (£7.95). TICs can provide a free brochure listing accommodation options.

Popular *Fort William Backpackers' Guest House* (☎ 700711, *Alma Rd*) is a short walk from the train station and costs £10 per night. Three miles from Fort William, up magical Glen Nevis, there's the *Glen Nevis Youth Hostel* (☎ 702336) which costs £12.25 and, across the river, *Ben Nevis Bunkhouse* (☎ 702240, *Achintee Farm*) for £9.

There are several other independent hostels in the area – the TIC has details. In beautiful Glencoe, 16 miles from Fort William, there's *Leacantuim Farm Bunkhouse* (☎ 01855-811256) and, close by in Glencoe village, the popular *Glencoe Youth Hostel* (☎ 01855-811219). Particularly favoured by mountain-climbers, Glencoe Youth Hostel is a 1½-mile walk from the main road, which is the Fort William to Glasgow bus route.

Getting There & Around Scottish Citylink (☎ 0870-550 5050) has four or five direct daily buses to Glasgow (£10.50, three hours) via Glencoe, with connections to London. See also the earlier Western Highlands Getting There & Around section.

You can hire bikes from Off-Beat Bikes (☎ 704008), 117 High St, for £12.50 a day.

Oban
☎ 01631 • pop 8500
As the most important ferry port on the west coast, Oban gets inundated with visitors, but it's on a beautiful bay and the harbour is interesting. By Highland standards it's quite large, but you can easily get around on foot. There isn't much to see or do in town, but there are some lovely coastal and hill walks in the vicinity.

The bus, train and ferry terminals are together beside the harbour. The TIC (☎ 563122), Argyll Square, one block behind the harbour, opens all year (until 9 pm in July and August).

Popular *Oban Backpackers Lodge* (☎ 562107, *Breadalbane St*) charges £9.50. There are numerous B&Bs in this area. *Oban Youth Hostel* (☎ 562025, *Corran Esplanade*), to the town's north (on the other side of the bay from the terminals), opens year-round.

For transport options, see the Scotland Getting Around section earlier in this chapter. Numerous CalMac (☎ 566688) boats link Oban with the Inner Hebridean islands and South Uist (Lochboisdale) in the Outer Hebrides (Western Isles). Up to seven ferries sail daily to Craignure on Mull (£3.45, 45 minutes).

NORTHERN HIGHLANDS & ISLANDS
Forget castles, forget towns, forget villages. The Highlands and northern Islands are all

BRITAIN

about mountains, sea, heather, moors, lochs – and wide, empty, exhilarating space. This is one of Europe's last great wildernesses, and it's more beautiful than you can imagine. The east coast is dramatic, but it's the north and west, where the mountains and sea collide, that exhaust superlatives. Orkney and Shetland are bleak and beautiful, and the Outer Hebrides are a stronghold of Gaelic culture and the old crofting ways.

Information

The Highlands of Scotland Tourist Board (☎ 01997-421160) publishes free accommodation guides for the Highlands north of Glencoe (including Skye). It's Web site is at www.host.co.uk. The Western Isles Tourist Board (☎ 01851-703088) does the same for the Outer Hebrides (Western Isles). Check the Web site at www.witb.co.uk. There are also separate tourist boards for Orkney (☎ 01856-872856) and Shetland (☎ 01595-693434). Their respective Web sites are found at www.orkney.com and www.shetland-tourism.co.uk.

Getting There & Around

This is a remote, sparsely populated region, so you need to be well organised and/or have plenty of time if you're relying on public transport. Transport services are drastically reduced after September so double-check timetables in the off season. Car rentals are available in Inverness, Oban and Stornoway; if you can get a group together, this can be a worthwhile option.

Air British Airways (☎ 0845-773 3377) and its partners British Regional Airlines and Loganair have daily flights between Benbecula, Stornoway and Inverness, and between Inverness and the Outer Hebrides. There are also daily scheduled flights from Glasgow to the beach airport at Barra, to Benbecula and to Stornoway on the Outer Hebrides, and regular flights between Glasgow and Inverness and between Edinburgh and Wick.

Bus Wick, Thurso, Ullapool and Kyle of Lochalsh can all be reached by regular buses from Inverness, or from Edinburgh and Glasgow via Inverness or Fort William; contact

Scottish Citylink (☎ 0870-550 5050) and Highland Country (☎ 01463-233371) in Inverness. In the far north-west, however, there's no straightforward link around the coast between Thurso and Ullapool; Highland Country buses and Royal Mail postbuses are the main options.

Train The Highland lines are justly famous. There are two routes from Inverness: up the east coast to Thurso, and west to Kyle of Lochalsh (see Inverness for details). There's also a regular train from Glasgow to Oban, Fort William and Mallaig (for Skye and the Inner Hebrides). Call ☎ 0845-748 4950 for more information.

Ferry CalMac (☎ 0870-565 0000) sails car and passenger ferries to all the major islands, but it can be expensive, especially if you're taking a vehicle. Consider its Island Rover tickets for unlimited travel between islands for eight or 15 days, or Island Hopscotch tickets that offer various route combinations at reduced rates. Inter-island ferry timetables depend on tides and weather, so check departures with TICs.

Inverness
☎ 01463 • pop 41,800

Inverness on the Moray Firth is the capital of the Highlands and the hub for Highlands transport. It's a pleasant place to while away a few days, although it lacks major attractions. In summer it's packed with visitors. Fortunately, most are intrepid monster hunters and their next stops will be Loch Ness and Fort William.

Orientation & Information The River Ness flows through the town from Loch Ness to Moray Firth. The bus and train stations, the TIC and the hostels are east of the river, within 10 minutes walk of each other. The TIC (☎ 234353), beside the museum on Castle Wynd, just off Bridge St, opens year-round. The Laundrette, 17 Young St just over the bridge, opens daily.

Places to Stay & Eat In peak season it's best to start looking for accommodation early; better still, book a bed ahead. The Inverness TIC charges £1.50 for local bookings.

Three hostels are clustered together, just 10 minutes from the train or bus station and just past the castle. *Inverness Student Hostel* (☎ *236556, 8 Culduthel Rd*) has the same owner as Edinburgh's High St Hostel – you can make phone bookings from there. It's a friendly, cosy place with a great view, and costs £9. Nearby, *Bazpackers Backpackers Hotel* (☎ *717663, 4 Culduthel Rd*) is clean and charges from £7.50, with linen. Possibly the best-equipped hostel in Scotland, *Inverness Millburn Youth Hostel* (☎ *231771, Victoria Drive*) is busy at Easter and in July and August (£12.75).

Along Old Edinburgh Rd and on Ardconnel St are lots of guesthouses and B&Bs. *Ivybank Guest House* (☎ *232796, 28 Old Edinburgh Rd*) costs £20 per person as does the graceful *Ardconnel House* (☎ *240455, 21 Ardconnel St*).

On Kenneth St, west of the river and adjoining Fairfield Rd, you'll find several B&Bs, including *Mardon* (☎ *231005*), No 37, which charges £15/28 a single/double.

Near the hostels, the *Castle Restaurant* (☎ *230925, 41 Castle St*) is a traditional cafe with plentiful food at low prices. *Littlejohn's* (☎ *713005, 28-30 Church St*) is bright and noisy with a very descriptive pasta-Mexican-burger menu. The busy *CHSS Coffee Shop* (*5 Mealmarket Close*) offers nourishing, healthy food in a relaxed atmosphere.

Getting There & Away See the introductory Getting Around sections for Scotland and Britain. Many people take tours from Inverness to Loch Ness, and there's a wide variety costing from £7.50.

Bus The Inverness bus station number is ☎ 233371. Scottish Citylink (☎ 0870-550 5050) has bus connections with major centres in England, including London via Perth and Glasgow. There are numerous daily buses to Glasgow (£12, 3½ hours) and Edinburgh via Perth (£12.50, four hours).

Two buses run daily to Ullapool (£5, 1½ hours), connecting with the CalMac ferry to Stornoway on Lewis (except Sunday). The 3½-hour ferry trip costs £12.70.

There are three or four daily Scottish Citylink services via Wick to Thurso and Scrabster (£9, from three hours) for ferries to

Orkney. The Citylink bus leaving Inverness at 1.30 pm connects at Wick with a Highland Country service to John o'Groats. There are connecting ferries from John o'Groats to Burwick and Kirkwall (both in Orkney). It costs £16 to John o'Groats, the same price to Kirkwall.

Citylink/Skeyways (☎ 01599-534328) operates three buses a day (two on Sunday) from Inverness to Kyle of Lochalsh and Portree (£7.50, three hours), on Skye.

It's possible to head to the north-west through Lairg. Stagecoach Inverness (☎ 239292) has a Monday to Saturday service to Lairg (Sunday too in summer). In summer, daily buses run through to Durness. There's also a Monday to Saturday postbus service (☎ 01246-546329), travelling Lairg-Tongue-Durness.

Train Trains from Glasgow or Edinburgh cost £29.90. The onward line from Inverness to Kyle of Lochalsh (£14.70, 2½ hours) offers one of the greatest scenic journeys in Britain and leaves you within walking distance of the pier for buses across the Skye Bridge. The line to Thurso (£12.50, 3½ hours) connects with the ferry to Orkney. There are three trains a day Monday to Saturday on both lines.

Car & Bicycle The TIC has a handy *Car Hire* leaflet. As well as the big boys, there's Sharp's Car Rental (☎ 236694), 1st floor, Highland Rail House, Station Square, where rates start at £24 (plus tax). There are some great cycling opportunities out of Inverness and several rental outlets, including Inverness Student Hostel (☎ 236556), 8 Culduthel Rd, where bikes cost £6/12 for a half/full day.

East Coast
The coast starts to get really interesting once you leave behind Invergordon's industrial development. Great heather-covered hills heave themselves out of the wild North Sea, with towns like Dornoch and Helmsdale moored precariously at its edge.

There are SYHA hostels at *Carbisdale Castle* (☎ *01549-421232*) and *Helmsdale* (☎ *01431-821577*). Book early for Helmsdale in July and August. Don't miss the wonderful heritage centre (☎ 01955-605393 June to September only) in **Wick**, otherwise, keep going to John o'Groats and beyond.

John o'Groats

The coast at the island's north-eastern tip isn't particularly dramatic, and John o'Groats is little more than a ramshackle tourist trap, but there's something inviting about the view across the water to Orkney. *John o'Groats Youth Hostel (☎ 01955-611424)* in Canisbay, 3 miles west of John o'Groats, opens late March to September. There are up to seven buses daily Monday to Saturday from Wick (£2.30) and Thurso (£2.50). From May to September, MV *Pentland Venture* (☎ 01955-611353) shuttles across to Burwick (Orkney).

Thurso & Scrabster

Thurso (population 9000) is a fairly large, fairly bleak place looking across Pentland Firth to Hoy, in Orkney. It's the end of the line, both for the east-coast railway and the big bus lines. The TIC (☎ 01847-892371), Riverside Rd, opens April to October (daily from late May).

The nearby coast has arguably the best, most regular **surf** in Britain. On the eastern side of town, in front of Lord Caithness' castle, there's a right-hand reef break. There's another shallow reef break 5 miles west at Brimms Ness.

Thurso Hostel (☎ 01847-896888, Ormlie Rd), also called Ormlie Lodge, charges £6/8 for dorm beds without/with sheets. In July and August *Thurso Youth Club Hostel (☎ 01847-892964, Old Mill, Millbank)* has basic dorm accommodation for £8, including linen. There are plenty of B&Bs around town. For a cheap bar meal, try the *Central Hotel (☎ 01847-893129, Traill St)*; mains are from £6.20.

Car ferries to Orkney depart from Scrabster, which is a 2-mile walk or a £1 bus ride from Thurso. Wheels Cycle Shop (☎ 01847-896124), The Arcade, 34 High St, rents mountain bikes from £10 a day.

Orkney Islands
☎ 01856

Just 6 miles off the north coast of Scotland, this magical group of islands is known for its dramatic coastal scenery (which ranges from 300m cliffs to white, sandy beaches) and abundant marine-bird life, and for a plethora

of prehistoric sites, including an entire 4500-year-old village at **Skara Brae**. If you're in the area around mid-June, don't miss the St Magnus Arts Festival.

Sixteen of these 70 islands are inhabited. **Kirkwall** (population 6100) is the main town, and **Stromness** the major port; both are on the largest island, which is known as Mainland. The land is virtually treeless, but lush and level rather than rugged. The climate, warmed by the Gulf Stream, is surprisingly moderate, with April and May being the driest months. Contact the TIC (☎ 872856), 6 Broad St, Kirkwall KW15 1NX, for more information.

Places to Stay There's a good selection of cheap B&Bs, six SYHA hostels and three independent hostels.

In Stromness, *Stromness Youth Hostel (☎ 850589, Hellihole Rd)*, a 10-minute walk from the ferry, charges £8.25. Also in Stromness, *Brown's Hostel (☎ 850661, 45 Victoria St)* is popular, and charges £8. On beautiful Papa Westray, the most northerly island, the excellent *Papa Westray Hostel (☎ 01857-644267, Beltane)* opens all year; £8.

Getting There & Away There's a car ferry from Scrabster, near Thurso, to Stromness operated by P&O (☎ 850655). There's at least one departure a day all year, with single fares costing £16. P&O also sails from Aberdeen (see that section earlier in this chapter).

John o'Groats Ferries (☎ 01955-611353) has a passenger ferry from John o'Groats to Burwick on South Ronaldsay from May to September. A one-way ticket is £16, but the company also offers an excellent special deal to Kirkwall (£27 return). In Thurso, a free bus meets the afternoon train from Inverness, and a bus for Kirkwall meets the ferry in Burwick (20 miles away).

Shetland Islands
☎ 01595 • pop 23,000

Sixty miles north of Orkney, the Shetland Islands remained under Norse rule until 1469, when they were given to Scotland as part of a Danish princess' dowry. Even today, these remote, windswept, treeless islands are almost as much a part of Scandinavia as of Britain. Lerwick, the capital, is less than 230 miles from Bergen in Norway.

BRITAIN

Much bleaker than Orkney, Shetland is famous for its varied bird life, its rugged coastline and 4000-year-old archaeological heritage. There are 15 inhabited islands. **Lerwick** is the largest town on Mainland Shetland, which is used as a base for the North Sea oilfields. Oil has brought a certain amount of prosperity to the islands – there are well-equipped leisure centres in many villages.

Small ferries connect a handful of the smaller islands. Contact the TIC (☎ 693434, ✉ shetland.tourism@zetnet.co.uk), Lerwick ZE1 0LU, for information on B&Bs and camping böds (barns). *Lerwick Youth Hostel* (☎ *692114, King Harald St*) opens from mid-April to October; £9.25.

Getting There & Away British Airways/Loganair (☎ 0845-773 3377) and Business Air (☎ 0500-341046) operate low-flying turboprop aircraft (with great views of the islands) daily between Orkney and Shetland. The standard fare is around £135 return.

Lerwick can be reached by P&O (☎ 01224-572615) ferries from Aberdeen (see the earlier Aberdeen Getting There & Away section), or from Orkney leaving Stromness on Tuesday morning and Sunday evening (£39/78 single/return, eight hours). See Scotland's introductory Getting There & Away section for ferry links to Scandinavia.

North Coast

The coast from Dounreay, with its nuclear power station, west around to Ullapool is mind-blowing. Everything is on a massive scale: vast emptiness, enormous lochs and snowcapped mountains. The unreliable weather and inadequate public transport are the only drawbacks.

Getting to Thurso by bus or train is no problem, but from there your troubles start. In July and August, Highland Country (☎ 01463-222244) runs a daily bus from Thurso to Durness. At other times of the year, Highland Country and Rapson's (☎ same) have Monday to Saturday services from Thurso to Bettyhill. There's also a postbus (☎ 01246-546329) from Tongue to Cape Wrath once daily, Monday to Saturday.

The alternative is to come north from Inverness via Lairg. There are trains daily to Lairg, from where Highland Country bus No

64 runs north to Durness daily (except Sunday). Monday to Saturday postbus services operate the Lairg-Talmine-Tongue and Lairg-Kinlochbervie-Durness routes. There are also services around the coast from Elphin to Scourie, Drumbeg to Lochinver, Shieldaig to Kishorn via Applecross, and Shieldaig to Torridon and Strathcarron, but often with gaps between towns.

Either renting cars or hitching are the other options.

Tongue Youth Hostel (☎ *01847-611301*) has a spectacular lochside location and *Durness Youth Hostel* (☎ *01971-511244*) is backed by the rocky Sutherland hills.

West Coast

Ullapool is the most northerly town of any significance and the jumping-off point for the Isle of Lewis. There's more brilliant coast round to Gairloch, along the incomparable Loch Maree and down to the Kyle of Lochalsh and Skye. From there onward you're back in the land of the tour bus; civilisation (and main roads) can be a shock after all the empty space.

Ullapool The small fishing village of Ullapool attracts the crowds because it's easily accessible along beautiful Loch Broom from Inverness. The TIC (☎ 01854-612987), 6 Argyle St, is one block inland, but most places are strung along the harbourfront, including *Ullapool Youth Hostel* (☎ *01854-612254*), open February to December; book ahead in Easter and summer; £9.25. There are a great many B&Bs. *Arch Inn* (☎ *01854-612454*) has rooms from £20.

See the Inverness Getting There & Away section.

Mallaig This fishing village makes a pleasant stopover between Fort William and Skye. From Mallaig the beautiful West Highland line train runs south four times daily Monday to Saturday to Fort William (£7.40, 1¼ hours), Oban and Glasgow. Mid-June to September, *The Jacobite* steam train (☎ 01524-732100) runs Monday to Friday between Fort William and Mallaig.

Kyle of Lochalsh Kyle, as it's known, is a small village that overlooks the lovely island of Skye across narrow Loch Alsh. There's a

BRITAIN

TIC (☎ 01599-534276) beside the seafront car park, but the nearest hostels are on Skye. The popular *Seagreen Restaurant & Bookshop* (☎ *01599-534388, Plockton Rd*) has wonderful wholefood.

Kyle can be reached by bus and train from Inverness (see that section), and by direct Scottish Citylink buses from Glasgow (£15.30, five hours), which continue across to Kyleakin and on to Uig (£7.20, 6½ hours) for ferries to Tarbert on Harris and Lochmaddy on North Uist.

Isle of Skye
pop 8847

Skye is a large, rugged island, 50 miles north to south and east to west. It's ringed by beautiful coastline and dominated by the Cuillin Hills, immensely popular for the sport of 'Munro bagging', climbing Scottish mountains of 3000 feet (914m) or higher. Tourism is a mainstay of the island economy, so you won't escape the crowds until you get off the main roads. You can contact the Portree TIC (☎ 01478-612137) for more information. Bicycles can be hired from Island Cycles (☎ 01478-613121) in Portree and Fairwinds Cycle Hire (☎ 01471-822270) in Broadford.

Places to Stay & Eat There are more than a dozen SYHA and independent hostels on the island and numerous B&Bs. The SYHA hostels most relevant to ferry users are at *Uig* (☎ 01470-542211) for the Outer Hebrides (Western Isles), open April to October; and *Armadale* (☎ *01471-844260*), for Mallaig, open April to September. There's also an SYHA hostel at *Kyleakin* (☎ *01599-534585*) which opens all year.

The pick of the independents is the friendly *Skye Backpackers* (☎ *01599-534510, Kyleakin*), a short walk from the Skye Bridge; beds cost from £10, and there are some double rooms. There's also *Fossil Bothy* (☎ *01471-82264, Lower Breakish*), and on the west coast there's *Croft Bunkhouse* (☎ *01478-640254*).

Portree is the main centre on the island and the *Ben Tianavaig Bistro* (☎ *01478-612152, 5 Bosville Terrace*) has an extensive vegetarian and seafood menu.

Getting There & Away There are still two ferries from the mainland to Skye. Mid-July to August, CalMac (☎ 01678-462403) operates between Mallaig and Armadale (£2.70, 30 minutes); it's wise to book. There's also a private Glenelg to Kylerhea service (☎ 01599-511302) from mid-April to late October (not always on Sunday), taking 10 minutes and costing 70p.

From Uig on Skye, CalMac has daily services to Lochmaddy on North Uist and (except Sunday) to Tarbert on Harris; both destinations take 1¾ hours and cost £8.30.

Outer Hebrides

The Outer Hebrides (Western Isles) are bleak, remote and treeless. The climate is fierce – the islands are completely exposed to the gales that sweep in from the Atlantic, and it rains more than 250 days of the year. Some people find the landscape mournful, but others find the stark beauty and isolated world of the crofters strangely unique and captivating.

The islands are much bigger than might be imagined (stretching in a 130-mile arc); those that do fall under the islands' spell will need plenty of time to explore. The Sabbath is strictly observed – nothing moves on a Sunday and it can be hard finding anything to eat. Tarbert (Harris) and Lochmaddy (North Uist) are reasonably pleasant villages, but the real attraction lies in the landscape.

See the earlier Skye and Kyle of Lochalsh sections for details of CalMac ferries to Tarbert and Lochmaddy, and the Oban section for ferries to Lochboisdale. All the TICs open for late ferry arrivals in summer but close between mid-October and early April.

Lewis & Harris Lewis (main town Stornoway, reached by ferry from Ullapool) and Harris (Tarbert, by ferry from Uig on Skye) are actually one island with a border of high hills between them. Lewis has low, rolling hills and miles of untouched moorland and freshwater lochs; Harris is rugged, with stony mountains bordered by meadows and sweeping, sandy beaches.

Stornoway (population 8100) is the largest town, but not particularly attractive. It does have a reasonable range of facilities, including a TIC (☎ 01851-703088) and several banks. It's also possible to rent cars, but they can't be taken off the islands; contact Arnol Motors (☎ 01851-710548) or Mackinnon Self-Drive (☎ 01851-702984).

Book a B&B by ringing around, or stay at the *Stornoway Backpackers Hostel (☎ 01851-703628)* for £9 a night. There's also *Garenin Crofters' Hostel (no ☎)*, open all year, 18 miles from Stornoway (buses twice daily). There's at least one bus a day between Tarbert and Stornoway (except Sunday). Alex Dan's Cycle Centre (☎ 01851-704025) hires bikes.

Tarbert has a TIC (☎ 01859-502011), open April to October only, a Bank of Scotland (no ATM) and two general stores. The nearest SYHA hostel is almost 7 miles south at *Stockinish (☎ 530373)*; there's one bus a day from Tarbert. At **Rhenigidale**, there's the SYHA *Rhenigidale Crofters' Hostel (no ☎)*, 10 miles north of Tarbert; a bus can take you to the end of the road at Maraig, but it's a two-hour walk from there; alternatively, walk the whole way, it's a great hike.

North & South Uist North Uist (main town Lochmaddy, reached by ferry from Uig on Skye, or from Tarbert or Leverburgh on Harris), Benbecula (by air from Inverness and Glasgow) and South Uist (Lochboisdale, by ferry from Oban or Mallaig) are joined by bridge and causeway. These are low, flat, green islands half-drowned by sinuous lochs and open to the sea and sky.

Barra (Castlebay, by ferry from Lochboisdale and, for passengers only, Ludag on South Uist) lies at the southern tip of the island chain and is famous for its wild flowers and glorious white, sandy beaches.

Lochmaddy has a TIC (☎ 01876-500321), open April to mid-October, a Bank of Scotland (no ATM) and a hotel. *Uist Outdoor Centre (☎ 01876-500480)* opens all year and has dorm accommodation from £7.

There's one postbus a day between Lochmaddy and Lochboisdale, which also has a bank and TIC (☎ 01878-700286). In Howmore, 15 miles north on the west coast, *Howmore Youth Hostel (no ☎)* opens all year. There's a bus from Lochboisdale.

Barra has a TIC (☎ 01871-810336) in Castlebay and about 20 scattered B&Bs, but no hostel.

Wales (Cymru)

There's a remarkably upbeat feeling in Wales today. In 1979 the majority of the people voted against home rule; yet in the 1997 referendum they said yes to a Welsh Assembly, and two years later its first members were elected and are currently based in Cardiff.

Wales has had the misfortune to be so close to England that it could not be allowed its independence, and yet to be far enough away to be conveniently forgotten. It sometimes feels rather like England's unloved back yard – a suitable place for mines, pine plantations and nuclear power stations.

It is almost miraculous that anything Welsh should have survived the onslaught of its dominating neighbour, but Welsh culture and language has proved enduring.

Although miles of coastline have been ruined by shoddy bungalows and ugly caravan parks, much of the most attractive countryside is now protected by national parks.

Wales' appeal lies in its countryside – the towns and cities are not particularly inspiring. The best way to appreciate the Great Welsh Outdoors is by walking, cycling, canal boating or hitching, or by some other form of private transport. Hay-on-Wye, Brecon, St David's, Dolgellau, Llanberis and Betws-y-Coed are noteworthy.

Many of Wales' magnificent medieval castles are within a mile of a train station: Caerphilly, north of Cardiff; Kidwelly, north of Llanelli; Harlech, south of Porthmadog; Caernarfon, in the north-west; and Conwy in the north.

FACTS ABOUT WALES
History
The Celts arrived from their European homeland sometime after 500 BC. Little is known about them, although it is to their Celtic forebears that the modern Welsh attribute national characteristics like eloquence, warmth and imagination.

The Romans invaded in AD 43, and for the next 400 years kept close control over the Welsh tribes from their garrison towns at Chester and Caerlon. From the 5th century to the 11th, the Welsh were under almost constant pressure from the Anglo-Saxon invaders

WALES

To Dublin &
Dun Laoghaire
(Ireland)

*Holyhead
Bay*

Amlwch

LIVERPOOL

Birkenhead
Widnes

Holyhead

Isle of Anglesey

ANGLESEY

A5

Mersey

Holy
Island

Llangefni

Menai
Bridge

*Conwy
Bay*

Llandudno

Rhyl

Conwy

Colwyn Bay

Dee

M56

Llanfairfechan

Abergele

A55

Holywell

Flint

Chester

*Caernarfon
Bay*

Bangor

Caernarfon

Llanberis

A487

CONWY

Llanrwst

Denbigh

FLINTSHIRE

Mold

A55

CHESHIRE

Betws-y-Coed

DENBIGHSHIRE

Ruthin

▲ Snowdon
(1085m)

Blaenau-
Ffestiniog

Wrexham

WREXHAM

Whitchurch

LLEYN

PENINSULA

Criccieth

Porthmadog

Ffestiniog

Bala

Dee

A5

Llangollen

Ellesmere

Pwllheli

**Snowdonia
National Park**

GWYNEDD

Oswestry

SHROPSHIRE

A49

*IRISH

SEA*

Barmouth

Dolgellau

Llanfyllin

Welshpool

Shrewsbury

Severn

A458

Pembrokeshire
Coast NP

Fishguard

St David's

PEMBROKE-
SHIRE

Tywyn

Machynlleth

Newtown

E N G L A N D

Church
Stretton

*CARDIGAN

BAY*

Haverfordwest

A487

Aberystwyth

A44

Llanidloes

Bishop's
Castle

Ludlow

To Rosslare

Milford
Haven

Pembroke

POWYS

Knighton

A49

Leominster

Pembrokeshire
Coast NP

Same Scale as Main Map

Aberaeron

New Quay

CEREDIGION

Tregaron

Wye

Llandrindod
Wells

A44

Kington

HEREFORDSHIRE

To
Rosslare
(Ireland)

Cardigan

Teifi

Lampeter

Llanwrtyd
Wells

Builth
Wells

Hay-on-
Wye

A487

Newcastle
Emlyn

CARMARTHENSHIRE

Llandovery

Llandeilo

Hereford

Fishguard

PEMBROKE-
SHIRE

Haverfordwest

A40

Carmarthen

Tywi

Brecon

A40

Brecon Beacons National Park

Abergavenny

Monmouth

A40

Narberth

Kidwelly

Ammanford

MERTHYR
TYDFIL

BLAENAU
GWENT

MONMOUTH-
SHIRE

Pembroke

Tenby

Llanelli

M4

NEATH &
PORT
TALBOT

Ebbw Vale

Blaenafon

Usk

A449

Chepstow

Pembrokeshire Coast
National Park

*Carmarthen

Bay*

Merthyr
Tydfil

Pontypool

Cwmbran

To Cork (Ireland)

GOWER
PENINSULA

SWANSEA

Swansea

Neath

Maesteg

Mountain Ash

RHONDDA
CYNON
TAFF

CAERPHILLY

Caerphilly

M4

Port
Talbot

Pontypridd

A470

Newport

NEWPORT

Porthcawl

BRIDGEND

Bridgend

Cowbridge

VALE OF
GLAMORGAN

CARDIFF

M4

Penarth

Mouth of the Severn

M5

Barry

BRISTOL   CHANNEL

BRITAIN

of England. In the 8th century, a Mercian king, Offa, constructed a dyke marking the boundary between the Welsh and the Mercians. Offa's Dyke can still be seen today, in fact you can walk its length.

The Celtic princes failed to unite Wales, and local wars were frequent. However, in 927, faced with the destructive onslaught of the Vikings, the Welsh kings recognised Athelstan, the Anglo-Saxon king of England, as their overlord in exchange for an alliance against the Vikings.

By the time the Normans arrived in England, the Welsh had returned to their warring, independent ways. To secure his new kingdom, William I set up powerful feudal barons along the Welsh borders. The Lords Marcher, as they were known, developed virtually unfettered wealth and power and began to advance on the lowlands of south and mid-Wales.

Edward I, the great warrior king, finally conquered Wales in a bloody campaign. In 1302 the title of Prince of Wales was given to the monarch's eldest son, a tradition that continues today. To maintain his authority, Edward built the great castles of Rhuddlan, Conwy, Beaumaris, Caernarfon and Harlech.

The last doomed Welsh revolt began in 1400 under Owain Glyndwr and was crushed by Henry IV. In 1536 and 1543, the Acts of Union made Wales, for all intents and purposes, another region of England.

From the turn of the 18th century, Wales, with its plentiful coal and iron, became the most important source of Britain's pig iron. By the end of the 19th century, almost a third of the world's coal exports came from Wales, and its enormous network of mining villages, with their unique culture of Methodism, rugby and male-voice choirs had developed.

The 20th century, especially the 1960s, '70s and '80s, saw the coal industry and the associated steel industry collapse. Large-scale unemployment persists as Wales attempts to move to more high-tech and service industries. After agriculture, tourism is now the second most important industry.

In 1997, the people of Wales voted to be governed by a Welsh Assembly rather than from the House of Commons in London. In a self-confident step towards greater political autonomy, the first Assembly was put in place in May 1999.

Geography

Wales has two major mountain systems: the Black Mountains and Brecon Beacons in the south, and the more dramatic mountains of Snowdonia in the north-west. The population is concentrated in the south-east along the coast between Cardiff and Swansea and the old mining valleys that run north into the Brecon Beacons. Wales is approximately 170 miles long and 60 miles wide. Cardiff is the capital.

Population

Wales has a population of 2.9 million, around 5% of the total population of Britain.

Language

Welsh is spoken by 20% of the population, mainly in the north, although a major effort has been made recently to reverse its slide into extinction. Although almost everyone speaks English, there is Welsh TV and radio, a more aggressive education policy and most signs are now bilingual.

At first sight, Welsh looks impossibly difficult to get your tongue around. Once you know that 'dd' is pronounced 'th', 'w' can also be a vowel pronounced 'oo', 'f' is 'v' and 'ff' is 'f', and you've had a native speaker teach you how to pronounce 'll' (roughly 'cl'), you'll be able to ask the way to Llanfairpwllgwyngyllgogerychwyrndrobwllllantysiliogogogoch (a village in Anglesey reputed to have Britain's longest place name – no joke) and be understood. Try the following (pronunciation in brackets):

Bore da (bora-da)	Good morning
Shw'mae (shoo-my)	Hello
Peint o gwrw (paint-o-guru)	Pint of beer
Diolch (diolkh)	Thank you
Da boch (da bokh)	Goodbye

FACTS FOR THE VISITOR
Activities

Hiking Wales has numerous popular walks; the most challenging are in the rocky Snowdonia National Park (around Llanberis and Betws-y-Coed) and the grassy Brecon Beacons National Park (around Brecon). There are seven long-distance walks, the most famous being the Pembrokeshire Coast Path and Offa's Dyke Path.

Most of the 189-mile Pembrokeshire Coast Path is in the Pembrokeshire Coast National Park, an area rich in coastal scenery and historical associations. From Amroth to Cardigan, there are wide, sandy beaches; rocky, windswept cliffs; and picturesque villages. Accommodation is widely available and it is easy to undertake shorter sections. The walk can be crowded on summer weekends. The National Park people publish an accommodation guide (£2.50); phone ☎ 01437-764636 for further information.

Offa's Dyke Path follows the English/Welsh border for 177 miles from Chepstow on the River Severn, through the beautiful Wye Valley and Shropshire Hills, ending on the North Wales coast at Prestatyn. The *Offa's Dyke Path Accommodation & Transport* guide is available from the Ramblers' Association (☎ 0207-339 8500) for £3.

See Lonely Planet's *Walking in Britain* for more information.

Surfing The south-west coast of Wales has a number of surf spots. From east to west, try Porthcawl, Oxwich Bay, Rhossili, Manorbier, Freshwater West and Whitesands.

GETTING AROUND

Distances in Wales are small, but, with the exception of links around the coast, public transport users have to fall back on infrequent and complicated bus timetables.

Sniff out a copy of *Wales Bus, Rail and Tourist Map & Guide*, sometimes available from TICs. This invaluable map lists bus and train routes, journey times and operators.

Bus

The major operators serving Wales are Arriva Cymru (☎ 0870-608 2608), for the north and west, and First Cymru (☎ 0870-608 2608) in the south. There are Day/Weekly Saver tickets available that can be very good value. For example, First Cymru has tickets for £4.80/16 covering all its services and also including some buses across the border in the Midlands.

Arriva has a particularly useful daily Traws Cambria service, but there's only one bus a day each way. The 701 (west coast) link runs between Cardiff, Swansea, Carmarthen, Aberystwyth, Porthmadog, Caernarfon and Bangor. Cardiff to Aberystwyth (four hours) costs £11.23; Aberystwyth to Porthmadog (two hours) costs £8.

The Backpacker Bus Company (☎ 029-2066 6900), 98 Neville St, Riverside, Cardiff CF1 8LS, offers tours and treks of Wales for three/six days for £99/119.

Train

Wales has some fantastic train lines both mainline services (☎ 0845-748 4950) and narrow-gauge survivors. Apart from the main lines along the north and south coasts to the Irish ferry ports, there are some interesting lines that converge on Shrewsbury (see Shrewsbury in the Central England section earlier in this chapter). The lines along the west coast and down the Conwy Valley are exceptional.

There are several Rover tickets: the North & Mid-Wales Rover gives seven days travel north of Aberystwyth and Shrewsbury plus Bus Gwynedd services (which means virtually all north-western buses) and the Blaenau Ffestiniog Railway for £40.90; and the Flexi Rover ticket for the same area allows travel on three days out of seven for £26.30. A railcard will get you a third off these prices but unfortunately it can't be used during summer.

The Freedom of Wales Rover gives eight days travel in any 15 days for £92, and you can use a railcard (one third off) year-round on this ticket.

SOUTH WALES

The valleys of the Usk and Wye, with their castles and **Tintern Abbey**, are beautiful, but can be packed with day-trippers. The south coast from Newport to Swansea is heavily industrialised, and the valleys running north into the Black Mountains and the Brecon Beacons National Park are still struggling to come to grips with the loss of the coal-mining industry.

Even so, the little villages that form a continuous chain along the valleys have their own stark beauty and the people are very friendly. The traditional market town of Abergavenny is also worth a look. The **Big Pit** (☎ 01495-790311), near Blaenafon, gives you a chance to experience life underground, and guided tours by former miners (£5.75/3.95) are highly recommended.

The Black Mountains and Brecon Beacons have very majestic, open scenery and their northern flanks overlook some of the most beautiful country in Wales.

Cardiff (Caerdydd)
☎ 029 • pop 285,000

The Welsh are proudly defensive of their capital, which has rapidly been transformed from a dull provincial backwater into a prosperous university city with an increasingly lively arts scene.

If you are planning to explore South Wales, stock up on maps and information from the excellent TIC (☎ 2022 7281, @ enquiries@cardifftic.co.uk), open daily, at the central train station. Free Internet access is available at Cardiff Central Library (☎ 382116) on Frederick St.

Cardiff Castle is worth seeing for its outrageous interior refurbishment. Revamped by the Victorians, it's more Hollywood than medieval. Nearby, the **National Museum of Wales** packs in everything Welsh but also includes one of the finest collections of impressionist art throughout Britain. The **Welsh Folk Museum**, at St Fagan's, 5 miles from the centre, is a popular open-air attraction with reconstructed buildings and craft demonstrations.

The *Youth Hostel* (☎ 2046 2303, *2 Wedal Rd, Roath Park*) is about 2 miles from the city centre. It operates seven days a week from March to October, opens at 3 pm and costs £13.50. *Cardiff Backpacker* (☎ 2034 5577, *98 Neville St, Riverside*) is an independent hostel less than a mile from the train and bus stations. The cheapest beds are £13.50 and there are also singles, doubles and dorms.

See the introductory Getting There & Away section at the start of the Britain chapter for details on transport to and from London.

Swansea
☎ 01792 • pop 190,000

Swansea is the second-largest town (it would be stretching the definition to call it a city), and the gateway to the **Gower Peninsula** and its superb coastal scenery (crowded in summer). Dylan Thomas grew up in Swansea and later called it an 'ugly, lovely town'. The town's position is certainly lovely, but there's no pressing reason to stay.

For more information, contact the TIC (☎ 468321, @ swantrsm@cableol.co.uk). Internet access is available at Swansea public library (☎ 516757) on Alexandra Rd. Moving

on west to the Gower Peninsula, the *Youth Hostel* (☎ 390706) is a converted lifeboat house, superbly situated right on the beach at Port Eynon. Bus No 18/A covers the 16 miles from Swansea.

Brecon Beacons National Park

The Brecon Beacons National Park covers 522 sq miles of high bare hills, surrounded on the northern flanks by a number of attractive market towns; Llandovery, Brecon, Crickhowell, Talgarth and Hay-on-Wye make good bases. The railhead is at Abergavenny. A 77-mile cycleway/footpath, the Taff Trail, connects Cardiff with Brecon.

There are three mountain ridges in the park: the popular Brecon Beacons in the centre, the Black Mountains in the east and the confusingly named Black Mountain in the west.

The National Park Visitor Centre (☎ 01874-623366) is in open countryside near Libanus, 5 miles south-west of Brecon. Other information offices are in Brecon (☎ 01874-623156), at the Cattle Market Car Park, and in Llandovery (☎ 01550-720693), Kings Rd. Both make B&B bookings. The **Monmouthshire & Brecon Canal**, which runs south-east from Brecon, is popular both with hikers (especially the 33 miles between Brecon and Pontypool) and canal boaters, and cuts through beautiful country.

Brecon
☎ 01874 • pop 7000

Brecon is an attractive, historic market town, with a **cathedral** dating from the 13th century. The market is held on Tuesday and Friday. There's a highly acclaimed **jazz festival** also in August. The TIC (☎ 622485, @ Brectic@powys.gov.uk) can organise B&Bs. The *Tymn-y-Caeau Youth Hostel* (☎ 665270) is 3 miles from town; ask directions from the TIC.

Brecon has no train station, but there are regular bus links. Stagecoach Red & White (☎ 01633-266336) has regular buses to Swansea, Abergavenny and Hereford via Hay-on-Wye.

Hay-on-Wye
☎ 01497 • pop 1600

At the north-eastern tip of the Black Mountains there's Hay-on-Wye, an eccentric market village that is now known as the world centre for **second-hand books** – there are over 26 shops and two million books, everything from first editions costing £1000 to books by the yard (literally).

Contact the TIC (☎ 820144) for information on the excellent restaurants and B&Bs in the neighbourhood. The *Capel-y-Ffin Youth Hostel (☎ 01873-890650)* is 8 miles south of Hay on the road to Abergavenny. The walk here from Hay follows part of Offa's Dyke and is highly recommended.

SOUTH-WEST WALES

The coastline north-east of St David's to Cardigan is particularly beautiful and, as it is protected by the national park, it remains unspoilt. The Pembrokeshire Coast Path begins at Amroth, north of Tenby, on the western side of Carmarthen Bay and continues to St Dogmaels to the west of Cardigan.

Carmarthen Bay is often referred to as Dylan Thomas Country; **Dylan's boathouse** at Laugharne (☎ 01994-427420), where he wrote *Under Milk Wood*, has been preserved exactly as he left it, and it is a moving memorial (£2.75/1). Llanstephan has a beautiful Norman castle overlooking sandy beaches. On west-facing beaches, there can be good surf; the Newgale filling station (☎ 01437-721398), Newgale, hires the necessary equipment and has daily surf reports.

Irish Ferries (☎ 0990-329129) leave Pembroke Dock for Rosslare in Ireland; ferries connect with buses from Cardiff and destinations east. Stena Line (☎ 0990-707070) has ferries to Rosslare from Fishguard; these connect with buses and trains. See the Ireland chapter for more details.

Pembroke Dock is a classically unpleasant ferry port and the surrounding region is not particularly inspiring either, although nearby **Pembroke Castle**, the home of the Tudors and birthplace of Henry VII, is magnificent. Tenby is attractive, however, and Fishguard is surprisingly pleasant.

Pembrokeshire Coast National Park

The national park protects a narrow band of magnificent coastline, broken only by the denser development around Pembroke and Milford Haven. The only significant inland

portion is the Preseli Hills to the south-east of Fishguard. There are National Park Information Centres and TICs at Tenby (☎ 01834-842402), St David's (☎ 01437-720392) and Fishguard (☎ 01348-873484), among others. Get a copy of their free paper, *Coast to Coast*, which has detailed local information. Apart from hostels, there are loads of B&Bs from around £15.

There's quite good public transport in the area (except on Sunday). Around Pembroke the main bus operator is Silcox Coaches (☎ 01646-683143), with buses from Pembroke and Pembroke Dock to Tenby; Richards Bros (☎ 01239-613756) is the main operator from St David's to Cardigan.

St David's
☎ 01437 • pop 1450

The linchpin for the south-west is beautiful St David's, one of Europe's smallest cities. There's a web of interesting streets, and, concealed in the Vale of Roses, beautiful **St David's Cathedral**. There is something particularly magical about this isolated, secretive, 12th-century building. But it's not an undiscovered secret.

Contact the TIC (☎ 720392, @ enquiries@stdavids.pembrokeshirecoast.org.uk) for more information. There are regular Richards Bros (☎ 01239-613756) buses to and from Fishguard (every two hours from Monday to Saturday). There's an interesting section of the coast path between St David's and Fishguard.

There are four handy *youth hostels*: near St David's *(☎ 720345)*, open from May to October except Thursday (daily from mid-July through August); near Newgale and Solva *(☎ 720959)*; at Trevine *(☎ 01348-831414)*, 11 miles from St David's; and at Pwll Deri *(☎ 01348-891233)*, 8 miles from Trevine and just over 4½ miles from Fishguard.

Fishguard
☎ 01348 • pop 3200

Fishguard stands out like a jewel among the depressing ranks of ugly ferry ports. It is on a beautiful bay, and the old part of town – Lower Fishguard – was the location for the 1971 film version of *Under Milk Wood*, which starred Richard Burton and Elizabeth Taylor. The train station and harbour (for Stena Line ferries to Rosslare) are at Goodwick, a 20-minute walk from the town proper.

The TIC (☎ 873484) is open daily in summer. *Hamilton Guest House & Backpackers Lodge (☎ 874797, 21 Hamilton St)* is near the TIC. It's a very friendly place, open 24 hours, with 20 beds in dormitories for £10 per person; £12 in a double room. By rail, Fishguard to London is £44 for a SuperSaver single or £27 Apex.

MID-WALES

Most visitors to Wales head either for the easily accessible south or the scenically more dramatic north, leaving the quiet valleys of mid-Wales to the Welsh.

This is unspoilt walking country: farming land interspersed with bare rolling hills and small lakes. The 120-mile **Glyndwr's Way** visits sites associated with the Welsh hero between Knighton (on Offa's Dyke Path) and Welshpool via Machynlleth. Leaflets are available from TICs in the area and are invaluable – route-finding is difficult in places.

Machynlleth is an attractive market town and a good base for exploring mid-Wales. The **Centre for Alternative Technology** (☎ 01654-702400) is an interesting working community that can be visited; it's open daily. The TIC (☎ 01654-702401), Owain Glyndwr Centre, is open year-round.

Aberystwyth, the only place of any size on the west coast, is a remarkably pleasant university town with good transport connections. **Steam trains** run through the Vale of Rheidol to Devil's Bridge, with spectacular views of the waterfall. *Borth Youth Hostel (☎ 871498)* is 8 miles north of Aberystwyth, near a wide sandy beach; open from April to November. Contact the TIC (☎ 01970-612125) for B&Bs and more information.

NORTH WALES

North Wales is dominated by the Snowdonia Mountains, which loom over the beautiful coastline. This is the holiday playground for much of the Midlands, so the coast is marred by tacky holiday villages and the serried ranks of caravan parks.

Heading east from Chester, the country is flat, industrialised and uninteresting until you reach Victorian resort, Llandudno – virtually contiguous with Conwy. From Llandudno and Conwy you can catch buses or trains to Betws-y-Coed or Llanberis, the main centres for exploring the Snowdonia National Park. From Betws-y-Coed there's a train to the bleak but strangely beautiful mining town of Blaenau Ffestiniog. One of Wales' most spectacular steam railways runs from Blaenau to the coastal market town of Porthmadog. From Porthmadog you can loop back to Shrewsbury, via Harlech and its castle.

The remote Lleyn Peninsula in the west escapes the crowds to a large extent; start from Caernarfon, with its magnificent castle, or Pwllheli. Near Porthmadog is whimsical Portmeirion, a holiday village built in the Italianate style – it's bizarrely attractive, but crowded in summer. Holyhead is one of the main Irish ferry ports.

The Red Rover day ticket (£4.60) is available on bus Nos 1 to 99 and covers most of the region. For information call ☎ 01286-679535.

Holyhead
☎ 01407 • pop 12,700

Holyhead is a grey and daunting ferry port. Both Irish Ferries (☎ 0990-329129) and Stena Line (☎ 0990-707070) run ferries to Ireland. Irish Ferries has services running directly to Dublin, Stena Line goes to Dun Laoghaire, just outside Dublin.

The TIC (☎ 762622) is in ferry terminal 1. Nearby there's a batch of B&Bs that are used to dealing with late ferry arrivals. The *Min-y-Don (☎ 762718)* is pleasant, with rooms for £15 per person. The TIC has a 24-hour information terminal in the train station. There are hourly trains east to Llandudno, Chester, Birmingham and London.

Llandudno
☎ 01492 • pop 13,500

Llandudno seethes with tourists in summer. It was developed as a Victorian holiday town and has retained much of its 19th-century architecture and antiquated atmosphere. There's a wonderful **pier and promenade** and donkeys on the beach.

Llandudno is on its own peninsula between two sweeping beaches, and is dominated by the spectacular limestone headland the **Great Orme** with the mountains of Snowdonia as a backdrop. The Great Orme, with its tramway, chair lift, superb views and Bronze Age mine, is quite fascinating.

There are hundreds of guesthouses, but it can be difficult to find somewhere in the peak July/August season. Contact the TIC (☎ 876413) for more information.

Getting There & Away There are numerous trains and buses between Llandudno and Chester, and between Llandudno and Holyhead.

Buses and trains run between Llandudno Junction, Betws-y-Coed (for Snowdonia National Park) and Blaenau Ffestiniog (for the brilliant narrow-gauge railway to Porthmadog). There are six trains a day from Monday to Saturday and the journey takes a bit over an hour. A North & Mid-Wales Rover ticket (£26.30) gives three days travel over one week and covers buses as well as trains. See the Shrewsbury Getting There & Away section for information on the complete Llandudno, Blaenau, Porthmadog, Dovey Junction, Shrewsbury loop.

Arriva Cymru (No 5/5B) has frequent services between Llandudno, Bangor and Caernarfon; there are plenty of buses from Bangor to Holyhead for the ferry.

Conwy
☎ 01492 • pop 3800

Conwy has been revitalised since the through traffic on the busy A55 was consigned to a tunnel which burrows under the estuary of the River Conwy and the town. It is now a picturesque and interesting little town, dominated by superb **Conwy Castle** (£3.50/2.50), one of the grandest of Edward I's castles and a medieval masterpiece.

The TIC (☎ 592248) is in the Conwy Castle Visitor Centre. Five miles west of Llandudno, Conwy is linked to Llandudno by several buses an hour and a few trains. There are, however, numerous trains from Llandudno to Llandudno Junction, a 15-minute walk from Conwy.

Snowdonia National Park

Although the Snowdonia Mountains are fairly compact, they loom over the coast and are definitely spectacular. The most popular region is in the north around Mt Snowdon, at 1085m the highest peak in Britain south of the Scottish Highlands. Hikers must be prepared to deal with hostile conditions at any time of the year.

There are National Park Information Centres at Betws-y-Coed (☎ 01690-710665), Blaenau Ffestiniog (☎ 01766-830360) and Harlech (☎ 01766-780658), among others; they all have a wealth of information, and all make B&B bookings.

Betws-y-Coed
☎ 01690 • pop 700

Betus (as it is known and pronounced) is a tourist village in the middle of the Snowdonia National Park. Despite bus loads of tourists it just can't help being beautiful. There's nothing to do except go for walks and take afternoon tea, which in this case is enough.

The TIC (☎ 710426) is useful, but the National Park Information Centre is excellent. Both are near the train station. There are plenty of B&Bs, and the two hostels are both about 5 miles away. *Capel Curig Youth Hostel* (☎ 720225) is to the west on the A5; *Ledr Valley Youth Hostel* (☎ 750202), Pont-y-Pant, is on the A470. There are numerous other hostels in the Snowdon area.

Snowdon Sherpa Buses, which is part of Bus Gwynedd, runs from Llandudno to Conwy, Betws-y-Coed, Capel Curig and Pen-y-Pas (for the hostels), and then on to Llanberis and Caernarfon. There are regular services daily from mid-May to late September. A Red Rover ticket (£4.60) can be bought on the bus.

Llanberis
☎ 01286 • pop 2000

This tourist town lies at the foot of Mt Snowdon and is packed with walkers and climbers. If you're neither, for a mere £15.80 you can take the Snowdon Mountain Railway (☎ 870223) for the ride to the top and back. The helpful TIC (☎ 870765, ✉ llanberis.tic@gwynedd.gov.uk) is in the High St.

The best hostel in the area is the *Pen-y-Pas Youth Hostel* (☎ 870428), 6 miles up the valley in a spectacular site at the start of one of the paths up Snowdon. Back in Llanberis there are numerous B&Bs. *Pete's Eats* (☎ 870358) is a warm cafe where hikers swap information over large portions of healthy food. In the evenings, climbers hang out in the **Heights** (*☎ 871179*), a hotel with a pub and restaurant that even has its own climbing wall.

Llangollen
☎ 01978 • pop 2600

In the north-east, 8 miles from the border with England, Llangollen is famous for its **International Musical Eisteddfod**. This six-day music and dance festival, held in July, attracts folk groups from around the world. Phone ☎ 860236 for details.

The TIC (☎ 860828, @ croeso@nwt.co.uk) is open daily in summer. The town makes an excellent base for outdoor activities – walks to ruined **Valle Crucis Abbey** and the Horseshoe Pass, horse-drawn canal-boat trips, and canoeing on the River Dee. **Plas Newydd** was the 'stately cottage' of the eccentric Ladies of Llangollen, fascinating as much for their unorthodox (for those days 1780-1831) lifestyle as for the building's striking black-and-white decoration.

The **Llangollen Youth Hostel & Activity Centre** (*☎ 860330*) is 1½ miles from the centre. Contact the TIC for B&Bs. There are frequent buses from Wrexham, but public transport to Snowdonia is limited.

France

France's most salient characteristic is its exceptional diversity. The largest country in Western Europe, France stretches from the rolling hills of the north to the seemingly endless beaches of the south; from the wild coastline of Brittany to the icy crags of the Alps, with cliff-lined canyons, dense forest and vineyards in between.

Over the centuries, France has received more immigrants than any other country in Europe. From the ancient Celtic Gauls and Romans to the more recent arrivals from France's former colonies in Indochina and Africa, these peoples have introduced new elements of culture, cuisine and art to France's unique and diverse civilisation.

Once on the western edge of Europe, today's France stands firmly at the crossroads: between England and Italy, Belgium and Spain, North Africa and Scandinavia. Of course, this is exactly how the French have always regarded their country – at the very centre of things.

AT A GLANCE

Capital	Paris
Population	60.2 million
Official Language	French
Currency	1 French franc (FF) = 100 centimes
Time	GMT/UTC+0100
Country Phone Code ☎	33

Facts about France

HISTORY
Prehistory to Medieval

Human presence in France dates from the middle Palaeolithic period, about 90,000 to 40,000 years ago. Around 25,000 BC the Stone Age Cro-Magnon people appeared and left their mark in the form of cave paintings and engravings.

The Celtic Gauls moved into what is now France between 1500 and 500 BC. Julius Caesar's Roman legions took control of the territory around 52 BC, and France remained under Roman rule until the 5th century, when the Franks (thus 'France') and other Germanic groups overran the country.

Two Frankish dynasties, the Merovingians and the Carolingians, ruled from the 5th to the 10th centuries. In 732, Charles Martel defeated the Moors at Poitiers, ensuring that France would not follow Spain and come under Muslim rule. Charles Martel's grandson, Charlemagne, extended the boundaries of the kingdom and was crowned Holy Roman Emperor in 800. During the 9th century, Scandinavian Vikings (the Normans) began raiding France's western coast and eventually founded the Duchy of Normandy.

Under William the Conqueror (the Duke of Normandy), Norman forces occupied England in 1066, making Normandy – and later, Plantagenet-ruled England – a formidable rival of the kingdom of France. A further third of France came under the control of the English Crown in 1154, when Eleanor of Aquitaine married Henry of Anjou (later King Henry II of England).

In 1415, French forces were defeated at Agincourt; in 1420, the English took control of Paris, and two years later King Henry IV

FRANCE

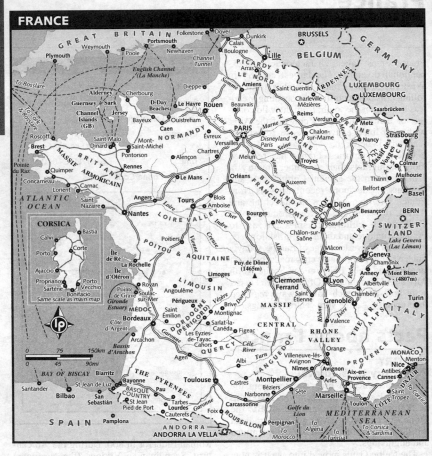

FRANCE

of England became king of France. But a 17-year-old peasant girl known to history as Jeanne d'Arc (Joan of Arc) surfaced in 1429 and rallied the French troops at Orléans. She was captured, convicted of heresy and burned at the stake two years later, but her efforts helped to turn the war in favour of the French.

Renaissance & Reformation

The ideals and aesthetics of the Italian Renaissance were introduced in the 15th century, partly by the French aristocracy returning from military campaigns in Italy. The influence was

most evident during the reign of François I, and the chateaux of Fontainebleau, near Paris, and Chenonceau in the Loire are good examples of Renaissance architectural style.

By the 1530s the Protestant Reformation had been strengthened in France by the ideas of the Frenchman John Calvin, an exile in Geneva. The Wars of Religion (1562-98) involved three groups: the Huguenots (French Protestants); the Catholic League, led by the House of Guise; and the Catholic monarchy. The fighting brought the French state close to disintegration. Henry of Navarra, a Huguenot who had embraced Catholicism, eventually became King Henry IV. In 1598, he promulgated the Edict of Nantes, which guaranteed the Huguenots many civil and political rights.

Louis XIV & the Ancien Régime

Louis XIV – also known as Le Roi Soleil (the Sun King) – ascended the throne in 1643 at the age of five and ruled until 1715. Throughout his long reign, he sought to extend the power of the French monarchy. He also involved France in a long series of costly wars and poured huge sums of money into his extravagant palace at Versailles.

His successor, Louis XV (ruled 1715-74), was followed by the incompetent – and later universally despised – Louis XVI. As the 18th century progressed, new economic and social circumstances rendered the old order (ancien régime) dangerously at odds with the needs of the country.

The Seven Years' War (1756-63), fought by France and Austria against Britain and Prussia, was one of a series of ruinous wars pursued by Louis XV, culminating in the loss of France's flourishing colonies in Canada, the West Indies and India to the British.

The French Revolution

By the late 1780s, Louis XVI and his queen, Marie-Antoinette, had managed to alienate virtually every segment of society. When the king tried to neutralise the power of reform-minded delegates at a meeting of the Estates General in 1789, the urban masses took to the streets and, on 14 July, a Parisian mob stormed the Bastille prison.

The Revolution began in the hands of the moderate, republican Girondists (Girondins in French), but they soon lost power to the radical Jacobins, led by Robespierre, Danton and Marat, who established the First Republic in 1792. In January 1793, Louis was guillotined in what is now place de la Concorde in Paris. Two months later the Jacobins set up the notorious Committee of Public Safety, which had near-dictatorial control during the Reign of Terror (September 1793 to July 1794).

In the resulting chaos, a dashing young general by the name of Napoleon Bonaparte chalked up a string of victories in the Italian campaign of the war against Austria, and his success soon turned him into an independent political force.

Napoleon

In 1799, when it appeared that the Jacobins were again on the ascendancy, Napoleon assumed power himself. Five years later he had himself crowned Emperor of the French by Pope Pius VII, and the scope and nature of Napoleon's ambitions became obvious to all.

In 1812, in an attempt to do away with his last major rival on the Continent, Tsar Alexander I, Napoleon invaded Russia. Although his Grande Armée (Grand Army) captured Moscow, it was wiped out shortly thereafter by the brutal Russian winter. Prussia and Napoleon's other enemies quickly recovered from earlier defeats, and less than two years later the Allied armies entered Paris. Napoleon abdicated and was exiled to his tiny Mediterranean island-kingdom of Elba.

At the Congress of Vienna (1814-15), the Allies restored the House of Bourbon to the French throne. But in March 1815, Napoleon escaped from Elba, landed in southern France and gathered a large army as he marched northward towards Paris. His 'Hundred Days' back in power ended when his forces were defeated by the English at Waterloo in Belgium. Napoleon was banished to the remote South Atlantic island of St Helena where he died in 1821.

19th Century

The 19th century was a chaotic one for France. Louis XVIII's reign (1815-24) was dominated by the struggle between extreme monarchists and those who saw the changes wrought by the Revolution as irreversible. Charles X (ruled 1824-30) handled the struggle between reactionaries and liberals with great ineptitude and was overthrown in the July Revolution of 1830. Louis-Philippe (ruled 1830-48), an ostensibly constitutional monarch of upper bourgeois sympathies and tastes, was then chosen by parliament to head what became known as the July Monarchy.

Louis-Philippe was in turn ousted in the February Revolution of 1848, in whose wake the Second Republic was established. In presidential elections held that year, Napoleon's undistinguished nephew Louis-Napoleon Bonaparte was overwhelmingly elected. A legislative deadlock led Louis-Napoleon to lead a coup d'etat in 1851, after which he was proclaimed Napoleon III, Emperor of the French.

The second empire lasted from 1852 until 1870, when the Prussian prime minister, Bismarck, goaded Napoleon III into declaring war on Prussia. Within months the thoroughly unprepared French army had been defeated and the emperor taken prisoner. When news of the debacle reached the French capital, the Parisian masses took to the streets and demanded that a republic be declared – the Third Republic.

WWI

Central to France's entry into WWI was the desire to regain Alsace and Lorraine, lost to Germany in 1871. This was achieved but at immense human cost: of the eight million French men who were called to arms, 1.3 million were killed and almost one million crippled. The war was officially ended by the Treaty of Versailles in 1919, which laid down severe terms (Germany was to pay US$33 billion in reparations).

WWII

During the 1930s the French, like the British, did their best to appease Hitler, but two days after the 1939 German invasion of Poland, the two countries reluctantly declared war on Germany. By June of the following year, France had capitulated. The British forces sent to help the French barely managed to avoid capture by retreating to Dunkirk and crossing the English Channel in small boats.

The Germans divided France into zones of direct occupation (in the north and along the west coast) and a puppet state based in the spa town of Vichy. Both the collaborationist government and French police forces in the German-occupied areas were very helpful to the Nazis in rounding up French Jews and other targeted groups for deportation to concentration camps.

General Charles de Gaulle, France's undersecretary of war, fled to London and set up a French government-in-exile. He also established the Forces Françaises Libres (Free French Forces), a military force dedicated to continuing the fight against Germany. The liberation of France began with the US, British and Canadian landings in Normandy on D-Day (6 June 1944). Paris was liberated on 25 August.

The Fourth Republic

De Gaulle soon returned to Paris and set up a provisional government, but in January 1946 he resigned as its president, miscalculating that this move would create a popular outcry for his return. A few months later, a new constitution was approved by referendum. The Fourth Republic was a period of unstable coalition cabinets, characterised by slow economic recovery fuelled by massive US aid, an unsuccessful war to reassert French colonial control of Indochina and an uprising by Arab nationalists in Algeria, whose population included over one million French settlers.

The Fifth Republic

The Fourth Republic came to an end in 1958; de Gaulle was brought back to power to prevent a military coup and even civil war. He soon drafted a new constitution that gave considerable powers to the president at the expense of the National Assembly.

In 1969, de Gaulle was succeeded as president by the Gaullist leader Georges Pompidou, who in turn was followed by Valéry Giscard d'Estaing in 1974. François Mitterrand, a Socialist, was elected president in 1981 and re-elected seven years later. The closely contested presidential election of May 1995 resulted in Jacques Chirac winning the mandate with 52% of the vote.

Chirac called a snap election in 1997 and remained president, but his party lost support to a coalition of Socialists, Communists and Greens, led by Lionel Jospin, who became prime minister. The popular Jospin remains the favourite to succeed Chirac in the next presidential ballot, scheduled for 2002.

GEOGRAPHY

France (551,000 sq km) is the largest country in Europe after Russia and Ukraine. It's shaped like a hexagon bordered by either mountains or water except for the relatively flat, north-east frontier that abuts Germany, Luxembourg and Belgium.

ECOLOGY & ENVIRONMENT

France has a rich variety of flora and fauna, including some 113 species of mammals (more than any other country in Europe).

About three-quarters of France's electricity is produced by nuclear power plants. France maintains an independent arsenal of nuclear weapons; in 1992, the government finally agreed to suspend nuclear testing on the Polynesian island of Moruroa and a nearby atoll. However, one last round of tests was concluded in January 1996 before France signed a nuclear test-ban treaty in April 1998.

GOVERNMENT & POLITICS

Despite a long tradition of highly centralised government, the country remains linguistically and culturally heterogeneous. There are even groups in the Basque Country, Brittany and Corsica who still demand complete independence from France.

France has had 11 constitutions since 1789. The present one, instituted by de Gaulle in 1958, established what is known as the Fifth Republic (see the previous History section). It gives considerable power to the president of the republic.

The 577 members of the National Assembly are directly elected in single-member constituencies for five-year terms. The 321 members of the rather powerless Sénat, who serve for nine years, are indirectly elected. The president of France is elected directly for a seven-year term (at the time of writing, a five-year term was under discussion).

Executive power is shared by the president and the Council of Ministers, whose members, including the prime minister, are appointed by the president but are responsible to parliament. The president, who resides in the Palais de l'Élysée in Paris, makes all major policy decisions.

France is one of the five permanent members of the UN Security Council. It withdrew from NATO's joint military command in 1966.

Local Administration

Regional names still exist, but for administrative purposes the country has been divided into units called *départements*, of which there are 96 in metropolitan France and another five abroad. The government in Paris is represented in each department by a *préfet* (prefect).

A department's main town, where the departmental government and the prefect are based, is known as a *préfecture*.

ECONOMY

After sluggish growth through much of the 1990s, the French economy has finally started to hum again. Some think tanks were predicting a rise of 3.5% or more in 2000, and unemployment – which was stuck around 12% in the late 1990s – has dropped to its lowest level in almost a decade and was seen falling below 9% by 2001.

The government has long played a significant interventionist *(dirigiste)* role in the French economy. More than 50% of GDP is still spent by the state, which employs one in every four French workers despite a series of heavyweight privatisations during the 1990s.

France is one of the world's most industrialised countries, with around 40% of the workforce employed in the industrial sector. But it's also the largest agricultural producer and exporter in the EU. Nearly one in 10 workers is engaged in agricultural production, which helps to account for the attention given by the government to French farmers during their periodic protests against cheaper imports.

POPULATION & PEOPLE

France has a population of 60.2 million, more than 20% of whom live in the Paris metropolitan area. During the last 150 years France has received more immigrants than any other European country (4.3 million between 1850 and 1945), including significant numbers of political refugees. In the late 1950s and early 1960s, as the French colonial empire collapsed, more than one million French settlers returned to France from Algeria, Morocco, Tunisia and Indochina. In recent years, there has been a racist backlash against France's non-white immigrant communities, led by the extreme-right Front National (FN) party.

ARTS
Architecture

A religious revival in the 11th century led to the construction of a large number of Romanesque churches, so called because their architects adopted elements from Gallo-Roman buildings. Romanesque buildings typically have round arches, heavy walls that let in very little light and a lack of ornamentation bordering on the austere.

The Gothic style originated in the mid-12th century in northern France, whose great wealth enabled it to attract the finest architects, engineers and artisans. Gothic structures are characterised by ribbed vaults, pointed arches and stained-glass windows, with the emphasis on space, verticality and light. The invention of the flying buttress meant that greater height and width were now possible. By the 15th century, decorative extravagance led to the Flamboyant Gothic style, so named because its wavy stone carving was said to resemble flames.

Painting

An extraordinary flowering of artistic talent took place in France during the late 19th and early 20th centuries. The impressionists, who endeavoured to capture the ever-changing aspects of reflected light, included Édouard Manet, Claude Monet, Edgar Degas, Camille Pissarro and Pierre-Auguste Renoir. They were followed by the equally creative post-impressionists, among whose ranks were Paul Cézanne, Paul Gauguin and Georges Seurat. A little later, the Fauves (literally, 'wild beasts'), the most famous of whom was Henri Matisse, became known for their radical use of vibrant colour. In the years before WWI Pablo Picasso, who was living in Paris, and Georges Braque pioneered cubism, a school of art which concentrated on the analysis of form through abstract and geometric representation.

Music

When French music comes to mind, most people hear accordions and *chansonniers* (cabaret singers) like Édith Piaf. But at many points in history, France has been at the centre of musical culture in Europe.

France's two greatest classical composers of the 19th century were the Romantic Hector Berlioz, the founder of modern orchestration, and César Franck, who specialised in organ compositions. Their output sparked a musical renaissance that would produce such greats as Gabriel Fauré and the impressionists Claude Debussy and Maurice Ravel.

Jazz hit Paris in the 1920s and has remained popular ever since. Violinist Stéfane Grappelli, pianist Michel Petrucciani and electric violinist Jean-Luc Ponty are among those who have left their mark on the world jazz scene.

Popular music has come a long way since the *yéyé* (imitative rock) of the 1960s sung by Johnny Halliday. Watch out for rappers MC Solaar, Doc Gynéco, Alliance Ethnik, and I Am from Marseille. Evergreen balladeers/folk singers include Francis Cabrel and Julien Clerc. The new age space music of Jean-Michel Jarre splits audiences around the globe.

France's claim to fame in recent years has been *sono mondial* (world music) – Algerian *raï*, Senegalese *mbalax* and West Indian *zouk*. Etienne Daho continues to top the charts with his trance numbers, and a recent development is Astérix rock, a homegrown folk-country sound based on accordions.

Literature

To get a feel for France and its literature of the 19th century, you might pick up a translation of novels by Victor Hugo *(Les Misérables or The Hunchback of Notre Dame)*, Stendahl *(The Red and the Black)*, Honoré de Balzac *(Old Goriot)*, Émile Zola *(Germinal)* or Gustave Flaubert *(A Sentimental Education or Madame Bovary)*.

After WWII, existentialism emerged – a significant literary movement based upon the philosophy that people are self-creating beings. Its most prominent figures – Jean-Paul Sartre *(Being and Nothingness)*, Simone de Beauvoir, and Albert Camus *(The Plague)* – stressed the importance of the writer's political commitment. De Beauvoir also wrote *The Second Sex*, which has had a profound influence on feminist thinking.

The *roman policier* (detective novel) has always been a great favourite with the French and among its greatest exponents has been the Belgian-born Georges Simenon and his novels featuring Inspector Maigret as well as Frédéric Dard (alias San Antonio), Léo Malet and Daniel Pennac, widely read for his witty crime fiction.

Other contemporary authors who enjoy a wide following include Françoise Sagan, Jean Auel, Emmanuel Carrère, Pascal Quignard and Stéphane Bourguignon.

Cinema

Film has always been taken very seriously as an art form in France. Some of the most innovative and influential filmmakers of the 1920s and 1930s were Jean Vigo, Marcel Pagnol and Jean Renoir.

After WWII, a new generation of directors burst onto the scene. Known as the *nouvelle vague* (new wave), this genre includes directors such as Jean-Luc Godard, François Truffaut, and Claude Chabrol, whose main tenet was that a film should be the conception of the filmmaker – not the product of a studio or a producer.

Despite the onslaught of American films, France is still producing commercially viable (albeit subsidised) films. Contemporary directors of note include Bertrand Blier *(Trop belle pour toi)*, Jean-Jacques Beineix *(Betty Blue)* and Olivier Assayas *(Les Destinées)*. The French film industry's main annual event is the Cannes Film Festival held in May.

SOCIETY & CONDUCT

Some visitors to France conclude that it would be a lovely country if it weren't for the French. The following tips might prove useful: Never address a waiter or bartender as *garçon* (boy); *s'il vous plaît* is the way it's done nowadays. Avoid discussing money, keep off the manicured French lawns and resist handling produce in markets. Always address people as *Monsieur* (Mr/sir), *Madame* (Mrs) and *Mademoiselle* (Miss); when in doubt use 'Madame'.

Finally, when you go out for the evening, it's a good idea to follow the local custom of dressing relatively well, particularly in a restaurant.

RELIGION

Some 80% of French people say they are Catholic, but although most have been baptised very few attend church. Protestants, who were severely persecuted during much of the 16th and 17th centuries, now number about one million.

France now has between four and five million Muslims, making Islam the second-largest religion in the country. The majority are immigrants (or their offspring) who came from North Africa during the 1950s and 1960s.

There has been a Jewish community in France almost continuously since Roman times. About 75,000 French Jews were killed during the Holocaust. The country's Jewish community now numbers some 650,000.

LANGUAGE

Around 122 million people worldwide speak French as their first language, and various forms of creole are used in Haiti, French Guiana and southern Louisiana. Thus the French tend to assume that all human beings should speak French; it was the international language of culture and diplomacy until WWI.

Your best bet is always to approach people politely in French, even if the only words you know are *'Pardon, Monsieur/Madame/ Mademoiselle, parlez-vous Anglais?'* ('Excuse me sir/madam/miss, do you speak English?').

See the Language chapter at the back of this book for pronunciation guidelines and useful words and phrases.

Facts for the Visitor

HIGHLIGHTS
Museums

Many of the country's most exceptional museums are in Paris. Besides the rather overwhelming Louvre, Parisian museums not to be missed include the Musée d'Orsay (late-19th and early-20th-century art), the Pompidou Centre (modern and contemporary art), the Musée Rodin, and the Musée National du Moyen Age (Museum of the Middle Ages) at the Hôtel de Cluny. Other cities known for their museums include Nice, Bordeaux, Strasbourg and Lyon.

Palaces & Chateaux

The royal palace at Versailles is the largest and most grandiose of the hundreds of chateaux located all over the country. Many of the most impressive ones, including Chambord, Cheverny, Chenonceau and Azay-le-Rideau, are in the Loire Valley around Blois and Tours. The cathedrals at Chartres, Strasbourg and Rouen are among the most beautiful in France.

FRANCE

Beaches

The Côte d'Azur – the French Riviera – has some of the best known beaches in the world, but you'll also find lovely beaches farther west on the Mediterranean.

SUGGESTED ITINERARIES

Two days
   Paris – the most beautiful city in the world.
One week
   Paris plus a nearby area, such as the Loire Valley, Champagne, Alsace or Normandy.
Two weeks
   As above, plus one area in the west or south, such as Brittany, the Alps or Provence.
One month
   As above, but spending more time in each place and visiting more of the west or south – Brittany, say, or the Côte d'Azur.

PLANNING
When to Go

France is at its best in spring, though wintry relapses aren't uncommon in April and the beach resorts only begin to pick up in mid-May. Autumn is pleasant, too, but by late October it's a bit cool for sunbathing. Winter is great for snow sports in the Alps and Pyrenees, but over Christmas, New Year and the February/March school holidays create surges in tourism. On the other hand, Paris always has all sorts of cultural activities during its rather wet winter.

In summer, the weather is warm and even hot, especially in the south, and the beaches, resorts and camping grounds get packed to the gills. Also, millions of French people take their annual month-long holiday *(congé)* in August. Resort hotel rooms and camp sites are in extremely short supply, while in the half-deserted cities many shops, restaurants, cinemas, cultural institutions and even hotels simply shut down. Avoid travelling in France during August.

Maps

For driving, the best road map is Michelin's *Motoring Atlas France* (1:200,000), which covers the whole country. Éditions Didier & Richard's series of 1:50,000 trail maps are adequate for most hiking and cycling excursions.

The Institut Géographique National (IGN) publishes maps of France in both 1:50,000 and 1:25,000 scale. Topoguides are little booklets for hikers that include trail maps and information (in French) on trail conditions, flora, fauna, villages en route and more.

TOURIST OFFICES
Local Tourist Offices

Every city, town, village and hamlet seems to have either an *office de tourisme* (a tourist office run by some unit of local government) or a *syndicat d'initiative* (a tourist office run by an organisation of local merchants). Both are an excellent resource and can almost always provide a local map at the very least. Many tourist offices will make local hotel reservations, usually for a small fee.

Details on local tourist offices appear under Information at the beginning of each city, town or area listing.

Tourist Offices Abroad

The French Government Tourist Offices in the following countries can provide brochures and tourist information.

Australia (☎ 02-9231 5244, fax 9221 8682,
   @ frencht@ozemail.com.au) 25 Bligh St, 22nd floor, Sydney, NSW 2000
Canada (☎ 514-288 4264, fax 845 4868,
   @ mfrance@mtl.net) 1981 McGill College Ave, Suite 490, Montreal, Que H3A 2W9
UK (☎ 020-7399 3500, fax 7493 6594,
   @ info@co.uk) 178 Piccadilly, London W1V OAL
USA (☎ 212-838 7800, fax 838 7855,
   @ info@francetourism.com) 444 Madison Ave, New York, NY 10020

VISAS & DOCUMENTS

Citizens of the USA, Canada, Australia and New Zealand, and most European countries can enter France for up to three months without a visa. South Africans, however, must have a visa to visit France (to avoid delays, apply before leaving home).

If you're staying in France for over three months to study or work, apply to the French consulate nearest where you live for a long-stay visa. If you're not an EU citizen, it's extremely difficult to get a work visa; one of the few exceptions allows holders of student visas to work part-time. Begin the paperwork several months before you leave home.

By law, everyone in France, including tourists, must carry identification with them. For visitors, this means a passport. A national identity card is sufficient for EU citizens.

Visa Extensions

Tourist visas *cannot* be extended. If you qualify for an automatic three-month stay upon arrival, you'll get another three months if you exit and then re-enter France. The fewer French entry stamps you have in your passport, the easier this is likely to be.

EMBASSIES & CONSULATES
French Embassies & Consulates

French embassies abroad include:

Australia (☎ 02-6216 0100, fax 6216 0127, ✉ embassy@france.net.au) 6 Perth Ave, Yarralumla, ACT 2600

Canada (☎ 613-789 1795, fax 562 3735, ✉ res@amba-Ottowa.fr) 42 Sussex Drive, Ottawa, Ont K1M 2C9

Germany (☎ 030-206 39000, fax 206 39010) Kochstrasse 6-7, D-10969 Berlin

Italy (☎ 06-686 011, fax 860 1360, ✉ france-italia@france-italia.it) Piazza Farnese 67, 00186 Rome

New Zealand (☎ 04-384 2555, fax 384 2577, ✉ consulfrance@actrix.gen.nz) Rural Bank Building, 34-42 Manners Street, Wellington

Spain (☎ 91-423 8900, fax 423 8901) Calle de Salustiano Olozaga 9, 28001 Madrid.

UK (☎ 020-7201 1000, fax 7201 1004, ✉ press@ambafrance.org) 58 Knightsbridge, London SW1X 7JT. Visa inquiries: ☎ 0891-887733

USA (☎ 202-944 6000, fax 944 6166, ✉ visaswashington@amb-wash.fv) 4101 Reservoir Rd, NW Washington, DC, 20007

Embassies & Consulates in France

Countries with embassies in Paris include:

Australia (☎ 01 40 59 33 00, fax 01 40 59 33 10, ✉ information.paris@dfat.gov.au) 4 rue Jean Rey, 15e (metro Bir Hakeim)

Canada (☎ 01 44 43 29 00, 01 44 43 29 99) 35 ave Montaigne, 8e (metro Franklin D Roosevelt)

New Zealand (☎ 01 45 00 24 11, 01 45 01 43 44) 7ter rue Léonard de Vinci, 16e (metro Victor Hugo)

Spain (☎ 01 44 43 18 00, fax 01 47 23 59 55, ✉ emba.espa@wanadoo.fr) 22 ave Marceau, 8e (metro Alma Marceau)

UK (☎ 01 44 51 31 00, fax 01 44 51 31 27, ✉ ambassade@amb-grandebretagne.fr) 35 rue du Faubourg St Honoré, 8e (metro Concorde)

USA (☎ 01 43 12 22, fax 01 42 66 97 83, ✉ ambassade@amb-usa.fr) 2 ave Gabriel, 1er (metro Concorde)

MONEY
Currency

One French franc (FF) equals 100 centimes. French coins come in denominations of five, 10 and 20 centimes and half, one, two, five, 10 and 20FF (the last two are two-tone). Banknotes are issued in denominations of 20, 50, 100, 200 and 500FF. The higher the denomination, the larger the bill.

Exchange Rates

country	unit		franc
Australia	A$1	=	4.21FF
Canada	C$1	=	4.89FF
euro	€1	=	6.55FF
Germany	DM1	=	3.35FF
Japan	¥100	=	6.68FF
New Zealand	NZ$1	=	3.26FF
Spain	100 ptas	=	3.94FF
UK	UK£1	=	10.9FF
USA	US$1	=	7.26FF

Exchanging Money

Cash & Travellers Cheques Generally you'll get a better exchange rate for travellers cheques than for cash. The most useful ones are issued by American Express in US dollars. Do not bring travellers cheques in Australian dollars as they are hard to change; US$100 bills can also be difficult.

Visa (Carte Bleue in France) is more widely accepted than MasterCard (Eurocard). Visa card-holders with a PIN number can get cash advances from banks and ATMs nationwide. American Express cards aren't very useful, except to get cash at American Express offices in big cities or to pay in upmarket shops and restaurants.

Many post offices make exchange transactions at a very good rate and accept American Express travellers cheques; there's no commission on US dollar travellers cheques (1.2% to 1.5% for ones in French francs).

The Banque de France, France's central bank, offers good rates on travellers cheques and take no commission (except 1% on French franc travellers cheques). Branches are open Monday to Friday but only offer currency services in the morning.

Commercial banks usually charge a stiff 20FF to 35FF per foreign currency transaction. In larger cities, exchange bureaus are faster, easier, open longer hours and often give better rates than the banks.

If your American Express travellers cheques are lost or stolen, call ☎ 0800 90 86 00, a 24-hour toll-free number. For lost or stolen Visa cards, call ☎ 0836 69 08 80 or 0800 90 20 33.

Costs
If you stay in hostels or the cheapest hotels and buy provisions from grocery stores rather than eating at restaurants, it's possible to tour France on as little as US$30 a day (US$35 in Paris). Eating out, lots of travel or treating yourself to France's many little luxuries can increase this figure dramatically.

Discounts Museums, cinemas, the SNCF, ferry companies and other institutions offer price breaks to people under the age of either 25 or 26; students with ISIC cards (age limits may apply); and seniors (people over 60 or, in some cases, 65.) Look for the words demi-tarif or tarif réduit (half-price tariff or reduced rate) on rate charts.

Tipping & Bargaining
It's not necessary to leave a pourboire (tip) in restaurants or hotels; under French law, the bill must already include a 15% service charge. Some people leave a few francs on the table for the waiter, but this isn't expected (especially for drinks). At truly posh restaurants, however, a more generous gratuity is expected. For a taxi ride, the usual tip is 2FF to 5FF no matter what the fare. Bargaining is rarely done in France except at flea markets.

Taxes & Refunds
France's VAT (value-added tax, ie, sales tax) is known in French as TVA (taxe sur la valeur ajoutée). The TVA is 19.6% on the purchase price of most goods (and for noncommercial vehicle rental). Prices that include TVA are often marked TTC (toutes taxes comprises), which means 'all taxes included'.

It's possible (though rather complicated) to get a reimbursement for TVA if you meet several conditions: you are not an EU national and are over 15 years of age; you have stayed in France less than six months; you are buying more than 1200FF worth of goods (not more than 10 of the same item); and the shop offers duty-free sales (vente en détaxe).

To claim a TVA, you fill out an export sales invoice (bordereau de vente) when you make your purchase, and this is stamped at your port of exit. The shop then reimburses you – by mail or bank transfer within 30 days – for the TVA you've paid. Note that duty-free shopping within the EU was abolished in mid-1999.

POST & COMMUNICATIONS
Postal Rates
La Poste, the French postal service, is fast, reliable and expensive. Postcards and letters up to 20g cost 3FF within the EU, 4.40FF to the USA, Canada and the Middle East, and 5.20FF to Australasia. Aerograms cost 5FF to all destinations. Overseas packages are now sent by air only, which is expensive.

Receiving Mail Mail to France must include the area's five-digit postcode, which begins with the two-digit number of the department. In Paris, all postcodes begin with 750 and end with the arrondissement number, eg, 75004 for the 4th arrondissement, 75013 for the 13th.

Poste restante mail is held alphabetically by family name, so make sure your last name is written in capital letters. If not addressed to a particular branch, poste restante mail ends up at the town's main post office (recette principale). In Paris, this means the central post office (☎ 01 40 28 20 00) at 52 rue du Louvre (1er; metro Sentier or Les Halles). There's a 3FF charge for every poste restante claimed.

You can also receive mail care of American Express offices, although if you don't have an American Express card or travellers cheques there's a 5FF charge each time you check to see if you have received any mail.

Telephone
Public Telephones Almost all public phones now require télécartes (phonecards), which are sold at post offices, tabacs (tobacco shops), Paris metro ticket counters and supermarket check-out counters. Cards worth 50/120 units cost 48.60/97.50FF. Each unit is good for one three-minute local call. To make a call with a phonecard, pick up the receiver,

insert the card and dial when the LCD screen reads 'Numérotez'. All telephone cabins can take incoming calls; give the caller the 10-digit number written after the words *'ici le'* on the information sheet next to the phone.

Domestic Dialling France has five telephone zones and all telephone numbers comprise 10 digits. Paris and Île de France numbers begin with 01. The other codes are: ☎ 02 for the north-west; ☎ 03 for the north-east; ☎ 04 for the south-east (including Corsica); and ☎ 05 for the south-west.

Numbers beginning with 0800 are free, but others in the series (eg, 0836) generally cost 2.23FF per minute. For directory assistance, dial ☎ 12.

International Dialling France's international country code is ☎ 33. When dialling from abroad, omit the initial '0' at the beginning of 10-digit phone numbers.

To place a direct call, dial ☎ 00 and then the country code, area code and local number. A three-minute call to the USA costs about 5/3FF peak/off-peak.

To make a reverse-charge call *(en PCV)* or person-to-person *(avec préavis)* from France to other countries, dial ☎ 00 (the international operator), wait for the second tone and then dial ☎ 33 plus the country code of the place you're calling (for the USA and Canada, dial 11 instead of 1).

For directory inquiries outside France, dial ☎ 00, and when the second tone sounds, dial 33, then 12, and finally the country code. For information on home-country direct calls, see the Telephones Appendix in the back of this book.

Telephone Cards You can buy prepaid phone cards in France that make calling abroad cheaper than with a standard télécarte. Carte Intercall Monde, Carte Astuce and Eagle Télécom International are among popular cards that give up to 60% off standard French international call rates. They're available in denominations of 50FF and 100FF from *tabacs*, newsagents, phone shops and other sales points.

Minitel Minitel is a computerised information service peculiar to France. Though useful, it can be expensive to use and the Internet is becoming a popular alternative. Minitel numbers consist of four digits (eg, 3611, 3614, 3615) and a string of letters. Most of the terminals in post offices are free for directory inquiries.

Fax
Virtually all French post offices can send and receive domestic and international faxes *(télécopies* or *téléfaxes)*. It costs around 12/60FF to send a one-page fax within France/to the USA.

Email & Internet Access
Email can be sent and received at cybercafes throughout France. La Poste has set up Internet centres at some 1000 post offices around France; a 50FF Cybercarte gives you an hour's access, and each 30FF 'recharge' is good for another hour. Commercial cybercafes charge about 20FF to 30FF for a half-hour's surfing.

INTERNET RESOURCES
Useful Web sites in English include the Paris Tourist Office (www.paris-touristoffice.com), the French Government Tourist Office (www.francetourism.com) and GuideWeb (www.guideweb.com), which has information about selected regions in France. Many towns have their own Web sites. Gay and lesbian travellers should check the Queer Resources Directory (www.france.qrd.org).

BOOKS
Lonely Planet
Lonely Planet's *France* guide has comprehensive coverage of France and includes chapters on Andorra and Monaco. *Paris Condensed* is a pocket companion with short visits in mind. Regional guides include *Provence & Côte D'Azur*, *The Loire*, *South-Western France* and *Corsica*. The *French phrasebook* is a complete guide to *la langue française*.

Guidebooks
Michelin's hardcover *Guide Rouge* (red guide) lists middle and upper-range hotels and rates France's greatest restaurants with the famous stars. Michelin's *guides verts* (green guides) cover all of France in 24 regional volumes (12 in English).

The best general French-language guides are by *Guide Bleu*. Its blue-jacketed all-France and regional guides provide accurate, balanced information on history, culture and architecture.

Travel

Paul Rambali's *French Blues* is a series of uncompromising yet sympathetic snapshots of modern France. *A Year in Provence* by Peter Mayle is an irresistible account of country life in southern France. *A Moveable Feast* by Ernest Hemingway portrays Bohemian life in 1920s Paris. Henry Miller also wrote some pretty dramatic stuff set in the French capital of the 1930s, including *Tropic of Cancer*. Gertrude Stein's *The Autobiography of Alice B Toklas* is an entertaining account of Paris' literary and artistic circles from WWI to the mid-1930s.

History & Politics

There are many excellent histories of France in English. Among the best is Fernand Braudel's two-volume *The Identity of France*, which recently went out of print. *France Today* by John Ardagh provides excellent insights into the way French society has evolved since WWII.

NEWSPAPERS & MAGAZINES

The excellent *International Herald Tribune* is sold at many news kiosks throughout France for 10FF. Other English-language papers you can find include the *Guardian*, the *Financial Times*, and the colourful *USA Today*. *Newsweek*, *Time* and the *Economist* are also widely available.

RADIO & TV

The BBC World Service can be picked up on 195kHz AM and 6195kHz, 9410kHz, 9760kHz and 12095kHz short wave. In northern France, BBC for Europe is on 648kHz AM. Upmarket hotels often offer cable TV access to CNN, BBC Prime, Sky and other networks. Canal+ (pronounced ka-NAHL pluce), a French subscription TV station available in many mid-range hotels sometimes shows undubbed English movies.

PHOTOGRAPHY & VIDEO

Be prepared to have your camera and film forced through the ostensibly film-safe x-ray machines at airports and when entering sensitive public buildings. Ask to have your film hand-checked, if not your whole camera. Film is widely available, and costs about 35/46FF for a 36-exposure roll of 100ASA print/slide film, excluding processing.

Note that French videotapes cannot be played on British, Australian or American video cassette recorders or TVs unless they are equipped with SECAM.

TIME

France is GMT/UTC plus one hour. Clocks are turned one hour ahead on the last Sunday in March and back again on the last Sunday in September.

LAUNDRY

Self-service laundrettes *(laveries libre service)* generally charge 18FF to 20FF a load and around 2FF for five minutes of drying. Bring lots of coins; few laundrettes have change machines.

TOILETS

Public toilets are scarce, though small towns often have one near the town hall *(mairie)*. In Paris, you're more likely to come upon one of the tan, self-disinfecting toilet pods. Many public toilets cost 2FF or even 2.50FF. Except in the most tourist-filled areas, cafe owners usually allow you to use their toilets provided you ask politely.

WOMEN TRAVELLERS

In general, women need not walk around in fear, although the French seem to have given little thought to sexual harassment – many men tend to stare hard at passing women, for instance. If you're subject to catcalls or hassled on the street, the best strategy is usually to walk on and ignore the comment. Making a cutting retort is ineffective in English and risky in French if your slang isn't proficient.

France's national rape crisis hotline, which is run by a women's organisation called Viols Femmes Informations, can be reached toll-free by dialling ☎ 0800 05 95 95 on weekdays from 10 am to 6 pm.

GAY & LESBIAN TRAVELLERS

Centre Gai et Lesbien (CGL; ☎ 01 43 57 21 47), 3 rue Keller (11e; metro Ledru Rollin),

500m east of place de la Bastille, is head-quarters for numerous organisations. Its bar, library and other facilities open 2 to 8 pm Monday to Saturday. Paris' Gay Pride parade is held on the last weekend in June. Gay publications include the monthlies *3 Keller*, *Action* and *Gay*. The monthly *Lesbia* gives a rundown of what's happening around the country.

DISABLED TRAVELLERS

France isn't well-equipped for *handicapés* – kerb ramps are few and far between, older public facilities and budget hotels often lack lifts, and the Paris metro is hopeless. Details of train travel for wheelchair users are available in SNCF's booklet *Guide du Voyageur à Mobilité Réduite*. You can also contact SNCF Accessibilité (the French rail company) toll-free at ☎ 0800 15 47 53.

Hostels in Paris that cater to disabled travellers include the Foyer International d'Accueil de Paris Jean Monnet and the Centre International de Séjour de Paris Kellermann (see Hostels & Foyers in the Paris section).

DANGERS & ANNOYANCES

The biggest crime problem for tourists in France is theft – especially of and from cars. Pickpockets are a problem, and women are a common target because of their handbags. Be especially careful at airports and on crowded public transport in cities.

France's laws regarding even small quantities of drugs are very strict, and the police have the right to search anyone at any time.

The rise in support for the extreme right-wing Front National in recent years reflects the growing racial intolerance in France. Especially in the south, entertainment places such as bars and discos are, for all intents and purposes, segregated.

Emergency national numbers include: ambulance ☎ 15, fire ☎ 18 and police ☎ 17.

BUSINESS HOURS

Most museums are closed on either Monday or Tuesday and on public holidays, though in summer some open daily. Most small businesses open 9 or 10 am to 6.30 or 7 pm daily except Sunday and perhaps Monday, with a break between noon and 2 pm or between 1 and 3 pm. In the south, midday closures are more like siestas and may continue until 3.30 or 4 pm.

Many food shops open daily except Sunday afternoon and Monday. Most restaurants open only for lunch (noon to 2 or 3 pm) and dinner (6.30 to about 10 or 11 pm); outside Paris, very few serve meals throughout the day. In August, lots of establishments simply close down for the annual month-long holiday.

Banque de France branches open Monday to Friday, but will change money and travellers cheques only in the morning (usually 8.45 am to 12.15 pm). Opening hours of other banks vary.

PUBLIC HOLIDAYS & SPECIAL EVENTS

National *jours fériés* (public holidays) in France include New Year's Day, Easter Sunday and Monday, 1 May (May Day), 8 May (1945 Victory Day), Ascension Thursday, Pentecost/Whit Sunday and Whit Monday, 14 July (Bastille Day), 15 August (Assumption Day), 1 November (All Saints' Day), 11 November (1918 Armistice Day) and Christmas Day.

Some of the biggest and best events in France include: the Festival d'Avignon (early July to early August), with some 300 daily music, dance and drama events; Bastille Day celebrations, spread over 13 and 14 July; Francofolies, a six-day dance and music festival held in mid-July in La Rochelle, with performers from all over the French-speaking world; the Festival Interceltique, a 10-day Celtic festival in early August held in the Breton town of Lorient; Lyon's Biennale de la Danse/d'Art Contemporain, a month-long festival (from mid-September) that's held in even-numbered years (in odd-numbered years the city holds a festival of contemporary art); and the Carnaval de Nice, held in Nice every spring around Mardi Gras (Shrove Tuesday).

ACTIVITIES
Skiing

The French Alps have some of the finest (and priciest) skiing in Europe, but there are cheaper, low-altitude ski stations in the Pyrenees; www.skifrance.fr provides information in English about ski resorts, services, conditions and more.

Surfing

The best surfing in France (and some of the best in all of Europe) is on the Atlantic coast around Biarritz.

Hiking

France has thousands of kilometres of hiking trails in every region of the country. These include *sentiers de grande randonnée*, long-distance hiking paths whose alphanumeric names begin with the letters GR and are sometimes hundreds of kilometres long (as in Corsica). These paths are run by an organisation called Fédération Française de Randonnée Pédestre (FFRP; ☎ 01 44 89 93 93, fax 01 40 35 85 67), which also publishes guides to these routes.

Canoeing

The Fédération Française de Canoë-Kayak (☎ 01 45 11 08 50) at 87 quai de la Marne, 94340 Joinville-le-Pont, can supply information on canoeing and kayaking clubs around the country. The sports are very popular in the Dordogne (Périgord) area.

Cycling

The French take their cycling very seriously, and whole parts of the country almost grind to a halt during the annual Tour de France.

A *vélo tout-terrain* (VTT; mountain bike) is a fantastic tool for exploring the countryside. Some GR and GRP hiking trails are open to mountain bikes; a *piste cyclable* is a bicycle path.

Mountain bike enthusiasts who can read French should look for the books of *Les Guides VTT,* a series of cyclists' topoguides published by Didier & Richard. Lonely Planet's *Cycling in France* is an essential resource when touring. *France by Bike: 14 Tours Geared for Discovery* by Karen and Terry Whitehall ($12) is a worthy rival.

Some of the best areas for cycling are around the Alpine resorts of Annecy and Chambery (see the French Alps & Jura section for details). The Loire Valley and coastal regions such as Brittany, Normandy and the Atlantic Coast offer a wealth of easier options.

Details on places that rent bikes appear at the end of individual city or town listings under Getting Around.

COURSES

For details on language and cooking courses, see Courses in the Paris section. Information on studying in France is available from French consulates and French Government Tourist Offices abroad. In Paris, you might also get in touch with the Ministry of Tourism-sponsored International Cultural Organisation (ICO; ☎ 01 42 36 47 18, fax 01 40 26 34 45, metro Châtelet) at 55 rue de Rivoli (1er), BP 2701, 75027 Paris CEDEX.

WORK

Getting a *carte de séjour* (temporary residence permit), which in most cases lets you work in France, is almost automatic for EU citizens; contact the Préfecture de Police in Paris or, in the provinces, the *mairie* (town hall) or nearest prefecture. For anyone else it's almost impossible, though the government tolerates undocumented workers helping out with agricultural work.

Working as an au pair is very common in France, especially in Paris. Single young people – particularly women – receive board, lodging and a bit of money in exchange for taking care of the kids and doing light housework. Knowing some French may be a prerequisite. For information on au pair placement, contact a French consulate or the Paris tourist office.

ACCOMMODATION
Camping

France has thousands of seasonal and year-round camping grounds. Facilities and amenities, reflected in the number of stars the site has been awarded, determine the price. At the less fancy places, two people with a small tent pay 20FF to 55FF a night. Campers without a vehicle can usually get a spot, even late in the day, but not in July and August, when most are packed with families.

Refuges & Gîtes d'Étape

Refuges (mountain huts or shelters) are basic dorms operated by national park authorities, the Club Alpin Français and other private organisations. They are marked on hiking and climbing maps. Some open year-round.

In general, refuges have mattresses and blankets but not sheets. Charges average 50FF to 70FF per night (more in popular areas), and meals are sometimes available. It's a good idea to call ahead and make a reservation.

Gîtes d'étape, which are usually better equipped and more comfortable than refuges, are found in less remote areas, often in villages. They also cost around 50FF to 70FF per person.

Hostels

In the provinces, *Auberges de Jeunesse* (hostels) generally charge 48FF to 73FF for a bunk in a single-sex dorm. In Paris, expect to pay 100FF to 140FF a night, including breakfast. In the cities, especially Paris, you'll also find *foyers*, student dorms used by travellers in summer. Most of France's hostels belong to one of three Paris-based organisations:

Fédération Unie des Auberges de Jeunesse (FUAJ; ☎ 01 44 89 87 27, fax 01 44 89 87 10, www.fuaj.org) 27 rue Pajol, 18e, 75018 Paris (metro La Chapelle)
Ligue Française pour les Auberges de la Jeunesse (LFAJ; ☎ 01 44 16 78 78, fax 01 44 16 78 80) 67 rue Vergniaud, 75013 Paris (metro Glacière)
Union des Centres de Rencontres Internationales de France (UCRIF; ☎ 01 40 26 57 64, fax 01 40 26 58 20, ✉ ucrif@aol.com) 27 rue de Turbigo, 2e, 75002 Paris (metro Étienne Marcel)

Only FUAJ is affiliated with the Hostelling International (HI) organisation.

Hotels

For two people sharing a room, budget hotels are often cheaper than hostels. Unless otherwise indicated, prices in this chapter refer to rooms in unrated or one-star hotels equipped with a washbasin. Most doubles, which generally cost the same or only marginally more than singles, have only one bed. Doubles with two beds usually cost a little more. A hall *douche* (shower) can be free or cost between 10FF and 25FF. If you'll be arriving after noon (after 10 am at peak times), it's wise to book ahead, though if you call on the day of your arrival, many will hold a room for you until a set hour. Local tourist offices also make reservations, usually for a small fee.

FOOD

A fully-fledged traditional French dinner – usually begun about 8.30 pm – has quite a few distinct courses: an apéritif or cocktail;

an *entrée* (first course); the *plat principal* (main course); *salade* (salad); *fromage* (cheese); *dessert*; *fruit* (fruit; pronounced fwee); *café* (coffee); and a *digestif* liqueur.

Restaurants usually specialise in a particular cuisine while brasseries – which look very much like cafes – serve quicker meals of more standard fare (eg, steak and chips/French fries or omelettes). Restaurants tend to open only for lunch (noon to 2 or 3 pm) and dinner (6.30 to about 10 or 11 pm); brasseries serve meals throughout the day.

Most restaurants offer at least one fixed-price, multicourse meal known in French as a *menu*. In general, *menus* cost much less than ordering each dish *a la carte* (separately).

Sitting in a cafe to read, write or talk with friends is an integral part of everyday life in France. A cafe located on a grand boulevard will charge considerably more than a place that fronts a side street. Once inside, progressively more expensive tariffs apply at the counter *(comptoir)*, in the cafe itself *(salle)* and outside on the *terrasse*. The price of drinks goes up at night, usually after 8 pm.

DRINKS
Nonalcoholic Drinks

Tap water in France is perfectly safe. Make sure you ask for *une carafe d'eau* (a jug of water) or *de l'eau du robinet* (tap water) or you may get costly *eau de source* (mineral water). A small cup of espresso is called *un café*, *un café noir* or *un express*; you can also ask for a *grand* (large) one. *Un café crème* is espresso with steamed cream. *Un café au lait* is espresso served in a large cup with lots of steamed milk. Decaffeinated coffee is *un café décaféiné* or simply *un déca*.

Other popular hot drinks include: *thé* (tea) – if you want milk you ask for *'un peu de lait frais'*; *tisane* (herbal tea); and *chocolat chaud* (hot chocolate).

Alcoholic Drinks

The French almost always take their meals with wine – *rouge* (red), *blanc* (white) or *rosé*. The least expensive wines cost less per litre than soft drinks. The cheapest wines are known as *vins ordinaires* or *vins de table* (table wines).

Alcoholic drinks other than wine include apéritifs, such as *kir* (dry white wine sweetened

FRANCE

with *cassis* – blackcurrant liqueur), *kir royale* (champagne with cassis), and *pastis* (anise-flavoured alcohol drunk with ice and water); and *digestifs* such as brandy or Calvados (apple brandy). A *demi* of beer (about 250ml) is cheaper *à la pression* (on draught) than from a bottle.

Getting There & Away

AIR
Air France and scores of other airlines link Paris with every part of the globe. Other French cities with international air links (mainly to places within Europe) include Bordeaux, Lyon, Marseille, Nice, Strasbourg and Toulouse. For information on Paris' two international airports, Orly and Roissy-Charles de Gaulle, see Getting There & Away in the Paris section.

Flights between London and Paris are sometimes available for as little as UK£50 return; with the larger companies expect to pay at least UK£88. One-way discount fares to Paris start at L229,000 from Rome, 55,000 dr from Athens, I£55 from Dublin, 1200FF from Istanbul, and 16,000 ptas from Madrid. Student travel agencies can supply details.

In France, inexpensive flights offered by charter clearing houses can be booked through many regular travel agents – look in agency windows and pamphlets advertising Go Voyages (☎ 01 53 40 44 29) or Look Voyages (☎ 01 55 49 49 60 or ☎ 0803 313 613). Web sites: www.govoyages.com and www.look-voyages.fr. Reliable travel agency chains include the French student travel company OTU (☎ 01 40 29 12 12) and Nouvelles Frontières (☎ 0803 33 33 33). Web sites: www.otu.fr and www.newfrontiers.com.

LAND
Britain
The highly civilised Eurostar (☎ 0990-186 186 in the UK; ☎ 0836 35 35 39 in France) links London's Waterloo Station with Paris' Gare du Nord via the Channel Tunnel, which passes through a layer of impermeable chalk marl 25m to 45m below the floor of the English Channel. The journey takes about three hours (including 20 minutes in the tunnel), not including the one-hour time change. Tickets for people aged 25 and under cost UK£45/75 one-way/return; return fares booked 14/seven days ahead cost UK£69/80. Student travel agencies often have youth fares not available direct from Eurostar. Web site: www.eurostar.com.

Eurotunnel shuttle trains (☎ 0990-35 35 35 in the UK; ☎ 03 21 00 61 00 in France) whisk buses and cars (and their passengers) from near Folkstone to Coquelles (just west of Calais) in 35 minutes. The regular one-way fare for a car and its passengers ranges from UK£109.50 (February and March) to UK£174.50 (July and August). For promotional fares you must book at least one day ahead. Web site: www.eurotunnel.com.

Elsewhere in Europe
Bus For details on Eurolines coach services (☎ 0836 69 52 52 in France) linking France with other European countries, see Getting There & Away in the Paris section. Web site: www.eurolines.fr.

Train Paris, France's main rail hub, is linked with every part of Europe. Depending on where you're coming from, you sometimes have to change train stations in Paris to reach the provinces. For details on Paris' six train stations, see Getting There & Away in the Paris section.

BIJ (Billets International de Jeunesse, ie, International Youth Tickets) tickets, available to people aged 25 or under, save you at least 20% on international 2nd class rail travel (one way or return); on some routes discounts – not available to Italy – are limited to night trains. BIJ tickets are not sold at train-station ticket windows – you have to go to an office of Voyages Wasteels or one of the student travel agencies. There's almost always at least one BIJ-issuer in the vicinity of major train stations.

On the super-fast *Thalys* trains that link Paris with Brussels, Amsterdam and Cologne, people aged 12 to 25 get significant discounts.

SEA
Ferry tickets are available from almost all travel agents.

Britain & the Channel Islands

Hoverspeed (☎ 0870-524 0 241 in the UK; ☎ 0820 00 35 55 in France) runs giant catamarans (SeaCats) from Folkestone to Boulogne (55 minutes). Foot passengers are charged UK£24 one-way (or return if you come back within five days). Depending on the season, a car with up to nine passengers is charged UK£109 to UK£175 one-way. Web site: www.hoverspeed.co.uk.

The Dover-Calais crossing is also handled by car ferries (one to 1½ hours, 44 a day) run by SeaFrance (☎ 0870-571 1711 in the UK; ☎ 0804 04 40 45 in France) and P&O Stena (☎ 0870-598 0980 in the UK; ☎ 0802 010 020 in France). Pedestrians pay UK£15/24 with SeaFrance/P&O Stena; cars are charged UK£122.50 to UK£170 one-way. Web sites: www.seafrance.com and www.posl.com.

If you're travelling to Normandy, the Newhaven-Dieppe route is handled by Hoverspeed's SeaCats (2¼ hours, one to three a day). Poole is linked to Cherbourg by Brittany Ferries (☎ 0870-536 0360 in the UK; ☎ 02 98 29 28 00 in France), which has one or two 4¼-hour crossings a day; the company also has ferries from Portsmouth to Caen (Ouistreham). On the Portsmouth-Cherbourg route, P&O Portsmouth (☎ 0870-598 0555 in the UK; ☎ 0803 013 013 in France) has three car ferries a day and, from mid-March to mid-October, two faster catamarans a day; the company also links Portsmouth with Le Havre. Web sites: www.brittany-ferries.com and www.poef.com.

If you're going to Brittany, Brittany Ferries links Plymouth with Roscoff (six hours, one to three a day) from mid-March to mid-November; the company also has services from Portsmouth to Saint Malo (8¾ hours). For information on ferries from Saint Malo to Weymouth, Poole, Portsmouth and the Channel Islands, see Getting There & Away in the Saint Malo (Brittany) section.

Ireland

Irish Ferries (☎ 01-638 3333 in Ireland; ☎ 02 33 23 44 44 in Cherbourg) has overnight runs from Rosslare to either Cherbourg (18 hours) or Roscoff (16 hours) every other day (three times a week from mid-September to October, with a possible break in service from November to February). Pedestrians pay I£40 to I£80 (I£32 to I£66 for students and seniors). Eurailpass holders are charged 50% of the adult pedestrian fare. Visit the Web site at www.irish-ferries.com.

Italy

For information on ferry services between Corsica and Italy, see Getting There & Away in the Corsica section.

North Africa

France's SNCM (☎ 0836 67 21 00) and the Compagnie Tunisienne de Navigation (CTN; ☎ 01-341 777 in Tunis) link Marseille with Tunis (about 24 hours; three or four a week). The standard adult fare is 900/1620FF one-way/return. Visit the Web site at www.sncm.fr.

Sète, 29km south-west of Montpellier, is linked with the Moroccan port of Tangier (Tanger; 36 hours, five to seven a month) by the Compagnie Marocaine de Navigation (☎ 04 99 57 21 21 in Sète; ☎ 09-94 23 50 in Tangier). The cheapest one-way berth costs 970FF. Discounts are available if you're under 26 or in a group of four or more.

Getting Around

AIR

France's long-protected domestic airline industry is being opened up to competition, though Air France still handles the majority of domestic flights. Web site: www.airfrance.fr.

Full-fare flying within France is extremely expensive, but very significant discounts are available to people aged 12 to 24, couples, families and seniors. The most heavily discounted flights may be cheaper than long-distance rail travel. Details on the complicated fare structures are available from travel agents.

BUS

Because the French train network is state-owned and the government prefers to operate a monopoly, the country has only very limited intercity bus service. However, buses (some run by the SNCF) are widely used for short distances, especially in rural areas with relatively few train lines (eg, Brittany and Normandy).

TRAIN

Eurail and Inter-Rail passes are valid in France.

France's excellent rail network, operated by the Société Nationale des Chemins de Fer Français (SNCF), reaches almost every part of the country. The most important train lines fan out from Paris like the spokes of a wheel. The SNCF's nationwide telephone number for inquiries and reservations (☎ 0836 35 35 39 in English) costs 2.23FF a minute. Web site: www.sncf.com.

The pride and joy of the SNCF is the high-speed TGV ('teh-zheh-veh'). There are now three TGV lines that go under a variety of names: the TGV Sud-Est and TGV Midi-Méditerranée link Paris' Gare de Lyon with the south-east, including Dijon, Lyon, the Alps, Avignon, Marseille, Nice and Mont-pellier; the TGV Atlantique Sud-Ouest and TGV Atlantique Ouest link Paris' Gare Montparnasse with western and south-western France, including Brittany, Tours, La Rochelle, Bordeaux, Biarritz and Toulouse; and the TGV Nord links Paris' Gare du Nord with Arras, Lille and Calais.

Reservation fees are optional unless you're travelling by TGV or want a couchette or special reclining seat. On popular trains (eg, on holiday weekends) you may have to reserve ahead to get a seat. Eurail-pass holders must pay all applicable reservation fees.

Before boarding the train, you must validate your ticket (and your reservation card, if it's separate) by time-stamping it in one of the *composteurs*, the bright orange posts that are located somewhere between the ticket windows and the tracks. Eurail and some other rail passes *must* be validated at a train station ticket window to initiate the period of validity.

Discounts
Passes for Nonresidents of Europe

The France Railpass allows unlimited rail travel within France for three to nine days over the course of a month. In 2nd class, the three-day version costs US$180 (US$145 each for two people travelling together); each additional day of travel costs US$30. The France Youthpass, available if you're 25 and under, costs US$164 for four days of travel over two months; additional days (up to a maximum of 10) cost US$20. In North America, Rail Europe (☎ 800-456 7245) has details. Web site: www.raileurope.com.

Passes for Residents of Europe

The Euro Domino France flexipass gives European residents who don't live in France three to eight days of midnight-to-midnight travel over a period of one month. The youth version (for people 25 and under) costs €120 three days and €24 each additional day; the adult version costs €150 three days and €30 each additional day.

Other Discounts

Discounts of 25% on one-way or return travel within France are available at all train station ticket windows to: people aged 12 to 25 (the Découverte 12/25 fare); one to four adults travelling with a child aged four to 11 (the Découverte Enfant Plus fare); people over 60 (the Découverte Senior fare); and – for return travel only – any two people who are travelling together (the Découverte À Deux fare).

No matter what age you are, the Découverte Séjour excursion fare gives you a 25% reduction for return travel within France if you meet two conditions: the total length of your trip is at least 200km; and you'll be spending a Saturday night at your destination.

The Découverte J30, which must be purchased 30 to 60 days before the date of travel, offers savings of 45% to 55%. The Découverte J8, which you must buy at least eight days ahead, gets you 20% to 30% off.

CAR & MOTORCYCLE

Travelling by car or motorcycle is expensive; petrol is costly and tolls can reach hundreds of francs a day if you're going cross-country in a hurry. Three or four people travelling together, however, may find that renting a car is cheaper than taking the train. In the centres of almost all French cities, parking is metered.

Unless otherwise posted, speed limits are 130km/h (110km/h in the rain) on *autoroutes* (dual carriageways/divided highways whose names begin with A); 110km/h (100km/h in the rain) on *routes nationales* (highways whose names begin with N) that have a divider down the middle; and 90km/h (80km/h if it's raining) on nondivided routes nationales and rural highways. When you pass a sign with a place name, you have entered the boundaries of a town or village; the speed limit automatically drops to 50km/h and stays there until you pass an identical sign with a red bar across it.

The maximum permissible blood-alcohol level in France is 0.05%.

Petrol *sans plomb* (unleaded) costs around 7FF a litre, give or take 10%. *Gasoil* or *gazole* (diesel) is about 5FF to 6FF a litre. Fuel is most expensive at the autoroute rest stops, and tends to be cheapest at the big supermarkets on the outskirts of towns.

If you don't live in the EU and need a car in France (or Europe) for 17 days (or a bit more) to six months, it's *much* cheaper to 'purchase' one from the manufacturer and then 'sell' it back than it is to rent one. The purchase-repurchase *(achat-rachat)* paperwork is not your responsibility. Both Renault's Eurodrive (☎ 1-800 221 1052 in the USA) and Peugeot's Vacation Plan/Sodexa (☎ 1-800-572 9655 or ☎ 1-800-223 1516 in the USA) offer great deals that – incredibly – include insurance with no deductible (excess). Web sites: www.eurodrive.renault.com and www.sodexa.com.

HITCHING

Hitching in France can be difficult, and getting out of big cities like Paris, Lyon and Marseille or travelling around the Côte d'Azur by thumb is well nigh impossible. Remote rural areas are your best bet, but few cars are likely to be going farther than the next large town. Women should not hitch alone.

It's an excellent idea to hold up a sign with your destination followed by the letters *s.v.p.* (for *s'il vous plaît* – 'please'). Some people have reported good luck hitching with truck drivers from truck stops. It's illegal to hitch on autoroutes but you can stand near the entrance ramps.

Organisations around France match people looking for rides with drivers going to the same destination. The best known is Allostop Provoya (☎ 01 53 20 42 42 or, from outside Paris; ☎ 01 53 20 42 43, @ allostop@ecritel .fr), based in Paris at 8 rue Rochambeau (9e; metro Cadet). If you're not a member (240FF for up to eight journeys over two years), there's a per-trip fee of between 30FF (for distances under 200km) and 70FF (for distances over 500km). Drivers charge 0.22FF per kilometre for expenses. Web site: www .ecritel.fr/allostop.

Paris

pop 2.2 million, metropolitan area 9.4 million

Paris has almost exhausted the superlatives that can reasonably be applied to a city. Notre Dame and the Eiffel Tower – at sunrise, at sunset, at night – have been described ad nauseam, as have the Seine and the subtle (and not-so-subtle) differences between the Left and Right banks. But what writers have been unable to capture is the grandness and even the magic of strolling along the city's broad, 19th-century avenues leading from impressive public buildings and exceptional museums to parks, gardens and esplanades. Paris is enchanting at any time, in every season.

ORIENTATION

In central Paris (which the French call Intra-Muros – 'within the walls'), the Rive Droite (Right Bank) is north of the Seine, while the Rive Gauche (Left Bank) is south of the river. For administrative purposes, Paris is divided into 20 *arrondissements* (districts) that spiral out from the centre. Paris addresses always include the arrondissement number, listed here after the street address, using the usual French notation, ie, 1er stands for *premier* (1st), 19e for *dix-neuvième* (19th), etc. When an address includes the full five-digit postal code, the last two digits indicate the arrondissement, eg, 75014 for the 14e.

Maps

Lonely Planet's *Paris City Map* includes central Paris, the Paris Métro, Montmartre, a walking tour and an index of all streets and sights.

INFORMATION
Tourist Offices

Paris' main tourist office (☎ 0836 68 31 12, fax 01 49 52 53 00, metro Georges V) at 127 Ave des Champs-Élysées, 8e, opens 9 am to 8 pm every day of the year, except 1 May and 25 December, (11 am to 6 pm on Sunday in winter). This is the best source of information on what's going on in the city. For a small fee and a deposit, the office can find you accommodation in Paris for that night or (up to eight days in advance) in the provinces. The tourist office has branches (☎/fax the same) in the Gare de Lyon open 8 am to 8 pm Monday to Saturday and at the base of the Eiffel Tower open 11 am to 6 pm daily (May to September).

Money

All of Paris' six major train stations have exchange bureaus open seven days a week until at least 7 pm. Avoid the big exchange-bureau chains like Chequepoint and ExactChange. Exchange offices at both airports are open until 11 pm.

Banque de France The best rate in town is offered by Banque de France, whose headquarters (☎ 01 42 92 22 27, metro Palais Royal) is three blocks north of the Louvre at 31 rue Croix des Petits Champs, 1er. The exchange service is open 9.30 am to 12.30 pm weekdays. The branch (☎ 01 44 61 15 30, metro Bastille) at 3 bis place de la Bastille, 4e, opens for exchange 9 am to 12.15 pm weekdays.

American Express Paris' landmark American Express office (☎ 01 47 77 77 75, metro Auber or Opéra) at 11 rue Scribe, 9e, faces the west side of Opéra Garnier. Exchange services are available 9.30 am to 6 pm (7 pm June to September) weekdays, and 10 am to 5 pm on the weekend.

Notre Dame (4e & 5e) Le Change de Paris (☎ 01 43 54 76 55, metro St Michel) at 2 place St Michel, 6e, has good rates. Open 10 am to 7 pm daily. Another exchange bureau (☎ 01 46 34 70 46), one block south of place St Michel at 1 rue Hautefeuille, 6e, is open 9 am to 9 pm daily.

Champs-Élysées (8e) Thanks to fierce competition, the Champs-Élysées is an excellent place to change money. The bureau de change (☎ 01 42 25 38 14, metro Franklin D Roosevelt) at 25 Ave des Champs-Élysées is open 9 am to 8 pm daily.

Montmartre (18e) The bureau de change (☎ 01 42 52 67 19, metro Abbesses) at 6 rue Yvonne Le Tac opens 10 am to 6.30 pm weekdays (10.30 am to 6 pm Saturday and Sunday, June to September).

Post & Communications

Paris' main post office (☎ 01 40 28 20 00, metro Sentier or Les Halles) at 52 rue du Louvre, 1er, is open 24 hours, 365 days. Foreign exchange is available during regular post office hours – 8 am to 7 pm weekdays, til noon on Saturday.

Email & Internet Access

Café Orbital (☎ 01 43 25 76 77, ✉ info@orbital.fr, metro Luxembourg), 13 rue de Médi-

cis, 6e, opens 9 am (noon on Sunday) to 10 pm Monday to Saturday. The Web Bar (☎ 01 42 72 66 55, ✉ webbar@webbar.fr, metro Temple or République) at 32 rue de Picardie, 3e, opens 8.30 am (11 am at the weekend) to 2 am weekdays.

Travel Agencies

Nouvelles Frontières (☎ 0825 00 08 25, metro Luxembourg) has 14 outlets around the city including one at 66 blvd St Michel, 6e, open 9 am to 7 pm Monday to Saturday. Voyageurs du Monde (☎ 01 42 86 16 00, metro Pyramides or Quartre Septembre), 55 rue Ste Anne, 2e, is a huge agency open 9.30 am to 7 pm Monday to Saturday.

Bookshops

The famous Shakespeare & Company (☎ 01 43 26 96 50, metro St Michel) English-language bookshop is at 37 rue de la Bûcherie, 5e, across the Seine from Notre Dame Cathedral.

WH Smith (☎ 01 44 77 88 99, metro Concorde) at 248 rue de Rivoli is the largest English-language bookshop in the city. At 29 rue de la Parcheminerie, 5e, the mellow, Canadian-run Abbey Bookshop (☎ 01 46 33 16 24, metro Cluny-La Sorbonne) has an eclectic selection of new and used fiction titles. Les Mots à la Bouche (☎ 01 42 78 88 30, metro Hôtel de Ville) at 6 rue Ste Croix de la Bretonnerie, 4e, is Paris' premier gay bookshop.

Cultural & Religious Centres

The British Council (☎ 01 49 55 73 00, metro Invalides), 9-11 rue de Constantine, 7e, has libraries and runs language courses. The American Church (☎ 01 47 05 07 99, metro Invalides) at 65 quai d'Orsay, 7e, is a place of worship and something of a community centre for English speakers; its announcement board is an excellent source of information regarding accommodation and employment.

Laundry

The laundrettes (laveries) mentioned here open daily and are near many of the places to stay listed later. Laverie Libre Service (metro Louvre Rivoli), 7 rue Jean-Jacques Rousseau, is near the BVJ hostels, or another branch at 25 rue des Rosiers (metro St Paul) in the Marais. There's a laundrette four blocks south-west of the Panthéon at 216 rue St

Jacques (metro Luxembourg). Lavomatique is at 63 rue Monge (metro Monge). Near Gare de l'Est is the Lav' Club (metro Gare de l'Est) at 55 blvd de Magenta, or try another Laverie Libre Service branch (metro Blanche) at 4 rue Burq, Montmartre.

Lost Property
Paris' Bureau des Objets Trouvés (Lost and Found Office; ☎ 01 55 76 20 20, metro Convention) is at 36 rue des Morillons, 15e. Since telephone inquiries are impossible, the only way to find out if a lost item has been located is to go there and fill in the forms. The office is open 8.30 am to 5 pm Monday, Wednesday and Friday, and to 8 pm Tuesday and Thursday. During July and August it closes at 3.45 pm. For items lost in the metro call ☎ 01 40 30 52 00.

Medical & Emergency Services
An easy *Assistance Publique* (public health service) to find is the Hôtel Dieu hospital (☎ 01 42 34 81 31, metro Cité), on the northern side of place du Parvis Notre Dame, 4e. A 24-hour emergency service (service des urgences) is provided.

Dangers & Annoyances
For its size, Paris is a safe city but you should always use common sense; for instance, avoid the large Bois de Boulogne and Bois de Vincennes parks after nightfall. And some stations are best avoided late at night, especially if you are on your own. These include Châtelet and its seemingly endless tunnels, Château Rouge in Montmartre, Gare du Nord, Strasbourg-St Denis, Montparnasse-Bienvenüe and Réaumur-Sébastopol.

THINGS TO SEE
The Carte Musées et Monuments museum pass gets you into some 75 museums and monuments without having to queue for a ticket. The card costs 80/160/240FF for one/three/five consecutive days and is on sale at the museums and monuments it covers, at some metro ticket windows and at the tourist office.

Left Bank
Île de la Cité (1er & 4e) Paris was founded sometime during the 3rd century BC when members of a tribe known as the Parisii set up a few huts on Île de la Cité. By the Middle Ages the city had grown to encompass both banks of the Seine, though Île de la Cité remained the centre of royal and ecclesiastical power.

Notre Dame (4e) Paris' cathedral (☎ 01 42 34 56 10, metro Cité or St Michel) is one of the most magnificent achievements of Gothic architecture. Begun in 1163 and completed around 1345, features include the three spectacular rose windows. One of the best views of Notre Dame's ornate flying buttresses can be had from the lovely little park behind the cathedral. The haunting **Mémorial des Martyrs de la Déportation**, in memory of the more than 200,000 people deported by the Nazis and French fascists during WWII, is close by.

Notre Dame is open 8 am to 6.45 pm daily. Entry is free, as are **guided tours** in English at noon on Wednesday and Thursday and at 2.30 pm on Saturday (daily in August). Concerts held here don't keep to a schedule but are advertised on posters around town. The **North Tower**, from which you can view many of the cathedral's most fierce-looking gargoyles, can be climbed via long, spiral steps (35/23FF).

Ste Chapelle (1er) The gem-like upper chapel of Ste Chapelle (☎ 01 53 73 78 51, metro Cité), illuminated by a veritable curtain of 13th-century stained glass, is inside the **Palais de Justice** (Law Courts) at 4 blvd du Palais, 1er. Consecrated in 1248, Ste Chapelle was built in three years to house a crown of thorns (supposedly worn by the crucified Christ) and other relics purchased by King Louis IX (later St Louis) earlier in the 13th century. Open daily, admission costs 35FF (23FF for those aged 12 to 25). A ticket valid for both Ste Chapelle and the Conciergerie costs 50/25FF.

Conciergerie (1er) The Conciergerie (☎ 01 53 73 78 50, metro Cité) was a luxurious royal palace when it was built in the 14th century. During the Reign of Terror (1793-94), it was used to incarcerate 'enemies' of the Revolution before they were brought before the tribunal, which met next door in what is now the

FRANCE

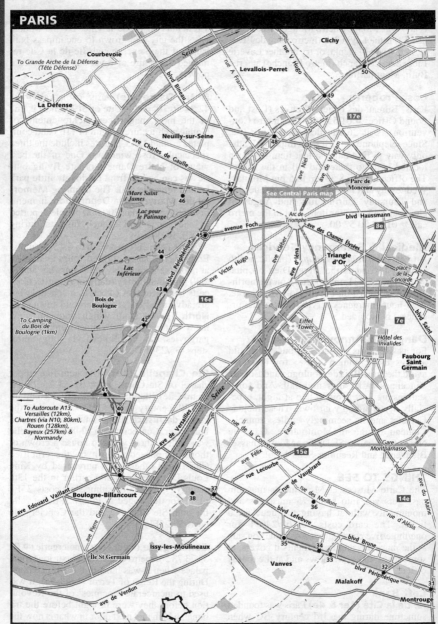

PARIS

Courbevoie

Seine

rue V Hugo

Clichy

To Grande Arche de la Défense
(Tête Défense)

rue A France

Levallois-Perret

blvd Bineau

50

La Défense

ave de Villiers

49

17e

ave Charles de Gaulle

Neuilly-sur-Seine

48

ave Niel

Parc de
Monceau

47

See Central Paris map

Mare Saint
James

46

Arc de
Triomphe

blvd Haussmann

ave des Champs Élysées

8e

Lac pour
le Patinage

45

avenue Foch

ave Kléber

ave d'Iéna

Triangle
d'Or

place
de la
Concorde

44

ave Victor Hugo

blvd Périphérique

Lac
Inférieur

43

16e

Eiffel
Tower

7e

blvd Saint

To Camping
du Bois de
Boulogne (1km)

42

Bois de
Boulogne

Hôtel des
Invalides

Faubourg
Saint
Germain

41

Seine

To Autoroute A13,
Versailles (12km),
Chartres (via N10, 80km),
Rouen (128km) &
Bayeux (257km) &
Normandy

40

ave de Versailles

rue de la Convention

Faure

Gare
Montparnasse

rue Félix

15e

ave du Maine

39

ave Edouard Vaillant

ave de Vaugirard

rue Lecourbe

rue des Morillons

36

14e

rue d'Alésia

Boulogne-Billancourt

38

37

blvd Lefebvre

ave Pierre Grenier

Issy-les-Moulineaux

blvd Brune

35

34

33

32

Île St Germain

Vanves

blvd Périphérique

31

Malakoff

ave de Verdun

Montrouge

FRANCE

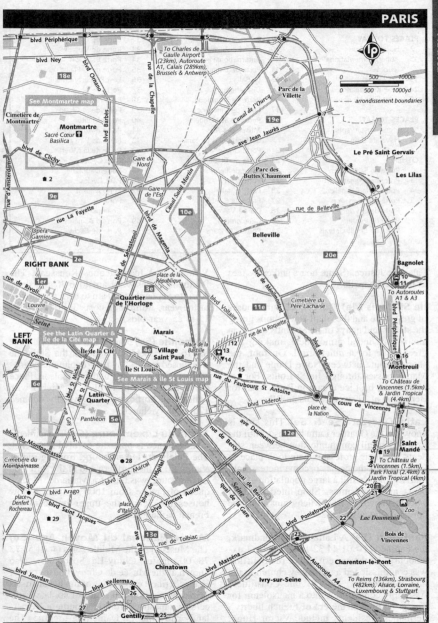

PARIS

To Charles de
Gaulle Airport
(23km), Autoroute
A1, Calais (289km),
Brussels & Antwerp

0   500   1000m
0   500   1000yd

--- arrondissement boundaries

blvd Périphérique

blvd Ney

18e

blvd Omano

rue de la Chapelle

blvd Barbès

Cimetière de
Montmartre

See Montmartre map

Montmartre
Sacré Cœur
Basilica

blvd de Clichy

rue d'Amsterdam

Gare du
Nord

2

9e

rue La Fayette

Opéra
Garnier

RIGHT BANK

2e

1er

rue de Rivoli

Louvre

Seine

**LEFT
BANK**

Germain

See the Latin Quarter &
Île de la Cité map

Île de la Cité

rue St Jacques

rue St Michel

6e

Île St Louis

See Marais & Île St Louis map

**Latin
Quarter**

Panthéon

5e

blvd du Montparnasse

Cimetière de
Montparnasse

30

place
Denfert
Rochereau

blvd Arago

blvd Saint Jacques

29

blvd Jourdan

27

Gare
de l'Est

blvd de Magenta

Canal Saint Martin

blvd de Sébastopol

10e

place de la
République

3e

**Quartier
de l'Horloge**

Marais

4e   **Village
Saint Paul**

blvd Saint Marcel

28

blvd de l'Hôpital

place
d'Italie

blvd Vincent Auriol

ave d'Italie

13e

rue de Tolbiac

Chinatown

blvd Kellermann

26

Parc de la
Villette

Canal de l'Ourcq

19e

ave Jean Jaurès

7

Parc des
Buttes Chaumont

Le Pré Saint Gervais

8

Les Lilas

9

rue de Belleville

Belleville

20e

blvd de Ménilmontant

blvd de Belleville

Cimetière du
Père Lachaise

blvd Voltaire

11e

rue de la Roquette

place de la
Bastille

12
13
14

15

rue du Faubourg St Antoine

rue de Charonne

blvd Diderot

place de
la Nation

ave Daumesnil

rue de Bercy

quai de Bercy

Seine

quai de la
Gare

blvd Masséna

24

Gentilly   25

blvd Poniatowski

23

Autoroute A4

Charenton-le-Pont

Ivry-sur-Seine

Bagnolet

10
11

To Autoroutes
A1 & A3

blvd Périphérique

16

Montreuil

To Château de
Vincennes (1.5km)
& Jardin Tropical
(4.4km)

cours de Vincennes

17

18

**Saint
Mandé**

blvd Soult

19

To Château de
Vincennes (1.5km),
Park Floral (2.4km) &
Jardin Tropical (4km)

20
21

Zoo

22   **Lac Daumesnil**

**Bois de
Vincennes**

To Reims (136km), Strasbourg
(482km), Alsace, Lorraine,
Luxembourg & Stuttgart

euro currency converter 1FF = €0.15

PARIS

PLACES TO STAY		9	Porte des Lilas	32	Porte de Châtillon
2	Hôtel des Trois	10	Gare Routière Internationale	33	Porte de Vanves
15	Auberge Internationale des		(International Bus Terminal)	34	Porte Brancion
	Jeunes	11	Porte de Bagnolet	35	Porte de la Plaine
19	CISP Ravel	13	Le Balajo	36	Lost Property Office
26	CISP Kellermann		Discothèque	37	Porte de Sèvres
29	FIAP Jean Monnet	16	Porte de Montreuil	38	Paris Heliport
		17	Porte de Vincennes	39	Porte de St Cloud
PLACES TO EAT		18	Porte de St Mandé	40	Porte Molitor
12	Ethnic Restaurants	20	Musée des Arts	41	Porte d'Auteuil
14	Havanita Café		d'Afrique et d'Océanie	42	Porte de Passy
		21	Porte Dorée	43	Porte de la Muette
OTHER		22	Porte de Charenton	44	Paris Cycles
1	Porte de Saint Ouen	23	Porte de Bercy	45	Porte Dauphine
3	Porte de Clignancourt	24	Porte d'Ivry	46	Paris Cycles
4	Porte de la Chapelle	25	Porte d'Italie	47	Porte Maillot
5	Porte d'Aubervilliers	27	Porte de Gentilly	48	Porte de
6	Porte de la Villette	28	Paris á Vélo		Champerret
7	Porte de Pantin	30	Catacombes	49	Porte d'Asnières
8	Porte du Pré St Gervais	31	Porte d'Orléans	50	Porte de Clichy

Palais de Justice. (Same hours and entry fees as the Ste Chapelle.)

Île St Louis (4e) The 17th-century houses of grey stone and the small-town shops lining the streets and quays of Île St Louis create an almost provincial atmosphere, making it a great place for a quiet stroll. On foot, the shortest route between Notre Dame and the Marais passes through Île St Louis. For reputedly the best ice cream in Paris, head for Berthillon at 31 rue St Louis en l'Île.

Latin Quarter (5e & 6e) This area is known as the Quartier Latin because, until the Revolution, all communication between students and their professors here took place in Latin. Whilst the 5e has become increasingly touristy, there's still a large population of students and academics. Shop-lined **Blvd St Michel**, known as 'Boul Mich', runs along the border of the 5e and the 6e.

Panthéon (5e) A Latin Quarter landmark, the Panthéon (☎ 01 44 32 18 00, metro Luxembourg), at the eastern end of rue Soufflot, was commissioned as an abbey church in the mid-18th century. In 1791, the Constituent Assembly converted it into a mausoleum for the 'great men of the era of French liberty'. Permanent residents include Victor Hugo,

Voltaire and Jean-Jacques Rousseau. The Panthéon opens 9.30 am to 6.30 pm daily April to September, 10 am to 6.15 pm the rest of the year. Admission costs 35FF (23FF for 12 to 25-year-olds).

Sorbonne (5e) Founded in 1253 as a college for 16 poor theology students, the Sorbonne was closed in 1792 by the Revolutionary government but reopened under Napoleon. **Place de la Sorbonne** links blvd St Michel with **Église de la Sorbonne**, the university's domed 17th-century church.

Jardin du Luxembourg (6e) The gardens' main entrance is opposite 65 blvd St Michel. The **Palais du Luxembourg**, fronting rue de Vaugirard at the northern end of the Jardin du Luxembourg, was built for Maria de' Medici, queen of France from 1600 to 1610. It now houses the Sénat, the upper house of the French parliament.

Musée National du Moyen Age (5e) The Museum of the Middle Ages (☎ 01 53 73 78 00, metro Cluny-La Sorbonne), also known as the Musée de Cluny, houses one of France's finest collections of medieval art. Its prized possession is a series of six late-15th-century tapestries from the southern Netherlands known as La Dame à la Licorne (The

Lady and the Unicorn). The museum is open 9.15 am to 5.45 pm daily, except Tuesday. Admission costs 38FF (28FF for those aged 18 to 25, and for everyone on Sunday).

Mosquée de Paris (5e) Paris' ornate central mosque (☎ 01 45 35 97 33, metro Monge) at place du Puits de l'Ermite was built between 1922 and 1926. There are tours 9 am to noon and 2 to 6 pm daily, except Friday. The mosque complex includes a small souk (marketplace), a *salon de thé* (tearoom), an excellent couscous restaurant and a **hammam** (Turkish bath; ☎ 01 43 31 18 14); enter at 39 rue Geoffroy St Hilaire. The hammam (85FF) opens to men from 2 to 9 pm on Tuesday and 10 am to 9 pm on Sunday only; on other days (10 am to 9 pm) it is reserved for women.

The mosque is opposite the **Jardin des Plantes** (Botanical Gardens), which includes a small **zoo** as well as the recently renovated **Musée d'Histoire Naturelle** (Museum of Natural History; ☎ 01 40 79 30 00, metro Monge), open weekdays, except Tuesday, 10 am to 6 pm (until 10 pm on Thursday). Admission 40/30FF.

Catacombes (14e) In 1785, the bones of millions of Parisians were exhumed from overflowing cemeteries and moved to the tunnels of three disused quarries. One such ossuary is the Catacombes (☎ 01 43 22 47 63, metro Denfert Rochereau). During WWII, these tunnels were used by the Résistance as headquarters. The route through the Catacombes begins from the small green building at 1 place Denfert Rochereau. The site is open 2 to 4 pm Tuesday to Friday, and 9 to 11 am and 2 to 4 pm on weekends. Tickets cost 33FF (22FF for students and seniors; 17FF for children). Take a flashlight (torch).

Musée d'Orsay (7e) The Musée d'Orsay (☎ 01 40 49 48 48, metro Musée d'Orsay), 1 rue de Bellechasse, exhibits works of art produced between 1848 and 1914. Spectacularly housed in a 1900 train station, it opens 10 am (9 am on Sunday and throughout summer) to 6 pm (to 9.45 pm on Thursday) Tuesday to Sunday from late Sepetmber to late June. Admission costs 40FF (30FF for those aged 18 to 25 and over 60, and everyone on Sunday; free for under 18s); tickets are valid all day.

Musée Rodin (7e) The Musée Auguste Rodin (☎ 01 44 18 61 10, metro Varenne), 77 rue Varenne, is one of the most pleasant museums in Paris. It is open 9.30 am to 5.45 pm daily from April to September (to 4.45 pm the rest of the year). Entrance costs 28FF (18FF for those aged 18 to 25 and over 60, and everyone on Sunday; free for under 18s). Visiting just the garden (5 pm close) costs 5FF.

Invalides (7e) The Hôtel des Invalides (metro Invalides for the Esplanade, metro Varenne or Latour Maubourg for the main building) was built in the 1670s by Louis XIV to provide housing for 4000 disabled veterans (*invalides*). It also served as the headquarters of the military governor of Paris, and was used as an armoury. On 14 July 1789 the Paris mob forced its way into the building and took all 28,000 firearms before heading for the Bastille prison.

The **Église du Dôme**, built between 1677 and 1735, is considered one of the finest religious edifices erected under Louis XIV. In 1861 it received the remains of Napoleon, encased in six concentric coffins.

The buildings on either side of the **Cour d'Honneur** (Main Courtyard) house the **Musée de l'Armée** (☎ 01 44 42 37 72), a huge military museum, and the light and airy **Tombeau de Napoléon 1er** (Napoleon's Tomb), both open 10 am to 4.45 pm (5.45 pm in summer) daily. Admission is 38/28FF.

Tour Eiffel (7e) The Tour Eiffel (☎ 01 44 11 23 23, metro Champ de Mars-Tour Eiffel) faced massive opposition from Paris' artistic and literary elite when it was built for the 1889 Exposition Universelle (World's Fair), held to commemorate the Revolution. It was almost torn down in 1909 but was spared for practical reasons – it proved an ideal platform for newfangled transmitting antennae. The Eiffel Tower is 320m high, including the television antenna at the very tip.

Three levels are open to the public. The lift (west and north pillars) costs 22FF for the 1st platform (57m), 47FF for the 2nd (115m) and 62FF for the 3rd (276m). Children four to 12 pay 13/23/32FF respectively; there are no other discounts. The escalator in the south pillar to the 1st and 2nd platforms costs 18FF.

FRANCE

Open 9.30 am to 11 pm (9 am till midnight mid-June to August) daily.

Champ de Mars (7e) The Champ de Mars, a grassy park around the Eiffel Tower, was once a parade ground for the 18th-century **École Militaire** (France's military academy) at the south-eastern end of the lawns.

Right Bank
Jardins du Trocadéro (16e) The Trocadéro gardens (metro Trocadéro), whose fountain and nearby sculpture park are grandly illuminated at night, are across the Pont d'Iéna from the Eiffel Tower. The colonnaded Palais de Chaillot, built in 1937, houses the anthropological and ethnographic Musée de l'Homme (Museum of Mankind; ☎ 01 44 05 72 72), open 9.45 am to 5.15 pm Wednesday to Monday (30/20FF); and the Musée de la Marine (Maritime Museum; ☎ 01 53 65 69 69), known for its beautiful model ships. The maritime museum opens 10 am to 5.45 pm Wednesday to Monday (38/28FF).

Musée Guimet (16e) The Guimet Museum (☎ 01 47 23 88 11, metro Iéna) at 6 place d'Iéna displays antiquities and art from throughout Asia. It opens 10.15 am to 1 pm and 2.30 to 6 pm Wednesday to Monday. Admission costs 16FF (12FF for 18 to 25-year-olds, students, and everyone on Sunday).

Louvre (1er) The Louvre Museum (☎ 01 40 20 53 17, or ☎ 01 40 20 51 51 for a recorded message, metro Palais Royal-Musée du Louvre), constructed around 1200 as a fortress and rebuilt in the mid-16th century as a royal palace, became a public museum in 1793. The collections on display have been assembled by French governments over the past five centuries and include works of art and artisanship from all over Europe as well as important collections of Assyrian, Egyptian, Etruscan, Greek, Coptic, Roman and Islamic art. The Louvre's most famous work is undoubtedly Leonardo da Vinci's *Mona Lisa*.

The Louvre is open 9 am to 6 pm (9.45 pm Monday and Wednesday) daily, except Tuesday. Ticket sales end 45 minutes before closing time. Admission to the permanent collections costs 45FF (26FF after 3 pm and all day Sunday); the first Sunday of every

month is free. There are no student/senior discounts, but under 18s get in free. Admission to temporary exhibits varies. Tickets are valid for the whole day, so you can leave and re-enter as you please. By advance purchasing your tickets at the *billeteries* (ticket office) at FNAC, or other department stores, for an extra 6FF, you can walk straight in without queuing at all.

For English-language guided tours (38/22FF) and audioguide tours (30FF), go to the mezzanine level beneath the glass pyramid.

Place Vendôme (1er) The 44m-high column in the middle of place Vendôme consists of a stone core wrapped in bronze from 1250 cannons captured by Napoleon at the Battle of Austerlitz (1805). The shops around the square are among Paris' most fashionable and expensive.

Musée de l'Orangerie (1er) This museum (☎ 01 42 97 48 16, metro Concorde), usually home to important impressionist works including a series of Monet's spectacular *Nymphéas* (Water Lilies), is being renovated and is due to reopen at the end of 2001.

Place de la Concorde (8e) This vast, cobbled square between the Jardin des Tuileries and the Champs-Élysées was laid out between 1755 and 1775. Louis XVI was guillotined here in 1793 – as were another 1343 people, including his wife Marie Antoinette, over the next two years. The 3300-year-old Egyptian **obelisk** in the middle of the square was given to France in 1829 by the ruler of Egypt, Mohammed Ali.

La Madeleine (8e) The church of St Mary Magdalene (metro Madeleine), built in the style of a Greek temple, was consecrated in 1842 after almost a century of design changes and construction delays.

Champs-Élysées (8e) The 2km-long Ave des Champs-Élysées links place de la Concorde with the Arc de Triomphe. Once popular with the aristocracy as a stage on which to parade their wealth, it has, in recent decades, been partly taken over by fast-food restaurants and overpriced cafes. The nicest bit is the park between place de la Concorde and Rond Point des Champs-Élysées.

Musée du Petit Palais (8e) The Petit Palais (☎ 01 42 65 12 73) will close in late 2000 for refurbishment.

West of the Petit Palais, the **Grand Palais** (☎ 01 44 13 17 17), 3 ave du Général du Eisenhower, built for the 1900 World Fair, is now used for temporary exhibitions. It is open 10 am to 8 pm (10 pm Wednesday) daily, except Tuesday. Admission varies.

Arc de Triomphe (8e) Paris' second most famous landmark, the Arc de Triomphe (☎ 01 55 37 73 77, metro Charles de Gaulle-Étoile) is 2.2km north-west of place de la Concorde in the middle of place Charles de Gaulle. Also called place de l'Étoile, this is the world's largest traffic roundabout and the meeting point of 12 avenues. Commissioned in 1806 by Napoleon to commemorate his imperial victories, it remained unfinished until the 1830s. An Unknown Soldier from WWI is buried under the arch, his fate and that of countless others like him commemorated by a memorial flame lit each evening at around 6.30 pm.

The platform atop the arch (lift up, steps down) is open 9.30 am to 11 pm daily from April to September, except on public holidays, and 10 am to 10.30 pm the rest of the year. It costs 40/25FF. The only sane way to get to the arch's base is via the underground passageways.

The **Voie Triomphale** (Triumphal Way) stretches 4.5km from the Arc de Triomphe along Ave de la Grande Armée to the sky-scraper district of **La Défense**, whose best known landmark, the **Grande Arche** (Grand Arch), is a hollow cube (112m to a side).

Centre Georges Pompidou (4e) Thanks in part to its outstanding temporary exhibitions, Centre Pompidou (☎ 01 44 78 12 33, metro Rambuteau or Châtelet-Les Halles) – also known as Centre Beaubourg – is by far the most frequented sight in Paris. **Place Igor Stravinsky**, south of the centre, and the large square to the west attract all kinds of street artists.

The **Musée National d'Art Moderne** (MNAM; National Museum of Modern Art)

on the 4th floor displays France's national collection of 20th-century art. It's open 11 am to 9 pm Wednesday to Monday and costs 30FF (20FF for 18 to 26-year-olds, students and seniors; free for under 18s). The **Bibliothèque Publique d'Information**, a huge, nonlending library, is on the 2nd floor.

Les Halles (1er) Paris' main wholesale food market, Les Halles, occupied this site from the 12th century until 1969, when it was moved out to the suburb of Rungis; a huge underground shopping mall (Forum des Halles) was built in its place. Just north of the grassy area on top of Les Halles is the mostly 16th-century **Église St Eustache**, noted for its wonderful pipe organ.

Hôtel de Ville (4e) Paris' city hall (☎ 01 42 76 40 40, metro Hôtel de Ville) at place de l'Hôtel de Ville was burned down during the Paris Commune of 1871 and rebuilt (1874-82) in the neo-Renaissance style. Enter at 29 rue de Rivoli; open 9.30 am to 6 pm Monday to Saturday.

Marais Area (4e) A marsh *(marais)* converted to agricultural use in the 13th century, this area was, during the 17th century – when the nobility erected luxurious but discreet mansions known as *hôtels particuliers* – the most fashionable part of the city. Eventually the Marais was taken over by ordinary Parisians and by the time renovation began in the 1960s, it had become a poor but lively Jewish neighbourhood. In the 1980s the area underwent serious gentrification and today it is the centre of Paris' gay life.

Place des Vosges (4e) Built in 1605 and originally known as place Royal, place des Vosges (metro Chemin Vert) is a square ensemble of 36 symmetrical houses. Duels were once fought in the elegant park in the middle. Today, the arcades around place des Vosges are occupied by upmarket art galleries, antique shops and salons de thé.

The nearby **Maison de Victor Hugo** is where the author lived from 1832 to 1848 (22/15FF; closed Monday).

Musée Picasso (3e) The Picasso Museum (☎ 01 42 71 25 21, metro St Paul or Chemin

FRANCE

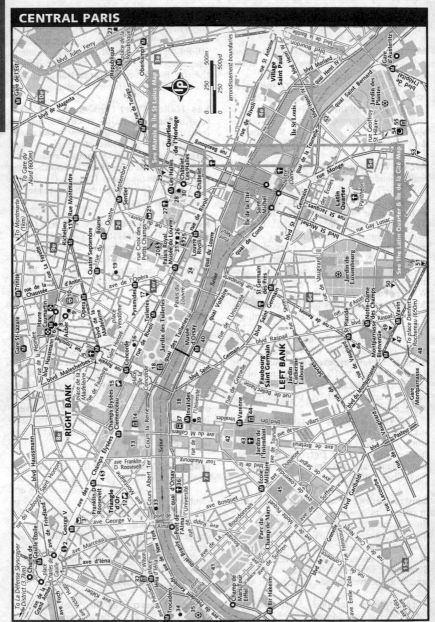

CENTRAL PARIS

CENTRAL PARIS

PLACES TO STAY		5	La Madeleine Church	30	Roue Libre
23	Auberge de Jeunesse	6	Au Printemps	32	Musée Guimet
	Jules Ferry		(Department Store)	33	Bateaux Mouches (Boat Tours)
26	Centre International BVJ	7	Galeries Lafayette	34	Palais de Chaillot
	Paris-Louvre & Laundrette		(Department Store)	35	Jardins du Trocadéro.
		8	Eurostar & Ferry Offices	36	American Church
PLACES TO EAT		9	American Express	37	Aérogare des Invalides
11	Chartier Restaurant	10	Opéra Garnier		(Buses to Orly)
17	Food Shops	12	Canadian Embassy	38	Palais Bourbon (National
29	Joe Allen	13	Grand Palais		Assembly Building)
31	Le Petit Mâchon	14	Musée du Petit Palais	39	British Council
47	Mustang Café	15	US Embassy	40	Musée d'Orsay
49	Le Caméléon Restaurant	16	WH Smith Bookshop	41	Eiffel Tower
50	CROUS Restaurant	18	Musée de l'Orangerie	42	Hôtel des Invalides
	Universitaire	19	Voyageurs du Monde	43	Église du Dôme
51	CROUS Restaurant	20	Banque de France	44	Musée Rodin
	Universitaire Bullier	21	Main Post Office	45	École Militaire
52	Founti Agadir	22	Rue Saint Denis Sex District	46	FNAC Store & Ticket Outlet
		24	Louvre Museum	48	Cimetière du
OTHER		25	Change du Louvre		Montparnasse
1	Arc de Triomphe		(Currency Exchange)	52	Institut du Monde Arabe
2	Main Tourist Office	27	Église Saint Eustache	53	Paris Mosque &
3	Post Office	28	Forum des Halles		Hammam
4	Bureau de Change		(Shopping Mall & Park)	54	Museum of Natural History

Vert) is just north-east of the Marais at 5 rue de Thorigny. Paintings, sculptures, ceramics, engravings and drawings donated to the French government by the heirs of Pablo Picasso (1881-1973) to avoid huge inheritance taxes are on display, as is Picasso's personal art collection (Braque, Cézanne, Matisse, Rousseau, etc). The museum opens 9.30 am to 6 pm (8 pm on Thursday) Wednesday to Monday; October to March it closes at 5.30 pm. Admission costs 30/20FF (free for under 18s).

Bastille (4e, 11e & 12e) The Bastille is the most famous nonexistent monument in Paris; the notorious prison was demolished shortly after the mob stormed it on 14 July 1789. The site is known as place de la Bastille. The 52m-high **Colonne de Juillet** in the centre was erected in 1830. The new (and rather drab) **Opéra Bastille** (☎ 01 44 73 13 99 or ☎ 0836 69 78 68, metro Bastille) is at 2-6 place de la Bastille.

Opéra Garnier (9e) Paris' renowned opera house (see Opera & Classical Music under Entertainment for contact details) was designed in 1860 by Charles Garnier. The **ceiling** of the auditorium was painted by Marc

Chagall in 1964. The building also houses the **Musée de l'Opéra**, open 10 am to 5 pm daily. Entrance is 30/20FF.

Montmartre (18e) During the 19th century Montmartre was a vibrant centre of artistic and literary creativity. Today it's an area of mimes, buskers, tacky souvenir shops and commercial artists. The **Moulin Rouge** (☎ 01 53 09 82 82, metro Blanche) at 82 blvd de Clichy, founded in 1889, is known for its twice-nightly revues of near-naked girls.

Basilique du Sacré Cœur Sacré Cœur (☎ 01 53 41 89 00, metro Anvers) was built to fulfil a vow taken by Parisian Catholics after the disastrous Franco-Prussian War of 1870-71. It is open 7 am to 11 pm daily (to 6 pm October to March). Admission is 15FF, students 8FF. The funicular up the hill's southern slope costs one metro/bus ticket each way.

Place du Tertre Just west of **Église St Pierre**, place du Tertre is filled with cafes, restaurants, portrait artists and tourists – though the real attractions of the area are the quiet, twisting streets. Look for the **windmills** on rue Lepic and Paris' last **vineyard**, on the corner of rue des Saules and rue St Vincent.

Pigalle (9e & 18e) Although the area along blvd de Clichy between the Pigalle and Blanche metro stops is lined with sex shops and striptease parlours, there are plenty of legitimate nightspots to choose from (see Entertainment).

Musée de l'Érotisme (Museum of Eroticism; ☎ 01 42 58 28 73, metro Blanche), 72 blvd de Clichy, tries to raise erotic art both antique and modern to a loftier plane – but we know why we visited. Open 10 am to 2 am daily (40FF, students 30FF).

Cimetière du Père Lachaise (20e) Père Lachaise Cemetery (☎ 01 43 70 70 33, metro Père Lachaise), final resting place of such notables as Chopin, Proust, Oscar Wilde and Édith Piaf, may be the most visited cemetery in the world. The best known tomb is that of 1960s rock star Jim Morrison, lead singer for The Doors, who died in 1971. The cemetery is free and open daily to at least 5.30 pm.

Bois de Vincennes (12e) Highlights of this 9.29-sq-km English-style park include the **Parc Floral** (Floral Garden; metro Château de Vincennes); the **Parc Zoologique de Paris** (Paris Zoo; ☎ 01 44 75 20 10, metro Porte Dorée); and the **Jardin Tropical** (Tropical Garden; RER stop Nugent-sur-Marne).

Château de Vincennes (12e) A *bona fide* royal chateau, the Château de Vincennes (☎ 01 48 08 31 20, metro Château de Vincennes) is at the northern edge of the Bois de Vincennes. You can walk around the grounds for free, but to see the Gothic **Chapelle Royale** and the 14th-century **donjon** (keep), you must take a tour (in French, with an information booklet in English). The chateau opens 10 am to 5 pm daily.

Musée des Arts d'Afrique et d'Océanie (12e) Specialising in art from Africa and the South Pacific, this museum (☎ 01 44 74 84 80, metro Porte Dorée) at 293 Ave Daumesnil opens 10 am to noon and 1.30 to 5.30 pm (6 pm on weekends) Wednesday to Monday. The admission fee is 40FF (reduced tariff 30FF, students 10FF).

Bois de Boulogne (16e) The 8.65-sq-km Bois de Boulogne is endowed with meandering trails, forests, cycling paths and *belle époque*-style cafes. Rowing boats can be rented at the **Lac Inférieur** (metro Ave Henri Martin).

Paris Cycles (☎ 01 47 47 76 50 for a recorded message or ☎ 01 47 47 22 37 to book) rents bicycles on ave du Mahatma Gandhi (metro Les Sablons) and at the northern end of the Lac Inférieur (metro Ave Foch). Rental costs 20/30FF for 30 minutes/one hour and 60/80FF for a half-day/day.

LANGUAGE COURSES

Alliance Française (☎ 01 45 44 38 28, metro St Placide) at 101 blvd Raspail, 6e, offers month-long French courses. Accord Language School (☎ 01 42 36 24 95, metro Les Halles) at 52 rue Montmartre, 1er, gets high marks from students.

ORGANISED TOURS
Bus

From April to late September, RATP's Balabus follows a 50-minute return route from Gare de Lyon to the Grande Arche in La Défense. Buses depart about every 20 minutes and cost one metro/bus ticket. L'Open Tour (☎ 01 43 46 52 06, fax 01 43 46 53 06) runs open-deck buses along three circuits year round, allowing you to jump on and off at more than 30 stops. Tickets cost 135/150FF for one/two days (less if you're holding a Carte Orange, Paris Visite or Batobus pass).

Bicycle

Both Roue Libre (☎ 01 53 46 43 77, fax 01 40 28 01 00, metro Les Halles), 95 bis rue Rambuteau, 1er, and Paris à Vélo C'est Sympa! (☎ 01 48 87 60 01, ✉ info@parisvelosympa .com, metro Bastille), 37 blvd Bourdon, 4e, offer bicycle tours on Saturday and Sunday (and during the week depending on demand). Paris à Vélo charges 185FF (160FF for under 26s) while Roue Libre's tours are 135FF and 85FF for children aged four to 12. Both include a guide, the bicycle and insurance. A 1½-hour Sunday morning Paris à Vélo tour costs 100/60FF.

Bullfrog Bike Tours (mobile/cellphone ☎ 06 09 98 08 60, ✉ bullfrogbikes@hotmail.com) head off from the Champ de Mars at 11 am and

3.30 pm from early May to late August (150FF). Night tours (170FF) leave at 8 pm.

Boat

Every 25 minutes, mid-April to early November, the Batobus river shuttle (☎ 01 44 11 33 99) docks at six places including Notre Dame and the Musée d'Orsay. A one/two day pass costs 60/80FF (35/40FF for children under 12). Bateaux Mouches (☎ 01 42 25 96 10 or for an English-language recording ☎ 01 40 76 99 99, metro Alma Marceau) makes a 1½-hour cruise for 40FF (20FF for under 14s) with commentary. Vedettes du Pont Neuf (☎ 01 46 33 98 38, metro Pont Neuf) operates one-hour boat circuits day and night for 50FF (25FF for under 12s).

PLACES TO STAY
Accommodation Services

Accueil des Jeunes en France (AJF; ☎ 01 42 77 87 80, metro Rambuteau) is at 119 rue St Martin, 4e, just west of the Centre Pompidou (open 10 am to 5.45 pm daily except Sunday). It makes same-day reservations at hostels, hotels and private homes for a 10FF fee; you pay at the office and take a voucher to the establishment. Prices start at 120FF per person (excluding 10FF fee).

The main tourist office (see Information earlier) and its Gare de Lyon annexe can also make same day bookings. It also has information on *pensions de famille*, similar to B&Bs, and homestays.

Camping

At the far western edge of the Bois de Boulogne, *Camping du Bois de Boulogne* (☎ 01 45 24 30 00, Allée du Bord de l'Eau, 16e) is Paris' only camping ground. Two people with a tent pay from 67/105FF with/without a vehicle. The Porte Maillot metro stop is linked to the camping ground by RATP bus No 244 (6 am to 8.30 pm) and, April to October, by privately operated shuttle bus (10FF).

Hostels & Foyers

Many hostels allow a three-night maximum stay, especially in summer. Only official *auberges de jeunesse* (youth hostels) require guests to present Hostelling International (HI) cards or equivalent. Curfew – if enforced – tends to be 1 or 2 am. Few hostels accept reservations by telephone.

Louvre Area (1er) *Centre International BVJ Paris-Louvre* (☎ 01 53 00 90 90, metro Louvre-Rivoli, 20 rue Jean-Jacques Rousseau) has bunks in single-sex rooms for 130FF, including breakfast.

Marais (4e) The Maison Internationale de la Jeunesse et des Étudiants *(MIJE; ☎ 01 42 74 23 45, fax 01 40 27 81 64)* runs three hostels in attractively renovated 17th and 18th-century Marais residences. Beds start at 145/240FF dorm/single, including breakfast. *MIJE Maubisson (12 rue des Barres, metro Hôtel de Ville)* is in our opinion the best. *MIJE Fourcy (6 rue de Fourcy, metro St Paul)*, the largest hostel, and *MIJE Fauconnier (11 rue du Fauconnier, metro Pont Marie)*, two blocks south of MIJE Fourcy, are the other options.

Panthéon Area (5e) The clean and friendly *Y&H Hostel* (☎ 01 45 35 09 53, fax 01 47 07 22 24, ✉ smile@youngandhappy.fr, 80 rue Mouffetard, metro Monge) is popular with a younger crowd. A bed in a three or four-bed room costs 117FF (137FF in a double).

11e Arrondissement *Auberge de Jeunesse Jules Ferry* (☎ 01 43 57 55 60, 8 blvd Jules Ferry, metro République) has dorm beds for 115FF (120FF in a double; 19FF extra without an HI card), including breakfast. Internet access costs 5FF.

The clean and friendly *Auberge Internationale des Jeunes* (☎ 01 47 00 62 00, fax 01 47 00 33 16, ✉ aijaijparis.com, 10 rue Trousseau, metro Ledru Rollin) attracts a young crowd and gets full in summer. Beds cost 81FF from November to February, 91FF from March to October, including breakfast.

12e Arrondissement *Centre International de Séjour de Paris (CISP) Ravel* (☎ 01 44 75 60 00, fax 01 43 44 45 30, ✉ 100616 .2215@compuserve.com, 4-6 Ave Maurice Ravel, metro Porte de Vincennes)* charges 126FF for a bed in a two to four-bed room, 156FF in a double and 206FF for a single, including breakfast.

FRANCE

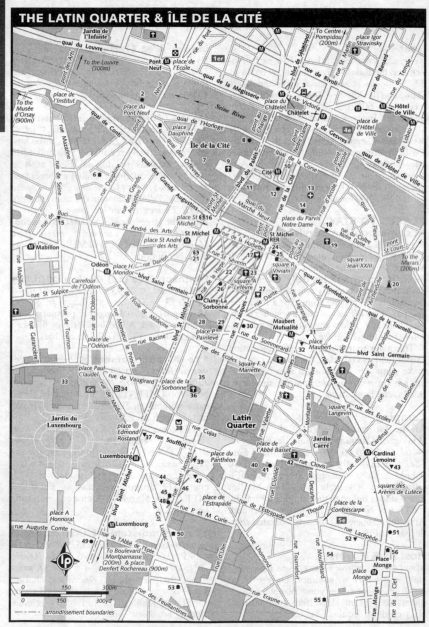

THE LATIN QUARTER & ÎLE DE LA CITÉ

euro currency converter €1 = 6.55FF

THE LATIN QUARTER & ÎLE DE LA CITÉ

PLACES TO STAY
5	Hôtel Henri IV
6	Hôtel de Nesle
25	Hôtel Esmeralda
45	Hôtel de Médicis
50	Hôtel Gay Lussac
53	Grand Hôtel du Progrès
55	Y & H Hostel
56	Hôtel Saint Christophe

PLACES TO EAT
15	Food Shops
22	Restaurants ('Bacteria Alley')
31	Food Shops
32	Fromagerie (Cheese Shop)
37	McDonald's
39	Perraudin
43	Le Petit Légume
44	Douce France Sandwich Bar
46	Food Shops
47	Tashi Delek Tibetan Restaurant
52	Ed l'Épicier Supermarket
54	Restaurants

OTHER
1	Samaritaine (Department Store)
2	Vedettes du Pont Neuf (Boat Tours)
3	Noctambus (All-Night Bus) Stops
4	Hôtel de Ville (City Hall)
7	Palais de Justice & Conciergerie
8	Conciergerie Entrance
9	Sainte Chapelle
10	Flower Market
11	Préfecture de Police
12	Préfecture Entrance
13	Hôtel Dieu (Hospital)
14	Hospital Entrance
16	Le Change de Paris
17	Caveau de la Huchette Jazz Club
18	Notre Dame Tower Entrance
19	Notre Dame Cathedral
20	WWII Deportation Memorial
21	Bureau de Change

23	Église Saint Séverin
24	Shakespeare & Co Bookshop
26	Abbey Bookshop
27	Le Cloître Pub; Polly Maggoo Pub
28	Musée du Moyen Age (Thermes de Cluny)
29	Musée du Moyen Age Entrance
30	Eurolines Bus Office
33	Palais du Luxembourg (French Senate Building)
34	Café Orbital
35	Sorbonne (University of Paris)
36	Église de la Sorbonne
38	Post Office
40	Panthéon
41	Panthéon Entrance
42	Église Saint Étienne du Mont
48	Laundrette
49	Nouvelles Frontières (Travel Agency)
51	Laundrette

13e & 14e Arrondissements The *Foyer International d'Accueil de Paris (FIAP) Jean Monnet* (☎ 01 43 13 17 00, fax 01 45 81 63 91, 30 rue Cabanis, metro Glacière) has modern rooms for five to eight/three to four/two people for 139/172/194FF per person, including breakfast. Rooms specially outfitted for disabled people (*handicapés*) are available. Reservations are accepted up to 15 days ahead.

The *Centre International de Séjour de Paris (CISP) Kellermann* (☎ 01 44 16 37 38, 17 blvd Kellermann, 13e, metro Porte d'Italie) has dorm beds for 113FF and singles for 156FF. Prices include sheets and breakfast. This place also has facilities for disabled people on the 1st floor. Reservations are accepted up to 48 hours in advance.

Hotels

Marais (4e) The friendly *Hôtel Rivoli* (☎ 01 42 72 08 41, 44 rue de Rivoli, metro Hôtel de Ville) is still a good deal with singles (no shower) starting at 200FF, doubles (with bath and toilet) at 300FF.

Hôtel de Nice (☎ 01 42 78 55 29, fax 01 42 78 36 07, 42 bis rue de Rivoli, metro Hôtel de Ville) is a family-run place with

singles/doubles/triples/quads for 380/450/550/680FF; some rooms have balconies. *Grand Hôtel Malher* (☎ 01 42 72 60 92, fax 01 42 72 25 37, 5 rue Malher, metro St Paul) has nice singles/doubles starting at 490/590FF (100FF more in the high season).

Notre Dame Area (5e) The *Hôtel Esmeralda* (☎ 01 43 54 19 20, fax 01 40 51 00 68, 4 rue St Julien, metro St Michel) is everybody's favourite. Its three simple singles (180FF) are booked well in advance. Doubles with bath and toilet start at 450FF.

Panthéon Area (5e) Basic singles at *Hôtel de Médicis* (☎ 01 43 54 14 66, 214 rue St Jacques, metro Luxembourg) start at 90FF; doubles/triples are 180/250FF.

A better deal is *Grand Hôtel du Progrès* (☎ 01 43 54 53 18, fax 01 56 24 87 80, 50 rue Gay Lussac, metro Luxembourg). Singles start at 160FF; larger doubles with a view at 240FF, including breakfast. The nearby, family-run *Hôtel Gay Lussac* (☎ 01 43 54 23 96, fax 01 40 51 79 49, metro Luxembourg) is a cut above, with small singles averaging 220FF; larger doubles/quads start at 360/450FF.

Hôtel St Christophe (☎ *01 43 31 81 54, fax 01 43 31 12 54,* ✉ *hotelstchristophe@compous erve.com, 17 rue Lacépède, metro place Monge)* is a classy small hotel with 31 well-equipped rooms at 550/680FF, although discounts are often available.

St Germain des Prés (6e) *Hôtel de Nesle* (☎ *01 43 54 62 41, 7 rue de Nesle, metro Odéon or Mabillon)* is a relaxed, colourfully decorated hotel in a quiet street. Singles/doubles with shower are 275/350FF (450FF for a double with bath and toilet). Reservations not accepted. The well-positioned *Hôtel Henri IV* (☎ *01 43 54 44 53, 25 place Dauphine, metro Pont Neuf)* at the western end of Île de la Cité has adequate singles/doubles starting at 125/200FF (hall showers 15FF). Book well ahead.

Montmartre (18e) Singles/doubles at the attractive *Hôtel des Arts* (☎ *01 46 06 30 52, fax 01 46 06 10 83, 5 rue Tholozé, metro Abessess)* start at 360/460FF. *Hôtel de Rohan* (☎ *01 42 52 32 57, fax 01 55 79 79 63, 90 rue Myrha, metro Château Rouge)* has basic, tidy singles/doubles for 120/150FF (hall showers 20FF). *Hôtel des Trois Poussins* (☎ *01 53 32 81 81, fax 01 53 32 81 82,* ✉ *h3p@les3po ussins.com, 15 rue Clauzel, metro St Georges)* is a lovely hotel due south of place Pigalle. Singles/doubles start at 680/780FF. Many of the rooms are small studios (from 780/880FF per single/double) with their own cooking facilities.

PLACES TO EAT
Restaurants
Except for those in the very touristy areas, most of the city's thousands of restaurants are pretty good value for money.

Forum des Halles *Le Petit Mâchon* (☎ *01 42 60 08 06, 158 rue St Honoré, metro Palais Royal)* bistro has Lyon-inspired specialities, with main courses from 68FF and a 98FF *menu*. American bar/restaurant *Joe Allen* (☎ *01 42 36 70 13, 30 rue Pierre Lescot, metro Étienne Marcel)* serves Californian wines and two/three course *menus* for 112/140FF.

Opéra Area (2e & 9e) *Chartier* (☎ *01 47 70 86 29, 7 rue du Faubourg Montmartre, metro Grands Boulevards)*, famous for its 330-seat *belle époque* dining room, has mains from 34FF and more elaborate two/three/four course *menus* for 74/110/190FF.

Marais (4e) Rue des Rosiers (metro St Paul), the heart of the old Jewish neighbourhood, has a few *kascher* (kosher) restaurants. Paris' best known Jewish (but not kosher) restaurant, founded in 1920, is *Restaurant Jo Goldenberg* at No 7, with main dishes for around 80FF. *Minh Chau* (*10 rue de la Verrerie, metro Hôtel de Ville)* is a tiny but welcoming Vietnamese place with tasty main dishes for about 30FF. For vegetarian fare head to *Aquarius* (*54 rue Ste Croix de la Bretonnerie, metro Rambuteau)*, where a tasty two-course lunch costs 64/92FF and a three-course dinner is 95FF.

Bastille (4e, 11e & 12e) While the area around Bastille has many ethnic restaurants, traditional French food is also available. *Havanita Café* (☎ *01 43 55 96 42, 11 rue de Lappe, metro Bastille)* serves Cuban-inspired food and drinks. Excellent main courses are 69FF to 94FF. *Bofinger* (☎ *01 42 72 87 82, 5-7 rue de la Bastille, metro Bastille)*, with an Art Nouveau interior, has *menus* for 119/178/189FF.

Latin Quarter (4e, 5e & 6e) This area has plenty of good Greek, North African and Middle Eastern restaurants – but avoid rue de la Huchette (aka 'bacteria alley') and its nearby streets, unless you're after shwarma (20FF), available at several places.

The Moroccan *Founti Agadir* (☎ *01 43 37 85 10, 117 rue Monge, metro Censier Daubenton)* has some of the best couscous, grills and tajines on the Left Bank. Lunch *menus* are 75/89FF. Or, if you fancy classics like *bœuf bourguignon* (59FF), try *Perraudin* (☎ *01 46 33 15 75, 157 rue St Jacques, metro Luxembourg)*, a reasonably priced traditional French restaurant.

Le Petit Légume (☎ *01 40 46 06 85, 36 rue des Boulangers, metro Cardinal Lemoine)*, a great choice for home-made vegetarian fare, has *menus* for 50/64/75FF.

Some of the best crepes in Paris are sold from a little stall opposite 68 rue Mouffetard. *Tashi Delek* (☎ *01 43 26 55 55, 4 rue St Jacques, metro Luxembourg)* offers good, cheap, Tibetan lunch/dinner *menus* for 65/105FF. *Douce France (7 rue Royer Collard, metro Luxembourg)* is a popular hole-in-the-wall selling great sandwiches.

Montparnasse (6e & 14e) For innovative food in a traditional setting, you couldn't do better than *Le Caméléon (☎ 01 43 20 63 43, 6 rue de Chevreuse, 6e, metro Vavin)*; the lobster ravioli (92FF) alone is worth a visit.

There are *creperies* at 20 rue d'Odessa and around the corner on rue du Montparnasse. *Mustang Café (☎ 01 43 35 36 12, 84 blvd du Montparnasse, metro Montparnasse-Bien-venüe)* serves passable Tex-Mex (platters and chilli from 47FF) until 5 am.

Montmartre (9e & 18e) Restaurants around place du Tertre tend to be touristy and overpriced – but there are alternatives. An old favourite is *Refuge des Fondus (☎ 01 42 55 22 65, 17 rue des Trois Frères, metro Abbesses)* where 92FF buys an apéritif, wine, and either cheese or meat fondue (meat: minimum of two). *Le Mono (☎ 01 46 06 99 20, 40 rue Véron)* serves West African dishes priced from 25FF to 70FF.

Il Duca (☎ 01 46 06 71 98, 26 rue Yvonne le Tac, metro Abbesses) serves good Italian food in an intimate setting. The lunch *menu* is 89FF and home-made pasta dishes are 55FF to 76FF.

University Restaurants Paris has 15 *restaurants universitaires* (student cafeterias) run by the Centre Régional des Œuvres Universitaires et Scolaires (CROUS; ☎ 01 40 51 36 00). Students with ID pay 14.50FF, guests about 24FF. Opening times vary, so check the schedule outside any of the following: *Assas (☎ 01 46 33 61 25, 92 rue d'Assas, 6e, metro Port Royal or Notre Dame des Champs)*; *Bullier (☎ 01 43 54 93 38, 39 ave Georges Bernanos, 5e, metro Port Royal)*; *Châtelet (☎ 01 43 31 51 66, 8 rue Jean Calvin, 5e, metro Censier Daubenton)*, just off rue Mouffetard; and *Mabillon (☎ 01 43 25 66 23, 3 rue Mabillon, 6e, metro Mabillon)*.

Self-Catering
Supermarkets are always cheaper than small grocery shops. The *Monoprix Supermarket (21 Avenue de l'Opéra)* opposite metro Pyramides is convenient for the Louvre area, or

try *Ed l'Épicier (37 rue Lacépède, metro Monge)* if you're in the Latin Quarter. For a different shopping experience altogether, head to *Fauchon (☎ 01 47 62 60 11, 26 place de la Madeleine, metro Madeleine)*, Paris' most famous gourmet-food shop.

Food Markets Paris' *marchés découverts* (open-air markets), open 7 am to 2 pm, pop up in various squares and streets two or three times a week. *Marchés couverts* (covered markets) open 8 am to about 1 pm and 4 to 7 or 7.30 pm Tuesday to Sunday. Ask at your hotel for the location of the nearest market.

Notre Dame Area (4e & 5e) There are a number of *fromageries* and *groceries* along rue St Louis en l'Île (metro Pont Marie) and place Maubert hosts a food market (Tuesday, Thursday, Saturday) and various other *food shops*.

St Germain des Prés (6e) *Food shops* are clustered on rue de Seine and rue de Buci (metro Mabillon) and at rue St Jacques. The covered *Marché St Germain* on rue Lobineau, just north of the eastern end of Église St Germain des Prés, has a huge array of produce and prepared foods.

Marais (4e) *Flo Prestige (10 rue St Antoine, metro Bastille)* has picnic supplies and, more importantly, delectable pastries and baked goods.

Montmartre (18e) Most of the *food shops* in this area are along rue Lepic and rue des Abbesses, about 500m south-west of Sacré Cœur.

ENTERTAINMENT
It's virtually impossible to sample the richness of Paris' entertainment scene without consulting *Pariscope* (3FF; includes an English-language insert) or *L'Officiel des Spectacles* (2FF), both published on Wednesday and available at any newsstand.

Tickets
Tickets can be reserved and bought at the ticket outlets in the FNAC stores at 136 rue de Rennes, 6e (☎ 01 49 54 30 00, metro St Placide) and at the 3rd underground level of

FRANCE

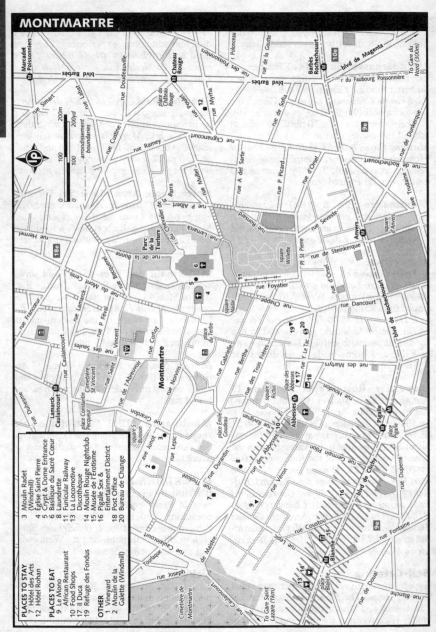

MONTMARTRE

PLACES TO STAY
7 Hôtel des Arts
12 Hôtel Rohan

PLACES TO EAT
9 Le Mono
  African Restaurant
10 Food Shops
17 Il Duca
19 Refuge des Fondus

OTHER
1 Vineyard
2 Moulin de la
  Galette (Windmill)

3 Moulin Radet
  (Windmill)
4 Eglise Saint Pierre
5 Crypt & Dôme Entrance
6 Basilique du Sacré Cœur
8 Laundrette
11 Funicular Railway
13 La Locomotive
  Discothèque
14 Moulin Rouge Nightclub
15 Musée de l'Erotisme
16 Pigalle Sex &
  Entertainment District
18 Post Office
20 Bureau de Change

euro currency converter €1 = 6.55FF

the Forum des Halles shopping mall (☎ 01 40 41 40 00, metro Châtelet-Les Halles) at 1-7 rue Pierre Lescot, 1er; and in the Virgin Megastores at 52-60 Ave des Champs-Élysées, 8e (☎ 01 49 53 50 00, metro Franklin D Roosevelt) and 99 rue de Rivoli, 1er (☎ 01 49 53 52 09, metro Franklin D Roosevelt).

Pubs
Unpretentious and relaxed, *Le Cloître* (*☎ 01 43 25 19 92, 19 rue St Jacques, 5e, metro St Michel*) seems to please the young Parisians who congregate there. Informal, friendly *Polly Maggoo* (*☎ 01 46 33 33 64, 11 rue St Jacques, metro St Michel*) was founded in 1967 and still plays music from that era.

Café Oz (*☎ 01 43 54 30 48, 18 rue St Jacques, metro Luxembourg*) is a casual, friendly pub with Foster's on tap. Anglophone and always crowded, *Stolly's* (*☎ 01 42 76 06 76, 16 rue de la Cloche Percée, 4e, metro Hôtel de Ville*) is on a tiny street just off rue de Rivoli.

Clubs & Dance Venues
The clubs and other dancing venues favoured by the Parisian 'in' crowd change frequently, and many are officially private, which means bouncers can deny entry to whomever they don't like the look of. For example, single men may not be admitted; women, on the other hand, get in free some nights.

Le Balajo (*☎ 01 47 00 07 87, 9 rue de Lappe, 11e, metro Bastille*), a mainstay of the Parisian dance-hall scene since 1935, is two blocks north-east of place de la Bastille. DJs play old-fashioned *musette* (accordion music) for retro tea dancing 2.30 to 6.30 pm on Thursday and 3 to 7 pm on Sunday (50FF). Night admission (100FF) includes one drink.

La Locomotive (*☎ 01 53 41 88 88, 90 blvd de Clichy, 18e, metro Blanche*), an enormous, ever popular disco open 11 pm (midnight on Monday) until 6 am, charges 70/100FF (including one drink) on weekdays/weekends. Women get in free before 12.30 am.

Jazz
A favourite for live Jazz, *Caveau de la Huchette* (*☎ 01 43 26 65 05, 5 rue de la Huchette, 5e, metro St Michel*) opens 9.30 pm to 2 am (later on weekends); entry costs 60FF

(students 55FF) during the week, 70FF (no discounts) at the weekend.

Opera & Classical Music
Paris plays host to dozens of concerts each week. The Opéra National de Paris splits its performances between Opéra Garnier (☎ 01 44 73 13 99), its original home built in 1875, and the modern Opéra Bastille (☎ 01 44 73 13 99), which opened in 1989. Both opera houses also stage ballets and concerts. Opera tickets (September to July only) cost 90FF to 670FF; ballets 70FF to 420FF; and concerts 85FF to 240FF. Check its Web site at www.opera-de-paris.fr. Unsold tickets are offered 15 minutes prior to showtime to students, under 25s or over 65s for about 100FF – ask for the *tarif spécial*.

Cinemas
Going to the movies in Paris is expensive (about 50FF), though most cinemas give discounts on Wednesday (and sometimes Monday). Check *Pariscope* and *L'Officiel des Spectacles* for listings: 'vo' (*version originale*) indicates subtitled movies.

SHOPPING
Fashion
Some of Paris' fanciest shops are along Ave Montaigne and rue du Faubourg St Honoré, 8e; rue St Honoré, 1er and 8e; and place Vendôme, 1er. Rue Bonaparte, 6e, offers a good choice of mid-range boutiques.

Department Stores
Paris' three main department stores, open 9.30 am to 7 pm Monday to Saturday (10 pm on Thursday) are: Au Printemps (☎ 01 42 82 50 00), 64 blvd Haussmann, metro Havre Caumartin; Galeries Lafayette (☎ 01 42 82 36 40), 40 blvd Haussmann, metro Auber or Chaussée; and Samaritaine (☎ 01 40 41 20 20), metro Pont Neuf, which provides an amazing view from the 10th-floor terrace of Building 2 at 19 rue de la Monnaie.

GETTING THERE & AWAY
Air
Paris has two major international airports. Aéroport d'Orly is 14km south of central Paris. For flight and other information call ☎ 01 49 75 15 15 or ☎ 0836 25 05 05. Aéroport Charles

FRANCE

MARAIS & ÎLE SAINT LOUIS

de Gaulle (☎ 01 48 62 22 80), also known as Roissy-Charles de Gaulle in the suburb of Roissy, is 23km north-east of central Paris. For airline information call ☎ 01 48 62 22 80 or ☎ 0836 25 05 05.

Telephone numbers for information at Paris' airline offices are:

Air France	☎ 0802 80 28 02
Air Liberté	☎ 0803 80 58 05
Air New Zealand	☎ 01 40 53 82 23
Air UK	☎ 01 44 56 18 08
American Airlines	☎ 0801 87 28 72
British Airways	☎ 0825 82 54 00
Continental	☎ 01 42 99 09 09
Lufthansa	☎ 0802 02 00 30
Northwest Airlines	☎ 01 42 66 90 00
Qantas	☎ 0803 84 68 46
Singapore Airlines	☎ 01 53 65 79 00
Thai	☎ 01 44 20 70 80
United	☎ 0801 72 72 72

Bus

Eurolines terminal, Gare Routière Internationale (☎ 0836 69 52 52, metro Gallieni), is at Porte de Bagnolet, 20e, on the eastern edge of Paris. Its ticket office in town (☎ 01 43 54 11 99, metro Cluny-La Sorbonne) at 55 rue St Jacques, 5e, opens 9.30 am to 6.30 pm week-

MARAIS & ÎLE SAINT LOUIS

PLACES TO STAY
9   Grand Hôtel Mahler
11 Hôtel Rivoli
13 Hôtel de Nice
15 MIJE Maubuisson
17 MIJE Fourcy
18 MIJE Fauconnier

PLACES TO EAT
4   Aquarius Vegetarian Restaurant
7   Restaurants
8   Restaurant Jo Goldenberg
12 Minh Chau
19 Food Shops

21 Ethnic Restaurants
22 Bofinger
23 Flo Prestige
32 Berthillon Ice Cream
33 Food Shops

OTHER
1   Web Bar
2   Accueil des Jeunes en France (AJF)
3   Centre Pompidou
5   Musée Picasso
6   Laundrette
10 Hôtel de Ville (City Hall)

14 Stolly's
16 Memorial to the Unknown Jewish Martyr
20 Maison de Victor Hugo
24 Banque de France
25 Colonne de Juillet
26 Entrance to Opéra-Bastille
27 Opéra-Bastille
28 Port de Plaisance de Paris Arsenal
29 Paris à Vélo C'est Sympa!
30 Notre Dame
31 Mémorial des Martyrs de la Déportation

days and 10 am to 5 pm on Saturday. There is no domestic, intercity bus service to or from Paris.

Train

Paris has six major train stations (*gares*), each handling traffic to different destinations. For information in English call ☎ 0836 35 35 35, 7 am to 10 pm. The metro station attached to each train station bears the same name as the gare. Paris' major train stations are:

Gare d'Austerlitz (13e) Loire Valley, Spain and Portugal and non-TGV trains to south-western France.

Gare de l'Est (10e) Parts of France east of Paris (Champagne, Alsace and Lorraine), Luxembourg, parts of Switzerland (Basel, Lucerne, Zürich), southern Germany (Frankfurt, Munich) and points farther east.

Gare de Lyon (12e) Regular and TGV Sud-Est trains to places south-east of Paris, including Dijon, Lyon, Provence, the Côte d'Azur, the Alps, parts of Switzerland (Bern, Geneva, Lausanne), Italy and points beyond.

Gare Montparnasse (15e) Brittany and places between (Chartres, Angers, Nantes) and the terminus of the TGV Atlantique serving Tours, Nantes, Bordeaux and other destinations in south-western France.

Gare du Nord (10e) Northern suburbs of Paris, northern France, the UK, Belgium, northern Germany, Scandinavia, Moscow etc; terminus of the TGV Nord (Lille and Calais), and the Eurostar to London.

Gare St Lazare (8e) Normandy, including Dieppe, Le Havre and Cherbourg.

GETTING AROUND

Paris' public transit system, most of which is operated by the RATP (Régie Autonome des Transports Parisians; ☎ 0836 68 77 14), is cheap and efficient. For information in English ring ☎ 0836 68 41 14.

To/From Orly Airport

Orly Rail is the quickest way to reach the Left Bank and the 16e. Take the free shuttle bus to the Pont de Rungis-Aéroport d'Orly RER station, which is on the C2 line, and get on a train heading into the city. Another fast way into town is the Orlyval shuttle train (57FF); it stops near Orly-Sud's Porte F and links Orly with the Antony RER station, which is on line B4. Orlybus (35FF) takes you to the Denfert-Rochereau metro station, 14e. Air France buses (45FF) go to/from Gare Montparnasse, 15e, (every 12 minutes) along Aérogare des Invalides in the 7e. RATP bus No 183 (8FF or one bus/metro ticket) goes to Porte de Choisy, 13e, but is very slow. Jetbus, the cheapest option, links both terminals with the Villejuif-Louis Aragon metro stop (26.50FF; 20 minutes). All services between Orly and Paris run every 15 minutes or so (less frequently late at night) from 5.30 or 6.30 am to 11 or 11.30 pm. A taxi to/from Orly costs from 120FF to 175FF, plus 6FF per piece of luggage over 5kg.

To/From Charles de Gaulle Airport

Roissyrail links the city with both of the airport's train stations (49FF, 35 minutes). To get to the airport, take any line B train whose four letter destination code begins with E (eg, EIRE). Regular metro ticket windows can't always sell these tickets, so you may have to buy one at the RER station where you board. Trains run every 15 minutes from 5.30 am to around 11 pm.

Air France bus No 2 will take you to Porte Maillot and the corner of Ave Carnot near the Arc de Triomphe for 60FF; bus No 4 to Gare Montparnasse costs 70FF.

RATP bus No 350 (24FF or three bus/metro tickets) links both aérogares with Porte de la Chapelle, 18e, and stops at Gare du Nord and Gare de l'Est, both in the 10e. RATP Bus No 351 goes to ave du Trône, on the eastern side of place de la Nation in the 11e and runs every half-hour or so until 8.20 pm (9.30 pm from the airport to the city). The trip costs 24FF or three bus/metro tickets.

Bus

Short trips cost one bus/metro/RER ticket (see Metro/RER/Bus Tickets below), while longer rides require two. Travellers without tickets can purchase them from the driver. Whatever kind of ticket (coupon) you have, you must cancel it in the little machine next to the driver. The fines are hefty if you're caught without a ticket or without a cancelled ticket. If you have a Carte Orange, Formule 1 or Paris Visite pass (see the following Metro & RER section), just flash it at the driver – do not cancel it in the machine.

After the metro shuts down at around 12.45 am, the Noctambus network, whose symbol is a black owl silhouetted against a yellow moon, links the Châtelet-Hôtel de Ville area with most parts of the city. Noctambuses begin their runs from Ave Victoria, 4e, between the Hôtel de Ville and place du Châtelet, every hour on the half-hour from 1.30 to 5.30 am seven days a week. A single ride costs 15FF and allows one immediate transfer onto another Noctambus.

Metro & RER

Paris' underground rail network consists of two separate but linked systems: the Métropolitain, known as the metro, which now has 14 lines and over 300 stations, and the RER which, along with certain SNCF lines, is divided into eight concentric zones. The whole system has been designed so that no point in Paris is more than 500m from a metro stop.

How it Works Each metro train is known by the name of its terminus; trains on the same line have different names depending on which direction they are travelling in. On lines that split into several branches and thus have more than one end-of-the-line station, the final destination of each train is indicated on the front, sides and interior of the train cars. In the stations, white-on-blue *sortie* signs indicate exits and black-on-orange *correspondance* signs show how to get to connecting trains. The last metro train sets out on its final run at 12.30 am. Plan ahead so as not to miss your connection. The metro starts up again at 5.30 am.

Metro/RER/Bus Tickets

The same tickets are valid on the metro, the bus and, for travel within the Paris city limits, the RER's 2nd-class carriages. They cost 8FF if bought individually and 55FF (half for children aged four to 11) for a *carnet* of 10. One ticket lets you travel between any two metro stations, including stations outside of the Paris city limits, no matter how many transfers are required. You can also use it on the RER system within zone 1.

For travel on the RER to destinations outside the city, purchase a special ticket *before* you board the train or you won't be able to get out of the station and could be fined. Always keep your ticket until you reach your destination and exit the station.

The cheapest and easiest way to travel the metro is with a Carte Orange, a bus/metro/RER pass whose accompanying magnetic coupon comes in weekly and monthly versions. You can get tickets for travel in up to eight urban and suburban zones; the basic ticket – valid for zones 1 and 2 – is probably sufficient.

The weekly ticket costs 82FF for zones 1 and 2 and is valid Monday to Sunday. Even if you'll be in Paris for only three or four days, it may very well work out cheaper than purchasing a carnet – you'll break even at 16 rides – and it will certainly cost less than buying a daily Mobilis or Paris Visite pass. The monthly Carte Orange ticket (255FF for zones 1 and 2) begins on the first day of each calendar month. Both are on sale in metro and RER stations and at certain bus terminals.

To get a Carte Orange, bring a passport-size photograph of yourself to any metro or

RER ticket counter (four photos for 25FF are available from automatic booths). Request a Carte Orange (which is free) and the kind of coupon you'd like. To prevent tickets being used by more than one person, you must write your surname *(nom)* and given name *(prénom)* on the Carte Orange, and the number of your Carte Orange on each weekly or monthly coupon you buy (next to the words Carte No).

Mobilis and Paris Visite passes, designed for tourists, are on sale in many metro and train stations and international airports. The Mobilis card (and its *coupon*) allows unlimited travel for one day in two to eight zones (32FF to 110FF). Paris Visite passes, providing discounts on entries to certain museums and activities as well as transport, are valid for one/two/three/five consecutive days of travel in either three, five or eight zones. The one to three-zone version costs 55/90/120/175FF for one/two/three/five days. Children aged four to 11 pay half-price. They can be purchased at larger metro and RER stations, at SNCF bureaus in Paris and at the airports.

Taxi
The *prise en* charge (flag fall) is 13FF. Within the city limits, it costs 3.53FF per kilometre for travel 7 am to 7 pm Monday to Saturday (tariff A). At night and on Sunday and holidays (tariff B), it's 5.83FF per kilometre. An extra 8FF is charged for taking a fourth passenger, but most drivers refuse to take more than three people because of insurance constraints. Luggage over 5kg costs 6FF extra and for pick-up from SNCF mainline stations there's a 5FF supplement. The usual tip is 2FF no matter what the fare.

There are 500 taxi stands *(tête de station)* in Paris. Radio-dispatched taxis include Taxis Bleus (☎ 01 49 36 10 10) and G7 Taxis (☎ 01 47 39 47 39). If you order a taxi by phone, the meter is switched on as soon as the driver gets your call.

Car & Motorcycle
Driving in Paris is nerve-wracking but not impossible. The fastest way to get across Paris is usually the Périphérique.

Street parking can cost 15FF an hour; large municipal parking garages usually charge 15/130/200FF per hour/10 hours/24 hours. Fines (75FF or 200FF) are dispensed by parking attendants with great abandon.

Renting a small car (Peugeot 106) for one day without insurance and no kilometres costs about 290FF, but cheaper deals from smaller agencies are available.

Rental agencies in Paris include:

Avis (☎ 0802 05 05 05 or ☎ 01 42 66 67 58)
Budget (☎ 0800 10 00 01)
Europcar (☎ 0803 35 23 52)
Hertz (☎ 01 39 38 38 38)
National/Citer (☎ 01 42 06 06 06)
Thrifty (☎ 0801 45 45 45)

Bicycle
There are 130km of bicycle lanes running throughout Paris. Some of them aren't particularly attractive or safe, but cyclists may be fined about 250FF for failing to use them. The tourist office distributes a free brochure-map called *Paris à Vélo*.

RATP-sponsored Roue Libre (see Bicycle under Organised Tours earlier) is the best place to rent bikes. Hire costs 20/75FF per hour/day or 115/225FF for a weekend/week, insurance included. See Bois de Boulogne (Things to See) for more information.

Around Paris

The region surrounding Paris is known as the Île de France (Island of France) because of its position between the rivers Aube, Marne, Oise and Seine.

DISNEYLAND PARIS
It took US$4.4 billion to turn beet fields 32km east of Paris into the much heralded Disneyland Paris. Now the most popular tourist attraction in Europe, it opens 365 days a year. From early September to March the hours are 10 am to 6 pm (8 pm on Saturday, some Sundays and perhaps during school holidays); in spring and early summer, the park opens 9 am to 8 pm (to 11 pm at the weekend and from early July to early September). Admission costs 220FF (170FF for those aged three to 11) from April to early November; the rest of the year, except during the Christmas holidays, prices drop to 165/135FF. Multiple-day passes are available.

FRANCE

VERSAILLES
pop 95,000

Versailles served as the country's political capital and the seat of the royal court from 1682 until 1789. After the Franco-Prussian War of 1870-71, the victorious Prussians proclaimed the establishment of the German empire from the chateau's Galerie des Glaces (Hall of Mirrors), and in 1919 the Treaty of Versailles was signed in the same room, officially ending WWI.

The chateau can be jammed with tourists, especially on weekends, in summer and most especially on summer Sundays. Arrive early to avoid the queues.

Information

The tourist office (☎ 01 39 24 88 88, ✉ touri sme@ot-versailles.fr) is just north of the Versailles-Rive Gauche train station at 2 bis ave de Paris. Open 9 am to 7 pm daily April to October (to 6 pm the rest of the year).

Château de Versailles

The enormous Château de Versailles (☎ 01 30 83 78 00 or ☎ 01 30 83 77 77) was built in the mid-17th century during the reign of Louis XIV (the Sun King). The chateau essentially consists of four parts: the main palace building; the vast 17th-century gardens; the late-17th-century Grand Trianon; and the mid-18th-century Petit Trianon.

Opening Hours & Tickets

The main building opens 9 am to 5.30 pm (6.30 pm May to September) daily, except Monday and public holidays. Admission to the **Grands Appartements** (State Apartments), including the 73m-long **Galerie des Glaces** (Hall of Mirrors) and the **Appartement de la Reine** (Queen's Suite), costs 45FF (after 3.30 pm daily 35FF, free for under 18s on Sunday). Tickets are on sale at Entrée A (Entrance A) off to the right from the equestrian statue of Louis XIV as you approach the building. You won't be able to visit other parts of the main palace unless you take one of the guided tours (see Guided Tours below). Entrée H has facilities for the disabled, including a lift.

The **Grand Trianon** (25FF; 15FF reduced rate) opens noon to 6.30 pm daily April to October; the rest of the year it closes at 5.30 pm. The **Petit Trianon**, open the same days and hours, costs 15/10FF. A combined ticket for both costs 30/20FF.

The gardens are open 7 am (8 am in winter) to nightfall daily (except if it's snowing). Entry is free, except on Saturday, July to September, and on Sunday early April to early October when the baroque fountains 'perform' the **Grandes Eaux**, 3.30 to 5 pm (30FF, students 20FF).

Guided Tours To make a reservation go to entrées C or D. A one-hour tour costs 25FF in addition to the regular entry fee; 80-minute audioguide tours available at entrée A for 35FF.

Getting There & Away

Bus No 171 (8FF or one metro/bus ticket, 35 minutes) links Pont de Sèvres in Paris with the place d'Armes and Versailles but it's faster to go by train. Each of Versailles' three train stations is served by RER and/or SNCF trains coming from a different group of Paris stations.

RER line C4 takes you from Paris' Left Bank RER stations to Versailles-Rive Gauche station (14.50FF). From Paris, catch any train whose four-letter code begins with the letter 'V'. There are up to 70 trains a day (half on Sunday), and the last train back to Paris leaves shortly before midnight.

RER line C5 links Paris' Left Bank with Versailles-Chantiers station (14.50FF). From Paris, take any train whose code begins with 'S'. Versailles-Chantiers is also served by some three dozen SNCF trains a day (20 on Sunday) from Gare Montparnasse (14.50FF, 15 minutes); all trains on this line continue on to Chartres.

From Paris' Gare St Lazare (20FF) and La Défense (12FF), the SNCF has about 70 trains a day to Versailles-Rive Droite, which is 1200m from the chateau. The last train to Paris leaves a bit past midnight.

CHARTRES
pop 40,300

The indescribably beautiful 13th-century cathedral of Chartres rises abruptly from the corn fields 88km south-west of Paris.

Orientation

The medieval sections of Chartres are situated along the Eure River and the hillside to the west. The cathedral is about 500m east of the train station.

Information

The tourist office (☎ 02 37 18 26 26, @ char tres.tourism@wanadoo.fr) is across place de la Cathédrale from the cathedral's main entrance. There's a Banque de France branch at 32 rue du Docteur Maunoury, and the main post office is at place des Épars.

Cathédrale Notre Dame

Chartres' 13th-century cathedral (☎ 02 37 21 75 02), unlike so many of its contemporaries, has not been significantly modified – construction of this early Gothic masterpiece took only 25 years, which is why the cathedral has a high degree of architectural unity.

The cathedral is open 7.30 am (8.30 am on Sunday) to 7.15 pm daily, except during Mass, weddings and funerals. Fascinating tours (35FF, students 25FF) are conducted by Englishman Malcolm Miller from Easter to November; audioguides (15FF to 30FF) are available from the cathedral bookshop. The 112m-high **Clocher Neuf** (new bell tower) is well worth the ticket price (25FF; 15FF for those aged 12 to 25) and the long, spiral climb.

Inside, the cathedral's most exceptional feature is its extraordinary **stained-glass windows**, most of which are 13th-century originals. The **trésor** (treasury) displays a piece of cloth given to the cathedral in 876 said to have been worn by the Virgin Mary.

The early-11th-century Romanesque **crypt**, the largest in France, can be visited by a half-hour guided tour in French (with a written English translation) for 11FF.

Old City

Streets with buildings of interest include **rue de la Tannerie**, which runs along the Eure, and **rue des Écuyers**, midway between the cathedral and the river. **Église St Pierre** at place St Pierre has a massive bell tower dating from around 1000 and some fine (often overlooked) medieval stained-glass windows.

Places to Stay

Camping *Les Bords de l'Eure* (☎ 02 37 28 79 43, 9 rue de Launay), about 2.5km southeast of the train station, is open May to early September. Bus No 8 (direction Hôpital) from the train station goes to the Vignes stop.

Hostel The pleasant and calm *Auberge de Jeunesse* (☎ 02 37 34 27 64, fax 02 37 35 75 85, 23 Ave Neigre) has beds for 68FF, including breakfast. From the train station, take bus No 5 (direction Mare aux Moines) to the Rouliers stop. Reception opens 2 to 10 pm daily.

Hotels Somewhat dingy rooms at *Hôtel de l'Ouest* (☎ 02 37 21 43 27, 3 place Pierre Sémard) start at 120FF. The eight-room *Hôtel Au Départ* (☎ 02 37 36 80 43, 1 rue Nicole) has singles/doubles/triples with washbasin and bidet for 120/190/300FF. Reception is at the Brasserie L'Ouest, 9 place Pierre Sémard (closed Sunday).

Hôtel de la Poste (☎ 02 37 21 04 27, fax 02 37 36 42 17, 3 rue du Général Koening), near place des Épars, has singles/doubles starting at 250/320FF.

Places to Eat

At *Café Serpente* (☎ 02 37 21 68 81, 2 rue du Cloître Notre Dame), across from the south porch of the cathedral, the plat du jour costs 78FF to 98FF. *La Vesuvio* (☎ 02 37 21 56 35, 30 place des Halles) serves pizzas (35FF to 60FF) and light meals; or there's always the *Monoprix* supermarket at 21 rue Noël Ballay, north-east of place des Épars.

Getting There & Around

Train There are three dozen trains a day (20 on Sunday) to/from Paris' Gare Montparnasse (72FF, 55 to 70 minutes) also stopping at Versailles' Chantiers station (61FF, 45 minutes). The last train back to Paris leaves Chartres a bit after 9 pm (7.40 pm on Saturday, after 10 pm on Sunday and holidays).

Alsace & Lorraine

The charming and beautiful region of Alsace, long a meeting place of Europe's Latin and Germanic cultures, is in France's far northeastern corner, nestled between the Vosges Mountains and, about 30km to the east, the Rhine River, marking the Franco-German border. The Alsatian language is a Germanic dialect similar to that spoken in nearby parts of Germany and Switzerland.

Most of Alsace became part of France in 1648 (Strasbourg, the region's largest city, retained its independence until 1681). But more than two centuries of French rule did little to dampen 19th and early-20th-century German enthusiasm for a foothold on the west bank of the southern Rhine, and the region (along with part of Lorraine) was twice annexed by Germany – from the Franco-Prussian War (1871) until the end of WWI, and again between 1939 and 1944.

STRASBOURG
pop 423,000

Strasbourg, just a few kilometres west of the Rhine, is Alsace's great metropolis and its intellectual and cultural capital. Towering above the restaurants and pubs of the lively old city is the marvellous cathedral, near which you'll find one of the finest ensembles of museums in France.

When it was founded in 1949, the Council of Europe decided to base itself in Strasbourg as a symbol of Franco-German (and pan-European) cooperation. The city is also the seat of the European Parliament (the legislative branch of the EU).

Orientation

The train station is 400m west of the Grande Île ('Large Island'), the city centre, which is delimited by the Ill River to the south and the Fossé du Faux Rempart to the north. place Kléber, the main public square on the Grande Île, is 400m north-west of the cathedral.

Information

The main tourist office (☎ 03 88 52 28 28, fax 03 88 52 28 29), 17 place de la Cathédrale, opens 9 am to 7 pm daily. There's a branch office (☎ 03 88 32 51 49) in front of the train station, in the underground complex beneath place de la Gare. Both offices sell the three-day Strasbourg Pass (58FF), which gets you a variety of discounts. Web site: www.strasbourg.com.

Money The Banque de France is at 3 place Broglie (open weekday mornings). The American Express office, 19 rue des Francs Bourgeois, opens weekdays and, from May to September, on Saturday.

Post & Communications The main post office, a neo-Gothic structure at 5 ave de la Marseillaise, is open 8 am to 7 pm weekdays and until noon Saturday. It has exchange services and a Cyberposte.

The Best Coffee Shop, 10 quai des Pêcheurs, offers cheap email access from 10 am (2 pm on weekends) to 11.30 pm.

Laundry On the Grande Île, there are laundrettes at 29 Grand' Rue (open until 8 pm) and 15 rue des Veaux (open until 9 pm).

Things to See

With its bustling public squares, busy pedestrianised areas and upmarket shopping streets, the **Grande Île** is a great place for aimless ambling.

Strasbourg's lacy Gothic cathedral, **Cathédrale Notre Dame**, was begun in 1176. The west facade was completed in 1284, but the spire (its southern companion was never built) wasn't in place until 1439. The interior can be visited daily until 7 pm; the astronomical clock goes through its paces at 12.30 pm (5FF). The 66m-high platform above the facade (from which the tower and its spire soar another 76m) can be visited daily – if you don't mind the 330 steps to the top (20/10FF).

Crisscrossed by narrow lanes, canals and locks, **Petite France**, in the south-west corner of the Grande Île, is the stuff of fairy tales, with half-timbered houses sprouting veritable thickets of geraniums.

The hugely expensive **European Parliament building** (☎ 03 88 17 20 07), inaugurated in 1999, and the Council of Europe's **Palais de l'Europe** (☎ 03 90 21 49 40), opened in 1977 – both about 2km north-east of the cathedral – can be visited on tours. Phone ahead for reservations.

Museums

Except for the Musée de l'Œuvre Notre-Dame and the Musée d'Art Moderne et Contemporain, which close on Monday, all of the city's museums open daily except Tuesday. Opening hours (except for the Musée d'Art Moderne) are 10 am to noon and 1.30 to 6 pm

(10 am to 5 pm on Sunday). Most museums (except the Musée d'Art Moderne, 30FF) charge 20/10FF.

The outstanding **Musée de l'Œuvre Notre Dame** is housed in several 14th and 15th-century buildings at 3 place du Château and displays one of France's finest collections of Romanesque, Gothic and Renaissance sculpture, including many of the cathedral's original statues.

The **Château des Rohan**, 2 place du Château, was built between 1732 and 1742 as a residence for the city's princely bishops. It now houses three museums (combined ticket 40/20FF): the **Musée Archéologique** covers the period from prehistory to 800 AD; the **Musée des Arts Décoratifs** give you a sense of the lifestyle of the rich and powerful during the 18th century; and the **Musée des Beaux-Arts** has paintings from the 14th to 19th centuries.

The new, superb **Musée d'Art Moderne et Contemporain** at place Hans Jean Arp has a diverse collection of works representing every major art movement of the past century or so.

The **Musée Alsacien** at 23 quai St Nicolas, housed in three 16th and 17th-century houses, affords a glimpse into Alsatian life over the centuries.

Organised Tours

Call to reserve a brewery tour at Kronenbourg (☎ 03 88 27 41 59, tram stop Duc d'Alsace), at 68 Route d'Oberhausbergen in the suburb of Cronenbourg, and Heineken (☎ 03 88 19 59 53), at 4 rue St Charles in Schiltigheim. Both are about 2.5km from the city centre. To get to Heineken, take bus No 4 to the Schiltigheim Mairie stop.

Places to Stay

It's *extremely* difficult to find last-minute accommodation from Monday to Thursday when the European Parliament is in plenary session one week each month (except August, and twice in October). Contact the tourist office for dates.

Camping The grassy *Camping de la Montagne Verte* (☎ 03 88 30 25 46, 2 rue Robert Forrer) opens mid-March to October. It's a few hundred metres from the *Auberge de Jeunesse René Cassin* (see Hostels), where you can pitch a tent for 42FF per person, including breakfast.

Hostels The modern *CIARUS* (☎ 03 88 15 27 88, fax 03 88 15 27 89, 7 rue Finkmatt) a 285-bed Protestant-run hostel about 1km north-east of the train station, has beds from 92FF, including breakfast. By bus, take Nos 4, 10, 20 or 72 to the place de Pierre stop.

The 286-bed *Auberge de Jeunesse René Cassin* (☎ 03 88 30 26 46, fax 03 88 30 35 16, 9 rue de l'Auberge de Jeunesse), 2km south-west of the train station, has beds for 73FF. To get there, take bus No 3 or 23 to the Auberge de Jeunesse stop.

Hotels The 15-room *Hôtel Le Colmar* (☎ 03 88 32 16 89, fax 03 88 21 97 17, 1 rue du Maire Kuss) has clean singles/doubles from 167/218FF. *Hôtel Weber* (☎ 03 88 32 36 47, fax 03 88 32 19 08, ☎ hotelpatricia@ hotmail.com, 22 blvd de Nancy) is hardly in the most attractive part of town, but quiet doubles start at 140FF.

The 16-room, family-run *Hôtel Michelet* (☎ 03 88 32 47 38, 48 rue du Vieux Marché aux Poissons) has simple singles/doubles from 145/170FF. The dark, rustic *Hôtel Patricia* (☎ 03 88 32 14 60, fax 03 88 32 19 08, ☎ hotelpatricia@hotmail.com, 1a rue du Puits) has ordinary but spacious doubles with great views from 180FF.

Facing the train station, the 61-room *Hôtel du Rhin* (☎ 03 88 32 35 00, fax 03 88 23 51 92, ☎ hotel-rhin@strasbourg.com, 7-8 place de la Gare) has doubles with washbasin starting at 200FF (360FF with shower and toilet). The 27-room, two-star *Hôtel de l'Ill* (☎ 03 88 36 20 01, fax 03 88 35 30 03, 8 rue des Bateliers) has tasteful doubles for 295FF.

Places to Eat

A *winstub* (pronounced VEEN-shtub) serves both wine and hearty Alsatian fare such as *choucroute* (sauerkraut) and *baeckeoffe* (pork, beef and lamb marinated in wine and cooked with vegetables).

Indulge yourself at *Au Crocodile* (☎ 03 88 32 13 02, 10 rue de l'Outre), with its three Michelin stars. It often plays host to visiting heads of state. The *menus* start at 410FF (including wine) for lunch on weekdays, otherwise 460FF (closed Sunday and Monday).

FRANCE

STRASBOURG

PLACES TO STAY
1 CIARUS Hostel
16 Hôtel du Rhin
17 Hôtel Le Colmar
36 Hôtel Michelet
41 Hôtel Weber
45 Hôtel de l'Ill
38 Hôtel Patricia

PLACES TO EAT
13 La Rose des Vins
21 Sidi Bou Saïd
27 Au Crocodile
28 Atac Supermarket
29 Winstub Le Clou
39 Au Pont Saint Martin
48 Le Bouchon
50 Adan Vegetarian Restaurant

MUSEUMS
33 Château des
   Rohan (Musée Archéologique,
   Musée des Arts Décoratifs
   & Musée des Beaux-Arts)
35 Musée de l'Œuvre
   Notre Dame

42 Musée d'Art Moderne et
   Contemporain
44 Musée Alsacien

PUBS & CLUBS
7 Le Griot
24 The Irish Times
40 Académie de la Bière
46 Café des Anges
47 La Salamandre

TRAM STOPS
12 Ancienne Synagogue Les
   Halles Tram Stop
14 Gare Centrale
   Tram Stop
22 Homme de Fer Tram &
   Bus Hub
25 Langstross Grand'
   Rue Tram Stop
43 Porte de l'Hôpital
   Tram Stop

OTHER
2 Église Saint Pierre-
   le-Jeune (Catholic)

3 Synagogue de la Paix
4 US Consulate
5 Église Saint Paul
6 Main Post Office
8 Banque de France
9 Hôtel de Police
10 Laundrette
11 Église Saint Pierre-
   le-Jeune (Prostestant)
15 Tourist Office Annexe
   (Galerie de l'En-Verre)
18 Pont Kuss Bus Stop
19 Église Saint Pierre-
   le-Vieux (Catholic
   & Protestant)
20 Laundrette
23 German Consulate
30 Eurolines Office
31 Best Coffee Shop
32 Cathédrale Notre Dame
34 Strasbourg Fluvial Boat
   Excursions
37 Main Tourist Office
49 Eurolines Coach Stops
51 Hôpital Civil

To Brasseries
Heineken (1.5km)

Place de
Haguenau

rue de Haguenau

rue de Bichheim

blvd Clemenceau

blvd de Président Poincaré

rue du Fossé des Treize

rue des Bonnes Gens

rue du Faubourg de Pierre

To'Hautepierre
Maillon Tram
Terminus

To
Kronenbourg
brewery (2km)

rue du Président Wilson

rue du Faubourg Saverne

rue du Marais Vert

Place des
Halles
Shopping
Mall

Kléber

quai Kellerman

11

Train
Station

place
de la
Gare

14 15

16

17

18

blvd du Président Wilson

rue Thiergarten

rue Kageneck

rue de Pâques

13

rue Kuhn

Public Library

Underground
Tramway

quai de Paris

12

quai Sébastopol

boulevard de Metz

rue Déserte

rue du Maire Kuss

rue de la Course

quai Saint-Jean

rue Desaix

Marché-aux Vins

rue du Vieux

rue de la Haute Montée

21

rue du Jeu des Enfants

Place
de l'Homme
de Fer

22

place
Kléber

rue du Faubourg National

quai Altorffer

quai Turckheim

19

40

20

rue du 21-Novembre

R des
Francs Bourgeois

Sainte-Hélène

rue du Fossé des Tanneurs

Grand' rue

24 25

rue Sainte Marguerite

R Adolph Seyboth

rue du Bain aux Plantes

rue du
Bouclier

rue
Salzmann

41

boulevard de Nancy

boulevard de Rosheim

place
Hans-Jean Arp

Petite
France

rue des
Moulins

39

rue Saint Martin
du Pont

place St
Thomas

Towers

Ponts
Couverts

rue de Wasselonne

rue d'Obernai

rue de Molsheim

42

Barrage
Vauban

Ill River

Hôtel
du
Département

rue Finkwiller

rue M Luther

quai Finkwiller

quai

boulevard de Lyon

To'La Laiterie
(200m)

To Auberge de Jeunesse
René Cassin (1.2km),
Camping de la Montagne Verte
(1.8km), Airport (12km) & Obernai

rue Humann

rue des Glacières

rue Kinchleger

euro currency converter **€1 = 6.55FF**

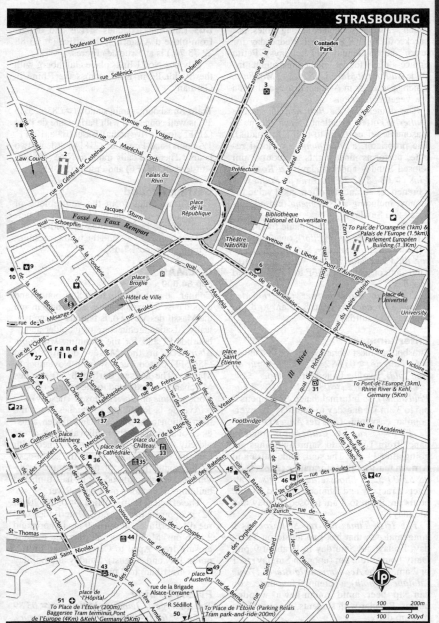

Winstub Le Clou (3 rue du Chaudron), which seats diners together at long tables, has baeckeoffe for 97FF (closed Wednesday for lunch and on Sunday and holidays). Petite France's many tourist-oriented restaurants include *Au Pont St Martin (15 rue des Moulins)*, which specialises in Alsatian dishes and has a few vegetarian options.

The dinner-only *Le Bouchon (6 rue Ste Catherine)* offers excellent French cuisine at reasonable prices (69FF to 125FF for mains). The proprietor, a *chansonnière* of local repute, performs most nights at about 9 pm (closed Sunday and Monday). *La Rose des Vins (☎ 03 88 32 74 40, 5 rue de Pâques)* is a French restaurant that offers good value for money, including a 98FF *menu* (closed Saturday and Sunday).

Self-service vegetarian-organic food is on offer at *Adan (6 rue Sédillot)*, open noon to 2 pm Monday to Saturday. *Sidi Bou Saïd (22 rue du Vieux Marché aux Vins)* has hearty Tunisian couscous for 60FF to 75FF (closed Monday).

The *Atac Supermarket (47 rue des Grandes Arcades)* is open 8.30 am to 8 pm Monday to Saturday.

Entertainment

Strasbourg's most vibrant venue for live music is *La Laiterie (☎ 03 88 23 72 37, 11-13 rue du Hohwald)*, near the Laiterie tram stop.

La Salamandre (☎ 03 88 25 79 42, 3 rue Paul Janet), an informal dance club, opens 9 pm to 3 am Wednesday to Saturday. At ever-popular, easygoing *Café des Anges (☎ 03 88 37 12 67, 5 rue Ste Catherine)*, you can dance from Tuesday to Saturday; things get going after 11 pm. The soul, funk, salsa and African music at the informal *Le Griot (☎ 03 88 52 00 52, 6 Impasse de l'Écrevisse)* attracts a racially and ethnically mixed crowd; hours are 9 pm to 4 am (closed Sunday and Monday).

The Irish Times (19 rue St Barbe) is a congenial pub that has live music on Tuesday, Friday and Saturday from about 9 pm. Daily hours are 2 pm (noon on Sunday) to 1 or 2 am. At the *Académie de la Bière (17 rue Adolphe Seyboth)*, a perennial favourite, you can sip beer amid rough-hewn wooden beams. Popular with students, it opens 9 am to 4 am daily.

Getting There & Away

Bus Eurolines coaches arrive and depart from place d'Austerlitz; the office (☎ 03 88 22 73 74) is at 5 rue des Frères.

City bus No 21 links place Gutenberg with the Stadthalle in Kehl, across the Rhine in Germany.

Train Strasbourg's train station (☎ 0836 35 35 39) is well connected with Paris' Gare de l'Est (215FF, four to five hours), Basel (Bâle; 103FF, 1½ hours) and Frankfurt (218FF, at least two hours). There are daily trains to Nice (468FF), Amsterdam (413FF) and Prague (593FF).

Getting Around

Three tram lines form the centrepiece of Strasbourg's excellent public transport network. Single bus/tram tickets, sold by bus (but not tram) drivers and the ticket machines at tram stops, cost 7FF.

COLMAR
pop 64,000

Colmar, an easy day trip from Strasbourg (and a good base for exploring the Route du Vin and the Massif des Vosges), is famous for the typically Alsatian architecture of its older neighbourhoods, and for the stunning *Issenheim Altarpiece* in the **Musée d'Unterlinden** (35/25FF; closed Tuesday from November to March). The **Musée Bartholdi**, 30 rue des Marchands, is dedicated to the creator of New York's *Statue of Liberty* (closed Tuesday).

Ave de la République stretches from the train station to the Musée d'Unterlinden, a distance of about 1km; the medieval streets of the old city (eg, **rue des Marchands**), lined with half-timbered buildings, are to the south-east. At the southern edge of the old city, **Petite Venise**, a neighbourhood of old, half-timbered buildings, runs along the Lauch River.

The efficient tourist office (☎ 03 89 20 68 92) is opposite the Musée d'Unterlinden at 4 rue d'Unterlinden. It opens 9 am to noon and 2 to 6 pm, Monday to Saturday (no midday closure from April to October; open until 7 pm in July and August). Sunday and holiday hours are 10 am to 2 pm.

Places to Stay

The *Auberge de Jeunesse Mittelhart (☎ 03 89 80 57 39, fax 03 89 80 76 16, 2 rue Pasteur)*,

2km north-west of the train station, has beds for 69FF, including breakfast. Reception is closed from 10 am to 5 pm. By bus, take No 4 to the Pont Rouge stop.

Near the train station, the cosy, 18-room *Hôtel La Chaumière* (☎ 03 89 41 08 99, 74 ave de la République) has simple and rather small doubles from 180FF (240FF with shower and toilet). The blush-pink (but fading) *Hôtel Primo* (☎ 03 89 24 22 24, fax 03 89 24 55 96, ✆ hotel-primo-99@rmcnet.fr, 5 rue des Ancêtres) has rooms with washbasin for up to three people for 159FF; doubles/quads with shower and toilet are 329/399FF.

Places to Eat
Alsatian specialities including spit-roasted ham (60FF) are served at *La Maison Rouge* (☎ 03 89 23 53 22, 9 rue des Écoles). A four-course Alsatian *menu* costs 84FF (closed on Sunday and Wednesday).

Djerba La Douce (☎ 03 89 24 17 12, 10 rue du Mouton) has Tunisian couscous for 53FF to 95FF (closed on Sunday).

There's a *Monoprix* supermarket across the square from the Musée d'Unterlinden (closed Sunday).

Getting There & Away
Colmar is served by frequent trains from Strasbourg (56FF, at least 30 minutes). Many destinations on the Route du Vin and in the Massif des Vosges are accessible by bus – check timetables at the tourist office and at the bus station next to the train station. Seven buses a day (three or four on weekends) go to the German university city of Freiburg (34FF or 10DM; 65 minutes).

ROUTE DU VIN
Meandering for some 120km along the eastern foothills of the Vosges, the Alsace Wine Route passes through picturesque villages guarded by ruined hill top castles. At places twee and touristy, it stretches from Marlenheim, about 20km west of Strasbourg, southward to Thann, about 35km south-west of Colmar.

Riquewihr, **Ribeauvillé** and **Kaysersberg** are perhaps the most attractive villages – and the most heavily touristed. Less touristy places include **Mittelbergheim**, **Eguisheim** and **Turkheim**. If you have your own transport, visit the imposing chateau of **Haut-Koenigsbourg**,

rebuilt early this century by Emperor Wilhelm II. The wine route is a good place to spot some of Alsace's famous storks.

Natzweiler-Struthof (☎ 03 88 97 04 49), the only Nazi concentration camp on French soil, is about 30km west of Obernai (open daily; closed 25 December to February).

The industrial city of **Mulhouse** (pronounced Moo-LOOZE), 43km south of Colmar, has a number of world-class museums dedicated to such subjects as historic motorcars, railways, firefighting, textile printing and wallpaper.

MASSIF DES VOSGES
The rounded mountaintops, deep forests, glacial lakes, rolling pastureland and tiny villages of the Vosges Mountains are a hiker's paradise, with an astounding 7000km of marked trails. In the winter, the area has 36 modest skiing areas with 170 ski lifts.

The **Route des Crêtes** (Route of the Crests), which begins in Cernay (36km south-west of Colmar), takes you to (or near) the Vosges' highest *ballons* (bald, rounded mountain peaks), as well as to several WWI sites. Mountaintop lookouts afford spectacular views of the Alsace plain, the Schwarzwald (Black Forest) across the Rhine in Germany, the Jura and – on clear days – the Alps. The highest point in the Vosges is the dramatic, windblown summit of the 1424m-high **Grand Ballon**.

NANCY
pop 102,000
Delightful Nancy has an air of refinement found nowhere else in Lorraine, the region that borders Alsace to the west. Thanks to the stunning, gilded **place Stanislas** (the central square), sumptuous cream-coloured buildings, and shop windows filled with fine glassware, the former capital of the dukes of Lorraine seems as opulent today as it did during the 16th to 18th centuries.

The **Musée de l'École de Nancy** houses a superb collection of the sinuous, dream-like works of the Art Nouveau movement, which once flourished here (30/20FF, closed Tuesday). It's about 2km south-west of the centre – by bus, take Nos 5 or 25 to the Nancy Thermal stop.

Other outstanding museums include the newly-reopened **Musée des Beaux-Arts** (Fine

Arts Museum) at place Stanislas (30/15FF), and the **Musée Historique Lorrain** (Lorraine Historical Museum) at 64 and 66 Grande Rue (30FF). Both are closed Tuesday.

Orientation & Information

The heart of Nancy is the beautifully proportioned place Stanislas. The train station, at the bottom of busy rue Stanislas, is 800m southwest of place Stanislas.

The tourist office (☎ 03 83 35 22 41) is inside the Hôtel de Ville on place Stanislas. It opens 9 am to 6 pm, Monday to Saturday (7 pm from April to October), and Sunday and holidays 10 am to 1 pm (5 pm from April to October).

Places to Stay

The 60-bed *Auberge de Jeunesse Remicourt* (☎ 03 83 27 73 67, fax 03 83 41 41 35, 149 rue de Vandœuvre in Villers-lès-Nancy), in an old chateau, is 4km south of the centre. A bed costs 80FF, including breakfast. By bus, take No 26 to the St Fiacre stop.

Two blocks south-west of place Stanislas, the welcoming and slightly off-beat, 29-room *Hôtel de l'Académie* (☎ 03 83 35 52 31, fax 03 83 32 55 78, 7 bis des Michottes) has singles/doubles with shower from 110/160FF. The friendly, two-star, 20-room *Hôtel des Portes d'Or* (☎ 03 83 35 42 34, fax 03 83 32 51 41, 21 rue Stanislas) has charming and well-kept doubles with upholstered doors from 280FF.

Places to Eat

Restaurant Le Gastrolâtre (☎ 03 83 35 51 94, 1 place Vaudémont) has Lorraine and Provençal *menus* from 95FF to 195FF (closed on Monday at midday and Sunday). Around the corner (and just a block from place Stanislas), rue des Maréchaux is lined with restaurants of all sorts.

The *covered market* (place Henri Mangin) opens 7 am to 6 pm Tuesday to Saturday. Across the square, inside the St Sébastien shopping centre, the *Casino* supermarket opens until 8.30 pm (closed Sunday).

Getting There & Away

From the train station on place Thiers there are direct services to Strasbourg (109FF, 70 to 95 minutes) and Paris' Gare de l'Est (206FF, three hours).

Far Northern France

Le Nord de France is made up of three historical regions: Flanders (Flandre or Flandres), Artois and Picardy (Picardie). Densely populated and laden with rustbelt industry, this is not one of the more fabled corners of France, but if you're up for a short trip from the UK, or inclined to do a little exploring, the region offers lots to do and some excellent dining.

LILLE
pop 1.1 million

Thanks to the Eurostar and other fast rail links, Lille – France's northern-most metropolis – is a popular first stop for visitors coming from across the Channel and Belgium. Long a major industrial centre, today's Lille has two renowned art museums and an attractive old town graced with ornate Flemish-style buildings.

Orientation & Information

Lille is centred around place du Général de Gaulle, place du Théâtre, and place Rihour. Vieux Lille (Old Lille) lies on the north side of the centre. Lille-Flandres train station is about 400m south-east of place du Général de Gaulle; the ultra-modern Lille-Europe train station is 500m farther east.

The tourist office (☎ 03 20 21 94 21, fax 03 20 21 94 20, ✆ ot.lille@wanadoo.fr), place Rihour, occupies a remnant of the 15th-century Palais Rihour. It is open 9.30 am to 6.30 pm Monday to Saturday; and 10 am to noon and 2 to 5 pm Sundays and holidays. Web site: www.cci-lille.fr.

Money The Banque de France at 75 rue Royale exchanges money 8.30 am to 12.15 pm weekdays. There's a Credit du Nord with an ATM on the corner of rue Jean Roisin and place Rihour.

Post & Communications The main post office, 8 place de la République, exchanges currency and has a Cyberposte. Net Arena Games (☎ 03 28 38 09 20), 10 rue des Bouchers, charges 20FF per half-hour of Web surfing.

Laundry The Laverie O'Claire, 57 rue du Molinel, lets you begin your last wash at 8 pm and the last dry cycle at 8.30 pm.

Things to See & Do

On place du Général de Gaulle, the ornate, Flemish Renaissance **Vieille Bourse** (Old Stock Exchange) consists of 24 separate buildings around a courtyard. Nearby, place du Théâtre is dominated by the neoclassical **Opéra** and the tower-topped neo-Flemish **Chambre de Commerce building**. North of place du Général de Gaulle, **Vieux Lille** gleams with nicely-restored 17th and 18th-century houses.

Lille's outstanding **Palais des Beaux-Arts** (Fine Arts Museum, metro République) has a superb collection of 15th to 20th-century paintings and exhibits of archaeology, medieval sculpture and ceramics. It opens noon (2 pm on Monday) to 6 pm (8 pm on Friday); it's closed Tuesday and bank holidays. Tickets cost 30/20FF.

North of Vieux Lille at 9 rue Princesse is the **Musée Charles de Gaulle** (☎ 03 20 31 96 03), where the premier-to-be was born in 1890. It opens 10 am to noon and 2 to 5 pm (closed Monday, Tuesday and holidays). Admission costs 15/5FF.

Special Events

The Braderie, a flea market extraordinaire covering most of the old town, is held on the first weekend of September. The Festival de Lille is a four-week series of concerts and other events held in September and October.

Places to Stay

Camping *Camping L'Image* (☎ 03 20 35 69 42, 140 rue Brune) 10km north-west of Lille in the suburb of Houplines, opens year-round. It charges 11/18FF per adult/tent site. By car, take the A25 towards Dunkerque and get off at exit No 8 (Chapelle d'Armentières).

Hostels The modern, 170-bed *Auberge de Jeunesse* (☎ 03 20 57 08 94, fax 03 20 63 98 93, ✉ lille@fuaj.org, 12 rue Malpart, metro République or Mairie de Lille) is in a former maternity hospital with dorm beds starting at 73FF, including breakfast. Reception opens 8 am to noon and 2 pm to 2 am. It's closed from 20 December to the end of January.

Hotels The place de la Gare has quite a few hotels. *Hôtel des Voyageurs* (☎ 03 20 06 43 14, fax 03 20 74 19 01) at No 10 has simple and clean singles/doubles, reached via a vintage lift, starting at 130/160FF (205/250FF with shower and toilet). A hall shower is 20FF.

The two-star *Hôtel de France* (☎ 03 20 57 14 78, fax 03 20 57 06 01, 10 rue de Béthune) has airy singles/doubles with washbasin for 150/170FF (200/240FF with shower and toilet). Hall showers are free. Drivers unloading luggage should take rue des Fossés.

Hôtel Moulin d'Or (☎ 03 20 06 12 67, fax 03 20 06 33 50, 15 rue du Molinel) has very simple, linoleum-floored doubles from 160FF, 280FF with shower, and 300FF with shower and toilet. There are no hall showers. Curfew is midnight.

Places to Eat

In Vieux Lille, the relaxed *La Pâte Brisée* (☎ 03 20 74 29 00, 63-65 rue de la Monnaie) has savoury and sweet *tartes*, salads, meat dishes and *gratin* in one/two/three-course *menus* for 47/69/84FF, including a drink. Try the great regional *menu* for 89FF at the intimate *La Tarterie de la Voûte* (☎ 03 20 42 12 16, 4 rue des Débris St Étienne), closed Monday night and Sunday.

The elegant *Le Hochepot* (☎ 03 20 54 17 59, 6 rue du Nouveau Siècle) serves Flemish dishes such as *coq à la bière*. The *menus* cost 125FF, including drinks. It's closed Saturday lunch and Sunday.

For a splurge, *À l'Huîtrière* (☎ 03 20 55 43 41, 3 rue des Chats Bossus), decorated with mosaics dating from 1928, has great seafood and traditional French cuisine. The lunch *menu* is 245FF; mains are about 170FF. It opens noon to 2.30 pm and 7 to 9.30 pm (closed Sunday evening and late July to late August). Reserve ahead.

Self-Catering The lively *Wazemmes food market* (*place Nouvelle Aventure, metro Gambetta*), 1.2km south-west of the centre, opens till 7 pm (closed Monday). There's a *Monoprix supermarket* at 31 rue du Molinel (closed Sunday).

Entertainment

Classical Music & Jazz Well-regarded *Orchestre National de Lille* (☎ 03 20 12 82 40) plays in the Palais de la Musique. *Le 30 (☎ 03 20 30 15 54, 30 rue de Paris)* has live jazz nightly (except Sunday); the audience sits on soft, modular couches in what looks like a 1960s airport VIP lounge.

Pubs & Bars *Café Oz (☎ 03 20 55 15 15, 33 place Louise de Bettignies)*, a branch of Paris' famous Australian bar, has Foster's on tap (18FF for 250mL) and good cocktails (45FF).

In Vieux Lille, the laid-back *Le Balatum (☎ 03 20 57 41 81, 13 rue de la Barre)* has numerous beers from 13FF. *L'Illustration Café (☎ 03 20 12 00 90, 18 rue Royale)* is a mellow Art Nouveau-style bar. Both open until 2 am.

Getting There & Away
Bus The Eurolines office (☎ 03 20 78 18 88), 23 parvis St Maurice, has direct buses to Brussels (50FF, 2½ hours), London (250FF, five hours) and other destinations. It opens 9 am to 6 or 8 pm (two-hour break at noon on Monday to Wednesday, closed Sunday).

Train Lille has frequent rail links to almost everywhere in France. Its two train stations (☎ 0836 35 35 35) are linked by metro line No 2.

Gare Lille-Flandres handles almost all regional services and most TGVs to Paris' Gare du Nord (208FF to 278FF, one hour, one to two per hour). The information office opens 9 am to 7 pm (closed Sunday and holidays).

Gare Lille-Europe is served by Eurostar trains to London (700FF at weekends, 1050FF on weekdays, 2 hours) and TGVs and Eurostars to Brussels (85FF to 98FF, 38 minutes, 15 a day). Other options include Calais (84FF, 1½ hours, eight to 15 a day).

Getting Around
Transpole (☎ 03 20 40 40 40) runs Lille's metro, trams and buses. Tickets (7.50FF) are sold on the bus but must be purchased (and validated in the orange posts) before boarding the metro or tram. A carnet of 10/weekly passes costs 64/71FF.

CALAIS
pop 78,000
Calais, only 34km from the English town of Dover, has long been a popular port for passenger travel between the UK and continental Europe. Its dominance of trans-Channel transport was sealed in 1994 when the Channel Tunnel was opened at Coquelles, 5km south-west of the town centre. Over 20 million people pass through Calais each year.

Orientation & Information
The centre of Calais, whose main square is place d'Armes, is encircled by canals and harbour basins, with Calais-Ville train station 650m to the south. The car ferry terminal is 1.7km north-east of place d'Armes; the hoverport is another 1.5km farther out.

The tourist office (☎ 03 21 96 62 40, fax 03 21 96 01 92, ☻ ot@ot-calais.fr), 12 blvd Georges Clemenceau, opens 9 am to 7 pm Monday to Saturday and Sunday morning. Web site: www.ot-calais.fr.

Money The Banque de France at 77 blvd Jacquard exchanges money 8.30 am to 12.10 pm weekdays. There are commercial banks along rue Royale.

Post & Communications The post office on place de Rheims opens until 6 pm weekdays and until noon on Saturday. It has a currency desk and a Cyberposte terminal.

Laundry The Lavorama on the eastern side of place d'Armes is open 7 am to 9 pm daily.

Things to See
A cast of Auguste Rodin's famous bronze statue of six emaciated but proud figures, known in English as **The Burghers of Calais**, stands in front of the Flemish Renaissance-style Hôtel de Ville, which is topped with an ornate 75m clock tower.

Across the street in Parc St Pierre is the **Musée de la Guerre** (☎ 03 21 34 21 57), an intriguing WWII museum housed in a 94m-long concrete bunker. You can begin your visit from 11 am to 4.15 pm (10 am to 5.15 pm from April to September). Admission costs 25/20FF.

The newly-renovated **Musée des Beaux-Arts et de la Dentelle** (Museum of Fine Arts & Lace; ☎ 03 21 46 48 40), 25 rue Richelieu, has exhibits on mechanised lacemaking (the first machines were smuggled to Calais from England in 1816). It opens 10 am to noon and 2 or 2.30 to 5.30 pm daily (6.30 pm at weekends; closed Tuesday). Admission costs 15FF/10FF (free on Wednesday).

Places to Stay

Camping The grassy but soulless *Camping Municipal* (☎ 03 21 97 89 79, ave Raymond Poincaré) opens all year. It charges 18.90/13.20FF per adult/tent or caravan site. From the train station, take bus No 3 to the Pluviose stop.

Hostels The modern and nicely furnished *Auberge de Jeunesse* (☎ 03 21 34 70 20, fax 03 21 96 87 80, ave Maréchal De Lattre de Tassigny), also called the Centre Européen de Séjour, is 200m from the beach. A spot in a two-bed double costs 94FF, and a single costs 136FF, including breakfast. Take bus No 3 to the Pluviose stop.

Hotels At Parc St Pierre near the train station, the nicely-renovated *Hôtel-Pension L'Ovale* (☎/fax 03 21 97 57 00, 38-40 ave Wilson) has bright, cheery rooms with high ceilings and sparkling new TVs. Singles or doubles cost 160FF, triples 180FF (all with private shower). The central and friendly *Hôtel Bristol* (☎/fax 03 21 34 53 24, 15 rue du Duc de Guise) has cosy singles/doubles from 150/160FF (180/220FF with shower and toilet); hall showers are free. Rooms for four and five people are also available.

The family-run *Hôtel Richelieu* (☎ 03 21 34 61 60, fax 03 21 85 89 28, 17 rue Richelieu) is a very quiet place. It has singles/doubles/quads with soft beds and a range of amenities for 250/254/314FF, including breakfast.

Places to Eat

Restaurants *Histoire Ancienne* (☎ 03 21 34 11 20, 20 rue Royale) is a Paris-style bistro specialising in meat dishes grilled over a wood fire. *Menus* go for 98FF to 158FF (closed Monday night and Sunday). Show a ferry or shuttle ticket and get a free bottle of takeaway wine.

The rustic *Au Coq d'Or* (☎ 03 21 34 79 05, 31 place d'Armes) serves grilled meat dishes and seafood daily. *Menus* run from 64FF to 245FF (closed Wednesday).

For a real treat, try the family-run *La Pléiade* (☎ 03 21 34 03 70, 32 rue Jean Quéhen), an elegant, mainly seafood restaurant whose *menus* cost 85FF to 160FF, plus dessert (closed Saturday midday and Monday).

Self-Catering Place d'Armes hosts a *food market* Wednesday and Saturday mornings. There's a *Match supermarket (place d'Armes)* that also opens Sunday morning in July and August.

Getting There & Away

For details on the Channel Tunnel and ferry fares and schedules, see Britain under Land and Sea in the Getting There & Away section.

Bus Bus Inglard (☎ 03 21 96 49 54) runs buses three times daily (except Sunday) from Calais-Ville train station and place du Théâtre to Boulogne (27FF, 1¼ hours). Cariane Littoral (☎ 03 21 34 74 40), 10 rue d'Amsterdam, has express BCD services to Boulogne (38FF, 35 minutes, six on weekdays and two on Saturday) and Dunkerque (40FF, 30 minutes, 11 weekdays and three on Saturday).

Train Calais has two train stations: Gare Calais-Ville (☎ 0836 35 35 35) and Gare Calais-Fréthun, 10km south-west of town near the Channel Tunnel entrance.

Calais-Ville has direct, non-TGV trains to Paris' Gare du Nord (182FF, 3½ hours, three to six a day), Boulogne (41FF, 35 minutes, hourly), and Lille-Flandres (84FF, 1½ hours, seven to 15 a day).

Calais-Fréthun is well-served by TGVs to Paris' Gare du Nord (215FF, 1½ hours, two a day) as well as the Eurostar to London (700FF to 1050FF, 1¾ hours, three a day). Calais-Fréthun is linked to the Calais-Ville station by Opale Bus No 7 (7.20FF).

Car To reach the Channel Tunnel's vehicle loading area, follow the road signs on the A16 to the 'Tunnel Sous La Manche'.

Boat P&O Stena and SeaFrance Sealink car ferries to/from Dover dock at the busy Terminal Est, just over 1km north-east of place d'Armes.

P&O Stena's office (☎ 0802 01 00 20) is at 41 place d'Armes. Nearby at No 2 is SeaFrance Sealink's office (☎ 0803 04 40 45). Both open weekdays and Saturday morning.

SeaCats to/from Dover, operated by Hoverspeed (☎ 0820 00 35 55 or ☎ 03 21 46 14 00), use the hoverport, 3km north-east of the town centre. Hovercraft no longer run on the Dover-Calais route.

Getting Around

Bus To reach the car ferry terminal, take a free shuttle run by SeaFrance Sealink and P&O Stena – they stop at the Calais-Ville train station and near each company's office at place d'Armes. Hoverspeed's buses to the hoverport (5FF) leave the train station about 45 minutes before each departure.

Opale Bus (☎ 03 21 00 75 75) operates local buses from place du Théâtre, which is 700m south of the train station. Almost all the lines stop at the Calais-Ville train station.

DUNKERQUE

pop 209,000

Dunkerque was flattened shortly before one of the dullest periods in Western architecture – 1950s brick low-rise. Unless you're planning to spend time on the beach or to join in the colourful pre-Lent carnival, there's little reason to spend the night here.

Orientation & Information

The train station is 600m south-west of Dunkerque's main square, place Jean Bart. The beach and its waterfront esplanade, Digue de Mer, are 2km north-east of the centre. The tourist office (☎ 03 28 26 27 28, fax 03 28 63 38 40, ✉ dunkerque@tourism.norsys.fr) is in the medieval belfry on rue de l'Amiral Ronarc.

Things to See & Do

The **Musée Portuaire** (Harbour Museum; ☎ 03 28 63 33 39), 9 quai de la Citadelle, housed in a former tobacco warehouse, has splendid ship models and exhibits on the history of Dunkerque as a port. Admission costs 25/20FF.

One-hour **boat tours** (☎ 03 28 58 85 12 for reservations) depart from place du Minck and afford views of the huge port and some of France's most important steel and petroleum works. Tickets cost 35FF (children 27FF).

Places to Stay & Eat

The *Auberge de Jeunesse* (☎ 03 28 63 36 34, fax 03 28 63 24 54, place Paul Asseman) is on the beach 3km north of the train station. Spots in eight-bed dorm rooms cost 48FF, plus 19FF for breakfast. Take bus No 3 to the 'Piscine' stop, walk past the pool and the hostel's on your right.

Opposite the tourist office, the two-star *Hôtel du Tigre* (☎/fax 03 28 66 75 17, 8 rue Clemenceau) has nice singles/doubles from 90/130FF (190/240FF with shower and toilet).

Kim Thanh Restaurant (☎ 03 28 51 22 98, 14 place Roger Salengro) 100m north-west of the tourist office, does Chinese-Vietnamese lunch *menus* (oodles of chicken) for 55FF (closed Tuesday and Saturday lunch).

Getting There & Away

BCD (☎ 03 21 83 51 51) runs buses to/from Dunkerque train station to Calais (40FF, 45 minutes, 11 on weekdays and three on Saturday). Dunkerque has frequent train links to Lille (73FF, 1¼ hours, 16 a day), Calais (83FF, 1¼ to 1¾ hours, 13 per day) and Paris Gare du Nord by TGV (280FF to 320FF, 1½ hours, hourly).

BATTLE OF THE SOMME MEMORIALS

The First Battle of the Somme, the WWI Allied offensive waged in the villages and woodlands north-east of Amiens, was designed to relieve pressure on the beleaguered French troops at Verdun (for more details see the Alsace & Lorraine chapter). On 1 July 1916, British, Commonwealth and French troops 'went over the top' in a massive assault along a 34km front. But German positions proved virtually unbreachable, and on the first day of the battle an astounding 20,000 British troops were killed and another 40,000 were wounded. Most casualties were infantrymen mowed down by German machine guns.

By the time the offensive was called off in mid-November, some 1.2 million lives had been lost on both sides. The British had advanced 12km, the French only 8km. The Battle of the Somme has become a metaphor for the meaningless slaughter of war, and its killing fields are a site of pilgrimage.

Commonwealth Cemeteries & Memorials

Over 750,000 soldiers from Canada, Australia, New Zealand, South Africa, the Indian subcontinent, the West Indies and other parts of the British Empire died on the Western Front, two-thirds of them in France. By Commonwealth tradition, they were buried where they fell, in over 1000 military cemeteries and 2000 civilian cemeteries. Today, hundreds of neatly-tended Commonwealth plots dot the landscape along a wide line running roughly from Albert and Cambrai north via Arras and Béthune to Armentières and Ypres (Ieper) in Belgium. Some 26 memorials (20 of them in France) bear the names of over 300,000 Commonwealth soldiers whose bodies were never recovered or identified. The French, Americans and Germans reburied their dead in large war cemeteries after the war.

Except where noted, all the monuments listed here are always open. Larger Commonwealth cemeteries usually have a plaque (often inside a little marble pavilion) with historical information in English. Touring the area is only really feasible by car or bicycle.

Maps & Brochures All of the memorials and cemeteries mentioned here (and hundreds of others) are indicated on Michelin's 1:200,000 scale maps. For more information, pick up Michelin's yellow maps Nos 51 and/or 52 overprinted by the Commonwealth War Graves Commission (☎ 03 21 21 77 00 in Beaurains) with all the Commonwealth cemeteries in the region (25FF). The brochure *The Somme – Remembrance Tour of the Great War* (5FF) is on offer at area tourist offices.

Normandy

Normandy (Normandie) derives its name from the Norsemen (Vikings) who took control of the area in the early 10th century. Modern Normandy is the land of the *bocage*, farmland subdivided by hedges and trees.

ROUEN
pop 107,000
The city of Rouen, for centuries the lowest bridging point on the Seine, is known for its many spires, church towers and half-timbered houses, not to mention its Gothic cathedral and excellent museums. Rouen can be visited on a day or overnight trip from Paris.

Orientation & Information
The train station (Gare Rouen-Rive Droite) is at the northern end of rue Jeanne d'Arc, the major thoroughfare running south to the Seine.

The tourist office (☎ 02 32 08 32 40, fax 02 32 08 32 44, ✆ otrouen@mcom.fr) is at 25 place de la Cathédrale. The office opens 9 am to 7 pm Monday to Saturday, and 9.30 am to 12.30 pm and 2.30 to 6 pm on Sunday, May to September; and 9 am to 6 pm Monday to Saturday, and 10 am to 1 pm on Sunday the rest of the year. Guided city tours (35FF) depart from the office in summer at 10.30 am and 3 pm daily.

Things to See
Rouen's main street, rue du Gros Horloge, runs from the cathedral to **place du Vieux Marché**, where 19-year-old Joan of Arc was burned at the stake for heresy in 1431. You'll learn more about her life from its stained-glass windows at the adjacent Église Jeanne d'Arc than at the tacky **Musée Jeanne d'Arc** across the square at No 33.

Rouen's **Cathédrale Notre Dame**, the subject of a series of paintings by Claude Monet, is a masterpiece of French Gothic architecture. There are several guided visits (15/10FF) a day to the crypt, ambulatory (containing Richard the Lion-Heart's tomb) and Chapel of the Virgin.

The **Musée Le Secq des Tournelles** on rue Jacques Villon (opposite 27 rue Jean Lecanuet) is devoted to the blacksmith's craft and displays some 12,000 locks, keys and tongs made between the 3rd and 19th centuries (15/10FF, closed Tuesday).

The **Musée des Beaux-Arts** facing the square at 26 bis rue Jean Lecanuet features some major paintings from the 16th to 20th centuries, including some of Monet's cathedral series (20/13FF, closed Tuesday).

La Tour Jeanne d'Arc on rue du Donjon, south of the train station, is the tower where Joan of Arc was imprisoned before her execution. There are two exhibition rooms (10FF, closed Tuesday).

Places to Stay
The year-round *Camping Municipal* (☎ 02 35 74 07 59, *rue Jules Ferry*), in the suburb of Déville-lès-Rouen, is 5km north-west of town. From the Théâtre des Arts or the nearby

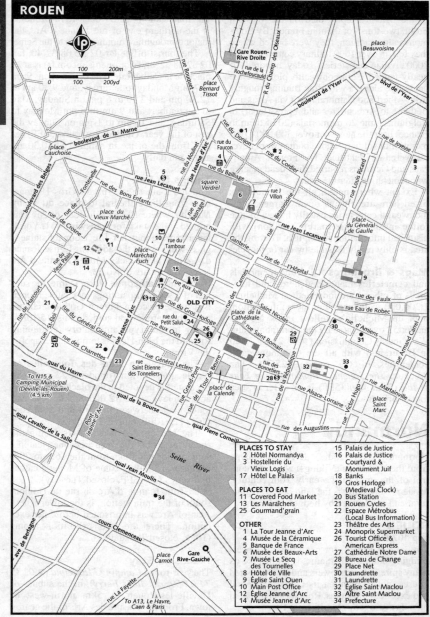

ROUEN

PLACES TO STAY
2 Hôtel Normandya
3 Hostellerie du
   Vieux Logis
17 Hôtel Le Palais

PLACES TO EAT
11 Covered Food Market
13 Les Maraîchers
25 Gourmand'grain

OTHER
1 La Tour Jeanne d'Arc
4 Musée de la Céramique
5 Banque de France
6 Musée des Beaux-Arts
7 Musée Le Secq
   des Tournelles
8 Hôtel de Ville
9 Église Saint Ouen
10 Main Post Office
12 Église Jeanne d'Arc
14 Musée Jeanne d'Arc

15 Palais de Justice
16 Palais de Justice
   Courtyard &
   Monument Juif
18 Banks
19 Gros Horloge
   (Medieval Clock)
20 Bus Station
21 Rouen Cycles
22 Espace Métrobus
   (Local Bus Information)
23 Théâtre des Arts
24 Monoprix Supermarket
26 Tourist Office &
   American Express
27 Cathédrale Notre Dame
28 Bureau de Change
29 Place Net
30 Laundrette
31 Laundrette
32 Église Saint Maclou
33 Aître Saint Maclou
34 Prefecture

euro currency converter €1 = 6.55FF

bus station, take bus No 2 and get off at the *mairie* (town hall) of Déville-lès-Rouen. It's 59FF for two people and a tent.

The spotless and friendly *Hôtel Normandya* (☎ 02 35 71 46 15, 32 rue du Cordier) is on a quiet street 300m south-east of the train station. Singles (some with shower) are 110FF to 140FF, doubles 10FF to 20FF more. The very French *Hostellerie du Vieux Logis* (☎ 02 35 71 55 30, 5 rue de Joyeuse), 1km east of the train station, has a pleasantly frayed atmosphere and a lovely garden out the back. Singles/doubles start at 100FF. The *Hôtel Le Palais* (☎ 02 35 71 41 40, 12 rue du Tambour), between the Palais de Justice and the Gros Horloge, has doubles with shower for 140FF.

Places to Eat
A *covered market* is held daily (except Monday) from 6 am to 1.30 pm at place du Vieux Marché. The bistro-style *Les Maraîchers* at No 37 is the pick of the Vieux Marché's many restaurants, with its terrace and varied *menus* from 69FF (89FF in the evening).

Gourmand'grain (☎ 02 35 98 15 74, 3 rue du Petit Salut) behind the tourist office, is a lunchtime vegetarian cafe with *menus* for 45FF and 69FF.

Getting There & Away
Buses to Dieppe (68FF, two hours) and Le Havre (84FF, three hours) are slower and more expensive than the train. The bus station (☎ 02 35 52 92 00) is at 25 rue des Charrettes near the Théâtre des Arts.

There are at least 20 trains a day to/from Paris' Gare St Lazare (124FF, 70 minutes). For train information, call ☎ 0836 35 35 39.

Getting Around
TCAR operates the local bus network and metro line. The metro links the train station with the Théâtre des Arts before crossing the Seine into the southern suburbs. Bus tickets cost 8FF, or 63FF for a magnetic card good for 10 rides.

BAYEUX
pop 15,000
Bayeux is celebrated for two trans-Channel invasions: the AD 1066 conquest of England by William the Conqueror (an event chronicled in the Bayeux Tapestry) and the Allied D-Day landings of 6 June 1944; Bayeux was the first town in France to be liberated from the Nazis.

Bayeux is an attractive – though fairly touristy – town with several excellent museums. It's also a good base for the D-Day beaches.

Orientation & Information
The cathedral, Bayeux's central landmark, is 1km north-west of the train station.

The tourist office (☎ 02 31 51 28 28, fax 02 31 51 28 29) is at Pont St Jean just off the northern end of rue Larcher. It opens 9 am to noon and 2 to 6 pm Monday to Saturday; and also on Sunday from 9.30 am to noon and 2.30 to 6 pm in July and August. A *billet jumelé* (multipass ticket) valid for most of Bayeux's museums (but not the Musée Mémorial) costs 38/22FF.

Things to See
The world-famous **Bayeux Tapestry** – a 70m-long strip of coarse linen decorated with woollen embroidery – was commissioned by Odo, bishop of Bayeux and half-brother to William the Conqueror, for the consecration of the cathedral in Bayeux in 1077. The tapestry recounts the story of the Norman invasion of 1066 – from the Norman perspective. Halley's Comet, which visited our solar system in 1066, also makes an appearance. The tapestry is housed in the **Musée de la Tapisserie de Bayeux** on rue de Nesmond, open 9 am to 7 pm daily (closed at lunch in off-season). Entry is 38/16FF.

Bayeux's **Cathédrale Notre Dame** is an exceptional example of Norman-Gothic architecture, dating from the 13th century.

The **Musée Mémorial 1944 Bataille de Normandie**, Bayeux's huge war museum on blvd Fabien Ware, displays a haphazard collection of photos, uniforms, weapons and life-like scenes associated with D-Day and the Battle of Normandy. An excellent 30-minute film is screened in English. Admission is 33/16FF.

The **Bayeux War Cemetery**, a British cemetery on blvd Fabien Ware, a few hundred metres west of the museum, is the largest of the 18 Commonwealth military cemeteries in Normandy. Many of the headstones are inscribed with poignant epitaphs.

FRANCE

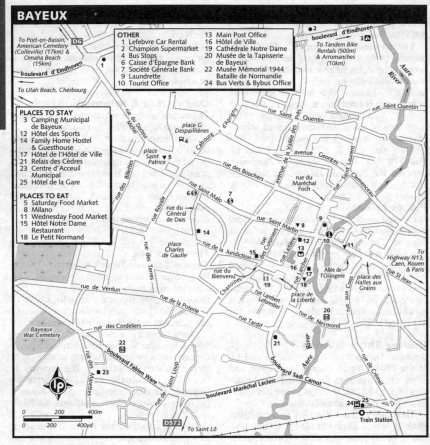

BAYEUX

OTHER
1 Lefebvre Car Rental
2 Champion Supermarket
4 Bus Stops
6 Caisse d'Épargne Bank
7 Société Générale Bank
9 Laundrette
10 Tourist Office
13 Main Post Office
16 Hôtel de Ville
19 Cathédrale Notre Dame
20 Musée de la Tapisserie de Bayeux
22 Musée Mémorial 1944 Bataille de Normandie
24 Bus Verts & Bybus Office

PLACES TO STAY
3 Camping Municipal de Bayeux
12 Hôtel des Sports
14 Family Home Hostel & Guesthouse
17 Hôtel de l'Hôtel de Ville
21 Relais des Cèdres
23 Centre d'Acceuil Municipal
25 Hôtel de la Gare

PLACES TO EAT
5 Saturday Food Market
8 Milano
11 Wednesday Food Market
15 Hôtel Notre Dame Restaurant
18 Le Petit Normand

To Port-en-Bassin, American Cemetery (Colleville) (17km) & Omaha Beach (15km)

boulevard d'Eindhoven

To Utah Beach, Cherbourg

To Tandem Bike Rentals (500m) & Arromanches (10km)

boulevard d'Eindhoven

Aure River

rue du Docteur Michel

place G Despaillières

rue Saint Prés Quentin

rue Saint Quentin

Cabourg

rue des Billettes

place Saint Patrice

avenue de la Vallée des

avenue Georges

rue des Bouchers

rue du Maréchal Foch

rue Saint Laurent

rue Clemenceau

rue Royale

rue Saint Malo

rue du Général de Dais

rue Saint Martin

rue des Cuisiniers

rue des Terres

place Charles de Gaulle

rue de la Juridiction

rue de Laitière

To Highway N13, Caen, Rouen & Paris

rue St Jean

Allée de l'Orangerie

rue aux Coqs

place des Halles aux Grains

rue du Bienvenu

Chanoines

rue de Verdun

rue de la Poterie

rue Lambert Leforestier

place de la Liberté

rue de Nesmond

rue des Cordeliers

rue Tardif

boulevard Sadi Carnot

Bayeaux War Cemetery

rue des Marettes

boulevard Fabien Ware

rue de Saint Loup

boulevard Maréchal Leclerc

Aure River

rue de Cremel

D572

To Saint Lô

Train Station

0 200 400m
0 200 400yd

Places to Stay
Camping *Camping Municipal de Bayeux* (☎ 02 31 92 08 43) is 2km north of town, just south of blvd d'Eindhoven. It's open mid-March to mid-November, and charges 9.20/17.10FF per tent/person. Bus Nos 5 and 6 from the train station stop here.

Hostels The *Family Home* hostel and guesthouse (☎ 02 31 92 15 22, fax 02 31 92 55 72, *39 rue du Général de Dais*) in three old buildings, is an excellent place to meet other travellers. Dorm beds are 100FF (95FF with HI card), singles 160FF. There's a kitchen, or

you can have a multicourse French dinner (with wine) for 65FF.

The modern, if slightly sterile, *Centre d'Accueil Municipal* (☎ 02 31 92 08 19, 21 rue des Marettes) is 1km south-west of the cathedral. Singles are good value at 90FF.

Hotels The old but well-maintained *Hôtel de la Gare* (☎ 02 31 92 10 70, fax 02 31 51 95 99, 26 place de la Gare), opposite the train station, has singles/doubles from 85/100FF. The central *Hôtel de l'Hôtel de Ville* (☎ 02 31 92 30 08, 31ter rue Larcher) has large and quiet rooms for 140/160FF.

Showers are free. Phone reservations are not accepted. A few hundred metres north, *Hôtel des Sports* (☎ 02 31 92 28 53, *19 rue St Martin*) has decent rooms (most with shower) starting at 160/200FF.

Places to Eat

There are *food markets* on rue St Jean (Wednesday morning) and on place St Patrice (Saturday morning).

Le Petit Normand (☎ 02 31 22 88 66, *35 rue Larcher*) specialises in traditional Norman food and has simple *menus* starting at 58FF (closed Sunday night and Wednesday, except in July and August). *Hôtel Notre Dame* restaurant (☎ 02 31 92 87 24) offers Norman fare at its best; lunch *menus* cost 60FF, dinner *menus* 95FF (closed Sunday lunch and Monday from November to March). *Milano* (☎ 02 31 92 15 10, *18 rue St Martin*) serves good pizza (closed Sunday from September to May).

Getting There & Away

The train station office (☎ 02 31 92 80 50) opens 7 am to 8.45 pm daily. Trains serve Paris' Gare St Lazare (171FF, via Caen), Cherbourg, Rennes and points beyond.

D-DAY BEACHES

The D-Day landings were the largest military operation in history. Early on the morning of 6 June 1944, swarms of landing craft – part of a flotilla of almost 7000 boats – ferried ashore 135,000 Allied troops along 80km of beaches north of Bayeux. The landings on D-Day were followed by the 76-day Battle of Normandy that began the liberation of Europe from Nazi occupation.

Things to See

Arromanches In order to unload the vast quantities of cargo necessary for the invasion, the Allies established two prefabricated ports. The remains of one of them, Port Winston, can be seen at Arromanches, a seaside town 10km north-east of Bayeux.

The **Musée du Débarquement** (Landing Museum; ☎ 02 31 22 34 31) explains the logistics and importance of Port Winston and makes a good first stop before visiting the beaches (35/20FF, closed Monday and in January).

Omaha Beach The most brutal combat of 6 June was fought 20km west of Arromanches at Omaha Beach. Today, little evidence of the war remains except the bunkers and munitions sites of a German fortified point to the west (look for the tall obelisk on the hill).

American Military Cemetery The remains of the Americans who lost their lives during the Battle of Normandy were either sent back to the USA or buried in the American Military Cemetery at Colleville-sur-Mer, containing the graves of 9386 American soldiers and a memorial to 1557 others whose bodies were never found.

Organised Tours

Tours of the D-Day beaches are offered by Bus Fly (☎ 02 31 22 00 08), based at the Family Home hostel in Bayeux (see Places to Stay in Bayeux). An afternoon tour to major D-Day sites costs 160/140FF, including museum entry fees.

Getting There & Away

Bus Bus Verts (☎ 02 31 92 02 92), with an office opposite Bayeux's train station (closed weekends and in July), sends bus No 70 west to the American cemetery at Colleville-sur-Mer and Omaha Beach. Bus No 74 serves Arromanches, and Gold and Juno beaches. In July and August only, Bus No 75 goes to Caen via Arromanches, Gold, Juno and Sword beaches and the port of Ouistreham. There are timetables posted in the train station and at place G Despallières.

Car For three or more people, renting a car can actually be cheaper than a tour, Lefebvre Car Rental (☎ 02 31 92 05 96) on blvd d'Eindhoven in Bayeux charges 350FF per day with 200km free.

MONT ST MICHEL
pop 42

It is difficult not to be impressed by Mont St Michel with its massive abbey anchored at the summit of a rocky island. Around the base are the ancient ramparts and a jumble of buildings that house the handful of people who still live there.

At low tide, Mont St Michel looks out over bare sand stretching into the distance. At high

FRANCE

tide – about six hours later – this huge expanse of sand is under water, though only the very highest tides cover the 900m causeway that connects the islet to the mainland. The French government is currently spending millions to restore Mont St Michel to its former glory, so parts of it may be scaffolded.

The Mont's major attraction is the **Abbaye du Mont St Michel** (☎ 02 33 89 80 00), at the top of the Grande rue, up the stairway. It opens 9 am to 5.30 pm daily (9.30 am to 5 pm from October to April). It's worth taking the guided tour (in English) included in the ticket price (40/25FF). There are also self-paced evening tours (60/35FF) at 9 or 10 pm (except Sunday) of the illuminated and music-filled rooms.

Pontorson The nearest town, Pontorson is 9km south and the base for most travellers. Route D976 from Mont St Michel runs right into Pontorson's main thoroughfare, rue du Couësnon.

Information

The tourist office (☎ 02 33 60 14 30, fax 02 33 60 06 75, @ ot.Mont.Saint.Michel@wanadoo .fr) is up the stairs to the left as you enter Mont St Michel at Porte de l'Avancée. It opens 9 am to noon and 2 to 5.45 pm Monday to Saturday. From Easter to September, it opens 9.30 am to noon and 1 to 6.30 pm daily. In July and August it opens 9 am to 7 pm daily.

There's another tourist office in Pontorson, open daily (closed Sunday in winter).

Places to Stay

Camping *Camping du Mont Saint Michel* (☎ 02 33 60 09 33), open mid-February to mid-November, is on the road to Pontorson (D976), 2km from the Mont. It charges 20/22FF per tent/person. Two-person bungalows with shower and toilet are 220FF.

Hostels Pontorson's *Centre Duguesclin* (☎ 02 33 60 18 65) operates as a 10-room hostel from Easter to mid-September. Beds are 48FF. The hostel is closed from 10 am to 6 pm, but there is no curfew. The hostel is 1km west of the train station on rue du Général Patton, which runs parallel to the Couësnon River north of rue du Couësnon. The hostel is on the left side in a three-storey stone building opposite No 26.

Hotels Mont St Michel has about 15 hotels but most are expensive. *La Mère Poulard* (☎ 02 33 60 14 01, fax 02 33 48 52 31), the first hotel on the left as you walk up the Grande rue, has doubles with shower from 300FF.

In Pontorson, across place de la Gare from the train station, there are a couple of cheap hotels. *Hôtel de l'Arrivée* (☎ 02 33 60 01 57, 14 rue du Docteur Tizon) has doubles for 95FF, or 165FF with shower.

Places to Eat

The tourist restaurants around the base of the Mont have lovely views but tend to be mediocre; *menus* start at about 80FF. A few places along the Grande rue sell sandwiches, quiches and such like. The nearest *supermarket* to the Mont is next to Camping du Mont St Michel on the D976.

In Pontorson, *La Crêperie du Couësnon* (☎ 02 33 60 16 67, 21 rue du Couësnon) has crepes and savoury galettes (10FF to 30FF). *La Tour de Brette* (☎ 02 33 60 10 69, 8 rue du Couësnon) across from the river, has good *menus* from 60FF.

Getting There & Away

STN (☎ 02 33 58 03 07) sends bus No 15 from Pontorson's train station to Mont St Michel daily year-round; most of the buses connect with trains to/from Paris, Rennes and Caen.

There are trains to Pontorson from Caen (via Folligny) and Rennes (via Dol). From Paris, take the train to Caen (from Gare St Lazare), Rennes (from Gare Montparnasse) or direct to Pontorson via Folligny (Gare Montparnasse).

Getting Around

Bikes can be rented at Pontorson's train station (55FF per day plus 1000FF deposit) and from E Videloup (☎ 02 33 60 11 40), 1 bis rue du Couësnon, which charges 50FF/80FF per day for one-speeds/mountain bikes.

Brittany

Brittany (Bretagne in French, Breizh in Breton), the westernmost region of France, is famous for its rugged countryside and wild coastline. Traditional costumes, including extraordinarily tall headdresses worn by the

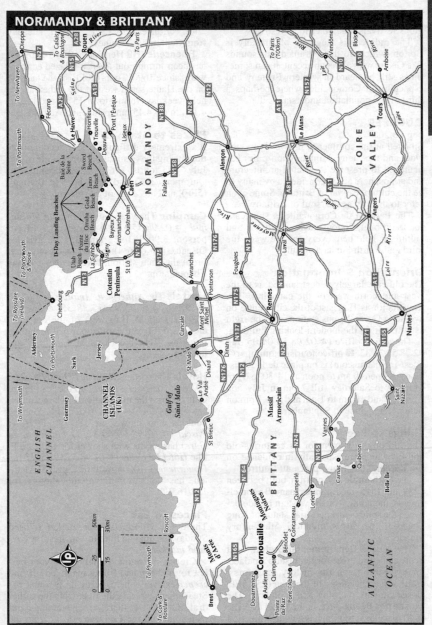

NORMANDY & BRITTANY

women, can still be seen at *pardons* (religious festivals) and other local festivals.

The indigenous language of Brittany is Breton, which, to the untrained ear, sounds like Gaelic with a French accent. It can sometimes still be heard in western Brittany and especially in Cornouaille, where perhaps a third of the population understands it.

QUIMPER
pop 63,200

Situated at the confluence of two rivers, the Odet and the Steïr, Quimper (cam-**pair**) has managed to preserve its Breton architecture and atmosphere and is considered by many to be the cultural capital of Brittany. Some even refer to the city as the 'soul of Brittany'.

The Festival de Cornouaille, a showcase for traditional Breton music, costumes and culture, is held here every year between the third and fourth Sundays in July.

Orientation & Information

The old city, largely pedestrianised, is to the west and north-west of the cathedral. The train station is 1km east of the city centre on ave de la Gare; the bus station is to the right as you exit, in the modern-looking building.

The tourist office (☎ 02 98 53 04 05, fax 02 98 53 31 33, ✆ office.tourisme.quimper@ouest-mediacap.com) is on place de la Résistance. It opens 9 am to noon and 1.30 to 6 pm Monday to Saturday (till 7 pm in July and August), and 10 am to 1 pm and 3 to 7 pm on Sunday, mid-June to September.

Things to See

The old city is known for its centuries-old houses, which are especially in evidence on **rue Kéréon** and around **place au Beurre**.

The **Cathédrale St Corentin**, built between 1239 and 1515, incorporates many Breton elements, including – on the western facade between the spires – an equestrian statue of King Gradlon, the city's mythical 5th-century founder.

The **Musée Départemental Breton**, next to the cathedral in the former bishop's palace, houses exhibits on the history, costumes, crafts and archaeology of the area (25/15FF, closed Sunday morning and Monday). The **Musée des Beaux-Arts**, in the Hôtel de Ville at 40 place St Corentin, has a wide collection

of European paintings from the 16th to early 20th centuries (25/15FF, closed Tuesday from September to June).

Faïenceries HB Henriot (☎ 02 98 90 09 36) has been turning out *faïence* (glazed earthenware) since 1690. Tours (20FF) of the factory, on rue Haute south-west of the cathedral, are held weekdays from 9 to 11.15 am and 1.30 to 4.15 pm (to 4.45 pm in July and August).

Places to Stay

It's extremely difficult to find accommodation during the Festival de Cornouaille in late July. The tourist office makes bookings in Quimper (2FF) and elsewhere in Brittany (5FF), and has a list of *private rooms*.

Camping The year-round *Camping Municipal* (☎ 02 98 55 61 09) charges 17.70FF per person, 3.90FF for a tent. It's on ave des Oiseaux just over 1km west of the old city. From the train station, take bus No 1 to the Chaptal stop.

Hostels The *Auberge de Jeunesse* (☎ 02 98 64 97 97, fax 02 98 55 38 37, 6 ave des Oiseaux) about 1km west of the old city, charges 67FF per dorm-room bed including breakfast. Take bus Nos 1 or 8 to the Chaptal stop.

Hotels The spotless *Hôtel de l'Ouest* (☎ 02 98 90 28 35, 63 rue Le Déan), up rue Jean-Pierre Calloch from the train station, has large, pleasant singles/doubles from 100/150FF. Singles/doubles with shower are 180/190FF. *Hôtel Pascal* (☎ 02 98 90 00 81, 17 bis ave de la Gare) has rooms with shower for 180/190FF. The *Hôtel Le Celtic* (☎ 02 98 55 59 35, 13 rue Douarnenez), 100m north of Église St Mathieu, has doubles without/with shower for 125/165FF.

Places to Eat

There's a *Monoprix* supermarket (closed Sunday) on quai du Port au Vin, near the *covered market*.

Crepes, a Breton speciality, are your best bet for a cheap and filling meal. You'll find *creperies* everywhere, particularly along rue Ste Catherine across the river from the cathedral. Otherwise there are several decent restaurants on rue Le Déan not far from the

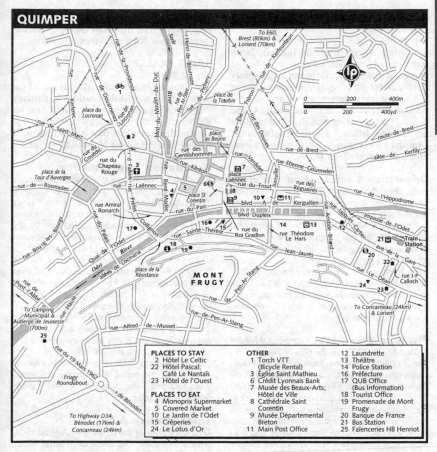

QUIMPER

PLACES TO STAY
2 Hôtel Le Celtic
22 Hôtel Pascal;
   Café Le Nantaïs
23 Hôtel de l'Ouest

PLACES TO EAT
4 Monoprix Supermarket
5 Covered Market
10 Le Jardin de l'Odet
15 Crêperies
24 Le Lotus d'Or

OTHER
1 Torch VTT
  (Bicycle Rental)
3 Église Saint Mathieu
6 Crédit Lyonnais Bank
7 Musée des Beaux-Arts;
  Hôtel de Ville
8 Cathédrale Saint
  Corentin
9 Musée Départemental
  Breton
11 Main Post Office

12 Laundrette
13 Théâtre
14 Police Station
16 Préfecture
17 QUB Office
  (Bus Information)
18 Tourist Office
19 Promenade de Mont
  Frugy
20 Banque de France
21 Bus Station
25 Faïenceries HB Henriot

train station, including Chinese-Vietnamese *Le Lotus d'Or* (☎ 02 98 53 02 54) at No 53 (closed Wednesday).

Le Jardin de l'Odet (☎ 02 98 95 76 76, 39 blvd Amiral de Kerguélen) is a good splurge, with tasty Lyonnais cuisine and *menus* from 80FF (closed Sunday).

Getting There & Away

A half-dozen companies operate out of the bus station (☎ 02 98 90 88 89). Destinations include Brest, Pointe du Raz, Roscoff (for ferries to Plymouth, England), Concarneau and Quimperlé.

Inquire at the train station for SNCF buses to Douarnenez, Camaret-sur-Mer, Concarneau and Quiberon. A one-way ticket on the TGV train to Paris' Gare Montparnasse costs 384FF (4 hours). You can also reach Saint Malo by train via Rennes. For rail information call ☎ 0836 35 35 35.

Getting Around

Bicycle Torch VTT (☎ 02 98 53 84 41) at 58 rue de la Providence rents out mountain bikes for 65/90FF per half-day/day (cheaper in winter). It's closed Sunday, Monday and Thursday morning.

FRANCE

AROUND QUIMPER
Concarneau
pop 19,500

Concarneau (Konk-Kerne in Breton), 24km south-east of Quimper, is France's third-most important trawler port. Concarneau is slightly scruffy and at the same time a bit touristy, but it's refreshingly unpretentious and is near several decent beaches. The **Ville Close** (walled city), built on a small island measuring 350m by 100m and fortified between the 14th and 17th centuries, is reached via a footbridge from place Jean Jaurès.

Orientation & Information Concarneau curls around the busy fishing port (Port de Pêche), with the two main quays running north-south along the harbour.

The tourist office (☎ 02 98 97 01 44, fax 02 98 50 88 81, ✉ otsi.concarneau@wanadoo.fr) is on quai d'Aiguillon, 200m north of the main (west) gate to the Ville Close. It opens 9 am to noon and 2 to 6 pm, Monday to Saturday, September to June; and 9 am to 8 pm in July and August. From April to June, it also opens 9 am to noon on Sunday. Web site: www.concarneau.org

Places to Stay & Eat *Camping Moulin d'Aurore* (☎ 02 98 50 53 08, 49 rue de Trégunc), open April to September, is 600m south-east of the Ville Close. The *Auberge de Jeunesse* (☎ 02 98 97 03 47, fax 02 98 50 87 57) is on the water at quai de la Croix, next to the Marinarium. From the tourist office, walk south to the end of quai Peneroff and turn right. Reception opens 9 am to noon and 6 to 8 pm, and beds are 48FF. *Hôtel des Halles* (☎ 02 98 97 11 41, fax 02 98 50 58 54, place de l'Hôtel de Ville) charges 220FF for a double with shower and TV.

L'Escale (☎ 02 98 97 03 31, 19 quai Carnot) is popular with local Concarnois – a hearty lunch or dinner *menu* costs just 51FF (closed Saturday night and Sunday). For excellent home-style crepes, try the unpretentious *Crêperie du Grand Chemin* (17 ave de la Gare).

Getting There & Away The bus station is in the parking lot north of the tourist office. Caoudal (☎ 02 98 56 96 72) runs up to four buses a day (three on Sunday) between

Quimper and Quimperlé (via Concarneau and Pont Aven). The trip from Quimper to Concarneau costs 26FF and takes 30 minutes.

SAINT MALO
pop 52,300

The Channel port of Saint Malo is one of the most popular tourist destinations in Brittany – and with good reason. It has a famous walled city and good nearby beaches, and is an excellent base for day trips to Mont St Michel (see the earlier Normandy section).

Orientation & Information

Saint Malo consists of the resort towns of St Servan, Saint Malo, Paramé and Rothéneuf. The old city, signposted as Intra-Muros ('within the walls') and also known as the Ville Close, is connected to Paramé by the Sillon Isthmus. The train station is 1.2km east of the old city along ave Louis Martin.

The tourist office (☎ 02 99 56 64 48, fax 02 99 56 67 00, ✉ office.de.tourisme.saint-malo@wanadoo.fr) is just outside the old city on Esplanade St Vincent. It opens 2 to 6 pm on Monday, and 9.30 am to 12.30 and 2 to 6 pm, Tuesday to Friday; and 9.30 to 1 pm and 2 to 5 pm on Saturday. In July and August, it opens 8.30 am to 8 pm Monday to Saturday, and 10 am to 7 pm on Sunday.

Cop Imprimu, 29 blvd des Talards, charges 30FF per half-hour of Web surfing and opens 9 am to 7 pm Monday to Friday, and 9 am to noon on Saturday.

Things to See & Do

Old City During the fighting of August 1944, which drove the Germans from Saint Malo, 80% of the old city was destroyed. After the war, the main historical monuments were lovingly reconstructed but the rest of the area was rebuilt in the style of the 17th and 18th centuries. The **ramparts**, built over the course of many centuries, are largely original. They afford superb views in all directions.

The **Musée de la Ville**, in the Château de Saint Malo at Porte St Vincent, deals with the history of the city and the Pays Malouin, the area around Saint Malo (27/13.50FF, closed Monday in winter).

The **Aquarium Intra-Muros** with over 100 tanks is built into the walls of the old city next to place Vauban (30/25FF). Europe's

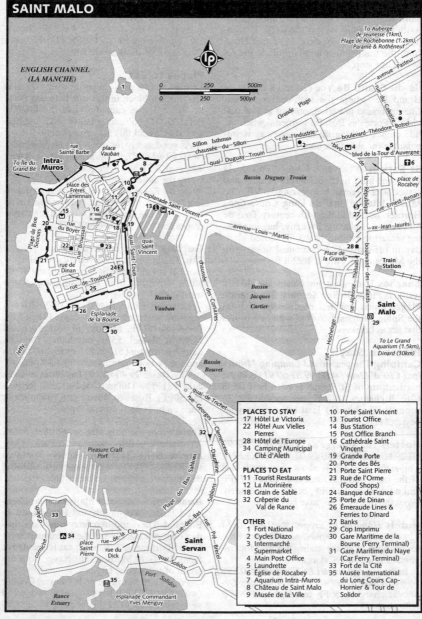

SAINT MALO

ENGLISH CHANNEL
(LA MANCHE)

To Auberge
de Jeunesse (1km),
Plage de Rochebonne (1.2km),
Paramé & Rothéneuf

To île du
Grand Bé

Intra-Muros

rue Sainte Barbe

place Vauban

place des Frères Lamennais

rue du Boyer

rue Broussais

rue de Dinan

rue de Toulouse

Plage de Bon Secours

quai Saint Vincent

quai Saint Louis

esplanade Saint Vincent

Bassin Duguay Trouin

Sillon Isthmus

chaussée-du-Sillon

quai Duguay-Trouin

Grande Plage

r de l'Industrie

boulevard-Théodore-Botrel

blvd

blvd de la-Tour d'Auvergne

place de Rocabey

rue-Ernest-Renan

av-Jean-Jaurès

avenue-Pasteur

rue-du-Calvaire

boulevard-des-Talards

avenue-Louis-Martin

Place de la Grande

rue-Alphonse-Thébault

rue-de-la-République

Train Station

Saint Malo

Bassin Jacques Cartier

Bassin Vauban

chaussée-des-Corsaires

Bassin Bouvet

rue-Hochelage

To Le Grand
Aquarium (1.5km),
Dinard (10km)

Esplanade de la Bourse

quai-de-Trichet

Pleasure Craft Port

quai-des-Bas-Sablons

rue-Georges-Clemenceau

rue-Dauphine

Plage des Bas Sablons

rue-Pré-Brécel

rue-des-Bas

rue-de-la-Cité

la Cité

rue du Dick

quai-Solidor

Saint Servan

corniche-d'Aleth

place Saint Pierre

rue-de-la-Cité

Port Solidor

esplanade Commandant Yves Menguy

Rance Estuary

jetty

PLACES TO STAY
17 Hôtel Le Victoria
22 Hôtel Aux Vielles Pierres
28 Hôtel de l'Europe
34 Camping Municipal Cité d'Aleth

PLACES TO EAT
11 Tourist Restaurants
12 La Morinière
18 Grain de Sable
32 Crêperie du Val de Rance

OTHER
1 Fort National
2 Cycles Diazo
3 Intermarché Supermarket
4 Main Post Office
5 Laundrette
6 Église de Rocabey
7 Aquarium Intra-Muros
8 Château de Saint Malo
9 Musée de la Ville

10 Porte Saint Vincent
13 Tourist Office
14 Bus Station
15 Post Office Branch
16 Cathédrale Saint Vincent
19 Grande Porte
20 Porte des Bés
21 Porte Saint Pierre
23 Rue de l'Orme (Food Shops)
24 Banque de France
25 Porte de Dinan
26 Émeraude Lines & Ferries to Dinard
27 Banks
29 Cop Imprimu
30 Gare Maritime de la Bourse (Ferry Terminal)
31 Gare Maritime du Naye (Car Ferry Terminal)
33 Fort de la Cité
35 Musée International du Long Cours Cap-Hornier & Tour de Solidor

euro currency converter 1FF = €0.15

first circular aquarium, **Le Grand Aquarium Saint Malo**, is on ave Général Patton 1.5km south of the train station (56/44FF in summer, 44/30FF off-season). Take bus No 5 from the train station and hop off at the La Madelaine stop.

Île du Grand Bé You can reach the Île du Grand Bé, where the 18th-century writer Chateaubriand is buried, on foot at low tide via the Porte des Bés. Be warned – when the tide comes rushing in, the causeway is impassable for about six hours.

St Servan St Servan's fortress, **Fort de la Cité**, was built in the mid-18th century and served as a German base during WWII. The **Musée International du Long Cours Cap-Hornier**, housed in the 14th-century Tour de Solidor on Esplanade Menguy, has interesting seafaring exhibits (20/10FF, closed Monday in off-season). A combined ticket with the Musée de la Ville is 40/20FF.

Beaches To the west, just outside the old city walls, is **Plage de Bon Secours**. The **Grande Plage**, which stretches north-eastward from the Sillon Isthmus, is spiked with tree trunks that act as breakers.

Places to Stay
Camping The year-round *Camping Municipal Cité d'Aleth* (☎ 02 99 81 60 91) is at the northern tip of St Servan next to Fort de la Cité. It charges 21/28FF per person/tent. In summer take bus No 1; at other times your best bet is bus No 6.

Hostels The *Auberge de Jeunesse* (☎ 02 99 40 29 80, fax 02 99 40 29 02, 37 ave du Père Umbricht, Paramé) is about 2km north-east of the train station. Dorm beds start at 72FF and doubles cost 170FF, breakfast included. From the train station, take bus No 5.

Hotels *Hôtel de l'Europe* (☎ 02 99 56 13 42, 44 blvd de la République) is across the roundabout from the train station. Modern, nondescript doubles start at 180FF.

In the old city, *Hôtel Le Victoria* (☎ 02 99 56 34 01, fax 02 99 40 32 78, 4 rue des Orbettes) charges 150FF for doubles (185FF with shower).

The friendly, family-run *Hôtel Aux Vieilles Pierres* (☎ 02 99 56 46 80) is in a quiet part of the old city at 4 rue des Lauriers. Doubles start at 140FF (170FF with shower); hall showers are free.

Places to Eat
Tourist restaurants, creperies and pizzerias are chock-a-block in the area between Porte St Vincent, the cathedral and the Grande Porte, but if you're after better food, and better value, avoid this area completely.

As good as any for seafood is *La Morinière* (☎ 02 99 40 85 77, 9 rue Jacques Cartier), with *menus* at 70FF and 90FF (closed Wednesday). Or try the more intimate *Grain de Sable* (☎ 02 99 56 68 72) at No 2, which serves an excellent fish soup. In St Servan, *Crêperie du Val de Rance* (11 rue Dauphine) serves Breton-style crepes and galettes (8FF to 42FF).

Getting There & Away
Bus The bus station, served by several operators, is at Esplanade St Vincent. Many of the buses departing from here also stop at the train station.

Courriers Bretons (☎ 02 99 19 70 70) has regular services to Cancale (21.50FF), Fougères (81FF, Monday to Saturday) and Mont St Michel (55FF, one hour). The first daily bus to Mont St Michel leaves at 9.50 am and the last one returns around 4.30 pm.

TIV (☎ 02 99 40 82 67) has buses to Cancale (21FF), Dinan (33FF), and Rennes (56.50FF). Buses to Dinard (20FF) run about once an hour until around 7 pm.

Train From the train station (☎ 0836 35 35 35) there is a direct service to Paris' Gare Montparnasse (315FF, 4¼ hours). Some go via Rennes (70FF). There are local services to Dinan (47FF) and Quimper (221FF).

Boat Ferries link Saint Malo with the Channel Islands, Weymouth and Portsmouth in England. There are two ferry terminals: hydrofoils, catamarans and the like depart from Gare Maritime de la Bourse; car ferries leave from the Gare Maritime du Naye. Both are south of the walled city.

From Gare Maritime de la Bourse, Condor (☎ 02 99 20 03 00) has catamaran and jetfoil services to Jersey (295FF, one-day excursion) and Guernsey (295FF) from mid-March to mid-November. Condor's service to Weymouth (270FF, 4 hours) operates daily from late May to mid-October.

Émeraude Lines (☎ 02 23 18 01 80) has ferries to Jersey, Guernsey and Sark from Gare Maritime du Naye. Service is most regular between late March and mid-November.

Between mid-March and mid-December, Brittany Ferries (☎ 0803 82 88 28) has boats to Portsmouth (passengers 270FF, 850FF to 1620FF with a car) three times a day from the Gare Maritime du Naye. In winter, ferries sail four or five times a week.

The Bus de Mer ferry (run by Émeraude Lines) links Saint Malo with Dinard (20/30FF single/return, 10 minutes) from April to September. In Saint Malo, the dock is just outside the Porte de Dinan; the Dinard quay is at 27 ave George V.

AROUND SAINT MALO
Dinard
pop 10,400

While Saint Malo's old city and beaches are geared towards middle-class families, Dinard attracts a well-heeled clientele – especially from the UK. Indeed, Dinard has the feel of an early-20th-century beach resort, with its candy-cane bathing tents and carnival rides.

Beautiful seaside trails extend along the coast in both directions from Dinard. The famous **Promenade du Clair de Lune** (Moonlight Promenade) runs along the Baie du Prieuré. The town's most attractive walk is the one that links the Promenade du Clair de Lune with Plage de l'Écluse via the rocky coast of **Pointe du Moulinet**. Bikes are not allowed.

The tourist office (☎ 02 99 46 94 12, fax 02 99 88 21 07, ✆ dinard.office.de.tourime@ wanadoo.fr) is in the colonnaded building at 2 blvd Féart. It opens 9 am to noon and 2 to 6 pm Monday to Saturday (9.30 am to 7.30 pm in July and August). Staying in Dinard can strain the budget, so consider making a day trip from Saint Malo (see that town's Getting There & Away section for details).

Loire Valley

From the 15th to 18th centuries, the fabled Loire Valley (Vallée de la Loire) was the playground of kings and nobles who expended vast fortunes and the wealth of the nation to turn it into a vast neighbourhood of lavish chateaux. Today, this region is a favourite destination of tourists seeking architectural glories from the Middle Ages and the Renaissance.

The earliest chateaux were medieval fortresses, thrown up in the 9th century to fend of marauding Vikings. As the threat of invasion diminished by the 15th century, chateaux architecture changed: fortresses gave way to pleasure palaces as the Renaissance ushered in whimsical, decorative features. From the 17th century onwards, grand country houses – built in the neoclassical style amid formal gardens – took centre stage.

BLOIS
pop 49,300

The medieval town of Blois (pronounced blwah) was a hub of court intrigue between the 15th and 17th centuries, and in the 16th century served as a second capital of France. Some dramatic events involving some of France's most important kings and historical figures took place inside the outstanding Château de Blois. The old city, seriously damaged by German attacks in 1940, retains its steep, twisting medieval streets.

Several of the Loire Valley's most rewarding chateaux, including Chambord and Cheverny, are a pleasant 20km-or-so cycle ride from Blois.

Orientation

Almost everything of interest is within walking distance of the train station, which is at the western end of ave Dr Jean Laigret. The old city lies south and east of Château de Blois, which towers over place Victor Hugo.

Information

Tourist Offices The tourist office (☎ 02 54 90 41 41, fax 02 54 90 41 49, ✆ blois.touri sm@wanadoo.fr), 3 ave Dr Jean Laigret, opens 9 am (10 am on Sunday) to 7 pm, May to September; and 9 am to 12.30 pm and 2 to 6 pm, Monday to Saturday, and 9.30 am to 12.30 pm on Sunday, the rest of the year.

Money & Post Banque de France, 4 ave Dr Jean Laigret, opens 9 am to 12.15 pm and

1.45 to 3.30 pm on weekdays. Several commercial banks face the river along quai de la Saussaye, near place de la Résistance.

The post office, rue Gallois, opens 8.30 am to 7 pm on weekdays, and 8 am to noon on Saturday.

Email & Internet Access The post office has Cyberposte. L'Étoile Tex (☎ 02 54 78 46 93, ✉ etoiletex.cybercafe@caramail.com), in the hotel of the same name at 7 rue du Bourg Neuf, is a busy bar charging 1FF per minute on its sole Internet terminal.

Things to See

Château de Blois Château de Blois (☎ 02 54 74 16 06) has a compellingly bloody history and an extraordinary mixture of architectural styles. Its four distinct sections are: early Gothic (13th century); Flamboyant Gothic (1498-1503), dating to the reign of Louis XII; early Renaissance (1515-24), from the reign of François I; and Classical (17th century). The chateau also houses an **archaeological museum** and the **Musée des Beaux-Arts** (Musem of Fine Arts), both open 9 am to noon and 2 to 5 pm, mid-October to mid-March; and 9 am to 6.30 pm (8 pm in July and August), the rest of the year (35/25FF). The chateau's evening **sound-and-light show** (60/30FF) runs May to September. For a chateau visit *and* show, buy the combination ticket (75/55FF).

Opposite, the **Maison de la Magie** (House of Magic) has magic shows, interactive exhibits and displays of clocks invented by the Blois-born magician Jean-Eugène Robert-Houdin (1805-71), after whom the great Houdini named himself. It opens 10.30 am to noon and 2 to 6.30 pm, July and August; 10 am to noon and to 6 pm, April to June and in September, October and November; and the same hours Wednesdays and at the weekend, February and March (48/42FF).

Old City Large brown signs in English pinpoint tourist sights around the predominantly-pedestrian, old city. **Cathédrale St-Louis** is named after Louis XIV, who had it rebuilt after a hurricane in 1678. There's a great view of Blois and the River Loire from the lovely **Jardins de l'Évêché** (Gardens of the Bishop's Palace), behind the cathedral.

The 15th-century **Maison des Acrobates** (House of Acrobats), 3 bis rue Pierre de Blois, is one of Blois' few medieval houses to survive the bombings of WWII. It's named after the cheeky characters carved in its timbers.

Places to Stay

Camping Two-star *Camping du Lac de Loire* (☎ 02 54 78 82 05), open April to mid-October, is in Vineuil, 4km south of Blois. It costs 49FF for two people and a tent. There's no bus service from town except in July and August (phone the camp site or the tourist office for details).

Hostels The *Auberge de Jeunesse* (☎/fax 02 54 78 27 21, 18 rue de l'Hôtel Pasquier) in Les Grouëts, is 4.5km south-west of Blois train station. It opens March to mid-November. Call first – it's often full. Dorm beds cost 68FF. The hostel closes 10 am to 6 pm. From place de la République, take bus No 4.

Hotels Near the train station, your best bet is *Hôtel St-Jacques* (☎ 02 54 78 04 15, fax 02 54 78 33 05, 7 rue Ducoux). Basic doubles cost upwards of 130FF. Opposite at No 6, family-run *Hôtel Le Savoie* (☎ 02 54 74 32 21, fax 02 54 74 29 58) has well-kept singles/doubles with shower, toilet and TV starting at 180/200FF.

North of the old city, 12-room *Hôtel du Bellay* (☎ 02 54 78 23 62, fax 02 54 78 52 04, 12 rue des Minimes) touts doubles costing 135FF to 160FF (185FF with bath or shower). *Hôtel L'Étoile Tex* (☎ 02 54 78 46 93, ✉ etoiletex .cybercafe@caramail.com, 7 rue du Bourg Neuf) has nine rooms costing 150FF to 180FF, and has Internet access (1FF per minute).

Places to Eat

In the old city, *Le Rond de Serviette* (☎ 02 54 74 48 04, 18 rue Beauvoir) claims to be Blois' most humorous and cheapest restaurant; its 49FF *menu* is unbeatable. Nearby, tuck into pasta and pizza at *La Scala* (☎ 02 54 74 88 19, 8 rue des Minimes). Its leafy summer terrace gets full fast.

La Mesa (☎ 02 54 78 70 70, 11 rue Vauvert) is a busy Franco-Italian joint, up an alleyway from 44 rue Foulerie. Its lovely courtyard is perfect for dining alfresco.

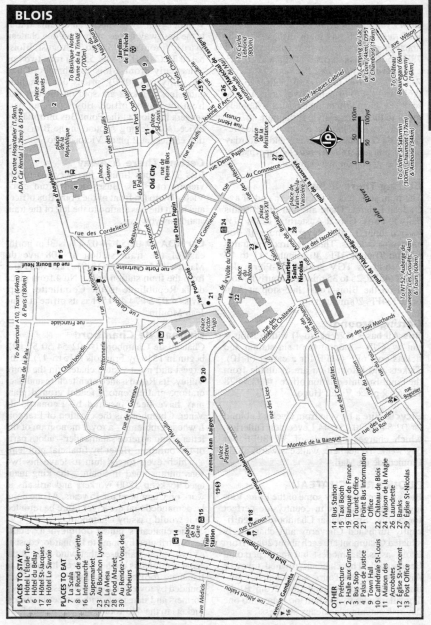

BLOIS

PLACES TO STAY
5 Hôtel L'Étoile Tex
6 Hôtel du Bellay
17 Hôtel St-Jacques
18 Hôtel Le Savoie

PLACES TO EAT
7 La Scala
8 Le Rond de Serviette
16 Intermarché Supermarket
23 Au Bouchon Lyonnais
25 La Mesa
28 Food Market
30 Au Rendez-Vous des Pêcheurs

OTHER
1 Préfecture
2 Halle aux Grains
3 Bus Stop
4 Palais de Justice
9 Town Hall
10 Cathédrale St-Louis
11 Maison de la Magie Acrobates
12 Église St-Vincent
13 Post Office
14 Bus Station
15 Taxi Booth
19 Banque de France
20 Tourist Office
21 Point Bus Information Office
22 Château de Blois
24 Maison de la Magie
26 Laundrette
27 Banks
29 Église St-Nicolas

euro currency converter 1FF = €0.15

Those seeking a splurge can try *Au Bouchon Lyonnais* (☎ 02 54 74 12 87, 25 rue des Violettes) which has main dishes of traditional French and Lyon-style cuisine costing 78FF to 128FF; *menus* are 118FF and 165FF.

Au Rendez-Vous des Pêcheurs (☎ 02 54 74 67 48, 27 rue du Foix) specialises in fish (96FF to 140FF) from the River Loire and the sea. The handwritten menu adds a homely touch to this cottage-style restaurant.

There's a *food market* on rue Anne de Bretagne on Tuesday, Thursday and Saturday until 1 pm, and an *Intermarché* supermarket near the station on ave Gambetta.

Getting There & Away

The train station is at the western end of ave Dr Jean Laigret. There are four direct trains daily to Paris' Gare d'Austerlitz (123FF, 1½ to two hours), plus several more if you change at Orléans. There are frequent trains to/from Tours (51FF, 40 minutes, 11 to 17 daily) and its TGV station, St-Pierre des Corps (49FF, 25 to 35 minutes, hourly). Most trains on the Blois-Tours line stop at Amboise (34FF, 20 minutes).

Getting Around

Bus All buses (except No 4) within Blois – run by TUB – stop at the train station and tickets cost 6FF (41FF for a carnet of 10). Tickets and information are available from the Point Bus information office (☎ 02 54 78 15 66), 2 place Victor Hugo.

Bicycle Hire a bicycle from Cycles Leblond (☎ 02 54 74 30 13), 44 Levée des Tuileries, which charges upwards of 30/180FF per day/week. To get here, walk eastwards along Promenade du Mail.

BLOIS AREA CHATEAUX

Blois is surrounded by some of the Loire Valley's finest chateaux in countryside perfect for cycling. Spectacular Chambord, magnificently furnished Cheverny and charmingly situated Chaumont are each about 20km from Blois, as is the modest but more personal Beauregard. The chateau-crowned town of Amboise (see the Tours Area Chateaux section) is also easily accessible from Blois. Travellers who try to cram too many into one day risk catching 'chateaux sickness'.

Organised Tours

Without your own wheels, an organised tour is the best way to see more than one chateau in a day. From mid-May to 31 August, Blois-based TLC (☎ 02 54 58 55 55) runs two bus tours daily from Blois to Chambord and Cheverny (65/50FF); prices don't include entry fees. Tickets are sold on the bus and from the tourist office. Buses pick up passengers in Blois at the Point Bus information office (see Getting Around in the Blois section earlier) at 2 place Victor Hugo.

Getting There & Away

Bus TLC runs limited bus services in the vicinity of Blois. Buses depart from place Victor Hugo (in front of the Point Bus office) and from the bus station to the left of the train station as you exit.

Car ADA (☎ 02 54 74 02 47) is 3km northeast of the train station at 108 ave du Maréchal Maunoury (D149). Take bus No 1 from the train station or bus No 4 from place de la République to the Cornillettes stop. Avis (☎ 02 54 74 48 15) has its office at 6 rue Jean Moulin.

Château de Chambord

Château de Chambord (☎ 02 54 50 50 02), begun in 1519 by François I (1515-47), is the largest and most visited chateau in the Loire Valley. Its Renaissance architecture and decoration, grafted onto a feudal ground plan, may have been inspired by Leonardo da Vinci. Chambord is the creation of François I, whose emblems – a royal monogram of the letter F and a fierce salamander – adorn parts of the building. Beset by financial problems – which even forced him to leave his two sons unransomed in Spain – the king managed to keep 1800 workers and artisans at work on Chambord for 15 years. At one point he demanded that the River Loire be rerouted so it would pass by Chambord.

The chateau's famed **double-helix staircase**, attributed by some to Leonardo, consists of two spiral staircases that wind around the same central axis but never meet. It leads to an Italianate **rooftop terrace**, where you're surrounded by towers, cupolas, domes, chimneys, dormers and slate roofs with geometric shapes. Tickets to the 440-room chateau are sold from

9.30 am to 4.45 pm, July and August; 9.30 am to 5.45 pm, April to June and September; and 9.30 am to 4.45 pm, October to March. Visitors already in the chateau can stay 45 minutes after ticket sales end (40/25FF).

From mid-July to mid-October, Chambord hosts a **light show** nightly. Tickets are sold from 10.30 pm until midnight in July, 10 to 11.30 pm in August, and 8.30 to 9.30 or 10 pm September to mid-October (80/50FF). Tickets covering show and chateau are available (100/55F).

Getting There & Away Chambord is 16km east of Blois and 20km north-east of Cheverny. During the school year, TLC bus No 2 average three return trips (two on Saturday, one on Sunday) from Blois to Chambord (18.50FF, 45 minutes). In July and August, your only bus option is TLC's guided tour (see the Blois Area Chateaux introduction).

Getting Around You can rent a bicycle from the Echapée Belle kiosk, next to Pont St-Michel in the castle grounds (25/70FF per hour/day).

Château de Cheverny

Château de Cheverny (☎ 02 54 79 96 29), the most magnificently furnished of the Loire Valley chateaux and still privately owned, was completed in 1634. Visitors wander through sumptuous rooms outfitted with the finest canopied beds, tapestries, paintings, painted ceilings and walls covered with embossed Córdoba leather. Three dozen panels illustrate the story of *Don Quixote* in the upstairs dining room.

The lush grounds shelter an 18th-century **Orangerie** where Leonardo da Vinci's *Mona Lisa* was hidden during WWII. The antlers of almost 2000 stags cover the walls of the **Salle des Trophées**, while the kennels keep a pack of 90 hunting hounds. Near the lake is a **balloon pad** where you can take to the skies in a hot-air balloon, mid-March to mid-October. The 10 to 12-minute ascent costs 47/43FF.

Cheverny (☎ 02 54 79 96 29, ✉ chateau .cheverny@wanadoo.fr) opens 9.15 or 9.30 am to 6.15 pm (6.30 pm July and August), April to September; and 9.15 or 9.30 am to noon and 2.15 to 5.30 pm (5 pm November to February), the rest of the year (35/24FF).

Getting There & Away Cheverny is 16km south-east of Blois and 20km south-west of Chambord.

The TLC bus from Blois to Villefranche-sur-Cher stops at Cheverny (14.60FF). Buses leave Blois at 6.50 am and 12.25 pm Monday to Saturday. The last bus back to Blois leaves at 6.58 pm. Times vary on Sunday and holidays; check schedules first.

Château de Beauregard

Built in the 16th century as a hunting lodge for François I, Beauregard is most famous for its **Galerie des Portraits**, which displays 327 portraits of notable faces from the 14th to 17th centuries.

Beauregard (☎ 02 54 70 36 74) opens from 9.30 am to noon and 2 to 5 or 6.30 pm, April to September (no break in July and August); and the same hours Thursday to Tuesday, February, March and October to January. Admission costs 40FF (students and children 30FF).

Getting There & Away

Beauregard is 6km south of Blois or a pleasant 15km cycle ride through forests from Chambord. There's road access to the chateau from the Blois-Cheverny D765 and the D956 (turn left at the village of Cellettes).

The TLC bus from Blois to St-Aignan stops at Cellettes (8.80FF), 1km south-west of the chateau, on Wednesday, Friday and Saturday; the first Blois-Cellettes bus leaves at 12.25 pm. There's no afternoon bus back except the Châteauroux-Blois line operated by Transports Boutet (☎ 02 54 34 43 95), which passes through Cellettes around 6.15 pm Monday to Saturday, and – except during August – at about 6 pm on Sunday.

Château de Chaumont

Château de Chaumont (☎ 02 54 51 26 26), set on a bluff overlooking the River Loire, resembles a feudal castle. Built in the late 15th century, it served as a booby prize for Diane de Poitier when her lover, Henry II, died in 1559, and hosted Benjamin Franklin several times when he served as ambassador to France after the American Revolution.

Its luxurious **stables** are the most famous feature, but the **Salle du Conseil** (Council Chamber) on the 1st floor, with its majolica tile floor and tapestries, and **Catherine de' Medici's bedroom** overlooking the chapel, are also remarkable. Tickets are sold from 9.30 am to 6 pm, mid-March to September; 10 am to 4.30 pm, the rest of the year (33FF).

Getting There & Away Château de Chaumont is 17km south-west of Blois and 20km north-east of Amboise in Chaumont-sur-Loire. The path leading up to the chateau begins at the intersection of rue du Village Neuf and rue Maréchal Leclerc (D751). Local trains run from Blois to Onzain (36FF, 10 minutes, eight or more daily), a 2km walk across the river from the chateau.

TOURS
pop 270,000

Lively Tours has the cosmopolitan and bourgeois air of a miniature Paris, with wide 18th-century avenues and cafe-lined boulevards. The city was devastated by German bombardment in June 1940, but much of it has been rebuilt since. The French spoken in Tours is said to be the purest in France.

Orientation

Tours' focal point is place Jean Jaurès, where the city's major thoroughfares – rue Nationale, blvd Heurteloup, ave de Grammont and blvd Béranger – join up. The train station is 300m east along blvd Heurteloup. The old city, centred around place Plumereau, is about 400m west of rue Nationale.

Information

Tourist Offices The tourist office (☎ 02 47 70 37 37, fax 02 47 61 14 22, ✉ info@ligeris.com), 78-82 rue Bernard Palissy, opens 8.30 am to 7 pm Monday to Saturday, 10 am to 12.30 pm and 2.30 to 5 pm on Sunday, May to October; and 9 am to 12.30 pm and 1.30 to 6 pm Monday to Saturday, 10 am to 1 pm on Sunday, the rest of the year.

Money Banque de France, 2 rue Chanoineau, has an exchange service, open 8.45 am to noon on weekdays. Commercial banks overlook place Jean Jaurès.

Post & Communications The post office, 1 blvd Béranger, opens 8 am to 7 pm on weekdays, and 8 am to noon on Saturday. It has a Cyberposte.

Alli@nce Micro (☎ 02 47 05 49 50), 7ter rue de la Monnaie, and Le Cyberspace (☎ 02 47 66 29 96), 13 rue Lavoisier, both charge around 25FF per hour to surf the Web; the latter is housed in a pub, open 2 pm to 5 am.

Things to See

Tours offers lovely quarters for strolling including the **old city** around place Plumereau, which is surrounded by half-timbered houses, as well as **rue du Grand Marché** and **rue Colbert**. The neighbourhood around the **Cathédrale St-Gatien**, built between 1220 and 1547 is renowned for its 13th- and 15th-century stained glass. Its Renaissance **cloister** can be visited.

The **Musée de l'Hôtel Goüin** at 25 rue du Commerce is an archaeological museum, housed in a splendid Renaissance mansion built around 1510 (21/16FF). The **Musée du Compagnonnage** (Guild Museum) overlooking the courtyard of **Abbaye St-Julien**, 8 rue Nationale, is a celebration of the skill of the French artisan (25/15FF). The **Musée des Vins de Touraine** (Museum of Touraine Wines) at No 16 is in the 13th-century wine cellars of Abbaye St-Julien (16/10FF).

The **Musée des Beaux-Arts** (Museum of Fine Arts), 18 place François Sicard, has a good collection of works from the 14th to 20th centuries (30/15FF).

Most museums in Tours close Tuesday.

Places to Stay

Camping Three-star *Camping Les Rives du Cher* (☎ 02 47 27 27 60, 63 rue de Rochpinard, St-Avertin), 5km south of Tours, opens April to mid-October. It charges 14/14/8FF per tent/person/car. From place Jean Jaurès, take bus No 5 to the St-Avertin bus terminal, then follow signs.

Hostels *Le Foyer* (☎ 02 47 60 51 51, fax 02 47 20 75 20, ✉ fjt.tours@wanadoo.fr, 16 rue Bernard Palissy), about 500m north of the train station, is a workers' dormitory. When there's space for travellers, singles/doubles cost 100/160FF. Reception closes Sunday.

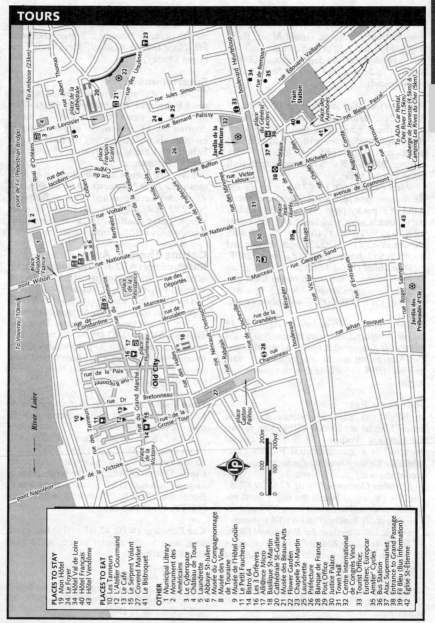

TOURS

PLACES TO STAY
19 Mon Hôtel
24 Le Foyer
34 Hôtel Val de Loire
40 Hôtel Français
43 Hôtel Vendôme

PLACES TO EAT
10 Les Tanneurs
12 L'Atelier Gourmand
13 Le Café
15 Le Serpent Volant
27 Covered Market
41 Le Bistroquet

OTHER
1   Municipal Library
2   Monument des Américains
3   Le Cyberspace
4   Château de Tours
5   Laundrette
6   Abbaye St-Julien
7   Musée du Compagnonnage
8   Musée des Vins de Touraine
9   Musée de l'Hôtel Goüin
11 Le Petit Faucheux
14 Bistro 64
16 Les 3 Orfèvres
17 All@nce Micro
18 Basilique St-Martin
20 Cathédrale St-Gatien
21 Musée des Beaux-Arts
22 Flower Garden
23 Chapelle St-Martin
25 Laundrette
26 Préfecture
28 Banque de France
29 Post Office
30 Justice Palace
31 Town Hall
32 Centre International de Congrès Vinci
33 Tourist Office;
    Eurolines; Europcar
35 Amster' Cycles
36 Bus Station
37 Atac Supermarket
38 Entrance to Grand Passage
39 Le Bleu (Bus Information)
42 Église St-Étienne

Tours' *Auberge de Jeunesse* (☎ 02 47 25 14 45, ave d'Atsnval) is 5km south of the train station in Parc de Grand Mont. Beds cost 48FF. Until 8.30 or 8.45 pm, take bus No 1 or 6 from place Jean Jaurès; from 9.20 pm to about midnight, take Bleu de Nuit bus N1 (southbound).

Hotels *Hôtel Val de Loire* (☎ 02 47 05 37 86, 33 blvd Heurteloup) looks almost like it did at the beginning of the 20th century. Basic singles/doubles with washbasin and bidet cost 100/150FF (130/180FF with shower, 200/250FF with bath and toilet). Hall showers cost 15FF.

Hôtel Français (☎ 02 47 05 59 12, 11 rue de Nantes) provides a cold welcome but is good for penny-pinchers: singles/doubles/triples/quads with washbasin and bidet cost 120/140/150/170FF (140/160/170/180 with shower or 155/190/220/250 with shower and toilet). A hall shower/breakfast costs 10/28FF.

Mon Hôtel (☎ 02 47 05 67 53, 40 rue de la Préfecture), 500m north of the train station, touts singles/doubles costing upwards of 100/115FF (170/200FF with shower and toilet).

Cheerful *Hôtel Vendôme* (☎ 02 47 64 33 54, @ hotelvendome.tours@wanadoo.fr, 24 rue Roger Salengro) is run by a friendly couple. Simple but decent singles/doubles start at 140/160FF (150/185FF with shower and toilet).

Places to Eat
In the old city, place Plumereau and rue du Frand Marché are loaded with places to eat. *Le Serpent Volant* (54 rue du Grand Marché) is a quintessential French cafe, while *Le Café* (39 rue du Dr Bretonneau) is a contemporary, funky favourite.

L'Atelier Gourmand (☎ 02 47 38 59 87, 37 rue des Cerisiers) boasts the city's most romantic courtyard terrace. It has a 49FF *plat du jour* (weekday lunches) and a 100FF *menu*.

Simple but attractive *Le Bistroquet* (☎ 02 47 05 12 76, 17 rue Blaise Pascal) specialises in paella but has French food *menus* for 44FF, 51FF and 62FF.

Les Tanneurs is a university resto-cum-cafe near the main university building on rue des Tanneurs. To dine you need a student ticket.

Sandwich stalls selling well-filled baguettes and pastries fill the Grand Passage shopping mall at 18 rue de Bordeaux. The *covered market* (place Gaston Pailhou) opens until 7 pm (1 pm Sunday).

Entertainment
Old-city cafe nightlife is centred around place Plumereau. *Les 3 Orfèvres* (☎ 02 47 64 02 73, 6 rue des Orfèvres) has live music starting at 11 pm most nights. Student nightlife abounds down tiny rue de la Longue Echelle and the southern strip of adjoining rue Dr Bretonneau.

Live jazz venues include alternative cafe-theatre *Le Petit Faucheux* (☎ 02 47 38 67 62, 23 rue des Cerisiers) and brilliant *Bistro 64* (☎ 02 47 38 47 40, 64 rue du Grand Marché) which plays Latin, Blues and *musique Française* in a 16th-century interior.

Getting There & Away
Bus Eurolines (☎ 02 47 66 45 56) has a ticket office next to the tourist office at 76 rue Bernard Palissy (closed Sunday).

The Tours bus station (☎ 02 47 05 30 49), opposite the train station on place du Général Leclerc, serves local destinations. The information desk (☎ 02 47 05 30 49) opens 7.30 am to noon and 2 to 6.30 pm Monday to Saturday. You can visit Chenonceau and Amboise in a day using CAT bus No 10 (study the schedules carefully).

Train Tours train station is on place du Général Leclerc. Several Loire Valley chateaux can be easily accessed by rail.

Paris' Gare Montparnasse is about 1¼ hours away by TGV (211FF to 277FF, 10 to 15 daily), often with a change at St-Pierre des Corps. Other services include to/from Paris' Gare d'Austerlitz (154FF, two to three hours), Bordeaux (224FF, 2¾ hours) and Nantes (135FF, 1½ to two hours).

Car Europcar (☎ 02 47 64 47 76) has an office, next to the tourist office, at 76 blvd Bernard Palissy.

Getting Around
Bus Local buses are run by Fil Bleu which has an information office (☎ 02 47 66 70 70) at 5 bis rue de la Dolve.

Bicycle From May to September, Amster'
Cycles (☎ 02 47 61 22 23, fax 02 47 61 28
48), 5 rue du Rempart, rents road and mountain bikes for 80/330FF per day/week.

TOURS AREA CHATEAUX

Several chateaux around Tours can be
reached by train, SNCF bus or bicycle. Several companies offer English-language tours
of the chateaux – reserve at the Tours tourist
office or contact the company directly.

Services Touristiques de Touraine (STT;
☎/fax 02 47 05 46 09, ◪ info@stt-millet.fr)
runs half/full-day coach tours, April to mid-
October, costing 190/300FF (including admission fees to three to four chateaux). STT's
Web site is at www.stt-millet.fr.

Château de Chenonceau

With its stylised moat, drawbridge, towers
and turrets straddling the River Cher, 16th-
century Chenonceau is everything a fairy-tale
castle should be, although its interior is only
of moderate interest.

Of the many remarkable women who created Chenonceau, Diane de Poitiers, mistress
of King Henri II, planted the garden to the
left (east) as you approach the chateau. After
Henri's death in 1559, his widow Catherine
de Médicis laid out the garden to the right
(west) as you approach the castle.

Between 1940 and 1942, the demarcation
line between Vichy-ruled France and the
German-occupied zone ran down the middle
of the Cher: the castle itself was under direct
German occupation, but southern entrance to
the 60m-long **Galerie** was in the area controlled by Marshal Pétain. For many trying to
escape the Vichy zone, this room served as
a crossing point.

Chenonceau (☎ 02 47 23 90 07, ◪ chateau
.de.chenonceau@wanadoo.fr) opens 9 am until
sometime between 4.30 pm (mid-November to
January) and 7 pm (mid-March to mid-September). Admission costs 50/40FF.

Getting There & Away

Château de Chen-
onceau, in the town of Chenonceaux (spelt
with an 'x') is 34km east of Tours. Between
Tours and Chenonceaux there are two or
three trains daily (32FF, 30 minutes); alternatively, trains on the Tours-Vierzon line
stop at Chisseaux (33FF, 24 minutes, six

daily), 2km east of Chenonceaux. In summer, take CAT bus No 10 to/from Tours
(13FF, one hour, one daily).

Château d'Azay-le-Rideau

Built on an island in the River Indre, Azay-
le-Rideau is among the most elegant of Loire
chateaux. The seven rooms open to the public are disappointing (apart from a few 16th-
century Flemish tapestries), but it's one of the
few chateaux which allows picnicking in its
beautiful park.

The chateau (☎ 02 47 45 42 04) opens
9.30 am to 6 pm, April to June and September; 9 am to 7 pm, July and August; and 9.30
am to 12.30 pm and to 5.30 pm, October to
March (35/23FF).

Getting There & Away

Azay-le-Rideau,
26km south-west of Tours, is on SNCF's
Tours-Chinon line (four or five daily Monday
to Saturday, one on Sunday). From Tours, the
30-minute trip (50 minutes by SNCF bus) costs
27FF; the station is 2.5km from the chateau.

Amboise

pop 11,000
Picturesque Amboise, an easy day trip from
Tours, is known for its **Château d'Amboise**
(☎ 02 47 57 00 98), perched on a rocky outcrop overlooking the town. The remains of
Leonardo da Vinci (1452-1519), who lived in
Amboise for the last three years of his life,
are supposedly under the chapel's northern
transept.

Inside the chateau walls, opposite 42 place
Michel Debré, is the innovative **Caveau des
Vignerons d'Amboise**, a wine cellar where
you can taste (for free) regional Touraine
wines, Easter to October. The chateau (☎ 02
47 57 00 98) opens 9 am to noon and 2 to 5
or 5.30 pm; April to October, hours are 9 am
to 6.30 pm (8 pm in July and August). Admission costs 40/33FF.

Da Vinci, who came to Amboise at the invitation of François I in 1516, lived and worked
in **Le Clos Lucé** (☎ 02 47 57 62 88) at 2 rue du
Clos Lucé, a 15th-century brick manor house
500m south-east of the chateau along rue Victor Hugo. The building contains restored rooms
and scale models of some 40 of Leonardo's
fascinating inventions. Le Clos Lucé opens 9
am to 7 pm (8 pm, July and August), March to

December; and 9 am to 6 pm (10 am to 5 pm in January), the rest of the year (39/32FF).

Information Amboise tourist office (☎ 02 47 57 09 28, fax 02 47 57 14 35, ✉ tourisme .amboise@wanadoo.fr) is next to the river, opposite 7 quai du Général de Gaulle (closed Sunday November to Easter).

Getting There & Away Several daily trains run to Amboise from both Tours (28FF, 20 minutes) and Blois (34km, 20 minutes). From Tours, you can also take CAT bus No 10 (19.60FF, 30 to 50 minutes).

South-Western France

The south-western part of France is made up of a number of diverse regions, ranging from the Bordeaux wine-growing area near the beach-lined Atlantic seaboard, to the Basque Country and the Pyrenees mountains in the south. The region is linked to Paris, Spain and the Côte d'Azur by convenient rail links.

LA ROCHELLE
pop 120,000
La Rochelle, a lively port city midway down France's Atlantic coast, is popular with middle-class French families and students on holiday. The ever-expanding Université de La Rochelle, opened in 1993, adds to the city's vibrancy. The nearby Île de Ré is ringed by long, sandy beaches.

Orientation & Information
The old city is north of the Vieux Port (old port), which is linked to the train station – 500m south-east – by ave du Général de Gaulle.

The tourist office (☎ 05 46 41 14 68) is in Le Gabut, the quarter on the south side of the Vieux Port. It opens 10 am to noon and 2 to 6 pm, Monday to Saturday (9 am to 7 pm in June and September, until 8 pm in July and August). Sunday hours are 10 am to noon (11 am to 5 pm in June and September, 9 am to 8 pm in July and August). Visit the Web site at www.ville-larochelle.fr

Things to See
To protect the harbour at night and defend it in times of war, a chain used to be stretched between the two 14th-century stone towers at the harbour entrance, the 36m **Tour St Nicolas** and **Tour de la Chaîne**; the latter houses displays on local history. West along the old city wall is **Tour de la Lanterne**, long used as a prison. All three towers are open daily; admission to each costs 25/15FF (45FF for combined ticket).

The **Musée Maritime Neptunea**, an excellent maritime museum at Bassin des Chalutiers, will soon be the permanent home of Jacques Cousteau's research ship *Calypso*. The entry fee (50/35FF) includes tours of a *chalutier* (fishing trawler). Next door, a vast, new **aquarium** is scheduled to open in early 2001.

Île de Ré
This flat, 30km-long island, fringed by beaches, begins 9km west of La Rochelle. It's connected to the mainland by a 3km toll bridge.

In July and August, and on Wednesdays, weekends and holidays in June, city buses Nos 1 or 50 (known as No 21 between the train station and place de Verdun) go to Sablanceaux (10FF, 25 minutes). Year-round, Rébus (☎ 05 46 09 20 15 in St Martin de Ré) links La Rochelle (the train station and place de Verdun) with St Martin de Ré and other island towns.

Places to Stay
Camping du Soleil (☎ 05 46 44 42 53, ave Marillac), about 1.5km south of the city centre, opens mid-May to mid-September and is often full. It's served by bus No 10.

The *Centre International de Séjour-Auberge de Jeunesse* (☎ 05 46 44 43 11, fax 05 46 45 41 48, ave des Minimes) is 2km south-west of the train station. A dorm bed costs 72FF, including breakfast. To get there, take bus No 10.

The two-star, 63-room *Hôtel Le Commerce* (☎ 05 46 41 08 22, fax 05 46 41 74 85, 6-10 place Verdun) has 11 doubles with washbasin for 135FF (165FF from May to September); doubles with shower and toilet are 235FF (290FF in season). In summer, breakfast (33FF) may be obligatory. In the pedestrianised old city, the friendly, 24-room

Hôtel Henri IV (☎ *05 46 41 25 79, fax 05 46 41 78 64, at place de la Caille)* has spacious doubles from 170FF (220FF with shower and toilet).

A few blocks from the train station, the 32-room *Terminus Hôtel* (☎ *05 46 50 69 69, fax 05 46 41 73 12, ✉ terminus@cdl-lr.com, 7 rue de la Fabrique)* offers comfortable doubles for 260FF to 300FF, depending on the season. One block north, the 22-room *Hôtel de Bordeaux* (☎ *05 46 41 31 22, fax 05 46 41 24 43, ✉ hbordeaux@free.fr, 43 rue St Nicolas)*, has quiet, pastel doubles from 175FF (285FF from June to September, including breakfast).

Places to Eat
The rustic *La Galathée (45 rue St Jean du Perot)* serves French *menus* for 65FF (weekday lunch), 85FF and 130FF (closed Tuesday and Wednesday except in July and August). The stylish *Bistrot l'Entracte (22 rue St Jean du Pérot)*, specialises in fish and seafood; the four-course *menu* costs 160FF (closed Sunday). There are dozens of other eateries along the northern side of the port and on nearby streets.

An all-you-can-eat Chinese and Vietnamese lunch/dinner buffet costs 69/75FF at *Loan Phuong (quai du Gabut)*. Couscous is on offer at *Shéhérazade (35 rue Gambetta)*, which is closed Monday at midday.

The lively *covered market (place du Marché)* opens 7 am to 1 pm daily. There's a *Prisunic* supermarket across from 55 rue du Palais (closed Sunday).

Getting There & Away
Eurolines ticketing is handled by Citram Littoral (☎ 05 46 50 53 57) at 30 cours des Dames (closed Saturday afternoon, Monday morning and Sunday).

You can take a TGV from Paris' Gare Montparnasse (320FF to 380FF, three hours) or a non-TGV from Gare d'Austerlitz (264FF). Other destinations include Bordeaux (134FF, two hours) and Tours (160FF).

Getting Around
The innovative local transport system, Autoplus (☎ 05 46 34 02 22), has its main bus hub at place de Verdun. Most lines run until sometime between 7.15 and 8 pm.

Autoplus' *Le Passeur* (4FF) ferry service links Tour de la Chaîne with the Avant Port. It runs whenever there are passengers – just press the red button on the board at the top of the gangplank.

Les Vélos Autoplus, a branch of the public transport company, will furnish you with a bike (lock included) for free for two hours (6FF per hour after that). Bikes are available daily at the Electrique Autoplus office at place de Verdun, open 6.45 am (1 pm on Sunday) to 7 pm. From May to September, they can also be picked up at the Vieux Port (across the street from 11 quai Valin).

The Electric Autoplus office at place de Verdun also rents electric motorcars with a range of 50km for 60/100FF per half-day/day. Electric Barigo scooters cost 40/70FF.

BORDEAUX
pop 650,000
Bordeaux is known for its neoclassical (if somewhat grimy) architecture, wide avenues and well-tended public parks. The city's cultural diversity (including 60,000 students), excellent museums and untouristy atmosphere make it much more than just a convenient stop between Paris and Spain. The marketing and export of Bordeaux wine are the town's most important economic activities.

Orientation
Cours de la Marne stretches for about 2km from the train station north-westward to place de la Victoire, which is linked to the tourist office area (1.5km farther north) by the pedestrians-only rue Ste Catherine. The city centre lies between place Gambetta and the Garonne River.

Information
The main tourist office (☎ 05 56 00 66 00, fax 05 56 00 66 01), 12 cours du 30 Juillet, opens 9 am to 7 pm, Monday to Saturday, and 9.45 am to 4.30 pm on Sunday. From May to September or October, it's open until 8 pm (7 pm on Sunday). Web site: www.bordeaux-tourisme.com

Money Banque de France, 15 rue de l'Esprit des Lois, changes money 9 am to noon on weekdays. There are commercial banks near the tourist office on cours de l'Intendance, rue

FRANCE

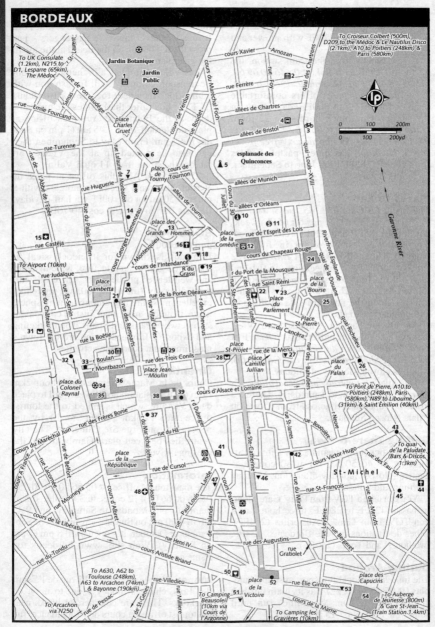

BORDEAUX

Jardin Botanique

Jardin Public

To UK Consulate
(1.2km), N215 to
D1, Lesparre (65km),
The Médoc

cours Xavier — Arnozan

rue Ferrère

cours du Maréchal Foch

cours de Verdun

rue de Fondaudège

rue Émile Fourcand

rue de Turenne

rue Huguerie

place
Charles
Gruet

allées de Chartres

allées de Bristol

esplanade des
Quinconces

allées de Munich

allées d'Orléans

place
de
Tourny

cours de
Tournon

allées de Tourny

place des
Grands
Hommes

place
de la
Comédie

cours de l'Esprit des Lois

cours du Chapeau Rouge

place
de la
Bourse

To Croiseur Colbert (500m),
D209 to the Médoc & Le Nautilus Disco
(2.1km), A10 to Poitiers (248km) &
Paris (580km)

quai des Chartrons

quai-Louis-XVIII

Garonne River

Riverfront Esplanade

quai de la Douane

quai Richelieu

To Airport (10km)

rue Castéja

place
Gambetta

cours Georges Clémenceau

cours de l'Intendance

R du Grassi

rue de la Porte Dijeaux

rue St-Rémi

place
du
Parlement

Place
St-Pierre

cours du Cancéra

place
du
Palais

To Pont de Pierre, A10 to
Poitiers (248km), Paris
(580km), N89 to Libourne
(31km) & Saint Émilion (40km)

place
St-Projet

place
Camille
Jullian

rue de la Merci

place
Jean
Moulin

cours d'Alsace et Lorraine

rue du Hâ

place de la
République

rue de Cursol

St-Michel

To quai
de la Paludate
(Bars & Discos,
1.3km)

cours Victor Hugo

rue St-François

place
du
Colonel
Raynal

rue des Frères Bonie

To A630, A62 to
Toulouse (248km),
A63 to Arcachon (74km)
& Bayonne (190km)

To Arcachon
via N250

To Camping
Beausoleil
(10km via
Cours
d'Argonne)

place
de la
Victoire

cours Aristide Briand

rue Henri IV

rue des Augustins

rue
Gratiolet

place des
Capucins

To Auberge
de Jeunesse (800m)
& Gare St-Jean
(Train Station 1.4km)

To Camping les
Gravières (10km)

cours de la Marne

euro currency converter €1 = 6.55FF

BORDEAUX

PLACES TO STAY		22	Calle Ocho	26	Porte Cailhau
8	Hôtel Touring & Hôtel Studio	50	The Down Under	28	Post Office Branch
9	Hôtel de Famille			29	Centre National JeanMoulin
20	Hôtel de la Tour Intendance	**OTHER**		30	Musée des Arts Décoratifs
33	Hôtel Boulan	1	Musée d'Histoire Naturelle	31	Main Post Office
		2	Musée d'Art Contemporain	32	Galerie des Beaux-Arts
PLACES TO EAT		3	Bord'Eaux Velos Loisirs	34	Jardin de la Mairie
7	Restaurant Baud et Millet	4	Halte Routière (Bus Station)	35	Musée des Beaux-Arts
13	Champion Supermarket	5	Girondins	36	Hôtel de Ville
	(Marché des Grands		Fountain-Monument	37	Tribunal de Grande Instance
	Hommes)	6	Laundrette		(Court; 1998)
18	La Chanterelle	10	Tourist Office	38	Cathédrale Saint André
23	Chez Édouard	11	Banque de France	39	Tour Pey-Berland (Belfry)
27	Claret's	14	Laundrette	40	Cyberstation
46	Champion Supermarket	15	Hôtel de Police	41	Musée d'Aquitaine
47	La Fournaise	16	Église Notre Dame	42	Porte de la GrosseCloche
51	Cassolette Café	17	Maison du Tourisme de la	43	Porte des Salinières
53	Fruit & Vegetable Stalls		Gironde	44	Église Saint Michel
54	Marche des Capucins	19	American Express	45	Tour Saint Michel
		21	Porte Dijeaux	48	Hôpital Saint André
ENTERTAINMENT		24	Bourse du Commerce	49	Synagogue
12	Grand Théâtre	25	Hôtel de la Douane	52	Porte d'Aquitaine

Esprit des Lois and cours du Chapeau Rouge. American Express (☎ 05 56 00 63 36) at 14 cours de l'Intendance is open on weekdays and, from June to September, also on Saturday morning.

Post & Communications The main post office, 37 rue du Château d'Eau, opens 8.30 am to 6.30 pm weekdays and until 12.30 pm on Saturday. The branch post office at place St Projet opens until 6.30 pm (noon on Saturday). Currency exchange and Cyberpostes are available at both.

Cyberstation (☎ 05 56 01 15 15), 23 Cour Pasteur, opens 11 am to 2 am (2 pm to midnight on Sunday).

Laundry The laundrettes at 5 rue de Fondaudège and 8 rue Lafaurie de Monbadon open 7 am to 9 pm.

Things to See
The following sights are listed roughly north to south. Admission to each museum costs 25/15FF (free for students and on the first Sunday of the month).

The excellent **Musée d'Art Contemporain** at 7 rue Ferrère hosts exhibits by contemporary artists (closed Monday). The **Jardin Public**, an 18th-century English-style park, is along cours de Verdun and includes Bordeaux's **botanical garden** and **Musée d'Histoire Naturelle** (Natural History Museum); closed Tuesday.

The most prominent feature of **Esplanade des Quinconces**, a vast square laid out in 1820, is a towering fountain-monument to the Girondins, a group of moderate, bourgeois legislative deputies executed during the French Revolution.

The neoclassical **Grand Théâtre** at place de la Comédie was built in the 1770s. **Porte Dijeaux**, which dates from 1748, leads from **place Gambetta**, which has a garden in the middle, to the pedestrianised commercial centre. A few blocks south, the **Musée des Arts Décoratifs** (Museum of Decorative Arts), 39 rue Bouffard, specialises in faïence, porcelain, silverwork, glasswork, furniture and the like; closed Tuesday.

In 1137, the future King Louis VII married Eleanor of Aquitaine in **Cathédrale St André**. Just east of the cathedral, there's the 15th-century, 50m-high belfry, **Tour Pey-Berland**, which can be climbed for 25/15FF (closed Monday). The **Centre National Jean Moulin** (Jean Moulin Documentation Centre), facing the north side of the cathedral, has exhibits on France during WWII; closed Monday.

At 20 cours d'Albert, the **Musée des Beaux-Arts** occupies two wings of the 18th-century Hôtel de Ville and houses a large collection of paintings, including 17th-century Flemish, Dutch and Italian works (closed Tuesday). The outstanding **Musée d'Aquitaine**, 20 cours Pasteur, illustrates the history and ethnography of the Bordeaux area (closed Monday).

The **Synagogue** (1882) on rue du Grand Rabbin Joseph Cohen (just west of rue Ste Catherine) is a mixture of Sephardic and Byzantine styles. During WWII the Nazis turned the complex into a prison. Visits are generally possible Monday to Thursday from 9 am to noon and 2 to 4 pm – ring the bell marked *gardien* at 213 rue Ste Catherine.

Places to Stay

The 150-spot *Camping Les Gravières* (☎ 05 56 87 00 36, place de Courréjean in Villenave d'Ornon), open all year, is 10km south-east of the city centre. By bus, take line B from place de la Victoire towards Corréjean and get off at the terminus.

About 700m west of the train station, the *Auberge de Jeunesse* (☎ 05 56 91 59 51, 22 cours Barbey) is being completely renovated and is scheduled to reopen in April 2001.

North of the centre near place de Tourny (from the station take bus Nos 7 or 8), *Hôtel Studio* (☎ 05 56 48 00 14, fax 05 56 81 25 71, 26 rue Huguerie) and three affiliated hotels offer charmless singles/doubles with shower, toilet and (in most cases) cable TV starting at an absolute minimum of 98/120FF. The hotel's mini-cybercafe charges guests 10FF an hour. Web site: www.hotel-bordeaux.com. *Hôtel de Famille* (☎ 05 56 52 11 28, fax 05 56 51 94 43, 76 cours Georges Clemenceau) has rather ordinary but homy doubles from 120FF (185FF with shower and toilet).

A few blocks south-west of place Gambetta, the quiet *Hôtel Boulan* (☎ 05 56 52 23 62, fax 05 56 44 91 65, 28 rue Boulan) has decent singles/doubles from 100/110FF (120/140FF with shower).

Just east of place Gambetta, you're assured of a warm welcome at the two-star *Hôtel de la Tour Intendance* (☎ 05 56 81 46 27, fax 05 56 81 60 90, 16 rue de la Vieille Tour), where ordinary doubles/triples cost 250/320FF. Another excellent deal is the two-star

Hôtel Touring (☎ 05 56 81 56 73, fax 05 56 81 24 55, 16 rue Huguerie), which has gigantic and spotless singles/doubles with shower for 180/220FF (220/240FF with toilet, too).

Places to Eat

La Chanterelle (3 rue de Martignac) serves moderately priced traditional French and regional cuisine; *menus* cost 75FF (lunch only) and 98FF (closed on Wednesday night and Sunday). Bistro-style cuisine and south-western French specialities are on offer at *Claret's* (☎ 05 56 01 21 21, place Camille Julien), whose *menus* cost 65FF (lunch only), 98 and 160FF (closed Saturday lunchtime and Sunday). The popular *Chez Édouard* (16 place du Parlement) purveys French bistro-style meat and fish dishes; *menus* cost 59FF (lunch except Sunday), 70FF and 99FF. There are lots of eateries along nearby rue du Parlement Ste Catherine, rue des Piliers de Tutelle and rue St Rémi.

Restaurant Baud et Millet (19 rue Huguerie) serves cheese-based cuisine (most dishes are vegetarian), including all-you-can-eat raclette for 110FF (closed Sunday).

The dinner-only *La Fournaise* (23 rue de Lalande) serves the delicious cuisine of Réunion; *menus* cost 80FF to 140FF (closed Sunday and Monday).

The inexpensive cafes and restaurants around place de la Victoire include the *Cassolette Café* (20 place de la Victoire), which serves family-style French food on small/large *cassolettes* (terracotta plates) that cost 11/33FF (open daily).

There's a *Champion* supermarket at place des Grands Hommes in the basement of the mirror-plated Marché des Grands Hommes (closed Sunday). Near *Marché des Capucins*, a covered food market just east of place de la Victoire (open 6 am to 1 pm, closed Monday), you'll find super-cheap *fruit and vegetable stalls* along rue Élie Gintrec (open until 1 pm, closed Sunday).

Entertainment

Bordeaux has a hopping nightlife scene. *The Down Under* (104 cours Aristide Briand), run by an ex-Aucklander, is a favourite of Anglophones; hours are 7 or 8 pm to 2 am daily. One of the really hot venues is a

Cuban-style bar called **Calle Ocho** (*24 rue des Piliers de Tutelle*), open 5 pm to 2 am (closed Sunday).

Among the best of the late-late dancing bars is tropical beach-themed **La Plage** (☎ 05 56 49 02 46, *40 quai de la Paludate*) along the river east of the train station, which opens from midnight to 5 am Wednesday to Saturday nights.

Getting There & Away

Buses to places all over the Gironde and nearby departments leave from the Halte Routière (☎ 05 56 43 68 43), in the north-east corner of esplanade des Quinconces; schedules are posted.

Bordeaux's train station, Gare St Jean (☎ 0836 35 35 39), is about 3km south-east of the city centre at the end of cours de la Marne. By TGV it takes only about three hours to/from Paris' Gare Montparnasse (352FF to 399FF). The trip to Bayonne (135FF) takes 1¾ hours.

BORDEAUX VINEYARDS

The Bordeaux wine-producing region, 1000 sq km in extent, is subdivided into 57 production areas called *appellations*, whose climate and soil impart distinctive characteristics to the wines grown there.

Over 5000 chateaux (also known as *domaines*, *crus* and *clos*) produce the region's highly regarded wines, which are mainly reds. Many smaller chateaux accept walk-in visitors (some are closed during the October grape harvest); the larger and better known ones usually require that you phone ahead.

Each vineyard has different rules about tasting – at some it's free, others charge entry fees, and others don't serve wine at all. Look for signs reading *dégustation* (wine tasting), *en vente directe* (direct sales), *vin à emporter* (wine to take away) and *gratuit* (free).

Opposite Bordeaux's main tourist office, the Maison du Vin de Bordeaux (☎/fax 05 56 00 22 66), open weekdays (and, in summer, on Saturday), has details on vineyard visits. It can also supply information on the many local *maisons du vin* (special wine-oriented tourist offices). Web site: www.vins-bordeaux.fr.

On Wednesday and Saturday (daily from May to October), the Bordeaux tourist office runs five-hour bus tours in French and English to local wine chateaux (160/140FF).

St Émilion
pop 400

The medieval village of St Émilion, 39km east of Bordeaux, is surrounded by vineyards renowned for their full-bodied, deeply coloured red wines. The most interesting historical sites – including the **Église Monolithe**, carved out of solid limestone from the 9th to the 12th centuries – can be visited only on the 45-minute guided tours (33/20FF) offered by the tourist office (☎ 05 57 55 28 28), which is at place des Créneaux (open daily). The 50 or so wine shops include the cooperative Maison du Vin (☎ 05 57 55 50 55) at place Pierre Meyrat, around the corner from the tourist office, which is owned by the 250 chateaux whose wines it sells (open daily).

From Bordeaux, St Émilion is accessible by train (44FF, 35 minutes, two or three a day) and bus (at least once a day, except on Sundays and holidays from October to April). The last train back usually departs at 6.27 pm.

THE MÉDOC

North-west of Bordeaux, along the western shore of the Gironde Estuary, lie some of Bordeaux's most celebrated vineyards. To the west, fine sandy beaches bordered by dunes stretch for some 200km from Pointe de Grave south along the **Côte d'Argent** (Silver Coast) to the Bassin d'Arcachon and beyond. The coastal dunes abut a vast pine forest planted in the 19th century to stabilise the drifting sands.

The most beautiful part of this renowned wine-growing area is north of **Pauillac**, along the D2 and the D204 (towards Lesparre). Vineyards around here include the **Château Lafitte Rothschild** (☎ 01 53 89 78 00 in Paris) and the equally illustrious **Château Mouton Rothschild** (☎ 05 56 73 21 29). Both places require advance reservations; the latter charges 30FF.

Seaside resorts include the beach resort of **Soulac-sur-Mer** (population 2800), where the two-star, 13-room **Hôtel La Dame de Cœur** (☎ 05 56 09 80 80, fax 05 56 09 97 47, ✉ la.dame.de.coeur@wanadoo.fr, *103 rue de la Plage*) has doubles from 250FF.

The relaxed naturist village of **Euronat** (☎ 05 56 09 33 33, fax 05 56 09 30 27), about 80km north of Bordeaux, covers 3.3 sq km (including 1.5km of dune-lined beachfront). The cheapest four-person bungalows range from 210FF a night (in winter) to 390FF a night (July and August), minimum three nights. Web site: www.euronat.fr.

Getting There & Away
The northern tip of the Médoc, Pointe de Grave, is linked to Royan by car ferries. Three to five Citram Aquitaine buses a day connect Bordeaux with Lesparre, Soulac-sur-Mer (two hours) and Point de Grave (76FF, 2¼ hours). SNCF bus-train combos linking Bordeaux with Margaux, Pauillac (54FF, one hour), Lesparre, Soulac (83FF, two hours) and Pointe de Grave (or nearby Le Verdon, 89FF) run five times a day (twice on weekends).

ARCACHON
pop 11,800
The beach resort of Arcachon, in the south-west corner of the triangular **Bassin d'Arcachon** (Arcachon Bay), became popular with bourgeois residents of Bordeaux at the end of the 19th century. Its major attractions are the sandy seashore and the extraordinary, 114m-high **Dune de Pyla**, Europe's highest sand dune, which is 8km south of town.

The flat area that abuts the **Plage d'Arcachon** (the town's beach) is known as the **Ville d'Été** (Summer Quarter). The liveliest section is around **Jetée Thiers**, one of the two piers, which is linked to pine-shaded **Cap Ferret** by boat. The **Ville d'Hiver** (Winter Quarter), on the tree-covered hillside south of the centre, was built about a century ago.

A few kilometres east of Arcachon, the oyster port of **Gujan Mestras** sprawls along 9km of coastline. Super-fresh and remarkably cheap oysters can be sampled at **Port de Larros**, one of the town's seven ports.

The tourist office (☎ 05 57 52 97 97, fax 05 57 52 97 77) is a few hundred metres from the train station at place Président Roosevelt (closed on Sunday and holidays except from April to September, when hours are 10 am to 1 pm). Web site: www.arcachon.com.

Places to Stay
The steep, inland side of the Dune de Pyla is gradually burying five large and rather pricey *camping grounds*, open about mid-April to mid-October.

Hotel rooms are nearly impossible to find in July and August. The 15-room *Hôtel Saint*

Christaud (☎/fax 05 56 83 38 53, 8 Allée de la Chapelle) has modern doubles for 99FF to 200FF, depending on the season. The down-to-earth *La Paix* (☎ 05 56 83 05 65, 8 ave de Lamartine), open late May to September, has simple doubles/quads from 171/283FF (25% more from mid-June to early September), including breakfast.

Getting There & Away
Some of the trains from Bordeaux to Arcachon (54FF, 55 minutes, 11 to 18 a day) – which also stop at Gujan Mestras near the Port de Larros – are coordinated with TGVs from Paris' Gare Montparnasse.

BAYONNE
pop 40,000
Bayonne is the most important city in the French part of the Basque Country (Euskadi in Basque, Pays Basque in French), a region straddling the French-Spanish border.

Its most important festival is the annual Fêtes de Bayonne, beginning on the first Wednesday in August. The festival includes a 'running of the bulls' like Pamplona's except that here they have cows rather than bulls.

Orientation & Information
The Adour and Nive Rivers split Bayonne into three: St Esprit, north of the Adour; Grand Bayonne, the oldest part of the city, on the west bank of the Nive; and the very Basque Petit Bayonne to its east.

The tourist office (☎ 05 59 46 01 46, fax 05 59 59 37 55, ❷ bayonne.tourisme@wanadoo.fr) is on place des Basques. It opens 9 am to 6.30 pm weekdays (10 am to 6 pm on Saturday). July and August hours are 9 am to 7 pm daily (10 am to 1 pm Sunday). Its brochure *Fêtes* is useful for cultural and sporting events while *Promenades and Discoveries*, in English, describes a self-guided walk around town.

You can log on at Cyber Net Café (☎ 05 59 55 78 98) on place de la République. Open 7 am to 2 am daily (from midday on Sunday), it charges 1FF per minute or 45FF an hour.

Things to See & Do
Construction of the Gothic **Cathédrale Ste Marie** on place Monseigneur Vansteenberghe began in the 13th century and was completed in 1451. The entrance to the

beautiful 13th-century **cloister** is on place Louis Pasteur.

The **Musée Bonnat** (20/10FF; closed Tuesday) at 5 rue Jacques Laffitte in Petit Bayonne, has a diverse collection, including a whole gallery of paintings by Rubens.

Places to Stay
Camping *Camping de Parme* (☎ 05 59 23 03 00, route de l'Aviation), 1.25km north-east of the Biarritz-La Négresse train station, charges 79FF for two people and tent. Open all year, it's usually booked during July and August.

Hostels The lively *Auberge de Jeunesse d'Anglet* (☎ 05 59 58 70 00, fax 05 59 58 70 07, ✆ biarritz@fuaj.fr, 19 route des Vignes) at 19 Route des Vignes in Anglet comes complete with a Scottish pub. Popular with surfers, it's open from mid-February to mid-November; reservations are essential in summer. B&B costs 73FF and you can also pitch a tent here for 48FF per person, including breakfast.

From Bayonne, take bus No 7 and get off at Moulin Barbot, a 10-minute walk away. From Biarritz, town or station, take bus No 9.

Hotels You can tumble off the train into hyperfriendly *Hôtel Paris-Madrid* (☎ 05 59 55 13 98, fax 05 59 55 07 22), just beside the station. Cheapest singles are 95FF, and pleasant doubles without/with shower start at 130/160FF. Big rooms with bathroom and cable TV which can take up to four cost from 210FF. Nearby at 1 rue Ste Ursule *Hôtel Monte Carlo* (☎ 05 59 55 02 68) has simple rooms from 90FF and larger ones with bathroom for two to four people from 170FF to 250FF.

In Petit Bayonne, *Hôtel des Basques* (☎ 05 59 59 08 02) on place Paul Bert has large, pleasant rooms with washbasin and toilet for between 135FF and 180FF and ones with full bathroom from 170FF. Showers cost 10FF.

The mid-range *Hôtel des Basses-Pyrénées* (☎ 05 59 59 00 29, fax 05 59 59 42 02, 12 rue Tour de Sault, closed January) is built around a 17th-century tower. Doubles/triples/quads with bathroom start at 300/330/350FF. It also has a few rooms with washbasin for 150FF to 170FF and private parking (30FF).

Places to Eat
Nowhere in town is more Basque than *Restaurant Euskalduna Ostatua*, near Hôtel des Basques at 61 rue Pannecau, where main dishes are a bargain 35FF to 50FF. It's open for lunch, weekdays only. Over the Nive River the family-run *Bar-Restaurant du Marché* (39 rue des Basques), where the cooking's homely and the owner's wife mothers everyone, will fill you to bursting for under 100FF. Open for lunch only.

A couple of blocks west, cheerful *Restaurant Dacquois* (48 rue d'Espagne) serves juicy sandwiches from 12FF and has a great value 65FF *menu*.

The central market, *Les Halles*, on the west quay (quai Amiral Jauréguiberry) of the Nive River, is open every morning except Sunday.

Entertainment
The greatest concentration of pubs and bars is in Petit Bayonne, especially along rue Pannecau and quai Galuperie. *La Pompe* (☎ 05 59 25 48 12, 7 rue des Augustins), a lively discotheque, throbs from 10 pm to dawn Thursday to Sunday.

Getting There & Away
Bus From place des Basques, ATCRB buses (☎ 05 59 26 06 99) run to St-Jean de Luz (22FF, 40 minutes, 10 daily) with connections for Hendaye (36FF, one hour). Two Transportes Pesa buses run to Irún and San Sebastián in Spain (38FF, 1¾ hours, daily except Sunday).

From the train station car park, RDTL (☎ 05 59 55 17 59) runs services northwards into Les Landes. For beaches north of Bayonne, such as Mimizan Plage and Moliets Plage, get off at Vieux Boucau (39FF, 1¼ hours). TPR (☎ 05 59 27 45 98) has three buses daily to Pau (85FF, 2¼ hours).

Bayonne is one of three hubs in South-West France for Eurolines, whose buses stop in place Charles de Gaulle, opposite the company office (☎ 05 59 59 19 33) at No 3.

Train The train station is just north of Pont St Esprit bridge. TGVs run to/from Paris' Gare Montparnasse (428FF, five hours). Two daily non-TGV trains go overnight to Paris' Gare d'Austerlitz (401FF or 471FF with couchette) in about eight hours.

There's a frequent service to Biarritz (13FF, 10 minutes), St-Jean de Luz (26FF, 25 minutes) and St-Jean Pied de Port (47FF, one hour), plus the Franco-Spanish border towns of Hendaye (37FF, 40 minutes) and Irún (45 minutes).

Some other destinations are Bordeaux (145FF, 2¼ hours, about 12 daily), Lourdes (126FF, 1¾ hours, six daily) and Pau (82FF, 1¼ hours, eight daily).

BIARRITZ
pop 30,000

The classy coastal town of Biarritz, 8km west of Bayonne, has fine beaches and some of Europe's best surfing. Unfortunately, it can be a real budget-buster – consider making it a day trip from Bayonne, as lots of French holidaymakers do. Many surfers camp or stay at one of the two excellent youth hostels – in Biarritz and in Anglet (see the Bayonne section).

Biarritz's Festival International de Folklore is held in early July.

Orientation & Information

Place Clemenceau, at the heart of Biarritz, is just south of Grande Plage, the main beach. The tourist office (☎ 05 59 22 37 10, fax 05 59 24 14 19, ✉ biarritz.tourisme@biarritz.tm.fr), 1 square d'Ixelles, is one block east of the square. It opens 9 am to 6.45 pm daily. In July and August it's open 8 am to 8 pm. It publishes Biarritzcope, a free monthly guide to what's on. In July and August, it has a branch at the train station.

Check your emails at Génius Informatique (1FF per minute, 50FF an hour).

Things to See & Do

The Grande Plage, lined in season with striped bathing tents, stretches from the Casino Bellevue to the stately Hôtel du Palais. North of the hotel is Plage Miramar and the 1834 Phare de Biarritz. Beyond this lighthouse the superb surfing beaches of Anglet extend for 4km (take bus No 9 from place Clemenceau).

The Musée de la Mer, Biarritz' sea museum, is on Pointe Atalaye overlooking Rocher de la Vierge, an islet reached by a short footbridge which offers sweeping coastal views. The museum (45/30FF) has a 24-tank aquarium plus seal and shark pools.

Places to Stay

Camping Biarritz Camping (☎ 05 59 23 00 12, 28 rue d'Harcet), open June to late September, is about 3km south-west of the centre and costs 105FF for two people and tent. Take bus No 9 to the Biarritz Camping stop.

Hostels For Biarritz's Auberge de Jeunesse (05 59 41 76 00, fax 05 59 41 76 07, ✉ auber gejeune.biarritz@wanadoo.fr, 8 rue Chiquito de Cambo), follow the railway westwards from the train station for 800m. B&B is 85FF and half-board, 120FF.

The otherwise expensive Hôtel Barnetche (☎ 05 59 24 22 25, fax 05 59 24 98 71, 5 avenue Charles Floquet) has dorm bunks for 100FF.

Hotels Nowhere is cheap in Biarritz, but prices drop by up to 25% outside summer.

In the Vieux Port area, trim Hôtel Palym (☎ 05 59 24 16 56, 7 rue du Port Vieux) has singles/doubles with toilet for 170/220FF (290FF with bathroom). Hôtel Atlantic (☎ 05 59 24 34 08) at No 10 has singles/doubles with washbasin for 195/215FF and doubles/triples/ quads with bathroom for 295/330/350FF.

Attractive Hôtel Etche-Gorria (☎ 05 59 24 00 74, 21 ave du Maréchal Foch) has doubles without/with bathroom for 180/290FF.

Places to Eat

Popular Le Bistroye (☎ 05 59 22 01 02, 6 rue Jean Bart), closed Wednesday evening and all Sunday, has delicious main dishes between 75FF and 95FF. Next door, La Mamounia (☎ 05 59 24 76 08) doles out couscous from 80FF and other Moroccan specialities from 95FF.

There are quite a few decent little restaurants around Les Halles. At Bistrot des Halles (☎ 05 59 24 21 22, 1 rue du Centre), for example, a three-course meal with wine from the chalkboard menu will set you back about 150FF.

The covered market off ave Victor Hugo is open 7 am to 1.30 pm daily.

Entertainment

Popular bar areas include the streets around rue du Port Vieux, the covered market area and around place Clemenceau. Two central discos are Le Caveau, 4 rue Gambetta and Le Flamingo inside the Casino.

Getting There & Away

Most local STAB buses stop beside the town hall, from where Nos 1 and 2 go to Bayonne's town hall and station.

Biarritz-La Négresse train station is 3km south of the centre and served by buses Nos 2 and 9. SNCF has a downtown office (☎ 05 59 24 00 94) at 13 ave du Maréchal Foch.

AROUND BIARRITZ
St-Jean Pied de Port
pop 1500

The walled Pyrenean town of St-Jean Pied de Port, 53km south-east of Bayonne, was once the last stop in France for pilgrims heading for the Spanish pilgrimage city of Santiago de Compostela. Nowadays it's a popular departure point for latter day hikers and bikers but can be hideously crowded in summer. The climb to the 17th-century **Citadelle** merits the effort with fine views.

The tourist office (☎ 05 59 37 03 57) is on place Charles de Gaulle. Riverside *Camping Municipal Plaza Berri* (☎ *05 59 37 11 19, ave du Fronton*), open Easter to September, charges 42FF for two people and tent. Cheerful *Hôtel des Remparts* (☎ *05 59 37 13 79, 16 place Floquet*) has rooms with bathroom from 210FF.

For lunch, *Chez Dédé* (☎ *05 59 37 16 40*), just inside the porte de France, has as many as seven good value, tasty *menus*, ranging from the modest *menu du routard* at 50FF to the *suggestion du chef* at 135FF.

Half the reason for coming to St-Jean Pied de Port is the scenic train trip from Bayonne (47FF, one hour, up to four daily).

LOURDES
pop 15,000

In 1858, 14-year-old Bernadette Soubirous saw the Virgin Mary within a small grotto in a series of 18 visions, later confirmed as bona fide apparitions by the Vatican. This simple peasant girl, who lived out her short life as a nun, was canonised as Ste Bernadette in 1933.

Some five million pilgrims annually, including many seeking cures for their illnesses, converge on Lourdes from all over the world.

In counterpoint to the fervent, almost medieval piety of the pilgrims is a tacky display of commercial exuberance.

Orientation & Information

Lourdes' two main east-west streets are rue de la Grotte and, 300m north, blvd de la Grotte. Both lead to the Sanctuaires Notre Dame de Lourdes. The principal north-south thoroughfare connects the train station with place Peyramale and the tourist office (☎ 05 62 42 77 40, fax 05 62 94 60 95, ✉ lourdes@sudfr.com), which opens 9 am to noon and 2 to 6 pm, Monday to Saturday (to 7 pm between Easter and mid-October, when it's also open 10 am to 6 pm on Sunday). From June to September, there is no midday closure.

The office sells the *Visa Passeport Touristique* (169FF), allowing entry to five museums in Lourdes.

Things to See

The huge religious complex that has grown around the cave where Bernadette saw the Virgin, is just west of the town centre. The main Pont St Michel entrance is open from 5 am to midnight.

Major sites include the **Grotte de Massabielle**, where Bernadette had her visions, its walls today worn smooth by the touch of millions of hands, the nearby **pools** in which 400,000 people immerse themselves each year; and the **Basilique du Rosaire** (Basilica of the Rosary). Dress modestly.

From the Sunday before Easter to mid-October, solemn **torch-lit processions** leave nightly at 8.45 pm from the Grotte de Massabielle while the **Procession Eucaristique** (Blessed Sacrament Procession) takes place daily at 5 pm.

Places to Stay

Camping Tiny *Camping de la Poste* (☎ *05 62 94 40 35, 26 rue de Langelle*), a few blocks east of the tourist office, is open Easter to mid-October. Charging 15/21FF per person/tent, it also has a few excellent value rooms with bathroom for 150FF.

Hotels Lourdes has plenty of budget hotels. Near the train station, friendly *Hôtel d'Annecy* (☎ *05 62 94 13 75, 13 ave de la Gare*) is open from Easter to October.

Singles/doubles/triples/quads with wash-basin are 95/152/176/198FF (140/195/215/223FF with bathroom). In the town centre, *Hôtel St Sylve* (*☎/fax 05 62 94 63 48, 9 rue de la Fontaine*) has large singles/doubles for 75/140FF (100/160FF with shower). Open April to October.

The stylish *Hôtel de la Grotte* (*☎ 05 62 94 58 87, fax 05 62 94 20 50, 66 rue de la Grotte*) has fine balconies and a gorgeous garden. Its singles/doubles with all mod-cons start at 390/420FF. Open April to October.

Places to Eat

Restaurants close early in this pious town; even *McDonald's* (*7 place du Marcadal*) is slammed shut at 10.30 pm. *Restaurant le Magret* (*10 rue des Quatre Frères Soulas*), opposite the tourist office, has excellent value *menus* at 80FF and 150FF. Next door, *La Rose des Sables* specialises in couscous (from 78FF). Both close Mondays. The covered *market* is on place du Champ Commun, south of the tourist office.

Getting There & Away

Bus The bus station, down rue Anselme Lacadé east of the covered market, serves regional towns including Pau (32FF, 1¼ hours, four to six daily). SNCF buses to the Pyrenean towns of Cauterets (39FF, one hour, five daily) and Luz-St-Sauveur (40FF, one hour, six daily) leave from the train station's car park.

Train The train station is 1km east of the sanctuaries. Trains connect Lourdes with many cities including Bayonne (106FF, 1¾ hours, three to four daily), Bordeaux (172FF, 2½ hours, six daily), Pau (39FF, 30 minutes, over 10 daily) and Toulouse (125FF, 2¼ hours, seven daily). There are five TGVs daily to Paris' Gare Montparnasse (478FF, 6 hours) and one overnight train to Gare d'Austerlitz (409FF, nine hours).

The Dordogne

The Dordogne (better known as Périgord in France) was one of the cradles of human civilisation, and a number of local caves, including the world-famous Lascaux, are adorned with extraordinary prehistoric paint-ings. The region is also renowned for its cuisine, which makes ample use of those quintessential French delicacies, *truffes du Périgord* (black truffles) and *foie gras*, the fatty liver of force-fed geese.

PÉRIGUEUX
pop 33,000

Founded over 2000 years ago on a curve in the gentle Isle River, Périgueux has one of France's best museums of prehistory, the **Musée du Périgord** at 22 cours Tourny (closed Tuesday and holidays). Admission costs 20/10FF.

The old city, known as **Puy St Front**, lies between blvd Michel Montaigne and the Isle River. The tourist office (*☎ 05 53 53 10 63, fax 05 53 09 02 50,* *✉ tourisme.perigueux@perigord.tm.fr*) is at 26 place Francheville, next to a fortified, medieval tower called **Tour Mataguerre**. It opens 9 am to 6 pm (closed Sunday). From mid-June to mid-September, daily hours are 9 am to 7 pm (10 am to 6 pm Sunday and holidays).

Places to Stay

The year-round *Barnabé Plage Campground* (*☎ 05 53 53 41 45*) is about 2.5km east of the train station along the Isle River. By bus, take line No 8 to the rue des Bains stop.

About 600m south of the cathedral, the *Foyer des Jeunes Travailleurs* (*☎ 05 53 53 52 05, rue des Thermes Prolongée*), just off blvd Lakanal, charges 73FF for a bed, including breakfast.

Near the train station, the cheapest hotel is the family-run, 16-room *Hôtel des Voyageurs* (*☎ 05 53 53 17 44, 26 rue Denis Papin*), where basic but clean doubles cost only 80FF (100FF with shower). Reception may be closed on weekend afternoons (hours posted).

Getting There & Away

The bus station (*☎ 05 53 08 91 06*), on place Francheville (just south-west of the tourist office), has buses to Sarlat (50.50FF, 1½ hours, one or two a day) via the Vézère Valley town of Montignac (35FF, 55 minutes).

The train station (*☎ 0836 35 35 39*), on rue Denis Papin (about 1km north-west of the tourist office), is served by local buses Nos 1, 4 and 5. Destinations include Bordeaux (99FF, 1¼ hours), Les Eyzies de Tayac (41FF,

30 minutes, two to four a day), Paris' Gare d'Austerlitz (268FF, four to five hours) and Sarlat (75FF).

SARLAT-LA-CANÉDA
pop 10,000

This beautiful town, situated between the Dordogne and Vézère Rivers, is graced by numerous Renaissance-style, 16th and 17th-century stone buildings. On Saturday mornings there's a colourful market on place de la Liberté and along rue de la République – edible (though seasonal) offerings include truffles, mushrooms, geese and parts thereof.

The main drag is known as rue de la République where it passes through the heart-shaped old town. The tourist office (☎ 05 53 59 27 67) occupies the 15th and 16th-century Hôtel de Maleville on place de la Liberté.

Places to Stay

The modest but friendly, 15-bed *Auberge de Jeunesse* (☎ 05 53 59 47 59 or ☎ 05 53 30 21 27, 77 ave de Selves) opens mid-March to mid-November. A bed costs 50FF; small tents can be pitched in the tiny back garden for 30FF a person (5FF more for the first night). Cooking facilities are available. Call ahead to check availability.

Doubles start at 250FF at the two-star places: *Hôtel de la Mairie* (☎ 05 53 59 05 71, 13 place de la Liberté), near the tourist office (open March to December); and *Hôtel Les Récollets* (☎ 05 53 31 36 00, fax 05 53 30 32 62, ✉ otelrecol@aol.com, 4 rue Jean-Jacques Rousseau), up an alley just west of rue de la République.

Getting There & Away

There are one or two buses a day (fewer in July and August) from place de la Petite Rigaudie to Périgueux (50.50FF, 1½ hours) via the Vézère Valley town of Montignac (35 minutes).

Sarlat's tiny train station (☎ 0836 35 35 39) is linked to Bordeaux (119FF, 2½ hours), Périgueux (75FF) and Les Eyzies de Tayac (47FF, 50 minutes, two a day).

VÉZÈRE VALLEY

Périgord's most important prehistoric sites are about 45km south-east of Périgueux and 20km north-west of Sarlat in the Vézère Valley,

mainly between Les Eyzies de Tayac and Montignac. Worthwhile caves not mentioned below include the **Grotte du Grand Roc** and **La Roque St Christophe**. For details on public transport, see Getting There & Away under Périgueux and Sarlat.

Les Eyzies de Tayac
pop 850

This dull, touristy village offers one of the region's best introductions to prehistory, the **Musée National de Préhistoire** (22/15FF), built into the cliff above the tourist office (closed Tuesday, except in July and August). Also of interest is the **Abri Pataud** (28/14FF), an impressive Cro-Magnon rock shelter in the cliff face (closed Monday, except in July and August).

The **Grotte de Font de Gaume**, a cave with 230 remarkably sophisticated polychrome figures of bison, reindeer and other creatures, and the **Grotte des Combarelles**, decorated with 600 often-superimposed engravings of animals, are 1km and 3km respectively north-east of Les Eyzies de Tayac on the D47. It charges 35/23FF for a tour, which must be reserved in advance on ☎ 05 53 06 86 00 (closed Wednesday).

Les Eyzies' tourist office (☎ 05 53 06 97 05, fax 05 53 06 90 79) is on the town's main street (closed on Sunday from October to February).

Montignac
pop 3100

Montignac, 25km north-east of Les Eyzies, achieved sudden fame thanks to the **Lascaux Cave**, 2km to the south-east, discovered in 1940 by four teenage boys who, it is said, were out searching for their dog. The cave's main room and a number of steep galleries are decorated with 15,000-year-old figures of wild oxen, deer, horses, reindeer and other creatures depicted in vivid reds, blacks, yellows and browns.

Lascaux has long been closed to the public to prevent deterioration, but you can get a good idea of the original at **Lascaux II**, a meticulous replica of the main gallery that opens daily (except on Monday from November to March) from 10 am to 12.30 pm and 1.30 to 6 pm (no midday closure from April to October; until 8 pm in July and August);

closed for three weeks in January. The last tour begins about an hour before closing time. Tickets, which from April to October are sold *only* in Montignac (next to the tourist office), cost 50FF (children 20FF).

SOUTH-WEST OF SARLAT
Along the Dordogne River about 15km south-west of Sarlat you'll find a number of lovely towns and spectacular fortified chateaux.

The trapezoid-shaped, walled village of **Domme**, set on a steep promontory high above the river, is one of the few bastides to have retained most of its 13th-century ramparts. The hamlet of **La Roque Gageac** is built halfway up the cliff face on the right bank of the river.

The 12th to 16th-century **Château de Castelnaud** (30FF) has everything you'd expect from a cliff-top castle. The interior is occupied by a **museum of medieval warfare** (open daily from March to mid-November). Across the river – also perched atop a sheer cliff – is Castelnaud's archrival, the dramatic **Château de Beynac** (40FF, open daily).

Quercy

South-east of the Dordogne department lies the warm, unmistakably southern region of Quercy. The dry limestone plateau in the north-east is covered with oak trees and cut by dramatic canyons created by the serpentine Lot River and its tributaries.

CAHORS
pop 21,432
Cahors, nestled in a bend of the Lot River, is a quiet town with a relaxed Midi atmosphere. The train station lies about 600m west of north-south oriented blvd Léon Gambetta, the main commercial thoroughfare.

A bit south of the train station is **Pont Valentré**, one of France's finest fortified medieval bridges. **Vieux Cahors** is the medieval quarter situated east of blvd Léon Gambetta.

The cavernous nave of the Romanesque-style **Cathédrale St Étienne**, consecrated in 1119, is crowned with two 18m-wide cupolas, the largest in France. The heavily mutilated, Flamboyant Gothic **cloître** (cloister) opens May to September.

The small, free **Musée de la Résistance** (☎ 05 65 22 14 25), on the north side of place Charles de Gaulle, has exhibits on the Resistance, the concentration camps and the liberation of France (open 2 to 6 pm daily).

Information
The tourist office (☎ 05 65 53 20 65, fax 05 65 53 20 74) is on place François Mitterrand. It opens 9 am to 12.30 pm and 1.30 to 6.30 pm, Monday to Saturday (6 pm on Saturday). In July and August, it's also open on Sunday and holidays from 10 am to noon.

About 500m south of the train station at 430 Allée des Soupirs, the municipal centre Les Docks offers Internet access from about 2 to 8 pm (until 6 pm at weekends, until 10 or 11 pm from Wednesday to Friday).

Places to Stay
The three-star *Camping Rivière de Cassebut* (☎ 05 56 30 06 30), on the left bank of the Lot about 1km north of Pont de Cassebut (the bridge just east of Vieux Cahors), is open April to October.

The *Auberge de Jeunesse* (☎ 05 65 35 64 71, fax 05 65 35 95 92, 20 rue Frédéric Suisse) is in the same building as the Foyer des Jeunes Travailleurs. Accommodation in four to 11-bed rooms cost 51FF. Telephone reservations are advisable.

In Vieux Cahors, *Hôtel de la Paix* (☎ 05 65 35 03 40, fax 05 65 35 40 88, place des Halles) has basic but clean doubles from 160FF (210FF with shower and toilet). Reception is closed on Sunday and holidays.

Places to Eat
Inexpensive restaurants around the Marché Couvert include the unpretentious *Restaurant Le Troquet des Halles* (*rue St Maurice*), where the four-course *menu* costs only 60FF, including wine. Except on Sunday, lunch is noon to 2 pm; dinner is available only from June to September.

Cahors' covered market, the *Marché Couvert (on place des Halles)*, opens 7.30 am to 12.30 pm and 3 to 7 pm, Tuesday to Saturday and Sunday mornings.

Getting There & Away
The train station (☎ 0836 35 35 39), on place Jouinot Gambetta (place de la Gare), is on the

main SNCF line linking Paris' Gare d'Austerlitz (314FF, 5¼ hours) with Toulouse (87FF, 1¼ hours). To get to Sarlat-la-Canéda, take a train to Souillac and an SNCF bus from there.

AROUND CAHORS

East of Cahors, the limestone hills between Cahors and Figeac are cut by the dramatic, cliff-flanked Lot and Célé Rivers. The **Grotte de Pech Merle** (☎ 05 65 31 27 05), 30km east of Cahors, has thousands of stalactites and dozens of paintings drawn by Cro-Magnon people over 16,000 years ago (open from the week before Easter until October). Arrive early as only 700 people a day are allowed to visit.

The village of **St Cirq Lapopie**, 25km east of Cahors, is perched on a cliff 100m above the Lot River. The harmonious riverside town of **Figeac** is on the Célé about 70km northeast of Cahors. Both are linked to Cahors by four to six SNCF buses a day.

Burgundy & the Rhône

DIJON
pop 230,000

Dijon, the prosperous capital of the dukes of Burgundy for almost 500 years, is one of France's most appealing provincial cities. Graced by elegant medieval and Renaissance residences, it has a distinctly youthful air, in part because of the major university situated there.

Dijon is a good starting point for visits to the vineyards of the Côte d'Or, arguably the greatest wine-growing region in the world (don't mention this when you're in Bordeaux).

Orientation & Information

Dijon's main thoroughfare runs eastward from the train station to Église St Michel: ave Maréchal Foch links the train station with the tourist office; rue de la Liberté continues eastward past the Palais des Ducs.

The tourist office (☎ 03 80 44 11 44, fax 03 80 42 18 83) is 300m east of the train station at place Darcy. It opens 9 am to 8 pm daily; from mid-October to April, hours are 10 am to 5.30 or 6 pm, until 1 pm on Sunday and holidays. The annexe, at 34 rue des Forges, faces the north side of the Palais des Ducs (closed Sunday and, from mid-October to April, on Saturday). Web site: www.ot-dijon.fr.

Money & Post The Banque de France, 2 place de la Banque, changes money on weekdays from 8.45 to 11.45 am.

The main post office, at place Grangier, open 8 am to 7 pm weekdays, Saturday to noon. Exchange services and a Cyberposte are available.

Laundry The laundrettes at 41 rue Auguste Comte and Nos 28 and 55 rue Berbisey are open until 8.30 or 9 pm daily.

Things to See

Dijon's major museums open daily except Tuesday, with the exception of the Musée National Magnin, which opens daily except Monday. Except where noted, entry is free for under 18s and students and, on the first Sunday of the month, for everyone. La Clé de la Ville combination ticket (45FF), available at the tourist office, gives access to all of Dijon's museums and to one of the tourist office's tours.

The **Palais des Ducs et des États de Bourgogne** (Palace of the Dukes and States General of Burgundy), remodelled in the neoclassical style in the 17th and 18th centuries, was once the home of the powerful dukes of Burgundy. The east wing houses the outstanding **Musée des Beaux-Arts**, one of the richest and most renowned fine arts museums in France. Hours are 10 am to 6 pm; admission costs 22FF.

Some of the finest of Dijon's many medieval and Renaissance townhouses are just north of the Palais des Ducs along **rue Verrerie** and **rue des Forges**, Dijon's main street until the 18th century. The splendid Flamboyant Gothic **Hôtel Chambellan** (1490) at 34 rue des Forges now houses the tourist office annexe.

Many great figures of Burgundy's history are buried in the Burgundian-Gothic **Cathédrale St Bénigne**, built in the late 13th century. **Église St Michel**, begun in 1499, is a Flamboyant Gothic church with an impressive Renaissance facade. The unusual **Église Notre Dame** was built in the Burgundian-Gothic

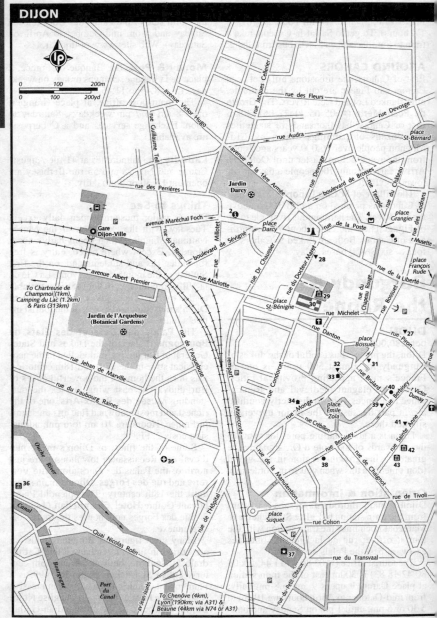

DIJON

To Chartreuse de
Champmol (1km),
Camping du Lac (1.2km)
& Paris (313km)

Jardin Darcy

Jardin de l'Arquebuse
(Botanical Gardens)

Gare
Dijon-Ville

avenue Victor Hugo

rue des Fleurs

rue Devosge

place
St-Bernard

rue Jacques Cellerier

rue Guillaume Tel

rue Audra

avenue de la 1ère Armée

rue Devosge

boulevard de Brosses

rue Temple

rue du Château

place
Grangier

rue des Godrans

rue des Perrières

avenue Maréchal Foch

place
Darcy

rue de la Poste

4

place
Grangier

5

r Musette

rue du Dr Remy

boulevard de Sévigné

rue Millotet

rue Dr Chaussier

3

28

rue du Docteur Maret

place
François
Rude

rue de la Liberté

avenue Albert Premier

rue Mariotte

place
St-Bénigne

30

29

rue Michelet

rue du Chapeau Rouge

rue Bossuet

rue de l'Arquebuse

rue Jehan de Marville

rue du Faubourg Raines

rempart

rue Danton

place
Bossuet

rue Piron

27

32

33

31

rue Brulard

40

39

r Berbisey

r Victor
Dumay

34

place
Émile
Zola

rue Monge

rue Crébillon

41

rue Sainte Anne

42

43

rue Berbisey

rue de la Manutention

38

rue du Chaignot

Ouche River

Canal

36

35

rue de l'Hôpital

Misericorde

rue de Tivoli

place
Suquet

rue Colson

Quai Nicolas Rolin

Bourgogne

de

Port
du
Canal

37

rue du Transvaal

av Jean Jaurès

rue du Petit Citeaux

To Chenôve (4km),
Lyon (190km; via A31) &
Beaune (44km via N74 or A31)

euro currency converter **€1 = 6.55FF**

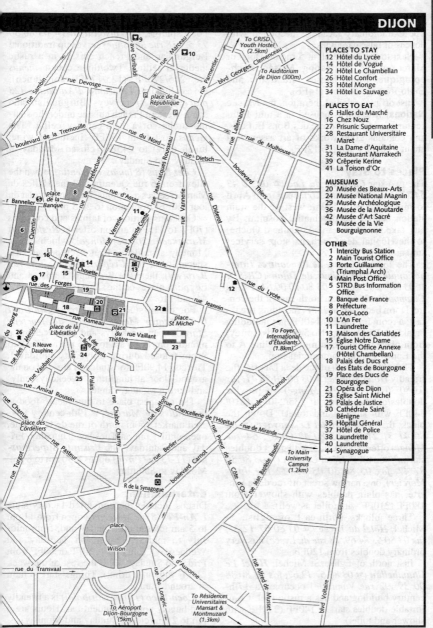

DIJON

PLACES TO STAY
12 Hôtel du Lycée
14 Hôtel de Vogüé
22 Hôtel Le Chambellan
26 Hôtel Confort
33 Hôtel Monge
34 Hôtel Le Sauvage

PLACES TO EAT
6 Halles du Marché
16 Chez Nouz
27 Prisunic Supermarket
28 Restaurant Universitaire Maret
31 La Dame d'Aquitaine
32 Restaurant Marrakech
39 Crêperie Kerine
41 La Toison d'Or

MUSEUMS
20 Musée des Beaux-Arts
24 Musée National Magnin
29 Musée Archéologique
36 Musée de la Moutarde
42 Musée d'Art Sacré
43 Musée de la Vie Bourguignonne

OTHER
1 Intercity Bus Station
2 Main Tourist Office
3 Porte Guillaume (Triumphal Arch)
4 Main Post Office
5 STRD Bus Information Office
7 Banque de France
8 Préfecture
9 Coco-Loco
10 L'An Fer
11 Laundrette
13 Maison des Cariatides
15 Église Notre Dame
17 Tourist Office Annexe (Hôtel Chambellan)
18 Palais des Ducs et des États de Bourgogne
19 Place des Ducs de Bourgogne
21 Opéra de Dijon
23 Église Saint Michel
25 Palais de Justice
30 Cathédrale Saint Bénigne
35 Hôpital Général
37 Hôtel de Police
38 Laundrette
40 Laundrette
44 Synagogue

style during the first half of the 13th century. The extraordinary facade is decorated with dozens of false gargoyles.

Next to the cathedral, at 5 rue du Docteur Maret, is the fascinating **Musée Archéologique**, which houses rare Celtic and Gallo-Roman artefacts (14FF).

Just off place de la Libération, the **Musée National Magnin** is housed in a mid-17th-century residence at 4 rue des Bons Enfants, and contains 2000 works of art assembled about a century ago (16/12FF).

Places to Stay

The two-star *Camping du Lac* (☎ *03 80 43 54 72, 3 blvd Chanoine Kir)*, open from April to mid-October, is 1.4km west of the train station behind the psychiatric hospital. By bus, take No 12 (towards Fontaine d'Ouche) to the Hôpital des Chartreux stop; services stop at around 8 pm.

The 260-bed *Centre de Rencontres Internationales et de Séjour de Dijon (CRISD; ☎ 03 80 72 95 20, fax 03 80 70 00 61, 1 blvd Champollion)* is 2.5km north-east of the centre. Dorm beds start at 72FF, including breakfast; a room for three is 140FF, not including breakfast. By bus, take No 5 (towards Épirey) from place Grangier; at night take line A to the Épirey Centre Commercial stop.

Three blocks south of rue de la Liberté, the friendly *Hôtel Monge* (☎ *03 80 30 55 41, fax 03 80 30 30 15, 20 rue Monge)* can provide doubles/quads starting at 135/240FF (210/ 340FF with shower and toilet). Down the block, the two-star *Hôtel Le Sauvage* (☎ *03 80 41 31 21, fax 03 80 42 06 07, 64 rue Monge)* offers good value, with quiet doubles starting at 240FF. *Hôtel Confort* (☎ *03 80 30 37 47, fax 03 80 30 03 43, 12 rue Jules Mercier)*, on a narrow street off rue de la Liberté, has plain doubles with shower from 180FF (210FF with toilet as well).

Three blocks north-east of Église St Michel, *Hôtel du Lycée* (☎ *03 80 67 12 35, fax 03 80 63 84 69, 28 rue du Lycée)* has very ordinary doubles from 120FF.

Just north of Église St Michel, *Hôtel Le Chambellan* (☎ *03 80 67 12 67, fax 03 80 38 00 39, 92 rue Vannerie)* occupies a 17th-century building and has a rustic feel. Comfortable doubles start at 140FF (220FF with shower and toilet).

Places to Eat

For a splurge, *La Toison d'Or* (☎ *03 80 30 73 52, 18 rue Ste Anne)* serves up traditional Burgundian and French cuisine in a rustic medieval setting. Two/three course *menus* are 215/270FF (125/170FF for lunch); closed Sunday. *La Dame d'Aquitaine (23 place Bossuet)* purveys Burgundian and south-western French cuisine under the soaring arches of a 13th-century cellar. The *menus* cost from 138FF (including wine; lunch only) to 245FF (closed Monday at midday and Sunday).

Chez Nous (8 Impasse Quentin), down the alley from 6 rue Quentin and the Halles du Marché, serves a copious, Burgundian plat du jour (60FF) from noon to 2.15 pm.

Generous portions of tajines and couscous (70FF to 115FF) are on offer at *Restaurant Marrakech (20 rue Monge)*, which closes Monday at midday. Breton crepes are the speciality of the *Crêperie Kerine (36 rue Berbisey)*; there are Brazilian, Tunisian and Egyptian places on the same street at Nos 42, 44 and 116.

For cheap student eats, try *Restaurant Universitaire Maret (3 rue du Docteur Maret)*, open weekdays and one weekend a month from 11.40 am to 1.15 pm and 6.40 to 8 pm (closed during university holidays). Tickets (14.90FF for students) are sold on the ground floor at lunchtime (weekdays only) and during Monday dinner.

The cheapest place to buy picnic food is the *Halles du Marché*, a 19th-century covered market 150m north of rue de la Liberté, open until 1 pm on Tuesday, Thursday, Friday and Saturday. The *Prisunic Supermarket (11-13 rue Piron)* opens 8.30 am to 8 pm, Monday to Saturday.

Entertainment

Discos include the converted-factory-style *L'An-Fer (8 rue Marceau)*, open from 11 pm to 5 am (closed on Monday and, from mid-July to mid-September, on Tuesday and Wednesday). Entry costs 50FF or 60FF from Friday to Sunday, 40FF the rest of the week (25FF without a drink). Things start to hum at around 1 am.

Coco-Loco (18 ave Garibaldi) is a friendly and hugely popular student bar. Hours are 6 pm to 2 am (closed Sunday and Monday).

Getting There & Away

Transco buses link the bus station (attached to the train station; ☎ 03 80 42 11 00) with some of the winemaking towns along the Côte d'Or, including Beaune.

The train station, Gare Dijon-Ville (☎ 0836 35 35 39), has TGV services to/from Paris' Gare de Lyon (227FF to 275FF, 1¾ hours). There are non-TGV trains to Lyon (133FF to 153FF, 1½ to two hours) and Nice (380FF, eight hours).

Getting Around

Dijon's extensive urban bus network is run by STRD (☎ 03 80 30 60 90). Bus lines are known by their number and the name of the terminus station. In the city centre, seven different lines stop along rue de la Liberté, and five more have stops around place Grangier. A Forfait Journée ticket, valid all day, costs 16FF at the STRD office at place Grangier (closed on Sunday).

CÔTE D'OR

Burgundy's finest vintages come from the vine-covered Côte d'Or, the eastern slopes of the limestone escarpment running for about 60km south from Dijon. The northern section, known as the Côte de Nuits, includes Gevrey-Chambertin, Vougeot, Vosne-Romanée and Nuits St Georges, known for their fine reds; the southern section, the Côte de Beaune, includes Pommard, Volnay, Meursault and Puligny-Montrachet. The tourist offices in Dijon and Beaune can provide details on *caves* (wine cellars) that offer tours and *dégustation* (wine tasting).

The Beaune tourist office handles ticketing for year-round, two-hour minibus tours of the Côte (190FF).

Beaune

pop 22,000

Beaune, a famous wine-making centre about 40km south of Dijon, makes an excellent day trip from Dijon. Its most notable historical site is the **Hôtel-Dieu**, France's most opulent medieval charity hospital (32/25FF). The tourist office (☎ 03 80 26 21 30), 1km west of the train station, is opposite the entrance to the Hôtel-Dieu. It opens 9 am (10 am in winter) to sometime between 6 pm (in winter) and 8 pm (from mid-June to late September, 7 pm on Sunday). Web site: www.ot-beaune.fr.

At the **Marché aux Vins**, on rue Nicolas Rolin 30m south of the tourist office, you can sample 18 wines for 50FF. **Patriarche Père et Fils** at 6 rue du Collège has one of the largest wine cellars in Burgundy; one-hour visits include sampling and begin from 10.30 am (9.30 am in the warm months) to 11 am and 2 to 5 pm.

Places to Stay & Eat The best deal in town is *Hôtel Rousseau* (☎ 03 80 22 13 59, 11 place Madeleine). Run by a friendly older woman, it has large, old-fashioned singles/doubles from 140/185FF; a room for five is 380FF. The 106-room, two-star *Hôtel Au Grand St Jean* (☎ 03 80 24 12 22, fax 03 80 24 15 43, ✉ hotel.saint.jean@netclic.fr, 18 rue du Faubourg Madeleine) has impersonal doubles/quads from 235/295FF.

Caves Madeleine (8 rue du Faubourg Madeleine) is a cosy wine bar with family-style Burgundian *menus* for 69FF and 115FF (closed on Thursday and Sunday). *Restaurant Maxime (3 place Madeleine)* offers reasonably priced Burgundian cuisine in a rustic but elegant dining room; *menus* range from 76FF to 150FF (closed Sunday night, Monday and, except from June to September, on Thursday night).

The refined *Restaurant Bernard & Martine Morillon (31 rue Maufoux)* has traditional French *menus* for 180FF to 480FF (closed Tuesday midday, Monday and in January).

Getting There & Away Beaune is linked to Dijon by train (38FF, 20 to 25 minutes, 18 to 24 a day) and Transco buses (☎ 03 80 42 11 00; 40FF, one hour, seven to nine a day, two on Sunday and holidays). The latter stop at a number of wine villages, including Vougeot, Nuits St Georges and Aloxe-Corton.

LYON

pop 415,500

The grand city of Lyon is part of a prosperous urban area of almost two million people, France's second-largest conurbation. Founded by the Romans over 2000 years ago, it has spent the last 500 years as a commercial, industrial and banking powerhouse. Lyon sports outstanding museums, a dynamic cultural life,

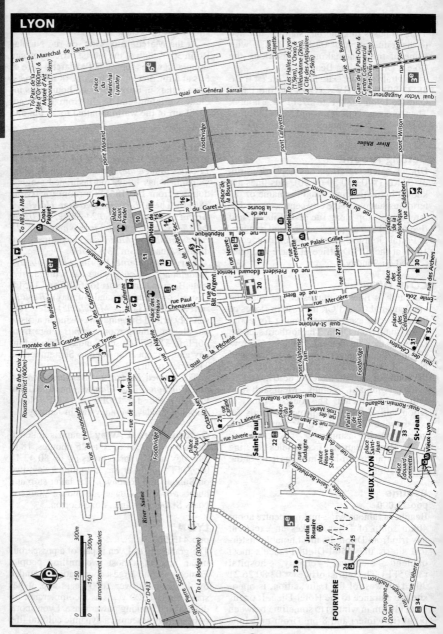

LYON

To Parc de la Tête d'Or (600m) & Musée d'Art Contemporain (1.3km)

ave du Maréchal de Saxe

place du Maréchal Lyautey

cours Lafayette

To Les Halles de Lyon (1km), Vivarais & Villeurbanne (2km), La Cité des Antiquaires (2.5km)

To Gare de la Part-Dieu & Centre Commercial La Part-Dieu (1.5km)

rue de Bonnel

rue Servient

quai du Général Sarrail

quai Victor Augagneur

pont Lafayette

pont Wilson

Footbridge

River Rhône

pont Morand

To N83 & N84

Croix Paquet

place Louis Pradel

rue Romarin

place de la Bourse

rue de la Bourse

rue du Président Carnot

place de la République

rue Childebert

R du Garet

Hôtel de Ville

rue de l'Arbre Sec

rue de la République

rue Grenette

rue Palais-Grillet

rue Neuve

rue Ferrandière

rue du Président Édouard Herriot

place des Jacobins

rue Émile Zola

rue des Archers

rue Burdeau

rue des Capucins

Ste-Catherine

place des Terreaux

rue Paul Chenavard

rue du Bât d'Argent

rue de Brest

rue Mercière

place Célestins

rue Terme

rue d'Algérie

quai de la Pêcherie

quai St-Antoine

quai des Célestins

montée de la Grande Côte

To the Croix Rousse District (400m)

rue de la Martinière

River Saône

Footbridge

pont Alphonse Juin

Footbridge

Octavio Mey

rue Carriand

r. Lainerie

rue Juiverie

place St-Paul

Saint-Paul

quai Romain-Rolland

place du Change

rue de Gadagne

rue du Bœuf

rue St-Jean

rue des Trois Maries

place Saint-Jean

place Neuve St-Jean

Palais de Justice

VIEUX LYON

montée Saint-Barthélemy

place Édouard Commette

St-Jean

Vieux Lyon

place Saint-Jean

rue de l'Annonciade

rue de la Martinière

quai Pierre Scize

To D433

To La Bodega (300m)

Jardin du Rosaire

FOURVIÈRE

To Campagne (200m)

rue Roger Radisson

rue du Cléberg

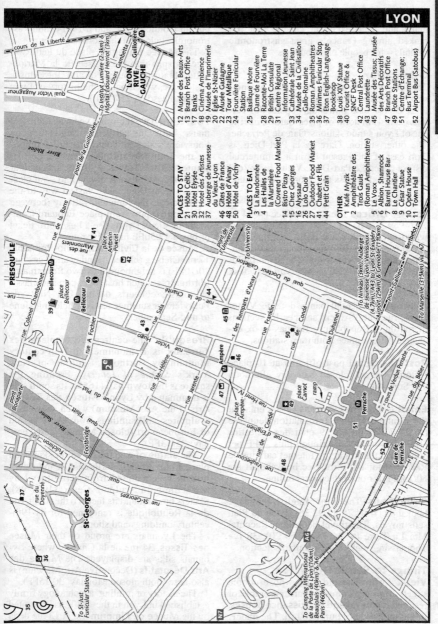

LYON

PLACES TO STAY
21 Hôtel Celtic
30 Hôtel Elysée
32 Hôtel des Artistes
37 Auberge de Jeunesse du Vieux Lyon
46 Gîtes de France
48 Hôtel d'Ainay
50 Hôtel de Vichy

PLACES TO EAT
3 La Randonnée
4 Les Halles de la Martinière
14 Bistro Pizay
15 Chez Georges
16 Alyssaar
26 Lolo Quoi
27 Outdoor Food Market
41 Chabert et Fils
44 Petit Grain

OTHER
1 Kafé Myzik
2 Amphithéâtre des Trois Gauls (Roman Amphitheatre)
5 Le Voxx
6 Albion, Shamrock
7 Barrel House Bar
8 Le Chantier
9 César Statue
10 Opéra House
11 Town Hall
12 Musée des Beaux-Arts
13 Branch Post Office
17 Banks
18 Cinéma Ambience
19 Musée de l'Imprimerie
20 Église St-Nizier
22 Musée Gadagne
23 Tour Métallique
24 Fourvière Funicular Station
25 Basilique Notre Dame de Fourvière
28 Raconte-Moi La Terre
29 British Consulate
31 Centre Régional Information Jeunesse
33 Cathédrale Saint Jean
34 Musée de la Civilisation Gallo-Romaine
35 Roman Amphitheatres
36 Minimes Funicular Stop
37 Eton English-Language Bookshop
38 Louis XIV Statue
40 Tourist Office & SNCF Desk
42 Central Post Office
43 Laundrette
45 Musée des Tissus; Musée des Arts Décoratifs
47 Branch Post Office
49 Police Stations
51 Centre d'Echange; Bus Terminal
52 Airport Bus (Satobus)

euro currency converter 1FF = €0.15

an important university, lively pedestrian malls and such excellent cuisine that it's ranked among France's great gastronomic capitals – for people of all budgets.

Orientation

The city centre is on the Presqu'île, a peninsula bounded by the Rhône and Saône Rivers. Place Bellecour is 1km south of place des Terreaux and 1km north of place Carnot, next to one of Lyon's train stations, Gare de Perrache. The other station, Gare de la Part-Dieu, is 2km east of the Presqu'île in a commercial district called La Part-Dieu. Vieux Lyon (old Lyon) sprawls across the Saône's west bank.

Information

Tourist Offices The tourist office (☎ 04 72 77 69 69, fax 04 78 42 04 32, ✉ lyoncvb@ lyon-france.com), place Bellecour, opens 10 am to 6 or 7 pm. Its Web site at www.lyon-france.com is worth a surf. The same building houses an SNCF reservations desk (closed Sunday).

Money Commercial banks dot rue Victor Hugo, rue Bât d'Argent and nearby sections of rue de la République. Thomas Cook exchange offices grace both train stations.

Post The central post office is at 10 place Antonin Poncet (closed Saturday afternoon and Sunday).

Email & Internet Access Check email at the Centre Régional Information Jeunesse (☎ 04 72 77 00 66), 9 quai des Célestins (10FF for initial subscription plus 10FF per 30 minutes). Rates at the Internet cafe inside Raconte-Moi La Terre (see bookshops) are 60/130FF for one/three hours online.

Bookshops The Eton English-language bookshop (☎ 04 78 92 92 36), 1 rue du Plat, sells novels. The travel bookshop, Raconte-Moi La Terre (☎ 04 78 92 60 20), 38 rue Thomassin, stocks a superb map selection.

Things to See & Do

Vieux Lyon The old city, whose cobble streets form a picture-postcard ensemble of restored **medieval and Renaissance houses**, lies at the base of Fourvière hill. The mainly

Romanesque **Cathédrale St Jean** has a Flamboyant Gothic facade and a 14th-century astronomical clock in the north transept.

The **Musée Gadagne**, place du Petit Collège, is split into the Musée de la Marionnette, featuring puppets, and the Musée Historique, which paints the history of Lyon (closed Tuesday, 25/13FF).

Fourvière Two thousand years ago, the Romans built the city of Lugdunum on Fourvière's slopes. Today the hill – topped by the **Tour Métallique** (1893), a sort of stunted Eiffel Tower – offers spectacular views of Lyon, its two rivers and – on clear days – Mont Blanc. The easiest way to the top is to ride the funicular railway (between 6 am and 10 pm) from place Édouard Commette in Vieux Lyon. Use a bus/metro ticket or buy a 12.50FF funicular return.

Musée de la Civilisation Gallo-Romaine, 17 rue Cléberg (closed Monday and Tuesday; 20/10FF) is neighboured by two **Roman amphitheatres** which host rock, pop and classical music concerts during Les Nuits de Fourvière, a summer festival held mid-June to mid-September.

Presqu'île The centrepiece of **place des Terreaux** is a monumental 19th-century fountain by Bartholdi, sculptor of New York's *Statue of Liberty*. Fronting the square is the **town hall** (1655). Its south side is dominated by Lyon's **Musée des Beaux-Arts** (Fine Arts Museum) which showcases sculptures and paintings from every period of European art (closed Monday and Tuesday; 25/13FF).

The **statue of a giant on roller skates** on place Louis Pradel, north-east of the **opera house**, was sculpted from scrap metal by Marseille-born sculptor César (1921-98). Skaters buzz around its feet. To the south, **rue de la République** is renowned for its 19th-century buildings and shops.

The Lyonnais are proud of their **Musée des Tissus**, 34 rue de la Charité, where Lyonnais silks are displayed. The **Musée des Arts Décoratifs** (Decorative Arts Museum) is also here (both closed Monday, 30/15FF).

The history of printing, a technology firmly established in Lyon in the 1480s, is illustrated by the **Musée de l'Imprimerie** at 13 rue de la

Poulaillerie (closed Monday and Tuesday; 25/13FF).

Other Attractions The main city park **Parc de la Tête d'Or** sits on the east bank of the Rhône, north of La Part-Dieu. The inspirational **Musée d'Art Contemporain** (Contemporary Art Museum), borders the river at 81 quai Charles de Gaulle and hosts fantastic modern art exhibitions. It also has a multimedia centre devoted to digital art (closed Monday and Tuesday, 25/13FF).

The **Institut Lumière** (☎ 04 78 78 18 95, ✉ contact@institut-lumiere.org) at 25 rue du Premier-Film brings to life the work of the motion-picture pioneers Auguste and Louis Lumière (closed Monday, 25/20FF). Classic and cult films are screened in its cinema. Program details are posted on its Web site at www.institut-lumiere.org.

Places to Stay

Camping *Camping International de la Porte de Lyon* (☎ 04 78 35 64 55) is some 10km north-west of Lyon in Dardilly. Open year round, it charges 80FF for two people with tent and car. Bus Nos 3 or 19 (towards Ecully-Dardilly) from the Hôtel de Ville metro station stop right out front.

Hostels *Auberge de Jeunesse du Vieux Lyon* (☎ 04 78 15 05 50, fax 04 78 15 05 51, ✉ lyon@fuaj.org, 40-45 montée du Chemin Neuf) in Vieux Lyon has dorm beds for 71FF including breakfast. Sheets cost 17FF. Non-HI members must buy a welcome stamp (19FF). Reception opens 24 hours.

Auberge de Jeunesse Lyon-Vénissieux (☎ 04 78 76 39 23, fax 04 78 77 51 11, ✉ lyonvenissieux@fuaj.fr, 51 rue Roger Salengro) is 5.5km south-east of Gare de Perrache in Vénissieux. A dorm bed costs 68FF including breakfast and reception opens 7.30 to 12.30 am. You can take bus No 35 from place Bellecour to the Georges Lévy stop or bus No 53 from Gare de Perrache to the États-Unis-Viviani stop.

Chambres d'Hôtes The *Gîtes de France* (☎ 04 72 77 17 55, fax 04 78 38 21 15, ✉ gites.rhone.alpes@wanadoo.fr, 1 rue Général Plessier) arranges B&B-type accommodation around Lyon and has lists of

gîtes (self-catering farms and cottages) to rent on a weekly basis.

Hotels At rock-bottom *Hôtel de Vichy* (☎ 04 78 37 42 58, 60 bis rue de la Charité) singles/doubles go for 140/150FF (180/200FF with shower and TV). Heading into town *Hôtel d'Ainay* (☎ 04 78 42 43 42, fax 04 72 77 51 90, 14 rue des Remparts d'Ainay) has basic singles/doubles for 165/175FF (205/215FF with shower and TV).

Old city lovers can try *Hôtel Celtic* (☎ 04 78 28 01 12, fax 04 78 28 01 34, 10 rue François Vernay) in Vieux Lyon. Singles/doubles are 135/160FF (170/200FF with shower).

Two-star spots include the hostelry-style *Hôtel Élysée* (☎ 04 78 42 03 15, fax 04 78 37 76 49, 92 rue du Président Édouard Herriot) which has singles/doubles from 340/360FF; and charming, three-star *Hotel des Artistes* (☎ 04 78 42 04 88, fax 04 78 42 93 76, 8 rue Gaspard André) which touts theatrically furnished, singles/doubles starting at 390/450FF.

Places to Eat

Fresh fruit, olives, cheese and bread are piled high at the *outdoor morning food market* (daily except Monday) on quai St Antoine. *Les Halles de la Martinière* (covered food market) in the northern Presqu'île at 24 rue de la Martinière and *Les Halles de Lyon*, walking distance from Gare de la Part-Dieu at 102 cours Lafayette, offer an equally tasty choice (both closed Sunday afternoon and Monday).

Piggy-part cuisine is the speciality of a traditional Lyonnais *bouchon* – literally 'traffic jam' elsewhere in France but a small, unpretentious bistro-style restaurant in Lyon. Bouchons worth a nibble include *Chez Georges* (☎ 04 78 28 30 46, 8 rue du Garet); *Bistro Pizay* (☎ 04 78 28 37 26, 4 rue Verdi); or *Chabert et Fils* (☎ 04 78 37 01 94, 11 rue des Marronniers). Both have good-value lunch deals (around 50FF).

Favoured for its elephant-sized portions is *La Randonnée* (☎ 04 78 27 86 81, 4 rue Terme) which has vegetarian platters (50FF), lunchtime/evening *formules* (which allows you to pick a set number of courses from 32/38FF) and *menus* (from 49/65FF).

Terraces great for lounging in the sun include *Campagne* (☎ 04 78 36 73 85, 20 rue

Cardinal Gerlier) atop Fourvière hill and any one of the *cafes* on place des Terreaux. On touristy rue Mercière *Lolo Quoi* (☎ *04 72 77 60 90, 40-4 rue Mercière)* is a chic spot, dressed in funky furnishings and it's not too wallet-crunching if you stick to a tasty bowl of pasta (50FF).

Syrian *Alyssaar* (☎ *04 78 29 57 66, 29 rue du Bât d'Argent)* has spicy *menus* for 78FF, 87FF and 105FF, while Vietnamese *Petit Grain* (☎ *04 72 41 77 85, 19 rue de la Charité)* sports salads, meats and vegetarian platters from 43FF. Rue Ste-Marie des Terreaux and rue Ste-Catherine are lined with Chinese, Turkish and other quick-eating joints.

Entertainment

Rue Ste-Catherine is cluttered with bars. At funky *Le Chantier* (☎ *04 78 39 05 56)*, at No 20, clubbers slide down bum-first – courtesy of a metal slide – to the basement dance floor. On the Saône's left bank *Le Voxx* (☎ *04 78 28 33 87, 1 rue d'Algérie)* lures live bands and a boisterous drinking crowd. On the right bank *La Bodéga* (☎ *04 78 29 42 35, 35 quai Pierre Scize)* also rocks 'til late.

Bands play at *Kafé Myzik* (☎ *04 72 07 04 26, 20 Montée St-Sébastien)*, a hole-in-the-wall club; at *Ninkasi* (☎ *04 72 76 89 09, 267 rue Marcel Mérieux)*, a micro-brewery next to the stadium which serves its own beer and runs a great-value food bar; and at *L'Oxxo* (☎ *04 78 93 62 03, 7 ave Albert Einstein)*, a student bar in Villeurbanne which sports a decor of recycled aeroplanes and cable cars.

Getting There & Away

Bus Most intercity buses depart from the terminal next to Gare de Perrache. Timetables are available from the TCL information office (☎ 04 78 71 70 00), on the middle level of the Centre d'Échange. Tickets are sold by the driver. Buses for destinations west of Lyon (☎ 04 78 43 40 74) leave from outside the Gorge de Loup metro station.

Train You can travel between Gare de Perrache and Gare de la Part-Dieu by metro (change at Charpennes) or by SNCF train. Lyon has direct rail links to all parts of France and Europe. Trains to/from Paris (318FF to 398FF, two hours) use the capital's Gare de Lyon.

Getting Around

Lyon's metro system has four lines (A to D), which run 5 am to midnight. Tickets (8FF) are valid for one-way travel on buses, trolleybuses, the funicular and the metro for one hour after time-stamping. A carnet of 10 tickets is 68FF. The Ticket Liberté (24FF; allows one day of unlimited travel) and the Ticket Liberté 2h (24FF; two hours of unlimited travel from 9 am to 4 pm) can be bought at metro ticket machines, or at the TCL information office (☎ 04 78 71 70 00) in the Centre d'Échange; at 43 rue de la République; or at the Vieux Lyon metro station.

The French Alps

The French Alps, where craggy, snowbound peaks soar above fertile, green valleys, is one of the most awe-inspiring mountain ranges in the world. In summer, visitors can take advantage of hundreds of kilometres of hiking trails and lots of other sporting activities, while the area's ski resorts attract enthusiasts from around the world in winter.

If you're going to ski or snowboard, expect to pay at least 260FF a day (including equipment hire, lifts and transport) at low-altitude stations, which usually operate from December to March. The larger, high-altitude stations cost 360FF to 460FF a day. The cheapest time to go skiing is in January, between the school holiday periods.

CHAMONIX
pop 9830

The town of Chamonix sits in a valley surrounded by the most spectacular scenery in the French Alps. The area is almost Himalayan in its awesomeness: deeply crevassed glaciers many kilometres long ooze down the valleys between the icy peaks and pinnacles around Mont Blanc, which soars almost four vertical kilometres above the valley floor.

There are some 330km of hiking trails in the Chamonix area. In winter, the valley offers superb skiing, with dozens of ski lifts and over 200km of downhill and cross-country ski runs.

Information

The tourist office (☎ 04 50 53 00 24, fax 04 50 53 58 90, @ info@chamonix.com) at

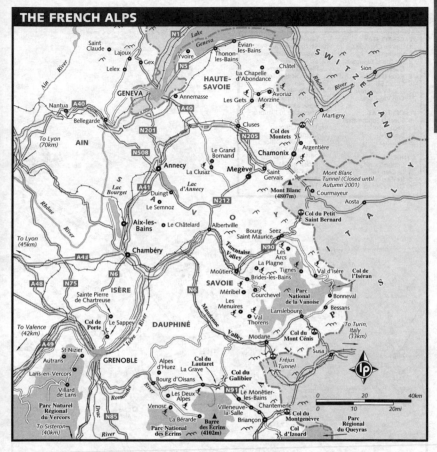

THE FRENCH ALPS

place du Triangle de l'Amitié, opposite place de l'Église, opens 8.30 am to 12.30 pm and 2 to 7 pm daily. Useful brochures on ski-lift hours and costs, refuges, camping grounds and parapente schools are available. In winter it sells a range of ski passes, valid for bus transport and all the ski lifts in the valley.

The Maison de la Montagne, near the tourist office at 109 place de l'Église, houses the Office de Haute Montagne (2nd floor; ☎ 04 50 53 22 08), which has information and maps for walkers and mountaineers (closed Sunday).

You can log onto the Internet at the busy cyBar (☎ 04 50 53 64 80), 81 rue Whymper,

or at the Santa Fe Bar & Restaurant (☎ 04 50 53 99 14), 148 rue du Docteur Paccard. Both charge 1FF per minute.

Climate Weather changes rapidly in Chamonix. Bulletins from *la météo* (the meteorological service) are posted in the window of the tourist office and at the Maison de la Montagne.

Things to See & Do
Aiguille du Midi The Aiguille du Midi (3842m) is a lone spire of rock 8km from the summit of Mont Blanc. The téléphérique

FRANCE

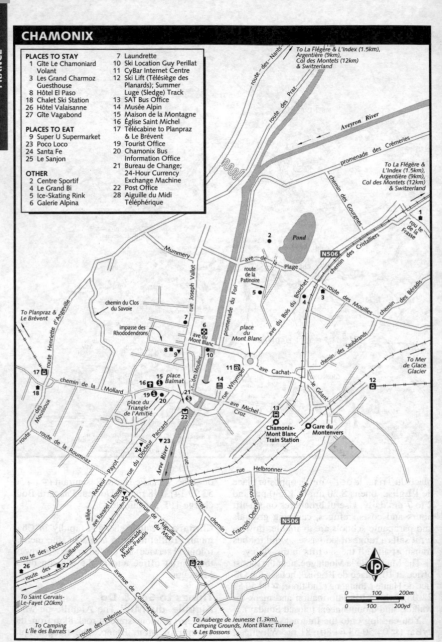

CHAMONIX

PLACES TO STAY
1 Gîte Le Chamoniard Volant
3 Les Grand Charmoz Guesthouse
8 Hôtel El Paso
18 Chalet Ski Station
26 Hôtel Valaisanne
27 Gîte Vagabond

PLACES TO EAT
9 Super U Supermarket
23 Poco Loco
24 Santa Fe
25 Le Sanjon

OTHER
2 Centre Sportif
4 Le Grand Bi
5 Ice-Skating Rink
6 Galerie Alpina

7 Laundrette
10 Ski Location Guy Perillat
11 CyBar Internet Centre
12 Ski Lift (Télésiège des Planards); Summer Luge (Sledge) Track
13 SAT Bus Office
14 Musée Alpin
15 Maison de la Montagne
16 Église Saint Michel
17 Télécabine to Planpraz & Le Brévent
19 Tourist Office
20 Chamonix Bus Information Office
21 Bureau de Change; 24-Hour Currency Exchange Machine
22 Post Office
28 Aiguille du Midi Téléphérique

euro currency converter €1 = 6.55FF

from Chamonix to the Aiguille du Midi (200FF) is the highest and probably scariest cable car in the world – the final leg rises almost vertically up to the Aiguille. In general, visibility is best early in the morning.

The Musée Alpin (☎ 04 50 53 25 93), just off ave Michel Croz in Chamonix, displays artefacts, lithographs and photos illustrating the history of mountain climbing and other Alpine sports. It's open from 2 to 7 pm from June to mid-October; its hours are 3 to 7 pm between Christmas and Easter. It's closed during the rest of the year. Entrance costs 20FF.

Between April and September, you can usually take a second cable car – depending on the winds – from the Aiguille du Midi across the glacier to **Pointe Helbronner** (3466m) and down to the Italian ski resort of **Courmayeur** (an extra 98FF return). A ride from Chamonix to the cable car's halfway point, **Plan de l'Aiguille** (2308m) – an excellent place to start hikes in summer – costs 66/85FF one way/return.

The téléphérique operates 8 am to 3.45 pm all year (6 am to 4.45 pm in July and August). To avoid long queues, arrive before 9.30 am when the buses start to arrive. You can make advance reservations 24 hours a day by calling ☎ 04 50 53 40 00. Pick up your boarding pass and ticket from the ticket office to the right.

Le Brévent Le Brévent (2525m), the highest peak on the west side of the valley, is known for its great views of Mont Blanc. It can be reached from Chamonix by a combination of *télécabine* (gondola) and téléphérique (☎ 04 50 53 13 18) for 57/84FF single/return. Services run from 8 am (9 am in winter) to 5 pm (an hour or so earlier in winter). Numerous hiking trails, including routes back to the valley, can be picked up at Le Brévent or at the cable car's midway station, **Planpraz** (1999m, 48/58FF one way/return).

Mer de Glace The heavily crevassed Mer de Glace (Sea of Ice), the second-largest glacier in the Alps, is 14km long, 1950m across at its widest point and up to 400m deep. It has become a popular tourist destination thanks to a cog-wheel railway, which has an upper terminus at an altitude of 1913m.

The train, which runs year-round (weather permitting), leaves from Gare du Montenvers

(☎ 04 50 53 12 54) in Chamonix. Tickets cost 79/42FF single/return. A combined ticket valid for the train, the gondola to the ice cave (Grotte de la Mer de Glace, 15FF return) and entry to the cave (14FF) costs 116FF. The ride takes 20 minutes each way.

Activities

Hiking In late spring and summer (mid-June to October), the Chamonix area has some of the most spectacular hiking trails anywhere in the Alps. The combined map and guide, *Carte des Sentiers du Mont Blanc* (Mountain Trail Map, 75FF), is ideal for straightforward day hikes. The best map of the area is the 1:25,000 scale IGN map (No 3630OT) entitled *Chamonix-Massif du Mont Blanc* (58FF). Lonely Planet publishes *Walking in France*, a useful guide for walks throughout the whole country.

The fairly level **Grand Balcon Sud** trail, which traverses the Aiguilles Rouges (western) side of the valley at about 2000m, offers great views of Mont Blanc and the glaciers to the east and south. If you'd prefer to avoid 1km of hard uphill walking, take either the Planpraz (46FF one way) or La Flégère lift (43FF one way).

From Plan de l'Aiguille, the midway point on the Aiguille du Midi cable car, the **Grand Balcon Nord** takes you to the Mer de Glace, from where you can hike down to Chamonix. There are a number of other trails from Plan de l'Aiguille.

Skiing & Snowboarding The Chamonix area has 160km of marked ski runs, 42km of cross-country trails and 64 ski lifts of all sorts. Count on paying around 39/220FF a day/week for regular skis or boots. Ski Location Guy Perillat (☎ 04 50 53 54 76) at 138 rue des Moulins is open daily and also rents out snowboards (100/150FF a day without/with boots or 600/700FF a week).

Places to Stay

Camping There are some 13 camp sites in the Chamonix region. In general, camping costs 25FF per person and 12FF to 26FF for a tent site. *L'Île des Barrats* open May to September, is near the base of the Aiguille du Midi cable car. The three-star *Les Deux Glaciers (route des Tissières)* in Les Bossons, 3km south of

FRANCE

Chamonix, is closed mid-November to mid-December. To get there, take the train to Les Bossons or Chamonix Bus to the Tremplin-le-Mont stop.

Refuges Most mountain refuges, which cost 90FF to 100FF a night, are accessible to hikers and are generally open mid-June to mid-September.

The easier-to-reach refuges include one at *Plan de l'Aiguille* (☎ 04 50 53 55 60) at 2308m, the intermediate stop on the Aiguille du Midi cable car, and another at *La Flégère* (☎ 04 50 53 06 13) at 1877m. It's advisable to reserve ahead.

Hostels *Chalet Ski Station* (☎ 04 50 53 20 25, 6 Route des Moussoux) is a gîte d'étape (next to the Planpraz/Le Brévent télécabine station). Beds cost 60FF a night. It's closed 10 May to 20 June and 20 September to 20 December.

The semi-rustic *Gîte Le Chamoniard Volant* (☎ 04 50 53 14 09, 45 Route de la Frasse) is on the north-eastern outskirts of town. A bunk in a cramped, functional room costs 66FF. An evening meal is available for 66FF. The nearest bus stop is La Frasse.

The *Auberge de Jeunesse* (☎ 04 50 53 14 52, fax 04 50 55 92 34, ❷ chamonix@fuaj.org, 127 Montée Jacques Balmat) is a few kilometres south-west of Chamonix in Les Pélerins. By bus, take the Chamonix-Les Houches line and get off at the Pélerins École stop. Beds are 74FF. In winter, only weekly packages are available, including bed, food, ski pass and ski hire for six days from 1450/2990FF in the low/high season.

The *GîteVagabond* (☎ 04 50 53 15 43, fax 04 53 68 21, 365 ave Ravanel le Rouge) is a neat little hostelry with a guest kitchen, bar/restaurant with Internet access, BBQ area, climbing wall and parking. A bed in a four or six person dorm costs 70FF or 149FF for half board.

Hotels At 468 Chemin des Cristalliers next to the railway tracks, *Les Grands Charmoz Guesthouse* (☎ 04 50 53 45 57) has doubles for 184FF. The lively *Hôtel El Paso* (☎ 04 50 53 64 20, fax 04 50 53 64 22, 37 Impasse des Rhododendrons) is great value. Doubles with shared bath in the low/high season cost

166/224FF, triples are 236/306FF. In summer a dorm bed costs 90FF.

Hôtel Valaisanne (☎ 04 50 53 17 98, 454 ave Ravanel Le Rouge) is a small, family-owned place 900m south-west of Chamonix town centre. It has doubles for 170/270FF in the low/high season.

Places to Eat

Handy *Poco Loco* (☎ 04 50 53 43 03, 47 rue du Docteur Paccard) has pizzas from 33FF to 45FF and *menus* from 50FF. It also serves great hot sandwiches (from 23FF), sweet crepes (from 8FF), and burgers to eat in or take àway.

Abuzz with hungry diners looking for salads, pizzas, vegetarian platters and Tex Mex specialities is the sometimes crowded *Santa Fe* (☎ 04 50 53 88 14, 148 rue du Docteur Paccard), a popular eating as well as meeting place. *Le Sanjon* (☎ 04 50 53 56 44, 5 ave Ravanel le Rouge) is a picturesque wooden chalet restaurant serving *raclette* (a block of melted cheese, usually eaten with potatoes and cold meats, 99FF) and fondue (69F).

The well-stocked *Super U* supermarket is at 117 rue Joseph Vallot.

Getting There & Away

Bus Chamonix' bus station is next to the train station. SAT Autocar (☎ 04 50 53 01 15) has buses to Annecy (95.30FF), Geneva (170FF, two hours), Grenoble (161FF). There are currently no services to Italy.

Train The narrow-gauge train line from St Gervais-Le Fayet (20km west of Chamonix) to Martigny, Switzerland (42km north of Chamonix), stops at 11 towns in the Chamonix Valley. You have to change trains at the Swiss border. From St Gervais there are trains to destinations all over France.

Chamonix-Mont Blanc train station (☎ 04 50 53 00 44) is on the east side of town. Major destinations include Paris' Gare de Lyon (469FF, six to seven hours), Lyon (186FF, 4½ hours) and Geneva (100FF, 2½ hours via St Gervais).

Getting Around

Bus transport in the valley is handled by Chamonix Bus (☎ 04 50 53 05 55), with an office at place de l'Église opposite the tourist office.

Between April and October, Le Grand Bi (☎ 04 50 53 14 16), 240 ave du Bois du Bouchet, rents three and 10-speed bikes for 65FF a day, mountain bikes for 100FF (closed Sunday).

ANNECY
pop 50,348

Annecy, situated at the northern tip of the incredibly blue Lac d'Annecy, is the perfect place to spend a relaxing holiday. Visitors in a sedentary mood can choose to sit along the lake and feed the swans or mosey around the geranium-lined canals of the old city. Museums and other sights are limited, but the town is an excellent base for water sports, hiking and biking.

Orientation & Information

The train and bus stations are 500m northwest of the old city, which is centred around the canalised Thiou River. The modern town centre is between the main post office and the Centre Bonlieu complex. The lake town of Annecy-le-Vieux is just east of Annecy.

The tourist office (☎ 04 50 45 00 33, fax 04 50 51 87 20, ✉ ancytour@cybercable.tm.fr) is in the Centre Bonlieu north of place de la Libération. It opens 9 am to 12.30 pm and 1.45 to 6 pm Monday to Saturday, 15 September to 15 May, and 9 am to 6.30 pm, May to September. Sunday openings vary.

The Emailerie (☎ 04 50 10 18 91) on Faubourg de Annonciades, opens 10 am to 10 pm daily (June to October) and 2 to 10 pm (closed Sunday) the rest of the year. Access charges are 25/45FF per 30 minutes/one hour.

Things to See & Do

The Vieille Ville, an area of narrow streets on either side of the Canal du Thiou, retains much of its 17th-century appearance despite recent gentrification. On the island in the middle, the Palais de l'Isle (a former prison) houses the Musée d'Histoire d'Annecy et de la Haute-Savoie (20/5FF, closed Tuesday).

The Musée d'Annecy (☎ 04 50 33 87 30), housed in the 16th-century Château d'Annecy overlooking the town, puts on innovative temporary exhibitions and has a permanent collection of local craftwork (30/10FF, closed Tuesday). The climb up to the chateau is worth it just for the view.

Beaches A kilometre north-east of the Champ de Mars there is a free beach, Plage d'Annecy-le-Vieux. Slightly closer to town, next to the casino, is the Plage de l'Impérial, which costs 18FF and is equipped with changing rooms. Perhaps Annecy's most pleasant stretch of lawn-lined swimming beach is the free Plage des Marquisats, 1km south of the old city along rue des Marquisats. The beaches are officially open from June to September.

Places to Stay

Camping *Camping Municipal Le Belvédère* (☎ 04 50 45 48 30, fax 04 50 45 55 56, Forêt du Crêt du Maure) is 2.5km south of the train station in a shaded forest. From mid-June to early September you can take bus No 91 (Ligne des Vacances) from the train station. It costs about 47/67FF for one/two people to pitch a tent.

Hostels The *Auberge de Jeunesse* (☎ 04 50 45 33 19, fax 04 50 52 77 52, 4 Route du Semnoz)* is 1km south of town in the Forêt du Semnoz. From mid-June to early September, bus No 91 goes there. Beds cost 72FF.

Hotels The small *Hôtel Rive du Lac* (☎ 04 50 51 32 85, fax 04 50 45 77 40, 6 rue des Marquisats)*, superbly located near the Vieille Ville and the lake, has one or two-bed rooms with shower for 146FF.

One of the cheapest places close to the Vieille Ville is the *Central Hôtel* (☎ 04 50 45 05 37, 6 bis rue Royale)* in a quiet courtyard. Doubles start at 160FF.

In the heart of the old city, the *Auberge du Lyonnais* (☎ 04 50 51 26 10, fax 04 50 51 05 04, 14 quai de l'Évêché)* occupies an idyllic setting next to the canal. Singles/doubles with toilet are 170/240FF.

One of the most oddly-placed hotels in Savoy is the *Hôtel de Savoie* (☎ 04 50 45 15 45, fax 04 50 45 11 99, ✉ hotel.savoie@mail.dotcom.fr, 1 place de St François)*, with its entrance on the left side of the Église St François de Sales – spooky. Simple rooms with washbasin cost from 150/220FF.

Places to Eat

In the new town centre, there are good pizzas (from 38FF), large salads (19FF to 43FF) and

FRANCE

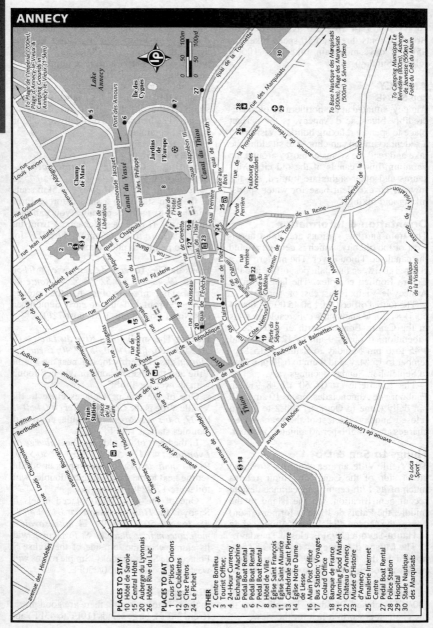

ANNECY

To Plage de l'Impérial (700m);
Plage d'Annecy-le-Vieux &
Camping Grounds in
Annecy-le-Vieux (1.5km)

Lake Annecy

Île des Cygnes

Pont des Amours

Jardins de l'Europe

Champ de Mars

To Base Nautique des Marquisats
(300m), Plage des Marquisats
(500m) & Sévier (5km)

To Camping Municipal Le
Belvédère (800m), Auberge
de Jeunesse (950m) &
Forêt du Crêt du Maure

Canal du Thiou

quai de la Tournette

quai des Marquisats

avenue de Trésum

Faubourg des Annonciades

quai aux Bois

Porte Perrière

Quai Perrière

place de l'Hôtel de Ville

rue de Grenette

rue de l'Isle

rue Perrière

boulevard de la Corniche

de la Reine

place du Château

chemin de la Tour

du Crêt du Maure

To Basilique
de la Visitation

rue Ste-Claire

quai de l'Evêché

quai J-J Rousseau

quai de la République

Côte Nemours

Porte du Sépulcre

Faubourg des Balmettes

River

Thiou

rue de la Gare

avenue de Chambéry

avenue du Rhône

avenue de Loverchy

To Loca
Sport

Train Station

place de la Gare

avenue Berthollet

avenue Brogny

avenue des Hirondelles

rue Louis Chaumontet

rue du Pâquier

quai E Chappuis

place de la Libération

rue Président Favre

rue Jean Jaurès

rue Guillaume Fichet

rue Louis Revon

avenue d'Aléry

rue Royale

rue Vaugelas

rue Carnot

rue Filaterie

rue du Lac

rue de l'Annexion

rue de la Poste

rue des Glières

rue F. St-Glières

rue Sommeiller

Champ de Mars

promenade Jacquet

quai Jules Philippe

quai Napoléon III

avenue de la Providence

rue de Bayreuth

avenue de la Visitation

euro currency converter €1 = 6.55FF

a children's *menu* (42FF) at *Lous P'tious Onions* (☎ *04 50 51 34 41, 36 rue Sommeiller*) in the Grand Passage. *Menus* start at 65FF. There are also inexpensive places along rue du Pâquier.

Les Oubliettes (☎ *04 50 45 39 78, 10 quai de l'Isle*), right next to the canal in the Old Town, has pizzas from 40FF to 55FF and a wide choice of other main courses such as an expansive *menu Savoyard* for 99FF. Just across the canal, *Le Pichet* (☎ *04 50 45 32 41, 13 rue Perrière*), has a big terrace and three-course *menus* for 66FF and 78FF.

Chez Petros (☎ *04 50 45 50 26, 13 Faubourg Ste Claire*) is a small but busy Greek restaurant with classic Greek *menus* from 65FF to 115FF, as well as excellent vegetarian dishes such as stuffed aubergines or peppers (40FF), haricot beans (42FF), or okra (54FF).

Getting There & Away
Bus The bus station, Gare Routière Sud, is on rue de l'Industrie next to the train station. Voyages Crolard (☎ 04 50 45 08 12) has regular services to Roc de Chère on the eastern shore of Lac d'Annecy and Bout du Lac at the far southern tip, as well as to Albertville and Chamonix.

Autocars Frossard (☎ 04 50 45 73 90) sells tickets to Geneva, Grenoble, Nice and elsewhere. Autocars Francony (☎ 04 50 45 02 43) has buses to Chamonix.

Train The train station (☎ 0836 35 35 35) is at place de la Gare. There are frequent trains to Paris' Gare de Lyon (451FF, 3¾ hours by TGV), Nice (404FF via Lyon, 352FF via Aix-les-Bains, eight to nine hours), Lyon (115FF, two hours), Chamonix (105FF, three hours) and Aix-les-Bains (39FF, 30 to 45 minutes).

GRENOBLE
pop 153,317
Grenoble is the intellectual and economic capital of the French Alps. Set in a broad valley surrounded by spectacular mountains, this spotlessly clean city has a Swiss feel to it.

Orientation & Information
The old city is centred around place Grenette, with its many cafes, and place Notre Dame.

Both are about 1km east of the train and bus stations.

The Maison du Tourisme at 14 rue de la République houses the tourist office (☎ 04 76 42 41 41, fax 04 76 00 18 98, @ office-de-tourism-de-grenoble@wanadoo.fr), an SNCF information counter and an information desk for the local bus network (TAG). The tourist office opens 9 am to 12.30 pm and 1.30 to 6 pm (closed Sunday). From June to mid-September, it opens Sunday from 10 am to noon.

Cybernet (☎ 04 76 51 73 18, @ services@neptune.fr), 8 rue Hache, charges 30/47FF for 30/60 minutes online. It opens noon to 2 pm and 10 pm to 1 am.

Things to See
Built in the 16th century to control the approaches to the city (and expanded in the 19th), **Fort de la Bastille** sits on the north side of the Isère River, 263m above the old city. The fort affords superb views of Grenoble and the surrounding mountain ranges. To reach the fort you can take the *téléphérique* (cable car; ☎ 04 76 44 33 65) from quai Stéphane Jay (24/35FF single/return, 19/28FF for students). Several hiking trails lead up the hillside to the fort.

Housed in a 17th-century convent at 30 rue Maurice Gignoux (at the foot of the Fort de la Bastille hill), the **Musée Dauphinois** has displays on the history of the Dauphiné region (20/10FF; closed Tuesday).

Grenoble's fine-arts museum, the **Musée de Grenoble**, 5 place de Lavalette, has a good collection of paintings and sculpture, including works by Matisse, Picasso and Chagall (25/15FF; closed Monday and Tuesday).

The **Musée de la Résistance et de la Déportation de l'Isère**, 14 rue Hébert, examines the region's role in the Resistance, and the deportation of Jews from Grenoble to Nazi concentration camps (20/10FF, closed Tuesday).

The double **Notre Dame** and **St Hugues Cathedral** on place Notre Dame and the adjoining 14th-century **Bishop's Palace** at 3 rue Très Cloîtres have had complete facelifts and now contain three museums: the **crypte archéologique**, with its Roman-era walls and baptistery dating from the 4th to 10th century; the **Musée d'Art Sacré**, containing liturgical and other religious objects; and the **Centre Jean Achard**, with exhibits

FRANCE

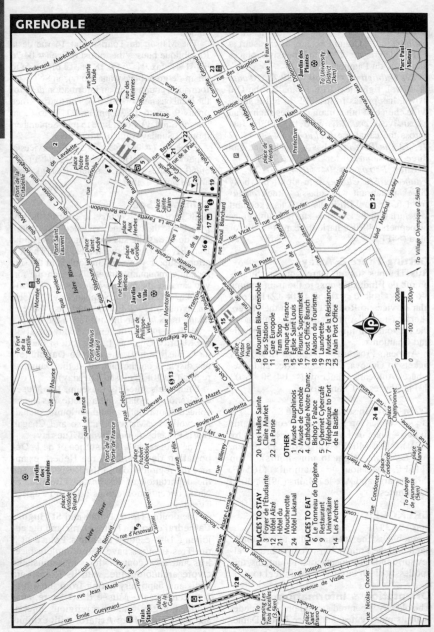

GRENOBLE

PLACES TO STAY
3 Foyer de l'Étudiante
12 Hôtel Alizé
21 Hôtel du
   Moucherotte
24 Hôtel Lakanal

PLACES TO EAT
6 Le Tonneau de Diogène
9 Restaurant
   Universitaire
14 Les Archers

20 Les Halles Sainte
   Claire Market
22 La Panse

OTHER
1 Musée Dauphinois
2 Musée de Grenoble
4 Cathédrale Notre Dame;
   Bishop's Palace
5 Cybermet Cybercafé
7 Téléphérique to Fort
   de la Bastille
8 Mountain Bike Grenoble
10 Bus Station
11 Gare Europole
13 Banque de France
15 Église Saint Louis
16 Prisunic Supermarket
17 Post Office Branch
18 Maison du Tourisme
19 Laundrette
23 Musée de la Résistance
25 Main Post Office

euro currency converter €1 = 6.55FF

of art from the Dauphiné region. Admission is 20FF.

Activities

Skiing & Snowboarding There are a number of inexpensive, low-altitude ski stations near Grenoble, including Col de Porte and Le Sappey (north of the city) and St Nizier du Moucherotte, Lans-en-Vercors, Villard-de-Lans and Méaudre (west of the city). The tourist office has comprehensive information, including accommodation lists.

Hiking The place to go for hiking information is Info-Montagne (☎ 04 76 42 45 90), on the 1st floor of the Maison du Tourisme. It sells hiking maps and has detailed info on gîtes d'étape and refuges (closed Sunday).

Places to Stay

Camping The year-round *Camping Les Trois Pucelles* (58 rue des Allobroges) is one block west of the Drac River in Grenoble's western suburb of Seyssins. From the train station, take the tram towards Fontaine and get off at the Maisonnat stop, then take bus No 51 to Mas des Îles and walk east on rue du Dauphiné.

Hostels The *Auberge de Jeunesse* (☎ 04 76 09 33 52, fax 04 76 09 38 99, **@** grenoble-echirolles@fuaj.org, 10 ave du Grésivaudan) is in Échirolles 5.5km south of the train station. From cours Jean Jaurès, take bus No 8 (direction Pont de Claix) and get off at the Quinzaine stop – look for the Casino supermarket. Reception opens 7.30 am to 11 pm, and beds cost 68FF.

Friendly and central *Foyer de l'Étudiante* (☎ 04 76 42 00 84, 4 rue Ste Ursule) accepts travellers of both sexes from the end of June to the end of September. Singles/doubles cost 90/130FF a day and, for those who want to linger longer, 450/700FF a week. It opens 7 to 12.30 am.

Hotels Near the train station, *Hôtel Alizé* (☎ 04 76 43 12 91, fax 04 76 47 62 79, 1 rue Amiral Courbet) has modern singles/doubles with washbasin for 138/202FF and doubles with shower for 162/212FF.

There are lots of inexpensive hotels in the place Condorcet area, about 800m south-east of the train station. One of the best is *Hôtel*

Lakanal (☎ 04 76 46 03 42, fax 04 76 17 21 24, 26 rue des Bergers). It attracts a young and friendly crowd and has simple singles/doubles with toilet for just 100/120FF. Rooms with shower and toilet cost 140/180FF. Breakfast is 20FF.

In the city centre, *Hôtel du Moucherotte* (☎ 04 76 54 61 40, fax 04 76 44 62 52, 1 rue Auguste Gaché) is a dark and rather old-fashioned place with huge, clean rooms. Its singles/doubles with shower start at 145/178FF. Breakfast is 30FF extra.

Places to Eat

Les Halles Ste Claire food market, near the tourist office, is open daily till 1 pm. The *Restaurant Universitaire* (5 rue d'Arsonval) opens 11.20 am to 1.15 pm and 6.20 to 7.50 pm weekdays between mid-September and mid-June. Tickets (about 15/30FF for students/nonstudents) are sold at lunchtime only.

For good food at reasonable prices, try *Le Tonneau de Diogène* (☎ 04 76 42 38 40, 6 place Notre Dame) which attracts a young, lively crowd. The plat du jour is 55FF, salads cost from 15FF to 38FF. It's open 8.30 am to 1 am.

La Panse (☎ 04 76 54 09 54, 7 rue de la Paix) offers a 50FF and 76FF lunch *menu* and a 100FF day and evening *menu* that are especially good value. It opens noon to 1.30 pm and 7.15 to 10 pm (closed Sunday).

Les Archers (☎ 04 76 46 27 76, 2 rue Docteur Bailly) is a brasserie-style restaurant with great outside seating in summer. The plat du jour is 57FF, *huîtres* (oysters) are 106FF a dozen, and it opens 10 am to 10 pm.

Getting There & Away

Bus The bus station (☎ 04 76 87 90 31) is next to the train station at place de la Gare. VFD (☎ 04 76 47 77 77) has services to Geneva (151FF, 2½ hours), Nice (311FF, five hours), Annecy (99FF, 1¾ hours), Chamonix (161FF, three hours), and to a number of ski resorts. Intercars (☎ 04 76 46 19 77, fax 04 76 47 96 34) handles long-haul destinations such as Budapest (580FF), Madrid (540FF), Lisbon (830FF), London (550FF), Prague (520FF) and Venice (260FF).

Train The train station (☎ 0836 35 35 39) is served by both tram lines (get off at the Gare

Europole stop). There's a regular fast service to Paris' Gare de Lyon (371FF, 3½ hours by TGV). There are three trains a day to Turin (246FF) and Milan (321FF) in Italy, and two trains a day to Geneva (118FF), and regular services to Lyon, Nice and Monaco.

Getting Around
Buses and trams take the same tickets (7.50FF, or 56FF for a carnet of 10), which are sold by bus (but not tram) drivers and by ticket machines at tram stops. They're valid for transfers within an hour of time-stamping, but not for return trips.

Mountain Bike Grenoble (☎ 04 76 47 58 76), 6 quai de France, has mountain bikes for 60/95FF for a half/full day, 170FF for two days, plus a 2000FF deposit (closed Sunday and Monday).

Provence

Provence was settled by the Ligurians, the Celts and the Greeks, but it was after its conquest by Julius Caesar in the mid-1st century BC that the region really began to flourish.

Many well-preserved amphitheatres, aqueducts and other buildings from the Roman period can still be seen in Arles and Nîmes (see the Languedoc-Roussillon section later). During the 14th century, the Catholic Church, then led by a series of French-born popes, moved its headquarters from feud-riven Rome to Avignon, thus beginning the most resplendent period in that city's history.

MARSEILLE
pop 1.23 million
The cosmopolitan and much maligned port of Marseille, France's second-largest city and third-most populous urban area, isn't a the least bit prettified for the benefit of tourists. Its urban geography and atmosphere derive from the diversity of its inhabitants, the majority of whom are immigrants (or their descendants) from the Mediterranean basin, West Africa and Indochina. Although Marseille is notorious for organised crime and racial tensions, the city is worth exploring for a day or two.

Orientation
The city's main street, La Canebière, stretches eastward from the Vieux Port. The train station is north of La Canebière at the top of blvd d'Athènes. The city centre is around rue Paradis, which becomes more fashionable as you move south.

Information
The tourist office (☎ 04 91 13 89 00, fax 04 91 13 89 20, ⓔ accueil@marseille-tourisme .com) is next to the Vieux Port at 4 La Canebière. It opens 9 am to 7 pm (Sunday from 10 am to 5 pm). From mid-June to mid-September, it opens till 7.30 pm daily. Staff can make hotel reservations. The annexe (☎ 04 91 50 59 18) at the train station opens weekdays only (Monday to Saturday in July and August).

The Le Rezo Cybercafé (☎ 04 91 42 70 02, ⓔ lerezo@lerezo.com), 68 cours Julien (6e) charges 30/50FF for 30 minutes/one hour access and opens 9.30 am to 8 pm Monday, 9.30 am to 10 pm Tuesday to Friday, and 10 am to 11 pm Saturday.

Dangers & Annoyances Despite its fearsome reputation, Marseille is probably no more dangerous than other French cities. As elsewhere, beware of bag-snatchers and pickpockets, especially at the train station. At night avoid the Belsunce area – the neighbourhood south-west of the train station and streets bordering La Canebière.

Things to See & Do
Marseille grew up around the **Vieux Port**, where Greeks from Asia Minor established a settlement around 600 BC. The quarter north of quai du Port (around the Hôtel de Ville) was blown up by the Germans in 1943 and rebuilt after the war. The lively **place Thiars** pedestrian zone, with its many late-night restaurants and cafes, is south of the quai de Rive Neuve.

If you like great panoramic views or overwrought mid-19th-century architecture, consider a walk up to the **Basilique Notre Dame de la Garde**, on a hill top 1km south of the Vieux Port – the highest point in the city. Bus No 60 will get you back to the Vieux Port.

Museums All the museums listed here charge 12FF to 18FF for admission; all admit students for half-price. The 'Passeport pour les musées' (50/25FF) is valid for 15 days and allows unlimited entry to all museums.

The **Centre de la Vieille Charité** is home to Marseille's Museum of Mediterranean Archaeology and has superb permanent exhibits on ancient Egypt and Greece (closed weekends). It's in the mostly North African Panier quarter (north of the Vieux Port) at 2 rue de la Charité.

The **Musée Cantini** off rue Paradis, at 19 rue Grignan, has changing exhibitions of modern and contemporary art (closed weekends).

Roman history buffs should visit the **Musée d'Histoire de Marseille** on the ground floor of the Centre Bourse shopping mall, just north of La Canebière (closed Tuesday). Its exhibits include the remains of a merchant ship that plied the waters of the Mediterranean in the late 2nd century AD.

Château d'If Château d'If (☎ 04 91 59 02 30), the 16th-century island fortress-turned-prison made infamous by Alexandre Dumas' *The Count of Monte Cristo*, can be visited daily from 9 am until 7 pm (closed Monday from October to March). Admission costs 22FF. Boats (20 minutes each way; 50FF return) depart from quai des Belges in the Vieux Port and continue to the nearby **Îles du Frioul** (80FF return for chateau and islands).

Places to Stay

Camping & Hostels Tents can usually be pitched (26FF per person) on the grounds of the *Auberge de Jeunesse Château de Bois Luzy* (☎ 04 91 49 06 18, fax 04 91 49 06 18, *Allées des Primevères*), 4.5km east of the city centre in the Montolivet neighbourhood. Otherwise dorm beds (HI card required) are 44FF. Take bus No 6 from near the Canebière-Réformés metro stop or bus No 8 from La Canebière.

The *Auberge de Jeunesse de Bonneveine* (☎ 04 91 73 21 81, fax 04 91 73 97 23, ✉ *mar seille@fuaj.org, Impasse du Docteur Bonfils (8e)*), 4.5km south of the Vieux Port, has beds for 72FF (closed in January). Take bus No 44 from the Rond-Point du Prado metro stop and get off at place Louis Bonnefon.

Hotels – Train Station Area The two-star *Hôtel d'Athènes* (☎ 04 91 90 12 93, fax 04 91 90 72 03, 37-39 blvd d'Athènes, 1er)* is at the foot of the grand staircase leading from the train station into town. Average but well-kept singles and doubles with shower and toilet cost 220FF to 300FF. Rooms in its adjoining annexe called the *Hôtel Little Palace* cost between 120FF and 280FF for singles/doubles.

Hotels – Around La Canebière *Hôtel Ozea* (☎ 04 91 47 91 84, 12 rue Barbaroux, 1er)* welcomes new guests 24 hours a day (at night just ring the bell to wake up the night clerk). Clean, old-fashioned doubles without/with shower are 120/150FF. There are no hall showers. There are well-kept singles and doubles at *Hôtel Pied-à-Terre* (☎ 04 91 92 00 95, 18 rue Barbaroux, 1er)* costing 120/150FF without/with shower.

A little more expensive but definitely worth the money is the homely and very clean *Hôtel Lutetia* (☎ 04 91 50 81 78, fax 04 91 50 23 52, 38 Allées Léon Gambetta)* with smallish rooms equipped with TV and phone for 230/260FF for singles/doubles.

Places to Eat

Fresh fruits and vegies are sold at the *Marché des Capucins*, one block south of La Canebière on place des Capucins, and at the *fruit and vegetable market* on cours Pierre Puget. Both are closed Sunday.

Restaurants along and near the pedestrianised cours Julien, a few blocks south of La Canebière, offer an incredible variety of cuisines: Antillean, Pakistani, Thai, Lebanese, Tunisian, Italian and more. An excellent value Caribbean-themed eatery with 'student dishes' for 29FF is the *Mosaic (38 cours Julien)*. Its *plat du jour* is only 19FF. *La Caucase (62 cours Julien)* specialising in Armenian dishes, is open nightly from about 6 pm and has *menus* from 88FF. *Le Resto Provençal (54 cours Julien)* does regional French cuisine and has outdoor tables; mains are around 115FF, the plat du jour is 43FF and the lunch *menu* is 65FF (closed Sunday and Monday). The West Indian *Restaurant Antillais (10 cours Julien)* has starters from 20FF, main dishes from 40FF, and a 100FF *menu* that includes house wine.

Countless cafes and restaurants line the pedestrian streets around place Thiars, which is on the south side of the Vieux Port. Though many offer bouillabaisse, the rich fish stew

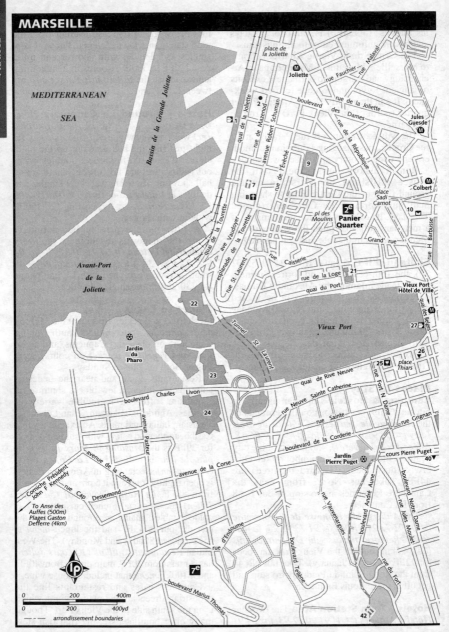

MARSEILLE

MEDITERRANEAN

SEA

Bassin de la Grande Joliette

Avant-Port
de la
Joliette

place de
la Joliette

Ⓜ Joliette

rue Fauchier

rue Malaval

boulevard des Dames

rue de la Joliette

Jules
Guesde
Ⓜ

rue de la République

Ⓜ Colbert

place Sadi Carnot

rue H Barbusse

quai de la Joliette

rue de Mazenod

avenue Robert Schuman

rue de l'Evêché

9

pl des Moulins

2e
Panier
Quarter

10

Grand' rue

quai de la Tourette

avenue Vaudoyer

esplanade de la Tourette

rue St Laurent

rue Caisserie

rue de la Loge

21

Vieux Port –
Hôtel de Ville

quai du Port

22

Ⓜ

Tunnel St Laurent

Vieux Port

27

Jardin
du
Pharo

23

quai de Rive Neuve

26

25

place
Thiars

boulevard Charles Livon

24

rue Neuve Sainte Catherine

rue Sainte

rue Fort N Dame

rue Grignan

avenue Pasteur

avenue de la Corse

boulevard de la Corderie

Jardin
Pierre Puget

cours Pierre Puget

40

Corniche Président
John F Kennedy

rue Cap

avenue de la Corse

rue Vauvenargues

boulevard André Aune

boulevard Notre Dame

L.rue Jules Moulet

Dessemond

To Anse des
Auffes (500m)
Plages Gaston
Defferre (4km)

rue d'Endoume

boulevard Tellene

rue du Fort

7e

42

boulevard Marius Thomas

0   200   400m
0   200   400yd

– – – arrondissement boundaries

euro currency converter €1 = 6.55FF

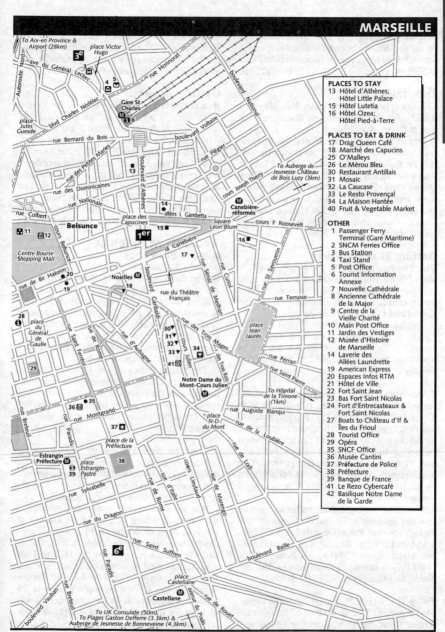

MARSEILLE

place Victor
Hugo

To Aix-en Province &
Airport (28km)

ave du Général
Leclerc

rue Honnorat

boulevard National

Autoroute Nord

blvd Charles Nédélec

Gare St
Charles

place
Jules
Guesde

rue Bernard du Bois

boulevard Voltaire

boulevard d'Athènes

rue Flégier

rue des Petites Maries

cours Joseph Thierry

To Auberge de
Jeunesse Château
de Bois Luzy (3km)

rue des Dominicaines

rue Nationale

Canebière-
réformés

rue Colbert

allées L Gambetta

cours F Roosevelt

place des
Capucines

Square
Léon Blum

cours Belsunce

Belsunce

la Canebière

Centre Bourse
Shopping Mall

rue de Bir Hakeim

Noailles

boulevard Garibaldi

rue du Théâtre
Français

rue St Savournin

rue Terrusse

place
du
Général
de Gaulle

rue Saint Ferréol

rue de Rome

rue d'Aubagne

rue des Trois Mages

place
Jean
Jaurès

rue Ferrari

cours Julien

rue des Trois Rois

Notre Dame du
Mont-Cours Julien

rue Saint Pierre

To Hôpital
de la Timone
(1km)

rue Montgrand

rue Auguste Blanqui

place
N-D
du Mont

rue de la Loubière

place de la
Préfecture

rue de Lodi

Estrangin
Préfecture

place
Estrangin-
Pastré

cours Lieutaud

cours d'Italie

rue de Rome

rue de Marengo

rue Sylvabelle

rue Paradis

rue du Dragon

rue Breteuil

rue Saint Suffren

place
Castellane

rue de Rouet

Castellane

avenue du Prado

To UK Consulate (50m),
To Plages Gaston Defferre (3.3km) &
Auberge de Jeunesse de Bonneveine (4.3km)

PLACES TO STAY
13   Hôtel d'Athènes;
     Hôtel Little Palace
15   Hôtel Lutetia
16   Hôtel Ozea;
     Hôtel Pied-à-Terre

PLACES TO EAT & DRINK
17   Drag Queen Café
18   Marché des Capucins
25   O'Malleys
26   Le Mérou Bleu
30   Restaurant Antillais
31   Mosaic
32   La Caucase
33   Le Resto Provençal
34   La Maison Hantée
40   Fruit & Vegetable Market

OTHER
1   Passenger Ferry
     Terminal (Gare Maritime)
2   SNCM Ferries Office
3   Bus Station
4   Taxi Stand
5   Post Office
6   Tourist Information
     Annexe
7   Nouvelle Cathédrale
8   Ancienne Cathédrale
     de la Major
9   Centre de la
     Vieille Charité
10   Main Post Office
11   Jardin des Vestiges
12   Musée d'Histoire
     de Marseille
14   Laverie des
     Allées Laundrette
19   American Express
20   Espaces Infos RTM
21   Hôtel de Ville
22   Fort Saint Jean
23   Bas Fort Saint Nicolas
24   Fort d'Entrecasteaux &
     Fort Saint Nicolas
27   Boats to Château d'If &
     Îles du Frioul
28   Tourist Office
29   Opéra
35   SNCF Office
36   Musée Cantini
37   Préfecture de Police
38   Préfecture
39   Banque de France
41   Le Rezo Cybercafé
42   Basilique Notre Dame
     de la Garde

FRANCE

for which Marseille is famous, it's difficult to find the real thing. Try **Le Mérou Bleu** *(32-36 rue St Saëns)*, a popular seafood restaurant with a lovely terrace. Bouillabaisse is 75FF to 145FF, other seafood dishes 72FF to 125FF.

Entertainment
Listings appear in the monthly *Vox Mag* and weekly *Taktik* and *Sortir*, all distributed for free at the tourist office.

One of Marseille's two Irish pubs, *O'Malleys (quai de Rive Neuve)* overlooks the old port on the corner of rue de la Paix. Camper than a row of tents and full of fun is the **Drag Queen Café** *(2 rue Sénac de Meilhan)*, which hosts live bands. For rock, reggae, country and other live music, try **La Maison Hantée** *(10 rue Vian)*, on a hip street between cours Julien and rue des Trois Rois.

Getting There & Away
Bus The bus station (☎ 04 91 08 16 40) at place Victor Hugo, 150m to the right as you exit the train station, offers services to Aix-en-Provence, Avignon, Cannes, Nice, Nice airport and Orange, among others.

Eurolines (☎ 04 91 50 57 55) has buses to Spain, Italy, Morocco, the UK and other countries. Its counter in the bus station is open from 8 am to noon and 2 to 6 pm (closed Sunday).

Train Marseille's passenger train station, served by both metro lines, is called Gare St Charles (☎ 0836 35 35 35). The information and ticket reservation office, one level below the tracks next to the metro entrance, is open from 9 am to 8 pm (closed on Sunday). Luggage may be left at the left-luggage office next to platform 1. The office is open from 6 am to 10 pm and it costs 20FF per piece of luggage per day.

From Marseille there are trains to more or less any destination in France. Some sample destinations are Paris' Gare de Lyon (379FF, 4¼ hours by TGV, 10 a day), Avignon (92FF, one hour), Lyon (209FF, 3¼ hours), Nice (149FF, 1½ hours), Barcelona (342FF, 8½ hours) and Geneva (262FF, 6½ hours).

Ferry The Société Nationale Maritime Corse-Méditerranée (SNCM; ☎ 0836 67 95 00) runs ferries from the *gare maritime* (passenger ferry terminal) at the foot of blvd des Dames to Corsica. The SNCM office, 61 blvd des Dames (closed Sunday), also handles ticketing for the Moroccan ferry company, Compagnie Marocaine de Navigation (COMANAV).

Getting Around
Bus & Metro Marseille has two easy-to-use metro lines, a tram line and an extensive bus network, which operate from 5 am to 9 pm. Night buses and tram No 68 run from 9 pm to 12.30 am. Tickets (9FF, 42FF for a carnet of six) are valid on all services for one hour (no return trips). Tram stops have modern blue ticket distributors that should be used to time-stamp your ticket before you board. For more information, visit the Espace Infos RTM (☎ 04 91 91 92 10), 6-8 rue des Fabres.

AROUND MARSEILLE
Aix-en-Provence
pop 134,222
One of the most appealing cities in Provence, Aix owes its atmosphere to the students who make up over 20% of the population. The city is renowned for its *calissons*, almond-paste confectionery made with candied melon, and for being the birthplace of post-impressionist painter Cézanne. Aix hosts the Festival International d'Art Lyrique each July.

The tourist office (☎ 04 42 16 11 61, fax 04 42 16 11 62, ✉ infos@aixenprovencetour ism.com) is on place Général de Gaulle. Aix is easy to see on a day trip from Marseille, and frequent trains (38FF) make the 35-minute trip.

Things to See The mostly pedestrianised old city is a great place to explore, with its maze of tiny streets full of ethnic restaurants and specialist food shops, intermixed with elegant 17th and 18th-century mansions.

Aix also has several interesting museums, the finest of which is the **Musée Granet** at place St Jean de Malte (10FF, closed Tuesday). The collection includes Italian, Dutch and French paintings from the 16th to 19th centuries as well as some of Cézanne's lesser known paintings. The **Musée des Tapisseries**, in the former bishop's palace at 28 place des Martyrs de la Résistance, is worth visiting for its tapestries and sumptuous costumes (15FF, closed Sunday).

AVIGNON
pop 85,935

Avignon acquired its ramparts and its reputation as a city of art and culture during the 14th century, when Pope Clement V and his court, fleeing political turmoil in Rome, established themselves here. From 1309 to 1377 huge sums of money were invested in building and decorating the popes' palace. Even after the pontifical court returned to Rome amid bitter charges that Avignon had become a den of criminals and brothel-goers, the city remained an important cultural centre.

Today, Avignon maintains its tradition as a patron of the arts, most notably through its annual performing arts festival. The city's other attractions include a bustling walled town and some interesting museums, including several across the Rhône in Villeneuve-lès-Avignon.

The world-famous Festival d'Avignon, held in the last three weeks of July, attracts many hundreds of artists who put on some 300 performances of all sorts each day. Avignon was Europe's first of the twelve Capitals of Culture in 2000.

Orientation

The main avenue in the walled city runs northward from the train station to place de l'Horloge; it's called cours Jean Jaurès south of the tourist office and rue de la République north of it. The island that runs down the middle of the Rhône between Avignon and Villeneuve-lès-Avignon is known as Île de la Barthelasse.

Information

The tourist office (☎ 04 32 74 32 74, fax 04 90 82 95 03, ✉ information@ot-avignon.fr), 41 cours Jean Jaurès, is 300m north of the train station. It opens 9 am to 6 pm (5 pm on Saturday, 10 am to midday on Sunday). During the Avignon Festival it opens 10 am to 8 pm daily (5 pm on Sunday).

The main post office is on cours Président Kennedy, which is through Porte de la République from the train station.

Cyberdrome (☎ 04 90 16 05 15, fax 04 90 16 05 14, ✉ cyberdrome@wanadoo.fr), on rue Guillaume Puy, charges 25FF for 30 minutes online access or 400FF for 10 hours and opens 7 am to 1 am.

Things to See & Do

Palais des Papes & Around Avignon's leading tourist attraction is the fortified Palace of the Popes, built during the 14th century. The seemingly endless halls, chapels, corridors and staircases were once sumptuously decorated, but these days they are nearly empty except for a few damaged frescoes. The palace opens 9 am to 7 pm (9 pm in July and 8 pm in August and September). Admission costs 45/37F.

At the far northern end of place du Palais, the **Musée du Petit Palais** houses an outstanding collection of 13th to 16th-century Italian religious paintings (30/15FF, closed Tuesday). Just up the hill is **Rocher des Doms**, a park with great views of the Rhône, Pont St Bénézet and Villeneuve-lès-Avignon.

Pont St Bénézet Originally built in the 12th century to link Avignon and Villeneuve-lès-Avignon, this is the 'Pont d'Avignon' mentioned in the French nursery rhyme. Once 900m long, the bridge was repaired and rebuilt several times until all but four of its 22 spans were washed away in the 17th century. Entry to the bridge (closed Monday) costs 17/9FF.

Museums Housed in an 18th-century mansion, the **Musée Calvet**, 65 rue Joseph Vernet, has a collection of ancient Egyptian, Greek and Roman artefacts as well as paintings from the 16th to 20th centuries (30/15FF). Its annexe, the **Musée Lapidaire**, 27 rue de la République, houses sculpture and statuary from the Gallo-Roman, Romanesque and Gothic periods (10FF, closed Tuesday).

At 17 rue Victor Hugo, the **Musée Louis Vouland** exhibits a fine collection of ceramics and some superb 18th-century French furniture (20/10FF, closed Sunday and Monday).

Villeneuve-lès-Avignon Avignon's picturesque sister city also has a few interesting sights, all of which are included in a 45FF combined ticket sold at the major sights. From Avignon, Villeneuve can be reached by foot or bus No 10 from the main post office.

The **Chartreuse du Val de Bénédiction**, 60 rue de la République, was once the largest and most important Carthusian monastery in France (32/21FF). The **Musée Pierre de**

FRANCE

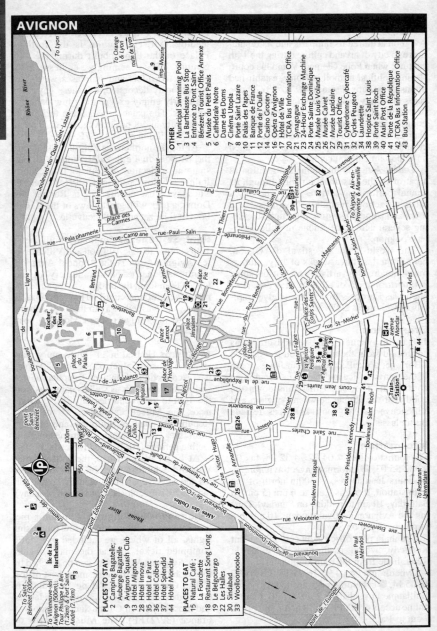

AVIGNON

OTHER
1 Municipal Swimming Pool
3 La Barthelasse Bus Stop
4 Entrance to Pont Saint Bénézet; Tourist Office Annexe
5 Musée du Petit Palais
6 Cathédrale Notre Dame des Doms
7 Cinéma Utopia
8 Porte Saint Lazare
10 Palais des Papes
11 Banque de France
12 Porte de l'Oulle
14 Casino Grocery
16 Opéra d'Avignon
17 Hôtel de Ville
20 TCRA Bus Information Office
21 Synagogue
23 24-Hour Exchange Machine
24 Porte Sainte Dominique
25 Musée Louis Voland
26 Musée Calvet
27 Musée Lapidaire
29 Tourist Office
31 Cyberdrome Cybercafé
32 Cycles Peugeot
34 Laundrette
38 Hospice Saint Louis
39 Porte Saint Roch
40 Main Post Office
41 Porte de la République
42 TCRA Bus Information Office
43 Bus Station

PLACES TO STAY
2 Camping Bagatelle; Auberge Bagatelle; Avignon Squash Club
9 Hôtel Mignon
13 Hôtel Innova
28 Hôtel Le Parc
35 Hôtel Colbert
36 Hôtel Splendid
37 Hôtel Splendid
44 Hôtel Monclar

PLACES TO EAT
15 Natural Café; La Fourchette
18 Restaurant Song Long
19 Le Belgocargo
22 Les Halles
30 Sindabad
33 Woolloomooloo

To Lyon
To Orange & Lyon
route de Lyon
imp-Mourre
Rhône River
boulevard du Quai Saint-Lazare
rue des Infirmières
rue-Louis-Pasteur
rue Carreterie
place des Carmes
rue Pala pharnerie
rue-Camp ane
rue-Paul-Sain
Guillaume Puy
rue Philonarde
rue Thiers
boulevard de la Ligne
Banasterie
f Bertrand
Rocher des Doms
boulevard du Rhône
place Campana
place Crillon
place de-la-Balance
r de-la-Balance
place du Palais
rue-des-Grottes
rue Grande Fusterie
rue-Joseph--Vernet
rue Vernet
rue St-Agricol
place de l'Horloge
place Jérusalem
place Carnot
place Pie
rue Carnot
rue Bonneterie
rue-du-Roi--René
rue St-Didier
rue-du Rempart-de-l'Oulle
boulevard--du-Rhône
Allées des Oulles
boulevard-de-Saint-Dominique
rue Velouterie
rue du-Rempart-de-l'Oulle
rue Victor Hugo
rue Annanelle
rue--Joseph
rue Saint Charles
rue de la République
rue Henri-Fabre
rue des Lices
rue des Teinturiers
rue St-Michel
rue du-Portail--Magnanen
boulevard-Saint--Michel
place des Corps Saints
rue Agricol Perdiguier
sq Agricol Perdiguier
cours Jean Jaurès
boulevard Saint Roch
cours Président Kennedy
boulevard Raspail
ave Paul Méindol
ave Eisenhower
pont de-l'Europe
avenue
To Airport, Aix-en-Provence & Marseille
To Arles
avenue Monclar
Train Station
To Restaurant Universitaire

To Saint-Bénézet (300m)
To Villeneuve-lès-Avignon (500m); Tour Philippe le Bel (1.2km) & Fort Saint André (2.1km)
Île de la Barthelasse
chemin des
pont Édouard-Daladier
pont Saint Bénézet

0 150 300m
0 150 300m

---

euro currency converter €1 = 6.55FF

Luxembourg on rue de la République has a fine collection of religious paintings (20/12FF, closed Mondays and in February).

The Tour Philippe le Bel, a defensive tower built in the 14th century at what was then the north-western end of Pont St Bénézet, has great views of Avignon's walled city, the river and the surrounding countryside. Admission costs 10FF. Another Provençal panorama can be enjoyed from the 14th-century Fort St André (25/15FF).

Special Events

The world-famous Festival d'Avignon is held every year during the last three weeks of July. Information on the official festival can be obtained by contacting the Bureau du Festival (☎ 04 90 27 66 50, fax 04 90 27 66 83), 8 bis rue de Mons, F-84000 Avignon. Tickets can be reserved from mid-June onwards.

Places to Stay

Camping The three-star *Camping Bagatelle* (*Île de la Barthelasse*) open year-round, is an attractive, shaded camping ground just north of Pont Édouard Daladier, 850m from the walled city. High season charges are 23.80FF per adult and 11FF to pitch a tent. Reception opens 8 am to 9 pm. Take bus No 10 from the main post office to the La Barthelasse stop.

Hostels The 210-bed *Auberge Bagatelle* (☎ 04 90 85 78 45, *Île de la Barthelasse*) is part of a large, park-like area that includes Camping Bagatelle. A bed in a room costs 60FF. See the Camping section for bus directions.

From April to September a bunk in a converted squash court at the *Avignon Squash Club* (☎ 04 90 85 27 78, *32 blvd Limbert*) costs 60FF. Reception opens 9 am to 10 pm (closed on Sunday from September to June; open 8 to 11 am and 5 to 11 pm in July and August). Take bus No 7 from the train station to the Université stop.

Hotels – Within the Walls There are three hotels all close to each other on the same street. *Hôtel Le Parc* (☎ 04 90 82 71 55, *18 rue Agricol Perdiguier*) has singles/doubles without shower for 145/175FF and 195/215FF with shower.

The friendly *Hôtel Splendid* (☎ 04 90 86 14 46, fax 04 90 85 38 55, *17 rue Agricol*

Perdiguier) has singles/doubles with shower for 130/200FF and rooms with shower and toilet for 170/280FF.

The third in the trio, the two-star *Hôtel Colbert* (☎ 04 90 86 20 20, fax 04 90 85 97 00, *7 rue Agricol Perdiguier*) has well-priced singles with shower for 160FF and doubles/triples with shower and toilet for 210/260FF.

The always busy *Hôtel Innova* (☎ 04 90 82 54 10, fax 04 90 82 52 39, *100 rue Joseph Vernet*) has bright, comfortable and soundproofed rooms ranging in price from 140FF to 220FF. Breakfast is 25FF.

Hôtel Mignon (☎ 04 90 82 17 30, fax 04 90 85 78 46, *12 rue Joseph Vernet*) has spotless, well-kept and soundproofed singles with shower for 150FF and doubles with shower and toilet for 220FF.

Hotels – Outside the Walls The noisy, family-run *Hôtel Monclar* (☎ 04 90 86 20 14, fax 04 90 85 94 94, @ hmonclar84@aol.com, *13 ave Monclar*) is in an 18th-century building just across the tracks from the train station. Comfortable doubles start at 165FF with sink and bidet. The hotel has its own parking lot (20FF) and a pretty, little back garden.

Places to Eat

Les Halles food market on place Pie is open daily (except Monday) from 7 am to 1 pm. *Restaurant Universitaire (ave du Blanchissage)*, south-west of the train station, opens October to June (closed Saturday dinner and Sunday, and during university holidays) from 11.30 am to 1.30 pm and 6.30 to 7.30 pm. People with student IDs can buy tickets (15FF to 30FF) at the CROUS office at 29 blvd Limbert, just east of the walled city on Monday, Tuesday, Wednesday and Friday from 10.30 am to 12.30 pm.

Restaurant Song Long (1 rue Carnot) offers a wide variety of excellent Vietnamese dishes, including 16 *plats végétariens* (vegetarian soups, salads, starters and main dishes from 28FF to 40FF). Lunch/dinner *menus* are 35FF, 40 and 45FF. Song Long opens daily.

Le Belgocargo (7 rue Armand de Pontmartin), a Belgian place tucked behind Église St Pierre, serves mussels 16 different ways for 49FF to 68FF and *waterzooi de volaille* (a creamy Belgian stew of chicken, leeks and herbs) for 58FF.

For hearty and healthy fodder in a rustic setting (tree trunks for benches etc) look no farther than the atmospheric **Natural Café** (*17 rue Racine*). It is closed on Sunday and Monday. Adjoining it is the more conventional **La Fourchette** (*17 rue Racine*), a Michelin-recommended place with *menus* for 150FF.

On the other side of town, a good choice is **Woolloomooloo** (*16 bis rue des Teinturiers*), a lively spot with vegetarian and Antillean dishes on offer (*menus* from 67FF to 89FF; closed Sunday and Monday). Nearby, the small bohemian **Sindabad** (*53 rue des Teinturiers*) offers good Tunisian, oriental and Provençal home cooking and has a 50FF *plat du jour* (closed Sunday).

Entertainment

Cinéma Utopia (*4 rue des Escaliers Ste Anne*) is a student entertainment/cultural centre with a jazz club, cafe and four cinemas screening nondubbed films.

From October to June, the **Opéra d'Avignon** (☎ 04 90 82 23 44, place de l'Horloge) stages operas, plays and concerts. The box office opens 11 am to 6 pm (closed Sunday).

Getting There & Away

Bus The bus station (☎ 04 90 82 07 35) is down the ramp to the right as you exit the train station. Tickets are sold on the buses, which are run by about 20 different companies. Destinations include Aix-en-Provence (86FF, one hour), Arles (38FF, 1½ hours), Nice (165FF), Nîmes (40FF), and Marseille (89FF, 35 minutes). Sunday services are less frequent.

Train The train station (☎ 0836 35 35 39) is across blvd St Roch from Porte de la République. There are frequent trains to Arles (36FF, 25 minutes), Nice (206FF, four hours), Nîmes (44FF, 30 minutes) and Paris (370FF, 3¼ hours via TGV).

Getting Around

TCRA municipal buses operate 7 am to about 7.40 pm. Tickets cost 6.50FF if bought from the driver; a carnet of five tickets (good for 10 rides) costs 48FF from TCRA offices in the walled city at porte de la République and at place Pie (closed Sunday).

Cycles Peugeot (☎ 04 90 86 32 49), 80 rue Guillaume Puy, has three-speeds and 10-speeds for 60/130/240FF for one/three/seven days (plus 1000FF deposit).

AROUND AVIGNON
Arles
pop 50,513

Arles began its ascent to prosperity in 49 BC when Julius Caesar, to whom the city had given its support, sacked Marseille, which had backed the Roman general Pompey. It soon became a major trading centre and by the late 1st century AD, needed a 20,000-seat amphitheatre and a 12,000-seat theatre. Now known as the **Arènes** and the **Théâtre Antique** respectively, they are still used to stage bullfights and cultural events.

Arles is also known for its **Église St Trophime** and **Cloître St Trophime**. Significant parts of both date from the 12th century and are in the Romanesque style. But the city is probably best known as the place where Van Gogh painted some of his most famous works, including *The Sunflowers*. The tourist office (☎ 04 90 18 41 20) is on esplanade des Lices.

There are regular bus services to Marseille (87FF, 2½ hours), Aix-en-Provence (68FF, 1¾ hours) and Avignon (40FF, 1½ hours).

Côte d'Azur

The Côte d'Azur, which includes the French Riviera, stretches along France's Mediterranean coast from Toulon to the Italian border. Many of the towns here – budget-busting St Tropez, Cannes, Antibes, Nice and Monaco – have become world-famous thanks to the recreational activities of the tanned and idle rich. The reality is rather less glamorous, but the Côte d'Azur still has a great deal to attract visitors: sunshine, 40km of beaches, all sorts of cultural activities and, sometimes, even a bit of glitter.

Unless you're camping or hostelling, your best bet is to stay in Nice, which has a generous supply of cheap hotels, and make day trips to other places. Note that theft from backpacks, pockets, cars and even laundrettes is a serious problem along the Côte d'Azur, especially at train and bus stations.

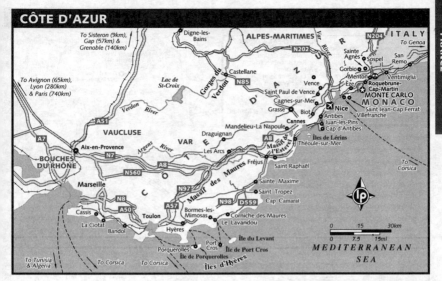

CÔTE D'AZUR

NICE
pop 342,738
Known as the capital of the Riviera, the fashionable yet relaxed city of Nice makes a great base from which to explore the entire Côte d'Azur. The city, which did not become part of France until 1860, has plenty of relatively cheap accommodation and is only a short train or bus ride away from the rest of the Riviera. Nice's beach may be nothing to write home about, but the city is blessed with a fine collection of museums.

Orientation
Ave Jean Médecin runs from near the train station to place Masséna. Vieux Nice is the area delineated by the quai des États-Unis, blvd Jean Jaurès and the 92m hill known as Le Château. The neighbourhood of Cimiez, home to several very good museums, is north of the town centre.

Information
The main tourist office (☎ 04 93 87 07 07, fax 04 93 16 85 16, ☻ otc@nice.coteazur.org) at the train station opens 8 am to 7 pm daily (to 8 pm July to September). The annexe at 5 promenade des Anglais (☎ 04 92 14 48 00) is open Monday to Saturday from 8 am to 6 pm.

The main post office is at 23 ave Thiers, one block from the train station. There are branch post offices at 4 ave Georges Clemenceau, on the corner of rue de Russie, and in the old city at 2 rue Louis Gassin.

Opposite the train station, Le Change (☎ 04 93 88 56 80) at 17 ave Thiers (to the right as you exit the terminal building) offers decent rates and is open from 7 am to midnight. American Express (☎ 04 93 16 53 53) is at 11 Promenade des Anglais (closed Sunday).

The Web Store (☎ 04 93 87 87 99, ☻ info@webstore.fr), 12 rue de Russie, charges 30/50FF for 30/60 minutes of Internet access and is open Monday to Saturday from 10 am to noon and 2 to 7 pm.

Things to See
An excellent-value museum pass (140/70FF), available at tourist offices and participating museums, gives free admission to some 60 Côte d'Azur museums. Unless otherwise noted, the following museums are open Wednesday to Monday from around 10 am to 5 or 6 pm (sometimes with a break for lunch in the off-season), and entry is around 25/15FF.

The **Musée d'Art Moderne et d'Art Contemporain** (Museum of Modern and Contemporary Art), ave St Jean Baptiste, specialises

FRANCE

NICE

PLACES TO STAY	PLACES TO EAT & DRINK
8 Backpackers Chez Patrick;	5 Flunch Cafétéria
Le Faubourg Montmartre	7 Cafétéria Casino
10 Hôtel du Piemont	9 Restaurant Le Toscan
11 Hôtel Belle Meunière	37 La Nissarda
14 Hôtel Les Orangers	38 Le Bistrot Saint Germain
19 Le Petit Louvre	47 Chez Wayne's
22 Centre Hébergement	51 William's Pub
Jeunesse	52 Jonathan's Live Music Pub
26 Hôtel Les Mimosas	55 Nissa Socca
34 Hôtel Little Masséna	56 Fruit & Vegetable Market
50 Hôtel au Picardie	

OTHER			
1 Fruit & Vegetable Market	18 Web Store Cybercafé	32 US Consulate	44 Post Office Branch
2 Musée Chagall	20 Prisunic Supermarket	33 Cycles Arnaud	45 Flower Market
3 Russian Orthodox Cathedral	21 Police Headquarters	35 UK Consulate	46 Palais de Justice
of Saint Nicholas	23 Airport Buses	36 24-Hour Currency	48 Boulangerie
4 Main Tourist Office	24 Public Showers & Toilets	Exchange Machine	49 Intercity Bus Station
6 Nicea Location Rent	25 Airport Buses	39 Banque de France	53 Cathédrale Sainte Réparate
12 Le Change	27 Laundrette	40 Station Centrale	54 Église Saint Jacques
13 Main Post Office	28 American Express	Terminus	le Majeur
15 Laundrette	29 Tourist Office Annexe	41 Théâtre de Nice	57 Buses to City Centre
16 Église Notre Dame	30 English-American	42 Musée d'Art Moderne	58 Tour Bellanda & Lift
17 Post Office	Library	et d'Art Contemporain	59 Ferry Terminal; SNCM Office
	31 Anglican Church	43 Opéra de Nice	

NICE

To Cimiez, Musée
Matisse & Musée
Archéologique (1.5km)

*VIEUX
NICE*

*Parc du
Château*

place
Saint
François

place
Garibaldi

place
Île de Beauté

To Auberge de
Jeunesse (2.5km)

*Bassin
Lympia*

To Monaco
via Corniche
Inférieure
(18km)

place
Magenta

place
Masséna

*Jardin
Albert
1er*

Square
Général
Leclerc

Espace
Masséna

place Pierre
Gautier

*VIEUX
NICE*

See inset

*Bassin
des
Amiraux*

*Bassin
du Commerce*

euro currency converter 1FF = €0.15

in eye-popping French and American avant-garde works from the 1960s to the present. It's served by bus Nos 3, 5, 7, 16 and 17.

The main exhibit at the **Musée Chagall**, opposite 4 ave Docteur Ménard, is a series of incredibly vivid Marc Chagall paintings illustrating stories from the Old Testament.

The **Musée Matisse**, with its fine collection of works by Henri Matisse (1869-1954), is at 164 ave des Arènes de Cimiez in Cimiez, 2.5km north-east of the train station. Many buses pass by, but No 15 is most convenient; get off at the Arènes stop.

The **Musée Archéologique** (Archaeology Museum) and nearby **Gallo-Roman Ruins** (which include public baths and an amphitheatre) are next to the Musée Matisse at 160 ave des Arènes de Cimiez.

Nice's **Russian Orthodox Cathedral of St Nicholas**, crowned by six onion-shaped domes, was built between 1903 and 1912; step inside and you'll be transported to Imperial Russia (15/10FF; closed Sunday morning). You'll need to dress appropriately: shorts or short skirts and sleeveless shirts are forbidden.

Activities

Nice's **beach** is covered with smooth pebbles, not sand. Between mid-April and mid-October, free public beaches alternate with private beaches (60FF to 70FF a day) that have all sorts of amenities (mattresses, showers, changing rooms, security etc). Along the beach you can hire paddle boats, sailboards and jet skis, and go parasailing (200FF for 15 minutes) and water-skiing (100FF to 130FF for 10 minutes). There are indoor showers (12FF) and toilets (2FF) open to the public opposite 50 Promenade des Anglais.

Places to Stay

There are quite a few cheap hotels near the train station and lots of places in a slightly higher price bracket along rue d'Angleterre, rue d'Alsace-Lorraine, rue de Suisse, rue de Russie and rue Durante, also near the station. In summer the inexpensive places fill up by late morning – book your bed by 10 am.

In summer, lots of backpackers sleep on the beach. Technically this is illegal, but the Nice police usually look the other way.

Hostels The *Auberge de Jeunesse* (☎ 04 93 89 23 64, fax 04 92 04 03 10, Route Forestière de Mont Alban) is 4km east of the train. Beds cost 68.50FF. There's a midnight curfew, and it's often full – call ahead. Take bus No 14 from the Station Centrale terminus on Square Général Leclerc, which is linked to the train station by bus Nos 15 and 17.

From mid-June to mid-September the *Centre Hébergement Jeunesse* (☎ 04 93 86 28 75, 31 rue Louis de Coppet) serves as a hostel. It's half a block north from rue de France. Beds are 50FF, and bags must be stored in the luggage room during the day (10FF). There's a midnight curfew.

The popular 21-bed *Backpackers Chez Patrick* (☎ 04 93 80 30 72, 32 rue Pertinax) is above the Faubourg Montmartre restaurant. Dorm beds are 80FF, and there's no curfew or daytime closure.

Hotels – Train Station Area *Hôtel Belle Meunière* (☎ 04 93 88 66 15, 21 ave Durante) is a clean, friendly place that attracts lots of young people. Dorm beds are 80FF, while doubles/triples with bath are 182/243FF. It's closed in December and January.

Across the street *Hôtel Les Orangers* (☎ 04 93 87 51 41, fax 04 93 82 57 82, 10 bis ave Durante) has dorm beds for 85FF, and great doubles and triples with shower, fridge and balcony for 210FF. The cheerful owner Marc speaks excellent English.

Rue d'Alsace-Lorraine is dotted with two-star hotels. One of the cheapest is the *Hôtel du Piemont* (☎ 04 93 88 25 15, fax 04 93 16 15 18, 19 rue d'Alsace-Lorraine), which has bargain singles/doubles with washbasin from 110/130FF. Singles/doubles with shower start at 140/170FF.

Hotels – Vieux Nice *Hôtel au Picardie* (☎ 04 93 85 75 51, 10 blvd Jean Jaurès) has single/double rooms from 120/150FF; there are also pricier rooms that include toilet and shower. Hall showers are 10FF.

Hotels – Elsewhere in Town The reception of the friendly *Hôtel Little Masséna* (☎ 04 93 87 72 34, 22 rue Masséna), is on the 5th floor (open until 8 pm). Doubles range in price from 140FF to 220FF. Rooms come with a hotplate and fridge. The relaxed, family-style

Hôtel Les Mimosas (☎ 04 93 88 05 59, *26 rue de la Buffa*) is two blocks north-east of the (currently closed) Musée Masséna. Utilitarian rooms of a good-size for one/two people cost 120/190FF.

Between the train station and the beach is the colourful *Le Petit Louvre* (☎ 04 93 80 15 54, fax 04 93 62 45 08, *10 rue Emma Tiranty*). Singles/doubles with shower, washbasin, fridge and hotplate are 180/205FF.

Places to Eat

In Vieux Nice, there's a *fruit and vegetable market* in front of the préfecture in cours Saleya from 6 am to 5.30 pm (closed Sunday afternoon and Monday). The no-name *boulangerie* at the south end of rue du Marché is the best place for cheap sandwiches, pizza slices and *michettes* (savoury bread stuffed with cheese, olives, anchovies and onions).

Cheap places near the train station include the *Flunch Cafétéria*, to the left as you exit the station building, and the *Cafétéria Casino* (*7 ave Thiers*) across the street. In the same vicinity, *Restaurant Le Toscan* (*1 rue de Belgique*), a family-run Italian place, offers large portions of home-made ravioli (closed Sunday).

There are Vietnamese and Chinese restaurants on rue Paganini, rue d'Italie and rue d'Alsace-Lorraine. Nearby, *Le Faubourg Montmartre* (*32 rue Pertinax*), beneath the Backpackers' Hotel, is always crowded. The house speciality is bouillabaisse (120FF for two), and there's a 68FF *menu*.

La Nissarda (*17 rue Gubernatis*) has specialities from Nice and Normandy. The *menus* are reasonably priced at 60FF (lunch only) and 78FF, 98FF and 138FF (closed Sunday and in August). Nearby, *Le Bistrot St Germain* (*9 rue Chauvain*) serves fresh, seasonal food at affordable prices.

In the old city, a perennial favourite with locals is *Nissa Socca* (*5 rue Ste Reparate*). Its Niçois specialities include *socca* (chickpea rissoles), *farcis* (stuffed vegetables) and ratatouille.

Entertainment

William's Pub (*4 rue Centrale*) has live music every night (except Sunday) starting at around 9 pm. There's pool, darts and chess in the basement. *Jonathan's Live Music Pub* (*1 rue de la Loge*) has live music every night in

summer. *Chez Wayne's*, (*15 rue de la Préfecture*) hosts a bilingual quiz on Tuesday, a ladies' night on Wednesday, karaoke on Sunday and live bands on Friday and Saturday. Happy hour is until 9 pm.

Getting There & Away

Bus The intercity bus station, opposite 10 blvd Jean Jaurès, is served by some two dozen bus companies. There are slow but frequent services daily until about 7.30 pm to Cannes (32FF, 1½ hours), Antibes (25.50FF, 1¼ hours), Monaco (20FF return, 45 minutes), and Menton (28.50FF return, 1¼ hours).

Train Nice's main train station, Gare Nice Ville, is 1.2km north of the beach on ave Thiers. There are fast, frequent services (up to 40 daily trains) to points all along the coast, including Monaco (20FF, 20 minutes), Antibes (20FF, 25 minutes) and Cannes (32FF, 40 minutes). The two or three TGVs that link Nice with Paris' Gare de Lyon (455FF, seven hours) are infrequent; it can be more convenient to travel via Marseille.

Trains for Digne-les-Bains make the scenic trip four times daily from Nice's Gare du Sud (☎ 04 93 82 10 17), 4 bis rue Alfred Binet, (109FF, 3¼ hours).

Getting Around

Local buses, run by Sunbus, cost 8/68FF for a single ticket/carnet of 10. Bus information and daily passes are available from the Sunbus information office (☎ 04 93 16 52 10) at the Station Centrale on ave Félix Faure. From the train station to Vieux Nice and the bus station, take bus No 2, 5 or 17. Bus No 12 links the train station with the beach.

Bicycles (80FF a day) can be rented from Nicea Location Rent (☎ 04 93 82 42 71), 9 ave Thiers. Cycles Arnaud (☎ 04 93 87 88 55), 4 place Grimaldi, has mountain bikes for 100/180FF a day/weekend (closed Monday morning and Sunday).

CANNES

pop 67,304

The harbour, the bay, Le Suquet hill, the beachside promenade, and the bronzed sun-worshippers on the beach provide more than enough natural beauty to make Cannes worth at least a day trip. It's also fun watching the

FRANCE

rich drop their money with such fashionable nonchalance.

Cannes is renowned for its many festivals and cultural activities, the most famous being the International Film Festival, which runs for two weeks in mid-May. People come to Cannes all year long, but the main tourist season runs from May to October. During the off season, however, the locals are more inclined to be friendly, prices are lower and there are no crowds to contend with.

Orientation

From the train station, follow rue Jean Jaurès west and turn left onto rue Vénizélos, which runs west into the heart of the Vieux Port. Place Bernard Cornut Gentille (formerly place de l'Hôtel de Ville), where the bus station is located, is on the north-western edge of the Vieux Port. Cannes' most famous promenade, the magnificent blvd de la Croisette, begins at the Palais des Festivals and continues eastward around the Baie de Cannes to Pointe de la Croisette.

Information

The main tourist office (☎ 04 93 39 24 53, fax 04 92 99 84 23, ✉ semoftou@palais-festivals-cannes.fr) is on the ground floor of the Palais des Festivals (closed Sunday from September to June). It opens 9 am to 7 pm (Monday to Friday) and 10 am to 6 pm on weekends. Daily hours in July and August are 9 am to 8 pm. *There's* an annexe (☎ 04 93 99 19 77) at the train station (closed Sunday); turn left as you exit the station and walk up the stairs next to Frantour Tourisme.

The main post office is at 22 rue Bivouac Napoléon, not far from the Palais des Festivals. Asher Cyber Espace (☎ 04 92 99 03 01, ✉ asher@riviera.net), 44 blvd Carnot, opens 9.30 am to 7 pm (Friday and Saturday from 9 am to midnight; closed Sunday).

Things to See & Do

Vieux Port Some of the largest yachts you'll ever see are likely to be sitting in the Vieux Port, a fishing port now given over to pleasure craft. The streets around the old port are particularly pleasant on a summer's evening, when the many cafes and restaurants light up the whole area with coloured neon.

The hill just west of the Vieux Port, **Le Suquet**, affords magnificent views of Cannes, especially in the late afternoon and on clear nights. The **Musée de la Castre**, housed in a chateau atop Le Suquet, has Mediterranean and Middle Eastern antiquities as well as objects of ethnographic interest from all over the world (10FF, free for students; closed Tuesday).

Beaches Each of the fancy hotels that line blvd de la Croisette has its own private section of the beach. Unfortunately, this arrangement leaves only a small strip of public sand near the Palais des Festivals. Other free public beaches – the **Plages du Midi** and **Plages de la Bocca** – stretch several kilometres westward from the old port.

Îles de Lérins The eucalyptus and pine-covered **Île Ste Marguerite**, where the Man in the Iron Mask (made famous in the novel by Alexandre Dumas) was held captive during the late 17th century, is just over 1km from the mainland. The island is crisscrossed by many trails and paths. The smaller **Île St Honorat** is home to Cistercian monks who welcome visitors to their monastery and the seven small chapels dotted around the island.

Compagnie Maritime Cannoise (CMC; ☎ 04 93 38 66 33) runs ferries to Île St Honorat (50FF return, 20 minutes) and Île Ste Marguerite (50FF return, 15 minutes). Both islands can be visited for 75FF. The ticket office is at the Vieux Port near the Palais des Festivals.

Places to Stay

Tariffs can be up to 50% higher in July and August – when you'll be lucky to find a room at any price – than in winter. During the film festival, all the hotels are booked up to a year in advance.

Hostels Cannes' *Centre International de Séjour at de la Jeunesse* (☎/fax 04 93 99 26 79, ✉ centre.sejour.youth.hostel.cannes@wanadoo.fr, 35 ave de Vallauris), in a small villa about 400m north-east of the train station, has dorm beds for 80FF (HI card required; available for 70/100FF for those under/over 26). Reception opens 8 am to 12.30 pm and 2.30 to 10.30 pm (3 to 10 pm on weekends); curfew is

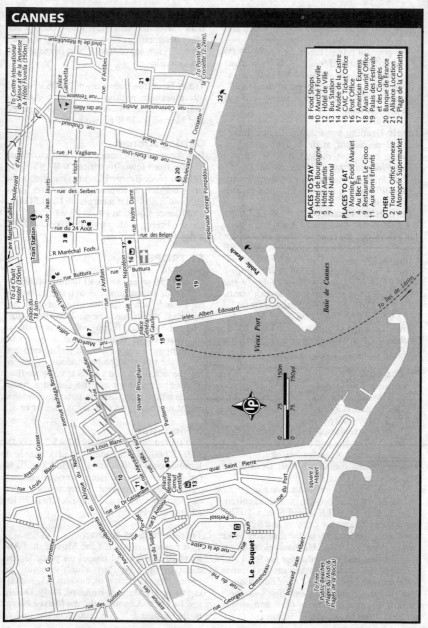

CANNES

PLACES TO STAY
3 Hôtel de Bourgogne
5 Hôtel Atlantis
7 Hôtel National

PLACES TO EAT
1 Morning Food Market
4 Ru Bec Fin
9 Restaurant Le Croco
11 Aux Bons Enfants

OTHER
2 Tourist Office Annexe
6 Monoprix Supermarket
8 Food Shops
10 Marché Forville
12 Hôtel de Ville
13 Bus Station
14 Musée de la Castre
15 CMC Ticket Office
16 Post Office
17 American Express
18 Main Tourist Office
19 Palais des Festivals et des Congrès
20 Banque de France
21 Alliance Location
22 Plage de la Croisette

To Centre International de Séjour et de la Jeunesse & Hôtel Florella (350m)

blvd de la République

place Gambetta

rue d'Antibes

rue Teisseire

rue des Alliés

rue Commandant André

To Pointe de la Croisette (2.2km)

rue Chabaud

rue H Vagliano

rue Hoche

rue des États-Unis

rue Macé

boulevard de la Croisette

ave Maréchal Galliéni

boulevard d'Alsace

Train Station

rue Jean Jaurès

rue des Serbes

rue du 24 Août

rue Notre Dame

rue des Belges

esplanade George Pompidou

To Le Chalit Hostel (350m)

R Maréchal Foch

rue Buttura

rue d'Antibes

rue Bivouac Napoléon

Buttura

Public Beach

place du 18 Juin

rue des Frères

rue d'Antibes

rue Maréchal Joffre

place Général de Gaulle

jetée Albert Édouard

Baie de Cannes

To Îles de Lérins

square Brougham

Vieux Port

rue Meynadier

La Pantiero

150m
150yd
0 75 150

rue Louis Blanc

avenue Badnaga Boualam

avenue de Grasse

rue Louis Blanc

rue du Nord

rue en Afrique

place Bernard Cornut Gentille

quai Saint Pierre

rue du Port

square J Hibert

rue du Dr Garagnaire

rue St Antoine

rue Félix Faure

rue du Suquet

Perissol

rue de la Castre

rue Georges Clemenceau

boulevard Jean Hibert

Le Suquet

rue G Guynemer

Anciens Combattants d'Afrique du Nord

avenue des

rue des Suisses

To Free Public Beaches (Plages du Midi & Plages de la Bocca) at midnight (2 am on weekends). To get there, follow blvd de la République for 300m and ave de Vallauris runs off to the right.

The pleasant private hostel *Le Chalit* (☎ *06 15 28 07 09, fax 04 93 99 22 11,* **☻** *le–chalit@ libertysurf.fr, 27 ave du Maréchal Galliéni)* is a five-minute walk north-west of the station. Beds are 90FF. Le Chalit opens year-round and there's no curfew.

Hotels Heading towards the Centre International de Séjour at de la Jeunesse, you pass the excellent-value but little known *Hôtel Florella* (☎/fax *04 93 38 48 11, 55 blvd de la République)*. Singles/doubles are 120/140FF, and doubles with shower and TV are 180FF.

Large *Hôtel Atlantis* (☎ *04 93 39 18 72, fax 04 93 68 37 65, 4 rue du 24 Août)* has a two-star rating but its cheapest singles/doubles with TV and minibar cost only 155/195FF during the low season. This rises to 195/220FF during July and August. *Hôtel de Bourgogne* (☎ *04 93 38 36 73, fax 04 92 99 28 41, 11 rue du 24 Août)* has singles/doubles with washbasin for 143/186FF. *Hôtel National* (☎ *04 93 39 91 92, fax 04 92 98 44 06, 8 rue Maréchal Joffre)* has singles/doubles from 130/220FF. Doubles/triples with shower and toilet are 250/300FF.

Places to Eat

A morning *food market* is held on place Gambetta, and at the *Marché Forville* north of place Bernard Cornut Gentille, both Tuesday to Sunday (daily in summer).

There are a few budget restaurants around the Marché Forville and many small (but not necessarily cheap) restaurants along rue St Antoine, which runs north-west from place Bernard Cornut Gentille.

Near the train station at *Au Bec Fin* (☎ *12 rue du 24 Août)*, choose from two excellent plats du jour for 55FF to 69FF or a 105FF *menu* (closed Saturday evening and Sunday). Another good choice is the popular *Aux Bons Enfants* (*80 rue Meynadier)*, with regional dishes and a plat du jour for 94FF.

One of the cheapest restaurants in Cannes is *Restaurant Le Croco* (*11 rue Louis Blanc)*, with pizzas, grilled meat and fish and shish kebabs. The *plat du jour* is 49FF and *menus* are 59FF (lunch) and 105FF (dinner).

Getting There & Away

Bus Buses to Nice (1½ hours; 32FF) and other destinations, most operated by Rapides Côte d'Azur, leave from place Bernard Cornut Gentille.

Train From the train station (☎ 0836 35 35 39) there are regular services to Antibes (13FF, 10 minutes), Nice (32FF, 40 minutes) and Marseille (133FF, two hours).

Getting Around

Bus Azur serves Cannes and destinations up to 7km from town. Its office (☎ 04 93 39 18 71) is at place Bernard Cornut Gentille, in the same building as Rapides Côte d'Azur. Tickets cost 7.70FF and a carnet of 10 is 51FF.

Alliance Location (☎ 04 93 38 62 62), 19 rue des Frères, rents mountain bikes for 80FF a day.

ST TROPEZ
pop 5444

Since 1956 when the small fishing village of St Tropez found fame through the patronage of French actor Brigitte Bardot and her acolytes, things have never been the same. The once isolated fishing village now draws in thousands of visitors a year. If you can, come by boat since the road traffic into and out of the town can be horrendous. If watching the rich dining on yachts is not your flute of Moët then there are the timeless backstreets where men still play pétanque and you might just bump into a famous face or two.

Information

The tourist office (☎ 04 94 97 45 21, fax 04 94 97 82 66, **☻** tourisme@nova.fr), quai Jean Jaurès, opens 9.30 am to 1 pm and 3 to 10.30 pm in high season. Hours vary slightly at other times of the year. It organises guided city tours in French and English (20/10FF for adults/children).

Things to See & Do

You might care to visit the **Musée de l'Annonciade**, a disused chapel on place Grammont in the Old Port which contains an impressive collection of modern art, including works by Matisse, Bonnard, Dufy, Derain and Rouault. Alternatively, the **Musée Naval** in the dungeon of the citadel at the end of

Montée de la Citadelle has displays on the town's maritime history and on the Allied landings in 1944.

For a decent beach you need to get 4km out of town to the excellent **Plage de Tahiti**. Naturists will need to get away from St Tropez to the beaches between the town and Le Lavandou to the west.

Places to Stay & Eat
Accommodation isn't cheap and even camping costs more than normal elsewhere. St Tropez's cheapest hotel is the dingy *Hôtel La Méditerranée* (☎ 04 94 97 00 44, fax 04 94 97 47 83, 21 blvd Louis Blanc). Doubles start at 200FF. One rung up the price ladder is *Hôtel Les Chimères* (☎ 04 94 97 02 90, fax 04 94 97 63 57, Port du Pilon) at the south-western end of ave du Général Leclerc. Singles/doubles with shower and breakfast cost 328/358FF.

Move away from the waterfront to eat. Extremely tasteful and not too expensive is the informal *Café Sud* (☎ 04 94 97 71 72, 12 rue Étienne Berny), tucked down a narrow street off Places des Lices. It has a *menu* for 140FF and tables are outside in a star-topped courtyard. Close by, the *Bistrot des Lices* (☎ 04 94 97 29 00, 3 Places des Lices) serves traditional Provençal cuisine, including wonderful *ratatouille*, with dishes from 120FF to 190FF.

Getting There & Away
St Tropez bus station, ave Général de Gaulle, is on the south-western edge of town on the one main road out of town. Frequent taxi boats run to Port Grimaud nearby and excursion boats run regularly to and from St Maxime and St Raphaël.

MENTON
pop 28,812
Reputed to be the warmest spot on the Côte d'Azur, Menton is encircled by mountains. The town is renowned for lemons and holds a two-week Fête du Citron (Lemon Festival) each year between mid-February and early March. The helpful tourist office (☎ 04 93 57 57 00) is in the Palais de l'Europe at 8 ave Boyer.

It's pleasant to wander around the narrow, winding streets of the Vieille Ville (old city) and up to the cypress-shaded **Cimetière du Vieux Château**, with the graves of English, Irish, North Americans, New Zealanders and others who died here during the 19th century. The view alone is worth the climb.

Église St Michel
The grandest baroque church in this part of France sits perched in the centre of the Vieille Ville. The **beach** along the promenade du Soleil is public and, like Nice's, carpeted with smooth pebbles. Better private beaches lie east of the old city in the port area, the main one being **Plage des Sablettes**.

Camping St Michel (☎ 04 93 35 81 23, Plateau St Michel), open from April to mid-October, is 1km north-east of the train station. The adjacent *Auberge de Jeunesse* (☎ 04 93 35 93 14, fax 04 93 35 93 07, Plateau St Michel) has beds for 68FF.

The bus station has services to Monaco (12.50FF return, 30 minutes) and Nice (28FF return, 1¼ hours). Take the train to get to Ventimiglia in Italy.

Monaco (Principauté de Monaco)

pop 30,000
The Principality of Monaco, a sovereign state whose territory covers only 1.95 sq km, has been ruled by the Grimaldi family for most of the period since 1297. Prince Rainier III (born in 1923), whose sweeping constitutional powers make him far more than a figurehead, has reigned since 1949. The citizens of Monaco (Monégasques), of whom there are only 5000 out of a total population of 30,000, pay no taxes. The official language is French, although efforts are being made to revive the country's traditional dialect. There are no border formalities and Monaco makes a perfect day trip from Nice.

Orientation
Monaco consists of four principal areas: Monaco Ville, also known as the old city or the Rocher de Monaco, perched atop a 60m-high crag overlooking the Port de Monaco; Monte Carlo, famed for its casino and its Grand Prix motor race, north of the harbour; La Condamine, the flat area surrounding the

FRANCE

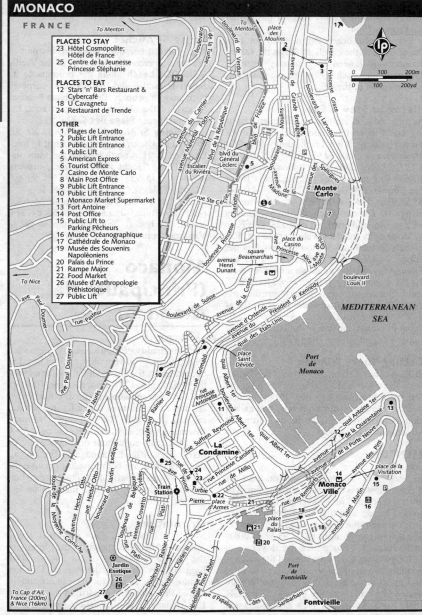

MONACO

FRANCE

To Menton

To Menton

place
des
Moulins

PLACES TO STAY
23 Hôtel Cosmopolite;
   Hôtel de France
25 Centre de la Jeunesse
   Princesse Stéphanie

PLACES TO EAT
12 Stars 'n' Bars Restaurant &
   Cybercafé
18 U Cavagnetu
24 Restaurant de Trende

OTHER
1 Plages de Larvotto
2 Public Lift Entrance
3 Public Lift Entrance
4 Public Lift
5 American Express
6 Tourist Office
7 Casino de Monte Carlo
8 Main Post Office
9 Public Lift Entrance
10 Public Lift Entrance
11 Monaco Market Supermarket
13 Fort Antoine
14 Post Office
15 Public Lift to
   Parking Pêcheurs
16 Musée Océanographique
17 Cathédrale de Monaco
19 Musée des Souvenirs
   Napoléoniens
20 Palais du Prince
21 Rampe Major
22 Food Market
26 Musée d'Anthropologie
   Préhistorique
27 Public Lift

N7

avenue Princesse Grace

boulevard du Larvotto

avenue de Grande Bretagne

blvd de France

boulevard du Jardin Exotique

avenue du Carnier

avenue Maréchal Foch

blvd de la République

blvd du
Général
Leclerc

Escalier
du Riviéra

rue Ste Cécile

boulevard Princesse Charlotte

**Monte
Carlo**

avenue des Spélugues

avenue de la
Madone

place du
Casino

square
Beaumarchais

avenue
Henri
Dunant

place du
Casino Princesse Alice

avenue de
Monte Carlo

boulevard
Louis II

**MEDITERRANEAN
SEA**

boulevard de Suisse

avenue de la Costa

avenue de l'Ostende

avenue du
avenue des États-Unis

quai des États-Unis

avenue du Président JF Kennedy

To Nice

ave Paul Doumer

rue Pasteur

ave Paul Doumer

rue Grimaldi

place Saint
Dévote

**Port
de
Monaco**

rue Princesse
Antoinette

boulevard Albert 1er

quai Albert 1er

quai Antoine 1er

avenue de la Quarantaine
avenue de la Porte Neuve

place de la
Visitation

**La
Condamine**

rue Suffren Reymond

rue Princesse Caroline

rue de Millo

avenue des Pins

**Monaco
Ville**

boulevard Rainier III

rue de la Turbie

Train
Station

rue
Plati

place
d'Armes

place
Pierre

rue des Remparts

avenue Saint Martin

place
du
Palais

**Port
de
Fontvieille**

avenue Hector Otto

ave Hector Otto

boulevard de Belgique

avenue Crovetto Frères

rue Plati

boulevard Rainier III

boulevard Charles III

**Jardin
Exotique**

Route de la Moyenne Corniche

avenue du
Héritière Prince Albert

ave de Papalins

ave d'Papalins

quai Jean-Charles Rey

Fontvieille

To Cap d'Ail,
France (200m)
& Nice (16km)

To Nice

harbour; and Fontvieille, an industrial area south-west of Monaco Ville and the Port de Fontvieille.

Information

Tourist Offices The Direction du Tourisme et des Congrès de la Principauté de Monaco (☎ 92 16 61 66, fax 92 16 60 00, ✉ dtc@monaco-congres.com), 2a blvd des Moulins, is across the public gardens from the casino. It opens 9 am to 7 pm (Sunday from 10 am to noon). From mid-June to mid-September, several tourist office kiosks open around the principality.

Money The currency of Monaco is the French franc. Both French and Monégasque coins are in circulation, but the latter are not widely accepted outside the principality.

In Monte Carlo, you'll find lots of banks in the vicinity of the casino. American Express (☎ 93 25 74 45), 35 blvd Princesse Charlotte, is near the main tourist office (closed Saturday and Sunday).

Post & Communications Monégasque stamps are valid only within Monaco, and postal rates are the same as in France. The main post office is at 1 ave Henri Dunant (inside the Palais de la Scala).

Calls between Monaco and the rest of France are treated as international calls. Monaco's country code is ☎ 377. To call France from Monaco, dial ☎ 00 and France's country code (☎ 33). This applies even if you are only making a call from the east side of blvd de France (in Monaco) to its west side (in France)!

Email & Internet Access Stars 'n' Bars (☎ 93 50 95 95, ✉ info@starsnbars.com), a bar and restaurant at 6 quai Antoine 1er, charges 40FF for 30 minutes of Internet access and opens 11 am to midnight (closed Monday).

Things to See & Do

Palais du Prince The changing of the guard takes place outside the Prince's Palace daily at 11.55 am. About 15 state apartments open to the public from 9.30 am to 6.20 pm daily, June to October. Entry is 30/15FF. Guided tours (35 minutes) in English leave every 15 or 20 minutes. A combined ticket

for entry to the **Musée des Souvenirs Napoléoniens** – a display of Napoleon's personal effects in the palace's south wing – is 40/20FF.

Musée Océanographique If you're going to go to one aquarium on your whole trip, the world-famous Oceanographic Museum, with its 90 sea-water tanks, should be it. The museum, which is on ave St Martin in Monaco Ville, opens 9 am to 7 pm daily (to 8 pm in July and August). The entry fee – brace yourself – is 60/30FF.

Cathédrale de Monaco The unspectacular 19th-century cathedral at 4 rue Colonel has one major draw – the grave of Grace Kelly (1929-1982). The Hollywood star married Prince Rainier III in 1956, but was killed in a car crash in 1982. The remains of other members of the royal family, buried in the church crypt since 1885, rest behind Princess Grace's tomb.

Jardin Exotique The steep slopes of the wonderful Jardin Exotique are home to some 7000 varieties of cacti and succulents from all over the world. The spectacular view is worth at least half the admission fee (40/19FF), which also gets you into the **Musée d'Anthropologie Préhistorique** and includes a half-hour guided visit to the **Grottes de l'Observatoire**, a system of caves 279 steps down the hillside. From the tourist office, take bus No 2 to the end of the line.

Places to Stay

Monaco's HI hostel, *Centre de la Jeunesse Princesse Stéphanie* (☎ 93 50 83 20, fax 93 25 29 82, 24 ave Prince Pierre) is 120m uphill from the train station. You must be aged between 16 and 31 to stay here. Beds (70FF) are given out each morning on a first-come, first-served basis – numbered tickets are distributed around 8 am and registration begins at 11 am.

Hôtel Cosmopolite (☎ 93 30 16 95, fax 93 30 23 05, ✉ hotel-cosmopolite@monte-carlo.mc, 4 rue de la Turbie) has decent singles/doubles with shower for 282/314FF, while doubles without shower are 228FF.

The two-star *Hôtel de France* (☎ 93 30 24 64, fax 92 16 13 34, ✉ hotel-france@monte-carlo.mc, 6 rue de la Turbie) has rooms with

FRANCE

shower, toilet and TV starting at 350/390FF, including breakfast.

Places to Eat
There are a few cheap restaurants in La Condamine along rue de la Turbie. Lots of touristy restaurants of more or less the same quality can be found in the streets leading off from place du Palais. The flashy *Stars 'n' Bars* (☎ 93 50 95 95, 6 Quai Antoine 1er) is a blues bar and restaurant with large portions of great salads (65FF to 75FF). It opens noon to 3 am daily (except Monday); the restaurant closes at midnight.

One of the few affordable restaurants specialising in Monégasque dishes is *U Cavagnetu* (☎ 93 30 35 80, 14 rue Comte Félix-Gastaldi) where a lunchtime *menu* is 85FF and in the evening jumps to between 115FF and 140FF. Very traditional and cosy is the small *Restaurant de Trende* (☎ 93 30 37 72, 19 rue de la Turbie). The decor is totally 1930s and the food absolutely Provençal.

Getting There & Away
There is no single bus station in Monaco – intercity buses leave from various points around the city.

The train station, which is part of the French SNCF network (☎ 0836 35 35 39), is on ave Prince Pierre. There are frequent trains to Menton (13FF, 10 minutes), Nice (42FF, 20 minutes) and Ventimiglia in Italy (21FF, 25 minutes).

Languedoc-Roussillon

Languedoc-Roussillon stretches in an arc along the coast from Provence to the Pyrenees. The plains of Bas Languedoc (Lower Languedoc) extend to the coast, where beaches are generally broad and sandy. The wine – Languedoc is France's largest wine-producing area – is red, robust and cheap. Inland are the rugged, sparsely populated mountains of Haut Languedoc (Upper Languedoc), a region of bare limestone plateaus and deep canyons.

Transport is frequent between cities on the plain but buses in the interior are about as rare as camels. For train information throughout the region, ring ☎ 0836 35 35 35.

MONTPELLIER
pop 228,000
Montpellier is one of the nation's fastest-growing cities. It's also one of the youngest, with students making up nearly a quarter of its population.

Montpellier hosts a popular theatre festival in June and a two-week international dance festival in June/July.

Orientation & Information
The Centre Historique has at its heart place de la Comédie, an enormous pedestrianised square. Westward from it sprawls a network of lanes between rue de la Loge and rue Grand Jean Moulin.

Montpellier's main tourist office (☎ 04 67 60 60 60) is at the south end of Esplanade Charles de Gaulle. It's open 9 am to 6.30 pm daily (reduced hours at weekends, later closing in summer).

To snack and surf, visit the Dimension 4 Cybercafé at 11 rue des Balances. It charges a bargain 35FF per hour.

Things to See
Musée Fabre, 39 blvd Bonne Nouvelle, has one of France's richest collections of French, Italian, Flemish and Dutch works from the 16th century onwards. **Musée Languedocien**, 7 rue Jacques Cœur, displays the region's archaeological finds. Both charge 20/10FF.

Beaches The closest beach is at **Palavas-les-Flots**, 12km south of the city. Take bus Nos 17 or 28.

Places to Stay
Camping *L'Oasis Palavasienne* (☎ 04 67 15 11 61, Route de Palavas), 4km south of town, open April to September, charges 106FF for two people and tent. Take bus No 17 to the Oasis stop.

Hostels A bed at the *Auberge de Jeunesse* (☎ 04 67 60 32 22, 2 Impasse de la Petite Corraterie), ideally located in the old city, costs 48FF. Take the tram from the bus or train station.

CHRISTOPHER WOOD

Window, Chateau d'Amboise, France

JOHN HAY

The Eiffel Tower at night, Paris

JOHN HAY

Monet's garden, full of colour, Giverny, France

JEAN-BERNARD CARILLET

Cathedral de la Major, Marseille, France

Kurhaus Wiesbaden, Hesse

Russian Orthodox Chapel, Darmstadt, Germany

Express train, Frankfurt/Main

Martin Luther Monument

Port of Hamburg on Elb River, Germany

Hotels At *Hôtel des Touristes (☎ 04 67 58 42 37, fax 04 67 92 61 37, 10 rue Baudin)*, just off place de la Comédie, there are roomy singles/doubles/triples with shower starting at 150/180/260FF.

Friendly *Hôtel des Étuves (☎ 04 67 60 78 19, 24 rue des Étuves)* has singles/doubles with bathroom from 130/160FF. Close by, *Hôtel Majestic (☎ 04 67 66 26 85, 4 rue du Cheval Blanc)* has basic singles/doubles for 110/140FF and doubles/triples/quads with bathroom for 200/300/350FF.

Places to Eat

Eating places abound in Montepellier's old quarter. Vegetarian *Tripti Kulai (20 rue Jacques Cœur)*, has *menus* for 69FF and 85FF. *La Tomate (6 rue Four des Flammes)* does great regional dishes, salads the size of a kitchen garden plus dessert for 50FF and *menus* from 50FF.

Entertainment

For a drink, try the bars flanking rue En-Gondeau, off rue Grand Jean Moulin. *Mash Disco Bar (5 rue de Girone)* is a popular student hangout.

Getting There & Away

Montpellier's bus station (☎ 04 67 92 01 43) is immediately south-west of the train station, itself 500m south of place de la Comédie.

Rail destinations include Paris' Gare de Lyon (379/452FF weekdays/weekends, four to five hours by TGV, about 10 a day), Carcassonne (113FF, 1¾ hours, at least 10 daily) and Nîmes (47FF, 30 minutes, more than 20 daily).

NÎMES
pop 135,000

Nîmes has some of Europe's best-preserved Roman buildings. **Les Arènes**, the amphitheatre (28/22FF), built around AD 100 to seat 24,000 spectators, is used to this day for theatre performances, music concerts and bullfights.

The rectangular **Maison Carrée**, a well-preserved 1st-century Roman temple, survived the centuries as a meeting hall, private residence, stable, church and archive.

Try to coincide with one of Nîmes' three wild *férias* (festivals) – Féria Primavera (Spring Festival) in February, Féria de Pentecôte (Whitsuntide Festival) in June, and the

Féria des Vendanges coinciding with the grape harvest in September.

The main tourist office (☎ 04 66 67 29 11) is at 6 rue Auguste.

To check your email, log on at Netgames, right beside the Maison Carrée.

Places to Stay

At year-round *Camping Domaine de la Bastide (☎ 04 66 38 09 21)*, 4km south of town on the D13, two people with tent pay 55FF. A dorm bed at the *Auberge de Jeunesse (☎ 04 66 23 25 04)* on Chemin de la Cigale, 3.5km north-west of the train station, costs 52FF.

In the old city, friendly *Hôtel de la Maison Carrée (☎ 04 66 67 32 89, 14 rue la Maison Carrée)* has singles/doubles/triples/quads with bathroom and TV for 180/220/330/350FF.

Places to Eat

La Truye qui Filhe (9 rue Fresque) blends self-service with a warm, homely atmosphere. Its *menu* is superb value at 52FF; open lunchtime only, closed August. *Le Portofino (3 rue Corneille)* serves great home-made pasta dishes.

Getting There & Away

Bus Nîmes' bus station is beside the train station. Destinations include Pont du Gard (35FF, 45 minutes, five to six daily), Avignon (65FF, 30 minutes, 10 or more daily) and Arles (34FF, 30 to 45 minutes, four to eight daily).

Train The train station is at the south-eastern end of ave Feuchères. Destinations include Paris' Gare de Lyon (366FF to 431FF, four hours by TGV, seven daily), Avignon (65FF, 30 minutes, 10 or more daily), Marseille (76FF, 1¼ hours, 12 daily) and Montpellier (66FF, 30 minutes, 15 or more daily).

AROUND NÎMES
Pont du Gard

The Roman general Agrippa slung the mighty Pont du Gard over the Gard River around 19 BC. You won't be alone; this three-tier aqueduct, 275m long and 49m high, receives over two million visitors a year.

There's a tourist kiosk on each bank and a brand new information centre on the left bank, set back from the river.

Buses from Avignon (26km) and Nîmes (23km) stop 1km north of the bridge.

CARCASSONNE
pop 45,000

From afar, the old walled city of Carcassonne looks like a fairy-tale medieval city. Once inside the fortified walls, however, the magic rubs off. Luring some 200,000 visitors in July and August alone, it can be a tourist hell in high summer. Purists may sniff at Carcassonne's 'medieval' Cité – whose impressive fortifications were extensively renovated and rebuilt in the 19th century – but what the heck; it *is* magic, one of France's greatest skylines.

The Ville Basse (lower town), a more modest stepsister to camp Cinderella up the hill, has cheaper eating places and accommodation and also merits a browse.

Orientation & Information

The Aude River separates the Ville Basse from the Cité on its hillock. The main tourist office (☎ 04 68 10 24 30) is in the Ville Basse opposite Square Gambetta.

Alerte Rouge (Red Alert), 73 rue Verdun, is a cybercafe where you can plug in 10 am to 1 am daily.

Things to See

The 1.7km-long double ramparts of **La Cité** (spectacularly floodlit at night) are spiked with 52 witches' hat towers. Within are narrow, medieval streets and the 12th-century **Château Comtal** (Count's Castle), visited by guided tour only (35/23FF). A 40-minute tour in English departs two or five times a day, according to season.

Places to Stay

Camping *Camping de la Cité* (☎ 04 68 25 11 77), on Route de St Hilaire about 3.5km south of the main tourist office, charges 75FF to 95FF for two people and tent. Take bus No 5 (hourly until 6.40 pm) from Square Gambetta to the route de Cazilhac stop.

Hostels In the heart of the Cité, the large, cheery *Auberge de Jeunesse* (☎ 04 68 25 23 16), on rue Vicomte Trencavel, has dorm beds for 70FF. There's a snack bar offering light meals and a great outside terrace.

The B&B at the *Centre International de Séjour* (☎ 04 68 11 17 00, 91 rue Aimé Ramon) in the Ville Basse, costs 68FF a night.

Hotels Handy for the train station is recommended *Hôtel Astoria* (☎ 04 68 25 31 38, 18 rue Tourtel) where basic singles/doubles cost 110/130FF (from 190FF with bathroom).

Pricing policy at welcoming *Relais du Square* (☎ 04 68 72 31 72, 51 rue du Pont Vieux) couldn't be simpler; large rooms, accommodating one to three people, cost 165FF, whatever their facilities. So in summer get there early if you want your own bathroom.

Places to Eat

In the Ville Basse, *Le Gargantua*, the restaurant of Relais du Square, has a weekday *menu* for 69FF and others from 128FF. *L'Italia* (*32 route Minervoise)*, handy for the station, is a pizza-plus joint that also does takeaways. Next door is the more stylish *Restaurant Gil* with Catalan-influenced *menus* from 100FF.

Getting There & Away

The train station is at the northern end of pedestrianised rue Georges Clemenceau. Carcassonne is on the main line linking Toulouse (74FF, 50 minutes, 10 or more daily) with Béziers (70FF, 50 minutes, five daily) and Montpellier (113FF, 1½ hours, 10 or more daily).

TOULOUSE
pop 690,000

Toulouse, France's fourth largest city, is renowned for its high-tech industries, especially aerospace; local factories have built the Caravelle, Concorde and Airbus passenger planes and also the Ariane rocket. Like Montpellier, it's a youthful place with over 110,000 students – more than any other French provincial city.

Most older buildings in the city centre are in rose-red brick, earning the city its nickname *la ville rose* (the pink city).

Orientation

The heart of Toulouse is bounded to the east by blvd de Strasbourg and its continuation, blvd Lazare Carnot and, to the west, by the Garonne River. Its two main squares are place du Capitole and, 300m eastwards, place Wilson.

Information

The busy **tourist office** (☎ 05 61 11 02 22) is in the Donjon du Capitole, a 16th-century tower on Square Charles de Gaulle. It's open 9 am to 6 pm weekdays (shorter hours and a lunch break at weekends), October to April. The rest of the year it opens 9 am to 7 pm, Monday to Saturday, plus 10 am to 1 pm and 2 to 5 pm on Sunday.

The OTU student travel agency (☎ 05 61 12 18 88) at 60 rue du Taur can help with cheap travel options.

Online time at Résomania cybercafe, 85 rue Pargaminières, is 40FF an hour.

Major annual events include Festival Garonne with riverside music, dance and theatre (July), Musique d'Été with music of all definitions around town (July and August) and Jazz sur Son 31, an international jazz festival (October).

Things to See & Do

Cité de l'Espace Space City (☎ 05 62 71 48 71) is a truly mind-boggling interactive space museum and planetarium (69FF). To get there, take bus No 15 from Allées Jean Jaurès to the end of the line, from where it's a 600m walk.

The **Galerie Municipale du Château d'Eau** (15/10FF) is a world-class photographic gallery inside a 19th-century water tower at the western end of Pont Neuf, just across the Garonne River.

Musée des Augustins (12FF, free for students), 21 rue de Metz, has a superb collection of paintings and stone artefacts.

Within the magnificent Gothic **Église des Jacobins**, the remains of St Thomas Aquinas (1225-74), an early head of the Dominican order, are interred on the north side.

The **Basilique St Sernin** is France's largest and most complete Romanesque structure. It's topped by a magnificent eight-sided 13th-century **tower**.

Places to Stay

Camping Year-round, the oft-packed *Camping de Rupé* (☎ 05 61 70 07 35, 21 chemin du Pont de Rupé), 6km north-west of the train station, charges 72FF for two people and tent. Take bus No 59 (last departure at 7.25 pm) from place Jeanne d'Arc to the Rupé stop.

Hotels Avoid the cheap hotels near the train station; most are fairly sordid.

The exceptionally friendly *Hôtel Beauséjour* (☎/fax 05 61 62 77 59, 4 rue Caffarelli), off Allées Jean Jaurès, is great value. Basic rooms start at 110FF and doubles/triples with bathroom are 150/190FF. *Hôtel Splendid* (☎/fax 05 61 62 43 02) at No 13, has simple rooms from 90FF while singles/doubles/triples with bathroom are 130/150/210FF.

Places to Eat

Fill yourself at lunchtime when there are some amazing deals. Look around – many places have lunch *menus* for 50FF to 60FF. Unmissable and an essential Toulouse experience are the small, spartan, lunchtime-only *restaurants* on the 1st floor of Les Halles Victor Hugo covered market (great in itself for atmosphere and fresh produce). They serve up generous quantities of hearty fare for 55FF to 85FF.

Place St Georges is almost entirely taken over by cafe tables. Both blvd de Strasbourg and place du Capitole are lined with restaurants and cafes.

Restaurant Saveur Bio (22 rue Maurice Fonvieille) serves tasty vegetarian food, including a 40FF lunchtime mixed plate, a great value 60FF buffet and three 85FF *menus*.

Entertainment

For what's on where, pick up a copy of *Toulouse Hebdo* (3FF) or Intramuros (free from the tourist office). For life after dark, ask at the tourist office for its free listing *Toulouse By Night*.

Cafes around place St-Pierre beside the Garonne pull in a mainly young crowd. Nearby, the *Why Not Café (5 rue Pargaminières)* has a beautiful terrace while *Café des Artistes (13 place de la Daurade)* is an art-student hangout.

Two hot discos near the centre are *La Strada (4 rue Gabriel Péri)* and *L'Ubu (16 rue St-Rome)*.

Getting There & Away

Bus Toulouse's bus station (☎ 05 61 61 67 67), just north of the train station, serves mainly regional destinations including Andorra (75FF, 4 hours, one to two daily). For longer distance travel, both Intercars (☎ 05 61 58 14 53) and

Eurolines (☎ 05 61 26 40 04) have offices in Toulouse.

Train The train station, Gare Matabiau, is on blvd Pierre Sémard, about 1km north-east of the city centre.

Destinations served by multiple daily direct trains include Bayonne (196FF, 3¾ hours), Bordeaux (165FF, 2½ hours) and Carcassonne (74FF, one hour).

The fare to Paris is 356FF by Corail (6½ hours, Gare d'Austerlitz) and 447FF by TGV (5½ hours, Gare Montparnasse via Bordeaux).

SNCF has an information and ticketing office at 5 rue Peyras.

Corsica (Corse)

Corsica, the most mountainous and geographically diverse of all the Mediterranean islands, has spent much of its history under foreign rule. From the 13th century it remained under Genoese control until the Corsicans, led by the extraordinary Pasquale Paoli, declared the island independent in 1755. But France took over in 1769 and has ruled Corsica since – except in 1794-96, when it was under English domination, and during the German and Italian occupation of 1940-43.

The island has 1000km of coastline, soaring granite mountains that stay snowcapped until July, a huge national park, flatland marshes, an uninhabited desert in the north-west and a 'continental divide' running down the middle of the island. It's a popular holiday destination for the French and increasingly for foreigner travellers who come for its exceptional hiking and diving opportunities.

AJACCIO (AIACCIU)
pop 52,880
The port city of Ajaccio, birthplace of Napoleon Bonaparte (1769-1821), is a great place to begin a visit to Corsica and a fine place for strolling. The many museums and statues dedicated to Bonaparte speak volumes – not about Napoleon himself, but about how the people of his native town prefer to think of him.

Orientation
Ajaccio's main street is cours Napoléon, which stretches from place du Général de Gaulle northward to the train station and beyond. The old city is south of place Foch. The ferry port is central to both the old and new town.

Information
Tourist Offices The tourist office (☎ 04 95 51 53 03, fax 04 95 51 53 01, ☻ ajaccio .tourisme@wanadoo.fr), 1 place Foch, is open 8 am to 6 pm daily (8 am to noon and 2 to 5 pm on Saturday). From July to mid-September it opens 8 am to 8.30 pm daily (9 am to 1 pm on Sunday). It closes at 7 pm from April to June and in October. The airport information counter (☎ 04 95 23 56 56) is open 6 am to 10.30 pm.

Money & Post The Banque de France is at 8 rue Sergent Casalonga. The main post office, which has an exchange service, is at 13 cours Napoléon.

Hiking The Maison d'Informations Randonnées (☎ 04 95 51 79 10, fax 04 95 21 88 17), 2 rue Major Lambroschini, provides information on the Parc Naturel Régional de la Corse and its hiking trails. It opens 8.30 am to 12.30 pm and 2 to 6 pm (5 pm on Friday; closed weekends).

Things to See & Do
Museums The house where Napoleon was born and raised, the **Maison Bonaparte** (☎ 04 95 21 43 89) on rue St Charles in the old city, was sacked by Corsican nationalists in 1793 but rebuilt later in the decade. It opens 9 am (10 am from October to April) to 11.45 am and 2 to 5.45 pm (4.45 pm from October to April), closed Sunday afternoon and Monday morning. Admission costs 22/15FF, including a guided tour in French.

The sombre **Salon Napoléonien** (☎ 04 95 21 90 15), on the 1st floor of the Hôtel de Ville at place Foch, exhibits memorabilia of the emperor. It opens 9 am to 11.45 am and 2 to 4.45 pm (closed weekends). Between 15 June and 15 September it opens until 5.45 pm and on Saturday. Entry is 5FF and visitors must be properly dressed.

The **Musée A Bandera** (☎ 04 95 51 07 34), 1 rue Général Lévie, deals with Corsican military history and costs 20/10FF. It's open 9 am to noon and 2 to 6 pm Monday to Saturday.

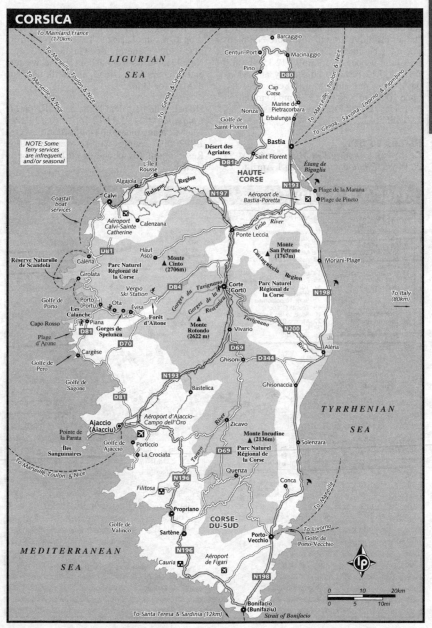

CORSICA

To Mainland France (170km)

LIGURIAN SEA

To Marseille, Toulon & Savona

To Marseille & Nice

NOTE: Some ferry services are infrequent and/or seasonal

Barcaggio

Centuri-Port • Macinaggio

Pino

D80

Cap Corse

Marine de Pietracorbara

Nonza • Erbalunga

Golfe de Saint-Florent

Bastia

Saint Florent

L'Île Rousse

Désert des Agriates

D81²

HAUTE-CORSE

Étang de Biguglia

N193

Algajola

Balagne Region

Aéroport de Bastia-Poretta

Plage de la Marana

Plage de Pineto

Coastal boat services

Calvi

N197

Aéroport Calvi-Sainte Catherine

Calenzana

Golo River

Ponte Leccia

D81

Haut Asco

▲ Monte Cinto (2706m)

Monte San Petrone (1767m)

Castagniccia Region

Moriani-Plage

Réserve Naturelle de Scandola

Galéria

Girolata

Parc Naturel Régional de la Corse

Vergio Ski Station

D84

Gorges du Tavignano

Corte (Corti)

Parc Naturel Régional de la Corse

N198

To Italy (80km)

Golfe de Porto

Porto (Portu)

Ota

Évisa

Forêt d'Aïtone

Gorges de la Restonica

Tavignano

N200

River

Aléria

Les Calanche

Piana

▲ Monte Rotondo (2622 m)

Vivario

Capo Rosso

D81

Gorges de Spelunca

D70

Plage d'Arone

Golfe de Pero

Cargèse

D69

Ghisoni

D344

Ghisonaccia

Golfe de Sagone

D81

Bastelica

N193

TYRRHENIAN SEA

Ajaccio (Aiacciu)

Aéroport d'Ajaccio-Campo dell'Oro

Porticcio

La Crociata

Golfe d'Ajaccio

River

Zicavo

▲ Monte Incudine (2136m)

Parc Naturel Régional de la Corse

Solenzara

Pointe de la Parata

Îles Sanguinaires

To Marseille, Toulon & Nice

D69

Taravo

River

Filitosa

N196

Quenza

Conca

To Marseille

Golfe de Valinco

Propriano

Sartène

CORSE-DU-SUD

Porto-Vecchio

To Livorno

Golfe de Porto-Vecchio

MEDITERRANEAN SEA

N196

Cauria

Aéroport de Figari

N198

To Marseille

Bonifacio (Bunifaziu)

Strait of Bonifacio

To Santa Teresa & Sardinia (12km)

0 10 20km

0 5 10mi

LP

FRANCE

Musée Fesch (☎ 04 95 21 48 17), 50-52 rue du Cardinal Fesch, has a fine collection of Italian primitive art and still more Napoleonia in the basement. Between September and mid-June it opens 9.15 am to 12.15 pm and 2.15 to 5.15 pm (closed Sunday and Monday); from mid-June to mid-September it's open 10 am to 5.30 pm (9.30 pm to midnight on Friday, closed Tuesday). Admission costs 25/15FF.

Places to Stay

Camping *Camping Les Mimosas* (☎ 04 95 20 99 85, Route d'Alata), open 1 April to 15

October, is about 3km north of the town centre. It costs 29/12FF per adult/tent site. Prices drop 10% out of season. Take bus No 4 from place du Général de Gaulle or cours Napoléon to the roundabout at the western end of cours Jean Nicoli, and walk up route d'Alata for 1km.

Hotels The best deal is the central *Hôtel le Colomba* (☎ 04 95 21 12 66, 8 ave de Paris) where clean, pleasant singles/doubles cost 140/200FF; doubles with shower are 180FF. Reservations (by phone or post) must be in French.

AJACCIO (AIACCIU)

PLACES TO STAY
1   Hôtel Kallisté
16 Hôtel Colomba

PLACES TO EAT
2   Monoprix Supermarket
7   Marché Municipal
21 La Pizza
23 U Scampi; Le Bosco
26 Café de Paris;
     Dolce Piacere

OTHER
3   Musée Fesch;
     Chapelle Impériale
4   Terminal Routier
5   Terminal Maritime
6   SNCM Ticketing Office

8   Main Post Office
9   Banque de France
10 Maison d'Information
     Randonnées
11 Préfecture
12 Musée A Bandera
13 Assemblée Régionale
     de la Corse
14 Laundrette
15 Relais des Gîtes Ruraux
17 TCA Boutique
18 Hôtel de Ville;
     Salon Napoléonien
19 Tourist Office
20 Boats to Îles Sanguinaires
22 Maison Bonaparte
24 Cathédrale
25 Taxi Rank

The friendly and efficiently run *Hôtel Kallisté* (☎ 04 95 51 34 45, fax 04 95 21 79 00, ✉ hotelkalliste@cyrnos.com, 51 cours Napoléon) has classy singles/doubles with shower and toilet for 240/280FF in low season; 320/360FF in June, July and September; and 380/430FF in August. Most rooms have both air-conditioning and mini-bar. Breakfast (38FF) is served in your room and there are English-speaking staff.

Places to Eat
Ajaccio's restaurants are mostly seasonal and mediocre. Cafes can be found along blvd du Roi Jérôme, quai Napoléon and the north side of place de Gaulle. *Café de Paris* and the neighbouring *Dolce Piacere*, on the west side of place du Général de Gaulle, both have giant terraces with good views of the sea and the square.

The best pizza (45FF to 59FF) is served at *La Pizza* (☎ 04 95 21 30 71, 2 rue des Anciens Fosées). Try the *quatre saisons* pizza, liberally sprinkled with chilli-laced olive oil.

The popular *U Scampi* (☎ 04 95 21 38 09, 11 rue Conventionnel Chiappe) serves fish and Corsican specialities – including octopus stew – on a flower-filled terrace. Lunch and dinner *menus* start at 85FF. It opens year-round (closed Friday night and Saturday lunchtime). *Le Bosco* (☎ 04 95 21 25 06) next door shares the same terrace as the Scampi and offers the same sort of *menus*, including a 195FF shellfish platter.

On Square Campinchi, the *Marché Municipal* open-air food market operates until 1 pm (closed Monday). There's a *Monoprix* supermarket opposite 40 cours Napoléon (closed Sunday).

Getting There & Away
Bus The Terminal Maritime et Routier on Quai l'Herminier houses Ajaccio's bus station. A dozen-odd companies have services, daily except Sunday and holidays, to Bastia (110FF, two a day), Bonifacio (110FF, two or three a day), Calvi (120FF, with a change at Ponte Leccia), Corte (60FF, two a day), Porto and Ota (70FF, 2½ hours, two a day), Sartène (70FF, two or three a day) and many small villages.

The bus station's information counter (☎ 04 95 51 55 45), which can provide schedules,

opens 7 am to 7 or 8 pm daily. Eurocorse (☎ 04 95 21 06 30 or 04 95 51 05 08), responsible for most of the long-distance lines, opens 8.30 am to 4 pm (closed Sunday).

Train The train station (☎ 04 95 23 11 03), blvd Sampiero (place de la Gare), is staffed 6.15 or 7.30 am to 6.30 pm daily (8 pm from late May to late September).

Ferry The Terminal Maritime is on quai l'Herminier next to the bus station. SNCM's ticketing office (☎ 04 95 29 66 99), across the street at 3 quai l'Herminier, opens 8 to 11.45 am and 2 to 6 pm (closed Saturday afternoon and Sunday). Ajaccio is connected to the mainland (Marseille, Toulon or Nice) by at least one daily ferry; the SNCM bureau in the ferry terminal opens two or three hours before the scheduled departure time.

Getting Around
Bus Local bus maps and timetables can be picked up at the TCA Boutique (☎ 04 95 51 43 23), 2 ave de Paris, open 8 am to noon and 2.30 to 6 pm (closed Sunday). Single tickets/carnet of 10 cost 7.50/58FF.

Taxi There's a taxi rank on place du Général de Gaulle, or call Radio Taxis Ajacciens (☎ 04 95 25 09 13).

Scooter The Hôtel Kallisté (see Places to Stay) rents scooters for 195/986FF per day/week. Prices drop between October and April.

BASTIA
pop 37,884
Bustling Bastia, Corsica's most important business and commercial centre, has rather an Italian feel to it. It was the seat of the Genoese governors of Corsica from the 15th century, when the *bastiglia* (fortress) from which the city derives its name was built. There's not all that much to see or do, but this pleasant place makes a good base for exploring **Cap Corse**, the wild, 40km-long peninsula to the north.

Orientation
The focal point of the town centre is 300m-long place St Nicolas. Bastia's main thoroughfares are the east-west ave Maréchal

Sébastiani, which links the ferry terminal with the train station, and the north-south blvd Paoli, a fashionable shopping street one block west of place St Nicolas.

Information

The tourist office (☎ 04 95 55 96 85, fax 04 95 55 96 00), place St Nicolas, opens 8 am to noon and 2 to 6 pm daily (closed on Sunday afternoon). In July and August it opens 8 am to 8 pm daily.

The Banque de France is at 2 bis cours Henri Pierangeli, half a block south of place St Nicolas. The main post office (with exchange services) is on the even-numbered side of ave Maréchal Sébastiani, a block west of place St Nicolas.

Things to See & Do

Bastia's **place St Nicolas**, a palm and plane tree-lined esplanade, was laid out in the late 19th century. The narrow streets and alleyways of **Terra Vecchia**, which is centred around place de l'Hôtel de Ville, lie just south. The 16th-century **Oratoire de l'Immaculée Conception** is opposite 3 rue Napoléon and was decorated in rich baroque style in the early 18th century.

The picturesque, horseshoe-shaped **Vieux Port** is between Terra Vecchia and the **Citadelle** and is probably the most colourful part of Bastia with its crumbling buildings and lively restaurants.

Places to Stay

Camping Small *Camping Les Orangers* (☎ 04 95 33 24 09), open from April to mid-October, is about 4km north of Bastia in Miomo. Fees are 13/10/25FF for a tent site/parking/per adult. Take the bus to Sisco from opposite the tourist office.

Hotels *Hôtel Le Riviera* (☎ 04 95 31 07 16, fax 04 95 34 17 39, 1 bis rue du Nouveau Port) has doubles with shower and toilet for 200/250FF in the low/high season. Reception is on the 1st floor. The family-run *Hôtel Central* (☎ 04 95 31 71 12, fax 04 95 31 82 40, 3 rue Miot) has basic singles/doubles with shower and toilet from 180/200FF and better-equipped rooms with TV from 230/250FF.

If your budget can handle it, the central, upmarket *Hôtel Napoléon* (☎ 04 95 31 60 30, fax 04 95 31 77 83, 43 blvd Paoli) has small but comfortable doubles equipped with all the amenities for around 290FF to 590FF. Prices rise early July to early September.

Places to Eat

Cafes and brasseries line the western side of place St Nicolas. More restaurants are on the north side of the Vieux Port, on quai des Martyrs de la Libération and on place de l'Hôtel de Ville in Terra Vecchia, where the *Café Pannini* sells great jumbo sandwiches.

Le Colomba (☎ 04 95 32 79 14, Vieux Port) is a large place serving 32 varieties of pizza (39FF to 57FF). The Brazilian pizza is the house speciality.

A bustling *food market* is held at place de l'Hôtel de Ville in Terra Vecchio every morning except Monday, and there's a *Spar supermarket* on the corner of rue César Campinchi and rue Capanelle.

Getting There & Away

Air France's fifth-busiest airport, Aéroport de Bastia-Poretta (☎ 04 95 54 54 54) is 20km south of the town. Municipal buses to the airport (50FF) depart from the roundabout opposite the train station about an hour before each flight's departure (eight or nine times a day). The tourist office has timetables.

Bus Rapides Bleus (☎ 04 95 31 03 79), 1 ave Maréchal Sebastiani, has buses to Porto-Vecchio and Bonifacio (via Porto-Vecchio) and handles tickets for Eurocorse buses to Corte and Ajaccio. The afternoon bus to Calvi run by Les Beaux Voyages (☎ 04 95 65 02 10) leaves from outside the train station.

Train The train station (☎ 04 95 32 60 06) is at the northern end of ave Maréchal Sébastiani. See Getting Around at the start of the Corsica section for more information.

Ferry Bastia is linked by ferry to both France and Italy. The ferry terminal is at the eastern end of ave Pietri. SNCM's office (☎ 04 95 54 66 81) across the roundabout handles ferries to mainland France, and opens 8 to 11.45 am and 2 to 5.45 pm daily (closed Sunday, and Saturday afternoon). The SNCM counter in the ferry terminal opens two hours before each sailing.

For Italy, Mobylines' office (☎ 04 95 34 84 94, fax 04 95 32 17 94), 4 rue du Commandant Luce de Casabianca, is 200m north of place St Nicolas. It opens 8 am to noon and 2 to 6 pm (until noon Saturday; closed Sunday). Corsica Ferries (☎ 04 95 32 95 95, fax 04 95 32 14 71), 15 bis rue Chanoine Leschi, opens 8.30 am to noon and 2 to 6.30 pm (closed on Sunday).

The cheapest low season fare to/from the mainland is around 184FF for passengers under 25 years of age.

CALVI
pop 5177
Calvi, where Admiral Horatio Nelson lost his eye, serves both as a military town and a rather upmarket holiday resort. The Citadelle, garrisoned by a crack regiment of the French Foreign Legion, sits atop a promontory at the western end of a beautiful half-moon shaped bay.

Orientation
The Citadelle – also known as the Haute Ville (upper town) – is north-east of the port. blvd Wilson, the main thoroughfare in the Basse Ville (lower town), is up the hill from quai Landry and the marina.

Information
The tourist office (☎ 04 95 65 16 67, fax 04 95 65 14 09) near the marina opens 9 am to 1.30 pm and 2 to 7 pm (closed Saturday afternoon and Sunday).

The Crédit Lyonnais, blvd Wilson, opens until 4.30 pm (closed on weekends) and sports a handy ATM. The main post office is about 100m to the south on the same street.

Things to See & Do
The Citadelle, set atop an 80m-high granite promontory and enclosed by massive Genoese ramparts, affords great views of the surrounding area. The 13th-century Église St Jean Baptiste was rebuilt in 1570; inside is a miraculous ebony icon of Christ. West of the church, a marble plaque marks the site of the house where, according to local tradition, Christopher Columbus was born. The imposing 13th-century Palais des Gouverneurs (Governors' Palace) is above the entrance to the citadel. Now known as Caserne Sampiero, it serves as a barracks

and mess hall for officers of the French Foreign Legion.

Beaches Calvi's 4km-long beach begins just south of the marina and stretches around the Golfe de Calvi. Other nice beaches, including one at Algajola, are west of town. The port and resort town of L'Île Rousse (Isula Rossa) east of Calvi is also endowed with a long, sandy beach with incredibly clean water.

Places to Stay
Camping & Studios Three-star *Camping Les Castors* (☎ 04 95 65 13 30, route de Pietra Maggiore), open from April to mid-October, is 800m south-east of the centre of town. Charges are 30/12FF per adult/tent site. Prices rise in July and August.

Farther south, the two-star *Camping La Clé des Champs* (☎ 04 95 65 00 86, route de Pietra Maggiore), open April to October, charges 25/10/12FF per adult/tent site/car.

Hostels The 130-bed *Auberge de Jeunesse BVJ Corsotel* (☎ 04 95 65 14 15, fax 04 95 65 33 72, ave de la République) opens from late March to October. Beds in two to eight-person rooms cost 120FF per person, including a filling breakfast.

Hotels *Hôtel du Centre* (☎ 04 95 65 02 01, 14 rue Alsace-Lorraine) is the cheapest place after the youth hostel. Open 1 June to 13 September, rooms with showers cost between 180FF and 250FF, depending on season.

Places to Eat
Calvi's attractive marina is lined with fairly pricey restaurants and cafes, but there are several budget places on rue Clemenceau, which runs parallel to blvd Wilson. *Best Of*, at the south end of the street, sells good sandwiches (around 25FF) including some with Corsican fillings.

Quai Landry's line-up of waterfront cafes and restaurants includes *Île de Beauté* (☎ 04 95 65 00 46), which specialises in fish and Corsican cuisine and has *menus* for 100FF and 150FF. *Callelu Restaurant* (☎ 04 95 65 22 18, quai Landry) does great fish dishes (110FF to 120FF).

The tiny *Marché Couvert* near Église Ste Marie Majeure opens 8 am to noon (closed

Sunday). The *Super U* supermarket is south of the town centre on ave Christophe Colomb.

Getting There & Away
Bus Buses to Bastia and Calenzana are run by Les Beaux Voyages (☎ 04 95 65 15 02), place de la Porteuse d'Eau. From mid-May to mid-October, an Autocars SAIB (☎ 04 95 26 13 70) bus serves the island's spectacular north-west coast from Calvi's Monument aux Morts (war memorial) to Galéria (1¼ hours) and Porto (three hours).

Train Calvi's train station (☎ 04 95 65 00 61), just off ave de la République, opens until 7.30 pm. From mid-April to mid-October, one-car shuttle trains *(navettes)* run by Tramways de la Balagne make 19 stops between Calvi and L'Île Rousse. The line is divided into three sectors and each costs one ticket (10FF).

Ferry SNCM ferries (☎ 04 95 65 01 38) sail to Calvi from Nice, Marseille and Toulon, but during winter they can be very infrequent. Between mid-May and mid-September, Corsica Ferries links Calvi with Genoa. You can also travel by the fast NGV *(Navire à Grande Vitesse)* boat back to the mainland.

PORTO (PORTU)
pop 460
The pleasant seaside town of Porto, nestled among huge outcrops of red granite and renowned for its sunsets, is an excellent base for exploring some of Corsica's natural wonders. **Les Calanche**, a spectacular mountain landscape of red and orange granite outcrops, towers above the azure waters of the Mediterranean slightly south of Porto along route D81. The **Gorges de Spelunca**, Corsica's most famous river gorge, stretches almost from the town of Ota, 5km east of Porto, to the town of Evisa, 22km away.

Orientation & Information
The marina is about 1.5km downhill from Porto's pharmacy – the local landmark – on the D81. The area, known as Vaïta, is spread out along the road linking the D81 to the marina. The Porto River just south of the marina is linked by an arched pedestrian bridge to a fragrant eucalyptus grove and a small, pebble beach.

The tourist office (☎ 04 95 26 10 55, fax 04 95 26 14 25) near the marina opens 9.30 am to noon and 2.30 to 6.30 pm Monday to Friday (9 am to 8 pm Monday to Saturday in July and August). Just around the corner is a Parc Naturel Régional de Corse office, open in summer. The only ATM between Ajaccio and Calvi is here at Porto.

Things to See & Do
A short trail leads to the 16th-century **Genoese tower** on the outcrop above the town. It's open 10 am and 6 pm, April to October (10FF).

From April to mid-October, the Compagnie des Promenades en Mer (☎ 04 95 26 15 16) runs **boat excursions** (170FF) to the fishing village of Girolata (passing by the Scandola Nature Reserve), and occasionally to Les Calanche in the evenings (80FF).

Places to Stay
Camping The friendly *Funtana al' Ora* (☎ 04 95 26 11 65), 2km east of Porto on the road to Évisa, charges 28FF per person and 11FF for a tent. It's open May to November.

Hostels In the nearby village of Ota, *Gîte d'Étape Chez Félix* (☎ 04 95 26 12 92) and *Gîte d'Étape Chez Marie* (☎ 04 95 26 11 37) both open year-round and charge 60FF for a dorm bed.

Hotels There are plenty of hotels in Vaïta and at the marina. One of the best deals is the *Hôtel du Golfe* (☎ 04 95 26 13 33) which charges 180FF for shower-equipped doubles with toilet (add 20FF per person in summer). *Hôtel Monte Rosso* (☎ 04 95 26 11 50, fax 04 95 26 12 30) nearby has doubles with shower and toilet for 240FF (300FF in July and August).

Getting There & Away
Autocars SAIB (☎ 04 95 22 41 99) has two buses a day linking Porto and nearby Ota with Ajaccio (2½ hours). From mid-May to mid-October a bus also goes from Porto to Calvi (three hours).

CORTE (CORTI)
pop 6329
When Pasquale Paoli led Corsica to independence in 1755, he made Corte, a fortified town at the geographical centre of the island,

the country's capital. To this day, the town remains a potent symbol of Corsican independence. In 1765, Paoli founded a national university there, but it was closed when his short-lived republic was taken over by France in 1769. The Università di Corsica Pasquale Paoli was reopened in 1981 and now has about 3000 students, making Corte the island's liveliest and least touristy town.

Ringed with mountains, snowcapped until as late as June, Corte is an excellent base for hiking; some of the island's highest peaks rise west of the town.

Information

The tourist office (☎ 04 95 46 26 70, fax 04 95 46 34 05, ✉ Corte.Tourisme@wanadoo.fr), La Citadelle, opens 9 am to noon and 2 to 5 pm (closed on weekends). In July and August it opens 9 am to 8 pm.

There are several banks with ATMs along the northern part of cours Paoli. The post office also has an ATM.

Things to See & Do

The **Citadelle**, built in the early 15th century and largely reconstructed during the 18th and 19th centuries, is perched on top of a hill, with the steep and twisted alleyways and streets of the **Ville Haute** and the Tavignanu and Restonica river valleys below.

The **Château** – the highest part, also known as the Nid d'Aigle (Eagle's Nest) – was built in 1419 by a Corsican nobleman and expanded by the French.

The impressive **Museu di a Corsica** (Musée de la Corse; ☎ 04 95 45 25 45) houses an outstanding exhibition on Corsican folk traditions, crafts, agriculture, economy and anthropology. It also has a small cinema and hosts temporary art and music exhibitions on the ground floor. Hours are 10 am to 8 pm in July and August; admission costs 35/20FF.

The **Gorges de la Restonica**, a deep valley cut through the mountains by the Restonica River, is a favourite with hikers. The river passes Corte, but some of the choicer trails begin about 16km south-west of town at the Bergeries Grotelle sheepfolds.

Places to Stay

Camping *Camping Alivetu* (☎ 04 95 46 11 09, *Faubourg de St Antoine*), open 1 April to 15 October, is just south of Pont Restonica. It charges 32/15FF per adult/tent site.

Hostels The quiet and very rural *Gîte d'Étape U Tavignanu* (☎ 04 95 46 16 85, fax 04 95 61 14 01, chemin de Baliri) opens all year and charges 80FF per person, including breakfast. From Pont Tavignanu (the first bridge on Allée du Neuf Septembre), walk westward along chemin de Baliri and follow the signs (almost 1km).

Hotels The 135-room *Hôtel HR* (☎ 04 95 45 11 11, fax 04 95 61 02 85, 6 allée du 9 Septembre) has clean, utilitarian rooms for one/two people for 135/250FF in low season and 135/400FF in high season.

Hôtel de la Poste (☎ 04 95 46 01 37, 2 place Padoue) has spacious, simple rooms with shower for between 140FF and 170FF (with toilet). The family-run *Hôtel du Nord et de L'Europe* (☎ 04 95 46 00 68, fax 04 95 47 40 72, 22 cours Paoli) accommodates students in winter but accepts travellers from April to October. Rooms with shower cost 180FF to 270FF.

Places to Eat

The *Restaurant Universitaire* on the main campus of the Università di Corsica on ave Jean Nicoli, in Résidence Pasquale Paoli, opens 11.30 am to 1.30 pm and 6.30 to 9 pm, October to June (closed at weekends). Meal tickets are sold 11 am to 1 pm.

Restaurant Le Bip's (☎ 04 95 46 06 26, 14 cours Paoli) is a nice cellar restaurant at the bottom of the flight of stairs 20m down the hill from *Brasserie Le Bip's* (☎ 04 95 46 04 48). The 80FF *menu* changes daily.

Corte's best restaurant is *U Museu* (☎ 04 95 61 08 36, Rampe Ribanella) which has an excellent range of tasty local fare. Unusual dishes include *civet de sanglier aux myrtes sauvages* (wild boar in myrtle).

There's a *Eurospar Supermarket* (7 ave Xavier Luciani) and a *Casino Supermarket* (allée du 9 Septembre).

Getting There & Away

Corte is on Eurocorse's Bastia-Ajaccio route, served by two buses a day in each direction (no Sunday service). The stop is at 3 ave Xavier Luciani where a schedule is posted.

The train station (☎ 04 95 46 00 97) is staffed 8 am to noon and 2 to 6.30 pm (closed on Sunday after 11 am, early September to late June).

BONIFACIO (BUNIFAZIU)
pop 2658

The famed **Citadelle** of Bonifacio sits 70m above the translucent waters of the Mediterranean, atop a long, narrow and easily defensible promontory – 'Corsica's Gibraltar'. On all sides, limestone cliffs sculpted by the wind and the waves drop almost vertically to the sea; the north side looks out on 1.6km-long Bonifacio Sound, at the eastern end of which is the **marina**. The southern ramparts afford views of the coast of Sardinia, 12km away.

Bonifacio was long associated with the Republic of Genoa. The local dialect – unintelligible to other Corsicans – is Genoese and many local traditions (including cooking methods) are Genoa-based.

Information

In the Citadelle, the tourist office (☎ 04 95 73 11 88, fax 04 95 73 14 97), 2 rue Fred Scamaroni, opens 9 am to 8 pm daily in summer and 9 am to noon and 2 to 6 pm Monday to Friday the rest of the year.

The Société Générale, outside the Citadelle at 38 rue St Érasme, has poor rates, charges 25FF commission (closed at weekends), and sports the only ATM in town. In summer, there are exchange bureaus along the marina.

Things to See & Do

Looking down the dramatic cliffs to the sea is a delight; the best views are to be had from **place du Marché** and from the walk west towards and around the cemetery. Don't miss **Porte de Gênes**, which is reached by a tiny 16th-century drawbridge, or the Romanesque **Église Ste Marie Majeure**, the oldest building in Bonifacio. **Rue des Deux Empereurs** (Street of the Two Emperors) is so-called because both Charles V and Napoleon slept there; look for the plaques at Nos 4 and 7. The **Foreign Legion Monument** east of the tourist office was brought back from Algeria in 1963 when that country won its independence.

Places to Stay

The olive-shaded **Camping Araguina** (☎ 04 95 73 02 96, ave Sylvère Bohn), open mid-March to October, is 400m north of the marina. It charges 31/34FF per person in the low/high season and 11FF for a tent.

The 32-room **Hôtel des Étrangers** (☎ 04 95 73 01 09, fax 04 95 73 16 97, ave Sylvère Bohn), 500m north of the marina, opens early April to October. Doubles with shower and toilet cost 220FF (280FF to 390FF from July to September).

In the Citadelle, the two-star **Hôtel Le Royal** (☎ 04 95 73 00 51, fax 04 95 73 04 68, rue Fred Scamaroni) has rooms for 225FF, 250FF and 290FF, October to April; prices double in July and August.

Places to Eat

In the Citadelle, **Pizzeria-Grill de la Poste** (☎ 04 95 73 13 31, 5 rue Fred Scamaroni) has Corsican dishes, pizza and pasta (45FF to 69FF). **Cantina Doria** (☎ 04 95 73 50 49, 27 rue Doria) is a neat, rustic hole-in-the-wall where you dine on wooden benches among old farming utensils. Their enormous soupe Corse (40FF) is enough for two people.

At the marina, **Super Marché Simoni** (93 quai Jérôme Comparetti) opens 8 am to 12.30 pm and 3.30 to 7.30 pm (closed Sunday afternoon). The **Coccinelle** supermarket next door has a fresh bakery counter.

Getting There & Away

Bus Eurocorse (☎ 04 95 70 13 83 in Porto-Vecchio) has buses to Ajaccio via Sartène. To Bastia, change buses at Porto-Vecchio, which is served by two buses daily (four in summer). All buses leave from the parking lot next to the Eurocorse kiosk at the east end of the marina.

Ferry Saremar (☎ 04 95 73 00 96) and Moby Lines (☎ 04 95 73 00) both offer a daily car and passenger ferry service year-round from Bonifacio's ferry port to Santa Teresa (50 minutes, two to seven per day).

Saremar charges 45/65FF for a one-way passenger fare in low/high season while Moby Lines charges 50/65FF. There's an additional 18.50FF port tax.

Germany

Few countries in Western Europe have such a fascinating and complicated past as Germany. Its reunification in 1990 was the beginning of yet another intriguing chapter. Much of this history is easily explored by visitors today, in a country of sheer beauty where outdoor activity is a way of life. There is a huge variety of museums, architecture from many historical periods and a heavy emphasis on cultural pursuits. Infrastructure is well organised, there is plenty of accommodation and the frothy beer, heady wine and hearty food are superb.

Though it's now one country, the cultural, social and economic differences of the formerly separate Germanys will take many years to disappear altogether. Visitors will notice the differences that persist between the east and the west despite over a decade of integration.

Facts about Germany

HISTORY

Events in Germany have often dominated the history of Europe. For many centuries, however, Germany was a patchwork of semi-independent principalities and city-states, preoccupied with internal quarrels and at the mercy of foreign conquerors. In the 18th and 19th centuries, these squabbling territories gradually came under the control of Prussia, a state created by the rulers of Brandenburg. Germany only became a nation-state in 1871 and, despite the momentous events that have occurred since, many Germans still retain a strong sense of regional identity.

Ancient & Medieval History

Germany west of the Rhine and south of the Main was part of the Roman Empire, but Roman legions never managed to subdue the warrior tribes beyond. As the Roman Empire crumbled, these tribes spread out over much of Europe, establishing small kingdoms. The Frankish conqueror Charlemagne, from his

AT A GLANCE

Capital	Berlin
Population	82.5 million
Official Language	German
Currency	1 Deutschmark = 100 pfennig
Time	GMT/UTC+0100
Country Phone Code	☎ 49

Also in Berlin
Berlin Mitte pp492-3
Tiergarten, Schöneberg & Kreuzberg p496
Charlottenburg & Wilmersdorf p500

DENMARK

Stralsund p540

Hamburg pp614-5   Schwerin p535

NETHERLANDS   Bremen p604

Potsdam p512   Greater Berlin p488   POLAND

Düsseldorf p600

BELGIUM   Cologne p594   Leipzig p521   Dresden p515

Erfurt p523   Weimar p526

Trier p582   Central Frankfurt p588   CZECH REPUBLIC

LUXEMBOURG   Heidelberg pp566-7   Nuremberg p556

Black Forest p571   Stuttgart p564

FRANCE   Freiburg p573

Central Munich pp544-5   AUSTRIA

SWITZERLAND

court in Aachen, forged a huge empire that covered most of Christian Western Europe, but it broke up after his death in 814.

The eastern branch of Charlemagne's empire developed in 962 into the Holy Roman Empire, organised under Otto I (Otto the Great). It included much of present-day Germany, Austria, Switzerland and Benelux. The term 'Holy Roman' was coined in an effort to assume some of the authority of the defunct Roman Empire.

The house of Habsburg, ruling from Vienna, took control of the shrinking empire in the 13th century, which became little more than a conglomerate of German-speaking states run by local rulers who paid mere lip

GERMANY

GERMANY (DEUTSCHLAND)

euro currency converter €1 = 1.95DM

service to the Habsburg emperor. A semblance of unity in northern Germany was maintained by the Hanseatic League, a federation of German and Baltic city-states with Lübeck as its centre. The League began to form in the mid-12th century and dissolved in 1669.

The Reformation

Things would never be the same in Europe after Martin Luther, a scholar from the monastery in Erfurt, nailed his *95 Theses* to the church door in Wittenberg in 1517. Luther opposed a Church racket involving the selling of so-called 'indulgences', which absolved sinners from temporal punishment. In 1521 he was condemned by the Church and went into hiding in Wartburg Castle in Eisenach. There he translated the Bible from the original Greek version into an everyday form of German. This Bible was printed on presses developed by Gutenberg in Mainz and was then read widely to the masses.

Luther's efforts at reforming the Church gained widespread support from merchants, wealthy townsfolk and, crucially, several ambitious German princes. This protest against the established Church began the Protestant movement and the Reformation. The Peace of Augsburg in 1555 declared that the religion of a state would be determined by its ruler.

Meanwhile the established Church, often called the 'Roman' Catholic Church, began a campaign known as the Counter-Reformation to stem the spread of Protestantism.

Thirty Years' War

The tensions between Protestant and Catholic states across Europe led to the catastrophic Thirty Years' War (1618-48). Germany, now the battlefield for the great powers of Europe, lost over a third of its population and many of its towns and cities. It took the country centuries to recover.

The Peace of Westphalia in 1648 established the rights of both faiths in Germany but also sealed the country's political division. The German-speaking states remained a patchwork of independent principalities within the loose framework of the Holy Roman Empire, but were weakened further by the loss of important territories.

Prussia Unites Germany

In the 18th century the Kingdom of Prussia, with its capital in Berlin, became one of Europe's strongest powers. Thanks to the organisational talents of Friedrich Wilhelm I (the Soldier King) and his son Friedrich II (Frederick the Great), it expanded eastwards at the expense of Poland, Lithuania and Russia.

In the early 19th century, the fragmented German states proved easy pickings for Napoleon. The Austrian emperor, Francis II, relinquished his crown as Holy Roman Emperor in 1806 following his defeat at Austerlitz. But the French never quite managed to subdue Prussia, which became the centre of German resistance. After his disastrous foray into Russia, Prussia led the war that put an end to Napoleon's German aspirations in a decisive battle at Leipzig in 1813.

In 1815 the Congress of Vienna again redrew the map of Europe. The Holy Roman Empire was replaced with a German Confederation of 35 states; it had a parliament in Frankfurt and was led by the Austrian chancellor Klemens von Metternich. The Confederation was shaken by liberal revolutions in Europe in 1830 and 1848, but the Austrian monarchy continued to dominate a divided Germany.

The well-oiled Prussian civil and military machine eventually smashed this arrangement. In 1866, Otto von Bismarck (the Iron Chancellor) took Prussia to war against Austria, and rapidly annexed northern Germany. Another successful war in 1870-71 saw Prussia defeat France and seize the provinces of Alsace and Lorraine. The Catholic, anti-Prussian states in southern Germany were forced to negotiate with Bismarck, who had achieved his dream of German unity. The Prussian king, Wilhelm I, became *Kaiser* (German emperor).

WWI & the Rise of Hitler

Wilhelm II dismissed Bismarck in 1890, but Germany's rapid growth overtaxed the Kaiser's political talents, and led to mounting tensions with England, Russia and France. When war broke out in 1914, Germany's only ally was a weakened Austria-Hungary.

Gruelling trench warfare on two fronts sapped the nation's resources and by late 1918 Germany sued for peace. The Kaiser abdicated and escaped to Holland. Anger on

GERMANY

the home front, which had been mounting during the fighting and deprivation, exploded when the troops returned home. A full-scale socialist uprising, based in Berlin and led by the Spartacus League, was put down and its leaders, Karl Liebknecht and Rosa Luxemburg, were murdered. A new republic, which became known as the Weimar Republic, was proclaimed.

The Treaty of Versailles in 1919 chopped huge areas off Germany and imposed heavy reparation payments. These were impossible to meet, and when France and Belgium occupied the Rhineland to ensure continued payments, the subsequent hyperinflation and miserable economic conditions provided fertile ground for political extremists. One of these was Adolf Hitler.

Led by Hitler, an Austrian drifter and German army veteran, the National (or Nazi) Socialist German Workers' Party staged an abortive coup in Munich in 1923. This landed Hitler in prison for nine months, during which time he wrote *Mein Kampf*.

From 1929 the worldwide economic depression hit Germany particularly hard, leading to massive unemployment, strikes and demonstrations. The Communist Party under Ernst Thälmann gained strength, but wealthy industrialists began to support the Nazis and police turned a blind eye to Nazi street thugs.

The Nazis increased their strength in general elections and in 1933 replaced the Social Democrats as the largest party in the Reichstag (parliament). Hitler was appointed chancellor and a year later assumed absolute control as *Führer* (leader) of what he called the Third Reich (the 'third empire'; the previous two being the Holy Roman Empire and Wilhelm I's German Empire).

WWII & the Division of Germany

From 1935 Germany began to rearm and build its way out of depression with strategic public works such as the autobahns. Hitler reoccupied the Rhineland in 1936, and in 1938 annexed Austria and parts of Czechoslovakia. Finally, in September 1939, after signing a pact that allowed both Stalin and himself a free hand in the east of Europe, Hitler attacked Poland, which led to war with Britain and France.

Germany quickly invaded large parts of Europe, but after 1942 began to suffer

increasingly heavy losses. Massive bombing reduced Germany's centres to rubble and the country lost 10% of its population. Germany accepted unconditional surrender in May 1945, soon after Hitler's suicide. Chief among the horrors of WWII was the extermination of millions of Jews, Roma (Gypsies), communists and others in history's first 'assembly-line' genocide. Camps were intended to rid Europe of people considered undesirable according to racist Nazi doctrine.

At conferences in Yalta and Potsdam, the Allies redrew the borders of Germany, making it a quarter smaller than it had already become after the Treaty of Versailles 26 years earlier. Some 6.5 million ethnic Germans migrated or were expelled to Germany from their homes in Eastern Europe, where they had lived for centuries. Germany was divided into four occupation zones and Berlin was occupied jointly by the four victorious powers.

In the Soviet zone, the communist Socialist Unity Party (SED) won the 1946 elections and began a rapid nationalisation of industry. In June 1948 the Soviet Union stopped all land traffic between Germany's western zones and Berlin. This forced the Western allies to mount a military operation known as the Berlin Airlift, which brought food and other supplies to West Berlin by plane until the Soviets lifted the blockade in May 1949.

In September 1949 the Federal Republic of Germany (FRG) was created out of the three western zones; in response the German Democratic Republic (GDR) was founded in the Soviet zone the following month, with (East) Berlin as its capital.

From Division to Unity

As the West's bulwark against communism, the FRG received massive injections of US capital, and experienced rapid economic development under the leadership of Konrad Adenauer. At the same time the GDR had to pay US$10 billion in war reparations to the Soviet Union and rebuild itself from scratch.

A better life in the west increasingly attracted skilled workers away from the miserable economic conditions in the east. As these were people the GDR could ill afford to lose, in 1961 it built a wall around West Berlin and sealed its border with the FRG. As the Cold War intensified, TV and radio stations in both

Germanys beamed programs heavy with propaganda to the other side.

Coinciding with a change to the more flexible leadership of Erich Honecker in the east, the *Ostpolitik* of FRG chancellor Willy Brandt allowed an easier political relationship between the two Germanys. In 1971 the four occupying powers – the Soviet Union, the USA, the UK and France – formally accepted the division of Berlin. Many western countries, but not West Germany itself, then officially recognised the GDR.

Honecker's policies produced higher living standards in the GDR, yet East Germany barely managed to achieve a level of prosperity half that of the FRG. After Mikhail Gorbachev came to power in the Soviet Union in March 1985, the East German communists gradually lost Soviet backing.

Events in 1989 rapidly overtook the East German government, which resisted pressure to introduce reforms. When Hungary relaxed its border controls in May 1989, East Germans began crossing to the west in their small Trabant cars. Tighter travel controls introduced by the Politburo resulted in would-be defectors taking refuge in the FRG's embassy in Prague. Meanwhile, mass demonstrations in Leipzig spread to other cities of the GDR and Honecker was replaced by his security chief, Egon Krenz, who introduced cosmetic reforms. Then suddenly on 9 November 1989, a Politburo decision to allow direct travel to the west was mistakenly interpreted as the immediate opening of all GDR borders with West Germany. That same night thousands of people streamed into the west past stunned border guards. Millions more followed in the next few days, and dismantling of the wall began soon thereafter.

The trend at first was to reform the GDR but, in East German elections held in early 1990, citizens voted clearly in favour of the Christian Democratic Union (CDU), thus paving the way for fast-track reunification. The wartime Allies signed the Two-Plus-Four Treaty which ended the postwar system of occupation zones, and a Unification Treaty was drawn up to integrate East Germany into the Federal Republic of Germany, which came about on 3 October 1990. All-German elections were held in late that year and, in the national euphoria, the CDU-led coalition, which strongly favoured reunification, soundly defeated the Social Democrat opposition. This earned its leader, Helmut Kohl, the epitaph of Germany's 'unification chancellor'.

The Land in the Middle

The Kohl era of German politics – synonymous with reunification but also with violent attacks on foreigners in the early 1990s – drew to a close in late 1998, when a coalition of Social Democrats and Bündnis 90/the Greens party took political office. Although actual support for Bündnis 90/the Greens has mostly waned since the mid-1990s, their current involvement in the coalition represents a new political highpoint.

In late 1999, it was revealed that during the term of Helmut Kohl, Germany's longest-serving chancellor, party slush funds had been maintained which are believed to have flowed into CDU election campaigns. The ensuing scandal tarnished the reputation of Kohl, who not only has earned a name for his services in promoting German unification and European integration, but also for flaunting German constitutional law.

Germany, the 'land in the middle', has assumed a more confident and assertive role in world affairs in recent times and is now a driving force behind plans to integrate its eastern neighbours into the European Union.

GEOGRAPHY

Germany covers 356,866 sq km and can be divided from north to south into several geographical regions.

The Northern Lowlands are a broad expanse of flat, low-lying land that sweeps across the northern third of the country from the Netherlands into Poland. The landscape is characterised by moist heaths interspersed with pastures and farmland.

The complex Central Uplands region divides northern Germany from the south. Extending from the deep schisms of the Rhineland massifs, to the Black Forest, the Bavarian Forest, the Ore Mountains and the Harz Mountains, these low mountain ranges are Germany's heartland. The Rhine and Main Rivers, important waterways for inland shipping, cut through the south-west of this region. With large deposits of coal and favourable transport conditions, this was one of the first regions in Germany to undergo industrialisation.

GERMANY

The Alpine Foothills, wedged between the Danube and the Alps, is typified by sub-alpine plateau and rolling hills, and by moors in eastern regions around the Danube.

Germany's Alps lie entirely within Bavaria and stretch from the large, glacially formed Lake Constance in the west to Berchtesgaden in Germany's south-eastern corner. Though lower than the mountains to their south, many summits are well above 2000m, rising dramatically from the Alpine Foothills to the 2966m Zugspitze, Germany's highest mountain.

CLIMATE

The German climate can be variable, so it's best to be prepared for all types of weather throughout the year. That said, the most reliable weather is from May to October. This, of course, coincides with the standard tourist season (except for skiing). The shoulder periods (late March to May and September to October) can bring fewer tourists and surprisingly pleasant weather.

Eastern Germany lies in a transition zone between the temperate maritime climate of Western Europe and the rougher continental climate of Eastern Europe – continental and Atlantic air masses meet here. The mean daily temperature in the capital of Berlin is 11°C, the average range of temperatures varying from -1°C in January to 18°C in July. The average annual precipitation is 585mm and there is no special rainy season. The camping season is from May to September.

ECOLOGY & ENVIRONMENT

Germans are fiercely protective of their natural surroundings. Households and businesses participate enthusiastically in waste-recycling programs. A refund system applies to a wide range of glass bottles and jars, while containers for waste paper and glass can be found in each neighbourhood. Though acid rain is a problem, German forests have lost little of their wonderful fairy-tale charm, whereas in eastern Germany regions around the Oder River and in parts of Mecklenburg and Western Pomerania have retained an intact Central European ecosystem.

Energy

Clashes between police and anti-nuclear demonstrators in Germany throughout the 1980s were the most violent and bloody in Europe since the 1968 Paris student riots: armed anarchists, armed police, and committed ordinary Germans were caught between revolutionary intent and a state of siege. In Germany, it was all about shutting down nuclear reactors and preventing new ones being built. Times have changed. Germany still generates about one-third of its energy from its 19 atomic plants, but a deal has been struck with the powerful energy lobby to close the plants over the next three decades. In the meantime, nuclear waste remains a sticky, unresolved issue.

FLORA & FAUNA

Few species of flora and fauna are unique to Germany. Unique, however, is the importance Germans place on their forests, the prettiest of which are mixed-species deciduous forests planted with beech, oak, maple and birch. You'll find that most cities even have their own city forest (Stadtwald). Alpine regions bloom in spring with orchids, cyclamen, gentians, edelweiss, and more; and the heather blossom on the Lüneburg Heath, north of Hanover, is stunning in August.

Apart from human beings, the most common large mammals are deer, wild pigs, rabbits, foxes and hares. The chances of seeing any of these in summer are fairly good, especially in eastern Germany. There's a particularly thriving wild pig population, and some pigs even wander occasionally into the suburbs of Berlin! On the coasts you will find seals and, throughout Germany, falcons, hawks, storks and migratory geese are a common sight.

Berchtesgaden (in the Bavarian Alps), the Wattenmeer parks in Schleswig-Holstein, Lower Saxony and Hamburg, and the Unteres Odertal, which is a joint German-Polish endeavour, are highlights among Germany's dozen or so national parks.

GOVERNMENT & POLITICS

Germany has a very decentralised governmental structure – a federal system based on regional states. Reunification saw eastern Germany's six original (pre-1952) states of Berlin, Brandenburg, Mecklenburg-Vorpommern (Mecklenburg-Western Pomerania), Sachsen (Saxony), Sachsen-Anhalt (Saxony-Anhalt) and Thüringen (Thuringia) all re-established. In the context of the Federal Republic of Germany they are called *Bundesländer* (federal states). The Bundesländer in western Germany are Schleswig-Holstein, Hamburg, Niedersachsen (Lower Saxony), Bremen, Nordrhein-Westfalen (North Rhine-Westphalia), Hessen (Hesse), Rheinland-Pfalz (the Rhineland-Palatinate), Saarland, Baden-Württemberg and Bayern (Bavaria). Germans commonly refer to the eastern states as the *neue Bundesländer* (new states) and to the western states as the *alte Bundesländer* (old states).

The Bundesländer have a large degree of autonomy in internal affairs and exert influence on the central government through the *Bundesrat* (upper house). The *Bundestag* (lower house) is elected by direct universal suffrage with proportional representation, although a party must have at least 5% of the vote to gain a seat. Germany's two major parties are the Christian Democrats (CDU, or CSU in Bavaria) and the Social Democrats (SPD). The Free Democrats (FDP), a small but influential liberal party, often holds the balance of power. The Democratic Socialists (PDS), the former East German SED, is a strong force in eastern Germany, whereas the popularity and fortunes of Bündnis 90/the Greens party have been mixed in recent years.

The current chancellor is Gerhard Schröder from the SPD, which governs in coalition with Bündnis 90/the Greens. In September 1999 the Bundestag resumed sitting in Berlin's restored Reichstag building, transferring the seat of government from Bonn.

ECONOMY

The Marshall Plan helped to produce West Germany's *Wirtschaftswunder* (economic miracle), which in the 1950s and 60s turned the FRG into the world's third-largest economy. Trade unions and industrial corporations developed a unique economic contract which involves employees in company decisions. Important industries include electrical manufacturing, precision and optical instruments, chemicals and vehicle manufacturing, and environmental technology.

East Germany's recovery was even more remarkable given the wartime destruction, postwar looting by the USSR, loss of skilled labour, and isolation from Western markets. The GDR was by any measure an important industrial nation, with major metallurgical, electrical, chemical and engineering industries. As a result of reunification, many industries were privatised but others were closed down, causing unemployment and hardship in some regions. Those most affected are women and older workers.

Eastern Germany now has a modern infrastructure, but little is being invested there. With the decline of traditional heavy industries in the region, tourism has become important; the region is also well-placed geographically to gain from restructured Eastern European markets or an expanded EU.

Unemployment remains a major problem throughout Germany, especially in eastern regions, where almost 18% of the work force is unemployed. The national figure is just over 10%.

Germany, though slow at first to adapt to the 'new economy' of the 1990s, now has thriving IT, online and telecommunications industries, though skilled labour shortages hamper its growth in some sectors, especially software development. Economic growth is slow in comparison to most other European countries – especially in eastern Germany – and ordinary Germans have lost much of their early enthusiasm for adopting the euro.

POPULATION & PEOPLE

Germany has a population of around 82.5 million, 15 million of whom live in eastern Germany, making the unified country the most populous in Europe apart from Russia. Germany's main native minority is the tiny group of Slavonic Sorbs in the far east of the country (Saxony and Brandenburg). In political and economic terms, Germany is Europe's most decentralised nation, but considerable variation in population density exists. The Ruhr district in the northern Rhineland has Germany's densest concentration of people and industry, while Mecklenburg-Western Pomerania in the north-eastern corner is relatively sparsely settled. About one-third of the population lives in 84 cities, each with over 100,000 people.

Over seven million foreigners also live in Germany. Most hail from Turkey, Italy, Greece and the former Yugoslavia, and have

GERMANY

arrived as 'guest workers' in the FRG since the early 1960s to work in lower-paid jobs. In 1999 archaic immigration laws dating back to 1913 were changed to make it easier for residents without German ancestry to gain citizenship. This now takes about seven years. Eastern Germany has fewer resident foreigners, though some of the roughly 200,000 workers who arrived in the GDR during the 1980s from 'fraternal socialist' countries remain. A strong immigrant tradition in Germany dates back to 1700, when around 30% of Berlin's population consisted of Huguenots who had fled religious oppression in France. Another large wave of immigrants moved to the Ruhr region from Poland in the late 19th century. In effect, Germany is a nation of immigration, which compensates for the extremely low birth rate among the established German population. (The number of Germans living in the country's eastern states has now dropped to levels last recorded in 1906!)

ARTS

Germany's meticulously creative population has made major contributions to international culture. Indeed Germans take their *Kultur* so seriously that visitors sometimes wonder how on earth they ever manage to actually enjoy it. The answer lies, perhaps, in a German musician's proverb: 'True bliss is absolute concentration'.

Architecture, Painting & Literature

The scope of German art is such that it could be the focus of an entire visit. The arts first blossomed during the Romanesque period (800–1200), of which examples can be found at the Germanisches Nationalmuseum in Nuremberg, Trier Cathedral, the churches of Cologne, the chapel of Charlemagne's palace in Aachen, and the Stiftskirche in Gernrode.

The Gothic style (1200–1500) is best viewed at Freiburg's Münster cathedral, Meissen Cathedral, Cologne's Dom and the Marienkirche in Lübeck. Artists from the Cologne school of painters and sculptor Peter Vischer and his sons produced Gothic sculpture and innovative paintings featuring rudimentary landscapes. One famous panel painting is a work by Meister Bertram (circa 1340), in Hamburg's Kunsthalle.

The Renaissance came late to Germany but flourished once it took hold. The draughtsman Albrecht Dürer of Nuremberg (1471–1528) was one of the world's finest portraitists, as was the prolific Lucas Cranach the Elder (1472–1553) who worked in Wittenberg for over 45 years.

The baroque period brought great sculpture, including works by Andreas Schlüter in Berlin. Balthasar Neumann's superb Residenz in Würzburg and the magnificent cathedral in Passau are foremost examples of baroque architecture.

The Enlightenment During the 18th century, the Saxon court at Weimar attracted some of the major cultural figures of Europe. Among them was Johann Wolfgang von Goethe (1749–1832), the poet, dramatist, painter, scientist, philosopher and perhaps the last European to achieve the Renaissance ideal of excellence in many fields. His greatest work, the drama Faust, is a masterful epic of all that went before him, as the archetypal human strives for meaning and knowledge.

Goethe's close friend, Friedrich Schiller (1759–1805), was a poet, dramatist and novelist. His most famous work is the dramatic cycle *Wallenstein*, based on the life of a treacherous general of the Thirty Years' War who plotted to make himself arbiter of the empire. Schiller's other great play, *William Tell*, dealt with the right of the oppressed to rise against tyranny. There are large museums in Weimar dedicated to both Schiller and Goethe.

The 19th & Early 20th Centuries Berlin too produced remarkable individuals, such as Alexander von Humboldt (1769–1859), an advanced thinker in environmentalism through his studies of the relationship of plants and animals to their physical surroundings. His contemporary, the philosopher Georg Wilhelm Friedrich Hegel (1770–1831), created an all-embracing classical philosophy that is still influential today. The neoclassical period in Germany was led by Karl Friedrich Schinkel and the Munich neoclassical school. The romantic period is best exemplified by the paintings of Caspar David Friedrich and Otto Runge.

Art Nouveau also made important contributions to German architecture, as exemplified by

Alfred Messel's Wertheim department store in Berlin. Expressionism followed, with great names like Paul Klee and the Russian-born painter Vasili Kandinsky. In 1919, Walter Gropius founded the Bauhaus movement in an attempt to meld the theoretical concerns of architecture with the practical problems faced by artists and craftspeople. With the arrival of the Nazis, Gropius accepted a chair at Harvard.

In the 1920s, Berlin was the theatrical capital of Germany, and its most famous practitioner was the Marxist poet and playwright Bertolt Brecht (1898–1956). Brecht introduced Marxist concepts into his plays, and his work was distinguished by the simplicity of its moral parables, its language and its sharp characterisation. Brecht revolutionised the theatre by detaching the audience from what was happening on stage, enabling them to observe the content without being distracted by the form. In 1933 Brecht fled the Nazis and lived in various countries, eventually accepting the directorship of the Berliner Ensemble in East Berlin, where his work has been performed ever since.

WWII & Beyond During the Third Reich, the arts were devoted mainly to propaganda, with grandiose projects and realist art extolling the virtues of German nationhood. Max Ernst, resident in France and the USA, was a prominent exponent of dada and surrealism who developed the technique of collage.

Postwar literature in both Germanys was influenced by the politically focused Gruppe 47. It included writers such as Günter Grass, whose modern classic, *Die Blechtrommel* (The Tin Drum), humorously traces German history through the eyes of Oskar, a young boy who refuses to grow. Christa Wolf, an East German novelist and Gruppe 47 writer, won high esteem in both Germanys. Her 1963 story *Der geteilte Himmel* (Divided Heaven) tells of a young woman whose fiance abandons her for life in the west.

Patrick Süskind's *Das Parfum* (The Perfume) is the extraordinary tale of a psychotic 18th-century perfume-maker with an obsessive genius. *Helden wie wir* (Heroes Like Us) by Thomas Brussig, an eastern German, tells the story of a man whose penis brings about the collapse of the Berlin Wall.

Music

Few countries can claim the impressive musical heritage of Germany. A partial list of household names includes Johann Sebastian Bach, Georg Friedrich Händel, Ludwig van Beethoven, Richard Wagner, Richard Strauss, Felix Mendelssohn-Bartholdy, Robert Schumann, Johannes Brahms and Gustav Mahler.

The two greatest baroque composers were born in Saxony in the same year. Johann Sebastian Bach (1685-1750) was born at Eisenach into a prominent family of musicians. During his time as court organist at Weimar and city musical director at Leipzig, Bach produced some 200 cantatas, plus masses, oratorios, passions and other elaborate music for the Lutheran service, as well as sonatas, concertos, preludes and fugues for secular use.

Georg Friedrich Händel (1685–1759) left his native Halle for Hamburg at 18. He composed numerous operas and oratorios, including his masterpiece *Messiah* (1742). The birthplaces of both Händel and Bach are now large museums.

In the 19th century, the musical traditions of Saxony continued with songwriter Robert Schumann (1810–56), born at Zwickau. In 1843 Schumann opened a music school at Leipzig in collaboration with composer Felix Mendelssohn-Bartholdy (1809–47), director of Leipzig's famous Gewandhaus Orchestra. Works by Richard Wagner (1813–83) represent a milestone in European classical music, and no composer since Wagner's time could ignore his attempts to balance all operatic forms to produce a 'total work of art'.

These musical traditions continue to thrive: the Dresden Opera and Leipzig Orchestra are known around the world, and musical performances are hosted almost daily in every major theatre in the country.

Germany has also contributed significantly to the contemporary music scene, with Kraftwerk creating the first 'techno' sounds, and through internationally known performers and bands such as Nina Hagen, Nena, the Scorpions, Fury in the Slaughterhouse and Die Toten Hosen.

You can hear jazz, folk, techno, house and other sounds in clubs in major cities. The Studio for Electronic Music in Cologne and Hamburg's Mojo club are two innovative venues. Traditional German oompah music is

GERMANY

still popular with some locals and tourists, while Schlager music, with its treacly lyrics, confounds foreigners with its popularity.

SOCIETY & CONDUCT

The unflattering image of Germans as overly disciplined and humourless is a stereotype rather than the reality. On the whole, you'll find Germans relaxed, personable and interested in enjoying life.

Tradition plays a surprisingly strong role despite or perhaps because of the country's modern industrial achievements. Hunters still wear green, many Bavarian women don the *Dirndl* (skirt and blouse), while some menfolk sport the typical Bavarian *Lederhosen* (leather shorts), a *Loden* (short jacket) and felt hat. In contrast, you might hear young Germans dismiss this sort of thing as *typisch deutsch* (typically German), a phrase that usually has negative connotations.

While Germans are generally not prudish or awkwardly polite, formal manners remain important. When making a phone call to anywhere in Germany, you'll find people more helpful if you first introduce yourself by name. Germans sometimes shake hands when greeting or leaving. Hugging and cheek kissing is common between males and females who know one another.

The Holocaust and WWII, while by no means taboo topics, should be discussed with tact and understanding in Germany. In western Germany these themes have been dealt with openly for decades, but Germans sometimes feel their country's postwar role as a prosperous democracy continues to be under-emphasised against its relatively short period under the Nazis. Germans understandably take great offence at the presumption that fascist ideas are somehow part of or even compatible with their national culture.

RELIGION

Most Germans belong to a church, and there are almost equal numbers of Catholics and Protestants; roughly speaking, Catholics predominate in the south, Protestants in the north and east. A majority of citizens pay contributions to their church, which the government collects along with their taxes, but in practice few Germans regularly attend church services.

Despite their bitter historical rivalry, conflict between Catholics and Protestants in Germany is not an issue these days. In eastern Germany, the Protestant Church, which claims support among the overwhelming majority of the population there, played a major role in the overthrow of German communism by providing a gathering place for anti-government protesters. Active church membership, however, remains even lower than in western Germany.

In 1933 some 530,000 Jews lived in Germany. Today Germany's Jewish citizens number around 50,000, with the largest communities in Berlin, Frankfurt and Munich. Their population is growing, though, with the recent influx of Russian Jews. There are also more than 1.7 million Muslims, most of them Turks.

LANGUAGE

It might come as a surprise to learn that German is a close relative of English. English, German and Dutch are all known as West Germanic languages. This means that you already know lots of German words – *Arm, Finger, Gold* – and you'll be able to figure out many others, such as *Mutter* (mother), *trinken* (drink), *gut* (good). A primary reason why English and German have grown apart is that when the Normans invaded England in 1066 they brought in many non-Germanic words. For this reason, English has many synonyms, usually with the everyday word being German, and the more literary or specialised one coming from French; for instance, 'start' and 'green' as opposed to 'commence' and 'verdant'.

German is spoken throughout Germany and Austria and in much of Switzerland. It is also useful in Eastern Europe, especially with older people. Although you will hear different regional dialects, the official language, *Hochdeutsch*, is universally understood. English is widely understood by young or educated Germans, but as soon as you try to meet ordinary people or move out of the big cities, especially in eastern Germany, the situation is rather different. Your efforts to speak the local language will be appreciated and will make your trip much more enjoyable.

Words that you'll often encounter on maps and throughout this chapter include: *Altstadt* (old city), *Bahnhof* (train station), *Brücke* (bridge), *Hauptbahnhof* (main train station), *Markt* (market, often the central square in old towns), *Platz* (square), *Rathaus* (town hall) and *Strasse* (street). German nouns are always written with a capital letter.

See the Language chapter at the back of the book for pronunciation guidelines and useful words and phrases.

Facts for the Visitor

HIGHLIGHTS
Museums & Galleries
Germany is a museum-lover's dream. Munich features the huge Deutsches Museum, and Frankfurt's Museumsufer (Museum Embankment) has enough museums for any addict. Berlin's Neue Bildergalerie and the Neue Meister gallery in Dresden are among the chief art museums, while cultural treasures are centred at Nuremberg's Germanisches Nationalmuseum.

Castles
Germany has castles of all periods and styles. If you're into castles, make sure to hit Heidelberg, Neuschwanstein, Burg Rheinfels on the Rhine River, Burg Eltz on the Moselle, the medieval Königstein and Wartburg Castles, Renaissance Wittenberg Castle, baroque Schloss Moritzburg and romantic Wernigerode Castle.

Historic Towns
Time stands still in parts of Germany, and some of the best towns in which to find this flavour are Wismar, Goslar and Regensburg. Meissen and Quedlinburg have a fairy-tale air, Weimar has a special place in German culture, and Lübeck is one of Europe's true gems. The old district (*Altstadt*) of many large cities also imparts this historic feel.

Roads & Rivers
Germany has many scenic theme roads, such as those in the Black Forest and the Fairy-Tale Road between Hanau and Bremen. The best way to explore them is by car. Check with local or regional tourist offices for maps and highlights of the route.

Important rivers such as the Rhine, Danube, Moselle and Elbe are well-serviced by boats in summer, and the Rhine and Moselle Rivers are especially suited to combined wine quaffing and cruising.

SUGGESTED ITINERARIES
Depending on the length of your stay, you might want to see and do the following things:

Two days
  Depending on where you enter the country, try to spend your two days in either Berlin or Munich.
One week
  Divide your time between Berlin and Munich, and throw in a visit to Dresden or Bamberg.
Two weeks
  Berlin (including Potsdam), Dresden or Bamberg, Munich, Freiburg and the Rhine or Moselle Valley.
One month
  Berlin (including Potsdam), Dresden or Bamberg, Meissen, the Harz Mountains, the Rhine or Moselle Valley, Munich, the Alps, Lake Constance, Freiburg or Lübeck.
Two months
  As for one month, plus Weimar, Regensburg, Passau, the Romantic Road, Cologne, and the North Frisian Islands.

PLANNING
When to Go
Unless frolicking in winter snow is your thing, the months from April to October offer the best possibilities. That said, a winter visit to Germany has its charms, especially in the Alps and in large cities like Berlin, Cologne, Hamburg and Munich. Things can get slushy, bitterly cold and bleak in mid-winter across the North German Plain, however, Schleswig-Holstein has a wonderful raw, winter mood at that time of year. The Baltic Sea coast is often deserted in the low season. Central Uplands regions, like the Harz Mountains and Black Forest, are good places to hike and relax year-round, especially at higher altitudes. Bring good winter gear and rain jackets, though!

TOURIST OFFICES
Don't hesitate to use the services of tourist offices in Germany, which are efficient, a mine of information and usually have useful free maps.

GERMANY

GERMANY

Local Tourist Offices

The German National Tourist Office (Deutsche Zentrale für Tourismus, DZT) is headquartered at Beethovenstrasse 69, 60325 Frankfurt/Main (☎ 069-97 46 40, fax 75 19 03, ✉ gnto–fra@compuserve.com). For local information, the office to head for in cities and towns in eastern and western Germany alike is the *Verkehrsamt* (tourist office) or *Kurverwaltung* (resort administration).

Tourist Offices Abroad

DZT representatives abroad include:

Australia & New Zealand German National Tourist Office (☎ 02-9267 8148, fax 9267 9035) c/o German-Australian Chamber of Industry and Commerce, P.O. Box A 980, Sydney, NSW 1235
Canada German National Tourist Office (☎ 416-968 1570, fax 968 1986, ✉ germanto@idirect.com) 175 Bloor St East, North Tower, 6th Floor, Toronto, Ont M4W 3R8
South Africa German National Tourist Office (☎ 011-646 1615, fax 484 2750) c/o Lufthansa German Airlines, PO Box 10883, Johannesburg 2000
UK German National Tourist Office (☎ 020-7317 09 08, fax 7495 61 29) PO Box 2695, London W1A 3TN
USA German National Tourist Office (☎ 212-661 72 00, fax 661 71 74, ✉ gntony@aol.com) 122 East 42nd St, 52nd floor, New York, NY 10168-0072
German National Tourist Office (☎ 310-234 02 50, fax 474 16 04, ✉ gntolax@aol.com) PO Box 641009, Los Angeles, CA 90064

There are also offices in Amsterdam, Brussels, Chicago, Copenhagen, Helsinki, Hong Kong, Madrid, Milan, Moscow, Oslo, Paris, São Paulo, Stockholm, Tel Aviv, Tokyo, Vienna and Zürich.

VISAS & DOCUMENTS

Americans, Australians, Britons, Canadians, New Zealanders and Japanese require only a valid passport (no visa) to enter Germany. Citizens of the EU and some other Western European countries can enter on an official identity card. Three months is the usual limit of stay; less for citizens of some developing countries. See Work later in this section for information on work permits.

EMBASSIES & CONSULATES
German Embassies & Consulates

Diplomatic representation abroad includes:

Australia (☎ 02-6270 1911, fax 6270 1951) 119 Empire Circuit, Yarralumla, ACT 2600
Canada (☎ 613-232 11 01, fax 594 93 30) 1 Waverley St, Ottawa, Ont K2P 0T8
France (☎ 01-53 83 45 00, fax 01-43 59 74 18) 13-15 ave Franklin D. Roosevelt, 75008 Paris
Netherlands (☎ 070-342 06 00, fax 365 19 57) Groot Hertoginnelaan 18-20, 2517 Den Haag
Ireland (☎ 01-269 30 11, fax 269 39 46) 31 Trimleston Ave, Booterstown, Dublin
New Zealand (☎ 04-473 6063, fax 473 6069) 90-92 Hobson St, Wellington
UK (☎ 020-7824 1300, fax 7824 1435) 23 Belgrave Square, London SW1X 8PZ
USA (☎ 202-298 4000, fax 298 4249) 4645 Reservoir Rd, NW Washington, DC 20007-1998

Embassies & Consulates in Germany

Some foreign embassies in Berlin are due to move in the next few years. For updated information in English, check the Web site: www.bau.berlin.de. The area code for Berlin is 030.

Australia (☎ 880 08 80, fax 880 08 80 351) Friedrichstrasse 200, 10117 Berlin
Austria (☎ 20 28 70, fax 22 90 569) Friedrichstrasse 60, 10117 Berlin
Canada (☎ 20 31 20, fax 20 31 25 90) Friedrichstrasse 95, 10117 Berlin
France (☎ 20 63 90 00, fax 20 63 90 10) Kochstrasse 6-7, 10969 Berlin
Ireland (☎ 22 07 20, fax 22 07 22 99) Friedrichstrasse 200, 10117 Berlin
Netherlands (☎ 20 95 60, fax 20 95 64 41) Friedrichstrasse 95, 10117 Berlin
New Zealand (☎ 20 62 10, fax 20 62 11 14) Friedrichstrasse 60, 10117 Berlin
South Africa (☎ 82 52 711, fax 82 66 543) Friedrichstrasse 60, 10117 Berlin
Switzerland (☎ 390 40 00, fax 391 10 30) Kirchstrasse 13, 10557 Berlin
UK (☎ 20 18 40, fax 20 18 41 59) Unter den Linden 32-34, 10117 Berlin
USA (☎ 238 51 74, fax 238 62 90 1) Neustädtische Kirchstrasse 4-5, 10117 Berlin

CUSTOMS

Most items you will need for personal use during a visit are duty free. In Germany, the usual allowances apply to duty-free and duty-paid goods if you are coming from a non-EU country.

MONEY

Until the euro is adopted in 2002, Germany will use the German Mark, or Deutschmark (DM), which consists of 100 pfennig (Pf). The easiest places to change cash in Germany are banks or foreign exchange counters at airports and train stations, particularly those of the Reisebank. Main banks in larger cities generally have automatic money-changing machines for after-hours use, but they don't give very good rates. The Reisebank charges a flat DM5 to change cash. Some local Sparkasse banks have good rates and low charges.

Travellers cheques can be cashed at any bank and the most widely accepted are American Express, Thomas Cook and Barclays. A percentage commission (usually a minimum of DM10) is charged by most banks on any travellers cheque, even those issued in Deutschmarks. The Reisebank charges 1% or a minimum of DM10 (DM5 on amounts below DM100) and DM7.50 for American Express. American Express charges no commission on its own cheques, but the exchange rates aren't great if the cheques have to be converted into Deutschmarks.

Eurocheques are widely accepted (up to DM400 per cheque). The Reisebank charges a commission of 1% or DM5 for cash payments on Eurocheques.

Credit cards are especially useful for emergencies, although they are often not accepted by hotels in the budget category and restaurants outside major cities. Cards most widely accepted for payment for goods and services are Eurocard (linked to Access and MasterCard), Visa and American Express.

There are ATMs in virtually all towns and cities and at some main train stations; most accept Visa, MasterCard, American Express, Eurocard, and bankcards linked to the Plus and Cirrus networks.

Typically, withdrawals over the counter against cards at major banks cost a flat DM10 per transaction. Check other fees and the availability of services with your bank before you leave home.

Having money sent to Germany is straightforward, if expensive. For emergencies,

Reisebank (Western Union) and Thomas Cook (MoneyGram) offer ready and fast international cash transfers through agent banks, but commissions are costly.

Currency

Coinage used until 2002 includes one, two, five, 10 and 50 Pf, as well as DM1, DM2 and DM5. There are banknotes of DM5, 10, 20, 50, 100, 200, 500 and 1000. Beware of confusing the old DM5 and current DM20 banknotes, which are the same colour and have similar designs, and watch out for counterfeit banknotes made on colour photocopy machines!

Travellers will notice goods priced in both euros and Deutschmarks until the introduction of the euro.

Exchange Rates

country	unit		Deutschmark
Australia	A$1	=	DM1.25
Canada	C$1	=	DM1.46
euro	€1	=	DM1.96
France	1FF	=	DM0.30
Japan	¥100	=	DM1.99
Netherlands	f1	=	DM0.89
New Zealand	NZ$1	=	DM0.97
UK	UK£1	=	DM3.25
USA	US$1	=	DM2.16

Costs

A tight budget can easily blow out in Germany. You can minimise costs by staying in hostels or private rooms, eating midday restaurant specials or through self-catering, and by limiting museum visits to days when they are free. Students pay the concession price mentioned in this chapter; the price for children is usually the same or marginally lower (often depending on age). Campers can expect to pay around DM15 per night, less if there are two of you. Add another DM20 for self-catering expenses and a beer or two from the supermarket, and your food, drinks and accommodation costs will be around DM35 per day. If travelling on a rail pass, but allowing for public transport costs and occasional expenses like toiletries, DM45 per day should be sufficient.

Tipping & Bargaining

Apart from restaurants and taxis, tipping is not widespread in Germany. In restaurants, rather than leave money on the table, tip when

GERMANY

you pay by stating a rounded-up figure or saying *es stimmt so* (that's the right amount). A tip of 10% is generally more than sufficient. Bargaining is usual only at flea markets.

Taxes & Refunds

Most German goods and services include a value-added tax (VAT, or *Mehrwertsteuer)* of 16% (7% for books and anything else involving copyright). Non-EU residents leaving the EU can have this tax refunded for any goods (not services) they buy.

At Frankfurt airport you should have your luggage labelled at the check-in and then take it to customs in area B6 of terminal 1, level 0.

POST & COMMUNICATIONS
Post

Standard post office hours are 8 am to 6 pm Monday to Friday and to noon on Saturday. Many train station post offices stay open later or offer limited services outside these hours.

Postal Rates Postcard rates are DM1 within Europe, DM2 to North America and Australasia; a 200g letter to anywhere in Europe costs DM1.10, a 50g letter DM3. Aerograms to North America and Australia cost DM2, and 20g letters by air to North America and Australasia cost DM3. Surface-mail parcels of up to 2kg to Europe/elsewhere cost DM12/15; the airmail cost is DM20/46.

Receiving Mail Mail can be sent poste restante *(Postlagernde Briefe)* to the main post office in your city (no fee for collection). German post offices will only hold mail for two weeks, so plan your drops carefully.

Telephone

Most pay phones in Germany accept only phonecards, available for DM12 and DM50 at post offices and some news kiosks, tourist offices and banks. One call unit costs just over DM0.12 from a private telephone and DM0.20 from a public phone (DM0.19 using a DM50 phonecard). Calling from a private phone is most expensive between 9 am and 6 pm, when a unit lasts 90 seconds for a city call, 45 seconds for a regional call (up to 50km) and 30 seconds for a Deutschland call (over 50km) during the peak period. From telephone boxes city calls cost DM0.20 per

minute. Calls to anywhere else in Germany from a phone box cost DM0.40 per minute.

To ring abroad from Germany, dial ☎ 00 followed by the country code, area code and number. A three-minute call to the USA from a public phone (DM12 Telekom phonecard) in Germany at peak time costs DM5.40, but you can reduce most international three-minute calls to less than DM1 by using prepaid telephone cards, such as those offered by ACC.

The country code for Germany is ☎ 49.

Home direct services whereby you reach the operator direct for a reverse charge call from Germany are only possible to some countries. The prefix is ☎ 0130 followed by the home direct number. For the USA and Canada dial 00 10 (AT&T), 00 12 (World Phone) or 00 13 (Sprint), or 00 14 for Canada. To Australia, dial 80 06 61 (Optus) or 80 00 61 (Telstra); to Britain dial 80 00 44 (BT).

For international information call ☎ 118 34 and for inland information call ☎ 118 33; both cost DM0.97 for the first 30 seconds and one unit per 3.8 seconds after that. See also the Telephones Appendix at the back of this book.

Fax

Most main post offices and main train stations have public fax-phones that operate with a phone card. The regular cost of the call, plus a DM2 service charge, will be deducted from your card on connection. Sending a telegram, though still possible, is costly, slow and has few advantages over using a telephone or fax.

Email & Internet Access

Internet cafes, where you can buy online time and send email, exist in many large cities. Locations change frequently, so check at tourist offices. The price in an Internet cafe is anything from around DM6 to DM20 per hour. If you wish to plug in your own laptop, you'll need a telephone plug adapter. Major Internet service providers have dial-in nodes in Germany. Because these usually vary from town to town, it's best to download a list from your provider's home page before setting out.

INTERNET RESOURCES

For up-to-date information about Germany on the Internet, try the German Information

Centre Web site at www.germany-info.org. Most of the information is in English and it also lists hyperlinks to other German information sites. The site offers travel information and homepages for various German cities. The Berlin tourist office maintains a useful Web site (www.berlin.de).

BOOKS

For a more detailed guide to the country, pick up a copy of Lonely Planet's *Germany*. Lonely Planet also publishes *Berlin* and *Munich* city guides.

The German literary tradition is strong and there are many works that provide excellent background to the German experience. Mark Twain's *A Tramp Abroad* is recommended for his comical observations on German life. For a more modern analysis of the German character and the issues facing Germany, dip into the Penguin paperback *Germany and the Germans* by John Ardagh.

NEWSPAPERS & MAGAZINES

Major British newspapers, the *International Herald Tribune* and *USA Today* are available from news kiosks at major train stations or throughout large cities, as are international editions of *Time*, *Newsweek* and the *Economist*. In smaller towns the choice may be limited.

The most widely read newspapers in Germany are *Die Welt*, *Bild*, *Frankfurter Allgemeine*, Munich's *Süddeutsche Zeitung* and the green-leaning *Die Tageszeitung (Taz)*. Germany's most popular magazines are *Der Spiegel*, *Focus* and *Stern*. *Die Zeit* is a weekly publication on culture and the arts.

RADIO & TV

Germany's two national TV channels are the government-funded ARD and ZDF. They are augmented by a plethora of regional and cable channels. You can catch English-language news and sports programs (Sky News, CNN and BBC World depending on the region) on cable or satellite TV in many mid-range hotels and pensions. The BBC World Service (on varying AM wavelengths depending on the region you happen to be in) and the Armed Forces Network (AM 873 around Frankfurt) broadcast in English.

LAUNDRY

You'll find a coin-operated laundry *(Münzwäscherei)* in most cities. Average costs are DM7 per wash, DM1 for optional spinning, plus DM1 per 15 minutes for drying. Some camping grounds and a few hostels also have laundry facilities. If you're staying in a private room, the host may take care of your washing for a reasonable fee. Most major hotels provide laundering services at fairly steep charges.

TOILETS

Finding a public toilet when you need one is usually not a problem in Germany, but it may cost anything from DM0.50 to DM2 for the convenience. All train stations and large public transit stations have toilets, and at some main stations you can even shower for around DM2 to DM10. The level of hygiene is usually very high, although some train stations and otherwise nice pubs can be surprisingly grotty. Public toilets also exist in larger parks, pedestrian malls and inner-city shopping areas, where ultra-modern self-cleaning pay toilets (with wide automatic doorways that allow easy wheelchair access) are increasingly being installed. Restaurant and pub owners rarely mind passers-by using their toilet in cases of emergency if you ask first.

WOMEN TRAVELLERS

Women should not encounter particular difficulties while travelling in Germany. The Lübeck-based organisation Frauen gegen Gewalt (☎ 0451-70 46 40), Marlesgrube 9, can offer advice if you are a victim of harassment or violence. Frauenhaus München (☎ 089-354 83 11, 24-hour service ☎ 089-35 48 30) in Munich also offers advice, and Frauennotruf (☎ 089-76 37 37) at Güllstrasse 3 in Munich can counsel victims of assault. Notice boards in student or alternative cafes and bookshops are good places to get local information on women's groups.

GAY & LESBIAN TRAVELLERS

Germans are generally fairly tolerant of homosexuality, but gays (who call themselves *Schwule*) and lesbians *(Lesben)* still don't enjoy quite the same social acceptance as in certain other northern European countries. Most progressive are the large cities, particularly Berlin and Frankfurt, where the

GERMANY

sight of homosexual couples holding hands is not uncommon, although kissing in public is rather less common. The age of consent is 18 years. Larger cities have many gay and lesbian bars as well as other meeting places for homosexuals. Berlin Pride is held on the last weekend in June. Other Pride festivals are held in mid-June in Bielefeld, Bochum, Hamburg and Wurzburg, in early July in Cologne and in late June in Mannheim.

DISABLED TRAVELLERS
Germany caters reasonably well to the needs of disabled travellers, with access ramps for wheelchairs and/or lifts where necessary in most public buildings, including toilets, train stations, museums, theatres and cinemas. But assistance is usually required when boarding any means of public transportation in Germany. On Deutsche Bahn distance services, you can arrange this when buying your ticket.

DANGERS & ANNOYANCES
Theft and other crimes against travellers are relatively rare in Germany. In the event of problems, the police are helpful and efficient.

Africans, Asians and southern Europeans may encounter racial prejudice, especially in eastern Germany where they have been singled out as convenient scapegoats for economic hardship, though the animosity is directed against immigrants, not tourists.

The emergency number for the police is ☎ 110 and the fire brigade/ambulance ☎ 112.

LEGAL MATTERS
The police in Germany are well trained and usually treat tourists with respect. You are required by law to prove your identity if asked by the police, so always carry your passport, or at least an identity card if you're an EU citizen.

BUSINESS HOURS
By law, shops in Germany may open 6 am to 8 pm on weekdays and until 4 pm on Saturday. In practice, however, only department stores and some supermarkets and fashion shops stay open until 8 pm; most open at 8 or 9 am. Bakeries are open 7 am to 6 pm on weekdays, until 1 pm on Saturday, and some open for the allowable maximum of three hours on Sunday.

Banking hours are generally 8.30 am to 1 pm and 2.30 pm to 4 pm Monday to Friday, but many banks remain open all day, and until 5.30 pm on Thursday. Government offices close for the weekend at 1 or 3 pm on Friday. Museums are generally closed on Monday; opening hours vary greatly, although many art museums are open later one evening per week.

Restaurants usually open 11 am to midnight (the kitchen often closes at 10 pm), with varying *Ruhetage* or closing days. Many restaurants close during the day from 3 to 6 pm. All shops and banks are closed on public holidays.

PUBLIC HOLIDAYS & SPECIAL EVENTS
Germany has many holidays, some of which vary from state to state. Public holidays include New Year's Day; Good Friday to Easter Monday; 1 May (Labour Day); Whit Monday, Ascension Day, Pentecost, Corpus Christi (10 days after Pentecost); 3 October (Day of German Unity); 1 November (All Saints' Day); 18 November (Day of Prayer and Repentance); and usually Christmas Eve to the day after Christmas.

There are many festivals, fairs and cultural events throughout the year. Famous and worthwhile ones include:

January
Carnival season (Shrovetide, known as Fasching in Bavaria) Many carnival events begin in large cities, most notably Cologne, Munich, Düsseldorf and Mainz; the partying peaks just before Ash Wednesday.

February
International Toy Fair Held in Nuremberg
International Film Festival Held in Berlin

March
Frankfurt Music Fair and **Frankfurt Jazz Fair**
Thuringian Bach Festival
Spring Fairs Held throughout Germany

April
Stuttgart Jazz Festival
Munich Ballet Days
Mannheim May Fair
Walpurgisnacht Festivals Held the night before May Day in the Harz Mountains

May
International Mime Festival Held in Stuttgart
Red Wine Festival Held in Rüdesheim
Dresden International Dixieland Jazz Festival

Dresden Music Festival Held in last week of May into first week of June

June
Moselle Wine Week Held in Cochem
Händel Festival Held in Halle
Sailing regatta Held in Kiel
Munich Film Festival
International Theatre Festival Held in Freiburg

July
Folk festivals Held throughout Germany
Berlin Love Parade
Munich Opera Festival
Richard Wagner Festival Held in Bayreuth
German-American Folk Festival Held in Berlin
Kulmbach Beer Festival
International Music Seminar Held in Weimar

August
Heidelberg Castle Festival
Wine festivals Held throughout the Rhineland area

September-October
Oktoberfest Held in Munich
Berlin Festival of Music & Drama

October
Frankfurt Book Fair
Bremen Freimarkt
Gewandhaus Festival Held in Leipzig
Berlin Jazzfest

November
St Martin's Festival Held throughout Rhineland and Bavaria

December
Christmas fairs Held throughout Germany, most famously in Munich, Nuremberg, Berlin, Essen and Heidelberg

ACTIVITIES
Germany, with its rugged Alps, picturesque uplands and fairy-tale forests, is ideal for hiking and mountaineering. Well-marked trails crisscross the country, especially popular areas like the Black Forest, the Harz Mountains, the so-called Saxon Switzerland area and the Thuringian Forest. The Bavarian Alps offer the most inspiring scenery, however, and are the centre of mountaineering in Germany. Good sources of information on hiking and mountaineering are: Verband Deutscher Gebirgs-und Wandervereine (Federation of German Hiking Clubs; ☎ 0561-938 73 12, fax 938 73 10, @ dt.wanderverband@t-online.de),

Wilhelmshöher Allee 157-9, 34121 Kassel; and Deutscher Alpenverein (German Alpine Club; ☎ 089-14 00 30, fax 140 03 98, @ info@alpenverein.de) at Von-Kahr-Strasse 2-4, 80997 Munich.

The Bavarian Alps are the most extensive area for winter sports. Cross-country skiing is also good in the Black Forest and Harz Mountains. Ski equipment starts at around DM20 per day, and daily ski-lift passes start at around DM30. Local tourist offices are the best sources of information.

Cyclists will often find marked cycling routes, and eastern Germany has much to offer cyclists in the way of lightly travelled back roads, especially in the flat and less-populated north. Offshore islands like Amrum and Rügen are also good for cycling. For more details and tips, see Cycling in the following Getting Around section.

Railway enthusiasts will be excited by the wide range of steam train excursions on old trains organised by the Deutsche Bahn. Ask for the free booklet *Nostalgiereisen* at any large train station in Germany. Historic steam trains ply a 132km integrated narrow-gauge network year-round in the eastern Harz. For more information, see Wernigerode in the Saxony-Anhalt section.

WORK
Germany currently offers limited employment prospects for anyone except computer programmers and software specialists, who can apply for so-called Green Cards, which will allow you to work and live in Germany for a restricted period. EU citizens may work in Germany, and special conditions apply for citizens of Canada, Israel, Japan, Switzerland and the USA. Germany also has a working holiday agreement with Australia, which allows tourists to work here for a limited period during their stay here.

Employment offices (*Arbeitsamt*) have an excellent data bank (SIS) of vacancies, or try major newspapers. Private language-teaching is another option. Street artists and hawkers are widespread in the cities, though you should ask the municipal authority about permits. The Arbeitsamt can also help with finding au pair work, and there are numerous approved au pair agencies throughout Germany.

GERMANY

An organisation that arranges unpaid cooperative work is the Christlicher Friedensdienst (☎ 069-45 90 72, fax 46 12 13), Rendeler Strasse 9-11, 60385 Frankfurt/Main.

ACCOMMODATION

Accommodation in Germany is well organised, though some cities are short on budget hotels; private rooms are one option in such situations. Accommodation usually includes breakfast. Look for signs saying *Zimmer frei* (rooms available) or *Fremdenzimmer* (tourist rooms) in house or shop windows of many towns. If you're after a hotel or especially a private room, head straight for the tourist office and use the room-finding service *(Zimmervermittlung)*, which is free or typically DM5. Staff will usually go out of their way to find something in your price range, although telephone bookings are not always available. TIBS (☎ 0761-88 58 10, fax 885 81 19, ✉ email@TIBS.de) handles accommodation bookings throughout Germany.

In official resorts and spas, displayed prices usually don't include *Kurtaxe* (resort tax) levies. Tourist offices can also help with farm stays.

Camping

Germany has over 2000 organised camping grounds. Most are open from April to September, but several hundred stay open throughout the year. Facilities range from the primitive to the over-equipped and overserviced. In eastern Germany camping grounds often rent out small bungalows. For camping on private property, permission from the landowner is required. The best overall source of information is the Deutscher Camping Club (☎ 089-380 14 20, fax 33 47 37), Mandlstrasse 28, 80802 Munich. Local tourist information sources can help too.

Hostels

The Deutsches Jugendherbergswerk or DJH (☎ 05231-740 10, fax 05231-74 01 49, or write to: DJH Service GmbH, 32754 Detmold), coordinates all affiliated Hostelling International (HI) hostels in Germany. Almost all hostels in Germany are open all year. Guests must be members of a HI-affiliated organisation, or join the DJH when checking in. The annual fee is DM20/35 juniors/seniors.

A dorm bed in a DJH hostel costs from around DM23 to DM45 for seniors; most charge less than DM32. Camping at a hostel (where permitted) is generally half-price. If you don't have a hostel-approved sleeping sheet, it usually costs from DM5 to DM7 to hire one (some hostels insist you hire one anyway). Breakfast is always included in the overnight price. Lunch or an evening meal will cost between DM6 and DM9.

Theoretically, visitors aged under 27 get preference, but in practice prior booking or arrival determines who gets rooms, not age. In Bavaria, though, the strict maximum age for anyone except group leaders or parents accompanying a child is 26. Check-in hours vary, but you usually must be out by 9 am. You don't need to do chores at the hostels and there are few rules. Most hostels have a curfew, which may be as early as 10 pm in small towns. The curfew is rarely before 11 pm in large cities; several have no curfew.

The DJH's *Jugendgästehäuser* (youth guesthouses) offer some better facilities, freer hours and two-bed to four-bed dormitory rooms from DM25 to DM45 per person, including sleeping sheet.

Pensions & Guesthouses

Pensions offer the basics of hotel comfort without asking hotel prices. Many of these are private homes with several rooms to rent, often a bit out of the centre of town. Some proprietors are a little sensitive about who they take in and others are nervous about telephone bookings – you may have to give a time of arrival and stick to it (many visitors have lost rooms by turning up late).

Hotels

Cheap hotel rooms are a bit hard to find during summer, but there is usually not much seasonal price variation. The cheapest hotels only have rooms with shared toilets (and showers) in the corridor. Average budget prices are DM60 for a single and DM90 for a double (without bathroom).

Expensive hotels provide few advantages for their upmarket prices. Some offer weekend packages, while spa towns are nice places to splurge on luxury hotels and healthy pursuits.

Rentals

Renting an apartment for a week or more is a popular form of holiday accommodation in Germany. Look in newspaper classifieds for *Ferienwohnungen* or *Ferien-Apartments*, or particularly if you want shared accommodation somewhere in an urban centre contact the local *Mitwohnzentrale* (the accommodation-finding service). Rates vary widely, but are lower than hotels and decrease dramatically with the length of stay.

FOOD

Germans are hearty eaters and this is truly a meat-and-potatoes kind of country, although vegetarians will usually find suitable restaurants or fast-food places. Restaurants always display their menus outside with prices, but watch for daily or lunch specials chalked onto blackboards. Beware of early closing hours, and of the *Ruhetag* (rest day) at some establishments. Lunch is the main meal of the day; getting a main meal in the evening is never a problem, but you may find that the dish or menu of the day only applies to lunch.

Students can eat cheaply – and well or badly, depending on the town – at university *Mensas* if they can show international student ID. This is not always checked.

A German breakfast in a pension or hotel is solid and filling. Germans at home might eat their heaviest meal at noon and then have lighter evening fare (*Abendbrot* or *Abendessen*, consisting of cheeses and bread).

Cafes & Bars

Much of the German daily and social life revolves around these institutions, which often serve meals and alcohol as well as coffee. Some attract a young or student crowd, stay open until late and are great places to meet people.

Snacks

If you're on a low budget, you can get a feed at stand-up food stalls (*Schnellimbiss* or *Imbiss*). The food is usually quite reasonable and filling, ranging from döner kebabs to traditional German sausages with beer.

Main Dishes

Sausage (*Wurst*), in its hundreds of forms, is by far the most popular main dish. Regional favourites include *Bratwurst* (spiced sausage), *Weisswurst* (veal sausage) and *Blutwurst* (blood sausage). Other popular choices include *Rippenspeer* (spare ribs), *Rotwurst* (black pudding), *gegrilltes Fleisch* or *Rostbrätl* (grilled meat) and many forms of *Schnitzel* (breaded pork or veal cutlet).

Potatoes feature prominently in German meals, either fried (*Bratkartoffeln*), mashed (*Kartoffelpüree*), grated and then fried (the Swiss *Rösti*), or as French fries (*Pommes Frites*); a Thuringian speciality is *Klösse*, a ball of mashed and raw potato which is then cooked to produce something like a dumpling. A similar Bavarian version is the *Knödel*. In Baden-Württemberg, potatoes are often replaced by *Spätzle* a local noodle variety.

Mid-priced Italian, Turkish, Greek and Chinese restaurants can be found in every town.

Desserts

Germans are keen on rich desserts. A popular choice is the *Schwarzwälder Kirschtorte* (Black Forest cherry cake), which is one worthwhile tourist trap. Desserts and pastries are also often enjoyed during another German tradition, the 4 pm coffee break.

Self-Catering

It's very easy and relatively cheap to put together picnic meals in any town. Simply head for the local market or supermarket and stock up on breads, sandwich meats, cheeses, wine and beer. Supermarkets such as Penny Markt, REWE and Plus are cheap and have quite a good range.

DRINKS

Buying beverages in restaurants is expensive. Make a point of buying your drinks in supermarkets if your budget is tight.

Nonalcoholic Drinks

The most popular choices are mineral water and soft drinks, coffee and fruit or black tea. Nonalcoholic beers are popular; Löwenbräu makes a nonalcoholic beer that is frequently served on tap in Bavaria.

Alcoholic Drinks

Beer is the national beverage and it's one cultural phenomenon that must be adequately explored. The beer is excellent and relatively

GERMANY

cheap. Each region and brewery has its own distinctive taste and body.

Beer-drinking in Germany has its own vocabulary. *Vollbier* is 4% alcohol by volume, *Export* is 5% and *Bockbier* is 6%. *Helles Bier* is light, while *dunkles Bier* is dark. Export is similar to, but much better than, typical international brews, while the *Pils* is more bitter. *Alt* is darker and more full-bodied. A speciality is *Weizenbier*, which is made with wheat instead of barley malt and served in a tall, half-litre glass with a slice of lemon.

Eastern Germany's best beers hail from Saxony, especially *Radeberger Pils* from near Dresden and *Wernesgrüner* from the Erzgebirge on the Czech border. *Berliner Weisse* is a foaming, low-alcohol wheat beer mixed with woodruff or raspberry syrup. The breweries of Cologne produce *Kölsch*; in Bamberg *Schlenkerla Rauchbier* is smoked to a dark-red colour.

German wines are exported around the world, and for good reason. They are inexpensive and typically white, light and intensely fruity. Germans usually ask for a *Schoppen* of whatever – a solid wine glass holding 200ml or 250ml. A *Weinschorle* or *Spritzer* is white wine mixed with mineral water. Wines don't have to be drunk with meals. The Rhine and Moselle Valleys are the classic wine-growing regions. The *Ebbelwei* of Hesse is a strong apple wine with an earthy flavour.

ENTERTAINMENT

The standard of theatre performances, concerts and operas is among the highest in Europe. Berlin is unrivalled when it comes to concerts and theatre and Dresden is famed for its opera.

Tickets can usually be purchased at short notice from tourist offices and directly from box offices.

Pubs & Beer Halls

The variety of pubs in Germany is enormous, ranging from vaulted-cellar bars through to theme pubs, Irish pubs, historic student pubs and clubs offering music or performances. Beer gardens are especially common in the south. It is worth experiencing the raucous atmosphere of a traditional Bavarian beer hall at least once during a visit to Germany.

Nightclubs

Germany's large cities throb with club and disco sounds. Berlin is a world techno capital, but you'll find a variety of lively clubs in most major cities. Posters around clubs, universities and cafes or city listing guides are good information sources.

Cinemas

Germans are avid movie-goers, but foreign films are usually dubbed into German. Original soundtrack versions (identifiable by the letter-codes OF, OV or OmU with subtitles) are mostly limited to university towns and bigger cities like Berlin, Munich, Hamburg and Frankfurt.

SPECTATOR SPORTS

Soccer is by far Germany's most popular sport and the country has been awarded the right to host the 2006 World Cup finals. Tickets to first-division games, usually played from Friday to Sunday, can be purchased at grounds and outlets. National knockout and European matches are mostly played during the week. The popularity of tennis has been boosted by the past achievements of Boris Becker and Steffi Graf, and motor racing is a national passion, due in no small part to Michael Schumacher. Exciting winter sports events are held annually in Oberstdorf and Garmisch-Partenkirchen.

SHOPPING

Products made in Germany are rarely cheap, but the higher prices are generally compensated for by high quality. Worthwhile industrial goods include optical lenses, fine crystal glassware (particularly from the Bavarian Forest), fine porcelain (particularly from Meissen) and therapeutic footwear, such as the sandals and shoes made by Birkenstock. Art reproductions, books and posters are sold in some museums and speciality shops. Germany's fine regional wines give you a real taste of the country to take back home. More predictable souvenirs include colourful heraldic emblems, cuckoo clocks from the Black Forest, Bavarian wooden carvings and traditional Bavarian clothing.

Giant robot, Frühlings-Dippemesse, Germany

Hessian parliament 'mascot', Frankfurt/Main

Brandenburg Gate, Berlin, Germany

Dawn hits the city, Frankfurt/Main, Germany

Fishing boats and buildings in Lautro Harbour, Crete

The Acropolis, Athens, Greece

Glistening blue ceramics, Greece

Ceremonial guard, Athens

Getting There & Away

AIR

The main arrival and departure points in Germany are Frankfurt, Munich, Düsseldorf and Berlin. Frankfurt is Europe's busiest airport after London's Heathrow. Flights are generally priced competitively among all major airlines, but Lufthansa (☎ 01803-80 38 03 within Germany) offers the most flexibility.

Flights to Frankfurt are usually cheaper than to other German cities. Regular flights from Western Europe to Germany tend to be more expensive than the train or bus. Airline deregulation within Europe has encouraged cheap, no-frills deals, especially between London and Frankfurt, Berlin or Düsseldorf. Ryanair and Buzz are cheap options. Look for ads in London or German newspapers.

From North America, Lufthansa, United Airlines, Air Canada, Delta Airlines, Singapore Airlines and Air Algerie have the most frequent flights. You can often get the best fare by flying another European carrier and changing planes for Germany at their home-country hub. The German charter company LTU makes regular scheduled international flights from North America, but these fill up quickly and usually force you to fly in and out of Düsseldorf.

The Asian carriers offer the cheapest – but often the most indirect – flights from Australia and New Zealand. Qantas and Lufthansa both fly via Asian hubs such as Singapore and Bangkok and continue on to Germany.

Lufthansa has many flights to the Eastern European nations, but the region's national carriers are cheaper.

LAND

Bus

If you're already in Europe, it's generally cheaper to get to/from Germany by bus than it is by train or plane but you trade price for speed. Return fares are noticeably cheaper than two one-way fares.

Eurolines is a consortium of national bus companies operating routes throughout the continent. Some sample one-way fares and travel times for routes include:

London-Frankfurt	DM127	14¼ hours
Amsterdam-Hamburg	DM75	7½ hours
Amsterdam-Frankfurt	DM75	5½ hours
Paris-Hamburg	DM108	14 hours
Paris-Cologne	DM70	6½ hours
Prague-Frankfurt	DM70	8½ hours
Barcelona-Frankfurt	DM172	20½ hours

Eurolines has a youth fare for those aged under 26 that saves around 10%. Tickets can be bought in Germany at most train stations. For information (but not bookings), contact Deutsche-Touring GmbH (☎ 069-7 90 30, fax 790 32 19) at Am Römerhof 17, 60486 Frankfurt/Main or check its Web site at: www.deutsche-touring.com.

Train

If you're already in Europe, a good way to get to Germany is by train, and it's a lot more comfortable (albeit more expensive) than the bus.

Generally the longer international routes are served by at least one day train and often a night train as well. Many night trains only carry sleeping cars, but a bunk is more comfortable than sitting up in a compartment and only adds DM38/26 to the cost of a 2nd class ticket in four-/six-berth compartments.

Major German cities with international train connections include: Berlin to/from Warsaw (DM57, six hours), Prague (DM96, five hours) and Budapest (DM184, 13 hours); Hamburg to/from Amsterdam (DM132, 4½ hours) and Paris (DM130, nine hours); Frankfurt to/from Paris (DM144, 10 hours), Vienna (DM166, 10 hours), Budapest (DM230, 13 hours), Zürich (DM161, four hours) and Milan (DM216, nine hours); and Munich to/from Paris (DM202, nine hours), Zürich (DM117, four hours), Milan (DM110, 7½ hours), Vienna (DM113, five hours), Zagreb (DM141, nine hours), Budapest (DM156, seven hours) and Prague (DM97, six hours). All prices are one way.

Car & Motorcycle

Germany is served by an excellent highway system. If you're coming from the UK, the quickest option is the Channel Tunnel. Ferries take longer, but are cheaper. Choices include hovercraft from Dover, Folkestone or Ramsgate to Calais in France. You can be in Germany three hours after the ferry docks.

GERMANY

Within Europe, autobahns and highways become jammed on weekends in summer and before and after holidays. This is especially true where border checks are still carried out, such as going to/from the Czech Republic and Poland.

You must have third-party insurance to enter Germany with a car or motorcycle.

Hitching & Ride Services

Hitchers may encounter delays getting to Germany via the main highways as hitching is becoming less popular both for riders and drivers. Aside from hitching, the cheapest way to get to Germany from elsewhere in Europe is as a paying passenger in a private car. Leaving Germany, or travelling within the country, such rides are arranged by *Mitfahrzentrale* agencies in many German cities. You pay a reservation fee to the agency and a share of petrol and costs to the driver. Local tourist offices can direct you to several such agencies, or call the city area code and ☎ 194 40 in large cities in Germany. Agencies for major cities are listed in the Getting There & Away sections for each city.

BOAT

If you're heading to or from the UK or Scandinavia, the port options are Hamburg, Lübeck, Rostock and Kiel. The Hamburg-Harwich service runs at least three times a week. The Puttgarden-Rødbyhavn ferry is popular with those heading to Copenhagen (see the Hamburg Getting There & Away section for details). In eastern Germany, there are five ferries in each direction daily all year between Trelleborg (Sweden) and Sassnitz near Stralsund (see the Rügen Island section) and another service to Klaipėda in Lithuania three times weekly

There are daily services between Kiel and Gothenburg (Sweden) and Oslo. A ferry between Travemünde (near Lübeck) and Trelleborg (Sweden) runs one to four times daily. Ferries also run several times a week between the Danish island of Bornholm and Sassnitz. Car-ferry service is also good from Gedser (Denmark) to Rostock. Silja runs fast ferries several times a week on the Rostock-Tallin-Helsinki route (up to 26 hours) from June to September. Finnlines has daily sailings from Lübeck to Helsinki. See the Kiel, Rostock,

Stralsund and Rügen Island Getting There & Away sections for more details.

DEPARTURE TAX

All security, airport and departure taxes are included in ticket prices. Be aware that some companies in Germany will advertise a flight *excluding* these charges, so check the fine print carefully. There is no departure tax if you depart by sea or land.

Getting Around

AIR

There are lots of flights within the country, but costs can be prohibitive compared to the train. Lufthansa has the most frequent air services within Germany. Deregulation has brought some competition. Lufthansa and Deutsche BA (☎ 01803-33 34 44) regularly offer special fares, mostly from around DM150 to DM200 for the longest routes.

Lufthansa also offers youth (under 27) fares for flights within Germany and Europe that generally save 25% on the high regular fares. Again it is worth checking these options with a travel agent.

BUS

The bus network in Germany functions primarily in support of the train network, going places where trains don't. Bus stations or stops are usually near the train station in any town. Schedule and route information is usually posted. Consider buses when you want to cut across two train lines and avoid long train rides to and from a transfer point. A good example of this is in the Alps, where the best way to follow the peaks is by bus.

In the Getting There & Away section for each city and town listing we note any bus services that are useful for reaching other places described in this chapter. Deutsche Bahn (DB) agents have information on certain key regional services, otherwise check with tourist offices.

Eurolines operates services within Germany as Deutsche-Touring GmbH, a subsidiary of the German Federal Railways (Deutsche Bahn). Eurolines (previously known as Europabus, a name you will still run into) services include the Romantic and Castle Roads buses in southern Germany, as well as organised bus tours of Germany lasting a week or more. See the Frankfurt and Romantic Road sections for details, or contact Deutsche-Touring GmbH (☎ 069-790 30, fax 790 32 19) at Am Römerhof 17, 60486 Frankfurt/Main (doesn't handle reservations).

TRAIN

Operated almost entirely by the Deutsche Bahn (DB), the German train system is arguably the best in Europe. Information is on the Internet at www.bahn.de.

The trains run on an interval system that means from the busiest to the quietest routes, you can count on service every one or two hours. The schedules are integrated throughout the country so that connections between trains are time-saving and tight, often only five minutes. Of course the obverse of this is that when a train is late – a not uncommon occurrence, especially during busy travel periods – connections are missed and you can find yourself stuck waiting for the next train. The moral here is that if you have to be somewhere at a specified time, say for your flight home, put some slack in your itinerary so you won't miss a connection and be really stranded.

Types of Trains

There is rarely ever a need to buy a 1st-class ticket on German trains; 2nd class is usually quite comfortable. German trains fall into specific classifications:

ICE

The InterCityExpress trains run at speeds up to 280km/h when they use special high-speed tracks. The trains are very comfortable and feature restaurant cars. The main routes link Hamburg to Munich, Cologne to Berlin, Frankfurt to Berlin, Frankfurt to Munich and Frankfurt to Basel. The trains carry a surcharge that varies by the route but usually adds at least 10% to the ticket.

IC/EC

Called InterCity, these are the premier conventional trains of DB. When trains are crowded, the open-seating coaches are much more comfortable than the older carriages with compartments. When these trains cross national borders they carry the EC designation for EuroCity. Travel on these trains requires a DM7 *Zuschlag* (extra fare) on a regular ticket. Buy this before boarding.

IR

Called InterRegio, these are fast trains that cover secondary routes and usually run at intervals of two hours. For journeys of over two hours' duration you can usually get to your destination faster by transferring from an IR train to an IC or ICE. The IR Zuschlag is DM3.

RE

RegionalExpress trains are local trains that make limited stops. They are fairly fast and run at one or two-hourly intervals.

SE

StadtExpress trains are found in metropolitan areas. They make few stops in urban areas and all stops in rural areas.

RB

RegionalBahn are the slowest DB trains, not missing a single cow town or junction of roads so sit back and enjoy the view.

S-Bahn

These DB-operated trains run frequent services in larger urban areas and sometimes run in tunnels under the city centre. Not to be confused with U-Bahns, which are run by local authorities who *don't* honour rail passes.

EN, ICN, D

These are night trains, although an occasional D may be an extra daytime train.

Tickets & Reservations

You often have the option of purchasing tickets with credit cards at ticket machines. Many have English-language options, but when in doubt consult the ticket window. For longer-distance trains it is always better to buy your ticket before boarding, since buying a ticket or Zuschlag from a conductor carries a penalty (DM5 to DM10). If you're really stuck you can *technically* use a credit card to buy a ticket on the train, but you're likely to get a better response, say, if you ask the conductor to launder your dirty clothes. Ticket agents, on the other hand, cheerfully accept credit cards, as do machines at some stations.

On some trains there are no conductors at all and roving teams of inspectors enforce compliance. If you are caught without a ticket the fine is DM60 and they accept *no* excuses.

During peak travel periods, a seat reservation (DM5) on a long-distance train can mean the difference between squatting near the toilet or relaxing in your own seat. Express reservations can be made at the last minute. If a crowded train is sold out or you don't have a reservation, try the end carriages.

Most waiting passengers mill about the middle of platforms like flocks of sheep.

Bunks on night trains cost DM38/26 extra in four-/six-berth compartments.

Fares

Standard DB ticket prices are distance-based at a rate of DM0.27 per kilometre. You will usually be sold a ticket for the shortest distance to your destination, so if for example you wish to travel from Munich to Frankfurt via Nuremberg (a slightly more expensive route than via Stuttgart), say so when you buy your ticket. At some stations tickets for anywhere in Germany can be bought from machines using a credit card.

Sample fares for one-way, 2nd-class ICE travel include: Hamburg to Munich DM268; Frankfurt to Berlin DM200; and Frankfurt to Munich DM147. Tickets are good for four days from the day you tell the agent your journey will begin and you can make unlimited stopovers along your route during that time.

There are hosts of special fares that allow you to beat the high cost of regular tickets. The following are the most popular special train fares offered by DB (all fares are for 2nd class):

Guten Abend
Literally 'Good Evening' tickets. They are valid for unlimited travel between 7 pm and 2 am the next day and cost DM59 (DM69 for ICE). They can offer significant reductions in price. For instance, you can take the 7.15 pm ICE from Hamburg to Munich, arriving at 1.26 am, for DM69 instead of the usual DM256.

Schönes Wochenende
These cheerful 'Good Weekend' tickets allow unlimited use of trains on a Saturday or Sunday for up to five people or one or both parents and all their children for DM35. The catch is that they are only good on RE, SE, RB and S-Bahns, so a money-saving trip from Cologne to Dresden can be a 12-hour ordeal of frequent train-changing or an adventure, depending on your outlook. They are best suited to weekend day trips from urban areas.

BahnCard
A DM260 card that entitles the owner to half-price travel on all trains (except S-Bahn). It's only worthwhile for extended visits to Germany.

In addition, ask about various 'Sparpreis' schemes that offer big savings on return tickets if one leg of the journey is on a weekend or a weekend falls between the forward and return trip. Most ticket agents are quite willing to help you find the cheapest options for your intended trip. For schedule and fare information (available in English), you can call ☎ 01805-99 66 33 from anywhere in Germany.

Rail Passes

Travel agents outside Germany sell German Rail Passes valid for unlimited travel on all DB trains for a given number of days within a 30-day period. The following prices (in US$), good for 2nd-class travel, are for adults/two adults travelling together/those under 26: five days $196/294/156; 10 days $306/459/210; and 15 days $416/624/366. The passes include some buses (like those on the Romantic Road route) and some ships (such as those plying the Rhine and Moselle Rivers). They do not include seat reservations. Eurail and Inter-Rail passes are also valid in Germany.

Stations

Almost all train stations have lockers (from DM2 depending on size). The few exceptions are noted in the Getting There & Away section for each city or town. Larger stations have DB Service Points counters that offer schedule information and are open long hours. Many have local maps that will help you find the tourist office.

Disabled passengers who need assistance must notify DB in advance of their needs. Train station platforms and the trains themselves are often not easily accessible.

CAR & MOTORCYCLE

German roads are excellent, and motorised transport can be a great way to tour the country. Prices for fuel vary from DM1.81 to DM1.92 per litre for unleaded super. Avoid buying fuel at more expensive autobahn filling stations.

The autobahn system of motorways runs throughout Germany. Road signs (and most motoring maps) indicate national autobahn routes in blue with an 'A' number, while international routes have green signs with an 'E' number. Though efficient, the autobahns are often busy, and literally present life in the fast lane. Tourists often have trouble coping with the very high speeds and the dangers involved in overtaking – don't underestimate the time it takes for a car in the rear-view mirror to close in at 180km/h. Secondary roads are easier on the nerves and much more scenic, but can be slow going.

Cars are impractical in urban areas. Vending machines on many streets sell parking vouchers which must be displayed clearly behind the windscreen. Leaving your car in a central *Parkhaus* (car park) costs roughly DM20 per day or DM2.50 per hour.

To find passengers willing to pay their share of fuel costs, drivers should contact the local Mitfahrzentrale (see Hitching & Ride Services in the Getting There & Away section).

Germany's main motoring organisation is the Allgemeiner Deutscher Automobil Club (ADAC, ☎ 089-767 60 or fax 089-76 76 28 01), whose main office is at Am Westpark 8, 81373 Munich; it also has offices in all major cities. Call the ADAC road patrol (☎ 0180-222 22 22) if your car breaks down.

Road Rules

Road rules are easy to understand and standard international signs are in use. The usual speed limits are 50km/h in built-up areas (in effect as soon as you see the yellow name board of the town) and 100km/h on the open road. The speed on autobahns is unlimited, though there's an advisory speed of 130km/h; exceptions are clearly signposted. The blood-alcohol limit for drivers is 0.05%. Obey the road rules carefully: the German police are very efficient and issue heavy on-the-spot fines; cameras are in widespread use and notices are sent to the car's registration address wherever that may be. If it's a rental company, they will bill your credit card.

Rental

Germany's four main rental companies are Avis (☎ 0180-555 77), Europcar (☎ 0180-580 00), Hertz (☎ 0180-533 35 35) and Sixt (☎ 0180-526 02 50), but there are numerous smaller local rental companies. Deals are usually better if you book at least a couple of days in advance. Weekend deals from noon Friday till 9 am Monday can be as low as DM125. To hire you usually must be at least 21 years of age.

Deals that include rental cars with train passes or airline tickets can be excellent value. Check with your travel agent.

Purchase

Due to the costs, paperwork and insurance hassles involved, buying a car in Germany tends to be an unwise option.

BICYCLE

Radwandern (bicycle touring) is very popular in Germany. In urban areas the pavement is often divided into separate sections for pedestrians and cyclists – be warned that these divisions are taken very seriously. Even outside towns and cities there are often separate cycling routes. Favoured routes include the Rhine, Moselle and Danube Rivers and the Lake Constance area. Of course, cycling is strictly *verboten* (forbidden) on the autobahns. Hostel-to-hostel biking is an easy way to go, and route guides are often sold at local DJH hostels. There are well-equipped cycling shops in almost every town, and a fairly active market for used touring bikes.

Simple three-gear bicycles can be hired from around DM15/60 per day/week, and more robust mountain bikes from DM18/90. Rental shops in many cities are noted in the Getting Around sections of the city and town listings. The DB publishes *Bahn&Bike* (DM9.80), an excellent annual handbook covering bike rental and repair shops, routes, maps and other resources.

A separate ticket must be purchased whenever you carry your bike on a train. These cost DM6/12 for distances under/over 100km. Most trains (excluding ICEs) have a 2nd-class carriage at one end with a bicycle compartment.

The central office of Germany's main cycling organisation is the Allgemeiner Deutscher Fahrrad Club (ADFC; ☎ 0421-34 62 90, fax 346 92 50, ✉ kontakt@adfc.de), Grünenstrasse 8-9, 28199 Bremen. Its Web site is at www.adfc.de (see also Activities in the earlier Facts for the Visitor section).

HITCHING

Lonely Planet does not recommend hitching *(Trampen)*. Though hitching is possible, Mitfahrzentrale ride-share services (see Hitching & Ride Services in the Getting There & Away section earlier), are a cheap, more reliable and safer option. That said, remember that hitching is absolutely not allowed on autobahns.

GERMANY

GERMANY

BOAT

Boats are most likely to be used for basic transport when travelling to or between the Frisian Islands, though tours along the Rhine and Moselle Rivers are also popular. In summer there are frequent services on Lake Constance but, except for the Constance to Meersburg and the Friedrichshafen to Romanshorn car ferries, these boats are really more tourist craft than a transport option. From April to October, excursion boats ply lakes and rivers throughout Germany and on a nice day can be a lovely way to see the country.

LOCAL TRANSPORT

Local transport is excellent within big cities and small towns, and is generally based on buses, trams, S-Bahn and/or U-Bahn (underground train system). The systems integrate all forms of transit; fares are determined by the zones or the time travelled, or sometimes both. Multiticket strips or day passes are generally available and offer better value than single-ride tickets. See the individual city and town Getting Around entries in this chapter for details.

Make certain you have a ticket before boarding; in some cases you will have to validate it in a little time-stamp machine on the platform or once aboard. Ticket inspections are frequent (especially at night and on holidays) and the fine is a non-negotiable DM60 payable on the spot. If you can't pay, the inspector will take your passport until you can.

Bus & Tram

Cities and towns operate their own services that can include buses, trolleybuses and/or trams. Bus drivers usually sell single-trip tickets as a service to forgetful passengers, but these are more expensive than tickets bought in advance. Large cities often have a limited night-bus system operating from about 1 to 4 am, when everything else has shut down.

Underground

Larger cities such as Berlin, Hamburg, Munich and Frankfurt have underground metro systems known as the U-Bahn. They have the same ticketing and validation requirements as the local buses and/or trams.

Train

Most large cities have a system of S-Bahn suburban trains. In places like Berlin, Hamburg, Munich and Frankfurt, they also serve the city centre. Tickets on these lines are integrated with other forms of local transport, however train pass-holders can ride S-Bahns (and only S-Bahns!) for free since they are operated by DB.

Taxi

Taxis (always bland beige sedans) are expensive and only really needed late, late at night. In fact, given traffic, they can actually take longer than public transport. For fast service, look up 'TaxiRuf' in the local telephone directory to find the nearest taxi rank. Taxis are metered and average DM4 flag fall and DM2.40 per kilometre; higher night tariffs apply.

ORGANISED TOURS

Local tourist offices offer various tour options, from short city sightseeing trips to multiday adventure, spa-bath and wine-tasting packages. Apart from city tours, other good sources for organised tours in and around Germany are Deutsche-Touring and DB.

There are scores of international and national tour operators with specific options. Your travel agent should have some details. Many airlines also offer tour packages with their tickets.

Berlin

☎ 030 • pop 3.4 million

Berlin, the largest city in Germany, has more to offer visitors than almost any city in Europe. Divided by a 162km wall until mid-1990, east and west Berlin remain an unfinished patchwork quilt. Some parts have been woven together, other parts remain isolated and separate. Eastern neighbourhoods near the wall, such as the Scheunenviertel, are the centres of artistic and cultural action in the city while outlying areas, with their grim communist-era high-rise housing, remain as bleak as ever.

The centre of 19th-century Prussian military and industrial might, this great city finally reached maturity in the 1920s, only to be bombed into rubble in WWII. After hibernating for the decades after the war, Berlin is now flexing its muscle as it adjusts to again playing the role of the heart of Germany. With hundreds of construction cranes dotting the city, the changes are breathtaking and it is a very exciting time to visit Berlin, once again the capital of the nation and one of Europe's most dynamic cities.

History

The first recorded settlement in present-day Berlin was a place named Cölln (1237) around the Spree River south of Museumsinsel (Museum Island), although Spandau, the junction of the Spree and the ponded Havel Rivers, is considered to be older. Medieval Berlin developed on the bank of the Spree around Nikolaikirche and spread northeast towards today's Alexanderplatz. In 1432, Berlin and Cölln, which were linked by the Mühlendamm, merged.

In the 1440s, Elector Friedrich II of Brandenburg established the rule of the Hohenzollern dynasty, which was to last until Kaiser Wilhelm II's escape from Potsdam in 1918. Berlin's importance increased in 1470 when the elector moved his residence here from Brandenburg and built a palace near the present Marx-Engels-Platz.

During the Thirty Years' War, Berlin's population was decimated, but in the mid-17th century the city was reborn stronger than before under the so-called Great Elector Friedrich Wilhelm. His vision was the basis of Prussian power and he sponsored Huguenot refugees seeking princely tolerance.

The Great Elector's son, Friedrich I, the first Prussian king, made the fast-growing Berlin his capital, and his daughter-in-law Sophie Charlotte encouraged the development of the arts and sciences and presided over a lively, intellectual court. Friedrich II sought greatness through building and was known for his political and military savvy. All this led to the city being nicknamed *Spreeathen* (Athens-on-Spree).

The Enlightenment arrived with some authority in the form of the playwright Gotthold Ephraim Lessing, and thinker and publisher Friedrich Nicolai; both helped make Berlin a truly international city.

The 19th century began on a low note with the French occupation of 1806-13, and in 1848 a bourgeois democratic revolution was suppressed, somewhat stifling the political development that had been set in motion by the Enlightenment. The population doubled between 1850 and 1870 as the Industrial Revolution, spurred on by companies such as Siemens and Borsig, took hold. In 1871 Bismarck united Germany under Kaiser Wilhelm I. The population of Berlin was almost two million by 1900.

Before WWI Berlin had become an industrial giant, but the war and its aftermath led to revolt throughout Germany. On 9 November 1918 Philipp Scheidemann, leader of the Social Democrats, proclaimed the German Republic from a balcony of the *Reichstag* (parliament) and hours later Karl Liebknecht proclaimed a free Socialist republic from a balcony of the Berliner Schloss. In January 1919 the Berlin Spartacists, Liebknecht and Rosa Luxemburg, were murdered by remnants of the old imperial army, which entered the city and brought the revolution to a bloody end.

On the eve of the Nazi takeover, the Communist Party under Ernst Thälmann was the strongest single party in 'Red Berlin', having polled 31% of the votes in 1932. Berlin was heavily bombed by the Allies in WWII and, during the 'Battle of Berlin' from August 1943 to March 1944, British bombers hammered the city every night. Most of the buildings you see today along Unter den Linden were reconstructed from the ruins. The Soviets shelled Berlin from the east, and after the last terrible battle buried 18,000 of their own troops.

In August 1945, the Potsdam Conference sealed the fate of the city by finalising plans for each of the victorious powers – the USA, Britain, France and the Soviet Union – to occupy a separate zone. In June 1948 the city was split in two when the three western Allies introduced a western German currency and established a separate administration in their sectors. The Soviets then blockaded West Berlin, but an airlift kept the city supplied and in the Western camp. In October 1949 East Berlin became the capital of the GDR. The construction of the Berlin Wall in August 1961 prevented the drain of skilled labour (between 1945 and 1961 four million East Germans were lured westwards by higher wages and political freedom).

GREATER BERLIN

When Hungary decided to breach the Iron Curtain in May 1989, the GDR government was back where it had been in 1961, but this time without Soviet backing. On 9 November 1989 the Wall opened and on 1 July 1990, when the Bundesrepublik's currency was adopted in the GDR, the Wall was being hacked to pieces. The Unification Treaty between the two Germanys designated Berlin the official capital of Germany, and in June 1991 the Bundestag voted to move the seat of government from Bonn to Berlin over the following decade at a cost of DM20 billion. A huge consortium of public and private organisations was charged with constructing the heart of a metropolis from scratch.

Orientation

Berlin sits in the middle of the region known from medieval times as the Mark and is surrounded by the new *Bundesland* (federal state) of Brandenburg. Roughly one-third of the city's municipal area is made up of parks, forests, lakes and rivers. In spite of WWII bombing, there are more trees here than in Paris and more bridges than in Venice. Much of the natural beauty of rolling hills and quiet shorelines is in the south-east and south-west of the city.

The Spree River winds across the city for over 30km, from the Grosser Müggelsee in the east to Spandau in the west. North and south of Spandau the Havel River widens into a series of lakes from Tegel to Potsdam. A network of canals links the waterways to each other and to the Oder River to the east, and there are beautiful walks along some of them.

Berlin has 23 independent administrative districts *(Bezirken)*, although most travellers will end up visiting only the eight 'core' ones. They are (clockwise from the west): Charlottenburg, Tiergarten, Mitte, Prenzlauer Berg, Friedrichshain, Kreuzberg, Schöneberg and Wilmersdorf. Kreuzberg itself, quite different in its eastern and western sections, is split in this chapter into Kreuzberg 36 and Kreuzberg 61 for clarity.

You can't really get lost within sight of the monstrous Fernsehturm (TV Tower). Unter den Linden, the fashionable avenue of aristocratic old Berlin, and its continuation, Karl-Liebknecht-Strasse, extend eastwards from the Brandenburger Tor (Brandenburg Gate)

to Alexanderplatz, once the heart of socialist Germany. Some of Berlin's finest museums are here, on Museumsinsel in the Spree. The cultural centre is around Friedrichstrasse, which crosses Unter den Linden. South of here, in areas once occupied by the Wall, the largest construction site in Europe continues hammering away. What used to be Checkpoint Charlie is now almost lost amid new construction. A new district has taken shape around Potsdamer Platz, which before the war had been the busiest intersection in Europe. Here and there a few sections of the wall have been preserved for public view but it is rapidly becoming impossible to tell where the historic barrier once stood.

The ruin and modern annexes of Kaiser-Wilhelm-Gedächtnis-Kirche, the shattered memorial church on Breitscheidplatz, a block away from Zoo station, form a most visible landmark. The tourist office and hundreds of shops are in the faded Europa-Center at the end of the square farthest from the station. The Kurfürstendamm (known colloquially as the 'Ku'damm') runs 3.5km south-west from Breitscheidplatz. To the north-east, between Breitscheidplatz and the Brandenburger Tor, is Tiergarten, a district named after the vast city park which was once a royal hunting domain. Nearby is another Brobdingnagian work site around the Lehrter Bahnhof, where the Spree has actually been rerouted to allow a vast underground tunnel that will become the new central train station for the city in 2007. Just north of the Hackescher Markt Bahnhof stretches the ancient neighbourhood of the Scheunenviertel (barn district). This was a centre of Jewish life before the war and is now attracting a lot of stylish businesses and residents.

While in central Berlin, keep in mind that the street numbers usually run sequentially up one side of the street and down the other (important exceptions are Martin-Luther-Strasse in Schöneberg, and Unter den Linden), although number guides appear on most corner street signs. Be aware, too, that a continuous street may change names several times and that on some streets (Pariser Strasse, Knesebeckstrasse) numbering sequences continue after interruptions caused by squares or plazas. The names of many major streets and other landmarks have been changed for political reasons and a few more will surely follow.

Information

Tourist Offices The main office of Berlin Touristen-Information is at Budapester Strasse 45 in the Europa-Center and is open 8 am to 10 pm Monday to Saturday and 9 am to 9 pm Sunday. This office also handles hotel reservations. There is another branch in the southern wing of the Brandenburger Tor (open 9.30 am to 6 pm daily). For telephone information and hotel reservations, call ☎ 25 00 25 from within Germany, or 1805-75 40 40 from outside Germany, fax 25 00 24 24 or @ reservation@btm.de.

The tourist office sells the Berlin Welcome Card (DM32), which entitles you to unlimited transport for three days and discounted admission to major museums, shows, attractions, sightseeing tours and boat cruises in both Berlin and Potsdam. It is also available at hotels and public transport ticket offices.

EurAide, the English-language travel information service, has an office in Zoo station. It offers train information, advice and reservations as well as a room-finding service (DM7.50) and is open 8 am to noon and 1 to 4 pm Monday to Saturday.

Money American Express cashes Amex travellers cheques without charging commission, but gives a very ordinary rate if you are converting. Its two offices are at Friedrichstrasse 172, across from Galeries Lafayette department store, and at Bayreuther Strasse 37. Thomas Cook has an exchange office at Friedrichstrasse 56 in Mitte.

Reisebank has an exchange office at Hardenbergplatz 1 outside Zoo station, open from 7.30 am to 10 pm daily. If you show a EurAide newsletter you'll pay less commission. There is another branch inside Ostbahnhof.

Post The main post office is at Budapester Strasse 142, just near the Europa-Center. It's open 8 am to midnight Monday to Saturday (and from 10 am Sunday). The poste restante service is here; letters should be clearly marked 'Hauptpostlagernd' and addressed to you at 10612 Berlin. Note that mail will only be held for two weeks. There are dozens of post offices all over Berlin, but most have more restricted opening hours.

Email & Internet Access Close to Zoo station, Café Website, Joachimstaler Strasse 41, has loads of computers hooked up for Internet access. You could also try Alpha Café, Dunckerstrasse 72 in Prenzlauer Berg (S8 or S10 to Prenzlauer Allee).

Travel Agencies Travel agencies offering cheap flights advertise in the *Reisen* (travel) classified section *(Kleinanzeigen)* of the city magazines *Zitty* and *Tip*. One of the better discount operators is Alternativ Tours (☎ 881 20 89), Wilmersdorfer Strasse 94 in Wilmersdorf (U7 to Adenauerplatz), which specialises in unpublished, discounted fares to anywhere in the world.

The following agencies are generally open between 9 am and 6 pm on weekdays and on Saturday until about 1 pm. Atlas Reisewelt is a big chain of travel agencies with several offices in Berlin. The most convenient branch is at Alexanderplatz 5 (☎ 242 73 70), inside the Kaufhof department store. Kilroy Travel (☎ 310 00 40) has especially good deals on air tickets, bus travel and car hire. There's a branch at Hardenbergstrasse 9 in Charlottenburg. STA Travel caters for young people and is at Gleimstrasse 28 (☎ 28 59 82 64) and Goethestrasse 73 (☎ 311 09 50). ISIC cards are issued here as well, provided you have proper and recognisable student and personal ID.

Newspapers & Magazines The quarterly English-German *Berlin Magazine* (DM3.50) has mainstream listings and is available at newsstands and tourist offices. To find out what's on in Berlin, check out *Zitty* (DM4) or *tip* (DM4.50). Both offer comprehensive listings (in German only) of all current events, including concerts, theatre, clubs, gallery exhibits, readings, movies etc. Also look for the free *030* in pubs and cafes which has the latest club and rave news (in German).

Bookshops There are a number of English-language bookstores in Berlin. The British Bookshop, Mauerstrasse 83-84 in Mitte, has a wide range of fiction and travel books including those by Lonely Planet. Books in

Berlin at Goethestrasse 69 has a good selection of English and American literature.

Large German bookshops with decent English-language sections include the vast Hugendubel at Tauentzienstrasse 13. Kiepert, Hardenbergstrasse 4-5, has many departments, from guidebooks to foreign-language dictionaries. Europa Presse Center at ground level in the Europa-Center has a big range of international papers and magazines.

Laundry The Schnell und Sauber Waschcenter chain has laundrettes (open from 6 am to 10 pm) at Uhlandstrasse 53 and Leibnizstrasse 72 in Charlottenburg, and on Mehringdamm on the corner of Gneisenaustrasse, right outside the Mehringdamm U-Bahn station exit in Kreuzberg 61. To wash and dry a load costs about DM10.

Medical & Emergency Services For 24-hour medical aid, advice and referrals, call the Kassenärztliche Bereitschaftsdienst (Public Physicians' Emergency Service; ☎ 31 00 31). If you need a pharmacy after hours, dial ☎ 011 41. For information on where you can find an emergency dentist *(Zahnarzt)*, dial ☎ 89 00 43 33.

The Zahnklinik Medeco has some English-speaking dentists. It's at Königin-Louise-Platz 1 (☎ 841 91 00) in Dahlem and at Klosterstrasse 17 (☎ 351 94 10) in Spandau and is open from 7 am to midnight daily. Most major hotels also have doctors or can refer you to one.

The general emergency number for a doctor *(Notarzt)* or fire brigade *(Feuerwehr)* throughout Berlin is ☎ 112.

Call ☎ 110 for police emergencies only. Otherwise, there are police stations all over the city, including City-Wache at Joachimstaler Strasse 14-19, south of Ku'damm. In eastern Berlin, there's a station at Otto-Braun-Strasse (formerly Hans-Beimler-Strasse) 27-37.

For mishaps on trains, your first recourse should be the *Bahnpolizei*, at ground level inside Zoo station. Police headquarters (☎ 69 95) and the municipal lost-and-found office (☎ 69 93 64 44) are at Platz der Luftbrücke 6 beside Tempelhof airport. If you've lost something on public transport, contact the BVG (☎ 25 62 30 40) at Potsdamer Strasse 180/182, 10783 Schöneberg.

Dangers & Annoyances Berlin is generally safe and tolerant. Walking alone at night on city streets shouldn't be considered a risk, bearing in mind the caveat that there is always safety in numbers in any urban environment. You may want to avoid the area along the Spree south of the Ostbahnhof, which has become the haunt of occasionally violent punks, urban drifters and druggies. There have also been reports of robberies in the area around Zoo station.

Things to See & Do

State museums (denoted by SMB) have free admission on the first Sunday of every month and are closed on Monday. Some require you to buy a day pass (DM8/4 adults/concession), valid for all SMB museums on that day. If you want to overindulge on museums, the Drei-Tages-Touristenkarte (DM16/8) gives unlimited access to SMB museums over three consecutive days.

Around Alexanderplatz Soaring above Berlin is the restored 368m **Fernsehturm** (1969), open 10 am to 1 am daily. If it's a clear day and the queue isn't too long, it's worth paying the DM9/4 to go up the tower or have a drink at the 207m-level Telecafé, which revolves twice an hour. The best thing about the view from the tower is that it is the one place in the city where you can't see it.

On the opposite side of the elevated train station from the tower is **Alexanderplatz** (or, affectionately, 'Alex'), the square named after Tsar Alexander I who visited Berlin in 1805. The area was redesigned several times in the late 1920s but little was ever actually built because of the Depression. It was bombed in WWII and completely reconstructed in the 1960s. The **World Time Clock** (1969) is nearby in case you want to check the time before making a telephone call home.

Museumsinsel Berlin's famed Museum Island is a scene of heavy construction as its grand buildings are restored. West of the Fernsehturm, on an island between two arms of the Spree River, is the GDR's **Palace of the Republic** (1976), which occupies the site of the bombed baroque Berliner Schloss that was demolished in 1950. During the communist era, the Volkskammer (People's Chamber)

GERMANY

GERMANY

BERLIN-MITTE

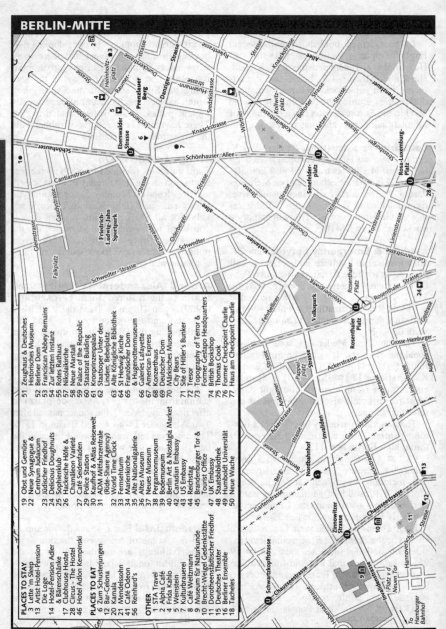

PLACES TO STAY
3   Lette 'm Sleep
8   Artist Hotel-Pension
    Die Loge
13 Hotel-Pension Adler
    & Bärenschänke
17 Clubhouse Hostel
28 Circus - The Hostel
46 Hotel Adlon Kempinski

PLACES TO EAT
6   Zum Schusterjungen
12 Bar-Celona
20 Kamala
21 Mendelssohn
41 Café Odeon
56 Reinhard's

OTHER
1   STA Travel
4   Alpha Café
5   Frida Kahlo
7   Kulturbrauerei
9   Café Weitzmann
10 Museum für Naturkunde
11 Brecht-Weigel Gedenkstätte
15 Dorotheenstädtischer Friedhof
16 Deutsches Theater
18 Berliner Ensemble
18 Tacheles

19 Obst und Gemüse
22 Neue Synagogue &
    Centrum Judaicum
23 Jüdischer Friedhof
24 Delicious Doughnuts
25 Sophienklub
26 Hackesche Höfe &
    Chamäleon Varieté
27 Café Seidenfaden
29 Police Station
30 Kaufhof & Atlas Reisewelt
31 ADM Mitfahrzentrale
    (Ride-Share Agency)
32 World Time Clock
33 Fernsehturm
34 Marienkirche
35 Alte Nationalgalerie
36 Altes Museum
37 Neues Museum
38 Pergamonmuseum
39 Bodemuseum
40 Berlin Art & Nostalgia Market
42 Canadian Embassy
43 US Embassy
44 Reichstag
45 Brandenburger Tor &
    Tourist Office
47 UK Embassy
48 Staatsbibliothek
49 Humboldt Universität
50 Neue Wache

51 Zeughaus & Deutsches
    Historisches Museum
52 Berliner Dom
53 Franciscan Abbey Remains
54 Zur letzten Instanz
55 Rotes Rathaus
56 Nikolaikirche
57 Neue Marstall
59 Palace of the Republic
60 Staatsrat Building
61 Kronprinzenpalais
62 Staatsoper Unter den
    Linden; Bebelplatz
63 Alte Königliche Bibliothek
64 St Hedwig Kirche
65 Französischer Dom
    & Hugenottenmuseum
66 Galeries Lafayette
67 American Express
68 Konzerthaus
69 Deutscher Dom
70 Märkisches Museum;
    City Bears
71 Site of Hitler's Bunker
72 Tresor
73 Topography of Terror &
    Former Gestapo Headquarters
74 British Bookshop
75 Thomas Cook
76 Former Checkpoint Charlie
77 Haus am Checkpoint Charlie

euro currency converter €1 = 1.95DM

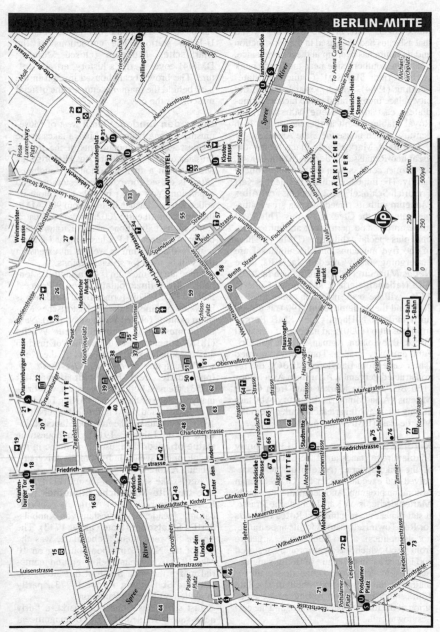

BERLIN-MITTE

GERMANY

euro currency converter 1DM = €0.51

used to meet in this monstrosity which faces Marx-Engels-Platz. In 1990 it was discovered that asbestos had been used in the construction and its future has been up in the air ever since.

On the southern side near the Spree bank is the former **Staatsrat** (Council of State) building (1964), with a portal from the old city palace incorporated in the facade. Immediately east are the **Neue Marstall** (New Royal Stables), built at the end of the 19th century, which house the State Archives.

North of Marx-Engels-Platz looms the great neo-Renaissance **Berliner Dom** (1904), the former court church of the Hohenzollern family. The imposing edifice beside it is Karl Friedrich Schinkel's 1829 neoclassical **Altes Museum** with its famed rotunda area featuring statues of the Greek divinities. This SMB museum boasts a permanent antiquities display plus special exhibitions (DM8/4). Three of the five museums on Museumsinsel are undergoing badly needed facelifts. The **Neues Museum** (1855) will reopen in 2005, **Alte Nationalgalerie** (Old National Gallery; 1876) will be back in action some time in 2001 and the **Bodemuseum** (1904) is closed until mid-2004. Happily, the SMB **Pergamonmuseum** (1930) and its feast of classical Greek, Babylonian, Roman, Islamic and Oriental antiquity is open. The world-renowned Ishtar Gate from Babylon (580 BC), the reconstructed Pergamon Altar from Asia Minor (160 BC) and the Market Gate from Greek Miletus (Asia Minor, 2nd century AD) are among the beautiful artefacts hauled from the Middle East (DM8/4 day pass).

Nikolaiviertel The rebuilt 13th-century **Nikolaikirche** stands amid the forced charms of the Nikolaiviertel (Nikolai quarter), conceived and executed under the GDR's Berlin restoration program. Another medieval church, **Marienkirche**, is on Karl-Liebknecht-Strasse. It stands near the monumental **Rotes Rathaus** (or Red Town Hall, named for its appearance, not its politics), a neo-Renaissance structure from 1860 which has been proudly restored and is once again the centre of Berlin's municipal government. Across Grunerstrasse, the remains of the bombed-out shell of the late 13th-century **Franciscan Abbey** mark the position of the former Spandauer Tor and the earliest town wall.

Märkisches Ufer Several interesting sights can be covered from the Märkisches Museum U-Bahn station. The collections of the **Märkisches Museum** (closed Monday; DM8/4) cover Berlin's history, art and culture. The brown bears housed in a pit in the park behind the main museum are the official mascots of the city.

Unter den Linden A stroll west of Museumsinsel along Unter den Linden takes in the greatest surviving monuments of the former Prussian capital. The **Deutsches Historisches Museum** in a former armoury (Zeughaus; 1706) is closed for extensive restoration and expansion. You won't be able to explore its collection on German history from 900 AD to the present until early 2002, but you can catch some of its exhibitions at the Kronprinzenpalais. Architect IM Pei has designed a glass roof for the museum as well as an extension that will be used for special exhibits.

Opposite the museum is the beautiful colonnaded **Kronprinzenpalais** (Crown Princes' Palace; 1732). This former royal residence is babysitting some Deutsches Historisches Museum exhibits (closed Wednesday; free). Next to the museum is Schinkel's **Neue Wache** (1818), a memorial to the victims of fascism and despotism, which harbours Käthe Kollwitz's sculpture *Mother and Her Dead Son* (open daily; free). **Humboldt Universität** (1753), the next building to the west, was originally a palace of the brother of King Friedrich II of Prussia and converted to a university in 1810. Beside this is the massive **Staatsbibliothek** (State Library; 1914). An equestrian **statue of Friedrich II**, usually at home in the middle of the avenue in front of the university, is being restored.

Across the street from the university, beside the **Alte Königliche Bibliothek** (Old Royal Library; 1780) with its curving baroque facade, is Wenzeslaus von Knobelsdorff's **Staatsoper** (State Opera; 1743). The square between them, **Bebelplatz**, was the site of the Nazis' first book-burning on 10 May 1933. A poignant, below-ground memorial marks the spot. South of this site is the Catholic **St Hedwig Kirche** (1773), partly modelled on Rome's Pantheon.

Just south lies Gendarmenmarkt, a fairly quiet square framed by a trio of magnificent buildings. The **Deutscher Dom** at the southern end of the square boasts a museum featuring an excellent exhibit on German history from 1800 to the present (closed Monday; free). The **Französischer Dom** contains the **Hugenottenmuseum** (closed Monday; DM3/2), which covers the exciting Huguenot contribution to Berlin life. The statuesque **Konzerthaus** (Concert Hall) completes the picture.

Tiergarten Unter den Linden ends at the **Brandenburger Tor**, or Brandenburg Gate (1791, by Karl Gotthard Langhans), a symbol of Berlin and once the boundary between east and west. It is crowned by the winged Goddess of Victory and a four-horse chariot. Pariser Platz is well on the way to resuming its former glory and the US, French and British embassies are under construction on their pre-war locations.

Beside the Spree, just north of the Brandenburger Tor, is the **Reichstag** (1894), where at midnight on 2 October 1990 the reunification of Germany was enacted. Again the home of the German parliament, the Reichstag has become Berlin's number one attraction, thanks to Sir Norman Foster's stunning reconstruction completed in 1999. The highlight is wending your way (and dodging blinding shards of light on a sunny day) to the top of the gleaming metal and glass dome. Get there early (and that means 8 am) to avoid the hordes awaiting their ascent during the day (it's open until midnight, though last admission is at 10 pm; free). While you're up there getting an eyeful of the city, have a look at the parliamentary office buildings taking shape to the north and east; to the west is the Federal Chancellery's new home-to-be on the northern edge of Tiergarten. Tours of the Reichstag are free but you must reserve in writing to: Deutscher Bundestag, Besucherdienst, 11011 Berlin.

Just west of the Reichstag, along the Spree River, is the **Haus der Kulturen der Welt** (House of World Cultures; 1957), nicknamed the 'pregnant oyster' for its shape. The arched roof collapsed in 1980 but has since been rebuilt. The photo and art exhibitions (often with Third World themes) are worth a look (closed Monday).

The huge city park, **Tiergarten**, stretches west from the Brandenburger Tor towards Zoo station and dates from the 18th century. Strasse des 17 Juni (named after the 1953 workers' uprising in East Berlin) leads west from the Brandenburger Tor through the park. On the north side of this street, just west of the gate, is the **Soviet War Memorial** flanked by the first Russian tanks to enter the city in 1945.

Farther west, in the middle of Strasse des 17 Juni, is the **Siegessäule** (Victory Column; 1873), which commemorates 19th-century Prussian military adventures. It is crowned by a gilded statue of the Roman victory goddess, Victoria, which is visible from much of Tiergarten. A spiral staircase leads to the top and affords a worthwhile view (DM1.50). Just north-east is **Schloss Bellevue** (1785), the official Berlin residence of the German president.

Potsdamer Platz One of the biggest attractions is the monumental construction site around Potsdamer Platz, the only area of Berlin which is neither east nor west. Sadly, the lipstick-red Infobox on stilts gazing over Leipziger Platz will have been demolished by the time you read this, so you'll have to experience the action and mushrooming modern architecture – like the **Sony-Center** and **DaimlerCity** complex – from the ground. Nearby, on the corner of Wilhelmstrasse and Vossstrasse, is the site of **Hitler's bunker**, now covered by a grassy area.

Kulturforum Area Plans for a cultural centre in the south-eastern corner of Tiergarten were born as early as the 1950s. One of the premier architects of the time, Hans Scharoun, was given the job of coming up with the design of what would become known as Kulturforum, a cluster of museums and concert halls. The first building erected was the gold-plated **Berliner Philharmonie** (1961). The **Musikinstrumenten-Museum** (Musical Instruments Museum), Tiergartenstrasse 1 in an annexe on the north-eastern side of the Philharmonie, focuses on the evolution of musical instruments from the 16th to the 20th centuries (closed Monday; DM4/2). The rich collection is beautifully displayed. The SMB **Kunstgewerbemuseum** (Museum of Decorative Arts) shows arts and crafts ranging from 16th-century chalices of gilded silver to Art Deco ceramics

GERMANY

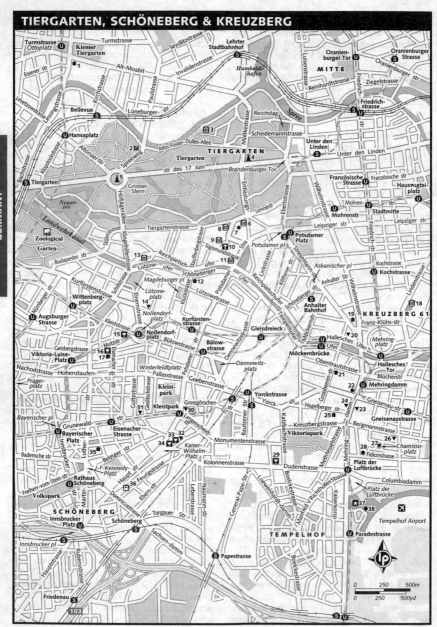

TIERGARTEN, SCHÖNEBERG & KREUZBERG

TIERGARTEN, SCHÖNEBERG & KREUZBERG

PLACES TO STAY					
1	Hotel Tiergarten	26	Barcomi's	10	St Matthäus Kirche
12	Jugendgästehaus Berlin	27	Deininger	11	Neue Nationalgalerie
17	Hotel Gunia	30	Tuk-Tuk	13	Bauhaus Archiv/Museum für
19	Hotel am Anhalter Bahnhof	31	Ousies		Gestaltung
21	Pension Kreuzberg	32	Pasodoble	15	KitKat@Metropolis
25	Hotel Transit			16	Tom's Bar; Hafen
35	Studentenhotel	**OTHER**		18	Jüdisches Museum
		2	Schloss Bellevue	22	Schnell und Sauber Laundrette
PLACES TO EAT		3	Haus der Kulturen der Welt	28	Friends of Italian Opera
14	Café Einstein	4	Soviet War Memorial	29	Golgatha
20	Grossbeerenkeller	5	Siegessäule	33	Leuchtturm
23	Naturkost Vegetarische	6	Musikinstrumenten-Museum	34	Café Mirell
	Buffet	7	Berliner Philharmonie	36	The Odeon Cinema
24	Restaurant Rissani II	8	Kunstgewerbemuseum	37	Police Headquarters
		9	Neue Gemäldegalerie	38	Municipal Lost & Found Office

and modern appliances (DM4/2). Its corridors seem endless but don't miss Carlo Bugatti's crazy suite of furniture (1885).

The SMB **Neue Gemäldegalerie** (New Picture Gallery) on Matthäiskirchplatz is an important post-Wende collaboration, bringing together stunning paintings previously split between the Bodemuseum and Dahlem's Gemäldegalerie. Focusing on European works from the 13th to the 18th centuries, its 1200-plus collection includes works by Dürer, Rembrandt, Botticelli and Goya (DM8/4 day pass).

To the south-east at Potsdamer Strasse 50 is the squat **Neue Nationalgalerie** (New National Gallery), with 19th and 20th-century paintings and sculptures by Picasso, Klee and many German expressionists (closed Monday; DM8/4 day pass).

Looking a bit forlorn amid the modern museums surrounding is the **St Matthäus Kirche** (1846). You can enjoy a panoramic view from the bell tower (DM1). The **Bauhaus Archiv/Museum für Gestaltung** (Bauhaus Archive/Museum of Design) at Klingelhöferstrasse 14 is dedicated to artists of the Bauhaus school, who developed the tenets of modern architecture of the 1950s and '60s. The building was designed by Bauhaus founder Walter Gropius (closed Tuesday; DM5/2.50).

Around Oranienburger Tor Known as the Scheunenviertel, this neighbourhood is one of the most vibrant in Berlin. The **Brecht-Weigel Gedenkstätte** at Chausseestrasse 125 is where the socialist playwright

Bertolt Brecht and his wife Helene Weigel lived from 1948 until his death in 1956 (closed Monday; DM6/3). Behind is **Dorotheenstädtischer Friedhof** with tombs of the illustrious, such as philosopher Georg Friedrich Hegel, poet Johannes Becher, and Brecht. There are two adjacent cemeteries here: you want the one closer to Brecht's house. The **Museum für Naturkunde** (Museum of Natural History; 1810), nearby at Invalidenstrasse 43, has the usual musty collection of dinosaur and mineral exhibits (closed Monday; 5/2.50).

Don't miss the magnificent **Neue Synagogue** at Oranienburger Strasse 28. Built in the Moorish-Byzantine style in 1866, it was desecrated by the Nazis and later destroyed by WWII bombing. The **Centrum Judaicum** has a permanent exhibition on Jewish life in Berlin (closed Saturday; DM5/3). Another legacy of the area's Jewish culture is the old **Jüdischer Friedhof** (Jewish Cemetery) on Rosenthaler Strasse. Although some 10,000 people are buried here including Moses Mendelssohn, the famous philosopher of the Enlightenment, few tombstones survived Nazi destruction in 1942.

If you travel west along Oranienburger Strasse you'll come across the rambling, crumbling **Tacheles** alternative art, culture and entertainment centre. Made famous by post-Wende squatters who gave the former department store a new lease of life, it's run by a self-governed, nonprofit organisation and boasts galleries, a theatre, studios – the whole shebang. It's under threat from developers (no surprises there) but was recently given a 10-year reprieve.

A big drawcard in the area is the **Hackesche Höfe** (1907), once owned by a Jewish businessman. This Art Nouveau cluster of buildings with eight interconnected courtyards is filled with galleries, shops and trendy cafes.

It's a joy wandering around the SMB **Hamburger Bahnhof**, a former train station cleverly converted into a top contemporary gallery (DM8/4 day pass). Lofty ceilings and streams of natural light make the collection, including works by Warhol, Lichtenstein and Rauschenberg, even more appealing.

Kreuzberg On Stresemannstrasse 110, parallel to a section of the Wall, is the site of the former SS-Gestapo headquarters where the open-air **Topography of Terror** exhibition (open daily; free) documents Nazi crimes. A new building for the exhibits should open here in 2001.

Almost nothing remains at the site of the famous **Checkpoint Charlie**, a major crossing between east and west during the Cold War. The history of the Wall is commemorated nearby in the **Haus am Checkpoint Charlie**, Friedrichstrasse 43-44, a tattered but fascinating private museum of escape memorabilia and photos (open daily; DM8/5).

The longest surviving stretch of the **Berlin Wall** is just west of the Warschauer Strasse terminus of the U1. This 300m section was turned over to artists who created the **East Side Gallery**, a permanent open-air art gallery along the side facing Mühlenstrasse. Be careful when you visit this area as it can be a bit seedy.

The Daniel Libeskind-designed **Jüdisches Museum** at Lindenstrasse 9-14 may not be due to open until late 2001, but that hasn't stopped tens of thousands of visitors coming to gawk at its provocative, zinc-clad shell or take an architectural tour (in English twice daily; DM8/5).

Kurfürstendamm Once the commercial heart of West Berlin, the 'Ku'damm' is showing a touch of age as creative and commercial energies are focused elsewhere in town. The area around Zoo station can become a stultifying tourist ghetto in summer.

The stark ruins of the **Kaiser-Wilhelm-Gedächtniskirche** (1895) in Breitscheidplatz, engulfed in the roaring commercialism all around, are a world-famous landmark. A British bombing on 22 November 1943 left only the broken west tower standing.

Adjacent to Zoo station, on the corner of Kantstrasse and Joachimstaler, is the **Erotik-Museum**, a surprisingly artistic creation of Beate Uhse, the German porno and sex toy queen (open from 9 am to midnight daily; DM10/8).

On the other side of Gedächtniskirche rises the **Europa-Center** (1965), a shopping and restaurant complex that's still bustling when other shops are closed. Situated north-east of the Europa-Center on Budapester Strasse is the elephant gate of Germany's oldest **Zoo and Aquarium** (over 150 years old). It contains some 1400 species and is open from 9 am to 5 pm daily, the aquarium till 6 pm. Admission for the zoo is DM14/7 for adults/children; a ticket also valid for the aquarium is DM22.50/11.

Charlottenburg Built as a summer residence for Queen Sophie Charlotte, **Schloss Charlottenburg** (1699) is an exquisite baroque palace on Spandauer Damm (U-Bahn to Sophie-Charlotte-Platz, then a 15-minute walk north along Schlossstrasse; or take bus No 145 from Zoo station right to the door). The palace was bombed in 1943 but has been completely rebuilt. Before the entrance is an equestrian statue of the Great Elector (1620-88), Sophie Charlotte's father-in-law. Along the Spree River behind the palace are extensive French and English gardens (free admission).

In the central building below the dome are the former royal living quarters. The winter chambers of Friedrich II, upstairs in the new wing (1746) to the east, are highlights, as well as the **Schinkel Pavilion**, the neoclassical **Mausoleum** and the rococo **Belvedere pavilion**. Huge crowds are often waiting for the guided tour of the palace and it may be difficult to get a ticket, especially on weekends and holidays in summer. If you can't get into the main palace, content yourself with the facades and gardens. A Day Card good for all the tours and attractions costs DM15/10.

Across the street at the beginning of Schlossstrasse is the SMB **Ägyptisches Museum** (Egyptian Museum), whose highlight is the 14th-century BC bust of Queen Nefertiti, an incredible sight to behold (DM8/4 day pass). Over the road from the museum is the **Sammlung Berggruen**, which is showing a collection called 'Picasso and His Time', on loan until 2006. As well as many Picasso paintings, drawings and sculptures, you'll be treated to works by Cézanne, Van Gogh, Gauguin, Braque and Klee (DM8/4 day pass).

Olympic Stadium Built by Hitler for the 1936 Olympic Games in which African-American runner Jesse Owens won four gold medals, this eerie 85,000-seat stadium lies south-west of Schloss Charlottenburg. It's one of the best examples of Nazi-era neoclassical architecture, and is still very much in use for sporting events, but you can visit it daily when there isn't something on (DM2/1). Take the U2 to Olympia-Stadion Ost, then it's a 10-minute walk along Olympische Strasse to Olympischer Platz.

Zehlendorf A mere shadow of their former selves, the **Dahlem Museums** in south-west Berlin (U1 to Dahlem-Dorf, then walk five minutes south on Iltisstrasse) have been massively affected by the ongoing reorganisation of Berlin museums. Some museums, like the Museum für Islamische Kunst (now in the Pergamonmuseum), have moved, while others like the Museum of East Asian Art and Museum of Indian Art won't reopen until at least 2001. The main area open is the SMB **Museum für Völkerkunde** (Museum of Ethnology), which takes you on a journey back in time to the early Americas, Australasia, Africa, and both South and East Asia (DM4/2).

Treptower Park The city's largest **Soviet Monument** (1949) is a grave site built to the heroic style and scale favoured by Stalin – some 5000 Soviet soldiers are buried here. It's a remarkable place, although somewhat faded since its days as a top attraction in East Berlin. It's open daily, and the Treptower Park S-Bahn station is served by several lines.

Organised Tours

Guide yourself for the price of a bus ticket (DM3.90) on bus No 100, which passes 18 major sights on its way from Zoo station to Michelangelostrasse in Prenzlauer Berg via Alexanderplatz, providing you with a great overview and cheap orientation to Berlin. The BVG even puts out a special brochure describing the route.

Walking Tours Among the best walking tours we've ever been on are the ones from Berlin Walks (☎ 301 91 94), which take between two and three hours and cost DM18/14 for those over/under 26 (DM13.50 with a Berlin Welcome Card). The Discover Berlin tour covers the heart of the city and leaves at 10 am and 2.30 pm daily from April to October and at 10 am only in November to January and March. A variation on this tour aimed at young people leaves at 9.45 am. It also offers tours of Third Reich sites and Berlin's Jewish heritage. Call for the latest schedules of the last two. The walks leave from outside the main entrance of Zoo station at the top of the taxi rank.

Insider Tours (☎ 692 31 49) has daily 3½-hour walking tours of the major sites in the city at 9.45 am and 2.15 pm daily from April to October (only 10 am from November to March). The walks (DM15/10) leave from in front of the Reisebank. It also has four-hour bike tours at 10 am and daily 3 pm (DM29/25). Both tours leave from opposite the main entrance to Zoo station next to McDonald's (underneath the giraffe).

Cruises One of the best ways to see Berlin's historic past is by boat. Reederei Bruno Winkler (☎ 349 95 95) runs a variety of tours on the Spree. The most popular is a three-hour cruise that leaves several times a day from mid-March to October. It departs from the Schlossbrücke over the Spree just east of Schloss Charlottenburg (DM22).

Central Berlin may be crowded with roads, office buildings and apartment blocks, but the south-eastern and south-western sections of the city are surprisingly green, with forests, rivers and lakes. In warmer months, tourist boats cruise the waterways, calling at picturesque villages, parks and castles. Stern und Kreis Schiffahrt (☎ 536 36 00) operates

GERMANY

GERMANY

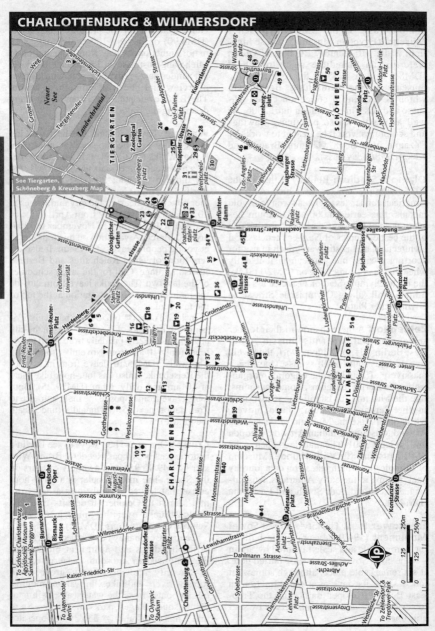

CHARLOTTENBURG & WILMERSDORF

See Tiergarten,
Schöneberg & Kreuzberg Map

CHARLOTTENBURG & WILMERSDORF

PLACES TO STAY			
5	Jugendgästehaus am Zoo	33	Pizzeria Amigo
13	Hotel-Pension Cortina	34	Café Kranzler
15	Pension Knesebeck	35	Aschinger
39	Hotel-Pension Alexandra	37	Zillemarkt
40	Hotel-Pension Majesty	38	Ali Baba
42	Hotel-Pension Modena		
44	Hotel-Pension Savoy	**OTHER**	
46	Pension Fischer	1	Deutsche Oper Berlin
49	Hotel Auberge	2	Kiepert Bookshop
		6	Kilroy Travel
PLACES TO EAT		8	STA Travel
3	Café am Neuen See	9	Books in Berlin
4	Technische Universität Mensa	11	Aldi Supermarket; Schnell
	(Student Cafeteria)		und Sauber Laundrette
7	Satyam	14	A-Trane Jazz Club
10	Il Pulcino	16	Gainsbourg
12	Good Friend	18	Dicke Wirtin
17	Cour Careé	19	Hegel
20	Schwarzes Café	21	Quasimodo
		22	Erotik-Museum

23	Reisebank
24	BVG Information Kiosk
25	Main Post Office
26	Aquarium
27	Tourist Office
28	Europa-Center
29	Euro-Change Office
30	Hugendubel Bookshop
31	Kaiser-Wilhelm-Gedächtnis-
	Kirche (Memorial Church)
32	Café Website
36	Australian Embassy
41	Alternativ Tours
43	Big Eden
45	City-Wache
	(Police Station)
47	KaDeWe Department Store
48	American Express
50	Connection Disco
51	Schnell und Sauber Laundrette

GERMANY

a number of cruises on the Wannsee and adjacent waters between April and October. The Kleine Havelrundfahrt (small Havel tour) runs from Wannsee to Kladow and Pfaueninsel to Potsdam and back. The journey is offered at least twice and up to five times daily, takes three hours if you go both ways, and costs DM12 (return DM16). The 7-Seen-Rundfahrt (seven lakes tour) operates six or seven times daily and takes you through various Havel lakes (including the Kleiner Wannsee and Glieniecker) over two hours (DM14). These and other tours leave from the docks near S-Bahn station Wannsee (S1 and S7). There are various student and child discounts.

For the price of a regular 3-zone BVG ticket (DM4.20) you can also use the ferry service between Wannsee and Kladow which operates hourly year-round, weather permitting.

Special Events
Berlin's calendar is filled with events. The best are:

February
International Film Festival Berlin Also known as the Berlinale, this is Germany's answer to the Cannes and Venice film festivals and attracts its own stable of stars (few) and starlets (plenty). For info call ☎ 25 48 90.

June
Berlin Pride Held on the last weekend in June, this is by far the largest gay event in Germany.

July
Love Parade The largest techno party in the world wends its way through the streets of Berlin in the middle of the month. In 1999 it attracted over 1.5 million people and is quickly challenging Oktoberfest as Germany's premier party event. Information on ☎ 390 66 60.

Places to Stay
If you're travelling to Berlin on weekends and between May and September, especially during big events like the Love Parade, be sure to make reservations at least several weeks ahead of time. From November to March, on the other hand, visitor numbers plunge significantly (except during the Christmas and New Year holidays) and you may be able to get very good deals at short notice.

The city's tourist information office, Berlin Tourismus Marketing (BTM; ☎ 25 00 25, fax 25 00 24 24), handles hotel reservations at no charge to guests. This is a convenient and fast way to find a room, however BTM can only make reservations for its partner hotels and pensions, and many good-value places are not represented.

Places to Stay – Budget Berlin has a
wide range of budget accommodation.

Camping Camping facilities in Berlin are
neither plentiful nor particularly good. All
are far from the city centre and complicated
to reach unless you have your own transport.
They fill up quickly, with a lot of space taken
up by caravans, and we strongly recommend
that you call ahead to inquire about vacancies. Charges are DM9.50 per person, plus
from DM7 for a small tent site to DM12.50
for a larger site with car space.

The only camping convenient to public
transport is *Campingplatz Kohlhasenbrück*
(☎ 805 17 37, Neue Kreisstrasse 36). Open
from April to September, it's in a peaceful location overlooking the Griebnitzsee in
Zehlendorf, about 15km south-west of the
centre. Take the S7 to Griebnitzsee station,
from here it's a 10-minute walk. Alternatively, get off at the previous stop, Wannsee,
and take bus No 118 directly to the camping
ground. If it's full, 2km east along the Teltow
Canal at Albrechts-Teerofen is *Campingplatz
Dreilinden* (☎ 805 12 01). Bus No 118 from
Wannsee station stops here as well.

DJH Hostels Berlin's hostels are very popular, especially on weekends and between
March and October; they are often booked out
by noisy school groups until early July. None
of them offers cooking facilities, but breakfast
is included in the overnight charge. To secure
yourself a bed, you should write several weeks
in advance to Deutsches Jugendherbergswerk,
Zentralreservierung, Kluckstrasse 3, 10785
Berlin. State precisely which nights you'll be
in Berlin and enclose an international postal
reply coupon so they can send back confirmation. They do not take phone reservations.

The only DJH hostel within walking distance of the city centre is the impersonal 364-
bed *Jugendgästehaus Berlin* (☎ 261 10 98,
fax 265 03 83, Kluckstrasse 3), which
charges DM24 for a dorm bed, DM34 per bed
in a three/four/five-bed room or DM84 for a
double room. It's in Schöneberg, near the
Landwehrkanal (U1 to Kurfürstenstrasse).

Jugendgästehaus am Wannsee (☎ 803 20
35, fax 803 59 08, Badeweg 1), on the corner
of Kronprinzessinnenweg, is pleasantly located
on Grosser Wannsee, the lake south-west of the

city. The hostel is a 10-minute walk from Niko-
lassee S-Bahn station (S1 and S7). From the
station, walk west over the footbridge and turn
left at Kronprinzessinnenweg. Beds cost
DM34/42 for juniors/seniors.

Jugendherberge Ernst Reuter (☎ 404 16
10, fax 404 59 72, Hermsdorfer Damm 48-
50) is in the far north-west of Berlin. Take the
U6 to Alt-Tegel, then bus No 125 right to the
door. You'll pay DM28/35 a bed.

Independent Hostels & Guesthouses All
hostels listed below are non-DJH and don't
have curfews. Some give discounts to students with ID.

In Charlottenburg, *Jugendgästehaus am
Zoo* (☎ 312 94 10, fax 31 25 50 30, Hardenbergstrasse 9a) is just three blocks from
Zoo station. The rates are DM47/85/35 for
singles/doubles/dorm (plus DM5 if you're
over 27).

Nearby is *Jugendhotel Berlin* (☎ 322 10
11, fax 322 10 12, Kaiserdamm 3). If you're
under 26, it's DM57/105 for singles/doubles
(DM92/143 for over-26s) with bath and toilet.
Take the U2 to Sophie-Charlotte-Platz.

In Mitte, *Circus – The Hostel* (☎ 28 39 14
33, fax 28 39 14 84, ✉ circus@mind.de, Rosa-
Luxemburg-Strasse 39-41), near Alexanderplatz, is a hugely popular place – and rightly
so. Comfortable singles/doubles/triples cost
DM50/80/105. Beds in larger rooms are
DM25 to DM39 per person. Breakfast is not
included. The Circus people jointly run *Clubhouse Hostel* (☎ 28 09 79 79, 28 09 79 77,
✉ mailto@clubhouse-berlin.de, Kalkscheune
2), just behind the Friedrichstadtpalast on
Friedrichstrasse, so both hostels have the same
prices and helpful, friendly staff.

In the heart of Prenzlauer Berg's nightlife,
Lette 'm Sleep (☎ 44 73 36 23, fax 44 73 36
25, ✉ info@backpackers.de, Lettestrasse 7)
receives rave reviews from travellers. You'll
pay DM25 to DM35 in three to six-bed rooms
or DM45 in doubles (with kitchenette).

Odyssee Globetrotter Hotel (☎ 29 00 00
81, Grünberger Strasse 23), in the 2nd back-
yard of a Friedrichshain apartment building,
has a good vibe. Colourful singles/doubles
are DM50/72, while dorm beds are DM24 to
DM32.

Two moderately priced hotels near Mehringdamm station (U6 or U7) have dormitory

accommodation. Friendly *Pension Kreuzberg* (☎ 251 13 62, fax 251 06 38, *Grossbeerenstrasse 64*) has beds for DM43, while plain singles/doubles go for DM75/98. *Hotel Transit* (☎ 789 04 70, fax 78 90 47 77, *Hagelberger Strasse 53-54*) provides multibed rooms with shower for DM33 per person and singles/doubles for DM90/105. This hostel often has noisy school groups.

In Kreuzberg 36, you'll find *Die Fabrik* (☎ 611 71 16, fax 618 29 74, ✆ info@ diefabrik.com, *Schlesische Strasse 18*) in a huge converted factory (U15 to Schlesisches Tor). Beds in a dormitory-style room on the ground floor go for DM30 per person. Singles/doubles/triples/quads are spread out over five floors (no lift) and cost DM66/ 94/120/144; breakfast is an extra DM10.

Jugendgästehaus Schreberjugend (☎ 615 10 07, fax 614 63 39, *Franz-Künstler-Strasse 10*) charges DM37 per night in two/three-bed rooms. Take the U6 or U15 to Hallesches Tor. In Schöneberg, you'll find the *Studentenhotel* (☎ 78 71 74 14, fax 78 71 74 12, ✆ info@stu dentenhotel.de, *Meininger Strasse 10*), which offers bed and breakfast for DM44 per person in a double room, DM40 in a quad (U4 to Rathaus Schöneberg).

If you're on a really tight budget, head for the *Internationales Jugendcamp Fliesstal* (☎ 433 86 40, fax 434 50 63), open in July and August only. From the U6 Alt-Tegel station take bus No 222 (direction: Lübars) four stops to the corner of Ziekowstrasse and Waidmannsluster Damm. Spaces in communal tents cost DM10 per person (blankets and foam mattresses provided); check-in is after 5 pm. No reservations are taken and officially this place is only for those aged 14 to 27, but usually no one gets turned away.

Hotels In Charlottenburg, *Hotel-Pension Majesty* (☎ 323 20 61, fax 323 20 63, *Mommsenstrasse 55*) charges from DM90/130 for simple singles/doubles. Rock-bottom prices are charged at *Pension Fischer* (☎ 218 68 08, fax 213 42 25, *Nürnberger Strasse 24a*), on the 2nd floor. Basic rooms cost DM50/80 without breakfast. *Hotel-Pension Cortina* (☎ 313 90 59, fax 312 73 96, *Kantstrasse 140*) has plenty of rooms from DM60/100.

Hotel-Pension Adler (☎ 282 93 52, *Friedrichstrasse 124*) is about as cheap as you're going to find in Mitte, with fairly average rooms with shared facilities costing DM69/89. *Hotel Gunia* (☎ 218 59 40, fax 218 59 44, *Eisenacher Strasse 10*) is in the heart of the gay district around Nollendorfplatz. It charges DM100/140 for simple rooms with bath (there's a single without bath for DM90).

Places to Stay – Mid-Range In Charlottenburg, excellent *Pension Knesebeck* (☎ 312 72 55, fax 313 95 07, *Knesebeckstrasse 86*) has basic singles/doubles for DM75/120 or DM85/140 with shower. Attractive *Hotel-Pension Alexandra* (☎ 881 21 07, fax 88 57 78 18, *Wielandstrasse 32*) has quiet, simple rooms for DM95/110 or DM120/125 with full facilities. At No 26, *Hotel-Pension Modena* (☎ 885 70 10, fax 881 52 94) charges from DM120/180 with own facilities (singles with shared shower go for DM80). *Hotel-Pension Savoy* (☎ 881 37 00, fax 888 37 46, *Meinekestrasse 4*) is in a beautiful building with a muralled, church-like entrance and an antique lift. Its 10 rooms vary greatly in price. Singles range from DM75 to DM125, doubles start at DM175.

In Kreuzberg, *Hotel am Anhalter Bahnhof* (☎ 251 03 42, fax 251 48 97, ✆ hotel-aab@ t-online.de, *Stresemannstrasse 36*) has simple, reasonably priced digs costing from DM120/170.

With far more personality than your average hotel, Mitte's *Artist Hotel-Pension Die Loge* (☎/fax 280 75 13, *Friedrichstrasse 115*), on the corner of Torstrasse, has a great deal with singles/doubles with shared bath from DM90/120. It caters for actors and artists. *Hotel Auberge* (☎ 235 00 20, fax 235 00 299, ✆ hotel-auberge@t-online.de, *Bayreuther Strasse 10*), in an interesting old building in Schöneberg, is a good place with large rooms from DM178/280.

Near the Tiergarten, family-run *Hotel Les Nations* (☎ 392 20 26/27, fax 392 50 10, *Zinzendorfstrasse 6*) is on a quiet side street. Comfortable, fully equipped rooms cost DM145/190. A special bonus: breakfast is served around the clock. *Hotel Tiergarten* (☎ 39 98 96 00, fax 393 86 92, ✆ hotel.tier garten@t-online.de, *Alt-Moabit 89*) is a contemporary business-style hotel in a bourgeois 19th-century house. Rates start at DM165/195.

GERMANY

Private Rooms Bed & Breakfast in Berlin (☎ 44 05 05 82, fax 44 05 05 83, 🅮 *bed breakfa@aol.com, Tietjenstrasse 36*) in Tempelhof can book singles, doubles and triples around the city.

Places to Stay – Top End Those holding generous expense accounts should head for *Hotel Adlon Kempinski* (☎ 226 10, fax 22 61 22 22, *Unter den Linden 77*), which offers front-row vistas of Brandenburger Tor. This replica of the famous historic hotel reopened to great fanfare in mid-1997 after a hiatus of more than half a century. It has 337 lavish rooms starting at DM390/460, *not* including the DM39 breakfast buffet.

Places to Eat

Berliners love eating out and have literally thousands of restaurants and cafes to choose from. There's no need to travel far, since every neighbourhood has its own cluster of eateries running the gamut of cuisines and price categories.

German In Charlottenburg is the old-fashioned Art Nouveau *Zillemarkt* (*Bleibtreustrasse 48a*), where you can indulge in huge portions at fair prices. German soul food is served up at the rustic *Grossbeerenkeller* (*Grossbeerenstrasse 90*) in Kreuzberg 61. The menu includes delicious artery-cloggers from DM12 to DM27. *Bärenschänke* (*Friedrichstrasse 124*) in Mitte is a smoky neighbourhood pub serving local specialities. There's a long bar where you can chat with Berliners as you swill your beer. *Aschinger* (*Kurfürstendamm 26*) is a cosy cellar serving dark beer brewed on the premises and huge lunch specials for DM9.80 to DM12.80. *Luisen-Bräu* (*Luisenplatz 1*) is another microbrewery and a good place to relax after a day of museum-hopping around Schloss Charlottenburg. Filling fare includes a daily dish for DM9.80. If you're in the mood for a hearty feed, head for *Zum Schusterjungen* (*Danziger Strasse 9*) in Prenzlauer Berg. Cheap classics include schnitzel with roast potatoes (DM13).

Asian Entering *Tuk-Tuk* (*Grossgörschenstrasse 2*) in Schöneberg feels like walking into an intimate bamboo den in Jakarta. Indonesian dishes from DM18 are accompanied

by soothing gamelan music. *Good Friend* (*Kantstrasse 30*), near restaurant-packed Savignyplatz, is short on decor but big in the popularity stakes (especially among the Russian Mafia). Most of its Chinese dishes cost less than DM22. Thai curries and noodles average around DM17 at *Kamala* (*Oranienburger Strasse 69*) in Mitte.

French *Cour Careé* (*Savignyplatz 5*) is a nice brasserie that is especially popular in summer. You can watch the goings-on in the square from the lovely garden until 2 am daily. *Reinhard's* (*Poststrasse 28*) is an island of sophistication in the touristy Nikolaiviertel. This chic brasserie serves Franco-German food, with plats du jour priced around DM19.

Greek Highly recommended is *Ousies* (*Grunewaldstrasse 16*), where the atmosphere is as boisterous as the waiters. The huge menu features treats like fried sardines stuffed with taramasalata (DM11.50).

International *Deininger* (*Friesenstrasse 23*) in Kreuzberg has an eclectic menu and different all-you-can-eat dishes (DM12) every Monday and Tuesday night, and a themed Sunday brunch. A hot tip for gourmet food lovers on a tight budget is friendly *Kiezküche* (*Waldenser Strasse 2-4*) near the Tiergarten. The chefs-in-training practise on you! Refined recipes such as poached salmon in sauce chantilly for a miraculous DM7 are typical.

Italian *Il Pulcino* (*Leibnizstrasse 74*) is a busy neighbourhood place in Charlottenburg. It's rustic and mid-priced, with wonderful pasta from DM13. The same neighbourhood's Bleibtreustrasse has several Italian joints, including *Ali Baba* at No 45 where the pizza (no more than DM12 for a large) is always fresh. You wouldn't call it stylish, but *Pizzeria Amigo* (*Joachimstaler Strasse 39*), near Zoo station, is a good place to pick up a quick pizza or bowl of pasta for less than DM10.

Spanish *Bar-Celona* (*Hannoversche Strasse 2*) is a friendly restaurant-bar near Brecht-Weigel Haus. If you can't decide between the endless incarnations of tortilla (all less than DM14.50), then choose a variety of tapas (under DM7). Delicious tapas (averaging

DM6), tortillas and paella are on the cards at *Pasodoble (Crellestrasse 39)* in Schöneberg.

Turkish The tastiest felafel we've ever eaten was from *Restaurant Rissani II (Mehringdamm 44)* in Kreuzberg. This casual eatery isn't the flashest place in the world, but who cares with food and prices (mains averaging DM7) like this?

Vegetarian Vegetarians hankering for an Indian fix should head for *Satyam (Goethestrasse 5)* in Charlottenburg. Try a big vegetarian platter for DM9.50. Homy *Naturkost Vegetarisches Büffet (Mehringdamm 48)* in Kreuzberg 61 (U6 or U7 to Mehringdamm) has takeaway or eat-in choices for under DM10.

Cafes The number and variety of cafes in Berlin are astonishing. They're wonderful places to relax over a cup of coffee, while ploughing through a newspaper or chatting with friends. Many of these places also honour the great Berlin tradition of serving breakfast all day.

Elegant *Café Einstein (Kurfürstenstrasse 58)* is a Viennese-style coffee house in a rambling villa. *Schwarzes Café (Kantstrasse 148)* in Charlottenburg is open around the clock, which is especially endearing if you roll into Berlin in the middle of the night. *Café Kranzler (Kurfürstendamm 18-19)* is one of Berlin's oldest coffee houses and a traditional *Konditorei* (cake shop). Popular with tourists and grandmas, it has a nice terrace for people-watching. On trendy Oranienburger Strasse, there are endless cafes to choose from. At No 39, *Mendelssohn's* footpath benches are pleasant places to slurp *Milchkaffee* on a sunny morning. A hearty German breakfast is DM9.80. *Barcomi's (Bergmannstrasse 21)* in Kreuzberg is a hole-in-the-wall place loved by locals for its great coffee and bagels.

In S-Bahn arch No 192, on Georgenstrasse near Museumsinsel, *Café Odéon* serves light meals like quiche lorraine and vegetable lasagne for DM6.50 to DM9. The walls are plastered with old-time, enamelled advertising signs. Balmy summer nights are the best time to be at the *Café am Neuen See (Lichtensteinallee 1)*, right in Tiergarten park. Service in the beer garden is pretty slow but that just gives you more time for people-watching and enjoying the view over the lake.

Student Cafeterias Anyone, student or not, may eat at the 1st-floor *Technische Universität Mensa (Hardenbergstrasse 34)*, three blocks from Zoo station. It's open 11 am to 2.30 pm, and you can fill your tray with a three-course lunch for around DM10. The *Humboldt Universität Mensa (Unter den Linden 6)* in Mitte has the same hours and can be found by entering the main portal, then taking the first door on your left, turning right at the end of the corridor and following your nose.

Snacks & Fast Food Berlin is paradise for snackers on the go, with Turkish (your best bet), Greek, Italian, Chinese, you name it specialities available at *Imbiss* (snack) stands throughout the city. Good areas to look for this sort of thing are along Budapester Strasse in Tiergarten, the eastern end of Kantstrasse near Zoo station, on Wittenbergplatz in Schöneberg, on Alexanderplatz in Mitte and around Schlesisches Tor station in Kreuzberg 36.

Self-Catering To prepare your own food, start your shopping at the discount Aldi, Lidl or Penny Markt supermarket chains, which have outlets throughout Berlin. An *Aldi* is on Joachimstaler Strasse, on the 1st floor opposite Zoo station.

Entertainment

Berliners take culture and fun seriously. The options are almost daunting and are always changing, so don't be surprised if the places we list are a bit different by the time you get to them. Put your faith in word-of-mouth tips for the most up-to-date, cutting-edge scenes.

For fancy, fairly upmarket venues, go to Savignyplatz and side streets like Bleibtreustrasse and northern Grolmannstrasse in Charlottenburg.

Kreuzberg 61 – around Mehringdamm, Gneisenaustrasse and Bergmannstrasse – is alternative but with some trendy touches, while Kreuzberg 36 along Oranienstrasse and

GERMANY

GERMANY

Wiener Strasse has a grungy, slightly edgy feel. Around Winterfeldtplatz in Schöneberg, you'll find few tourists and lots of thirty-somethings with alternative lifestyles and young families.

In the eastern districts, the nightlife is far more earthy and experimental. The energy is electric, with an abundance of new bars and restaurants opening and previously dull streets erupting into life, seemingly overnight. The most dynamic scene is in Prenzlauer Berg (locals say Prenzl'berg), especially around Käthe-Kollwitz-Platz and its side streets but also on Knaackstrasse and the streets north of Danziger Strasse. Simon-Dach-Strasse in Friedrichshain has an emerging bar scene. More established are the nightclubs and cafes/pubs in Mitte along Oranienburger Strasse, Rosenthaler Platz, Hackescher Markt and adjacent streets in the Scheunenviertel.

Pubs & Bars *Gainsbourg (Savignyplatz 5)* speaks to a thirty-something artsy crowd that enjoys its warmly lit, clubby atmosphere. Nearby, *Hegel (Savignyplatz 2)* is the preferred watering hole of academics and the more cultured of Berlin's expat Russians. Gentrifying Kreuzberg 36 is *Morgenland (Skalitzer Strasse 35)*, which is good for long conversations at oddly shaped designer tables. A longtime hang-out is *Flammende Herzen (Flaming Hearts; Oranienstrasse 170)*, which is dark, romantic and, occasionally, gay.

Plenty of popular cafe-pubs with outdoor tables in warm weather are clustered around Käthe-Kollwitz-Platz in Prenzlauer Berg, including *Café Weitzmann (Husemannstrasse 2)*. That suburb's Lynchener Strasse also boasts the fun, Spanish-themed *Frida Kahlo* (with plenty of pictures by the monobrowed one) and cosy *Weinstein* wine bar. Dark and retro, *Astro (Simon-Dach-Strasse 40)* is a cool techno bar in Friedrichshain. There are lots of interesting pubs and cafes on Crellestrasse in Schöneberg, including the inexpensive *Café Mirell* at No 46 and *Leuchtturm* (Lighthouse) at No 17, which has walls plastered in kitsch oil paintings. *Obst und Gemüse (Oranienburger Strasse 48)* in Mitte is a pretty hip and popular bar.

Berliner Kneipen Typical Berlin pubs have their own tradition of hospitality: good food (sometimes rustic daily dishes or stews only), beer, humour and *Schlagfertigkeit* (quick-wittedness). In Charlottenburg, *Dicke Wirtin (Carmerstrasse 9)* is an earthy place off Savignyplatz with daily stews for under DM6. Historic *Zur letzten Instanz (The Final Authority; Waisenstrasse 14)* in Mitte claims traditions dating back to the 1600s and is next to a chunk of medieval town wall. *Alte Berliner Kneipe (Schlesische Strasse 6)* in Kreuzberg 36 is especially authentic, as is nearby *Oberbaum-Eck* on the corner of Oberbaumstrasse and Bevernstrasse.

Beer Gardens As soon as the last winter storms have blown away, pallid Berliners reacquaint themselves with the sun. A cult place is the open-air *Golgatha (Dudenstrasse 48-64)* in Viktoriapark, Kreuzberg 61. In the south-western district of Zehlendorf is *Loretta am Wannsee (Kronprinzessinenweg 260)*, a huge garden with seating for over 1000 (S1, S3 or S7 to Wannsee).

Clubs Berlin has a reputation for unbridled and very late nightlife. Usually nothing happens until 11 pm at the earliest, though there's a growing trend for 'after-work' clubs and raves, so those hip, hard-working, hard-clubbing types don't have to kiss their partying lifestyle goodbye. Cover charges (when they apply) range from DM5 to DM20 and usually don't include a drink.

Berlin *is* techno music and you'll be hard pressed to find a nightclub that plays anything else. One of the oldest techno temples is *Tresor (☎ 609 37 02, Leipziger Strasse 126a)*, housed inside the actual money vault of a former department store in Mitte. It also has a summer beer garden.

Popular and always packed is *Delicious Doughnuts (☎ 28 09 92 74, Rosenthaler Strasse 9)*, an acid jazz club in Mitte. *SO 36 (☎ 61 40 13 07, Oranienstrasse 190)* is one of Berlin's longest-running techno nightclubs. The Kreuzberg club has theme nights, ranging from techno to punk to gay and lesbian.

A great example of the wild scene in Berlin is the *KitKat Club@Metropolis (☎ 217 36 80, Nollendorf Platz 5)* in Schöneberg. During Sex Trance Bizarre parties on Friday and Saturday nights you only get in wearing your 'sexual fantasy outfit' (meaning erotic or basically no clothes!).

A great club in Mitte is *Sophienklub* (☎ 282 45 52, *Sophienstrasse 6*) off Rosenthaler Strasse, especially if you're tired of techno. Chances are you'll hear Britpop, 70s and 80s music, disco and Indie.

The nightclubs around the Ku'damm are generally more mainstream and are avoided by most Berliners. Places tend to be packed with tourists, especially German high-school kids, who usually disappear with the last U-Bahn train. Typical is *Big Eden* (☎ 882 61 20, *Kurfürstendamm 202*).

Gay & Lesbian

Pardon our presumption, but if you're reading this, you probably don't need to be told that Berlin is about the gayest city in Europe. For listings and one-off parties, check the gay and lesbian freebie *Siegessäule* or the strictly gay *Sergej Szene Berlin*. For tips and advice, contact Mann-O-Meter (☎ 216 80 08), Motzstrasse 5, in Schöneberg.

Hafen (*Motzstrasse 19*), near legendary Nollendorfplatz, is full of gay yuppies fortifying themselves before they move on to the legendary *Tom's Bar*, next door on the corner of Eisenacher Strasse, with its famous dark and active cellar. *Connection* (*Fuggerstrasse 33*) is arguably the best gay nightclub in town.

Interesting places in Kreuzberg 36 include the *O-Bar* (*Oranienstrasse 168*) with a good mixed crowd and *Schoko-Café* (*Mariannenstrasse 6*), a convivial meeting place for lesbians. A pleasant lesbian cafe is the smoke and alcohol-free *Café Seidenfaden* (*Dircksenstrasse 47*) in Mitte.

Jazz

The *A-Trane* (☎ 313 25 50, *Bleibtreustrasse 1*) in Charlottenburg, is still *the* place in Berlin for jazz. The cover charge is DM10 to DM20 but on some nights (usually Tuesday and Wednesday) admission is free. *Quasimodo* (☎ 312 80 86, *Kantstrasse 12a*) has live jazz, blues or rock acts in the basement every night. The stylish cafe on the ground floor is a good place for a pre-show drink.

Classical Music

The *Berliner Philharmonie* (☎ 25 48 81 32, *Herbert-von-Karajan Strasse 1*) is famous for its supreme acoustics. All seats are excellent, so just take the cheapest. The lavish *Konzerthaus* (☎ 203 09 21 01) on Gendarmenmarkt in Mitte is home to the renowned Berlin Symphony Orchestra.

Cinemas

Films cost as much as DM17 and foreign films are usually dubbed into German. If the film is shown in the original language with German subtitles, it will say 'OmU' on the advertisement. If the film is screened in the original language without German subtitles, it will say 'OF' or 'OV'.

Cinemas with frequent original-language showings include *The Babylon* (☎ 61 60 91 93, *Dresdner Strasse 126*) in Kreuzberg 36 (U1, U8, or U15 to Kottbusser Tor), *The Odeon* (☎ 78 70 40 19, *Hauptstrasse 116*) – take the U4 to Innsbrucker Platz or S1, S45 or S46 to Schöneberg, and the new *Cinemaxx* (☎ 44 316 316, *Potsdamer Strasse 5*) at Potsdamer Platz.

Theatre

Berlin has more than 100 theatres, so there should be something for everybody. In the former eastern section, they cluster around Friedrichstrasse; in the western part they're concentrated along Ku'damm. The *Deutsches Theater* (☎ 28 44 12 25, *Schumannstrasse 13a*) goes from strength to strength with its classic and modern productions. Nearby, the *Berliner Ensemble* (☎ 28 40 81 55, *Bertolt-Brecht-Platz 1*) performs classic Brecht plays. *Friends of Italian Opera* (☎ 693 56 92, *Fidicinstrasse 40*) in Kreuzberg is Berlin's only English-language ensemble.

Opera

The *Staatsoper Unter den Linden* (☎ 208 28 61, *Unter den Linden 5-7*) in Mitte hosts lavish productions with international talent in an exquisite building dating from 1743. Tickets cost between DM6 and DM190.

The *Deutsche Oper Berlin* (☎ 343 84 01, *Bismarckstrasse 35, Charlottenburg*) has classical works of mostly Italian and French composers. Tickets range from DM17 to DM142 (U2 to Deutsche Oper).

Cabaret

A number of venues are trying to revive the lively and lavish variety shows of 1920s Berlin. Programs include dancers, singers, jugglers, acrobats and other entertainers, who each perform a short piece. Expect to pay at least DM20. Don't confuse

GERMANY

cabaret with *Kabarett*, political and satirical revues.

Chamäleon Varieté (☎ *282 71 18*), in the Hackesche Höfe in Mitte, has a variety show which includes comedy and slapstick, juggling acts, singing and more.

Cultural Centres The hottest venue in Prenzl'berg is the **Kulturbrauerei** *(Cultural Brewery;* ☎ *441 92 69, Knaackstrasse 97)*, where artists from around the world work in a space of 8000 sq metres. The Kulturbrauerei, closed for renovation at the time of writing, attracts people from all walks of life with events as diverse as post-Love Parade raves to poetry readings.

Shopping

Berlin's decentralised character is reflected in the fact that it doesn't have a clearly defined shopping artery like London's Oxford Street or New York's Fifth Avenue. Rather, the numerous shopping areas are in various neighbourhoods, many of which have a local speciality and 'feel'. For art galleries and haute couture, for instance, you should head for posh Charlottenburg, while multiethnic Kreuzberg is known for its eclectic second-hand and junk stores.

The closest Berlin gets to an international shopping strip is the area along Kurfürstendamm and its extension, Tauentzienstrasse. The star of this area is KaDeWe at Tauentzienstrasse 21. This is truly one of Europe's grand stores, the Harrods of Germany. Every year, about 30 million shopping fetishists have a field day on its six floors. The gourmet food halls on the 6th floor are not to be missed!

The Wilmersdorfer Strasse stop of the U7 will put you in the thick of pedestrian streets filled with affordable shops and department stores patronised by real Berliners. Much more upmarket is the chic indoor shopping complex right outside the U6 Französische Strasse in Mitte. Anchored by Galeries Lafayette, a branch of the famous Parisian department store, it is connected by an underground tunnel to smallish malls filled with international designer boutiques.

Markets The Berlin Art and Nostalgia Market is held at the north-eastern end of Museumsinsel 8 am to 5 pm on weekends.

The selection here is heavy on collectibles, books, ethnic crafts and possibly authentic GDR memorabilia. From U/S-Bahn station Friedrichstrasse, walk east along Georgenstrasse for about 10 minutes.

Getting There & Away

Air There are hardly any direct flights to Berlin from overseas and, depending on the airline you use, you're likely to fly first into another European city like Frankfurt, Amsterdam, Paris or London and catch a connecting flight from there.

For now, Berlin has three airports. Tegel (TXL; ☎ 41 01 23 07) primarily serves destinations within Germany and Europe. Schönefeld (SXF; ☎ 609 10) mostly operates international flights to/from Europe, Asia, Africa and Central America. Berlin-Tempelhof (THF; ☎ 695 11) became famous as the main landing hub for Allied airlifts during the Berlin blockade of 1948-49. Today it is the main hub for domestic departures and flights to Central Europe, but is scheduled to close by 2002; its services will be taken over by Tegel. Then, by 2007, Tegel will be closed, leaving a revamped and expanded Schönefeld as Berlin's airport hub.

Bus Berlin is well connected to the rest of Europe by long-distance bus. Most buses arrive at and depart from the Zentraler Omnibusbahnhof (ZOB) at Messedamm 8 in Charlottenburg, opposite the stately Funkturm radio tower (U2 to Kaiserdamm or S45 to Witzleben). The ZOB Reisebüro (☎ 301 80 28 for information, ☎ 302 52 94 for reservations) is open weekdays from 9 am to 5.30 pm. Tickets are also available from many travel agencies in Berlin. The left-luggage office at the bus station is open 5.30 am to 9.30 pm daily.

Train Until the opening of the huge new Lehrter Bahnhof in 2007 (the current station is just for local trains), train services to and from Berlin will remain confusing because of the extensive construction around town which affects several stations. Trains scheduled to leave from or arrive at one station may be spontaneously rerouted to another.

Many trains serve Zoo station as well as Ostbahnhof (the former main train station). These trains may also stop at Friedrichstrasse and Alexanderplatz stations. Finally, many long-distance and night trains use Lichtenberg station in eastern Berlin. Check your schedules carefully and be aware that you may need to switch stations, usually an easy feat on the appropriate S-Bahn line. The S5 and S7 travel directly between Zoo and Lichtenberg, two stations you're likely to arrive at or depart from. The journey takes about 35 to 45 minutes. Conventional train tickets to and from Berlin are valid for all trains on the S-Bahn, which means that you can use your train ticket to ride the S-Bahn to/from your train station.

Zoo station is the principal station for long-distance travellers going to/from the west. It has scores of lockers (from DM2) and a large Reisezentrum (reservation and information office) that is open 5.15 am to 11 pm. Lichtenberg station, on Weitlingstrasse in Lichtenberg, generally handles trains to/from the old east as well as the countries beyond. It has lockers and a Reisezentrum. Ostbahnhof station is gaining importance as the train system is revised.

ICE and IC trains have hourly services to every major city in Germany. There are night trains to the capitals of most major Central European countries.

Hitching Lonely Planet does not encourage hitching for all the obvious reasons. Having said that, if you do want to hitch a ride, it's best to head to one of the service areas on the city autobahns. If you're destination is Leipzig, Nuremberg, Munich and beyond, make your way to the Dreilinden service area on the A115. Take the U1 to Krumme Lanke, then bus No 211 to Quantzstrasse, then walk down to the rest area. For Dresden, take the S9 or S45 to Altglienicke and position yourself near the autobahn on-ramp. Those headed to Hamburg or Rostock should go to the former border checkpoint Stolpe by catching the U6 to Alt-Tegel and then bus No 224 to Stolpe.

Mitfahrzentralen (ride-share agencies) organise lifts and charge a fixed amount payable to the driver, plus commission ranging from DM7 for short distances to DM20 for longer trips. Generally, a ride to Leipzig costs DM19, Frankfurt/Main is DM49, Munich DM53, Cologne DM50, Budapest DM90 and

Paris DM84. All prices include commission. One central agency is ADM Mitfahrzentrale in Zoo station (☎ 194 40), on the Vinetastrasse platform of the U2. It is open 9 am to 8 pm weekdays and 10 am to 6 pm weekends. A second branch, in the Alexanderplatz U-Bahn station as you cross from U2 to U8, is open 10 am to 6 pm weekdays and 11 am to 4 pm weekends.

Getting Around

Much of central Berlin is currently one gigantic construction site, which certainly has an effect on the flow of traffic. Gridlock, mysteriously rerouted roads and sudden dead ends that weren't there yesterday are among the obstacles you'll have to navigate when driving through the core districts. The area around Potsdamer Platz and Brandenburger Tor should be avoided.

However, Berlin's public transport system is excellent, so use it. Roughly one billion passengers each year ride the huge network of U-Bahn and S-Bahn trains, buses, trams and ferries which extends pretty much into every corner of Berlin and the surrounding areas.

To/From the Airports Tegel airport is connected by bus No 109 to Zoo station, a route that travels via Kurfürstendamm and Luisenplatz. Express bus X9 (DM9.90/6.60) goes to Lützowplatz and Kurfürstenstrasse via Budapester Strasse and Zoo station. The trip between the airport and the western centre takes 30 minutes. A taxi between Tegel and Zoo station costs about DM35.

Schönefeld airport is easily reached in 29 minutes by the Airport Express train leaving from Zoo station every 30 minutes. The train also stops at the rest of the stations along the central train line including Friedrichstrasse and Ostbahnhof. The station is about 300m from the terminal and is connected by a free shuttle bus. A taxi to Zoo station costs between DM50 and DM70.

Tempelhof airport is closer in and is served by the U6 (Platz der Luftbrücke) and by bus No 119 from Kurfürstendamm via Kreuzberg. A taxi to/from Zoo station will cost about DM30.

Public Transport Berlin's public transport system offers services provided by Berliner Verkehrsbetriebe (BVG; ☎ 194 49, 6 am to

GERMANY

11 pm daily), which operates the U-Bahn, buses, trams and ferries, and the Deutsche Bahn (DB; ☎ 01805-99 66 33) which runs the S-Bahn and regional RE, SE and RB trains (rail pass-holders can use the DB trains for free). Since the system is jointly operated, one type of ticket is valid on all forms of transport (with the few exceptions noted below). The BVG kiosk on Hardenbergplatz in front of Zoo station has free route maps and general information on buses, U-Bahns, trams and ferries. It's open 8 am to 10 pm daily and also sells tickets and passes. For information on S-Bahn, RE and RB connections, visit the Reisezentrum office inside Zoo station.

Berlin's metropolitan area is divided into three tariff zones: A, B and C. Tickets are valid in at least two zones (AB or BC), or in all three zones. Unless you're venturing to Potsdam or the very outer suburbs, you'll only need the AB ticket. Taking a bicycle in specially marked carriages of the S-Bahn or U-Bahn costs DM2.50 (free if you hold a monthly ticket). On the U-Bahn, bikes are allowed only between 9 am and 2 pm and from 5.30 pm to closing time on weekdays (any time at the weekend). The following types of tickets and passes are available:

Kurzstrecke (Short Trip) – This ticket (DM2.50) allows you to travel any three stops by U-Bahn or S-Bahn or six stops by bus or tram.

Langstrecke (Long Trip) – With this ticket (DM3.90) you can travel on all forms of public transport (except RE, SE and RB trains) for two hours within two of the three zones (AB or BC) with unlimited transfers.

Ganzstrecke (Entire Route System) – This ticket (DM4.20) also allows unlimited travel for two hours, but in all three zones (ABC). It's also valid on RE, SE and RB trains.

Tageskarte (Day Pass) – This excellent value ticket gives you unlimited travel until 3 am the following day and costs only DM7.80 (zones AB or BC) or DM8.50 (zones ABC).

Bus drivers sell single and day tickets, but tickets for U/S-Bahn trains and other multiple day tickets must be purchased in advance. Most types of tickets are available from the orange vending machines (which feature instructions in English) in U/S-Bahn stations. Tickets must be stamped (validated) in a red

machine *(Entwerter)* at the platform entrances to U/S-Bahn stations or at bus stops before boarding. If you're using a timed ticket like the Langstrecke, validate it just as your train or bus arrives to ensure full value. If you're caught without a ticket (or with an unvalidated one), there's a DM60 fine.

The most efficient way to travel around Berlin is by U/S-Bahn. The lines operate from 4 am until just after midnight, but most S-Bahns continue to operate hourly between midnight and 4 am on Saturday and Sunday.

If you're in a hurry and need to travel across town, don't take the bus! Traffic congestion makes travelling rather slow. Bus stops are marked with a large 'H' and the name of the stop. Some 70 bus lines operate between 1 am and about 4 am, when regular service resumes. Buses leave from the major nightlife areas like Zoo station, Hackescher Markt in Mitte and Nollendorfplatz in Schöneberg, and cover the entire Berlin area, including the outer districts. Normal fares apply. About 30 tram lines crisscross the entire eastern half of Berlin and a network map is available at the BVG office.

Car & Motorcycle You'll soon want to ditch your wheels in Berlin. Parking in garages is expensive (about DM2 to DM3 per hour) but it'll often be your only cho ice if you want to be near the main shopping areas or attractions. Free street parking, while impossible to find in these central areas, is usually available in residential streets, especially in the eastern districts. If you're staying at a hotel, keep in mind that most don't have their own garages.

Taxi Taxi stands with call columns are located beside all main train stations and throughout the city; just look for the sign. Flag fall is DM4.20; then it's DM2.20 per kilometre for the first 6km and DM2 thereafter. Night (11 pm to 6 am) and weekend charges are higher by DM0.20 per kilometre, and a fifth passenger costs DM2.50 on top of the fare. If you order a taxi by phone (☎ 194 10, ☎ 21 01 01 or ☎ 21 02 02), flag fall goes up to DM6.

Bicycle Fahrradstation is the largest bike-rental agency with branches all over the city, including at the left-luggage office in Zoo station (☎ 29 74 93 19). Bikes cost from DM18 to DM23 a day.

Brandenburg

The state of Brandenburg surrounds the city-state of Berlin and is a flat region of lakes, marshes, rivers and canals. In 1618, the electors of Brandenburg acquired the eastern Baltic duchy of Prussia, eventually merging the two states into a powerful union called the Kingdom of Prussia. By 1871, this kingdom brought all the German states under its control, leading to the establishment of the German Empire.

Many Berliners will warn you about the 'Wild East', advising you not to stray too far afield in what they consider to be a backward and sometimes violent region. But Brandenburgers, ever *korrekt* in the Prussian style, sniff and ask what can you expect from a bunch of loud-mouthed and brash upstarts like the Berliners. However, some small towns in Brandenburg have seen occasional extremely violent attacks against African and Asian foreigners recently. In 1996 the dichotomy was set in stone when a referendum to merge Brandenburg with the city-state of Berlin failed at the polls.

POTSDAM
☎ 0331 • pop 130,500
Potsdam, on the Havel River just beyond the south-western tip of Greater Berlin, is the capital of Brandenburg state. In the mid-18th century Friedrich II (Frederick the Great, 1740-86) built many of the marvellous palaces in Sanssouci Park, to which visitors flock today.

In April 1945, British bombers devastated the historic centre of Potsdam, including the City Palace on Alter Markt, but fortunately most of the palaces in the park escaped undamaged. The Allies chose Schloss Cecilienhof for the Potsdam Conference of August 1945, which set the stage for the division of Berlin and Germany into occupation zones.

Only 24km from Berlin and easily accessible by S-Bahn, Potsdam is an ideal day trip.

Orientation & Information
The main train station and last stop for the S-Bahn is Potsdam-Stadt. From here, it is about a 3km walk over the Lange Brücke and through the town centre to the gates of Sanssouci Park. You can also take a bus or tram (see Getting Around later in this section). The town itself is an interesting mix of bad GDR-era architecture, newly restored buildings exuding charm, and old classics that have been mouldering away for decades.

Potsdam-Information (☎ 27 55 80, fax 27 55 99), beside the Alter Markt at Friedrich-Ebert-Strasse 5, has varying opening hours: 9 am to 8 pm weekdays (to 6 pm Saturday and 4 pm Sunday) April to October, and 10 am to 6 pm weekdays (to 2 pm weekends) November to March. It has a smaller branch situated at Brandenburger Strasse 18, while Sanssouci-Information, near the old windmill opposite Schloss Sanssouci, has details on the palaces in the park and is usually open the same hours as the Schloss.

Sanssouci Park This large park is open from dawn till dusk with no admission charge. The palaces and outbuildings all keep separate hours and charge separate admission prices. A day ticket allowing entry to all palaces and other sights in the park costs DM20/15 and a family card is DM25, but you have to work pretty fast to make it pay off. Note that some sites have different days of closure.

Covering the whole circuit of sites means walking several kilometres. Begin your tour of the park with Georg Wenzeslaus von Knobelsdorff's **Schloss Sanssouci** (1747), the celebrated rococo palace with glorious interiors. You have to take the guided tour, so arrive early and avoid weekends and holidays, or you may not get a ticket. They're usually sold out by 2.30 pm – even in the shoulder seasons. The palace is open 9 am to 5 pm Tuesday to Sunday April to mid-October (to 4 pm November to April).

The late-baroque **Neues Palais** (1769), the summer residence of the royal family, is one of the most imposing buildings in the park and the one to see if your time is limited. It keeps the same hours as Schloss Sanssouci but is closed on Friday instead of Monday.

The following sites are closed on Monday and November to April. The **Bildergalerie** (1764) contains an extensive collection of 17th-century paintings. The Renaissance-style

GERMANY

GERMANY

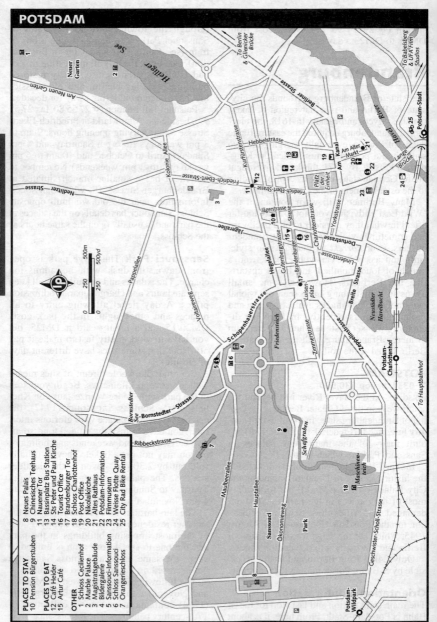

POTSDAM

PLACES TO STAY
10 Pension Bürgerstuben

PLACES TO EAT
12 Café Heider
15 Artur Café

OTHER
1 Schloss Cecilienhof
2 Marble Palace
3 Magistratsgebäude
4 Bildergalerie
5 Sanssouci-Information
6 Schloss Sanssouci
7 Orangerieschloss
8 Neues Palais
9 Chinesisches Teehaus
11 Nauener Tor
13 Bassinplatz Bus Station
14 Sts Peter und Paul Kirche
16 Tourist Office
17 Brandenburger Tor
18 Filmmuseum
19 Post Office
20 Nikolaikirche
21 Altes Rathaus
22 Potsdam-Information
23 Filmmuseum
24 Weisse Flotte Quay
25 City Rad Bike Rental

Orangerieschloss (1864) was built as a guesthouse for foreign royalty. Although it's the largest palace on the grounds, it is not the most interesting. The **Schloss Charlottenhof** (1826) is a must and can be visited on a 30-minute German-language tour. However, the exterior is more interesting than the interior.

Take some time to wander around the royal grounds and use up some film on the **Chinesisches Teehaus** (1757), also closed Friday.

Altstadt From the baroque **Brandenburger Tor** (1770) on Luisenplatz at the western end of the old town, pedestrian Brandenburger Strasse runs east to **Sts Peter und Paul Kirche** (1868). North-west of here, on Friedrich-Ebert-Strasse, is the **Nauener Tor** (Nauen Gate; 1755), another monumental arch. The **Holländisches Viertel** (Dutch Quarter) to the south-east, bounded by Friedrich-Ebert-Strasse, Hebbelstrasse, Kurfürstenstrasse and Gutenbergstrasse, has some 134 gabled red-brick houses built for Dutch workers in the 1730s.

South-east of central Platz der Einheit is the great neoclassical dome of Schinkel's **Nikolaikirche** (1850) on Alter Markt. On the eastern side of the square is Potsdam's **Altes Rathaus** (Old Town Hall; 1753), which now contains several art galleries upstairs (closed Monday; DM4/2).

West of the Alter Markt on Breite Strasse and housed in the **Marstall**, the former royal stables designed by Knobelsdorff in 1746, is the **Filmmuseum** (closed Monday; DM4/2). It contains exhibits on the history of the UFA and DEFA movie studios in Babelsberg and some excellent footage from Nazi-era and postwar communist propaganda films.

Neuer Garten, the winding lakeside park on the west bank of the Heiliger See, north-east of the city centre, is home to **Schloss Cecilienhof**, an English-style country manor (closed Monday; DM4). This was the site of the 1945 Potsdam Conference. The park is also home to the lovely **Marble Palace** (1792).

The **UFA film studios**, Germany's one-time response to Hollywood, are east of the city centre on August-Bebel-Strasse (enter from Grossbeerenstrasse). This is where silent movie epics such as Fritz Lang's *Metropolis* were made, along with some early Greta Garbo films. For a look behind the scenes you can take the commercial and expensive tour

from March to October between 10 am and 6 pm (DM29/26).

Cruises Weisse Flotte (☎ 275 92 10) operates boats on the Havel River and the lakes around Potsdam, departing regularly from April to early October from the dock below the Hotel Mercure near Lange Brücke. There are frequent boats to Wannsee (DM16.50 return).

Places to Stay & Eat
Potsdam's proximity to Berlin and the dearth of cheap accommodation make staying overnight an unappealing option. However, should you end up here for the night, *Pension Bürgerstuben (☎ 280 11 09, fax 280 48 54, Jägerstrasse 10)* has singles/doubles with facilities at DM90/150.

Cosy *Artur Café (Dortustrasse 16)*, a cafe-cum-antique shop, has light meals for under DM7. For breakfast, lunch or dinner try *Café Heider (Friedrich-Ebert-Strasse 29)*, a lively meeting and eating place adjacent to Nauener Tor.

Getting There & Away
Potsdam-Stadt train station is just south-east of the town centre across the Havel River. The next two stops after Potsdam-Stadt are Potsdam-Charlottenhof and then Potsdam-Wildpark, which are closer to Sanssouci Park and all the palaces but are served only by RegionalBahn (RB) trains, not the Regional Express (RE) or S-Bahn Nos 3 and 7, which is how most people get here from Berlin.

Potsdam-Stadt station is also served by ICE and IC trains linking Berlin with points west, so you can stop off on your way to or from the big metropolis.

Getting Around
To reach Schloss Charlottenhof and the Neues Palais from Lange Brücke, take bus No 606; tram No 98 is also good for the former. Bus No 695 goes past Schloss Sanssouci, the Orangerieschloss and the Neues Palais. Catch bus No 694 to Schloss Cecilienhof.

City Rad (☎ 61 90 52) rents bikes from Bahnhofsplatz just north of the Potsdam-Stadt train station. It's open daily from May to September and rental is from DM15 per day.

GERMANY

GERMANY

SACHSENHAUSEN CONCENTRATION CAMP

In 1936 the Nazis opened a 'model' concentration camp near the town of Oranienburg, about 35km north of Berlin. By 1945 about 220,000 men from 22 countries had passed through the gates of Sachsenhausen labelled, as at Auschwitz in south-western Poland, *Arbeit Macht Frei* (Work Sets You Free); about 100,000 died here. After the war, the Soviets and the communist leaders of the GDR used the camp for *their* undesirables.

Plan on spending at least two hours at Sachsenhausen, which is easily reached from Berlin. Among the many museums and monuments within the triangular-shaped, walled grounds are **Barracks 38 and 39**. Rebuilt after an arson attack by neo-Nazis in 1992, they contain excellent displays of the camp's history. An information office (☎ 03301-80 37 15) sells maps, brochures and books, including several very useful English-language guides.

The camp is open 8.30 am to 6 pm from April to September, closing at 4.30 pm the rest of the year (closed Monday; free).

From Berlin take the S1 to Oranienburg (DM4.20, 40 minutes). The camp is 2km north-east of the station, but it's an easy, signposted 20-minute walk. Follow Stralsunder Strasse north and turn east (right) onto Bernauer Strasse. After about 600m turn left at Strasse der Einheit and then right on Strasse der Nationen to the main entrance.

Saxony

The Free State of Saxony (Sachsen) is the most densely populated and industrialised region in eastern Germany. Germanic Saxon tribes originally occupied large parts of north-western Germany, but in the 10th century they expanded south-eastwards into the territory of the pagan Slavs.

The medieval history of the various Saxon duchies and dynasties is complex, but in the 13th century the Duke of Saxony at Wittenberg obtained the right to participate in the election of Holy Roman emperors. Involvement in Poland weakened Saxony in the 18th century, and ill-fated alliances, first with Napoleon and then with Austria, led to the ascendancy of Prussia over Saxony in the 19th century.

In the south, Saxony is separated from Czech Bohemia by the Erzgebirge, eastern Germany's highest mountain range. The Elbe River cuts north-west from the Czech border through a picturesque area known as the 'Saxon Switzerland' towards the capital, Dresden. Leipzig, a great educational and commercial centre on the Weisse Elster River, rivals Dresden in historic associations. Quaint little towns like Görlitz and Meissen punctuate this colourful, accessible corner of Germany.

DRESDEN

☎ 0351 • pop 463,500

In the 18th century the Saxon capital Dresden was famous throughout Europe as 'the Florence of the north'. During the reigns of Augustus the Strong (ruled 1694-1733) and his son Augustus III (ruled 1733-63), Italian artists, musicians, actors and master craftsmen, particularly from Venice, flocked to the Dresden court. The Italian painter Canaletto depicted the rich architecture of the time in many paintings which now hang in Dresden's Alte Meister Gallery, alongside countless masterpieces purchased for Augustus III with income from the silver mines of Saxony.

In February 1945 much of Dresden was devastated by Anglo-American fire-bombing raids. At least 35,000 people died at a time when the city was jammed with refugees and the war was almost over. This horrific attack is the basis for the book *Slaughterhouse Five* by Kurt Vonnegut, who was a POW in Dresden at the time. Quite a number of Dresden's great baroque buildings have been restored, but the city's former architectural masterpiece, the Frauenkirche, is still in the midst of a laborious and enormously expensive reconstruction.

The Elbe River cuts a curving course between the low, rolling hills. In spite of modern rebuilding in concrete and steel, this city invariably wins visitors' affections. With its numerous museums and many fine baroque palaces, a stay of two nights is the minimum required to fully appreciate Dresden. Its annual International Dixieland Festival takes place in the first half of May.

Orientation

Dresden has two important train stations: the main station, or Dresden-Hauptbahnhof, on the southern side of town; and Dresden-Neustadt,

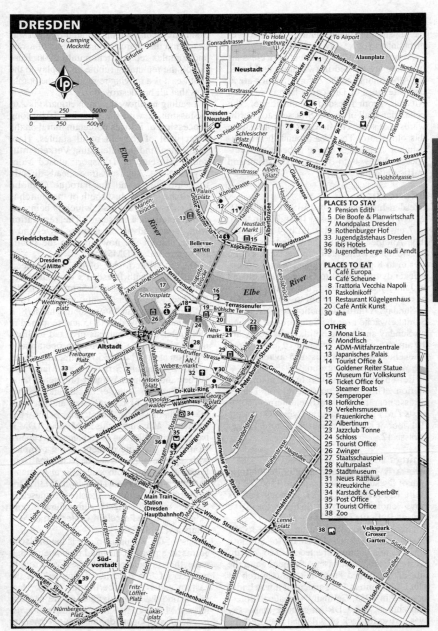

DRESDEN

PLACES TO STAY
2 Pension Edith
5 Die Boofe & Planwirtschaft
7 Mondpalast Dresden
9 Rothenburger Hof
33 Jugendgästehaus Dresden
36 Ibis Hotels
39 Jugendherberge Rudi Arndt

PLACES TO EAT
1 Café Europa
4 Café Scheune
8 Trattoria Vecchia Napoli
10 Raskolnikoff
11 Restaurant Kügelgenhaus
20 Café Antik Kunst
30 aha

OTHER
3 Mona Lisa
6 Mondfisch
12 ADM-Mitfahrzentrale
13 Japanisches Palais
14 Tourist Office &
   Goldener Reiter Statue
15 Museum für Volkskunst
16 Ticket Office for
   Steamer Boats
17 Semperoper
18 Hofkirche
19 Verkehrsmuseum
21 Frauenkirche
22 Albertinum
23 Jazzclub Tonne
24 Schloss
25 Tourist Office
26 Zwinger
27 Staatsschauspiel
28 Kulturpalast
29 Stadtmuseum
31 Neues Rathaus
32 Kreuzkirche
34 Karstadt & Cyberb@r
35 Post Office
37 Tourist Office
38 Zoo

GERMANY

euro currency converter 1DM = €0.51

north of the river. Most trains stop at both, but the ramshackle Hauptbahnhof is more convenient unless you're staying in Neustadt.

At present most of Dresden's priceless art treasures are housed in two large buildings, the Albertinum and the Zwinger, which are at opposite sides of Dresden's largely restored Altstadt. From Dresden Hauptbahnhof, the pedestrian mall of Prager Strasse leads northwards past some classic GDR monoliths into this old centre. The area around the Hauptbahnhof and Prager Stasse is being redeveloped with new high-rises and pedestrian and traffic underpasses.

Information

Dresden-Information (☎ 49 19 20, fax 49 19 21 16) is at Prager Strasse 10 and open 9 am to 7 pm weekdays and 9 am to 4 pm Saturday. Another office in the underpass below the Goldener Reiter statue in Neustadt is open 10 am to 8 pm weekdays and 9 am to 6 pm weekends from April to October. It's closed in January and February, but during the rest of the year it's open 10 am to 4 pm Tuesday to Sunday. A third information counter, in the Schinkelwache near the Semperoper, is open on Sunday and public holidays; its hours are 10 am to 6 pm weekdays and 10 am to 4 pm weekends. Information is also available on the Web site www.dresden.de.

Reisebank has a branch in the main train station. There is a post office on Prager Strasse near the tourist office. Internet access costs DM5 per half-hour at Cyberb@r on the 3rd floor of Karstadt department store, Prager Strasse 12.

Things to See & Do

Altstadt The Altmarkt area is the historic hub of Dresden. To the east you'll see the rebuilt **Kreuzkirche** (1792), famous for its boys' choir, and in the distance the 1912 **Neues Rathaus** (New Town Hall).

Cross the wide Wilsdruffer Strasse to the **Stadtmuseum** (closed Friday to Sunday; DM4/2) in a building erected in 1776. Northwest up Landhausstrasse is Neumarkt and the site of the ruined **Frauenkirche** (Church of Our Lady) built in 1738 and, until it was badly bombed in 1945, Germany's greatest Protestant church. The GDR, in a move many say was a ruse for lack of will, had declared the

ruins a war memorial to remain untouched. Soon after reunification, popular opinion was heard and the church is in the midst of a vast and complex reconstruction until 2006. Ruse or not, the remaining rubble on display to the south-east is a moving reminder of the bombings that all but destroyed it.

Leading north-west from Neumarkt is Augustusstrasse, with the stunning 102m-long **Procession of Princes** porcelain mural on the outer wall of the old royal stables. Here you'll also find the interesting **Verkehrsmuseum** (Museum of Transport; closed Monday; DM4/2). Augustusstrasse leads directly to Schlossplatz and the baroque Catholic **Hofkirche** (1755). Just south of the church is the Renaissance **Schloss**, which is being reconstructed as a museum. The restoration work is well advanced, and the tower and a palace exhibit are now open to the public (closed Monday; DM5/2).

On the western side of the Hofkirche is Theaterplatz, with Dresden's glorious opera house, the neo-Renaissance **Semperoper**. The first opera house on the site opened in 1841 but burned down in 1869. Rebuilt in 1878, it was again destroyed in 1945 and reopened in 1985 after the communists invested millions in the restoration. The Dresden opera has a tradition going back 350 years, and many works by Richard Strauss, Carl Maria von Weber and Richard Wagner premiered here.

The baroque **Zwinger** (1728) and its museums are one of Dresden's stars and occupies the southern side of Theaterplatz. The **Historisches Museum** (closed Monday; DM3) has a superb collection of ceremonial weapons. Housed in opposite corners of the complex with separate entrances are the **Mathematisch-Physikaler Salon** with scientific instruments and timepieces (closed Thursday; DM3/2), the **Museum für Tierkunde** (zoological museum; closed Tuesday; DM2/1), with natural history exhibits, and the **Porcelain Collection** (closed Thursday; DM3/2).

East of the Augustusbrücke is the **Brülsche Terrasse**, a pleasant elevated riverside promenade that is saddled with the overwrought moniker of 'the Balcony of Europe'. At the eastern end is the **Albertinum** (1885). Here you'll find the **Gemäldegalerie Alte Meister** (closed Monday), which boasts Raphael's *Sistine Madonna*, **Gemäldegalerie Neue Meister** (closed Tuesday), with renowned 19th and 20th-century paintings, and the **Grünes Gewölbe** (Green Vault), hosting a collection of jewel-studded precious objects (closed Tuesday). Eventually the Grünes Gewölbe will be relocated to its original site in the Schloss. You can visit all three with a combined ticket (DM7/4).

South-east of the Altstadt is the Grosser Garten, enchanting in summer and home to a fine **zoo** (DM10/5), open daily and with more than 400 species. In the garden's north-western corner are the **Botanical Gardens** (free). The hothouse is especially lovely during a freezing Dresden winter.

Neustadt Neustadt is an old part of Dresden largely untouched by the wartime bombings. After unification it became the centre of the city's alternative scene, but as entire street blocks are renovated it's losing its hard-core feel and instead has become the centre of Dresden's nightlife.

The **Goldener Reiter** statue (1736) of Augustus the Strong stands at the northern end of the Augustusbrücke, leading to Hauptstrasse, a pedestrian mall. At the mall's northern end, on Albertplatz, there's an evocative marble monument to the poet Schiller. Just west is Königstrasse, lined with renovated buildings and shops. Other museums near the Goldener Reiter include the **Museum für Volkskunst** (Museum of Folk Art; closed Monday; DM3/1.50), Grosse Meissner Strasse 1, and the **Japanisches Palais** (1737), Palaisplatz, which contains **Landesmuseum für Vorgeschichte** (Museum of Pre-History) with displays on the evolution of humans (closed Monday; DM4/2).

Elbe River Excursions From May to November, Sächsische Dampfschifffahrts GmbH (☎ 86 60 90), which prides itself on having the world's oldest and largest fleet of paddle-wheel steamers, has frequent excursions on the Elbe River. A one-hour tour costs DM20. You can also use the boats to reach Pillnitz Palace (DM23, 1½ hours) and even as far as lovely Meissen (DM27, two hours). Schedules vary and you may need to book, so check with the ticket office, in a small glass building on the waterfront just east of Augustusbrücke.

Places to Stay

The tourist office (☎ 49 19 22 22 for booking) can arrange *private rooms* for a DM6 fee.

Camping The closest place to pitch your tent is *Camping Mockritz* (☎ 471 52 50), open March to December, 5km south of the city. Take the frequent No 76 Mockritz bus from behind the Dresden train station. It has bungalows, but like the camping ground itself they're often full in summer.

Hostels In a former Communist Party training centre, central *Jugendgästehaus Dresden* (☎ 49 26 20, fax 492 62 99, Maternistrasse 22) is a 15-minute walk north-west of the main train station (or take tram No 7, 9, 10 or 26 to the corner of Ammonstrasse and Freiberger Strasse). Beds cost DM33/38 junior/senior in basic twin or triple rooms (DM7 extra for rooms with shower and toilet). The non-DJH *Jugendherberge Rudi Arndt* (☎ 471 06 67, fax 472 89 59, Hübnerstrasse 11) is 10 minutes' walk south of the main train station and offers dorm beds for DM25/30.

In the heart of Neustadt nightlife are two hostels enjoyed by readers; their prices exclude breakfast. *Die Boofe* (☎ 801 33 61, fax 801 33 62, ✉ boofe@t-online.de, Louisenstrasse 20) charges DM49.50/79 for singles/doubles (including breakfast) and DM27 per person in larger rooms (not including breakfast). Close by, *Hostel Mondpalast Dresden* (☎/fax 8 04 60 61, ✉ mondpalast@t-online.de, Katherinenstrasse 11-13) is DM40/64, or DM25 per bed in a dorm.

Hotels Average hotel rates in Dresden are among the highest in Germany, with few genuine budget places near the centre. Pickings south of the Elbe are especially slim.

Five minutes north of the main train station and along Prager Strasse are *Hotel Ibis Bastei* (☎ 48 56 66 61), *Hotel Ibis Königstein* (☎ 48 56 66 62) and *Hotel Ibis Lilienstein* (☎ 48 56 66 63). Their 1960s-style architecture hides no surprises and they have similar rates, with rooms from DM110/130.

Pension Edith (☎ 802 83 42, Priesnitzstrasse 63), in a quiet backstreet, has rooms with private shower for DM79/109; it only has a few, so you need to book well ahead. The small but pleasant *Hotel Ingeburg*

(☎ 809 12 00, fax 809 11 99, Dammweg 16) charges from DM97/133. **Rothenburger Hof** (☎ 88 12 60, fax 812 62 22, ❷ kontakt@dres den-hotel.de, Rothenburger Strasse 15-17) has classy rooms with bath (and an incredible breakfast buffet) for DM95/165.

Places to Eat
Head straight to Neustadt for food and fun (interesting restaurants are the inverse of architectural gems on the pedestrian streets around Altstadt). Close to Augustusbrücke and below the Museum of Early Romanticism, **Restaurant Kügelgenhaus** (Hauptstrasse 13) has a good range of local Saxon dishes, and there's a beer cellar below the restaurant. The menu at **Raskolnikoff** (Böhmische Strasse 34) divides dishes into the four corners of Central Europe: the East boasts cheap Russian dishes like borscht (beetroot soup) and wareniki (dough baked with potatoes and mushrooms).

Italian is the dominant cuisine on Alaunstrasse. **Trattoria Vecchia Napoli** (Alaunstrasse 33) has oven-fresh pizza and enticing pasta dishes (from DM9) that demand to be washed down with red wine. In the surrounding streets, there are scores of late-night restaurant-bars that include **Planwirtschaft**, in a beer cellar below Die Boofe hostel on Louisenstrasse, and **Café Scheune** (Alaunstrasse 36), with excellent Indian food; the tasty vegetarian thali meal for two (DM28) is good value. **Café Europa** (Königsbrücker Strasse 68) is open 24 hours.

You really don't need help in choosing any of the places near the Brühlsche Terrace as long as you're happy with high prices, marginal food and excellent people-watching. But **Café Antik Kunst** on Terrassengasse is an exception: sit on and amid antique furniture and drink good coffee. A real Altstadt find that's both stylish and tasty (and possibly hence the name) is **aha** (Kreuzstrasse 7), just off Altmarkt. Staff serve inventive organic fare daily, with a DM7 vegetarian lunch special on weekdays.

Entertainment
Sax (DM2.50) is a comprehensive German-language listings guide available at newsstands throughout the city.

Dresden is synonymous with opera, and performances at the **Semperoper** are brilliant.

Dresden's two other great theatres are the **Staatsschauspiel** (☎ 4913555), also near the Zwinger, and the **Staatsoperette** (☎ 207 99 29, Pirnaer Landstrasse 131) in Leuben in the far east of the city. Tickets for all three theatres can be bought from Dresden-Information, or an hour before each performance at the appropriate theatre's box office. Tickets for the Semperoper cost from DM35, but they're usually sold out well in advance. Many theatres close from mid-July to the end of August.

A variety of musical events are presented in the **Kulturpalast** (☎ 486 62 50, Schlossstrasse 2). **Jazzclub Tonne** (☎ 802 60 17, Am Brauhaus 3) has live jazz five nights per week (entry DM12 to DM20).

For a drink, the choices in the cafe-laden blocks around Alaunstrasse and Louisenstrasse are many (and include those listed under Places to Eat earlier), from dark, eclectic **Mondfisch** (Louisenstrasse 37) to **Mona Lisa**, a quasi-Caribbean cocktail bar, down the street at No 77.

Getting There & Around
Hourly IC trains link Dresden to the Berlin-Ostbahnhof (DM59, two hours) and Leipzig (DM40, 1¼ hours), where you can connect to major cities all over Germany. IC trains every two hours to Hanover (DM111, 4½ hours) and Cologne (DM198, 7½ hours) allow more connection possibilities, especially with fast ICE trains at Hanover. There are trains to Budapest (DM142), Vienna (DM123), Warsaw (DM135) and Prague (DM98). There's an ADM-Mitfahrzentrale (☎ 194 40) at Antonstrasse 41.

For travel on Dresden's local trains and trams, a one-hour ticket in one zone is DM2.90, a day ticket is DM8 and a weekly ticket is DM21.

AROUND DRESDEN
Schloss Pillnitz
From 1765 to 1918, Schloss Pillnitz was the summer residence of the kings and queens of Saxony. The most romantic way to get to this palace, on the Elbe about 10km south-east of Dresden, is on one of Dresden's old steamers. Otherwise, take tram No 9 or 14 to the end of the line, then walk a few blocks down to the riverside and cross the Elbe on the small

GERMANY

ferry, which operates year-round. The museum at Pillnitz (open May to mid-October, except Monday) closes at 5.30 pm, but the gardens (which stay open until 8 pm) and the palace exterior with its Oriental motifs are far more interesting than anything inside, so don't worry if you arrive too late to get in.

Schloss Moritzburg

This palace rises impressively from its lake 14km north-west of Dresden. Erected as a hunting lodge for the Duke of Saxony in 1546, Moritzburg was completely remodelled in baroque style in 1730 and has an impressive interior. Entry costs DM7/5 and it's open from 9 am to 5.30 pm daily from April to October, with guided tours the rest of the year (☎ 035207-87 30). You can catch a bus or train from Dresden-Hauptbahnhof.

Meissen

☎ 03521 • pop 32,000

Just 27km north-west of Dresden, Meissen is a perfectly preserved old German town and the centre of a rich wine-growing region. Augustus the Strong of Saxony created Europe's first porcelain factory at the Albrechtsburg palace in 1710. Meissen straddles the Elbe, with the old town on the western bank and the train station on the eastern bank. The train-pedestrian bridge behind the station is the quickest way across (and presents a picture-postcard view). From the bridge, continue up Obergasse then bear right through Hahnemannsplatz and Rossplatz to Markt, the town's central square.

At Markt 3 is Meissen-Information (☎ 03521-419 49, fax 41 94 19), open 10 am to 6 pm weekdays (to 5 pm November to March) and 10 am to 3 pm weekends. Also on Markt are the restored **Rathaus** (1472) and the 15th-century **Frauenkirche** (open daily from May to October). The church's tower (1549), with a porcelain carillon that chimes every quarter-hour, is well worth climbing (DM2/1) for fine views of the Altstadt; pick up the key in the church or from the adjacent Pfarrbüro (parish office).

Various steeply stepped lanes lead up to **Al-brechtsburg**, whose towering medieval **Dom** with its altarpiece by Lucas Cranach the Elder, is visible from afar (DM3.50/2.50; open daily). Beside the cathedral is the remarkable

15th-century Albrechtsburg **palace** (DM6/4; open daily but closed 1 to 19 January). Constructed with an ingenious system of internal arches, it was the first palace-style castle built in Germany.

Meissen has long been famous for its chinaware, with its trademark blue crossed-swords insignia. The **porcelain factory** is now at Talstrasse 9, 1km south-west of town. There are often long queues for the workshop demonstrations (DM9/7), but you can view the fascinating porcelain collection in the museum at your leisure (a further DM5).

Pension Burkhardt (☎ 45 81 98, fax 45 81 97, Neugasse 29) has attractive rooms with full facilities from DM70/110 for its singles/doubles. *Kartoffelkäfer (Marktgasse 1)*, next to the tourist bureau, is all things spud to all spud-lovers, with hearty meals from DM9.20. The courtyard at *Zollhof (Elbstrasse 7)* is a pleasant place to eat Saxon dishes (light meals under DM10 and mains for under DM20) or slurp that rarity, good coffee.

Half-hourly S-Bahns travel to Meissen from both Dresden train stations (DM8.70, 40 minutes), but it's far nicer, between May and September, to travel by steamer (see Cruises in the earlier Dresden section).

LEIPZIG

☎ 0341 • pop 437,000

Since the discovery of rich silver mines in the nearby Erzgebirge (Ore Mountains) in the 16th century, Leipzig has enjoyed almost continual prosperity. Today Leipzig is a major business and transport centre, and the second-largest city in eastern Germany. It has a strong cultural tradition and still offers plenty for book and music lovers (Johann Sebastian Bach's time here is celebrated by a museum and an active choir).

Since medieval times Leipzig has hosted annual trade fairs, and during the communist era these provided an important exchange window between East and West. After unification, the city spent a huge amount of money on a new ultramodern fairground to re-establish itself as one of Europe's great 'fair cities'. Never as heavily bombed as nearby Dresden, in recent years central Leipzig has undergone a restoration and construction boom that has brought new life to its many fine old buildings.

Orientation

With its 23 platforms, the impressive Leipzig train station (1915) is the largest terminal station in Europe. It has been lavishly renovated and is home to many shops and restaurants. To reach the city centre, head through the underpass below Willy-Brandt-Platz and continue south for five minutes; the central Markt square is just a couple of blocks south-west. Ring roads surround the old city centre, more or less where the former city walls once stood.

Information

Leipzig-Information (☎ 710 42 65, fax 710 42 71), Richard-Wagner-Strasse 1, is directly opposite the train station. It is open 9 am to 7 pm weekdays (to 4 pm Saturday and 2 pm Sunday). The Web site www.leipzig.de has tourist information in English, German and French.

There is a Reisebank at the main train station. The main post office is at Augustusplatz 1. Sip coffee and watch your dirty clothes spin at Maga Pon, a laundrette-cafe at Gottschedstrasse 3. You can surf the Internet (DM5 for half an hour) at Cyberb@r on the top floor of Karstadt, Neumarkt 38.

Things to See & Do

The Renaissance **Altes Rathaus** (1556) on Markt is one of Germany's most beautiful town halls. Behind it is the **Alte Börse** (1687), with a monument to Goethe (1903) in front. The former Leipzig University law student called the town a 'little Paris' in his drama *Faust*. **Nikolaikirche** (1165), between Markt and Augustusplatz, has a truly remarkable interior.

Just south-west of Markt is **Thomaskirche** (1212), with Bach's tomb in front of the altar. Bach worked in Leipzig from 1723 until his death in 1750, and the St Thomas Boys' Choir which he once led is still going strong. Opposite the church, at Thomaskirchhof 16, is the **Bach Museum** (DM6/4).

Although the building's origins date back to the 16th century, the baroque-style **Neues Rathaus**, with its impressive 108m tower, was completed as recently as 1905. North along Dittrichring where it intersects with Goerdelerring, is the former East German *Stasi* (secret police) headquarters (diagonally opposite the Schauspielhaus). It is home to the **Museum in der Runden Ecke**, with exhibits outlining

Stasi methods of investigation and intimidation – some appalling, some worthy of Inspector Clouseau (closed Monday; free entry).

The best of Leipzig's fine museums, **Museum der bildenden Künste** (Museum of Fine Arts), is in temporary quarters until a new building is completed in 2002. The excellent collection of old masters is at Grimmaische Strasse 1-7 (DM5/2.50).

Wide Augustusplatz, three blocks east of Markt, is ex-socialist Leipzig, with the space-age (in the sense of the battered Russian Mir) **universität** (1975) and **Gewandhaus** concert hall (1983) juxtaposed with the functional **Opernhaus** (opera house; 1960). Leipzig's dazzling **Neue Messe** (trade fairgrounds) are 5km north of the train station (take tram No 16).

The city has long been a major publishing and library centre, and the **Deutsche Bücherei**, at Deutscher Platz 1, houses millions of books (including most titles published in German since 1913) as well as a **book and printing museum** (free). Farther to the south-east is Leipzig's most impressive sight, the **Völkerschlachtdenkmal** (Battle of Nations Monument), a 91m monument erected in 1913 to commemorate the decisive victory by combined Prussian, Austrian and Russian armies over Napoleon's forces here in 1813 (open daily; DM5/2.50).

Places to Stay

During trade fairs many of Leipzig's hotels raise their prices and it can be hard to find a room. Leipzig-Information runs a free *room-finding service* (☎ 710 42 55).

Campingplatz Am Auensee (☎ 465 16 00, Gustav-Esche-Strasse 5) is in a pleasant wooded spot on the city's north-western outskirts (take tram No 11 to Wahren; from here it's an eight-minute walk). Camping costs DM12 per person plus DM5 for a car/tent site.

Two youth hostels are about 5km east of the centre. The *Jugendpension* (☎ 194 30, Rudolf-Breitscheid-Strasse 39) is near the Völkerschlachtdenkmal (tram No 15). It charges DM22/30 for juniors/seniors. The larger *Jugendherberge* (☎ 245 70 11, Volksgartenstrasse 24) costs DM25/30. Take tram No 17, 27 or 31 (direction: Schönefeld) to Löbauer Strasse and walk five minutes further north.

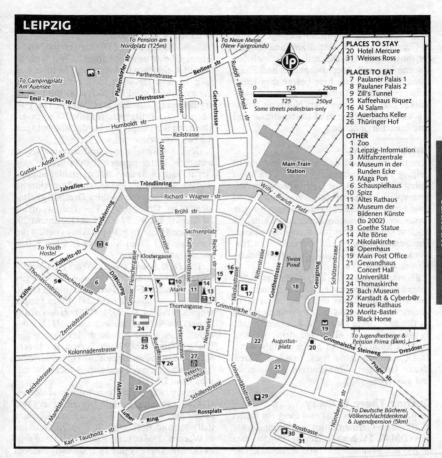

LEIPZIG

PLACES TO STAY
20 Hotel Mercure
31 Weisses Ross

PLACES TO EAT
7 Paulaner Palais 1
8 Paulaner Palais 2
9 Zill's Tunnel
15 Kaffeehaus Riquez
16 Al Salam
23 Auerbachs Keller
26 Thüringer Hof

OTHER
1 Zoo
2 Leipzig-Information
3 Mitfahrzentrale
4 Museum in der Runden Ecke
5 Maga Pon
6 Schauspielhaus
10 Spizz
11 Altes Rathaus
12 Museum der Bildenen Künste (to 2002)
13 Goethe Statue
14 Alte Börse
17 Nikolaikirche
18 Opernhaus
19 Main Post Office
21 Gewandhaus Concert Hall
22 Universität
24 Thomaskirche
25 Bach Museum
27 Karstadt & Cyberb@r
28 Neues Rathaus
29 Moritz-Bastei
30 Black Horse

0 125 250m
0 125 250yd
Some streets pedestrian-only

GERMANY

North-west of the main train station is **Pension am Nordplatz** (☎ 960 31 43, fax 564 98 71, Nordstrasse 58), with basic rooms from DM80/100. Other reasonable options include the family-run **Weisses Ross** (☎ 960 59 51, Rossstrasse 20) from DM70/95. Farther east of the city centre, **Pension Prima** (☎ 688 34 81, Dresdner Strasse 82) has simple offerings for DM50/70. Live like a member of the politburo at the GDR-era **Hotel Mercure Leipzig** (☎ 214 60, fax 960 49 16, Augustusplatz 5-6), with large rooms decently priced at DM130/180.

Places to Eat
The train station mall is filled with eateries and supermarkets. Food like *Mutti* (mum) used to make averages DM15 at one of the two **Paulaner Palais** restaurants at Klostergasse 3 and 5. **Al Salam** (Nikolaistrasse 33) has Middle Eastern food to die for. Doners are DM3 while the vegetarian platter is DM7.50. Luther's favourite pub was **Thüringer Hof** (Burgstrasse 19), where great dishes cost from DM13. Another place with a long tradition is **Zill's Tunnel** (☎ 960 20 78, Barfussgässchen 9), with typical German specialities (from about DM18). Founded in

1525, *Auerbachs Keller*, just south of the Altes Rathaus in the Mädler Passage, is one of Germany's classic restaurants and another for those on the Goethe trail. *Faust* includes a scene in which Mephistopheles and Faust carouse with students here before they leave riding on a barrel. *Kaffeehaus Riquez*, an up-market cafe in a superb Art Nouveau building, stands on the corner of Reichsstrasse and Schuhmachergässchen.

Entertainment

Live theatre and music are major features in Leipzig's cultural offerings. With a tradition dating back to 1743, the *Gewandhaus* on Augustusplatz has Europe's longest established civic orchestra; one of its conductors was the composer Mendelssohn-Bartholdy. Leipzig's modern *Opernhaus* is just across the square. The *Schauspielhaus (Bosestrasse 1)*, a few blocks west of Markt, mixes classic theatre with modern works.

Moritz-Bastei (Universitätsstrasse 9), spread over three underground floors, has live music or disco most nights, but in summer really comes into its own as a cultural venue. *Spizz (Markt 9)* is a trendy cafe by day and slick place for drinking and dancing by night. Both of these clubs have music ranging from rock to jazz. *Black Horse* Irish pub *(Rossstrasse 12)* is cosy and gay-friendly.

Getting There & Away

Leipzig is linked by fast and frequent trains to all major German cities, including Dresden (DM40, 1¼ hours), Berlin (DM58, two hours) and Munich (DM140, 5½ hours). The Mitfahrzentrale (☎ 194 40) is at Goethestrasse 7-10; sample fares (including booking fee) include: Berlin DM22 and Munich DM44.

Getting Around

Trams are the main form of public transport in Leipzig, with the most important lines running via Willy-Brandt-Platz in front of the train station. Fares are both time and zone-based, eg, a 15-minute ticket in the inner city is DM1.70 while an hour ticket on the whole system is DM3. Strip tickets valid for five rides are DM8/16 for 15/60-minute trips.

GÖRLITZ
☎ 03581 • pop 63,000

Situated 100km east of Dresden on the Neisse River, Görlitz emerged from WWII with its beautiful old town undamaged. The town was split in two, however, under the Potsdam Treaty, which used the Neisse as the boundary between Germany and Poland. The Polish part of Görlitz was renamed Zgorzelec. The town is an important border stop between the two countries.

Görlitz's Renaissance and baroque architecture is better preserved than that of any city its size in Saxony. Of particular interest are the **Rathaus** (1537), the **Peterskirche** (1497) and the 16th-century **Dreifaltigkeitskirche** on Obermarkt. The tourist office (☎ 475 70, fax 47 57 27) is at Obermarkt 29. It is open 10 am to 6.30 pm daily (until 4 pm Saturday and 1 pm Sunday) and has a free room-finding service.

The *DJH hostel (☎/fax 40 65 10, Goethestrasse 17)*, south of the station, charges DM21. Central *Gästehaus Lisakowski (☎ 40 05 39, Landeskronstrasse 23)* offers simple singles/doubles for DM60/90. *Hotel Bon-Apart (☎ 480 80, Elisabethstrasse 41)* is a delightful place with a stained-glass facade and charges from DM90 per person for lovely rooms. *Zum alten Brauhaus (Bruderstrasse 3)* has a beer garden and serves local specialities from DM10.

Hourly RB trains run to/from Dresden (DM29, two hours), while IR trains every two hours take 90 minutes. There are four IR trains daily to/from Berlin (3½ hours). Night trains to Warsaw (DM80) and Kraków (DM86) stop in Görlitz. There is one IR train daily to/from Wroclaw (DM27, 2½ hours).

Thuringia

The state of Thuringia (Thüringen) occupies a basin cutting into the heart of Germany between the Harz Mountains and the hilly Thuringian Forest. The Germanic Thuringians were conquered by the Franks in 531 and converted to Christianity by St Boniface in the 8th century. The Duke of Saxony seized the area in 908 and for the next 1000 years the region belonged to one German principality or another. Only in 1920 was Thuringia reconstituted as a state with something approaching its original borders. Under the communists it was again split into separate districts, but since 1990 it has been a single unit once again.

ERFURT
☎ 0361 • pop 200,000

This trading and university centre, founded as a bishop's residence by St Boniface in 742, is the lively capital of Thuringia. Erfurt was only slightly damaged during WWII and, because of the numerous burgher town houses, churches and monasteries that grace its surprisingly well-preserved medieval

quarter, the city is on Unesco's world cultural heritage listing.

Orientation & Information

Bahnhofstrasse leads north from the train station to Anger, a large square in the heart of the city. Continue straight ahead, following tram tracks along Schlösserstrasse to Fischmarkt. The friendly and efficient tourist office (☎ 664 00, fax 664 02 90, ✉ service@erfurt-tourist-info.de) is just east of Fischmarkt and the Rathaus (town hall) at Benediktsplatz 1. It is open 10 am to 7 pm weekdays (till 6 pm from January to March),

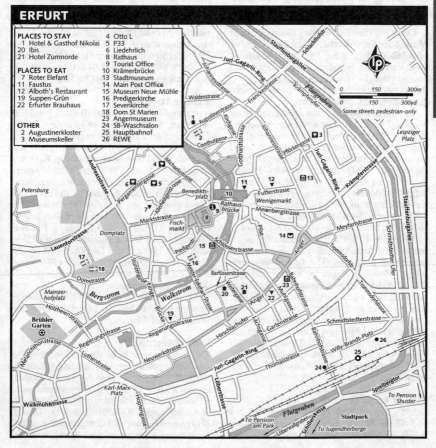

ERFURT

PLACES TO STAY
1 Hotel & Gasthof Nikolai
20 Ibis
21 Hotel Zumnorde

PLACES TO EAT
7 Roter Elefant
11 Faustus
12 Alboth's Restaurant
19 Suppen-Grün
22 Erfurter Brauhaus

OTHER
2 Augustinerkloster
3 Museumskeller

4 Otto L
5 P33
6 Liederhirch
8 Rathaus
9 Tourist Office
10 Krämerbrücke
13 Stadtmuseum
14 Main Post Office
15 Museum Neue Mühle
16 Predigerkirche
17 Severikirche
18 Dom St Marien
23 Angermuseum
24 SB-Waschsalon
25 Hauptbahnhof
26 REWE

weekends till 4 pm. It sells Erfurt's three-day ClassicCard (DM25), which allows unlimited use of public transportation and entry to museums. Web site: www.erfurt-tourist-info.de

There's a Reisebank at Erfurt's Hauptbahnhof (closed Sunday) and the main post office is on Anger. You'll find a convenient laundrette (SB-Waschsalon) at Bahnhofstrasse 22, below the rail bridge.

Things to See & Do

The numerous interesting backstreets and laneways in Erfurt's surprisingly large Altstadt make this a fascinating place to explore on foot. Pick up the tourist office's *A Tour of the Historical City* booklet (DM2.50), which has a map and good descriptions of numbered sights.

Don't miss the 13th-century Gothic **Dom St Marien** and **Severikirche**, which stand together on a hillock dominating the central square of Domplatz. The wooden stools (1350) and stained glass (1410) in the choir, and figures on the portals, make the cathedral one of the richest medieval churches in Germany.

Around Fischmarkt you will find numerous historical buildings. The eastbound street beside the town hall leads to the medieval restored **Krämerbrücke** (1325), which is lined on each side with timber-framed shops. This is the only such bridge north of the Alps. Further north, on the same side of the River Gera, is **Augustinerkloster**, a late-medieval monastery that was home to Martin Luther early in the 16th century (open cdaily, only by arrangement from November to March; DM5.50/4).

Although Erfurt's main attraction is its magnificent Alstadt buildings, it also has some interesting museums. The **Anger Museum** (closed Monday), Anger 18, has regional medieval art, frescoes and faience; the **Stadtmuseum** (open daily), Johannesstrasse 169, focuses mainly on Erfurt's Stone Age and medieval history; whereas the **Museum Neue Mühle** (closed Monday) is an old streamside millhouse (the last of some 60 water mills that Erfurt once had) with working machinery dating from the early 1880s. Entry to each museum is DM3/1.50.

Places to Stay

Erfurt's *Jugendherberge* (☎ 562 67 05, fax 562 67 06, ✉ jugendherberge-erfurt@t-onl ine.de, Hochheimer Strasse 12) is south-west of the centre and costs DM25/30 for juniors/seniors. Take tram No 5 from Erfurt train station southbound to the terminus.

The tourist office arranges private accommodation from around DM40/80 (plus a booking fee of DM5 per person).

Pension Schuster (☎ 373 50 52, Rubenstrasse 11) has clean, bright rooms for DM65/70 (breakfast DM5 extra) with a bathroom. *Pension am Park* (☎ 345 34 71, fax 345 33 44, Löberwallgraben 22) has fairly good rooms with shared facilities for DM75/100 (check-in is after 2 pm). *Ibis* (☎ 664 10, fax 664 11 11, ✉ h1648@accor-hotels.com, Barfüsserstrasse 9) is central and standard, but good value at DM120 for doubles without breakfast (singles cost the same). *Hotel & Gasthof Nikolai* (☎ 59 81 70, fax 59 81 71 20, Augustinerstrasse 30) has nice rooms from DM115/169 with pleasant views. *Hotel Zumnorde* (☎ 568 00, fax 568 04 00, Anger 50-51) is a quality option for DM170/230.

Places to Eat

You should have no trouble finding good eats in Erfurt. *Suppen-Grün* (Regierungsstrasse 70) serves up wholesome organic-vegetarian broths (from DM6.50) until 3 pm daily except Sunday. The microbrewery *Erfurter Brauhaus* (Anger 21) offers cheap, hearty fare to accompany its own-brew pilsener and *Schwarzbier*. *Roter Elefant* on the corner of Turnierstrasse and Allerheiligenstrasse is a trendy cafe-restaurant that does tasty meals for under DM20 (closed Sunday). *Faustus* (Wenigemarkt 5) is a glitzier version of this, with main dishes from DM17 to DM27. *Alboth's Restaurant* (☎ 568 82 07, Futterstrasse 15-16) is top of the gourmet range – with prices to match.

There's a convenient *REWE* supermarket near the train station in the InterCity Hotel on Willy-Brandt-Platz.

Entertainment

The best nightlife is in the Andreasviertel, a few paces north-west of Fischmarkt. *Liedehrlich* (Pergamentergasse 6) gets a student crowd. *P33* (☎ 210 87 14, Pergamentergasse 33) serves meals, a Sunday brunch with music, and also stages Kabarett and jazz. *Otto L* (Pergamentergasse 30) completes the triumvirate on an aeronautical note. *Museumskeller*

(☎ 562 49 94, Juri-Gagarin-Ring 140a) is a popular rock venue. For an overview of events, jazz, rock and classical music, or theatre and cabaret, pick up the free monthly *Erfurt Magazine* from the tourist office and hotels around town.

Getting There & Away

Every two hours a direct IR train connects Frankfurt (DM72, 3½ hours) and Erfurt. The same train goes to/from Berlin (DM81, 3½ hours) and to/from Weimar (DM8, 14 minutes) and Eisenach (DM15, 40 minutes). Regional trains also run to/from Weimar and Eisenach. IC trains go to/from Leipzig (DM54, 2 hours) every two hours.

WEIMAR
☎ 03643 • pop 61,000

Not a monumental city, nor a medieval one, Weimar appeals to more refined tastes. As a repository of German humanistic traditions it is unrivalled. Many famous people lived and worked here, including Lucas Cranach the Elder, Johann Sebastian Bach, Christoph Martin Wieland, Friedrich Schiller, Johann Gottfried von Herder, Johann Wolfgang von Goethe, Franz Liszt, Friedrich Nietzsche, Walter Gropius, Lyonel Feininger, Vasili Kandinsky, Gerhard Marcks and Paul Klee. From 1919 to 1925 it was the focal point of the Bauhaus movement, which laid the foundations of modern architecture, and today is a centre for architecture, music and media studies.

Weimar is also known as the place where the German republican constitution was drafted after WWI (hence, the 1919-33 Weimar Republic). The ruins of the Buchenwald concentration camp, near Weimar, are haunting evidence of the terrors of the Nazi regime (see the Around Weimar section).

Orientation & Information

The centre of town is just west of the Ilm River and a 20-minute walk south of the train station. Buses run fairly frequently between the station and Goetheplatz, from where it's a short walk east along small streets to Herderplatz or Markt.

Weimar-Information (☎ 240 00, fax 24 04 40, ✉ tourist-info@weimar.de), Markt 10, is open 9.30 am to 7 pm weekdays, till 5 pm

Saturday and till 4 pm Sunday. It opens 10 am to 6 pm weekdays and till 2 pm weekends from November to March. A smaller tourist office (☎ 24 00 45, fax 24 00 46) inside Weimar Hauptbahnhof is open 10 am to 8 pm daily. Available from both offices is the three-day Weimar Card (DM20), providing entry to most of Weimar's museums, unlimited travel on city buses and other benefits. Web site: www.weimar.de

Most of Weimar's museums and many cultural activities are managed by a trust foundation, the Stiftung Weimarer Klassik (☎ 54 51 02, fax 41 98 16, ✉ tobisch@weimar-klassik.de), whose information centre is at Frauentorstrasse 4.

The central post office is on the corner of Heinrich-Heine-Strasse and Schwanseestrasse. Times Square, inside Weimar Hauptbahnhof, is not only one of Germany's more tasteful train station cafe-bars, it's also a great Internet cafe (open daily; DM3 per 15 minutes). There's a convenient laundry at Graben 47.

Things to See & Do

A good place to begin your visit is on Herderplatz. The **Herderkirche** (1500) has an altarpiece (1555) by Lucas Cranach the Elder, who died before he could finish it. His son, Lucas Cranach the Younger, completed the work and included a portrait of his father (to the right of the crucifix, between John the Baptist and Martin Luther).

A block east of Herderplatz towards the Ilm River is Weimar's main art museum, the **Schlossmuseum** (closed Monday; DM6/3) on Burgplatz. The large collection, with masterpieces by Cranach, Dürer and others, occupies three floors of this castle, which was formerly the residence of the Elector of the Duchy of Saxony-Weimar. The **Neues Museum Weimar** at Rathenauplatz, north of the centre has excellent changing exhibitions of modern art (closed Monday; DM5/2.50).

Platz der Demokratie, with the renowned music school founded in 1872 by Franz Liszt, is south of the Sclossmuseum. This square spills over into Markt, where you'll find the neo-Gothic **Rathaus** (1841) and the **Cranachhaus**, in which Lucas Cranach the Elder spent his last two years and died (in 1553). West of Markt via some narrow lanes is Theaterplatz, with **Goethe and Schiller statues** (1857), and

GERMANY

GERMANY

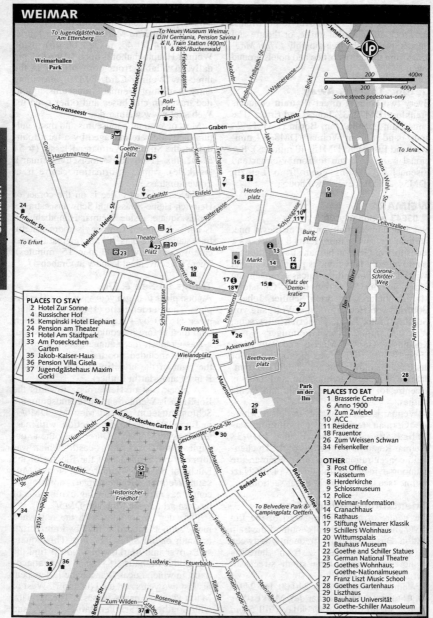

WEIMAR

To Jugendgästehaus Am Ettersberg

To Neues Museum Weimar, DJH Germania, Pension Savina I & II, Train Station (400m) & B85/Buchenwald

To Jena

To Erfurt

To Belvedere Park & Campingplatz Oettern

PLACES TO STAY
2 Hotel Zur Sonne
4 Russischer Hof
15 Kempinski Hotel Elephant
24 Pension am Theater
31 Hotel Am Stadtpark
33 Am Poseckschen Garten
35 Jakob-Kaiser-Haus
36 Pension Villa Gisela
37 Jugendgästehaus Maxim Gorki

PLACES TO EAT
1 Brasserie Central
6 Anno 1900
7 Zum Zwiebel
10 ACC
11 Residenz
18 Frauentor
26 Zum Weissen Schwan
34 Felsenkeller

OTHER
3 Post Office
5 Kasseturm
8 Herderkirche
9 Schlossmuseum
12 Police
13 Weimar-Information
14 Cranachhaus
16 Rathaus
17 Stiftung Weimarer Klassik
19 Schillers Wohnhaus
20 Wittumspalais
21 Bauhaus Museum
22 Goethe and Schiller Statues
23 German National Theatre
25 Goethes Wohnhaus;
    Goethe-Nationalmuseum
27 Franz Liszt Music School
28 Goethes Gartenhaus
29 Liszthaus
30 Bauhaus Universität
32 Goethe-Schiller Mausoleum

Some streets pedestrian-only

euro currency converter €1 = 1.95DM

the **German National Theatre**, where the constitution of the Weimar Republic was drafted in 1919. Opposite the theatre on this same square are the **Bauhaus Museum** (closed Monday; DM5/3) and the **Wittumspalais** (closed Monday; DM6/4), a museum dedicated to the poet Christoph Martin Wieland (1733-1813), who first translated Shakespeare's works into German.

Houses & Tombs From Theaterplatz, the elegant Schillerstrasse curves around to the **Schillers Wohnhaus** at No 12 (closed Tuesday; DM5/3). Schiller lived in Weimar from 1799 to 1805. Goethe, his contemporary, spent the years 1775 to 1832 here. **Goethes Wohnhaus** (DM8/5; closed Monday), a block ahead and then to the right along Frauentorstrasse, is where the immortal work *Faust* was written. Attached to the house is the **Goethe-Nationalmuseum** (open daily; DM8/5) with exhibits on Schiller, Goethe and their life and times.

The **Liszthaus** (closed Monday; entry DM4/3) is south on Marienstrasse by the edge of Park an der Ilm. Liszt resided in Weimar during 1848 and from 1869 to 1886, and here he wrote his *Hungarian Rhapsody* and *Faust Symphony*. In the yellow complex across the road from the Liszthaus, Walter Gropius laid the groundwork for modern architecture. The buildings themselves, erected by the famous architect Henry van de Velde between 1904 and 1911, now house Weimar's **Bauhaus Universität**.

The tombs of Goethe and Schiller lie side by side in a neoclassical crypt in the **Historischer Friedhof** (Historical Cemetery), two blocks west of the Liszthaus.

Parks & Palaces Weimar boasts three large parks, each replete with monuments, museums and attractions. Most accessible is **Park an der Ilm**, which runs right along the eastern side of Weimar and contains **Goethes Gartenhaus** (closed Tuesday; DM4/3). Goethe himself landscaped the park.

Several kilometres farther south is **Belvedere Park**, with its baroque castle housing the **Rokokomuseum** and the **Historic Coach Collection** (☎ 54 61 62; both open from April to October, closed Monday; combined entry DM6/3.50). The surrounding park is beautiful and very spacious. Take bus No 12 from Goetheplatz.

Places to Stay

For a flat fee of DM5 Weimar-Information arranges private rooms (from about DM40 per person).

Camping The closest camping ground is the *Campingplatz Oettern* (☎ 036453-802 64), open from May to November, at Oettern in the scenic Ilm Valley, 7km south-east of Weimar. Charges are DM5 per person, DM4 per vehicle, plus DM5 for a site.

Hostels Weimar has four DJH hostels. *Jugendherberge Germania* (☎ 85 04 90, fax 85 04 91, Carl-August-Allee 13), in the street running south (downhill) from the station, charges DM25/30 for juniors/seniors. *Am Poseckschen Garten* (☎ 85 07 92, fax 85 07 93, Humboldtstrasse 17) is more central but least comfortable. Beds are DM25/30.

Jugendgästehaus Maxim Gorki (☎ 85 07 50, fax 85 07 49, Zum Wilden Graben 12) on the southern uphill side of town (bus No 8 from the station), costs DM26/31. *Jugendgästehaus Am Ettersberg* (☎ 42 11 11, fax 42 11 12) at Ettersberg-Siedling (bus No 6 from the main train station to Obelisk) costs the same.

Pensions & Hotels *Savina II* (☎ 51 33 52, fax 86 69 11, ✉ pensionsavina@compuserve .com, Meyerstrasse 60) has bright rooms near the station (with attached kitchen) from DM78/138 for singles/doubles. Its sister, the tiny *Pension Savina I* (Rembrandtweg 13) charges DM59/104 for rooms without a shower and toilet (same contact details; breakfast served at Savina II). *Pension am Theater* (☎ 889 40, fax 88 94 32, Erfurter Strasse 10) has nice rooms with all facilities for DM85/125.

Pension Villa Gisela (☎ 886 80, fax 886 89, Wilhelm-Külz-Strasse 35) is in a quiet neighbourhood south of town and charges DM85/125. *Jakob-Kaiser-Haus* (☎ 246 30, fax 24 63 15, Wilhelm-Külz-Strasse 22), in an Art Nouveau style suburban villa, is DM95/140/160 single/double/triple, but book early as seminars are held here. For both of these take bus No 6 from the train station.

GERMANY

Hotel Zur Sonne (☎ 80 04 10, fax 86 29 32, Rollplatz 2) offers cramped but otherwise quite reasonable rooms for DM100/150. *Hotel Am Stadtpark* (☎ 248 30, fax 51 17 20, Amalienstrasse 19) specialises in twins and doubles for DM165.

Russischer Hof (☎ 77 40, fax 77 48 40, ℮ russischerhof@deraghotels.de, Goetheplatz 2) is at the top-end, with rooms for DM210/240. The historic *Kempinski Hotel Elephant* (☎ 80 20, fax 80 26 10, Markt 19) has standard-class accommodation for DM280/330.

All prices include breakfast.

Places to Eat

Anno 1900 (Geleitstrasse 12a), in a restored late 19th-century winter garden, has mains from DM14 to DM25 and also a couple of vegetarian dishes on the menu. *Zum Zwiebel* (Teichgasse 6) serves cheap hearty meals. *Brasserie Central* (☎ 85 27 74, Rollplatz 8a) is open till late and serves generous main dishes such as lamb goulash in wine sauce for DM18. *Frauentor* (Schillerstrasse 2) is a modern, swish and stylish cafe-restaurant. Main dishes here cost around DM15 to DM25. *Zum Weissen Schwan*, next to the Goethemuseum on Frauenplan, is a classic Weimar eating house whose patrons included Goethe, Schiller and Liszt. Quality main dishes are fairly well-priced at DM17 to DM36.

Another Weimar institution is the *Felsenkeller* (☎ 85 03 66, Humboldtstrasse 37) run by the local Felsenbräu brewery. The atmosphere is great, the beer is cheap, the food is good and well priced – no wonder it's often full.

The *Residenz* (Grüner Markt 4) has average, if well-priced, fare but some nice wines on offer. A young crowd gathers here to drink until late. *ACC* (☎ 85 11 61, Burgplatz 2) is right next door. This cafe-bar stays open till late, serves well-priced food, has occasional music, and houses an exhibition gallery upstairs.

Entertainment

The *German National Theatre* (☎ 755 334) on Theaterplatz is the main stage for Weimar's cultural activities. Goethe's theatrical works are regularly performed here along with many other productions. Tickets to the German National Theatre and other events can be bought at the tourist office.

The *Kasseturm*, a beer cellar in the round tower on Goetheplatz, has live music, disco or cabaret most nights.

Getting There & Away

There are frequent direct IR trains to Berlin-Zoo (DM75, three hours) via Naumburg and Halle, and to Frankfurt/Main (DM78, three hours) via Erfurt and Eisenach. IC/EC trains go to Dresden (DM65, 2½ hours) and Leipzig (DM31, 1¼ hours).

AROUND WEIMAR
Buchenwald

The Buchenwald museum and memorial are on Ettersberg Hill, 7km north-west of Weimar. You first pass the memorial with mass graves of some of the 56,500 WWII victims from 18 nations, including German antifascists, Jews, and Soviet and Polish prisoners of war. The concentration camp and museum are 1km beyond the memorial. Many prominent German communists and Social Democrats, Ernst Thälmann and Rudolf Breitscheid among them, were murdered here. On 11 April 1945, as US troops approached, the prisoners rebelled at 3.15 pm (the clock tower above the entrance still shows that time), overcame the SS guards and liberated themselves.

After the war the Soviet victors turned the tables by establishing Special Camp No 2, in which thousands of (alleged) anticommunists and former Nazis were worked to death.

The main Buchenwald museum and concentration camp (☎ 46 43) are open 9.45 am to 6 pm daily except Monday (8.45 am to 5 pm from October to April). Last entry is 45 minutes before closing. Bus No 6 runs via Goetheplatz and Weimar train station to Buchenwald roughly every 40 minutes. Admission is free.

EISENACH
☎ 03691 • pop 45,000

The birthplace of Johann Sebastian Bach, Eisenach is a small picturesque city on the edge of the Thuringian Forest. Its main attraction is the Wartburg castle, from where the landgraves (German counts) ruled medieval Thuringia. Martin Luther went into hiding here under the assumed name of Junker

Jörg after being excommunicated and put under a papal ban.

Orientation & Information

Markt, Eisenach's central square, is reached on foot in 15 minutes from the train station by following Bahnhofstrasse west to Karlsplatz and then continuing west along the pedestrianised Karlstrasse. Wartburg is 2km south-west of town.

The friendly and well-organised Eisenach-Information (☎ 194 33, fax 67 09 60, @ tou rist-info@eisenach-tourist.de) is on Markt at No 2. It's open 10 am to 6 pm Monday, 9 am to 6 pm Tuesday to Friday, and 10 am to 2 pm on weekends. Its three-day Classic-Card (DM24) provides free admission to the castle, most museums and use of public transport.

Wartburg

The superb old castle, on a forested hill overlooking Eisenach, is world famous. Martin Luther translated the New Testament from Greek into German while in hiding here (1521-22), thus making an enormous contribution to the development of the written German language. You can only visit the castle's interior with a guided tour (most tours are in German), which includes the museum, Luther's study room and the amazing Romanesque great hall. Tours run continuously 8.30 am to 5 pm, March to October (9 am to 3.30 pm in winter) and cost DM11/6; arrive early to avoid the crowds. Guided tours in English are only possible by prior reservation (at least two weeks beforehand in summer) through Wartburg-Information (☎ 7 70 73) at Am Schlossberg 2. A free English-language leaflet set out in the sequence of the tour is available.

To get to the Wartburg castle on foot, go one block west of Markt to Wydenbrugkstrasse and a steep signposted lane called Schlossberg, which leads 2km south-west through forest to the castle. Between April and October there's also a shuttle bus running up to the castle; it leaves from the terminal in front of the train station roughly every hour (DM2.50 return).

Places to Stay & Eat

The nearest camping ground is the **Camping-platz Altenberger See** (☎ 21 56 37, Neubau 24), 7km south of town in Wilhelmsthal. Charges are DM5 for a site plus DM7 per per-

son and DM2 per car. **Jugendherberge Artur Becker** (☎ 74 32 59, fax 74 32 60, Mariental 24) is in the valley below Wartburg. The cost for juniors/seniors is DM25/30. Take bus No 3 from the station to Liliengrund.

Eisenach-Information has a free room-finding service (for around DM45 per person). **Gasthof Storchenturm** (☎/fax 21 52 50, Georgenstrasse 43) has small rooms for DM53/85 with shower and toilet. **Pension Mahret** (☎ 74 27 44, fax 750 33, Neustadt 30) offers apartments with shower and toilet for DM78/116 (discounts on longer stays; without breakfast). The small **Pension Christine Kilian** (☎/fax 21 11 22, Kapellenstrasse 8) is in Eisenach's southern suburbs. It has doubles from DM90 with shower and toilet. The historic **Hotel Thuringer Hof** (☎ 280, fax 28 19 00, @ thueringer–hof@t-online.de, Karlsplatz 11) is central and has pleasant rooms starting at DM150/195 with breakfast.

The **Kartoffelkeller** (Sophienstrasse 44) serves quite good dishes with a spud focus for about DM10 to DM20.

Getting There & Away

Use the frequent regional or IR services to Erfurt (DM15, 40 minutes) and Weimar (DM19, 50 minutes) rather than the IC as they are far cheaper and take only a few minutes longer. IR services run direct to Frankfurt/Main and Berlin-Zoo.

Saxony-Anhalt

The State of Saxony-Anhalt (Sachsen-Anhalt) comprises the former East German districts of Magdeburg and Halle. Originally part of the duchy of Saxony, medieval Anhalt was split into smaller units by the sons of various princes. In 1863 Leopold IV of Anhalt-Dessau united the three existing duchies, and in 1871 his realm was made a state of the German Reich.

The mighty Elbe River flows north-west across Saxony-Anhalt, past Lutherstadt Wittenberg and Magdeburg on its way to the North Sea at Hamburg. On the Saale River south of Magdeburg is Halle.

The Harz Mountains fill the south-western corner of Saxony-Anhalt and spread across into Lower Saxony to Goslar (see the Harz

GERMANY

Mountains map in the Lower Saxony section). Historical towns like Quedlinburg and Wernigerode lie near the gentle, wooded slopes and are highly recommended. Its two largest cities, Magdeburg and Halle, are only of limited interest to visitors.

WERNIGERODE
☎ 03943 • pop 35,500
Wernigerode is flanked by the foothills of the Harz Mountains. A romantic ducal castle rises above the old town, which contains some 1000 half-timbered houses from five centuries in various states of repair. Summer throngs of tourists have brought cash that has all but erased any trace of the old GDR. The century-old steam-powered, narrow-gauge Harzquerbahn runs a gorgeous 60km route south to Nordhausen and also to Brocken, the highest mountain in northern Germany (1142m).

Orientation & Information
From Bahnhofsplatz, Rudolf-Breitscheid-Strasse leads south-east to Breite Strasse, which runs south-west to Markt, the old town centre. The tourist office (☎ 194 33, fax 63 20 40, @ wernigerod-tg@netco.de) is near Markt at Nicolaiplatz 1 (open 9 am to 7 pm weekdays, 10 am to 3 pm Saturday and 10 am to 3 pm Sunday; closing at 6 pm weekdays from October to April).

Things to See & Do
It's nice to wander along the streets of the medieval old town centre. The **Rathaus** (1277) on Markt, with its pair of pointed black-slate towers, is a focal point. From here it's just a short climb to the neo-Gothic **castle**. First built in the 12th century, the castle has been renovated and enlarged over the centuries and got its current fairy-tale facade from Count Otto of Stolberg-Wernigerode in the 19th century. The castle's museum (open daily from May to October; otherwise closed Monday; DM8/7) has a nice chapel and Great Hall.

Activities
There are plenty of short walks and day hikes nearby. The beautiful deciduous forest behind the castle is highly recommended. The more serious might tackle the 30km route (marked by blue crosses) from Mühlental south-east of the town centre to Elbingerode,

Königshütte, with its 18th-century wooden church, and the remains of medieval Trageburg castle at Trautenstein. The tourist office can make suggestions and you'll need a good topographic map for some of them. Or explore the region by mountain bike, available from Hallermann (☎ 63 25 08), Breite Strasse 27, for DM15 per day.

Wernigerode is the major northern terminus for steam train services throughout the Harz Mountains and Hochharz National Park. For information contact Harzer Schmalspurbahnen (☎ 55 81 43, fax 55 81 48), Marktstrasse 3. Services to Brocken from Wernigerode cost DM26/42 one way/return (1¾ hours), and to Nordhausen-Nord DM17/27 (three hours). There is a three-day steam-train pass for DM80 and a one-week pass for DM100. Web site: www.hsb-wr.de.

Places to Stay
The non-DJH *Jugendgästaehaus* (☎/fax 63 20 61, Friedrichstrasse 53) has dorm beds for DM27. Take bus No 1 or 4 to Kirchstrasse.

Rooms booked through the tourist office's free room-finding service cost around DM45. *Hotel zur Tanne* (☎ 63 25 54, fax 67 37 35, Breite Strasse 59) charges DM40/60 for basic singles/doubles or DM80/95 with bathroom. *Hotel zur Post* (☎ 690 40, fax 69 04 30, Marktstrasse 17) has rooms with a bathroom for DM95/160. *Pension Schweizer Hof* (☎/fax 63 20 98, Salzbergstrasse 13) caters to hikers, with route information and charges from DM65/100. *Gothisches Haus* (☎ 67 50, fax 67 55 37, @ gothisches-haus@travelcharme.com, Am Markt 1) is the place to splurge, with rates of DM170/250 and lower off-peak prices.

Places to Eat
Altwernigerode Kartoffelhaus (*Marktstrasse 14*) serves well-priced traditional and potato dishes. *Nonnenhof* at Am Markt adjoining Gothisches Haus has regional specialties for around DM15 and there's also a good up-market restaurant in Gothisches Haus itself. *d.a.g. Guinnesskneipe* (*Kleine Bergstrasse 13*) does only light snacks but is a great place to drink in the evening.

Getting There & Away
For details on bus services in the western Harz, see the Getting Around section under

Western Harz Mountains in Lower Saxony. There are frequent trains to Goslar (DM12, 30 minutes), which connect with services to Hanover (DM36, 2½ hours). Direct trains go to Halle (DM31, two hours), and also to Halberstadt (DM8, 30 minutes) with connections to Magdeburg (DM22, 1½ hours), where you can change for Berlin (DM62, three hours).

QUEDLINBURG
☎ 03946 • pop 26,000

One of Germany's true gems, Quedlinburg dates back over 1000 years. It once exercised considerable power in German affairs through a collegiate foundation for widows and daughters of the nobility. Almost all buildings in the centre are half-timbered, street after cobbled street of them, earning Quedlinburg the honour of being a Unesco World Heritage site.

Orientation & Information
The centre of the old town is a 10-minute walk from the train station down Bahnhofstrasse. Quedlinburg-Information (☎ 90 56 24, fax 90 56 29, ✉ Q.T.M@t-online.de) is at Markt 2. It opens 9 am to 7 pm weekdays from May to September, 10 am to 4 pm weekends. It closes an hour earlier in March, April, October and December, and in November, January and February it's open till 5 pm weekdays only.

Things to See & Do
The Renaissance **Rathaus** (1615) on Markt has its own Roland statue (1426), however, the real focal point for visitors is the hill just south-west with the old castle district, known as **Schlossberg**. The area features the Romanesque **Church of St Servatii** (1129) or 'Dom' (closed Monday; DM6/4), with a 10th-century crypt and priceless reliquaries and early Bibles. In 1938 SS meetings were held in the Dom – a 'Germanic solemn shrine'. On a more contemporary note, try visiting the **Lyonel-Feininger-Galerie** (closed Monday; DM6/3) where you can view brilliant works by this Bauhaus artist who fled the Nazis and settled in America.

To get in some hiking, take a bus or train 10km south-west to Thale, the starting point for hikes along the lovely Bode Valley in the Harz Mountains. From here it's just a short walk to Hexentanzplatz, site of a raucous celebration during *Walpurgisnacht* every 30 April, believed in German folklore to be the night of a witches' sabbath. Also worthwhile is a visit to Gernrode and its delightful **Church of St Cyriakus**, just 8km south of Quedlinburg.

Places to Stay & Eat
Hotel and private rooms can be booked free of charge through Quedlinburg-Information. The central *Familie Klindt* (☎ 70 29 11, *Hohe Strasse 19*) has budget, basic rooms for DM30/50. *Hotel Zum Augustinern* (☎ 77 16 11, *fax 70 12 35, Reichenstrasse 35a*) has good rooms for DM70/110 with facilities. *Hotel am Dippeplatz* (☎ 77 14 11, fax 91 59 92, *Breite Strasse 16*) is bright and clean and the rates are DM80/140. *ROMANTIK Hotel Theophano* (☎ 963 00, fax 96 30 36, ✉ theophano@t-online.de, *Markt 13/14*) is top of the range, with prices from DM120/160 and there's a good upmarket restaurant in the adjacent cellar.

Kartoffelhaus No 1 (*Breite Strasse 37*) serves filling meals for all budgets. *Brauhaus Lüdde* (*Blasiistrasse 14*) has hearty pub food from DM14 to DM22 and brews its own pilsener, *Altbier* and the sweetish low-alcohol Pubarschknall.

Getting There & Away
There are hourly trains to/from Halberstadt (DM6, 17 minutes) where you can connect to Wernigerode (DM12, one hour). Direct trains go to Magdeburg (DM19, 1¼ hours), where you can change for Berlin-Zoo (DM60, three hours). Going to/from Halle (DM24, two hours), you must change at the hamlet of Wegeleben. Trains leave hourly for Gernrode (DM3, 14 minutes).

MAGDEBURG
☎ 0391 • pop 240,000

Magdeburg, on the Elbe River, lies at a strategic crossing of transport routes from Thuringia to the Baltic and Western Europe to Berlin. It was severely damaged by wartime bombing and much of it is now an unfortunate example of the worst GDR post-war reconstruction. The main reason for visiting Magdeburg, the capital of Saxony-Anhalt, is for its splendid churches and Gothic cathedral.

GERMANY

Orientation & Information

From the broad square in front of the train station, take Ernst-Reuter-Allee east towards a bridge over the Elbe. After two large blocks, turn left (north) into Breiter Weg to Alter Markt. Tourist Information Magdeburg (☎ 540 49 01, fax 540 49 10), Julius-Bremer-Strasse 10, is just north of Alter Markt. It's open 10 am to 6 pm weekdays and 10 am to 1 pm Saturday.

Things to See & Do

The centre of the old town is **Alter Markt**, with a copy of the bronze **Magdeburger Reiter** (Magdeburg Rider; 1240) of Otto the Great facing the high-Renaissance **Rathaus** (1698). South of the bridge is Magdeburg's oldest building, the 12th-century Romanesque convent **Unser Lieben Frauen**, now a museum (closed Monday; DM4/2, although you can enter the cloister and church for free). A little farther south is the soaring Gothic **Dom** (open from 10 am to 4 pm daily). The cathedral, the second tallest in Germany after Cologne, has evocative and moody cloisters.

Places to Stay & Eat

The simple but pleasant *Campingplatz Barleber See* (☎ 50 32 44) is 8km north of town right on a lake. Take tram No 10 to the last stop. The DJH *Jugendgästehaus Magdeburg* (☎ 53 21 01, fax 53 21 02, ✉ jugendher bergemagdeburg@gmx.de, Leiterstrasse 10) charges DM34/39 junior/senior. Go right for 50m out of the station, then turn left on Hasselbachstrasse. You can get good private rooms from about DM40 through the tourist office, for a DM5 fee. The *Bildungshotel* (☎ 251 50 40, fax 251 50 65, Lorenzweg 56) charges DM75/95 for quite good singles/doubles. The *InterCity Hotel* (☎ 596 20, fax 499, Bahnhofstrasse 69), with rooms for DM95/130, is a good option in the centre of town.

The *Deneckes Kartoffelhaus* (Otto-v.-Guericke-Strasse 57) has filling mains from DM12 to DM26. There is a produce market on Alter Markt daily except Sunday

Getting There & Away

There are frequent regional trains to/from Berlin-Zoo (DM40, 1½ hours) and trains to Leipzig (DM34, 1½ hours), Hanover (DM44, 1½ hours) and Quedlinburg (DM20, 1¼

hours); and IC/ICE connections to Frankfurt (DM153, 3¾ hours) with a change in Braunschweig. Change trains in Halberstadt for Wernigerode (DM22, 1¼ hours).

LUTHERSTADT WITTENBERG
☎ 03491 • pop 52,000

Wittenberg is where Martin Luther did most of his work, including launching the Protestant Reformation in 1517 which changed the face of Europe. Ever quotable, Luther hurled vitriol at the corrupt church in Rome, even calling the Vatican a 'gigantic, bloodsucking worm'. Wittenberg can be seen in a day from a Berlin base, but is worth a longer look.

Orientation & Information

Hauptbahnhof Lutherstadt Wittenberg, the stop for all the fast trains, is a 15-minute walk from the city centre. Go under the tracks and on to Collegienstrasse. Wittenberg-Information (☎ 49 86 10, fax 49 86 11, ✉ wb–info@wit tenberg.de), Schlossplatz 2, is open 9 am to 6 pm weekdays, 10 am to 3 pm Saturday, and 11 am to 4 pm Sunday. It opens 10 am to 4 pm weekdays from November to February, and closes an hour earlier on weekends. The Historic Mile (DM4.80) is a very good English-language guide to the city. Check the Web site at www.wittenberg.de.

Things to See & Do

The **Lutherhaus** (DM7/3) is a Reformation museum inside Lutherhalle, a former monastery at Collegienstrasse 54. It contains an original room furnished by Luther in 1535. He stayed here in 1508 while teaching at Wittenberg University and made the building his home for the rest of his life after returning in 1511.

The large altarpiece in **Stadtkirche St Marien** was created jointly by Renaissance painter Lucas Cranach the Elder and his son in 1547. It shows Luther, his friend and supporter Melanchthon and other Reformation figures, as well as Cranach the Elder himself, in Biblical contexts. In June 1525 Luther married ex-nun Katharina von Bora in this church, where he also preached. The town recalls the nuptials in a marriage festival each June that's ripe for reform. The **Luthereiche**, the site where Luther burnt the papers that threatened his

GERMANY

excommunication, is on the corner of Luther-strasse and Am Bahnhof.

Imposing monuments to Luther and Melanchthon stand in front of the impressive **Altes Rathaus** (1535) on Markt. On one corner of Markt is the **Cranachhaus**, Schlosstrasse 1, which has a picturesque courtyard.

At the western end of town is **Wittenberg Castle** (1499) with its huge, rebuilt church onto whose door Luther allegedly nailed his *95 Theses* on 31 October 1517. His tombstone lies below the pulpit, and Melanchthon's is opposite.

Places to Stay & Eat

The camping ground *Bergwitz* (☎ *034921-282 28*), in the village of Kemberg, is some 11km south of town on Lake Bergwitz. There are hourly trains. The often-mobbed *Jugendherberge* (☎ */fax 40 32 55*) is upstairs in Wittenberg Castle (DM22/27 juniors/seniors, sheets DM6).

Wittenberg-Information finds private rooms from DM40 per person. *Gasthaus Central* (☎*/fax 41 15 72, Mittelstrasse 20*) has clean singles/doubles for DM58/92 with bathroom. The *Best Western Stadtpalais* (☎ *42 50, fax 42 51 00*, ✉ *info@stadtpalais.bestwestern.de, Collegienstrasse 56-7*) has good rooms with breakfast from DM145/185.

Most of the town's food options are on or near Collegienstrasse.

Getting There & Away

Wittenberg is on the main train line between Berlin (DM39, one hour) and Leipzig (DM23, 45 minutes) and has direct trains to/from Halle (DM16, one hour). Every two hours IC trains run to/from Berlin-Ostbahnhof, stopping at Schönefeld airport (DM31, 50 minutes).

HALLE

☎ 0345 • pop 262,000

The former state capital and largest city in Saxony-Anhalt, Halle is as untouristy as you might expect of a city that was the centre of the GDR chemical industry. Halle is a university town, a modest cultural centre and, unfortunately, has Germany's highest crime rate.

Orientation & Information

To walk to the city centre from the Hauptbahnhof, head through the underpass and down the pedestrian Leipziger Strasse past the 15th-century Leipziger Turm to Markt, Halle's central square. Halle-Information (☎ 202 33 40, fax 50 27 98) is in the unmistakable elevated gallery built around the 1506 Roter Turm on the Markt. It's open 10 am to 6 pm weekdays, and also 10 am to 2 pm weekends from May to September.

Things to See & Do

The Markt has a statue (1859) of the great composer Georg Friedrich Händel, who was born in Halle in 1685. The four tall towers of **Marktkirche** (1529) loom above the square, and you can climb one for a view of the city. Don't miss the exquisitely decorated Gothic interior.

The **Händelhaus** (open daily; DM5/3) at Grosse Nikolai Strasse 5 was the composer's birthplace and now houses a major collection of musical instruments. Nearby on Friedemann Bachplatz is the imposing 15th-century **Moritzburg** castle (closed Monday; DM5/3), a former residence of the archbishops of Magdeburg that now contains a museum of 19th and 20th-century art, including GDR art and some impressive German expressionist works. Look for the goofy workers' monument, **Die Fäuste** (The Fists), on Riebeck Platz, looking like a pulled tooth; and the GDR-built **Trabant** car atop the Neues Theater.

Places to Stay & Eat

The municipal *Am Nordbad Campingplatz* (☎ *523 40 85, Am Nordbad 12*) is near the Saale River (open from early May until late September; take tram No 2 or 3 to Am Nordbad). The central *Jugendherberge* (☎ *202 47 16, fax 202 51 72, August-Bebel-Strasse 48a*) charges DM24/29 for juniors/seniors.

The tourist office can find private rooms from DM35 per person. The small *Pension Am Alten Markt* (☎ *521 14 11, fax 523 29 56, Schmeerstrasse 3*) charges DM95/110 with shower and WC.

Zum Kleinen Sandberg (☎ *202 31 09, fax 202 54 88, Kleiner Sandberg 5*) is very central and has rustic singles/doubles for DM120/180, and basic rooms for DM100/ 160. The restaurant downstairs serves good food in the DM20 to DM35 range and a cheaper lunch special.

India Gate (☎ *202 11 35, Grosse-Ulrich-Strasse 36*) has cheap student menus for less than DM12 and other dishes from about DM15 to DM25.

Getting There & Away

Several trains an hour go to/from Leipzig (DM10, 30 minutes). Direct IR trains go to/from Berlin-Zoo (DM48, two hours).

NAUMBURG
☎ 03445 • pop 32,000

Naumburg is one of those pretty little medieval towns for which Germany is famous. It is strategically located between Halle/Leipzig and Weimar, and the scenic Unstrut Valley lies to the north-west. It can be hurriedly seen in a two-hour break between trains but really deserves a day.

Orientation & Information

The main train station (Naumburg/Saale) is 1.5km north-west of the old town. Out of the station take Markgrafenweg to Rossbacher Strasse, then turn left and walk to Bauernweg, which heads up the hill. From here, follow the curving road to the cathedral. Markt, the central square, is five minutes from the cathedral along the pedestrian quarter. Alternatively, bus Nos 1 and 2 run frequently from the train station to Markt or nearby Theaterplatz.

Naumburg's helpful tourist office (☎ 20 16 14, fax 26 60 47, ✉ stadt.naumburg@t-onli ne.de), Markt 6, is open 9 am to 6 pm weekdays and 9 am to 4 pm on Saturday. You can visit Naumburg's major sights using the free *A Walk Through Town* brochure. There is a souvenir store posing as a tourist office across from the cathedral.

Things to See & Do

In the ancient western quarter of the town stands the magnificent late-Romanesque/early-Gothic **Dom Sts Peter and Paul**, filled with art treasures like the famous 13th-century statues of Uta and Ekkehard in the west choir. Don't miss the 1972 bronze handrails on the stairs to the east choir. It's open 9 am to 6 pm Monday to Saturday and noon to 6 pm Sunday (slightly shorter hours from October to February; DM6/3). Ask for an information sheet in English. Naumburg's picturesque **Rathaus** (1528) and Gothic **Stadtkirche St Wenzel**, built between 1218 and 1523, rise above Markt. Friedrich Nietzsche fans will want to make a

pilgrimage to **Nietzsche-Haus**, Weingarten 18 (DM3/1.50).

Naumburg is an ideal base for hiking, cycling and kayaking in the picturesque Saale-Unstrut region. The tourist office can help you with places to rent gear.

Places to Stay & Eat

Campingplatz Blütengrund (☎ 20 27 11), 1.5km north-east of Naumburg at the confluence of the Saale and Unstrut Rivers, charges DM7 per person. The large *Jugendherberge* (☎ /fax 70 34 22), Am Tennisplatz 9, 1.5km south of the town centre, has double rooms at DM28/34 juniors/seniors. Multibed rooms go for DM24/29.

The tourist office organises private rooms; expect to pay around DM30 per person for somewhere central. *Gasthaus St Othmar* (☎/fax 20 12 13, Othmarsplatz 7) is a restored historic hotel with rooms from DM50/90 with shower and WC. *St Wenzel* (☎ 717 90, fax 717 93 01, Fr-Nietsche-Strasse 21a), a 10-minute walk from Markt, charges DM60/90 with facilities. *Hotel Stadt Aachen* (☎ 24 70, fax 24 71 30, Markt 11) has clean, quality rooms for DM95/155.

The *Magnus Carolus* restaurant in Hotel Stadt Aachen is excellent value with traditional main courses for under DM25. The *Gerichtsklause am Dom* (Domplatz 12a) serves well-priced and tasty dishes in a lilac-bedecked beer garden.

Getting There & Away

Frequent IR trains stop at Naumburg going to/from Berlin (DM64, 2½ hours), Weimar (DM12, 30 minutes) and Frankfurt (DM89, 3½ hours). Regular IC trains go to/from Leipzig (DM22, 45 minutes).

Mecklenburg-Western Pomerania

The state of Mecklenburg-Western Pomerania (Mecklenburg-Vorpommern) is a low-lying, postglacial region of lakes, meadows, forests and Baltic Sea (Ostsee) beaches, stretching across northern Germany from Schleswig-Holstein to Poland. Most of the state is historic Mecklenburg; only the island of Rügen and the area from Stralsund to the Polish border traditionally belong to Western Pomerania, or Vorpommern.

In 1160 the Duke of Saxony, Heinrich (Henry the Lion), Christianised the region and made the local Polish princes his vassals. Germanisation gradually reduced the Slavonic element, and in 1348 the dukes of Mecklenburg became princes of the Holy Roman Empire. Sweden entered the scene during the Thirty Years' War (1618-48). In 1867 the whole region joined the North German Confederation and, in 1871, the German Reich.

Offshore islands like Poel and Hiddensee are largely untouched, while others, including Rügen, are popular resorts. Just keep in mind the very short swimming season (July and August usually).

SCHWERIN
☎ 0385 • pop 105,000
Schwerin's surrounding lakes make this one of the most picturesque towns in eastern Germany. The town gets its name from a Slavic castle known as Zaurin (animal pasture) on the site of the present Schloss. This former seat of the Grand Duchy of Mecklenburg – now the capital of Mecklenburg-Western Pomerania – is an interesting mix of renovated 16th and 17th-century half-timbered houses and 19th-century architecture.

Orientation & Information
Down the hill to the east of the train station is Pfaffenteich, the lake whose southern end is at the beginning of Schwerin's main street, Mecklenburgstrasse. Markt is one block east of here. Farther south, around Alter Garten on the Schweriner See, are the monumental Marstall (the former royal stables), the Schloss (ducal castle), and the museums, parks, tour boats and other treats. Schwerin-Information (☎ 592 52 13, fax 55 50 94, ✉ stadtmarketing-schwerin@t-online.de), Am Markt 10, is open 10 am to 6 pm weekdays. It closes at 2 pm on weekends (closed Sunday from May to September).

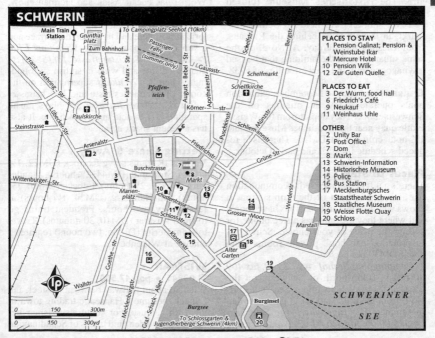

SCHWERIN

PLACES TO STAY
1 Pension Galinat; Pension & Weinstube Ikar
4 Mercure Hotel
10 Pension Wilk
12 Zur Guten Quelle

PLACES TO EAT
3 Der Wurm; food hall
6 Friedrich's Café
9 Neukauf
11 Weinhaus Uhle

OTHER
2 Unity Bar
5 Post Office
7 Dom
8 Markt
13 Schwerin-Information
14 Historisches Museum
15 Police
16 Bus Station
17 Mecklenburgisches Staatstheater Schwerin
18 Staatliches Museum
19 Weisse Flotte Quay
20 Schloss

Things to See & Do

Above **Markt** rises the tall 14th-century Gothic **Dom** (open daily, usually at least from 11 am to 3 pm); you can climb the 219 steps up the 19th-century church tower (DM2) for the view. The cathedral is a superb example of north German red and glazed-black brick architecture.

South-east of Alter Garten, over the causeway, is Schwerin's neo-Gothic **Schloss**, on an island connected to the **Schlossgarten** by a further causeway. Admission to the superb interior costs DM8/6. On the city side of Alter Garten is the **Staatliches Museum** (DM7 /3.50), which has an excellent collection of works by old Dutch masters. All these sights are open 10 am to 8 pm Tuesday and 10 am to 6 pm Wednesday to Sunday, closing one hour earlier November to March. A special ticket for these and other attractions is available from Schwerin-Information for DM9.50.

The dramatic cream-coloured building next to the art museum is the **Mecklenburgisches Staatstheater Schwerin**, or state theatre. The **Historisches Museum** (closed Monday; DM3) is at Grosser Moor 38.

Town **markets** are held on Schlachtermarkt, in the old town behind the Rathaus, from Tuesday to Saturday. At No 3, on the same square, stands the building that housed a synagogue until the Nazi atrocities of 1938.

Cruises From May to September, excursion boats operate every 30 minutes on the Schweriner See. They depart from the Weisse Flotte quay near the Staatliches Museum, and 1½-hour cruises cost DM15. There is a reduced schedule in April and early October.

Places to Stay

There's a nifty computerised accommodation list and map in front of the train station. It shows which hotels and pensions have rooms and where they are, and has a free phone for calling the place of your choice. Schwerin-Information can book private rooms from about DM30 per person.

Campingplatz Seehof (☎ *51 25 40, fax 409 40 68*) is 10km north of Schwerin on the western shore of Schweriner See (take bus No 8 from the train station). It gets crowded in summer. The *Jugendherberge Schwerin* (☎ *326 00 06, fax 326 03 03, Waldschulweg*

3) is about 4km south of the city centre (take bus No 14 from Marienplatz; DM25/DM30 juniors/seniors).

The central *Pension Wilk* (☎ *550 70 24, Buschstrasse 13*) has simple doubles for DM70. Also central, *Pension Galinat* (☎ *73 34 61, Steinstrasse 1*) has nice basic rooms for DM50/75, or DM75/110 with a bathroom. Next door, *Pension & Weinstube Ikar* (☎ *73 44 73, fax 758 88 50,* ✉ *info@pension-ikar.de, Steinstrasse 3*) is also reasonable, with rates of DM75/110 with bathroom. *Zur Guten Quelle* (☎ *56 59 85, Schusterstrasse 12*) charges DM105/140 for rooms with facilities and has a good restaurant downstairs. The *Mercure Hotel* (☎ *595 50, fax 59 55 59,* ✉ *mercure .schwerin@t-online.de, Wismarsche Strasse 107-9*) has helpful staff and good singles/ doubles from DM150/170 (breakfast DM23) and cheaper weekend deals.

Places to Eat

The *food hall* in the shopping centre on Wittenburger Strasse known as *Der Wurm* (The Worm) has cheap Asian and German chow. *Friedrich's Café (Friedrichstrasse 2)* serves mid-priced traditional dishes in a warm, historic atmosphere and has a popular terrace and a superb view of the water. *Weinhaus Uhle* (☎ *56 29 56, Schusterstrasse 13-15*) offers quality cuisine and wine in stylish surroundings. There's a *Neukauf* supermarket on the corner of Schmiedestrasse and Buschstrasse. *Unity Bar (Arsenalstrasse 36)* plays music spanning jazz to acid and is open late. It also has a decent snack menu.

Getting There & Away

Various IR trains serve Rostock (DM22, 1¼ hours), Stralsund (DM44, 2¼ hours), Magdeburg (DM52, 2½ hours), Lübeck (DM20, 1¼ hours) and Hamburg (DM34, 1¼ hours) at least every two hours. Frequent trains go to/from Wismar (DM10, 30 minutes). Travel to/from Berlin (DM65, two hours) requires a change at Wittenberge.

WISMAR

☎ 03841 • pop 47,500

Wismar, about halfway between Rostock and Lübeck, became a Hanseatic trading town in the 13th century. For centuries Wismar belonged to Sweden, and traces of Scandinavian rule can still be seen (and heard). It's less hectic than Rostock or Stralsund and is a pretty little town worth seeing for its historic centre and crumbling architectural gems.

Information
Wismar-Information (☎ 258 15, fax 25 18 19, @ touristinfo@wismar.de) at Am Markt 11 is very helpful. The office is open 9 am to 6 pm daily.

Things to See & Do
Of the three great red-brick churches that once rose above the rooftops, only **St Nikolai** survived the Anglo-American bombing raids during WWII intact. The massive red shell of **St Georgenkirche** is under long-term restoration. Cars now park where the 13th-century **St Marienkirche** once stood, although the great brick steeple (1339), partly restored, still towers above. Apart from this, it's hard to believe that Wismar's gabled houses were badly bombed.

In a corner of Markt is the Dutch Renaissance **Wasserkunst** waterworks (1602) and the **Rathaus** (1819), whose basement houses the town's historical museum (DM2/1). The Renaissance **Schabbellhaus** (1571), at Schweinsbrücke 8 near St Nikolai, has art exhibitions and special displays, including a horrific display of rotted teeth yanked by a local dentist.

Busy town **markets** are held on Tuesday, Thursday and Saturday on Am Markt. On Saturday, a lively fish market takes place at Alter Hafen.

Wismar is the gateway to **Poel Island**, a beach resort that is renowned for its preserved natural beauty. Take bus No 430 from Grossschmiedestrasse, just off Marktplatz, to Kirchdorf (DM3.80), where there's a Kurverwaltung (☎ 038425-203 47) at Wismarsche Strasse 2.

Places to Stay & Eat
The nearest *camping ground* ☎ 64 23 77, Am Strand 19c) is 9km north-west of Wismar in Zierow. Take bus No 401 or the B105. The *Jugendherberge* (☎ 326 80, fax 32 68 68, Juri-Gagarin-ring 30a) is a 15 minute walk from the centre in Friedenshof or can be reached with bus D from the main train station (DM29/34 juniors/seniors).

Wismar-Information arranges private rooms from DM40 per person (DM5 booking fee).

The central *Pension Chez Fasan* (☎ 21 34 25, fax 20 22 85, Bademutterstrasse 19) offers good value at DM40/80 (breakfast DM7.50 extra).

Historic *Hotel Altes Brauhaus* (☎ 21 14 16, fax 28 32 23, Lübsche Strasse 37) has rooms from DM90/120 with bathroom. *New Orleans Hotel* (☎ 268 60, fax 26 86 10, Runde Grube 3), a modern hotel and restaurant on the waterfront, offers southern comforts from DM85/120 with facilities. *Hotel Stadt Hamburg* (☎ 23 90, fax 23 92 39, @ hotelsthh@aol.com, Am Markt 24) has pleasant rooms for DM155/195, rising to DM215/255 for top of the range.

A string of restaurants and bars line the car-free Am Lohberg near the fishing harbour. *Brauhaus am Lohberg* (☎ 25 02 38) brews its own beer and serves traditional dishes from around DM6 to DM35. *Pier 10* (☎ 21 01 25, Am Lohberg 10) is a seafood place with a comfy outdoor area. Markt and the nearby pedestrian streets have cafes and some fast-food places. *Alter Schwede* (☎ 28 35 52, Alter Markt 19) is an upmarket option in Wismar's oldest burgher house.

Getting There & Away
Regional trains run to/from Rostock every hour (DM15, 1¼ hours) and regularly to/from Schwerin (DM10, 30 minutes). Buses run daily except Sunday to Lübeck from beside the train station (DM10, two hours).

ROSTOCK
☎ 0381 • pop 211,500
Rostock, the largest city in lightly populated north-eastern Germany, is a major Baltic port and shipbuilding centre. In the 14th and 15th centuries Rostock was an important Hanseatic city trading with Rīga, Bergen and Bruges. Rostock University, founded in 1419, was the first in northern Europe.

The years after reunification were difficult in Rostock – unemployment soared and neo-Nazis engaged in attacks on foreign workers which brought national and worldwide condemnation. Now, however, the city is working hard to improve conditions. The city centre along Kröpeliner Strasse and the former dock area on the Warnow have been redeveloped into pleasant pedestrian quarters. The sights can easily occupy a day and

GERMANY

the beach resort of Warnemünde is only 12km north.

Orientation & Information

Rostock-Information (☎ 194 33, 381 22 22, fax 381 26 01, ✉ touristinfo@rostock.de) is in the old post office building at Neuer Markt 3-8, about 1.5km from the train station. It's open 10 am to 7 pm weekdays and till 4 pm weekends from May to September. The rest of the year it closes at 6 pm weekdays. Take tram No 11 or 12 from outside the station. The tourist office sells the 48-hour Rostock Card (DM15), which entitles holders to a free tour of town, various reductions for sights and performances, and free public transport (including the S-Bahn to/from Warnemünde). Rostock's main post office is in the same building. Web information on Rostock is at www.rostock.de.

Things to See & Do

Rostock's splendid 13th-century **Marien-kirche** (DM2/1), Am Ziegenmarkt, survived WWII unscathed. This huge brick edifice contains a functioning astronomical clock (1472), a Gothic bronze baptismal font (1290), a Renaissance pulpit (1574) and a baroque organ (1770). For a bird's-eye view of town, however, scale the stairs or take the lift up the tower of the **Petrikirche** on Alter Markt (DM3.50/2.50).

Kröpeliner Strasse, a broad pedestrian mall lined with 15th and 16th-century burgher houses, runs west from the **Rathaus** on Neuer Markt to the 14th-century **Kröpeliner Tor** (closed Monday and Tuesday; DM4/2) near a stretch of old city wall. Halfway along, off the south-western corner of Universitätsplatz, is the **Kloster 'Zum Heiligen Kreuz' Museum** (DM4/2; closed Monday) in an old convent (1270).

Rostock's interesting **Schifffahrtsmuseum** (closed Monday; DM4/2), August-Bebel-Strasse 1, tells the story of shipping on the Baltic Sea. You'll find it near the **Steintor** city gate.

Places to Stay

The 85-berth *Jugendgästeschiff Traditionsschiff* (☎ 71 62 24, fax 71 40 14) is in the converted 10,000 tonne freighter *Dresden* on the harbour at Schmarl-Dorf, between Rostock and Warnemünde. Take the S-Bahn to Lütten Klein station, then bus No 35 (direction: Schmarl-Fähre) to avoid the walk past the unwelcoming apartment blocks. If you do hoof it, be cautious. Walk east on Warnower Allee for 30 minutes, turn left at the three-way intersection and go past the lighthouse and the car parks to the far gangway. It's a good deal at DM27.50/39 for juniors/seniors – the setting is delightful and it even has a shipbuilding museum. But you are a long way from anything else and the connecting bus stops running at about 8 pm.

Rostock-Information can book private singles/doubles from around DM30/60 for a DM5 counter fee. After hours, you can call ☎ 194 14 for a recorded message (in German only) about vacant hotel rooms.

The small *City-Pension* (☎ 459 07 04, fax 25 22 60, Krönkenhagen 3) is central and quiet, with rooms for DM75/115 with facilities. It is charming but the pension is on a busy street and doesn't have double-glazed windows. Ask for a quiet room, which will cost from DM109/139 with facilities. The upmarket *Hotel Sonne* (☎ 497 30, fax 497 33 51, ✉ info@hotel-sonne-rostock.de) is much the same story but its windows are better. The cheapest prices are DM195/235. Higher rates are charged for rooms not fronting busy Steinstrasse.

Places to Eat

Burger King and *Jimmy's Hamburger* jostle for position on the corner of Kröpeliner Strasse and Briete Strasse. *Kölsch-& Altbierhaus* (Wokrenter Strasse 36), between Lange Strasse and the harbour, has a woodsy, pub atmosphere – expect to pay around DM12 to DM24 for main dishes, but lunches are much cheaper (open till late). *Salsalitos* (☎ 519 35 65, Am Leuchtturm 9), a few blocks to the west, pulls a young crowd of eaters in the evening (around DM15 to DM30 for mains). The *Spar* supermarket in the Hanse Passage on the corner of Schickmannstrasse and an der Oberkannte has a good range.

Getting There & Away

There are hourly trains from Wismar (DM15, 1¼ hours), and frequent IR trains to/from Berlin-Zoo (DM75, three hours), Stralsund

(DM20, one hour), Schwerin (DM22, 1¼ hours) and Hamburg (DM54, 2¼ hours).

Vehicle-passenger ferries cross to Trelleborg (Sweden) and Gedser (Denmark) from Rostock Seaport (take tram No 19 or 21 to Seehafen Fähre). Scandlines (☎ 673 12 17, 01805-72 26 35 46) has services daily between Rostock and Trelleborg for DM20 to DM30 per passenger (5¾ hours; bikes DM5 extra). Its Web site is at www.scandlines.de. TT-Line (☎ 040-360 14 42, fax 360 14 07) departs from Rostock for Trelleborg several times daily using fast and slow boats. The crossing takes three to six hours and costs from DM50 to DM100 one way, depending on the season. Bicycles are DM10 to DM20 extra and cars are much more. See its Web site at www.TTLine.de for more information. To Gedser, Scandlines charges DM6 to DM10 per person for trips that take up to two hours. Tickets and timetable information are available at the train station. Silja runs fast ferries several times a week between Rostock-Tallinn-Helsinki (up to 26 hours) from June to September from DM150 peak period price.

Getting Around

Day tickets (*Tageskarte*) cost DM4.50. For two zones (covering Rostock and Warnemünde), single rides cost DM3.20 and day tickets DM6.30. The double-decker S-Bahn north to Warnemünde departs from the main train station on various platforms, so check the departure board carefully.

AROUND ROSTOCK
Warnemünde

This popular beech resort and fishing village on the Baltic Sea at the mouth of the Warnow River is actually part of greater Rostock. In winter it offers a quiet, picturesque alternative as a place to stay, while in summer or on warm days it is jammed with Berlin's funseekers. But Warnemünde also has a small and picturesque fishing harbour, where stallholders sell the daily catch – fresh, smoked or in bread rolls...it's delicious!

The beach **promenade** to the north of the harbour offers a nice stroll. Warnemünde's broad, sandy beach stretches west from the **lighthouse** (1898) and is chock-a-block with bathers on a hot summer day.

Finding good, cheap accommodation here is not difficult in winter, and it makes a wonderful alternative to Rostock. Warnemünde-Information charges DM5 for its room-finding service; the tourist office in Rostock can also help. In summer, accommodation is as scarce as hen's teeth.

It's easy to get to Warnemünde station on the double-decker S-Bahn from Rostock station (see Getting Around in the Rostock section) every 15 minutes during the day, every 30 minutes in the evenings, and hourly from midnight to dawn. The trains are reportedly very safe at night.

STRALSUND
☎ 03831 • pop 61,500

Stralsund, an enjoyable city on the Baltic Sea north of Berlin, is almost completely surrounded by lakes and the sea, which once contributed to its defence. It was a Hanseatic city in the Middle Ages and later formed part of the Duchy of Pommern-Wolgast. From 1648 to 1815 it was under Swedish control. Today it's an attractive historic town with fine museums and buildings, pleasant walks and a restful, uncluttered waterfront. The island of Rügen is just across the Strelasund, and in summer the ferry to Hiddensee Island leaves from here.

Orientation & Information

The old town and port are connected by causeways to their surrounds; the main train station is across the Tribseer Damm causeway, west of the old town. Neuer Markt is the south-western hub and the bus station is a few blocks south, past the Marienkirche. The post office is on Neuer Markt, opposite the Marienkirche.

Stralsund-Information (☎ 246 90, fax 24 69 49) is at Alter Markt 9, near the northern focus of the old town. It's open 9 am to 7 pm weekdays, 9 am to 2 pm Saturday and 10 am to 2 pm Sunday from May to September; 10 am to 5 pm weekdays and to 2 pm Saturday the rest of the year.

Things to See & Do

On Alter Markt is the medieval **Rathaus**, where you can stroll through the vaulted and pillared structures and around to the impressive **Nikolaikirche**. The 14th-century **Marienkirche**

GERMANY

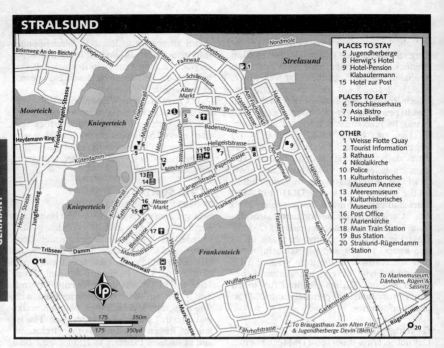

STRALSUND

PLACES TO STAY
5 Jugendherberge
8 Herwig's Hotel
9 Hotel-Pension Klabautermann
15 Hotel zur Post

PLACES TO EAT
6 Torschliesserhaus
7 Asia Bistro
12 Hansekeller

OTHER
1 Weisse Flotte Quay
2 Tourist Information
3 Rathaus
4 Nikolaikirche
10 Police
11 Kulturhistorisches Museum Annexe
13 Meeresmuseum
14 Kulturhistorisches Museum
16 Post Office
17 Marienkirche
18 Main Train Station
19 Bus Station
20 Stralsund-Rügendamm Station

on Neuer Markt is a massive red-brick edifice typical of north German Gothic architecture. You can climb the 350 steps of the tower (on a daunting network of steep ladders) for a sweeping view of Stralsund (DM2).

There are organ recitals on the 1659 instrument in Marienkirche and in the Gothic splendour of Nikolaikirche, on alternating Wednesdays in summer at 8 pm; the bill is occasionally filled by chamber music. Performances cost DM8/5.

There are two excellent museums on Mönchstrasse. **Meeresmuseum**, an oceanic complex and aquarium in a 13th-century convent church, is open 10 am to 5 pm daily from May to October (10 am to 6 pm in July and August; DM7/3.50). Some aquariums in the basement contain tropical fish and coral, while others display creatures of the Baltic and North Seas. The **Kulturhistorisches Museum** (closed Monday; DM6/3) has a large collection which is housed in the cloister of an old convent (and an annexe for local history at Böttcherstrasse 23; one ticket admits

you to both). A further addition, the **Marinemuseum** (☎ 29 73 27), covers the colourful history of Baltic seafaring. It's located on the island of Dänholm, off the B96 towards Rügen (closed Monday; DM6/3).

Many fine buildings have been restored on the showpiece **Mühlenstrasse** near Alter Markt. The old harbour is close by and you can stroll along the sea wall, then west along the waterfront park for a great view of Stralsund's skyline.

Cruises From May to September, Weisse Flotte ferries (☎ 268 10) depart from the old harbour for Neuendorf on Hiddensee Island (DM14/24 one way/return). Check beforehand if you want to take a bike (DM10). There are also short crossings to Altefähr (on Rügen; DM3.50) and one-hour harbour cruises at 2.30 pm daily from May to October (DM8).

Places to Stay
See the following Rügen Island section for camping grounds. The excellent Stralsund

Jugendherberge (☎ *29 21 60, fax 29 76 76, Am Kütertor 1*) is in the 17th-century waterworks. Take bus No 4 or 5 from the main train station (DM25/30 juniors/seniors; closed in December and January). The *Jugendherberge Devin* (☎ *49 02 89, fax 40 02 91, Strandstrasse 219*) is 8km from town off the Greifswald road in Devin. Take bus No 3 from the main train station (closed in January and February).

Stralsund-Information handles reservations for private rooms, pensions and hotels (DM5 fee). *Hotel-Pension Klabautermann* (☎ *29 36 28, fax 28 06 12, Am Querkanal 2*) is near the port and has a view of the city. It charges DM70/120. *Herwig's Hotel* (☎ *266 80, fax 26 68 23, Heilgeiststrasse 50*) has quite good rooms for DM75/120 with facilities. The historic *Hotel zur Post* (☎ *20 05 00, fax 20 05 10, ✉ info@hotel-zur-post-stralsund.de, Tribseer Strasse 22*) charges from DM145/175 for stylish rooms.

Places to Eat

Asia Bistro (☎ *70 36 78, Heilgeistrasse 389*) does budget meals that are mostly under DM15. *Torschliesserhaus* (☎ *29 30 32*) is next to the youth hostel and has dishes for less than DM11. The *Hansekeller* (☎ *70 38 40, Mönchstrasse 48*) serves hearty regional dishes in the earthy atmosphere of a vaulted cellar for under DM27. *Braugasthaus Zum Alten Fritz* (☎ *25 55 00, Greifswalder Chausee 84-5*) is worth the trek out of town (take bus No 3 from the main train station), with good beer and some tasty and well-priced dishes; open daily.

Getting There & Away

Frequent IR trains run to/from Rostock (DM20, one hour), Berlin (DM65, three hours), Schwerin (DM44, 2¼ hours) and Hamburg (DM73, 3¼ hours).

International trains between Berlin and Stockholm or Oslo use the car ferry connecting Fährhafen Sassnitz on Rügen Island with Trelleborg and Malmö (Sweden). If you're heading to Sweden, be sure to travel in a carriage labelled for Malmö, as the train may split up at Sassnitz. Two or three daily connections to Stockholm (changing at Malmö) are available (see also Rügen Island following, and the Getting There & Away section at the beginning of this chapter).

From Stralsund, there are about 20 daily trains to Sassnitz (DM15, one hour) on Rügen Island, most of which connect at Lietzow for Binz (DM15, 1¼ hours).

RÜGEN ISLAND

Germany's largest island, Rügen, is just north-east of Stralsund and connected by a causeway. The island's highest point is Königsstuhl (117m), reached by car or bus from Sassnitz. The **chalk cliffs** that tower above the sea are the main attraction. Much of Rügen and its surrounding waters are either national park or protected nature reserves. The **Bodden** inlet area is a bird refuge and is popular with birdwatchers.

The main resort area is around Binz, Sellin and Göhren, on a peninsula on Rügen's eastern side. A lovely hike from Binz to Sellin skirts the cliffs above the sea through beech and pine forest and offers great coastal views. Another destination is **Jagdschloss Granitz** (1834), also surrounded by lush forest.

Tourismus Verband Rügen (☎ 03838-807 70, fax 25 44 40) is at Am Markt 4 in Bergen and publishes a huge magazine listing all accommodation on the island along with other useful information. In Sassnitz, the tourist office (☎ 038392-51 60, fax 516 16, ✉ fvb-sassnitz@t-online.de), Seestrasse 1, handles inquiries and also books hotel and private rooms for an outrageous fee of DM15 by telephone, or DM8 over-the-counter. It's open 9 am to 7 pm Monday to Friday, 10 am to 7 pm Saturday and 2 pm to 7 pm Sunday from April to October. The rest of the year it's open 9 am to 5 pm weekdays only. Binz Information (☎ 038393-27 82, fax 307 17, ✉ fremdenverkehrsverein binz@t-online.de), Heinrich-Heine-Strasse 7, books rooms over-the-counter (free) and is open from 9 am to 6 pm weekdays (till 4 pm from November to March).

Places to Stay

Rügen has 21 camping grounds – the largest concentration of them is at Göhren.

In Binz, the *Jugendherberge* (☎ *038393-325 97, fax 325 96, ✉ jugendherberge-binz@t-online.de, Strandpromenade 35*) is across from the beach (DM36/43.50 juniors /seniors). The *Jugendherberge Prora* (☎ *038393-328 44, fax 328 45, ✉ jh-prora@t-online .de, Strandstrasse 12*) is at Prora-Ost, five minutes from

GERMANY

the Prora-Ost station (DM27/32 for juniors/ seniors). It is in the 2km-long workers' retreat built by Hitler before the war – a sight in itself.

Binz is the premier resort on the island and its hotels charge top prices. *Hotel-Pension Granitz* (☎ 038393-26 78, fax 324 03, *Bahnhofstrasse 2*) has rooms for DM80/140 with facilities. *Deutsche Flagge* (☎ 038393-2805, *fax 462 99, Schillerstrasse 9*) charges DM150/ 190 for comfortable accommodation.

Getting There & Away
Local trains run almost hourly from 8 am to 9 pm between Stralsund and Sassnitz (DM15, one hour). From Sassnitz to Binz (DM8, 1¼ hours), you must usually change in Lietzow. A historic and fun narrow-gauge train links Putbus to Göhren via Binz.

Scandlines (☎ 038392-644 20, 01805-72 26 35 46) runs five passenger-vehicle ferries daily from the vast Sassnitz ferry terminal, 5km south of town, to/from Trelleborg (Sweden; DM20 to DM30 one way). Cars are DM155 to DM165, which includes passengers. A six-berth cabin on the service to Klaipéda in Lithuania costs from DM120 to DM140 (19 hours, thrice weekly).

If you're taking a train to the Sweden-bound ferry, find out whether it ends at Sassnitz's main station or goes right to the quay (to Fährhafen Sassnitz station). You'll need to catch a bus or walk from the main station to the harbour if you're not on a through train.

Scandlines also has at least three services weekly to/from Rønne on Bornholm (Denmark) for DM20 to DM30.

HIDDENSEE ISLAND
Hiddensee is a narrow 17km-long island off Rügen's west coast, north of Stralsund. No cars are allowed on Hiddensee and there are no camping grounds or hostels. The tourist office in Vitte (☎ 038300-642 26, fax 642 25, ✉ insel .information@t-online.de), Norderende 162, has accommodation information and a free booking service. It's open 7 am to 5 pm Monday to Friday (also 10 am to noon on Saturday from May to September).

Ferries (☎ 0180-321 21 50) from Schaprode on Rügen's west coast run frequently across to Hiddensee (DM11/21 one way/return to Neuendorf, DM14/24 to Kloster and Vitte, DM10 for bicycles). Buses link Schaprode to Bergen, which is on the main Rügen train line. In summer there are also ferries from Stralsund (see Cruises in the Stralsund section).

Bavaria

For many visitors to Germany, Bavaria (Bayern) is a microcosm of the whole country. Here you will find fulfilled the German stereotypes of *Lederhosen*, beer halls, oompah bands and romantic castles.

Yet Bavarians are proudly independent and often think of themselves as citizens of a separate country only tenuously linked to the rest of Germany.

Bavaria was ruled for centuries as a duchy under the line founded by Otto I of Wittelsbach, and eventually graduated to the status of kingdom in 1806. The region suffered amid numerous power struggles between Prussia and Austria and was finally brought into the German Empire in 1871 by Bismarck. The last king of Bavaria was Ludwig II (1845-86), who earned the epithet the 'mad king' due to his obsession for building fantastic fairy-tale castles at enormous expense. He was found drowned in Starnberger See in suspicious circumstances and left no heirs.

Bavaria draws visitors all year. If you only have time for one part of Germany after Berlin, this is it. Munich, the capital, is the heart and soul. The Bavarian Alps, Nuremberg and the medieval towns on the Romantic Road are other important attractions.

MUNICH
☎ 089 • pop 1.3 million
Munich (München) is the Bavarian mother lode. But this beer-quaffing, sausage-eating city can be as cosmopolitan as anywhere in Europe. Munich residents have figured out how to enjoy life and are perfectly happy to show outsiders, as a visit to a beer hall will confirm. There's much more to Munich, however, than beer. Decide on one of the many fine museums and take a leisurely look.

Munich has been the capital of Bavaria since 1503, but really achieved prominence under the guiding hand of Ludwig I in the 19th century. It has seen many turbulent times, but the 20th century was particularly rough. The city almost starved during WWI, the Nazis got their start here in the 1920s and WWII brought bombing and more than 6000 civilian deaths. Today it is the centre of Germany's burgeoning high-tech industries and has less unemployment than many other regions.

Orientation

The main train station is just west of the centre. Although there's extensive public transport, old-town Munich is enjoyable for walking. From the station, head east along Bayerstrasse, through Karlsplatz, and then along Neuhauser Strasse and Kaufingerstrasse to Marienplatz, the hub of Munich.

North of Marienplatz are the Residenz (the former royal palace), Schwabing (the famous student section) and the parklands of the Englischer Garten. East of Marienplatz is the Platzl quarter for beer houses and restaurants, as well as Maximilianstrasse, a fashionable street that's fun for strolling and window-shopping.

Information

Tourist Offices The main tourist office (☎ 23 33 02 56, fax 23 33 02 57, ☻ tourismus@ muenchen.btl.de) is at the main train station, to the right as you exit via the eastern entrance. Its hours are 9 am to 8 pm Monday to Saturday and 10 am to 6 pm Sunday. You can expect to stand in line during summer. Its room-finding service is free and you must apply in person, call ☎ 23 33 03 00 or write to: Fremdenverkehrsamt München, D-80313 München. Another branch on Marienplatz is open from 10 am to 8 pm weekdays and to 4 pm Saturday.

EurAide (☎ 59 38 89, ☻ euraide@comp userve.com), near platform 11 at the main train station, is an excellent source of information in English. The office gives advice on local and European train travel, and its room-finding service (DM7.50 per booking) is at least as skilful as the tourist office's. It's open 7.45 am to noon and 1 to 4.30 pm daily from May to mid-October (these hours on weekdays plus Saturday morning mid-October to April).

Yet another useful office is the Jugendinformationszentrum (Youth Information Centre; ☎ 51 41 06 60) on the corner of Paul-Heyse-Strasse and Landwehrstrasse. Open from noon to 6 pm Monday to Friday (until 8 pm on Thursday), it has a wide range of information for young people as well as an extensive library of periodicals and cheap Internet access.

The excellent *Young People's Guide* (DM1) is available from information offices. The English-language monthly *Munich Found* (DM4.50) is also useful. There is a useful Web site at www.munich-tourist.de.

Money Reisebank has two offices at the main train station; if you show a EurAide newsletter, your commission will be cheaper. You'll find American Express at Promenadeplatz 6 and Thomas Cook at Petersplatz 10.

Post & Communications Munich's main post office at Bahnhofplatz 1 is open from 8 am to 8 pm weekdays and until noon Saturday. The poste restante address is: Hauptpostlagernd (Poste Restante), Bahnhofplatz 1, 80074 Munich.

Internet Café, Nymphenburger Strasse 145, offers an hour's free access if you order a dish of its so-so Italian food costing more than DM10; otherwise it's DM7 for 30 minutes at this popular traveller hang-out. Karstadt am Dom, Neuhauser Strasse 21, has Internet terminals on its 4th floor for DM3 a half-hour.

Travel Agencies ABR Reisebüro (☎ 120 40) is in the main train station. Council Travel (☎ 39 50 22), near the university at Adalbertstrasse 32, is a good budget agency.

Bookshops The best travel bookshop in town is Geobuch, opposite Viktualienmarkt, at Rosental 6. The widest cultural book range is available at Hugendubel on Marienplatz, with a good selection of Lonely Planet guides and tons of English-language offerings.

Laundry Close to the main train station and open from 7 am to 11 pm daily, City SB-Waschcenter is at Paul-Heyse-Strasse 21. Loads cost DM6 and the last wash must be in by 10 pm.

Medical & Emergency Services Medical help is available at the Kassenärztlicher Notfalldienst; call ☎ 55 14 71. For ambulances call ☎ 112. An English-speaking pharmacy is in the main train station. There is also a police station in the main train station on the Arnulfstrasse side (emergency number ☎ 110).

GERMANY

GERMANY

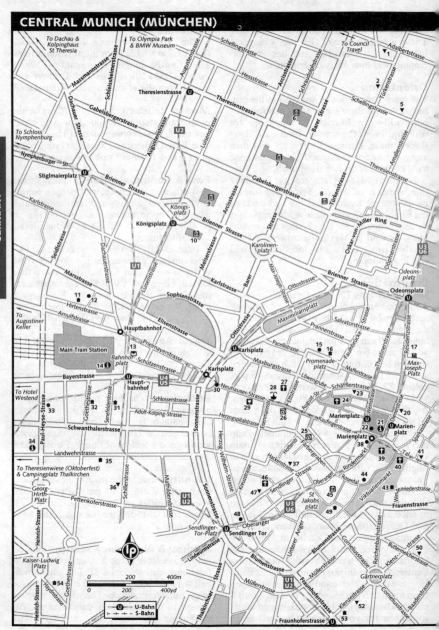

CENTRAL MUNICH (MÜNCHEN)

euro currency converter €1 = 1.95DM

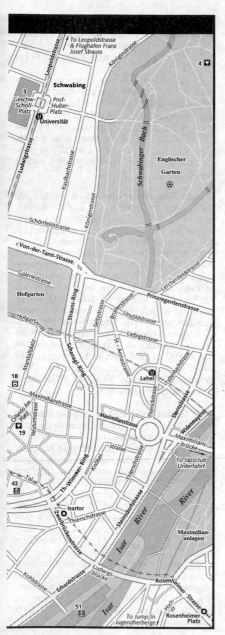

CENTRAL MUNICH

PLACES TO STAY
11 4 you münchen
16 Hotel Bayerischer Hof
32 Jugendhotel Marienherberge
35 Pension Marie-Luise
43 Hotel-Pension am Markt
53 Am Gärtnerplatz-Theater
54 Pension Haydn

PLACES TO EAT
1 Vorstadt Café
2 Alter Simpl
5 Schall und Rauch
20 Alois Dallmayr
23 Münchner Suppenküche
36 Jinny's Thai Food
37 Prinz Myschkin
41 Weisses Brauhaus
47 Cipriani
50 Bei Carla
52 Morizz

OTHER
3 Universität
4 Chinesischer Turm
6 Neue Pinakothek
7 Alte Pinakothek
8 Pinakothek der Moderne
9 Glyptothek
10 Antikensammlungen
12 ADM-Mitfahrzentrale
13 Main Post Office
14 Main Tourist Office
15 American Express
17 Residenz
18 Nationaltheater
19 Hofbräuhaus
21 Tourist Office
22 Altes Rathaus & Glockenspiel
24 Frauenkirche
25 Internet Café
26 Karstadt am Dom
27 Michaelskirche
28 Richard Strauss Fountain
29 Augustiner Bierhalle
30 Karlstor
31 Euro Youth Hostel
33 City SB-Waschcenter
34 Jugendinformationszentrum
38 Hugendubel
39 Peterskirche
40 Heiliggeistkirche
42 Zentrum für Aussergewöhnliche Museen
44 Geobuch
45 Stadtmuseum & Stadtcafé
46 Asamkirche
48 Sendlinger Tor
49 Hotel Blauer Bock
51 Deutsches Museum

GERMANY

Dangers & Annoyances Crime and staggering drunks leaving the beer halls are major problems in Munich. Watch valuables carefully around touristy areas and the streets around the main train station. A common trick is to steal your gear if you strip off in the Englischer Garten (don't let that stop you, just watch your stuff!).

Things to See & Do
Except where otherwise noted, museums and galleries are closed on Monday.

The pivotal **Marienplatz** is a good starting point. Dominating the square is the towering neo-Gothic **Altes Rathaus** (old town hall), with its incessantly photographed **Glockenspiel** (carillon) which does its number at 11 am and noon (also at 5 pm from May to October). Two important churches are on this square: **Peterskirche** and, behind the Altes Rathaus, the **Heiliggeistkirche**. Head west along the shopping street Kaufingerstrasse to the late-Gothic **Frauenkirche** (Church of Our Lady), the landmark church of Munich; the monotonous red brick is Bavarian in its simplicity. Continue west on Kaufingerstrasse to **Michaelskirche**, Germany's grandest Renaissance church.

Farther west is the **Richard Strauss Fountain** and then the medieval **Karlstor**, an old city gate. Double back towards Marienplatz and turn right onto Eisenmannstrasse, which becomes Kreuzstrasse and converges with Herzog-Wilhelm-Strasse at the medieval gate of **Sendlinger Tor**. Go down the left side of the shopping street Sendlinger Strasse to the **Asamkirche**, a remarkable church designed by brothers Cosmas Damian and Egid Quirin Asam. It shows a rare unity of style, with scarcely a single unembellished surface.

Continue along Sendlinger Strasse and turn right on Hermann-Sack-Strasse to reach the **Stadtmuseum** (DM5/4) on St-Jakobs-Platz, where the outstanding exhibits cover beer brewing, fashion, musical instruments, photography and puppets.

Palaces The huge **Residenz** housed Bavarian rulers from 1385 to 1918 and features more than 500 years of architectural history. Apart from the palace itself, the **Residenzmuseum** (open daily; DM8/6) has an extraordinary array of 100 rooms containing the Wittelsbach house's belongings, while the **Schatzkammer** (DM8/6) exhibits a ridiculous quantity of jewels, crowns and ornate gold. See both on a combined ticket (DM14/11).

If this doesn't satisfy your passion for palaces, visit **Schloss Nymphenburg** (general admission DM8/5, or for everything including the museum and gallery DM15/12) northwest of the city centre via tram No 17 from the northern side of the main train station. This was the royal family's equally impressive summer home. The surrounding park is worth a long, regal stroll.

Deutsches Museum A vast science and technology museum, this is like a combination of Disneyland and the Smithsonian Institute all under one huge roof that covers 13km of corridors on eight floors. You can explore anything from the depths of coal mines to the stars, but it's definitely too large to see everything so pursue specific interests. Note that some of the areas are musty, dusty and out of date while others, such as the hair-raising electricity demonstration, are a thrill. The museum (☎ 2179-1) is open 9 am to 5 pm daily (DM12/5 for adults/children). A visit to the planetarium costs DM3 extra. To get to the museum, take the S-Bahn to Isartor or tram No 18 to Deutsches Museum. Visit the Web site at www.deutsches-museum.de.

Art Galleries The **Alte Pinakothek**, on Barer Strasse, is a veritable treasure house of European masters from the 14th to 18th centuries. Highlights include Dürer's Christ-like *Self Portrait* and his *Four Apostles*, Rogier van der Weyden's *Adoration of the Magi* and Botticelli's *Pietà* (DM7/4).

Immediately north, at No 29, is the **Neue Pinakothek**, which contains mainly 19th-century works, including Van Gogh's *Sunflowers*, and sculpture and is open daily (DM7/4, free on Sunday). A combined card costing DM12/6 gets you into both.

The huge new **Pinakothek der Moderne**, a block east of the Alte Pinakothek, is planned to open in October 2001. It will bring together four collections of modern art, graphic art, applied art and architecture from galleries and museums around the city.

Other Museums On Königsplatz, the **Glyptothek** and the **Antikensammlungen** have some of Germany's best antiquities collections (mostly Greek and Roman). To visit either museum costs DM6, to visit both is DM10, but on Sunday it's free.

North of the city, auto-fetishists can thrill to the **BMW Museum** (open daily; DM5.50/4), at Peutelring 130. Take the U3 direct from Marienplatz to Olympiazentrum.

It's a mixed bag and that's the delight of the **Zentrum für Aussergewöhnliche Museen** (Centre for Unusual Museums), Westenriederstrasse 26, where you can find displays on everything from chamber pots and the Easter Bunny to Austrian Empress Elisabeth, known to her pals as 'Sisi' (open daily; DM8/5).

Englischer Garten One of the largest city parks in Europe, this is a great place for strolling, especially along the Schwabinger Bach. In balmy summer weather, nude sunbathing is the rule rather than the exception. It's not unusual for hundreds of naked people to be in the park on a normal business day, with their clothes stacked primly on the grass.

Olympiaturm If you like heights, go up the lift of the 290m Olympiaturm (tower) in the Olympia Park complex (open until midnight; DM5/2.50).

Dachau This was the first Nazi concentration camp, built in March 1933. Jews, political prisoners, homosexuals and others deemed 'undesirable' by the Third Reich were imprisoned in the camp. More than 200,000 people were sent here; over 30,000 died at Dachau and countless others died after being transferred to other death camps. An English-language documentary is shown at 11.30 am and 3.30 pm. A visit includes camp relics, a memorial and a very sobering museum (a new section of which opens in 2001). It's open 9 am to 5 pm (closed Monday; free). Take the S2 to Dachau and then bus No 726 or 724 (Sunday and holidays) to the camp. A two-zone ticket (DM7.20) is needed for the trip.

Organised Tours
Munich Walks (☎ 235 90 20) runs excellent English-language tours from April to November (two to three hours; DM18/14 for se-

niors/juniors). Both tours – one covering the heart of the city, the other Third Reich sites – leave from in front of the EurAide office.

Mike's Bike Tours (☎ 25 54 39 87) runs guided city cycling tours in English (DM36/46 for half/full-day tours). Half-day tours (four hours) leave at least once daily from March to October, while all-day tours run daily from June to August. Tours depart from the archway in front of the Altes Rathaus on Marienplatz.

Radius Bike Rental (☎ 59 61 13) offers 2½ hour bicycle tours in English (DM25) from its store near Track 27 in the main train station. Tours leave at 10.30 am from May to early October.

A new tour option, the bike and walk company (☎ 58 95 89 33) runs bike (DM31/27 for over/under 26s) and walking tours (DM15) from April to October. Tours meet outside the Glockenspiel on Marienplatz.

Oktoberfest
Hordes come to Munich for the **Oktoberfest**, one of the continent's biggest and most drunken parties, running the 15 days before the first Sunday in October (that's 22 September to 7 October 2001 and 21 September to 6 October 2002). Reserve accommodation well ahead and go early in the day so you can grab a seat in one of the hangar-sized beer 'tents'. The action takes place at the Theresienwiese grounds, about a 10-minute walk south-west of the main train station. While there is no entrance fee, those DM12 litres of beer add up fast.

Places to Stay
Munich can be jammed with tourists year-round. Without reservations you may have to throw yourself at the mercy of the tourist office or EurAide room-finding services (see Information earlier).

Camping The most central camping ground is *Campingplatz Thalkirchen* (☎ 723 17 07, *Zentralländstrasse 49*), south-west of the city centre and close to the hostel on Miesingstrasse. Closed from November to mid-March, it can be incredibly crowded in summer, but there always seems to be room for one more tent. Take the U3 to Thalkirchen and then bus No 57 (about 20 minutes). It charges DM7 for a tent site plus DM8.40 per person.

GERMANY

GERMANY

Youth Hostels Munich's youth hostels that are DJH and HI affiliated do not accept guests over age 26.

The most central is the *Jugendherberge München (☎ 13 11 56, fax 167 87 45, Wendl-Dietrich-Strasse 20)*, north-west of the city centre (U1 to Rotkreuzplatz). It's large, loud and busy. Beds cost from DM30. Still decently close, and a better deal, is the modern *Jugendgästehaus München (☎ 723 65 50, fax 724 25 67, Miesingstrasse 4)*, south-west of the city centre in the suburb of Thalkirchen. Take the U3 to Thalkirchen, and then follow the signs. Beds are DM32.50 in dorms, with higher prices for smaller rooms. Both hostels have a 1 am curfew. *Jugendherberge Burg Schwaneck (☎ 74 48 66 72, fax 74 48 66 80, Burgweg 4-6)* is in a great old castle in the southern suburbs, 10 minutes' walk from the Pullach station on the S7. Dorm beds cost from DM23.

Munich's summer budget favourite is *'The Tent' (☎ 51 41 06 16)*, less famously known as Jugendlager am Kapuziner Hölzl. This mass camp is open from late June to early September. There's no curfew and priority is given to those under age 24. Take tram No 17 from the main train station to Botanischer Garten, then walk straight on Franz-Schrank-Strasse to In den Kirschen. A thermal mattress and blanket in the big tent costs DM13, including a small breakfast and a shower.

Other Hostels Munich has quite a few non-DJH hostels or hotels that offer cheaper dormitory accommodation as well as simple rooms. People over 26 often have to pay a surcharge (call it a 'maturity tax').

Newcomer to the hostel scene, *Jump-In Jugendherberge (☎ 48 95 34 37, Hochstrasse 51)* is recommended by readers and has beds from DM29. Catch the S-Bahn to Karlsplatz and then tram No 27 to Ostfriedhof). Call before arriving as you can only check in during certain hours.

Just near the main train station, *Euro Youth Hotel (☎ 59908811, fax 59908877, ✉ info@euro-youth-hotel.de, Senefelderstrasse 5)* offers dorm beds for DM29, beds in three to four-bed rooms for DM36 and doubles for DM42.

4 you münchen (☎ 552 16 60, fax 55 21 66 66, Hirtenstrasse 18) has ecologically correct

lodging. The downstairs 'hostel' section where, unfortunately, the under-27 rule also applies, costs from DM24 for dorm beds and from DM61.50/92 for singles/doubles; the organic high-fibre breakfast costs an extra DM7.50. Oldsters over 26 pay DM69/99 in the adjoining hotel section.

Kolpinghaus St Theresia (☎ 12 60 50, fax 12 60 52 12, Hanebergstrasse 8) charges DM36/43/49 for beds in triple/double/single rooms. Take the U1 to Rotkreuzplatz, then walk north for 10 minutes.

Women under 26 can try the *Jugendhotel Marienherberge (☎ 55 58 05, Goethestrasse 9)*, where dorm beds start at DM30 and singles/doubles cost only DM40/70.

Hotels There are plenty of fairly cheap, if scruffy, places near the station. The cramped *Pension Marie-Luise (☎ 55 42 30, Landwehrstrasse 35)* offers rooms from DM55/80.

An ideal compromise of location, price and cleanliness is *Pension Haydn (☎ 53 11 19, Haydnstrasse 9)*, near the Goetheplatz U-Bahn station and within walking distance of the main train station. Rooms without bath are DM75/110. Friendly *Hotel Westend (☎ 508 09 00, fax 502 58 96, Landsberger Strasse 20)* is a fabulous deal with nice rooms from DM70/100. It's a 10-minute walk west of the main train station or three stops on tram No 18 or 19.

Another value-for-money deal is *Hotel-Pension am Markt (☎ 22 50 14, Heilig geiststrasse 6)*, just off the Viktualienmarkt. Prices start at DM64/110, including a peaceful breakfast amid classical music in a grand room. Central *Hotel Blauer Bock (☎ 23 17 80, fax 23 17 82 00, Sebastiansplatz 9)* has reasonably spacious singles/doubles/triples starting at DM70/110/195, including a buffet breakfast and garage parking.

Escape the tourist rabble at *Am Gärtnerplatz-Theater (☎ 202 51 70, fax 20 25 17 22, Klenzestrasse 45)*, which offers antique-filled rooms from DM120/150 in a cool part of town close to the gay and lesbian scene. The best mid-priced deal is *Hotel Petri (☎ 58 10 99, fax 580 86 30, Aindorferstrasse 82)* in Westend. Rooms have distinctive antiques and there's also a garden and a small indoor swimming pool. Singles/doubles with private facilities start at DM110/170.

For utter opulence, *Hotel Bayerischer Hof* (☎ 212 00, fax 212 09 06, ❸ hbh@compuserve.com, Promenadeplatz 2-6) serves it up on an over-the-top, gold-leaf platter. Your life (or night) of luxury starts from DM330/430.

Places to Eat

At *Viktualienmarkt*, just south of Marienplatz, you can put together a picnic feast to take to the Englischer Garten. Or you can grab a tasty snack like *Fischsemmel* (a roll stuffed with pickled herring and raw onion) and a beer, and chat to regulars in the lively, leafy beer garden. More prosperous picnickers might prefer the legendary *Alois Dallmayr (Dienerstrasse 14)*, one of the world's greatest (and priciest) delicatessens, with an amazing range of exotic foods imported from every corner of the earth.

Student card-holders can fill up for around DM4 in any of the university *Mensas*, at Leopoldstrasse 13, Arcisstrasse 17 and Helene-Mayer-Ring 9. *Münchner Suppenküche (Schäfflerstrasse 7)* has meaty and vegetarian soups averaging DM8.

Weisses Brauhaus (Tal 7), serves the classic Munich Weisswürste (sausage) as well as other dainty delicacies like *Kalbskopf* (calf head, and don't ask any more questions) for DM17.50. In Schwabing, *Alter Simpl (Türkenstrasse 57)* is something of an institution, with good jazz and a menu with reasonable vegetarian options (mains average DM15).

If you feel another sausage or potato will tip you over the edge, try the spicy soups (from DM5.90) and curries (from DM15.90) at *Jinny's Thai Food (Schillerstrasse 32)*. For imaginative vegetarian cuisine, nothing beats stylish *Prinz Myschkin (Hackenstrasse 2)*. Its food blends South-East Asian, Indian and Italian influences, with changing daily menus and main courses for as little as DM16. Italian food is a good deal in Munich. *Cipriani (Sendlinger Strasse 28)* in the Asam-Hof, a small courtyard just off Sendlinger Strasse, has great panini. Its patio is a calm oasis amid the urban din.

Cafes Central cafes cater largely to tourists and therefore tend to be rather expensive, though it's fun hanging out at *Stadtcafé* at the Stadtmuseum, a popular haunt for Munich's intellectual types.

You'd be best to head to Schwabing for cafe culture, which ranges from techno-soundtracked chill-out places to *Schicki-Micki* heaven. *Vorstadt Café (Türkenstrasse 83)* is one of many lively student hang-outs and is open till late. Schellingstrasse has some cool cafe-bars, like *Schall und Rauch* at No 22.

Entertainment

Beer Halls & Beer Gardens Beer drinking is an integral part of Munich's entertainment scene. Germans drink an average of 130L of the amber liquid each per year, while Munich residents manage to drink much more than this!

Several breweries run their own beer halls, so try at least one large, frothy, litre mug (called a *Mass*) of beer before heading off to another hall. Most famous is the enormous and tourist-packed *Hofbräuhaus (Am Platzl 9)*. That there is a Planet Hollywood across the street should tell you everything you need to know about the place. Far better is the *Augustiner Bierhalle (Neuhauser Strasse 27)*, an authentic example of an old-style Munich beer hall that is filled with happy locals munching plates full of cheap chow.

On a summer day there's nothing better than sitting and sipping among the greenery at one of Munich's beer gardens. In the Englischer Garten is the classic *Chinesischer Turm* beer garden, although the nearby *Hirschau* beer garden on the banks of the Kleinhesseloher See is less crowded. The *Augustiner Keller (Arnulfstrasse 52)*, five minutes from the main train station, has a large and leafy beer garden. Its beer hall is a fine place when the weather keeps you indoors. Join thousands of locals at *Hirschgarten*, a beautiful beer garden set in woods adjoining a fenced deer enclosure. Take the S-Bahn west to Laim, exit the station north and turn right on Winfried Strasse. Enter the park and follow your ears.

Performing Arts, Cinemas & Jazz Munich is one of the cultural capitals of Germany; the publications listed in the earlier Information section can guide you to the best events. The *Nationaltheater* on Max-Joseph-Platz is the home of the Bavarian State Opera and the site

GERMANY

of many cultural events (particularly during the opera festival in July). You can buy tickets at Maximilianstrasse 11 or call ☎ 21 85 19 20.

You can catch films in English at both **Museum-Lichtspiele** (☎ 48 24 03, Lilienstrasse 2) and **Cinema** (☎ 55 52 55, Nymphenburger Strasse 31).

Munich is also a hot scene for jazz. **Jazzclub Unterfahrt** (☎ 448 27 94, Kirchenstrasse 96), near the Ostbahnhof station, has live music from 9 pm (except Monday) and jam sessions open to everyone on Sunday night.

Gay & Lesbian Much of Munich's gay and lesbian nightlife is in the area just south of Sendlinger Tor, especially around Gärtnerplatz. There's good food and cocktails at **Morizz** (Klenzestrasse 43), which looks a lot like a Paris bar and is popular with gay men of all ages. **Bei Carla** (Buttermelcherstrasse 9) is a small, friendly, lesbian cafe.

Shopping
Christkindlmarkt (Christmas Market) on Marienplatz in December is large and well stocked but often expensive, so buy a warm drink and just wander around. The Auer Dult, a huge flea market on Mariahilfplatz, has great buys and takes place during the last weeks of April, July and October.

Getting There & Away
Air Munich is second in importance only to Frankfurt for international and national connections. Flights will take you to all major destinations worldwide. Main German cities are serviced by at least half a dozen flights daily.

Train Train services to/from Munich are excellent. There are rapid connections at least every two hours to all major cities in Germany, as well as frequent EC trains to other European cities such as Innsbruck (two hours), Vienna (five hours), Prague (six hours), Zürich (4¼ hours), Verona (5½ hours) and Paris (eight hours).

High-speed ICE services from Munich include Frankfurt (DM147, 3½ hours), Hamburg (DM268, six hours) and Berlin (DM277, 6½ hours).

Bus Munich is linked to the Romantic Road by the Deutsche-Touring (also known as the

Europabus) Munich-Frankfurt service (see Getting Around in the following Romantic Road section). Inquire at Deutsche-Touring (☎ 545 87 00, fax 54 58 70 21), near platform 26 of the main train station, about its international services to destinations such as Prague and Budapest. Buses stop along the northern side of the train station.

Car & Motorcycle Munich has autobahns radiating outwards on all sides. Take the A9 to Nuremberg, the A92 to Passau, the A8 east to Salzburg, the A95 to Garmisch-Partenkirchen and the A8 west to Ulm or Stuttgart. The main rental companies have counters together on the second level of the main train station. For arranged rides, the ADM-Mitfahrzentrale (☎ 1 94 40) is near the main train station at Lämmerstrasse 4. Destinations and sample charges (including booking fees) include: Berlin DM52, Frankfurt-am-Main DM40 and Leipzig DM42.

Getting Around
To/From the Airport Munich's gleaming Flughafen Franz Josef Strauss is connected by the S8 to Marienplatz and the main train station (DM14). The service takes 40 minutes and runs every 20 minutes from 4 am until around 12.30 am. The airport bus also runs at 20-minute intervals from Arnulfstrasse on the north side of the main train station (DM15, 45 minutes) between 6.50 am and 7.50 pm. Forget taxis (at least DM80!).

Public Transport Getting around is easy on Munich's excellent public transport network (MVV). The system is zone-based, and most places of interest to tourists (except Dachau and the airport) are within the 'blue' inner zone (Innenraum). MVV tickets are valid for the S-Bahn, U-Bahn, trams and buses, but must be validated before use. The U-Bahn ends around 12.30 am on weekdays and 1.30 am on weekends, but there are some later buses and S-Bahns. Rail passes are valid only on the S-Bahn. Bicycle transport is free, but forbidden on weekdays during the morning and evening rush hours.

Short rides (Kurzstrecke) cost DM1.80 and are good for no more than four stops on buses and trams and two stops on the U and S-Bahns. Longer trips cost DM3.60. It's cheaper to buy a strip-card of 10 tickets *(Mehrfahrtenkarte)* for DM15 and stamp one strip per adult on short rides, two strips for longer rides in the inner zone. Day passes *(Tageskarte)* for the inner zone cost DM9, while three-day tickets cost DM22, or DM32 for two adults.

Taxi Taxis are expensive (more than DM5 flag fall, plus DM2.20 per kilometre) and not much more convenient than public transport. For a radio-dispatched taxi dial ☎ 216 10.

Car & Motorcycle It's not worth driving in the city centre – many streets are pedestrian only. The tourist office has a map which shows city parking places (DM3 or more an hour).

Bicycle Pedal power is popular in relatively flat Munich. Radius Bike Rental (see the Organised Tours section earlier) rents out two-wheelers from DM25/75 per day/week.

AUGSBURG
☎ 0821 • pop 260,000
Originally established by the Romans, Augsburg later became a centre of Luther's Reformation and is now a lively provincial city crisscrossed by small streams. For some it will be a day trip from Munich, for others an ideal base (especially during Oktoberfest) or a gateway to the Romantic Road.

Augsburg's tourist offices are at Bahnhofstrasse 7 (☎ 502 07 22), open 9 am to 6 pm Monday to Friday; and at Rathausplatz (☎ 502 07 35), open 9 am to 6 pm weekdays and 10 am to 1 pm weekends.

Things to See & Do
The onion-shaped towers of the modest, 16th-century **St Maria Stern Kloster** in Elias-Holl-Platz started a fashion which spread throughout southern Germany. More impressive are those on the **Rathaus**, the adjacent **Perlachturm** and the soaring tower of **St Ulrich und Afra Basilika** (on Ulrichsplatz near the southern edge of the old town). The **Dom Mariae Heimsuchung**, on Hoher Weg north of Rathausplatz, is more conventionally styled. One of Martin Luther's more colourful anti-papal documents was posted here after he was run out of town in 1518. Dramatist Bertolt Brecht's family home was on the stream at Am Rain 7 and is now the **Bertolt-Gedänkstätte**, a museum dedicated to Brecht and the work of young artists (closed Monday and Tuesday; DM3.50/2).

Places to Stay & Eat
Campers should head to *Campingplatz Augusta* (☎ 70 75 75), 7km north-east of the centre near the Augsburg Ost autobahn interchange (take bus No 301, 302 or 305). The worn but central *DJH Hostel* (☎ 3 39 09, fax 15 11 49), at Beim Pfaffenkeller 3 just east of St Mary's Cathedral, charges DM20. *Hotel Von den Rappen* (☎ 21 76 40, *Äussere Uferstrasse 3)* has modern singles/doubles with shower for DM54/85, plus a Bavarian restaurant downstairs.

With nice outdoor tables, *Bauerntanz (Bauerntanz-Gässchen 1)*, just past Barfusgasse, has been serving cheap local food and beer since 1572. South of the Fuggerei houses, an early welfare settlement, *3 Königinnen (Meister-Veits-Gässchen 32)* has a cool beer garden on a quiet street.

Getting There & Away
Trains between Munich and Augsburg are frequent (DM16, 40 minutes). Regular ICE/IC trains also serve Ulm (DM36, 40 minutes), Stuttgart (DM66, 1½ hours) and Nuremberg (DM45, one hour). Connections to/from Regensburg take two hours via Ingolstadt. The Deutsche-Touring Romantic Road bus stops at the train station.

ROMANTIC ROAD
Originally conceived as a way of promoting tourism in western Bavaria, the Romantic Road (Romantische Strasse) links a series of picturesque Bavarian towns and cities. The trip has become one of the most popular in Germany and you will have to decide if you want to fall for the sales pitch and join the throngs – you won't be disappointed though.

The Romantic Road runs north-south through western Bavaria, from Würzburg to Füssen near the Austrian border, passing through Rothenburg ob der Tauber, Dinkelsbühl and Augsburg. The main places for information about the Romantic Road are the tourist offices in Würzburg and Augsburg.

Locals get their cut of the Romantic Road hordes through, among other things, scores of good-value private accommodation offerings.

GERMANY

Look for the *'Zimmer Frei'* signs and expect to pay around DM25 to DM40 per person. Tourist offices are efficient at finding accommodation in almost any price range. DJH hostels listed in this section only accept people aged under 27.

Getting There & Away

In the north of the Romantic Road route, Würzburg is well-served by trains. To start at the southern end, take the hourly RE train from Munich to Füssen (two hours, some services change at Buchloe, DM35). Rothenburg is linked by train to Würzburg, Nuremberg and Munich via Steinach. To reach Dinkelsbühl, take a train to Ansbach and from there a frequent bus onwards. Nördlingen has train connections to Stuttgart and Munich.

There are four daily buses between Füssen and Garmisch-Partenkirchen (DM13; all stop at Hohenschwangau and Oberammergau), as well as several connections between Füssen and Oberstdorf (DM14; via the Tirolean town of Reutte and/or Pfronten). Deutsche-Touring runs a daily 'Castle Road' coach service in each direction between Mannheim and Rothenburg via Heidelberg (DM52, 5½ very long hours).

Getting Around

It is possible to do this route using train connections, local buses or by car (just follow the brown 'Romantische Strasse' signs), but most train pass-holders prefer to take the Deutsche-Touring (also known as Europabus) bus. From April to October Deutsche-Touring runs one coach daily in each direction between Frankfurt and Munich (12 hours), and another in either direction between Dinkelsbühl and Füssen (4½ hours). The bus makes short stops in some towns, but it's both silly and mind-numbing to do the whole trip in one go, since you can break the journey at any point and continue the next day (reserve a seat for the next day as you disembark).

The full fare from Frankfurt to Füssen is DM129 (change buses in Dinkelsbühl). Eurail and German Rail passes are valid and Inter-Rail pass-holders receive a 50% discount, but you must pay a ridiculous DM10 'registration fee' plus DM3 for each piece of luggage. Those over 60 save 50% and those under 26 save 10%. Tickets are available for

short segments and reservations are only necessary on summer weekends. For information and reservations, contact Deutsche-Touring GmbH (☎ 089-59 38 89, fax 089-550 39 65) at Am Römerhof 17, 60486 Frankfurt/Main.

With its gentle gradients and an ever-changing scenery, the Romantic Road makes a good bike trip. Radl-Tour (☎ 08191-4 71 77 or 09341-53 95) offers nine-day cycling packages along the entire route from Würzburg to Füssen for DM860.

Rothenburg ob der Tauber

☎ 09861 • pop 12,000

The route's main attraction, Rothenburg was granted the status of a 'free imperial city' in 1274. It's full of cobbled lanes and picturesque old houses and enclosed by towered walls, all of which are worth exploring. It is absolutely mobbed in summer and its museums only open in the afternoon from November to March. The tourist office (☎ 404 92, fax 8 68 07, **@** info@rothenburg.de) is at Markt 1 and open 9 am to 6 pm (with a half-hour break at 12.30 pm) weekdays and 10 am to 1 pm weekends.

Things to See The **Rathaus** on Markt was commenced in Gothic style in the 14th century but completed in Renaissance style. The tower gives a majestic view over the town and the Tauber Valley. According to legend, the town was saved during the Thirty Years' War when the mayor won a challenge by the Imperial general Tilly and downed more than 3L of wine at a gulp. The **Meistertrunk** scene is re-enacted by the clock figures on the tourist office building (eight times daily in summer).

The **Puppen und Spielzeugmuseum** of dolls and toys at Hofbronnengasse 13 is the largest private collection in Germany (DM6/ 2.50 for adults/children). The **Reichsstadt Museum** in the former convent (DM5/3) features the superb *Rothenburger Passion* in 12 panels (by Martinus Schwarz, 1494) and the Judaika room, with a collection of gravestones with Hebrew inscriptions.

Places to Stay & Eat Camping options are a kilometre or two north of the town walls at Detwang, west of the road on the river. There are signs to ***Tauber-Romantik*** (☎ 61 91), open from Easter to late October. Rothenburg's jammed **Youth Hostel** (*☎ 941 60, fax 94 16 20*), housed in two enormous renovated old buildings at Mühlacker 1, has beds for DM22. Inside the old town, **Gasthof Butz** (*☎ 22 01, ✉ gasthofbutz@rothenburg.com, Kapellenplatz 4*) offers rooms from DM60/120. The **Reichs-Küchenmeister** (*☎ 97 00, Kirchplatz 8*) is a half-timbered house in the centre with rooms from DM110/140 and a traditional restaurant with a leafy outdoor area.

You can eat cheaply at **Doner Kebab** (*Hafengasse 2*), where Turkish kebabs cost from DM5. In a lovely old timber building, **Altfrankische Weinstube** (*Klosterhof 7*) has good-value meals for between DM9.80 and DM19.80. Avoid the temptation to buy a *Schneeball*, a crumbly ball of bland dough with the taste and consistency of chalk that is surely one of Europe's worst 'local specialties'.

Dinkelsbühl
☎ 09581 • pop 11,000

South of Rothenburg, Dinkelsbühl is another walled town of cobbled streets. It celebrates the **Kinderzeche** (Children's Festival) in mid-July, commemorating a legend from the Thirty Years' War that the children of the town successfully begged the invading Swedish troops to leave Dinkelsbühl unharmed. The hour-long walk around the town's **walls** and its almost 30 **towers** is the scenic highlight. The tourist office (*☎ 902 40, fax 902 79, ✉ touristik.service@dinkelsbuehl.de*) is at Marktplatz 1 and open 9 am to 6 pm weekdays, 10 am to 4pm Saturday and 10 am to 1 pm Sunday.

DCC-Campingplatz Romantische Strasse (*☎/fax 78 17*) is open all year. Dinkelsbühl's **Youth Hostel** (*☎ 95 09, fax 48 74, Koppengasse 10*) charges DM18. **Fränkischer Hof** (*☎ 579 00, fax 57 90 99, Nördlinger Strasse 10*) has rooms from DM45/80. The ornate facade of **Deutsches Haus** (*☎ 60 59, Weinmarkt 3* is one of the town's attractions. The hotel has a cosy restaurant serving Franconian dishes for under DM20, plus rooms costing from DM85/130.

Nördlingen
☎ 09081 • pop 21,000

Nördlingen is encircled by its original 14th-century walls and lies within the basin of the **Ries**, a huge crater created by a meteor more

than 15 million years ago. The crater is one of the largest in existence (25km in diameter) and the **Rieskrater Museum** gives details (closed Monday; DM5/2.50). For a bird's-eye view of the town, climb the tower of **St Georg Kirche**. You'll find the tourist office (*☎ 43 80, fax 8 41 13, ✉ stadt.noerdlingen@t-online.de*) at *Marktplatz 2*. The **Youth Hostel** (*☎ 841 09, Kaiserwiese 1*) charges DM19; follow the many signs. **Altreuter Garni** (*☎ 43 19, Markt 11*) has simple but pleasant singles/doubles with bath and WC for DM65/95.

Füssen
☎ 08362 • pop 17,000

Just short of the Austrian border, Füssen has a monastery, castle and splendid baroque architecture, but it is primarily visited for the two castles in nearby Schwangau associated with King Ludwig II. Its tourist office (*☎ 70 77, fax 391 81, ✉ kurverwaltung@fussen .de*) is at Kaiser-Maximilian-Platz 1. The office is open 8.30 am to 6 pm weekdays, 9.30 am to 2.30 pm Saturday (open 10 am to noon from November to May) and 10 am to noon Sunday (closed Sunday from November to May).

Neuschwanstein & Hohenschwangau Castles The castles provide a fascinating glimpse into the king's state of mind (or lack thereof). Hohenschwangau is where Ludwig lived as a child, but more interesting is the adjacent Neuschwanstein, his own creation (albeit with the help of a theatrical designer). Although it was unfinished at the time of his death in 1886, there is plenty of evidence of Ludwig's twin obsessions: swans and Wagnerian operas. The sugary pastiche of architectural styles reputedly inspired Disney's Fantasyland castle. There's a great view of Neuschwanstein from the Marienbrücke (bridge) over a waterfall and gorge just above the castle. From here you can hike the Tegelberg for even better vistas.

Take the bus from Füssen train station (DM2.50), share a taxi (DM14) or walk the 5km. Both castles are open daily and entry is only by guided tour (DM12/9): Neuschwanstein opens from 9 am to 5.30 pm (10 am to 4 pm from October to March) and Hohenschwangau is open from 8.30 am to 5.30 pm (9.30 am to 4.30 pm from mid-October to mid-March). Go early to avoid the massive crowds.

GERMANY

Places to Stay & Eat The *Youth Hostel* (☎ 77 54, fax 27 70, Mariahilferstrasse 5) is by the train line, 10 minutes west of the station. Dorm beds cost DM20, curfew is a draconian 10 pm and the hostel is closed from mid-November to Christmas. The tourist office has lists of *private rooms* from DM30 per person. Central *Hotel Alpenhof* (☎ 32 32, Theresienstrasse 8) has attractive rooms from DM50/120. *Infooday* (Ritterstrasse 6), open until 6.30 pm weekdays and until 1 pm Saturday, has excellent buffet food (DM2.53 per 100g for hot dishes) to take away or eat in. *Weitzen* (Schrannengasse 10) has a beer garden where you can relax with a nice frothy mug.

WÜRZBURG
☎ 0931 • pop 127,000

Surrounded by forests and vineyards, the charming city of Würzburg straddles the upper River Main. Rebuilt after bombings late in the war, Würzburg is a centre of art, beautiful architecture and delicate wines.

The tourist office (☎ 37 23 98, **ℯ** touris mus@wuerzburg.de), in the rococo masterpiece Haus zum Falken on Oberer Markt, is open 10 am to 6 pm weekdays and to 2 pm weekends (closed Sunday November to March). In the same building, the Stadtbücherei (☎ 37 34 38) has Internet access for DM3 a half-hour, but you'd be wise to book.

Things to See & Do
Spread all along the Balthasar-Neumann-Promenade, the magnificent **Residenz**, a baroque masterpiece by Neumann (he's also on the DM50 note), took a generation to build and is well worth the DM8/6 admission. The open **Hofgarten** at the back is a favourite spot. The **Dom St Kilian** interior and the adjacent **Neumünster** in the old town continue the baroque themes of the Residenz.

Neumann's fortified **Alter Kranen** (old crane), which serviced a dock on the river bank south of Friedensbrücke, is now the **Haus des Frankenweins**, where you can taste Franconian wines (for around DM2 per glass).

The fortress **Marienberg**, across the river on the hill, is reached by crossing the 15th-century stone **Alte Mainbrücke** (bridge) from the city. It encloses the **Fürstenbau Museum**, featuring the episcopal apartments (DM4/3)

and the regional **Mainfränkisches Museum** (DM5/2.50). Both museums (combined card DM6) are closed on Monday. For a dizzy thrill, look down the well in the courtyard. For a simple thrill, wander the walls enjoying the panoramic views.

A **museum** celebrating Würzburg's most important son – Wilhelm Conrad Röntgen, discoverer of the X-ray – at Röntgenring 8 is open on weekdays (free).

Places to Stay & Eat
Kanu-Club camping ground (☎ 725 36, Mergentheimer Strasse 13b), on the west bank of the Main, has two-man tents for DM3 plus DM4 per person; take tram No 3 or 5 to Jugendbühlweg. *Jugendgästehaus Würzburg* (☎ 425 90, fax 41 68 62, Burkarderstrasse 44), below the fortress, charges DM25 for beds (tram No 3 or 5 from the train station).

No-frills *Pension Spehnkuch* (☎ 547 52, fax 547 60, Röntgenring 7) has clean singles/doubles/triples for DM50/94/135. *Gasthof Goldener Hahn* (☎ 519 41, fax 519 61, Marktgasse 7) offers perhaps the best value for a central location with singles/doubles with facilities from DM85/150.

Sternbäck on Sternplatz is a student hangout with a 1920s feel and 19 varieties of baked potato from DM5.90. One of Würzburg's most popular eating and drinking spots is *Bürgerspital* (Theaterstrasse 19). Originally a medieval hospice, it offers a wide selection of Franconian wines (including its own vintages) and serves excellent house specialities averaging DM16.

Getting There & Away
Würzburg is 80 minutes by frequent IC/EC trains from Frankfurt (DM54) and an hour from Nuremberg (DM42). It's a major stop-off for the ICE trains on the Hamburg-Munich line. It is also on the Deutsche-Touring Romantic Road bus route (2½ hours to/from Rothenburg by bus). The main bus station is next to the train station off Röntgenring.

BAMBERG
☎ 0951 • pop 70,000

Tucked away from the main routes in northern Bavaria, Bamberg is practically a byword for magnificence – an untouched monument to the Holy Roman Emperor Heinrich II (who conceived it), to its prince-bishops and clergy and to its patriciate and townsfolk. It is a fun and beautiful town recognised by Unesco as a World Heritage site.

The tourist office (☎ 87 11 61, fax 87 19 60, ☻ info@bamberg.de) is at Geyerswörth-strasse 3 on the island in the River Regnitz. It's open 9 am to 6 pm weekdays and 9 am to 3 pm Saturday (plus 10 am to 2 pm Sunday from May to October).

Things to See & Do

Bamberg's main appeal is its fine buildings; their sheer number, their jumble of styles and the ambience this helps create. Most attractions are spread either side of the River Regnitz, but the colourful **Altes Rathaus** is actually in it, precariously perched on its own islet. The princely and ecclesiastical district is centred on Domplatz, where the Romanesque and Gothic **cathedral**, housing the statue of the chivalric king-knight, the *Bamberger Reiter*, is the biggest attraction. Above Domplatz is the former Benedictine monastery of St Michael, at the top of Michaelsberg. The **Kirche St Michael** is a must-see for its baroque art and the herbal compendium painted on its ceiling. The garden terraces afford another marvellous overview of the city's splendour. There is also the **Fränkisches Brauereimuseum** (closed Monday; DM3.50/2.50), which shows how the monks brewed their robust *Benediktiner Dunkel* beer.

Places to Stay & Eat

Jugendherberge Wolfsschlucht (☎ 560 02, fax 552 11, Oberer Leinritt 70) is on the west bank; turn south off Münchener Ring towards the clinic complex, east at Bamberger Strasse, then north along the river. Beds are DM20. The hostel is closed mid-December to February.

The brewery hotel *Gasthof Fässla* (☎ 265 16, fax 20 19 89, Obere Königstrasse 19-21) has rooms for DM63/98 as well as an earthy restaurant downstairs. *Hotel Alt-Bamberg* (☎ 98 61 50, fax 20 10 07, Habergasse 11), in a quiet location near the Rathaus, charges DM58 for simple singles or DM68/115 for singles/doubles with all facilities. The 17th-century *Wirtshaus zum Schlenkerla (Dominikanerstrasse 6)* provides Franconian specialities, along with its own house-brewed

Rauchbier, a dark-red local speciality that has a startling smoky flavour.

Getting There & Away

There are hourly RE and RB trains to/from both Würzburg (DM27) and Nuremberg (DM16.40), taking one hour. Bamberg is also served by IC trains running between Munich (DM78, 2½ hours) and Berlin (DM125.60, 5½ hours) every two hours.

NUREMBERG

☎ 0911 • pop 488,000

Nuremberg (Nürnberg) is the largest city of the Franconia region of northern Bavaria. Though the flood of tourists to this historical town never seems to cease – especially during its world-famous Christmas market – it's still worth the trip. Nuremberg played a major role during the Nazi years and during the war crimes trials afterwards. The city was rebuilt after Allied bombs reduced it to rubble on 2 January 1945.

Orientation & Information

The main train station is just outside the city walls of the old town. The main artery, the mostly pedestrian Königstrasse, takes you through the old town and its major squares. There are tourist offices in the train station's main hall (☎ 233 61 32, fax 233 61 66), open 9 am to 7 pm Monday to Saturday, and on Hauptmarkt (☎/fax 233 61 35), open 9 am to 6 pm Monday to Saturday (10 am to 1 pm and 2 to 4 pm Sunday from May to September and during the Christmas market).

The main post office is at Bahnhofplatz 1 by the station and a Reisebank is inside the station. There's a central laundrette at Fünferplatz 2. Maximum Internet cafe, Färberstrasse 11, offers one hour of surfing between noon and 3 pm for DM5; at other times your fiver gets you 30 minutes.

Things to See & Do

The spectacular **Germanisches National-museum**, Kartäusergasse 1, is the most important general museum of German culture. It displays works by German painters and sculptors, an archaeological collection, arms and armour, musical and scientific instruments and toys. It's open 10 am to 5 pm Tuesday to Sunday (to 9 pm Wednesday;

GERMANY

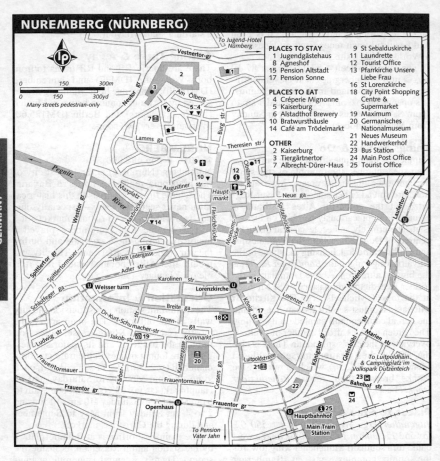

NUREMBERG (NÜRNBERG)

PLACES TO STAY
1 Jugendgästehaus
8 Agneshof
15 Pension Altstadt
17 Pension Sonne

PLACES TO EAT
4 Créperie Mignonne
5 Kaiserburg
6 Alstadthof Brewery
10 Bratwursthäusle
14 Café am Trödelmarkt

OTHER
2 Kaiserburg
3 Tiergärtnertor
7 Albrecht-Dürer-Haus
9 St Sebalduskirche
11 Laundrette
12 Tourist Office
13 Pfarrkirche Unsere
   Liebe Frau
16 St Lorenzkirche
18 City Point Shopping
   Centre &
   Supermarket
19 Maximum
20 Germanisches
   Nationalmuseum
21 Neues Museum
22 Handwerkerhof
23 Bus Station
24 Main Post Office
25 Tourist Office

DM6/3). Close by, the **Neues Museum**, Luitpoldstrasse 5, opened its modern art and design collection, contained in a sleek, streamlined building, to the public in April 2000 (closed Monday; DM6/4).

The scenic **Altstadt** is easily covered on foot. The **Handwerkerhof**, a re-creation of the crafts quarter of old Nuremberg, is walled in opposite the main train station. It's about as quaint (read 'over-priced') as they can possibly make it. On Lorenzer Platz is the **St Lorenzkirche**, noted for the 15th-century tabernacle that climbs like a vine up a pillar to the vaulted ceiling.

To the north is the bustling **Hauptmarkt**, where the most famous *Christkindlmarkt* (Christmas market) in Germany is held from the Friday before Advent to Christmas Eve. The church here is the ornate **Pfarrkirche Unsere Liebe Frau**; the clock's figures go strolling at noon. Near the Rathaus is **St Sebalduskirche**, Nuremberg's oldest church (dating from the 13th century), with the shrine of St Sebaldus.

It's not a bad climb up Burgstrasse to the **Kaiserburg** castle area for a good view of the city. You can visit the palace complex, chapel, well and tower on a DM10 ticket. The walls spread west to the tunnel-gate of **Tiergärtnertor**, where you can stroll behind the castle to the gardens. Nearby is the well renovated **Albrecht-Dürer-Haus** (DM5), where Dürer, Germany's renowned Renaissance draughtsman, lived from 1509 to 1528.

Nuremberg's role during the Third Reich is well known. The Nazis chose this city as their propaganda centre and for mass rallies, which were held at **Luitpoldhain**, a (never completed) sports complex of megalomaniac proportions. After the war, the Allies deliberately chose Nuremberg as the site for the trials of Nazi war criminals. A chilling documentary film, *Fascination and Force*, can be seen in the museum at the rear of the Zeppelin stand (on the Zeppelin field) at Luitpoldhain; the museum is open from 10 am to 6 pm daily from May to October (closed Monday; DM2/1). Take tram No 4 to Dutzendteich or No 9 to Luitpoldhein. A new museum called the **Dokumentationszentrum** covering the entire Nazi era is scheduled to open in 2002.

Places to Stay

Campingplatz im Volkspark Dutzendteich (☎ *81 11 22, Hans-Kalb-Strasse 56*) is near the lakes in the Volkspark, south-east of the city centre (U1 to Messezentrum). It charges DM10 per site plus DM8 per person, and is open from May to September.

The excellent *Jugendgästehaus* (☎ *230 93 60, fax 23 09 36 11*) is in the historical Kaiserstallung next to the castle. Dorm beds including sheets cost DM29 (juniors only). The cheapest option for those aged over 27 is the remote *Jugend-Hotel Nürnberg* (☎ *521 60 92, Rathsbergstrasse 300*), north of the city (take U2 to Ziegelstein, then bus No 21 to Buchenbühl). Dorm beds start at DM27 and there are singles/doubles from DM37/58; prices exclude breakfast.

Simple, friendly *Pension Vater Jahn* (☎ *44 45 07, Jahnstrasse 13*), south-west of the main train station, has rooms from DM50/80. For reasonable accommodation in the city centre, *Pension Altstadt* (☎ *22 61 02, Hintere Ledergasse 4*) and *Pension Sonne* (☎ *22 71 66, Königstrasse 45*) are good options. The former has basic singles/doubles from DM55/90, while the latter lives up to its name with sunny rooms for DM57/95. Lovely *Ag-*

neshof (☎ *21 44 40, fax 21 44 41 44, Agnessgasse 10*) is near the castle and charges DM165/198.

Places to Eat

A top draw is the *Bratwursthäusle* (*Rathausplatz 1*), where you can try Nuremberg's justly famous *Bratwurstl* (small grilled sausages). Be sure to order at least a dozen with both the *Meerrettich* (horseradish) and the *Kartoffelsalat* (potato salad).

Kaiserburg (*Ubere Krämersgasse 20*) has an old blackened wood interior and hot dishes from DM9.80. Just around the corner, *Créperie Mignonne* (*Untere Schmiedgasse 5*) has French bistro music and crepes from DM12.50. The *Altstadthof Brewery* (*Bergstrasse 19*) is a rambling place which brews its own beer and serves hearty meals from DM9. Some nights there's live theatre.

Probably the loveliest place to sit on a sunny day is *Café am Trödelmarkt* (☎ *20 88 77*), on an island overlooking the covered bridge and half-timbered houses; continental breakfasts cost from DM7. There is a *supermarket* in the basement of the City Point shopping complex on the corner of Breite Gasse and Pfannenschmiedsgasse.

Getting There & Around

IC trains run hourly to/from Frankfurt (DM73, 2½ hours) and Munich (DM61, 1½ hours). IR trains run every two hours to Stuttgart (DM54, two hours) and IC trains every two hours to Berlin (DM144, 5½ hours). Several daily EC trains travel to Vienna and Prague (both six hours). Buses to regional destinations including Rothenburg leave from the station just east of the main train station.

Tickets on the bus, tram and U-Bahn system cost DM2.50/3.30 for each short/long ride in the central zone. A day pass is DM6.60.

REGENSBURG
☎ 0941 • pop 141,000

On the Danube River, Regensburg has relics of all periods, yet lacks the packaged feel of some other German cities. It escaped the carpet bombing, and here, as nowhere else in Germany, you enter the misty ages between the Roman and the Carolingian.

GERMANY

From the main train station walk up Maximillianstrasse for 10 minutes to reach the centre. The tourist office (☎ 507 44 10, fax 507 44 19, ✉ tourismus@info.regensburg.baynet.de) is in the Altes Rathaus and is open 8.30 am to 6 pm weekdays and 9 am to 4 pm weekends (to 2.30 pm Sunday). C@fe Netzblick, Am Römling 9, is a bar-cum-Internet cafe offering half an hour's access for DM5.

Things to See

Dominating the skyline are the twin spires of the Gothic **Dom St Peter**, built during the 14th and 15th centuries from unusual green limestone. It has striking original stained-glass windows above the choir on the eastern side. The **Altes Rathaus** was progressively extended from medieval to baroque times and remained the seat of the Reichstag for almost 150 years. There are tours in English at 3.15 pm daily (DM5; not Sunday) from May to September. The **Roman wall**, with its **Porta Praetoria** arch, follows Unter den Schwibbögen onto Dr-Martin-Luther-Strasse.

Lavish **Schloss Thurn und Taxis** is near the train station and is divided into three separate sections: the castle proper (Schloss), the monastery (Kreuzgang) and the royal stables (Marstall). A ticket for all three costs DM18/14. Nearby is **St Emmeram Basilika**, a baroque masterpiece containing untouched Carolingian and episcopal graves and relics (free).

Places to Stay & Eat

Camp at *Azur-Camping* (☎ 27 00 25, Weinweg 40) and you'll pay a DM11.50 site fee plus DM8.50 per adult. Bus No 6 from the train station goes to the entrance. The *Youth Hostel* (☎ 574 02, fax 524 11, Wöhrdstrasse 60) costs DM27 (juniors only; closed December). Take bus No 3, 8 or 9 to the Eisstadion stop. In the town centre, *Diözesanzentrum Obermünster* (☎ 597 02, fax 597 22 30, Obermünsterplatz 7) charges DM50/90 for singles/doubles; ring ahead if you can't arrive before 5 pm. *Bischofshof Hotel* (☎ 584 60, fax 584 61 46, ✉ info@hotel-bischofshof.de, Krauterermarkt 3) is in a gorgeous courtyard; its lovely rooms are good value at DM125/225.

The arty *Hinterhaus* bar-restaurant (*Rote-Hahnen-Gasse 2*), in a covered alley, has fresh fare with good vegetarian choices from DM7.

Just across the river, *Alte Linde (Müllerstrasse 1)* serves German dishes from DM6.50 in its large, leafy beer garden with great views of the cathedral. One of the oldest eateries in the world, *Historische Wurstküche* has been serving Bratwurstl for centuries from its spot at the southern end of the Steinerne Brücke.

Getting There & Away

Regensburg is on the train line between Nuremberg (DM34, one hour) and Austria and there are EC/IC trains in both directions every two hours, as well as IR trains to Munich (DM38, 1½ hours). EC/IC services run every two hours south-east to Passau (DM39, one hour). Regensburg is a major stop on the Danube bike route.

PASSAU
☎ 0851 • pop 51,000

As it exits Germany for Austria, the Danube River flows through the lovely baroque town of Passau, where it is joined by the rivers Inn and Ilz. Passau is not only at a confluence of inland waterways, but also forms the hub of long-distance cycling routes.

The city's two tourist offices are contactable on ☎ 95 59 80, fax 351 07 or ✉ tourist-info@passau.de. The main one at Rathausplatz 3 is open 9 am to 5 pm weekdays (to 4 pm Friday); until 6 pm weekdays and 9.30 am to 3 pm weekends from Easter to mid-October. The tourist centre for the region at Bahnhofstrasse 36, virtually opposite the train station, is especially useful for info about bicycle and boat travel along the Danube.

Things to See & Do

You'll notice that the Italian-baroque essence has not doused the medieval feel as you wander through the narrow lanes, tunnels and archways of the old town and monastic district to Ortspitze, where the rivers meet. The 13th-century **Veste Oberhaus** (closed Monday and during February; DM7/4) has a great view over the city from the castle tower (DM2). The imposing cathedral **Dom St Stephan**, built between 1680 and 1890, houses the world's largest church organ (17,774 pipes). The daily half-hour concerts, at noon, from May to October (DM4/2), are acoustically stunning. The glockenspiel in the colourful **Rathaus** chimes several times daily and wall markings show historical flood levels.

Places to Stay & Eat

There's camping at *Zeltplatz Ilzstadt* (☎ *414 57, Halser Strasse 34*), with a DM10 fee per adult and no tent price (over the Ilz River bridge on bus No 2 or 4). It's a wheezy climb up to the castle across the Danube which contains the *Youth Hostel* (☎ *413 51, fax 437 09*); it accepts juniors only (DM18). A bus runs from the Rathaus to the castle from Easter to mid-October. A good budget option from May to late October, especially for cyclists, is *Rotel Inn* (☎ *951 60*) on the Danube at Donaugelände; rooms cost DM35/50. *Pension Rössner* (☎ *93 13 50, fax 931 35 55, Bräugasse 19*) has clean rooms from DM60/100.

For cheap eats, Ludwigstrasse is the place, with a large *marketplace* at No 16, complete with fruit stalls, meat and fish stands. *Peschl-Terrasse* (*Rossränke 4*) is a pub-brewery with a terrace on the Danube and home-style German dishes from DM6.20 for light meals and DM14.80 for mains.

Getting There & Away

Trains run direct to/from Munich (DM52, two hours), Regensburg (DM39, one hour) and Nuremberg (DM67, two hours). EC trains serve Austria, including Linz (DM28, 1¼ hours) and Vienna (DM52, three hours). From May to October Wurm + Köck (☎ 92 92 92), Höllgasse 26, sails down the Danube to Linz (DM38, five hours) twice daily.

BAVARIAN ALPS

While not quite as high as their sister summits farther south in Austria, the Bavarian Alps (Bayerlsche Alpen) rise so abruptly from the rolling hills of southern Bavaria that their appearance seems all the more dramatic. Stretching westward from Germany's southeastern corner to the Allgäu region near Lake Constance, the Alps take in most of the mountainous country fringing the southern border with Austria.

Activities

The Bavarian Alps are extraordinarily well organised for outdoor pursuits, with skiing, snowboarding and hiking being the most popular. The ski season usually begins in mid-December and continues into April. Ski gear is available for hire in all the resorts, with the lowest daily/weekly rates including skis, boots and stocks at around DM15/90 (downhill), DM12/60 (cross-country) and DM30/110 (snowboard). Five-day skiing courses cost around DM150.

The hiking season runs from late May right through to November, but the higher trails may be icy or snowed-over before mid-June or after September. Canoeing and rafting on the lakes and rivers, mountain biking and paragliding are popular summer activities.

Accommodation

Most of the resorts have plenty of reasonably priced guesthouses and private rooms, though it's still a good idea to reserve accommodation. Tourist offices can help you find a room; otherwise look out for *'Zimmer Frei'* signs. In most resorts a local tax (or *Kurtaxe*, usually an extra DM3 per night) is levied, although this usually gives free local transport and other deals. Be warned that rates can be higher in July and August, and that hotel and pension owners may not be keen to let rooms for just one or two nights.

Getting Around

While the public transport network is very good, the mountain geography means there are few direct routes between main centres; sometimes a short cut via Austria is quicker (such as between Füssen and Oberstdorf). Road rather than rail routes are often more practical. For those driving, the German Alpine Road (Deutsche Alpenstrasse) is a scenic way to go, though obviously much slower than the autobahns and highways that fan out across southern Bavaria.

Regional RVO bus passes giving free travel on the network between Füssen, Garmisch and Mittenwald are excellent value; the day pass is DM13 and a pass for five days' travel within one month costs DM40.

Berchtesgaden

☎ 08652 • pop 8200

Berchtesgaden is perhaps the most romantically scenic place in the Bavarian Alps. To reach the centre from the train station, cross the footbridge and walk uphill up Bahnhofstrasse. The tourist office (☎ 96 70, fax 96 74 00,

@ info@berchtesgaden.de), just across the river from the train station at Königsseer Strasse 2, is open 8 am to 6 pm weekdays and 8 am to 5 pm Saturday (plus 9 am to 3 pm Sunday from mid-June to September). Outside of these months, it is open 8 am to 5 pm weekdays and 9 am to noon Saturday.

Things to See & Do A tour of the **Salzbergwerk** combines history with a carnival (rides and games to amuse you). Visitors descend into the salt mine for a 1½-hour tour. It's open 9 am to 5 pm daily from May to mid-October and 12.30 to 3.30 pm Monday to Saturday during the rest of the year (DM21/11 for adults/children).

Nearby **Obersalzberg** is a deceptively innocent-looking place with a creepy legacy as the second seat of government for the Third Reich. Hitler, Himmler, Goebbels and the rest of the Nazi hierarchy all maintained homes here. The new **Dokumentation Obersalzberg museum** documents the evil bunch's time in the area (don't miss the photo of the fun-loving Führer relaxing in *Lederhosen*), as well as the horrors their policies produced, through photos, audio and film. Ask for the free brochure in English as the explanatory captions and audio are in German. The DM5/3 entry also gets you into the eerie **Hitler's bunker**. Catch bus No 9538 (DM7.90 return) from the Nazi-constructed Berchtesgaden train station to Obersalzberg-Hintereck. Take the first major street on the right after alighting from the bus and follow it for five minutes.

Kehlstein, a spectacular meeting house seldom used by Hitler, despite its reputation as the **'Eagle's Nest'**, is a popular destination. The views are stunning and the history bracing. Entrance (open mid-May to October; DM22) includes transport on special buses linking the summit with Hintereck/Obersalzberg as well as the 120m lift through solid rock to the peak. Be sure to reserve a spot on a bus going down when you leave the one going up. Alternatively you can make the steep ascent or descent on foot in two to three hours.

The best way to see Obersalzberg and Kehlstein is with Berchtesgaden Mini Bus Tours (☎ 08652-649 71), whose **English-language tours** last four hours and cover the entire history of the area during WWII

(DM55, including entrance to Kehlstein). These are the only historical tours of the area; local authorities won't allow any German-language tours for fear they will attract Nazi-sympathising pilgrims.

You can forget the horrors of war at the **Königssee**, a beautiful alpine lake 5km south of Berchtesgaden (linked by hourly buses in summer). There are frequent boat tours (from DM19) across the lake to the quaint chapel at St Bartholomä.

The wilds of Berchtesgaden National Park unquestionably offer some of the best **hiking** in Germany. A good introduction to the area is a 2km path up from St Bartholomä beside the Königssee to the Watzmann-Ostwand, a massive 2000m-high rock face – scores of mountaineers have died attempting to climb it. Another popular hike goes from the southern end of the Königssee to the Obersee. Berchtesgaden's **skiing** centre is the Jenner area at Königssee. Daily/weekly (six days out of seven) ski-lift passes cost DM39.50/165.70.

Places to Stay & Eat Of the five camping grounds in the Berchtesgaden area, the nicest are up at Königssee: *Grafenlehen* (☎ 41 40) and *Mühleiten* (☎ 45 84). Both charge DM10 per site plus DM8 per person. The *Youth Hostel* (☎ 21 90, fax 663 28, Gebirgsjägerstrasse 52) is DM23 for bed and breakfast. From the train station, take bus No 9539 to Strub, then continue a few minutes on foot. The hostel is closed in November and December.

Hotel Watzmann (☎ 20 55, fax 5174, Franziskanerplatz 2) is just opposite the chiming church in the old town, but closed in November and December. Simple singles/doubles cost from DM33/66. Watzmann is popular for its superb food served at outdoor tables. *Hotel Floriani* (☎ 660 11, fax 634 53, Königsseer Strasse 37) is a friendly place near the station with modern rooms from DM65/110. *Alt Berchtesgaden* (Bahnhofstrasse 3) bills itself as a 'schnitzel paradise' and it truly is, with 15 kinds for a mere DM9.95 each.

Getting There & Away For the quickest train connections to Berchtesgaden it's usually best to take a Munich-Salzburg IC/EC/IR train and change at Freilassing (DM48). It's a 2½-hour train trip from Munich, but less than an hour from Salzburg.

Garmisch-Partenkirchen

☎ 08821 • pop 27,000

The combined towns of Garmisch and Partenkirchen were merged by Hitler for the 1936 Winter Olympics. Munich residents' favourite getaway spot, this often-snooty, year-round resort is also a big draw for skiers, snowboarders, hikers and mountaineers.

The huge **ski stadium** outside town hosted the Olympics. From the pedestrian Am Kurpark, walk up Klammstrasse, cross the tracks and veer left on the first path to reach the stadium and enjoy the spectacular views. The tourist office (☎ 18 07 00, fax 18 07 55, ☻ tourist-info@garmisch-partenkirchen.de), Richard Strauss Platz 2, is open 8 am to 6 pm Monday to Saturday as well as 10 am to noon Sunday.

Twenty kilometres north of Garmisch lies over-touristed **Oberammergau**. The town becomes a focus of world attention every 10 years when a good portion of the local populace perform day-long Passion plays. The next series of performances, which date back to the 17th century, will be in 2010.

A great short hike from Garmisch is to the **Partnachklamm gorge**, via a winding path above a stream and underneath waterfalls. Take the Graseck cable car and follow the signs.

An excursion to the **Zugspitze** summit, Germany's highest peak (2963m), is the most popular outing from Garmisch. There are various ways up, including a return trip by rack-railway (just west of the main train station), summit cable car and Eibsee cable car for DM76, or you can scale it in two days. For information on guided hiking or mountaineering courses, check with Bergsteigerschule Zugspitze (☎ 589 99), Dreitorspitz Strasse 13, Garmisch.

Garmisch is bounded by four separate ski areas: **Zugspitze plateau** (the highest), **Alpspitze/Hausberg** (the largest), **Eckbauer** (the cheapest) and **Wank** (the most evocative, despite its name). Day ski passes range from DM30 for Eckbauer to DM62 for Zugspitze. The Happy Ski Card covers all four areas and is valid for a minimum of three days (DM144). A web of cross-country ski trails run along the main valleys.

Flori Wörndle (☎ 583 00) has ski-hire outlets at the Alpspitze and Hausbergbahn lifts.

For skiing information and instruction (downhill), contact the Skischule Garmisch-Partenkirchen (☎ 49 31), Am Hausberg 4, or (cross-country) the Skilanglaufschule (☎ 15 16), Olympia-Skistadion.

Places to Stay & Eat The camping ground nearest to Garmisch, *Zugspitze (☎ 31 80)*, is along highway B24. Take the *weiss-blaue* (literally: white-and-blue) bus (outside the train station and left across the street) in the direction of the Eibsee. Sites cost DM5 plus DM9.50/5 per person/car and DM4 Kurtaxe. The *Youth Hostel (☎ 29 80, fax 585 36, Jochstrasse 10)*, in the suburb of Burgrain, charges DM21 per bed and is closed from November until Christmas. From the train station take bus No 3, 4 or 5 to the Burgrain stop.

Five minutes' walk from the station is the quiet *Hotel Schell (☎ 957 50, fax 95 75 40, Partnachauenstrasse 3)*, while in the town centre is *Gästehaus Becherer (☎ 547 57, Höllentalstrasse 4)* with sunny, clean rooms. Both charge from DM45/90 and don't mind you staying only one night.

On Griesstrasse is *Gasthaus zur Schranne*, an old tavern with daily specials from DM7.50. *Peer's Antipasti (Klammstrasse 10a)* has delicious filled ciabatta rolls from DM6. Outside the main entrance to the train station, *Ciao (Bahnhofstrasse 26)* does superb pasta and pizza from DM10.

Getting There & Away Garmisch is serviced from Munich by hourly trains (DM27, 1½ hours). Trains from Garmisch to Innsbruck (1½ hours) pass through Mittenwald (DM7.60, 20 minutes). RVO bus No 1084, from in front of the train station, links Garmisch with Füssen (DM13, two hours) four times daily via Oberammergau. There is a daily bus to Oberstdorf (DM29).

Mittenwald

☎ 08823 • pop 8500

Mittenwald is a less-hectic alternative to nearby Garmisch-Partenkirchen. At Dammkarstrasse 3, the tourist office (☎ 339 81, fax 27 01, ☻ kurverwaltung@mittenwald.de) is open 8 am to noon and 3 to 5 pm weekdays and 10 am to noon Saturday.

Popular local hikes with cable-car access go to the Alpspitze (2628m), the Wank

(1780m), Mt Karwendel (2384m) and the Wettersteinspitze (2297m). The Karwendel ski area has the longest run (7km) in Germany. Combined day ski passes covering the Karwendel and nearby Kranzberg ski areas cost DM38. For ski hire and instruction, you should contact Erste Skischule (☎ 35 82) on Bahnhofsplatz.

The camping ground closest to Mittenwald is *Am Isarhorn* (☎ 52 16, fax 80 91), 2km north of town off the B2 highway. The *Youth Hostel* (☎ 17 01, fax 29 07, Buckelwiesen 7) is in a beautiful spot 4km outside Mittenwald. It charges DM18 per night and is closed in November and December.

Gasthaus Bergfrühling (☎ 80 89, Dammkarstrasse 12) has basic but bright rooms from DM50/120. *Gasthof Alpenrose* (☎ 927 00, Obermarkt 1) offers rooms for DM77/128, as well as affordable, old-style eating and live Bavarian music. *Hochland-klause* (Albert-Schott-Strasse 5) has a nice outdoor area and dishes up hearty mountain fare from DM9.

For information on getting to/from Mittenwald, see the earlier Garmisch-Partenkirchen entry.

Oberstdorf
☎ 08322 • pop 11,000

Over in the western part of the Bavarian Alps, Oberstdorf is a car-free resort. Like Garmisch, it is surrounded by towering peaks and offers superb hiking.

The tourist office (☎ 70 00, fax 70 02 36, 🄴 info@oberstdorf.de) is at Marktplatz 7 and open from 8 am to noon and 2 pm to 6 pm weekdays and 9.30 am to noon Saturday. A convenient room-finding service on Bahnhofplatz at the train station is open daily.

For an exhilarating day **hike**, ride the Nebelhorn cable car to the upper station then walk down via the Gaisalpseen, two lovely alpine lakes. In-the-know skiers value Oberstdorf for its friendliness, lower prices and generally uncrowded pistes. The village is surrounded by several ski areas: the **Nebelhorn, Fellhorn/Kanzelwand** and **Söllereck**. Combined daily/weekly ski passes that include all three areas (plus the adjoining Kleinwalsertal lifts on the Austrian side) cost DM58/295. For ski hire and tuition, try

the Neue Skischule, which has convenient outlets at the valley stations of the Nebelhorn (☎ 27 37) and Söllereck (☎ 51 54) lifts.

The local *camping ground* (☎ 65 25, Rubingerstrasse 16) is 2km north of the station beside the train line. The *Youth Hostel* (☎ 22 25, fax 804 46, Kornau 8), on the outskirts of town near the Söllereck chairlift, charges DM20 per night (full pension is a bargain at DM31); take the Kleinwalsertal bus to the Reute stop.

Gasthaus Binz Otto (☎ 44 55, Bachstrasse 14) is a central and quaint wooden inn with simple rooms for DM38 per person. Basic *Zum Paulanerbräu* (☎ 23 43, fax 96 76 13), in the heart of the Altstadt, charges DM62/126. Its restaurant serves up hearty Bavarian fare, averaging DM16. *Zum wilde Männle* (Oststrasse 15) serves similar food but is a bit classier, and the extra you pay is worth it.

There are hourly RB trains to/from Immenstadt where you can connect to Lindau (DM24.60, two hours) and Munich (DM47, 2½ hours). Direct RE trains to/from Ulm run every two hours (DM35, 1¾ hours). Several daily bus connections to Füssen operate via Reutte in Austria and/or Pfronten.

Baden-Württemberg

Baden-Württemberg is one of Germany's main tourist regions. With recreational centres such as the Black Forest and Lake Constance, medieval towns like Heidelberg and the health spa of Baden-Baden, it's one of the most varied parts of Germany.

The prosperous modern state of Baden-Württemberg was created in 1951 out of three smaller regions: Baden, Württemberg and Hohenzollern. Baden was first unified and made a grand duchy by Napoleon, who was also responsible for making Württemberg a kingdom in 1806. Both areas, in conjunction with Bavaria and 16 other states, formed the Confederation of the Rhine under French protection. Baden and Württemberg sided with Austria against Prussia in 1866, but were ultimately drafted into the German Empire in 1871.

STUTTGART

☎ 0711 • pop 630,500

Stuttgart enjoys the status of being Baden-Württemberg's state capital and the hub of its industries. At the forefront of Germany's economic recovery from the ravages of WWII, Stuttgart started life less auspiciously in 950 AD as a horse stud farm. Lacking historical monuments, the city attracts visitors with its air of relaxed prosperity amid the vineyard-covered hills.

Information

The tourist office (☎ 222 82 40, fax 222 82 53), Königstrasse 1a, is opposite the main train station and on the main pedestrian strip. It's open 9.30 am to 8.30 pm weekdays, 9.30 am to 6 pm Saturday and 10.30 am to 6 pm Sunday (1 to 6 pm Sunday from November to April). Room reservations can be made here for no fee.

The main post office is at Bolzstrasse 3. You'll find a Reisebank at the main train station. The Königstrasse department stores Karstadt and Kaufhof have Internet terminals on their top floors – the former, at No 1, charges DM5 per half-hour and the latter, at No 6, asks for DM6.

Things to See

Stretching south-west from the Neckar River to the city centre is the **Schlossgarten**, an extensive strip of parkland divided into three sections (Unterer, Mittlerer and Oberer), complete with ponds, swans, street entertainers and modern sculptures. At their northern edge the gardens take in the **Wilhelma** zoo and botanical gardens (open daily; DM14/7). At their southern end they encompass the sprawling baroque **Neues Schloss** and the Renaissance **Altes Schloss**. Adjoining the park, at Konrad-Adenauer-Strasse 30, you'll find the **Staatsgalerie** (closed Monday; DM9/5) housing an excellent collection from the Middle Ages to the present. In the Mittlerer Schlossgarten, the **Carl Zeiss Planetarium** (open daily; DM9/5) is named after the company that invented the planetarium.

Motor Museums The motor car was first developed by Gottlieb Daimler and Carl Benz at the end of the 19th century. The impressive **Mercedes-Benz Museum** (☎ 172

25 78) in the suburb of Sindelfingen is open 9 am to 4 pm Tuesday to Sunday (free); take S-Bahn No 1 to Neckarstadion. Mercedes-Benz also runs free weekday tours of its Sindelfingen plant, but you must reserve a spot in advance (☎ 07031-90 24 93; children under 14 not allowed). For even faster cars, cruise over to the **Porsche Museum**, open from 9 am to 4 pm daily (to 5 pm weekends; free); take S-Bahn No 6 to Neuwirtshaus. Sadly, neither place offers free samples.

Places to Stay

You can camp at *Campingplatz Stuttgart* (☎ 55 66 96, fax 55 74 54, Mercedesstrasse 40), by the river and 500m from the Bad Cannstatt S-Bahn station. Adults pay DM9 each plus DM4 for the site. The DJH *Youth Hostel* (☎ 24 15 83, fax 236 10 41, Haussmannstrasse 27) is a signposted 15-minute walk east of the main train station. Beds cost DM24/29 for juniors/seniors, and the curfew is from midnight. The non-DJH *Jugendgästehaus* (☎ 24 11 32, Richard-Wagner-Strasse 2), south-east of the centre, charges DM40/70/90 for singles/doubles/triples. Take U-Bahn No 15 to Bubenbad. The cheapest deal for those between 16 and 27 is *Tramper Point Stuttgart* (☎ 817 74 76, fax 237 28 10, Wiener Strasse 317), which has portable beds in a communal room for DM13. It's open from late June to early September (check in between 5 pm and 11 pm); take U-Bahn No 6 to Sportpark Feuerbach.

Hotel Espenlaub (☎ 21 09 10, fax 210 91 55, Charlottenstrasse 27) has pleasant singles/doubles, starting at DM60/90 without bathroom. Rooms at the *Gasthof Alte Mira* (☎ 222 95 02, fax 222 95 03 29, Büchsenstrasse 24) start at DM60/100. Just around the corner is the smaller *Museumstube* (☎ 29 68 10, Hospitalstrasse 9), with simple rooms from DM63/98.

The best value in the city centre is offered by *Holl's Arche* (☎ 24 57 59, fax 24 30 44, Bärenstrasse 2), in a great spot opposite the Markthalle, with rooms with private facilities for DM80/130.

Places to Eat

The *Markthalle*, a superb Art Nouveau-style market gallery on Dorotheenstrasse, is the perfect place to pick up fresh treats for a

GERMANY

GERMANY

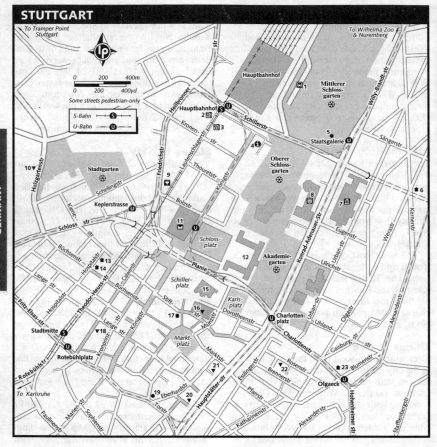

STUTTGART

picnic in the nearby parks; it's open 7 am to 6 pm weekdays and to 2 pm on Saturday. For a really cheap lunch, though, try the university *Mensa (Holzgartenstrasse 11)*. The upstairs dining hall is for students, while the ground-floor cafeteria and the small *Mensa Stüble* in the basement are open to the un-educated masses.

Otherwise, join the natural-fibre-clad mobs at *iden (Eberhardtstrasse 1)*, a spacious vege-tarian restaurant with a tasty spread of whole-food selections. The *Weinstube Stetter (☎ 24 01 63, Rosenstrasse 32)*, in the Bohnenviertel (Bean Quarter), has Swabian specialities like

Maultaschen (similar to ravioli) from DM8.20 plus a good assortment of regional wines. *Lit-fass (Schwabenzentrum Block 3)*, in a sunken courtyard, is a popular cafe that has live music on many nights and serves some of the best Turkish food in town, with a good vegetarian selection. On a street lined with restaurants and nightclubs, *Calwer Eck Bräu (Calwerstrasse 31)* brews its own excellent beer and serves a wide range of dishes from about DM15.

Entertainment

Lift Stuttgart is a comprehensive free guide to local entertainment and events. The

STUTTGART

PLACES TO STAY				OTHER	
6	DJH Youth Hostel	18	Calwer Eck Braü	4	Tourist Office
13	Museumstube	20	Litfass	5	Carl Zeiss
14	Gasthof Alte Mira	21	iden		Planetarium
17	Holl's Arche	22	Weinstube	7	Staatsgalerie
23	Hotel Espenlaub		Stetter	8	Staatstheater
				9	Palast de Republic
PLACES TO EAT		OTHER		11	Main Post Office
10	University Mensa	1	Bus Station	12	Neues Schloss
16	Markthalle	2	Karstadt	15	Altes Schloss
		3	Kaufhof	19	Hans-im-Glück Platz

GERMANY

Staatstheater (☎ *20 20 90*), in the Oberer Schlossgarten near Konrad-Adenauer-Strasse, holds regular symphony, ballet and opera performances.

On the corner of Friedrichstrasse and Lautenschlagerstrasse is the grandly named *Palast de Republic*, a busy bar that's grown from a kiosk into an institution. Probably the coolest place for bars is tiny Geissstrasse, just a block from Eberhardstrasse, where there are several places that pour out onto a small square unofficially called Hans-im-Glück Platz. For leafy fun, there's a *beer garden* in the Mittlerer Schlossgarten, north-east of the main train station.

Getting There & Around
Stuttgart's international airport is south of the city and is served by S-Bahn Nos 2 and 3 (DM4.80, 30 minutes from the main train station). There are frequent train departures for all major German and many international cities. ICE trains run to Frankfurt (DM88, 80 minutes), Berlin (DM256, six hours) and Munich (DM87, two hours). Regional and long-distance buses leave from the station next to the main train station.

Single fares on Stuttgart's public transport network are DM2/2.90 for short/long trips within the central zone. A four-ride strip ticket costs DM10.80 and a day pass is DM12.

AROUND STUTTGART
Tübingen
☎ 07071 • pop 8000
This gentle, picturesque university town is a perfect place to spend a day wandering winding alleys and enjoying the views of half-timbered houses and old stone walls. It's an ideal day trip from Stuttgart, 35km north – catch one of the hourly regional trains (DM16.40, one hour). On **Marktplatz**, the centre of town, is the 1435 **Rathaus** with its ornate baroque facade and astronomical clock. The nearby late-Gothic **Stiftkirche** houses tombs of the Württemberg dukes and has excellent medieval stained-glass windows. From the heights of the Renaissance **Schloss Hohentübingen** (now part of the university) there are fine views over the steep, red-tiled rooftops of the old town. The tourist office (☎ 913 60, fax 350 70, ✉ mail@tuebingen-info.de) is by the main bridge, Neckarbrücke. It is open 9 am to 7 pm weekdays and until 5 pm Saturday (and 2 to 5 pm Sunday from May to September).

The *DJH hostel* (☎ 230 02, fax 250 61, Gartenstrasse 22/2) charges DM26/31 for juniors/seniors. Central *Hotel Am Schloss* (☎ 929 40, fax 92 94 10, ✉ info@hotelam-schloss.de, Burgsteige 18) has simple singles/doubles from DM72/130. Its restaurant's *Maultaschen* are a local institution. The Turkish food at *Restaurant Istanbul* (Karl-strasse 1) is fighting fresh (felafel with salad in bread cooked on the premises is DM6).

HEIDELBERG
☎ 06221 • pop 140,000
The French destroyed Heidelberg in 1693; they may have been the last visitors to dislike this charming town on the Neckar River. Its magnificent castle and medieval town are irresistible drawcards for most travellers in Germany. Mark Twain began his European travels here and recounted his comical observations in *A Tramp Abroad*. Britain's JMW Turner loved Heidelberg and it inspired him to produce some of his finest landscape paintings.

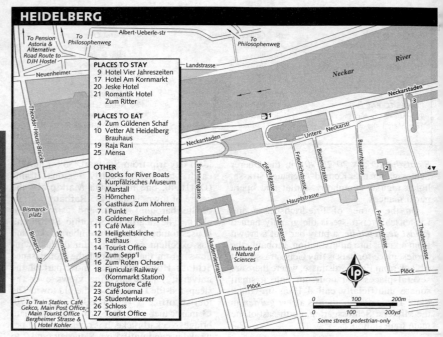

HEIDELBERG

PLACES TO STAY
9 Hotel Vier Jahreszeiten
17 Hotel Am Kornmarkt
20 Jeske Hotel
21 Romantik Hotel
   Zum Ritter

PLACES TO EAT
4 Zum Güldenen Schaf
10 Vetter Alt Heidelberg
   Brauhaus
19 Raja Rani
25 Mensa

OTHER
1 Docks for River Boats
2 Kurpfälzisches Museum
3 Marstall
5 Hörnchen
6 Gasthaus Zum Mohren
7 i Punkt
8 Goldener Reichsapfel
11 Café Max
12 Heiligkeitskirche
13 Rathaus
14 Tourist Office
15 Zum Sepp'l
16 Zum Roten Ochsen
18 Funicular Railway
   (Kornmarkt Station)
22 Drugstore Café
23 Café Journal
24 Studentenkarzer
26 Schloss
27 Tourist Office

Heidelberg's sizable student population (attending the oldest university in the country) makes it a lively city. But be warned; this place is chock-a-block with tourists during July and August, so try to avoid coming then or you might start to empathise with the French...

Orientation & Information

Arriving in Heidelberg can be something of an anticlimax. Expectations of a quaint old town clash with the modern and less interesting western side of the city near the train station. To find out what this city is really about continue down Kurfürsten-Anlage to Bismarckplatz, where old Heidelberg begins to reveal itself. Hauptstrasse is the pedestrian way leading eastwards through the heart of the old city from Bismarckplatz via Marktplatz to Karlstor.

The main tourist office (☎ 194 33, fax 14 22 22, ❷ cvb@heidelberg.de), outside the train station at Willy-Brandt-Platz 1, is open for abrupt service 9 am to 7 pm Monday to

Saturday (10 am to 6 pm Sunday between mid-March and mid-November). Smaller offices at the funicular train station near the castle and on Neckarmünzplatz keep reduced hours.

The main post office is to the right as you leave the train station. You'll find a Reisebank in the train station. Café Gecko, Bergheimer Strasse 8, charges DM4 for 30 minutes on the Internet.

Things to See & Do

Heidelberg's large **Schloss** is one of Germany's finest examples of grand Gothic-Renaissance architecture. The building's half-ruined state actually adds to its romantic appeal. Seen from anywhere in the Altstadt, the striking red-sandstone castle (open daily) dominates the hillside. Entry costs DM4/2, which covers the castle, the **Grosses Fass** (Great Vat; an enormous 18th-century keg capable of holding 221,726L) and **Deutsches Apothekenmuseum** (German Pharmaceutical Museum). It

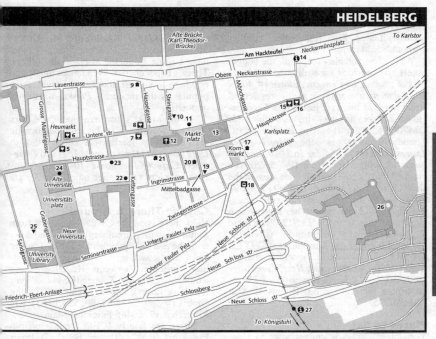

HEIDELBERG

costs nothing to wander the grounds and garden terraces.

You can take the funicular railway to the castle from lower Kornmarkt station (DM3 return), or enjoy an invigorating 10-minute walk up steep, stone-laid lanes. The funicular continues up to the **Königstuhl**, where there's a TV and lookout tower (DM8.50 return, including a castle stop).

Dominating Universitätsplatz are the 18th-century **Alte Universität** and the **Neue Universität**. The **Studentenkarzer** (students' jail) is on Augustinergasse (closed Sunday and Monday; DM1.50/1). From 1778 to 1914 this jail was used for uproarious students. Sentences (usually two to 10 days) were earned for heinous crimes such as drinking, singing and womanising (no word as to whether 'manising' was *verboten*). The **Marstall** is the former arsenal, now a student refectory. The **Kurpfälzisches Museum** (Palatinate Museum) on Hauptstrasse contains paintings, sculptures and the jawbone of the 600,000-year-old Heidelberg

Man (closed Monday; DM5/3, DM3/2 on Sunday).

A stroll along the **Philosophenweg**, north of the Neckar River, gives a welcome respite from Heidelberg's tourist hordes. Leading through steep vineyards and orchards, the path offers the great views of the Altstadt and castle that inspired German philosopher Hegel.

Places to Stay

You don't get very good value for your money here, and finding any accommodation in the high season can be difficult. Arrive early in the day or book ahead.

Camping Haide (☎ 06223-21 11) is also on the river and charges DM8.50 per person and from DM6 per site. Take bus No 35 to Orthopädische Klinik. The local *DJH hostel* (☎ 41 20 66, fax 40 25 59, Tiergartenstrasse 5) is across the river from the train station. The rates are DM24/29 for juniors/seniors. If you want a chance at a room, fax your reservation at least a week in advance. To get there from the station or Bismarckplatz, take bus No 33 towards Ziegelhausen. The veteran *Jeske Hotel* (☎ 2 37 33, Mittelbadgasse 2) is ideally situated. Frau Jeske offers doubles without breakfast for DM48.

With a few notable exceptions, the budget hotels and pensions are well outside the old part of town. Tiny *Pension Astoria* (☎ 40 29 29, Rahmengasse 30) is in a quiet residential street north of the river just across Theodor-Heuss-Brücke, and has singles/doubles for DM70/115. Near the Alte Brücke (Karl-Theodor-Brücke) is the *Hotel Vier Jahreszeiten* (☎ 241 64, fax 16 31 10, Haspelgasse 2), with rooms from DM85/120. It's claimed that Goethe himself once creased the sheets here. *Hotel Kohler* (☎ 97 00 97, fax 97 00 96, Goethestrasse 2), east and within walking distance of the station, has high season singles/doubles from DM115/170 (but these are much cheaper at other times). Also in the old town is *Hotel Am Kornmarkt* (☎ 243 25, fax 282 18, Kornmarkt 7), which charges from DM90/140. *Romantik Hotel Zum Ritter* (☎ 13 50, fax 13 52 30, Hauptstrasse 178) is an ornate top-end option. Rooms start at DM175/295.

Places to Eat

You might expect a student town to have plenty of great budget eats but, unfortunately, free-spending tourists outweigh frugal scholars. A meal at the *Mensa* will cost students about DM5. *Raja Rani* (Mittelbadgasse 5) is an Indian stehcafe (stand-up cafe) and takeaway with simple, tasty (and often vegetarian) curries from DM5 a plate.

Many student pubs (see Entertainment) have main courses priced from around DM14. They make their own sausage and beer at *Vetter Alt Heidelberg Brauhaus* (Steingasse 9), which is bustling year round. A large old tavern, *Zum Güldenen Schaf* (Hauptstrasse 115) has an extensive menu, with vegetarian fare from DM14 and local specialities from around DM16.

Entertainment

Backstreet pubs and cafes are a feature of the nightlife in this thriving university town. *Zum Roten Ochsen* (Hauptstrasse 217) and *Zum Sepp'l* next door are historic student pubs, now mostly frequented by tourists and avoided by students. Better are *Gasthaus*

Zum Mohren (Untere Strasse 5-7) and *Hörnchen*, with outdoor tables on Heumarkt.

The *Goldener Reichsapfel* on Untere Strasse is an original students' hang-out that hasn't quite gone the way of the others. There's noisy chatter, even louder music and nowhere to sit just about every night. Also popular is the modern *i Punkt*, diagonally opposite.

On the Markt's northern side, *Café Max* is a big favourite. It's a bit more democratic than the posey 'intellectual' cafes, although *Café Journal* (Hauptstrasse 162) and *Drugstore Café* (Kettengasse 10), for serious chess-players (and other quiet guests), are good.

Getting There & Around

Heidelberg is on the Castle Road route from Mannheim to Nuremberg. From mid-May until the end of September Deutsche-Touring has a daily coach service, with one bus in either direction between Heidelberg and Rothenburg ob der Tauber (DM47, a very long five hours); contact Deutsche-Touring GmbH (☎ 089-59 38 89, fax 550 39 65), Am Römerhof 17, 60486 Frankfurt/Main.

There are hourly ICE/IC trains to/from Frankfurt (DM22.40, one hour), Stuttgart (DM38, 40 minutes) and Munich (DM104, three hours). Mannheim, 12 minutes to the west by frequent trains, has connections to cities throughout Germany. You can arrange a lift through the local Citynetz Mitfahr-Service (☎ 194 44) at Bergheimer Strasse 125.

Bismarckplatz is the main local transport hub. The bus and tram system in and around Heidelberg is extensive and efficient. Single tickets are DM3.30 and a 24-hour pass costs DM10.

BADEN-BADEN
☎ 07221 • 53,000

Baden-Baden's natural hot springs have attracted visitors since Roman times, but this small city only really became fashionable in the 19th century when the likes of Victor Hugo came to bathe in and imbibe its therapeutic waters. Today Baden-Baden is Germany's premier (and ritziest) health spa and offers many other salubrious activities in a friendly and relaxed atmosphere.

Orientation & Information

The train station is 7km north-west of town. Bus Nos 201, 205 and 216 run frequently to/from Leopoldsplatz, the heart of Baden-Baden. From here, Sophienstrasse leads eastwards to the more historic part of town. North of Sophienstrasse are the baths, the Stiftskirche and the Neues Schloss. Across the river to the west you'll find the Trinkhalle (pump room) and tourist office, and past Goetheplatz the Kurhaus and Spielhalle (casino).

The tourist office (☎ 27 52 00, fax 27 52 02) is in the Trinkhalle; collect some info and sample the local drop (see later). It's open 9.30 am to 5 pm weekdays (to 3 pm Saturday). There is a spa Kurtaxe (visitors' tax) of DM5, entitling you to a Kurkarte from your hotel which brings various discounts. The tax doesn't apply to those staying at the hostel.

Things to See & Do

The ancient **Römische Badruinen** (Roman Bath Ruins) on Römerplatz are worth a quick look, but for a real taste of Baden-Baden head for the ornate and grand **Trinkhalle** at Kaiserallee 3. You can have a free drink of the spa water piped in hot right from the ground. Next door is the 1820s **Kurhaus**, which houses the opulent **casino** where Dostoyevsky was inspired to write **The Gambler** (guided tours between 9.30 and noon daily; DM6).

The **Merkur Cable Car** takes you up to the 660m summit (DM7 return; 10 am to 10 pm daily), where there are fine views and numerous walking trails (bus No 204 or 205 from Leopoldplatz takes you to the cablecar station). A good hiking-driving tour is to the wine-growing area of **Rebland**, 6km to the west.

Spas On either side of Römerplatz are the two places where you can take the waters: **Friedrichsbad** (☎ 27 59 20), Römerplatz 1, and **Caracalla-Therme** (☎ 27 59 40), Römerplatz 11. Don't leave town without a visit to one or both.

The 19th-century Friedrichsbad is decadently Roman in style and offers a Roman-Irish bathing program for DM36. Your three hours of humid bliss comprises 16 steps of hot and cold baths, saunas, steam rooms and showers that leave you feeling scrubbed, sparkling and loose as a goose. An extra DM12 gets you a soap-and-brush massage which covers just about every nook and cranny. No clothing is allowed inside, and several of the bathing sections are mixed on most days, so leave your modesty at the reception desk. Friedrichsbad is open 9 am to 10 pm Monday to Saturday and noon to 8 pm Sunday. Mixed bathing hours change almost every day.

Modern Caracalla-Therme is a vast complex of outdoor and indoor pools, hot and cold-water grottoes and many more delights. Two hours of watery bliss cost DM19. It's open from 8 am to 10 pm daily. You must wear a bathing costume and bring your own towel.

Places to Stay & Eat

The closest camping ground is **Campingplatz Adam** (☎ 07223-2 31 94), at Bühl-Oberbruch, about 12km outside town. Baden-Baden's **DJH hostel** (☎ 522 23, fax 600 12, Hardbergstrasse 34) lies 3km north-west of the centre; it costs DM24/29 for juniors/seniors. Take bus No 201 to Jugendherberge stop.

The tourist office may be able to find you a private room for no commission. Otherwise, **Gästehaus Löhr** (☎ 330 29, Adlerstrasse 2), just off Augustaplatz, is a good deal by Baden-Baden standards. The reception is in Café Löhr at Lichtentaler Strasse 19. A single with no shower is DM35, while rooms with shower are DM60/110. **Hotel Am Markt** (☎ 227 47, Marktplatz 17), up by the Stiftskirche, charges DM54/110 for simple rooms. Despite brusque service (unless you look like a million dollars), **Hotel Römerhof** (☎ 234 15, fax 39 17 07, Sophienstrasse 25) has pleasant rooms with bathroom from DM85/170.

Amadeus on Leopoldsplatz will rock you with vegetarian and Italian specials from DM7 to DM22. For reasonable regional specialties like *Flammkuchen* (a sort of Alsatian pizza) and a nice patio, head for **Warsteiner Brasserie** on Hindenburgplatz.

Kaiser's supermarket (*Lichtentaler 15*) is close to the lush and picnic-friendly parks.

Getting There & Away

Baden-Baden is on the busy Mannheim-Basel train line. Fast trains in either direction stop every two hours. Frequent local trains serve Karlsruhe and Offenburg, from where you can make connections to much of Germany.

BLACK FOREST

Home of the cuckoo clock, the Black Forest (Schwarzwald) gets its name from the dark canopy of evergreens. The fictional Hansel and Gretel encountered their wicked witch in these parts, but modern-day hazards are more likely to include packs of tourists in buses. However, 20 minutes' walk from even the most crowded spots will put you in quiet countryside dotted with huge traditional farmhouses and patrolled by amiable dairy cows.

Orientation & Information

The Black Forest lies east of the Rhine between Karlsruhe and Basel. It's roughly triangular in shape, about 160km long and 50km wide. Baden-Baden, Freudenstadt, Titisee and Freiburg act as convenient information posts for Black Forest excursions. Even smaller towns in the area generally have tourist offices.

Freudenstadt's tourist office is a good place for information on the northern part of the region. Open 10 am to 5 pm weekdays and 10 am to 1 pm Saturday, the office (☎ 07441-86 40, fax 8 51 76, @ touristinfo@freudenstadt .de) is on Am Marktplatz.

Titisee's office (☎ 07651-98 04 0, fax 98 04 40, @ touristinfo@titisee.de), inside the Kurhaus at Strandbadstrasse 4, also covers neighbouring Neustadt and the rest of the southern Black Forest. It's open 8 am to noon and 1.30 to 5.30 pm weekdays and 10 am to noon weekends from May to October. The Feldberg office (☎ 07655-80 19, fax 801 43, @ tourist-info@feldberg-schwarz.de) is at Kirchgasse 1 and is open 9 am to 6 pm weekdays, and during the ski season on weekend mornings.

Things to See

Enjoying the natural countryside will be the main focus, although you can take a plunge in a lake or down a ski slope, or lose yourself in shops full of cuckoo clocks.

Halfway between Baden-Baden and Freudenstadt along the Schwarzwald-Hochstrasse (Black Forest Highway), the first major tourist sight is the **Mummelsee**, south of the Hornisgrinde peak. It's a small, deep lake steeped in folklore (legend has it that an evil sea king inhabits the depths). If you want to escape the bus loads, hike down the hill to the peaceful **Wildsee**.

Farther south, **Freudenstadt** is mainly used as a base for excursions into the countryside, however the central marketplace, the largest in Germany, is worth a look.

The area between Freudenstadt and Freiburg is cuckoo-clock country, a name that takes on new meaning when you see the prices people are willing to pay. A few popular stops are **Schramberg**, **Triberg** and **Furtwangen**. In Furtwangen, visit the **Deutsches Uhrenmuseum** (German Clock Museum; DM5/3) for a look at the traditional Black Forest skill of clock-making.

Titisee boasts its namesake natural lake where you can take a cruise (DM6, 25 minutes) or rent a boat in summer. The engines are all electric to preserve the lake's serenity and some time on the water can soothe even the most frenzied backpacker's soul.

Activities

Summer With over 7000km of marked trails, the possibilities are, almost literally, endless. Hiking maps are everywhere and any tourist office can set you off on anything from easy one-hour jaunts to multiday treks. Three classic long-distance **hiking trails** run south from the northern Black Forest city of Pforzheim as far as the Swiss Rhine: the 280km Westweg to Basel; the 230km Mittelweg to Waldhut-Tiengen; and the 240km Ostweg to Schaffhausen.

The southern Black Forest, especially the area around the 1493m Feldberg summit, offers some of the best hiking; small towns like Todtmoos or Bonndorf serve as useful bases for those wanting to get off the more heavily trodden trails. The 10km **Wutachschlucht** (Wutach Gorge) outside Bonndorf is justifiably famous. You can also try windsurfing, boating or swimming on the highland lakes, though some may find the water a bit cool. Titisee boasts several beaches.

Winter The Black Forest ski season runs from late December to March. While there is some good downhill skiing, the Black Forest is more suited to cross-country skiing. The Titisee area is the main centre for winter sports, with uncrowded downhill runs at Feldberg (day passes DM38; rental

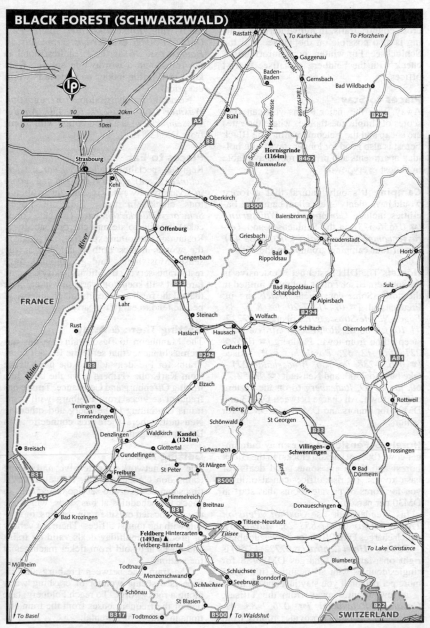

BLACK FOREST (SCHWARZWALD)

GERMANY

To Karlsruhe
To Pforzheim
Rastatt
Gaggenau
Baden-Baden
Gernsbach
Bad Wildbach
Bühl
Hornisgrinde (1164m)
Mummelsee
Oberkirch
Baiersbronn
Griesbach
Freudenstadt
Offenburg
Horb
Gengenbach
Bad Rippoldsau
Sulz
Lahr
Bad Rippoldsau-Schapbach
Alpirsbach
Steinach
Wolfach
Oberndorf
Rust
Haslach
Hausach
Schiltach
Gutach
Elzach
Rottweil
Teningen
Emmendingen
Triberg
Schönwald
St Georgen
Denzlingen
Waldkirch
Kandel (1241m)
Glottertal
Furtwangen
Villingen-Schwenningen
Trossingen
Breisach
Gundelfingen
St Peter
Freiburg
St Märgen
Bad Dürrheim
Himmelreich
Breitnau
Donaueschingen
Bad Krozingen
Titisee-Neustadt
Feldberg (1493m)
Hinterzarten
Titisee
To Lake Constance
Feldberg-Bärental
Müllheim
Todtnau
Schluchsee
Blumberg
Menzenschwand
Schluchsee
Seebrugg
Bonndorf
Schönau
St Blasien
SWITZERLAND
To Basel
Todtmoos
To Waldshut

FRANCE
Rhine River
Strasbourg
Kehl

Schwarzwald-Hochstrasse
Talerstrasse

B294
A5
B3
B462
B500
B33
A81
B294
B33
B500
B31
A5
B31
B315
B317
B500
B22

0 10 20km
0 5 10mi

Höllental Route
Breg River
Brend River

euro currency converter 1DM = €0.51

equipment available) and numerous graded cross-country trails. In midwinter, ice skating is also possible on the Titisee and the Schluchsee. For winter sports information, check with the Feldberg or Titisee tourist offices.

Places to Stay

Away from the major towns you can find scores of simple guesthouses where the rates are cheap and the welcome warm. The Black Forest is also good for longer stays, with holiday apartments and private rooms available in almost every town.

Camping It's only natural that a forest would have plenty of excellent camping. Facilities include *Campingplatz Wolfsgrund* (☎ 07656-573) on the Schluchsee and *Terrassencamping Sandbank* (☎ 07651-82 43), one of four camping grounds on the Titisee.

Hostels The DJH hostel net is extensive in the southern Black Forest, but more limited in the north. Some convenient *hostels* are in: Freudenstadt (☎ 07441-77 20, fax 8 57 88, Eugen-Nägele-Strasse 69); Triberg (☎ 07722-41 10, fax 66 62, Rohrbacher Strasse 3), a steep climb from town; Feldberg (☎ 07676-221, fax 12 32, Passhöhe 14); Titisee (☎ 07652-238, fax 756, Bruderhalde 27) – take bus No 7300; and Neustadt (☎ 07652-73 60, fax 42 99, Rudenberg 6) on the eastern edge of town. All charge between DM23 and DM24 for juniors and DM28 and DM29 for seniors.

Hotels & Pensions Lodges may outnumber cows (but not cuckoo clocks) in the Black Forest and there are some good deals for basic rooms. Tourists offices can also direct you to scores of private rooms that start at DM30 per person.

In Freudenstadt is *Gasthof Pension Traube* (☎/fax 07441-853 28, Markt 41), which charges DM50/100 for singles/doubles.

Triberg's *Hotel Central* (☎ 07722-43 60) is right on Markt and charges DM50/88 for singles/doubles with all facilities (it's DM5 more per person if you stay just one night).

A few minutes away from the Titisee, *Gasthaus Rehwinkel* (☎ 07651-83 41, Neustädter Strasse 7) provides rooms from DM39/78. In neighbouring Neustadt, the family-run *Romantik-Hotel Adler-Post* (☎ 07651-50 66, ✉ adler-post@romantik.de, Hauptstrasse 16) is the friendliest hotel in the forest and a worthwhile splurge from DM138/198 (the indoor pool alone is worth the price).

Near the Feldberg slopes, *Berggasthof Wasmer* (☎ 07676-230, fax 430, An der Wiesenquelle 1) is a good option with rooms from DM42/84.

Places to Eat

Regional specialities include *Schwarzwälderschinken* (ham), which is smoked and served in a variety of ways. Rivalling those ubiquitous clocks in fame (but not price), *Schwarzwälderkirschtorte* (Black Forest cake) is a chocolate and cherry concoction. Restaurants are often expensive so a picnic in the woods makes both fiscal and scenic sense. Most hotels and guesthouses have restaurants serving traditional hearty German fare that will keep you warm in winter. Note that all the fresh air takes its toll on diners and people tend to eat fairly early.

Getting There & Away

The Mannheim to Basel train line has numerous branches that serve the Black Forest. Trains for Freudenstadt and the north leave from Karlsruhe. Triberg is on the busy line linking Offenburg and Constance. Titisee has frequent services from Freiburg with some trains continuing to Feldberg and others to Neustadt, where there are connections to Donaueschingen.

Getting Around

The rail network is extensive and where trains don't go, buses do. However travel times can be slow and service infrequent, so check the schedules at bus stops, which are usually located outside train stations, or consult with the tourist offices. There's a variety of group and multiday deals valid on trains and buses and sold from ticket machines at the stations.

The train line between Freiburg and Titisee is a scenic wonder of crashing water along a rocky gorge. To reach Feldberg, take one of the frequent buses from the train stations in Titisee or Bärental.

Drivers enjoy flexibility in an area that rewards it. The main tourist road, the Schwarzwald-Hochstrasse (B500), runs from Baden-Baden to Freudenstadt and from Triberg to Waldshut. Other thematic roads with maps provided by tourist offices include Schwarzwald-Bäderstrasse (spa town route), Schwarzwald-Panoramastrasse (panoramic view route) and Badische Weinstrasse (wine route).

FREIBURG
☎ 0761 • pop 203,000

The gateway to the southern Black Forest, Freiburg im Breisgau is a fun place, thanks to the city's large and thriving university community. Ruled for centuries by the Austrian Habsburgs, Freiburg has retained many traditional features, although major reconstruction was necessary following severe bombing damage during WWII. The monumental 13th-century cathedral is the city's key landmark but the real attractions are the vibrant cafes, bars and street-life, plus the local wines. The best times for tasting are early July for the four days of *Weinfest* (Wine Festival), or mid-August for the nine days of *Weinkost* (loosely meaning 'wine as food').

Orientation & Information

The city centre is a convenient 10-minute walk from the train station. Walk east along Eisenbahnstrasse to the tourist office, then continue through the bustling pedestrian zone to Münsterplatz, dominated by the red stone cathedral.

The tourist office (☎ 3 88 18 80, fax 3 70 03, @ touristik@fwt-online.de), Rotteckring 14, is open 9.30 am to 6 pm weekdays, 9.30 am to 2 pm Saturday and 10 am to noon Sunday. From May to October it is open until 8 pm weekdays and 5 pm Saturday. It has piles of information on the Black Forest.

The main post office is on Eisenbahnstrasse 58-62, while Volksbank Freiburg is opposite the train station. PingWing Internet Center, Niemensstrasse 3, offers half an hour's Internet access for DM5. Café Fleck

GERMANY

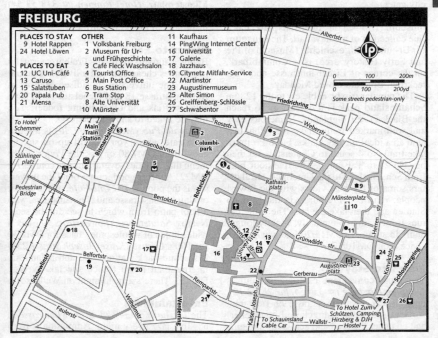

FREIBURG

PLACES TO STAY	OTHER	11 Kaufhaus
9 Hotel Rappen	1 Volksbank Freiburg	14 PingWing Internet Center
24 Hotel Löwen	2 Museum für Ur-	16 Universität
	und Frühgeschichte	17 Galerie
PLACES TO EAT	3 Café Fleck Waschsalon	18 Jazzhaus
12 UC Uni-Café	4 Tourist Office	19 Citynetz Mitfahr-Service
13 Caruso	5 Main Post Office	22 Martinstor
15 Salatstuben	6 Bus Station	23 Augustinermuseum
20 Papala Pub	7 Tram Stop	25 Alter Simon
21 Mensa	8 Alte Universität	26 Greiffenberg-Schlössle
	10 Münster	27 Schwabentor

Waschsalon, Predigerstrasse 3, has a laundrette (open until 1 am daily) and a cafe.

Things to See & Do

The major sight in Freiburg is the 700-year-old **Münster** (cathedral), a classic example of both high and late-Gothic architecture looming over Münsterplatz, Freiburg's market square. Check out the stone and wood carvings, the stained-glass windows and the western porch. Ascend the tower to the stunning pierced spire (DM2.50/1.50) for great views of Freiburg and, on a clear day, the Kaiserstuhl and the Vosges. South of the Münster stands the picturesque **Kaufhaus**, the 16th-century merchants' hall.

While you're admiring the pavement mosaics on the pedestrian streets make sure you sidestep the old drainage system, the **Bächle** (tiny, permanently flowing canals which run throughout the centre). Tourist lore claims that dolts who step in the water have to marry a local. The bustling **university quarter** is north-west of the Martinstor (one of the old city gates).

Freiburg's main museum, the **Augustinermuseum** (DM4/2) on Augustinerplatz, has a fine collection of medieval art. The **Museum für Ur- und Frühgeschichte** (Museum of Pre and Early History; free) is in Columbipark, on the corner of Eisenbahnstrasse and Rotteckring. Both are closed Monday.

The popular trip by cable car to the 1286m **Schauinsland** peak is a quick way to reach the Black Forest highlands. Numerous easy and well-marked trails make the Schauinsland area ideal for day walks. From Freiburg take tram No 4 south to Günterstal and then bus No 21 to Talstation. The five-hour hike from Schauinsland to the Untermünstertal offers some of the best views with the fewest people; return to Freiburg via the train to Staufen and then take the bus. The cable car runs from 9 am to 5 pm daily, slightly longer hours in summer (DM13/20 one way/return, concession DM10/17).

Places to Stay

The most convenient camping ground is *Camping Hirzberg* (☎ 350 54, fax 28 92 12), open all year at Kartäuserstrasse 99. Take tram No 1 to Messeplatz (direction: Littenweiler) and go under the road and across the stream.

Freiburg's *DJH hostel* (☎ 676 56, fax 603 67, Karthäuserstrasse 151), on the eastern edge of the city, is often full with German school groups, so phone ahead. Take tram No 1 to Römerhof (direction: Littenweiler) and follow the signs down Fritz-Geiges-Strasse. A bed costs DM26/31 for juniors/seniors. There is an 11.30 pm curfew, but you can ask for an extension (they make it clear, however, that you will not be welcome if you come back drunk!).

The tourist office has access to a limited supply of *private rooms* (DM5 charge). One of the cheapest places in central Freiburg is *Hotel Schemmer* (☎ 20 74 90, Eschholzstrasse 63), behind the train station, with basic singles/doubles for DM65/95. Historic *Hotel Zum Schützen* (☎ 72 02 10, Schützenallee 12), on the way to the youth hostel, is also a reasonable compromise for location and value with rooms from DM65/95.

In the Altstadt, *Hotel Löwen* (☎ 331 61, Herrenstrasse 47) is near the Schwabentor and has simple rooms for DM65/90. Right on Münsterplatz, *Hotel Rappen* (☎ 313 53 54) has charming rooms from DM100/130 and an inspirational breakfast buffet.

Places to Eat

Being a university town, Freiburg virtually guarantees cheap eats and a lively restaurant scene. The university-subsidised *Mensas* at Rempartstrasse 18 and Hebelstrasse 9a have salad buffets and other filling fodder. You may be asked to show student ID.

Papala Pub (Moltkestrasse 30) is a retro-style cafe where you can fill up on starchy chow from DM7.80 or risk the *Volles Risiko* menu that includes several surprise courses for DM22. Another good joint around the university is the popular *UC Uni-Café*, on the corner of Universitätsstrasse and Niemanstrasse, with a cool patio from which to see and be seen. Nearby *Salatstuben (Löwenstrasse 1)* has a wide choice of wholesome salads for DM2.30 per 100g. *Caruso (Kaiser Joseph Strasse 258)* has a laid-back Latino vibe and a fantastic international menu (lunch specials average DM13). There's a sushi night on Wednesday.

Entertainment

The *Jazzhaus* (☎ 349 73, Schnewlinstrasse 1) has live jazz every night. Admission is from

DM5 (it rises quickly when a famous musician is playing).

Galerie (Milchstrasse 7) has a cosy seating area warmed by a wood stove in winter, and a lilac-scented patio in summer. Everybody is happy at *Alter Simon (Konvikstrasse 43)*, where the merry scene spills onto the street until well past midnight.

If the weather is nice, walk over the pedestrian bridge at the Schwabentor and head up the hill to *Greiffenberg-Schlössle*, a vast beer garden with stunning views over the town to France and back to the Black Forest. Go for the fun and froth but not the food.

Getting There & Around

Freiburg lies on the Mannheim-Basel train corridor and is served by numerous ICE and EC trains in both directions. The trains to Titisee leave every 30 minutes (DM16). The regional bus station is next to Track 1. For ride-sharing information contact the Citynetz Mitfahr-Service (☎ 194 44) at Belfortstrasse 55.

Single rides on the efficient local bus and tram system cost DM3.30. A 24-hour pass costs DM8. Trams depart from the bridge over the train tracks.

DANUBE RIVER

The Danube (Donau), one of Europe's great rivers, rises in the Black Forest. In Austria, Hungary and Romania it is a mighty almost intimidating waterway, but in Germany it's narrower and more tranquil, making it ideal for hiking and biking tours. In fact, Donaueschingen is the gateway to the **Donauradwanderweg (Danube Bike Trail)**, a beautiful and level trail that stretches 583km east through cities that include Ulm and Regensburg, to Passau on the Austrian border. From there you can continue on to Vienna and beyond.

The booklet *Donauradwanderführer* provides maps and descriptions of the German route and is available from bookshops and tourist offices for DM18.80. Tourist offices also have a free brochure in English called *Tips, Info and Facts for Carefree Travels along the German Danube*, which gives useful information about riverside towns, along with listings of camping facilities, hostels and bike-rental places.

To exploit its location right at the source of the Danube, **Donaueschingen** boasts the

Donauquelle (Danube Source) monument in the park of the Fürstenberg Schloss. However, the river really begins 1km east where two tributaries – the Brigach and the Breg – meet at a site dominated by a charmless highway bridge. Among the town's few highlights are the plaques around the Donauquelle sent by former eastern bloc countries far downstream; these are heavy on platitudes and read like EU applications.

Donaueschingen's tourist office (☎ 0771-85 72 21, fax 85 72 28) at Karlstrasse 58 is open 8 am to 5 pm weekdays, and also 9 am to noon Saturday from May to September. Staff have lots of information on Danube cycling. Rothweiler (☎ 0771-131 48), Max-Egan-Strasse 14, rents out bikes from DM20 per day. Trains runs to/from Offenburg (DM24.60), Constance (DM22.40) and Neustadt (DM10) in the Black Forest.

ULM
☎ **0731 ● pop 165,000**

A city well worth a visit, Ulm is famous for its Münster tower, the highest cathedral spire in Europe. It's also the birthplace of Albert Einstein. It was a trading city in the 12th century and barges with local goods floated down the Danube as far as the Black Sea.

Greater Ulm is actually two cities in two *Länder* (states), a state of affairs that dates back to Napoleon's influence on the region: he decreed that the middle of the river would divide Baden-Württemberg and Bavaria. On the southern side of the Danube, the Bavarian city of Neu Ulm is bland and modern. On the other side is Ulm, with the main attractions. Ulm is a hub for frequent fast trains to Lindau, Munich, Stuttgart and the north.

Orientation & Information

Ulm's tourist office (☎ 161 28 30, fax 161 16 41, ✉ unt@tourismus.ulm.de) is in a remarkably harmonious modern building on Münsterplatz and is open 8 am to 6 pm Monday to Saturday (to 8 pm Thursday) and 11 am to 6 pm Sunday. Internet access costs DM7 a half-hour and DM11 an hour at connect onlinecafe, Frauenstrasse 31.

Things to See & Do

The main reason for coming to Ulm is to see the huge **Münster**, famous for its 161m-high

GERMANY

steeple. Though begun in 1377, it took over 500 years for the entire structure to be completed. Climbing to the top (DM4) via the 768 spiralling steps yields great views and a dizzy head. A stained-glass window above the entrance recalls the Holocaust. The cathedral is open daily: 9 am to 4:45 pm November to February (to 5.45 pm in March and October) and 8 am to 6.45 pm April to September (to 7.45 pm in July).

Schwörmontag (Oath Monday), the second-last Monday in July, has been going on since 1397. After the mayor makes an oath, at the **Schwörhaus** (Oath House), the populace moves down to **Fischerviertel**, a charming old quarter built around streams flowing into the Danube, for a raucous procession of rafts and barges. Later, all-night parties take place on the town's streets and squares. The next day is a local holiday as everybody sleeps it off.

Places to Stay & Eat

The **DJH hostel** (☎ 38 44 55, fax 38 45 11, Grimmelfinger Weg 45) charges juniors/seniors DM20/24 with breakfast. From the train station, take tram No 1 to Ehinger Tor, then bus No 4 to Schulzentrum; from here it's a five-minute walk. Across the river in Neu-Ulm, the **Rose** (☎ 778 03, Kasernstrasse 42a) has singles/doubles from DM35/70. Close enough to Münsterplatz to keep time by the Münster bells, **Hotel-Restaurant Bäumle** (☎ 622 87, fax 602 26 04, Kohlgasse 6) has good rooms from DM55/75. Its restaurant downstairs has creative regional fare. Quaff the local dark beer at **Drei Kannen** (Hafenbad 31), a historic restaurant and beer garden. **Lloyd**, a bar-cafe on Dreiköniggasse, is a great place to linger, especially on summer nights.

LAKE CONSTANCE

Lake Constance (Bodensee) is a perfect cure for travellers stranded in landlocked southern Germany. Often jokingly called the 'Swabian Ocean', this giant bulge in the sinewy course of the Rhine offers a choice of water sports, relaxation or cultural pursuits. The lake itself adds special atmosphere to the many historic towns around its periphery, which can be explored by boat or bicycle and on foot.

The lake's southern side belongs to Switzerland and Austria, whose snow-capped mountain tops provide a perfect backdrop

when viewed from the northern (German) shore. The German side of Lake Constance features three often-crowded tourist centres in Constance, Meersburg and the island of Lindau. It's essentially a summer area, when it abounds with liquid joy, and is too often foggy or at best hazy in winter.

Cycling

A 270km international bike track circumnavigates Lake Constance through Germany, Austria and Switzerland, tracing the often steep shoreline beside vineyards and pebble beaches. The route is well signposted, but you may want one of the many widely sold cycling maps. The tourist booklet *Rad Urlaub am Bodensee* lists routes, rental places and a wealth of other information for the region.

In Constance, Velotours (☎ 07531-982 80), Fritz-Arnold-Strasse 2b, rents out bikes (DM20/100 daily/weekly) and organises cycling tours.

Accommodation

The lake's popularity pushes up accommodation prices; fortunately excellent hostel and camping facilities exist around the lake. During summer the hostels roar with mobs, so call ahead.

See tourist offices for apartments and private rooms away from the tourist mobs (and often set among vineyards overlooking the lake).

Getting There & Away

Constance has train connections every one to two hours to Offenburg (DM50) and Stuttgart (DM56). Meersburg is easily reached by bus No 7395 from Friedrichshafen (DM5, every 30 minutes), or by Weisse Flotte (☎ 07531-28 13 98) boats from Constance (DM5.80, several times a day in season). The Constance to Meersburg car ferry (☎ 07531-80 34 75) runs every 15 minutes all year from the north-eastern Constance suburb of Staad (DM5.60 per person, DM5 per bicycle and from DM9.50 for cars). Lindau has trains to/from Ulm (DM35, every two hours), Munich (DM54) and Bregenz (DM3.80, hourly, 15 minutes), where you can connect to the rest of Austria.

Getting Around

Trains link Lindau, Friedrichshafen and Constance, and buses fill in the gaps. By car, the

B31 hugs the northern shore of Lake Constance, but it can get rather busy. The most enjoyable, albeit slowest, way to get around is on the Weisse Flotte boats (☎ 07531-28 13 98) which, from Easter to late October, call several times a day at the larger towns along both sides of the lake; there are discounts for rail pass-holders. The seven-day Bodensee-Pass costs DM57 and gives one free day of travel on the boats plus six days at half-price on all boats, buses, trains and mountain cableways on and around Lake Constance (including its Austrian and Swiss shores).

Constance
☎ 07531 • pop 76,000

The town of Constance (Konstanz) achieved historical significance in 1414 when the Council of Constance convened to try to heal huge rifts in the Church. The consequent burning at the stake of the religious reformer Jan Hus as a heretic, and the scattering of his ashes over the lake, failed to block the impetus of the Reformation.

In the west, Constance straddles the Swiss border, a good fortune that spared it from Allied bombing in WWII. The tourist office (☎ 13 30 30, fax 13 30 60, ✉ info@touristinf ormation.stadt.konstanz.de) is at Bahnhofplatz 13 (150m to the right from the station exit) and open between 9 am and 6.30 pm weekdays and to 1 pm Saturday, April to October. Its hours are 9.30 am to 12.30 pm and 2 to 6 pm weekdays from November to March.

Things to See & Do The city's most visible feature is the Gothic spire of the **cathedral**, added only in 1856 to a church that was started in 1052, which gives excellent views over the old town. Visit the old **Niederburg** quarter or relax in the parklands of the **Stadtgarten**. If you have time, head across to **Mainau Island** (DM18.50/9.50), with its baroque castle set among vast and gorgeous gardens that include a butterfly house. Take a ferry or bus No 4. Five public beaches are open from May to September, including the Strandbad Horn with shrub-enclosed nude bathing. Take bus No 5 or walk for 20 scenic minutes around the shore.

Places to Stay & Eat You can pitch a tent at *Campingplatz Litzelstetten-Mainau* (☎ 94 30 30), a 20-minute walk towards Mainau Island from Constance. The *DJH Hostel* (☎ 322 60, fax 311 63, Zur Allmannshöhe 18) charges DM22/27 for juniors/seniors; take bus No 4 from the station to the Jugendherberge stop. Many people prefer the *HI Hostel* (☎ 41-71-688 26 63, fax 688 47 61), a 20-minute walk along the lake from the train station to Kreuzlingen in Switzerland. This palatial hostel charges about DM27 a night (they accept Deutschmarks).

In Constance's old town, *Pension Gretel* (☎ 232 83, Zollernstrasse 6-8) has simple rooms from DM55/95. *Seekuh* is a mellow cafe with a cool patio on the corner of Zollernstrasse and Konzilstrasse. It dishes up salads, pasta and pizza from around DM11, is open late and has live music on most summer Saturdays.

Meersburg
☎ 07532 • pop 5200

Meersburg is across the lake from Constance and an ideal base for exploring the long northern shore. The helpful tourist office (☎ 43 11 10, fax 43 11 20, ✉ info@ meersburg.de) is in the city museum building at Kirchstrasse 4; it's open 9 am to 6 pm weekdays and 10 am to 2 pm Saturday from March to September (it is only open weekdays from October to April and closes at 4.30 pm).

It's a pretty town right on the lake, with terraced streets and vineyard-patterned hills. The **Steigstrasse** is lined with lovely half-timbered houses that each boasts a gift shop. The 11th-century **Altes Schloss** is the oldest structurally intact castle in Germany (open daily; DM10/8). The baroque **Neues Schloss** houses the town's art collection (open daily from April to October; DM6/5).

Meersburg is a good base for watery pursuits and is popular with windsurfers. Rudi Thum's (☎ 55 11) at the yacht harbour rents out equipment and offers sailing courses.

Gasthaus zum Letzten Zeller (☎ 61 49, Daisendorferstrasse 41) has good rooms for DM60/98 as well as a popular restaurant. The town has no shortage of expensive restaurants – a good one in the Oberstadt is *Winzerstube zum Becher* on Höllgasse which serves traditional dishes infused with an international flavour.

GERMANY

Lindau
☎ 08382 • pop 24,000

Most of the German part of Lake Constance lies within Baden-Württemberg, but Lindau in the east is just inside Bavaria, near the Austrian border. The tourist office (☎ 91 80, fax 91 82 90), directly opposite the station, is open 9 am to 6 pm weekdays and 9 am to 1 pm Saturday from April to October.

Connected to the nearby lakeshore by bridges, key sights of this oh-so-charming island town are the muralled **Altes Rathaus** on Reichsplatz, the **city theatre** on Barfüsserplatz and the harbour's **Seepromenade**, with its Bavarian Lion monument and lighthouse. When the haze clears, the Alps provide a stunning backdrop for a zillion photos.

Lindau's water isn't as crowded as the land. Windsurf-Schule Kreitmeir (☎ 233 30) at Strandbad Eichwald has a windsurfing school and equipment rental. For boat rental contact Grahneis (☎ 55 14).

You can camp along the shore at *Park Camping Lindau am See* (☎ 722 36), 3km south-east of Lindau. The posh *DJH Hostel* (☎ 967 10, fax 96 71 50, Herbergsweg 11) charges DM29 (juniors and families only). Family-run *Pension Noris* (☎ 960 85, fax 96 08 25, Brettermarkt 13) has recommended rooms for DM40/80.

Lindau's broad parks, shady benches and fine views all but demand picnicking. The main pedestrian drag, Maximilianstrasse, is lined with supermarkets and delis. *Gasthaus zum Sünfzen (Maximilianstrasse 1)* is an island institution, serving Swabian-Bavarian fare from DM15.

Friedrichshafen, Überlingen & Birnau

Friedrichshafen, the largest and most 'central' city on the lake's northern shore, has its tourist office (☎ 07541-300 10, fax 7 25 88) near the Stadtbahnhof train station at Bahnhofsplatz 2. Count Zeppelin built his first explodable cigar-shaped airships here, an endeavour commemorated in that town's superb **Zeppelin Museum** (DM12/6; closed Monday) on the lakeside promenade. The *DJH hostel* (☎ 07541-724 04, fax 749 86, Lindauer Strasse 3) is 15 minutes from the harbour and charges DM26/31 for juniors/ seniors.

Überlingen features the astonishing **Cathedral of St Nicholas**, which boasts a dozen side altars and a wooden four-storey central altar dating from the 17th century. Another impressive **baroque church** can be found at Birnau.

Rhineland-Palatinate

Rhineland-Palatinate (Rheinland-Pfalz) has a rugged topography characterised by thinly populated mountain ranges and forests cut by deep river valleys. Created after WWII from parts of the former Rhineland and Rhenish Palatinate regions, its turbulent history saw the area settled by the Romans and later hotly contested by the French and a variety of German states. The state capital is Mainz.

This land of wine and great natural beauty, with its highlight the Moselle Valley, is a little quieter than the Rhine River tourist route.

THE MOSELLE VALLEY
Exploring the vineyards and wineries of the Moselle (Mosel) Valley is an ideal way to get a taste of German culture and people – and, of course, the wonderful wines. Take the time to slow down and do some sipping.

The Moselle is also bursting at the seams with historical sites and picturesque towns built along the river below steep rocky cliffs planted with vineyards (they say locals are born with one leg shorter than the other so that they can easily work the vines). It's one of the country's most romantically scenic regions. Though the entire route is packed with visitors from June to October, getting off the beaten path is always easy.

Orientation & Information
The most scenic section of the Moselle Valley runs 195km north-east from Trier to Koblenz. At Koblenz, the tourist office (☎ 0261-30 38 80, fax 303 88 11, ✉ touris tik@koblenz.de) is at Bahnhofsplatz in front of the main train station. In the Moselle Valley proper, staff are helpful in Cochem's tourist office (☎ 02671-600 40, fax 60 04 44, ✉ verkehrsamt.Cochem@lcoc.de), on Endertplatz next to the bridge. There are also useful tourist offices in Bernkastel-Kues (06531-40 23, fax 79 53), Am Gestade

5; and in Traben-Trarbach (☎ 06541-8 39 80, fax 83 98 39, ❷ info@traben-trarbach.de) at Bahnstrasse 22. Almost all other towns along the river have a visitor information centre.

Things to See

Koblenz While not to be compared with Trier or Cochem, Koblenz is a nice enough place to spend half a day or so. The Deutsches Eck is a park at the sharp confluence of the Rhine and Moselle rivers dedicated to German unity.

Immediately across the Rhine is the impressive Festung Ehrenbreitstein fortress, which houses the DJH hostel and the Landesmuseum (% 0261-970 31 50).

Burg Eltz Not to be missed is a visit to Burg Eltz (02672-13 00; open daily from April to 1 November) at the head of the beautiful Eltz Valley. Towering over the surrounding hills, this superb medieval castle has frescoes, paintings, furniture and ornately decorated rooms. Burg Eltz is best reached by train to Moselkern, from where it's a 50-minute walk up through the forest. Alternatively, you can drive via Münster-Maifeld to the nearby car park. Entry is allowed only with regular guided tours (DM9/6), but the **Schatzkammer** (treasure chamber; DM4/2) can be visited without one.

Cochem This pretty picture-postcard German town has narrow alleyways and gates. It's also a good base for hikes into the hills. For a great view, head up to the **Pinnerkreuz** with the chairlift on Endertstrasse (DM6.90). **Reichsburg Castle** (☎ 02671-255) is a 15-minute walk up the hill from town. There are regular daily tours between 9 am and 5 pm from mid-March to mid-November (DM7). English translation sheets are available.

Bernkastel-Kues, Traben-Trarbach & Beilstein A bit further upstream, visit Beilstein, Traben-Trarbach or Bernkastel-Kues for a look at typical Moselle towns that survive on more than the tourist trade.

Activities

Wine Tasting The main activities along the Moselle Valley are eating and wine tasting. Just pick out a winery and head inside. Note that most wineries are closed from November to March. Cochem's HH Hieronimi (☎ 02671-221), just across the river at Stadionstrasse 1-3, is a friendly, family-run winery that offers tours for DM9, including two tastings, a complimentary bottle of its own wine and a souvenir glass. Also in Cochem is Weingut Rademacher (☎ 02671-41 64), diagonally behind the train station at Pinnerstrasse 10, whose tours of the winery and cellar (an old WWII bunker) cost DM9.50/13 with four/six wine tastings.

In Bernkastel-Kues, the Weingut Dr Willkomm (☎ 06531-80 54), Gestade 1, is in a lovely old arched cellar; the winery also distils its own brandy.

Hiking & Cycling The Moselle Valley is particularly scenic walking country, but expect some steep climbs if you venture away from the river. The views are worth the sore muscles. Tourist offices sell good maps showing trails and paths, and usually have tips on short hikes.

Places to Stay

There are camping grounds, hostels and rooms with classic views all along the Moselle Valley. Many wine-makers also have their own small pensions and, as usual, local tourist offices operate well-organised room-finding services. In May, on summer weekends or during the local wine harvest (mid-September to mid-October), accommodation is hard to find.

Koblenz The camping ground *Rhein Mosel* (☎/fax 0261-80 24 89), open April to mid-October, is on Schartwiesenweg at the confluence of the Moselle and Rhine Rivers opposite the Deutsches Eck. The daytime passenger ferry across the Moselle puts the camping ground within five minutes' walk of town.

Koblenz has a wonderful *DJH hostel* (☎ 0261-97 28 70, fax 972 87 30, ❷ jh-koblenz@djh-info.de) in the old Ehrenbreitstein fortress (at a flat rate of DM25.20), but it's advisable to book ahead in summer. From the main train station take bus No 7, 8 or 9; there's also a chairlift (DM7/10 up/return) from Ehrenbreitstein station by the river. *Hotel*

Jahn van Werth (☎ *0261-365 00, fax 365 06, van Werth Strasse 9*) offers good value in small basic singles/doubles for DM40/85; larger basic rooms are DM65/100 and rooms with shower and WC are DM75/120.

Cochem The riverside *Campingplatz Am Freizeitszentrum* (☎ *02671-44 09*) is in Stadionstrasse, downstream from the northern bridge; open from 10 days before Easter to the end of October. Cochem's *DJH hostel* (☎ *02671-86 33, fax 85 68,* ✆ *jh-cochem@ djh-info.de, Klottener Strasse 9*) charges a flat DM23.80. The large *Hotel Noss* (☎ *02671-36 12, fax 53 66, Moselpromenade 17*) is on the waterfront and has quite good rooms for DM85/150 with shower and WC.

Bernkastel-Kues *Campingplatz Kueser Werth* (☎ *06531-82 00*) has pleasant tent sites by the river. The *DJH hostel* (☎ *06531-23 95, fax 15 29,* ✆ *jh-bernkastel-kues@djh-info.de, Jugendherbergsstrasse 1*) is near the castle (a flat DM22.80). *Hotel zur Post* (☎ *06531-967 00, fax 96 70 50, Gestade 17*) has rooms from DM87/152.

Traben-Trarbach For campers, there's the *Rissbach* (☎ *06541-31 11, Rissbacher Strasse 170*), open April to mid-October. The *DJH hostel* (☎ *06541-92 78, fax 37 59,* ✆ *jh-traben-trarbach@djh-info.de, Hirtenpfad 6*) has beds in small dorms for DM26.90. *Central-Hotel* (☎ *06541-6238, Bahnstrasse 43*) is clean, friendly and provides a good breakfast for DM60/110 with toilet and WC.

Places to Eat
Good wine often means good food and this is true all along the Moselle, with dozens of inexpensive family places to choose from. The Moselle is also an ideal place for peaceful riverside picnics with good local food and wine.

Koblenz Altenhof and the area around Münzplatz in the Altstadt offer many good eating options. The stylish *Osteria Novecento* (☎ *0261-914 46 20, Münzplatz 3*) serves tasty pizza and pasta for about DM15 and other dishes from DM19 to DM28. *Café Miljöö* (☎ *0261-142 37, Gemüsegasse 8-10*) does light dishes in a cafe atmosphere till late.

Cochem A cheap fast-food choice is *Kochlöffel (Am Markt 10)*, where you can eat well for under DM10 (chicken halves DM4.50). *Zom Stoffje* (☎ *02671-72 60, Oberbachstrasse 14*) is a traditional eating house with main dishes for around DM25 to DM35.

Traben-Trarbach Unusual and popular with locals is *Alte Zunftscheune* (☎ *06541-97 37*) in Neue Rathausstrasse (behind the tourist office), where steak with horseradish sauce, salad and fried potato costs DM27.

Getting There & Away
It's most practical to begin your Moselle Valley trip from either Trier or Koblenz. If you have private transport and are coming from the north, however, you might head up the Ahr Valley and cut through the scenic Eifel Mountain area between the A61 and A48.

Getting Around
The Moselle Valley can be explored on foot or by bike, car, boat or other public transport. One easy way through is by train between Koblenz and Traben-Trarbach, using buses between Traben-Trarbach and Bernkastel-Kues, and taking the excellent bus-train connection from Kues to Wittlich and on to Trier or Koblenz.

Bus A scheduled bus service along the Moselle runs between Trier and Bullay, about three-fifths of the way towards Koblenz. (In this stretch of the valley the train line is too far from the river for convenience.) Moselbahn (☎ *0651-2 10 76*) runs eight buses on weekdays in each direction; fewer on weekends (DM13, three hours each way). It's a very scenic route, following the river's winding course and passing through numerous quaint villages along the way. Buses leave from outside the train stations in Trier, Traben-Trarbach and Bullay. Frequent buses run between Kues (Alter Bahnhof) and Wittlich main train station (about 5km from the town of Wittlich), connecting with trains to Koblenz and Trier.

Train Local and fast trains run every hour between Trier and Koblenz (DM30, 1½ hours), but the only scenic stretch on this line is between Cochem and Koblenz. A scenic Moselweinbahn line runs from Bullay to Traben-Trarbach (DM4.60, 20 minutes).

Car & Motorcycle Driving along the Moselle is ideal, though drivers will risk cramped necks (not to mention nervous passengers) from looking up at the majestic slopes. One possibility is to rent a car in either Koblenz or Trier and drop it off at the other end.

Bicycle The Moselle is a popular area among cyclists, and for much of the river's course there's a separate 'Moselroute' bike track. Touren-Rad (☎ 0261-911 60 16), Hohenzollernstrasse 127, near the main train station in Koblenz, rents quality mountain and touring bicycles from DM15/12 per day. It has a deal with the rental shop at Trier's main train station (☎ 0651-14 88 56), so you can pick up or return bikes at either. In Bernkastel, Fun-Bike Team (06531-940 24), Schanzstrasse 22, rents standard bikes from DM12 per day.

Boat A great way to explore the Moselle is by boat. While much of the river's charm comes from its winding course, this does make water travel particularly slow. To get from Koblenz to Trier using scheduled ferry services takes two days.

Between early May and mid-October, Köln-Düsseldorfer (KD) Line (☎ 0221-208 8318) ferries sail daily between Koblenz and Cochem (DM37 one way, 4½ hours). From Cochem, the Gebrüder Kolb Line (☎ 02673-15 15) runs boats upriver to Trier and back (DM71/96 one way/return) between May and mid-October. Various smaller ferry companies also operate on the Moselle.

Eurail and German Rail passes are valid for all normal KD Line services, and travel on your birthday is free. There are numerous other possible excursions, ranging from short return cruises to multiday wine-tasting packages.

TRIER
☎ 0651 • pop 100,000

Trier is touted as Germany's oldest town. Although settlement of the site dates back to 400 BC, Trier itself was founded in 15 BC as Augusta Treverorum, the capital of Gaul, and was second in importance only to Rome in the Western Roman Empire. You'll find more Roman ruins here than anywhere else north of the Alps. There's a university too, and the city is quite lively.

Orientation & Information

From the main train station head west along Bahnhofstrasse and Theodor-Heuss-Allee to the Porta Nigra, where you'll find Trier's tourist office (☎ 97 80 80, fax 447 59, ✉ info@tit.de). It is open 9 am to 6.30 pm Monday to Saturday (to 3 pm Sunday) from April to October. The rest of the year it closes at 5 pm weekdays, 1 pm Saturday and is also closed Sunday. It has a free and efficient room-finding service. Ask here about daily guided city walking tours in English (DM10), and the three-day Trier-Card (DM17), a combined ticket for the city's main sights and museums (DM25 including public transport). From Porta Nigra, walk along Simeonstrasse's pedestrian zone to Hauptmarkt, the heart of the old city. Most of the sights are within this area of roughly 1 sq km. There's a convenient and cheap Wasch Center laundrette at Brückenstrasse 19-21. The main post office is near the station.

Things to See

The town's chief landmark is the **Porta Nigra**, the imposing city gate on the northern edge of the town centre, which dates back to the 2nd century (DM4/2). The interesting **Rheinisches Landesmuseum**, Weimarer Allee 1, has works of art dating from Palaeolithic, Roman and modern times. It's open 9.30 am to 5 pm Tuesday to Friday and 10.30 am to 5 pm weekends (DM7).

Trier's massive Romanesque **Dom** shares a 1600-year history with the nearby and equally impressive **Konstantin Basilika**. Also worth visiting are the ancient **Amphitheater**, the **Kaiserthermen** and **Barbarathermen** (Roman baths). The early-Gothic **Dreikönigenhaus**, Simeonstrasse 19, was built around 1230 as a protective tower; the original entrance was on the second level, accessible only by way of a retractable rope ladder. History buffs and nostalgic socialists can visit the **Karl Marx Museum** (☎ 430 11; DM3/2), in the house where a star was born on Brückenstrasse 10 (but

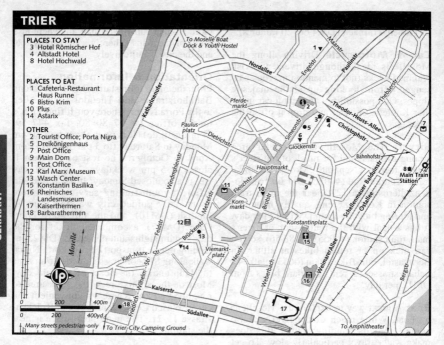

TRIER

PLACES TO STAY
3 Hotel Römischer Hof
4 Altstadt Hotel
8 Hotel Hochwald

PLACES TO EAT
1 Cafeteria-Restaurant
  Haus Runne
6 Bistro Krim
10 Plus
14 Astarix

OTHER
2 Tourist Office; Porta Nigra
5 Dreikönigenhaus
7 Post Office
9 Main Dom
11 Post Office
12 Karl Marx Museum
13 Wasch Center
15 Konstantin Basilika
16 Rheinisches
   Landesmuseum
17 Kaiserthermen
18 Barbarathermen

Many streets pedestrian-only   To Trier-City Camping Ground

don't expect to view anything particularly
revolutionary).

Places to Stay

The municipal camping ground *Trier-City*
(☎ 8 69 21, *Luxemburger Strasse 81*) is
nicely positioned on the Moselle and open all
year. It charges DM4 for a tent, DM8 per
person and DM4 for a car. The *DJH Jugendgästehaus* (☎ 14 66 20, fax 146 62 30,
ⓔ jh-trier@djh-info.de, *An der Jugendherberge 4*) is also down by the riverside. It
charges DM29 per person in four-bed dorms,
DM39 in doubles and DM54 in single rooms.

   Hotel Hochwald (☎ 758 03, fax 743 54,
Bahnhofplatz 5) is opposite the train station
and charges DM48 for very plain singles.
Rooms with shower and WC cost DM66/130.
Altstadt Hotel (☎ 480 41, fax 412 93) at Am
Porta-Nigra-Platz in the centre has spacious
singles/doubles from DM110/190. *Hotel
Römischer Hof* (☎ 977 00, fax 97 70 99) is
across the road and offers even better rooms
from DM110/170.

Places to Eat

Trier is a great place to sample some Franco-
German cooking. The bustling *Bistro Krim*
(☎ 739 43, *Glockenstrasse 7*) offers generous
Mediterranean-inspired dishes at affordable
prices. There are also several set menus such
as its three-course 'Mediterranean' menu for
DM39.50. *Astarix* (☎ 722 39, *Karl-Marx-
Strasse 11*) is a favourite student hang-out
back in an arcade that serves large salads and
some main dishes for under DM10 (open till
late). *Cafeteria-Restaurant Haus Runne*
(☎ 209 26 77, *Engelstrasse 25*) serves good
cafeteria-style lunches.

   Plus (*Brotstrasse 23*) is a central supermarket. The narrow Judengasse, near Markt,
has several bars and cafes for tipples and nib-
bles, whereas a slicker crowd gravitates towards a cluster of bars on Viehmarktplatz.

Getting There & Away

Trier has hourly local and fast trains to/from
Saarbrücken (DM22, 1½ hours) and Koblenz
(DM30, 1½ hours), as well as services to

Luxembourg (DM16, 45 minutes) and Metz (in France; DM34, 2½ hours). For information on river ferries, see Getting There & Away in the previous Moselle Valley section.

RHINE VALLEY – KOBLENZ TO MAINZ

A trip along the Rhine is on the itinerary of most travellers. The section between Mainz and Koblenz offers the best scenery, especially the narrow tract downriver from Rüdesheim. Spring and autumn are the best times to visit; in summer it's over-run and in winter most towns go into hibernation.

Orientation & Information

The best sources of information are local tourist offices along the way. The tourist office in Mainz (☎ 06131-28 62 10, fax 286 21 55, ✉ tourist@info-mainz.de) is at Brücken-turm am Rathaus (bus No 7, 13, 17, 19 or 27 to Rheingoldhalle). In Koblenz the tourist office (☎ 0261-30 38 80, fax 303 88 11, ✉ touristik@koblenz.de) is at Bahnhofsplatz.

C@fé Enterprise, at Bilhildisstrasse 2 (on Münsterplatz) in Mainz, has Internet facilities.

Things to See

Where the slopes along the Rhine aren't covered with vines, you can bet they built a castle. One of the most impressive is **Burg Rheinfels** in St Goar. Across the river, just south of St Goarshausen, is the Rhine's most famous sight: the **Loreley Cliff**. Hackneyed legend has it that a maiden sang sailors to their deaths against its base. It's worth the trek to the top of the Loreley for the view, but try to get up there early in the morning before the hordes ascend.

Rüdesheim Rolling drunk on tourism, this town is worth a visit only if you are studying mass tourism at its worst, or seeking out the bucolic paths in the hills above. To get some perspective on the area take the **Weinlehrpfad** walking route (from above Drosselgasse). It leads through vineyard slopes to the **Brömserburg**, an old riverside castle that houses an interesting wine museum (DM5/3). Assmannshausen is a prettier and calmer town a few kilometres downriver.

Mainz Half an hour's ride by train from Frankfurt, Mainz has an attractive old town.

Of special interest are the massive **St Martins** cathedral and the **Stephanskirche**, with stained-glass windows by Marc Chagall. Mainz's museums include the **Gutenberg Museum** (closed Monday; DM6/3), which contains the first printed Bible.

Activities

Wine Tasting As with the Moselle Valley, the Koblenz-to-Mainz section of the Rhine Valley is great for wine tasting. Oberwesel and Bacharach, respectively 40km and 45km south of Koblenz are the best towns for a true Rhine wine-tasting experience. For tastings in other towns, ask for recommendations at the tourist offices or just follow your nose.

Hiking Though the trails here may be a bit more crowded with day-trippers than those along the Moselle, hiking along the Rhine is also excellent. The slopes and trails around Bacharach are justly famous.

Places to Stay

Camping Camping facilities line the Rhine, but amenities and views vary greatly. Good possibilities include: Oberwesel's *Schönburg* (☎ 06744-245), open May to October and right beside the river; Bacharach's *Sonnenstrand* (☎ 06743-17 52), open from April to mid-November and offering riverside camping just 500m south of the centre; and St Goarshausen's *Auf der Loreley* (☎ 06771-4 30), right on the legendary rock and open all year (call if it is unattended).

Hostels There are *DJH hostels* in: Oberwesel (☎ 06744-933 30, fax 74 46, Auf dem Schönberg, ✉ jh-oberwesel@djh-info.de); St Goar (☎ 06741-388, fax 28 69, ✉ jh-st-goar@djh-info.de, Bismarckweg 17); in St Goarshausen (☎ 06771-2619, fax 81 89), right on top of the Loreley; Bacharach (☎ 06743-12 66, fax 26 84, ✉ jh-bacharach@djh-info-de), a legendary facility housed in the Burg Stahleck castle; Rüdesheim (☎ 06722-27 11, fax 482 84, ✉ ruedesheim@djh-hessen.de), at Am Kreuzburg; and in Mainz, *Jugendgästehaus* (☎ 06131-853 32, fax 824 22, ✉ jh-mainz@djh-info.de, Otto-Brunfels-Schneise 4).

Hotels & Pensions In St Goar, *Knab's Mühlenschänke* (☎ 06741-16 98, fax 16 78,

Gründelbachtal 73) is about 1.5km out of town beyond the castle. Singles/doubles cost DM65/100 and you can sip the house wine here in a rural atmosphere. *Schlosshotel Rheinfels* (☎ 06741-80 20, fax 80 28 02) in the castle is the top address in town, with rooms from DM155/230 and a fine restaurant with prices to match. In Bacharach, *Irmgaard Orch* (☎ 06743-15 53, Spurgasse 2) offers good budget rooms for DM35/50. In Rüdesheim, the large, riverside *Parkhotel Deutscher Hof* (☎ 06722-30 16, fax 17 17, ☺ info@parkhotel-ruedesheim.de, Rheinstrasse 21-23) charges DM110/140. *Hotel Stadt Coblenz* (☎ 06131-22 76 02, fax 22 33 07, Rheinstrasse 499), in Mainz, has basic rooms for DM75/100 and DM100/130 with facilities (ask for one away from the street). For accommodation in Koblenz, see Places to Stay in the previous Moselle Valley section.

Places to Eat

Whether you put together a modest picnic by the river or dine in one of the numerous local restaurants, this is the place to savour unique Rhine wine and food.

In Bacharach, *Kurpfälzische Münze* (06743-1375, Oberstrasse 72) serves traditional dishes from DM20 to DM30, including game. Avoid eating anywhere in Rüdesheim's Drosselgasse, an oversold row of touristy shops and restaurants. In Mainz, *Hof Ehrenfels* (Grebenstrasse 5-7) serves quality regional dishes.

Getting There & Away

Koblenz or Mainz are the best starting points. The Rhine Valley is also easily accessible from Frankfurt on a long day trip, but that won't do justice to the region.

Getting Around

Each mode of transport has its own advantages and all are equally enjoyable. Try combining several of them by going on foot one day, cycling the next, and then taking a boat for a view from the river.

Boat The Köln-Düsseldorfer (KD) Line (☎ 0221-20 88 318) earns its bread and butter on the Rhine, with many slow and fast boats daily between Koblenz and Mainz. The most scenic stretch is between Koblenz and

Rüdesheim; the journey takes about four hours downstream, about 6½ hours upstream (DM42.40). See Getting Around in the previous Moselle Valley section for information about concessions. Boats stop at many riverside towns along the way.

Train Train services operate on both sides of the Rhine River, but are more convenient on the left bank. You can travel non-stop on IC/EC trains or travel by regional RB or SE services (DM25, 1½ hours).

Car Touring the Rhine Valley by car is also ideal. The route between Koblenz and Mainz is short enough for a car to be rented and returned to either city. There are no bridge crossings between Koblenz and Rüdesheim, but there are several ferry crossings.

Saarland

In the late 19th century, Saarland's coal mines and steel mills fuelled the burgeoning German economy. Since WWII, however, the steady economic decline of coal and steel has made Saarland the poorest region in western Germany. Though distinctly German since the early Middle Ages, Saarland was ruled by France for several periods during its turbulent history. Reoccupied by the French after WWII, it only joined the Federal Republic of Germany in 1957, after the population rejected French efforts to turn it into an independent state.

SAARBRÜCKEN

☎ 0681 • pop 185,000

Saarbrücken, capital of Saarland, has an interesting mixed French and German feel. While lacking major tourist sights, this city is a matter-of-fact place where people go about their daily business and where tourists are treated as individuals. It's also an easy base for day trips to some of the beautiful little towns nearby, such as Ottweiler, Saarburg, Mettlach and St Wendel.

Orientation & Information

The main train station is in the north-western corner of the old town, which stretches out on both sides of the Saar River. The tourist office

(☎ 93 80 90, fax 938 09 39), Reichstrasse 1, is a two-minute walk from the station. It opens 9 am to 8 pm weekdays and 10 am to 4 pm Saturday. It's closed for one hour from noon on Saturday.

The Reisebank in the main train station is open daily. There's also a post office here and another in the city centre at Dudweiler-strasse 17. The Waschhaus laundry at Nauwieserstrasse 22 opens from 8 am to 10 pm daily.

Things to See & Do

Start your visit by strolling along the lanes around lively **St Johanner Markt** in the central pedestrian zone. A flea market is held here every second Saturday from April to November. Not far away beside the Saar River are the **Saarländische Staatstheater**, a neoclassical structure built by the Nazis, and the **Saarland-Museum** (closed Monday; DM8/4), the city's main art gallery.

Cross the 1549 **Alte Brücke** (Old Bridge) to **Schloss Saarbrücken**, the former palace on Schlossplatz designed by King Wilhelm Friedrich's court architect, Friedrich Joachim Stengel, in the 18th century.

There are several museums around Schloss-platz; the most interesting is the **Abenteuer Museum** (Adventure Museum), with a hotch-potch of weird souvenirs and photos collected since 1950 by solo adventurer extraordinaire, Heinz Rox-Schulz. It is open 9 am to 1 pm Tuesday and Wednesday and 3 pm to 7 pm Thursday and Friday (DM3/2).

The nearby **Ludwigsplatz**, a baroque square that is also the work of Stengel, is dominated by the Lutheran **Ludwigskirche**. It is often closed, but you can peer through the glass doorway.

Places to Stay & Eat

The *Campingplatz Saarbrücken* (☎ 517 80) at Am Spicherer Berg is out on the French border, south of the city; take bus No 42 to Spicherer Weg from where it's a five-minute walk. The cost is DM8 per person and DM10 for a tent. The excellent *Jugendherberge* (☎ 330 40, fax 37 49 11, Meerwiesertalweg 31) is a half-hour walk north-east of the train station. Or take bus No 49 or 69 to Prinzen-weiher. Beds cost DM29 in four-person dorms, or DM36 in two-person rooms.

Hotel zur Klause (☎ 92 69 60, fax 926 96 50, Deutschherrnstrasse 72) charges DM70/120 for rooms with a shower and WC. *Hotel Stadt Hamburg* (☎ 330 53, fax 37 43 30, Bahnhofstrasse 71-73) has clean rooms for DM95/140. *Hotel im Fuchs* (☎ 93 65 50, fax 936 55 36, Kappenstrasse 12) has quite nice rooms for DM110/160 with facilities.

In Saarbrücken's eateries, your taste-buds get to visit France while enjoying hearty German servings. *Gasthaus Zum Stiefel* (☎ 93 54 50, Am Stiefel 2) is in an old brewery just off St Johanner Markt. It has an upmarket restaurant at the front specialising in fine meat and fish dishes, with main courses from DM25. The pub out the back (enter from Froschengasse) has house beers on tap and serves less-expensive food. Also try some of the other bistros and fast-food places along Froschengasse.

You'll find many restaurants and student pubs along the streets running off Max-Ophüls-Platz. The *Café Kostbar (Nauwieser-strasse 19)*, in an attractive backstreet courtyard, has well-priced set menus. *Tomate 2 (Schlossstrasse 2)* is a Mediterranean-style bistro across the river, near Schlossplatz, with meals in the DM20 to DM30 range.

Getting There & Away

There are frequent trains to the connecting cities of Mannheim (DM76, 2¼ hours), Koblenz (DM55, 2½ hours), Mainz (DM46, two hours) and Frankfurt (DM60, 2½ hours), as well as services across the border to Metz.

The ADM-Mitfahrzentrale (☎ 194 40) is at Grossherzog-Friedrich-Strasse 59

Hesse

The Hessians, a Frankish tribe, were among the first people to convert to Lutheranism in the early 16th century. Apart from a brief period of unity in that same century under Philip the Magnanimous, Hesse (Hessen) remained a motley collection of principalities and, later, of Prussian administrative districts until it was proclaimed a state in 1945. Its main cities are Frankfurt, Kassel and the capital, Wiesbaden.

As well as being a transportation hub, the very un-German city of Frankfurt can also be

GERMANY

used as a base to explore some of the smaller towns in Hesse. The beautiful Taunus and Spessart regions offer quiet village life and hours of scenic walks.

FRANKFURT/MAIN
☎ 069 • pop 650,000

They call it 'Bankfurt', 'Mainhattan' and much more. It's on the Main (pronounced mine) River, and is generally referred to as Frankfurt-am-Main, or Frankfurt/Main, since there's another large city called Frankfurt (Frankfurt/Oder) near the Polish border.

Frankfurt/Main is the financial and geographical centre of western Germany, as well as the host of important trade fairs. Thanks to generous funding in the 1980s and early 1990s, Frankfurt also has some excellent museums.

It is Germany's most important transport hub for air, train and road connections so you'll probably end up here at some point. Don't be surprised if you find this cosmopolitan melting pot more interesting than you had expected.

Orientation
The airport is 11 minutes by train south-west of the city centre. The Hauptbahnhof (main train station) is on the western side of the city, but within walking distance of the old city centre.

The safest route to the city centre through the sleazy train station area is along Kaiserstrasse. This leads to Kaiserplatz and then to a large square called An der Hauptwache. The area between the former lockup (Hauptwache), and the Römerberg, in the tiny vestige of Frankfurt's original old city, is the centre of Frankfurt. The Main River runs just south of the Altstadt, with several bridges leading to one of the city's livelier areas, Sachsenhausen. Its north-eastern corner, behind the youth hostel (see Places to Stay), is known as Alt Sachsenhausen and is full of quaint old houses and narrow alleyways.

Information
Tourist Offices Frankfurt's most convenient tourist office (☎ 21 23 88 49/51, fax 212 37 88) is in the main hall of the train station. It's open 8 am to 9 pm weekdays, and 9 am to 6 pm on weekends and holidays. For its efficient room-finding service there's a charge of DM5.

People with particular needs or those staying longer in Frankfurt should contact Tourismus + Congress (☎ 21 23 03 96, fax 21 23 07 76, @ info@tcf.frankfurt.de), Kaiserstrasse 56. This office handles room reservations (free of charge) and is open till 5.30 pm weekdays. Call ☎ 21 23 08 08 to reserve by telephone.

In the centre of the city, the Römer tourist office (☎ 21 23 87 08/09) at Römerberg 27 (north-west corner of the square) is open 9.30 am to 5.30 pm weekdays, 10 am to 4 pm weekends.

The head office of the German National Tourist Office (☎ 97 46 40, fax 75 19 03, @ gnto–fra@compuserve.com), north of the main train station at Beethovenstrasse 69, is a good place to visit if you're still planning your trip to Germany; it has brochures on all areas of the country.

One and two-day Frankfurt cards (DM12/19) give 50% reductions on admission to all of the city's important museums, the airport terraces, the zoo and Palmengarten, as well as unlimited travel on public transport.

Money The main train station has a branch of the Reisebank, near the southern exit at the head of platform No 1, which is open 6.30 am to 10 pm daily. There are banks and numerous ATMs at the airport, including a Reisebank in Terminal 1, arrival hall B (open 6 am to 11 pm daily).

American Express and Thomas Cook are opposite each other on Kaiserstrasse at Nos 10 and 11 respectively.

Post & Communications The main post office is on the ground floor of the Hertie department store at Zeil 90 (standard shop hours). A post office inside the main train station is open 6.30 am to 9 pm weekdays, 8 am to 6 pm Saturday and 11 am to 6 pm Sunday. The airport post office (waiting lounge, departure hall B) is open 7 am to 9 pm daily.

Email & Internet Access Cyberyder (☎ 91 39 67 54), Töngesgasse 31, charges DM6.50 for half an hour online.

Bookshops The train station has several good international press shops. Hugendubel, on Beibergasse between the Hauptwache and

Rathenauplatz, stocks Lonely Planet guides and has a cafe downstairs. The English Bookshop at Börsenstrasse 15 has a wide range of English-language fiction and nonfiction.

Laundry The Wasch Center chain has a laundrette in Frankfurt at Wallstrasse 8 in Sachsenhausen. It charges DM6 per wash, DM1 for (optional) use of the spinner, and DM1 (per 15 minutes) for the tumble dryer. In Bockenheim, the SB-Waschcenter, Grosse Seestrasse 46, charges DM8 per wash and DM1 dryers (10 minutes).

Medical Services The Uni-Klinik (☎ 630 11) at Theodor Stern Kai in Sachsenhausen is open 24 hours a day. For medical queries, contact the doctor service on ☎ 192 92, 24 hours a day.

Dangers & Annoyances The area around the main train station is a base for Frankfurt's sex and illegal drug trades. Frequent police patrols of the station and the surrounding Bahnhofsviertel keep things under control, but it's advisable to exercise 'big city' sense.

Things to See & Do
Eighty per cent of the old city was wiped off the map by two Allied bombing raids in March 1944, and postwar reconstruction was subject to the demands of the new age. Rebuilding efforts were more thoughtful, however, in the **Römerberg**, the old central area of Frankfurt west of the cathedral, where restored 14th and 15th-century buildings provide a glimpse of the beautiful city this once was. The old town hall, or **Römer**, is in the north-western corner of Römerberg and consists of three 15th-century houses topped with Frankfurt's trademark stepped gables.

East of Römerberg, behind the Historischer Garten (Historical Garden), which has the remains of Roman and Carolingian foundations, is the **Dom**, the coronation site of Holy Roman emperors from 1562 to 1792. It's dominated by the elegant 15th-century Gothic **tower** (completed in the 1860s) – one of the few structures left standing after the 1944 raids. The small **Wahlkapelle** (Voting Chapel) on the cathedral's southern side is where the seven electors of the Holy Roman Empire chose the emperor

from 1356 onwards; the adjoining **choir** has beautiful wooden stalls.

Anyone with an interest in German literature should visit **Goethe Haus**, Grosser Hirschgraben 23-25. Johann Wolfgang von Goethe was born in this house in 1749. The museum is open 9 am to 6 pm weekdays (till 4 pm from October to March), 10 am to 4 pm weekends (DM7/3).

A bit farther afield, the botanical **Palmengarten** (DM7/3) and the creative **Frankfurt Zoo** (DM11/5) are good places to unwind. It is also a nice 40-minute walk east along the south bank of the Main River to the **lock** in Offenbach – just before it is a good beer garden.

There's a great **flea market** along the Museumsufer between 8 am and 2 pm every Saturday.

Museums Most of Frankfurt's museums are closed on Monday and offer free entry on Wednesday. Unless otherwise indicated, the ones below are open 10 am to 5 pm Tuesday to Sunday (to 8 pm Wednesday).

The **Museum für Moderne Kunst**, north of the cathedral at Domstrasse 10, features works of modern art by Joseph Beuys, Claes Oldenburg and many others (DM10/5). Also on the north bank is the **Jüdisches Museum** (DM5/2.50, free on Saturday).

Numerous museums line the south bank of the Main River along the so-called **Museumsufer** (Museum Embankment). Pick of the crop is the **Städelsches Kunstinstitut**, Schaumainkai 63, with a world-class collection of paintings by artists from the Renaissance to the 20th century, including Botticelli, Dürer, Van Eyck, Rubens, Rembrandt, Vermeer, Cézanne and Renoir (DM10/8). Other highlights are: **Deutsches Filmmuseum** (open 2 to 8 pm Saturday; DM5/2.50) and the **Kunsthandwerkmuseum** (Museum of Applied Arts; DM8/4).

Places to Stay
Camping The most recommended camping ground is *Campingplatz Heddernheim* (☎ 57 03 32, An der Sandelmühle 35) in the Heddernheim district north-west of the city centre. It's open all year and charges DM5.50 for tent sites, DM2 per car and DM9.50 per person, and is a 15-minute ride on the U1, U2 or U3

GERMANY

GERMANY

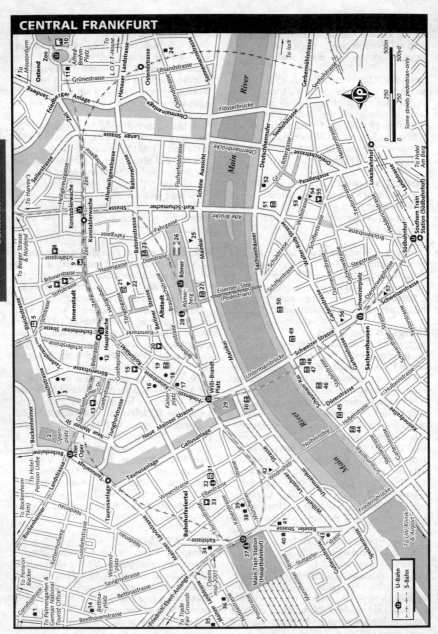

CENTRAL FRANKFURT

CENTRAL FRANKFURT

PLACES TO STAY
1 Hotel-Pension Gölz; Pension Sattler
11 Hotel am Zoo
14 Hotel-Pension Bruns
17 Steigenberger Frankfurter Hof
24 Hotel-Garni Diplomat
34 Hotel Carlton
35 Hotel Glockshuber
36 Hotel Topas
38 Hotel Münchner Hof
39 Hotel Eden
40 Hotel Tourist
41 Hotel Wiesbaden; Gaylord Indian Restaurant
52 Haus der Jugend

PLACES TO EAT
3 Blaubart Gewölbekeller
22 Kleinmarkthalle
25 Metropol
42 Ginger Brasserie
54 Fichte-Kränzi

56 HL Supermarket
57 Zum Gemalten Haus

OTHER
2 Alte Oper (Old Opera House)
4 English Bookshop
5 Turm-Palast Cinema
6 The Cave
7 Sinkkasten
8 Zum Schwejk
9 Post Office; Hertie Department Store
10 Zoo
12 Hugendubel
13 Jazzkeller
15 U60311
16 American Express
18 Thomas Cook
19 Goethe Haus
20 Jazz-Kneipe
21 Cyberyder
23 Museum für Moderne Kunst

26 Dom
27 Historisches Museum
28 Römer Tourist Office
29 Städtische Bühnen/Frankfurter Oper
30 Jüdisches Museum
31 English Theater
32 Tourismus + Congress
33 Jazz-Kneipe
37 Tourist Office
43 ADM-Mitfahrzentrale
44 Liebighaus (Museum of Ancient Sculpture)
45 Städelsches Kunstinstitut
46 Museum für Post und Kommunikation
47 Deutsches Architekturmuseum
48 Deutsches Filmmuseum
49 Museum für Völkerkunde
50 Kunsthandwerkmuseum
51 Ikonen-Museum
53 Wasch Center
55 Stereo Bar

from the Hauptwache U-Bahn station – get off at Heddernheim.

Hostels The big, bustling and crowded *Haus der Jugend* (☎ 610 01 50, fax 61 00 15 99, *Deutschherrnufer 12*) is within walking distance of the city centre and Sachsenhausen's nightspots. Rates (including breakfast) for beds in large dorms are DM27/34 for members under/over 20 years, DM39.50 in four-person rooms. Singles/doubles cost DM54/44 per person. Evening meals of several courses cost DM8.90. From the train station take S-Bahn No 2, 3, 4, 5 or 6 to Lokalbahnhof, then walk north for 10 minutes. Check-in begins at 2 pm and there's a midnight to 6 am curfew (postcode for bookings: 60594 Frankfurt/Main).

Hotels & Pensions In this city, 'cheap' can mean paying over DM100 for a spartan double room. During the many busy trade fairs even that price is unrealistic, with scarce rooms commanding a 50% to 100% premium.

Predictably, most of Frankfurt's lower-budget accommodation is in the sleazy Bahnhofsviertel surrounding the station. *Hotel*

Eden (☎ 25 19 14, fax 25 23 37, *Münchener Strasse 429*) has reasonable rooms for DM85/125 with WC and shower. *Hotel Münchner Hof* (☎ 23 00 66, fax 23 44 28, *Münchener Strasse 46*) has fairly good basic offerings for DM80/100, or DM100/140 with WC and shower. *Hotel Carlton* (☎ 23 20 93, fax 23 36 73, *Karlstrasse 11*) charges DM110/140 for rooms with facilities. *Hotel Tourist* (☎ 23 30 95/96/97, fax 23 69 86, *Baseler Strasse 23-25*) is similar and costs DM95/140. *Hotel Wiesbaden* (☎ 23 23 47, fax 25 28 45, *Baseler Strasse 52*) is one of the better options in the area, with rooms from DM115/150.

Hotel Glockshuber (☎ 74 26 28, fax 74 26 29, *Mainzer Landstrasse 120*), north of the main train station, is another pleasant option. Basic rates here start at DM65/110. *Hotel Topas* (☎ 23 08 52, fax 417 06 54, *Niddastrasse 88*) has quite nice rooms for DM100/130 with a bathroom.

Sachsenhausen has few budget places. *Hotel Am Berg* (☎ 61 20 21, fax 61 51 09, *Grethenweg 23*), in the quiet backstreets a few minutes' walk south-east from Südbahnhof, has rooms from DM65/95 without a bathroom, doubles from DM125 with bathroom, and several more expensive choices.

Some of the best pensions are in Frankfurt's posh Westend. *Pension Backer* (☎ 74 79 92, fax 74 79 00, Mendelssohnstrasse 92) has basic rooms for DM50/70. *Hotel-Pension Bruns* (☎ 78 88 96, fax 74 88 46) at No 42 charges DM70/90 for simple rooms and DM100/130 for rooms with shower and WC. The pleasant *Hotel-Pension Gölz* (☎ 74 67 35, fax 74 61 42, ✉ hotelgoelz@aol.com, Beethovenstrasse 44) has basic rooms for DM69, and singles/doubles with a bathroom for DM85/130. *Pension Sattler* (☎ 74 60 91) at No 46 charges DM110/160 for quite good singles/doubles with a bathroom. The friendly and clean *Hotel-Pension Uebe* (☎ 59 12 09, Grüneburgweg 3) costs DM129 for doubles with facilities, but without breakfast.

In Bockenheim, *Hotel West* (☎ 247 90 20, fax 707 53 09, Gräfstrasse 81) has quite good rooms for DM90/150 with facilities. *Hotel Falk* (☎ 70 80 94, fax 70 80 17, Falkstrasse 38A), in a quiet but still central neighbourhood, is one notch higher at DM120/160.

East of Konstablerwache, *Hotel-Garni Diplomat* (☎ 430 40 40, fax 430 40 22, Ostendstrasse 24-26) has nice rooms with all facilities for DM80/120. *Hotel am Zoo* (☎ 94 99 30, fax 94 99 31 99, ✉ Hotel–am–Zoo@t-online.de, Alfred-Brehm-Platz 6) is a reasonable options for DM135/199.

The quality *Steigenberger Frankfurter Hof* (☎ 215 02, fax 21 59 00, ✉ infoline@frankfurter-hof.steigenberger.de) at Am Kaiserplatz, charges DM415/470 for rooms excluding breakfast, but at DM245/310 with breakfast it's a good bet on the weekend.

Places to Eat

The area around the main train station has lots of ethnic eating options. Baseler Strasse in particular has a Middle Eastern tone. *Gaylord (Baseler Strasse 54)* is an Indian restaurant with lunch curry specials from about DM15 and evening main dishes for around DM22. The pan-Asian *Ginger Brasserie (Windmühlstrasse 14)* has everything Eastern on the menu from Sichuan to sushi, tandoori to Thai with most main courses between DM19 and DM29.

Known to locals as Fressgass (Munch-Alley), the Kalbächer Gasse and Grosse Bockenheimer Strasse area, between Opernplatz and Börsenstrasse, has some medium-priced restaurants and fast-food places with outdoor tables in summer. *Blaubart Gewölbekeller (Kaiserhofstrasse 18)* serves well-priced hearty dishes in a beer cellar atmosphere. It's also a lively place to drink until late. The *Kleinmarkthalle* off Hasengasse, is a great produce market with loads of fruit, vegetables, meats and hot food. *Metropol (Weckmarkt 13-15)*, near the Dom, serves well-priced, filling salads, casseroles and the like, but the service is notoriously slow – four hours for a cup of coffee that never arrived is our record. Still, it remains a nice place to eat and tipple till late.

Apple-wine taverns are a Frankfurt eating and drinking tradition, serving *Ebbelwoi* (Frankfurt dialect for *Apfelwein*), an alcoholic apple cider, along with local specialities like *Handkäse mit Musik* (literally, 'hand-cheese with music'). This is a round cheese soaked in oil and vinegar and topped with onions; you supply the music. Some good Ebbelwoi are in Alt-Sachsenhausen – the area directly behind the DJH hostel – which bulges with eateries and pubs. *Fichte-Kränzi (Wallstrasse 5)* is highly recommended for its friendly atmosphere and well-priced food. It also serves beer. *Zum Gemalten Haus (Schweizer Strasse 67)* is a lively place full of paintings of old Frankfurt. *Zur Sonne* (☎ 45 93 96, Berger Strasse 312), in Bornheim, is authentic and has a gorgeous yard for summer tippling (open from around 4 pm daily).

Wallstrasse and the surrounding streets in Alt-Sachsenhausen also have lots of ethnic mid-priced restaurants.

Another good place for ravenous hunters and gatherers is the cosmopolitan Berger Strasse and Nordend areas north of the Zeil. *Café Gegenwart (Berger Strasse 6)* is a large bar/restaurant serving large, hearty dishes from DM14; if the weather cooperates you can sit outside. *Eckhaus (Bornheimer Landstrasse 45)* is a relaxed restaurant and bar that serves well-priced salads and main dishes in the evening. For both of these, take the U-4 to Merianplatz. *Strandcafé (Koselstrasse 46)* serves delicious felafel and salads and other Middle-Eastern dishes for under DM20 in a pleasant atmosphere. No alcohol can be drunk here (take the U-5 to

Musterschule). *Grössenwahn* (☎ *59 93 56, Lenau-Strasse 97*) is a wonderful upmarket pub where, if you choose carefully, you can eat for under DM25. Take the U-5 to Glauburgstrasse. Follow Lenaustrasse north until you think you've reached the end – and keep going north.

In Bockenheim, *Stattcafé (Grempstrasse 21)* offers vegetarian and meat dishes from around DM13, as well as good coffee and cakes. *Pielok (Jordanstrasse 3)* looks like your grandmother had a hand in the decorations; it's cosy and the food is traditional, filling and extremely well-priced.

Fresh produce markets are held 8 am to 6 pm on Thursday and Friday at Bockenheimer Warte and Südbahnhof respectively. There are supermarkets in the basements at Hauptwache and Hertie on Zeil. A HL supermarket is in the basement of Woolworths on Schweizer Strasse in Sachsenhausen.

Entertainment

Ballet, opera and theatre are strong features of Frankfurt's entertainment scene. For information and bookings, ring Städtische Bühnen (☎ 21 23 79 99, Willy-Brandt-Platz), or the Hertie concert and theatre-booking service on ☎ 29 48 48 (Zeil 90; commission charged). *Journal Frankfurt* (DM3.30) has good listings in German of what's on in town, and the MainCity series of guides is worth browsing.

The *Turm-Palast* (☎ 28 17 87), Am Eschenheimer Turm, is a multi-screen cinema showing films in English. English-language plays and musicals are staged every evening (except Monday) by the *English Theater* (☎ 24 23 16 20), Kaiserstrasse 52.

Frankfurt also has a couple of very good jazz venues. *Blues & Beyond* (☎ 46 99 09 87, *Berger Strasse 159*) is a small venue for blues and jazz bands; the *Jazzkeller* (☎ 28 85 37, *Kleine Bockenheimer Strasse 18a*) and the *Jazz-Kneipe* (☎ 28 71 73, *Berliner Strasse 70*) also get top acts. *Sinkkasten* (☎ 28 03 85, *Brönnerstrasse 5*) has live bands. *Mousonturm* (☎ 40 58 95 20, *Waldschmidtstrasse 4*) in a converted soap factory in Bornheim offers music, dance performances and politically oriented cabaret.

The *Cave* (Brönnerstrasse 11) is a club that usually has indie and punk; *U60311* on Rossmarkt has techno and house music; *L.O.F.T.*

– House (☎ 934 48 41, Hanauer Landstrasse 181-85) gets a young crowd for various styles; *Stereo Bar (Abtgässchen 7),* in Sachsenhausen, has a 1970s feel. A popular gay bar is *Zum Schwejk* at Schäffergasse 20, while *Harvey's*, a restaurant and bar on Friedberger Platz, is a favoured meeting place for Frankfurt's gay and lesbian yuppies.

Getting There & Away

Air Flughafen Frankfurt/Main is Germany's largest airport, with the highest freight and second highest passenger turnover in Europe. This high-tech town has two terminals linked by an elevated railway. Departure and arrival halls A, B and C are in Terminal 1, with Lufthansa flights handled in hall A; halls D and E are in the new Terminal 2. The airport train station has two sections: platforms 1 to 3 (below Terminal 1, hall B) handle regional and S-Bahn connections, whereas IR, IC and ICE connections are in the long-distance train station. Signs point the way. Hourly IC or EC trains go to Cologne (DM66, two hours) and Nuremberg (DM76, 2½ hours) and six direct ICEs run to/from Hamburg on weekdays (DM196, four hours).

The airport information number is ☎ 69 03 05 11.

Bus Long-distance buses leave from the southern side of the main train station, where there's a Europabus office (☎ 23 07 35/6) that handles bookings. It caters for most European destinations, but the most interesting possibility is the Romantic Road bus (see the Bavaria section earlier in the chapter). Also see the introductory Getting There & Away section.

Train The main train station handles more departures and arrivals than any other station in Germany, so finding a train to or from almost anywhere is not a problem. For rail information, call ☎ 01805-99 66 33. The DB Lounge above the information office is a comfortable retreat open 6 am to 11 pm daily for anyone with a valid train ticket.

Car Frankfurt features the famed Frankfurter Kreuz, the biggest autobahn intersection in the country. All main car rental companies have offices in the main hall of the train station and at the airport.

GERMANY

The ADM-Mitfahrzentrale (☎ 194 40) is on Baselerplatz, three minutes' walk south of the train station. A sample of fares (including fees) is: Berlin DM54, Hamburg DM49, Cologne DM23, Dresden DM49 and Munich DM41.

Getting Around
To/From the Airport The S-Bahn's S8/S9 train runs every 15 minutes between the airport and Frankfurt Hauptbahnhof (11 minutes), usually continuing via Hauptwache and Konstablerwache to Offenbach; a fixed fare of DM5.90 applies. Taxis (about DM45 and taking 30 minutes without traffic jams) or the frequent airport bus (from Südbahnhof; DM5.90) take longer.

Public Transport Frankfurt's excellent transport network (RMV) integrates all bus, tram, S-Bahn and U-Bahn lines. Single or day tickets can be purchased from automatic machines (press the flag button for explanations in English) at almost any stop. Press *Einzelfahrt Frankfurt* for destinations in zone 50, which takes in most of Frankfurt (a plane symbol indicates the button for the airport). *Peak* period short-trip tickets (*Kurzstrecken*) cost DM2.90, single tickets cost DM3.60 and a *Tageskarte* (24-hour ticket; also valid for the airport trip) is DM8.20.

Car Traffic flows smoothly in Frankfurt, but the extensive system of one-way streets can be extremely frustrating. You might want to park your vehicle in an outlying area or one of the many car parks and proceed on foot or by public transport.

Taxi Taxis are slow compared with public transport and expensive at DM3.80 flag fall plus a minimum of DM2.15 per km. There are taxi ranks throughout the city, or you can ring ☎ 23 00 01/33, ☎ 25 00 01 or ☎ 54 50 11 to book a cab.

MARBURG
☎ 06421 • pop 77,000
Situated 90km north of Frankfurt, Marburg is known for its charming Altstadt with the splendid **Elizabethkirche** and the **Philipps-Universität**, Europe's very first Protestant university (founded in 1527). Wander up to

the museum in the **castle**, from where there are nice views of the old town.

Places to Stay & Eat
Marburg's *DJH hostel* (☎ 234 61, fax 121 91, ✉ Marburg@djh-hessen.de, Jahnstrasse 1) is about 10 minutes' walk upstream along the river from Rudolfsplatz in the Altstadt (DM24.50/29.50 juniors/seniors). For other budget accommodation drop in at the tourist office (99 12 23, fax 99 12 12, ✉ mtm@ scm.de), Pilgrimstein 26; it has a free room-finding service. *Barfuss* (☎ 253 49, Barfüsserstrasse 33) is a lively eatery with moderately priced food.

North Rhine-Westphalia

The North Rhine-Westphalia (Nordrhein-Westfalen) region was formed in 1946 from a hotchpotch of principalities and bishoprics, most of which had belonged to Prussia since the early 19th century. A quarter of Germany's population lives here. The Rhine-Ruhr industrial area is the country's economic powerhouse and one of the most densely populated conurbations in the world. Though the area is dominated by bleak industrial centres connected by a maze of train lines and autobahns, some of the cities are steeped in history and their attractions warrant an extensive visit.

COLOGNE
☎ 0221 • pop 965,000
Located at a major crossroads of European trade routes, Cologne (Köln) was an important city even in Roman times. It was then known as Colonia Agrippinensis, the capital of the province of Germania, and had no fewer than 300,000 inhabitants. In later years it remained one of northern Europe's main cities (the largest in Germany until the 19th century), and it is still the centre of the German Roman Catholic church. Almost completely destroyed in WWII, it was quickly rebuilt and many of its old churches and monuments have been meticulously restored.

It's worth making the effort to visit this lively, relaxed city, especially for its famous cathedral, interesting museums and vibrant nightlife.

Orientation

Situated on the Rhine River, the skyline of Cologne is dominated by the cathedral. The pedestrianised Hohe Strasse runs straight through the middle of the old town from north to south and is Cologne's main shopping street. The main train station is just north of the cathedral. The main bus station is just behind the train station, on Breslauer Platz.

Maps The DB Service Point has useful free maps of the central area and the tourist office sells an excellent map (DM1) with a street key.

Information

Tourist Office The helpful tourist office (☎ 22 12 33 45, fax 22 12 33 20, ℮ koelnt ourismus@stadt-koeln.de) is opposite the cathedral's main entrance at Unter Fettenhennen 19. In summer it's open 8 am to 10.30 pm Monday to Saturday, from 9 am Sunday and public holidays; opening hours are 8 am to 9 pm Monday to Saturday and 9.30 am to 7 pm Sunday and public holidays from November to April. Browse through the guide booklets before deciding which one to buy. *Monatsvorschau*, the monthly what's-on booklet, is a good investment at DM2. The room-finding service (DM5) is a bargain when the city is busy with trade fairs, but you cannot book by telephone.

Money The Reisebank at the train station is open 7 am to 10 pm daily. American Express is at Burgmauer 14 and the Thomas Cook office is at Burgmauer 4, near the tourist office.

Post & Communications The main post office is upstairs in Ludwig im Bahnhof bookshop inside the main train station. It opens 6 am to 11 pm Monday to Saturday and from 8 am Sunday.

Email & Internet Access Moderne Zeiten (☎ 206 72 51), Richmodstrasse 13, is a very hip place where you can surf the web for DM8 per 30 minutes. It also serves food and drinks. It opens from 8 to 1 am daily (Sunday from 10 am).

Bookshops Ludwig im Bahnhof, inside the main train station, stocks the international press and also has Lonely Planet titles.

Laundry The Öko-Express Waschsalon (closed Sunday) is on the corner of Händelstrasse and Richard-Wagner-Strasse.

Medical & Emergency Services The police are on ☎ 110; for fire and ambulance call ☎ 112. An on-call doctor can be contacted on ☎ 192 92.

Things to See

Cologne has a large town centre and the cathedral (Dom) is its heart, soul and tourist draw. Combined with the excellent museums next door, plan to spend at least one full day inside and around the Dom.

Dom Head first to the southern side of the Dom for an overall view. The structure's sheer size, with spires rising to 157m, is overwhelming. Building began in 1248 in the French Gothic style. The huge project was stopped in 1560 but started again in 1842, in the style originally planned, as a symbol of Prussia's drive for unification. It was finally finished in 1880. Miraculously, it survived WWII's heavy night bombing intact.

The Dom is open 7 am to 7.30 pm daily. When you reach the transept you'll be overwhelmed by the sheer size and magnificence of it all. The five **stained-glass windows** along the north aisle depict the lives of the Virgin and St Peter. Behind the high altar you can see the **Magi's Shrine** (circa 1150-1210), believed to contain the remains of the Three Wise Men, which was brought to Cologne from Milan in the 12th century. On the south side, in a chapel off the ambulatory, is the 15th-century **Adoration of the Magi altarpiece**. Guided tours in English are held at 10.30 am and 2.30 pm Monday to Saturday (at 2.30 pm only on Sunday) and cost DM7/4; meet inside the main portal. Tours in German are more frequent and cost DM6/3.

For a fitness fix, pay DM3/1.50 (closes at 4 pm from November to February) to climb 509 steps up the Dom's south tower to the base of the stupendous steeples, which towered over all of Europe until the Eiffel Tower was erected. Look at the 24-tonne **Peter Bell**, the

GERMANY

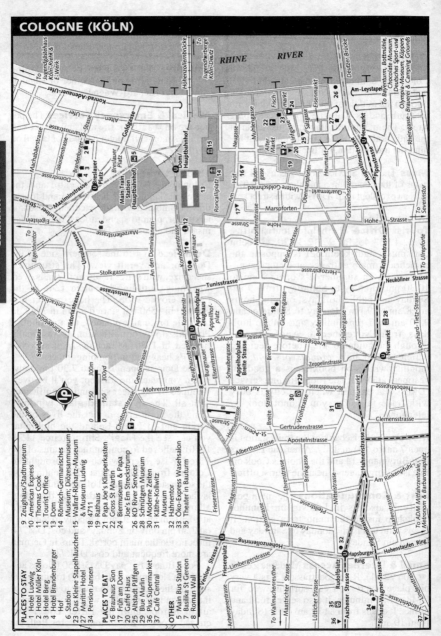

COLOGNE (KÖLN)

PLACES TO STAY
1 Hotel Ludwig
2 Hotel Müller Köln
3 Hotel Berg
4 Hotel Brandenburger Hof
6 Station
23 Das Kleine Stapelhäuschen
27 Maritim Hotel
34 Pension Jansen

PLACES TO EAT
16 Brauhaus Sion
17 Früh am Dom
20 Gaffel Haus
25 Altstadt Päffgen
29 Blue Marlin
30 Moderne Zeiten
37 Café Central

OTHER
5 Main Bus Station
7 Basilika St Gereon
8 Roman Wall

9 Zeughaus/Stadtmuseum
10 American Express
11 Thomas Cook
12 Tourist Office
13 Dom
14 Römisch-Germanisches
   Museum; Diözesanmuseum
15 Wallraf-Richartz-Museum
   & Museum Ludwig
18 4711
19 Rathaus
21 Papa Joe's Klimperkasten
22 Gross St Martin
24 Biermuseum & Papa
   Joe's Em Streckstrump
26 KD River Services
28 Schnütgen Museum
31 Käthe-Kollwitz
   Museum
33 Hahnentor
33 Öko-Express Waschsalon
35 Theater in Bauturm

euro currency converter €1 = 1.95DM

largest working bell in the world, on your way up. At the end of your climb, the view from the vantage point, 98.25m up, is absolutely stunning: on a clear day you can see all the way to the Siebengebirge Mountains beyond Bonn. The cathedral **treasury** (DM3.50/1.50) has a small but valuable collection of reliquaries. It is open 9 am to 5 pm Monday to Saturday, from April to October (to 4 pm in winter), 1 pm to 4 pm Sunday. Cologne's archbishops are interred in the crypt.

Other Churches Many other churches are worth a look, particularly Romanesque ones that have been restored since WWII bombing. The most handsome from the outside is **Gross St Martin**, near Fischmarkt, while the most stunning interior is that of the **Basilika St Gereon** on Christophstrasse, with its incredible four-storey decagon (open 9 am to 12.30 pm and 1.30 to 6 pm weekdays, and Saturday morning and Sunday afternoon; enter from Gereonkloster).

Museums The **Römisch-Germanisches Museum**, next to the cathedral at Roncalliplatz 4, displays artefacts from all aspects of the Roman settlement in the Rhine Valley. Highlights are the giant Poblicius grave monument and the Dionysos mosaic around which the museum was built. The museum is open 10 am to 5 pm Tuesday to Sunday (DM5/2.50).

The **Wallraf-Richartz-Museum & Museum Ludwig** at Bischofsgartenstrasse 1 (open 10 am to 6 pm Wednesday to Friday, until 8 pm Tuesday, from 11 am weekends; DM10/5) is one of the country's finest art galleries, making brilliant use of natural light. One floor is devoted to the Cologne Masters of the 14th to 16th centuries, known for their distinctive use of colour. Also look for familiar names like Rubens, Rembrandt and Dürer. The contemporary art collection provides a wonderful contrast. Catch some prime Kirchner, Kandinsky and Max Ernst, as well as pop-art works by Rauschenberg and Andy Warhol. The building also houses a unique photography collection from the former Agfa Museum in Leverkusen.

At Cäcilienstrasse 29, the former church of St Cecilia houses the **Schnütgen Museum**, an overwhelming display of church riches,

including many religious artefacts and early ivory carvings (open 10 am to 5 pm Tuesday to Friday, from 11 am weekends; DM5/2.50). At the **Diözesanmuseum** on Roncalliplatz, admission is free to see the religious treasures (closed Thursday).

The multi-media **Deutsches Sport- und Olympia-Museum**, Rheinaufen 1, is a great place to find out all about the history of sport from ancient times to the present day. It opens from 10 am to 6 pm Tuesday to Friday, 11 am to 7 pm weekends (till 8 pm Friday; DM8/4).

Other museums worth visiting are the **Käthe Kollwitz Museum**, Neumarkt 18-24, with some fine sculpture and graphics (DM5/2.50); the **Zeughaus** on Zeughaus strasse, restored as the **Stadtmuseum** (DM5/2.50), which has a model of Cologne and a good armoury collection; and the **Chocolate Museum**, on the river in the Rheinauhafen near the Altstadt (DM10/5), where you will learn everything about the history of making chocolate – as if you cared beyond the taste (all closed Monday).

Activities
Guided Tours The summer daily city tour in English lasts two hours and departs from the tourist office at 10.30 am, 11 am and 2.30 pm (at 11 am and 2 pm from November to March). The cost is a steep DM26. You can also make day trips to nearby cities with KD River Cruises (see Getting There & Away later in this section). A trip down the Rhine to Bonn is DM22.20, to Koblenz DM92 one way.

Historical Walks You can give yourself a free tour of ancient and medieval Cologne by walking around its restored monuments with a free city-sights map from the tourist office. If you walk west from the Dom along Komödienstrasse over Tunisstrasse, you reach the Zeughaus museum, the Burgmauer side of which was built along the line of the **Roman wall**. Continue west until you find a complete section of the north wall, which leads to a corner tower standing among buildings on the street corner at St-Apern-Strasse. One block south of here is another tower ruin near Helenenstrasse.

You can also take a lift down and walk through the **Roman sewer** and see the remains of the palace of the Praetorium under the medieval town hall (entry on Kleine Budengasse; closed Monday; DM3/1.50). The **Rathaus** (town hall) itself is open 7.30 am to 4.45 pm weekdays (to 2 pm only on Friday); the facades, foyer and tower have been restored.

The city's medieval towers and gates complement its Romanesque churches. The Bayenturm on the Rhine bank at the eastern end of Severinswall is completely rebuilt, but along the street to the west the vine-bedecked Bottmühle and the mighty main south gate of Severinstor have more of the original basalt and tuff stones. To the north-west along Sachsenring is the vaulted Ulrepforte towergate and a section of wall with two more towers. North of the city centre is the gate of Eigelsteintor on Eigelstein, suspended from which is a boat from the MS *Schiff Cöln*, which sank off Heligoland in 1914. The main west gate, Hahnentor, is at Rudolfplatz.

Special Events

Try to visit Cologne during the wild and crazy period of the Cologne Carnival (Karneval), rivalled only by Munich's Oktoberfest. People dress in creative costumes, clown suits, as popular personalities, and whatever else their alcohol-numbed brains may invent. The streets explode with activity on the Thursday before the seventh Sunday before Easter. On Friday and Saturday evening the streets pep up, Sunday is like Thursday and on Monday (*Rosenmontag*) there are formal and informal parades, and much spontaneous singing and celebrating.

Places to Stay

Cheap accommodation in Cologne is not plentiful, but there are a couple of good pensions around the city, and you should be able to get private rooms unless there's a trade fair on.

Camping The most convenient camping ground is *Campingplatz der Stadt Köln* (☎ 83 19 66) on Weidenweg in Poll, 5km south-east of the city centre. Take U16 to Marienburg and cross the bridge (open from May to the end of September). It charges DM8 per person, DM4 for a car and DM4 for a small tent. *Campingplatz Berger* (☎ 39 22 11, *Uferstrasse 53*), 7km south of the city in Rodenkirchen, is open all year. Take the U16

to Marienburg and from there bus No 130. It charges DM8 per person and DM8 for a car.

Hostels Cologne has two DJH hostels. The bustling *Jugendherberge Köln-Deutz* (☎ 81 47 11, fax 88 44 25, ✉ JH-DEUTZ@t-online .de, Siegesstrasse 5a) in Deutz is a 15-minute walk east from the main train station over the Hohenzollernbrücke or three minutes from Bahnhof Köln-Deutz (sometimes called Messe-Osthallen). The charge for juniors/ seniors is DM32/37 while double rooms cost DM46 per person and singles DM53.

The *Jugendgästehaus Köln-Riehl* (☎ 76 70 81, fax 76 15 55, ✉ jgh-koeln-riehl@t-on line.de, An der Schanz 14) is north of the city in Riehl. It's more pleasant and has one to six-bed rooms between DM39 and DM65. Take the U15 or U16 to Boltensternstrasse. The gaudy backpackers' hostel *Station* (☎ 912 53 01, fax 912 53 03, ✉ station@t-on line.de, Marzellenstrasse 44-48) has singles for DM40 and beds in large dorms for DM27.

Hotels & Pensions Accommodation prices in Cologne increase by at least 20% when fairs are on. If you have private transport, inquire about parking – a night in a car park will set you back DM25 or more (and not all of them operate 24 hours). The tourist office room-finding service can help with hotel rooms in the lower price range.

Pension Jansen (☎ 25 18 75, fax 25 18 75, Richard-Wagner-Strasse 18) provides basic singles/doubles from DM55/100 and is convenient to the restaurant quarter of town.

A lot of other budget and mid-range hotels cluster in the streets north of the main train station. *Hotel Brandenburger Hof* (☎ 12 28 89, fax 13 53 04, Brandenburger Strasse 2) has basic rooms from DM75/90, DM95/120 with shower and WC. *Hotel Berg* (☎ 12 11 24, fax 139 00 11, ✉ hotel@hotel-berg.com, Brandenburger Strasse 6) has some fairly good rooms without shower and WC from DM75/95, or DM110/130 with bathroom. *Hotel Müller Köln* (☎ 912 83 50, fax 13 71 56, ✉ Hotel-Mueller-Koeln@t-online.de, Brandenburger Strasse 20) has reasonable singles/ doubles for DM115/145 with shower and WC. *Hotel Ludwig* (☎ 16 05 40, fax 16 05 44 44, ✉ hotel@hotelludwig.com, Brandenburger Strasse 22-24) is a fairly good option in the mid-price range, with decent rooms for DM145/185; some have a view to the Dom and there are also weekend deals.

Das Kleine Stapelhäuschen (☎ 257 78 62, fax 257 42 32, @ stapelhaeuschen@comp userve.com, Fischmarkt 1-3), in the middle of the Altstadt, has pleasant rooms from DM75/ 125 and rooms with facilities for DM125/ 195. This rises to DM135/235 for the larger singles/doubles. The *Maritim Hotel* (☎ 202 70, fax 202 78 26, @ reservierung@kolmar itim.de, Heumarkt 20) caters largely to a trade fair and business clientele. Rooms here start at DM274/314.

Places to Eat

Cologne's beer halls serve cheap and filling (though often bland) meals to go with their home brew (see Beer Halls for details).

Brauhaus Sion (Unter Taschenmacher 9) is a big beer hall, packed most nights and for good reason: you'll eat your fill for well under DM20, including a couple of beers. *Altstadt Päffgen* (Heumarkt 62) at the northern or Salzgasse end is more upmarket but authentic. It serves meals for around DM22. *Gaffel Haus* (Alter Markt 20-22) is another nice place to eat and sample the local brew.

The Internet cafe Moderne Zeiten (see Email & Internet Access) has a *restaurant* attached where you can eat pasta and the like while surfing. Across the street, *Blue Marlin* (Wolfstrasse 4) does delicious sushi from DM15 for eight pieces or from DM2 a piece.

The Belgisches Viertel (Belgian Quarter) around and west of Hahnentor is packed with restaurants of all descriptions. You'll find a couple of moderately priced Asian eating houses on Händelstrasse.

Café Central (Jülicher Strasse 1), on the corner of Händelstrasse, is open till late and has an adjoining restaurant called *o.T.* that serves mains in the DM25 to DM30 range; the cafe itself does breakfast and light dishes.

To put together a picnic, visit a *market*; the biggest is held on Tuesday and Friday at Aposteln-Kloster near Neumarkt. The supermarket *Plus* (Aachener Strasse 64) is in the Belgisches Viertel.

Entertainment

Evenings and weekends in the Altstadt are like miniature carnivals, with bustling crowds

and lots to do. The beverage of choice is beer, and there are plenty of places to enjoy it. The best source of information on bars and restaurants is *Tag und Nacht* (DM9.80; one of the *Stadt Revue* series), available at newsagents and kiosks around town.

Papa Joe's Klimperkasten (Alter Markt 50) is a lively jazz pub with a wonderful pianola. *Papa Joe's Em Streckstrump* (Buttermarkt 37) is more intimate. *Metronom* (Weyerstrasse 59), near the Kwartier Latäng (Latin Quarter), is Cologne's most respected evening bar for jazz enthusiasts, with live performances mainly weekdays.

Wallmachenreuther (Brusseler Platz 9) is an off-beat bar in the Belgisches Viertel which also serves food. The gay scene also centres on the Belgisches Viertel.

E-Werk (☎ 96 27 90, Schanzenstrasse 28-36), in a converted power station in Mülheim, is Cologne's usual venue for rock concerts. It turns into a huge techno club on Friday and Saturday nights.

Köln Ticket (☎ 28 01), at Roncalliplatz next to the Römisch-Germanisches Museum, has tickets and information on classical music and theatre performances in town. *Theater im Bauturm* (☎ 52 42 42, Aachener Strasse 24) is one of Cologne's more innovative theatres.

Beer Halls As in Munich, beer in Cologne reigns supreme. There are more than 20 local breweries, all producing a variety called Kölsch, which is relatively light and slightly bitter. The breweries run their own beer halls and serve their wares in skinny glasses holding a mere 200ml, but you'll soon agree it's a very satisfying way to drink the stuff. See Places to Eat for other suggestions. *Früh am Dom* (Am Hof 12-14) is famous for its own-brew beer; the *Biermuseum* (Buttermarkt 39) – beside Papa Joe's – has 18 varieties on tap. *Küppers Brauerei* (☎ 934 78 10, Alteburger Strasse 157) is in Bayenthal, south of the city (take the U16 to Bayenthalgürtel). It has a nice beer garden and there's also a beer museum which you can visit if you call ahead.

Shopping

A good Cologne souvenir might be a small bottle of *eau de Cologne*, which is still produced in its namesake city. The most famous

GERMANY

brand is called 4711, after the house number where it was invented. There's still a perfumery and gift shop by that name at the corner of Glockengasse and Schwertnergasse. Try to catch the Glockenspiel, with characters from Prussian lore parading above the store hourly from 9 am to 9 pm.

Getting There & Away

Air Cologne/Bonn airport has many connections within Europe and to the rest of the world. For flight information ring ☎ 02203-40 40 01/02.

Bus Deutsche Touring's Eurolines (☎ 13 52 52) offers overnight trips to Paris (DM58, 6½ hours). The office is at the main train station at the Breslauer Platz exit.

Train There are frequent services to both nearby Bonn (DM9, 18 minutes) and Düsseldorf (DM12, 20 minutes) as well as to Aachen (DM20, one hour). Frequent direct IC/EC (DM93, 3¼ hours) and ICE (DM104, 2¾ hours) trains go to Hanover. There are IC/EC links with Frankfurt/Main (DM68, 2¼ hours) – a new ICE line is being built to Frankfurt's airport – and ICE trains to Berlin (DM190, 4½ hours). The Thalys high-speed train connects Paris and Cologne via Aachen and Brussels (DM108/128 weekdays/weekends, four hours, seven times daily; with only a small discount for rail pass-holders!).

Car The city is on a main north-south autobahn route and is easily accessible for drivers and hitchhikers. The ADM Mitfahrzentrale (☎ 194 40) is at Triererstrasse 47 near Barbarossaplatz.

Boat An enjoyable way to travel to/from Cologne is by boat. KD River Cruises (☎ 208 83 18), which has its headquarters in the city at Frankenwerft 1, has services all along the Rhine.

Getting Around

To/From the Airport Bus No 170 runs between Cologne/Bonn airport and the main bus station every 15 minutes from 5.30 am to 10.30 pm daily (DM8.90, 20 minutes).

Public Transport Cologne offers a convenient and extensive mix of buses, trams and local trains – trams go underground in the inner city, and trains handle destinations up to 50km around Cologne. Ticketing and tariff structures are complicated. The best ticket option is the one-day pass: DM9.60 if you're staying near the city (one or two zones); DM15.30 for most of the Cologne area (four zones); and DM21.40 including Bonn (seven zones). Single city trips cost DM2.20 and 90-minute two-zone tickets are DM3.50.

Taxi To order a taxi call ☎ 194 10 or ☎ 28 82 (an extra DM1 is charged on the normal rates).

AROUND COLOGNE
Bonn
☎ 0228 • pop 300,000

This friendly, relaxed city on the Rhine south of Cologne became West Germany's temporary capital in 1949 and is mainly an administrative centre now that the seat of government and embassies are in Berlin. Settled in Roman times, Bonn was the seat of the electors of Cologne in the 18th century, and some of their baroque architecture survived the ravages of WWII and the postwar demand for modern government buildings. Organise a day trip out here and to the nearby spa town of Bad Godesberg. Classical music buffs can pay homage to Bonn's most famous son, Ludwig van Beethoven.

The tourist office (☎ 77 50 00 or 194 33, fax 77 50 77, ◎ bonninformation@bonn.de) is behind the Karstadt department store in Windeckstrasse, a three-minute walk along Poststrasse from the Hauptbahnhof (open daily, closes at 4 pm weekends).

Bonn is a city that lives and breathes Beethoven. You can visit the **Beethoven-Haus**, Bonngasse 20, where the composer was born in 1770. The house contains much memorabilia concerning his life and music, including his last piano, specially made with an amplified sounding board to accommodate his deafness. It is open 10 am to 6 pm Monday to Saturday from April to October (till 5 pm in winter), 11 am to 4 pm Sunday (DM8/6). The Beethoven Festival is held every two to three years (the last was in September 2000).

The **Münsterbasilika** on Münsterplatz has a splendid interior and honours Saints Cassius and Florentius, two martyred Roman officers who became the patron saints of Bonn.

Bonn also has several interesting museums. The **Frauenmuseum**, Im Krausfeld 10, promotes and exhibits art created by women in an environment that combines history, mythology and contemporary artistic expressions (DM8/5). Opening hours are 2 to 5 pm Tuesday to Saturday, 11 am to 5 pm Sunday. Take bus No 624 or 634 to Kaiser-Karl-Ring.

The **Haus der Geschichte der Bundesrepublik Deutschland**, Adenauerallee 250, covers the history of Germany from 1945 (open 9 am to 7 pm, closed Monday; free entry); it is part of the **Museumsmeile**, a row of four museums that also includes the **Museum Alexander Koenig**, a natural history museum; the **Kunstmuseum** with its collection of 20th-century art; and exhibitions at the **Kunst- und Ausstellungshalle der Bundesrepublik Deutschland**.

There are frequent trains to Cologne in the north and to Koblenz (DM22, 30 minutes) in the south. See the Cologne Activities section for river cruises to/from Bonn. The Bonn transit system is linked with Cologne's and a one-way train ride between the two cities costs only DM9 (see the Cologne Getting Around section for passes covering both).

DÜSSELDORF
☎ 0211 • pop 571,000

Though not particularly strong in historical sights, this elegant and wealthy capital of North Rhine-Westphalia is an important centre for fashion and commerce, and a charming example of big-city living along the Rhine River.

Information
The tourist office (☎ 17 20 20, fax 16 10 71, @ vvd@t-online.de) is opposite the main exit of the train station towards the northern end of Konrad-Adenauer-Platz. It's open 8 am to 8 pm Monday to Saturday and 4 to 8 pm Sunday. The main post office is across the street. The Reisebank in the train station's main hall is open till 10 pm Monday to Friday and till 9 pm weekends. There's a convenient SB Waschsalon laundry at Charlotenstrasse 87.

Email & Internet Access
G@rden Internet cafe (☎ 86 61 60) is behind the town hall at Rathausufer 8.

Things to See & Do
To catch a glimpse of Düsseldorf's swish lifestyle, head for the famed Königsallee, or 'Kö', with its stylish (and pricey) boutiques and arcades. Stroll north along the Kö to the **Hofgarten**, a large park in the city centre.

The city has several interesting museums. These include the **Kunstmuseum Düsseldorf** at Ehrenhof north of the Oberkasseler Brücke (10 am to 6 pm Tuesday to Sunday; DM5/2.50), with a comprehensive European collection, and the incorporated **Glasmuseum Hentrich** (10 am to 6 pm Tuesday to Sunday). The **Kunstsammlung Nordrhein-Westfalen**, Grabbeplatz 5 (10 am to 6 pm Tuesday to Thursday and on weekends, to 8 pm Friday; DM12/8), has a huge modern art collection.

The **Goethe-Museum Düsseldorf** in Schloss Jägerhof, Jacobistrasse 2, pays tribute to the life and work of one of Europe's great men of letters. The large collection includes books, first drafts, letters, medals and much more (closed Monday and also Saturday morning; DM4/2). German-literature buffs will also want to visit the **Heinrich-Heine-Institut** at Bilker Strasse 12-14, which documents the Düsseldorfer's career (11 am to 5 pm Tuesday to Friday and on Sunday, 1 to 5 pm Saturday; DM4/2), or his house at Bolkerstrasse 53, now a literary pub.

On Marktplatz, the restored **Rathaus** (town hall) looks out onto the **statue of Prince Elector Johann Wilhelm**, known in local speech as 'Jan Wellem'. He lies buried in the ornate early-baroque **St Andreas Kirche** at the corner of Kay-und-Lore-Lorentz-Platz and Andreasstrasse, now in the care of a Dominican monastery. Another church worth visiting is the 13th-century **St Lambertus Basilika** on Stiftsplatz.

Nearby, the reconstructed **Schlossturm** of the long-destroyed Residenz stands on Burgplatz as a forlorn reminder of the Palatine elector's glory. In summer, the town's youth congregate on the steps below the tower. From here the pedestrian-only **Rheinuferpromenade** provides perfect strolling along the river. **Schloss Benrath** (☎ 899 72 71; open daily), a late-baroque pleasure palace with park, makes for a lovely excursion. Take tram No 701 from Jan-Wellem-Platz.

GERMANY

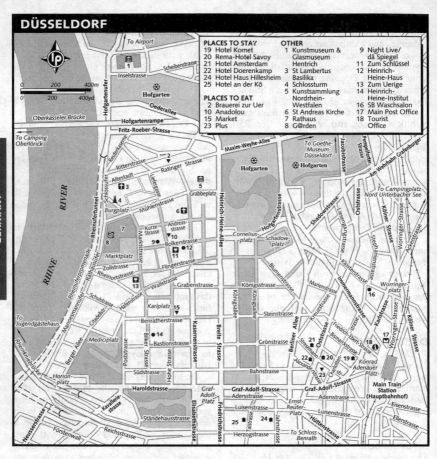

DÜSSELDORF

PLACES TO STAY	OTHER	
19 Hotel Komet	1 Kunstmuseum &	9 Night Live/
20 Rema-Hotel Savoy	Glasmuseum	dä Spiegel
21 Hotel Amsterdam	Hentrich	11 Zum Schlüssel
22 Hotel Doerenkamp	3 St Lambertus	12 Heinrich-
24 Hotel Haus Hillesheim	Basilika	Heine-Haus
25 Hotel an der Kö	4 Schlossturm	13 Zum Uerige
	5 Kunstsammlung	14 Heinrich-
PLACES TO EAT	Nordrhein-	Heine-Institut
2 Brauerei zur Uer	Westfalen	16 SB Waschsalon
10 Anadolou	6 St Andreas Kirche	17 Main Post Office
15 Market	7 Rathaus	18 Tourist
23 Plus	8 G@rden	Office

Places to Stay

There are two camping grounds quite close to the city. **Campingplatz Nord Unterbacher See** (☎ 899 20 38) is at Kleiner Torfbruch in Düsseldorf-Unterbach (take S-Bahn No 7 to Düsseldorf-Eller, then bus No 735 to Kleiner Torfbruch). It's open 4 April to 30 September. **Camping Oberlörick** (☎ 59 14 01) is at Lutticherstrasse, just beside the Rhine in Düsseldorf-Lörick (U-Bahn No 70, 74, 76 or 77 to Belsenplatz, and then bus No 828 or 838). It's open mid-April to mid-September. The trek to the Altstadt is very inconvenient from either camping ground.

The **Jugendgästehaus** (☎ 55 73 10, fax 57 25 13, ✉ jgh-duesseldorf@t-online.de, Düsseldorfer Strasse 1) is in posh Oberkassel across the Rhine from the Altstadt. It charges DM38 in small dorms and has some singles (DM47) and doubles (DM43 per person). Take U-Bahn No 70, 74, 75, 76, or 77 from the main train station to Luegplatz. From there it's a short walk.

Düsseldorf frequently hosts trade shows that inflate its already high hotel and pension prices. The tourist office can help with finding big discounts offered by many of the comfortable business hotels on weekends and when no fair is in town. It levies DM5 for bookings made on the day of check-in.

Hotel Amsterdam (☎ *840 58, fax 840 50, Stresemannstrasse 20)* has rooms with private shower from DM80/145. *Hotel Komet* (☎ *17 87 90, fax 178 79 50, Bismarckstrasse 93)* has reasonable singles/doubles for DM69/98 with bathroom (breakfast from DM7). *Hotel Haus Hillesheim* (☎ *38 68 60, fax 386 86 33, ✆ rezeption@hotel-hillesheim.de, Jahnstrasse 19)* charges DM80/110 for quite nice accommodation, or DM120/140 with facilities. *Hotel Doerenkamp* (☎ *32 80 11, fax 13 45 82, Stresemannstrasse 25)* has fine rooms with facilities for DM115/150 (ask for a quiet one) and pet rabbits to thrill the kids.

Hotel an der Kö (☎ *37 10 48, fax 37 08 35, Talstrasse 9)* charges DM160/230 for nice bright rooms with all facilities. The *Rema-Hotel Savoy* (☎ *36 03 36, 0800-800 36 33, fax 35 66 42, Oststrasse 128)* has impressive corridors but fairly ordinary rooms at DM190/240. Ask for a quiet, renovated one.

Places to Eat

The *Brauerei zur Uer* (*Ratinger Strasse 16)* is a rustic place to eat your fill for under DM20. Ratinger Strasse is also home to a couple of other pub-style places where you can eat and drink. *Zum Schlüssel* (*Bolkerstrasse 43-7)* is popular for its beer, but also has good food for around DM14 to DM25. *Anadolou* (*Mertensgasse 10)* serves delicious Anatolian sit-down and takeaway food including vegetarian dishes.

You can replenish supplies at the *Plus* supermarket at Stresemannstrasse 31, near Hotel Doerenkamp. A fresh produce *market* is held daily except Sunday on Karlplatz.

Entertainment

Besides walking and museum-hopping, one of the best things to do in Düsseldorf is (surprise!) drink beer. There are lots of bars (for drinking and eating) in the Altstadt, affectionately referred to as the 'longest bar in the world'. On evenings and weekends, the best places overflow onto the pedestrian-only streets. Favoured streets include Bolkerstrasse, Kurze Strasse, Andreasstrasse and the surrounding side streets.

The beverage of choice is Alt beer, a dark and semisweet brew typical of Düsseldorf. Try Gatzweilers Alt in *Zum Schlüssel* (see Places to Eat). The spartan *Zum Uerige* on Berger Strasse is the only place where you can buy Uerige Alt beer. It's DM2.50 per quarter-litre glass, and the beer flows so quickly that the waiters just carry around trays and give you a glass when you're ready. *Night Live* (*Bolkerstrasse 22)* has live bands; it's upstairs from *dä Spiegel*, itself a popular bar.

Getting There & Away

Düsseldorf's Lohausen airport (S-Bahn trains run every 20 minutes between the airport and the main train station) is busy with many national and international flights. Düsseldorf is part of a dense S-Bahn and train network in the Rhine-Ruhr region and regular IC/EC services run to/from Hamburg (DM123, 3¾ hours), ICE services to Hanover (DM95, 2¾ hours), and trains to Cologne (DM12, 30 minutes), IR trains to Frankfurt (DM82, 3½ hours) and most other major German cities.

Getting Around

As Düsseldorf is very spread out, it's easiest to get around by public transport. Buy your ticket from one of the orange machines at stops, although bus drivers will sell singles, and validate it before boarding. A short-trip ticket up to 1.5km (destinations are listed on the machines) costs DM2.10. A single ticket for zone A, which includes all of Düsseldorf proper, is DM3.20. Better value is the 24-hour TagesTicket for DM11.30, valid for up to five people in zone A.

AACHEN
☎ 0241 • pop 250,000

Aachen was famous in Roman times for its thermal springs. The great Frankish conqueror Charlemagne was so impressed by their revitalising qualities that he settled here and made it the capital of his kingdom in 794. Ever since, Aachen has held special significance among the icons of German nationhood. It is now an industrial and commercial centre and home to the country's largest technical university.

Orientation

Aachen's compact old centre is contained within two ring roads that roughly follow the old city walls. The inner ring road, or

GERMANY

GERMANY

Grabenring, changes names – most ending in 'graben' – and encloses the old city proper. To get to the tourist office from the Hauptbahnhof, turn left on leaving the main entrance, cross Römerstrasse, follow Bahnhofstrasse north and then go left along Theaterstrasse to Kapuzinergraben. Pick up an excellent free city map from the DB Service Point counter in the train station.

Information

The efficient tourist office (☎ 1 80 29 60/1, fax 1 80 29 30, ✉ mail@aachen-tourist.de) is at Atrium Elisenbrunnen on Kapuzinergraben. It is open 9 am to 6 pm Monday to Friday, until 2 pm Saturday. The Sparkasse bank opposite the tourist office at Friedrich-Wilhelm-Platz 1-4 stays open till 1 pm on Saturday. The main post office is temporarily inside the main train station but should be back at Kapuzinergraben 19 by early 2001. The bus station is at the north-eastern edge of Grabenring on the corner of Kurhausstrasse and Peterstrasse.

Email & Internet Access Vision Internet Café is at Neupforte 25.

Things to See & Do

Dom Aachen's drawing card is its cathedral (Dom, Kaiserdom or Münster), open 7 am to 7 pm daily. The cathedral's subtle grandeur, its historical significance and interior serenity make a visit almost obligatory – it's on Unesco's world cultural heritage list. No fewer than 30 Holy Roman emperors were crowned here from 936 to 1531.

The heart of the cathedral is a Byzantine-inspired **octagon**, built on Roman foundations, which was the largest vaulted structure north of the Alps when consecrated as Charlemagne's court chapel in 805. He lies buried here in the golden **shrine**, and the cathedral became a site of pilgrimage after his death, not least for its religious relics. The Gothic **choir** was added in 1414; its massive stained-glass windows are impressive even though some date from after WWII. The octagon received its **folded dome** after the city fire of 1656 destroyed the original tent roof. The **western tower** dates from the 19th century.

Worth noting is the huge brass **chandelier**, which was added to the octagon by Emperor Friedrich Barbarossa in 1165; the **high altar** with its 11th-century gold-plated Pala d'Oro (altar front) depicting scenes of the Passion; and the gilded copper ambo, or **pulpit**, donated by Henry II. Unless you join a German-language tour (DM3), you'll only catch a glimpse of Charlemagne's white-marble **throne** on the upper gallery of the octagon on the western side, where the nobles sat.

The entrance to the **Domschatzkammer** (cathedral treasury), with one of the richest collections of religious art north of the Alps, is on nearby Klostergasse (open 10 am to 1 pm Monday, 10 am to 6.30 pm Tuesday to Sunday, to 9 pm Thursday; DM5/4, includes pamphlet).

Other Attractions North of the cathedral, the 14th-century **Rathaus** overlooks Markt, a lively gathering place in summer, with its fountain statue of Charlemagne. The eastern tower of the Rathaus, the Granusturm, was once part of Charlemagne's palace. The Rathaus is open 10 am to 5 pm weekdays (closed at 1 pm for an hour on weekends; DM3/1.50). History buffs will be thrilled by the grand Empire Hall upstairs, where Holy Roman emperors enjoyed their coronation feasts.

Foremost among Aachen's worthwhile museums is the **Ludwig Forum for International Art**, Jülicherstrasse 97-109, with works by Warhol, Lichtenstein, Baselitz and others (open 10 am to 5 pm Tuesday and Thursday, till 8 pm Wednesday and Friday, 11 am to 5 pm weekends; DM6/3).

Thermal Baths Aachen was known for its thermal springs as early as Roman times, and the 8th-century Franks called the town 'Ahha', which is supposed to mean water. A visit to the new, city-owned **Carolus Thermen** (☎ 180 29 00), due to open in late 2000, will cost DM14 for two hours (DM24 with the sauna), or DM26 for up to five hours of splashy activity (DM40 with sauna). It's on Passstrasse in the city garden, north-east of the centre. Web site: www.carolus-thermen.de

Places to Stay

The nearest camping ground is *Hoeve de Gastmolen* (☎ *0031 43306 5755*) in the Dutch town of Vaals, about 6km outside

Aachen at Lemierserberg 23. Take bus No 15 or 65 and get off at the 'Heuvel' stop.

The DJH *Jugendgästehaus* (☎ *71 10 10, fax 711 01 20, Maria-Theresia-Allee 280)* is 4km south-west of the train station on a hill overlooking the city. Take bus No 2 to Ronheide, or bus No 12 to the closer Colynshof at the foot of the hill. It charges DM38.50 in dorms, and has some singles/doubles for DM63.50/77.

Hotels & Pensions The tourist office arranges private rooms from DM30/50, but ask for something within walking distance of the city centre. For budget rooms it's best to call the reservation service well in advance on ☎ 180 29 50/1.

Hotel Marx (☎ *375 41, fax 267 05,* @ *Hotel-Marx@gmx.de, Hubertusstrasse 33-35)* offers good rooms for DM60/100, but at that price you'll have to perform your ablutions acrobatically in the basin. Rooms with facilities start at DM85/140. The central *Hotel Drei Könige* (☎ *483 93, fax 361 52, Büchel 5)* has a few basic rooms for DM65/105, DM100/130 with shower and WC. *Hotel am Marschiertor* (☎ *319 41, fax 319 44,* @ *hotel.marschiertor@t-online.de, Wallstrasse 1-7),* near the train station, has quite nice singles/doubles from DM105/130 (breakfast DM15 extra). The historic *Dorint Select Quellenhof* hotel (☎ *913 20, fax 913 21 00,* @ *info.AAHQUE@dorint.com, Monheimsallee 52),* near the city park, charges DM320/370 (breakfast an extra DM32).

Places to Eat
Being a university town, Aachen is full of spirited cafes, restaurants and pubs, especially along Pontstrasse, referred to by locals as the 'Quartier Latin'. *Café Kittel (Pontstrasse 39)* is a popular student hang-out with a lively garden area. It serves reasonably priced light meals, including vegetarian dishes. *Gaststätte Labyrinth (Pontstrasse 156-158)* is a rambling beer-hall type place that lives up to its name. Good, filling meals range from DM10 to DM16. *Chico Mendes* café/bar *(Pontstrasse 74-76)* in the Katakomben Studentenzentrum serves cheap organic dishes.

Alt Aachener Kaffeestuben (Büchel 18) is a coffee house (wine also served) with old-world charm that does a traditional lunchtime dish for DM12.50. *Pasta (Jakobstrasse 1)* actually sells fresh pasta, but it also has several tables where you can eat delicious pasta dishes till 7 pm (4 pm Saturday, closed Sunday) for under DM15.

Plus (Bahnhofstrasse 18) is a fairly central supermarket for self-caterers.

Entertainment
The best source of information on bars, clubs and restaurants in Aachen and the Maas-Rhine region is the free *euroview* guide in English – the tourist office keeps copies. *Domkeller (Hof 1)* has been a student pub since the 1950s and usually features jazz or blues on Monday. *B9 (Blondelstrasse 9)* is one club that gets a young crowd. The style changes nightly. *Club Voltaire (Friedrichstrasse 9)* attracts an older, mixed crowd. The *City Theatre* (☎ *478 42 44)* on Theaterplatz has concerts and opera most nights; Aachen Ticket (☎ 180 29 65) in the tourist office has information and sells tickets.

Getting There & Away
Aachen is well served by road and rail. There are fast trains almost every hour to Cologne (43 minutes, DM20) and Liège (40 minutes, DM16). The high-speed Thalys passes through seven times daily on its way to Brussels and Paris. There's also a frequent bus service to Maastricht (55 minutes, DM9).

Getting Around
Aachen's points of interest are clustered around the city centre, which is covered easily on foot. Those arriving with private transport can park their cars in one of the many car parks. City bus tickets bought from the driver cost DM1.70, batches of six purchased from outlets go for DM8.70. A 24-hour Familienkarte und Gruppenkarte is valid for up to five people and costs DM8.80. You can buy it on buses and from machines and outlets.

Bremen

The federal state of Bremen covers only the 404 sq km comprising the two cities of Bremen (the state capital) and Bremerhaven. In medieval times Bremen was for a period Europe's northernmost archbishopric. The city was ruled by the Church until it joined the Hanseatic League in the 14th century. Controlled by the French from 1810 to 1813, Bremen went on to join the German Confederation in 1815. In 1871 the city was made a state of the German Empire. In 1949 Bremen was officially declared a state of the Federal Republic of Germany.

BREMEN

☎ 0421 • pop 545,000

Bremen is, after Hamburg, the most important harbour in Germany, even though the open sea lies 113km to the north. Its Hanseatic past and congenial Altstadt area around Am Markt and Domsheide make it an enjoyable place to explore on foot.

Orientation & Information

The heart of the city is Am Markt, but its soul is the port. The tourist office (☎ 30 80 00, fax 308 00 30, ✉ btz@bremen-tourism.de) before the main train station is open 9.30 am to 6.30 pm Monday to Wednesday, till 8 pm Thursday

and Friday and till 4 pm weekends. There is also a booth at the Rathaus opposite the smaller of the main Altstadt churches, Unser Lieben Frauen Kirche. City walks (English explanations provided) leave at 2 pm daily from the tourist office at the station (DM10). A Bremen tourist card (from DM19.50 for two days) offers unlimited public transport and substantial discounts on city sights. There's a Reisebank inside the train station. The main post office is also on Domsheide and there's another one near the train station. Its Web site is at www.bremen-tourism.de.

Things to See & Do

Around Am Markt don't miss the splendid and ornate **Rathaus** (town hall), the cathedral **St-Petri-Dom**, which has a tower lookout (Easter to October; DM1) and museum (DM3/2; both closed Sunday until 2 pm), and the large statue of **Roland**, Bremen's sentimental protector, erected in 1404.

Walk down **Böttcherstrasse**, a re-creation of a medieval alley, complete with tall brick

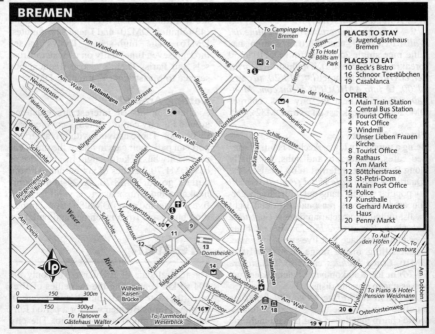

BREMEN

PLACES TO STAY
6 Jugendgästehaus Bremen

PLACES TO EAT
10 Beck's Bistro
16 Schnoor Teestübchen
19 Casablanca

OTHER
1 Main Train Station
2 Central Bus Station
3 Tourist Office
4 Post Office
5 Windmill
7 Unser Lieben Frauen Kirche
8 Tourist Office
9 Rathaus
11 Am Markt
12 Böttcherstrasse
13 St-Petri-Dom
14 Main Post Office
15 Police
17 Kunsthalle
18 Gerhard Marcks Haus
20 Penny Markt

euro currency converter €1 = 1.95DM

houses, shops, galleries, restaurants and three museums (closed Monday; DM8/4 for all three). The **Paula-Becker-Modersohn-Haus**, at No 8, has works by its namesake contemporary painter, and varied exhibits of the **Bernhard Hoetger Collection**; Hoetger's striking sculptures grace much of the Böttcherstrasse. The **Roselius-Haus** is at No 6, with a collection of paintings and applied arts from the 12th through to the 19th centuries. The **Glockenspiel**, active in summer hourly from noon to 6 pm (in winter at noon, 3 and 6 pm), plays an extended tune between rooftops and an adjacent panel swivels to reveal reliefs of fearless sea dogs (the best known here being Columbus).

The nearby **Schnoorviertel** area features fishing cottages that are now a tourist attraction, with shops, cafes and tiny lanes.

An excellent walk around the Altstadt is along the **Wallanlagen**, peaceful parks stretching along the old city walls and moat. Backing onto the parkland is Bremen's **Kunsthalle** art gallery (10 am to 5 pm Wednesday to Sunday, to 9 pm Tuesday; DM8/4). **Gerhard Marcks Haus** (10 am to 6 pm Tuesday to Sunday; DM6/4) contains a good collection of sculpture by its namesake. Both museums are closed on Monday.

Beck's Brewery (☎ 50 94 5555), Am Deich 18-19 (take tram No 1 or 8 from the train station to Am Brill), runs its German-language tours hourly from 10 am to 5 pm Tuesday to Saturday, to 3 pm Sunday, and tours in English at 1.30 pm on the same days. It costs DM5 and includes a tasting.

One good reference around which to frame a Bremen trip is the **Fairy-Tale Road** between Hanau, the birthplace of the Brothers Grimm, and Bremen (see the Fairy-Tale Road section later in this chapter).

Places to Stay

The closest camping ground is *Camping-platz Bremen* (☎ 21 20 02, *Am Stadtwaldsee 1*). It charges DM7.50 per person, the same for a tent, and DM2.50 for a car. Take tram No 5 from the train station to Kuhlenkamp-fallee, then bus No 28 to the Campingplatz stop.

Jugendgästehaus Bremen (☎ 17 13 69, *fax 17 11 02, Kalkstrasse 6*) is across from Beck's brewery. Take tram No 1 or 8 from

the train station to Am Brill (DM30/35 juniors/seniors).

The friendly *Hotel Garni Gästehaus Walter* (☎ 55 80 27, *fax 55 80 29, Buntentorstein-weg 86-88*) has pleasant rooms from DM45/75, from DM65/98 with shower and WC. Take tram No 4 or 5 from the main train station. *Hotel-Pension Weidmann* (☎ 498 44 55, *Am Schwarzen Meer 35*) charges DM50/100 for basic accommodation. Take tram No 2 from Domsheide or No 10 from the station. The Art Nouveau *Hotel Bölts am Park* (☎ 34 61 10, *fax 34 12 27, Slevogtstrasse 23*) has very nice rooms from DM95/155 with facilities. You get a nifty view at *Turmhotel Weserblick* (☎ 79 19 79, *fax 49 42 33, Oster-deich 53*) for DM145/190.

Places to Eat

A prowl around Ostertorsteinweg (near Am Dobben) will offer all sorts of gastronomic possibilities. *Casablanca (Ostertorsteinweg 59)* has cheap baked potatoes, soups and salads. *Piano (Fehrfeld 64)*, just east of Am Dobben, serves tasty baked casseroles for around DM12 to DM16 and Mediterranean-inspired cuisine.

Auf den Höfen, north of Ostertorsteinweg, has several restaurants and bars. *Zum Hofheurigen* does schnitzel for around DM16. *Savarin* serves good casseroles; *Dos Mas* offers well-priced Mexican chow.

On Markt, *Beck's Bistro (Markt 9)* has traditional dishes a la carte, and lunch specials for around DM12. *Schnoor Teestübchen (Wüstestätte 1)* specialises in tea and cakes, but always serves vegetarian soups and quiche for around DM10 at lunchtime. Bremen's *Ratskeller* has 650 varieties of wine but no Beck's beer.

The *Penny Markt* on Ostertorsteinweg is one convenient supermarket.

Getting There & Away

There are frequent regional and IC trains servicing Hamburg (DM40, one hour). There are hourly IC trains to Cologne (DM100, three hours). A couple of ICE trains run direct to Frankfurt (DM172, 3½ hours) and Munich (DM241, six hours) daily. Change trains in Hanover for Berlin (DM135, 3½ hours). For Amsterdam (four hours), change in Osnabrück.

Getting Around
To get to Am Markt follow the tram route from directly in front of the train station. The tourist office keeps good public transport maps. Short trips on buses and trams cost DM1.70, a four-trip transferable ticket DM10.40 and a day pass DM8.50.

Lower Saxony

Lower Saxony (Niedersachsen) has much to offer, and it's a quick train ride or autobahn drive from the tourist centres down south. The scenic Harz Mountains, the old student town of Göttingen, and the picturesque towns along the Fairy-Tale Road are the most popular tourist attractions. British occupation forces created the federal state of Lower Saxony in 1946, when the states of Braunschweig (Brunswick), Schaumburg-Lippe and Oldenburg were amalgamated with the Prussian province of Hanover.

HANOVER
☎ 0511 • pop 520,000
Hanover (Hannover), the capital of Lower Saxony, has close links with the English-speaking world. In 1714, the eldest son of Electress Sophie of Hannover a granddaughter of James I of England and VI of Scotland ascended the British throne as King George I. This Anglo-German union lasted through several generations until 1837. Savaged by heavy bombing in 1943, Hanover was rebuilt into a prosperous city known throughout Europe for its trade fairs.

Information
The tourist office (☎ 16 84 97 11, fax 16 84 97 08) is at Ernst-August-Platz 2, next to the main post office and near the main train station. It's open 9 am to 7 pm weekdays, 9.30 am to 3 pm Saturday. The HannoverCard, which entitles you to unlimited public transportation and discount admission to museums and other attractions, costs DM14 for one day, DM22 for three days and is valid after 9 am each day.

Things to See & Do
One way to pick out most city sights on foot is to follow the numbered attractions with the help of the *Red Thread Guide* (DM4) from the tourist office. The chief attractions are the glorious parks of **Herrenhäuser Gärten**, especially the baroque **Grosser Garten** and the **Berggarten** (open till 8 pm on summer evenings; DM5), and their museums (take tram No 4 or 5). The gardens are open from 8 am year-round and close at 4.30 pm from November to January; opening hours get longer as the weather warms up, with the gardens closing at 8 pm from May to August. The **Fürstenhaus** (DM6/3.50) shows what treasures remain from the Guelph palaces, and the **Wilhelm-Busch-Museum** of caricature and satirical art (both closed Monday; DM4/2) contains the work of Wilhelm Busch and others.

The **Sprengel Museum** (open till 8 pm on Tuesday, closed Monday; DM8/6) on Kurt-Schwitters-Platz exhibits contemporary works, the highlights being Picasso and Max Beckmann. The **Niedersächsisches Landesmuseum** (closed Monday; DM3/1.50), Willy-Brandt-Allee 5, has displays of natural history and European paintings.

At Am Markt in the old town, the 14th-century **Marktkirche**, apart from its truncated tower, is characteristic of the northern red-brick Gothic style; the original stained-glass windows are particularly beautiful. The **Altes Rathaus** across the marketplace was built in various sections over a century. Around **Burgstrasse** some of the half-timbered town houses remain, as well as the **Ballhof**, originally built for badminton-type games of the 17th century but today offering theatrical plays.

On Breite Strasse the ruin of the **Aegidienkirche**, smashed in 1943, is an eloquent memorial; the peace bell inside is a gift from one of Hanover's sister-cities Hiroshima.

Places to Stay
The tourist office only offers a private room-finding service during trade fairs. The *Jugendherberge* (☎ 131 76 74, fax 185 55, Ferdinand-Wilhelm-Fricke-Weg 1) is 3km out of town. Take the U3 or U7 from Hauptbahnhof to Fischerhof, then cross the river on the Lodemannbrücke bridge and turn right. The price for juniors/seniors is DM27/32.

Hotel Flora (☎ 38 39 10, fax 383 91 91, Heinrichstrasse 36) provides quite pleasant singles/doubles from DM70/120, or with a bathroom for DM90/140. *Hotel Gildehof* (☎ 36 36 80, fax 30 66 44, *Joachimstrasse 6*) charges DM85/125 for clean rooms, or DM112/147 with a bathroom. The restaurant downstairs serves well-priced traditional dishes. *Hotel am Thielenplatz* (☎ 32 76 91, fax 32 51 88, ✉ hotel.am.thielenplatz@t-online.de, *Thielenplatz 2*) has rooms with shower and WC from DM110/180. The *Hotel Alpha* (☎ 34 15 35, *Friesenstrasse 19*) offers all facilities for DM138/178. *Congress Hotel am Stadtpark* (☎ 280 50, fax 81 46 52, ✉ rezeption@congress-hotel-hannover.de, *Clausewitzstrasse 6*) gets congress and trade fair visitors. Prices start at DM190/298.

Places to Eat

The Altstadt area behind Marktkirche has plenty of well-priced restaurants offering German cuisine. The *Markthalle* food hall, on the corner of Karmarschstrasse and Leinestrasse, is a gourmand's paradise – it roughly keeps normal shop hours and has lots of budget ethnic food stalls, some vegetarian offerings and fresh produce. *Brauhaus Ernst August* (*Schmiedestrasse 13A*) brews its own Hannöversch beer and serves German dishes from around DM11 to DM31. *Sawaddi* (☎ 34 43 67, *Königstrasse 7*) behind the station has a cheap lunch menu, and mains for about DM25.

Getting There & Away

Hanover's spruced-up train station is a major hub. ICE trains to/from Hamburg (DM67, 1½ hours), Munich (DM215, 4½ hours), Frankfurt (DM140, 2½ hours) and Cologne (DM104, 2¾ hours) leave hourly, and every two hours to Berlin-Zoo (DM101, 1¾ hours). A web of regional services fills in the gaps locally.

Getting Around

The city centre is fairly compact and can be easily covered on foot. Single journeys on the combined tram/U-Bahn system for one zone cost DM3.20 and day passes cost DM6. Bus No 60 (20 minutes, DM10) departs for the airport every 20 to 30 minutes from the rear entrance of the train station. The S5 connects the airport with the fairgrounds via the main train station in 25 minutes. For the Messe, the U1 or U18 also run from the main train station.

FAIRY-TALE ROAD

The Fairy-Tale Road (Märchenstrasse), so called because of the number of legends and fairy tales which sprang from this region, is well worth a day or two. The route begins at Hanau and runs to Kassel and Göttingen, passes near Hanover and ends in Bremen. The stretch between Hanover and Göttingen is the most historical section of the route. Among the most interesting towns here are Hamelin (Hameln) of Pied Piper fame, Bodenwerder where the great adventurer Baron von Münchhausen made his home, and the surprising town of Bad Karlshafen.

Information

Every town, village and hamlet along the Fairy-Tale Road has an information office of some sort. The Fremdenverkehrsverband Weserbergland-Mittelweser E.V. (☎ 930 00, fax 93 00 33) at Inselstrasse 3 in Hamelin has a free regional room finding service and is the best place to obtain brochures on activities and sights all along the middle Weser. Weserdampfschiffahrt GmbH ferries is in the same building.

The tourist office in Hamelin (☎ 20 26 18, fax 20 25 00) is at Deisterallee 1. In Bodenwerder, the tourist office (☎ 405 41, fax 61 52) is at Weserstrasse 3. In Bad Karlshafen it is in the Kurverwaltung (☎ 99 99 24, fax 99 99 25) by the 'harbour'.

The telephone area codes are Hamelin ☎ 05151, Bodenwerder ☎ 05533 and Bad Karlshafen ☎ 05672.

Things to See

Hamelin Among the most interesting sights is the **Rattenfängerhaus** ('Rat Catcher's House') on Osterstrasse, the old town's main street, built at the beginning of the 17th century. On the Bungelosenstrasse side is an inscription that tells how, in 1284, 130 children of Hamelin were led past this site and out of town by a piper wearing multicoloured clothes, never to be seen again. Also have a look at the Rattenfänger **Glockenspiel** (chime display) at the Weser Renaissance **Hochzeitshaus** at the Markt end of Osterstrasse (daily at 1.05, 3.35 and 5.35 pm). More of the story is at the museum in the ornate **Leisthaus** (closed Monday; DM3). For the other beauties of Hamelin – the restored

GERMANY

16th to 18th-century half-timbered houses with inscribed dedications – stroll through the south-eastern quarter of the old town, around Alte Marktstrasse and Grossehofstrasse or Kupferschmiedestrasse.

Bodenwerder The **Rathaus** is said to be the house in which the legendary Baron von Münchhausen was born. The baron became known for telling outrageous tales, the most famous of which was how he rode through the air on a cannonball. This very cannonball is in a room dedicated to the baron in the Rathaus. Also interesting is the statue of the baron, riding half a horse, in the garden outside the Rathaus. This was, of course, another of his stories.

There is a rather pleasant **walking track** along the Weser River in both directions from Bodenwerder.

Bad Karlshafen After passing through towns like Hamelin and Bodenwerder, the last thing you expect is this whitewashed, meticulously planned, baroque village. Originally the city was planned with an impressive harbour and a canal connecting the Weser River with the Rhine in the hope of diverting trade away from Hanover and Münden in the north. The plans were laid by a local earl with help from Huguenot refugees. The earl's death in 1730 prevented completion of the project, but even today his incomplete masterpiece and the influence of the Huguenots is too beautiful to miss.

Places to Stay & Eat
In Hamelin the camping ground *Fährhaus an der Weser* (☎ 611 67) is on Uferstrasse, across the Weser River from the old town and 10 minutes' walk north. Also in Hamelin, there's the *DJH hostel* (☎ 34 25, fax 423 16, Fischbeckerstrasse 33); in Bodenwerder, the *DJH hostel* (☎ 26 85, fax 62 03) is on Richard-Schirrmann-Weg; in Bad Karlshafen, the hostel is *Hermann Wenning* (☎ 338, fax 83 61, Winnefelderstrasse 7).

Hotel Altstadtwiege (☎ 278 54, Neue Marktstrasse 10) in Hamelin charges from DM65/130. *Hotel-Garni Christinenhof* (☎ 950 80, fax 436 11, Alte Marktstrasse 18) offers stylish rooms from DM150/195. The

Gaststätte Rattenfängerhaus in the Rat Catcher's House, serves main courses averaging DM26.

Getting Around
The easiest way to follow the Fairy-Tale Road is by car. There are frequent regional trains between Hanover and Hamelin (DM15, 45 minutes). From Hamelin's train station, direct bus No 520 follows the Weser River to Holzminden via Bodenwerder several times daily. Bus No 221 from Holzminden (board at Hafendamm) runs to Höxter bus station, which connects with bus No 220 to Bad Karlshafen, from where trains go to Göttingen.

GÖTTINGEN
☎ 0551 • pop 130,000

This leafy university town is an ideal stopover on your way north or south; it's on the direct train line between Munich and Hamburg. Though small, Göttingen is a lively town, mostly because of its large student population. A legion of notables, including Otto von Bismarck and the Brothers Grimm, studied and worked here, and the university has produced over 40 Nobel Prize winners.

Information
The main tourist office is in the old Rathaus on Markt 9 (☎ 49 98 00, fax 499 80 10, ✉ tourismus@goettingen.de). It is open 9.30 am to 6 pm weekdays, 10 am to 4 pm weekends (closed from 1 to 2 pm weekdays, after 1 pm Saturday and all day Sunday in winter). A smaller tourist office is in the round building in front of the train station (☎ 499 80 40). There's a post office just to the left (north) and another near Wilhelmsplatz at Friedrichstrasse 3. A Waschcenter laundry is at Ritterplan 4.

Things to See
The tourist office sells the excellent brochure *A Walk through the City* (DM2). At Markt, don't miss the **Great Hall** in the Rathaus where colourful frescoes cover every inch of wall space. Just outside, students mill about the **Gänseliesel** fountain, the town's symbol. The bronze beauty has a reputation as 'the most kissed girl in the world' because every student who obtains a doctor's degree must plant a kiss on her cheek.

The 15th-century **Junkernschänke** at Barfüsserstrasse 5, with its colourful carved facade, is the most stunning of the town's half-timbered buildings. A walk on top of the old **town wall** along Bürgerstrasse takes you past **Bismarckhäuschen**, a modest building where the Iron Chancellor lived in 1833 during his wild student days (open 10 am to 1 pm Tuesday and 3 to 5 pm Thursday and Saturday; free) and the pretty **Botanical Gardens**.

Places to Stay

Camping am Hohen Hagen (☎ 05502-21 47), about 10km west of town in Dransfeld (bus No 120), is open year-round. It charges DM10.50 per tent and DM8.50 per person. The *Jugendherberge* (☎ 576 22, fax 438 87, Habichtsweg 2) costs DM27/32 for juniors/seniors. From the train station main entrance, cross Berliner Strasse, go right to Groner-Tor-Strasse and take bus No 6 or 9 from across the street.

The friendly *Hotel Garni Gräfin von Holtzenorff* (☎ 639 87, fax 63 29 85, Ernst-Ruhstrat-Strasse 4) charges DM49/85 for basic rooms and DM75/120 with bathroom. Take bus No 13 to Florenz-Sartorius-Strasse. *Berliner Hof* (☎ 38 33 20, fax 383 32 32, ✉ berlinerhof.goettingen@t-online.de, Weender Landstrasse 43) has rooms with shower and WC for DM75/100. The homely *Hotel Kasseler Hof* (☎ 720 81, 770 34 29, Rosdorfer Weg 26), on the edge of the old town, has simple rooms from DM60/115 or DM95/145 with bathroom. *Hotel Central* (☎ 571 57, fax 571 05, Jüdenstrasse 12) in the middle of town charges from DM80 for basic singles and from DM95/150 for rooms with bathroom.

Places to Eat

Nikolaistrasse and Goethe Allee offer loads of takeaway options, while a filling lunchtime meal at the *Zentralmensa*, through the arch off Weender Landstrasse, costs DM6 or less. There's another Mensa on Wilhelmsplatz. *Salamanca* (Gartenstrasse 21b) offers tasty, well-priced food in a student atmosphere. *Diwan* (Rote Strasse 11) is a good Turkish restaurant in the mid-price range.

A convenient *Plus* supermarket is on the corner of Prinzenstrasse and Stumpfebiel.

Entertainment

Göttingen's bars and clubs give this small university town a lively, big-city atmosphere. *Apex (Burgstrasse 46)* is a nice place for a nibble and drink. The *Irish Pub (Mühlenstrasse 4)* offers a few dishes and has live music (no cover charge). *Nörgelbuff (☎ 438 85, Groner Strasse 23)* has live blues, rock and jazz in a vaulted cellar. The dance club *Blue Note (Wilhelmsplatz 3)* is popular with students and non-students alike; *Tangente* (☎ 463 76, Goetheallee 8a) gets an older student crowd. *Die Oper (☎ 48 79 98, Nikolaistrasse 1b)* is for young boppers and it has a couple of bars downstairs which draw a mixed crowd.

Getting There & Away

Hourly ICE trains pass through on their way to/from Hanover (DM51, 30 minutes), Berlin, Hamburg, Frankfurt and Munich. Direct RB trains depart every two hours from Göttingen for Goslar in the Harz Mountains (DM23, 1¼ hours).

GOSLAR
☎ 05321 • pop 48,000

Goslar is a centre for Harz Mountains tourism, but this 1000-year-old city with its beautifully preserved half-timbered buildings has plenty of charm in its own right. The town and the nearby Rammelsberg Mine is listed as a world cultural heritage site by Unesco.

Information

The tourist office (☎ 780 60, fax 78 06 44, ✉ goslarinfo@t-online.de), Markt 7, can help when the area's accommodation is packed. It is open 9.15 am to 6 pm Monday to Friday, 9.30 am to 4 pm Saturday, and 9.30 am to 2 pm Sunday. It closes at 5 pm weekdays, 2 pm Saturday and all day Sunday from November to April. For information on the Harz Mountains visit the Harzer Verkehrsverband (☎ 3 40 40, fax 34 04 66, ✉ harzerverkehrsverband@t-online.de) at Marktstrasse 45 (open weekdays).

Things to See & Do

The **Marktplatz** has several photogenic houses. The one opposite the Gothic **Rathaus** has a chiming clock depicting four scenes

GERMANY

from the history of mining in the area. It struts its stuff at 9 am, noon, 3 and 6 pm. The **market fountain** dates from the 13th century and is crowned by an eagle.

The **Kaiserpfalz** (DM8/4) is a reconstructed Romanesque 11th-century palace usually jammed with tour-bus visitors. It was closed for restoration at the time of research but should be open again by the time you read this. Just below is the restored **Domvorhalle** which displays the 11th-century 'Kaiserstuhl' throne, used by German emperors. At the **Rammelsberger Bergbaumuseum**, about 1km south of the town centre on Rammelsberger Strasse, you can delve into the mining history of the area and descend into the shafts on a variety of tours costing from DM10 to DM35.

Places to Stay

The pretty *Jugendherberge* (☎ *222 40, fax 413 76, Rammelsberger Strasse 25)* is situated behind the Kaiserpfalz (take bus C to Theresienhof from the train station). It charges DM22/27 for juniors/seniors and is often full of high school students.

Another option is *Hotel und Campingplatz Sennhütte* (☎ *225 02, Clausthaler Strasse 28)*, 3km south on Route B241. Take bus No 434 from the train station to Sennhütte. Camping charges are DM5.50 per person, DM4.50 per tent and DM3.50 per car. It's closed on Thursday. Several clean, simple rooms with nice views start at DM40/80 and you'll find lots of trails nearby.

The tourist office can help with room bookings, especially on busy weekends and in summer. *Haus Bielitza* (☎ *207 44, Abzuchtstrasse 11)* has passable rooms for DM35/55 (hall shower DM3.50). *Gästehaus Schmitz* (☎ *234 45, fax 30 60 39, Kornstrasse 1)* offers the best value with bright singles/doubles for DM55/70 with shower/WC, and single apartments from DM55. *Gästehaus Verhoeven* (☎ *238 12, Hoher Weg 12)* has clean, simple rooms from DM65/102 or with facilities for DM100/130. The upmarket *Hotel Kaiserworth* (☎ *70 90, fax 70 93 45,* ❻ *hotel@kaiserworth.de, Markt 3)*, in a magnificent 500-year-old building, has singles/doubles starting from DM99/199.

Places to Eat

The *Altdeutsches Kartoffelhaus*, in the Kaiserpassage shopping arcade on Breite Strasse, offers generous portions of potato dishes for between DM7 and DM25. *Brauhaus Wolpertinger (Marstallstrasse 1)*, a restaurant with whimsical decor, serves main dishes for around DM15 to DM30. *Didgeridoo (Hoher Weg 13)* specialises in well-priced kangaroo burgers and barbecue meals (and has some good Australian wines). *Restaurant Aubergine* (☎ *421 36, Marktstrasse 4)* charges from DM20 to DM40 for delicious Mediterranean cuisine.

Getting There & Away

Goslar is regularly connected by train to Göttingen (DM23, 1¼ hours), Hanover DM23, 1½ hours) and Wernigerode (30 minutes). For information on getting to/from the eastern Harz region, see Getting Around in the following Western Harz Mountains section and the Getting There & Away sections under Quedlinburg and Wernigerode earlier in this chapter.

WESTERN HARZ MOUNTAINS

Known mostly to Germans and Scandinavians, the Harz Mountains (Harzgebirge) don't have the dramatic peaks and valleys of the Alps, but they offer a great four-seasons sports getaway without some of the Alpine tackiness and tourism. Silver, lead and copper mines in the area have been largely exhausted, and many can now be visited.

Orientation & Information

Pick up the booklet *Grüner Faden* (Green Thread; DM3), available at any tourist office in the Harz and at many hotels. For weather reports and winter snow information (in English), contact the Harzer Verkehrsverband in Goslar (☎ 340 40).

The Goslar tourist office has information on the Harz Mountains. Hahnenklee's tourist office (☎ 05325-510 40, fax 51 04 20) is at Kurhausweg 7; in Bad Harzburg, the tourist office (☎ 05322-753 30, fax 753 29) is at Herzog-Wilhelm-Strasse 86; in Clausthal-Zellerfeld, the tourist office (☎ 05323-810 24, fax 839 62) is at Bahnhofstrasse 5a.

Things to See

Hahnenklee is proud of its Norwegian-style **'stave' church**, but most remarkable is

Clausthal-Zellerfeld's 17th-century wooden church **Zum Heiligen Geist** at Hindenburgplatz, built to accommodate over 2000 worshippers! Nearby, the technical university's **mineral collection** at Römerstrasse 12a (DM1) is of particular interest to geology buffs.

For a fine view, take the **Bergbahn** car up to the castle ruins above Bad Harzburg (DM4/6 one-way/return, less with resort card). The embarkation point is 2km uphill from the train station, so you can promenade among German wealth and ambition and check the array of furs and other luxury goods flaunted in this health resort.

Activities

Despite 400km of groomed **hiking** trails in the National Park Harz, its beauty hasn't suffered. Maps and information are abundant, and most hikes are under 10km. Trails through the wildly romantic Okertal (just outside Goslar), and the 15km to Hahnenklee from Goslar, are especially picturesque. From the cable-car station in Bad Harzburg paths lead to Sennhütte (1.3km), Molkenhaus (3km) and to the scenic Rabenklippe (7km) overlooking the Ecker Valley. All have restaurants: a blackboard inside the cable-car station indicates which ones are open. From Bad Harzburg you can also pick up the medieval Kaiserweg route, which joins the Goetheweg to Torfhaus (11km) and the Brocken (7km from Torfhaus).

Cycling is popular in summer among those seeking a hilly challenge, and in winter the Harz Mountains offers excellent conditions for **cross-country skiing**. Snow enthusiasts will find **downhill skiing** conditions average, but slopes can be quite good in Hahnenklee, St Andreasberg and Braunlage. Rental equipment is easy to find. Downhill and cross-country gear starts at about DM15 a day. Tourist offices in most towns keep a list of places that hire bikes and ski equipment.

The Harz Mountains also has a healthy number of spa towns where **spa activities** are offered. Most spa towns have indoor swimming facilities and all have *Kurzentren* (spa centres) which offer massages and other physical therapies to soothe an aching body after an all too brisk hike, ride or ski through hilly terrain.

Places to Stay

Many of the 30 or so camping grounds in the Harz Mountains are open all year – pick up the free *Der Harz Camping* brochure. There is no shortage of budget rooms in hotels and pensions. Tourist offices in each town have useful listings and can help with bookings. For extended stays ask about apartments or holiday homes, which become good deals when staying a week or more. In spa resorts you will pay about a DM2.50 *Kurtaxe* (resort tax) per day on hotel accommodation (less in hostels and at camping grounds).

Hahnenklee *Campingplatz am Kreuzeck* (☎ 05325-25 70) is 2km north of Hahnenklee (bus No 434 from Goslar or Hahnenklee). The *Jugendherberge* (☎ 22 56, fax 35 24, Hahnenkleer Strasse 11) is near the Bockswiese bus stop (same bus) on the road from Goslar (DM22/27 for juniors/seniors).

Bad Harzburg *Campingplatz Wolfenstein* (☎ 05322-35 85) is about 3km east of town at Wolfstein on Ilsenburger Strasse (bus No 74 or 77 from the train station). The youth hostel *Braunschweiger Haus* (☎ 45 82, fax 18 67, Waldstrasse 5) provides beds for DM23/27 juniors/seniors. Take bus No 73 from the train station.

Clausthal-Zellerfeld *Campingplatz Waldweben* (☎ 05323-817 12, Spiegeltaler Strasse 31) is around 1km west of Zellerfeld. The *Jugendherberge* (☎ 842 93, fax 838 27, Altenauer Strasse 55) charges DM22/27 for juniors/seniors (bus No 408). The hostel is usually closed on the first weekend of the month from mid-September to mid-May.

Getting Around

Frequent regional trains link Goslar with Wernigerode. Four direct trains depart daily for Göttingen via Bad Harzburg. Bus No 77 shuttles several times daily between Bad Harzburg and Wernigerode (just under an hour; DM6). It stops on the far side of Am Bahnhofsplatz at Bad Harzburg train station and next to the main station in Wernigerode.

Bus Nos 408 and 432 run between Goslar and Altenau, while Nos 408 and 434 connect Goslar with Clausthal-Zellerfeld (No 434 via Hahnenklee).

GERMANY

Hamburg

☎ 040 • pop 1.7 million

The first recorded settlement on the present site of Hamburg was the moated fortress of Hammaburg, built in the first half of the ninth century. The city that developed around it became the northernmost archbishopric in Europe, to facilitate the conversion of the northern peoples.

The city was burned down many times, but in the 13th century it became the Hanseatic League's gateway to the North Sea and was second in importance and influence only to Lübeck. With the decline of the Hanseatic League in the 16th century, Lübeck faded into insignificance but Hamburg continued to thrive.

Hamburg strode confidently into the 20th century but WWI stopped all trade and most of Hamburg's merchant shipping fleet (almost 1500 ships) was forfeited to the Allies as reparation payment. In WWII, over half of Hamburg's residential areas and port facilities were demolished and 55,000 people killed in Allied air raids that spawned horrific firestorms.

Today it is a sprawling port city and a separate state of Germany, with a stylish shopping district, numerous waterways (with more bridges than Venice), and even a beach (in Blankenese, Germany's most exclusive suburb).

Orientation

The Hauptbahnhof (main train station) is very central, near Aussenalster lake and fairly close to most of the sights. These are south of Aussenalster and north of the Elbe River, which runs all the way from the Czech Republic to Hamburg before flowing into the North Sea. The city centre features the Rathaus and the beautiful Hauptkirche St Michaelis. The port is west of the city centre, facing the Elbe.

Information

The small tourist office in the main train station (☎ 30 05 12 00, fax 30 05 13 33, ✉ info@hamburg-tourism.de) at the Kirchenallee exit offers limited brochures and a room-finding service. It has great hours (7 am to 11 pm daily) and friendly staff. There's also an office at St Pauli harbour, between piers 4 and 5, open 10 am to 7 pm daily, and till 5.30 pm from October to March. You can view its official Web site at www.hamburg-tourism.de.

Both tourist offices stock the Hamburg Card, which offers unlimited public transportation and free or discounted admission to most attractions, museums and cruises. The 'day card' is valid after 6 pm on the day of purchase and throughout the next day and costs DM12.80 (single) or DM24.50 (groups of up to five people). The 'multi-day card' is valid on the day of purchase and the following two days (DM26.50/43). An even better deal is the Hamburg Jugend Pass, only available at youth hostels, which gives even steeper discounts to anyone under 27 for a mere DM12.50 (extendable for an extra DM5.50 per day).

Money There is a Reisebank above the Kirchenallee exit of the main train station (open 7.30 am to 10 pm daily), and others at Altona train station (closed Sunday) and in terminal 4 at the airport (open 6 am to 10 pm daily).

Post & Communications There's a small post office with a poste-restante service (four weeks for international mail) near the Kirchenallee exit of the train station (open 8 am to 8 pm Monday to Friday, 9 am to 6 pm Saturday and 10 am to 6 pm Sunday). The main post office is on the corner of Dammtorstrasse at Stephansplatz.

Email & Internet Access Surf-In (☎ 33 30 75 34) in the Lust for Life store at Mönchebergstrasse 1 charges DM3 for 30 minutes online.

Newspapers & Magazines For cultural events and lifestyle information, look for *Max City Guide* (DM9.80) and the magazines *Szene* (DM5) and *Oxmox* (DM2). For classified ads of all sorts, pick up a copy of *Avis*, published on Tuesday (DM3.50) and Friday (DM4.10).

Bookshops Dr Götze Land & Karte, Bleichenbrücke 9 in the Bleichenhof arcade claims to be the biggest specialist map and travel bookshop in Europe and has a smattering of guidebooks in English. A second, smaller shop is in the Wandelhalle shopping arcade at the main train station. The branch of Thalia Bücher on Grosse Bleichen 19 has a large selection of English-language books and some guidebooks. Second-hand books can be bought at the English Bookstore, Stresemannstrasse 169 (S-Bahn to Holstenstrasse).

Laundry The Schnell & Sauber chain has a laundrette at Nobistor 34, near the Safeway store; an SB Wasch-Center is on the eastern side of Neuer Pferdemarkt (U-Bahn to Feldstrasse).

Medical & Emergency Services For an ambulance call ☎ 112. A medical emergency service is available on ☎ 22 80 22. For urgent dental treatment call ☎ 115 00. The police are on ☎ 110; there is one station in St Georg at Steindamm 82 and another in St Pauli at Spielbudenplatz 31, on the corner of Davidstrasse.

Dangers & Annoyances Overall, Hamburg is a very safe city, but you should take special care in the seedy drug and prostitution area in St Georg.

Things to See & Do
Altstadt Much of Hamburg's old city centre was lost in WWII, but it's still worth a walking tour. The area is laced with wonderful canals (called 'fleets') running from the Alster lakes to the Elbe.

The Altstadt centres on Rathausmarkt, where the large **Rathaus** and huge clock tower overlook the lively square. This is one of the most interesting city halls in Germany, and the 40-minute tour is worthwhile at DM2/1. It's in English hourly from 10.15 am to 3.15 pm Monday to Thursday, to 1.15 pm Friday to Sunday. The building has 647 rooms – six more than Buckingham Palace.

It is a moving experience to visit the remaining tower of the devastated **St-Nikolai-Kirche**, now an antiwar memorial, nearby on Ost-West-Strasse. From there, walk a few blocks west to the baroque **Hauptkirche St Michaelis** and take the lift up the tower (DM4.50/2, enter through portal No 3) for a great view of the city and the port. Inside, the beautiful interiors and the crypt (a donation

of DM1 is requested) are open for viewing. The tower is open 9 am to 6 pm Monday to Saturday, from 11.30 am Sunday (slightly shorter hours November to March).

Port After exploring the Altstadt, stroll down to one of the busiest ports in the world. It boasts the world's largest carpet warehouse complex, while the Free Port Warehouses stockpile goods from all continents.

The **port cruises** are touristy but still worthwhile. There are many options; for details see Organised Tours later in this section.

If you're in the port area early on a Sunday (5 to 10 am, October to March from 7 am), head for **Fischmarkt** (Fish Market) in St Pauli, right on the Elbe. Hamburg's oldest market (established 1703) is popular with locals and tourists alike and everything under the sun is sold here. Cap your morning with a visit to the live jazz session at the Fischauktionshalle (Fish Auction Hall), Grosse Elbstrasse 9.

Reeperbahn Among Hamburg's biggest tourist attractions is the famous Reeperbahn red-light district. It is 600m long and is the heart of the St Pauli entertainment district, which includes shows, bars, cabarets, clubs, theatres and a casino. In recent years, the Reeperbahn sex establishments have been gradually moving over for popular restaurants and bars, with a dwindling number of peep shows and sex shops plying a 'traditional' trade.

If you venture into one of these haunts, make sure you understand costs before going in. Ask for the price list if it's not posted by the entrance. Entry is sometimes free or DM5 to DM10, but there might be a minumum purchase of DM40 or more – about enough for a campari and soda in some places. On **Grosse Freiheit**, Safari is one of the more famous clubs. **Herbertstrasse** is the notorious street where the prostitutes pose in windows offering their wares. It is fenced off at each end by a metal wall and men under 18 and women are not allowed in. Ironically, the hustling is much more aggressive on the surrounding regular streets.

Other Attractions Hamburg's **Kunsthalle**, on Glockengiesserwall, has old masters and a

GERMANY

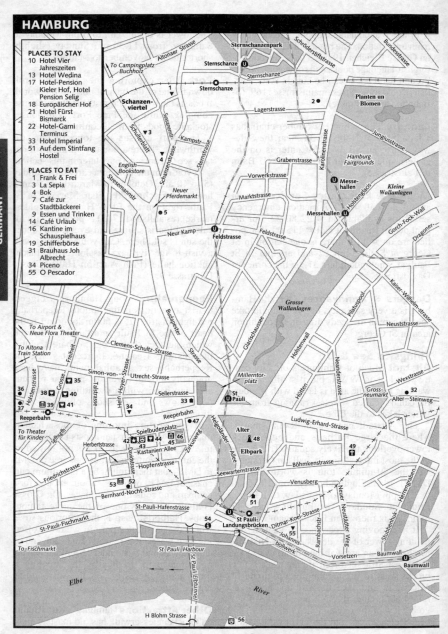

HAMBURG

PLACES TO STAY
10 Hotel Vier
     Jahreszeiten
13 Hotel Wedina
17 Hotel-Pension
     Kieler Hof, Hotel
     Pension Selig
18 Europäischer Hof
21 Hotel Fürst
     Bismarck
22 Hotel-Garni
     Terminus
33 Hotel Imperial
51 Auf dem Stintfang
     Hostel

PLACES TO EAT
1   Frank & Frei
3   La Sepia
4   Bok
7   Café zur
     Stadtbäckerei
9   Essen und Trinken
14 Café Urlaub
16 Kantine im
     Schauspielhaus
19 Schifferbörse
31 Brauhaus Joh
     Albrecht
34 Piceno
55 O Pescador

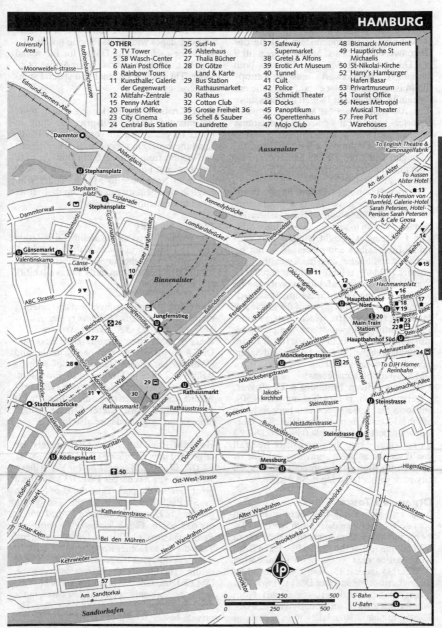

large collection of German paintings from the 19th and 20th centuries. Contemporary art is housed next door in the modern **Galerie der Gegenwart** (both closed Monday, open till 9 pm Thursday; DM15/9 entry includes both museums). The waxworks museum **Panoptikum** is an unusual place and fun for the entire family. Founded in 1879, it contains more than 100 well-known (at least to Germans) historical, political and show-business celebrities. It's at Spielbudenplatz 3 and is open 11 am to 9 pm weekdays, Saturday till midnight, and from 10 am Sunday (closed from mid-January to early February). Admission costs DM7/4.

Harry's Hamburger Hafen Basar, Bernhard-Nocht-Strasse 89-91, is a fascinating 'shop': it's the life's work of Harry, a bearded character known to seamen all over the world, who for decades bought trinkets and souvenirs from sailors and others. Now run by Harry's daughter, the shop has a wealth of curiosities (DM4/2; refunded with a purchase). You'll find changing exhibitions on the theme of erotica at the **Privartmuseum**, Bernhard-Nocht-Strasse 69. This is part of the **Erotic Art Museum**, Nobistor 10a, which contains some 1800 paintings, drawings and sculptures by artists from Delacroix to Picasso (open 10 am to midnight daily, till 1 am Friday and Saturday; entry to each museum is DM15/10, or DM20/10 for both museums).

The view from Hamburg's **TV Tower**, Lagerstrasse 2-8, is breathtaking (DM6.50), but for a real scream, you can bungee jump off the 130m-high platform (DM250), Germany's tallest jump. Call ☎ 089-60 60 89 23 for bookings. From the tower or in free fall you'll see the adjacent sprawling gardens of **Planten un Blomen**, a gorgeous landscaped city park with a large Japanese garden.

Organised Tours

Basic city sightseeing bus tours in English operate at least twice daily from April to October, and every 15 minutes from 9.30 am to 4.45 pm the rest of the year. They leave from Kirchenallee next to the main train station (DM22/11) and last 1¾ hours; you can add a harbour cruise for an extra DM11. Two-hour 'Fleet' (inner canal) cruises depart from Jungfernstieg three times daily (DM23/14). The 50-minute Alster lakes tour departs at least three times daily from Jungfernstieg and costs DM16/8. Or you can cover the Alster lakes in stages with boats leaving hourly; it's DM2 for each stop or DM13 for the round trip. Both of these operate from April to October. There are also canal and special summer cruises.

Port Cruises The Barkassen launch tours (60 minutes; DM15, half-price for children up to 16 years) run all year from St Pauli-Landungsbrücken, piers 1 to 9. They depart half-hourly from 9 am to 6 pm from April to October, and hourly from 10.30 am to 3.30 pm from November to March. Tours with English commentary run at 11 am daily from April to September from pier 1.

Places to Stay

The tourist office at the main train station charges DM6 for accommodation bookings. You can also call the Hamburg-Hotline (☎ 30 05 13 00) 8 am to 8 pm daily for availability and reservations.

Camping Though inconvenient and catering mainly for caravans, *Campingplatz Buchholz* (☎ 540 45 32, Kieler Strasse 374) charges DM7 per person, DM12.50 and DM14.50 for one or two-person tents, and DM6 per car. From Hauptbahnhof take S-Bahn No 2 or 3 to Stellingen or Eidelstedt. You can also take bus No 183 from Hamburg-Altona train station towards Schnelsen. It runs straight down Kieler Strasse, where other camping grounds are also located.

Hostels Hamburg's two DJH hostels are large. *Auf dem Stintfang* (☎ 31 34 88, fax 31 54 07, ✉ jh-stintfang@t-online.de, Albert-Wegener-Weg 5) charges DM27/32 and has a great view of the port. Take the U or S-Bahn to St Pauli-Landungsbrücken. The youth guesthouse *Horner Rennbahn* (☎ 651 16 71, fax 655 65 16, ✉ jgh-hamburg@t-online.de, Rennbahnstrasse 100) is less convenient. Take the U3 to Horner Rennbahn and walk 10 minutes north past the racecourse and leisure centre (DM30/35.50 juniors/seniors). A DM2.50 discount per night for stays of three nights or more only applies if you check in for three nights, not if you extend your stay. The private hostel *Schanzenstern* (☎ 439 84 41, *fax 439 34 13, Bartelsstrasse 12)*, in the lively Schanzenviertel, has beds in clean dorms for DM33 and singles/doubles/triples for DM60/90/115 excluding breakfast (it's just off Susannenstrasse).

Hotels & Pensions Most budget hotels are along Steindamm and a few blocks east of the main train station along Bremer Reihe. *Hotel-Pension Selig* (☎ 24 46 89, fax 24 98 45, Bremer Reihe 23) has reasonable basic rooms for DM60/120. *Hotel-Pension Kieler Hof* (☎ 24 30 24, fax 24 60 18, Bremer Reihe 15) has rooms with shower cabins for DM60/100 (both excluding breakfast). *Hotel-Garni Terminus* (☎ 280 31 44, fax 24 15 80, Steindamm 5) charges from DM75/100, or DM90/120 with a bathroom.

Lange Reihe is less sleazy than other streets in St Georg. *Hotel-Pension von Blumfeld* (☎ 24 58 60, fax 24 32 82, Lange Reihe 54) is a vast improvement on all the above. It has nice basic rooms for DM60/90, or DM80/110 with a bathroom, and a dishevelled parrot called Jakob. *Galerie-Hotel Sarah Petersen* (☎/fax 24 98 26, Lange Reihe 50) is a classic art-scene Hamburg hotel, with rooms decorated in different styles. The cheapest single/double costs DM85/120, rising to DM275/290 with video, fax and other useful comforts. *Hotel Fürst Bismarck* (☎ 280 10 91, fax 280 10 96, Kirchenallee 49) is more conventional from DM118/160 with all facilities. The *Europäischer Hof* (☎ 24 82 48, fax 24 82 47 99, Kirchenallee 45) has rooms from DM190/250, but ask for one that's quiet and has been renovated.

Hotel Wedina (☎ 24 30 11, fax 280 38 94, ✉ wedina@oal.com, Gurlittstrasse 23) charges DM195/240 for quality, spacious rooms. *Aussen Alster Hotel* (☎ 24 15 57, fax 280 32 31, Schmilinskystrasse 11), just one block north, offers the same high standard from DM170/260, rising to DM210/320. Both are in quiet streets a bit away from the sleaze.

The family-run *Hotel Imperial* (☎ 31 17 20, fax 319 60 21, ✉ hotel-imperial@t-online.de, Millerntorplatz 3-5) charges DM95/150 for singles/doubles during the week and from DM115/165 on weekends. Rooms face away from the Reeperbahn, and are spacious and

well-furnished. It's an excellent mid-range option in the throbbing heart of St Pauli.

Hotel Vier Jahreszeiten (☎ 349 40, fax 34 94 26 00, ✉ vier-jahreszeiten@hvj.de, Neuer Jungfernstieg 9-14) is Hamburg's premier address with rooms ranging from DM400 a single to the DM3100 Jahreszeiten Suite ... umm, yes, that's per night.

Places to Eat
Hauptbahnhof Area Hamburg is one of the best spots in Germany for fish. *Schifferbörse (Kirchenallee 46)* offers a truly fishy Hamburg experience. Here, you sit amid original ship furniture and beneath a giant wooden ship dangling from the ceiling. But expect to pay about DM35, including one drink. *Kantine im Schauspielhaus*, downstairs in the Deutsches Schauspielhaus on Kirchenallee, is one of the best kept secrets in this part of town, with plain but filling lunches for DM10. The student *Café Urlaub (Lange Reihe 63)*, which is open from breakfast until 2 am, is a good cafe eating and drinking option. Here you can find good salads and pasta dishes for around DM14. *Cafe Gnosa (Lange Reihe 93)* is especially popular among gays and lesbians. It has good lunch specials and is nice for an evening meal or drink. The Aussen Alster Hotel (see Places to Stay) serves quality Mediterranean inspired main dishes for around DM20 to DM25.

Gänsemarkt & Around You'll find a wide choice around Gänsemarkt and Jungfernstieg near the Binnenalster lake. *Essen und Trinken (Gänsemarkt 21)* is a food hall in an arcade where you can choose from Asian, Mediterranean and German cuisine at budget prices. *Café zur Stadtbäckerei* is a bakery which also supplies shoppers and workers with warm drinks and filling, tasty snacks. *Brauhaus Joh. Albrecht (Adolfsbrücke 7)* is a bustling microbrewery where most dishes cost under DM20.

Schanzenviertel The lively Schanzenviertel neighbourhood lies west of the TV Tower and north of St Pauli (take the U-Bahn or S-Bahn to Sternschanze) and is shared by students and immigrants. Lots of cosy cafes and restaurants string along Schanzenstrasse and

Susannenstrasse; *Frank and Frei* on the corner of the two, is a student hang-out with a small menu. *La Sepia (Schulterblatt 36)* serves terrific seafood in a Mediterranean atmosphere for around DM26, sometimes with live music. *Bok (Susannenstrasse 15)* draws a young sushi-eating crowd. A delicious 18-piece Bento III sushi platter costs DM30.

St Pauli/Port Area There's a cluster of good Portuguese and Spanish restaurants along Ditmar-Koel-Strasse and Reimarus-Strasse near St Pauli Landungsbrücken. *O Pescador*, on the corner of the two, serves a variety of mid-priced meat and fish dishes. Just off the Reeperbahn, *Picenò (Hein-Hoyer-Strasse 8)* is good for Italian fare at reasonable prices in a cosy, relaxed atmosphere.

Self-Catering Head for one of the *Penny Markt* budget groceries. There's one on Baumeisterstrasse, one on the corner of Lange Reihe and Schmilinskystrasse to the east of the main train station, and one near the corner of Königstrasse and Holstenstrasse at the western end of the Reeperbahn (a Safeway store across the road offers a wider variety). Really good fresh fare is offered at Grossneumarkt on market days (Wednesday and Saturday).

Entertainment

The jazz scene in Hamburg is hot. The hip *Mojo Club (☎ 43 52 32, Reeperbahn 1)* should absolutely *not* be missed by aficionados of jazz or avante garde music, or by anyone else for that matter who has more than a passing interest in music. Its Web site is at www.mojo.de. The *Cotton Club (34 38 78, Alter Steinweg 10)* has more traditional jazz flavours. Get there before 8.30 pm if you've reserved seats.

The *English Theatre (☎ 227 70 89, Lerchenfeld 14)* is good for a language fix; *Theater für Kinder (☎ 38 25 38, Max-Brauer-Allee 76)* in Altona is great for kids – their language is more international. The cinema complex *City (☎ 24 44 63, Steindamm 9)* screens English-language films in the original.

Hamburg has an excellent alternative and experimental theatre scene. *Kampnagelfabrik (☎ 27 09 49 49, Jarrestrasse 20-24)* is a good place to start. Take bus No 172 or 173

from U-Bahn station Mundsburg (www.kampnagel.de). *Schmidt Theater (☎ 31 77 88 99, Spielbudenplatz 27)* is much loved for its wild variety shows and casual atmosphere. See its Web site at www.tivoli.de.

Among Hamburg's musicals are: *Cats* at the *Operettenhaus (Spielbudenplatz 1)*; *Das Phantom der Oper* at the *Neue Flora Theater*, on the corner of Alsenstrasse and Stresemannstrasse (take the S-Bahn to Holstenstrasse); and the *Buddy Holly Story* at the *Neues Metropol Musical Theater (Norderelbstrasse 6)*. Take the shuttle service from Pier 1 of the St Pauli Landungsbrücken. Tickets, which start at around DM60, can be reserved at the tourist offices or on the hotline ☎ 30 05 13 00.

For central theatre or concert bookings, go to the Last Minute Theaterkasse on the 4th floor of the Alsterhaus shopping complex in Poststrasse (open during regular shopping hours).

Not surprisingly, St Pauli is the flash point for nightclubs. *Tunnel (Grosse Freiheit 10)* usually serves up techno and house; *Cult (Grosse Freiheit 2)* is another favourite of that ilk; *Docks (☎ 31 78 83 11, Spielbudenplatz 19)* sometimes has live bands; as does the hip *Grosse Freiheit 36 (Grosse Freiheit 36)*. At *Gretel & Alfons* across the street, you can have a drink where the Beatles once quaffed.

Getting There & Away

Air Hamburg's international airport (☎ 50 75 25 57) in Fuhlsbüttel has frequent flights to domestic destinations as well as cities in Scandinavia and elsewhere in Europe.

Bus International destinations not served directly by train from Hamburg, such as Amsterdam (DM80, 6½ hours) and London (DM136, 17½ hours), are served by Eurolines buses.

A good option for getting to London is Rainbow Tours (☎ 32 09 33 09, fax 32 09 30 99), Gänsemarkt 45, which offers return trips without an overnight stay from DM69 – a cheap way to get to London, even if you don't use the return portion of the ticket. The central bus station is south-east of the main train station on Adenauerallee.

Train Hamburg's Hauptbahnhof is one of the busiest in Germany, although it does not handle all the through traffic. There are frequent RE/RB trains to Lübeck (DM16, 45 minutes) and Kiel (DM30, 1¼ hours), various services to Hanover (DM50, 1½ hours) and Bremen (DM33, 1¼ hours), as well as IC trains to Berlin (DM88, 2½ hours) and ICE trains to Frankfurt (DM191, 3½ hours) via Hanover. Almost hourly trains depart for Copenhagen (4½ hours). There are overnight services to Munich, Vienna and Paris as well as Zurich via Basel. Hamburg-Altona station is quieter but has a monopoly on some services to the north. Trains run to/from Kiel, and Westerland on Sylt (DM71, three hours). Carefully read the timetables when booking to/from Hamburg stations or you could finish up at the wrong station at the wrong time. Hamburg-Harburg handles some regional services (for instance to/from Cuxhaven, the main port for Heligoland).

Car & Motorcycle The autobahns of the A1 (Bremen-Lübeck) and A7 (Hanover-Kiel) cross south of the Elbe River. A convenient Mitfahr-Zentrale (☎ 194 40) is at Ernst-Merck-Strasse 8 near the train station. Sample one-way prices are Cologne DM44, Frankfurt/Main DM49, Amsterdam DM47 and Berlin DM31.

Ferry Hamburg is 20 hours by car ferry from the English port of Harwich. DFDS Seaways (☎ 389 03 71, fax 38 90 31 41) runs services at least three times a week in either direction. The Fischereihafen terminal is at Van-der-Smissen-Strasse 4, about 1km west of the Fischmarkt (S1 to Königstrasse, or bus No 383 to/from Altona station). It is open 10 am to 4.30 pm weekdays, just before departure at weekends (exchange money before you reach the terminal or on board). The one-way passenger fare to Harwich ranges from DM106 to DM674, depending on the season, the day of the week and cabin comforts. A car costs an extra DM88 to DM143 and a bicycle will cost DM5.

Scandlines (☎ 01805-72 26 35 46 37) operates a busy car and passenger ferry from Puttgarden to Rødby, which leaves every half-hour 24 hours a day and takes 45 minutes. The cost is DM85 each way for a car including up to five people all year. A bicycle costs DM13 including one person. A single

passenger pays DM5 (DM10 mid-June to August) each way. If you're travelling by train, the cost of the ferry is included in your ticket.

Getting Around
To/From the Airport A taxi from the main train station costs around DM30 (one easy number to use is ☎ 21 12 11). A better airport option is to take the U1 from the main train station to Ohlsdorf and from there the No 110 express bus (DM4.20). Airport buses (DM8.50, return DM12.50) make the 25-minute trip to the airport from the train station every 25 minutes between 5 am and 9.20 pm.

Public transport buses, the U-Bahn and the S-Bahn operate in Hamburg. A day pass for travel after 9 am in most of Hamburg is DM8 (DM12.90 if you include the surrounding area) and there are various family passes. Single journeys cost DM2.70 for the city tariff area, DM4.20 for the city and surrounding area, and DM6.80 within the outer tariff area. Children pay a basic DM1.50. For the Schnellbus or 1st-class S-Bahn the day supplements are DM2. A three-day travel-only pass is DM23.30, and weekly cards range from DM24.50 to DM49.50 depending on your status and the distance you want to travel (check the diagrams with the oval-shaped zones marked in yellow). From midnight to dawn the night-bus network takes over from the trains, converging on the main metropolitan bus station at Rathausmarkt. For transport options with a Hamburg Card see the Information section.

Hamburg's bicycle tracks are extensive and reach almost to the centre of the city.

Schleswig-Holstein

Schleswig-Holstein is Germany's northernmost state and borders Denmark at the southern end of the Jutland Peninsula. Among the many attractions here are the North Frisian Islands and the historical city of Lübeck.

Schleswig and Holstein began breaking away from Denmark with the help of Sweden in the mid-17th century, a process which took until 1773. When Holstein joined the German Confederation in 1815, Denmark tried to lure Schleswig back to the motherland.

GERMANY

Three wars were fought over the region between Germany and Denmark: the first in 1848–50; a second in 1864; and a third in 1866, when Bismarck annexed it to unify Germany. Under the conditions of the Treaty of Versailles in 1919, North Schleswig was given to Denmark. Finally, in 1946, the British military government formed the state of Schleswig-Holstein from the Prussian province of the same name.

LÜBECK
☎ 0451 • pop 215,000

Medieval Lübeck was known as the Queen of the Hanseatic League, as it was the capital of this association of towns that ruled trade on the Baltic Sea from the 12th to the 16th centuries. This beautiful city, with its red-stone buildings, is a highlight of the region and well worth taking the time to explore.

Orientation & Information

Lübek's old town is set on an island ringed by the canalised Trave River, a 15-minute walk east from the main train station. To get there, take Konrad-Adenauer-Strasse across the pretty Puppenbrücke (Doll Bridge) to Holstentor, the city's western gateway. Then follow Holstenstrasse east from An der Untertrave to Kohlmarkt, from where Breite Strasse leads north to Markt and the historic Rathaus.

The city runs two tourist offices. Lübeck-Werbung (☎ 1 22 19 09; fax 1 22 12 02), just off An der Untertrave at Beckergrube 95, is open 8 am to 4 pm weekdays only. Lübeck-Information (☎ /fax 1 22 54 19) is near the Rathaus at Breite Strasse 62. It is open 9.30 am to 6 pm weekdays and 10 am to 2 pm weekends. Both city tourist offices run a room-finding service. The private room-finding office at the train station (☎ 86 46 75, fax 86 30 24) charges DM5. Web site: www.Luebeck-info.de.

The Lübeck-Travemünde Card entitles you to unlimited travel and discounts on cruises, museums, cinema and other attractions. It costs DM9 for 24 hours and DM18 for three days and is available at tourist offices, hotels, youth hostels and museums.

The central post office is on Königstrasse 46, across from the Katarinenkirche. There's a police station near the youth hostel at Mengstrasse 20.

Things to See & Do

The landmark **Holstentor** (☎ 122 41 29), a fortified gate with huge twin towers, serves as the city's symbol as well as its museum (closed Monday; DM5/3), but for a literary kick, visit the recently refurbished **Buddenbrookhaus**, Mengstrasse 4, the family house where Thomas Mann was born and which he made famous in his novel *Buddenbrooks*. The literary works and philosophical rivalry of the brothers Thomas and Heinrich are commemorated here (open daily; DM8/5). The **Marienkirche** on Markt contains a stark reminder of WWII; a bombing raid brought the church bells crashing to the stone floor and the townspeople have left the bell fragments in place, with a small sign saying, 'A protest against war and violence'. Also on Markt is the imposing **Rathaus** which covers two full sides of the square. It can be toured – three times on weekdays – for DM4/2.

Lübeck's **Marionettentheater** (Puppet Theatre; ☎ 700 60), on the corner of Am Kolk and Kleine Petersgrube, is an absolute must (closed Monday). Usually there is an afternoon performance for children (3 pm) and an evening performance for adults, but times vary. Afternoon seats cost DM8 and evening seats DM13 to DM22 depending on the play. It's best to book ahead. The **Museum für Puppentheater** (☎ 786 26), a survey of all types of dolls and puppetry, is just around the corner from the theatre at Kleine Petersgrube 4. It is open from 10 am to 6 pm daily (DM6/5/3 for adults/students/children.

The tower lift at the partly restored **Petrikirche** costs DM3.50/2 and affords a superb view over the Altstadt. It is usually open 9 am to 6 pm daily from May to October (closed January and February), and shorter hours in other months.

Places to Stay

The nearest camping ground is *Campingplatz Schönböcken* (☎ 89 30 90, *Steinrader Damm 12*), in a western suburb of Lübeck. It is open from April to October and charges DM7 per person, DM6 for a tent and DM2 per car. The tourist office can help with information on camping grounds in the nearby coastal resort of Travemünde.

Lübeck has two DJH hostels. The *Jugendgästehaus Lübeck* (☎ 702 03 99, fax

GERMANY

770 12, Mengstrasse 33) is clean, comfortable and well situated in the middle of the old town, 15 minutes' walk from the train station (DM28.50/37 for juniors/seniors in dorms). It also has single and twin-bed rooms for DM42 per person. The *Folke-Bernadotte-Heim* (☎ 334 33, fax 345 40, Am Gertrudenkirchhof 4) is a little outside the old town. Take bus No 1, 3, 11 or 12 to Gustav-Radbruch-Platz (DM28/33 for juniors/seniors). The YMCA's *Sleep-Inn* (☎ 719 20, fax 789 97, Grosse Petersgrube 11) charges DM15 per bed in dorms, DM40 per double, and there are apartments from DM30 per person. Breakfast is DM7 and sheets DM8 extra (closed mid-December to mid-January).

The *Hotel Stadt Lübeck* (☎ 838 83, fax 86 32 21, Am Bahnhof 21) is just outside the main train station. Fairly good rooms with shower and WC cost DM79/129. The *Altstadt Hotel* (☎ 720 83, fax 737 78, Fischergrube 52) is convenient and pleasant, with rooms for DM135/195, and double suites for DM240. The *Mövenpick Hotel* (☎ 150 40, fax 150 41 11, Willy-Brandt-Allee 1-3), opposite the Holstentor, has singles from DM175 to DM260 and doubles from DM215 to DM300.

Places to Eat

The best eating and drinking options are in the area directly east of the Rathaus. *Tipasa (Schlumacherstrasse 12-14)* serves specials on weekday afternoons for around DM10. It's also a great place to eat and drink in the evening. *Hieronymus* (☎ 706 30 17, Fleischhauerstrasse 81) is a relaxed and rambling restaurant spread over three floors of a 15th-century building. Most dishes on the creative menu cost DM10 to DM20 and are quite filling. Lunch specials are good value. The *Schiffergesellschaft (Breite Strasse 2)* has a unique maritime atmosphere and a menu starting at around DM30 for main dishes. *Amadeus (Königstrasse 26)* is a lively cafe with a limited menu.

Save room for a dessert or a snack of marzipan, which was invented in Lübeck (local legend has it that the town ran out of flour during a long siege and resorted to grinding almonds to make bread). *JG Niederegger (Breite Strasse 89)*, a shop and cafe directly opposite the Rathaus, is

Lübeck's mecca of marzipan. The supermarket *Co-op (Sandstrasse 24)* is conveniently located near Kohlmarkt.

Getting There & Away

Lübeck is close to Hamburg, with at least one train every hour (DM16, 45 minutes). There are also frequent services to Kiel (DM22, 1¼ hours) and Schwerin (DM20, 1¼ hours). Trains to/from Copenhagen also stop here.

The central bus station is next to the main train station. Services to/from Wismar stop here, as well as Autokraft buses to/from Hamburg, Schwerin, Kiel, Rostock and Berlin.

Getting Around

Frequent double-decker buses run to Travemünde (DM3.50, 45 minutes) from the central bus station. City buses also leave from here; a single journey costs DM3.50. The Lübeck-Karte (a day card for transport only) costs DM10 and includes the Travemünde area.

KIEL

☎ 0431 • pop 246,000

Kiel, the capital of Schleswig-Holstein, was seriously damaged by Allied bombing during WWII, but is now a vibrant and modern city. At the end of a modest firth, it has long been one of Germany's most important Baltic Sea harbours and was the host of Olympic sailing events in 1936 and 1972.

Orientation & Information

Kiel's main street is Holstenstrasse, a colourful, pedestrian street near the fjord. It runs north-south from the Nikolaikirche to Sophienhof, a large indoor shopping mall connected to the main train station by an overpass. The tourist office (☎ 67 91 00, fax 679 10 99, ✉ info@kiel-tourist.de) is at Andreas-Gayk-Strasse 31, a northern extension of Sophienblatt and just five minutes by foot from the main train station. It's core opening hours are 9 am to 6.30 pm Monday to Friday, till 1 pm Saturday (till 4.30 pm on Saturday from May to September). In June and July it opens till 2 pm Sunday. Edit(ha's) Internet cafe at Alter Markt 13 is a good place to surf the web on the fjord. Web site: www.kiel-tourist.de.

Things to See & Do

Kiel's most famous attraction is the **Kieler Woche** (Kiel Week) in the last full week in June, a festival revolving around a series of yachting regattas attended by over 4000 of the world's sailing elite and half a million spectators. Even if you're not into sailing, the atmosphere is electric – just make sure you book a room in advance if you want to be in on the fun.

To experience Kiel's love for the sea in a less energetic fashion, take a ferry ride to the village of **Laboe** at the mouth of the firth. Ferries leave hourly from Bahnhofbrücke pier behind the train station. They take around one hour to reach Laboe, hopping back and forth across the firth along the way. In Laboe, you can visit **U995**, a wartime U-boat, on the beach, which is now a technical museum (open daily; DM3.50/2.50). Nearby is the **Marine-Ehrenmal** (Naval Memorial) with a navigation museum (open daily; DM5/3).

Kiel is also the point at which the shipping canal from the North Sea enters the Baltic Sea. Some 60,000 ships pass through the canal every year, and the **locks** (*Schleusen;* ☎ 360 30), at Holtenau 6km north of the city centre, are worth a visit. Admission to the viewing platform is DM3/2; tours of the locks are offered at 9 and 11 am and 1 and 3 pm daily (DM4.50/3).

The open-air **Schleswig-Holstein Freilicht-museum** (☎ 65 96 60) in nearby Molfsee (take Autokraftbus No 500) is also worth seeing. More than 60 historical houses typical of the region have been relocated here, giving you a thorough introduction to the northern way of life. The museum is open 9 am to 6 pm daily from April to October (DM8/5) and 11 am to 4 pm only on Sunday from November to March (DM3).

Places to Stay

Kiel's *Campingplatz Falckenstein* (☎ 39 20 78, *Palisadenweg 171)* is in the northern suburb of Friedrichsort and open from April to October. It charges DM7 per person, from DM8 to DM12 for tents and DM3.50 per car. The *Jugenherberge* (☎ 73 14 88, fax 73 57 23, *Johannesstrasse 1)* is in the suburb of Gaarden. You can walk across the pretty drawbridge behind the train station, or take

the Laboe ferry to Gaarden, from where it's a 10-minute walk; or take bus No 11 or 12 from the main train station to Kieler Strasse (DM28/33 for juniors/seniors).

The tourist office charges DM3.50 for accommodation bookings and stocks an excellent free brochure listing private rooms and apartments.

Hotel Runge (☎ 733 33 96, 73 19 92, *Elisabethstrasse 16)* in Gaarden charges DM60/100 or DM75/120 with shower and WC. Take bus No 11 or 12 to Augustern from the main train station. The central *Hotel Schweriner Hof* (☎ 614 16, fax 67 41 34, *Königsweg 13)* has good singles/doubles from DM70/110, and DM110/140 with shower and WC. *Muhl's Hotel* (☎ 997 90, fax 997 91 79, *Lange Reihe 5)* is central and costs DM110/150 for nice rooms with facilities. *Steigenberger Hotel Conti-Hansa* (☎ 511 50, fax 511 54 44, *Schlossgarten 7)* has standard-class rooms for DM250/300.

Places to Eat

The woodsy *Friesenhof (Fleethörn 9)* in the Rathaus building has daily lunch specials for around DM10; otherwise main dishes range from DM16 to DM32, and between 3 and 5 pm all dishes are half price plus DM2.

The *Klosterbrauerei (Alter Markt 9)* is a private brewery with good beer, well-priced food and a great atmosphere Lunch specials are served here for around DM10. You'll find lots of cheap take-away options in the Turkish quarter around the hostel in Gaarden. *Ça va (Holtenauer Strasse 107)* is a popular gay cafe-bar that does light dishes in the evening (open late).

Getting There & Away

Regional buses run to/from Lübeck, Schleswig and Puttgarden from the bus station on Auguste-Viktoria-Strasse, just north of the main train station. Numerous RE trains run every day between Kiel and Hamburg-Altona or Hamburg Hauptbahnhof (DM30, 1¼ hours). The trains to Lübeck leave every hour (DM22, 1¼ hours). The ADM Mitfahrzentrale (☎ 194 40) is at Sophienblatt 52a.

The daily Kiel-Gothenburg ferry (14 hours) leaves from Schwedenkai and is run by Stena Line (☎ 0180-533 36 00). One-way passenger prices go from DM70 to DM160 depending

GERMANY

on the season (DM18 to DM28 for bikes). Web site: www.stenaline.de.

Color Line ferries (☎ 730 03 00) run direct to/from Kiel and Oslo daily (19½ hours). Non-cabin space is only available from mid-June to mid-August (DM168/182 during the week/weekend). Otherwise, basic double cabins cost from DM120 to DM182 per person depending on the season. There are 50% off-peak student concessions. Ferries depart from the Norwegenkai across the fjord in Gaarden (use the footbridge). Web site: www.color-line.de.

Getting Around
City buses leave from Sophienblatt, in front of the train station. To get to the North-Baltic Sea Canal and the locks, take bus No 11 to Wik; the locks are about five minutes' walk from the terminus.

NORTH FRISIAN ISLANDS
Sylt ☎ 04651 • pop 21,000
Amrum ☎ 04682 • pop 2100
The Frisian Islands reward those who make the trek; with sand dunes, sea, pure air and every so often sunshine. Friesland itself covers an area stretching from the northern Netherlands along the coast up into Denmark. North Friesland (Nordfriesland) is the western coastal area of Schleswig-Holstein up to and into Denmark. The sea area forms the National Park of Wattenmeer, and the shifting dunes, particularly on the islands of Amrum, Föhr and Langeness, are sensitive and cannot be disturbed – paths and boardwalks are provided for strolling. The most popular of the North Frisian Islands is the glamorous resort of Sylt, which gets very crowded from June to August; the neighbouring islands of Föhr and Amrum are far more relaxed and less touristy.

Orientation & Information
The excellent tourist office inside Westerland's train station on Sylt (☎ 99 88, fax 99 81 00) can help with information and accommodation. Its minimum opening hours are 9 am to 6 pm Monday to Friday, to 4.30 pm Saturday, and to 2 pm Sunday (closed Sunday from November to April). The Bädergemeinschaft Sylt (☎ 820 20, fax 82 02 22), near the Westerland Rathaus at Stephanstrasse 6, and Sylt

Tourismus Zentrale (☎ 60 26, fax 281 80), Keitumer Landstrasse 10b just outside of town in Tinnum, are other useful sources of information. On Amrum, the friendly tourist office (☎ 940 30, fax 94 03 20) is at the harbour car park. The spa administrations *(Kurverwaltungen)* at the various resorts are also useful sources of information.

All communities charge visitors a so-called *Kurtaxe*, a resort tax of about DM4 to DM6 a day, depending on the town and the season. Paying the tax gets you a *Kurkarte* which you need on Sylt even just to get onto the beach. Day passes are available from kiosks at beach entrances, but if you're spending more than one night, your hotel can obtain a pass for you for the length of your stay (not included in the room rate).

Things to See
Nature is the prime attraction on the North Frisian Islands; the different moods of the rough North Sea and the placid Wattenmeer lend the region its unique character. Beautiful dunes stretch out for miles, red and white cliffs border wide beaches, and bird lovers will be amply rewarded. The reed-roofed *Friesenhäuser* are typical of the region. But of course, civilisation has also taken hold here, especially in Westerland on Sylt. After WWII, the German jet-set invaded the island, which explains the abundance of luxury homes, cars and expensive restaurants, particularly around Kampen.

On Amrum, you'll find signs of traditional Frisian life around the village of **Nebel**. The **lighthouse**, the tallest in northern Germany at 63m, affords a spectacular view of the dunes from the south-west of the island and over to the islands of Sylt, Föhr and Langeness. It's open 8.30 am to 12.30 pm weekdays from April to October; Wednesday morning only the rest of the year (DM3).

Activities
In Westerland, a visit to the indoor water park and health spa **Sylter Welle** (☎ 99 82 42) is fun, especially when it's too cold for the beach. It includes saunas, solariums, a wave pool and a slide and is open from 10 am to either 9 or 10 pm daily (DM17, DM25 with sauna; no time limit). For a real thrill, though, visit one of Sylt's beach saunas –

GERMANY

the tourist office can point you in the right direction.

Heikos Reiterwiese in Westerland (☎ 56 00) on Sylt, and Reiterhof Jensen (☎ 20 30) on Amrum offer **horse-riding**. One of several excellent **hikes** on Amrum (8km return) is from Norddorf along the beach to the tranquil Ood **nature reserve**. The tourist office can help with information on guided hikes in summer across the Watt to Föhr. The flat terrain of the islands is also suited to **cycling**. On Amrum, the tourist office keeps a list of rental places. In Westerland on Sylt, Fahrrad am Bahnhof (☎ 58 03; DM9 per day) is conveniently situated at the train station.

Places to Stay

Low-budget accommodation is hard to find on the islands, but the tourist offices can help with private rooms from DM25 per person. Another option may be to rent an apartment, which can cost as little as DM60 in the low season and DM85 in the high season. Unless it's a particularly slow time proprietors may be reluctant to rent for fewer than three days.

Sylt Sylt has seven camping grounds. *Campingplatz Kampen* (☎ 420 86, Möwenweg 4) is set beautifully amid dunes near the small town of Kampen (open from Easter to mid-October). In Hörnum, there's the *Jugendherberge* (☎ 88 02 94, fax 88 13 92, Friesenplatz 2) in the south of the island. There's also a *Jugendherberge* (☎ 87 03 97, fax 87 10 39) in List. Both charge DM24/29 juniors/seniors and neither is very central, but bus services bring you close.

Hotel Garni Diana (☎ 988 60, fax 98 86 86, Elisabethstrasse 19) charges DM70/130 for basic rooms and DM100/180 with a bathroom. The lovely *Landhaus Nielsen* (☎ 986 90, fax 98 69 60, Bastianstrasse 5) charges DM90/130 for singles/doubles. Winter prices are lower.

Amrum *Campingplatz Schade* (☎ 22 54) is at the northern edge of Wittdün. The *Jugendherberge* (☎ 20 10, fax 17 47, Mittelstrasse 1) has 218 beds but it's best to book ahead, even in the low season (DM24/29 juniors/seniors). The historic *Hotel Ual Öömrang* (☎ 836, fax 14 32, Bräätlun 4) in Norddorf charges DM90/180 for rooms with a bathroom (closed January and February).

Places to Eat

Sylt Picnics are a fine option on the islands. In Westerland, ***Toni's Restaurant*** *(Norderstrasse 3)* serves good, inexpensive fare from DM11 to DM30; it also has a pleasant garden. *Blum's (Neue Strasse 4)* has soup from DM6.50, main dishes from DM18 and some of the freshest fish in town. The *Alte Friesenstube* (☎ 12 28, Gaadt 4) is in a 17th-century building. It specialises in northern German and Frisian cooking but expect to pay around DM60 per head for a three-course meal with wine. Kampen's *Kupferkanne* (☎ 410 109) in Stapelhooger Wai is a beautiful stop during a bike tour. You'll end up paying DM15.50 for a giant cup of coffee and a slice of cake with cream, but the view of the Wattenmeer is free.

List's harbour sports a number of colourful kiosks. *Gosch*, prides itself on being Germany's northernmost fish kiosk, and is an institution well known beyond Sylt.

Amrum Amrum has only a few restaurants and many of them close in the low season. The *Hotel Ual Öömrang* (see Places to Stay) serves filling traditional dishes for around DM27. The *Burg Haus*, built on an old Viking hill-fort above the eastern beach at Norddorf, has a teahouse atmosphere and home-made cakes.

Note that restaurants can close as early as 7 pm in the low season.

Getting There & Away

Sylt Sylt is connected to the mainland by a scenic train-only causeway right through the Wattenmeer. Around seven IC trains leave from Hamburg-Hauptbahnhof daily for Westerland, but the regional trains from Hamburg-Altona are faster and less expensive (DM64, 2¾ hours). If you are travelling by car, you must load it onto a train in the town of Niebüll near the Danish border. There are about 26 crossings in both directions every day and no reservations can be made. The cost per car is a shocking DM144 return, but that includes all passengers.

Amrum To get to Amrum and the island of Föhr, you must board a ferry in Dagebüll Hafen. To get there, take the Sylt-bound train from Hamburg-Altona and change in Niebüll.

In summer, there are also some through trains. A day-return from Dagebüll costs DM23.50 (45 minutes one way), which allows you to visit both islands. If you stay overnight, return tickets cost DM27.40 (bicycle DM7.50). The trip to Amrum takes around two hours, stopping at Föhr on the way.

There are daily flights between Westerland airport and Hamburg, Munich and Berlin, and several flights weekly from other German cities.

Getting Around

Sylt's two north-south bus lines run every 20 to 30 minutes, and three other frequent lines cover the rest of the island. There are seven price zones, costing from DM2.30 to DM11. Some buses have bicycle hangers. On Amrum, a bus runs from the ferry terminal in Wittdün to Norddorf and back every 30 to 60 minutes, depending on the season. The slow, fun inter-island options are the day-return cruises to Föhr (Wyk) and Amrum (Wittdün) from the harbour at Hörnum on Sylt. Day-return cruises through shallow banks that attract seals and sea birds are offered by Adler-Schiffe (☎ 04651-987 00 in Westerland; DM35). Bicycles are an extra DM8.50. WDR ferries also run on day-return trips in the summer from Wittdün on Amrum to Föhr (DM13) and the two nearby islands of Hallig Hooge and Nordmarsch-Langeness (both DM17).

HELIGOLAND
☎ 04725 • pop 1650

Not technically part of the Frisian Islands, Heligoland (Helgoland) lies 70km out to sea and is a popular day trip from the islands. Oddly, Heligoland is economically not part of the EU and therefore remains a duty-free port. Because of the North Sea's strong currents and unpredictable weather, however, the passage will be most enjoyed by people with iron stomachs. From April to October, WDR ferries (☎ 04681-801 40) sail from Hörnum on Sylt twice weekly and from Amrum and Dagebüll (all DM44 day return).

Seasick crowds flock like lemmings to this unlikely chunk of red rock sticking up out of the sea. It was used as a submarine base in WWII, and it's still possible to tour the strong bunkers and underground tunnels. The island was heavily bombed and all of the houses are new. Take a walk along Lung Wai ('long way'), filled with duty-free shops, and then up the stairway of 180 steps to Oberland for what view there is. There's also a scenic trail around the island. Small boats run from Heligoland to neighbouring **Düne**, a tiny island filled with beaches and nudists.

GERMANY

Greece

The first travel guide to Greece was written 1800 years ago by the Greek geographer and historian Pausanias, so the tourism industry isn't exactly in its infancy.

The country's enduring attraction is its archaeological sites; those who travel through Greece journey not only through the landscape but also through time, witnessing the legacy of Europe's greatest ages – the Mycenaean, Minoan, classical, Hellenistic and Byzantine.

You cannot wander far in Greece without stumbling across a broken column, a crumbling bastion or a tiny Byzantine church, each perhaps neglected and forgotten but still retaining an aura of former glory.

Its culture is a unique blend of East and West, inherited from the long period of Ottoman rule and apparent in its food, music and traditions. The mountainous countryside is a walker's paradise crisscrossed by age-old donkey tracks leading to stunning vistas.

The magnetism of Greece is also due to less tangible attributes – the dazzling clarity of the light, the floral aromas that permeate the air, the spirit of places – for there is hardly a grove, mountain or stream which is not sacred to a deity, and the ghosts of the past still linger.

Then again, many visitors come to Greece simply to get away from it all and relax in one of Europe's friendliest and safest countries.

Facts about Greece

HISTORY

Greece's strategic position at the crossroads of Europe and Asia has resulted in a long and turbulent history.

During the Bronze Age, which lasted from 3000 to 1200 BC in Greece, the advanced Cycladic, Minoan and Mycenaean civilisations flourished. The Mycenaeans were eventually swept aside by the Dorians in the 12th century BC. The next 400 years are often referred to as the 'age of darkness' (1200-800 BC), which sounds a bit unfair for

AT A GLANCE

Capital	Athens
Population	10.6 million
Official Language	Greek
Currency	1 drachma = 100 lepta
Time	GMT/UTC+0200
Country Phone Code ☎	30

a period that saw the arrival of the Iron Age and emergence of geometric pottery. Homer's *Odyssey* and *Iliad* were composed at this time.

By 800 BC, when Homer's works were first written down, Greece was undergoing a cultural and military revival with the evolution of the city-states, the most powerful of which were Athens and Sparta. Greater Greece – Magna Graecia – was created, with southern Italy as an important component. The unified Greeks repelled the Persians twice, at Marathon (490 BC) and Salamis (480 BC). The period which followed was an unparalleled time of growth and prosperity, resulting in what is called the classical (or golden) age.

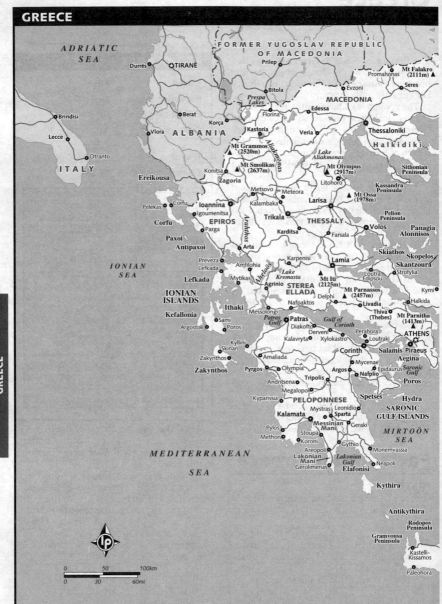

GREECE

The Golden Age

This is the period when the Parthenon was commissioned by Pericles, Sophocles wrote *Oedipus the King*, and Socrates taught young Athenians to think. At the same time, the Spartans were creating a military state. The golden age ended with the Peloponnesian War (431-404 BC) in which the militaristic Spartans defeated the Athenians. So embroiled were they in this war that they failed to notice the expansion of Macedonia under King Philip II, who easily conquered the war-weary city-states.

Philip's ambitions were surpassed by those of his son Alexander the Great, who marched triumphantly into Asia Minor, Egypt, Persia and what are now parts of Afghanistan and India. In 323 BC he met an untimely death at the age of 33, and his generals divided his empire between themselves.

Roman Rule & the Byzantine Empire

Roman incursions into Greece began in 205 BC, and by 146 BC Greece and Macedonia had become Roman provinces. After the subdivision of the Roman Empire into eastern and western empires in AD 395, Greece became part of the eastern (Byzantine) Empire, based at Constantinople.

In the centuries that followed, Venetians, Franks, Normans, Slavs, Persians, Arabs and, finally, Turks took their turns to chip away at the Byzantine Empire.

The Ottoman Empire & Independence

The end came in 1453, when Constantinople fell to the Turks. Most of Greece soon became part of the Ottoman Empire. Crete was not captured until 1670, leaving Corfu the only island never occupied by the Turks. By the 19th century the Ottoman Empire had become the 'sick man of Europe'. The Greeks, seeing nationalism sweep Europe, fought the War of Independence (1821-32). The great powers – Britain, France and Russia – intervened in 1827, and Ioannis Kapodistrias was elected the first Greek president.

Kapodistrias was assassinated in 1831 and the European powers stepped in again, declaring that Greece should become a monarchy. In January 1833 Otho of Bavaria was installed as king. His ambition, called the

Great Idea, was to unite all the lands of the Greek people to the Greek motherland. In 1862 he was peacefully ousted and the Greeks chose George I, a Danish prince, as king.

In WWI, Prime Minister Venizelos allied Greece with France and Britain. King Constantine (George's son), who was married to the Kaiser's sister Sophia, disputed this and left the country.

Smyrna & WWII

After the war, Venizelos resurrected the Great Idea. Underestimating the new-found power of Turkey under the leadership of Atatürk, he sent forces to occupy Smyrna (the present-day Turkish port of İzmir) which had a large Greek population. The army was repulsed and many Greeks were slaughtered. This led to a brutal population exchange between the two countries in 1923.

In 1930 George II, Constantine's son, was reinstated as king and he appointed the dictator General Metaxas as prime minister. Metaxas' grandiose ambition was to take the best from Greece's ancient and Byzantine past to create a Third Greek Civilisation. What he actually created was more a Greek version of the Third Reich. His chief claim to fame is his celebrated *okhi* (no) to Mussolini's request to allow Italian troops into Greece in 1940.

Despite Allied help, Greece fell to Germany in 1941. Resistance movements polarised into royalist and communist factions, leading to a bloody civil war which lasted until 1949. The country was left in chaos. More people were killed in the civil war than in WWII, and 250,000 people were homeless. The sense of despair became the trigger for a mass exodus. Almost a million Greeks headed off in search of a better life elsewhere, primarily to Australia, Canada and the USA. Villages – whole islands even – were abandoned as people gambled on a new start in cities such as Melbourne, Toronto, Chicago and New York. While some have drifted back, the majority have stayed away.

The Colonels

Continuing political instability led to the colonels' coup d'etat in 1967. King Constantine (son of King Paul, who succeeded George II) staged an unsuccessful counter coup, then fled the country. The colonels' junta then distinguished itself by inflicting appalling brutality, repression and political incompetence upon the people. In 1974 they attempted to assassinate Cyprus' leader, Archbishop Makarios. When Makarios escaped, the junta replaced him with the extremist Nikos Samson, prompting Turkey to occupy Northern Cyprus. The continued occupation remains one of the most contentious issues in Greek politics. The junta, now discredited, had little choice but to hand back power to civilians. In November 1974 a plebiscite voted against restoration of the monarchy, and Greece became a republic. An election brought the right-wing New Democracy (ND) party into power.

The Socialist 1980s

In 1981 Greece entered the then EC (European Community, now the EU). Andreas Papandreou's Panhellenic Socialist Movement (PASOK) won the next election, giving Greece its first socialist government. PASOK promised removal of US air bases and withdrawal from NATO, which Greece had joined in 1951. Instead Papandreou presided over seven years of rising unemployment and spiralling debt.

He was forced to step aside in 1989 while an unprecedented conservative and communist coalition took over to investigate a scandal involving the Bank of Crete. Papandreou and four ministers were ordered to stand trial, and the coalition ordered fresh elections for October 1990.

The 1990s

The elections brought New Democracy back to power with a majority of two. Tough economic reforms introduced by Prime Minister Konstantinos Mitsotakis soon made his government deeply unpopular. By late 1992, allegations began to emerge about the same sort of corruption and dirty tricks that had brought Papandreou unstuck. Mitsotakis himself was accused of having a secret horde of Minoan art, and he was forced to call an election in October 1993.

Greeks again turned to PASOK and the ailing Papandreou, who eventually had been cleared of all charges. He had little option but to continue with the austerity program begun by Mitsotakis, quickly making his government equally unpopular.

Papandreou was forced to step down in January 1996 after a lengthy spell in hospital. His departure produced a dramatic change of direction for PASOK, with the party abandoning its leftist policies and electing experienced economist and lawyer Costas Simitis as its new leader. Cashing in on his reputation as the Mr Clean of Greek politics, Simitis romped to a comfortable majority at a snap poll called in October 1996.

His government has focussed almost exclusively on the push for further integration with Europe, which has meant more tax reform and more austerity measures. While unpopular at the time, Simitis appears to have accomplished his objectives. At the time of writing, Greece was expecting to be admitted to the single European currency in mid-2001.

The electorate showed its appreciation of his achievements by handing Simitis a mandate for another four years at elections held in April 2000.

Foreign Policy

Greece's foreign policy is dominated by its extremely sensitive relationship with Turkey, its giant Muslim neighbour to the east.

At the time of writing, these two uneasy NATO partners appeared to be trying hard to be friends. It's a dramatic turnaround after years of mutual antagonism, when even the smallest incident brought talk of all-out war. The trigger was the massive earthquake that struck western Turkey in August 1999. Television images of the devastation prompted Greece to join the rescue effort. Its rescue teams were greeted like heroes, and grateful Turks were quick to return the favour following the earthquake that struck northern Athens a month later. The two have kept talking ever since.

The break-up of former Yugoslavia and the end of the Stalinist era in Albania have given Greece two new issues to worry about.

GEOGRAPHY

Greece consists of the southern tip of the Balkan peninsula and about 2000 islands, only 166 of which are inhabited. The land mass is 131,900 sq km and Greek territorial waters cover a further 400,000 sq km.

Most of the country is mountainous. The Pindos Mountains in Epiros are the southern extension of the Dinaric Alps, which run the length of former Yugoslavia. The range continues down through Central Greece and the Peloponnese, and re-emerges in the mountains of Crete. Less than a quarter of the country is suitable for agriculture.

CLIMATE

The climate is typically Mediterranean with mild, wet winters followed by very hot, dry summers.

There are regional variations. The mountains of Northern Greece have a climate similar to the Balkans, with freezing winters and very hot, humid summers, while the west coast and the Ionian Islands have the highest rainfall.

Mid-October is when the rains start in most areas, and the weather stays cold and wet until February – although there are also occasional winter days with clear blue skies and sunshine. Crete stays warm the longest – you can swim off its southern coast from mid-April to November.

ECOLOGY & ENVIRONMENT

Looking at the harsh, rocky landscapes today, it's hard to believe that in ancient times Greece was a fertile land with extensive forests. The change represents an ecological disaster on a massive scale. The main culprit has been the olive tree. In ancient times, native forest was cleared on a massive scale to make way for a tree whose fruit produced an oil that could be used for everything from lighting to lubrication. Much of the land cleared was hill country that proved unsuitable for olives. Without the surface roots of the native trees to bind it, the topsoil quickly disappeared. The ubiquitous goat has been another major contributor to ecological devastation.

The news from the Aegean Sea is both good and bad. According to EU findings, it is Europe's least polluted sea – apart from areas immediately surrounding major cities. Like the rest of the Mediterranean, it has been overfished.

FLORA & FAUNA
Flora
The variety of flora is unrivalled in Europe. The wild flowers are spectacular. They continue to thrive because much of the land is too poor for agriculture and has escaped the ravages of modern fertilisers. The best places to see the amazing variety are the mountains of Crete and the southern Peloponnese.

Fauna
You won't encounter many animals in the wild, mainly due to the macho habit of blasting to bits anything that moves. Wild boar are still found in reasonable numbers in the north and are a favourite target for hunters. Squirrels, rabbits, hares, foxes and weasels are all fairly common on the mainland; less common is the cute European suslik – a small ground squirrel. Reptiles are well represented. The snakes include several viper species, which are poisonous.

Bird-watchers have more chance of coming across something unusual than animal spotters. Lake Mikri Prespa in Macedonia has the richest colony of fish-eating birds in Europe, while the Dadia Forest Reserve in Thrace numbers such majestic birds as the golden eagle and the giant black vulture among its residents.

Endangered Species
The brown bear, Europe's largest land mammal, still survives in very small numbers in the mountains of Northern Greece, as does the grey wolf.

Europe's rarest mammal, the monk seal, was once very common in the Mediterranean, but is now on the brink of extinction in Europe. There are about 400 left in Europe, half of which live in Greece. There are about 40 in the Ionian Sea and the rest are found in the Aegean.

The waters around Zakynthos are home to the last large sea turtle colony in Europe, that of the loggerhead turtle (*Careta careta*). The Sea Turtle Protection Society of Greece (☎/fax 01-523 1342, ❷ stps@compulink .gr), Solomou 57, Athens 104 32, runs monitoring programs and is always looking for volunteers.

National Parks
Visitors who expect Greek national parks to provide facilities on a par with those in countries like Australia and the USA will be very disappointed. Although they all have

refuges and some have marked hiking trails, Greek national parks have little else by way of facilities.

The most visited parks are Mt Parnitha, just north of Athens, and the Samaria Gorge on Crete. The others are Vikos-Aoös and Prespa national parks in Epiros; Mt Olympus on the border of Thessaly and Macedonia; and Parnassos and Iti national parks in Central Greece.

If you want to see wildlife, the place to go is the Dadia Forest Reserve in eastern Thrace.

There is also a National Marine Park off the coast of Alonnisos, and another around the Bay of Laganas area off Zakynthos.

GOVERNMENT & POLITICS

Since 1975, democratic Greece has been a parliamentary republic with a president as head of state. The president and parliament, which has 300 deputies, have joint legislative power. Prime Minister Simitis heads a 43-member cabinet.

ECONOMY

Traditionally, Greece has been an agricultural country, but the importance of agriculture in the economy is declining. Tourism is by far the biggest industry; shipping comes next.

POPULATION & PEOPLE

The population of Greece is 10.6 million. Women outnumber men by more than 200,000. Greece is now a largely urban society, with 68% of people living in cities. By far the largest is Athens, with more than 3.7 million in the greater Athens area – which includes Piraeus (171,000). Other major cities are Thessaloniki (750,000), Patras (153,300), Iraklio (127,600), Larisa (113,400) and Volos (110,000). Less than 15% of the population live on the islands. The most populous are Crete (537,000), Evia (209,100) and Corfu (107,592).

Contemporary Greeks are a mixture of all of the invaders who have occupied the country since ancient times. There are a number of distinct ethnic minorities – about 300,000 ethnic Turks in Thrace; about 100,000 Britons; about 5000 Jews; Vlach and Sarakatsani shepherds in Epiros; Roma (Gypsies); and lately, a growing number of Albanians.

ARTS

The arts have been integral to Greek life since ancient times. In summer, Greek dramas are staged in the ancient theatres where they were originally performed.

The visual arts follow the mainstream of modern European art, and traditional folk arts such as embroidery, weaving and tapestry continue.

The *bouzouki* is the most popular musical instrument, but each region has its own speciality of instruments and sounds. *Rembetika* music, with its themes of poverty and suffering, was banned by the junta, but is now enjoying a revival. Rembetika is the music of the working classes and has its roots in the sufferings of the refugees from Asia Minor in the 1920s. Songs are accompanied by bouzouki, guitar, violin and accordion.

The blind bard Homer composed the narrative poems *Odyssey* and *Iliad*. These are tales of the Trojan war and the return to Greece of Odysseus, King of Ithaki, linking together the legends sung by bards during the dark age. Plato was the most devoted pupil of Socrates, writing down every dialogue he could recall between Socrates, other philosophers and the youth of Athens. His most widely read work is the *Republic*, which argues that the perfect state could only be created with philosopher-rulers at the helm.

Nikos Kazantzakis, author of *Zorba the Greek* and numerous other novels, plays and poems, is the most famous of 20th-century Greek novelists. The Alexandrian, Constantine Cavafy (1863-1933), revolutionised Greek poetry by introducing a personal, conversational style. He is considered the TS Eliot of Greek literary verse. Poet George Seferis (1900-71) won the Nobel Prize for literature in 1963, and Olysseus Elytis (1911-96) won the same prize in 1979.

Theophilos (1866-1934) is famous for his primitive style of painting. The country's most famous painter was a young Cretan painter called Domenikos Theotokopoulos, who moved to Spain in 1577 and became known as the great El Greco.

SOCIETY & CONDUCT

Greece is steeped in traditional customs. Name days (celebrated instead of birthdays),

GREECE

weddings and funerals all have great significance. On someone's name day there is an open house and refreshments are served to well-wishers who stop by with gifts. Weddings are highly festive, with dancing, feasting and drinking sometimes continuing for days.

If you want to bare all, other than on a designated nude beach, remember that Greece is a conservative country, so take care not to offend the locals.

MYTHOLOGY
The myths are accounts of the gods whom the Greeks worshipped in ancient times. The main characters are the 12 principle deities, who lived on Mt Olympus – which the Greeks thought to be at the exact centre of the world.

The supreme deity was **Zeus**, who was also god of the heavens. He was the possessor of an astonishing libido and mythology is littered with his offspring. Zeus was married to his sister, **Hera**, who was the protector of women and the family. She was able to renew her virginity each year by bathing in a spring. She was the mother of **Ares**, the god of war, and **Hephaestus**, god of the forge.

Demeter was the goddess of earth and fertility, while the goddess of love (and lust) was the beautiful **Aphrodite**. The powerful goddess of wisdom and guardian of Athens was **Athena**, who is said to have been born (complete with helmet, armour and spear) from Zeus' head.

Poseidon, the brother of Zeus, was god of the sea and preferred his sumptuous palace in the depths of the Aegean to Mt Olympus. **Apollo**, god of the sun, was also worshipped as the god of music and song. His twin sister, **Artemis**, was the goddess of childbirth and the protector of suckling animals.

Hermes, messenger of the gods, completes the first XI – the gods whose position in the pantheon is agreed by everyone. The final berth is normally reserved for **Hestia**, goddess of the hearth. She was too virtuous for some, who promoted the fun-loving **Dionysos**, god of wine, in her place.

Other gods included **Hades**, god of the underworld; **Pan**, god of the shepherds; **Asclepius**, the god of healing; and **Eros**, the god of love.

Heroes such as **Heracles** and **Theseus** were elevated almost to the ranks of the gods.

Xena, sadly, does not feature anywhere. The strapping warrior princess of TV fame is a script writer's invention – not a myth!

RELIGION
About 97% of Greeks nominally belong to the Greek Orthodox Church. The rest of the population is split between the Roman Catholic, Protestant, Evangelist, Jewish and Muslim faiths. While older Greeks and those in rural areas tend to be deeply religious, most young people are decidedly more interested in the secular.

LANGUAGE
Greeks are naturally delighted if you can speak a little of their language, but you don't need to be able to speak Greek to get around. English is almost a second language, especially with younger people. You'll also find many Greeks have lived abroad, usually in Australia or the USA, so even in remote villages there are invariably one or two people who can speak English.

See the Language chapter at the back of this book for pronunciation guidelines and useful Greek words and phrases.

Transliteration
Travellers in Greece will frequently encounter confusing and seemingly illogical English transliterations of Greek words. Transliteration is a knotty problem – there are six ways of rendering the vowel sound 'ee' in Greek, and two ways of rendering the 'o' sound and the 'e' sound.

This guidebook has merely attempted to be consistent within itself, not to solve this long-standing difficulty.

As a general rule, the Greek letter gamma (γ) appears as a 'g' rather than a 'y'; therefore it's *agios*, not *ayios*. The letter delta (δ) appears as 'd' rather than 'dh', so it's *domatia*, not *dhomatia*. The letter phi (φ) can be either 'f' or 'ph'. Here, we have used the general rule that classical names are spelt with a 'ph' and modern names with an 'f' – so it's Phaestos (not Festos), but Folegandros, not Pholegandros. Please bear with us if signs in Greek don't agree with our spelling. It's that sort of language.

Facts for the Visitor

HIGHLIGHTS
Islands

Many islands are overrun with visitors in summer. For tranquillity, try lesser-known islands such as Kassos, Sikinos and Kastellorizo. If you enjoy mountain walks, Naxos, Crete, Samothraki and Samos are all very rewarding. If you prefer the beach, try Paros.

Museums & Archaeological Sites

Greece has more ancient sites than any other country in Europe. It's worth seeking out some of the lesser lights where you won't have to contend with the crowds that pour through famous sites like the Acropolis, Delphi, Knossos and Olympia.

The leading museum is the National Archaeological Museum in Athens, which houses Heinrich Schliemann's finds from Mycenae and Minoan frescoes from Akrotiri on Santorini (Thira). The Thessaloniki Museum contains treasures from the graves of the Macedonian royal family, and the Iraklio Museum houses a vast collection from the Minoan sites of Crete.

Museums and sites are free for card carrying students and teachers from EU countries. An International Student Identification Card (ISIC) gets non-EU students a 50% discount.

Historic Towns

Two of Greece's most spectacular medieval cities are in the Peloponnese. The ghostly Byzantine city of Mystras, west of Sparta, clambers up the slopes of Mt Taygetos, its winding paths and stairways leading to deserted palaces and churches. In contrast, Byzantine Monemvasia is still inhabited, but equally dramatic and full of atmosphere.

There are some stunning towns on the islands. Rhodes is the finest surviving example of a fortified medieval town, while Naxos' *hora* (main village) is a maze of narrow, stepped alleyways of whitewashed Venetian houses, their tiny gardens ablaze with flowers.

SUGGESTED ITINERARIES

Depending on the length of your stay, you might want to see and do the following:

One day
   Spend the day in Athens seeing its museums and ancient sites.
One week
   Spend one day in Athens, two days in the Peloponnese visiting Nafplio/Mycenae and Olympia, and four days in the Cyclades.
Two weeks
   Spend two days in Athens, two days in the Peloponnese, and two days in Central Greece visiting Delphi and Meteora. Follow up with a week of island-hopping through the Cyclades.
One month
   Spend two days in Athens, two days in the Peloponnese; catch an overnight ferry from Patras to Corfu for two days; head to Ioannina and spend two days exploring the Zagorohoria villages of northern Epiros; spend three days travelling back to Athens via Meteora and Delphi. Take a ferry from Piraeus to Chios and spend two weeks island-hopping back through the North-Eastern Aegean Islands, the Dodecanese and the Cyclades.

PLANNING
When to Go

Spring and autumn are the best times to visit. Winter is pretty much a dead loss, unless you're going to take advantage of the cheap skiing. The islands go into hibernation between late November and early April. Hotels and restaurants close up, and buses and ferries operate on drastically reduced schedules.

The cobwebs are dusted off in time for Easter, and conditions are perfect until the end of June. Everything is open, public transport operates normally, but the crowds have yet to arrive. From July until mid-September, it's on for young and old as northern Europe heads for the Mediterranean en masse. If you want to party, this is the time to go. The flip side is that everywhere is packed out, and rooms can be hard to find.

The pace slows down again by about mid-September, and conditions are ideal once more until the end of October.

Maps

Unless you are going to trek or drive, the free maps given out by tourist offices will probably suffice. The best motoring maps are

GREECE

produced by local company Road Editions, which also produces a good trekking series.

What to Bring
In summer, bring light cotton clothing, a sun hat and sunglasses; bring sunscreen too – it's expensive in Greece. In spring and autumn, you will need light jumpers (sweaters) and thicker ones for the evenings.

In winter, thick jumpers and a raincoat are essential. You will need to wear sturdy walking shoes for trekking in the country, and comfortable shoes are a better idea than sandals for walking around ancient sites. An alarm clock for catching early-morning ferries, a torch (flashlight) and a small daypack will also be useful.

TOURIST OFFICES
The Greek National Tourist Organisation (GNTO) is known as EOT in Greece. There is either an EOT office or a local tourist office in almost every town of consequence and on many islands. Most do no more than give out brochures and maps. Popular destinations have tourist police, who can often help in finding accommodation.

Local Tourist Offices
The EOT head office (☎ 01-321 0561/62, fax 325 2895, ✆ gnto@eexi.gr) is at Amerikis 2, Athens 105 64. Other tourist offices are listed through the book.

Tourist Offices Abroad
Australia (☎ 02-9241 1663) 51 Pitt St, Sydney, NSW 2000
Canada (☎ 416-968 2220) 1300 Bay St, Toronto, Ont M5R 3K8
  (☎ 514-871 1535) 1233 Rue de la Montagne, Suite 101, Montreal, Que H3G 1Z2
France (☎ 01 42 60 65 75) 3 Ave de l'Opéra, Paris 75001
Germany (☎ 069-237 735) Neue Mainzer-strasse 22, 60311 Frankfurt
  (☎ 089-222 035) Pacellistrasse 2, W 80333 Munich 2
  (☎ 040-454 498) Abteistrasse 33, 20149 Hamburg 13
  (☎ 030-217 6262) Wittenplatz 3A, 10789 Berlin 30
Italy (☎ 06-474 4249) Via L Bissolati 78-80, Rome 00187
  (☎ 02-860 470) Piazza Diaz 1, 20123 Milan

Japan (☎ 03-3505 5911) Fukuda Bldg West, 5th Floor 2-11-3 Akasaka, Minato-ku, Tokyo 107
UK (☎ 020-7499 4976) 4 Conduit St, London W1R ODJ
USA (☎ 212-421 5777) Olympic Tower, 645 5th Ave, New York, NY 10022
  (☎ 312-782 1084) Suite 160, 168 North Michigan Ave, Chicago, Illinois 60601
  (☎ 213-626 6696) Suite 2198, 611 West 6th St, Los Angeles, California 92668

VISAS & DOCUMENTS
Nationals of Australia, Canada, EU countries, Israel, New Zealand and the USA are allowed to stay in Greece for up to three months without a visa. For longer stays, apply at a consulate abroad or at least 20 days in advance to the Aliens Bureau (☎ 01-770 5711), Leoforos Alexandros 173, Athens. Elsewhere in Greece, apply to the local police authority. Singapore nationals can stay in Greece for 14 days without a visa.

In the past, Greece has refused entry to those whose passport indicates that they have visited Turkish-occupied North Cyprus, though there are reports that this is less of a problem now. To be on the safe side, however, ask the North Cyprus immigration officials to stamp a piece of paper rather than your passport. If you enter North Cyprus from the Greek Republic of Cyprus, no exit stamp is put in your passport.

Driving Licence & Permits
Greece recognises all national driving licences, provided the licence has been held for at least one year. It also recognises an International Driving Permit, which should be obtained before you leave home.

Hostel Card
A Hostelling International (HI) card is of limited use in Greece. The only place you will be able to use it is at the Athens International Youth Hostel.

Student & Youth Cards
The most widely recognised (and thus the most useful) form of student ID is the International Student Identity Card (ISIC). Holders qualify for half-price admission to museums and ancient sites and for discounts at some budget hotels and hostels.

Seniors Cards

See the Senior Travellers section later in this chapter.

EMBASSIES & CONSULATES
Greek Embassies Abroad

Greece has diplomatic representation in the following countries:

Australia (☎ 02-6273 3011) 9 Turrana St, Yarralumla, Canberra, ACT 2600
Canada (☎ 613-238 6271) 76-80 Maclaren St, Ottawa, Ont K2P 0K6
France (☎ 01 47 23 72 28) 17 Rue Auguste Vaquerie, 75116 Paris
Germany (☎ 0228-83010) Koblenzer St 103, 5300 Bonn 2
Italy (☎ 06-854 9630) Via S Mercadante 36, Rome 00198
Japan (☎ 03-340 0871/72) 16-30 Nishi Azabu, 3-chome, Minato-ku, Tokyo 106
New Zealand (☎ 04-473 7775) 5-7 Willeston St, Wellington
South Africa (☎ 021-24 8161) Reserve Bank Bldg, St George's Rd, Cape Town
Turkey (☎ 312-446 5496) Ziya-ul-Rahman Caddesi 9-11, Gazi Osman Pasa 06700, Ankara
UK (☎ 020-7229 3850) 1A Holland Park, London W11 3TP
USA (☎ 202-667 3169) 2221 Massachusetts Ave NW, Washington, DC, 20008

Foreign Embassies in Greece

The following countries have diplomatic representation in Greece:

Australia (☎ 01-644 7303) Dimitriou Soutsou 37, Athens 115 21
Canada (☎ 01-725 4011) Genadiou 4, Athens 115 21
France (☎ 01-339 1000) Leoforos Vasilissis Sofias 7, Athens 106 71
Germany (☎ 01-728 5111) Dimitriou 3 & Karaoli, Kolonaki 106 75
Italy (☎ 01-361 7260) Sekeri 2, Athens 106 74
Japan (☎ 01-775 8101) Athens Tower, Leoforos Messogion 2-4, Athens 115 27
New Zealand (honorary consulate; ☎ 01-771 0112) Semitelou 9, Athens 115 28
South Africa (☎ 01-680 6645) Kifissias 60, Maroussi, Athens 151 25
Turkey (☎ 01-724 5915) Vasilissis Georgiou B 8, Athens 106 74
UK (☎ 01-723 6211) Ploutarhou 1, Athens 106 75
USA (☎ 01-721 2951) Leoforos Vasilissis Sofias 91, Athens 115 21

CUSTOMS

Duty-free allowances in Greece are the same as for other EU countries. Import regulations for medicines are strict; if you are taking medication, make sure you get a statement from your doctor before you leave home. It is illegal, for example, to take codeine into Greece. The export of antiques is prohibited. You can bring in as much foreign currency as you like, but if you want to leave with more than US$1000 in foreign banknotes the money must be declared on entry. It is illegal to bring in more than 100,000 dr, and to leave with more than 20,000 dr.

MONEY

Banks will exchange all major currencies, in either cash or travellers cheques and also Eurocheques. Post offices charge less commission than banks, but won't cash travellers cheques.

All major credit cards are accepted, but only in larger establishments. You'll find ATMs everywhere, particularly in tourist areas.

Currency

The Greek unit of currency is the drachma (dr). Coins come in denominations of five, 10, 20, 50 and 100 dr, while banknotes come in 50, 100, 500, 1000, 5000 and 10,000 dr denominations.

Exchange Rates

country	unit		drachma
Australia	A$1	=	216.27 dr
Canada	C$1	=	251.62 dr
euro	€1	=	337.20 dr
France	1FF	=	51.41 dr
Germany	DM1	=	172.41 dr
Japan	¥100	=	343.81 dr
New Zealand	NZ$1	=	167.89 dr
UK	UK£1	=	560.86 dr
USA	US$1	=	373.22 dr

Costs

Greece is still a cheap country by European standards. A rock-bottom daily budget would be about 7000 dr, which would mean staying in hostels, self-catering and seldom taking buses or ferries. Allow at least 12,000 dr per day if you want your own room and plan to eat out regularly, as well as travelling and seeing the sites. If you want a real holiday – comfortable rooms and restaurants all the way – reckon on 20,000 dr per day.

Tipping & Bargaining

In restaurants the service charge is included on the bill, but it is the custom to leave a small tip – just round off the bill. Accommodation is nearly always negotiable outside peak season, especially if you are staying more than one night. Souvenir shops are another place where substantial savings can be made. Prices in other shops are normally clearly marked and non-negotiable.

Taxes & Refunds

Value-added tax (VAT) varies from 15% to 18%. A tax-rebate scheme applies at a restricted number of shops and stores; look for a Tax Free sign in the window. You must fill in a form at the shop and present it with the receipt at the airport on departure. A cheque will (hopefully) be sent to your home address.

POST & COMMUNICATIONS
Post

Postal rates for cards and small airmail letters (up to 20g) are 140 dr to EU destinations, and 170 dr elsewhere. The service is slow but reliable – five to eight days within Europe and about 10 days to the USA, Australia and New Zealand.

Post offices are usually open 7.30 am to 2 pm. In major cities they stay open until 8 pm and also open 7.30 am to 2 pm on Saturday. Do not wrap up a parcel until it has been inspected at the post office.

Mail can be sent poste restante to any main post office and is held for up to one month. Your surname should be underlined and you will need to show your passport when you collect your mail. Parcels are not delivered in Greece – they must be collected from a post office.

Telephone

The phone system is modern and efficient. All public phone boxes use phonecards, sold at OTE offices and *periptera* (kiosks). Four cards are available: 100 units (1000 dr), 200 units (1800 dr), 500 units (4200 dr) and 1000 units (8200 dr). The 'i' at the top left hand of the dialling panel on public phones brings up the operating instructions in English.

Direct-dial long-distance and international calls can also be made from public phones. Many countries participate in the Home Country Direct scheme, which allows you to access an operator in your home country for reverse-charge calls. A three-minute call to the USA costs 708 dr.

If you're calling Greece from abroad, the country code is ☎ 30. If you're making an international call from Greece, the international access code is ☎ 00.

Fax

Main city post offices have fax facilities.

Email & Internet Access

Greece was slow to embrace the wonders of the Internet, but is now striving to make up for lost time. Internet cafes are springing up everywhere, and are listed under the Information section for cities and islands where available.

There has also been a huge increase in the number of hotels and businesses using email, and addresses also have been listed where available.

INTERNET RESOURCES

There has also been a huge increase in the number of Web sites providing information about Greece.

A good place to start is the 500 Links to Greece listed at www.viking1.com/corfu/link.htm. It has links to a huge range of sites covering everything from accommodation to Zeus. One site that it doesn't provide a link to is www.greektravel.com, front door for an assortment of interesting sites by Matt Barrett.

The Greek Ministry of Culture has put together an excellent site at www.culture.gr with loads of information about museums and ancient sites.

BOOKS
Lonely Planet

Lonely Planet's *Greece* contains more comprehensive information on all the areas covered by this chapter as well as coverage of less-visited areas, particularly in Central and Northern Greece. *Greek Islands* is especially tailored for island-hoppers; if you want to concentrate on specific regions, pick up Lonely Planet's *Corfu & the Ionians* or *Crete* guides. In mid-2001, guides to *Athens* and *Rhodes & the Dodecanese* will be published.

Travel

The ancient Greek traveller Pausanias is acclaimed as the world's first travel writer. His *Guide to Greece* was written in the 2nd century AD and still makes fascinating reading.

History

A Traveller's History of Greece by Timothy Boatswain & Colin Nicholson is probably the best choice for the layperson who wants a good general reference.

General

There are numerous books to choose from if you want to get a feel for the country. *Zorba the Greek* by Nikos Kazantzakis may seem an obvious choice, but read it and you'll understand why it's the most popular of all Greek novels translated into English.

English writer Louis de Bernières has become almost a cult figure following the success of *Captain Corelli's Mandolin*, which tells the emotional story of a young Italian army officer sent to the island of Kefallonia during WWII.

Other modern authors to look out for include Anne Michaels *(Fugitive Pieces)* and Gillian Bouras *(A Foreign Wife* and *Aphrodite and the Others)*.

NEWSPAPERS & MAGAZINES

The main English-language newspaper is the daily *Athens News* (300 dr). The Athens edition of the *International Herald Tribune* (400 dr) carries an eight-page English translation of the popular Greek daily *Kathimerini*.

Foreign newspapers are widely available, although only between April and October in smaller resort areas.

RADIO & TV

There are plenty of radio stations to choose from, especially in Athens, but not many broadcast in English. If you have a shortwave radio, the best frequencies for the World Service are 618, 941 and 1507MHz.

The nine TV channels offer nine times as much rubbish as one channel. You'll find the

occasional American action drama in English (with Greek subtitles). News junkies can get their fix with CNN and Euronews.

PHOTOGRAPHY

Major brands of film are widely available, but quite expensive outside major towns and on the islands.

Never photograph military installations or anything else with a sign forbidding pictures.

TIME

Greece is two hours ahead of GMT/UTC, and three hours ahead on daylight-saving time, which begins at 12.01 am on the last Sunday in March, when clocks are put forward one hour. Clocks are put back an hour at 12.01 am on the last Sunday in September.

Out of daylight-saving time, at noon in Greece it is also noon in Istanbul, 10 am in London, 2 am in San Francisco, 5 am in New York and Toronto, 8 pm in Sydney and 10 pm in Auckland. These times do not make allowance for daylight saving in the other countries.

LAUNDRY

Large towns and some islands have laundrettes. Most charge about 2000 dr to wash and dry a load, whether you do it yourself or leave it to them.

TOILETS

You'll find public toilets at all major bus and train stations, but they are seldom very pleasant. You will need to supply your own paper. In town, a cafe is the best bet, but the owner won't be impressed if you don't buy something.

Warning

Greek plumbing cannot handle toilet paper; always put it in the bin provided.

WOMEN TRAVELLERS

Many foreign women travel alone in Greece. Hassles occur, but they tend to be a nuisance rather than threatening. Violent offences are very rare. Women travelling alone in rural areas are usually treated with respect. In rural areas it's sensible to dress conservatively; it's perfectly OK to wear shorts, short skirts etc in touristy places.

GREECE

GAY & LESBIAN TRAVELLERS

In a country where the church still plays a major role in shaping society's views on issues such as sexuality, it should come as no surprise that homosexuality is generally frowned upon. Although there is no legislation against homosexual activity, it is wise to be discreet and to avoid open displays of togetherness.

This has not prevented Greece from becoming a popular destination for gay travellers. Athens has a busy gay scene, but most people head for the islands – Mykonos and Lesvos in particular. Paros, Rhodes, Santorini and Skiathos also have their share of gay hang-outs.

DISABLED TRAVELLERS

If mobility is a problem, the hard fact is that most hotels, museums and ancient sites are not wheelchair accessible. Lavinia Tours (☎ 031-23 2828), Egnatia 101 (PO Box 11106), Thessaloniki 541 10, has information for disabled people coming to Greece.

SENIOR TRAVELLERS

Elderly people are shown great respect in Greece. There are some good deals available for EU nationals. For starters, those over 60 qualify for a 50% discount on train travel plus five free journeys per year. Take your ID card or passport to a Greek Railways (OSE) office and you will be given a Senior Card. Pensioners also get a discount at museums and ancient sites.

DANGERS & ANNOYANCES

Greece has the lowest crime rate in Europe. Athens is developing a bad reputation for petty theft and scams, but elsewhere crimes are most likely to be committed by other travellers. Drug laws are very strict.

BUSINESS HOURS

Banks are open 8.30 am to 2.30 pm Monday to Thursday, to 2 pm Friday. Some city banks also open 3.30 to 6.30 pm and on Saturday morning. Shops are open 8 am to 1.30 pm and 5.30 to 8.30 pm on Tuesday, Thursday and Friday, and 8 am to 2.30 pm on Monday, Wednesday and Saturday, but these times are not always strictly adhered to. Periptera (kiosks) are open from early morning to midnight. All banks and shops, and most museums and archaeological sites, close during holidays.

PUBLIC HOLIDAYS & SPECIAL EVENTS

Public holidays are as follows:

New Year's Day 1 January
Epiphany 6 January
First Sunday in Lent February
Greek Independence Day 25 March
Good Friday/Easter Sunday March/April
Spring Festival/Labour Day 1 May
Feast of the Assumption 15 August
Okhi Day 28 October
Christmas Day 25 December
St Stephen's Day 26 December

Easter is Greece's most important festival, with candle-lit processions, feasting and firework displays. The Orthodox Easter is 50 days after the first Sunday in Lent.

A number of cultural festivals are also held during the summer months. The most important is the Athens Festival, when plays, operas, ballet and classical music concerts are staged at the Theatre of Herodes Atticus. The festival is held in conjunction with the Epidaurus Festival, which features ancient Greek dramas at the theatre at Epidaurus.

ACTIVITIES
Windsurfing

Sailboards are widely available for hire, priced from 2000 dr an hour. The top spots for windsurfing are Hrysi Akti on Paros, and Vasiliki on Lefkada – reputedly one of the best places in the world to learn.

Skiing

Greece offers some of the cheapest skiing in Europe. There are 16 resorts dotted around the mainland, most of them in the north. They have all the basic facilities and are a pleasant alternative to the glitzy resorts of northern Europe. What's more, there are no package tours. More information is available from the Hellenic Ski Federation (☎ 01-524 0057, fax 524 8821), PO Box 8037, Omonia, Athens 100 10, or from the EOT.

Hiking

The mountainous terrain is perfect for trekkers who want to get away from the crowds.

The popular routes are well marked and well maintained, including the E4 and E6 trans-European treks, which both end in Greece.

If you want someone to do the organising for you, Trekking Hellas (☎ 01-323 4548, fax 325 1474, ✉ trekking@compulink.gr), Filellinon 7, Athens 105 57 offers a range of treks and other adventure activities throughout the country.

LANGUAGE COURSES

If you are serious about learning Greek, an intensive course at the start of your stay is a good way to go about it. Most of the courses are in Athens and are covered in the Athens section later in this chapter. More information about courses is available from EOT offices and Greek embassies.

WORK

Your best chance of finding work is to do the rounds of the tourist hotels and bars at the beginning of the season. The few jobs available are hotly contested, despite the menial work and dreadful pay. EU nationals don't need a work permit, but everyone else does.

ACCOMMODATION

There is a range of accommodation in Greece to suit every taste and pocket. All places to stay are subject to strict price controls set by the tourist police. By law, a notice must be displayed in every room, which states the category of the room and the price for each season. If you think you've been ripped off, contact the tourist police. Prices quoted in this book are for the high season, unless otherwise stated. Prices are about 40% cheaper between October and May.

Camping

Greece has almost 350 camping grounds. Prices vary according to facilities, but reckon on about 1500 dr per person and about 1200 dr for a small tent. Many sites close in winter. Freelance camping is officially forbidden, but often tolerated in remoter areas.

Refuges

Greece has 55 mountain refuges, which are listed in the booklet *Greece Mountain Refuges & Ski Centres*, available free of charge at EOT and EOS (Ellinikos Orivatikos Syndesmos, the Greek Alpine Club) offices.

Hostels

You'll find youth hostels in most major towns and on half a dozen islands. The only place affiliated to Hostelling International (HI) is the excellent Athens International Youth Hostel (☎ 01-523 4170).

Most other youth hostels in Greece are run by the Greek Youth Hostel Organisation (☎ 01-751 9530, fax 751 0616, ✉ y-hostels@otenet.gr), Damareos 75, Athens 116 33. There are affiliated hostels in Athens, Olympia, Patras and Thessaloniki on the mainland, and on the islands of Crete and Santorini. Rates vary from 1600 dr to 2000 dr and you don't have to be a member *to* stay in any of them.

There is a XEN (YWCA) hostel for women in Athens.

Domatia

Domatia are the Greek equivalent of the British bed and breakfast, minus the breakfast. Once upon a time, domatia consisted of little more than spare rooms that families would rent out in summer to supplement their income. Nowadays many domatia are purpose-built appendages to the family house. Rates start at about 6000/9000 dr for singles/doubles.

Hotels

Hotels are classified as deluxe, A, B, C, D or E class. The ratings seldom seem to have much bearing on the price, but expect to pay 6000/9000 dr for singles/doubles in D and E class, and from 10,000/15,000 dr in a decent C-class place with private bathroom.

Some places are classified as pensions and rated differently. Both are allowed to levy a 10% surcharge for stays of less than three nights, but they seldom do. It normally works the other way – you can bargain if you're staying more than one night.

Apartments

Self-contained family apartments are available in some hotels and domatia, particularly on the islands.

Traditional Settlements

Traditional settlements are old buildings of architectural merit that have been converted

GREECE

into tourist accommodation. They are terrific places to stay if you can afford 10,000 dr to 15,000 dr for a double.

Houses & Flats

For long-term rental accommodation in Athens, check the advertisements in the English-language newspapers. In rural areas, ask around in *tavernas*.

FOOD

If Greek food conjures up an uninspiring vision of lukewarm *moussaka* collapsing into a plate of olive oil, take heart – there's a lot more on offer.

Snacks

Greece has a great range of fast-food options for the inveterate snacker. Foremost among them are the *gyros* and the *souvlaki*. The gyros is a giant skewer laden with seasoned meat that grills slowly as it rotates, the meat being steadily trimmed from the outside. Souvlaki are small, individual kebabs. Both are served wrapped in pitta bread with salad and lashings of *tzatziki* (a yogurt, cucumber and garlic dip). Other snacks are pretzel rings, *spanakopitta* (spinach and cheese pie) and *tyropitta* (cheese pie). Dried fruits and nuts are also very popular.

Starters

Greece is famous for its appetisers, known as *mezedes* (literally, 'tastes'). Standards include tzatziki, *melitzanosalata* (aubergine dip), *taramasalata* (fish-roe dip), *dolmades* (stuffed vine leaves), *fasolia* (beans) and *oktapodi* (octopus). A selection of three or four represents a good meal and can be a good option for vegetarians. Most dishes cost between 600 dr and 1000 dr.

Main Dishes

You'll find moussaka (layers of aubergine and mince, topped with bechamel sauce and baked) on every menu, alongside a number of other taverna staples. They include *moschari* (oven-baked veal and potatoes), *keftedes* (meatballs), *stifado* (meat stew), *pastitsio* (macaroni with mince meat and bechamel sauce, baked) and *yemista* (either tomatoes or green peppers stuffed with mince meat and rice). Most main courses cost between 1000 dr and 1600 dr.

The most popular fish are *barbouni* (red mullet) and *ksifias* (swordfish), but they don't come cheap. Prices start at about 3000 dr for a serve. *Kalamaria* (fried squid) is readily available and cheap at about 1400 dr.

Fortunately for vegetarians, salad is a mainstay of the Greek diet. The most popular is *horiatiki salata*, normally listed on English menus as Greek or country salad. It's a mixed salad of cucumbers, peppers, onions, olives, tomatoes and feta (sheep or goat's-milk white cheese).

Desserts

Turkish in origin, most desserts are variations on pastry soaked in honey. Popular ones include *baklava* (thin layers of pastry filled with honey and nuts) and *kadaifi* (shredded wheat soaked in honey).

Restaurants

There are several varieties of restaurants. An *estiatoria* is a straightforward restaurant with a printed menu. A taverna is often cheaper and more typically Greek, and you'll probably be invited to peer into the pots. A *psistaria* specialises in charcoal-grilled dishes. *Ouzeria* (ouzo bars) often have such a good range of mezedes that they can be regarded as eating places.

Kafeneia

Kafeneia are the smoke-filled cafes where men gather to drink coffee, play backgammon and cards and engage in heated political discussion. They are a bastion of male chauvinism. Female tourists tend to avoid them, but those who venture in invariably find they are treated courteously.

Self-Catering

Buying and preparing your own food is easy in Greece. Every town of consequence has a supermarket, as well as fruit and vegetable shops.

DRINKS
Nonalcoholic Drinks

Bottled mineral water is cheap and available everywhere, as are soft drinks and packaged juices.

Alcohol

Greece is traditionally a wine-drinking society. If you're spending a bit of time in the country, it's worth acquiring a taste for retsina (resinated wine). The best (and worst) flows straight from the barrel in the main production areas of Attica and Central Greece. Tavernas charge from 800 dr to 1500 dr for 1L. Retsina is available by the bottle everywhere. Greece also produces a large range of regular wines from traditional grape varieties.

Mythos and Alpha are two Greek beers to look out for. Amstel is the most popular of several northern European beers produced locally under licence. Expect to pay about 200 dr in a supermarket, or 500 dr in a restaurant. The most popular aperitif is the aniseed-flavoured ouzo.

ENTERTAINMENT

The busy nightlife is a major attraction for many travellers. Nowhere is the pace more frenetic than on the islands in high season; Ios and Paros are famous for their raging discos and bars. Discos abound in all resort areas. If you enjoy theatre and classical music, Athens and Thessaloniki are the places to be.

Greeks are great film-goers. Cinemas show films in the original language (usually English) with Greek subtitles.

SPECTATOR SPORTS

Greek men are sports mad. Basketball has almost overtaken soccer as the main attraction. If you happen to be eating in a taverna on a night when a big match is being televised, expect indifferent service.

SHOPPING

Greece produces a vast array of handicrafts, including woollen rugs, ceramics, leather work, hand-woven woollen shoulder bags, embroidery, copperware and carved-wood products.

Getting There & Away

AIR

There are no less than 16 international airports, but most of them handle only summer charter flights to the islands. Athens handles the vast majority of international flights, including all intercontinental flights. Athens has regular scheduled flights to all the European capitals, and Thessaloniki is also well served.

Most flights are with the national carrier, Olympic Airways, or the flag carrier of the country concerned.

Europe

Flying is the fastest, easiest and cheapest way of getting to Greece from northern Europe. What's more, scheduled flights are so competitively priced that it's hardly worth hunting around for charter cheapies.

Olympic Airways, British Airways and Virgin Atlantic all offer 30-day return tickets from London for about UK£240 (midweek departures) in high season, and Olympic and British Airways offer returns to Thessaloniki for about UK£225.

At the time of writing, the cheapest fares were being offered by EasyJet (☎ 0870 600 0000), which was offering London (Luton) to Athens from UK£69 one way.

Charter flights from London to Athens are readily available for UK£99/189 one way/return in high season, dropping to UK£79/129 in low season. Fares are about UK£109/209 to most island destinations in high season. Similar deals are available from charter operators throughout Europe.

Athens is a good place to buy cheap air tickets. Examples of one-way fares include London (25,000 dr), Madrid (73,000 dr), Paris (55,000 dr) and Rome (42,000 dr). Remember to add the international departure tax of 6800 dr.

The USA & Canada

Olympic Airways has daily flights to Athens from New York and up to three a week from Boston. Delta also has daily flights from New York. Apex fares range from US$960 to US$1550. It's worth shopping around for cheaper deals from the major European airlines.

You should be able to get to Athens from Toronto and Montreal for about C$1150 or from Vancouver for C$1500. Olympic has up to five flights a week to Athens from Toronto via Montreal.

Australia

Olympic flies to Athens twice a week from Sydney via Melbourne. Fares range from A$1595 to A$2400.

LAND
Northern Europe

Overland travel between northern Europe and Greece is virtually a thing of the past. Buses and trains can't compete with cheap air fares, and the turmoil in the former Yugoslavia has cut the shortest overland route. All bus and train services now go via Italy and take the ferries over to Greece.

Train Unless you have a Eurail pass, travelling to Greece by train is prohibitively expensive. Greece is part of the Eurail network, and passes are valid on ferries operated by Adriatica di Navigazione and Hellenic Mediterranean Lines from Brindisi to Corfu, Igoumenitsa and Patras.

Neighbouring Countries

Bus The Hellenic Railways Organisation (OSE) has buses from Athens to Istanbul (23,000 dr, 22 hours) at 11 pm every day, and to Tirana (12,600 dr, 21 hours) at 8.30 am every day except Sunday.

Train There are daily trains between Athens and Istanbul for 20,000 dr, leaving Athens at 11.15 pm. The trip takes 23 hours.

Car & Motorcycle The crossing points into Turkey are at Kipi and Kastanies, the crossings into the Former Yugoslav Republic of Macedonia (FYROM) are at Evzoni and Niki, and the Bulgarian crossing is at Promahonas. All are open 24 hours a day. The crossing points to Albania are at Kakavia and Krystallopigi.

Hitching If you want to hitchhike to Turkey, look for a through-ride from Alexandroupolis because you cannot hitchhike across the border.

SEA
Italy

The most popular crossing is from Brindisi to Patras (18 hours), via Corfu (nine hours) and Igoumenitsa (10 hours). There are numerous services. Deck-class fares start at about 7500

dr one way in low season, 12,000 dr in high season. Eurail pass-holders can travel free with both Adriatica di Navigazione and Hellenic Mediterranean. You still need to make a reservation and pay port taxes – L8000 in Italy and 1800 dr in Greece.

There are also ferries to Patras from Ancona, Bari, Trieste and Venice, stopping at either Corfu or Igoumenitsa on the way. In summer there are also ferries from Bari and Brindisi to Kefallonia.

Turkey

There are five regular ferry services between the Greek islands and Turkey: Lesvos-Ayvalık, Chios-Çeşme, Samos-Kuşadası, Kos-Bodrum and Rhodes-Marmaris. All are daily services in summer, dropping to weekly in winter. Tickets must be bought a day in advance and you will be asked to hand over your passport. It will be returned on the boat.

Cyprus & Israel

Salamis Lines and Poseidon Lines operate services from Piraeus to the Israeli port of Haifa, via Rhodes and Lemessos (formerly Limassol) on Cyprus. Deck-class fares from Piraeus are 19,000 dr to Lemessos and 28,000 dr to Haifa. Given the amount of time you'll be spending on board, it's worth getting a cabin – 34,000 dr to Lemessos and 47,000 dr to Haifa. Port tax costs an additional 3000 dr.

Students and travellers aged under 30 qualify for a 20% discount on these fares.

LEAVING GREECE

An airport tax of 6800 dr for international flights is included in air fares. Port taxes are 1800 dr to Italy and 3000 dr to Turkey, Cyprus and Israel.

Getting Around

AIR

Most domestic flights are operated by Olympic Airways and its offshoot, Olympic Aviation. They offer a busy schedule in summer with flights from Athens to 25 islands and a range of mainland cities. Sample fares include Athens-Iraklio for 21,400 dr, Athens-Rhodes for 23,400 dr and Athens-Santorini for 22,200 dr. There are also flights from Thessaloniki to the islands. It is advisable to book at least two weeks in advance, especially in summer. Services to the islands are fairly skeletal in winter. Aegean Air, Air Greece and Cronus Airlines provide competition on a few major routes. Air Manos specialises in package deals to the islands.

These fares include the 3400 dr tax on domestic flights, paid when you buy your ticket.

BUS

Buses are the most popular form of public transport. They are comfortable, they run on time and there are frequent services on all the major routes. Almost every town on the mainland (except in Thrace) has at least one bus a day to Athens. Local companies can get you to all but the remotest villages. Reckon on paying about 1200 dr per hour of journey time. Sample fares from Athens include 8700 dr to Thessaloniki (7½ hours) and 3650 dr to Patras (three hours). Tickets should be bought at least an hour in advance to ensure a seat.

Major islands also have comprehensive local bus networks. In fact, every island with a road has a service of some sort, but they tend to operate at the whim of the driver.

TRAIN

Trains are generally looked on as a poor alternative to bus travel. The main problem is that there are only two main lines: to Thessaloniki and Alexandroupolis in the north and to the Peloponnese. In addition there are a number of branch lines, such as Pyrgos-Olympia and the spectacular Diakofto-Kalavryta mountain railway.

If there are trains going in your direction, they are a good way to travel. Be aware that there are two distinct levels of service: the painfully slow, dilapidated trains that stop at all stations and the faster, modern intercity trains.

The slow trains represent the cheapest form of transport. It may take five hours to crawl from Athens to Patras, but the 2nd-class fare is only 1580 dr. Intercity trains do the trip in just over three hours for 2980 dr – still cheaper than the bus.

Inter-Rail and Eurail passes are valid in Greece, but you still need to make a reservation. In summer, make reservations at least two days in advance.

CAR & MOTORCYCLE

Car is a great way to explore areas that are off the beaten track. Bear in mind that roads in remote regions are often poorly maintained. You'll need a good road map.

You can bring a vehicle into Greece for four months without a carnet – only a Green Card (international third-party insurance) is required.

Average prices for fuel are 255 dr per litre for super, 240 dr for unleaded and 170 dr for diesel.

Most islands are served by car ferries, but they are expensive. Sample fares for small cars from Piraeus include 19,600 dr to Crete and 24,000 dr to Rhodes.

Road Rules

Greek motorists are famous for ignoring the road rules, which is probably why the country has one of the highest road fatality rates in Europe. No casual observer would ever guess that it is compulsory to wear seat belts in the front seats of vehicles, nor that it is compulsory to wear a crash helmet on motorcycles of more than 50cc – always insist on a helmet when renting a motorcycle.

The speed limit for cars is 120km/h on toll roads, 90km/h outside built-up areas and 50km/h in built-up areas. For motorcycles, the speed limit outside built-up areas is 70km/h. Speeding fines start at 30,000 dr.

Drink-driving laws are strict – a blood alcohol content of 0.05% incurs a penalty and over 0.08% is a criminal offence.

Rental

Car hire is expensive, especially from the multinational hire companies. High-season weekly rates with unlimited mileage start at about 110,000 dr for the smallest models, dropping to 90,000 dr in winter – and that's without tax and extras.

You can generally do much better with local companies. Their advertised rates are 25% lower and they're often willing to bargain.

Mopeds, however, are cheap and available everywhere. Most places charge about 3000 dr per day.

Warning If you plan to hire a motorcycle or moped, check that your travel insurance

GREECE

covers you for injury resulting from motorbike accidents. Many policies don't.

Lonely Planet receives a lot of letters complaining about companies hiring out poorly maintained machines. Most insurance policies won't pay out for injuries caused by defective machines.

Automobile Association
The Greek automobile club, ELPA, offers reciprocal services to members of other national motoring associations. If your vehicle breaks down, dial ☎ 104.

BICYCLE
People do cycle in Greece, but you'll need strong leg muscles to tackle the mountainous terrain. You can hire bicycles, but they are not nearly as widely available as cars and motorcycles. Prices range from about 1000 dr to 3000 dr. Bicycles are carried free on most ferries.

HITCHING
The further you are from a city, the easier hitching becomes. Getting out of major cities can be hard work, and Athens is notoriously difficult. In remote areas, people may stop to offer a lift even if you aren't hitching.

BOAT
Ferry
Every island has a ferry service of some sort. They come in all shapes and sizes, from the state-of-the-art 'superferries' that run on the major routes to the ageing open ferries that operate local services to outlying islands.

The hub of the vast ferry network is Piraeus, the main port of Athens. It has ferries to the Cyclades, Crete, the Dodecanese, the Saronic Gulf Islands and the North-Eastern Aegean Islands. Patras is the main port for ferries to the Ionian Islands, while Volos and Agios Konstantinos are the ports for the Sporades.

Some of the smaller islands are virtually inaccessible in winter, when schedules are cut back to a minimum. Services start to pick up in April and are running at full steam from June to September.

Fares are fixed by the government. The small differences in price you may find between ticket agencies are the result of some agencies sacrificing part of their designated commission to qualify as a 'discount service'. The discount seldom amounts to more than 50 dr. Tickets can be bought at the last minute from quayside tables set up next to the boats. Prices are the same, contrary to what you will be told by agencies.

Unless you specify otherwise, you will automatically be sold deck class, which is the cheapest fare. Sample fares from Piraeus include 4800 dr to Mykonos and 5900 dr to Santorini (Thira).

Hydrofoil
Hydrofoils offer a faster alternative to ferries on some routes, particularly to islands close to the mainland. They take half the time, but cost twice as much. Most routes operate only during high season.

Catamaran
High-speed catamarans have rapidly become an important part of the island travel scene. They are just as fast as the hydrofoils – if not faster, and much more comfortable. They are also much less prone to cancellation in rough weather.

Yacht
It's hardly a budget option, but *the* way to see the islands is by yacht. There are numerous places to hire boats, both with and without crew. If you want to go it alone, two crew members must have sailing certificates. Prices start at about US$1300 per week for a four-person boat. A skipper will cost an extra US$800 per week.

LOCAL TRANSPORT
You'll find taxis almost everywhere. Flag fall is 200 dr, followed by 66 dr per kilometre in towns and 120 dr per kilometre outside towns. The rate doubles from midnight to 5 am. There's a surcharge of 300 dr from airports and 160 dr from ports, bus stations and train stations. Luggage is charged at 55 dr per item over 10kg. Taxis in Athens and Thessaloniki often pick up extra passengers along the way (yell out your destination as they cruise by; when you get out, pay what's on the meter, minus what it read when you got in, plus 200 dr).

In rural areas taxis don't have meters, so make sure you agree on a price with the driver before you get in.

GREECE - MAIN FERRY ROUTES

ORGANISED TOURS

Greece has many companies which operate guided tours, predominantly on the mainland, but also on larger islands. The major operators include CHAT, Key Tours and GO Tours, all based in Athens. It is cheaper to travel independently – tours are only worthwhile if you have extremely limited time.

STREET NAMES

Odos means street, *plateia* means square and *leoforos* means avenue. These words are often omitted on maps and other references, so we have done the same throughout this chapter, except when to do so would cause confusion.

Athens Αθήνα

☎ 01 • pop 3.7 million

Ancient Athens ranks alongside Rome and Jerusalem for its glorious past and its influence on Western civilisation, but the modern city is a place few people fall in love with.

However inspiring the Acropolis might be, most visitors have trouble coming to terms with the surrounding urban sprawl, the appalling traffic congestion and the pollution.

However, the city is not without its redeeming features. The Acropolis is but one of many important ancient sites, and the National Archaeological Museum has the world's finest collection of Greek antiquities.

Culturally, Athens is a fascinating blend of East and West. King Otho and the middle class that emerged after independence may have been intent on making Athens a European city, but the influence of Asia Minor is everywhere – the coffee, the kebabs, the raucous street vendors and the colourful markets.

ORIENTATION

Although Athens is a huge, sprawling city, nearly everything of interest to travellers is located within a small area bounded by Omonia Square (Plateia Omonias) to the north, Monastiraki Square (Plateia Monastirakiou) to the west, Syntagma Square (Plateia Syntagmatos) to the east and the Plaka district to the south. The city's two major landmarks, the Acropolis and Lykavittos Hill, can be seen from just about everywhere in this area.

Syntagma is the heart of modern Athens. Flanked by luxury hotels, banks and fast-food restaurants, the square is dominated by the old royal palace – home of the Greek parliament since 1935.

Omonia is slowly being cleaned up following the completion of metro construction, but is still better known for its prostitutes and pickpockets than its neoclassical architecture. The major streets of central Athens all meet here. Panepistimiou (El Venizelou) and Stadiou run parallel south-east to Syntagma, while Athinas leads south to the market district of Monastiraki. Monastiraki is in turn linked to Syntagma by Ermou – home to some of the city's smartest shops – and Mitropoleos.

Mitropoleos skirts the northern edge of Plaka, the delightful old Turkish quarter which was virtually all that existed when Athens was declared the capital of independent Greece. Its labyrinthine streets are nestled on the north-eastern slope of the Acropolis, and most of the city's ancient

sites are close by. It may be touristy, but it's the most attractive and interesting part of Athens and the majority of visitors make it their base.

Streets are clearly signposted in Greek and English. If you do get lost, it's very easy to find help. A glance at a map is often enough to draw an offer of assistance. Anyone you ask will be able to direct you to Syntagma (say SYN-tag-ma).

INFORMATION
Tourist Offices

The main EOT tourist office (☎ 331 0561/62, fax 325 2895, ✉ gnto@eexi.gr) is close to Syntagma at Amerikis 2. It has a useful free map of Athens as well as information about public transport in Athens, including ferry departures from Piraeus. The office is open 9 am to 7 pm Monday to Friday and 9.30 am to 2 pm Saturday.

The EOT office (☎ 969 4500) at the East airport terminal is open 9 am to 7 pm Monday to Friday and 11 am to 5 pm Saturday.

The tourist police (☎ 924 2700) are open 24 hours a day at Dimitrakopoulou 77, Koukaki. Take trolleybus No 1, 5 or 9 from Syntagma. They also have a 24-hour information service (☎ 171).

Money

Most of the major banks have branches around Syntagma, open 8 am to 2 pm Monday to Thursday and 8 am to 1.30 pm Friday. The National Bank of Greece has an automatic exchange machine.

American Express (☎ 324 4975) is at Ermou 2, and Eurochange (☎ 322 0155) has an office nearby at Karageorgi Servias 4. It changes Thomas Cook travellers cheques without commission.

In Plaka, Acropole Foreign Exchange, Kydathineon 23, is open 9 am to midnight daily. The banks at the East and West airport terminals are open 7 am to 9 pm.

Post & Communications

The main post office is at Eolou 100, Omonia (postcode 102 00), which is where mail addressed to poste restante will be sent unless specified otherwise. If you're staying in Plaka, it's best to get mail sent to the Syntagma post office (postcode 103 00). Both are open 7.30 am to 8 pm Monday to Friday, to 2 pm Saturday, and 9 am to 1.30 pm Sunday. Parcels over 2kg going abroad must be posted from the parcels office at Stadiou 4 (in the arcade). They should not be wrapped until they've been inspected.

The OTE telephone office at 28 Oktovriou-Patission 85 is open 24 hours a day. There are also offices at Stadiou 15, Syntagma, and at Athinas 50, south of Omonia. They are open 7 am to 11.30 pm daily.

Email & Internet Access

Internet cafes are popping up like mushrooms all over Athens. Most charge from 1000 dr to 1500 dr per hour of computer time, whether you log on or not. They include:

Skynet Internet Centre
  At the corner of Voulis and Apollonos, Plaka, open 9.30 am to 8.30 pm Monday to Friday and 10 am to 8.30 pm Saturday
Sofokleus.com Internet Café
  Stadiou 5, Syntagma, open 10 am to 10 pm Monday to Saturday and 1 to 11 pm Sunday
Museum Internet Café
  Oktovriou-Patission 46, open 9 am to 2.30 am daily

Travel Agencies

The bulk of the city's travel agencies are around Syntagma square, particularly in the area just south of the square on Filellinon, Nikis and Voulis.

Reputable agencies include STA Travel (☎ 321 1188, fax 321 1194, ✆ robissa@spark.net.gr), Voulis 43, and Etos Travel (☎ 324 1884, fax 322 8447, ✆ usit@usitetos.gr), Filellinon 1. Both these places also issue International Student Identity Cards.

Bookshops

Athens has three good English-language bookshops. The biggest is Eleftheroudakis, which has branches at Panepistimiou 17 and Nikis 4. The others are Pantelides Books, Amerikis 11, and Compendium Books, Nikis 28. Compendium also has a second-hand books section.

Cultural Centres

The British Council (☎ 363 3215), Plateia Kolonaki 17, and the Hellenic American Union (☎ 362 9886), Massalias 22, hold frequent concerts, film shows, exhibitions etc. Both also have libraries.

Laundry

Plaka has a convenient laundry at Angelou Geronta 10, just off Kydathineon near the outdoor restaurants.

Medical & Emergency Services

For emergency medical treatment, ring the tourist police (☎ 171) and they'll tell you where the nearest hospital is. Don't wait for an ambulance – get a taxi. Hospitals give free emergency treatment to tourists. For hospitals with outpatient departments on duty, ring ☎ 106. For first-aid advice, ring ☎ 166. You can get free dental treatment at the Evangelismos Hospital, Ipsilandou 45.

Dangers & Annoyances

Athens has its share of petty crime.

Pickpockets Pickpockets have become a major problem. Their favourite hunting grounds are the metro system and the crowded streets around Omonia, particularly Athinas. The Sunday market on Ermou is another place where it pays to take extra care of your valuables.

Taxi Touts Taxi drivers working in league with some overpriced C-class hotels around Omonia are a problem. The scam involves taxi drivers picking up late-night arrivals, particularly at the airport and Bus Terminal A, and persuading them that the hotel they want to go to is full. The taxi driver will pretend to phone the hotel of choice, announce that it's full and suggest an alternative. You can ask to speak to your chosen hotel yourself, or insist on going where you want.

Bar Scams Lonely Planet receives a steady flow of letters warning about bar scams, particularly around Syntagma. The most popular version runs something like this: friendly Greek approaches solo male traveller and discovers that the traveller knows little about Athens; friendly Greek then reveals that he, too, is from out of town. Why don't they go to this great little bar that he's just discovered and have a beer? They order a drink, and the equally friendly owner then offers another

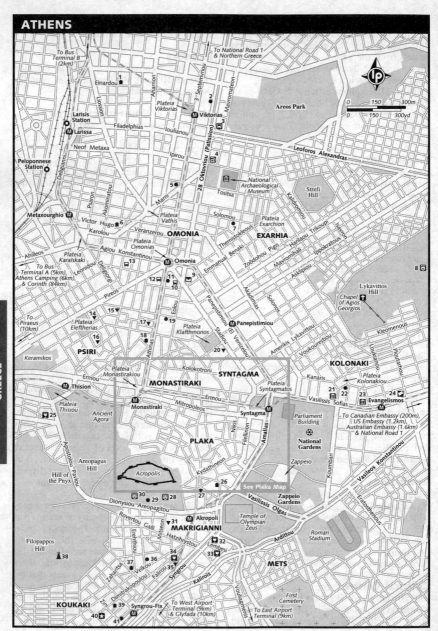

ATHENS

To Bus
Terminal B
(2km)

To National Road 1
& Northern Greece

Areos Park

Einardou   1

Larisis
Station

Larissa

Filadelphias

Ioulianou

Plateia
Viktorias

2

Viktorias

3

Peloponnese
Station

Neof Metaxa

Ipirou

28 Oktovriou (Patission)

Leoforos Alexandras

Strefi
Hill

Metaxourghio

Victor Hugo   6

Karolou

Marni

5

Plateia
Vathis

Tositsa

National
Archaeological
Museum

Solomou

Plateia
Exarchion

Veranzerou   OMONIA

Plateia
Omonias

EXARHIA

Ahilleos

Plateia
Karaiskaki

To Bus
Terminal A (5km),
Athens Camping (6km)
& Corinth (84km)

Agiou Konstantinou

13

Omonia

Pireos

Emmanual Benaki

Zoodohou Pigis

Harilaou Trikoupi

Ippokratous

Lykavittos
Hill

Chapel
of Agios
Georgios

8

To
Piraeus
(10km)

14

15

Plateia
Eleftherias

16

PSIRI

17

18

19

11
10

12

9

Eolou

Panepistimiou (E Venizelou)

Plateia
Klafthmonos

Stadiou

Panepistimiou

Akadimias

Solonos

Amerikis Lykavittou

Voukourestiou

Kleomenous

KOLONAKI

Keramikos

Athinas

20

Plateia
Monastirakiou

Kolokotroni

SYNTAGMA

Plateia
Syntagmatos

Plateia
Kolonakiou

Ermou

Thision

Plateia
Thisiou

25

Ancient
Agora

MONASTIRAKI

Monastiraki

Mitropoleos

Ermou

Nikis

Filellinon

Syntagma

Kanaris

Vasilissis Sofias

21   22

24

Evangelismos

To Canadian Embassy (200m),
US Embassy (1.2km),
Australian Embassy (1.6km)
& National Road 1

Aeropagus
Hill

Hill of
the Pnyx

Acropolis

PLAKA

Kydathineon

Amalias

Parliament
Building

National
Gardens

Zappeio

See Plaka Map

Vasileos Konstantinou

Filopappos
Hill

38

Dionysiou Areopagitou

30   29   28

27

26

Zappeio
Gardens

Vasilissis Olgas

Temple of
Olympian
Zeus

Rovertou Galli

31

MAKRIGIANNI

Akropoli

Hatzihrystou

Roman
Stadium

Ardittou

METS

Erehthiou

37   36

34

35

32

33

Lembesi

Veikou

Syngrou

Kalirois

KOUKAKI

39

Syngrou-Fix

40

41

Dimitrakopoulou

Zin

Falirou

To West Airport
Terminal (9km)
& Glyfada (10km)

To East Airport
Terminal (9km)

First
Cemetery

0   150   300m
0   150   300yd

GREECE

ATHENS

PLACES TO STAY		31	Socrates Prison Taverna	21	Benaki Museum
1	Hostel Aphrodite	35	To 24 Hours	22	British Council
6	Athens International Youth			23	Goulandris Museum of
	Hostel	**OTHER**			Cycladic & Ancient Greek Art
18	Hotel Cecil	2	OTE	24	UK Embassy
26	Hotel Dioskouros	3	Mavromateon Bus Terminal	25	Stavlos
37	Art Gallery Hotel	4	Museum Internet Café	28	Ancient Theatre of Dionysos
39	Marble House Pension	5	Rodon Club	29	Stoa of Eumenes
		7	AN Club	30	Theatre of Herodes Atticus
PLACES TO EAT		8	Lykavittos Theatre	32	Lamda Club
14	Bengal Garden	9	Main Post Office	33	Granazi Bar
15	Pak Bangla Indian Restaurant	10	Bus 091 to Airport	34	Porta Bar
16	Embros	11	Marinopoulos Supermarket	36	Hellaspar Supermarket
17	Fruit & Vegetable Market	12	Bus 049 to Piraeus	38	Monument of Filopappos
20	Vasilopoulou Delicatessen	13	Bus 051 to Bus Terminal A	40	Tourist Police
27	Daphne Restaurant	19	Rembetika Stoa Athanaton	41	Olympic Airways Head Office

drink. Women appear, more drinks are provided and the visitor relaxes as he realises that the women are not prostitutes, just friendly Greeks. The crunch comes at the end of the evening when the traveller is presented with an exorbitant bill and the smiles disappear. The con men who cruise the streets playing the role of the friendly Greek can be very convincing – some people have been taken in more than once.

ACROPOLIS
Most of the buildings now gracing the Acropolis were commissioned by Pericles during the golden age of Athens in the 5th century BC. The site had been cleared for him by the Persians, who destroyed an earlier temple complex on the eve of the Battle of Salamis.

The entrance to the Acropolis is through the **Beule Gate**, a Roman arch that was added in the 3rd century AD. Beyond this is the **Propylaia**, the monumental gate that was the entrance in ancient times. It was damaged by Venetian bombing in the 17th century, but it has since been restored. To the south of the Propylaia is the small, graceful **Temple of Athena Nike**, which is not accessible to visitors.

Standing supreme over the Acropolis is the monument which more than any other epitomises the glory of ancient Greece – the **Parthenon**. Completed in 438 BC, this building is unsurpassed in grace and harmony. To achieve perfect form, its lines were ingeniously curved to counteract unharmonious optical illusions. The base curves upwards slightly towards the ends, and the columns become slightly narrower towards the top, with the overall effect of making them both look straight.

Above the columns are the remains of a Doric frieze, which was partly destroyed by Venetian shelling in 1687. The best surviving pieces are the controversial Elgin Marbles, carted off to Britain by Lord Elgin in 1801. The Parthenon, dedicated to Athena, contained an 11m-tall gold-and-ivory statue of the goddess completed in 438 BC by Phidias of Athens (only the statue's foundations exist today).

To the north is the **Erechtheion** and its much-photographed Caryatids, the six maidens who support its southern portico. These are plaster casts – the originals (except for the one taken by Lord Elgin) are in the site's museum.

The site and museum are open 8 am to 8 pm daily. The combined admission fee is 2000 dr.

SOUTH OF THE ACROPOLIS
The importance of theatre in the life of the Athenian city-state can be gauged from the dimensions of the enormous **Theatre of Dionysos**, just south of the Acropolis. Built between 342 and 326 BC on the site of an earlier theatre, it could hold 17,000 people spread over 64 tiers of seats, of which about 20 survive. The entrance is on Dionysiou Areopagitou. It's open 8.30 am to 2.30 pm daily; admission is 500 dr.

GREECE

The **Stoa of Eumenes**, built as a shelter and promenade for theatre audiences, runs west from the Theatre of Dionysos to the **Theatre of Herodes Atticus**, built in Roman times. It is used for performances during the Athens Festival, but is closed at other times.

TEMPLE OF OLYMPIAN ZEUS
Begun in the 6th century BC, this massive temple took more than 700 years to complete. The Emperor Hadrian eventually finished the job in AD 131. It was the largest temple in Greece, impressive for the sheer size of its 104 Corinthian columns (17m high with a base diameter of 1.7m). The site is just south-east of Plaka, and the 15 remaining columns are a useful landmark for travellers arriving in the city by bus or taxi from the airport. The site is open 8.30 am to 2.30 pm Tuesday to Sunday; admission is 500 dr.

ROMAN STADIUM
The stadium, just east of the temple, hosted the first Olympic Games of modern times in 1896. It was originally built in the 4th century BC as a venue for the Panathenaic athletic contests. The seats were rebuilt in Pentelic marble by Herodes Atticus in the 2nd century AD, and faithfully restored in 1895.

ANCIENT AGORA
The Agora was the marketplace of ancient Athens and the focal point of civic and social life. Socrates spent much time here expounding his philosophy. The main monuments are the well-preserved **Temple of Hephaestus**, the 11th-century **Church of the Holy Apostles** and the reconstructed **Stoa of Attalos**, which houses the site's museum.

The site is open 8 am to 8 pm Tuesday to Sunday (to 5 pm in winter); admission is 1200 dr.

ROMAN AGORA
The Romans built their agora just west of its ancient counterpart. Its principle monument is the wonderful **Tower of the Winds**, built in the 1st century BC by a Syrian astronomer named Andronicus. Each side represents a point of the compass, and has a relief carving depicting the associated wind. The site is open 8.30 am to 2.30 pm Tuesday to Sunday; admission is 500 dr.

MUSEUMS
Athens has no less than 28 museums, displaying everything from ancient treasures to old theatre props. You'll find a complete list at the tourist office. These are the highlights:

National Archaeological Museum
This is the undoubted star of the show – the most important museum in the country, with finds from all the major sites. The crowd-pullers are the magnificent, exquisitely detailed gold artefacts from Mycenae and the spectacular **Minoan frescoes** from Santorini (Thira), which are here until a suitable museum is built on the island. The museum is at 28 Oktovriou-Patission 44, open 8.30 am to 8 pm Tuesday to Sunday and noon to 8 pm on Monday; admission is 2000 dr.

Benaki Museum
This museum, on the corner of Vasilissis Sofias and Koumbari, houses the collection of Antoine Benaki, the son of an Alexandrian cotton magnate named Emmanual Benaki. The collection includes ancient sculpture, Persian, Byzantine and Coptic objects, Chinese ceramics, icons, two El Greco paintings and a superb collection of traditional costumes.

Goulandris Museum of Cycladic & Ancient Greek Art
This private museum was custom-built to display a fabulous collection of Cycladic art, with an emphasis on the early Bronze Age. Particularly impressive are the beautiful marble figurines. These simple, elegant forms, mostly of naked women with arms folded under their breasts, inspired 20th-century artists such as Brancusi, Epstein, Modigliani and Picasso.

It's at Neofytou Douka 4 and is open 10 am to 4 pm daily, except Tuesday and Sunday; admission is 1000 dr.

LYKAVITTOS HILL
Pine-covered Lykavittos is the highest of the eight hills dotted around Athens. From the summit there are all-embracing views of the city, the Attic basin and the islands of Salamis and Aegina – pollution permitting.

The southern side of the hill is occupied by the posh residential suburb of Kolonaki. The main path to the summit starts at the top of

Loukianou, or you can take the funicular railway from the top of Ploutarhou (500 dr).

WHAT'S FREE
Changing of the Guard
Every Sunday at 11 am a platoon of traditionally costumed *evzones* (guards) marches down Vasilissis Sofias, accompanied by a band, to the Tomb of the Unknown Soldier in front of the parliament building on Syntagma.

LANGUAGE COURSES
Try the Athens Centre (☎ 701 2268, fax 701 8603, @ athenscr@compulink.gr), Arhimidous 48, Mets, or the Hellenic American Union (☎ 362 9886, fax 363 3174, @ dtolias@hau.gr), Massalias 22, Pefkakia.

ORGANISED TOURS
Key Tours (☎ 923 3166), Kallirois 4; CHAT Tours (☎ 322 3137), Stadiou 4; and GO Tours (☎ 322 5951), Voulis 31-33, are the main operators. You'll see their brochures everywhere, offering identical tours and prices. They include a half-day bus tour (10,000 dr), which does no more than point out major sights.

SPECIAL EVENTS
The Athens Festival is the city's most important cultural event, running from mid-June to the end of August. It features plays, ballet and classical-music concerts at venues like the Theatre of Herodes Atticus and the Lykavittos Theatre. Information and tickets are available from the Festival Box Office, Stadiou 4.

PLACES TO STAY
Camping
The closest camping ground is *Athens Camping* (☎ 581 4114, 581 1562/63), 7km west of the city centre at Athinon 198 – on the road to Corinth. There are several camping grounds south-east of Athens on the coast road to Cape Sounion.

Hostels
There are a few places around town making a pitch for the hostelling market by tagging 'youth hostel' onto their name. There are some dreadful dumps among them.

There are only a couple of youth hostels worth knowing about. They include the

excellent HI-affiliated *Athens International Youth Hostel* (☎ 523 4170, fax 523 4015, Victor Hugo 16). Location is the only drawback, otherwise the place is almost too good to be true. The spotless rooms, each with bathroom, sleep two to four people. Rates are 1720 dr per person for HI members. If you're not a member, you can either pay 4200 dr to join or 700 dr for a daily stamp.

XEN (YWCA; ☎ 362 4291, Amerikis 11) is an option for women only. Singles/doubles with bathroom are 10,000/12,000 dr. Annual membership costs 1000 dr.

Hotels
Athens is a noisy city and Athenians keep late hours, so an effort has been made to select hotels in quiet areas. Plaka is the most popular place to stay, and it has a good choice of accommodation right across the price spectrum. Rooms fill up quickly in July and August, so it's wise to make a reservation.

Plaka *Student & Travellers' Inn* (☎ 324 4808, fax 321 0065, @ students-inn@ath.forthnet.gr)* right in the heart of Plaka at Kydathineon 16 is a well-run place with spotless rooms. It has beds in large dorms for 4000 dr, four-person dorms for 4500 dr and three-person dorms for 5000 dr. There are also singles/doubles for 8000/11,000 dr. All rooms share communal bathrooms. The place stays open all year, and rooms are heated in winter.

Festos Youth & Student Guest House (☎ 323 2455, @ consolas@hol.gr, Filellinon 18), Filellinon 18, has dorm beds priced from 3000 dr to 3500 dr. The owners have better rooms nearby at *Hotel Dioskouros* (☎ 324 8165, Pittakou 6), where doubles with shared bathroom are 9000 dr.

Plaka also has some good mid-range accommodation. *Acropolis House Pension* (☎ 322 2344, fax 322 6241, Kodrou 6-8) is a beautifully preserved 19th-century house. Singles/doubles with private bathroom are 15,000/18,000 dr. *Hotel Adonis* (☎ 324 9737, fax 323 1602, Kodrou 3), opposite, is a comfortable modern hotel with air-con singles/doubles from 12,000/17,000 dr. It has good views of the Acropolis from the 4th-floor rooms, and from the rooftop bar.

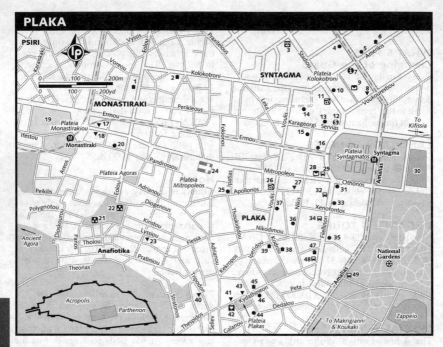

PLAKA

Monastiraki The friendly, family-run *Hotel Tempi* (☎ 321 3175, fax 325 4179, ✉ tempiho tel@travelling.gr, Eolou 29) is a quiet place on the pedestrian precinct part of Eolou. Rooms at the front overlook a small square with a church and a flower market. It's 6000/10,000 dr for singles/doubles with shared bathroom, or 11,500 dr for doubles with private bathroom. It has a small communal kitchen where the guests can prepare breakfast.

The nearby *Hotel Carolina* (☎ 324 3551/52, fax 324 3550, Kolokotroni 55) has singles/doubles with outside bathroom for 7000/11,000 dr, or 8000/12,000 dr with inside bathroom. All the rooms have air-con available.

Hotel Cecil (☎ 321 8005, fax 321 9606, Athinas 39) occupies a fine old classical building with beautiful high, moulded ceilings. It looks immaculate after a complete refit, and singles/doubles with private bathroom are good value at 10,000/15,000 dr, including breakfast.

Koukaki *Marble House Pension* (☎ 923 4058, fax 922 6461, Zini 35A) is a quiet place tucked away on a small cul-de-sac. Rates are 5500/9500 dr for singles/doubles with shared bathroom, or 6500/11,000 dr with private bathroom. All rooms come equipped with bar fridge, ceiling fans and safety boxes for valuables.

Art Gallery Hotel (☎ 923 8376, fax 923 3025, ✉ ecotec@otenet.gr, Erehthiou 5) is a friendly place that's always brimming with fresh flowers. It offers comfortable singles/doubles/triples for 14,000/16,500/19,800 dr with balcony and private bathroom.

Both these places are just a short ride from Syntagma on trolleybus No 1, 5, 9 or 18.

Omonia & Surrounds There are dozens of hotels around Omonia, but most of them are either bordellos masquerading as cheap hotels or uninspiring, overpriced C-class hotels.

Hostel Aphrodite (☎ 881 0589, fax 881 6574, ✉ hostel-aphrodite@ath.forthnet.gr, Einardou 12) is a fair way north of Omonia,

PLAKA

PLACES TO STAY		41	Plaka Psistaria	22	Tower of the Winds
1	Hotel Tempi	43	Byzantino	24	Athens Cathedral
2	Hotel Carolina			25	National Welfare Organisation
6	XEN (YWCA) Hostel	**OTHER**		26	Skynet Internet Centre
38	Hotel Adonis	3	OTE	28	Syntagma Post Office
39	Acropolis House Pension	4	Eleftheroudakis Books	29	Buses to Airport
45	Student & Travellers' Inn	5	Pantilides Books	30	Parliament
47	Festos Youth & Student	7	Tourist Office (EOT)	31	ETOS Travel
	Guest House	9	Parcel Post Office	32	Bus 040 to Piraeus
		10	Athens Festival Box Office	33	Olympic Airways
PLACES TO EAT		11	Sofokleos.com Internet Café	34	Buses to Cape Sounion
8	Brazil Coffee Shop	12	National Bank of Greece	35	OSE Office (Train Tickets)
17	Savas	13	Eurochange	36	Compendium Books
18	Thanasis	14	Pan Express Travel	37	STA Travel
23	Eden Vegetarian	15	Eleftheroudakis Books	42	Brettos (bar)
	Restaurant	16	American Express	44	Laundrette
27	Furin Kazan Japanese	19	Flea Market	46	Acropole Foreign Exchange
	Restaurant	20	Centre of Hellenic Tradition	48	Trolley Stop for Plaka
40	Ouzeri Kouklis	21	Roman Agora	49	Bus 024 to Bus Terminal B

but it's only 10 minutes from the train stations. It's a long-standing favourite with travellers, with Internet access and a bar. Dorm beds are priced from 3500 dr. There are also singles/doubles with shared bathroom for 6000/10,000 dr, and doubles with private bathroom for 11,000 dr.

PLACES TO EAT
Plaka
For most people, Plaka is the place to be. It's hard to beat the atmosphere of dining out beneath the floodlit Acropolis.

You do, however, pay for the privilege – particularly at the outdoor restaurants around the square on Kydathineon. The best of this bunch is *Byzantino (Kydathineon 20)*, which prices its menu more reasonably and is popular with Greek family groups. The nearby *Plaka Psistaria (Kydathineon 28)* has a range of gyros and souvlakia to eat there or take away.

Ouzeri Kouklis (Tripodon 14) is an old-style ouzeri with an oak-beamed ceiling, marble tables and wicker chairs. It serves only mezedes, which are brought round on a large tray for you to take your pick. They include flaming sausages – ignited at your table – and cuttlefish for 1200 dr, as well as the usual dips for 600 dr. The whole selection, enough for four hungry people, costs 9800 dr.

Vegetarian restaurants are thin on the ground in Athens. *Eden Vegetarian Restaurant (Lyssiou 12)* is one of only three. The Eden has been around for years, substituting soya products for meat in tasty vegetarian versions of moussaka and other Greek favourites. Reckon on 8000 dr for two people.

For a real treat, head to *Daphne Restaurant (☎ 322 7971, Lysikratous 4)*. It's an exquisitely restored 1830s neoclassical mansion decorated with frescoes from Greek mythology. The menu includes regional specialities like rabbit cooked in mavrodaphne wine. Reckon on about 10,000 dr per person. It's open every night from 7 pm.

Syntagma
Fast food is the order of the day around busy Syntagma with an assortment of Greek and international offerings.

Anyone suffering from a surfeit of Greek salad and souvlaki should head for *Furin Kazan Japanese Fast-Food Restaurant (Apollonos 2, Syntagma)*. It has noodle dishes from 1800 dr and rice dishes from 1600 dr. It's open 11.30 am to 5.30 pm Monday to Saturday.

Follow your nose to the *Brazil Coffee Shop* on Voukourestiou for the best coffee in town.

South of the Acropolis
To 24 Hours (Syngrou 44) is a great favourite with Athenian night owls. As the name suggests, it's open 24 hours. It calls itself a *patsadakia*, which means that it specialises in

GREECE

patsas (tripe soup), but it always has a wide selection of taverna dishes.

Socrates Prison *(Mitseon 20)* is not named after the philosopher, but after the owner – who reckons the restaurant is his prison. It's a stylish place with an imaginative range of mezedes from 850 dr and main dishes from 1500 dr.

Monastiraki

There are some excellent cheap places to eat around Monastiraki, particularly for gyros and souvlaki fans. **Thanasis** and **Savas**, opposite each other at the bottom end of Mitropoleos, are the places to go.

Psiri

There are loads of possibilities in Psiri, just north-west of Monastiraki. Once rated as 'Athens at its most clapped out', the district has undergone an amazing transformation in the past two years. The narrow streets are now dotted with numerous trendy ouzeris, tavernas and music bars, particularly the central area between Plateia Agion Anargyron and Plateia Iroön.

If none of the places grabs your attention as you wander around, try **Embros** *(Plateia Agion Anargyron 4)*. It's a popular spot with seating in the square, and a choice of about 20 mezedes. They include delicious cheese croquettes (1150 dr) and chicken livers wrapped in bacon (1600 dr).

The streets north of Psiri, around Plateia Eletherias, have been adopted by the city's Bangladeshi community and it's the place to head for a good curry and a cold beer. Try **Bengal Garden** *(Korinis 12)* or the smarter **Pak Bangla Indian Restaurant** *(Menandrou 13)*.

Self-Catering

Supermarkets are few and far between in central Athens. Those that do exist are marked on the main Athens map. **Vasilopoulou** *(Stadiou 19)* is an excellent delicatessen with a good selection of cold meats and cheeses. For the best range of fresh fruit and vegetables, head for the **markets** on Athinas.

ENTERTAINMENT

Friday's edition of the *Athens News* carries a 16-page weekly entertainment guide, while the *Kathimerini* supplement that accompa-

nies the *International Herald Tribune* has daily listings.

Discos & Bars

Discos operate in central Athens only between October and April. In summer, the action moves to the coastal suburbs of Glyfada and Ellinikon.

Most bars around Plaka and Syntagma are places to avoid, especially if there are guys outside touting for customers. One place that's recommended is **Brettos** *(Kydathineon 41)*, a delightful old family-run place right in the heart of Plaka. Huge old barrels line one wall, and the shelves are stocked with an eye-catching collection of coloured bottles.

Most bars in Athens have music as a main feature. Thisio is a good place to look, particularly on Iraklidon. **Stavlos** *(Iraklidon 10)* occupies an amazing old rabbit warren of a building.

Gay Bars

The greatest concentration of gay bars is to be found on the streets off Syngrou, south of the Temple of Olympian Zeus. Popular spots include the long-running **Granazi Bar** *(Lembesi 20)* and the more risque **Lamda Club** *(Lembesi 15)*. Lesbians should check the nearby **Porta Bar** *(Falirou 10)*.

Rock & Jazz Concerts

The **Rodon Club** *(Marni 24)*, north of Omonia, hosts touring international rock bands, while local bands play at the **AN Club** *(Solomou 20, Exarhia)*.

Rembetika Clubs

Rembetika Stoa Athanaton *(☎ 321 4362, Sofokleous 19)* above the meat market is a good place to check, although it's closed from mid-May to the end of September. For the rest of the year, it's open 3 to 7.30 pm daily, except Sunday, and from midnight to 6 am.

Folk Dancing

The **Dora Stratou Dance Company** performs at its theatre on Filopappos Hill at 10.15 pm every night from mid-May to October, with additional performances at 8.15 pm on Wednesday. Tickets are 1500 dr. Filopappos

Hill is west of the Acropolis, off Dionysiou Areopagitou. Bus No 230 from Syntagma will get you there.

Sound-and-Light Show

Athens' endeavour at this spectacle is not one of the world's best. There are shows in English every night at 9 pm from April to October at the theatre on the *Hill of the Pnyx* (☎ 322 1459). Tickets are 1500 dr. The Hill of the Pnyx is opposite Filopappos Hill, and the show is timed so that you can cross straight to the folk dancing.

SPECTATOR SPORTS

Almost half of the 18 soccer teams in the Greek first division are based in Athens or Piraeus. The most popular are Olympiakos (Piraeus), Panathinaikos (Athens), which plays at the Olympic Stadium on alternate Sundays, AEK (Athens), and PAOK (Thessaloniki). Fixtures and results are listed in the *Athens News*.

SHOPPING

The National Welfare Organisation shop, on the corner of Apollonos and Ipatias, Plaka, is a good place to go shopping for handicrafts. It has top-quality goods and the money goes to a good cause – the organisation was formed to preserve and promote traditional Greek handicrafts.

The Centre of Hellenic Tradition, Pandrossou 36, Plaka, has a display of traditional and modern handicrafts from each region of Greece. Most of the items are for sale.

GETTING THERE & AWAY
Air

Athens' dilapidated airport, Ellinikon, is 9km south of the city. There are two main terminals: West for all Olympic Airways flights, and East for all other flights. The airport's old military terminal is dusted off for charter flights in peak season.

Facilities are equally primitive at all the terminals. Nothing is likely to change, however, until the new international airport at Spata (21km east of Athens) opens in 2002.

The Olympic Airways head office (☎ 926 7251/54) is at Syngrou 96. Much more convenient is the office at Filellinon 13, near Syntagma.

Bus

Athens has two main intercity bus stations. The EOT gives out schedules for both with departure times, journey times and fares.

Terminal A, north-west of Omonia at Kifissou 100, has departures to the Peloponnese, the Ionian Islands and western Greece. To get there, take bus No 051 from the junction of Zinonos and Menandrou, near Omonia. Buses run every 15 minutes from 5 am to midnight.

Terminal B is north of Omonia off Liossion and has departures to Central and Northern Greece as well as to Evia. To get there, take bus No 024 from outside the main gate of the National Gardens on Amalias. EOT misleadingly gives the terminal's address as Liossion 260, which turns out to be a small workshop. Liossion 260 is where you should get off the bus. Turn right onto Gousiou and you'll see the terminal at the end of the road.

Buses for Attica leave from the Mavromateon terminal at the junction of Alexandras and 28 Oktovriou-Patission.

Train

Athens has two train stations, about 200m apart on Deligianni, about 1km north-west of Omonia. Trains to the Peloponnese leave from the Peloponnese station, while trains to the north leave from Larisis station – as do all international services.

Services to the Peloponnese include eight trains to Patras, four of which are intercity express (2980 dr, 3½ hours), while services north include 10 trains a day to Thessaloniki, five of which are intercity express (8250 dr, six hours). The 7 am service from Athens is express right through to Alexandroupolis, arriving at 7 pm. There are also trains to Volos and Halkida on Evia.

The easiest way to get to the stations is on Metro Line 2 to Larissa, outside Larisis station. The Peloponnese station is across the footbridge at the southern end of Larisis station. Tickets can be bought at the stations or at the OSE offices at Filellinon 17, Sina 6 and Karolou 1.

Car & Motorcycle

National Rd 1 is the main route north from Athens. It starts at Nea Kifissia. To get there from central Athens, take Vasilissis Sofias from Syntagma and follow the signs. National

Rd 8, which begins beyond Dafni, is the road to the Peloponnese. Take Agiou Konstantinou from Omonia.

The northern reaches of Syngrou, just south of the Temple of Olympian Zeus, are packed solid with car-rental firms.

Hitching

Athens is the most difficult place in Greece to hitchhike from. Your best bet is to ask the truck drivers at the Piraeus cargo wharves. Otherwise, for the Peloponnese, take a bus from Panepistimiou to Dafni, where National Rd 8 begins. For Northern Greece, take the metro to Kifissia, then a bus to Nea Kifissia and walk to National Rd 1.

Ferry

See the Piraeus section later in this chapter for information on ferries to/from the islands.

GETTING AROUND
To/From the Airport

There is a 24-hour express-bus service between central Athens and both the East and West terminals, also calling at the special charter terminal when in use.

Service No E91 leaves Stadiou, near Omonia, every 20 minutes from 6 am to 9 pm, every 40 minutes from 9 pm until 12.20 am, and then hourly through the night. It stops at Syntagma (outside the post office) five minutes later. The trip takes from 30 minutes to an hour, depending on traffic. The return service is No E92. The fare is 250 dr (500 dr from midnight to 6 am), and you pay the driver. There are also express buses between the airport and Plateia Karaïskaki in Piraeus.

A taxi from the airport to Syntagma should cost from 1500 dr to 2500 dr, depending on the time of day.

Bus & Trolleybus

Blue-and-white suburban buses operate from 5 am to midnight and charge a flat rate of 120 dr. Route numbers and destinations, but not the actual routes, are listed on the free EOT map.

The map does, however, mark the routes of the yellow trolleybuses, making them easy to use. They also run from 5 am to midnight and cost 120 dr.

There are special buses that operate 24 hours a day to Piraeus. Bus No 040 leaves from the corner of Syntagma and Filellinon, and No 049 leaves from the Omonia end of Athinas. They run every 20 minutes from 6 am to midnight, and then hourly.

Tickets can be bought from ticket kiosks and regular periptera. Once on a bus, you must validate your ticket by putting it into a machine; the penalty for failing to do so is 4800 dr.

Metro

Although sections of the long-awaited new metro system finally came on line in late 1999, much work remains to be done before the system becomes fully operational – supposedly before the Olympics in 2004.

Line 1 runs from Piraeus (Great Harbour) to the northern suburb of Kifissia, with useful stops at Monastiraki, Omonia (city centre) and Plateia Viktorias (National Archaeological Museum).

Line 2 has useful stops at Larissa (for the train stations), Omonia, Panepistimiou and Syntagma (city centre). Line 3 will eventually run north-east from Monastiraki to Stavros, where it will connect with trains to the international airport at Spata.

Ticket prices are 150 dr for most journeys, including Monastiraki-Piraeus. There are ticket machines and ticket booths at all stations, and validating machines at platform entrances. The penalty for travelling without a validated ticket is 4800 dr.

Trains operate between 5 am and midnight.

Taxi

Athenian taxis are yellow. The flag fall is 200 dr, with a 160 dr surcharge from ports and train and bus stations, and a 300 dr surcharge from the airport. After that, the day rate (tariff 1 on the meter) is 66 dr per kilometre. The rate doubles between midnight and 5 am (tariff 2 on the meter). Baggage is charged at the rate of 55 dr per item over 10kg. The minimum fare is 500 dr, which covers most journeys in central Athens.

Around Athens

PIRAEUS Πειραιάς
☎ 01 • pop 171,000
Piraeus has been the port of Athens since classical times. These days it's little more

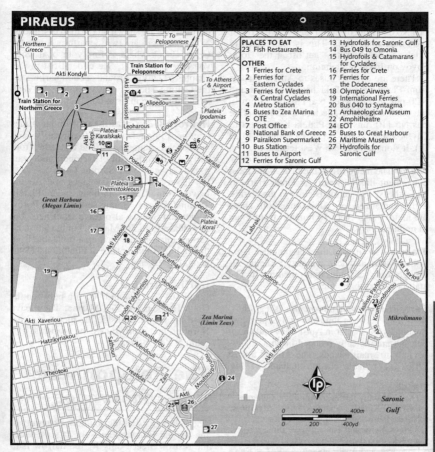

PIRAEUS

To Northern Greece

To Peloponnese

Train Station for Peloponnese

Akti Kondyli

To Athens & Airport

Train Station for Northern Greece

Akti Kalimassioti

Alipedou

Plateia Ipodamias

Gounari

Leoharous

Plateia Karaiskaki

Akti Tzelepi

Poseidonos

Aristateos

Karaoli

Plateia Themistokleous

Tsamadou

Vasileos Georgiou

Filonos

Sotiros

Plateia Korai

Great Harbour (Megas Limin)

Akti Miaouli

Notara

Kolokotroni

Merarhias

Bouboulinas

Sotiros

Labraki

Skouze

Filellinon

Indón Polytehniou

Tríkoupi

Zea Marina (Limin Zeas)

Akti Xaveriou

Kantharou

Plateia Korai

Hatzikyriakou

Afendouli

Akti

Theotoki

Freatidas

Zan

Akti Koundouroti

Moutsopoulou

Sahtouri

Akti Koundourou

Vas Pavlou

Vasilisis Pavlou

Akti Koundourou

Mikrolimano

Saronic Gulf

GREECE

0   200   400m
0   200   400yd

PLACES TO EAT
23 Fish Restaurants

OTHER
1   Ferries for Crete
2   Ferries for Eastern Cyclades
3   Ferries for Western & Central Cyclades
4   Metro Station
5   Buses to Zea Marina
6   OTE
7   Post Office
8   National Bank of Greece
9   Pairaikon Supermarket
10 Bus Station
11 Buses to Airport
12 Ferries for Saronic Gulf
13 Hydrofoils for Saronic Gulf
14 Bus 049 to Omonia
15 Hydrofoils & Catamarans for Cyclades
16 Ferries for Crete
17 Ferries for the Dodecanese
18 Olympic Airways
19 International Ferries
20 Bus 040 to Syntagma
22 Archaeological Museum
24 EOT
25 Buses to Great Harbour
26 Maritime Museum
27 Hydrofoils for Saronic Gulf

than an outer suburb of the space-hungry capital, linked by a mish-mash of factories, warehouses and apartment blocks. The streets are every bit as traffic-clogged as Athens, and behind the veneer of banks and shipping offices most of Piraeus is pretty seedy. The only reason to come here is to catch a ferry or hydrofoil.

Orientation & Information

Piraeus consists of a peninsula surrounded by harbours. The most important of them is the Great Harbour. All ferries leave from here, as well as hydrofoil and catamaran services to

Aegina and the Cyclades. There are dozens of shipping agents around the harbour, as well as banks and a post office.

Zea Marina, on the other side of the peninsula, is the main port for hydrofoils to the Saronic Gulf Islands (except Aegina). North-east of here is the picturesque Mikrolimano (small harbour), lined with countless fish restaurants. There's a tourist office (☎ 452 2586) at Zea Marina.

Getting There & Away

Bus There are two 24-hour bus services between central Athens and Piraeus. No 049

runs from Omonia to the Great Harbour, and bus No 040 runs from Syntagma to the tip of the Piraeus peninsula. This is the service to catch for Zea Marina – get off at the Hotel Savoy on Iroön Politehniou.

There are express buses to Athens airport from Plateia Karaïskaki between 5 am and 8.20 pm, and between 6 am and 9.25 pm in the other direction. The fare is 250 dr. Blue bus No 110 runs from Plateia Karaïskaki to Glyfada and Voula every 15 minutes (120 dr). It stops outside the West terminal.

Metro The metro offers the fastest and most convenient link between the Great Harbour and Athens. The station is close to the ferries, at the northern end of Akti Kalimassioti. There are metro trains every 10 minutes from 5 am to midnight.

Train All services to the Peloponnese from Athens start and terminate at Piraeus, although some schedules don't mention it. The station is next to the metro.

Ferry The following information is a guide to departures between June and mid-September. Schedules are similar in April, May and October, but are radically reduced in winter – especially to small islands. The Athens tourist office has a reliable schedule, updated weekly.

Cyclades
    There are daily ferries to Amorgos, Folegandros, Ios, Kimolos, Kythnos, Milos, Mykonos, Naxos, Paros, Santorini, Serifos, Sifnos, Sikinos, Syros and Tinos; two or three ferries a week to Iraklia, Shinoussa, Koufonisi, Donoussa, and Anafi; none to Andros or Kea.
Dodecanese
    There are daily ferries to Kalymnos, Kos, Leros, Patmos and Rhodes; three a week to Karpathos and Kassos; and weekly services to the other islands.
North-Eastern Aegean
    There are daily ferries to Chios, Lesvos (Mytilini), Ikaria and Samos; and two a week to Limnos.
Saronic Gulf Islands
    There are daily ferries to Aegina, Poros, Hydra and Spetses all year.
Crete
    There are two boats a day to Iraklio; daily services to Hania and Rethymno; and three a week to Agios Nikolaos and Sitia.

The departure points for the various ferry destinations are shown on the map of Piraeus. Note that there are two departure points for Crete. Check where to find your boat when you buy your ticket. See under Boat in this chapter's Getting Around section earlier and the Getting There & Away sections for each island for more information.

Hydrofoil & Catamaran Minoan Lines operate Flying Dolphins (hydrofoils) and high-speed catamarans to the Cyclades from early April to the end of October, and year-round services to the Saronic Gulf.

All services to the Cyclades and Aegina leave from Great Harbour, near Plateia Themistokleous. Some services to Poros, Hydra and Spetses also leave from here, but most leave from Zea Marina. For the latest departure information, pick up a timetable from the Flying Dolphin office at Filellinon 3 (Syntagma) in Athens.

Getting Around
Local bus Nos 904 and 905 run between the Great Harbour and Zea Marina. They leave from the bus stop beside the metro at Great Harbour, and drop you by the maritime museum at Zea Marina.

The Peloponnese
Η Πελοπόννησος

The Peloponnese is the southern extremity of the rugged Balkan peninsula. It's linked to the rest of Greece only by the narrow Isthmus of Corinth, and this has long prompted people to declare the Peloponnese to be more an island than part of the mainland. It technically became an island after the completion of the Corinth Canal across the isthmus in 1893, and it is now linked to the mainland only by road and rail bridges.

The Peloponnese is an area rich in history. The principal site is Olympia, which is the birthplace of the Olympic Games, but there are many other sites which are worth seeking out. Epidaurus, Corinth and Mycenae in the north-east are all within easy striking distance of the pretty Venetian town of Nafplio.

In the south are the magical old Byzantine towns of Monemvasia and Mystras. The rugged Mani Peninsula is famous for its spectacular wild flowers in spring, as well as for the bizarre tower settlements sprinkled across its landscape.

The beaches south of Kalamata are some of the best in Greece.

PATRAS Πάτρα
☎ 061 ● pop 153,300
Patras is Greece's third-largest city and the principal port for ferries to Italy and the Ionian Islands. It's not particularly exciting and most travellers hang around only long enough for transport connections.

Orientation & Information
The city is easy to negotiate and is laid out on a grid stretching uphill from the port to the old *kastro* (castle). Most services of importance to travellers are to be found along the waterfront, known as Othonos Amalias, in the middle of town and Iroön Politehniou to the north. All the various shipping offices are to be found along here. The train station is right in the middle of town on Othonos Amalias, and the bus station is close by.

PATRAS

PLACES TO STAY
20 Hotel Rannia
23 Pension Nicos

PLACES TO EAT
7 Europa Centre

OTHER
1 Customs
2 Tourist Police
3 EOT
4 OTE
5 Minoan Lines
6 Kronos Supermarket
8 Adriatica
9 Boats to Ionian Islands
10 Superfast Ferries
11 Strintzis
12 Med Link Lines
13 First-Aid Centre
14 Main Bus Station
15 ANEK
16 Olympic Airways
17 Archaeological Museum
18 Post Office
19 Laundrette
21 National Bank of Greece
22 Buses to Zakynthos
24 Kronos Supermarket
25 Rocky Racoon Music Bar
26 Kastro

GREECE

The tourist office (☎ 620 353) is inside the port fence off Iroön Politehniou, and the tourist police (☎ 451 833) are upstairs in the embarkation hall.

Money The National Bank of Greece on Plateia Trion Symahon has a 24-hour automatic exchange machine.

Post & Communications The post office is on the corner of Zaïmi and Mezonos. There's a telephone office opposite the tourist office at the port. For Internet access, head inland to the Rocky Racoon Music Bar, Gerokostopoulou 56. It's open 9 am to 3 am daily.

Things to See & Do
There are great views of Zakynthos and Kefallonia from the Venetian **kastro**, which is reached by the steps at the top of Agiou Nikolaou.

Places to Stay & Eat
Most travellers go to *Pension Nicos (☎ 623 757)*, up from the waterfront on the corner of Patreos and Agiou Andreou 121. Its doubles with shared facilities are 6500 dr, and singles/doubles with bathroom are 4000/7000 dr.

C-class *Hotel Rannia (☎ 220 114, fax 220 537, Riga Fereou 53)* facing Plateia Olgas has comfortable air-con singles/doubles with TV for 10,000/15,000 dr – 8000/12,000 dr outside peak season.

The *Europa Centre (Othonos Amalias 10)* is a convenient cafeteria-style place close to the international ferry dock. It has a range of taverna dishes as well as spaghetti (from 900 dr) and a choice of vegetarian meals (900 dr).

Getting There & Away
For transport from Athens, see that city's Getting There & Away section earlier in this chapter.

The best way to travel to Athens is by train. The buses may be faster, but they drop you a long way from the city centre at Terminal A on Kifissou. This can be a real hassle if you're arriving in Athens after midnight – when there are no connecting buses to the city centre, leaving newcomers at the mercy of the notorious Terminal A taxi drivers.

The trains take you close to the city centre, five minutes from Syntagma on the new metro system.

Bus Buses to Athens (3650 dr, three hours) run every 30 minutes, with the last at 9.45 pm. There are also 10 buses a day to Pyrgos (for Olympia) and two to Kalamata.

Train There are nine trains a day to Athens. Four are slow trains (1580 dr, five hours) and five are intercity express (2580 dr, 3½ hours). The last intercity train leaves at 6 pm. Trains also run south to Pyrgos and Kalamata.

Ferry There are daily ferries to Kefallonia (3450 dr, four hours), Ithaki (3500 dr, six hours) and Corfu (6000 dr, 10 hours). Services to Italy are covered in the Getting There & Away section at the start of this chapter. Ticket agents line the waterfront.

DIAKOFTO-KALAVRYTA RAILWAY
This spectacular rack-and-pinion line climbs up the deep gorge of the Vouraikos River from the small coastal town of Diakofto to the mountain resort of **Kalavryta**, 22km away. It is a thrilling journey, with dramatic scenery all the way. There are four trains a day in each direction.

Diakofto is one hour east of Patras on the main train line to Athens.

CORINTH
☎ 0741 • pop 27,400
Modern Corinth is an uninspiring town which gives the impression that it has never quite recovered from the devastating earthquake of 1928. It is, however, a convenient base from which to visit nearby ancient Corinth.

Places to Stay & Eat
Corinth Beach Camping (☎ 27 967) is about 3km west of town. Buses to ancient Corinth can drop you there.

Corinth's budget hotels are a grim bunch. The least awful of them is *Hotel Apollon (☎ 22 587, Pirinis 18)* near the train station, even though it doubles as a brothel. From the outside the place looks to be on the verge of collapse, but the rooms have been redecorated and are reasonable value at 5000/7000 dr for singles/doubles with bathroom.

If you can afford it, head for the friendly family-run *Hotel Ephira* (☎ 24 021, fax 24 514, *Ethnikis Antistaseos 52*). It costs 9000/14,500 dr for clean air-con singles/doubles with bathroom.

Taverna O Theodorakis near the port on the side street next to the Hotel Corinthos is a lively place specialising in fish.

Getting There & Away

Bus Corinth has two main bus stations. There are buses to Athens (1500 dr, 1½ hours) every 30 minutes from the bus station on the corner of Ermou and Koliatsou, on the south-eastern side of the park in the city centre. Buses to Nafplio leave from the junction of Ethnikis Antistaseos and Aratou, while buses to other parts of the Peloponnese leave from a new bus station on the southern side of town. Hourly buses to ancient Corinth (240 dr, 20 minutes) leave from Koliatsou, north-west of the central park.

Train There are 14 trains a day to Athens, five of them intercity services. There are also trains to Kalamata, Nafplio and Patras.

ANCIENT CORINTH & ACROCORINTH

The sprawling ruins of ancient Corinth lie 7km south-west of the modern city. Corinth (Κόρινθος) was one of ancient Greece's wealthiest and most wanton cities. When Corinthians weren't clinching business deals, they were paying homage to Aphrodite in a temple dedicated to her, which meant they were frolicking with the temple's sacred prostitutes. The only ancient Greek monument remaining here is the imposing **Temple of Apollo**; the others are Roman. Towering over the site is Acrocorinth, the ruins of an ancient citadel built on a massive outcrop of limestone.

Both sites are open 8 am to 6 pm daily. Admission is 1200 dr for ancient Corinth and free for Acrocorinth.

NAFPLIO Ναύπλιο
☎ 0752 • pop 11,900

Nafplio ranks as one of Greece's prettiest towns. The narrow streets of the old quarter are filled with elegant Venetian houses and neoclassical mansions.

There's a small municipal tourist office (☎ 24 444) on 25 Martiou in the modern part

of town. It's open 9 am to 1.30 pm and 4.30 to 9 pm daily. The bus station is on Syngrou, the street which separates the old town from the new.

Palamidi Fortress

There are terrific views of the old town and the surrounding coast from this ruined hill-top fortress. The climb is strenuous – there are almost 1000 steps – so start early and take water with you. The fortress is open 8 am to 4.30 pm Monday to Friday, and 8 am to 2.30 pm weekends; admission is 800 dr.

Places to Stay & Eat

The cheapest rooms are in the new part of town along Argous, the road to Argos.

Hotel Economou (☎ 23 955, *Argonafton 22*) is run by the manager of the former youth hostel, now closed. Two rooms have been set up as dorms, with beds for 2500 dr. Argonafton runs off Argous.

Most people prefer to stay in the old part of town, where there are numerous signs for domatia. Singles/doubles cost from 5000/8000 dr. Stylish *Hotel Byron* (☎ 22 351, fax 26 338, *e byronhotel@otenet.gr, Platanos 2*) has beautifully furnished singles for 13,000 dr, and doubles range from 16,000 dr to 22,000 dr.

The old town has dozens of restaurants. Most close in winter, when the choice shrinks to a few long-standing favourites like *Taverna Paleo Arhontiko* (☎ 22 449) on the corner of Ypsilandou and Sofroni. Reservations are essential on Friday and Saturday nights. Reckon on 6000 dr for two, plus wine.

Another popular spot is the *Mezedopoleio O Noulis*. It serves a fabulous range of mezes (snacks) which can easily be combined into a meal. Check the *saganaki flambé*, ignited with Metaxa (brandy) as it reaches your table.

Getting There & Away

There are hourly buses to Athens (2650 dr, 2½ hours) via Corinth, as well as services to Argos (for Peloponnese connections), Mycenae and Epidaurus.

EPIDAURUS Επίδαυρος

The crowd-puller at this site is the huge and well-preserved **Theatre of Epidaurus**, but don't miss the more peaceful **Sanctuary of Asclepius** nearby. Epidaurus was regarded as

GREECE

the birthplace of Asclepius, the god of healing, and the sanctuary was once a flourishing spa and healing centre. The setting alone would have been enough to cure many ailments.

The site is open 8 am to 5 pm daily, to 7 pm in summer; admission is 1500 dr.

You can enjoy the theatre's astounding acoustics first-hand during the Epidaurus Festival from mid-June to mid-August.

Getting There & Away
There are two buses a day from Athens (2250 dr, 2½ hours), as well as three a day from Nafplio (600 dr, 40 minutes). During the festival, there are excursion buses from Nafplio and Athens.

MYCENAE Μυκήνες
Mycenae was the most powerful influence in Greece for three centuries until about 1200 BC. The rise and fall of Mycenae is shrouded in myth, but the site was settled as early as the sixth millennium BC. Historians are divided as to whether the city's eventual destruction was wrought by invaders or internal conflict between the Mycenaean kingdoms. Described by Homer as 'rich in gold', Mycenae's entrance, the **Lion Gate**, is Europe's oldest monumental sculpture.

Excavations have uncovered the palace complex and a number of tombs. The so-called **Mask of Agamemnon**, discovered by Heinrich Schliemann in 1873, now holds pride of place at the National Archaeological Museum in Athens along with other finds from the site.

The site is open 8 am to 7 pm daily; admission is 1500 dr.

Places to Stay
Most people visit on day trips from Nafplio, but there are several hotels in the modern village below the site. The *Belle Helene Hotel* (☎ 76 255, fax 76 179) has singles/doubles for 5000/7500 dr.

Getting There & Away
There are buses from Argos and Nafplio.

SPARTA Σπάρτη
☎ 0731 • pop 14,100
The bellicose Spartans sacrificed all the finer things in life to military expertise and left no monuments of any consequence. Ancient Sparta's forlorn ruins lie amid olive groves at the northern end of town. Modern Sparta is a neat, unspectacular town, but it's a convenient base from which to visit Mystras.

Orientation & Information
Sparta is laid out on a grid system. The main streets are Paleologou, which runs north-south through the town, and Lykourgou, which runs east-west. The tourist office (☎ 24 852) is in the town hall on the main square, Plateia Kentriki. It's open 8 am to 2.30 pm Monday to Friday.

Places to Stay & Eat
Camping Paleologou Mystras (☎ 22 724), 2km west of Sparta on the road to Mystras, is a friendly, well-organised site with good facilities – including a swimming pool. It's open all year. Buses to Mystras can drop you off there.

There's a good choice of hotels back in town. The popular family-run *Hotel Cecil* (☎ 24 980, fax 81 318, Palaeologou 125) has singles/doubles with bathroom and TV for 8000/10,000 dr.

The *Restaurant Elysse* (Palaeologou 113) offers Lakonian specialities like *chicken bardouniotiko* (1300 dr), which is chicken cooked with onions and feta cheese.

Getting There & Away
The bus terminal is at the eastern end of Lykourgou. There are 10 buses a day to Athens (3900 dr, four hours), three to Monemvasia and two to Kalamata. There are also frequent buses to Mystras (250 dr, 30 minutes).

MYSTRAS Μυστράς
Mystras, 7km from Sparta, was once the shining light of the Byzantine world. Its ruins spill from a spur of Mt Taygetos, crowned by a mighty fortress built by the Franks in 1249. The streets of Mystras are lined with palaces, monasteries and churches, most of them dating from the period between 1271 and 1460, when the town was the effective capital of the Byzantine Empire.

The site is open 8 am to 7 pm daily. Admission is 1200 dr, which includes entrance to the museum (closed Monday). You'll need to take an entire day to do this vast

GREECE

place justice. Take a taxi or hitch a ride to the upper Fortress Gate and work your way down. Take some water.

MONEMVASIA Μονεμβασία
☎ 0732

Monemvasia is no longer an undiscovered paradise, but mass tourism hasn't lessened the impact of one's first encounter with this extraordinary old town – nor the thrill of exploring it.

Things to See

Monemvasia occupies a great outcrop of rock that rises dramatically from the sea opposite the village of Gefyra. It was separated from the mainland by an earthquake in AD 375 and access is by a causeway from Gefyra. From the causeway, a road curves around the base of the rock for about 1km until it comes to a narrow L-shaped tunnel in the massive fortifying wall. You emerge, blinking, in the **Byzantine town**, hitherto hidden from view.

The cobbled main street is flanked by stairways leading to a complex network of stone houses with tiny walled gardens and courtyards. Steps (signposted) lead to the ruins of the **fortress** built by the Venetians in the 16th century. The views are great, and there is the added bonus of being able to explore the Byzantine **Church of Agia Sophia**, perched precariously on the edge of the cliff.

Places to Stay & Eat

There is no budget accommodation in Monemvasia, but there are domatia in Gefyra as well as cheap hotels.

Basic *Hotel Akrogiali* (☎ 61 360), opposite the National Bank of Greece, has singles/doubles with shower for 6000/9000 dr.

If your budget permits, treat yourself to a night in one of the beautifully restored traditional settlements in Monemvasia. The pick of them is *Malvasia Guest Houses* (☎ 61 113, fax 61 722), with singles for 9000 dr, and doubles from 12,000 dr to 15,000 dr. Prices include a generous breakfast.

The *Taverna O Botsalo* is the place to go for a hearty meal in Gefyra, while *To Kanoni*, on the right of the main street in Monemvasia, has an imaginative menu.

Getting There & Away

Bus There are four buses a day to Athens (5800 dr, six hours), travelling via Sparta, Tripolis and Corinth.

Ferry In July and August, there are at least two hydrofoils a day to Piraeus via the Saronic Gulf Islands.

GYTHIO Γύθειο
☎ 0731 • pop 4900

Gythio, once the port of ancient Sparta, is an attractive fishing town at the head of the Lakonian Gulf. It is the gateway to the rugged Mani Peninsula to the south.

The main attraction is the picturesque islet of **Marathonisi**, linked to the mainland by a causeway. According to mythology it is ancient Cranae, where Paris (a prince of Troy) and Helen (the wife of Menelaus of Sparta) consummated the love affair that sparked the Trojan War. An 18th-century tower on the islet has been turned into a **museum** of Mani history.

Places to Stay & Eat

Meltemi Camping (☎ 22 833) is the pick of the sites along the coast south of town. Buses to Areopoli can drop you there.

You'll find plenty of domatia signs around town. They include *Xenia Rooms to Rent* (☎ 22 719), opposite the causeway to Marathonisi. It has singles/doubles with bathroom for 4000/6000 dr. The nearby *Saga Pension* (☎ 23 220, fax 24 370) charges 7000/10,000 dr for singles/doubles with TV and breakfast.

The waterfront is lined with countless fish tavernas with very similar menus. For something completely different, head inland to the tiny *General Store & Wine Bar* (☎ 24 113, Vasileos Georgiou 67). You'll find an unusually varied and imaginative menu featuring dishes like orange and pumpkin soup (600 dr) and fillet of pork with black pepper and ouzo (2800 dr).

Getting There & Away

Bus There are five buses a day to Athens (4700 dr, 4¼ hours) via Sparta (750 dr, one hour), five to Areopoli (500 dr, 30 minutes), two to Gerolimenas (1150 dr, two hours), and one to the Diros Caves (700 dr, one hour).

GREECE

Ferry There are daily ferries to Kythira (1600 dr, two hours) in summer, continuing twice a week to Kastelli-Kissamos on Crete (5100 dr, seven hours). Tickets are sold at Golden Ferries (☎ 22 996, fax 22 410) opposite the tourist office on Vasileos Pavlou.

THE MANI

The Mani is divided into two regions, the Lakonian (inner) Mani in the south and Messinian (outer) Mani in the north-west below Kalamata.

Lakonian Mani
☎ 0733

The Lakonian Mani is wild and remote, its landscape dotted with the dramatic stone tower houses that are a trademark of the region. They were built as refuges from the clan wars of the 19th century. The best time to visit is in spring, when the barren countryside briefly bursts into life with a spectacular display of wild flowers.

The region's principal village is **Areopoli**, about 30km south-west of Gythio. There are a number of fine towers on the narrow, cobbled streets of the old town at the lower end of the main street, Kapetan Matapan.

Just south of here are the magnificent **Diros Caves**, where a subterranean river flows. The caves are open 8 am to 5.30 pm from June to September, closing at 2.30 pm from October to May. Admission is 3500 dr.

Gerolimenas, 20km farther south, is a tiny fishing village built around a sheltered bay. **Vathia**, a village of towers built on a rocky peak, is 11km south-east of Gerolimenas. Beyond Vathia, the coastline is a series of rocky outcrops sheltering pebbled beaches.

Places to Stay & Eat There are no camping grounds in the Lakonian Mani.

In Areopoli, there are basic singles/doubles for 4000/6000 dr at *Perros Bathrellos Rooms* (☎ 51 205) on Kapetan Matapan. It's above the popular *Taverna Barbar Petros*. The *Hotel Kouris* (☎ 51 340) on the main square charges 7500/9500 dr with bathroom.

In Gerolimenas, comfortable singles/doubles with bathroom at *Hotel Akrogiali* (☎ 54 204) go for 8000/12,000 dr. It also has a good restaurant.

Getting There & Around There are five buses a day from Areopoli to Sparta via Gythio.

Areopoli is the focal point of the local bus network. There are three buses a day to Itilo, two a day to the Diros Caves and Gerolimenas, and occasional buses to Vathia.

Crossing to the Messinian Mani involves changing buses at Itilo.

Messinian Mani
☎ 0721

The Messinian Mani runs north along the coast from Itilo to Kalamata. The beaches here are some of the best in Greece, set against the dramatic backdrop of the Taygetos mountains.

Itilo, the medieval capital of all the Mani, is split by a ravine that is the traditional dividing line between inner and outer Mani.

The picturesque coastal village of **Kardamyli**, 37km south of Kalamata, is the starting point for walks up the **Taygetos Gorge**. It takes about 2½ hours to walk to the deserted **Monastery of the Saviour**. Strong footwear is essential and take plenty of water.

Stoupa, 10km south of Kardamyli, has a great beach and is a popular package destination in summer.

Places to Stay & Eat There are several camping grounds along the coast, including two at Stoupa.

There are numerous domatia around Kardamyli with singles/doubles for 5000/8000 dr. *Stavros Bravacos* (☎ 73 326) has doubles with kitchen facilities for 9000 dr. The popular *Taverna Perivolis* is one of nine tavernas around the village.

Accommodation in Stoupa is monopolised by package operators in summer. *Hotel Stoupa* (☎ 54 308) on the road into town has doubles with bathroom for 11,000 dr. *Taverna Akrogiali* has a great setting overlooking the main beach.

Getting There & Away There are two buses a day from Kalamata to Itilo, stopping at Kardamyli and Stoupa.

OLYMPIA Ολυμπία
☎ 0624

The site of ancient Olympia lies 500m beyond the modern town, surrounded by the green foothills of Mt Kronion. There is a well-

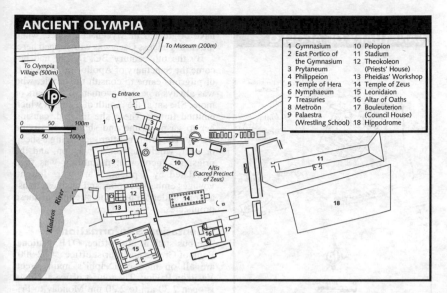

ANCIENT OLYMPIA

To Museum (200m)

To Olympia
Village (500m)

Entrance

1 Gymnasium	10 Pelopion
2 East Portico of	11 Stadium
the Gymnasium	12 Theokoleon
3 Prytaneum	(Priests' House)
4 Philippeion	13 Pheidias' Workshop
5 Temple of Hera	14 Temple of Zeus
6 Nymphaeum	15 Leonidaion
7 Treasuries	16 Altar of Oaths
8 Metroön	17 Bouleuterion
9 Palaestra	(Council House)
(Wrestling School)	18 Hippodrome

0   50   100m
0   50   100yd

Kladeos River

Altis
(Sacred Precinct
of Zeus)

organised municipal tourist office on the main street, open 9 am to 9 pm daily between June and September, and 8 am to 2.45 pm Monday to Saturday the rest of the year. It also changes money.

Things to See

In ancient times, Olympia was a sacred place of temples, priests' dwellings and public buildings, as well as being the venue for the quadrennial Olympic Games. The first Olympics were staged in 776 BC, reaching the peak of their prestige in the 6th century BC. The city-states were bound by a sacred truce to stop fighting for three months and compete.

The site is dominated by the immense, ruined **Temple of Zeus**, to whom the games were dedicated. The site is open 8 am to 7 pm Monday to Friday, and 8.30 am to 3 pm weekends. Admission is 1200 dr. There's also a **museum** north of the archaeological site. It keeps similar hours and admission is also 1200 dr. Allow a whole day to see both.

Places to Stay & Eat

There are three good camping grounds to choose from. The most convenient is *Camping Diana* (☎ 22 314), 250m west of town. It has excellent facilities and a pool.

The *youth hostel* (☎ 22 580, Praxitelous Kondyli 18) has dorm beds for 1700 dr, including hot showers.

Pension Achilleys (☎ 22 562, Stefanopoulou 4) has singles/doubles with shared bathroom for 3000/6000 dr.

Fast Food Vassilakis at the corner of Spiliopoulou and Karamanli is better value than most places in town with pasta from 1000 dr and grilled meats from 1500 dr.

Getting There & Away

There are four buses a day to Olympia from Athens (5900 dr, 5½ hours). There are also regular buses and trains to Olympia from Pyrgos, 24km away on the coast.

Central Greece

Central Greece has little going for it in terms of attractions – with the notable exceptions of Delphi and surroundings.

DELPHI Δελφοί
☎ 0265 • pop 2400

Like so many of Greece's ancient sites, the setting at Delphi – overlooking the Gulf of Corinth from the slopes of Mt Parnassos – is

GREECE

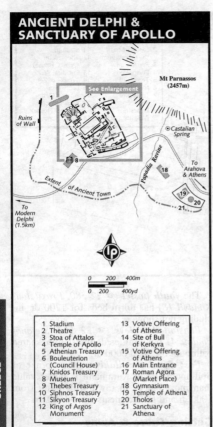

ANCIENT DELPHI & SANCTUARY OF APOLLO

1 Stadium	13 Votive Offering
2 Theatre	of Athens
3 Stoa of Attalos	14 Site of Bull
4 Temple of Apollo	of Kerkyra
5 Athenian Treasury	15 Votive Offering
6 Bouleuterion	of Athens
(Council House)	16 Main Entrance
7 Knidos Treasury	17 Roman Agora
8 Museum	(Market Place)
9 Thebes Treasury	18 Gymnasium
10 Siphnos Treasury	19 Temple of Athena
11 Sikyon Treasury	20 Tholos
12 King of Argos	21 Sanctuary of
Monument	Athena

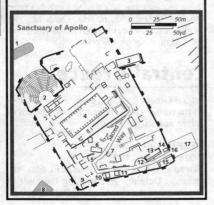

stunning. The Delphic oracle is thought to have originated in Mycenaean times, when the earth goddess Gaea was worshipped here.

By the 6th century BC, Delphi had become the Sanctuary of Apollo and thousands of pilgrims came to consult the oracle, who was always a peasant woman of 50 years or more. She sat at the mouth of a chasm which emitted fumes. These she inhaled, causing her to gasp, writhe and shudder in divine frenzy. The pilgrim, after sacrificing a sheep or goat, would deliver a question, and the priestess' incoherent mumbling was then translated by a priest. Wars were fought, voyages embarked upon, and business transactions undertaken on the strength of these prophecies.

Orientation & Information

The bus station, post office, OTE, National Bank of Greece and tourist office (☎ 82 900) are all on modern Delphi's main street, Vasileon Pavlou. The tourist office at No 44 is open 7.30 am to 2.30 pm Monday to Friday. The ancient site is 1.5km east of modern Delphi.

Sanctuary of Apollo

The **Sacred Way** leads up from the entrance of the site to the **Temple of Apollo**. It was here that the oracle supposedly sat, although no chasm, let alone vapour, has been detected. The path continues to the theatre and stadium. Opposite this sanctuary is the **Sanctuary of Athena** (free admission) and the much-photographed **tholos**, a 4th-century BC columned rotunda of Pentelic marble.

The site is open 7.30 am to 7.15 pm Monday to Friday, and 8.30 am to 2.45 pm weekends and public holidays. The museum is open similar hours. Entry to each is 1200 dr.

Places to Stay & Eat

There are lots of hotels in town, starting with *Hotel Tholos* (*☎/fax 82 268, Apollonos 31*). It has singles/doubles with bathroom for 5000/9000 dr. It's open from March to November and on Friday and Saturday in winter. *Hotel Parnassos* (*☎ 82 321, Vasileon Pavlou and Frederikis 32*) charges 8000/10,000 dr with breakfast.

The food is good value at *Taverna Vakhos* next to the Hotel Tholos.

Getting There & Away

There are five buses a day to Delphi from Athens (2900 dr, three hours).

Northern Greece

Northern Greece covers the regions of Epiros, Thessaly, Macedonia and Thrace. It includes some areas of outstanding natural beauty, such as the Zagoria region of north-western Epiros.

IGOUMENITSA Ηγουμενίτσα
☎ 0665 • pop 6800

Igoumenitsa, opposite the island of Corfu, is the main port of north-western Greece. Few people stay any longer than it takes to buy a ticket out. The bus station is on Kyprou. To get there from the ferries, follow the waterfront (Ethnikis Antistasis) north for 500m and turn up El Venizelou. Kyprou is two blocks inland and the bus station is on the left.

Places to Stay & Eat

If you get stuck for the night, you'll find signs for *domatia* around the port. The D-class *Egnatia* (☎ 23 648, Eleftherias 2) has comfortable rooms for 8500/11,500 dr with private bathroom.

Bilis (☎ 26 214, Agion Apostolon 15) opposite the Corfu ferry quay is handy for a quick meal.

Getting There & Away

Bus Services include nine buses a day to Ioannina (1900 dr, two hours), and four a day to Athens (8850 dr, 8½ hours).

Ferry There are international services to the Italian ports of Ancona, Bari, Brindisi, Trieste and Venice. Ticket agents are opposite the port.

Ferries to Corfu (1400 dr, 1½ hours) operate every hour between 5 am and 10 pm.

IOANNINA Ιωάννινα
☎ 0651 • pop 90,000

Ioannina is the largest town in Epiros, sitting on the western shore of Lake Pamvotis. In Ottoman times, it was one of the most important towns in the country.

Orientation & Information

The town centre is around Plateia Dimokratias where the main streets of the new town meet. All facilities of importance to travellers are nearby.

The helpful EOT office (☎ 25 086) is set back on a small square at Napoleon Zerva 2, 100m to the south-west along Dodonis. It's open 7.30 am to 2.30 pm and 5.30 to 8.30 pm Monday to Friday, and 9 am to 1 pm Saturday. Robinson Travel (☎ 29 402), 8th Merarhias Gramou 10, specialises in treks in the Zagoria region.

For Internet access, try the Giannena Club, 100m from the tourist office at Stoa Saka 30-32.

Things to See

The **old town** juts out into the lake on a small peninsula. Inside the impressive fortifications lies a maze of winding streets flanked by traditional Turkish houses.

The **Nisi** (island) is a serene spot in the middle of the lake, with four monasteries set among the trees. Ferries to the island leave from just north of the old town. They run half-hourly in summer and hourly in winter. The fare is 200 dr.

Places to Stay & Eat

Camping Limnopoula (☎ 25 265) is on the lakeside 2km north of town.

The cheapest hotel is *Agapi Inn* (☎ 20 541, Tsirigoti 6) near the bus station. Basic singles/doubles cost 5000/7000 dr. Next door is the co-owned *Hotel Paris*, which has more comfortable singles/doubles for 6000/9000 dr. There are *domatia* on the island.

There are several restaurants outside the entrance to the old town. *To Manteio Psistaria* is recommended.

Getting There & Away

Ioannina has two flights a day to Athens (18,400 dr) and one servicing Thessaloniki (12,100 dr).

The main bus terminal is 300m north of Plateia Dimokratias on Zossimadon, the northern extension of Markou Botsari. Services include 12 buses a day to Athens (7700 dr, seven hours), nine to Igoumenitsa, five to Thessaloniki and three to Trikala via Kalambaka.

GREECE

ZAGORIA & VIKOS GORGE
☎ 0653

The Zagoria (Zagória) region covers a large expanse of the Pindos Mountains north of Ioannina. It's a wilderness of raging rivers, crashing waterfalls and deep gorges. Snowcapped mountains rise out of dense forests. The remote villages that dot the hillsides are famous for their impressive grey-slate architecture.

The fairytale village of **Monodendri** is the starting point for treks through the dramatic **Vikos Gorge**, with its awesome sheer limestone walls. It's a strenuous 7½-hour walk from Monodendri to the twin villages of **Megalo Papingo** and **Mikro Papingo**. The trek is very popular and the path is clearly marked. Ioannina's EOT office has information.

Other walks start from **Tsepelovo**, near Monodendri.

Places to Stay & Eat

There are some wonderful places to stay, but none of them come cheap. The options in Monodendri include the traditional *Monodendri Pension & Restaurant* (☎ 71 300). Doubles are 9000 dr. *Pension Gouris* (☎ 094-789 909) in Tsepelovohas is a delightful place with doubles for 12,000 dr. The owner, Alexis, also runs a shop and restaurant and can advise on treks.

Xenonas tou Kouli (☎ 41 138) is one of several options in Megalo Papingo. Rates start at 12,000 dr for doubles. The owners are official EOS guides. The only rooms in Mikro Papingo are at *Xenonas Dias* (☎ 41 257), a beautifully restored mansion with doubles for 11,000 dr. It has a restaurant specialising in charcoal grills.

Getting There & Away

Buses to the Zagoria leave from the main bus station in Ioannina. There are buses to Monodendri on weekdays at 6 am and 4.15 pm; to Tsepelovo on Monday, Wednesday and Friday at 6 am and 3 pm; and to the Papingo villages on Monday, Wednesday and Friday at 6 am and 2.30 pm.

TRIKALA Τρίκαλα

Trikala is a major transport hub, but otherwise has little of interest. Eight buses a day run between Trikala and Athens (5400 dr, 5½ hours).

There are also six buses a day to Thessaloniki, two to Ioannina and hourly buses to Kalambaka (for Meteora).

METEORA Μετέωρα
☎ 0432

Meteora is an extraordinary place. The massive, sheer columns of rock that dot the landscape were created by wave action millions of years ago. Perched precariously atop these seemingly inaccessible outcrops are monasteries that date back to the late 14th century.

Meteora is just north of the town of Kalambaka, on the Ioannina-Trikala road. The rocks behind the town are spectacularly floodlit at night. **Kastraki**, 2km from Kalambaka, is a charming village of red-tiled houses just west of the monasteries.

Things to See

There were once monasteries on each of the 24 pinnacles, but only five are still occupied. They are Megalou Meteorou (Metamorphosis, open 9 am to 1 pm and 3 to 6 pm, closed Tuesday), Varlaam (open 9 am to 1 pm and 3.30 to 6 pm, closed Friday), Agiou Stefanou (open 9 am to 1 pm and 3 to 5 pm daily), Agias Triados (open 9 am to 5 pm, closed Thursday), Agiou Nikolaou (open 9 am to 5 pm daily) and Agias Varvaras Rousanou (open 9 am to 6 pm, closed Wednesday). Admission is 500 dr for each monastery; free for Greeks.

Meteora is best explored on foot, following the old paths where they exist. Allow a whole day to visit all of the monasteries and take food and water. Women must wear skirts that reach below their knees, men must wear long trousers, and arms must be covered.

Places to Stay & Eat

Kastraki is the best base for visiting Meteora. *Vrachos Camping* (☎ 22 293), on the edge of the village, is an excellent site.

There are dozens of *domatia* in town, charging from 4000/6000 dr for singles/doubles. *Hotel Sydney* (☎/fax 23 079) on the road into town from Kalambaka has comfortable doubles with bathroom for 9000 dr.

In Kalambaka, *Koka Roka Rooms* (☎ 24 554) at the beginning of the path to Agia Triada is a popular travellers place. Doubles

METEORA

Ypapanti
(closed to the public)

0   250   500m
0   250   500yd

Megalou Meteorou
(Grand Meteora)

Varlaam

Agiou Nikolaou Anapafsa

Agias Varvaras
Rousanou   Psaropetra

Boufidis
Camping

Agiou Antoniou
(closed to
the public)

Kastraki

Panagia

Bantovas

Agias Triados
(Holy Trinity)

Agiou Stefanou

Vrachos
Camping

Kalambaka

To
Ioannina

To
Trikala

with bath are 8000 dr; the taverna downstairs is good value. Telephone for a lift from the bus or train station.

Getting There & Away

Kalambaka is the hub of the transport network. There are frequent buses to Trikala and two a day to Ioannina. Local buses shuttle constantly between Kalambaka and Kastraki; five a day continue to Metamorphosis.

Trains between Kalambaka and Volos weren't operating at the time of research. The line was being upgraded and services were scheduled to resume in 2001. These trains connect with trains from Athens and Thessaloniki at Paleofarsalos.

THESSALONIKI Θεσσαλονίκη
☎ 031 • pop 750,000

Thessaloniki, also known as Salonica, is Greece's second-largest city. It's a bustling, sophisticated place with good restaurants and a busy nightlife. It was once the second city of Byzantium, and there are some magnificent Byzantine churches, as well as a scattering of Roman ruins.

Orientation

Thessaloniki is laid out on a grid system. The main thoroughfares – Tsimiski, Egnatia and Agiou Dimitriou – run parallel to Nikis, on the waterfront. Plateias Eleftherias and Aristotelous, both on Nikis, are the main squares. The city's most famous landmark is the White Tower (no longer white) at the eastern end of Nikis.

The train station is on Monastiriou, the westerly continuation of Egnatia beyond Plateia Dimokratias, and the airport is 16km to the south-east. The old Turkish quarter is north of Athinas.

Information

Tourist Offices The EOT office (☎ 271 888), Plateia Aristotelous 8, is open 8.30 am to 8 pm Monday to Friday, and 8.30 am to 2 pm Saturday. The tourist police (☎ 554 871) are at Dodekanisou 4, 5th floor, open 7.30 am to 11 pm daily.

Money The National Bank and the Commercial Bank have branches on Plateia Dimokratias. The branch of the National Bank of Greece at Tsimiski 11 is open at weekends for currency exchange. American Express (☎ 269 521) is at Tsimiski 19.

Post & Communications The main post office is at Aristotelous 26 and the OTE telephone office is at Karolou Dil 27.

Email & Internet Access Globus Internet Café (☎ 232 901) is a long-established place near the Roman Agora at Amynta 12.

Laundry Bianca Laundrette, just north of the Arch of Galerius on Antoniadou, charges 1400 dr to wash and dry a load.

Medical Services There is a first-aid centre (☎ 530 530) at Navarhou Koundourioti 6.

Things to See

The **archaeological museum**, at the eastern end of Tsimiski, houses a superb collection of treasures from the royal tombs of Philip II. It is open 8 am to 7 pm Tuesday to Friday

GREECE

THESSALONIKI

GREECE

KASTRA

University
Campus

Hospital

To Pilgrims'
Office (250m)

International
Exhibition
Fairground

To Airport
(16km)

Angelaki-

Ethniki Amynis

Plateia
Navarinou

Alex Svolou

Agias Sofias

Karolou Dil

Aristotelous

Ermou

Venizelou

Ionos Dragoumi

Tsimiski

Plateia
Aristotelous

Plateia
Eleftherias

Navarinou Koundourioti

Plateia
Dimokratias

Dodekanisou

Karaoli & Dimitriou

Tandalidou

Plateia
Dimokratias

Polytehniou

26 Oktovriou

Gulf of Thessaloniki

To Lesvos, the Sporades,
Cyclades & Crete

Port

Mitropoleos-

Proxenou Koromila

Nikis-

Egnatia

Filippou

Olympiados

Agiou Dimitriou

Olympou

Amynta

Iasonidou

Athinas

Antigonidon

Langada

Anegenseos-

Train Station

Monastiriou

To Kavala (169km),
Alexandroupolis
(349km) & Turkey

To Evzoni (63km)
& Edessa (89km)

To Larisa (303km)
& Athens (513km)

Ethnikis Aminis

Nik Germanou

Tilis Sep#mvriou

0   100   200m
0   100   200yd

Minor Streets not Depicted

THESSALONIKI

PLACES TO STAY		9	Alexandroupolis Bus Station	31	First-Aid Centre
14	Hotel Acropol	10	Airport Bus Terminal	32	Ferry Departure Point
16	Hotel Averof	11	Athens & Trikala Bus Station	33	Car Parking
17	Hotel Atlas	12	Katerini Bus Station	34	UK Consulate
46	Youth Hostel	13	Tourist Police	35	Molho Bookshop
		18	Local Bus Station	36	National Bank of Greece
PLACES TO EAT		19	Roman Agora	37	American Express
15	Ta Nea Ilysia	20	Globus Internet Café	39	Train Tickets Office
38	O Loutros Fish Taverna	21	Church of Panagia		(OSE)
			Ahiropiitos	40	OTE
OTHER		22	Rotonda	41	US Consulate
1	Kavala Bus Station	23	Bianca Laundrette	42	Foreign Newspapers Kiosk
2	Church of Osios David	24	Arch of Galerius	43	Olympian Cinema
3	Monastery of Vlatadon	25	Main Post Office	44	EOT
4	Atatürk's House	26	Olympic Airways Office	45	Church of Agia Sofia
5	Turkish Consulate	27	Hydrofoil Departure Point	47	White Tower
6	Show Avantaz	28	Olympic Airways	48	Archaeological
7	Church of Agios Dimitrios	29	Ta Ladadika (area)		Museum
8	Ministry of Macedonia &	30	Karaharsis Travel & Shipping	49	Museum of Byzantine
	Thrace		Agency		Culture

and 12.30 to 7 pm Monday; admission is 1500 dr.

The **White Tower** is the city's most prominent landmark. It houses a **Byzantine Museum**, with splendid frescoes and icons. It's open 8 am to 2.30 pm Tuesday to Sunday; admission is free.

Places to Stay & Eat

The *youth hostel* (☎ 225 946, Alex Svolou 44) has dorm beds for 2000 dr. To get there, take bus No 10 from outside the train station to the Kamara stop.

The best budget hotel in town is *Hotel Acropol* (☎ 536 170) on Tandalidou, a quiet side street off Egnatia. Clean singles/doubles with shared bath are listed at 6000/9000 dr, but most of the time it charges a bargain 5000 dr per room. You'll find similar prices at the quiet *Hotel Averof* (☎ 538 498, Leontos Sofou 24).

Hotel Atlas (☎ 537 046, Egnatia 40) has singles/doubles with shared bathroom for 6000/9000 dr and doubles with bath for 12,000 dr. The rooms at the front get a lot of traffic noise.

Ta Nea Ilysia opposite the Hotel Averof on Leontos Sofou is a popular place, with main dishes priced from 1300 dr.

O Loutros Fish Taverna, which occupies an old Turkish hammam near the flower market on Komninon, is a lively place full of local colour. Most dishes cost from 2000 dr to 3000 dr.

Entertainment

You will find live bouzouki and folk music every night at *Show Avantaz*, opposite the Turkish consulate at Agiou Dimitriou 156. It opens at 11 pm.

A good area to check is *Ta Ladadika*, near the ferry quay, where former shipping warehouses have been converted into numerous trendy cafes, bars and restaurants.

Getting There & Away

Air There are up to 20 flights a day to Athens, priced from 19,400 dr with Air Greece to 23,400 dr with Olympic. Olympic has daily flights to Ioannina, Lesvos and Limnos, and occasional flights to Chios, Mykonos and Rhodes. Aegean Airlines has two flights a day to Iraklio. Olympic Airways (☎ 230 240) is at Nav Koundourioti 3.

Bus There are several bus terminals, most of them near the train station. Buses to Athens, Igoumenitsa and Trikala leave from Monastiriou 65 and 67; buses to Alexandroupolis leave from Koloniari 17; and buses to Litihoro (for Mt Olympus) leave from Promitheos 10. Buses to the Halkidiki Peninsula leave from

GREECE

Karakasi 68 (in the eastern part of town; it's marked on the free EOT map). To get there, take local bus No 10 from Egnatia to the Botsari stop.

The OSE has two buses a day to Athens from the train station, as well as international services to Istanbul and Tirana (Albania).

Train There are nine trains a day to Athens, five of them intercity express services (8250 dr, six hours). There are also five trains to Alexandroupolis, two of which are express services (4990 dr, 5½ hours). All the international trains from Athens stop at Thessaloniki. You can get more information from the OSE office at Aristotelous 18, or from the train station.

Ferry & Hydrofoil There's a Sunday ferry to Lesvos, Limnos and Chios throughout the year. In summer there are at least three ferries a week to Iraklio (Crete), stopping in the Sporades and the Cyclades on the way. In summer there are daily hydrofoils to Skiathos, Skopelos and Alonnisos. Karaharisis Travel & Shipping Agency (☎ 524 544, fax 532 289), Koundourioti 8, handles tickets for both ferries and hydrofoils.

Getting Around

There is no bus service from the Olympic Airways office to the airport. Take bus No 78 from the train station (150 dr). A taxi from the airport costs about 2000 dr.

There is a flat fare of 100 dr on bus services within the city.

HALKIDIKI Χαλκιδική

Halkidiki is the three-pronged peninsula south-east of Thessaloniki. It's the main resort area of Northern Greece, with superb sandy beaches right around its 500km of coastline. **Kassandra**, the south-western prong of the peninsula, has surrendered irrevocably to mass tourism. **Sithonia**, the middle prong, is not as over-the-top and has some spectacular scenery.

Mt Athos

Halkidiki's third prong is occupied by the all-male Monastic Republic of Mt Athos (also called the Holy Mountain), where monasteries full of priceless treasures stand amid an impressive landscape of gorges, wooded mountains and precipitous rocks.

Obtaining a four-day visitors permit involves a bit of work. Start early, because only 10 foreign adult males may enter Mt Athos per day and there are long waiting lists in summer. You can start the process from outside Thessaloniki, but you will have to pass through Thessaloniki anyway to pick up your reservation.

You must first book a date for your visit with the Mount Athos Pilgrims' Office (☎ 031-861 611, fax 861 811), Leoforos Karamanli 14, just east of the Exhibition Site (off map) in Thessaloniki. This office is open 8.30 am to 1.30 pm and 6 to 8 pm weekdays (except Wednesday). Call first and make a telephone booking.

Letters of recommendation are no longer required, but you must declare your intention to be a pilgrim. You need to supply a photocopy of your passport details and, if you are Orthodox, a photocopied certificate showing your religion.

You must then call at the Pilgrims' Office in person to collect the forms confirming your reservation. You can then proceed from Thessaloniki to the port of Ouranoupolis, departure point for boats to Mt Athos, where you will be given your actual permit.

Armed at last with your permit, you can explore, on foot, the 20 monasteries and dependent religious communities of Mt Athos. You can stay only one night at each monastery.

MT OLYMPUS Ολυμπος Ορος
☎ 0352

Mt Olympus is Greece's highest and mightiest mountain. The ancients chose it as the abode of their gods and assumed it to be the exact centre of the Earth. Olympus has eight peaks, the highest of which is Mytikas (2917m). The area is popular with trekkers, most of whom use the village of **Litohoro** as a base. Litohoro is 5km inland from the Athens-Thessaloniki highway.

The EOS office (☎ 81 944) on Plateia Kentriki has information on the various treks and conditions. The office is open 9 am to 1 pm and 6 to 8.30 pm Monday to Friday, and 9 am to 1 pm Saturday.

The main route to the top takes two days, overnighting at one of the refuges on the mountain. Good protective clothing is essential, even in summer.

Places to Stay & Eat

The cheapest rooms are at *Hotel Markesia* (☎ *81 831*) near Plateia Kentriki. It has clean singles/doubles with bathroom for 6500/ 7500 dr. It's open from June to October. At other times, try the cheery *Hotel Enipeas* (☎/fax *81 328*) on Plateia Kentriki, where you'll find singles/doubles for 9000/ 12,000 dr. *Olympus Taverna* on Agiou Nikolaou serves standard fare at reasonable prices.

There are four *refuges* on the mountain at altitudes ranging from 940m to 2720m. They are open from May to September.

Getting There & Away

There are eight buses a day to Litohoro from Thessaloniki and three from Athens (7500 dr, six hours).

ALEXANDROUPOLIS

Αλεξανδρούπολη

☎ 0551 • pop 37,000

Dusty Alexandroupolis doesn't have much going for it, but if you're going to Turkey or Samothraki, you may end up staying overnight here. There's a tourist office (☎ 24 998) in the town hall on Dimokratias.

Places to Stay & Eat

Hotel Lido (☎ *28 808, Paleologou 15*), one block north of the bus station, is a great budget option. It has singles/doubles with shared bathroom for 4000/5000 dr, and doubles with private bathroom for 6500 dr.

Neraida Restaurant on Kyprou has a good range of local specialities priced from 1600 dr. Kyprou starts opposite the pier where ferries leave for Samothraki.

Getting There & Away

There are five flights a day to Athens (19,700 dr) from the airport 7km west of town. There are five trains and five buses (5400 dr) a day to Thessaloniki. There's also a daily train and a daily OSE bus to Istanbul.

In summer there are at least two boats a day to Samothraki (2300 dr, two hours), dropping to one in winter. There are also hydrofoils to Samothraki and Limnos.

Saronic Gulf Islands

Νησιά του Σαρωνικού

The Saronic Gulf Islands are the closest island group to Athens. Not surprisingly, they are a very popular escape for residents of the congested capital. Accommodation can be hard to find between mid-June and September, and on weekends year-round.

Getting There & Away

Ferries to all four islands, and hydrofoils to Aegina, leave from the Great Harbour in Piraeus. Hydrofoils to the other islands run from Zea Marina in Piraeus.

AEGINA Αίγινα

☎ 0297 • pop 11,000

Aegina is the closest island to Athens and a popular destination for day-trippers. Many make for the lovely **Temple of Aphaia**, a well-preserved Doric temple 12km east of Aegina town. It is open 8.15 am to 7 pm weekdays (to 5 pm in winter) and 8.30 am to 3 pm weekends. Admission is 800 dr. Buses from Aegina town to the small resort of **Agia Marina** can drop you at the site. Agia Marina has the best beach on the island, which isn't saying much.

Most travellers prefer to stay in Aegina town, where the *Hotel Plaza* (☎ *25 600*) has singles/doubles overlooking the sea for 4500/7500 dr.

POROS Πόρος

pop 4000

Poros is a big hit with the Brits, but it's hard to work out why. The beaches are nothing to write home about and there are no sites of significance. The main attraction is pretty Poros town, draped over the Sferia Peninsula. Sferia is linked to the rest of the island, known as Kalavria, by a narrow isthmus. Most of the package hotels are here. There are a few *domatia* in Poros town, signposted off the road to Kalavria.

The island lies little more than a stone's throw from the mainland, opposite the Peloponnesian village of Galatas.

HYDRA Ύδρα
☎ 0298 • pop 3000
Hydra is the island with the most style and is famous as the haunt of artists and jet-setters. Its gracious stone mansions are stacked up the rocky hillsides that surround the fine natural harbour. The main attraction is peace and quiet. There are no motorised vehicles on the island – apart from a garbage truck and a few construction vehicles.

Accommodation is expensive, but of a high standard. *Hotel Dina* (☎ 52 248) has singles/doubles overlooking the harbour for 10,000/12,000 dr, less on weekdays.

SPETSES Σπέτσες
☎ 0298 • pop 3700
Pine-covered Spetses is perhaps the most beautiful island in the group. It also has the best beaches, so it's packed with package tourists in summer. The **old harbour** in Spetses town is a delightful place to explore.

Orloff Apartments (☎ 72 246) has well-equipped studios behind the harbour for 6000/10,000 dr.

Cyclades Κυκλάδες

The Cyclades, named after the rough circle they form around Delos, are quintessential Greek islands with brilliant white architecture, dazzling light and golden beaches.

Delos, historically the most important island of the group, is uninhabited. The inhabited islands of the archipelago are Mykonos, Syros, Tinos, Andros, Paros, Naxos, Ios, Santorini (Thira), Anafi, Amorgos, Sikinos, Folegandros and the tiny islands of Koufonisi, Shinousa, Iraklia and Donousa, lying east of Naxos. A further six – Kea, Kythnos, Serifos, Sifnos, Kimolos and Milos (all with small permanent populations) – are referred to as the Western Cyclades.

Some of the Cyclades, like Mykonos, Ios and Santorini, have embraced tourism, filling their coastlines with bars and their beaches with sun lounges. Others, like Anafi, Sikinos and the tiny islands east of Naxos, are little more than clumps of rock, each with a village, secluded coves and few tourists.

To give even the briefest rundown on every island is impossible in a single chapter.

For more detailed information, see Lonely Planet's *Greek Islands*.

History
The Cyclades enjoyed a flourishing Bronze Age civilisation (3000 to 1100 BC), more or less concurrent with the Minoan civilisation.

By the 5th century BC, the island of Delos had been taken over by Athens, which kept its treasury there.

Between the 4th and 7th centuries AD, the islands, like the rest of Greece, suffered a series of invasions and occupations. During the Middle Ages they were raided by pirates – hence the labyrinthine character of their towns, which was meant to confuse attackers. On some islands the whole population would move into the mountainous interior to escape the pirates, while on others they would brave it out on the coast. Hence on some islands the hora (main town) is on the coast and on others it is inland.

The Cyclades became part of independent Greece in 1827.

Getting There & Away
Air Mykonos and Santorini have international airports that receive charter flights from northern Europe. There are daily flights from Athens to Milos, Syros, Naxos, Paros, Mykonos and Santorini. In addition there are direct flights between Santorini and Mykonos. Both islands have direct connections with Rhodes and Thessaloniki, and there are two flights a week from Santorini to Iraklio (Crete).

Ferry There are daily boats from Piraeus to most islands, but in winter, services are severely curtailed. A daily ferry travels between Mykonos, Paros, Naxos, Ios and Santorini. In summer, hydrofoils and catamarans link Paros, Naxos, Syros, Tinos, Ios and Santorini. In July, August and September, the Cyclades are prone to the *meltemi*, a ferocious north-easterly wind which can disrupt ferry schedules.

MYKONOS Μύκονος
☎ 0289 • pop 6170
Mykonos is perhaps the most visited – and most expensive – of all Greek islands. It has the most sophisticated nightlife and is a mecca for gay travellers.

MYKONOS

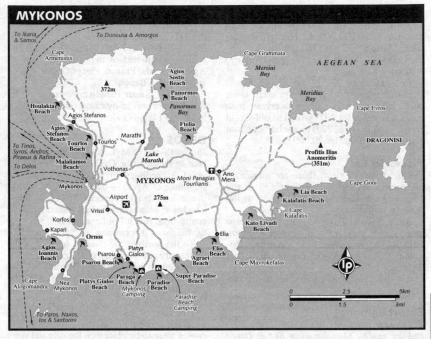

Orientation & Information

There is no tourist office. The tourist police
(☎ 22 482) are at the port, in the same building as the hotel reservation office (☎ 24 540),
the association of rooms and apartments office (☎ 26 860), and the camping information
office (☎ 22 852). The post office is not far
from the south bus station, and the OTE is
near the north bus station. There's slow and
expensive Internet access at Porto Market,
opposite the port. A useful Web site is
www.mykonosgreece.com.

Things to See

The island's capital and port is warren-like
Mykonos town, with chic boutiques, houses
with brightly painted wooden balconies, and
flowering plants cascading down dazzling
white walls.

The **archaeological museum** and **maritime museum** are OK. The **folklore museum**, near the Delos quay, is well stocked
with local memorabilia. It's open 5.30 to 8.30
pm daily; admission is free.

The most popular beaches are **Platys Gialos**, with wall-to-wall sun lounges, the mainly
nude **Paradise** and mainly gay **Super Paradise**, **Agrari** and **Elia**. The less crowded ones
are **Panormos**, **Kato Livadi** and **Kalafatis**.

Places to Stay

Paradise Beach Camping (☎ 22 852, fax 24
350, ✉ paradise@paradise.myk.forthnet.gr)
charges 1500 dr per person and 1100 dr per
tent. Two-person beach cabins with shared facilities are 10,000 dr; cabins for four with private bath cost 22,000 dr. **Mykonos Camping**
(☎ 24 578) near Platys Gialos beach charges
2000/1100 dr per person/tent. Minibuses for
these sites usually meet the ferries and there are
regular buses into town.

Rooms fill up quickly in summer, so it's
prudent to succumb to the first domatia owner
who accosts you. Outside of the high season
(July and August), you can get some excellent
bargains.

Kalogera is a good street to seek out lodgings – there are a number of mid-range hotels

here, including *Hotel Philippi (☎ 22 294, fax 24 680)*, offering simple doubles/triples with bath for 17,000/22,000 dr. Nearby, *Rooms Chez Maria (☎ 22 480)* has attractive rooms for 15,000/20,000 dr. There's a good (pricey) restaurant here as well.

Hotel Delos (☎ 22 517, fax 22 312, ℮ ero stravel@myk.forthnet.gr) on the small town beach has spotless doubles with private bath and water views for 20,000 dr. The old-world *Hotel Apollon (☎ 22 223)* on the harbourfront also offers doubles for 20,000 dr.

Places to Eat

For food with a view, there are numerous restaurants around the harbour and in the charming area known as Little Venice, on the western waterfront.

Busy *Niko's Taverna*, near the Delos quay, serves fresh seafood. *Sesame Kitchen*, next to the maritime museum on Matogianni, offers a variety of vegetarian dishes. *Antonini's Taverna*, on Taxi Square, is popular with locals for its good-value traditional fare.

Entertainment

Troubador (formerly the Down Under Bar) and the nearby *Skandinavian Bar & Disco* are very popular. *Rhapsody* in Little Venice plays jazz and blues. Next door, *Montparnasse Piano Bar* plays classical music at sunset.

Cavo Paradiso, 300m above Paradise Beach, has all-night raves starting at 3 am. Entry is 5000 dr.

Porta, *Kastro Bar*, *Icaros* and *Manto* are among the many popular gay haunts. *Pierro's* is the place for late-night dancing.

Getting There & Away

Daily flights from Mykonos to Athens cost 19,100 dr and to Santorini 15,400 dr. In summer there are also flights to/from Rhodes and Thessaloniki. The Olympic Airways office (☎ 22 490) is on Plateia Louka, by the south bus station.

There are ferries daily to Mykonos from Piraeus (4800 dr). From Mykonos there are daily ferries and hydrofoils to most Cycladic islands, and weekly services to Crete, the North-Eastern Aegean and the Dodecanese. For the port police, call ☎ 22 218.

Getting Around

The north bus station is near the port, behind the OTE office. It serves Agios Stefanos, Elia, Kalafatis and Ano Mera. The south bus station, south-east of the windmills, serves Agios Yiannis, Psarou, Platys Gialos, Ornos and Paradise Beach.

Paradise, Super Paradise, Agrari and Elia Beaches are served by caïque from Mykonos town and Platys Gialos.

DELOS Δήλος

Just south-east of Mykonos, the uninhabited island of Delos is the Cyclades' archaeological jewel. According to mythology, Delos was the birthplace of Apollo – the god of light, poetry, music, healing and prophecy. The island flourished as an important religious and commercial centre from the 3rd millennium BC, reaching the height of its power in the 5th century BC.

To the north of the island's harbour is the **Sanctuary of Apollo**, containing temples dedicated to him, and the **Terrace of the Lions**. These proud beasts were carved in the 7th century BC from marble from Naxos, and their function was to guard the sacred area. (At the time of research the marble lions had been moved to the island's museum and copies were to be placed on the original site.) The **Sacred Lake** (dry since 1926) is where Leto supposedly gave birth to Apollo. The **museum**, with impressive but poorly labelled artefacts, is east of this section.

South of the harbour is the **Theatre Quarter**, where private houses were built around the **Theatre of Delos**. East of here are the **Sanctuaries of the Foreign Gods**. Climb **Mt Kynthos** (113m) for a spectacular view of Delos and the surrounding islands.

Excursion boats leave Mykonos for Delos (30 minutes) between 9 and 10.15 am daily except Monday, when the site is closed. The round trip is 1900 dr; entrance to the site is 1200 dr. The boat schedule allows you only about three hours on the island – for full appreciation of the site, it's worth investing in a guidebook or, better still, a guided tour. There is a cafeteria on the island.

PAROS Πάρος
☎ 0284 • pop 9591

Paros is an attractive island, although less dramatically so than Naxos, 16km to the east. Its

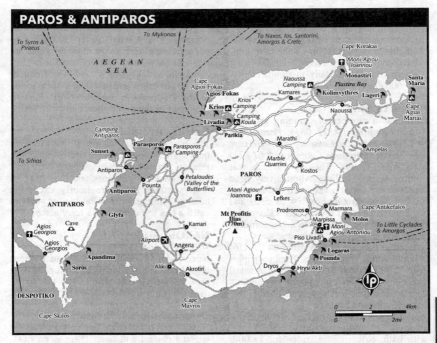

PAROS & ANTIPAROS

softly contoured and terraced hills culminate in one central mountain, Profitis Ilias. It has some of the finest beaches in the Cyclades, and is famous for its pure white marble – no less than the *Venus de Milo* herself was created from it.

Orientation & Information

Paros' main town and port is Parikia, on the west coast. Agora, also known as Market St, is Parikia's main commercial thoroughfare running south-west from the main square, Plateia Mavrogenous (opposite the ferry terminal). There is no tourist office but countless agencies can help with information. The OTE is on the south-west waterfront; turn right from the ferry pier. The post office is also on the waterfront, but to the north of the pier.

Wired Cafe is on Market St, while just north of the quay is Memphis.net, a bar-cum-cybercafe. A good Web site is at parosweb.com.

Things to See & Do

One of the most notable churches in Greece is Parikia's **Panagia Ekatontapyliani** (Our Lady of the Hundred Gates), which features a beautiful, highly ornate interior. Visitors must be 'modestly attired' (ie, no shorts).

Petaloudes, 8km from Parikia, is better known as the Valley of the Butterflies. In summer, huge swarms of the creatures almost conceal the copious foliage.

The charming village of **Naoussa**, filled with white houses and labyrinthine alleyways, is still a working fishing village, despite an enormous growth in tourism over the last few years. Naoussa has good beaches served by caïque, including popular **Kolimvythres**, with bizarre rock formations; **Monastiri**, a mainly nude beach; and **Santa Maria**, which is good for windsurfing. Paros' longest beach, **Hrysi Akti** (Golden Beach) on the south coast, is also popular with windsurfers.

The picturesque inland villages of **Lefkes**, **Marmara** and **Marpissa** are all worth a visit and offer good walking opportunities. The Moni Agiou Antoniou (Monastery of St Anthony), on a hill above Marpissa, offers breathtaking views.

GREECE

Antiparos This small island, less than 2km from Paros, has superb beaches but is becoming too popular for its own good. One of the chief attractions in Antiparos is the **cave**, considered one of Europe's most beautiful (open 9.45 am to 4.45 pm daily in summer only; entry 600 dr).

Places to Stay

Paros has a number of camping grounds. *Koula Camping* (☎ 22 081), *Parasporas* (☎ 22 268) and *Krios Camping* (☎ 21 705) are near Parikia. *Antiparos Camping* (☎ 61 221) is on Agios Giannis Theologos Beach, just north of Antiparos village. Alternatively, head for Naoussa, which has two camp sites nearby: *Naoussa Camping* (☎ 51 595) and *Surfing Beach* (☎ 51 013). There's also an information office at Naoussa's bus terminal which can help with accommodation.

Back in Parikia, *Rooms Mike* (☎ 22 856) is popular with backpackers. Doubles/triples cost 12,000/15,000 dr, with use of a small kitchen. Walk 50m left from the pier and it's next to Memphis.net cybercafe. Mike also has self-contained studios.

The very friendly owners of *Rooms Rena* (☎/fax 21 427) offer spotless doubles/triples with bath, balcony and fridge for 13,000/16,000 dr; turn left from the pier then right at the ancient cemetery.

Hotel Argonauta (☎ 21 440, fax 23 442) on the main square offers comfortable rooms for 18,000/21,000 dr.

Places to Eat

There are countless tavernas and cafes lining the waterfront and surrounding the main square. If you're after a cheap, quick fix, *Zorba's* on the main square does a mean gyros. Just off Market St is the oddly named *Happy Green Cow*, dishing up good vegetarian fare. For something more upmarket, try *I Trata* or *Porphyra*, on opposite sides of the ancient cemetery, north of the pier. Both offer excellent seafood at reasonable prices.

Entertainment

There are a few good bars tucked away in the old town, including the mellow *Pirate* jazz and blues bar. The far southern end of Parikia's waterfront has *Slammers*, *Comma Club* and *The Dubliner Irish Bar* to keep you going.

Getting There & Away

Flights to/from Athens cost 18,900 dr. Paros is a major transport hub for ferries. Daily connections with Piraeus cost 4900 dr. There are frequent ferries and hydrofoils to Naxos, Ios, Santorini and Mykonos, and less frequent ones to Amorgos and Astypalea, then across to the Dodecanese and the North-Eastern Aegean. For the port police, call ☎ 21 240.

Getting Around

The bus station is 100m north of the ferry quay. There are frequent buses to Aliki, Pounta, Naoussa, Lefkes, Piso Livadi and Hrysi Akti. For Petaloudes, take the Aliki bus.

In summer there are hourly excursion boats to Antiparos from Parikia, or you can catch a bus to Pounta and a ferry across.

NAXOS Νάξος
☎ 0285 • pop 16,703

Naxos, the biggest, greenest and perhaps most beautiful island of the archipelago, is popular but big enough to allow you to escape the hordes.

Orientation & Information

Naxos town (Chora), on the west coast, is the island's capital and port. There is no EOT, but the privately owned Naxos Tourist Information Centre (NTIC; ☎ 25 201, fax 25 200) opposite the quay makes up for this, thanks to the inimitable Despina. The office is open 8 am to midnight daily and offers many services, including luggage storage and laundry.

To find the OTE, turn right from the quay and it's on the waterfront, 150m past the National Bank of Greece. The post office is three blocks farther on. Internet access is available at Rental Centre on Plateia Protodikiou, also known as Central Square.

Things to See & Do

The winding alleyways of **Naxos town**, lined with immaculate whitewashed houses, clamber up to the crumbling 13th-century kastro walls. The well-stocked archaeological museum is here, housed in a former school where Nikos Kazantzakis was briefly a pupil. It's open 8 am to 2.30 pm Tuesday to Sunday; admission is 600 dr.

After the town beach of Agios Georgios, south beyond the harbourfront, sandy **beaches**

NAXOS & THE MINOR ISLANDS

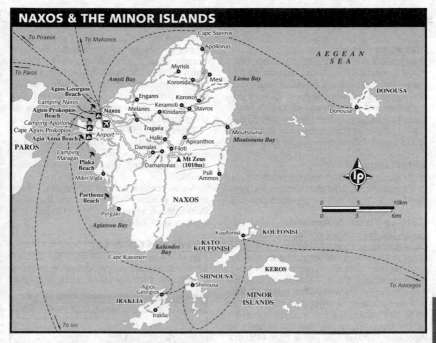

– which become progressively less crowded – continue southwards as far as Pyrgaki Beach.

On the north coast, **Apollonas** has a rocky beach and a pleasant sheltered bay. If you're curious about the *kouros* statues, you can see the largest one, 10.5m long and dating from the 7th century BC, just outside of Apollonas, lying abandoned and unfinished in an ancient marble quarry.

The gorgeous **Tragaea region** is a vast Arcadian olive grove with Byzantine churches and tranquil villages. **Filoti**, the largest settlement, perches on the slopes of **Mt Zeus** (1004m). It takes three hours to climb the trail to the summit. The village of **Apiranthos** is a gem, with many old houses of uncharacteristically bare stone.

Minor Islands This string of tiny islands is off the east coast of Naxos. Of the seven, only Koufonisi, Donousa, Shinousa and Iraklia are inhabited. They see few tourists and have few amenities, but each has some domatia. They are served by two or three ferries

a week from Piraeus via Naxos, some of which continue to Amorgos.

Places to Stay

Naxos' three camping grounds are ***Camping Naxos*** (☎ 23 500), 1km south of Agios Georgios Beach; ***Camping Maragas*** (☎ 24 552), Agia Anna Beach; and ***Camping Apollon*** (☎ 24 117), 700m from Agios Prokopios Beach.

Dionyssos Youth Hostel (☎ 22 331) is the best budget choice, with dorm beds for 2000 dr, doubles/triples with private bath for 4000/5000 dr and cooking facilities for guests. It's signposted from Agiou Nikodemou, also known as Market St. Book through the NTIC.

Pension Irene (☎ 23 169), south-east of the town centre, has doubles for around 14,000 dr. Near the kastro, ***Hotel Panorama*** (☎ 24 404) has lovely quiet doubles/triples for 15,000/18,000 dr.

There are also some good accommodation options by Agios Giorgios Beach, including

Hotel St George (☎ 23 162), with very pleasant doubles/triples for 18,000/20,000 dr.

Places to Eat
Popi's Grill on the waterfront serves good-value souvlaki for 1700 dr. *Taverna Galini* out by Pension Irene is a favourite with locals and serves up delicious seafood. In the winding streets and alleys around the kastro, you'll find *Manolis Garden* serving excellent Greek fare. If you're hankering for curry in this part of the world, follow the signs for *Dolfini*.

Entertainment
Nightlife is centred around the southern end of the waterfront; *Med Bar*, *Cream*, *Veggera* and *Day & Night* will keep you entertained.

Getting There & Around
Naxos has daily flights to Athens (20,100 dr), daily ferries to Piraeus (4900 dr) and good ferry and hydrofoil connections with most islands in the Cyclades. At least once a week there are boats to Crete, Thessaloniki, Rhodes and Samos. For the port police, call ☎ 22 300.

Buses run to most villages and the beaches as far as Pyrgaki. The bus terminal is in front of the quay. There are four buses daily to Apollonas (1200 dr) and five to Filoti (450 dr).

IOS Ιος
☎ 0286 • pop 2000
Ios epitomises the Greece of sun, sand and sex; in high season it's the *enfant terrible* of the islands. Come here if you want to bake on a beach all day and drink all night. Yet it's not only young hedonists who holiday on Ios – the island is also popular with the older set (anyone over 25) – but the two groups tend to be polarised. The young stay in 'the village' and others at the Ormos port. Nonravers should avoid the village from June to September.

Ios has a tenuous claim to being Homer's burial place. His tomb is supposedly in the island's north, although no one seems to know exactly where.

Gialos Beach, at the port, is OK. **Koumbara Beach**, a 20-minute walk west of Gialos, is less crowded and mainly nudist. **Milopotas**, 1km east, is a superb long beach. Vying with Milopotas for best beach is **Manganari**, on the south coast, reached by bus or, in summer, by excursion boats from the port.

Orientation & Information
The capital, Ios town ('the village', also known as the Hora), is 2km inland from the port of Ormos. The bus terminal in Ormos is straight ahead from the ferry quay on Plateia Emirou. To walk from Ormos to Ios town, turn left from Plateia Emirou, then immediately right and you'll see the stepped path leading up to the right after 100m. The walk takes about 20 minutes.

There is no EOT tourist office, but information is available at the port from travel agents, most of which offer free luggage storage and free use of safes to reduce thefts.

An increasing number of venues – from hotels (Francesco's, Far Out) and bars (Fun Pub) to travel agents – are now offering Internet access to their patrons.

Places to Stay & Eat
Far Out Camping (☎ 91 468, fax 92 303, ✉ farout@otenet.gr) on Milopotas Beach is a seriously slick operation, attracting up to

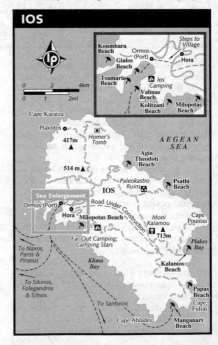

IOS

2000 people a night in summer. Open from May to October, camping costs 1600 dr per person; tents can be hired for 400 dr. Bungalows cost from 2500 dr to 4000 dr per person. There are loads of features – pools, bar, restaurants, minimarket, travel agency, safe boxes, sports facilities. Next door is *Far Out Village Hotel* (☎ 92 305), with lovely double rooms and access to all the Far Out facilities for 20,000 dr.

If you prefer a quieter camp site, try *Camping Stars* (☎ 91 302), also in Milopotas, or *Camping Ios* (☎ 91 050) in Ormos.

There is a wonderful view of the bay from *Francesco's* (☎/fax 91 223, ✉ fragesco@otenet.gr) in the village. Dorm beds cost 2500 dr; doubles/triples with private bath are 10,000/12,000 dr. It's a lively meeting place with a bar and terrace.

In the port, head right from the ferry quay to *Hotel Poseidon* (☎ 91 091) for lovely rooms (18,000 dr for a double) with great views across the harbour.

In the village, *Taverna Lord Byron*, *Pithari Taverna* and *Fun Pub* are the most popular eateries. For a seafood treat, head to *Filippos* on the road between the port and Koumbara Beach. At the port, try *The Octopus Tree*, a quaint, authentic eatery by the fishing boats (so you know the fish is fresh!).

Entertainment

The party crowd reckons the port is dull, while the older set thinks the village is crazy, so take your pick. At night the tiny central square has so many party-goers that it can take 30 minutes to get from one side to the other. Surprisingly, bars in the square charge competitive prices.

Scorpions, *Dubliners* and *Sweet Irish Dreams* are perennial favourites in the village; *Blue Note* and *Red Bull* are also very popular.

Getting There & Around

Ios has daily connections with Piraeus (5300 dr), and there are frequent hydrofoils and ferries to the major Cycladic islands. For up-to-date schedules contact the port police (☎ 91 264).

There are regular buses between the port, the village and Milopotas Beach.

SANTORINI (THIRA)

Σαντορίνη (Θήρα)

☎ 0286 • pop 9360

Around 1450 BC, the volcanic heart of Santorini exploded and sank, leaving an extraordinary landscape. Today the startling sight of the malevolently steaming core almost encircled by sheer cliffs remains – this is certainly the most dramatic of all Greek islands. It's possible that the catastrophe destroyed the Minoan civilisation, but neither this theory nor the claim that the island was part of the lost continent of Atlantis has been proven.

Orientation & Information

The capital, Fira, perches on top of the caldera (submerged crater) on the west coast. The port of Athinios is 12km away. There is no EOT or tourist police, but the helpful Dakoutros Travel Agency (☎ 22 958 or 24 286, fax 22 686) makes up for this. It's in the southern part of the main square (Plateia Theotokopoulou) opposite the taxi station and is open 8 am to 9 or 10 pm daily. The post office is a block south of the taxi station, the OTE is 200m north of the main square, and the Lava Internet Cafe is just north of the main square.

Things to See & Do

Fira The commercialism of Fira has not quite reduced its all-pervasive dramatic aura. The best of the town's museums is the exceptional new **Museum of Prehistoric Thera**, with wonderful displays of well-preserved, well-labelled artefacts predominantly from ancient Akrotiri. The large-scale wall paintings from the 17th century BC are a highlight. The museum is open 8.30 am to 3 pm Tuesday to Sunday; at the time of writing the admission price had not been determined – expect to pay around 1200 dr. To get there, walk south from the main square, past the bus station and take the next street on the right.

The **Megaron Gyzi Museum**, behind the Catholic monastery, houses local memorabilia, including fascinating photographs of Fira before and immediately after the 1956 earthquake. Opening hours are erratic; check the notice on the door.

Around the Island Excavations in 1967 uncovered the remarkably well-preserved Minoan settlement of **Akrotiri**. There are remains

GREECE

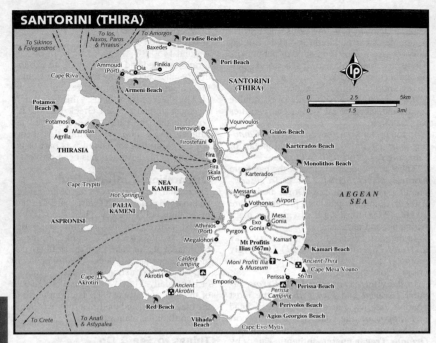

SANTORINI (THIRA)

of two and three-storey buildings, and evidence of a sophisticated drainage system. The site is open 8.30 am to 3 pm Tuesday to Sunday; admission is 1200 dr.

Less impressive than Akrotiri, the site of **Ancient Thira** is still worth a visit for the stunning views. **Moni Profiti Ilia**, a monastery built on the island's highest point, can be reached along a path from Ancient Thira; the walk takes about one hour.

Santorini's **beaches** are of black volcanic sand that becomes very hot, making a beach mat essential. Kamari and Perissa get crowded – those near Oia and Monolithos are quieter. Red Beach, a 10-minute walk from Akrotiri, is popular.

From Imerovigli, just north of Fira, a 12km coastal path leads to the picturesque village of **Oia** (pronounced **ee**-ah), famed for postcard-perfect sunsets. On a clear day there are breathtaking views of neighbouring islands.

Of the surrounding islets, only **Thirasia** is inhabited. At Palia Kameni you can bathe in hot springs, and on Nea Kameni you can clamber around on volcanic lava. A six-hour tour to these three islands by either caïque or glass-bottom boat costs 5500 dr. Tickets are available from most agencies in town.

Places to Stay
Beware of the aggressive accommodation owners who meet boats and buses and claim that their rooms are in Fira when in fact they're in Karterados. Ask to see a map to check their location.

Camping Santorini (☎ 22 944), 1km east of the main square, has many facilities including a restaurant and swimming pool. The cost is 1000 dr per person and 1000 dr per tent.

Thira Hostel (☎ 23 864), 200m north of the square, is a good place to meet people and sleeps as many as 145. It has dorms with up to 10 beds for 3000 dr per person, roof beds for 2000 dr, plus doubles/triples with private bath for 10,000/12,000 dr. It also has a very cheap restaurant.

There are plenty of rooms to rent near the main square and on the road running east towards Camping Santorini, including *Pension Petros* (☎ 22 573), offering basic but pleasant doubles for 17,000 dr. The location can be a bit noisy, however.

A short walk north-east of the centre of town will take you to a quiet rural area with plenty of domatia. *Pension Stella* has doubles/triples for 16,000/19,000 dr, *Pension Horizon* charges 17,000/20,000 dr and *Villa Gianna* – which has a pool – charges 21,000/25,000 dr. All have private bath, some have balcony. To book any of these, ring Dakoutros Travel (see Orientation & Information earlier in this section). The same agent has properties in Oia on its books; most are in traditional houses with fine views. Double studios cost from 25,000 dr; a house for four starts at 35,000 dr.

Places to Eat
Toast Club, on the square, is a fast-food operation (pizza and pasta) and a favourite with budget travellers. *Restaurant Stamna*, just east of the square, has good-value daily specials. *Naoussa*, not far from the cable-car station, is excellent. The food served by other restaurants in this area does not always represent good value for money, but you may not mind given the million-dollar view. For something special, visit upmarket *Kukumavlos*, by the Orthodox cathedral, where you can enjoy fine dining while admiring the sunset.

Entertainment
Bars and clubs are clustered along one street, Erythrou Stavrou. From the main square, facing north, turn left at George's Snack Corner then take the first right. *Koo Club*, *Enigma* and *Murphy's* are all popular, and *Kira Thira Jazz Bar* is an old favourite.

Getting There & Away
Flights cost 22,200 dr to Athens, 22,900 dr to Rhodes, 15,400 dr to Mykonos and to Iraklio (Crete). The Olympic Airways office (☎ 22 493) is 200m south of the hospital.

Daily ferries to Piraeus cost 5900 dr. There are frequent connections with Crete, Ios, Paros and Naxos. Ferries travel less frequently to/from Anafi, Sikinos, Folegandros,

Sifnos, Serifos, Kimolos, Milos, Karpathos and Rhodes. For the port police call ☎ 22 239.

Getting Around
There are daily boats from Athinios and Fira Skala to Thirasia and Oia. The islets surrounding Santorini can only be visited on excursions from Fira.

Large ferries use Athinios port, where they are met by buses. Small boats use Fira Skala, which is served by donkey or cable car (1000 dr each); otherwise it's a clamber up 600 steps. The cable car runs every 20 minutes from 6.40 am to 9 pm.

The bus station is just south of Fira's main square. Buses go to Oia, Kamari, Perissa, Akrotiri and Monolithos frequently. Port buses usually leave Fira, Kamari and Perissa 90 minutes to an hour before ferry departures.

Crete Κρήτη

Crete, Greece's largest island, is divided into four prefectures: Hania, Rethymno, Iraklio and Lassithi. All of Crete's large towns are on the north coast, and it's here that the package tourist industry thrives – Crete has the dubious distinction of playing host to a quarter of all visitors to Greece. You can escape the hordes by visiting the undeveloped west coast, heading into the rugged mountainous interior, or staying in one of the villages of the Lassithi Plateau which, when the tour buses depart, return to rural tranquillity.

Crete has many opportunities for superb trekking and climbing. It's also the best place in Greece for buying high-quality, inexpensive leather goods.

For more detailed information, see Lonely Planet's *Crete*.

History
Crete was the birthplace of Minoan culture, Europe's first advanced civilisation, which flourished from 2800 to 1450 BC. Very little is known of Minoan civilisation, which came to an abrupt end, possibly destroyed by Santorini's volcanic eruption.

Later, Crete passed from the warlike Dorians to the Romans, and then to the Genoese,

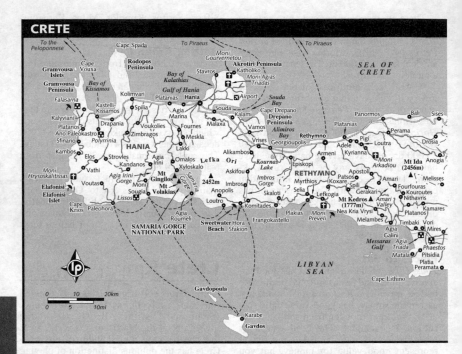

CRETE

who in turn sold it to the Venetians. Under the Venetians, Crete became a refuge for artists, writers and philosophers who fled Constantinople after it fell to the Turks. Their influence inspired the young Cretan painter Domenikos Theotokopoulos, who moved to Spain and there won immortality as the great El Greco.

The Turks finally conquered Crete in 1670. It became a British protectorate in 1898 after a series of insurrections and was united with independent Greece in 1913. There was fierce fighting during WWII when a German airborne invasion defeated Allied forces in the 10-day Battle of Crete. An active resistance movement drew heavy reprisals from the German occupiers.

Getting There & Away

Air The international airport is at Iraklio, Crete's capital. Hania and Sitia have domestic airports. There are several flights a day from Athens to Iraklio and Hania, and weekly flights to Sitia. In summer there are three flights a week to Rhodes from Iraklio and two to Santorini.

Ferry Kastelli-Kissamos, Rethymno, Hania, Iraklio, Agios Nikolaos and Sitia have ferry ports. Ferries travel most days to Piraeus from Hania (5900 dr), Rethymno and Iraklio (7000 dr); less frequently from Agios Nikolaos and Sitia (7600 dr). There are at least two boats a week from Iraklio to Santorini and on to other Cycladic islands.

In summer there's at least one ferry a week from Iraklio to Rhodes (6200 dr) via Kassos and Karpathos and at least three a week from Agios Nikolaos to Rhodes via Sitia, Kassos and Karpathos. In summer, a twice-weekly boat sails from Iraklio to Cyprus via Rhodes and then on to Israel.

Getting Around

Frequent buses run between towns on the north coast, and less frequently to the south

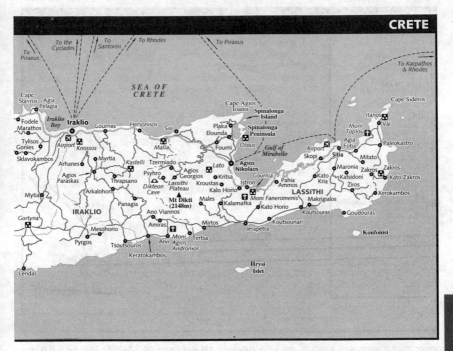

CRETE

To Piraeus | To the Cyclades | To Santorini | To Rhodes | To Piraeus

To Karpathos & Rhodes

SEA OF CRETE

Cape Stavros Agia Pelagia

Fodele Iraklio Bay Iraklio Gournes Hersonisos Sisi Plaka Spinalonga Island Cape Agios Ioanis Spinalonga Island Cape Sideros

Marathos

Tylisos Gonies Airport Knossos Malia Fourni Elounda Spinalonga Peninsula Olous Gulf of Mirabello Itanos Vai Moni Toplou

Sklavokambos Arhanes Kastelli Tzermiado Agios Georgios Lato Agios Nikolaos Gournia Airport Agia Fotia Sitia Mitato Paleokastro

Agios Paraskas Myrtia Psyhro Thrapsano Dikteon Cave Lassithi Plateau Kritsa Kroustas Istron Pahia Ammos Skopi Maronia Katsidoni Zakros Zakros Kato Zakros

Mytia Arkalohori Panagia Mt Dikti (2148m) Males Kalo Horio Kato Kria Ziros Xerokambos

IRAKLIO Ano Viannos Moni Faneromenis Makrigialos

Gortyna Mesohorio Amiras Mirtos Kalamafka Kato Horio Koutsouras Goudouras

Pyrgos Tsoutsouros Arvi Moni Agios Andronios Tertsa Ierapetra Koutsounari Koufonisi

Keratokambos LASSITHI

Lendas Hrysi Islet

---

coast and mountain villages. For more information, visit the long-distance bus Web site at www.ktel.org .

Parts of the south coast are without roads, so boats are used to connect villages.

IRAKLIO Ηράκλειο
☎ 081 • pop 127,600

Iraklio, Crete's capital, lacks the charm of Rethymno or Hania, its old buildings swamped by modern apartment blocks. Its neon-lit streets do exude a certain dynamism, but apart from its archaeological museum and proximity to Knossos, there's little point in lingering here.

Orientation & Information

Iraklio's two main squares are Plateia Venizelou and Plateia Eleftherias. Dikeosynis and Dedalou run between them, and 25 Avgoustou is the main thoroughfare leading from the waterfront to Plateia Venizelou. The EOT (☎ 228 225), open 8 am to 2.30 pm

weekdays, and Olympic Airways (☎ 229 191) are on Plateia Eleftherias. The tourist police (☎ 283 190) are at Dikeosynis 10.

Most of the city's banks are on 25 Avgoustou. The American Express representative, Adamis, is at 25 Avgoustou 23.

The central post office is on Plateia Daskalogiani, and there is a temporary post office by El Greco Park in summer. The OTE is just north of El Greco Park. You can access the Internet at Netcafe, on 1878, or Istos Cyber Cafe, Malikouti 2.

There is a laundrette and left-luggage storage area at Washsalon, Handakos 18.

Things to See

Don't leave Iraklio without seeing the magnificent collection at the **archaeological museum**. Opening times are 8 am to 7 pm Tuesday to Sunday, 12.30 to 7 pm Monday. Admission is 1500 dr.

Close to the waterfront is the **Historical Museum of Crete**, covering the island's

GREECE

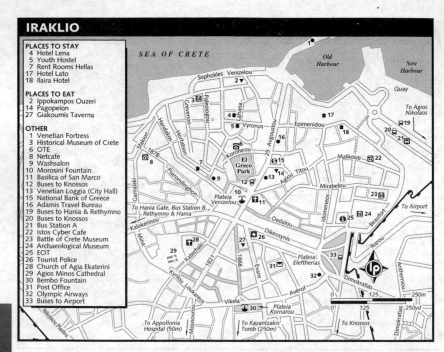

more recent past. It's open 9 am to 5 pm weekdays, to 2 pm Saturday. Admission is 1000 dr.

You can pay homage to the great writer Nikos Kazantzakis by visiting his grave. To get there, walk south on Evans and turn right onto Plastira.

Places to Stay

Beware of taxi drivers who tell you that the pension of your choice is dirty, closed or has a bad reputation. They're paid commissions by the big hotels.

There's few domatia in Iraklio and not much budget accommodation. **Rent Rooms Hellas** (☎ 288 851, Handakos 24) is a hostel popular with backpackers despite the number of draconian rules posted in the rooftop reception and bar. Singles/doubles/triples are 4500/6000/7500 dr; dorm beds are 2000 dr. As a last resort there's also the **youth hostel** (☎ 286 281, Vyronos 5) off 25 Avgoustou, where beds in small, crowded dorms cost 1800 dr.

Hotel Lena (☎ 223 280, Lahana 10) is one of the nicer budget hotels. Singles/doubles with shared facilities cost 6500/9000 dr; with private bath 8500/11,000 dr.

Ilaira Hotel (☎ 227 103, Epimenidou 1) near the old harbour and bus stations is situated among a cluster of decent mid-range hotels. It has hints of the 1970s (lots of brown and orange), but it offers clean, comfortable singles/doubles for 10,000/14,000 dr, plus it has a rooftop terrace. Across the road is the very upmarket **Hotel Lato** (☎ 228 103, Epimenidou 15) with rooms for 25,000/31,000 dr.

Places to Eat

Plateia Venizelou has countless fast-food outlets and cafe-bars, while Theosadaki, the little street between 1866 and Evans, is lined with traditional tavernas. One of the best is **Giakoumis Taverna** (Theosadaki 5).

Ippokampos Ouzeri, on the waterfront just west of 25 Avgoustou, offers a huge range of good-value mezedes and is always packed. Go early to get a table.

Pagopeion, by Agios Titos church, has good food with imaginative titles, and the toilets alone are worth a visit.

There's a bustling, colourful *market* all the way along 1866.

Getting There & Away

For air and ferry information, see Getting There & Away at the start of the Crete section. For the port police, call ☎ 244 912.

Iraklio has two bus stations. Bus station A, just inland from the new harbour, serves eastern Crete (Agios Nikolaos, Ierapetra, Sitia, Malia and the Lassithi Plateau). Bus station B, 50m beyond the Hania Gate, serves the south (Phaestos, Matala, Anogia). The Hania/Rethymno terminal is opposite bus station A.

Getting Around

Bus No 1 goes to/from the airport (180 dr) every 15 minutes between 6 am and 1 am; it stops at Plateia Eleftherias adjacent to the archaeological museum. Local bus No 2 goes to Knossos (260 dr) every 10 minutes from bus station A and also stops on 25 Avgoustou.

Car and motorcycle-rental firms are mostly along 25 Avgoustou.

KNOSSOS Κνωσσός

Knossos, 8km south-east of Iraklio, is the most famous of Crete's Minoan sites and is the inspiration for the myth of the Minotaur. According to legend, King Minos of Knossos was given a bull to sacrifice to the god Poseidon, but instead decided to keep it. This enraged Poseidon, who punished the king by causing his wife Pasiphae to fall in love with the animal. The result of this bizarre union was the Minotaur – half-man and half-bull – who lived in a labyrinth beneath the king's palace, feeding on youths and maidens.

In 1900 the ruins of Knossos were uncovered by Arthur Evans. Although archaeologists tend to disparage Evans' reconstruction, the buildings – an immense palace, courtyards, private apartments, baths and more – give a good idea of what a Minoan palace may have looked like. The delightful frescoes depict plants and animals, as well as people participating in sports, ceremonies and festivals, and generally enjoying life, in contrast to the battle scenes found in the art of classical Greece.

A whole day is needed to see the site, and a guidebook is immensely useful. The site is open 8 am to 7 pm daily from April to October; entry is 1500 dr. Arrive early to avoid the crowds. See Getting Around under Iraklio, earlier, for transport details.

PHAESTOS & OTHER MINOAN SITES

Phaestos (Φαιστός), Crete's second-most important Minoan site, is not as impressive as Knossos but worth a visit for its stunning views of the plain of Mesara. The palace was laid out on the same plan as Knossos, but excavations have not yielded many frescoes. The site is open 8 am to 7 pm daily; entry is 1200 dr.

Crete's other important Minoan sites are **Malia**, 34km east of Iraklio, where there is a palace complex and adjoining town, and **Zakros**, 40km from Sitia. This was the smallest of the island's palatial complexes. The site is rather remote and overgrown, but the ruins are on a more human scale than at Knossos, Phaestos or Malia.

HANIA Χανιά
☎ 0821 • pop 65,000

Lovely Hania, the old capital of Crete, has a harbour with crumbling, softly hued Venetian buildings. It oozes charm; it also oozes package tourists.

Orientation & Information

Hania's bus station is on Kydonias, a block south-west of Plateia 1866, the town's main square. Halidon runs from here to the old harbour. The fortress separates the old harbour from the new. Hania's port is at Souda, 10km from town.

The EOT office (☎ 92 943) is at Kriari 40, 20m from Plateia 1866. It's open 7.30 am to 2 pm weekdays. The central post office is at Tzanakaki 3 and the OTE is next door. Internet access is available at Vranas Studios on Agion Deka, or from e-Kafe.com, Theotokopoulou 53.

Things to See

The **archaeological museum** at Halidon 30 is housed in the former Venetian Church of San Francesco; the Turks converted it into a mosque. It's open 8 am to 7 pm Tuesday to

HANIA

PLACES TO STAY	12 Tholos Restaurant	16 Buses to Souda
3 Hotel Meltemi		17 EOT
7 Rooms for Rent George	OTHER	18 Buses to Western Beaches
13 Vranas Studios	1 e-Kafe.com	19 Main Bus Station
14 Pension Fidias	2 Naval Museum	20 National Bank of Greece
	4 Mosque of the Janissaries	21 Post Office
PLACES TO EAT	5 Archaeological Site	22 OTE
8 Tsikoydadiko	6 Cafe Crete	23 Olympic Airways
9 Tamam	11 Archaeological Museum	24 EOS
10 Suki Yaki	15 Orthodox Cathedral	25 War Museum

Sunday. Admission is 500 dr. There's also the **naval museum**, by the fortress, and the **war museum** at Tzanakaki 23.

Places to Stay

The nearest camping ground is *Camping Hania* (☎ 31 138), 3km west of town, on the beach. Take a Kalamaka bus from Plateia 1866.

The budget choice is *Pension Fidias* (☎ 52 494, Sarpaki 6), behind the Orthodox cathedral, which offers beds in three-bed dorms for 2500 dr. Doubles, some with bath, cost from 5500 dr.

The most interesting rooms are in the ancient Venetian buildings around the old harbour. *Hotel Meltemi* (☎ 92 802, Agelou 2) next to the fortress is quite run-down but has character and a great location. Doubles cost from 7000 dr. *Rooms for Rent George* (☎ 88 715, Zambeliou 30), one block from the waterfront, has singles/doubles/triples for 4000/7000/9000 dr.

Vranas Studios (☎/fax 58 618, 🅔 vranas@ yahoo.com, Agion Deka 10) by the cathedral has lovely, spacious studios sleeping up to three and costing 17,000 dr in August but considerably less (11,000 dr) at other times.

Places to Eat

The lively central *food market* houses a few inexpensive tavernas.

For alfresco dining, try *Tsikoydadiko (Zambeliou 31)*, or the lovingly preserved ruins at the classy *Tholos Restaurant (Agion Deka 36)*. Both serve good Greek cuisine at reasonable prices. Another good choice is the excellent *Tamam (Zambeliou 51)*, while atmospheric *Suki Yaki (Halidon 26)*, under the archway, serves up authentic – albeit pricey – Chinese and Thai meals.

Entertainment

The authentic *Cafe Crete (Kalergon 22)* has live Cretan music every evening.

There are numerous cafes and bars around the harbour, particularly near the fortress.

Getting There & Away

For air and ferry information, see Getting There & Away at the start of the Crete section. Olympic Airways (☎ 40 268) is at Tzanakaki 88. For the port police at Souda, call ☎ 89 240.

There are frequent buses to Iraklio, Rethymno and Kastelli-Kissamos, and less frequent ones to Paleohora, Omalos, Hora Sfakion, Lakki and Elafonisi from the bus station on Kydonias. Buses for Souda (the port) leave frequently from outside the food market, and for beaches just west of Hania from the south-eastern corner of Plateia 1866.

THE WEST COAST

This is Crete's least developed coastline. At Falasarna, 16km west of Kastelli-Kissamos, there's a magnificent sandy beach and a few tavernas and domatia. There are buses in summer from Kastelli-Kissamos and Hania. South of Falasarna there are good sandy beaches near the villages of Sfinario and Kambos.

Farther south you can wade out to more beaches on beautiful Elafonisi islet. Travel agents in Hania and Paleohora run excursions to the area.

SAMARIA GORGE
Φαράγγι της Σαμαριάς

It's a wonder the rocks underfoot haven't worn away completely as so many people trample through the Samaria Gorge. But it is one of Europe's most spectacular gorges, and

worth seeing. You can do it independently by taking a bus from Hania to the head of the gorge at Omalos and walking the length of the gorge (16km) to Agia Roumeli, from where you take a boat to Hora Sfakion and then a bus back to Hania. Or you can join one of the daily excursions from Hania (many companies also offer an 'easy' option, which starts from Agia Roumeli and goes about 4km into the gorge).

The first public bus leaves Hania at 6.15 am and excursion buses also leave early so that people get to the top of the gorge before the heat of the day. The walk takes about five or six hours, and you need good walking shoes and a hat, as well as water and food. The gorge is open early May to mid-October; admission is 1200 dr.

LEFKA ORI Λευκά Ορι

Crete's rugged White Mountains are south of Hania. For information on climbing and trekking, contact the EOS (☎ 24 647), Tzanakaki 90, Hania. Alpine Travel (☎ 53 909, ✉ info@alpine.gr), in Hania, offers many trekking programs; check its comprehensive Web site at www.alpine.gr. Also based in Hania is Trekking Plan (☎ 60 861), which rents mountain bikes and organises bike tours into the mountains. Its Web site is at www.cycling.gr.

PALEOHORA & THE SOUTH-WEST COAST
☎ 0823

Paleohora (Παλαιοχώρα) was discovered by hippies back in the 1960s and from then on its days as a tranquil fishing village were numbered. It remains a relaxing, if overrated, resort favoured by backpackers. There's a helpful tourist office three blocks south of the bus stop.

Farther east, along Crete's south-west coast, are the resorts of Sougia, Agia Roumeli, Loutro and Hora Sfakion; of these, Loutro is the most appealing and is the least developed.

Places to Stay & Eat

Camping Paleohora (☎ 41 120) is 1.5km north-east of the town, near the pebble beach. There's also a restaurant and nightclub here.

In Paleohora, *Homestay Anonymous* (☎ 41 509) is a great place for backpackers. It has clean rooms set around a small courtyard; singles/doubles are 4000/5500 dr and there is a communal kitchen. *Oriental Bay Rooms* (☎ 41 076) at the northern end of the pebble beach (on the road to the camping ground), has comfortable doubles/triples with bath for 7000/8000 dr.

There are numerous domatia and taverna along the harbourfront. There's a good vegetarian restaurant, *The Third Eye*, close to the sandy beach.

Getting There & Away

There are at least three buses a day between Hania and Paleohora (1600 dr).

There's no road linking the coastal resorts, but they are connected by boats from Paleohora in summer. Twice weekly the boat goes to Gavdos Island (Europe's southernmost point).

Coastal paths lead from Paleohora to Sougia and from Agia Roumeli to Loutro. Both walks take five to six hours.

RETHYMNO Ρέθυμνο

☎ 0831 • pop 24,000

Although similar to Hania, with its Venetian and Turkish buildings (not to mention its package tourists), Rethymno is smaller and has a distinct character.

The EOT (☎ 29 148) is on the beach side of El Venizelou and is open 8 am to 2 pm weekdays. The tourist police (☎ 28 156) occupy the same building.

The post office is at Moatsou 21 and the OTE is at Kountouriotou 28. There's Internet access upstairs at Galero cafe, beside the Rimondi fountain.

Things to See & Do

The imposing **Venetian fortress** is open 8 am to 8 pm daily except Monday; entry is 900 dr. The **archaeological museum** opposite the fortress entrance is open 8.30 am to 3 pm Tuesday to Sunday; entry is 500 dr. The **historical and folk art museum** on Vernardou has a well-presented display of Cretan crafts. Its opening hours are 9.30 am to 1.30 pm Monday to Saturday; entry is 600 dr.

The Happy Walker (☎ 52 920), Tombazi 56, has a program of daily walks in the countryside costing from 7000 dr per person.

Places to Stay

The nearest camping ground is *Elisabeth Camping* (☎ 28 694) on Myssiria beach, 3km east of town.

The *youth hostel* (☎ 22 848, Tombazi 45) is a friendly place; beds are 1800 dr in dorms or on the roof. *Olga's Pension* (☎ 53 206, Souliou 57) in the heart of town is colourful and eclectically decorated, with rooms spread off a network of terraces bursting with greenery. Doubles/triples with private bath are 9000/12,000 dr. The tranquil *Rent Rooms Garden* (☎ 28 586, Nikiforou Foka 82) is an old Venetian house with a delightful garden; rooms are 10,000/15,000 dr.

Places to Eat

Stella's Kitchen, beneath Olga's Pension, offers hearty breakfasts and cheap snacks. *Taverna Kyria Maria (Diog Mesologiou 20)*, tucked behind the Rimondi fountain, is a cosy family-run taverna.

Gounakis Restaurant & Bar (Koroneou 6) has live Cretan music every evening and reasonably priced food.

The area east of Rimondi fountain is a good place to investigate. Arabatzoglou and Radamanthios have a number of upmarket places, including *Avli* and *Taverna Larenzo*. The *Punch Bowl* Irish bar is also here.

Getting There & Away

For ferries, see Getting There & Away at the start of the Crete section. For the port police, call ☎ 22 276.

There are frequent buses to Iraklio (1800 dr) and Hania (1600 dr), and less frequent ones to Agia Galini, Arkadi Monastery and Plakias.

LASSITHI PLATEAU Οροπέδιο Λασιθίου

The first view of this mountain-fringed plateau, laid out like an immense patchwork quilt, is breathtaking. The plateau, 900m above sea level, is a vast expanse of orchards and fields, dotted by some 7000 metal windmills with white canvas sails.

Lassithi's major sight, the **Dikteon Cave**, on the side of Mt Dikti, is where, according to mythology, the Titan Rhea hid the newborn Zeus from Cronos, his offspring-gobbling father. It's open 8 am to 4 pm daily and entry is 800 dr.

Places to Stay & Eat

Psyhro is the best place to stay; it's near the cave and has the best views. **Zeus Hotel** (☎ *0844-31 284)* has singles/doubles with private bath for 5000/8000 dr. On the main street, **Stavros** and **Platanos** tavernas serve decent food at similar prices.

Getting There & Away

There are daily buses to the area from Iraklio and three a week from Agios Nikolaos.

SITIA Σητεία
☎ 0843 • pop 8000

Back on the north coast, the manifestations of package tourism gather momentum as they advance eastwards, reaching a crescendo in Agios Nikolaos. The tourist overkill dies down considerably by the time you reach Sitia, an attractive town with a hotel-lined bay and long sandy beach.

The municipal tourist office is on the waterfront just before the town beach. The post office is on Dimokratou, off El Venizelou, and the OTE is on Kapetan Sifis, which runs inland from Plateia El Venizelou, the main square. The ferry port is a bit of a hike; it's signposted from the main square.

Places to Stay & Eat

There are no camping grounds near Sitia, but it's possible to camp in the grounds of the **youth hostel** (☎ *22 693, Therissou 4)* on the road to Iraklio for 1200 dr. Dorm beds cost 1500 dr; doubles/triples with shared facilities are 3500/5000 dr.

There is no shortage of domatia behind the waterfront. The immaculate **Hotel Arhontiko** (☎ *28 172, Kondylaki 16)* has doubles/triples for 5000/6500 dr. To find it, walk towards the ferry dock along El Venizelou, turn left up Filellinon and then right onto Kondylaki.

The waterfront is buzzing with tavernas and bars; inland you'll find **Kali Kardia Taverna** *(Foundalidhou 20)* and **O Mixos** *(Kournarou 15)*. Both are excellent value and popular with locals.

Getting There & Away

For air and ferry information, see Getting There & Away at the start of the Crete section. To contact the port police, call ☎ 22 310.

There are at least three buses daily to Ierapetra and five to Iraklio via Agios Nikolaos. In summer there are two or three buses daily to Vaï and Zakros.

AROUND SITIA

The reconstructed **Toplou Monastery**, 15km from Sitia, houses some beautifully intricate icons and other relics. To get there, take a Vaï bus from Sitia, get off at the fork for the monastery and walk the last 3km.

Superb **Vaï Beach**, famous for its palm trees, gets crowded, but it's well worth a visit.

Dodecanese
Δωδεκάνησα

The Dodecanese are more verdant and mountainous than the Cyclades and have comparable beaches. And here, more than other islands, you get a sense of Greece's proximity to Asia. Ancient temples, massive crusader fortifications, mosques and imposing Italian-built neoclassical buildings stand juxtaposed, vestiges of a turbulent past.

There are 16 inhabited islands in the group; the most visited are Rhodes, Kos, Patmos and Symi.

RHODES Ρόδος

According to mythology, the sun god Helios chose Rhodes as his bride and bestowed light, warmth and vegetation upon her. The blessing seems to have paid off, for Rhodes produces flowers in profusion and enjoys more sunny days than most Greek islands.

The ancient sites of Lindos and Kamiros are legacies of Rhodes' importance in antiquity. In 1291 the Knights of St John, having fled Jerusalem under siege, came to Rhodes and established themselves as masters. In 1522 Süleyman I, sultan of the Ottoman Empire, staged a massive attack on the island and took Rhodes City. The island, along with the other Dodecanese, then became part of the Ottoman Empire.

In 1912 it was the Italians' turn and in 1944 the Germans took over. The following year Rhodes was liberated by British and Greek commandos. In 1948 the Dodecanese became part of Greece.

GREECE

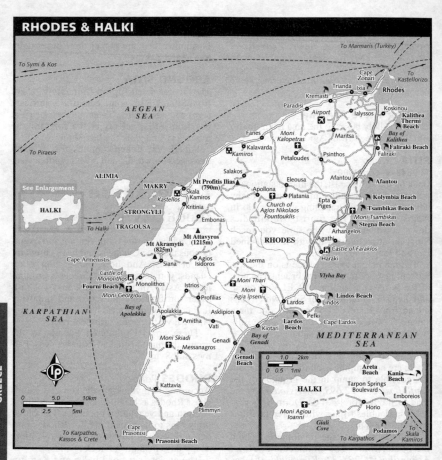

RHODES & HALKI

Rhodes City
☎ 0241 • pop 43,500

Rhodes' capital and port is Rhodes City, on the northern tip of the island. Almost everything of interest here lies in the old town. The main thoroughfares are Sokratous, Pythagora, Agiou Fanouriou and Ipodamou, with mazes of narrow streets between them. The new town to the north is a monument to package tourism.

The main port is east of the old town, and north of here is Mandraki Harbour, supposed site of the Colossus of Rhodes, a giant bronze statue of Apollo (built in 292-280 BC) – one

of the Seven Wonders of the World. The statue stood for a mere 65 years before being toppled by an earthquake.

Information The EOT office (☎ 23 255, *e* eot-rodos@otenet.gr) is on the corner of Makariou and Papagou. It's open 7.30 am to 3 pm weekdays. The tourist police (☎ 27 423) are next door. In summer there is also a municipal tourist office on Plateia Rimini, open longer hours than the EOT.

The main post office is on Mandraki and the OTE is at Amerikis 91. There is a cyber-cafe, Rock Style, at Dimokratias 7, just south of the old town, and Minoan Internet Cafe is at Iroön Politehniou 13 (new town).

Things to See & Do In the old town, the 15th-century Knights' Hospital is a splendid building. It was restored by the Italians and is now the **archaeological museum**, housing an impressive collection, including the exquisite statue of *Aphrodite of Rhodes*. Opening times are 8.30 am to 3 pm Tuesday to Sunday. Admission is 800 dr.

Odos Ippoton – the Avenue of the Knights – is lined with magnificent medieval buildings, the most imposing of which is the **Palace of the Grand Masters**, restored, but never used, as a holiday home for Mussolini. It's open 8.30 am to 3 pm daily except Monday. Admission is 1200 dr.

The old town is reputedly the world's finest surviving example of medieval fortification. The 12m-thick walls are closed to the public, but you can take a **guided walk** along them on Tuesday and Saturday, starting at 2.45 pm in the courtyard at the Palace of the Grand Masters (1200 dr).

The 18th-century **Turkish bath** on Plateia Arionos (signposted from Ipodamou) offers a rare opportunity to bathe Turkish-style in Greece. It's open 1 to 6 pm Tuesday, 11 am to 6 pm Wednesday, Thursday and Friday, and 8 am to 6 pm Saturday. Entry is 500 dr (300 dr on Wednesday and Saturday).

Places to Stay *Faliraki Camping* (☎ 85 358) about 15km south of Rhodes City near Faliraki Beach, has good facilities including a pool and charges 1500/800 dr per person/tent. Take a bus from the east-side bus station.

The old town is well supplied with accommodation. The unofficial *Rodos Youth Hostel* (☎ 30 491, Ergiou 12) off Agiou Fanouriou is popular and has a lovely garden. Dorm beds cost 1500 dr, doubles with shared facilities are 3500 dr; with bath 6000 dr. There is a kitchen available for self-caterers and during the summer there are roof beds (1000 dr) and barbecue facilities.

Sunlight Hotel (☎ 21 435, Ipadomou 32) above Stavros Bar has doubles/triples with private bath and fridge for 10,000/12,000 dr. The friendly *Pension Andreas* (☎ 34 156, fax 74 285, Omirou 28D) has a terrace bar with terrific views, and email facilities for guests.

Clean, pleasant doubles with shared bathroom cost 10,000 dr, doubles/triples/quads with private bath are 12,500/15,500/18,000 dr.

Other good choices include the *Pink Elephant* (☎ 22 469, Irodotou 42) and *Hotel Spot* (☎ 34 737, Perikleous 21). Both have clean, bright doubles with private bath for 12,000 dr.

Sara from Kafe Besara (see Places to Eat) has well located, self-contained *apartments* set around a lovely courtyard. Apartments sleeping two/four cost 20,000/30,000 dr a night. Visit the cafe (📧 cafe_besara@yahoo.com) or call ☎ 30 363.

Most of Rhodes' other villages have hotels or a few domatia.

Places to Eat Away from the venues with tacky photo menus, you'll find some good eateries.

For the best Greek coffee in town and a game of backgammon or chess, try *Kafekopteion* (*Sokratous 76*). Head to *Kringlan Swedish Bakery* (*I Dragoumi 14*) in the new town for exceptional sandwiches and delicious pastries.

One of the best-value places to eat in the old town is the *Fisherman's Ouzeria* on Sofokleous. *Taverna Kostas* (*Pythagora 62*) and *Yiannis Taverna* on Platanos are highly popular and also good value.

If you're tired of Greek food, however, there are some excellent options. *Le Bistrot de L'Auberge* (*Praxitelous 21*) in a beautifully restored medieval house serves terrific French dishes. Indian food fans should visit *India Restaurant* (*Konstantopedos 16*) opposite the Swedish bakery. *Kasbah* (*Platonos 4*) serves huge Moroccan-influenced meals; the delicious couscous mains (3800 dr) are enough to satisfy two hungry people. For a seafood treat, head to the upmarket *Alexis* (*Sokratous 18*).

The funky *Kafe Besara* (*Sofokleous 11*), run by Australian expat Sara, and *Marco Polo Cafe* (*Agiou Fanouriou 40*) are both popular for daytime coffees and evening drinks.

Entertainment There is a distinctly average *sound-and-light show* at the Palace of the Knights, depicting the Turkish siege. A noticeboard outside gives the times for performances

GREECE

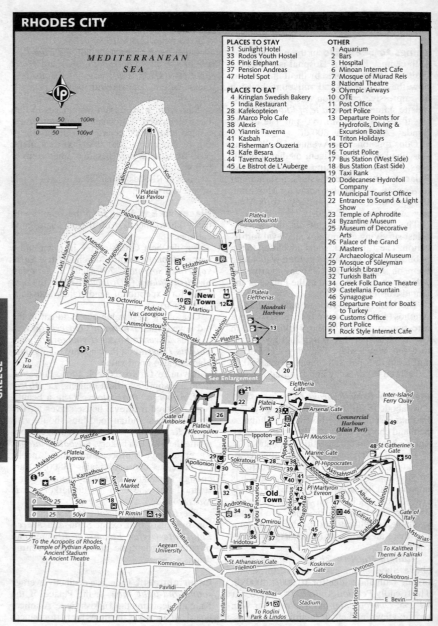

RHODES CITY

MEDITERRANEAN SEA

PLACES TO STAY
31 Sunlight Hotel
33 Rodos Youth Hostel
36 Pink Elephant
37 Pension Andreas
47 Hotel Spot

PLACES TO EAT
4 Kringlan Swedish Bakery
5 India Restaurant
28 Kafekopteion
35 Marco Polo Cafe
38 Alexis
40 Yiannis Taverna
41 Kasbah
42 Fisherman's Ouzeria
43 Kafe Besara
44 Taverna Kostas
45 Le Bistrot de L'Auberge

OTHER
1 Aquarium
2 Bars
3 Hospital
6 Minoan Internet Cafe
7 Mosque of Murad Reis
8 National Theatre
9 Olympic Airways
10 OTE
11 Post Office
12 Port Police
13 Departure Points for
   Hydrofoils, Diving &
   Excursion Boats
14 Triton Holidays
15 EOT
16 Tourist Police
17 Bus Station (West Side)
18 Bus Station (East Side)
19 Taxi Rank
20 Dodecanese Hydrofoil
   Company
21 Municipal Tourist Office
22 Entrance to Sound & Light
   Show
23 Temple of Aphrodite
24 Byzantine Museum
25 Museum of Decorative
   Arts
26 Palace of the Grand
   Masters
27 Archaeological Museum
29 Mosque of Süleyman
30 Turkish Library
32 Turkish Bath
34 Greek Folk Dance Theatre
39 Castellania Fountain
46 Synagogue
48 Departure Point for Boats
   to Turkey
49 Customs Office
50 Port Police
51 Rock Style Internet Cafe

in different languages, or you can check the schedule with the EOT. Admission is 1200 dr.

The **Greek Folk Dance Theatre** (☎ 29 085) on Andronikou gives first-rate performances, beginning at 9.20 pm. Admission is 3500 dr.

The old town has some great bars, but a popular place for big-time bar-hopping is Orfanidou in the city's north-west, lined with bars representing almost every nationality.

Around the Island

The imposing **Acropolis of Lindos**, Rhodes' most important ancient city, shares a rocky outcrop with a **crusader castle**. The site is open 8 am to 7 pm Tuesday to Friday, and 8.30 am to 3 pm weekends. Admission is 1200 dr. Below the site is Lindos town, with labyrinths of winding streets full of whitewashed, elaborately decorated houses. It's undeniably beautiful but very touristy. The bus to Lindos from Rhodes City's east-side station costs 1000 dr.

The extensive ruins of **Kamiros**, an ancient Doric city on the west coast, are well preserved, with the remains of houses, baths, a cemetery and a temple, but the site should be visited as much for its lovely setting on a gentle hillside overlooking the sea.

Between Rhodes City and Lindos the **beaches** are crowded. If you prefer isolation, venture south to the bay of Lardos. Even farther south, between Genadi and Plimmyri, you'll find good stretches of deserted sandy beach. On the west coast, beaches tend to be pebbly and the sea is often choppy.

Getting There & Away

Air There are daily flights from Rhodes to Athens (23,400 dr) and Karpathos (12,800 dr). In summer there are regular services to Iraklio, Mykonos, Santorini, Kassos and Kastellorizo. The Olympic Airways office (☎ 24 571) is at Ierou Lohou 9.

For information and efficient service, Triton Holidays (☎ 21 690, fax 31 625, ✉ info@ tritondmc.gr) near the New Market at Plastira 9 is hard to beat.

Ferry There are daily ferries from Rhodes to Piraeus (9000 dr). Most sail via the Dodecanese north of Rhodes, but at least three times a week there is a service via Karpathos, Kassos, Crete and the Cyclades. The EOT gives out a schedule.

There are daily excursion boats to Symi (5000 dr return), as well as a hydrofoil (3000 dr one way) and regular ferry service (1600 dr). Similar services also run to Kos, Kalymnos, Nysiros, Tilos, Patmos and Leros.

Between April and October there are regular boats from Rhodes to Marmaris (Turkey); one-way tickets cost 11,000 dr (13,500 dr return). There is an additional US$10 Turkish port tax each way.

From March to August there are regular ferries to Israel (from 28,000 dr) via Cyprus (17,000 dr). Prices do not include foreign port tax.

For the port police, call ☎ 27 695.

Getting Around

To/From the Airport There are frequent buses between the airport and Rhodes City's west-side bus station (450 dr). A taxi to the airport costs about 3500 dr.

Bus Rhodes City has two bus stations. The west-side bus station, next to the New Market, serves the airport, the west coast, Embona and Koskinou; the east-side station, nearby on Plateia Rimini, serves the east coast and inland southern villages. The EOT has a schedule.

Car & Motorcycle You'll be tripping over independent car and motorcycle-rental outlets in Rhodes City's new town, particularly on and around 28 Oktovriou. Try to bargain – competition is fierce.

Many parts of the old town are prohibited to cars, but there are car parks around the periphery.

SYMI Σύμη
☎ 0241 • pop 2332

Symi town is outstandingly attractive, with pastel-coloured neoclassical mansions surrounding the harbour and covering the surrounding hills. The island is easily accessible by boat from Rhodes, but you'll have more fun if you stay over when the day-trippers have gone.

There is no tourist office or tourist police. Perhaps the best source of information is the English-language *Symi Visitor* newspaper, widely available and free of charge. It includes useful maps of the town, which is divided into

GREECE

two parts: Gialos, the harbour, and Horio, above it, crowned by the kastro.

There is little by way of budget accommodation on the island; double rooms average about 14,000 dr. *Catherinettes Rooms to Let* (☎ 72 698), *Hotel Glafkos* (☎ 71 358) and *Rooms to Let Helena* (☎ 71 931), all scattered around the harbour, are some good options. The bulk of the restaurants are at the end of the harbour. *O Meraklis* and *Taverna Neraida* are cheap and cheerful eateries; at night, the *Sunflower* sandwich and salad bar turns into an excellent vegetarian restaurant. *Hellenikon* has a cellar of 140 different Greek wines, while *Tholos*, a five-minute walk from the harbour towards the tiny town beach, offers well-prepared, imaginative fare.

Aside from the excursion boats, a number of ferries and hydrofoils between Rhodes and Kos also call at Symi. The port police are on ☎ 71 205.

KARPATHOS Κάρπαθος
☎ 0245 • pop 5323
The picturesque, elongated island of Karpathos lies midway between Crete and Rhodes. It's a relaxed place, with little of the hype that surrounds more touristed islands.

Orientation & Information
The main port and capital is Pigadia, and there's a smaller port at Diafani. There's no EOT or tourist police; your best bet is to see one of the travel agencies. Karpathos Travel (☎ 22 148) is on Dimokratias. There is Internet access at Caffe Galileo, two doors from the Olympic Airways office on Apodimon Karpathou, the main thoroughfare running parallel to the waterfront.

Things to See & Do
Karpathos has glorious **beaches**, particularly at Apella, Kira Panagia and Lefkos.

The northern village of **Olymbos** is like a living museum and is endlessly fascinating to ethnologists. Women wear brightly coloured and embroidered skirts, waistcoats and headscarves and goatskin boots. Interiors of houses are decorated with embroidered cloth and their facades with brightly painted moulded-plaster reliefs, and the inhabitants speak a dialect which retains some

Doric words. A two-hour uphill walking trail leads from Diafani to Olymbos, and there are infrequent local buses between these two towns. There are excursions to Olymbos from Pigadia, but these leave you with an excessive 4½ hours in the small town.

Places to Stay & Eat
There's plenty of accommodation and owners usually meet the boats. *Harry's Rooms* (☎ 22 188), just off 28 Oktovriou, has spotless singles/doubles with shared bathroom for 4500/5500 dr. *Hotel Avra* (☎ 22 388, 28 Oktovriou) has comfortable doubles with/without private bath for 8000/6000 dr. Basic accommodation is also available at Diafani, Olymbos and several other villages.

To sample traditional local dishes, head for busy *Taverna Karpathos*, near the quay. On Apodimon Karpathou there is a wonderful *taverna* that serves great mezedes and often has locals playing music. The place has no sign – it's a white and blue building just up from the National Bank of Greece.

Getting There & Away
Karpathos has an international airport that receives charter flights from northern Europe. There are daily flights to Rhodes (12,700 dr) and three a week to Kassos (6800 dr) and Athens (25,900 dr).

There are three ferries a week to Rhodes (4400 dr) and to Piraeus (7900 dr) via the Cyclades and Crete. In bad weather, ferries do not stop at Diafani. There is also a weekly high-speed catamaran on the Kassos-Karpathos-Halki-Rhodes route. For the port police, call ☎ 22 227.

KOS Κως
☎ 0242 • pop 26,379
Kos is renowned as the birthplace of Hippocrates, father of medicine. Kos town manifests the more ghastly aspects of mass tourism, and the beaches are pretty horrendous, with wall-to-wall sun lounges and beach umbrellas. The island is crowded but there are a few areas where you can try to escape the masses.

Orientation & Information
Kos town, on the north-east coast, is the main town and port. The municipal tourist office

(☎ 24 460, 🖃 dotkos@hol.gr), Vasileos Georgiou 1, is near the hydrofoil pier. The post office is on Vasileos Pavlou; the OTE is on the corner of Vironos and Xanthou. Internet access is available at Cafe Del Mare, Megalou Alexandrou 4.

Things to See

Before you beat a hasty retreat from Kos town, check the 13th-century **fortress** and the **archaeological museum**, open 8 am to 3 pm Tuesday to Sunday. Entry is 800 dr. The **ancient agora** and the **odeion** are also worth seeing.

On a pine-clad hill, 4km from Kos town, stand the extensive ruins of the renowned healing centre of **Asclepion**, where Hippocrates practised medicine. The site is open 8 am to 3 pm Tuesday to Sunday; admission is 800 dr.

The villages in the **Asfendion** region of the Dikeos Mountains are reasonably tranquil. There is a long stretch of beach along Kefalos Bay. **Paradise** is the most appealing of these beaches, but don't expect to have it to yourself.

Places to Stay & Eat

Kos Camping (☎ 23 910) is 3km along the eastern waterfront. There are frequent buses from the harbourfront in town; take any heading to Agios Fokas.

Otherwise, head for the convivial *Pension Alexis* (☎ 28 798, 25 594, Irodotou 9) close to the harbour (the entrance is on Omirou). Singles/doubles/triples with shared bath cost 5000/7500/9000 dr. The friendly English-speaking Alexis is a font of information. He is also the owner of *Hotel Afendoulis* (☎ 25 321, Evripilou 1), where comfortable, well-kept singles/doubles/triples with private bath cost 7500/11,000/13,0000 dr.

Olympiada behind the Olympic Airways office, and *Filoxenia Taverna* on the corner of Pindou and Alikarnassou, are popular with locals. *Creta Corner* on the corner of Artemisias and Korai serves excellent, well-priced food, and there's often live Greek music.

Entertainment

Kos town is well known for its nightlife. The streets of Diakon and Nafklirou are lined with bars that are jam-packed in high season.

Getting There & Away

Apart from European charter flights, there are daily flights from Kos to Athens (21,400 dr). The Olympic Airways office (☎ 28 331) is at the southern end of Vasileos Pavlou.

There are frequent ferries from Rhodes that continue on to Piraeus (7700 dr) via Kalymnos, Leros and Patmos. There are less frequent connections to Nisyros, Tilos, Symi, Samos and Crete. Daily excursion boats also go to Nisyros, Kalymnos and Rhodes. Ferries travel daily in summer to Bodrum in Turkey costing 9000 dr one way (10,000 dr return). A particularly helpful agency is Pulia Tours (☎ 26 388), Vasileos Pavlou 3.

For the port police, call ☎ 26 594.

Getting Around

Buses for Asclepion, Agios Fokas (for the camping ground) and Lampi leave from opposite the town hall on the harbourfront; all other buses leave from the station behind the Olympic Airways office.

PATMOS Πάτμος
☎ 0247 • pop 2663

Starkly scenic Patmos gets crowded in summer, but manages to remain remarkably tranquil. Orthodox and Western Christians have long made pilgrimages to this holy island.

Orientation & Information

The tourist office (☎ 31 666), post office and police station are all in the white Italianate building at the island's port and capital of Skala. There is an Internet cafe, Millennium, a few blocks inland from the port, just up from the OTE.

Things to See

The **Monastery of the Apocalypse**, on the site where St John wrote the book of Revelations, is between the port and the hora. The attraction here is the cave where the saint lived and dictated his revelations. Opening times are 8 am to 1 pm daily and 4 to 6 pm on Tuesday, Wednesday and Sunday.

The hora's whitewashed houses huddle around the fortified **Monastery of St John the Theologian**, which houses a vast collection of monastic treasures, including embroidered robes, Byzantine jewellery and early manuscripts and icons. It's open the same hours as

GREECE

the Monastery of the Apocalypse. Admission to the monastery is free, but it costs 1200 dr to see the treasury.

Appropriate dress (ie, no shorts) is requested for visitors to the holy sites.

Patmos' indented coastline provides numerous secluded coves, mostly with pebble beaches. The best is Psili Ammos in the south, reached by excursion boat.

Places to Stay & Eat

Stefanos Camping (☎ *31 821*) is on Meloi Beach, 2km north-east of Skala. Someone usually meets the ferries, but call ahead to make sure.

There are a few budget pensions along the hora road, including *Pension Maria Paskeledi* (☎ *32 152*), where singles/doubles/triples with shared bathroom cost 4000/7000/9000 dr.

There is a cluster of mid-range hotels about 500m to the right of the port as you disembark. *Hotel Australis* (☎ *31 576*) and *Villa Knossos* (☎ *32 189*), next to each other, offer pleasant singles/doubles for 10,000/15,000 dr, and both have wonderful gardens. Hotel Australis also has pricier studio apartments.

O Pantelis Taverna, one block back from the waterfront, and *Grigoris Taverna*, opposite the passenger-transit port building, are popular eateries. *Restaurant Pisofani* serves up good fresh fish.

Cafe Aman, a five-minute walk from the port (turn left facing inland), offers excellent salads and pastas in a lovely setting. Aman and its neighbouring bars are popular for late-night drinks.

Getting There & Around

Frequent ferries travel between Patmos and Piraeus (7200 dr), and to Rhodes (4400 dr) via Leros, Kalymnos and Kos. There are also frequent boats to Samos. For the port police, call ☎ 34 131. Skala, Hora, Grikos and Kambos are connected by buses which depart from the port. In summer there are frequent excursion boats to the various beaches and to the islets of Arki and Marathi.

KASTELLORIZO Καστελλόριζο (MEGISTI)

☎ 0241 • pop 275

Tiny Kastellorizo lies 116km east of Rhodes, its nearest Greek neighbour, and only 2.5km

from the southern coast of Turkey. Its **Blue Grotto** is spectacular and comparable to its namesake in Capri. The name derives from the blue appearance of the water in the grotto, caused by refracted sunlight. Excursion boats will take you to the cave, and also to some of the surrounding islets, all of which are uninhabited. The island's remoteness is drawing a steady trickle of visitors, but as yet it remains pristine. There are plenty of rooms for rent – owners usually meet the boats. Three flights (10,900 dr) and two ferries (3700 dr) a week operate between Rhodes and Kastellorizo.

North-Eastern Aegean Islands

These islands are less visited than the Cyclades and the Dodecanese. There are seven major islands in this group: Chios, Ikaria, Lesvos, Limnos, Samos, Samothraki and Thasos.

SAMOS Σάμος

☎ 0273 • pop 32,000

Samos was an important centre of Hellenic culture and is reputedly the birthplace of the philosopher and mathematician Pythagoras. Lush and humid, its mountains are skirted by pine, sycamore and oak-forested hills.

Orientation & Information

Samos has three ports: Vathy (Samos town) and Karlovasi on the north coast, and Pythagorio on the south-east coast.

Vathy's unhelpful EOT office (☎ 28 530) is in a side street one block north of Plateia Pythagora. A better bet is ITSA Travel (☎ 23 605/06, ✉ itsa@otenet.gr), directly opposite the port. Friendly staff here can help with ferries, excursions and accommodation, plus there's free luggage storage.

The post office is on Smyrnis, four blocks from the waterfront. The OTE is on Plateia Iroön, behind the municipal gardens. There is a cybercafe on the waterfront, 250m from Plateia Pythagora and next to the police station.

Things to See & Do

Very little is left of the **ancient city** of Samos, on which the town of Pythagorio now stands. The Sacred Way, once flanked by

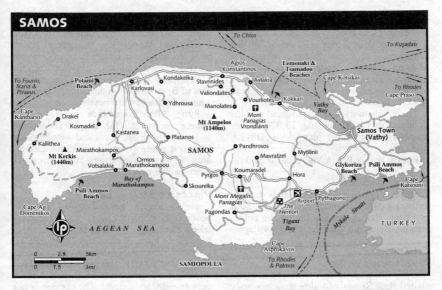

SAMOS

To Chios

To Kuşadası

To Fourni,
Ikaria &
Piraeus

Potami
Beach

Kondakeïka

Agios
Konstantinos

Stavrinides

Avlakia

Lemonaki &
Tsamadou
Beaches

Cape Kotsikas

To Rhodes
Cape Praso

Karlovasi

Valiondates

Vourliotes

Kokkari

Cape
Kanthario

Drakeï

Ydhrousa

Manolates

Moni
Panagias
Vrondianis

Vathy
Bay

Samos Town
(Vathy)

Kosmadeï

Kastanea

Mt Ampelos
(1140m)

Platanos

SAMOS

Pandhrosos

Mytilinii

Kallithea

Marathokampos

Mt Kerkis
(1440m)

Votsalakia

Ormos
Marathokampou

Pyrgos

Koumaradeï

Mavratzeï

Hora

Glykoriza
Beach

Psili Ammos
Beach

Cape
Katsouni

Bay of
Marathokampos

Skoureïka

Psili Ammos
Beach

Moni Megalis
Panagias

Airport

Pythagorio

TURKEY

Cape Ag
Domenikos

AEGEAN SEA

Pagondas

The
Hereon

Tigani
Bay

Mykale Straits

0   2.5   5km
0   1.5   3mi

SAMIOPOULA

Cape
Asprokavos

To Rhodes
& Patmos

2000 statues, has now metamorphosed into the airport's runway.

The extraordinary **Evpalinos Tunnel**, built in the 6th century BC, is the site's most impressive surviving relic. The 1km tunnel was dug by political prisoners and used as an aqueduct to bring water from the springs of Mt Ampelos. Part of it can still be explored. It's 2km north of Pythagorio and is open 8.30 am to 3 pm daily, except Monday. Entry is 800 dr.

Vathy's **archaeological museum**, by the municipal gardens, is outstanding, the highlight being a 4.5m kouros statue. It's open 8.30 am to 3 pm daily, except Monday. Admission is 800 dr.

The villages of **Manolates** and **Vourliotes** on the slopes of Mt Ampelos are excellent walking territory, as there are many marked pathways. There's also good walking in the area north-east of Vathy. Quiet beaches can be found on the south-west coast in the Marathokampos area.

Places to Stay & Eat

Pythagorio, where you'll disembark if you've come from Patmos, is touristy and expensive. Vathy, 20 minutes away by bus, is cheaper. *Pythagoras Hotel* (☎ 28 422, fax 28 893, ✉ smicha@otenet.gr) is a good budget option.

Doubles/triples in high season go for 9000/11,000 dr, but considerably less at other times. There's also a good-value restaurant here. The hotel is 800m to the left of the quay. Call ahead to be met at the port.

The friendly *Pension Vasso* (☎ 23 258) is open year-round and has singles/doubles/triples for 5000/9000/12,000 dr with balcony and bath. To get there from the quay, turn right onto the waterfront, left onto Stamatiadou and walk up the steps. Nearby, *Hotel Ionia* (☎ 28 782) is cheap. Singles/doubles with shared bathroom are 4000/6000 dr.

Hotel Samos (☎ 28 377, fax 23 771, ✉ hotsamos@otenet.gr) on the waterfront just near the port is a decent choice, offering singles/doubles/triples for 9900/12,600/17,450 dr. The hotel has lots of facilities, including rooftop pool, bar and restaurant.

The popular *Taverna Gregoris*, near the post office, serves good food at reasonable prices. *O Kipos* (The Garden), one block back from the waterfront on Kalomiri, offers good traditional food in a lovely outdoor setting.

Getting There & Away

Samos has an international airport receiving European charter flights. There are also daily flights to Athens (17,400 dr) and two flights a week to Thessaloniki (25,400 dr).

There are daily ferries to Piraeus (6700 dr), some via Paros and Naxos, others via Mykonos, and two ferries a week to Chios (3000 dr). There are ferries to Patmos (3100 dr one way) or excursion boats for day-trippers (8000 dr return).

There are daily boats to Kuşadası (for Ephesus) in Turkey, costing 13,000 dr one way (14,000 dr return), plus US$10 Turkish port tax.

For the port police in Vathy call ☎ 27 318.

Getting Around

To get to Vathy's bus station, follow the waterfront and turn left onto Lekadi, 250m south of Plateia Pythagora (just before the police station). Buses run to all the island's villages.

CHIOS Χίος
☎ 0271 • pop 54,000

'Craggy Chios', as Homer described it, is less visited than Samos and almost as riotously fertile. It is famous for its mastic trees, which produce a resin still used in chewing gum.

In 1822 an estimated 25,000 inhabitants of the island were massacred by the Turks after an uprising against Turkish rule.

Orientation & Information

The main town and port is Chios town, which is unattractive and noisy; only the old Turkish quarter has any charm. It is, however, a good base from which to explore the island.

The municipal tourist office (☎ 44 389) is at Kanari 18, the main street running from the waterfront to Plateia Vounakiou in the town centre. Manos Center (☎ 20 002), right by the ferry dock, can help with accommodation and transport arrangements and is open to meet the 4 am ferry from Piraeus.

The OTE is 100m beyond the tourist office, and the post office is on Rodokanaki, a block back from the waterfront. On the southern waterfront at Egeou 98 is Enter Internet Café (the cafe is upstairs; enter from the side street).

Things to See

The **Philip Argenti Museum**, in the same building as the Korais library near the cathedral in Chios town, contains exquisite embroideries and traditional costumes. It's open 8 am to 2

pm weekdays (also 5 to 7.30 pm Friday) and 8 am to 12.30 pm Saturday. Admission is 300 dr.

The **Nea Moni** (New Monastery), 14km west of Chios town, houses some of Greece's most important mosaics. They date from the 11th century and are among the finest examples of Byzantine art in the country. It's open 8 am to 1 pm and 4 to 8 pm daily; entry is free.

Pyrgi, 24km from Chios town, is one of Greece's most beautiful villages. The facades of its dwellings are decorated with intricate grey and white geometric patterns. **Emboreios**, 6km south of Pyrgi, is an attractive black-pebble beach.

Places to Stay & Eat

There's a *camping ground* (☎ 74 111) on the beach 14km north of Chios town. To reach it, take a Kardamyla or Langada bus.

In Chios town, *Rooms Alex* (☎ 26 054, Livanou 29) offers good budget accommodation. Rooms cost 8000 dr with private bath, there's a lovely roof terrace and the owner, Alex, is very friendly and helpful. The pension is one block back from the waterfront, about 500m south of the quay. *Chios Rooms* (☎ 20 196) at the opposite end of the harbour to the ferry dock, has clean, simple rooms in a lovely old building. Singles/doubles with shared bath are 5000/9000 dr, with private bathroom 7000/11,000 dr.

By the police station, 50m to the right of the ferry disembarkation point, is *Ouzeri Theodosiou*, a popular establishment serving delectable mezedes. Opposite Rooms Alex is *Ta Duo Aderfi* (The Two Brothers), with a pleasant garden and good food.

There's an astonishing number of bars lining the waterfront, catering largely to the 2000 students from the island's university.

Getting There & Away

There are daily flights from Chios to Athens (15,800 dr) and twice-weekly flights to Thessaloniki (22,400 dr) and Lesvos (10,900 dr).

Ferries sail at least twice a week to Samos (3000 dr) and Piraeus (5800 dr) via Lesvos, and once a week to Thessaloniki (8400 dr) via Lesvos and Limnos. There are a few boats to the small islands of Psara, west of Chios, and Inousses, to the east. In summer daily boats travel to Çeşme in Turkey; tickets cost 15,000 dr one way (20,000 dr return), plus

US$10 Turkish port tax. For the port police call ☎ 44 433.

Getting Around

There are two bus stations. Blue buses go to local villages (Vrontados, Karyes, Karfas) and leave from the right side (coming from the waterfront) of Plateia Vounakiou, by the garden. Green, long-distance buses (to Pyrgi and Mesta) leave from the station one block to the left of Plateia Vounakiou.

LESVOS (MYTILINI) Λέσβος
(Μυτιλήνη)

Lesvos is the third largest Greek island. It has always been a centre of artistic and philosophical achievement and creativity, and it remains a spawning ground for innovative ideas in the arts and politics.

A useful source of information on the island is the Web site www.greeknet.com.

Mytilini
☎ 0251 • pop 23,970

Mytilini, the capital and port of Lesvos, is a large working town built around two harbours. All passenger ferries dock at the southern harbour. The tourist police (☎ 22 776) are at the entrance to the quay; the EOT (☎ 42 511) is 50m up the road at Aristarhou 6. The post office is on Vournazon, west of the southern harbour, and the OTE is on the same street. Internet access is available at Net Club, 200m south of the southern harbour on Eliti; it's open from 4 pm weekdays, from 10 am Saturday and Sunday.

Things to See Mytilini's imposing **castle**, built in early Byzantine times and renovated in the 14th century, opens 8.30 am to 3 pm daily, except Monday. The new **archaeological museum**, signposted north of the quay, is open 8.30 am to 3 pm Tuesday to Sunday. Don't miss the **Theophilos Museum**, which houses the works of the prolific primitive painter Theophilos. It's 4km from Mytilini in the village of Varia (take a local bus) and is open 9 am to 2.30 pm and 6 to 8 pm Tuesday to Sunday. Entry to each of these attractions costs 500 dr.

Places to Stay & Eat Domatia owners belong to a cooperative called Sappho Room

Finding Service; most of these domatia are in little side streets off Ermou, near the northern harbour. *Salina's Garden Rooms* (☎ 42 073, Fokeas 7) has doubles from 6500 dr with shared facilities; nearby, *Thalia Rooms* (☎ 24 640, Kinikiou 1) has doubles from 7500 dr with private bath. Nearest to the quay is *Iren* (☎ 22 787, Komninaki 41), where clean but simple doubles/triples cost 9000/11,000 dr.

The ramshackle but atmospheric *Ermis Ouzeri* has yet to be discovered by the tourist crowd. It's at the northern end of Ermou on the corner with Kornarou. There are popular tavernas spilling over the pavement south of the harbour; *Stratos Psarotaverna* offers good fish dishes.

The Lazy Fish (*Imvrou 5*) is an atmospheric place for a drink.

Around the Island

Northern Lesvos is best known for its exquisitely preserved traditional town of **Mithymna** (also known as Molyvos), which is a good place to spend a few days. The neighbouring beach resort of **Petra**, 6km south, is affected by low-key package tourism, while the villages surrounding **Mt Lepetymnos** are authentic, picturesque and worth a day or two of exploration.

Western Lesvos is a popular destination for lesbians who come on a kind of pilgrimage in honour of Sappho, one of the greatest poets of ancient Greece. The beach resort of **Skala Eresou** is built over ancient Eresos, where she was born in 628 BC.

Southern Lesvos is dominated by **Mt Olympus** (968m), with pine forests decorating its flanks. **Plomari**, a large traditional coastal village, is popular with visitors, and the picturesque village of **Agiasos** is a favourite day-trip destination.

Getting There & Away

There are daily flights from Lesvos to Athens (19,900 dr), and less frequent services to Thessaloniki (20,900 dr), Limnos (13,400 dr) and Chios (10,900 dr). The Olympic Airways office (☎ 28 659) is at Kavetsou 44.

In summer there are daily boats to Piraeus (7200 dr), some via Chios. There are three a week to Kavala (6500 dr) via Limnos and two a week to Thessaloniki (8400 dr). Ferries to Ayvalik, Turkey cost 16,000 dr one

GREECE

way (21,000 dr return). The port police (☎ 28 827) are 75m from the port on Pavlou Kountouriotou.

Getting Around

There are two bus stations in Mytilini. The one for long-distance buses is just beyond the south-western end of Pavlou Kountouriotou. For local buses go to the harbour's northern-most section.

SAMOTHRAKI Σαμοθράκη
☎ 0551 • pop 2800

This wild, alluring island has only recently been discovered by holiday-makers and is deservedly popular with walkers. Experienced trekkers can climb **Mt Fengari** (1611m), the highest mountain in the Aegean.

Samothraki's big attraction is the **Sanctuary of the Great Gods**, an ancient site at Paleopolis shrouded in mystery. No one knows quite what went on here, only that it was a place of initiation into the cult of the Kabeiroi, the gods of fertility. They were believed to help seafarers, and to be initiated into their mysteries was seen as a safeguard against shipwreck and other misfortune. The site's winding pathways lead through lush shrubbery to extensive ruins. The site's most celebrated relic, the *Winged Victory of Samothrace*, which now has pride of place in Paris' Louvre, was discovered here in 1863. Both the site and its small museum are open 8.30 am to 3 pm Tuesday to Sunday. Admission to each is 500 dr.

Samothraki's port is Kamariotissa on the north-west coast. The island's capital, the hora (also called Samothraki), is 5km inland. Most people stick to the resorts of Kamariotissa, Loutra (Therma) and Pahia Ammos, leaving the rest of the island untouched.

There are two camping grounds at Loutra and a number of domatia in the port and hora. Ferries link Samothraki with Limnos, and with Kavala and Alexandroupolis on the mainland.

Sporades Σποράδες

The Sporades group comprises the lush, pine-forested islands of Skiathos, Skopelos and Alonnisos, south of the Halkidiki Peninsula, and far-flung Skyros, off Evia.

Getting There & Away

Air Skiathos receives many charter flights from northern Europe. In summer there are daily flights from Athens to Skiathos (16,700 dr) and two a week between Athens and Skyros (14,200 dr).

Ferry Skiathos, Skopelos and Alonnisos have frequent ferry services to the mainland ports of Volos and Agios Konstantinos, as well as one or two a week to Kymi (Evia), via Skyros. In high season there are also connections to Thessaloniki.

There is an extensive hydrofoil service from these mainland ports and between the islands. The hydrofoils are more frequent, faster and more convenient, but fares are double those for the ferries.

In summer, three hydrofoils a week connect Skyros with other islands in the Sporades.

SKIATHOS Σκίαθος
☎ 0427 • pop 4100

Skiathos is tagged the Mykonos of the Sporades, which means it's crowded and expensive, but it does have good beaches, particularly on the south coast. However, the island lacks the charm of Skopelos and Alonissos.

Orientation & Information

There is a tourist information booth and helpful touch-screen computer to the left as you disembark from the boats. Skiathos town's main thoroughfare is Papadiamanti, running inland from opposite the port. Here you'll find the post office, the OTE and the tourist police (☎ 23 172). Around the corner from the post office, on Evangelistrias, is Internet Zone Cafe. A good source of information is the Web site at www.n-skiathos.gr.

Places to Stay & Eat

There is a Rooms to Let kiosk on the waterfront, to the right as you disembark, or you can wander Papadiamanti and its side streets looking for hotels or domatia. Be warned that accommodation is hard to come by in July and August.

There is a *camping ground* (☎ 49 250) at Koukounaries Beach on the south coast. In town, the best value is at *Hotel Karafelas* (☎ 21 235) at the end of Papadiamanti. Quite comfortable single/doubles are available for 10,000/14,000 dr.

Numerous fast-food outlets, cafes and bars line Papadiamanti. *Niko's Cafe Bar* offers an extensive menu at reasonable prices. The waterfront restaurants are much of a muchness, catering to the tourist trade. A notable exception is popular *Ta Psaradiki Ouzeri* at the far end of the old harbour by the fish market.

Getting There & Around

See earlier for information about flights to/from Skiathos.

There are frequent ferries to Volos (2700 dr) and Agios Konstantinos (3300 dr) and regular connections to Skopelos, Alonissos and Skyros. The port police are on ☎ 22 017.

Crowded buses ply the south-coast road between Skiathos town and Koukounaries Beach every 20 to 30 minutes, stopping at the beaches along the way.

SKOPELOS Σκόπελος
☎ 0424 • pop 5000

Skopelos is less commercialised than Skiathos, but following hot on its trail.

Information

There is no tourist office or tourist police in Skopelos town. The post office is well hidden in the labyrinth of alleyways behind the waterfront. To find it, walk up the road opposite the bus station, take the first left, the first right, the first left again, and it's on the right. The OTE is signposted from the middle of the waterfront, and there's a cybercafe, Click & Surf, one block back from the waterfront on Nirvana.

Things to See

Attractive **Skopelos town**, with white houses built on a hillside, hides mazes of narrow streets and stairways leading up to the kastro. **Glossa**, the island's other town, lying inland in the north, is similarly appealing with fewer concessions to tourism.

Staphylos, 4km from Skopelos town, is a decent beach that gets very crowded; over a headland is **Velanio**, the island's designated nudist beach. The 2km stretch of tiny pebbles at **Milia**, 10km farther on, is considered the island's best beach.

Places to Stay & Eat

The Rooms & Apartments Association of Skopelos (☎ 24 567), in a small office on the waterfront, can help you find accommodation.

Pension Sotos (☎ 22 549) in a charming old building in the middle of the waterfront has charming doubles/triples with private bath for 10,000/15,000 dr. There's also a communal kitchen and courtyard garden.

A 10-minute walk from the port is *Pension Soula* (☎ 22 930) with rooms for 12,000/15,000 dr, a communal kitchen and garden. To find it, walk right from the port and turn left at Hotel Amalia. Follow the road, bearing right after about 200m, and the pension is on the right.

Zio Peppe on the waterfront has excellent pizza from 700 dr. For a cheap, basic and popular restaurant, try *O Platanos*, just in from the bus station. *Restaurant Alexander*, beyond the OTE (follow the signs), is more upmarket but offers good, reasonably priced fare in a lovely garden setting.

Getting There & Around

There are frequent ferries to Volos (3400 dr) and Agios Konstantinos (4100 dr). These boats also call at Alonnisos and Skiathos. Large ferries dock behind the bus station; other boats at the quay to the harbour's north. Many hydrofoil services to Skopelos also call at Loutraki, the port for Glossa. You can contact the port police on ☎ 22 180.

The bus station is on the waterfront. There are frequent buses from Skopelos town to Glossa, stopping at the beaches on the way.

ALONNISOS Αλόννησος
☎ 0424 • pop 3000

Alonnisos is the least visited of these islands and is green and serene. The water surrounding the island has been declared a marine park and is the cleanest in the Aegean.

The harbour town is Patitiri; the hora is a few kilometres inland. A winding path starting from just beyond Pension Galini in Patitiri leads within 40 minutes to the hora. Alonnisos is an ideal island for walking and there is a network of well-signposted trails, as well as guided walks offered by many of the travel agencies.

Kokkinokastro and **Hrysia Milia** are among the good beaches lining the coast.

GREECE

Places to Stay & Eat

There are two camping grounds: large, shady *Camping Rocks* (☎ 65 410) in Patitiri and smaller *Ikaros Camping* (☎ 65 258) on the east coast at Steni Vala beach. There is a Rooms to Let service (☎ 65 577) opposite the quay.

Pension Galini (☎ 65 573, fax 65 094) is a good choice: doubles/triples cost 15,000/17,000 dr with private bath. Spacious, well-equipped apartments for four/six people are also available for 20,000/25,000 dr. The pension is 400m up Pelasgon, on the left beside the lobster restaurant (there's no sign).

For imaginatively prepared local cuisine, try *To Kamaki Ouzeri*, on Ikion Dolopon.

Getting There & Away

There are frequent ferries to Volos (3800 dr) and Agios Konstantinos (4400 dr) via Skiathos and Skopelos. The port police can be reached at ☎ 65 595.

Ionian Islands
Τα Επτάνησα

The Ionian Islands stretch down the west coast of Greece from Corfu in the north to remote Kythira, situated off the southern tip of the Peloponnese.

Getting There & Away

Air There are lots of charter flights to Corfu from northern Europe in summer, as well as a few flights to Kefallonia and Zakynthos. Olympic has daily flights from Athens to Corfu, Zakynthos, Kefallonia and Kythira.

Ferry Most ferries between Italy and Patras call at Corfu. In summer, there are also services from Brindisi to Kefallonia, Zakynthos and Paxi.

CORFU Κέρκυρα

Corfu is the most important island in the group, with a population of 107,592.

Corfu Town

☎ 0661 • pop 36,000

The old town of Corfu, wedged between two fortresses, occupies a peninsula on the is-land's east coast. The narrow alleyways of high shuttered tenements in mellow ochres and pinks are an immediate reminder of the town's long association with Venice.

Orientation & Information The town's old fortress (Palaio Frourio) stands on an eastern promontory, separated from the town by an area of parks and gardens known as the Spianada. The new fortress (Neo Frourio) lies to the north-west. Ferries dock at the new port, just west of the new fortress. The long-distance bus station is on Avrami, just inland from the port.

The EOT office (☎ 37 520) is on Rizospaston Voulefton, between the OTE and the post office, and the tourist police (☎ 30 265) are at Samartzi 4. All the major Greek banks are in town, including the National Bank on the corner of Voulgareos and Theotoki. American Express is represented by Greek Skies Tours (☎ 30 883), Kapodistriou 20A.

Things to See The **archaeological museum**, Vraili 5, houses a collection of finds from Mycenaean to classical times. The star attraction is the pediment from the Temple of Artemis, decorated with gorgons. Opening times are 8.45 am to 3 pm Tuesday to Saturday and 9.30 am to 2.30 pm Sunday; admission is 800 dr.

The **Church of Agios Spiridon**, Corfu's most famous church, has an elaborately decorated interior. Pride of place is given to the remains of St Spiridon, displayed in a silver casket; four times a year they are paraded around the town.

Places to Stay & Eat There are no decent budget places in town. A lot of people wind up at the *Hotel Evropi* (☎ 39 304), but only because it's close to the port – it's signposted off Xenofondos Stratigou. It charges 5500/6000 dr for singles/doubles.

The cheapest reasonable rooms are at the *Hotel Ionian* (☎ 30 628), also near the port at Xenofondos Stratigou 46. It charges 8500/11,000 dr for singles/doubles with bathroom. The C-class *Hotel Konstantinopolis* (☎ 48 716, fax 48 718, Zavitsianou 3) is a splendid Art Nouveau hotel. Singles/doubles are 12,500/18,600 dr.

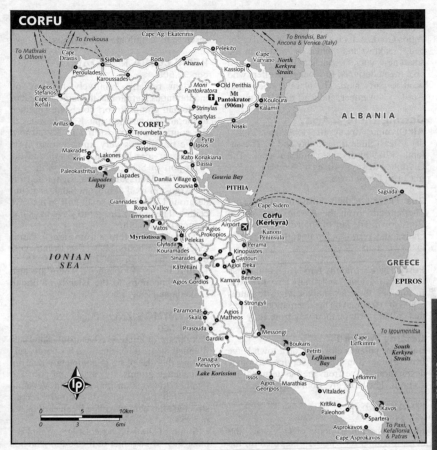

CORFU

There are several cheap restaurants near the new port. The tiny *O Thessalonikios* on Xenofondos Stratigou does succulent spit-roast chicken (1200 dr). In town, try *Hrysomalis (Nik Theotaki 6)* near the Spianada.

Around the Island
There's hardly anywhere in Corfu that hasn't made its play for the tourist dollar, but the north is totally over the top. The only real attraction there is the view from the summit of **Mt Pantokrator** (906m), Corfu's highest mountain. There's a road to the top from the village of **Strinila**.

The main resort on the west coast is **Paleo-kastritsa**, which is built round a series of pretty bays. Farther south, there are good beaches around the small village of **Agios Gordios**. Between Paleokastritsa and Agios Gordios is the hill-top village of **Pelekas**, supposedly the best place on Corfu to watch the sunset.

Places to Stay
Accommodation on Corfu is dominated by package groups. Most backpackers head straight for the *Pink Palace* (☎ *53 103/04, fax 53 025,* ✉ *pink-palace@ker.forthnet.gr),* a

GREECE

huge complex of restaurants, bars and budget rooms that tumbles down a hillside outside Agios Gordios. It charges 6500 dr per day for bed, breakfast and dinner, or 7500 dr in the smart new wing. Debauchery is the main item on a menu designed for young travellers who want to party hard. The place is open from April to November, and staff meet the boats.

Getting There & Away
Air Olympic Airways flies to Athens (23,400 dr) at least three times a day and to Thessaloniki (20,900 dr) three times a week. The Olympic Airways office (☎ 38 694) is at Polila 11 in Corfu town.

Bus There are daily buses to Athens and Thessaloniki from the Avrami terminal in Corfu town. The fare of 8650 dr to Athens includes the ferry to Igoumenitsa. The trip takes 11 hours.

Ferry There are hourly ferries to Igoumenitsa (1400 dr, 1½ hours) and a daily ferry to Paxoi. In summer, there are daily services to Patras (5800 dr, 10 hours) on the international ferries that call at Corfu on their way from Italy.

Getting Around
Buses for villages close to Corfu town leave from Plateia San Rocco. Services to other destinations leave from the bus terminal on Avrami. The EOT gives out a schedule.

ITHAKI Ιθάκη
pop 3100
Ithaki is the fabled home of Odysseus, the hero of Homer's *Odyssey*, who pined for his island during his journeys to far-flung lands. It's a quiet place with some isolated coves. From the main town of Vathy you can walk to the **Fountain of Arethousa**, the fabled site of Odysseus' meeting with the swineherd Eumaeus on his return to Ithaki. Take water with you, as the fountain dries up in summer.

Ithaki has daily ferries to the mainland ports of Patras and Astakos, as well as daily services to Kefallonia and Lefkada.

KEFALLONIA Κεφαλλονιά
pop 32,500
Tourism remains relatively low-key on mountainous Kefallonia, the largest island of the Ionian group. Resort hotels are confined to the areas near the capital, the beaches in the south-west, Argostoli and the airport. Public transport is very limited, apart from regular services between Argostoli and the main port of Sami, 25km away on the east coast. The **Melissani Cave**, signposted off the Argostoli road 4km from Sami, is an underground lake lit by a small hole in the cave ceiling. The nearby **Drogarati Cave** has some impressive stalactites.

There are daily ferries from Sami to Patras (3450 dr, four hours), as well as from Argostoli and the south-eastern port of Poros to Kyllini in the Peloponnese. There are also ferry connections to the islands of Ithaki, Lefkada and Zakynthos.

ZAKYNTHOS Ζάκυνθος
pop 32,560
Zakynthos, or Zante, is a beautiful island surrounded by great beaches – so it's hardly surprising that the place is completely overrun by package groups. Its capital and port, Zakynthos town, is an imposing old Venetian town that has been painstakingly reconstructed after being levelled by an earthquake in 1953.

Some of the best beaches are around the huge **Bay of Laganas** in the south, which is where endangered loggerhead turtles come ashore to lay their eggs in August – at the peak of the tourist invasion. Conservation groups are urging people to stay away and the Greek government has declared this area a National Marine Park.

There are regular ferries between Zakynthos and Kyllini in the Peloponnese.

Ireland

This chapter covers the independent Republic of Ireland and Northern Ireland, which forms part of the United Kingdom (UK).

Ireland is one of Western Europe's least populated, least industrialised and, in a word, least 'spoilt' countries. It also has one of the longest and most tragic histories in Europe.

That long history is easy to trace through Stone Age passage tombs and ring forts, medieval monasteries and castles, and the stately homes and splendid Georgian architecture of the 18th and 19th centuries. The tragic side is almost as easy to spot; the reminders of Ireland's long and difficult relationship with Britain are ubiquitous.

WHAT'S IN A NAME?

The north-eastern corner of Ireland is part of the UK and its official name is Northern Ireland. It is also referred to as 'the North', or Ulster, a reference to the historical province of Ulster that, following the partition of Ireland in 1921, was ceded to Britain. The rest of Ireland is known as the Republic of Ireland, although on your travels you may hear it referred to as Éire, the Irish Republic, the Republic, Southern Ireland or 'the South'.

Facts about Ireland

HISTORY
Celts & Vikings

Fierce Celtic warriors probably reached Ireland from mainland Europe around 300 BC and were well ensconced by 100 BC. Christian monks, including St Patrick, arrived in Ireland around the 5th century AD and as the Dark Ages enveloped Europe, Ireland became an outpost of European civilisation; a land of saints, scholars and missionaries, its thriving monasteries produced beautiful illuminated manuscripts, some of which survive to this day.

From the end of the 8th century, the rich monasteries were targets of raids by Vikings until they, too, began to settle. At the height of their power the Vikings ruled Dublin, Waterford and Limerick, but they were eventually defeated by the legendary Celtic hero

Brian Ború, the king of Munster, at the battle of Clontarf in 1014.

The British Arrive

In 1169 the Norman conquest of England, by then more than a century old, spread to Ireland when Henry II, fearful of the growing power of the Irish kingdoms, dispatched his forces to the island – the legendary figure Strongbow among them. Yet just as the Vikings had first raided then settled and assimilated, so did the

709

Anglo-Norman intruders. Over the centuries, English control gradually receded to an area around Dublin known as 'the Pale'.

In the 1500s, the Protestant Henry VIII moved once again to enforce English control over his unruly neighbour, but real entanglement in Irish affairs was left to his daughter and successor, Elizabeth I. Under Elizabeth the oppression of the Catholic Irish got seriously under way. Huge swathes of Irish land were confiscated and given to trustworthy Protestant settlers, sowing the seeds of the divided Ireland that exists today. The English forces put down a series of rebellions and in 1607 the disheartened Irish lords departed for France in the 'Flight of the Earls'.

In 1641 a Catholic rebellion in Ulster led to violent massacres of Protestant settlers. Later in the decade, the English Civil War ended in victory for Oliver Cromwell and defeat for the Catholic sympathiser Charles I. Once again English attention was turned to sorting out Ireland. Cromwell rampaged through the country for two years, starting in 1649, leaving a trail of blood and smoke behind him.

Less than a decade later, the Restoration saw Charles II on the English throne. His Catholic sympathies were kept firmly in check, but in 1685 his brother James II (a Scotsman) succeeded him. James' more outspoken Catholicism raised the ire of English Protestants, and he was forced to flee the country, intending to raise an army in Ireland and regain his throne, which had been handed over to the Protestant William of Orange (a Dutchman) and his wife Mary (James' daughter). In March 1689 James II arrived from France at Kinsale, near Cork, and marched north to Dublin and then Derry (Londonderry). Unfortunately for James II, William of Orange landed in 1690 at Carrickfergus, just north of Belfast, with an army of up to 36,000 men. The ensuing Battle of the Boyne took place on 12 July 1690; William's victory was a turning point, and is commemorated to this day by northern Protestants as a pivotal triumph over 'popes and popery'.

By early in the 18th century, the dispirited Catholics in Ireland held less than 15% of the land and suffered a host of brutal restrictions in employment, education, land ownership and religion. An organisation known as the United Irishmen, originally formed by Belfast Presbyterians, began agitating for Irish civil rights under the leadership of a young Dublin Protestant and republican, Theobald Wolfe Tone (1763-98). The United Irishmen started out with high ideals of bringing together men of all creeds to reform and reduce England's power in Ireland. Its attempts at gaining power through straightforward politics were fruitless, and when war broke out between Britain and France, the United Irishmen tried to organise a French invasion of Ireland. In 1796 a French fleet with thousands of troops approached Bantry Bay in County Cork but was repelled by poor weather. A few years later Wolfe Tone attempted an invasion with another French fleet, but he was captured by the British and later committed suicide in jail.

Ireland's Protestant gentry, alarmed at the level of unrest, was much inclined to cuddle back up to the security of Britain. In 1800 the Act of Union, joining Ireland politically with Britain, was passed. The Irish parliament duly voted itself out of existence, and around 100 of the Irish MPs moved to the House of Commons in London.

In the first half of the 19th century Daniel O'Connell (1775-1847) seemed to be succeeding in moving Ireland towards greater independence by peaceful means. In 1828 O'Connell stood for a seat representing County Clare in the British parliament, even though being a Catholic meant that he could not legally take the seat. O'Connell won easily, and rather than risk a Catholic rebellion the British parliament passed the 1829 Act of Catholic Emancipation, allowing Catholics limited voting rights and the right to be elected as MPs. After this great victory, O'Connell settled down to the business of securing further reforms. He unfortunately died just as Ireland was suffering its greatest tragedy.

Introduced from South America, the easily grown potato was the staple food of a rapidly growing but desperately poor Irish population. From 1800 to 1840 the population had rocketed from four to eight million, but successive failures of the potato crop between 1845 and 1851, the so-called Great Famine, resulted in mass starvation and emigration. The lack of support from Britain during the famine was (and remains) a national disgrace; during these years there were excellent harvests of other crops such as wheat, but

IRELAND

Counties

1 Derry	9 Sligo	17 Meath	25 Tipperary
2 Antrim	10 Mayo	18 Louth	26 Ladis
3 Tyrone	11 Roscommon	19 Offaly	27 Kilkenny
4 Fermanagh	12 Galway	20 Kildare	28 Carlow
5 Armagh	13 Longford	21 Dublin	29 Wicklow
6 Down	14 Cavan	22 Clare	30 Cork
7 Donegal	15 Monaghan	23 Kerry	31 Waterford
8 Leitrim	16 Westmeath	24 Limerick	32 Wexford

euro currency converter IR£1 = €1.26

these were too expensive for the poor to purchase and Britain continued to export food from Ireland. As a result, about one million people died, many of disease rather than straight starvation, and another million emigrated. Emigration continued to reduce the population during the next 100 years.

In the late 19th and early 20th centuries, the British parliament finally began to contemplate Irish home rule, but WWI interrupted the process. Ireland might still have moved, slowly but peacefully, towards some sort of accommodation were it not for a bungled uprising in 1916. Though it is now celebrated as a glorious bid for freedom, the so-called Easter Rising was, in fact, heavy with rhetoric, light on planning and decidedly lacking in public support. The British response was just as badly conceived. After the insurrection had been put down, a long, drawn-out series of trials and executions (15 in all) transformed all the ringleaders from troublemakers to martyrs and roused international support for Irish independence.

The Road to Independence

In the 1918 general election, Irish republicans stood under the banner of Sinn Féin (We Ourselves or Ourselves Alone) and won a majority of the Irish seats. Ignoring London's parliament, where technically they were supposed to sit, the newly elected Sinn Féin deputies, many of them veterans of the 1916 Easter Rising, declared Ireland independent and formed the first Dáil Éireann (Irish assembly or lower house), lead by Eamon de Valera. While the Irish had declared independence, the British had by no means conceded it, and a confrontation was imminent.

The Anglo-Irish War (1919-21), pitted Sinn Féin and its military wing, the Irish Republican Army (IRA), against the British. The increasingly harsh responses of Britain's notorious Black and Tans infantry further roused anti-British sentiment, and atrocity was met with atrocity. This was the period when Michael Collins came to the fore, a charismatic and ruthless leader who masterminded the IRA's campaign of violence against the British (while serving as minister for finance in the new Dáil).

After months of negotiations in London, an Irish delegation led by Michael Collins and Arthur Griffith signed the Anglo-Irish Treaty on 6 December 1921. The treaty gave 26 counties of Ireland independence and allowed six largely Protestant counties in Ulster the choice of opting out (a foregone conclusion).

The treaty was ratified by the Irish Dáil in January 1922, but passions were so inflamed that within weeks a civil war broke out. The issue at the time was not so much the future of Protestant Ulster, but rather that, under the terms of the Anglo-Irish Treaty, the British king remained the (nominal) head of the new Irish Free State and Irish MPs were required to swear an oath of allegiance to the British crown. To de Valera and many Irish Catholics, these compromises were a betrayal of IRA and republican principles. In the violence that followed Michael Collins was assassinated in Cork by anti-Treaty forces, while the Free State government briefly imprisoned De Valera.

By 1923 the civil war had ground to a halt, and for nearly 50 years development in the Republic of Ireland was slow and relatively peaceful. After boycotting the Dáil for a number of years, de Valera founded a new party called Fianna Fáil (Warriors of Ireland), which won a majority in the 1932 election. De Valera introduced a new constitution in 1937 that abolished the oath of British allegiance and claimed sovereignty over the six counties of Ulster. In 1948 the Irish government declared the country a republic at last and, in 1949, left the British Commonwealth.

The Troubles

While the Anglo-Irish Treaty granted independence to 26 counties, six counties in the north were governed by a Northern Irish parliament that sat at Stormont, near Belfast, from 1920 until 1972. The Protestant majority made sure its rule was absolute by systematically excluding Catholics from power. This led to the formation of an initially nonsectarian civil rights movement in 1967, to campaign for fairer representation for Northern Irish Catholics. In January 1969 a civil rights march from Belfast to Derry was organised to demand a fairer division of jobs and housing. Just outside Derry a Protestant mob attacked the mostly Catholic marchers. Further marches and protests followed but, increasingly, exasperation on one side was met with violence from the other. And far from keeping the two sides apart, Northern

Ireland's mainly Protestant police force, the Royal Ulster Constabulary (RUC), was becoming part of the problem.

Finally in August 1969 British troops were sent into Derry and, two days later, Belfast, to maintain law and order. Though the Catholics initially welcomed the British army, it soon came to be seen as a tool of the Protestant majority. The peaceful civil rights movement lost ground and the IRA, which had been hibernating, found itself with new and willing recruits for an armed independence struggle.

Thus the so-called Troubles rolled back and forth throughout the 1970s and into the 1980s. Passions reached fever pitch in 1972 when 13 unarmed Catholics were shot dead by British troops in Derry on 'Bloody Sunday' (30 January). Then again in 1981 when IRA prisoners in Northern Ireland went on a hunger strike to demand the right to be recognised as political prisoners (rather than as terrorists). Ten of them fasted to death, the best known being an elected MP, Bobby Sands.

The waters were further muddied by the IRA splitting into 'official' and 'provisional' wings, from which sprang even more violent republican organisations. Protestant paramilitary organisations such as the Ulster Volunteer Force (UVF) sprang up in opposition to the IRA and its splinter groups, and so violence was met with violence.

Giving Peace a Chance

In 1985 the Anglo-Irish Agreement gave the Dublin government an official consultative role in Northern Irish affairs for the first time. The Downing Street Declaration of December 1993, signed by Britain and the Republic, moved matters forward, with Britain declaring that it had no 'selfish, economic or military interest' in preserving the division of Ireland.

In August 1994 the announcement of a 'permanent cessation of violence' on behalf of the IRA by Sinn Féin's leader, Gerry Adams, offered the almost unimagined prospect of peace in Ulster. When Protestant paramilitary forces responded with their own cease-fire in October 1994, most British troops were withdrawn to barracks and roadblocks were removed.

In 1995 the British and Irish governments published two 'framework documents' to lay the groundwork for all-party peace talks. The

subsequent negotiations stalled when Britain's Conservative prime minister, John Major, refused to allow all-party talks to start until the IRA first decommissioned its weapons. The negotiations were shattered in February 1996 by an IRA bomb in the Docklands area of east London. In June 1996, with the IRA's refusal to restore its cease-fire, 'all-party' talks on Ulster's future convened without the participation of Sinn Féin.

At this point the peace process regained momentum. In the British general election of May 1997, Tony Blair's Labour Party won a landslide victory, enabling it to act with a much freer hand than the previous Conservative government. In June 1997 Britain's new Northern Ireland Secretary, Dr Mo Mowlam, promised to admit Sinn Féin to all-party talks following any new cease-fire. Encouraged by this, the IRA declared another cease-fire on 20 July 1997.

To worldwide acclaim these talks produced the Good Friday Agreement on 10 April 1998. This complex agreement allows the people of Northern Ireland to decide their political future by majority vote, and commits its signatories to 'democratic and peaceful means of resolving differences on political issues'. It further established a new Northern Irish parliament and high-level political links between the Republic and Northern Ireland. In May 1998, the agreement was approved by 71% of voters in referendums held simultaneously on both sides of the Irish border. However, despite these moves towards peace, later that year a bomb planted by the 'Real IRA' killed 28 people in Omagh.

Since the Good Friday Agreement the peace process has stopped and started, the new parliament being suspended then reinstated. In Derry there is an official inquiry into the events surrounding Bloody Sunday, which some say is a token gesture. And although at times it seems that the Troubles have been reduced to political banter between the parties, one thing is for sure – Ireland, the island, has an optimistic future and most agree that the 'war' is over.

GEOGRAPHY & ECOLOGY

Ireland is divided into 32 counties: 26 in the Republic and six in Northern Ireland. The island measures 84,421 sq km (about 83% is the Republic) and stretches 486km north to south and 275km east to west. The jagged coastline extends for 5631km. The midlands of Ireland are flat, generally rich farmland and huge swaths of brown peat (which is rapidly being depleted for fuel).

Carrantuohill (1038m) on the Iveragh Peninsula, County Kerry, is the highest mountain on the island. The River Shannon, the longest in Ireland, flows for 259km before emptying into the Atlantic west of Limerick.

Ireland's rivers and lakes are well-stocked with fish such as salmon and trout, and the island is home to some three dozen mammal species, including the Irish hare and Irish stoat. The Office of Public Works (OPW) maintains five national parks and 75 nature reserves in the Republic; the National Trust oversees 26 nature reserves in Northern Ireland.

CLIMATE

Ireland has a relatively mild climate with a mean annual temperature of 10°C. In January and February, average temperatures range from 4° to 7°C. Average maximums in July and August are from 14° to 16°C. June, July and August are the sunniest months; December and January are the gloomiest. The sea around Ireland is surprisingly warm for the latitude, due to the influence of the Gulf Stream. Snow is relatively scarce – perhaps one or two flurries in winter in higher areas.

It does tend to rain a lot in Ireland, often every day for weeks on end. Annual rainfall is about 1000mm.

GOVERNMENT & POLITICS

The Republic of Ireland has a parliamentary system of government. The lower house of parliament (Oireachtas) is known as the Dáil and its 166 members are elected by a system of proportional representation. The prime minister's official title is Taoiseach (pronounced tea shock); the current Taoiseach is Bertie Ahern. The 60-strong upper house is called the Seanad (Senate), and it basically rubber-stamps Dáil legislation. The president (an tuachtaran) of Ireland is elected for seven years. Though the post lacks political power and is limited to two terms, Mary Robinson, the president from 1991-97 and the current UN High Commissioner on Human Rights, injected a healthy dose of liberalism into an

otherwise highly conservative political structure. The current president is Mary McAleese.

The main political parties in the Republic are Fianna Fáil and Fine Gael, although the Labour Party has managed to capitalise on the growing disenchantment with these two traditional power-brokers. Two other parties of note are the Liberal Progressive Democrats, which split from Fianna Fáil in the mid-1980s, and the socialist Democratic Left.

Northern Ireland, governed from London since its ineffective parliament at Stormont was abolished in 1972, elected a new parliament in 1998 as part of the Good Friday Agreement. Northern Ireland's main Protestant parties are the Ulster Unionist Party (UUP) led by David Trimble, and Ian Paisley's hard-line Democratic Unionist Party (DUP). Catholic parties are John Hume's middle-of-the-road Social Democratic and Labour Party (SDLP), and Sinn Féin, the political wing of the IRA led by Gerry Adams. At present, Trimble is the First Minister of the new Northern Ireland parliament.

ECONOMY

The Irish economy is one of Europe's most buoyant, and although small, is exciting international interest. Inflation at present is low, running at around 2%, but experts can't agree if it will go under that mark or through the roof. Exports, mainly to Britain, the European Union (EU) and the USA, continue at record levels. Ireland is a major exporter of computer software, and information technology is now contributing more to the economy than agriculture. In the last five years the economy has grown by an annual average of around 8%. The continuing growth has reduced unemployment figures, now sitting around 5%, although wages are still below EU standards.

Northern Ireland's shipbuilding and other great industrial activities have declined dramatically, but new industries have developed and, of course, the region is heavily supported financially by Britain. Almost 30% of the working population is employed in one way or another by the government. Northern Ireland's unemployment rate has been dropping and now sits at less than 7%.

The first cease-fire, in 1994, brought an almost instant dividend in the shape of a 20% boom in tourism, especially from Britain and the Republic, and the Good Friday Agreement may eventually produce similar results. In 1997-98 foreign investment was a record £522 million, and international companies continue to show interest.

POPULATION & PEOPLE

The total population of Ireland is around 5.2 million: 3.6 million in the Republic and 1.6 million in Northern Ireland. Prior to the 1845-51 Great Famine the population was around eight million; death and emigration reduced it to around six million, and emigration continued at a high level for the next 100 years. It wasn't until the 1960s that Ireland's population finally began to increase again.

ARTS
Music

Traditional Irish music, played on instruments such as the *bodhrán* (a flat, goatskin drum), *uilleann* (or 'elbow') pipes, flute and fiddle, is an aspect of Irish culture that visitors are most likely to encounter. Almost every town and village in Ireland seems to have a pub renowned for its traditional music. Of the Irish music groups, perhaps the best-known are the Chieftains, the Dubliners, Clannad, Altan, De Danann and the wilder Pogues. Among popular Irish singers/musicians who have made it on the international stage are Van Morrison, Enya, Sinéad O'Connor, Bob Geldof, U2, the Cranberries and, more recently, The Corrs, Boyzone, Ash and B*wiched.

Literature

The Irish have made a great impact on world literature. Important writers include Jonathan Swift, Oscar Wilde, WB Yeats, George Bernard Shaw, James Joyce, Sean O'Casey, Samuel Beckett and, more recently, Roddy Doyle, whose *Paddy Clarke Ha Ha Ha* won the Booker Prize in 1993. The Ulster-born poet Séamus Heaney was awarded the Nobel Prize for Literature in 1995. Earlier Irish Nobel laureates include Shaw (1925), Yeats (1938) and Beckett (1969). Presently Frank McCourt is a world favourite with his autobiographical *Angela's Ashes* and *'Tis*.

Architecture

Ireland is packed with archaeological sites, prehistoric graves, ruined monasteries, crumbling fortresses, abandoned manor houses and many other firm reminders of its long and often dramatic history. You may encounter the following terms on your travels:

cashel – a stone ring fort or *rath*
dolmen – a portal tomb or Stone Age grave consisting of stone 'pillars' supporting a stone roof or capstone
ogham stone – a memorial stone of the 4th to 9th centuries, marked on its edge with groups of straight lines or notches to represent the Latin alphabet
passage tomb – a megalithic mound-tomb with a narrow stone passage leading to a burial chamber
ring fort or *rath* – is a circular fort, originally constructed of earth and timber, later made of stone
round tower – a tall tower or belfry built as a lookout and place of refuge from the Vikings

SOCIETY & CONDUCT

The Irish are an easy-going, loquacious, fun-loving people. They are used to tourists and there are few social taboos. In Northern Ireland people have been wary of discussing the Troubles, while in the Republic the subject is more likely to produce resigned indifference – but this is changing. Do not take humorous Irish scepticism or sarcasm too seriously.

Irish society is very homogeneous and people have relatively little experience with those of different races, cultures and sexual orientations. Most people, especially in the countryside, tend to be socially conservative.

RELIGION

Religion has always played a major role in Irish history. Almost everybody is either Catholic or Protestant, with the Republic 95% Catholic and Northern Ireland about 60% Protestant. The Jewish community in Ireland is tiny but long-established.

The Catholic Church has always opposed attempts to liberalise laws governing contraception, divorce and abortion. Today, condom machines can be found in all parts of Ireland, divorce is legal, but abortion remains illegal in the Republic. The Catholic Church still wields considerable power in the Republic. There is, however, a curious ambivalence towards it. Attending Mass is often more a social obligation than a spiritual experience.

IRELAND

LANGUAGE

Officially the Republic of Ireland is bilingual. English is spoken throughout the island, but there are still parts of western and southern Ireland known as the Gaeltacht where Irish – a Celtic language closely related to Scottish Gaelic and less so to Welsh – is still the native language.

It's an attractive but difficult tongue with an orthographic (spelling) system that would have given Charles Berlitz apoplexy. For example, 'mh' is pronounced like 'v', 'bhf' is a 'w', and 'dh' is like 'g'.

Facts for the Visitor

HIGHLIGHTS
Scenery, Beaches & Coastline

There's a lot of natural beauty in Ireland, but among the best is the scenery around the Ring of Kerry and the Dingle Peninsula, the barren stretches of the Burren, the rocky Aran Islands, and the Glens of Antrim in Northern Ireland.

Favourite stretches of coast include the Cliffs of Moher, the Connemara and Donegal coasts, and the Causeway Coast of Northern Ireland.

Museums & Castles

In Dublin, Trinity College's Old Library with the ancient *Book of Kells* is a must-see, and there are extensive collections at the National Museum and National Gallery. Belfast has the Ulster Museum and the Ulster Folk Museum just outside the city.

Ireland is littered with castles and forts of various types and in various stages of ruin. The Stone Age forts on the Aran Islands are of particular interest, but there are other ancient ring forts all over Ireland. Prime examples of castles can be found at Kilkenny, Blarney, and, in Northern Ireland, Carrickfergus and Dunluce.

Religious Sites

The passage tomb at Newgrange, near Dublin, is the most impressive relic of pre-Christian Ireland. Early Christian churches and ruined monastic sites, some well over 1000 years old,

are scattered throughout Ireland. Glendalough, Jerpoint Abbey and the Rock of Cashel are all recommended.

SUGGESTED ITINERARIES

Depending on the length of your stay, you might want to see and do the following things:

Two days
  Visit Dublin and perhaps one place nearby – Powerscourt and Glendalough to the south, or Newgrange to the north.
One week
  Visit Dublin, Glendalough, Kilkenny, the Burren and Galway.
Two weeks
  As for one week, plus the Ring of Kerry (Iveragh Peninsula), Killarney and Cork.
One month
  With your own car you can cover all the main attractions around the coast. This is more difficult to achieve in the same time by bicycle or on public transport.

PLANNING
When to Go

The tourist season begins the weekend before the much celebrated St Patrick's Day (17 March) and is in full swing from Easter onward.

In July and August the crowds are at their biggest and that's when prices are at their highest. Many tourist facilities close or have shorter opening hours in the quieter winter months.

Maps

There are many good-quality maps of Ireland, including the Michelin *Ireland Motoring Map* No 405 (1:400,000) and the four-part Ordnance Survey Holiday Map series (1:250,000).

What to Bring

The Irish climate is changeable and even at the height of summer you should be prepared for cold weather and sudden rainfall. A raincoat and/or umbrella is an absolute necessity.

Walkers should be particularly well prepared if they are crossing open country. Otherwise, Ireland presents few surprises. Dress is usually casual even in the cities.

IRELAND

TOURIST OFFICES

The Irish tourist board, Bord Fáilte (pronounced bord fawlcha), and the Northern Ireland Tourist Board (NITB) operate separate offices. Both are usually well organised and helpful, though Bord Fáilte will not provide any information on places (such as B&Bs and camping grounds) that it has not approved.

Every town big enough to have half-a-dozen pubs will have a tourist office. Most will find you a place to stay for a fee of IR£1 to IR£2. Many of the smaller offices are closed in winter.

Tourist Offices Abroad

Overseas offices of Bord Fáilte include:

Australia (☎ 02-9299 6177) 5th Floor, 36 Carrington St, Sydney, NSW 2000
Canada (☎ 416-929 2777) 160 Bloor St East, Suite 1150, Toronto, Ont M4W 1B9
Netherlands (☎ 020-622 3101) Spuistraat 104, 1012 VA Amsterdam
New Zealand (☎ 09-379 3708) Dingwall Bldg, 87 Queen St, Auckland 1
UK (☎ 020-7766 9920) Ireland House, 24 Haymarket, London SW14 4DG
USA (☎ 212-418 0800) 345 Park Ave, New York, NY 10154

Tourist information for Northern Ireland abroad is usually handled by the British Tourist Authority (BTA), though there are a few offices of the NITB:

Canada (☎ 416-925 6368) 2 Bloor St West, Suite 1501, Toronto, Ont M5R 3J8
New Zealand (☎ 09-379 3708) Dingwall Bldg, 87 Queen St, Auckland 1
UK (☎ 020-7839 8416) British Travel Centre, 12 Lower Regent St, London SW1Y 4PQ
USA (☎ 212-922 0101) 551 5th Ave, Suite 701, New York, NY 10176

VISAS & DOCUMENTS

For citizens of the EU and most other Western countries, no visa is required to visit either the Republic or Northern Ireland. EU nationals are allowed to stay indefinitely, while other visitors can usually remain for three to six months.

UK nationals born in Britain or Northern Ireland do not need a passport, but it's advisable to carry some form of identification.

EMBASSIES & CONSULATES

Irish Embassies & Consulates

Irish diplomatic offices overseas include:

Australia (☎ 02-6273 3022) 20 Arkana St, Yarralumla, ACT 2600
Canada (☎ 613-233 6281) 130 Albert St, Ottawa, Ont K1A 0L6
Japan (☎ 03-3263 0695) 2-10-7 Kojimachi, Chiyoda-ku, Tokyo 102
South Africa (☎ 012-342 5062) Delheim Suite, Tulbach Park, 1234 Church St, 0083 Colbyn, Pretoria
UK (☎ 020-7235 2171) 17 Grosvenor Place, London SW1X 7HR
USA (☎ 202-462 3939) 2234 Massachusetts Ave NW, Washington DC 20008. In addition there are consulates in Boston, Chicago, New York and San Francisco.

Foreign Embassies in Ireland

Foreign embassies in Dublin include:

Australia (☎ 01-676 1517) 6th floor, Fitzwilton House, Wilton Terrace, Dublin 2
Canada (☎ 01-478 1988) 65-68 St Stephen's Green, Dublin 2
France (☎ 01-260 1666) 36 Ailesbury Rd, Dublin 4
UK (☎ 01-205 3742) 29 Merrion Rd, Dublin 4
USA (☎ 01-668 9946) 42 Elgin Rd, Dublin 4

In Northern Ireland, nationals of most countries other than the USA should contact their embassy in London.

USA (☎ 028-9032 8239) Queens House, 14 Queen St, Belfast

MONEY

Currency

The Irish pound or punt (IR£), like the British pound sterling (£), is divided into 100 pence (p). Banks offer the best exchange rates. Exchange bureaus are open longer than banks, but the rate is not as good and the commission higher. Most of the post offices provide currency-exchange facilities and are open on Saturday morning.

Pounds sterling are used in Northern Ireland, though several banks also issue their own Northern Irish pound notes, which are equivalent to sterling but not readily accepted in Britain.

Most major currencies and types of travellers cheques are readily accepted in Ireland. Eurocheques can also be cashed here.

IRELAND

Exchange Rates

country	unit		Irish pound
Australia	A$1	=	IR£0.51
Canada	C$1	=	IR£0.59
euro	€1	=	IR£0.79
France	1FF	=	IR£0.12
Germany	DM1	=	IR£0.40
Japan	¥100	=	IR£0.80
New Zealand	NZ$1	=	IR£0.39
UK	UK£1	=	IR£1.32
USA	US$1	=	IR£0.87

Costs

Ireland is an expensive place, marginally more costly than Britain, but prices vary around the island. Many places to stay, particularly hostels (but also hotels and some B&Bs) have low and high-season prices. Entry prices to sites and museums are usually 20% to 50% lower for children, students and senior citizens (OAPs).

For the budget traveller, IR£40 per day should cover hostel accommodation, getting around, a meal in a restaurant and possibly something for the folks at home – leaving just enough for a pint at the end of the day.

ATMs & Credit/Charge Cards

Major credit cards, particularly Visa and MasterCard (often called Access), are widely accepted, even at B&Bs. You can obtain cash advances on your card from banks and from automatic teller machines (ATMs). Even small towns have ATMs that accept foreign cards affiliated with the Star, Plus and Eurocard networks.

Tipping

Fancy hotels and restaurants usually add a 10% or 15% service charge onto the bill. Simpler places usually do not add service; if you decide to tip, just round up the bill (or add 10% at most). Taxi drivers do not have to be tipped, but if you're feeling flush 10% is more than generous.

Consumer Taxes

Value-added tax (VAT) applies to most goods and services in Ireland. People residing in EU countries are not entitled to a VAT refund. Other visitors can claim back the VAT on purchases that are being taken out of the EU. If you buy something from a so-called Cashback Store (they have signs), you will be given a voucher that can be refunded at most international airports or stamped at ferry ports and mailed back for refund.

POST & COMMUNICATIONS

Post

Post offices (An Post) in the Republic are open 9 am (9.30 am on Tuesday or Wednesday) to 5.30 pm weekdays, 9 am to 1 pm Saturday; smaller offices close for lunch.

Postcards cost 28p to EU countries and 38p outside Europe, while aerograms cost 32p to EU countries, 52p outside Europe.

Post-office hours and postal rates in Northern Ireland are the same as in Britain. Mail can be addressed to poste restante at post offices, but is officially held for only two weeks. Writing 'hold for collection' on the envelope may help.

Telephone

Phonecards are almost essential these days in the Republic, where Telecom Éireann sells Callcards of 10/20/50/100 units for IR£2/3.50/8/16.

In Northern Ireland, telephone booths (boxes) accepting British Telecom (BT) phonecards are few and far between outside Belfast. International calls can be dialled directly from pay phones.

See the Telephones appendix at the back of this book for information about making international calls to or from the Republic or Northern Ireland (ie, the UK). The important difference is that to call Northern Ireland from the Republic, you do not use ☎ 0044 as for the rest of the UK. Instead, you dial ☎ 028 and then the local number.

Direct Home Calls You can dial direct to your home country operator and then reverse charges or charge the call to a local phone-credit card. Dial the following codes then the area code and number you want. Your home-country operator will come on the line before the call goes through:

Australia	☎ 1800 5500 61 + number
France	☎ 1800 5500 33 + number
New Zealand	☎ 1800 5500 64 + number
UK BT	☎ 1800 5500 44 + number
UK Mercury	☎ 1800 5500 04 + number

USA AT&T	☎ 1800 5500 00 + number
USA MCI	☎ 1800 5510 01 + number
USA Sprint	☎ 1800 5520 01 + number

Fax, Telegraph, Email & Internet Access

Faxes can be sent from post offices or other specialist offices. To send international telegrams, phone ☎ 196 in the Republic or ☎ 0800-190190 in Northern Ireland. Internet cafes are slowly springing up all over the country. The rate for email and Internet access is about IR£5 per hour.

INTERNET RESOURCES

The World Wide Web is a major source of information, although sites vary widely in accuracy. Your first stop should be the award-winning Lonely Planet site (www .lonelyplanet.com.au/dest/eur/ire.htm). For an overview of travelling and tourism in Ireland you can try the Dublin Tourism Centre (www.visit.ie/dublin), Bord Fáilte (www .ireland.travel.ie) or the Northern Irish Tourism Board (www.ni-tourism.com).

The *Irish Times* (www.irish-times.ie) has an award-winning site with Irish news, arts features and its much-loved crossword puzzles. Travel Ireland (www.travel-ireland .com) is a reservation service dressed up with some information on sights.

BOOKS

Lonely Planet's *Ireland*, *Dublin* and *Walking in Ireland* guides offer comprehensive coverage of the island and its most visited city.

One of the better books about Irish history is *The Oxford Companion to Irish History* (1998) edited by SJ Connolly.

NEWSPAPERS

The main papers in the Republic are the Dublin-based *Irish Times* and *Irish Independent* and the *Cork Examiner*. In Northern Ireland there's the *Belfast Telegraph* and the staunchly Protestant *News Letter* tabloid. British newspapers are available as is the *International Herald Tribune* and *USA Today*.

RADIO & TV

Ireland has two state-controlled television channels (RTÉ 1 and Network 2) and three radio stations. Northern Ireland's two TV channels are BBC Northern Ireland and Ulster Television. With the right aerial, Britain's BBC and other stations can now be picked up in most parts of the country. Raidió na Gaeltachta (92.5/96 FM or 540/828/963 MW) is the national Irish-language service.

PHOTOGRAPHY

Ireland and its people are very photogenic, but the sky is often overcast, so photographers should bring high-speed film (eg, 200 or 400 ASA). A roll of 24-exposure print film costs around IR£5 or so to process.

TIME

Ireland is on the same time as Britain and advances the clock by one hour from late March to late October. During the summer months it stays light until after 10 pm.

LAUNDRY

Most towns have several laundrettes, usually with an attendant who washes, dries and neatly folds your clothes for around IR£5. Hostel laundries are usually good value.

TOILETS

Public toilets in the Republic are often marked *fir* for men and *mná* for women.

WOMEN TRAVELLERS

Women travellers will find Ireland a blissfully relaxing experience, with little risk of hassle on the street or anywhere else. Nonetheless, walking alone at night, especially in certain parts of Dublin, is unwise. Hitching is not recommended, even though it's probably safer than anywhere else in Europe.

There's little need to worry about what you wear in Ireland. Nor is finding contraception the problem it once was, although anyone on the pill should bring adequate supplies with them.

GAY & LESBIAN TRAVELLERS

Despite the 1993 decriminalisation of homosexuality for people over the age of 17 in the Republic (1982 in Northern Ireland), gay life is generally not acknowledged or understood. Only Dublin, and to a certain extent Belfast and Cork, have open gay communities. The *Gay Community News*, a free tabloid published monthly in Dublin, is available at bars

IRELAND

and cafes or by subscription to GCN at 6 South William St, Dublin 2 (☎ 01-671 0939/9076, ✉ gcn@tinet.ie). The bi-monthly events magazine *In Dublin* has a gay and lesbian section with club and resource-centre listings. Information is also available from the following:

OUThouse Community Centre (☎ 01-670 6377) 6 South William St, Dublin 2) Web site: //indigo.ie/~outhouse
Northern Ireland Gay Rights Association (NIGRA; ☎ 028-9066 4111) Cathedral Buildings, Lower Donegall St, Belfast
Rainbow Project Northern Ireland (☎ 028-9031 9030) 33 Church Lane, Belfast

DISABLED TRAVELLERS

Guesthouses, hotels and sights throughout Ireland are increasingly being adapted for people with disabilities. Bord Fáilte's various accommodation guides indicate which places are wheelchair accessible, and the NITB publishes *Accessible Accommodation in Northern Ireland*. The National Rehabilitation Board and Dtour have put together a Web site at www.iol.ie/infograf/dtour that lists accessibility information for accommodation in both the Republic and Northern Ireland.

National Rehabilitation Board (☎ 01-874 7503) 44 North Great George's St, Dublin 1
Disability Action (☎ 028-9049 1011) 2 Annadale Ave, Belfast BT7 3JH

DANGERS & ANNOYANCES

Ireland is probably safer than most countries in Europe, but the usual precautions should be observed. Drug-related crime is on the increase, and Dublin has its fair share of pickpockets. Be careful with your belongings when you visit pubs and cafes.

If you're travelling by car note that Dublin is notorious for car break-ins and petty theft. Car theft is also a problem in Belfast. Cyclists should always lock their bicycles and be cautious about leaving bags attached.

The emergency number in both the Republic and Northern Ireland is ☎ 999.

BUSINESS HOURS

Offices are open 9 am to 5 pm weekdays, shops a little later. On Thursday and/or Friday, shops stay open later. Many are also open on Saturday. In winter, tourist attractions are often open

shorter hours, fewer days per week or may be shut completely. In Northern Ireland the main thing to remember is that many tourist attractions are closed on Sunday morning, rarely opening until around 2 pm – well after church services (and Sunday lunch) have ended.

PUBLIC HOLIDAYS & SPECIAL EVENTS

Public holidays in Ireland (IR), Northern Ireland (NI) or both are:

New Year's Day 1 January
St Patrick's Day 17 March
Easter March/April – Good Friday, Easter Monday
May Holiday (IR) – first Monday in May
May Bank Holidays (NI) – first and last Mondays in May
June Bank Holiday (IR) – first Monday in June
Orangemen's Day (NI) – 12 July, or 13th if 12th is a Sunday
August Holiday (IR) – first Monday in August
August Bank Holiday (NI) – last Monday in August
October Holiday (IR) – last Monday in October
Christmas Day 25 December
St Stephen's Day/Boxing Day 26 December

The All-Ireland hurling and football finals both take place in Dublin in September. There are some great regional cultural events around the island, like the Galway Arts Festival in late July. In Dublin, Leopold Bloom's Joycean journey around the city is marked by various events on Bloomsday (16 June). The Dublin International Film Festival in April is also a highlight. In Northern Ireland, July is marching month and every Orangeman in the country hits the streets on the 'glorious 12th'. Other events include the Ould Lammas Fair at Ballycastle in August, and the Belfast Festival at Queen's in November.

ACTIVITIES

Ireland is a great place for outdoor activities, and the tourist boards put out a wide selection of information sheets covering bird-watching (the Hook area of County Wexford), surfing (great along the west coast), scuba diving, hang-gliding, trout and salmon fishing, ancestor tracing, horse riding, sailing, canoeing and many other activities.

Walking is particularly popular although, as usual, you must come prepared for wet weather. There are now well over 20 way-marked trails, varying in length from the 26km Cavan Way to the 900km Ulster Way.

WORK

At present Ireland is good for casual employment; many pubs and restaurants advertise positions in their windows. Citizens of EU countries can work in Ireland without special papers. For information contact an Irish embassy or consulate in your own country.

ACCOMMODATION

Bord Fáilte's dedicated guides to camping grounds, B&Bs, hotels etc cost IR£1.50 and IR£4. There are also a great many excellent places that aren't 'tourist-board approved'. NITB publishes *Where to Stay* (£3.99), which covers similar ground for Northern Ireland.

Bord Fáilte offices book local accommodation for a fee of IR£1 (or IR£2 to book in another town). This can be handy when it may take numerous phone calls to find a free room. The NITB provides a similar booking service.

All accommodation prices in this chapter are high-season rates (generally June to August); at other times of year, subtract 15% to 25% from the listed prices.

Camping

Camping grounds are not as common in Ireland as they are elsewhere in Europe, but there are still plenty of them around. Some hostels also have space for tents. At commercial camping grounds, costs are typically IR£6 to IR£8 for a tent and two people.

Hostels

There are hordes of hostels in Ireland, but in summer they can be heavily booked.

An Óige (meaning 'youth'), the Irish branch of Hostelling International (HI), has 37 hostels scattered round the country, and there are another seven in Northern Ireland administered by the Youth Hostel Association of Northern Ireland (YHANI). These hostels are open to members of HI, members of An Óige/YHANI (annual membership IR£10), or to any overseas visitor for an additional nightly charge of IR£1. If you pay the extra charge six times, you become a member.

Two other associations with reliable accommodation include the Independent Holiday Hostels (IHH), a cooperative group with 137 associated hostels in both Northern Ireland and the Republic; and the 'back-to-basics' Independent Hostels Owners (IHO) association, with 82 members around Ireland.

From June to September nightly costs at most hostels are IR£7 to IR£10, except for the more expensive hostels in Dublin, Belfast and a few other places. Rates are cheaper in the low season.

An Óige (☎ 01-830 4555, ✉ anoige@iol.ie) 61 Mountjoy St, Dublin 7
Youth Hostel Association of Northern Ireland (YHANI; ☎ 028-9031 5435) 22-32 Donegall Rd, Belfast
Independent Holiday Hostels (IHH; ☎ 01-836 4700, ✉ ihh@iol.ie) 57 Gardiner St Lower, Dublin 1
Independent Hostels Owners in Ireland (IHO; ☎ 073-30130) Dooey Hostel, Glencolumbcille, County Donegal

B&Bs

The bed and breakfast is as Irish a form of accommodation as there is. It sometimes seems every other house is a B&B, and you'll stumble upon them in the most unusual and remote locations. Typical costs are IR£16 to IR£20 per person a night, though more-luxurious B&Bs can cost from IR£25 a head. Most B&Bs are very small, so in summer they can quickly fill up. Breakfast at an Irish B&B is almost inevitably cereal followed by 'a fry', which means fried eggs, bacon and sausages, plus toast and/or brown-bread and butter.

FOOD

Traditional meals (like Irish Stew, often found in pubs) are hearty and cheap. There are also some more obscure recipes that any traveller worth their salt should try. Fast food is everywhere, from traditional fish and chips to more recent arrivals like burgers, pizzas and kebabs. A bowl of the day's soup and some excellent soda or brown bread can be a cheap lunch. Seafood, long neglected in Ireland, is often excellent, especially in the west, and there are some good vegetarian restaurants. For an interesting and entertaining view of eating and drinking in Ireland see Lonely Planet's *World Food Ireland*.

IRELAND

DRINKS

In Ireland a drink means a beer, either lager or stout. Stout is usually Guinness, the famous black beer of Dublin, although in Cork it can mean a Murphy's or a Beamish. If you don't develop a taste for stout, a wide variety of lagers are available, including Harp and Smithwicks. Simply asking for a Guinness will get you a pint (570ml, IR£2 to IR£2.25 in a pub). If you want a half-pint (285ml, IR£1 to IR£1.20), ask for a 'glass' or a 'half'.

In the Republic, pub hours are 10.30 am to 11.30 pm Monday to Saturday, and 12.30 to 2 pm and 4 to 11 pm Sunday. A bill for longer drinking hours was before parliament at the time of writing. In Northern Ireland, pub hours are 11.30 am to 11 pm Monday to Saturday, 12.30 to 2 pm and 7 to 10 pm Sunday.

ENTERTAINMENT

Listening to traditional music in a pub while nursing a pint of Guinness is the most popular form of entertainment in Ireland. If someone suggests visiting a particular pub for its good 'crack' (from the Irish *craic*), it means a good time, convivial company, sparkling conversation and scintillating music. Music sessions usually begin at around 9 or 9.30 pm at pubs. Theatre is popular, and a 'medieval banquet' (a sort of Irish theatre-restaurant performance in an old castle) finds its way onto many tourist itineraries.

An impressive Web site for what's happening in Ireland is at www.entertainmentireland .ie where there are reviews, festival information and listings for music, clubs, theatre, exhibitions and comedy.

SHOPPING

Clothing, especially anything woollen and hand-knitted or woven, is the most authentically Irish purchase. Celtic-inspired jewellery and fine Waterford crystal and glassware are other popular buys.

Getting There & Away

AIR

Aer Lingus is the Irish national airline with international connections to other countries in Europe and to the USA. Ryanair is the next largest Irish carrier, with routes to Europe and the USA.

Britain

Dublin, Shannon and Cork are linked by a variety of airlines to many cities in Britain, including London's five airports. There are also flights to various regional cities in the Republic of Ireland. The standard return economy fare from London to Dublin is around £155, but advance-purchase fares are available, offering return tickets for as low as £60. These usually must be booked well in advance because seats are often limited. Ryanair has some of the best deals to Dublin from London's Stansted airport, sometimes as low as £20 one-way. Virgin Atlantic Airways flies from London City airport to Dublin.

Belfast is also linked with several cities in Britain, including London (Heathrow), by the British Airways Express shuttle service. Costs on the shuttle range from £50 off-peak one-way to £150 for an advance-purchase return.

Continental Europe

Dublin is connected with other major centres in Europe; there are also flights to Cork, Shannon and Belfast. From Paris, the standard return fare to Dublin is around 1700FF, to Belfast (via London) 2200FF, but prices for both can reach 4000FF in peak times.

The USA

Aer Lingus (from New York and other centres) and Delta (from Atlanta) fly direct to Dublin and Shannon. Because competition on flights to London is so much fiercer, it is usually cheaper to fly to London first. During the summer high season, the return fare between New York and Dublin with Aer Lingus is around US$850, though advance-purchase fares sit just under US$650 return. In the low season, discount return fares from New York to London are about US$500, and in the high season between US$600 and US$700.

Australia & New Zealand

Advance-purchase excursion fares from Australia or New Zealand to Britain (see the Britain chapter) can have a return flight to Dublin tagged on at no extra cost. Return fares from Australia vary from around

A\$1700 (low season) to A\$2500 (high season), but special deals often are available.

LAND

Because of cheap flights, getting to Ireland by land (including ferry) is not very popular. Bus Éireann and National Express operate Eurolines and Supabus services direct from London and other UK centres to Dublin, Belfast and other cities. For details in London, contact Eurolines (☎ 0870-514 3219), or National Express (☎ 0870-580 8080). London to Dublin by bus takes about 12 hours and costs £20/38 to £30/55 one-way/return. To Belfast it's 13 hours and slightly more expensive.

SEA

There's a great variety of ferry services from Britain and France to Ireland. Prices vary drastically, depending on season, time of day, day of the week and length of stay. One-way fares for an adult foot passenger can be as little as IR£20, but nudge close to £50 in summer. For a car plus driver and up to four adult passengers, prices can range from IR£170 to IR£300. There are often special deals, discounted return fares and other money savers worth investigating.

Britain

There are ferry services from Scotland (Cairnryan and Stranraer), England (Fleetwood, Heysham and Liverpool), Wales (Fishguard, Holyhead, Pembroke and Swansea) and the Isle of Man (Douglas) to ports in the Republic (Dublin, Cork, Rosslare Harbour and Dun Laoghaire) and Northern Ireland (Belfast and Larne).

Following is a list of shipping lines:

Irish Ferries
(☎ 0870-517 1717) For services from Holyhead to Dublin (3¼ hours by ferry), and Pembroke to Rosslare Harbour (four hours by ferry)
Isle of Man Steam Packet Company and SeaCat Services
(☎ 0870-552 3523) For catamaran services from Douglas (Isle of Man) to Belfast (2¾ hours, May to September) and Dublin (2¾ hours, May to September), Liverpool to Dublin (four hours), and Heysham (four hours), Stranraer (1½ hours) and Troon (2½ hours) to Belfast

Norse Irish Ferries
(☎ 028-9077 9090) For services from Liverpool to Belfast (8½ hours by ferry)
P&O European Ferries
(☎ 0870-242 4777) For services from Cairnryan to Larne (one hour by fast ferry, 2½ hours by ferry), Fleetwood to Larne (eight hours by ferry) and Liverpool to Dublin (eight hours by ferry)
Stena Line
(☎ 0870-570 7070) For services from Holyhead to Dublin (3¾ hours by ferry) and Dun Laoghaire (1¾ hours by fast ferry), Fishguard to Rosslare Harbour (3½ hours by ferry, 1¾ hours by catamaran), and Stranraer to Belfast (3¼ hours by ferry, 1¾ hours by catamaran)
Swansea Cork Ferries
(☎ 01792-456116) For services from Swansea to Cork (10 hours, mid-May to mid-September)

France

Eurail passes are valid for ferry crossings between Ireland and France on Irish Ferries only; Inter-Rail passes give reductions. Either way you must book in advance to receive the discount – don't just walk on the ferry.

Irish Ferries run from Roscoff and Cherbourg to Rosslare Harbour, April to January, taking 14 and 18½ hours respectively.

Brittany Ferries (☎ 021-27 7801 in Cork) sails from Roscoff to Cork once weekly, the trip taking 14 hours (Friday from Roscoff, Saturday from Cork) from April to early October.

Getting Around

Travelling around Ireland looks very simple, as the distances are short and there's a dense network of roads and railways. But in Ireland, from A to B is seldom a straight line, and public transport can be expensive (particularly trains), infrequent or both. For these reasons having your own transport – car or bicycle – can be a major advantage.

PASSES & DISCOUNTS

Eurail passes are valid for train travel in the Republic of Ireland but not in Northern Ireland and entitle you to a reduction on Bus Éireann's three-day Irish Rambler tickets. They are also valid on some ferries between France and the Republic. Inter-Rail passes offer a 50% reduction on train travel within

IRELAND

Ireland and discounts on some ferries to/from France and Britain.

For IR£7 students can have a Fairstamp affixed to their ISIC card by any usit CAMPUS agency. This gives a 50% discount on Iarnród Éireann (Irish Rail) services. Irish Rambler tickets are available from Bus Éireann for bus-only travel within the Republic. They cost IR£30 (for travel on three out of eight consecutive days), IR£70 (eight out of 15 days) or IR£100 (15 out of 30 days).

For train-only travel within the Republic, the Irish Explorer ticket (IR£90) is good for five travel days out of 15. In Northern Ireland, the Freedom of Northern Ireland pass allows unlimited travel on Ulsterbus and Northern Irish railways for one day (£10) or seven consecutive days (£35). The Irish Rover ticket combines services with Bus Éireann and Ulsterbus for three days (IR£40), eight days (IR£90) or 15 days (IR£140).

BUS

Bus Éireann is the Republic's national bus line, with services all over the Republic and into Northern Ireland. Fares are much cheaper than regular rail fares. Return fares are usually only a little more expensive than one-way fares, and special deals (eg, same-day returns) are often available. Most intercity buses in Northern Ireland are operated by Ulsterbus.

TRAIN

Iarnród Éireann, the Republic of Ireland's railway system, operates trains on routes that fan out from Dublin. Distances are short in Ireland and fares are often twice as expensive as the bus, but travel times can be dramatically reduced. As with buses, special fares are often available, and a midweek return ticket is often not much more than the single fare. First-class tickets cost from IR£3 to IR£15 more than the standard fare for a single journey.

Northern Ireland Railways has four routes from Belfast, one of which links up with the Republic's rail system.

CAR & MOTORCYCLE
Road Rules

As in Britain, driving is on the left and you should only overtake (pass) to the right of the vehicle ahead of you. The driver and front-seat passengers must wear safety belts; in Northern Ireland passengers in the rear must also wear them. Motorcyclists and their passengers must wear helmets; headlights should be dipped. Minor roads may sometimes be potholed and will often be very narrow, but the traffic is rarely heavy except as you go through popular tourist or busy commercial towns.

Speed limits in both Northern Ireland and the Republic appear in kilometres, miles or both, and are generally the same as in Britain: 112km/h (70mph) on motorways, 96km/h (60mph) on other roads and 48km/h (30mph) or as signposted in towns. On quiet, narrow, winding rural roads it's simply foolish to speed. Ireland's blood-alcohol limit is 0.08% and strictly enforced.

Parking in car parks or other specified areas in Ireland is regulated by 'pay and display' tickets or disc parking. You buy a disc, available from newsstands, on which you punch out or tick the time you park. Discs usually cost around 50p each and are valid for between one and three hours. In Northern Ireland beware of Control Zones in town centres where, for security reasons, cars absolutely must not be left unattended. Double yellow lines by the roadside mean no parking at any time; single yellow lines warn of restrictions, which will be signposted.

The Automobile Association (AA) has offices in Belfast (☎ 028-9088 7766), Dublin (☎ 01-677 9481) and Cork (☎ 021-50 5155). The AA breakdown number in the Republic is ☎ 1800-667788; in Northern Ireland it's ☎ 0800-887766. In Northern Ireland, members of the Royal Automobile Club (RAC) can call ☎ 028-9033 1133 for information; its breakdown number is ☎ 0800-828282.

Rental

Car rental in Ireland is expensive so you will often be better off booking a package deal from your home country. In high season it's wise to book ahead. In the off season, some companies simply discount all rates by about 25%, and there are often special deals. Some smaller companies charge an extra daily fee if you go across the border, to Northern Ireland or the Republic.

People under 21 are not allowed to hire a car; for the majority of rental companies you must be at least 23 and have had a valid driving licence for a minimum of 12 months.

Some companies will not rent to those over 70 or 75. Your own local licence is usually sufficient to hire a car for up to three months.

In the Republic, the typical weekly high-season rental rates with insurance, collision-damage waiver, VAT and unlimited distance, are around IR£250 for a small car (Ford Fiesta), IR£330 for a medium-sized car (Toyota Corolla 1.3) and IR£360 for a larger car (Ford Mondeo). In Northern Ireland similar cars would cost about 10% less.

The international rental companies Avis, Budget, Hertz, Eurodollar and Thrifty have offices all over Ireland. There are many Dublin-based operators with rates from as low as IR£140 a week, including Murray's Europcar (☎ 01-614 2800), Argus Rent-A-Car (☎ 01-490 4444) and Malone Car Rental (☎ 01-670 7888).

BICYCLE

A large number of visitors explore Ireland by bicycle. Although the distances are relatively short, the weather is often wet, and the most interesting parts of Ireland can be very hilly. Despite these drawbacks, it's a great place for bicycle touring, and facilities are good.

You can either bring your bike with you on the ferry or plane or rent one in Ireland. Typical rental costs are IR£7 to IR£10 a day or IR£30 to IR£40 a week. Bags and other equipment can also be rented. Raleigh Rent-a-Bike (☎ 01-626 1333), Raleigh House, Kylemore Rd, Dublin 10, has dozens of outlets around the country, some of which offer one-way rentals for IR£40 a week.

Bicycles can be transported on some Bus Éireann and Ulsterbus routes; the charges vary. By train the cost ranges from IR£2 to IR£6 for a one-way journey, depending on the distance.

HITCHING

While we don't recommend hitching – it's never entirely safe in any country – hitching in Ireland is commonplace and generally hassle-free. The major exceptions are in busy tourist areas where the competition from other hitchers is stiff and the cars are often full. In the Republic there are usually large numbers of local people on the road who use hitching as an everyday means of travel. Women should travel with someone else (even though many local women appear to hitch alone with-out problems). If you feel at all doubtful about an offered ride, turn it down.

ORGANISED TOURS

Bord Fáilte has details of general tour operators and specialist companies that include angling, walking, cycling, cultural holidays and tours for the disabled. Ulsterbus and Bus Éireann run day trips to major tourist sites.

Tír na nÓg Tours (☎ 01-836 4684, @ tnn@indigo.ie), 57 Gardiner St Lower, Dublin 1, specialises in off-the-tourist-trail tours. Prices start at IR£99 (for three days) and include transport, accommodation and site entry fees.

If you're going to be staying in hostels, it's worth considering the Slow Coach (☎ 01-679 2684, @ slocoach@star.co.uk), 6 South William St, Dublin 2, which is operated in association with An Óige and the IHH. For IR£95 you can travel by bus around Ireland from hostel to hostel with no time limit on when you complete your trip.

To beat the windy-sick feeling of bus tours, Rail Tours Ireland (☎ 01-856 0045), next door to Tír na nÓg Tours in Dublin, uses the rail network for its guided tours, with stops synchronised with the train timetable. Day tours start from around IR£39.

Dublin

☎ 01 • pop 952,692

Dublin (Baile Átha Cliath) is Ireland's capital and largest, most cosmopolitan city, although it still is one of the smallest capitals in the EU. Dublin is growing at a furious pace; the city centre is an intricate mass of shops, restaurants, pubs and people. Travellers returning after several years will find a somewhat changed city. Cybercafes and world-class restaurants now sit happily next to smoky pubs and chophouses.

And in spite of rapid changes, Dublin remains a city of character and characters. Dublin's literary history seems to bump against you at every corner, and many pubs are still filled with old-timers swapping stories over an afternoon pint of Guinness.

Orientation

Dublin is neatly divided by the River Liffey into the more affluent 'south side' and the

IRELAND

DUBLIN

PLACES TO STAY
1 Dublin International Youth Hostel; An Óige Head Office
2 The Frederick Guest House
3 Waverley House
4 Barry's Hotel
5 Belvedere Hotel
6 MEC Budget Accommodation Centre
8 Charles Stewart
19 Marlborough Hostel
20 Park House B&B; Gardiner Lodge
21 Backpackers Ireland: Eurohostel; Abraham House
22 Jacobs Inn
24 Isaac's Hostel
26 Backpackers Citi Hostel
27 Globetrotters Tourist Hostel; Townhouse
28 Cardijn House
32 Ashfield House
37 Wynn's Hotel Dublin
40 Abbey Hostel
41 Arlington Hotel
47 Brewery Hostel
55 Avalon House
74 Shelbourne Hotel

PLACES TO EAT
17 Bewley's Oriental Café
29 101 Talbot
33 Bewley's Oriental Café
42 The Epicurean Food Hall
44 Winding Stair Bookshop & Café
46 Brazen Head
57 Pasta Fresca
59 Rajdoot Tandoori
60 Bewley's Oriental Café
63 Café Java
65 Café en Seine
72 La Stampa

PUBS
16 Slatterys
31 John Mulligan's
43 Pravda
45 Handel's
53 The Long Hall
54 Jute
61 McDaid's
64 John Kehoe's
76 O'Donoghue's
77 Doheny & Nesbitt

OTHER
7 James Joyce Centre
9 Dublin Writers Museum; Chapter One
10 Hugh Lane Municipal Gallery
11 Gate Theatre
12 Laundry Shop
13 Imax Cinema; Virgin Multiplex
14 The Chimney; Ceol - The Irish Traditional Music Centre
15 Old Jameson Distillery
18 Dublin Bus (Bus Átha Cliath)
23 Busáras
25 Rail Tours Ireland; Tír na nÓg Tours
30 Abbey Theatre; Peacock Theatre
34 usit CAMPUS Travel Office
35 Global Internet Café
36 Iarnród Éireann Travel Centre
38 Eason
39 General Post Office
48 Guinness Hopstore
49 Dublinia
50 Christ Church Cathedral
51 St Patrick's Cathedral
52 Marsh's Library
56 Royal College of Surgeons; Buses to Glendalough
58 Gaiety Theatre
62 Post Office
66 Northern Ireland Tourist Board
67 The Dublin Experience
68 Book of Kells
69 National Gallery
70 Natural History Museum
71 National Museum
73 Aer Lingus
75 Irish Ferries

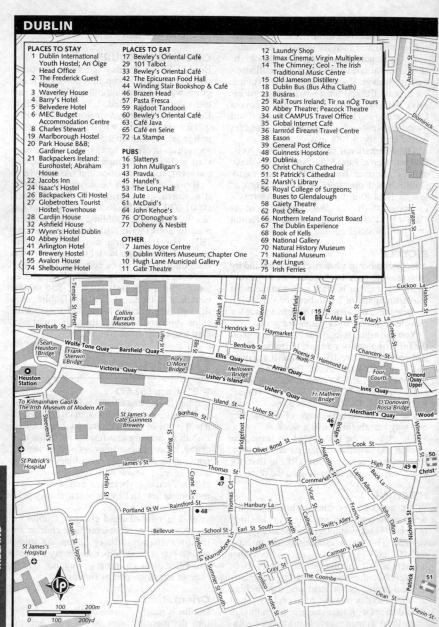

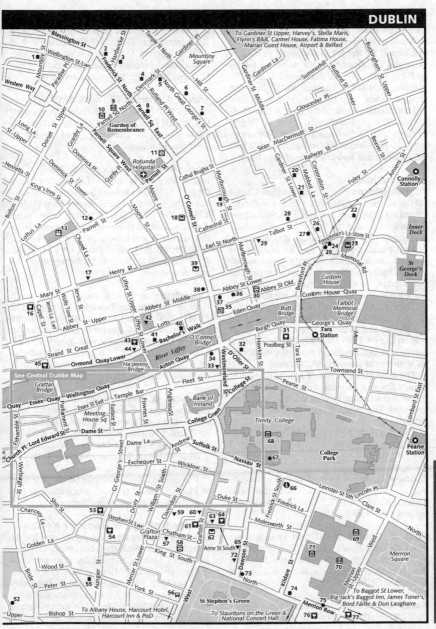

DUBLIN

To Gardiner St Upper, Harvey's, Stella Maris,
Flynn's B&B, Carmel House, Fatima House,
Marian Guest House, Airport & Belfast

Mountjoy
Square

Garden of
Remembrance

Rotunda
Hospital

Connolly
Station

Inner
Dock

St
George's
Dock

Custom
House

Talbot
Memorial
Bridge

Custom House Quay

Butt
Bridge

Tara
Station

Poolbeg St

See Central Dublin Map

Grattan
Quay

Bank of
Ireland

Meeting
House Sq

College Green

Trinity College

College
Park

Pearse
Station

Merrion
Square

St Stephen's Green

To Albany House, Harcourt Hotel,
Harcourt Inn & PoD

To Stauntons on the Green &
National Concert Hall

To Baggot St Lower,
Big Jack's Baggot Inn, James Toner's,
Bord Fáilte & Dun Laoghaire

IRELAND

euro currency converter IR£1 = €1.26

less prosperous 'north side' (where the 1991 film *The Commitments* was set).

North of the river important landmarks are O'Connell St, the major shopping thoroughfare, and Gardiner St, with its many B&Bs and guesthouses. Pedestrianised Henry St, running west off O'Connell St, is the main shopping area.

Immediately south of the river is the often-raucous Temple Bar district, Dame St, Trinity College and St Stephen's Green. For shopping, the pedestrianised Grafton St and its surrounding streets and lanes are always busy.

Information

Tourist Offices The Dublin Tourism Centre (✆ information@dublintourism.ie) is in the de-sanctified St Andrew's Church on St Andrew St, west of Trinity College. Services include accommodation bookings, car rentals, maps, concert tickets and more. In July and August (when it can be a madhouse) the centre is open 9 am to 7 pm Monday to Saturday, 9 am to 3.30 pm Sunday. At other times of year the hours are 9 am to 5.30 pm Monday to Saturday.

There are also Dublin Tourism offices at the airport and on the waterfront at Dun Laoghaire, and all three share a 24-hour information line (✆ 1850 230 330). Dublin Tourism is so-so about answering email queries, but try its Web site at www.visitdublin.com.

The head office of Bord Fáilte at Baggot St Bridge has an information desk and, although it is less conveniently situated, it is much less crowded. The office is open 9.30 am to 5 pm weekdays.

The NITB (✆ 679 1977), 16 Nassau St, is open 9 am to 5.30 pm weekdays, 10 am to 5 pm Saturday.

Money American Express has an exchange bureau in the Dublin Tourism Centre, and Thomas Cook (✆ 677 1721) is opposite the entrance to Trinity College.

Post & Communications Dublin's famous General Post Office (GPO) is situated on O' Connell St, north of the river. South of the river there are post offices on Anne St South and St Andrew St.

Email & Internet Access Planet Cyber Cafe (✆ 679 0583) has two locations: 23 South Great George's St and 13 St Andrews St. Both are open until at least 10 pm daily, and charge IR£5 per hour. Does Not Compute (✆ 670 4464), opposite Dublin's Viking Adventure, and Global Internet Café, just north of the O'Connell Bridge, are other alternatives.

Travel Agencies The usit CAMPUS travel office (✆ 679 8833), 19 Aston Quay, near O'Connell Bridge, opens 9 am to 6 pm weekdays (to 8 pm Thursday), and 10 am to 5.30 pm Saturday.

Bookshops Directly opposite Trinity College is Eason's excellent Hanna's Bookshop (✆ 677 1255), 1 Dawson St. Around the corner is the well-stocked Hodges Figgis (✆ 677 4754), 56-58 Dawson St, with a large selection of books on things Irish. Facing it across the road is Waterstone's (✆ 679 1415).

North of the Liffey, Eason (✆ 873 3811), 40 O'Connell St, has a big selection of books and magazines.

Laundry Convenient laundries in north Dublin include the Laundry Shop (✆ 872 3541), 191 Parnell St, and the Laundrette (✆ 830 0340), 110 Dorset St Lower, near An Óige's Dublin International Youth Hostel. The cheerful All American Laundrette (✆ 677 2779), 40 South Great George's St, is opposite the Long Hall pub.

Medical & Emergency Services The Eastern Health Board Dublin Area (✆ 679 0700), Doctor Stevens Hospital, 138 Thomas St, Dublin 8, can advise you on a suitable doctor from 9 am to 5 pm weekdays. There is a Well Women clinic at 35 Lower Liffey St (✆ 872 8051).

For emergency assistance phone ✆ 999 or ✆ 112 for *gardai* (police), ambulance or fire brigade. Both numbers are free.

Trinity College & Book of Kells

Ireland's premier university was founded by Elizabeth I in 1592. Its full name is the University of Dublin, but Trinity College is the institution's sole college. Until 1793 Trinity's students were all Protestants, but today the majority of its 9500 students are Catholic. Women were first admitted to the college in 1903, earlier than at most British universities.

IRELAND

In summer, walking tours depart regularly from the main gate on College Green, Monday to Saturday from 9.30 am to 4.30 pm, Sunday from noon to 4 pm. The tour costs IR£5.50 and is good value since it includes the fee to see the *Book of Kells*, an illuminated manuscript dating from around AD 800, and one of Dublin's prime attractions. It's on display in the East Pavilion of the Colonnades together with the 9th-century *Book of Armagh*, the even older *Book of Durrow* (AD 675) and Brian Ború's harp. Opening hours are 9.30 am to 5 pm Monday to Saturday, noon to 4.30 pm Sunday. Entry is IR£4.50.

Trinity's other big attraction is the **Dublin Experience**, a 45-minute audiovisual introduction to the city. Late May to October shows take place daily on the hour from 10 am to 5 pm. Entry is IR£3.

Museums

The highlight of the exhibits at the **National Museum** (☎ 667 7444) on Kildare St is the Treasury, with its superb collection of Bronze Age, Iron Age and medieval gold objects. Other exhibits focus on the Viking period, the 1916 Easter Rising and the struggle for Irish independence. The museum is free and open 10 am to 5 pm Tuesday to Saturday, from 2 pm Sunday. While you're there check the taxidermal treasures at the adjoining **Natural History Museum**.

The small **Dublin Civic Museum** (☎ 679 4260), 58 William St South, focuses on Dublin's long and tumultuous history. A notable display is the stone head from O'Connell St's Lord Nelson's Pillar, which was blown up by the IRA in 1966. The museum is open 10 am to 6 pm Tuesday to Saturday, 11 am to 2 pm Sunday, and entry is free.

Dublin Writers Museum (☎ 872 2077), 18-19 Parnell Square, celebrates the city's long and continuing role as a literary centre, with displays on Joyce, Swift, Yeats, Wilde, Beckett and others. It's open 10 am to 5 pm (from 11 am Sunday), and entry is IR£3.10. The nearby **James Joyce Centre**, 35 North Great George's St, is a must for avid Joyceans. Entry is IR£2.75.

Galleries

The **National Gallery** (☎ 661 5133), Merrion Square West, has an excellent collection with a strong Irish content. Opening 10 am to 5.30 pm Monday to Saturday (to 8.30 pm Thursday), 2 to 5 pm Sunday, there are guided tours on Saturday (3 pm) and Sunday (2.15, 3 and 4 pm). Entry is free.

On Parnell Square, north of the river, **Hugh Lane Municipal Gallery** (☎ 874 1903) has works by contemporary Irish artists, as well as retrospectives and a large impressionist collection. It's open 9.30 am to 5 or 6 pm Tuesday to Saturday, 11 am to 5 pm Sunday and entry is free.

The **Irish Museum of Modern Art** (IMMA) at the old Royal Hospital Kilmainham is renowned for its conceptual installations and temporary exhibits. It opens 10 am to 5.30 pm Tuesday to Saturday, noon to 5.30 pm Sunday. Entry is free.

In Temple Bar, around Meeting House Square, is the **National Photographic Archive** (☎ 603 0200) and the **Gallery of Photography** (☎ 670 9293). In fact, in and around Meeting House Square is a cauldron of cultural activities, including the **Irish Film Archive**, the multimedia centre **Arthouse**, galleries, studios, an open-air cinema and image gallery, and a Saturday food market and book fair. For information call the Temple Bar Culture Line (☎ 671 5717).

Christ Church Cathedral & Around

On Christ Church Place, Christ Church Cathedral was a simple structure of wood until 1169, when the present stone church was built. In the south aisle is a monument to the 12th-century Norman warrior Strongbow. Note the church's precariously leaning north wall (it's been that way since 1562). Christ Church is open 10 am to 5 pm daily, and entry is IR£2.

On Essex St West is **Dublin's Viking Adventure** (☎ 679 6040), where costumed 'Norse' guides lead visitors through life-size mock-ups of Viking-era Dublin. The adventure opens 10 am to 4.30 pm Tuesday to Saturday, and entry is IR£4.95.

St Patrick's Cathedral & Around

A church stood on the site of St Patrick's Cathedral, on Patrick's Close, as early as the 5th century, but the present building dates from 1191. It's noted for its connections with Jonathan Swift, author of *Gulliver's Travels*

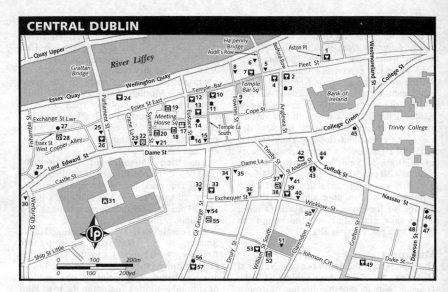

CENTRAL DUBLIN

and dean of St Patrick's from 1713 to 1745. Swift and his beloved companion 'Stella' (Esther Johnson) are both interred here. Entry is IR£2.30, and it is open 9 am to 6 pm daily, but closed at times of worship.

Just south of the cathedral is the not-to-be-missed **Marsh's Library** (☎ 454 3511), dating from 1701 and boasting some 25,000 volumes lovingly stacked in dark oak bookcases. Note the wire cages where readers were once locked in with precious manuscripts. Open weekdays (except Tuesday) and Saturday morning, entry is IR£1.

Dublin Castle

Though much of it has been rebuilt over the centuries, Dublin Castle (☎ 677 7129), more a palace than a castle, dates back to the 13th century. The city got its modern name from the black pool (*dubh linn*) beneath the castle gardens. Entry is IR£3, but there's not much to see, since many of the castle's rooms are reserved for government functions. The castle is open 10 am to 5 pm weekdays and 2 to 5 pm weekends.

Guinness Brewery

Very little of the vast Guinness Brewery is open to the public. Rather than a tour of the

brewery, the main attraction is the **Guinness Hopstore** (☎ 408 4800) on Crane St, in a scruffy neighbourhood south-east of the city centre. Historical displays and a lame audio-visual program (although an upgrade is planned late 2000) preface a free half-pint of fresh, creamy Guinness. Guinness was first brewed by Arthur Guinness in 1759 and is now produced worldwide at the rate of 10 million pints a day.

Entry to the Hopstore is IR£5. It's open 9.30 am to 5 pm Monday to Saturday, 10.30 am to 4.30 pm Sunday from April to September. The rest of the year it opens 9.30 am to 4 pm Monday to Saturday, noon to 4 pm Sunday. Take bus No 51B or 78A from Aston Quay.

Kilmainham Gaol

The grey, sombre Kilmainham Gaol (☎ 453 5984) played a key role in Ireland's struggle for independence and was the site of mass executions following the 1916 Easter Rising. The tour includes a great audiovisual introduction to the prison from its opening in 1796 until its closure in 1924. The gaol is on Inchicore Rd near the IMMA, west of Christ Church Cathedral; take bus No 51 or 79 from Aston Quay. It's open 9.30 am to 4.45 pm daily from April to September; the rest of the

CENTRAL DUBLIN

PLACES TO STAY
3   Oliver St John Gogarty Hostel
11   Barnacles Temple Bar House
16   River House Hotel
29   Kinlay House;
     Dublin Bike Tours

PLACES TO EAT
5   Elephant & Castle
6   La Paloma
8   The Chameleon
9   Cafe Irie; Juste Pasta
15   La Mezza Luna
21   Mermaid Café
23   Les Frères Jacques
25   Poco Loco
30   Leo Burdock's
32   Yamamori
34   Odessa Lounge & Grill
35   Stag's Head
36   Boulevard Café
37   QV2
40   Cornucopia

41   Trocadero; Café Rouge
44   O'Neill's
50   Alpha Café
51   Blazing Salads II; Powerscourt
     Townhouse Shopping
     Centre
54   Good World Restaurant

PUBS
1   Palace Bar
2   Oliver St John Gogarty
4   Auld Dubliner
7   Quays Bar
10   Temple Bar
12   Norseman
24   Clarence;
     Clarence Hotel
26   Front Lounge
33   The Globe; Rí Rá
39   International Bar
49   Davy Byrne's
53   Grogan's Castle Lounge
57   Hogan's

OTHER
13   Temple Bar Music Centre
14   Arthouse
17   Irish Film Centre (IFC)
18   Gallery of Photography
19   National Photographic
     Archive
20   Irish Film Archive
22   Olympia Theatre
27   Dublin's Viking Adventure
28   Does Not Compute
31   Dublin Castle
38   Planet Cyber Cafe
42   Post Office
43   Dublin Tourism Centre;
     American Express
45   Thomas Cook
46   Eason: Hanna's Bookshop
47   Waterstone's
48   Hodges Figgis
52   Dublin Civic Museum
55   Planet Cyber Cafe
56   All American Laundrette

year it opens 9.30 am to 4 pm weekdays and 10 am to 4.45 pm Sunday. Entry is IR£3.50.

Other Attractions

Dublin's finest **Georgian architecture**, including its famed doorways, is found around **St Stephen's Green** and **Merrion Square**, both of which are prime picnic spots whenever the sun shines.

The 1815 **General Post Office** (GPO) building on O'Connell St is an important landmark, both physically and historically. During the 1916 Easter Rising the Irish Volunteers used the GPO as a base for attacks against the British army. After a fierce battle the GPO was almost totally destroyed. Upon surrendering, the leaders of the Irish rebellion and 13 others were taken to Kilmainham Gaol and executed.

The **Old Jameson Distillery** (☎ 807 2355) on Bow St, north of the Liffey, is a defunct brewery with displays on the whiskey-making process. The audiovisual show is a dud, but the free whiskey-tasting is a big hit. Tours are held from 9.30 am to 5 pm daily for IR£3.95.

At the back of the distillery is **The Chimney** (☎ 676 9575), Smithfield Village, a modern viewing platform with a glass-and-steel lift tacked onto an old chimneystack. Pick your days and it's a view of Dublin unparalleled. Open 9.30 am to 6 pm daily (10.30 am to 6 pm Sunday), entry is IR£3. In the same complex is **Ceol – The Irish Traditional Music Centre** (☎ 817 3820), a must for lovers of jigs, reels and lonely ballads, and for those who just don't get it. The centre is full of interactive displays tracing the roots of Irish music. Opening times are the same as The Chimney's, except on Sunday when the centre opens at noon. Entry is IR£4.95.

Organised Tours

Gray Line (☎ 670 8822), with a kiosk at the Dublin Tourism Centre, has three-hour Dublin bus tours for around IR£7. Dublin Bus (☎ 873 4222) has a variety of coach tours; a three-hour open-deck bus journey is IR£7. A hop-on hop-off service that does a 75-minute city circuit with commentary runs daily from mid-April to late September. The IR£5 ticket lets you travel all day.

The Heart of Dublin Tour (☎ 278 1626), a 90-minute on-foot tour of central Dublin, leaves from the Dublin Tourism Centre on Friday and Saturday. Two-hour walks of 'revolutionary' Dublin, focusing on the years 1916-23, are offered by Footsoldiers (☎ 662 9976).

Other theme tours are The Dublin Literary Pub Crawl (☎ 670 5602) on which you are

IRELAND

accompanied by actors performing pieces from Irish literature; the Musical Pub Crawl (☎ 478 0193); The Walk Macabre (☎ 677 1512) for tales of horror from Dublin's past; and the more scholarly 'seminar on the street' Historical Walking Tours of Dublin (☎ 878 0227). Each lasts about two hours and costs around IR£6. Bookings can be made via Dublin Tourism, hostels or by calling direct.

Places to Stay

At unexpected times Dublin can be bedless for a radius of up to 60km. So we recommend advance reservations any time, even for hostels. For B&Bs and hotels, Dublin Tourism will do the work for a small fee. Contact it in person, by email (✉ reservations@dublintourism.ie) or phone (☎ 1800 668 668).

Hostels North of the Liffey Two affiliated hostels are a stone's throw from the Busáras bus and Connolly train stations: the 212-bed *Jacobs Inn* (☎ 855 5660, 21-28 Talbot Place) and the often noisy 210-bed *Isaac's Hostel* (☎ 836 3877, 2-5 Frenchman's Lane). Dorm beds at Jacobs are IR£9.25 to IR£11.25; doubles/triples/quads cost up to IR£21.50/18.50/17.50 per person. Isaac's charges IR£7.50 to IR£9.95 for dorms and up to IR£19.95/42 for singles/doubles. Both have cafes and kitchen facilities and the dorms are closed from 11 am to 3 pm.

IHH *Cardijn House* (☎ 878 8484, 15 Talbot St), also known as 'Goin' My Way', is an older 42-bed hostel east of O'Connell St. The nightly cost is IR£9. Breakfast is included and there are good cooking facilities.

Gardiner St Lower is a goldmine of hostels. At No 47, the welcoming IHH *Globetrotters Tourist Hostel* (☎ 873 5893) is a modern place with good security. The dorm beds cost IR£12/14 in low/high season, with full Irish breakfast. The simple IHO *Backpackers Ireland: Eurohostel* (☎ 836 4900) at No 80 has dorm beds for IR£8/10 midweek/weekend. Adjacent is IHH *Abraham House* (☎ 855 0600) at No 82. It's well run and clean, with beds in small/large dorms for IR£9/13 (add IR£2 for peak times) and singles/doubles for IR£22/30. The IHO's pleasant *Backpackers Citi Hostel* (☎ 855 0035) at No 61-62 charges IR£8 to IR£11 for dorm beds and IR£35 to IR£50 for private doubles.

If you don't mind street noise, the central *Abbey Hostel* (☎ 878 0700, 29 Bachelor's Walk) overlooks the River Liffey, has new facilities, good security and a friendly vibe. Dorms from IR£11 to IR£16, quads IR£18 per head.

IHH *Marlborough Hostel* (☎ 874 7629, 81-82 Marlborough St) is noisy and some staff can be slothful, but it's popular nonetheless. It's IR£8.50 in the dorms, IR£15 per person for private rooms.

IHH *MEC Budget Accommodation Centre* (☎ 878 0071, 42 North Great George's St) is a sprawling 100-bed hostel in an old Georgian townhouse. It's nice but a tad drab. Dorm beds cost from IR£8.50 to IR£13.50.

At *Charles Stewart* (☎ 878 0350, 5-6 Parnell Square East) there are no dorms as such, but if you can find six friends you can share a spick-and-span room for IR£16 each. Fully equipped singles/doubles cost IR£20/50, Irish breakfast included.

An Óige's 363-bed *Dublin International Youth Hostel* (☎ 830 1766, 61 Mountjoy St) suffers from its rough-and-tumble surroundings. Although the hostel is very safe, after dark it's an unsavoury walk from the city centre. From Dublin airport, bus No 41A stops on Dorset St Upper, a short walk away. Beds are IR£10 to IR£11 including continental breakfast.

Not quite a hostel, *The Frederick Guest House* (☎ 874 2277, 13 Frederick St) above a cafe has dorm beds for IR£15 and singles from IR£20.

Hostels South of the Liffey The big, well-equipped IHH *Kinlay House* (☎ 679 6644, 2-12 Lord Edward St), beside Christ Church Cathedral, is central, but some rooms can fill with traffic noise. Rates are IR£10 per person in four-bed dorms, and IR£16/24 a single/double. Continental breakfast is included and cooking facilities are available.

IHH's *Avalon House* (☎ 475 0001, 55 Aungier St) is in a renovated Georgian building nicely positioned just west of St Stephen's Green. It has some cleverly designed rooms with mezzanine levels. Beds in standard dorms are IR£8 to IR£12 including continental breakfast.

Just north of Trinity College, *Ashfield House* (☎ 679 7734, 19-20 D'Olier St) has all the amenities of a semideluxe hotel but fills up quickly. Dorm beds are IR£11 to IR£14, singles/doubles IR£35/46.

Although staying in the Temple Bar district is plenty of fun, street noise is a serious drawback. A good choice is the IHH *Barnacles Temple Bar House* (☎ 671 6277, *19 Temple Lane*), with dorms for IR£9 to IR£11 and doubles from IR£50. *Oliver St John Gogarty Hostel* (☎ 671 1822, *18-21 Anglesea St*) adjoins a boisterous pub but is surprisingly quiet. The facilities include a cafe and restaurant. Dorm beds cost IR£12 to IR£17, doubles IR£38.

The IHH *Brewery Hostel* (☎ 453 8600, *22-23 Thomas St*) is close to the Guinness Hopstore and has top-drawer facilities, including a secure car park. Unfortunately the neighbourhood is scruffy and it's a longish walk to the centre. Dorm beds start at IR£8.50, doubles IR£38, including breakfast.

B&Bs If you want something close to the city centre, Gardiner Sts Upper and Lower are the places to look. They're not the prettiest parts of Dublin and can be noisy, but they are relatively cheap.

The friendly *Harvey's* (☎ 874 5140, *11 Gardiner St Upper*) has singles/doubles for IR£25/35. There are several more B&Bs nearby, including *Stella Maris* (☎ 874 0835) next door at No 13, *Flynn's B&B* (☎ 874 1702) at No 15, *Carmel House* (☎ 874 1639) at No 16 and *Fatima House* (☎ 874 5410) at No 17. The cheapest is *Marian Guest House* (☎ 874 4129) at No 21 with rooms for IR£20 per person, though the plumbing can be a little loud at times.

Nicer B&Bs along Gardiner St Lower include *Gardiner Lodge* (☎ 836 522) at No 87, *Park House B&B* (☎ 855 0034) at No 90 and the highly recommended *Townhouse* (☎ 878 8808) joined to Globetrotters hostel at No 47-48. All three charge IR£35 to IR£37.50 per person.

Hardwicke St, only a short walk from Gardiner St Upper, has a few B&Bs including the Joycean haunt *Waverley House* (☎ 874 6132) at No 4, which was then known as 'The Boarding House'. Singles cost IR£30, doubles IR£46 to IR£70.

Hotels *River House Hotel* (☎ 670 7655, *23-24 Eustace St*) in Temple Bar opposite the Irish Film Centre, charges IR£60/90 for fully equipped singles/doubles.

South-west of St Stephen's Green, in a Georgian townhouse, *Albany House* (☎ 475 1092, *84 Harcourt St*) is good value at IR£60/100. Farther down at No 60, in the erstwhile residence of George Bernard Shaw, is *Harcourt Hotel* (☎ 478 3677), with 53 deluxe rooms costing IR£70/90. With similar standards is the nearby *Harcourt Inn* (☎ 478 3927) at No 27; rooms cost IR£60/100.

Two top-tier hotels overlook leafy St Stephen's Green: *Stauntons on the Green* (☎ 478 2300, *83 St Stephens Green South*), and Dublin's most exclusive hotel, the *Shelbourne* (☎ 676 6471, *27 St Stephens Green North*). The former charges IR£69/110, while the latter is a hefty IR£185/230 in high season, or you could pay IR£950 for the Presidential Suite (breakfast not included).

North of the Liffey are four mid-range options. The *Arlington Hotel* (☎ 804 9100, *23-25 Bachelor's Walk*) is a stylish Georgian inn overlooking the river and charges IR£69/110, and on weekends £95/130. *Wynn's Hotel Dublin* (☎ 874 5131, *35-39 Abbey St Lower*) is an older hotel with plenty of charm, though the facilities are somewhat basic; rates are IR£65/95. You can save a few pounds at two older hotels on Great Denmark St: *Belvedere Hotel* (☎ 874 1413) at No 5 and *Barry's Hotel* (☎ 874 6943) at No 1-2; both charge around IR£45/80.

Places to Eat

Around Temple Bar Although at times a mecca for tourists and rowdy rugby rogues, the Temple Bar district is convenient and caters to all tastes and budgets. *La Mezza Luna* (☎ 671 2840) on Dame St near the corner of Temple Lane is enormously popular; book or be prepared to wait. It has vegetarian dishes starting at IR£4.95 and pasta that will make you burst. *Les Frères Jacques* (☎ 679 4555, *74 Dame St*) is one of Temple Bar's fancier French restaurants and only for those that can afford to splurge; mains are IR£17 and up. *Mermaid Café* (*70 Dame St*) is renowned for creative seafood dishes and decadent desserts; mains start at IR£12.95, the majority around the mid to high teens.

Omelettes (from IR£6.50) are a speciality at the popular and bustling but somewhat overpriced *Elephant & Castle (18 Temple Bar)*. It stays open until midnight on Friday and Saturday, until 11.30 pm on other days. *The Chameleon (1 Fownes St)*, just off Wellington Quay, specialises in Indonesian dishes such as *rijstaffel* and *gado gado* for around IR£6; it's open in the evening. *Cafe Irie*, upstairs at 12 Fownes St, has fried tofu for IR£3.20 and a huge selection of sandwiches starting at IR£2.50. Next door, the cute *Juste Pasta* does pasta from IR£5.95 and 'not pasta' from IR£6.50 to IR£10.50. *La Paloma*, on Asdill's Row, around the corner from the Quays Bar, has a wide range of Spanish *tapas* and mains for around IR£12.

Poco Loco (32 Parliament St) offers straightforward Tex-Mex, and its combination plates are great value at IR£6.95.

Although it's not in Temple Bar proper, *Leo Burdock's (2 Werburgh St)* doles out Dublin's best fish and chips. There aren't any tables, but you can eat picnic-style down the road beside St Patrick's Cathedral.

Around Grafton St Popular *Café Java (5 Anne St South)* does excellent brunches (bagels and egg scrambles) at around IR£4.95. *Cornucopia (19 Wicklow St)* is a popular wholefood cafe, catering for special diets with all sorts of creative concoctions for less than IR£7 (closed Sunday). *Alpha Café*, upstairs on the corner of Wicklow and Clarendon Sts, is cheap, simple and has fried everything (grills from IR£3). A bit to the west, the fashionable *Boulevard Café (27 Exchequer St)* does grilled meats, gourmet pizzas and pastas (IR£5.50 to IR£12) daily to midnight. The nearby Powerscourt Townhouse Shopping Centre is stuffed with eating places and makes a great stop for lunch; notables include *Blazing Salads II*, a popular vegetarian restaurant on the top level, with a variety of salads for around IR£1 each (closed Sunday).

Straightforward preparation, large helpings and late opening hours are the selling points at *Trocadero (3 St Andrew's St)*, where mains cost around IR£10. The adjacent *Café Rouge*, part of a French-theme chain, serves great coffees and pastries and has good-value lunches (IR£5.95) and dinner specials (IR£7.95). Across the road, *QV2*, at No 14-15, is an elegant Dublin institution that looks more expensive than it is.

There are lunch and earlybird specials for IR£7.50.

Pasta Fresca (3-4 Chatham St), just off Grafton St's southern end, has authentic pasta dishes for IR£5.95 to IR£8.95 and antipasta from IR£2.50. *Rajdoot Tandoori (26-28 Clarendon St)*, in the Westbury Centre behind the Westbury Hotel, has superb tandoori dishes from IR£8.60.

On South Great George's St, *Yamamori*, No 71-72, serves sushi and delicious Japanese noodle soups from IR£5. Dublin's finest Chinese dishes are cooked up at the *Good World Restaurant* at No 18; a full meal will set you back at least IR£12.

Stylish *Odessa Lounge & Grill (13-14 Dame Court)*, next to the Rí Rá dance club, is great for steaks and preclubbing cocktails, as well as for massive weekend brunch plates at IR£5.50 to IR£7.95.

La Stampa (☎ 677 8611, 35 Dawson St) serves European cuisine in an attractive Georgian dining area. It's open from lunch until late and main courses are around IR£15.

North of the Liffey Although fast-food chains and cafes are well represented north of the Liffey, especially on O'Connell St, you won't find many good full-service restaurants. A major exception is the hidden, *101 Talbot*, oddly enough at 101 Talbot St, does adventurous pastas from IR£5.50 and interesting mains from IR£8.50 to IR£12.50 (closed Sunday and Monday). *Chapter One*, downstairs from the Dublin Writers Museum, is worth a look, particularly if on your way to or from the Gate theatre. Steaks, pastas and meal-size salads are IR£5 to IR£12.

Pubs Don't leave Dublin without having at least one pub lunch. Full meals are offered weekdays from 11.30 am to 2 pm or so, and the going rate is IR£5 to IR£7 for a major feast of meat, vegies and potatoes. The wonderfully old-looking *Stag's Head* on Dame Court, apart from being an extremely popular drinking spot, turns out simple, well-prepared meals. The lunch buffet at *O'Neill's*, opposite the Dublin Tourism Centre, is highly recommended. *The Brazen Head* on Bridge St, always packed at lunchtime, offers everything from sandwiches to a carvery buffet.

euro currency converter €1 = IR£0.78

Cafes There are three branches of *Bewley's Oriental Cafés* around the centre. Bewley's, something of a Dublin institution, has above-average cafeteria-style breakfasts (IR£3), sandwiches (to IR£3) and full meals (to IR£5). The people-watching is first rate, and you can sit all day reading the paper without feeling guilty. The 78 Grafton St branch is the flagship, open to 1 am daily (to 7 pm Sunday). The branch at 11-12 Westmoreland St is open to 9 pm daily. There is a smaller branch north of the Liffey at 40 Mary St.

Café en Seine (40 Dawson St) is a swanky Parisian-style cafe-cum-bar with light lunches.

The *Winding Stair Bookshop & Café*, on Ormond Quay Lower, north of the Liffey, opposite Ha'penny Bridge, is a rambling bookshop with teas, pastries and sandwiches.

The Epicurean Food Hall, with entrances on Lower Liffey and Middle Abbey Sts, has several cafes, but the highlights here are the delis, celebrating world food from Japanese to Eastern European. It's open 8.30 am to 7 pm Monday to Saturday, 10 am to 6 pm Sunday.

Entertainment

For events, reviews and particularly for club listings, get a free copy of the fortnightly *Event Guide*, available from music venues, cafes, hostels etc. Its Web site is at www.eventguide.ie.

The *Temple Bar Music Centre* (☎ 670 9105) on Curved St is a venue to watch. There is music seven days a week, with something to suit most tastes.

Pubs Dublin has some 850 pubs, so there's no possibility of being caught too far from a Guinness should a terrible thirst strike you. The Temple Bar district is choc-a-block with pubs that feature live music. Notables here include the *Temple Bar* on Temple Lane, the *Norseman* on the corner of Temple Bar and Eustace St, the restored *Oliver St John Gogarty Bar (57-58 Fleet St)*, the *Quays Bar* overlooking Temple Square, and the *Auld Dubliner (24-25 Temple Bar)*.

Other atmospheric spots for a pint include the *Stag's Head* on Dame Court, *The Long Hall* on South Great George's St, the *Palace Bar* on Fleet St, *John Kehoe's* on Anne St South, *John Mulligan's (8 Poolbeg St)*, *Grogan's Castle Lounge* on the corner of William and Castle Sts, and *James Toner's* and *Doheny & Nesbitt* on Baggot St – also popular for lunch.

Davy Byrne's (21 Duke St), off Grafton St, has been famous ever since Leopold Bloom dropped in for a sandwich. It's now an anaemic yuppie bar.

Pubs with live music from blues to rock to traditional Irish include the *International Bar (23 Wicklow St)*; *McDaid's (3 Harry St)*; touristy *O'Donoghue's (15 Merrion Row)*, one of the most renowned music pubs in Ireland; and *Big Jack's Baggot Inn* on Baggot St.

North of the river on Capel St, both *Slatterys* and *Handel's* are busy music pubs.

Dublin's very 'hip' pubs attract fashion-conscious crowds worthy of London and New York. Hipster spots include *Front Lounge* on Parliament St, *The Globe* and *Hogan's* on South Great George's St, *Jute (2 Aungier St)*, the *Clarence (6-8 Wellington Quay)* inside the U2-owned Clarence Hotel, and the northside's Russianesque *Pravda* on Liffey St.

Clubs The reality of clubbing in a city like Dublin is that trends change. Check club listings or just ask; cafes usually give good advice. Some stayers include *Rí Rá* on Dame Court with an eclectic mix of world beats; the bit-too-fab-o 'Kitchen Club' inside the *Clarence Hotel* on Wellington Quay; the 'Palace of Dance', *PoD (35 Harcourt St)*; and the *Gaiety Theatre* on King St South which usually has a club night when there's nothing else on.

Theatre & Classical Music The famous *Abbey Theatre* (☎ 878 7222) and the smaller *Peacock Theatre* are on Abbey St Lower near the river. The *Gate Theatre* (☎ 874 4045) is on Parnell Square East. The *Olympia Theatre* (☎ 677 7744) on Dame St has plays and international music acts. The *Gaiety Theatre* (☎ 677 1717) is on King St South.

Concerts take place at the *National Concert Hall* (☎ 671 1888), Earlsfort Terrace, just south of St Stephen's Green.

Cinema The *Irish Film Centre* (IFC; ☎ 679 5744, 6 Eustace St) has two screens in the Temple Bar showing off-beat and art films. The complex also has a bar, cafe and bookshop. The Parnell Centre, at the west end of

IRELAND

Parnell St, has an *Imax Cinema* (☎ *817 4200*) with a 25m-wide screen for quantity cinema, and the *Virgin Multiplex* (☎ *872 8444*) has all the hits for quality-with-a-question-mark cinema.

Getting There & Away

Air Aer Lingus (☎ 886 8888 for reservations, ☎ 886 6705 for flight information) has an office at 13 St Stephen's Green North.

Bus Busáras (☎ 836 6111), Bus Éireann's central bus station, is just north of the Liffey on Store St. Standard one-way fares from Dublin include Cork (IR£13, 3½ hours, four daily), Galway (IR£9, 3¾ hours, five daily), and Rosslare Harbour (IR£10, three hours, six daily). Buses to Belfast depart from the Busáras up to seven times a day Monday to Saturday (three times on Sunday) and cost IR£11.50.

Slightly cheaper private bus companies have many services daily to Galway, but are less frequent to other locations. Try Nestor Travel (☎ 671 9822) or City Link (☎ 626 6888).

Train Connolly station (☎ 836 3333), just north of the Liffey, is the station for Belfast, Derry, Sligo, other points north and Wexford. Heuston station (☎ 836 5421), south of the Liffey and well west of the centre, is the station for Cork, Galway, Killarney, Limerick, Waterford and most other points to the west, south and south-west. For travel information and tickets, the Iarnród Éireann Travel Centre (☎ 836 6222) is at 35 Abbey St Lower. Regular one-way fares from Dublin include Belfast (IR£19, 2¼ hours, six daily), Cork (IR£33.50, 3¼ hours, up to eight daily), Galway (IR£22, three hours, four daily), and Limerick (IR£26.50, 2¼ hours, up to 13 daily).

Boat There are two direct services from Holyhead on the north-western tip of Wales, one to Dublin Port, and the other to Dun Laoghaire at the southern end of Dublin Bay. Stena Lines (☎ 204 7777), in Dun Laoghaire, and Irish Ferries (☎ 661 0715), 2-4 Merrion Row, are the main carriers. See the Getting There & Away section earlier in this chapter for more details.

Getting Around

To/From the Airport Dublin airport (☎ 844 4900) is 10km north of the centre. There's an Airlink Express service to/from Busáras for IR£3 and to/from Heuston train station for IR£3 (both 30 minutes). Alternatively, the slower bus (one hour) Nos 41 and 41A (the latter on weekends only), costs IR£1.10. A taxi to the centre should cost about IR£15.

To/From the Ferry Terminals Buses go to Busáras from the Dublin Ferryport terminal (☎ 855 2222), Alexandra Rd, after all ferry arrivals. Buses also run from Busáras to meet ferry departures. To travel between Dun Laoghaire's ferry terminal (☎ 880 1905) and Dublin, take bus No 46A to Fleet St in Temple Bar, bus No 7 to Eden Quay, or bus No 7A or 8 to Burgh Quay. Alternatively, take the Dublin Area Rapid Transport (DART) rail service to Pearse station (for south Dublin) or Connolly station (for north Dublin).

Local Transport Dublin Bus (Bus Átha Cliath; ☎ 873 4222) has an office at 59 O'Connell St. Buses cost IR£1.20 for one to three stages, up to a maximum of IR£2.60. These tickets give you two trips valid for a month, and single fares can be bought on the bus. One-day passes cost IR£3.50 for bus, or IR£5.20 for bus and DART. Late-night Nitelink buses (IR£3) operate from the College St/Westmoreland St/D'Olier St triangle until 3 am on Friday and Saturday nights.

DART provides quick rail access to the coast as far north as Howth (IR£1.10) and south to Bray (IR£1.30). Pearse station is handy for central Dublin.

Taxis in Dublin are expensive, with flagfall at IR£1.80. To order a taxi, ring City Cabs (☎ 872 2688) or National Radio Cabs (☎ 677 2222).

Car All the major companies have offices at Dublin airport and in the city centre. Three cheaper options are Murray's Europcar (☎ 614 2800) on Baggot St Bridge; Argus Rent-A-Car (☎ 490 4444), with a desk at the Dublin Tourism Centre; and Malone Car Rental (☎ 670 7888), 26 Lombard St East. The cheapest rates are around IR£140 per week, a substantial savings over the big-name agencies.

IRELAND

Bicycle Dublin Bike Tours (☎ 679 0899), Lord Edward St, has bike rental for IR£10 per day and tours year-round. Other rental places open during high season; contact Dublin Tourism for details.

AROUND DUBLIN
Dun Laoghaire
☎ 01

Dun Laoghaire (pronounced dun leary), only 13km south of central Dublin, is both a popular resort and a busy harbour with ferry connections to Britain. There is a hostel in Dun Laoghaire, as well as many B&Bs; they're a bit cheaper than in central Dublin, and the fast and frequent rail connections make it convenient to stay out here.

On the southern side of the harbour is the **Martello Tower**, where James Joyce's epic novel *Ulysses* opens. It now houses the **James Joyce Museum** (☎ 280 9265).

The tower is open 10 am to 5 pm Monday to Saturday, 2 to 6 pm Sunday from April to October. Phone in advance at other times of the year. Entry is IR£2.70.

Bus No 7, 7A, 8 or 46A, or the DART rail service (IR£1.10, 20 minutes), will take you from Dublin to Dun Laoghaire.

Places to Stay The small *Marina House* (☎ 284 1524) on Old Dunleary Rd (turn left at the Salthill & Monkstown DART station) has dorm beds for IR£12.

The Rosmeen Gardens area is packed with B&Bs. To get there, walk south along George's St, the main shopping street; Rosmeen Gardens is the first street after Glenageary Rd Lower, directly opposite People's Park.

Malahide Castle
☎ 01

Despite the vicissitudes of Irish history, the Talbot family managed to keep **Malahide Castle** (☎ 846 2184) under its control from 1185 to 1973. The castle is packed with furniture and paintings, and Puck, the family ghost, is still in residence. The extensive **Fry Model Railway** (☎ 846 3779) in the castle grounds covers 240 sq metres and authentically displays much of Dublin and Ireland's rail and public transport system (it's better than it sounds). The castle is open in summer

10 am to 5 pm Monday to Saturday, 11 am to 6 pm Sunday; slightly shorter hours apply the rest of the year. Entry is IR£3.15. The railway (IR£2.90, combined tickets available) has similar opening hours.

To reach Malahide, take bus No 42 from beside Busáras, or a Drogheda-bound train from Connolly station. Malahide is 13km north-east of Dublin.

Newgrange
☎ 041

The Boyne Valley has the finest Celtic passage-tomb in Europe, a huge flattened mound faced with quartz and granite, at Newgrange on the N51. The tomb is believed to date from around 3200 BC, predating the great pyramids of Egypt by some six centuries. You can follow a guide down the narrow passage to the tomb chamber about a third of the way into the colossal mound. Around 8 am on the mornings of the winter solstice, the rising sun's rays shine directly down the long passage and illuminate the tomb chamber for 17 minutes. Tours leave from the Brú na Bóinne visitor centre (☎ 988 0300), 2km west of Donore, from 9.30 am to 5.30 pm June to September (to 4.30 pm the rest of the year). Entry is IR£4.

The South-East

COUNTY WICKLOW
County Wicklow, less than 20km south of Dublin, has three contenders for the 'best in Ireland': best garden (at Powerscourt), best monastic site (at Glendalough) and best walk (the Wicklow Way). Its main towns, many of them dormitory communities for Dublin, follow the coast south. Between Bray and Arklow sit pleasant seaside resorts and beaches, especially at Brittas Bay. West towards Sally Gap is a sublime mountainous wasteland, which includes the black waters of Lough Tay.

Powerscourt
In 1974, after major renovations, the 18th-century mansion at Powerscourt Estate was burned to the ground when a bird's nest in a chimney caught fire. One wing of the building remains, now internally revamped with exhibition room, cafe and shop, but people

IRELAND

come for the 19th-century, 20-hectare formal gardens. There are five strollable terraces extending for over 500m down to Triton Lake, with views east to the Great Sugar Loaf Mountain.

The estate is only 500m south of Enniskerry's main square and about 22km south of Dublin. It is open 9.30 am to 5.30 pm daily from March to October and 9.30 am until dusk the rest of the year. Admission to the gardens and visitor centre is IR£5; to the gardens alone it's IR£4. In winter prices are considerably less. Bus No 44 runs regularly from Hawkins St in Dublin to Enniskerry.

From the estate, a scenic 6km trail leads to **Powerscourt Waterfall**, at 130m the highest in Ireland. You can reach the waterfall by road (5km), following signs from the estate entrance. The waterfall can be viewed daily; in summer 9.30 am to 7 pm and in winter 10.30 am until dusk. Entry is IR£2.

Glendalough
☎ 0404

Glendalough (Gleann dá Loch), pronounced glen-da-lock, was founded in the late 6th century by St Kevin, an early Christian bishop who established a monastery on the Upper Lake's south shore. It is said that St Kevin stood in one of the lakes long enough for birds to nest in his hands and, apparently, the humble fellow made his bed in the hollow of a tree.

During the Middle Ages, when Ireland was known as 'the island of saints and scholars', Glendalough became a monastic city catering to thousands of students and teachers. The site is entered through the only surviving monastic gateway in Ireland.

The Glendalough Visitor Centre (☎ 45325), opposite the Lower Lake car park (free), overlooks a round tower, a ruined cathedral, and the tiny Church of St Kevin. It has historical displays, an audiovisual program, and is open 9.30 am to 5 pm daily. Admission is IR£2. From here a trail leads 1km west to the panoramic Upper Lake, with a car park (IR£1.50) and more ruins nearby.

Glendalough attracts heaps of tourists. In summer the secret is to arrive early and/or to stay late, as the site is free and open 24 hours. The lower car park gates are locked when the visitor centre closes.

Places to Stay An Óige's *Glendalough Hostel* (☎ 45342), 600m west of the visitor centre, is open year-round and has excellent facilities. Dorms cost up to IR£10.50. At the village of Laragh, 3km east of the monastic site, the basic *Wicklow Way Hostel* (☎ 45345), beside Lynham's 'The Laragh Inn' Bar, charges IR£7 for a dorm bed and IR£25 per person for a private room year-round. The Glendalough area also has plenty of moderately priced B&Bs.

Getting There & Away St Kevin's Bus Service (☎ 01-281 8119) runs daily to Glendalough from outside Dublin's College of Surgeons, across from St Stephen's Green. Buses leave daily at 11.30 am and 6 pm, returning to Dublin at 4.15 pm. It's recommended to stay the night and return on the 7.20 am or 9.45 am service (9.45 am only on weekends). The one-way/return fare is IR£6/10.

The Wicklow Way

Running for 132km, from County Dublin through to County Carlow, the Wicklow Way is the most popular of Ireland's long-distance walks. The route is clearly signposted and documented in leaflets and guidebooks; one of the better ones is *The Complete Wicklow Way* by JB Malone. Much of the trail traverses countryside above 500m, so pack boots with grip, a walking stick and clothing for Ireland's fickle weather.

The most attractive section of the walk is from Enniskerry to Glendalough (three days). *Glencree* (☎ 01-286 4037) and *Knockree* (☎ 01-286 4036) hostels are both at Enniskerry. Prices for dorm beds are IR£7.

WEXFORD
☎ 053

Little remains of Wexford's Viking past – apart from its narrow streets and name, Waesfjord, or 'Ford of Mud Flats'. Cromwell was in one of his most destructive moods when he included Wexford on his 1649-50 Irish tour, destroying the churches and 'putting to the sword' three-quarters of the town's 2000 inhabitants.

Wexford is a convenient stopover for those travelling to France or Wales via the Rosslare Harbour ferry port, 21km southeast of Wexford.

IRELAND

Orientation & Information

The train and bus stations are at the northern end of town, on Redmond Place. Follow the River Slaney 700m south along the often-bleak waterfront quays to reach the tourist office (☎ 23111), on The Crescent. It is open 9 am to 6 pm Monday to Saturday from March to October, and 9.30 am to 5.30 pm the rest of the year. The curiously tight North Main and South Main Sts are a block inland and parallel to the quays.

The main post office is north-west of the tourist office, between the quays and Nth Main St on Anne St. Wash your clothes at Padraig's Laundry, next to the hostel.

Things to See & Do

Of the six original town gates only the 14th-century **West Gate** on Slaney St survives. The **Westgate Heritage Centre** (☎ 46506), beside the gate, has an audiovisual display on the history of Wexford. It's open May to September. Admission is IR£1.50.

Nearby **Selskar Abbey** was founded by Alexander de la Roche in 1190 after a crusade to the Holy Land. Its present ruinous state is a result of Cromwell's visit in 1649. The **Bullring**, on the corner of Cornmarket and North Main St, was the site of one of Cromwell's massacres, but gets its name from the now-defunct sport of bull-baiting. Today a market is held on Friday and Saturday mornings.

About 5km north-west of Wexford, beside the Dublin-Rosslare (N11) road at Ferrycarrig, the **Irish National Heritage Park** (☎ 20733) is an outdoor theme-park condensing Irish history from the Stone Age to the early Norman period. The 14 reconstructed sights are enlivened by a not-to-be-missed free guided tour. Entry is IR£5, and the park opens 9.30 am to 6.30 pm daily from March to November (last admission at 5.30 pm).

Places to Stay

The *Ferrybank Camping & Caravan Park* (☎ 44387) is open from Easter to late September and costs from IR£5 to IR£10 for a tent site (75p for a shower). From the quays, cross the River Slaney via the Wexford Bridge (R741) and walk straight for five minutes.

The IHH *Kirwan House* (☎ 21208) on Mary St is a small and friendly hostel. It has Internet access, dorm beds for IR£8 and private rooms for IR£12 per person. From the tourist office, go right at Henrietta St, then right at South Main St, take a quick left at Allen St, right at High St and left at Mary St.

An elegant if stuffy B&B is *Westgate House* (☎ 22167), 150m south of the train station, with rates from IR£25 per person. Other places can be found along Redmond Rd, right from the train station.

Places to Eat

North and South Main Sts have something for most tastes, including sandwiches and picnic supplies at *Greenacres Food Hall (54 North Main St)*; Chinese at *Chan's Restaurant (90 North Main St)*; and pub grub at *Tim's Tavern (51 South Main St)*. The more upmarket *La Riva*, on The Crescent, serves pastas and grilled meats and has a good wine list. For traditional fish and chips try *Premier (104 South Main St)*.

Entertainment

Many of Wexford's pubs are strung along North and South Main Sts. Just around the corner on Cornmarket is the small and warm *Thomas Moore Tavern*, where the poet's mother was born. For music try *Wren's Nest* on Customs House Quay; *Mooney's (12 Commercial Quay)*; *Tack Room* on South Main St or the tiny *Crown Bar* on Monck St. *The Sky and the Ground*, on the far end of South Main St, has traditional music, good meals and a roaring youthful crowd at night.

Wexford hosts the country's biggest opera festival in late October and theatre and dance are performed year-round at the *Wexford Arts Centre* (☎ 23764), on Cornmarket.

Getting There & Away

Wexford's O'Hanrahan train station (☎ 33114 or 33162), on the Dublin-Rosslare line, is served by three trains daily in each direction; the three-hour trip to Dublin costs IR£11. There are also trains to Rosslare Harbour (IR£4, 25 minutes, three daily). Bus Éireann runs from the train station to Rosslare Harbour (IR£2.50, 20 minutes, seven daily), Dublin (IR£7.50, three hours, six daily) and beyond.

IRELAND

ROSSLARE HARBOUR
☎ 053

Rosslare Harbour has frequent ferry services to France and Wales (see the Getting There & Away section earlier in this chapter). There is absolutely no reason to linger at Rosslare Harbour, so catch the first bus or train to Wexford or points beyond. If you do stay, An Óige's **Rosslare Harbour Hostel** (☎ 33399) is on Goulding St, across the park at the back of the Hotel Rosslare, just uphill from the ferry terminal. It opens early and late for ferry departures. Beds in dorms range from IR£8 to IR£10.50. The tourist office (☎ 33622) is inside the ferry terminal. The bus and train stations are just outside.

WATERFORD
☎ 051 • pop 42,540

Although Waterford (Port Láirge) is a busy port and modern commercial centre, it also retains vestiges of its Viking and Norman past. Strongbow took the city in 1170, and in later centuries it was the most powerful political centre in Ireland.

Today Waterford is famed for its crystal, but it's also a college town, and during the academic year the crowded pubs are plenty of fun.

Orientation & Information

The main shopping street runs directly back from the River Suir, beginning as Barronstrand St and changing names as it runs south to intersect with Parnell St, which runs north-east back up to the river, becoming The Mall on the way. Reginald's Tower (at the top of The Mall) and the Clocktower (at the top of Barronstrand St) are handy landmarks.

The tourist office (☎ 87 5823), in The Granary, is near the river at 41 Merchant's Quay. It is open 9 am to 5 pm Monday to Saturday, and until 6 pm April to October; it's also open 11 am to 5 pm Sunday in July and August. Hidden away in Parnell Court, off Parnell St, Voy@ger Internet Cafe (☎ 84 3900) is open to 10 pm daily. The laundrette Duds 'n' Suds, is next to a big grey church on Parnell St.

Waterford Crystal Factory

The first Waterford glass factory was established in 1783 but closed in 1851 as a result of punitive taxes imposed by the British government. The business wasn't revived until 1947.

The visitor centre (☎ 33 2500) is 2km out on the road to Cork (N25). A guided tour (IR £3.50) takes you through the factory, where you can see big-cheeked glass blowers and fragile exhibits. In summer you can buy a ticket from the tourist office to avoid long queues at the factory. Public transport runs from the top of the mall at Broard St to the factory every 10 minutes (IR£1.50 return). The factory is open 8.30 am to 4 pm daily (shorter hours out of season).

Other Attractions

Good for a stroll, the **old quarter** is strangely quiet and separate from the main shopping areas to the west. Several handsome sections of the old city wall still stand, including **Reginald's Tower**, on the corner of The Mall and Parade Quay. The tower, built in 1003, has a museum (entry IR£1.50), open Easter to October.

Around the corner is the ruinous **French Church** (1240). If you want to take a peek inside, there is a sign on the fence explaining how to get the key.

On Merchants Quay, **The Granary** (☎ 30 4500), a gutted old grain store sleekly redesigned, houses the tourist office and the Waterford Treasures. The exhibition is tastefully designed and documents 1000 years of the city's history with artefacts, art and interactive and audiovisual presentations. It's open 9.30 am to 9 pm daily from June to August, 10 am to 5 pm the rest of the year. Entry is IR£4.

Places to Stay

Budget accommodation is in short supply in Waterford. It is wise to book ahead or try nearby Tramore, 12km to the south. Tramore has a hostel, **The Monkey Puzzel** (☎ 38 6754), and camping at the **Newtown Cove Caravan & Camping Park** (☎ 38 1121). There are regular buses from Waterford.

Waterford's hostel is the IHH **Barnacles Viking House** (☎ 85 3827) on Coffee House Lane, off Parade Quay one block west of Reginald's Tower. Dorm beds cost IR£7.50 to IR£9, including breakfast and a personal security locker. Doubles are IR£14.50 to IR£16.50.

The Mall and Parnell St have several cheap B&Bs, but traffic noise can be a problem. You could try **Derrynane House** (☎ 87 5179, 19 The Mall), where singles/doubles

IRELAND

cost IR£16/32. Attractively positioned near the Christ Church Cathedral, *Beechwood* (☎ 87 6677, *7 Cathedral Square*) has rooms for IR£18/32.

Places to Eat

Haricot's Wholefood (*11 O'Connell St*) has vegetarian and meaty dishes for IR£5 to IR£7. It's relaxed and boasts 'Nu-tron friendly food'. On John St, *Cafe Luna* has thick coffee and is popular after pub closing time. *The Brasserie*, an excellent bistro on the edge of the City Square mall, does moderately priced pizzas and is open seven days for breakfast, lunch and dinner. Lunch starts at IR£3 and dinner at IR£6. In the snug old-quarter is the more expensive *The Wine Vault* (*2 High St*), with over 300 wines to choose from.

Entertainment

On O'Connell St behind the tourist centre *The Roxy* has music alternating nightly between indie and techno. The venerable *T & H Doolan* (*32 George's St*) is packed on weekends, with the best traditional music in town. On John St is the popular *Geoff's*, but bypass *Pulpit* next door. Just up the street at the junction with Manor Rd, *Peig's Bar* has music sessions and is the pick of the four or so pubs that are there.

Garter Lane Art Centre (☎ 85 5038, *22A O'Connell St*) hosts contemporary and cutting edge films and exhibitions, and stages plays.

Getting There & Away

The train station (☎ 87 3401) is across the river from the town centre. There are regular rail connections to Dublin (IR£13, 2½ hours, four daily), Rosslare Harbour (IR£6, 80 minutes, twice daily), Kilkenny and Wexford. Bus Éireann (☎ 87 9000) has a new depot opposite the tourist office and sends buses to Dublin (IR£7), Wexford (IR£7.30), Rosslare Harbour (IR£8.80) and Cork (IR£9). The usit CAMPUS office (☎ 87 2601) is at 36-37 George's St.

Getting Around

Wright's Cycle Depot (☎ 87 4411), 19-20 Henrietta St, around the corner from Viking House hostel, rents bikes at around IR£10 per day during the warmer months.

KILKENNY

☎ 056 • pop 18,696

Despite the occasional heavy brewery-waft through its main streets, Kilkenny (Cill Chainnigh) is perhaps the most attractive large town in the country. Even though it was ransacked by Cromwell during his 1650 campaign, Kilkenny retains some of its medieval ground-plan, particularly the narrow streets. Overlooking a sweeping bend in the River Nore, Kilkenny Castle is a must for visitors.

Orientation & Information

Most places of interest can be found on or close to Parliament St and its continuation (High St), which runs parallel to the River Nore; or along Rose Inn St, which changes its name to John St, and leads away from the river to the north-east. The tourist office (☎ 51500), open Monday to Saturday all year, is in Shee Alms House on Rose Inn St, a short walk from the castle. Access the Internet at Compustore, in the Market Cross Shopping Centre on James St, 10 am to 6 pm daily.

Kilkenny Castle

Stronghold of the powerful Butler family, Kilkenny Castle (☎ 21450) has a history dating back to 1172, though the present castle is a more recent structure. The **Long Gallery**, with its vividly painted ceiling and extensive portrait collection of Butler family members over the centuries, is quite remarkable. Guided castle-tours are compulsory and cost IR£3.50. In summer the castle is open 10 am to 7 pm daily; hours are slightly shorter the rest of the year.

The castle also hosts contemporary art exhibitions in the **Butler Gallery**, which is free and open whenever the castle is.

St Canice's Cathedral

The approach on foot from Parliament St leads over Irishtown Bridge and up **St Canice's Steps**, which date from 1614; the wall at the top contains fragmentary medieval carvings. Around the cathedral is a **round tower** (which you can climb for IR£1) and an 18th-century bishop's palace. Although the present cathedral dates from 1251, it has a much longer history and contains some remarkable tombs and monuments that are decoded on a board in the south aisle.

IRELAND

Other Attractions

On Parliament St, **Rothe House** is a restored Tudor merchant's house dating from 1594. It's open 10.30 am to 5 pm Monday to Saturday from April to October, 3 to 5 pm Sunday. The rest of the year the rooms are open daily but hours vary. Entry is IR£2.

Smithwicks Brewery, also on Parliament St, shows a video and has tastings on weekdays at 3 pm from June to September. Free tickets are available at the tourist office. Tynan **walking tours** (☎ 65929) has one-hour walking tours of Kilkenny, taking in some of the more interesting low-key sites. The tours cost IR£3 and leave from the tourist office several times a day throughout the year.

Places to Stay

The small *Tree Grove Caravan & Camping Park* (☎ 70302) is 1.5km south of Kilkenny on the New Ross (R700) road. If you've come up the hill from Kilkenny on foot, a tent for two costs IR£6; if you're in a car it's IR£7. Hot, high-pressure showers are free for all.

Open year-round, the IHH *Kilkenny Tourist Hostel* (☎ 63541, 35 Parliament St) is central and has helpful staff who can guide you to the best things to do around town. Dorm beds cost IR£8 to IR£9 and private rooms IR£11 to IR£12 per person.

Well worth the hassle getting there is An Óige's *Foulksrath Castle Hostel* (☎ 67674), beautifully situated in a 16th-century Norman castle 13km north of Kilkenny in Jenkinstown, near Ballyragget (watch for the sign). Buggy's Buses (☎ 41264) has a service between The Parade in Kilkenny and the hostel (IR£1, 20 minutes), leaving at 11.30 am and 5.30 pm Monday to Saturday.

There are plenty of B&Bs, especially south of the city along Patrick St and north of the city on Castlecomer Rd. The central *Bregagh Guesthouse* (☎ 22315) on Dean St, near St Canice's Cathedral, has rooms at IR£25 per head. A few doors down, *Kilkenny B&B* (☎ 64040) has a variety of rooms from IR£16 a head. Near the train station on Dublin Rd is *Knockavon House* (☎ 64294), with a friendlier approach than the previous two. Singles/doubles are IR£20/36.

Places to Eat

Italian Connection (38 Parliament St) has good-value pizzas from IR£4.75 and pasta from IR£7. *Edward Langton's (69 John St)* is a stylish, award-winning pub with affordable lunches but pricey set dinners. For simpler pub grub try **Caisleán Uí Cuain**, opposite the castle. *Paris Texas* on High St has a decent bar and Mexican dishes at around IR£8. *Kytelers*, home of Kilkenny's most famous witch, Dame Alice Kyteler, is a multilevel old building with a good restaurant, and bar meals.

Entertainment

The best pub in town for traditional Irish music is *Maggie's* on St Keiran St. Others include *Ryan's* on Friary St and *John Cleere's* and *Fennelly's*, on Parliament St. At most of these you'll find music Wednesday to Saturday. *The Pumphouse* is popular with travellers and locals alike, and *The Cat Laughs*, on Dean St, has comedy.

The *Watergate Theatre* (☎ 61674), Parliament St, hosts musical and theatrical productions throughout the year.

Getting There & Around

McDonagh train station (☎ 22024) is on Dublin Rd, east of the town centre via John St. Four trains a day (five on Friday, three on Sunday) link Dublin's Heuston station to Kilkenny (IR£12) and then on to Waterford (IR£5).

Bus Éireann (☎ 051-87 9000) operates out of the train station. There are six buses a day (five on Sunday) to Dublin (IR£7), three to Cork (IR£5.30), up to five to Galway and one or two to Wexford, Waterford and Rosslare Harbour.

JJ Wall (☎ 21236), 88 Maudlin St, rents bikes for IR£7 per day.

AROUND KILKENNY
Kells Priory

Only 13km south of Kilkenny, Kells Priory is one of Ireland's most impressive and romantic monastic sites. The earliest remnants of the priory date from the late 12th century, with the bulk of the present ruins from the 15th century. Inside the walls are the remains of an Augustinian abbey and the foundations of some chapels and houses. Extraordinarily it's free and there are no set opening hours,

IRELAND

which makes it ideal for a private monastic adventure. Unfortunately, unless you've got a car, the site is difficult to get to. A taxi will cost about IR£10 from Kilkenny.

Jerpoint Abbey

Dating from the 12th century, Jerpoint Abbey (☎ 056-24623) is Ireland's finest Cistercian monastery. It's just south of Thomastown, about 20km south of Kilkenny. The fragments of the monastery's cloister are particularly notable, and there are some intriguing stone carvings on the church walls and tombs. Entry is IR£2, and it's open 9.30 am to 6.30 pm daily from mid-June to September. In the off season, the hours are shorter; if no one is there, appointments can be made.

CASHEL
☎ 062

The **Rock of Cashel** (☎ 61437), in the town of Cashel, 18km north of Cahir, is one of Ireland's most spectacular archaeological sites. On the outskirts of town rises a huge lump of limestone bristling with ancient fortifications. Mighty stone walls encircle a complete round-tower, a roofless abbey and the country's finest 12th-century **Romanesque chapel**. The complex is open 9 am to 4.30 pm daily (to 7.30 pm in summer), and admission is IR£3.50.

If you chose to stay the night, the IHH *Cashel Holiday Hostel* (☎ 62330, 6 John St) has dorm beds for IR£8.50 and doubles from IR£12 per person. The tourist office (☎ 61333), open daily April to September (weekdays only for the other months), is in the town hall, on Cashel's main street. Buses on line 8 (Dublin to Cork) pass through Cashel.

The South-West

CORK
☎ 021 • pop 180,000

Cork (Corcaigh), the Irish Republic's second-largest city, is home to a major university and prides itself on its heady mix of pubs, cafes, restaurants, and love of the arts.

The Cork International Jazz Festival and the International Film Festival both take place in October.

The Black and Tans were at their most brutal in Cork and much of the town was burnt down during the Anglo-Irish War. Cork was also a centre for the civil war that followed independence (Irish leader Michael Collins was ambushed and killed nearby). Today Cork is noted for its hurling and Gaelic-football teams, and its fierce rivalry with Dublin.

Orientation & Information

The city centre is an island between two channels of the River Lee. Oliver Plunkett St and the curve of St Patrick's St are the main shopping/eating/drinking areas. The train station and several hostels are north of the river; MacCurtain St and Glanmire Rd Lower are the main thoroughfares there.

The less-than-helpful tourist office (☎ 427 3251), really a big gift-shop, is on Grand Parade. It's open 9.15 am to 5.30 pm Monday to Saturday (closed 1 to 2.15 pm), and open daily in July and August. There is a post office on Oliver Plunkett St.

Internet access is available at i dot Café (☎ 427 3544) in the Gate Multiplex centre, North Main St. There are laundrettes at 14 MacCurtain St (across from Isaac's Hostel), and on Western Rd opposite the gates of University College Cork.

Things to See

Cork's notable churches include the imposing 1879 **St Finbarr's Cathedral**, south of the centre; particularly impressive are the huge pulpit and colourful chancel ceiling. North of the river there's a fine view from the tower of the 18th-century **St Anne's Church, Shandon** (☎ 450 5906). The quirky salmon-shaped weathervane was apparently chosen because the local monks reserved for themselves the right to fish for salmon in the river. The church is open 10 am to 5 pm Monday to Saturday. It costs IR£3.50 to climb the tower, ring the Shandon Bells, view the interior and its small collection of 17th-century books and watch an audiovisual presentation about the Shandon area.

The ground floor of the small **Cork Public Museum** is mostly devoted to Cork's role in the fight for Irish independence, while the 1st floor has archaeological displays. Entry is free on weekdays and 75p Sunday afternoon.

IRELAND

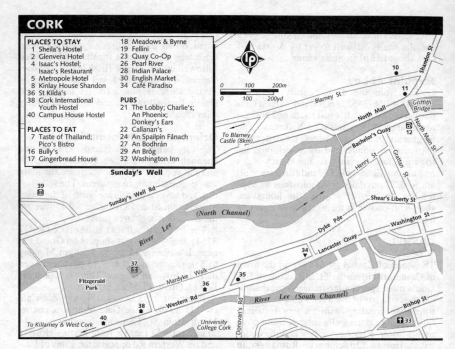

CORK

PLACES TO STAY
1 Sheila's Hostel
2 Glenvera Hotel
4 Isaac's Hostel;
  Isaac's Restaurant
5 Metropole Hotel
8 Kinlay House Shandon
36 St Kilda's
38 Cork International
  Youth Hostel
40 Campus House Hostel

PLACES TO EAT
7 Taste of Thailand;
  Pico's Bistro
16 Bully's
17 Gingerbread House

18 Meadows & Byrne
19 Fellini
23 Quay Co-Op
26 Pearl River
28 Indian Palace
30 English Market
34 Café Paradiso

PUBS
21 The Lobby; Charlie's;
  An Phoenix;
  Donkey's Ears
22 Callanan's
24 An Spailpín Fánach
27 An Bodhrán
29 An Bróg
32 Washington Inn

Cork City Gaol (☎ 430 5022) received its first prisoners in 1824 and its last in 1923. The 35-minute taped tour around the restored cells, and the 20-minute audiovisual on the prison's history are quite moving. Upstairs, the **National Radio Museum** has a collection of beautiful old radios. The complex is off Sunday's Well Rd, and opens 9.30 am to 6 pm daily, March to October (reduced hours the rest of the year). It costs IR£3.50 to see either the radios or the gaol (joint tickets are available).

Crawford Art Gallery (☎ 427 3377), with its new bellied-out-brickwork, glass and steel, is an impressive example of cutting-edge architecture melding into an existing 18th-century building. The permanent collection has works by Irish artists like Jack Yeats and Seán Keating, as well as works of the British Newlyn and St Ives' schools. The revamped gallery spaces display most of the collection, as well as contemporary shows and retrospectives. The gallery has an excellent cafe and is closed on Sunday; admission is free.

Places to Stay

Camping Opposite the entrance to the airport, on the N27, is *Bienvenue Ferry Caravan and Camping* (☎ 431 2711). Tent sites are IR£8 for two people and the airport bus, 500m away, will take you to Cork for IR£2.50.

Hostels Across the river from the bus station, IHH *Isaac's Hostel* (☎ 450 0011, 48 MacCurtain St) has beds in large/small dorms for IR£7.95/9.25. It's a smart-looking place with modern facilities, but can be a tad impersonal.

Back from MacCurtain St, off Wellington Rd, is clean and friendly *Sheila's Hostel* (☎ 450 5562, 4 Belgrave Place). The facilities are superb: laundry, cafe, foreign exchange, bike hire – even a sauna. Dorm beds start at IR£7.50, doubles IR£22.

Behind St Anne's Church is the modern *Kinlay House Shandon* (☎ 450 8966), Bob & Joan's Walk. Beds in mixed dorms of up to 12 people cost IR£8, doubles are IR£25, all including light breakfast.

IRELAND

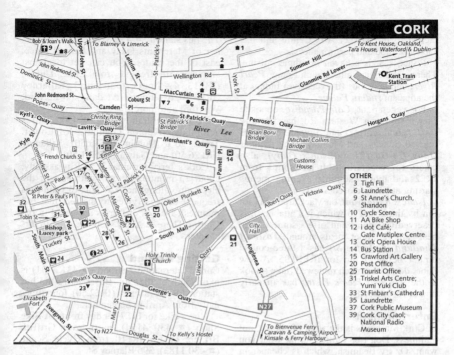

CORK

OTHER
3 Tigh Fili
6 Laundrette
9 St Anne's Church, Shandon
10 Cycle Scene
11 AA Bike Shop
12 i dot Café; Gate Mutiplex Centre
13 Cork Opera House
14 Bus Station
15 Crawford Art Gallery
20 Post Office
25 Tourist Office
31 Triskel Arts Centre; Yumi Yuki Club
33 St Finbarr's Cathedral
35 Laundrette
37 Cork Public Museum
39 Cork City Gaol; National Radio Museum

South of the river, **Kelly's Hostel** (☎ *431 5612, 25 Summerhill South*) has beds from IR£6.50 and boasts the best showers in Cork.

Out by the university, to the west of the centre, the An Óige **Cork International Youth Hostel** (☎ *454 3289, 1-2 Western Rd*) has had an expensive make-over, and is excellent value at IR£9 for dorm beds. The much smaller **Campus House Hostel** (☎ *434 3531, 3 Woodland View*) just a few doors down has beds for IR£8. Bus No 8 from the bus station stops outside the An Óige hostel.

B&Bs & Hotels Glanmire Rd Lower, a short distance east of the train station, is lined with economical B&Bs. **Kent House** (☎ *450 4260*) at No 47 has singles/doubles starting at IR£23.50/38; **Oakland** (☎ *450 0578*) at No 51 charges IR£25/40; and rates at **Tara House** (☎ *450 0294*) at No 52 start at IR£21/35.

The quiet **Glenvera Hotel** (☎ *450 2030*), Wellington Rd, charges IR£27 per person for B&B-style service.

On the opposite side of town, Western Rd also has plenty of more-exclusive (and therefore expensive) B&Bs, including **St Kilda's** (☎ *427 3095*), a big blue house with its own car park. It charges IR£70 for a double.

The old-world **Metropole Hotel** (☎ *450 8122, fax 450 6450*) on MacCurtain St, has ritzy red carpets, and rooms from IR£74/99.

Places to Eat

For self-catering, head straight for the well-stocked food stalls inside the **English Market**, off the western end of St Patrick's St.

Between St Patrick's St and the pedestrianised area of Paul St are several narrow lanes packed with restaurants. For coffees and light meals, try the popular **Gingerbread House**, or **Fellini**, with its French film paraphernalia. Both are on Carey's Lane.

Meadows & Byrne on French Church St is often full; and trendy, mid-range **Bully's** (*40 Paul St*) has candles and low lighting, tasty pizzas and pastas.

IRELAND

The Yumi Yuki Club on Tobin St is attached to the Triskel Arts Centre and has Japanese food and performances.

Princess St is a haven of ethnic cuisine. There's authentic Chinese at mid-range *Pearl River*, and delicious (if expensive) Indian at the adjacent *Indian Palace*.

For vegetarians, *Café Paradiso*, opposite Jury's Hotel on Western Rd, has friendly staff, good coffee and inventive dishes (closed Sunday and Monday). The popular *Quay Co-Op (24 Sullivan's Quay)*, also caters for vegetarians. It has soups from IR£2 and more elaborate evening menus starting at IR£5 (closed Sunday).

Isaac's Restaurant, on MacCurtain St (not run by the hostel to which it's attached), is deservedly popular and offers some of the best-value gourmet meals around. *Taste of Thailand (8 Bridge St)* has a three-course dinner before 7 pm for IR£10.95. A few doors down, the much reviewed (take a look at the window) *Pico's Bistro* has an early dinner for IR£10.85.

Entertainment

In Cork Murphy's is the stout of choice, not Guinness. Don't be bullied; drink what you want. Or try Beamish, which is cheaper in most pubs. But entertainment in Cork goes further than pints, jigs and reels; *Cork's List*, a free fortnightly publication available from pubs, cafes and the like, lists it all.

On Union Quay *The Lobby*, *Charlie's*, *An Phoenix* and *Donkey's Ears* are all side by side, and at least one of them has live music (from rock to traditional) most nights.

An Bodhrán (42 Oliver Plunkett St) regularly features music, as does *An Bróg* at No 78. More subdued is *An Spailpín Fánach (28 South Main St)*, with traditional music four nights a week. Students hang out at *Washington Inn* on Washington St. For a real Cork drinking experience visit tiny *Callanan's*, or any of the other small pubs on George's Quay.

Cork's cultural institutions include the *Cork Opera House* (☎ 427 0022), on Emmet Place, and the *Triskel Arts Centre* on Tobin St, just off South Main St, an important venue for films, theatre, music, and other media arts. *Tigh Fili* (☎ 450 9274) on MacCurtain St has a poets' platform, exhibitions and workshops.

Getting There & Away

The bus station (☎ 450 8188) is on the corner of Merchants Quay and Parnell Place, east of the centre. You can get to almost anywhere in Ireland from Cork: Dublin (IR£13, 4½ hours, four daily), Killarney (IR£9.40, two hours, five daily), Waterford, Wexford and more.

Cork's Kent train station (☎ 450 6766) is across the river on Glanmire Rd Lower. Trains go to Dublin (IR£33.50), Kilkenny (IR£26.50) and Galway (IR£31.50).

Cork's ferry terminal is at Ringaskiddy, about 15 minutes by car south-east of the city centre along the N28. Bus Éireann runs frequent daily services to the terminal (45 minutes). Details of ferries are listed in the Getting There & Away section earlier in this chapter.

Getting Around

Cork's international airport (☎ 431 3131) is 6km south of the city. Buses leave the bus station for the airport (IR£2.50) four times daily from April to September.

Hire a bike for IR£7 per day from AA Bike Shop (☎ 430 4154), north over Griffith Bridge; or for IR£10 from Cycle Scene (☎ 430 1183), 396 Blarney St.

AROUND CORK
Blarney
☎ 021

Just north-west of Cork, Blarney (An Bhlarna) is a village with one overwhelming drawcard – the 15th-century **Blarney Castle** (☎ 438 5252). Even the most jaded visitor will feel compelled to kiss the **Blarney Stone** and get the 'gift of the gab'. It was Queen Elizabeth I, exasperated with Lord Blarney's ability to talk endlessly without ever actually agreeing to her demands, who invented the term. Bending over backwards to kiss the sacred rock requires a head for heights, though you're unlikely to fall since there's someone there to hold you in position.

The castle's opening times are all over the place: 9 am to 6.30 or 7 pm Monday to Saturday, or to sundown in winter; 9.30 am to 5.30 pm Sunday. Entry is IR£3.50.

There are myriad B&Bs surrounding the castle, plus an unaffiliated *Blarney Tourist Hostel* (☎ 438 5580), which has basic but good facilities. It is a few kilometres west of

Blarney on the road to Killarney. Dorm beds are IR£7, doubles IR£17.

Buses run regularly from the Cork bus station (IR£2.50 return, 30 minutes).

Kinsale
☎ 021

Kinsale (Cionn tSáile) is the quintessential Irish seaside town. People come for the coastal scenery and a promise that Kinsale is the undisputed gourmet capital of Ireland.

The tourist office (☎ 477 2234, 1 Pier Rd) is open March to October.

South-east of Kinsale, a scenic 2.5km walk from the town centre, stand the brawny ruins of 17th-century **Charles Fort** (☎ 477 2263), one of the best preserved star forts in Europe (IR£2.50). It was built in the 1670s and remained in use until 1921, when the retreating British army destroyed much of it. On a sunny day the views from the hill-top battlements are stunning. The site is open 10 am to 6 pm daily from mid-March to October; weekends only for other times of the year.

Buses connect Kinsale with Cork (IR£5.50 return, 45 minutes) five times daily and stop near the tourist office. To head west by bus you'll have to go back to Cork.

Places to Stay To get to the modern hostel at *Castlepark Marina Centre* (☎ 477 4959) walk from the tourist office for 20 minutes along Pier Rd to the Trident Hotel, from which ferries run to the hostel June to September on the hour, starting at 8 am. Alternatively take a cab (IR£4) or call and ask nicely for a pick-up. Dorm beds cost up to IR£9, doubles IR£22. The hostel is closed November to 17 March, and there's an on-site cafe and a pub next door.

The scruffy IHH *Dempsey's Hostel* (☎ 477 2124) is closer to town but its location, behind the Texaco petrol station on the Cork road, is nothing to write home about. Dorm beds are IR£6, doubles IR£16.

Places to Eat Café Palermo on Pearse St does reasonably priced gourmet pizzas and pastas. Some of the upmarket places, like Max's Wine Bar (☎ 477 2443) and Cottage Loft (☎ 477 2803), both on Main St, serve close-to-affordable lunches and early-

evening meals. Mary's Lane Steak and Seafood Bistro (☎ 477 4708) near the corner of High and Market Sts has a three course special for IR£13.95, including a song or two by Mary.

WEST COUNTY CORK

Travelling west by public transport from Cork can be tough. There are at least two daily bus services (more in summer) connecting towns. The trick is to plan ahead at Cork, have the timetables committed to memory, and be prepared to change buses and backtrack.

Baltimore & Clear Island
☎ 028

Just 13km down the River Ilen from Skibbereen, sleepy Baltimore has a population of around 200 that swells enormously during summer. The small tourist office (☎ 21766) at the harbour opens in high season, but otherwise has details for fishing, sailing cruises, buses and ferries on the door. The Baltimore Diving Centre (☎ 20300) arranges diving expeditions.

Baltimore has plenty of B&Bs, plus the excellent IHH *Rolf's Hostel* (☎ 20289); follow the signs up a hill 700m east of town. Dorm beds start at IR£8, doubles IR£23.

Baltimore's main attraction is its proximity to Clear Island, the most southerly point of Ireland (apart from Fastnet Rock, 6km to the south-west). Clear Island is a Gaeltacht area with about 150 Irish-speaking inhabitants, one shop and three pubs. From June to September, ferries (☎ 39135) leave Baltimore (weather permitting) at 2.15 and 7 pm Monday to Saturday and at noon, 2.15, 5 and 7 pm on Sunday. In July and August there is an extra service at 11 am (12 pm on Sunday). At other times of year boats leave Monday to Saturday at 2.15 pm. The trip takes 45 minutes and return fare is IR£8, with no extra charge for bikes. In summer, boats to Clear Island also leave from Schull (see the Mizen Head Peninsula section).

A *camping ground* (☎ 39119), signposted from the shop, costs IR£3 per person and opens from June to mid-September. An Óige's basic *Cape Clear Island Hostel* (☎ 39198), a short walk from the pier, costs IR£7.50 and is open March until the end of November.

IRELAND

Mizen Head Peninsula

☎ 028

Mizen Head is a scenic alternative to the better known and much more touristy Ring of Kerry and Dingle Peninsula.

At least two buses a day leave Cork (via Skibbereen) for the small village of **Schull** at the foot of Mt Gabriel (407m). In summer, Schull's pubs and restaurants are packed with tourists, but the rest of the year it's blissfully quiet. The IHH's excellent, cedar-panelled *Schull Backpackers' Lodge* (☎ 28681), with dorm beds at IR£7.50 and doubles starting at IR£22, is on Colla Rd. If you're headed to Clear Island, note that boats also leave from Schull's pier in June and September at 2.30 pm and return at 5.30 pm; in July and August they leave at 10 am, 2.30 and 4.30 pm and return at 11 am, 3.30 and 5.30 pm. The return fare is IR£9.

The road west from Schull leads to the small village of **Goleen**, home to a few cafes and pubs, plus a pottery and arts workshop called The Ewe (☎ 35492), which runs 'creative escape courses'. From Goleen, one road leads to Barleycove Beach and onwards to the small village of **Crookhaven**, with its handful of B&Bs and pubs.

The other road leads south, past fields with crumbling dry-stone fences, to **Mizen Head** and its 1910 signal station, now a lame visitors centre (☎ 35115), which is on a small island connected to the mainland by a 45m-high suspension bridge. People come to see the stunning layered vista of rocks as they cross the bridge, clench their teeth at the bitter wind and gaze out to sea. The station is open to the public daily from April to October, but only on weekends from November to March. Admission is IR£2.50.

Bantry

☎ 027

Famed for its mussels and wedged between hills and the waters of Bantry Bay, Bantry's major attraction is colourful old **Bantry House** (☎ 50047), superbly situated overlooking the bay. The gardens are beautifully kept, and the house is noted for its French and Flemish tapestries. Entry to the gardens is IR£2, to the house an extra IR£4. Both are open 9 am to 6 pm daily. In the courtyard a French Armada exhibit (entry IR£3) recounts the sorry saga of France's attempt in 1796 to aid the Irish independence struggle.

From Bantry's central pier, boats run to nearby **Whiddy Island** from May to September. Bantry's tourist office (☎ 50229) on the east end of Wolfe Tone Square is open from April to October. Frequent buses to Cork (three daily), Killarney, Glengarriff and beyond stop just off the main square at Barry Murphy's pub.

The IHH *Bantry Independent Hostel* (☎ 51050) is on Bishop Lucey Place just off Glengarriff Rd, about 600m north-east of the town centre. Dorm/double beds cost IR£8/20 in the high season. The *Small Independent Hostel* (☎ 51140), right beside the harbour on the north bank, has dorm beds for IR£6.50. There are plenty of B&Bs in Bantry, including a few around Wolfe Tone Square.

The Beara Peninsula

☎ 027

From Bantry the N71 follows the coast northwest to Glengarriff from where the R572 runs south-west to the Beara Peninsula, a harsh, rocky landscape ideal for walking and cycling. It's possible to drive the 137km 'Ring of Beara' in one day, however, that would be missing the point.

Coming from Glengarriff, the first village on the peninsula is **Adrigole**, a quiet place with lots of rocks and *Hungry Hill Lodge* (☎ 60228). The new facilities include camping for IR£4 per person, dorm beds from IR£8, doubles from IR£20 and a cafe boasting to be the only place in Adrigole to get something to eat.

Other peninsula hostels include *Beara Hostel* (☎ 70184), 3km west of Castletownbere, with dorm beds for IR£7 and camping for IR£4. *Garranes Hostel* (☎ 73147), between Castletownbere and Allihies, has a superb location overlooking Bantry Bay. The surrounds have a meditative quiet, not surprising seeing as it's owned by the Dzogchen Buddhist retreat (☎ 73032) next door. Guests have the option of joining daily meditation sessions. It's IR£7.50 for a dorm bed.

In the village of **Allihies**, the IHH *Village Hostel* (☎ 73107) is open April to the end of October and charges IR£8.50 for dorm beds, IR£4 for tent sites. In among the surrounding copper mines is An Óige's *Allihies Hostel*

(☎ 73014), with beds for IR£7; it's open June to the end of September. An Óige's *Glanmore Lake Lodge* (☎ 064-83181), open Easter to the end of September, is in an old schoolhouse 5km from Lauragh, and has dorm beds for IR£7.

The West Coast

KILLARNEY
☎ 064 • pop 7250

By the time you reach Killarney (Cill Airne) you will have seen plenty of touristy Irish towns, but nothing will prepare you for a Killarney summer weekend chock-a-block with tour coaches. Cynics may find Killarney to be little more than a charmless Irish theme-park. Still, with a national park and three lakes right on its doorstep, there are easy escapes for walkers and cyclists. Killarney is also a convenient base for touring the Ring of Kerry (see that section later in this chapter).

Information

Killarney's busy tourist office (☎ 31633), open Monday to Saturday (closed 1 to 2.15 pm) year-round and on Sunday from June to August, is on Beech Rd. The main post office is on New St. Gleeson's Laundrette is behind the Spar supermarket where Plunkett St meets College St. Web Talk on High St and Café Internet on New St provide daily Internet access.

Around Town

Most of Killarney's attractions are just outside the town, not actually in it. The 1855 **St Mary's Cathedral**, on Cathedral Place, is worth a look, as is the **National Museum of Irish Transport**, set back from East Avenue Rd. The latter has an interesting assortment of old cars, bicycles, automotive smells and pasty mannequins. The museum is open 10 am to 6 pm daily from April to October. Entry is IR£3.

Killarney National Park

Killarney's 10,236-hectare national park has a pedestrian entrance immediately opposite St Mary's Cathedral, and a drivers entrance off the N71. Within the park there are beautiful Lough Leane, Muckross Lake and the Upper Lake. In 1981 the park was designated a Unesco Biosphere Reserve.

Generally, sites within the park are interesting, but if you're starting to get bored with ruins and ex-gentry housing, the park is exceptional for some self-motivated exploring.

The restored 14th-century **Ross Castle** is a 2.5km walk from St Mary's Cathedral. Entry to the castle is IR£2.50. Hour-long **cruises of Lough Leane** leave the castle daily in summer; make bookings at the tourist office. From late September to May boats depart on weekends only.

Inisfallen Island, Lough Leane's largest, is where the 13th-century *Annals of Inisfallen* were written. The annals, now in the Bodleian Library at Oxford, remain a vital source of information about early Irish history. From Ross Castle you can hire a boat and row to the island to inspect the ruins of a 12th-century oratory. Alternatively, boatmen charge passengers IR£4 each for the crossing.

The core of Killarney National Park is **Muckross Estate**, donated to the government in 1932 by Arthur Bourn Vincent. The estate is 5km from Killarney and you can walk around the estate's rooms, and view their faded 19th-century fittings, daily year-round for IR£4.

Gap of Dunloe

In summer the Gap, a heather-clad valley at the foot of Purple Mountain (832m), is Killarney tourism at its worst. Rather than paying over IR£30 for a one-hour horse-and-trap ride through the Gap, consider hiring a bike and cycling to Ross Castle. From here take a boat across to Lord Brandon's Cottage and cycle down through the Gap and back into town via the N72 and a path through the golf course. Including bike hire, this should cost you about IR£14. The 90-minute boat trip alone justifies the trip.

Places to Stay

Wherever you stay, book ahead from June to August.

Camping About 1.5km out along the Cork road (N22) is *Fleming's White Bridge Caravan & Camping Park* (☎ 31590) while *Flesk Muckross Caravan Park* (☎ 31704) is 1.5km out on the Kenmare road (N71). Tent sites at

IRELAND

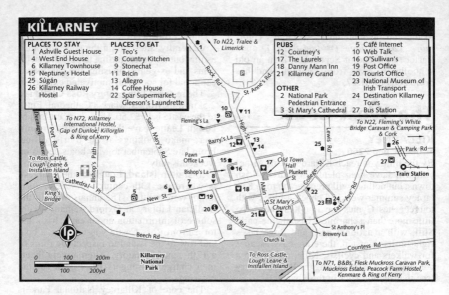

KILLARNEY

PLACES TO STAY	PLACES TO EAT	PUBS	5 Café Internet
1 Ashville Guest House	7 Teo's	12 Courtney's	10 Web Talk
4 West End House	8 Country Kitchen	17 The Laurels	16 O'Sullivan's
6 Killarney Townhouse	9 Stonechat	18 Danny Mann Inn	19 Post Office
15 Neptune's Hostel	11 Bricin	21 Killarney Grand	20 Tourist Office
25 Súgán	13 Allegro		23 National Museum of
26 Killarney Railway	14 Coffee House	OTHER	Irish Transport
Hostel	22 Spar Supermarket;	2 National Park	24 Destination Killarney
	Gleeson's Laundrette	Pedestrian Entrance	Tours
		3 St Mary's Cathedral	27 Bus Station

both are IR£5 per person and are available mid-March to October.

Hostels Just off Park Rd and closest to the bus and train station, the modern, well-equipped *Killarney Railway Hostel* (☎ 35299) has dorm beds for IR£8.50, private rooms for IR£15 and doubles IR£25.

Off New St, in the town centre, Bishop's Lane leads to the much-recommended *Neptune's Hostel* (☎ 35255). Dorm beds start at IR£7.50, and singles/doubles are IR£19/24.

The small *Súgán* (☎ 33104) on Lewis Rd has a big kitchen, a cosy dining room, bikes for hire and a rack of guitars, but there are often queues for the two toilets and outdoor shower. Ask for a map of the town and Killarney will come alive. Dorms are IR£9.

An Óige's large *Killarney International Hostel* (☎ 31240) has a full range of services and is 2km west of town; a hostel bus meets trains from Dublin and Cork. Dorm beds range from IR£7.50 to IR£8.50. But for the real out-of-town experience, the IHH *Peacock Farm Hostel* (☎ 33557), a quiet rural oasis, is 7km away in Gortdromakiery, call to arrange a free pick-up. It has impressive views of Loch Guitane, a great sunroom, and cute sea-motif showers. It's open from April

until the end of September, and dorm beds are IR£7.

B&Bs In high season finding a room can be tricky, so it's worth paying the IR£1 booking fee and letting the tourist office do the hunting. Both *West End House* (☎ 32271) along New St beside the Shell petrol station, and *Killarney Townhouse* a bit farther down New St, have singles/doubles for IR£30/45. Within walking distance of the centre of town on Rock Rd is *Ashville Guest House* (☎ 36405), with plenty of rooms starting at IR£39 for a double. Otherwise, the road to Muckross is a good place to look.

Places to Eat

For good coffee try *Coffee House*, on High St. On New St, *Country Kitchen* has breakfast and lunchtime sandwiches and salads. Duck down Flemings Lane, off High St, to the *Stonechat*, which has a good choice of soups, sandwiches and cakes and a courtyard if the weather is kind. *Allegro*, on High St, does basic pizza, pasta and burgers, and has a specials menu of traditional meals for IR£4.95.

The inviting *Bricín*, above a craft shop on High St, does seafood and stews, and has vegetarian options. Mains cost IR£10 to

IR£15, and lunchtime specials cost IR£4.50. For a cheap meal, *Teo's* on New St has a half-pizza and chips for IR£2.

Entertainment

Killarney has plenty of music pubs, but much of what's played is tourist-oriented, like at *The Laurels* on Main St. The musical part (IR£4 cover charge) is actually behind the main pub and reached by a side alley. Pubs with more authentic music include the *Danny Mann Inn*, on New St; and *Courtney's*, on High St. But the most popular is the *Killarney Grand* on Main St, which has nights of poetry readings, and interesting takes on the traditional thing.

Getting There & Around

Bus Éireann (☎ 34777) operates from outside the small train station (☎ 31067), with regular services to Cork (IR£10), Galway (via Limerick, IR£13.50), Dublin (IR£15) and Rosslare Harbour (IR£16). Travelling by train to Cork (IR£10) usually involves changing at Mallow, but there is a direct route to Dublin (IR£34) via Limerick Junction.

In the same lane as Neptune's Hostel is O'Sullivan's (☎ 31282) which rents bikes for IR£6 per day.

THE RING OF KERRY
☎ 066

The Ring of Kerry, a 179km circuit around the Iveragh Peninsula, with its dramatic coastal scenery, is one of Ireland's premier tourist attractions.

Most travellers tackle the Ring by bus on a guided day trip from Killarney. Tourist coaches approach the Ring in an anticlockwise direction and in summer it's hard to know which is more unpleasant – driving/cycling behind the buses or travelling in the opposite direction and meeting them on blind corners.

Eliminate some of these frustrations by getting off the main highway. The **Ballaghbeama Pass** cuts across the peninsula's central highlands and has spectacular views and remarkably little traffic. The shorter **Ring of Skellig**, at the end of the peninsula, has fine views of the Skellig Rocks and is also less touristy. You can forgo roads completely by walking the **Kerry Way**, which winds through the Macgillycuddy's Reeks mountains past Carrantuohill (1038m), the highest mountain in Ireland.

Things to See

Daniel O'Connell was born near **Cahirciveen**, one of the Ring's larger towns. The excellent Barracks Heritage Centre (☎ 947 2589) off Bridge St occupies what was once an intimidating Royal Irish Constabulary (RIC) barracks. Exhibits focus on Daniel O'Connell and 20th-century Irish history. Entry is IR£3.

South of Cahirciveen the R565 branches west to the 11km-long **Valentia Island**, a jumping-off point for the **Skellig Rocks**, two tiny islands 12km off the coast. Boats run from Portmagee, just before the bridge to Valentia, to uninhabited Skellig Michael, with its superb monastery ruins and abundant bird life. The standard fare is IR£20 return. Booking is essential; contact Joe Roddy (☎ 947 4268) or Des Lavelle (☎ 947 6124).

The **Skellig Experience Centre** (☎ 947 6306), on Valentia Island across from Portmagee, has exhibits on the life and times of the monks who lived on Skellig Michael from the 7th to the 12th centuries. Entry is IR£3, and the centre opens daily March to October.

The pretty pastel-coloured town of **Kenmare** is an excellent alternative base for exploring the Ring of Kerry. Kenmare is somewhat touristy, but it's nothing like Killarney.

Places to Stay

It's wise to book your next night as you make your way around the Ring; some places are closed out of season, others fill up quickly. Ring of Kerry hostels typically charge IR£8 to IR£9 for dorm beds.

Cycling hostel-to-hostel around the Ring, there's the IHH *Laune Valley Farm* (☎ 976 1488), 2km east of Killorglin; the IHO *Caitin Baiters Hostel* (☎ 947 7614) in Kells; the IHH *Sive Hostel* (☎ 947 2717) in Cahirciveen; the IHO *Ring Lyne Hostel* (☎ 947 6103) in Chapeltown and An Óige's *Valentia Island* (☎ 947 6154) in Knightstown on Valentia Island; the An Óige *Baile an Sceilg* (☎ 947 9229) in Ballinskelligs; and the IHH *Fáilte Hostel* (☎ 064-42333) in Kenmare.

An Óige's *Black Valley Hostel* (☎ 064-34712) in the Macgillycuddy's Reeks mountains is a good starting point for walking the Kerry Way. It's open from March to late November.

Getting There & Around

If you're not up to cycling, Bus Éireann operates a Ring of Kerry bus service daily from mid-May to mid-September. In June buses leave Killarney at 8.30 am, 1.30 and 3.45 pm (Sunday at 9.40 am and noon), stopping at Killorglin, Glenbeigh, Kells, Cahirciveen, Waterville, Caherdaniel and Sneem before returning to Killarney. (The 3.45 pm service terminates at Waterville.) For more details ring ☎ 064-34777.

Travel agents in Killarney, including Destination Killarney Tours (☎ 064-32638) on East Avenue Rd, offer daily tours of the Ring for about IR£10. Hostels in Killarney arrange tours for around IR£8.

THE DINGLE PENINSULA

☎ 066

The Dingle Peninsula is just as beautiful as and far less crowded than the Ring of Kerry, with narrow roads that discourage heavy bus-traffic.

The region's main hub, Dingle Town (An Daingean), is a workaday fishing village with a dozen good pubs. The western tip of the peninsula, noted for its extraordinary number of ring forts and high crosses, is predominantly Irish-speaking.

Dingle Town

In the winter of 1984 fisherfolk noticed a solitary bottlenose dolphin that followed their vessels and sometimes leapt over their boats. Boats (☎ 915 2626) leave Dingle's pier for a one-hour trip to find **Fungie the dolphin**. The cost is IR£6 (free if Fungie doesn't show, but he usually does). You can swim with him for IR£10; wetsuit hire is extra.

Open daily, **Dingle Oceanworld** (☎ 915 2111), opposite the harbour, has a walkthrough tunnel and touch pool for IR£4.50. You can **ride a horse** through the peninsula with Dingle Horse Riding (☎ 915 2018).

East of Dingle Town

From Tralee the N86 heads west along the coast. The 'quick' route to Dingle Town is south-west from Camp via Anascaul and the N86. The scenic route follows the R560 north-west and crosses the wildly scenic **Connor Pass** (456m).

West of Dingle Town

From Dingle follow signs for the 'Slea Head Drive', a scenic coastal stretch of the R559. First stop is the village of **Ventry** and its excellent post office-cum-delicatessen-cum-wineshop. A few kilometres south-west, **Slea Head** offers some of the peninsula's best views.

Ferries run to the bleak **Blasket Islands** (IR£10 return, 20 minutes) (☎ 915 6444 or 915 6533), off the tip of the peninsula, from Dunquin. Dunquin's **Blasket Centre** (☎ 56444), open daily from Easter to September, focuses on the hearty islanders who lived on Great Blasket until 1953. Entry is IR£2.50.

Places to Stay

The going rate for a dorm bed in and around Dingle is IR£7 to IR£9.50.

In Dingle Town, the inviting *Grapevine Hostel* (☎ 915 1434) on Dykegate St has beds in dorms and four-bed rooms. For a more rural setting try the popular *Rainbow Hostel* (☎ 915 1044), 1km west of town (call for free pick-up from the bus stop); camping is also available. East along the Tralee road, the IHH *Ballintaggart Hostel* (☎ 915 1454) in a spacious 19th-century house has a free shuttle service to/from town, plus bike hire. If these places are full, the clean, friendly but basic *Marina Hostel* (☎ 915 1065) is near the pier.

Hostels east of Dingle include the IHH *Fuchsia Lodge* (☎ 915 7150), in Anascaul; and the IHH *Connor Pass Hostel* (☎ 713 9179) in Stradbally, near Castlegregory. The former is open year-round, the latter from mid-March to November.

West of Dingle, look for An Óige's year-round *Dunquin Hostel* (☎ 915 6121) near the Blasket ferry and the IHO *Black Cat Hostel* (☎ 915 6286) in Ballyferriter, open May to October.

Getting There & Around

Buses stop outside the car park at the back of the Super Valu store in Dingle Town. Buses for Dingle Town leave Tralee four times daily from Monday to Saturday. Two buses daily depart from Killarney for Dingle in the summer. Note that there are few services on Sunday.

There are several bike-rental places in Dingle. Paddy Walsh (☎ 915 2311) on Dykegate

IRELAND

St near the Grapevine Hostel has bikes for IR£6 (IR£5 with a student card).

LIMERICK
☎ 061 • pop 79,000

Limerick (Luimneach) is the Irish Republic's third-largest city and for a long time it was regarded by travellers as one of the dullest spots in the country. In recent years it has become a place of interest in its own right, with all sorts of eating establishments and a lively music scene. That said, if you're pressed for time, skip Limerick and head straight for the Irish countryside.

Orientation & Information

The main street through town changes name from Rutland St to Patrick St, O'Connell St, The Crescent and Quinlan St as it runs south. The train and bus station lie to the south-east, off Parnell St.

The tourist office (☎ 31 7522), on Arthur's Quay near the River Shannon, is open Monday to Saturday and on Sunday in summer. There is Internet access at Webster's (☎ 31 2066) on Thomas St. There is a laundrette at 19 Ellen St, near where it meets Patrick St.

Things to See

Across the Shannon is **King John's Castle** (☎ 41 1201). The dummies in the action exhibits are a bit frightening, but the audiovisual, focusing on the castle's 800-year history, is informative. The castle is open all year, and entry is IR£4.50.

The adjacent **Limerick Museum** (☎ 41 7826), open 10 am to 1 pm and 2.15 to 5 pm Tuesday to Saturday, seems cluttered and unimaginative, but is far more interesting if you read the old letters. A short walk south is Limerick's oldest building, the 12th-century **St Mary's Cathedral**. Continue south on Bridge St to the fascinating **Hunt Museum** on Rutland St, where there are contemporary art shows, 2000 artefacts and the finest collection of Bronze Age, Celtic and medieval treasures outside of Dublin. It's open 10 am to 5 pm daily, except Sunday when it opens 2 to 5 pm. Entry is IR£4.50.

Places to Stay

An Óige's **Limerick Hostel** (☎ 31 4672, 1 Pery Square) is a short walk across People's Park from the bus and train station, and has dorm beds for IR£8. At the IHH **Barringtons Lodge & Hostel** (☎ 41 5222) on Georges Quay you can have one of the 88 beds for IR£7.50. **Broad Street Hostel** (☎ 31 7222) has dorms for IR£9, including a light breakfast.

There are cheap B&Bs on Davis St, directly opposite the train station. **Alexandra** (☎ 31 8472, 6 Alexandra Terrace) off O'Connell Ave is fairly close to the centre and has singles/doubles from IR£25/50.

Places to Eat

There is a **Tesco** supermarket in the Arthur's Quay Shopping Centre beside the tourist office. For a good coffee, try **Java's – The Beat Café** (5 Catherine St), near the corner of Thomas St. On O'Connell St (between Cecil and Shannon Sts), **La Romana** does mostly pastas for around IR£7. Open when its museum namesake is, **The Hunt Museum Restaurant** has views of the River Shannon and is popular for lunch.

Getting There & Away

Bus Éireann (☎ 31 3333) services operate from Colbert train station. There are regular bus connections to Dublin (IR£11), Cork, Galway, Killarney and other centres. By train (☎ 31 5555) it costs IR£26.50 to Dublin and IR£14 to Cork. Specials are often available for early trains to Dublin.

Shannon airport (☎ 47 1444), 24km from Limerick, handles domestic and international flights.

Getting Around

Buses connect the airport with the bus and train station for IR£3.70. There are also direct buses from the airport to Dublin.

Bicycles are available for hire at Emerald Alpine Cycles (☎ 41 6983), 1 Patrick St, for IR£12 per day.

THE BURREN

County Clare's greatest attraction is the Burren, a harsh and inhospitable stretch of country battered by the cranky Atlantic Ocean. *Boireann* is Irish for 'Rocky Country', and the name is no exaggeration. One of Cromwell's generals concluded that in the Burren there was 'neither water enough to drown a man, nor a tree to hang him, nor soil enough to bury him.'

IRELAND

Despite its unwelcoming look, the Burren is an area of major interest, with many ancient dolmens, ring forts, round towers and high crosses. There's also some stunning scenery, a good collection of hostels and some of Ireland's best music pubs.

For the nitty-gritty on the Burren get a copy of Tim Robinson's *Burren Map & Guide* at bookshops or tourist offices. From Galway both Lally Coaches (☎ 091-56 2905) and O'Neachtain Tours (☎ 091-55 3188) arrange guided bus-tours to the Burren and Cliffs of Moher for IR£10, leaving the Galway tourist office at 10 am daily and returning by 4.30 pm. Rambler Guided Walks (☎ 091-58 2525) explores the Burren by bus and foot for IR£12.

Doolin
☎ 065

Tiny Doolin, famed for its music pubs, is a convenient base for exploring the Burren and the awesome Cliffs of Moher. It's also a gateway for boats to Inisheer, the easternmost and smallest of the Aran Islands.

Doolin's popularity among backpackers has skyrocketed over the past few years, and at night the three or so pubs are packed with a cosmopolitan crowd. In summer it can be difficult to get a bed, so book ahead. Some of the hostels rent bikes for around IR£8 a day plus deposit.

Places to Stay Situated down by the harbour, *O'Connors Riverside Camping & Caravan Park* (☎ 707 4314) charges IR£4 to IR£6 for a tent plus IR£1.50 per person. It's open April to September. Both the Aille River and Rainbow hostels allow camping for around IR£4 per person.

Doolin's hostels charge around IR£8 for dorm beds. *Paddy Moloney's Doolin Hostel* (☎ 707 4006), a large and modern IHH hostel in the lower village, has two doubles for IR£20 apiece. The upper village has three IHH hostels: 16-bed *Rainbow Hostel* (☎ 707 4415), 30-bed *Aille River Hostel* (☎ 707 4260), and 24-bed *Flanagan's Village Hostel* (☎ 707 4564). Aille River, in a converted farmhouse, is the nicest of the bunch.

Getting There & Away There are direct buses to Doolin from Limerick, Ennis, Galway and even Dublin; the main Bus Éireann stop is across from Paddy Moloney's Doolin Hostel. See the Aran Islands section later in this chapter for information on ferries to and from the islands.

Cliffs of Moher

Eight kilometres south of Doolin are the towering Cliffs of Moher (203m), one of Ireland's most famous natural features. In summer the cliffs are overrun by day-trippers, so consider staying in Doolin and hiking along the Burren's quiet country lanes where the views are just as good and crowds are never a problem. Either way, be careful walking along these sheer cliffs, especially in wet or windy weather.

Near the Cliffs of Moher visitor centre (☎ 065-708 1171) is **O'Brien's Tower**. Apparently, local landlord Cornelius O'Brien (1801-57) raised it to impress 'lady visitors'. Today's visitors pay IR£1 to climb the tower. From here walk south or north and the crowds soon disappear.

The Cliffs of Moher are free and never close. The visitor centre is open daily, there is an adjacent shop/cafe and it costs IR£1 to use the car park.

GALWAY
☎ 091 ● pop 57,000

The city of Galway (Gaillimh) is a pleasure, with its narrow streets, fast-flowing river, old stone and wooden shop-fronts, and good restaurants and pubs. On weekends people come from as far as Dublin for the nightlife, and during the city's festivals the streets are bursting. Galway is one of Europe's fastest growing cities, and Ireland's fourth-largest, and is also a departure point for the rugged Aran Islands.

Orientation & Information

Galway's tightly packed town-centre is spread evenly on both sides of the River Corrib. The bus and train stations are within a stone's throw of Eyre Square.

The tourist office (☎ 56 3081) on Victoria Place just off Eyre Square is open 9 am to 5.45 pm weekdays, 9 am to 12.45 pm Saturday; its hours are extended and it opens daily from Easter to September. In summer there can be a delay of an hour or more in making accommodation bookings.

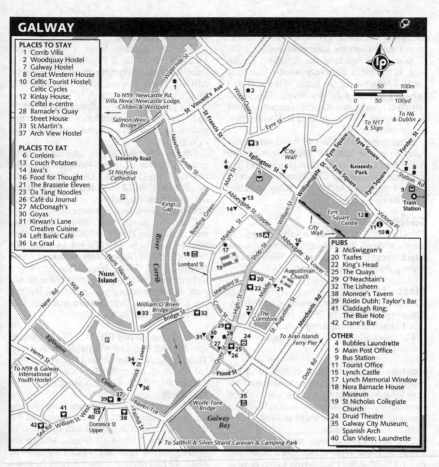

GALWAY

PLACES TO STAY
1 Corrib Villa
2 Woodquay Hostel
7 Galway Hostel
8 Great Western House
10 Celtic Tourist Hostel;
Celtic Cycles
12 Kinlay House;
Celtel e-centre
28 Barnacle's Quay
Street House
33 St Martin's
37 Arch View Hostel

PLACES TO EAT
6 Conlons
13 Couch Potatoes
14 Java's
16 Food for Thought
21 The Brasserie Eleven
23 Da Tang Noodles
26 Café du Journal
27 McDonagh's
30 Goyas
31 Kirwan's Lane
Creative Cuisine
34 Left Bank Café
36 Le Graal

PUBS
3 McSwiggan's
20 Taafes
22 King's Head
25 The Quays
29 O'Neachtain's
32 The Lisheen
38 Monroe's Tavern
39 Róisín Dubh; Taylor's Bar
41 Claddagh Ring;
The Blue Note
42 Crane's Bar

OTHER
4 Bubbles Laundrette
5 Main Post Office
9 Bus Station
11 Tourist Office
15 Lynch Castle
17 Lynch Memorial Window
18 Nora Barnacle House
Museum
19 St Nicholas Collegiate
Church
24 Druid Theatre
35 Galway City Museum;
Spanish Arch
40 Clan Video; Laundrette

To N59, Newcastle Rd,
Villa Nova, Newcastle Lodge,
Clifden & Westport

To N17
& Sligo

To N6
& Dublin

Kennedy
Park

Eyre Square
Centre

Train
Station

To Aran Islands
Ferry Pier

To N59 & Galway
International
Youth Hostel

Flood St

To Salthill & Silver Strand Caravan & Camping Park

Galway
Bay

The main post office is on Eglington St. Bubbles laundrette is on Mary St and another laundrette is over the river on Dominick St. Nearby, at Clan Video you can access the Web, although Celtel e-centre near the entrance to Kinlay House, has better facilities.

Things to See

Galway is a great place to wander around, and a copy of the *Tourist Guide of Old Galway*, available from the tourist office, points out many curiosities.

Eyre Square is the uninspired focal point of the eastern part of the city centre. In the cen-

tre of the square is **Kennedy Park**, honouring a visit by John F Kennedy in 1963. To the north of the square is a controversial statue to the Galway-born writer and hell-raiser Pádraic O'Conaire (1883-1928). South-west of the square, on Shop St, **St Nicholas Collegiate Church** dates from 1320 and has several interesting tombs.

Also on Shop St, parts of **Lynch Castle**, now a bank, date back to the 14th century. Lynch, so the story goes, was a mayor of Galway in the 15th century who, when his son was condemned for murder personally acted as hangman, since nobody else was

IRELAND

willing to do the job. The stone facade that is the **Lynch Memorial Window**, on Market St, marks the spot of the sorrowful deed.

Across the road, in the Bowling Green area, is the **Nora Barnacle House Museum** (☎ 56 4743), the former home of the wife and life-long muse of James Joyce. The small museum, dedicated to the couple, opens daily, except Sunday, from mid-May to mid-September, for IR£1.

Little remains of Galway's old city walls apart from the **Spanish Arch**, right by the river mouth. Next to the arch is the small and unimpressive **Galway City Museum**, open 10 am to 1 pm and 2 to 5 pm Monday to Saturday (IR£1).

Special Events

The Galway Arts Festival in July is huge. For information on the festival's music, arts, and street spectaculars check its Web site at www.galwayartsfestival.com.

Places to Stay

Camping The *Silver Strand Caravan & Camping Park* (☎ 59 2040) is on the coast just beyond Salthill. Large/small tents are IR£7/6 plus 50p per adult, and the site opens Easter to September.

Hostels There are legions of hostels in and around Galway. All are open year-round except for the An Óige hostel. It's wise to book your hostel during summer, festivals and on weekends. Prices range from IR£8 in winter to IR£12 in peak times.

The modern and well maintained IHH *Great Western House* (☎ 56 1139 or free call 1800 425929), Frenchville Lane, is adjacent to the bus and train station. It has a sauna, restaurant and 190 beds.

On the same street but closer to the square is the happiest hostel in Galway, the 50-bed *Galway Hostel* (☎ 56 6959). Prices include a light breakfast.

Despite the four flights of stairs, the IHH *Kinlay House* (☎ 56 5244), opposite the tourist office, is well equipped and offers a light breakfast. Around the corner on Queen St there's the scruffy IHO *Celtic Tourist Hostel* (☎ 56 6606).

Barnacle's Quay Street House (☎ 56 8644, 10 Quay St) is a justly popular IHH

property with 98 beds, and is surrounded by good pubs and cafes.

Near the Salmon Weir Bridge, *Corrib Villa* (☎ 56 2892, 4 Waterside St) is in a three-storey townhouse with good kitchen facilities. There are no private rooms, only smallish dorms.

The independent *Woodquay Hostel* (☎ 56 2618, 23-24 Woodquay) has a decent kitchen and eating area but cramped washrooms and rickety bunks.

On the other side of the river, at the junction of Upper and Lower Dominick Sts, is the possibly too-laid-back *Arch View Hostel* (☎ 58 6661). At IR£6 to IR£7, this hostel is the cheapest in Galway. It also offers a IR£30-per-week rate in winter.

Continue north-west from Upper Dominick St along Henry and St Helen Sts, then turn left onto St Mary's Rd to reach An Óige's 200-bed *Galway International Youth Hostel* (☎ 52 7411). It's on the St Mary's College campus and opens from June to August, but ring before you make the journey out there. From Eyre Square you can take bus No 1 straight to the college.

B&Bs Expect to pay IR£20 to IR£25 per person for B&B accommodation in Galway. There are not many around the city centre, but it's worth trying *St Martin's* (☎ 56 8286, 2 Nuns Island St), which is situated right on the Corrib.

Otherwise, walk 10 minutes from the centre on Newcastle Rd, which is west of the river and runs in a north-south direction (it becomes the N59 to Clifden). Among the many choices here are *Villa Nova* (☎ 52 4849, 40 Lower Newcastle Rd), and *Newcastle Lodge* (☎ 52 7888) at No 28.

Places to Eat

Among old books and library lighting, *Café du Journal* on Quay St serves light but filling meals and good espresso. For bagels, large sandwiches and desserts, daily to midnight, head to *Java's* on Abbeygate St Upper. Across the road *Couch Potatoes* has big spuds stuffed with all manner of fillings for about IR£4.

Food for Thought on Lower Abbeygate St is a budget wholefood restaurant that also serves chicken and fish. Nobody does fish and chips (from IR£4.45) better than *Conlons*, on Eglington St. *Left Bank Café*, on Dominick St Lower, is basic but complements hefty sandwiches and IR£4.50 mains with strong coffees.

The Brasserie Eleven (19 Middle St) has pizza, a good salad-bar and lunch specials that include vegetarian dishes from IR£4.95. Also on Middle St *Da Tang Noodles* serves Japanese-style noodle soups, meat and vegie, for less than IR£5.50.

McDonagh's on Quay St is excellent for seafood, with mains starting from IR£11, lunch specials at IR£5.50, and fish and chips too.

On the other side of the Corrib, *Le Graal (13 Dominick St Lower)* is a charming dinner-only spot with nightly vegetarian and fish specials and mains from IR£6.95. It opens at 6 pm and has music, including jazz nights.

Travellers desperate for an epicurean adventure should try *Kirwan's Lane Creative Cuisine (☎ 56 8266)* at the end of Kirwan's Lane. This place could happily sit in any stylish area of New York or London, and has the prices to match. Across the road, *Goyas* is similarly dressed, but cafe-like.

Entertainment

The fortnightly *Galway & Mayo List* has listings of what's on in and around Galway. It is available free from hostels, cafes and pubs.

Galway has dozens of good pubs, among them *O'Neachtain's* (17 Upper Cross St) which is over 100 years old. *King's Head*, farther north on High St, has a carnivalesque execution scene in the front window and music most nights in summer. Almost next door, the enormously popular and much recommended *Taafes* is a music and sports bar.

McSwiggan's on Daly's Place is big, always busy, and has good meals for IR£6.95. *The Quays* on Quay St draws a crowd on weekends and in summer and has an eclectic mix of music, many levels and an intriguing if not overdone timber interior. *The Lisheen (5 Bridge St)* is one of the better traditional-music venues in Galway.

Across the river the choice spot for traditional music is *Monroe's Tavern*, on the corner of Dominick St Upper and Fairhill St. The nearby *Róisín Dubh* is good for alternative music and often has international acts. *Taylor's Bar* next door and, around the corner on Sea Rd, *Crane's Bar*, have music in summer. So too does *Claddagh Ring* on William St West while nearby *The Blue Note (3 William St West)* has live jazz and rock a few nights a week.

The small *Druid Theatre (☎ 56 8617)* on Chapel Lane puts on two or three, often experimental, productions per year.

Getting There & Away

The bus station (☎ 56 2000) is behind the Great Southern Hotel, off Eyre Square, next to the Ceannt train station (☎ 56 4222). Bus Éireann has services to Doolin (IR£8.50), Dublin (IR£9), Killarney (IR£14.50), Limerick, Sligo and beyond. The Dublin services operate up to eight times daily.

Private bus companies, generally a bit cheaper than Bus Éireann, also operate from Galway. Bus Nestor (☎ 79 7144) runs five buses a day (seven on Friday) to Dublin's Tara St DART station via Dublin airport. Often there are specials (IR£5 at the time of writing).

From Galway there are four or more trains to and from Dublin (IR£16 for a single, IR£22 from Friday to Sunday; 2¾ hours). Connections with other train routes can be made at Athlone.

Getting Around

Most of the hostels rent bikes. Celtic Cycles (☎ 56 6606) on Queen St rents bikes for IR£7/30 a day/week.

ARAN ISLANDS
☎ 099

In recent years the windswept, starkly beautiful Aran Islands have become one of western Ireland's major attractions. Apart from natural beauty, the Irish-speaking islands have some of the country's oldest Christian and pre-Christian ruins.

On the islands the Irish passion for stone walls is almost absurd, with countless kilometres of stone walls separating even the tiniest patches of rocky land. Inhospitable though these rocky patches may appear, the islands were settled at a much earlier date than the mainland, since agriculture was easier to pursue here than in the densely forested Ireland of the pre-Christian era.

There are three main islands in the group, all inhabited year-round. Most visitors head

IRELAND

for long and narrow (14.5km by a maximum 4km) Inishmór (or Inishmore). The land slopes up from the relatively sheltered northern shores of the island and plummets on the southern side into the raging Atlantic. Inishmaan and Inisheer are much smaller and receive far fewer visitors.

Although many visitors make day trips to the islands from Galway and Doolin, Inishmór alone is worth a few days of exploration. The islands can get crowded at holiday times (St Patrick's Day, Easter) and in July and August, when accommodation is at a premium and advance reservations are advised.

Orientation & Information

April to mid-September, a tourist office (☎ 61263) operates on the waterfront at Kilronan, the arrival point and major village of Inishmór. You can change money there and at some of the local shops. A couple of hundred metres to the north is a small post office and a Wednesday-only branch of the Bank of Ireland. There are no ATMs on the islands.

J M Synge's *The Aran Islands* is the classic account of life on the islands and is readily available in paperback. A much less accessible (but more recent) tribute to the islands is map-maker Tim Robinson's *Stones of Aran*. For detailed exploration, pick up a copy of his *The Aran Islands: A Map and Guide*.

Inishmór

The 'Big Island' has four impressive stone forts of uncertain age, though 2000 years is a good guess. Halfway down the island, about 8km west of Kilronan, semicircular **Dún Aengus**, perched terrifyingly on the edge of the sheer southern cliffs, is the best-known of the four. If you see only one sight on Inishmór, let it be Dún Aengus.

About 1.5km north is **Dún Eoghanachta**, while halfway back to Kilronan is **Dún Eochla**; both are smaller but perfectly circular ring forts. Directly south of Kilronan and dramatically perched on a promontory is another fort, **Dún Dúchathair**.

Ionad Árann (☎ 61355), just off the main road leading out of Kilronan, introduces the landscape and traditions of the islands. It opens 10 am to 5 pm daily, April to October (until 7 pm June to August); admission is IR£2.50.

Inishmaan

The least visited of the three islands is Inishmaan (Inis Meáin, or 'Middle Island'). High stone walls border its fields, and it's a delight to wander along the lanes and take in some of the tranquillity. The main archaeological site here is **Dún Chonchúir**, a massive oval-shaped stone-fort built on a high point and offering good views of the island.

Inisheer

The smallest island, only 8km off the coast from Doolin, is Inisheer (Inis Oírr, or 'Eastern Island'). The 15th-century **O'Brien Castle** (Caislea'n Uí Bhriain) overlooks the beach and harbour. It was built within the remains of a ring fort called **Dún Formna** dating from as early as the 1st century AD.

Places to Stay

Hostels throughout the islands charge IR£7 to IR£10 for dorm beds. Although most are open year-round, it's a good idea to ring ahead in the off season.

Inishmór In Kilronan, the modern, justly popular *Kilronan Hostel* (☎ 61255), also known as Tí Joe Mac's Hostel, is a short walk from the pier. *St Kevin's Hostel*, between Tí Joe Mac's and the Spar supermarket, is a bit run-down and opens only in summer; inquire at the *Dormer House B&B* (☎ 61125) opposite. Small and basic, *Aharla Hostel* (☎ 61305) is just off the road to Kilmurvey.

A few kilometres north-west of Kilronan, the IHO *Mainistir House Hostel* (☎ 61169 or 61322) has breakfast included and transport that meets the ferry. Also with a pick-up facility, the IHO *Dún Aengus Hostel* (☎ 61318), open April to October, is near the beach on the west side of Kilmurvey Bay, 7km from Kilronan.

The numerous B&Bs in and around Kilronan include the large *Dormer House* (☎ 61125), behind Tí Joe Mac's. Open year-round, it has rooms starting at IR£18 per person.

Inishmaan There are no hostels on Inishmaan, but B&Bs are relatively cheap, at about IR£14 per person. Try *Angela Uí Fátharta's* (☎ 73012) in Creigmore, about 500m north-west of the pier. It's open March to October.

IRELAND

Inisheer The *Inisheer Camp Site* (☎ 75008), by the Strand, opens May to September. It charges IR£2.50 per tent and has basic facilities. *Brú Radharc Na Mara* (☎ 75087 or 75024) is an IHH hostel near the pier.

Getting There & Away

Air If time is important or seasickness a concern on the often-rough Atlantic, you can fly to the islands and back with Aer Árann (☎ 091-59 3034) for IR£35. Flights operate to all three islands four times a day (hourly in summer) and take less than 10 minutes. The mainland departure point is Connemara regional airport at Minna, near Inverin, 38km west of Galway. A connecting bus from outside the Galway tourist office costs IR£2.50 each way.

Boat Island Ferries (☎ 091-56 8903 in Galway) serves Inishmór year-round (IR£15 return, 40 minutes). Unfortunately the boat leaves from Rossaveal, 37km west of Galway, which means it's an extra IR£4 to catch an Island Ferries bus from outside the tourist office in Galway. Buses leave 1½ hours before ferry departure time and are scheduled to meet arriving ferries. If you have a car you can go straight to Rossaveal.

From April to October, Island Ferries sails daily to Inishmór at 10.30 am, 1.30 pm and 6.30 pm; from November to March times are 10.30 am and 5.30 pm.

Between June and September, Island Ferries has daily direct services to Inishmór from Galway's docks (IR£18 return). The 46km sea crossing takes 1½ hours, which can be a bit hard on sensitive stomachs. From May to September boats also sail twice daily to Inishmaan and Inisheer. During this period there are ferries connecting the islands; call for details.

Another option is to leave from Doolin in County Clare (see The Burren section earlier in this chapter). Doolin Ferries (☎ 065-74455 in Doolin) runs three routes daily: Doolin-Inisheer (IR£15 return, 30 minutes, mid-April to September), Doolin-Inishmaan (IR£18 return, 40 minutes, mid-April to September) and Doolin-Inishmór (IR£20 return, 55 minutes, mid-May to August).

Getting Around

Inisheer and Inishmaan are small enough to explore on foot, but on larger Inishmór, bikes

are definitely the way to go. Aran Cycle Hire (☎ 61132), just up from Kilronan's pier, charges IR£5 per day. The islands are tough on bikes, so check your cruiser carefully before renting it.

Plenty of small operators offer speedy bus tours to some of the island's principal sights for around IR£5; they'll find you as you get off the ferry.

CONNEMARA
☎ 095

The north-west corner of County Galway is the wild and barren region known as Connemara. It's a stunning patchwork of bogs, lonely valleys, pale-grey mountains and small lakes that shimmer when the sun shines. Connemara's isolation has allowed Irish to thrive and the language is widely spoken here; the lack of English signposting can be a little confusing at times.

By car or bicycle the most scenic routes through Connemara are Oughterard-Recess (via the N59), Recess-Kylemore Abbey (via the R344) and Leenane-Louisburgh (via the R335). From Galway, Lally Coaches (☎ 091-56 2905) and O'Neachtain Tours (☎ 091-55 3188) arrange day-long tours of Connemara for around IR£10.

Things to See

Aughanure Castle (☎ 55 2214), 3km east of Oughterard, is a 16th-century tower house on a rocky outcrop overlooking Lough Corrib. It opens daily mid-June to mid-September; entry is IR£2.

Just west of **Recess** (Straith Salach) on the N59, the turn north at the R334 takes you through the stunning Lough Inagh Valley. At the end of the R334 is the equally scenic **Kylemore Abbey** (☎ 41146) and its adjacent lake. The neo-Gothic 19th-century abbey is run by nuns, with some sections open to the public daily year-round.

From Kylemore you can take the N59 east to Leenane (An Líonán), then detour north on the R335 to Louisburgh and onwards to Westport (see the following Westport section); or you can travel 17km south-west along the N59 to **Clifden** (An Clochán), Connemara's largest town. Clifden has a few good pubs but is otherwise dull. The Clifden Walking Centre (☎ 21379) at Island House

IRELAND

on Market St runs guided walking trips for around IR£15.

Places to Stay

Oughterard has numerous B&Bs and a good hostel. *Canrawer House Hostel* (☎ *55 2388*) is at the Clifden end of town, just over 1km down a signposted turning. It has dorm beds starting at IR£8, and bike hire.

An Óige's excellent *Ben Lettery Hostel* (☎ *51136*) on the N59 halfway between Recess and Clifden is open Easter to September.

In Clifden, the IHH *Clifden Town Hostel* (☎ *21076*) is on Market St in the centre of town and charges IR£8 to IR£10 for a dorm bed. The IHH/IHO *Brookside Hostel* (☎ *21812*), down by the Owen Glin River on Hulk St, charges IR£7 to IR£8 for a bed and is open January until the end of October. Ask for a map of the Sky Road and the 'Eighth Wonder of the World' and you won't be disappointed.

Getting There & Away

Buses link Clifden with Galway via Oughterard and Maam Cross, or via Cong and Leenane. In summer there are three express buses a day to/from Galway.

WESTPORT
☎ 098

Westport (Cathair na Mairt) is a popular stop on the way to/from Sligo and Donegal. It has a pleasant main street and a handful of good pubs.

North over the River Carrowbeg, there's a small year-round tourist office (☎ 25711).

Things to See

Westport's major attraction, **Croagh Patrick**, about 7km west of the town, is the hill from which St Patrick performed his snake expulsion act (Ireland has been serpent-free ever since). Climbing the 765m peak is a ritual for thousands of pilgrims on the last Sunday of July.

Places to Stay

There are two IHH hostels: the *Old Mill Hostel* (☎ *27045*) in a courtyard off James St, and the almost-luxurious *Club Atlantic Holiday Hostel* (☎ *26644*) on Altamount St near the train station. Both are open year-round and charge IR£7 to IR£8 for dorm beds. The IHO

Granary Hostel (☎ *25903*), on The Quay, opens March to October. Beds here are IR£6.

Getting There & Away

There are bus connections to Belfast, Cork, Galway, Limerick, Shannon, Sligo and Waterford. Buses depart from the Octagon at the end of James St. The train station (☎ 25253) is on Altamount St, south-east of the town centre. There are three daily rail connections to Dublin (3½ hours) via Athlone.

The North-West

County Sligo and County Donegal comprise Ireland's rural north-western corner. The coastal scenery is unparalleled, yet the region's distance from Dublin (and the lack of convenient rail links) keeps crowds to a minimum. Tourism in the north-west, especially County Donegal, is extremely seasonal, and many attractions and tourist offices close from October to March.

SLIGO
☎ 071 • pop 18,000

William Butler Yeats (1865-1939) was educated in Dublin and London, but his poetry is muddied with the county of his mother's family. He returned to Sligo (Sligeach) many times, and there are plentiful reminders of his presence in this sleepy (some would say boring) town and in the rolling green hills around it.

The tourist office (☎ 61201), open weekdays year-round and on weekends in July and August, is on Temple St, just south of the centre. The main post office is on Wine St east of the train and bus station. Cygo Internet Café is at 19 O'Connell St.

Things to See

Sligo's two major attractions are outside town. **Carrowmore**, 5km to the south-west, is the site of a megalithic cemetery (☎ 61534) with over 60 stone rings, passage tombs and other Stone Age remains. It's the largest Stone Age necropolis in Europe. The visitor centre here is open daily from May to October, and entry is IR£1.50.

A few kilometres north-west of Carrowmore is the hill-top cairn-grave known as

Knocknarea. About 1000 years younger than Carrowmore, the huge cairn is said to be the grave of the legendary Maeve, Queen of Connaught in the 1st century AD. Several trails lead to the top of the 328m-high grassy hill.

Places to Stay & Eat
The excellent IHH *Eden Hill Holiday Hostel* (☎ 43204) on Pearse Rd is a 10-minute walk south-east of the centre via the Dublin road. It costs IR£7.80 for a dorm bed. Just north of the town centre on Markievicz Rd, the IHH *White House Hostel* (☎ 45160) costs IR£7. The smaller and more basic IHO *Yeats County Hostel* (☎ 46876) is opposite the bus and train station at 12 Lord Edward St, and costs IR£6.50. All three are open year-round.

Sligo's less expensive B&Bs are on the various approaches to town. *Renate House* (☎ 62014) in the centre on Upper John St is a small B&B with singles/doubles from IR£23.50/34.

Bar Bazzar: Coffee Culture, on Market St, near the monument, has coffee, snacks and second-hand books. *Bistro Bianconi (44 O'Connell St)* serves decent Italian dishes for around IR£11, salads and pizzas from IR£8.

Getting There & Around
Bus Éireann (☎ 60066) has three services a day to/from Dublin (IR£10, four hours). There's also a Galway-Sligo-Donegal-Derry service three times daily. Buses operate from below the train station (☎ 69888), which is just west of the centre along Lord Edward St. Trains leave three times a day for Dublin via Boyle, Carrick-on-Shannon and Mullingar.

Hire a bike from Gary's Cycles (☎ 45418) on Lower Quay St.

DONEGAL
☎ 073 • pop 3000
Donegal Town (Dún na nGall) is not the major centre in County Donegal, but it's a pleasant and laid-back place and well worth a visit.

The triangular Diamond is the centre of Donegal; a few steps south along the River Eske is the tourist office (☎ 21148), open June to September on weekdays only.

Donegal Castle, on a rocky outcrop over the River Eske, stands in ruins but is impressive all the same. Notice the floral decoration on the corner turret and the decorated fireplace

on the 1st floor. The castle is open daily from March to October. Admission is IR£3.

Places to Stay & Eat
The comfortable IHH/IHO *Donegal Town Independent Hostel* (☎ 22805), open year-round, is 1km north-west of town on the Killybegs road (N56). Dorm beds are IR£7, private rooms IR£8.50 per person. Camping in the grounds is IR£4 per person.

An Óige's *Ball Hill Hostel* (☎ 21174) has an absolutely stunning setting at the end of a quiet road, right on the shores of Donegal Bay. To get here, take the Killybegs road (N56) and, 5km out, look for the signs on the left-hand side of the road. Beds are IR£7.50, and it's open from Easter to September. The location is pretty remote, so stock up on food before arriving.

The *Blueberry Tearoom* is busy and often smoky, but has good meals from IR£3.95. The *Atlantic Restaurant* on Main St and *Errigal Restaurant* farther east are inexpensive, with meals from IR£3.95.

Getting There & Away
From Donegal there are Bus Éireann (☎ 21101) connections to Derry, Enniskillen and Belfast to the north; Sligo and Galway to the west; and Limerick and Cork to the south. The bus stop is on the Diamond, outside the Abbey Hotel. McGeehan's Coaches (☎ 075-46150) does a Donegal-Dublin return trip three times a day (more in summer) departing from the police station opposite the tourist office.

AROUND DONEGAL
The cliffs at **Slieve League**, dropping some 300m straight into the Atlantic Ocean, are a recommended two or three-day side trip from Donegal. To drive to the cliff edge, take the Killybegs-Glencolumbcille road (R263) and, at Carrick, take the turn-off signposted 'Bunglas'. Continue beyond the narrow track signposted for Slieve League (this trail is good for hikers) to the one signposted for Bunglas. Starting from Teelin, experienced walkers can spend a day walking via Bunglas and the somewhat terrifying One Man's Path to Malinbeg, near Glencolumbcille.

If you're walking, a convenient base is the IHH's year-round *Derrylahan Hostel* (☎ 38079), 2km south-east of Carrick and

IRELAND

3km north-west of Kilcar. Beds are IR£7, and there's a small food shop. Call for free pick-up from Kilcar.

McGeehan's Coaches (☎ 075-46150) serves Carrick and Kilcar once daily (more frequently in summer) on its Dublin-Donegal-Glencolumbcille route. Otherwise, there are daily Bus Éireann coaches from Donegal to Killybegs, with onward buses to Kilcar and Carrick.

Northern Ireland

☎ 028

More than a quarter-century of internal strife has seriously affected tourism in Northern Ireland. Though this was understandable in the dark days of the late 1960s and early '70s, wanton violence was never a serious threat to visitors here. In 1995, following the declaration of the first IRA cease-fire, the numbers of visitors from abroad jumped dramatically. Although the numbers fell in 1996 after hostilities resumed, ratification in 1998 of the Good Friday Agreement provided a dose of positive international press, and tourism figures are once again rising.

The accent here is distinctly different, the currency is pounds sterling and distances are measured in miles; otherwise, cross-border differences are insignificant. If anything, the Northern Irish are friendlier to foreign visitors than their counterparts in the Republic, perhaps to compensate for years of bad publicity.

Northern Ireland has plenty going for it: the Causeway Coast road, the Glens of Antrim, the old walls of Derry, cosmopolitan Belfast. But even with the coming of peace and the end of military roadblocks, the signs of the Troubles can't be ignored: the street murals in Belfast and Derry, shuttered shopfronts, deserted fortified police-stations, and the occasional armoured car and circling helicopter are still as much a part of Northern Ireland as green fields and smoke-filled pubs.

BELFAST
pop 279,240

Had the Troubles never happened, the capital of Northern Ireland would simply be a big, rather ugly industrial city, pleasantly situated and with some impressive Victorian archi-tecture, but well past its prime. As it is, Belfast (Béal Feirste) has been deformed by violence for nearly 30 years, and until recently its residents were forced to incorporate bomb threats and army checkpoints into their daily routines.

Yet if your only view of the city has been through the media's lens, you may be surprised to find that Belfast is actually busy and bustling - clean and prosperous in parts, the city has become much livelier and far more cheerful than its grim reputation leads visitors to expect.

Orientation & Information

The city centre is a compact area with the imposing City Hall as the central landmark. Belfast's principal shopping district is north of the square. To the south lies the Golden Mile, a restaurant and pub-filled stretch of Dublin Rd, Shaftesbury Square, Bradbury Place and Botanic Ave.

The helpful NITB (☎ 9024 6609), 59 North St (a new location is planned, but undecided at the time of writing), is open 9 am to 5.15 pm Monday to Saturday (in summer to 7 pm), and noon to 4 pm on Sunday in July and August. Bord Fáilte (☎ 9032 7888), 53 Castle St, has information on the Irish Republic. The Youth Hostel Association of Northern Ireland (YHANI; ☎ 9032 4733), 22-32 Donegall Rd, has its offices at the Belfast International Youth Hostel.

The main post office is on Castle Place, and there's a smaller branch on Shaftesbury Square. There's a laundrette in the university area at 160 Lisburn Rd, and The Laundry Room is at 37 Botanic Ave. Bronco's Web Cafe is at 122 Great Victoria St.

Around the City

At the north-eastern corner of **City Hall** (1906) is a statue of Sir Edward Harland, the Yorkshire-born engineer who founded Belfast's Harland & Wolff shipyards. The yard's most famous construction was the ill-fated *Titanic*, the 'unsinkable' boat that sank in 1912. A memorial to the disaster and its victims stands on the east side of City Hall.

City Hall is fronted by a dour statue of Queen Victoria. To the north-east between High St and Queen's Square, the queen's consort, Prince Albert, also makes his Belfast

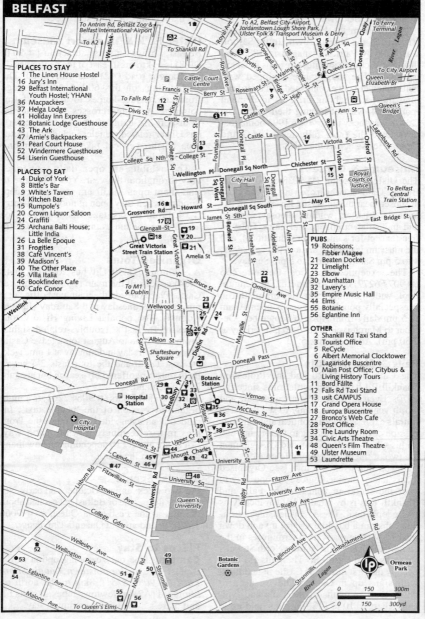

BELFAST

PLACES TO STAY
1 The Linen House Hostel
16 Jury's Inn
29 Belfast International
   Youth Hostel; YHANI
36 Macpackers
37 Helga Lodge
41 Holiday Inn Express
42 Botanic Lodge Guesthouse
43 The Ark
47 Arnie's Backpackers
51 Pearl Court House
52 Windermere Guesthouse
54 Liserin Guesthouse

PLACES TO EAT
4 Duke of York
8 Bittle's Bar
9 White's Tavern
14 Kitchen Bar
15 Rumpole's
24 Crown Liquor Saloon
25 Graffiti
25 Archana Balti House;
   Little India
26 La Belle Epoque
31 Frogities
38 Cafe Vincent's
39 Madison's
40 The Other Place
45 Villa Italia
46 Bookfinders Cafe
50 Cafe Conor

PUBS
19 Robinsons;
   Fibber Magee
21 Beaten Docket
23 Limelight
23 Elbow
30 Manhattan
32 Lavery's
35 Empire Music Hall
44 Elms
55 Botanic
56 Eglantine Inn

OTHER
2 Shankill Rd Taxi Stand
3 Tourist Office
5 ReCycle
6 Albert Memorial Clocktower
7 Laganside Buscentre
10 Main Post Office; Citybus &
   Living History Tours
11 Bord Fáilte
12 Falls Rd Taxi Stand
13 usit CAMPUS
17 Europa Opera House
18 Europa Buscentre
27 Bronco's Web Cafe
28 Post Office
33 The Laundry Room
34 Civic Arts Theatre
48 Queen's Film Theatre
49 Ulster Museum
53 Laundrette

IRELAND

0   150   300m
0   150   300yd

appearance at the slightly leaning **Albert Memorial Clocktower** (1867).

Across from the Europa Hotel on Great Victoria St, the famed **Crown Liquor Saloon** was built by Patrick Flanagan in 1885 and displays Victorian architecture at its most extravagant. The snugs come equipped with bells that were once connected to a board behind the bar, enabling drinkers to demand more drink without leaving their seats. The Crown was lucky to survive a 1993 bomb that devastated the (now fully restored) **Grand Opera House** across the road.

Museums & Gardens

The **Ulster Museum** (☎ 9038 3000) in the Botanic Gardens (which open at 8 am and close at sunset) near the university has excellent exhibits on Irish art, wildlife, dinosaurs, steam and industrial machines, and more. Entry is free (except for some major exhibitions), and the museum is open 10 am to 5 pm weekdays, 1 to 5 pm Saturday, and 2 to 5 pm Sunday.

The exceptionally good **Belfast Zoo** (☎ 9077 6277) is on Antrim Rd. The penguin pool, with its underwater viewing-platform, is especially popular. The zoo is open 10 am to 5 pm daily from April to September; October to March it closes at 3.30 pm (Friday at 2.30 pm). Admission is £5.10.

Falls & Shankill Rds

The Catholic Falls Rd and the Protestant Shankill Rd have been battlefronts since the 1970s. Even so, these areas are quite safe and worth venturing into, if only to see the large **murals** expressing local political and religious passions. King Billy riding to victory in 1690 on his white steed, and hooded IRA gunmen are two of the more memorable images.

If you don't fancy a tour (see Organised Tours later), the ideologically sound way to visit the sectarian zones of the Falls and Shankill Rds is by what is known locally as the 'people taxi'. These recycled, black London cabs run a bus-like service up and down their respective roads from terminuses in the city. Shankill Rd taxis go from North St, Falls Rd taxis from Castle St. The Falls Rd taxis occupy the first line at the Castle St taxi park, with signs up in Gaelic. They're used to doing tourist circuits of the Falls and typically charge £10 to £12 (the cabs hold up to

five people) for a one-hour tour that takes in the main points of interest.

Ulster Folk & Transport Museum

Belfast's biggest tourist attraction (☎ 9042 8428) is 11km north-east of the centre beside the Bangor road (A2) near Holywood. The 30 buildings on this 60-hectare site range from city terrace-homes to thatched farm-cottages. A bridge crosses the A2 to the Transport Museum, where you can see various Ulster-related vehicles including a prototype of the vertical take-off and landing (VTOL) aircraft.

The exhibits are open daily, but times vary throughout the year. You'll be sure to find them open 10.30 am to 5 pm except Sunday, when they open at noon. Joint entry is £4. From Belfast take Ulsterbus No 1 or any Bangor-bound train that stops at Cultra station.

Organised Tours

A 3½-hour, £8.50 Citybus tour (☎ 9045 8484) covers all the main sights. It begins at Castle Place outside the main post office at 1 pm every Wednesday and Saturday (June to August). The popular Living History tour takes in Belfast's Troubles-related sights. From mid-June to August tours leave Castle Place on Thursday and Sunday at 1 pm. Tickets cost £8.50 and the tour lasts 2½ hours. Both tours are offered off-season but are subject to demand.

Black Taxi Tours (☎ 9064 2264) is a more organised version of the 'people taxi'. Included is an even-sided account of the Troubles in a refreshingly down-to-earth way. Prices are about £10 depending on how many people are in the cab.

Special Events

For two weeks in late October and early November the people of Belfast get excited about the arts at the Festival at Queen's (☎ 9066 7687), in and around Queen's University.

Places to Stay

Camping The only camping option in the Belfast area is *Jordanstown Lough Shore Park* (☎ 9086 8751), 8km to the north on Shore Rd (A2) in Newtownabbey. It costs £7, and there's a two-night maximum stay.

Hostels At *Arnie's Backpackers* (☎ 9024 2867, 63 Fitzwilliam St) dorm beds cost from £7 to £8.50. Arnie's has laundry and cooking facilities and two attention-seeking dogs but, with only 22 beds, demand for space far exceeds supply.

The YHANI *Belfast International Youth Hostel* (☎ 9031 5435, 22-32 Donegall Rd) is large (112 beds), modern and very clean. There's a laundry and small cafe, but no kitchen facilities. Dorm beds cost up to £9, private/twin rooms £16/22.

The Ark (☎ 9032 9626, 18 University St) has 31 beds. Dorms cost £6.50 to £7.50 and twins are £12 per person. *Macpackers* (☎ 9022 0845, 1 Cameron St), linked to Steve's Backpackers in Derry, has beds for £7.50 per night (fifth night is free), including breakfast and free half-hour of Internet access per day. At the other end of the central city area is *The Linen House Hostel* (☎ 9058 6400, 18-20 Kent St) with dorm beds for £6.50 to £8.50, and singles/doubles for £10/24.

From June to the end of September, *Queen's Elms* (☎ 9038 1608, 78 Malone Rd), run by the university, offers excellent accommodation. Rooms cost £8.20/9.64/12 for UK/international/nonstudents. Twin rooms cost £21. There are cooking and laundry facilities.

B&Bs The NITB office makes B&B reservations for a minimal fee; credit-card bookings can be made over the phone (☎ 0800-317153). Many B&Bs are in the university area, which is close to the centre, safe and well-stocked with restaurants and pubs. Botanic Ave, Malone Rd, Wellington Park and Eglantine Ave are good hunting grounds.

The large and comfortable *Helga Lodge* (☎ 9032 4820, 7 Cromwell Rd) has singles/doubles from £22/40. Nearby is the handsome *Botanic Lodge Guesthouse* (☎ 9032 7682, 87 Botanic Ave), where the rooms all have TV and cost £25/40. Also in the popular university area, *Windermere Guesthouse* (☎ 9066 2693), Wellington Park, has small but comfy rooms overlooking a quiet street for £24 per person.

The basic *Pearl Court House* (☎ 9066 6145, 11 Malone Rd) charges £23.50 per person. *Liserin Guesthouse* (☎ 9066 0769,

17 Eglantine Ave) charges £20/40 for a room with a shower and TV.

Hotels The *Holiday Inn Express* (☎ 9031 1909, 106A University St) charges £64.95 for a room, including continental breakfast. Its weekend rate is great value at £49.95 a night.

In the city centre, *Jury's Inn* (☎ 9053 3500), College Square, is a moderately priced three-star hotel with rooms that accommodate three adults for only £65.

Places to Eat

Pubs At the *Crown Liquor Saloon* on Great Victoria St you can get oysters and Irish stews, and at the same time take in the magnificent decor.

Keeping a low profile is *Rumpole's* (81 Chichester St) which is good for steak-and-spud lunches. A block farther north, *Bittle's Bar* is a small pub entered from 70 Upper Church Lane. It specialises in traditional dishes like sausages and *champ* (an Ulster speciality of mashed potatoes and spring onions).

White's Tavern on Wine Cellar Entry between Rosemary and High Sts is one of Belfast's most historic taverns and a popular lunchtime meeting spot.

The *Duke of York* is another oldie, serving sandwiches starting from £1.50 and excellent solid lunches for around £5.50. It's hidden away down Commercial Court, off Donegall St, and has faded signs directing the way. *Kitchen Bar*, on Victoria Square, is another popular lunch spot.

Restaurants There are numerous budget restaurants along the Golden Mile from Dublin Rd south to University Rd and Botanic Ave.

Graffiti (50 Dublin Rd) serves excellent, filling pasta dishes for under £6.75. There are often queues for tables at *Villa Italia* (37-41 University Rd), a vibrant Italian restaurant and pizzeria.

The upstairs *Archana* (53 Dublin Rd) prides itself as the only Balti House in Belfast. It serves Balti curries from £5.50. Downstairs the superb *Little India* dishes up Belfast's best fauna-free curries from £5.50. There's also a £2.50 lunch special of two vegie dishes and rice.

Belfast's most authentic and expensive French cuisine can be sampled at stylish *La Belle Epoque* *(61 Dublin Rd)*, but there also are lunch specials for £6.25. It's closed Sunday. French food is fairly cheap at friendly *Frogities* *(10 Bradbury Place)*, with tasty crepes for less than £5.

Botanic Ave has lots of cafes. Try *The Other Place* *(79 Botanic Ave)*, which is lively and good for coffee. More on the ritzy side is *Madison's* *(59-63 Botanic Ave)*, which welcomes you for coffee, snacks, lunch specials (£4.95), dinner, drinks, dancing and sleeping. Across the road you'll find a range of ethnic cuisines from Thai to Mexican and French at *Café Vincent's*. Main dishes are £6 to £10.

Bookfinders Cafe *(47 University Rd)* is at the back of a pleasantly musty second-hand bookshop. *Cafe Conor* *(11A Stranmillis Rd)* in the building where artist William Conor once had his studio is perfect for a coffee or post-Ulster Museum meal.

Entertainment

Belfast's guide to what's on is the *Big List*, available at cafes, pubs and the like.

Pubs in the city centre are often packed at lunch but empty out after dark, when pubs along the Golden Mile come alive. An exception to this rule is *Robinsons* on Great Victoria St, with its many bars, historic paraphernalia (including personal-hygiene products) and a walk-through to *Fibber Magee* on Blackstaff Square. Across the road the often rowdy *Beaten Docket* on Great Victoria St is also busy at night.

A major landmark along the Golden Mile at Bradbury Place, *Lavery's* is intensely popular with students, bikers and hardened drinkers, hence the weekend-night cover charge. More comfortable is the student-filled *Elms* *(36 University Rd)*. Farther south and facing each other across Malone Rd are the *Eglantine Inn* and the *Botanic*, two student-bars known as the 'Egg and Bott'. If you crave a quiet pint try the *Elbow* on Dublin Rd.

Limelight *(17 Ormeau Ave)* is a stayer in the Belfast nightclub world. Hyper-trendy *Manhattan* on Bradbury Place has a sharp mosaic and usually a queue at the entrance. *Empire Music Hall* *(42 Botanic Ave)*, a barn-like pub inside a former church, has live music three nights a week and a stand-up comedy night.

The *Queen's Film Theatre* *(toll-free 0800 3 28 28 11)* on University Square Mews, has independent, classic, cult and arthouse films. There's often a musical, opera or ballet on at the *Grand Opera House* (☎ 9024 1919), and something less formal at the *Civic Arts Theatre* (☎ 9031 6900) on Botanic Ave.

Getting There & Away

The usit CAMPUS/Belfast Student Travel office (☎ 9032 4073) is at 13B Fountain Centre, College St. For security reasons there are no left-luggage facilities at Belfast train or bus stations. For all Ulsterbus, Northern Ireland Railways (NIR) and local bus information call ☎ 9089 9411 or 9033 3000.

Air There are flights from some regional airports in Britain to the convenient Belfast City airport (☎ 9045 7745), Airport Rd, but everything else goes to Belfast International airport (☎ 9442 2888), 30km north of the city in Aldergrove by the M2.

Bus Belfast has two separate bus stations. The smaller of the two is the Laganside Buscentre, on Oxford St near the river, with bus connections to counties Antrim, Down and Derry. Buses to everywhere else in Northern Ireland, the Republic, the international airport and the Larne ferries, leave from the bigger Europa Buscentre on Glengall St.

Pick up regional bus timetables for free at the bus stations. Ulsterbus produces an excellent free *Exploring Ulster* booklet with services and fares to major attractions accessible from Belfast.

There are seven daily Belfast-Dublin buses (three on Sunday) that take about three hours and start at £10.50 one way. For connections to Derry and Donegal, contact the Lough Swilly Bus Company (☎ 7126 2017) in Derry.

Train Belfast has two main train stations – Great Victoria St, next to the Europa Buscentre, and Belfast Central, east of the city centre on East Bridge St.

Destinations served from Belfast Central include Derry and Dublin. Dublin-Belfast trains (£19/29 one way/return, two hours) run up to six times a day (three on Sunday). From Belfast Central a free (with your bus or train ticket) Centrelink bus to Donegall Square in the city centre leaves every 10 minutes. A local train also connects with Great Victoria St.

Great Victoria St station has services to Derry and Larne Harbour.

For tickets and information contact the NIR at Great Victoria St station; it opens 9 am to 5 pm weekdays, 9 am to noon Saturday.

Boat See the Getting There & Away section at the beginning of this chapter for more details on ferries to/from Northern Ireland.

From Belfast there are three main ferry routes connecting Belfast to Stranraer, Liverpool and the Isle of Man.

Belfast's ferry terminal, on Donegall Quay a short walk north of the city centre, is used only by boats to Stranraer and the Isle of Man.

Norse Irish ferries to Liverpool leave from Victoria terminal, 5km north of central Belfast; take a bus from Europa Buscentre or catch a taxi (£7 to £10).

Getting Around

Airbus buses link Belfast International airport with the Europa Buscentre every half-hour (£5, 35minutes). A taxi costs about £20.

The Belfast City airport is only 6km north-east of the centre, and you can cross the road from the terminal to the Sydenham Halt station, from which trains run to Botanic station for less than £1.

A short trip on a bus costs 50p to 90p. Most local bus services depart from Donegall Square, near the City Hall, where there is a ticket kiosk.

If you're driving, be fastidious about where you park; car theft is a serious problem here. The tourist office has a free leaflet showing all the multistorey car parks.

ReCycle (☎ 9031 3113, 1-4 Albert Square) hires bikes for £6.50/30 per day/week.

THE BELFAST-DERRY COASTAL ROAD

Ireland isn't short of fine stretches of coast, but the Causeway Coast from Portstewart in County Derry to Ballycastle in County Antrim, and the Antrim Coast from Ballycastle to Belfast, are as magnificent as they come.

From late May to late September, Ulsterbus' Antrim Coaster bus No 252 operates twice daily (except Sunday) between Belfast and Coleraine (four hours), stopping at all the main tourist sights. Also, its open-topped Bushmills Bus (No 177) is a double-decker that runs from the Giant's Causeway to Coleraine five times daily in July and August. The trip takes just over an hour. Bus No 162 runs year-round along the Antrim coast between Larne and Cushendun.

Carrickfergus

Only 13km north-east of Belfast is Carrickfergus and its impressive Norman **castle** (☎ 9335 1273) which was built in 1180 by John de Courcy and overlooks the harbour where William III landed in 1690. A small museum documents the castle's long history (it was occupied up until 1928). The castle is open year-round, 10 am to 6 pm Monday to Saturday, 2 to 6 pm Sunday; October to March it closes at 4 pm and is not open Sunday. Entry is £2.70.

There are no hostels in Carrickfergus; the cheapest B&B (£20 per person) is *Langsgarden* (☎ 9336 6369, 70-72 Scottish Quarter).

Glens of Antrim

Between Larne and Ballycastle, the nine Glens of Antrim are extremely picturesque stretches of woodland where streams cascade into the sea. The picture-perfect port of **Cushendall** has been dubbed the 'Capital of the Glens', while **Glenariff**, a few kilometres to the south, lays claim to the title 'Queen of the Glens'. Between Cushendun and Ballycastle, eschew the main A2 road for the narrower and more picturesque B92, and take the turn-off down to sweeping Murlough Bay.

The YHANI *Cushendall Youth Hostel* (☎ 2177 1344) is open from March to mid-December and is 1km north of the village. Dorm beds cost £8.25.

Ballycastle

Ballycastle, where the Atlantic Ocean meets the Irish Sea, is a quiet harbour town and a natural base for exploring the coasts to the west or south.

The IHH/IHO *Castle Hostel* (☎ 2076 2337, 62 Quay Rd), just past the Marine Hotel, charges £7 a night. It's clean, welcoming and spacious. The IHO *Ballycastle Backpackers* (☎ 2076 3612), 4 North St), near the waterfront and the main bus stop, charges £6.

IRELAND

Carrick-a-Rede Island

Open from May to mid-September, but closed any time the wind is too strong, the 20m rope bridge connecting Carrick-a-Rede Island to the mainland is a heart-stopper, swaying some 25m above the furious sea. The island is the site of a salmon fishery and a nesting ground for gulls and fulmars. You can cross the bridge for free, but the National Trust car park costs £2; it's a 1.25km walk from there to the bridge.

Giant's Causeway

Chances are you've seen pictures of the Giant's Causeway (Clochán an Aifir), Northern Ireland's main tourist attraction. The hexagonal basalt columns are impressive and do look as if a giant might have accidentally tipped out all 37,000 of them (that's counting the ones under the water). According to legend, the giant in question, Finn McCool, fancied a female giant on the Scottish island of Staffa and built some stepping stones to the island where, indeed, similar rock formations are found.

The more prosaic explanation is that lava erupted from an underground fissure and crystallised some 60 million years ago. Although the phenomenon is very clearly explained in the **Causeway Visitors Centre** (☎ 2073 1855) by a new exhibition and audiovisual for £1.50, skip the tourist garb and head straight for the natural wonder.

It costs nothing to make the pleasant 1.5km pilgrimage to the actual site, and two circular footpaths start from outside the visitors centre. About four buses a day (fewer on Sunday) between Portrush and Ballycastle pass the Giant's Causeway.

A recommended walk is from the Giant's Causeway 16km east along the coast (not the highway), past Dunseverick Castle to the beach at Whitepark Bay, where you'll find the year-round YHANI *Whitepark Bay Hostel* (☎ 2073 1745), with beds from £10.50.

Bushmills

Bushmills, 4km south-west of the Giant's Causeway, is a small town just off the A2 between Portrush and Ballycastle. The town itself is grimy and grey; the real attraction, 500m south of the main square, is the **Old Bushmills Distillery** (☎ 2073 3272), the only place in the world where Bushmills whiskey is distilled. Whiskey was first officially bottled here in 1608, but records indicate that the activity was going on for hundreds of years before that. After a noisy tour of the industrial process (it's quieter on weekends, when production is halted), you're rewarded with a whiskey-tasting session.

From April to October distillery tours leave every 20 minutes from 9.30 am to 4 pm daily (Sunday from noon). In the off season, tours leave weekdays at 10.30 and 11.30 am and 1.30, 2.30 and 3.30 pm. Admission is £3.50.

Dunluce Castle

Abandoned back in 1641, the ruins of 14th-century Dunluce Castle (☎ 2073 1938), dramatically sited overlooking the sea between Bushmills and Portrush, still bear a hint of the castle's former eminence. The south wall, facing the mainland, has two openings cut into it to hold cannons salvaged from the wreck of the *Girona*, a Spanish Armada vessel that foundered nearby in 1588. Perched 30m above the sea, the castle was of obvious military value, and there are extensive remains inside the walls, giving a good idea of life here.

Entry to the castle is £1.50 and guided tours are available. It opens 10 am (2 pm on Sunday) to 6 pm daily April to September (closed Tuesday); the rest of the year it closes at 4 pm.

Portstewart & Portrush

These twin seaside resorts are only 6km apart. Portstewart, the nicer of the two, has a slightly decayed, early 20th century feel to it. A day can easily be passed visiting the excellent beaches in the vicinity.

Portstewart's *Causeway Coast Hostel* (☎ 83 3789, 4 Victoria Terrace) at the eastern end of town charges £7 per person. In Portrush, the IHO *Macools* (☎ 82 4845, 5 Causeway View Terrace) is a clean 20-bed hostel with sea views. Beds in single-sex dorms cost £7 a head.

DERRY
pop 72,330

Derry or Londonderry – even choosing what you call Northern Ireland's second-largest city can be a political statement. In practice it's better known as Derry whatever your politics.

Doire, the original Irish name, means 'oak grove', and the 'London' prefix was added as

Sea sponges for sale, Hania market, Greece

WB Yeats statue, Sligo, Ireland

A young Celtic traveller, Dublin, Ireland

Window cleaning, Eyeries, County Cork, Ireland

High Cross, Ireland

The Anchor Inn, Cork

La Tene Stone, Castlestrange

Rolling hills in the Fooey River Valley, County Galway, Ireland

Venice Carnival (Carnevale)

Face mask, Venice, Italy

Wine cellar, Altesino, Italy

a reward for the town's central role in the struggle between Protestant King William III and Catholic King James II.

In the '60s, resentment at the long-running domination and gerrymandering of the city council by Protestants boiled over in the (Catholic dominated) civil rights marches of 1968. Simultaneously, attacks by Protestants on the Catholic Bogside district began, leading to a veritable siege. The British government decided that open warfare could only be prevented by military intervention, and on 14 August 1968 British troops entered Derry. In January 1972, 'Bloody Sunday' saw the deaths of 14 unarmed Catholic civil rights marchers in Derry at the hands of the British army, an event that marked the beginning of the Troubles in earnest.

Today Derry is as safe to visit as anywhere else in Northern Ireland. The arts are alive, and festivals, such as the Banks of the Foyle Halloween Carnival and the Foyal Film Festival, draw crowds from everywhere.

Orientation

The old centre of Derry is the small, walled city on the west bank of the River Foyle. The heart of the walled city is The Diamond, intersected by four main roads: Shipquay St, Ferryquay St, Bishop St Within and Butcher St. The Catholic Bogside area is below the walls to the north-west. To the south is a Protestant estate known as the Fountain. The Waterside district across the river is mostly Protestant.

Information

Derry's NITB tourist office (☎ 7126 7284) and Bord Fáilte (☎ 7136 9501) share an impressive, modern stone office just outside the walled city at the Tourist Information Centre, 44 Foyle St. Together they cover the whole of Ireland, are tirelessly helpful and are open 9 am to 5 pm weekdays year-round. The NITB office has extended hours in summer.

The main post office is on Custom House St just north of the Tower Museum.

At Central Library (☎ 7127 2300), 35 Foyle St, you can access the Internet until 1 pm (£2.50 per hour after). It's wise to book ahead. Duds 'n Suds laundrette, 141 Strand Rd, has while-you-wait facilities like a pool table, video games and a snack bar.

Things to See

Until the mid-1990s, the presence of the army and protective iron gates made Derry's magnificent **city walls** hard to appreciate. The gates are still there, but now they're open and it's possible to walk all round the walls, built between 1613 and 1618. They're about 8m high, 9m thick, and go around the old city for a length of 1.5km. A major highlight for the traveller, and a must-walk, the gates give an excellent overview of Bogside and its defiant **murals**, one notably proclaiming 'You Are Now Entering Free Derry'. From the city walls between Butcher's Gate and the army barracks, you can see many of the in-your-face building-side murals.

Just inside Coward's Bastion to the north, O'Doherty's Tower houses the excellent **Tower Museum** (☎ 7137 7633), which traces the story of Derry from the days of St Columbcille to the present. The museum is open 10 am to 5 pm Tuesday to Saturday year-round, 10 am to 5 pm daily (Sunday from 2 pm) in July and August. Admission is £3.50.

The fine red-brick **Guildhall** was originally built in 1890, reconstructed after a fire in 1908 and bombed by the IRA in 1972. It's just outside the city walls and is noted for its stained-glass windows. At present the inquiry into Bloody Sunday is being held here and entry to the building is restricted, but you can sneak into the foyer to take a peek at the windows.

Austere **St Columb's Cathedral** dates from 1628 and stands at the southern end of the walled city, off Biship St Within. Entry is £1 (add an extra £2 if you want to take photos).

Organised Tours

Both Derry City Guided Walking Tours (☎ 7127 1996), 11 Carlisle Rd, and the Derry Visitor & Convention Bureau, in the Tourist Information Centre (☎ 7126 7284), have walking tours of the City Walls and around for about £3.

Places to Stay

There are only two hostels in Derry, so consider booking ahead. The larger of the two is the YHANI *Derry City Hostel* (☎ 7128 4100, 6 Magazine St), in the walled city near Butcher's Gate, just 150m from the bus station. The cheapest dorm beds without breakfast are £6.50 and the most expensive £8; doubles cost £30.

Not as formal is **Steve's Backpackers** (☎ *7137 7989, 4 Asylum Rd*), a small, friendly, year-round hostel north of the walled city. From Butchers Gate follow Waterloo St until it turns into Strand Rd, walk for about 500m and turn left onto Asylum Rd. Beds are £7.50, there is no check-out time and the fifth night is free.

Within walking distance of the bus station, the friendly **Acorn House** (☎ *7127 1156, 17 Aberfoyle Terrace, Strand Rd*) has singles/doubles from £20/32. **Clarence House** (☎ *7126 5342, 15 Northland Rd*) charges £19/50; the double comes with an *en suite*. Farther along, **Florence House** (☎ *7126 8093, 16 Northland Rd*) is cheaper at £17 per person.

Places to Eat

Just outside the Ferryquay Gate, south-east of the walled city, modern **Fitzroy's** has entrances at 3 Carlisle Rd and 2-4 Bridge St, and moves from cool cafe to sophisticated mains at night. *The Sandwich Company* on The Diamond, and *The Bailey*, a few doors along on Bishop St, are handy for a simple lunch.

In the made-for-tourists Craft Village on Shipquay St, **Thran Maggies** is one of the few places to eat in the walled city after dark – at least until 9.15 pm. Whenever it's sunny the outdoor tables are packed, and there are fish mains from £4.95.

On Shipquay St, **Townsman** serves above-average pub food. *The Strand Bar*, on Strand Rd about 200m from the northern corner of the walled city, has meals upstairs from £8.95, along with a pub, nightclub and live music.

Entertainment

Derry's liveliest pubs are those situated along Waterloo St: *The Gweedore Bar*; *Dungloe*; *Tracy's*; and *Peadar O'Donnell's*, which is good for traditional music. *Castle Bar*, also on Waterloo St, has a back wall as part of the city wall – if you dare to look. The *Metro Bar* (*3-4 Bank Place*), just inside the walls, is Derry's trendiest (and most crowded) pub.

There are several theatres in Derry, with something for most tastes. Try *The Playhouse* (☎ *7126 8027, 5-7 Artillery St*) for

community theatre, or the **Rialto Entertainment Centre** (☎ *7126 0516, 5 Market St*) for larger productions.

In the **Calgach Centre** (☎ *7137 3177*) on Butcher St, inside the walled city, is *The Fifth Province*, a Celtic journey through the ages. Informative and entertaining, but at times over-the-top, this multimedia extravaganza has shows several times a day (£3).

The **Orchard Gallery** (☎ *7126 9675*) on Orchard St has contemporary art shows with works from Ireland and elsewhere. *The Verbal Arts Centre* (☎ *7126 6946*) on Stable Lane, near Bishop's Gate, focuses on the literary tradition of Derry and its surrounds.

The Oscar-nominated **The Nerve Centre** (☎ *7126 0562, 7-8 Magazine St*) is a multimedia venue with music, art-house cinema and cafe and bar. It also has workshops and studios for the development of creative technologies, including animation, film, and music. It's also a melting pot for digitally orientated minds.

Getting There & Away

The Ulsterbus station (☎ *7126 2261*) is just outside the city walls, on Foyle St near the Guildhall. There are frequent services between Belfast and Derry. Bus No 212, the *Maiden City Flyer*, is the fastest (one hour 40 minutes); a one-way ticket costs £7.10. There are also semifrequent connections to Portrush and Portstewart. Each day at 9 am a bus leaves Derry for Cork in the Republic, arriving at 7.15 pm. Bus Éireann operates a Derry-Galway service three times daily, via Donegal and Sligo.

Lough Swilly Bus Service (☎ *7126 2017*), with an office upstairs at the Ulsterbus station, serves County Donegal across the border, and has an £18 eight-day unlimited travel offer. Celtic Connection (☎ *0131-225 3330* in Edinburgh) can get you to Scotland (either Edinburgh or Glasgow) for £29.

Derry's Waterside train station (☎ *7134 2228*) is across the River Foyle from the centre, but is connected to it by a free Linkline bus. There are seven trains daily to Belfast (three on Sunday; three hours) via Portrush.

ENNISKILLEN & LOUGH ERNE

Enniskillen, the main town of County Fermanagh, is a handy centre for activities on

Upper and Lower Lough Erne. Enniskillen itself is rather bland, with only one notable sight – **Enniskillen Castle** (☎ 6632 5000), home to the Fermanagh History & Heritage Centre and a museum dedicated to the Royal Inniskilling Fusiliers. The castle and museums are open 10 am to 5 pm Tuesday to Friday and 2 to 5 pm Monday year-round, on weekends in July and August (2 to 5 pm), and Saturday only in May, June and September (2 to 5 pm). Entry is £2.

The town centre is on an island in the River Erne, which connects the upper and lower lakes. The tourist office (☎ 6632 3110), open daily Easter to September (weekdays the rest of the year), is on Wellington Rd about 100m from the centre; staff are knowledgeable about **boating** and **fishing** on Lough Erne.

Between May and September from the Round 'O' Jetty at Brook Park, the MV *Kestrel* waterbus (☎ 6632 2882) operates 90-minute tours (£5) of the lower lough, including a visit to **Devenish Island**, with its 9th-century church and one of the best round-towers in Ireland.

White Island, close to the eastern shore of the lough, has a line of eight mysterious statues, dating from around the 6th century. From April to September, a ferry runs across to White Island from the Castle Archdale marina, 20km north of Enniskillen on the Kesh road. Return fare is £3.

Marble Arch Caves (☎ 6634 8855), 16km south-west of Enniskillen via the A4 and A32, is Ireland's most extensive cave network. The 90-minute tours (£6) are popular and it's wise to book ahead. The caves are open 10.30 am to 4.30 pm daily from mid-March to September.

If you're driving through County Fermanagh to/from Derry, don't miss the excellent **Ulster-American Folk Park** (☎ 8224 3292) on the A5 in Castletown, 8km north-west of Omagh. This open-air museum has impressive life-size exhibits: a forge, weaver's cottage, a 19th-century Ulster street, and an early street from the US state of Pennsylvania (where many Ulster emigrants settled). Admission is £4. It opens daily from April to September, and on weekdays only the rest of the year.

Places to Stay

In Enniskillen there is hostel-style accommodation and a camp site at *Lakeland Canoe Centre* (☎ 6632 4250), on Castle Island, which is reached by free ferry from the Fermanagh Lakeland Forum south-east of the tourist office. It costs £8 to pitch your tent, or £9 for a dorm bed.

The YHANI *Castle Archdale Youth Hostel* (☎ 6862 8118), 19km north-west of Enniskillen near the White Island ferry, charges £8.25 and is open March to October.

Getting There & Around

Enniskillen's Ulsterbus station (☎ 6632 2633) is across from the tourist office, on Shore Rd. There are up to 10 services a day to Belfast via Dungannon (two hours). Buses also run to Derry (3¼ hours) and Cork (11¼ hours) via Omagh (one hour). From Omagh, there are express buses to Dublin.

Bicycles can be hired at the Lakeland Canoe Centre for about £10 a day.

Italy

During a visit to Italy, an 18th-century English traveller wrote: 'Of all the countries in the world, Italy is the most adorned by the arts. Of all the countries in the world, she has the least need of them.' As inspiring today as it was then, Italy is a magnificently complex – if unevenly woven – tapestry of natural splendour and human achievement.

Centuries ago, well-to-do northern Europeans were drawn to the Mediterranean light, and so the Grand Tour (of Europe) was born. What they found in Italy was an extraordinary cocktail: next to the awe-inspiring artistic wealth of Rome, Venice and Florence they often encountered squalid decadence, poverty and spivs on the make.

The economic miracles of the past decades have transformed the country, but beneath all the style, fine food and delicious wine, there remains, happily, a certain chaotic air. Not everything is wonderful – expanding industry, poor urban planning, unchecked resort construction and what at times seems like an almost wilful indifference to the nation's art treasures have too often blighted the cities and countryside.

You could not hope to experience all the wonders of the country in even a year's non-stop travel. From the grandeur of the Dolomites to the rainbow-coloured sea of Sardinia, there is much more to the country than St Peter's and the Uffizi.

AT A GLANCE

Capital	Rome
Population	57.8 million
Official Language	Italian
Currency	1 Italian lira (L) = 100 centesimi
Time	GMT/UTC+0100
Country Phone Code	☎ 39

Facts about Italy

HISTORY

The traditional date for the founding of Rome by Romulus is 753 BC, but the country had already been inhabited for thousands of years. Palaeolithic Neanderthals lived in Italy during the last Ice Age more than 20,000 years ago, and by the start of the Bronze Age, around 2000 BC, the peninsula had been settled by several Italic tribes.

From about 900 BC the Etruscan civilisation developed until these mysterious people, whose origins are still controversial, dominated the area between the Arno and Tiber Valleys. After the foundation of Rome, Etruscan civilisation continued to flourish until the end of the 3rd century BC, when the Romans overwhelmed the last Etruscan city.

The Roman Republic

The new Roman republic, after recovering from the invasion of the Gauls in 390 BC, began its expansion into southern Italy. Rome claimed Sicily following the First Punic War against Hannibal in 241 BC, after his legendary crossing of the Alps. Rome defeated Carthage in 202 BC and within a few years claimed Spain and Greece as colonies.

ITALY (ITALIA)

Expansion & Empire

In the 1st century BC, under Julius Caesar, Rome conquered Gaul and moved into Egypt. After Caesar's assassination by his nephew, Brutus, on the Ides of March in 44 BC, a power struggle began between Mark Antony and Octavius, leading to the deaths of Antony and Cleopatra in Egypt in 31 BC and the establishment of the Roman Empire in 27 BC. Octavius, who had been adopted by Julius Caesar as his son and heir, took the title of Augustus Caesar and became the first emperor. Augustus ruled for 45 years, a period of great advancement in engineering, architecture, administration and literature.

The Eastern & Western Empires

By the end of the 3rd century, the empire had grown to such an extent that Emperor Diocletian divided it between east and west for administrative purposes. His successor, Constantine, declared religious freedom for Christians and moved the seat of power to the eastern capital, Byzantium, which he renamed Constantinople. During the 4th century, Christianity was declared the official state religion and grew in power and influence.

By the early 5th century, German tribes had entered Rome, and in 476 the Western Roman Empire ended when the German warrior, Odoacer, deposed the emperor and declared himself ruler of Italy. The south and Sicily were dominated by Muslim Arabs until the Normans invaded in 1036.

The City-States & the Renaissance

The Middle Ages in Italy were marked by the development of powerful city-states in the north. This was the time of Dante, Petrarch and Boccaccio, Giotto, Cimabue and Pisano.

In the 15th century the Renaissance, which began in Florence, spread throughout the country, fostering genius of the likes of Brunelleschi, Donatello, Bramante, Botticelli, da Vinci, Masaccio, Lippi, Raphael and, of course, Michelangelo.

By the early 16th century much of the country was under Spanish rule. This lasted until 1713 when, following the War of Spanish Succession, control of Italy passed to the Austrians. It was not until after the invasion by Napoleon in 1796 that a degree of unity was introduced into Italy, for the first time since the fall of the Roman Empire.

The Risorgimento

In the 1860s Italy's unification movement, known as the Risorgimento, gained momentum, and in 1861 the Kingdom of Italy was declared under the rule of King Vittorio Emanuele. Venice was wrested from Austria in 1866 and Rome from the papacy in 1870.

Mussolini & WWII

In the years after WWI, Italy was in turmoil. In 1921 the Fascist Party, formed by Benito Mussolini in 1919, won 35 of the 135 seats in parliament. In October 1921, after a period of considerable unrest and strikes, the king asked Mussolini to form a government, whereupon he became prime minister with only 7% representation in parliament.

Mussolini formed the Rome-Berlin axis with Hitler in 1936 and Italy entered WWII as an ally of Germany in June 1941. After a series of military disasters and an invasion by the Allies in 1943, the king led a coup against Mussolini and had him arrested. After being rescued by the Germans, Mussolini tried to govern in the north, but was fiercely opposed by Italian partisans, who finally shot him in April 1945.

The Italian Republic

In 1946, following a referendum, the constitutional monarchy was abolished and the republic established. Italy was a founding member of the European Economic Community in 1957 and was seriously disrupted by terrorism in the 1970s following the appearance of the Red Brigades, who kidnapped and assassinated the Christian Democrat prime minister, Aldo Moro, in 1978.

In the decades that followed WWII, Italy's national government was dominated by the centre-right Christian Democrats, usually in coalition with other parties (excluding the Communists). Italy enjoyed significant economic growth in the 1980s, but the 1990s heralded a new period of crisis for the country, both economically and politically.

The 1990s

Against the backdrop of a severe economic crisis, the very foundations of Italian politics

ITALY

were shaken by a national bribery scandal known as *tangentopoli* (bribesville). Investigations eventually implicated thousands of politicians, public officials and businesspeople, and left the main parties in tatters, effectively demolishing the centre of the Italian political spectrum.

After a period of right-wing government, new elections in 1996 brought a centre-left coalition known as the Olive Tree to power. Led by economist Romano Prodi, it included the communists for the first time in Italian history. A program of fiscal austerity was ushered in to guarantee Italy's entry into Europe's economic and monetary union (EMU), which occurred in 1998. Although the prime minister has been replaced three times (the government is currently led by socialist Giuliano Amato, who inherited the poisoned chalice from Prodi's successor Massimo d'Alema in March 2000) the Olive Tree coalition is holding on. If it survives until the planned elections of 2001 it will be the first government to serve out a full five-year term.

The Mafia
The 1990s have also seen Italy moving more decisively against the Sicilian Mafia, prompted by the 1992 assassinations of two prominent anti-Mafia judges. A major offensive in Sicily, plus the testimonies of several *pentiti* (informers or supergrasses), led to several important arrests – most notably of the Sicilian godfather, Salvatore 'Toto' Riina, who is now serving a life sentence. The man believed to have taken power after Riina's arrest, Giovanni Brusca, was arrested in May 1996 and implicated in the murders of anti-Mafia judges, Giovanni Falcone and Paolo Borsellino. A number of subsequent high profile arrests have undoubtedly dented the Mafia's confidence, but the battle is far from won.

GEOGRAPHY
Italy's boot shape makes it one of the most recognisable countries in the world. The country, incorporating the islands of Sicily and Sardinia, is bound by the Adriatic, Ligurian, Tyrrhenian and Ionian seas, which all form part of the Mediterranean Sea. About 75% of the Italian peninsula is mountainous, with the Alps dividing the country from France, Switzerland and Austria, and the

Apennines forming a backbone which extends from the Alps into Sicily. There are four active volcanoes: Stromboli and Vulcano (in the Aeolian Islands), Vesuvius (near Naples) and Etna (Sicily).

CLIMATE
Italy lies in a temperate zone, but the climates of the north and south vary. Summers are uniformly hot, but are often extremely hot and dry in the south. Winters can be severely cold in the north – particularly in the Alps, but also in the Po Valley – whereas they are generally mild in the south and in Sicily and Sardinia.

ECOLOGY & ENVIRONMENT
The countryside can be dramatically beautiful, but the long presence of humans on the peninsula has had a significant impact on the environment. Aesthetically the result is not always displeasing – much of the beauty of Tuscany, for instance, lies in the interaction of olive groves with vineyards, fallow fields and stands of cypress and pine. Centuries of tree clearing, combined with illegal building have also led to extensive land degradation and erosion. The alteration of the environment, combined with the Italians' passion for hunting *(la caccia)*, has led to many native animals and birds becoming extinct, rare or endangered. Under laws progressively introduced this century, many animals and birds are now protected.

There are numerous national parks in Italy. Among the most important are the Parco Nazionale del Gran Paradiso and the Parco Nazionale dello Stelvio, both in the Alps, and the Parco Nazionale d'Abruzzo.

Central and southern Italy are sometimes subject to massive earthquakes. A series of quakes devastated parts of the Appenine areas of Umbria and the Marche in September 1997. There was an earthquake after four days of tremors in central Italy in April 1998.

GOVERNMENT & POLITICS
For administrative purposes Italy is divided into 20 regions, each of which have some degree of autonomy. The regions are then subdivided into provinces and municipalities.

The country is a parliamentary republic, headed by a president who appoints the prime minister. The parliament consists of a senate and chamber of deputies, both of which have equal legislative power. The seat of national government is in Rome. Until reforms were introduced in 1994, members of parliament were elected by what was probably the purest system of proportional representation in the world. Two-thirds of both houses are now elected on the basis of who receives the most votes in their district, basically the same as the first-past-the-post system in the UK. The old system generally produced unstable coalition governments – Italy had 53 governments in the 48 years between the declaration of the republic and the introduction of electoral reforms.

ECONOMY

Italy has the fifth-largest economy in the world, thanks to some spectacular growth in the 1980s. However, the severe economic crisis of 1992-93 prompted a succession of governments to pull the economy into line with draconian measures such as the partial privatisation of the country's huge public sector. The Olive Tree coalition worked hard to meet the Maastricht criteria for entry into the European Monetary Union (EMU), cutting the budget deficit and lowering inflation in time to be included in the first intake of countries in May 1998.

Despite years of effort and the expenditure of trillions of lire, a significant economic gap still exists between Italy's northern and southern regions. The fact remains that Italy's richest regions (Piedmont, Lombardy, Veneto and Emilia-Romagna) are all northern, and its poorest (Calabria, Campania and Sicily) are all southern.

POPULATION & PEOPLE

The population of Italy is 57.8 million. The country has the lowest birthrate in Europe – a surprising fact considering the Italians' preoccupation with children and family. Foreigners may like to think of Italy as a land of passionate, animated people who gesticulate wildly when speaking, love to eat, drive like maniacs and don't like to work. However, it will take more than a holiday in Italy to understand its vigorous and remarkably diverse inhabitants. Overall the people remain fiercely protective of their regional customs, including their dialects and cuisine.

ARTS
Architecture, Painting & Sculpture

Italy has often been called a living art museum and certainly it is not always necessary to enter a gallery to appreciate the country's artistic wealth – it is all around you as you walk through Florence or Venice, or a medieval hill-top village in Umbria. In the south of Italy and in Sicily, where Greek colonisation preceded Roman domination, there are important Greek archaeological sites such as the temples at Paestum, south of Salerno, and at Agrigento in Sicily. Pompeii and Herculaneum give an idea of how ancient Romans actually lived.

Byzantine mosaics adorn churches throughout Italy, most notably at Ravenna, in the Basilica of San Marco in Venice, and in Monreale cathedral near Palermo. There are also some interesting mosaics in churches in Rome. In Apulia, you can tour the magnificent Romanesque churches, a legacy of the Normans (the region's medieval rulers) and their successors, the Swabians.

The 15th and early 16th centuries in Italy saw one of the most remarkable explosions of artistic and literary achievement in recorded history – the Renaissance. Patronised mainly by the Medici family in Florence and the popes in Rome, painters, sculptors, architects and writers flourished and many artists of genius emerged. The High Renaissance (about 1490-1520) was dominated by three men – Leonardo da Vinci (1452-1519), Michelangelo Buonarrotti (1475-1564) and Raphael (1483-1520).

The baroque period (17th century) was characterised by sumptuous, often fantastic architecture and richly decorative painting and sculpture. In Rome there are innumerable works by the great baroque sculptor and architect Gianlorenzo Bernini (1598-1680).

Neoclassicism in Italy produced the sculptor, Canova (1757-1822). Of Italy's modern artists, Amedeo Modigliani (1884-1920) is perhaps the most famous. The early 20th century also produced an artistic movement known as the Futurists, who rejected the sentimental art of the past and were infatuated by new technology, including modern warfare. Fascism produced its own style of architecture in Italy, characterised by the EUR satellite city and the work of Marcello Piacentini

ITALY

(1881-1960), which includes the *Stadio dei Marmi* at Rome's Olympic Stadium complex.

Music
Few modern Italian singers or musicians have made any impact outside Italy – one exception is Zucchero (Adelmo Fornaciari), who has become well known in the USA and UK as Sugar. Instead, it is in the realms of opera and instrumental music where Italian artists have triumphed. Antonio Vivaldi (1675-1741) created the concerto in its present form. Verdi, Puccini, Bellini, Donizetti and Rossini, composers from the 19th and early 20th centuries, are all stars of the modern operatic era. Tenor Luciano Pavarotti (1935-) is today's (fading) luminary of Italian opera. Not so with Andrea Bocelli (1958-) who soared to international stardom in the 1990s.

Literature
Before Dante wrote his *Divina Commedia* (Divine Comedy) and confirmed vernacular Italian as a serious medium for poetic expression, Latin was the language of writers. Among the greatest writers of ancient Rome were Cicero, Virgil, Ovid and Petronius.

A contemporary of Dante was Petrarch (1304-74). Giovanni Boccaccio (1313-75), author of the *Decameron*, is considered the first Italian novelist.

Machiavelli's *The Prince*, although a purely political work, has proved the most lasting of the Renaissance works.

Italy's richest contribution to modern literature has been in the novel and short story. Cesare Pavese and Carlo Levi both endured internal exile in southern Italy during Fascism. Levi based *Christ Stopped at Eboli* on his experiences in exile in Basilicata. Umberto Eco shot to fame with his first and best-known work, *The Name of the Rose*.

Theatre
At a time when French playwrights ruled the stage, the Venetian Carlo Goldoni (1707-93) attempted to bring Italian theatre back into the limelight with the *commedia dell'arte*, the tradition of improvisational theatre. Luigi Pirandello (1867-1936), author of *Six Characters in Search of an Author*, won the Nobel Prize in 1934. Modern Italian theatre's most enduring representative is actor/director Dario Fo, who won the Nobel Prize in 1998.

Cinema
From 1945 to 1947, Roberto Rossellini produced three neorealist masterpieces, including *Rome Open City* starring Anna Magnani. Vittorio de Sica produced another classic in 1948, *Bicycle Thieves*. Schooled with the masters of neorealism, Federico Fellini in many senses took the creative baton from them and carried it into the following decades, with films such as *La Dolce Vita*. The career of Michelangelo Antonioni reached a climax with *Blow-up* in 1967. Bernardo Bertolucci had his first international hit with *Last Tango in Paris*. He made the blockbuster *The Last Emperor* in 1987, *The Sheltering Sky* (1990), *Stealing Beauty* (1995) and *Beseiged* (1998). Franco Zeffirelli's most recent film was *Tea with Mussolini*. Other notable directors include the Taviani brothers, Giuseppe Tornatore, Nanni Moretti and Roberto Benigni, director of the Oscar-winning *Life is Beautiful* (1998).

SOCIETY & CONDUCT
It is difficult to make blanket assertions about Italian culture, if only because Italians have lived together as a nation for little over 100 years. Prior to unification, the peninsula was long subject to a varied mix of masters and cultures. This lack of unity contributed to the survival of local dialects and customs. Even today many Italians tend to identify more strongly with their region or home town than with the nation. An Italian is first and foremost a Tuscan or Sicilian, or even a Roman or Neapolitan.

In some parts of Italy, especially in the south, women might be harassed if they wear skimpy or see-through clothing. Modest dress is expected in all churches. Those that are major tourist attractions, such as St Peter's in Rome, strictly enforce dress codes (no shorts, bare arms or shoulders).

RELIGION
Around 85% of Italians profess to be Catholic. The remaining 15% includes about 700,000 Muslims, 500,000 evangelical Protestants, 140,000 Jehovah's Witnesses and smaller communities of Jews, Waldenses and Buddhists.

LANGUAGE

English is most widely understood in the north, particularly in major centres such as Milan, Florence and Venice. Staff at most hotels and restaurants usually speak a little English, but you will be better received if you attempt to communicate in Italian.

Italian, a Romance language, is related to French, Spanish, Portuguese and Romanian. Modern literary Italian developed in the 13th and 14th centuries, predominantly through the works of Dante, Petrarch and Boccaccio, who wrote chiefly in the Florentine dialect. Although many dialects are spoken in everyday conversation, so-called standard Italian is the national language of schools, media and literature, and is understood throughout the country.

Many older Italians still expect to be addressed by the third person formal, ie, *Lei* instead of *Tu*. It is not polite to use the greeting *ciao* when addressing strangers, unless they use it first; use *buongiorno* and *arrivederci*.

See the Language chapter at the back of this book for pronunciation guidelines and useful words and phrases.

Facts for the Visitor

HIGHLIGHTS

Coming up with a Top 10 list for Italy is a little like trying to find the 10 shiniest gold ingots in Fort Knox. Bearing that in mind, you could try the following:

1. Florence
2. Aeolian Islands
3. Amalfi Coast
4. Siena
5. Italian food
6. The Cinque Terre
7. Ancient ruins of Rome, Pompeii & Paestum
8. Venice
9. Parco Naturale di Fanes-Sennes-Braies (in the Dolomites)
10. Carnevale in Ivrea (Piemonte)

SUGGESTED ITINERARIES

Depending on the length of your stay, you might want to see and do the following things:

Two days
  Visit Rome to see the Forum, the Colosseum, St Peter's Basilica and the Vatican museums.

One week
  Visit Rome and Florence, with detours in Tuscany to Siena and San Gimignano. Or visit Rome and Naples, with detours to Pompeii, Vesuvius and the Amalfi Coast.

Two weeks
  As above, plus Bologna, Verona, Ravenna and at least three days in Venice.

PLANNING
When to Go

The best time to visit Italy is in the off season, particularly April-June and September-October, when the weather is good, prices are lower and there are fewer tourists. During July and August (the high season) it is very hot, prices are inflated, the country swarms with tourists and hotels by the sea and in the mountains are usually booked out. Note that many hotels and restaurants in seaside areas close down for the winter months.

Maps

Michelin map No 988 (1:1,000,000) covers the entire country. There is also a series of area maps at 1:400,000 – Nos 428 to 431 cover the mainland, No 432 covers Sicily and No 433 Sardinia.

If you're driving, the AA's *Big Road Atlas – Italy* (UK£9.99) is scaled at 1:250,000 and includes 39 town maps.

What to Bring

A backpack is a definite advantage in Italy, but if you plan to use a suitcase and portable trolley, be warned about the endless flights of stairs at train stations and in many of the smaller medieval towns, as well as the petty thieves who prey on tourists who have no hands free because they are carrying too much luggage. A small pack (with a lock) for use on day trips and for sightseeing is preferable to a handbag or shoulder bag, particularly in the southern cities where motorcycle bandits are very active. A money belt is absolutely essential in Italy, particularly in the south and in Sicily, but also in the major cities, where groups of dishevelled-looking women and children prey on tourists with bulging pockets.

In the more mountainous areas the weather can change suddenly, even in high summer, so remember to bring at least one item of warm clothing. Most importantly, bring a pair of hardy, comfortable, worn-in walking shoes.

ITALY

In many cities, pavements are uneven and often made of cobblestones.

TOURIST OFFICES
Local Tourist Offices
There are three main categories of tourist office in Italy: regional, provincial and local. Their names vary throughout the country. Provincial offices are sometimes known as the Ente Provinciale per il Turismo (EPT) or, more commonly, the Azienda di Promozione Turistica (APT). The Azienda Autonoma di Soggiorno e Turismo (AAST) and Informazioni e Assistenza ai Turisti (IAT) offices usually have information only on the town itself. In some of the very small towns and villages the local tourist office is called a Pro Loco, and is often little more than a room with a desk. At most offices you should be able to get an *elenco degli alberghi* (a list of hotels), a *pianta della città* (map of the town) and information on the major sights. Staff speak English in larger towns, but in the more out-of-the-way places you may have to rely on sign language. Tourist offices are generally open 8.30 am to 12.30 or 1 pm and 3 to 7 pm Monday to Friday and on Saturday morning. Hours are usually extended in summer.

The Centro Turistico Studentesco e Giovanile (CTS) has offices all over Italy and specialises in discounts for students and young people, but is also useful for travellers of any age looking for cheap flights and sightseeing discounts. It is linked with the International Student Travel Confederation. You can get a student card here if you have documents proving that you are a student.

Tourist Offices Abroad
Information about Italy can be obtained at Italian State Tourist Offices (Web site www.enit .it) throughout the world, including:

Australia (☎ 02-9262 1666, fax 9262 5745) c/o Italian Chamber of Commerce, Level 26, 44 Market St, Sydney, NSW 2000
Canada (☎ 514-866 7668, ✉ initaly@ican.net) Suite 1914, 1 Place Ville Marie, Montreal, Quebec H3B 2C3
UK (☎ 020-7408 1254, ✉ enitlond@globalnet.co.uk) 1 Princes St, London W1R 8AY
USA (☎ 212-245 4822, ✉ enitny@bway.net) Suite 1565, 630 Fifth Ave, New York, NY

10111; (☎ 310-820 1819) Suite 550, 12400 Wilshire Blvd, Los Angeles, CA 90025; (☎ 312-644 0996, ✉ enitch@italiantouism.com) 500 North Michigan Ave, Chicago, IL 60611

Sestante CIT (Compagnia Italiana di Turismo), Italy's national travel agency, also has offices throughout the world (known as CIT outside Italy). It can provide extensive information on Italy, as well as book tours and accommodation. It can also make train bookings. Offices include:

Australia (☎ 03-9650 5510) Level 4, 227 Collins St, Melbourne, Vic 3000; (☎ 02-9267 1255), 263 Clarence St, Sydney, NSW 2000
Canada (☎ 514-845 4310, 800 361 7799) Suite 750, 1450 City Councillors St, Montreal, Quebec H3A 2E6 (☎ 905-415 1060, 800 387 0711) Suite 401, 80 Tiverton Court, Markham, Toronto, Ontario L3R 0G4
UK (☎ 020-8686 0677, 8686 5533, ✉ ciao@citalia.co.uk) Marco Polo House, 3/5 Lansdown Rd, Croydon CR9 1LL
USA (☎ 212-730 2121, ✉ citnewyork@msn.com) 10th floor, 15 West 44th Street, New York, NY 10036 (☎ 310-338 8615, ✉ citlax@email.msm.com) 6033 West Century Blvd, suite 980, Los Angeles, CA 90045

VISAS & DOCUMENTS
EU citizens require only a national identity card or a passport to stay in Italy for as long as they like and since Italy is now a member of the Schengen Area, EU citizens can enter the country without passport controls.

Citizens of many other countries including the USA, Australia, Canada and New Zealand do not need to apply for visas before arriving in Italy if they are entering the country as tourists only. If you are entering the country for any reason other than tourism, you should insist on having your passport stamped. Visitors are technically obliged to report to a *questura* (police station) if they plan to stay at the same address for more than one week, to receive a *permesso di soggiorno* – in effect, permission to remain in the country for a nominated period up to the three-month limit. Tourists who are staying in hotels or youth hostels are not required to do this since proprietors need to register their guests with the police. A permesso di soggiorno only becomes a necessity (for non-EU citizens) if you plan to study, work (legally) or live in Italy.

EMBASSIES & CONSULATES
Italian Embassies & Consulates
Italian diplomatic missions abroad include:

Australia
Embassy: (☎ 02-6273 3333, fax 6273 4223, ✉ ambital2@dynamite.com.au) 12 Grey St, Deakin, Canberra, ACT 2600
Consulate: (☎ 03-9867 5744, fax 9866 3932, ✉ itconmel@netlink.com.au) 509 St Kilda Rd, Melbourne, Vic 3004
Consulate: (☎ 02-9392 7900, fax 9252 4830, ✉ itconsyd@armadillo.com.au) Level 43, The Gateway, 1 Macquarie Place, Sydney, NSW 2000

Canada
Embassy: (☎ 613-232 2401, fax 233 1484, ✉ italcomm@trytel.com) 21st floor, 275 Slater St, Ottawa, Ontario K1P 5H9
Consulate: (☎ 514-849 8351, fax 499 9471, ✉ consitmtl@cyberglobe.net) 3489 Drummond St, Montreal, Quebec H3G 1X6
Consulate: (☎ 416-977 1566, ✉ consolato.it@toronto.italconsulate.org) 136 Beverley St, Toronto, Ontario M5T 1Y5

France
Embassy: (☎ 01 49 54 03 00, fax 01 45 49 35 81, ✉ stampa@dial.oleane.com) 7 rue de Varenne, Paris 75007
Consulate: (☎ 01 44 30 47 00, fax 01 45 66 41 78) 5 blvd Augier, Paris 75116

New Zealand
Embassy: (☎ 04-473 53 39, fax 472 72 55, ✉ ambwell@xtra.co.nz) 34 Grant Rd, Thorndon, Wellington

UK
Embassy: (☎ 020-7312 2209, fax 7312 2230, ✉ emblondon@embitaly.org.uk) 14 Three Kings Yard, London W1Y 2EH
Consulate: (☎ 020-7235 9371, fax 7823 1609) 38 Eaton Place, London SW1X 8AN

USA
Embassy: (☎ 202-328 5500, fax 328 5593, ✉ itapress@ix.netcom.com) 1601 Fuller St, NW Washington, DC 20009
Consulate: (☎ 213-820 0622, fax 820 0727, ✉ cglos@aol.com) Suite 300, 12400 Wilshire Blvd, West Los Angeles, CA 90025
Consulate: (☎ 212-737 9100, fax 249 4945, ✉ italconsny@aol.com) 690 Park Ave, New York, NY 10021-5044
Consulate: (☎ 415-931 4924, fax 931 7205) 2590 Webster St, San Francisco, CA 94115

Embassies & Consulates in Italy
The headquarters of most foreign embassies are in Rome, although there are generally British and US consulates in other major cities. The following addresses and phone numbers are for Rome:

Australia (☎ 06 85 27 21) Via Alessandria 215
Austria (☎ 06 844 01 41) Via Pergolesi 3
  Consulate: (☎ 06 855 29 66) Viale Liegi 32
Canada (☎ 06 44 59 81) Via G B de Rossi 27
  Consulate: (☎ 06 44 59 81) Via Zara 30
France (☎ 06 68 60 11) Piazza Farnese 67
  Consulate: (☎ 06 68 80 21 52) Via Giulia 251
Germany (☎ 06 88 47 41) Via Po 25c
  Consulate: (☎ 06 88 47 41) Via Francesco Siacci 2c
New Zealand (☎ 06 440 29 28) Via Zara 28
Spain (☎ 06 687 81 72) Largo Fontanella Borghese 19
  Consulate: (☎ 06 687 14 01) Via Campo Marzio 34
Switzerland (☎ 06 808 36 41) Via Barnarba Oriani 61
  Consulate: (☎ 06 808 83 61) Largo Elvezia 15
UK (☎ 06 482 54 41) Via XX Settembre 80a
USA (☎ 06 467 41) Via Vittorio Veneto 119a-121

For a complete list of all foreign embassies in Rome and other major cities throughout Italy, look in the local telephone book under *ambasciate* or *consolati*, or ask for a list at the tourist office.

CUSTOMS
As of 1 July 1999, duty-free sales within the EU were abolished. Under the rules of the single market, goods bought in and exported within the EU incur no additional taxes, provided duty has been paid somewhere within the EU and the goods are for personal consumption.

Travellers coming from outside the EU, on the other hand, can import, duty free: 200 cigarettes, 1L of spirits, 2L of wine, 60mls of perfume, 250mls of *eau de toilet*, and other goods up to a total value of L340,000 (€175); anything over this limit must be declared on arrival and the appropriate duty paid (it is advisable to carry all receipts).

MONEY
A combination of travellers cheques and credit cards is the best way to take your

ITALY

money. If you buy travellers cheques in lire there should be no commission charged for cashing them. There are exchange offices at all major airports and train stations, but it is advisable to obtain a small amount of lire before arriving to avoid problems and queues at the airport and train stations.

Major credit cards, including Visa, MasterCard and American Express, are widely accepted in Italy and can be used for purchases for payment in hotels and restaurants (although smaller places might not accept them). They can also be used to get money from ATMs (*bancomats*) or, if you don't have a PIN, over the counter in major banks, including the Banca Commerciale Italiana, Cassa di Risparmio and Credito Italiano. If your credit card is lost, stolen or swallowed by an ATM, you can telephone toll-free (☎ 167-82 20 56) to have it cancelled. To cancel a MasterCard the number in Italy is ☎ 167-86 80 86, or you can make a reverse-charge call to St Louis in the USA (☎ 314-275 66 90). To cancel a Visa card in Italy, phone ☎ 167-82 10 01. The toll-free emergency number to report a lost or stolen American Express card varies according to where the card was issued. Check with American Express in your country or contact American Express in Rome (☎ 06 722 82) which has a 24-hour card-holders' service.

The fastest way to receive money is through Western Union (☎ 167-01 38 39 toll-free). This service functions in Italy through the Mail Boxes Etc chain of stores, which you will find in the bigger cities. The sender and receiver have to turn up at a Western Union outlet with passport or other form of ID and the fees charged for the virtually immediate transfer depend on the amount sent.

Currency

Until the euro notes and coins are in circulation, Italy's currency will remain the lira (plural: lire). Notes come in denominations of L1000, L2000, L5000, L10,000, L50,000, L100,000 and L500,000. Coin denominations are L50, L100 (two types of silver coin), L200, L500 and L1000.

Remember that, like other continental Europeans, Italians indicate decimals with commas and thousands with points.

Exchange Rates

country	unit		lire
Australia	A$1	=	L1241.85
Canada	C$1	=	L1444.84
euro	€1	=	L1936.27
France	1FF	=	L295.182
Germany	DM1	=	L989.999
Ireland	£IR1	=	L2458.56
Japan	¥100	=	L1972.57
New Zealand	NZ$1	=	L964.079
UK	UK£1	=	L3222.28
USA	US$1	=	L2143.12

Costs

A *very* prudent traveller could get by on L80,000 per day, but only by staying in youth hostels, eating one meal a day (at the hostel), buying a sandwich or pizza by the slice for lunch and minimising the number of galleries and museums visited, since the entrance fee to most major museums is cripplingly expensive at around L12,000. You save on transport costs by buying tourist or day tickets for city bus and underground services. When travelling by train, you can save money by avoiding the fast Eurostars which charge a *supplemento rapido*. Italy's railways also offer a few cut-price options for students, young people and tourists for travel within a nominated period (see the Getting Around section in this chapter for more information).

Museums and galleries usually give discounts to students, but you will need a valid student card which you can obtain from CTS offices if you have documents proving you are a student.

A basic breakdown of costs during an average day could be: accommodation L25,000 (youth hostel) to L60,000; breakfast (coffee and croissant) L3000; lunch (sandwich and mineral water) L6000; public transport (bus or underground railway in a major town) L6000; entry fee for one museum L12,000; a sit-down dinner L14,000 to L30,000.

Tipping & Bargaining

You are not expected to tip on top of restaurant service charges, but it is common practice among Italians to leave a small amount, say around 10%. In bars they will leave any small change as a tip, often only L100 or L200. You can tip taxi drivers if you wish but it's not obligatory.

Bargaining is common throughout Italy in the various flea markets, but not normally in shops. You can try bargaining for the price of a room in a *pensione*, particularly if you plan to stay for more than a few days or out of season.

POST & COMMUNICATIONS
Post

Stamps *(francobolli)* are available at post offices and authorised tobacconists (look for the official *tabacchi* sign: a big 'T', often white on black). Since letters often need to be weighed, what you get at the tobacconist's for international air mail will occasionally be an approximation of the proper rate. Main post offices in the bigger cities are generally open from around 8 am to 6 pm. Many open on Saturday morning too.

Postcards and letters up to 20g sent air mail cost L1400 to Australia and New Zealand, L1300 to the USA and L800 to EU countries (L900 to the rest of Europe). Aerograms are a cheap alternative, costing only L900 to send anywhere. They can be purchased at post offices only.

A new service, *posta prioritaria* (priority post – a little like the UK's 1st class post), began in 1999. For L1200, postcards and letters up to 20g posted to destinations within Italy, the EU, Switzerland and Norway are supposed to arrive the following day.

Sending letters express *(espresso)* costs a standard extra L3600, but may help speed a letter on its way.

Telephone & Fax

Italy's country code is ☎ 39. Area codes are an integral part of the telephone number, even if you're dialling a local number. Not content to make the area code part of the phone number, it is planned to convert the initial 0 into a 4 by the end of 2000. Thus any number in Rome will begin with 46.

Local and long distance calls can be made from any public phone, or from a Telecom office in larger towns. Italy's rates, particularly for long-distance calls, are among the highest in Europe. Local calls cost a minimum of L200. Most public phones accept only phonecards, sold in denominations of L5000, L10,000 and L15,000 phonecards at tobacconists and newsstands, or from vending machines at Telecom offices.

To make a reverse-charge (collect) call from a public telephone, dial ☎ 170. All operators speak English. Numbers for this Home Country Direct service are displayed in the first pages of Italian phone books and include: Australia (☎ 172 10 61, Telstra), Canada (☎ 172 10 01, Teleglobe), New Zealand (☎ 172 10 64), UK (☎ 172 01 44, BT Automatic) and USA (☎ 172 10 11, AT&T). For international directory inquiries call ☎ 176.

International faxes can cost L8000 for the first page and L5000 per page thereafter. You can transmit faxes from specialist fax/photocopy shops, post offices and from some tabacchi. Some Telecom public phones can also send faxes.

Email & Internet Access

Italy has a growing number of Internet cafes, where you can send and receive email or surf the Net for around L10,000 to L15,000 an hour.

INTERNET RESOURCES

There is an Italy page at Lonely Planet's Web site at www.lonelyplanet.com. The following are just a few of the huge number of useful Web sites for travellers to Italy.

Alfanet at www.alfanet.it has a Welcome Italy page, with a link to information about a number of cities; CTS at www.cts.it has useful information (but in Italian only) from Italy's leading student travel organisation; Rome at www.informaroma.it has information on the city's monuments and museums, virtual tours and links to other pertinent sites.

Travel Italy at www.travel.it provides useful tourist information; and Il Vaticano at www.christusrex.org has detailed information about the Vatican City, including virtual tours of the main monuments and the Musei Vaticani.

BOOKS

For a more comprehensive guide to Italy, pick up a copy of Lonely Planet's *Italy*. If you want to concentrate on specific regions, pick up Lonely Planet's new *Rome, Venice, Tuscany & Umbria* and *Sicily* guides. Also useful are the *Italian phrasebook, World Food Italy* and *Rome City Map*. If you're a

ITALY

hiking enthusiast, a good companion is Lonely Planet's *Walking in Italy*.

For a potted history of the country, try the *Concise History of Italy* by Vincent Cronin. *A History of Contemporary Italy – Society and Politics 1943-1988* by Paul Ginsborg is well written and absorbing. Luigi Barzini's classic *The Italians* is a great introduction to Italian people and culture, while *Excellent Cadavers: The Mafia and the Death of the First Italian Republic* by Alexander Stille is a shocking and fascinating account of the Mafia in Sicily.

Interesting introductions to travelling in Italy include *A Traveller in Italy* by HV Morton, who also wrote similar guides to Rome and southern Italy.

NEWSPAPERS & MAGAZINES

Major English-language newspapers available in Italy are the *Herald Tribune,* the English *Guardian,* the *Times* and the *Telegraph.* *Time* magazine, *Newsweek* and the *Economist* are available weekly.

TIME

Italy is one hour ahead of GMT/UTC, and two hours ahead during summer. Daylight-saving time starts on the last Sunday in March, when clocks are put forward an hour. Clocks are put back an hour on the last Sunday in September. Remember to make allowances for daylight-saving time in your own country. Note that Italy operates on a 24-hour clock.

LAUNDRY

Coin laundrettes, where you can do your own washing, are catching on in Italy. You'll find them in most of the main cities and towns. A load will cost around L8000. Many camping grounds have laundry facilities.

WOMEN TRAVELLERS

Italy is not a dangerous country for women, but women travelling alone will often find themselves plagued by unwanted attention from men. Most of the attention falls into the nuisance/harassment category and it is best simply to ignore the catcalls, hisses and whistles. However, women touring alone should use common sense. Avoid walking alone in dark and deserted streets and look for centrally located hotels that are within easy walking distance of places where you can eat at night. In the south, including Sicily and Sardinia, the unwelcome attention paid to women travelling alone can border on the highly intrusive, particularly in the bigger cities. Women should also avoid hitchhiking alone.

GAY & LESBIAN TRAVELLERS

Homosexuality is legal in Italy and generally well tolerated in major cities, though overt displays of affection might get a negative response in smaller towns and villages, particularly in the south.

The national organisation for gays (men and women) is AGAL (☎ 051 644 70 54, fax 051 644 67 22) in Bologna.

DISABLED TRAVELLERS

The Italian travel agency CIT can advise on hotels which have special facilities. The UK-based Royal Association for Disability and Rehabilitation, or RADAR (☎ 020-7250 3222), publishes a useful guide called *Holidays & Travel Abroad; A Guide for Disabled People*.

DANGERS & ANNOYANCES

Theft is the main problem for travellers in Italy, mostly in the form of petty thievery and pickpocketing, especially in the bigger cities. Although not something you should be particularly worried about, a few precautions are necessary to avoid being robbed. Always carry your cash in a money belt and avoid flashing your dough in public. Pickpockets operate in crowded areas, such as markets and on buses.

Watch out for groups of dishevelled-looking kids, who can be lightening fast as they empty your pockets. Motorcycle bandits are a minor problem in Rome, Naples, Palermo and Syracuse. If you are using a shoulder bag, make sure that you wear the strap across your body and have the bag on the side away from the road.

Never leave valuables in a parked car – in fact, try not to leave anything in the car if you can help it.

It is a good idea to park your car in a supervised car park if you are leaving it for any amount of time. Car theft is a major problem in Rome and Naples. Throughout Italy you can call the police (☎ 113) or *carabinieri* (☎ 112) in an emergency.

BUSINESS HOURS

Business hours can vary from city to city, but generally shops and businesses are open 8.30 am to 1 pm and 5 to 7.30 pm Monday to Saturday, and some are also open on Sunday mornings. Banks are generally open 8.30 am to 1.30 pm and from 2.30 to 4.30 pm Monday to Friday, but hours vary between banks and cities. Large post offices are open 8 am to 6 or 7 pm Monday to Saturday. Most museums close on Monday, and restaurants and bars are required to close for one day each week.

All of this has become more flexible since opening times were liberalised under new trading hours laws that went into effect in April 1999. At the time of writing it was difficult to determine what effect this would have on day to day practicalities, as Italians tend to value their time off and are not necessarily rushing to keep their shops open throughout the week.

PUBLIC HOLIDAYS & SPECIAL EVENTS

National public holidays include: 6 January (Epiphany); Easter Monday; 25 April (Liberation Day); 1 May (Labour Day); 15 August (*Ferragosto* or Feast of the Assumption); 1 November (All Saints' Day); 8 December (Feast of the Immaculate Conception); 25 December (Christmas Day); and 26 December (Feast of St Stephen).

Individual towns also have public holidays to celebrate the feasts of their patron saints. Some of these are the Feast of St Mark in Venice on 25 April; the Feast of St John the Baptist on 24 June in Florence, Genoa and Turin; the Feast of St Peter and St Paul in Rome on 29 June; the Feast of St Januarius in Naples on 19 September; and the Feast of St Ambrose in Milan on 7 December.

Annual events in Italy worth keeping in mind include:

Carnevale During the 10 days before Ash Wednesday, many towns stage carnivals. The one held in Venice is the best known, but there are also others, including at Viareggio in Liguria and Ivrea near Turin.

Holy Week There are important festivals during this week everywhere in Italy, in particular the colourful and sombre traditional festivals of Sicily. In Assisi the rituals of Holy Week attract thousands of pilgrims.

Scoppio del Carro Literally 'Explosion of the Cart', this colourful event held in Florence in Piazza del Duomo on Easter Sunday features the explosion of a cart full of fireworks and dates back to the Crusades. If all goes well, it is seen as a good omen for the city.

Corso dei Ceri One of the strangest festivals in Italy, this is held in Gubbio (Umbria) on 15 May, and features a race run by men carrying enormous wooden constructions called *ceri*, in honour of the town's patron saint, Sant'Ubaldo.

Il Palio On 2 July and 16 August, Siena stages this extraordinary horse race in the town's main piazza.

ACTIVITIES
Hiking

It is possible to go on organised treks in Italy, but if you want to go it alone you will find that trails are well marked and there are plenty of refuges in the Alps, in the Alpi Apuane in Tuscany and in the northern parts of the Appennines. The Dolomites in particular provide spectacular walking and trekking opportunities. In Sardinia head for the eastern mountain ranges between Oliena and Urzulei and along the coastal gorges between Dorgali and Baunei (see the Sardinia section for details). If you plan on hiking, a good companion guide is Lonely Planet's *Walking in Italy*.

Skiing

The numerous excellent ski resorts in the Alps and the Apennines usually offer good skiing conditions from December to April.

Cycling

This is a good option if you can't afford a car but want to see the more isolated parts of the country. Classic cycling areas include Tuscany and Umbria.

ACCOMMODATION

The prices mentioned here are intended as a guide only. There is generally a fair degree of fluctuation throughout the country, depending on the season. Prices usually rise by 5% to 10% each year, although sometimes they remain fixed for years, or even drop.

Camping

Facilities throughout Italy are usually reasonable and vary from major complexes with swimming pools, tennis courts and restaurants, to simple camping grounds. Average prices are around L8000 per person and L11,000 or more for a site. Lists of camping grounds in and near major cities are usually available at tourist information offices.

The Touring Club Italiano (TIC) publishes an annual book on all camping sites in Italy, *Campeggi e Villaggi Turistici in Italia* (L32,000). Free camping is forbidden in many of the more beautiful parts of Italy, although the authorities seem to pay less attention in the off season.

Hostels

Hostels in Italy are called *ostelli per la gioventú* and are run by the Associazione Italiana Alberghi per la Gioventú (AIG), which is affiliated with Hostelling International (HI). Prices, including breakfast, range from L16,000 to L24,000. Closing times vary, but are usually from 9 am to 3 or 5 pm and curfews are around midnight. Men and women are often segregated, although some hostels have family accommodation.

An HI membership card is not always required, but it is recommended that you have one. Membership cards can be purchased at major hostels, from student and youth travel centre (CTS) offices and from AIG offices throughout Italy. Pick up a list of all hostels in Italy, with details of prices, locations etc from the AIG office (☎ 06 487 11 52) in Rome, Via Cavour 44.

Pensioni & Hotels

Establishments are required to notify local tourist boards of prices for the coming year and by law must then adhere to those prices (although they do have two legal opportunities each year to increase charges). If tourists believe they are being overcharged, they can make a complaint to the local tourist office. The best advice is to confirm hotel charges before you put your bags down, since many proprietors employ various methods of bill padding. These include charges for showers (usually around L2000), a compulsory breakfast (up to L14,000 in the high season) and compulsory half or full board, although this can often be a good deal in some towns.

The cheapest way to stay in a hotel or pensione is to share a room with two or more people: the cost is usually no more than 15% of the cost of a double room for each additional person. Single rooms are uniformly expensive in Italy (from around L45,000) and quite a number of establishments do not even bother to cater for the single traveller.

There is often no difference between an establishment that calls itself a pensione and one that calls itself an *albergo* (hotel); in fact, some use both titles. *Locande* (similar to pensioni) and *alloggi*, sometimes also known as *affittacamere*, are generally cheaper, but not always.

Rental Accommodation

Finding rental accommodation in the major cities can be difficult and time-consuming and you will often find the cost prohibitive, especially in Rome, Florence, Milan and Venice. In major resort areas, such as the Aeolian Islands and other parts of Sicily, and in the Alps, rental accommodation is reasonably priced and readily available and many tourist offices will provide information by mail or fax.

One organisation which publishes booklets on villas and houses in Tuscany, Umbria, Veneto, Sicily and Rome is Cuendet. Write to Cuendet & Cie spa, Strada di Strove 17, 53035 Monteriggioni, Siena (☎ 0577 57 63 10, fax 0577 30 11 49, ✉ cuende@mbox .vol.it) and ask for a catalogue (US$17). Prices, however, are expensive. CIT offices throughout the world also have lists of villas and apartments for rent in Italy.

Agriturismo

This is basically a farm holiday and is becoming increasingly popular in Italy. Traditionally, the idea was that families rented out rooms in their farmhouses. For detailed information on all facilities in Italy contact Agriturist (☎ 06 68 52 33 37), Corso Vittorio Emanuele 89, 00186 Rome; Web site: www.agriturist.it. It publishes a book (L40,000) listing establishments throughout Italy which is available at its office and in selected bookshops.

Refuges

Before you go hiking in any part of Italy, obtain information about refuges *(rifugi)* from the local tourist offices. Some refuges have private rooms, but many offer dorm-style accommodation, particularly those which are more isolated. Average prices are from L18,000 to L40,000 per person for B&B. A meal costs around the same as at a trattoria. The locations of refuges are marked on good hiking maps and most open only from late June to September. The alpine refuges of CAI (Italian Alpine Club) offer discounts to members of associated foreign alpine clubs.

FOOD & DRINK

Eating is one of life's great pleasures for Italians. Cooking styles vary notably from region to region and significantly between the north and south. In the north the food is rich and often creamy; in central Italy the locals use a lot of olive oil and herbs and regional specialities are noted for their simplicity, fine flavour and the use of fresh produce. As you go further south the food becomes hotter and spicier and the *dolci* (cakes and pastries) sweeter and richer.

Vegetarians will have no problems eating in Italy. Most eating establishments serve a selection of *contorni* (vegetables prepared in a variety of ways).

If you have access to cooking facilities, buy fruit and vegetables at open-air markets and salami, cheese and wine at *alimentari* or *salumerie* (a cross between a grocery store and a delicatessen). Fresh bread is available at a *forno* or *panetteria*.

Restaurants are divided into several categories. A *tavola calda* (literally 'hot table') usually offers inexpensive, pre-prepared meat, pasta and vegetable dishes in a self-service style. A *rosticceria* usually offers cooked meats, but also often has a larger selection of takeaway food. A pizzeria will of course serve pizza, but usually also a full menu. An *osteria* is likely to be either a wine bar offering a small selection of dishes, or a small *trattoria*. Many of the establishments that are in fact restaurants (*ristoranti*) call themselves trattoria and vice versa for reasons best known to themselves.

Most eating establishments charge a *coperto* (cover charge) of around L2000 to L3000, and a *servizio* (service charge) of 10% to 15%. Restaurants are usually open for lunch from 12.30 to 3 pm, but will rarely take orders after 2 pm. In the evening, opening hours vary from north to south. In the north they eat dinner earlier, usually from 7.30 pm, but in Sicily you will be hard-pressed to find a restaurant open before 8.30 pm. Very few restaurants stay open after 11.30 pm.

A full meal will consist of an antipasto, which can vary from *bruschetta*, a type of garlic bread with various toppings, to fried vegetables, or *prosciutto e melone* (ham wrapped around melon). Next comes the *primo piatto*, a pasta dish or risotto, followed by the *secondo piatto* of meat or fish. Italians often then eat an *insalata* (salad) or contorni and round off the meal with dolci and *caffé*, often at a bar on the way home or back to work.

Italian wine is justifiably world-famous. Fortunately, wine is reasonably priced, so you will rarely pay more than L12,000 for a bottle of drinkable wine and as little as L6000 will still buy something of reasonable quality. Try the famous chianti and *brunello* in Tuscany, but also the *vernaccia* of San Gimignano, the *barolo* in Piedmont, the *lacrima christi* or *falanghina* in Naples and the *cannonau* in Sardinia. Beer is known as *birra* and the cheapest local variety is Peroni.

ENTERTAINMENT

Whatever your tastes, there should be some form of entertainment in Italy to keep you amused, including opera, theatre, classical music concerts, rock concerts and traditional festivals. Major entertainment festivals are also held, such as the Festival of Two Worlds in June/July at Spoleto, Umbria Jazz in Perugia in July, Rome's Estate Romana in July, and the Venice Biennale every odd-numbered year. Operas are performed in Verona and Rome throughout summer (for details see the Entertainment sections under both cities) and at various times of the year throughout the country, notably at the opera houses in Milan and Rome.

SPECTATOR SPORTS

Soccer (*calcio*) is the national passion and there are stadiums in all the major towns. If you'd rather watch a game than visit a Roman ruin, check newspapers for details of who's playing where, although tickets for the bigger matches can be hard to find. The Italian Formula One Grand Prix races are held at Monza, just north of Milan in September. The San Marino Grand Prix is held at Imola in May. Good luck finding a ticket, though.

SHOPPING

Italy is synonymous with elegant, fashionable and high-quality clothing, leather goods, glass and ceramics. The problem is that most are very expensive. However, if you happen to be in the country during the summer sales in July and August and the winter sales in January and February, you can pick up incredible bargains.

Getting There & Away

AIR

Although paying full fare to travel by plane in Europe is expensive, there are various discount options, including cut-price fares for students and people aged under 25 or 26 (depending on the airline). There are also standby fares which are usually around 60% of the full fare. Several airlines offer cut-rate fares on legs of international flights between European cities. These are usually the cheapest fares available, but the catch is that they are often during the night or very early in the morning, and the days on which you can fly are severely restricted. Some examples of cheap one-way fares at the time of writing are: Rome-Paris L220,000 (L360,000 return); Rome-London L210,000 (L258,000 return); and Rome-Amsterdam L329,000 return.

Another option is to travel on charter flights. There are several companies throughout Europe which operate these, and fares are usually cheaper than for normal scheduled flights. Italy Sky Shuttle (☎ 020-8748 1333), part of the Air Travel Group, 227 Shepherd's Bush Rd, London W6 7AS, specialises in charter flights, but also offers scheduled flights.

Look in the classified pages of the London Sunday newspapers for information on other cheap flights. Campus Travel (☎ 020-7730 3402), 52 Grosvenor Gardens, SW1W OAG, and STA Travel (☎ 020-7361 6161), 86 Old Brompton Rd, London SW7 3LH, both offer reasonably cheap fares. Within Italy, information on discount fares is available from CTS and Sestante CIT offices (see the earlier Tourist Offices section).

LAND

If you are travelling by bus, train or car to Italy it will be necessary to cross various borders, so remember to check whether you require visas for those countries before leaving home.

Bus

Eurolines is the main international carrier in Europe, with representatives in Italy and throughout the continent. Its head office (☎ 020-7730 8235) is at 52 Grosvenor Gardens, Victoria, London SW1. In Italy the main bus company operating this service is Lazzi, with offices in Florence (☎ 055 35 71 10) at Piazza Adua and in Rome (☎ 06 884 08 40) at Via Tagliamento 27b. Buses leave from Rome, Florence, Milan, Turin, Venice and Naples, as well as numerous other Italian towns, for major cities throughout Europe including London, Paris, Barcelona, Madrid, Amsterdam, Budapest, Prague, Athens and Istanbul. Some ticket prices are Rome-Paris L187,000 (L297,000 return), Rome-London L260,000 (L398,000 return) and Rome-Barcelona L211,000 (L376,000 return).

Train

Eurostar (ES) and Eurocity (EC) trains run from major destinations throughout Europe direct to major Italian cities. On overnight hauls you can book a *cuccetta* (known outside Italy as a couchette or sleeping berth).

Travellers aged under 26 can take advantage of Billet International de Jeunesse tickets (BIJ, also known in Italy as BIGE), which can cut fares by around 50%. They are sold at Transalpino offices at most train stations and at CTS and Sestante CIT offices in Italy, Europe and overseas. Examples of one-way 2nd-class fares are: Rome-Amsterdam L218,900, Rome-Paris L170,000 and Rome-London L284,300. Throughout Europe and in Italy it is worth paying extra for a couchette on night trains. A couchette from Rome to Paris is an extra L48,000.

You can book tickets at train stations or at CTS, Sestante CIT and most travel agencies. Eurostar and Eurocity trains carry a supplement (determined by the distance you are travelling and the type of train).

Car & Motorcycle

Travelling with your own vehicle certainly gives you more flexibility. The drawbacks in Italy are that cars can be inconvenient in larger cities where you'll have to deal with heavy traffic, parking problems, the risk of car theft, the exorbitant price of petrol and toll charges on the autostrade.

If you want to rent a car or motorcycle, you will need a valid EU driving licence, an International Driving Permit, or your driving permit from your own country. If you're driving your own car, you'll need an international insurance certificate, known as a Carta Verde (Green Card), which can be obtained from your insurer.

Hitching

Hitching is never safe in any country and we don't recommend it. Your best bet is to inquire at hostels throughout Europe, where you can often arrange a lift. The International Lift Centre in Florence (☎ 055 28 06 26) and Enjoy Rome (☎ 06 445 18 43) might be able to help organise lifts. It is illegal to hitch on the autostrade.

SEA

Ferries connect Italy to Spain, Croatia, Greece, Turkey, Tunisia and Malta. There are also services to Corsica (from Livorno) and Albania (from Bari and Ancona). See Getting There & Away under Brindisi (for ferries to/from Greece), Ancona (to/from Greece, Albania and Turkey), Venice (to/from Croatia) and Sicily (to/from Malta and Tunisia).

Getting Around

AIR

Travelling by plane is expensive within Italy and it makes much better sense to use the efficient and considerably cheaper rail and bus services. The domestic airlines are Alitalia, Meridiana and Air One. The main airports are in Rome, Pisa, Milan, Bologna, Genova, Torino, Naples, Catania, Palermo and Cagliari, but there are other, smaller airports throughout Italy. Domestic flights can be booked directly with the airlines or through Sestante CIT, CTS and other travel agencies.

Alitalia offers a range of discounts for students, young people and families, and for weekend travel.

BUS

Numerous bus companies operate within Italy. It is usually necessary to make reservations only for long trips, such as Rome-Palermo or Rome-Brindisi. Otherwise, just arrive early enough to claim a seat.

Buses can be a cheaper and faster way to get around if your destination is not on major rail lines, for instance from Umbria to Rome or Florence, and in the interior areas of Sicily and Sardinia.

TRAIN

Travelling by train in Italy is simple, relatively cheap and generally efficient. The Ferrovie dello Stato (FS) is the partially privatised state train system and there are several private railway services throughout the country.

There are several types of trains: Regionale (R), which usually stop at all stations and can be very slow; interRegionale (iR), which run between the regions; Intercity (IC) or Eurocity (EC), which service only the major cities; and Eurostar Italia (ES), which serves major Italian and European cities.

To go on the Intercity, Eurocity and Eurostar Italia trains, you have to pay a *supplemento*, an additional charge determined by the distance you are travelling and the type of train.

All tickets must be validated in the yellow machines at the entrance to all train platforms.

It is not worth buying a Eurail or Inter-Rail pass if you are going to travel only in Italy. The FS offers its own discount passes for travel within the country. These include the Cartaverde for those aged 26 years and under. It costs L40,000, is valid for one year, and entitles you to a 20% discount on all train travel. You can also buy a *biglietto chilometrico* (kilometric ticket), which is valid for two months and allows you to cover 3000km, with a maximum of 20 trips. It costs L214,000 (2nd class) and you must pay the supplement if you catch an Intercity or Eurostar train. Its main attraction is that it can be used by up to five people, either singly or together.

Some examples of 2nd-class fares (plus IC supplement) are Rome-Florence L26,600

(IC L13,100) and Rome-Naples L18,600 (IC L13,200).

CAR & MOTORCYCLE

Roads are generally good throughout the country and there is an excellent system of autostrade (freeways). The main north-south link is the Autostrada del Sole, which extends from Milan to Reggio di Calabria (called the A1 from Milan to Naples and the A3 from Naples to Reggio).

In Italy people drive on the right-hand side of the road and pass on the left. Unless otherwise indicated, you must give way to cars coming from the right. It is compulsory to wear seat belts if they are fitted to the car (front seat belts on all cars and back seat belts on cars produced after 26 April 1990). If you are caught not wearing your seat belt, you will be required to pay a L62,500 on-the-spot fine.

Helmets are now compulsory for every motorcycle and moped rider and passenger.

Some of the Italian cities, including Rome, Bologna, Florence, Milan and Turin have introduced restricted access to both private and rental cars in their historical centres. The restrictions, however, do not apply to vehicles with foreign registrations. *Motorini* (mopeds) and scooters (such as Vespas) are able to enter the zones without any problems.

Speed limits, unless otherwise indicated by local signs, are: on autostrade 130km/h for cars of 1100cc or more, 110km/h for smaller cars and motorcycles under 350cc; on all main, nonurban highways 100km/h; on secondary nonurban highways 90km/h; and in built-up areas 50km/h.

Petrol prices are high in Italy – around L1950 per litre. Petrol is called *benzina*, unleaded petrol is *benzina senza piombo* and diesel is *gasolio*.

The blood-alcohol limit is 0.08% and random breath tests have now been introduced.

Call the Automobile Club d'Italia (ACI) on ☎ 116 for roadside assistance.

BOAT

Navi (large ferries) service the islands of Sicily and Sardinia, and *traghetti* (smaller ferries) and *aliscafi* (hydrofoils) service areas such as Elba, the Aeolian Islands, Capri and Ischia. The main embarkation points for Sicily and Sardinia are Genoa, La Spezia, Livorno, Civitavecchia, Fiumicino and Naples.

Tirrenia Navigazione is the major company servicing the Mediterranean and it has offices throughout Italy. Most long-distance services travel overnight and all ferries carry vehicles (you can usually take a bicycle free of charge).

BICYCLE

Bikes are available for rent in most Italian towns – the cost can be up to L25,000 a day and up to L110,000 a week (see the Getting Around section in each city). However, if you are planning to do a lot of cycling, consider buying a bike in Italy; you can buy a decent second-hand bicycle for L200,000. Bikes can travel in the baggage compartment of some Italian trains (not on the Eurostars or Intercity trains).

Rome

pop 2.6 million

A phenomenal concentration of history, legend and monuments coexist in chaotic harmony in Rome (Roma), as well as an equally phenomenal concentration of people busily going about their everyday lives. It is easy to pick the tourists because they are the only ones to turn their heads as the bus passes the Colosseum.

Rome's origins date to a group of Etruscan, Latin and Sabine settlements on the Palatine, Esquiline, Quirinal and surrounding hills, but it is the legend of Romulus and Remus – the twins raised by a she-wolf – which has captured the popular imagination. The myth says Romulus killed his brother during a battle over who should govern, and then established the city on the Palatine (Palatino), one of the famous Seven Hills of Rome. From the legend grew an empire that eventually controlled almost the entire world known to Europeans at the time.

In Rome there is visible evidence of the two great empires of the western world: the Roman Empire and the Christian Church. On the one hand is the Forum and Colosseum, and on the other St Peter's and the Vatican. In between, in almost every piazza, lies history on so many levels that what you see is only the tip of the iceberg – this is exemplified by

St Peter's Basilica, which stands on the site of an earlier basilica built by the Emperor Constantine over the necropolis where St Peter was buried.

ORIENTATION

Rome is a vast city, but the historical centre is relatively small. Most of the major sights are west – and within walking distance – of the central train station, Stazione Termini. Invest L6000 in the street map and bus guide *Roma*, with a red-and-blue cover; it's available at any newsstand in Stazione Termini.

Plan an itinerary if your time is limited. Many of the major museums and galleries open all day until 5 or 7 pm, and some remain open until 10 pm. Many museums are closed on Monday, but it is a good idea to check.

The main bus terminus is in Piazza del Cinquecento, directly in front of the train station. Many intercity buses arrive and depart from the Piazzale Tiburtina, in front of the Stazione Tiburtina, accessible from Termini on the Metropolitana Linea B.

INFORMATION
Tourist Offices

There is an APT tourist information office (☎ 06 487 12 70) at Stazione Termini, open 8.15 am to 7.15 pm daily. It's in the central courseway.

The main APT office (☎ 06 48 89 92 53/55) is at Via Parigi 5 and opens 8.15 am to 7.15 pm Monday to Friday and until 1.45 pm on Saturday. Walk north-west from Stazione Termini, through Piazza della Repubblica. Via Parigi runs to the right from the top of the piazza, about a five-minute walk from the station. The office has information on hotels and museum opening hours and entrance fees. Staff can also provide information about provincial and Intercity bus services, but you need to be specific about where and when you want to go (see the Getting Around section for further information).

It's likely that you'll get all the information and assistance you need at Enjoy Rome (☎ 06 445 18 43, fax 06 445 07 34) Via Varese 39 (five minutes north-east of the station). Check out the Web site at www.enjoyrome.com. This is a privately run tourist office that offers a free hotel-reservation service. The English-speaking staff can also organise alternative

accommodation such as apartments. They have extensive up-to-date information about Rome and good information about accommodation in other cities. The office is open 8.30 am to 1 pm and 3.30 to 6 pm Monday to Friday and 8.30 am to 1 pm on Saturday.

Money

Banks are open 8.30 am to 1.30 pm and usually from 2.45 to 3.45 pm Monday to Friday. You will find a bank and exchange offices at Stazione Termini. There is also an exchange office (Banco di Santo Spirito) at Fiumicino airport, to your right as you exit from the customs area.

Numerous other exchange offices are scattered throughout the city, including American Express (☎ 06 676 41), at Piazza di Spagna 38, and Thomas Cook (☎ 06 4 82 81 82), at Piazza Barberini 21.

Otherwise, go to any bank in the city centre. The Banca Commerciale Italiana, Piazza Venezia, is reliable for receiving money transfers and will give cash advances on both Visa and MasterCard. Credit cards can also be used in automatic teller machines (ATMs), known as bancomats, to obtain cash 24 hours a day. You'll need to get a PIN from your bank.

Post & Communications

The main post office is at Piazza San Silvestro 19, just off Via del Tritone, and is open 9 am to 6 pm Monday to Sunday (Saturday to 2 pm). *Fermo posta* (poste restante) is available here. You can send telegrams from the office next door (open 24 hours).

The Vatican post office (☎ 06 69 88 34 06) in Piazza di San Pietro (St Peter's Square) is open 8 am to 7 pm Monday to Saturday (8.30 am to 2.15 pm Monday to Saturday, July and August). The service is faster and more reliable, but there's no fermo posta. The postcode for central Rome is 00100, although for fermo posta at the main post office it is 00186.

There is a Telecom office at Stazione Termini, from where you can make international calls direct or through an operator. Another office is near the station, on Via San Martino della Battaglia opposite the Pensione Lachea. International calls can easily be made with a phonecard from any public telephone. Phonecards can be purchased at tobacconists and newspaper stands.

ROME (ROMA)

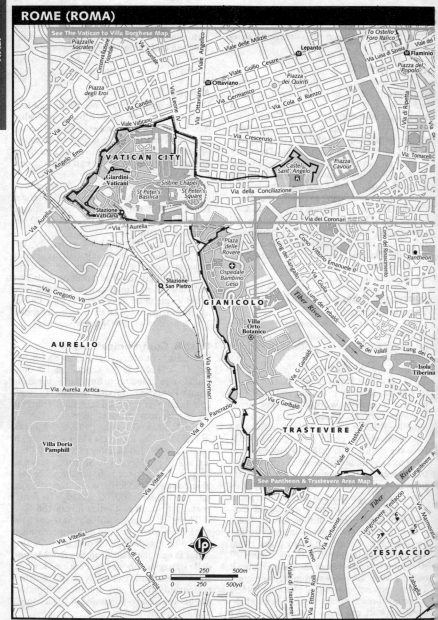

See The Vatican to Villa Borghese Map

Piazzalle
Socrates

Piazza
degli Eroi

VATICAN CITY

Giardini
Vaticani

Sistine Chapel

St Peter's
Basilica

St Peter's
Square

Stazione
Vaticana

To Ostello
Foro Italico

Lepanto

Piazza
del
Popolo

Flaminio

Ottaviano

Piazza
dei Quiriti

Castel
Sant' Angelo

Piazza
Cavour

Via della Conciliazione

Via dei Coronari

AURELIO

Plaza
delle
Rovere

Ospedale
Bambino
Gesù

Stazione
San Pietro

GIANICOLO

Villa
Orto
Botanico

Pantheon

**Isola
Tiberina**

Tiber River

Villa Doria
Pamphili

TRASTEVERE

See Pantheon & Trastevere Area Map

TESTACCIO

0   250   500m

0   250   500yd

euro currency converter €1 = L1936

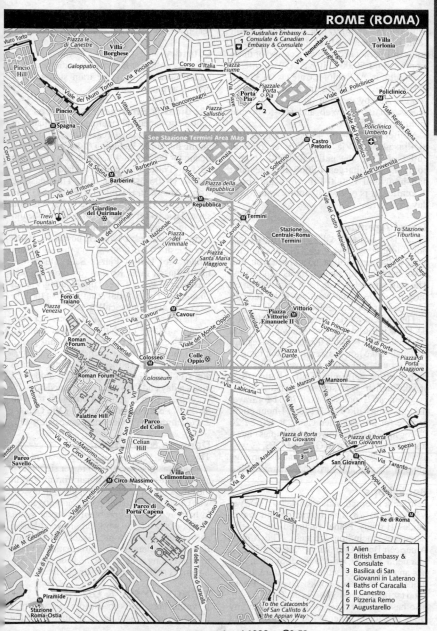

ROME (ROMA)

To Australian Embassy &
Consulate & Canadian
Embassy & Consulate

Muro Torto

Piazza le
di Canestre

Villa
Borghese

Villa
Torlonia

Via Nomentana

Galoppatio

Via Regina
Margherita

Pincio
Hill

Via Pinciana

Corso d'Italia

Piazza
Fiume

Piazzale
Porta
Pia

Policlinico

Via del Policlinico

Viale del Muro Torto

Via Boncompagni

Porta
Pia

Pincio

Via Vittorio Veneto

Piazza
Sallustio

Via del Policlinico

Policlinico
Umberto I

M Spagna

Via Sistina

Via Piave

Viale Regina Elena

See Stazione Termini Area Map

Castro
Pretorio

Il Corso

Via del Tritone

M
Barberini

Via Barberini

Barberini

Via Orlando

Via Cernaia

Via Solferino

Viale del Castro Pretorio

Viale dell'Università

Trevi
Fountain

Giardino
del Quirinale

Piazza della
Repubblica

Via del Corso

Via del Quirinale

Repubblica

M Termini

To Stazione
Tiburtina

Via Nazionale

Piazza
del
Viminale

Stazione
Centrale-Roma
Termini

Piazza
Santa Maria
Maggiore

Via Cavour

Via Tiburtina

Via dei Sardi

Foro di
Traiano

Via Cavour

Via Carlo Alberto

Piazza
Venezia

Via dei Fori Imperiali

M Cavour

Piazza
Vittorio
Emanuele II

Vittorio
M

Via Principe
Eugenio

Via di Porta
Maggiore

Roman
Forum

Colosseo
M

Colle
Oppio

Piazza
Dante

Via Manzoni

Piazza di
Porta
Maggiore

Roman Forum

Viale del Monte Oppio

Colosseum

Via Merulana

Via Labicana

Viale Manzoni

Manzoni
M

Palatine Hill

Via di San Gregorio VII

Parco
del Celio

Via Claudia

Viale Manzoni

Via Emanuele Filiberto

Parco
Savello

Via del Circo Massimo

Celian
Hill

Piazza di Porta
San Giovanni

Piazza di Porta
San Giovanni

Via La Spezia

3

San Giovanni
M

Via Taranto

Via Appia Nuova

Villa
Celimontana

Via di Amba Aradam

M Circo Massimo

Viale Aventino

Parco di
Porta Capena

Re di Roma
M

Via delle Terme di Caracalla

Via Druso

Via Gallia

4

Via delle Terme di Caracalla

1	Alien
2	British Embassy & Consulate
3	Basilica di San Giovanni in Laterano
4	Baths of Caracalla
5	Il Canestro
6	Pizzeria Remo
7	Augustarello

Piramide
M

Stazione
Roma-Ostia

To the Catacombs
of San Callisto &
the Appian Way

Email & Internet Access

Bibli (☎ 06 588 40 97), at Via dei Fienaroli 28 in Trastevere, is a bookshop that offers 10 hours of Internet access over a period of three months for L50,000. It has a Web site at www.bibli.it. At Explorer Café (☎ 06 324 17 57), Via dei Gracci 85 (near the Vatican), you can pay by the hour (about L12,000) to access email, the Web and CD-Rom and multimedia libraries.

Nolitel Italia (☎ 06 42 00 70 01) at Via Sicilia 54 near Via Veneto, is an official outlet of TIM, the national mobile phone company. It charges L8000 for the first half-hour and L7000 for every half-hour thereafter. It is open 9.30 am to 7 pm Monday to Saturday.

Travel Agencies

There is a Sestante CIT office (Italy's national tourist agency; ☎ 06 474 65 55) at Piazza della Repubblica 65, where you can make bookings for planes, trains and ferries. The staff speak English, have information on fares for students and young people, and can arrange tours of Rome and surrounds.

The student tourist centre, CTS (☎ 06 462 04 31, ✉ info@cts.it), Via Genova 16 off Via Nazionale, offers much the same services and will also make hotel reservations, but focuses on discount and student travel. There is a branch office at Termini. Staff at both offices speak English. Web site: www.cts.it.

American Express (☎ 06 6 76 41 for travel information; ☎ 06 7 22 82 for 24-hour client service for lost or stolen cards; ☎ 167 87 20 00 for lost or stolen travellers cheques) has a travel service similar to CIT and CTS, as well as a hotel-reservation service, and can arrange tours of the city and surrounding areas.

Bookshops

Feltrinelli International (☎ 06 487 01 71), Via VE Orlando 78, has literature and travel guides (Lonely Planet included) in several languages, including Japanese. The Anglo-American Book Company (☎ 06 679 52 22), Via della Vite 27, off Piazza di Spagna, also has an excellent selection of literature, travel guides and reference books. The Lion Bookshop (☎ 06 32 65 04 37), Via dei Greci 33-36, also has a good range, as does the Economy Book & Video Center (☎ 06 474 68 77), Via

Torino 136, off Via Nazionale, which also has second-hand books.

Laundry

There is an Onda Blu coin laundrette at Via Lamarmora 10, near the train station. It is open 8 am to 10 pm daily.

Medical & Emergency Services

Emergency medical treatment is available in the *pronto soccorso* (casualty sections) at public hospitals, including Ospedale San Gallicano (☎ 06 588 23 90), Via di San Gallicano 25/a in Trastevere; and Ospedale Fatebenefratelli (☎ 06 5 87 31), Isola Tiberina. The Rome American Hospital (☎ 06 2 25 51), Via E Longoni 81, is a private hospital and you should use its services only if you have health insurance and have consulted your insurance company. Rome's paediatric hospital is Bambino Gesú (☎ 06 6 85 91) on the Janiculum (Gianicolo) Hill at Piazza Sant' Onofrio 4. From Piazza della Rovere (on the Lungotevere near St Peter's) head uphill along Via del Gianicolo. The hospital is at the top of the hill.

For an ambulance call ☎ 118.

There is a pharmacy in Stazione Termini, open 7 am to 11 pm daily (closed in August). Otherwise, closed pharmacies should post a list in their windows of others open nearby.

The *questura* (police headquarters; ☎ 06 468 61) is at Via San Vitale 15. It's open 24 hours a day and thefts can be reported here. Its Foreigners Bureau (Ufficio Stranieri; ☎ 06 46 86 29 77) is around the corner at Via Genova 2. For immediate police attendance call ☎ 113.

Dangers & Annoyances

Thieves are very active in the areas in and around Stazione Termini, at major sights such as the Colosseum and Roman Forum, and in the city's most expensive shopping streets, eg, Via Condotti, although police activity seems to have reduced the problem in recent years. Pickpockets like to work on crowded buses, particularly No 40 from St Peter's to Termini. For more comprehensive information on how to avoid being robbed, see the Dangers & Annoyances section earlier in this chapter.

THINGS TO SEE & DO

It would take years to explore every corner of Rome, months to begin to appreciate the incredible number of monuments and weeks for a thorough tour of the city. You can, however, cover most of the important monuments in five days, or three at a minimum.

Piazza del Campidoglio

Designed by Michelangelo in 1538, the piazza is on the Capitolino (Capitoline Hill), the most important of Rome's seven hills. Formerly the seat of the ancient Roman government, it is now the seat of Rome's municipal government. Michelangelo also designed the facades of the three palaces that border the piazza. A modern copy of the bronze equestrian statue of Emperor Marcus Aurelius stands at its centre: the original is now on display in the ground-floor portico of the Palazzo Nuovo (also called Palazzo del Museo Capitolino). This and the other two palaces flanking the piazza (Palazzo del Museo Capitolino and Palazzo dei Conservatori) make up the **Musei Capitolini**, well worth visiting for their collections of ancient Roman sculpture, including the famous *Capitoline Wolf*, an Etruscan statue dating from the 6th century BC. They are open 10 am to 9 pm Tuesday to Sunday. Admission is L12,000.

Walk to the right of the Palazzo del Senato to see a panorama of the Roman Forum. Walk to the left of the same building to reach the ancient Roman **Carcere Mamertino**, where St Peter was believed to have been imprisoned.

The **Chiesa di Santa Maria d'Aracoeli** is between the Campidoglio and the Monumento Vittorio Emanuele II at the highest point of the Capitoline Hill. It is built on the site where legend says the Tiburtine Sybil told the Emperor Augustus of the coming birth of Christ.

Piazza Venezia

This piazza is overshadowed by a neoclassical monument dedicated to Vittorio Emanuele II, often referred to by Italians as the *macchina da scrivere* (typewriter) because it resembles one. Built to commemorate Italian unification, the piazza incorporates the **Altare della Patria** and the tomb of the unknown soldier, as well as the **Museo del Risorgimento**. Also in the piazza is the 15th-century **Palazzo Venezia**, which was Mussolini's official residence and now houses a museum.

Roman Forum & Palatine Hill

The commercial, political and religious centre of ancient Rome, the Forum stands in a valley between the Capitoline and Palatine (Palatino) hills. Originally marshland, the area was drained during the early republican era and became a centre for political rallies, public ceremonies and senate meetings. Its importance declined along with the empire after the 4th century, and the temples, monuments and buildings constructed by successive emperors, consuls and senators over a period of 900 years fell into ruin, eventually to be used as pasture.

The area was systematically excavated in the 18th and 19th centuries, and excavations are continuing. You can enter the Forum from Via dei Fori Imperiali, which leads from Piazza Venezia to the Colosseum. Entrance to the Forum is free, but it costs L12,000 to head up to the Palatine. The Forum and Palatine Hill are open 9 am to 7 pm Monday to Saturday in summer (to 4 pm in winter), and 9 am to 1 pm on Sunday year-round.

As you enter the Forum, to your left is the **Tempio di Antonino e Faustina**, erected by the senate in 141 AD and transformed into a church in the 8th century. To your right are the remains of the **Basilica Aemilia**, built in 179 BC and demolished during the Renaissance, when it was plundered for its precious marble. The Via Sacra, which traverses the Forum from north-west to south-east, runs in front of the basilica. Towards the Campidoglio is the **Curia**, once the meeting place of the Roman senate and converted into a Christian church in the Middle Ages. The church was dismantled and the Curia restored in the 1930s. In front of the Curia is the **Lapis Niger**, a large piece of black marble which legend says covered the grave of Romulus. Under the Lapis Niger is the oldest known Latin inscription, dating from the 6th century BC.

The **Arco di Settimo Severo** was erected in 203 AD in honour of this emperor and his sons, and is considered one of Italy's major triumphal arches. A circular base stone beside the arch marks the *umbilicus urbis*, the symbolic centre of ancient Rome. To the south is the **Rostrum**, used in ancient times by public speakers and once decorated by the rams of captured ships.

South along the Via Sacra is the **Tempio di Saturno**, one of the most important temples in ancient Rome. Eight granite columns remain. The **Basilica Julia**, in front of the temple, was the seat of justice, and nearby is the **Tempio di Giulio Cesare** (Temple of Julius Caesar), which was erected by Augustus in 29 BC on the site where Caesar's body was burned and Mark Antony read his famous speech. Back towards the Palatine Hill is the **Tempio dei Castori**, built in 489 BC in honour of the Heavenly Twins, or Dioscuri. It is easily recognisable by its three remaining columns.

In the area south-east of the temple is the **Chiesa di Santa Maria Antiqua**, the oldest Christian church in the Forum. It is closed to the public. Back on the Via Sacra is the **Case delle Vestali**, home of the virgins who tended the sacred flame in the adjoining **Tempio di Vesta**. If the flame went out, it was seen as a bad omen. The next major monument is the vast **Basilica di Costantino**. Its impressive design inspired Renaissance architects. The **Arco di Tito**, at the Colosseum end of the Forum, was built in 81 AD in honour of the victories of the emperors Titus and Vespasian against Jerusalem.

From here climb the Palatino, where wealthy Romans built their homes and where legend says that Romulus founded the city. Archaeological evidence shows that the earliest settlements in the area were on the Palatine. Like the Forum, the buildings of the Palatine fell into ruin and in the Middle Ages the hill became the site of convents and churches. During the Renaissance, wealthy families established their gardens here. The Farnese gardens were built over the ruins of the Domus Tiberiana, which is now under excavation.

Worth a look is the impressive **Domus Augustana**, which was the private residence of the emperors; the **Domus Flavia**, the residence of Domitian; the **Tempio della Magna Mater**, built in 204 BC to house a black stone connected with the Asiatic goddess Cybele; and the **Casa di Livia**, thought to have been the house of the wife of Emperor Augustus, and decorated with frescoes.

Colosseum

Originally known as the Flavian Amphitheatre, Rome's most famous monument was begun by Emperor Vespasian in 72 AD in the grounds of Nero's Golden House, and completed by his son Titus. The massive structure could seat 80,000 and featured bloody gladiatorial combat and wild beast shows that resulted in thousands of human and animal deaths.

In the Middle Ages the Colosseum became a fortress and was later used as a quarry for travertine and marble for the Palazzo Venezia and other buildings. Restoration works have been underway since 1992. Opening hours are 9 am to 7 pm daily in summer (to one hour before sunset in winter). Entry is L10,000.

Arch of Constantine

On the west side of the Colosseum is the triumphal arch built to honour Constantine following his victory over his rival Maxentius at the battle of Milvian Bridge (near the present-day Zona Olimpica, north-west of the Villa Borghese) in 312 AD. Its decorative reliefs were taken from earlier structures.

Circus Maximus

There is not much to see here apart from the few ruins that remain of what was once a chariot racetrack big enough to hold 300,000 spectators.

Baths of Caracalla

The huge Terme di Càracalla complex, covering 10 hectares, could hold 1600 people and included shops, gardens, libraries and entertainment. Begun by Antonius Caracalla and inaugurated in 217 AD, the baths were used until the 6th century. From the 1930s to 1993 they were an atmospheric venue for opera performances in summer. These performances have now been banned to prevent further damage to the ruins. The baths are open 9 am to 7 pm Monday to Saturday and to 2 pm on Sunday in summer; in winter until 3 pm daily. Entry is L8000.

Some Significant Churches

Down Via Cavour from Stazione Termini is **Santa Maria Maggiore**, built in the 5th century. Its main baroque facade was added in the 18th century, preserving the 13th-century mosaics of the earlier facade. Its bell tower is Romanesque and the interior is baroque. There are 5th-century mosaics decorating the triumphal arch and nave.

Follow Via Merulana to reach **Basilica di San Giovanni in Laterano**, Rome's cathedral.

The original church was built in the 4th century, the first Christian basilica in Rome. Largely destroyed over a long period of time, it was rebuilt in the 17th century.

Basilica di San Pietro in Vincoli, just off Via Cavour, is worth a visit because it houses Michelangelo's *Moses* and his unfinished statues of Leah and Rachel, as well as the chains worn by St Peter during his imprisonment before being crucified.

Chiesa di San Clemente, Via San Giovanni in Laterano, near the Colosseum, defines how history in Rome exists on many levels. The 12th-century church at street level was built over a 4th-century church which was, in turn, built over a 1st-century Roman house containing a temple dedicated to the pagan god Mithras.

Santa Maria in Cosmedin, north-west of Circus Maximus, is regarded as one of the finest medieval churches in Rome. It has a seven-storey bell tower and its interior is heavily decorated with Cosmatesque inlaid marble, including the beautiful floor. The main attraction for the tourist hordes is, however, the **Bocca della Verità** (Mouth of Truth). Legend has it that if you put your right hand into the mouth and tell a lie, it will snap shut.

Baths of Diocletian

Started by Emperor Diocletian, these baths were completed in the 4th century. The complex of baths, libraries, concert halls and gardens covered about 13 hectares and could house up to 3000 people. After the aqueduct that fed the baths was destroyed by invaders in 536 AD, the complex fell into decay. Parts of the ruins are now incorporated into the Basilica di Santa Maria degli Angeli.

Basilica di Santa Maria degli Angeli

Designed by Michelangelo, this church incorporates what was the great central hall and *tepidarium* (lukewarm room) of the original baths. During the following centuries his work was drastically changed and little evidence of his design, apart from the great vaulted ceiling of the church, remains. An interesting feature of the church is a double meridian in the transept, one tracing the polar star and the other telling the precise time of the sun's zenith. The church is open from

7.30 am to 12.30 pm and from 4 to 6.30 pm. Through the sacristy is an entrance to a stairway leading to the upper terraces of the ruins.

Museo Nazionale Romano

This museum, located in three separate buildings, houses an important collection of ancient art, including Greek and Roman sculpture. The museum is largely housed in the restored Palazzo Altemps, Piazza Sant'Apollinare 44, near Piazza Navona. It contains numerous important pieces from the Ludovisi collection, including the *Ludovisi Throne*. Entry is L10,000. Another part of the same museum is in the Palazzo Massimo alle Terme, in Piazza dei Cinquecento. It contains a collection of frescoes and mosaics from the Villa of Livia, excavated at Prima Porta. Entry is L12,000. Both sections open 9 am to 6.45 pm Tuesday to Saturday (to 7.45 pm on Sunday).

Via Vittorio Veneto

This was Rome's hot spot in the 1960s, where film stars could be spotted at the expensive outdoor cafes. These days you will find only tourists, and the atmosphere of Fellini's *La Dolce Vita* is long dead.

Piazza di Spagna & Spanish Steps

This piazza, church and famous staircase (Scalinata della Trinitá dei Monti) have long provided a major gathering place for foreigners. Built with a legacy from the French in 1725, but named after the Spanish Embassy to the Holy See, the steps lead to the church of Trinitá dei Monti, which was built by the French.

In the 18th century the most beautiful men and women of Italy gathered there, waiting to be chosen as artists' models. To the right as you face the steps is the house where Keats spent the last three months of his life, and where he died in 1821. In the piazza is the boat-shaped fountain of the **Barcaccia**, believed to be by Pietro Bernini, father of the famous Gian Lorenzo. One of Rome's most elegant shopping streets, **Via Condotti**, runs off the piazza towards Via del Corso.

Piazza del Popolo

This vast piazza was laid out in the 16th century and redesigned in the early 19th century by Giuseppe Valadier. It is at the foot of the

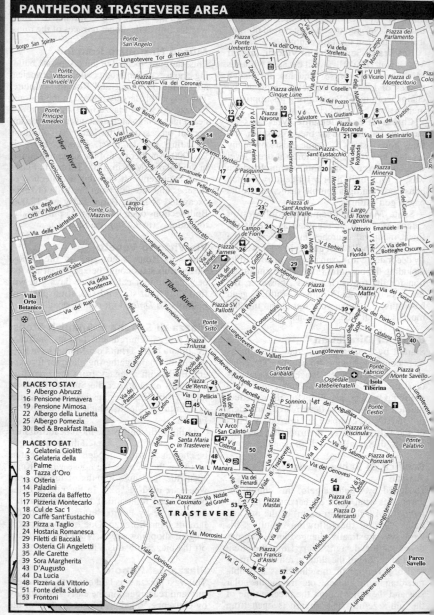

PANTHEON & TRASTEVERE AREA

PLACES TO STAY
9 Albergo Abruzzi
16 Pensione Primavera
19 Pensione Mimosa
22 Albergo della Lunetta
25 Albergo Pomezia
30 Bed & Breakfast Italia

PLACES TO EAT
2 Gelateria Giolitti
3 Gelateria della
   Palme
8 Tazza d'Oro
13 Osteria
14 Paladini
15 Pizzeria da Baffetto
17 Pizzeria Montecarlo
20 Caffè Sant'Eustachio
24 Hostaria Romanesca
29 Filetti di Baccalà
33 Osteria Gli Angeletti
35 Alle Carette
39 Sora Margherita
43 D'Augusto
44 Da Lucia
48 Pizzeria da Vittorio
51 Fonte della Salute
53 Frontoni

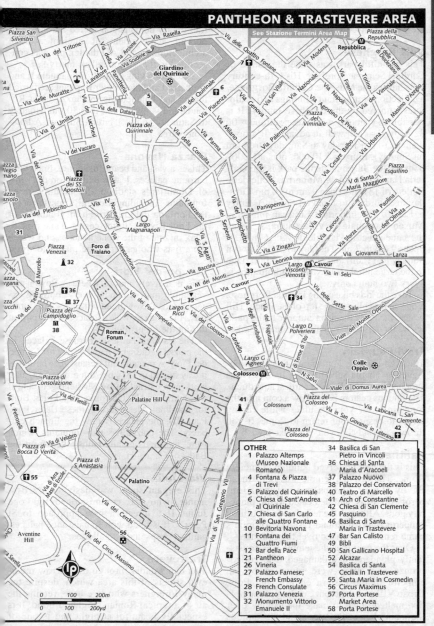

PANTHEON & TRASTEVERE AREA

See Stazione Termini Area Map

OTHER

1 Palazzo Altemps (Museo Nazionale Romano)
4 Fontana & Piazza di Trevi
5 Palazzo del Quirinale
6 Chiesa di Sant'Andrea al Quirinale
7 Chiesa di San Carlo alle Quattro Fontane
10 Bevitoria Navona
11 Fontana dei Quattro Fiumi
12 Bar della Pace
21 Pantheon
26 Vineria
27 Palazzo Farnese; French Embassy
28 French Consulate
31 Palazzo Venezia
32 Monumento Vittorio Emanuele II

34 Basilica di San Pietro in Vincoli
36 Chiesa di Santa Maria d'Aracoeli
37 Palazzo Nuovo
38 Palazzo dei Conservatori
40 Teatro di Marcello
41 Arch of Constantine
42 Chiesa di San Clemente
45 Pasquino
46 Basilica di Santa Maria in Trastevere
47 Bar San Calisto
49 Bibli
50 San Gallicano Hospital
52 Alcazar
54 Basilica di Santa Cecilia in Trastevere
55 Santa Maria in Cosmedin
56 Circus Maximus
57 Porta Portese Market Area
58 Porta Portese

Pincio Hill, from where there is a panoramic view of the city.

Villa Borghese

This beautiful park was once the estate of Cardinal Scipione Borghese. His 17th-century villa houses the **Museo e Galleria Borghese,** a collection of important paintings and sculptures gathered by the Borghese family. It is possible to visit only with a reservation (☎ 06 32 81 01), so call well in advance. It's open 9 am to 10 pm Tuesday to Saturday (to 8 pm on Sunday). Entry is L10,000, plus a L2000 booking fee. Just outside the park is the **Galleria Nazionale d'Arte Moderna**, Viale delle Belle Arti 131. It's open 9 am to 10 pm Tuesday to Saturday (to 8 pm on Sunday). Entry is L8000. The important Etruscan museum, **Museo Nazionale di Villa Giulia**, is along the same street in Piazzale di Villa Giulia. It opens 9 am to 7 pm Tuesday to Saturday (on Sunday to 11 am) and entry is L10,000. Due to the large numbers of visitors admittance is every two hours only.

Take the kids bike riding in Villa Borghese. You can hire bikes at the top of the Pincio Hill or near the Porta Pinciana entrance to the park, where there is also a small amusement park.

Trevi Fountain

The high-baroque Fontana di Trevi was designed by Nicola Salvi in 1732. Its water was supplied by one of Rome's earliest aqueducts. The famous custom is to throw a coin into the fountain (over your shoulder while facing away) to ensure your return to Rome. If you throw a second coin you can make a wish.

Pantheon

This is the best preserved building of ancient Rome. The original temple was built in 27 BC by Marcus Agrippa, son-in-law of Emperor Augustus, and dedicated to the planetary gods. Although the temple was rebuilt by Emperor Hadrian around 120 AD, Agrippa's name remains inscribed over the entrance.

Over the centuries the temple was consistently plundered and damaged. The gilded-bronze roof tiles were removed by an emperor of the eastern empire, and Pope Urban VIII had the bronze ceiling of the portico melted down to make the canopy over the main altar of St Peter's and 80 cannons

for Castel Sant'Angelo. The Pantheon's extraordinary dome is considered the most important achievement of ancient Roman architecture. In 608 AD the temple was consecrated to the Virgin and all martyrs.

The Italian kings Vittorio Emanuele II and Umberto I and the painter Raphael are buried there. The Pantheon is in Piazza della Rotonda and is open 9 am to 6.30 pm Monday to Saturday and to 1 pm on Sunday. Admission is free.

Piazza Navona

This is a vast and beautiful square, lined with baroque palaces. It was laid out on the ruins of Domitian's stadium and features three fountains, including Bernini's masterpiece, the **Fontana dei Quattro Fiumi** (Fountain of the Four Rivers), in the centre. Take time to relax on one of the stone benches and watch the artists who gather in the piazza to work.

Campo de' Fiori

This is a lively piazza where a flower and vegetable market is held every morning except Sunday. Now lined with bars and trattorias, the piazza was a place of execution during the Inquisition.

The **Palazzo Farnese** (Farnese Palace), in the piazza of the same name, is just off Campo de' Fiori. A magnificent Renaissance building, it was started in 1514 by Antonio da Sangallo, work was carried on by Michelangelo and it was completed by Giacomo della Porta. Built for Cardinal Alessandro Farnese (later Pope Paul III), the palace is now the French embassy. The piazza has two fountains, which were enormous granite baths taken from the Baths of Caracalla.

Via Giulia

This elegant street was designed by Bramante, who was commissioned by Pope Julius II to create a new approach to St Peter's. It is lined with Renaissance palaces, antique shops and art galleries.

Trastevere

You can wander through the narrow medieval streets of this area which, despite the many foreigners who live here, retains the air of a typical Roman neighbourhood. It is especially beautiful at night and is one of

Market stallholder, Basilicata, Italy

The famous leaning bell tower, Pisa, Italy

Gondolas are a renowned mode of transport, Venice, Italy

MARTIN MOOS

Nightlife abounds on Lijnbaansgracht, Amsterdam, Netherlands

AMERENS HEDWICH

Overlooking Amsterdam's centre

ELLIOT DANIEL

A short black and a long joint

MARTIN MOOS

Some of Amsterdam's 550,000 bicycles

the more interesting areas for bar-hopping or a meal.

Of particular note here is the **Basilica di Santa Maria in Trastevere**, in the lovely piazza of the same name. It is believed to be the oldest church dedicated to the Virgin in Rome. Although the first church was built on the site in the 4th century, the present structure was built in the 12th century and features a Romanesque bell tower and facade, with a mosaic of the Virgin. Its interior was redecorated during the baroque period, but the vibrant mosaics in the apse and on the triumphal arch date from the 12th century. Also take a look at the **Basilica di Santa Cecilia** in Trastevere.

Gianicolo

Go to the top of the Gianicolo (Janiculum), the hill between St Peter's and Trastevere, for a panoramic view of Rome.

Catacombs

There are several catacombs in Rome, consisting of miles of tunnels carved out of volcanic rock, which were the meeting and burial places of early Christians in Rome. The largest are along the Via Appia Antica, just outside the city and accessible on bus No 660 (from Piazza dei Cinquecento). The **Catacombs of San Callisto** and **Catacombs of San Sebastiano** are almost next to each other on the Via Appia Antica. San Callisto is open 8.30 am to noon and 2.30 to 5.30 pm (closed Wednesday and all of February). San Sebastiano is open 8.30 am to noon and 2.30 to 5 pm (closed Sunday and all of November). Admission to each costs L8000 and is with a guide only.

Vatican City

After the unification of Italy, the papal states of central Italy became part of the new kingdom of Italy, causing a considerable rift between church and state. In 1929, Mussolini, under the Lateran Treaty, gave the pope full sovereignty over what is now the Vatican City.

The tourist office (☎ 06 69 88 44 66), in Piazza San Pietro to the left of the basilica, is open 8.30 am to 7 pm Monday to Saturday. Guided tours of the Vatican City gardens (L18,000) can be organised here. A few doors up is the Vatican post office (☎ 06 69 88 34 06), said to offer a much more reliable service

than the normal Italian postal system. It is open 8 am to 7 pm Monday to Saturday (8.15am to 2.15 pm Monday to Saturday, July and August).

The city has its own postal service, currency, newspaper, radio station, train station and army of Swiss Guards.

St Peter's Basilica & Square The largest and most famous church in the Christian world, **San Pietro** (St Peter's) stands on the site where St Peter was buried. The first church on the site was built during Constantine's reign in the 4th century, and in 1506 work started on a new basilica, designed by Bramante.

Although several architects were involved in its construction, it is generally held that St Peter's owes more to Michelangelo, who took over the project in·1547 at the age of 72 and was particularly responsible for the design of the dome. He died before the church was completed. The cavernous interior contains numerous treasures, including Michelangelo's superb *Pietá*, sculpted when he was only 24 years old and the only work to carry his signature (on the sash across the breast of the Madonna). It has been protected by bulletproof glass since an attack in 1972 by a hammer-wielding vandal.

Bernini's huge, baroque *Baldacchino* (a heavily sculpted bronze canopy over the papal altar) stands 29m high and is an extraordinary work of art. Another point of note is the red porphyry disc near the central door, which marks the spot where Charlemagne and later emperors were crowned by the pope.

Entrance to Michelangelo's soaring dome is to the right as you climb the stairs to the atrium of the basilica. Make the entire climb on foot for L7000, or pay L8000 and take the elevator for part of the way (recommended).

The basilica is open 7 am to 7 pm daily (6 pm in winter) and dress rules are stringently enforced – no shorts, miniskirts or sleeveless tops. Prams and strollers must be left in a designated area outside the basilica.

Bernini's **Piazza San Pietro** (St Peter's Square) is considered a masterpiece. Laid out in the 17th century as a place for Christians of the world to gather, the immense piazza is bound by two semicircular colonnades, each of which is made up of four rows of Doric

ITALY

columns. In the centre of the piazza is an obelisk that was brought to Rome by Caligula from Heliopolis (in ancient Egypt). When you stand on the dark paving stones between the obelisk and either of the fountains, the colonnades appear to have only one row of columns.

The Pope usually gives a public audience at 10 or 11 am every Wednesday in the Papal Audience Hall. You must make a booking, either in person or by fax to the Prefettura della Casa Pontifica (☎ 06 69 88 30 17, fax 06 69 88 58 63), on the Monday or Thursday before the audience between 9 am and 1 pm. Go

through the bronze doors under the colonnade to the right as you face the basilica.

Vatican Museums From St Peter's follow the wall of the Vatican City (to the right as you face the basilica) to the museums, or catch the regular shuttle bus (L2500) from the piazza in front of the tourist office. The museums are open 8.45 am to 3.45 pm Monday to Friday (to 12.45 on Saturday). Admission is L15,000. The museums are closed on Sunday and public holidays, but open on the last Sunday of every month from 9 am to 1 pm (free admission, but queues are always very

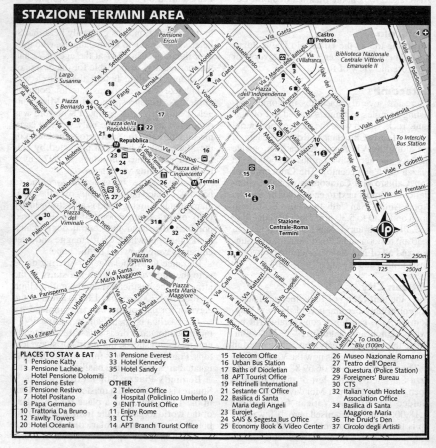

STAZIONE TERMINI AREA

PLACES TO STAY & EAT			
1 Pensione Katty	31 Pensione Everest	15 Telecom Office	26 Museo Nazionale Romano
3 Pensione Lachea;	33 Hotel Kennedy	16 Urban Bus Station	27 Teatro dell'Opera
Hotel Pensione Dolomiti	35 Hotel Sandy	17 Baths of Diocletian	28 Questura (Police Station)
5 Pensione Ester		18 APT Tourist Office	29 Foreigners' Bureau
6 Pensione Restivo	**OTHER**	19 Feltrinelli International	30 CTS
7 Hotel Positano	2 Telecom Office	21 Sestante CIT Office	32 Italian Youth Hostels
8 Papa Germano	4 Hospital (Policlinico Umberto I)	22 Basilica di Santa	Association Office
10 Trattoria Da Bruno	9 ENIT Tourist Office	Maria degli Angeli	34 Basilica di Santa
12 Fawlty Towers	11 Enjoy Rome	23 Eurojet	Maggiore Maria
20 Hotel Oceania	13 CTS	24 SAIS & Segesta Bus Office	36 The Druid's Den
	14 APT Branch Tourist Office	25 Economy Book & Video Center	37 Circolo degli Artisti

long). Guided visits to the Vatican gardens cost L18,000 and can be booked by calling ☎ 06 69 88 44 66.

The Vatican museums contain an incredible collection of art and treasures collected by the popes, and you will need several hours to see the most important areas and museums. The Sistine Chapel comes towards the end of a full visit; otherwise, you can walk straight there and then work your way back through the museums.

The **Museo Pio-Clementino**, containing Greek and Roman antiquities, is on the ground floor near the entrance. Through the tapestry and map galleries are the **Stanze di Rafaello**, once the private apartments of Pope Julius II, decorated with frescoes by Raphael. Of particular interest is the magnificent **Stanza della Segnatura**, which features **Raphael's masterpieces** *The School of Athens* and *Disputation on the Sacrament*.

From Raphael's rooms, go down the stairs to the sumptuous **Appartamento Borgia**, decorated with frescoes by Pinturicchio, then go down another flight of stairs to the **Sistine Chapel**, the private papal chapel built in 1473 for Pope Sixtus IV. Michelangelo's wonderful frescoes of the *Creation* on the barrel-vaulted ceiling and *Last Judgment* on the end wall have both been restored to their original brilliance. It took Michelangelo four years, at the height of the Renaissance, to paint the ceiling; 24 years later he painted the extraordinary *Last Judgment*. The other walls of the chapel were painted by artists including Botticelli, Ghirlandaio, Pinturicchio and Signorelli. To best enjoy the ceiling frescoes, a pocket mirror is recommended so that you don't have to strain your neck.

ORGANISED TOURS

Enjoy Rome (☎ 06 445 18 43, 167-27 48 19 toll-free), Via Varese 39, offers walking or bike tours of Rome's main sights for L35,000 per person and a shuttle service for Pompeii. ATAC bus No 110 leaves daily at 3.30 pm (2.30 pm in winter) from Piazza dei Cinquecento, in front of Stazione Termini, for a three-hour tour of the city. The cost is L15,000. Vastours (☎ 06 481 43 09), Via Piemonte 34, operates half-day coach tours of Rome from L48,000 and full-day coach tours

of the city from L130,000, as well as tours to Tivoli, the Castelli Romani and other Italian cities. American Express (☎ 06 676 41) in Piazza di Spagna 38 and the CIT office in Piazza della Repubblica also offer guided tours of the city.

SPECIAL EVENTS

Although Romans desert their city in summer, particularly in August when the weather is relentlessly hot and humid, cultural and musical events liven up the place. The Comune di Roma coordinates a diverse series of concerts, performances and events throughout summer under the general title Estate Romana (Roman Summer). The series usually features major international performers. Information is published in Rome's daily newspapers.

A jazz festival is held in July and August in the Villa Celimontana, a park on top of the Celian Hill (access from Piazza della Navicella).

The Festa de' Noantri is held in Trastevere in the last two weeks of July in honour of Our Lady of Mt Carmel. Street stalls line Viale di Trastevere, but head for the backstreets for live music and street theatre.

At Christmas the focus is on the many churches of Rome, each setting up its own nativity scene. Among the most renowned is the 13th-century crib at Santa Maria Maggiore. During Holy Week, at Easter, the focus is again religious and events include the famous procession of the cross between the Colosseum and the Palatino on Good Friday, and the Pope's blessing of the city and the world in St Peter's Square on Easter Sunday.

The Spanish Steps become a sea of pink azaleas during the Spring Festival in April.

PLACES TO STAY
Camping

About 15 minutes from the centre by public transport is *Village Camping Flaminio* (☎ 06 333 26 04, Via Flaminia Nuova 821). It costs L16,000 per person and L22,000 for a site. Tents and bungalows are available for rent. From Stazione Termini catch bus No 910 to Piazza Mancini, then bus No 200 to the camping ground. At night, catch bus No 24n from Piazzale Flaminio (just north of Piazza del Popolo).

ITALY

THE VATICAN TO VILLA BORGHESE

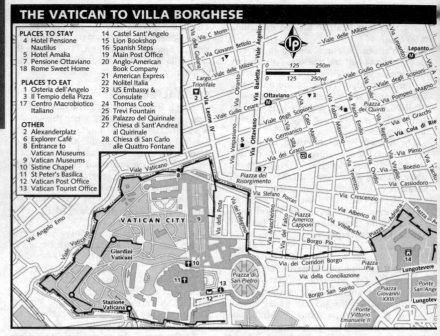

PLACES TO STAY
4 Hotel Pensione
   Nautilus
5 Hotel Amalia
7 Pensione Ottaviano
18 Rome Sweet Home

PLACES TO EAT
1 Osteria dell'Angelo
3 Il Tempio della Pizza
17 Centro Macrobiotico
   Italiano

OTHER
2 Alexanderplatz
6 Explorer Café
8 Entrance to
   Vatican Museums
9 Vatican Museums
10 Sistine Chapel
11 St Peter's Basilica
12 Vatican Post Office
13 Vatican Tourist Office

14 Castel Sant'Angelo
15 Lion Bookshop
16 Spanish Steps
19 Main Post Office
20 Anglo-American
   Book Company
21 American Express
22 Nolitel Italia
23 US Embassy &
   Consulate
24 Thomas Cook
25 Trevi Fountain
26 Palazzo del Quirinale
27 Chiesa di Sant'Andrea
   al Quirinale
28 Chiesa di San Carlo
   alle Quattro Fontane

Hostels

The HI *Ostello del Foro Italico* (☎ 06 323 62 67, *Viale delle Olimpiadi 61)* costs L25,000 a night, breakfast and showers included. Take Metro Linea A to Ottaviano, then bus No 32 to Foro Italico. The head office of the Italian Youth Hostels Association (☎ 06 487 11 52) is at Via Cavour 44, 00184 Rome. It will provide information about all the hostels in Italy. You can also join HI here.

B&Bs

This type of accommodation in private houses is a recent addition to Rome's accommodation options for budget travellers. *Bed & Breakfast Italia* (☎ 06 687 86 18, fax 06 687 86 19, 📧 md4095@mclink.it, Corso Vittorio Emanuele II 282)* is one of several B&B networks. Central singles/doubles with shared bathroom cost L50,000/95,000, or L70,000/130,000 with private bath. Also well worth checking is *Rome Sweet Home* (☎/fax 06 69 92 48 33, 📧 romesweethome@tisc alinet.it, Via della Vite 32)*. Prices are more expensive (L70,000/

100,000) but the B&Bs are stunning. It has a Web site at www.romesweethome.it.

Hotels & Pensioni

North of Stazione Termini To reach the pensioni in this area, head to the right as you leave the train platforms onto Via Castro Pretorio. The excellent *Fawlty Towers* (☎ 06 445 48 02, Via Magenta 39)* offers hostel-style accommodation at L40,000 per person, or L45,000 with a shower. Run by the people at Enjoy Rome, it offers lots of information about Rome and added bonuses are the sunny terrace and satellite TV.

Nearby in Via Palestro are several reasonably priced pensioni. *Pensione Restivo* (☎ 06 446 21 72, 📧 info@enjoyrome.com, Via Palestro 55)* has reasonable singles/doubles at L70,000/110,000, including the cost of showers. There's a midnight curfew. *Pensione Katty* (☎ 06 444 12 16, Via Palestro 35)* has basic rooms from L55,000/90,000. Around the corner is *Pensione Ester* (☎ 06 495 71 23, Viale Castro Pretorio 25)* with comfortable

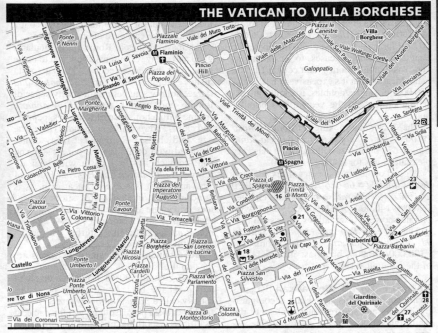

THE VATICAN TO VILLA BORGHESE

doubles/triples for L70,000/100,000. *Hotel Positano* (☎ 06 49 03 60, *Via Palestro 49*) is a more expensive option. Very pleasant rooms with bathroom, TV and other comforts cost L120,000/160,000.

Two good pensioni are in the same building. *Pensione Lachea* (☎ 06 495 72 56, *Via San Martino della Battaglia 11*) has large rooms for L70,000/90,000. *Hotel Pensione Dolomiti* (☎ 06 49 10 58) has singles/doubles for L65,000/95,000.

Papa Germano (☎ 06 48 69 19; **ⓔ** info@ hotelpapagermano.it, *Via Calatafimi 14a*) is one of the more popular budget places in the area. It has singles/doubles for L55,000/ 80,000, or a double with private bathroom for L100,000.

Across Via XX Settembre, about 1km from the station, *Pensione Ercoli* (☎ 06 474 54 54, *Via Collina 48*) has rooms for L90,000/140,000.

South of Stazione Termini This area is seedier, but prices remain the same. As you

exit to the left of the station, follow Via Gioberti to Via G Amendola, which becomes Via F Turati. This street, and the parallel Via Principe Amedeo, harbours a concentration of budget pensioni, so you should easily find a room. The area improves as you get closer to the Colosseum and Roman Forum.

On Via Cavour, the main street running south-west from the piazza in front of Termini, is *Everest Pensione* (☎ 06 488 16 29, *Via Cavour 47*), with clean and simple singles/doubles for L60,000/90,000. *Hotel Sandy* (☎ 06 445 26 12, *Via Cavour 136*) has dormitory beds for L35,000 a night.

Better quality hotels in the area include *Hotel Oceania* (☎ 06 482 46 96, *Via Firenze 50*), which can take up to five people in a room; it has doubles for up to L260,000. *Hotel Kennedy 2* (☎ 06 446 53 73, *Via F Turati 62*) has good quality singles/doubles with bath for up to L149,000/249,000.

City Centre At *Pensione Primavera* (☎ 06 68 80 31 09, *Piazza San Pantaleo 3*) on a square just off Via Vittorio Emanuele II, there are immaculate doubles with bathroom for up to L180,000. The *Albergo Abruzzi* (☎ 06 679 20 21, Piazza della Rotonda 69) overlooks the Pantheon – which excuses, to an extent, its very basic, noisy rooms. You couldn't find a better location, but it's expensive at L105,000/150,000 for singles/doubles. Bookings are essential throughout the year at this popular hotel.

The strictly nonsmoking *Pensione Mimosa* (☎ 06 68 80 17 53, fax 683 35 57, Via Santa Chiara 61), off Piazza della Minerva, has very pleasant rooms for L90,000/110,000.

A good choice in this category is *Albergo della Lunetta* (☎ 06 686 10 80, fax 06 689 20 28, Piazza del Paradiso 68), which charges L90,000/140,000, or L110,000/190,000 with private shower. Reservations are essential.

The *Albergo Pomezia* (☎/fax 06 686 13 71, Via dei Chiavari 12) has rooms for L120,000/170,000, breakfast included. Use of the communal shower is free.

Near St Peter's & the Vatican

Bargains do not abound in this area, but it is comparatively quiet and still reasonably close to the main sights. Bookings are an absolute necessity as rooms are often filled with people attending conferences and so on at the Vatican. The simplest way to reach the area is on the Metropolitana Linea A to Ottaviano. Bus No 64 from Termini stops at St Peter's.

The best bargain in the area is *Pensione Ottaviano* (☎ 06 39 73 72 53, ✉ gi.costantini@agora.stm.it, Via Ottaviano 6), near Piazza Risorgimento. It has beds in dormitories for L35,000 per person. *Hotel Pensione Nautilus* (☎ 06 324 21 18, Via Germanico 198) offers basic singles/doubles for L90,000/110,000; or L130,000/160,000 with private bathroom. *Hotel Amalia* (☎ 06 39 72 33 56, fax 39 72 33 65, ✉ hotelamalia@iol.it, Via Germanico 66) has a beautiful courtyard entrance and clean, sunny rooms. Rooms are L105,000/140,000 and include breakfast and use of the communal shower. Triples are L182,000.

PLACES TO EAT

Rome bursts at the seams with trattorias, pizzerias and restaurants – and not all of them overrun by tourists. Eating times are generally from 12.30 to 3 pm and 8 to 11 pm. Most Romans head out for dinner around 9 pm, so it's better to arrive earlier to claim a table.

Antipasto dishes in Rome are particularly good and many restaurants allow you to make your own mixed selection. Typical pasta dishes include *bucatini all'Amatriciana* (large, hollow spaghetti with a salty sauce of tomato and bacon), *penne all'arrabbiata* (penne with a hot sauce of tomatoes, peppers and chilli) and *spaghetti carbonara* (pancetta, eggs and cheese). Romans eat many dishes prepared with offal. Try the *paiata* – if you can stomach it – it's pasta with veal intestines. *Saltimbocca alla Romana* (slices of veal and ham) is a classic meat dish, as is *straccetti con la rucola*, fine slices of beef tossed in garlic and oil and topped with fresh rocket. In winter you can't go past *carciofi alla Romana* (artichokes stuffed with garlic and mint or parsley).

Good options for cheap, quick meals are the hundreds of bars, where *panini* (sandwiches) cost L2500 to L5000 if taken *al banco* (at the bar), or takeaway pizzerias, usually called *pizza a taglio*, where a slice of freshly cooked pizza, sold by weight, can cost as little as L2000. Bakeries are numerous and are another good choice for a cheap snack. Try a huge piece of *pizza bianca*, a flat bread resembling focaccia, costing from around L2000 a slice (sold by weight).

Try *Paladini* (Via del Governo Vecchio 29) for sandwiches, and *Pizza a Taglio* on Via Baullari for takeaway pizza.

There are numerous outdoor **markets**, notably the lively daily market in Campo de' Fiori. Other, cheaper food markets are held in Piazza Vittorio Emanuele, near the station, and in Via Andrea Doria, near Largo Trionfale, north of the Vatican.

Restaurants, Trattorias & Pizzerias

The restaurants near Stazione Termini are generally to be avoided if you want to pay reasonable prices for good food. The side streets around Piazza Navona and Campo de' Fiori harbour many budget trattorias and pizzerias, and the areas of San Lorenzo (to the east of Termini, near the university) and Testaccio (across the Tiber near Piramide) are popular local eating districts. Trastevere offers an excellent selection of rustic eating places hidden in tiny piazzas, and pizzerias where it doesn't cost the earth to sit at a table on the street.

City Centre The *Pizzeria Montecarlo (Vicolo Savelli 12)* is a very traditional pizzeria, with paper sheets for tablecloths. A pizza with wine or beer will cost as little as L17,000. The *Pizzeria da Baffetto (Via del Governo Vecchio 11)* is a Roman institution. The pizzas are huge and delicious. Expect to join a queue if you arrive after 9 pm and don't be surprised if you end up sharing a table. Pizzas cost around L10,000 to L15,000, a litre of wine costs L9000 and the cover charge (coperto) is only L2000. Farther along the street at No 18 is a tiny, nameless *osteria* where you can eat an excellent, simple meal for around L25,000. There's no written menu, but don't be nervous – the owner/waiter will explain slowly (in Italian). Back along the street towards Piazza Navona is *Cul de Sac 1 (Piazza Pasquino 73)*, a wine bar which also has light meals at reasonable prices.

Centro Macrobiotico Italiano (Via della Vite 14), is a vegetarian restaurant which also serves fresh fish in the evenings. It charges an annual membership fee (which reduces as the year goes by), but tourists can usually eat there and pay only a small surcharge.

There are several small restaurants in Campo de' Fiori. *Hostaria Romanesca* is tiny, so arrive early in winter. In summer there are numerous tables outside. A dish of pasta will cost around L12,000, a full meal around L40,000.

Just off Campo de' Fiori is *Filetti di Baccalá* in the Largo dei Librari, which serves only deep-fried cod fillets for L6500 and wine for L9000 a litre. Across Via Arenula in the Jewish quarter is *Sora Margherita (Piazza delle Cinque Scole 30)*. Open only at lunchtime, it serves traditional Roman and Jewish food and a full meal will cost around L38,000.

West of the Tiber On the west bank of the Fiume Tevere (Tiber River), good-value restaurants are concentrated in Trastevere and the Testaccio district, past Piramide. Many of the establishments around St Peter's and the Vatican are geared for tourists and can be very expensive. There are, however, some good options. Try *Il Tempio della*

Pizza (Viale Giulio Cesare 91) or the highly recommended *Osteria dell'Angelo (Via G Bettolo 24)*, along Via Leone IV from the Vatican City, although this place can be difficult to get into if you get there after 8 pm.

In Trastevere, try *Frontoni*, on Viale di Trastevere opposite Piazza Mastai, for fantastic panini made with pizza bianca. *D'Augusto*, in Piazza dei Renzi just around the corner from the Basilica di Santa Maria in Trastevere (turn right as you face the church and walk to Via della Pelliccia), is a very popular cheap eating spot. The food might be average, but the atmosphere, especially in summer with tables outside in the piazza, is as traditionally Roman as you can get. A meal with wine will cost around L29,000. *Da Lucia (Vicolo del Mattinato 2)* is more expensive at around L50,000 a full meal, but the food is good and the owners are delightful. In summer you'll sit beneath the neighbours' washing.

For a Neapolitan-style pizza, try *Pizzeria da Vittorio (Via San Cosimato 14)*. You'll have to wait for an outside table if you arrive after 8.30 pm, but the atmosphere is great. A bruschetta, pizza and wine will cost around L30,000.

You won't find a cheaper, noisier, more chaotic pizzeria in Rome than *Pizzeria Remo (Piazza Santa Maria Liberatrice 44)* in Testaccio. Nearby is *Il Canestro* on Via Maestro Giorgio, which specialises in vegetarian food and is relatively expensive; you won't get much change out L60,000. *Augustarello (Via G Branca 98)*, off the piazza, specialises in the very traditional Roman fare of offal dishes. The food is reasonable and a meal will cost around L25,000.

Between Termini & the Forum If you have no option but to eat near Stazione Termini, try to avoid the tourist traps offering overpriced full menus. *Trattoria da Bruno (Via Varese 29)* has good food at reasonable prices – around L8500 for pasta and up to L17,000 for a second course. Home-made gnocchi are served on Thursday. A decent pizzeria is *Alle Carrette (Vicolo delle Carrette 14)*, off Via Cavour near the Roman Forum. A pizza and wine will cost around L16,000. Just off Via Cavour is *Osteria Gli Angeletti (Via dell'Angeletto)*, an excellent little restaurant with prices at the higher end of the budget range. You'll pay L10,000 to

L14,000 for a pasta and around L16,000 for a second course.

Cafes

Remember that prices skyrocket in bars as soon as you sit down, particularly near the Spanish Steps, in the Piazza della Rotonda and in Piazza Navona, where a *cappuccino a tavola* (at a table) can cost L5000 or more. The same cappuccino taken at the bar will cost around L1800 – but passing an hour or so watching the world go by over a cappuccino, beer or wine in any of the above locations can be hard to beat!

For the best coffee in Rome head for *Tazza d'Oro*, on Via degli Orfani just off Piazza della Rotonda; and *Caffé Sant'Eustachio* (*Piazza Sant'Eustachio 82*). Try the *granita di caffé* at either one.

Gelati

Both *Gelateria Giolitti* (*Via degli Uffici del Vicario 40*) near the Pantheon and *Gelateria della Palme* (*Via della Maddalena 20*) just around the corner have a huge selection of flavours. In Trastevere, *Fonte della Salute* (*Via Cardinale Marmaggi 2-6*) also has excellent gelati.

ENTERTAINMENT

Rome's best entertainment guide is the weekly *romac'é* (L2000), available at all newsstands. It has an English-language section. Another good entertainment guide is *Trovaroma*, a weekly supplement in the Thursday edition of the newspaper *La Repubblica*. It provides a comprehensive listing of what's happening in the city, but in Italian only. The newspaper also publishes a daily listing of cinema, theatre and concerts.

Metropolitan is a fortnightly magazine for Rome's English-speaking community (L1500). It has good entertainment listings and is available at outlets including the Economy Book & Video Center, Via Torino 136, and at newsstands in the city centre, including Largo Argentina.

Cinema

There are a handful of cinemas in Trastevere that show English-language movies. There are daily shows at *Pasquino* (☎ *06 580 36 22, Vicolo del Piede 19*), just off Piazza Santa Maria. *Alcazar* (☎ *06 588 00 99, Via Merry del Val 14*) shows an English-language film every Monday. *Nuovo Saucer* (☎ *06 581 81 16, Largo Ascianghi*) shows films in their original language on Monday and Tuesday.

Nightclubs

Among the more interesting and popular Roman live music clubs is *Radio Londra* (*Via di Monte Testaccio 67*), on the Testaccio area. On the same street are the more sedate music clubs *Caruso Caffé* at No 36 and *Caffé Latino* at No 96, both generally offering jazz or blues. More jazz and blues can be heard at *Alexanderplatz* (*Via Ostia 9*) and *Big Mama* (*Via San Francesco a Ripa 18*) in Trastevere. *Circolo degli Artisti* (*Via Lamarmora 28*), near Piazza Vittorio Emanuele, is a lively club, popular among Rome's hip set.

Roman discos are outrageously expensive. Expect to pay up to L30,000 to get in, which may or may not include one drink. Perennials include *Alien* (*Via Velletri 13*), *Piper '90* (*Via Tagliamento 9*) and *Gilda-Swing* (*Via Mario de' Fiori 97*). The best gay disco is *L'Alibi* (*Via di Monte Testaccio 44*).

Exhibitions & Concerts

From November to May, opera is performed at the *Teatro dell'Opera* (☎ *06 481 70 03, Piazza Beniamino Gigli*). A season of concerts is held in October and November at the *Accademia di Santa Cecilia* (*Via della Conciliazione 4*) and the *Accademia Filarmonica* (*Via Flaminia 118*). A series of concerts is held from July to the end of September at the *Teatro di Marcello* (*Via Teatro di Marcello 44*) near Piazza Venezia. For information call ☎ 06 482 74 03.

Rock concerts are held throughout the year. For information and bookings, contact the ORBIS agency (☎ 06 482 74 03) in Piazza Esquilino near Stazione Termini.

Bars

Vineria in Campo de' Fiori, also known as Giorgio's, has a wide selection of wine and beers. In summer it has tables outside, but prices are steep – better to stand at the bar. *Bar della Pace* (*Via della Pace 3-7*) is big with the trendy crew, but being hip has a price. *Bevitoria Navona* (*Piazza Navona 72*) has wine by the glass. In Trastevere, the slacker-alternative set seems to prefer *Bar San Calisto (Piazza San Calisto)*, probably because you don't have to pay extra to sit at the outside tables. Near Piazza Santa Maria Maggiore, *The Druid's Den (Via San Martino ai Monti 28)* is a popular Irish pub, which means you can get Guinness and Kilkenny on tap.

SHOPPING

It is probably advisable to stick to window-shopping in the expensive Ludovisi district, the area around Via Veneto. The major fashion shops are in Via Sistina and Via Gregoriana, heading towards the Spanish Steps. Via Condotti and the parallel streets heading from Piazza di Spagna to Via del Corso are lined with moderately expensive clothing and footwear boutiques, as well as shops selling accessories.

It is cheaper, but not as interesting, to shop along Via del Tritone and Via Nazionale. There are some interesting second-hand clothes shops along Via del Governo Vecchio.

If clothes don't appeal, wander through the streets around Via Margutta, Via Ripetta, Piazza del Popolo and Via Frattina to look at the art galleries, artists' studios and antiquarian shops. Antique shops line Via Coronari, between Piazza Navona and Lungotevere di Tor di Nona.

Everyone flocks to the famous Porta Portese market every Sunday morning. Hundreds of stalls selling anything you can imagine line the streets of the Porta Portese area parallel to Viale di Trastevere, near Trastevere. Take time to rummage through the piles of clothing and bric-a-brac and you will find some incredible bargains. Catch tram No 8 from Largo Argentina and ask the driver where to get off (it's a 10-minute ride).

The market on Via Sannio, near Porta San Giovanni, sells new and second-hand clothes and shoes at bargain prices.

GETTING THERE & AWAY
Air

The main airline offices are in the area around Via Veneto and Via Barberini, north of Stazione Termini. Qantas, British Airways, Alitalia, Air New Zealand, Lufthansa and Singapore Airlines are all on Via Bissolati. The main airport is Leonardo da Vinci, at Fiumicino (see the Getting Around section).

Bus

The main terminal for intercity buses is in Piazzale Tiburtina, in front of the Stazione Tiburtina. Catch the Metropolitana Linea B from Termini to Tiburtina. Buses connect with cities throughout Italy. Numerous companies, some of which are listed here, operate these services. For information about which companies operate services to which destinations and from where, go to the APT office, or Enjoy Rome (see Tourist Offices). At Eurojet (☎ 06 481 74 55, fax 06 474 45 21, @ eurojet@adv.it), Piazza della Repubblica 54, you can buy tickets for and get information about several bus services. Otherwise, there are ticket offices for all of the companies inside the Tiburtina station. COTRAL buses, which service Lazio, depart from numerous points throughout the city, depending on their destinations.

Some useful bus lines are:

COTRAL (☎ 167-43 17 84) Via Ostiense 131 – services throughout Lazio
Lazzi (☎ 06 884 08 40) Via Tagliamento 27b – services to other European cities (Eurolines) and the Alps
Marozzi (information at Eurojet) – services to Bari and Brindisi, as well as to Pompeii, Sorrento and the Amalfi Coast and Matera in Basilicata
SAIS & Segesta (☎ 06 481 96 76) Piazza della Repubblica 42 – services to Sicily
SENA (information at Eurojet) – service to Siena
SULGA (information at Eurojet) – services to Perugia and Assisi

Train

Almost all trains arrive at and depart from Stazione Termini. There are regular connections to all major cities in Italy and throughout Europe. For train timetable information phone ☎ 147 88 80 88 (from 7 am to 9 pm), or go to the information office at the station (English is spoken). Timetables can be bought at most newsstands in and around Termini and are particularly useful if you are travelling mostly by train. Services at Termini include telephones, money exchange (see the earlier Information section) and luggage storage (☎ 147 30 62 75; L5000 per piece every six hours, beside track 22). Some trains depart from the stations Ostiense and at Tiburtina.

ITALY

Car & Motorcycle

The main road connecting Rome to the north and south is the Autostrada del Sole A1, which extends from Milan to Reggio di Calabria. On the outskirts of the city it connects with the Grande Raccordo Anulare (GRA), the ring road encircling Rome. If you are entering or leaving Rome, use the Grande Raccordo and the major feeder roads which connect it to the city; it might be longer, but it is simpler and faster. From the Grande Raccordo there are 33 exits into Rome. If you're approaching from the north, take the Via Salaria, Via Nomentana or Via Flaminia exits. From the south, Via Appia Nuova, Via Cristoforo Colombo and Via del Mare (which connects Rome to the Lido di Ostia) all provide reasonably direct routes into the city. The A12 connects the city to Civitavecchia and to Fiumicino airport.

Car rental offices at Stazione Termini in Rome include Avis (☎ 06 419 99/98), Hertz (☎ 06 321 68 31) and Maggiore (☎ 147 86 70 67). All have offices at both airports. Happy Rent (☎ 06 481 81 85), Via Farini 3, rents scooters and bicycles (with baby seats available), as well as some cars and video cameras. It also offers a free baggage deposit and a free email service to its customers. It has a Web site at www.happyrent.com. Another option for scooters and bicycles is I Bike Rome (☎ 06 322 52 40), Via Veneto 156.

Boat

Tirrenia and the Ferrovie dello Stato (FS) ferries leave for various points in Sardinia (see Sardinia's Getting There & Away section) from Civitavecchia. A Tirrenia fast ferry leaves from Fiumicino, near Rome, and Civitavecchia. Bookings can be made at Sestante CIT, or any travel agency displaying the Tirrenia or FS sign. You can also book directly with Tirrenia (☎ 06 474 20 41), Via Bissolati 41, Rome; or at the Stazione Marittima (ferry terminal) at the ports. Bookings can be made at Stazione Termini for FS ferries.

GETTING AROUND
To/From the Airport

The main airport is Leonardo da Vinci (☎ 06 65 95 36 40 for flights only) at Fiumicino. Access to the city is via the airport-Stazione Termini direct train (follow the signs to the station from the airport arrivals hall), which costs L16,000. The train arrives at and leaves from platform No 22 at Termini and there is a ticket office on the platform. The trip takes 35 minutes. The first train leaves the airport for Termini at 7.37 am and the last at 10.07 pm. Another train makes stops along the way, including at Trastevere and Ostiense, and terminates at Stazione Tiburtina (L8000). The trip takes about 50 minutes. A night bus runs from Stazione Tirburtina to the airport from 12.30 to 3.45 am, stopping at Termini at the corner of Via Giolitti about 10 minutes later. The airport is connected to Rome by an autostrada, accessible from the Grande Raccordo Anulare (ring road).

Taxis are prohibitively expensive from the airport – don't even bother.

The other airport is Ciampino, which is used for most domestic and international charter. Blue COTRAL buses (running from 6.50 am to 11.40 pm) connect with the Metropolitana (Linea A at Anagnina), where you can catch the subway to Termini or the Vatican. But if you arrive very late at night, you could end up being forced to catch a taxi. A metropolitan train line, the FM4, connects Termini with the Ciampino airport and Albano Laziale. The airport is connected to Rome by Via Appia Nuova.

Bus

The city bus company is ATAC (☎ 167 43 17 84 for information in English). Details on which buses head where are available at the ATAC information booth in the centre of Piazza dei Cinquecento. Another central point for main bus routes in the centre is Largo Argentina, on Corso Vittorio Emanuele south of the Pantheon. Buses run from 5.30 am to midnight, with limited services throughout the night on some routes. A fast tram service, the No 8, connects Largo Argentina with Trastevere, Porta Portese and the suburb of Monte Verde.

Rome has an integrated public transport system, so you can use the same ticket for the bus, subway and suburban railway. Tickets cost L1500 and are valid for 75 minutes. They must be purchased *before* you get on the bus and validated in the orange machine as you enter. The fine for travelling without a ticket is L100,000, to be paid on the spot, and there is no sympathy for 'dumb tourists'.

Tickets can be purchased at any tobacconist, newsstand, or at the main bus terminals. Daily tickets cost L6000 and weekly tickets cost L24,000.

Metropolitana

The Metropolitana (Metro) has two lines, A and B. Both pass through Stazione Termini. Take Linea A for Piazza di Spagna, the Vatican (Ottaviano) and Villa Borghese (Flaminio), and Linea B for the Colosseum, Circus Maximus and Piramide (for Testaccio and Stazione Ostiense). Tickets are the same as for city buses (see under Bus in this section). Trains run approximately every five minutes between 5.30 am and 11.30 pm (12.30 am on Saturday).

Taxi

Taxis are on radio call 24 hours a day in Rome. Cooperativa Radio Taxi Romana (☎ 06 35 70) and La Capitale (☎ 06 49 94) are two of the many operators. Major taxi ranks are at the airports, Stazione Termini and Largo Argentina in the historical centre. There are surcharges for luggage (L2000 per item), night service (L5000), Sunday and public holidays (L2000) and travel to/from Fiumicino airport (L14,000/11,500). The flag fall is L4500 (for the first 3km), then L1200 for every kilometre. There is a L5000 supplement from 10 pm to 7 am and L2000 from 7 am to 10 pm on Sunday and public holidays.

Car & Motorcycle

Negotiating Roman traffic by car is difficult enough, but you are taking your life in your hands if you ride a motorcycle in the city. The rule in Rome is to watch the vehicles in front and never take for granted that the vehicles behind are watching you. Pedestrians should watch out for motorcycles, which never seem to stop at red lights.

If your car goes missing after being parked illegally, check with the traffic police (☎ 06 676 91). It will cost about L180,000 to get it back plus L15,600 for each day it has been in the police yard.

A major parking area close to the centre is at the Villa Borghese. Entrance is from Piazzale Brasile at the top of Via Veneto. There is a supervised car park at Stazione Termini. There are large car parks at Stazione Tiburtina and Piazza dei Partigiani at Stazione Ostiense

(both accessible to the centre of Rome by the Metro). See the preceding Getting There & Away section for information about car, scooter and bike rental.

Around Rome

OSTIA ANTICA

The Romans founded this port city at the mouth of the Tiber in the 4th century BC and it became a strategically important centre of defence and trade. It was populated by merchants, sailors and slaves, and the ruins of the city provide a fascinating contrast to a place such as Pompeii. It was abandoned after barbarian invasions and the appearance of malaria, but Pope Gregory IV re-established the city in the 9th century.

The Rome EPT office or Enjoy Rome can provide information about the ancient city, or call the ticket office on ☎ 06 56 35 80 99.

Things to See

Of particular note in the excavated city are the mosaics of the **Terme di Nettuno** (Baths of Neptune); a **Roman theatre** built by Augustus; the **forum** and **temple**, dedicated to Jupiter, Juno and Minerva; and the **Piazzale delle Corporazioni**, where you can see the offices of Roman merchants, distinguished by mosaics depicting their trades. The site is open 9 am to 7 pm (last admission 6 pm) Tuesday to Sunday and entry is L8000.

Getting There & Away

To get to Ostia Antica take the Metropolitana Linea B to Magliana and then the Ostia Lido train (getting off at Ostia Antica). By car, take the SS8bis (aka Via del Mare) or Via Ostiense.

TIVOLI

pop 52,372

Set on a hill by the Anio River, Tivoli was a resort town of the ancient Romans and became popular as a summer playground for the rich during the Renaissance. It is famous today for the terraced gardens and fountains of the Villa d'Este and the ruins of the spectacular Villa Adriana, built by the Roman emperor Hadrian.

The local tourist office (☎ 0774 33 45 22) is in Largo Garibaldi near the COTRAL bus stop.

ITALY

Things to See

Hadrian built his summer villa, **Villa Adriana**, in the 2nd century AD. Its construction was influenced by the architecture of the famous classical buildings of the day. It was successively plundered by barbarians and Romans for building materials and many of its original decorations were used to embellish the Villa d'Este. However, enough remains to give an idea of the incredible size and magnificence of the villa. You will need about four hours to wander through the vast ruins.

Highlights include La Villa dell'Isola (the Villa of the Island) where Hadrian spent his pensive moments, the Imperial Palace and its Piazza d'Oro (Golden Square), and the floor mosaics of the Hospitalia. The villa is open 9 am to about one hour before sunset daily (around 7.30 pm; last entry at 6.30 pm) between April and September. Entry is L8000.

The Renaissance **Villa d'Este** was built in the 16th century for Cardinal Ippolito d'Este on the site of a Franciscan monastery. The villa's beautiful gardens are decorated with numerous fountains, which are its main attraction. Opening hours are the same as for Villa Adriana and entry is L8000. Both villas are closed on Monday.

Getting There & Away

Tivoli is about 40km east of Rome and accessible by COTRAL bus. Take Metro Linea B from Stazione Termini to Ponte Mammolo; the bus leaves from outside the station every 20 minutes. The bus also stops near the Villa Adriana, about 1km from Tivoli. Otherwise, catch local bus No 4 from Tivoli's Piazza Garibaldi to Villa Adriana.

TARQUINIA
pop 14, 020

Believed to have been founded in the 12th century BC and to have been the home of the Tarquin kings who ruled Rome before the creation of the republic, Tarquinia was an important economic and political centre of the Etruscan League. The major attractions here are the painted tombs of its *necropoli* (burial grounds). The IAT tourist information office (☎ 0766 85 63 84) is at Piazza Cavour 1.

Things to See

The 15th-century Palazzo Vitelleschi houses the **Museo Nazionale Tarquiniense** and an excellent collection of Etruscan treasures, including frescoes removed from the tombs. There are also numerous sarcophagi that were found in the tombs. The museum is open 9 am to 7 pm Tuesday to Sunday. Entry is L8000 and the same ticket covers entry to the **necropolis**, a 15 to 20-minute walk away (or catch one of four daily buses). The necropolis has the same opening hours as the museum. Ask at the tourist office for directions. The tombs are richly decorated with frescoes, though many are seriously deteriorated.

Places to Stay & Eat

Tarquinia has limited (and overpriced) accommodation, so it is best visited as a day trip from Rome. If you must stay, remember to book well in advance. The nearest camp site is *Tusca Tirrenica* (☎ 0766 86 42 94), Viale Nereidi, 5km from the town. *Hotel Miramare* (☎ 0766 86 40 20, Viale dei Tirreni 36) is in the newer part of town, about a 10-minute walk downhill from the medieval centre. Singles/doubles with private bath cost L90,000/140,000.

For a good, cheap meal, try *Cucina Casareccia* (*Via G Mazzini 5*), off Piazza Cavour, or the *Trattoria Arcadia* opposite at No 6.

Getting There & Away

Buses leave approximately every hour for Tarquinia from Via Lepanto in Rome, near the Metropolitana Linea A Lepanto stop, arriving at Tarquinia a few steps away from the tourist office. You can also catch a train from Ostiense, but Tarquinia's station is at Tarquinia Lido (beach), approximately 3km from the centre. You will then need to catch one of the regular local buses.

CERVETERI

Ancient Caere was founded by the Etruscans in the 8th century BC and enjoyed a period of great prosperity as a maritime centre from the 7th to 5th centuries BC. The main attractions here are the tombs known as *tumoli*, great mounds with carved stone bases. Treasures taken from the tombs can be seen in the Vatican Museums, the Villa Giulia Museum and the Louvre. The Pro Loco tourist office is at Piazza Risorgimento 19.

The main necropolis area, **Banditaccia**, is open 9 am to 6 pm daily, while in winter it closes one hour before sunset. Entry is L8000. You can wander freely once inside the area, though it is best to follow the recommended routes in order to see the best preserved tombs. Banditaccia is accessible by local bus in summer only from the main piazza in Cerveteri, but it is also a pleasant 3km walk west from the town.

Cerveteri is accessible from Rome by COTRAL bus from Via Lepanto, outside the Lepanto stop on Metropolitana Linea A.

Northern Italy

Italy's affluent north is capped by the Alps and bound by the beaches of Liguria and lagoons of Venice, with the gently undulating Po River plain at its heart. Venice and Milan are the big drawcards, but leave room for the historic cities and towns of Piedmont, Lombardy, Emilia-Romagna and the Veneto.

GENOA
pop 950,849

Travellers who write off Genoa (Genova) as simply another seedy port town, bypassing the city for the coastal resorts, do the town a disservice. This once-powerful maritime republic, birthplace of Christopher Columbus (1451-1506) and now capital of the region of Liguria, can still carry the title La Superba. It is a city of contrasts, where humble backstreets lead onto grand thoroughfares and piazzas lined with marble and stucco palaces.

Orientation

Most trains stop at Genoa's two main stations, Principe and Brignole. The area around Brignole is closer to the city centre and a better bet for accommodation than Principe, which is close to the port. Women travelling alone should avoid the port area at night.

From Brignole walk straight ahead along Via Fiume to get to Via XX Settembre and the historical centre. Walking around Genoa is easier than using the local ATM bus service, but most useful buses stop outside both stations.

Information

Tourist Offices The main IAT tourist information office (☎ 010 24 87 11, fax 010 246 76 58, @ aptgenova@apt.genova.it) is on the waterfront at Via del Porto Antico, in the Palazzina Santa Maria building. It's open 9 am to 6.30 pm daily. There are branches at Stazione Principe and the airport (open 8 am to 8 pm Monday to Saturday; the Stazione Principe office also opens 9 am to noon on Sunday).

Post & Communications The main post office is in Via Dante, just off Piazza de Ferrari. You'll also find public phones here. There is a Telecom office to the left of Stazione Brignole on Piazza Verdi, open from 8 am to 9 pm daily. Genoa's postcode is 16100.

Medical & Emergency Services The Ospedale San Martino (☎ 010 55 51) is in Via Benedetto XV. In an emergency, call ☎ 118 for an ambulance and ☎ 113 for the police.

Things to See & Do

Start by wandering around the labyrinthine old port area, searching out the 12th-century, black-and-white marble **Cattedrale di San Lorenzo** and the **Palazzo Ducale** in Piazza Matteotti. The palaces of the Doria family, one of the city's most important families in the 14th and 15th centuries, can be found in **Piazza San Matteo**. To see some of the city's other palaces, take a walk along **Via Garibaldi**, which is lined with grand buildings. Several are open to the public and contain art galleries, including the 16th-century **Palazzo Bianco** and 17th-century **Palazzo Rosso**. Italian and Flemish Renaissance works are displayed in the **Galleria Nazionale di Palazzo Spinola**, Piazza Superiore di Pellicceria 1. The gallery is open 9 am to 7 pm Tuesday to Saturday (from 2 pm on Sunday); entry is L8000.

Genoa's **aquarium** is Europe's biggest, and well worth a visit. It's on the waterfront at Ponte Spinola and opens 9.30 am to 7 pm Monday to Friday and until 8 pm on weekends (11 pm on Thursday in summer and closed on Monday in winter). Admission is L19,000.

Places to Stay

The HI *Ostello Genova* (☎ 010 242 24 57, @ hostelge@iol.it) is at Via Costanzi 120 in Righi, just outside Genoa. B&B costs L23,000 and an evening meal of pasta is L5000. Catch bus No 40 from Stazione Brignole.

On the 3rd floor of a gracious old palazzo near Stazione Brignole, *Carola* (☎ *010 839 13 40, Via Gropallo 4*) has a family atmosphere and pleasant singles/doubles/triples with shower for L45,000/75,000/100,000. To get there, turn right as you leave the station, walk up Via de Amicis to Piazza Brignole and turn right onto Via Gropallo. *Albergo Rita* (☎*/fax 010 87 02 07*), a few doors up at No 8, has singles for L50,000/75,000 and doubles for L75,000/90,000 without/with bathroom.

Splash out a little at *Hotel Bel Soggiorno* (☎ *010 54 28 80, fax 010 58 14 18, Via XX Settembre 19*), where chintzy rooms with bathroom, TV and minibar start at L85,000/ 110,000. One of the city's grandest establishments is the *Bristol Palace* (☎ *010 59 25 41, fax 010 56 17 56, Via XX Settembre 35*), where rooms with all the trimmings are L185,000/330,000.

Places to Eat

Don't leave town without trying *pesto genovese*, *pansoti* (ravioli in walnut sauce), *farinata* (a Tuscan torte made with chickpea flour) and, of course, *focaccia*. Plenty of shops sell sandwiches and pizza by the slice in the Brignole and port areas. For seafood, head to the *Via Sottoripo arcades* on the waterfront; at No 113 the takeaway fried calamari, sardines and zucchini cost around L4000.

The basic but authentic *Trattoria Da Maria* (*Vico Testa d'Oro 14*), off Via XXV Aprile, offers a full meal including wine for L13,000. Hidden away at Vico degli Orefici 5, *La Santa* has a reputation for good regional cooking; the tourist menu is L20,000 (not including drinks) and pasta starts at L8000.

Entertainment

The Genoa Theatre Company performs at the *Politeama Genovese* (☎ *010 839 35 89*) and the *Teatro della Corte* (☎ *010 534 22 00*). *Teatro della Tosse in Sant'Agostino* (☎ *010 247 07 93, Piazza R Negri 4*) has a season of diverse shows from October to May.

Getting There & Away

Air Cristoforo Colombo airport at Sestri Ponente, 6km west of the city, has regular domestic and international connections. The Volabus (☎ 010 558 24 14) airport bus service leaves from Piazza Verdi, just outside Stazione Brignole, and also stops at Stazione Principe. Service is half-hourly from 5.30 am to 11 pm.

Bus Buses for Rome, Florence, Milan and Perugia leave from Piazza della Vittoria, south of Stazione Brignole. Eurolines buses leave from the same piazza for Barcelona, Madrid and Paris. Book at Geotravels (☎ 010 58 71 81) in the piazza.

Train Genoa is connected by train to major cities. For train information call ☎ 147 88 80 88.

Boat The city's busy port is a major embarkation point for ferries to Sicily, Sardinia and Corsica. Major companies are Corsica Ferries (☎ 019 21 55 11 in Savona); Moby Lines (☎ 010 25 27 55) at Ponte Asserato (for Corsica); Tirrenia (☎ 010 254 30 58) at the Stazione Marittima, Ponte Colombo (for Sicily and Sardinia); and Grandi Navi Veloci and Grandi Traghetti (☎ 010 58 93 31) at Via Fieschi 17 (for Sardinia, Sicily, Malta and Tunisia). For more information, see the Getting There & Away sections under Sicily and Sardinia, and under Corsica in the France chapter.

RIVIERA DI LEVANTE

The Ligurian coastal region from Genoa to La Spezia (on the border with Tuscany) rivals the Amalfi Coast in its spectacular beauty. Several of the resorts have managed to remain relatively unspoiled, despite attracting thousands of summer tourists. There's a chance of suitable beach weather in both spring and autumn.

There are IAT tourist offices in most of the towns, including Santa Margherita Ligure (☎ 0185 28 74 86, fax 0185 29 02 22), Via XXV Aprile 4 in the town centre, and in La Spezia (☎ 0187 77 09 00, fax 0187 77 09 08), near the waterfront at Via Mazzini 45. They can advise on accommodation, which is often hard to find.

Things to See & Do

Pretty Santa Margherita Ligure is a good base from which to explore the nearby resorts of **Portofino**, a haunt of the rich and famous, and **Camogli**, a fishing village turned resort town, just a short bus ride away. The medieval Benedictine monastery of **San Fruttuoso** is a 2½-hour hilly walk from Camogli or Portofino, with sensational views along the way; you may want to catch the ferry back.

The five tiny coastal villages of the **Cinque Terre** – Riomaggiore, Manorola, Corniglia, Vernazza and Monterosso – are easily reached by train from La Spezia. Linked by unforgettably scenic walking and hiking tracks, these once-secluded mountainside fishing and wine-growing villages are attracting increasing numbers of visitors.

Places to Stay & Eat
Santa Margherita's *Nuova Riviera* (*☎/fax 0185 28 74 03,* **@** *gisabin@tin.it, Via Belvedere 10)* is an immaculate, nonsmoking, family-run hotel 15 minutes or so from the station (follow Via Roma to Piazza Mazzini). Singles/doubles/triples are around L110,000/ 125,000/155,000 (negotiable) with shower and breakfast; B&B accommodation is also offered. Nearby, *Albergo Annabella* (*☎ 0185 28 65 31, Via Costasecca 10)* has large rooms for L60,000/80,000. Right by the station, *Albergo Azalea* (*☎ 0185 28 81 60, Via Roma 60)* has rooms from L65,000/95,000 with bathroom.

The orderly and well-run *Ostello 5 Terre* (*☎ 0187 92 02 15,* **@** *ostello@cdh.it, Via B Riccobaldi 21)* in Manorola has B&B from L25,000, and an evening meal for around L12,000; book well ahead.

In La Spezia, *Albergo Parma* (*☎ 0187 74 30 10, fax 0187 74 32 40, Via Fiume 143)* is opposite the station, with rooms from L75,000/ 90,000 with shower, TV and phone.

In Santa Margherita, *Trattoria San Siro (Corso Matteotti 137)* is about 15 minutes from the beach; a full meal costs around L35,000. La Spezia's many good trattorias include *La Tavernetta (Via Fiume 57)*, with pizza or pasta for L9000, and *Dino (Via Da Passano 17)*, for reasonably priced seafood near the seafront.

Getting There & Away
The entire coast is served by train and all points are accessible from Genoa. Buses leave from Santa Margherita's Piazza Martiri della Libertà for Portofino.

Boats leave from near the bus stop in Santa Margherita for Portofino (L10,000 return),

San Fruttuoso (L20,000) and the Cinque Terre (L35,000); from La Spezia to the Cinque Terre by boat it's L33,000.

TURIN
pop 962,507
Turin (Torino) is the capital of the Piedmont region. The House of Savoy, which ruled this region for hundreds of years (and Italy until 1945), built a gracious baroque city of boulevards, porticoes and arcades. Italy's industrial expansion began here with companies such as Fiat and Olivetti.

Orientation & Information
The Porta Nuova train station is the point of arrival for most travellers. To reach the city centre, cross Corso Vittorio Emanuele II and walk straight ahead through the grand Carlo Felice and San Carlo piazzas until you come to Piazza Castello. The tourist office is at Piazza Castello 161 (☎ 011 53 51 81, fax 011 53 00 70), open 9.30 am to 7 pm Monday to Saturday, and Sunday to 3 pm. There's also a branch at the Porta Nuova train station (☎ 011 53 13 27, fax 011 561 70 95).

Things to See
Piazza San Carlo, known as Turin's drawing room, is capped by the baroque churches of **San Carlo** and **Santa Cristina**. The centre of historical Turin is **Piazza Castello**, which features the sumptuous **Palazzo Madama**, home to the **Museo Civico d'Arte Antica**. The gardens of the adjacent 17th-century **Palazzo Reale** (Royal Palace) were designed in 1697 by Louis le Nôtre, whose other works include the gardens at Versailles.

The **Cattedrale di San Giovanni Battista**, west of the Palazzo Reale and off Via XX Settembre, houses the **Shroud of Turin**, the linen cloth believed to have been used to wrap the crucified Christ. Scientists have established that the shroud dates from the 12th century. The shroud is displayed for only a few days each year; for further details call ☎ 800 329 329. A reasonable copy is displayed in the cathedral, and a museum devoted to the legend of the shroud is at Via San Domenico 28, open 9 am to noon and 3 to 7 pm daily (L9000).

Turin's **Museo Egizio** (☎ 011 561 77 76), Via Accademia delle Scienze 6, is considered one of the best museums of ancient Egyptian art after those in London and Cairo. It opens 9 am to 7 pm Tuesday to Saturday (to 2 pm on Sunday); admission is L12,000.

Places to Stay & Eat

Turin has plenty of cheap, if a little run-down, accommodation.

Campeggio Villa Rey (☎ *011 819 01 17, Strada Superiore Val San Martino 27)* opens March to October. *Ostello Torino* (☎ *011 660 29 39, Via Alby 1)*, on the corner of Via Gatti, is in the hills east of the Po River. Catch bus No 52 from the Porta Nuova station (No 64 on Sunday). B&B is L22,000 and a meal is L14,000.

The one-star *Canelli* (☎ *011 54 60 78, Via San Dalmazzo 5b)*, off Via Garibaldi, has bare singles/doubles/triples with shower for L40,000/55,000/66,000. The two-star *Albergo Magenta* (☎ *011 54 26 49, fax 011 54 47 55, Corso Vittorio Emanuele II 67)* is near Porta Nuova station, and has singles/doubles for L50,000/75,000 or L90,000/120,000 with bathroom. In a great location, *San Carlo* (☎ *011 562 78 46, fax 011 53 86 53, Piazza San Carlo 197)* has rooms with bathroom, TV and old-world style for L85,000/120,000. Not far away near Piazza Castello, *Hotel Venezia* (☎ *011 562 30 12, fax 011 562 37 26, Via XX Settembre 70)* offers three-star luxury for L180,000/230,000.

One of Turin's better self-service restaurants is *La Grangia* (*Via Garibaldi 21)*, where a full meal costs around L15,000.

At *Pizzeria alla Baita dei 7 Nani* (*Via A Doria 5)* you can grab a pizza and a beer for around L12,000. For gelati, head for *Caffè Fiorio* (*Via Po 8)*; try the gooey *gianduia* (chocolate; L2500).

Getting There & Away

Turin is serviced by Caselle international airport (☎ 011 567 63 61), with flights to European and national destinations. Sadem (☎ 011 311 16 16) buses run to the airport every 45 minutes from the corner between Via Sacchi and Corso Vittorio Emanuele II, on the western side of the Porta Nuova train station. Sadem's intercity buses terminate at the main bus station at Corso Inghilterra 1, near Porta Susa train station. Buses serve the Valle d'Aosta, most of the towns and ski resorts in Piedmont and major Italian cities. Regular trains connect with Milan, Aosta, Venice, Genoa and Rome.

Getting Around

The city is well serviced by a network of buses and trams. A map of public-transport routes is available at the station information office.

MILAN
pop 1,308,000

The economic and fashion capital of Italy, Milan (Milano) has long been an elegant and cultural city. Its origins are believed to be Celtic, but it was conquered by the Romans in 222 BC and became a major trading and transport centre. From the 13th century the city flourished under the rule of two powerful families: the Visconti, followed by the Sforza.

Milan closes down almost completely in August, when most of the city's inhabitants take their annual holidays.

Orientation

From Milan's central train station (Stazione Centrale), it's easy to reach the centre of town on the efficient underground railway (known as the Metropolitana Milanese, or MM). The city of Milan is huge, but most sights are in the centre. Use the Duomo and the Castello Sforzesco as your points of reference; the main shopping areas and sights are around and between the two.

Information

Tourist Offices The main branch of the APT tourist office (☎ 02 72 52 43 01/02/03, fax 02 72 52 43 50) is at Via Marconi 1, in Piazza del Duomo, where you can pick up the useful city guides *Milan is Milano* (with a good map), *Hello Milan* and *Milano Mese*. The office is open 8.30 am to 7 pm Monday to Friday, 9 am to 1 pm and 2 to 6 pm on Saturday, and to 5 pm on Sunday. The branch office at Stazione Centrale (☎ 02 72 52 43 60), near the Telecom office, has useful listings in English posted outside.

Milan City Council operates an information office in Galleria Vittorio Emanuele II, open 8.30 am to 5 pm Monday to Friday, to 2.30 pm on Saturday.

Foreign Consulates Foreign consulates include Australia (☎ 02 777 04 21) at Via Borgogna 2, Canada (☎ 02 675 81) at Via Vittorio Pisani 19, France (☎ 02 655 91 41) at Via Mangili 1, the UK (☎ 02 72 30 01) at Via San Paolo 7 and the USA (☎ 02 29 03 51) at Via P Amedeo 2/10.

Money Banks in Milan open 8.30 am to 1.30 pm and 2.45 to 3.45 pm Monday to Friday. Exchange offices on Piazza Duomo include Banca Ponti at No 19, and there are offices open daily at Stazione Centrale. The American Express office (☎ 02 87 66 74) is at Via Brera 3 and opens 9 am to 5 pm Monday to Friday.

Post & Communications The main post office is at Via Cordusio 4, off Via Dante, near Piazza del Duomo, and is open 8 am to 7 pm Monday to Friday and 9.30 am to 1 pm on Saturday. Fermo posta is open from 8.15 am to 12.30 pm. There are also post offices at the station and at Linate airport.

There is a Telecom Italia telephone office in the upper level of Stazione Centrale, open 8 am to 8 pm daily; it has international telephone directories. The Telecom office in the Galleria has Internet access (L200 per minute), a fax machine and phonecards; it closes at 9.30 pm. Milan's postcode is 20100.

The Hard Disk Cafe at Corso Sempione 44 (www.hdc.it) was Milan's first cybercafe and it's still the best in town, with snacks, cocktails and 60 screens. For basic Internet access closer to the station, Boomerang on the corner of Via Gasparotto and F Filzi charges L3000 for 10 minutes, L8000 per half-hour.

Bookshops The American Bookstore, Via Campiero 16, provides a good selection of English-language books.

Laundry The Lavanderia Self-Service on Via Tadino charges L5000 or L10,000 for a megaload. It's open 7.30 am to 9.30 pm daily.

Medical & Emergency Services For an ambulance call ☎ 118. The public hospital, Ospedale Maggiore Policlinico (☎ 02 550 31), is at Via Francesco Sforza 35, close to the centre. There is an all-night pharmacy (☎ 02 669 09 35) in Stazione Centrale. In an emergency call the police on ☎ 113. The questura (police headquarters) for foreigners is at Via Montebello (☎ 02 62 26 34 00); English is spoken. For lost property call the Milan City Council (☎ 02 546 52 99) at Via Friuli 30.

Dangers & Annoyances Milan's main shopping areas are popular haunts for groups of thieves, who are as numerous here as in Rome and just as lightning-fast. They use the same technique of waving cardboard or newspaper in your face to distract you while they head for your pockets or purse. Be particularly careful in the piazza in front of the Stazione Centrale. Don't hesitate to make a racket if you are hassled.

Things to See & Do

Start with the extraordinary **Duomo**, begun in 1386 to an unusual French Gothic design. With its spiky marble facade shaped into pinnacles, statues and pillars, this tumultuous structure is certainly memorable – as is the view from the roof (stairs L6000, lift L9000).

Join the throngs and take a *passeggiata* through the magnificent **Galleria Vittorio Emanuele II** to **La Scala**, Milan's famed opera house. The theatre's **museum** is open 9 am to noon and 2 to 5.30 pm daily (closed on Sunday from November to April). Admission is L6000.

At the end of Via Dante is the immense **Castello Sforzesco**, originally a Visconti fortress and entirely rebuilt by Francesco Sforza in the 15th century. Its museum collections include furniture, artefacts and sculpture, notably Michelangelo's unfinished *Pietà Rondanini*. The castle is open 9.30 am to 5.30 pm Tuesday to Sunday. Admission is free.

Nearby on Via Brera is the 17th-century Palazzo di Brera, home to the **Pinacoteca di Brera**. This gallery's vast collection includes Mantegna's masterpiece, the *Dead Christ*, and is open 9 am to 5.45 pm Tuesday to Saturday, and on Sunday to 8 pm. Admission is L12,000.

Leonardo da Vinci's *Last Supper* can be viewed by prior appointment in the Cenacolo Vinciano, Piazza Santa Maria delle Grazie 2; phone ☎ 199 199 100 to make a booking. After centuries of damage from floods, heavy-handed restorations, bombing and decay, the recently restored fresco was unveiled in 1999

ITALY

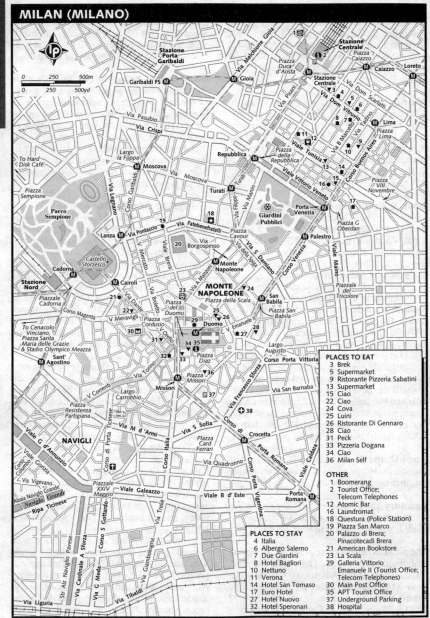

MILAN (MILANO)

0 250 500m
0 250 500yd

To Hard
Disk Café

Stazione
Porta
Garibaldi

Garibaldi FS

Piazza
Duca
d'Aosta

Stazione
Centrale

Stazione
Centrale

Piazza
Caiazzo

Caiazzo

Loreto

Piazza
Sempione

Parco
Sempione

Castello
Sforzesco

Stazione
Nord

Piazzale
Cadorna

Cadorna

To Cenacolo
Vinciano,
Piazza Santa
Maria delle Grazie
& Stadio Olympico Meazza

Sant'
Agostino

Lanza

Moscova

Turati

Repubblica

Piazza
della
Repubblica

Viale Tunisia

Piazza
Lima

Lima

Piazza
VIII
Novembre

Porta
Venezia

Giardini
Pubblici

Piazza
Cavour

Questura

Piazza
Borgospesso

Monte
Napoleone

MONTE
NAPOLEONE

Piazza della Scala

San
Babila

Piazza San
Babila

Duomo

Piazza
del Duomo

Piazza
Diaz

Piazza
Missori

Missori

Palestro

Piazza G
Oberdan

Piazzale
del
Tricolore

Largo
Augusto

Corso Porta Vittoria

Via San Barnaba

NAVIGLI

Piazza
Resistenza
Partigiana

Largo
Carrobbio

Piazza
Card
Ferrari

Piazza
XXIV
Maggio

Viale Galeazzo

Viale B d' Este

Piazza
S Sofia

Piazza di
Crocetta

Porta
Romana

Porta
Romana

Via Liguria

PLACES TO EAT
3   Brek
5   Supermarket
9   Ristorante Pizzeria Sabatini
13 Supermarket
15 Ciao
22 Ciao
24 Cova
25 Luini
26 Ristorante Di Gennaro
28 Ciao
31 Peck
33 Pizzeria Dogana
34 Ciao
36 Milan Self

OTHER
1   Boomerang
2   Tourist Office;
    Telecom Telephones
12 Atomic Bar
16 Laundromat
18 Questura (Police Station)
19 Piazza San Marco
20 Palazzo di Brera;
    Pinacotecadi Brera
21 American Bookstore
23 La Scala
29 Galleria Vittorio
    Emanuele II (Tourist Office;
    Telecom Telephones)
30 Main Post Office
35 APT Tourist Office
37 Underground Parking
38 Hospital

PLACES TO STAY
4   Italia
6   Albergo Salerno
7   Due Giardini
8   Hotel Bagliori
10 Nettuno
11 Verona
14 Hotel San Tomaso
17 Euro Hotel
27 Hotel Nuovo
32 Hotel Speronari

euro currency converter €1 = L1936

to a mixed reception: judge for yourself. The building is open Tuesday to Saturday from 9 am to 7 pm, Sunday to 8 pm. Admission is L12,000.

Special Events
St Ambrose's Day (7 December) is Milan's major festival, with celebrations at the Fiera di Milano (MM1: Amendola Fiera).

Places to Stay
Hostels The HI *Ostello Piero Rotta* (*☎/fax 02 39 26 70 95, Viale Salmoiraghi 1*) is north-west of the city centre; B&B is L26,000. Take the MM1 to the QT8 stop. The hostel is closed between 9 am and 3.30 pm, and lights out is 12.30 am. *Protezione della Giovane* (*☎ 02 29 00 01 64, Corso Garibaldi 123*) is run by nuns for single women aged 16 to 25 years. Beds cost from L37,000 a night. Pre-booking is required.

Hotels Milan's hotels are among the most expensive and heavily booked in Italy, particularly due to trade fairs held in the city, so it's strongly recommended to book in advance. There are numerous budget hotels around Stazione Centrale, but the quality varies. The tourist office will make bookings, held by hotels for one hour.

Stazione Centrale & Corso Buenos Aires
One of Milan's nicest one-star hotels is *Due Giardini* (*☎ 02 29 52 10 93, fax 02 29 51 69 33, Via B Marcello 47*), with rooms overlooking a tranquil back garden; comfortable doubles are L150,000 with bathroom and TV. To get there turn right off Via D Scarlatti, which is to the left as you leave the station.

Budget options nearby on busy Via Dom Vitruvio, off Piazza Duca d'Aosta, include *Albergo Salerno* (*☎ 02 204 68 70*) at No 18, with clean singles/doubles for L65,000/90,000 (add L30,000 for a bathroom). *Italia* (*☎ 02 669 38 26*) at No 44 has less attractive rooms for L55,000/85,000; L90,000/130,000 with bathroom.

The no-frills *Nettuno* (*☎ 02 29 40 44 81, Via Tadino 27*) has rooms with bathroom for L75,000/115,000. Near Piazza della Repubblica, *Verona* (*☎ 02 66 98 30 91, Via Carlo Tenca 12*) has rooms for L80,000/150,000 with shower, satellite TV and telephone.

Just off Corso Buenos Aires, the friendly *Hotel San Tomaso* (*☎ 02 29 51 47 47, ✉ hotelsantomaso@tin.it, Viale Tunisia 6*) on the 3rd floor has singles/doubles/triples for L60,000/100,000/135,000, all with shower and TV.

Closer to the centre, off Piazza G Oberdan, *Euro Hotel* (*☎ 02 20 40 40 10, ✉ eurohotel.viasirtori@tin.it, Via Sirtori 26*) is a good bet, with modern rooms with shower, satellite TV and breakfast for L110,000/140,000/180,000.

For some three-star comfort, try the *Hotel Bagliori* (*☎ 02 29 52 68 84, fax 02 29 52 68 42, Via Boscovich 43*). Singles range seasonally from L140,000 to L220,000, doubles from L220,000 to L320,000.

The Centre In a great location near Piazza del Duomo, *Hotel Speronari* (*☎ 02 86 46 11 25, fax 02 72 00 31 78, Via Speronari 4*) has comfortable singles/doubles for L75,000/110,000; L95,000/160,000 with bathroom. *Hotel Nuovo* (*☎ 02 86 46 05 42, Piazza Beccaria 6*) is also in the thick of things, just off Corso Vittorio Emanuele II and the Duomo. Basic rooms cost L60,000/80,000, and a double with bathroom is L120,000.

Places to Eat
There are plenty of fast-food outlets and sandwich bars in the station and Duomo areas, extremely popular during the lunchtime rush.

For something less hectic, try one of the many trattorias or fill up on the snacks served in bars from around 5 pm.

Restaurants If you're looking for a traditional trattoria, try the side streets south of the station and along Corso Buenos Aires.

Around Stazione Centrale The *Ciao* outlet (*Corso Buenos Aires 7*) is part of a self-service chain (there are a multitude of others, including those surrounding the Duomo, on Corso Europa and at Via Dante 5), but the food is pretty good and relatively cheap. Pizza and pasta dishes cost from L5000 and salads start at around L4500. The *Brek* chain is a similar but superior alternative.

Ristorante Pizzeria Sabatini (*Via Boscovich 54*), around the corner from Corso Buenos

Aires, serves imaginative pasta dishes such as gorgonzola with nuts (L13,000), as well as traditionally prepared meat and fish dishes; pizza is a speciality (from L9000).

City Centre The *Ristorante Di Gennaro (Via Santa Radegonda 14)* is reputed to be one of the city's first pizzerias, and the pizzas and focaccias are still excellent. *Pizzeria Dogana*, on the corner of Via Capellari and Via Dogana near the Duomo, has outside tables and pasta and pizza for around L10,000.

For a more authentic self-service experience, join the city workers at *Milan Self (Via Baracchini 9)*, with pasta for L6000 and salad at L4500. It's open for lunch Monday to Friday.

Cafes & Sandwich Bars The popular *Luini (Via Santa Radegonda 16)*, just off Piazza del Duomo, is one of Milan's oldest fast-food outlets and a favourite haunt of teenagers and students.

For a classy cuppa in elegant surroundings, head to *Cova (Via Monte Napoleone 8)*, established in 1817.

The best gourmet takeaway is *Peck*. Its rosticceria is at Via Cesare Cantù 3, where you can buy cooked meats and vegetables, and there's another outlet near the Duomo at Via Spadari 7-9.

Self-Catering There's a reasonable *supermarket* inside the station, as well as those close by at Via D Vitruvio 32 and on the corner of Via Lecco and F Casati.

Entertainment

Music, theatre and cinema dominate Milan's entertainment calendar. The opera season at *La Scala* opens on 7 December. For tickets go to the box office (☎ 02 72 00 37 44) in the portico in Via Filodrammatici, open noon to 6 pm daily, but don't expect a good seat unless you book well in advance.

Milan has a reasonable selection of bars, from the disco-pubs and wine bars surrounding Piazza San Marco to pricey bars such as *Atomic (Via Casati 24)*.

For football fans a visit to *Stadio Olympico Meazza* (in San Siro) is a must, with AC Milan and Inter Milan drawing crowds of up to 85,000. Ticket prices start at

around L25,000, and can be bought at branches of Cariplo (AC Milan) and Banca Popolare di Milano (Inter) banks.

Shopping

Looking good is more than just a Milanese pastime, but designer threads don't come cheap. Hit the main streets behind the Duomo around Corso Vittorio Emanuele II for clothing, footwear and accessories, or dream on and window-shop for couturier fashions in Via Monte Napoleone, Via Borgospesso and Via della Spiga.

The areas around Via Torino, Corso Buenos Aires and Corso XXII Marzo are less expensive. Markets are held around the canals (south-west of the centre), notably on Viale Papiniano on Tuesday and Saturday morning. A flea market is held in Viale Gabriele d'Annunzio each Saturday, and there's an antique market in Brera at Via Fiori Chiari every third Saturday of the month.

Getting There & Away

Air Most international flights use Malpensa airport, about 50km north-west of Milan. Domestic and European flights use Linate airport, about 7km east of the city. For flight information for the two airports call ☎ 02 74 85 22 00.

Bus Bus stations are scattered throughout the city, although some major companies use Piazza Castello as a terminal. Check with the APT.

Train Regular trains go from Stazione Centrale to Venice, Florence, Bologna, Genoa, Turin and Rome, as well as major cities throughout Europe. For timetable information call ☎ 147 88 80 88 or go to the busy office in Stazione Centrale (English is spoken), open from 7 am to 11 pm. Regional trains stop at Stazione Porta Garibaldi and Stazione Nord in Piazzale Cadorna on the MM2 line.

Car & Motorcycle Milan is the major junction of Italy's motorways, including the Autostrada del Sole (A1) to Rome, the Milano-Torino (A4), the Milano-Genova (A7) and the Serenissima (A4) for Verona and Venice, and the A8 and A9 north to the lakes and the Swiss border.

All these roads meet with the Milan ring road, known as the Tangenziale Est and Tangenziale Ovest (the east and west bypasses). From here follow the signs which lead into the centre. The A4 in particular is an extremely busy road, where an accident can hold up traffic for hours. In winter all roads in the area become extremely hazardous because of rain, snow and fog.

Getting Around
To/From the Airport STAM airport shuttle buses leave for Linate airport from Piazza Luigi di Savoia, on the east side of Stazione Centrale, every 30 minutes from 5.40 am to 9 pm (25 minutes, L5000). Airpullman Service runs shuttle buses from the same piazza to Malpensa airport every 20 minutes from 5.20 am to 10 pm (50 minutes, L13,000). Buses link the airports hourly from 4 am to 11.30 pm.

The Malpensa Express train links Malpensa airport with Cadorna underground station in the centre of Milan. Trains leave Cadorna from 5 am to 11.10 pm, and Malpensa from 6 am to 1.30 am. The journey takes 40 minutes and tickets cost L15,000.

Bus & Metro Milan's public transport system is extremely efficient, with underground (MM), tram and bus services. Tickets are L1500, valid for one underground ride and/or 75 minutes on buses and trams.

You can buy tickets in the MM stations, as well as at authorised tobacconists and newsstands.

Taxi Taxis won't stop if you hail them in the street – head for the taxi ranks, all of which have telephones. A few of the radio taxi companies serving the city are Radiotaxidata (☎ 02 53 53), Prontotaxi (☎ 02 52 51), Autoradiotaxi (☎ 02 85 85) and Arco (☎ 02 67 67).

Car & Motorcycle Entering central Milano by car is a hassle. The city is dotted with expensive car parks (look for the blue sign with a white 'P'). A cheaper alternative is to use one of the supervised car parks at the last stop on each MM line. In the centre there are private garages that charge around L4000 per hour (L6000 first hour). Hertz, Avis, Maggiore and Europcar all have offices at Stazione Centrale.

MANTUA
pop 53,065
Mantua (Mantova) is closely associated with the Gonzaga family, who ruled from the 14th to 18th centuries. The powerful family embellished the city with sumptuous palaces, built to impress and amuse, making Mantua a byword for courtly excess. As a result, the city is also known for its master works by painter Andrea Mantegna and architect Giulio Romano, who were summoned to work for the Gonzaga. You can easily visit the city on a day trip from Milan, Verona or Bologna.

Information
The APT tourist office (☎ 0376 32 82 53), Piazza Andrea Mantegna 6, is a 10-minute walk from the station along Corso Vittorio Emanuele, which becomes Corso Umberto 1. The office is open 8.30 am to 12.30 pm and 3 to 6 pm Monday to Saturday and 9.30 am to 12.30 pm on Sunday.

Things to See
Mantua's **Piazza Sordello** is surrounded by impressive buildings, including the eclectic **cattedrale**, which combines a Romanesque tower, baroque facade and Renaissance interior. The piazza is dominated by the massive **Palazzo Ducale**, former seat of the Gonzaga family. The palace has more than 500 rooms and courtyards, but its showpieces are the Gonzaga apartments and art collection, and the **Camera degli Sposi** (Bridal Chamber), with frescoes by Mantegna. The palace is open 9 am to 6 pm Tuesday to Sunday. Admission is L12,000.

Don't miss the Gonzaga's lavishly decorated summer palace, **Palazzo del Tè**, completed in 1534 by the master of Mannerism, Giulio Romano. It's open 9 am to 5.30 pm Tuesday to Sunday. Admission is L12,000.

Places to Stay & Eat
There are camping sites 2km from Mantua at **Corte Chiara** (☎ 0376 39 08 04) and 7km from town at **Sacchini** (☎ 0376 44 87 63), priced at around L20,000 per person. In Mantua, **Albergo ABC** (☎ 0376 32 33 47, Piazza Don Leoni 25) has singles/doubles with bathroom and breakfast for L100,000/140,000.

For cheap but good pizza or pasta head to **Pizzeria Capri** (Via Bettinelli 8), opposite the

ITALY

station, or **La Masseria** *(Piazza Broletto 7)*. For finer dining, **Ristorante Pavesi** *(Piazza delle Erbe 13)* serves full meals for around L40,000.

Getting There & Away

Mantua is accessible by train and bus from Verona (about 40 minutes), and by train from Milan and Bologna with a change at Modena.

VERONA
pop 255,824

Forever associated with Romeo and Juliet, Verona has much more to offer than the fabricated relics of a tragic love story. Once an important Roman city, Verona reached its peak under the rule of the della Scala (also known as the Scaligeri) family in the 13th and 14th centuries, a period noted for the savage family feuding on which Shakespeare based his play.

Orientation & Information

Buses leave for the historical centre from outside the train station; otherwise, it's a 20-minute walk, heading right to leave the bus station, crossing the river and walking along Corso Porta Nuova to Piazza Brà. From there take Via Mazzini and turn left at Via Cappello to reach Piazza delle Erbe.

The main APT tourist office (☎ 045 806 86 80, ✆ veronapt@tin.it) is at Via degli Alpina 9, facing Piazza Brà. It's open 9 am to 6 pm Monday to Saturday (to 8 pm and on Sunday to 2.30 pm from July to September). The branch at the train station (☎ 045 800 08 61) is open from 7 am to 9 pm.

The main post office is on Piazza Viviani. The Ospedale Civile Maggiore (☎ 045 807 11 11) is at Piazza A Stefani.

Things to See & Do

Piazza Brà's Roman amphitheatre, known as the **Arena**, was built in the 1st century and is now Verona's opera house.

Walk along Via Mazzini to Via Cappello and **Juliet's House** (Casa di Giulietta), its entrance smothered with lovers' graffiti. Further along the street to the right is **Porta Leoni**, one of the gates to the old Roman Verona; **Porta Borsari**, the other gate to the city, is north of the Arena at Corso Porta Borsari.

Piazza delle Erbe, the former site of the Roman forum, is lined with Verona's characteristic pink marble palaces and filled with market stalls. The piazza remains the lively heart of the city. Just off the square is the elegant **Piazza dei Signori**, flanked by the medieval town hall, the Renaissance **Loggia del Consiglio** and the della Scala (Scaligeri) residence, partly decorated by Giotto and nowadays known as the **Governor's Palace**. Take a look at the **Duomo**, on Via Duomo, for its Romanesque main doors and Titian's glorious *Assumption*.

Places to Stay & Eat

The lovingly restored HI **Ostello Villa Francescatti** *(☎ 045 59 03 60, fax 800 91 27, Salita Fontana del Ferro 15)* has B&B for L22,000 (including sheets) and dinner for L14,000. An HI or student card is necessary. The **camping ground** (L10,000 per person with your own tent) next door is run by the hostel management. To get there catch bus No 73 from the station to Piazza Isolo and follow the signs.

Albergo Castello *(☎/fax 045 800 44 03, Corso Cavour 43)* has singles/doubles with shower for L90,000/140,000; the entrance is around the corner. **Albergo Ciopeta** *(☎ 045 800 68 43, ✆ ciopeta@iol.it, Vicolo Teatro Filarmonico 2)*, just off Piazza Brà, has quaint rooms for L80,000/130,000. For some three-star luxury, **Antica Porta Leona** *(☎ 045 59 54 99, fax 045 59 52 14, Corticella Leoni 3)* has well-appointed rooms for around L140,000/200,000.

Boiled meats are a Veronese speciality, as is the crisp Soave white wine. Both the Castello and Ciopeta hotels have well-priced restaurants. **Pizzeria Liston** *(Via dietro Liston 19)* has good pizzas from L11,000 and a full meal for around L35,000. **Brek** in Piazza Brà has a view of the Arena and the usual cheap dishes from L8000.

Entertainment

Verona hosts musical and cultural events throughout the year, culminating in a season of opera and drama from July to September at the *Arena* (tickets from around L40,000). There is a lyric-symphonic season in winter at the 18th-century *Teatro Filarmonico* *(☎ 045 800 28 80, Via dei Mutilati 4)*, just off

Piazza Brà. Information is available from the Fondazione Arena di Verona (☎ 045 805 18 11), Piazza Brà 28. The box office (☎ 045 800 51 51) is at Via dietro Anfiteatro 6b, or book on the Web at www.arena.it.

Getting There & Away
The Verona-Villafranca airport (☎ 045 809 56 66) is just outside town and accessible by bus and train.

The main APT bus station is in the piazza in front of the train station, known as Porta Nuova. Buses leave for surrounding areas, including Mantua, Ferrara and Brescia.

Verona is on the Brenner Pass railway line to Austria and Germany, and is directly linked by train to Milan, Venice, Florence and Rome.

The city sits at the intersection of the Serenissima A4 (Milan-Venice) and the Brennero A22 autostrade.

Getting Around
The APT airport bus leaves from Porta Nuova and from Piazza Cittadella, off Corso Porta Nuova near Piazza Brà. Bus Nos 11, 12 and 13 connect the station with Piazza Brà, and Nos 72 and 73 go to Piazza delle Erbe.

If you arrive by car, you should have no trouble reaching the centre – simply follow the 'centro' signs. There are also signs marking the directions to most hotels. There's a free car park in Via Città di Nimes (near the train station) – a good bet, as parking in the centre is limited.

PADUA
pop 215,137
Although famous as the city of St Anthony and for its university, which is one of the oldest in Europe, Padua (Padova) is often merely seen as a convenient and cheap place to stay while visiting Venice. In fact the city offers a rich collection of art treasures, and its many piazzas and porticoed streets are a stress-free pleasure to explore.

Orientation & Information
It's a 15-minute walk from the train station to the centre of town, or you can take bus No 3 or 8 along Corso del Popolo (which becomes Corso Garibaldi).

The IAT tourist office (☎ 049 875 20 77, fax 049 875 50 08) at the station opens

9.15 am to 6.30 pm Monday to Saturday and 9 am to noon on Sunday.

The post office is at Corso Garibaldi 33 and there's a telephone office nearby (open 8 am to 9.30 pm). Padua's postcode is 35100.

Things to See
Thousands of pilgrims arrive in Padua every year to visit the **Basilica del Santo** in the hope that St Anthony, patron saint of Padua and of lost things, will help them find whatever it is they are looking for. The saint's tomb is in the basilica, along with artworks including the 14th-century frescoes and bronze sculptures by Donatello which adorn the high altar. Donatello's bronze equestrian statue, known as the *Gattamelata* (Honeyed Cat), is outside the basilica.

The **Musei Civici agli Eremitani** and **Cappella degli Scrovegni** are at Piazza Eremitani 8. The chapel's emotionally charged frescoes depicting the life of Christ were painted by Giotto between 1303 and 1305. The transcendent 38 panels are considered one of the world's greatest works of figurative art. The museum and chapel are open 9 am to 7 pm (to 6 pm in winter) Tuesday to Sunday; it's advisable to book in summer, and a combined ticket to both costs L10,000.

A combined L15,000 ticket (L10,000 for students) allows entry to the city's monuments and can be bought at any of the main sights.

Places to Stay & Eat
Padua has no shortage of budget hotels, but they fill up quickly in summer. The non-HI *Ostello della Città di Padova* (☎ 049 875 22 19, fax 049 65 42 10, Via A Aleardi 30) has B&B for L23,000. Take bus No 3, 8 or 12 from the station to Prato della Valle (a piazza about five minutes away) and then ask for directions.

Verdi (☎ 049 875 57 44, Via Dondi dell' Orologio 7) has clean singles/doubles for L40,000/64,000 and is in the university district off Via Dante. The two-star *Sant'Antonio* (☎ 049 875 13 93, fax 049 875 25 08, Via Santo Fermo 118), near the river and the northern end of Via Dante, has comfortable rooms with TV and phone for L95,000/120,000. In the heart of the old city, the *Leon Bianco* (☎ 049 875 08 14, fax 049 875 61 84, Piazetta Pedrocchi 12) has three-star rooms for L115,000/170,000.

Grab a snack at **Dalla Zita** *(Via Gorizia 16)*, off Piazza Pedrocchi, where you'll be spoilt for choice with more than 100 sandwich fillings on offer. **Birroteca da Mario** *(Via Breda 3)*, off Piazza della Frutta, is a good choice for panini and pizza. **Trattoria al Pero** *(Via Santa Lucia 72)*, near Piazza dei Signori, serves delectable regional dishes for around L15,000. Daily food **markets** are held in Piazza delle Erbe and Piazza della Frutta.

Getting There & Away

Padua is directly linked by train to Milan, Venice and Bologna, and is easily accessible from most other major cities. Regular buses serve Venice, Milan, Trieste and surrounding towns. The bus terminal is in Piazzale Boschetti, off Via Trieste, near the train station. There is a large public car park in Prato della Valle, a massive piazza near the Basilica del Santo.

VENICE
pop 309,422

La Serenissima, the Most Serene Republic, perhaps no other city in the world has inspired the superlatives heaped upon Venice (Venezia) by great writers and travellers through the centuries. Byron's 'fairy city of the heart, rising like water-columns from the sea' was, and forever will be, an inspired phenomenon.

The secret to discovering its romance and beauty is to *walk*. Parts of Dorsoduro and Castello see few tourists even in the high season (July to September), and it's here that you'll appreciate just how seductive Venice can be. It's easy to happily lose yourself for hours in the narrow winding streets between the Accademia and the train station, where the signs pointing to San Marco and the Rialto never seem to make any sense – but what a way to pass the time!

The islands of the lagoon were first settled during the barbarian invasions of the 5th and 6th centuries AD, when the people of the Veneto sought refuge in the marshy region, gradually building the unique city on a raft of wooden posts driven into the subsoil. The waters that today threaten the city's existence once protected it from its enemies. Following centuries of Byzantine rule, Venice evolved into a republic ruled by a succession of doges (chief magistrates) and enjoyed a period of

independence that lasted 1000 years. It was the point where east met west, and the city eventually grew in power to dominate half the Mediterranean, the Adriatic and the trade routes to the Levant. It was from Venice that Marco Polo set out on his voyage to China.

Today, Venice is increasingly being left to the tourists – the regular floods (caused by high tides) and soaring property values make it impractical as a place of residence. Most of the 'locals' live in industrial Mestre, which is linked to the city by the 4km-long bridge across the lagoon.

Orientation

Venice is built on 117 small islands and has some 150 canals and 400 bridges. Only three bridges cross the Grand Canal (Canal Grande): the Rialto, the Accademia and, at the train station, the Scalzi. The city is divided into six *sestieri* (quarters): Cannaregio, Castello, San Marco, Dorsoduro, San Polo and Santa Croce. A street can be called a *calle*, *ruga* or *salizzada*; a street beside a canal is a *fondamenta*; a canal is a *rio*; and a quay is a *riva*. The only square in Venice called a *piazza* is San Marco – all the others are called *campo*.

If all that isn't confusing enough, Venice also has its own style of street numbering. Instead of a system based on individual streets, each sestiere has a long series of numbers. There are no cars in the city and all public transport is via the canals, on *vaporetti* (water buses). To cross the Grand Canal between the bridges, use a *traghetto* (basically a public gondola, but much cheaper). Signs will direct you to the various traghetto points. Of course the other mode of transportation is *a piedi* (on foot).

To walk from the *ferrovia* (train station) to San Marco along the main thoroughfare, Lista di Spagna (whose name changes several times), will take a good half-hour – follow the signs to San Marco. From San Marco the routes to other main areas, such as the Rialto, the Accademia and the ferrovia, are well signposted but can be confusing, particularly in the Dorsoduro and San Polo areas.

It's worth buying the street-referenced *Venezia* map published by FMB, as the free tourist office map provides only a vague guide to the complicated network of streets.

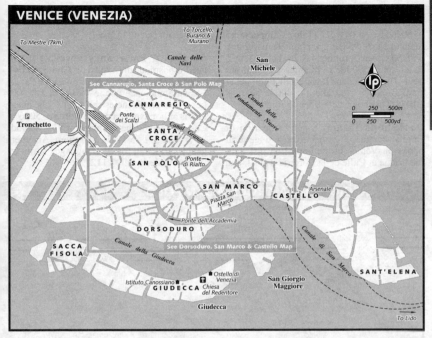

VENICE (VENEZIA)

Information

Tourist Offices Venice has three APT tourist office branches: at the train station (☎ 041 529 87 27), open 8 am to 7 pm daily; at Piazza San Marco 71f (☎ 041 520 89 64), open from 9.30 am to 3.30 pm daily and the Venice Pavilion (☎ 041 522 63 56), on the waterfront next to the Giardini Ex Reali (turn right from San Marco), open 10 am to 6 pm daily. Hours can vary a little seasonally.

Visitors aged between 14 and 29 can buy a Rolling Venice card (L5000), which offers significant discounts on food, accommodation, shopping, transport and entry to museums. It is available from tourist offices July to September, and from a number of private offices at other times; check at the tourist offices for details.

Foreign Consulates The British consulate (☎ 041 522 72 07) is in the Palazzo Querini near the Accademia, Dorsoduro 1051.

Money Most of the main banks have branches in the area around the Rialto and San Marco.

The American Express office at Salizzada San Moisè (exit from the western end of Piazza San Marco onto Calle Seconda dell'Ascensione) will exchange money without charging commission. Its opening hours are 9 am to 5.30 pm Monday to Friday and to 12.30 pm at weekends. There's an ATM for card-holders.

Thomas Cook, Piazza San Marco 141, is open 9.10 am to 7.45 pm Monday to Saturday and 9.30 am to 5 pm on Sunday. There is also a bank at the train station, or you can change money at the train ticket office between 7 am and 9.30 pm daily.

Post & Communications The main post office is on Salizzada del Fontego dei Tedeschi, just near the Ponte di Rialto (Rialto Bridge) on the main thoroughfare to the station. Stamps are sold at window Nos 9 and 10 in the central courtyard. There's a branch post office just off the western end of Piazza San Marco, and at the train station.

There are several Telecom offices in the city, including those at the post office, near the Rialto and on Strada Nova. Venice's post-code is 30100.

Nethouse (☎ 041 277 11 90), Campo Santo Stefano 2967-2958, is open from 9 am to 2 am, with 60 screens, printing, fax and helpful staff. Rates are L4500 for 15 minutes, L18,000 per hour. The smaller and less frenetic Puntonet at Campo Santa Margherita 3002 charges L10,000 per hour, L3000 for 15 minutes.

Bookshops There is a good selection of English-language guidebooks and general books on Venice in the bookshop just over the bridge at Calle de la Cortesia 3717d, and at Studium, behind St Mark's Basilica on the corner of Calle de la Canonica, on the way from San Marco to Castello.

Medical & Emergency Services If you need a hospital, the Ospedale Civile (☎ 041 529 45 17) is on Campo SS Giovanni e Paolo. For an ambulance phone ☎ 041 523 00 00. For police emergencies call ☎ 113. The questura is at Fondamenta di San Lorenzo 5056 in Castello, and on the mainland at Via Nicolodi 22 (☎ 041 271 55 11) in Marghera. An emergency service in foreign languages is run by the carabinieri; call ☎ 112.

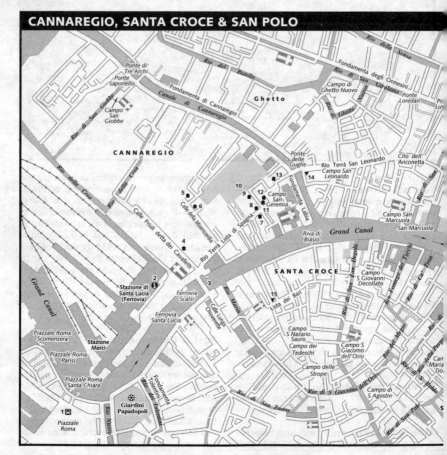

CANNAREGIO, SANTA CROCE & SAN POLO

Things to See & Do

Before you visit Venice's principal monuments, churches and museums, you should catch the No 1 vaporetto along the Grand Canal, lined with Gothic, Moorish, Renaissance and rococo palaces. Then you can stretch your legs by taking a long walk: start at **San Marco** and either delve into the tiny lanes of tranquil **Castello** or head for the **Accademia Bridge** (Ponte dell'Accademia) to reach the narrow streets and squares of **Dorsoduro** and **San Polo**.

Remember that most museums are closed on Monday.

Piazza & Basilica di San Marco San Marco's dreamlike, 'can this be real' quality has you pinching yourself no matter how many times you visit. Napoleon felt so at home he called it the finest drawing room in Europe. The piazza is enclosed by the basilica and the elegant arcades of the Procuratie Vecchie, Procuratie Nuove and Libreria Sansoviniana. San Marco hosts flocks of pigeons and tourists, and both compete for space in the high season. While you're standing gob-smacked you might be lucky enough to see the bronze *mori* (Moors) strike the bell of the 15th-century Torre dell'Orologio (clock tower).

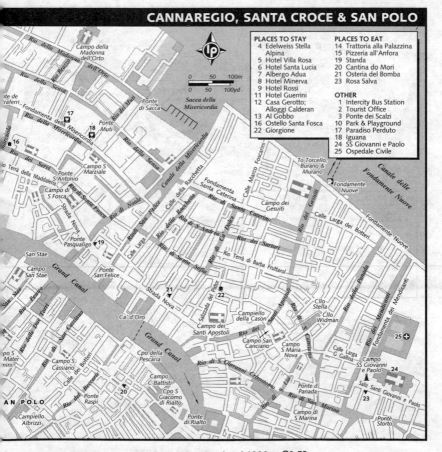

CANNAREGIO, SANTA CROCE & SAN POLO

PLACES TO STAY
4 Edelweiss Stella Alpina
5 Hotel Villa Rosa
6 Hotel Santa Lucia
7 Albergo Adua
8 Hotel Minerva
9 Hotel Rossi
11 Hotel Guerrini
12 Casa Gerotto; Alloggi Calderan
13 Al Gobbo
16 Ostello Santa Fosca
22 Giorgione

PLACES TO EAT
14 Trattoria alla Palazzina
15 Pizzeria all'Anfora
19 Standa
20 Cantina do Mori
21 Osteria del Bomba
23 Rosa Salva

OTHER
1 Intercity Bus Station
2 Tourist Office
3 Ponte dei Scalzi
10 Park & Playground
17 Paradiso Perduto
18 Iguana
24 SS Giovanni e Paolo
25 Ospedale Civile

With its spangled spires, Byzantine domes and seething facade of mosaics and marble, the Basilica di San Marco is the western counterpart of Constantinople's Santa Sophia. The elaborately decorated basilica was built to house the body of St Mark, stolen from its burial place in Egypt by two Venetian merchants and carried to Venice in a barrel of pork. The saint has been reburied several times in the basilica (at least twice the burial place was forgotten) and his body now lies under the high altar. The present basilica was built in the 11th century and richly decorated with mosaics, marbles, sculpture and a jumble of other looted embellishments over the ensuing five centuries. The bronze horses prancing above the entrance are replicas of the famous statues liberated in the Sack of Constantinople in 1204. The originals can be seen in the basilica's **museum** (entry is L3000).

Don't miss the **Pala d'Oro** (L3000), a stunning gold altarpiece decorated with silver, enamels and precious jewels. It is behind the basilica's altar.

The basilica's 99m freestanding **bell tower** dates from the 10th century, although it suddenly collapsed on 14 July 1902 and had to be rebuilt. It costs L8000 to get to the top.

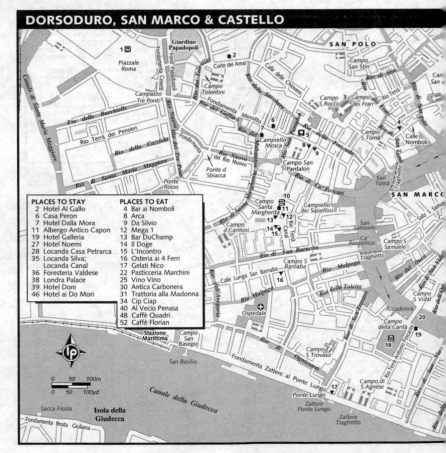

DORSODURO, SAN MARCO & CASTELLO

PLACES TO STAY
2 Hotel Al Gallo
6 Casa Peron
7 Hotel Dalla Mora
11 Albergo Antico Capon
19 Hotel Galleria
27 Hotel Noemi
28 Locanda Casa Petrarca
35 Locanda Silva;
   Locanda Canal
36 Foresteria Valdese
38 Londra Palace
39 Hotel Doni
46 Hotel ai Do Mori

PLACES TO EAT
4 Bar ai Nomboli
8 Arca
9 Da Silvio
12 Mega 1
13 Bar DuChamp
14 Il Doge
15 L'Incontro
16 Osteria ai 4 Ferri
17 Gelati Nico
22 Pasticceria Marchini
25 Vino Vino
30 Antica Carbonera
31 Trattoria alla Madonna
34 Cip Ciap
40 Al Vecio Penasa
48 Caffè Quadri
52 Caffè Florian

ITALY

Palazzo Ducale The official residence of the doges and the seat of the republic's government, this palace also housed many government officials and the prisons. The original palace was built in the 9th century and later expanded, remodelled and given a Gothic tracery facade. Visit the **Sala del Maggior Consiglio** to see the paintings by Tintoretto and Veronese. The palace is open 9 am to 7 pm daily (to 5 pm November to March) and the ticket office closes 1½ hours beforehand. Admission is L18,000 and the same ticket covers entry to the nearby Museo Correr, Biblioteca Marciana and Museo Archeologico, as well as the Palazzo Mocenigo (San Stae area), and Burano and Murano museums.

The **Bridge of Sighs** (Ponte dei Sospiri) connects the palace to the old prisons. The bridge evokes romantic images, probably because of its association with Casanova, a native of Venice who spent some time in the prisons. In fact it was the thoroughfare for prisoners being led to the dungeons.

Galleria dell'Accademia The Academy of Fine Arts' collection traces the development of Venetian art, and includes masterpieces by Bellini, Carpaccio, Tintoretto,

DORSODURO, SAN MARCO & CASTELLO

OTHER
1 Intercity Bus Station
3 Frari
5 Cafe Blue
10 Puntonet
18 Galleria dell'Accademia
20 Ponte dell'Accademia
21 Nethouse
23 Collezione Peggy Guggenheim
24 Chiesa di Santa Maria della Salute
26 American Express
29 Bookshop
32 Ponte di Rialto
33 Main Post Office; Telecom Telephones
37 Questura (Police Station)
41 Bridge of Sighs
42 Palazzo Ducale
43 Basilica di San Marco
44 Studium Bookshop
45 Torre dell'Orologio (Clock Tower)
47 Thomas Cook
49 Procuratie Vecchie
50 Tourist Office
51 Procuratie Nuove
53 Bell Tower
54 Libreria Sansoviniana
55 Tourist Office; Venice Pavilion

Titian, Giorgione and Veronese. The gallery is open 9 am to 7 pm Tuesday to Saturday, to 8 pm on Sunday and to 2 pm on Monday. Admission is L12,000.

For a change of pace, visit the nearby **Collezione Peggy Guggenheim**, displayed in the former home of the American heiress. The collection runs the gamut of modern art from Bacon to Pollock, and the palazzo is set in a sculpture garden where Miss Guggenheim and her many pet dogs are buried. It is open 10 am to 6 pm Wednesday to Monday (to 10 pm on Saturday). Admission is L12,000.

Churches Venice has many gorgeous churches, and most of them boast an art treasure or two. The **Chiesa del Redentore** (Church of the Redeemer) on Giudecca Island was built by Palladio to commemorate the end of the great plague of 1576, and is the scene of the annual Festa del Redentore (see the Special Events section). Longhena's **Chiesa di Santa Maria della Salute** guards the entrance to the Grand Canal and contains works by Tintoretto and Titian. Be sure to visit the great Gothic churches **SS Giovanni e Paolo**, with glorious stained-glass, and the **Frari**, home to Titian's tomb and his uplifting *Assumption*. Entry to each is L3000, or you can buy the Chorus Pass (L15,000) which gets you into 13 of the city's most famous churches.

The Lido This thin strip of land, east of the centre, separates Venice from the Adriatic and is easily accessible by vaporetto Nos 1, 6, 14 and 61. Once *the* most fashionable beach resort – and still very popular – it's almost impossible to find a space on its long beach in summer.

Islands The island of **Murano** is the home of Venetian glass. Tour a factory for a behind-the-scenes look at its production, or visit the Glassworks Museum to see some exquisite historical pieces. Despite the constant influx of tourists, **Burano** is still a relatively sleepy fishing village, renowned for its lace-making. **Torcello**, the republic's original island settlement, was abandoned due to malaria. Just about all that remains on the hauntingly deserted island is the Byzantine cathedral, its exquisite mosaics intact. Excursion boats travel to the three islands from San Marco (L30,000 return). Vaporetto

No 12 goes to all three from Fondamenta Nuove (L6000 one way).

Gondolas These might represent the quintessential romantic Venice, but at around L120,000 (L150,000 after 8 pm) for a 50-minute ride, they are very expensive. It is possible to squeeze up to six people into one gondola and still pay the same price. Prices are set for gondolas, so check with the tourist office if you have problems.

Organised Tours
The Associazione Guide Turistiche (☎ 041 520 90 38), Castello 5327, arranges group tours in various languages for a hefty L200,000. Shop around the various travel agencies for the best deals on guided walks and collective gondola rides with serenade (around L50,000 per person).

Special Events
The major event of the year is Venice's famed Carnevale, held during the 10 days before Ash Wednesday, when Venetians don spectacular masks and costumes for what is literally a 10-day street party. At its decadent height in the 18th century, the Carnevale lasted for six months!

The Venice Biennale, a major exhibition of international visual arts, is held every odd-numbered year, and the Venice International Film Festival is held every September at the Palazzo del Cinema, on the Lido.

The most important celebration on the Venetian calendar is the Festa del Redentore (Festival of the Redeemer), held on the third weekend in July and featuring a spectacular fireworks display. The Regata Storica, a gondola race on the Grand Canal, is held on the first Sunday in September.

Places to Stay
Simply put, Venice is expensive. The average cost of a basic single/double without bath in a one-star hotel is around L90,000/120,000; prices quoted in this section are high season. Some hotels include breakfast, which allows their proprietors to charge a little more. Prices skyrocket in peak periods (Christmas, Carnevale, Easter etc), but can drop dramatically at other times of the year. It is advisable to make a booking

before you arrive. As Venice does not have a traditional street numbering system, the best idea is to ring your hotel when you arrive and ask for specific directions.

Camping Litorale del Cavallino, north-east of the city along the Adriatic coast has numerous camping grounds, many with bungalows. The tourist office has a full list, but you could try *Marina di Venezia* (☎ *041 530 09 55,* @ *camping@marinave.it, Via Montello 6, Punta Sabbioni)*, which is open from mid-April to the end of August.

Hostels The HI *Ostello di Venezia* (☎ *041 523 82 11, fax 041 523 56 89, Fondamenta delle Zitelle 86)* is on the island of Giudecca. It is open to members only, though you can buy a card there. B&B is L27,000 and full meals are available for L14,000. Take vaporetto No 82 from the station (L6000 one way) and get off at Zitelle; curfew is 11.30 pm. *Istituto Canossiano* (☎/*fax 041 522 21 57, Ponte Piccolo 428)* is nearby on Giudecca, with dorm beds for women only at L23,000 per night. Take vaporetto No 82 and get off at Palanca.

Foresteria Valdese (☎/*fax 041 528 67 97, Castello 5170)* has dorm beds for L30,000 and doubles from L85,000 per night. Follow Calle Lunga from Campo Santa Maria Formosa. Students will feel at home at *Ostello Santa Fosca* (☎ *041 71 57 75,* @ *cpu@iuav.unive.it, Cannaregio 2372)*, less than 15 minutes from the station through Campo Santa Fosca. Dorm beds are L30,000 and check-in is 4 to 7 pm.

Hotels Not surprisingly, bargain hotels are few and far between in Venice.

Cannaregio The two-star *Edelweiss Stella Alpina* (☎ *041 71 51 79,* @ *stelalpina@tin.it, Calle Priuli detta dei Cavalletti 99d)*, near the station on the first street on the left after the Scalzi church, has decent singles/doubles for L110,000/160,000; with bathroom they're L150,000/235,000. The next street on the left is Calle della Misericordia, with two recommended hotels. *Hotel Santa Lucia* (☎/*fax 041 71 51 80)*, at No 358, is a newish building (ie, 20th century) with a strip of terrace garden. Doubles with shower and breakfast go for L170,000 (L140,000 without shower),

and singles without shower or breakfast are L80,000. At No 389, the friendly *Hotel Villa Rosa* (☎/*fax 041 71 89 76)* has pleasant, well-furnished singles/doubles/triples/quads with bathroom, breakfast and satellite TV for L130,000/190,000/240,000/280,000.

On Lista di Spagna, the main drag, *Albergo Adua* (☎ *041 71 61 84, fax 041 244 01 62)* at No 233a has clean singles/doubles with shower for L130,000/200,000. Across the road at No 230, *Hotel Minerva* (☎ *041 71 59 68,* @ *lchecchi@tin.it)* has modest rooms for L70,000/95,000.

Hotel Rossi (☎ *041 71 51 64, fax 041 71 77 84)* is just off Lista di Spagna (via a Gothic archway) at the end of tiny Calle de le Procuratie. Singles/doubles/triples/quads with bathroom and bare essentials are L100,000/160,000/195,000/230,000. On the same street, the two-star *Hotel Guerrini* (☎ *041 71 53 33, fax 041 71 51 14)* has comfortable singles without/with bathroom for L80,000/120,000, and doubles for L160,000/230,000. Around the corner, *Casa Gerotto* (☎/*fax 041 71 53 61, Campo San Geremia 283)* and the neighbouring *Alloggi Calderan* together offer singles/doubles in a hostel atmosphere for around L110,000/140,000. *Al Gobbo* (☎ *041 71 50 01)*, at No 312 in the same campo, provides sparkling-clean rooms with bathroom and breakfast for L120,000/150,000.

For a multistar splurge in this less touristy area, the 15th-century *Giorgione* (☎ *041 522 58 10, fax 041 523 90 92, Calle Larga dei Proverbi 4587)*, just off Campo dei SS Apostoli, has tranquil doubles with the lot starting at around L235,000.

San Marco Although this is the most touristy area of Venice, it has some surprisingly good-quality (relatively) budget pensioni. *Hotel Noemi* (☎ *041 523 81 44,* @ *hotelnoemi@tin.it, Calle dei Fabbri 909)* is only a few steps from Piazza San Marco and has simple singles/doubles for L90,000/130,000.

Locanda Casa Petrarca (☎ *041 520 04 30, Calle delle Schiavine 4386)* is one of the area's nicest cheaper hotels, with singles for L75,000 and doubles without/with shower for L140,000/170,000. To get there, find Campo San Luca, go along Calle dei Fusari, then take the second street on the left and turn right onto Calle delle Schiavine; the hotel is at the end of Schiavine, overlooking a canal.

Just off Piazza San Marco, **Hotel ai Do Mori** (☎ *041 520 48 17, fax 041 520 53 28, Calle Larga San Marco 658)* has pleasant singles/doubles, some with views of St Mark's basilica, for L120,000/150,000.

Castello This area is to the east of Piazza San Marco. Although close to the piazza it's less touristy, and eerily reminiscent of the atmospheric movie *Don't Look Now*. **Locanda Silva** (☎ *041 522 76 43, fax 041 528 68 17, Fondamenta del Rimedio 4423)* has rather basic singles/doubles for L70,000/110,000, and **Locanda Canal** (☎ *041 523 45 38, fax 041 241 91 38)*, next door at No 4422c, has better doubles with bathroom for L160,000. To get there, head off from Campo Santa Maria Formosa towards San Marco.

Hotel Doni (☎*/fax 041 522 42 67, Fondamenta del Vin 4656)* is a little establishment off Salizzada San Provolo. It has clean, quiet rooms without bathroom for L75,000/95,000; a double with bathroom is L140,000.

On the waterfront, live like a doge at the **Londra Palace** (☎ *041 520 05 33, fax 041 522 50 32, Riva degli Schiavoni 4171)*, where views and pampering up the rates to L375,000 (and upwards) a double.

Dorsoduro, San Polo & Santa Croce This is the most authentic area of Venice, in which you can still find the atmosphere of a living city. **Hotel Al Gallo** (☎ *041 523 67 61, fax 041 522 81 88, Corte dei Amai 197g)*, off Fondamenta Tolentini heading down from the station, has excellent doubles with shower for L115,000. **Casa Peron** (☎ *041 71 00 21, fax 041 71 10 38, Salizzada San Pantalon 84)* has clean singles/doubles with shower for L100,000/150,000 including breakfast. To get to the Casa Peron from the station, cross Ponte dei Scalzi and follow the signs to San Marco and Rialto till you reach Rio delle Muneghette, then cross the wooden bridge. Nearby, **Hotel Dalla Mora** (☎ *041 71 07 03, fax 041 72 30 06, Santa Croce 42a)* is on a lovely small canal just off Salizzada San Pantalon. It has airy rooms, some with canal views and a common open terrace. Singles/doubles/triples/quads with bathroom are L95,000/150,000/190,000/230,000. Bookings are a must.

In one of the nicest squares in Venice, **Albergo Antico Capon** (☎*/fax 041 528 52 92, Campo Santa Margherita 3004b)* provides singles/doubles with bathroom for L120,000/150,000.

Hotel Galleria (☎ *041 523 24 89,* ✉ *galleria@tin.it, Dorsoduro 878a)* has elegant rooms in a 17th-century palace facing the Grand Canal at Ponte dell'Accademia. But don't panic: this must be the last remaining affordable hotel on the Grand Canal. A double with bathroom costs L180,000, and singles/doubles without facilities are L100,000/150,000.

Mestre Mestre makes an economical if somewhat drab alternative to staying in Venice. There are a number of good hotels as well as plenty of cafes and places to eat around the main square. If you're travelling by car, the savings on car-parking charges are considerable. The two-star **Albergo Roberta** (☎ *041 92 93 55, fax 041 93 09 83, Via Sernaglia 21)* has good-sized, clean singles/doubles with bathroom for L90,000/130,000. The one-star **Albergo Giovannina** (☎ *041 92 63 96, fax 041 538 84 42, Via Dante 113)* has decent singles for L50,000 and doubles with bathroom for L90,000.

Places to Eat
Unless you choose carefully, eating in Venice can be an expensive business.

Bars serve a wide range of tasty panini, *tramezzini* (sandwiches) and rolls with every imaginable filling. They cost around L2500 to L5000 if you eat them while standing at the bar. Head for one of the many *bacari* (traditional wine bars) for wine by the glass *(ombra)* and interesting bite-sized snacks *(cichetti)*. The staples of the Veneto region's cucina are rice and beans. Try the *risi e bisi* (risotto with peas), followed by a glass of *fragolino*, the Veneto's fragrant strawberry wine.

Restaurants Avoid the tourist traps around San Marco and near the train station, where prices are high and the quality is poor.

Cannaregio Heading from the station, **Trattoria alla Palazzina** *(Cannaregio 1509)* is just over the first bridge after Campo San Geremia. It has a garden at the rear and serves good if pricey pizzas for L13,000 to L20,000. A full meal will cost around L50,000. The authentic *Osteria del Bomba (Calle de l'Oca 4297)*, parallel to Strada Nova near Campo dei SS Apostoli, has pasta from L8000 and a mouthwatering array of cichetti.

Around San Marco & Castello The popular bar/osteria *Vino Vino (San Marco 2007)* is at Ponte Veste near Teatro La Fenice. The good-quality menu changes daily, with pasta or risotto for L10,000 and a main dish for around L15,000. Wine is sold by the glass. *Antica Carbonera*, on Calle Bembo (a continuation of Calle dei Fabbri), is an atmospheric old trattoria with pasta from L13,000 and a full meal for around L60,000. Just off Campo Santa Maria Formosa and over Ponte del Mondo Novo, *Cip Ciap* serves filling pizza by the slice for L3000 to L5000.

Dorsoduro, San Polo & Santa Croce This is the best area for small, authentic trattorias and pizzerias. The pizzas are particularly good at *Pizzeria all'Anfora*, across the Ponte dei Scalzi from the station at Lista dei Bari 1223, with a garden at the rear. Pizzas cost L7500 to L14,000.

L'Incontro (Rio Terrà Canal 3062a), between Campo San Barnaba and Campo Santa Margherita, serves excellent food, with a full meal around L45,000.

Cantina do Mori, on Sottoportego dei do Mori, off Ruga Rialto, is a small, very popular wine bar which also serves sandwiches. *Trattoria alla Madonna*, Calle della Madonna, two streets west of the Rialto, specialises in seafood – a full meal costs up to L70,000, but it's worth the extra lire.

The stylish *Arca (Calle San Pantalon 3757)*, past Campo San Pantalon, has pasta and pizza for L9000 to L16,000.

Around the corner is *Da Silvio (Crosera San Pantalon 3817)*, which is a good-value pizzeria/trattoria with outside tables in a garden setting.

Cafes & Bars If you can cope with the idea of paying L15,000 for a cappuccino, spend an hour or so sitting at an outdoor table in Piazza San Marco, listening to the orchestra at either *Caffè Florian* or *Caffè Quadri*. For a cheaper alternative, try Campo Santa Margherita's

Bar DuChamp, a student favourite where panini cost around L6000 and you can sit outside at no extra charge.

Bar ai Nomboli, between Campo San Polo and the Frari on the corner of Calle dei Nomboli and Rio Terrà dei Nomboli, has a huge selection of gourmet sandwiches and tramezzini. In the Castello area you can choose from an extensive range of cheap panini at the bar *Al Vecio Penasa (Calle delle Rasse 4585)*.

If you're looking for a typical osteria serving Venetian cichetti, try *Osteria ai 4 Ferri* on Calle Lunga San Barnaba, off Campo San Barnaba in Dorsoduro.

Gelati & Pastries Some of the best gelati in Venice is served at *Gelati Nico (Fondamenta Zattere ai Gesuati 922)*. You can join the locals taking their evening stroll along the fondamenta or take a seat at an outside table. *Il Doge*, Campo Santa Margherita, also has excellent gelati. A popular place for cakes and pastries is *Pasticceria Marchini (Calle del Spezier 2769)*, just off Campo Santo Stefano. *Rosa Salva*, on Campo SS Giovanni e Paolo, is frequented by locals for its gelati and extra special pastries. Try the hot chocolate.

Self-Catering For fruit and vegetables, as well as delicatessens, head for the *market* in the streets on the San Polo side of the Rialto Bridge. There's a *Standa* supermarket on Strada Nova and a *Mega 1* supermarket just off Campo Santa Margherita.

Entertainment

The free weekly booklet *Un Ospite di Venezia*, available at hotels and tourist offices, has entertainment listings, or buy a copy of the monthly *Venezia News* from newsagents for L4000. The tourist office also has brochures listing events and performances for the entire year.

Venice lost its opera house, the magnificent Teatro La Fenice, to a fire in January 1996. Reconstruction is slowly under way, and in the interim performances are held at *PalaFelice (☎ 041 521 01 61)*, a tentlike structure on the car-park island of Tronchetto.

Major art exhibitions are held at *Palazzo Grassi* (San Samuele vaporetto stop), and smaller exhibitions are held at various venues in the city throughout the year.

In Cannaregio, *Paradiso Perduto (Fondamenta della Misericordia 2539)* has live music and outdoor tables; the food's good too. A few doors up at No 2515, *Iguana* pumps out live and loud Latino music, with burritos on the side. In Dorsoduro, there's *Café Blue (Salizzada San Pantalon 3778)*, a pub-like drinking den near trendy Campo Santa Margherita.

Shopping

For many visitors, Venice is synonymous with its elaborate glassware. There are several workshops and showrooms in Venice, particularly in the area between San Marco and Castello and on the island of Murano, designed mainly for tourist groups. If you're interested in buying some Venetian glass, shop around carefully because quality and prices can vary dramatically.

Venice is a trinket box of jewellery, crystals, grotesque Carnevale masks and bronze lions. You'll find them in shops throughout the city. Lace is another characteristic product of the Venetian lagoon, produced mainly on the island of Burano and available in Venice at Annelie Pizzi e Ricami, at Calle Lunga San Barnaba 2748. Marbled paper and luscious velvet fabrics are other Venetian specialities. Window-shop at Venice's oldest traditional papermaking establishment, Legatoria Piazzesi, Campiello della Feltrina 2551c, San Marco.

The main shopping area for designer-label clothing, shoes, accessories and jewellery is in the narrow streets between San Marco and the Rialto, particularly the Merceria and the area around Campo San Luca. Luxury items can be found in the area near La Fenice.

Getting There & Away

Air Marco Polo airport (☎ 041 260 92 60) is just east of Mestre and services domestic and European flights. It is accessible by regular *motoscafo* (motorboat) from San Marco and the Lido (L17,000). From Piazzale Roma there are also ATVO buses (☎ 041 520 55 30) for L5000 or the ACTV city bus No 5 for L1500. A water taxi from San Marco will cost around L110,000.

Bus ACTV buses (☎ 041 528 78 86) leave from Piazzale Roma for surrounding areas including Mestre and Chioggia, a fishing port at the southernmost point of the lagoon. Buses also go to Padua and Treviso. Tickets and information are available at the office in Piazzale Roma.

Train The train station, Stazione Santa Lucia (☎ 147 88 80 88), is directly linked to Padua, Verona, Trieste, Milan and Bologna, and so is easily accessible for Florence and Rome. You can also head to major points in Germany, Austria and the former Yugoslavia. The Venice Simplon *Orient Express* runs between Venice and London, via Innsbruck, Zürich and Paris, twice weekly. Ask at any travel agent or phone ☎ 041 528 58 11.

Boat Minoan Lines (☎ 041 271 23 45), Porto Venezia, Zona Santa Marta, runs ferries to Greece four times a week in winter and daily in summer. Deck class costs L126,000 one way in the high season.

Getting Around

Once you cross the bridge from Mestre, cars must be left at the car park on the island of Tronchetto or at Piazzale Roma (cars are allowed on the Lido – take car ferry No 17 from Tronchetto). The car parks are not cheap at around L25,000 a day. A cheaper alternative is to leave the car at Fusina, near Mestre, and catch the vaporetto to Zattere and then the No 82 either to Piazza San Marco or the train station. Ask for information at the tourist information office just before the bridge to Venice.

As there are no cars in Venice, vaporetti are the city's mode of public transport. From Piazzale Roma, vaporetto No 1 zigzags its way along the Grand Canal to San Marco and then to the Lido. There is the faster No 82 if you are in a hurry to get to San Marco. The No 12 vaporetto leaves from Fondamenta Nuove for the islands of Murano, Burano and Torcello. A full timetable is available at vaporetto ticket offices. A single vaporetto ticket costs L6000 (plus L6000 for luggage), even if you only ride to the next station; a return is L10,000. A 24-hour ticket costs L18,000 for unlimited travel, a 72-hour ticket is L35,000 (worthwhile) and a one-week ticket costs L60,000.

Water taxis are exorbitant, with a set charge of L27,000 for a maximum of seven minutes, then L500 every 15 seconds. It's an extra L8000 if you phone for a taxi, and various other surcharges add up to make a gondola ride seem cheap.

FERRARA
pop 138,015

The seat of the Este dukes from the 13th century to the end of the 16th century, Ferrara retains much of the austere splendour of its heyday. Graceful palaces line the city's streets, which radiate from the imposing Castello Estense and are largely traffic-free.

Information

The tourist information office (☎ 0532 20 93 70, ✆ infotur.comfe@fe.nettuno.it) is inside the Castello Estense. It opens 9 am to 1 pm and 2 to 6 pm daily.

Things to See

The small historical centre encompasses medieval Ferrara, to the south of the **Castello Estense** and the area to the north. The castle – complete with moat and drawbridges – was begun by Nicolò II d'Este in 1385. It now houses government offices, and the areas open to the public have a suitably chilling atmosphere.

The pink-and-white striped **Duomo** dates from the 12th century, with Gothic and Renaissance additions and an unusual triple facade. Its museum has a superb collection of Renaissance art. The Renaissance Palazzo dei Diamanti, along Corso Ercole I d'Este, contains the **Pinacoteca Nazionale** and exhibitions of modern art. The gallery is open 9 am to 2 pm Tuesday to Saturday (Sunday to 1 pm). Entry is L8000.

The **Palazzo Schifanoia**, Via Scandiana 23, is one of the city's earliest major Renaissance buildings and another of the Este palaces. It features the 'Room of the Months', decorated with Ferrara's finest Renaissance frescoes, portraying courtly life. The palace, whose name means 'chase your cares away', is open 9 am to 7 pm daily; entry is L8000.

Places to Stay & Eat

Ferrara is a cheap alternative to Bologna, and can be used as a base for visiting Venice. *Albergo Centro Storico* (☎ 0532 20 33 74, *Via Vegri 15*) is central but basic, with singles/

doubles for L40,000/60,000. South of the cathedral, *Pensione Artisti* (☎ 0532 76 10 38, *Via Vittoria 66*) has singles for L30,000 and doubles without/with bathroom for L60,000/85,000. Better rooms are available at the two-star *Albergo Nazionale* (☎ 0532 20 96 04, *Corso Porta Reno 32*) for L80,000/120,000 with bathroom. Opposite the cathedral, the four-star *Annunziata* (☎ 0532 20 11 11, *fax 0532 20 32 33, Piazza Repubblica 5*) combines period features with modern themes. Comfortable rooms cost L220,000/320,000.

Pizzeria il Ciclone (*Via Vignatagliata 11*) has pizzas for around L10,000. Closer to the cathedral at Via Adelardi 11, *Al Brindisi* serves up traditional dishes like salami cooked in red wine for L15,000. Next door, *Pappagallo* is a simple but satisfying self-service where a meal including wine costs L12,000. In the medieval quarter, *Angeli (Via delle Volte 4)* is a rustic but stylish osteria, with roast beef for L19,000 and tortellini for L12,000.

Getting There & Away

Ferrara is on the Bologna-Venice train line, with regular trains to both cities. It is 40 minutes from Bologna and 1½ hours from Venice. Regular trains also run directly to Ravenna. Buses run from the train station to Modena (also in the Emilia-Romagna region).

BOLOGNA
pop 404,378

Bologna is not only an elegant, wealthy and intellectual centre, it's also one of Italy's more attractive larger cities. The regional capital of Emilia-Romagna, it is famous for its porticoed streets, harmonious rusty-hued architecture, university (the oldest in Europe) and, above all, its gastronomic tradition. The Bolognese have given the world tortellini, lasagne, mortadella and the inescapable spaghetti bolognese – known in Bologna as *spaghetti al ragù* – hence one of the city's nicknames, Bologna la Grassa (Bologna the Fat).

Information

The IAT tourist office (☎ 051 23 96 60, fax 051 23 14 54), at Piazza Maggiore 6, under the portico of the town hall, is open 9 am to 7 pm Monday to Saturday, to 2 pm on Sunday. There are branch offices at the train station and airport. Pick up a map and the useful booklet *Welcome to Bologna*.

The main post office is in Piazza Minghetti. Telecom telephones are at Piazza VIII Agosto 24, and at the train station. In a medical emergency call ☎ 118, or Ospedale Maggiore on ☎ 051 647 81 11. For the police call ☎ 113.

Things to See & Do

Perfect for a stroll, Bologna's traffic-free centre is formed by **Piazza Maggiore**, the adjoining **Piazza del Nettuno** and **Fontana di Nettuno** (Neptune's Fountain), sculpted in bronze by the French artist who became known as Giambologna, and **Piazza di Porta Ravegnana**, with its two leaning towers to rival Pisa's (originally there were 42).

The **Basilica di San Petronio** in Piazza Maggiore is dedicated to the city's patron saint, Petronius. It was here that Charles V was crowned emperor by the pope in 1530. The incomplete red-and-white marble facade displays the colours of Bologna, and the chapels inside contain notable works of art. The adjacent **Palazzo Comunale** (town hall) is a huge building combining several architectural styles in remarkable harmony. It features a bronze statue of Pope Gregory XIII (a native of Bologna, and the creator of the Gregorian calendar), an impressive staircase attributed to Bramante and Bologna's collection of art treasures.

The **Basilica di Santo Stefano** is a group of four churches (originally there were seven) and includes the 11th-century Chiesa del Crocefisso, which houses the bones of San Petronio.

The **Basilica di San Domenico**, erected in the early 16th century, houses the elaborate sarcophagus of St Dominic, the founder of the Dominican order. The chapel was designed by Nicoló Pisano and its shrine features figures carved by a young Michelangelo.

The **Museo Civico Archeologico**, **Pinacoteca Nazionale**, French Gothic **Basilica di San Francesco** and Romanesque **Basilica di Santo Stefano** are also well worth a visit.

Places to Stay

Budget hotels in Bologna are virtually nonexistent and it is almost impossible to find a single room. The city's busy trade-fair calendar means that hotels are often heavily booked, so always book in advance.

The best options are the two HI hostels: *Ostello San Sisto* (☎ 051 51 92 02, *Via Viadagola 14*) charges L18,000 with breakfast and *Ostello Due Torri* (☎/fax 051 50 18 10), on the same street at No 5, charges L21,000. Take bus Nos 93 or 20b from Via Irnerio (off Via dell'Indipendenza south of the station), ask the bus driver where to alight, then follow the signs to the hostel.

Right in the historic centre, *Albergo Garisenda* (☎ 051 22 43 69, *fax 051 22 10 07, Galleria del Leone 1*) looks onto the two towers and Via Rizzoli, and provides decent singles/doubles without shower for L70,000/ 100,000. *Apollo* (☎ 051 22 39 55, *fax 051 23 87 60, Via Drapperie 5*) nearby has singles/ doubles for L60,000/95,000, and doubles/ triples with bathroom for L130,000/165,000. Away from the centre, *Albergo Marconi* (☎ 051 26 28 32, *Via G Marconi 22*) provides rather anonymous single/double rooms for L55,000/70,000, with shower for L88,000/ 110,000.

Bologna has plenty of two and three-star hotels, although standards are disappointing. *Accademia* (☎ 051 23 23 18, *fax 051 26 35 90, Via delle Belle Arti 6*) is a good two-star midway between the train station and old centre, with rooms for L130,000/190,000. Closer to the station, the three-star *Donatello* (☎/fax 051 24 81 74, *Via dell'Indipendenza 65*) offers cut-price rates if there are no trade fairs happening, with roomy doubles for L160,000.

Places to Eat

Pizzeria Bella Napoli (*Via San Felice 40*) serves some of Bologna's best pizzas at reasonable prices. *Pizzeria Altero* (*Via Ugo Bassi 10*) has good pizza by the slice for only L1500. Grab a coffee and cake at *Zanarini* (*Via Luigi Carlo Farini 2*), the city's grandest tearoom. The self-service *Due Torri* (*Via dei Giudei 4*) is excellent value for lunch, with mains from L13,000 and pasta or salad for L4000 to L9000. For something fancier, try the elegant and airy *Diana* (*Via dell'Indipendenza 24a*) or the traditional, wood-lined *Cesari* (*Via Carbonesi 8*), where a sampling of the local cuisine will set you back around L70,000.

Shop at *Mercato Ugo Bassi* (*Via Ugo Bassi 27*), a covered market offering all the

BOLOGNA

PLACES TO STAY
3 Donatello
5 Accademia
7 Albergo Marconi
16 Apollo
17 Albergo Garisenda

PLACES TO EAT
6 Diana
8 Pizzeria Bella Napoli
9 Mercato Ugo Bassi
11 Pizzeria Altero
18 Due Torre
24 Zanarini
25 Cesari

OTHER
1 Tourist Office
2 Intercity Bus Terminal
4 Pinacoteca Nazionale
10 Basilica di San Francesco
12 Questura (Police Station)
13 Palazzo Comunale
14 IAT Tourist Office
15 Fontana di Nettuno
19 Le Due Torri
   (Leaning Towers)
20 Basilica di Santo Stefano
21 Main Post Office
22 Museo Civico Archeologico
23 Basilica di San Petronio
26 Basilica di San Domenico

local fare. There's also a *market* in the streets
south-east of Piazza Maggiore.

Getting There & Away
Bologna is a major transport junction for
northern Italy and trains from virtually all
major cities stop here. Buses to major cities
depart from the terminal in Piazza XX Settembre, around the corner from the train station in Piazza delle Medaglie d'Oro.

The city is linked to Milan, Florence and
Rome by the A1 (Autostrada del Sole). The
A13 heads directly for Venice and Padua, and
the A14 goes to Rimini and Ravenna.

Getting Around
Traffic is restricted in the city centre, so it's
best to park at one of the many public car
parks outside the city walls. Bus No 25 will
take you from the train station to the historical centre.

RAVENNA
pop 135,844
Ravenna is best known for its exquisite mosaics, relics of the time it was capital of the
Western Roman Empire, stronghold of
Theodoric the Great (king of the Ostrogoths)
and western seat of the Byzantines, notably

ITALY

under Justinian and Theodora. The town is easily accessible from Bologna and is worth a day trip, at the very least.

Information
The IAT tourist office (☎ 0544 354 04, fax 0544 48 26 70) is at Via Salara 8 and is open 8.30 am to 6 pm Monday to Saturday and 10 am to 4 pm on Sunday. The Ospedale Santa Maria delle Croci (☎ 0544 40 91 11) is at Via Missiroli 10. In a police emergency call ☎ 113.

Things to See
The pick of Ravenna's mosaics are found in the **Basilica di Sant'Apollinare Nuovo**, the **Basilica di San Vitale**, the **Mausoleo di Galla Placidia** (these are the oldest) and the **Battistero Neoniano**. These buildings are all in the town centre and an admission ticket to the four, as well as to the **Museo Arcivescovile**, costs L10,000. The mosaics in the **Basilica di Sant'Apollinare in Classe**, 5km away, are also notable.

Special Events
Ravenna hosts a music festival from late June to early August, featuring international artists. An annual theatre and literature festival is held in September in honour of Dante, who spent his last 10 years in the city and is buried here. In winter, opera and dance are staged at the *Teatro Alighieri (☎ 0544 325 77, Piazza Garibaldi 5)*.

Places to Stay & Eat
The HI *Ostello Dante (☎ 0544 42 11 64, Via Aurelio Nicolodi 12)* opens March to November. Take bus No 1 from Viale Pallavacini, to the left of the train station. B&B is L23,000 and family rooms are available for L25,000 per person. An evening meal is L14,000. *Al Giaciglio (☎/fax 0544 394 03, Via Rocca Brancaleone 42)* is Ravenna's sole one-star establishment, with singles/doubles and shower for L55,000/80,000. To find it, go straight ahead from the station along Viale Farini and turn right onto Via Rocca Brancaleone. Two-star *Ravenna (☎ 0544 21 22 04, fax 0544 21 20 77, Via Maroncelli 12)*, just outside the train station, has rooms for around L80,000/100,000. In the heart of the city's historic centre, the three-star *Hotel Centrale Byron (☎ 0544 334*

79, fax 0544 341 14, Via IV Novembre 14) has classy rooms from L90,000/126,000, including breakfast.

For a quick meal, you can try the *Bizantino* self-service restaurant in the city's fresh-produce market in Piazza Andrea Costa. *Cá de Vén (Via Corrado Ricci 24)* is a popular place for a regional dish or glass of wine in medieval surroundings.

Getting There & Away
Ravenna is accessible by train from Bologna, sometimes with a change at Castel Bolognese. The trip takes around 1½ hours.

Getting Around
Cycling is a popular way to get around the sights. Rental is L15,000 per day or L2000 per hour from COOP San Vitale, Piazza Farini, to the left as you leave the station.

SAN MARINO
The world's oldest surviving republic, San Marino was founded in 300 AD by a stonemason said to have been escaping religious persecution. The tiny state (only 61 sq km) strikes its own coins, has its own postage stamps and army – and is an unashamed tourist trap. The main attraction is the splendid view of the mountains and coast. You can also wander along the city walls and visit the two fortresses.

The tourist office (☎ 0549 88 29 98) is in the Palazzo del Turismo at Contrada Omagnano 20. San Marino is accessible from Rimini by bus.

The Dolomites

The limestone Dolomites (Dolomiti) stretch across Trentino-Alto Adige and into the Veneto. This spectacular Alpine region is the Italians' favoured area for skiing and there are excellent hiking trails.

Information
Information about Trentino-Alto Adige can be obtained in Trent at the APT del Trentino (☎ 0461 83 90 00, ✉ apt@provincia.tn.it), Via Romagnosi 3; in Rome (☎ 06 36 09 58 42, fax 06 320 24 13), Via del Babuino 20; and in Milan (☎ 02 86 46 12 51, fax 02 72 00

21 88), Piazza Diaz 5. Bolzano's tourist office (☎ 0471 30 70 00, ✉ bolzano@ sudtirol.com), Piazza Walther 8, also has information on the region, and there's a telephone information service on ☎ 0471 41 38 08.

The APT Dolomiti at Cortina (☎ 0436 27 11) can provide information on trekking and skiing in the Veneto.

Skiing

The Dolomites' numerous ski resorts range from expensive and fashionable Cortina d'Ampezzo in the Veneto to family-oriented resorts such as those in the Val Gardena in Trentino-Alto Adige. All the resorts have helpful tourist offices with loads of information on facilities, accommodation and transport.

The high season is generally from Christmas to early January and from early February to April, when prices increase considerably. A good way to save money is to buy a *settimana bianca* (literally, 'white week'), a package-deal ski holiday available through travel agencies throughout Italy. This covers accommodation, food and ski passes for seven days.

If you want to go it alone, but plan to do a lot of skiing, invest in a ski pass. Most resort areas offer their own passes for unlimited use of lifts at several resorts for a nominated period. The cost in the 2000-01 high season for a six-day pass was around L270,000. The Superski Dolomiti pass (☎ 0471 79 53 97), which allows access to 460 lifts and 1200km of ski runs in 12 valleys, costs L300,000. The average cost of ski and boot hire in the Alps is around L25,000 a day for downhill and L20,000 for cross-country.

Trekking

Without doubt, the Dolomites provide the most breathtaking opportunities for walking in the Italian Alps – from a half-day stroll with the kids to demanding treks that combine walking with mountaineering skills. The walking season is roughly from July to late September. Alpine refuges (*rifugi*) usually close around 20 September.

Buy a map of the hiking trails which also shows the locations of Alpine refuges. The best maps are the Tabacco 1:25,000 series, which can be bought in newsagents and bookshops in the area where you plan to hike,

and often in major bookshops in larger cities. Lonely Planet's *Walking in Italy* outlines several treks in detail and the *Italy* guide also details some suggested treks.

Hiking trails are generally well marked with numbers on red-and-white painted bands (which you will find on trees and rocks along the trails), or by numbers inside different coloured triangles for the Alte Vie (the four High Routes through the Dolomites which link a chain of rifugi and can take up to two weeks to walk – the APT in Trent has a booklet).

Recommended hiking areas include:

Alpe di Siusi
  A vast plateau above the Val Gardena, at the foot of the spectacular Sciliar.
Cortina area
  Featuring the magnificent Parco Naturale di Fanes-Sennes-Braies.
Pale di San Martino
  Accessible from San Martino di Castrozza.

Warning Remember that even in summer the weather is extremely changeable in the Alps: although it might be sweltering when you set off, you should be prepared for very cold and wet weather on even the shortest of walks. Essentials include a pair of good-quality, worn-in walking boots, an anorak or pile/wind jacket, a lightweight backpack, a warm hat and gloves, a waterproof poncho, light food and plenty of water.

Getting There & Away

The region has an excellent public transport network – the two principal bus companies are SAD in Alto Adige and the Veneto, and Atesina in Trentino. There's a network of long-distance buses operated by a number companies (eg, Lazzi, SITA, Sena, STAT and ATVO) connecting the main towns and many of the ski resorts with major cities such as Rome, Florence, Venice, Bologna, Milan and Genoa. Information is available from tourist offices and *autostazioni* (bus stations) in the region. For long-distance travel information, Lazzi Express (☎ 06 884 08 40, fax 06 841 23 96) is at Via Tagliamento 27b in Rome, and in Florence (☎ 055 28 71 18, fax 055 21 43 28) at Piazza Stazione 47r. SITA (☎ 055 21 47 21, fax 055 48 36 51) is at Via Santa Caterina da Siena 17 in Florence.

Getting Around

If you are planning to hike in the Alps during the warmer months, you'll find that hitchhiking is no problem, especially near the resort towns. The areas around the major resorts are well serviced by local buses, and tourist offices will be able to provide information on local bus services. During winter, most resorts have 'ski bus' shuttle services from the towns to the main ski facilities.

CORTINA D'AMPEZZO
pop 1200

Italy's most fashionable and expensive ski resort, Cortina is also one of the best equipped and certainly the most picturesque. The area is very popular for trekking and climbing, with well-marked trails and numerous rifugi.

The main APT tourist office (☎ 0436 27 11) has information on Cortina's (expensive!) accommodation. *International Camping Olympia* (☎ 0436 50 57) is north of Cortina at Fiames and is open year-round. *Casa Tua* (☎ 0436 22 78, ✉ casatua@tin.it, Zuel 100) in Cortina charges L50,000 to L90,000 per person, depending on the season. SAD buses connect Cortina with Bolzano, via Dobbiaco, and long-distance services are operated by ATVO, Zani, Lazzi and SITA.

CANAZEI
pop 1730

Set in the Fassa Dolomites, the resort of Canazei has more than 100km of trails and is linked to the challenging network of runs known as the **Sella Ronda**. Canazei also offers cross-country skiing and summer skiing on Marmolada, which at 3342m is the highest peak in the Dolomites.

The Marmolada *camping ground* (☎ 0462 60 16 60) is open all year, and there is also a choice of hotels, furnished rooms and apartments. Contact the AAST tourist office (☎ 0462 60 11 13, fax 0462 60 25 02) for full details. The resort is accessible by Atesina bus from Trent and SAD bus from Bolzano.

VAL GARDENA

This is one of the most popular skiing areas in the Alps, due to its reasonable prices and first-class facilities for downhill, cross-country and Alpine skiing. There are superb walking trails in the Sella Group and the Alpe di Siusi. The Vallunga, behind Selva, is great for family walks and cross-country skiing.

The valley's main towns are Ortisei, Santa Cristina and Selva, all offering plenty of accommodation and easy access to runs. The tourist offices at Santa Cristina (☎ 0471 79 30 46, fax 0471 79 31 98) and Selva (☎ 0471 79 51 22, fax 0471 79 42 45) have extensive information on accommodation and facilities. Staff speak English and will send details on request. The Val Gardena is accessible from Bolzano by SAD bus, and is connected to major Italian cities by coach services (Lazzi, SITA and STAT).

SAN MARTINO DI CASTROZZA

Located in a sheltered position beneath the Pale di San Martino, this resort is popular among Italians and offers good facilities and ski runs, as well as cross-country skiing and a toboggan run. The APT office (☎ 0439 76 88 67, fax 0439 76 88 14) will provide a full list of accommodation, or try *Garni Suisse* (☎ 0439 680 87, Via Dolomiti 1), where singles/doubles with breakfast cost L43,000/86,000. Buses travel regularly from Trent, Milan, Venice, Padua and Bologna.

Central Italy

Miraculously, the rolling hills and soft golden light of Tuscany, and rugged hill towns of Umbria and the Marches – so familiar to us through the works of the Renaissance artists – seem virtually unchanged today. The locals remain close to the land, but in each of the regions there is a strong artistic and cultural tradition – even the smallest medieval hill town can harbour extraordinary works of art.

FLORENCE
pop 403,294

Cradle of the Renaissance, home of Dante, Machiavelli, Michelangelo and the Medici. Florence's (Firenze) dazzling wealth of art, culture and history overwhelms most visitors, making it one of the most enticing cities in Italy – as the throngs of visitors attest.

Florence was founded as a colony of the Etruscan city of Fiesole in about 200 BC and later became the strategic Roman garrison settlement of Florentia. In the Middle Ages the city developed a flourishing economy based on banking and commerce, which sparked a period of building and growth previously unequalled in Italy. It was a major focal point for the Guelph and Ghibelline struggle of the 13th century, which saw Dante banished from the city. But Florence truly flourished in the 15th century under the Medici, reaching the height of its cultural, artistic and political development as it gave birth to the Renaissance.

The Grand Duchy of the Medici was succeeded in the 18th century by the House of Lorraine (related to the Austrian Habsburgs). Following the Risorgimento unification, Florence was the capital of the new kingdom of Italy from 1865 to 1871. During WWII parts of the city were destroyed by bombing, including all of the bridges except the Ponte Vecchio, and in 1966 a devastating flood destroyed or severely damaged many important works of art.

Orientation

Whether you arrive by train, bus or car, the main train station, Santa Maria Novella, is a good reference point. Budget hotels and pensioni are concentrated around Via Nazionale to the east of the station, and Piazza Santa Maria Novella to the south. The main thoroughfare to the centre is Via de' Panzani and then Via de' Cerretani, about a 10-minute walk. You'll know you've arrived when you first glimpse the Duomo.

Once at Piazza del Duomo you will find Florence easy to negotiate, with most of the major sights within easy walking distance. Most museums stay open until 10 pm (virtually all are closed on Monday), but Florence is a living art museum and you won't waste your time by just strolling through its streets. Take the city ATAF buses for longer distances such as to Piazzale Michelangelo or the nearby suburb of Fiesole, both of which offer panoramic views of the city.

Information

Tourist Offices The Florence City Council (Comune di Firenze) operates a tourist information office (☎ 055 21 22 45, fax 055 238 12 26) opposite the main train station at Piazza della Stazione 4, next to the Chiesa di Santa Maria Novella; there's another office at Borgo Santa Croce 29r (☎ 055 234 04 44). Opening hours are 8.30 am to 5.30 pm Monday to Saturday (to 1.30 pm on Sunday). The main APT office (☎ 055 29 08 32/33, fax 055 276 03 83) is just north of the Duomo at Via Cavour 1r, open 8.15 am to 7.15 pm Monday to Saturday and Sunday to 1.30 pm. At all offices you can pick up a map of the city, a list of hotels and other useful information.

The Consorzio ITA, inside the station on the main concourse, has a computerised system for checking the availability of hotel rooms and can book you a night for a small fee; there are no phone bookings. A good map of the city, on sale at newsstands, is the one with the white, red and black cover called *Firenze: Pianta della Città*.

Foreign Consulates The US consulate (☎ 055 239 82 76) is at Lungarno Vespucci 38, the UK's (☎ 055 28 41 33) is at Lungarno Corsini 2 and the French consulate (☎ 055 230 25 56) is at Piazza Ognissanti 2.

Money The main banks are concentrated around Piazza della Repubblica. You can also use the service at the information office in the station, but it has poor exchange rates.

Post & Communications The main post office is on Via Pellicceria, off Piazza della Repubblica, and is open 8.15 am to 7 pm Monday to Saturday. Poste restante mail can be addressed to 50100 Firenze. There is a Telecom office at Via Cavour 21r, open 7 am to 11 pm daily, and another at the station.

Internet Train has 10 branches in Florence, including offices not far from the station at Via Guelfa 24r (☎ 055 21 47 94) and in Santa Croce at Via dei Benci 36 (☎ 055 263 85 55). It charges L6000/12,000 per half-hour/hour and also offers postal and money-transfer services. The lively Caffè Mambo at Via G Verdi 49 has a separate Internet area and charges L2500 for 15 minutes.

Bookshops The Paperback Exchange, Via Fiesolana 31r (closed Sunday), offers a vast selection of new and second-hand English-language books. Internazionale Seeber, Via de' Tornabuoni 70r; and Feltrinelli International, Via Cavour 12 20r, also have good selections.

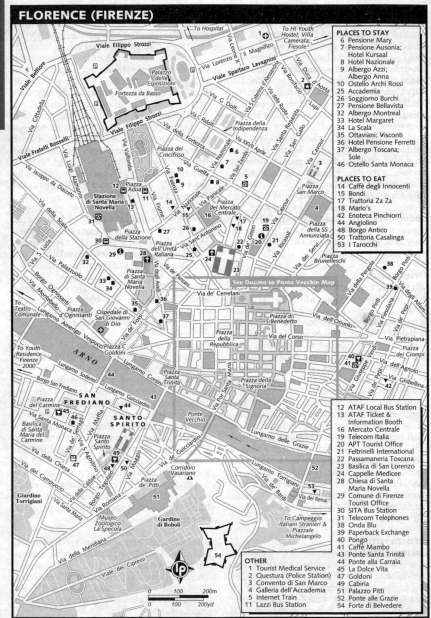

FLORENCE (FIRENZE)

PLACES TO STAY
6 Pensione Mary
7 Pensione Ausonia;
  Hotel Kursaal
8 Hotel Nazionale
9 Albergo Azzi;
  Albergo Anna
10 Ostello Archi Rossi
25 Accademia
26 Soggiorno Burchi
27 Pensione Bellavista
32 Albergo Montreal
33 Hotel Margaret
34 La Scala
35 Ottaviani; Visconti
36 Hotel Pensione Ferretti
37 Albergo Toscana;
  Sole
46 Ostello Santa Monaca

PLACES TO EAT
14 Caffè degli Innocenti
15 Bondi
17 Trattoria Za Za
18 Mario's
42 Enoteca Pinchiorri
44 Angiolino
48 Borgo Antico
50 Trattoria Casalinga
53 I Tarocchi

OTHER
1 Tourist Medical Service
2 Questura (Police Station)
3 Convento di San Marco
4 Galleria dell'Accademia
5 Internet Train
11 Lazzi Bus Station
12 ATAF Local Bus Station
13 ATAF Ticket &
  Information Booth
16 Mercato Centrale
19 Telecom Italia
20 APT Tourist Office
21 Feltrinelli International
22 Passamaneria Toscana
23 Basilica di San Lorenzo
24 Cappelle Medicee
28 Chiesa di Santa
  Maria Novella
29 Comune di Firenze
  Tourist Office
30 SITA Bus Station
31 Telecom Telephones
38 Onda Blu
39 Paperback Exchange
40 Pongo
41 Caffè Mambo
43 Ponte Santa Trinità
44 Ponte alla Carraia
45 La Dolce Vita
47 Goldoni
49 Cabiria
51 Palazzo Pitti
52 Ponte alle Grazie
54 Forte di Belvedere

See Duomo to Ponte Vecchio Map

Laundry Onda Blu, east of the Duomo at Via degli Alfani 24bR and at Via Guelfa 22a rosso, is self-service and charges L5500 to wash and L5500 to dry.

Medical & Emergency Services For an ambulance call ☎ 118. The main public hospital is Ospedale Careggi (☎ 055 427 71 11), Viale Morgagni 85, north of the city centre. Tourist Medical Service (☎ 055 47 54 11), Via Lorenzo il Magnifico 59, can be phoned 24 hours and the doctors speak English, French and German. An organisation of volunteer interpreters (English, French and German) called the Associazione Volontari Ospedalieri (☎ 055 234 45 67, ☎ 055 40 31 26) will translate free of charge once you've found a doctor. Hospitals have a list of volunteers. All-night pharmacies include the Farmacia Comunale (☎ 055 28 94 35), inside the station; and Molteni (☎ 055 28 94 90) in the city centre at Via dei Calzaiuoli 7r.

Call ☎ 113 for the police. The questura (☎ 055 497 71) is at Via Zara 2. There is an office for foreigners where you can report thefts etc. For information about lost property call ☎ 055 328 39 42. Towed-away cars (☎ 055 30 82 49) can be collected from Via dell'Arcovata 6 (south-west of the centre).

Dangers & Annoyances Crowds, heavy traffic, noisy Vespas and summer heat can combine to make Florence unpleasant. Air pollution can be a problem for small children, people with respiratory problems and the elderly. Pickpockets are active in crowds and on buses: beware of the groups of dishevelled women and children carrying newspapers and cardboard, whose trick is to distract you while others rifle through your bag and pockets.

Things to See & Do
Duomo With its nougat facade and sykline-dominating dome, the Duomo is one of Italy's most famous monuments, and the world's fourth-largest cathedral. Named the Cattedrale di Santa Maria del Fiore, the breathtaking structure was begun in 1294 by the Sienese architect Arnolfo di Cambio but took almost 150 years to complete.

The Renaissance architect Brunelleschi won a public competition in 1420 to design the enormous dome, the first of its kind since antiquity. The octagonal dome is decorated with frescoes by Vasari and Zuccari, and stained-glass windows by Donatello, Paolo Uccello and Lorenzo Ghiberti. For a bird's-eye view of Florence, climb to the top of the cupola (open 8.30 am to 7.30 pm Monday to Friday and to 5 pm on Saturday; entry L10,000). The Duomo's marble facade is a 19th-century replacement of the unfinished original, which was pulled down in the 16th century.

Giotto designed and began building the graceful **bell tower** next to the cathedral in 1334, but died before it was completed. The campanile is 82m high and you can climb its stairs daily between 9 am and 7.30 pm; entry is L10,000.

The Romanesque **baptistry**, believed to have been built between the 5th and 11th centuries on the site of a Roman temple, is the oldest building in Florence. Dante was baptised here, and it is particularly famous for its gilded-bronze doors. The celebrated *Gates of Paradise* by Lorenzo Ghiberti face the Duomo to the east; Ghiberti also designed the north door. The south door, by Andrea Pisano, dates from 1336 and is the oldest. Most of the doors are copies – the original panels are being removed for restoration and placement in the Museo dell'Opera del Duomo. The baptistry is open noon to 6.30 pm Monday to Saturday and 8.30 am to 1.30 pm on Sunday; entry costs L5000.

Uffizi Gallery The Palazzo degli Uffizi, built by Vasari in the 16th century, contains some of the world's best-loved Renaissance paintings. The collection is Italy's most important, and represents the huge legacy of the Medici family. Be prepared to swoon – and to join a lengthy queue.

The gallery's inordinate number of masterpieces include 14th-century gems by Giotto and Cimabue; Botticelli's *Birth of Venus* and *Allegory of Spring* from the 15th century; and works by Filippo Lippi, Fra Angelico and Paolo Uccello. *The Annunciation* by Leonardo da Vinci is also here, along with Michelangelo's *Holy Family*, Titian's *Venus of Urbino* and renowned works by Raphael, Andrea del Sarto, Tintoretto, Caravaggio and Tiepolo. The gallery is open 8.30 am to 10 pm daily except Monday (Sunday to 8 pm). Entry is L12,000.

Piazza della Signoria & Palazzo Vecchio

Designed by Arnolfo di Cambio and built between 1298 and 1340, the Palazzo Vecchio is the traditional seat of the Florentine government. In the 16th century it became the ducal palace of the Medici (before they moved to the Palazzo Pitti), and was given an interior facelift by Vasari. Visit the Michelozzo courtyard just inside the entrance and the lavishly decorated apartments upstairs. The palazzo is open 9 am to 7 pm (Thursday and Sunday to 2 pm) daily. Admission is L11,000.

The palace's turrets, battlements and bell tower form an imposing backdrop to Piazza della Signoria, scene of many pivotal political events in the history of Florence, including the execution of the religious and political reformer Savonarola; a bronze plaque marks the spot where he was burned at the stake in 1498. The **Loggia della Signoria**, at right angles to the Palazzo Vecchio, displays sculptures such as Giambologna's *Rape of the Sabine Women*, but Cellini's famous *Perseus* has been relocated to the Uffizi. The statue of *David* is a fine copy of Michelangelo's masterpiece; the original was installed on the site in 1504, and is now safely indoors in the Galleria dell'Accademia.

Ponte Vecchio

This famous 14th-century bridge, lined with gold and silversmiths' shops, was the only one to survive Nazi bombing in WWII. Originally, the shops housed butchers, but when a corridor along the 1st floor was built by the Medici to link the Palazzo Pitti and Palazzo Vecchio, it was ordered that goldsmiths rather than noisome butchers should trade on the bridge.

Palazzo Pitti

This immense and imposing palazzo was built for the Pitti family, great rivals of the Medici, who moved in a century later. The **Galleria Palatina** has works by Raphael, Filippo Lippi, Titian and Rubens, hung in lavishly decorated rooms. The gallery and gloriously over-the-top **royal apartments** are open 8.30 am to 10 pm Tuesday to Saturday and to 8 pm on Sunday; entry L12,000. The palace also houses the **Museo degli Argenti** (Silver Museum) and **Galleria d'Arte Moderna**, open 8.30 am to 2 pm Tuesday to Sunday.

Don't leave without visiting the Renaissance **Giardino di Boboli** (Boboli Gardens), with grottoes, fountains, leafy walkways and panoramic city views. Entry is L4000.

Museo del Bargello

Also known as the Palazzo del Podestà, the medieval Palazzo del Bargello has a grim history as the seat of the local ruler and, later, of the chief of police. The palace now houses Florence's rich collection of sculpture, notably Michelangelo's *Bacchus*, Donatello's bronze *David*, Giambologna's *Mercury* and works by Benvenuto Cellini and the della Robbias. The Bargello is at Via del Proconsolo 4, and is open 8.30 am to 2 pm Tuesday to Sunday; entry is L8000.

Galleria dell'Accademia

Michelangelo's *David* is housed in this gallery, as are four of the artist's unfinished *Slaves*. Early Florentine works are on show in the gallery upstairs. The Accademia is at Via Ricasoli 60, and opens 8.30 am to 10 pm Tuesday to Saturday and Sunday to 8 pm. Entry is L12,000.

Convento di San Marco

The Monastery of St Mark pays homage to the work of Fra Angelico, who decorated many of the monks' cells with sublime frescoes and lived here from 1438 to 1455. Don't miss the peaceful cloisters (depicted in his *Annunciation*). The monastery also contains works by Fra Bartolomeo and Ghirlandaio, as well as the cell of the monk Savonarola. It's open 8.30 am to 2 pm Tuesday to Sunday, and entry is L8000.

Basilica di San Lorenzo & Cappelle Medicee

The basilica was built by Brunelleschi in the early 15th century for the Medici and includes his mathematically precise **Sagrestia Vecchia** (Old Sacristy), with sculptural decoration by Donatello. The cloister leads to the **Biblioteca Laurenziana**, the huge library built to house the Medici collection of some 10,000 manuscripts and entered via Michelangelo's flowing Mannerist stairway.

The Cappelle Medicee (Medici Chapels) are around the corner in Piazza Madonna degli Aldobrandini. The **Cappella dei Principi**, sumptuously decorated with marble and semiprecious stones, was the principal burial

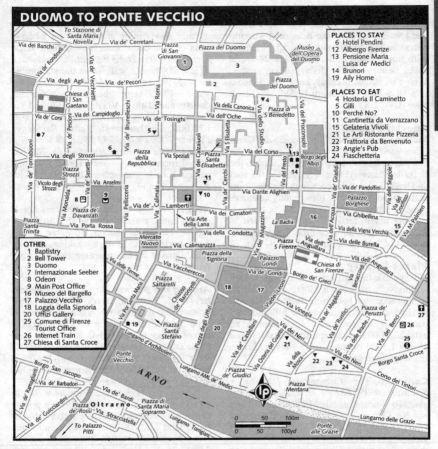

DUOMO TO PONTE VECCHIO

PLACES TO STAY
6 Hotel Pendini
12 Albergo Firenze
13 Pensione Maria Luisa de' Medici
14 Brunori
19 Aily Home

PLACES TO EAT
4 Hosteria Il Caminetto
5 Gilli
10 Perché No?
11 Cantinetta da Verrazzano
15 Gelateria Vivoli
21 Le Arti Ristorante Pizzeria
22 Trattoria da Benvenuto
23 Angie's Pub
24 Fiaschetteria

OTHER
1 Baptistry
2 Bell Tower
3 Duomo
7 Internazionale Seeber
8 Odeon
9 Main Post Office
16 Museo del Bargello
17 Palazzo Vecchio
18 Loggia della Signoria
20 Uffizi Gallery
25 Comune di Firenze Tourist Office
26 Internet Train
27 Chiesa di Santa Croce

place of the Medici grand dukes. The incomplete **Sagrestia Nuova** was Michelangelo's first architectural effort, and contains his *Medici Madonna*, *Night & Day* and *Dawn & Dusk* sculptures, which adorn the Medici tombs. The chapels are open 8.30 am to 5 pm Tuesday to Sunday, and admission is L11,000.

Other Attractions The Tuscan Gothic **Chiesa di Santa Maria Novella** was constructed for the Dominican Order during the 13th and 14th centuries; its white-and-green marble facade was designed by Alberti in the 15th century. The church features Masaccio's *Trinity*, a masterpiece of perspective, and is decorated with frescoes by Ghirlandaio (who was perhaps assisted by a very young Michelangelo). **Cappella di Filippo Strozzi** has frescoes by Filippino Lippi, and those in the cloisters are by Paolo Uccello.

Head up to **Piazzale Michelangelo** for unparalleled views of Florence. To reach the piazzale from the city centre, cross the Ponte Vecchio, turn left and walk along the river, then turn right at Piazza Giuseppe Poggi; if you're footsore, take bus No 13 from the station.

Cycling

I Bike Italy (☎ 055 234 23 71) offers single and two-day guided bike rides (and walking tours) in the countryside around Florence, with stops at vineyards. It supplies 24-speed bikes, helmets and English-speaking guides; Web site: www.ibikeitaly.com. The Fiesole ride costs US$65, Chianti US$80 and Siena (two days) US$235.

Special Events

Major festivals include the Scoppio del Carro (Explosion of the Cart), held in front of the Duomo on Easter Sunday; and, on 24 June, the Festa del Patrono (Feast of St John the Baptist) and lively Calcio Storico, which features football matches played in 16th-century costume. Maggio Musicale Fiorentino, Italy's longest-running music festival, runs from April to June. For information call the Teatro Comunale (☎ 055 21 11 58, fax 055 277 94 10).

Places to Stay

Always ask the full price of a room before putting your bags down. Hotels and pensioni in Florence are becoming increasingly expensive and are notorious for bill-padding, particularly in summer. Many require an extra L10,000 for a compulsory breakfast and charge L3000 or more for a shower. Prices listed are high season.

Camping The *Campeggio Italiani e Stranieri* (☎ 055 681 19 77, Viale Michelangelo 80) is near Piazzale Michelangelo. Take bus No 13 from the station. *Villa Camerata* (☎ 055 60 03 15, fax 055 61 03 00, Viale Augusto Righi 2-4) is next to the HI hostel (see the next section). *Campeggio Panoramico* (☎ 055 59 90 69, fax 055 591 86, Via Peramonda 1), in Fiesole, also has bungalows. Take bus No 7 from the station.

Hostels The HI *Ostello Villa Camerata* (☎ 055 60 14 51, fax 055 61 03 00, Viale Augusto Righi 2-4) charges L26,000 for B&B and L14,000 for dinner; there is also a bar. Take bus No 17, which leaves from the right of the station as you leave the platforms and takes 20 minutes. Daytime closing is 9 am to 2 pm. It is open to HI members only and reservations can be made by mail (essential in summer).

The private *Ostello Archi Rossi* (☎ 055 29 08 04, fax 055 230 26 01, Via Faenza 94r) is another good option at L30,000 for a bed in a six or nine-bed dorm room. *Ostello Santa Monaca* (☎ 055 26 83 38, Via Santa Monaca 6) is a 20-minute walk from the station: go through Piazza Santa Maria Novella, along Via de' Fossi, across the Ponte alla Carraia, directly ahead along Via de' Serragli, and Via Santa Monaca is on the right. A bed costs L25,000. Further west, *Youth Residence Firenze 2000* (☎ 055 233 55 58, ✉ scatizzi@dada.it, Via le Raffaello Sanzio 16) has shared rooms with *en suite* for L55,000 per person. It lacks atmosphere, but the warm indoor pool is a big plus.

Hotels With more than 150 budget hotels in Florence, you should be able to find a room even in peak season. However, it is always advisable to make a booking, and you should arrive by late morning to claim your room.

Around the Station Tiny *Pensione Bellavista* (☎ 055 28 45 28, fax 055 28 48 74, Largo Alinari 15), at the start of Via Nazionale, has simple singles/doubles for L90,000/130,000; two of the doubles have balconies and a view of the Duomo. *Albergo Azzi* (☎/fax 055 21 38 06, Via Faenza 56) has rooms with breakfast for L70,000/110,000. The owners are helpful, and they also run *Albergo Anna* upstairs.

Across Via Nazionale, *Soggiorno Burchi* (☎ 055 41 44 54, Via Faenza 20) is a private house with eccentric but comfortable rooms for around L90,000/110,000 with bathroom. *Hotel Nazionale* (☎ 055 238 22 03, fax 055 238 17 35, Via Nazionale 22) has rooms with shower for L100,000/150,000, breakfast included. A few doors up at No 24, the recently renovated *Pensione Ausonia* (☎ 055 49 65 47, fax 055 462 66 15) has something for everyone. Run by a young couple who go out of their way to help travellers, the accommodation ranges from standard singles/doubles/triples with breakfast for L90,000/145,000/190,000 to rooms with bathroom for L115,000/165,000/220,000; downstairs in their two-star *Hotel Kursaal* (☎ 055 49 63 24), superior doubles/triples with balcony, air-con and satellite TV are L210,000/255,000. *Pensione Mary* (☎/fax 055 49 63 10, Piazza dell'Indipendenza 5) has singles/doubles with bathroom and breakfast for L120,000/160,000.

Closer to the station, the two-star *Accademia* (☎ 055 29 34 51, fax 055 21 97 71, Via Faenza 7) is housed in an 18th-century palace, replete with magnificent stained-glass doors and carved wooden ceilings. Singles are L140,000 and doubles with bathroom go for L230,000, including breakfast and satellite TV.

Around Piazza Santa Maria Novella Via della Scala, which runs north-west off the piazza, is lined with pensioni. *La Scala* (☎ 055 21 26 29) at No 21 has small doubles/triples for L85,000/150,000. *Hotel Margaret* (☎ 055 21 01 38), at No 25, has pleasantly furnished singles/doubles with bathroom for L95,000/120,000. At No 43, the no-frills *Albergo Montreal* (☎ 055 238 23 31, fax 055 28 74 91) has clean singles for L85,000 and doubles/triples/quads with bathroom for L110,000/150,000/185,000.

Sole (☎/fax 055 239 60 94, Via del Sole 8) charges L70,000/100,000 for basic singles/doubles; a double with bathroom costs L120,000. Ask for a quiet room, as the street can be noisy. *Albergo Toscana* (☎/fax 055 21 31 56), in the same building, has pretty rooms with bathroom for L90,000/150,000. Slightly north, the family-run *Hotel Pensione Ferretti* (☎ 055 238 13 28, fax 055 21 92 88, Via delle Belle Donne 17) has comfortable singles for L70,000; rooms with bathroom are L90,000/140,000, including breakfast.

Ottaviani (☎ 055 239 62 23, fax 055 29 33 55, Piazza Ottaviani 1), just off Piazza Santa Maria Novella, has singles/doubles for a reasonable L70,000/90,000, breakfast included. *Visconti* (☎/fax 055 21 38 77), in the same building, has statues galore and a pleasant breakfast terrace. Singles are L65,000, and doubles are L90,000/140,000 without/with bathroom.

The Duomo to Ponte Vecchio This area is a 15-minute walk from the station and is right in the heart of old Florence. One of the best deals is the small *Aily Home* (☎ 055 239 65 05, Piazza Santo Stefano 1), overlooking the Ponte Vecchio. Its singles are L40,000 and doubles (three of which overlook the bridge) go for L70,000 a night. *Albergo Firenze*

(☎ 055 21 42 03, fax 055 21 23 70, Piazza dei Donati 4), just south of the Duomo, offers singles/doubles with bathroom and breakfast for L100,000/140,000. *Brunori* (☎ 055 28 96 48, Via del Proconsolo 5) has doubles for L96,000, with bathroom for L124,000. *Pensione Maria Luisa de' Medici* (☎/fax 055 28 00 48, Via del Corso 1) is in a 17th-century palace. It has no singles, but its large rooms cater for up to five people. A double starts at L80,000.

Up several notches, the three-star *Hotel Pendini* (☎ 055 21 11 70, fax 055 28 18 07, Via degli Strozzi 2) is just around the corner from Piazza della Repubblica. Light and airy rooms on the 4th floor are L180,000/260,000. A family suite for six is L570,000.

Villa Experience life in an old villa at *Bencistà* (☎/fax 055 591 63, ✉ bencista@uol.it, Via Benedetto da Maiano 4), about 1km from Fiesole in the hills overlooking Florence. Compulsory half-board is a budget-breaking L270,000/300,000 without/with bathroom.

Places to Eat

Tuscany is known for its simple but fine cuisine. At its most basic, how can you beat a thick slice of crusty bread drizzled with olive oil and downed with a glass of ripe Chianti? Try the *ribollita*, a very filling soup of vegetables and white beans, reboiled with chunks of bread and garnished with olive oil. Another traditional dish is *bistecca alla Fiorentina* (steak Florentine), big enough for two.

The *covered market* in San Lorenzo, open 7 am to 2 pm Monday to Friday, offers fresh produce, cheeses and meat at reasonable prices.

Restaurants – City Centre At the *Trattoria da Benvenuto* (Via Mosca 16r), on the corner of Via dei Neri, a full repast will cost around L45,000 and a quick meal of pasta, bread and wine L16,000. For more atmospheric surroundings, there's the attractively timbered *Le Arti Ristorante Pizzeria* (Via dei Neri 57). The menu is more varied than most, with good pizza for around L10,000 and pasta for L13,000. At No 35r on the same street, *Angie's Pub* has focaccia for around L6000, as well as hamburgers and hot dogs, swilled down with beer on tap; there's no extra charge to sit. *Fiaschetteria* (Via dei Neri 17r) has a good range of panini from L2500 and value-for-money pastas for around L8000.

At *Hosteria Il Caminetto (Via dello Studio 34)*, just south of Piazza del Duomo, pasta for L14,000 or a full meal for around L45,000 can be enjoyed on its small vine-covered terrace. *Enoteca Pinchiorri (☎ 24 27 77, Via Ghibellina 87)*, just north of Chiesa di Santa Croce, is arguably the city's finest restaurant. The cuisine is Italian-style nouvelle, the surroundings are palatial and, at more than L150,000 per head, the prices are prohibitive.

Restaurants – Around San Lorenzo
Tiny but popular *Mario's (Via Rosina 2r)*, near the Mercato Centrale, is open at lunchtime only, and serves delicious pasta for around L7000. Around the corner at Piazza del Mercato Centrale 24, *Trattoria Za Za* is another local favourite, with outdoor seating and reasonable prices. *Bondi (Via dell'Ariento 85)* specialises in focaccia and pizza from L3000.

Restaurants – In the Oltrarno
Trattoria Casalinga (Via dei Michelozzi 9r) is a bustling place popular with the locals. The food is great and a filling meal of pasta, meat or contorni, and wine will cost around L15,000 to L20,000. *I Tarocchi (Via de' Renai 16)* serves superior pizza from L7500 to L10,000, as well as regional dishes including a good range of pasta from L9000 to L11,000 and plenty of salads for around L8000. *Angiolino (Via Santo Spirito 36r)* is an excellent trattoria where a full meal will cost around L40,000. In trendy Piazza Santo Spirito, *Borgo Antico* is a great summer retreat for alfresco dining, but at L25,000 for spaghetti vongole it's not cheap.

Cafes & Snack Bars
Perhaps the city's finest cafe is the wonderfully intact *belle époque Gilli*, on Piazza della Repubblica. If you can't resist the bountiful display of mouthwatering sweet and savoury delights, you'll save lire if not calories by eating and drinking at the bar.

Caffè degli Innocenti (Via Nazionale 57), near the Mercato Centrale, has a selection of pre-prepared panini and good cakes for around L2500 to L4500. The streets between the Duomo and the Arno harbour many pizzerias where you can buy takeaway pizza by the slice for around L2000 to L4000, depending on the weight.

Cantinetta da Verrazzano (Via dei Tavolini 18r) wine bar/cafe is a tight fit and deservedly popular. Grab a snack from the takeaway bakery, have a meal or quaff some memorable Chianti.

Gelati Two of the city's best outlets for gelati are *Gelateria Vivoli* in Via dell'Isola delle Stinche, south of Via Ghibellina, and *Perché No? (Via dei Tavolini 19r)*, off Via dei Calzaiuoli. Tiny tubs cost L3000, but at Vivoli it's well worth it for the comfy seats and welcome bathroom.

Entertainment
Hotels and tourist offices should have copies of the various free publications listing the theatrical and musical events and festivals held in the city and surrounding areas. Look out for the bimonthly *Florence Today* and the monthly *Florence Concierge Information*. The monthly *Firenze Spettacolo* entertainment guide is available from newsstands, where you can also pick up English-language publication *Vista*.

Concerts, opera and dance are performed year-round at the *Teatro Comunale (Corso Italia 16)*, with the main seasons running from September to December and January to April. Contact the theatre's box office (☎ 055 277 92 36).

English films are screened at a number of cinemas: the *Astro* in Piazza San Simone, near Santa Croce (every night except Monday); the *Odeon* in Piazza Strozzi (Monday and Wednesday); and the *Goldoni*, Via de' Serragli (Wednesday).

Nightclubs include *La Dolce Vita*, spilling onto Piazza del Carmine, south of the Arno, and *Pongo (Via Giuseppe Verdi 59r)*, with an assortment of live music. The tiny but noisy *Cabiria* bar in Piazza Santo Spirito is popular, especially in summer.

A more sedate pastime is the nightly *passeggiata* (stroll) in Piazzale Michelangelo, overlooking the city (take bus No 13 from the station or the Duomo).

Shopping
The main shopping area is between the Duomo and the Arno, with boutiques concentrated

ITALY

along Via Roma, Via dei Calzaiuoli and Via Por Santa Maria, leading to the goldsmiths lining the Ponte Vecchio. Window-shop along Via de' Tornabuoni, where top designers such as Gucci, Prada and Ferragamo hawk their wares.

The open-air market (open Monday to Saturday) held in the streets surrounding San Lorenzo near the Mercato Centrale offers leather goods, clothing and jewellery at low prices but often dodgy quality. Check carefully before you buy. You can bargain, but not if you use a credit card. The flea market at Piazza dei Ciompi, off Borgo Allegri and north of Santa Croce, is not as extensive but there are often some great bargains. It opens from around 9 am to 6 pm Monday to Saturday and on the last Sunday of the month.

Florence is renowned for its beautifully patterned paper, which is stocked in the many *cartolerie* (stationer's shops) throughout the city and at the markets. Lovers of Florentine velvet cushions, tapestries and decorative tassels should head for Passamaneria Toscana, Piazza San Lorenzo 12r.

Getting There & Away
Air Florence is served by two airports, Amerigo Vespucci and Galileo Galilei. Amerigo Vespucci (☎ 055 37 34 98, flight info ☎ 055 306 17 00/02), a few kilometres north-west of the city centre, serves domestic and European flights. Galileo Galilei (☎ 055 21 60 73, Firenze Air Terminal at Santa Maria Novella station), just under an hour away from Florence near Pisa, is one of northern Italy's main international and domestic airports.

Bus The SITA bus station (☎ 055 21 47 21, fax 055 48 36 51), Via Santa Caterina da Siena 17, is just west of the train station. Buses leave for Siena, San Gimignano and Volterra. Lazzi (☎ 055 28 71 18, fax 055 21 43 28) is at Piazza Stazione 47r.

Train Florence is on the main Rome-Milan line. Most of the trains are the fast Eurostars, for which you have to book and to pay a *rapido* supplement. Regular trains also go to/from Venice (three hours) and Trieste. For train information ring ☎ 147 88 80 88.

Car & Motorcycle Florence is connected by the Autostrada del Sole (A1) to Bologna and Milan in the north and Rome and Naples to the south. The Firenze-Mare motorway links Florence with Prato, Pistoia, Lucca, Pisa and the Versilia coast, and a *superstrada* (dual carriageway) joins the city to Siena. Exits from the autostrade into Florence are well signposted, and either one of the exits marked 'Firenze nord' or 'Firenze sud' will take you to the centre of town. There are tourist information offices on the A1 both to the north and south of the city.

Getting Around
To/From the Airport Regular trains to Pisa airport leave from platform No 5 at Florence's Santa Maria Novella station daily from 6.46 am to 5 pm. Check your bags in at the air terminal (☎ 055 21 60 73) near platform 5, at least 15 minutes before train departure time.

You can get to Amerigo Vespucci airport by ATAF bus No 62 from the train station (every 20 minutes from 6.30 am to 10.20 pm) or, more directly, by SITA coach from the depot in Via Santa Caterina da Siena (every hour or so from 8.15 am to 7.30 pm).

Bus ATAF buses service the city centre and Fiesole. The terminal for the most useful buses is in a small piazza to the left as you go out of the station onto Via Valfonda. Bus No 7 leaves from here for Fiesole and also stops at the Duomo. Tickets must be bought before you get on the bus and are sold at most tobacconists and newsstands or from automatic vending machines at major bus stops (L1500 for one hour, L2500 for three hours, L6000 for 24 hours).

Car & Motorcycle If you're spending the day in Florence, use the underground parking areas at the train station or in Piazza del Mercato Centrale (L4000 an hour). Less expensive parking is available from November to February at the Fortezza da Basso (L3000 an hour).

To rent a car, try Hertz (☎ 055 28 22 60), Via M Finiguerra 33r, or Avis (☎ 055 21 36 29), Borgo Ognissanti 128r. For motorcycles and bicycles try Alinari (☎ 055 28 05 00), Via Guelfa 85r. Ask at the station for information about the city council's free bicycles for use between 8 am and 7.30 pm.

ITALY

PISA
pop 98,928

Once a maritime power to rival Genoa and
Venice, Pisa now makes the most of its one
remaining claim to fame: its leaning tower.
The busy port city was also the site of an important university and the home of Galileo
Galilei (1564-1642). Pisa was devastated by
the Genoese in the 13th century, and its history eventually merged with that of Florence.
Like that city, Pisa straddles the Arno River;
unlike Florence, however, the city has a
pleasing intimacy and charm so far intact despite the many day-trippers.

Orientation & Information

The focus for visitors is the Campo dei Miracoli, a 1.5km walk from the train station across
the Arno. Bus No 4 will save you the walk.
The medieval town centre around Borgo
Stretto is a kilometre or so from the station.

There are APT tourist information offices
at the station (☎ 050 422 91), the airport and
at Via Carlo Cammeo 2, west of Campo dei
Miracoli. The offices open 9 am to 7 pm
Monday to Saturday, and 9.30 am to 1.30 pm
Sunday. Pisa's postcode is 56100.

Things to See & Do

The Pisans can justly claim that their **Campo
dei Miracoli** (Field of Miracles) is one of the
most beautiful squares in the world, whether
by day or by night. A welcome expanse of
well-kept lawns provides the perfect setting
for the dazzling white marble cathedral, baptistry and bell tower – all of which lean to
varying degrees.

The striped Pisan-Romanesque **cathedral**,
begun in 1063, has a graceful facade of tiered
arches and a cavernous column-lined interior.
The transept's bronze doors, facing the leaning tower, are by Bonanno Pisano, while the
16th-century bronze doors of the main entrance are by Giambologna. The cathedral's
cupcake-like **baptistry**, which was started in
1153 and took two centuries to complete,
contains a pulpit sculpted by Nicola Pisano.

The famous leaning **bell tower** found itself
in trouble from the start, because of the marshy
nature of the land on which it was built. Its

architect, Bonanno Pisano, managed to complete only three of the tower's eventual seven
tiers before it started to lean. It has continued
to lean by an average 1mm a year, and today
it is almost 5m off the perpendicular. The
tower has been closed for over a decade, and
is braced by strengthening cables, weighted
with more than 1000 tons of lead and undergoing a ground-levelling process – all in all, it
resembles a construction site. It's hoped that
the weights and steel cables will be removed
in 2001, leaving the tower still leaning but
without the risk of collapse, and open to a limited number of visitors.

The pricing structure for the Campo is
staggered; in essence, it costs L3000 to see
the cathedral, and from L18,000 to L10,000
for all or just a few of the sights.

After taking in the Campo dei Miracoli,
wander down Via Santa Maria, along the
Arno and into the Borgo Stretto to explore the
old city.

Places to Stay & Eat

Pisa has a range of reasonably priced hotels.
Many of the budget places double as residences for students during the school year, so
it can sometimes be difficult to find a cheap
room.

The non-HI *Ostello per la Gioventù* (☎/fax
050 89 06 22, Via Pietrasantina 15) has dorm
beds for L24,000, and is closed between 9 am
and 6 pm. Take bus No 3 from the station.
Right by the Campo dei Miracoli, *Albergo
Gronchi* (☎ 050 56 18 23, Piazza Arcivesco-
vado 1) has modern singles/doubles for
L35,000/58,000. The two-star *Hotel di Stefano* (☎ 050 55 35 59, fax 050 55 60 38, Via
Sant'Apollonia 35) is not far away and offers
good-quality rooms with shower for
L100,000/125,000. *Albergo Milano* (☎ 050
231 62, fax 050 442 37, Via Mascagni 14) is
just outside the station, with pleasant rooms
and a friendly owner. Basic rooms go for
L60,000/80,000; rooms with shower cost
L85,000/115,000.

Splash out with a view of the Arno at the
grand *Royal Victoria* (☎ 050 94 01 11, fax
050 94 01 80, Lungarno Pacinotti 12), which
dates from 1839 and offers lovely rooms for
L145,000/175,000.

Being a university town, Pisa has a number of cheap eating places. Head for Borgo

Stretto and the university area. **Trattoria da Matteo** *(Via l'Arancio 46)* is a good choice for cheap pizza and pasta. **Antica Trattoria il Campano**, in an old tower near the market at Vicolo Santa Margherita, is full of medieval atmosphere; a meal costs around L35,000. **Spaghetteria alle Bandierine** *(Via Mercanti 4)* has a rustic farmhouse feel and serves a multitude of delicious spaghetti dishes, particularly seafood. Leave room for the *panna cotta* with strawberries (L5000). Head to **La Bottega del Gelato** in Piazza Garibaldi for gelati, or grab a cocktail and bar snack at **Krott** *(Lungarno Pacinotti 2)*. There's an open-air food *market* in Piazza delle Vettovaglie, off Borgo Stretto.

Getting There & Away

The airport, with domestic and European flights, is only a few minutes away by train, or by bus No 3 from the station. Lazzi (☎ 050 462 88) buses run to Florence via Lucca; somewhat surprisingly, there's an original Keith Haring mural opposite its office in Piazza Vittorio Emanuele. CPT (☎ 050 50 55 11) operates buses to Livorno via Tirrenia. Pisa is linked by direct train to Florence, Rome and Genoa. Local trains head for Lucca and Livorno.

SIENA

pop 56,956

Italy's best preserved medieval town, Siena, is built on three hills and surrounded by its historic ramparts. The maze-like historic centre is jam-packed with majestic Gothic buildings in various shades of the colour known as burnt sienna; it's also usually crammed to bursting with visitors.

According to legend, Siena was founded by the sons of Remus (one of the founders of Rome). In the Middle Ages the city became a free republic, but its success and power led to serious rivalry with Florence, both politically and culturally. Painters of the Sienese School produced significant works of art, and the city was home to St Catherine and St Benedict.

Siena is divided into 17 *contrade* (districts) and each year 10 are chosen to compete in the Palio, a tumultuous horse race and pageant held in the shell-shaped Piazza del Campo on 2 July and 16 August.

Orientation

Leaving the train station, cross the concourse to the bus stop opposite and catch bus No 9 or 10 to Piazza Gramsci, then walk into the centre along Via dei Termini (it takes about five minutes to reach Piazza del Campo). From the intercity bus station in Piazza San Domenico, it's a five-minute walk along Via della Sapienza and then turn right onto Via delle Terme. Visitors' cars are not allowed into the medieval centre.

Information

Tourist Office The APT office (☎ 0577 28 05 51, fax 0577 27 06 76) is at Piazza del Campo 56. It opens 8.30 am to 7.30 pm Monday to Saturday (8.30 am to 1 pm and 3 to 7 pm Monday to Friday and to 1 pm on Saturday from 11 November to 21 March).

Post & Communications The main post office is at Piazza Matteotti 1. Telecom is at Via dei Termini 40.

There is a branch of the Internet Train at di Città 121, with 20 screens.

Laundry Onda Blu, at Via Casato di Sotto 17, charges L10,000 to wash and dry.

Medical & Emergency Services For an ambulance, call ☎ 118. The public hospital (☎ 0577 58 51 11) is on Viale Bracci, just north of Siena at Le Scotte.

For police attendance call ☎ 113. The questura is at Via del Castoro 23 and its Foreigners' Bureau is in Piazza Jacopo della Quercia (facing the Duomo).

Things to See

Siena's uniquely shell-shaped **Piazza del Campo** (known simply as Il Campo) has been the city's focus since the 14th century. The piazza's sloping base is formed by the nobly proportioned **Palazzo Pubblico** (town hall), considered one of Italy's most graceful Gothic buildings. Its Sienese art treasures include Simone Martini's *Maestà* and Ambrogio Lorenzetti's *Allegories of Good & Bad Government*. The town hall is open 10 am to 7 pm daily (to 11 pm in July and August), and entry is L10,000 (L5000 for students).

The spectacular **Duomo** is another Gothic masterpiece, and one of the most enchanting

ITALY

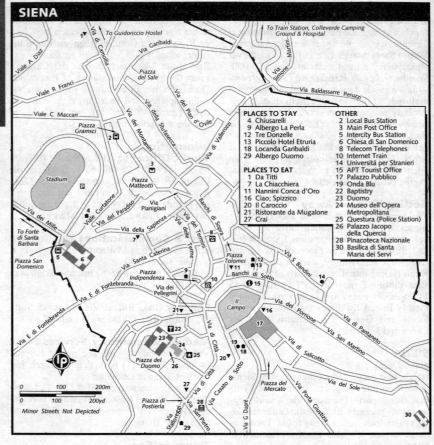

SIENA

To Guidoriccio Hostel
Via di Camollia
Via Garibaldi
Viale A. Diaz
Piazza del Sale
Via della Sturalsecca
Via del Pian d'Ovile
Via Simone Martini
To Train Station, Colleverde Camping Ground & Hospital
Viale R. Franci
Via Baldassarre Peruzzi
Viale C. Maccari
Piazza Gramsci
Via dei Montanini
Via di Vallerozzi

Stadium

Piazza Matteotti
Via Pianigiani
Banchi di Sopra

Viale Curtatone
Via del Paradiso
Via della Sapienza
Via dei Termini

To Forte di Santa Barbara
Via dei Mille

Piazza San Domenico
Via Santa Caterina
Via delle Terme
Banchi di Sotto
Via S. Bandini

Via E. di Fontebranda
Piazza Indipendenza
Via dei Pellegrini
Piazza Tolomei
Il Campo

Via di Città
Via del Pontone
Via di Pantaneto
Via San Martino

Piazza del Duomo
Via di Città
Via di Salicotto

Piazza del Mercato
Via del Sole

Piazza di Postierla
Via San Pietro
Via Casato di Sotto
Via Porta Giustizia
Via G. Dupré

0 100 200m
0 100 200yd
Minor Streets Not Depicted

PLACES TO STAY
4 Chiusarelli
9 Albergo La Perla
12 Tre Donzelle
13 Piccolo Hotel Etruria
18 Locanda Garibaldi
29 Albergo Duomo

PLACES TO EAT
1 Da Titti
7 La Chiacchiera
11 Nannini Conca d'Oro
16 Ciao; Spizzico
20 Il Caroccio
21 Ristorante da Mugalone
27 Crai

OTHER
2 Local Bus Station
3 Main Post Office
5 Intercity Bus Station
6 Chiesa di San Domenico
8 Telecom Telephones
10 Internet Train
14 Università per Stranieri
15 APT Tourist Office
17 Palazzo Pubblico
19 Onda Blu
22 Baptistry
23 Duomo
24 Museo dell'Opera Metropolitana
25 Questura (Police Station)
26 Palazzo Jacopo della Quercia
28 Pinacoteca Nazionale
30 Basilica di Santa Maria dei Servi

cathedrals in Italy; plans to enlarge it were stymied by the arrival of the Black Death in 1348. Its black-and-white striped marble facade has a Romanesque lower section, with carvings by Giovanni Pisano, and the inlaid-marble floor (largely covered) features various works depicting biblical stories. The marble and porphyry **pulpit** was carved by Nicola Pisano, father of Giovanni; other artworks include a bronze statue of St John the Baptist by Donatello, and statues of St Jerome and Mary Magdalene by Bernini.

A door in the north aisle leads to the **Libreria Piccolomini**, built by Pope Pius III to house the magnificent illustrated books of his uncle, Pope Pius II. It features frescoes by Pinturicchio and a Roman statue of the Three Graces. Entry is L2000.

The **Museo dell'Opera Metropolitana** (Duomo Museum) is in Piazza del Duomo. Its many works of art formerly adorned the cathedral, including the *Maestà* by Duccio di Buoninsegna and the 12 marble statues by Giovanni Pisano, which once graced the Duomo's facade; other works include those by Ambrogio Lorenzetti, Simone Martini and Taddeo di Bartolo. From mid-March to the end of September the museum is open 9 am to 7.30 pm daily. In October it closes at 6 pm and during the rest of the year at 1.30 pm. Entry is L6000.

The **baptistry**, behind the cathedral, has a Gothic facade and is decorated with 15th-century frescoes. The highlight is the font by Jacopo della Quercia, with sculptures by Donatello and Ghiberti. It opens 9 am to 7.30 pm daily (in October it closes at 6 pm and during the rest of the year its hours are 10 am to 1 pm and 2.30 to 5 pm); entry is L3000.

The 15th-century Palazzo Buonsignori houses the **Pinacoteca Nazionale** (National Picture Gallery), whose Sienese masterpieces include Duccio di Buoninsegna's *Madonna dei Francescani*, *Madonna col Bambino* by Simone Martini and a series of Madonnas by Ambrogio Lorenzetti. The gallery is open 9 am to 7 pm Tuesday to Saturday, Monday to 1.30 pm and 8 am to 1 pm on Sunday. Admission is L8000.

Places to Stay

It is always advisable to book a hotel in Siena, particularly in August and during the Palio, when accommodation is impossible to find for miles around.

Colleverde camping ground (☎ 0577 28 00 44, fax 0577 33 32 98) is outside the historical centre at Strada di Scacciapensieri 47 (take bus No 3 from Piazza Gramsci). It opens 21 March to 10 November and costs L15,000 for adults, L8000 for children and L15,000 for a site.

Guidoriccio (☎ 0577 522 12, Via Fiorentina) hostel is about 3km out of the centre in Stellino. B&B is L29,000 and an evening meal is L16,000. Take bus No 3 from Piazza Gramsci.

In the heart of the old town, *Tre Donzelle* (☎ 0577 28 03 58, fax 0577 22 39 33, Via delle Donzelle 5) offers serviceable singles/doubles for L50,000/80,000 and doubles with shower for L100,000. Nearby, the two-star *Piccolo Hotel Etruria* (☎ 0577 28 80 88, fax 0577 28 84 61, Via delle Donzelle 1) has renovated rooms for L75,000/120,000 with bathroom. *Albergo La Perla* (☎ 0577 471 44, Via delle Terme 25) has small but clean rooms with shower for L80,000/110,000. Behind the town hall, *Locanda Garibaldi* (☎ 0577 28 42 04, Via Giovanni Dupré 18) has rooms for L45,000/85,000. Its small trattoria is reasonably priced.

The three-star *Duomo* (☎ 0577 28 90 88, fax 0577 430 43, Via Stalloreggi 38) has rooms with views for L150,000/220,000. *Chiusarelli* (☎ 0577 28 05 62, fax 0577 27 11 77, Viale Curtatone 15) is well placed for drivers near the Stadio Comunale car park; pleasant singles are L95,000, while singles/doubles with bathroom are L125,000/185,000.

Agriturismo is well organised around Siena. The tourist office can provide a list of establishments.

Places to Eat

The ubiquitous self-service *Ciao* and ready-to-go *Spizzico* are right on the Campo at No 77. For a traditional hostaria, try *Il Caroccio*, off the Campo at Via Casato di Sotto 32, where a meal costs around L35,000 and bistecca alla Fiorentina is L40,000 a kilogram. *Ristorante da Mugalone* (Via dei Pellegrini 8) is another good place for local specialities. Pasta is around L12,000, second courses L16,000 and bistecca is L6000 per 100gms.

Tiny *La Chiacchiera* (Costa di Sant'Antonio 4), off Via Santa Caterina, serves local specialities. Pasta dishes cost from L7000 and a bottle of house wine is L5000. A full meal will cost L30,000. There are several trattorias further north of here, in a less frenetic neighbourhood. *Da Titti* (Via di Camollia 193) is a no-frills establishment with big wooden bench tables where a full meal with wine costs around L28,000.

Supermarkets in the town centre include *Crai* (Via di Città 152-156) and *Consorzio Agrario*, Via Piani Giani. *Nannini Conca d'Oro* (Banchi di Sopra 22) is one of the city's finest cafes and a good place to stock up on panforte.

Getting There & Away

Regular Tra-In buses run from Florence to Siena, arriving at Piazza San Domenico. Buses also go to San Gimignano, Volterra and other points in Tuscany, and there's a daily bus to Rome. For timetable information about buses to Perugia, ask at the Balzana travel agency (☎ 0577 28 50 13); these buses leave from the train station.

Siena is not on a main train line, so from Rome it is necessary to change at Chiusi and from Florence at Empoli, making buses a better alternative.

SAN GIMIGNANO
pop 6956

Few places in Italy rival the beauty of San Gimignano, a town which has barely changed since medieval times. Set on a hill overlooking the misty pink, green and gold Tuscan landscape, the town is best known for its huge pockmarked towers (13 of the original 72 remain), the 11th-century fortified homes of its leading feuding families.

The tiny town is packed with tourists on weekends, so try to visit during the week. The Pro Loco tourist information office (☎ 0577 94 00 08, ✉ prolocosg@tin.it) is at Piazza del Duomo 1 in the town centre.

Things to See & Do

Climb San Gimignano's tallest tower, **Torre Grossa** (also known as the town hall tower), off Piazza del Duomo, for a memorable view of the Tuscan hills. The tower is reached from within the **Palazzo del Popolo**, which houses the **Museo Civico**, whose star attraction is Lippo Memmi's 14th-century *Maestà*. The **Duomo** has a Romanesque interior, frescoes by Ghirlandaio in the **Cappella di Santa Fina** and a particularly gruesome *Last Judgment* by Taddeo di Bartolo. The city's most impressive piazza is **Piazza della Cisterna**, named for the 13th-century well at its centre.

Places to Stay & Eat

San Gimignano offers few options for budget travellers. The nearest camping ground is *Il Boschetto di Piemma* (☎ 0577 94 03 52, fax 0577 94 19 82), about 3km from San Gimignano at Santa Lucia. It costs L9000 a night for adults, L7000 for children and L12,000 for a tent site. It is open from April to mid-October and there is a bus service to the site. The non-HI *hostel* (☎ 0577 94 19 91, Via delle Fonti 1) opens 1 March to 31 October and charges L29,000 for B&B, L16,000 for a meal.

Hotels in town are expensive but there are numerous rooms for rent in private homes, and agriturismo is well organised in this area. For information, contact the tourist office. If you can afford a treat, soak up the medieval ambience at *Hotel La Cisterna* (☎ 0577 94 03 28,

fax 0577 94 20 80, Piazza dell Cisterna 24), where singles/doubles are L120,000/200,000.

Friendly *Trattoria Chiribiri (Piazzetta della Madonna 1)*, off Via San Giovanni, has hearty minestrone for L8000 and ravioli for L10,000. A fresh-produce *market* is held on Thursday morning in Piazza del Duomo.

Getting There & Away

Regular buses connect San Gimignano with Florence and Siena. Buses arrive at Porta San Giovanni and timetables are posted outside the tourist office. Enter through the Porta and continue straight ahead to reach Piazza del Duomo.

CERTALDO
pop 15,942

Located in the Val d'Elsa between Florence and Siena, this small medieval town is definitely worth a visit. Giovanni Boccaccio, one of the fathers of the Italian language, was born here in 1313.

Fattoria Bassetto (☎ 0571 66 83 42, ✉ bassetto@dedalo.com), 2km east of the town on the road to Siena, is a former 14th-century Benedictine convent, surrounded by a garden with swimming pool. Dorm-style accommodation is L35,000 and a private room is L65,000.

Umbria

Mountainous Umbria is characterised by its many medieval hill towns, and noted for its Romanesque and Gothic architecture. Towns such as Assisi, Gubbio, Spello, Spoleto, Todi and Orvieto are accessible by bus or train from Perugia, the region's capital.

PERUGIA
pop 144,732

Perugia is one of Italy's best-preserved medieval hill towns, with panoramic views at every turn. The city has a lively and bloody past, due to the internal feuding of the Baglioni and Oddi families, and the violent wars waged against its neighbours during the Middle Ages. Perugia also has a strong artistic and cultural tradition: it was the home of the painter Perugino, and Raphael, his student, also worked here. Its University for Foreigners, established in 1925, attracts thousands of students from all over the world, and the Umbria Jazz festival is held here in July.

Orientation & Information

Perugia's hub is the old town's central main drag, Corso Vannucci, running north-south from Piazza Italia, through Piazza Repubblica and ending at Piazza IV Novembre and the Duomo.

The IAT tourist office (☎ 075 572 33 27, fax 075 573 93 86) is opposite the Duomo at Piazza IV Novembre 3, and is open 8.30 am to 1.30 pm and 3.30 to 6.30 pm Monday to Saturday (9 am to 1 pm on Sunday). The main post office is in Piazza Matteotti. The monthly magazine *Viva Perugia: What, Where, When* (L1000 at newsstands) has events listings and other useful information.

Things to See

Perugia's austere **Duomo** has an unfinished facade in the characteristic Perugian red-and-white marble. Inside are frescoes and decorations by artists from the 15th to 18th centuries. The **Palazzo dei Priori**, just down from the Duomo on Corso Vannucci, is a rambling 13th-century palace which houses

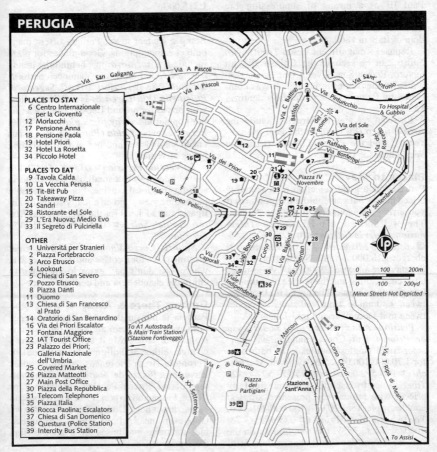

PERUGIA

PLACES TO STAY
6 Centro Internazionale per la Gioventù
12 Morlacchi
17 Pensione Anna
18 Pensione Paola
19 Hotel Priori
32 Hotel La Rosetta
34 Piccolo Hotel

PLACES TO EAT
9 Tavola Calda
10 La Vecchia Perusia
15 Tit-Bit Pub
20 Takeaway Pizza
24 Sandri
28 Ristorante del Sole
29 L'Era Nuova; Medio Evo
33 Il Segreto di Pulcinella

OTHER
1 Università per Stranieri
2 Piazza Fortebraccio
3 Arco Etrusco
4 Lookout
5 Chiesa di San Severo
7 Pozzo Etrusco
8 Piazza Danti
11 Duomo
13 Chiesa di San Francesco al Prato
14 Oratorio di San Bernardino
16 Via dei Priori Escalator
21 Fontana Maggiore
22 IAT Tourist Office
23 Palazzo dei Priori; Galleria Nazionale dell'Umbria
25 Covered Market
26 Piazza Matteotti
27 Main Post Office
30 Piazza della Repubblica
31 Telecom Telephones
35 Piazza Italia
36 Rocca Paolina; Escalators
37 Chiesa di San Domenico
38 Questura (Police Station)
39 Intercity Bus Station

Minor Streets Not Depicted

the impressively frescoed **Sala dei Notari** and the **Galleria Nazionale dell'Umbria**, with works by Perugino and Fra Angelico. Between the two buildings, in Piazza IV Novembre, is the 13th-century **Fontana Maggiore**, designed by Fra Bevignate in 1278 and carved by Nicola and Giovanni Pisano.

At the other end of Corso Vannucci is the **Rocca Paolina** (Paolina Fortress), the ruins of a massive 16th-century fortress built upon the foundations of the palaces and homes of powerful families of the day, notably the Baglioni. The homes were destroyed and the materials used to build the fortress under orders of Pope Paul III as a means of suppressing the Baglioni. The fortress itself was destroyed by the Perugians after the declaration of the kingdom of Italy in 1860.

Raphael's magnificent fresco *Trinity with Saints* can be seen in the **Chiesa di San Severo**, Piazza San Severo. One of the last works by the painter in Perugia, it was completed by Perugino after Raphael's death in 1520.

Etruscan remains in Perugia include the **Arco Etrusco** (Etruscan Arch), near the university, and the **Pozzo Etrusco** (Etruscan Well), near the Duomo.

Places to Stay

Perugia has a good selection of reasonably priced hotels, but you could have problems if you arrive unannounced in July or August. The well-located non-HI **Centro Internazionale per la Gioventù** (☎ 075 572 28 80, @ ostello@edisons.it, *Via Bontempi 13*) charges L18,000 a night. Sheets (for the entire stay) are an extra L2000. Its TV room has a frescoed ceiling and the terrace has some of Perugia's best views. The hostel is closed between 9.30 am to 4 pm and shuts down between mid-December and mid-January.

Pensione Anna (☎/fax 075 573 63 04, *Via dei Priori 48*), off Corso Vannucci, has character-filled singles/doubles with bathroom for L70,000/100,000. The two-star **Morlacchi** (☎ 075 572 03 19, fax 075 573 50 84, *Via Tiberi 2*) nearby is a little better but similarly priced, with attractively presented singles/doubles/triples for L70,000/100,000/130,000. The two-star **Hotel Priori** (☎ 075 572 33 78, fax 075 572 32 13, *Via Vermiglioli 3*), on the corner of Via dei Priori, has a delightful breakfast terrace and small but serviceable singles/doubles for L90,000/140,000, including breakfast.

Pensione Paola (☎ 075 572 38 16, *Via della Canapina 5*) is down the escalator from Via dei Priori, with pleasant rooms without bathroom for L43,000/65,000. Off the Piazza Italia end of Corso Vannucci, **Piccolo Hotel** (☎ 075 572 29 87, *Via Luigi Bonazzi 25*) has small doubles without/with bathroom for L60,000/75,000.

If you're feeling flush, the four-star **La Rosetta** (☎/fax 075 572 08 41, *Piazza Italia 19*) has palatial period-detailed rooms from L215,000.

Places to Eat

Being a student town, Perugia offers many budget eating options. Good places for pizza include **L'Era Nuova**, just behind the trendy **Medio Evo** bar on Corso Vannucci, and **Tit-Bit Pub**, Via dei Priori 105. **Il Segreto di Pulcinella** (*Via Larga 8*) is another option, with pizzas for around L9000. There's a tiny but popular *takeaway pizza place* at Via dei Priori 3. **Tavola Calda** (*Piazza Danti 16*) has cheap sandwiches and hot dishes, including heaps of vegies.

La Vecchia Perusia (☎ 075 572 59 00, *Via Ulisse Rocchi 9*) is a small old-style trattoria serving fine local cuisine. For unforgettable panoramic views and an equally stunning antipasto spread, head for the ever-popular **Ristorante del Sole** (☎ 075 573 50 31, *Via Oberdan 28*).

Sandri (*Corso Vannucci 32*) is a great meeting place for a coffee and delicious cake, where you don't pay extra to sit down to enjoy the chandeliers and ceiling frescoes.

Getting There & Away

Perugia is not on the main Rome-Florence railway line, but there are some direct trains from both cities. Most services require a change, either at Foligno (from Rome) or Terontola (from Florence). Intercity buses leave from Piazza dei Partigiani (at the bottom of the Rocca Paolina escalators) for Rome, Fiumicino airport, Florence, Siena and cities throughout Umbria including Assisi, Gubbio and nearby Lake Trasimeno. Timetables for trains and buses are available from the tourist office.

Getting Around

The main train station is a few kilometres downhill from the historical centre. Catch any bus heading for Piazza Italia. Tickets cost L1200 and must be bought before you get onboard.

Most of the historical centre is closed to normal traffic, but tourists are allowed to drive to their hotels. It is probably wiser not to do this, as driving in central Perugia is a nightmare because of the extremely narrow, winding streets, most of which are one way. The solution is to park at one of the large car parks downhill, and take the pedestrian elevator up to the old centre. There is a supervised car park (L13,000 for the first two days, then L8500 per day) at Piazza dei Partigiani, from where you can catch the Rocca Paolina escalator leading to Piazza Italia. There are two major car parks at the foot of the Via dei Priori escalator.

ASSISI

pop 24,626

Home of St Francis, Assisi retains a modicum of spirituality despite attracting millions of visitors each year. Away from the hullabaloo, tranquillity can still be found in the medieval laneways. Assisi's inhabitants have been aware of the visual impact of their city since Roman times, perched halfway up Mt Subasio. From the valley its pink-and-white marble buildings shimmer in the sunlight. In September 1997, a strong earthquake rocked the town, causing part of the vault of the upper church of the Basilica di San Francesco to collapse. While the upper basilica has since reopened, the painstaking task of restoration continues.

The APT tourist office (☎ 075 81 25 34, ✉ aptas@krenet.it), Piazza del Comune, has all the information you need on hotels, sights and events in Assisi. It's open 8 am to 2 pm and 3.30 to 6.30 pm Monday to Friday, 9 am to 1 pm and 3.30 to 6.30 pm on Saturday and 9 am to 1 pm Sunday.

Things to See

Most people come to Assisi to visit its religious monuments. Dress rules are applied rigidly – absolutely no shorts, miniskirts or low-cut dresses/tops are allowed.

St Francis' Basilica is composed of two churches, one built on top of the other. The lower church is decorated with frescoes by Simone Martini, Cimabue and a pupil of Giotto, and contains the crypt where St Francis is buried. The Italian Gothic upper church has a stone-vaulted roof, and was decorated by the great painters of the 13th and 14th centuries, in particular Giotto and Cimabue. The frescoes in the apse and entrance received the most damage in the 1997 earthquake.

The impressively frescoed 13th-century **Basilica di Santa Chiara** contains the remains of St Clare, friend of St Francis and founder of the Order of Poor Clares.

For spectacular views of the valley below, head to the massive 14th-century **Rocca Maggiore** fortress. You'll easily be able to spot the huge **Basilica di Santa Maria degli Angeli**, built around the first Franciscan monastery. St Francis died in its **Cappella del Transito** in 1226.

Places to Stay & Eat

Assisi is well geared for tourists and there are numerous budget hotels and *affittacamere* (rooms for rent). Peak periods, when you will need to book well in advance, are Easter, August and September, and the Feast of St Francis on 3 and 4 October. The tourist office has a full list of affittacamere and religious institutions.

The small HI *Ostello della Pace* (☎/fax 075 81 67 67, Via Valecchi 177) is open all year; B&B is L25,000. The hostel is on the bus line between Santa Maria degli Angeli and Assisi. The non-HI hostel *Fontemaggio* and camping ground (☎ 075 81 36 36, fax 075 81 37 49) has B&B for L25,000 and singles/doubles for L50,000/100,000. From Piazza Matteotti, at the far end of town from the basilica, it's a 30-minute uphill walk along Via Eremo delle Carceri to No 8.

Albergo Italia (☎ 075 81 26 25, fax 075 804 37 49, Vicolo della Fortezza), just off Pizza del Comune, has rooms with shower for L45,000/69,000. Nearby, the three-star *Dei Priori* (☎ 075 81 22 37, fax 075 81 68 04, Corso Mazzini 15) has comfortable rooms for L75,000/100,000.

For a snack of pizza by the slice for around L2000, head for *Pizza Vincenzo*, just off Piazza del Comune at Via San Rufina 1a. A good self-service in the same area is *Il Foro Romano* (Via Portico 23). *Il Pozzo Romano (Via*

Santa Agnese 10), off Piazza Santa Chiara, has pizzas for around L9000 and a tourist menu for L22,000. Dine under ancient architraves at *Dal Carro (Vicolo dei Nepis 2)*, off Corso Mazzini, with superior pasta dishes from L7000. If you want to splash some cash, try the stylish *Medio Evo (Via Arco dei Priori 4)*.

Getting There & Away

Buses connect Assisi with Perugia, Foligno and other local towns, leaving from Piazza Matteotti. Buses for Rome and Florence leave from Piazzale dell'Unità d'Italia. Assisi's train station is in the valley, in the suburb of Santa Maria degli Angeli. It's on the same line as Perugia and a shuttle bus runs between the town and the station.

ANCONA
pop 101,285

The main reason to visit Ancona, a largely unattractive and industrial port city in the Marches, is to catch a ferry to Croatia, Greece or Turkey.

The easiest way to get from the train station to the port is by bus No 1. There are tourist information offices at the train station and the stazione marittima (seasonal). The main APT office (☎ 071 35 89 91, ✉ aptancona@tin.it) is out of the way at Via Thaon de Revel 4. It has a good Web site at www.comune.ancona.it. The main post office is at Piazza XXIV Maggio, open 8.15 am to 7 pm Monday to Saturday.

If you're stuck here waiting for a ferry, there are a couple of options for dining and accommodations. Many backpackers choose to bunk down at the ferry terminal, although the city has many cheap hotels. The relatively new *Ostello della Gioventú (☎/fax 071 4 22 57, Via Lamaticci)* has B&B for L24,000.

In the old town, *Trattoria da Dina (☎ 523 39, Vicolo ad Alto 3)* has full meals for L19,000.

Getting There & Away

Buses depart from Piazza Cavour for towns throughout the Marches region. Rome is served by Marozzi (☎ 0734 85 91 18). Ancona is on the Bologna-Lecce train line and thus easily accessible from major towns throughout Italy. It is also directly linked to Rome via Foligno.

All ferry operators have information booths at the ferry terminal, off Piazza Kennedy. Most lines offer discounts on return fares. Prices listed are for one-way deck class in the 2000 high season.

Companies include Superfast (☎ 071 207 02 40) to Patras in Greece (L136,000), Minoan Lines (☎ 071 20 17 08) to Igoumenitsa and Patras (L124,000) and Adriatica (☎ 071 20 49 15) to Durrës in Albania (L155,000) and to Split in Croatia (L80,000).

URBINO
pop 15,114

This town in the Marches can be difficult to reach, but it is worth the effort to see the birthplace of Raphael and Bramante – little changed since the Middle Ages and still a centre of art, culture and learning.

The IAT tourist information office (☎ 0722 27 88, ✉ iat@comune.urbino.ps.it) is at Piazza Duca Federico 35 and is open 9 am to 1 pm Monday to Saturday. The Banca Nazionale del Lavoro on Via Vittorio Emanuele has an ATM, as do most banks spread about the town centre. The main post office is at Via Bramante 18. There are Telecom offices at Via Puccinotti 4 and at Piazza San Francesco 1.

Things to See

Urbino's main sight is the huge **Palazzo Ducale**, designed by Laurana and completed in 1482. The best view is from Corso Garibaldi to the west, from where you can appreciate the size of the building and see its towers and loggias. Enter the palace from Piazza Duca Federico and visit the **Galleria Nazionale delle Marches**, featuring works by Raphael, Paolo Uccello and Verrocchio. The palace is open 9 am to 7 pm Tuesday to Saturday, to 9 pm on Sunday and to 2 pm Monday. Between February and May visits must be arranged in advance by calling ☎ 0722 32 90 57. Entry is L8000. Also visit the **Casa di Rafaello**, Via Raffaello 57, where the artist Raphael was born, and the **Oratorio di San Giovanni Battista**, with 15th-century frescoes by the Salimbeni brothers.

Places to Stay & Eat

Urbino is a major university town and most cheap beds are taken by students during the school year. The tourist office has a full list of affittacamere. The *Pensione Fosca* (☎ *0722 32 96 22, Via Raffaello 61*) has singles/doubles for L42,000/60,000.

There are numerous bars around Piazza della Repubblica in the town centre and near the Palazzo Ducale which sell good panini. Try *Pizzeria Galli*, Via Vittorio Veneto 19, for takeaway pizza by the slice. *Ristorante Da Franco*, just off Piazza del Rinascimento, next to the university, has a self-service section where you can eat a full meal for around L22,000.

Getting There & Away
There is no train service to Urbino, but it is connected by SAPUM and Bucci buses on weekdays to cities including Ancona, Pesaro and Arezzo. There is a bus link to the train station at the town of Fossato di Vico, on the Rome-Ancona line. There are also buses to Rome twice a day. All buses arrive at Borgo Mercatale, down Via Mazzini from Piazza della Repubblica. The tourist office has timetables for all bus services.

Southern Italy

Although much poorer than the north, the land of the *mezzogiorno* (midday sun) is rich in history and cultural traditions. The attractions here are simpler and more stark, the people more vibrant and excitable, and myths and legends are inseparable from official history. Campania, Apulia and Basilicata cry out to be explored and absolutely nothing can prepare you for Naples.

NAPLES
pop 1,067,365
Crazy and confusing, but also seductive and fascinating, Naples (Napoli), capital of the Campania region, has an energy that is palpable. Beautifully positioned on the Bay of Naples and overshadowed by Mt Vesuvius, it is one of the most densely populated cities in Europe. The city's homegrown mafia, the Camorra, is not as internationally infamous as its Sicilian counterpart, but in Naples it is just as pervasive.

While in the city, look out for its famous *presepi* (nativity cribs).

Orientation
Both the Stazione Centrale (central train station) and the main bus terminal are just off the vast Piazza Garibaldi. Naples is divided into *quartieri* (districts). The main shopping thoroughfare into the historical centre, Spaccanapoli, is Corso Umberto I, which heads south-west from Piazza Garibaldi to Piazza Bovio. West on the bay are Santa Lucia and Mergellina, both fashionable and picturesque and a far cry from the chaotic, noisy historical centre. South-west of Mergellina is Posillipo, where the ultra-wealthy live, and in the hills overlooking the bay is the residential Vomero district, a natural balcony across the city and bay to Vesuvius.

Information
Tourist Offices The EPT office at the station (☎ 081 26 87 79) will make hotel bookings, but make sure you give specific details on where you want to stay and how much you want to pay. Some staff speak English. Ask for *Qui Napoli* (Here Naples), published monthly in English and Italian, which lists events in the city, as well as information about transport and other services. The office is open 8.30 am to 8 pm Monday to Saturday and 9 am to 2 pm on Sunday.

There's an AAST office in Piazza del Gesú Nuovo (☎ 081 552 33 28), near Piazza Dante, open 8.30 am to 7.30 pm Monday to Saturday and until 3.30 pm on Sunday. The student travel centre, CTS (☎ 081 552 79 60), is at Via Mezzocannone 25.

Money There is a branch of the Banca Nazionale del Lavoro at Via Firenze 39; otherwise, there are plenty of exchange booths throughout the city which often offer lower rates than the banks.

Post & Communications The main post office is in Piazza G Matteotti, off Via Armando Diaz. It's open 8.15 am to 7.30 pm Monday to Friday and to 1 pm on Saturday. There is a Telecom office at Via A Depretis 40, open 9 am to 10 pm daily. Internetbar, Piazza Bellini 74, provides Internet access. The postcode for central Naples is 80100.

Medical & Emergency Services For an ambulance call ☎ 081 752 06 96. Each city

ITALY

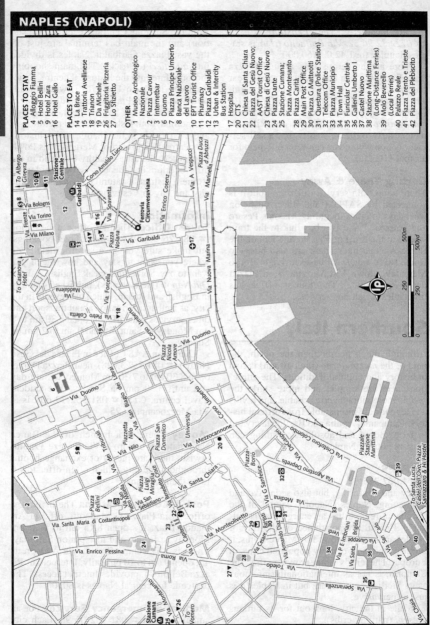

NAPLES (NAPOLI)

PLACES TO STAY
4 Alloggio Fiamma
5 Hotel Bellini
9 Hotel Zara
16 Hotel Gallo

PLACES TO EAT
14 La Brace
15 Trattoria Avellinese
18 Trianon
19 Da Michele
26 Friggitoria Pizzeria
27 Lo Sfizietto

OTHER
1 Museo Archeologico
  Nazionale
2 Piazza Cavour
3 Internetbar
6 Duomo
7 Piazza Principe Umberto
8 Banca Nazionale
  del Lavoro
10 EPT Tourist Office
11 Pharmacy
12 Piazza Garibaldi
13 Urban & Intercity
  Bus Station
17 Hospital
20 CTS
21 Chiesa di Santa Chiara
22 Piazza del Gesù Nuovo;
  AAST Tourist Office
23 Chiesa di Gesù Nuovo
24 Piazza Dante
25 Stazione Cumana;
  Piazza Montesanto
28 Piazza Carità
29 Main Post Office
30 Piazza G Matteotti
31 Questura (Police Station)
32 Telecom Office
33 Piazza Municipio
34 Town Hall
35 Funicular Centrale
36 Galleria Umberto I
37 Castel Nuovo
38 Stazione Marittima
  (Long-Distance Ferries)
39 Molo Beverello
  (Local Ferries)
40 Palazzo Reale
41 Piazza Trento e Trieste
42 Piazza del Plebiscito

district has a Guardia Medica (after hours medical service); check in *Qui Napoli* for details. The Ospedale Loreto-Mare (☎ 081 20 10 33) is near the station on Via A Vespucci. The pharmacy in the central station is open 8 am to 8 pm daily.

The questura (☎ 081 794 11 11) is at Via Medina 75, just off Via A Diaz, and has an office for foreigners where you can report thefts and so on. To report a stolen car call ☎ 081 794 14 35.

Dangers & Annoyances The petty crime rate in Naples is extremely high, particularly of the bag-snatching kind. Car theft is also a major problem, so think twice before bringing a vehicle to the city. Women should be careful at night near the station and around Piazza Dante. The area west of Via Toledo and as far north as Piazza Caritá can be particularly threatening.

Naples' legendary traffic is less chaotic these days, but you will still need to take care when crossing roads.

Things to See & Do

Start by walking around Spaccanapoli, the historic centre of Naples. From the station and Corso Umberto I turn right onto Via Mezzocannone, which will take you to Via Benedetto Croce, the main street of the quarter. To the left is Piazza del Gesú Nuovo, with the Neapolitan baroque **Chiesa di Gesú Nuovo** and the 14th-century **Chiesa di Santa Chiara**, restored to its original Gothic-Provençal style after it was severely damaged by bombing during WWII. The beautiful **Chiostro delle Clarisse** (Nuns' Cloisters) should not be missed.

The **Duomo** has a 19th-century facade but was built by the Angevin kings at the end of the 13th century, on the site of an earlier basilica. Inside is the **Cappella di San Gennaro**, which contains the head of St Januarius (the city's patron saint) and two vials of his congealed blood. The saint is said to have saved the city from plague, volcanic eruptions and other disasters. Every year the faithful gather to pray for a miracle, namely that the blood will liquefy and save the city from further disaster (see under Special Events).

Turn off Via Duomo onto **Via Tribunali**, one of the more characteristic streets of the area, and head for Piazza Dante, through the 17th-century **Port'Alba**, one of the gates to the city. Via Roma, the most fashionable street in old Naples, heads to the left (becoming Via Toledo) and ends at Piazza Trento e Trieste and the **Piazza del Plebiscito**.

In the piazza is the **Palazzo Reale**, the former official residence of the Bourbon and Savoy kings, now a museum. It is open 9 am to 1.30 pm Tuesday to Sunday and also from 4 to 7.30 pm on weekends. Admission is L8000. Just off the piazza is the **Teatro San Carlo**, one of the most famous opera houses in the world thanks to its perfect acoustics and beautiful interior.

The 13th-century **Castel Nuovo** overlooks Naples' ferry port. The early-Renaissance triumphal arch commemorates the entry of Alfonso I of Aragon into Naples in 1443. It is possible to visit the **Museo Civico** in the castle. Situated south-west along the waterfront at Santa Lucia is the **Castel dell'Ovo**, originally a Norman castle, which is surrounded by a tiny fishing village, the **Borgo Marinaro**.

The **Museo Archeologico Nazionale** is in Piazza Museo, north of Piazza Dante. It contains one of the most important collections of Graeco-Roman artefacts in the world, mainly the rich collection of the Farnese family, and the art treasures that were discovered at Pompeii and Herculaneum. The museum opens 9 am to 10 pm Tuesday to Saturday (Sunday to 8 pm). Admission is L12,000.

To escape the noisy city centre, catch the Funicolare Centrale (funicular), on Via Toledo, to the suburb of **Vomero** and visit the Certosa di San Martino, a 14th-century Carthusian monastery, rebuilt in the 17th century in Neapolitan-baroque style. It houses the **Museo Nazionale di San Martino**. The monastery's church is well worth a visit, as are its terraced gardens, which afford spectacular views of Naples and the bay. The monastery is open 9 am to 2 pm Tuesday to Sunday. Entry is L8000.

Special Events

Religious festivals are lively occasions in Naples, especially the celebration of St Januarius, the patron saint of the city, held three times a year (the first Sunday in May, 19 September and 16 December) in the Duomo.

ITALY

Places to Stay

Hostel The HI *Ostello Mergellina Napoli* (☎ *081 761 23 46, Salita della Grotta 23*), in Mergellina, is modern and safe. B&B is L26,000. It's open all year and imposes a maximum three-night stay in summer. Take the Metropolitana to Mergellina, and signs will direct you to the hostel from the waterfront.

Hotels Most of the cheap hotels are near the station and Piazza Garibaldi in a rather unsavoury area, and some of the cheaper hotels double as brothels. It is best to ask the tourist office at the station to recommend or book a room.

Station Area The following hotels are safe and offer a reasonable standard of accommodation. The *Hotel Zara* (☎ *081 28 71 25*, ✉ hotelzar@tin.it, *Via Firenze 81*) is clean, with singles/doubles for L35,000/60,000. Via Firenze is off Corso Novara, to the right as you leave the train station. *Albergo Ginevra* (☎ *081 28 32 10, Via Genova 116*), about 300m from the station, is another reliable and well-kept place with rooms for L42,000/67,000. The *Casanova Hotel* (☎ *081 26 82 87, Corso Garibaldi 333*) is quiet and safe. Rooms are L35,000/70,000; triples with shower are L95,000. *Hotel Gallo* (☎ *081 20 05 12, fax 081 28 18 49, Via Spaventa 11*), to the left out of the train station, has rooms of different standards (ask to see them first) for L110,000/160,000.

Around Spaccanapoli The best option in this area is the popular *Hotel Bellini* (☎ *081 45 69 96, Via San Paolo 44*), which offers singles/doubles for L70,000/120,000. *Alloggio Fiamma* (☎ *081 45 91 87, Via Francesco del Giudice 13*) has pretty basic doubles/triples for L80,000/110,000.

Out of the Centre In Santa Lucia, *Pensione Astoria* (☎ *081 764 99 03, Via Santa Lucia 90*) has basic singles/doubles for L45,000/70,000. In the same building is *Albergo Teresita* (☎ *081 764 01 05*), with rooms for L45,000/70,000. At Vomero, just near the funicular station, *Pensione Margherita* (☎ *081 556 70 44, Via D Cimarosa 29*) charges L60,000/110,000; ask for a room with a bay view. Have a L50 coin on hand for the lift.

Places to Eat

Naples is the home of pasta and pizza. In fact, once you have eaten a good Neapolitan pizza, topped with fresh tomatoes, oregano, basil and garlic, no other pizza will taste the same. Try a *calzone*, a filled version of a pizza, or *mozzarella in carozza* (mozzarella deep-fried in bread) which is sold at tiny street stalls. Also sold at street stalls is the *misto di frittura* (deep-fried vegetables). Don't leave town without trying the *sfogliatelle* (light, flaky pastry filled with ricotta).

Restaurants There are several inexpensive places to eat in and around Naples' centre.

City Centre According to the locals the best pizza in Naples (and Italy) is served at *Da Michele* (*Via Cesare Sersale 1*). The place is always crowded and you'll need to queue with a numbered ticket. Another excellent option is the nearby *Trianon* (*Via Pietro Colletta 46*) near Via Tribunali, where there's a wide selection from L5000. *La Brace* (*Via Spaventa 14*) is also recommended. You can eat well for around L25,000. Down the same street at Nos 31-35 is *Trattoria Avellinese*, Via Silvio Spaventa 31-35, just off Piazza Garibaldi, which specialises in cheap seafood.

Mergellina & Vomero For a good meal, Neapolitans head for the area around Piazza Sannazzaro, south-west of the centre, which is also handy to the HI hostel. *Pizzeria da Pasqualino* (*Piazza Sannazzaro 79*) has outdoor tables and serves good pizzas and seafood. A meal will cost around L20,000 with wine. *Daniele* (*Via A Scarlatti 104*) is a bar with a restaurant upstairs. *Cibo Cibo* (*Via Cimarosa 150*) is another good budget spot. In Vomero, *Trattoria da Sica* (*Via Bernini 17*) has excellent local dishes – try the spaghetti *alle vongole e pomodorini* (clams and cherry tomatoes).

Food Stalls On the corner of Vico Basilico Puoti and Via Pignasecca is *Lo Sfizietto*. *Friggitoria Pizzeria* is at Piazza Montesanto. Both offer lots of cheap goodies.

Entertainment

The monthly *Qui Napoli* and the local newspapers are the only real guides to what's on.

In July there is a series of free concerts called Luglio Musicale a Capodimonte held outside the archaeological museum. The ***Teatro San Carlo*** (☎ *081 797 21 11*) has year-round performances of opera, ballet and concerts. Tickets start at L20,000.

Getting There & Away

Air Capodichino airport (☎ 081 789 62 68), Viale Umberto Maddalena, is 5km north-east of the city centre. There are connections to most Italian and several European cities. Bus No 14 or 14R leaves from Piazza Garibaldi every 30 minutes for the airport (20 minutes).

Bus Buses leave from Piazza Garibaldi, just outside the train station, for destinations including Salerno, Benevento, Caserta (every 20 minutes) and Bari, Lecce and Brindisi in Apulia.

Train Naples is a major rail-transport centre for the south, and regular trains for most major Italian cities arrive and depart from the Stazione Centrale. There are up to 30 trains a day for Rome.

Car & Motorcycle Driving in Naples is not recommended. The traffic is chaotic, and car and motorcycle theft is rife. However, the city is easily accessible from Rome on the A1. The Naples-Pompeii-Salerno road connects with the coastal road to Sorrento and the Amalfi Coast.

Boat *Traghetti* (small ferries), *aliscafi* (hydrofoils) and *navi veloce* (fast ships) leave for Capri, Sorrento, Ischia and Procida from the Molo Beverello, in front of the Castel Nuovo. Some hydrofoils leave for the bay islands from Mergellina, and ferries for Ischia and Procida also leave from Pozzuoli. All operators have offices at the various ports from which they leave.

Tickets for the hydrofoils cost around double those for ferries, but the trip takes half the time.

Ferries to Palermo and Cagliari (Tirrenia ☎ 147 89 90 00) and to the Aeolian Islands (Siremar ☎ 091 761 36 88) leave from the Stazione Marittima on Molo Angioino, next to Molo Beverello (see the Getting There & Away sections under Sicily and Sardinia).

SNAV (☎ 081 761 23 48) runs regular ferries and, in summer, hydrofoils to the Aeolian Islands.

Getting Around

You can make your way around Naples by bus, tram, Metropolitana (underground) and funicular. City buses leave from Piazza Garibaldi in front of the central station bound for the centre of Naples, as well as Mergellina. Tickets cost L1500 for 90 minutes and are valid for buses, trams, the Metropolitana and funicular services. Day tickets cost L4500. Useful buses include No 14 or 14R to the airport; Nos R2 and R1 to Piazza Dante; and No 110 from Piazza Garibaldi to Piazza Cavour and the archaeological museum. Tram No 1 leaves from east of Stazione Centrale for the city centre. To get to Molo Beverello and the ferry terminal from the train station, take bus No R2 or 152, a bus called 'La Sepsa', or the M1.

The Metropolitana station is downstairs at the train station. Trains head west to Mergellina, stopping at Piazza Cavour, Piazza Amedeo and the funicular to Vomero, and then head on to the Campi Flegrei and Pozzuoli. Another line, now under construction, will eventually connect Piazza Garibaldi and Piazza Medaglie d'Oro, with stops including the Museo Archeologico Nazionale.

The main funicular connecting the city centre with Vomero is the Funicolare Centrale in Piazza Duca d'Aosta, next to Galleria Umberto I, on Via Toledo.

The Ferrovia Circumvesuviana operates trains for Herculaneum, Pompeii and Sorrento. The station is about 400m south-west of Stazione Centrale, in Corso Garibaldi (take the underpass from Stazione Centrale). The Ferrovia Cumana and the Circumflegrei, based at Stazione Cumana in Piazza Montesanto, operate services to Pozzuoli, Baia and Cumae every 20 minutes.

AROUND NAPLES

From Naples it's only a short distance to the **Campi Flegrei** (Phlegraean Fields) of volcanic lakes and mud baths, which inspired both Homer and Virgil in their writings. Today part of suburban Naples, the area is dirty and overdeveloped, but still worth a day trip. The Greek colony of **Cumae** is certainly

ITALY

worth visiting, particularly to see the Cave of the Cumaean Sybil, home of one of the ancient world's greatest oracles. Also in the area is **Lake Avernus**, the mythical entrance to the underworld, and **Baia** with its submerged Roman ruins visible from a glass-bottomed boat.

Reached by CPTC bus from Naples' Piazza Garibaldi or by train from the Stazione Centrale is the **Palazzo Reale** at Caserta (☎ 0823 32 11 37), usually called the Reggia di Caserta. Built by the Bourbon king Charles III, this massive 1200-room palace is set in gardens modelled on Versailles.

Pompeii & Herculaneum

Buried under a layer of lapilli (burning fragments of pumice stone) during the devastating eruption of Mt Vesuvius in 79 AD, **Pompeii** provides a fascinating insight into how the ancient Romans lived. It was a resort town for wealthy Romans, and among the vast ruins are impressive temples, a forum, one of the largest known Roman amphitheatres, and streets lined with shops and luxurious houses. Many of the site's mosaics and frescoes have been moved to Naples' Museo Archeologico Nazionale. The exception is the Villa dei Misteri, where the frescoes remain *in situ*. Many houses and shops are closed, but efforts are under way to open more of Pompeii to the public.

There are tourist offices (AACST) at Via Sacra 1 (☎ 081 850 72 55) in the new town, and just outside the excavations at Piazza Porta Marina Inferiore 12 (☎ 167 01 33 50 toll-free). Both offer information for visitors, notes on guided tours and a simple map of the ancient city. The ruins are open from 9 am to one hour before sunset; entry is L12,000.

Catch the Ferrovia Circumvesuviana train from Naples and get off at the Pompeii-Villa dei Misteri stop; the Porta Marina entrance is close by.

Herculaneum (Ercolano) is closer to Naples and is also a good point from which to visit Mt Vesuvius. Legend says the city was founded by Hercules. First Greek, then Roman, it was also destroyed by the 79 AD eruption, buried under mud and lava. Most inhabitants of Herculaneum had enough warning and managed to escape. The ruins here are smaller and the buildings, particularly the private houses, are

remarkably well preserved. Here you can see better examples of the frescoes, mosaics and furniture that used to decorate Roman houses.

Herculaneum is also accessible on the Circumvesuviana train from Naples. The ruins are open daily from 9 am to one hour before sunset. Entry is L12,000.

If you want to have a look into the huge crater of Mt Vesuvius, catch the Trasporti Vesuviani bus (☎ 081 739 28 33) from the piazza in front of the Ercolano train station or from Pompeii's Piazza Anfiteatro. The return ticket costs L7000 from Ercolano and L12,000 from Pompeii. The first bus leaves Pompeii at 8.30 am and takes 30 minutes to reach Herculaneum. You'll then need to walk about 1.5km to the summit, where you must pay L9000 to be accompanied by a guide to the crater. See Lonely Planet's *Walking in Italy* guide for detailed information on walking circuits on Vesuvius. The last bus returns to Pompeii from Herculaneum's Quota 1000 car park at 5.45 pm in summer and at 5 pm in winter.

SORRENTO
pop 16,459

This major resort town is in a particularly beautiful area, but is heavily overcrowded in summer with package tourists and traffic. However, it is handy to the Amalfi Coast and Capri.

Information

The centre of town is Piazza Tasso, a short walk from the train station along Corso Italia. The AAST tourist office (☎ 081 807 40 33), Via Luigi de Maio 35, is located inside the Circolo dei Forestieri complex. It is open 8.45 am to 2.30 pm and 4 to 6.45 pm Monday to Saturday.

The post office is at Corso Italia 210 and the Telecom telephone office is at Piazza Tasso 37. The Deutsche Bank on Piazza Angelina Laura has an ATM. Sorrento's postcode is 80067.

For medical assistance contact the Ospedale Civile (☎ 081 533 11 11).

Places to Stay & Eat

There are several camping grounds, including *Nube d'Argento* (☎ 081 878 13 44, Via del Capo 21), which costs L12,000 per person and up to L15,000 for a tent site.

ITALY

The HI *Ostello La Caffeteria* (☎ *081 807 29 25, Via degli Aranci 160*), near the train station, offers B&B for L26,000.

Hotel City (☎ *081 877 22 10, Corso Italia 221*) has singles/doubles with bathroom for L75,000/105,000. *Pensione Linda* (☎ *081 878 29 16, Via degli Aranci 125*) has very pleasant rooms with bathroom for L60,000/100,000.

You can get a cheap meal at *Self-Service Angelina Lauro* in Piazza Angelino Lauro. *Giardinello* (*Via dell'Accademia 7*) has pizzas from about L6500. On Via San Cesareo, off Piazza Tasso are several *alimentari* (grocery shops) where you can buy food for picnics.

Getting There & Away
Sorrento is easily accessible from Naples on the Circumvesuviana train line. SITA buses leave from outside the train station for the Amalfi Coast. Hydrofoils and ferries leave from the port, along Via de Maio and down the steps from the tourist office, for Capri and Napoli year-round and Ischia in summer only.

In summer, traffic is heavy along the coastal roads to Sorrento.

CAPRI
pop 7075
This beautiful island, an hour by ferry from Naples, retains the mythical appeal that attracted Roman emperors, including Augustus and Tiberius, who built 12 villas here, although the steady flow of summer tourists have somewhat spoilt its tranquil exclusivity. A short bus ride will take you to Anacapri, the town uphill from Capri – a good alternative if rooms are full in Capri. The island is famous for its grottoes, but is also a good place for walking. There are tourist offices at Marina Grande (☎ 081 837 06 34), where all the ferries arrive; in Piazza Umberto I (☎ 081 837 06 86, fax 081 837 09 18, @ touristoffice@capri.it) in the centre of town; and at Piazza Vittoria 4 in Anacapri (☎ 081 837 15 24). Online information can be found at www.capri.it.

Things to See & Do
There are expensive boat tours of the grottoes, including the famous **Grotta Azzurra** (Blue Grotto). Boats leave from the Marina Grande and a return trip will cost L26,500 (which includes the cost of a motorboat to the grotto, rowing boat into the grotto and entrance fee). It is cheaper to catch a bus from Anacapri (although the rowboat and entrance fee still total around L16,000). It is possible to swim into the grotto before 9 am and after 5 pm, but do so only in company and when the sea is very calm. You can walk to most of the interesting points on the island. Sights include the **Giardini d'Augusto**, in the town of Capri, and **Villa Jovis**, the ruins of one of Tiberius' villas, along the Via Longano and Via Tiberio. The latter is a one-hour walk uphill from Capri. Also visit Axel Munthe's wonderful **Villa San Michele** at Anacapri, home of the Swedish writer at the end of the 19th century.

Places to Stay & Eat
The *Stella Maris* (☎ 081 837 04 52, Via Roma 27), just off Piazza Umberto I, is right in the noisy heart of town. Doubles range from L100,000 to L160,000, depending on the season. *Villa Luisa* (☎ 081 837 01 28, Via D Birago 1) is a private house with a couple of doubles for rent at L95,000; the views are terrific.

In Anacapri near the town centre, the *Loreley* (☎ 081 837 14 40, @ loreley@caprinet.it, Via G Orlandi 16) has singles/doubles with bathroom starting at L80,000/135,000. *Caesar Augustus* (☎ 837 14 21, Via G Orlandi 4) is a beautiful hotel that becomes a knockout bargain in the off season and when there are empty rooms – in season, rooms start at L150,000/200,000. It opens from 1 May to the end of October.

In Capri, try *La Cisterna* (Via M Serafina 5) for a pizza. In Anacapri try the *Trattoria il Solitario* (Via G Orlandi 54), in a garden setting. Another good place is *Il Saraceno*, Via Trieste e Trento 18, where a full meal could cost up to L30,000. Try the lemon liqueur.

Getting There & Away
Getting to Capri is no problem, as there are hydrofoils and ferries virtually every hour from Naples' Molo Beverello and Mergellina, at least in summer. The Naples daily *Il Mattino* has all sailing times.

Several companies make the trip, including Caremar (☎ 081 551 3882), which runs ferries for L12,000 one way; and Linee Marittime Veloci (☎ 081 552 7209 in Beverello and

ITALY

☎ 081 761 2348 in Mergellina), which runs hydrofoils for L20,000 one way.

Getting Around

From Marina Grande, the funicular directly in front of the port takes you to the town of Capri (L1700), which is at the top of a steep hill some 3km from the port up a winding road. Small local buses connect the port with Capri, Anacapri and other points around the island (L1700 for one trip).

AMALFI COAST

The 50km-stretch of the Amalfi Coast swarms with rich tourists in summer and prices are correspondingly high. However, it remains a place of rare and spectacular beauty and if you can manage to get there in spring or autumn, you will be surprised by the reasonably priced accommodation and peaceful atmosphere.

There are tourist information offices in the individual towns, including in Positano (☎ 089 87 50 67) at Via Saracino 2, and Amalfi (☎ 089 87 11 07), on the waterfront at Corso Roma 19.

Positano

pop 3638

This is the most beautiful town on the coast, but for exactly this reason it has also become the most fashionable. It is, however, still possible to stay here cheaply.

Villa Maria Luisa (☎ 089 87 50 23, Via Fornillo 40) is the pick of the budget options, with double rooms with terraces for L100,000 in the low season and L130,000, breakfast included, in August. The *Villa delle Palme* (☎ 089 87 51 62), around the corner in Via Pasitea, is run by the same management and charges L125,000 for a double in the low season, L140,000 at the height of summer. Next door is the pizzeria *Il Saraceno d'Oro*.

Around Positano

The hills behind Positano offer some great walks if you tire of lazing on the beach. The tourist office at Positano has a brochure listing four routes, ranging in length from two to four hours. Visit **Nocelle**, a tiny, isolated village above Positano, accessible by walking track from the end of the road from Positano. Have lunch at *Trattoria Santa Croce* (☎ 089

81 12 60), which has a terrace with panoramic views. It is open for both lunch and dinner in summer, but at other times of the year it is best to telephone and check in advance. From Nocelle, a walking track leads directly up into the hills overlooking the Amalfi Coast. Nocelle is accessible by local bus from Positano, via Montepertuso.

On the way from Positano to Amalfi is the town of **Praiano**, which is not as scenic but has more budget options, including the only camping ground on the Amalfi Coast. *La Tranquillitá* (☎ 089 87 40 84, ✉ contraq@ contraqpraiano.com) has a pensione, bungalows and a small camping ground. It costs L25,000 per head to camp there if you have your own tent. For a double room or bungalow it is L100,000 (with breakfast) and in summer there is compulsory half-pension at L105,000 per head including room, private bathroom, breakfast and dinner. The SITA bus stops outside the pensione. The entire establishment closes down in winter, reopening at Easter.

Amalfi

pop 5589

One of the four powerful maritime republics of medieval Italy, Amalfi today is a popular tourist resort. It has an impressive **Duomo**, and nearby is the **Grotta dello Smeraldo**, which rivals Capri's Grotta Azzurra.

In the hills behind Amalfi is **Ravello**, accessible by bus and worth a visit if only to see the magnificent 11th-century **Villa Rufolo**, once the home of popes and later of the German composer Wagner. The 20th-century **Villa Cimbrone** is set in beautiful gardens, which end at a terrace offering a spectacular view of the Gulf of Salerno. There are numerous walking paths in the hills between Amalfi and Ravello. Pick up *Walks from Amalfi – The Guide to a Web of Ancient Italian Pathways* (L12,000) in Amalfi.

Places to Stay & Eat The HI *Ostello Beato Solitudo* (☎ 081 802 50 48, Piazza G Avitabile) is in Agerola San Lazzaro, a village just 16km west of Amalfi. It charges L17,500 for bed only. A bus leaves every 45 minutes from Amalfi, the last at 8.50 pm.

For a room in Amalfi, *Albergo Proto* (☎ 089 87 10 03, Salita dei Curiali 4) has doubles/triples from L125,000/175,000, breakfast included. *Hotel Lidomare* (☎ 87 13 32, *Via Piccolomini 9*) provides homy singles/doubles for L80,000/135,000 – just follow the signs from Piazza del Duomo and go left up a flight of stairs.

Ristorante al Teatro (*Via E Marini 19*) offers good food in very pleasant surroundings; you should get a main for around L8500. To get there, follow the signs to the left from Via Pietro Capuana, the main shopping street off Piazza del Duomo. *Pizzeria da Maria* (*Via Lorenzo d'Amalfi 14*) has pizzas for around L6000 and a good set menu for L28,000.

Getting There & Away
Bus The coast is accessible by regular SITA buses, which run between Salerno (a 40-minute train trip from Naples) and Sorrento (accessible from Naples on the Circumvesuviana train line). Buses stop in Amalfi at Piazza Flavio Gioia, from where you can catch a bus to Ravello.

Car & Motorcycle The coastal road is narrow and in summer it is clogged with traffic, so be prepared for long delays. At other times of the year you should have no problems. Hire a motorcycle in Sorrento, Salerno or Maiori.

Boat Hydrofoils and ferries also service the coast, leaving from Salerno and stopping at Amalfi and Positano. From Positano in summer you can catch a boat to Capri.

PAESTUM
The evocative image of three Greek temples standing in fields of poppies is not easily forgotten and makes the trek to this archaeological site well worth the effort. The three temples, just south of Salerno, are among the world's best preserved monuments of the ancient Greek world. There is a tourist office (☎ 0828 81 10 16) open 9 am to 2 pm daily and an interesting museum (L8000) at the site, open 9 am to 7 pm (to 10 pm in summer) daily (except the first and third Monday of the month). The ruins are open daily from 9 am to two hours before sunset and entry is L8000.

Paestum is accessible from Salerno by ATACS bus or by train.

MATERA
pop 20,000
This ancient city in the region of Basilicata evokes powerful images of a peasant culture which existed until just over 30 years ago. Its famous *sassi* (the stone houses built in the two ravines that slice through the city) were home to more than half of Matera's population until the 1950s, when the local government built a new residential area just out of Matera and relocated the entire population. The wards are now a major tourist attraction, and have been designated a World Heritage Site by Unesco – a far cry from the days when Matera struggled against poverty, deprivation and malaria. Francesco Rosi's excellent film *Cristo si é fermato a Eboli* (Christ stopped at Eboli) is a poignant illustration of what life was like in Basilicata.

There is a tourist office (☎ 0835 33 19 83) at Via de Viti De Marco 9, off the main Via Roma. Itinera (☎ 0835 26 32 59, ✆ arttur@tin.it) organises guided tours in English of the sassi wards for around L50,000 an hour (maximum five people). There is online information about Matera at www.materanet.com.

Things to See
The two main sassi wards, known as **Barisano** and **Caveoso**, had no electricity, running water or sewerage until well into last century. The oldest sassi are at the top of the ravines, and the dwellings which appear to be the oldest were established in the 20th century. As space ran out in the 1920s, the population started moving into hand-hewn or natural caves, an extraordinary example of civilisation in reverse. The sassi zones are accessible from Piazza Vittorio Veneto and Piazza del Duomo in the centre of Matera. Be sure to see the rock churches, **Santa Maria d'Idris** and **Santa Lucia alla Malve**, both with amazingly well-preserved Byzantine frescoes. The 13th-century Apulian-Romanesque **cathedral**, overlooking Sasso Barisano, is also worth a visit. In Sasso Caveoso you could be approached by young children wanting to act as tour guides.

Some parts of the wards are now being restored and some people have begun to move back into the area. Excavations in Piazza Vittorio Veneto have revealed the ruins of parts of **Byzantine Matera**, including a castle and a rock church decorated with frescoes. The excavations are ongoing but the site is now open to the public.

Places to Stay & Eat

There are few options for budget accommodation here and it is best to book in advance. The fairly bare *Albergo Roma (☎ 0835 33 39 12, Via Roma 62)* offers singles/doubles for L45,000/65,000.

The local fare is simple and the focus is on vegetables. *Da Aulo (Via Padre Minozzo 21)* is economical and serves typical dishes of Basilicata. There is a fruit and vegetable *market* near Piazza V Veneto, between Via Lucana and Via A Persio.

Getting There & Away

SITA buses connect Matera with Potenza, Taranto and Metaponto. The town is on the private Ferrovie Apulo-Lucane train line, which connects with Bari, Altamura and Potenza. There are also three Marozzi buses a day from Rome to Matera. Buses arrive in Piazza Matteotti, a short walk down Via Roma to the town centre.

APULIA

The province of Apulia, the thin heel of the Italian peninsula, has long been isolated from the rest of the country and dismissed as a rural backwater with endemic poverty and not much else. Yet for centuries the 400-km strip of territory that makes up the province has been fought over by virtually every major colonial power, from the Greeks to the Spanish, who were intent on establishing a strategic foothold right on the Mediterranean. Each culture left its distinctive architectural mark, still in evidence today, albeit crumbling, untended and often ruined.

Brindisi

pop 95,383

As the major embarkation point for ferries to Greece, the city swarms with travellers in transit. There is not much to do here, other than wait, so most backpackers gather at the train station or at the port in the Stazione Marittima. The two are connected by Corso Umberto I – which becomes Corso Garibaldi – and are a 10-minute walk from each other; otherwise, you can take bus No 3 or 9.

The EPT tourist information office (☎ 0831 56 21 26) is at Lungomare Regina Margherita 12. Another information office is inside the ferry terminal. Be careful of bag snatchers and pickpockets in the area around the train station and the port.

If you need to bunk down for the night while awaiting a ferry, the non-HI *Ostello per la Gioventú (☎ 0831 56 80 24, Via N Brandi 4, Casale)* is about 2km out of town. B&B costs L20,000. Take bus No 3 from Via Cristoforo Colombo near the train station. *Hotel Venezia (☎ 0831 52 75 11, Via Pisanelli 4)* has singles/doubles for L27,000/50,000. Turn left off Corso Umberto I onto Via S Lorenzo da Brindisi to get there.

There are numerous takeaway outlets along the main route between the train and boat stations, but if you want a meal, head for the side streets. The *Vecchio Vicolo (Vicolo D'Orimini 13)* between the station and the port has good-value meals for around L20,000.

Getting There & Away Marozzi runs several buses a day to/from Rome (Stazione Tiburtina), leaving from Viale Regina Margherita in Brindisi. Appia Travel (☎ 0831 52 16 84), Viale Regina Margherita 8-9, sells tickets (L65,000; nine hours). There are rail connections to the major cities of northern Italy, as well as Rome, Ancona and Naples.

Boat Ferries leave Brindisi for Greek destinations including Corfu, Igoumenitsa, Patras and Cefalonia. Adriatica (☎ 0831 52 38 25), Corso Garibaldi 85-87, is open from 9 am to 1 pm and 4 to 7 pm; you must check in here until 7 pm (after 8 pm check-in is in front of the ship). Other major ferry companies are Hellenic Mediterranean Lines (☎ 0831 52 85 31), Corso Garibaldi 8; and Italian Ferries (☎ 0831 59 03 21), Corso Garibaldi 96-98.

Adriatica and Hellenic are the most expensive, but also the most reliable. They are also the only lines which can officially accept Eurail and Inter-Rail passes, which means you pay only L20,500 to travel deck class. For a *poltrona* (airline-type chair) you'll pay L32,000, and L48,000 for a 2nd-class cabin. If you want to use your Eurail or Inter-Rail pass, it is important to reserve some weeks in advance in summer. Even with a booking in summer, you must still go to the Adriatic or

Hellenic embarkation office in the Stazione Marittima to have your ticket checked.

Discounts are available for travellers under 26 years of age and holders of some Italian rail passes. Note that fares increase by 40% in July and August. Ferry services are also increased during this period. Average prices in the 2000 high season for deck class were: Adriatica and Hellenic to Corfu, Igoumenitsa, Cefalonia or Patras cost L120,000 (L100,000 return); Med Link to Patras cost L70,000 on deck. Prices go up by an average L25,000 for a poltrona, and for the cheapest cabin accommodation prices jump by L40,000 to L65,000. Bicycles can be taken aboard free, but the average high-season fare for a motorcycle is L60,000 and for a car around L130,000.

The port tax is L12,000, payable when you buy your ticket. It is essential to check in at least two hours prior to departure.

Lecce
pop 100,884

Baroque can be grotesque, but never in Lecce. The style here is so refined and particular to the city that the Italians call it Barocco Leccese (Lecce baroque). Lecce's numerous bars and restaurants are a pleasant surprise in such a small city.

There is an APT information office (☎ 0832 24 80 92) at Via Vittorio Emanuele 24 near Piazza Duomo. Take bus No 2 from the station to the town centre.

Things to See & Do The most famous example of Lecce baroque is the **Basilica di Santa Croce**. Artists worked for 150 years to decorate the building, creating an extraordinarily ornate facade. In the **Piazza del Duomo** are the 12th-century **cathedral** (which was completely restored in the baroque style by the architect Giuseppe Zimbalo of Lecce) and its 70m-high **bell tower**; the **Palazzo del Vescovo** (Bishop's Palace); and the **Seminario**, with its elegant facade and baroque well in the courtyard. In Piazza Sant'Oronzo are the remains of a **Roman amphitheatre**.

Places to Stay & Eat Cheap accommodation is not abundant in Lecce, but camping facilities abound in the province of Salento. *Torre Rinalda* (☎ 0832 38 21 62), near the sea at Torre Rinalda is accessible by STP bus

from the terminal in Lecce's Via Adua. It costs L12,000/16,000 per person/site.

In Lecce try *Hotel Cappello* (☎ 0832 30 88 81, Via Montegrappa 4) near the station. Singles/doubles are L57,000/90,000 with bathroom.

A good snack bar is *Da Guido e Figli (Via Trinchese 10)*. A more traditional eating place is *Angiolino (Via Principi di Savoia)* near Porta Napoli. A full meal could cost L20,000.

Getting There & Away STP buses connect Lecce with towns throughout the Salentine peninsula, leaving from Via Adua. Lecce is directly linked by train to Brindisi, Bari, Rome, Naples and Bologna. The Ferrovie del Sud Est runs trains to all major points in Apulia.

Sicily

Sicily, the largest island in the Mediterranean, is a land of Greek temples, Norman churches and castles, Arab and Byzantine domes and splendid baroque churches and palaces. Its landscape, dominated by the volcano Mt Etna (3323m) on the east coast, ranges from fertile coast to mountains in the north to a vast, dry plateau at its centre.

Sicily, with a population of about five million, has a mild climate in winter. Summer can be relentlessly hot, when the beaches swarm with holidaying Italians and other Europeans. The best times to visit are in spring and autumn, when it is hot enough for the beach, but not too hot for sightseeing.

Most ferries from Italy arrive at Sicily's capital, Palermo, which is a convenient jumping-off point. If you're short on time, spend a day in Palermo and then perhaps head for Taormina and Agrigento. Syracuse is another highlight.

The Mafia remains a powerful force in Sicily, despite taking a hammering from the authorities throughout the 1990s. But the 'men of honour' are little interested in the affairs of tourists, so there is no need to fear you will be the target in a gang war while in Sicily.

Getting There & Away
Air There are flights from major cities in Italy and throughout Europe to Palermo and

Catania. The easiest way to get information is from any Sestante CIT or Alitalia office.

Bus & Train Bus services from Rome to Sicily are operated by Segesta (in Rome ☎ 06 481 96 76), which has two departures daily from Rome's Piazza Tiburtina. The buses service Messina (L55,000; 9 hours), Palermo (L66,000; 12 hours) and Syracuse (L66,000; 12 hours). SAIS Trasporti (in Palermo ☎ 091 617 11 41) also has a daily service to Catania and Palermo (L75,000).

One of the cheapest ways to reach Sicily is to catch a train to Messina. The cost of the ticket covers the 3km-ferry crossing from Villa San Giovanni (Calabria) to Messina.

Boat Sicily is accessible by ferry from Genova, Livorno, Naples, Reggio di Calabria and Cagliari, and also from Malta and Tunisia. The main companies servicing the Mediterranean are Tirrenia (in Palermo ☎ 091 33 33 00; in Rome ☎ 06 474 20 41); and Grimaldi (in Palermo ☎ 091 58 74 04; in Rome ☎ 06 42 81 83 88), which runs Grandi Traghetti and Grandi Navi Veloci. Prices are determined by the season and jump considerably in the summer period (July to September). Timetables can change each year and it's best to check at a travel agency that takes ferry bookings. Be sure to book well in advance during summer, particularly if you have a car.

At the time of writing, high-season fares for a poltrona were Genoa-Palermo with Grimaldi Grandi Navi Veloci (L150,000; 20 hours); Naples-Palermo with Tirrenia (L88,000; 10 hours); and Cagliari-Palermo with Tirrenia, (L70,000; 10 hours). A bed in a shared cabin with four beds costs an additional L25,000 to L35,000. Cars cost upwards of L130,000.

Other ferry lines servicing the island are Grandi Traghetti for Livorno-Palermo and Gozo Channel for Sicily-Malta. For information on ferries going from the mainland directly to Lipari, see the Getting There & Away section under Aeolian Islands.

Getting Around

Bus is the most common mode of public transport in Sicily. Numerous companies run services between Syracuse, Catania and Palermo as well as to Agrigento and towns in the interior. The coastal train service between Messina and Palermo and Messina to Syracuse is efficient and reliable.

PALERMO
pop 730,000

An Arab emirate and later the seat of a Norman kingdom, Palermo was once regarded as the grandest and most beautiful city in Europe. Today it is in a remarkable state of decay, due to neglect and heavy bombing during WWII, yet enough evidence remains of its golden days to make Palermo one of the most fascinating cities in Italy.

Orientation

Palermo is a large but easily manageable city. The main streets of the historical centre are Via Roma and Via Maqueda, which extend from the central station to Piazza Castelnuovo, a vast square in the modern part of town.

Information

Tourist Offices The main APT tourist office (☎ 091 58 61 22) is at Piazza Castelnuovo 35. It's open 8.30 am to 2 pm and 2.30 to 6 pm Monday to Friday (to 2 pm on Saturday). There are branch offices at the Stazione Centrale (☎ 091 616 59 14) and airport (☎ 091 59 16 98) with the same opening hours as the main office.

Money The exchange office at the Stazione Centrale is open 8 am to 8 pm daily. American Express is represented by Ruggieri & Figli (☎ 091 58 71 44), Via Emerico Amari 40, near the Stazione Marittima.

Post & Communications The main post office is at Via Roma 322 and the main Telecom telephone office is opposite the station in Piazza G Cesare, open 8.30 am to 9.30 pm daily. The postcode for Palermo is 90100.

Medical & Emergency Services For an ambulance call ☎ 091 30 66 44. The public hospital, Ospedale Civico (☎ 091 666 22 07), is at Via Carmelo Lazzaro. The all-night pharmacy, Lo Cascio (☎ 091 616 21 17), is near the train station at Via Roma 1. The questura (☎ 091 21 01 11) is at Piazza della Vittoria and is open 24 hours a day.

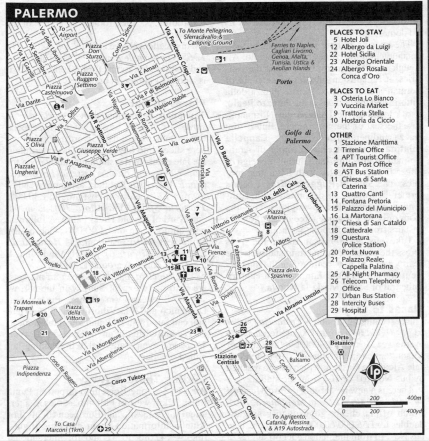

PALERMO

PLACES TO STAY
5 Hotel Joli
12 Albergo da Luigi
22 Hotel Sicilia
23 Albergo Orientale
24 Albergo Rosalia
   Conca d'Oro

PLACES TO EAT
3 Osteria Lo Bianco
7 Vucciria Market
9 Trattoria Stella
10 Hostaria da Ciccio

OTHER
1 Stazione Marittima
2 Tirrenia Office
4 APT Tourist Office
6 Main Post Office
8 AST Bus Station
11 Chiesa di Santa
   Caterina
13 Quattro Canti
14 Fontana Pretoria
15 Palazzo del Municipio
16 La Martorana
17 Chiesa di San Cataldo
18 Cattedrale
19 Questura
   (Police Station)
20 Porta Nuova
21 Palazzo Reale;
   Cappella Palatina
25 All-Night Pharmacy
26 Telecom Telephone
   Office
27 Urban Bus Station
28 Intercity Buses
29 Hospital

Dangers & Annoyances Contrary to popular opinion, Palermo is not a hotbed of thievery, but you will have to watch your valuables, which may attract pickpockets and bag snatchers. The historical centre can be a little dodgy at night, especially for women walking alone. Travellers should also avoid walking alone in the area north-east of the station, between Via Roma and the port (though there is safety in numbers).

Things to See

The intersection of Via Vittorio Emanuele and Via Maqueda marks the **Quattro Canti** (four corners of historical Palermo). The four 17th-century Spanish baroque facades are each decorated with a statue. Nearby is **Piazza Pretoria**, with a beautiful fountain, **Fontana Pretoria**, created by Florentine sculptors in the 16th century. Locals used to call it the Fountain of Shame because of its nude figures. Also in the piazza are the baroque **Chiesa di Santa Caterina** and the **Palazzo del Municipio** (town hall). Just off the piazza is Piazza Bellini and Palermo's most famous church, **La Martorana**, with a beautiful Arab-Norman bell tower and an interior decorated with Byzantine mosaics. Next to it is the Norman **Chiesa** di San Cataldo, which also mixes Arab and Norman styles and is easily recognisable by its red domes.

The huge **cattedrale** is along Via Vittorio Emanuele, on the corner of Via Bonello. Although modified many times over the centuries, it remains an impressive example of Norman architecture. Opposite Piazza della Vittoria and the gardens is the **Palazzo Reale**, also known as the Palazzo dei Normanni, now the seat of the government. Enter from Piazza Indipendenza to see the **Cappella Palatina**, a magnificent example of Arab-Norman architecture, built during the reign of Roger II and decorated with Byzantine mosaics. The **Sala di Ruggero** (King Roger's former bedroom), is decorated with 12th-century mosaics. It is possible to visit the room only with a guide (free of charge). Go upstairs from the Cappella Palatina.

Take bus No 8/9 from under the trees across the piazza from the train station to the nearby town of **Monreale** to see the magnificent mosaics in the famous 12th-century cathedral of **Santa Maria la Nuova**.

Places to Stay

The best camping ground is **Trinacria** (☎ 091 53 05 90, Via Barcarello 25), at Sferracavallo by the sea. It costs L9000/L9500/L500 per person/tent/car. Catch bus No 616 from Piazzale Alcide de Gasperi, which can be reached by bus Nos 101 or 107 from the station.

There is a new hostel called **Casa Marconi** (☎ 091 657 06 11, Via Monfenera 140), which offers cheap, good quality singles/doubles for L35,000/60,000. To get there, take bus No 246 from the station. Get off at Piazza Montegrappa; the hostel is 300m away.

Near the train station try **Albergo Orientale** (☎ 091 616 57 27, Via Maqueda 26), in an old and somewhat decayed palace; rooms are L35,000/55,000. Around the corner is **Albergo Rosalia Conca d'Oro** (☎ 091 616 45 43, Via Santa Rosalia 7), with rather basic singles/doubles/triples from L40,000/60,000/90,000 without bath.

The **Hotel Sicilia** (☎ 091 616 84 60, Via Divisi 99), on the corner of Via Maqueda, has singles/doubles of a higher standard at L50,000/75,000 with bath. **Albergo da Luigi** (☎ 091 58 50 85, Via Vittorio Emanuele 284), next to the Quattro Canti, has rooms from

L30,000/50,000, or L40,000/60,000 with bathroom. Ask for a room with a view of the fountain.

An excellent choice is **Hotel Joli** (☎ 091 611 17 65, Via Michele Amari 11), which has clean and comfortable rooms for L60,000/90,000. It is a popular choice so book early.

Places to Eat

A popular Palermitan dish is *pasta con le sarde* (pasta with sardines, fennel, peppers, capers and pine nuts). Swordfish is served here sliced into huge steaks. The Palermitani are late eaters and restaurants rarely open for dinner before 8 pm. At **Osteria Lo Bianco** (Via E Amari 104), at the Castelnuovo end of town, a full meal will cost around L30,000. **Trattoria Stella** (Via Alloro 104) is in the courtyard of the old Hotel Patria. A full meal will come to around L40,000. One of the city's best-loved restaurants is **Hostaria da Ciccio** (Via Firenze 6), just off Via Roma. A meal will come to around L30,000.

The **Vucciria**, Palermo's open-air markets, are held daily except Sunday in the narrow streets between Via Roma, Piazza San Domenico and Via Vittorio Emanuele. Here you can buy fresh fruit and vegetables, meat, cheese and virtually anything else you want. There are even stalls that sell steaming-hot boiled octopus.

Getting There & Away

Air The Falcone-Borsellino airport at Punta Raisi, 32km west of Palermo, serves as a terminal for domestic and European flights. For Alitalia information about domestic flights, ring ☎ 147 86 56 41 and for international flights ring ☎ 147 86 56 42.

Bus The main (Intercity) terminal for destinations throughout Sicily and the mainland is in the area around Via Paolo Balsamo, to the right (east) as you leave the station. Offices for the various companies are all in this area, including SAIS Traporti (☎ 091 616 60 28), Via Balsamo 16; and Segesta (☎ 091 616 79 19), Via Balsamo 26.

Train Regular trains leave from the Stazione Centrale for Milazzo, Messina, Catania and Syracuse, as well as for nearby towns such as Cefalú. Direct trains go to Reggio di Calabria,

Naples and Rome. For a one-way ticket to Rome you pay L73,200 in 2nd class plus a L26,000 Intercity supplement.

Boat Boats leave from the port (Molo Vittorio Veneto) for Sardinia and the mainland (see the earlier Sicily Getting There & Away section). The Tirrenia office (☎ 091 33 33 00) is at the port.

Getting Around

Taxis to/from the airport cost upwards of L70,000. The cheaper option is to catch one of the regular blue buses that leave from outside the station roughly every 45 minutes from 5 am to 9.45 pm. The trip takes one hour and costs L6500. Palermo's buses are efficient and most stop outside the train station. Bus No 7 runs along Via Roma from the train station to near Piazza Castelnuovo and No 39 goes from the station to the port. You must buy tickets before you get on the bus; they cost L1500 and are valid for one hour.

AEOLIAN ISLANDS

Also known as the Lipari Islands, the seven islands of this archipelago just north of Milazzo are volcanic in origin. They range from the well-developed tourist resort of Lipari and the understated jet-set haunt of Panarea, to the rugged Vulcano, the spectacular scenery of Stromboli (and its fiercely active volcano), the fertile vineyards of Salina, and the solitude of Alicudi and Filicudi, which remain relatively undeveloped. The islands have been inhabited since the Neolithic era, when migrants sought the valuable volcanic glass, obsidian. The Isole Eolie (Aeolian Islands) are so named because the ancient Greeks believed they were the home of Aeolus, the god of wind. Homer wrote of them in the *Odyssey*.

Information

The main AAST tourist information office (☎ 090 988 00 95) for the islands is on Lipari at Corso Vittorio Emanuele 202. Other offices are open on Vulcano, Salina and Stromboli during summer.

Things to See & Do

On **Lipari** visit the citadel (castello), with its archaeological park and museum. You can also go on excellent walks on the island.

Catch a local bus from the town of Lipari to the hill-top village of Quattrocchi for a great view of Vulcano. Boat trips will take you around the island – contact the tourist office for information.

Vulcano, with its ever-present, rotten-egg smell of sulphur (you'll get used to it), is a short boat trip from Lipari's port. The main volcano, Vulcano Fossa, is still active, though the last recorded period of eruption was 1888-90. You can make the one-hour hike to the crater, or take a bath in the therapeutic hot muds.

Stromboli is the most spectacular of the islands. Climb the cone (924m) at night to see the Sciara del Fuoco (Trail of Fire), lava streaming down the side of the volcano, and the volcanic explosions from the crater. Many people make the trip (four to five hours) without a guide during the day, but at night you should go with a guided group. The AGAI and GAE official guides (☎/fax 090 98 62 54, ✉ stromboli@iol.it) organise guided tours which depart at around 5 pm and return at 11.30 pm. It's best to contact them in advance to make a booking, since they only depart if groups are large enough. Remember to take warm clothes, wear heavy shoes and carry a torch and plenty of water.

Places to Stay & Eat

Camping facilities are available on Salina and Vulcano. Most accommodation in summer is booked out well in advance on the smaller islands, particularly on Stromboli, and most hotels close during winter.

Lipari Lipari provides the best options for a comfortable stay. It has numerous budget hotels, affittacamere and apartments, and the other islands are easily accessible by regular hydrofoil. When you arrive on Lipari you will be approached by someone offering accommodation. This is worth checking because the offers are usually genuine. The island's camping ground, *Baia Unci* (☎ 090 981 19 09), is at Canneto, about 3km out of Lipari town. It costs L18,000 a night per person. The HI *Ostello per la Gioventú Lipari* (☎ 090 981 15 40, *Via Castello 17*) is inside the walls of the citadel. A bed costs L14,500 a night, plus L1000 for a hot shower and L3000 for breakfast. A meal costs L15,000, but you can cook your own. It's open March to October.

Lo Nardo Maria (☎ *090 988 0431, fax 090 981 31 63, Vicolo Ulisse)* is a private home with four comfortable double rooms costing L50,000 between October and April but double that amount during the summer. from L25,000 to L40,000 per person, depending on the season.

You can eat surprisingly cheaply on Lipari. *Da Bartolo* (*Via Garibaldi 53)* is a good choice for seafood; a full meal costs around L35,000. At *Nenzyna* (*Via Roma 2)* you can eat well for L25,000.

Stromboli On Stromboli the popular *Casa del Sole* (☎ *090 98 60 17, Via Soldato Cincotta)*, on the road to the volcano, has singles/doubles for L35,000/40,000. If you want to splurge, try the hotel *La Sirena* (☎ *090 988 99 97, Via Pecorini Mare)*, which charges L70,000/120,000 for rooms with bath.

Vulcano On Vulcano, try *Pensione Agostino* (☎ *090 985 23 42, Via Favaloro 1)*, close to the mud bath, which has doubles with bathroom from L50,000 to L100,000 depending on the season. *Hotel Arcipelago* (☎ *090 985 20 02)* is beautifully positioned on Vulcano's northern coast and costs L185,000 for half-board.

Alicudi & Filicudi If you want seclusion, head for Filicudi or Alicudi. However, the hotels aren't exactly cheap. Alicudi's *Ericusa* (☎ *090 988 99 02)* costs L105,000 for half-board in summer and Filicudi's *La Canna* (☎ *090 988 99 56, Via Rosa 53)* charges L115,000 for half-board.

Getting There & Away
Ferries and hydrofoils leave for the islands from Milazzo (which is easy to reach by train from Palermo and Messina) and all ticket offices are along Via Rizzo at the port. SNAV runs hydrofoils (L19,500 one way). Siremar also runs hydrofoils, but its ferries are half the price. If arriving at Milazzo by train, you will need to catch a bus to the port. If arriving by bus, simply make the five-minute walk back along Via Crispi to the port area. SNAV also runs hydrofoils from Palermo twice a day in summer and three times a week in the off season.

You can travel directly to the islands from the mainland. Siremar runs regular ferries from Naples and SNAV runs hydrofoils from Naples (see the Naples Getting There & Away section), Messina and Reggio di Calabria. Note that occasionally the sea around the islands can be very rough and sailings are cancelled, especially out of season to the outer islands.

Getting Around
Regular hydrofoil and ferry services operate between the islands. Both Siremar and Aliscafi SNAV have offices at the port on Lipari, where you can get full timetable information.

TAORMINA
pop 10,500
Spectacularly located on a hill overlooking the sea and Mt Etna, Taormina was long ago discovered by the European jet set, which has made it one of the more expensive and touristy towns in Sicily. But its magnificent setting, its Greek theatre and the nearby beaches remain as seductive now as they were for the likes of Goethe and DH Lawrence. The AAST tourist office (☎ *0942 2 32 43)* in Palazzo Corvaja, just off Corso Umberto near Largo Santa Caterina, has extensive information on the town.

Things to See & Do
The **Greek theatre** (entry L4000) was built in the 3rd century BC and later greatly expanded and remodelled by the Romans. Concerts and theatre are staged here in summer and it affords a wonderful view of Mt Etna. From the beautiful **Trevelyan Gardens** there is a panoramic view of the sea. Along Corso Umberto is the **Duomo**, with a Gothic facade. The local beach is **Isola Bella**, a short bus ride from Via Pirandello or by the *funivia* (cable car), which costs L5000 return.

Trips to Mt Etna can be organised through CST (☎ *0942 2 33 01)*, Corso Umberto 101. In nearby Catania, Natura e Turismo (NeT; ☎ *095 33 35 43, fax 095 53 79 10,* ✉ natetur@tin.it, *Via Quartararo 11)* organises guided walks and excursions on Mt Etna and in surrounding areas.

Places to Stay & Eat
You can camp near the beach at *Campeggio San Leo* (☎ *0942 2 46 58, Via Nazionale)* at

Capo Taormina. The cost is L10,000 per person per night, and L14,000 for a tent site.

There are numerous *affittacamere* (room rentals) in Taormina and the tourist office has a full list. *Il Leone* (☎ *0942 2 38 78, Via Bagnoli Croce 127*), near the Trevelyan Gardens, charges L45,000 per person with breakfast. *Pensione Svizzera* (☎ *0942 237 90,* ✉ *sviz zera@tau.it, Via Pirandello 26*), on the way from the bus stop to the town centre, has very pleasant singles/doubles for L80,000/120,000 with private bathroom.

Ristorante La Piazzetta (*Via Paladini 5*) has excellent full meals for around L30,000. *Da Rita* (*Via Calapitrulli 3*) serves pizza, bruschetta and lots of big salads. To drink a good Sicilian wine or sangria, go to *Arco Rosso* (*Via Naumachie 7*). Eat a typical Sicilian summer breakfast at *Bam Bar* (*Via Di Giovanni 45*); order a granita of crushed ice with fresh fruit or almonds.

Getting There & Away
Bus is the easiest way to get to Taormina. SAIS buses leave from Messina, Catania and also from the airport at Catania. Taormina is on the main train line between Messina and Catania, but the station is on the coast and regular buses will take you to Via Pirandello, near the centre; bus services are heavily reduced on Sunday.

ETNA
Dominating the landscape in eastern Sicily between Taormina and Catania, Mt Etna (3323m) is Europe's largest live volcano. It has four live craters at its summit and its slopes are littered with crevices and extinct cones. Eruptions of slow lava flows can occur, but are not really dangerous. Etna's most recent eruption was in 1999. You can climb to the summit (it's a seven-hour hike), but the handiest way is to take the cable car (SITAS ☎ 095 91 41 41) from the **Rifugio Sapienza** on the Nicolosi side of the mountain. The all-in price for the cable car, a 4WD vehicle to near the tip of the crater and a guide is L65,000. From the north side, there is a 4WD minibus (Le Betulle/STAR; ☎ 095 64 34 30) from Piano Provenzana. A three-hour guided tour costs L60,000.

Mt Etna is best approached from Catania by AST bus (☎ 095 53 17 56), which departs Via L Sturzo (in front of the train station) at 8.15 am, returning from Rifugio Sapienza at 4.30 pm (L7000 return). A private Circumetnea train line (☎ 095 37 48 42) circles Mt Etna from Giarre-Riposto to Catania. It starts from Catania at Stazione Borgo, Corso delle Province 13 (take bus Nos 29 or 36 from Catania's main train station). From Taormina, you can take an FS train to Giarre, where you can catch the Circumetnea.

SYRACUSE
pop 125,900
Once a powerful Greek city to rival Athens, Syracuse (Siracusa) is one of the highlights of a visit to Sicily. Founded in 743 BC by colonists from Corinth, it became a dominant sea power in the Mediterranean, prompting Athens to attack the city in 413 BC. Syracuse was the birthplace of the Greek mathematician and physicist Archimedes, and Plato attended the court of the tyrant Dionysius, who ruled from 405 to 367 BC.

Orientation & Information
The main sights of Syracuse are in two areas: on the island of Ortygia and at the archaeological park 2km across town. There are two tourist information offices. The AAT (☎ 0931 46 42 55), Via Maestranza 33 on Ortygia, opens 9 am to 1 pm and 4.30 to 8.30 pm weekdays (morning only on Saturday). The APT (☎ 0931 6 77 10), Via San Sebastiano 45, opens 8.30 am to 1.30 pm Monday to Saturday. There is a branch office of the APT, with the same opening hours, at the archaeological park.

Things to See
Ortygia On the island of Ortygia the buildings are predominantly medieval, with some baroque palaces and churches. The **Duomo** was built in the 7th-century on top of the Temple of Athena, incorporating most of the original columns in its three-aisled structure. The splendid **Piazza del Duomo** is lined with baroque palaces. Walk down Via Picherali to the waterfront and the **Fonte Aretusa** (Fountain of Arethusa), a natural freshwater spring. According to Greek legend, the nymph Arethusa, pursued by the river-god Alpheus, was turned into a fountain by the goddess Diana. Undeterred, Alpheus turned himself into the river which feeds the spring.

Neapolis-Parco Archeologico To get to this archaeological zone, catch bus No 1 from Riva della Posta on Ortygia. The main attraction here is the 5th-century BC **Greek theatre**, its seating area carved out of solid rock. Nearby is the **Orecchio di Dionisio**, an artificial grotto in the shape of an ear which the tyrant of Syracuse, Dionysius, used as a prison. The 2nd-century **Roman amphitheatre** is impressively well preserved. The park opens daily from 9 am to one hour before sunset. Admission is L4000.

The **Museo Archeologico Paolo Orsi** (☎ 0931 46 40 22), about 500m east of the archaeological zone, off Viale Teocrito, contains Sicily's best-organised and most interesting archaeological collection. The museum is open 9 am to 1 pm and 3.30 to 6.30 pm Tuesday to Sunday. Admission is L8000.

Places to Stay
Camping facilities are at *Agriturist Rinaura* (☎ 0931 72 12 24), about 4km from the city near the sea. Camping costs L8000 per person and L19,000 for a site. Catch bus Nos 21, 22 or 24 from Corso Umberto. The non-HI *Ostello della Gioventú* (☎ 0931 71 11 18, Viale Pepoli 45) is 8km west of town on SS115; catch bus Nos 11 or 25 from Piazzale Marconi. Beds cost L25,000; full board is L42,000.

Hotel Gran Bretagna (☎ 0931 6 87 65, Via Savoia 21), just off Largo XXV Luglio on Ortygia, has very pleasant singles/doubles for L63,000/99,000 with bath or L53,000/87,000 without. *Hotel Aretusa* (☎ 0931 2 42 11, Via Francesco Crispi 75) is close to the train station; comfortable and clean rooms cost L45,000/70,000.

Places to Eat
On Ortygia, *Ristorante Osteria da Mariano* (Vicolo Zuccalá 9) serves typical Sicilian food. *Pizzeria Trattoria Zsa Zsa* (Via Roma 73) serves 65 different kinds of pizza, antipasti and pasta. At both places a full meal will cost less than L25,000. A good pizzeria is *Il Cenacolo* (Via del Consiglio Reginale 10).

At *Pasticceria Cassarino* (Corso Umberto 86) you can try scrumptious Sicilian sweets including *cannoli di ricotta* and *arancini*.

There is an open-air, fresh produce *market* in the streets behind the Temple of Apollo, open daily (except Sunday) until 1 pm. You will find several *alimentari* and *supermarkets* along Corso Gelone.

Getting There & Away
SAIS buses leave from Riva della Posta on Ortygia for Catania, Palermo, Enna and surrounding small towns. The SAIS service for Rome also leaves from the piazza, connecting with the Rome bus at Catania. AST buses also service Palermo from Piazza della Posta. Syracuse is easy to reach by train from Messina and Catania. Boat services from Syracuse to Malta remain in a state of flux and it is best to check with the tourist offices.

AGRIGENTO
pop 55,200

Founded in approximately 582 BC as the Greek Akragas, Agrigento is today a pleasant medieval town, but the Greek temples in the valley below are the real reason to visit. The Italian novelist and dramatist Luigi Pirandello (1867-1936) was born here, as was the Greek philosopher and scientist Empedocles (circa 490-430 BC).

The AAST tourist office (☎ 0922 2 04 54), Via Cesare Battisti 15, opens 8.30 am to 1.30 pm and 4.30 to 7 pm Monday to Friday (to 1 pm on Saturday).

Things to See & Do
Agrigento's **Valley of the Temples** is one of the major Greek archaeological sights in the world. Its five main Doric temples were constructed in the 5th century BC and are in various states of ruin because of earthquakes and vandalism by early Christians. The only temple to survive relatively intact is the **Tempio della Concordia**, which was transformed into a Christian church. The **Tempio di Giunone**, a five-minute walk uphill to the east, has an impressive sacrificial altar. The **Tempio di Ercole** is the oldest of the structures. Across the main road which divides the valley is the massive **Tempio di Giove**, one of the most imposing buildings of ancient Greece. Although now completely in ruins, it used to cover an area measuring 112m by 56m, with columns 18m high. **Telamoni**, colossal statues of men, were also used in the structure. The remains of one of them are in the **Museo Archeologico**, just north of the temples on Via dei Templi (a copy lies at the archaeological site).

Close by is the **Tempio di Castore e Polluce**, which was partly reconstructed in the 19th century. The temples are lit up at night and are open until one hour before sunset. To get to the temples from the town, catch bus No 1, 2 or 3 from the train station.

Places to Stay & Eat
The **Bella Napoli** (☎ *0922 2 04 35, Piazza Lena 6)*, off Via Bac Bac at the end of Via Atenea, has clean and comfortable singles/doubles for L25,000/55,000 (L44,000/75,000 with private bathroom). For a decent, cheap meal try the excellent **La Forchetta** *(Piazza San Francesco 9);* the spaghetti *al pesce di spada* (swordfish) is delicious at L8000.

Getting There & Away
Intercity buses leave from Piazza Rosselli, just off Piazza Vittorio Emanuele, for Palermo, Catania and surrounding small towns.

Sardinia

The second-largest island in the Mediterranean, Sardinia (Sardegna) was colonised by the Phoenicians and Romans, followed by the Pisans, Genoese and finally the Spaniards. But it is often said that the Sardinians, known on the island as Sardi, were never really conquered – they simply retreated into the hills.

The landscape of the island ranges from the 'savage, dark-bushed, sky-exposed land' described by DH Lawrence, to the beautiful gorges and valleys near Dorgali and the unspoiled coastline between Bosa and Alghero. Try to avoid the island in August, when the weather is hot and the beaches are overcrowded.

Getting There & Away
Air Airports at Cagliari, Olbia and Alghero link Sardinia with major Italian and European cities. For information contact Alitalia or the Sestante CIT or CTS offices in all major towns.

Boat The island is accessible by ferry from Genoa, Livorno, Fiumicino (the port of Rome), Civitavecchia, Naples, Palermo, Trapani, Bonifacio (Corsica) and Tunis. The departure points in Sardinia are Olbia, Golfo Aranci and Porto Torres in the north, Arbatax on the east coast and Cagliari in the south.

The main company, Tirrenia, runs a service between Civitavecchia and Olbia, Arbatax or Cagliari, and between Genoa and Porto Torres, Olbia, Arbatax or Cagliari. There are fast ships between Fiumicino and Golfo Aranci/Arbatax, La Spezia and Golfo Aranci, and Civitavecchia and Olbia. The national railway, Ferrovie dello Stato (FS), runs a slightly cheaper service between Civitavecchia and Golfo Aranci. Moby Lines (which also runs Navarma Lines and Sardegna Lines) and Sardinia Ferries (also known as Elba and Corsica Ferries) both operate services from the mainland to Sardinia, as well as to Corsica and Elba. They depart from Livorno, Civitavecchia and arrive at either Olbia or Golfo Aranci. Grandi Navi Veloci runs a service between Genova and Olbia or Porto Torres from late June to late September. Most travel agencies in Italy have brochures on the various companies' services.

Timetables change and prices fluctuate with the season. Prices for a poltrona on Tirrenia ferries in the 2000 high season were: Genoa to Cagliari (L102,000; 20 hours); Genoa to Porto Torres or Olbia (L83,000; 13 hours); Naples to Cagliari (L78,000; 16 hours); and Palermo to Cagliari (L73,000; 14 hours); Civitavecchia to Olbia, (L40,400; seven hours); Civitavecchia to Cagliari (L77,000; 13½ hours). The cost of taking a small car ranged from L134,100 to L180,000, and for a motorcycle from L40,100 to L53,900.

For online information including departures, timetables and fares, check Tirrenia's Web site at www.tirrenia.com. Moby Lines has a Web site at www.mobylines.it (Italian only).

Getting Around
Bus The two main bus companies are the state-run ARST, which operates extensive services throughout the island, and the privately owned PANI, which links main towns.

Train The main FS train lines link Cagliari with Oristano, Sassari and Olbia. The private railways that link smaller towns throughout the island can be very slow. However, the *trenino* (little train), which runs from Cagliari to Arbatax through the Barbagia, is a very

ITALY

relaxing way to see part of the interior (see the Cagliari Getting There & Away section).

Car & Motorcycle The only way to explore Sardinia properly is by road. Rental agencies are listed under Cagliari and some other towns around the island.

Hitching You might find hitchhiking laborious once you get away from the main towns because of the light traffic. Women should not hitchhike in Sardinia under any circumstances.

CAGLIARI
pop 204,237

This attractive city offers an interesting medieval section, the beautiful beach of Poetto, and salt lakes with a population of pink flamingoes.

Orientation
If you arrive by bus, train or boat, you will find yourself at the port area of Cagliari. The main street along the harbour is Via Roma, and the old city stretches up the hill behind it to the castle. Most of the budget hotels and restaurants are in the area near the port.

Information
Tourist Offices The AAST information booth (☎ 070 66 92 55), Piazza Matteotti 9, is open 8 am to 8 pm daily in July and August and 8 am to 2 pm in other months. There are also information offices at the airport and in the Stazione Marittima.

The Ente Sardo Industrie Turistiche office (ESIT; ☎ 167 01 31 53 or 070 6 02 31, fax 070 66 46 36), Via Goffredo Mameli 97, is open 8 am to 8 pm daily during the summer (reduced hours the rest of the year). It has information on the whole island.

Post & Communications The main post office (☎ 070 6 03 11) is on Piazza del Carmine, up Via La Maddalena from Via Roma. The Telecom office is at Via G M Angioj, north of Piazza Matteotti. The postcode for Cagliari is 09100.

Medical & Emergency Services For an ambulance ring ☎ 070 28 62 00, and for medical attention go to the Ospedale Civile (☎ 070 609 22 67), Via Ospedale. Contact the police on ☎ 113, or go to the questura (☎ 070 6 02 71), Via Amat 9.

Things to See
The **Museo Archeologico Nazionale**, Piazza Arsenale, in the Citadella dei Musei, has a fascinating collection of Nuraghic bronzes. It's open 9 am to 2 pm and 3 to 8 pm daily, April to September (9 am to 7 pm Tuesday to Sunday the rest of the year). Admission is L4000.

It's enjoyable enough to wander through the medieval quarter. The Pisan-Romanesque **Duomo** was built in the 13th century, but later remodelled. It has an interesting Romanesque pulpit.

From the **Bastione di San Remy**, which is in the centre of town in Piazza Costituzione and once formed part of the fortifications of the old city, there is a good view of Cagliari and the sea.

The Pisan **Torre di San Pancrazio**, in Piazza Indipendenza, is also worth a look. The **Roman amphitheatre**, on Viale Buon Cammino, is considered the most important Roman monument in Sardinia. During summer opera is performed here.

Spend a day on the **Spiaggia di Poetto**, east of the centre, and wander across to the salt lakes to see the flamingoes.

Special Events
The Festival of Sant'Efisio, a colourful festival mixing the secular and the religious, is held annually for four days from 1 May.

Places to Stay & Eat
There are numerous budget pensioni near the station. Try the *Locanda Firenze* (☎ 070 66 85 05, Corso Vittorio Emanuele 149), which has comfortable singles/doubles for L43,000/58,000. *Locanda Miramare* (☎ 070 66 40 21, Via Roma 59) has rooms for L56,000/75,000. Nearby is *Albergo La Perla* (☎ 66 94 46, Via Sardegna 18), with rooms for L46,000/58,000.

Several reasonably priced trattorias can be found in the area behind Via Roma, particularly around Via Sardegna and Via Cavour. *Trattoria da Serafino (Via Lepanto 6)*, on the corner of Via Sardegna, has excellent food at reasonable prices. *Trattoria Gennargentu (Via Sardegna 60)* has good pasta and seafood and a full meal costs around L33,000. *Trattoria Ci Pensa Cannas*, down the street at No

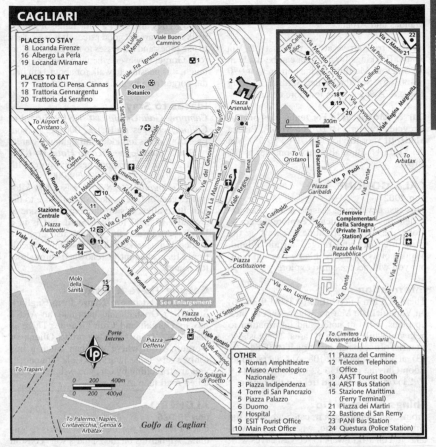

CAGLIARI

PLACES TO STAY
8 Locanda Firenze
16 Albergo La Perla
19 Locanda Miramare

PLACES TO EAT
17 Trattoria Ci Pensa Cannas
18 Trattoria Gennargentu
20 Trattoria da Serafino

OTHER
1 Roman Amphitheatre
2 Museo Archeologico Nazionale
3 Piazza Indipendenza
4 Torre di San Pancrazio
5 Piazza Palazzo
6 Duomo
7 Hospital
9 ESIT Tourist Office
10 Main Post Office
11 Piazza del Carmine
12 Telecom Telephone Office
13 AAST Tourist Booth
14 ARST Bus Station
15 Stazione Marittima (Ferry Terminal)
21 Piazza dei Martiri
22 Bastione di San Remy
23 PANI Bus Station
24 Questura (Police Station)

37, is another good choice, with meals for around L26,000. On Via Sardegna there are also grocery shops and bakeries.

Getting There & Away

Air Cagliari's airport (☎ 070 24 02 00) is to the north-west of the city at Elmas. ARST buses leave regularly from Piazza Matteotti to coincide with flight arrivals and departures. The Alitalia office (☎ 070 24 00 79 or 147 86 56 43) is at the airport.

Bus & Train ARST buses (☎ 070 409 83 24; or in Sardinia ☎ 800 86 50 42) leave from Piazza Matteotti for nearby towns, the Costa del Sud and the Costa Rei. PANI buses (☎ 070 65 23 26) leave from further along Via Roma at Piazza Darsena for towns such as Sassari, Oristano and Nuoro. The main train station is also in Piazza Matteotti. Regular trains leave for Oristano, Sassari, Porto Torres and Olbia. The private Ferrovie della Sardegna (FdS) train station is in Piazza della Repubblica. For information about the *Trenino Verde* which runs along a scenic route between Cagliari and Arbatax, contact ESIT (see Information), or the FdS directly (☎ 070 58 02 46). The most interesting and picturesque section of the route is between Mandas and Arbatax.

Boat Ferries arrive at the port just off Via Roma. Bookings for Tirrenia can be made at the Stazione Marittima in the port area (☎ 070 66 60 65). See the earlier Sardinia Getting There & Away section for more details.

Car & Motorcycle For rental cars or motorcycles try Hertz (☎ 070 66 81 05), Piazza Matteotti 1; or Ruvioli (☎ 070 65 89 55), Via dei Mille 11. Both also have branches at the airport.

CALA GONONE
pop 1002
This fast-developing seaside resort is an excellent base from which to explore the coves along the eastern coastline, as well as the Nuraghic sites and rugged terrain inland. Major points are accessible by bus and boat, but you will need a car to explore.

Information
There is a Pro Loco office (☎ 0784 9 36 96) on Viale del Blu Marino, where you can pick up maps, a list of hotels and information to help you while visiting the area. There is also a tourist office in nearby Dorgali (☎ 0784 9 62 43), at Via Lamarmora 108. At Cala Gonone, Coop Ghivine (☎ 0336 32 69 57, fax 0784 9 67 21) organises guided treks in the region.

Things to See & Do
From Cala Gonone's port, catch a boat to the **Grotta del Bue Marino**, where a guide will take you on a 1km walk to see vast caves with stalagmites, stalactites and lakes. Sardinia's last colony of monk seals once lived here, but have not been sighted in several years. Boats also leave for **Cala Luna**, an isolated beach where you can spend the day by the sea or take a walk along the fabulous gorge called **Codula di Luna**. However, the beach is packed with day-tripping tourists in summer. The boat trip to visit the grotto and beach costs L35,000.

A **walking track** along the coast links Cala Fuili, south of Cala Gonone, and Cala Luna (about three hours one way).

If you want to descend the impressive **Gorropu Gorge**, ask for information from the team of young expert guides based in Urzulei

– Societá Gorropu (☎ 0782 64 92 82, 0347 775 27 06). They also offer a wide range of guided walks in the area at good prices. It is necessary to use ropes and harnesses to traverse the Gorropu Gorge; however, when it doesn't rain too much, it is possible to walk for about 1km into the gorge from its northern entrance.

Places to Stay
Camping Gala Gonone (☎ 0784 931 65, Via Collodi) charges up to L27,000 per person. Free camping is forbidden throughout the area.

Hotels include the *Piccolo Hotel* (☎ 0784 932 32, Via C Colombo) near the port, with singles/doubles for L60,000/99,000.

Su Gologone (☎ 28 75 12) is a few kilometres east of Oliena, near the entrance to the Lanaittu valley. It's on the expensive side at around L155,000 for half-board, but is in a lovely setting and the owners also organise guided tours, treks and horse-riding expeditions. Its restaurant is renowned throughout the island.

Getting There & Away
Catch a PANI bus to Nuoro from Cagliari, Sassari or Oristano and then take an ARST bus to Dorgali and Cala Gonone. There is also a bus from Olbia's port to Oliena or Dorgali, from where you can catch a bus (only every three hours) to Cala Gonone. If you are travelling by car, you will need a detailed road map of the area.

ALGHERO
pop 39,026
One of the most popular tourist resorts in Sardinia, Alghero is on the island's west coast in the area known as the Coral Riviera. The town is a good base from which to explore the magnificent coastline linking it to Bosa in the south, and the famous Grotte di Nettuno (Neptune's Caves) on the Capocaccia to the north.

Information
The train station is on Via Don Minzoni, some distance from the centre, and is connected by a regular bus service to the centre of town.

The AAST tourist office (☎ 079 97 90 54) is at Piazza Porta Terra 9, near the port and just across the gardens from the bus station. The old city and most hotels and restaurants are in the area west of the tourist office.

The main post office is at Via XX Settembre 108. There is a bank of public telephones on Via Vittorio Emanuele at the opposite end of the gardens from the tourist office. The postcode for Alghero is 07041.

In an emergency ring the police on ☎ 113; for medical attention ring ☎ 079 93 05 33, or go to the Ospedale Civile (☎ 079 99 62 33) on Via Don Minzoni.

Things to See & Do

It's worth wandering through the narrow streets of the old city and around the port. The most interesting church is the **Chiesa di San Francesco**, Via Carlo Alberto. The city's **cathedral** has been ruined by constant remodelling, but its bell tower remains a fine example of Gothic-Catalan architecture.

Near Alghero at the beautiful **Capocaccia** are the **Grotte di Nettuno**, accessible by hourly boats from the port (L18,000), or three time a day by the FS bus from Via Catalogna (L4500 one way, 50 minutes).

If you have your own transport, don't miss the **Nuraghe di Palmavera**, about 10km out of Alghero on the road to Porto Conte.

The coastline between Alghero and Bosa is stunning. Rugged cliffs fall down to isolated beaches, and near **Bosa** is one of the last habitats of the griffon vulture. It's quite an experience if you are lucky enough to spot one of these huge birds. The best way to see the coast is by car or motorcycle. If you want to rent a bicycle or motorcycle to explore the coast, try Cicloexpress (☎ 079 98 69 50), Via Garibaldi, at the port.

Special Events

In summer Alghero stages the Estate Musicale Algherese (Alghero's Summer Music Festival) in the cloisters of the church of San Francesco, Via Carlo Alberto. A festival, complete with fireworks display, is held on 15 August for the Feast of the Assumption.

Places to Stay & Eat

It is virtually impossible to find a room in August unless you book months in advance. At other times of the year you should have little trouble. Camping facilities include *Calik* (☎ *079 93 01 11*) in Fertilia, about 6km out of town (L24,000 per person). The HI *Ostello dei Giuliani* (☎ *079 93 03 53, Via Zara 1*) is also in Fertilia. Take the hourly bus 'AF' from Via Catalogna to Fertilia. B&B costs L15,000, a shower is L1000 and a meal costs L15,000. The hostel is open all year.

In the old town is the *Hotel San Francesco* (☎ *079 97 92 58, Via Ambrogio Machin 2*) with singles/doubles for L55,000/90,000.

A pleasant place to eat is *Trattoria Il Vecchio Mulino* (*Via Don Deroma 7*). A full meal will cost around L45,000.

Getting There & Away

Alghero is accessible from Sassari by train. The main bus station is on Via Catalogna, next to the public park. ARST (☎ 079 95 01 79) buses leave for Sassari and Porto Torres. FS buses (☎ 95 04 58) also service Sassari, Macomer and Bosa.

Liechtenstein

Blink and you might miss Liechtenstein; the country measures just 25km from north to south, and an average of 6km from west to east. In some ways you could be forgiven for mistaking it for a part of Switzerland. The Swiss franc is the legal currency, all travel documents valid for Switzerland are also valid for Liechtenstein, and the only border regulations are on the Austrian side. Switzerland also represents Liechtenstein abroad, subject to consultation.

But a closer look reveals that Liechtenstein is quite distinct from its neighbour. The ties with Switzerland began only in 1923 with the signing of a customs and monetary union. Before that, it had a similar agreement with Austria-Hungary.

Although Liechtenstein shares the Swiss postal system, it issues its own postage stamps.

Unlike Switzerland, Liechtenstein joined the United Nations (1990) and, in 1995, the European Economic Area (EEA). Despite going separate ways over the EEA issue, the open border between Liechtenstein and Switzerland will remain intact. Liechtenstein has no plans to seek full EU membership.

Liechtenstein is a very prosperous country. In 1998 it suffered from an unusually high level of unemployment: 2% – 482 people!

AT A GLANCE

Capital	Vaduz
Population	31,325
Official Language	German
Currency	1 Swiss franc (Sfr) = 100 centimes
Time	GMT/UTC+0100
Country Phone Code	☎ 423

Facts about Liechtenstein

Liechtenstein was created by the merger of the domain of Schellenberg and the county of Vaduz in 1712 by the powerful Liechtenstein family. It was a principality under the Holy Roman Empire from 1719 to 1806 and, after a spell in the German Confederation, it achieved full sovereign independence in 1866. A modern constitution was drawn up in 1921 but even today, the prince retains the power to dissolve parliament and must approve every act before it becomes law. Prince Franz Josef II was the first ruler to live in the castle above the capital city of Vaduz. He died in 1989 after a reign of 51 years, and was succeeded by his son, Prince Hans-Adam II. Prince Hans-Adam is currently agitating for constitutional reforms that will actually limit his own powers in some respects.

Liechtenstein has no military service and its minuscule army (80 men!) was disbanded in 1868. It is a country known for its wines, postage stamps, dentures (an important export) and its status as a tax haven. In 2000, Liechtenstein's financial and political institutions were rocked by allegations that money laundering is rife in the country.

Despite its small size, Liechtenstein has two political regions (upper and lower) and three distinct geographical areas: the Rhine

LIECHTENSTEIN

valley in the west, the edge of the Tirolean Alps in the south-east, and the northern lowlands. The current population is 31,320, with a third of that total made up of foreign residents.

Facts for the Visitor

Sightseeing highlights are few. Many tourists come to Liechtenstein only for the stamps – a stamp in the passport and stamps on a postcard for the folks back home. But it's worth lingering to appreciate the art collection, and to enjoy the scenery.

See the Switzerland chapter for details on entry regulations, currency etc. The same emergency numbers apply as in Switzerland: dial ☎ 117 for the police, ☎ 144 for an ambulance, or ☎ 118 in the event of a fire.

Liechtenstein's telephone country code is ☎ 423. There are no regional telephone codes.

Getting There & Away

Liechtenstein has no airport (the nearest is in Zürich), and only a few trains stop within its borders, at Schaan. Getting there by postbus is easiest. There are usually three buses an hour from the Swiss border towns of Buchs (Sfr2.40) and Sargans (Sfr3.60) which stop in Vaduz. Buses run every 30 minutes from the Austrian border town of Feldkirch; you sometimes have to change at Schaan to reach Vaduz (the Sfr3.60 ticket is valid for both buses).

By road, route 16 from Switzerland passes through Liechtenstein via Schaan and terminates at Feldkirch. The N13 follows the Rhine along the Swiss/Liechtenstein border; minor roads cross into Liechtenstein at each motorway exit.

Getting Around

Postbus travel within Liechtenstein is cheap and reliable; all fares cost Sfr2.40 or Sfr3.60, and a weekly/monthly pass is only Sfr10/20 (half-price for students and senior citizens).

The only drawback is that some services finish early; the last of the hourly buses from Vaduz to Malbun, for example, leaves at 6.20 pm (takes 35 minutes). Get a timetable from the Vaduz tourist office.

Vaduz

Although it's the capital of Liechtenstein, Vaduz is little more than a village, with a population of 5100.

Orientation & Information

Two adjoining streets, Äulestrasse and the pedestrian-only Städtle, enclose the town centre. Everything of importance is within this small area, including the bus station.

The Vaduz tourist office (☎ 232 14 43, fax 392 16 18, @ touristinfo@lie-net.li), Städtle 37, has a free room-finding service and information on the whole country. It is open 8 am to noon and 1.30 to 5.30 pm Monday to Friday. From May to October it's also open until

4 pm on Saturday. Staff members are kept busy putting surprisingly dull souvenir entry stamps in visitors passports (Sfr2). Pick up the excellent *Tourist Guide*, which tells you everything you might want to know about the country.

The main post office (postcode FL-9490), Äulestrasse 38, is open 8 am to 6 pm Monday to Friday, and 8 to 11 am Saturday. Postal rates are the same as in Switzerland. The post office has an adjoining philatelic section, open 8.30 am to noon and 1.30 to 4.30 pm weekdays only. The Telecom FL shop, Austrasse 77, 1km south of Vaduz, provides free Internet access.

The hospital, Krankenhaus Vaduz (☎ 235 44 11), is at Heiligkreuz 25.

Bikes can be rented from Melliger AG (☎ 232 16 06), Kirchstrasse 10, for Sfr20 per day; they can be picked up the evening before rental begins.

Things to See & Do

Although the **castle** is not open to the public, it is worth climbing the hill for a closer look. There's a good view of Vaduz and the mountains, and a network of marked walking trails along the ridge.

The **Liechtenstein Art Museum**, or Kunstmuseum, is opposite the tourist office in a new building purpose-built in 2000. It comprises a range of works, including parts of the prince's art collection. Opening hours are 10 am to 5 pm (8 pm Thursday), closed Monday, and entry costs Sfr8 (students Sfr5). The **Postage Stamp Museum**, next to the tourist office, contains 300 frames of national stamps issued since 1912 (free; open daily). A **Ski Museum** awaits at Bangarten 10, open weekday afternoons (Sfr5). The **National Museum**, Städtle 43, will be closed until about 2003.

Look out for processions and fireworks on 15 August, Liechtenstein's national holiday.

Places to Stay

Hotel Falknis (☎ 232 63 77, Landstrasse 92) is a 15-minute walk (or take the postbus) from the centre of Vaduz towards Schaan. Reasonable singles/doubles are Sfr50/100 with a shower on each floor. *Gasthof Au* (☎ 232 11 17, fax 232 11 68, Austrasse 2) is the only other budget option in Vaduz. Singles/doubles

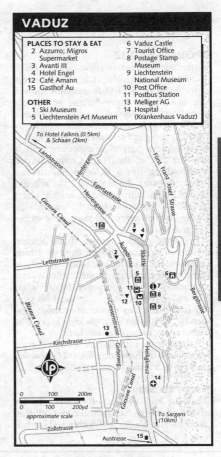

VADUZ

PLACES TO STAY & EAT	6	Vaduz Castle
2	Azzurro; Migros	7	Tourist Office
	Supermarket	8	Postage Stamp
3	Avanti III		Museum
4	Hotel Engel	9	Liechtenstein
12	Café Amann		National Museum
15	Gasthof Au	10	Post Office
		11	Postbus Station
OTHER	13	Melliger AG
1	Ski Museum	14	Hospital
5	Liechtenstein Art Museum		(Krankenhaus Vaduz)

are Sfr80/120 with private shower, or Sfr60/95 without; triples are Sfr145. Eating is pleasant and fairly inexpensive in the garden restaurant here.

Places to Eat

Most restaurants are pricey in Vaduz, so look out for lunchtime specials. *Hotel Engel (Städtle 13)* has good meals from Sfr17, with vegetarian choices. *Avanti III (Städtle 5)* provides cheap but basic fodder. On Äulestrasse, try *Café Amann* (closes 7 pm weekdays, noon Saturday, and all day Sunday), or *Azzurro*, next to the *Migros* supermarket. Azzurro is a

LIECHTENSTEIN

stand-up place with pizzas from Sfr10, open until 7 or 8 pm (5 pm Sunday).

AROUND VADUZ

Northern Liechtenstein is dotted with small communities. There's little to do except enjoy the quiet pace of life and view the village churches. Pottery-making is demonstrated on weekdays at Schaedler Keramik (☎ 373 14 14) in **Nendeln** (admission free). The Rofenberg in **Eschen-Nendeln** was formerly a place of public execution and is now the site of the Holy Cross Chapel. **Schellenberg** has a Russian monument, commemorating the night in 1945 when a band of 500 heavily armed Russian soldiers crossed the border. They had been fighting for the German army, but they came to defect, not attack.

Triesenberg, on a terrace above Vaduz, commands an excellent view over the Rhine valley and has a pretty onion-domed church. There's also a museum devoted to the Walser community, which journeyed from Valais (Switzerland) to settle here in the 13th century (closed Sunday except in summer, and Monday; admission Sfr2, students Sfr1). The Walser dialect is still spoken here.

Balzers, in the extreme south of the country, is dominated by the soaring sides of Gutenberg Castle, which is closed to the public.

Places to Stay

Check the Vaduz tourist office hotel list for private rooms or cheaper accommodation that is outside Vaduz, but within a short bus ride of the capital. Schaan, for example, has **Hotel Post** (☎ *232 17 18, fax 233 35 44*) by the bus station, providing singles/doubles from Sfr45/90 with shower, and small singles for Sfr38 without.

The **SYHA hostel** (☎ *232 50 22, fax 232 58 56, Untere Rütigasse 6*), 10 minutes' walk from Schaan towards Vaduz, is open from March to November. Beds cost Sfr28.30 including breakfast. From 9.30 am to 5 pm reception is closed and the doors are locked.

Triesenberg has a **camp site** (☎ *392 26 86*), with dorm beds for Sfr12.

MALBUN

Liechtenstein's ski resort, Malbun, lies at 1600m amid the mountains in the south-east. It has some good runs for novices (and two ski schools) as well as more difficult runs. A one-day pass for all ski lifts costs Sfr35 (students/seniors Sfr29). Skis, shoes and poles cost Sfr43 for a day, and can be hired from the sports shop (☎ 263 37 55).

The road from Vaduz terminates at Malbun. The tourist office (☎ 263 65 77, fax 263 73 44, ✉ malbuninfo@lie-net.li) is by the first bus stop and is open daily, except Sunday, 9 am to noon and 1.30 to 5 pm (1 to 4 pm on Saturday). It's closed between seasons.

Places to Stay & Eat

The village has six hotels, each with a restaurant. Singles/doubles start at Sfr45/90 at **Alpenhotel Malbun** (☎ *263 11 81, fax 263 96 46*), or Sfr70/110 at **Turna** (☎ *232 34 21, fax 263 51 73*, ✉ lampert1@bluewin).

Luxembourg

The Grand Duchy of Luxembourg (Luxemburg, Letzeburg) has long been a transit land. For centuries ownership passed from one European superpower to the other; and for decades travellers wrote it off as merely an expensive stepping stone to other destinations.

While it's true that this tiny country is more a tax shelter for financial institutions than a budget haven for travellers, many people miss the best by rushing through. Its beautiful countryside is dotted with feudal castles, deep river valleys and quaint winemaking towns, while the capital, Luxembourg City, is often described as the most dramatically situated in Europe.

Facts about Luxembourg

HISTORY

Luxembourg's history reads a little like the fairy tale its name evokes. More than 1000 years ago, in 963, a count called Sigefroi (or Siegfried, Count of Ardennes) built a castle high on a promontory, laying the foundation stone of the present-day capital and the beginning of a dynasty which spawned rulers throughout Europe.

By the end of the Middle Ages, the strategically placed, fortified city was much sought after – the Burgundians, Spanish, French, Austrians and Prussians all waging bloody battles to conquer and secure it. Besieged, devastated and rebuilt more than 20 times in 400 years, it became the strongest fortress in Europe after Gibraltar, hence its nickname, 'Gibraltar of the north'.

Listed as a French 'forestry department' during Napoleon's reign, it was included in the newly formed United Kingdom of the Netherlands, along with Belgium, in 1814. It was cut in half 16 years later when Belgium severed itself from the Netherlands and Luxembourg was split between them. This division sparked the Grand Duchy's desire for independence, and in 1839 the Dutch portion became present-day Luxem-

Capital	Andorra la Vella
Population	66,000
Official Language	Catalan
Currency	1 French franc (FF) = 100 centimes 1 peseta (pta) = 100 centimos
Time	GMT/UTC+0100
Country Phone Code ☎ 376	

bourg. Later, after the country declared itself neutral, many of the fortifications were dismantled.

Luxembourg entered the 20th century riding on the wealth of its iron-ore deposits. When this industry slumped in the mid-1970s, the Grand Duchy not only survived but prospered by introducing favourable banking and taxation laws, which made it a world centre of international finance.

GEOGRAPHY

On the maps of Europe, Luxembourg commonly gets allocated a 'Lux' tag – and even

that abbreviation can be too big to fit the space it occupies on the map between Belgium, Germany and France. At only 82km long, 57km wide, and riddled with rivers, its 2586 sq km are divided between the forested Ardennes highlands to the north, and farming and mining country to the south.

CLIMATE

Luxembourg has a temperate climate with warm summers and cold winters – it's especially cold in the Ardennes, which sometimes gets snow. The sunniest months are May to August, although April and September can be pretty nice as well. Precipitation is spread evenly over the year.

ECOLOGY & ENVIRONMENT

About a third of Luxembourg is covered by forests which are home to wild boar, fox and deer. The main environmental concerns are air and water pollution in urban areas.

Luxembourg has no national parks. The so-called Parc Naturel de la Haute Sûre (Upper Sûre Nature Park) in the country's north-west is a group of communes which have banded together to promote and protect their region. The Maison du Parc Naturel (☎ 89 93 31 1) at

15 Rte de Lultzhausen (about 500m from the village of Esch-sur-Sûre) is the park's impressive information centre-cum-museum.

GOVERNMENT & POLITICS

One of Europe's smallest sovereign states, Luxembourg is a constitutional monarchy headed by Grand Duke Jean, who came to the throne after his mother's abdication in 1964. On 28 September 2000, Grand Duke Jean is expected to abdicate in favour of his eldest son, Henri. The main political parties are the Christian-Social, Democratic and Workers-Socialist.

The prime minister, Jean-Claude Jüncker, was re-elected in 1999; he has led the government since 1995.

ECONOMY

Luxembourg's strong economy rides on its banking and insurance sectors. Agriculture and the steel and tourism industries are also important. GDP in 1998 was US$13.9 billion. Unemployment is the lowest in Europe at 2.6%.

POPULATION & PEOPLE

A motto occasionally seen carved in stone walls sums up the people's character: *Mir wëlle bleiwe wat mir sin* – We want to remain what we are. Despite a history of foreign domination, Luxembourg's 429,000 inhabitants steadfastly retain an independent character.

ARTS

Few Luxembourgers are internationally known in the arts, which is probably why Edward Steichen, one of the pioneers of American photography, is held in such high regard in his native land. The expressionist painter Joseph Kutter introduced modern art to Luxembourg. Roger Manderscheid is a respected contemporary author who often writes in Letzeburgesch, the national language.

RELIGION

Christianity was established early, and today Catholicism reigns supreme. More than 95% of the population are Roman Catholic, with the church dominating many facets of life, including politics, the media and education. About 3% of the population are Protestant or Jewish.

LANGUAGE

There are three official languages in Luxembourg: French, German and Letzeburgesch. The latter is most closely related to German and was proclaimed as the national tongue in 1984. English is widely spoken in the capital and by younger people around the countryside.

Luxembourgers speak Letzeburgesch to each other but generally switch to French when talking to foreigners. A couple of Letzeburgesch words often overheard are *moien* (good morning/hello) and *äddi* (goodbye). Like French speakers, Luxembourgers say *merci* for 'thank you'. In the business world, politics, the judiciary and the press, French or German are mainly used. For a rundown on these two languages, see the Language Guide at the back of this book.

Facts for the Visitor

HIGHLIGHTS

Luxembourg's highlights include: strolling along the capital's Chemin de la Corniche; spending a lazy afternoon visiting wineries along the Moselle Valley; hiking almost anywhere in the north; and taking in the expansive view from Bourscheid Castle.

SUGGESTED ITINERARIES

Depending on the length of your stay, you might want to see and do the following things (although if you're relying on public transport, you will need a few more days to cover these areas):

Two days
  Spend one day in Luxembourg City and the other in either Echternach or Vianden.
One week
  Spend two days in Luxembourg City, two days exploring the centre and north (Vianden, Clervaux or Diekirch), two days in the Müllerthal region (Echternach and Beaufort) and a day along the Moselle Valley.

PLANNING
When to Go

The countryside in spring can be a riot of wildflowers and blossoms, summer is the warmest time and, in autumn, wine-making

LUXEMBOURG

villages are celebrating their grape harvests. For climate considerations, see the Climate section earlier in this chapter.

Maps
Good road maps include those published by Geoline (scale: 1:140,000) and Michelin (No 924; scale: 1:150,000).

TOURIST OFFICES
The Office National du Tourisme headquarters (☎ 42 82 82 10, fax 42 82 82 38, ✉ tourism@ont.smtp.etat.lu), PO Box 1001, L-1010, Luxembourg City, will send you information. Its Web site is at www.etat.lu /tourism.

Tourist Offices Abroad
Luxembourg tourist offices abroad include:

UK (☎ 020-7434 2800, fax 020-7734 1205, ✉ tourism@luxembourg.co.uk) 122 Regent St, London W1R 5FE

USA (☎ 212-935 88 88, fax 212-935 58 96, ✉ luxnto@aol.com) 17 Beekman Place, New York, NY 10022

VISAS & DOCUMENTS
Visitors from many countries need only a valid passport for three-month visits. Regulations are basically the same as for entering the Netherlands (for more details, see the Facts for the Visitor section in that chapter).

EMBASSIES & CONSULATES
Luxembourg Embassies Abroad
In countries where there is no representative, contact the Belgian or Dutch diplomatic missions. Luxembourg embassies and consulates include:

UK (☎ 020-7235 6961, fax 7235 9734) 27 Wilton Crescent, London SW1X 8SD

USA (☎ 202-265 41 71/72, fax 328-82 70) 2200 Massachusetts Ave, NW Washington, DC 20008

Foreign Embassies in Luxembourg
The nearest Australian, Canadian and New Zealand embassies are in Belgium (see the Belgium Facts for the Visitor section). The following embassies are all in Luxembourg City:

Belgium (☎ 44 27 46 1, fax 45 42 82) 4 Rue des Girondins, L-1626

France (☎ 45 72 71 1, fax 72 71 22 7) 8 Blvd Joseph II, L-1840

Germany (☎ 45 34 45 1, fax 45 56 04) 20-22 Ave Émile Reuter, L-2420

Ireland (☎ 45 06 10, fax 45 88 20) 28 Route d'Arlon, L-1140

Netherlands (☎ 22 75 70, fax 40 30 16) 5 Rue CM Spoo, L-2546

UK (☎ 22 98 64, fax 22 98 67) 14 Blvd Roosevelt, L-2450

USA (☎ 46 01 23, fax 46 14 01) 22 Blvd Emmanuel Servais, L-2535

CUSTOMS
Petrol, alcohol, tobacco and perfume products are relatively cheap in Luxembourg and people from neighbouring countries often come here to stock up. The usual allowances apply to duty-free goods if you are coming from a non-EU country and to duty-paid goods if you're arriving from within the EU.

MONEY
Currency
The unit of currency is the Luxembourg franc – written as 'f' or 'flux' – which is issued in f1, f5, f20 and f50 coins, and f100, f1000 and f5000 notes. It's equal to the Belgian franc (for exchange rates, see the Belgium Facts for the Visitor section), but while Belgian currency is commonly used in Luxembourg the reverse does not apply. Banks are the main exchange bureaus and charge about f200 commission. All major credit cards are commonly accepted; ATMs are located at the airport and around Luxembourg City.

Costs
Prices are slightly more expensive than Belgium – except petrol, which is much cheaper.

Those really keen on exploring the Grand Duchy should consider the Luxembourg Card. Valid from Easter to 31 October, it gives free admission to many attractions throughout the country plus unlimited use of public transport. It's available from tourist offices and costs f350/600/850 for an adult for one/two/three days; family cards cost f700/1200/1700. Alternatively, the Stater Museeskaart is a two-day card allowing free admission to the major sights in Luxembourg City and costs f250/400 for an adult/family. It can be purchased year-round.

Many museums offer a concession price for children.

Tipping & Bargaining
Tipping is not obligatory and bargaining is downright impossible.

Taxes & Refunds
Value-added tax (abbreviated in French as TVA) is calculated at 15%, except for hotel, restaurant and camping ground prices, which enjoy only a 3% levy. The procedure for claiming the tax back is tedious unless you buy from shops affiliated with the Tax Cheque Refund Service. These shops will give you a stamped Tax Refund Cheque which can be cashed at your port of exit.

POST & COMMUNICATIONS
Post
Post offices (except in Luxembourg City) are open 9 am to 5.30 pm weekdays. It costs f21 to send a letter (under 20g) within Europe and f30 outside. Mail to Australia, Canada, New Zealand and the USA takes at least a week. To the UK and within Europe, it'll take around two or three days. There's a f16 fee (sometimes waived) for poste restante – letters should be addressed to: Post Office, Poste Restante, L-1118 Luxembourg 2.

Telephone
For making international telephone calls to Luxembourg, the country code is ☎ 352. To telephone abroad, the international access code is ☎ 00 (see the Telephone Appendix). There are no telephone area codes in Luxembourg.

Local telephone calls are time-based and cost a minimum of f10. International phone calls can be made using f125, f250 or f550 phonecards. The cost of a three-minute phone call in peak time to the USA is f111. Numbers prefixed with 0800 are toll-free numbers.

Mobile phone users will find Luxembourg works on GSM 900/1800, which is compatible with elsewhere in Europe and Australia but not with the North American GSM 1900 or the system used in Japan.

Fax
Faxes can be sent from post offices and cost f180/280/350 for the first page to the UK/USA/Australia, plus f30/130/200 for each additional page. It costs f80 to receive a fax.

Email & Internet Access
Public Internet access facilities are very limited and you will only find cybercafes in Luxembourg City.

INTERNET RESOURCES
Upcoming tourist events in Luxembourg City are listed on the city's Web site at www.luxembourg-city.lu/touristinfo. For general information – weather, cinema listings, regional events – head to www.luxweb.lu.

BOOKS
For a humorous look at Luxembourg ways, get hold of *How to Remain What You Are* by George Müller, a Luxembourg psychologist. An excellent multilingual publication for walkers is *182 x Luxembourg*, which describes 182 of the country's most charming hiking trails. *40 Cycle Routes* is the cyclist's equivalent. Both are published by Éditions Guy Binsfield and widely available in bookstores.

NEWSPAPERS & MAGAZINES
The *Lëtzebuerger Journal* and *Luxemburger Wort* are the two main daily newspapers. The only English-language newspaper is the weekly *Luxembourg News* (f90), which gives a brief rundown of local news and has entertainment listings. Foreign newspapers and magazines are readily available.

RADIO & TV
Den Neie Radio (DNR; 102.9kHz) concentrates on classical music and news. Radio Lëtzebuerg (RTL; 93.3kHz) plays commercial pop.

There's a plethora of international TV stations from which to choose. RTL, one of the main national stations, broadcasts in Letzeburgesch from 7 pm to midnight.

TIME
Luxembourg operates on Central European Time. Noon in Luxembourg is 3 am in San Francisco, 6 am in New York and Toronto, 11 am in London, 9 pm in Sydney and 11 pm in Auckland. The 24-hour clock is commonly

LUXEMBOURG

used. Daylight-saving time comes into effect at 2 am on the last Sunday in March, when clocks are moved an hour forward; they're moved an hour back at 2 am on the last Sunday in October.

LAUNDRY

Most larger towns have a self-service *laverie*. A 5kg wash costs about f300; dryers are f35 for 10 minutes.

TOILETS

Public toilets in Luxembourg are not common. Those that have an attendant charge between f10 and f40; those that don't are usually ill-kept and best avoided.

WOMEN TRAVELLERS

Women should face few problems travelling around Luxembourg. However, in the event of attack, contact the women's crisis organisation Waisse Rank (☎ 40 20 40), 84 Rue Adolphe Fischer, Luxembourg City.

GAY & LESBIAN TRAVELLERS

Luxembourg's national homosexual and lesbian organisation is Rosa Lëtzebuerg (mobile/cellphone ☎ 091-31 10 37), 94 Blvd Patton, L-2316 Luxembourg. Attitudes to homosexuality are quite relaxed and in the capital, Luxembourg City, you will find a couple of gay bars. The age of consent is 16. Luxembourg Pride is a small festival held in mid-June. A gay Luxembourg Web site is www.ogayane.com.

DISABLED TRAVELLERS

Disabled travellers will find little joy getting around Luxembourg – lifts are not commonplace, ramps are few, and pavements are uneven. For information it's best to contact Info-Handicap (☎ 36 64 66), 20 Rue de Contern, L-5955 Itzig.

SENIOR TRAVELLERS

Only Luxembourg citizens are entitled to discounts for seniors on local transport, and there are no discounts for the elderly at museums.

TRAVEL WITH CHILDREN

Kids usually enjoy exploring any old castle, a boat trip on the Moselle and riding the toy train in Luxembourg City.

DANGERS & ANNOYANCES

Luxembourg is a safe country to travel around. In the event of an emergency, call ☎ 113 for the police or ☎ 112 for medical assistance.

LEGAL MATTERS

Should you need (free) legal advice, contact the Service d'Accueil et d'Information Juridique (☎ 22 18 46), Côte d'Eich in Luxembourg City.

BUSINESS HOURS

Trading hours are 9 am to 5.30 pm weekdays (except Monday when some shops open about noon), and a half or full day on Saturday. Many shops close for lunch between noon and 2 pm. Banks have shorter hours: 8.30 am to 4.30 pm weekdays and, in the capital, on Saturday mornings – country branches close for lunch.

PUBLIC HOLIDAYS & SPECIAL EVENTS

Public holidays include New Year's Day, Easter Monday, May Day (1 May), Ascension Day, Whit Monday, National Day (23 June), Assumption Day (15 August), All Saints' Day (1 November) and Christmas Day.

For a small country, Luxembourg is big on festivals. Pick up the tourist office's *Calendar of Events* brochure for local listings. The biggest national events are carnival, held six weeks before Easter, and Bonfire Day (Bürgsonndeg), one week later. National Day is held on 23 June, however festivities take place on the evening of 22 June.

ACTIVITIES

With a dense network of marked walking paths, the Grand Duchy is a hiker's haven. National routes are indicated by yellow signposts. Tracks, marked by white triangles, connect the 11 Hostelling International (HI) hostels. Most bookshops sell hiking maps (also see the previous Books section), and local tourist offices always stock regional walking maps.

WORK

Seasonal grape picking is possible in the Moselle Valley for about six weeks from mid-September. No permit is needed, but the work is popular with locals.

ACCOMMODATION
In summer it's wise to reserve all accommodation. The national tourist office has free hotel and camping brochures, and charges f20 to book a hotel room. For accommodation in B&Bs or *gîtes ruraux* (rural houses), contact the Association for Rural Tourism (☎ 95 71 84, fax 95 71 85, @ tourural@pt.lu), Château de Wiltz, L-9516 Wiltz. It publishes a free brochure (in English) listing many options.

Camping grounds are abundant, although mainly in the central and northern regions. Rates are f50 to f65 per adult at 'Category 3' grounds, and f100 to f280 in the more plentiful (and better equipped) 'Category 1' grounds. In general, children are charged half the adult rate, and a tent site is equivalent to an adult rate.

There are 11 hostels – most close irregularly throughout the year, so ring ahead. The nightly dorm rate, including breakfast, varies from f375 to f575 for members under 26 years, and f455 to f670 for older members. Sheets cost f125, and nonmembers must pay an extra f110 a night. For more details contact Hostelling International (HI; ☎ 22 55 88, fax 46 39 87, @ information@youthhostels.lu), 2 Rue du Fort Olisy, L-2261 Luxembourg City.

B&Bs, mainly in rural areas, usually go for between f1200 and f1600 for two people, while the cheapest hotels charge f1000/1400 for a basic single/double room with breakfast.

FOOD & DRINKS
Luxembourg's cuisine is similar to that of Belgium's Wallonia region – plenty of pork, freshwater fish and game meat – but with a German influence in local specialities like liver dumplings with sauerkraut. The national dish is *judd mat gaardebounen* (smoked pork with beans). Strict vegetarians will find little joy. A *plat du jour* (dish of the day) in the cheapest cafe costs about f260. Beer, both local (Mousel) and Belgian, is plentiful, and the Moselle Valley white wines are highly drinkable.

ENTERTAINMENT
Nightlife outside Luxembourg City is very tame. In summer, terrace cafes take over town squares and are the place for people-watching, especially during local festivals. Cinemas generally screen films in their original language with French, and sometimes German, subtitles.

SHOPPING
White wines and local liqueurs (made from plums, pears, nuts and cherries) are popular purchases. Look for the Marque Nationale label, which indicates quality vintages.

Getting There & Away

AIR
The international airport, Findel, is 6km east of the capital, and is serviced by frequent buses (see the Luxembourg City Getting Around section). The national carrier, Luxair, flies to a number of European destinations, including London, Paris and Frankfurt. Its main office (☎ 4798 1 for general information, ☎ 4798 50 50 for arrivals/departures) is at the airport. There's a f120 departure tax when leaving Findel (it's included in ticket prices).

LAND
Bus
Eurolines buses do not pass through Luxembourg; Busabout buses from the UK do (see Getting Around at the start of this book for details).

Train
The Benelux Tourrail pass (see the Belgium Getting Around section) costs f6600/4400 for a 1st/2nd-class ticket for people above 26 years and f3300 (2nd-class only) for those under 26. It's also valid for travelling on national (CFL) buses.

Train services include to Brussels (f890, 2¾ hours, hourly for a one-way 2nd-class ticket), Amsterdam (f1634, 5½ hours, hourly), Paris (f1550, four hours, six trains per day) and Trier in Germany (f306, 40 minutes, 11 per day). The station office (☎ 49 90 49 90) in Luxembourg City is open 24 hours.

Car & Motorcycle
The E411 is the major route to Brussels; the A4 leads to Paris and the E25 to Metz; the main route to Germany is the E44 via Trier.

LUXEMBOURG

RIVER

It's possible to take a cruise boat from points along the Moselle to destinations in Germany. Two boats ply these waters from Easter to October. From Remich to Konz (three hours) it costs f490/590 one-way/return. For more details, see the Moselle Valley section.

Getting Around

BUS & TRAIN

Unlike its Benelux partners, Luxembourg does not have an extensive rail system, so getting around once you leave the main north-south train line can take time. The bus network (operated by CFL) is comprehensive and the fare system for both train and bus is simple: f40 for a 'short' (about 10km or less) trip, or f160 for a 2nd-class unlimited day ticket (known as a *Billet Reseau*), which is also good for travelling on inner-city buses. It's valid from the time of purchase until 8 am the next day.

More information can be obtained from either the CFL bus information kiosk (☎ 49 90 55 44) or train information office (☎ 49 90 49 90), both inside the Luxembourg City train station.

In most train stations, you'll find either a luggage room (f100 per article for 24 hours) or luggage lockers (f80 to f150 for 48 hours).

CAR & MOTORCYCLE

Road rules are easy to understand and standard international signs are in use. The blood-alcohol limit for drivers is 0.08%. The speed limit on motorways is 120km. Fuel prices are among the cheapest in Western Europe: lead-free/diesel costs f33/26 per litre (leaded petrol is virtually impossible to find). For all other motoring information, contact the Club Automobile de Luxembourg (☎ 45 00 45 1), 54 Route de Longwy, L-8007 Bertrange.

Car rental costs from f2900 per day (including insurance, VAT and unlimited kilometres) for a small Peugeot.

BICYCLE

Cycling is more a popular pastime than the way of life it is elsewhere in the Benelux. Bikes can be hired for about f400 per day in Luxembourg City. It costs f40 to take your bike on a train.

HITCHING

Hitching is not common. Note that it is illegal on motorways.

BOAT

Special train-boat-bus combo tickets (f400) are available on weekends (Easter until 31 October) to tour the Moselle Valley. From Luxembourg City, you take the train to Wasserbillig, a boat to Remich and return to the capital by bus. The national tourist office at the train station in Luxembourg City has details.

For more information on passenger boat services, see the Moselle Valley section.

LOCAL TRANSPORT

Luxembourg City has a good local bus network. Elsewhere there is little public transport besides taxis. Taxis cost f35 per kilometre plus a 10% night surcharge; 25% extra on Sunday.

ORGANISED TOURS

A half-day trip by bus from Luxembourg City takes in Vianden and the Müllerthal region. It runs from May to September; for details ask the tourist office for the *Sightseeing Luxembourg* brochure.

Luxembourg City

pop 80,176

Strikingly situated high on a promontory overlooking the Pétrusse and Alzette Valleys, the Grand Duchy's 1000-year-old capital is a composed blend of old and new. One of Europe's financial leaders, it's a wealthy city with an uncommonly tranquil air and unusually clean streets. The historical value of the city's remaining fortifications and older quarters were acknowledged in 1994 when Unesco added them to its list of World Heritage sites.

Orientation

The city centre has three main sections – the largely pedestrianised old town, the train station area and the Grund. The old town is north of the valleys and based around two large squares – Place d'Armes and Place Guillaume II. To the south – across Pont Adolphe and Pont Passerelle, two impressive bridges that span the Pétrusse Valley – is the train station quarter. The station itself is 1.25km from Place d'Armes. The Grund, or lower town, is a picturesque, cobblestoned quarter, built well below the fortifications, and home these days to some brisk nightlife. Across the Alzette Valley rise the modern towers of the European Centre (Centre Européen) on the Kirchberg Plateau.

Information

Tourist Offices The Luxembourg City tourist office (☎ 22 28 09, fax 46 70 70, ✉ touristinfo@luxembourg-city.lu), Place d'Armes, is open 9 am to 7 pm daily (until 6 pm Sunday) from 1 April to 31 September. The rest of the year it's open 9 am to 6 pm (10 am to 6 pm Sunday). It hands out free city maps, a comprehensive walking tour pamphlet and the handy *Luxembourg Weekly* events guide.

The national tourist office (☎ 42 82 82 20, fax 42 82 82 30, ✉ tourism@ont.smtp.etat.lu) is inside the train station.

It's open 9 am to 7 pm daily (closed for lunch on Sunday) between 1 June and 30 September. The rest of the year it's open 9.15 am to 12.30 pm and 1.45 to 6 pm daily. It provides city and national information and reserves rooms.

At the airport and at main highway entrances there are interactive touch screens for information.

Money The Kredietbank Luxembourg, Place de la Gare, next to the station, is a convenient bank. Outside banking hours, exchange offices (with poorer rates) are open at the train station 8.30 am to 9 pm daily, and at the airport 6 am to 10 pm.

Post & Communications The main post office, 25 Rue Aldringen, is open 7 am to 7 pm weekdays, and until 5 pm Saturday. The post office branch (fax 49 11 75), 38 Place de la Gare near the train station, is open 6 am to 7 pm weekdays and until noon Saturday.

For Internet access, there are two options. The Café Chiggeri (☎ 22 82 36), 15 Rue du Nord, is a stylish, laid-back cafe with just one computer terminal. It's open until 1 am (3 am on weekends). CDROMWorld (☎ 26 48 03 12, ✉ info@cdromworld.lu), 41 Ave de la Gare in the Galerie Mercure, is a computer shop with a few terminals for surfing. It's open 10 am to 7 pm weekdays and until 5pm Saturday. It charges f100 for 30 minutes.

Travel Agencies Sotours (☎ 46 15 14 1), 15 Place du Théâtre, specialises in student and youth fares. Nouvelles Frontières (☎ 46 41 40), Rue des Bains, has occasional discount air fares.

Bookshops Librairie Bourbon (☎ 49 22 06), 11 Rue du Fort Bourbon, has a decent selection of books relating to Luxembourg, English-language novels, travel guides and maps. It's open 9 am to 6 pm weekdays and until 5 pm Saturday. Magasin Anglais (☎ 22 49 25), 19 Allée Scheffer, is an all-round 'English' shop (magazines, Hobnob biscuits, videos etc) with a wall of English-language books. It's a 15-minute walk north-west of Place d'Armes.

Laundry There's a Quick Wash on Place de Strasbourg and a Self Wash at 2 Rue du Fort Wallis. Both are open Monday to Saturday.

Medical Services In the case of a medical emergency or if you need a pharmacy outside normal working hours call ☎ 112. For a hospital, head to Clinique Ste Thérèse (☎ 49 77 61) on Rue Ste Zithe.

Things to See & Do

Luxembourg is best covered on foot, indeed, the city seems made for leisurely wandering.

From Place d'Armes, head south down Rue Chimay to **Place de la Constitution**, where you will have excellent views over the Pétrusse Valley and of the spectacular bridges that span it. East along Blvd Roosevelt, the gardens which cover the 17th-century **Citadelle du St Esprit** offer superb panoramas up both valleys and over the Grund.

Follow the natural curve north to the **Chemin de la Corniche** – a pedestrian promenade hailed as 'Europe's most beautiful balcony' – which winds along to the **Bock**, the cliff on which Count Sigefroi built his mighty fort. The castle and much of the fortifications

LUXEMBOURG

LUXEMBOURG CITY

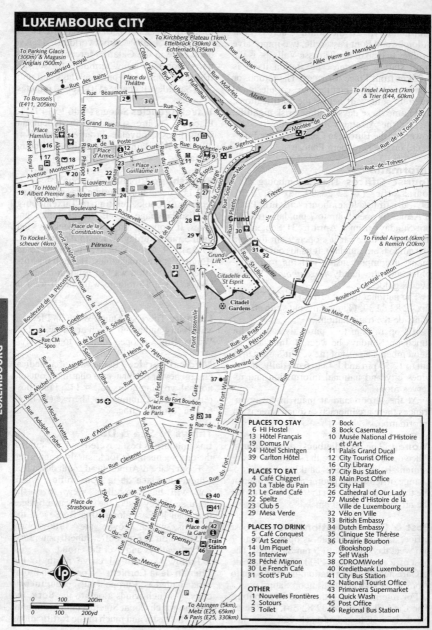

To Kirchberg Plateau (1km),
Ettelbrück (30km) &
Echternach (35km)

To Parking Glacis
(300m) & Magasin
Anglais (500m)

To Brussels
(E411, 205km)

To Findel Airport (7km)
& Trier (E44, 60km)

Allée Pierre de Mansfeld

Boulevard Royal

Rue des Bains

Place du
Théâtre

Rue Beaumont

Côte d'Eich

Montée de Pfaffenthal

Rue Vauban

Rue Mohrfels

Alzette

Blvd U Uelveling

Blvd Victor Thorn

Rue - du - Rost

Montée - de - Clausen

Rue - de - la - Tour-Jacob

Place
Hamilius

Grand Rue

Neuve

Rue Aldringen

Rue de la Poste

Rue du Curé

Rue Boucherie

Rue Sigefroi

Rue - de - Trèves

Blvd Royal

Avenue Monterey

Rue Philippe II

Place
d'Armes

Rue du Marché aux Herbes

Rue Notre Dame

Place
Guillaume II

Rue Large

Rue du St-Esprit

Rue Sosthène Weis

Rue de Trèves

To Hôtel
Albert Premier
(500m)

Boulevard

Roosevelt

Place de la
Constitution

de la Constitution

Rue Plaetis

Grund

Rue de la Comète

To Kockel-
scheuer (4km)

Pétrusse

Pont Adolphe

Grund
Lift

Rue St-Ulric

Alzette

To Findel Airport (6km)
& Remich (20km)

Citadelle du
St Esprit

Citadel
Gardens

Boulevard Général-Patton

Rue Marie et Pierre Curie

Avenue de la Pétrusse

Avenue de la Liberté

Rue Goethe

Rue Sainte

R de la Grève

R Schiller

Boulevard de la Pétrusse

Rue Heine

R Dicks

Rue de Prague

Montée de la Pétrusse

Boulevard - d'Avranches

Rue du Laboratoire

Pont Passerelle

Rue CM
Spoo

Rue Renert

Rodange

Zithe

R du Fort Elisabeth

Gare

Rue du Fort Wallis

Neipperg

Rue Michel

Rue Adolphe Fisher

Rue Michel Wetter

R du Fort Bourbon

Place
de Paris

R du Fort

Avenue de la Gare

Rue - de - Bonnevoie

Rue du Fort

Rue Glesener

Place de
Strasbourg

Rue 1900

Rue d'Anvers

Rue Joseph Junck

Rue de Strasbourg

Rue du Fort Wedell

Rue du Fort Reims

Place de
la Gare

Train
Station

Rue d'Epernay

Rue du Commerce

Rue - Mercier

To Alzingen (5km),
Metz (E25, 65km)
& Paris (E25, 330km)

0   100   200m
0   100   200yd

PLACES TO STAY
6 HI Hostel
13 Hôtel Français
19 Domus IV
24 Hôtel Schintgen
39 Carlton Hôtel

PLACES TO EAT
4 Café Chiggeri
20 La Table du Pain
21 Le Grand Café
22 Speltz
23 Club 5
29 Mesa Verde

PLACES TO DRINK
5 Café Conquest
9 Art Scene
14 Um Piquet
15 Interview
28 Péché Mignon
30 Le French Café
31 Scott's Pub

OTHER
1 Nouvelles Frontières
2 Sotours
3 Toilet

7 Bock
8 Bock Casemates
10 Musée National d'Histoire
   et d'Art
11 Palais Grand Ducal
12 City Tourist Office
16 City Library
17 City Bus Station
18 Main Post Office
25 City Hall
26 Cathedral of Our Lady
27 Musée d'Histoire de la
   Ville de Luxembourg
32 Vélo en Ville
33 British Embassy
34 Dutch Embassy
35 Clinique Ste Thérèse
36 Librairie Bourbon
   (Bookshop)
37 Self Wash
38 CDROMWorld
40 Kredietbank Luxembourg
41 City Bus Station
42 National Tourist Office
43 Primavera Supermarket
44 Quick Wash
45 Post Office
46 Regional Bus Station

euro currency converter €1 = f40.33

were dismantled between 1867 and 1883 following the treaty of London. There's little left – the main attractions are the view and the nearby entrance to the Bock Casemates, a 23km network of underground passages spared from destruction because of their delicate position in relation to the town.

The **Grund** district lies in the valley directly below, accessible from the other side of the Bock or by a free **lift** dug in the cliff near the citadel at Place du St Esprit.

From the Bock, it's a short walk to Rue du Marché aux Herbes where you'll find the **Palais Grand Ducal**. Originally a town hall, the palace was built in the 1570s during Spanish rule and later expanded; the royal family took up residence here at the end of the 19th century. It has been extensively restored in recent years and is open to visitors from mid-July to 31 August only. The nearby **Place Guillaume II** is lined with formal government edifices.

Bock Casemates The Bock Casemates are a honeycomb of damp, rock rooms carved out under the Bock. Long ago, they housed bakeries, slaughterhouses and thousands of soldiers; during WWI and WWII they were used as a bomb shelter for 35,000 people. They are open 10 am to 5 pm daily from 1 March to 31 October; entry costs f70 (concession f40).

Museums The **Musée National d'Histoire et d'Art**, Place Marché aux Poissons, contains a mixture of Roman and medieval relics, fortification models and art from the 13th century up to the present day. However, 80% of it is closed for renovations until late 2001. It's open 10 am to 5 pm Tuesday to Sunday; admission is f100 (concession f50). The **Musée d'Histoire de la Ville de Luxembourg**, Rue du St Esprit 14, is a state-of-the-art complex covering the history of the city. It's open 10 am to 6 pm Tuesday to Sunday; entry costs f200 (free for children).

Market On Wednesday and Saturday morning, there's a food market on Place Guillaume II. On the second and fourth Saturday morning of each month, it's bric-a-brac time on Place d'Armes.

Organised Tours

Guided walks are a marvellous way of discovering the city's many nooks and crannies, and theme walks – following in the footsteps of Vauban or nature trails for example – are also popular. The tourist office has details on all possibilities.

The *Pétrusse Express* is a toy train that runs from Place de la Constitution down to the Grund. It operates daily from Easter to 31 October and costs f230 (concession f160). Alternatively, Sales-Lentz/Segatos operates 2¼-hour city bus trips for f450 (concession f250); inquiries and bookings can be made at the tourist office.

Special Events

Two festivals are worth catching: Octave, a Catholic pilgrimage held from the third to fifth Sunday after Easter, which climaxes with a street parade headed by the Grand Duke; and Schueberfouer, a fortnight-long fun fair in late August, during which decorated sheep take to the streets.

Places to Stay

Luxembourg has a dearth of cheap options – most accommodation here is geared for business travellers.

Camping About 4km south of the city is *Kockelscheuer* (☎ 47 18 15, *22 Route de Bettembourg*) in Kockelscheuer (take bus No 2 from the train station). It's open from Easter to 31 October.

Hostel The HI *hostel* (☎ 22 68 89, *fax 22 33 60*, 📧 *luxembourg@youthhostels.lu, 2 Rue du Fort Olizy*) is located in a valley below the old city. Bus No 9 from the airport or train station stops nearby, otherwise it's a 30-minute walk from the station. It's open all year, and charges f650/1140 for a single/double for members aged under 26 and f750/1340 for members over 26. Dorms start at f435/520. Nonmembers pay an extra f110 a night.

Hotels The big, old *Carlton Hôtel* (☎ 29 96 60, *fax 29 96 64*, 📧 *carlton@pt.lu, 9 Rue de Strasbourg*) has clean singles from f750 to f2500, and doubles between f1400 and f3000; breakfast is f150 extra.

Hôtel Schintgen (☎ *22 28 44, fax 46 57 19, 6 Rue Notre Dame*) is well located and has decent single/double/triple rooms starting at f2600/3200/3500.

The most delightful mid-range option is *Hôtel Français* (☎ *47 45 34, fax 46 42 74, 14 Place d'Armes*). It's small, modern, superbly sited and dotted with *objets d'art* – all in all a winning combination. Prices begin at f3400/4400. Its Web site is www .hotelfrancais.lu.

Domus IV (☎ *46 78 78 1, fax 46 78 79, 37 Ave Monterey*) is a new hotel with gaily decorated, innovative rooms. Those without kitchenettes cost f4300, f4800 with. Breakfast is f400.

Undoubtedly the city's most charming hotel is the brand-new *Hotel Albert Premier* (☎ *44 24 42 1, fax 44 74 41,* ✆ *hotel-albert-premier@resto.lu, 2a Rue Albert 1er*). About 750m due west of Place d'Armes, it has 10 opulent rooms – all individually styled – ranging from f8000 to f14,000. Check it out at www.albert1er.lu.

Places to Eat

Restaurants The *Club 5* (☎ *46 17 63, 5 Rue Chimay*) is a trendy downstairs brasserie and 1st-floor restaurant. The brasserie is open daily until 1 am and does a good-value plat du jour (f350); the restaurant's a bit dearer.

Le Grand Café (☎ *47 14 36, 9 Place d'Armes*) is a lively establishment with an eclectic line-up of meals (f450 to f650). It's popular with tourists and locals alike.

The only purely vegetarian option is *Mesa Verde* (☎ *46 41 26, 11 Rue du St Esprit*), an exotically colourful restaurant that's often full. Mains are in the f650 to f950 range.

One of the best addresses in town is *Speltz* (☎ *47 49 50, 8 Rue Chimay*). Seafood and French *haute cuisine* are the staples, and mains go from f900 to f1200.

Cafes A convivial cafe-cum-bakery with no-smoking surroundings is *La Table du Pain* (☎ *24 16 08, 19 Ave Monterey*). It covers two floors and serves salads (f250) and open sandwiches (f160 to f200) from 7 am to 7 pm daily.

The *Café Chiggeri* (☎ *22 82 36, 15 Rue du Nord*) draws a hip crowd with its range of international meals, including vegetarian fare (f320).

Self-Catering For picnic supplies, there's a *Primavera* supermarket in the Galerie Kons.

Entertainment

The Grund area is one of the most popular nightlife spots and, when the cliffs are lit up in summer, it's a pleasant stroll down to the taverns which huddle here. *Le French Café (Rue de Trèves)* has a moody ambience and a great line-up of international beers. *Scott's Pub (Bisserweg)* is popular with lovers of loud (weekend) blues and rock; it's calmer on weekdays.

In the old centre, *Art Scene (6 Rue Sigefroi)* has live jazz or blues from 10 pm every Friday and Saturday night. There's no cover charge, but drink prices are hiked up on these nights. *Pêché Mignon (17 Rue du St Esprit)* is a trendy cafe with musical and literary evenings. The raw *Interview (19 Rue Aldringen)* is popular with young people while the nearby *Um Piquet (30 Rue de la Poste)* has a cosier feel. The city's gay scene revolves around the lively *Café Conquest* (☎ *22 21 41, 7 Rue du Palais de Justice)*. There are a few nightclubs around the station and along Rue Joseph Junck – this area is a bit seedy.

Getting There & Away

For information on international flights and train services, see the Getting There & Away section at the beginning of this chapter. For national destinations, see the Getting There & Away section for each place. Turn left as you leave the train station to find CFL buses heading to towns within Luxembourg.

Getting Around

To/From the Airport Bus No 9 (three services hourly) connects Findel airport with the HI hostel, Place Hamilius and the train station; it costs f40 (f50 extra for luggage). Alternatively the Luxair bus (f150) picks up at the station and Place Hamilius. A taxi to Findel costs about f800.

Bus City buses depart from in front of the train station and from Place Hamilius in the old town. Free bus route maps are handed out at the tourist office. For ticket information, see the Getting Around section earlier in this chapter.

Car The cheapest car park is Glacis, about 800m north-west of Place d'Armes. Street parking is difficult to find.

For car rental try: Autolux (☎ 22 11 81), 33 Blvd Prince Henri; Avis (☎ 43 51 71), Findel airport; Budget (☎ 43 75 75), Findel airport; or Hertz (☎ 43 46 45), Findel airport.

Bicycle Vélo en Ville (☎ 47 96 23 83), 8 Bisserweg, rents out bikes for f250 per half-day, f400 a day or f2000 a week (20% off for those aged under 26).

Around Luxembourg

MOSELLE VALLEY

Less than half an hour's drive east of the capital, the Luxembourg section of the Moselle Valley is one of Europe's smallest wine regions. More than a dozen towns line the **Route du Vin** (Wine Road), which follows the Moselle from Wasserbillig, through the region's capital at Grevenmacher, past the popular, waterfront playground of Remich, to the small, southern border town of Schengen.

There are only two tourist offices en route: at Grevenmacher (☎ 75 82 75), 10 Route du Vin, and Remich (☎ 69 84 88), in the bus station on the Esplanade.

Things to See & Do

Wine tasting is the obvious attraction and there are several *caves* (cellars) where you can sample the fruity, white vintages. Try the **Caves Bernard-Massard** in Grevenmacher or **St Martin** in Remich. Both are open daily from 1 April to 31 October and run tours (f100) which end with a drink.

From Easter to October, it's possible to enjoy a **boat cruise** on the Moselle on board either the new *MS Princesse Marie-Astrid* or the *Musel*. They call in at Remich, Wormeldange, Grevenmacher and Wasserbillig, before continuing to Konz and Saarburg in Germany. A sample fare is f390/490 one-way/return between Remich and Grevenmacher (two hours). For more details contact Navitours (☎ 75 84 89) at 1 Rue de Luxembourg, Grevenmacher. Also check out the train-boat-bus combo from Luxembourg City (see Boat in Getting Around for details).

Special Events

The wine festivals start in August and climax with November's 'New Wine' festival in Wormeldange; each village celebrates nearly all stages of the wine-making process.

Places to Stay

Next to the butterfly garden in Greven-macher, there's *Camping de la Route du Vin* (☎ 75 02 34, Route du Vin) open from April to September. In Remich, *Camping Europe* (☎ 69 80 18, Rue du Camping) is 100m from the bus station. It's open from Easter to mid-September.

Remich has several riverfront hotels. The cheapest is *Beau Séjour* (☎ 69 81 26, fax 66 94 82, 30 Quai de la Moselle) which has rooms (shared toilet) from f1100/1900, or with private facilities for f1800/2600. In Wormeldange, *Relais du Postillon* (☎ 76 84 85, fax 76 81 86, 113 Rue Principale) offers pleasant rooms from f1700/2100. *Bamberg's* (☎ 76 00 22, fax 76 00 56, ✉ bamberg@pt.lu, Route du Vin) in the village of Ehnen is best known for its restaurant (delicious French and seafood cuisine) but it also has well-priced accommodation for f2400/2800.

Getting There & Away

The region is difficult to explore without your own transport. Trains stop at Wasserbillig only; buses from Luxembourg City go to Grevenmacher (twice daily) from where there are connections to other towns.

CENTRAL LUXEMBOURG

While there's not much to keep you in central Luxembourg, the area can make a good exploration base. The town of Ettelbrück is the nation's central rail junction and from here it's easy to get a train to the nearby town of Diekirch, which is home to the country's main wartime museum.

The tourist office in Diekirch (☎ 80 30 23), 1 Esplanade, is a 10-minute walk from the station. It's open 9 am to noon and 2 to 5 pm weekdays (it's also open 10 am to noon and 2 to 4 pm weekends, from 1 July to 15 August).

LUXEMBOURG

Things to See & Do

The **Musée National d'Histoire Militaire**, 10 Rue Barmertal in Diekirch, details the 1944 Battle of the Bulge and the liberation of Luxembourg by US troops. Its excellent collection of wartime artefacts is well presented. The museum is open 10 am to 6 pm daily from 1 April to 1 November, and 2 pm to 6 pm the rest of the year. Admission is f200 (concession f120).

With a car, it's well worth taking the winding drive north-west of Diekirch to the 1000-year-old **Bourscheid Castle**, which is situated on a plateau overlooking farmland and the Sûre River. The castle is open daily from April to October, and on weekends from November to March. Admission is f80 (concession f30).

Places to Stay

Diekirch offers a decent choice of accommodation but if you want to overnight in a hostel you'll need to stay in Ettelbrück.

Camping de la Sûre (☎ 80 94 25, *34 Route de Gilsdorf*) is by the river and open from 1 April to 30 September. The Ettelbrück *hostel* (☎ 81 22 69, fax 81 69 35, *Rue G D Joséphine-Charlotte*) is a 20-minute walk from the station; closed December and January. *B&B Weber-Posing* (☎ 80 32 54, *74 Rue Principale*) in Gilsdorf, about 2km west from central Diekirch, has large, old-fashioned rooms for f700 per person. *Hiertz* (☎ 80 35 62, fax 80 88 69, *1 Rue Clairefontaine*) in the heart of Diekirch has one of the region's best restaurants, and has decent rooms for f2300/2900.

Getting There & Away

Hourly trains from Luxembourg City to Ettelbrück take 30 minutes; to Diekirch, it takes 40 minutes.

MÜLLERTHAL

The Müllerthal region lies north-east of the capital, based around the old, Christian town of Echternach. The area is often referred to as *Petite Suisse* (Little Switzerland), due to its extensive woodlands and fascinating sandstone plateaus. Outdoor enthusiasts love this area – it's great for hiking, cycling and rock climbing, and is one of Luxembourg's prime tourist spots.

The tourist information office in Echternach (☎ 72 02 30) at Porte St Willibrord, is open 9 am to noon and 2 to 5 pm Monday to Friday (also on weekends in July and August). There are smaller offices in the villages of Beaufort (☎ 83 60 81), 9 Rue de l'Église, and Berdorf (☎ 79 06 43), 7 Rue Laach.

Things to See & Do

If you happen to be in Echternach on Whit Sunday, look out for the handkerchief pageant in honour of St Willibrord, a missionary who died in the town centuries ago. If not, you can visit the **basilica** where St Willibrord's remains lie in a white, marble sarcophagus. Behind the basilica, there's a **Benedictine abbey**.

You can also head west to the walking paths which wind through wonderful rocky chasms and past waterfalls to **Berdorf**, situated on the tableland 6km away, and on to the hidden castle of **Beaufort**, open 9 am to 6 pm daily from 1 April to 25 October.

Places to Stay

Camping grounds are abundant throughout this region, and the loveliest ones of course are away from the towns. If you're stuck for transport, *Camping Officiel* (☎ 72 02 72, *5 Route de Diekirch*), is about 200m from the bus station in Echternach. In Beaufort, the big *Camping Plage* (☎ 83 60 99, *Grand Rue*) is open all year.

There are two *hostels* – one in Echternach (☎ 72 01 58, fax 72 87 35, **@** echternach@youthhostels.lu, *9 Rue André Duchscher*) and the other at Beaufort (☎ 83 60 75, fax 86 94 67, *6 Rue de l'Auberge*). Room rates start at f375/455 for those under/over 26 years.

Hotels are plentiful in Echternach: try *Aigle Noir* (☎ 72 03 83, fax 72 05 44, *54 Rue de la Gare*), about 40 steps from the bus station, which has basic accommodation for f1250/1500, or *Hôtel Le Pavillon* (☎ 72 98 09, fax 72 86 23, **@** diedling@pt.lu, *2 Rue de la Gare*). It's a sweet little corner hotel with just 10 well-equipped rooms for f1800/2400 (f2100/2700 from May to September).

Getting There & Away

Only buses connect Echternach with Luxembourg City – the trip takes 40 minutes. From Echternach, buses head out to other towns.

THE ARDENNES

The Grand Duchy's northern region is known as the Luxembourg Ardennes. It's spectacular country – winding valleys with fast-flowing

LUXEMBOURG

rivers cut deep through green plateaus crowned by castles. Of the three main towns, Clervaux, in the far north, is the most accessible; while Vianden, in the east, is arguably Luxembourg's most touristy town. To the west, Wiltz holds no special appeal, though the tiny nearby hamlet of Esch-sur-Sûre attracts a staggering number of tourists simply because of its picturesque location.

Clervaux

Clervaux's tourist office (☎ 92 00 72) is ensconced in its castle and is open 2 to 5 pm weekdays from Easter to 30 June, 9.45 to 11.45 am and 2 to 6 pm daily from 1 July to 31 August, and 9.45 to 11.45 am and 1 to 5 pm September through October.

The town has two main sights: its feudal **castle**, in the town centre, and the turreted **Benedictine abbey**, high in the forest above. The castle houses Edward Steichen's famous photography collection, *Family of Man*, which is open 10 am to 6 pm from Tuesday to Sunday (closed January and February). Admission is f150.

Vianden

Vianden's new tourist office (☎ 83 42 57), 1 Rue du Vieux Marché, is open from 9.30 am to noon and 1 to 6 pm daily from 1 April to 30 October. The rest of the year it's open weekdays only.

The town's most noted feature is its impeccably restored **chateau**, open 10 am to 4 pm daily (to 6 pm in summer). Admission is f180 (concession f80). The chateau's striking position can be photographed from the **télésiège** (chair lift), which climbs the nearby hill daily from Easter to mid-October.

Vianden was home to author, Victor Hugo, during his exile from France in 1870-71. There are plans to turn the house where he lived (across the river from the tourist office and denoted with a plaque) into a museum.

Wiltz

The tourist office (☎ 95 74 44) is in the chateau. Its opening hours are 10 am to 6 pm daily in July and August, and 10 am to noon and 2 to 5 pm weekdays from September to June.

Built on the side of a small plateau, Wiltz is more spacious, but less picturesque, than Clervaux or Vianden. It's divided in two: the Ville Haute (High Town), where most of the sights are found, is situated on a crest, while the Ville Basse and the train station flank the river below. The rather sterile **chateau** sits on the edge of the Ville Haute and is home to an exhibition on the 1944 Battle of the Bulge. It's open from 10 am to noon and 1 to 5 pm daily from 1 June to mid-September.

Esch-sur-Sûre

The tiny village of Esch-sur-Sûre is off the Wiltz-Ettelbrück road. It's built on a rocky peninsula skirted by the Sûre River and is lorded over by steep cliffs and a ruined castle. It's all very picturesque and, in summer, tourists come here in vast numbers.

A worthwhile detour is to the **Maison du Parc Naturel** (see the Ecology & Environment section), which contains a wonderful working collection of old looms and other textile-making machines, as well as environmental displays.

Places to Stay

Clervaux In Clervaux the closest camping ground is *Camping Officiel* (☎ 92 00 42, 33 Klatzewé), open April to mid-November. There's no hostel in Clervaux; the nearest *hostel* (☎ 99 80 18, fax 97 96 24, 24 Rue de la Gare) is 6km away in Troisvierges. The *Hôtel du Parc* (☎ 92 06 50, fax 92 10 68, 2 Rue du Parc) occupies a lovely, old mansion and has just seven rooms from f1650/2600.

Vianden There are several camping grounds in Vianden. *Op dem Deich* (☎ 83 43 75) is on the river to the south of town, about 200m from the bus station. It's open from Easter to 31 September. Vianden's *hostel* (☎ 83 41 77, fax 84 94 27, @ vianden@youthhostels.lu, 3 Montée du Château) sits in the shadow of the chateau. It has rooms with between two and 16 beds and prices start at f375/455 for those under/over 26 years.

There are heaps of hotels, many open from Easter to October only. The most expensive ones line the Grand Rue. For something cheaper try the friendly *Auberge de l'Our* (☎ 83 46 75, fax 84 91 94, 35 Rue de la Gare) with bright rooms starting at f950/1600 (bathroom facilities are communal).

Wiltz The *Camping Kaul* (☎ 95 00 79, *Rue Jos Simon*), about 800m from the train station, is open from 1 May to 31 October. The *hostel* (☎ 95 80 39, fax 95 94 40, ✉ *wiltz@you thhostels.lu, 6 Rue de la Montagne*) is a 1km climb from the train station, behind the Ville Haute. Prices start at f375/455 for those under/over 26 years.

Auberge la Ballade (☎ 95 73 24, fax 95 92 27, *144 Rue du X Septembre*) is a rustic little inn with just four modern rooms, about 1km from the train station in the Ville Basse. Rates are f800/1200 without private facilities, or f1000/1600 with. The most engaging hotel is

Aux Anciennes Tanneries (☎ 95 75 99, fax 95 75 95, ✉ *tannerie@pt.lu, 42a Rue Jos Simon*) in the Ville Basse. Modern rooms overlook a babbling stream, and there's also an excellent restaurant. Prices start at f2800/3000.

Getting There & Away

There are trains every two hours to Clervaux (one hour) from Luxembourg City. To reach Vianden, take the Luxembourg City-Ettelbrück train and then take a connecting bus. To get to Wiltz (1½ hours) take the Luxembourg City-Clervaux train to Kautenbach, and another train from there.

euro currency converter €1 = f40.33

The Netherlands

A small country with a big reputation for liberalism, the Netherlands (Nederland, or Holland as it's commonly, but incorrectly, known) swims in a sea of familiar images. A land of bikes, dikes, blazing flower fields, mills and few hills – these quintessential images of the Netherlands do exist outside the major cities and the once-radical, still exuberant, capital of Amsterdam.

While Amsterdam tops most travellers' itineraries, there is plenty to entice you away from the 'anything goes' capital. The countryside's endlessly flat landscape, broken only by slender church steeples in scenes that inspired the nation's early artists, is a cyclist's nirvana. And while you may be pressed to find untouched spaces and solitude, you'll discover a hard-fought-for land with proud people and farmers who, yes, still wear traditional clogs.

Facts about the Netherlands

HISTORY

The Netherlands' early history is linked with Belgium and Luxembourg: the three were known as the Low Countries until the 16th century, when the present-day Netherlands' boundaries were roughly drawn. Originally the land was inhabited by tribal groups: the Germanic Batavi drained the sea lagoons while the Frisii lived on mounds in the remote north.

In the late 16th century, the region's northern provinces united to fight the Spanish (see the Belgium History section). The most powerful of these provinces was Holland with its main city of Amsterdam, and to the outside world, Holland became synonymous with the independent country that was to emerge in this corner of Europe (a bit like saying England when you mean Britain).

Led by Prince William of Orange, nicknamed William the Silent for his refusal to enter into religious arguments, the Revolt of the Netherlands lasted 80 years, ending in 1648 with a treaty that recognised the 'United Provinces' as an independent republic. As part

AT A GLANCE

Capital	Amsterdam
Population	15.65 million
Official Languages	Dutch (Netherlandic)
Currency	1 Netherlands guilder or gulden (f or Dfl) = 100 cents
Time	GMT/UTC+0100
Country Phone Code ☎ 31	

The Randstad p927
Leiden p925   ⊙ Central Amsterdam p918
The Hague Centre p931   ◻ Delft p933

GERMANY

BELGIUM   ◻ Maastricht p941

of the deal, the Schelde River was closed to all non-Dutch ships. This destroyed the trade of the largest port in that time, Antwerp, but ensured the prosperity of its rival, Amsterdam.

Amsterdam stormed onto the European scene in what was the province of Holland's most glorified period: the Golden Age from about 1580 to about 1740, after which the British began dominating the world seas. The era's wealth was generated by the Dutch East India Company, which sent ships to the Far East in search of spices and other exotic goods, while colonising the Cape of Good Hope and Indonesia and establishing trading posts throughout Asia. Later the West Indies

Company sailed to West Africa and the Americas, creating colonies in Surinam, the Antilles and New Amsterdam (today's New York).

Meanwhile, Amsterdam's bourgeoisie indulged in fine, gabled canal houses and paintings of themselves and the remains of last night's dinner. This in turn stimulated the arts and brought renown to painters such as Rembrandt.

But it didn't last. In 1795 the French invaded and Napoleon appointed his younger brother Louis as king. When the largely unpopular French occupation came to an end, the United Kingdom of the Netherlands – incorporating Belgium and Luxembourg – was born. The first king, King William I of Orange, was crowned in 1814, and the House of Orange rules to this day. In 1830 the Belgians rebelled and became independent; Luxembourg did the same soon after.

While the Netherlands stayed neutral in WWI, it was unable to do so in WWII. The Germans invaded on 10 May 1940, obliterating much of Rotterdam in a bombing blitz four days later. Although a sound Dutch resistance movement formed, only a small minority of the country's Jews survived the war.

In 1949, despite military attempts to hold on to Indonesia, the colony won independence. Surinam followed much later, gaining a peaceful handover of sovereignty in 1975. The Antilles still have close ties with the Netherlands but are self-ruled.

In 1953 one of the country's worst disasters hit when a high spring tide coupled with a severe storm breached the dikes in Zeeland, drowning 1835 people. To ensure the tragedy would never be repeated, under the Delta Plan a network of dams and dikes was constructed (see the Delta Region section later in this chapter).

The social consciousness of the 1960s found fertile ground in the Netherlands, especially in Amsterdam, which became the radical heart of Europe. The riotous squatter's movement stopped the demolition of much cheap inner-city housing, the lack of which is a problem that has continued into the 21st century.

GEOGRAPHY

Bordered by the North Sea, Belgium and Germany, the Netherlands occupies 33,920 sq km. It is largely artificial, its lands reclaimed from the sea over many centuries and the drained polders protected by dikes. More than half of the country lies below sea level. Only in the south-east Limburg province will you find hills.

The south-west province of Zeeland is the combined delta area of the Schelde, Maas, Lek and Waal Rivers; the Lek and Waal are branches of the Rhine, carrying most of its water to the sea – the mighty Rhine itself peters out in a pathetic little stream (the Oude Rijn, or Old Rhine) at the coast near Katwijk.

CLIMATE

The Netherlands has a temperate maritime climate with cool winters and mild summers. The wettest months are July and August, though precipitation is spread pretty evenly throughout the year. The sunniest months are May to August, and the warmest are June to September. Because it's such a flat country, wind has free reign – something you'll soon notice if you take to cycling.

ECOLOGY & ENVIRONMENT

On the whole, the Dutch public takes environmental issues such as pollution very seriously, and sound legislation has been set up to help preserve and protect the environment. The nation's most pressing environmental problems are water and air pollution, and the contamination of groundwater by high levels of nitrates and phosphates used in agriculture.

There are 15 national parks dotted around the countryside. As you'd expect in a nation of this size, they're not enormous, but invaluable for preserving fauna and flora. The Hoge Veluwe and nearby Veluwezoom were the first parks to be declared in the 1930s. Other major parks are Schiermonnikoog (5400 hectares; mainly dunes), the Biesbosch (7100 hectares; wetlands) and Dwingelderveld (3600 hectares; heather fields).

GOVERNMENT & POLITICS

Against the European trend, the Netherlands developed from a republic to a constitutional monarchy, headed today by Queen Beatrix who took over from her mother, Juliana, in 1980. The country's political scene is often compared with the physical landscape – flat and often dull – with coalition governments pursuing policies of compromise. The three

THE NETHERLANDS (NEDERLAND)

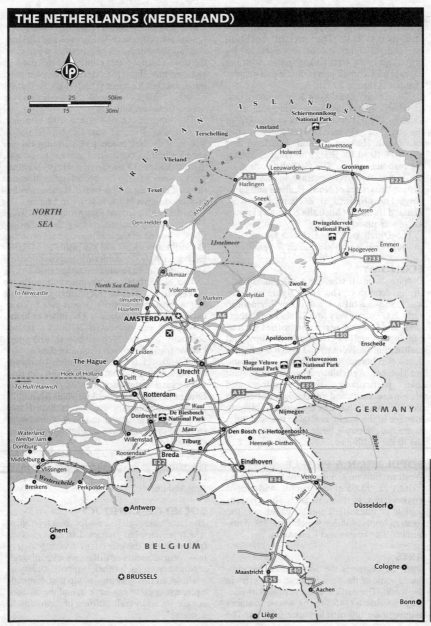

NETHERLANDS

main parties are the socialist PvdA, the conservative Liberal VVD and the Catholic-Protestant CDA. The present coalition government comprises the socialists, led by prime minister, Wim Kok, together with the liberals and a small party, the D66. The next election is due in 2002.

The country consists of 12 provinces, one of which, Flevoland, only came into existence in 1967 after it had been claimed from the sea. The province of Holland was split into North Holland (capital: Haarlem) and South Holland (capital: The Hague) during the Napoleonic era. The Catholic portion of the population lives mainly in the southeastern provinces of North Brabant and Limburg. The province of Zeeland gave New Zealand its name (Australia once was known as New Holland).

The Dutch view the EU as a fact of life, and further integration is taken for granted.

ECONOMY

Despite its small size, the Netherlands has a strong economy. The GDP figure in 1998 was US$348.6 billion, and unemployment in early 2000 was a very low 2.7%. The Netherlands is a leader in service industries such as banking, as well as electronics (Philips) and multimedia (Polygram) and also has a highly developed horticultural industry – bulbs and cut flowers. Agriculture plays an important role, particularly dairy farming and glasshouse fruits and vegetables. Rotterdam harbour, which handles the largest shipping tonnage in the world, is vital to the economy, as are the country's large supplies of natural gas in the north-east.

POPULATION & PEOPLE

Western Europe's most densely populated country has 15.65 million people, and a lot of Frisian cows, in its small area. This concentration is intensified in the Randstad, the western hoop of cities which includes Amsterdam, The Hague and Rotterdam.

ARTS

Over the centuries the Netherlands has produced some of the most influential painters in the world. The earliest artist of note was Hieronymus Bosch (1450-1516), whose macabre paintings are full of religious allegories. The greatest artist of 17th-century Dutch painting was Rembrandt (1606-69), who excelled in religious art, portraiture, landscapes and still life – ie, all the categories of paintings popular at the time. Other notable painters of this golden age are Frans Hals (1582-1666), master of portraits, and Jan Vermeer (1632-75), who meticulously crafted balanced compositions of scenes from ordinary life.

The nation's best-known 19th-century painter was Vincent van Gogh (1853-90), whose short but productive painting career ended when he committed suicide to escape mental illness. Van Gogh's early, sombre works were done in his homeland, and stand in stark contrast to the frenzied paintings he produced in his last few years in France.

In the 20th century Piet Mondrian (1872-1944), with his abstract rectangular compositions, was one of the leading exponents of the De Stijl movement, and the prints of Maurits Escher (1902-72) depicting impossible images continue to fascinate mathematicians.

The Netherlands shines internationally in other artistic fields, including jazz (The Hague hosts the world's largest jazz festival each summer) and dance. The latter is highlighted by the respected Nationaal Ballet company and the Nederlands Danstheater, known for its innovative modern dance.

Though relatively little Dutch literature has been translated into English you can find some classic tales such as *Max Havelaar* by Eduard D Dekker, better known as Multatuli. Noted contemporary authors include Harry Mulisch *(The Assault)* and Cees Nooteboom *(A Song of Truth and Semblance* and *In the Dutch Mountains).*

The Diary of Anne Frank, an autobiography written by a Jewish teenager, movingly describes life while hiding in Nazi-occupied Amsterdam.

SOCIETY & CONDUCT

The Dutch are well known for their tolerance, which perhaps has stemmed from *verzuiling* (pillarisation), the custom of dividing society into compartments or pillars which, although separate from each other, support society as a whole. In this way any group that demands a place in society can have it, and the balance is kept by an overall attitude of 'agreeing to disagree'.

NETHERLANDS

It's customary to greet shopkeepers and bar/cafe owners when entering their premises.

In red-light districts, 'No photo' stickers often adorn windows and should be taken seriously.

RELIGION

The number of former churches that now house art galleries is the most obvious sign of today's attitude to religion – and art. Catholics are the largest religious grouping, accounting for 19% of the population. The Dutch Reformed Church, to which half the population belonged 100 years ago, attracts about 15% today, though it's still the official church of the royal family.

LANGUAGE

Most English speakers use the term 'Dutch' to describe the language spoken in the Netherlands, and 'Flemish' for that spoken in the northern half of Belgium and a tiny northwestern corner of France. Both are in fact the same language, the correct term for which is Netherlandic, or *Nederlands*, a West Germanic language spoken by about 25 million people worldwide.

The people of the northern Fryslân (Friesland) province speak their own language. Although Frisian is actually the nearest relative of the English language, you won't be able to make much sense of it when you hear it spoken.

The differences between Dutch and Flemish *(Vlaams)*, in their spoken as well as written forms, are similar to those between UK and North American English.

Like many other languages, Netherlandic gives its nouns genders. There are three genders: masculine, feminine (both with *de* for 'the') and neuter (with *het*). Where English uses 'a' or 'an', Netherlandic uses *een* (pronounced *ern*), regardless of gender.

Netherlandic also has a formal and informal version of the English 'you'. The formal version is *U* (written with a capital letter and pronounced *ü*), the informal version is *je* (pronounced *yer*). As a general rule, people who are older than you should still be addressed with *U*. See the Language chapter at the back of the book for pronunciation guidelines and useful words and phrases.

Facts for the Visitor

HIGHLIGHTS

After Amsterdam, the Keukenhof gardens (see The Randstad section) are a must, especially for flower aficionados, while anyone with a bit of dirt should investigate *wadlopen* – mud-flat-walking (see The North section). Museum and cycling buffs will be in their element throughout the Netherlands – a visit to the Kröller-Müller Museum (see the Arnhem & the Hoge Veluwe section) superbly combines the two.

SUGGESTED ITINERARIES

Depending on the length of your stay, you might want to see and do the following:

Two days
  Visit Amsterdam.

One week
  Spend two days in Amsterdam, one day each in The Hague, Leiden, the Keukenhof gardens, and the Hoge Veluwe national park, and the remaining day visiting Rotterdam (Kinderdijk windmills) or Waterland Neeltje Jans (see the Delta Region section).

Two weeks
  Spend three days in Amsterdam, two days in The Hague, one day each in Maastricht, Leiden, the Keukenhof gardens, Delft, Rotterdam (Kinderdijk), a day in the Delta Region (Waterland Neeltje Jans and Middelburg) and another in the Hoge Veluwe national park, and if you have any time left over, head to Schiermonnikoog, Den Bosch or Alkmaar.

One month
  This should give you enough time to have a look around the whole country.

PLANNING
When to Go

Spring is the ideal time to visit, as there's less chance of rain and the bulbs are in bloom – daffodils from about early to late April, and tulips from about late April to mid-May.

Maps

The Lonely Planet *Amsterdam City Map* is plastic-coated to make it rainproof and has a handy street index. Excellent road maps of the Netherlands include those produced by

NETHERLANDS

Michelin (scale: 1:400,000) and the ANWB (scale: 1:300,000). The ANWB also puts out provincial maps detailing cycling paths and picturesque road routes (scale: 1:100,000).

TOURIST OFFICES
Local Tourist Offices
The ubiquitous VVV – the national tourist organisation – sells brochures on everything and maps for everywhere. Its offices are generally open 8 or 9 am to 5 or 6 pm Monday to Friday, and 10 am to 4 pm Saturday, and sometimes on Sunday as well. Staff will book accommodation for a fee of f4.50 to f6 per person. In larger cities, and during the summer months of July and August, opening hours are extended. Some VVV offices have telephone numbers prefixed by ☎ 0900 (these numbers cost f1 a minute) and are answered by recorded messages in Dutch – wait for the message to end to be answered personally.

The Netherlands Board of Tourism (NBT; ✉ info@nbt.nl), Vlietweg 15, Postbus 458, 2260 MG Leidschendam, takes postal and email inquiries only.

Tourist Offices Abroad
NBT has offices overseas, including the following:

Belgium (☎ 02-543 0800, ✉ info@nbt.be) Louizalaan 89, 1050 Brussels
Canada (☎ 416-363 1577) 25 Adelaide St East, suite 710, Toronto, Ont M5C 1Y2
France (☎ 01 43 12 34 27, ✉ balie@hollande-tourisme.fr) 9 rue Scribe, 75008 Paris
Germany (☎ 0221-9257 1727) Friesenplatz 1, Postfach 270580, 50672 Cologne 1
Japan (☎ 03-3222 1112) NK Shinwa Building 5F, 5-1 Kojimachi, Chiyoda-ku, Tokyo 102-0083
UK (☎ 020-7802 8108, ✉ information@nbt.org.uk) PO Box 523, London, SW1E 6NT
USA (☎ 212-370 7360, ✉ info@goholland.com) 355 Lexington Ave, New York, NY 10017

VISAS & DOCUMENTS
Travellers from Australia, Canada, Israel, Japan, New Zealand, the USA and many other countries need only a valid passport – no visa – for a stay of up to three months. EU nationals can enter for three months with just their national identity card or a passport expired for not more than five years. Nationals of most other countries need a so-called Schengen Visa valid for 90 days. After three months, extensions can be applied for through the Vreemdelingenpolitie (Aliens' Police), but you'll need a good reason for an extension to be granted.

EMBASSIES & CONSULATES
Dutch Embassies & Consulates
Dutch embassies and consulates abroad include the following:

Australia (☎ 02-6273 3111) 120 Empire Circuit, Yarralumla, Canberra, ACT 2600
Canada (☎ 613-237 5030) Suite 2020, 350 Albert St, Ottawa, Ont K1R 1A4
New Zealand (☎ 04-471 6390) 10th floor, Investment House, corner Ballance and Featherston Sts, Wellington
UK (☎ 020-7590 3200) 38 Hyde Park Gate, London SW7 5DP
USA (☎ 202-244 5300) 4200 Linnean Ave, NW Washington, DC 20008

Embassies & Consulates in the Netherlands
Embassies (in The Hague) and consulates (in Amsterdam) of other countries in the Netherlands include:

Australia
(☎ 070-310 82 00) Carnegielaan 4, 2517 KH The Hague
Belgium
(☎ 070-312 34 56) Lange Vijverberg 12, 2513 AC The Hague
Canada
(☎ 070-311 16 00) Sophialaan 7, 2514 JP The Hague
France
Embassy: (☎ 070-312 58 00) Smidsplein 1, 2514 BT The Hague
Consulate: (☎ 020-530 69 71) Vijzelgracht 2, 1017 HR Amsterdam
Germany
Embassy: (☎ 070-342 06 00) Groot Hertoginnelaan 18, 2517 EG The Hague
Consulate: (☎ 020-673 62 45) De Lairessestraat 172, 1075 HM Amsterdam
Ireland
(☎ 070-363 09 93) Dr Kuyperstraat 9, 2514 BA The Hague
New Zealand
(☎ 070-346 93 24) Carnegielaan 10, 2517 KH The Hague

NETHERLANDS

UK
  Embassy: (☎ 070-427 04 27) Lange Voorhout 10, 2514 ED The Hague
  Consulate: (☎ 020-676 43 43) Koningslaan 44, 1075 AE Amsterdam
USA
  Embassy: (☎ 070-310 92 09) Lange Voorhout 102, 2514 EJ The Hague
  Consulate: (☎ 020-575 53 09) Museumplein 19, 1071 DJ Amsterdam

CUSTOMS

In the Netherlands, the usual allowances apply to duty free goods if you are coming from a non-EU country and to duty paid goods if you're arriving from within the EU.

MONEY

The Netherlands is participating in the euro, the European single currency (see the boxed text 'The Euro' in the introductory Facts for the Visitor chapter).

Currency

The currency is the guilder, divided into 100 cents and symbolised as 'Dfl' or 'f' (originally 'florin'). There are 5c, 10c, 25c, f1, f2.50 and f5 coins, and f10, f25, f50, f100, f250 and f1000 notes.

Exchange Rates

country	unit		guilder
Australia	A$1	=	f1.41
Canada	C$1	=	f1.64
euro	€1	=	f2.20
France	1FF	=	f0.34
Germany	DM1	=	f1.13
Japan	¥100	=	f2.24
New Zealand	NZ$1	=	f1.10
UK	UK£1	=	f3.67
USA	US$1	=	f2.44

Exchanging Money

Banks stick to official exchange rates and charge 2.50% to 2.75% (with a minimum of f7.50) for exchanging cash, and f10 commission for travellers cheques. The national exchange organisation, De Grenswisselkantoren (GWK; literally 'The Border Exchange Offices'), has similiar rates but the commissions are usually slightly cheaper. You'll find GWK branches at all major border posts and train stations, open 7 or 8 am to 8 or 10 pm daily. The branches at Amsterdam's Centraal Station and Schiphol airport operate 24 hours. With a student card there's 25% less commission on cash.

In larger cities there are many private exchange bureaus that close late but generally ask high commissions or offer lousy rates, as well as exchange services at the post office. Although all major credit cards are recognised, the Netherlands is still very much a cash-based society. ATMs are located at Schiphol airport and at Centraal Station in Amsterdam.

Costs

Living in hostels and eating in cheap cafes, you'll be looking at spending at least f60 a day. Getting around costs relatively little due to the country's size.

Avid museum goers should buy the Museumjaarkaart (Museum Year Card), which gives free entry into 440 museums and art galleries. It costs f55 for adults (f25 for those aged under 24) and is issued at museums or tourist information (VVV) offices (you'll need a passport photo). Unless stated otherwise, all the museums and art galleries mentioned in this chapter are free with the Museumjaarkaart. Many museums offer concession prices for children (and often for seniors and students also). Children's concession prices are mentioned throughout this chapter.

Tipping & Bargaining

Tipping is not compulsory, but 'rounding up' the bill is always appreciated in taxis, restaurants and pubs with table or pavement service. Forget about bargaining, though the Dutch themselves get away with it at flea markets.

Taxes & Refunds

The value-added tax (BTW in Dutch) is calculated at 17.5% for most goods except consumer items like food, for which you pay 6%. Travellers from non-EU countries can have it refunded on goods over f300 providing they're bought from one shop on one day and are exported within three months.

To claim back the tax, ask the shop owner to provide an export certificate when you make the purchase. When you leave for a non-EU country, get the form endorsed by the Dutch customs, then send the certificate to the supplier, who in turn refunds the tax

NETHERLANDS

by cheque or money order. If you want the tax before you leave the country, it's best to buy from shops affiliated with the Tax Cheque Refund Service. These shops will give you a stamped Tax Refund Cheque which can be cashed at your port of exit (but because of red tape, you'll lose about 5% of the refund). You'll need to show the customs officers the goods, the bill and your passport.

POST & COMMUNICATIONS
Post
In general, post offices are open 9 am to 5 or 6 pm Monday to Friday, and until noon or 1 pm Saturday. Letters cost f0.80 within the Netherlands, f1.80 for up to 20g within Europe, f2.80 outside, and will take about a week to the USA and Canada, six to 10 days to Australia and New Zealand, and two to three days to the UK.

Telephone
For making international telephone calls to the Netherlands, the country code is ☎ 31. To telephone abroad, the international access code is ☎ 00 (see the Telephones appendix at the back of this book).

Local telephone calls are time-based – the minimum charge from a Telecom phone is f0.25, then roughly f0.20 per minute. Telephone numbers prefixed with ☎ 0900 are more expensive (between f0.50 and f1 a minute). Numbers starting with ☎ 0800 are free calls, and those prefixed with ☎ 06-5 or ☎ 06-6 are mobile and pager numbers. In local telephone books, similar surnames are listed alphabetically by address, not by initials.

Telephones take f10 and f25 phonecards and, sometimes, credit cards. Coin-operated telephones are rare. International calls can be made from public phones and post offices, using phonecards designed specifically for international calls. Alternatively, you can use a Lonely Planet eKno Communication Card (see the Lonely Planet Web site at www.lonelyplanet.com.au for details). A three-minute phone call to the USA costs f0.51.

For travellers with mobile phones, the Netherlands uses GSM 900/1800, which is compatible with the rest of Europe and Australia but not with the North American GSM 1900 or the system used in Japan.

Fax
International faxes can be sent (but not received) from post offices but they are very expensive – f25 for the first page plus f3/5 to countries within/outside Europe for each additional page. Much cheaper is Kinko's, which has two branches – one in Amsterdam (☎ 020-589 09 10, fax 589 09 20) at Overtoom 62, and the other in Rotterdam (☎ 010-411 63 44, fax 213 19 40), Vasteland 92. Both are open 24 hours daily, charge f3.50/4.50 per page for sending faxes within/outside Europe, and f1 per page to receive a fax.

Email & Internet Access
Cybercafes are plentiful. In major towns they're open until about 11 pm, and charge f2.50 to f3.50 for 20 minutes. The local *bibliotheek* (library) in most towns is also good for Internet access. In Amsterdam you'll also find public Internet terminals that use phonecards located at various points around town.

INTERNET RESOURCES
The Dutch are digital-media leaders. The best place to start a virtual visit to the Netherlands is the Netherlands Board of Tourism site at www.visitholland.com. Also good is the Amsterdam city site at www.amsterdam.nl or you could try DDS (De Digitale Stad – The Digital City – www.dds.nl).

BOOKS
Lonely Planet's *The Netherlands* guide is a must for those intending in-depth exploration. If you're concentrating on the capital, there's Lonely Planet's *Amsterdam* city guide. For a humorous look at Dutch ways, pick up *The UnDutchables* by the non-Dutch Colin White & Laurie Boucke or, more seriously, *Culture Shock! Netherlands* by Hunt Janin.

FILMS
Two Dutch films have won an Oscar for best foreign film – *De Aanslag* (The Assault) by Fons Rademakers in 1986, and *Karakter* (Character) by Mike Van Diem in 1997. The 1973 film *Turks Fruit* by Paul Verhoeven is also well-known internationally.

NEWSPAPERS & MAGAZINES
There's no English-language newspaper, but international papers and magazines are easy

NETHERLANDS

to find. The largest national newspaper is *De Telegraaf.*

RADIO & TV

London's BBC radio World Service can be tuned to on 648kHz medium wave. Cable TV has reached the majority of homes, meaning there is no shortage of English-language programs on Dutch TV.

TIME

The Netherlands is in the Central European Time zone. Noon is 11 am in London, 6 am in New York, 3 am in San Francisco, 6 am in Toronto, 9 pm in Sydney, and 11 pm in Auckland. The 24-hour clock is commonly used. Daylight-saving time comes into effect at 2 am on the last Sunday in March, when clocks are moved an hour forward, and ends at 2 am on the last Saturday in October, when they're moved an hour back again.

LAUNDRY

If you can push past all the piles of clothes in a typical Dutch *wassalon*, you're lucky – at least you're in the front door. Self-service laundrettes are often no more than a few machines put aside for do-it-yourselfers in staffed laundries. In large cities, you'll also find the traditional unattended laundrette. A 5kg wash costs an average of f10 to f12 including drying.

TOILETS

Public toilets are not abundant, which is why most people tend to duck into a cafe, pub or department store. Toilet attendants require tips of f0.25 to f1.

WOMEN TRAVELLERS

The women's movement has a strong foothold and women travellers will find *vrouwen* (women's) cafes, bookshops and help centres in many cities. Het Vrouwenhuis (Women's House; ☎ 020-625 20 66, ✉ info@vrouwenhuis.nl), Nieuwe Herengracht 95, 1011 RX Amsterdam, is well known.

Unwanted attention from men is not a big problem in the Netherlands. However, in the event of rape or attack, De Eerste Lijn (☎ 020-613 02 45) is an Amsterdam-based help line, open 10.30 am to 11 pm weekdays and 4 to 11 pm weekends.

GAY & LESBIAN TRAVELLERS

The Netherlands has long had the reputation of being the most liberal country in Europe where attitudes to homosexuality are concerned. The age of consent is 16, discrimination on the basis of sexual orientation is illegal, and gay and lesbian couples can legally marry. Most provincial capitals have at least one gay and lesbian bar or cafe, as well as a branch of COC, a gay and lesbian information service. In Amsterdam, COC (☎ 020-626 30 87) is at Rozenstraat 14.

If you're wanting information on gay or lesbian venues, the best place to start is the Gay & Lesbian Switchboard (☎ 020-623 65 65), an Amsterdam-based information and help line staffed from 10 am to 10 pm daily. *Gay News Amsterdam* and *Gay & Night* are just two of the many free publications available that list gay hotels, bars etc throughout the Netherlands. The Amsterdam Pride parade is in the first week of August. On the Internet, head to www.dds.nl/plein/homo for gay listings and information.

DISABLED TRAVELLERS

Travellers with a mobility problem will find the Netherlands fairly well equipped to meet specialised needs. A large number of government buildings, museums, hotels and restaurants have lifts and/or ramps. Many trains and some taxis have wheelchair access, and most train stations have a toilet for the handicapped.

For the visually impaired, train timetables are published in Braille, and Dutch bank notes have raised symbols on the corners for identification.

For more information contact the Nederlands Instituut voor Zorg & Welzijn (☎ 030-230 66 03, fax 231 96 41), Postbus 19152, 3501 DD Utrecht. It's at www.nizw.nl on the Web.

SENIOR TRAVELLERS

Senior travellers should encounter few problems when travelling around the Netherlands. Many buildings have lifts or ramps, and public transport is quite accessible. Some museums offer discounts to seniors. The Gilde Amsterdam (☎ 020-625 13 90), Hartenstraat 18 in Amsterdam, is a group of volunteers aged 50 and over that organises interesting

NETHERLANDS

walks (2½ hours; f5) around the capital. It's open 1 to 4 pm weekdays.

TRAVEL WITH CHILDREN

The Dutch are pretty relaxed where kids are concerned and you'll find plenty to occupy children. Keep in mind that there's a lot of open water (ie, canals and rivers) in Dutch cities and around the countryside. Some popular activities include biking in the countryside, taking the kids to Vondelpark or the Tropenmusem in Amsterdam, or heading to the beach at Zandvoort near Haarlem.

DANGERS & ANNOYANCES

The number of tales of travellers in Amsterdam having their wallets swiped could fill a book. Pickpockets often use distraction as their key tool, so keep your hands on your valuables, especially at Centraal Station in Amsterdam, the post office, and other tourist strongholds. Cyclists too should be warned: the stolen bicycle racket is rife. Locals use two chains to lock up their bikes, and even that's no guarantee.

Despite popular belief to the contrary, drugs are illegal. Possession of more than 5g of marijuana or hash can, strictly speaking, get you a large fine and/or land you in jail – hard drugs can definitely land you in jail. Small amounts of 'soft' drugs for personal use are generally, though not officially, tolerated, but could complicate matters if you're already in trouble with the police over something else. Don't buy drugs from street dealers – you'll end up getting ripped off or mugged.

In the event of an emergency, the national telephone number for police, ambulance and fire brigade is ☎ 112.

LEGAL MATTERS

Police in the Netherlands are generally polite and helpful. If you've broken the law, they can hold you for six hours for questioning. Should you need legal assistance, the Buro voor Rechtshulp (☎ 020-520 51 00), Spuistraat 10 in Amsterdam, can give free legal advice during business hours.

BUSINESS HOURS

The working week starts leisurely at around lunchtime on Monday. For the rest of the week most shops open at 8.30 or 9 am and close at 5.30 or 6 pm, except Thursday or Friday when many close at 9 pm, and on Saturday at 4 pm. In Amsterdam and tourist centres you will find many shops open on Sunday, too. Supermarkets often have extended trading hours. Banks are generally open 9 am to 4 or 5 pm Monday to Friday. Many museums are closed on Monday.

PUBLIC HOLIDAYS & SPECIAL EVENTS

Public holidays are held on New Year's Day, Good Friday (but most shops stay open), Easter Sunday and Monday, Queen's Day (30 April), Ascension Day, Whit Sunday and Monday, Christmas Day and Boxing Day.

The Holland Festival brings many of the top names in music, opera, dance and theatre to Amsterdam for performances throughout June. Another big event in Amsterdam is Koninginnedag (Queen's Day), the 30 April national holiday held on the former Queen Juliana's birthday. On this day the whole central city becomes a huge street-market/party where people sell whatever they've dug out of their attics.

Religious celebrations like carnival are confined to the south-eastern provinces of North Brabant and Limburg.

Floriade is a huge horticultural exhibition staged every 10 years – the next will run from mid-April to mid-October in 2002.

ACTIVITIES

Cycling, windsurfing, sailing and boating are some of the most popular Dutch pastimes, especially in the waterlogged provinces of Fryslân and Zeeland.

WORK

Australian, New Zealand and US citizens are legally allowed to work in the Netherlands. However, there is a mound of red tape to get through before you can do so, and the bottom line is that you must be filling a job that no Dutch or EU national has the skill to do. In other words, there are few legal openings for non-EU nationals. Illegal jobs (working 'in the black') are also very rare these days, although some travellers still manage to pick up work in the bulb fields near Leiden.

ACCOMMODATION

Rarely cheap and often full, accommodation is best booked ahead, especially in Amsterdam or if you're going to be in the Randstad during the Keukenhof season. You can book hotel accommodation (no deposit required) through the Netherlands Reservation Centre which has a Web site at www.hotelres.nl, or via the Amsterdam Reservation Center (☎/fax 777 000 888, ✆ reservations@amsterdamtourist.nl).

Once you're in the country, the VVV tourist offices and the GWK money exchange offices usually handle bookings for a fee (f4 to f6).

Camping grounds are copious but prices vary – on average f7/8/4.50 per adult/tent/car. The NBT has a selective list of sites, or there's the ANWB's annual camping guide (f19.95), both available from some VVVs or bookshops.

The country's official hostel organisation is the Nederlandse Jeugdherberg Centrale (NJHC; ☎ 020-551 31 55, fax 639 01 99, ✆ info@njhc.org), Prof Tulpstraat 2, 1018 HA Amsterdam. It's at www.njhc.org on the Web. The NJHC has four categories of hostels, with nightly rates in a dorm varying from f22.50 to f28 for members (f25.50 to f31.50 in July and August), including breakfast. Category four hostels (those in Amsterdam, The Hague and Maastricht) charge f34.25 to f38.75. At all hostels, a nonmember pays f5 extra. Some hostels have private rooms – expect to pay between f75 to f90 for a single, and f100 to f135 for a double. In Amsterdam you'll find similarly priced unofficial hostels.

B&Bs start at f35 per person a night. Local VVVs have lists, or you can book through Bed & Breakfast Holland (☎ 020-615 75 27, fax 669 15 73, ✆ bbrholland@hetnet.nl), Theophile de Bockstraat 3, 1058 TV Amsterdam. If you go through this organisation, you must book a minimum of two nights and there's a f10 administration fee (f20 for bookings by fax or email).

Hotels start at f75/100 for basic single/double rooms that are rarely flash, with continental breakfast included. In the mid-range, prices start from f120/200, and at the top-end the sky's the limit. Prices sometimes rise during the high season (roughly 15 March to 15 November); prices quoted throughout this chapter are for the high season.

FOOD

While gastronomical delights are not a Dutch forte, you won't go hungry. And what the traditional cuisine lacks in taste sensation, it makes up for in quantity. Thanks also to the sizable Indonesian, Surinamese and Turkish communities – and to the culinary revolution that has taken over Amsterdam in recent years – there are plenty of spicy or interesting options. Vegetarians will find that many *eetcafés* (eating pubs) have at least one meat-free dish.

Snacks

On the savoury side, the national fast-food habit is *frites* – chips or French fries – usually sold from a *frituur* (chip shop). *Kroketten*, or croquettes (crumbed fried concoctions), are sold hot from vending machines; *broodjes* (open sandwiches) are everywhere; and mussels, raw herrings and deep-fried fish are popular coastal snacks.

As for sweets, *appelgebak* (apple pie) ranks up there with frites, while *poffertjes* (miniature pancakes sprinkled with icing sugar) are sure-fire tourist food, as are *pannekoeken* (pancakes) and *stroopwafels* (hot wafers glued together with syrup).

Main Dishes

Dinner traditionally comprises thick soups and meat, fish or chicken dishes fortified with potatoes. Most restaurants have a *dagschotel* (dish of the day) for between f15 and f20, while eetcafés serve meals or cheap snacks. Otherwise, the Indonesian *rijsttafel* ('rice table') of boiled rice with oodles of side dishes is pricey but worth a try, as are Zeeland mussels, best during months with an 'r' in their name (or so local tradition has it).

Self-Catering

The national Albert Heijn chain has saturated the country with supermarkets.

DRINKS

Tap water in the Netherlands is fine, though many people prefer bottled mineral water. Beer is the staple alcoholic drink, served cool and topped by a two-finger-thick head of froth (a sight that can horrify Anglo-Saxon drinkers). Popular brands include Heineken

NETHERLANDS

and Amstel. Many Belgian beers – such as Duvel and Westmalle Triple – have become immensely popular in the Netherlands, and are reasonably priced.

Dutch *genever* (gin) is made from juniper berries; a common combination, known as a *kopstoot* ('head butt'), is a glass of genever with a beer chaser – two or three of those is all most people can handle. There are plenty of indigenous liqueurs, including *advocaat* (a kind of eggnog) and the herb-based Beerenburg.

ENTERTAINMENT

You'll rarely have to search for nightlife. Bars and cafes abound, from popular pavement terraces to old brown cafes thick with conversation and smoke. In summer, parks come alive with festivals while city squares reverberate with the sounds of street musicians. Movies screen in their original language with Dutch subtitles.

SHOPPING

Diamonds and flowers are the specialities, the latter cheap and plentiful all year. For flower bulbs, it's easiest to buy through one of the specialist mail-order companies. They'll handle all the red tape, including the 'health certificate' many countries require for importing bulbs. As for diamonds, if you've got the budget to buy them, you probably don't need advice.

Getting There & Away

AIR

The Netherlands has just one main international airport, Schiphol, 18km south-west of central Amsterdam. It's one of Western Europe's major international hubs, and services flights from airlines worldwide as well as the national carrier, KLM Royal Dutch Airlines. Most foreign airlines have offices in Amsterdam (see the Amsterdam Getting There & Away section). The airport is linked directly to the Dutch rail network. Schiphol airport tax (f33) is always included in the price of a plane ticket – there's no other departure tax to pay.

LAND

Bus

Eurolines is the main international bus company servicing the Netherlands. It has regular buses from Amsterdam to a crop of European destinations, as well as to Scandinavia and North Africa. Depending on the service, there are stops in Breda, Rotterdam, The Hague and Utrecht. Eurolines buses cross the Channel either on ferries departing from Calais in France or via the Eurotunnel. Members of Hostelling International (HI) get a 10% discount on Eurolines tickets.

For more detailed information, see the Amsterdam (or other relevant city) Getting There & Away section.

Train

Nederlandse Spoorwegen (NS; Netherlands Railways) operates regular and efficient train services to all its neighbouring countries. For international train information and reservations, call ☎ 0900-92 96.

The main line south from Amsterdam passes through The Hague and Rotterdam and on to Antwerp (f52.50, two hours, hourly trains) and Brussels (f62.50, 2¾ hours, hourly trains) in Belgium. The line south-east runs to Cologne (f91, 2¾ hours, every two hours) and farther into Germany. The line east goes to Berlin, with a branch north to Hamburg. All these fares are one way in 2nd class; people aged under 26 get a 25% discount (bring your passport). The *Weekendretour* (weekend return) ticket gives a 40% discount on return fares to Belgium or Germany when travelling between Friday and Monday.

The high-speed *Thalys* train runs five times per day between Amsterdam and Paris-Nord (f161/132 on weekdays/weekends, 4¼ hours). At present, this train runs on normal tracks between Amsterdam and Brussels, with the new high-speed lines not expected to be finished until 2005. Those aged under 26 get a 45% discount and seniors with a Rail Plus (formerly Rail Europe Senior) card are entitled to a discount on return fares. Thalys is at www.thalys.com on the Web.

The UK The only train-ferry route is via Hook of Holland (Hoek van Holland) near Rotterdam to Harwich in England and on to London's Liverpool St station. The Channel is crossed using Stena Line's high-speed vessel *Stena HSS*. The fare is f137/55 for adults/children and the total journey takes six hours.

Alternatively, you can get a train to Brussels and connect there with Eurostar trains which operate through the Channel Tunnel. From Amsterdam, the one-way trip to London's Waterloo station takes about six hours and costs f280, or f250 for return Apex fares (these must be reserved eight days in advance). Those under 25 pay f110. There are nine services per day.

Car & Motorcycle

The main entry points from Belgium are the E22 (Antwerp-Breda) and the E25 (Liège-Maastricht). From Germany there are many crossings, but the main links are the E40 (Cologne-Maastricht), the E35 (Düsseldorf-Arnhem), and the A1 (Hannover-Amsterdam). For details about car ferries from England, see the following section.

SEA

Three companies operate car/passenger ferries between the Netherlands and England. For information on train-ferry combos, see the earlier Train section. Most travel agents have information on the following services.

Stena Line's high-speed *Stena HSS* sails from Hook of Holland to Harwich in 3¾ hours. One-way fares for a car with driver range from f520 to f830 depending on the day of the week and the season. There are also special five-day return tickets for between f370 and f690. A one-way passenger ticket costs f140/100 for an adult/child.

P&O/North Sea Ferries operates an overnight boat (14½ hours) between Europoort (near Rotterdam) and Hull. Basic one-way rates for cars start at f200/250 in the low/high season, adult tickets are f125/160, child fares go for f37/48 and cabins start at f49 per person.

DFDS Seaways sails daily from Ijmuiden (near Amsterdam) to Newcastle. The journey takes 15 hours. Rates for cars in the low/mid/high season are f110/135/215; passenger fares start at f85/110/160. Cabins begin at f120/150/200 per person.

RIVER

Several companies offer round-trip riverboat cruises from either Rotterdam or Arnhem along the Schelde to Belgium (four to six days) or via the Rhine and Moselle Rivers to Germany (eight to 14 days). Most travel agents have brochures.

Getting Around

The Netherlands' public transport system is excellent. For all national train/bus/tram information, call ☎ 0900-92 92 (f0.75 per minute).

AIR

Internal flights are of little interest to visitors, owing to the country's small size and excellent train services.

BUS

Buses are used for regional transport rather than for long distances, which are better travelled by train. They provide a vital service, especially in parts of the north and east, where trains are less frequent or nonexistent. The national *strippenkaart* (see the following Local Transport section) is used on many regional buses.

TRAIN

NS trains are fast and efficient, with at least one InterCity train every 15 minutes between major cities, and half-hourly trains on branch lines. Most stations have small/large luggage lockers which cost f5/8 respectively for 24 hours.

Costs

If you're returning on the same day, it's cheaper to buy a *dagretour* (day return) rather than two single tickets.

There's a melange of discount fares but you'd have to live on the trains to make most of them worthwhile. A One-Day Ticket gives unlimited 2nd/1st-class travel and costs f75/117. With this ticket you can also buy a Public Transport Day Card for f9 which gives unlimited use of city buses, trams and metros. The Meermans Kaart, or Group Ticket, gives two to six people (f114 to f192) unlimited travel on weekends or after 9 am on weekdays (except in July and August when there is no weekday restriction). The Euro Domino Holland pass entitles adults to three/five days' travel within

NETHERLANDS

one month for f130/196. Those under 26 years pay f104/158. If you're travelling with children, there's a f2.50 Railrunner ticket which gives one days' unlimited travel for three children.

For the full list, get the *Exploring Holland by Train* brochure, which also details discount 'Rail Idee' or day excursion tickets.

CAR & MOTORCYCLE

Foreign drivers need a Green Card as proof of insurance. Road rules are basically stick to the right and give way to the right (except at major crossroads and roads with right of way). Watch out for cyclists – they're abundant. Speed limits are 50km/h in built-up areas, 80km/h in the country, 100km/h on major through roads and 120km/h on motorways. Fuel prices per litre are f2.53 to f2.59 for *loodvrij* (lead-free), f2.65 for leaded and f1.75 for diesel. The maximum permissible blood-alcohol concentration is 0.05%. For other motoring information, contact the Royal Dutch Touring Association (ANWB; ☎ 020-673 08 44), Museumplein 5, 1071 DJ Amsterdam.

BICYCLE

With 10,000km of cycling paths, a *fiets* (bicycle) is *the* way to go. The ANWB publishes cycling maps for each province. Major roads have separate bike lanes, and, except for motorways, there's virtually nowhere bicycles can't go. That said, in places such as the Delta region and along the coast you'll need muscles to combat the North Sea headwinds. To take a bicycle on a train (not allowed in peak hours) costs f10 for up to 80km, f15 for greater distances, or f25 for a *dagkaart* (day card). While about 85% of the population own bikes and there are more bikes than people, they're also abundantly available for hire. In most cases you'll need to show your passport, and leave an imprint of your credit card or a deposit (from f50 to f200). Private operators charge about f15/50 per day/week. Hire shops at train stations charge f9.50/38. You must return the bike to the same station.

Alternatively, it can work out much cheaper to buy a 'second-hand' bike from a street market for upwards of f25, bearing in mind it's probably part of the stolen bike racket.

HITCHING

Hitching is no longer common in the Netherlands and it is illegal on motorways. Be wary of the usual dangers and risks.

BOAT

Ferries connect the mainland with the five Frisian Islands (see The North section for details) and are also used as road connections in Zeeland.

LOCAL TRANSPORT
Bus & Tram

Buses and/or trams operate in most cities, and Amsterdam and Rotterdam also have metro systems.

Fares operate nationally. Buy a strippenkaart (strip card), valid throughout the country, and stamp off a number of strips depending on how many zones you cross. The ticket is then valid on all buses, trams, metro systems and city trains for an hour, or longer depending on the number of strips you've stamped. Around central Amsterdam, for example, you'll use two strips – one for the journey plus one for the zone. A zone farther will cost three strips, and so on. When riding on trams it is up to you to stamp your card; on buses the drivers stamp strips as you get on. Bus and tram drivers sell two/three-strip cards for f3/4.50. More economical are 15/45-strip cards for f12/35.25, which you must purchase in advance at train or bus stations, post offices or some VVV offices. If all this sounds too complicated, simply invest in a dagkaart (day card), available in some large cities.

Taxi

Usually booked by phone (officially you're not supposed to wave them down on the street), taxis also hover outside train stations and hotels and cost roughly f20 for 5km. There are also *treintaxis* (train taxis) which charge a flat rate of f7.50 a person to anywhere within a certain radius (it varies from city to city) of the train station. You can buy your treintaxi voucher at most train stations. They do not operate in Amsterdam, The Hague, Rotterdam or from Schiphol airport.

ORGANISED TOURS

It's possible to whip through windmills, visit cheese markets and take in nearby towns all

NETHERLANDS

in a day trip from Amsterdam (see Around Amsterdam for details). Local tourist offices can advise on bus, canal, bike or walking tours available in their own town or city.

Amsterdam

☎ 020 • pop 725,000

For many travellers, Amsterdam is a city of preconceived ideas. Personal freedom, liberal drug laws, the gay centre of Europe – these are images synonymous with the Dutch capital since the heady 1960s and 1970s when it was Europe's most radical city.

While the exuberance dimmed somewhat during the 1980s, it was not extinguished. In the year 2000 tolerance still holds pride of place although it's being increasingly tested with a chronic housing shortage and growing numbers of homeless. More obvious, however, is the rich and lively mix of the historical and contemporary that you'll experience when exploring the myriad art galleries and museums, relaxing in the canal-side cafes or enjoying the open-air entertainment that pulsates throughout the summer.

ORIENTATION

By capital-city standards, Amsterdam is small. Its major sights, accommodation and nightlife are scattered around a web of concentric canals (*grachten*) known as the canal belt, which gives the city an initially confusing, yet ultimately orderly and unique feel.The centre, easily and enjoyably covered on foot, has two main parts: the old, medieval core and the 'newer', 17th-century canal-lined quarters that surround it. Corked to the north by Centraal Station, the old city centre is encased by the Kloveniersburgwal and Singel canals. After Singel come Herengracht, Keizersgracht and Prinsengracht, the newer canals dug to cope with Amsterdam's Golden Age expansion. The city's central point is Dam Square, five minutes' walk straight down Damrak from Centraal Station. Main streets bisect the canal belt like spokes in a wheel.

INFORMATION
Tourist Offices

The VVV has four offices around town. The two busiest are at Centraal Station: one is on platform two and is open 8 am to 8 pm Monday to Saturday and 9 am to 5 pm Sunday; the other, outside at Stationsplein 10, is open 9 am to 5 pm daily. A third tourist office at Leidseplein operates 9 am to 5 pm daily, and the Stadionplein tourist office (good for motorists entering the city from the west or south) is open 9 am to 5 pm Monday to Saturday. During peak summer months, some of these opening hours may be extended. There's also an office at Schiphol airport, open 7 am to 10 pm daily. For telephone information, call ☎ 0900-400 40 40 (f1.05 per minute) from 9 am to 5 pm weekdays, or you can send an email to ✆ info@amsterdamtourist.nl.

The VVVs sell a f39.50 Amsterdam Culture & Leisure Pass which gives free entry to several museums and discounts on a range of things from canal boats to restaurants.

Money

There are 24-hour GWK offices at Centraal Station and Schiphol airport, and another GWK office (open 8 am to 11 pm daily) next to the VVV at Leidseplein; otherwise, there's a throng of midnight-trading *bureaux de change* along Damrak and Leidsestraat. The main post office also handles foreign exchange. There are ATMs at the ABN-AMRO bank on Dam Square and on Leidseplein.

American Express is at Damrak 66; to report lost or stolen cards, call ☎ 504 80 00, or for travellers cheques, ☎ 06-022 01 00. Thomas Cook has offices at Damrak 1-5 (☎ 620 32 36) and at Leidseplein 31a (☎ 626 70 00).

Post & Communications

The main post office is at Singel 250, and is open 9 am to 6 pm weekdays (until 8 pm Thursday), and 10 am to 1.30 pm Saturday.

Email & Internet Access

For those on a tight budget, In de Waag (☎ 422 77 72) on Nieuwmarkt is a pleasant cafe with a couple of computers and free Internet access (you must buy a drink). Alternatively, book a free half-hour session at the Openbare Bibliotheek (Public Library) at Prinsengracht 587.

The Internet Cafe (☎ 627 10 52, ✆ info @internet.nl), Martelaarsgracht 11, has 34 terminals, a trendy clientele, and charges f2.50 for 20 minutes.

NETHERLANDS

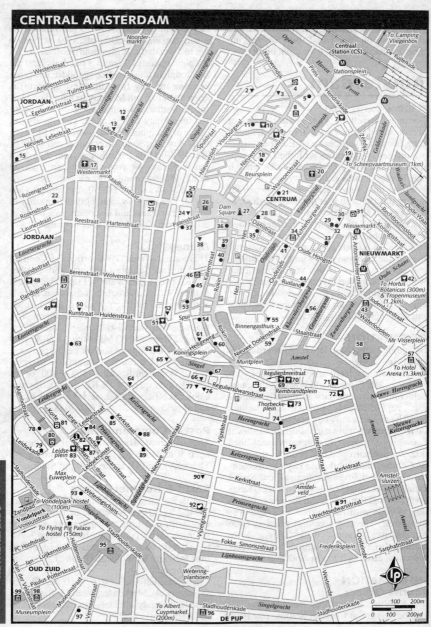

CENTRAL AMSTERDAM

euro currency converter €1 = f2.20

CENTRAL AMSTERDAM

PLACES TO STAY
12 Canal House Hotel
15 Hotel van Onna
19 The Crown
28 Grand Hotel
    Krasnapolsky
29 The Shelter
33 Zosa
56 Stadsdoelen Hostel
75 Seven Bridges
79 American Hotel
89 Hans Brinker Hostel
91 Hotel Prinsenhof
94 Smit Hotel

PLACES TO EAT
1 Bolhoed
2 De Keuken van 1870
3 Dorrius
13 Christophe
24 Albert Heijn Food Plaza
30 AH Supermarket
38 Supper Club
50 Miramare
52 Kantijl en de Tijger
55 Atrium
59 Café De Jaren
61 Vlaams Frites Huis
64 Metz & Co
65 AH Supermarket
66 Gary's Muffins
76 Rose's Cantina
77 Le Pêcheur
84 Shoarma/Felafel
   Eateries
86 Bojo
90 Hollandse Glorie

PLACES TO DRINK
7 In den Olofspoort
9 De Kuil
10 In de Wildeman
14 Café 't Smalle
42 Bimhuis
48 Saarein
49 La Tertulia
51 Hoppe
62 The Odeon
69 Escape
70 De Kroon
71 Sinners in Heaven
72 iT
73 Schiller
83 The Bulldog
87 Jazz Café Alto

OTHER
4 The Internet Cafe
5 Thomas Cook
6 Tourist Office
8 Sexmuseum De Venustempel
11 Yellow Bike
16 Anne Frankhuis
17 Westerkerk
18 American Express
20 Oude Kerk
21 Condomerie Het
   Gulden Vlies
22 COC Cafe
23 Main Post Office
25 Magna Plaza
26 Koninklijk Paleis
27 Nationaal Monument
31 In de Waag
32 Webers Holland

34 Hash Marihuana Hemp
   Museum
35 Damstraat Rent-a-Bike
36 Eurolines Amsterdam
37 Vrolijk Bookshop
39 Budget Air
40 NBBS Reizen
41 Laundry
43 Rembrandthuis
44 The Book Exchange
45 Schuttersgalerij
46 Amsterdams Historisch
   Museum
47 Woonbootmuseum
53 Begijnhof
54 Waterstones Bookshop
57 Joods Historisch
   Museum
58 City Hall/Muziektheater
60 American Book Centre
63 Public Library & Cafe
67 Bloemenmarkt
68 Tuschinskitheater
74 Bridge of 15 Bridges
78 Melkweg
80 Stadsschouwburg
81 Boom Chicago
82 Tourist Office
85 The Clean Brothers Laundry
88 Conscious Dreams
92 French Consulate
93 Paradiso
95 Rijksmuseum
96 Heineken Museum
97 ANWB
98 Van Gogh Museum
99 Stedelijk Museum

Travel Agencies
Amsterdam is a major European centre for cheap fares to anywhere in the world. A few of the better-known budget agencies are Budget Air (☎ 627 12 51) at Rokin 34; Eurolines Amsterdam (☎ 560 87 88) at Rokin 10; and NBBS Reizen (☎ 624 09 89) at Rokin 66 which is a nationwide 'student' travel agency.

Bookshops
English-language books are plentiful but horribly expensive. Recommended bookshops include the American Book Centre (☎ 625 55 37), Kalverstraat 185, which gives 10% discounts to students; The Book Exchange (☎ 626 62 66), Kloveniersburgwal 58, a rabbit warren of second-hand books; Vrolijk (☎ 623 51 42), Paleisstraat 135, a lesbian and gay bookshop; and Waterstones (☎ 638 38 21), Kalverstraat 152, which is strong on guides, maps and novels, and stocks translated Dutch literature.

Laundry
The Clean Brothers have a laundrette at Kerkstraat 56 near Leidseplein, open 7 am to 9 pm daily. There's also a big laundrette at Oude Doelenstraat 12.

Medical & Emergency Services
The Central Doctors Service (☎ 0900-503 20 42) handles 24-hour medical, dental and pharmaceutical emergencies and inquiries. The closest hospital to the centre is Onze Lieve

NETHERLANDS

Vrouwe Gasthuis (☎ 599 91 11), 1e Ooster-parkstraat 279, near the Tropenmuseum. For police, ambulance and fire brigade, the national emergency number is ☎ 112. The main police station (☎ 559 91 11) is at Elandsgracht 117.

THINGS TO SEE & DO

With 141 art galleries and 40-odd museums, Amsterdam is justly famed for its cultural proliferation.

The best place to start a walking tour is **Dam Square** (the 'Dam'), where the Amstel River was dammed in the 13th century, giving the city its name. Today it's the crossroads for the crowds surging along the pedestrianised Kalverstraat and Nieuwendijk shopping streets, and the pivotal point for trips to interesting outer quarters. Here too is the **Nationaal Monument**, a 22m-high obelisk dedicated to those who died in WWII and, on the western side, the **Koninklijk Paleis** (Royal Palace), which is occasionally used by the royal family (and occasionally open to the public – check with the VVV).

Heading west from Dam Square along Raadhuisstraat, you'll cross the main canals to the **Westerkerk**, whose 85m-high tower is the highest in the city. In the church's shadow stands a **statue of Anne Frank**, the young Jewish diarist who hid for years with her family in a nearby house, only to be tragically discovered near the end of WWII. Across Prinsengracht from here spreads the **Jordaan**, an area built up in the 17th century to house the city's lower class. Revived in the 1960s as a student ghetto, today its many renovated gabled houses sit atop canal-front cafes in Amsterdam's trendiest quarter.

South from the Dam along NZ Voorburgwal, the quaint **Spui Square** acts as a facade to hide one of the inner city's most tranquil spots, the **Begijnhof**. Such *hofjes*, or groupings of almshouses, were built throughout the Low Countries in the Middle Ages to house Catholic women, the elderly and poor. From the Begijnhof you can walk though the **Schuttersgalerij** (Civic Guard Gallery), a glass-covered passageway adorned with enormous group portraits of dignitaries from the 16th to 18th centuries, to the interesting **Amsterdams Historisch Museum**.

Continuing south-west from Spui, Leidsestraat ends where the city's nightlife takes off at **Leidseplein**. From there it's just a few minutes' walk south-east past **Vondelpark** – a summer-long entertainment venue – to the ever-inundated **Museumplein** where you'll find the Rijksmuseum, Van Gogh Museum and Stedelijk Museum (see the following section). Follow Singelgracht two blocks east to the **Heineken Museum**.

Back across the canals at the northern end of Vijzelstraat, the **Muntplein tower** denotes the colourful **Bloemenmarkt** (flower market). To the south-east is **Rembrandtplein**, one of the nightlife hubs, and the **'Bridge of 15 Bridges'**, so called because from here you can see 15 bridges (they're best viewed at night when lit up). Farther north, the sleaze of the **red-light district** extends along the parallel OZ Voorburgwal and OZ Achterburgwal canals past **Oude Kerk**, the city's oldest church, to **Zeedijk**, once the heroin nerve centre. It's been given a face-lift in the last decade but plenty of drugs are still going down in the alleys leading to the stark **Nieuwmarkt**.

South-east of here is the city's Jewish quarter, or **Jodenhoek**, and the **Joods Historisch Museum**. The nearby Rembrandthuis and Waterlooplein market attract hordes. Farther east, the **Hortus Botanicus** (Botanical Garden) is home to the world's oldest pot plant.

Museums & Galleries

Amsterdam's museums are expensive and if you intend visiting more than a few, it's worth buying the Museumjaarkaart (see Money in the Facts for the Visitor section in this chapter).

The **Rijksmuseum**, Stadhouderskade 42, is the Netherlands' largest art collection, concentrating on Dutch artists from the 15th to 19th centuries and housing Rembrandt's famous *Night Watch*. It occupies a palatial 19th-century building and is the best introduction you'll get to Dutch art. Opening hours are 10 am to 5 pm daily, and entry costs f15 (concession f7.50). Visit the museum's Web site at www.rijksmuseum.nl.

The **Van Gogh Museum**, Paulus Potterstraat 7, boasts the world's largest collection of Vincent's works, including hundreds of drawings and some 200 paintings. Highlights include the dour *Potato Eaters*, the famous *Sunflowers* and the ominous *Wheatfield with Crows*, one of his last paintings. It's open 10

NETHERLANDS

am to 5 pm daily, and entry is f12.50 (concession f5). The museum is at www.van goghmuseum.nl on the Web. The **Stedelijk Museum**, next door at Paulus Potterstraat 13, has the country's best collection of modern and contemporary Dutch art, and is open 11 am to 5 pm daily; admission is f9 (concession f4.50). It's at www.stedelijk.nl on the Web.

The **Anne Frankhuis**, at Prinsengracht 263, is arguably the city's most famous canal house; come early to avoid the queues. Anne wrote her famous diary here, and excerpts from it are used to describe the persecution of the Jews during WWII. It's open 9 am to 9 pm daily from April to August, and until 5 pm from September through March. Entry is f10 (concession f5); the Museumjaarkaart is not accepted.

For a wider picture, the **Joods Historisch Museum**, Jonas Daniël Meijerplein 2, details Jewish society and the Holocaust. It's open 11 am to 5 pm daily and costs f8 (concession f2); take tram No 9 from the Centraal Station or the metro to Waterlooplein.

The **Rembrandthuis**, Jodenbreestraat 4-6, displays sketches by the master in his former home. It's open 10 am to 5 pm Monday to Saturday, from 1 to 5 pm Sunday, and costs f12.50 (concession f7.50). Take the metro to Waterlooplein.

The **Amsterdams Historisch Museum**, Kalverstraat 92, explores the city's rich history via an impressive collection of paintings, models and archaeological finds. It occupies a former orphanage and is attached to the Civic Guard Gallery with its impressive portraits. The museum is open 10 am to 5 pm weekdays and from 11 am on weekends. Admission is f12.

The highlight of the excellent **Scheepvaartmuseum** (Maritime Museum), Kattenburgerplein 1, is the superb replica of the 18th-century East Indiaman, *Amsterdam*, moored alongside. It's open 10 am to 5 pm Tuesday to Saturday, from noon Sunday, and from June to September also on Monday; admission costs f14.50 (concession f8). The museum is about a 15 minute walk east of Centraal Station, or take bus No 22.

The **Tropenmuseum** (Museum of the Tropics), Linnaeusstraat 2, realistically depicts African, Asian and Latin American lifestyles. It's open 10 am to 5 pm weekdays, from noon to 5 pm weekends, and costs

f12.50 (concession f7.50); take tram No 9 or bus No 22 from Centraal Station.

For a peak at life on a houseboat, head to the **Woonbootmuseum's** *Hendrika Maria* on Prinsengracht opposite No 296. Built in 1914, it's open 10 am to 5 pm Tuesday to Saturday and admission is f3.75 (concession f2.50).

Beer production stopped in 1988 but the **Heineken Museum**, in the 130-year-old former brewery building at Stadhouderskade 78, still coerces beer buffs to its weekday tours (f2) at 9.30 and 11 am (also 2.30 pm from 1 June to 15 September). In July and August, there are extra tours on Saturday at 11 am and 2.30 pm.

As is to be expected, Amsterdam has a handful of museums that you'd probably find nowhere else in the world. The name says it all at the **Hash Marihuana Hemp Museum** at OZ Achterburgwal 148. It's open 11 am to 10 pm daily. The **Sexmuseum De Venustempel**, Damrak 18, is the first museum most people encounter upon arriving in the city by train. All things pornographic are extolled here – what a start to Amsterdam!

Canal Cruises

For details on the various options for seeing Amsterdam from the water, see Canal Boat, Bus & Bike in the following Getting Around section.

Markets

Most street markets are open 9 or 10 am to 5 pm daily except Sunday. The biggest flea market is **Waterlooplein**, good for cheap bikes and locks. The **Bloemenmarkt** on Singel is a floating flower market, established in 1862. **Albert Cuypmarkt** at Albert Cuypstraat, four blocks south of the Heineken Museum, has general goods like food and clothes.

ORGANISED TOURS

Yellow Bike (☎ 620 69 40), Nieuwezijds Kolk 29 (just off NZ Voorburgwal), organises bicycle tours of the city (f32, three hours) or a countryside tour taking in a windmill and clog factory (f42.50, six hours, bring your own lunch). Tours run from April to November only.

Several companies organise bus tours (3½ hours) around Amsterdam for between f30 and f45; ask at the VVV for details.

NETHERLANDS

PLACES TO STAY

Amsterdam is popular all year but in peak times it's overrun – bookings are essential.

Camping

The closest ground is *Vliegenbos* (☎ 636 88 55, *Meeuwenlaan 138*) across the harbour from Centraal Station. It's open April to September and charges f14.75 for one person with a tent plus f7.75/15.50 for a motorbike/car. Take bus No 32 or 36 from Centraal Station, or use the free ferry from behind Centraal Station and then walk 20 minutes.

Hostels & Youth Hotels

Most of the private hostels and youth hotels don't take advance bookings, so turn up early.

Old City Centre Accurately advertised as the 'cheapest B&B in town', *The Shelter* (☎ 625 32 30, *Barndesteeg 21*) is a Christian hostel in the red-light district. It has single-sex dorms, midnight curfews, and charges f23 per night (maximum age 35). Five minutes' walk south is *Stadsdoelen* (☎ 624 68 32, *fax 639 10 35, Kloveniersburgwal 97*), one of the city's two official NJHC hostels. It charges f31.25 (non-members f5 more); the closest metro is Nieuwmarkt. In the heart of the red-light district is the lively *Kabul* (☎ 623 71 58, *fax 620 08 69, Warmoesstraat 38*). Singles/doubles/triples go for f90/125/150 (or f110/175/225 on weekends) and dorm beds cost between f35 and f55 (weekends f40 to f60).

Beyond the Old City Centre The main NJHC hostel, *Vondelpark* (☎ 589 89 99, *fax 589 89 55*, @ *fit.vondelpark@njhc.org, Zandpad 5*), is one of Europe's largest hostels. It's newly renovated, well-run and is open all year. Dorm rates range from f35.50 to f40 depending on the season (nonmembers pay f5 extra), and there are singles from f75 to f90, and doubles from f100 to f135. Get tram No 1, 2 or 5 to Leidseplein, from where it's a five-minute walk. Nearby is the *Flying Pig Palace* (☎ 400 41 87, *fax 421 08 02, Vossiusstraat 46*), a popular backpackers abode. A bed in a three/four/12-bed dorm costs f50/48/34, and there are double rooms for f110. There's a small kitchen for guests to use. Check out its Web site at www.flyingpig.nl.

The huge, modern *Hans Brinker* (☎ 622 06 87, *fax 638 20 60, Kerkstraat 136*) is popular with well-off visiting students and has singles/twins/triples from f115/125/195. It's at www.hans-brinker.com on the Web.

Hotels

The following rates, unless stated otherwise, include breakfast. Many hotels lower their prices in winter.

Old City Centre Situated on one of the main red-light canals is *The Crown* (☎ 626 96 64, *fax 420 64 73, OZ Voorburgwal 21*). It has a lively bar, and singles/doubles start at f80/130.

Zosa (☎ 330 62 41, *fax 330 62 42*, @ *info @zosa-online.com, Kloveniersburgwal 20*) is an innovative little hotel/restaurant with just six ultra-modern rooms for f200/250.

The *Grand Hotel Krasnapolsky* (☎ 554 91 11, *fax 622 86 07*, @ *info@krasnapolsky.nl, Dam 9*), right on Dam Square, is one of the city's historic showpieces. Rooms start at f550/628; breakfast costs f38.

Beyond the Old City Centre A sage choice on a quiet canal is *Seven Bridges* (☎ 623 13 29, *Reguliersgracht 31*). Every room is furnished differently and its singles/doubles start at f120/230. It's already been discovered, so book well ahead.

Another good option is *Hotel Prinsenhof* (☎ 623 17 72, *fax 638 33 68*, @ *prinshof @xs4all.nl, Prinsengracht 810*). Rooms with beamed ceilings start at f85/125, or f160/165 with private shower. Triples go for f175.

The large *Smit Hotel* (☎ 671 47 85, *fax 662 91 61*, @ *hotel.smit@wxs.nl, PC Hooftstraat 24*) has decent rooms for f155/210. It's close to the major museums. Tram No 2 or 5 stops nearby.

In the Jordaan, the efficient *Hotel van Onna* (☎ 626 58 01, *fax 623 68 62, Bloemgracht 104*) has small, sparsely-decorated modern rooms for f80/160; book ahead.

Hotel Arena (☎ 694 74 44, *fax 663 26 49*, @ *info@hotelarena.nl, 's-Gravesandestraat 51*) has metamorphosed many times over the years. It's now a big hotel with pristine white rooms, all with private facilities. Doubles go from f150 to f210, and a triple/quad is f200/250. Breakfast is f15 extra. Take the

NETHERLANDS

metro to Weesperplein then follow the signs for about 600m.

The *Canal House Hotel* (☎ 622 51 82, fax 624 13 17, ✉ canalhousehotel@compuserve .com, Keizersgracht 148) has 26 rooms, all furnished in an ornate, 17th-century style. Prices range from f285 to f365. The hotel's Web site is www.canalhouse.nl.

Overlooking Leidseplein is the *American Hotel* (☎ 556 30 00, fax 556 30 01, ✉ ameri can@interconti.com, Leidsekade 97). Built in 1901, the hotel has touches of Art Nouveau, with Art-Deco-style rooms starting at f395/550. Breakfast is f35 extra.

PLACES TO EAT

Restaurants abound: try the neon-lit streets off Leidseplein for a veritable diner's market, the Jordaan for discreet eetcafés, or the city centre for fast-food factories, student cafeterias and vegetarian hideaways.

Restaurants

Amsterdam's restaurants beckon with variety and a casual approach.

Old City Centre The *De Keuken van 1870* (☎ 624 89 65, Spuistraat 4) is an unpretentious Dutch diner that began last century as a soup kitchen. Open until 9 pm, it offers a basic three-course meal for f12. For much classier Dutch, try *Dorrius* (☎ 420 22 24, Nieuwezijds Voorburgwal 5). Traditional main courses range from f30 to f45, and it does a very good herring with apple salad.

Kantijl en de Tijger (☎ 620 09 94, Spuistraat 291) is an Indonesian restaurant with modern, minimalist decor. Mains hover in the f22 to f30 bracket; the *bami goreng* (f24) is delicious. Reservations are essential at the *Supper Club* (☎ 638 05 13, Jonge Roelensteeg 21). This ultra-trendy restaurant occupies one big, stark, white room where you dine on mattresses – novel to say the least. The four-course set meal costs f95.

Beyond the Old City Centre Greek and Italian cuisine compete fiercely with steak houses and Dutch fare in the streets off Leidseplein. Here you'll find *Bojo* (☎ 622 74 34, Lange Leidsedwarstraat 51), a cheap, Indonesian eatery open until the early hours of the morning.

The *Hollandse Glorie* (☎ 624 47 64, Kerkstraat 222) is laced and intimate, with Dutch mains from f28. *Rose's Cantina* (☎ 625 97 97, Reguliersdwarsstraat 38) is a big, everpopular, Mexican restaurant with even bigger pitchers of sangria. Main courses range from f26 to f44.

In the Jordaan, the amiable *Miramare* (☎ 625 88 95, Runstraat 6) has tasty pizzas from f11.50. *Bolhoed* (☎ 626 18 03, Prinsengracht 60) is a colourful vegetarian haunt serving excellent organic and vegan food – mains range from f24 to f35 and a threecourse meal is f35. You'll need to reserve for dinner.

Le Pêcheur (☎ 624 31 21, Reguliersdwarsstraat 32) is a stylish seafood restaurant with a pleasant terrace garden out back. Mains hover around f40. It's closed Sunday.

For French *haute cuisine*, head to *Christophe* (☎ 625 08 07, Leliegracht 46). A Michelin star, refined modern decor, frogs' legs, truffles, pigeon and *foie gras* all combine to make this a top-end dining experience. Mains range from f55 to f65.

Cafes & Eetcafés

Amsterdam has a plethora of cafes where you can have a coffee, beer or a snack, and an increasing number of pubs that also serve meals.

The huge *Café de Jaren* (☎ 625 57 71, Nieuwe Doelenstraat 20) has a popular sun deck and English newspapers. Reservations are necessary for the 1st-floor section and its all-you-can-eat salad bar (f18).

For late-night munchies, try *Gary's Muffins* (☎ 420 24 06, Reguliersdwarsstraat 53), open until 1 am (3 am on weekends).

The university's (smoke-free) student cafeteria, *Atrium (OZ Achterburgwal 237)* attracts a wide assortment of diners (not just students) and does cheap, self-service meals for f10. It's open noon to 2 pm and 5 to 7 pm weekdays only.

Metz & Co (☎ 520 70 48, Leidsestraat 34) is a chic department store with a 6thfloor cafe open until 5 or 6 pm daily (to 9 pm on Thursday). Breakfast, soup, salad and sandwiches are the go, and the view is superb.

There are inexpensive, authentic *Chinese* and *Thai eateries* at Nieuwmarkt, and *Surinamese cafes* near Albert Cuypmarkt.

NETHERLANDS

Fast Food

Amsterdam's favourite frituur, the **Vlaams Frites Huis** (*Voetboogstraat 33*) is open until 6 pm daily.

There's a clutch of little **shoarma/felafel eateries** on Leidsestraat. Most are open until about 4 am and do excellent, all-you-can-eat felafels for f6.

Self-Catering

The **Albert Heijn Food Plaza** on NZ Voorburgwal is open 8 am to 10 pm Monday to Saturday and 11 am to 7 pm Sunday. Other **Albert Heijn** supermarkets are at Vijzelstraat 119, on Nieuwmarkt, and on the corner of Singel and Leidsestraat.

ENTERTAINMENT

While the infamous youth clubs, 'smoking' coffee shops and red-light district live on, the radical air is largely gone. These days you'll see groups of elderly tourists herded en masse past the windowed women while the younger set head for the music cafes, designer bars and nightclubs dotted throughout the city.

Classical music, theatre and ballet are high on the priorities, as are African and world music. Pick up the monthly *What's On* guide (f4) from the VVV or from the Amsterdam Uit Buro (AUB; ☎ 0900-01 91) ticket shop at Leidseplein 26.

Gay nightlife is centred on Reguliersdwarsstraat, Kerkstraat and the streets off Rembrandtplein; the COC (see the Gay & Lesbian Travellers section earlier in this chapter) has venue lists.

Pubs

Pubs, bars, brown cafes, cafes – call them what you like, but places to drink abound. For the intimate atmosphere of the old brown cafe, try **Hoppe** (*Spui 18*) – it's been enticing drinkers behind its thick curtain for more than 300 years (the entrance is to the right of the pub-with-terrace of the same name). **In de Wildeman** (*Kolksteeg 3*) attracts beer connoisseurs with its sizable beer menu. **In den Olofspoort** (*Nieuwebrugsteeg 13*) is a typical genever-tasting house.

In the Jordaan, **Café 't Smalle** (*Egelantiersgracht 12*) has the quaintest floating terrace you're ever likely to see. The trendy **De Kroon** (*Rembrandtplein 17*) and the smooth **Schiller** (*Rembrandtplein 26*) are both recommended.

There's a throng of gay bars and cafes, although not nearly as many options for lesbians. **Saarein** (*Elandsstraat 119*) is the most popular women's bar, open until about 1 am (closed Monday). **COC Café** (*Rozenstraat 14*) is a gay and lesbian cafe open evenings only.

Live Music

The Dutch favour live jazz, and Amsterdam's no exception. There are plenty of venues. **Jazz Café Alto** (☎ 626 32 49, *Korte Leidsedwarsstraat 115*) is a little bar with nightly sessions from 9.30 pm. A larger jazz venue is the **Bimhuis** (☎ 623 13 61, *Oude Schans 73*).

The legendary **Melkweg** (*Milky Way;* ☎ 531 81 81, *Lijnbaansgracht 234a*) moves from late until early with live rock, reggae and African rhythm. The equally hallowed **Paradiso** (☎ 626 45 21, *Weteringschans 6*) has everything from dance parties to world music or classical.

'Smoking' Coffee Shops

You'll have little difficulty pinpointing the 350-odd coffee shops whose trade is marijuana and hash rather than tea and tart. One of the most famous and expensive is **The Bulldog** (*Leidseplein 13-17*). **La Tertulia**, on the corner of Prinsengracht and Oude Looiersstraat, is candid and colourful; **De Kuil**, (*Oudebrugsteeg 27*) is popular and central.

Nightclubs

One of the oldest clubs in town is **The Odeon** (*Singel 460*), a big student haunt open nightly. **Escape** (*Rembrandtplein 11*) is capable of drawing 2000 people on a Saturday night. **iT** (*Amstelstraat 24*) is the largest gay/mixed nightclub – it's open Thursday to Sunday and there's usually a queue. The place to be seen is **Sinners in Heaven** (*Wagenstraat 3*), open Thursday to Sunday. The club at **Hotel Arena** (see Places to Stay) has '60 to '90s dance music on Friday and Saturday nights.

Cinema

The 80-year-old Art Deco **Tuschinskitheater** (☎ 0900-93 63, *Reguliersbreestraat 26*) is the city's cinematic showpiece. For foreign and art films try **Desmet** (☎ 627 34 34, *Plantage Middenlaan 4a*) behind the Hortus Botanicus.

NETHERLANDS

Theatre & Dance

Premier performing arts venues are the *Stadsschouwburg* (☎ 624 23 11, *Leidseplein 26*) and the *Muziektheater* (☎ 625 54 44, *Waterlooplein 22*).

The comedy club Boom Chicago (☎ 530 73 00, Leidseplein 12) has an English-language program.

SHOPPING

Amsterdam is a shopper's city, and there are exclusive outlets everywhere. *Mike's Guide*, available free from the VVV, gives a snapshot of the most zany shops. *Art & Antiques in Amsterdam* (also free) pinpoints enticing shops in the so-called Spiegelkwartier (Nieuwe Spiegelstraat and nearby side-streets). Shops with leading fashion designer labels are dotted along PC Hooftstraat.

Some interesting shops include Condomerie Het Gulden Vlies (☎ 627 41 74), Warmoesstraat 141, which is well situated for its trade; Webers Holland (☎ 638 17 77), Kloveniersburgwal 26, with avant-garde fashion; Conscious Dreams (☎ 626 69 07), Kerkstraat 17, trades in magic mushrooms and aphrodisiacs; and Magna Plaza, a grandiose shopping complex on Nieuwezijds Voorburgwal.

GETTING THERE & AWAY
Air

Amsterdam has long been known for its cheap air tickets (see Travel Agencies in the Amsterdam Information section). Airline offices in Amsterdam include KLM (☎ 474 77 47 for 24-hour reservations and information), Postbus 7700, 1117 ZL Schiphol; Malaysia Airlines (☎ 626 24 20), Weteringschans 24a, 1017 SG Amsterdam; and Qantas (☎ 683 80 81), Stadhouderskade 6, 1054 ES Amsterdam.

Bus

Eurolines operates from Amstel Station, which is connected to Centraal Station by metro.

Tickets can be bought from the Eurolines office (☎ 560 87 88) at Rokin 10. High season prices come into effect from 1 July to 31 August.

To London (f90/100 in the low/high season, 10 to 11 hours) there are three or four

services per day, with buses stopping at Utrecht, The Hague, Rotterdam and Breda.

Other Eurolines services include Antwerp (f35, 3½ hours), Brussels (f35, five hours), Cologne (f55/65, 4½ hours), Copenhagen (f145/155, 13 hours) and Paris (f75/95, 8½ hours).

Train

The international information and reservations office at Centraal Station is open 6.30 am to 10 pm daily; for all international information call ☎ 0900-92 96. For national information, ask at the ticket windows or call ☎ 0900-92 92.

For fares and journey times to other destinations in the Netherlands, check the Getting There & Away sections in those places. For information on trains to neighbouring countries, including train/ferry services to London, see the Getting There & Away section earlier in this chapter.

Car & Motorcycle

Local companies have the cheapest car rental – about f70 per day plus kilometre fees. Try the following: Avis (☎ 683 60 61), Nassaukade 380; Diks Autohuur (☎ 662 33 66), Van Ostadestraat 278; Europcar (☎ 683 21 23), Overtoom 197; and Budget (☎ 612 60 66), Overtoom 121.

For motorbikes, Motor-Way (☎ 679 85 07), Stadionweg 279, rents Honda 500/Yamaha 900 machines for f90/135 per day, or f515/730 per week (plus f29 per day insurance). A deposit of f650 is required.

Hitching

For Groningen and northern Germany, take the metro to Amstel Station and get onto Gooiseweg; to hitch to Utrecht, Belgium and central/southern Germany, take tram No 25 to Nieuwe Utrechtseweg; to hitch to Schiphol, Leiden and The Hague, get tram No 6, 16 or 24 to Stadionplein and head out on Amstelveenseweg; to hitch to Haarlem and Alkmaar, get tram No 12 or bus No 15 to Haarlemmerweg.

Ferry

For details on train-ferry services to the UK, see the Getting There & Away section earlier in this chapter.

NETHERLANDS

GETTING AROUND
To/From the Airport
There are trains every 10 minutes between Schiphol and Amsterdam Centraal Station (f6.50, 20 minutes). Taxis cost about f60.

Bus, Tram & Metro
Amsterdam's comprehensive public transport network is operated by the Gemeentevervoer-bedrijf (GVB), which has an information office next to the VVV on Stationsplein, open 7 am to 9 pm weekdays and from 8 am weekends. Pick up the free transport map.

Buses, trams and the metro use strip cards (see Local Transport in the Getting Around section earlier in this chapter), or you can buy one/two/three-day daycards for f11/17/22 (f5 per day extra up to nine days) from the GVB (one to eight-day tickets are sold from some VVV offices also). All services run from about 5 or 6 am until midnight, when the more limited night buses takes over.

The Circle Tram 20 is designed to meet the needs of tourists. It operates 9 am to 6 pm daily and departs every 12 minutes from Centraal Station. One/two/three-day tickets cost f10/15/19, or f6/10/12.50 for children.

For all information, the national public transport number is ☎ 0900-92 92.

Taxi & Watertaxi
Both are expensive, but watertaxis, with their half/one-hour rental fee of f125/200, prohibitively so. For watertaxi information and bookings, call ☎ 530 10 90; for road taxis ☎ 677 77 77.

Car & Motorcycle
A 17th-century city enmeshed by waterways is hardly the place for motorised transport. Anti-car feelings are strong and the city council has done much to restrict access and parking. The *Amsterdam by Car* leaflet, free from the VVV, pinpoints parking areas and warns of dire penalties – a wheel clamp and a f130 fine – for nonconformists. If you do bring your car, the best place to park is the 'Transferium' parking garage at Amsterdam Arena stadium, which charges f12.50 per day and includes two return metro tickets to the city centre (20 minutes).

Motorcycles can usually be parked on pavements providing they don't obstruct pedestrians, but security is a big problem with any parked vehicle, irrespective of the time of day. For any queries, contact the Parking Control Department (☎ 555 03 33).

Moped
The Moped Rental Service (☎ 422 02 66), Marnixstraat 208, charges f15 for the first hour plus f12.50 for each extra hour, f50 for six hours or f80 per day. No driving licence is required but there's a hefty f1000 deposit.

Bicycle
Tram tracks and the other 400,000 bikes are the only real obstacle to cycling; local cyclists can get very impatient when pedestrians block cycle paths. It's advisable to book rental bikes ahead in summer. Try Damstraat Rent-a-Bike (☎ 625 50 29), Damstraat 20, which charges f15/68 per day/week plus a f50 deposit or credit card imprint. The Rijwiel Shop (☎ 624 83 91), to the left out of Centraal Station, charges f9.50/38 with a f200 deposit or credit card imprint.

Canal Boat, Bus & Bike
Canal cruises (f12 an hour) leave from in front of Centraal Station, along Damrak and Rokin and near the Rijksmuseum. They're a very touristy thing to do but they're also a great way to see the city from a different perspective. Night cruises are especially enchanting, as many of the bridges are illuminated and the whole scene takes on something of an unreal quality.

The Canal Bus (☎ 623 98 86) stops at the tourist enclaves between Centraal Station and the Rijksmuseum, and has a day ticket for f25. Better value is the Amsterdam Transport Pass (f31.50), which gives one days' travel on the Canal Bus plus discounts at selected museums and restaurants.

The Museumboot (☎ 530 10 90) offers a f25 day ticket (f20 if bought after 1 pm) good for unlimited travel. In summer, canal 'bikes' can be hired from kiosks at Centraal Station and Leidseplein, with two/four-seaters costing f12.50/22.50 per hour (plus a f50 deposit).

AROUND AMSTERDAM
Bus tours to nearby sights can be booked through the VVV, and include trips to

NETHERLANDS

Aalsmeer, Alkmaar (f45), The Hague, Delft and Fryslân via the Afsluitdijk (f62). For information on the Keukenhof, see The Randstad section.

The world's biggest flower auction is held Monday to Friday at **Aalsmeer**, south of Amsterdam; take bus No 172 from Centraal Station. Bidding starts early, so arrive between 7.30 and 9 am. Admission costs f7.50.

To get to the once typical, but now tourist-filled, fishing village of **Volendam**, take bus No 110 from Centraal Station (35 minutes). To the similar village and former island of **Marken**, now connected to the mainland by a dike, get bus No 111 (45 minutes) or go to Volendam and take the ferry (summer only).

The **Alkmaar cheese market**, which is staged at 10 am every Friday in summer in the town's main market square, attracts droves. Arrive early if you want to get more than a fleeting glimpse of the famous round cheeses being weighed and whisked away. There are two trains per hour from Centraal Station

(f11.50, 30 minutes) and it's a 10-minute walk at the other end.

The Randstad

The Netherlands' most densely populated region, the Randstad (literally, 'Urban Agglomeration') spreads in a circle from Amsterdam which incorporates The Hague, Rotterdam and Utrecht, and smaller towns like Haarlem, Leiden, Delft and Gouda. A compact area, its many sights are highlighted by the bulb fields which explode in intoxicating colours between March and May.

HAARLEM
☎ 023 • pop 147,873
Less than 15 minutes by train from Amsterdam, Haarlem is a small but vibrant town, close to the wealthy seaside resort of Zandvoort. The Haarlem VVV (☎ 0900-616 16 00) is at Stationsplein 1 next to the train station.

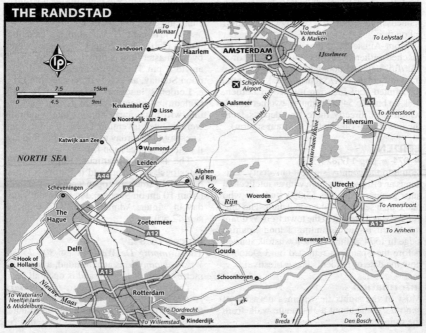

THE RANDSTAD

NETHERLANDS

The **Frans Hals Museum**, Groot Heiligland 62, features portraits by Frans Hals, the town's favourite 17th-century artist. The **Teyler Museum**, Spaarne 16, is the country's oldest museum, housing a curious collection including drawings by Michelangelo and Raphael. Also worth a look is the **St Bavokerk** on Grote Markt – this church houses the Müller organ which Mozart played as a youngster.

From Amsterdam, there are trains every 15 minutes to Haarlem (f6.50).

KEUKENHOF

Near the town of Lisse between Haarlem and Leiden, the Keukenhof, the world's largest garden, attracts a staggering 800,000 people in a mere eight weeks every year. Its beauty is something of an enigma, combining nature's talents with artificial precision to create a garden where millions of bulbs – tulips, daffodils and hyacinths – bloom every year, perfectly in place and exactly on time.

It's open late March to late May but exact dates vary each year, so check with the VVV at Leiden or the Keukenhof (☎ 0252-46 55 55, ✉ info@keukenhof). Admission costs f19 (concession f9.50). It's at www.keukenhof .nl on the Web.

From Amsterdam, the Keukenhof can be reached either by a bus tour (f47/75 for a half/full day and booked at the VVV) or by train to Leiden (f13.75 return, or ask about the discounted Rail Idee fare). Once in Leiden, pick up bus No 54 (25 minutes, two per hour), which runs directly there, and departs from the bus station (in front of the train station).

LEIDEN

☎ 071 • pop 117,821

Home to the country's oldest university, Leiden is an effervescent town with an intellectual aura generated by the 15,000 students who make up a seventh of the population. The university was a present to the town from William the Silent for withstanding a long Spanish siege in 1574. A third of the townsfolk starved before the Spaniards retreated on 3 October, now the date of Leiden's biggest festival.

Information

Most of the sights lie within a network of central canals, about a 10-minute walk from the train station.

The main post office, at Schipholweg 130, is about 300m north-east of the station, or there's a central branch at Breestraat 46. There's a Zelf Was (laundry) at Morsstraat 50. For Internet access head to the Centrale Bibliotheek (☎ 514 99 43), Nieuwstraat 4.

Tourist Offices The VVV (☎ 0900-222 23 33, fax 516 12 27), Stationsweg 2D, is open 10 am to 6.30 pm weekdays and to 4.30 pm Saturday (also 11 am to 3 pm Sunday from April to 15 September).

Things to See & Do

In summer **canal cruises** leave from near the bridge at Beestenmarkt. To tour the town's many **hofjes** (almshouses), pick up the walking tour booklet from the VVV.

The **Rijksmuseum van Oudheden** (National Museum of Antiquities), Rapenburg 28, tops Leiden's list of museums. Its striking entrance hall contains the Temple of Taffeh, a gift from Egypt for the Netherlands' help in saving ancient monuments from inundation when the Aswan High Dam was built. It's open 10 am to 5 pm Tuesday to Friday, from noon on weekends, and costs f7 (concession f6).

The 17th-century **Museum De Lakenhal** (Cloth Hall), Oude Singel 28, houses works by old masters and period rooms. It's open 10 am to 5 pm Tuesday to Saturday and from noon Sunday, and costs f8 (concession f5).

Leiden's landmark windmill, **De Valk** (Falcon), Binnenvestgracht 1, is a museum that will blow away notions that windmills were a Dutch invention. Open 10 am to 5 pm Tuesday to Saturday and from 1 pm Sunday, it costs f5 (concession f3).

The **Hortus Botanicus**, Rapenburg 73, dates back 400 years and is Europe's oldest botanical garden. It's open 9 am to 5 pm daily (from 10 am on Sunday), but is closed Saturday in winter. Admission costs f5 (concession f2.50).

Places to Stay

The *Camping De Wasbeek* (☎ 301 13 80, Wasbeeklaan 5b) is at Warmond, a few kilometres north of Leiden, and is open all year.

The nearest NJHC hostel, *De Duinark* (☎ 0252-37 29 20, fax 37 70 61, Langevelderlaan 45), is in Noordwijkerhout, 45 minutes away near Noordwijk an Zee – take bus No

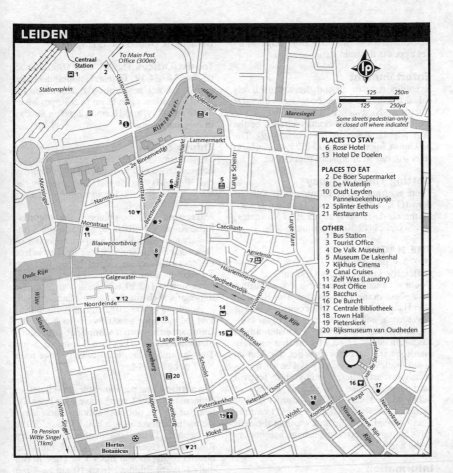

LEIDEN

PLACES TO STAY
6 Rose Hotel
13 Hotel De Doelen

PLACES TO EAT
2 De Boer Supermarket
8 De Waterlijn
10 Oudt Leyden
   Pannekoekenhuysje
12 Splinter Eethuis
21 Restaurants

OTHER
1 Bus Station
3 Tourist Office
4 De Valk Museum
5 Museum De Lakenhal
7 Kijkhuis Cinema
9 Canal Cruises
11 Zelf Was (Laundry)
14 Post Office
15 Bacchus
16 De Burcht
17 Centrale Bibliotheek
18 Town Hall
19 Pieterskerk
20 Rijksmuseum van Oudheden

Some streets pedestrian-only or closed off where indicated

60 (two per hour) to Sancta Maria hospital and walk 10 minutes.

The canal-front ***Pension Witte Singel*** (*☎ 512 45 92, fax 514 28 90, Witte Singel 80*), south of the town centre, has singles/doubles for f60/92, or f85/120 with private bath facilities. It's 20 minutes' walk from the station.

The ***Rose Hotel*** (*☎ 514 66 30, fax 521 70 96, Beestenmarkt 14*) is central and popular with young travellers, but a bit scruffy. Rooms cost f90/135. Alternatively, near the Rijksmuseum is the stately ***Hotel De Doelen*** (*☎ 512 05 27, fax 512 84 53, ☏ info@dedoelen.com, Rapenburg 2*). All rooms have a shower and toilet, and prices start at f100/150 (breakfast costs f12.50).

Places to Eat

The ***Oudt Leyden Pannekoekenhuysje*** (*☎ 513 31 44, Steenstraat 51*) does enormous pancakes for f8 to f18. The predominantly vegetarian ***Splinter Eethuis*** (*☎ 514 95 19, Noordeinde 30*) has organic two-course meals for f18.50 (closed Monday to Wednesday).

De Waterlijn (*☎ 512 12 79, Prinsessekade 5*) is a floating cafe that's popular with locals craving a coffee or cake. If you have guilders to burn, there is a lane of expensive, candle-lit

NETHERLANDS

restaurants behind Pieterskerk on Kloksteeg. Self-caterers will find a *De Boer Supermarket* opposite the train station.

Entertainment

Evenings revolve around the town's lively cafes. Check the notice boards at either *De Burcht* on Nieuwstraat, a literary bar next to the remains of a 12th-century citadel, or the ever popular *Bacchus (Breestraat 49)*. The *Kijkhuis Cinema (☎ 566 15 85, Vrouwenkerksteeg 10)* has an alternative film circuit.

Getting There & Away

There are trains every 15 minutes to Amsterdam (f13.25, 35 minutes), Haarlem (f9.50, 30 minutes), The Hague (f5.50, 15 minutes) and Schiphol (f9.50, 17 minutes).

THE HAGUE
☎ 070 • pop 445,000

Officially known as 's-Gravenhage ('the Count's Domain') because a count built a castle here in the 13th century, The Hague – Den Haag in Dutch – is the country's seat of government and residence of the royal family, though the capital city is Amsterdam. It has a refined air, created by the many stately mansions and palatial embassies that line its green boulevards. The city is known for its prestigious art galleries, a huge jazz festival held annually near the seaside suburb of Scheveningen, and the miniature town of Madurodam. There is a poorer side to all the finery, though, and the area south of the centre is far removed from its urbane neighbours to the north.

Information

Trains stop at Station Hollands Spoor (HS), a 20-minute walk south of the city, or at Centraal Station, five minutes from the centre. The area between Spui and Centraal Station has recently experienced a massive face-lift in order to create The Hague's New Centre – a prestigious commercial and residential area.

There's a GWK money exchange bureau in Centraal Station. The main post office is on Kerkplein. There's a laundry to the east behind Centraal Station at Theresiastraat 250. Internet users should head to either Cafe Tweeduizendvijf (☎ 364 40 94), Denneweg

7f, or to the bank of terminals at the Centrale Bibliotheek (☎ 353 44 55), Spui 68.

Tourist Offices The VVV (☎ 0900-340 35 05, fax 346 24 12, @ reservations@denhaag. com for hotel reservations), Koningin Julianaplein 30, is open 9 am to 5.30 pm Monday to Saturday, and 10 am to 2 pm on Sunday in July and August.

Things to See

Those interested in the city's eclectic **architecture** can take a two-hour guided tour (Saturday only from May to August) organised by the VVV. The cost is f30 for an adult plus child.

Museums The showpiece is the **Mauritshuis**, Korte Vijverberg 8, an exquisite 17th-century mansion housing a superb collection of Dutch and Flemish masterpieces and a touch of the contemporary. It's open 10 am to 5 pm Tuesday to Saturday (from 11 am Sunday); admission is f12.50 (concession f6.50). The museum's Web site is at www.mauritshuis.nl.

Admirers of De Stijl, and in particular of Piet Mondrian, won't want to miss the **Gemeentemuseum** (Municipal Museum), Stadhouderslaan 41. Open 11 am to 5 pm Tuesday to Sunday, it costs f10 – take tram No 7 or bus No 14.

Binnenhof The parliamentary buildings, or Binnenhof (Inner Court), have long been the heart of Dutch politics, although nowadays the parliament meets in a building outside the Binnenhof. Tours take in the 13th-century Ridderzaal (Knight's Hall) and must be booked in advance at the VVV. They're run daily (except Sunday) from 10 am to 4 pm and cost f6.50 (concession f5).

Koninklijk Paleis There are three royal palaces but the only one accessible to the public is the **Lange Voorhout Paleis Museum**, which stages temporary art exhibitions. You can pass the palaces on a two-hour 'Royal Tour' which leaves from the VVV at 1 pm (Tuesday to Saturday from May through August). It costs f30 for one adult plus child.

Peace Palace Home of the International Court of Justice, the Peace Palace *(Vredepaleis)* on Carnegieplein can be visited by

THE HAGUE (DEN HAAG) CENTRE

To Peace Palace (800m) &
Gemeentemuseum (2.2km)

To Madurodam
(2km) &
Scheveningen
(4km)

To Camping
Duinhorst (4km)

To Amsterdam (A4,45km),
Utrecht (A12,50km) &
Rotterdam (A13,20km)

To Bellevue
Appartementenhotel
(2.5km)

To Laundry (1.3km)

Hofvijver

Kerkpl

Koningin
Julianaplein

Centraal
Station

To Hollands Spoor
Train Station (600m)

To City
Hostel (500m)

PLACES TO STAY
18 Hotel Corona

PLACES TO EAT
1 De Wankele Tafel
2 Benkei
11 Schlemmer
22 Le Perroquet
24 Hema Supermarket

OTHER
3 Cafe Tweeduizendvijf
4 Stairs
5 Lange Voorhout Paleis Museum
6 French Embassy
7 US Embassy
8 British Embassy
9 Koninklijk Paleis
10 Belgian Embassy
12 Tourist Office
13 Babylon Centre
14 Poten Still
15 Mauritshuis
16 Ridderzaal
17 Binnenhof
19 Main Post Office
20 Grote Kerk
21 Old Town Hall
23 New City Hall & Centrale Bibliotheek
25 Paard van Troje
26 Haags Filmhuis
27 Danstheater Lucent

0   100   200m
0   100   200yd

---

guided tours only, which cost f5 (concession f3) and must be booked – inquire at the VVV. To get there, take tram No 7 or bus No 4 from Centraal Station.

Madurodam Everything that's quintessential Netherlands is in this tiny 'town' that's big with tourists. It's at George Maduroplein 1 and is open 9 am to 6 pm daily (until 8 pm from March to June, and until 11 pm from July to August). Admission is f21 (concession f14). Take tram Nos 1 and 9 or bus No 22 from the Centraal Station. It's at www.madurodam.nl on the Web.

Places to Stay

While diplomats and royalty may call The Hague home, few travellers on a budget will.

Camping Duinhorst (☎ 324 22 70, *Buurtweg 135*) is to the east of Scheveningen and is open April to September.

The modern NJHC *City Hostel* (☎ 315 78 88, fax 315 78 77, ℮ denhaag@njhc.org, *Scheepmakerstraat 27*) is the only bright spot on the budget scene. Singles range from f80 to f85, doubles from f90 to f109, and dorms from f35.50 to f40. It's a five-minute walk from Station HS, or take tram No 1, 9 or 12 from Centraal Station to the stop 'Rijswijkseplein'.

NETHERLANDS

The pleasant *Bellevue Appartementenhotel* (☎ *360 55 52, fax 345 35 08, Beeklaan 417)* has self-contained singles/doubles from f65/120 (f12.50 extra for breakfast), and street parking. Take tram No 3 (direction 'Kijkduin') and get off at Valkenbosplein, from where it's a 300m walk. For a diplomat-style splurge there's *Hotel Corona* (☎ *363 79 30, fax 361 57 85, @ corona@greenpark.nl, Buitenhof 39)*. It has charming rooms from f285/330; on weekends, these prices drop to f185/220. Breakfast costs f30.

Places to Eat

Fortunately there's more variety for eating than sleeping. The cobbled streets off Denneweg are lively. Here you'll find *De Wankele Tafel* (☎ *364 32 67, Mauritskade 79)*, a cheerful little vegetarian haunt with three-course meals from f12.50 to f21 (closed Sunday). The nearby *Benkei* (☎ *364 79 99, Denneweg 142)* is a long-established and well-respected Japanese restaurant, with main courses from f25 to f55 (closed Monday).

The ever-popular *Le Perroquet* (☎ *363 97 86, Lange Poten 12)* serves satay specials for f19. It's also good for the ubiquitous *koffie met appelgebak* (coffee with apple pie). *Schlemmer* (☎ *360 90 00, Lange Houtstraat 17)* is a tastefully decorated brasserie with a limited international menu (mains from f20 to f30).

Self-caterers should head to *Hema* on Grote Marktstraat.

Entertainment

Although it's more a city for fine dining than raging, there are a few lively cafes, and in the second week of July the North Sea Jazz Festival considerably invigorates the music scene. If you're into ballet, be sure to catch a performance by the renowned Nederlands Danstheater in the *Danstheater Lucent* (☎ *360 49 30)* on Spui. Casual dress will do; no performances in July and August.

On a daily level, there's *Poten Still* (*Herenstraat 15)*, a small Irish pub on a grungy nightlife street. *Stairs* (*Nieuwe Schoolstraat 21)* is a gay bar/disco.

The *Haags Filmhuis* (☎ *365 99 00, Spui 191)* screens foreign and art movies. The *Paard van Troje* (☎ *360 16 18, Prinsegracht 12)* is The Hague's answer to Amsterdam's Melkweg and Paradiso 'cultural activity centres'. It's expected to reopen in mid-2001 after extensive renovations.

Getting There & Away

Eurolines buses stop at the bus station above Centraal Station. Tickets can be bought at Broere Reizen (☎ 382 40 51) travel agent inside the Babylon Centre. London services originate in Amsterdam, arriving in The Hague about one hour later. For more details, see the Amsterdam Getting There & Away section.

From Centraal Station, there are trains to Amsterdam (f17.25, 45 minutes), Gouda (f8.50, 20 minutes), Leiden (f5.50, 15 minutes), Rotterdam (f7.50, 20 minutes) and Schiphol airport (f13.25, 40 minutes). Just 9km away, Delft can be reached by tram No 1 (30 minutes) which departs from next to Centraal Station.

Getting Around

There's a public transport information kiosk inside Centraal Station. Buses and some trams leave from above Centraal Station, while other trams take off from the side. Tram No 8 goes to Scheveningen via the Peace Palace, while tram Nos 1 and 9 follow Nieuwe Parklaan past Madurodam to the coast. Tram No 9 links Centraal Station and HS.

DELFT

☎ 015 • pop 95,116

Had the potters who lived in Delft long ago not been such accomplished copiers, today's townsfolk would probably live in relative peace. But the distinctive blue-and-white pottery which the 17th-century artisans duplicated from Chinese porcelain became famous worldwide as delftware. If you're here in summer, the number of tourists will probably make you wish you weren't; in winter its old-world charm and narrow, canal-lined streets make it a pleasant overnight stay.

Information

The train and neighbouring bus station are a 10-minute stroll south of the central Markt. The VVV (☎ 212 61 00, fax 215 86 95), Markt 85, is open 9 am to 5.30 pm Monday to Saturday, and 11 am to 3 pm on Sunday in summer. The post office is on Hippolytusbuurt. Internet users should head to the Centrale Bibliotheek (☎ 212 34 50), Kruisstraat 71.

NETHERLANDS

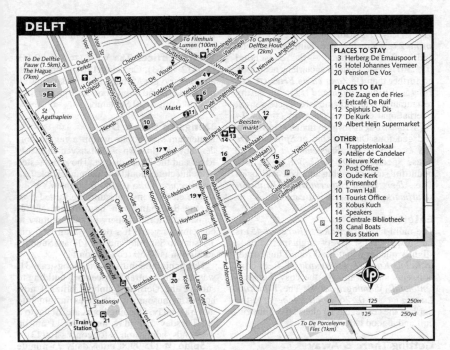

DELFT

To Filmhuis Lumen (100m)
To Camping Delftse Hout (2km)
To De Delftse Pauw (1.5km) & The Hague (7km)
To De Porceleyne Fles (1km)

PLACES TO STAY
3 Herberg De Emauspoort
16 Hotel Johannes Vermeer
20 Pension De Vos

PLACES TO EAT
2 De Zaag en de Fries
4 Eetcafé De Ruif
12 Spijshuis De Dis
17 De Kurk
19 Albert Heijn Supermarket

OTHER
1 Trappistenlokaal
5 Atelier de Candelaer
6 Nieuwe Kerk
7 Post Office
8 Oude Kerk
9 Prinsenhof
10 Town Hall
11 Tourist Office
13 Kobus Kuch
14 Speakers
15 Centrale Bibliotheek
18 Canal Boats
21 Bus Station

Things to See & Do

There are several places where you can see delftware being made and/or painted. The most central outfit is **Atelier de Candelaer**, Kerkstraat 14, a small painting studio and shop. The town's two main delftware factories are outside the centre. **De Delftse Pauw**, Delftweg 133, is the smaller, employing painters who work mainly from their homes; take tram No 1 to Pasgeld, walk up Broekmolenweg to the canal and turn left. It has free, daily tours. **De Porceleyne Fles**, Rotterdamseweg 196 to the south, is the only original factory, operating since 1653. It's charges f5 for tours; bus No 63 from the train station stops nearby, or it's a 25-minute walk from the town centre.

The 14th-century **Nieuwe Kerk** on the Markt houses the crypt of the Dutch royal family as well as the mausoleum of William the Silent. The church is open Monday to Saturday; admission is f4 (concession f1.50). The Gothic **Oude Kerk**, with 140 years' seniority and a 2m tilt in its tower, is at Heilige Geestkerkhof.

The **Prinsenhof**, St Agathaplein 1, is where William the Silent held court until assassinated here in 1584. It now houses historical and contemporary art, and is open 10 am to 5 pm Tuesday to Saturday (from 1 pm Sunday). Admission is f5 (concession f2.50).

During summer, **canal boats** leave from Koornmarkt.

Places to Stay

The closest camping ground is *Delftse Hout* (☎ 213 00 40, Korftlaan 5) just to the northeast of town. It's open all year; get bus No 64 from the station. *Pension De Vos* (☎ 212 32 58, Breestraat 5) is homy and has doubles only for f70. *Herberg De Emauspoort* (☎ 219 02 19, fax 214 82 51, ✉ emauspoort@ emauspoort.nl, Vrouwenregt 11) is excellent value, with lovely rooms from f85/135, plus two gorgeous, Roma-style (gypsy) caravans for f135/150. The brand new and very likable *Hotel Johannes Vermeer* (☎ 212 64 66, fax 213 48 35, ✉ hotelvermeer@hotelnet.nl, Molslaan 18) has 25 modern rooms costing f175.

NETHERLANDS

Places to Eat

The *Eetcafé De Ruif* (☎ 214 22 06, *Kerkstraat 23*) is a rustic eatery with hearty meals and a floating terrace – the dagschotel (f15.50) is good value. Vegetarians need look no further than *De Zaag en de Fries* (☎ 213 70 15, *Vrouw Juttenland 17*), an earthy restaurant serving organic fare. There's great international cuisine at *De Kurk* (☎ 214 14 74, *Kromstraat 20*) where mains start at f30, and generous Dutch dishes at *Spijshuis De Dis* (☎ 213 17 82, *Beestenmarkt 36*). The house speciality, *De Bokkepot* (f29), is a bountiful stew of rabbit, chicken and beef. The *Albert Heijn Supermarket* (*Brabantseturfmarkt 41*) services self-caterers.

Entertainment

The multi-faceted *Speakers* (*Burgwal 45*) is the town's most lively nightspot. For a slightly quieter haunt head round the corner to *Kobus Kuch* (*Beestenmarkt 1*). Beer connoisseurs should aim for the cosy *Trappistenlokaal* (*Vlamingstraat 4*). The *Filmhuis Lumen* (☎ 214 02 26, *Doelenplein 5*), to the north of the centre, has an alternative film circuit and a good cafe.

Getting There & Away

It's 10 minutes by train to Rotterdam (f5.50), even less to The Hague (f4.25). Tram No 1 leaves for The Hague (30 minutes) every 10 minutes from in front of the train station.

ROTTERDAM

☎ 010 • pop 592,471

Rotterdam is not your quintessential Dutch city. Bombed to oblivion on 14 May 1940, its centre is ultra-modern, with mirrored skyscrapers and some extraordinarily innovative buildings. The city prides itself on this experimental architecture, as well as having the world's largest port and many festivals that attract a young crowd throughout summer. In 2001, Rotterdam, along with Porto, will be the European City of Culture.

Information

Central Rotterdam is not compact and getting orientated takes time. The heart of the city is the pedestrianised shopping streets based around Lijnbaan. The main post office is at Coolsingel 42, opposite the VVV. Internet users should head to Time2surf, Stadhuisplein 32, around the corner from the VVV.

Tourist Offices The VVV (☎ 414 00 00, fax 412 17 63), Coolsingel 67, is open 9.30 am to 5 or 6 pm Monday to Saturday (until 9 pm Friday), and from noon to 5 pm Sunday from 1 April to 30 September.

Things to See & Do

Rotterdam's sights lie within a region bordered by the old town of Delfshaven, the Maas River and the Blaak district. Those interested in architecture should buy the guidebook *Two Architecture Walks* (f9.95) from the VVV.

The city's many museums are lorded over by the **Boijmans van Beuningen**, Museumpark 18, a rich gallery of 14th-century to contemporary art. It's open 10 am to 5 pm Tuesday to Saturday and from 11 am Sunday; admission is f7.50 (concession f4).

Het Schielandshuis, Korte Hoogstraat 31, was the only central 17th-century building to survive the German bombing blitz. It now houses a museum which gives insight into that tragic day. Opening hours are 10 am to 5 pm Tuesday to Friday, and from 11 am on weekends; admission is f6 (concession f3).

Spido (☎ 275 99 88) runs daily 75-minute harbour cruises which cost f16 (concession f9.50), and day trips (summer only) for f42 (concession f31) to the harbour's heart at Europoort. Departure is from Leuvehoofd (take the metro to Leuvehaven).

The **Euromast**, a 185m-high tower, pricks the skyline at Parkhaven 20; admission is f15.50 (concession f10). Take tram No 6 or 9 or the metro to Dijkzigt. A combination ticket for a Spido harbour cruise and the Euromast costs f27 (concession f17).

With an Escher-like design, the **Kijkkubus** (Cube Houses), Overblaak 70, offers a new angle on modern living. The display house is open 11 am to 5 pm daily. Admission is f3.50 (concession f2.50); take the metro to Blaak.

Delfshaven, Rotterdam's old town, is most famed for its **Oude Kerk**, Aelbrechtskolk 20, where the Pilgrim Fathers set sail to the New World – get the metro to Delfshaven.

The **Kunsthal**, Westzeedijk 341, is the city's premier venue for temporary art exhibitions – take tram No 5 to Westzeedijk.

NETHERLANDS

Places to Stay

The *Stadscamping* (☎ *415 34 40, Kanaalweg 84)* is 40 minutes' walk north-west of the station, or you can take bus No 33.

The NJHC *hostel* (☎ *436 57 63, fax 436 55 69,* ✉ *rotterdam@njhc.org, Rochussenstraat 107)* is 20 minutes' walk from the station, or get the metro to Dijkzigt.

The best budget hotel option is *Hotel Bienvenue* (☎ *466 93 94, fax 467 74 75, Spoorsingel 24)* which has pleasant singles/doubles, all with TV, from f81/100. It's two blocks straight up the canal from the rear entrance of Centraal Station.

The name says it all at *Hotel Bazar* (☎ *206 51 51, fax 206 51 59, Witte de Withstraat 16)* in the heart of town. It's an original hotel/restaurant with lantern-lit rooms starting at f115/135.

Maritime romantics might enjoy a night at the *Hotel New York* (☎ *439 05 00, fax 484 27 01, Koninglnnenhoofd 1)*. This palatial building once was the headquarters of the Holland-America shipping line; rooms with great harbour views start at f200.

Places to Eat

The *Westerpaviljoen* (☎ *436 26 45, Mathenesserlaan 155)* is a large cafe popular with all types – basic meals cost between f12 and f17. *Dudok* (☎ *433 3102, Meent 88)* is a pricier but more central version of the same. Named after a well-known Dutch architect, this brasserie is said to have Rotterdam's best appelgebak. *Blaeu* (☎ *433 07 75, Wijnstraat 20)* has a view of the Kijk-Kubus and reasonably-priced Dutch specialities. *De Pijp* (☎ *436 68 96, Gaffelstraat 90)* is over a century old (and looks every bit of it) and is still going strong. Mains range from f27 to f34, and reservations are essential. Self-caterers will find an *Albert Heijn* supermarket on Lijnbaan, the main shopping street.

Entertainment

The many terrace cafes on Stadhuisplein and at Oude Haven near the Kijk-Kubus are popular with a young crowd. Rotterdam is home to one of the country's biggest music venues, the *Ahoy'* (☎ *293 33 00)* – check the monthly *R'uit* guide (free from the VVV) for listings.

Getting There & Away

Eurolines buses stop at Conradstraat (to the right as you leave the train station) where Eurolines also has an office (☎ 412 44 44) at No 20. Services to London leave from Amsterdam, arriving in Rotterdam 1½ hours later.

Trains run every 15 minutes to Amsterdam (f23.25, one hour), Delft (f5.50, 10 minutes), The Hague (f7.50, 20 minutes) and Utrecht (f15.25, 40 minutes). Half-hourly services run to Middelburg (f33, 1½ hours), Gouda (f7.50, 18 minutes) and Hook of Holland (f8.50, 30 minutes).

For information on the ferries from Hook of Holland and Europoort to England, see the Getting There & Away section at the beginning of this chapter. P&O/North Sea Ferries' bus (f12.50) leaves daily at 4 pm from Conradstraat (next to Centraal Station) to connect with the ferry at Europoort.

Getting Around

Trams leave from in front of the train station; the metro from underneath. Both run until about midnight; on Friday and Saturday, night buses then take over. A one/two-day public transport card costs f12/18.

AROUND ROTTERDAM

The **Waterland Neeltje Jans** (see Around Middelburg in the Delta Region section) can be reached from Centraal Station by taking the metro to Spijkenesse Centraal and then bus No 104 (2¼ hours in total). The **Kinderdijk**, the Netherlands' picture-postcard string of 19 working windmills, sits between Rotterdam and Dordrecht near Alblasserdam. On Saturday afternoons in July and August the mills' sails are set in motion. One windmill is open daily from 1 April to 30 September – get the metro to Zuidplein then bus No 154 (1¼ hours).

GOUDA

☎ 0182 • pop 72,282

Think Dutch cheese, and most people will say Gouda (or Edam). This pretty little town, 25km north-east of Rotterdam, is best known for its cheese market, held at 10 am every Thursday morning in July and August. Enormous rounds of cheese – some weighing up to 25kg – are brought to the Markt where they're weighed and sold. Surprisingly, the

NETHERLANDS

Markt is the largest in the country, as Gouda was a major player in the cloth trade in the Middle Ages. For more information, the VVV (☎ 0182-51 36 66) is at Markt 27.

Regular trains connect Gouda with Rotterdam (f7.50, 18 minutes) and Amsterdam (f17.25, one hour).

UTRECHT
☎ 030 • pop 233,632

Lorded over by the Dom, the country's tallest church tower, Utrecht is an antique frame surrounding an increasingly modern interior. Its 14th-century sunken canals, once-bustling wharfs and cellars now brim with chic restaurants and cafes.

Information

The most appealing quarter lies between Oudegracht and Nieuwegracht and the streets around the Dom.

The VVV (☎ 0900-414 14 14, fax 233 14 17), Vredenburg 90, is five minutes from the train station; it's open 9 am to 6 pm weekdays and until 5 pm Saturday.

Things to See & Do

During summer, **canal cruises** leave from Oudegracht.

The 112m-high **Dom Tower** has 465 steps leading up to excellent views. From 1 April to 31 October the tower is open 10 am to 5 pm weekdays and from noon at weekends. The rest of the year it's open weekends only. Entry costs f7.50 (concession f4.50).

The **Museum Van Speelklok tot Pierement**, Buurkerkhof 10, has a colourful collection of musical clocks and street organs. It's open 10 am to 5 pm Tuesday to Saturday, from noon Sunday, and costs f12 (concession f7.50).

For religious and medieval art buffs, **Het Catharijneconvent Museum**, Nieuwegracht 63, winds through a 15th-century convent and has the country's largest collection of medieval Dutch art. It's open 10 am to 5 pm Tuesday to Friday and from 11 am weekends; entry is f10 (concession f5).

Places to Stay

Camping De Berekuil (☎ 271 38 70, Ariënslaan 5) is 1.5 km from the centre, open all year and easily reached by bus No 57 from the station.

The **Strowis Hostel** (☎/fax 238 02 80, ☻ strowis@xs4all.nl, Boothstraat 8) is a colourful budget option right in the heart of town. Double rooms cost f80 and dorms (four to 14 beds) are f20 to f25. There's a kitchen for guests to use. It's a 15 minute walk from Centraal Station or take bus No 54 to Janskerkhof then walk 200m.

The **Park Hotel** (☎ 251 67 12, fax 254 04 01, Tolsteegsingel 34) has homy rooms with private shower and toilet for f125, and parking. It's about 25 minutes' walk from the station, or take bus No 2.

The **Hotel Tulip Inn Centre** (☎ 231 31 69, fax 231 01 48, ☻ reservations@utrecht.goldentulip.nl, Janskerkhof 10) is a comfortable central hotel with an atmospheric cafe and a charming brasserie. Rooms cost f210/275.

Places to Eat

The Oudegracht is lined with outdoor restaurants and cafes. **De Winkel van Sinkel** (☎ 230 30 30, Oudegracht 158) is a huge cafe occupying an old warehouse. Pasta dishes start at f18.50 and there are various vegetarian options. The multifaceted **Oudaen** (☎ 231 18 64, Oudegracht 99) houses a small brewery, a proeflokaal (tasting house) and a plush restaurant serving French cuisine.

De Baas (☎ 231 51 85, Lijnmarkt 8) is a cheap, colourful eatery, open Tuesday to Saturday (evenings only). **Moby Dick** (☎ 670 03 00, Kromme Nieuwegracht 16) does meat, fish and vegetarian dishes for between f24 and f36.

Shoarma (pitta-bread) eateries are plentiful along Voorstraat. **Eettafel Veritas** (Kromme Nieuwe Gracht 54) is a student mensa open weeknights from 5 to 8 pm.

For self-caterers, there's an **Albert Heijn Supermarket** in Hoog Catharijne (the huge shopping centre next to the train station), and another at Voorstraat 38.

Getting There & Away

Eurolines buses stop at Jaarbeursplein out the back of the train station; tickets can be bought from Wasteels (☎ 293 08 70), a travel agent at Jaarbeurstraverse 6 (on the covered walkway which joins the station to Jaarbeursplein). Buses arrive in Utrecht 45 minutes after leaving Amsterdam – for more details, see the Amsterdam Getting There & Away section.

As Utrecht is the national rail hub, there are frequent trains to Amsterdam (f11.50, 30 minutes), Arnhem (f17.25, 40 minutes), Den Bosch (f13.25, 30 minutes), Gouda (f9.50, 22 minutes), Maastricht (f42, two hours), Rotterdam (f15.25, 40 minutes) and The Hague (f17.25, 45 minutes).

Getting Around

Buses leave from underneath Hoog Catharijne (the shopping complex adjoining the train station).

Arnhem & the Hoge Veluwe

☎ 026

About an hour's drive east of Amsterdam, the Hoge Veluwe is the Netherlands' best-known national park and home of the prestigious Kröller-Müller Museum. To the south, the town of Arnhem was the site of fierce fighting between the Germans and British and Polish airborne troops during the failed Operation Market Garden in WWII. Today it's a peaceful town, the closest base to the nearby war museum and the national park.

INFORMATION

The VVV (☎ 0900-202 40 75, fax 442 26 44), Willemsplein 8, is one block to the left out of Arnhem's train station. Buses leave from the right as you exit the station. The town's pedestrianised centre, based around the well-hidden Korenmarkt, is five minutes' walk from the station.

THINGS TO SEE

In Arnhem itself, the main attraction is the **Museum voor Moderne Kunst** (Modern Art Museum), Utrechtsestraat 87, which occupies a neoclassical building overlooking the Rhine. It's a 10-minute walk from the station. Outside the town, Oosterbeek's wartime **Airborne Museum**, Utrechtseweg 232, is open 11 am to 5 pm weekdays and from noon on Sunday – get there on bus No 1.

Hoge Veluwe

Stretching for nearly 5500 hectares, the Hoge Veluwe is a mix of forests and woods, shift-

ing sands and heathery moors. It's home to red deer, wild boar, moufflon (a Mediterranean goat), and the **Kröller-Müller Museum** with its vast collection of Van Gogh paintings. The museum is open 10 am to 5 pm, Tuesday to Sunday.

The park is best seen on foot or bicycle – the latter are available free of charge at the park entrances or from the visitors centre inside the park.

To get to the park, take the special bus (No 12) which leaves from Stationsplein in Arnhem at least four times daily from 1 April to 30 October. A return ticket costs f9 (concession f5.50).

The park is open 8 am to sunset daily and costs f8 (concession f4) and f8.50 for a car. A combination ticket for the park and the museum costs f16 (concession f8). The yearly Museumjaarkaart is not valid.

PLACES TO STAY & EAT

The **Alteveer Hostel** (☎ 442 01 14, Diepenbrocklaan 27) is to the north of town, 10 minutes on bus No 3. **Pension Parkzicht** (☎ 442 06 98, fax 443 62 02, Apeldoornsestraat 16) is 10 minutes' walk downhill from the station and has singles/doubles for f52.50/95. Almost opposite the train station is **Hotel Haarhuis** (☎ 442 74 41, fax 442 74 49, Stationsplein 1), a chain hotel with comfortable rooms for f175/240.

Terrace cafes rim the Korenmarkt – **Wampie** is the oldest and trendiest. **Mozaïk** (☎ 351 55 65, Ruiterstraat 43) is a popular Turkish restaurant, and has some vegetarian meals (f30).

GETTING THERE & AWAY

Trains to Amsterdam (f25, 65 minutes) and Rotterdam (f30.50, 75 minutes) go via Utrecht (f17.25, 40 minutes), while the line south passes Den Bosch (f17.25, 45 minutes) and continues to Maastricht (f36, two hours).

The Delta Region

The Netherlands' aptly named province of Zeeland ('Sea Land') makes up most of the Delta region. Spread over the south-west corner of the country, it was until recent

NETHERLANDS

decades a solitary place, where isolated islands were battered by howling winds and white-capped seas, and where little medieval towns, nestled somewhere in a protected nook, were seemingly lost in time. But after the 1953 flood (see the History section at the beginning of this chapter) came the decision to defend Zeeland from the sea – and thus bring it into the present day. One by one the islands were connected by causeways and bridges, and the Delta Project (see the Around Middelburg section that follows) became a reality.

The region's main town, Middelburg, makes a good base for exploration or, for something more quaint, head to Willemstad.

MIDDELBURG
☎ 0118 • pop 44,309
Middelburg is the long-time capital of Zeeland. It makes for a pleasant overnight stop and has a handful of worthy sights. The VVV (☎ 65 99 44) is centrally located at Nieuwe Burg 40.

Things to See & Do
Near the VVV is the Gothic **Stadhuis** (Town Hall) which, like much of the central district, was destroyed during the 1940 German blitz that flattened Rotterdam. Dating back to the mid-15th century, it was convincingly restored. A few streets away is **Lange Jan**, the town's other distinctive tower, which rises from the former 12th-century **Abdij** (Abbey) complex. The tower can be climbed from mid-April to 31 October. For insight into the province's history, visit the **Zeeuws Museum** (Zeeland Museum) inside the Abbey.

Places to Stay & Eat
The nearest NJHC hostel, *Kasteel Westhove* (☎ 58 12 54), is in a medieval castle about 15km west between the villages of Domburg and Oostkapelle. It's open mid-March to mid-October – from Middelburg station, take the hourly ZWN bus No 53. In town, *B&B De Kaepstander* (☎ 64 28 48, Koorkerkhof 10) is a quaint place with rooms for f50/90. *Hotel Roelant* (☎ 62 76 59, fax 62 89 73, Koepoortstraat 10) has functional rooms starting at f57/115. A nice spot for a light meal is *Sint Jan* (☎ 62 89 95, St

Janstraat 40), a cosy cafe next to the 16th-century fish market.

Getting There & Away
Trains run regularly to Amsterdam (f48, 2½ hours) and Rotterdam (f33, 1½ hours).

AROUND MIDDELBURG
The disastrous 1953 flood was the impetus for the Delta Project, in which the south-west river deltas were blocked using a network of dams, dikes and a remarkable 3.2km storm-surge barrier. Lowered only in rough conditions, this barrier was built following environmental opposition to plans to dam the Eastern Schelde (Oosterschelde). It can be dropped during abnormally high tides but generally remains open to allow normal tidal movements and the survival of the region's shellfish.

Finished in 1986, the project is explained at **Waterland Neeltje Jans** (☎ 0111-65 27 02), a theme park constructed next to the storm-surge barrier's command centre. Admission to Neeltje Jans includes entry to the Delta Expo and to a dolphin rehabilitation centre, and also allows for a walk on the storm-surge barriers. Open 10 am to 5.30 pm daily (closed Monday and Tuesday from 1 November to 31 March), it costs f20/15 for adults/children. To get there from Middelburg, take the ZWN bus No 104 (30 minutes, twice hourly). If you are driving or hitching, head onto the N57 in the direction of 'Burgh-Haamstede'.

WILLEMSTAD
☎ 0168 • pop 3500
Sitting on the edge of the Delta region but officially part of Brabant province, Willemstad is a picturesque fortified village. Built in the mid-16th century, the village was given to the nation's saviour, William the Silent, in 1582 as compensation for his expenses in leading the Revolt of the Netherlands.

The VVV (☎ 47 60 55, fax 476 054) is at Hofstraat 1. Overnighters will find two mid-range hotels: *Willemstad* (☎ 47 22 50, Voorstraat 42) and *Het Wapen van Willemstad* (☎ 47 34 50, Benedenkade 12).

Public transport to Willemstad is limited to an hourly bus from Roosendaal or Breda, or buses from Rotterdam (45 minutes).

The North

The Netherlands' northern region is made up of several provinces, including Fryslân and Groningen. Capped by the Frisian Islands, the region's shores are washed by the shallow Waddenzee which is home to a small number of seals and the unique Dutch sport of wadlopen (see the Groningen section).

Even to the Dutch, the lake-land province of Fryslân is a bit 'different' from the rest of the Netherlands. Here the people have their own flag, anthem and language – Frysk (Frisian). The province's name was officially changed from Friesland to Fryslân (as it is spelt in Frysk) in 1996.

AFSLUITDIJK

The 30km long Afsluitdijk, or 'Enclosing Dyke', connects the provinces of North Holland and Fryslân and transformed the old Zuiderzee into the IJsselmeer lake. Driving along the dike's A7 motorway, you'll pass the Stevinsluizen, sluices named after the 17th-century engineer Henri Stevin, who first mooted the idea of reclaiming the Zuiderzee.

Tours to Fryslân from Amsterdam usually take in the Afsluitdijk. Otherwise, without your own wheels, you can cross it on the hourly bus No 350 from Alkmaar to Leeuwarden, but not by train.

LEEUWARDEN

☎ 058 • 88,717

As the economic and cultural capital of Fryslân, Leeuwarden radiates an air of proud independence. The city developed from three *terp* (artificial dwelling mound) settlements which merged in the 15th century, though it's better remembered as the birthplace of Mata Hari, the dancer executed by the French in 1917 on suspicion of spying for the Germans.

The VVV (☎ 0900-202 40 60, fax 215 35 93), Stationsplein 1, has city and provincial information. More can be gained from the Frisian Museum, Turfmarkt 11, as well as at the Frisian Literair Museum, Grote Kerkstraat 21, a literary museum occupying Mata Hari's former house.

For a cheap hotel, head to *De Pauw* (☎ 212 36 51, fax 216 07 93, Stationsweg 10), conveniently located near the train and bus stations.

More central and comfortable is *Hotel 't Anker* (☎ 212 52 16, fax 212 82 93, Eewal 69) with rooms for f85/120.

From Amsterdam there are hourly trains to Leeuwarden (f48, two hours), or you can take bus No 350 from Alkmaar across the Afsluitdijk.

GRONINGEN

☎ 050 • pop 169,044

This lively provincial capital has been an important trading centre since the 13th century. Its prosperity increased with the building in 1614 of the country's second oldest university and, later, the discovery of natural gas. The VVV (☎ 313 97 74, fax 313 63 58), Gedempte Kattendiep 6, is halfway between the train station and the city centre.

The city's colourful Groninger Museum, Museumeiland 1, is opposite the train station. It's open 10 am to 5 pm Tuesday to Sunday.

Groningen is the best place to arrange wadlopen, a serious pastime – strenuous and at times dangerous – involving kilometres-long, low-tide walks in mud that can come up to your thighs. To get into the thick of it, contact Dijkstra Wad Walking Tours (☎ 0595-528 300) at Pieterburen to the north of town.

For overnighters, there's the clean *Simplon* (☎ 313 52 21, Boterdiep 73). This youth centre (take bus No 1 from the train station) has large dorms for f21.50 per person. More centrally, *Hotel Friesland* (☎ 312 13 07, Kleine Pelsterstraat 4) has doubles for f77.

Hourly trains depart from Amsterdam to Groningen (f51, 2½ hours) and from Groningen to Leeuwarden (f15.25, 50 minutes).

FRISIAN ISLANDS

The Netherlands is capped by the Frisian (or Wadden) Islands, a group of five islands including Texel, Ameland and Schiermonnikoog. They are important bird-breeding grounds, as well as being an escape for stressed southerners. Ferries connect the islands to the mainland, and bikes can be hired for getting around.

Texel

☎ 0222

The largest and most populated island, Texel's 30km of beach can seem overrun all summer but even more so in June when the

NETHERLANDS

world's largest catamaran race is staged here. The biggest village is Den Burg where you'll find the VVV (☎ 31 47 41, fax 31 00 54) at Emmalaan 66.

Campers can head to *De Krim Vakantiecentrum* (☎ *39 01 11, fax 39 01 21, Roggeslootweg 6)* in Cocksdorp; it's open all year. The main NJHC hostel (open summer only) is the pleasant *Panorama* (☎ *31 54 41, Schansweg 7)*. *Hotel 't Koogerend* (☎ *31 33 01, fax 31 59 02, Kogerstraat 94)* in Den Burg is moderately priced.

Trains from Amsterdam to Den Helder (f23.25, 1½ hours) are met by a bus that whips you to the awaiting, hourly car ferry. The voyage takes 20 minutes, and costs f10 (concession f5); cars/bicycles are charged f48.50/6.

Ameland
☎ 0519

Ameland is noted for its birds and four quaint villages. The main one, Nes, is home to the VVV (☎ 54 65 46, fax 54 29 32), Rixt van Doniastraat 2.

Camping Duinoord (☎ *54 20 70, fax 54 21 46, Jan van Eijckweg 4)* is in Nes. The NJHC *hostel* (☎ *55 53 53, Oranjeweg 59)* is near the lighthouse at Hollum – get bus No 130 from Nes. *Hotel Nobel* (☎ *55 41 57, fax 55 45 15, ⓔ nobel@xs4all.nl, Kosterweg 16)*, in the quiet village of Ballum, has rooms for f75/110.

From Leeuwarden, take bus No 60 to the port at Holwerd. On weekdays there are six boats a day; weekends have four (hourly services from 1 June to 31 August). Returns cost f20.50 (concession f10.80) and f9.70 for bikes, and cars start at f140. The journey takes 45 minutes.

Schiermonnikoog
☎ 0519

With one of the nation's most tongue-tying names, Schiermonnikoog is the smallest island of the group and off-limits to cars. In the only village, about 3km from the ferry terminus, you'll find the VVV (☎ 53 12 33), Reeweg 5.

Two accomodation options are *Camping Seedune* (☎ *53 13 98, Seeduneweg 1)*, or *Hotel Tjattel* (☎ *53 11 33, Langestreek 94)* which has singles/doubles for f120/240.

There are four ferries (three on Sunday) from the village of Lauwersoog, between

Leeuwarden and Groningen. To get there from Leeuwarden take bus No 50; from Groningen, use bus No 63. The voyage takes 45 minutes each way and return tickets cost f21.70 (concession f12) and f10 for a bike.

The South-East

Sprinkled with woods, heather and the odd incline, the Netherlands' south-eastern corner is made up of the North Brabant and Limburg provinces. Its two main towns, Den Bosch and Maastricht, are intimate and energetic.

DEN BOSCH
☎ 073 ● pop 127,200

Den Bosch (officially known as 's-Hertogenbosch, 'The Count's Forest') is the capital of North Brabant. The town's pedestrianised centre is based around the Markt, a 10-minute walk east of the train station. The VVV (☎ 0900-112 23 34), Markt 77, is housed in the town's oldest building.

Things to See

The **Noordbrabants Museum**, Verwersstraat 41, features exhibits about Brabant life and art from earlier times. It's open 10 am to 5 pm Tuesday to Friday, from noon on weekends.

The **St Janskathedraal** is one of the most ornate churches in the Netherlands. It's a few minutes' walk from the Markt at the end of Kerkstraat, the main shopping thoroughfare.

Places to Stay & Eat

For accommodation there's *Hotel All Inn* (☎/*fax 613 40 57, Gasselstraat 1)*, one block east of the Markt, with basic rooms for f45 per person (breakfast is f10). Considerably more upmarket is *Hotel Central* (☎ *692 69 26, fax 614 56 99, ⓔ info@hotel-central.nl, Burg Leofffplein 98)*. This place overlooks the Markt (though the entrance is round the rear) and has modern rooms for f210/260 (breakfast f25).

Van Puffelen (☎ *689 04 14, Molenstraat 4)* is a spacious eetcafé (closed Monday) with eclectic cuisine (including vegetarian dishes). *De Leeuwenborgh* (☎ *692 69 26, Markt 51)* is more refined and does good local cuisine (mains are f30 to f46). For a sweet local snack try a *Bossche Bol*, a big chocolate-coated blob bought from bakeries.

Getting There & Away

Trains run regularly to Amsterdam (f23.25, one hour) via Utrecht (f13.25, 30 minutes), and to Arnhem (f17.25, 45 minutes) and Maastricht (f33, 1½ hours).

MAASTRICHT

☎ 043 • pop 120,796

The Netherlands' oldest city, Maastricht sits at the bottom end of the thin finger of land that juts down between Belgium and Germany – and is influenced by them both. Capital of the largely Catholic Limburg province, its history stretches back to 50 BC, when the Romans set up camp on a bank of the Maas River.

Today, spanning both banks, this lively city has a reputation even in its own country as being something a little 'foreign'.

Information

The west bank of the Maas is the city's main hub. Here you'll find the old, now largely pedestrianised, centre and its trendy Stokstraat quarter. On the east bank there's the Wyck, an area of 17th-century houses, intimate cafes and bars and, further south, Céramique, the new showpiece quarter.

The GWK money exchange office at the train station is open 8 am to 9 pm daily. The main post office is at Grote Staat 5. There's a (serviced) laundry, Wasserij Huysmans, at Boschstraat 82. For Internet access go to the Stadsbibliotheek (☎ 350 56 00) in the Centre Céramique, Ave Céramique 50.

Tourist Offices The VVV (☎ 325 21 21) is housed in Het Dinghuis ('The Thing House') on the corner of Kleine Staat and Jodenstraat. It's open 9 am to 5 or 6 pm Monday to Saturday (from May to October also 11 am to 3 pm Sunday).

Things to See & Do

The VVV has a brochure on a walk around the fortification walls which still partly surround the city.

The premier museum, **Bonnefanten**, Ave Céramique 250 in Céramique, features art

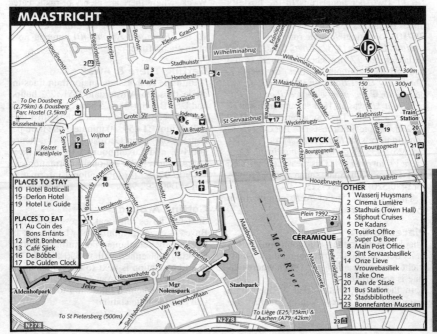

MAASTRICHT

PLACES TO STAY
10 Hotel Botticelli
15 Derlon Hotel
19 Hotel Le Guide

PLACES TO EAT
11 Au Coin des Bons Enfants
12 Petit Bonheur
13 Café Sjiek
16 De Böbbel
17 De Gulden Clock

OTHER
1 Wasserij Huysmans
2 Cinema Lumière
3 Stadhuis (Town Hall)
4 Stiphout Cruises
5 De Kadans
6 Tourist Office
7 Super De Boer
8 Main Post Office
9 Sint Servaasbasiliek
14 Onze Lieve Vrouwebasiliek
18 Take One
20 Aan de Stasie
21 Bus Station
22 Stadsbibliotheek
23 Bonnefanten Museum

NETHERLANDS

and architecture from the Limburg area, and is open 11 am to 5 pm Tuesday to Sunday. Admission costs f10 (concession f7.50). Visit its Web site at www.bonnefantenmuseum.nl.

The main basilica is the 10th-century **Sint Servaasbasiliek** on Vrijthof (entrance on Keizer Karelplein). It's large and somewhat stark, but has a rich treasure house of religious artefacts. Open 10 am to 4 or 5 pm daily (to 6 pm in July and August), entry to the treasury costs f4/1 for adults/children.

Farther south, on the Onze Lieve Vrouweplein, is **Onze Lieve Vrouwebasiliek**, a smaller Gothic structure.

Stiphout Cruises (☎ 351 53 00), Maaspromenade 27, operates 50-minute boat trips along the Maas River for f11 (concession f7).

Places to Stay

The closest camping ground is the four-star **De Dousberg** (☎ 343 21 71, Dousbergweg 102). It's 700m from **Dousberg Parc Hostel** (☎ 346 67 66, fax 346 67 55, Dousbergweg 4), which is 5km west of the train station. Bus No 11 (two per hour) runs to the hostel's front door. At night a Call-Bus will get you there. It charges f34 for a bed in a dorm, or f93/108 for a single/double room.

Hotel Le Guide (☎ 321 61 76, fax 325 99 13, Stationsstraat 17) has cheerful rooms (some with private bathroom facilities) for f98/117. The lovely **Hotel Botticelli** (☎ 352 63 00, fax 352 63 36, ✉ reception@botticellihotel.nl, Papenstraat 11) was an 18th-century mansion of a wine merchant. The rooms range from f130 to f275, and breakfast costs f22. For even more comfort there's the **Derlon Hotel** (☎ 321 67 70, fax 325 19 33, ✉ derlon@hospitality.nl, Onze Lieve Vrouweplein 6). This pleasant hotel is on the city's most charming square and has rooms for f420/520; breakfast is f37.

The VVV has a list of **B&Bs** ranging from f55 to f80 per person.

Places to Eat

Thanks mainly to the gastronomic influences of its Belgian and German neighbours, Maastricht ranks high among the Dutch where cuisine is concerned.

In the centre, Platielstraat is lined with restaurants and cafes. Nearby, there's **De** **Bóbbel** (☎ 321 74 13, Wolfstraat 32), a charming brown cafe with decent snacks for about f12. A range of regional specialities (mains from f31) is offered by the **De Gulden Clock** (☎ 325 27 09), Wycker Brugstraat 54.

For fabulous food and informal dining (reservations not taken) head to **Café Sjiek** (☎ 321 01 58, St Pieterstraat 13), an atmospheric little eetcafé that has been around for years. Two options for good French food are **Petit Bonheur** (☎ 321 51 09, Achter de Molens 2) or the more expensive **Au Coin des Bons Enfants** (☎ 321 23 59, Ezelmarkt 4), where mains range from f40 to f60.

Picnic supplies can be bought from **Super de Boer** supermarket on Kleine Staat.

Entertainment

If the weather's good, Vrijthof and the more intimate Onze Lieve Vrouweplein are taken over by people-watching terrace cafes. **De Kadans** (☎ 326 17 00, Kesselkade 62), a big bistro-cum-disco, is the most happening spot in town. Alternatively, cross the river to the Wyck, where there are plenty of rustic cafes including **Take One** (Rechtstraat 28), a beer specialist's haven. **Cinema Lumière** (☎ 321 40 80, Bogaardenstraat 40) screens non-mainstream films.

Getting There & Away

Within the Netherlands, major train lines include those to Amsterdam (f51, 2½ hours) and Den Bosch (f33, 1½ hours). Major international connections include those to Liège in Belgium (f14.50, 30 minutes, one train per hour), Cologne in Germany (f38, 1½ hours, hourly), and Luxembourg City (f59, three hours, hourly). For national information call ☎ 0900-92 92; for international information call ☎ 0900-92 96.

Getting Around

Stadsbus buses run local routes, as do Call-Buses – evening minibuses which must be booked by telephone. For information or bookings on either, call ☎ 350 57 07. The main bus station is next to the train station. Bikes can be hired at Aan de Stasie (☎ 321 11 00), Stationsplein, a bike shop to the left as you exit the train station.

Portugal

Spirited yet unassuming, Portugal has a dusty patina of faded grandeur; the quiet remains of a far-flung colonialist realm. Even as it flows towards the economic mainstream of the European Union (EU) it still seems to gaze nostalgically over its shoulder and out to sea.

For visitors, this far side of Europe offers more than beaches and port wine. Beyond the crowded Algarve, one finds wide appeal: a simple, hearty cuisine based on seafood and lingering conversation, an enticing architectural blend wandering from the Moorish to Manueline to surrealist styles, and a changing landscape that occasionally lapses into impressionism. Like the *emigrantes* (economically inspired Portuguese who eventually find their way back to their roots), *estrangeiros* (foreigners) who have tasted the real Portugal can only be expected to return.

Facts about Portugal

HISTORY

The early history of Portugal goes back to the Celts who settled the Iberian Peninsula around 700 BC. A subsequent pattern of invasion and reinvasion was established by the Phoenicians, Greeks, Romans and Visigoths.

In the 8th century the Moors crossed the Strait of Gibraltar and commenced a long occupation which introduced Islamic culture, architecture and agricultural techniques to Portugal. The Moors were ejected in the 12th century by powerful Christian forces in the north of the country who mobilised attacks against them with the help of European Crusaders.

In the 15th century Portugal entered a phase of conquest and discovery inspired by Prince Henry the Navigator. Explorers such as Vasco da Gama, Ferdinand Magellan and Bartolomeu Diaz discovered new trade routes and helped create an empire that, at its peak, extended to Africa, Brazil, India and the Far East. This period of immense power and wealth ended in 1580 when Spain occupied

AT A GLANCE	
Capital	Lisbon
Population	10 million
Official Language	Portuguese
Currency	1 Portuguese escudo = 100 centavos
Time	GMT/UTC+0100
Country Phone Code ☎	351

the Portuguese throne. The Portuguese regained it within 90 years, but their imperial momentum had been lost.

At the close of the 18th century Napoleon mounted several invasions of Portugal, but was eventually trounced by the troops of the Anglo-Portuguese alliance.

A period of civil war and political mayhem in the 19th century culminated in the abolition of the monarchy in 1910 and the founding of a democratic republic.

A military coup in 1926 set the stage for the dictatorship of António de Oliveira Salazar, who clung to power until his death in 1968. General dissatisfaction with his regime and a ruinous colonial war in Africa led to the

PORTUGAL

To Tuy

Valença
Arcos de
Valdevez
Parque Nacional da
Peneda-Gerês
Verin
Viana do Castelo
Montalegre
Bragança
Ponte
de Lima
Caldas do
Gerês
Chaves
Barcelos
Braga
Guimarães
Amarante
Mirandela
TRÁS-OS-MONTES
Miranda
do Douro
To Zamora
Porto
Vila Real
Peso da
Régua
Douro
Pocinho
SPAIN
DOURO
Rio
Lamego
BEIRA ALTA
ATLANTIC
OCEAN
Aveiro
Viseu
Guarda
Vilar Formoso
Luso &
Buçaco
Forest
Seia
Gouveia
Manteigas
To Salamanca
BEIRA
Pampilhosa
Torre
(1993m)
Penhas da Saúde
Covilhã
Figueira da Foz
Coimbra
Serra da
Estrela
Parque Natural
da Serra da Estrela
LITORAL
Lousã
BEIRA BAIXA
Monsanto
Leiria
Castelo
Branco
Nazaré
Batalha
Fátima
Tomar
Alcobaça
Entroncamento
To Cáceres
Peniche
Santarém
Tejo
Castelo de Vide
Marvão
Óbidos
Rio
Portalegre
Ericeira
Mafra
RIBATEJO
ALTO ALENTEJO
Sintra
Vila Franca
de Xira
Estremoz
Badajoz
Cascais
Queluz
LISBON
Arraiolos
Vila
Viçosa
To Seville
Estoril
Évora
Parque Natural
da Arrábida
Setúbal
Reserva Natural do
Estuário do Sado
Monsaraz
SPAIN
Sines
Beja
Serpa
BAIXO
ALENTEJO
To Seville
ATLANTIC
OCEAN
0   50   100km
0   30   60mi
Monchique
Silves
Lagos
ALGARVE
Vila Real de
Santo António
Sagres
Albufeira
Faro
Tavira
To Seville

so-called Revolution of the Carnations, a peaceful military coup on 25 April 1974.

The granting of independence to Portugal's African colonies in 1974-75 produced a flood of nearly a million refugees into the country. The 1970s and early 1980s saw extreme swings between political right and left, and strikes over state versus private ownership.

Portugal's entry into the EU in 1986 and its acceptance as a member of the European Monetary System in 1992 secured a measure of stability, although the 1990s were troubled by recession, rising unemployment and continuing backwardness in agriculture and education.

Expo '98, which attracted eight million visitors, triggered some vast infrastructure projects and launched Portugal into a new era of economic success. Ensuring further attention (and development) are Porto's status as a European Capital of Culture in 2001, and Portugal's role as host of the European football championships in 2004.

GEOGRAPHY & ECOLOGY

Portugal is about twice the size of Switzerland, just 560km from north to south and 220km from east to west.

The northern and central coastal regions are densely populated. The northern interior is characterised by lush vegetation and mountains; the highest range, the Serra da Estrela, peaks at Torre (1993m). The south is less populated and, apart from the mountainous backdrop of the Algarve, flatter and drier.

CLIMATE

Midsummer heat is searing in the Algarve and Alentejo, and in the upper Douro Valley, but tolerable elsewhere. The north is rainy and chilly in winter. Snowfall is common in the Serra da Estrela.

ECOLOGY & ENVIRONMENT

Portugal has one international-standard national park (70,290-hectare Peneda-Gerês), 11 *parques naturais* (natural parks, of which the biggest and best known is 101,060-hectare Serra da Estrela), eight nature reserves and several other protected areas. The government's Instituto da Conservação da Natureza (ICN; Information Division ☎ 213 523 317), Rua Ferreira Lapa 29-A, Lisbon,

manages them all, though information is best obtained from each park's headquarters.

GOVERNMENT & POLITICS

Portugal has a Western-style democracy based on the Assembleiada República, a single-chamber parliament with 230 members and an elected president. The two main parties are the Socialist Party (Partido Socialista or PS) and the right-of-centre Social Democratic Party (Partido Social Democrata or PSD). Other parties include the Communist Party (PCP) and the new Left Bloc (BE). In October 1999 the Socialist Party under the popular António Guterres was re-elected for a second four-year term.

ECONOMY

After severe economic problems in the 1980s, Portugal has tamed inflation to around 2% and enjoys an annual growth rate of around 3.5%, thanks largely to infrastructure investment and privatisation. Agriculture plays a decreasing role compared with industry and services (eg, telecommunications, banking and tourism). Portugal benefits from low labour costs, a young population and massive EU funding which has helped improve its infrastructure dramatically. In 1999 the country made the grade for European monetary union and smoothly joined the euro currency zone.

POPULATION & PEOPLE

Portugal's population of 10 million does not include the estimated three million Portuguese living abroad as migrant workers.

ARTS
Music

The best-known form of Portuguese music is the melancholy, nostalgic songs called *fado*, popularly considered to have originated with the yearnings of 16th-century sailors. Much on offer to tourists in Lisbon is overpriced and far from authentic. The late Amália Rodrigues was the star of Portuguese fado; her recordings are sold in most record shops in Portugal.

Literature

In the 16th century, Gil Vicente, master of farce and religious drama, set the stage for Portugal's dramatic tradition. Later in that century Luís de Camões wrote *Os Lusíadas,* an

PORTUGAL

epic poem celebrating the age of discovery (available in translation as *The Lusiads*). Camões is considered Portugal's national poet.

Two of Portugal's finest 20th-century writers are poet-dramatist Fernando Pessoa (1888-1935), author of the 1934 *Message*; and the 1998 Nobel Prizewinning novelist José Saramago, whose novels (notably *Baltasar and Blimunda* and *The Year of the Death of Ricardo Reis*) weave together the real and imaginary. Others to try are Eça de Queiroz *(The Maias)* and Fernando Namora *(Mountain Doctor)*. A contemporary Portuguese 'whodunnit', close to the political bone, is *The Ballad of Dog's Beach* by José Cardoso Pires.

Architecture

Unique to Portugal is Manueline architecture, named after its patron King Manuel I (1495-1521). It symbolises the zest for discovery of that era and is characterised by boisterous spiralling columns and nautical themes.

Crafts

The most striking Portuguese craft is the decorative tiles called *azulejos,* based on Moorish techniques of the 15th century. Superb examples are to be seen all over the country. Lisbon has its own azulejos museum.

SOCIETY & CONDUCT

Despite prosperity and foreign influence, the Portuguese have kept a firm grip on their culture. Folk dancing remains the pride of villages everywhere, and local festivals are celebrated with gusto. TV soccer matches, a modern element of male Portuguese life, ensure the continuation of the traditional long lunch break.

The Portuguese tend to be very friendly but socially conservative: win their hearts by dressing modestly outside of the beach resorts, and by greeting and thanking them in Portuguese. Shorts and hats are considered offensive inside churches.

RELIGION

Portugal is 99% Roman Catholic, with fewer than 120,000 Protestants and about 5000 Jews.

LANGUAGE

Like French, Italian, Spanish and Romanian, Portuguese is a Romance language, derived from Latin. It's spoken by over 10 million people in Portugal and 130 million in Brazil, and is the official language of five African nations. Nearly all turismo staff speak English. In Lisbon, Porto and the Algarve it's easy to find English-speakers, but they are rare in the countryside, and among older folk. In the north, you'll find returned emigrant workers who speak French or German.

See the Language Guide at the back of the book for pronunciation guidelines and useful words and phrases. For more, pick up Lonely Planet's *Portuguese phrasebook*.

Facts for the Visitor

HIGHLIGHTS

Tops for scenery are the mountain landscapes of the Serra da Estrela and Peneda-Gerês National Park. Architecture buffs should visit the monasteries at Belém and Batalha, and the palaces of Pena (Sintra) and Buçaco. Combining the best of both worlds are Portugal's old walled towns such as Évora and Marvão. In Lisbon don't miss the Gulbenkian museum, and Europe's largest Oceanarium.

SUGGESTED ITINERARIES

Depending on the length of your stay, you might want to see and do the following:

Two days
  Lisbon
One week
  Devote four or five days to Lisbon and Sintra and the rest to Óbidos and Nazaré.
Two weeks
  As for one week, plus two days in Évora and the rest in the Algarve (including one or two days each in Tavira, Lagos and Sagres).
One month
  As above, plus a day each in Castelo de Vide and Marvão, two in Coimbra, five in the Douro Valley (Porto plus a Douro River cruise) and the remainder in either the Serra da Estrela or the Peneda-Gerês National Park.

PLANNING
When to Go

Peak tourist season is June to early September. Going earlier (late March or April) or later (late September to early October) gives you fewer crowds, milder temperatures, spectacular foliage, and seasonal discounts including up to 50% for accommodation (prices in this chapter are for peak season). The Algarve tourist season lasts from late February to November.

Maps

Michelin's No 940 *Portugal; Madeira* map is accurate and useful even if you're not driving. Maps by the Automóvel Club de Portugal (ACP) are marginally less detailed but more current. For maps and information on the national/natural parks it's best to visit the information offices at or near each park, though even here trekkers will find little of use.

Topographic maps are published (and sold) by two mapping agencies in Lisbon: the civilian Instituto Português de Cartográfia e Cadastro (☎ 213 819 600, fax 213 819 697, ✉ ipcc@ipcc.pt), at Rua Artilharia Um 107, and the military Instituto Geográfico do Exército (☎ 218 520 063, fax 218 532 119, ✉ igeoe@igeoe.pt), on Avenida Dr Alfredo Bensaúde. Porto Editora, Praça Dona Filipa de Lencastre 42, in Porto, stocks the (better) military versions.

TOURIST OFFICES
Local Tourist Offices

Called *postos de turismo* or just *turismos,* local tourist offices are found throughout Portugal and offer information, maps and varying degrees of assistance.

Tourist Offices Abroad

Portuguese tourist offices operating abroad under the administrative umbrella of ICEP (Investimentos, Comércio e Turismo de Portugal) include:

Canada Portuguese Trade & Tourism Commission (☎ 416-921-7376, fax 921-1353, ✉ iceptor@idirect.com) 60 Bloor St West, Suite 1005, Toronto, Ontario M4W 3B8

Spain Oficina de Turismo de Portugal (☎ 91-522 4408, fax 522 2382, ✉ acarrilho@mail2.icep.pt) Gran Via 27, 1st floor, 28013 Madrid

UK Portuguese Trade & Tourism Office (☎ 020-7494 1441, fax 7494 1868, ✉ iceplondt@aol.com) 22-25a Sackville St, London W1X 1DE

USA Portuguese National Tourist Office (☎ 212-354 4403, fax 764 6137, ✉ tourism@portugal.org) 590 Fifth Ave, 4th floor, New York, NY 10036-4785

VISAS & DOCUMENTS
Visas

No visa is required for any length of stay by nationals of EU countries. Those from Canada, Israel, New Zealand and the USA can stay up to 60 days in any half-year without a visa. Others, including nationals of Australia and South Africa, need visas (and should try to get them in advance) unless they're spouses or children of EU citizens.

Portugal is a signatory of the Schengen Convention on the abolition of mutual border controls (see Visas in the introductory Facts for the Visitor chapter), but unless you're a citizen of the UK, Ireland or a Schengen country, you should check visa regulations with the consulate of each Schengen country you plan to visit. You must apply in your country of residence.

Outside Portugal, visa information is supplied by Portuguese consulates. In Portugal, contact the Foreigners Registration Service (Serviço de Estrangeiros e Fronteiras; ☎ 213 585 545), Rua São Sebastião da Pedreira 15, Lisbon, for information. It's open 9 am to noon and 2 to 4 pm weekdays.

EMBASSIES & CONSULATES
Portuguese Embassies & Consulates

Portuguese embassies abroad include:

Australia (☎ 02-6290 1733) 23 Culgoa Circuit, O'Malley, ACT 2606
Canada (☎ 613-729-0883) 645 Island Park Drive, Ottawa, Ont K1Y 0B8
France (☎ 01 47 27 35 29) 3 Rue de Noisiel, 75116 Paris
Ireland (☎ 01-289 4416) Knock Sinna House, Knock Sinna, Fox Rock, Dublin 18
Spain (☎ 91-561 78 00) Calle Castello 128, 28006 Madrid
UK (☎ 020-7235 5331) 11 Belgrave Square, London SW1X 8PP
USA (☎ 202-328 8610) 2125 Kalorama Rd NW, Washington, DC 20008

Embassies & Consulates in Portugal

Foreign embassies in Portugal include:

Canada (☎ 213 164 600) Avenida da Liberdade 196, Lisbon
Consulate: (☎ 289 803 757) Rua Frei Lourenço de Santa Maria 1, Faro

France (☎ 213 939 100) Calçada Marquês de Abrantes 123, Lisbon
(☎ 226 094 805) Rua Eugénio de Castro 352, Porto
Ireland (☎ 213 929 440) Rua da Imprensa à Estrela 1, Lisbon
Spain (☎ 213 472 381) Rua do Salitre 1, Lisbon
(☎ 225 101 685) Rua de Dom João IV 341, Porto
Consulates: (☎ 251 822 122) Avenida de Espanha, Valença do Minho
(☎ 281 544 888) Avenida Ministro Duarte Pacheco, Vila Real de Santo António
UK (☎ 213 924 000) Rua de São Bernardo 33, Lisbon
(☎ 226 184 789) Avenida da Boavista 3072, Porto
Consulate: (☎ 282 417 800) Largo Francisco A Maurício 7, Portimão
USA (☎ 217 273 300) Avenida das Forças Armadas, Lisbon
(☎ 222 080 061) Rua da Reboleira 7, Porto

There are no embassies for Australia or New Zealand. New Zealand has an honorary consul in Lisbon (☎ 213 509 690; from 9 am to 1 pm weekdays); the nearest embassy is in Rome (☎ 39-6-440 29 28). Australian citizens can call the Australian Policy Liaison Office at the Canadian Embassy (or the Australian Embassy in Paris, ☎ 33-1 40 59 33 00).

MONEY
Currency
The unit of Portuguese currency is the escudo, further divided into 100 centavos. Prices are written with a $ sign between escudos and centavos; eg, 25 escudos 50 centavos is 25$50. There are 200$00, 100$00, 50$00, 20$00, 10$00, 5$00, 2$50 and 1$00 coins. Notes currently in circulation are 10,000$00, 5000$00, 2000$00, 1000$00 and 500$00.

There is no limit on the importation of currency. If you leave Portugal with more than 100,000$00 in escudos or 500,000$00 in foreign currency you must prove that you brought in at least this much.

From 1 January 1999, when Portugal joined the European Monetary Union, goods and services were priced in both escudos and euros. The escudo will be withdrawn on 1 July 2002.

Exchange Rates

country	unit		escudos
Australia	A$1	=	128$58
Canada	C$1	=	149$60
euro	€1	=	200$48
France	1FF	=	30$56
Germany	DM1	=	102$51
Japan	¥100	=	204$24
New Zealand	NZ$1	=	99$82
Spain	100 ptas	=	120$49
UK	UK£1	=	333$64
USA	US$1	=	221$90

Exchanging Money
Portuguese banks can change most foreign cash and travellers cheques but charge a commission of around 2500$00. Better deals for travellers cheques are at private exchange bureaus in Lisbon, Porto and tourist resorts.

Better value (and handier) are the 24-hour Multibanco ATMs at most banks. Exchange rates are reasonable and normally the only charge is a handling fee of about 1.5% to your home bank. Few tourist centres have automatic cash-exchange machines.

Major credit cards – especially Visa and MasterCard – are widely accepted by shops, hotels and a growing number of guesthouses and restaurants.

Costs
Portugal remains one of the cheapest places to travel in Europe. On a rock-bottom budget – using hostels or camping grounds, and mostly self-catering – you can squeeze by on US$20 to US$25 a day. With bottom-end accommodation and cheap restaurant meals, figure around US$30. Travelling with a companion and taking advantage of the off-season discounts (see When to Go earlier in this section), two can eat and sleep well for US$60 to US$70 per day. Outside major tourist areas, and in low season, prices dip appreciably.

Concessions are often available on admission fees etc if you're over 65, under 26 or hold a student card.

Tipping & Bargaining
A reasonable restaurant tip is 10%. For a snack, a bit of loose change is sufficient. Taxi drivers appreciate 10% of the fare, and petrol station attendants 50$00 to 100$00.

Good-humoured bargaining is acceptable in markets but you'll find the Portuguese tough opponents! Off season, you can sometimes bargain down the price of accommodation.

Taxes & Refunds

IVA is a sales tax levied on a wide range of goods and services; in most types of shops it's 17%. Tourists from non-EU countries can claim an IVA refund on goods from shops belonging to Europe Tax-Free Shopping Portugal. The minimum purchase for a refund is 11,700$00 in any one shop. The shop assistant fills in a cheque for the refund (minus an administration fee). When you leave Portugal you present goods, cheque and your passport at customs for a cash, postal-note or credit-card refund.

This service is available at Lisbon, Porto and Faro airports (postal refund only at Faro). If you're leaving overland, contact customs at your final EU border point, or call Europe Tax-Free Shopping Portugal (Lisbon ☎ 218 408 813).

POST & COMMUNICATIONS
Post

Postcards and letters up to 20g cost 52$00 within Portugal, 90$00 to Spain, 100$00 to European destinations and 140$00 to destinations outside Europe. For delivery to North America or Australasia allow eight to 10 days; delivery within Europe averages four to six days.

For parcels, 'economy air' (or surface airlift, SAL) costs about a third less than airmail and usually arrives a week or so later. Printed matter is cheapest to send in batches of under 2kg. The post office at Praça dos Restauradores in Lisbon and Porto's main post office are open into the evening and at weekends. Most major towns have a post office with *posta restante* service, though it's not always the main branch. In Lisbon and Porto a charge of 65$00 is levied for each item claimed.

Addresses in Portugal are written with the street name first, followed by the building address and often a floor number with a ° symbol, eg, 15-3°. An alphabetical tag on the address, eg, 2-A, indicates an adjoining entrance or building. R/C (*rés do chão*) means ground floor.

Telephone

In 1999 Portugal completely revised its telephone numbering system. Aside from a few assistance numbers, all domestic numbers now have nine digits. All digits must be dialled from any location, effectively rendering area codes obsolete.

Local calls from public coin telephones start at 30$00, but as the largest acceptable coin is 50$00, these are impractical for long-distance and international calls. Handier and cheaper are 'Credifones', which accept cards sold at newsagents, tobacconists and telephone offices. The cards come in 650$00, 1300$00 or 1900$00 denominations; a youth/student card should get you a 10% discount.

Domestic charges drop by 50% from 9 pm to 9 am on weekdays, and all day Saturday and Sunday. International charges drop by around 10% to 25% from 9 pm to 9 am, and 20% to 50% during the weekend. Hotels typically charge over *three times* the economy/Credifone rate!

A three-minute direct-dial (IDD) evening/weekend call from Portugal using a Credifone costs about 180/90$00 within the EU, 200/90$00 to the USA or Canada, and 360/360$00 to Australia or New Zealand.

To call Portugal from abroad, dial the international access code, then ☎ 351 (the country code for Portugal) and the number. From Portugal, the international access code is ☎ 00. For operator help or to make a reverse-charge (collect) call from Portugal, dial ☎ 172. For domestic inquiries, dial ☎ 118; for numbers abroad, dial ☎ 177. Multilingual operators are available.

For more information on telephoning in Europe, see the Telephones Appendix at the back of this book.

Fax

Post offices operate a domestic and international service called Corfax, costing 820$00 for the first page to Europe and 1250$00 to North America or Australia. Some private shops offer much cheaper services.

Email & Internet Access

Many towns have a branch of the Instituto Português da Juventude or IPJ, a state-funded youth-centre network. Most of these offer free Internet access during certain hours.

Some municipal libraries also have free access. Some newer youth hostels have access for around 500$00 per hour. Internet cafes in bigger towns charge 100$00 to 600$00 (or more) per hour.

INTERNET RESOURCES
Three useful Web sites on Portugal are: A Collection of Home Pages about Portugal (www.well.com/user/ideamen/portugal.html; Portugal Info (www.portugal-info.net); and Excite City.Net (www.city.net/countries/portugal).

BOOKS
Rose Macaulay's *They Went to Portugal* and *They Went to Portugal Too* follow a wide variety of visitors from medieval times to the 19th century. Marion Kaplan's *The Portuguese: The Land and Its People* offers a fine overview of Portugal and its place in the modern world.

Walkers and car tourers should pack the *Landscapes of Portugal* series by Brian & Aileen Anderson, including books on the Algarve, Sintra/Estoril and the Costa Verde. More detailed is *Walking in Portugal* by Bethan Davies and Ben Cole.

NEWSPAPERS & MAGAZINES
Portuguese-language newspapers include the dailies *Diário de Notícias, Público* and *Jornal de Notícias,* and weeklies *O Independente* and *Expresso.* For entertainment listings, check local dailies or seasonal cultural-events calendars from tourist offices.

English-language newspapers published in Portugal include *The News,* with regional editions featuring local news and classified pages, and *Anglo-Portuguese News.* Newspapers and magazines from abroad are widely available in major cities and tourist resorts.

RADIO & TV
Portuguese radio is represented by the state-owned stations *Antena 1, 2* and *3,* by *Rádio Renascença* and by a clutch of local stations. BBC World Service is at 12.095MHz or 15.485MHz short-wave, but reception is poor.

Portuguese TV includes state-run channels RTP-1 (or Canal 1) and RTP-2 (or TV2) and two private channels, SIC and TVI. Soaps *(telenovelas)* take up the lion's share of broadcasting time.

LAUNDRY
There are *lavandarias* everywhere, most specialising in dry-cleaning *(limpeza à seco).* They'll often do wash-and-dry *(lavar e secar)* too, though it may take a day or two. Figure 1500$00 to 2500$00 for a 5kg load.

TOILETS
The rare public toilets are of the sit-down variety, generally clean and usually free. Coin-operated toilet booths are increasingly common in bigger cities. Most people, however, go to the nearest cafe for a drink or pastry and use the facilities there.

WOMEN TRAVELLERS
Outside Lisbon and Porto, an unaccompanied foreign woman is an oddity, and older people may fuss over you as if you were in need of protection. Women travelling on their own or in small groups report few hassles. In Lisbon and Porto, women should be cautious about where they go alone after dark. Hitching is not recommended for solo women anywhere in Portugal.

GAY & LESBIAN TRAVELLERS
In this predominantly Catholic country, there is little understanding or acceptance of homosexuality. But Lisbon has a flourishing gay scene, with an annual Gay Pride Festival (around June 28) and a Gay & Lesbian Community Center (Centro Comunitário Gay e Lésbico de Lisboa; ☎ 218 873 918), Rua de São Lazaro 88, open 4 to 9 pm daily. For information on gay-friendly bars, restaurants and clubs in Lisbon and Porto, check the Web sites www.ilga-portugal.org and www.portugalgay.pt.

DISABLED TRAVELLERS
The Secretariado Nacional de Rehabilitação (☎ 217 936 517, fax 217 965 182), Avenida Conde de Valbom 63, Lisbon, publishes the Portuguese-language *Guia de Turismo* with sections on barrier-free accommodation, transport, shops, restaurants and sights in Portugal. It's only available at its offices.

Turintegra, part of the Cooperativa Nacional Apoio Deficientes (CNAD; ☎/fax 218 595 332), Praça Dr Fernando Amado, Lote

566-E, 1900 Lisbon, keeps a keener eye on developments and arranges holidays and transport for disabled travellers.

DANGERS & ANNOYANCES

The most widespread crime against foreigners is theft from rental cars, followed by pickpocketing, and pilfering from camping grounds. On the increase are armed robberies, mostly in the Algarve, Estoril Coast, parts of Lisbon and a few other cities. But with the usual precautions (use a money belt or something similar, bag your camera when not in use and don't leave valuables in cars or tents) there's little cause for worry. For peace of mind take out travel insurance.

Avoid swimming on beaches which are not marked as safe: Atlantic currents are notoriously dangerous (and badly polluted near major cities).

The national emergency number is ☎ 112 for police, fire and other emergencies anywhere in Portugal.

BUSINESS HOURS

Most banks are open 8.30 am to 3 pm weekdays. Most museums and other tourist attractions are open 10 am to 5 pm weekdays but are often closed at lunchtime and all day Monday. Shopping hours generally extend from 9 am to 7 pm on weekdays, and 9 am to 1 pm on Saturday. Lunch is given serious and lingering attention between noon and 3 pm.

PUBLIC HOLIDAYS & SPECIAL EVENTS

Public holidays in Portugal include New Year's Day, Carnival (Shrove Tuesday; February/March), Good Friday and the following Saturday, Liberty Day (25 April), May Day, Corpus Christi (May/June), National Day (10 June), Feast of the Assumption (15 August), Republic Day (5 October), All Saints' Day (1 November), Independence Day (1 December), Feast of the Immaculate Conception (8 December) and Christmas Day.

Portugal's most interesting cultural events include:

Holy Week Festival Easter week in Braga features colourful processions including Ecce Homo, with barefoot penitents carrying torches.

Festas das Cruzes Held in Barcelos in May, the Festival of the Crosses is known for processions, folk music and dance, and regional handicrafts.

Feira Nacional da Agricultura In June, Santarém hosts the National Agricultural Fair, with bullfighting, folk singing and dancing.

Festa do Santo António The Festival of Saint Anthony fills the streets of Lisbon on 13 June.

Festas de São João Porto's big street bash is the St John's Festival, from 16 to 24 June.

Festas da Nossa Senhora da Agonia Viana do Castelo's Our Lady of Suffering Festival, for three days nearest to 20 August, is famed for folk arts, parades and fireworks.

ACTIVITIES

Off-road cycling (BTT or *bicyclete tudo terrano,* all-terrain bicycle) is booming in Portugal, with bike trips on offer at many tourist destinations (see Tavira, Setúbal, Évora and Peneda-Gerês National Park).

Despite some fine rambling country, walking is not a Portuguese passion. Some parks are establishing trails, though, and some adventure travel agencies offer walking tours (see Lisbon, Serra da Estrela, Porto and Peneda-Gerês National Park).

Popular water sports include surfing, windsurfing, canoeing, white-water rafting and water-skiing. For information on local specialists see Lagos, Sagres and Peneda-Gerês National Park.

Alpine skiing is possible at Torre in the Serra da Estrela from January through March.

The Instituto Português da Juventude (see Lisbon for more on the IPJ) offers holiday programs for 16 to 30-year-olds (visitors too), including BTT, canoeing and rock climbing. Private organisations with activities including these plus trekking, horse riding, caving and hydrospeed (running white-water without a boat) are listed under Lisbon, Porto and Peneda-Gerês National Park.

COURSES

Interlingua in Portimão (☎/fax 282 416 030, ✉ interlingua@mail.telepac.pt) runs a two-hour fun course in Portuguese language basics for 4000$00. Longer courses are offered by Centro de Línguas in Lagos (☎/fax 282 761 070, ✉ cll@mail.telepac.pt); Cambridge School in Lisbon (☎ 213 124 600, fax 213 534 729, ✉ cambridge@mail.telepac.pt), with Porto and Coimbra branches too; Lisbon-based IPFEL (☎ 213 154 116, fax 213 154 119, **@** instituto@ipfel.pt), with a Porto branch; and CIAL-Centro de Linguas in Lisbon (☎ 217 940 448, fax 217 960 783, **@** portuguese@cial.pt), Porto (☎ 223 320 269) and Faro (☎ 289 807 611).

ACCOMMODATION

Most tourist offices have lists of accommodation to suit a range of budgets, and can help you find and book it. Although the government uses stars to grade some types of accommodation, criteria seem erratic.

Camping

Camping is popular, and easily the cheapest option. The multilingual, annually updated *Roteiro Campista* (900$00), sold in larger bookshops, contains details of nearly all Portugal's camping grounds. Depending on facilities and season, most prices per night run to about 300$00 to 600$00 per adult, 300$00 to 500$00 for a small tent and 300$00 to 500$00 per car. Many camping grounds close in the low season.

Hostels

Portugal has 38 *pousadas da juventude* (youth hostels), all part of the Hostelling International (HI) system. Low rates are offset by segregated dorms, midnight curfews and partial daytime exclusion at most (but not all) of them.

In high season, dorm beds cost 1700$00 to 2900$00, and most hostels also offer basic doubles for 3800$00 to 4600$00 (without bath) or 4100$00 to 6500$00 (with). Bed linen and breakfast are included. Many hostels have kitchens where you can do your own cooking, plus TV rooms and social areas.

Advance reservations are essential in summer. Most hostels will call ahead to your next stop at no charge, or you can pay 300$00 per set of bookings (with three days' notice) through the country's central HI reservations office, Movijovem (☎ 213 524 072, fax 213 528 621, **@** movijovem@mail.telepac.pt), Avenida Duque d'Ávila 137, Lisbon.

If you don't already have a card from your national hostel association, you can join HI by paying an extra 400$00 (and having a 'guest card' stamped) at each of the first six hostels where you stay.

Private Rooms

Another option is a private room (*quarto particular*), usually in a private house, with shared facilities. Home-owners may approach you at the bus or train station; otherwise watch for 'quartos' signs or ask at tourist offices. Rooms are usually clean, cheap (4500$00 to 6000$00 for a double in summer) and free from hostel-style restrictions. A variant is a rooming house (*dormida*), where doubles are about 4500$00. You may be able to bargain in the low season.

Guesthouses

The most common types of guesthouse, the Portuguese equivalent of B&Bs, are the *residencial* and the *pensão* (plural *pensões*). Both are graded from one to three stars, and the best are often cheaper and better-run than some hotels. High-season pensão rates for a double start around 5000$00; a residencial, where breakfast is normally included, is a bit more. Many have cheaper rooms with shared bathrooms.

Hotels

The government grades hotels with one to five stars. For a high-season double figure on 15,000$00 to as much as 50,000$00. *Estalagem* and *albergaria* refer to upmarket inns. Prices drop spectacularly in low season. Breakfast is usually included.

Other Accommodation

Pousadas de Portugal are government-run former castles, monasteries or palaces, often in spectacular locations. For details contact tourist offices, or Pousadas de Portugal (☎ 218 481 221, fax 218 405 846), Avenida Santa Joana Princesa 10, 1749 Lisbon.

Private counterparts are operated under a scheme called Turismo de Habitação and a number of smaller schemes (often collectively called 'Turihab'), which allow you to stay in anything from a farmhouse to a manor house; some also have self-catering cottages. Tourist offices can tell you about local Turihab properties.

A double in high season costs a minimum of 16,300$00 in a Pousada de Portugal but just 10,000$00 in a Turihab farmhouse.

FOOD

Eating and drinking get serious attention in Portugal. The fast-food era has been ignored in favour of leisurely dining and devotion to wholesome ingredients.

The line between snacks and meals is blurred. Bars and cafes offer snacks or even a small menu. For full meals try a *casa do pasto* (a simple, cheap eatery), *restaurante*, *cervejaria* (bar-restaurant) or *marisqueira* (seafood restaurant). Lunchtime typically lasts from noon to 3 pm, evening meals from 7 to 10.30 pm.

The *prato do dia* (dish of the day) is often a bargain at around 800$00; the *ementa turística* (tourist menu) rarely is. A full portion or *dose* is ample for two decent appetites; a *meia dose* (half-portion) is a quarter to a third cheaper. The *couvert* – the bread, cheese, butter, olives and other titbits at the start of a meal – cost extra.

Common snacks are *pastéis de bacalhau* (codfish cakes), *prego em pão* (meat and egg in a roll) and *tosta mista* (toasted cheese and ham sandwich). Prices start around 300$00.

Seafood offers exceptional value, especially *linguado grelhado* (grilled sole), *bife de atum* (tuna steak) and the omnipresent *bacalhau* (dried cod) cooked in dozens of ways. Meat is hit-or-miss, but worth sampling are local *presunto* (ham), *borrego* (roast lamb) and *cabrito* (kid). Main-dish prices start around 900$00.

Cafes and *pastelarias* (pastry shops) offer splendid desserts and cakes. Cheeses from Serra da Estrela, Serpa and the Azores are good but pricey.

Local markets offer fresh seafood, vegetables and fruit. Big cities have grocery shops *(minimercadoes)* and many now have vast *hipermercados*.

DRINKS

Coffee is a hallowed institution with its own nomenclature. A small black espresso is a *bica*. Half-and-half coffee and milk is *café com leite*. For coffee with lots of milk at breakfast, ask for a *galão*. Tea *(chá)* comes with lemon *(com limão)* or with milk *(com leite)*. Fresh orange juice is common. Mineral water *(água mineral)* is carbonated *(com gás)* or still *(sem gás)*.

Local beers *(cerveja)* include Sagres in the south and Super Bock in the north. A 20cL draught is called *um imperial*; *uma garrafa* is a bottle.

Portuguese wine *(vinho)* offers great value in all varieties: red *(tinto)*, white *(branco)* and semi-sparkling young *(vinho verde)*, which is usually white but occasionally red. Restaurants often have *vinho da casa* (house wine) for as little as 350$00 per 350ml jug. You can please the most discerning taste buds for under 800$00 a bottle. Port, synonymous with Portugal, is produced in the Douro Valley east of Porto and drunk in three forms: ruby, tawny and white.

ENTERTAINMENT

Portugal has many local festivals and fairs, often centred on saints' days and featuring music, dance, fireworks, parades, handicraft fairs or animal markets. See the earlier Public Holidays & Special Events section.

Fado, the melancholy Portuguese equivalent of the blues (see Music under Facts about Portugal), is offered in *casas de fado* in Lisbon, Coimbra and Porto. More conventional bars, pubs and clubs abound in Lisbon, Porto and the Algarve.

Some bigger towns sponsor summer cultural programs, especially music (rock, jazz and classical) and dance. Ask at tourist offices for free what's-on publications, or see the local newspaper for listings.

Cinemas cost around 800$00 a ticket, with prices often reduced once weekly to lure audiences from their homes. Foreign films are usually subtitled.

SPECTATOR SPORTS

Football (soccer) dominates the sporting scene. The season lasts from August to May and most villages and towns have a team. The three best are Lisbon's Benfica and Sporting, and Porto's FC Porto. Ask the tourist office about forthcoming matches. The fever will peak in 2004 when Portugal hosts the European football championships.

Bullfighting remains popular despite pressure from international animal-rights activists. The season runs from March to October. Portuguese rules prohibit a public kill, though bulls are often dispatched in private afterwards. In Lisbon, bullfights are held at Campo Pequeno on Thursday. Less touristy versions can be seen at the June agricultural fair in Vila Franca de Xira and Santarém.

SHOPPING

Leather goods, especially shoes and bags, are good value, as are textiles such as lace and embroidered linen. Handicrafts range from inexpensive pottery and basketwork to substantial purchases like Arraiolos rugs, filigree jewellery and made-to-order azulejos.

Getting There & Away

AIR

British Airways (BA), TAP Air Portugal and the no-frills carrier Go have daily direct flights from London to Lisbon; BA and TAP also go to Porto and Faro. On most days there are direct links to Lisbon and Porto from Paris, Frankfurt, Amsterdam, Brussels and Madrid.

From the UK, high-season London-Lisbon return fares start about UK£160 with Go (☎ 0845-605 4321). London-Porto via a third-country carrier can be as low as UK£150, and charter fares to Lisbon or Faro start about UK£170. TAP (☎ 0845-601 0932) and BA (☎ 0845-722 2111) both offer youth/ student fares, but the best such deals are with agencies such as Trailfinders (☎ 020-7937 1234), usit CAMPUS (☎ 0870-240 1010) and STA (☎ 020-7361 6161).

France has frequent Portugal connections at reasonable prices. TAP (☎ 08 02 31 93 20) and Air France (☎ 08 02 80 28 02) have youth/student fares but you're better off with agencies like AJF (☎ 01 42 77 87 80), usit CONNECT (☎ 01 43 29 69 50) or Wasteels (☎ 08 03 88 70 00).

For prices from Portugal, ask youth travel agencies usit TAGUS (Lisbon ☎ 213 525 986, Porto ☎ 226 094 146) or Wasteels (Lisbon ☎ 218 869 793, Porto ☎ 225 370 539). TAP (☎ 808 205 700) and BA (☎ 808 212 125) can be contacted at local rates from anywhere in Portugal.

LAND
Bus

Portugal's main Eurolines agents are Internorte (Porto ☎ 226 052 420), Intercentro (Lisbon ☎ 213 571 745) and Intersul (Faro ☎ 289 899 770), serving north, central and southern Portugal, respectively.

UK-based Busabout (☎ 020-7950 1661) is a Europe-wide hop-on-hop-off coach network with stops near hostels and camping grounds, and passes that let you travel as much as you want within a set period. Its Portugal stops are in Porto, Lisbon and Lagos.

Spain Spanish connections of Eurolines (Madrid ☎ 91 327 1381) include Madrid-Lisbon (5700 ptas/6860$00), Madrid-Porto (4560 ptas/5490$00) and Seville-Lisbon (4870 ptas/5870$00), all at least three times weekly; and Seville-Lagos (2630 ptas/3170$00) four to six times weekly.

Spanish operators with Portugal links include AutoRes (☎ 902-19 29 39) and ALSA (Madrid ☎ 91 754 6502), each with twice-daily Madrid-Lisbon services; and Damas (Huelva ☎ 959 25 69 00), running twice daily from Seville to Faro, jointly with the Algarve line EVA. Three times weekly, Transportes Agobe (☎ 902-15 45 68) runs from Granada via Seville and the Algarve to Lisbon, continuing on Saturday to Coimbra and Porto.

The UK & France Eurolines (UK ☎ 08705-143219) runs a variety of services from London (Victoria coach station) via the Channel ferry, with a 7½ hour stopover and change of coach in Paris. These include at least four weekly to Porto (UK£105/770FF one way from London/Paris, 40 hours); five to Lisbon (UK£108/735FF, 42 hours); and two to Faro/Lagos (UK£113/785FF, 45 hours).

The independent line IASA (Paris ☎ 01 43 53 90 82, Porto ☎ 222 084 338, Lisbon ☎ 213 143 979) runs five coaches weekly on four routes: Paris-Viana do Castelo; Paris-Braga; Paris-Porto; and Paris-Coimbra-Lisbon. Its one-way/return fares range from 640/990FF to 695/995FF.

Train
Spain The main rail route is Madrid-Lisbon on the *Talgo Lusitânia* via Valência de Alcántara. The nightly express takes 10½ hours, and a 2nd-class reserved seat costs 6700 ptas/8000$00, a sleeper berth 9300 ptas/11,200$00.

A popular northern route is Vigo-Porto (three expresses daily). Badajoz-Elvas-Lisbon is tedious (two regional services daily, with a change at Entroncamento) but the scenery is grand. There are no direct southern trains: from Seville you can ride to Huelva, change for Ayamonte, bus across the border to Vila Real de Santo António, and catch frequent trains to Faro and Lagos.

The daily Paris-Lisbon train (see the following UK & France section) goes via Salamanca, Valladolid, Burgos, Vitória and San Sebastian.

The UK & France In general, it's only worth taking the train if you can use under-26 rail passes such as Inter-Rail (see the Getting Around chapter at the beginning of this book).

All services from London to Portugal go via Paris, where you change trains (and stations) for the *TGV Atlantique* to Irún in Spain (change trains again). From Irún there are two standard routes: the *Sud-Expresso* across Spain to Coimbra in Portugal, where you can continue to Lisbon or change for Porto; and an express service to Madrid, changing there to the *Lusitânia* to Lisbon. Change at Lisbon for the south of Portugal.

Buying a one-way, 2nd-class, adult/youth London-Lisbon ticket (seat only) for the cheapest route, via the channel ferry, costs UK£166/88; allow at least 30 hours. Tickets for this route are available from bigger train stations or from Connex South Eastern (☎ 0870-001 0174). The Eurostar service to Paris via the Channel Tunnel cuts several hours off the trip but bumps up the cost.

Car & Motorcycle

The quickest routes from the UK are by ferry via northern Spain: from Portsmouth to Bilbao with P&O Stena Line (☎ 08706-003300) and from Plymouth to Santander with Brittany Ferries (☎ 08705-360360). In winter, Brittany sails from Poole or Portsmouth.

Alternatively, motor through France via Bordeaux, and through Spain via Burgos and Salamanca.

DEPARTURE TAX

Airport taxes for return flights between Portugal and other European countries range from about 3000 ptas/3600$00 for Spain to UK£25/9200$00 for the UK. Taxes are included in the ticket price with a scheduled carrier, but payable at check-in with charter flights.

Getting Around

AIR

Flights within Portugal are poor value unless you have a youth/student card. Both PGA Portugália Airlines (Lisbon ☎ 218 425 559) and TAP (☎ 808 205 700) have multiple daily Lisbon-Porto and Lisbon-Faro links, for about 17,100$00 and 16,300$00 respectively; Portugália offers a 50% youth discount. TAP has a daily Lisbon-Faro service connecting with its international arrivals and departures at Lisbon.

BUS

A welter of regional bus companies together operate a network of comfortable, direct intercity *expressos,* fast regional *rápidas,* and *carreiras* which stop at every crossroad. Local weekend services can thin out to nothing, especially up north and when school is out.

A Lisbon-Porto express (3½ hours) costs 2300$00 and Lisbon-Faro (about five hours) costs 2500$00. A youth card should get you discounts of about 20%.

TRAIN

Caminhos de Ferro Portugueses (CP), the state railway company, operates three main services: *rápido* or *intercidade* (IC on timetables), *interregional* (IR) and *regional* (R). Intercidade and interregional tickets cost at least twice the price of regional services, with reservations either mandatory or recommended. A special fast IC service called Alfa links Lisbon, Coimbra and Porto. If you can match your itinerary and pace to a regional service, rail travel is cheaper, if slower, than by bus.

Sample 2nd-class IC/IR fares include 2650/2080$00 for Lisbon-Porto and 2100/1930$00 for Lisbon-Faro.

Children aged four to 12 and adults over 65 travel at half-price. Youth-card holders get 30% off R and IR services (except at weekends). There are also family discounts. One/two/three-week tourist tickets (*bilhetes turísticos)* at 18,500/31,000/43,300$00 are good for 1st-class travel, but worthwhile only if you're practically living on Portuguese trains.

Frequent train travellers may want to buy the *Guia Horário Oficial* (350$00), with all domestic and international timetables, from ticket windows at most stations.

CAR & MOTORCYCLE
ACP (Automóvel Clube de Portugal), Portugal's representative for various foreign car and touring clubs, provides medical, legal and breakdown assistance for members. But anyone can get road information and maps from its head office (☎ 213 180 100, fax 213 180 227), Rua Rosa Araújo 24, Lisbon. ACP emergency help numbers are ☎ 219 429 103 for southern Portugal and ☎ 228 340 001 for northern Portugal.

Petrol is pricey – eg, 185$00 and up for 1L of 95-octane unleaded fuel *(sem chumbo)*, which is readily available.

Road Rules
There are indeed rules, though Portuguese drivers are among Europe's most accident-prone. Although city driving (and parking) is hectic, rural roads have surprisingly little traffic. EU subsidies have paid for major upgrades of the road system, and there are now long stretches of motorway, some of them toll roads.

Driving is on the right. Speed limits for cars and motorcycles are 50km/h in cities and public centres, 90km/h on normal roads and 120km/h on motorways (but 50, 70 and 100km/h for motorcycles with sidecars). Drivers and front passengers in cars must wear seat belts. Motorcyclists and passengers must wear helmets, and motorcycles must have headlights on day and night.

Drink-driving laws are strict, with a maximum legal blood-alcohol level of 0.05%.

Car Rental
Portugal has dozens of local car-rental firms, many offering lower daily rates than international firms. To rent a small car for a week in high season, figure on about UK£200 from the UK or at least 45,000$00 from Portugal (with tax, insurance and unlimited mileage). However, fly-drive packages from international firms or TAP Air Portugal can be good value. You must be at least 25 and have held your licence for over a year (some companies allow younger drivers at higher rates).

BICYCLE
A growing number of towns have bike rental outfits (1500$00 to 3500$00 a day). If you're bringing your own machine, pack plenty of spares. Bikes can no longer be taken with you on trains, though most bus lines will accept them as accompanied baggage, subject to space and sometimes for an extra fee.

LOCAL TRANSPORT
Except in Lisbon or Porto there's little reason to take a municipal bus. Lisbon's underground system is handy for getting around the city centre and out to Parque das Nações, the former Expo site (see the Lisbon section for details). Porto is building its own underground system.

Taxis offer good value over short distances, especially for two or more people, and are plentiful in towns. Fares go up at night and at weekends, and if your trip leaves the city limits.

Enthusiasts for stately progress shouldn't miss the trams in Lisbon and Porto, an endangered species, and the *elevadores* (funiculars and elevators) of Lisbon, Bom Jesus (Braga) and Nazaré. Commuter ferries cross the Rio Tejo all day to/from Lisbon.

ORGANISED TOURS
Gray Lines (☎ 213 522 594, fax 213 560 668), Avenida Praia da Vitória 12-B, Lisbon, organises multiday coach tours throughout Portugal, through local agents or upper-end tourist hotels. The AVIC coach company (☎ 258 806 180), Avenida dos Combatentes 206, Viana do Castelo, offers short tours of the Douro and Lima Valleys. Miltours (☎ 289 890 600), Veríssimo de Almeida 14, Faro, has day trips in the Algarve and elsewhere.

Among unusual offerings by UK agencies are art, music and history tours by Martin Randall Travel (☎ 020-8742 3355) and wine tours by Arblaster & Clarke (☎ 01730-893344). Two of the UK agencies with Portugal hiking holidays are Explore Worldwide (☎ 01252-760000) and Ramblers Holidays (☎ 01707-331133). For references to the adventure-travel specialists within Portugal, see Activities under Facts for the Visitor in this chapter.

Lisbon

pop 663,000

Although it has the crowds, noise and traffic of a capital city, Lisbon's low skyline and breezy position beside the Rio Tejo (River Tagus) lend it a small, manageable feel. Its unpretentious atmosphere, pleasant blend of architectural styles and diverse attractions appeal to a wide range of visitors. Furthermore, Lisbon (Lisboa to the Portuguese) is one of Europe's most economical destinations.

Orientation

Activity centres on the Baixa district, focused at Praça Dom Pedro IV, known by all as the Rossio. Just north of the Rossio is Praça dos Restauradores, at the bottom of Avenida da Liberdade, Lisbon's park-like 'main street'. West of the Rossio it's a steep climb to the Bairro Alto district, traditional centre of Lisbon's nightlife. East of the Rossio, it's another climb to the Castelo de São Jorge and the adjacent Alfama district, a maze of ancient lanes. Several kilometres west is Belém with its cluster of attractions. Parque das Nações, the former Expo '98 site with its grand Oceanarium, lies on the revamped north-eastern waterfront.

Information

Tourist Offices Turismo de Lisboa (☎ 213 433 672, fax 213 610 359) has a new information centre, CRIA (Centro de Representação, Informação e Animação), in Praça do Comércio, dealing specifically with Lisbon inquiries.

A tourist office (☎ 213 463 314, fax 213 468 772) run by ICEP, the national tourist organisation, in the Palácio Foz on Praça dos Restauradores, deals only with national inquiries. Both offices are open 9 am to 8 pm daily.

Other Turismo de Lisboa kiosks are at Rua Augusta, on Largo Martim Moniz and at Belém. A branch (☎ 218 450 660) at the airport is open 6 am to midnight daily. All have free maps and the bimonthly *Follow me Lisboa,* listing sights and current events. All sell the Lisboa Card, good for unlimited travel on nearly all city transport and free or discounted admission to many museums and monuments; a 24/48/72-hour card costs 2100/3500/4500$00.

Money Banks with 24-hour cash-exchange machines are at the airport, Santa Apolónia train station and Rua Augusta 24. A better deal is the exchange bureau Cota Câmbios, Rossio 41, open 9 am to 9 pm daily. Nearly every bank has an ATM machine.

Top Tours (☎ 213 155 885, fax 213 155 873), Avenida Duque de Loulé 108, offers American Express card or travellers-cheque holders commission-free currency exchange, help with lost cards or cheques and holding/forwarding of mail and faxes. It's closed at weekends.

Post & Communications The central post office is on Praça do Comércio. Mail addressed to Posta Restante, Central Correios, Terreira do Paço, 1100 Lisboa, comes here. A telephone office at Rossio 68 is open until 11 pm daily. A more convenient post and telephone office on Praça dos Restauradores is open until 10 pm on weekdays and to 6 pm at weekends. Planet Megastore (see Email & Internet Access) has a cheap fax service.

Email & Internet Access Portugal Telecom's Net Center (☎ 213 522 292), Avenida Fontes Pereira de Melo 38, offers Internet access at 200$00 per half-hour, 9 am to 5 pm weekdays. Access costs 100$00 per quarter-hour at Espaço Ágora (☎ 213 940 170), Rua Cintura, Armazém 1 (behind Santos train station), open 2 pm to 1 am daily; and 175$00 per quarter-hour at a bar called the Web Café (☎ 213 421 181), Rua do Diário de Notícias 126, 4 pm to 2 am daily. Planet Megastore (☎ 217 928 100), Avenida da República 41-B, open 8 am to midnight daily, charges 200$00 per quarter-hour.

Travel Agencies Trusty youth-travel agencies are usit TAGUS (☎ 213 525 986, fax 213 532 715), Rua Camilo Castelo Branco 20; and Wasteels (☎ 218 869 793, fax 218 869 797), Rua dos Caminhos do Ferro 90, by Santa Apolónia train station.

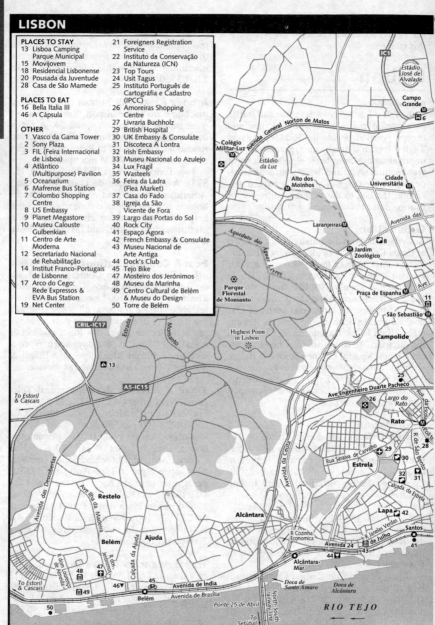

LISBON

PLACES TO STAY
13 Lisboa Camping Parque Municipal
15 Movijovem
18 Residencial Lisbonense
20 Pousada da Juventude
28 Casa de São Mamede

PLACES TO EAT
16 Bella Italia III
46 A Cápsula

OTHER
1 Vasco da Gama Tower
2 Sony Plaza
3 FIL (Feira Internacional de Lisboa)
4 Atlântico (Multipurpose) Pavilion
5 Oceanarium
6 Mafrense Bus Station
7 Colombo Shopping Centre
8 US Embassy
9 Planet Megastore
10 Museu Calouste Gulbenkian
11 Centro de Arte Moderna
12 Secretariado Nacional de Rehabilitação
14 Institut Franco-Portugais de Lisbonne
17 Arco do Cego: Rede Expressos & EVA Bus Station
19 Net Center

21 Foreigners Registration Service
22 Instituto da Conservação da Natureza (ICN)
23 Top Tours
24 Usit Tagus
25 Instituto Português de Cartográfia e Cadastro (IPCC)
26 Amoreiras Shopping Centre
27 Livraria Buchholz
29 British Hospital
30 UK Embassy & Consulate
31 Discoteca A Lontra
32 Irish Embassy
33 Museu Nacional do Azulejo
34 Lux Fragil
35 Wasteels
36 Feira da Ladra (Flea Market)
37 Casa do Fado
38 Igreja da São Vicente de Fora
39 Largo das Portas do Sol
40 Rock City
41 Espaço Ágora
42 French Embassy & Consulate
43 Museu Nacional de Arte Antiga
44 Dock's Club
45 Tejo Bike
47 Mosteiro dos Jerónimos
48 Museu da Marinha
49 Centro Cultural de Belém & Museu do Design
50 Torre de Belém

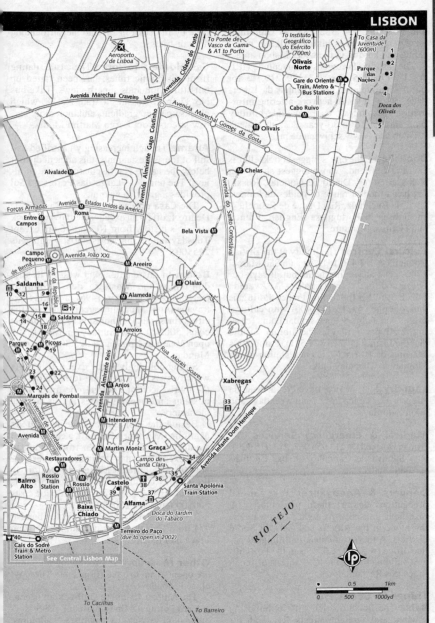

euro currency converter 1 escudo = €0.004

Cabra Montêz (mobile/cellphone ☎ 917 446 668, fax 214 382 285, @ cabramon tez@ip.pt) organises biking, walking, horse riding and karting in the wider Lisbon area.

The Instituto Português da Juventude (IPJ; ☎ 213 179 235, fax 213 179 219, @ ipj .infor@mail.telepac.pt), Avenida da Liberdade 194, is a youth network offering information resources, courses and holiday programs for 16 to 30-year-olds; also check its Web site (www.sejuventude.pt).

Bookshops The city's biggest bookseller is Livraria Bertrand, whose biggest shop is at Rua Garrett 73. Diário de Notícias, Rossio 11, has a modest range of guides and maps. Livraria Buchholz, Rua Duque de Palmela 4, specialises in Portuguese, English, French and German literature.

Cultural Centres The library at the British Council (☎ 213 476 141), Rua de São Marçal 174, opens at varying hours but always between noon and 6 pm weekdays. At Avenida Luis Bivar 91 is the Institut Franco-Portugais de Lisbonne (☎ 213 111 400) with cultural events and a library open similar hours (closing 2.30 pm Friday). The library at the Goethe Institut (☎ 218 824 511), Campo dos Mártires da Pátria 37, is open similar hours Monday to Thursday only.

Laundry Self-service Lave Neve, Rua da Alegria 37, is open until 7 pm weekdays and noon Saturday.

Medical & Emergency Services The British Hospital (☎ 213 955 067, 213 976 329), Rua Saraiva de Carvalho 49, has English-speaking staff.

Dangers & Annoyances Take normal precautions against theft, particularly on rush-hour transport. At night avoid wandering alone in the Alfama and Cais do Sodré districts. A tourist-oriented, multilingual police office (☎ 213 421 634) is in the Foz Cultura building beside the ICEP tourist office in Praça dos Restauradores.

Things to See & Do
Baixa The Baixa district, with its imposing squares and straight streets, is ideal for strolling. From the Rossio, ascend at a stately pace by funicular or lift into the surrounding hilly districts.

Castelo de São Jorge The castle, dating from Visigothic times, has been tarted up but still commands superb views. Take bus No 37 from Rossio, or tram No 28, which clanks up steep gradients and incredibly narrow streets from Largo Martim Moniz.

Alfama Though increasingly gentrified and full of tourist restaurants, this ancient district below the castle is a fascinating maze of alleys. The terrace at **Largo das Portas do Sol** provides a great viewpoint.

The **Casa do Fado**, Largo do Chafariz de Dentro 1, offers an excellent audiovisual look at fado's history from 10 am to 6 pm except Tuesday; admission costs 450$00 (students 225$00).

Belém In this quarter 6km west of Rossio, don't miss the **Mosteiro dos Jerónimos** (Jerónimos Monastery, 1496), a soaring extravaganza of Manueline architecture and the city's finest sight. Admission to the cloisters costs 500$00 (free Sunday morning). It's open 10 am to 1 pm and 2 to 5.30 pm except Monday.

Sitting obligingly in the river a 10-minute walk away is the Manueline **Torre de Belém**, *the* tourist icon of Portugal; the tower's admission and opening times are as for the monastery.

Beside the monastery is the **Museu da Marinha** (Maritime Museum), a collection of nautical paraphernalia open from 10 am to 6 pm except Monday (to 5 pm in winter), for 500$00. The brilliant **Museu do Design**, in the Centro Cultural de Belém opposite, is open 11 am to 7.15 pm daily; admission costs 500$00 (students 250$00).

To reach Belém take the train (or bus No 43) from Cais do Sodré or tram No 15 from Praça da Figueira.

Other Museums The following museums are open 10 am to 6 pm (from 2 pm Tuesday; closed Monday).

The **Museu Calouste Gulbenkian** is considered Portugal's finest museum. Allow several hours to view its paintings, sculptures, jewellery and more. The adjacent **Centro de Arte Moderna** exhibits a cross section of modern Portuguese art. Entry to each costs 500$00 (free to students, children and seniors, and to all on Sunday). The handiest metro station is São Sebastião.

One of Lisbon's most attractive museums is the **Museu Nacional do Azulejo** (National Azulejos Museum) in the former convent of Nossa Senhora da Madre de Deus. Entry costs 400$00. Take bus No 104 from Praça do Comércio (weekdays) or No 59 from Rossio (weekends).

The **Museu Nacional de Arte Antiga** (Antique Art Museum), Rua das Janelas Verdes, houses the national collection of works by Portuguese painters. Admission costs 500$00 (students 250$00; free to all on Sunday morning). From Praça da Figueira take bus No 40 or 60 or tram No 15.

Parque das Nacões The former Expo '98 site, a revitalised 2km-long waterfront area in the north-east, has a range of attractions, notably a magnificent **Oceanarium**, Europe's largest. It's open 10 am to 6 pm daily; entry costs 1500$00 (800$00 seniors and those under 16). Take the metro to Oriente station, an equally impressive Expo project.

Organised Tours

Carris (☎ 213 613 000) offers tours by open-top bus (2000$00) and tram (2800$00). Transtejo (☎ 218 820 348) runs cruises on the Tejo for 3000$00 from the Terreiro do Paço ferry terminal.

Places to Stay

Camping *Lisboa Camping – Parque Municipal* (☎ 217 623 100, Parque Florestal de Monsanto) is 6km north-west of Rossio. Take bus No 43 from Cais do Sodré.

Hostels The central *pousada da juventude* (☎ 213 532 696, Rua Andrade Corvo 46) is open 24 hours a day.

The closest metro station is Picoas, or take bus No 46 from Santa Apolónia station or Rossio.

The newer *casa da juventude* (☎ 218 920 890, Via de Moscavide) is 1km north of Gare do Oriente. Take bus No 44 from Praça dos Restauradores or Oriente to the Avenida da

Boa Esperança roundabout; the hostel is 250m down the road.

Reservations are essential at both hostels.

Hotels & Guesthouses In high season – and for central hotels at any time – advance bookings are imperative.

Baixa & Restauradores Adequate doubles with shared bath start around 4000$00 at homely *Pensão Santo Tirso* (☎ 213 470 428, Praça Dom Pedro IV 18, 3rd floor) and 5000$00 at *Pensão Prata* (☎ 213 468 908, Rua da Prata 71, 4th floor) and *Pensão Arco da Bandeira* (☎ 213 423 478, Rua dos Sapateiros 226, 3rd floor).

Slightly pricier are Pensão Duque (☎ 213 463 444, Calçada do Duque 53) and Pensão Norte (☎ 218 878 941, Rua dos Douradores 159, 2nd floor).

More salubrious, with doubles around 7000$00, are *Pensão Imperial* (☎ 213 420 166, Praça dos Restauradores 78, 4th floor) and friendly *Hospedaria Bons Dias* (☎ 213 471 918, Calçada do Carmo 25, 5th floor). Old-fashioned *Pensão Residencial Alcobia* (☎ 218 865 171, fax 218 865 174, Poço do Borratém 15) has doubles for 8000$00 with breakfast. Brighter, security-conscious *Pensão Residencial Gerês* (☎ 218 810 497, fax 218 882 006, Calçada do Garcia 6) charges 9000$00 (without breakfast).

Bairro Alto & Rato Near the Elevador da Glória, pleasant *Pensão Globo* (☎ 213 462 279, Rua do Teixeira 37) has doubles without bath from 4500$00. *Pensão Londres* (☎ 213 462 203, fax 213 465 682, Rua Dom Pedro V 53) has spacious rooms, the upper ones with great views; doubles start at 7200$00. *Casa de São Mamede* (☎ 213 963 166, fax 213 951 896, Rua Escola Politécnica 159) has doubles in an elegant old house for 15,000$00.

Marquês de Pombal & Saldanha The *Residencial Lisbonense* (☎ 213 544 628, Rua Pinheiro Chagas 1) has bright doubles from 8000$00.

A three-star hotel with the facilities of a four-star is *Hotel Presidente* (☎ 213 539 501, fax 213 520 272, Rua Alexandre Herculano 13) with doubles for 16,000$00.

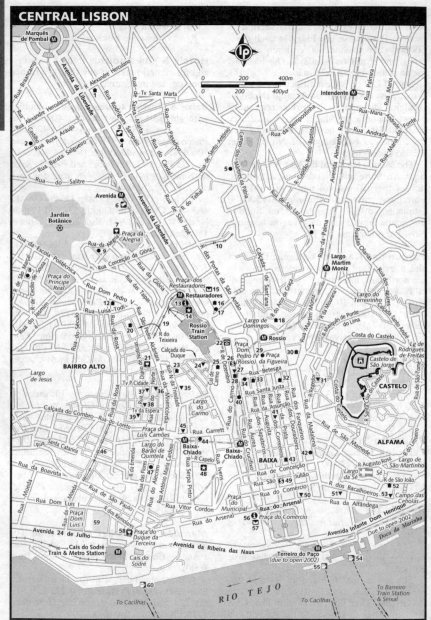

CENTRAL LISBON

CENTRAL LISBON

	PLACES TO STAY	39	Adega do Ribatejo	15	Post & Telephone Office
1	Hotel Presidente		(Casa de Fado)	17	ABEP Ticket Kiosk
12	Pensão Londres	41	Adega Regional da Beira	19	Elevador da Glória
16	Pensão Imperial	45	Café A Brasileira	21	Web Café
18	Pensão Residencial Gerês	50	Martinho da Arcada	22	Telephone Office
20	Pensão Globo	51	Hua Ta Li	26	Cota Câmbios
23	Pensão Duque	53	Solar do Vez	29	Carris Kiosk
25	Hospedaria Bons Dias			34	Diário de Notícias
28	Pensão Santo Tirso		OTHER	40	Elevador de Santa Justa
30	Pensão Residencial Alcobia	2	Automóvel Clube de Portugal	42	Santos Ofícios
32	Pensão Norte		(ACP)	44	Livraria Bertrand
33	Pensão Arco da Bandeira	3	Canadian Embassy	46	Elevador da Bica
43	Pensão Prata	4	Instituto Português da	47	Fabrica Sant'Ana
52	Pensão São João da Praça &		Juventude (IPJ)	48	Police Sation
	Sé Guest House	5	Goethe Institut	49	24-Hour Cash Exchange
		6	Spanish Embassy		Machine
	PLACES TO EAT	7	Hot Clube de Portugal	54	Terreiro do Paço Ferry Terminal
24	Restaurante O Sol	8	British Council	55	Cais de Alfândega Ferry
27	Nicola	9	Lave Neve		Terminal
31	São Cristóvão	10	Elevador de Lavra	56	Turismo de Lisboa (CRIA)
35	Cervejaria da Trindade	11	Gay & Lesbian Community	57	Central Post Office
36	Sinal Vermelho		Centre	58	Ó Gilíns Irish Pub
37	Adega Machado (Casa de	13	ICEP National Tourist Office	59	Mercado da Ribeira
	Fado)		& Turismo de Lisboa	60	Cais do Sodré Car Ferry
38	A Primavera	14	Tourist Police Post		Terminal

Alfama Behind the cathedral, at Rua São João da Praça 97, popular *Pensão São João da Praça* (*☎/fax 218 862 591*) on the 2nd floor and genteel *Sé Guest House* (*☎ 218 864 400*) on the 1st floor have doubles from 6000$00 to 12,000$00 (with breakfast).

Places to Eat

There are dozens of restaurants and cafes in the Baixa (best for lunchtime bargains) and Bairro Alto (pricier evening venues). A trendier restaurant and bar zone is riverside Doca de Santo Amaro, near Alcântara-Mar station. The main market, Mercado da Ribeira, is near Cais do Sodré station.

Baixa & Alfama *Adega Regional da Beira* (*☎ 213 467 014, Rua dos Correeiros 132*) is one of many reasonably priced places along this street. Vegetarian *Restaurante O Sol* (*☎ 213 471 944, Calçada do Duque 23*) offers set meals for under 1000$00. A bargain Chinese restaurant is *Hua Ta Li* (*☎ 218 887 91 70, Rua dos Bacalhoeiros 109*).

Among several restaurants with outdoor seating in lower Alfama, *Solar do Vez* (*☎ 218 870 794, Campo das Cebolas 48*) has an ap-

pealing simplicity. *São Cristóvão* (*☎ 218 885 578, Rua de São Cristóvão 30*) is famous for its Cape Verdean dishes.

For a coffee or a meal, two late 19th/early 20th century cafes are *Nicola* (*☎ 213 460 579, Rossio 24*) and *Martinho da Arcada* (*☎ 218 879 259, Praça do Comércio 3*). The literary pedigree of *Café A Brasileira* (*☎ 213 469 547, Rua Garrett 120*) is symbolised by the bronze figure of Fernando Pessoa outside.

Bairro Alto & Saldanha Tiny *Restaurante A Primavera* (*☎ 213 420 477, Travessa da Espera 34*) has a family ambience complemented by honest cooking. Smarter and pricier (with great desserts) is *Restaurante Sinal Vermelho* (*☎ 213 461 252, Rua das Gáveas 89*).

Cervejaria da Trindade (*☎ 213 423 506, Rua Nova da Trindade 20-C*) is a converted convent decorated with azulejos. Main dishes start at around 1400$00.

Bright and cheerful *Bella Italia III* (*☎ 213 528 636, Avenida Duque d'Ávila 40-C*) is a pastelaria-cum-restaurant, with pizzas and half-portions of Portuguese fare for under 1000$00.

Belém A row of attractive restaurants in Belém with outdoor seating includes *A Cápsula* (☎ *213 648 768, Rua Vieira Portuense 72*).

Entertainment

For current listings, pick up the free bimonthly *Follow me Lisboa* or monthly *Agenda Cultural* from the tourist office, or *Público* from a newsstand.

Music Many Lisbon *casas de fado* (which are also restaurants) produce pale tourist imitations of fado at high prices. All have a minimum charge of 2000$00 to 4500$00. In the Bairro Alto, try *Adega Machado* (☎ *213 224 640, Rua do Norte 91*) or the simpler *Adega do Ribatejo* (☎ *213 468 343, Rua Diário de Notícias 23*). The tourist offices can suggest others.

Hot Clube de Portugal (☎ *213 467 369, Praça da Alegria 39*) is at the centre of a thriving jazz scene, with live music three or four nights weekly. It's open 10 pm to 2 am (closed Sunday and Monday).

Ó Gilíns Irish Pub (☎ *213 421 899, Rua dos Remolares 8-10*) is open 11 am to 2 am daily, with live Irish tunes most Saturday nights and jazz with Sunday brunch.

Disco clubs come and go. Try *Luanda* (☎ *213 633 959, Travessa de Teixeira Júnior 6*) or the good *Lux Fragil* (☎ *218 820 890, Avenida Infante Dom Henrique, Cais da Pedra à Santa Apolónia*), both raving from midnight until 5 am. Other bar-discos are by the river: *Rock City* (☎ *213 428 640, Rua Cintura do Porto de Lisboa, Armazém 225*) has live rock nightly except Monday; *Dock's Club* (☎ *213 950 856, Rua da Cintura do Porto de Lisboa 226*) carries on until 4 am nightly except Sunday.

The African music scene (predominantly Cape Verdean) thrives in bars around Rua de São Bento; one of the best known is *Discoteca A Lontra* (☎ *213 956 968, Rua de São Bento 155*), open until 4 am nightly except Monday.

Cinemas Lisbon has dozens of cinemas, including multiscreen ones at *Amoreiras* (☎ *213 878 752*) and *Colombo* (☎ *217 113 222*) shopping complexes. Tickets cost 800$00 (550$00 Monday).

Spectator Sports Lisbon's football teams are Benfica and 2000 national champions Sporting. The tourist offices can advise on match dates and tickets. Bullfights are staged at Campo Pequeno between April and October. Tickets are available at ABEP ticket agency on Praça dos Restauradores.

Shopping

For azulejos, try Fabrica Sant'Ana at Rua do Alecrim 95. The Museu Nacional do Azulejo also has a small shop. Santos Ofícios at Rua da Madalena 87 has an eclectic range of Portuguese folk art. On Tuesday and Saturday, visit the Feira da Ladra, a huge open-air market at Campo de Santa Clara in the Alfama.

Getting There & Away

Air Lisbon is connected by daily flights to Porto, Faro and many European centres (see the introductory Getting There & Away and Getting Around sections of this chapter). For arrival and departure information call ☎ 218 413 700.

Bus A dozen different companies, including Renex (☎ 218 874 871), operate from Gare do Oriente. The Arco do Cego terminal (☎ 213 545 439), Avenida João Crisóstomo, is the base for Rede Expressos (☎ 213 103 111) and EVA (☎ 213 147 710), whose networks cover the whole country.

Train Santa Apolónia station (☎ 218 884 025/027) is the terminus for northern and central Portugal, and for all international services (trains also stop en route at the better-connected Gare do Oriente). Cais do Sodré station is for Belém, Cascais and Estoril. Rossio station serves Sintra.

Barreiro station, across the river, is the terminus for southern Portugal; connecting ferries leave frequently from the pier at Terréiro do Paço.

The North-South railway line, over the Ponte de 25 Abril, goes to suburban areas and will eventually carry farther to southern Portugal.

Ferry Cais da Alfândega is the terminal for several ferries including to Cacilhas (110$00), a transfer point for some buses to Setúbal. A car ferry (for bikes too) runs from Cais do Sodré terminal.

Getting Around

To/From the Airport The AeroBus runs every 20 minutes from 7 am to 9 pm, taking 30 to 45 minutes between the airport and Cais do Sodré, including a stop by the ICEP tourist office. A 460/1075$00 ticket is good for one/three days on all buses, trams and funiculars. Local bus Nos 8, 44, 45 and 83 also run near the ICEP tourist office; No 44 links the airport with Gare do Oriente too. A taxi into town is about 1500$00, plus 300$00 if your luggage needs to go in the boot.

Bus & Tram Individual bus and tram tickets are 80$00 from Carris kiosks, most conveniently at Praça da Figueira and the Santa Justa elevador; tickets bought on board cost 160$00. A four/seven-day Passe Turístico, valid for all trams and buses and the metro, costs 1720/2430$00.

Buses and trams run from 6 am to 1 am, with some night services. Pick up a transport map, *Planta dos Transportes Públicas da Carris*, from tourist offices or Carris kiosks.

Wheelchair users can call the Cooperativa Nacional Apoio Deficientes (☎ 218 595 332) for assistance to hire adapted transport. The clattering, antediluvian trams (*eléctricos*) are an endearing component of Lisbon; try No 28 to Alfama from Largo Martim Moniz.

Metro The metro is useful for hops across town and to the Parque das Nações. Individual tickets cost 100$00; a *caderneta* of 10 tickets is 850$00. A day ticket (*bilhete diário*) is 270$00. The metro operates from 6.30 am to 1 am. Beware of pickpockets during rush hour.

Taxi Lisbon's taxis are plentiful. Flagging them down can be tricky: they're best hired from taxi ranks. Some at the airport are less than scrupulous.

Car & Bicycle Car rental companies in Lisbon include Avis (☎ 800 201 002) and Europcar (☎ 219 407 790). Rupauto (☎ 217 933 258, fax 217 931 768) has cheap rates. Tejo Bike (☎ 218 871 976), 300m east of Belém, rents bikes for 750$00 an hour to ride along the waterfront.

Around Lisbon

SINTRA
pop 20,000

If you take only one trip from Lisbon, make it Sintra. Beloved by Portuguese royalty and English nobility, its thick forests and startling architecture provide a complete change from Lisbon. The tourist office (☎ 219 231 157, fax 219 235 176), at Praça da República 23 in the historic centre, has a good map and accommodation information.

At weekends and during the annual July music festival, expect droves of visitors. In high season it's wise to book accommodation ahead.

Things to See

The **Palácio Nacional de Sintra**, Manueline and Gothic, with Moorish origins, dominates the town with its twin chimneys. It's open 10 am to 5.30 pm except Wednesday; admission costs 600$00 (students 300$00).

One of Sintra's best museums is the **Museu do Brinquedo** on Rua Visconde de Monserrate, with 20,000 toys from around the world. It's open 10 am to 6 pm except Monday, and costs 500/300$00.

An easy 3km climb from the centre leads to the ruined **Castelo dos Mouros** with a fine view over the town and surroundings. It's open 9 am to 7 pm daily. Twenty minutes on is the exuberantly Romantic **Palácio da Pena**, built in 1839. It's open 10 am to 6.30 pm (5 pm in winter) except Monday, for 600/300$00. Cars are prohibited; Stagecoach bus No 434 (600$00) runs regularly from the station via the tourist office.

Rambling, romantic **Monserrate Gardens**, 4km from town, are open 10 am to 5 pm daily (admission free). En route is an extraordinary, mystical mansion, **Quinta da Regaleira**, open 10 am to 6 pm (4 pm in winter) daily, for 2000/1000$00.

Places to Stay

The nearest decent camping ground is *Camping Praia Grande* (☎ 219 290 581), on the coast 11km from Sintra and linked by a frequent bus service. A *pousada da juventude* (☎ 219 241 210) is at Santa Eufémia, 4km from the centre; reservations are essential.

PORTUGAL

Casa de Hóspedes Adelaide (☎ 219 230 873, Rua Guilherme Gomes Fernandes 11), a 10-minute walk from the station, has reasonable doubles without bath from 4000$00. Better-value private rooms are around 4500$00 (the tourist office has a list). Across the tracks, friendly *Piela's (☎ 219 241 691, Rua João de Deus 70 – due to move in 2001 to Avenida Desiderio Cambournac 1-3)* has doubles without bath from around 6000$00.

Places to Eat

Close to the tourist office is the recommended *Tulhas (☎ 219 232 378, Rua Gil Vicente 4-6)*. Simple *A Tasca do Manel (☎ 219 230 215, Largo Dr Vergilio Horta 5)* serves up standards for around 900$00 a dish. Behind the station, *Restaurante Parririnha (☎ 219 231 207, Rua João de Deus 41)* serves great grilled fish. Cavernous *Bistrobar Ópera Prima (☎ 219 244 518, Rua Consiglieri Pedroso 2-A)* has live jazz, soul and blues several nights weekly.

Getting There & Away

The Lisbon-Sintra railway terminates in the district of Estefânia, 1.5km north-east of the historic centre. Sintra's bus station, and another train station, are a further 1km east in the new-town district of Portela de Sintra. Frequent shuttle buses run to the historic centre from the bus terminal.

Trains run every 15 minutes all day from Lisbon's Rossio station. Buses run regularly from Sintra to Estoril and Cascais.

Getting Around

A taxi to Pena or Monserrate costs around 2000$00 return. Horse-drawn carriages are a romantic alternative: figure on 10,000$00 to Monserrate and back. Old trams run from Ribeira de Sintra (1.5km from the centre) to Praia das Maças, 12km to the west.

CASCAIS
pop 30,000

Cascais, the 'in' beach resort on the coast west of Lisbon, is packed with tourists in summer. The tourist office (☎ 214 868 204, fax 214 672 280), Rua Visconde de Luz 14, has accommodation lists and bus timetables; there's also a police post (☎ 214 863 929) here.

Smartprint (☎ 214 866 776), at Rua Frederico de Arouca 45, has Internet access for 155$00 per five minutes.

Things to See & Do

Two kilometres east of Cascais, **Estoril** is an old-fashioned resort with Europe's biggest casino, open 3 pm to 3 am daily. Estoril's Praia Tamariz beach (beside the train station) has an ocean swimming pool.

The sea roars into the coast at **Boca do Inferno** (Hell's Mouth), 2km west of Cascais. Spectacular, windy **Cabo da Roca**, Europe's westernmost point, is 16km from Cascais and Sintra (served by buses from both towns). Long, wild **Guincho** beach, 3km from Cascais, is a popular surfing venue.

Transrent (☎ 214 864 566) at Centro Comercial Cisne, Avenida Marginal (near the post office), rents bicycles and motorcycles.

Places to Stay & Eat

Camping Orbitur do Guincho (☎ 214 871 014, fax 214 872 167) is 7km from Cascais near Guincho beach. *Residencial Avenida (☎ 214 864 417, Rua da Palmeira 14)* has doubles without bath for 6000$00. The tourist office can recommend private rooms from around 5000$00. *Casa da Pergola (☎ 214 840 040, fax 214 834 791, Avenida Valbom 13)* has fancy doubles from 17,000$00.

A Económica (☎ 214 833 524, Rua Sebastião J C Melo 11) serves standard fare at low prices. Try delicious fish kebabs at *A Tasca (Rua Afonso Sanches 61)*.

Getting There & Away

Trains run frequently all day to Estoril and Cascais from Cais do Sodré station in Lisbon.

SETÚBAL
pop 80,000

This refreshingly untouristy city, an easy 50km south of Lisbon, has fine beaches and seafood restaurants, and is a good base for exploring nearby Parque Natural da Arrábida and Reserva Natural do Estuário do Sado.

The tourist office (☎/fax 265 534 402), Praça do Quebedo, is a five-minute walk east from the bus terminal at Avenida 5 de Outubro. A regional tourist office (☎ 265 539 120, fax 265 539 127) is at Travessa Frei Gaspar 10.

The Instituto Português da Juventude (IPJ; ☎ 265 532 707) at Largo José Afonso has free Internet access for limited periods on weekdays. Ciber Centro (☎ 265 234 800), Avenida Bento Gonçalves 21-A, charges 250$00 for 15 minutes. It's open 9 am to 11 pm weekdays.

Things to See

The town's main cultural attraction is the 15th-century **Igreja de Jesus** in Praça Miguel Bombarda, with early Manueline decoration inside. The **Galeria da Pintura Quinhentista** around the corner displays a renowned collection of 16th-century paintings; it's open 9 am to noon and 2 to 5 pm except Sunday and Monday (admission free).

Good **beaches** west of town include Praia da Figuerinha (accessible by bus in summer). Across the estuary at Tróia is a more developed beach, plus the ruins of a Roman settlement. On the ferry trip across you may see some of the estuary's 30 or so bottle-nosed dolphins.

Activities

The Sistemas de Ar Livre (☎ 265 227 685, mobile/cellphone 919 361 725) organises Sunday walks for 1000$00 per person; ask at the tourist office. For jeep safaris, hiking and biking in the Serra da Arrábida, or canoe trips through the Reserva Natural do Estuário do Sado, contact Planeta Terra (☎ 265 532 140), Praça General Luís Domingues 9. Vertigem Azul (☎ 265 238 000), Avenida Luísa Todi 375, offers dolphin-spotting and canoeing trips.

Places to Stay & Eat

A municipal *camping ground (☎ 265 522 475)* is 1.5km west of town. The *pousada da juventude (☎ 265 534 431, Largo José Afonso)* has doubles with bath as well as dorm beds.

Residencial Todi (☎ 265 220 592, Avenida Luísa Todi 244) has doubles without/with bath from 3000/4000$00. *Casa de Hóspedes Bom Amigo (☎ 265 526 290)*, in Praça de Bocage, has well-adorned doubles without bath for around 5000$00. Smarter *Residencial Bocage (☎ 265 543 080, fax 265 543 089, Rua São Cristovão 14)* has doubles for 7500$00.

Cheap restaurants east of the regional tourist office include *Triângulo (☎ 265 233 927, Rua Arronches Junqueiro 76)*. Seafood restaurants line the western end of Avenida Luísa Todi; friendly *Casa do Chico (☎ 265 239 502)* at No 490 is less touristy than most. Popular *Restaurante Antóniu's (☎ 265 523 706, Rua Trabalhadores do Mar 31)* is also recommended.

Getting There & Away

Buses leave frequently from Lisbon's Gare do Oriente and from Cacilhas, a short ferry ride from Lisbon's Cais de Alfândega. Ferries shuttle across the estuary to Tróia regularly; the tourist office has the latest timetable.

The Algarve

Boisterous and full of foreigners, the Algarve is about as far from traditional Portugal as one can get. The focus is on Albufeira and Lagos, with sun, sand and golf (and surfing along the west coast) the draw cards, but there are other attractions: the forested slopes of Monchique, the fortified village of Silves and windswept, historic Sagres. The district capital and largest town is Faro.

Information

The expat-oriented, English-language newspapers with information on entertainment and coming events include the *Algarve News*, *APN* and *Algarve Resident*.

Dangers & Annoyances Theft is a significant problem in the Algarve. Don't leave anything valuable unattended in your vehicle, tent or on the beach.

Swimmers should beware of dangerous currents, especially on the west coast. Beaches are marked by coloured flags: red means no bathing, yellow means yes to wading but no to swimming, green means anything goes.

Shopping

Few souvenirs are actually made in the Algarve, but woollens (cardigans and fishing pullovers) and Moorish-influenced ceramics are good value. Algarviana is a local *amaretto* (bitter almond liqueur), and the salubrious bottled waters of Monchique are sold everywhere.

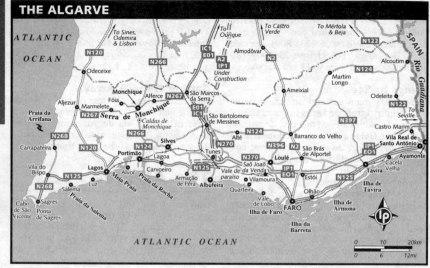

THE ALGARVE

Getting Around

Rede Expressos and EVA together run an efficient network of bus services throughout the Algarve. The IP1/EO1 superhighway, to run the length of the coast, is nearly complete. Bicycles, scooters and motorcycles can be rented everywhere; see town listings.

FARO

pop 40,000

Pleasantly low-key Faro is the main transport hub and commercial centre. The tourist office (☎ 289 803 604, fax 289 800 453) on Rua da Misericórdia has leaflets on just about every Algarve community.

Things to See & Do

The **waterfront** around Praça de Dom Francisco Gomes has pleasant gardens and cafes. Faro's beach, **Praia de Faro**, is 6km southwest of the city on Ilha de Faro; take bus No 16 from opposite the bus station or, from May to September, a ferry from Arco da Porta Nova, close to Faro's port.

At Estói, 12km north of Faro, the romantically ruined **Estói Palace** has a surreal garden of statues, balustrades and azulejos; take the Faro to São Brás de Alportel bus which goes via Estói.

Places to Stay & Eat

A big, cheap **municipal camping ground** (☎ 289 817 876) is on Praia de Faro. The **pousada da juventude** (☎ 289 826 521, Rua da Polícia de Segurança Pública 1) provides double rooms (4200/4600$00 without/with bath) as well as 1900$00 dorm beds. It's open 6 pm to midnight.

Residencial Adelaide (☎ 289 802 383, fax 289 826 870, Rua Cruz dos Mestres 7) is a friendly budget pensão with doubles without/with bath for 5000/6000$00. Close to the bus and train stations is **Pensão Residencial Filipe** (☎/fax 289 824 182, Rua Infante Dom Henrique 55), which has doubles without/with bath for around 6000/7500$00.

Lively **Sol e Jardim** (☎ 289 820 030, Praça Ferreira de Almeida 22) serves good seafood. **A Garrafeira do Vilaça** (☎ 289 802 150, Rua São Pedro 33) is popular for budget meals.

Getting There & Away

Faro airport has both domestic and international flights (see the introductory Getting There & Away section of this chapter).

From the bus station, just west of the centre, there are at least a dozen daily express coaches to Lisbon (about four hours) and frequent buses to other coastal towns.

The train station is a few minutes' walk west of the bus station. Two IR and three IC trains run daily to Lisbon (Barreiro), and about half a dozen each to Albufeira and Portimão.

Getting Around

The airport is 6km from the centre. The Aero-Bus runs into town in summer only (free to those with airline tickets). Bus Nos 14 and 16 run into town until 9 pm (but infrequently in winter). A taxi costs about 1300$00.

TAVIRA

pop 12,000

Tavira is one of the Algarve's oldest and handsomest towns. The tourist office (☎ 281 322 511) is at Rua da Galeria 9. Bicycles and scooters can be rented from Loris Rent next door (☎ 281 325 203). For walking or bike tours call Exploratio (☎/fax 281 321 973, mobile/cellphone 919 338 226). PostNet (☎ 281 320 910), Rua Dr Silvestre Falcão, Lote 6, has Internet access for 200$00 per 15 minutes.

Things to See & Do

In the old town the Igreja da Misericórdia has a striking Renaissance doorway and interior azulejos. From there, it's a short climb to the castle dominating the town.

Ilha da Tavira, 2km from Tavira, is an island beach connected to the mainland by ferry. Walk 2km beside the river to the ferry terminal at Quatro Águas or take the (summer only) bus from the bus station.

For a look at the old Algarve, take a bus to near Cacela Velha, an unspoilt hamlet 8km from Tavira. Another worthwhile day trip is to the fishing centre of Olhão, 22km west of Tavira.

Places to Stay & Eat

Ilha da Tavira has a *camping ground*, but the ferry stops running at 11 pm (usually 1 am from July to September). Popular *Pensão Residencial Lagoas* (☎ 281 322 252, *Rua Almirante Cândido dos Reis 24)* has doubles without bath from 5000$00. Central *Residencial Imperial* (☎ 289 322 234, *Rua José Pires Padinha 24)* has doubles with bath and breakfast for 8000$00. Riverside *Pensão Residencial Princesa do Gilão*

(☎ 289 325 171, *Rua Borda d'Água de Aguiar 10)* charges 8000$00.

Good budget restaurants on riverside Rua Dr José Pires Padinha include *Restaurante Regional Carmina* (☎ 281 322 236) at No 96 and *Casa de Pasto A Barquinha* (☎ 281 322 843) at No 142. *Cantinho do Emigrante* (☎ 281 323 696, *Praça Dr Padinha 27)* also has bargain fare.

At Olhão, enjoy a delicious seafood lunch at *Restaurante Isidro* (☎ 289 714 124, *Rua 5 de Outubro 68)*, opposite the market; it's closed Wednesday.

Getting There & Away

Some 15 trains and at least four express buses run daily between Faro and Tavira (30 to 50 minutes).

LAGOS

pop 20,000

This tourist resort has some of the Algarve's finest beaches. The tourist office (☎ 289 763 031) is 1km north-east of the centre, at the Situo São João roundabout; it's closed at weekends during winter. The pousada da juventude (see Places to Stay) has Internet access at 300$00 per half-hour.

Things to See & Do

In the old town, the municipal museum houses an assortment of archaeological finds, ecclesiastical treasures, handicrafts and animal foetuses. The adjacent Igreja de Santo António has some intricate baroque woodwork.

The beach scene includes Meia Praia, a vast strip to the east; and to the west Praia da Luz and the more secluded Praia do Pinhão.

Espadarte do Sul (☎ 289 761 820) operates boat trips from Docapesca harbour, including snorkelling and game fishing. On the seaside promenade, local fishermen offer motorboat jaunts to the nearby grottoes.

Places to Stay

Two nearby camping grounds are *Trindade* (☎ 289 763 893), 200m south of the town walls, and *Imulagos* (☎ 289 760 031), with a shuttle bus from the waterfront road. The *pousada da juventude* (☎ 289 761 970) is at Rua Lançarote de Freitas 50.

Residencial Marazul (☎ 289 769 749, *Rua 25 de Abril 13)* has smart doubles from

PORTUGAL

around 11,000$00. *Private rooms* are plentiful, for around 5500$00.

Places to Eat
For good Algarve specialities, try *O Cantinho Algarvio* (☎ 289 761 289, *Rua Afonso d'Almeida 17*). A local favourite is *Restaurante Bar Barros* (☎ 282 762 276, *Rua Portas de Portugal 83*). *Mullens (Rua Cândido dos Reis 86)* is a wood-panelled pub with good food.

Getting There & Away
Bus and train services depart frequently for other Algarve towns and around a dozen times daily to Lisbon; by train, change at Tunes for Lisbon.

Getting Around
You can rent bicycles, mopeds and motorcycles from Motoride (☎ 289 761 720), Rua José Afonso 23, or agents in town. Figure about 1000$00 a day for a mountain bike or 7000$00 for a motorbike.

MONCHIQUE
pop 4000
This quiet highland town in the forested Serra de Monchique offers a quiet alternative to the discos and beach life on the coast.

Things to See & Do
Monchique's **Igreja Matriz** has an amazing Manueline portal, its stone seemingly tied in knots! Follow the brown pedestrian signs up from the bus station, around the old town's narrow streets.

Caldas de Monchique, 6km south, is a revamped but still charming hot-spring hamlet. Some 8km west is the Algarve's 'rooftop', the 902m **Fóia** peak atop the Serra de Monchique, with terrific views through a forest of radio masts.

Monchique's tourist office (☎ 289 911 189) has details of walking, horseback and mountain-bike trips in the hills.

Places to Stay & Eat
Central *Residencial Estrela de Monchique* (☎ 289 913 111, *Rua do Porto Fundo 46*) has doubles with bath for 5000$00. *Restaurante A Charrete* (☎ 289 912 142, *Rua Dr Samora Gil 30*) is the best in town.

Getting There & Away
Over a dozen buses run daily from Lagos to Portimão, from where five to nine services run daily to Monchique.

SILVES
pop 10,500
Silves was the capital of Moorish Algarve, rivalling Lisbon for influence. Times are quieter now, but the huge castle is well worth a visit.

The tourist office (☎ 289 442 255), Rua 25 de Abril, is open weekdays and Saturday morning.

Places to Stay & Eat
Residencial Sousa (☎ 289 442 502, *Rua Samoura Barros 17*) has doubles without bath for around 5000$00. *Residencial Ponte Romana* (☎ 289 443 275) beside the old bridge has doubles with bath from 6000$00.

Restaurante Rui (☎ 289 442 682, *Rua C Vilarinho 27*), Silves' best fish restaurant, serves a memorable *arroz de marisco* (shellfish rice). For cheaper meals, try the riverfront restaurants opposite the old bridge.

Getting There & Away
Silves train station is 2km from town; trains from Lagos (35 minutes) stop six times daily (from Faro, change at Tunes), to be met by local buses. Six buses run daily to Silves from Albufeira (40 minutes).

SAGRES
pop 2500
Sagres is a small fishing port perched on dramatic cliffs in Portugal's south-western corner. The tourist office (☎ 289 624 873), just beyond the central Praça da República on Rua Comandante Matoso, is open weekdays and Saturday morning. Turinfo (☎ 289 620 003), open daily on Praça da República, rents cars and bikes, books hotels and arranges jeep and fishing trips.

Things to See & Do
In the **fort**, on a wide windy promontory, Henry the Navigator established his school of navigation and primed the explorers who later founded the Portuguese empire.

Among several beaches close to Sagres, a good choice is at the small village of **Salema**, 17km east.

No Sagres visit would be complete without a trip to **Cabo de São Vicente** (Cape St Vincent), 6km to the west. A solitary lighthouse stands on this barren cape, Europe's southwesternmost point.

Places to Stay & Eat

Parque de Campismo Sagres (☎ *289 624 351*) is 2km from town, off the Vila do Bispo road. Many Sagres folk rent rooms for around 5000$00 a double. Cheap, filling meals can be had at *Restaurante A Sagres* at the roundabout as you enter the village, and at cafes in Praça da República.

Getting There & Away

About 15 buses run daily to Sagres from Lagos (45 to 65 minutes), fewer on Sunday. Three continue out to Cabo de São Vicente on weekdays.

Central Portugal

Central Portugal, good for weeks of desultory rambling, deserves more attention than it receives. From the beaches of the Costa de Prata to the lofty Serra da Estrela and the sprawling Alentejo plains, it is a landscape of extremes.

Some of Portugal's finest wines come from the Dão region, while farther south, the hills and plains are studded with equally famous cork oaks. The mountainous centre is graced with scores of fortresses and walled cities with cobbled streets, clean air and grand panoramas.

ÉVORA

pop 54,000

One of Portugal's architectural gems and a Unesco World Heritage Site, the walled town of Évora is the capital of Alentejo province, a vast landscape of olive groves, vineyards and wheat fields. The town's charm lies in the narrow streets of the well-preserved inner town.

Orientation & Information

The focal point is Praça do Giraldo, from where you can wander through backstreets until you meet the city walls. An annotated map is available from the tourist office (☎ 266 702 671) at Praça do Giraldo 73. For other guides and maps go to Nazareth bookshop, Praça do Giraldo 46.

Outside the tourist office is an automatic cash-exchange machine. Oficin@ bar (☎ 266 707 312) at Rua da Moeda 27 has Internet access for 100$00 per 10 minutes.

Things to See & Do

On Largo do Marquês de Marialva is the **Sé**, Évora's cathedral, with cloisters and a museum of ecclesiastical treasures, both closed Monday. Admission costs 450$00.

The **Museu de Évora** features fantastic 16th-century Portuguese and Flemish painting. Admission costs 350$00. Opposite is the Roman-era **Temple of Diana**, subject of Évora's top-selling postcard.

The **Igreja de São Francisco**, south of Praça do Giraldo, includes the ghoulish Capela dos Ossos (Chapel of Bones), constructed with the bones and skulls of several thousand people. Admission costs 100$00.

Évora's big bash, and one of Alentejo's biggest country fairs, is the Feira de São João, held from approximately 22 June to 2 July.

Places to Stay

Accommodation gets tight in Évora in summer; booking ahead is essential.

An *Orbitur camping ground* (☎ *266 705 190*) is about 2km south of town (buses to Alcaçovas stop there). Évora's *pousada da juventude* (☎ *266 744 848*) is at Rua Miguel Bombarda 40.

Recommended *private rooms* are those at Rua Romão Ramalho 27 (☎ 266 702 453) with doubles costing 5000$00. *Residencial O Alentejo* (☎ *266 702 903, Rua Serpa Pinto 74*) has doubles with bath for 6000$00. Rooms at handsome *Pensão Policarpo* (☎/*fax 266 702 424, Rua da Freiria de Baixo 16*) start at 9500$00. *Residencial Solar Monfalim* (☎ *266 750 000, Largo da Misericórdia 1*) is a mini-palace with doubles from 14,500$00.

Places to Eat

O Portão (☎ *266 703 325, Rua do Cano 27*), by the aqueduct, is a popular budget choice with dishes from 700$00. *Café Restaurant O Cruz* (☎ *266 744 779, Praça 1 de Maio 20*) offers traditional fare at reasonable prices.

Jovial *Taberna Tipica Quarta-Feira* (☎ *266 707 530, Rua do Inverno 16*) packs

PORTUGAL

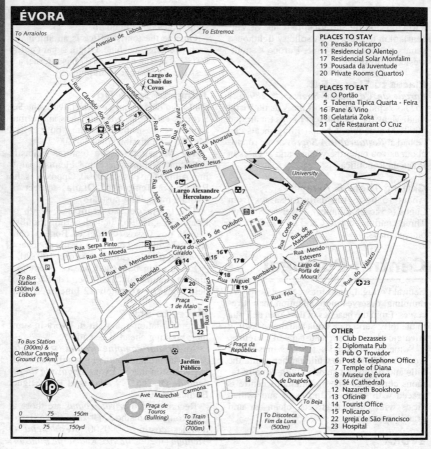

ÉVORA

PLACES TO STAY
10 Pensão Policarpo
11 Residencial O Alentejo
17 Residencial Solar Monfalim
19 Pousada da Juventude
20 Private Rooms (Quartos)

PLACES TO EAT
4 O Portão
5 Taberna Tipica Quarta - Feira
16 Pane & Vino
18 Gelataria Zoka
21 Café Restaurant O Cruz

OTHER
1 Club Dezasseis
2 Diplomata Pub
3 Pub O Trovador
6 Post & Telephone Office
7 Temple of Diana
8 Museu de Évora
9 Sé (Cathedral)
12 Nazareth Bookshop
13 Oficin@
14 Tourist Office
15 Policarpo
22 Igreja de São Francisco
23 Hospital

them in for its speciality creamed spinach and pork dishes. *Pane & Vino* (☎ *266 746 960, Páteo do Salema 22)* has great pasta and pizzas. Ice-cream fans will appreciate *Gelataria Zoka* (*Largo de São Vicente 14*).

Entertainment
Student hang-outs include several bars north-west of the centre: *Club Dezasseis* (☎ *266 706 559, Rua do Escrivão da Cámara 16)*; *Diplomata Pub* (☎ *266 705 675, Rua do Apóstolo 4)*, with frequent live music; and *Pub O Trovador* (☎ *266 707 370, Rua da Mostardeira 4)*. *Discoteca Fim da Luna*

(☎ *266 701 719, Avenida Combatentes da Grande Guerra 56)* is near the train station.

Getting There & Away
Évora has six weekday express coach connections to Lisbon (1¼ hours) and two to Faro (four to five hours), departing from the terminal off Avenida Túlio Espanca (700m south-west of the centre). Fast trains run from Lisbon (2½ hours, three daily).

Getting Around
Bike Lab (☎ 266 735 500) rents bikes for 250/2000$00 per hour/day. Policarpo (☎ 266

746 970, fax 266 746 984, ✉ viagenspol icarpo@ip.pt), Alcárcova de Baixo 43, organises city tours and half-day jaunts to megaliths and other nearby attractions.

MONSARAZ
pop 150

This walled village high above the plain is well worth the trip for its medieval atmosphere, clear light and magnificent views. Of architectural interest is the **Museu de Arte Sacra**, probably a former tribunal, with a rare 15th-century fresco. The **castle's** parapets have the best views.

Places to Stay & Eat

Several places along the main Rua Direita have doubles for around 5000$00. The tourist office (☎ 266 557 136) on the main square has details of Turihab and other elegant places. There are several tourist-geared restaurants and a grocery store near the main gate. Eat before 8 pm: the town goes to bed early.

Getting There & Away

On weekdays only, buses run to/from Reguengos de Monsaraz (35 minutes, 17km, two to four daily), which is connected to Évora (one hour, six daily). The last one back from Monsaraz leaves at 5 pm.

ESTREMOZ
pop 9000

The Estremoz region is dominated by huge mounds of marble from its quarries. The town's architectural appeal lies in its elegant, gently deteriorating buildings, liberally embellished with marble.

Information

The tourist office (☎ 268 333 541, fax 268 401 089) is at Largo da República 26 just south of the main square (known as the Rossio).

Things to See & Do

Upper Estremoz is crowned by the 14th-century **Torre de Menagem** with fine views of the town and countryside, and now a luxury pousada. Opposite is the **Museu Municipal**, specialising in unique Estremoz pottery figurines, and open daily except Monday; entry costs 180$00.

The focus of the lower town is the Rossio, with a lively **market** on Saturday morning. The nearby **Museu Rural**, a charming one-room museum of rural Alentejan life, is open daily except Sunday for 100$00. The bell-tower of the **Museu de Arte Sacra**, open daily (admission 200$00), offers great views of the Rossio.

Vila Viçosa, another marble town 17km from Estremoz, is centred on the **Palácio Ducal**, ancestral home of the dukes of Bragança, and full of period furnishings and artwork. It's open daily except Monday for a steep 1000$00 (plus 500$00 for the armoury museum).

Places to Stay & Eat

Friendly *Pensão-Restaurante Mateus* (☎ 268 322 226, Rua Almeida 41) has doubles for 4500/6000$00 without/with bath. Nearby *Adega do Isaias* (☎ 268 223 18, Rua Almeida 21) is a popular tavern serving great grills.

Getting There & Away

On weekdays Estremoz is linked to Évora by four local buses (1¼ hours) and two expressos (45 minutes). Daily expressos include two to Portalegre (one hour) and five to Elvas (50 minutes)

CASTELO DE VIDE & MARVÃO
pop 3000

From Portalegre it's a short hop to **Castelo de Vide**, noted for its picturesque houses clustered below a castle. Highlights are the **Judiaria** (Old Jewish Quarter) in a well-preserved network of medieval backstreets, and the view from the castle. Try to spend a night here or in **Marvão**, a mountaintop medieval walled village (population 190) 12km from Castelo de Vide, with grand views across large chunks of Spain and Portugal.

Information

The tourist offices at Castelo de Vide (☎ 245 901 361, fax 245 901 827), Rua de Bartolomeu Álvares da Santa 81, and at Marvão (☎ 245 993 886, fax 245 993 526), Largo de Santa Maria, can help with accommodation.

Getting There & Away

On weekdays only, three buses run from Portalegre to Castelo de Vide (20 minutes) and two to Marvão (45 minutes). One daily bus links the two villages (with a change at Portagem, a junction 5km from Marvão).

NAZARÉ
pop 13,000

This once-peaceful 17th-century fishing village was 'discovered' by tourism in the 1970s. Fishing skills and distinctive local dress have gone overboard and in high season it's a tourist circus, but the beautiful coastline and fine seafood still make it worthwhile.

The tourist office (☎ 262 561 194), at the end of Avenida da República by the funicular, is open 10 am to 10 pm daily in high season.

Things to See & Do

Lower Nazaré's beachfront retains a core of narrow streets now catering to tourists. The cliff-top section, O Sítio, is reached by a vintage funicular railway, and the view is superb.

The beaches attract huge summer crowds. Beware of dangerous currents. The tourist office will tell you which beaches are safe.

Places to Stay & Eat

Two good campsites are the well-equipped *Vale Paraíso* (☎ 262 561 546) off the Leiria road, and an *Orbitur* (☎ 262 561 111) off the Alcobaça road, both 2.5km from Nazaré. Many townspeople rent out rooms; doubles start about 4500$00. Among budget pensões is *Residencial Marina* (☎ 262 551 541, Rua Mouzinho de Albuquerque 6), with doubles around 6000$00. Room prices rocket in August.

Seafront restaurants are expensive. For cheaper fare in simple surroundings, try *Casa Marques* (☎ 262 551 680, Rua Gil Vicente 37). Friendly *A Tasquinha* (☎ 262 551 945, Rua Adrião Batalha 54) does good *carne de porco à Alentejana* (pork and clams). Popular *Casa O Pescador* (☎ 262 553 326, Rua António Carvalho Laranjo 18-A) is also reasonably priced.

Getting There & Away

The nearest train station, 6km away at Valado, is connected to Nazaré by frequent buses. Nazaré has numerous bus connections to Lisbon, Alcobaça, Óbidos and Coimbra.

ALCOBAÇA
pop 6000

Alcobaça's attraction is the immense **Mosteiro de Santa Maria de Alcobaça**, founded in 1178. The original Gothic has undergone Manueline, Renaissance and baroque additions. Of interest are the tombs of Pedro I and Inês de Castro, the cloisters, the kings' room and the kitchens. It's open 9 am to 7 pm daily (to 5 pm in winter); entry costs 400$00 (free admission to the church).

The tourist office (☎ 262 582 377) is opposite the monastery.

Getting There & Away

There are frequent buses to/from Nazaré and Batalha. The closest train station is 5km north-west at Valado dos Frades, connected to Alcobaça by regular buses.

BATALHA

Batalha's single highlight is its monastery, the **Mosteiro de Santa Maria de Vitória**, a colossal Gothic masterpiece constructed between 1388 and 1533. Earthquakes and vandalism by French troops have taken their toll, but restoration was completed in 1965. Highlights include the Founder's Chapel (with the tomb of Henry the Navigator), the Royal Cloisters, the Chapter House and the Unfinished Chapels. It's open 9 am to 6 pm daily; entry to the Cloisters and Unfinished Chapels costs 400$00.

The tourist office (☎ 244 765 180) is next to the abbey, on Largo Paulo VI.

Getting There & Away

There are frequent bus connections to Alcobaça and Nazaré, and at least three direct buses to Lisbon daily.

ÓBIDOS
pop 500

This charming walled village is one of the prettiest (and most touristy) in Portugal. Highlights include the **Igreja de Santa Maria**, with fine azulejos, and **views** from the walls. The tourist office (☎ 262 959 231, fax 262 959 014) is on Rua Direita.

Places to Stay & Eat

Private rooms are available for around 4500$00 a double. Among several Turihab properties is romantic *Casa do Poço* (☎ 262 959 358, Travessa da Mouraria) where doubles cost around 11,500$00. *Residencial Martim de Freitas* (☎ 262 959 185, Estrada

Nacional 8), outside the walls, has doubles from 6000$00.

Cheap cafes outside the walls include *Café Snack Bar O Aqueduto*. Inside, *Café-Restaurante 1 de Dezembro* (☎ 262 959 298), next to the Igreja de São Pedro, has pleasant outdoor seating. There's a small *grocery* just inside the town gate.

Getting There & Away
There are regular bus connections from Lisbon, directly (two hours) or via Caldas da Rainha, 10 minutes away. From the train station, outside the walls at the foot of the hill, there are five services daily to Lisbon (four with a change at Cacém).

COIMBRA
pop 150,000
Coimbra is famed for its 13th-century university, and for its traditional role as a centre of culture and art, complemented in recent times by industrial development.

The regional tourist office (☎ 239 855 930, fax 239 825 576), Largo da Portagem, has pamphlets and cultural-events information, but a municipal tourist office (☎ 239 832 591) on Praça Dom Dinis, and another (☎ 239 833 202) on Praça da República, are more useful. The Centro de Juventude (☎ 239 790 600) at Rua Pedro Monteiro 73 offers free Internet access on weekdays, with a half-hour maximum.

Coimbra's annual highlight is Queima das Fitas, a boozy week of fado and revelry beginning on the first Thursday in May, when students celebrate the end of the academic year.

Things to See
Lower Coimbra's main attraction is the **Mosteiro de Santa Cruz** with its ornate pulpit and medieval royal tombs. In the upper town, visit the **old university** with its baroque library and Manueline chapel, and the **Machado de Castro Museum**, with a fine collection of sculpture and painting. The back alleys of the university quarter are filled with student hangouts and an exuberant atmosphere.

At **Conimbriga**, 16km south of Coimbra, are the well-preserved ruins of a Roman town (open 9 am to 1 pm and 2 to 8 pm daily in summer, and to 6 pm in winter), including mosaic floors, baths and fountains. The good site museum (with a restaurant) is open 10 am to 1 pm and 2 to 6 pm except Monday. Entry costs 350$00. Frequent buses run to Condeixa, 2km from the site; direct buses depart at 9.05 or 9.35 am (only 9.35 am at weekends) from the AVIC terminal at Rua João de Ruão 18, returning at 1 and 6 pm (only 6 pm at weekends).

Activities
Daily from April to October, O Pioneiro do Mondego (☎ 239 478 385 from 8 to 10 am, 1 to 3 pm and 8 to 10 pm) rents kayaks at 3000$00 for paddling the Rio Mondego. At 10 am a free minibus collects you from Parque Dr Manuel Braga and takes you to Penacova for the 25km river journey.

Places to Stay
For Coimbra's *pousada da juventude* (☎ 239 822 955, Rua António Henriques Seco 12-14), take northbound bus No 46 from Coimbra A train station.

Near Coimbra A, *Pensão Lorvanense* (☎ 239 823 481, Rua da Sota 27) has doubles without/with bath for 4000/5000$00. Those at *Pensão Residencial Rivoli* (☎ 239 825 550, Praça do Comércio 27) cost 5500/6000$00, with shared toilets. Very central *Pensão Residencial Larbelo* (☎ 239 829 092, fax 239 829 094, Largo da Portagem 33) has doubles with bath for 6500$00.

Pensão Flôr de Coimbra (☎ 239 823 865, fax 239 821 545, Rua do Poço 5) has doubles for 5000$00 (6000/7000$00 with shower and without/with toilet), and a small daily (except Sunday) vegetarian menu. Quiet doubles with bath at *Residência Coimbra* (☎ 239 837 996, fax 239 838 124, Rua das Azeiteiras 55) start at 7000$00.

In a lane near the university, Dutch-run *Casa Pombal Guesthouse* (☎ 239 835 175, fax 239 821 548, Rua das Flores 18) has everything from 7000$00 bathless doubles to bird's-eye views at 8200$00 with bath, and a huge breakfast.

Places to Eat
The lanes west of Praça do Comércio, especially Rua das Azeiteiras, feature a concentration of good-value fare; a zero-frills eatery at No 5, *Refeição Económica* ('cheap eats'),

has hearty specials from just 600$00. *Restaurante Democrática* (☎ 239 823 784, *Travessa da Rua Nova*) has Portuguese standards, with some half-portions under 900$00.

Self-service *Restaurante Jardim da Manga*, behind the fountains at the back of the Mosteiro de Santa Cruz, has a few basic dishes from 700$00; it's closed Saturday. *Zé Manel* (☎ 239 823 790, *12 Beco do Forno*) has crazy decor and huge servings; go by 8 pm to beat the crowds.

East of the university, *Bar-Restaurante ACM* (☎ 239 823 633, *Rua Alexandre Herculano 21A*) has plain fare from 700$00 per dish; it's open daily except Saturday. Downstairs behind the *Centro de Juventude* (*Rua Pedro Monteiro 73*) is a clean canteen with a few main dishes under 800$00 and lots of salads.

Vaulted *Café Santa Cruz* beside the Mosteiro de Santa Cruz is great for coffee breaks.

Entertainment
Bar Diligência (☎ 239 827 667, *Rua Nova 30*) and *Boémia Bar* (☎ 239 834 547, *Rua do Cabido 6*) are popular casas de fado. *Café-Galeria Almedina* (☎ 239 836 192, *Arco de Almedina*) offers fado and other live sounds. A good dance bar is *Aqui Há Rato* (☎ 239 824 804, *Largo da Sé Velha 20*). Two popular discos are *João Ratão* (☎ 239 404 047, *Avenida Afonso Henriques 43*) and *Via Latina* (☎ 239 833 034, *Rua Almeida Garrett 1*).

Getting There & Away
At least a dozen buses and as many trains run daily from Lisbon and Porto, plus frequent express buses from Faro and Évora. The main long-distance train stations are Coimbra B, 2km north-west of the centre, and central Coimbra A (on timetables this is called just 'Coimbra'). Most long-distance trains call at both. Other useful connections are to Figueira da Foz and to Luso/Buçaco (from Coimbra A).

LUSO & THE BUÇACO FOREST
pop 2000
Walkers will appreciate the Buçaco Forest, chosen by 16th-century monks as a retreat, and relatively untouched ever since. It begins about 1km from the spa resort of Luso, where the tourist office (☎/fax 231 939 133) on Avenida Emídio Navarro has a general map

of the forest, and leaflets about trails and over 700 tree and shrub species.

Places to Stay & Eat
The Luso tourist office has accommodation lists. *Pensão Central* (☎ 231 939 254, *Avenida Emídio Navarro*) has doubles from 4500$00. Hearty meals are available at *Restaurante O Cesteiro* (☎ 231 939 360) on the N234, 500m north from the tourist office.

The elegant five-star *Palace Hotel do Buçaco* (☎ 231 930 101, fax 231 930 509), a former royal hunting lodge in the forest, is as fine an expression of Manueline style as any in Portugal. Singles/doubles start at 29,000/34,000$00. Figure on at least 2500$00 per dish in the restaurant or 5000$00 for the set menu.

Getting There & Away
Five buses daily go to Luso/Buçaco from Coimbra and Viseu (two at weekends). Just one train, departing around 10.30 am from Coimbra B, gives you enough time for a day trip.

SERRA DA ESTRELA
The forested Serra da Estrela is Portugal's highest mainland mountain range (topping out at the 1993m Torre), and the core of a designated *parque natural*. With its outlying ranges it stretches nearly across Portugal, and offers some of the country's best hiking.

Orientation & Information
The best place for information on the Parque Natural da Serra da Estrela is the main park office in Manteigas (☎ 275 980 060, fax 275 980 069); other offices are at Seia, Gouveia and Guarda. Other good sources for regional information are the tourist offices at Guarda (☎ 271 212 115) and Covilhã (☎ 275 319 560).

The park administration publishes *À Descoberta da Estrela*, a walking guide with maps and narratives. Park offices and some tourist offices sell an English edition (850$00), plus a detailed topographic map of the park (1100$00).

Places to Stay
The *pousada da juventude* (☎ 275 335 375, fax 275 335 109) at Penhas da Saúde, 10km

above Covilhã, offers meals (or you can cook your own), dorms and a few functional doubles. Buses come from Covilhã twice daily in August only, and hitching is fairly safe and easy. The only other options are your feet or bike, or a taxi (about 1600$00). This makes a good base for excursions.

Guarda also has a *pousada da juventude* (☎/fax 271 224 482), and Seia, Gouveia, Guarda and Covilhã have some modestly priced guesthouses. Manteigas, though most central of all, tends to be pricey.

Getting There & Away
Several buses run each day from Coimbra, along the park's perimeter to Seia, Gouveia, Guarda or Covilhã, plus others from Porto and Lisbon to Guarda and Covilhã. Twice-daily IC trains link Lisbon and Coimbra to Guarda, and two daily IC trains run from Lisbon to Covilhã on the Lisbon-Paris line.

Getting Around
No buses cross the park, though you can go around it: Seia-Covilhã takes two hours via Guarda. At least one or two buses link Seia, Gouveia and Guarda every day, and considerably more run between Guarda and Covilhã.

The North

Most visitors are surprised to discover Portugal's northern tier, with its wine country, great forests, mountainous Peneda-Gerês National Park and a strand of undeveloped beaches. The urban scene focuses on Porto, with its medieval centre by the Rio Douro. Within easy reach of Porto are three historical cities: Braga, the country's religious heart; finely situated Viana do Castelo; and Guimarães, which declares itself Portugal's birthplace.

PORTO
pop 270,000
Porto is Portugal's second-largest city, and the focus of the port-wine trade. Its reputation as an industrial centre belies considerable charm; indeed its old centre has been declared a Unesco World Heritage Site, and the city was, with Rotterdam, named European City of Culture for 2001.

Orientation
The city clings to the north bank of the Rio Douro, spanned here by five bridges. On the far bank is Vila Nova de Gaia and its port wine lodges, a major attraction.

Central Porto's axis is Avenida dos Aliados. Major shopping areas are eastward around the Bolhão Market and Rua Santa Catarina, and westward along Rua dos Clérigos. At the southern end of Avenida dos Aliados, Praça da Liberdade and São Bento train station are major local bus hubs. Another is Jardim da Cordoaria (called Jardim de João Chagas on some maps), about 400m westward.

The picturesque Ribeira district lies along the waterfront, in the shadow of the great Ponte de Dom Luís I bridge.

Information
Tourist Offices The main municipal tourist office (☎ 222 052 740, fax 223 323 303) at Rua Clube dos Fenianos 25 is open 9 am to 5.30 pm on weekdays. A smaller office (☎ 222 009 770) at Rua Infante Dom Henriques 63 is open during these hours and 9.30 am to 4.30 pm at weekends. From July to September both are open 9 am to 7 pm weekdays and 9.30 am to 4.30 pm at weekends.

A national (ICEP) tourist office (☎ 222 057 514, fax 222 053 212) at Praça Dom João I 43 is open 9 am to 7 pm daily in July and August, and 9 am to at least 7 pm weekdays and 9.30 am to 3.30 pm at weekends the rest of the year.

Money Banks with ATMs and exchange desks are everywhere. Better rates for travellers cheques are at the exchange bureaus Portocâmbios, Rua Rodrigues Sampaio 193, and Intercontinental, Rua de Ramalho Ortigão 8. Top Tours (☎ 222 074 020, fax 222 074 039), Rua Alferes Malheiro 96, is Porto's American Express representative.

Post & Communications The main post office (the place for poste-restante mail) is across Praça General Humberto Delgado from the main tourist office. A telephone office at Praça da Liberdade 62 is open 10 am to 10 pm daily. Faxes can be sent from the post office, and domestic ones from the telephone office.

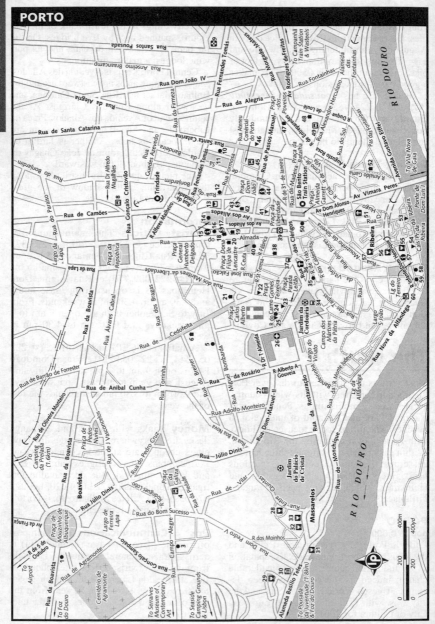

PORTO

euro currency converter €1 = 200 escudo

PORTO

	PLACES TO STAY				
6	Pensão Estoril	3	usit TAGUS	31	Maré Alta
18	Residencial Vera Cruz	4	Internorte Tickets	32	Club Mau-Mau
19	Pensão Pão de Açucar		and Buses	33	Mexcal
20	Pensão Porto Rico	5	Lavandaria Olimpica	34	Cordoaria Bus Stand
21	Pensão São Marino	7	Top Tours & American	35	Casa Oriental
38	Residencial União		Express	36	Torre dos Clérigos
42	Pensão Chique	8	REDM; AV Minho; Carlos	37	Renex Tickets and Buses
47	Residencial Santo André		Soares Tickets & Buses	39	Telephone Office
48	Residencial Afonso	9	Central Shopping	40	Livraria Porto Editora
52	Pensão Astória	10	STCP Kiosk		(bookshop)
		11	Bolhão Market	43	Portocambios Exchange
	PLACES TO EAT	12	Casa Januário	44	National (ICEP)
22	Restaurante Romão	13	Main Post Office		Tourist Office
23	Café Ancôra Douro	14	Town Hall	45	Rodonorte Bus Station
25	Restaurante A Tasquinha	15	Main Municipal Tourist	49	Rede Expressos
41	Café Embaixador		Office; Tourism Police		Bus Station
46	Café Majestic	16	Portweb	50	STCP Kiosk
53	Casa Filha da Mãe Preta	17	Intercontinental Exchange	51	Sé
54	Pub-Petisqueira O Muro	24	Garrafeira do Carmo	55	Meia-Cave
		26	Santo António Hospital	56	Academia
	OTHER	27	Soares dos Reis National	57	Municipal Tourist Office
1	STCP Kiosk		Museum	58	Arte Facto
2	Instituto Português da	28	Solar do Vinho do Porto	59	Lavandaria São
	Juventude	29	Voice Bar		Nicolau
		30	Tram Museum	60	Tram Terminus

Email & Internet Access The Instituto Português da Juventude (☎ 226 003 173), Rua Rodrigues Lobo 98, offers free Internet access 9 am to 8 pm weekdays. At Portweb (☎ 222 005 922), Praça General Humberto Delgado 291, access costs 100$00 per hour from 9 am to 4 pm daily, and 240$00 from then to 2 am.

Travel Agencies Two youth-oriented agencies are usit TAGUS (☎ 226 094 146, fax 226 094 141), Rua Campo Alegre 261, and Wasteels (☎ 225 370 539, fax 225 373 210), Rua Pinto Bessa 27/29 near Campanhã station. See also Top Tours under Money earlier.

Local adventure-tour operators with northern Portugal experience include Montes d'Aventura (☎ 228 305 157, fax 228 305 158) for trekking, cycling and canoeing, and Trilhos (☎/fax 225 504 604) for canyoning and hydrospeed.

Laundry Lavandaria Olimpica, Rua Miguel Bombarda, and Lavandaria 5 à Sec in the Central Shopping centre have laundry and dry-cleaning services. A cheaper municipal service, Lavandaria São Nicolau, is on Rua Infante Dom Henrique. All are closed Sunday.

Medical Services & Emergency Santo António Hospital (☎ 222 077 500), Rua Vicente José Carvalho, has English-speaking staff. Direct any request for police help to the 'tourism police' office (☎ 222 081 833) at Rua Clube dos Fenianos 11, open 8 am to 2 am daily.

Things to See & Do
The riverfront **Ribeira** district is the city's beating heart, with narrow lanes, grimy bars, good restaurants and river cruises.

The 225 steps of the **Torre dos Clérigos** on Rua dos Clérigos lead to the best panorama of the city (200$00; open 10 am to noon and 2 to 5 pm daily).

The **Sé**, the cathedral dominating central Porto, is worth a visit for its mixture of architectural styles and ornate interior (250$00; open 9 am to 12.30 pm and 2.30 to 5.30 pm except Sunday morning).

The **Soares dos Reis National Museum**, Rua Dom Manuel II 44, offers masterpieces of 19th and 20th-century Portuguese painting and sculpture (350$00; open 10 am to 12.30 pm and 2 to 6 pm, closed all day Monday and Tuesday morning).

Porto's finest new museum is the **Serralves Museum of Contemporary Art**, Rua de Serralves 947/999 (800$00; open 10 am to 7 pm, except to 10 pm Thursday, closed Monday).

The **Museu dos Carros Eléctricos** (Tram Museum), Cais do Bicalho, is a cavernous old tram warehouse with dozens of restored cars. It's open 9.30 am to 1 pm and 3 to 6 pm except Monday, for 350$00.

At the **Bolhão market**, east of Avenida dos Aliados, you can get anything from seafood to herbs and honey. It's open weekdays until 5 pm and Saturday to 1 pm.

Across the river in Vila Nova de Gaia, some two dozen **port-wine lodges** are open for tours and tastings on weekdays and Saturday, and a few on Sunday. The tourist office (☎ 223 751 902) there has details. Or select from a huge port-wine list at the **Solar do Vinho do Porto** (☎ 226 097 793), Rua Entre Quintas 220 in Porto. This bar is open 10 am to 11.45 pm weekdays and 11 am to 10.45 pm on Saturday.

Special Events
Porto's big festival is the Festa de São João (St John's Festival) in June. Also worth catching are several music festivals, including Celtic music in April-May, rock in August, and fado in October.

Places to Stay
Camping *Camping da Prelada* (☎ 228 312 616, Rua Monte dos Burgos) is 4km northwest of the centre (take bus No 6 from Praça de Liberdade or bus No 50 from Jardim da Cordoaria).

Three camping grounds near the sea in Vila Nova de Gaia are *Campismo Salgueiros* (☎ 227 810 500, fax 227 810 136, Praia de Salgueiros), *Campismo Marisol* (☎ 227 135 942, fax 227 126 351, Praia de Canide) and *Campismo Madalena* (☎ 227 122 520, fax 227 122 534, Praia da Madalena). Bus No 57 runs to all of them from São Bento station.

Note that the sea at all these places is far too polluted for swimming.

Hostels The fine *pousada da juventude* (☎ 226 177 257, fax 226 177 247, Rua Paulo da Gama 551), 4km west of the centre, is open 24 hours a day. Doubles and dorm-style quads are available, and reservations are essential. Take bus No 35 from Largo dos Lóios (a block west of Praça da Liberdade), or No 1 from São Bento station.

Guesthouses Porto's cheapest guesthouses are around Praça da Batalha, east and uphill from São Bento station. Some are dodgy, but two reliable ones where doubles with bath start at 4000$00 are *Residencial Afonso* (☎ 222 059 469, Rua Duque de Loulé 233) and *Residencial Santo André* (☎ 222 055 869, Rua Santo Ildefonso 112). Down towards the river, *Pensão Astória* (☎ 222 008 175, Rua Arnaldo Gama 56) has elegant old doubles, some with river views, for 5000$00 with bath and breakfast.

Plain doubles with shower at central *Residencial União* (☎ 222 003 078, Rua Conde de Vizela 62) and *Pensão Porto Rico* (☎ 223 394 690, Rua do Almada 237) start at 5000$00; the former also has cheaper rooms with shared bath. *Pensão Chique* (☎ 223 322 963, Avenida dos Aliados 206) offers small doubles for 6500$00 with breakfast. Those at *Residencial Vera Cruz* (☎ 223 323 396, fax 223 323 421, Rua Ramalho Ortigão 14) are 8000$00. *Pensão Pão de Açucar* (☎ 222 002 425, fax 222 050 239, Rua do Almada 262) has handsome doubles with shower from 9500$00; bookings are essential.

Near the university, *Pensão Estoril* (☎ 222 002 751, fax 222 082 468, Rua de Cedofeita 193) and the better-value *Pensão São Marino* (☎ 223 325 499, Praça Carlos Alberto 59) offer doubles with shower from 6500$00, with breakfast.

Places to Eat
Excellent value in the centre can be found at the self-service mezzanine at *Café Embaixador* (☎ 222 054 182, Rua Sampaio Bruno 5), with grills, salads and vegetables; it's open 6.30 am to 10 pm except Sunday.

Near the university, *Restaurante A Tasquinha* (☎ 223 322 145, Rua do Carmo 23) has well-prepared regional dishes for 1000$00 to 2000$00. Cheerfully downmarket *Restaurante Romão* (☎ 222 005 639, Praça Carlos Alberto 100) has northern specialities for around 900$00 per dish. A lively student haunt at lunchtime is *Café Ancôra Douro* (☎ 222 081 201, Praça de Parada Leitão 49).

An exception to the Ribeira's many overpriced, touristy eateries is *Pub-Petisqueira O*

Muro (☎ *222 083 426, Muro dos Bacal-hoeiros 88*), with decor from dried bacalhau to Che Guevara, and good *feijoado de marisco* (a rich bean and seafood stew) for 850\$00; it's open noon to 2 am daily. Congenial *Casa Filha da Mãe Preta* (☎ *222 055 515, Cais da Ribeira 39*) has Douro views, and main dishes mostly under 2000\$00.

Café Majestic (☎ *222 003 887, Rua Santa Catarina 112*) is an extravagant Art Nouveau relic with expensive coffees and afternoon teas.

Entertainment

Lively pubs in the Ribeira include *Academia* (☎ *222 005 737, Rua São João 80*), *Ryan's Irish Pub* (☎ *222 005 366, Rua Infante Dom Henrique 18*) and *Meia-Cave* (☎ *223 323 214, Praça da Ribeira 6*).

A newer generation of clubs in the riverfront area called Massarelos, 2km west of the Ribeira, includes *Mexcal* (☎ *226 009 188*) and *Club Mau-Mau* (☎ *226 076 660*), on Rua da Restauração; *Maré Alta* (☎ *226 162 540, Rua do Ouro*); and *Voice* (☎ *226 067 815, Rua do Capitão Eduardo Romero 1*). All are on the No 1 bus line from São Bento station.

Shopping

Port is, of course, a popular purchase. Shops with a broad selection include Garrafeira do Carmo, Rua do Carmo 17; Casa Januário, Rua do Bonjardim 352; and Casa Oriental, Campo dos Mártires de Pátria 111. Other good buys are shoes and gold-filigree jewellery. For handicrafts, visit Arte Facto at Rua da Reboleira 37 in the Ribeira (closed Monday).

Getting There & Away

Air Porto is connected by daily flights from Lisbon and London, and almost-daily direct links from other European centres (see the introductory Getting There & Away and Getting Around sections of this chapter). For flight information call ☎ 229 412 141.

Bus Renex (☎ 222 003 395), with a 24-hour ticket office at Rua das Carmelitas 32, is the choice for Lisbon and the Algarve. From a terminal at Rua Alexandre Herculano 370, Rede Expressos (☎ 222 006 954) goes all over Portugal. From or near Praceto Régulo Magauanha, off Rua Dr Alfredo Magalhães, REDM (☎ 222 003 152) goes to Braga, AV Minho

(☎ 222 006 121) to Viana do Castelo, and Carlos Soares (☎ 222 051 383) to Guimarães. Rodonorte (☎ 222 005 637) departs from its own terminal at Rua Ateneu Comércial do Porto 19, mainly to Vila Real and Bragança.

Northern Portugal's main international carrier is Internorte (see the introductory Getting There & Away section of this chapter), whose coaches depart from the booking office (☎ 226 052 420, fax 226 099 570) at Praça da Galiza 96.

Train Porto, a northern Portugal rail hub, has three stations. Most international trains, and all intercidade links, start at Campanhã, 2km east of the centre. Interregional and regional services depart from either Campanhã or the central São Bento station (bus Nos 34 and 35 run frequently between these two). For Guimarães, go to Trindade station.

At São Bento you can book tickets for services to any destination from any Porto station; for information call ☎ 225 364 141 between 8 am and 11 pm daily.

Getting Around

To/From the Airport The AeroBus (☎ 808 200 166) runs between Avenida dos Aliados and the airport via Boavista every half-hour from 7 am to 7.30 pm. The 500\$00 ticket, purchased on the bus, also serves as a free bus pass until midnight of the day you buy it.

City bus Nos 56 and 87 run about every half-hour until 8.30 pm to/from Jardim da Cordoaria, and until about 12.30 am to/from Praça da Liberdade.

A taxi costs around 2500\$00 plus a possible 300\$00 baggage charge.

Bus Central hubs of Porto's extensive bus system include Jardim da Cordoaria, Praça da Liberdade and São Bento station (Praça Almeida Garrett). Tickets are cheapest from STCP kiosks (eg, opposite São Bento station, beside Bolhão market and at Boavista) and many newsagents and tobacconists: 90\$00 for a short hop, 125\$00 to outlying areas or 320\$00 for an airport return trip. Tickets bought on the bus are always 180\$00. Also available is a 400\$00 day pass.

Tram Porto has one remaining tram, the No 1E, trundling daily from the Ribeira to the

PORTUGAL

coast at Foz do Douro and back to Boavista every half-hour all day.

Metro Work has begun on Porto's own 'underground', a combination of upgraded and new track that will reach Campanhã, Vila Nova de Gaia and several coastal resorts to the north.

Taxi To cross town, figure on about 600$00. An additional charge is made to leave the city limits, including across the Ponte Dom Luís I to Vila Nova de Gaia.

ALONG THE DOURO

The Douro Valley is one of Portugal's scenic highlights, with 200km of expansive panoramas from Porto to the Spanish border. In the upper reaches, port-wine vineyards wrap around every hillside.

The river, tamed by eight dams and locks since the late 1980s, is navigable right across Portugal. Highly recommended is the train journey from Porto to Peso da Régua (about a dozen trains daily, 2½ hours), the last 50km clinging to the river's edge; four trains continue daily to Pocinho (4½ hours). Douro Azul (☎ 223 393 950, fax 222 083 407) and other companies run one and two-day river cruises, mostly from March to October. Cyclists and drivers can choose river-hugging roads along either bank, though they're crowded at weekends.

The elegant, detailed colour map *Rio Douro* (600$00) is available from Porto bookshops.

VIANA DO CASTELO
pop 18,000

This attractive port at the mouth of the Rio Lima is renowned for its historic old town and its promotion of folk traditions. The tourist office (☎ 258 822 620, fax 258 827 873) on Rua Hospital Velho has information on festivals and the region in general.

In August Viana hosts the Festas de Nossa Senhora da Agonia (see the Facts for the Visitor section at the start of this chapter for details).

Things to See

The town's focal point is Praça da República, with its delicate fountain and el-egant buildings, including the 16th-century **Misericórdia**.

Atop Santa Luzia Hill, the **Templo do Sagrado Coração de Jesus** offers a grand panorama across the river. A funicular railway climbs the hill from 9 am to 6 pm (hourly in the morning, every 30 minutes in the afternoon) from behind the train station.

Places to Stay

Viana's *pousada da juventude* (☎ 258 800 260, fax 258 820 870), on Rua da Argaçosa, is about 1km east of the town centre.

Pensão Vianense (☎ 258 823 118, Avenida Conde da Carreira 79) and *Casa de Hóspedes Guerreiro* (☎ 258 822 099, Rua Grande 14) have plain doubles with shared facilities from 5000$00. Doubles with bath (breakfast included) are about 6000$00 at central *Pensão Dolce Vita* (☎ 258 824 860, Rua do Poço 44) and 7500$00 at *Pensão-Restaurant Alambique* (☎ 258 821 364, Rua Manuel Espregueira 86).

The tourist office has listings of *private rooms*.

Places to Eat

Most pensões have good-value restaurants, open to nonguests too. *A Gruta Snack Bar* (☎ 258 820 214, Rua Grande 87) has lunchtime salads for under 500$00. *Adega do Padrinho* (☎ 258 826 954, Rua Gago Coutinho 162) offers traditional dishes for under 1100$00 per half-portion. Seafood is pricey, but try the cervejaria part of *Os Três Arcos* (☎ 258 824 014, Largo João Tomás da Costa 25), with half-portions from 1000$00. *Viana's Restaurante* (☎ 258 824 797, Rua Frei Bartolomeu dos Mártires 179), near the fish market, specialises in *bacalhau*, in all its forms.

Getting There & Away

Half a dozen express coaches go to Braga and to Porto every day (fewer at weekends), with daily express services on to Coimbra and Lisbon. Daily train services run north to Spain and south to Porto and Lisbon.

BRAGA
pop 80,000

Crammed with churches, Braga is considered Portugal's religious capital. During

Easter week, huge crowds attend its Holy Week Festival.

The tourist office (☎ 253 262 550) on Praça da República can help with accommodation and maps.

Things to See & Do
In the centre of Braga is the **Sé**, an elegant cathedral complex. Admission to its treasury museum and several tomb chapels costs 300$00.

At Bom Jesus do Monte, a hilltop pilgrimage site 5km from Braga, is an extraordinary stairway, the **Escadaria do Bom Jesus**, with allegorical fountains, chapels and a superb view. Buses run frequently from Braga to the site, where you can climb the steps or ascend by funicular railway.

It's an easy day trip to **Guimarães**, considered the cradle of the Portuguese nation, with a medieval town centre and a palace of the dukes of Bragança.

Places to Stay
The *pousada da juventude (☎ 253 616 163, Rua de Santa Margarida 6)* is a 10-minute walk from the city centre. A bargain in the centre is *Hotel Francfort (☎ 253 262 648, Avenida Central 7)*, where well-kept old doubles start at 3500$00. *Casa Santa Zita (☎ 253 618 331, Rua São João 20)* is a hostel for pilgrims (and others) with doubles from 4500$00. *Grande Residência Avenida (☎ 253 609 020, fax 253 609 028, Avenida da Liberdade 738)* offers good value with doubles from 6000$00.

Places to Eat
Lareira do Conde (☎ 253 611 340, Praça Conde de Agrolongo 56) specialises in inexpensive grills. Around the corner from the bus station, *Retiro da Primavera (☎ 253 272 482, Rua Gabriel Pereira de Castro 100)* has good half-portions for under 900$00. *Casa Grulha (☎ 253 262 883, Rua dos Biscaínhos 95)* serves good-value *cabrito assado* (roast kid, a local speciality). *Taberna do Felix (☎ 253 617 701, Praça Velha 17)* has simple, imaginative dishes from 1000$00.

For people-watching over coffee or beer, settle down at *Café Vianna* on Praça da República.

Getting There & Away
The motorway from Porto puts Braga within easy day trip reach. Intercidade trains arrive twice daily from Lisbon, Coimbra and Porto, and there are daily connections north to Viana do Castelo and Spain. Daily bus services link Braga to Porto and Lisbon.

PENEDA-GERÊS NATIONAL PARK
This wilderness park along the Spanish border has spectacular scenery and a wide variety of fauna and flora. Portuguese daytrippers and holiday-makers tend to stick to the main villages and camping areas, leaving the rest of the park to hikers.

The park's main centre is **Vila do Gerês** (or Caldas do Gerês, or just Gerês), a sleepy, hot-spring village.

Orientation & Information
Gerês' tourist office (☎ 253 391 133, fax 253 391 282) is in the colonnade at the upper end of the village. For park information go around the corner to the park office (☎ 253 390 110).

Other park offices are at Arcos de Valdevez, Montalegre and the head office (☎ 253 203 480, fax 253 613 169) is on Avenida António Macedo in Braga. All have a map of the park (530$00) with some roads and tracks (but not trails), and a free English-language booklet on the park's features.

Activities
Hiking A long-distance footpath is being developed, mostly following traditional roads or tracks between villages where you can stop for the night. Park offices sell map-brochures (300$00) for two sections available so far.

Day hikes around Gerês are popular; at weekends and all summer the Miradouro walk at **Parque do Merendas** is crowded. A more strenuous option is the old Roman road from Mata do Albergaria (10km up-valley from Gerês by taxi or hitching), past the **Vilarinho das Furnas** reservoir to Campo do Gerês. More distant destinations include **Ermida** and **Cabril**, both with simple accommodation and cafes.

Guided walks are organised by PlanAlto (☎/fax 253 351 005) at Cerdeira camping ground in Campo do Gerês, and Trote-Gerês (☎/fax 253 659 860) at Cabril.

Cycling Mountain bikes can be hired from Água Montanha Lazer (☎ 253 391 779, fax 253 391 598, ✉ aguamontanha@mail.telepac.pt) in Rio Caldo, Pensão Carvalho Araújo (☎ 253 391 185) in Gerês, or PlanAlto.

Horse Riding The national park operates facilities (☎ 253 391 181) from beside its Vidoeiro camping ground, near Gerês. Trote-Gerês also has horses for hire.

Water Sports Rio Caldo, 8km south of Gerês, is the base for water sports on the Caniçada reservoir. Água Montanha Lazer rents canoes and other boats. For paddling the Salamonde reservoir, Trote-Gerês rents canoes from its camping ground at Cabril.

Gerês' Parque das Termas (170$00 admission) has a swimming pool, open for 700/1100$00 on weekdays/weekends.

Organised Tours
Agência no Gerês (☎ 253 391 141), at Hotel Universal in Gerês, runs two to 5½-hour minibus trips around the park in summer, for 1000$00 to 2000$00 per person.

Places to Stay
The *pousada da juventude* (☎/fax 253 351 339) and *Cerdeira Camping Ground* (☎/fax 253 351 005) at Campo do Gerês make good hiking bases. Trote-Gerês runs its own *Parque de Campismo Outeiro Alto* (☎/fax 253 659 860) at Cabril. The park runs a *camping ground* (☎ 253 391 289) 1km north of Gerês at Vidoeiro, and others at Lamas de Mouro and Entre-Ambos-os-Rios.

Gerês has plenty of pensões, though many are block-booked by spa patients in summer. Try *Pensão da Ponte* (☎ 253 391 121) beside the river, with doubles from 6000/7500$00 without/with bath. At the top of the hill, *Pensão Adelaide* (☎ 253 390 020, fax 253 390 029) provides doubles with bath from 7000$00.

Trote-Gerês runs the comfortable *Pousadinha de Paradela* (☎ 276 566 165) in Paradela, with doubles from 5000$00.

Places to Eat
Most Gerês pensões serve hearty meals, to guests and nonguests. There are several *restaurants*, plus shops in the main street for picnic provisions. The *Cerdeira Camping Ground* at Campo do Gerês has a good-value restaurant.

Getting There & Away
From Braga, 10 coaches daily run to Rio Caldo and Gerês, and seven to Campo do Gerês (fewer at weekends). Coming from Lisbon or Porto, change at Braga.

Spain

Spaniards approach life with such exuberance that most visitors have to stop and stare. In almost every town in the country, the nightlife will outlast the foreigners. Then just when they think they are coming to terms with the pace, they are surrounded by the beating drums of a fiesta, with day and night turning into a blur of dancing, laughing, eating and drinking. Spain also holds its own in cultural terms with formidable museums like the Prado and Thyssen-Bornemisza art galleries in Madrid, the wacky Dalí museum in Figueres, and Barcelona's Picasso and Miró museums.

Then, of course, you have the weather and the highly varied landscape. From April to October the sun shines with uncanny predictability on the Mediterranean coast and the Balearic Islands. Elsewhere you can enjoy good summer weather in the more secluded coves of Galicia, in the Pyrenees or the mountains of Andalucía, or on the surf beaches of western Andalucía or the País Vasco (Basque Country).

A wealth of history awaits the visitor to Spain: fascinating prehistoric displays at the archaeological museums in Teruel and Madrid; and from Roman times the aqueduct in Segovia, the seaside amphitheatre in Tarragona and the buried streets of Roman Barcelona made accessible via an underground walkway. After Roman times, the Moorish era left perhaps the most powerful cultural and artistic legacy, focused on Granada's Alhambra, Córdoba's mosque and Seville's *alcázar* (fortress) but evident in monuments throughout much of the country. Christian Spain also constructed hundreds of impressive castles, cathedrals, monasteries, palaces and mansions, which still stand across the length and breadth of the country.

AT A GLANCE

Capital	Madrid
Population	39 million
Official Language	Spanish (Castilian)
Currency	1 peseta (pta) = 100 centimos
Time	GMT/UTC+0100
Country Phone Code	☎ 34

Facts about Spain

HISTORY
Ancient History

Located at the crossroads between Europe and Africa, the Iberian Peninsula has always been a target for invading peoples and civilisations. From around 8000 to 3000 BC, people from North Africa known as the Iberians crossed the Strait of Gibraltar and settled the peninsula. Around 1000 BC Celtic tribes entered northern Spain, while Phoenician merchants were establishing trading settlements along the Mediterranean coast. They were followed by Greeks and Carthaginians who arrived around 600 to 500 BC.

The Romans arrived in the 3rd century BC, but took two centuries to subdue the peninsula. Christianity came to Spain during the 1st century AD, but was initially opposed by the Romans, leading to persecution and martyrdoms. In AD 409 Roman Hispania was invaded by Germanic tribes and by 419 the Christian Visigoths, another Germanic

SPAIN

people, had established a kingdom which lasted until 711, when the Moors – Muslim Berbers and Arabs from North Africa – crossed the Strait of Gibraltar and defeated Roderic, the last Visigoth king.

Muslim Spain & the Reconquista

By 714, the Muslim armies had occupied the entire peninsula, apart from some northern mountain regions. Muslim dominion was to last almost 800 years in parts of Spain. In Islamic Spain – known as al-Andalus – arts and sciences prospered, new crops and agricultural techniques were introduced, and palaces,

mosques, schools, gardens and public baths were built.

In 722 a small army under the Visigothic leader Pelayo inflicted the first defeat on the Muslims (known to Christians as Moros, or Moors) at Covadonga in northern Spain. This marked the beginning of the Reconquista, the spluttering reconquest of Spain by the Christians. By the early 11th century, the frontier between Christian and Muslim Spain stretched from Barcelona to the Atlantic.

In 1085, Alfonso VI, king of León and Castile, took Toledo. This prompted the Muslim leaders to request help from northern

Africa, which arrived in the form of the Almoravids. They recaptured much territory and ruled it until the 1140s. The Almoravids were followed by the Almohads, another North African dynasty, which ruled until 1212. By the mid-13th century, the Christians had taken most of the peninsula except for the state of Granada.

In the process the kingdoms of Castile and Aragón emerged as Christian Spain's two main powers, and in 1469 they were united by the marriage of Isabel, princess of Castile, and Fernando, heir to the throne of Aragón. Known as the Catholic Monarchs, they united Spain and laid the foundations for the Spanish golden age. They also revived the notorious Inquisition, which expelled and executed thousands of Jews and other non-Christians. In 1492 the last Muslim ruler of Granada surrendered to them, marking the completion of the Reconquista.

The Golden Age

Also in 1492, while searching for an alternative passage to India, Columbus stumbled on the Bahamas and claimed the Americas for Spain. This sparked a period of exploration and exploitation that was to yield Spain enormous wealth while destroying the ancient American empires. For three centuries, gold and silver from the New World were used to finance the rapid expansion and slow decline of the Spanish empire.

In 1516, Fernando was succeeded by his grandson Carlos, of the Habsburg dynasty. Carlos was elected Holy Roman Emperor in 1519 and ruled over an empire that included Austria, southern Germany, the Netherlands, Spain and the American colonies. He and his successors were to lead Spain into a series of expensive wars that ultimately bankrupted the empire. In 1588, Sir Francis Drake's English fleet annihilated the mighty Spanish Armada. The Thirty Years' War (1618-48) saw Spain in conflict with the Netherlands, France and England. By the reign of the last Habsburg monarch, Carlos II (1655-1700), the Spanish empire was in decline.

The 18th & 19th Centuries

Carlos II died without an heir. At the end of the subsequent War of the Spanish Succession (1702-13), Felipe V, grandson of French king Louis XIV, became the first of Spain's Bourbon dynasty. A period of stability, enlightened reforms and economic growth ensued, and was ended by events after the French Revolution of 1789.

When Louis XVI was guillotined in 1793, Spain declared war on the French republic, but then turned to alliance with France and war against Britain, in which the Battle of Trafalgar (1805) ended Spanish sea power. In 1807-08 French troops entered Spain and Napoleon convinced Carlos IV, the Spanish king, to abdicate, in whose place he installed his own brother Joseph Bonaparte. The Spaniards fought a five-year war of independence. In 1815 Napoleon was defeated by Wellington and a Bourbon, Fernando VII, was restored to the Spanish throne.

Fernando's reign was a disastrous advertisement for monarchy: the Inquisition was reestablished, liberals and constitutionalists were persecuted, free speech was repressed, Spain entered a severe recession and the American colonies won their independence. After his death in 1833 came the First Carlist War (1834-39), fought between conservative forces led by Don Carlos, Fernando's brother, and liberals who supported the claim of Fernando's daughter Isabel (later Isabel II) to the throne. In 1868 the monarchy was overthrown during the Septembrina Revolution and Isabel II was forced to flee. The First Republic was declared in 1873, but within 18 months the army had restored the monarchy, with Isabel's son Alfonso XII on the throne. Despite political turmoil, Spain's economy prospered in the second half of the 19th century, fuelled by industrialisation.

The disastrous Spanish-American War of 1898 marked the end of the Spanish empire. Spain was defeated by the USA and lost its last overseas possessions; Cuba won a qualified independence and Puerto Rico, Guam and the Philippines passed to the USA.

The 20th Century

The early 20th century was characterised by military disasters in Morocco and growing instability as radical forces struggled to overthrow the established order. In 1923, with Spain on the brink of civil war, Miguel Primo de Rivera made himself military dictator, ruling until 1930. In 1931 Alfonso XIII fled the country, and the Second Republic was declared.

Like its predecessor, the Second Republic fell victim to internal conflict. The 1936 elections told of a country split in two, with the Republican government (an uneasy alliance of leftist parties known as the Popular Front) and its supporters on one side, and the right-wing Nationalists (an alliance of the army, Church and the fascist-style Falange Party) on the other.

Nationalist plotters in the army rose against the government in July 1936. During the subsequent Spanish Civil War (1936-39), the Nationalists, led by General Francisco Franco, received heavy military support from Nazi Germany and fascist Italy, while the elected Republican government received support only from Russia and, to a lesser degree, from the International Brigades made up of foreign leftists.

By 1939 Franco had won and an estimated 350,000 Spaniards had died. After the war, thousands of Republicans were executed, jailed or forced into exile. Franco's 35-year dictatorship began with Spain isolated internationally and crippled by recession. It wasn't until the 1950s and 1960s, when the rise in tourism and a treaty with the USA combined to provide much needed funds, that the country began to recover. By the 1970s Spain had the fastest-growing economy in Europe.

Franco died in 1975, having named Juan Carlos, grandson of Alfonso XIII, his successor. King Juan Carlos is widely credited with having overseen Spain's transition from dictatorship to democracy. The first elections were held in 1977, a new constitution was drafted in 1978, and a failed military coup in 1981 was seen as a futile attempt to turn back the clock. Spain joined the then EC in 1986, and celebrated its return to the world stage in style in 1992, with Expo '92 in Seville and the Olympic Games in Barcelona. In 1997 it became fully integrated in the North Atlantic Treaty Organisation and in 1999 Spain met the criteria for launching the new European currency, the euro. By the time of the 2000 general election, Spain had the fastest growing economy in the EU.

GEOGRAPHY & ECOLOGY

Spain is probably Europe's most geographically diverse country, with landscapes ranging from the near-deserts of Almería to the green, Wales-like countryside and deep coastal inlets of Galicia, and from the sun-baked plains of Castilla-La Mancha to the rugged mountains of the Pyrenees.

The country covers 84% of the Iberian Peninsula and spreads over nearly 505,000 sq km, more than half of which is high tableland, the *meseta*. This is supported and divided by several mountain chains. The main ones are the Pyrenees along the border with France; the Cordillera Cantábrica backing the north coast; the Sistema Ibérico from the central north towards the middle Mediterranean coast; the Cordillera Central from north of Madrid towards the Portuguese border; and three east-west chains across Andalucía, one of which is the highest range of all, the Sierra Nevada.

The major rivers are the Ebro, Duero, Tajo (Tagus), Guadiana and Guadalquivir, each draining a different basin between the mountains and all flowing into the Atlantic Ocean, except for the Ebro which reaches the Mediterranean Sea.

CLIMATE

The meseta and the Ebro basin have a continental climate: scorching in summer, cold in winter and dry. Madrid regularly freezes in December, January and February and temperatures climb above 30°C in July and August. The Guadalquivir basin in Andalucía is only a little wetter and positively broils in high summer, with temperatures in Seville that kill people every year. This area doesn't get as cold as the meseta in winter.

The Pyrenees and the Cordillera Cantábrica backing the Bay of Biscay coast bear the brunt of cold northern and north-western airstreams. Even in high summer you never know when you might get a shower. The Mediterranean coast as a whole, and the Balearic Islands, get a little more rain than Madrid and the south can be even hotter in summer. The Mediterranean also provides Spain's warmest waters (reaching 27°C or so in August) and you *can* swim as early as April or even late March in the south-east.

In general you can rely on pleasant or hot temperatures just about everywhere from April to early November (plus March in the south, but minus a month at either end on the northern and north-western coasts). Snowfalls in the mountains start as early as October and some snow cover lasts all year on the highest peaks.

FLORA & FAUNA

The brown bear, wolf, lynx and wild boar all survive in Spain, although only the boar exists in healthy numbers. Spain's high mountains harbour the goat-like chamois and Spanish ibex (the latter is rare) and big birds of prey such as eagles, vultures and the lammergeier. The marshy Ebro delta and Guadalquivir estuary are important for waterbirds, the spectacular greater flamingo among them. Many of Spain's 5500 seed-bearing plants occur nowhere else in Europe because of the barrier of the Pyrenees. Spring wildflowers are spectacular in many country and hill areas.

The conservation picture has improved by leaps and bounds in the past 20 years and Spain now has 25,000 sq km of protected areas, including 10 national parks. But overgrazing, reservoir creation, tourism, housing developments, agricultural and industrial effluent, fires and hunting all still threaten plant and animal life.

GOVERNMENT & POLITICS

Spain is a constitutional monarchy. The 1978 constitution restored parliamentary government and grouped the country's 50 provinces into 17 autonomous communities, each with its own regional government. From 1982 to 1996 Spain was governed by the centre-left PSOE party led by Felipe González. In the 1996 election the PSOE, weakened by a series of scandals and long-term economic problems, was finally unseated by the right-of-centre Partido Popular, led by José María Aznar. Aznar was handily re-elected in 2000 in the first-ever overall parliamentary majority for a right-of-centre party in democratic Spain.

ECONOMY

Spain has experienced an amazing economic turnabout in the 20th century, raising its living standards from the lowest in Western Europe to a level comparable with the rest of the continent. Its booming economy came back to earth with a thud in the early 1990s, though an initially slow recovery sped up by the end of the decade. The official figure for those registered for unemployment benefits has dropped to 9.1%, although EU estimates put the real figure

at 15%. Either way, it is one of the higher rates in Western Europe. Service industries employ over six million people and produce close to 60% of the country's GDP. The arrival of over 50 million tourists every year brings work to around 10% of the entire labour force. Industry accounts for about one-third of both workforce and GDP, but agriculture accounts for only 4% of GDP compared to 23% in 1960, although it employs one in 10 workers.

POPULATION & PEOPLE

Spain has a population of just under 40 million, descended from all the many peoples who have settled here over the millennia, among them Iberians, Celts, Romans, Jews, Visigoths, Berbers and Arabs. The biggest cities are Madrid (3.1 million), Barcelona (1.5 million), Valencia (739,000) and Seville (701,000). Each region proudly preserves its own unique culture, and some – Catalonia and the País Vasco in particular – display a fiercely independent spirit.

ARTS
Cinema

Early Spanish cinema was hamstrung by a lack of funds and technology, and perhaps the greatest of all Spanish directors, Luis Buñuel, made his silent surrealist classics *Un Chien Andalou* (1928) and *L'Age d'Or* (1930) in France. Buñuel, however, returned to Spain to make *Tierra sin Pan* (Land without Bread, 1932), a film about rural poverty in the Las Hurdes area of Extremadura.

Under Franco there was strict censorship, but satirical and uneasy films like Juan Antonio Bardem's *Muerte de un Ciclista* (Death of a Cyclist, 1955) and Luis Berlanga's *Bienvenido Mr Marshall* (Welcome Mr Marshall, 1953) still managed to appear. Carlos Saura, with films like *Ana y los Lobos* (Anna and the Wolves, 1973), and Victor Erice, with *El Espiritu de la Colmena* (Spirit of the Beehive, 1973) and *El Sur* (The South, 1983), looked at the problems of young people scarred by the Spanish Civil War and its aftermath.

After Franco, Pedro Almodóvar broke away from this serious cinema dwelling on the past with his humorous films set amid the social and artistic revolution of the late 1970s and 1980s notably *Mujeres al Borde de un Ataque de Nervios* (Women on the Verge of

SPAIN

a Nervous Breakdown, 1988). In 1995, Ken Loach produced a moving co-production on the Spanish Civil War, *Tierra y Libertad* (Land and Freedom).

Painting

The golden age of Spanish art (1550-1650) was strongly influenced by Italy but the great Spanish artists developed their talents in unique ways. The giants were the Toledo-based El Greco (originally from Crete), and Diego Velázquez, perhaps Spain's most revered painter. Both excelled with insightful portraits. Francisco Zurbarán and Bartolomé Esteban Murillo were also prominent. The genius of the 18th and 19th centuries was Francisco Goya, whose versatility ranged from unflattering royal portraits and anguished war scenes to bullfight etchings.

Catalonia was the powerhouse of early-20th-century Spanish art, engendering the hugely prolific Pablo Picasso (born in Andalucía), the colourful symbolist Joan Miró, and Salvador Dalí, who was obsessed with the unconscious and weird. Works by these and other major Spanish artists can be found in galleries throughout the country.

Architecture

The earliest architectural relics are the prehistoric monuments on Menorca. Reminders of Roman times include the ruins of Mérida and Tarragona, and Segovia's amazing aqueduct. The Muslims left behind some of the most splendid buildings in the entire Islamic world, including Granada's Alhambra, Córdoba's mosque and Seville's alcázar – the latter an example of *mudéjar* architecture, the name given to Moorish work done throughout Christian-held territory.

The first main Christian architectural movement was Romanesque, in the north in the 11th and 12th centuries, which has left countless lovely country churches and several cathedrals, notably that of Santiago de Compostela. Later came the many great Gothic cathedrals (Toledo, Barcelona, León, Salamanca and Seville) of the 13th to 16th centuries, as well as Renaissance styles, such as the plateresque work so prominent in Salamanca and the austere work of Juan de Herrera, responsible for El Escorial. Spain then followed the usual path to baroque (17th and 18th centuries) and neoclassicism (19th century) before Catalonia produced its startling modernist (roughly Art Nouveau) movement around the turn of the 20th century, of which Antoni Gaudí's La Sagrada Família church is the most stunning example. More recent architecture is only likely to excite specialists.

Literature

One of the earliest works of Spanish literature is the *Cantar de mío Cid*, an anonymous epic poem describing the life of El Cid, an 11th-century Christian knight. Miguel de Cervantes' novel *Don Quixote de la Mancha* is the masterpiece of the literary flowering of the 16th and 17th centuries, and one of the world's great works of fiction. The playwrights Lope de Vega and Pedro Calderón de la Barca were also leading lights of the age.

The next high point, in the early 20th century, grew out of the crisis of the Spanish-American War that spawned the intellectual 'Generation of '98'. Philosophical essayist Miguel de Unamuno was prominent, but the towering figure was poet and playwright Federico García Lorca, whose tragedies *Blood Wedding* and *Yerma* won international acclaim before he was murdered in the civil war for his Republican sympathies. Camilo José Cela, author of the civil war aftermath novel *The Family of Pascal Duarte*, won the 1989 Nobel Prize for literature. Juan Goytisolo is probably the major contemporary writer; his most approachable work is his autobiography *Forbidden Territory*. There has been a proliferation of women – particularly feminist writers – in the past 25 years, among whose prominent representatives are Adelaide Morales, Ana María Matute and Rosa Montero.

SOCIETY & CONDUCT

Most Spaniards are economical with etiquette but this does not signify unfriendliness. They're gregarious people, on the whole very tolerant and easy-going towards foreigners. It's not easy to give offence. Disrespectful behaviour including excessively casual dress in churches won't go down well though.

Siesta

Contrary to popular belief, most Spaniards do not sleep in the afternoon. The siesta is

SPAIN

generally devoted to a long leisurely lunch and lingering conversation. Then again, if you've stayed out until 5 am ...

Flamenco

Getting to see real, deeply emotional, flamenco can be hard, as it tends to happen semi-spontaneously in little bars. Andalucía is its traditional home. You'll find plenty of clubs there and elsewhere offering flamenco shows; these are generally aimed at tourists and are expensive, but some are good. Your best chance of catching the real thing is probably at one of the flamenco festivals in the south, usually held in summer.

RELIGION

Only about 20% of Spaniards are regular churchgoers, but Catholicism is deeply ingrained in the culture. As the writer Unamuno said: 'Here in Spain we are all Catholics, even the atheists'.

Many Spaniards have a deep-seated scepticism of the Church; during the civil war, churches were burnt and clerics shot because they represented repression, corruption and the old order.

LANGUAGE

Spanish, or Castilian (*castellano*) as it is often and more precisely called, is spoken by just about all Spaniards, but there are also three widely spoken regional languages: Catalan (another Romance language, closely related to Spanish and French) is spoken by about two-thirds of people in Catalonia and the Balearic Islands and half the people in the Valencia region; Galician (another Romance language that sounds like a cross between Spanish and Portuguese) is spoken by many in the northwest; and Basque (of obscure, non-Latin origin) is spoken by a minority in the País Vasco and Navarra.

English isn't as widely spoken as many travellers seem to expect. In the principal cities and tourist areas it's much easier to find people who speak at least some English, though generally you'll be better received if you at least try to communicate in Spanish.

See the Language chapter at the back of the book for pronunciation guidelines and useful words and phrases.

Facts for the Visitor

HIGHLIGHTS

Beaches

Yes, it's still possible to have a beach to yourself in Spain. In summer it may be a little tricky, but spots where things are bound to be quiet are such gems as the beaches of Cabo Favàritx in Menorca, and some of the secluded coves on Cabo de Gata in Andalucía. There are also good, relatively uncrowded beaches on the Costa de la Luz, between Tarifa and Cádiz. On the Galician coast, between Noia and Pontevedra, are literally hundreds of beaches where even in mid-August you won't feel claustrophobic.

Museums & Galleries

Spain is home to some of the finest art galleries in the world. The Prado in Madrid has few rivals, and there are outstanding art museums in Bilbao, Seville, Barcelona, Valencia and Córdoba. Fascinating smaller galleries, such as the Dalí museum in Figueres and the abstract art museum in Cuenca, also abound. Tarragona and Teruel have excellent archaeological museums.

Buildings

Try not to miss Andalucía's Muslim-era gems – the Alhambra in Granada, the alcázar in Seville and the Mezquita in Córdoba – or Barcelona's extraordinary La Sagrada Família church. The fairy-tale alcázar in Segovia has to be seen to be believed.

For even more exciting views, and loads of medieval ghosts, try to reach the ruined castle in Morella, Valencia province. Or you can fast-forward to 1997 and Bilbao's spectacular Guggenheim museum, whose wavy exterior steals the show from the contemporary art within.

Scenery

There's outstanding mountain scenery often coupled with highly picturesque villages in the Pyrenees and Picos de Europa in the north and in parts of Andalucía such as the Alpujarras. On the coasts, the rugged inlets of Galicia and stark, hilly Cabo de Gata in Andalucía stand out.

SPAIN

SUGGESTED ITINERARIES

If you want to whiz around as many places as possible in limited time, the following itineraries might suit you:

Two days
Fly to Madrid, Barcelona or Seville, or nip into Barcelona or San Sebastián overland from France.
One week
Spend two days each in Barcelona, Madrid and Seville, allowing one day for travel.
Two weeks
As above, plus San Sebastián, Toledo, Salamanca and/or Cuenca, Córdoba and/or Granada, and maybe Cáceres and/or Trujillo.
One month
As above, plus some of the following: side trips from the cities mentioned above; an exploration of the north, including Santiago de Compostela and the Picos de Europa; visits to Teruel, Mallorca, Formentera, Segovia, Ávila, or some smaller towns and more remote regions such as North-East Extremadura or Cabo de Gata.

PLANNING
When to Go

For most purposes the ideal months to visit Spain are May, June and September (plus April and October in the south). At these times you can rely on good weather, yet avoid the sometimes extreme heat and main crush of Spanish and foreign tourists of July and August, when temperatures may climb to 45°C in parts of Andalucía and when Madrid is unbearably hot and almost deserted.

The summer overflows with festivals, including Sanfermines, with the running of the bulls in Pamplona, and Semana Grande all along the north coast (dates vary from place to place), but there are excellent festivals during the rest of the year too.

In winter the rains never seem to stop in the north, except when they turn to snow. Madrid regularly freezes in December, January and February. At these times Andalucía is the place to be, with temperatures reaching the mid-teens in most places and good skiing in the Sierra Nevada.

Maps

Some of the best maps for travellers are published by Michelin, which produces a 1:1 million *Spain Portugal* map and six 1:400,000

regional maps. The country map doesn't show railways, but the regional maps do.

What to Bring

You can buy anything you need in Spain, but some articles, such as sun-screen lotion, are more expensive than elsewhere. Books in English tend to be expensive and are hard to find outside main cities.

A pair of strong shoes and a towel are essential. A moneybelt or shoulder wallet can be useful in big cities. Bring sunglasses if glare gets to you. If you want to blend in, don't just pack T-shirts, shorts and runners – Spaniards are quite dressy and many tourists just look like casual slobs to them.

TOURIST OFFICES

Most towns (and many villages) of any interest have a tourist office *(oficina de turismo)*. These will supply you with a map and brochures with basic information on local sights, attractions, accommodation, history etc. Some can also provide information on other places too. Their staff are generally helpful and often speak some English. There is also a nationwide phone line with information in English (☎ 901-30 06 00), daily from 9 am to 6 pm.

Tourist Offices Abroad

Spain has tourist information centres in 19 countries including:

Canada (☎ 416-961-3131, @ toronto@tourspain.es) 2 Bloor St W, 34th floor, Toronto M4W 3E2
France (☎ 01 45 03 82 57, @ paris@tourspain.es) 43, rue Decamps, 75784 Paris, Cedex 16
Portugal (☎ 01-357 1992, @ lisboa@tourspain.es) Avenida Sidónio Pais 28 3 Dto, 1050 Lisbon
UK (☎ 020-7486 8077, brochure request ☎ 0891 669920 at 50p a minute, @ londres@tourspain.es) 22-23 Manchester Square, London W1M 5AP
USA (☎ 212-265 8822, @ oetny@tourspain.es) 666 Fifth Ave, 35th floor, New York, NY 10103

VISAS & DOCUMENTS

Citizens of EU countries can enter Spain with their national identity card or passport. UK citizens must have a full passport – a British visitor passport won't do. Non-EU nationals must take their passport.

EU, Norway and Iceland citizens require no visa. Nationals of Australia, Canada, Israel, Japan, New Zealand, Switzerland and the USA need no visa for stays of up to 90 days but must have a passport valid for the whole visit. Keep in mind this 90 day limit applies throughout the EU, so don't overstay your time in the EU even if Spain is only part of your trip. South Africans are among nationalities who do need a visa for Spain.

It's best to obtain the visa in your country of residence to avoid possible bureaucratic problems. Both 30-day and 90-day single-entry, and 90-day multiple-entry visas are available, though if you apply in a country where you're not resident the 90-day option may not be available. Multiple-entry visas will save you a lot of time and trouble if you plan to leave Spain say to Gibraltar or Morocco then re-enter it.

The Schengen System

Spain is one of the Schengen Area countries; the others are Portugal, Italy, France, Germany, Austria, the Netherlands, Belgium and Luxembourg, Sweden, Finland, Denmark and Greece. They have theoretically done away with passport control on travel between them. (In fact, checks have been known to occur at airports and on Lisbon-Madrid trains.) It is illegal to enter Spain without a visa (if you require one) and doing so can lead to deportation.

One good thing about the system is that a visa for one Schengen country is valid for others too. Compare validity periods, prices and the number of permitted entries before you apply, as these can differ between countries.

Stays of Longer than 90 Days

EU, Norway and Iceland nationals planning to stay in Spain more than 90 days are supposed to apply during their first month in the country for a residence card. This is a lengthy, complicated procedure; if you intend to subject yourself to it, consult a Spanish consulate before you go to Spain, as you'll need to take certain documents with you.

Other nationalities on a Schengen visa are flat out of luck when it comes to extensions. For stays of longer than 90 days you're supposed to get a residence card. This is a nightmarish process, starting with a residence visa issued by a Spanish consulate in your country of residence; start the process well in advance.

EMBASSIES & CONSULATES
Spanish Embassies & Consulates

Spanish embassies include:

Australia (☎ 02-6273 3555,
  @ embespau@mail.mae.es) 15 Arkana St, Yarralumla, Canberra, ACT 2600; consulates in Brisbane, Melbourne, Perth and Sydney
Canada (☎ 613-747-2252,
  @ spain@DocuWeb.ca) 74 Stanley Avenue, Ottawa, Ont K1M 1P4
  Consulate in Toronto: (☎ 416-977-1661)
  Consulate in Montreal: (☎ 514-935-5235)
France (☎ 01 44 43 18 00,
  @ ambespfr@mail.mae.es) 22 avenue Marceau, 75008 Paris, Cedex 08
Portugal (☎ 01-347 2381,
  @ embesppt@mail.mae.es) Rua do Salitre 1, 1250 Lisbon
UK (☎ 020-7235 5555, @ espemblon@ espemblon.freeserve.co.uk, 39 Chesham Place, London SW1X 8SB
  Consulate: (☎ 020-7589 8989) 20 Draycott Place, London SW3 2RZ and in Edinburgh and Manchester
USA (☎ 202-452 0100) 2375 Pennsylvania Ave NW, Washington, DC 20037; consulates in Boston, Chicago, Houston, Miami, Los Angeles, New Orleans, New York and San Francisco

Embassies & Consulates in Spain

Some 70 countries have embassies in Madrid, including:

Australia (☎ 91 441 93 00) Plaza del Descubridor Diego de Ordás 3-2, Edificio Santa Engrácia 120
Canada (☎ 91 431 45 56) Calle de Núñez de Balboa 35
France (☎ 91 310 11 12) Calle del Marqués Ensenada 10
Germany (☎ 91 557 90 00) Calle de Fortuny 8
Ireland (☎ 91 436 40 95) Paseo de la Castellana 46
Japan (☎ 91 590 13 21), Calle de Serrano 109
Morocco (☎ 91 563 79 28) Calle de Serrano 179
  Consulate: (☎ 91 561 21 45) Calle de Leizaran 31
New Zealand (☎ 91 523 02 26, 91 531 09 97) Plaza de la Lealtad 2
Portugal (☎ 91 561 47 23) Calle de Castelló 128
  Consulate: (☎ 91 577 35 38) Calle Lagasca 88
UK (☎ 91 308 06 18) Calle de Fernando el Santo 16

SPAIN

Consulate: (☎ 91 308 53 00) Calle del Marqués Ensenada 16
USA (☎ 91 577 40 00) Calle de Serrano 75

CUSTOMS

From outside the EU you are allowed to bring in duty-free one bottle of spirits, one bottle of wine, 50ml of perfume and 200 cigarettes. From within the EU you can bring 2L of wine *and* 1L of spirits, with the same limits on the rest. Duty-free allowances for travel between EU countries were abolished in 1999.

MONEY
Currency

Spain's currency for everyday transactions until early in 2002 is the peseta (pta). The legal denominations are coins of one, five (known as a *duro*), 10, 25, 50, 100, 200 and 500 ptas. There are notes of 1000, 2000, 5000 and 10,000 ptas. Take care not to confuse the 500 ptas coin with the 100 ptas coin.

Exchange Rates

Banks mostly open 8.30 am to 2 pm Monday to Friday, 8.30 am to 1 pm Saturday and tend to give better exchange rates than currency-exchange offices. Travellers cheques attract a slightly better rate than cash. ATMs accepting a wide variety of cards are common.

country	unit		pesetas
Australia	A$1	=	106.71 ptas
Canada	C$1	=	124.16 ptas
euro	€1	=	166.38 ptas
France	1FF	=	25.36 ptas
Germany	DM1	=	85.07 ptas
Japan	¥100	=	169.5 ptas
New Zealand	NZ$1	=	82.84 ptas
UK	UK£1	=	276.89 ptas
USA	US$1	=	184.16 ptas

Costs

Spain is one of Western Europe's more affordable countries. If you are particularly frugal, it's possible to scrape by on 3000 ptas to 4000 ptas a day; this would involve staying in the cheapest possible accommodation, avoiding eating in restaurants or going to museums or bars, and not moving around too much. Places like Madrid, Barcelona, Seville and San Sebastián will place a greater strain on your moneybelt.

A more reasonable budget would be 6000 ptas a day. This could allow you 1500 ptas to 2000 ptas for accommodation; 300 ptas for breakfast (coffee and a pastry); 1000 ptas to 1500 ptas for lunch or dinner; 600 ptas to 800 ptas for another, lighter meal; 250 ptas for public transport; 500 ptas to 1000 ptas for entry fees to museum, sights or entertainment; and a bit over for a drink or two and intercity travel.

Tipping & Bargaining

In restaurants, menu prices include a service charge, and tipping is a matter of personal choice – most people leave some small change and 5% is plenty. It's common to leave small change in bars and cafes. The only places in Spain where you are likely to bargain are markets and, occasionally, cheap hotels – particularly if you're staying for a few days.

Consumer Taxes & Refunds

In Spain, VAT (value-added tax) is known as IVA *(impuesto sobre el valor añadido)*. On accommodation and restaurant prices, there's a flat rate of 7% IVA which is usually, but not always, included in quoted prices. To check, ask if the price is 'con IVA' (with VAT) or 'sin IVA' (without VAT).

On retail goods, alcohol, electrical appliances etc, IVA is 16%. Visitors are entitled to a refund of IVA on any item costing more than 15,000 ptas that they are taking out of the EU. Ask the shop for a Europe Tax-Free Shopping Cheque when you buy, then present the goods and cheque to customs when you leave. Customs stamps the cheque and you then cash it at a booth with the 'Cash Refund' sign. There are booths at all main Spanish airports, the border crossings at Algeciras, Gibraltar and Andorra, and similar refund points throughout the EU.

POST & COMMUNICATIONS
Post

Main post offices in provincial capitals are usually open about 8.30 am to 8.30 pm Monday to Friday, and about 9 am to 1.30 pm Saturday. Stamps are also sold at *estancos* (tobacconist shops with the 'Tabacos' sign in yellow letters on a maroon background). A standard airmail letter or card costs 70 ptas to Europe, 115 ptas to the

USA or Canada, and 185 ptas to Australia or New Zealand. Aerograms cost 85 ptas regardless of the destination.

Mail to/from Europe normally takes up to a week, and to North America, Australia or New Zealand around 10 days, but there may be some unaccountable long delays.

Poste-restante mail can be addressed to you at either poste restante or *lista de correos*, the Spanish name for it, in the city in question. It's a fairly reliable system, although you must be prepared for mail to arrive late. American Express card or travellers cheque holders can use the free client mail service (see the Facts for the Visitor chapter at the beginning of this book).

Common abbreviations used in Spanish addresses are 1, 2, 3 etc, which mean 1st, 2nd, 3rd floor, and s/n *(sin número)*, which means the building has no number.

Telephone & Fax

Area codes in Spain are an integral part of the phone number; all numbers are nine digits long, without area codes.

Public pay phones are blue, common and easy to use. They accept coins, phonecards *(tarjetas telefónicas)* and, in some cases, credit cards. Phonecards come in 1000 and 2000 ptas denominations and are available at main post offices and estancos. A three-minute call from a pay phone costs 25 ptas within a local area, 65 ptas to other places in the same province, 110 ptas to other provinces, or 230 ptas to another EU country. Provincial and inter-provincial calls, except those to mobile phones, are around 50% cheaper between 8 pm and 8 am and all day Saturday and Sunday; local and international calls are around 10% cheaper between 6 pm and 8 am and all day Saturday and Sunday.

International reverse-charge (collect) calls are simple to make: from a pay phone or private phone dial ☎ 900-99 00 followed by ☎ 61 for Australia, ☎ 44 for the UK, ☎ 64 for New Zealand, ☎ 15 for Canada, and for the USA ☎ 11 (AT&T) or ☎ 14 (MCI).

A three-minute call to the USA at peak rates will cost 280 ptas, and to Australia 820 ptas.

Most main post offices have a fax service, but you'll often find cheaper rates at shops or offices with 'Fax Público' signs.

INTERNET RESOURCES

Cybercafes are beginning to spring up in major Spanish cities. Charges for an hour online range anywhere from 200 ptas to 900 ptas.

An Internet search under 'Spain, Travel' will reveal dozens of sites.

BOOKS

The New Spaniards by John Hooper is a fascinating account of modern Spanish society and culture. For a readable and thorough, but not over-long, survey of Spanish history, *The Story of Spain* by Mark Williams is hard to beat.

Classic accounts of life and travel in Spain include Gerald Brenan's *South from Granada* (1920s), Laurie Lee's *As I Walked Out One Midsummer Morning* (1930s), George Orwell's *Homage to Catalonia* (the civil war), and *Iberia* by James Michener (1960s). Among the best of more recent books are *Homage to Barcelona* by Colm Toíbín, *Spanish Journeys* by Adam Hopkins and *Cities of Spain* by David Gilmour.

Of foreign literature set in Spain, Ernest Hemingway's civil war novel *For Whom the Bell Tolls* is a must.

If you're planning in-depth travels in Spain, get hold of Lonely Planet's *Spain*.

NEWSPAPERS & MAGAZINES

The major daily newspapers in Spain are the solid liberal *El País*, the conservative *ABC*, and *El Mundo*, which specialises in breaking political scandals. There's also a welter of regional dailies, some of the best being in Barcelona, the País Vasco and Andalucía.

International press such as the *International Herald Tribune*, *Time* and *Newsweek*, and daily papers from Western European countries reach major cities and tourist areas on the day of publication; elsewhere they're harder to find and are a day or two late.

RADIO & TV

There are hundreds of radio stations, mainly on the FM band – you'll hear a substantial proportion of British and American music. The national pop/rock station, Radio 3, has admirably varied programming.

Spaniards are Europe's greatest TV watchers after the British, but do a lot of their watching in bars and cafes which makes it more of a social activity. Most TVs receive

SPAIN

SPAIN

six channels: two state-run (TVE1 and La2), three privately run (Antena 3, Tele 5 and Canal+), and one regional channel. Apart from news, TV seems to consist mostly of game and talk shows, sport, soap operas, sitcoms, and English-language films dubbed into Spanish.

PHOTOGRAPHY & VIDEO

Main brands of film are widely available and processing is fast and generally efficient. A roll of print film (36 exposures, 100 ASA) costs around 700 ptas and can be processed for around 1700 ptas though there are often better deals if you have two or three rolls developed together. The equivalent in slide film is around 850 ptas plus the same for processing. Nearly all pre-recorded videos in Spain use the PAL image-registration system common to Western Europe and Australia. These won't work on many video players in France, North America and Japan.

TIME

Spain is one hour ahead of GMT/UTC during winter, and two hours ahead from the last Sunday in March to the last Sunday in September.

LAUNDRY

Self-service laundrettes are rare. Laundries (*lavanderías*) are common but not particularly cheap. They will usually wash, dry and fold a load for 1000 ptas to 1200 ptas.

TOILETS

Public toilets are not very common in Spain. The easiest thing to do is head for a cafe. It is polite to buy something in exchange for the toilet service.

WOMEN TRAVELLERS

The best way for women travellers to approach Spain is simply to be ready to ignore stares, cat calls and unnecessary comments. However, Spain has one of the lowest incidences of reported rape in the developed world, and even physical harassment is much less frequent than you might expect. The Asociación de Asistencia a Mujeres Violadas, at Calle de O'Donnell 42 in Madrid (☎ 91 574 01 10, Monday to Friday from 10 am to 2 pm and 4 to 7 pm; recorded message in Spanish at other times) offers advice and

help to rape victims, and can provide details of similar centres in other cities, though only limited English is spoken.

GAY & LESBIAN TRAVELLERS

Attitudes towards gays and lesbians are pretty tolerant, especially in the cities. Madrid, Barcelona, Sitges, Ibiza and Cádiz all have active gay and lesbian scenes. A good source of information on gay places and organisations throughout Spain is Coordinadora Gai-Lesbiana (☎ 93 298 00 29, fax 93 298 06 18), Carrer de Finlandia 45, 08014 Barcelona. Its Web site is www.pangea .org/org/cgl. In Madrid, the equivalent is Cogam (☎/fax 91 532 45 17), Calle del Fuencarral 37, 28004 Madrid.

DISABLED TRAVELLERS

Spanish tourist offices in other countries can provide a basic information sheet with some useful addresses, and give information on accessible accommodation in specific places. INSERSO (☎ 91 347 88 88), Calle de Ginzo de Limea 58, 28029 Madrid, is the government department for the disabled, with branches in all of Spain's 50 provinces.

You'll find some wheelchair-accessible accommodation in main centres, but it may not be in the budget category – although 25 Spanish youth hostels are classed as suitable for wheelchair users.

SENIOR TRAVELLERS

There are reduced prices for people over 60, 63 or 65 (depending on the place) at some attractions and occasionally on transport.

USEFUL ORGANISATIONS

The travel agency TIVE, with offices in major cities throughout Spain, specialises in discounted tickets and travel arrangements for students and young people. Its Madrid office (☎ 91 543 74 12, fax 91 544 00 62) is at Calle de Fernando El Católico 88.

DANGERS & ANNOYANCES

It's a good idea to take your car radio and any other valuables with you any time you leave your car. In fact it's best to leave nothing at all – certainly nothing visible – in a parked car. In youth hostels, don't leave belongings unattended as there is a high incidence of theft. Beware of pickpockets in cities and tourist resorts (Barcelona and Seville have bad reputations). There is also a relatively high incidence of mugging in such places, so keep your wits about you. Emergency numbers for the police throughout Spain are ☎ 091 (national police) and ☎ 092 (local police).

Drugs

In 1992 Spain's liberal drug laws were severely tightened. No matter what anyone tells you, it is not legal to smoke dope in public bars. There is a reasonable degree of tolerance when it comes to people having a smoke in their own home, but not in hotel rooms or guesthouses.

BUSINESS HOURS

Generally, people work Monday to Friday from 9 am to 2 pm and then again from 4.30 or 5 pm for another three hours. Shops and travel agencies are usually open these hours on Saturday too, though some may skip the evening session. Museums all have their own unique opening hours; major ones tend to open for something like normal business hours (with or without the afternoon break), but often have their weekly closing day on Monday, not Sunday.

PUBLIC HOLIDAYS & SPECIAL EVENTS

Spain has at least 14 official holidays a year, some observed nationwide, some very local. When a holiday falls close to a weekend, Spaniards like to make a *puente* (bridge) meaning they take the intervening day off too. The following holidays are observed virtually everywhere:

New Year's Day 1 January
Epiphany or Three Kings' Day (when children receive presents) 6 January
Good Friday
Labour Day 1 May
Feast of the Assumption 15 August
National Day 12 October
All Saints' Day 1 November
Feast of the Immaculate Conception 8 December
Christmas 25 December

The two main periods when Spaniards go on holiday are Semana Santa (the week leading up to Easter Sunday) and the month of August.

At these times accommodation in resorts can be scarce and transport heavily booked, but other cities are often half-empty.

Spaniards indulge their love of colour, noise, crowds and partying at innumerable local fiestas and *ferias* (fairs); even small villages will have at least one, probably several, during the year. Many fiestas are based on religion but still highly festive. Local tourist offices can always supply detailed information.

Among festivals to look out for are La Tamborada in San Sebastián on 20 January, when the whole town dresses up and goes berserk; *carnaval*, a time of fancy-dress parades and merrymaking celebrated around the country about seven weeks before Easter (wildest in Cádiz and Sitges); Valencia's week-long mid-March party, Las Fallas, with all-night dancing and drinking, first-class fireworks, and processions; Semana Santa with its parades of holy images and huge crowds, notably in Seville; Seville's Feria de Abril, a week-long party held in late April, a kind of counterbalance to the religious peak of Semana Santa; Sanfermines, with the running of the bulls, in Pamplona in July; Semana Grande, another week of heavy drinking and hangovers, all along the north coast during the first half of August; and Barcelona's week-long party, the Festes de la Mercè, around 24 September.

ACTIVITIES
Surfing & Windsurfing

The País Vasco has good surf spots – San Sebastián, Zarauz and the legendary left at Mundaca, among others. Tarifa, Spain's southernmost point, is a windsurfers' heaven, with constant breezes and long, empty beaches.

Skiing

Skiing in Spain is cheap and the facilities and conditions are good. The season runs from December to May. The most accessible resorts are in the Sierra Nevada (very close to Granada), the Pyrenees (north of Barcelona) and in the ranges north of Madrid. Contact tourist offices in these cities for information. Affordable day trips can be booked through travel agents.

Cycling

Bike touring isn't as common as in other parts of Europe because of deterrents such as the often-mountainous terrain and summer heat. It's a more viable option on the Balearic Islands than on much of the mainland, although plenty of people get on their bikes in spring and autumn in the south. Mountain biking is increasingly popular and areas like Andalucía and Catalonia have many good tracks. Finding bikes to rent is a hit-and-miss affair so if you're set on the idea it's best to bring your own.

Hiking

Spain is a trekker's paradise, so much so that Lonely Planet has published a guide to some of the best treks in the country, *Walking in Spain*. See also the Mallorca and Picos de Europa sections of this chapter.

Walking country roads and paths, between settlements, can also be highly enjoyable and a great way to meet the locals.

Two organisations publish detailed close-up maps of small parts of Spain. The CNIG covers most of the country in 1:25,000 (1cm to 250m) sheets, most of which are recent. The CNIG and the Servicio Geográfico del Ejército (SGE, Army Geographic Service) each publishes a 1:50,000 series; the SGE's tends to be more up to date as the maps were published in the mid-1980s. Also useful for hiking and exploring some areas are the *Guía Cartográfica* and *Guía Excursionista y Turística* series published by Editorial Alpina. The series combines information booklets in Spanish (or sometimes Catalan) with detailed maps at scales ranging from 1:25,000 to 1:50,000, which are well worth their price (around 500 ptas). You may well find CNIG, SCE and Alpina publications in local bookshops but it's more reliable to get them in advance from specialist map or travel shops like La Tienda Verde in Madrid, and Altaïr and Quera in Barcelona.

If you fancy a really long walk, there's the Camino de Santiago. This route, which has been followed by Christian pilgrims for centuries, can be commenced at various places in France. It then crosses the Pyrenees and runs via Pamplona, Logroño and León all the way to the cathedral in Santiago de Compostela. There are numerous guidebooks explaining the route, and the best map is published by CNIG.

COURSES

The best place to take a language course in Spain is generally at a university. Those with the best reputations include Salamanca, Santiago de Compostela and Santander. It can also be fun to combine study with a stay in one of Spain's most exciting cities such as Barcelona, Madrid or Seville. There are also dozens of private language colleges throughout the country; the Instituto Cervantes (☎ 020-7235 0353), 102 Eaton Square, London SW1 W9AN, can send you lists of these and of universities that run courses. Some Spanish embassies and consulates also have information.

Other courses available in Spain include art, cookery and photography. Spanish tourist offices can help with information.

WORK

EU, Norway and Iceland nationals are allowed to work in Spain without a visa, but if they plan to stay more than three months, they are supposed to apply within the first month for a residence card (see Visas & Documents earlier in this chapter). Virtually everyone else is supposed to obtain, from a Spanish consulate in their country of residence, a work permit and, if they plan to stay more than 90 days, a residence visa. These procedures are even more difficult (see Visas & Documents). That said, quite a few people do manage to work in Spain one way or another – though with Spain's unemployment rate running at around 15%, don't rely on it. Teaching English is an obvious option – a TEFL certificate will be a big help. Another possibility is gaining summer work in a bar or restaurant in a tourist resort. Quite a lot of these are run by foreigners.

ACCOMMODATION
Camping

Spain has more than 800 camping grounds. Facilities and settings vary enormously, and grounds are officially rated from 1st class to 3rd class. You can expect to pay around 500 ptas each per person, car and tent. Tourist offices can direct you to the nearest camping ground. Many are open all year, though quite a few close from around October to Easter. With certain exceptions (such as many beaches and environmentally protected areas), it is legal to camp outside camping grounds. You'll need permission to camp on private land.

Hostels

Spain's youth hostels (albergues juveniles) are often the cheapest place to stay for lone travellers, but two people can usually get a double room elsewhere for a similar price. With some notable exceptions, hostels are only moderate value. Many have curfews and/or are closed during the day, or lack cooking facilities (if so they usually have a cafeteria). They can be lacking in privacy, and are often heavily booked by school groups. Most are members of the country's Hostelling International (HI) organisation, Red Española de Albergues Juveniles (REAJ), whose head office (☎ 91 347 77 00, fax 91 401 81 60) is at Calle de José Ortega y Gasset 71, 28006 Madrid.

Prices often depend on the season or whether you're under 26; typically you pay 900 ptas to 1700 ptas. Some hostels require HI membership, others don't but may charge more if you're not a member. You can buy HI cards for 1800 ptas at virtually all hostels.

Other Accommodation

Officially, all the establishments are either hoteles (from one to five stars), hostales (one to three stars) or pensiones. In practice, there are all sorts of overlapping categories, especially at the budget end of the market. In broad terms, the cheapest are usually fondas and casas de huéspedes, followed by pensiones. All these normally have shared bathrooms, and singles/doubles for 1250/2500 ptas to 3000/4000 ptas. Some hostales and hostal-residencias come in the same price range, but others have rooms with private bathroom costing anywhere up to 8000 ptas or so. Hoteles are usually beyond the means of budget travellers. The luxurious state-run paradores, often converted historic buildings, are prohibitively expensive.

Room rates in this chapter are generally high-season prices, which in most resorts and other heavily touristed places means July and August, Semana Santa and sometimes Christmas and New Year. At other times prices in many places go down by 5% to 25%. In many cases you have to add 7% IVA.

FOOD

It's a good idea to reset your stomach's clock in Spain, unless you want to eat alone or only with other tourists. Most Spaniards start the day with a light breakfast (desayuno), perhaps coffee with a tostada (piece of buttered toast) or pastel (pastry). Churros con chocolate (long, deep-fried doughnuts with thick hot chocolate) are a delicious start to the day and unique to Spain. Lunch (almuerzo or comida) is usually the main meal of the day, eaten between about 1.30 and 4 pm. The evening meal (cena) is usually lighter and may be eaten as late as 10 or 11 pm. It's common (and a great idea!) to go to a bar or cafe for a snack around 11 am and again around 7 or 8 pm.

Spain has a huge variety of local cuisines. Seafood as well as meat is prominent almost everywhere. One of the most characteristic dishes, from the Valencia region, is paella – rice, seafood, the odd vegetable and often chicken or meat, all simmered up together, traditionally coloured yellow with saffron. Another dish, of Andalucían origin, is gazpacho, a soup made from tomatoes, breadcrumbs, cucumber and/or green peppers, eaten cold. Tortillas (omelettes) are an inexpensive stand-by and come in many varieties. Jamón serrano (cured ham) is a treat for meat-eaters.

Cafes & Bars

If you want to follow Spanish habits, you'll be spending plenty of time in cafes and bars. In almost all of them you'll find tapas available. These saucer-sized mini-snacks are part of the Spanish way of life and come in infinite varieties from calamari rings to potato salad to spinach with chickpeas to a small serving of tripe. A typical tapa costs 100 ptas to 250 ptas (although sometimes they will come free with your drinks), but check before you order because some are a lot dearer. A ración is a meal-sized serving of these snacks; a media ración is a half-ración.

The other popular snacks are bocadillos, long filled white bread rolls. Spaniards eat so many bocadillos that some cafes sell nothing else. Try not to leave Spain without sampling a bocadillo de tortilla de patata, a roll filled with potato omelette.

You can often save 10% to 20% by ordering and eating food at the bar rather than at a table.

Restaurants

Throughout Spain, there are plenty of restaurants serving good, simple food at affordable prices, often featuring regional specialities.

Many restaurants offer a *menú del día* – the budget traveller's best friend. For around 850 ptas to 1500 ptas, you typically get a starter, a main course, dessert, bread and wine – often with a choice of two or three dishes for each course. The *plato combinado* is a near relative of the *menú*. It literally translates as 'combined plate' – maybe a steak and egg with chips and salad, or fried squid with potato salad. You'll pay more for your meals if you order a la carte, but the food will be better.

Vegetarian Food

Finding vegetarian fare can be a headache. It's not uncommon for 'meatless' food to be flavoured with meat stock. But in larger cities and important student centres there's a growing awareness of vegetarianism, so that if there isn't a vegetarian restaurant, there are often vegetarian items on menus. A good vegetarian snack at almost any place with bocadillos or sandwiches is a bocadillo (or sandwich) *vegetal*, which has a filling of salad and, often, fried egg (*sin huevo* means without egg).

Self-Catering

Every town of any substance has a *mercado* (food market). These are fun and great value. Even big eaters should be able to put together a filling meal of bread, *chorizo* (spiced sausage), cheese, fruit and a drink for 500 ptas or less. If you shop carefully you can eat three healthy meals a day for as little as 700 ptas.

DRINKS

Coffee in Spain is strong. Addicts should specify how they want their fix: *café con leche* is about 50% coffee, 50% hot milk; *café solo* is a short black; *café cortado* is a short black with a little milk.

The most common way to order a beer (*cerveza*) is to ask for a *caña* (pronounced can-ya), which is a small draught beer. *Corto* and, in the País Vasco, *zurrito*, are other names for this. A larger beer (about 300ml) is often called a *tubo*, or in Catalonia a *jarra*. All these words apply to draught beer (*cerveza de barril*) – if you just ask for a cerveza you're likely to get bottled beer, which is more expensive.

Wine (*vino*) comes in white (*blanco*), red (*tinto*) or rosé (*rosado*). Tinto de verano, a

kind of wine shandy, is good in summer. There are also many regional grape specialities such as *jerez* (sherry) in Jerez de la Frontera and *cava* (like champagne) in Catalonia. *Sangría*, a sweet punch made of red wine, fruit and spirits, is refreshing and very popular with tourists.

The cheapest drink of all is, of course, water. To specify tap water (which is safe to drink almost everywhere), just ask for *agua del grifo*.

ENTERTAINMENT

Spain has some of the best nightlife in Europe; wild and *very* late nights, especially on Friday and Saturday, are an integral part of the Spain experience. Many young Spaniards don't even think about going out until midnight or so. Bars, which come in all shapes, sizes and themes, are the main attractions until around 2 or 3 am. Some play great music that will get you hopping before – if you can afford it – you move on to a disco till 5 or 6 am. Discos are generally expensive, but not to be missed if you can manage to splurge. Spain's contributions to modern dance music are *bakalao* and *makina*, kinds of frenzied (150bpm to 180bpm) techno.

The live music scene is less exciting. Spanish rock and pop tends to be imitative, though the bigger cities usually offer a reasonable choice of bands. See the earlier Society & Conduct section for information on flamenco.

Cinemas abound and are good value, though foreign films are usually dubbed into Spanish.

SPECTATOR SPORTS

The national sport is *fútbol* (soccer). The best teams to see for their crowd support as well as their play are usually Real Madrid and Barcelona, although the atmosphere can be electric anywhere. The season runs from September to May.

Bullfighting is enjoying a resurgence despite continued pressure from international animal-rights activists. It's a complex activity that's regarded as much as an art form as a sport by aficionados. If you decide to see a *corrida de toros*, the season runs from March to October. Madrid, Seville and Pamplona are among the best places to see one.

SPAIN

SHOPPING

Many of Spain's best handicrafts are fragile or bulky and inconvenient unless you're going straight home. Pottery comes in a great range of attractive regional varieties. Some lovely rugs and blankets are made in places like the Alpujarras and Níjar in Andalucía. There's some pleasing woodwork available too, such as Granada's marquetry boxes and chess sets. Leather jackets, bags and belts are quite good value in many places.

Getting There & Away

AIR

Spain has many international airports including Madrid, Barcelona, Bilbao, Santiago de Compostela, Seville, Málaga, Almería, Alicante, Valencia, Palma de Mallorca, Ibiza and Maó (Menorca). In general, the cheapest destinations are Málaga, the Balearic Islands, Barcelona and Madrid.

Australia

In general, the best thing to do is to fly to London, Paris, Frankfurt or Rome, and then make your way overland. Alternatively, some flight deals to these centres include a couple of short-haul flights within Europe, and Madrid or Barcelona are usually acceptable destinations for these. Some round-the-world (RTW) fares include stops in Spain. STA Travel should be able to help you out with a good price. Generally speaking, a return fare to Europe for under A\$1700 is too good to pass up.

North America

Return fares to Madrid from Miami, New York, Atlanta or Chicago range from US\$780 to US\$830 on Iberia or Delta. From the west coast you are usually looking at about US\$100 more.

The UK

Scheduled flights to Spain are generally expensive, but with the huge range of charter, discount and low-season fares, it's often cheaper to fly than to take a bus or train. Check the travel sections of *TNT* or *Time Out* magazines or the weekend newspapers. The following are examples of short-notice low-season return fares from London:

Dest'n	Fare (UK£)	Agent Phone
Barcelona	129	Charter Flight Centre ☎ 020-7565 6755
Ibiza	119	Go ☎ 0845-605 4321
Madrid	109	EasyJet ☎ 0870-600 0000
Málaga	109	Spanish Travel Services ☎ 020-7387 5337

From Spain

For northern Europe, check the ads in local English-language papers in tourist centres like the Costa del Sol, the Costa Blanca and the Balearic Islands. You may pick up a one-way fare to London for around 12,000 ptas. The youth and student travel agency TIVE, and the general travel agency Halcón Viajes, both with branches in most main cities, have some good fares: generally you're looking at around 13,000 ptas to 15,500 ptas one way to London, Paris or Amsterdam, and at least 30,000 ptas to the USA.

LAND
Bus

There are regular bus services to Spain from all major centres in Europe, including Lisbon, London and Paris. In London, Eurolines (☎ 0870-514 3219) has services at least three times a week to Barcelona (UK£84 one way, 23 to 25 hours), Madrid (UK£77 one way, at least 27 hours) and Málaga (UK£79 one way, 34 hours). Tickets are sold by major travel agencies, and people under 26 and senior citizens qualify for a 10% discount. There are also bus services to Morocco from some Spanish cities.

Train

Reaching Spain by train is more expensive than bus unless you have a rail pass, though fares for those under 26 come close to the bus price. Normal one-way fares from London (using the ferry, not Eurostar) to Madrid (via Paris) are UK£104. For more details, contact the Rail Europe Travel Centre in London (☎ 08705-848 848) or a travel agent. See the introductory Getting Around chapter for more on rail passes and train travel through Europe.

SPAIN

Car & Motorcycle

If you're driving or riding to Spain from England, you'll have to choose between going through France (check visa requirements) or taking a direct ferry from England to Spain (see the following section). The cheapest way is one of the shorter ferries from England to France, then a quick drive down through France.

SEA
The UK

There are two direct ferry services. Brittany Ferries (in England ☎ 0870 536 0360) runs Plymouth-Santander ferries twice weekly from about mid-March to mid-November (24 hours), and a Portsmouth-Santander service (30 hours), usually once a week, in other months. P&O European Ferries (in England ☎ 08702 424 999) runs Portsmouth-Bilbao ferries twice weekly almost all year (35 hours). Prices on all services are similar: one-way passenger fares range from about UK£50 in winter to UK£85 in summer (cabins extra); a car and driver costs from UK£152 to UK£275, or you can take a vehicle and several passengers for UK£233 to UK£403.

Morocco

Ferry services between Spain and Morocco include Algeciras-Tangier, Algeciras-Ceuta, Gibraltar-Tangier, Málaga-Melilla, Almería-Melilla and Almería-Nador. Those to/from Algeciras are the fastest, cheapest and most frequent, with up to 20 ferries and hydrofoils a day to Ceuta (1½ hours/40 minutes) and 14 to Tangier (two hours/one hour). One-way passenger fares on the ferry/hydrofoil are 1801/2945 ptas (Ceuta) and 2960/3440 ptas (Tangier). A car to Ceuta/Tangier costs 9300/8223 ptas. You can buy tickets at Algeciras harbour, but it's more convenient to go to one of the many agencies on the waterfront. The price doesn't vary, so just look for the place with the shortest queue.

Don't buy Moroccan currency until you reach Morocco, as you will get ripped off in Algeciras.

LEAVING SPAIN

Departure taxes on flights out of Spain, which vary, are factored directly into tickets.

Getting Around

AIR

Spain has four main domestic airlines: Iberia (with subsidiary Binter Mediterráneo, both on ☎ 902-40 05 00), Air Europa (☎ 902-40 15 01) and Spanair (☎ 902-13 14 15). They and a couple of smaller airlines compete to produce some fares that can make flying worthwhile if you're in a hurry, especially for longer or return trips.

The return fare between Madrid and Barcelona can be as high as 30,000 ptas. To Palma de Mallorca, Santiago de Compostela, or Málaga you are looking at around 29,000 ptas return. All these fares can be cut in half if you comply with certain restrictions.

Among travel agencies, TIVE and Halcón Viajes are always worth checking for fares. There are some useful deals if you're under 26 (or, in some cases, over 63).

BUS

Spain's bus network is operated by dozens of independent companies and is more extensive than its train system, serving remote towns and villages as well as the major routes. The choice between bus and train depends on the particular trip you're taking; for the best value, compare fares, journey times and frequencies each time you move. Buses to/from Madrid are often cheaper than (or barely different from) cross-country routes. For instance Seville to Madrid costs 2745 ptas while the shorter Seville-Granada trip is 2700 ptas.

Many towns and cities have one main bus station where most buses arrive and depart, and these usually have an information desk giving information on all services. Tourist offices can also help with information but don't sell tickets.

TRAIN

Trains are mostly modern and comfortable, and late arrivals are now the exception rather than the rule. The main headache is deciding which compartment on which train gives you best value for money.

RENFE, the national railway company, runs numerous types of train, and travel times can vary a lot on the same route. So can fares, which may depend not just on the type of train but also the day of the week and time of day. *Regionales* are all-stops trains which are cheap and slow. *Cercanías* provide regular services from major cities to the surrounding suburbs and hinterland, sometimes even crossing regional boundaries.

Among long-distance *(largo recorrido)* trains the standard daytime train is the *diurno* (its night-time equivalent is the *estrella*). Quicker is the InterCity (mainly because it makes fewer stops), while the *Talgo* is the quickest and dearest.

Best of all is the AVE high-speed service that links Madrid and Seville in just 2½ hours. The *Talgo 200* uses part of this line to speed down to Málaga from Madrid. The *Euromed* is an AVE-style train that speeds south from Barcelona to Valencia and Alicante. A *Tren Hotel* is a 1st-class sleeper-only express.

There's also a bewildering range of accommodation types, especially on overnight trains (fares quoted in this chapter are typical 2nd-class seat fares). Fortunately ticket clerks understand the problem and are usually happy to go through a few options with you. The cheapest sleeper option is usually a *litera*, a bunk in a six-berth 2nd-class compartment.

You can buy tickets and make reservations at stations, RENFE offices in many city centres, and travel agencies that display the RENFE logo.

Train Passes

Rail passes are valid for all RENFE trains, but Inter-Rail users have to pay supplements on Talgo and InterCity services, and full fare on the high-speed AVE service between Madrid and Seville. All pass-holders making reservations for long-distance trains pay a fee of between 500 ptas and 1500 ptas.

RENFE's Tarjeta Turística (also known as the Spain Flexipass) is a rail pass for non-Europeans, valid for three to 10 days travel in a two-month period: in 2nd class, three days costs US$155, and 10 days is US$365. It can be purchased from agents outside Europe, or a few main train stations and RENFE offices in Spain. Students and under 26s can also buy an ExploreRail card valid for seven, 15 or 30 days of unlimited travel. It's a real bargain, costing just 19,000/23,000/30,000 ptas, and available at agents such as usit UNLIMITED (☎ 902-32 52 75). Web site: www.unlimited.es.

CAR & MOTORCYCLE

If you're driving or riding around Spain, consider investing 2600 ptas in the *Michelin Atlas de Carreteras España Portugal*. It's a handy atlas with detailed road maps as well as maps of all the main towns and cities.

Spain's roads vary enormously but are generally quite good. Fastest are the *autopistas*, multilane freeways between major cities. On some, mainly in the north, you have to pay hefty tolls (from the French border to Barcelona, for example, it's 1580 ptas). Minor routes can be slow going but are usually more scenic. Petrol is relatively expensive at around 114 ptas for a litre of unleaded.

The head office of the Spanish automobile club Real Automovil Club de España (RACE; ☎ 900-20 00 93) is at Calle de José Abascal 10, 28003 Madrid. For the RACE's 24-hour, nationwide, on-road emergency service, call the toll free number ☎ 900-11 22 22.

Road Rules

Although a little hairy, driving in Spain is not too bad and locals show at least some respect for the rules. Speed limits are 120km/h on the autopistas, 90km/h or 100km/h on other country roads and 50km/h in built-up areas. The maximum allowable blood-alcohol level is 0.05%. Seat belts must be worn, and all motorcyclists must always wear a helmet and keep headlights on day and night.

Trying to find a parking spot can be a nightmare in larger towns and cities. Spanish drivers park anywhere to save themselves the hassle of a half-hour search, but *grúas* (tow trucks) will tow your car if given the chance. The cost of bailing out a car can be as high as 10,000 ptas.

Rental

Rates vary widely from place to place. The best deals tend to be in major tourist areas, including at their airports. At Málaga airport you can rent a small car for under 20,000 ptas a week. More generally, you're looking at anything up to 9000 ptas for a day with unlimited kilometres, plus insurance, damage waiver and taxes. Hiring for several days can bring the average daily cost down a great deal – a small car for a week might cost 40,000 ptas all up. Local companies often have better rates than the big firms.

SPAIN

BICYCLE

See Cycling in the Activities section earlier in this chapter.

HITCHING

It's still possible to thumb your way around parts of Spain, but large doses of patience and common sense are necessary. Women should avoid hitching alone. Hitching is illegal on autopistas and difficult on major highways. Your chances are better on minor roads, although the going can still be painfully slow.

BOAT

For information on ferries to, from and between the Balearic Islands, see that section of this chapter.

LOCAL TRANSPORT

In many Spanish towns you will not need to use public transport, as transport terminals and accommodation are centralised and within walking distance of most tourist attractions.

Most towns in Spain have an effective local bus system. In larger cities, these can be complicated, but tourist offices can advise on which buses you need. Barcelona and Madrid both have efficient underground systems which are faster and easier to use than the bus systems.

Taxis are still pretty cheap. If you split a cross-town fare between three or four people, it can be a decidedly good deal. Rates vary slightly from city to city: in Barcelona, they cost 295 ptas flag fall, plus about 100 ptas per kilometre; in Madrid they're a bit cheaper (190 ptas flag fall). There are supplements for luggage and airport trips.

Madrid

pop 3.1 million

Whatever apprehensions you may have about Madrid when you first arrive, Spain's capital is sure to grow on you. Madrid may lack the glamour or beauty of Barcelona and the historical richness of so many Spanish cities (it was insignificant until Felipe II made it his capital in 1561), but it more than makes up for this with a remarkable collection of museums and galleries, some lovely parks and gardens and wild nightlife.

ORIENTATION

The area of most interest to visitors lies between Parque del Buen Retiro in the east and Campo del Moro in the west. These two parks are more or less connected by Calle de Alcalá and Calle Mayor, which meet in the middle at Puerta del Sol. Calle Mayor passes the main square, Plaza Mayor, on its way from Puerta del Sol to the Palacio Real in front of Campo del Moro.

The main north-south thoroughfare is Paseo de la Castellana, which runs (changing names to Paseo de los Recoletos and finally Paseo del Prado) all the way from Chamartín train station in the north to Madrid's other big station, Atocha.

INFORMATION
Tourist Offices

The main tourist office (☎ 91 429 49 51) is at Calle del Duque de Medinaceli 2. It opens 9 am to 7 pm Monday to Friday, and 9 am to 1 pm Saturday. The office at Barajas airport (☎ 91 305 86 56) is open 8 am to 8 pm Monday to Friday and 8 am to 1 pm Saturday. The one at Chamartín train station (☎ 91 315 99 76) keeps the same hours.

Yet another Oficina de Turismo (☎ 91 364 18 76), Ronda de Toledo 1, is located in the Centro Comercial de la Puerta de Toledo. It opens 9 am to 7 pm Monday to Friday and 9.30 am to 1.30 pm Saturday.

Money

Large banks like the Caja de Madrid usually have the best rates, but check commissions first. Banking hours vary but it is generally safe to assume they will be open 9 am to 2 pm weekdays (to 1 pm Saturday). American Express (☎ 91 527 03 03 open 24 hours, ☎ 900-99 44 26 for replacing lost travellers cheques) is at Plaza de las Cortes 2 and has reasonable rates. It's open 9 am to 5.30 pm Monday to Friday and 9 am to noon Saturday.

If you're desperate there are plenty of *bureaux de change* around Puerta del Sol and Plaza Mayor, which offer appalling rates but are often open until midnight.

Post & Communications

The main post office is in the gigantic Palacio de Comunicaciones on Plaza de la Cibeles. Poste restante (lista de correos) is at windows 78 to 80 and is open 8 am to 9.30 pm weekdays and 8.30 am to 2 pm Saturday.

The Telefónica *locutorio* (phone centre) at Gran Vía 30 has phone books for the whole country and cabins where you can make calls in relative peace. It's open 9.30 am to midnight daily. Keep an eye out for private phone companies, whose offices can undercut Telefónica by 50%.

Email & Internet Access

Dozens of cafes and shops offer Internet connections, including Aroba52, on Calle de los Reyes (metro: Plaza de España) which charges 300 ptas an hour, or La Casa de Internet, Calle de Luchana 20 (metro: Bilbao) at 900 ptas an hour.

Travel Agencies

For cheap travel tickets try Viajes Zeppelin (☎ 91 542 51 54), Plaza de Santo Domingo 2; or TIVE (☎ 91 543 74 12), the student and youth travel organisation, at Calle de Fernando el Católico 88 or in the Instituto de la Juventud (☎ 91 347 77 78) at Calle de José Ortega y Gasset 71. Both open 9 am to 1 pm Monday to Friday.

Bookshops

La Casa del Libro, Gran Vía 29-31, has a broad selection of books on all subjects, including books in English and other languages. For English-language books, you could also try Booksellers, Calle de José Abascal 48. Librería de Mujeres, Calle de San Cristóbal 17, is a women's bookshop. La Tienda Verde, Calle de Maudes 38 (metro: Cuatro Caminos), specialises in walking guides and maps for many parts of Spain.

Laundry

Laundrettes include Lavandería España on Calle del Infante, Lavomatique on Calle de Cervantes, and Lavandería Alba at Calle del Barco 26.

Medical & Emergency Services

If you have medical problems pop into the nearest Insalud clinic often marked 'Centro de Salud'. A handy one in the centre is at Calle de las Navas de Tolosa 10. You can also get help at the Anglo-American Medical Unit (☎ 91 435 18 23), Calle del Conde de Aranda

1. For an ambulance call the Cruz Roja on ☎ 522 22 22 or Insalud on ☎ 061. There is a 24-hour pharmacy, Farmacia del Globo (☎ 91 369 20 00), at Plaza de Antón Martín 46.

In police emergency you can call the Policía Nacional on ☎ 091 or the Guardia Civil on ☎ 062.

THINGS TO SEE & DO

Madrid will make a lot more sense if you spend some time walking around before you get into the city's cultural delights. The following walking tour could take anywhere from a few hours to a few days – it's up to you. You'll find more detail on the major sights in following sections.

Unless you want to hit the big art galleries first, the most fitting place to begin exploring Madrid is the **Puerta del Sol**, the official city centre.

Walk up Calle de Preciados and take the second street on the left, which will bring you out to Plaza de las Descalzas. Note the **baroque doorway** in the Caja de Madrid building; it was built for King Felipe V in 1733 and faces the **Monasterio de las Descalzas Reales**.

Moving south down Calle de San Martín you come to the **Iglesia de San Ginés**, one of Madrid's oldest churches. Behind it is the wonderful **Chocolatería de San Ginés**, generally open 7 to 10 am and 1 to 7 pm.

Continue down to and cross Calle Mayor, and then into Madrid's most famous square, **Plaza Mayor**. After a coffee on the plaza, head west along Calle Mayor until you come to the historic **Plaza de la Villa**, with Madrid's 17th-century *ayuntamiento* (town hall). On the same square stand the 16th-century **Casa de Cisneros** and the Gothic-mudéjar **Torre de los Lujanes**, one of the city's oldest buildings, dating from the Middle Ages.

Take the street down the left side of the Casa de Cisneros, cross the road at the end, go down the stairs and follow the cobbled Calle del Cordón out onto Calle de Segovia. Almost directly in front of you is the mudéjar tower of the **Iglesia de San Pedro**. Proceeding down Costanilla de San Pedro you reach the **Iglesia de San Andrés**.

From here you cross Plaza de la Puerta de Moros and head south-west to the **Basílica de San Francisco El Grande**, or east past the

SPAIN

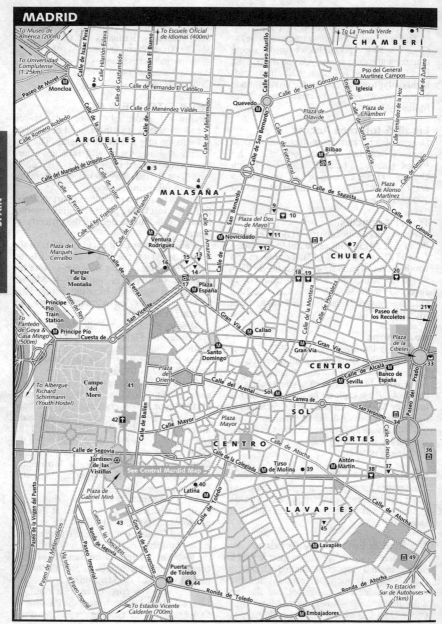

SPAIN

MADRID

To Museo de América (200m)
To Universidad Complutense (1.25km)
To Escuele Oficial de Idiomas (400m)
To La Tienda Verde ● 1

CHAMBERÍ

Calle de Isaac Peral
Calle Hilarión Eslava
Calle de Gaztambide
Guzmán El Bueno
Calle de Bravo Murillo
Pso del General Martínez Campos
Calle de Zurbano

Paseo de Moret
Ⓜ Moncloa
2 ●
Calle de Fernando El Católico
Calle de Eloy Gonzalo
Ⓜ Iglesia

Calle Romero Robledo
Calle de Menéndez Valdés
Quevedo
Calle de San Bernardo
Plaza de Olavide
Plaza de Chamberí
Calle de Santa Engracia
Calle Fernández de la Hoz
Calle de Almagro

ARGÜELLES
Calle de la Princesa
Calle del Marqués de Urquijo
Calle de Vallehermoso
Calle de Fuencarral
Bilbao ●
5 ▣
Plaza de Alonso Martínez
Calle de Génova

3 ●
Calle de Tudor
Calle de Ferraz
Calle del Rey Francisco
Calle de Luisa Fernanda
MALASAÑA
4 ●
San Bernardo
Calle de Amaniel
Calle de Sagasta

Plaza del Marqués Cerralbo
Ventura Rodríguez Ⓜ
9 ▼
10 ▣
Plaza del Dos de Mayo
6 ▣

Parque de la Montaña
16 ●
15 ▼ 13 ▼
14 ▼
Ⓜ Noviciado
11 ▼
12 ▼
8 ▥
7 ●
CHUECA

Príncipe Pío Train Station
17 ▣ Plaza España Ⓜ
18 ▼ 19 ▼
20 ▼

To Panteón de Goya & Casa Mingo (500m)
Ⓜ Príncipe Pío
Cuesta de
Gran Vía
Calle de la Montera
Calle de Hortaleza
Paseo de los Recoletos
21 ▼

Santo Domingo Ⓜ
Ⓜ Callao
Gran Vía
Ⓜ Gran Vía
Plaza de la Cibeles

To Albergue Richard Schirrmann (Youth Hostel)
Campo del Moro
41 ●
Plaza de Oriente
CENTRO
Calle de Alcalá
Banco de España
33 ●

Calle de Bailén
Calle del Arenal
Sol Ⓜ
Ⓜ Sevilla
Paseo del Prado

42 ▣
Calle Mayor
Plaza Mayor
Carrera de San Jerónimo
34 ▥

Calle de Segovia
Jardines de las Vistillas
CENTRO
Calle de Atocha
SOL
CORTES
Calle de Jesús
36 ▥

Plaza de Gabriel Miró
See Central Mardid Map
Calle de la Colegiata
Tirso de Molina ●
39 ●
Antón Martín Ⓜ
38 ▼
37 ▼

43 ●
40 ●
Latina
Calle de Toledo
LAVAPIÉS
45 ●
49 ▥

Puerta de Toledo Ⓜ
ⓘ 44
Gran Vía de San Francisco
Cuesta de las Descargas
Ronda de Segovia
Calle de Atocha
Ⓜ Lavapiés

To Estadio Vicente Calderón (700m)
Ronda de Toledo
Ⓜ Embajadores
To Estación Sur de Autobuses (1km)

Paseo de la Virgen del Puerto
Paseo de los Melancólicos
Vía Inferial al Paseo Imperial

euro currency converter €1 = 166 ptas

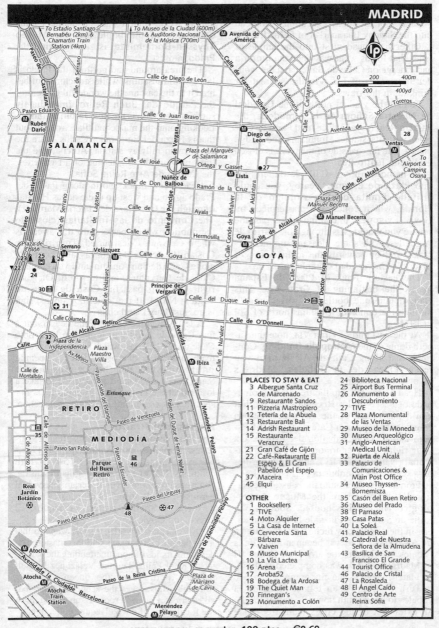

MADRID

To Estadio Santiago
Bernabéu (2km) &
Chamartín Train
Station (4km)

To Museo de la Ciudad (600m)
& Auditorio Nacional
de la Música (700m)

Avenida de
América

Paseo de la Castellana

Calle de Serrano

Calle de Diego de León

Calle de Francisco Silvela

Calle de Cartagena

los Toreros

28

Paseo Eduardo Data

Rubén
Darío

Calle de Juan Bravo

Calle de Ardemans

Avenida de

Ventas

To
Airport &
Camping
Osuna

SALAMANCA

de Vergara

Plaza del Marqués
de Salamanca

Diego de
León

Plaza de
Manuel Becerra

Paseo de la Castellana

Calle de Serrano

Calle de Lagasca

Calle del Príncipe

Calle de José

Núñez de
Balboa

Ortega y Gasset

Calle de Don Balboa

Lista

27

Ramón de la Cruz

Calle de Alcalá

Manuel Becerra

Calle de

Ayala

Calle de Alcántara

Plaza de Colón

Serrano

Velázquez

Hermosilla

Calle de Goya

Goya

Calle de Alcalá

GOYA

Calle Fuente del Berro

23
22

25
26

24

30

31

Calle de Vilanuava

Calle de Velázquez

Príncipe de
Vergara

Calle del Duque de Sesto

29

O'Donnell

Calle del Doctor Esquerdo

Calle Columena

Calle de Alcalá

Retiro

Calle de O'Donnell

32

Plaza de la
Independencia

Calle

Av Méjico

Plaza
Maestro
Villa

Avenida

Calle de Narváez

Ibiza

Calle de
Montalbán

Estanque

RETIRO

Salón de Estanque

Paseo del Duque de Fernán Núñez

Paseo de Venezuela

Paseo de Menéndez Pelayo

MEDIODÍA

35

Paseo San Pablo

Parque
del Buen
Retiro

46

Paseo del Ecuador

Real
Jardín
Botánico

Paseo del Urugay

47

Paseo del Duque

48

Paseo de la Reina Cristina

Avenida de Menéndez Pelayo

Atocha

Atocha

Avenida de la Ciudade de Barcelona

Atocha
Train
Station

Plaza de
Mariano
de Cavia

Menéndez
Pelayo

PLACES TO STAY & EAT		
3	Albergue Santa Cruz de Marcenado	
9	Restaurante Sandos	
11	Pizzeria Mastropiero	
12	Tetería de la Abuela	
13	Restaurante Bali	
14	Adrish Restaurant	
15	Restaurante Veracruz	
21	Gran Café de Gijón	
22	Café-Restaurante El Espejo & El Gran Pabellón del Espejo	
37	Maceira	
45	Elqui	

OTHER	
1	Booksellers
2	TIVE
4	Moto Alquiler
5	La Casa de Internet
6	Cervecería Santa Bárbara
7	Vaiven
8	Museo Municipal
10	La Vía Lactea
16	Arena
17	Aroba52
18	Bodega de la Ardosa
19	The Quiet Man
20	Finnegan's
23	Monumento a Colón

24	Biblioteca Nacional
25	Airport Bus Terminal
26	Monumento al Descubrimiento
27	TIVE
28	Plaza Monumental de las Ventas
29	Museo de la Moneda
30	Museo Arqueológico
31	Anglo-American Medical Unit
32	Puerta de Alcalá
33	Palacio de Comunicaciones & Main Post Office
34	Museo Thyssen-Bornemisza
35	Casón del Buen Retiro
36	Museo del Prado
38	El Parnaso
39	Casa Patas
40	La Soleá
41	Palacio Real
42	Catedral de Nuestra Señora de la Almudena
43	Basílica de San Francisco El Grande
44	Tourist Office
46	Palacio de Cristal
47	La Rosaleda
48	El Ángel Caído
49	Centro de Arte Reina Sofía

SPAIN

0   200   400m
0   200   400yd

market along Plaza de la Cebada – once a popular spot for public executions – to head into the Sunday flea market of **El Rastro**.

Otherwise, head west into the tangle of lanes that forms what was once the **morería** and emerge on Calle de Bailén and the wonderful *terrazas* of Las Vistillas – great for drinking in the views.

Follow the viaduct north to the **Catedral de Nuestra Señora de la Almudena**, the **Palacio Real** (royal palace) and Plaza de Oriente, with its statues, fountains and hedge mazes. The far east side of the plaza is closed off by the **Teatro Real**.

At its northern end, Calle de Bailén runs into **Plaza de España**. Nearby, you could visit the **Ermita de San Antonio de la Florida**, which contains a masterpiece by Goya. If you were to continue north past the square you would pass through the Barrio de Argüelles, with some pleasant summer terrazas, and on towards the main centre of Madrid's Universidad Complutense.

The eastern flank of Plaza de España marks the beginning of **Gran Vía**. This Haussmannesque boulevard was slammed through the tumbledown slums north of Sol in 1911.

At the east end of Gran Vía, note the superb dome of the **Metropolis Building**. Continue east along Calle de Alcalá until you reach **Plaza de la Cibeles**, Madrid's favourite roundabout.

Head north (left) up the tree-lined promenade of Paseo de los Recoletos. On the left you'll pass some of the city's best known cafes, including Gran Café de Gijón, El Espejo and El Gran Pabellón del Espejo. On your right is the enormous **Biblioteca Nacional** (National Library), and a little farther on a statue of Columbus in Plaza de Colón.

From here walk around the back of the National Library, where the **Museo Arqueológico Nacional** is housed. South along Calle de Serrano is Plaza de la Independencia, in the middle of which stands the **Puerta de Alcalá**. The gate was begun at Plaza de la Cibeles to celebrate the arrival of Carlos III in Madrid in 1769, was completed in 1778, and later moved as the city grew.

Turn right and then left at Plaza de la Cibeles to head south down Paseo del Prado, an extension of the city's main tree-lined boulevard, and you'll soon reach the art gallery with which it shares its name. On the other side of the boulevard, the **Museo Thyssen-Bornemisza** is, along with the **Prado**, a must.

The area around and north of the Prado is laced with museums, while stretching out behind it to the east are the wonderful gardens of the **Parque del Buen Retiro**. Immediately south of the Prado is the **Real Jardín Botánico**. Looking onto the manic multilane roundabout that is Plaza del Emperador Carlos V are the city's main railway station, **Atocha**, and the third in Madrid's big league of art galleries, the **Centro de Arte Reina Sofía**.

Head a few blocks north along Paseo del Prado again and west up Calle de las Huertas (through the tiny Plaza de Platería Martínez). The **Convento de las Trinitarias** (closed to the public), which backs onto this street, is where Cervantes lies buried. Turn right up Costanilla de las Trinitarias and continue along Calle de San Agustín until you come to Calle de Cervantes, and turn left. On your right you will pass the **Casa de Lope de Vega** at No 11. If the '*abierto*' ('open') sign is up, just knock and enter.

A left turn at the end of Calle de Cervantes into Calle de León will bring you back onto Calle de las Huertas, which you may have already noticed is one of Madrid's happening streets. Anywhere along here or up on Plaza de Santa Ana will make a great place to take a load off at the end of this gruelling tour! For specific tips, consult the Entertainment section.

Museo del Prado

The Prado is one of the world's great art galleries. Its main emphasis is on Spanish, Flemish and Italian art from the 15th to 19th centuries, and one of its strengths lies in the generous coverage given to certain individual geniuses. Whole strings of rooms are devoted to three of Spain's greats, Velázquez, El Greco and Goya.

Of Velázquez's works, it's *Las Meninas* that most people come to see, and this masterpiece depicting maids of honour attending the daughter of King Felipe IV, and Velázquez himself painting portraits of the queen and king (through whose eyes the scene is witnessed) takes pride of place in room 12 on the 1st floor, the focal point of the Velázquez collection.

Virtually the whole south wing of the 1st floor is given over to Goya. His portraits, in rooms 34 to 38, include the pair *Maja Desnuda* and *Maja Vestida*; legend has it that the woman depicted here is the Duchess of Alba, Spain's richest woman in Goya's time. Goya was supposedly commissioned to paint her portrait for her husband and ended up having an affair with her so he painted an extra portrait for himself. In room 39 are Goya's great war masterpieces, crowned by *El Dos de Mayo 1808* (2 May 1808) and, next to it, *Los Fusilamientos de Moncloa*, also known as *El Tres de Mayo 1808* (3 May 1808), in which he recreates the pathos of the hopeless Madrid revolt against the French. There are more Goya works in rooms 66 and 67 on the ground floor.

Other well-represented artists include El Greco, the Flemish masters Hieronymus Bosch and Peter Paul Rubens, and the Italians Tintoretto, Titian and Raphael.

The Prado is open 9 am to 7 pm Tuesday to Saturday, and until 2 pm on Sunday and holidays. Tickets are 500 ptas (half-price for students) and includes the Casón del Buen Retiro, a subsidiary a short walk east that contains the collection's 19th-century works. Entry is free on Sunday and Saturday afternoon (2.30 to 7 pm), as well as on selected national holidays.

Centro de Arte Reina Sofia

At Calle de Santa Isabel 52, opposite Atocha station, the Reina Sofia museum houses a superb collection of predominantly Spanish modern art. The exhibition focuses on the period 1900 to 1940, and includes, in room 7, Picasso's famous *Guernica*, his protest at the German bombing of the Basque town of Guernica during the Spanish Civil War in 1937. The day of the bombing, 26 April, had been a typical market day in the town of 5000 people. Because of the market there were another 5000 people selling their wares or doing their weekly shopping. The bombs started to drop at 4 pm. By the time they stopped, three hours later, the town and thousands of the people in it had been annihilated.

Guernica was painted in Paris. Picasso insisted that it stay outside Spain until Franco and his cronies were gone and democracy had been restored. It was secretly brought to Spain

in 1981, and moved here from the Casón del Buen Retiro in 1992. It's displayed with a collection of preliminary sketches and paintings which Picasso put together in May 1937.

The museum also contains further works by Picasso, while room 9 is devoted to Salvador Dalí's surrealist work and room 13 contains a collection of Joan Miró's late works, characterised by their remarkable simplicity.

The gallery opens 10 am to 9 pm Monday to Saturday (except Tuesday, when it is closed), and 10 am to 2.30 pm Sunday. Entry is 500 ptas (half-price for students), but free on Sunday and Saturday afternoon (2.30 to 7 pm).

Museo Thyssen-Bornemisza

Purchased by Spain in 1993 for something over US$300 million (a snip), this extraordinary collection of 800 paintings was formerly the private collection of the German-Hungarian family of magnates, the Thyssen-Bornemiszas. Starting with medieval religious art, it moves on through Titian, El Greco and Rubens to Cézanne, Monet and Van Gogh, then from Miró, Picasso and Gris to Pollock, Dalí and Lichtenstein, thereby offering one of the best and most comprehensive art-history lessons you'll ever have. The museum is at Paseo del Prado 8, almost opposite the Prado, and opens 10 am to 7 pm Tuesday to Sunday. Entry is 700 ptas (400 ptas for students). Separate temporary exhibitions generally cost more.

Palacio Real

Madrid's 18th-century Royal Palace is a lesson in what can happen if you give your interior decorators a free hand. You'll see some of the most elaborately decorated walls and ceilings imaginable, including the sublime Throne Room (and other rooms of more dubious merit). This over-the-top palace hasn't been used as a royal residence for some time and today is only used for official receptions and, of course, tourism.

The first series of rooms you strike after buying your ticket is the Farmacia Real (Royal Pharmacy), an unending array of medicine jars and stills for mixing royal concoctions. The Armería Real (Royal Armoury) is a shiny collection of mostly 16th and 17th-century weapons and royal suits of armour. Elsewhere are a good selection of Goyas, 215 absurdly ornate clocks from the Royal Clock

SPAIN

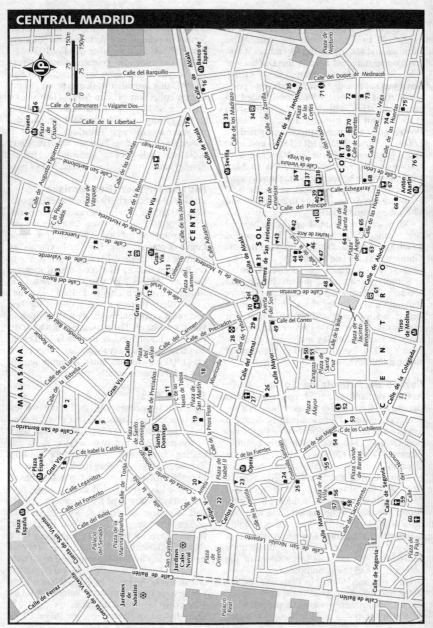

CENTRAL MADRID

CENTRAL MADRID

PLACES TO STAY
1 Hostal Alcázar Regis
4 Hostal Medieval
7 Hostal Ginebra
8 Hotel Laris
9 Hostal Lamalonga
19 Hostal Paz
24 Hostal Mairu
25 Hostal Pinariega
29 Hostal Cosmopolitan
31 Hostal Centro Sol
44 Hostal Tineo
49 Hostal Riesco
51 Hostal Santa Cruz
54 Hostal La Macarena
62 Hostal Persal
64 Hostal Delvi
65 Hostal Vetusta
66 Hostal Matute
72 Hostal Dulcinea
73 Hostal Gonzalo
75 Hostal López

PLACES TO EAT
13 Restaurante Integral Artemisa
20 Restaurante La Paella Real
21 Taberna del Alabardero
23 Café del Real

32 La Finca de Susana
36 Restaurante Integral
   Artemisa
40 La Trucha
43 Museo del Jamón
45 La Casa del Abuelo
46 La Trucha
47 Las Bravas
53 Restaurante Sobrino de Botín
76 Restaurante La Sanabresa

OTHER
2 Morocco Disco
3 Lavandería Alba
5 Cruising Bar
6 Rimmel Bar
10 Viajes Zeppelin
11 Centro de Salud
12 La Casa del Libro
14 Telefónica Phone Centre
15 Cock Bar
16 RENFE Train Booking Office
17 Edificio Metropolis
18 Monasterio de las Descalzas
   Reales
22 Teatro Real
26 Chocolatería de San Ginés
27 Iglesia de San Ginés

28 El Corte Inglés Department
   Store
30 Police Station
33 Police Station
34 Teatro de la Zarzuela
35 American Express
37 La Venencia Bar
38 Carbones Bar
39 Viva Madrid
41 Teatro de la Comedia
42 Suristán
48 Torero
50 Librería de Mujeres
52 Tourist Office
55 Mercado de San Miguel
56 Torre de los Lujanes
57 Ayuntamiento
58 Casa de Cisneros
59 Iglesia de San Pedro
60 Iglesia de San Andrés
61 Teatro Calderón
63 Café Central
67 Café Populart
68 Lavandería España
69 Lavomatique
70 Casa de Lope de Vega
71 Tourist Office
74 Convento de las Trinitarias

Collection, and five Stradivarius violins, still used for concerts and balls. Most of the tapestries in the palace were made in the Royal Tapestry Factory. All the chandeliers are original and no two are the same.

The palace is open 9.30 am to 6 pm (5 pm October to April), Monday to Saturday, and 9 am to 2.30 pm (2 pm October to April) on Sunday and holidays. Admission costs 900 ptas (1000 ptas if you join a guided tour), or 400 ptas for students. All EU citizens get in free on Wednesday (bring your passport). The nearest metro station is Opera.

Monasterio de las Descalzas Reales

The Convent of the Barefoot Royals, on Plaza de las Descalzas, was founded in 1559 by Juana of Austria, daughter of the Spanish king Carlos I, and became one of Spain's richest religious houses thanks to gifts from noblewomen. Much of the wealth came in the form of art; on the obligatory guided tour you'll be confronted by a number of tapestries based on

works by Rubens, and a wonderful painting entitled *The Voyage of the 11,000 Virgins*. Juana of Austria is buried here. The convent is open 10.30 am to 12.45 pm Tuesday to Saturday and again (except Friday) from 4 to 5.30 pm. On Sunday and holidays it opens from 11 am to 1.45 pm. Admission costs 700 ptas (300 ptas for students), but is free on Wednesday for EU citizens.

Panteón de Goya

Also called the Ermita de San Antonio de la Florida, this little church contains not only Goya's tomb, directly in front of the altar, but also one of his greatest works – the entire ceiling and dome, beautifully painted with religious scenes (and recently restored). The scenes on the dome depict the miracle of St Anthony. The panteón is the first of two small churches 700m north-west along Paseo de la Florida from Príncipe Pío metro station. The chapel opens 10 am to 2 pm and 4 to 8 pm Tuesday to Friday (mornings only in July and August), and 10 am to 2 pm weekends.

Entry is 300 ptas, half for students (free on Wednesday and Sunday).

Museo Arqueológico

This museum on Calle de Serrano traces the history of the peninsula from the earliest prehistoric cave paintings to the Iberian, Roman, Carthaginian, Greek, Visigothic, Moorish and Christian eras. Exhibits include mosaics, pottery, fossilised bones and a partial reconstruction of the prehistoric Altamira cave paintings. It's open 9.30 am to 8.30 pm Tuesday to Saturday, and 9.30 am to 2 pm Sunday. Entry costs 500 ptas (students pay half), but is free on Sunday and from 2.30 pm on Saturday.

Other Museums

Madrid almost has more museums than the Costa del Sol has high-rise apartments. They include: the **Museo Municipal**, with assorted art including some Goyas, and some beautiful old maps, scale models, silver, porcelain and period furniture; the **Museo de la Moneda**, which follows the history of coinage in great detail and contains a mind-boggling collection of coins and paper money; the **Museo de América** with stuff brought from the Americas from the 16th to 20th centuries; and even the **Museo de la Ciudad**, perfectly described by one traveller as 'a must for infrastructure buffs!', which rather drily traces the growth of Madrid. Check the tourist office's *Enjoy Madrid* brochure for more details.

Real Jardín Botánico

The perfect answer to an overdose of art and history could be this beautiful botanic garden next door to the Prado. The eight-hectare gardens are open daily from 10 am to dark and entrance costs 250 ptas.

Parque del Buen Retiro

This is another great place to escape hustle and bustle. On a warm spring day walk between the flowerbeds and hedges or just sprawl out on one of the lawns.

Stroll along **Paseo de las Estatuas**, a path lined with statues originally from the Palacio Real. It ends at a lake overlooked by a **statue of Alfonso XII**. There are rowing boats for rent at the northern end when the weather is good.

Perhaps the most important, and certainly the most controversial, of the park's other monuments is *El Ángel Caído* (The Fallen Angel). First-prize winner at an international exhibition in Paris in 1878, this is said to be the first statue in the world dedicated to the devil.

You should also visit some of the park's gardens, such as the exquisite **La Rosaleda** (rose garden), and the **Chinese Garden** on a tiny island near the Fallen Angel. The all-glass **Palacio de Cristal** in the middle of the park occasionally stages modern-art exhibitions.

Campo del Moro

This stately garden is directly behind the Palacio Real, and the palace is visible through the trees from just about all points. A couple of fountains and statues, a thatch-roofed pagoda and a carriage museum provide artificial diversions, but nature is the real attraction.

El Rastro

If you get up early on a Sunday morning you'll find the city almost deserted, until you get to El Rastro. It is one of the biggest flea markets you're ever likely to see, and if you're prepared to hunt around, you can find almost anything. The market spreads along and between Calle de Ribera de Curtidores and Calle de los Embajadores (metro: Latina). It's said to be the place to go if you want to buy your car stereo back. Watch your pockets and bags.

ORGANISED TOURS

You can pick up a Madrid Vision bus around the centre of Madrid up to 10 times a day. There are only three on Sunday and holidays. A full round trip costs 1700 ptas and you can board the bus at any of 14 clearly marked stops. Taped commentaries in four languages, including English, are available, and the bus stops at several major monuments, including the Prado and near Plaza Mayor. If you buy the 2200 ptas ticket, you can use the buses all day to get around (2900 ptas buys you the same right for two days running).

SPECIAL EVENTS

Madrid's major fiesta celebrates its patron saint, San Isidro Labrador, throughout the third week of May. There are free music performances around the city and one of the country's top bullfight seasons at the Plaza Monumental de las Ventas. The Malasaña district, already busy enough, has its biggest party on 2 May, and the Fiesta de San Juan is held in the Parque del Buen Retiro for the seven days leading up to 24 June. The few locals who haven't left town in August will be celebrating the consecutive festivals of La Paloma, San Cayetano and San Lorenzo. The last week of September is Chamartín's Fiesta de Otoño (Autumn Festival), about the only time you would go to Chamartín other than to catch a train.

PLACES TO STAY
Finding a place to stay in Madrid is never really a problem.

Camping
There is one camping ground within striking distance of central Madrid. To reach *Camping Osuna* (☎ 91 741 05 10) on Avenida de Logroño near the airport, take metro No 5 to Canillejas (the end of the line), from where it's about 500m. It charges 660 ptas per person, car and tent.

Hostels
There are two HI youth hostels in Madrid. The *Albergue Richard Schirrman* (☎ 91 463 56 99) is in the Casa de Campo park (metro: El Lago; bus No 33 from Plaza Ópera), B&B in a room of four costs 1200 ptas (under 26) or 1700 ptas.

The *Albergue Santa Cruz de Marcenado* (☎ 91 547 45 32, Calle de Santa Cruz de Marcenado 28, metro: Argüelles; bus Nos 1, 61 and Circular), has rooms for four, six and eight people. B&B costs the same as in the other hostel. This is one of the few Spanish hostels in HI's International Booking Network.

Hostales & Pensiones
These tend to cluster in three or four parts of the city and the price-to-quality ratio is fairly standard. In summer the city is drained of people, thanks to the horrific heat, so if you are mad enough to be here then, you may well be able to make a hot deal on the price. At other times it's only worth trying to bargain if you intend to stay a while.

Around Plaza de Santa Ana Santa Ana is one of Madrid's 'in' districts – and so budget places are starting to disappear. Close to Sol and within walking distance of the Prado and Atocha train station, it's also home to countless bars, cafes and restaurants of all classes.

On the square itself at No 15, *Hostal Delvi* (☎ 91 522 59 98, 3rd floor) is friendly enough with OK rooms, including tiny singles. You will pay from 2000/2500 ptas for its singles/doubles without bath or 4000 ptas for *en-suite* doubles.

West off the square, *Hostal Persal* (☎ 91 369 46 43, fax 91 369 19 52, Plaza del Ángel 12) is edging out of budgeteers range. Comfortable rooms with bath, TV and phone cost 5800/8700 ptas, including breakfast.

Hostal Vetusta (☎ 91 429 64 04, Calle de las Huertas 3) has small but cute rooms with own shower starting at 3000/4500 ptas; try for one looking onto the street. *Hostal Matute* (☎/fax 91 429 55 85, Plaza de Matute 11) has spacious, somewhat musty singles/doubles for 3500/5000 ptas without own bath and 4500/6000 ptas with.

Hostal Gonzalo (☎ 91 429 27 14, Calle de Cervantes 34) is in sparkling nick. Singles/doubles with private shower and TV are 5000/6200 ptas. The staff will take a few hundred pesetas off the bill if you stay at least three days. Across the road at No 19, *Hostal Dulcinea* (☎ 91 429 93 09, fax 91 369 25 69, ✉ donato@telelline.es) has well-maintained if simply furnished rooms and is often full. Rooms cost 5500/6000 ptas.

Roughly halfway between Atocha train station and Santa Ana, *Hostal López* (☎ 91 429 43 49, Calle de las Huertas 54) is a good choice. Singles/doubles start at 3600/4500 ptas without own bath, or 4200/5200 ptas with.

Around Puerta del Sol & Plaza Mayor
You can't get more central than Plaza de la Puerta del Sol. This and Plaza Mayor, Madrid's true heart, are not major budget accommodation areas, but there are a few good options scattered among all the open-air cafes, tapas bars, ancient restaurants and souvenir shops.

The pick of the cheaper bunch is *Hostal Riesco* (☎ 91 522 26 92, Calle de Correo 2, 3rd floor). Singles/doubles with full bath cost 4000/5800 ptas. *Hostal Tineo* (☎ 91 521 49 43, Calle de la Victoria 6) charges a standard 3500/5500 ptas for singles/doubles with washbasin only. They range up to 5000/6500 ptas for rooms with private bathroom.

SPAIN

Hostal Santa Cruz (☎ 91 522 24 41, Plaza de Santa Cruz 6) is in a prime location. Rooms here start from about 3600/5200 ptas. If you don't mind the traffic, *Hostal Cosmopolitan (☎ 91 522 66 51, Puerta del Sol 9, 3rd floor)* has basic singles/doubles with washbasin for just 1800/3300 ptas.

The more upmarket *Hostal La Macarena (☎ 91 365 92 21, fax 91 366 61 11, Cava de la Cava de San Miguel 8)* has excellent rooms with private bath, TV and phone – pricey but worth it. Singles/doubles/triples cost 6500/8500/10,500 ptas. *Hostal Centro Sol (☎ 91 522 15 82, fax 91 522 57 78, Carrera de San Jerónimo 5)* offers smallish rooms in top order with own bath, TV, phone, heating and air-con, and mini-bar. They are good value at 6000/7500/9500 ptas for singles/doubles/triples.

Around Gran Vía The hostales on and around Gran Vía tend to be a little more expensive. All the same, it's another popular area.

Gran Vía itself is laden with accommodation. *Hostal Lamalonga (☎ 91 547 26 31, Gran Vía 56)* is reliable. Rooms with private bath start at 4500/6500 ptas. *Hostal Alcázar Regis (☎ 91 547 93 17, fax 91 559 07 85)*, No 61, is not a bad choice at the cheaper end of the scale. Singles/doubles cost 4000/6000 ptas.

Calle de Fuencarral is similarly choked with hostales and pensiones, especially at the Gran Vía end. *Hostal Ginebra (☎ 91 532 10 35, Calle de Fuencarral 17)* is a reliable choice not far from Gran Vía. All rooms have TV and phone; singles with washbasin only start at 3200 ptas, while singles/doubles with full bathroom cost 4200/5000 ptas. *Hostal Medieval (☎ 91 522 25 49, Calle de Fuencarral 46)* has spacious and bright singles/doubles with shower for 3000/4500 ptas. Doubles with full private bathroom cost 5500 ptas.

Hotel Laris (☎ 91 521 46 80, fax 91 521 46 85, Calle del Barco 3) is nudging middle range but has decent rooms with all the extras for 5800/8700 ptas.

Around Ópera The tiny *Hostal Paz (☎ 91 547 30 47, Calle de la Priora Flora 4)* looks horrible from the outside, but the cheap rooms inside are reasonable value if a little cramped at 2600/4000 ptas. Quietly tucked away *Hostal Mairu (☎ 91 547 30 88, Calle del Es-pejo 2)* is a simple place with singles/doubles for 2600/4200 ptas. Doubles with own bath cost 4400 ptas. Nearby, *Hostal Pinariega (☎/fax 91 548 08 19, Calle de Santiago 1)* is a sunnier alternative with rooms starting at 3500/4800 ptas.

Rental
Many of the hostales mentioned above will do a deal on long stays. This may include a considerable price reduction, meals and laundry. It is simply a matter of asking. For longer stays, check the rental pages of *Segundamano* magazine or notice boards at universities, the Escuela Oficial de Idiomas and cultural institutes like the British Council or Alliance Française.

PLACES TO EAT
Around Santa Ana
There are tons of Gallego seafood restaurants in this area, but the best is the newly opened *Maceira*, away from the main tourist hubbub at Calle de Jesús 7. Splash your *pulpo a la gallega* down with a crisp white Ribeiro.

In *La Casa del Abuelo (Calle de la Victoria 14)*, on a back street south-east of Puerta del Sol, you can sip a *chato* (small glass) of the heavy El Abuelo red wine while munching on heavenly king prawns, grilled or with garlic. Next, duck around the corner to *Las Bravas (Callejón de Álvarez Gato)* for a caña and the best *patatas bravas* in town. The antics of the bar staff are themselves enough to merit a pit stop and the distorting mirrors are a minor Madrid landmark.

La Trucha (Calle de Núñez de Arce 6) is one of Madrid's great bars for tapas. It's just off Plaza de Santa Ana, and there's another nearby at Calle de Manuel Fernández y González 3. You could eat your fill at the bar or sit down in the restaurant. It closes on Sunday and Monday.

Something of an institution is the *Museo del Jamón*. Walk in to one of these places and you'll understand the name. Huge clumps of every conceivable type of ham dangle all over the place. You can eat plates and plates of ham – the Spaniards' single most favoured source of nutrition. There's one at Carrera de San Jerónimo 6.

If it's just plain cheap you want, *Restaurante La Sanabresa (Calle del Amor de Dios 12)* has a very good *menú* for just 900 ptas.

La Finca de Susana (Calle de Arlabán 4) is a great new spot. Soft lighting and a veritable jungle of greenery create a soothing atmosphere for a meal that doesn't have to cost more than about 2000 ptas.

Vegetarians generally do not have an easy time of it Spain, but Madrid offers a few safe ports. *Elqui (Calle de Buenavista 18)* is a self-service buffet-style place open daily, but Monday for lunch (until 4 pm) and Friday and Saturday evening for dinner (a la carte). *Restaurante Integral Artemisa (Calle de Ventura de la Vega 4)*, is excellent. A full meal will cost around 2000 ptas, and there is another branch off Gran Vía at Calle de las Tres Cruces 4.

Around Plaza Mayor

You know when you're getting close to Plaza Mayor when you see signs in English saying 'Typical Spanish Restaurant' and 'Hemingway Never Ate Here'. Nevertheless, when the sun's shining (or rising) there's not a finer place to be than at one of the outdoor cafes in the plaza.

Calle de la Cava San Miguel and Calle de Cuchilleros are packed with *mesones* that aren't bad for a little tapas hopping. A cut above the rest is *Restaurante Sobrino de Botín (Calle de Cuchilleros 17)*, one of Europe's oldest restaurants (established in 1725), where the set *menú* costs 4050 ptas – it's popular with those who can afford it.

Other Areas

Just about anywhere you go in central Madrid, you can find cheap restaurants with good food.

Casa Mingo (Paseo de la Florida 34), near the Panteón de Goya, is a great old place for chicken and cider. A full roast bird, salad and bottle of cider – enough for two – comes to less than 2000 ptas.

If you're after paella at all costs, head for *Restaurante La Paella Real (Calle de Arrieta 2)* near Plaza de Oriente, which does a whole range of rice-based dishes from 1800 ptas. For a really excellent meal in a cosy atmosphere try *Taberna del Alabardero (Calle de Felipe V 6)* nearby. Expect little change from 6000 ptas per person. If this is a bit steep, consider a couple of the mouthwatering tapas at the bar.

In the Malasaña area around Plaza del Dos de Mayo, *Restaurante Sandos (Plaza del Dos de Mayo 8)* can do you a cheap outdoor pizza and beer, or a set *menú* from 850 ptas. Better still is the crowded *Pizzeria Mastropiero (Calle de San Vicente Ferrer 34)* on the corner of Calle del Dos de Mayo. This is a justifiably popular Argentine-run joint where you can get pizza by the slice.

The Plaza de España area is a good hunting ground for non-Spanish food, though you're looking at 2000 ptas to 2500 ptas for a meal in the better places. *Restaurante Bali (Calle de San Bernardino 6)* has authentic Indonesian fare at around 6000 ptas for two. The *Adrish*, virtually across the street at No 1, is about Madrid's best Indian restaurant. The long-established *Restaurante Veracruz (Calle de San Leonardo de Dios 5)* has a set *menú* (including a bottle of wine) for 950 ptas. It's closed Sunday.

Cafes

Madrid has so many fine places for a coffee and a light bite that you'll certainly find your own favourites. Ours include: the historic, elegant *Café-Restaurante El Espejo (Paseo de Recoletos 31)* where you can also sit at the early-20th-century-style *El Gran Pabellón del Espejo* outside; the equally graceful *Gran Café de Gijón* just down the road; *Café del Real (Plaza de Isabel II)* with a touch of faded elegance – good for breakfast and busy at night too; or *Nuevo Café Barbieri (Calle del Ave María 45)*, a wonderful old place, once the haunt of the artistic and hopefully artistic. An enchanting teahouse with a hint of the 1960s is the *Tetería de la Abuela (Calle del Espíritu Santo 19)*. Along with the great range of teas you can indulge in scrummy crepes.

ENTERTAINMENT

A copy of the weekly *Guía del Ocio* (125 ptas at newsstands) will give you a good rundown of what's on in Madrid. Its comprehensive listings include music gigs, art exhibitions, cinema, TV and theatre. It's very handy even if you can't read Spanish.

Bars

The epicentres of Madrid's nightlife are the Santa Ana-Calle de las Huertas area, and the

SPAIN

Malasaña-Chueca zone north of Gran Vía. The latter has a decidedly lowlife element.

Any of the bars on Plaza de Santa Ana makes a pleasant stop, especially when you can sit outside in the warmer months. *Viva Madrid (Calle de Manuel Fernández y González 7)* gets hellishly crowded at weekends, but take a look at its tiles and heavy wooden ceilings. On the same street, *Carbones* is a busy place open till about 4 am with good mainstream music on the jukebox. *La Venencia (Calle de Echegaray 7)* is an ill-lit, woody place that looks as if it hasn't been cleaned in years – perfect for sampling one of its six varieties of sherry.

Café Populart (Calle de las Huertas 22) often has music, generally jazz or Celtic. For more jazz with your drinks, *Café Central (Plaza del Ángel 10)* is another good choice. Just beyond the hubbub of Huertas is *El Parnaso*, a quirky but engaging bar at Calle de Moratín 25. The area around the bar is jammed with an odd assortment of decorative paraphernalia.

In Malasaña, *Cervecería Santa Bárbara (Plaza de Santa Bárbara 8)* is a classic Madrid drinking house and a good place to kick off a night out. You can sip on a vermouth drawn from the barrel at the wonderful, dimly lit *Bodega de la Ardosa (Calle de Colón 13)*. *La Vía Lactea (Calle de Velarde 18)* is a bright place with thumping mainstream music, a young crowd and a good drinking atmosphere.

Irish pubs are very popular in Madrid: two good ones are *The Quiet Man (Calle de Valverde 44)*, and *Finnegan's (Plaza de las Salesas 9)*.

Calle de Pelayo Campoamor is lined with an assortment of bars, graduating from noisy rock bars at the north end to gay bars at the south end, where you've reached the Chueca area, the heart of Madrid's gay nightlife. *Rimmel (Calle de Luis de Góngora 4)* and *Cruising (Calle de Pérez Galdós 5)* are among the more popular gay haunts. The latter has a dark room and puts on occasional shows.

The quaintly named *Cock Bar (Calle de Reina 16)*, once served as a discreet salon for high-class prostitution. The ladies in question have gone but this popular bar retains plenty of atmosphere.

Live Music & Discos

Latin rhythms have quite a hold in Madrid. A good place to indulge is *Vaiven (Travesía de San Mateo 1)* in Malasaña. Entry is free but a beer is about 600 ptas. *Morocco (Calle del Marqués de Leganés 7)* in Malasaña is still a popular stop on the Madrid disco circuit. It gets going about 1 am.

Near Plaza de Santa Ana, Calle de la Cruz has a couple of good dance spaces; try to pick up fliers for them before you go – they may save you queueing. *Suristán* at No 7 pulls in a wide variety of bands, from Cuban to African, usually starting at 11.30 pm, sometimes with a cover charge up to 1000 ptas. *Torero* at No 26 has Spanish music upstairs and international fare downstairs.

Arena (Calle de la Princesa 1) near Plaza de España offers music for all tastes – funky, house, techno and acid jazz – until 6.30 am from Wednesday to Sunday.

For a taste of the authentic, *La Soleá (Calle de la Cava Baja 27)* is regarded by some as the last real flamenco bar in Madrid. *Casa Patas (Calle de Cañizares 10)* hosts recognised masters of flamenco song, guitar and dance. Bigger flamenco names also play some of Madrid's theatres – check listings.

Cinemas

Cinemas are reasonably priced, with tickets around 850 ptas. Films in their original language (with Spanish subtitles) are usually marked VO *(versión original)* in listings. A good part of town for these is on and around Calle de Martín de los Heros and Calle de la Princesa, near Plaza de España. The *Renoir*, *Alphaville* and *Princesa* complexes here all screen VO movies.

Classical Music, Theatre & Opera

There's plenty happening, except in summer. The city's grandest stage, the recently reopened *Teatro Real (☎ 91 516 06 06)* is the scene for opera. If you can't get into the Teatro Real, the *Teatro Calderón (☎ 91 369 14 34, Calle de Atocha 18)* plays second fiddle. The beautiful old *Teatro de la Comedia (☎ 91 521 49 31, Calle del Príncipe 14)*, home to the Compañía Nacional de Teatro Clásico, stages gems of classic Spanish and European theatre. The *Centro Cultural de la Villa (☎ 91 575 60 80)*, under the waterfall at Plaza de

Colón, stages everything from classical concerts to comic theatre, opera and even classy flamenco. Also important for classical music is the **Auditorio Nacional de Música**, (☎ 91 337 01 40, Avenida del Príncipe de Vergara 146, metro: Cruz del Rayo).

SPECTATOR SPORTS

Spending an afternoon or evening at a football (soccer) match provides quite an insight into Spanish culture. Tickets can be bought on the day of the match, starting from around 2500 ptas, although big games may be sold out. Real Madrid's home is the huge Estadio Santiago Bernabéu (metro: Santiago Bernabéu). Atlético Madrid plays at Estadio Vicente Calderón (metro: Pirámides).

Bullfights take place most Sundays between March and October – more often during the festival of San Isidro Labrador in May, and in summer. Madrid has Spain's largest bullring, the Plaza Monumental de las Ventas (metro: Ventas), and a second bullring by metro Vista Alegre. Tickets are best bought in advance, from agencies or at the rings, and cost from under 2000 ptas.

SHOPPING

For general shopping needs, start at either the markets or the large department stores. The most famous market is El Rastro (see Things to See & Do earlier in this Madrid section). The largest department store chain is El Corte Inglés, with a central branch just north of Sol on Calle de Preciados.

The city's premier shopping street is Calle de Serrano, a block east of Paseo de la Castellana. Calle del Almirante off Paseo de Recoletos has a wide range of engaging, less mainstream shops. For guitars and other musical instruments, hunt around the area near the Palacio Real. For leather try the shops on Calle del Príncipe and Gran Vía, or Calle de Fuencarral for shoes. For designer clothing, try the Chueca area.

GETTING THERE & AWAY
Air
Scheduled and charter flights from all over the world arrive at Madrid's Barajas airport, 13km north-east of the city. With nowhere in Spain more than 12 hours away by bus or train, domestic flights are generally not good value unless you're in a burning hurry. Nor is Madrid the budget international flight capital of Europe. That said, you *can* find bargains to popular destinations such as London, Paris and New York. For an idea on domestic fares, see the Getting Around section earlier in this chapter. See also Travel Agencies under Information earlier in this Madrid section.

Airline offices in Madrid include:

Air France (☎ 91 330 04 12, bookings ☎ 901-11 22 66), Torre de Madrid, Plaza de España 18
American Airlines (☎ 91 453 14 00), Calle de Orense 4
British Airways (☎ 91 387 43 00, ☎ 902-11 13 33), Calle de Serrano 60
Iberia (☎ 91 587 75 36, 902-40 05 00 for bookings), Calle de Velázquez 130
Lufthansa (☎ 902-22 01 01), Calle del Cardenal Marcelo Spinola 2

Bus
There are eight bus stations dotted around Madrid, serving many different bus companies. Tourist offices can tell you which one you need for your destination. Most buses to the south, and some to other places (including a number of international services), use the Estación Sur de Autobuses (☎ 91 468 42 00), Calle de Méndez Álvaro (metro: Méndez Álvaro). The choice between bus and train depends largely on where you're going. More detail on services to/from Madrid is given in other city sections in this chapter.

Train
Atocha station, south of the centre, is used by most trains to/from southern Spain and many destinations around Madrid. Some trains from the north also terminate here, passing through Chamartín, the other main station (in the north of the city), on the way. Chamartín (metro: Chamartín) is smaller and generally serves destinations north of Madrid, although this rule is not cast-iron; some trains to the south use Chamartín and don't pass through Atocha.

The main RENFE booking office (☎ 91 328 90 20) is at Calle de Alcalá 44 and is open 9.30 am to 8 pm Monday to Friday.

For information on fares, see the Getting There & Away section under the city you are going to.

SPAIN

Car & Motorcycle

Madrid is surrounded by two ring-road systems, the older M-30 and the M-40, considerably further out (a third, the M-50, is also planned). Roads in and out of the city can get pretty clogged at peak hours (around 8 to 10 am, 2 pm, 4 to 5 pm and 8 to 9 pm), and on Sunday night.

Car-rental companies in Madrid include Avis (☎ 91 547 20 48), Budget (☎ 91 577 63 63), Europcar (☎ 91 541 88 92) and Hertz (☎ 91 542 58 03). All these have offices at the airport, in the city centre, and often at the main train stations. Robbery on hire-cars leaving the airport is a problem, so be careful.

You can rent motorbikes from Moto Alquiler (☎ 91 542 06 57), Calle del Conde Duque 13, but it's pricey, starting at 4500 ptas plus 16% IVA per day for a 50cc Honda Sky. Rental is from 8 am to 8 pm and you have to leave a refundable deposit of 50,000 ptas on your credit card. Something like a Yamaha 650 will cost you 16,000 ptas a day plus tax and the deposit is 175,000 ptas.

GETTING AROUND
To/From the Airport

The metro runs right into town from the airport, at the upper level of the T2 terminal. Alternatively, an airport bus service runs to/from an underground terminal in Plaza de Colón every 12 to 15 minutes. The trip takes 30 minutes in average traffic and costs 385 ptas. A taxi between the airport and city centre should cost around 2000 ptas.

Bus

In general, the underground (metro) is faster and easier than city buses for getting around central Madrid. Bus route maps are available from tourist offices.

A single ride costs 135 ptas. A 10-ride *Metrobus* ticket (705 ptas) can be used on buses and metro. Night owls may find the 20 bus lines, running from midnight to 6 am, useful. They run from Puerta del Sol and Plaza de la Cibeles.

Metro

Madrid has a very efficient, safe and simple underground system. Trains run from 6.30 am to 1.30 am and the fares are the same as on buses.

Taxi

Madrid's taxis are inexpensive by European standards. They're handy late at night, although in peak hours it's quicker to walk or get the metro. Flag fall is 190 ptas, after which it's 90 ptas per kilometre (120 ptas between 10 pm and 6 am).

Car & Motorcycle

There's little point subjecting yourself to Madrid's traffic just to move from one part of the city to another, especially at peak hours. Most on-street parking space in central Madrid is designated for people with special permits, but almost everybody ignores this – ignoring the 12,000 parking tickets slapped on vehicles every day. But you risk being towed if you park in a marked no-parking or loading zone, or if you double-park. There are plenty of car parks across the city, costing about 200 ptas an hour.

Around Madrid

EL ESCORIAL

The extraordinary 16th-century monastery-palace complex of San Lorenzo de El Escorial lies one hour north-west of Madrid, just outside the town of the same name.

El Escorial was built by Felipe II, king of Spain, Naples, Sicily, Milan, the Netherlands and large parts of the Americas, to commemorate his victory over the French in the battle of St Quentin (1557) and as a mausoleum for his father Carlos I, the first of Spain's Habsburg monarchs. Felipe began searching for a site in 1558, deciding on El Escorial in 1562. The last stone was placed in 1584, and the next 11 years were spent on decoration. El Escorial's austere style, reflecting not only Felipe's wishes but also the watchful eye of architect Juan de Herrera, is loved by some, hated by others. Either way, it's a quintessential monument of Spain's golden age.

Almost all visitors to El Escorial make it a day trip from Madrid. It opens 10 am to 6 pm Tuesday to Sunday (to 5 pm from October to March); entry 900 ptas, 400 ptas for students.

Information

You can get information on El Escorial from tourist offices in Madrid, or from the tourist

SPAIN

office (☎ 91 890 15 54) close to the monastery at Calle de Floridablanca 10. It's open 10 am to 2 pm and 3 to 5 pm Monday to Friday, and 10 am to 2 pm Saturday.

Things to See

Above the monastery's main gateway, on its west side, stands a **statue of San Lorenzo**, holding a symbolic gridiron, the instrument of his martyrdom (he was roasted alive on one). Inside, across the Patio de los Reyes, stands the restrained **basílica**, a cavernous church with a beautiful white-marble crucifixion by Benvenuto Cellini, sculpted in 1576. At either side of the altar stand bronze statues of Carlos I and his family (to the left), and Felipe II with three of his four wives and his eldest son (on the right).

From the basílica, follow signs to the ticket office *(taquilla)*, where you must pay 900 ptas (students 400 ptas) to see the other open parts of El Escorial. The price includes an optional guided tour of the *panteones* and one or two other sections.

The route you have to follow leads first to the **Museo de Arquitectura**, detailing in Spanish how El Escorial was constructed, and the **Museo de Pintura**, with 16th and 17th-century Spanish, Italian and Flemish fine art. You then head upstairs to the richly decorated **Palacio de Felipe II**, in one room of which the monarch died in 1598; his bed was positioned so that he could watch proceedings at the basílica's high altar. Next you descend to the **Panteón de los Reyes**, where almost all Spain's monarchs since Carlos I, and their spouses, lie in gilded marble coffins. Three empty sarcophagi await future arrivals. Backtracking a little, you find yourself in the **Panteón de los Infantes**, a larger series of chambers and tunnels housing the tombs of princes, princesses and other lesser royalty.

Finally, the **Salas Capitulares** in the southeast of the monastery house a minor treasure trove of El Grecos, Titians, Tintorettos and other old masters.

When you emerge, it's worth heading back to the entrance, where you can gain access to the **biblioteca** (library), once one of Europe's finest and still a haven for some 40,000 books. You can't handle them, but many historic and valuable volumes are on display.

Getting There & Away

The Herranz bus company runs up to 30 services a day from the Intercambiador de Autobuses at the Moncloa metro station in Madrid to San Lorenzo de El Escorial (405 ptas one way). Only about 10 run on Sunday and during holidays.

Up to 20 sluggish *cercanías* trains (line C-8a) serve El Escorial from Atocha station (via Chamartín) in Madrid (430 ptas). Seven of these go on to Ávila. Local buses will take you the 2km from the train station up to the monastery.

Castilla y León

The one-time centre of the mighty Christian kingdom of Castile, Castilla y León is one of Spain's most historic regions. From Segovia's Roman aqueduct to the walled city of Ávila, and from León's magnificent cathedral to the lively old centre of Salamanca, it is crowded with reminders of its prominent role in Spain's past.

SEGOVIA
pop 54,750

Segovia is justly famous for its magnificent Roman aqueduct but also has a splendid ridgetop old city worthy of more than a fleeting visit.

Originally a Celtic settlement, Segovia was conquered by the Romans around 80 BC. The Visigoths and Moors also left their mark before the city ended up in Castilian hands in the 11th century.

The main tourist office (☎ 921 46 03 34) is on Plaza Mayor, with another branch (☎ 921 46 29 06) beside the aqueduct. Both are open daily.

Things to See

You can't help but notice the 1st-century AD **aqueduct**, stretching away from the east end of the old city. It's over 800m long, up to 29m high, has 163 arches – and not a drop of mortar was used in its construction.

At the heart of the old city is the 16th-century Gothic **catedral** on the pretty Plaza Mayor. Its sombre interior is anchored by an imposing choir and enlivened by 20-odd chapels. Of these, the Capilla del Cristo del

Consuelo houses a magnificent Romanesque doorway preserved from the original church.

Rapunzel towers, turrets topped with slate witch's hats and a moat deep enough to drown Godzilla (well, almost) make the **Alcázar** a most memorable monument. A 15th-century fairy-tale castle, perched on a craggy cliff top at the west end of the old city, it was virtually destroyed by fire in 1862. What you see today is an evocative over-the-top reconstruction of the original. You can tour the inside for 400 ptas, but don't leave without climbing the Torre de Juan II for magnificent views.

Places to Stay

About 2km along the road to La Granja is *Camping Acueducto* (☎ 921 42 50 00), open April to September.

Fonda Aragón (☎ 921 46 09 14) and *Fonda Cubo* (☎ 921 46 09 17), both at Plaza Mayor 4, are shabby but the cheapest accommodation in town. Both have singles only, costing 1600 ptas at the Aragón and 1300 ptas at the Cubo.

More pleasant is *Hostal Plaza* (☎ 921 46 03 03, Calle del Cronista Lecea 11) where singles/doubles start at 3100/4500 ptas. Also central and good is *Hostal Juan Bravo* (☎ 921 46 34 13, Calle de Juan Bravo 12), which charges 3800 ptas for doubles without or 4800 ptas for those with bath.

Outside the old town, but close to the aqueduct, is the spick-and-span *Hostal Don Jaime* (☎ 921 44 47 87, Calle de Ochoa Ondategui 8). Doubles with private bath and TV cost 5600 ptas; singles (shared facilities only) are 3200 ptas.

Places to Eat

The simple *Bar Ratos (Calle de los Escuderos)* makes generously stuffed sandwiches from 350 ptas. *Cueva de San Esteban (Calle de Valdeláguila 15)* has delicious set lunches for 1000 ptas. Segovia's speciality is *cochinillo asado* (roast suckling pig); a good place to sample this is in the timber-laden dining room of *Mesón José María (Calle del Cronista Lecea 11)*, a favourite among Segovians.

For meatless fare, try *La Almuzara (Marqués del Arco 3)*, which has a warm, artsy ambience and prices that won't break the bank (closed Monday, and Tuesday lunchtime).

Getting There & Away

Up to 30 buses daily run to Madrid (825 ptas, 1½ hours), and others serve Ávila and Salamanca. The bus station is 500m south of the aqueduct, just off Paseo Ezequiel González. Trains to Madrid leave every two hours (790 ptas, 1¾ hours).

Getting Around

Bus No 2 connects the train station with the aqueduct and Plaza Mayor. Otherwise, walking is the best way to get about.

AROUND SEGOVIA

In the mountain village of San Ildefonso de la Granja, 12km south-east, you can visit the royal palace and glorious gardens of **La Granja**, a Spanish version of Versailles built by Felipe V in 1720. The 300-room Palacio Real, restored after a fire in 1918, is impressive but perhaps the lesser of La Granja's jewels. You can visit about half of the rooms, including its Museo de Tapices (Tapestry Museum; 700/300 ptas). A highlight of the gardens is its 28 fountains, some of which are switched on in summer (325 ptas).

Regular buses run from Segovia to San Ildefonso.

About 50km north-west of Segovia, **Castillo de Coca** is also well worth a visit. This beautiful all-brick castle was built in 1453 by the powerful Fonseca family and is surrounded by a deep moat. Guided tours operate daily (300 ptas). Up to five buses daily make the trip from Segovia.

ÁVILA

pop 38,200

Ávila deservedly lays claims to being one of the world's best preserved, and most impressive, walled cities. Constructed during the 11th and 12th centuries, its imposing *muralla* consists of no fewer than eight monumental gates and 88 towers.

Ávila is also distinguished by being the highest city in Spain (1130m) and the birthplace of St Teresa of Ávila, the 16th-century mystical writer and reformer of the Carmelite order. Less to be boasted about, however, is that Tomás de Torquemada orchestrated the most brutal phase of the Spanish Inquisition in Ávila, sending off 2000 people to be burnt at the stake in the late 15th century.

The tourist office (☎ 920 21 13 87), Plaza de la Catedral 4, is open daily.

Things to See & Do
Of Ávila's many convents, museums and monuments, the **catedral** (open daily) is perhaps the most interesting. Not merely a house of worship, it was also an ingenious fortress; its stout granite apse forms the central bulwark in the eastern wall of the town, the most open to attack and hence the most heavily fortified.

Around the western side, the main facade conceals the Romanesque origins of what is essentially the earliest Gothic church in Spain. You can catch a partial peek inside for free, but proceeding to the inner sanctum – plus the cloister, sacristy and small museum – costs 250 ptas.

Just outside the walls, the Romanesque **Basílica de San Vicente** (open daily; 200 ptas) is striking. Gothic modifications in granite contrast with the warm sandstone of the Romanesque original. Work started in the 11th century.

About 500m east of the old town, the **Monasterio de Santo Tomás** (open daily; 100 ptas) is thought to be Torquemada's burial place. Built hastily in 1482 as a royal residence, it is formed by three interconnecting cloisters and the church.

The **Convento de Santa Teresa** (1636) was built over the saint's birthplace. The room where she was allegedly born is now a chapel smothered in gold. The souvenir shop next door gives access to a small room crammed with Teresa relics, including her ring finger (complete with ring). Both are open daily (free).

Los Cuatro Postes, a lookout point around 1km west of the city gates on the Salamanca road, has the best view of the city and its perfectly preserved walls.

Places to Stay
Hostal Jardín (☎ 920 21 10 74, Calle de San Segundo 38) has scruffy but adequate singles/doubles from 3000/4000 ptas. Better is *Hostal El Rastro (☎ 920 21 12 18, Plaza del Rastro 1)*, which is full of character and also has a good *restaurant*. Rooms start at 3880/5560 ptas. Even more comfortable is *Hostal San Juan (☎ 920 25 14 75, Calle de los Comuneros de Castilla 3)* where rooms with telephone, TV, shower and WC cost 3800/7000 ptas.

Places to Eat
Restaurante Los Leales (Plaza de Italia 4) has a solid *menú* for 1000 ptas. Pleasant *Posada de la Fruta (Plaza de Pedro Dávila 8)* serves cheap and informal meals in its cafeteria/bar and more substantial fare in its traditional dining room.

Italiano (Calle de San Segundo 30) makes salads, pizza and pasta for under 1000 ptas, as does *Siglo Doce* just inside Puerta de los Leales. *Cafe del Adarve (Calle de San Segundo 50)* is a hip hang-out and good place for a drink, as is the wine and tapas bar *Bodeguita de San Segundo* across the street.

Gimeco (Calle Eduardo Marquina 18) is the most central supermarket.

Getting There & Away
Buses to Madrid leave up to eight times on weekdays, down to three on weekends (930 ptas, 1½ hours), while Salamanca is served four times on weekdays (700 ptas, 1½ hours) and Segovia up to seven times (550 ptas, one hour).

There are up to 30 trains a day to Madrid (865 ptas, 1½ hours); trains to Salamanca cost the same. The bus and train stations are, respectively, 700m and 1.5km east of the old town. Bus No 1 links the train station with the old town.

BURGOS
pop 161,500
A mighty chilly place in winter, Burgos is famous for being home to one of Spain's greatest Gothic cathedrals.

Just outside of town lie a couple of remarkable monasteries.

Information
The regional tourist office (☎ 947 20 31 25; closed Sunday) is on Plaza de Alonso Martínez 7. Another branch (☎/fax 947 27 87 10; closed Sunday afternoon) is inside the Teatro Principal on Paseo de Espolón. The main post office is on Plaza del Conde de Castro. The Ciber-Cafe at Calle de la Puebla 21 provides Internet access.

SPAIN

Things to See

It is difficult to imagine that on the site of the majestic Gothic cathedral (1261), there once stood a modest Romanesque church. Twin towers, each representing 84m of richly decorated fantasy, lord over this truly dizzying masterpiece. Inside, the highlight is the **Escalera Dorada** (gilded staircase) by Diego de Siloé. El Cid lies buried beneath the central dome, and you can visit the cloisters and church treasures for 400 ptas.

Of Burgos' two monasteries, the **Monasterio de las Huelgas** is the more interesting. About a half-hour walk west of the town centre along the south bank of the Río Arlanzón, it was founded in 1187 by Eleanor of Acquitaine and is still home to 35 Cistercian nuns. Highlights of the guided tour include Las Claustrillas, an elegant Romanesque cloister, and a museum with preserved garments once worn by Eleanor and other medieval royals (closed Monday; 700/300 ptas).

About 4km east of the centre, the **Cartuja de Miraflores** is a functioning Carthusian monastery rich in treasure. The walk along the Río Arlanzón and through a lush park is particularly pleasant.

Places to Stay & Eat

Camping Fuentes Blancas (☎/fax 947 48 60 16) is about 4km from the centre on the road to the Cartuja de Miraflores. It's open April to September and served by hourly bus No 26.

Beg, borrow and/or steal to secure a bed at *Pensión Peña* (☎ 947 20 62 23, Calle de la Puebla 18). Completely refurbished singles/doubles with washbasin cost 1700/2900 ptas. *Pensión Victoria* (☎ 947 20 15 42, Calle de San Juan 3) comes reader-recommended and has OK rooms with washbasin for 2800/4000 ptas. *Hostal Joma* (☎ 947 20 33 50, Calle de San Juan 26) is basic but in the heart of the action. Rooms go for 1750/3100 ptas.

Cervecería Morito on Calle de la Sombrerería is popular with locals for its cheap drinks and budget-friendly hot dishes. *Royal* (Plaza de Huerto del Rey 23) serves a wide range of salads, burgers and sandwiches well under 1000 ptas.

Getting There & Away

The bus station is a Calle de Miranda 3. Continental Auto runs up to 12 buses daily to Madrid (1950 ptas). Buses also go to Santander, San Sebastián, Vitoria and Bilbao.

Trains to Madrid depart up to nine times daily (3060 ptas, four hours) and to Bilbao six times (2000 ptas, three hours). Others go to León, Salamanca and other major cities.

SALAMANCA
pop 160,500

If any major Castillian city can be said to jump with action, it's Salamanca. Year round, its countless bars, cafes and restaurants are jam-packed with students and young visitors from around the world. This is one of Spain's most inspiring cities, both in terms of the beauty of its architecture and its modern, laid-back lifestyle.

Information

The municipal tourist office (☎ 923 21 83 42) on Plaza Mayor, open daily, concentrates on city information. A second branch (☎ 923 26 85 71) in the Casa de las Conchas focuses on the wider region (closed Saturday afternoon and Sunday).

The post office is situated at Gran Vía 25. For Internet access try Campus Cibermático at Plaza Mayor 10. There's a coin-operated laundrette at Pasaje Azafranal 18.

Things to See

As in many Spanish cities, one of the joys of Salamanca is to simply wander the streets. At the heart of the old centre is the harmonious **Plaza Mayor** (1755), designed by José Churriguera, which is ringed by medallions of sundry famous figures; until the 19th century, bullfights took place here.

Salamanca's **University** was founded in 1218. Its main facade on Calle de los Libreros is a tapestry in sandstone, bursting with images of mythical and historical figures ... and the famously elusive frog. Join the throngs trying to find the little creature.

Brace yourself for the **Catedral Nueva** (New Cathedral) on Rúa Mayor. This incredible Gothic structure, completed in 1733, took 220 years to build. As you try to take in the detailed relief around the entrance, you may wonder how they did it so fast. From inside the cathedral, you can enter the adjacent **Catedral Vieja** (Old Cathedral) for 300 ptas. A Romanesque construction begun in 1120, this church

SPAIN

SALAMANCA

PLACES TO STAY
9 Pensión Los Angeles;
Campus Cibermático
13 Pensión Las Vegas
15 Hostal La Perla
Salamantina
16 Le Petit Hotel
25 Pensión Feli

PLACES TO EAT
2 La Regenta
11 MusicArte
Café
14 El Patio Chico
17 El Grillo Azul
19 El Bardo
22 Café El Ave

OTHER
1 Camelot
3 O'Neill's Irish Pub
4 Captain Haddock
5 Posada de las Almas
6 Laundrette
7 Post Office
8 Tio Vivo
10 Oficina Municipal
de Turismo
12 Café El Corrillo
18 El Gran Café Moderno
20 Casa de las Conchas;
Tourist Office
21 Irish Rover
23 Patio de las
Escuelas Menores
24 University
26 Catedral Vieja
27 Catedral Nueva
28 Convento de
las Dueñas
29 Convento de
San Esteban

SPAIN

is a bit of a hybrid, with some elements of Gothic; the ribbed cupola shows a Byzantine influence. Both cathedrals are open daily.

Other major sights include the **Convento de San Esteban** and the **Convento de las Dueñas**. The 15th-century **Casa de las Conchas**, named for the scallop shells clinging to its facade, is a symbol of Salamanca.

Places to Stay

Salamanca is always in season, so book ahead when possible. The central HI *Albergue Juvenil* (☎ 923 26 91 41, @ esterra@mmteam .disbumad.es, Calle Escoto 13-15) charges 1750 ptas per bunk, including bed linen and breakfast. Bus No 16 connects the hostel with the centre.

Pensión Los Angeles (☎ 923 21 81 66, *Plaza Mayor 10*) has low-frills singles/doubles with washbasin for 1900/2900 ptas. A favourite of young travellers is the tiny *Pensión Las Vegas* (☎ 923 21 87 49, *Calle de Meléndez 13*), where clean rooms cost 2000/3500 ptas. *Hostal La Perla Salamantina* (☎/fax 923 21 76 56, *Calle de Sánchez Barbero 7*) has bright rooms with washbasin for 2100/3500 ptas. Rooms at *Pensión Feli* (☎ 923 21 60 10, *Calle de los Libreros 58*), near the university, are cheerful and rent for 2400/3400 ptas.

For more comfort, try *Le Petit Hotel* (☎ *923 26 55 67, Ronda de Sancti-Spíritus 39*) whose small but tidy rooms with phone, TV and private bath cost 4000/6500 ptas.

Places to Eat
For good and filling breakfasts from 375 ptas, go to *Café Unamuno (Calle Zamora 55)*. *MusicArte Café (Plaza del Corrillo 22)* is a hip hang-out for coffee, pizza and sandwiches at budget prices.

El Patio Chico (Calle de Meléndez 13) is a lively place for beers and filling tapas (400 ptas each), plus a set *menú* for 1500 ptas. At *Café El Ave (Calle de los Libreros 24)* full meals can be had from 700 ptas. For more atmosphere, go to the bustling *El Bardo (Calle de la Compañia 8)*, which does decent paella for 1100 ptas. *El Grillo Azul* (☎ *923 21 92 33, Calle Grillo 1*) has inexpensive vegetarian fare.

La Regenta (Calle de Espoz y Mina 19-20) is a frilly coffeehouse with velvet curtains, polished antiques and yummy cakes.

Entertainment
Salamanca, with its myriad bars, is the perfect after-dark playground. A drink at *Tío Vivo (Calle de Clavel 3)* is a must, if only to experience the whimsical decor. A long-time favourite is *El Gran Café Moderno (Gran Vía 75)*, made to resemble an early-20th-century Parisian street. *Café El Corrillo (Calle de Meléndez 8)* is great for a beer and live jazz. *O'Neill's (Calle de Zamora 14)* and *The Irish Rover* by the Casa de las Conchas are Salamanca's popular Irish pubs.

Captain Haddock is a romantic, candlelit haunt with a muted nautical theme. It's in a courtyard off Calle Consejo.

Great discos include *Camelot* inside an actual convent on Calle de la Companía, and *Posada de las Almas* on Plaza de San Boal, a fantasy world inhabited by life-sized papier-mâché figures and doll houses.

Getting There & Away
Bus Salamanca's bus station is at Avenida de Filiberto Villalobos 85, about 1km north-west of Plaza Mayor. AutoRes has frequent express service to Madrid (2250 ptas, 2½ hours), as well as a few nonexpress buses (1750 ptas, 3¾

hours). Other destinations served regularly include Santiago de Compostela, Cáceres, Ávila, Segovia, León and Valladolid.

Train Four trains leave daily for Madrid (2130 ptas, 2½ hours) via Ávila (865 ptas, 1¾ hours). A train for Lisbon leaves at 4.41 am.

Getting Around
Bus No 4 runs past the bus station and round the old town perimeter to Gran Vía. From the train station, the best bet is bus No 1, which heads down Calle de Azafranal. Going the other way, it can be picked up along Gran Vía.

LEÓN
pop 147,300
León is far too often left off travellers itineraries. For those who get here, a fresh and pleasant city awaits, with long boulevards, open squares, excellent nightlife and one of Spain's greatest cathedrals. León was at its mightiest from the 10th to 13th centuries, as capital of the expanding Christian kingdom of the same name.

The tourist office (☎ 987 23 70 82, fax 987 27 33 91), opposite the cathedral, is open daily.

Things to See
León's breathtaking 13th-century **catedral** is a wonder of Gothic architecture. It has an extraordinarily intricate facade with a rose window, three richly sculptured doorways and two muscular towers. The most outstanding feature, though, awaits inside – 128 radiant stained-glass windows (with a surface of 1800 sq metres) give the place an ethereal quality.

About 500m north-west of here is a great monument from the earlier Romanesque period – the **Real Basílica de San Isidoro**. It contains the **Panteón Real** where Leonese royalty lie buried beneath a canopy of some of the finest frescoes in all of Spain. It can only be seen on a guided tour (400 ptas).

The last in León's trio of major sights is the **Hostal de San Marcos**, at the end of the Gran Vía de San Marcos. This former pilgrim's hospital, with its golden-hued 100m-long facade (1513), now houses a parador (luxury hotel) and the Museo de León.

Also of interest is the **Casa de Botines** on Plaza de San Marcelo, designed by famed

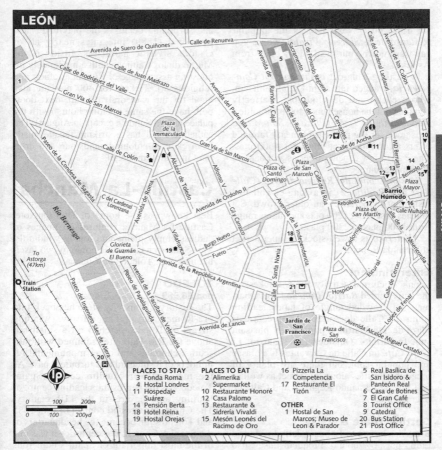

LEÓN

SPAIN

PLACES TO STAY
3 Fonda Roma
4 Hostal Londres
11 Hospedaje Suárez
15 Pensión Berta
18 Hotel Reina
19 Hostal Orejas

PLACES TO EAT
2 Alimerika Supermarket
10 Restaurante Honoré
12 Casa Palomo
13 Restaurante & Sidrería Vivaldi
15 Mesón Leonés del Racimo de Oro

16 Pizzeria La Competencia
17 Restaurante El Tizón

OTHER
1 Hostal de San Marcos; Museo de Leon & Parador

5 Real Basílica de San Isidoro & Panteón Real
6 Casa de Botines
7 El Gran Café
8 Tourist Office
9 Catedral
20 Bus Station
21 Post Office

Catalan architect Antoni Gaudí, although it's rather conservative by his standards.

Places to Stay

Pensión Berta (☎ *987 25 70 39, Plaza Mayor 8*) has rickety but clean doubles for 3000 ptas. The decidely no-frills ***Fonda Roma*** (☎ *987 22 46 63, Avenida de Roma 4*) is in an attractive old building and has rooms for 900/1500 ptas. ***Hospedaje Suárez*** (☎ *987 25 42 88, Calle de Ancha 7*) offers the same standard and prices.

    Hotel Reina (☎ *987 20 52 12, Calle de Puerta de la Reina 2*) has rooms with wash-basin for 1870/3365 ptas and others with full bath costing 4000/5000 ptas. For more comfort, try the friendly ***Hostal Londres*** (☎ *987 22 22 74, Avenida de Roma 1*) where charming doubles with TV, shower and WC start at 4500 ptas. ***Hostal Orejas*** (☎/fax *987 25 29 09, Calle de Villafranca 8*) has rooms with similar amenities for 5500/6500 ptas; those with washbasin go for 4000/5000 ptas.

Places to Eat

Restaurante Honoré (*Calle de los Serradores 4*) has a good *menú* for 950 ptas. ***Casa Palomo***, on tiny Calle de la Escalerilla, is a quality establishment with a lunch *menú* for 1300 ptas. Next door is the popular *Restaurante & Sidrería Vivaldi*, where you can wash down your meal with a cider from Asturias.

A bustling hang-out is *Pizzeria La Competencia*, wedged into tight Calle Mulhacín, whose cheap and delicious pies perfectly complement the house wine (400 ptas/bottle). *Restaurante El Tizón (Plaza de San Martín 1)* is good for big portions of meaty fare and offers an abundant set lunch for 1600 ptas. There are a few decent pizzerias and bars on the same square.

Mesón Leonés del Racimo de Oro (Calle de Caño Badillo 2) is a long-established restaurant favoured by an older crowd. Set lunches cost about 1200 ptas and mains range from 1500 ptas to 2300 ptas.

Alimerika is a well-stocked supermarket at Avenida Roma 2.

Entertainment
León's nocturnal activity flows thickest in the aptly named *Barrio Húmedo* (Wet Quarter), the crowded tangle of lanes leading south off Calle de Ancha. Its epicentre is Plaza de San Martín, a particularly pleasant spot for drinks. Outside of the Barrio, *El Gran Café* on Calle de Cervantes is a classy and popular spot, but there are plenty of other possibilities along this street as well as on Calle de Fernando Regueral and Calle de Sacramento.

Getting There & Away
Bus Alsa has up to 12 buses daily to Madrid (2665 ptas, 3½ hours). Frequent buses also run to Astorga (405 ptas, 30 minutes) and Oviedo (1015 ptas, 1¾ hours). Other destinations include Bilbao, Salamanca, Burgos and San Sebástian.

Train Up to 10 trains daily leave for Madrid (3600 ptas, 4¼ hours) and three go to Barcelona (5700 ptas, 11 hours). Plenty of trains head west to Astorga (410 ptas, 45 minutes), north to Oviedo (1700 ptas, two hours) and east to Burgos (2100 ptas, two hours).

AROUND LEÓN
A more extravagant example of Gaudí's work is in the town of **Astorga**, 47km south-

west of León. Fairy-tale turrets, frilly facades and surprising details – the playful Palacio Episcopal (1889) integrates nearly all of Gaudí's stylistic hallmarks. Inside is the Museo de los Caminos with a moderately interesting assemblage of Roman artefacts and religious art. Tickets for 400 ptas are also good for the cathedral museum next door; both have the same opening hours (with the palace closed Sunday, except in August). The cathedral itself has a striking facade, made from caramel-coloured sandstone and dripping in sculptural detail.

Castilla-La Mancha

Best known as the home of Don Quixote, Castilla-La Mancha conjures up images of endless empty plains and lonely windmills. This Spanish heartland is home to two fascinating cities, Toledo and Cuenca.

TOLEDO
pop 66,989
The history of this city stretches back into pre-Roman days. The narrow, winding streets of Toledo, perched on a small hill above the Río Tajo, are crammed with museums, churches and other monumental reminders of a splendid and turbulent past. As the main city of Muslim central Spain, Toledo was the peninsula's leading centre of learning and the arts in the 11th century. The Christians wrested control of it in 1085 and Toledo soon became the headquarters of the Spanish Church. For centuries it was one of the most important of Spain's numerous early capitals. Until 1492, Christians, Jews and Muslims coexisted peaceably here, for which Toledo still bears the label 'Ciudad de las Tres Culturas' (City of the Three Cultures). Its unique architectural combinations, with Arabic influences everywhere, are a strong reminder of Spain's mixed heritage. El Greco lived here from 1577 to 1614 and many of his works can still be seen in the city.

Toledo is quite expensive and packed with tourists and souvenir shops. Try to stay here at least overnight, since you can enjoy the street and cafe life after the tour buses have headed north in the evening.

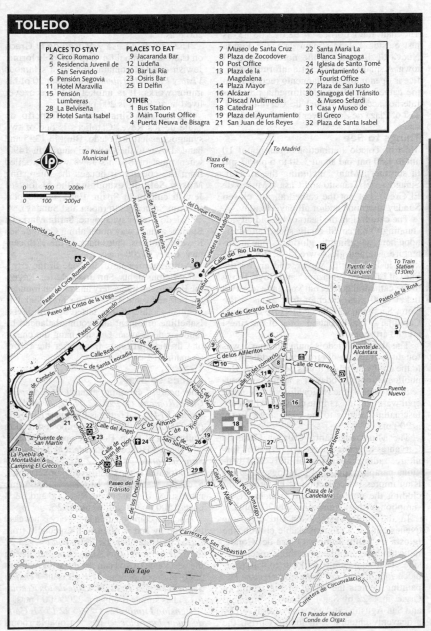

TOLEDO

PLACES TO STAY
2   Circo Romano
5   Residencia Juvenil de San Servando
6   Pensión Segovia
11 Hotel Maravilla
15 Pensión Lumbreras
28 La Belviseña
29 Hotel Santa Isabel

PLACES TO EAT
9   Jacaranda Bar
12 Ludeña
20 Bar La Ría
23 Osiris Bar
25 El Delfin

OTHER
1   Bus Station
3   Main Tourist Office
4   Puerta Neuva de Bisagra

7   Museo de Santa Cruz
8   Plaza de Zocodover
10 Post Office
13 Plaza de la Magdalena
14 Plaza Mayor
16 Alcázar
17 Discad Multimedia
18 Catedral
19 Plaza del Ayuntamiento
21 San Juan de los Reyes

22 Santa María La Blanca Sinagoga
24 Iglesia de Santo Tomé
26 Ayuntamiento & Tourist Office
27 Plaza de San Justo
30 Sinagoga del Tránsito & Museo Sefardi
31 Casa y Museo de El Greco
32 Plaza de Santa Isabel

SPAIN

Information

The main tourist office (☎ 925 22 08 43) is just outside Toledo's main gate, the Puerta Nueva de Bisagra, at the northern end of town. A smaller, more helpful information office is open in the ayuntamiento (across from the cathedral). Discad Multimedia provides Internet access at Miguel de Cervantes 17, east of Plaza de Zocodover towards the river.

Things to See

Most of Toledo's attractions open about 10 am to 1.30 pm and about 3.30 to 6 pm (7 pm in summer). Many, including the alcázar, Sinagoga del Tránsito and Casa y Museo de El Greco, but not the cathedral, are closed Sunday afternoon and/or all day Monday.

The **catedral**, in the heart of the old city, is stunning. You could easily spend an afternoon here, admiring the glorious stone architecture, stained-glass windows, tombs of kings in the Capilla Mayor, and art by the likes of El Greco, Velázquez and Goya. Entry to the cathedral is free, but you have to buy a ticket (700 ptas) to enter four areas – the Coro, Sacristía, Capilla de la Torre and Sala Capitular – which contain some of the finest art and artisanry.

The **alcázar**, Toledo's main landmark, was fought over repeatedly from the Middle Ages to the civil war, when it was besieged by Republican troops. Today it's a military museum, created by the Nationalist victors of the civil war, with most of the displays which are fascinating relating to the 1936 siege. Entry is 200 ptas.

The **Museo de Santa Cruz** on Calle de Cervantes contains a large collection of furniture, fading tapestries, military and religious paraphernalia, and paintings. Upstairs is an impressive collection of El Grecos including the masterpiece *La Asunción* (Assumption of the Virgin). Entry is 200 ptas.

In the south-west of the old city, the queues outside an unremarkable church, the **Iglesia de Santo Tomé** on Plaza del Conde, indicate there must be something special inside. That something is El Greco's masterpiece *El Entierro del Conde de Orgaz*. The painting depicts the burial of the Count of Orgaz in 1322 by San Esteban (St Stephen) and San Agustín (St Augustine), observed by a heavenly entourage, including Christ, the Virgin, John the Baptist and Noah. Entry is 200 ptas.

The so-called **Casa y Museo de El Greco** on Calle de Samuel Leví, in Toledo's former Jewish quarter, contains the artist's famous *Vista y Plano de Toledo*, plus about 20 of his minor works. It is unlikely El Greco ever lived here. Entry is 200 ptas.

Nearby, the **Sinagoga del Tránsito** on Calle de los Reyes Católicos is one of two synagogues left in Toledo. Built in 1355 and handed over to the Catholic church in 1492, when most of Spain's Jews were expelled from the country, it houses the interesting **Museo Sefardí**, examining the history of Jewish culture in Spain. Entry is 400 ptas (free on Saturday afternoon and Sunday).

Toledo's other synagogue, **Santa María La Blanca**, a short way north along Calle de los Reyes Católicos, dates back to the 12th century. Entry is 200 ptas.

A little farther north lies one of the city's most visible sights, **San Juan de los Reyes**, the Franciscan monastery and church founded by Fernando and Isabel. The prevalent late Flemish-Gothic style is tarted up with lavish Isabelline ornament and counterbalanced by mudéjar decoration. Outside hang the chains of Christian prisoners freed after the fall of Granada in 1492.

Places to Stay

The nearest camping ground is *Camping Circo Romano* (☎ 925 22 04 42, *Avenida de Carlos III 19*), but better is *Camping El Greco* (☎ 925 22 00 90), well signposted 2.5km south-west of town. Both are open all year.

Toledo's HI hostel, *Residencia Juvenil de San Servando* (☎ 925 22 45 54), is beautifully located in the Castillo de San Servando, a castle that started life as a Visigothic monastery. It's east of the Río Tajo and B&B costs 1200 ptas if you're under 26.

Cheap accommodation in the city is not easy to come by and is often full, especially from Easter to September. *La Belviseña* (☎ 925 22 00 67, *Cuesta del Can 5*), is basic but among the best value (if you can get in), with rooms at 1500 ptas per person. The pleasant *Pensión Segovia* (☎ 925 21 11 24, *Calle de los Recoletos 2*) has simple rooms for 2200/3000 ptas.

Pensión Lumbreras (☎ 925 22 15 71, *Calle de Juan Labrador 9*) has reasonable rooms and pleasant courtyard for 1700/3200/4500 ptas. *Hotel Santa Isabel* (*☎/fax 925 25 31 36, Calle de Santa Isabel 24*) is a good mid-range hotel well placed near the cathedral, yet away from the tourist hordes. Pleasant rooms with air-con are 3925/6075 ptas plus IVA. *Hotel Maravilla* (*☎ 925 22 83 17, Plaza de Barrio Rey 5*), just off the Zocodover, has rooms with private bath for 4000/6500 ptas.

Places to Eat

Among the cheap lunch spots, *El Delfin* (*Calle del Taller del Moro*) has a set *menú* for 950 ptas. For outdoor dining, the *Osiris Bar* on the shady Plaza del Barrio Nuevo is a decent choice, with set lunches from 1300 ptas.

If you just want to pick at a pâté and cheese platter over a beer, try the chilled-out *Jacaranda Bar* (*Callejón de los Dos Codos 1*). For Toledo's best seafood, the tiny *Bar La Ría* (*Callejón de los Bodegones 6*) is hard to beat at 2000 ptas for a good meal. An excellent little place for a full meal (1500 ptas *menú*) or simply a beer and tapas is *Ludeña* (*Plaza de la Magdalena 13*).

Getting There & Away

To reach most major destinations from Toledo, you need to backtrack to Madrid (or at least Aranjuez). Toledo's bus station (*☎ 925 22 36 41*) is on Avenida de Castilla-La Mancha. There are buses (585 ptas) every half-hour from about 6 am to 10 pm to/from Madrid (Estación Sur). The Aisa line has a service from Toledo to Cuenca at 5.30 pm, Monday to Friday.

Trains from Madrid (Atocha) are more pleasant than the bus, but there are only nine of them daily. The first from Madrid departs at 7.05 am, the last from Toledo at 8.56 pm (660 ptas one way). Toledo's train station is 400m east of the Puente de Azarquiel.

Bus No 5 links the train and bus stations with Plaza de Zocodover.

CUENCA
pop 43,733

Cuenca's setting is hard to believe. The high old town is cut off from the rest of the city by the Júcar and Huécar Rivers, sitting at the top of a deep gorge. Most of its famous monuments appear to teeter on the edge – a photographer's delight.

The Infotur office (*☎ 969 23 21 19*) at Calle de Alfonso VIII 2, just before the arches of Plaza Mayor, is especially helpful. La Repro, close to the train and bus stations, provides Internet access.

Things to See & Do

Cuenca's **Casas Colgadas** (Hanging Houses), originally built in the 15th century, are precariously positioned on a cliff top, their balconies literally hanging over the gorge. A footbridge across the gorge provides access to spectacular views of these buildings (and the rest of the old town) from the other side. Inside one of the Casas Colgadas is the **Museo de Arte Abstracto Español**. This exciting collection includes works by Fernando Zobel, Sempere, Millares and Chillida. Initially a private initiative of Zobel to unite works by fellow artists of the 1950s Generación Abstracta, it now holds works up to the present day. Entry is 500 ptas, and the museum opens from 11 am to 2 pm and 4 to 6 pm (to 8 pm on Saturday).

Nearby, on Calle del Obispo Valero, is the **Museo Diocesano** (200 ptas). Of the religious art and artefacts inside, the 14th-century Byzantine diptych is the jewel in the crown. Hours are the same as the Museo de Arte Abstracto Español.

South of Plaza Mayor in a former convent is the **Museo de Las Ciencias** (science museum). Displays range from a time machine to the study of the resources of Castilla-La Mancha (closed Sunday afternoon; free).

On Plaza Mayor you'll find Cuenca's strange **catedral**. The lines of the unfinished facade are Norman-Gothic and reminiscent of French cathedrals, but the stained-glass windows look like they'd be more at home in the abstract art museum.

As you wander the old town's beautiful streets, check the **Torre de Mangana**, the remains of a Moorish fortress in a square west of Calle de Alfonso VIII, overlooking the plain below.

Places to Stay & Eat

Up at the top of the *casco* is the clean and simple *Pensión La Tabanqueta* (*☎ 969 21 12 90, Calle de Trabuco 13*) costing 2000 ptas per person. Ask for a room with views of the Júcar gorge.

Down in the new town, there are several places on Calle de Ramón y Cajal, which runs from near the train station towards the old town. The friendly *Pensión Marín* (☎ *969 22 19 78, Calle de Ramón y Cajal 53*), a short walk from the train station, has rooms for 1300/2400 ptas.

At the foot of the casco is the *Posada de San Julián* (☎ *969 21 17 04, Calle de las Torres 1*), a cavernous old place with doubles for 3000 ptas (4000 ptas with own bathroom) and the *Pensión Tintes* (☎ *969 21 23 98, Calle de los Tintes 7*) which has basic rooms for about 1500 ptas a head in summer.

Most restaurants and cafes around Plaza Mayor are better for a drink and people-watching than for good-value eating. A decent establishment for solid La Manchan food is the *Restaurante San Nicolás (Calle de San Pedro 15)*. Mains range between 2000 ptas and 3000 ptas.

Getting There & Away
There are up to nine buses a day to Madrid (1325 ptas to 1650 ptas, 2½ hours), and daily buses to Barcelona, Teruel and Valencia. There are five trains a day direct to Madrid (Atocha), taking 2½ hours and costing 1405 ptas one way. There are also four trains a day to Valencia.

Bus No 1 or 2 from near the bus and train stations will take you up to Plaza Mayor in the old town.

Catalunya

BARCELONA
pop 1.5 million
If you only visit one city in Spain, it probably should be Barcelona. After hosting the Olympic Games in 1992, it has finally taken its place on the list of the world's great cities. Catalonia's modernist architecture of the late 19th and early 20th centuries – a unique melting pot of Art Nouveau, Gothic, Moorish and other styles – climaxes here in the inspiring creations of Antoni Gaudí, among them La Sagrada Família church and Parc Güell. Barcelona also has world-class museums including two devoted to Picasso and Miró, a fine old quarter (the Barri Gòtic) and nightlife as good as anywhere in the country.

Orientation
Plaça de Catalunya is Barcelona's main square, and a good place to get your bearings when you arrive. The main tourist office is right here. Most travellers base themselves in Barcelona's old city (Ciutat Vella), the area bordered by the harbour Port Vell (south), Plaça de Catalunya (north), Ronda de Sant Pau (west) and Parc de la Ciutadella (east).

La Rambla, the city's best known boulevard, runs through the heart of the old city from Plaça de Catalunya down to the harbour. On the east side of La Rambla is the medieval quarter (Barri Gòtic), and on the west the seedy Barri Xinès. North of the old city is the gracious suburb L'Eixample, where you'll find the best of Barcelona's modernist architecture.

Information
Tourist Offices The main tourist office is the Centre d'Informació Turisme de Barcelona (☎ 906-30 12 82) at Plaça de Catalunya 17-S (actually underground). It opens from 9 am to 9 pm daily.

Handy offices are located at Estació Sants, the main train station, and the EU passengers arrivals hall at the airport and both open daily (mornings only on Sunday and holidays).

Money Banks usually have the best rates for both cash and travellers cheques. Banking hours are usually 8 am to 2 pm weekdays. The American Express office at Passeig de Gràcia 101 is open 9.30 am to 6 pm weekdays and 10 am to noon Saturday. There is another branch on La Rambla dels Capuxtins 74. The rates are reasonable. For after-hours emergencies, currency-exchange booths throng La Rambla.

Post & Communications The main post office is on Plaça d'Antoni López. For most services including poste restante (lista de correos), it's open Monday to Saturday from 8 am to 9.30 pm.

Email & Internet Access Among dozens of options, you can use the Internet for 600 ptas a half-hour (or 800 ptas an hour for students) upstairs at El Café de Internet (☎ 93 302 11 54), Gran Via de les Corts Catalanes 656.

SPAIN

Travel Agencies Usit UNLIMITED (☎ 93 412 01 04), at Ronda de l'Universitat 16, sells youth and student air, train and bus tickets. It has a branch in the Turisme Juvenil de Catalunya office at Carrer de Rocafort 116-122. Halcón Viatges (☎ 902-30 06 00) is a reliable chain of travel agents with a branch at Carrer de Pau Claris 108.

Bookshops In the Barri Gòtic, Quera, at Carrer de Petritxol 2, specialises in maps and guides. Próleg, at Carrer de la Dagueria 13, is a good women's bookshop.

In L'Eixample, Altaïr, Carrer de Balmes 71, is a superb travel bookshop; Librería Francesa at Passeig de Gràcia 91 has French language books, and Come In, at Carrer de Provença 203, is good for novels and books on Spain, and dictionaries. The English Bookshop, Carrer d'Entença 63, has a good range of literature.

Laundry Lavomatic, at Carrer del Consolat de Mar 43-45, is a rare self-service laundrette. A 7kg load costs 575 ptas and drying costs 105 ptas for five minutes.

Emergency The Guàrdia Urbana (City Police; ☎ 092) has a station at La Rambla 43, opposite Plaça Reial. For an ambulance or emergency medical help call ☎ 061. Hospital Creu Roja (☎ 93 300 20 20), Carrer del Dos de Maig 301, has an emergency room. There's a 24-hour pharmacy at Carrer d'Aribau 62 and another at Passeig de Gràcia 26.

Dangers & Annoyances Watch your pockets, bags and cameras on the train to/from the airport, on La Rambla, in the Barri Gòtic south of Plaça Reial and in the Barri Xinès especially at night. These last two areas have been somewhat cleaned up in recent years but pickpockets, bag-snatchers and intimidating beggars still stalk the unsuspecting.

Things to See

La Rambla The best way to introduce yourself to Barcelona is by a leisurely stroll from Plaça de Catalunya down La Rambla, the magnificent boulevard of a thousand faces. This long pedestrian strip, shaded by leafy trees, is an ever-changing blur of activity, lined with newsstands, bird and flower stalls, and cafes. It's populated by artists, buskers, human statues, shoe-shine merchants, beggars, and a constant stream of people promenading and just enjoying the sights.

About halfway down La Rambla is the wonderful **Mercat de la Boqueria**, which is worth going to just for the sights and sounds, but is also a good place to stock up on fresh fruit, vegetables, nuts, bread, pastries – everything you'll need for a park picnic. Just off La Rambla, farther south, **Plaça Reial** was, until a few years ago, a seedy square of ill repute, but it's now quite pleasant, with numerous cafes, bars and a couple of music clubs. Just off the other side of La Rambla at Carrer Nou de la Rambla 3-5 is Gaudí's moody **Palau Güell**, open 10 am to 1.30 pm and 4 to 6.30 pm daily, except Sunday (400 ptas, students 200 ptas). This is also the place to pick up **Ruta del Modernisme** tickets, which allow you to see others Gaudí efforts around the city.

Down at the end of La Rambla stands the **Monument a Colom**, a statue of Columbus atop a tall pedestal. A small lift will take you to the top of the monument (250 ptas). Just west is the **Museu Marítim**, in the beautiful 14th-century Royal Shipyards, with an impressive array of boats, models, maps and more. If you like boats and the sea, you won't be disappointed. It's open 10 am to 7 pm daily (800 ptas, 600 ptas for students and seniors).

Barri Gòtic Barcelona's serene Gothic **catedral** is open 8.30 am to 1.30 pm and 4 to 7.30 pm daily (from 5 pm on weekends). Be sure to visit the lovely cloister. Each Sunday at noon, crowds gather in front of the cathedral to dance the Catalan national dance, the *sardana*. Just east of the cathedral is the fascinating **Museu d'Història de la Ciutat** (City History Museum) composed of several buildings around **Plaça del Rei**, the palace courtyard of the medieval monarchs of Aragón. From the royal chapel, climb the multitiered Mirador del Rei Martí for good views. The museum also includes a remarkable subterranean walk through excavated portions of Roman and Visigothic Barcelona. It's all open 10 am to 2 pm and 4 to 8 pm Tuesday to Saturday, and 10 am to 2 pm Sunday. Entrance is 500 ptas.

A few minutes walk west of the cathedral, **Plaça de Sant Josep Oriol** is a hang-out for

SPAIN

SPAIN

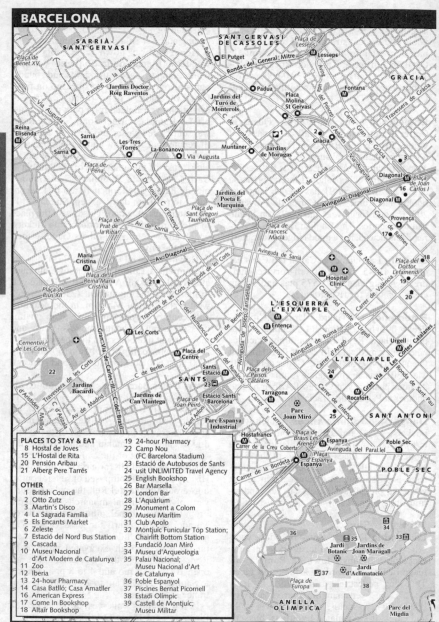

BARCELONA

PLACES TO STAY & EAT
8 Hostal de Joves
15 L'Hostal de Rita
20 Pensión Aribau
21 Alberg Pere Tarrés

OTHER
1 British Council
2 Otto Zutz
3 Martin's Disco
4 La Sagrada Família
5 Els Encants Market
6 Zeleste
7 Estació del Nord Bus Station
9 Cascada
10 Museu Nacional
   d'Art Modern de Catalunya
11 Zoo
12 Iberia
13 24-hour Pharmacy
14 Casa Batlló; Casa Amatller
16 American Express
17 Come In Bookshop
18 Altaïr Bookshop

19 24-hour Pharmacy
22 Camp Nou
   (FC Barcelona Stadium)
23 Estació de Autobusos de Sants
24 usit UNLIMITED Travel Agency
25 English Bookshop
26 Bar Marsella
27 London Bar
28 L'Aquàrium
29 Monument a Colom
30 Museu Marítim
31 Club Apolo
32 Montjuïc Funicular Top Station;
   Chairlift Bottom Station
33 Fundació Joan Miró
34 Museu d'Arqueologia
35 Palau Nacional;
   Museu Nacional d'Art
   de Catalunya
36 Poble Espanyol
37 Piscines Bernat Picornell
38 Estadi Olímpic
39 Castell de Montjuïc;
   Museu Militar

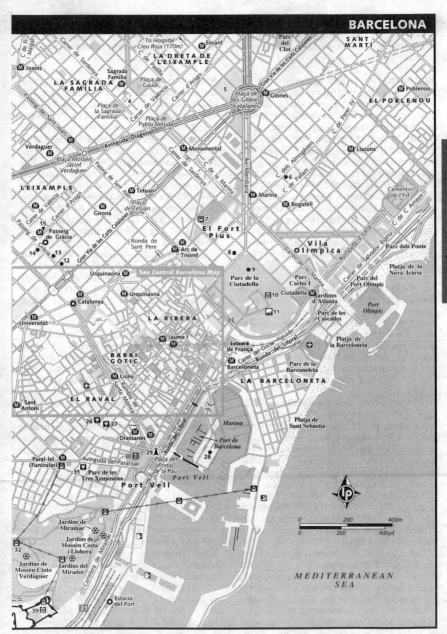

bohemian musicians and buskers. The plaza is surrounded by cafes and towards the end of the week becomes an outdoor art and craft market.

Waterfront For a look at the new face of Barcelona, take a stroll along the once-seedy waterfront. From the bottom of La Rambla you can cross the Rambla de Mar footbridge to the **Moll d'Espanya**, a former wharf in the middle of the old harbour, Port Vell. There you'll find **L'Aquàrium**, one of Europe's best aquariums, open 9.30 am to 9 pm daily, but not cheap at 1450 ptas. North-east of Port Vell, on the far side of the drab La Barceloneta area, the city **beaches** begin. Along the beachfront, after 1.25km you'll reach the **Vila Olímpica**, site of the 1992 Olympic village, which is fronted by the impressive **Port Olímpic**, a large marina with dozens of rather touristy bars and restaurants (you won't find too many locals here).

La Sagrada Família Construction on Gaudí's principal work and Barcelona's most famous building (metro: Sagrada Família) began in 1882 and is taking a *long* time. The church is not yet half-built and it's anyone's guess whether it will be finished by 2082. Many feel that it should not be completed but left as a monument to the master, whose career was cut short when he was hit by a tram in 1926.

Today there are eight towers, all over 100m high, with 10 more to come – the total of 18 representing the 12 Apostles, the four Evangelists and the mother of God, with the tallest tower (170m) standing for her son. Although La Sagrada Família is effectively a building site, the awesome dimensions and extravagant yet careful sculpting of what has been completed make it probably Barcelona's greatest highlight. The north-east Nativity Facade was done under Gaudí's own supervision; the very different north-west Passion Facade has been built since the 1950s.

You can climb high inside some of the towers by spiral staircases for a vertiginous overview of the interior and a panorama to the sea, or you can opt out and take a lift some of the way up. Entry to La Sagrada Família, which is on Carrer de Sardenya, on the corner of Carrer de Mallorca is 800 ptas for everyone.

It's open 9 am to 8 pm daily from April to the end of August; 9 am to 7 pm in March, September and October; and 9 am to 6 pm from November to February.

More Modernism Many of the best modernist buildings are in L'Eixample, including Gaudí's beautifully coloured **Casa Batlló** at Passeig de Gràcia 43 and his **La Pedrera** at No 92, an apartment block with a grey stone facade that ripples round the corner of Carrer de Provença. Next door to Casa Batlló at No 41 is **Casa Amatller**, by another leading modernist architect, Josep Puig i Cadafalch.

Another modernist highpoint is the **Palau de la Música Catalana** concert hall at Carrer de Sant Pere mes alt 11 in the La Ribera area east of the Barri Gòtic – a marvellous concoction of tile, brick, sculpted stone and stained glass.

You can visit La Pedrera, with its giant chimney pots looking like multicoloured medieval knights, independently. It is open 10 am to 8 pm daily and entry costs 600 ptas. Guided visits take place at 6 pm; 11 am on weekends and holidays.

Museu Picasso & Around The Museu Picasso, in a medieval mansion at Carrer de Montcada 15-19 in La Ribera, houses the most important collection of Picasso's work in Spain – more than 3000 pieces, including paintings, drawings, engravings and ceramics. It concentrates on Picasso's Barcelona periods (1895-1900 and 1901-04) early in his career, and shows how the precocious Picasso learned to handle a whole spectrum of subjects and treatments before developing his own forms of expression. There are also two rooms devoted to Picasso's 1950s series of interpretations of Velázquez's masterpiece *Las Meninas*. The museum is open 10 am to 8 pm Tuesday to Saturday, and 10 am to 3 pm Sunday. Entry is 725 ptas, free on the first Sunday of each month.

The **Museu Textil i d'Indumentària** (Textile and Costume Museum), opposite the Museu Picasso, has a fascinating collection of tapestries, clothing and other textiles from centuries past and present. Opening hours are 10 am to 8 pm Tuesday to Saturday and 10 am to 3 pm Sunday. Entrance is 400 ptas (or 700 ptas if you combine it with the Museu Barbier-Mueller d'Art Precolombí next door).

The **Museu Barbier-Mueller d'Art Pre-colombí** holds one of the most prestigious collections of pre-Columbian art in the world. It opens 10 am to 8 pm Tuesday to Saturday and 10 am to 3 pm Sunday. Admission costs 500 ptas.

At the south end of Carrer de Montcada is the **Església de Santa Maria del Mar**, probably the most perfect of Barcelona's Gothic churches.

Parc de la Ciutadella As well as being ideal for a picnic or stroll, this large park east of the Ciutat Vella has some more specific attractions. Top of the list are the monumental **cascada** (waterfall), a dramatic combination of statuary, rocks, greenery and thundering water created in the 1870s with the young Gaudí lending a hand; and **Museu Nacional d'Art Modern de Catalunya**, with a good collection of 19th and early-20th-century Catalan art, open 10 am to 7 pm Tuesday to Saturday, until 2.30 pm Sunday; entry is 500 ptas. At the southern end of the park is Barcelona's **zoo**, open 10 am to 7 pm daily (1550 ptas) and famed for its albino gorilla.

Parc Güell This park, in the north of the city, is where Gaudí turned his hand to landscape gardening. It's a strange, enchanting place where Gaudí's passion for natural forms really took flight to the point where the artificial almost seems more natural than the natural.

The main, lower gate, flanked by buildings with the appearance of Hansel and Gretel's gingerbread house, sets the mood in the park, with its winding paths and carefully tended flower beds, skewed tunnels with rough stone columns resembling tree roots, and the famous dragon of broken glass and tiles. The house in which Gaudí lived most of his last 20 years has been converted into a museum, open 10 am to 8 pm daily from April to August; the rest of the year 10 am to 2 pm and 4 to 6 pm Sunday to Friday (300 ptas). The simplest way to Parc Güell is to take the metro to Lesseps then walk 10 to 15 minutes; follow the signs north-east along Travessera de Dalt then left up Carrer de Larrard. The park is open from 9 am daily: to 9 pm June to September, to 8 pm April, May and October, to 7 pm March and November, and other months to 6 pm (free).

Montjuïc This hill overlooking the city centre from the south-west is home to some of Barcelona's best museums and attractions, some fine parks, and the main 1992 Olympic sites – well worth some of your time.

On the north side of the hill, the impressive **Palau Nacional** houses the **Museu Nacional d'Art de Catalunya**, with a great collection of Romanesque frescoes, wood-carvings and sculpture from medieval Catalonia. Opening hours are 10 am to 7 pm Tuesday to Saturday (to 9 pm Thursday), 10 am to 2.30 pm Sunday and holidays. Entry is 800 ptas.

Nearby is the **Poble Espanyol** (Spanish Village), by day a tour group's paradise with its craft workshops, souvenir shops and creditable copies of famous Spanish architecture; after dark it becomes a nightlife jungle, with bars and restaurants galore. It's open from 9 am daily (to 8 pm Monday; to 2 am Tuesday to Thursday; to 4 am Friday and Saturday; to midnight Sunday). Entry is 975 ptas (students and children aged seven to 14 pay 550 ptas). After 9 pm on days other than Friday and Saturday, it's free.

Downhill east of the Palau Nacional, the **Museu d'Arqueologia** (Archaeological Museum) has a good collection from Catalonia and the Balearic Islands. Opening hours are 9.30 am to 7 pm Tuesday to Saturday, 10 am to 2.30 pm Sunday (400 ptas, free on Sunday).

Above the Palau Nacional is the **Anella Olímpica** (Olympic Ring), where you can swim in the Olympic pool, the **Piscines Bernat Picornell**, open 7 am until midnight Monday to Friday, to 9 pm Saturday, and 7.30 am to 4.30 pm Sunday for 650 ptas, and wander into the main **Estadi Olímpic** (open 10 am to 6 pm daily; admission free).

The **Fundació Joan Miró**, a short distance downhill east of the Estadi Olímpic, is one of the best modern art museums in Spain. Aside from many works by Miró, there are both permanent and changing exhibitions of other modern art. It's open 10 am to 7 pm Tuesday to Saturday (to 9.30 pm Thursday), and 10 am to 2.30 pm Sunday and holidays. Entry is 800 ptas.

At the top of Montjuïc is the **Castell de Montjuïc**, with a military museum and great views.

To get to Montjuïc you can either walk or take a bus from Plaça d'Espanya (metro:

SPAIN

CENTRAL BARCELONA

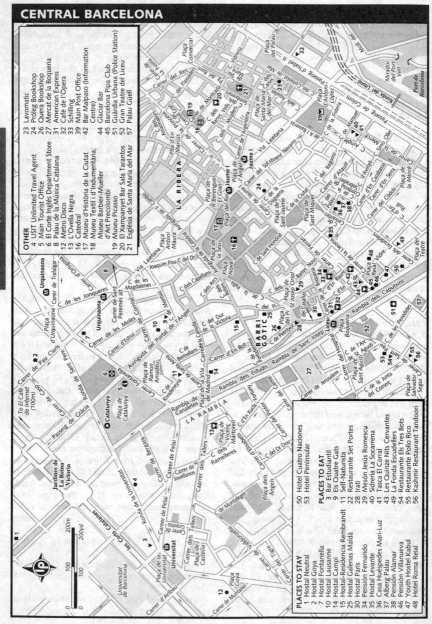

OTHER
- 4 USIT Unlimited Travel Agent
- 5 Main Tourist Office
- 8 El Corte Inglés Department Store
- 8 Palau de la Música Catalana
- 12 Metro Disco
- 13 L'Ovella Negra
- 16 Catedral
- 17 Museu d'Història de la Ciutat
- 18 Museu Tèxtil i d'Indumentària; Museu Barbier-Mueller d'Art Precolombí
- 19 Museu Picasso
- 20 El Xampanyet Bar Sala Tarantos
- 21 Església de Santa Maria del Mar
- 23 Lavomatic
- 24 Pròleg Bookshop
- 26 Quera Bookshop
- 27 Mercat de la Boqueria
- 31 American Express
- 32 Cafè de l'Òpera
- 33 Schilling
- 39 Main Post Office
- 42 Bar Malpaso (Information Centre)
- 44 Glaciar Bar
- 45 Barcelona Pipa Club
- 51 Guàrdia Urbana (Police Station)
- 52 Gran Teatre del Liceu
- 57 Palau Güell

PLACES TO STAY
- 1 Hostal Neutral
- 2 Hostal Goya
- 6 Hostal Fontanella
- 7 Hostal Lausanne
- 10 Hostal Campi
- 14 Hostal-Residència Rembrandt
- 15 Hostal Galerías Maldà
- 25 Hostal Paris
- 30 Hostal Levante
- 35 Casa Huéspedes Mari-Luz
- 36 Alberg Palau
- 37 Pensión Alamar
- 46 Pensión Villanueva
- 47 Youth Hostel Kabul
- 48 Hotel Roma Reial
- 50 Hotel Cuatro Naciones
- 53 Hotel Peninsular

PLACES TO EAT
- 3 Bar Estudiantil
- 9 Els Quatre Gats
- 11 Self-Naturista
- 22 Restaurante Set Portes
- 28 Irati
- 29 Mesón Jesús Romescu
- 40 Sidrería La Socarrena
- 41 Tasca El Corral
- 43 Les Quinze Nits Cervantes
- 49 La Fonda Escudellers
- 54 Restaurante Els Tres Bots
- 55 Restaurante Pollo Rico
- 56 Kashmir Restaurant Tandoori

euro currency converter €1 = 166 ptas

Espanya). Bus No 61 from here links most of the main sights and ends at the foot of a chairlift (475 ptas) up to the castle. A funicular railway (250 ptas) from Paral.lel metro station also runs to the chairlift. From November to mid-June, the chairlift and funicular run only on weekends and holidays.

Tibidabo At 542m, this is the highest hill in the wooded range that forms the backdrop to Barcelona – a good place for a change of scene, some fresh air and, if the air's clear, 70km views. At the top are the Temple del Sagrat Cor, a church topped by a giant Christ statue, and the Parc d'Atraccions funfair. A short distance along the ridge is the 288m Torre de Collserola telecommunications tower, with a hair-raising external glass lift (it opens 11 am to 2.30 pm and 3.30 to 6 pm Wednesday to Friday, to 8 pm in summer, and weekends all day; tickets cost 500 ptas).

The fun way to Tibidabo is to take a suburban train from Plaça de Catalunya to Avinguda de Tibidabo (10 minutes), then hop on the *tramvia blau* tram (275 ptas) across the road, which will take you up to the foot of the Tibidabo funicular railway. The funicular climbs to the church at the top of the hill for 300 ptas. All these run every 10 or 15 minutes from at least 9 am to 9.30 pm.

Els Encants Market This good second-hand market by Plaça de les Glòries Catalanes, is open between 8 am and 6 pm (8 pm in summer) on Monday, Wednesday, Friday and Saturday.

Organised Tours
The Bus Turístic service covers two circuits (24 stops) linking virtually all the major tourist sights. Tourist offices and many hotels have leaflets explaining the system, or you can call ☎ 93 423 18 00. Tickets, available on the bus, are 2000 ptas for one day's unlimited rides, or 2500 ptas for two consecutive days. Service is about every 20 minutes from 9 am to 9.30 pm. Tickets entitle you to discounts of up to 300 ptas on entry fees and tickets to more than 20 sights along the route.

A walking tour of the Ciutat Vella on Saturday and Sunday mornings departs from the Oficina d'Informació de Turisme de Barcelona on Plaça de Catalunya (English at 10 am; Spanish and Catalan at noon). The price is 1000 ptas.

Special Events
Barcelona's biggest festival is the Festes de la Mercè, several days of merrymaking around 24 September including *castellers* (human-castle builders), dances of giants and *correfocs* – a parade of firework-spitting dragons and devils. There are many others – tourist offices can clue you in.

Places to Stay
Camping The closest camping ground to Barcelona is *Camping Cala Gogó* (☎ 93 379 46 00), 9km south-west, which can be reached by bus No 65 from Plaça d'Espanya. About 2km to 3km farther out in Viladecans, on Carretera C-246, *El Toro Bravo* (☎ 93 637 34 62) and *La Ballena Alegre* (☎ 93 658 05 04) are much more pleasant, and there are several more camping grounds within a few more kilometres on Carretera C-246. To get to any of these, take bus No L95 from the corner of Ronda de la Universitat and Rambla de Catalunya. All charge upwards of 3400 ptas.

Hostels A handful of places in Barcelona provide dormitory accommodation. For two people they're not great value, but they're certainly good places to meet other travellers. All require you to rent sheets, at 150 ptas to 350 ptas for your stay, if you don't have them (or a sleeping bag). Ring before you go as the hostels can get booked up.

Youth Hostel Kabul (☎ 93 318 51 90, Plaça Reial 17) is a rough-and-ready place but it has no curfew and is OK if you're looking for somewhere with a noisy party atmosphere; it has 130 places and charges 2000 ptas a night (no card needed). Security is slack but there are safes available for your valuables. Bookings are not taken.

Alberg Palau (☎ 93 412 50 80, Carrer del Palau 6) has just 40 places and is more pleasant. It charges 1600 ptas a night including breakfast and has a kitchen. It's open 7 am to midnight. No card is needed.

Hostal de Joves (☎ 93 300 31 04, Passeig de Pujades 29), near metro Arc de Triomf, is small and rather grim, with 68 beds and a kitchen, and charges 1500 ptas including breakfast; there's a 1 or 2 am curfew. A hostel

SPAIN

card is only needed during the six peak weeks in summer.

Alberg Mare de Déu de Montserrat (☎ 93 210 51 51, Passeig Mare de Déu del Coll 41-51) is the biggest and most comfortable hostel, but is 4km north of the centre. It has 180 beds and charges 1900 ptas if you're under 25 or have an ISIC or IYTC card, 2500 ptas otherwise (breakfast included). A hostel card is needed. It's closed during the day and you can't get in after 3 am. It's a 10-minute walk from Vallcarca metro or a 20-minute ride from Plaça de Catalunya on bus No 28.

Alberg Pere Tarrés (☎ 93 410 23 09, Carrer de Numància 149), about a five-minute walk from Les Corts metro, has 90 beds from 1500 ptas to 2000 ptas, depending on age and whether or not you have a hostel card (rates include breakfast). It has a kitchen, but is closed during the day and you can't get in after 2 am.

Pensiones & Hostales Most of the cheaper options are scattered through the old city, on either side of La Rambla. Generally, the areas closer to the port and on the west side of La Rambla are seedier and cheaper, and as you move north towards Plaça de Catalunya standards (and prices) rise.

Hostal Galerias Maldà (☎ 93 317 30 02, Carrer del Pi 5) is upstairs in an arcade, and about as cheap as you'll find. It's a rambling family-run establishment with basic singles/doubles for 1500/3000 ptas, and one great little single set aside in a kind of tower. The rambling *Hostal Paris (☎/fax 93 301 37 85, Carrer del Cardenal Casañas 4)* caters to backpackers, with 42 mostly large rooms for between 3000 ptas for a single and 7500 ptas a double with bath.

Casa Huéspedes Mari-Luz (☎ 93 317 34 63, Carrer del Palau 4) is both bright and sociable, with dorms for 2000 ptas a bed and doubles 5500 ptas to 5800 ptas.

Pensión Alamar (☎ 93 302 50 12, Carrer de la Comtessa de Sobradiel 1) has 12 singles for 2500 ptas, and one double room for 5000 ptas. *Hostal Levante (☎ 93 317 95 65, Baixada de Sant Miquel 2)* is a good family-run place with singles for 3500 ptas, or doubles for 5500/6500 ptas with/without private bath. Ask about apartments for longer stays.

If you want a nice double on the square, head to *Pension Villanueva (☎ 91 301 50 84,*

Plaça Reial 2). Prices start at 2500/3500 ptas for basic singles/doubles and range up to 7500 ptas for the best rooms.

Hostal Fontanella (☎/fax 93 317 59 43, Via Laietana 71) is a friendly, immaculate place, with 10 (in some cases smallish) rooms costing 3000/5000 ptas or 4000/6900 ptas with bathroom. An excellent deal is the friendly *Hostal Campi (☎ 93 301 35 45, fax 93 301 41 33, Carrer de la Canuda 4)*. Singles/doubles without private bath cost 2700/5000 ptas, or roomy doubles with shower and toilet cost 6000 ptas.

Up near Plaça de Catalunya is the excellent *Hostal Lausanne (☎ 93 302 11 39, Avinguda Portal de l'Àngel 24, 1st floor)*, with good security and rooms (mostly doubles) from 5500 ptas. *Hostal-Residencia Rembrandt (☎ 93 318 10 11, Carrer Portaferrissa 23)* charges 3000/5000 ptas, or 4000/7000 ptas with shower or bath, but is often fully booked.

Once-grand *Hotel Peninsular (☎ 93 302 31 38, Carrer de Sant Pau 34)* has singles/doubles from 3500/6000 ptas, although the rooms don't quite live up to the impressive foyer and central atrium. *Pensión Fernando (☎ 93 301 79 93, Carrer de l'Arc del Remedio 4)* is on Carrer de Ferran, in spite of the address. Dorm beds go for 2300 ptas, and there are doubles and triples for 7000/8500 ptas. You can catch some rays on the roof.

A few cheapies are spread strategically across the upmarket L'Eixample area, north of Plaça de Catalunya. *Hostal Goya (☎ 93 302 25 65, fax 93 412 04 35, Carrer de Pau Claris 74)* has 12 nice, good-sized rooms starting at 3100/4500 ptas. Doubles with private shower and toilet cost 5600 ptas. *Pensión Aribau (☎ 93 453 11 06, Carrer d'Aribau 37)* offers reasonable singles/doubles for 3500/6500 ptas. The singles only have a basin but do come with a TV, while the doubles have shower, toilet, TV and even a fridge.

A leafier location is *Hostal Neutral (☎ 93 487 63 90, fax 93 487 68 48, Rambla de Catalunya 42)*. En suite doubles cost 6530 ptas, rooms without are 5460 ptas. There are no singles.

Hotels Higher up the scale, but good value, is the *Hotel Roma Reial (☎ 93 302 03 66, Plaça Reial 11)*. Modern singles/doubles with bath cost 6000/9000 ptas in high season.

euro currency converter €1 = 166 ptas

At *Hotel Jardi* (☎ 93 301 59 00, *Plaça de Sant Josep Oriol 1*) doubles with a balcony over this lovely square cost around 8000 ptas. Refurbishments underway at the time of writing should soon make this good little place even better. If you want to be right on La Rambla, *Hotel Cuatro Naciones* (☎ 93 317 36 24, fax 93 302 69 85, *La Rambla 40*) has adequate rooms for 7490/10,700 ptas; a century ago this was Barcelona's top hotel.

Places to Eat

For quick food, the *Bocatta* and *Pans & Company* chains, with numerous branches around the city, do good hot and cold baguettes with a range of fillings for 360 ptas to 700 ptas.

The greatest concentration of cheaper restaurants is within walking distance of La Rambla. There are a few good-value ones on Carrer de Sant Pau, west off La Rambla. *Kashmir Restaurant Tandoori*, at No 39, does tasty curries and biryanis from around 800 ptas. *Restaurante Pollo Rico*, at No 31, has a somewhat seedy downstairs bar where you can have a quarter chicken or an omelette, with chips, bread and wine, for 500 ptas; the restaurant upstairs is more salubrious and only slightly more expensive. *Restaurante Els Tres Bots*, at No 42, is grungy but cheap, with a *menú* for 875 ptas.

There are lots more places in the Barri Gòtic. *Self-Naturista* (*Carrer de Santa Anna 13*), a self-service vegetarian restaurant, does a good lunch *menú* for 965 ptas. *Mesón Jesús Romescu* (*Carrer dels Cecs de la Boqueria 4*) is a cosy, homy place with a good lunch *menú* for 1400 ptas.

Carrer de la Mercè, running roughly west from the main Correus i Telègrafs (post office) is a good place to find little northern Spanish cider houses. *Tasca El Corral* at No 19 and *Sidrería La Socarrena* at No 21 are both worth checking, but there are many others. A Basque favourite is *Irati* (*Carrer del Cardenal Cassanyes 17*). The set *menú* is 1500 ptas, or you can enjoy the great tapas and a zurrito of beer or six.

For something a bit more upmarket, *Les Quinze Nits Cervantes* (*Plaça Reial 6*) and *La Fonda Escudellers* (*Carrer dels Escudellers*) are two stylish bistro-like restaurants, under the same management, with a big range

of good Catalan and Spanish dishes at reasonable prices, which can mean long queues in summer and at weekends. Three courses with wine and coffee will be about 2500 ptas.

Carrer dels Escudellers also has a couple of good night-time takeaway felafel joints at around 300 ptas a serve.

Or there's *Restaurante Set Portes* (☎ 93 319 30 33, *Passeig d'Isabel II 14*), a classic dating from 1836 and specialising in paella (1475 ptas to 2225 ptas). It's essential to book. Another famous institution is *Els Quatre Gats* (*Carrer Montsió 3*), Picasso's former hang-out, and now a bit pricey.

L'Eixample has a few good restaurants to offer as well. *Bar Estudiantil* (*Plaça de la Universitat*) does economical plats combinats, eg, chicken, chips and *berenjena* (aubergine), or *botifarra*, beans and red pepper, each for around 600 ptas. This place is open until late into the night and is a genuine student hangout. *L'Hostal de Rita* (*Carrer d'Aragó 279*), a block east of Passeig de Gràcia, is an excellent mid-range restaurant with a four-course lunch *menú* for 995 ptas, and a la carte mains for 700 ptas to 1000 ptas.

Entertainment

Barcelona's entertainment bible is the weekly *Guía del Ocio* (125 ptas at newsstands). Its excellent listings (in Spanish) include films, theatre, music and art exhibitions.

Bars Barcelona's huge variety of bars are mostly at their busiest from about 11 pm to 2 or 3 am, especially Thursday to Saturday. *Cafè de l'Òpera* (*La Rambla 74*), opposite the Liceu opera house, is the liveliest place on La Rambla. It gets packed with all and sundry at night. *Glaciar* (*Plaça Reial 3*) is busy with a young crowd of foreigners and locals. Tiny *Bar Malpaso* (*Carrer d'En Rauric 20*), just off Plaça Reial, plays great Latin and African music. Another hip low-lit place with a more varied (including gay) clientele is *Schilling* (*Carrer de Ferran 23*).

El Xampanyet (*Carrer de Montcada 22*), near the Museu Picasso, is another small place, specialising in cava (Catalan champagne, around 500 ptas a bottle), with good tapas too.

West of La Rambla, *L'Ovella Negra* (*Carrer de les Sitges 5*) is a noisy, barn-like tavern

SPAIN

with a young crowd. *Bar Marsella (Carrer de Sant Pau 65)* specialises in absinthe (absenta in Catalan), a potent but mellow beverage with supposed narcotic qualities. If by 2.30 am you still need a drink and you don't want a disco, your best bet (except on Sunday) is the *London Bar (Carrer Nou de la Rambla 36)* which sometimes has live music and opens until about 5 am.

Live Music & Discos Many music places have dance space and some discos have bands on around midnight or so, to pull in some custom before the real action starts about 3 am. If you go for the band, you can normally stay for the disco at no extra cost and avoid bouncers' whims about what you're wearing etc. Women and maybe male companions may get in free at some discos if the bouncers like their looks. Count on 300 ptas to 800 ptas for a beer in any of these places. Cover charges can be anything from zero to 3000 ptas, which may include a drink.

Barcelona Pipa Club (Plaça Reial 3) has jazz Thursday to Saturday around midnight (ring the bell to get in). Entry is around 1000 ptas. *Jamboree (Plaça Reial 17)* has jazz, funk, and a disco later, from about 1.30 am. *Club Apolo (Carrer Nou de la Rambla 113)* has live world music several nights a week, followed by live salsa or a varied disco. Expect entry of around 2000 ptas for both of these.

Otto Zutz (Carrer de Lincoln 15) is for the beautiful people dressed in black. The crowd's cool and the atmosphere's great.

Zeleste (Carrer dels Almogàvers 122), in Poble Nou, is a cavernous warehouse-type club, regularly hosting visiting bands. *Mirablau*, at the foot of the Tibidabo funicular, is a bar with great views and a small disco floor; it's open till 5 am.

The two top gay discos are *Metro (Carrer de Sepúlveda 185)* and *Martin's (Passeig de Gràcia 130)*. Metro attracts some lesbians and heteros as well as gay men; Martin's is for gay men only.

Cinemas For films in their original language (with Spanish subtitles), check listings for those marked VO (versión original). A ticket is usually 600 ptas to 750 ptas but many cinemas reduce prices on Monday or Wednesday.

Classical Music & Opera The *Gran Teatre del Liceu* opera house on La Rambla, gutted by fire in 1994, reopened in October 1999. For information on opera, dance and concerts, call ☎ 93 485 99 13.

There are other fine theatres, among them the lovely *Palau de la Música Catalana* (☎ *93 295 72 00, Carrer de Sant Pere més alt 11)*, the city's chief concert hall.

Getting There & Away

Air Barcelona's airport, 14km south-west of the city centre at El Prat de Llobregat, caters to international as well as domestic flights. It's not a European hub, but you can often dig up specials and cheap youth fares.

Iberia (☎ 902-40 05 00) is at Passeig de Gràcia 30; Spanair (24 hours ☎ 902-13 14 15) and Air Europa (☎ 902-40 15 01) are at the airport.

Bus The terminal for virtually all domestic and international buses is the Estació del Nord at Carrer d'Alí Bei 80 (metro: Arc de Triomf). Its information desk (☎ 93 265 65 08) is open 7 am to 9 pm daily. A few international buses go from Estació d'Autobuses de Sants beside Estació Sants train station.

Several buses a day go to most main Spanish cities. Madrid is seven or eight hours away (3400 ptas), Zaragoza 4½ hours (1655 ptas), Valencia 4½ hours (2900 ptas) and Granada 13 to 15 hours (7915 ptas). Buses run several times a week to London (14,075 ptas), Paris (11,975 ptas) and other European cities.

Train Virtually all trains travelling to/from destinations within Spain stop at Estació Sants (metro: Sants-Estació); most international trains use Estació de França (metro: Barceloneta).

For some international destinations you have to change trains at Montpellier or the French border. There are direct trains daily to Paris, Zürich and Milan.

Daily trains run to most major cities in Spain. To Madrid there are seven trains a day (5100 ptas, 6½ to 9½ hours); to San Sebastián two (4600 ptas, eight to 10 hours); to Valencia 10 (4600 ptas, as little as three hours on high-speed Euromed train) and to Granada (6400 ptas, eight hours).

Tickets and information are available at the stations or from the RENFE office in

Passeig de Gràcia metro/train station on Passeig de Gràcia, open 7 am to 10 pm daily (Sunday 9 pm).

Car & Motorcycle Tolls on the A-7 autopista to the French border are around 1500 ptas. The N-II to the French border and the N-340 southbound from Barcelona are toll-free but slower. The fastest route to Madrid is via Zaragoza on the A-2 (around 2300 ptas), which heads west off the A-7 south of Barcelona, then the toll-free N-II from Zaragoza.

Getting Around
To/From the Airport Trains link the airport to Estació Sants and Catalunya station on Plaça de Catalunya every half-hour. They take 15 to 20 minutes and a ticket is 355 ptas. The A1 Aerobús does the 40-minute run between Plaça de Catalunya and the airport every 15 minutes, or every half-hour at weekends. The fare is 500 ptas. A taxi from the airport to Plaça de Catalunya is around 2500 ptas.

Bus, Metro & Train Barcelona's metro system spreads its tentacles around the city in such a way that most places of interest are within a 10-minute walk of a station. Buses and suburban trains are only needed for a few destinations but note the Bus Turístic under Organised Tours earlier in this Barcelona section.

A single metro, bus or suburban train ride costs 150 ptas, but a T-1 ticket, valid for 10 rides, costs only 825 ptas, while a T-DIA ticket (625 ptas) gives unlimited city travel in one day.

Car & Motorcycle While traffic flows smoothly thanks to an extensive one-way system, navigating can be frustrating. Parking a car is also difficult and, if you choose a parking garage, quite expensive. It's better to ditch your car and rely on public transport.

Taxi Barcelona's black-and-yellow taxis are plentiful, reasonably priced and especially handy for late-night transport. Flagfall is 300 ptas, after which it's about 105 ptas per kilometre. From Plaça de Catalunya, it costs around 700 ptas to Estació Sants.

MONESTIR DE MONTSERRAT
Unless you are on a pilgrimage, the prime attraction of Montserrat, 50km north-west of Barcelona, is its setting. The Benedictine Monastery of Montserrat sits high on the side of an amazing 1236m mountain of truly weird rocky peaks, and is best reached by cable car. The monastery was founded in 1025 to commemorate an apparition of the Virgin Mary on this site. Pilgrims still come from all over Christendom to pay homage to its Black Virgin (La Moreneta), a 12th-century wooden sculpture of Mary, regarded as Catalonia's patroness.

Information
Montserrat's information centre (☎ 93 877 77 77), to the left along the road from the top cable-car station, is open 10 am to 6 pm daily. It has a good free leaflet/map on the mountain and monastery.

Things to See & Do
If you are making a day trip to Montserrat, come early. Apart from the monastery, exploring the mountain is a treat.

The two-part **Museu de Montserrat**, on the plaza in front of the monastery's basílica, has an excellent collection ranging from an Egyptian mummy to art by El Greco, Monet and Picasso. It's open 9.30 am to 6 pm daily, for 600 ptas (students 400 ptas).

Opening times when you can file past the image of the Black Virgin, high above the main altar of the 16th-century **basílica**, vary according to season. The Montserrat Boys' Choir (Escolania) sings in the basílica Monday to Saturday at 1 and 7 pm (1 pm only on Sunday), except in July. The church fills up quickly, so try to arrive early.

You can explore the mountain above the monastery on a web of paths leading to small chapels and some of the peaks. The Funicular de Sant Joan (580/925 ptas one way/return) will lift you up the first 250m from the monastery.

Places to Stay & Eat
There are several accommodation options (all ☎ 93 877 77 77) at the monastery. The cheapest rooms are in the *Cel.les de Montserrat*, blocks of simple apartments, with showers, for up to 10 people. A two-person apartment

SPAIN

costs up to 5990 ptas in high season. Overlooking Plaça de Santa Maria is the comfortable *Hotel Abat Cisneros*, with rooms from 6725/11,650 ptas in high season. The Cisneros has a four-course *menú* for 2700 ptas.

The *Snack Bar* near the top cable-car station has platos combinados from 875 ptas and bocadillos from about 350 ptas. *Bar de la Plaça*, in the Abat Oliva cel.les building, has similar prices. *Cafeteria Self-Service*, near the car park, has great views but is dearer.

Getting There & Away

Trains run from Plaça d'Espanya station in Barcelona to Aeri de Montserrat up to 18 times a day (most often on summer weekdays), a 1½-hour ride. Return tickets for 1905 ptas include the cable car between Aeri de Montserrat and the monastery.

There's also a daily bus to the monastery from Estació d'Autobuses de Sants in Barcelona at 9 am (plus 8 am in July and August) for a return fare of 1400 ptas. It returns at 5 pm.

COSTA BRAVA

The Costa Brava ranks with Spain's Costa Blanca and Costa del Sol among Europe's most popular holiday spots. It stands alone, however, in its spectacular scenery and proximity to northern Europe, both of which have sent prices skyrocketing in the most appealing places.

The main jumping-off points for the Costa Brava are the inland towns of Girona (Gerona in Castilian) and Figueres (Figueras). Both places are on the A-7 autopista and the toll-free N-II highway which connect Barcelona with France. Along the coast the most appealing resorts are, from north to south, Cadaqués, L'Escala (La Escala), Tamariu, Llafranc, Calella de Palafrugell and Tossa de Mar.

Tourist offices along the coast are very helpful, with information on accommodation, transport and other things; they include Girona (☎ 972 22 65 75), Figueres (☎ 972 50 31 55), Palafrugell (☎ 972 30 02 28), and Cadaqués (☎ 972 25 83 15).

Coastal Resorts

The Costa Brava (Rugged Coast) is all about picturesque inlets and coves. Some longer beaches at places like L'Estartit and Empúries are worth visiting out of season, but there has been a tendency to build tall buildings wherever engineers think it can be done. Fortunately, in many places it just can't.

Cadaqués, about one hour's drive east of Figueres at the end of an agonising series of hairpin bends, is perhaps the most picturesque of all Spanish resorts, and haunted by the memory of the artist Salvador Dalí, who lived here. It's short on beaches, so people spend a lot of time sitting at waterfront cafes or wandering along the beautiful coast. About 10km north-east of Cadaqués is **Cap de Creus**, a rocky peninsula with a single restaurant at the top of a craggy cliff. This is paradise for anyone who likes to scramble around rocks risking life and limb with every step.

Farther down the coast, past L'Escala and L'Estartit, is Palafrugell, itself a few kilometres inland with little to offer, but near three beach towns that have to be seen to be believed. The most northerly of these, **Tamariu,** is also the smallest, least crowded and most exclusive. **Llafranc** is the biggest and busiest, and has the longest beach. **Calella de Palafrugell**, with its truly picture-postcard setting, is never overcrowded and always relaxed. If you're driving down this coast, it's worth stopping at some of these towns, particularly out of season.

Other Attractions

When you have had enough beach for a while, make sure you put the **Teatre-Museu Dalí**, on Plaça Gala i Salvador Dalí in Figueres, at the top of your list. This 19th-century theatre was converted by Dalí himself and houses a huge and fascinating collection of his strange creations. From July to September the museum is open 9 am to 7.15 pm daily. Queues are long on summer mornings. From October to June it's open 10.30 am to 5.15 pm daily (closed Monday until the end of May, and on 1 January and 25 December). Entry is 1000 ptas (800 ptas October to May).

Historical interest is provided by **Girona**, with a lovely medieval quarter centred on a Gothic cathedral, and the ruins of the Greek and Roman town of **Empúries**, 2km from L'Escala.

For a spectacular stretch of coastline, take a drive north from Tossa de Mar to San Feliu de Guíxols. There are 360 curves in this

20km stretch of road, which, with brief stops to take in the scenery, can take a good two hours.

Among the most exciting attractions on the Costa Brava are the Illes Medes, off the coast from the package resort of L'Estartit. These seven islets and their surrounding coral reefs, with a total land area of only 21.5 hectares, have been declared a natural park to protect their extraordinarily diverse flora and fauna. Almost 1500 different life forms have been identified on and around the islands. You can arrange glass-bottom boat trips and diving.

Places to Stay

Most visitors to the Costa Brava rent apartments. If you are interested in renting an apartment for a week or so, contact local tourist offices in advance for information.

Figueres Figueres' HI hostel, the *Alberg Tramuntana (☎ 972 50 12 13, Carrer Anicet Pagès 2)* is two blocks from the tourist office. It charges 1700 ptas if you're under 26 or have an ISIC or IYTC card, 2275 ptas otherwise (breakfast included). Alternatively, *Pensión Isabel II (☎ 972 50 47 35, Carrer de Isabel II 16)* has reasonable rooms with bath for 2800 ptas. Don't sleep in Figueres' Parc Municipal – people have been attacked here at night.

Girona *Pensión Viladomat (☎ 972 20 31 76, Carrer dels Ciutadans 5)* has comfortable singles/doubles starting at 2000/4000 ptas.

Cadaqués *Camping Cadaqués (☎ 972 25 81 26)* is at the top of the town as you head towards Cabo de Creus. Two adults with a tent and a car pay 2880 ptas plus IVA. At these prices, a room in town in probably a better bet. *Hostal Marina (☎ 972 25 81 99, Carrer de Frederico Rahola 2)* has doubles at up to 5500 ptas plus IVA, or 8000 ptas with private bath.

Near Palafrugell There are camping grounds at all three of Palafrugell's satellites, all charging similar hefty rates. In Calella de Palafrugell try *Camping Moby Dick (☎ 972 61 43 07)*; in Llafranc, *Camping Kim's (☎ 972 30 11 56)*; and in Tamariu, *Camping Tamariu (☎ 972 62 04 22)*.

Hotel and pensión rooms are relatively thin on the ground here, as many people come on package deals and stay in apartments. In Calella de Palafrugell, the friendly *Hostería del Plancton (☎ 972 61 50 81)* is one of the best deals on the Costa Brava, with rooms at 2200 ptas per person, but it's only open from June to September. *Residencia Montaña (☎ 972 30 04 04, Carrer de Cesàrea 2)* in Llafranc is not a bad deal at 6300 ptas plus IVA. In Tamariu, the *Hotel Sol d'Or (☎ 972 30 04 24, Carrer de Riera 18)* near the beach, has doubles with bathroom for 6550 ptas.

Getting There & Away

A few buses run daily from Barcelona to Tossa del Mar, L'Estartit and Cadaqués, but for the small resorts near Palafrugell you need to get to Girona first. Girona and Figueres are both on the railway connecting Barcelona to France. The dozen or so trains daily from Barcelona to Portbou at the border all stop in Girona, and most in Figueres. The fare from Barcelona to Girona is 790 ptas to 910 ptas, to Figueres 1125 ptas to 1290 ptas.

Getting Around

There are two or three buses a day from Figueres to Cadaqués and three or four to L'Escala. Figueres bus station (☎ 972 67 42 98) is across the road from the train station.

Several buses daily run to Palafrugell from Girona (where the bus station is behind the train station), and there are buses from Palafrugell to Calella de Palafrugell, Llafranc and Tamariu. Most other coastal towns (south of Cadaqués) can be reached by bus from Girona.

TARRAGONA
pop 112,795

Tarragona makes a perfect contrast to the city life of Barcelona. Founded in 218 BC, it was for a long time the capital of much of Roman Spain, and Roman structures figure among its most important attractions. Other periods of history are also well represented, including the medieval cathedral and 17th-century British additions to the old city walls. The city's archaeological museum is one of the most interesting in Spain. Today, Tarragona is a modern city with a large student population and a lively beach scene and Spain's answer to Disneyland Paris, Port Aventura, is just a few kilometres south.

SPAIN

SPAIN

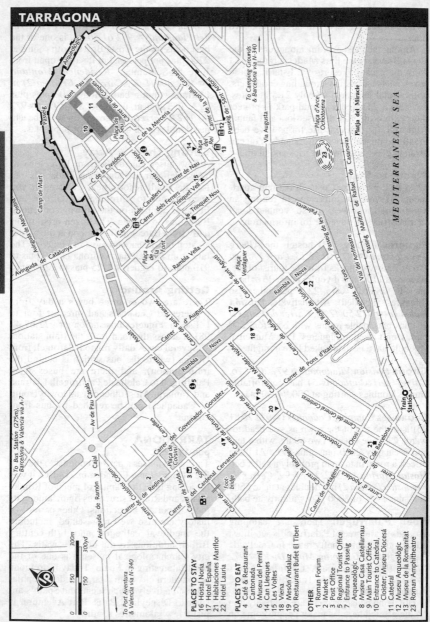

TARRAGONA

PLACES TO STAY
16 Hostal Noria
17 Hotel España
21 Habitaciones Mariflor
22 Hotel Lauria

PLACES TO EAT
4 Café & Restaurant Cantonada
6 Museu del Pernil
14 Can Llesques
15 Les Voltes
18 Viena
19 Mesón Andaluz
20 Restaurant Bufet El Tiberi

OTHER
1 Roman Forum
2 Market
3 Post Office
5 Regional Tourist Office
7 Entrance to Passeig Arqueològic
8 Museu Casa Castellarnau
9 Main Tourist Office
10 Entrance to Catedral, Cloister; Museu Diocesà
11 Catedral
12 Museu Arqueològic
13 Museu de la Romanitat
23 Roman Amphitheatre

euro currency converter €1 = 166 ptas

Orientation & Information

Tarragona's main street is Rambla Nova, which runs approximately north-west from a cliff top overlooking the Mediterranean. A couple of blocks to the east, parallel to Rambla Nova, is Rambla Vella, which marks the beginning of the old town. To the south-west, on the coast, is the train station.

Tarragona's main tourist office (☎ 977 24 50 64) is at Carrer Major 39. There is also a regional tourist office at Carrer de Fortuny 4.

Things to See & Do

The **Museu d'Història de Tarragona** comprises four separate Roman sites around the city, plus the 14th-century noble mansion now serving as the **Museu Casa Castellarnau**, Carrer dels Cavallers 14. A good site to start with is the **Museu de la Romanitat** on Plaça del Rei, which includes part of the vaults of the Roman circus, where chariot races were held. Nearby and close to the beach is the well-preserved Roman **amphitheatre**, where the gladiators battled each other, or wild animals, to the death. On Carrer de Lleida, a few blocks west of Rambla Nova, are remains of a **Roman forum**. The **Passeig Arqueològic** is a peaceful walkway along a stretch of the old city walls, which are a combination of Roman, Iberian and 17th-century British efforts.

From June to September, all these places open 9 or 10 am to 8 pm Tuesday to Saturday (the Passeig Arqueològic to midnight) and 10 am to 2 pm Sunday. In other months, they tend to open 10 am to 1.30 pm and at least two afternoon hours (10 am to 2 pm Sunday and holidays). Admission to each is 300 ptas.

Tarragona's **Museu Arqueològic** on Plaça del Rei gives further insight into the city's rich history. The carefully presented exhibits include frescoes, mosaics, sculpture and pottery dating back to the 2nd century BC. The museum is open 10 am to 1 pm and 4.30 to 7 pm Tuesday to Saturday (10 am to 8 pm in July and August), 10 am to 2 pm Sunday and holidays. Entry is 400 ptas, free on Tuesday.

The **catedral** sits grandly at the highest point of Tarragona, overlooking the old town. Some parts of the building date back to the 12th century AD. It's open for tourist visits Monday to Friday for hours that vary with the season (longest in summer) but always include 10 am to 1 pm and (except from mid-November to mid-March) 3 to 6 pm. Entrance is through the beautiful cloister with the excellent Museu Diocesà.

If you're here in summer, Platja del Miracle is the main city beach. It is reasonably clean but can get terribly crowded. Several other beaches dot the coast north of town, but in summer you will never be alone.

Port Aventura

Port Aventura (☎ 902-20 22 20), which opened in 1995 7km west of Tarragona, near Salou, is Spain's biggest and best funfair-adventure park, with a noticeable American influence. If you have 4600 ptas to spare (3400 ptas for children aged from five to 12), it makes a fun day out with never a dull moment although it only opens from Semana Santa to October. There are hair-raising experiences like a virtual submarine and the Dragon Khan, claimed to be Europe's biggest roller coaster. It is open daily during its season from 10 am to 8 pm, and from around mid-June to mid-September until midnight. Night tickets, valid from 7 pm, are 3400 ptas.

Trains run to Port Aventura's own station, about a 1km walk from the site, several times a day from Tarragona and Barcelona (1305 ptas return).

Places to Stay

Camping Tàrraco (☎ 977 23 99 89) is near Platja Arrabassada beach, off the N-340 road 2km north-east of the centre. There are more, better camping grounds on Platja Larga beach, a couple of kilometres farther on.

If you intend to spend the night in Tarragona in summer, you would be wise to call ahead to book a room. *Hostal Noria* (☎ 977 23 87 17, Plaça de la Font 53) is decent value at 2700/4600 ptas but is often full. *Habitaciones Mariflor* (☎ 977 23 82 31, Carrer del General Contreras 29) occupies a drab building near the station, but has clean rooms for 2100/4000 ptas.

Hotel España (☎ 977 23 27 12, Rambla Nova 49) is a well-positioned, but unexciting, one-star hotel where rooms with bath cost 3300/6000 ptas plus IVA. The three-star *Hotel Lauria* (☎ 977 23 67 12, Rambla Nova 20) is a worthwhile splurge at 5500/8500 ptas plus IVA, with a good location and a pool.

SPAIN

Places to Eat

For Catalan food, head for the stylish *Restaurant Bufet El Tiberi* (*Carrer de Martí d'Ardenya 5*), which offers an all-you-can-eat buffet for 1450 ptas per person. Nearby *Mesón Andaluz* (*Carrer de Pons d'Icart 3, upstairs*), is a backstreet local favourite, with a good three-course *menú* for 1500 ptas.

The *Museu del Pernil* (*Plaça de la Font 16*) is the place to dig into porcine delights. A platter of mixed meats and sausages will cost about 1700 ptas. Or if cheese is your thing, try a platter (*taula de formatges*) at *Can Llesques* (*Carrer de Natzaret 6*), a pleasant spot looking onto Plaça del Rei.

Café Cantonada (*Carrer de Fortuny 23*) is a popular place for tapas; next door, *Restaurant Cantonada* has pizzas and pasta from around 850 ptas. Rambla Nova has several good places, either for a snack or a meal. *Viena* (*Rambla Nova 50*) has good croissants and a vast range of *entrepans* from 300 ptas.

Tucked under the vaults of the former Roman circus, *Les Voltes* (*Carrer de Trinquet Vell 12*) is a little overpriced, but the *menú* is not bad at 1500 ptas.

Getting There & Away

Over 20 regional trains a day run from Barcelona to Tarragona (660 ptas, one to 1½ hours). There are about 12 trains daily from Tarragona to Valencia, taking two to 3½ hours and costing 2095 ptas. To Madrid, there are four trains each day – two via Valencia – taking seven hours, and two via Zaragoza taking six hours. Fares start at 4900 ptas.

Balearic Islands

Floating out in the Mediterranean waters off the east coast of Spain, the Balearic Islands (Islas Baleares) are invaded every summer by a massive multinational force of hedonistic party animals. Not surprising really, when you consider the ingredients on offer: fine beaches, relentless sunshine and wild nightlife.

Despite all this, the islands have managed, to a degree, to maintain their individuality and strong links with their past. Beyond the bars and beaches are Gothic cathedrals, Stone Age ruins, small fishing villages, some spectacular bushwalks and endless olive groves and orange orchards.

Most place names and addresses are given in Catalan, the main language spoken in the islands. High-season prices are quoted here. Out of season, you will often find things are much cheaper and accommodation especially can be as much as half the quoted rates here.

Getting There & Away

Air Scheduled flights from the major cities on the Spanish mainland are operated by several airlines, including Iberia, Air Europa and Spanair. The cheapest and most frequent flights are from Barcelona and Valencia.

Standard one-way fares from Barcelona are not great value hovering around 10,000 ptas to Palma de Mallorca and more to the other islands. At the time of writing, however, you could get a return, valid for up to a month, for 13,000 ptas with Spanair. Booking at least four days ahead brought the price down to about 10,000 ptas return. In low season the occasionally truly silly offer, such as 4000 ptas one way, comes up. From Valencia, Ibiza is marginally cheaper by air.

When in the islands keep your eyes peeled for cheap charter flights to the mainland. At the time of writing one-way charters were going for 14,900 ptas to places like Seville and Vigo, 10,900 ptas for Málaga and 7500 ptas to Alicante.

Interisland flights are expensive (given the flying times involved), with Palma to Maó or Ibiza costing 9400 ptas (return flights cost double).

Boat Trasmediterránea (information and ticket purchases on ☎ 902-45 46 45, or www.trasmediterranea.com) is the major ferry company for the islands, with offices in (and services between) Barcelona (☎ 93 295 90 00), Valencia (☎ 96 367 65 12), Palma de Mallorca (☎ 971-40 50 14), Maó (☎ 971-36 60 50) and Ibiza city (☎ 971-31 51 00).

Scheduled services are: Barcelona-Palma (eight hours, seven to nine services weekly); Barcelona-Maó (nine hours, two to six services weekly); Barcelona-Ibiza city (9½ hours or 14½ hours via Palma, three to six services weekly); Valencia-Palma (8½ hours, six to seven services weekly); Valencia-Ibiza city (seven hours, six to seven services weekly); Palma-Ibiza city (4½ hours, one or two services weekly); and Palma-Maó (6½ hours, one service weekly).

Prices quoted below are the one-way fares during summer; low and mid-season fares are considerably cheaper.

Fares from the mainland to any of the islands are 6920 ptas for a Butaca Turista (seat); a berth in a cabin ranges from 11,410 ptas (four-share) to 18,690 ptas (twin-share) per person. Taking a small car costs 19,315 ptas, or there are economy packages (Paquete Ahorro) available.

Inter-island services (Palma-Ibiza city and Palma-Maó) both cost 3540 ptas for a Butaca Turista, and 9875 ptas for a small car. Ask, too, about economy packages.

During summer, Trasmediterránea also operates the following Fast Ferry services (prices quoted are for a Butaca Turista): Barcelona-Palma (8990 ptas, 4¼ hours, up to three services a week); Valencia-Palma (6920 ptas, 6¼ hours, four services weekly); Valencia-Ibiza (6920 ptas, 3¼ hours, four services weekly); Palma-Ibiza city (5750 ptas, 2¼ hours, four services weekly).

Another company, Balearia (☎ 902-16 01 80) operates two or three daily ferries from Denia (on the coast between Valencia and Alicante) to Sant Antoni de Portmany and one to Ibiza city (6295 ptas one way, four hours). Another service links Ibiza to Palma (3245 ptas, three hours).

Iscomar (☎ 902-11 91 28) has from one to four daily car ferries (depending on the season) between Ciutadella on Menorca and Port d'Alcúdia on Mallorca (4400 ptas one way). Cape Balear (☎ 902-10 04 44) operates up to three daily fast ferries to Ciutadella from Cala Ratjada (Mallorca) in summer for around 8000 ptas return. The crossing takes 75 minutes.

MALLORCA

Mallorca is the largest of the Balearic Islands. Most of the five million annual visitors to the island are here for the three *s* words: sun, sand and sea. There are, however, other reasons for coming. Palma, the capital, is worth exploring and the island offers a number of attractions away from the coast.

Orientation & Information

Palma de Mallorca is on the southern side of the island, on a bay famous for its brilliant sunsets. The Serra de Tramuntana mountain range, which runs parallel with the northwest coastline, is trekkers heaven. Mallorca's best beaches are along the north-east and east coasts; so are most of the big tourist resorts.

All of the major resorts have at least one tourist office. Palma has four on Plaça d'Espanya (☎ 971-75 43 29), at Carrer de Sant Domingo 11 (☎ 971-72 40 90), on Plaça de la Reina and at the airport. Palma's post office is on Carrer de la Constitució.

Things to See & Do

The enormous **catedral** on Plaça Almoina is the first landmark you will see as you approach the island by ferry. It houses an excellent museum, and some of the cathedral's interior features were designed by Antoni Gaudí; entry costs 500 ptas.

In front of the cathedral is the **Palau de l'Almudaina**, the one-time residence of the Mallorcan monarchs. Inside is a collection of tapestries and artworks, although it's not really worth the 450 ptas entry. Instead, visit the rich and varied **Museu de Mallorca** (300 ptas).

Also near the cathedral are the interesting **Museu Diocesà** and the **Banys Àrabs** (Arab baths), the only remaining monument to the Muslim domination of the island. Also worth visiting is the collection of the **Fundació Joan Miró**, housed in the artist's Palma studios at Carrer de Joan de Saridakis 29, 2km west of the centre.

Mallorca's north-west coast is a world away from the concrete jungles on the other side of the island. Dominated by the Serra de Tramuntana mountains, it's a beautiful region of olive groves, pine forests and small villages with stone buildings; it also has a rugged and rocky coastline.

There are a couple of highlights for drivers: the hair-raising road down to the small port of **Sa Calobra** and the amazing trip along the peninsula leading to the island's northern tip, **Cap Formentor**.

If you don't have your own wheels, take the **Palma to Sóller train** (see Getting Around later in this section). It's one of the most popular and spectacular excursions on the island. Sóller is also the best place to base

SPAIN

PALMA DE MALLORCA

yourself for trekking. The easy three-hour return walk from here to the beautiful village of **Deiá** is a fine introduction to trekking on Mallorca. The tourist office's *Hiking Excursions* brochure covers 20 of the island's better walks, or for more detailed information see Lonely Planet's *Walking in Spain*.

Most of Mallorca's best beaches have been consumed by tourist developments, although there are exceptions. The lovely **Cala Mondragó** on the south-east coast is backed by a solitary hostal, and a little farther south the attractive port town of **Cala Figuera** and nearby **Cala Santanyi** beach have both escaped many

of the ravages of mass tourism. There are also some good quiet beaches near the popular German resort of **Colonia San Jordi**, particularly Ses Arenes and Es Trenc, both a few kilometres back up the coast towards Palma.

Places to Stay

Palma The *Pensión Costa Brava* (☎ 971 71 17 29, *Carrer de Ca'n Martí Feliu 16*), is a backstreet cheapie with reasonable rooms from 2000/3300 ptas. The cluttered 19th-century charm of *Hostal Pons* (☎ 971 72 26 58, *Carrer del Vi 8*), overcomes its limitations (spongy beds, only one bathroom); it charges 2500 ptas

PALMA DE MALLORCA

PLACES TO STAY		13	Bon Lloc	18	Tourist Office
7	Pensión Costa Brava	14	Abaco	19	Post Office
9	Hotel Born			20	Main Tourist Office
12	Hostal Pons	**OTHER**		21	Ayuntamiento
15	Hostal Apuntadores	1	Bus Station; Airport Bus	22	Església de Santa Eulàlia
16	Hostal Ritzi	2	Tourist Office	23	Basílica de Sant Francesc
		4	Hospital	24	Palau de l'Almudaina
PLACES TO EAT		5	Església de Santa Magadalena	25	Catedral
3	Restaurant Celler Sa Premsa	6	Mercat de l'Olivar	26	Museu Diocesà
10	Celler Pagès	8	Teatro Principal	27	Museu de Mallorca
11	Bar Martín	17	American Express	28	Banys Àrabs (Arab Baths)

SPAIN

per person. *Hostal Apuntadores (☎ 971 71 34 91, Carrer dels Apuntadores 8)* has smartly renovated singles/doubles at 2700/4200 ptas, doubles with bathroom at 4800 ptas, or hostel beds at 1800 ptas. Next door, *Hostal Ritzi (☎ 971 71 46 10)* has good security and comfortable rooms at 3500/5000 ptas with shower, or doubles with shower/bath for 5500 ptas and 7500 ptas. It offers laundry and kitchen facilities and satellite TV in the lounge.

The superb *Hotel Born (☎ 971 71 29 42, Carrer de Sant Jaume 3)* in a restored 18th-century palace has B&B at up to 13,375/17,655 ptas.

Other Areas After Palma, you should head for the hills. In Deià, the charming *Fonda Villa Verde (☎ 971 63 90 37)* charges 6000/8300 ptas, while *Hostal Miramar (☎ 971 63 90 84)*, overlooking the town, has B&B at 4500/8500 ptas. Beside the train station in Sóller, the popular *Hotel El Guía (☎ 971 63 02 27)* has rooms for 5405/8415 ptas, or nearby (go past El Guía and turn right) the cosy *Casa de Huéspedes Margarita (☎ 971 63 42 14)* has singles/doubles/triples for 2800/3800/4500 ptas.

If you want to stay on the south-east coast, the large *Hostal Playa Mondragó (☎ 971 65 77 52)* at Cala Mondragó has B&B for 3800 ptas per person. At Cala Figuera, *Hostal Ca'n Jordi (☎ 971 64 50 35)* has rooms from 3200/5000 ptas.

You can also sleep cheaply at several quirky old monasteries around the island – the tourist offices have a list.

Places to Eat

For Palma's best range of eateries, wander through the maze of streets between Plaça de la Reina and the port. Carrer dels Apuntadores is lined with restaurants – seafood, Chinese, Italian and even a few Spanish restaurants! Around the corner on Carrer de Sant Joan is the amazing *Abaco*, the bar of your wildest dreams (with the drinks bill of your darkest nightmares).

For a simple cheap meal with the locals, head for *Bar Martín (Carrer de la Santa Creu 2)*. It has a no-nonsense set *menú* for 950 ptas. You can also eat well in the tiny *Celler Pagès (Carrer de Felip Bauçà 2)* where the 1250 ptas *menú* sometimes includes *sopa de pescado* (fish soup).

The rustic *Restaurant Celler Sa Premsa (Plaça del Bisbe Berenguer de Palou 8)* is an almost obligatory stop. The hearty *menú* costs 1335 ptas (plus IVA). For vegetarian food, try *Bon Lloc (Carrer de Sant Feliu 7)*.

Getting Around

Bus No 17 runs every half-hour between the airport and Plaça Espanya in central Palma (300 ptas, 30 minutes). Alternatively, a taxi will cost around 2000 ptas.

Most parts of the island are accessible by bus from Palma. Buses generally depart from or near the bus station at Plaça Espanya – the tourist office has details. Mallorca's two train lines also start from Plaça Espanya. One goes to the inland town of Inca and the other goes to Sóller (380 ptas one way, or 735 ptas for the 10.40 am 'Parada Turística'; both highly picturesque jaunts).

The best way to get around the island is by car – it's worth renting one just for the drive along the north-west coast. There are about 30 rental agencies in Palma (and all the big companies have reps at the airport). If you want to compare prices, then many of them have harbourside offices along Passeig Marítim.

IBIZA

Ibiza (Eivissa in Catalan) is the most extreme of the Balearic Islands, both in terms of its landscape and the people it attracts. Hippies, gays, fashion victims, nudists, party animals – this is one of the world's most bizarre melting pots. The island receives over a million visitors each year. Apart from the weather and the desire to be 'seen', the main drawcards are the notorious nightlife and the many picturesque beaches.

Orientation & Information

The capital, Ibiza (Eivissa) city, is on the south-eastern side of the island. This is where most travellers arrive (by ferry or air; the airport is to the south) and it's also the best base. The next largest towns are Santa Eulària des Riu on the east coast and Sant Antoni de Portmany on the west coast. Other big resorts are scattered around the island.

In Ibiza city, the tourist office (☎ 971 30 19 00) is on Passeig des Moll opposite the Estación Marítima. The post office is at Carrer de Madrid s/n, or you can go online for 900 ptas an hour at Ibiform (☎ 971 31 58 69), Avinguda de Ignacio Wallis 8 (1st floor).

Things to See & Do

Shopping seems to be a major pastime in Ibiza city. The port area of **Sa Penya** is crammed with funky and trashy clothes boutiques and hippy market stalls. From here you can wander up into **D'Alt Vila**, the old walled town, with its upmarket restaurants, galleries and the **Museu d'Art Contemporani**. There are fine views from the walls and from the **catedral** at the top, and the **Museu Arqueològic** next door is worth a visit.

The heavily developed **Platja de ses Figueretes** beach is a 20-minute walk south of Sa Penya – you'd be better off taking the half-hour bus ride (125 ptas) south to the beaches at **Ses Salines**.

If you're prepared to explore, there are still numerous unspoiled and relatively undeveloped beaches around the island. On the north-east coast, **Cala de Boix** is the only black-sand beach in the islands, while farther north are the lovely beaches of

S'Aigua Blanca. On the north coast near Portinatx, **Cala Xarraca** is in a picturesque, semiprotected bay, and near Port de Sant Miquel is the attractive **Cala Benirras**. On the south-west coast, **Cala d'Hort** has a spectacular setting overlooking two rugged rock-islets, Es Verda and Es Verdranell.

Places to Stay

Ibiza City There are quite a few hostales in the streets around the port, although in mid-summer cheap beds are scarce. The *Hostal-Residencia Ripoll* (☎ 971 31 42 75, Carrer de Vicent Cuervo 14) has singles/doubles for 3800/5800 ptas. You get clean rooms and friendly hosts nearby at *Hostal Sol y Brisa* (☎ 971 31 08 18, Avinguda de Bartomeu Vicent Ramón 15). Singles/doubles with shared bathrooms cost from 3500/6000 ptas. On the waterfront (officially at Carrer de Barcelona 7), *Hostal-Restaurante La Marina* (☎ 971 31 01 72) has good doubles with harbour views for 5000 ptas to 7000 ptas. Outside peak season some rooms are let as singles for about half (back rooms are noisy).

One of the best choices is *Casa de Huéspedes La Peña* (☎ 971 19 02 40, Carrer de la Virgen 76) at the far end of Sa Penya. There are 13 simple and tidy doubles with shared bathrooms at rates up to 4000 ptas.

Hostal-Residencia Parque (☎ 971 30 13 58, Carrer de Vicent Cuervo 3) is quieter than most of the other hostales. Singles without private bath cost 5000 ptas, while singles/doubles with bath cost between 8000 ptas and 12,000 ptas.

Hotel Montesol (☎ 971 31 01 61, Passeig de Vara de Rey 2) is a comfortable one-star place. Singles/doubles range up to 8700/16,300 ptas. Many of the singles are too pokey for the price.

Other Areas One of the best of Ibiza's half-dozen camping grounds is *Camping Cala Nova* (☎ 971 33 17 74), 500m north of the resort town of Cala Nova and close to a good beach.

If you want to get away from the resort developments the following places are all worth checking. Near the Ses Salines beach (and bus stop), *Hostal Mar y Sal* (☎ 971 39 65 84) has doubles at 5500 ptas (plus IVA). Near the S'Aigua Blanca beaches, *Pensión Sa Plana* (☎ 971 33 50 73) has a pool and rooms with bath from 5000/6500 ptas, including breakfast. Or you could stay by the black-sand beach, Cala Boix, at *Hostal Cala Boix* (☎ *971 33 52 24)*, where B&B costs 2500 ptas per person.

Places to Eat

Bland, overpriced eateries abound in the port area, but there are a few exceptions. The no-frills *Comidas Bar San Juan (Carrer Montgri 8)* is outstanding value with main courses from 500 ptas to 850 ptas. *Ca'n Costa (Carrer de la Cruz 19)* is another family-run eating house with a *menú* for 900 ptas to 1100 ptas.

Moving up the ladder, *Lizarran (Avinguda de Bartomeu Rosselló 15)* is part of a Basque chain that has a firm foothold in Barcelona and has now made a hop across the sea. The tapas are good. If you're looking for somewhere intimate and romantic, head for the candle-lit *La Scala (Carrer de sa Carrossa 6)* up in D'Alt Vila.

Entertainment

Ibiza's nightlife is renowned. The gay scene is wild and the dress code expensive. Dozens of bars keep Ibiza city's port area jumping until the early hours – particularly on Carrer de Barcelona and Carrer de Garijo Cipriano. After they wind down you can continue on to one of the island's world-famous discos – if you can afford the 4000 ptas to 7000 ptas entry, that is. The big names are *Pacha*, on the north side of Ibiza city's port; *Privilege* and *Amnesia*, both 6km out on the road to Sant Antoni; *El Divino*, across the water from the town centre (hop on one of its boats); and *Space*, south of Ibiza city in Platja d'En Bossa.

Getting Around

Buses run between the airport and Ibiza city hourly (125 ptas); a taxi costs around 1800 ptas. Buses to other parts of the island leave from the series of bus stops along Avenida d'Isidoro Macabich. Pick up a copy of the timetable from the tourist office.

If you are intent on getting to some of the more secluded beaches you will need to rent wheels. In Ibiza city, Autos Isla Blanca (☎ 971 31 54 07) at Carrer de Felipe II will hire out a Renault Twingo for 18,000 ptas for three days all inclusive, or a scooter for around 1300 ptas a day.

FORMENTERA

A short boat ride south of Ibiza, Formentera is the smallest and least developed of the four main Balearic Islands. It offers fine beaches and some excellent short walking and cycling trails. A popular day trip from Ibiza, it can get pretty crowded in midsummer, but most of the time it is still possible to find a strip of sand out of earshot of other tourists.

Orientation & Information

Formentera is about 20km from east to west. Ferries arrive at La Savina on the north-west coast; the tourist office (☎ 971 32 20 57) is behind the rental agencies you'll see when you disembark. Three kilometres south is the island's pretty capital, Sant Francesc Xavier, where you'll find most of the banks. From here, the main road runs along the middle of the island before climbing to the highest point (192m). At the eastern end of the island is the Sa Mola lighthouse. Es Pujols is 3km east of La Savina and is the main tourist resort (and the only place with any nightlife to speak of).

Things to See & Do

Some of the island's best and most popular beaches are the beautiful white strips of sand along the narrow promontory which stretches north towards Ibiza. A 2km walking trail leads from the La Savina-Es Pujols road to the far end of the promontory, from where you can wade across a narrow strait to **S'Espalmador**, a tiny islet with beautiful, quiet beaches. Along Formentera's south coast, **Platja de Migjorn** is made up of numerous coves and beaches. Tracks lead down to these off the main road. On the west coast is the lovely **Cala Saona** beach.

The tourist office's *Green Tours* brochure outlines 19 excellent walking and cycling trails that take you through some of the island's most scenic areas.

Places to Stay

Camping is not allowed on Formentera. Sadly, the coastal accommodation places mainly cater to German and British package-tour agencies and are overpriced and/or booked out in summer. In Es Pujols you could try *Hostal Tahiti* (☎ *971 32 81 22)*, with B&B at 7000/10,075 ptas. If you prefer peace and quiet you are better off in Es Caló. *Fonda*

SPAIN

Rafalet (☎ 971 32 70 16) has good rooms on the waterfront for 5000/9000 ptas in August, or across the road the tiny and simple *Casa de Huéspedes Miramar (☎ 971 32 70 60)* charges 4000 ptas.

Perhaps the best budget bet is to base yourself in one of the small inland towns and bike it to the beaches. In Sant Ferran (1.6km south of Es Pujols), the popular *Hostal Pepe (☎ 971 32 80 33)* has B&B with bath at 3375/6090 ptas. In Sant Francesco Xavier, doubles at the amiable *Restaurant Casa Rafal (☎ 971 32 22 05)* go for 7000 ptas. La Savina isn't the most thrilling place, but *Hostal La Savina (☎ 971 32 22 79)* has rooms for up to 7500/9000 ptas, including breakfast.

Getting There & Away
There are 20 to 25 ferries daily between Ibiza city and Formentera. The trip takes about 25 minutes by jet ferry (2085 ptas one-way), or about an hour by car ferry (2300 ptas return, 9500 ptas for a small car).

Getting Around
A string of rental agencies line the harbour in La Savina. Bikes start at 650 ptas a day (900 ptas for a mountain bike). Scooters start at 1300 ptas and head up to 4000 ptas for more powerful motorbikes. Cars, though superfluous, go for 5000 ptas to 7000 ptas. A regular bus service connects all the main towns.

MENORCA
Menorca is perhaps the least overrun of the Balearics. In 1993, it was declared a Biosphere Reserve by Unesco, with the aim of preserving important environmental areas such as the Albufera d'es Grau wetlands and its unique collection of archaeological sites.

Orientation & Information
The capital, Maó (Mahón in Spanish), is at the eastern end of the island. Its busy port is the arrival point for most ferries, and Menorca's airport is 7km south-west. The main road runs down the middle of the island to Ciutadella, Menorca's second-largest town, with secondary roads leading north and south to the resorts and beaches.

The main tourist office is in Maó (☎ 971 36 37 90) at Plaça de S'Esplanada 40. During summer there are offices at the airport and in Ciutadella on Plaça des Born. Maó's post office is on Carrer del Bon Aire.

Things to See & Do
Maó and Ciutadella are both harbour towns, and from either place you'll have to commute to the beaches. Maó absorbs most of the tourist traffic. While you're here you can take a boat cruise around its impressive harbour and sample the local gin at the **Xoriguer distillery**. Ciutadella, with its smaller harbour and historic buildings, has a more distinctively Spanish feel about it.

In the centre of the island, the 357m-high **Monte Toro** has great views of the whole island, and on a clear day you can see as far as Mallorca.

With your own transport and a bit of footwork you'll be able to discover some of Menorca's off-the-beaten-track beaches. North of Maó, a drive across a lunar landscape leads to the lighthouse at **Cap de Favàritx**. If you park just before the gate to the lighthouse and climb up the rocks behind you, you'll see a couple of the eight beaches that are just waiting for scramblers like yourself to grace their sands.

On the north coast, the picturesque town of **Fornells** is on a large bay popular with windsurfers. Farther west at the beach of Binimella, you can continue (on foot) to the unspoilt Cala Pregonda.

North of Ciutadella is **La Vall**, another stretch of untouched beach backed by a private nature park (700 ptas entry per car). On the south coast are two good beaches either side of the Santa Galdana resort – Cala Mitjana to the east and Macarella to the west.

Menorca's beaches aren't its only attractions. The interior of the island is liberally sprinkled with reminders of its rich and ancient heritage. Pick up a copy of the tourist office's *Archaeological Guide to Minorca*.

Places to Stay
Menorca's two *camping grounds* are near the resorts of Santa Galdana, about 8km south of Ferreries, and Son Bou, south of Alaior. They open in summer only.

Maó and Ciutadella both have a handful of good budget options. In Maó, *Hostal Orsi (☎ 971 36 47 51, Carrer de la Infanta 19)* is run by a Glaswegian and American who are a mine of information. It's bright, clean and well located. Singles/doubles with only a washbasin cost 2600/4400 ptas. *Hostal La Isla* (☎ *971 36 64 92, Carrer de Santa Catalina 4)* has excellent rooms with bath at 2300/4100 ptas plus IVA.

In Ciutadella *Hostal Oasis* (☎ *971 38 21 97, Carrer de Sant Isidre 33)* is set around a spacious courtyard and has its own Italian restaurant; doubles with bath and breakfast are 5500 ptas (no singles). *Hotel Geminis* (☎ *971 38 46 44, Carrer Josepa Rossinyol 4)* is a friendly and stylish two-star place with excellent rooms for 5000/8000 ptas plus IVA.

In Fornells, *Hostal La Palma* (☎ *971 37 66 34, Plaça S'Algaret 3)* has singles (not available in summer) for 4000 ptas and doubles for 7250 ptas (in high season).

Places to Eat

Maó's waterfront road, Andén de Levante, is lined with restaurants with outdoor terraces. *Ristorante Roma* at No 295 is a stylish Italian eatery; it's surprisingly good value with pizzas and pastas for around 900 ptas and several set *menú* choices ranging from 1500 ptas to 2300 ptas. For a mix of dishes ranging from gazpacho to felafel, you could try the wholesome food at *La Sirena*, at No 199.

Ciutadella's port is also lined with restaurants, and you won't have any trouble finding somewhere to eat. After dinner, check *Sa Clau*, a hip little jazz and blues bar set in the old city walls.

Getting Around

From the airport, a taxi into Maó costs around 1200 ptas; there are no buses.

TMSA (☎ 971 36 03 61) runs six buses a day between Maó and Ciutadella (560 ptas), with connections to the major resorts on the south coast. In summer there are also daily bus services to most of the coastal towns from both Maó and Ciutadella.

If you're planning to hire a car, rates vary seasonally from around 3500 ptas to 8000 ptas a day; during the summer, minimum hire periods sometimes apply. In Maó, places worth trying include Autos Valls (☎ 971 36 84 65), Plaça d'Espanya 13, and Autos Isla (☎ 971 36 65 69), Avinguda de Josep Maria

Quadrado 28. Motos Menorca (☎ 971 35 47 86), at Andén de Llevant 35-36, hires out mountain bikes (1400 ptas per day), scooters and Vespas (from 3200 ptas a day).

Valencia

Although perhaps best known for the package resorts of the Costa Blanca, this region also includes Spain's lively third city, Valencia – and some rare undiscovered secrets if you penetrate inland.

VALENCIA
pop 739,000

Vibrant Valencia, birthplace of paella, is blessed with great weather and hosts the country's wildest party – Las Fallas (12-19 March), an exuberant blend of fireworks, music, all-night partying and over 350 *fallas*, giant sculptures which all go up in flames on the final night.

Orientation

The action part of the city is oval, bounded by the old course of the Turia River and the sickle-shaped inner ring road of Calles Colón, Játiva and Guillem de Castro. These trace the walls of the old city, demolished in 1865 as – believe it or not – a job-creation project which dismantled one of the Mediterranean coastline's major monuments.

Within the oval are three major squares: Plazas del Ayuntamiento, de la Reina (also known as Plaza de Zaragoza) and de la Virgen.

Many Valencian streets now have signs only in Catalan rather than Spanish, but the difference between the two is rarely confusing.

Information

The main tourist office is at Calle Paz 48 (☎ 96 398 64 22, fax 96 398 64 21). It's open 10 am to 6.30 pm weekdays (to 2 pm Saturday). Three smaller ones are at the train station, town hall and Teatro Principal. All have reams of information in English.

The imposing neobaroque main post office is on Plaza del Ayuntamiento. Poste restante is on the 1st floor.

American Express is represented by Viajes Duna (☎ 96 374 15 62, Calle Cirilo Amorós 88).

SPAIN

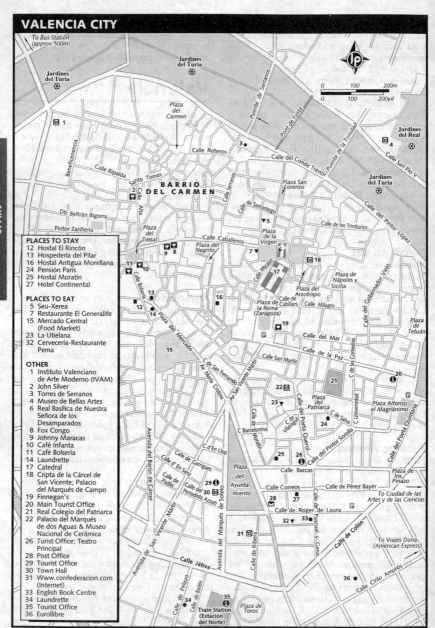

VALENCIA CITY

To Bus Station
(approx 500m)

Jardines
del Turia

Jardines
del Turia

Jardines
del Real

Plaza
del
Carmen

Calle Roteros

Calle del Conde Trénor

Calle San Pio V

Beneficencia

Calle Ripalda

Santo Tomas

Calle Serranos

**BARRIO
DEL CARMEN**

Plaza San
Lorenzo

Jardines
del Turia

Dtr. Beltrán Bigorra

Calle de Samaniego

Calle del Pintor López

Pintor Zariñena

Calle Alta

Plaza
del
Tossal

Calle Caballeros

Plaza de
la Virgen

Calle de los Trinitarios

Plaza del
Negrito

Plaza de
Nápoles y
Sicilia

Plaza del
Arzobispo

Calle del Gobernador Viejo

Plaza
de
Tetuán

Plaza de
la Reina
(Zaragoza)

Calle de Cabillars

Calle Milagro

Calle del Mar

Calle de la Paz

Calle del Mercado

C de San Fernando

Av María Cristina

Av San Vicente Mártir

Calle San Martín

Calle de las Comedias

Calle San Martín

Plaza Alfonso
el Magnánimo

Plaza de
los
Pinazo

To Ciudad de las
Artes y de las Ciencias

Avenida del Barón de Cárcer

C d'En Llop

Calle de Garrigues

Calle d'En Sanz

Calle de
Padilla

Plaza del
Patriarca

C de Salvá

C de
Vilaragut

C de Poeta Querol

Calle del Pintor Sorolla

C Universidad

Plaza
del
Ayunta-
miento

C Barcelonina

Calle de
Moratín

Calle Barcas

Calle Correos

Calle de Pérez Bayer

C de
Periodista Azzati

Avenida del Marqués de Sotelo

Avenida de San Vicente Mártir

Calle de Ribera

Calle de Roger de Lauria

Calle de Pascual y Genís

Calle de Colón

To Viajes Duna
(American Express)

Calle Cirilo Amorós

Calle Játiva

Calle de Pelayo

Calle de Bailén

Train Station
(Estación
del Norte)

Plaza de
Toros

PLACES TO STAY
12 Hostal El Rincón
13 Hospedería del Pilar
16 Hostal Antigua Morellana
24 Pensión Paris
25 Hostal Moratín
27 Hotel Continental

PLACES TO EAT
5 Seu-Xerea
7 Restaurante El Generalife
15 Mercado Central
   (Food Market)
23 La Utielana
32 Cervecería-Restaurante
   Pema

OTHER
1 Instituto Valenciano
  de Arte Moderno (IVAM)
2 John Silver
3 Torres de Serranos
4 Museo de Bellas Artes
6 Real Basílica de Nuestra
  Señora de los
  Desamparados
8 Fox Congo
9 Johnny Maracas
10 Café Infanta
11 Café Bolsería
14 Laundrette
17 Catedral
18 Cripta de la Cárcel de
   San Vicente; Palacio
   del Marqués de Campo
19 Finnegan's
20 Main Tourist Office
21 Real Colegio del Patriarca
22 Palacio del Marqués
   de dos Aguas & Museo
   Nacional de Cerámica
26 Turist Office; Teatro
   Principal
28 Post Office
29 Tourist Office
30 Town Hall
31 Www.confederacion.com
   (Internet)
33 English Book Centre
34 Laundrette
35 Tourist Office
36 Eurollibre

SPAIN

euro currency converter €1 = 166 ptas

Among several cybercafes in town is the noisy, 48-terminal www.confederacion.com (yes, that's the name) at Calle Ribera 8. Just off Plaza del Ayuntamiento, it charges 500 ptas per hour.

Valencia has two good predominantly English-language bookshops: the English Book Centre, Calle Pascual y Genís 16 and Eurollibre, Calle Hernán Cortés 18.

There are two central laundrettes at Plaza del Mercado 12, close to the covered market, and Calle Pelayo 11, near the train station.

Things to See & Do
The city of Valencia merits, as a minimum, a couple of days of your life.

The aesthetically stunning, ultramodern **Ciudad de las Artes y de las Ciencias** promises to become Valencia's premier attraction. Already open to the public is the **Hemisfèric** (☎ 96 399 55 77), at once planetarium, IMAX cinema and laser show (admission to each, 1100 ptas). An interactive science museum, the **Museo de las Ciencias Príncipe Felipe**, is scheduled to open in 2001.

The **Museo de Bellas Artes** (Fine Arts Museum) ranks among Spain's best, with works by El Greco, Goya, Velázquez, Ribera, Ribalta and artists such as Sorolla and Pinazo of the Valencian impressionist school. It's open 10 am to 2.15 pm and 4 to 7.30 pm Tuesday to Saturday (continuously on Sunday). Admission is free.

The **Instituto Valenciano de Arte Moderno** (IVAM, pronounced eebam) beside Puente de las Artes, houses an impressive permanent collection of 20th-century Spanish art and hosts excellent temporary exhibitions. Admission is 350 ptas, free Sunday.

Valencia's **cathedral** boasts three magnificent portals – one Romanesque, one Gothic and one baroque. Climb the Miguelete bell tower (200 ptas) for a sweeping view of the sprawling city. The cathedral's museum also claims – among several others contenders – to be home to the Holy Grail (Santo Cáliz), which you can see in a side chapel. As for the past thousand years, the **Tribunal de las Aguas** (Water Court) meets every Thursday at noon outside the cathedral's Plaza de la Virgen doorway to resolve any irrigation disputes between farmers.

Nearby on Plaza del Arzobispo is the crypt of a Visigoth chapel, reputedly prison to the 4th-century martyr, San Vicente. It's well worth taking in the free 25-minute multimedia show, which presents Valencia's history and the saint's life. Book at the **Palacio del Marqués de Campo** just opposite and ask for a showing in English.

The baroque **Palacio del Marqués de dos Aguas**, on Calle del Poeta Querol, is fronted by an extravagantly sculpted facade. It houses the **Museo Nacional de Cerámica**, which has ceramics from around the world – and especially the renowned local production centres of Manises, Alcora and Paterna. It's open 10 am to 2 pm and 4 to 8 pm, Tuesday to Saturday plus Sunday morning (admission free).

Valencia city's beach is the broad **Playa de la Malvarrosa**, bordered by the **Paseo Marítimo** promenade and a string of restaurants. **Playa El Salér**, 10km south, is backed by shady pinewood. Autocares Herca (☎ 96 349 12 50) buses (150 ptas, 30 minutes) run hourly (every half-hour in summer) from the junction of Gran Vía de las Germanias and Calle Sueca.

Special Events
Las Fallas de San José is an exuberant, anarchic swirl of fireworks, music, festive bonfires and all-night partying. If you're in Spain from 12-19 March, head for Valencia. Accommodation is at a premium – but you can always do like thousands of others and lay your head in the old riverbed.

Places to Stay
Camping The nearest camp ground, *Devesa Gardens* (☎/fax 96 161 11 36), is 13km south of Valencia near El Saler beach. *Alberge Las Arenas* (☎/fax 96 356 42 88, Calle Eugenia Viñes 24)* is a pebble's throw from Malvarrosa beach and within earshot of its wild summer nightlife. Take bus No 32 from Plaza del Ayuntamiento. Both are open year-round.

Central and near the covered market, *Hospedería del Pilar* (☎ 96 391 66 00, Plaza del Mercado 19) has clean basic singles/doubles/triples at 1600/2995/3900 ptas (2140/3850/4815 ptas with shower). Nearby, most rooms at the vast *Hostal El Rincón* (☎ 96 391 79 98, Calle de la Carda 11) are small but nicely priced at 1500/2800 ptas. It also

SPAIN

provides eight spacious renovated rooms with bathroom and air-con – excellent value at 2000/3600 ptas.

Near Plaza del Ayuntamiento, **Pensión París** (*☎/fax 96 352 67 66, Calle Salvá 12*) has spotless singles/doubles/triples without shower at 2500/3600/5400 ptas (doubles/triples with shower at 4200/6000 ptas). At recently renovated and welcoming **Hostal Moratín** (*☎/fax 96 352 12 20, Calle Moratín 15*) singles/doubles with shower are 2900/4500 ptas (3500/5500 ptas with bathroom).

Newly opened, **Hostal Antigua Morellana** (*☎/fax 96 391 57 73, Calle en Bou 2*) in a renovated 18th-century building has cosy singles/doubles with bathroom at 4000/6000 ptas.

Hotel Continental (*☎ 96 353 52 82, Calle Correos 8*) is modern and friendly, and its singles cost 7000 ptas to 9000 ptas, doubles 9000 ptas to 15,000 ptas according to season. All have air-con and satellite TV.

Places to Eat

You can eat local and well for around 1500 ptas at unpretentious **La Utielana**, tucked away off Calle Prócida, just east of Plaza del Ayuntamiento. At **Cervecería-Restaurante Pema** (*Calle Mosén Femades 3*) choose anything from a simple tapa to a full-blown meal. Its weekday lunch *menú* at 1100 ptas, including a drink and coffee, must be central Valencia's best deal.

Restaurante El Generalife (*Calle Caballeros 5*) has an excellent value *menú* for 1200 ptas. Nearby, **Seu-Xerea** (*☎ 96 392 40 00, Calle del Conde de Almodóvar 4*) has an inventive a la carte menu and does a warmly recommended lunchtime *menú* for 2200 ptas.

For authentic paella, head for Las Arenas, just north of the port, where a long line of restaurants all serve up the real stuff, and enjoy a three-course waterfront meal for around 1500 ptas.

And everyone, not only self-caterers, can have fun browsing around the bustling **Mercado Central**, Valencia's *modernista* covered market.

Entertainment

Valencia has four main nightlife zones, each bursting with bars: Barrio del Carmen (El Carmé), the old quarter; in vogue Mercado de Subastos on the west side of town; Plaza de Canovas for young up-and-comers; and the student haunt, Plaza de Xuquer.

In El Carmé, Calle Caballeros has swanky bars such as **Johnny Maracas**, a suave salsa place, or **Fox Congo** and others more modest in tone and price. On and around Plaza del Tosal are some of the most sophisticated bars this side of Barcelona, including **Café Infanta** and **Café Bolsería**, and cheap and cheerful places like **John Silver** on Calle Alta.

To continue partying, head for the university zone 2km east (500 ptas to 600 ptas by taxi from the centre). Along Avenida Blasco Ibáñez and particularly around Plaza de Xuquer are enough bars and discos to keep you busy beyond sunrise.

Finnegan's, an Irish pub on Plaza de la Reina, draws English-speakers.

Getting There & Away

Bus The bus station (*☎ 96 349 72 22*) is beside the old riverbed on Avenida de Menéndez Pidal. Bus No 8 connects it to Plaza del Ayuntamiento.

Major destinations include Madrid (2875 ptas to 3175 ptas, up to 12 daily), Barcelona (2900 ptas, up to 12 daily) and Alicante (1980 ptas, 2¼ hours).

Train Express trains run from Estación del Norte (*☎ 96 352 02 02* or *☎ 902-24 02 02*) to/from Madrid (5700 ptas, 3½ hours, up to 10 daily), Barcelona (mostly 4500 ptas, three to five hours, 12 daily) and Alicante (1400 ptas to 3200 ptas, 1½ to two hours, up to eight daily).

Boat In summer, Trasmediterránea (reservations *☎ 902-45 46 45*) operates daily car and passenger ferries to Mallorca and Ibiza and has a weekly run to Menorca. During the rest of the year, sailings are less frequent.

Getting Around

EMT (*☎ 96 352 83 99*) buses run until about 10 pm with night services continuing on seven routes until around 1 am. You can pick up a route map from one of the tourist offices. Tickets cost 125 ptas, a one-day pass is 500 ptas and a 10-trip *bono*, 700 ptas.

Estoí Palace, the Algarve, Portugal

Castelo de Vide, Alto Alentejo, Portugal

Detail of a tiled wall mural, Aveiro, Portugal

Model village, Sobreiro, Portugal

Traditional clothes, Estremadura, Portugal

Rio Douro, Porto, Portugal

CHRISTOPHER GROENHOUT

La Sagrada Familia, Barcelona, Spain

DAMIEN SIMONIS

Easter candles, Barcelona

DAMIEN SIMONIS

Town Hall door, Alicante, Spain

MASON FLORENCE

Vineyard in Andalucia, Spain

DAMIEN SIMONIS

La Pedura, designed by Gaudi, Barcelona

The smart highspeed tram is a pleasant way to get to the beach, paella restaurants of Las Arenas and the port. Metro lines primarily serve the outer suburbs.

Ergobike (☎ 96 392 32 39, Calle Museo), just off Plaza del Carmen, rents town bikes and recumbents.

INLAND VALENCIA
Morella
pop 2850

Perched on a hill top, crowned by a castle and completely enclosed by a wall over 2km long, the fairy-tale town of Morella, in the north of the Valencia region, is one of Spain's oldest continually inhabited towns.

The tourist office (☎ 964 17 30 32, closed Sunday afternoon and Monday) is just behind the Torres de San Miguel which flank the main entrance gate.

Things to See & Do

Morella's **castle**, although in ruins, remains imposing and gives breathtaking views of the town and surrounding countryside. The castle grounds (300 ptas) are open 10.30 am until 6.30 pm daily (to 7.30 pm from May to August).

The old town itself is easily explored on foot. Three small museums, set in the towers of the ancient walls, have displays on local history, photography and the 'age of the dinosaurs'. Each costs 300 ptas or you can buy a combined ticket, including admission to the castle, for 1000 ptas.

Places to Stay & Eat

The cheapest option is friendly *Fonda Moreno (☎ 964 16 01 05, Calle de San Nicolás 12)* which has six quaint and basic doubles at 2350 ptas. Its upstairs restaurant does a hearty *menú* for 950 ptas.

Freshly refurbished *Hostal El Cid (☎ 964 16 01 25, Puerta de San Mateo 2)* has spruce singles/doubles with bathroom for 3400/5500 ptas.

Hotel Cardenal Ram (☎ 964 17 30 85, Cuesta de Suñer 1), occupying a 16th-century cardinal's palace, has singles/doubles with all facilities for 5350/8550 ptas.

Restaurante Vinatea (Calle Blasco de Alagón 17, closed Monday) does a *menú* (1250 ptas) which is rich in local dishes. Or go a la carte and order a plateful of its scrummy *garbanzos en salsa de almendra* (chick peas in almond sauce) for 600 ptas.

Getting There & Away

On weekdays, Autos Mediterráneo (☎ 964 22 05 36) runs two buses a day to/from both Castellón and Vinarós. There's also one Saturday bus to/from Castellón.

Guadalest

A spectacular route runs west from just south of Calpe (see later in this section) to the inland town of **Alcoy**, famous for its Moros y Cristianos fiesta in April. About halfway to Alcoy, stop at the old Muslim settlement of **Guadalest**, dominated by the Castillo de San José and besieged nowadays by coach parties from the coast.

Elche (Elx)
pop 200,000

Just 20km south-west of Alicante, Elche is famed for its extensive palm groves, planted by the Muslims. Visit the **Huerto del Cura** with its tended lawns, colourful flowerbeds and a freakish eight pronged palm tree. The gardens (admission 300 ptas), opposite the hotel of the same name, are open 9 am to 6 pm daily.

The major festival is the Misteri d'Elx, a two-part medieval mystery play and lyric drama. It's performed in the Basílica de Santa María on 14 and 15 August (with public rehearsals the three previous days).

Budget accommodation options are very limited. One little gem is the friendly, spotlessly clean *Hotel Faro (☎ 96 546 62 63)* where simple singles/doubles are 1800/3600 ptas (2000/4000 ptas from July to September).

Elche, on the Alicante-Murcia train line, has frequent services (235 ptas) to Alicante, to which AM Molla runs up to 30 buses (205 ptas) daily.

ALICANTE (ALACANT)
pop 285,000

Alicante is a dynamic town with an interesting old quarter, good beach and frenetic nightlife. It becomes even wilder for the Fiesta de Sant Joan, 24 June, when Alicante stages its own version of Las Fallas (see Special Events under Valencia city earlier in this chapter).

ALICANTE

Same Scale as Main Map

Estación de Madrid
(RENFE Train Station)

To Youth Hostel
& Madrid

Joins Main Map

See Inset

To Youth Hostel
& Madrid

0   100   200m
0   100   200yd

Av de Salamanca

Av de Salamanca

Calle de San Juan Bosco

Av de la Estación

Av de Maisonnave

Calle del Pintor Cabrera

Calle del General Lacy

General Pintor O'Donnell

Calle del Portugal

Calle del Arquitecto Morell

Calle de los Reyes Católicos

Calle Oscar Esplá

Calle de Italia

Calle del Arzobispo Loaces

Calle del Pintor Aguirre

Calle del Pintor Lorenzo Casanova

Calle de Alemania

Av del Doctor Gadea

Av del Doctor Ramón y Cajal

To Elche

Av C. Calvo

Calle de Pablo Iglesias

Av de Benito
Pérez Galdos

Calle del Poeta Quintana

Calle de Segura

Av de General Marvá

Plaza de
los Luceros

C de Álvarez Sereix

C de Ángel Lozano

Av del Federico Soto

Plaza de
Calvo Sotelo

Calle de San Juan Bosco

Calle de Capitán Segarra

Calle de Calderón de la Barca

Calle de San Vicente

Calle de la Constitución

Av Alfonso X El Sabio

Calle de las Navas

Calle de Médico Pascual Pérez

Calle del Teatro

Plaza
Ildefonso

Calle de Jerusalén

Calle de Gerona

Calle del Barón de Finestrat

Calle de San Francisco

Calle Canalejas

Calle de Jauría

Calle de Valdés

Av Jaime II

Future Parque
de la Ereta

Calle de Toledo

Plaza del
Carmen

Plaza de
San Cristóbal

Plaza del
Ayuntamiento

C Maldonado

Monges

C de los Labradores

Rambla de Méndez Núñez

Calle Mayor

C de Rafael
Altamira

Calle de San Fernando

Plaza de
Gabriel
Miró

Paseo del Conde de Vallellano

MEDITERRANEAN SEA

2

3

4

5

6

7

8

14

15

16

17

21

22

23

13

9

12

11

10

SPAIN

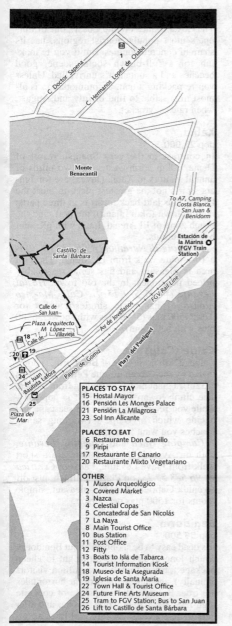

PLACES TO STAY
15 Hostal Mayor
16 Pensión Les Monges Palace
21 Pensión La Milagrosa
23 Sol Inn Alicante

PLACES TO EAT
6 Restaurante Don Camillo
9 Piripi
17 Restaurante El Canario
20 Restaurante Mixto Vegetariano

OTHER
1 Museo Arqueológico
2 Covered Market
3 Nazca
4 Celestial Copas
5 Concatedral de San Nicolás
7 La Naya
8 Main Tourist Office
10 Bus Station
11 Post Office
12 Fitty
13 Boats to Isla de Tabarca
14 Tourist Information Kiosk
18 Museo de la Asegurada
19 Iglesia de Santa María
22 Town Hall & Tourist Office
24 Future Fine Arts Museum
25 Tram to FGV Station; Bus to San Juan
26 Lift to Castillo de Santa Bárbara

Of its five tourist offices, the main one (☎ 965 20 00 00) is at Rambla de Méndez Núñez 23.

Things to See & Do

The **Castillo de Santa Bárbara**, a 16th-century fortress, overlooks the city. Take the lift (400 ptas return), reached by a footbridge opposite Playa del Postiguet, or walk via Avenida Jaime II or the new Parque de la Ereta. Admission is free.

The **Museo de la Asegurada** on Plaza Santa María houses an excellent collection of modern art, including a handful of works by Dalí, Miró and Picasso. Admission is free.

At the time of writing, the **Museo Arqueológico** was awaiting its transfer to a new permanent home off Calle Doctor Sapen. Also in preparation was the new **Museo de Bellas Artes**, Alicante's fine arts museum, which will occupy an 18th-century mansion on Calle Gravina.

Playa del Postiguet is Alicante's city beach. Larger and less crowded beaches are at **Playa de San Juan**, easily reached by buses 21 and 22.

Most days, Kontiki (☎ 96 521 63 96) runs boat trips (1800 ptas return) to the popular **Isla de Tabarca**, an island where there's good snorkelling and scuba diving from quiet beaches.

Be sure to fit in a stroll along Explanada de España, rich in cafes and running parallel to the harbour.

Places to Stay

About 10km north of Alicante, *Camping Costa Blanca*, outside Campello and 200m from the beach, has a good pool. Alicante's youth hostel, *La Florida* (☎ 96 511 30 44, *Avenida de Orihuela 59*), is 2km west of the centre and open to all only between July and September.

At the outstanding *Pensión Les Monges Palace* (☎ 96 521 50 46, *Calle de Monges 2*) rooms cost 3900/4200/5000 ptas with wash-basin/shower/full bathroom and have satellite TV and air-con (700 ptas supplement).

Pensión La Milagrosa (☎ 96 521 69 18, *Calle de Villavieja 8*) has clean, basic rooms for 1500 ptas to 2000 ptas per person according to season and a small guest kitchen. *Hostal Mayor* (☎ 96 520 13 83, *Calle Mayor 5*) has

SPAIN

pleasant singles/doubles/triples with full bathroom at 3000/6000/9000 ptas (cheaper out of season).

Sol Inn Alicante (☎ *96 521 07 00, fax 96 521 09 76,* ✉ *sol.alicante@solmelia.es, Calle de Gravina 9*) is a modern, stylish three-star place with rooms for 9600/11,350 ptas (cheaper at weekends).

Places to Eat

Restaurante El Canario (Calle de Maldonado 25) is a no-frills eatery with a hearty *menú* for 950 ptas. Nearby, *Restaurante Mixto Vegetariano (Plaza de Santa María 2)* is a simple place with vegetarian and meat *menús* for 1000 ptas. *Restaurante Don Camillo (Plaza del Abad Penalva 2)* has above-average pasta dishes.

Highly regarded *Piripi* (☎ *96 522 79 40, Calle Oscar Esplá 30)* is the place for stylish tapas or fine rice and seafood dishes. Expect to pay about 3500 ptas a head.

Entertainment

Alicante's nightlife zone clusters around the cathedral – look out for *Celestial Copas*, *La Naya*, *Nazca* and *Fitty*. In summer the disco scene at Playa de San Juan is thumping. There are also dozens of discos in the coastal resorts between Alicante and Denia; FGV 'night trains' ferry partygoers along this notorious stretch.

Getting There & Away

There are daily services from the bus station on Calle de Portugal to Almería (2570 ptas, 4½ hours), Valencia (1980 ptas, 2¼ hours), Barcelona (4650 ptas, eight hours), Madrid (3345 ptas, five hours) and towns along the Costa Blanca.

From the train station on Avenida de Salamanca there's frequent service to Madrid (4700 ptas, four hours), Valencia (1400 ptas to 3200 ptas, two hours) and Barcelona (6500 ptas, around five hours).

From Estación de la Marina, the Ferrocarriles de la Generalitat Valenciana (FGV) station at the north-eastern end of Playa del Postiguet, a narrow-gauge line follows an attractive coastal route northwards as far as Denia (995 ptas) via Playa de San Juan (125 ptas), Benidorm (445 ptas) and Calpe (680 ptas).

COSTA BLANCA

The Costa Blanca (White Coast), one of Europe's most popular tourist regions, has its share of concrete jungles. But if you're looking for a full-blown social scene, good beaches and a suntan, it's unrivalled. Unless you're packing a tent, accommodation is almost impossible to find in July and August, when rates skyrocket.

Xàbia
pop 22,000

In contrast to the very Spanish resort of Denia, 10km north-west, over two-thirds of annual visitors to Xàbia (Jávea) are foreigners so it's not the greatest place to meet the locals. This laid-back resort is in three parts: the old town (3km inland), the port, and the beach zone of El Arenal, lined with pleasant bar-restaurants.

Camping El Naranjal (☎ *96 579 10 70)* is a 10-minute walk from El Arenal. The port area is pleasant and has some reasonably priced *pensiones*. In the old town, *Hostal Levante* (☎ *96 579 15 91, Calle Maestro Alonso 5)* has basic singles/doubles for 2700/4500 ptas (5500 ptas with shower, 6500 ptas with bathroom).

Calpe (Calp)

Calpe, 22km north-east of Benidorm, is dominated by the Gibraltaresque **Peñon de Ilfach** (332m), a giant molar protruding from the sea. The climb towards the summit is popular – while you're up there, enjoy the seascape and decide which of Calpe's two long sandy beaches you want to laze on.

Camping Ifach and *Camping Levante*, both on Avenida de la Marina, are a short walk from Playa Levante. *Pensión Céntrica* (☎ *96 583 55 28)* on Plaza de Ilfach, just off Avenida Gabriel Miró, has pleasant, simple rooms for 1500 ptas per person.

Benidorm
pop 56,500

It's dead easy to be snobbish about Benidorm, which long ago sold its birthright to cheap package tourism (nearly five million visitors annually), and indeed many of the horror tales are true. But beneath the jungle of concrete high-rises are 5km of white beaches and after dark there's a club scene to rival Ibiza's.

SPAIN

Almost everyone here is on a package deal and major hotels can be reasonable value out of high season, but there's no truly budget accommodation. *Hotel Nou Calpí (☎/fax 96 681 29 96, Plaza Constitución 5)* provides singles/doubles with full bathroom for 2700/5000 ptas (3000/6500 ptas, July to October), including breakfast.

Andalucía

The stronghold of the Muslims in Spain for nearly eight centuries, Andalucía is perhaps Spain's most exotic and colourful region. The home of flamenco, bullfighting and some of the country's most brilliant fiestas, it's peppered with reminders of the Muslim past from treasured monuments like the Alhambra in Granada and the Mezquita in Córdoba to the white villages clinging to its hillsides. The regional capital, Seville, is one of Spain's most exciting cities.

Away from the cities and resorts, Andalucía is surprisingly untouristed. Its scenery ranges from semideserts to lush river valleys to gorge-ridden mountains. Its long coastline stretches from the relatively remote beaches of Cabo de Gata, past the crowds of the Costa del Sol, to come within 14km of Africa at Tarifa before opening up to the Atlantic Ocean on the Costa de la Luz with its long, sandy beaches.

SEVILLE
pop 701,000
Seville (Sevilla) is one of the most exciting cities in Spain, with an atmosphere both relaxed and festive, a rich history, some great monuments, beautiful parks and gardens, and a large, lively student population. Located on the Río Guadalquivir, which is navigable to the Atlantic Ocean, Seville was the leading Muslim city in Spain in the 11th and 12th centuries. It reached its greatest heights in the 16th and 17th centuries, when it held a monopoly on Spanish trade with the Americas.

Seville is quite an expensive place, so it's worth planning your visit carefully. In July and August, the city is stiflingly hot and not a fun place to be. It's best during its unforgettable spring festivals, though rooms then (if you can get one) are expensive.

Information
The main tourist office (☎ 95 422 14 04) at Avenida de la Constitución 21 is open 9 am to 7 pm Monday to Friday, 10 am to 7 pm Saturday, 10 am to 2 pm Sunday. It's often extremely busy, so you might try the other offices at Paseo de las Delicias 9 (☎ 95 423 44 65), open 8.30 am to 2.45 pm Monday to Friday, and Calle de Arjona 28 (☎ 95 450 56 00), open 8 am to 8.45 pm Monday to Friday, 8.30 am to 2.30 pm weekends.

Seville has heaps of public Internet/email services. A typical rate is 300 ptas an hour. One good-value place is Cibercafé Torredeoro.net (☎ 95 450 28 09), Calle Núñez de Balboa 3A. Librería Beta at Avenida de la Constitución 9 and 27 has guidebooks and novels in English. Tintorería Roma, Calle de Castelar 2C, will wash, dry and fold a load of washing for 1000 ptas.

Things to See & Do
Cathedral & Giralda Seville's immense cathedral, one of the biggest in the world, was built on the site of Muslim Seville's main mosque between 1401 and 1507. The structure is primarily Gothic, though most of the internal decoration is in later styles. The adjoining tower, La Giralda, was the mosque's minaret and dates from the 12th century. The climb up La Giralda affords great views and is quite easy as there's a ramp (not stairs) all the way up inside. One highlight of the cathedral's lavish interior is Christopher Columbus' supposed tomb inside the south door (no one's 100% sure that his remains didn't get mislaid somewhere in the Caribbean). The four crowned sepulchre-bearers represent the four kingdoms of Spain at the time of Columbus' sailing. The entrance to the Catedral and Giralda for nongroup visitors at our last check was the Puerta del Perdón on Calle Alemanes. Hours are 11 am to 5 pm Monday to Saturday (700 ptas; students and pensioners 200 ptas) and 2 to 7 pm Sunday (free).

Alcázar Seville's alcázar, a residence of Muslim and Christian royalty for many centuries, was founded in AD 913 as a Muslim fortress. It has been adapted by Seville's rulers in almost every century since, which makes it a mishmash of styles, but adds to its fascination. The highlights are the **Palacio de**

SPAIN

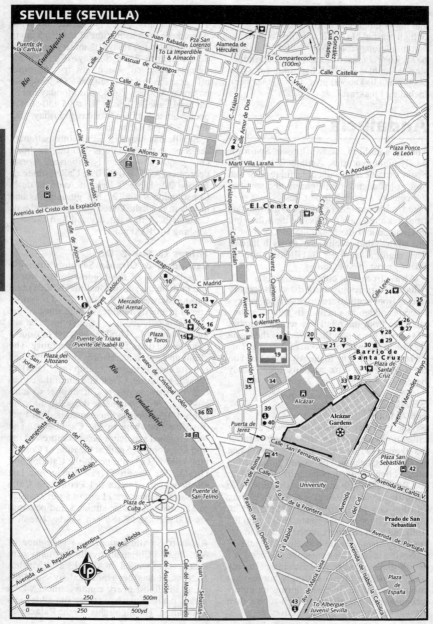

SEVILLE (SEVILLA)

Puente de la Cartuja

Río Guadalquivir

C Juan Rabadán
Pza San Lorenzo
To La Imperdible & Almacén
Alameda de Hércules
To Compartecoche (100m)

C Gonzalez Cua dradro
Calle Castellar

C del Torneo
C Pascual de Gayangos
Calle de Baños
Calle Golos
Calle Alfonso XII
Calle Marqués de Paradas

C Trajano
C Viriato
Calle Amor de Dios

Plaza Ponce de León

Calle de Aiona

Avenida del Cristo de la Expiación

2

4 ▲
▼ 3
5 ▲

6

7 ▼ ▲ 8

Marti Villa Laraña

C A Apodaca

El Centro

9 ●

C Pérez Galdós

Calle Velázquez

Calle Tetuán

Álvarez Quintero

C Zaragoza
10 ▼

C Madrid
13 ▼

Calle Reyes Católicos
11 ●

Mercado del Arenal

Calle de Castela
12 ▲
14 ▲ 16 ●
15 ▲

17 ●
C Alemanes
18 ▲

20 ▼
22 ▲
21 ▼
23 ▼

24 ▲
Calle Leyes

25 ▲
26 ●
28 ▼
27 ●
29 ▲
30 ●

Barrio de Santa Cruz
31 ▲
33 ▼ ▲ 32

Plaza de Santa Cruz

Avenida de la Constitución

19

34

Alcázar

35

36

Plaza de Toros

Paseo de Cristóbal Colón

Río Guadalquivir

Plaza del Altozano

Puente de Triana (Puente de Isabel II)

C San Jorge

Calle Pages

Calle Evangelista

Calle Betis

del Corro

37

38

39 ●
40

Puerta de Jerez

Alcázar Gardens ✼

Calle San Fernando

41

Av de Roma
Calle
Palos de la Frontera

University

Avenida del Cid

Avenida Menéndez Pelayo

Plaza San Sebastián

42

Avenida de Carlos V

Prado de San Sebastián

Avenida de Portugal

Calle del Trabajo

Puente de San Telmo

Plaza de Cuba

Avenida de la República Argentina

Calle de Niebla

Calle de Asunción

Calle del Monte Carmelo

Calle Juan Sebastián

Paseo de las Delicias

C La Rábida

Av de María Luisa

Avenida de Isabel la Católica

Plaza de España

43 ●
To Albergue Juvenil Sevilla

LP

0   250   500m
0   250   500yd

euro currency converter €1 = 166 ptas

SEVILLE (SEVILLA)

PLACES TO STAY		13	Bodega Paco Góngora	18	Giralda
2	Hostal Unión, Hostal Pino	20	Cervecería Giralda	19	Cathedral
5	Hostal Rmero	21	Bodega Santa Cruz	24	La Carbonería
7	Hostal Lis II	23	Pizzeria San Marco	31	Los Gallos
10	Hostal Central	28	Carmela	34	Archivo de Indias
12	Hotel La Rábida	33	Corral del Agua	35	Main Post Office
22	Hostal Goya			36	Cibercafé Torredeoro.net
25	Hostal La Montoreña	**OTHER**		37	Alambique, Mui d'Aqui &
26	Las Casas de la Judería	1	Fun Club		Big Ben
27	Hostal Bienvenido	4	Museo de Bellas Artes	38	Torre del Oro, Cruceros
29	Pensión San Pancraclo	6	Plaza de Armas Bus Station		Turísticos
30	Pensión Cruces	9	El Mundo	39	Main Tourist Office
32	Hostería del Laurel	11	Tourist Office	40	Librería Beta
		14	Arena	41	Airport Bus Stop
PLACES TO EAT		15	A3	42	Prado de San Sebastián Bus
3	Bodegón Alfonso XII	16	Tintorería Roma (Laundry)		Station
8	Patio San Eloy	17	Librería Beta	43	Tourist Office

Don Pedro, exquisitely decorated by Muslim artisans for the Castilian king Pedro the Cruel in the 1360s, and the large, immaculately tended **gardens**, the perfect place to ease your body and brain after some intensive sightseeing. The Alcázar is open 9.30 am to 7 pm Tuesday to Saturday (to 5 pm from October to March), 9.30 am to 5 pm Sunday and holidays. Entry is 700 ptas (free for students and pensioners).

Walks & Parks If you're not staying in the **Barrio de Santa Cruz**, the old Jewish quarter immediately east of the cathedral and alcázar, make sure you take a stroll among its quaint streets and lovely plant-bedecked plazas. Another enjoyable walk is along the **riverbank**, where the 13th-century Torre del Oro contains a small, crowded maritime museum. Nearby is Seville's famous bullring, the **Plaza de Toros de la Real Maestranza**, one of the oldest in Spain (begun in 1758). Interesting 300-ptas tours are given in English and Spanish, about every 20 minutes from 9.30 am to 2 pm and 3 to 6 or 7 pm daily (bullfight days 10 am to 3 pm).

South of the centre, large **Parque de María Luisa** is a pleasant place to get lost in, with its maze of paths, tall trees, flowers, fountains and shaded lawns.

Museums The **Archivo de Indias**, beside the cathedral, houses over 40 million documents dating from 1492 through to the decolonisation of the Americas. There are changing displays of fascinating maps and documents, open 10 am to 1 pm Monday to Friday (free).

The **Museo de Bellas Artes**, on Plaza del Museo, has an outstanding, beautifully housed collection of Spanish art, focusing on Seville artists like Murillo and Zurbarán. It's open Tuesday to Sunday (250 ptas, free for EU citizens).

Organised Tours

One-hour river cruises (1700 ptas) by Cruceros Turísticos Torre del Oro go at least hourly from 11 am to 7 pm from the Torre del Oro.

Special Events

The first of Seville's two great festivals is Semana Santa, the week leading up to Easter Sunday. Throughout the week, long processions of religious brotherhoods (*cofradías*), dressed in strange penitents' garb with tall, pointed hoods, accompany sacred images through the city, watched by huge crowds. The Feria de Abril, a week in late April, is a kind of release after this solemnity: the festivities involve six days of music, dancing, horse riding and traditional dress on a site in the Los Remedios area west of the river, plus daily bullfights and a general city-wide party.

Places to Stay

The summer prices given here can come down substantially from October to March, but around Semana Santa and the Feria de Abril they typically rise about 50%.

Camping Sevilla (☎ 95 451 43 79), 6km out on the N-IV towards Córdoba, charges 1790 ptas for two people with a car and tent, and runs a shuttle bus to/from Avenida de Portugal in the city.

Seville's recently-renovated HI hostel, *Albergue Juvenil Sevilla* (☎ 95 461 31 50, *Calle Isaac Peral 2*), has 277 places, all in twins or triples. It's about 10 minutes south by bus No 34 from opposite the main tourist office. Bed and breakfast is 1605/2140 ptas for under/over 26s most of the year.

The Barrio de Santa Cruz has some good-value places to stay. *Hostal Bienvenido* (☎ 95 441 36 55, *Calle Archeros 14*) provides singles/doubles from 1900/3700 ptas. Clean *Hostal La Montoreña* (☎ 95 441 24 07, *Calle San Clemente 12*) charges 2000/3000 ptas. *Pensión San Pancracio* (☎ 95 441 31 04, *Plaza de las Cruces 9*) has small singles for 2000 ptas and bigger doubles for 3400 ptas (4000 ptas with bath). *Pensión Cruces* (☎ 95 422 60 41, *Plaza de las Cruces 10*) has a few dorm beds at 1500 ptas and singles/doubles starting at 2000/4000 ptas. Sociable *Hostal Goya* (☎ 95 421 11 70, *Calle Mateos Gago 31*) has nice clean rooms with bath or shower from 4300/6000 ptas. Attractive *Hostería del Laurel* (☎ 95 422 02 95, ✉ host-laurel@eintec.es, *Plaza de los Venerables 5*) charges 7000/9500 ptas plus IVA. *Las Casas de la Judería* (☎ 95 441 51 50, fax 95 442 21 70, *Callejón de Dos Hermanas 7*) is a group of charming old houses around patios and fountains, charging 12,500/18,000 ptas plus IVA.

The area north of Plaza Nueva, only a 10-minute walk from all the hustle and bustle, has some good value too. Friendly *Hostal Unión* (☎ 95 422 92 94, *Calle Tarifa 4*) has nine good clean rooms at 2000/3500 ptas (3000/4500 ptas with bath). *Hostal Pino* (☎ 95 421 28 10, *Calle Tarifa 6*), next door, is similarly priced. Little *Hostal Romero* (☎ 95 421 13 53, *Calle Gravina 21*) offers clean, bare rooms for 2000/3500 ptas. *Hostal Lis II* (☎ 95 456 02 28, ✉ lisII@sol.com, *Calle Olavide 5*) in a pretty house charges 2300/4500 ptas for basic rooms or 5000 ptas for doubles with bath. *Hostal Central* (☎ 95 421 76 60, *Calle Zaragoza 18*) has well-kept rooms with bath

for 4500/6500 ptas. Impressive *Hotel La Rábida* (☎ 95 422 09 60, *Calle Castelar 24*) charges 6100/9300 ptas plus IVA.

Places to Eat

The Barrio de Santa Cruz is a good area for decent-value eating. *Hostería del Laurel* (*Plaza de los Venerables 5*) has an atmospheric old bar with good media raciónes (550 ptas to 1500 ptas) and raciónes. *Cervecería Giralda* (*Calle Mateos Gago 1*) is a good spot for breakfast. Tostadas are from 120 ptas to 480 ptas, or there's bacon and scrambled eggs for 630 ptas. *Bodega Santa Cruz* on the same street, a bar popular with visitors and locals, serves a big choice of decent-sized tapas, most at 175 ptas to 200 ptas. *Pizzeria San Marco* (*Calle Mesón del Moro 6*) does highly popular pizzas and pastas around 850 ptas (closed Monday). Calle Santa María La Blanca has several places with outdoor tables: at the *Carmela* a media ración of *tortilla Alta-Mira* (with potatoes and vegetables) is almost a meal in itself for 700 ptas. For something classier, the cool courtyard of *Corral del Agua* (*Callejón del Agua 6*) is great on a hot day, if you can get a table. Main courses (1900 ptas to 2500 ptas) include good fish choices.

West of Avenida de la Constitución, *Bodega Paco Góngora* (*Calle Padre Marchena 1*) has a huge range of good seafood at decent prices – media raciónes of fish *a la plancha* (grilled) are mostly 675 ptas. Farther north, bright, busy *Patio San Eloy* (*Calle de San Eloy 9*) serves heaps of good tapas for 175 ptas to 215 ptas. *Bodegón Alfonso XII* (*Calle Alfonso XII 33*) is excellent value with deals like scrambled eggs (*revuelto*) with cheese, ham and spinach for 550 ptas, or a bacon, eggs and coffee breakfast for 400 ptas.

Mercado del Arenal on Calle Pastor y Landero is the main food market in the central area.

Entertainment

Seville's nightlife is among the liveliest in Spain. On fine nights throngs of people block the streets outside popular bars. Seville has some great music bars, often with space for a bit of dancing. As in most places in Spain, the real action begins around midnight on Friday and Saturday.

Drinking & Dancing Until about 1 am, Plaza del Salvador is a popular spot for an open-air drink, with a studenty crowd and a couple of little bars selling carry-out drinks.

There are some hugely popular bars just north of the cathedral, but the crowds from about midnight around Calle de Adriano, west of Avenida de la Constitución, have to be seen to be believed. Busy music bars on Adriano itself include *A3* and *Arena*. Nearby on Calle de García de Vinuesa and Calle del Dos de Mayo are some quieter *bodegas* (traditional wine bars), some with good tapas, that attract a more mature crowd. Plaza de la Alfalfa is another good area; there are some great tapas bars east along Calle Alfalfa, and at least five throbbing music bars north on Calle Pérez Galdós.

The *Fun Club* (Alameda de Hércules 86) is a small, busy dance warehouse, open Thursday to Sunday – live bands play some nights. Several good pub-like bars line the same street a little farther north. The *Almacén* bar at *La Imperdible* arts centre (*Plaza San Antonio de Padua 9*) stages free music from around 11 pm Thursday to Saturday – from blues to psychedelic punk to beat-beat DJs.

In summer there's a lively scene along the east bank of the Guadalquivir, which is dotted with temporary bars. On the far bank, *Alambique*, *Mui d'Aqui* and *Big Ben*, side by side on Calle del Betis, all play good music year-round, attracting an interesting mix of students and travellers.

Flamenco Seville is arguably Spain's flamenco capital and you're most likely to catch spontaneous atmosphere (of unpredictable quality) in one of the bars staging regular nights of flamenco with no entry charge. These include the sprawling *La Carbonería* (*Calle Levíes 18*), thronged nearly every night from about 11 pm to 4 am, and *El Mundo* (*Calle Siete Revueltas 5*), with flamenco at 11 pm Tuesday. There are also several tourist-oriented venues with regular shows – of these, *Los Gallos* (*☎ 95 421 69 81, Plaza de Santa Cruz 11*) is a cut above the average, with two shows nightly (3500 ptas).

Spectator Sports
The bullfight season runs from Easter to October, with fights most Sundays about 6.30

pm, and every day during the Feria de Abril and the preceding week. The bullring is on Paseo de Cristóbal Colón. Tickets start around 1500 ptas or 3000 ptas depending on who's fighting.

Getting There & Away
Air Seville airport (☎ 95 444 90 00) has quite a range of domestic and international flights. Air Europa flies to Barcelona from 16,500 ptas.

Bus Buses to Extremadura, Madrid, Portugal and Andalucía west of Seville leave from the Plaza de Armas bus station (☎ 95 490 80 40). Numerous daily buses run to/from Madrid (2745 ptas, six hours); to/from Lisbon there are five direct buses a week (4800 ptas, eight hours). Daily buses run to/from places on the Algarve such as Faro, Albufeira and Lagos.

Buses to other parts of Andalucía and eastern Spain use Prado de San Sebastián bus station (☎ 95 441 71 11). Daily services include nine or more each to Córdoba (1225 ptas, 1¾ hours), Granada (2400 ptas, three hours) and Málaga (1900 ptas, 2½ hours).

Train Seville's Santa Justa train station is 1.5km north-east of the centre on Avenida Kansas City. To/from Madrid, there are 14 superfast AVE trains each day, covering the 471km in just 2½ hours and costing 8400 ptas to 9900 ptas in the cheapest class (*turista*); a few other trains take 3¼ hours to 3¾ hours for 6600 ptas to 8300 ptas.

Other daily trains include about 20 to Córdoba (1090 ptas to 2800 ptas, 45 minutes to 1¼ hours) and three or more each to Granada (2415 ptas to 2665 ptas, three hours) and Málaga (2130 ptas, 2½ hours). For Lisbon (7000 ptas, 16 hours) you must change at Cáceres.

Car Pooling Compartecoche (☎ 95 490 75 82), Calle de González Cuadrado 49, is an intercity car-pooling service. Its service is free to drivers, while passengers pay an agreed transfer rate.

Getting Around
The airport is 7km from the centre, off the N-IV Córdoba road. Amarillos Tour (☎ 902-21 03 17) runs buses to/from Puerta de Jerez in the city at least nine times daily (350 ptas).

Bus No C1, in front of Santa Justa train station, follows a clockwise circuit via Avenida de Carlos V, close to Prado de San Sebastián bus station and the city centre; No C2 does the same route anticlockwise. No C4, south down Calle de Arjona from Plaza de Armas bus station, goes to Puerta de Jerez in the centre; returning, take No C3.

CÓRDOBA
pop 310,000

Roman Córdoba was the capital of Baetica province, covering most of Andalucía. Following the Muslim invasion in AD 711 it soon became the effective Muslim capital on the peninsula, a position it held until the Córdoban Caliphate broke up after the death of its ruler Al-Mansour in 1002. Muslim Córdoba at its peak was the most splendid city in Europe, and its Mezquita (Mosque) is one of the most magnificent of all Islamic buildings. From the 11th century Córdoba was overshadowed by Seville and in the 13th century both cities fell to the Christians in the Reconquista.

Córdoba is at its best from about mid-April to mid-June, when the weather is warm but not too warm and it stages most of its annual festivals.

Orientation

Immediately north of the Río Guadalquivir is the old city, a warren of narrow streets focused on the Mezquita. The main square of the modern city is Plaza de las Tendillas, 500m north of the Mezquita.

Information

The helpful regional tourist office (☎ 957 47 12 35) faces the Mezquita at Calle de Torrijos 10. It's open 10 am to 6, 7 or 8 pm (according to season) Monday to Saturday, 10 am to 2 pm on Sunday and holidays. The municipal tourist office (☎ 957 20 05 22) is on Plaza de Judá Leví, a block west of the Mezquita.

Most banks and ATMs are around Plaza de las Tendillas. One ATM handier to the old city is at the corner of Calles San Fernando and Lucano.

Things to See & Do

The inside of the famous **Mezquita**, begun by emir Abd ar-Rahman I in AD 785 and enlarged by subsequent generations, is a mesmerising sequence of two-tier arches in stripes of red brick and white stone. From 1236 the mosque was used as a church and in the 16th century a cathedral was built right in its centre – somewhat wrecking the effect of original Muslim building, in many people's opinion. Opening hours are 10 am to 7.30 pm Monday to Saturday (to 5.30 pm October to March), 3.30 to 7.30 Sunday and holidays (2 to 5.30 pm October to March). Entry is 800 ptas.

The Judería, Córdoba's medieval Jewish quarter north-west of the Mezquita, is an intriguing maze of narrow streets and small plazas. Don't miss the beautiful little **Sinagoga** on Calle Judíos, one of Spain's very few surviving medieval synagogues (open daily except Monday). Nearby are the **Casa Andalusí**, Calle Judíos 12, a 12th-century house with exhibits on Córdoba's medieval Muslim culture, and the **Museo Taurino** (Bullfighting Museum) on Plaza de Maimónides, celebrating Córdoba's legendary matadors such as El Cordobés and Manolete.

South-west of the Mezquita stands the **Alcázar de los Reyes Cristianos** (Castle of the Christian Monarchs), with large and lovely gardens. Entry is 300 ptas (free on Friday).

The **Museo Arqueólogico**, Plaza de Jerónimo Páez 7, is also worth a visit (250 ptas, free for EU citizens). On the south side of the river, across the **Puente Romano**, is the **Torre de la Calahorra** with a museum highlighting the intellectual achievements of Islamic Córdoba, with excellent models of the Mezquita and Granada's Alhambra – open daily (500 ptas).

Places to Stay

Most people look for lodgings close to the Mezquita. Córdoba's excellent youth hostel, *Albergue Juvenil Córdoba* (☎ 957 29 01 66), is perfectly positioned on Plaza de Judá Leví. It has no curfew. Most of the year, bed and breakfast is 1605/2140 ptas for under/over 26s.

Many Córdoba lodgings are built around charming patios. One such place is friendly *Huéspedes Martínez Rücker* (☎ 957 47 25 62, ✉ hmrucker@alcavia.net, Calle Martínez Rücker 14), a stone's throw east of the Mezquita. It has clean singles/doubles for 2000/3500 ptas. *Hostal Rey Heredia* (☎ 957

CÓRDOBA

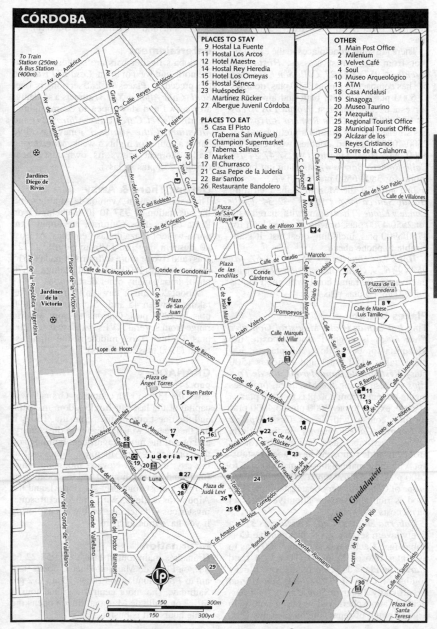

PLACES TO STAY
9 Hostal La Fuente
11 Hostal Los Arcos
12 Hotel Maestre
14 Hostal Rey Heredia
15 Hotel Los Omeyas
16 Hostal Séneca
23 Huéspedes
   Martínez Rücker
27 Albergue Juvenil Córdoba

PLACES TO EAT
5 Casa El Pisto
   (Taberna San Miguel)
6 Champion Supermarket
7 Taberna Salinas
8 Market
17 El Churrasco
21 Casa Pepe de la Judería
22 Bar Santos
26 Restaurante Bandolero

OTHER
1 Main Post Office
2 Milenium
3 Velvet Café
4 Soul
10 Museo Arqueológico
13 ATM
18 Casa Andalusí
19 Sinagoga
20 Museo Taurino
24 Mezquita
25 Regional Tourist Office
28 Municipal Tourist Office
29 Alcázar de los
   Reyes Cristianos
30 Torre de la Calahorra

euro currency converter 100 ptas = €0.60

47 41 82, Calle Rey Heredia 26) has rooms around a plant-filled patio from 1500/3000 ptas.

There are some good places to the east, farther from the tourist masses. *Hostal La Fuente (☎ 957 48 78 27, Calle San Fernando 51)* has compact singles at 3500 ptas, doubles at 6000 ptas – all with bath and air-con; it serves a decent breakfast. *Hostal Los Arcos (☎ 957 48 56 43, Calle Romero Barros 14)* has singles/doubles around a pretty patio for 2500/4000 ptas, and doubles with bath for 5000 ptas. *Hotel Maestre (☎ 957 47 24 10, Calle Romero Barros 4)* has plain but bright rooms for 3800/6500 ptas plus IVA.

Just north of the Mezquita, the charming *Hostal Séneca (☎/fax 957 47 32 34, Calle Conde y Luque 7)* has rooms with shared bath for 2550/4700 ptas, or with attached bath for 4750/5900 ptas, including breakfast. It's advisable to phone ahead.

Hotel Los Omeyas (☎ 957 49 22 67, fax 957 49 16 59, Calle Encarnación 17) is an attractive middle-range hotel, with good rooms for 5000/8500 ptas plus IVA.

Places to Eat

Tiny *Bar Santos (Calle Magistral González Francés 3)* is a good stop opposite the Mezquita for bocadillos (200 ptas to 300 ptas), tapas (150 ptas) and raciónes (500 ptas). *Restaurante Bandolero (Calle de Torrijos 6)*, also facing the Mezquita, provides media raciónes from 250 ptas to 1000 ptas; a la carte, expect to pay 3000 ptas to 4000 ptas for three courses with drinks. *Casa Pepe de la Judería (Calle Romero 1)* in the Judería serves tasty tapas and raciónes in rooms around its little patio, and has a good restaurant with most main dishes from 1600 ptas to 2400 ptas. *El Churrasco (Calle Romero 16)* is one of Córdoba's very best restaurants. The food is rich and service attentive. The set *menú* costs 3500 ptas.

Taberna Salinas (Calle Tundidores 3) is a lively tavern serving good, inexpensive Córdoban fare. Raciónes cost around 700 ptas to 800 ptas (closed Sunday). There's a food *market* on Plaza de la Corredera, two blocks south-east. *Casa El Pisto (Plaza San Miguel 1)*, officially *Taberna San Miguel*, is a particularly atmospheric old watering hole with a good range of tapas, media raciónes (500

ptas to 1000 ptas) and raciónes. You can sit at tables behind the bar (closed Sunday).

Entertainment

Córdoba's livelier bars are scattered around the north and west of town. *Casa El Pisto* (see the preceding Places to Eat section) is one. *Soul (Calle Alfonso XIII 3)* attracts a studenty/ arty crowd and stays open to 3 am nightly. Nearby *Velvet Café (Calle Alfaros 29)* and *Milenium (Calle Alfaros 33)* may have live bands a couple of nights a week. *Magister* on Calle Morería brews its own tasty beer (around 250 ptas a glass).

Getting There & Away

The train station on Avenida de América, and the bus station (☎ 957 40 40 40) behind it on Plaza de las Tres Culturas, are about 1km north-west of Plaza de las Tendillas. At least 10 buses a day run to/from Seville (1225 ptas) and five or more to/from Granada (1515 ptas), Madrid (1600 ptas) and Málaga (1570 ptas), among many other destinations.

About 20 trains a day run to/from Seville, taking between 45 and 75 minutes for 1090 ptas to 2800 ptas. Options to/from Madrid range from several AVEs (6100 ptas to 7200 ptas, 1¾ hours) to a middle-of-the-night Estrella (3700 ptas, 6¼ hours).

GRANADA
pop 241,000

From the 13th to 15th centuries, Granada was capital of the last Muslim kingdom in Spain, and the finest city on the peninsula. Today it has the greatest Muslim legacy in the country, and one of the most magnificent buildings on the continent – the Alhambra. South-east of the city, the Sierra Nevada mountain range (mainland Spain's highest and the location of Europe's most southerly ski slopes), and the Alpujarras valleys, with their picturesque, mysterious villages, are well worth exploring if you have time to spare.

Information

Granada's main tourist office (☎ 958 22 66 88), on Plaza de Mariana Pineda, opens 9.30 am to 7 pm Monday to Friday, 10 am to 2 pm Saturday. The more central regional tourist office on Calle de Mariana Pineda opens the same hours but is busier.

SPAIN

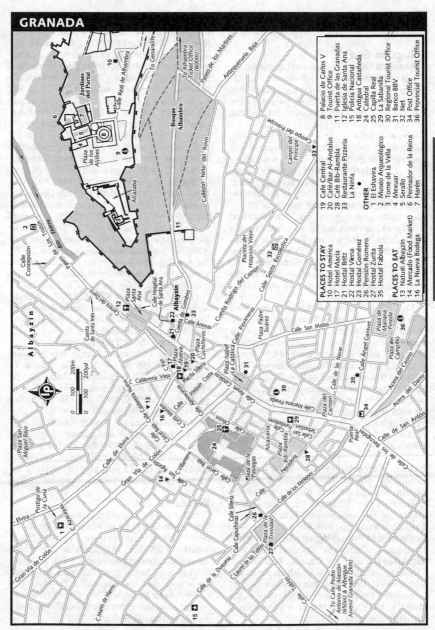

GRANADA

PLACES TO STAY
10 Hotel América
17 Hotel Macía
21 Hostal Britz
22 Hostal Viena
23 Hostal Gomérez
26 Pensión Romero
27 Hostal Zurita
35 Hostal Fabiola

PLACES TO EAT
13 Natturi Albayzín
14 Mercado (Food Market)
16 La Nueva Bodega

19 Cafe Central
20 Café/Bar Al-Andalus
28 Café Bib-Rambla
33 Restaurante Pizzería
    La Ninfa

OTHER
1 El Eshavira
2 Museo Arqueológico
3 Tome de la Vela
4 Mexuar
5 Serallo
6 Peinador de la Reina
7 Harén

8 Palacio de Carlos V
9 Tourist Office
11 Puerta de las Granadas
12 Iglesia de Santa Ana
15 Policía Nacional
18 Antigua Castañeda
24 Catedral
25 Capilla Real
29 La Sabanilla
30 Regional Tourist Office
31 Banco BBV
32 Net
34 Post Office
36 Provincial Tourist Office

euro currency converter 100 ptas = €0.60

Net, Calle Santa Escolástica 13, open daily, offers Internet access for 200 ptas an hour.

Things to See
Alhambra One of the greatest accomplishments of Islamic art and architecture, the Alhambra is simply breathtaking. Much has been written about its fortress, palace, patios and gardens, but nothing can really prepare you for what you will see.

The **Alcazaba** is the Alhambra's fortress, dating from the 11th to the 13th centuries. The views from the tops of the towers are great. The **Palacio Nazaries** (Nasrid Palace), built for Granada's Muslim rulers in their 13th to 15th-century heyday, is the centrepiece of the Alhambra. The beauty of its patios and intricacy of its stucco and woodwork, epitomised by the Patio de los Leones (Patio of the Lions) and Sala de las Dos Hermanas (Hall of the Two Sisters), are stunning. Don't miss the **Generalife**, the soul-soothing palace gardens – a great spot to relax and contemplate the rest of the Alhambra from a little distance.

The Alhambra and Generalife are open 8.30 am to 8 pm daily (to 6 pm October to March) for 1000 ptas. The 8000 tickets for each day can sell out fast, especially from May to October. You can book ahead, for an extra 125 ptas, at any branch of Banco BBV (in many Spanish cities), or by calling ☎ 902-22 44 60 between 9 am and 6 pm and paying by Visa or MasterCard. Any tickets available for same-day visits are sold at the Alhambra ticket office and, 9 am to 2 pm Monday to Friday, at Banco BBV on Plaza Isabel la Católica.

Other Attractions
Simply wandering around the narrow, hilly streets of the **Albayzín**, the old Muslim district across the river from the Alhambra (not too late at night), or the area around **Plaza de Bib-Rambla** is a real pleasure. On your way, stop by the **Museo Arqueológico** (Archaeological Museum) on Carrera del Darro at the foot of the Albayzín, and the **Capilla Real** (Royal Chapel) on Calle Oficios in which Fernando and Isabel, the Christian conquerors of Granada in 1492, are buried. Next door to the chapel is Granada's **catedral**, which dates in part from the early 16th century.

Places to Stay
Camping Sierra Nevada (☎ 958 15 00 62, Avenida de Madrid 107), 200m from the estación de autobuses, is the closest camping ground to the centre. It closes from November to February. Granada's modern youth hostel, *Albergue Juvenil Granada* (☎ 958 27 26 38, Calle Ramón y Cajal 2) is 1.7km west of the centre and a 600m walk south-west of the train station. Most of the year, bed and breakfast is 1605/2140 ptas for under/over 26s.

Close to Plaza Nueva (well placed for the Alhambra and Albayzín), *Hostal Gomérez* (☎ 958 22 44 37, Cuesta de Gomérez 10) has well-kept singles/doubles at 1600/2700 ptas. *Hostal Britz* (☎/fax 958 22 36 52, Cuesta de Gomérez 1) provides clean, adequate rooms for 2340/3900 ptas, or 4000/5400 ptas with bath. *Hostal Viena* (☎ 958 22 18 59, Calle Hospital de Santa Ana 2) has rooms for 3000/4000 ptas. *Hotel Macía* (☎ 958 22 75 36, fax 958 22 75 33, Plaza Nueva 4) offers good value among the more expensive hotels, with singles/doubles for 6820/10,275 ptas.

Hostal Fabiola (☎ 958 22 35 72, Calle de Ángel Ganivet 5) is a good, family-run place. You pay 1800/4000/5000 ptas for singles/doubles/triples with bath.

The Plaza de la Trinidad area is another with plenty of choice. Family-run *Pensión Romero* (☎ 958 26 60 79, Calle Sillería 1) has rooms for 1700/2900 ptas. *Hostal Zurita* (☎ 958 27 50 20, Plaza de la Trinidad 7) is good value at 2000/4000 ptas (5000 ptas for doubles with bathroom).

Hotel América (☎ 958 22 74 71, fax 958 22 74 70, Calle Real de Alhambra 53) is only open from March to October but has a magical position within the walls of the Alhambra; doubles are 13,375 ptas and you need to reserve well ahead.

Places to Eat
Popular *Cafe Central* on Calle de Elvira offers everything from good breakfasts to *menús* (from 1100 ptas) to fancy coffees. Nearby *Café/Bar Al Andalus* on Plaza Nueva has good cheap Arabic food. Tasty felafel in pitta bread costs 300 ptas and spicy meat main dishes are around 1000 ptas.

La Nueva Bodega (Calle Cetti Meriém 3) has reliable and economical food, with daily *menús* starting at 950 ptas.

SPAIN

The *teterías* (Arabic-style teahouses) on Calle Calderería Nueva, a picturesque pedestrian street west of Plaza Nueva, are expensive but can be enjoyable. *Naturii Albayzín (Calle Calderería Nueva 10)* is a good vegetarian restaurant.

Café Bib-Rambla on Plaza Bib-Rambla is great for breakfast. Coffee and toast with butter and excellent marmalade cost 400 ptas at its tables on the plaza. *Restaurante-Pizzería La Ninfa (Campo del Príncipe 14)* is an excellent Italian eatery on a plaza south of the Alhambra that buzzes at night.

For fresh fruit and vegies, the large covered *mercado* (market) is on Calle San Agustín.

In Granada's bars, tapas are often free at night.

Entertainment
The highest concentration of music bars is on and around Calle Pedro Antonio de Alarcón. To get there, walk south on Calle de las Tablas from Plaza de la Trinidad. After 11 pm at weekends, you can't miss it.

Bars in the streets west of Plaza Nueva get very lively on weekend nights. The *Antigua Castañeda* on Calle de Elvira is one of the most famous bars in Granada and an institution among locals and tourists alike, serving great tapas – which will probably come free if you're standing at the bar after about 8 pm. Bars north of Plaza Nueva on Carrera del Darro and Paseo de los Tristes get fun after midnight.

Granada's oldest bar, *La Sabanilla (Calle de San Sebastían 14)*, though showing its age, is worth a visit. Don't miss *El Eshavira (Postigo de la Cuna 2)*, a roomy jazz and flamenco club down a dark alley off Calle Azacayas (open from 10 pm nightly).

In the evening some travellers go to the Sacromonte caves to see flamenco, but it's touristy and a bit of a rip-off.

Getting There & Away
Granada's bus station (☎ 958 18 54 80) is at Carretera de Jáen s/n, on the continuation of Avenida de Madrid, 3km north-west of the centre. At least nine daily buses serve Madrid (1950 ptas, five to six hours), and others run to Barcelona, Valencia and destinations across Andalucía.

The train station is about 1.5km west of the centre, on Avenida de Andaluces. Of the two trains daily to Madrid, one takes 9½ hours overnight (3600 ptas), the other six hours (3800 ptas). To Seville, there are three trains a day (from 2415 ptas, three hours). For Málaga and Córdoba, you have to change trains in Bobadilla. There's one train daily to Valencia and Barcelona.

COSTA DE ALMERÍA
The coast east of Almería city in eastern Andalucía is perhaps the last section of Spain's Mediterranean coast where you can have a beach to yourself (not in high summer, admittedly). This is Spain's sunniest region – even in late March it can be warm enough to take in some rays and try out your new swimsuit.

The most useful tourist offices are in Almería (☎ 950 62 11 17), San José (☎ 950 38 02 99) and Mojácar (☎ 950 47 51 62).

Things to See & Do
The **Alcazaba**, an enormous 10th-century Muslim fortress, is the highlight of Almería city. In its heyday the city was more important than Granada.

The best thing about the region is the wonderful coastline and semidesert scenery of the **Cabo de Gata** promontory. All along the 50km coast from El Cabo de Gata village to Agua Amarga, some of the most beautiful and empty beaches on the Mediterranean alternate with precipitous cliffs and scattered villages. Roads or paths run along or close to this whole coastline. The main village is laid-back **San José**, with excellent beaches such as **Playa de los Genoveses** and **Playa de Mónsul** within 7km south-west.

Mojácar, 30km north of Agua Amarga, is a white town of Muslim origin, with cube-shaped houses perched on a hill 2km from the coast. Although a long resort strip, Mojácar Playa, has grown up below, Mojácar is still a pretty place and it's not hard to spend time here, especially if you fancy a livelier summer beach scene than Cabo de Gata offers.

Places to Stay & Eat
Almería Near the bus and train stations, *Hostal Americano (☎ 950 28 10 15, Avenida de la Estación 6)* offers well-kept singles/doubles from 2850/5540 ptas to 3915/6410 ptas.

SPAIN

Cabo de Gata In high summer it's a good idea to ring ahead about accommodation, as some places fill up. In San José *Camping Tau* (☎ *950 38 01 66)* and the friendly non-HI youth hostel *Albergue Juvenil de San José* (☎ *950 38 03 53, Calle Montemar s/n)*, with bunks for 1300 ptas, both open from April to September. *Hostal Bahía* (☎ *950 38 03 07)* on Calle Correo has attractive singles/doubles with bathroom for 5000/7500 ptas. *Restaurante El Emigrante* across the road does good fish and meat mains around 850 ptas to 1400 ptas, and omelettes for 400 ptas to 500 ptas.

Mojácar The better-value places are mostly up in the old town. *Pensión Casa Justa* (☎ *950 47 83 72, Calle Morote 7)* is reasonable value with singles/doubles from 2500/5000 ptas. *Hostal La Esquinica* (☎ *950 47 50 09, Calle Cano 1)* charges 2500/4500 ptas. Charming *Hostal Mamabel's* (☎ *950 47 24 48, Calle Embajadores 5)* has eight big rooms with sea views and bath, for 9630 ptas a double, and a good restaurant with a three-course *menú* for 1800 ptas, plus drinks and IVA. *Restaurante El Viento del Desierto* on Plaza del Frontón is good value with main courses such as beef Bourguignon for 650 ptas to 800 ptas.

Getting There & Away
Almería has an international and domestic airport and is accessible by bus and train from Madrid, Granada and Seville, and by bus from Málaga, Valencia and Barcelona. Buses run from Almería bus station to El Cabo de Gata village and (except nonsummer Sundays) to San José. Mojácar can be reached by bus from Almeriá, Murcia, Granada and Madrid.

MÁLAGA
pop 528,000
The large port city of Málaga, a major entry point into Spain thanks to its international airport feeding the nearby Costa del Sol, has a bustling street life and a thumping nightlife in the narrow streets behind Plaza de la Constitución. It also boasts a 16th-century cathedral, and a Muslim palace/fortress, the Alcazaba, from which the walls of the Muslim Castillo de Gibralfaro climb to the top of the hill dominating the city. A major new museum devoted to the work of Málaga-born artist Pablo Picasso is due to open in Málaga

in late 2002. The helpful regional tourist office (☎ 95 221 34 45), in the centre at Pasaje Chinitas 4, opens daily.

The Costa del Sol, a string of tightly packed resorts running south-west from Málaga towards Gibraltar, is best avoided if you're more interested in Spain than foreign package tourists.

Places to Stay & Eat
The friendly, central *Pensión Córdoba* (☎ 95 221 44 69, Calle Bolsa 9) has singles/doubles at 1500/3000 ptas. *Hotel Carlos V* (☎ 95 221 51 20, Calle Císter 10) near the cathedral offers comfortable doubles for 8300 ptas.

Café Central on Plaza de la Constitución is a noisy local favourite; food prices are reasonable, with plenty of choice. A short walk north-east, *La Posada (Calle Granada 33)* is great for tapas and raciónes of *carnes a la brasa* (grilled meats). It's 1600 ptas for lamb chops.

Getting There & Away
Málaga airport has a good range of domestic as well as international flights. Trains and buses run every half-hour from the airport to the city centre The city is also linked by train and bus to all major Spanish centres. The bus and train stations are round the corner from each other, 1km west of the city centre.

RONDA
pop 34,500
One of the prettiest and most historic towns in Andalucía, Ronda is a world apart from the nearby Costa del Sol. The town straddles the savagely deep El Tajo gorge, at the heart of some lovely hill country dotted with white villages.

The regional tourist office (☎ 95 287 12 72) is at Plaza de España 1.

Things to See & Do
Ronda is a pleasure to wander around, but during the day you'll have to contend with busloads of day-trippers from the coast.

The **Plaza de Toros** (1785) is considered the home of bullfighting and is a mecca for aficionados; inside is the small but fascinating **Museo Taurino**. Entry is 400 ptas. Vertiginous cliff-top views open out from the nearby Alameda del Tajo park.

SPAIN

The 18th-century **Puente Nuevo** (New Bridge), an amazing feat of engineering, crosses the gorge to the originally Muslim old town (La Ciudad), which is littered with ancient churches, monuments and palaces. At the **Casa del Rey Moro**, Calle Santo Domingo 17, you can climb down a Muslim-era stairway cut inside the rock right to the bottom of the gorge (open daily, 600 ptas). Try not to miss the **Iglesia de Santa María la Mayor**, a church whose tower was once the minaret of a mosque; the **Museo del Bandolero**, Calle Armiñán 65, dedicated to the banditry for which central Andalucía was once renowned; or the beautiful **Baños Arabes** (Arab Baths), open Wednesday to Sunday.

Places to Stay & Eat

Camping El Sur (☎ 95 287 59 39) is a good small site 2km out on the Algeciras road.

The bright *Pensión La Purísima* (☎ 95 287 10 50, Calle Sevilla 10) has nine rooms at 2000/3000 ptas. *Hotel Morales* (☎/fax 95 287 15 38, Calle Sevilla 51) has pleasant rooms with bath for 3500/6000 ptas and is full of information on exploring the town and surrounding country.

El Molino on Plaza del Socorro is popular for its pizzas, pasta and platos combinados from 550 ptas to 775 ptas, and varied breakfasts. *Restaurante Hermanos Macías (Calle Pedro Romero 3)* is a reliable mid-range eatery with meat and fish main dishes from 800 ptas to 1600 ptas.

Getting There & Away

Several buses run daily to Seville (1285 ptas, 2½ hours), Málaga (1075 ptas, two hours) and Cádiz. One goes to Algeciras (1010 ptas) Monday to Friday. The bus station is on Plaza Concepción García Redondo.

A few direct trains go to Granada (1775 ptas, 2¼ hours), Málaga (1175 ptas, two hours), Algeciras, Córdoba and Madrid. For Seville, and further trains to/from the above destinations, change at Bobadilla or Antequera. The station is on Avenida de Andalucía.

ALGECIRAS

pop 102,000

Algeciras, an unattractive industrial and fishing town between Tarifa and Gibraltar, is the major port linking Spain with Morocco. Keep your wits about you, and ignore offers from the legions of money-changers, drug-pushers and ticket-hawkers. The tourist office (☎ 956 57 26 36) on Calle Juan de la Cierva near the ferry port, opens 9 am to 2 pm Monday to Friday.

If you need a room, there's loads of budget accommodation in the streets behind Avenida de la Marina, the street the port is on. Beware early-hours market noise, though. Friendly *Hostal González* (☎ 956 65 28 43, Calle José Santacana 7) has good, clean singles/doubles with private bath at 2000/4000 ptas.

Getting There & Away

Bus Comes, on Calle San Bernardo, about 400m inland from the port, runs frequent buses to/from La Línea, and several daily to/from Tarifa, Cádiz and Seville. Portillo, Avenida Virgen del Carmen 15, 200m north of the port, runs to/from Málaga, the Costa del Sol and Granada. Bacoma, inside the port, runs to/from Valencia, Barcelona, France, Germany and Holland.

Train Direct daily trains run to/from Madrid and Granada, passing through Ronda and through Bobadilla where you can change for Málaga, Córdoba and Seville.

Boat Trasmediterránea (☎ 902-45 46 45), EuroFerrys (☎ 956 65 11 78) and other companies operate frequent ferries to/from Tangier in Morocco and Ceuta, the Spanish enclave on the Moroccan coast. Usually at least 20 daily go to Tangier and 40 or more to Ceuta. From late June to September there are ferries almost round the clock. Buy your ticket in the port or at agencies on Avenida de la Marina – prices are the same. To Tangier, adults pay 3500 ptas one-way by ferry (2½ hours), or 4440 ptas by hydrofoil (one hour). Cars cost 10,750 ptas. To Ceuta, it's 1945 ptas by ferry (90 minutes) or 3095 ptas by 'fast ferry' (40 minutes). Cars are 8930 ptas. Buquebus (☎ 902-41 42 42) crosses to Ceuta in 30 minutes for 2945 ptas (cars 8223 ptas).

CÁDIZ, TARIFA & THE COSTA DE LA LUZ

The historic port of Cádiz is squeezed on to an island just off Andalucía's Atlantic coast, joined to the mainland by a causeway. Ninety kilometres to its south is windy Tarifa,

SPAIN

perched at continental Europe's most southerly point and with a lively windsurfing scene. Between the two places stretch the long, sandy beaches of the Costa de la Luz (Coast of Light), where laid-back villages such as Los Caños de Meca, Zahara de los Atunes and Bolonia have fairly plentiful middle-range accommodation – they're unfortunately a little hard to reach without your own wheels.

Things to See & Do

Cádiz Check the **Torre Tavira**, an old watchtower with a *cámara oscura* projecting moving images of the city on to a screen (open daily); the **Museo de Cádiz**, with archaeological and art collections (closed Monday); the **Castillo de Santa Catalina**, built in 1598 (open daily); and the large 18th-century **cathedral** (closed to tourist visits on Sunday). From Cádiz you can easily visit the historic sherry-making towns of El Puerto de Santa María and Jerez de la Frontera by bus or train (or boat, to El Puerto).

Tarifa A 10km-long beach beloved of windsurfers, **Playa de los Lances** stretches northwest from Tarifa. For windsurf rental and classes try places along here such as Club Mistral at the Hurricane Hotel or Spin Out in front of Camping Torre de la Peña II. In Tarifa town, enjoy exploring the winding old streets and visit the castle, **Castillo de Guzmán**, dating from the 10th century.

Places to Stay & Eat

Cádiz's excellent independent youth hostel *Quo Qádiz* (☎/fax 956 22 19 39, Calle Diego Arias 1) has accommodation from 1000 ptas a person including breakfast. Friendly, clean *Hostal Fantoni* (☎ 956 28 27 04, Calle Flamenco 5) has singles/doubles at 2000/3700 ptas. Plaza de San Juan de Dios and the Plaza de Mina area are full of varied places to eat.

In Tarifa, a good choice is *Pensión Africa* (☎ 956 68 02 20, Calle María Antonia Toledo 12) with bright, comfy rooms for 2500/4000 ptas (3500/5000 ptas with private bath). There are plenty of eating options on and near the central Calle Sancho IV El Bravo.

Getting There & Away

The Comes company (☎ 956 21 17 63), on Cádiz's Plaza de la Hispanidad, runs buses to/from Seville (1385 ptas, 1¾ hours), Tarifa and Málaga. Up to 15 daily trains chuff to/from Seville (1290 ptas, two hours), with others heading for Córdoba and beyond. Comes also links Tarifa (Calle Batalla del Salado) with Algeciras, La Línea, Seville and Málaga.

Gibraltar

pop 29,000

The British colony of Gibraltar occupies a huge lump of limestone, almost 5km long and over 1km wide, near the mouth of the Mediterranean Sea. It's a curious and interesting port of call if you're in the region. Gibraltar has certainly had a rocky history: it was the bridgehead for the Muslim invasion of Spain in AD 711 and Castile didn't finally wrest it from the Muslims until 1462. In 1704 an Anglo-Dutch fleet captured Gibraltar after a one-week siege. Spain gave up military attempts to regain it from Britain after the failure of the Great Siege of 1779-83, but during the Franco period Gibraltar was an extremely sore point between Britain and Spain, and the border was closed for years.

Gibraltar is internally self-governing and an overwhelming majority of Gibraltarians – many of whom are of Genoese or Jewish ancestry – want to retain British sovereignty. Spain has offered Gibraltar autonomous-region status within Spain, but Britain and the Gibraltarians reject any compromise over sovereignty.

Information

To enter Gibraltar you need a passport or EU national identity card. EU, US, Canada, Australia, New Zealand, Israel, South Africa and Singapore passport-holders are among those who do *not* need visas for Gibraltar, but anyone who needs a visa for Spain should have at least a double-entry Spanish visa if they intend to return to Spain from Gibraltar.

Gibraltar has a helpful tourist office at the border. The main office (☎ 45000) is in Duke of Kent House, Cathedral Square, open 9 am to 5.30 pm Monday to Friday; another is at The Piazza (☎ 74982), Main St, open 9 am to 5.30 pm Monday to Friday, 10 am to 4 pm weekends.

The currency is the Gibraltar pound or pound sterling. You can use pesetas, however currency conversion rates aren't in your favour. But exchange rates for buying pesetas are a bit better than in Spain. Change any unspent Gibraltar pounds before you leave.

To phone Gibraltar from Spain, the telephone code is ☎ 9567; from other countries dial the international access code, then ☎ 350 (the code for Gibraltar) and the local number. To phone Spain from Gibraltar, just dial the nine-digit Spanish number.

Gibraltar is better than anywhere in Spain – except Palma de Mallorca – for finding (unpaid) yacht crew work. Ask around at Marina Bay harbour.

Gibraltar has lots of British high street shops, including a Safeway supermarket, in the Europort area.

Things to See & Do

Central Gibraltar is nothing special – you could almost be in Bletchley or Bradford – but the **Gibraltar Museum**, on Bomb House Lane, has a very interesting historical, architectural and military collection and includes a Muslim-era bathhouse. It's open 10 am to 6 pm Monday to Friday, 10 am to 2 pm Saturday (£2). Many graves in the **Trafalgar Cemetery** are of those who died at Gibraltar from wounds received in the Battle of Trafalgar (1805) off Los Caños de Meca.

The large **Upper Rock Nature Reserve**, covering most of the upper rock, has spectacular views and several interesting spots to visit. It's open 9.30 am to 7 pm daily. Entry, at £5 an adult and £1.50 a vehicle, includes all the following sites, which are open to 6.15 or 6.30 pm. Cable-car tickets (see Getting Around later in this section) include entry to the reserve, the Apes' Den and St Michael's Cave.

The rock's most famous inhabitants are its colony of **Barbary macaques**, the only wild primates (apart from *Homo sapiens*) in Europe. Some of these hang around the **Apes' Den** near the middle cable-car station, others can often be seen at the top station or Great Siege Tunnels.

From the top cable-car station, you can see Morocco in decent weather. **St Michael's Cave**, a 20-minute downhill walk south from here, is a big natural grotto renowned for its stalagmites and stalactites. Apart from attracting tourists in droves, it's used for concerts, plays and even fashion shows. The

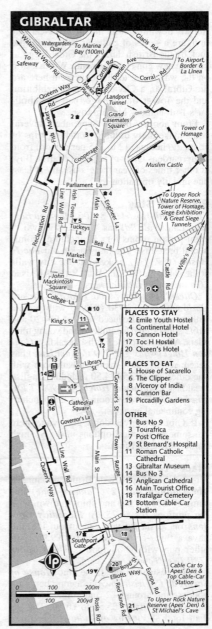

GIBRALTAR

PLACES TO STAY
2 Emile Youth Hostel
4 Continental Hotel
10 Cannon Hotel
17 Toc H Hostel
20 Queen's Hotel

PLACES TO EAT
5 House of Sacarello
6 The Clipper
8 Viceroy of India
12 Cannon Bar
19 Piccadilly Gardens

OTHER
1 Bus No 9
3 Tourafrica
7 Post Office
9 St Bernard's Hospital
11 Roman Catholic Cathedral
13 Gibraltar Museum
14 Bus No 3
15 Anglican Cathedral
16 Main Tourist Office
18 Trafalgar Cemetery
21 Bottom Cable-Car Station

SPAIN

Great Siege Tunnels, a 30-minute walk north (mostly downhill) from the top cable-car station, are a series of galleries hewn from the rock by the British during the Great Siege to provide new gun emplacements. Worth a stop on the way down to the town from here are the Gibraltar, a City under Siege exhibition and the Tower of Homage, part of Gibraltar's 14th-century Muslim castle.

From about April to September, several boats make daily dolphin-watching trips of about 2½ hours (£12 to £15 per person) from Watergardens Quay or adjacent Marina Bay; at other times of year there's usually at least one in daily operation.

Places to Stay

Emile Youth Hostel (☎ 51106, Montagu Bastion, Line Wall Rd) has 43 places in two to eight-person rooms for £12 including continental breakfast. The ramshackle old Toc H Hostel (☎ 73431), tucked into the city walls at the south end of Line Wall Rd, has beds at £6 a night and cold showers.

Queen's Hotel (☎ 74000, 1 Boyd St) has singles/doubles at £20/30 (£36/40 with private bath or shower). Reduced rates of £14/20 and £16/24 are offered for students and young travellers. All rates include English breakfast. Cannon Hotel (☎/fax 51711, 9 Cannon Lane) has decent rooms, each sharing a bathroom with one other, for £22.50/34.50 including English breakfast. Continental Hotel (☎ 76900, 1 Engineer Lane) has cosy rooms at £42/55 including continental breakfast.

If Gibraltar prices don't grab you, there are some economical options in the Spanish border town, La Línea.

Places to Eat

Most of the many pubs do British pub meals. The Cannon Bar (27 Cannon Lane) has some of the best fish and chips in town, with big portions for £4.75. At Piccadilly Gardens on Rosia Rd you can sit outside and have a three-course dinner for £9.95. Another pub with good food is The Clipper (78B Irish Town).

For a restaurant meal, the chic House of Sacarello (57 Irish Town) is a good bet, with good soups around £2 and some excellent daily specials from £5.50 to £6.10. The Indian food at Viceroy of India (9/11 Horse

Barrack Court) is usually pretty good. It has a three-course lunch special for £6.75.

Getting There & Away

Air GB Airways (☎ 79300, UK ☎ 0345-222111) flies daily to/from London. Return fares from London range from around £175 to £275, depending on the season. Monarch Airlines (☎ 47477, UK ☎ 08700-405040) flies daily to/from Luton, with return fares from £100 to £250. Morocco's Regional Air Lines (☎ 79300) flies Gibraltar to Casablanca most days for £104 return.

Bus There are no regular buses to Gibraltar, but La Línea bus station is only a five-minute walk from the border.

Car & Motorcycle Vehicle queues at the border often make it less time-consuming to park in La Línea, then walk across the border. To take a car into Gibraltar you need an insurance certificate, registration document, nationality plate and driving licence. You do not have to pay any fee, despite what con artists might try to tell you.

Ferry There are normally two ferries a week to/from Tangier, taking two hours for £18/30 one way/return per person and £40/80 per car. Tourafrica (☎ 77666), ICC Building, Main St, sells tickets.

Getting Around

The frequent bus Nos 3 and 9 run direct from the border into town. Few buses run after 2 pm Saturday and none on Sunday – but the 1.5km walk is quite interesting as it crosses the airport runway.

All of Gibraltar can be covered on foot, but there are other options. Weather permitting, the cable car leaves its lower station on Red Sands Rd every few minutes from 9.30 am to 5.15 pm, Monday to Saturday. The one-way/return fares are £3.65/4.90. For the Apes' Den, disembark at the middle station.

Extremadura

Extremadura, a sparsely populated tableland bordering Portugal, is far enough from the most beaten tourist trails to give you a genuine sense of exploration, something that *extremeños* themselves have a flair for. Many epic 16th-century *conquistadores* including Francisco Pizarro (who conquered the Incas) and Hernán Cortés (who did the same to the Aztecs) sprang from this land.

Trujillo and Cáceres are the two not-to-be-missed old towns, and Mérida has Spain's biggest collection of Roman ruins. A spot of hiking, or just relaxing, in the valleys of North-East Extremadura makes the perfect change from urban life. If you can, avoid June to August, when Extremadura is *uncomfortably* hot.

TRUJILLO
pop 9000
Trujillo can't be much bigger now than in 1529, when its most famous son Francisco Pizarro set off with his three brothers and a few local buddies for an expedition that culminated in the bloody conquest of the Inca empire three years later. Trujillo is blessed with a broad and fine Plaza Mayor, from which rises its remarkably preserved old town, packed with aged buildings exuding history. If you approach from the Plasencia direction you might imagine that you've driven through a time warp into the 16th century. The tourist office (☎ 927 32 26 77) is on Plaza Mayor.

Things to See
A statue of Pizarro, by American Charles Rumsey, dominates the Plaza Mayor. On the plaza's south side, the Palacio de la Conquista (closed to visitors) sports the carved images of Francisco Pizarro and the Inca princess Inés Yupanqui.

Two noble mansions you *can* visit are the 16th-century Palacio de los Duques de San Carlos, also on the Plaza Mayor (100 ptas), and Palacio de Orellana-Pizarro, through the alley in the plaza's south-west corner.

Up the hill, the Iglesia de Santa María la Mayor is an interesting hotchpotch of 13th to 16th-century styles, with some fine paintings by Fernando Gallego of the Flemish school. Higher up, the Casa-Museo de Pizarro has informative displays (in Spanish) on the lives and adventures of the Pizarro family. At the top of the hill, Trujillo's castillo is an impressive though empty structure, primarily of Moorish origin. Entry is 200 ptas for each.

Places to Stay & Eat
Camas Boni (☎ 927 32 16 04, Calle Domingo de Ramos 7) is good value with small but well-kept singles/doubles from 2000/3000 ptas, and doubles with bathroom for 4500 ptas. *Casa Roque* (☎ 927 32 23 13, Calle Domingo de Ramos 30) has rooms at 3000/3500 ptas. *Hostal Nuria* (☎ 927 32 09 07, Plaza Mayor 27) has nice rooms with bath for 3300/5500 ptas. The friendly *Hostal La Cadena* (☎ 927 32 14 63, Plaza Mayor 8) is also good, at 5500 ptas for doubles with bath.

Don't miss *Restaurante La Troya* on Plaza Mayor if you're a meat-eater. The *menú* costs 1990 ptas, but it will save you from eating much else for the next few days. Portions are gigantic and you also get a large omelette and a salad for starters, and an extra main course later on! There are great tapas here too. Elsewhere on Plaza Mayor *Cafetería Nuria* has various dishes starting at 550 ptas. *Café-Bar El Escudo* on Plaza de Santiago is also moderately priced.

Getting There & Away
The bus station (☎ 927 32 12 02) is 500m south of Plaza Mayor, on Carretera de Mérida. At least six buses run daily to/from Cáceres (390 ptas, 45 minutes), Badajoz and Madrid (2350 ptas, 2½ to four hours), and four or more to/from Mérida (1020 ptas, 1¼ hours).

CÁCERES
pop 77,768
Cáceres is larger than Trujillo and has an even bigger old town, created in the 15th and 16th centuries and so perfectly preserved that it can seem lifeless at times. The old town is worth two visits – one by day to look around and one by night to soak up the atmosphere of accumulated ages.

The tourist office (☎ 927 24 63 47) is on Plaza Mayor. Ciberjust, on Calle Diego Maria Crehuet 7, is a good Internet cafe.

Things to See
The old town is still surrounded by walls and towers raised by the Almohads in the 12th century. Entering it from Plaza Mayor, you'll see ahead the fine 15th-century Iglesia de Santa María, Cáceres' cathedral. Any time from February to September, Santa María's tower will be topped by the ungainly nests of

SPAIN

SPAIN

the large storks which make their homes on every worthwhile vertical protuberance in the old city.

Many of the old city's churches and imposing medieval mansions can only be admired from outside, but you *can* enter the good **Museo de Cáceres** on Plaza de Veletas, housed in a 16th-century mansion built over a 12th-century Moorish cistern *(aljibe)* the museum's prized exhibit (closed Monday, 200 ptas, free for EU citizens). Also worth a look is the **Casa-Museo Árabe Yussuf Al-Borch** at Cuesta del Marqués 4, a private house decked out with oriental and Islamic trappings to capture the feel of Moorish times (200 ptas). The **Arco del Cristo** at the bottom of this street is a Roman gate.

Places to Stay

The best area to stay is around Plaza Mayor, though it gets noisy at weekends. *Pensión Márquez* (☎ 927 24 49 60, Calle de Gabriel y Galán 2), just off the low end of the plaza, is a friendly place with clean rooms at 1500/3000 ptas. *Hostal Castilla* (☎ 927 24 44 04, Calle de los Ríos Verdes 3), one block west, has rooms for 2000/4000 ptas. *Hostal Plaza de Italia* (☎ 927 24 77 60), away from the centre at Calle Constancia 12, has clean, pleasant rooms with shower for 3500/5500 ptas.

Places to Eat

Cafetería El Puchero (Plaza Mayor 33) is a popular hang-out with a huge variety of eating options, from good bocadillos (around 400 ptas) and raciónes to a la carte fare. *Cafetería El Pato*, a block down the arcade, has an upstairs restaurant with good three-course *menús*, including wine, for 1200 ptas to 2000 ptas plus IVA.

Restaurante El Figón de Eustaquio (Plaza de San Juan 12) serves good traditional extremeño food. The three-course *menú de la casa*, with wine, is 1700 ptas plus IVA.

Getting There & Away

Bus Minimum daily services from the bus station (☎ 927 23 25 50) include at least six to Trujillo (450 ptas) and Madrid (2420 ptas, 3½ hours); five each to Mérida (675 ptas, 1¼ hours) and Plasencia; three each to Salamanca (1705 ptas, three to four hours), Zafra and

Seville (2090 ptas, four hours) and two to Badajoz.

Train Three to five trains a day run to/from Madrid (from 2385 ptas, 3½ to five hours) and Mérida (one hour) and two or three each to/from Plasencia (1¼ hours), Badajoz (two hours) and Barcelona. The single daily train to Lisbon (from 4475 ptas, six hours) leaves in the middle of the night.

MÉRIDA
pop 51,830

Once the biggest city in Roman Spain, Mérida is home to more ruins of that age than anywhere else in the country. The tourist office (☎ 924 31 53 53) is at Avenida de José Álvarez Saenz de Buruaga, by the gates to the Roman theatre. Ware Nostrum is a funky Internet cafe on Calle del Baños.

Things to See

For 800 ptas (half-price for students and EU citizens) you can get a ticket that gives you entry to the **Teatro Romano**, **Anfiteatro**, the **Casa del Anfiteatro**, the **Casa Romana del Mithraeo**, the **Alcazaba**, **Iglesia de Santa Eulalia** and the **Arqueologica de Moreria**. Entry to just the Teatro Romano and Anfiteatro is 600 ptas. The theatre was built in 15 BC and the gladiators' ring, or Anfiteatro, seven years later. Combined they could hold 20,000 spectators. Various other reminders of imperial days are scattered about town, including the **Puente Romano**, at 792m one of the longest the Romans ever built.

Places to Stay & Eat

Pensión El Arco (☎ 924 31 83 21, Calle de Miguel de Cervantes 16) is great value and deservedly popular with backpackers; rooms cost 1800/3500 ptas with shared bathroom. *Hostal Bueno* (☎ 924 30 29 77, Calle Calvario 9) is also good at 2500/4500 ptas.

Casa Benito, on Calle de San Francisco, is a great old-style wood-panelled bar and restaurant, decked with bullfighting memorabilia, serving local fare at reasonable prices.

Three good eateries line up on Calle de Felix Valverde Lillo. *Restaurante El Briz*, at No 5, does a great *montado de lomo* (pork loin sandwich) for 350 ptas and has a restaurant at the back with a *menú* for 1350 ptas.

Next door, there's the upmarket *Restaurante Nicolás* with a 2000 ptas *menú*. *Restaurante Antillano* at No 15 is popular with locals and has a *menú* for just 1200 ptas.

Getting There & Away

From the bus station (☎ 924 37 14 04) at least seven daily buses run to Badajoz (680 ptas), Seville (1550 ptas to 1590 ptas) and Madrid (from 2755 ptas), and at least four to Cáceres (675 ptas) and Trujillo (820 ptas).

At least four trains run a day to Badajoz, and two or more to Cáceres, Ciudad Real, Madrid (2945 ptas, five to six hours).

NORTH-EAST EXTREMADURA

From Plasencia, the green, almost Eden-like valleys of La Vera, Valle del Jerte and Valle del Ambroz stretch north-east into the Sierra de Gredos and its western extensions. Watered by rushing mountain streams called *gargantas*, and dotted with medieval villages, these valleys offer some excellent walking routes and attract just enough visitors to provide a good network of places to stay.

Information

The Editorial Alpina booklet *Valle del Jerte, Valle del Ambroz, La Vera* includes a 1:50,000 map of the area showing walking routes. Try to get it from a map or bookshop before you come; if not, the tourist office in Cabezuela del Valle may have copies.

There are tourist offices at Plasencia (☎ 927 42 21 59), Jaraíz de la Vera (☎ 927 17 05 87), Jarandilla de la Vera (☎ 927 56 04 60), Cabezuela del Valle (☎ 927 47 25 58) and Hervás (☎ 927 47 36 18). Most sizable villages have banks.

Things to See & Do

La Vera About halfway up the valley, **Cuacos de Yuste** has its share of narrow village streets with half-timbered houses leaning at odd angles. Up a side road, 2km north-west, is the **Monasterio de Yuste**, to which in 1557 Carlos I, once the world's most powerful man, retreated for his dying years. Guided tours of the simple royal chambers and the monastery church in Spanish are 100 ptas.

The road continues past the monastery to **Garganta la Olla**, another typically picturesque village, from where you can head

over the 1269m **Puerto del Piornal** pass into the Valle del Jerte.

Jarandilla de la Vera is a bigger village, with a 15th-century fortress-church on the main square (below the main road), and a parador occupying a castle-palace where Carlos I stayed while Yuste was being readied for him. Of the longer hikes, the Ruta de Carlos V (see the following Valle del Jerte section) is one of the most enticing. If you want to do it in reverse, ask for directions at Camping Jaranda.

Valle del Jerte This valley grows half of Spain's cherries and turns into a sea of white at blossom time in April. **Piornal**, high on the south flank, is a good base for walks along the Sierra de Tormantos. In the bottom of the valley, **Cabezuela del Valle** has a particularly medieval main street. A 35km road crosses from just north of here over the 1430m Puerto de Honduras pass to Hervás in the Valle del Ambroz. For hikers, the PR-10 trail climbs roughly parallel, to the south. From **Jerte** you can walk into the beautiful **Parque Natural de la Garganta de los Infiernos**.

Tornavacas, near the head of the valley, is the starting point of the **Ruta de Carlos V**, a 28km marked trail following the route by which Carlos I (who was also Carlos V of the Holy Roman Empire) was carried over the mountains to Jarandilla on the way to Yuste. It can be walked in one long day just as Carlos' bearers did.

Valle del Ambroz Towards the head of the valley, **Hervás**, a small pleasant town, has the best surviving 15th-century Barrio Judío (Jewish quarter) in Extremadura, where many Jews took refuge in hope of avoiding the Inquisition.

Places to Stay & Eat

There are *camping grounds* – many with fine riverside positions – in several villages including Cuacos de Yuste, Hervás, Jarandilla de la Vera and Jerte. Most are only open from March/April to September/October. There are free *zonas de acampada*, camping areas with no facilities, at Garganta la Olla and Piornal.

In Plasencia, *Hostal La Muralla* (☎ 927 41 38 74, Calle de Berrozana 6) charges from 2000/2500 ptas to 3500/4000 ptas plus IVA for a range of rooms. On the main road in Cuacos de Yuste, *Pensión Sol* (☎ 927 17 22 41) has good rooms for 1900/2900 ptas, and a restaurant. In Jarandilla de la Vera, **Hostal Jaranda** (☎ 927 56 02 06, *Aventda de Soledad Vega Ortiz 101*), on the main road, has rooms with bath for 45000/7400 ptas plus IVA, and an excellent-value three-course *menú* with wine for 1200 ptas plus IVA.

In Piornal, **Pensión Los Piornos** (☎ 927 47 60 55, *Plaza de las Eras*), near the bus stop, charges 2000/4000 ptas.

In Cabezuela del Valle, the good **Hotel Aljama** (☎ 927 47 22 91, *Calle de Federico Bajo s/n*), almost touching the church across the street, has nice rooms for 3000/4900 ptas plus IVA. There are numerous places to eat and drink on nearby Calle del Hondón. **Hostal Puerto de Tornavacas** (☎ 927 19 40 97), a couple of kilometres up the N-110 from Tornavacas, is an inn-style place with rooms for 2500/4600 ptas, and a restaurant specialising in extremeño food.

Getting There & Away

Your own wheels are a big help but if you do use buses, you can walk over the mountains without worrying about how to get back to your vehicle! The following bus services run Monday to Friday, with much reduced services on weekends.

A Mirat bus from Cáceres and Plasencia to Talayuela, stopping at the villages on the C-501 in La Vera. One or two Mirat buses run from Plasencia to Garganta la Olla and Losar de la Vera. From Madrid's Estación Sur de Autobuses, Doaldi runs daily buses to La Vera.

From Plasencia, a daily bus heads for Piornal, and four a day run up the Valle del Jerte to Tornavacas.

Los Tres Pilares runs two buses between Plasencia and Hervás. Enatcar has a few services between Cáceres, Plasencia and Salamanca via the Valle del Ambroz, stopping at the Empalme de Hervás junction on the N-630, 2km from the town.

Galicia, Asturias & Cantabria

Galicia has been spared the mass tourism that has reached many other parts of Spain. Its often wild coast is indented with a series of majestic estuaries – the Rías Altas and Rías Bajas – which hide some of the prettiest and least known beaches and coves in Spain. Inland are rolling green hills dotted with picturesque farmhouses.

In winter, Galicia can be freezing, but in summer it has one of the most agreeable climates in Europe, although you must expect some rain.

The coasts of the still greener and at least as beautiful Asturias and Cantabria regions, east of Galicia, are dotted with fine sandy beaches and some picturesque villages and towns. Inland are the beautiful Picos de Europa mountains.

SANTIAGO DE COMPOSTELA
pop 87,000

This beautiful small city marks the end of the Camino de Santiago, a name given to several major medieval pilgrim routes from as far away as France, still followed today by plenty of the faithful – and plenty who just fancy a good long walk or bike ride. Thanks to its university, Santiago is a lively city almost any time, but it's at its most festive around 25 July, the Feast of Santiago (St James). Its regional tourist office (☎ 98158 40 81) at Rúa do Vilar 43 opens 10 am to 2 pm and 4 to 7 pm Monday to Friday, 11 am to 2 pm and 5 to 7 pm Saturday, and 11 am to 2 pm Sunday.

Things to See & Do

The goal of the Camino de Santiago is the **cat-edral** on magnificent **Praza do Obradoiro**. Under the main altar lies the supposed tomb of Santiago Apóstol (St James the Apostle). It's believed the saint's remains were buried here in the 1st century AD and rediscovered in 813, after which he grew into the patron saint of the Christian Reconquista, his tomb attracting streams of pilgrims from all over Western Europe. The cathedral is a superb Romanesque creation of the 11th to 13th centuries, with later decorative flourishes, and its masterpiece is the Pórtico de la Gloria inside the west facade.

Santiago's compact old town is a work of art, and a walk around the cathedral will take you through some of its most inviting squares. It's also good to stroll in the beautifully landscaped **Carballeira de Santa Susana** park

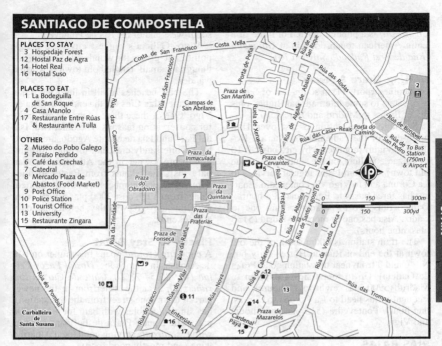

SANTIAGO DE COMPOSTELA

PLACES TO STAY
3 Hospedaje Forest
12 Hostal Paz de Agra
14 Hotel Real
16 Hostal Suso

PLACES TO EAT
1 La Bodeguilla
de San Roque
4 Casa Manolo
17 Restaurante Entre Rúas
& Restaurante A Tulla

OTHER
2 Museo do Pobo Galego
5 Paraíso Perdido
6 Café das Crechas
7 Catedral
8 Mercado Plaza de
Abastos (Food Market)
9 Post Office
10 Police Station
11 Tourist Office
13 University
15 Restaurante Zingara

SPAIN

south-west of the cathedral. Just north-east of the old city, off Porta do Camino, an impressive old convent houses the **Museo do Pobo Galego**, covering Galician life from fishing through music and crafts to traditional costume (open daily, free).

Places to Stay

Santiago is jammed with cheap pensiones, but many are full with students. A quiet central option with decent rooms is *Hospedaje Forest* (☎ 981 57 08 11, Callejón de Don Abril Ares 7) where singles/doubles start at 1600/2900 ptas. The attractive *Hostal Paz de Agra* (☎ 981 58 90 45, Rúa da Calderería 37) is a spotless old house with rooms for 2500/4000 ptas (3500/5000 ptas with private bath) – inquire at Restaurante Zingara, Rúa de Cardenal Payá. The popular little *Hostal Suso* (☎ 981 58 66 11, Rúa do Vilar 65) has comfortable modern doubles with bath for 5350 ptas. *Hotel Real* (☎ 981 56 92 90, Rúa da Calderería 49) provides good-sized singles/doubles with mod cons for 7500/10,500 ptas.

Places to Eat

Popular with readers of travel guides is *Casa Manolo (Rúa Travesa 27)*, which has a good-value set meal for 750 ptas.

A couple of medium-priced places that have some good dishes are *Restaurante Entre Rúas* and *Restaurante A Tulla*, in the tiny square on the lane Entrerúas. You should get away with having to spend around 1500 ptas.

The highly popular *La Bodeguilla de San Roque (Rúa de San Roque 13)* offers excellent, eclectic and moderately-priced fare, including enormous salads (550 ptas) and good *revoltos* (scrambled egg) concoctions.

Entertainment

For traditional Celtic music, Galician-style (sometimes live), head for *Café das Crechas (Via Sacra 3)*. *Paraíso Perdido* on the tiny square of Entrealtares is one of Santiago's oldest bars. The local drinking and dancing scene is centred in the new town, especially around Praza Roxa about 800m south-west of the cathedral. *Black* (*Avenida de Rosalía de Castro s/n*) is a popular disco. For more of a Latin American touch, look in at *Guiayaba* (*Rúa de Frei Rodendo Salvado 16*).

Getting There & Away

Lavacolla airport, 11km south-east of Santiago, caters to some international flights, plus direct flights to Madrid and Barcelona.

Santiago's bus station is just over 1km north-east of the cathedral, on Rúa de Rodriguez Viguri (connected by city bus No 10 to Praza de Galicia, on the south edge of the old town). Castromil runs regular services to La Coruña and to Vigo via Pontevedra. Enatcar has three buses to Barcelona (8½ hours). Dainco runs two to Salamanca and one to Cádiz. Alsa has one or more to Madrid (5135 ptas, nine hours).

The train station is 600m south of the old town at the end of Rúa do Horreo (city bus Nos 6 and 9 from near the station go to Praza de Galicia). Up to four trains a day run to Madrid (5900 ptas, eight to 11 hours), and frequent trains head to La Coruña (515 ptas, one hour), Pontevedra (515 ptas, one hour) and Vigo.

RÍAS BAJAS

The grandest of Galicia's estuaries are the four Rías Bajas, on its west-facing coast. From north to south these are the Ría de Muros, Ría de Arousa, Ría de Pontevedra and Ría de Vigo. All are dotted with low-key resorts, fishing villages and good beaches.

Tourist offices in the region include one at Calle del General Mola 3, Pontevedra (☎ 986 85 08 14) and another by the Estación Marítima (port) in Vigo (☎ 986 43 05 77).

Things to See & Do

On Ría de Arousa, **Isla de Arousa** is connected to the mainland by a long bridge. Its inhabitants live mainly from fishing and some of the beaches facing the mainland are very pleasant and protected, with comparatively warm water. **Cambados**, a little farther south, is a peaceful seaside town with a magnificent plaza surrounded by evocative little streets.

The small city of **Pontevedra** has managed to preserve a classic medieval centre backing on to the Río Lérez, ideal for wandering around. There are some good, tranquil beaches

around the villages of **Aldán** and **Hío**, near the south-west end of the Ría de Pontevedra.

Vigo, Galicia's biggest city, is a disappointment given its wonderful setting, although its small, tangled old town is worth a wander.

The best beaches of all in the Rías Bajas are on the **Islas Cíes** off the end of the Ría de Vigo. One of these three islands is off limits for conservation reasons. The other two, Isla del Faro and Isla de Monte Agudo, are linked by a white sandy crescent, together forming a 9km breakwater in the Atlantic. You can only visit the islands from Easter to mid-September, and numbers are strictly limited. Boats from Vigo cost 2000 ptas return; from mid-June they go every day, before that, only at weekends.

Places to Stay & Eat

A *camping ground* opens in summer on Isla de Arousa. In Cambados, *Hostal Pazos Feijoo* (☎ 986 54 28 10, *Calle de Curros Enríquez 1*), near the waterfront in the newer part of town (one street from the bus station), has singles/doubles with bath for 4000/6000 ptas. The square Praza de Fefiñáns swarms with *restaurants* serving good local Albariño wine (and mostly good food).

In Pontevedra, *Casa Alicia* (☎ 986 85 70 79, *Avenida de Santa María 5*) and *Casa Maruja* (☎ 986 85 49 01, *Praza de Santa María 12*), round the corner, are good. The former has homy doubles for around 3000 ptas; the latter charges 3000/4000 ptas for spotless rooms. You can eat cheaply at *O' Merlo* (*Avenida de Santa María 4*), with an unbeatable 1000-ptas *menú*.

Hostal Stop (☎ 986 32 94 75) in tiny Hío has rooms for 3000/5000 ptas in summer.

In Vigo, *Hotel Pantón* (☎ 986 22 42 70, *Rúa de Lepanto 18*) has rooms with bath and TV for 3300/5900 ptas plus IVA in high summer. Old Vigo is laced with tapas bars and eateries of all descriptions. *Restaurante Fay-Bistes* (*Rúa Real 7*) has a set lunch for 1000 ptas and good tapas.

Camping is the only option to stay on the Islas Cíes. You must book (575 ptas per person and per tent, plus IVA) at the office in the *estación marítima* in Vigo. Places are limited. You can then organise a round-trip boat ticket for the days you require.

Getting There & Away

Pontevedra and Vigo are the area's transport hubs, with a reasonable network of local buses fanning out from them. Both are well served by buses and trains from Santiago de Compostela and La Coruña, and Vigo has services from more distant places like Madrid and Barcelona, as well as Iberia flights from those cities. Three trains a day run from Vigo to Porto in Portugal (3½ hours).

LA CORUÑA

pop 252,000

La Coruña (A Coruña in Galician) is an attractive port city with decent beaches and a wonderful seafront promenade, the Paseo Marítimo. The older part of town, the **Ciudad Vieja**, is huddled on the headland north of the port, while the most famous attraction, the **Torre de Hércules** lighthouse, originally built by the Romans (open 10 am to 6 pm or later, daily), caps the headland's northern end. The north-west side of the isthmus joining the headland to the mainland is lined with sandy **beaches**, more of which stretch along the 30km sweep of coast west of the city.

Places to Stay & Eat

Calle de Riego de Agua, a block back from the waterfront Avenida de la Marina on the southern side of the isthmus, is a good spot to find lodgings. *Pensión La Alianza (☎ 981 22 81 14, Calle de Riego de Agua 8)* charges 2200/3800 ptas for average singles/doubles. A step up is nearby *Hostal La Provinciana (☎ 981 22 04 00, Rúa Nueva 7-9)*, with rooms for 4500/6500 ptas plus IVA.

Calle de la Franja has several good places to eat. *Casa Jesusa* at No 8 offers a tasty set lunch for 1350 ptas.

Getting There & Away

Daily trains and buses run to Santiago de Compostela, Vigo, Santander, León, Madrid and Barcelona.

RÍAS ALTAS

North-east of La Coruña stretches the alternately pretty and awesome coast called the Rías Altas. This has some of the most dramatic scenery in Spain, and beaches that in good weather are every bit as inviting as those on the better known Rías Bajas. Spots to head for include the medieval towns of **Betanzos**, **Pontedeume** and **Viveiro** (all with budget accommodation), the tremendous cliffs of **Cabo Ortegal** and the **beaches** between there and Viveiro. Buses from La Coruña and Santiago de Compostela will get you into the area. After that you'll need local buses and the occasional walk or lift.

PICOS DE EUROPA

This small region straddling Asturias, Cantabria and Castilla y León has some of the finest walking country in Spain. The spectacular mountain and gorge scenery ensures a continual flow of visitors from all over Europe and beyond. The Picos begin only 20km from the coast, and are little more than 40km long and 25km wide. They comprise three limestone massifs: the eastern Macizo Ándara, with a summit of 2444m, the western Macizo El Cornión, rising to 2596m, and the central Macizo Los Urrieles, reaching 2648m.

The Picos are a national park, with its main information office (☎ 985 84 86 14) at Casa Dago, Avenida de Covadonga 43, Cangas de Onís. Plenty of information on walks is available here and at several other tourist and information offices around the Picos. Trekkers will find Lonely Planet's *Walking in Spain* useful. Good maps available locally are Adrados Ediciones' *Picos de Europa* (1:80,000) and *Picos de Europa Macizos Central y Oriental* and *Picos de Europa Macizo Occidental* (1:25,000).

The main access towns for the Picos are Cangas de Onís, Arenas de Cabrales and Potes. A good starting point for walks is **Lago Enol**, a lake 7km up from Covadonga, above Cangas de Onís in the north-west Picos. Another, though without public transport, is **Sotres** in the north-east.

Places to Stay & Eat

A few hundred metres from Lago de Enol, *Refugio Vega de Enol (☎ 985 84 85 76)* has bunks for 500 ptas and meals. You can camp free nearby. In Sotres, *Pensión La Perdiz (☎ 985 94 50 11)* charges 3100/4000 ptas for singles/doubles with private bath (less without). *Casa Cipriano (☎ 985 94 50 24)*, across the road, is a little more expensive. The good clean *Albergue Peña Castil (☎ 985 94 50 70)* offers bunks for 1100 ptas

SPAIN

to 1300 ptas and, like the Cipriano, has a restaurant.

In Espinama (for a southern approach), the attractive *Hostal Puente Deva* (☎ *942 73 66 58*) has rooms for 3400/5000 ptas and a restaurant.

Cangas de Onís, Arenas de Cabrales and Potes all have a wide range of accommodation.

Getting There & Away

From the roads encircling the Picos, three main routes lead into the heart of the mountains: from Cangas de Onís to Covadonga and Lago Enol; from Arenas de Cabrales to Poncebos and Sotres; and from Potes to Espinama and Fuente Dé.

A few buses from Santander, Oviedo and León serve the three main access towns. Buses also run from Cangas de Onís to Covadonga, from Covadonga to Lago de Enol (July, August only), and (late June to mid-September) from Potes to Espinama and Fuente Dé.

SANTANDER
pop 192,000

Santander, capital of Cantabria, is a modern, cosmopolitan city with wide waterfront boulevards, leafy parks and crowded beaches. The Semana Grande fiesta in late July is a pretty wild party, but accommodation all along the north coast in the second half of July and August needs to be booked ahead.

The city tourist office (☎ 942 21 61 20) is in the harbourside Jardines de Pereda, and the regional one (☎ 942 31 07 08) is nearby at Plaza Porticada 5.

Things to See & Do

Santander's main attractions are its beaches and its bars. As you come round to the main beach, El Sardinero, on bus No 1 from the central post office, you may notice an uncanny resemblance to Bondi Beach in Australia, with surfers out in force by mid-March, despite the cold. The streets behind El Sardinero are lined with some of Spain's most expensive real estate.

Places to Stay

Camping Bellavista (☎ *942 39 15 30, Avenida del Faro s/n*), out near the lighthouse about 1.5km beyond El Sardinero beach, is open all year.

The high-season rates given here fall a lot from October to May/June. *Pensión La Porticada* (☎ *942 22 78 17, Calle Méndez Núñez 6*), near the train and bus stations and ferry dock, has reasonable rooms for 4000/5000 ptas. Try for one overlooking the bay. Nearby and much smarter is *Hotel México* (☎ *942 21 24 50, Calle Calderón de la Barca 3*), charging 8000/12,800 ptas plus IVA.

Pensión La Corza (☎ *942 21 29 50, Calle Hernán Cortés 25*) is nicely located on a pleasant square, Plaza de Pombo. Sizable, quirkily furnished rooms cost from 4750 ptas to 6000 ptas a double. Just behind Playa del Sardinero, a good-value choice is *Hostal Carlos III* (☎/*fax 942 27 16 16, Avenida Reina Victoria 135*), costing 6500/8500 ptas plus IVA.

Places to Eat

The older part of town has lots of highly atmospheric old mesones, which here refers to traditional wine bars also serving food. *Mesón Goya* (*Calle Daóiz y Velarde 25*) is typical and one of the more economical – salmon or a beef fillet *a la plancha* will cost you 800 ptas to 1000 ptas. A cavernous classic, with no name outside and more expensive, is *La Conveniente* (*Calle Gómez Oreña 9*). Near the latter on Plaza de Cañadio, *Bar Cañadio* serves first-class seafood and local specialities, with raciónes from 700 ptas to 1100 ptas in the bar and main dishes in its restaurant behind starting at 1500 ptas.

Near El Sardinero beach, *La Caña* (*Calle Joaquin Costa 45*) has an excellent *menú* for 1400 ptas.

Entertainment

In the old town, Calle Río de la Pila – and to a marginally lesser extent Plaza de Cañadio – teem with bars of all descriptions. In summer, there's quite a good scene in El Sardinero along the main drag.

Getting There & Away

Santander is one of the major entry points to Spain, thanks to its ferry link with Plymouth, England (see Getting There & Away at the start of this chapter).

The ferry terminal and train and bus stations are all in the centre of Santander, within 300m of each other. Several daily buses head east to

Bilbao, San Sebastián (1790 ptas, 2½ hours) and Irún, and west to Oviedo (1710 ptas) and Gijón. Some stop at lesser places along the coast. Six a day go to Madrid (3300 ptas) via Burgos. Others run to Pamplona, Zaragoza, Barcelona, Salamanca and elsewhere.

Trains to Bilbao (925 ptas, 2½ hours, three daily) and Oviedo are run by FEVE, a private line which does not accept rail passes. From Oviedo FEVE continues into north-east Galicia. Trains to Madrid, Castilla y León and the rest of Galicia are run by RENFE, so rail passes are valid. To Madrid there are three trains most days (from 4300 ptas, 5½ to 8¾ hours), via Ávila.

SANTILLANA DEL MAR
pop 1030
Despite good, sandy beaches and some appealing villages along the coasts, the least missable other destination in Cantabria or Asturias is the marvellously preserved medieval village of Santillana del Mar, 30km west of Santander.

The Romanesque carvings in the cloister of the **Colegiata de Santa Julia** church are Santillana's finest works of art. There's also a **Museo de la Inquisición** (Inquisition Museum) with an alarming collection of instruments of torture and death.

Two kilometres south-west of Santillana are the world-famous **Cuevas de Altamira**, full of wonderful 14,000-year-old Stone Age animal paintings. A maximum of 20 people a day are allowed into the caves and the waiting list is three years long.

Contact the regional tourist office in Santander to find out how to join the waiting list, but for those of us who can't wait so long, a new museum at the caves, complete with full-scale replica of the caves, was due to open in 2001.

Places to Stay & Eat
Santillana has heaps of accommodation but little in the real budget range. An excellent choice is *Hospedaje Octavio* (☎ 942 81 81 99, Plaza Las Arenas 6), where charming rooms with timber-beam ceilings and private bath are 3500/5500 ptas.

Casa Cossío, about the nearest restaurant to the Colegiata, serves a good range of fare, with a *menú* for 1150 ptas.

Getting There & Away
Several daily buses call in at Santillana en route between Santander and San Vicente de la Barquera, farther west.

País Vasco, Navarra & Aragón

The Basque people have lived in Spain's País Vasco (Basque Country, or Euskadi in the Basque language), Navarra and the adjoining Pays Basque in south-western France for thousands of years. They have their own ancient language (Euskara), a distinct physical appearance, a rich culture and a proud history.

Along with this strong sense of identity has come, among a significant minority of Basques in Spain, a desire for independence. The Basque nationalist movement was born in the 19th century. During the Franco years the Basque people were brutally repressed and Euskadi ta Askatasuna (ETA), a separatist movement, began its terrorist activities. With Spain's changeover to democracy in the late 1970s, the País Vasco was granted a large degree of autonomy, but ETA has pursued its violent campaign.

ETA terrorism may be a deterrent to tourism but the País Vasco is a beautiful region. Although the Bilbao area is heavily industrialised, the region has a spectacular coastline, a green and mountainous interior and the elegance of San Sebastián and the Guggenheim museum in Bilbao itself. Another great reason to visit is to sample the delights of Basque cuisine, considered the best in Spain.

South-east of the País Vasco, the Navarra and Aragón regions reach down from the Pyrenees into drier, more southern lands. Navarra has a high Basque population and its capital is Pamplona, home of the Sanfermines festival with its running of the bulls.

The Aragón Pyrenees offer the best walking and skiing on the Spanish side of this mountain range. There are half a dozen decent ski resorts. The most spectacular walking (day hikes included) is in the Parque Nacional de Ordesa y Monte Perdido, whose main access point is the village of Torla. During Easter week and from July to September you are

SPAIN

forbidden to drive the few kilometres from Torla into the park – a shuttle bus service for a maximum 1800 people a day is provided instead (there's no limit on people walking into the park). Weatherwise the best months up there are late June to mid-September.

SAN SEBASTIÁN
pop 180,000

San Sebastián (Donostia in Basque) is a stunning city. Famed as a ritzy resort for wealthy Spaniards, it has also been a stronghold of Basque nationalist feeling since well before Franco. The surprisingly relaxed town curves round the beautiful Bahía de la Concha. Those who live here consider themselves the luckiest people in Spain, and after spending a few days on the perfect crescent-shaped beaches in preparation for the wild evenings, you may begin to understand why.

Information

The municipal tourist office (☎ 943 48 11 66) is at Boulevard Reina Regente 8 (closed Sunday afternoon). The regional tourist office (☎ 943 02 31 50) at Paseo de los Fueros 1 is open daily.

The main post office is on Calle de Urdaneta, behind the cathedral. Donosti-Net, Calle de Embeltrán 2 in the old town *(Parte Vieja)*, is a good Internet cafe. Lavomatique, Calle de Iñigo 14, is a rarity in Spain – a good self-service laundrette. A full load of washing and drying costs about 1000 ptas.

Things to See

The **Playa de la Concha** and **Playa de Ondarreta** are among the most beautiful city beaches in Spain. You can reach **Isla de Santa Clara**, in the middle of the bay, by boat from the harbour. In summer, you can also swim out to rafts anchored in the bay. The Playa de la Zurriola (also known as Playa de Gros), east of the Río Urumea, is less crowded and popular with both swimmers and surfers.

San Sebástian's revamped **Aquarium** has 10 large tanks teeming with tropical fish, morays, sharks and other finned creatures. There are also exhibits on pirates, Basque explorers and related themes. It's open 10 am to 10 pm daily (to 8 pm in winter); 1100 ptas. The nearby **Museo Naval** is interesting too

but you need to read Spanish to fully appreciate the displays (200 ptas).

Museo de San Telmo, in a 16th-century monastery on Plaza de Zuloaga, has a varied collection with a heavy emphasis on Basque paintings. A highlight is the chapel whose lavish wall frescoes chronicle Basque history. Museum hours are 10.30 am to 1.30 pm and 4 to 8 pm, closed Sunday afternoon and Monday; free.

Overlooking Bahía de la Concha from the east is **Monte Urgull**, topped with a statue of Christ that enjoys sweeping views. It only takes 30 minutes to walk up – a stairway starts from Plaza de Zuloaga in the old town.

The views from the summit of Monte Igueldo are better still. You can save your legs by catching the funicular to the **Parque de Atracciones** (amusement park). At the foot of the hill, at Punta Torrepea, right in the bay, is Eduardo Chillida's abstract iron sculpture *Peine de los Vientos* (Wind Combs).

Places to Stay

As in much of northern Spain, rooms are hard to find in July and August, so arrive early or book ahead, and be aware of huge seasonal price differences. Prices given here are for peak periods.

Camping Igueldo (☎ 943 21 45 02), open year-round, is out beyond Monte Igueldo but connected to the centre by bus No 16. The HI hostel *Albergue La Sirena* (☎ 943 31 02 68, ✆ udala-youthhostel@donostia.org, Paseo de Igueldo 25) offers bed and breakfast for 2000/2255 ptas children/adults. Curfew is midnight during the week, 2 am on weekends.

In the lively Parte Vieja, consider yourself lucky to score a room at the superfriendly *Pensión San Lorenzo* (☎ 943 42 55 16, Calle de San Lorenzo 2) whose nicely decorated doubles with bath cost 3500 ptas. Other assets include metered Internet access and kitchen use (off-season only). Also good is *Pensión Loinaz* (☎ 943 42 67 14, Calle de San Lorenzo 17), which has updated bathrooms and charges 4000/5500 ptas singles/doubles.

Pensión Aussie (☎ 943 42 28 74, Calle San Jerónimo 23) works pretty much like a hostel. Beds in two to four-bed rooms, some quite nicely decorated, are 2000 ptas. It's popular with backpackers, as is *Pensión San*

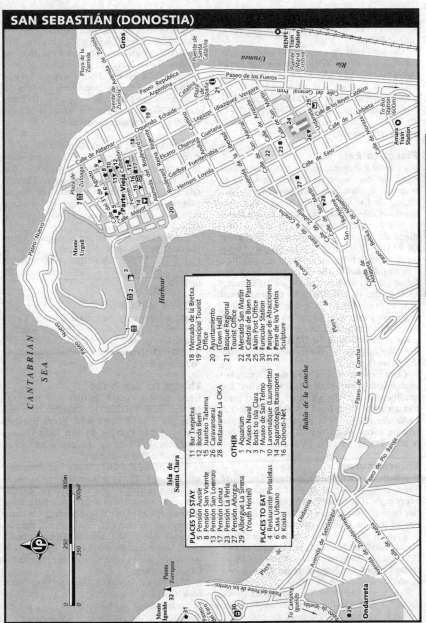

SAN SEBASTIÁN (DONOSTIA)

PLACES TO STAY
5 Pensión Aussie
8 Pensión San Vicente
13 Pensión San Lorenzo
17 Pensión Loinaz
23 Pensión La Perla
27 Pensión Añorga
29 Albergue La Sirena
   (Youth Hostel)

PLACES TO EAT
4 Restaurante Portaletas
6 Casa Urbano
9 Koskol
11 Bar Txepetxa
12 Borda Berri
15 Juantxo Taberna
26 Caravanserai
28 Restaurante La OKA

OTHER
1 Aquarium
2 Museo Naval
3 Boats to Isla Clara
7 Museo de San Telmo
10 Lavomatique (Laundrette)
14 Sagardotegia Itxaropena
16 Donosti-Net

18 Mercado de la Bretxa
19 Municipal Tourist
   Office
20 Ayuntamiento
   (Town Hall)
21 Basque Regional
   Tourist Office
22 Mercado San Martín
24 Catedral de Buen Pastor
25 Main Post Office
30 Funicular Station
31 Parque de Atracciones
32 Peine de los Vientos
   Sculpture

Vicente (☎ 943 42 29 77, Calle San Vicente 7) where rather bare-bone rooms cost 3000/5000 ptas.

The area near the cathedral is more peaceful than the Parte Vieja. *Pensión La Perla (☎ 943 42 81 23, Calle de Loyola 10)* has excellent rooms with shower and WC for 3500/5500 ptas; some overlook the cathedral. Also recommended is *Pensión Añorga (☎ 943 46 79 45, Calle de Easo 12)* whose motherly owner rents rooms for 4000/5000 ptas.

Places to Eat

It's almost a shame to sit down in a restaurant when the bars have such good tapas, or as they are known here, *pinchos*. Many bars cluster in the Parte Vieja, where *Bar Txepetxa (Calle Pescadería 5)* and *Borda Berri (Calle Fermín Calbetrón 12)* are recommended. Also here is *Juantxo Taberna (☎ 943 42 74 05, Calle de Embeltrán 6)*, famous for its cheap, super-sized sandwiches. The tiny *Koskol (Calle de Iñigo 5)* has a delicious, generous lunch *menú* for 1000 ptas.

A young crowd flocks to *Caravanserai* next to the cathedral, a trendy bistro whose extensive menu runs the gamut from burgers to pasta to sandwiches. A fun vegetarian place is *Restaurante La OKA (Calle de San Martín 43)*, open for lunch daily (plus Saturday dinner).

Casa Urbano at No 17 is a more upmarket choice with a well-entrenched reputation for quality seafood. The set lunch is 3000 ptas. *Restaurante Portaletas (☎ 943 42 42 72, Calle del Puerto 8)* is popular with locals. Dining takes place beneath heavy timber beams. The set lunch is 1500 ptas.

Entertainment

San Sebastián's nightlife is great. The Parte Vieja comes alive at around 8 pm nearly every night. The Spanish habit of bar-hopping has been perfected here and one street alone has 28 bars in a 300m stretch!

Typical drinks are a zurrito (beer in a small glass) and *txacolí* (a tart Basque wine). If you'd like to have a swig of Basque cider (*sidra*), head for *Sagardotegia Itxaropena (Calle de Embeltran 16)*.

Whenever the Parte Vieja quietens down around 1 or 2 am, the crowd heads to Calle de los Reyes Católicos behind the cathedral.

Getting There & Away

Bus The bus station is a 20-minute walk south of the Parte Vieja on Plaza de Pío XII; ticket offices are along the streets north of the station. Buses leave for destinations all over Spain. PESA has half-hourly express service to Bilbao (1120 ptas, one hour), while La Roncalesa goes to Pamplona up to 10 times daily (790 ptas, two hours). Buses to Madrid (3800 ptas) run nine times daily.

Train The RENFE train station is across the river on Paseo de Francia. There are daily trains to Madrid (6400 ptas, eight hours) and to Barcelona (5000 ptas, 8¼ hours). There is one daily direct train to Paris and several others that require a change at Hendaye (France). Other destinations include Salamanca and Lisbon.

Eusko Tren is a private company (international passes not valid) running trains to Hendaye (115 ptas) and Bilbao (900 ptas, 2¾ hours) departing from Amara station on Calle de Easo.

COSTA VASCA

Spain's ruggedly beautiful Costa Vasca (Basque Coast) is one of its least touristy coastal regions. A combination of rainy weather, chilly seas and terrorism tends to put some people off.

Things to See & Do

Between the French border and San Sebastián, **Fuenterrabia** (Hondarribia) is a picturesque fishing town with good beaches nearby, while **Pasajes de San Juan** (Pasaia Donibane) has a pretty old section and some good-value fish restaurants.

The coastal stretch between San Sebastián and Bilbao to the west is considered some of the finest **surfing** territory in Europe. **Zarauz** (Zarautz), about 15km west of San Sebastián, stages a round of the World Surfing Championship each September. Farther west, the picturesque village of **Guetaria** (Getaria) has a small beach, but the main attraction is just in wandering around the narrow streets and the fishing harbour.

Mundaca (Mundaka), 12km north of Guernica (Gernika), is a surfing town. For much of the year, surfers and beach bums hang around waiting for the legendary 'left-hander' to

Limestone cliffs, Prades, Catalunya, Spain

JON DAVISON

Fisherman, Mallorca, Spain

JON DAVISON

Castell de Belver, Mallorca, Spain

JON DAVISON

San Salvador, Arta, Balearic Islands

JON DAVISON

DAMIAN SIMONIS

Plaza de España, Seville, Spain

DAN HERRICK

Moorings in Cala Figuera harbour, Spain

MARK HONAN

International Balloon Week, Vaud, near Lake Geneva, Switzerland

MARTIN MOOS

Schauffhausen, Switzerland

MARTIN MOOS

The start of Swiss chocolate

MARTIN MOOS

Wine restaurant, Zürich

CHRIS MELLOR

The Matterhorn and surrounds, Swiss Alps

break. When it does, it's one of the longest you'll ever see! The Mundaka Surf Shop rents gear and also gives surfing lessons. Food and accommodation are hopelessly overpriced in this town, even in the off-season. Your best bet is *Camping Portuondo* (☎/fax 94 687 77 01), about 1km south of town, which has lovely terraced grounds and also rents bungalows.

Getting Around
The coastal road is best explored by car. If you don't have your own transport, there are buses from San Sebastián to Zarauz and Guetaria, and from Bilbao to Guernica. From Guernica you can take a bus to Bermeo which will drop you in Mundaca. Eusko Tren from Bilbao and San Sebástian also serves a few coastal towns.

BILBAO
pop 360,000
Once the industrial heart of the north, Bilbao has spruced itself up and, since 1997, created for itself a tourist gold mine – the US$100 million **Museo Guggenheim de Arte Contemporáneo**. Designed by US architect Frank Gehry, this fantastical, swirling structure was inspired in part by the anatomy of a fish and the hull of a boat – both allusions to Bilbao's past and present economy. The interior makes wonderful use of space, with light pouring in through a central glass atrium of cathedral proportions. The permanent exhibit of modern and contemporary art is still small but choice with artists like Picasso, Mondrian and Kandinsky among those represented. All the other galleries are used for high-calibre temporary exhibits.

Museum hours are 10 am to 8 pm Tuesday to Sunday (daily in July and August); 1200/600 ptas. Arrive early and ask about free guided English-language tours.

Some 300m up the street, excellent **Museo de Bellas Artes** has works by El Greco, Velázquez and Goya, as well as 20th-century masters like Gauguin. Basque artists are shown as well (closed Monday; 600/300 ptas).

The main tourist office (☎ 94 479 57 60) is on Paseo Arenal 1 and there's also an information kiosk by the Guggenheim (closed Monday). For Internet access, go to El Señor de la Red, Calle Rodríguez Arias 69.

Places to Stay & Eat
Albergue Bilbao Aterpetxea (☎ 94 427 00 54, @ aterpe@albergue.bilbao.net, Carretera Basurto-Kastrexana Errep 70) is a 10-minute direct bus ride (No 58) away from the centre and charges from 1900 ptas to 2500 ptas, including breakfast.

Pensión Méndez (☎ 94 416 03 64, Calle de Santa María 13) is central but can be a bit noisy. Singles/doubles cost 3000/4000 ptas. *Hostal La Estrella* (☎ 94 416 40 66, Calle de María Múñoz 6) is a charming, brightly painted place where rooms with washbasin cost 2700/4800 ptas and those with bath are 4000/6500 ptas.

Las Siete Calles (Seven Streets), the nucleus of Bilbao's old town, brims with tapas bars and restaurants. *Rio-Oja (Calle de Perro 6)* is among the many places for cheap food and drink. *Cafe Boulevard (Calle de Arenal 3)*, Bilbao's oldest coffeehouse (1871) nearby, has breakfasts, full meals and tapas at wallet-friendly prices. *Café Iruña (Calle de Colón Larreátegui)* is Bilbao's most celebrated cafe.

Getting There & Away
Bus Buses to Madrid (3400 ptas) and Barcelona (4850 ptas) depart from Calle de la Autonomía 17. Most other buses use the huge Termibus lot in the south-west corner of town (metro: San Mamés).

Train Four daily trains to Madrid (5800 ptas, 6¼ hours) and two to Barcelona (4900 ptas, nine hours) leave from RENFE's central Abando train station. The Eusko Tren station with regional services is about 1km south of the centre.

Boat P&O ferries leave for Portsmouth from Santurtzl, about 14km north-west of Bilbao's city centre. The voyage takes about 35 hours from England and 29 hours the other way.

PAMPLONA
pop 182,500
The madcap festivities of Sanfermines in Pamplona (Iruñea in Basque) run from 6-14 July and are characterised by nonstop partying and, of course, the running of the bulls. The safest place to watch the *encierro* (running) is on TV. If this is far too tame for you, see if you can sweet-talk your way on to a

SPAIN

balcony in one of the streets where the bulls run. The bulls are let out at 8 am, but if you want to get a good vantage point you will have to be there around 6 am.

If you visit at any other time of year, you'll find a pleasant and modern city, with lovely parks and gardens, and a compact old town with a lively bar and restaurant scene.

The tourist office (☎ 948 22 07 41) is on Plaza San Francisco and open weekdays only (plus Saturday morning in July and August).

Places to Stay & Eat

The nearest camping ground is *Camping Ezcaba* (☎ *948 33 03 15*), 7km north of the city. It fills up a few days before Sanfermines. A bus service (direction Arre/Oricain) runs four times daily from Calle de Teovaldos (near the bullring).

For Sanfermines you need to book well in advance (and pay as much as triple the regular rates). During the festival, beds are also available in *casas particulares* (private houses) – check with the tourist office or haggle with the locals at the bus and train stations. Otherwise, join the many who sleep in one of the parks, plazas or shopping malls. There's a left-luggage office *(consigna)* at the bus station.

Pamplona's old centre is filled with cheap pensions renting basic singles/doubles for around 2000/3500 ptas. Contenders on the Calle San Nicolás include *Fonda Aragonesa* (☎ *948 22 34 28*) at No 32, *Habitaciones San Nicolás* (☎ *948 22 13 19*) at No 13 and *Habitaciones Otano* (☎ *948 22 50 95*) at No 5. Near the tourist office, *Camas Escaray Lozano* (☎ *948 22 78 25, Calle Nueva 24*) has probably the nicest rooms in this range. Right by the indoor market and next to the bull running route is *Habitaciones Redin* (☎ *948 22 21 82, Calle de Mercado 5*).

Calle de San Nicolás is packed with tapas bars, with *Baserri* at No 32 offering the best quality. Almost as good is *Otano* (☎ *948 22 26 38*) across the street.

Bar Anaitasuna (Calle de San Gregorio 58) has uncluttered, modern decor and is busy from breakfast to midnight. The set lunch costs 1600 ptas, platos combinados around 1000 ptas.

Getting There & Away

The bus station is on Avenida de Yangüas y Miranda, a five-minute walk south of the old town. There are 10 buses daily to San Sebastián (790 ptas) and eight to Bilbao (1580 ptas). Four daily head for Madrid (3220 ptas) and two to Barcelona (2190 ptas).

Pamplona is on the San Sebastián-Zaragoza railway line, but the station is awkwardly situated north of town. If you arrive this way, catch bus No 9 to the centre.

ZARAGOZA
pop 603,000

Zaragoza, capital of Aragón and home to half its 1.2 million people, is often said to be the most Spanish city of all. Once an important Roman city, under the name Caesaraugusta, and later a Muslim centre for four centuries, it is today primarily a hub of industry and commerce, but with a lively and interesting old heart on the south side of the Río Ebro.

The city tourist office (☎ 976 20 12 00), in a surreal-looking glass cube on Plaza del Pilar, opens 10 am to 8 pm daily.

Things to See

Zaragoza's focus is the vast 500m-long main square, **Plaza de Nuestra Señora del Pilar** (Plaza del Pilar for short). Dominating the north side is the **Basílica de Nuestra Señora del Pilar**, a 17th-century church of epic proportions. People flock to the church's Capilla Santa to kiss a piece of marble pillar believed to have been left by the Virgin Mary when she appeared to Santiago (St James) in a vision here in AD 40.

At the south-east end of the plaza is **La Seo**, Zaragoza's brooding 12th to 16th-century cathedral. Its north-west facade is a mudéjar masterpiece. The inside, reopened in 1998 after 18 years of restoration, features an impressive 15th-century main altarpiece in coloured alabaster.

The odd trapezoid structure in front of La Seo is the outside of a remarkable museum housing the **Roman forum** of ancient Caesaraugusta. Well below modern ground level you can visit the remains of shops, porticos and a great sewerage system, all brought to life by an imaginative audiovisual show. The forum is open 10 am to 2 pm and 5 to 8 pm Tuesday to Saturday, 10 am to 2 pm Sunday (400 ptas).

SPAIN

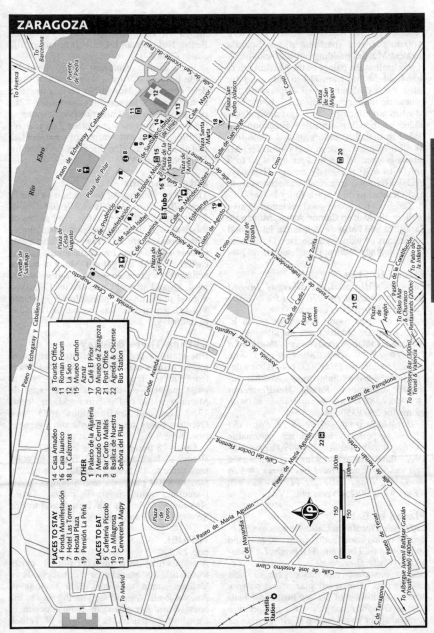

ZARAGOZA

SPAIN

PLACES TO STAY
4 Fonda Manifestación
7 Hotel Las Torres
9 Hostal Plaza
19 Pensión La Peña

PLACES TO EAT
5 Cafetería Piccolo
10 La Milagrosa
13 Cervecería Mapy

14 Casa Amadeo
16 Casa Juanico
18 La Calzorras

OTHER
1 Palacio de la Aljafería
2 Mercado Central
3 Bar Corto Maltés
6 Basílica de Nuestra
   Señora del Pilar

8 Tourist Office
11 Roman Forum
12 La Seo
15 Museo Camón
   Aznar
17 Café El Prior
20 Museo de Zaragoza
21 Post Office
22 Agreda & Oscense
   Bus Station

euro currency converter   100 ptas = €0.60

A little over 1km west of the plaza, the **Palacio de la Aljafería**, today housing Aragón's *cortes* (parliament), is Spain's greatest Muslim building outside Andalucía. It was built as the palace of the Muslim rulers who held the city from 714 to 1118, and the inner Patio de Santa Isabel displays all the geometric mastery and fine detail of the best Muslim architecture. The upstairs palace, added by the Christian rulers Fernando and Isabel in the 15th century, boasts some fine Muslim-inspired mudéjar decoration. The Aljafería is open 10 am to 2 pm and 4.30 to 8 pm (4 to 6.30 pm) daily except Thursday, Friday afternoon and Sunday afternoon from mid-October to mid-April. Entry is free.

Zaragoza has some good museums. Three of them, the **Museo Camón Aznar**, **Museo de Zaragoza** and **Patio de la Infanta**, have good collections of work by Francisco Goya, who was born 30km south at Fuendetodos, in 1746.

Places to Stay

Zaragoza's HI hostel, the **Albergue Juvenil Baltasar Gracián** (*☎ 976 55 13 87, Calle Franco y López 4*), is open all year.

The cheapest rooms elsewhere are in El Tubo, the maze of busy lanes and alleys south of Plaza del Pilar. A good choice is *Pensión La Peña* (*☎ 976 29 90 89, Calle Cinegio 3*) with singles/doubles for 1500/3000 ptas. It has a decent little *comedor* (dining room). Another reasonable cheapie is *Fonda Manifestación* (*☎ 976 29 58 21, Calle Manifestación 36*) with rooms for 2500/3500 ptas.

Hostal Plaza (*☎ 976 29 48 30, Plaza del Pilar 14*), perfectly located, has reasonable rooms with shower for 4300/4900 ptas plus IVA – the rooms overlooking the plaza are the best value in town. *Hotel Las Torres* (*☎ 976 39 42 50, Plaza del Pilar 11*) has modern rooms for 6000/7500 ptas plus IVA.

Places to Eat

Cafetería Piccolo on Calle Prudencio serves decent platos combinados from 800 ptas and stays open till 1 or 2 am. The bright *La Milagrosa* (*Calle Don Jaime I 43*) serves inexpensive breakfasts, and raciónes for 300 ptas to 700 ptas. The small plazas and narrow streets south-west of La Seo host some brilliant tapas bars, among them the inexpensive seafood spot *Casa Amadeo* (*Calle Jordán de Urríes 3*), *Cervecería Mapy* (*Plaza Santa Marta 8*), *La Calzorras* on Plaza de San Pedro Nolasco and *Casa Juanico* (*Calle Santa Cruz 21*).

For classier restaurant eating, head for Calle Francisco Vitoria, 1km south of Plaza del Pilar. *Risko Mar* at No 16 is a fine fish restaurant with an excellent *menú* for 4250 ptas plus IVA (minimum two people). Across the street, *Churrasco* is another Zaragoza institution, with a wide variety of meat and fish and an excellent-value three-course lunch for 1300 ptas plus IVA.

Entertainment

There's no shortage of bars in and around El Tubo. *Bar Corto Maltés* (*Calle del Temple 23*) is one of a string of rather cool places on this lane. All the barmen sport *corto maltés* (sideburns). *Café El Prior* on Calle Santa Cruz is a good place for a little dancing in the earlier stages of a night out. Much of the bar action takes place about 1km farther southwest, on and around Calle Doctor Cerrada – a good place to start at is *Morrissey* (*Gran Vía 33*), which often has live bands Thursday to Saturday.

Getting There & Away

Bus stations are scattered all over town; tourist offices can tell you what goes where from where. The Agreda company runs to most major Spanish cities from Paseo de María Agustín 7. The trip to Madrid costs 1750 ptas and to Barcelona 1655 ptas. Oscense buses head towards the Pyrenees from here, too.

Up to 15 trains daily run from El Portillo station to both Madrid (3100 ptas to 4000 ptas, three to 4½ hours) and Barcelona (2900 ptas to 4100 ptas, 3½ to 5½ hours). Some Barcelona trains go via Tarragona. Trains also run to Valencia via Teruel, and to San Sebastián via Pamplona.

TERUEL
pop 29,300

Aragón's hilly deep south is culturally closer to Castilla-La Mancha or the backlands of Valencia than to some other regions of Aragón itself. A good stop on the way to the coast from Zaragoza, or from Cuenca in Castilla-La Mancha, is the town of Teruel, which has a flavour all its own thanks to four centuries of Muslim domination in the Middle Ages and some remarkable mudéjar architecture dating from after its capture by the Christians in 1171.

The tourist office (☎ 978 60 22 79) is at Calle Tomás Nogués 1.

Things to See

Teruel has four magnificent mudéjar towers, on the cathedral of **Santa María** (12th and 13th centuries) and the churches of **San Salvador** (13th century), **San Martín** and **San Pedro** (both 14th century). These, and the painted ceiling inside Santa María, are among Spain's best mudéjar architecture and artisanry. Note the complicated brickwork and colourful tiles on the towers, so typical of the style. The **Museo Provincial de Teruel** on Plaza Padre Polanco is well worth a visit, mainly for its fascinating archaeological section going back to *Homo erectus*.

Places to Stay & Eat

Fonda del Tozal (☎ 978 60 10 22, Calle del Rincón 5) is great value. It's an amazing rick-

ety old house run by a friendly family, and most of the rooms have cast-iron beds, enamelled chamber pots and exposed ceiling beams. Singles/doubles cost 1500/3000 ptas. In winter, you might prefer *Hostal Aragón* (☎ *978 60 13 87, Calle de Santa María 4*), which is also charming but has mod cons such as heating. Rooms are 2150/3200 ptas, or 3200/4860 ptas with private bath, all plus IVA. Both places are just a couple of minutes walk from the cathedral.

Teruel is famed for its ham. If you can't fit a whole leg of it in your backpack, at least sample a *tostada con jamón*, with tomato and olive oil. One of the best places for hamming up is *La Taberna de Rokelin* (*Calle de Tozal 33*), a narrow bar with a beautiful rack of smoked pig hocks.

Getting There & Away

The bus station is on Ronda de Ambeles. Daily buses head to Barcelona (6½ hours), Cuenca (2¾ hours), Valencia (two hours) and Madrid (2415 ptas, 4½ hours).

By rail, Teruel is about midway between Valencia and Zaragoza, with three trains a day to both places.

SPAIN

Switzerland

Switzerland (Schweiz, Suisse, Svizzera, Svizzra) offers its fair share of cliches – from irresistible chocolates, kitsch cuckoo clocks, and yodelling Heidis, to humourless bankers – but plenty of surprises, too. The visitor will find flavours of Germany, France and Italy, but always seasoned with a unique Swissness.

Goethe described Switzerland as a combination of 'the colossal and the well-ordered', a succinct reference to the indomitable and majestic alpine terrain set against tidy, efficient, watch-precision towns and cities. Together, these elements provide a peerless attraction.

Prices are high in Switzerland, and you may be tempted to rush through the country faster than you would like. It doesn't have to be that way. You can enjoy some of the best scenery and hiking in Europe without paying a thing, so find yourself a friendly base in the mountains and take it all in at your leisure.

Facts about Switzerland

HISTORY

The first inhabitants of the region were from a Celtic tribe, the Helvetii. The Romans appeared on the scene in 107 BC by way of the Great St Bernard Pass, but because of the difficulty of the terrain, their attempted conquest of the area was never decisive. They were gradually driven back by the Germanic Alemanni tribe, which settled in the region in the 5th century. Burgundians and Franks also came to the area, and Christianity was gradually introduced.

The territory was united under the Holy Roman Empire in 1032 but central control was never very tight, allowing neighbouring nobles to contest each other for local influence. That was changed by the Germanic Habsburg family, which became the most powerful dynasty in Central Europe. Habsburg expansion was spearheaded by Rudolph I, who gradually brought the squabbling nobles to heel.

Language Areas p1100

GERMANY
LIECHTENSTEIN
FRANCE
Basel p1148
Zürich p1135
Bern p1112
Lucerne p1141
AUSTRIA
Lausanne p1124
Geneva p1118
FRANCE
ITALY

The Swiss Confederation

Upon Rudolph's death in 1291, local leaders saw a chance to gain independence. The forest communities of Uri, Schwyz and Nidwalden formed an alliance on 1 August 1291. Their pact of mutual assistance is seen as the origin of the Swiss Confederation, and their struggles against the Habsburgs are idealised in the familiar legend of William Tell. Duke Leopold responded by dispatching his powerful Austrian army in 1315, which was routed by the Swiss at Morgarten. The effective action of the union soon prompted other communities to join. Lucerne (1332) was followed by Zürich (1351), Glarus and Zug

SWITZERLAND

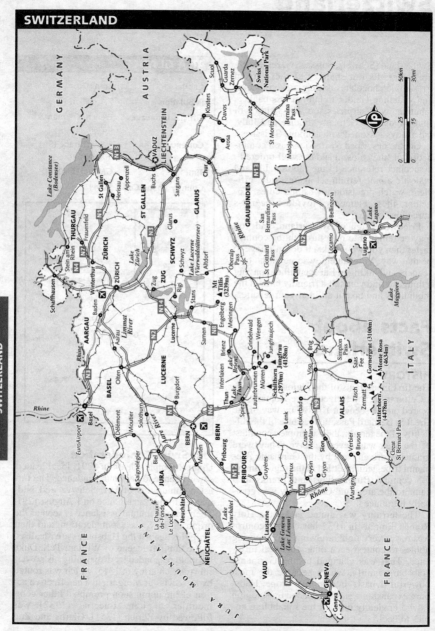

(1352), and Bern (1353). There were further defeats of the Habsburgs at Sempach (1386) and Näfels (1388).

Encouraged by these successes, the Swiss gradually acquired a taste for territorial expansion. More land was seized from the Habsburgs. They took on Charles the Bold, the Duke of Burgundy, and defeated him at Grandson and Morat. Fribourg, Solothurn, Basel, Schaffhausen and Appenzell joined the confederation, and the Swiss gained independence from Holy Roman Emperor Maximilian I after their victory at Dornach in 1499. Finally the Swiss over-reached themselves. They took on a superior force of French and Venetians at Marignano in 1515 and lost. The defeat prompted them to withdraw from the international scene. Realising they could no longer compete against larger powers with better equipment, they renounced expansionist policies and declared their neutrality. Even so, Swiss mercenaries continued to serve in other armies for centuries, and earned an unrivalled reputation for skill and courage.

The Reformation in the 16th century caused upheaval throughout Europe. The Protestant teachings of Luther, Zwingli and Calvin spread quickly, although the inaugural cantons remained Catholic. This caused internal unrest that dragged on for centuries, but the Swiss did at least manage to avoid international disputes. At the end of the Thirty Years' War in 1648 they were recognised in the Treaty of Westphalia as a neutral state. Switzerland was free to prosper as a financial and intellectual centre.

The French Republic invaded Switzerland in 1798 and established the Helvetic Republic. The Swiss vehemently resisted such centralised control, which caused Napoleon to restore the former confederation of cantons in 1803. Yet France retained overall jurisdiction. Further cantons also joined the confederation: Aargau, St Gallen, Graubünden, Ticino, Thurgau and Vaud. Napoleon was finally sent packing after his defeat by the British and Prussians at Waterloo. The ensuing Congress of Vienna guaranteed Switzerland's independence and permanent neutrality, as well as adding the cantons of Valais, Geneva and Neuchâtel.

The Modern State

Throughout the gradual move towards one nation, each canton remained fiercely independent, even to the extent of controlling its own coinage and postal services. The cantons lost these powers in 1848, when a new federal constitution was agreed upon (still largely in place, albeit revised in 1874 and 1999). Bern was established as the capital and the Federal Assembly was set up to take care of national issues. The cantons retained legislative (Grand Council) and executive (States Council) powers to deal with local matters.

Having achieved political stability, Switzerland could concentrate on economic and social matters. Relatively poor in mineral resources, it developed industries predominantly dependent on highly skilled labour. A network of railways and roads was built, opening up previously inaccessible regions of the Alps and helping the development of tourism. The Red Cross was founded in Geneva in 1863 by Henri Dunant, and compulsory free education was enshrined in the 1874 constitution.

The Swiss have carefully guarded their neutrality in the 20th century. Their only involvement in WWI was organising Red Cross units. Switzerland joined the League of Nations after peace was won and under the proviso that its involvement would be purely financial and economic rather than entailing any possible military sanctions. Apart from some accidental bombing, WWII also left Switzerland largely unscathed, and its territory proved to be a safe haven for escaped Allied prisoners.

While the rest of Europe underwent the painful process of rebuilding from the ravages of war, Switzerland expanded its already powerful commercial, financial and industrial base. Zürich developed as an international banking and insurance centre. Many international bodies, such as the World Health Organisation (WHO), based their headquarters in Geneva. Workers and employers struck agreements, under which industrial weapons such as strikes and lockouts were renounced. Social reforms, such as old-age pensions (1948), were also introduced.

Afraid that its neutrality would be compromised, Switzerland declined to become a member of the United Nations (though it has 'observer' status, ie, it gives money but it doesn't have a vote) or the North Atlantic Treaty Organisation (NATO). It did, however, join the European Free Trade Association (EFTA). In the face of other EFTA nations applying for EU (then known as the European Community) membership, Switzerland finally made an application in 1992. As a prelude to full EU membership Switzerland was to join the EEA (European Economic Area), yet the government's strategy lay in ruins after citizens rejected the EEA in a December 1992 referendum. Switzerland's EU application has consequently been frozen while the government seeks closer integration with the EU. A bilateral agreement covering transport and labour movements between Switzerland and the EU was ratified in 1999.

Switzerland's WWII record has come under critical scrutiny in recent years. Allegedly, many Jewish refugees were turned back from Switzerland's border, and left to face their fate in Nazi Germany. Moreover, Swiss banks were major conduits for Nazi plunder during WWII – at least US$400 million (US$3.8 billion in today's values) was deposited. The banks also held on to huge sums deposited by Jews who subsequently became victims of the Holocaust. In 1998, upon facing a class action lawsuit in the USA by Holocaust survivors, the banks agreed to pay US$1.25 billion to settle all outstanding claims relating to these deposits.

Defence

Despite its long-standing neutrality, Switzerland maintains a 400,000-strong civilian army. Every able-bodied male undergoes national service at 20 and stays in the reserves for 22 years, all the while keeping his rifle and full kit at home. An infrastructure is in place to repel any invasion, including the planned destruction of key roads and bridges. All new buildings must have a substantial air-raid capacity, and underground car parks can be instantly converted to bunkers. Emergency hospitals, unused yet fully equipped, await underneath ordinary hospitals. It's a sobering thought, as you explore the countryside, to realise that those apparently undisturbed mountains and lakes hide a network of military installations and storage depots. Potential invaders would be well advised not to mess with the Swiss.

GEOGRAPHY & ECOLOGY

Mountains make up 70% of Switzerland's 41,290 sq km. The land is 45% meadow and pasture, 24% forest and 6% arable. Farming of cultivated land is intensive and cows graze on the upper slopes in the summer as soon as the retreating snow line permits.

The Alps occupy the central and southern regions of the country. The Dufour summit (4634m) of Monte Rosa is the highest point, although the Matterhorn (4478m) is more famous. A series of high passes in the south provides overland access into Italy. Glaciers account for an area of 2000 sq km, most notably the Aletsch Glacier, which at 169 sq km is the largest valley glacier in Europe.

The St Gotthard Massif in the centre of Switzerland is the source of many lakes and rivers, such as the Rhine and the Rhône. The Jura Mountains straddle the border with France. These mountains peak at around 1700m and are less steep and less severely eroded than the Alps.

Between the two mountain systems is the Mittelland, also known as the Swiss Plateau, a region of hills crisscrossed by rivers, ravines and winding valleys. This area has spawned the most populous cities and is also where much of the agricultural activity takes place.

Switzerland has long been an environmentally aware nation. Citizens diligently recycle household waste and cities encourage the use of public transport. The policy in the mountains is to contain rather than expand existing resorts.

CLIMATE

Ticino in the south has a hot, Mediterranean climate, and Valais in the south-west is noted for being dry. Elsewhere the temperature is typically from 20° to 25°C in summer and 2° to 6°C in winter, with spring and autumn temperatures hovering around the 7° to 14°C mark. Summer tends to bring a lot of sunshine, but also the most rain. You will need to be prepared for a range of temperatures depending on your altitude.

Look out for the *Föhn*, a hot, dry wind that sweeps down into the valleys and can be oppressively uncomfortable. It can strike at any time of year. Daily weather reports covering 25 resorts are displayed in major train stations.

GOVERNMENT & POLITICS

The modern Swiss Confederation is made up of 23 cantons; three are subdivided, bringing the total to 26. Each has its own constitution and legislative body for dealing with local issues. The Jura achieved full cantonal status as late as 1979.

National legislative power is in the hands of the Federal Assembly, which has two chambers. The lower chamber, the National Council, has 200 members elected by proportional representation. The upper chamber, the States Council, has 46 members, two per full canton. The Federal Assembly elects seven members to form the Federal Council, which holds executive power. All elections are for a four-year term except the posts of president and vice-president of the confederation, which are rotated annually. The vice-president always succeeds the president, meaning the governing body is not dominated by any one individual.

Under the 1874 constitution, Swiss citizens enjoy direct democracy: 50,000 signatories are needed to force a full referendum on proposed laws, and 100,000 to initiate legislation. Citizens regularly vote in referenda on national, local and communal issues. Yet surprisingly, women only won the right to vote in federal elections in 1971. It was 1991 before women gained a cantonal vote in Appenzell, the last remaining canton that still conducts votes by a show of hands in an open-air parliament *(Landsgemeinde)*.

ECONOMY

Switzerland has a mixed economy with an emphasis strongly on private ownership. The state still runs postal services and the federal railway, though telecommunications were privatised in 1998. The economy is efficient, despite generally high prices (there's a problem with price-fixing cartels). At least for the Swiss, high prices are matched by high wages, and a good proportion of the wealth generated is channelled back into the community via social welfare programs. Unemployment, at a negligible level for decades, crept to a record 5.2% in 1997 before dropping back to below 3%. Inflation is generally below 1%.

In the absence of other raw materials, hydroelectric power has become the main source of energy. Chemicals, machine tools and watches and clocks are the most important exports. Silks and embroidery, also

significant, are produced to a high quality. Swiss banks are a magnet for foreign funds attracted to political and monetary stability. Tourism, although dented by the recently strong Swiss franc, is still the country's third-biggest industry and the excellent infrastructure makes life easy for visitors (it's especially easy to spend too much money!). Swiss breakthroughs in science and industry include vitamins, DDT, gas turbines and milk chocolate. They also, for their sins, developed the modern formula for life insurance.

POPULATION & PEOPLE

With a population of 7.1 million, Switzerland averages 172 people per sq km. The alpine districts are sparsely populated, meaning that the Mittelland is very densely settled, especially round the shores of the larger lakes. Zürich is the largest city, with 354,000 people, and next comes Basel (177,000), Geneva (175,000) and Bern (132,000). Most of the people are of Germanic origin, as reflected in the breakdown of the four national languages (see Language later in this chapter). One-fifth of people living in the country are residents but not Swiss citizens; the foreign influx started after WWII, particularly from southern Europe.

ARTS

Switzerland does not have a very strong tradition in the arts, even though many foreign writers and artists have visited and settled, attracted by the beauty and tranquillity of the mountains and lakes. Among them were Voltaire, Byron and Shelley.

Paul Klee is the best-known native painter. He created abstract works which used colour, line and form to evoke a variety of sensations. The 18th-century writings of Rousseau in Geneva played an important part in the development of democracy. Carl Jung, with his research in Zürich, was instrumental in developing modern psychoanalysis. Arthur Honegger is the only Swiss composer of note. But music plays a big role, with a full symphony orchestra based in every main city.

Gothic and Renaissance architecture are evident in urban areas, especially Bern. Rural Swiss houses vary according to region, but are generally characterised by ridged roofs with wide, overhanging eaves, and balconies and verandas usually enlivened by colourful floral displays, especially geraniums.

SOCIETY & CONDUCT

The Swiss are law-abiding people; even minor transgressions such as littering can cause offence. Always shake hands when being introduced to a Swiss, and again when leaving. Formal titles should also be used – in German, *Herr* for men and *Frau* for women. It is also customary to greet shopkeepers when entering their shops. Public displays of affection are OK, but are more common in French and Italian Switzerland than in the slightly more formal German-speaking parts.

In a few mountain regions such as Valais, people still wear traditional rural costumes, but dressing up is usually reserved for festivals. Every spring hardy herders climb to alpine pastures with their cattle and live in summer huts while tending their herds. They gradually descend to village level as the grassland is grazed. Both their departure and return is a cause for celebrations and processions.

Yodelling and playing the alp horn are also part of the alpine tradition, as is Swiss wrestling. Visitors are advised to leave such activities to the experts, no matter how tempting the idea of joining in may seem after a few too many beers.

RELIGION

Protestantism and Roman Catholicism are equally widespread, though their concentration varies between cantons. Strong Protestant areas are Bern, Vaud and Zürich, whereas Valais, Ticino and Uri are mostly Catholic. Some churches are supported entirely by donations from the public, while others receive state subsidies.

LANGUAGE

Located in the corner of Europe where the German, French and Italian language areas meet, Switzerland is a linguistic melting pot with three official federal languages: German (spoken by 64% of the population), French (19%) and Italian (8%). A fourth language, Rhaeto-Romanic, or Romansch, is spoken by less than 1% of the population, mainly in the canton of Graubünden. Derived from Latin, it's a linguistic relic which, along with Friulian and Ladin across the border in Italy, has survived in the isolation of mountain valleys. Romansch was recognised as a national language by referendum in 1938 and given federal protection in 1996.

Though German-speaking Swiss have no trouble with standard High German, they use Swiss German, or *Schwyzertütsch*, in private conversation and most nonofficial situations. Swiss German covers a wide variety of melodic dialects that can differ quite markedly from High German. Visitors will probably note the frequent use of the suffix *-li* to indicate the diminutive, or as a term of endearment.

English speakers will have few problems being understood in the German-speaking parts. However, it is simple courtesy to greet people with the Swiss-German *Grüezi* (Hello) and to inquire *Sprechen Sie Englisch?* (Do you speak English?) before launching into English.

In French Switzerland you shouldn't have too many problems either, though the locals' grasp of English will probably not be as good as the German speakers'. Italian Switzerland is where you will have the greatest difficulty. Most locals speak some French and/or German in addition to Italian. English has a lower priority, but you'll still find that the majority of hotels and restaurants have at least one English-speaking staff member.

See the Language chapter at the back of the book for German, French and Italian pronunciation guidelines and useful words and phrases.

LANGUAGE AREAS

- Romansch
- German
- French
- Italian

Basel · Zürich · Lucerne · Bern · Chur · St Moritz · Lausanne · Bellinzona · Geneva

Facts for the Visitor

HIGHLIGHTS

Endless, beautiful vistas greet you in this country. The views from Schilthorn or its neighbour, Jungfrau, are unforgettable. Zermatt combines inspiring views of the Matterhorn and quality skiing. Be sure to take a boat trip: Lake Lugano reveals the sunny side of Switzerland's Italian canton, and Lake Thun offers snowcapped scenery and several castles. Excursions are also excellent on lakes Lucerne and Geneva.

The Château de Chillon near Montreux is justifiably the most famous castle in Switzerland. Bern, Lucerne, St Gallen and Stein am Rhein have picturesque town centres. Zürich, Basel and Geneva are bursting with fine museums and art galleries. Lausanne features a unique collection of bizarre 'outsider' art. You can see Swiss cheese being made at 'showcase dairies' in Gruyères and elsewhere.

The Swiss Museum Passport will save you money if you plan to visit more than a handful of museums. It costs Sfr30 (Sfr25 for students and those with the Euro<26 card), is valid for one month, and gets free entry to 250 museums. Buy it from Switzerland Tourism or the museums concerned. Details are at www.museums.ch.

SUGGESTED ITINERARIES

Depending on the length of your stay, you could see and do the following things:

Two days
  Visit the sights in Geneva and take a trip on the lake. Don't miss Château de Chillon in Montreux.
One week
  Visit Geneva, Lausanne and Montreux. En route to Lucerne, spend a couple of days exploring Interlaken and the Jungfrau Region.
Two weeks
  As above, but spend longer in the mountains. Visit Bern, Basel and Zürich.
One month
  As above, but after Zürich, explore St Gallen and eastern Switzerland before looping down to take in Graubünden, Ticino and Valais.
Two months
  As above, but take your time. Visit Neuchâtel and the Jura Mountains from Bern.

PLANNING
When to Go

Switzerland is visited throughout the year – from December to April for winter sports, and May to October for general tourism and hiking. Alpine resorts all but close down in May and November.

Maps

Michelin covers the whole country with four maps. The *Landeskarte der Schweiz* (Topographical Survey of Switzerland) series is larger in scale and especially useful for hiking. Kümmerly + Frey maps are also good for hikers. All these maps are sold throughout Switzerland. Swiss banks, especially the UBS branches, are a good source of free maps.

What to Bring

Take a sturdy pair of boots if you intend to walk in the mountains, and warm clothing for those cold nights at high altitude. Hostel membership is invaluable and it's cheaper to join before you get to Switzerland.

TOURIST OFFICES
Local Tourist Offices

Tourist offices (*Verkehrsbüro*) are extremely helpful. They have plenty of literature to give out, including maps (nearly always free), and somebody invariably speaks English. Local offices can be found everywhere tourists are likely to go and will often book hotel rooms and organise excursions. If you're staying in resorts, ask the local tourist office if there's a Visitor's Card, as these are good for discounts.

Tourist Offices Abroad

A free-phone number for Switzerland Tourism that works worldwide (in countries where it has an office) is 00800-100 200 30. Switzerland Tourism offices can be found in:

Canada (☎ 416-695 2090, fax 695 2774, ✉ sttoronto@switzerlandtourism.com) 926 The East Mall, Etobicoke, Toronto, Ontario M9B 6K1
UK (☎ 020-7734 1921, fax 7437 4577, ✉ stlondon@switzerlandvacation.ch) Swiss Centre, Swiss Court, London W1V 8EE
USA (☎ 212-757 59 44, fax 262 61 16, ✉ stnewyork@switzerlandtourism.com) Swiss Center, 608 Fifth Ave, New York, NY 10020

Switzerland Tourism also has offices in Los Angeles, Chicago, Paris, Milan, Munich and Vienna. It has no office in Australia, but you can get information from Swissair in Sydney (☎ 02-9231 3744, fax 9251 6531, ✉ swissair@ tiasnet.com.au).

VISAS & DOCUMENTS

Visas are not required for passport holders of the UK, the USA, Canada, Australia or New Zealand. A maximum three-month stay applies although passports are rarely stamped. The few developing world and Arab nationals who require visas should have a passport valid for at least six months after their intended stay.

EMBASSIES & CONSULATES
Swiss Embassies & Consulates

Swiss embassies can be found in:

Australia (☎ 02-6273 3977, fax 6273 3428, ✉ swissembcan@dynamite.com.au) 7 Melbourne Ave, Forrest, Canberra, ACT 2603
Canada (☎ 613-235 1837, fax 563 1394, ✉ swissemott@compuserve.com) 5 Marlborough Ave, Ottawa, Ontario K1N 8E6
New Zealand (☎ 04-472 1593, fax 472 1593) 22 Panama St, Wellington
UK (☎ 020-7616 6000, fax 7724 7001, ✉ vertretung@lon.rep.admin.ch) 16-18 Montague Place, London W1H 2BQ
USA (☎ 202-745 7900, fax 387 2564, ✉ vertretung@was.rep.admin.ch) 2900 Cathedral Ave NW, Washington, DC 20008-3499

Embassies & Consulates in Switzerland

All embassies are in Bern (the Bern tourist office has a complete list). They include:

Canada (☎ 031-357 32 00) Kirchenfeldstrasse 88
France (☎ 031-359 21 11) Schosshaldenstrasse 46
Germany (☎ 031-359 41 11) Willadingweg 83
Italy (☎ 031-352 41 51) Elfenstrasse 14
UK (☎ 031-359 77 00) Thunstrasse 50
USA (☎ 031-357 70 11) Jubiläumsstrasse 93

Foreign consulates include:

Austria (☎ 01-283 27 00) Seestrasse 161, Zürich
Australia (☎ 022-799 91 00) 2 Chemin des Fins, Geneva (there's no embassy)
Canada (☎ 022-919 92 00), 5 Ave de l'Ariana, Geneva

France (☎ 022-311 34 41) 11 Rue J Imbert Galloix, Geneva
Germany (☎ 01-265 65 65) Kirchgasse 48, Zürich
New Zealand (☎ 022-929 03 50) 2 Chemin des Fins, Geneva (there's no embassy)
UK (☎ 022-918 24 00) 37-39 Rue de Vermont, Geneva
   (☎ 01-383 65 60) Minervastrasse 117, Zürich
USA (☎ 022-798 16 05) 29 Route de Pré-Bois, Geneva
   (☎ 01-422 25 66) Dufourstrasse 101, Zürich

CUSTOMS

Visitors from Europe may import 200 cigarettes, 50 cigars or 250g of pipe tobacco. Visitors from non-European countries may import twice as much. The allowance for alcoholic beverages is the same for everyone: 1L of alcohol above 15% and 2L below 15%. Tobacco and alcohol may only be brought in by people aged 17 or older.

MONEY
Currency

Swiss francs (Sfr – written CHF locally) are divided into 100 centimes, which are usually called *Rappen* in German-speaking Switzerland. There are 10, 20, 50, 100, 500 and 1000 franc notes, and five, 10, 20 and 50 centime coins, as well as ones for one, two and five francs.

All major travellers cheques and credit cards are equally accepted. Virtually all train stations have money-exchange facilities open daily. Commission is not usually charged for changing cash or cheques but it's gradually creeping in. Shop around for the best exchange rates. Hotels usually have the worst rates.

Getting money sent to Switzerland should be straightforward. No charge is made at Swiss American Express (AmEx) offices for receiving Moneygram transfers. Likewise for money sent to Western Union offices, of which there are many, particularly at larger train stations. Encashing money transfers sent to Swiss banks can be problematic, as this is usually only possible for account-holders of that bank. Automatic teller machines (ATMs or Bancomats) for credit card advances are numerous, though some don't accept Visa cards. ATMs at post offices (called Postomats) do allow Visa cash advances.

SWITZERLAND

There are no restrictions on the amount of currency that can be brought in or taken out of Switzerland.

Exchange Rates

country	unit		Swiss franc
Australia	A$1	=	Sfr0.99
Canada	C$1	=	Sfr1.16
euro	€1	=	Sfr1.55
France	1FF	=	Sfr0.24
Germany	DM1	=	Sfr0.79
Japan	¥100	=	Sfr1.58
New Zealand	NZ$1	=	Sfr0.77
UK	UK£1	=	Sfr2.58
USA	US$1	=	Sfr1.72

Costs

Prices are higher in Switzerland than anywhere else in Western Europe. Some travellers can scrimp by on about Sfr55 a day after buying a rail pass. This is survival level – camping or hostelling, self-catering when possible and allowing nothing for nonessentials. If you want to stay in pensions and have a beer, count on spending twice as much. Minimum prices per person are around Sfr22/38 in a hostel/hotel and Sfr9/15 for lunch/dinner (excluding drinks). Taking cable cars is a major expense; if you're fit enough, walk instead.

Tipping & Bargaining

Tipping is not strictly necessary as hotels, restaurants and bars are required by law to include a 15% service charge on bills (though locals often 'round up'). Even taxis often have a service charge included. Prices are fixed, but travellers have successfully haggled for lower hotel rates in the low season.

Consumer Taxes

VAT (MWST or TVA) on goods and services is levied at a rate of 7.5% (3.5% for hotel bills). Nonresidents can claim the tax back on purchases over Sfr500. Ask for the documentation when making the purchase.

Switzerland has a motorway tax (see the Getting There & Away section later in this chapter).

POST & COMMUNICATIONS
Post

Postcards and letters to Europe cost Sfr1.30/1.20 priority/economy; to elsewhere they cost Sfr1.80/1.40. The term poste restante is used nationwide or you could use the German term, *Postlagernde Briefe*. Mail can be sent to any town with a post office and is held for 30 days; show your passport to collect mail. AmEx also holds mail for one month for people who use its cheques or cards.

Post office opening times vary but typically are 7.30 am to noon and 2 to 6.30 pm Monday to Friday and until 11 am Saturday. The largest post offices offer services outside normal hours (to late evening daily), but some transactions are subject to a Sfr1 to Sfr2 surcharge.

Telephone & Fax

Swisscom, the privatised former monopoly, is the main telecommunications provider. With Swisscom pay phones the minimum charge is a massive Sfr0.60, though per minute rates are low. For Swisscom local/national calls, there are three tariff levels. Normal rates (Sfr0.07/0.12 per minute) apply from 8 am to 5 pm Monday to Friday; rates are cheapest from 10 pm to 6 am every night of the week.

The country code for Switzerland is ☎ 41. Drop the initial zero on the area code when dialling from overseas. For Swisscom international calls, normal rate applies on weekdays (day or night), and rates are 20% lower on weekends. A normal-rate call to the USA/Australia/UK costs Sfr0.58/0.78/0.78 per minute. Prepaid calling cards can be even cheaper – the post office sells a range of cards. Many telephone boxes no longer take coins; the Swisscom *taxcard* comes in values of Sfr5, Sfr10 and Sfr20. Hotels can charge as much as they like for telephone calls, and they usually charge a lot, even for direct-dial calls.

To send a fax at post offices costs Sfr4 plus the telephone call time.

INTERNET RESOURCES

Most large towns have an Internet cafe. Occasionally you can find free places (eg, some

Phone Code Changes

Regional telephone codes in Switzerland will disappear before April 2002. Instead, the current regional code will form part of the subscriber number.

post offices). Addresses/prices are quoted in this chapter, or ask at local tourist offices. The Web site www.MySwitzerland.com has useful links, eg, to rail/Swissair timetables. For current news, try www.sri.ch.

BOOKS

See Lonely Planet's *Switzerland* and *Walking in Switzerland* guides for more detailed information on Switzerland and its walks. *Living and Working in Switzerland* by David Hampshire is an excellent practical guide. *Why Switzerland?* by Jonathan Steinberg looks at the country's history and culture, and enthusiastically argues that Switzerland is *not* a boring country. *The Xenophobe's Guide to the Swiss* by Paul Bilton is an informative and sometimes amusing small volume. *The Swiss, the Gold and the Dead* by Jean Ziegler details shady banking deals in WWII. Fiction about Switzerland is surprisingly scarce, but Anita Brookner won the Booker Prize in 1984 for *Hotel du Lac*, a novel set around Lake Geneva.

English-language books are widely available in Switzerland, though for foreign titles you always pay more in francs than the cover price. Check second-hand bookshops in cities.

NEWSPAPERS & MAGAZINES

Various English-language newspapers and magazines *(The Times, International Herald Tribune, Newsweek)* are widely available and cost around Sfr3 to Sfr6.

RADIO & TV

Swiss Radio International broadcasts in English. Pick it up on 3985kHz, 6165kHz and 9535kHz. The English-language World Radio Geneva is on the FM band at 88.4mHz. Multichannel, multilingual cable TV is widespread; nearly all hotels have it.

PHOTOGRAPHY & VIDEO

Allow plenty of film for those mountain views. Film (36 exposures) is around Sfr7.50 for Kodak Gold and Sfr17.90 for Kodachrome. The Inter Discount chain has low prices. Switzerland uses the PAL video system.

TIME

Swiss time is GMT/UTC plus one hour. Daylight savings comes into effect at midnight on the last Saturday in March, when the clocks are moved forward one hour; they go back again on the last Saturday in October.

LAUNDRY

There is no shortage of coin-operated or service laundrettes in cities. It usually costs about Sfr10 to wash and dry a 5kg load. Many hostels also have washing machines (around Sfr8).

TOILETS

Public toilets are invariably spick-and-span. Urinals are free but there's often a pay slot for cubicles.

WOMEN TRAVELLERS

Women travellers should experience few problems with sexual harassment in Switzerland. However, some Ticino males suffer from the same machismo leanings as their Italian counterparts, so you may experience unwanted attention in the form of whistles and catcalls. It's best to ignore the perpetrators.

GAY & LESBIAN TRAVELLERS

Attitudes to homosexuality are reasonably tolerant. The age of consent is 16. The *Cruiser* magazine (☎ 01-261 82 00, ✉ info@cruiser.ch, Postfach, Zürich CH-8025) has extensive listings of gay and lesbian organisations, bars and events in Switzerland (Sfr4.50). Also check the Web site at www.pinkcross.ch. There are pride parades in Geneva (early July) and Zürich (mid-July).

DISABLED TRAVELLERS

Switzerland Tourism can provide useful information. Many hotels have disabled access and most train stations have a mobile lift for boarding trains. The Swiss Invalid Association (☎ 062-212 12 62, fax 206 88 89), or Schweizerischer Invalidenverband, is at Froburgstrasse 4, Olten CH-4600. Its Web site (www.siv.ch) is in German, French and Italian.

DANGERS & ANNOYANCES

Crime rates may be low but don't neglect security. Some people might find congregations of young drug addicts in cities unsettling. Emergency telephone numbers are: police ☎ 117; fire brigade ☎ 118; and ambulance (most areas) ☎ 144. Take special care in the mountains as helicopter rescue (☎ 1414) is extremely expensive, so make sure your travel insurance covers alpine sports.

BUSINESS HOURS

Most shops are open 8 am to 6.30 pm, Monday to Friday, with a 90-minute or two-hour break for lunch at noon. In towns there's often a late shopping day till 9 pm, typically on Thursday or Friday. Closing times on Saturday are usually 4 or 5 pm. At some places (eg, large train stations) you may find shops open daily. Banks are open 8.30 am to 4.30 pm weekdays, with some local variations.

PUBLIC HOLIDAYS & SPECIAL EVENTS

National holidays are 1 January, Good Friday, Easter Monday, Ascension Day, Whit Monday, 1 August (National Day), and 25 and 26 December. Some cantons observe 2 January, 1 May (Labour Day), Corpus Christi and All Saints' Day. Numerous events take place at a local level throughout the year, so it's worth checking with the local tourist office. Most dates vary from year to year. This is just a brief selection:

January
Costumed Sleigh Rides Experience archetypal Swiss kitsch in the Engadine in January.

February
Carnival The *Fasnacht* spring carnival is celebrated throughout the country in February; it's particularly lively in Basel and Lucerne.

March
Engadine Skiing Marathon Features professionals and amateurs – a great spectacle.

March to October
Combats de Reines From March to October (except in June and July) you can see cow fights in lower Valais.

April
Landsgemeinde Unique show of hands vote in Appenzell, on the last Sunday of April.

May
May Day Celebrated everywhere, though especially in St Gallen and Vaud.

July
Montreux Jazz Festival Big-name rock/jazz acts hit town.

August
National Day Expect celebrations and fireworks on 1 August.

October
Vintage Festivals Down a couple during October in wine-growing regions such as Neuchâtel and Lugano.

November
Onion Market Late November in Bern – there's a real carnival atmosphere.

December
Escalade Festival This historical festival in Geneva celebrates deliverance from would-be conquerers.

ACTIVITIES
Water Sports

Water-skiing, sailing and windsurfing are possible on most lakes. Courses are usually available, especially in Graubünden and central Switzerland. There are over 350 lake beaches. Anglers should contact the local tourist office for a fishing permit valid for lakes and rivers. The Rotsee near Lucerne is a favourite place for rowing regattas. Rafting is possible on many alpine rivers, including the Rhine and the Rhône. Canoeing is mainly centred on the Muota in Schwyz canton and on the Doubs in the Jura.

Skiing

There are dozens of ski resorts throughout the Alps, the pre-Alps and the Jura, incorporating some 200 ski schools. Those resorts favoured by the package-holiday companies do not necessarily have better skiing facilities, but they do tend to have more diversions off the slopes in terms of sightseeing and nightlife.

Equipment can always be hired at resorts; for one day you'll pay about Sfr43/20 for downhill/cross-country gear. You can buy new equipment at reasonable prices, or try asking to buy ex-rental stock – affluent Swiss spurn such equipment, so you might pick up real bargains.

Ski passes (Sfr35 to Sfr60 for one day, but multiday passes are cheaper per day) allow unlimited use of mountain transport.

Hiking & Mountaineering

For information contact the Swiss Alpine Club (SAC; ☎ 031-370 1818, fax 370 18 00),

Monbijoustrasse 61, Bern. Walking is popular and an exhilarating activity in rural areas. There are 50,000km of designated footpaths, often with a convenient inn or cafe en route. Yellow signs marking the trail make it difficult to get lost; each gives an average walking time to the next destination. Slightly more strenuous mountain paths have white-red-white markers instead. Lonely Planet's *Walking in Switzerland* contains track notes for walking in the Swiss countryside. Zermatt is a favourite destination for mountaineers, but you should never climb on your own or without proper equipment.

Adventure Sports

Bungy-jumping, paragliding, canyoning and other high-adrenalin activities are now widely available in Switzerland, especially in the Interlaken area.

WORK

Switzerland's new bilateral agreement with the EU will ensure regulations for EU citizens will ease over the next few years. Non-EU citizens officially need special skills to work legally but people still manage to find casual work in ski resorts – anything from snow clearing to washing dishes. Hotel work has the advantage of including meals and accommodation.

In theory, jobs and work permits should be sorted out before arrival, but if you find a job once there the employer may well have unallocated work permits. The seasonal 'A' permit (Permis A, Saisonbewilligung) is valid for up to nine months, and the elusive and much sought-after 'B' permit (Permis B, Aufenthaltsbewilligung) is renewable and valid for a year. Many resort jobs are advertised in the Swiss weekly newspaper, *hotel + tourismus revue*. Casual wages are higher than in most other European countries.

ACCOMMODATION
Camping

There are about 450 camping grounds, which are classified from one to five stars depending upon amenities and convenience of location. Charges per night are around Sfr7 per person plus Sfr5 to Sfr10 for a tent, and from Sfr3 for a car. Many sites offer a slight discount if you have a Camping Carnet (earned by membership of a camping club). Free camping is discouraged and should be discreet. The Swiss Camping & Caravanning Federation (☎ 041-210 48 22), or Schweizerischer Camping und Caravanning-Verband (SCCV), is at Habsburgerstrasse 35, Lucerne CH-6004.

Hostels

There are 60 official Swiss Youth Hostels (*Jugendherberge, auberge de jeunesse, alloggio per giovani*) which are automatically affiliated to the international network. Nearly all youth hostels include breakfast and sheets in the price. Most also charge Sfr2.50 less during the low season (this chapter quotes high season prices). Some places have double or family rooms available (with single or bunk beds). Around half of the Swiss hostels have kitchen facilities. Membership cards must be shown at hostels. Nonmembers pay a Sfr5 'guest fee' to stay in Swiss hostels; six of these add up to a full international membership card. Buying international membership before you depart home would be cheaper.

Hostels do get full, and telephone reservations are not accepted. Write, or ask your Swiss hostel to reserve ahead for your next one (Sfr1 plus a Sfr9 refundable deposit). Better yet, book on the Web site at www.youthhostel.ch. Booking via the IBN network costs Sfr7.50. A map, giving full details of all hostels on the reverse, is available free from hostels and some tourist offices. The Swiss Youth Hostel Association (SYHA; ☎ 01-360 14 14, fax 360 14 60, ✉ bookingoffice@youthhostel.ch), or Schweizer Jugendherbergen, is at Schaffhauserstrasse 14, Zürich CH-8042.

In the last few years there's been a welcome growth in independent 'backpacker hostels' – they're listed in *Swiss Backpacker News*, free from hostels and some tourist offices. Check the Web site at www.backpacker.ch. They tend to be slightly pricier than youth hostels as breakfast/sheets are often extra, but they are less regulated and allow you to escape the bane of hostel living – noisy school groups. Many offer double rooms and kitchens; some have a bar. Membership is not required.

In ski resorts, some hotels have an annexe with a dormitory (*Touristenlager* or *Massenlager* in German, *dortoir* in French).

The Swiss Alpine Club maintains around 150 dormitory-style mountain huts at higher altitudes.

Hotels

Swiss accommodation is geared towards value for money rather than low costs, so even budget rooms are fairly comfortable (and pricey). The high-season prices quoted in this chapter could be reduced by 10% (towns) to 40% (alpine resorts) during the low season. Hotels are star rated. Prices start at around Sfr45/75 for a basic single/double. Count on at least Sfr10 more for a room with a private shower. Rates generally include breakfast, which tends to be a buffet in mid-range and top-end hotels. Half-board (ie, including dinner) is common in ski resorts. 'Hotel Garni' means a B&B establishment without a restaurant. Note that some train stations have hotel information boards with a free telephone. The Swiss Hotel Association (☎ 031-370 41 11), or Schweizer Hotelier-Verein (SHV), is at Monbijoustrasse 130, Bern CH-3001.

Other Accommodation

Private houses in rural areas sometimes offer inexpensive rooms; look out for signs saying *Zimmer frei* (room(s) vacant). Some farms also take paying guests. Self-catering accommodation is available in holiday chalets, apartments or bungalows. Local tourist offices have full lists of everything on offer in the area.

FOOD

The Swiss emphasis on quality extends to meals. Basic restaurants and taverns *(Stübli)* provide simple but well-cooked food although prices are generally high. Many budget travellers rely on picnic provisions from supermarkets, but even here prices can be a shock, with cheese costing over Sfr20 a kilogram!

The main supermarket chains (closed Sunday, except at some train stations) are Migros and Coop. Larger branches have good quality self-service restaurants, which are typically open until around 6.30 pm on weekdays and to 4 or 5 pm on Saturday. These, along with EPA department store restaurants, are usually the cheapest places for hot food, with dishes starting at around Sfr9. Likewise at university restaurants *(mensas)* – when mentioned in this chapter they are open to everyone, but note that serving times are limited, and they're usually closed during university holidays. Buffet-style restaurant chains, like Manora and Inova, offer freshly cooked food at low prices. Fast-food joints are proliferating.

The best value is a fixed-menu dish of the day *(Tagesteller, plat du jour*, or *piatto del giorno)*. Main meals are eaten at noon. Cheaper restaurants (except pizzerias) tend to be fairly rigid about when they serve. Go to a hotel or more upmarket restaurant for more flexible, later eating. Dedicated vegetarian restaurants can be hard to come by, though many places offer vegetarian choices. Restaurants tend to have a closing day, often Monday.

Swiss food borrows characteristics from its larger neighbours. *Müsli* (muesli) was invented in Switzerland at the end of the 19th century. Soups are popular and often very filling. Cheese is important, particularly in French Switzerland. Emmental and Gruyère are combined with white wine to create *fondue*, which is served up in a vast pot and eaten with bread cubes. *Raclette* is melted cheese, served with potatoes. *Rösti* (fried, shredded potatoes) is German Switzerland's national dish. Veal is highly rated throughout the country; in Zürich it is thinly sliced and served in a cream sauce *(Geschnetzeltes Kalbsfleisch)*. *Bündnerfleisch* is dried beef, smoked and thinly sliced. As in other Germanic countries, a wide variety of *Wurst* (sausage) is available.

Finally, Switzerland makes some of the most delectable chocolate in the world – you may find yourself eating a lot of it here!

DRINKS

Mineral water is readily available but tap water is fine to drink. Note that milk from alpine cows contains a high level of fat.

Alcohol is pricey in bars and clubs. Lager comes in 0.5L or 0.3L bottles, or on draught *(vom Fass* or *à la pression)* with measures ranging from 0.2L to 0.5L. Fortunately, beer and wine prices in supermarkets are relatively low.

Wine is considered an important part of the meal even though it is rather expensive. The local wines are generally good but you might never have heard of them, as they are rarely exported. The main growing regions are the Italian and French-speaking areas, particularly in Valais and by lakes Neuchâtel and Geneva. Both red and white wines are produced, and each region has its speciality (eg, merlot in Ticino). There is also a choice of locally produced fruit brandies, often served with or in coffee.

ENTERTAINMENT

Cinemas usually show films in their original language. Check posters for the upper-case letter: for instance, E/d/f indicates English with German and French subtitles. In French Switzerland you might see 'VO' instead, which signifies 'original version'. The nightlife is not all it could be in the cities and is generally expensive. Geneva has late nightclubs (boîtes), although Zürich is also lively. Several cheaper, alternative-style venues are mentioned in this chapter. In ski resorts the 'après ski' atmosphere can keep things lively until late. Listening to music is popular. Classical, folk, jazz and rock concerts are performed in all major cities.

SHOPPING

Watches and chocolates are on many people's shopping lists. Swiss army knives range from simple blades (Sfr10) to mini-toolboxes (Sfr100 or more); the larger youth hostels sell them at below-list price. A grotesquely tacky cuckoo clock with a girl bouncing on a spring will set you back at least Sfr25 – Interlaken is a good place to find one. Should you want a cowbell with a decorative band, to adorn yourself or a suitable pet, they'll cost from Sfr8 to a fortune depending on the size. If you're after textiles and embroidery look around St Gallen, and for woodcarvings go to Brienz.

Getting There & Away

AIR

The main entry points for flights are Zürich and Geneva. Each has several nonstop flights a day to major transport hubs such as London, Paris and Frankfurt. Both airports are linked directly to the Swiss rail network. EuroAirport, near Mulhouse in France, serves

Basel. Bern has a small airport with some international flights (eg, direct to/from London City airport by Air Engiadina). Swissair luggage check-in facilities are at major Swiss train stations. For Swissair reservations throughout Switzerland, call ☎ 0848-800 700 (local rate).

LAND
Bus

Eurolines buses go to both Zürich (one to three per week, via Basel; UK£53/48 adults/youths one-way) and Geneva (three to six per week; UK£59/53) from London's Victoria coach station – about a 20-hour journey. Geneva also has bus connections to Chamonix and Barcelona, and Zürich has various services to Eastern Europe. See Geneva and Zürich for details.

Train

Located in the heart of Europe, Switzerland has excellent and frequent train connections to the rest of the continent. Zürich is the busiest international terminus. It has two direct day trains and one night train to Vienna (nine hours). There are several trains daily to both Geneva and Lausanne from Paris (three to four hours by superfast TGV). Travelling from Paris to Bern takes 4½ hours by TGV. Most connections from Germany pass though Zürich or Basel. Nearly all connections from Italy pass through Milan before branching off to Zürich, Lucerne, Bern or Lausanne. Reservations on international trains are subject to a surcharge of Sfr5 to Sfr33, depending on the service.

Car & Motorcycle

Roads into Switzerland are good despite the difficulty of the terrain, but special care is needed to negotiate mountain passes. Some, such as the N5 route from Morez (France) to Geneva are not recommended if you have not had previous experience. Upon entering Switzerland you will need to decide whether you wish to use the motorways (there is a one-off charge of Sfr40). Organise this money beforehand, since you might not always be able to change money at the border. Better still, buy it in advance from Switzerland Tourism or a motoring organisation. The sticker (called a vignette) you receive is valid for a year and must be displayed on the windscreen. A separate fee must be paid for trailers and caravans (motorcyclists must pay, too). Some alpine tunnels incur additional tolls.

BOAT

Basel can be reached by Rhine steamer from Amsterdam or other towns en route; the journey time is more than four days. Switzerland can also be reached by lake steamers: from Germany via Lake Constance (Bodensee); from Italy via Lake Maggiore; and from France via Lake Geneva (Lac Léman).

DEPARTURE TAX

Swiss airport taxes of around Sfr15 are always included in the ticket price – there is no other departure tax to pay.

Getting Around

PASSES & DISCOUNTS

Swiss public transport is a fully integrated and comprehensive system incorporating trains, buses, boats and funiculars. Some say it's the most efficient network in the world. Various special tickets make the system even more attractive.

The best deal for people planning to travel extensively is the Swiss Pass, entitling the holder to unlimited travel on Swiss Federal Railways, boats, most alpine postbuses and also on trams and buses in 35 towns. Reductions of 25% apply on funiculars and mountain railways. These passes are valid for four days (Sfr230), eight days (Sfr320), 15 days (Sfr380), 21 days (Sfr440) and one month (Sfr500); prices are for 2nd-class tickets. The Swiss Flexi Pass allows free, unlimited trips for three to nine days within a month and costs Sfr220 to Sfr430 (2nd class). With either pass, two people travelling together get 15% off.

The Swiss Card allows a free return journey from your arrival point to any destination in Switzerland, 50% off rail, boat and bus excursions, and reductions on mountain railways. It costs Sfr150 (2nd class) or Sfr200 (1st class) and it is valid for a month. The Half-Fare Card is a similar deal minus the free return trip. It costs Sfr90 for one month or Sfr150/222 for one/two years.

Except for the Half-Fare Card, these passes are best purchased before arrival in Switzerland from Switzerland Tourism or a travel agent, as they can be bought at only a few major transport centres once you're there.

The Family Card gives free travel for your children (50% off for other children) aged under 16 if they're accompanied by you. Most vendors of the various Swiss travel passes will supply this free to pass purchasers; if not, the Family Card can be bought from major Swiss train stations for Sfr20.

Regional passes, valid for a specific tourist region, provide free travel on certain days and half-price travel on other days within a seven or 15-day period.

All the larger lakes are serviced by steamers, for which rail passes are usually valid (including Eurail; Inter-Rail often gets 50% off). A Swiss Navigation Boat Pass costs Sfr35 and entitles the bearer to 50% off fares of the main operators. It is valid year-round, but few boats sail in winter.

AIR

Internal flights are not of great interest to most visitors, owing to the high prices and excellent ground transport. Crossair, a subsidiary of Swissair, is the local carrier and links major towns and cities several times daily.

BUS

Yellow postbuses are a supplement to the rail network, following postal routes and linking towns to the more inaccessible regions in the mountains. In all, routes cover some 8000km of terrain. They are extremely regular, and departures tie in with train arrivals. Postbus stations are next to train stations.

TRAIN

The Swiss rail network covers 5000km and is a combination of state-run and private lines. Trains are clean, reliable, frequent and as fast as the terrain will allow. Prices are high, though the travel passes mentioned earlier will cut costs. All fares quoted are for 2nd class; 1st-class fares are about 65% higher. In general, Eurail passes are not valid for private lines and Inter-Rail pass holders get a 50% discount. All major stations are connected by hourly departures, but services stop from around midnight to 6 am.

SWITZERLAND

Train stations invariably offer luggage storage, either at a counter (usually Sfr5 per piece) or in 24-hour lockers (Sfr2 to Sfr5). They also have excellent information counters which give out free timetable booklets and advice on connections. Single/return train tickets over 80/160km are valid for two days/one month; you can break the journey but tell the conductor of your intentions. Train schedules are revised yearly, so double-check details before travelling. Phone ☎ 0900-300 300 for train information (Sfr1.19 per minute).

CAR & MOTORCYCLE

Be prepared for winding roads, high passes and long tunnels. Normal speed limits are 50km/h in towns, 120km/h on motorways, 100km/h on semi-motorways (roadside rectangular pictograms show a white car on a green background) and 80km/h on other roads. Don't forget you need a vignette to use motorways and semi-motorways (see the Getting There & Away section earlier in this chapter). Mountain roads are good but stay in low gear whenever possible and remember that ascending traffic has right of way over descending traffic, and postbuses always have right of way. Snow chains are recommended in winter. Use dipped lights in *all* road tunnels. Some minor alpine passes are closed from November to May – check with tourist offices or motoring organisations. The Swiss Touring Club (TCS; ☎ 022-417 2727) is at 4 Chemin de Blandonnet, Case postale 820, CH-1214, Geneva. Its Web address is www.tcs.ch.

Ring ☎ 140 for the national 24-hour breakdown service. Switzerland is tough on drink-driving, so don't risk it; if your blood alcohol level is over 0.05% you face a large fine or imprisonment.

Rental

For the best deals, you have to prebook – see the Getting Around chapter. One-way drop-offs are usually free of charge within Switzerland, though collision damage waiver costs extra. All the multinationals have similar rates – around Sfr130 for one day's rental (unlimited kilometres), with reductions beyond three days. Look out for special weekend deals (Europcar charges Sfr259 including 1500km) or a cheaper 'local tariff'. Local operators may have lower prices (the local

tourist office will have details), though you won't get a 'one-way drop-off' option.

BICYCLE

Despite the hilly countryside, cycling is popular in Switzerland. Cycles can be hired from most train stations and returned to any station with a rental office, though there is a Sfr6 surcharge if you don't return it to the same station (declare your intentions at the outset). The cost is Sfr20 per day or Sfr80 per week. Bikes can be transported on most trains; get a one-day bike pass for Sfr15 (Sfr10 with Swiss travel pass). Local tourist offices often have good cycling information. Bern, Basel, Geneva and Zürich offer free bike loans – see the city sections.

HITCHING

Although illegal on motorways, hitching is allowed on other roads. It can be alternatively fairly easy or quite slow. Indigenous Swiss are not all that sympathetic towards hitchers and you'll find that most of your lifts will come from foreigners. A sign is helpful. Make sure you stand in a place where vehicles can stop. To try to get a ride on a truck, ask around the customs post at border towns.

LOCAL TRANSPORT
City Transport

All local city transport is linked together on the same ticketing system and you need to buy tickets before boarding. One-day passes are usually available and are much better value than paying per trip. There are regular checks for fare dodgers; those caught without a ticket pay an on-the-spot fine of Sfr40 to Sfr60.

Taxis are always metered and tend to wait around train stations, but beware – they are expensive!

Mountain Transport

There are five main modes of transport used in steep alpine regions. A funicular (*Standseilbahn* or *funiculaire*) is a pair of counterbalancing cars on rails, drawn by cables. A cable car (*Luftseilbahn* or *téléphérique*) is dramatically suspended from a cable high over a valley. A gondola (*Gondelbahn* or *télécabine*) is a smaller version of a cable car except that the gondola is hitched onto a continuously running cable as soon as the passengers are inside. A cable chair *(Sessel-bahn* or *télésiège)* is likewise hitched onto a cable but is unenclosed. A ski lift *(Schlepplift* or *téléski)* is a T-bar hanging from a cable, which the skiers hold onto while their feet slide along the snow.

The terms 'gondola' and 'cable car' are more or less interchangeable and T-bars are gradually being phased out.

ORGANISED TOURS

Tours are booked through local tourist offices. The country is so compact that excursions to the major national attractions are offered from most towns. A trip up to Jungfraujoch, for example, is available from Zürich, Geneva, Bern, Lucerne or Interlaken. Most tours represent reasonable value.

Bern

☎ 031 • pop 132,000

Founded in 1191 by Berchtold V, Bern (Berne in French) is Switzerland's capital and fourth-largest city. The story goes that the city was named for the bear *(Bärn* in local dialect) that was Berchtold's first kill when hunting in the area. Even today the bear remains the heraldic mascot of the city. Despite playing host to the nation's politicians, Bern retains a relaxed, small-town charm. A picturesque old town contains 6km of covered arcades and 11 historic fountains, as well as the descendants of the city's first casualty who perform tricks for tourists. The world's largest Paul Klee collection is housed in the Museum of Fine Arts.

Orientation

The compact centre of the old town is contained within a sharp U-bend of the Aare River. The main train station is within easy reach of all the main sights and has bicycle rental (daily from 6.10 am to 11 pm), Swissair check-in and expensive showers.

Information

Tourist Offices Bern Tourismus (☎ 328 12 12, fax 312 12 33, ✉ info-res@bernetourism .ch) is in the train station and open 9 am to 8.30 pm daily. From 1 October to 31 May it shuts two hours earlier and Sunday hours are

reduced to 10 am to 5 pm. Services include hotel reservations (or use the free hotel phone outside) and excursions. There's another office by the bear pits.

The tourist office's free booklet, *Bern aktuell*, contains much practical and recreational information in three languages. Some small shops are shut on Monday morning, and many stay open till 9 pm on Thursday.

Money The SBB exchange office is in the lower level of the train station and open from 6.15 am to 8.45 pm (until 9.45 pm in summer) daily.

Post & Communications The main post office (Schanzenpost 3001) is on Schanzenstrasse; it is open 7.30 am to 6.30 pm Monday to Friday and 7.30 to 11 am on Saturday.

Email & Internet Access Free terminals are at the Medienhaus, Zeughausgasse 14, open 8 am to 6 pm weekdays, 9 am to 11 pm Saturday. The Loeb department store on Spitalgasse has an Internet cafe in the 2nd-level basement.

Travel Agencies The budget and student travel agency SSR (☎ 302 03 12) has two offices: Falkenplatz 9 and Rathausgasse 64. They're open weekdays and Saturday morning.

Bookshops Stauffacher, Neuengasse 25, has many English-language books. Check Rathausgasse or Kramgasse for second-hand bookshops.

Medical & Emergency Services The university hospital (☎ 632 21 11) is on Fribourgstrasse. For help in locating a doctor or pharmacy, call ☎ 311 22 11. Important phone numbers are: police ☎ 117; fire brigade ☎ 118; and ambulance ☎ 144.

Things to See

The free city map from the tourist office details a picturesque walk through the old town. The core of the walk is Marktgasse and Kramgasse, with their covered arcades, colourful fountains, and cellars containing shops, bars and theatres. The best fountain is the ogre fountain, Kornhausplatz, depicting a giant enjoying a repast of wriggling children.

SWITZERLAND

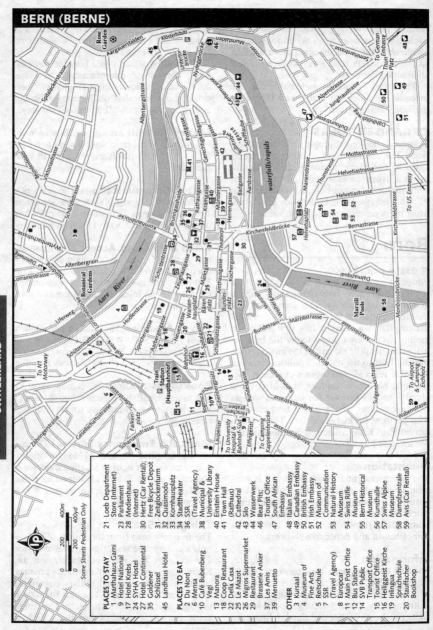

BERN (BERNE)

PLACES TO STAY
1 Marthahaus Garni
9 Hotel National
17 Hotel Krebs
24 SYHA Hostel
27 Hotel Continental
35 Goldener Schlüssel
45 Landhaus Hotel

PLACES TO EAT
6 Mensa
10 Café Bubenberg Vegi
13 Manora
18 Coop Restaurant
22 Della Casa
26 Le Mazot
29 Migros Supermarket Restaurant
32 Brasserie Anker
37 Les Amis
39 Menuetto

OTHER
3 Kursaal
4 Museum of Fine Arts
5 Reitschule
7 SSR (Travel Agency)
8 Europcar
11 Main Post Office
12 Bus Station
14 SVB Public Transport Office
15 Tourist Office
16 Heiliggeist Kirche
19 Inlingua Sprachschule
20 Stauffacher Bookshop
21 Loeb Department Store (Internet)
23 Parliament
28 Medienhaus (Internet)
30 Hertz (Car Rental); Free Bicycle Depot
31 Zeitglockenturm
33 Kornhausplatz
34 Stadttheater
36 SSR (Travel Agency)
38 Municipal & University Library
40 Town Hall (Rathaus)
41 Cathedral
42 Silo
43 Wasserwerk
44 Bear Pits;
46 Tourist Office
47 South African Embassy
48 Italian Embassy
49 Canadian Embassy
50 British Embassy
51 Irish Embassy
52 Museum of Communication
53 Natural History Museum
54 Swiss Rifle Museum
55 Bern Historical Museum
56 Kunsthalle
57 Swiss Alpine Museum
58 Dampfzentrale
59 Avis (Car Rental)

SWITZERLAND

Dividing Marktgasse and Kramgasse there's the **Zeitglockenturm**, a clock tower on which revolving figures herald the chiming hour. People congregate a few minutes before the hour on the eastern side to see them twirl. Originally a city gate, the clock was installed in 1530. The **Einstein House**, Kramgasse 49, is where the physicist developed his special theory of relativity, but there's little to see (Sfr3; closed Sunday and Monday).

The unmistakably Gothic, 15th-century **cathedral** *(Münster)* is noted for its stained-glass windows and elaborate main portal. Just over the Aare River are the **bear pits** *(Bärengraben)*. Bears have been at this site since 1857, although records show that as far back as 1441 the city council bought acorns to feed the ancestors of these overgrown pets. The adjoining Tourist Center has an informative free multimedia show (till 4 or 5 pm daily; closed Monday to Thursday in winter). Up the hill is the **Rose Garden**, which has 200 varieties of roses and an excellent view of the city.

Parliament It's well worth visiting the Bundeshäuser, home of the Swiss Federal Assembly. There are free daily tours when the parliament is not in session (watch from the public gallery when it is). Arrive early and reserve a place for later in the day. A multilingual guide takes you through the impressive chambers and highlights the development of the Swiss constitution.

Museums There is no shortage of museums. The **Museum of Fine Arts** (Kunstmuseum), Hodlerstrasse 8-12, holds the Klee collection and an interesting mix of Italian masters, Swiss and modern art. It is open 10 am to 9 pm on Tuesday and 10 am to 5 pm from Wednesday to Sunday (Sfr6, students Sfr4).

Many museums are grouped together on the southern side of the Kirchenfeldbrücke. The best is the **Bern Historical Museum** (Bernisches Historisches Museum), Helvetiaplatz 5, open 10 am to 5 pm Tuesday to Sunday (to 8 pm Wednesday; Sfr5, students Sfr3). Highlights include the original sculptures from the Münster doorway depicting the Last Judgment, Niklaus Manuel's macabre *Dance of Death* panels, and the ridiculous codpiece on the William Tell statue upstairs. The interactive **Museum of Communication**, Helvetia-

platz 16, is open 10 am to 5 pm Tuesday to Sunday (Sfr5).

Also worthwhile is the **Natural History Museum** (Naturhistorisches Museum) on Bernastrasse, with animals depicted in realistic dioramas. It is open 9 or 10 am to 5 pm daily (closed Monday morning). Entry costs Sfr5, students Sfr3.

Markets An open-air vegetable, fruit and flower market is held at Bärenplatz on Tuesday and Saturday mornings, or daily in summer. On the fourth Monday in November, Bern hosts its famous onion market.

Organised Tours

Inquire at the tourist office about tours. The two-hour city tour by coach (Sfr23) has informative commentary; the on-foot version costs Sfr12.

Places to Stay

Camping Near the river, south of town is *Camping Eichholz* (☎ 961 26 02, Strandweg 49). Take tram No 9 from the station to Wabern. The site is open from 1 May to 30 September, and charges Sfr6.90 per person, from Sfr5 for a tent and Sfr2 for parking. It also has cheap bungalows. Prices are about the same at *Camping Kappelenbrücke* (☎ 901 10 07), except during July and August when they rise to Sfr8.35 per adult, Sfr6.50 for a tent and Sfr3 for a car. It's open year-round except for three weeks in late January. Take the Hinterkappelen postbus to Eymatt.

Hostels The SYHA *hostel* (☎ 311 63 16, fax 312 52 40, Weihergasse 4) is in a good location below Parliament (signposted). It is usually full in summer. The reception shuts from 10 am to 3 pm (summer) or 5 pm (winter), but bags can be left in the common room during the day. Dorm beds are Sfr27.25; add Sfr13 for single rooms. There's lunch (Sr12), dinner (Sfr11), lockers and washing machines (Sfr4 to wash and from Sfr1 to dry).

Hotels There's a limited choice of budget rooms in Bern. *Bahnhof-Süd* (☎ 992 51 11, fax 991 95 91, Bümplizstrasse 189), to the west of town (take bus No 13), has singles/doubles with hall showers from Sfr50/90. Telephone ahead as it's often full. Take bus No 20 from

Bahnhofplatz for *Marthahaus Garni* (☎ *332 41 35, fax 333 33 86,* ✉ *pension.marthahaus@ bluewin.ch, Wyttenbachstrasse 22a*). It's a friendly place with comfortable rooms, TV lounges and a kitchen. Singles/doubles are Sfr60/95 and triples/quads are Sfr120/150. Prices for singles/doubles/triples with private shower/WC and TV are Sfr90/120/150.

Convenient to the train station is *National* (☎ *381 19 88, fax 381 68 78,* ✉ *info@natio nalbern.ch, Hirschengraben 24*). It has good-value singles/doubles from Sfr60/100, or Sfr85/130 with private shower and toilet.

Near the bear pits is *Landhaus Hotel* (☎ *331 41 66, fax 332 69 04,* ✉ *landhaus@spectraweb .ch, Altenbergstrasse 4*). Dorms (Sfr30) are split into two-person cubicles; modern, minimalist doubles are Sfr140 with shower or Sfr110 without (Sfr95/75 single occupancy). Bedding and breakfast cost extra in dorms only. There's a kitchen, and in the restaurant there's free jazz on Thursday, except during summer. It's closed Sunday evening.

In the old town, *Goldener Schlüssel* (☎ *311 56 88, fax 311 02 16,* ✉ *info@goldener schluessel.ch, Rathausgasse 72*) has rooms with TV, radio and telephone. Singles/doubles are Sfr102/145 with shower/WC or Sfr78/114 without. Prices are 10% higher at *Hotel Krebs* (☎ *320 15 15, fax 311 10 35,* ✉ *hotel-krebs@ thenet.ch, Genfergasse 8*), but guests get free tea and coffee.

The three-star *Hotel Continental* (☎ *329 21 21, fax 329 21 99,* ✉ *continental@hote lbern.ch, Zeughausgasse 27*) has new fittings and lower rates Friday to Sunday: Sfr105/150 instead of Sfr130/180.

Places to Eat

The *Coop*, in Ryfflihof on Neuengasse, and *Migros* supermarket (*Marktgasse 46*) both have a cheap self-service restaurant with late opening to 9 pm on Thursday. Also good value is the university *mensa* (*Gesellschaftsstrasse 2*), on the 1st floor. Meals cost around Sfr10 to Sfr14, with reductions for students. It is open 11.30 am to 1.45 pm and 5.45 to 7.30 pm Monday to Friday (closed Friday evening). It closes from mid-July to early August. There's also a ground-floor cafe.

Manora (*Bubenbergplatz 5a*) is a busy buffet-style restaurant with tasty dishes for Sfr9 to Sfr16. The pile-it-on-yourself salad is

Sfr4.20 to Sfr8.90 per plate. Nearby is *Café Bubenberg Vegi* (*1st floor, Bubenbergplatz 8*) which has terrace seating and good vegetarian food for Sfr14 to Sfr20, and regular Indian buffets from Sfr23.80. Slightly more expensive but also recommended for vegetarian food is *Menuetto* (☎ *311 14 48, Münstergasse 47*), open daily except Sunday.

Several pleasant restaurants with outside seating line Bärenplatz, though there's little to choose between them. Go to *Le Mazot* at No 5 to try Swiss specialities such as Rösti (Sfr13.50) and fondue (Sfr20.50). *Restaurant Brasserie Anker* (*Zeughausgasse 1*) has standard Swiss food for a similar price (closed Sunday evening). Its front section is popular with beer drinkers (only Sfr4 for 0.5L).

Du Nord (☎ *332 23 38, Lorrainestrasse 2*) is a bar-restaurant attracting a youngish clientele. Swiss and Italian food costs Sfr14 to Sfr35 (closed Wednesday). At *Les Amis* (☎ *311 51 87, Rathausgasse 63*), main courses (around Sfr30) have a French-Italian influence. It's below a bar and closed on Sunday and Monday.

The dingy exterior of *Della Casa* (☎ *311 21 42, Schauplatzgasse 16*) hides a good quality restaurant within. The local speciality, *Bernerplatte* (a selection of hot meats with sauerkraut, potatoes and beans), costs Sfr40, but perhaps you can find it on the excellent three-course daily *menu* for Sfr23 (lunch to 2 pm, dinner to 9 pm; not available in the plusher upstairs section). It's closed Saturday evening and Sunday.

Entertainment

On Monday, cinemas charge Sfr11 instead of the usual Sfr15. Open-air swimming pools, such as those at Marzili, have free entry (open May to September). A favoured activity in the summer is to walk upriver then float in the swift current of the Aare back to Marzili.

There are various late-night clubs in the centre but entry and drink prices are high. Young people with fewer francs go to places like *Wasserwerk* (*Wasserwerkgasse 5*). There's a bar (open 8 pm) with pool tables and a relaxed view on dope smokers, a Friday and Saturday disco (entry up to Sfr15; from 10 pm) and live music (Sfr18 to Sfr30). *Silo*, a nearby bar on the 1st floor of Mühleplatz 11, has dancing on Friday and Saturday (cheap or free entry). *Quasimodo (Rathausgasse 75)* is a dimly-lit bar with DJs on Friday and Saturday (free entry).

Dampfzentrale (☎ 311 63 37, Marzilis-trasse 47) is a venue for jazz and other music, plus art exhibitions. The *Reitschule (☎ 306 69 69)* on Schützenmattstrasse is a centre for alternative arts, offering reasonable admission prices for dance, theatre, cinema and live music, as well as a bar, restaurant (open from 5 pm; closed Sunday) and women's centre. The place looks a bit seedy, but it's generally a safe place to hang out.

Getting There & Away
Air There are daily flights to/from London, Paris, Lugano, Brussels and other European destinations from the small airport.

Bus Postbuses depart from the western side of the train station.

Train There are at least hourly connections to most Swiss towns, including Geneva (Sfr50, 1¾ hours), Basel (Sfr37, 70 minutes), Interlaken (Sfr25, 50 minutes) and Zürich (Sfr48, 70 minutes).

Car & Motorcycle There are three motorways which intersect at the northern part of the city. The N1 is the route from Neuchâtel in the west and Basel and Zürich in the northeast. The N6 connects Bern with Thun and the Interlaken region in the south-east. The N12 is the route from Geneva and Lausanne in the south-west.

Getting Around
To/From the Airport Belp airport is 9km south-east of the city centre. A small white bus links the airport to the train station (Sfr14). It takes 20 minutes and is coordinated with flight arrivals and departures.

Bus Getting around on foot is easy enough if you're staying in the city centre. Bus and tram tickets cost Sfr1.50 (maximum six stops) or Sfr2.40. A day pass for the city and regional network is Sfr7.50. A 24/48/72-hour pass for the city only costs Sfr6/9/12. Buy single-journey tickets at stops and passes from the tourist office or the SVB public transport office at Bubenbergplatz 5.

Taxi Many taxis wait by the train station. They charge Sfr6.50 plus Sfr2.80 (Sfr3 on Sunday and after 8 pm) per kilometre.

Bicycle From May to October there's *free* daily loans of city bikes at Casinoplatz and by the LOEB department store. ID and Sfr20 deposit are required.

AROUND BERN
There are some excellent excursions close to Bern. **Fribourg**, south-west of Bern and 30 minutes away by train (Sfr11.80), has an old town-centre, fine views and a well-presented Art & History Museum. Farther south is **Gruyères**, about an hour away from either Fribourg or Montreux. Note the 13th-century castle on the hill, and next to the train station is a dairy (☎ 026-921 14 10) offering daily free cheese-making tours. About 30km west of Bern is **Murten** (Morat in French), a historic walled town overlooking a lake (hourly trains from Fribourg and Bern).

Neuchâtel

☎ 032 • pop 32,000

Neuchâtel is inside the French-speaking region of Switzerland, on the north-west shore of the lake that shares its name. This relaxing town offers easy access to the mountain areas of the Jura, where there's good cross-country skiing and hiking.

Orientation & Information
The train station (Gare CFF) changes money daily and rents bikes. The central pedestrian zone and Place Pury (the hub of local buses) are about 1km away down the hill along Ave de la Gare. The tourist office (☎ 889 68 90, fax 889 62 96, @ tourisme.neuchatelois@ ne.ch) is nearby in the main post office (Poste, 2001) by the lake. It's open 9 am to noon and 1.30 to 5.30 pm Monday to Friday, 9 am to noon Saturday; it's open daily in summer.

Things to See & Do
The centrepiece of the old town is the 12th century **castle**, now housing cantonal offices, and the adjoining **Collegiate Church**. The church contains a striking cenotaph of 15 statues dating from 1372. Nearby, the **Prison**

SWITZERLAND

Tower (Sfr0.50; closed October to March) offers a good view of the area and has interesting models showing the town during the 15th and 18th centuries.

One of the town's several museums, the **Museum of Art and History** (Musée d'Art et d'Histoire), Esplanade Léopold Robert 2, is especially noted for three 18th-century clockwork figures. They're always on display but are only activated on the first Sunday of each month. Entry is Sfr7, or Sfr4 for students; the museum is shut on Monday and free on Thursday.

The tourist office has information on nearby walking trails and boat trips on the lake.

Places to Stay

Oasis Neuchâtel (☎ *731 31 90, fax 730 37 09, Rue du Suchiez 35)* is over 2km from the town centre; take bus No 1 to Vauseyon then follow the signs towards Centre sportive. This small, friendly independent hostel offers vegetarian meals and kitchen facilities; check-in is from 5 to 9 pm. Beds are Sfr24 in dorms, or Sfr30 in doubles, or Sfr20 (own sleeping bag needed) in a garden tepee. It's usually open from 1 April to 31 October. La Chaux-de-Fonds (see Around Neuchâtel later in this chapter) has a SYHA *hostel* (☎ *968 43 15, fax 968 25 18, Rue de Doubs 34)*, which is closed in December.

Hôtel-Restaurant du Poisson (☎ *753 30 31, fax 753 06 25, Ave Bachelin 7, Marin)* has singles/doubles for Sfr50/100 with shower or Sfr45/90 without; take bus No 1 from Place Pury. In central Neuchâtel, *Hôtel Marché* (☎ *724 58 00, fax 721 47 42, Place des Halles 4)* provides variable singles/doubles for Sfr70/100 with TV and hall shower. *Hôtel Alpes et Lac* (☎ *723 19 19, fax 723 19 20,* **ⓔ** *hotel@alpesetlac.ch)*, opposite the train station, has refurbished rooms with bathroom and TV from Sfr98/148.

Places to Eat

Cheap self-service restaurants are at *Coop* (Rue de la Treille 4), *EPA* on Rue des Epancheurs, and at *Cité Universitaire* on Ave de Clos-Brochet (open for weekday lunches). *La Crêperie* is at Rue de l'Hôpital 7. If you don't like thin pancakes you'll think this place is a load of crepe, because that's all it serves, but they're tasty, affordable and varied. *Appareils de Chauffage* (Rue des Moulins 37) is a youngish place for drinks and good lunches (from Sfr13.50).

A unique feature of Neuchâtel is its *restaurants de nuit*, open from around 9 pm to 6 am. They provide an excellent opportunity for revellers to eat, drink and dance all night. *Garbo Café (Rue des Chavannes 7)* is one such place (weekend cover charge; closed Monday).

Getting There & Around

There are hourly fast trains to Geneva (Sfr42, 70 minutes), Bern (Sfr17.20, 35 minutes) and many other destinations. Postbuses leave from outside the station. Local buses cost Sfr1.60 to Sfr2.60 per trip, or Sfr6 for a 24-hour pass.

AROUND NEUCHÂTEL

Six kilometres to the east of Neuchâtel at Marin (take bus No 1 from Place Pury) is **Papiliorama**, with over 1000 butterflies of all sizes and hues, and **Nocturama**, with Latin American night creatures. They're in the Marin Centre and open daily (combined ticket Sfr11).

Twenty kilometres north-west of Neuchâtel and accessible by train in 30 minutes (Sfr10), is **La Chaux-de-Fonds**. This watchmaking town is worth visiting for its Horology Museum (Sfr8, students Sfr4; closed Monday) at Rue des Musées 29.

The Jura canton is known for **horse riding**; contact Jura Tourisme (☎ 032-952 19 52, fax 952 19 55, **ⓔ** crs@jura.ch), Rue de la Gruère 1, Saignelégier. Costs are relatively low in this part of Switzerland.

Geneva

☎ 022 • pop 175,000

Geneva (Genève, Genf, Ginevra) is Switzerland's third-largest city, comfortably encamped on the shore of Lake Geneva (Lac Léman). Geneva belongs not so much to French-speaking Switzerland as to the whole world. It is truly an international city, a destination where belligerents worldwide come to settle their differences by negotiation. Over 40% of residents are non-Swiss and many world organisations are based here, not least the United Nations (European headquarters).

Geneva won respite from the Duke of Savoy in 1530 and was ripe for the teachings of John Calvin two years later. It soon became known as the Protestant Rome, during which time fun became frowned upon. Thankfully this legacy barely lingers and today Geneva offers a varied nightlife. In 1798 the French annexed the city and held it for 16 years before it was admitted to the Swiss Confederation as a canton in 1815.

Orientation

The Rhône River runs through the city, dividing it into *rive droite* (north of the Rhône) and *rive gauche* (the south). Conveniently in the centre of town on the northern side is the main train station, Gare de Cornavin. To the south of the river lies the old part of town and many important buildings. In the summer, Geneva's most visible landmark is the Jet d'Eau, a giant fountain on the southern shore.

In France, **Mont Salève** yields an excellent view of the city and Lake Geneva. Take bus No 8 to Veyrier and walk across the border. The cable car up costs Sfr19 return and runs daily in summer, but infrequently in winter.

Information

Tourist Offices The main tourist office (☎ 909 70 00, fax 909 70 11, ✉ info@gene ve-tourisme.ch), 18 Rue du Mont-Blanc, is open 8 am to 6 pm daily from mid-June to 31 August. At other times it closes on Sunday and opens 9 am to 6 pm Monday to Saturday. Hotel reservations cost Sfr5. There's another tourist office in the airport (10 am to 3 pm daily) and a city information office (☎ 311 99 70) in the old town on Pont de la Machine (closed Monday morning and Sunday).

The Centre d'Accueil et de Renseignements (CAR; ☎ 731 46 47) has youth-oriented information dispensed from a bus parked at the station end of Rue du Mont-Blanc. It's open 9 am to 11 pm daily from mid-June to 31 August.

Ask any of the above places for the excellent, free *Vélo-Cité* map.

Money The exchange office in Gare de Cornavin is open 6.45 am to 8 pm daily (9.30 pm in summer). The best rates we saw were at the Bureau de Change Michel at 32 Rue de Zürich, open on weekdays and Saturday morning. Some exchange offices in the air-port charge Sfr5 commission on cash exchanges, but you can do this commission-free at the adjoining train station.

Post & Communications The main post office is at 18 Rue du Mont-Blanc, 1211 Genève 1. It is open 7.30 am to 6 pm Monday to Friday and 8.30 am to noon Saturday.

Email & Internet Access Good rates for Internet access (Sfr1/5 for 10/60 minutes) are at Club Videorom, 19 Rue des Alpes (closed Sunday morning).

Travel Agencies American Express (☎ 731 76 00) is at 7 Rue du Mont-Blanc, near many other travel agents and airline offices. The budget and student travel agency SSR (☎ 329 97 34) is at 3 Rue Vignier.

Bookshops Librairie des Amateurs, 15 Grand-Rue, has some second-hand English-language books from Sfr3. Artou (☎ 818 02 40), 8 Rue de Rive, is good for travel books and maps.

Medical Services Ring ☎ 111 (premium rate) for medical information. The Cantonal Hospital (☎ 372 33 11) is at 24 Rue Micheli du Crest. Permanence Médico Chirurgicale (☎ 731 21 20), 1-3 Rue de Chantepoulet, is a private clinic open 24 hours. Emergency dental treatment (☎ 733 98 00) is available at 60 Ave Wendt.

Things to See

The city centre is so compact that it is easy to see many of the main sights on foot. Start a scenic walk through the old town at the **Île Rousseau**, noted for a statue in honour of the celebrated free thinker.

Turn right (west) along the southern side of the Rhône until you reach the 13th-century **Tour de L'Île**, once part of the medieval city fortifications. Walk south down the narrow, cobbled Rue de la Cité until it becomes Grand-Rue. At No 40 is Rousseau's birthplace. A short detour off Grand-Rue there's the part-Romanesque, part-Gothic **Cathedral St Pierre**. John Calvin preached here from 1536 to 1564. There is a good view from the tower, which is open daily until at least 5 pm (Sfr3). The cathedral is on a significant but unspectacular

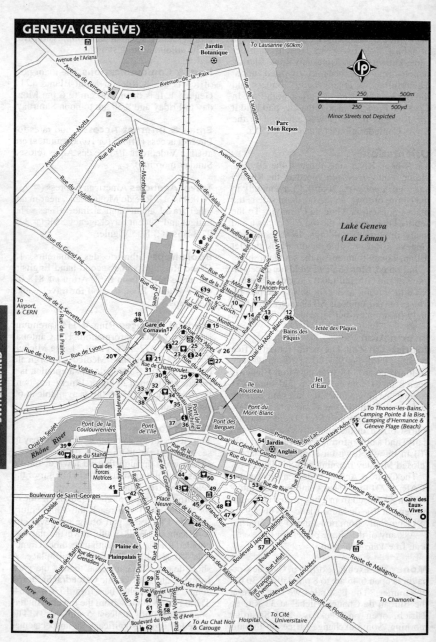

GENEVA (GENÈVE)

To Lausanne (60km)

Jardin
Botanique

Avenue de l'Ariana

Avenue de Ferney

Avenue de-la-Paix

Parc
Mon Repos

Avenue de France

Lake Geneva
(Lac Léman)

Rue de Lausanne

Rue de Montbrillant

Avenue Giuseppe-Motta

Rue de Vermont

Rue du Vidollet

Rue du Grand Pré

Rue des Gares

To Airport,
& CERN

Rue de la Servette

Rue de la Prairie

Rue de Lyon

Rue Voltaire

Gare de
Cornavin

Bains des
Pâquis

Jetée des Pâquis

Île
Rousseau

Jet
d'Eau

To Thonon-les-Bains,
Camping Pointe à la Bise,
Camping d'Hermance &
Genève Plage (Beach)

Pont du
Mont-Blanc

Pont des
Bergues

Promenade du Lac

Jardin
Anglais

Pont de la
Coulouvrenière

Rhône River

Pont de l'Ile

Quai des
Forces
Motrices

Boulevard de Saint-Georges

Place
Neuve

Grand Rue

Plaine de
Plainpalais

Boulevard des Philosophes

Arve River

Boulevard du Pont d'Arve

To Au Chat Noir
& Carouge

Hospital

To Cité
Universitaire

To Chamonix

Gare des
Eaux-
Vives

Route de Malagnou

SWITZERLAND

GENEVA (GENÉVE)

PLACES TO STAY
- 4 Centre Masaryk
- 5 SYHA Hostel
- 6 City Hostel
- 13 Hôtel de la Cloche
- 15 L'Aiglon
- 16 Bernina
- 30 Excelsior
- 41 Hôtel Beau-Site
- 58 Hôtel le Prince
- 59 Forget Me Not
- 62 Hôtel Carmen

PLACES TO EAT
- 8 Migros
- 10 Le Blason
- 11 Edelweiss Restaurant; Sixt
- 14 Auberge de Savièse
- 19 Kong Restaurant
- 20 La Trattoria
- 32 Restaurant Manora
- 33 Auberge de Coutance
- 35 Sugar Hut
- 38 Buffet de Chine

- 42 Victoria
- 47 Chez Ma Cousine
- 51 EPA Department Store
- 52 La Tête dans le Sable
- 55 l'Amiral
- 61 Café Universal

OTHER
- 1 International Red Cross & Red Crescent Museum
- 2 Palais des Nations (UN)
- 3 Place des Nations
- 7 Horizon Motos
- 9 Bureau de Change Michel
- 12 Free Bicycle Rental
- 17 Place de Cornavin
- 18 Genev' Roule
- 21 Notre-Dame
- 22 CAR Information Centre
- 23 Post Café
- 24 Main Tourist Office; Main Post Office
- 25 Club Videorom
- 26 Place des Alpes

- 27 International Bus Terminal
- 28 American Express
- 29 Permanence Médico Chirurgicale
- 31 Place des 22 Cantons
- 34 Mulligans
- 36 City Information Office
- 37 Tour de l'Île
- 39 L'Usine
- 40 Le 2e Bureau
- 43 Flanagan's Irish Bar
- 44 Librairie des Amateurs
- 45 Rousseau's Birthplace
- 46 Reformation Monument
- 48 Cathedral St Pierre
- 49 Maison Tavel
- 50 Alhambar
- 53 Artou Bookshop
- 54 CGN Ticket Booth
- 56 Museum of Natural History
- 57 Museum of Art & History
- 60 SSR Travel Agency
- 63 Centre Sportif des Vernets

archaeological site (Sfr5, students Sfr3; closed Monday). Grand-Rue terminates at **Place du Bourg-de-Four**, the site of a medieval market-place which now has a fountain and touristy shops.

Take Rue de la Fontaine to reach the lakeside. Anti-clockwise round the shore is the **Jet d'Eau**. Calling this a fountain is something of an understatement. The water shoots up with incredible force (200km/h, 1360 horsepower) to create a 140m-high plume. At any one time, seven tonnes of water is in the air, and much of it, depending on the whims of the wind, falls on spectators who venture out on the pier. It's not activated in winter or in high winds.

Parks & Gardens On the lakefront near the old town, the **Jardin Anglais** features a large clock composed of flowers. Colourful flower gardens and the occasional statue line the promenade on the northern shore of the lake (well worth a stroll) and lead to two relaxing parks. One of these, the **Jardin Botanique**, features exotic plants, llamas and an aviary. Entry is free and it is open until 7.30 pm (5 pm in winter) daily. South of Grand-Rue is

Promenade des Bastions. This park contains a massive monument to the Reformation: the giant figures of Bèze, Calvin, Farel and Knox are flanked by smaller statues of other important figures, and depictions in relief of events instrumental to the spread of the movement.

Museums Geneva is not a bad place on a rainy day as there are plenty of museums, many of which are free. The most important is the **Museum of Art and History** (Musée d'Art et d'Histoire), 2 Rue Charles Galland, with a vast and varied collection including paintings, sculpture, weapons and archaeological displays. The nearby **Museum of Natural History** (Musée d'Histoire Naturelle) on Route de Malagnou has dioramas, minerals and anthropological displays. In the old town, **Maison Tavel**, 6 Rue du Puits Saint Pierre, is notable for a detailed relief map of Geneva in 1850, covering 35 sq metres. These museums have free entry and are open 9.30 or 10 am to 5 pm Tuesday to Sunday.

By the UN's Palais des Nations there's the **International Red Cross & Red Crescent Museum**, a vivid multimedia illustration of the history of these two humanitarian organisations. It's open 10 am to 5 pm Wednesday to Monday (Sfr10, students/seniors Sfr5).

United Nations The European arm of the UN is in the Palais des Nations, former home of its deceased parent, the League of Nations, and the focal point for a resident population of 3000 international civil servants. The hour-long tour of the interior is pricey and only moderately interesting (Sfr8.50, students and seniors Sfr6.50). The pleasant gardens have a towering grey monument coated with heat-resistant titanium, donated by the former USSR to commemorate the conquest of space, but you can't go into the grounds unless you take the interior tour.

It's open on weekdays from November to March and daily from April to October. Guided tours are held from 10 am to noon and 2 to 4 pm (9 am to 6 pm in July and August). You need to show your passport to get in.

Activities

Centre Sportif des Vernets (☎ 418 40 00), 4 Rue Hans Wilsdorf, has swimming (Sfr5, students Sfr2) and ice skating (same price) and is open from 9 am daily except Monday. On weekends in summer Lake Geneva is alive with the bobbing white sails of sailing boats. Swim in the lake at Genève Plage (Sfr7, including entry to a large pool with waterslide) or at Bains des Pâquis (Sfr2), which is also a great place to hang out on summer evenings.

Organised Tours

CERN, near the north-western Geneva suburb of Meyrin, is a particle physics research laboratory which has an interesting free exhibition (with English text; closed Sunday and Monday morning). This was the first lab to create anti-matter (in 1996). On Saturday, three-hour guided tours of the site and 27km-long particle accelerator are free (take your passport); book about two weeks ahead on ☎ 767 84 84 or ✆ visits-service@cern.ch. Take bus No 15 from the station.

Special Events

The Geneva Festival, held on the second weekend in August, is a time of fun, fireworks and parades. L'Escalade (around 12 December) celebrates the foiling of an invasion by the Duke of Savoy in 1602.

Places to Stay

Camping Seven kilometres north-east of the city centre on the southern lakeshore is *Camping Pointe à la Bise* (☎ 752 12 96), Vesenaz; it costs Sfr6 per person, plus from Sfr9 for tents. Take bus E from Rive. Farther (at the terminus of bus E) and cheaper is *Camping d'Hermance* (☎ 341 05 05, *Chemin des Glerets*). Both sites are open from around April to October and prices include car parking.

Hostels A good selection of dormitory accommodation is listed in the *Info-jeunes* leaflet issued by the tourist office, including some that take women only.

North of the Rhône The SYHA *hostel* (☎ 732 62 60, fax 738 39 87, 28-30 Rue Rothschild), is big, modern and busy, with helpful staff. Large dorms are Sfr24, doubles are Sfr65 and dinners are Sfr12.50, and there's a TV room, laundry, Internet and kitchen facilities. The hostel is closed from 10 am to 4 pm (to 2 pm in summer) and there is a midnight curfew.

Centre Masaryk (☎ 733 07 72, 11 Ave de la Paix) provides dorms for Sfr30. Singles/doubles/triples cost Sfr45/80/105 and you can get a key for late access. Take bus No 5 or 8 from Gare de Cornavin.

City Hostel (☎ 901 15 60, ✆ info@cityhostel.ch, 2 Rue Ferrier), is a new backpacker hostel. Reception is open all day to 10 pm. Its four-bed dorms are Sfr24 and singles/doubles are Sfr50/70. There's a kitchen but no breakfast.

South of the Rhône The *Cité Universitaire* (☎ 839 22 22, fax 839 22 23, 46 Ave Miremont) has many beds, but dorms (Sfr17) are only available in July and August. Take bus No 3 from Gare de Cornavin to the terminus at Champel, south of the city centre. Singles/doubles cost Sfr45/61, or Sfr38/55 for students. A double studio with kitchen, toilet and shower is Sfr68. Breakfast is Sfr6. Reception is open 8 am to noon (9 to 11 am on Sunday) and 2 pm (6 pm on weekends) to 10 pm.

Forget Me Not (☎ 320 93 55, fax 781 46 45, 8 Rue Vignier) has simple, student-style rooms with sink for Sfr45/80. Dorms are Sfr25 and there's kitchens but no breakfast.

Hotels In addition to the affordable choices mentioned here, there are many high-cost high-class hotels.

North of the Rhône The *Hôtel de la Cloche* (☎ 732 94 81, fax 738 16 12, 6 Rue de la Cloche) is small, old-fashioned, friendly and liable to be full unless you call ahead. Its big singles/doubles using hall shower are Sfr55/85; doubles with shower/WC are Sfr120.

L'Aiglon (☎ 732 97 60, fax 732 87 71, 16 Rue Sismondi) has varying, sizable doubles for Sfr100 with shower or Sfr130 with shower/WC and TV. Breakfast is Sfr10 per head and it's in a colourful, slightly seedy street.

There's not much to choose between the tourist-class hotels clustered near the train station. *Bernina* (☎ 908 49 50, fax 908 49 51, 22 Place de Cornavin) has renovated rooms with TV and telephone and charges Sfr105/150 with shower and Sfr80/105 without. *Excelsior* (☎ 732 09 45, fax 738 43 69, 32 Rue Rousseau), has dull but decently equipped singles/doubles from Sfr115/180.

South of the Rhône The *Hôtel Beau-Site* (☎ 328 10 08, fax 329 23 64, 3 Place du Cirque) is a good deal, with kitchen facilities, free tea and coffee, and sizable, old-fashioned rooms with high ceilings and creaky wood floors. Singles/doubles/triples cost from Sfr60/82/100 using hall shower or Sfr70/90/110 with private shower.

Big rooms with TV in *Hôtel Carmen* (☎ 329 11 11, fax 781 59 33, @ hotelcarmen .gasser@bluewin.ch, 5 Rue Dancer) are Sfr76/92 with shower or Sfr53/72 without. Breakfast costs Sf8. *Hôtel le Prince* (☎ 807 05 00, fax 807 05 29, 16 Rue des Voisins) has comfortable if smallish rooms with shower, TV and telephone. Singles/doubles are Sfr75/95, or Sfr85/105 with private toilet.

Places to Eat

Fondue and raclette are widely available. Also popular is locally caught perch, but it costs well over Sfr20 unless you can find it as a plat du jour. Fruit and vegetable markets are scattered around, eg, at Plaine de Plainpalais.

North of the Rhône Migros supermarket on Rue des Pâquis has a cheap self-service restaurant. *Aperto*, a supermarket in the train station, is open 6 am to 10 pm daily. Buffet-style *Restaurant Manora (4 Rue de Cornavin)* has tasty daily dishes from Sfr10 and extensive salad and dessert bars. It is open 7 am (9 am on Sunday) to 9 pm daily. Opposite, *Auberge de Coutance* (☎ 732 79 19, 5 Rue de Coutance) is recommended for exquisite south-western French specialities from Sfr25 (Sfr15 at lunch). It's an atmospheric restaurant, closed on Sunday.

La Trattoria (1 Rue de la Servette) near the station, has excellent Italian food from Sfr15 (closed Sunday). Along the road at No 31 is *Kong Restaurant*, providing tasty Chinese dishes for Sfr20. Visit at lunchtime on weekdays, when there are meals for Sfr12 including rice and starter, and (Tuesday to Friday) Sfr17.50 secures an all-you-can-eat buffet. Another good Chinese option is *Buffet de Chine (5 Rue de Grenus)*, with daily plates for Sfr10 (open 11 am to 9 pm, Monday to Saturday).

Le Blason (23 Rue des Pâquis) looks like a typical bar-restaurant by day, with meals from Sfr14, but it also courts late-night clubbers by opening from 4 am to 8 am and noon to 2 am daily (4 am to 10 am on weekends). *Auberge de Savièse (20 Rue des Pâquis)* opposite has lunchtime plats du jour from Sfr13 and Swiss specialities such as fondue from Sfr19.50 (closed lunchtime at weekends). Sometimes the air is so thick with cheese that people on a diet could dine on the scent alone. Fondue is Sfr23 at *Edelweiss* (☎ 731 49 40), but there's a free folklore show (from 7 pm nightly).

Take advantage of the international flavour of Geneva to vary your diet. Explore the streets north of Rue des Alpes for cheapish Oriental and Asian food. South of Rue des Alpes, *Sugar Hut (16 Rue des Etuves)* has good Thai food from about Sfr20 (closed Saturday lunchtime and Sunday).

South of the Rhône For the cheapest eating in the old town, head for the restaurant in the *EPA* department store on Rue de la Croix d'Or. Meals cost from Sfr8 to Sfr14.

Chez Ma Cousine (6 Place du Bourg-de-Four) is a tiny place offering just one dish – half-chicken, potatoes and salad for Sfr12.90.

SWITZERLAND

It's closed Sunday. Nearby, *La Tête dans le Sable* (☎ *310 25 50, 9 Rue Verdaine*) is a trendy place with several small rooms. Meals are anything from Sfr16 to Sfr55 and there's a good salad buffet. *Victoria* at Place du Cirque is a stylish mid-priced brasserie owned by two gourmet chefs. Dishes are above Sfr20 and it's open daily.

Café Universal (*26 Blvd du Pont d'Arve*) is atmospheric, French and smoky, with theatrical patrons. Plats du jour are from Sfr16 and dinners are mostly above Sfr25 (closed Sunday and Monday). Another good place for those with slightly larger budgets is *l'Amiral* (☎ *735 18 08, 24 Quai Gustave-Ador*), near the Jet d'Eau. The three-course *menu touristique* for Sfr32 includes fillet of perch (open daily).

Entertainment

Geneva has a good selection of nightclubs but unless you have money to burn, steer clear. These, along with dance, music and theatre events, are listed in *Genève Agenda*, free from the tourist office.

Alternative arts flourish in the city: ask locally about in-vogue (and often short-lived) squats that put on various events. *L'Usine* (☎ *781 34 90, 4 Place des Volontaires*) is a converted old factory (hence the name), now a centre for cinema, theatre, concerts and homeless art objects. It has a bar and an inexpensive restaurant (limited choice but great food from Sfr12, Tuesday to Friday evenings). Nearby, *Le 2e Bureau* (☎ *320 24 49, 9 Rue du Strand*) is a bar with a relaxed ambience and free concerts (closed Sunday).

A good international bar is *Post Café* (*7 Rue de Berne*), with draught cider and Guinness, and British sports on TV. Similar places are *Mulligans* (*14 Rue Grenus*) and *Flanagan's Irish Bar* in the old ◆own at Rue du Cheval-Blanc. *Alhambar* (☎ *312 20 36*) on the 1st floor at 10 Rue de la Rôtisserie has good lunches, drinks and free live music. *Au Chat Noir* (☎ *343 49 98, 13 Rue Vautier*) has live music (mostly jazz, entry Sfr15) and DJs.

Getting There & Away

Air Geneva airport is an important transport hub and has frequent connections to every major European city. Swissair, by the station on Rue de Lausanne, has youth fares (under 26) and one-off offers; the office is open 8.30 am to 6.30 pm Monday to Friday.

Bus International buses depart from Place Dorcière (☎ 732 02 30), off Rue des Alpes. There are four buses a week to London (Sfr150, 17 hours), three weekly to Barcelona (Sfr100, 10 hours) and several daily to Chamonix (Sfr43, 1½ hours).

Train There are more or less hourly connections to most Swiss towns; the Zürich trip takes three hours (Sfr77), as does Interlaken (Sfr65), both via Bern. There are regular international trains to Paris (Sfr103 by TGV, 3½ hours; reservations essential), Hamburg (Sfr273, 10 hours), Milan (Sfr81, four hours) and Barcelona (Sfr100, 10 hours). Gare des Eaux-Vives is the best station for Annecy and Chamonix. To get there from Gare de Cornavin, take any bus going to Bel Air and then tram No 12 or 16.

Car & Motorcycle An autoroute bypass skirts Geneva, with major routes intersecting south-west of the city: the N1 from Lausanne joins with the E62 to Lyon (130km) and the E25 heading south-east towards Chamonix. Toll-free main roads follow the course of these motorways.

Sixt (☎ 738 13 13), 1 Place de la Navigation, has the best daily car rental rates (from Sfr99 per day with unlimited kilometres). Its weekend deal for 72 hours is Sfr149. Horizon Motos (☎ 732 29 90), 51 Rue de Lausanne, has motorcycles (weekend rates from Sfr104, unlimited kilometres).

Boat Compagnie Générale de Navigation (CGN; ☎ 312 52 23), on Quai du Mont-Blanc and by Jardin Anglais, operates a steamer service to all towns and major villages bordering Lake Geneva, including those in France. Most boats only operate between May and September, such as those to Lausanne (Sfr33, 3½ hours) and Montreux (Sfr38.80, 4½ hours).

Eurail and Swiss passes are valid on CGN boats, or there are CGN boat day passes for Sfr52. CGN also has circular excursions and dancing cruises.

Getting Around

To/From the Airport Getting from Cointrin airport is easy with 200 trains a day into Gare de Cornavin (Sfr5, six minutes). Bus No 10 (Sfr2.20) does the same 5km trip. A taxi would cost Sfr25 to Sfr35.

Bus The city is efficiently serviced by buses, trolley buses and trams. There are ticket dispensers at stops. A ticket for multiple rides within one hour costs Sfr2.20, or a ticket valid for three stops within 30 minutes is Sfr1.50. A day pass costs Sfr5 for the city or Sfr8.50 for the whole canton. Get a small discount on fares with a prepaid 'Carte@bus' card, available from the Transports Publics Genevois offices, eg, in Gare de Cornavin.

Taxi The cost for most taxis is Sfr6.30 plus Sfr2.70 per kilometre, though some operators have higher prices.

Bicycle Bike rental is at Gare de Cornavin, though they're cheaper (Sfr8 per day) from Genev' Roule (☎ 740 13 43), 17 Place de Montbrillant. From May to October Genev' Roule even has bikes *free of charge*, available here and at Bains des Pâquis, Place du Rhône and Plaine de Plainpalais. Some ID and Sfr50 deposit is required.

Boat In addition to CGN (see the previous Getting There & Away section) smaller companies operate excursions on the lake between April and October but no passes are valid. Ticket offices and departures are along Quai du Mont-Blanc and by the Jardin Anglais. Trips range from half an hour (Sfr8, several departures a day) to two hours (Sfr20), with commentary in English.

Lake Geneva Region

LAUSANNE

☎ 021 • pop 125,000

Capital of the canton of Vaud, this hilly city is Switzerland's fifth largest. Don't miss the Musée de l'Art Brut, one of Europe's most unusual art collections.

Orientation & Information

In the train station is a tourist office (open 9 am to 7 pm daily) and bicycle rental and money-changing facilities. Opposite, behind McDonald's, is the Quanta video games arcade, with Internet access (Sfr4 for 30 minutes). The main post office (Poste Principale 1001) is by the station. The cathedral, shopping streets and Place St François (the main hub for local transport) are up the hill to the north.

The principal tourist office (☎ 613 73 21, fax 616 86 47, ✉ information@lausanne-tourisme.ch) is in the Ouchy metro station by the lake. It's open 9 am to 6 pm daily (to 8 pm from April to September). Commission is charged for hotel reservations.

Things to See & Do

The fine Gothic **cathedral** was built in the 12th and 13th centuries and has an impressive main portal and attractive stained-glass windows. Extensive renovations, including the famous rose window, were completed in 1998. The church and tower are open daily.

The **Musée de l'Art Brut**, 11 Ave de Bergières, should take at least two hours of your time. It's a fascinating amalgam of art created by untrained artists – the mentally unhinged, eccentrics and incarcerated criminals. Some of the images created are startling, others are merely strange. Biographies and explanations are in English and the collection is open 11 am to 1 pm and 2 to 6 pm Tuesday to Sunday (Sfr6, students Sfr4).

Lausanne is the headquarters of the International Olympic Committee, so it is perhaps inevitable that there's a museum devoted to the games. The lavish and impressive **Musée Olympique** (Olympic Museum), 1 Quai d'Ouchy, is open daily, except Monday in winter (Sfr14, students Sfr9), and tells the Olympic story using videos, archive film, interactive computers and memorabilia.

The large **Palais de Rumine**, near the Place de la Riponne, contains several museums, covering natural history and other sciences; all are free the first Sunday in the month. Its Fine Arts (Beaux-Arts) collection exhibits many works by Swiss artists (Sfr6, students Sfr4; closed Monday).

The lake provides plenty of sporting opportunities. Vidy Sailing School (☎ 617 90 00) offers courses on and rental equipment

SWITZERLAND

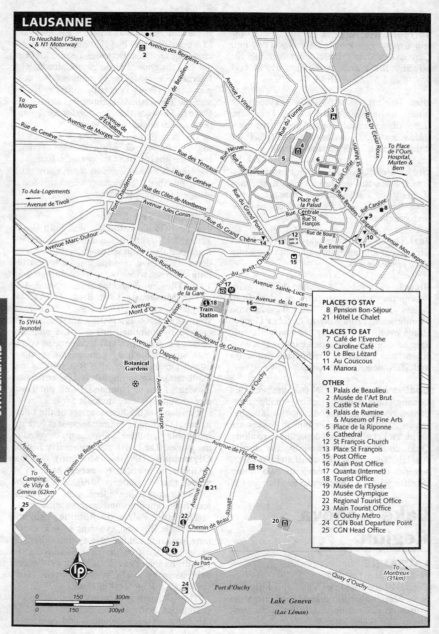

LAUSANNE

To Neuchâtel (75km) & N1 Motorway
Avenue des Bergières
To Morges
Avenue de Beaulieu
Avenue A Vinet
Avenue d'Echallens
Avenue de Morges
Rue de Genève
Rue du Tunnel
To Place de l'Ours, Hospital, Murten & Bern
Rue des Terreaux
Rue Neuve
Rue Saint Laurent
Rue Dr César Roux
Rue St Martin
Rue Louis Curtat
Rue de Genève
Rue des Côtes-de-Montbenon
To Ada-Logements
Avenue de Tivoli
Port Chauderon
Avenue Jules Gonin
Rue du Grand Pont
Place de la Palud
Rue Centrale
Rue St François
Rue de Bourg
Rue Caroline
Rue Pépinet
Avenue Mon Repos
Avenue Marc-Dufour
Avenue Louis-Ruchonnet
Rue du Grand Chêne
Rue Enning
Rue du Petit-Chêne
Avenue Sainte-Luce
Place de la Gare
Train Station
Avenue de la Gare
To SYHA Jeunotel
Avenue Mont d'Or
Avenue W Fraisse
Boulevard de Grancy
Avenue Dapples
Botanical Gardens
Avenue de la Harpe
Avenue d'Ouchy
Avenue de l'Elysée
To Camping de Vidy & Geneva (62km)
Avenue de Rhodanie
Chemin de Bellerive
Chemin de Beau-Rivage
Place du Port
Port d'Ouchy
Quay d'Ouchy
To Montreux (31km)
Lake Geneva
(Lac Léman)

PLACES TO STAY
8 Pension Bon-Séjour
21 Hôtel Le Chalet

PLACES TO EAT
7 Café de l'Everche
9 Caroline Café
10 Le Bleu Lézard
11 Au Couscous
14 Manora

OTHER
1 Palais de Beaulieu
2 Musée de l'Art Brut
3 Castle St Marie
4 Palais de Rumine & Museum of Fine Arts
5 Place de la Riponne
6 Cathedral
12 St François Church
13 Place St François
15 Post Office
16 Main Post Office
17 Quanta (Internet)
18 Tourist Office
19 Musée de l'Elysée
20 Musée Olympique
22 Regional Tourist Office
23 Main Tourist Office & Ouchy Metro
24 CGN Boat Departure Point
25 CGN Head Office

0   150   300m
0   150   300yd

SWITZERLAND

for windsurfing, water-skiing and sailing. For less athletic entertainment, try a tour of the nearby wine growers' cellars, centring on Lavaux and Chablais to the east and La Côte to the west. Get details from the tourist office.

Places to Stay

Year-round lakeside camping is possible at *Camping de Vidy* (☎ 624 20 31, *3 Chemin du Camping*), west of the city centre (take bus No 2). It also has two/four person bungalows for about Sfr55/90.

Nearby on the same bus route, the SYHA *Jeunotel* (☎ 626 02 22, *fax 626 02 26*, *❷ jeun otel@urbanet.ch, 36 Chemin du Bois-de-Vaux*) is intended as a cross between a youth hostel and a hotel. It offers no-frills accommodation in dorms (Sfr25), singles/doubles (Sfr76/92 with shower and WC or Sfr52/76 without), and triples/quads (Sfr87/116 without). The self-service restaurant serves cheap meals.

Also west of the city centre there's *Ada-Logements* (☎/fax 625 71 34, *60 Ave de Tivoli*). It's student oriented but takes tourists if there's space. Singles/doubles are Sfr50/70. *Pension Bon-Séjour* (☎ 323 59 52, *10 Rue Caroline*) in a residential block is more central. Rooms cost Sfr40/66, some with shower; phone ahead. Much cosier is the small *Hôtel Le Chalet* (☎ 616 52 06, *49 Ave d'Ouchy*) with singles/doubles/triples for Sfr62/88/99. Young people may get a discount. There are hall showers, a garden, and breakfast is Sfr9.

Places to Eat

The buffet-style *Manora* (*17 Place St François*) has a good choice of vegetables, salad and fruit, and main dishes are around Sfr10. *Cafe de l'Everche* (*4 Rue Louis Curtat*) by the cathedral has a lunch and evening two-course *menu* for Sfr15, and a pleasant garden at the back. It is closed Sunday lunchtime.

Au Couscous (*2 Rue Enning*), on the 1st floor, has a wide menu including Tunisian, vegetarian and macrobiotic food. Meals mostly cost above Sfr17 and it's closed at lunchtime on weekends. Nearby, *Le Bleu Lézard* (*10 Rue Enning*) has inexpensive food and a cellar bar with free live music or DJs most nights. Opposite is *Caroline Café*, which is a food hall in the Coop Centre with

a range of cheap meals till 10.30 pm (closed Sunday).

Getting There & Away

There are three trains hourly to/from Geneva (Sfr20, 50 minutes), and one or two hourly to Bern. Trains to Interlaken Ost cost Sfr54 via Bern (two hours); the picturesque route via Montreux/Zweisimmen is Sfr58 (three hours). For boat services, see the Geneva section.

MONTREUX

☎ 021 • pop 19,700

Centrepiece of the so-called Swiss Riviera, Montreux offers marvellous lakeside walks and access to the ever-popular Château de Chillon. Nearby Vevey is an equally good base.

Orientation & Information

The train station and main post office are on Ave des Alpes, with the town centre to the left (south). The tourist office (☎ 962 84 36, fax 963 81 13, ❷ tourism@montreux.ch) is a few minutes away in the pavillon on the lakeshore (descend the stairs or lift opposite the post office). It is open 8.30 am to 5.30 pm Monday to Friday and 9 am to noon Saturday, or 9 am to 7 pm daily in summer.

Things to See

Montreux is known for the **Château de Chillon** (pronounced sheeyoh), which receives more visitors than any other historical building in Switzerland. In a stunning position on Lake Geneva, the fortress caught the public imagination when Lord Byron wrote about the fate of Bonivard, a follower of the Reformation, who was chained to the fifth pillar in the dungeons for four years in the 16th century. Byron etched his own name on the third pillar.

The castle, still in excellent condition, dates from the 11th century and has been much modified and enlarged since. Allow at least two hours to view the tower, courtyards, dungeons and numerous rooms containing weapons, utensils, frescoes and furniture. Entry costs Sfr7.50 for adults, Sfr6 for students and Sfr3.50 for children. The castle is open daily, but hours range from 10 am to 5 pm in winter to 9 am to 7 pm in summer. The castle is a pleasant 45-minute walk along the

SWITZERLAND

lakefront from Montreux (15 minutes from the hostel), or it's also accessible by local train (stop: Veytaux-Chillon) or bus No 1 (Sfr2.60; stop: Veytaux). **Vevey**, to the west, has several interesting museums and is easily reached by bus No 1.

Montreux's other claim to fame is the **Jazz Festival** in early July. The program is announced in late April; inquire then for tickets on ☎ 963 82 82. Visit the Web site at www.montreuxjazz.com.

Places to Stay

The SYHA *hostel* (☎ *963 49 34, fax 963 27 29, 8 Passage de l'Auberge, Territet)* is a 30-minute walk along the lake clockwise from the tourist office (or take the local train to Territet, or bus No 1). It's near the waterfront, under the railway line, and is closed in December and January. Dorms are Sfr29 and doubles (bunk beds) are Sfr76.

A good alternative is *Yoba Riviera Lodge* (☎ *923 80 40, fax 923 80 41,* **ⓔ** *rivier alodge@bluewin.ch, 5 Grande-Place)* in the centre of Vevey. Beds are Sfr35 in double rooms or Sfr25 (Sfr20 without sheets) in dorms. Breakfast is Sfr7, or use the kitchen. Reception is closed from noon to 4 pm.

Pension Wilhelm (☎ *963 14 31, fax 963 32 85, 13 Rue de Marché)* charges Sfr55/100 for rooms without shower in an old-fashioned, family-run hotel. Doubles with own shower are Sfr110. *Hostellerie du Lac* (☎ *963 32 71, fax 963 18 35, 12 Rue du Quai)* is the only affordable choice right by the lake. Rooms vary in style and facilities – some have lakeside balconies, all have TV and radio. Doubles start at Sfr85 with hall shower or Sfr130 with shower and WC. Subtract about Sfr15 for single occupancy (closed mid-December to mid-February).

Places to Eat

The *Migros* supermarket, in the Forum shopping centre by the lake, has a takeaway section. *Paradise (58 Grand-Rue)* has fast food but is best for its extensive salad buffet (Sfr2.60 per 100g). Across the street is *Metropole*, with idyllic outside seating overlooking the lake. Meals, including pizzas, start about Sfr14.

Brasserie des Alpes (23 Ave des Alpes) provides good French and Italian fare from

Sfr14 and is open daily. *Hostellerie du Lac* has a decent restaurant serving fish and other meals (Sfr13 to Sfr38).

Budget options in Vevey include *Manora* by the station and a *Migros* restaurant on Rue de Lausanne.

Getting There & Away

Hourly trains run to/from Geneva and take 70 minutes (Sfr29). From Lausanne, there are three trains an hour (Sfr9.40, 25 minutes). Interlaken can be reached via a scenic rail route, with changeovers at Zweisimmen and Spiez (rail passes valid, though there is a Sfr6 supplement for 'Panoramic Express' trains only). The track winds its way up the hill for an excellent view over Lake Geneva. For boat services, see the Geneva Getting There & Away section earlier in this chapter.

VAUD ALPS

If you're in this region in late January, don't miss the International Hot Air Balloon Week, a visually spectacular event in **Château d'Oex**, on the Montreux-Interlaken railway line. Contact the tourist office (☎ *924 25 25, fax 924 25 26,* **ⓔ** *chateau-d oex@bluewin.ch)*.

To get off the beaten track, consider staying in quiet, untouristed **Gryon** (1130m), south-east of Montreux. It is scenically situated, close to the Villars ski area and 30 minutes by train from Bex (on the Lausanne-Sion rail route). There are several cheap places to stay – ask at the tourist office (☎ 024-498 14 22).

Swiss Alp Retreat (☎ *024-498 33 21, fax 498 35 31)*, based in the Chalet Martin, is favoured by young backpackers. Beds cost Sfr18 in dorms or from Sfr28 in doubles; add Sfr3 for the first night. There's a kitchen (no breakfast) and check-in is from 9 am to 9 pm (phone ahead). Check the Web site at www.gryon.com.

Leysin is accessible from Aigle on the Lausanne-Sion route and is a skiing and hiking centre. Stay at the *Hiking Sheep Guesthouse* (☎/*fax 024-494 35 35,* **ⓔ** *hsgl@o media.ch)* where there's a kitchen and friendly staff. Beds are Sfr30/35 in dorms/doubles, without breakfast (reductions in low season). Reception is closed from noon to 5 pm.

Valais

The dramatic alpine scenery of Valais (Wallis in German) once made it one of the most inaccessible regions of Switzerland. Nowadays the mountains and valleys have been opened up by an efficient network of roads, railways and cable cars. It is an area of great natural beauty and, naturally enough, each impressive panorama has spawned its own resort. Skiing (47 listed centres) in the winter and hiking in the summer are primary pursuits, but angling, swimming, mountaineering, even tennis, are widely enjoyed.

Valais is also known for its Combats de Reines (Kuhkämpfe in German) – cow fights organised in villages to determine which beast is most suited to lead the herd up to the summer pastures. They usually take place on selected Sundays, starting in late March, and are accompanied by much celebration and consumption of Valais wine. The combatants rarely get hurt. There is a grand final in Aproz round about Ascension Day (40 days after Easter) and the last meeting of the season is at the Martigny Fair in October.

SION

☎ 027 • pop 26,200

Sion, the capital of the Lower Valais, merits a perusal en route from Montreux to Zermatt (all trains stop here). Two ancient fortifications dominate the town, Tourbillon Castle and, on the neighbouring hill, the Valère church. Both provide a fine view of the Rhône Valley. The Valais regional museums are here too. If you want to stop over, there's an SYHA *hostel* (☎ 323 74 70, fax 323 74 38, Rue de l'Industrie 2), behind the station – exit left and turn left under the tracks.

ZERMATT

☎ 027 • pop 5340

Skiing, hiking and mountaineering are the main attractions in this resort, all overseen by the Matterhorn (4478m), the most famous peak in the Alps.

Orientation & Information

Zermatt is car-free except for electric taxis, and street names are rarely used. The tourist office (☎ 967 01 81, ✆ zermatt@wallis.ch),

beside the train station, is open 8.30 am to noon and 1.30 to 6 pm Monday to Friday, and 8.30 am to noon Saturday. During the high season it is also open Saturday afternoon and Sunday. Next door is a travel agent, which changes money. The Alpin Center (☎ 966 24 60) on the main street near the post office is another good information source.

Activities

Zermatt has many demanding slopes to test the experienced skier; beginners have fewer possibilities. February to April is peak time, but in early summer the snow is still good and the lifts are less busy. There are excellent views of mountain panoramas, including Monte Rosa and the Matterhorn, from the network of cable cars and gondolas.

The cog-wheel railway to Gornergrat (3100m; Sfr63 return) is a particular highlight. The Klein Matterhorn is topped by the highest cable station in Europe (3820m); it provides access to summer skiing slopes, as well as the ski route down to Cervinia in Italy (don't forget your passport). There are footpaths to and from many of the cable-car terminals. A day pass for all ski lifts, excluding Cervinia, costs Sfr62. Ski shops open daily for rental – for one day, hire prices are Sfr28 for skis and stocks and Sfr15 for boots.

A walk in the cemetery is a sobering experience for would-be mountaineers, as numerous monuments tell of deaths on Monte Rosa and the Matterhorn. Also wander around the traditional Valais wooden huts in the Hinter Dorf area, just north of the church.

Places to Stay & Eat

Some hotels and restaurants close between seasons.

Camping Matterhorn (☎ 967 39 21), to the left of the train station, is open from June to early September.

The SYHA *hostel* (☎ 967 23 20, fax 967 53 06) has an excellent view of the Matterhorn. Turn left at the church, cross the river and take the second right. Dorm beds at halfboard are Sfr46. To wash and dry laundry costs Sfr8. The hostel is shut between seasons. Nearby, *Matterhorn Hostel* (☎ 968 19 19, fax 968 10 15, ✆ info@matterhornhostel .com) is open year-round. Dorms (four to eight beds) are Sfr24/29 in low/high season, and basic doubles are Sfr34/36 per person. Optional breakfast/dinner is Sfr6/12. In both hostels, doors stay open during the day though check-in is from 4 pm.

Opposite the train station and popular with mountaineers is the renovated *Hotel Bahn-hof* (☎ *967 24 06, fax 967 72 16,* ✉ *hotel_ba hnhof@hotmail.com*) with 12-bed dorms for Sfr30 and compact singles/doubles from Sfr54/84. Prices are without breakfast but there's a kitchen. *Hotel Gabelhorn* (☎ *967 22 35*) in the Hinter Dorf area of the village is small and friendly, charging from Sfr50/88; doubles with shower are Sfr98. Nearby, *Hotel Mischabel* (☎ *967 11 31, fax 967 65 07,* ✉ *mischabel.zermatt@reconline.ch*) is a wooden chalet with balconies and a garden. There are singles with shower/WC for Sfr67, and singles/doubles/triples at Sfr57 per person using hall shower.

North Wall Bar, near the hostels, is one of the cheapest and best bars in the village, popular with resort workers. It has ski videos, music, good pizzas from Sfr10 and beer for Sfr4.50 (0.50L). The bar is closed between seasons, otherwise it's open 6 pm to midnight daily. Down the hill, the more expensive *Papperla Pub* is also popular.

Beyond the church on the main street, *Restaurant Weisshorn* and the *Café du Pont* next door are both good places for food. Also recommended is *Walliserkanne* by the post office which has fondue, raclette, and Valais specialities from Sfr14.

Getting There & Away
Hourly trains depart from Brig, calling at Visp en route. The steep and scenic journey takes 80 minutes and costs Sfr37 one way, Sfr63 return. It is a private railway; Swiss Passes are valid, Eurail passes are not, and Inter-Rail passes earn 50% off for those under 26. See the St Moritz Getting There & Away section later in this chapter for information on the *Glacier Express*. The valley is a cul-de-sac, but if you're going to Saas Fee you can divert there from Stalden-Saas.

As Zermatt is car-free, you need to park cars at Täsch (Sfr4.50 to Sfr11 per day) and take the train from there (Sfr7.40). Parking is free near Visp station if you take the Zermatt train.

SAAS FEE
☎ 027 • pop 1670
In an off-shoot from the Zermatt valley, Saas Fee is ringed by 4000m peaks and has summer skiing. The highest metro in the world operates all year to Mittelallalin at 3500m, where there's an ice pavilion (Sfr7) and fabulous views. The tourist office (☎ 958 18 58, ✉ to@saas-fee.ch) is opposite the bus station, and can tell you about various affordable accommodation options. These include *Albana*, offering beds in shared rooms from Sfr33. The reception is in the adjoining *Hotel Mascotte* (☎ *957 27 24, fax 957 12 16*), which has singles/doubles for Sfr55/110 with private toilet and shower.

Getting There & Away
Car-free Saas Fee cannot be reached by train. Hourly buses depart from Brig via Visp, take one hour and cost Sfr17.40; reserve the return trip two hours in advance. There are car parks at the village entrance.

OTHER RESORTS
The best known resort in west Valais is **Verbier**, with 400km of ski runs. Ski passes cost Sfr56 for one day or Sfr318 for a week. Lesser-known resorts can have perfectly adequate skiing yet be much cheaper. For example, ski passes in **Leukerbad**, west of Brig, are Sfr41 (students Sfr34) for one day. Leukerbad is also a health spa with hot springs.

Ticino

South of the Alps and enjoying a Mediterranean climate, Ticino (Tessin in German) gives more than just a taste of Italy. Indeed, it belonged to Italy until the Swiss Confederation seized it in 1512. The people are darker skinned than their compatriots, and the cuisine, architecture and vegetation reflect that found farther south. Italian is the official language of the canton. Many people also speak French and German but you will find English less widely spoken than in the rest of Switzerland. The region offers mountain hikes and dramatic gorges in the north, and water sports and relaxed, leisurely towns in the south. A two/15-day fishing permit for Ticino's lakes and rivers costs Sfr40/100 at tourist offices.

Free open-air music festivals include Bellinzona's Piazza Blues (late June), and Lugano's Estival Jazz (early July) and Blues to Bop Festival (end of August). There are others – check with local tourist offices.

BELLINZONA
☎ 091 • pop 17,100

The capital of Ticino is a city of castles. Bellinzona is set in a valley of lush mountains, and stands at the southern side of two important alpine passes, San Bernardino and St Gotthard. You can roam the ramparts of the two larger castles, **Castelgrande** or **Castello di Montebello**, and visit the museums inside (Sfr4 each, closed Monday). The smallest castle, **Castello di Sasso Corbaro** high on the hill, hosts temporary exhibitions.

The tourist office (☎ 825 21 31, fax 825 38 17, ✆ bellinzona.turismo@bluewin.ch), Viale Stazione 18, is on the main street, in the post office. It is open weekdays and Saturday morning.

Places to Stay & Eat
There are a few budget hotels in town. A convenient choice is *Garni Moderno (☎/fax 825 13 76, Viale Stazione 17b)*, part of Caffè della Posta (closed Sunday). It has new-looking rooms for Sfr55/90, and doubles with a small bathroom for Sfr120. *Tsui-Fok (☎/fax 825 13 32, Via Nocca 20)* offers oldish rooms with hall showers for Sfr45/70; add Sfr5 per person for breakfast. Reception and the restaurant are closed till 6.30 pm on Monday and 2.30 to 6.30 pm on other days.

As you might expect, Bellinzona has plenty of affordable pizzerias, or check the self-service restaurants at *Coop*, on Via H Guisan, the nearby *Migros*, or *Inova*, in the Innovazione department store on Viale Stazione. *Pedemonte (☎ 825 33 33, Via Pedemonte 12)* is a great place for mid-price food (closed Monday).

Getting There & Away
Bellinzona is on the train route connecting Locarno (Sfr6.80, 25 minutes) and Lugano (Sfr10.80, 30 minutes). It is also on the Zürich-Milan route. Postbuses head northeast to Chur; you need to reserve your postbus seat the day before on ☎ 825 77 55, or at the train station. There is a good cycling

track along the Ticino River to Lake Maggiore and Locarno.

LOCARNO
☎ 091 • pop 15,000

Locarno lies at the northern end of Lake Maggiore. At 205m above sea level, it's Switzerland's lowest town.

Orientation & Information
Piazza Grande is the centre of town and the location of the main post office (Posta 1, 6600). Nearby is the tourist office (☎ 751 03 33, fax 751 90 70, ✆ locarno@ticino.com), Largo Zorzi, within the casino complex. It has brochures on many parts of Switzerland, and opens 9 am to 6 pm Monday to Friday and (mid-March to mid-October) 10 am to 4 pm Saturday, 10 am to 2 pm Sunday.

A five-minute walk east is the train station, where money exchange and bike rental is available daily. Pardo Bar, Via della Motta 3, has Internet access (Sfr4 for 20 minutes).

Things to See & Do
The principal attraction is the **Madonna del Sasso**, up on the hill with a good view of the lake and the town. The sanctuary was built after the Virgin Mary appeared in a vision in 1480. It contains some 15th-century paintings, a small museum and several distinctive statue groups. There is a funicular from the town centre, but the 20-minute walk up is not demanding (take Via al Sasso off Via Cappuccini) and you pass some shrines on the way.

In the town, explore the Italianate piazzas and arcades. There are a couple of churches worth a look, including the 17th-century **Chiesa Nuova** on Via Cittadella, with an ornate ceiling and frolicking angels.

Locarno has more hours of sunshine than anywhere else in Switzerland, just right for strolls round the lake. **Giardini Jean Arp** is a small lakeside park off Lungolago Motta, where sculptures by the surrealist artist are scattered among the palm trees and tulips.

Places to Stay
Delta Camping (☎ 751 60 81) is very expensive at Sfr20 (Sfr30 in high season) plus Sfr10 (Sfr17) per person.

The SYHA *hostel (☎ 756 15 00, fax 756 15 01, Via Varenna 18)*, 500m west of Piazza

Grande, has a range of rooms and prices, starting at Sfr31 for dorms and Sfr57/66 for singles/doubles. Check in from 3 pm.

Pensione Città Vecchia (☎/fax 751 45 54, *e* cittavecchia@datacomm.ch, *Via Toretta 13*), uphill from Piazza Grande via a side street by Innovazione, is an independent hostel without curfew or daytime closing. Beds in different-sized dorms are Sfr24, plus Sfr4.50 each for sheets or breakfast; both are provided in singles/doubles at Sfr35 per person. It is open from March to November. *Osteria Reginetta* (☎/fax 752 35 53, *e* reginetta.locarno@bluewin.ch, *Via della Motta 8*) is 200m west of the pensione and open the same months. It provides singles/doubles/triples for Sfr42 per person, or Sfr49 including breakfast.

Convenient for the station is *Garni Montaldi* (☎ 743 02 22, fax 743 54 06, *Piazza Stazione*). Modern singles/doubles with telephone and cable TV cost from Sfr60/120 with shower or Sfr55/100 without. You can get some great deals out of season. The reception is also here for *Stazione*, an older building to the rear where singles/doubles with shower are Sfr47/88. Stazione closes from 1 November to 31 March.

Places to Eat

A *Coop* supermarket is on Piazza Grande; opposite there's the *Migros De Gustibus* snack bar. *Inova* (*Via Stazione 1*) by the train station has good self-service dishes from Sfr9, help-yourself salad plates from Sfr4.20 to Sfr9.90, and cheap beer. It is open until 10 pm daily.

Lungolago on Lungolago Motta has pizzas from only Sfr10.50 and outside tables (open daily). It's a popular evening drinking venue for youngish locals (beer Sfr3.50) and is open daily.

Try fish and French specialities (Sfr35 to Sfr50) in the upstairs section at *Ristorante Cittadella* (*Via Cittadella 18*). Downstairs, there are pizzas from Sfr12 (closed Sunday in summer). The restaurant at *Hotel Ristorante Zurigo* (*Via Verbano 9*) serves good, mid-range food.

Getting There & Away

The St Gotthard Pass provides the road link (N2) to central Switzerland. There are trains every one to two hours from Brig, passing through Italy en route (Sfr50, three hours). You change trains at Domodóssola across the border, so bring your passport.

One-day travel passes for boats on Lake Maggiore cost Sfr11 to Sfr20 depending upon the validity range. For more information, contact Navigazione Lago Maggiore (NLM; ☎ 751 18 65). There is a regular boat and hydrofoil service from Italy (except in winter).

LUGANO
☎ 091 • pop 29,000
Switzerland's southernmost tourist town offers an excellent combination of lazy days, watery pursuits and hillside hikes.

Orientation & Information

The train station has money-exchange, bike rental and an Aperto supermarket, all open daily. The old town lies down the hill to the east (10 minutes' walk), where you'll find the tourist office (☎ 913 32 32, fax 922 76 53, *e* infor@lugano-tourism.ch), Riva Giocondo Albertolli, on the lake side of the Municipio building. Opening hours are 9 am to 6.30 pm Monday to Friday, 9 am to 12.30 pm and 1.30 to 5 pm Saturday, and 10 am to 2 pm Sunday. In winter, opening hours reduce to 9 am to 12.30 pm and 1.30 to 5.30 pm weekdays only.

The main post office (Posta 1, 6900) is in the centre of the old town at Via della Posta 7. Internet access is at City Disc, Via P Peri; charges are Sfr4/8/10 for 20/40/60 minutes.

Things to See & Do

Winding alleyways, pedestrian-only piazzas and colourful parks make Lugano an ideal town for walking around. The **Santa Maria degli Angioli** church, Piazza Luini, has a vivid fresco of the Crucifixion by Bernardino Luini dating from 1529.

The **Thyssen-Bornemisza Gallery**, Villa Favorita, Castagnola, is a famous private art collection. It covers every modern style from abstract to photorealism, though the Old Masters were removed to Spain in 1992. Admission is Sfr10 for adults or Sfr6 for students, and it's open 10 am to 5 pm Friday to Sunday, from April to November only. The **Cantonal Art Museum**, Via Canova 10, also has a worthwhile modern selection (Sfr7, students Sfr5). It's open 10 am to 5 pm Wednesday to Sunday and 2 to 5 pm Tuesday. Exhibitions cost extra in both places.

The **Lido**, east of the Cassarate River, offers a swimming pool and sandy beaches for Sfr7 a day, and it's open daily from 1 May to mid-September. A boat tour of **Lake Lugano** is a very enjoyable excursion. There are boat and bus departures approximately every 90 minutes to nearby Melide, where **Swissminiatur** displays 1:25 scale models of national attractions (Sfr11, children Sfr7; closed in winter, otherwise open daily). Picturesque villages, reachable by boat, are Gandria (visit the customs museum across the shore) and Morcote.

The tourist office has hiking information, and conducts free guided walks of the town on Monday from April to October (book the day before). There are excellent hikes and views from **Monte San Salvatore** and **Monte Brè**. The funicular from Paradiso up Monte San Salvatore operates from mid-March to mid-November only and costs Sfr12 to go up or Sfr18 return. To ascend Monte Brè, you can take the year-round funicular from Cassarate (Sfr13 up, Sfr19 return).

Places to Stay

The relaxed SYHA *hostel* (☎ 966 27 28, fax 968 23 63, Via Cantonale 13), is a hard 20-minute walk uphill from the train station (signposted), or take bus No 5 to Crocifisso (Sfr1.20). Dorm beds are Sfr23 and doubles are Sfr56. Optional breakfast is Sfr7, and reception is closed from 12.30 to 3 pm. The hostel has private grounds and a swimming pool and closes from 1 November to mid-March.

Two stops earlier on bus No 5 is *Ristorante Bar Romano* (☎/fax 966 22 17, Via San Gottardo 103) with simple but pleasant rooms for only Sfr38/76. Reservations are advised, especially for Sunday when the bar is closed.

Close to the train station is *Hotel Montarina* (☎ 966 72 72, fax 966 00 17, ✉ asbest@ tinet.ch, Via Montarina 1) in two buildings with a garden, kitchen and swimming pool. Beds in large dorms are Sfr20, plus Sfr4 if you need sheets. Singles/doubles are Sfr50/80 and triples/quads are Sfr105/140. Singles/doubles with own shower/WC are Sfr65/120. Prices exclude breakfast, and the hotel is closed from 31 October to pre-Easter.

Hotel Ristorante Pestalozzi (☎ 921 46 46, fax 922 20 45, Piazza Indipendenza 9) has singles/doubles/triples for Sfr92/144/206 with own shower/WC or Sfr60/100/140 without. In Paradiso (bus No 1) try *Hotel Dischma* (☎ 994 21 31, fax 994 15 03, ✉ dischma@swissonline.ch, Vicolo Geretta 6). It has a jolly hostess and singles/doubles with shower and toilet for Sfr65/110.

Places to Eat

There is a large *Migros* supermarket and restaurant on Via Pretorio opposite Via Emilio Bossi. The *EPA department store* (Via Nassa 22) also has a cheap restaurant. Similarly priced is *Ristorante Inova*, up the stairs on the northern side of Piazza Cioccaro, with excellent buffet-style food (open until 10 pm daily). Also good and cheap for Italian and vegetarian food is alcohol-free *Hotel-Restaurant Pestalozzi* (see Places to Stay), which is open 6 am to 11 pm daily.

As you might expect, pizza and pasta abound. *Sayonara* on the southern side of Piazza Cioccaro has both, as well as local dishes (open daily). The popular *La Tinèra*, Via dei Gorini, off Piazza della Riforma, is also good for Ticinese food and has meals for Sfr11 to Sfr27 (closed Sunday). For drinks and pittas, try *Ethnic* in the pedestrian-only Quartiere Maghetti (closed Saturday lunch and Sunday).

Getting There & Away

Lugano is on the same road and rail route as Bellinzona. Two postbuses run to St Moritz daily in summer, with one making the trip in winter (and only on Friday, Saturday and Sunday during some weeks). It costs Sfr63 (plus a Sfr10 supplement) and takes four hours. You need to reserve your seat the day before at the bus station or the train information office, or by phoning ☎ 807 85 20. Buses leave from the bus station on Via Serafino Balestra, though the St Moritz bus also calls at the train station. A seven-day regional holiday pass costs Sfr92 and is valid for all regional public transport, including funiculars and boats on Lake Lugano.

Graubünden

Tourists in Switzerland once were a summer phenomenon. Then in 1864, Johannes Badrutt, the owner of the Engadiner Kulm Hotel in St Moritz, offered four English summer guests free accommodation if they returned for winter. He told them they were missing the best time of the year. Although dubious of the claim, the English could not refuse a free offer. They returned, enjoyed themselves and winter tourism was born.

Present-day Graubünden (Grisons, Grigioni, Grishun) has some of the most developed and best-known winter sports centres in the world, including Arosa, Davos, Klosters, Flims and, of course, St Moritz. Away from the international resorts, Graubünden is a relatively unspoiled region of rural villages, alpine lakes and hill-top castles. The people speak German, Italian or Romansch.

CHUR
☎ 081 • 33,500

Chur is the canton's capital and largest town, yet it has a compact centre. It has been continuously inhabited since 3000 BC.

Orientation & Information

From the train station, walk down Bahnhofstrasse and turn left for the tourist office (☎ 252 18 18, fax 252 90 76, ✉ info@churtourismus.ch), Grabenstrasse 5, open 8.30 am to noon and 1.30 to 6 pm on weekdays, except Monday morning, and 9 am to noon Saturday. The regional tourist office (☎ 254 24 24, ✉ contact@graubuenden.ch), Alexanderstrasse 24, has information on the canton (open 8 am to 6 pm weekdays).

Things to See

Chur has an attractive old town with 16th-century buildings, fountains and alleyways. Augusto Giacometti designed three of the windows in the 1491 **Church of St Martin**. In the impressive **cathedral**, built from 1150, take note of the crypt, the high altar and the carved heads on the choir stalls. The **Kunstmuseum** on Postplatz is closed on Monday (Sfr10, students Sfr7) and contains modern art, including a generous gathering of stuff by the three Giacomettis: Alberto, Augusto and Giovanni. Note also the sci-fi work by local artist HR Giger, who created the monsters in the *Alien* films. If you like sci-fi themes, then you should visit Giger's creatively decorated bar at Comercialstrasse 23.

Places to Stay & Eat

Camp Au (☎ 284 22 83) by the sports centre, is open year-round.

Hotel Schweizerhaus (☎ 252 10 96, fax 252 27 31, Kasernenstrasse 10) has dorms for Sfr30, and singles/doubles for Sfr55/110 with shower and Sfr40/80 without. Breakfast is Sfr5. *Hotel Pizzeria Collina delle Rose* (☎/fax 252 23 88, Malixerstrasse 32) has rooms with shower and TV from Sfr70/130, or Sfr45/90 without. Both hotels are a five-minute walk south-west of the old town. Greater comfort and arty decor can be found at *Hotel Drei Könige* (☎ 252 17 25, fax 252 17 26, Reichsgasse 18). Singles/doubles with TV start from Sfr85/130 with shower/WC or Sfr65/100 without.

Self-service restaurants are at *Coop* on Bahnhofstrasse and at *Migros* on Gürtelstrasse, both open till 9 pm on Friday. *Speise Restaurant Zollhaus* (Malixerstrasse 1) has two parts (open daily). Bierschwemme is the downstairs bar and serves meals and lunch specials for around Sfr12. Upstairs is the calmer and more cultured Bündnerstube, where there's a larger range of meals and prices (from Sfr12.50). Also good is the atmospheric restaurant in *Hotel Zunfthaus zur Rebleuten* (Kupfergasse 1), where meals start at around Sfr16.50 (closed Tuesday until 5 pm).

Getting There & Away

Postbuses leave from the depot above the train station, including the express service to Bellinzona (reserve ahead on ☎ 256 31 66). There are rail connections to Davos, Klosters and Arosa, and fast trains to Sargans (the station for Liechtenstein, only 25 minutes away) and Zürich (Sfr38, 90 minutes). Chur can be visited on the *Glacier Express* route (see the St Moritz Getting There & Away section later in this chapter).

ST MORITZ
☎ 081 • pop 5600

The playground of today's international jet-setters, St Moritz needs little introduction. The curative properties of this resort's waters have been known for 3000 years.

Orientation & Information

St Moritz exudes health and wealth. The train station near the lake rents out bikes and

SWITZERLAND

changes money from 6.50 am to 8.10 pm daily. Just up the hill is the post office (7500) and five minutes farther on is the tourist office or *Kurverein* (☎ 837 33 33, fax 837 33 77, ✉ information@stmoritz.ch) at Via Maistra 12. It's open 9 am to 6 pm Monday to Saturday; in the low season, it closes for lunch and on Saturday afternoon. To the southwest, 2km around the lake from the main town, St Moritz Dorf, lies St Moritz Bad; buses run between the two. Not much stays open during November, May and early June.

Bobby's Pub, Via dal Bagn, has Internet access (10 am to 1 am daily, Sfr2 for 10 minutes)

Activities

In the St Moritz region there are 350km of downhill runs, although the choice for beginners is limited. A one-day ski pass costs Sfr55, and ski and boot rental is about Sfr43 for one day. There are also 160km of cross-country trails (equipment rental Sfr20) and 120km of marked hiking paths.

Numerous other sporting activities are on offer: golf (including on the frozen lake in winter), tennis, squash, fishing, horse riding, sailing, windsurfing and river rafting, to mention just a few. The tourist office has a list of the inevitably high prices. If you can't afford to partake in the activities, people-watching, at least, is fun and free.

Buying a health treatment in the spa is another way to spend money, or you could pop into the **Engadine Museum** or the **Segantini Museum**.

Places to Stay

The *Olympiaschanze* camping ground (☎ 833 40 90) is 1km south-west of St Moritz Bad and opens late May to late September.

The SYHA *Stille Hostel* (☎ 833 39 69, fax 833 39 69, Via Surpunt 60, St Moritz Bad) has good, modern facilities. Compulsory half-board per person is Sfr43.50 in four-bed dorms or Sfr56 in double rooms. Laundry costs Sfr4 per load and there's mountain bike rental for Sfr15 per day. Reception is closed from 9 am to 4 pm but the downstairs doors stay open, and the hostel is open year-round. If it's full, try the *Sporthotel Stille* (☎ 833 69 48, fax 833 07 08, ✉ hotel.stille@bluewin.ch) next door. Singles/doubles are Sfr65/110 in summer; doubles are Sfr166 for half-board in winter.

Bellaval (☎ 833 32 45, fax 833 04 06), right by the train station on the southern side, has bare singles/doubles using hall shower for Sfr67/130. *Hotel Sonne* (☎ 833 03 63, fax 833 60 90, ✉ hotelsonne@swissonline.ch, Via Sela 11, St Moritz Bad) has singles/doubles/triples with shower/WC and TV, starting at Sfr95/160/210 in summer or Sfr105/180/225 in winter, plus a few cheaper rooms with hall facilities.

Hotels in the centre of St Moritz Dorf sport three stars or more. *Hotel Languard Garni* (☎ 833 31 37, fax 833 45 46, ✉ languard@bluewin.ch) is a good family hotel, charging from Sfr100/180, or about Sfr125/225 in winter. It's on Via Veglia near the tourist office.

Places to Eat

Eating can be affordable, even in pricey hotels, if you stick to lunch specials. This is the best bet in St Moritz Dorf, or go to *Hotel Steinbock* (Via Serlas 12), down from the post office, where meals start at Sfr17.

A *Coop* supermarket is on Via dal Bagn, St Moritz Bad. Next door there's *La Fontana*, a rustic-type bar/restaurant with candle lighting, and mostly Italian meals from Sfr12.

Down the road there's *Veltlinerkeller* at No 11. It has a wide-ranging menu (Sfr12 to Sfr40) and hunting trophies on the wall. It's closed on Sunday in the off season. The popular *Hotel Sonne* (see Places to Stay) serves pasta, salads and tasty pizzas from Sfr12.

Getting There & Away

Two postbuses run to Lugano daily in summer and one runs in winter (and only on Friday, Saturday and Sunday during some weeks). You must reserve a seat the day before on ☎ 837 67 64. A train-bus combination will get you to Landeck in Austria.

Nine daily trains travel south to Tirano in Italy with connections to Milan. The famous *Glacier Express* connects St Moritz to Zermatt via the 2033m Oberalp Pass, taking 7½ hours to cover 290 scenic kilometres and crossing 291 bridges (Sfr138). Novelty drink glasses in the dining car have sloping bases to compensate for the hills – but you must remember to keep turning them around! Beware of the Sfr9 reservation fee that's payable only on some trains.

AROUND ST MORITZ

The Engadine Valley, running north-east and south-west of St Moritz, offers a combination of plush resorts and unspoilt villages. In the latter category are **Guarda** and **Zuoz,** where you can see homes displaying traditional **sgraffito** designs (patterns scratched on wall plaster) that are characteristic of the Engadine. The annual cross-country ski marathon between Maloja and Zuoz is on the second Sunday in March. The route crosses ice-covered lakes and passes by St Moritz Lake. Trains run and buses run regularly along the valley.

Flora and fauna abound in the 169 sq km of the **Swiss National Park** (open June to October). The park information centre (☎ 081-856 13 78) near Zernez has details of hiking routes and the best places to see particular animals. Check the Web site at www.nationalpark.ch.

Other Ski Resorts

In the **Davos/Klosters** region there are 320km of ski runs, mostly medium to difficult, including one of the hardest runs in the world, the Gotschnawang. **Arosa** is another top-notch resort, easily reached by a scenic train ride from Chur. Most other ski resorts in Graubünden have predominantly easy to medium runs. Ski passes for the top resorts average Sfr50 for one day (cheaper by the week); passes for smaller places cost less.

Zürich

☎ 01 • pop 354,000

Switzerland's most populous city offers an ambience of affluence and plenty of cultural diversions. Banks and art galleries will greet you at every turn in a strange marriage of finance and aesthetics. If you've got the money, there's plenty to do. At night, the pin-stripe brigade yields the streets to bar-hoppers and techno-party clubbers.

Zürich started life as a Roman customs post and graduated to the status of a free city under the Holy Roman Empire in 1218. The city's reputation as a cultural and intellectual centre began after it joined the Swiss Confederation in 1351. Zwingli helped things along with his teachings during the Reformation. In the 19th century, Zürich's international status as an industrial and business centre was given impetus by the energetic administrator and railway magnate Alfred Escher. WWI saw the influx of luminaries such as Lenin, Trotsky, James Joyce; and Tristan Tzara and Hans Arp, key figures in the founding of Dadaism in 1916 at the Cabaret Voltaire.

Orientation

Zürich is at the northern end of Lake Zürich (Zürichsee), with the city centre split by the Limmat River. Like many Swiss cities, it is compact and conveniently laid out. The main train station (Hauptbahnhof) is on the western or left bank of the river, close to the old centre.

Information

Tourist Offices The Zürich Tourist Service (☎ 215 40 00, fax 215 40 44, ✉ information@zurichtourism.ch) is in the train station's main hall. It arranges hotel reservations (no commission; ☎ 211 40 44), car rentals and excursions, and stocks country-wide brochures. Opening hours are 8.30 am to 8.30 pm Monday to Friday and 8.30 am to 6.30 pm Saturday and Sunday, except from 1 April to 31 October when it closes at 7 pm weekdays and hours are 9 am to 6.30 pm weekends. Staff charge for city maps but you can get them free from one of the larger city banks instead.

Money There's no shortage of choice when exchanging money in this banking city. Banks are open 8.15 am to 4.30 pm Monday to Friday (until 6 pm Thursday). The exchange office in the main train station is open 6.30 am to 10.45 pm daily. In the airport, change money in terminal A to avoid paying commission on cash.

Post & Communications The main post office is Sihlpost (☎ 296 21 11), Kasernenstrasse 95-97, 8021. It is open 7.30 am to 8 pm Monday to Friday and 8 am to 4 pm Saturday. Like many other large Swiss post offices, it also has a counter open till late daily but some transactions incur a Sfr1 surcharge outside normal hours. Another post office is at the main train station.

Email & Internet Access Stars Bistro, in the main hall of the train station, charges Sfr5

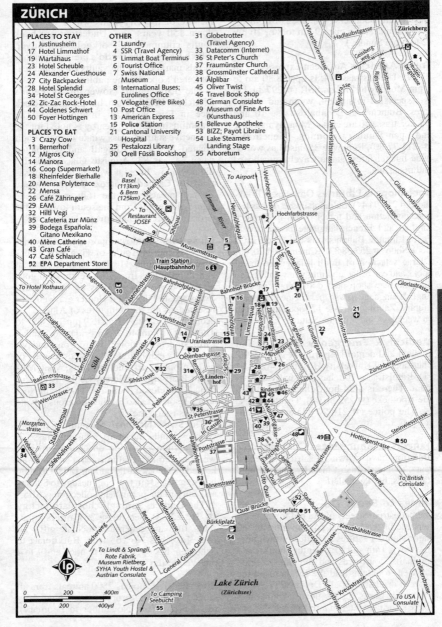

ZÜRICH

PLACES TO STAY
1 Justinusheim
17 Hotel Limmathof
19 Martahaus
23 Hotel Scheuble
24 Alexander Guesthouse
27 City Backpacker
28 Hotel Splendid
34 Hotel St Georges
42 Zic-Zac Rock-Hotel
44 Goldenes Schwert
50 Foyer Hottingen

PLACES TO EAT
3 Crazy Cow
11 Bernerhof
12 Migros City
14 Manora
16 Coop (Supermarket)
18 Rheinfelder Bierhalle
20 Mensa Polyterrace
22 Mensa
26 Café Zähringer
29 EAM
32 Hiltl Vegi
35 Cafeteria zur Münz
39 Bodega Española;
    Gitano Mexikano
40 Mère Catherine
43 Gran Café
47 Café Schlauch
52 EPA Department Store

OTHER
2 Laundry
4 SSR (Travel Agency)
5 Limmat Boat Terminus
6 Tourist Office
7 Swiss National
   Museum
8 International Buses;
   Eurolines Office
9 Velogate (Free Bikes)
10 Post Office
13 American Express
15 Police Station
21 Cantonal University
   Hospital
25 Pestalozzi Library
30 Orell Füssli Bookshop

31 Globetrotter
   (Travel Agency)
33 Datacomm (Internet)
36 St Peter's Church
37 Fraumünster Church
38 Grossmünster Cathedral
41 Älplibar
45 Oliver Twist
46 Travel Book Shop
48 German Consulate
49 Museum of Fine Arts
   (Kunsthaus)
51 Bellevue Apotheke
53 BIZZ; Payot Libraire
54 Lake Steamers
   Landing Stage
55 Arboretum

SWITZERLAND

for 20 minutes (11 am to midnight daily). Datacomm, Badenerstrasse 29, is Sfr5/8 for 30/60 minutes; it's open 9 am to 8 or 10 pm (2 to 6 pm Sunday).

Travel Agencies American Express (☎ 228 77 77), Uraniastrasse 14, is open 8.30 am to 6 pm Monday to Friday. SSR (☎ 297 11 11) is a specialist in student, youth and budget fares. Branches at Leonhardstrasse 10 and Bäckerstrasse 40 are closed Monday morning and open Saturday morning. Globetrotter (☎ 211 77 80), Rennweg 35, also has worldwide budget fares, and a travel noticeboard and magazine.

Bookshops & Libraries Orell Füssli Bookshop (☎ 211 04 44), Bahnhofstrasse 70, has fiction, nonfiction and travel books in English. English and French-language books are at Payot Libraire, Bahnhofstrasse 9. The Travel Book Shop (☎ 252 38 83), Rindermarkt 20, has a large selection of English-language travel books and can order anything you want. It also runs the map shop next door. You can read English-language newspapers in the Pestalozzi Library, Zähringerstrasse 17 (open until 8 pm on weekdays and 5 pm on Saturday).

Medical & Emergency Services For medical and dental help, ring ☎ 261 61 00. The Cantonal University Hospital (☎ 255 11 11), Rämistrasse 100, has a casualty department. There is a 24-hour chemist at Bellevue Apotheke (☎ 252 56 00), Theaterstrasse 14. The police (☎ 216 71 11) are at Bahnhofquai 3.

Dangers & Annoyances Crime and drug addiction have grown in Zürich in recent years. Crime still isn't high by international standards, but keep alert.

Things to See & Do

The pedestrian streets of the old town on either side of the Limmat contain most of the major sights. Features to notice are winding alleyways, 16th and 17th-century houses and guildhalls, courtyards and fountains. Zürich has 1030 fountains and the locals insist the water is drinkable in all. Don't be surprised if a waiter heads for the nearest fountain if you ask for tap water in a restaurant!

The elegant **Bahnhofstrasse** was built on the site of the city walls which were torn down 150 years ago. Underfoot are bank vaults crammed full of gold and silver. Zürich is one of the world's premier precious metals markets but the vaults (for some reason) aren't open to the public.

The 13th-century tower of **St Peter's Church**, St Peterhofstatt, has the largest clock face in Europe (8.7m in diameter). The **Fraumünster Church** nearby is noted for the distinctive stained-glass windows in the choir created by Marc Chagall and completed when he was 83. Augusto Giacometti also did a window here, as well as in the **Grossmünster Cathedral** across the river where Zwingli preached in the 16th century. The figure glowering from the south tower of the Grossmünster is Charlemagne.

Museums The most important of many museums is the **Museum of Fine Arts** (Kunsthaus), Heimplatz 1. The large permanent collection ranges from 15th-century religious art to the various schools of modern art. Swiss artists Füssli and Hodler are well represented, as are the sculptures of Alberto Giacometti. It's open 10 am to 9 pm Tuesday to Thursday, 10 am to 5 pm Friday to Sunday (Sfr6, students/seniors Sfr4, free on Sunday). Temporary exhibitions always cost extra. For non-European art and artefacts, visit **Museum Rietberg**, Gablerstrasse 15 (Sfr5, students Sfr3; closed Monday). Take tram No 7 south. Look out also for the numerous private galleries round the city.

The **Swiss National Museum** (Schweizerisches Landesmuseum), Museumstrasse 2, has a definitive section on church art, plus weapons, coins, costumes and utensils all housed in a mock castle built in 1898. Opening hours are 10.30 am to 5 pm Tuesday to Sunday and entry to the permanent collection is Sfr5.

The **Lindt & Sprüngli chocolate factory** (☎ 716 22 33), Seestrasse 204, offers a museum, film and generous chocolate gift – all free! Take bus No 165 from Bürkliplatz to Schooren. It's open 10 am to noon and 1 to 4 pm Wednesday to Friday.

Zoo The large zoo has 2500 animals from all around the world; it's open 8 am to 6 pm daily (until 5 pm from November to February).

Entry costs Sfr14 (students Sfr7) and you can get there by tram No 5 or 6. The zoo backs on to Zürichberg, a large wood ideal for walks away from the noise of the city.

Other Attractions Tourist Office guides give informative walks around the old town (two hours; Sfr18). Walks around the Zürichsee are pleasant: the concrete walkways give way to trees and lawns in the Arboretum on the west bank, and there's a flower clock at nearby Bürkliplatz. On the eastern bank, the Zürichhorn park has sculptures. Take the S10 train to Uetliberg (813m) for good views and hikes.

Special Events

On the third Monday in April, Zürich holds its spring festival, Sechseläuten. Guild members parade the streets in historical costume and tour the guildhalls, playing music. A fireworks-filled 'snowman' (the Böögg) is ignited at 6 pm. Another local holiday is Knabenschiessen, a shooting competition for 12 to 16-year-olds, on the second weekend of September.

Fasnacht brings lively musicians and a large, costumed procession. The carnival commences with typical Swiss precision at 11.11 am on 11 November, though the biggest parades are in February. Less traditionalist is the techno Street Parade in August. A huge fairground takes over central Zürich during the Züri Fäscht, usually every third year (2001 etc) in early July. The Zürcher festspiele, mid-June to mid-July, concentrates on music and the arts, and the Züri Jazz Woche takes place in early September.

Places to Stay

Accommodation can be a problem, particularly from August to October. Cheaper hotels fill early. Book ahead, or use the information board and free phone in the train station. The tourist office can sometimes get lower rates (no booking fee). Private rooms are virtually nonexistent.

Budget *Camping Seebucht* (☎ 482 16 12, Seestrasse 559) is on the west shore of the lake, 4km from the city centre (signposted). Take bus No 161 or 165 from Bürkliplatz. It is open from around May to September and has good facilities including a shop and cafe.

Prices are Sfr8.50 per adult, Sfr12 for a tent, Sfr3 for parking or Sfr16 for a camper van.

The SYHA *hostel* (☎ 482 35 44, fax 480 17 27, Mutschellenstrasse 114, Wollishofen) has 24-hour service. To get there, take tram No 6 or 7 to Morgental, or the S-Bahn to Wollishofen. Four or six-bed dorms (with lockers; own padlock needed) are Sfr31, and doubles are Sfr90. There's a restaurant and laundry facilities (Sfr8 to wash and dry).

City Backpacker (☎ 251 90 15, fax 251 90 24, ✉ backpacker@access.ch, Niederdorfstrasse 5), also known as Hotel Biber, is more convenient. Singles/doubles are Sfr65/88 and triples/quads are Sfr120/156, all with sheets. Dorms are Sfr29, plus Sfr3 if you need sheets. Prices are without breakfast but there are kitchens, Internet, a rooftop area and hall showers. Reception is closed noon to 3 pm.

Also very central is *Martahaus* (☎ 251 45 50, fax 251 45 40, ✉ info@martahaus.ch, Zähringerstrasse 36). Singles/doubles/triples cost Sfr70/98/120, and Sfr35 gets you a place in a six-bed dorm which is separated into individual cubicles by partitions and curtains. There is a comfortable lounge and breakfast room, and a shower on each floor. Book ahead (telephone reservations OK), particularly for single rooms.

Foyer Hottingen (☎ 256 19 19, fax 256 19 00, ✉ reservation@foyer-hottingen.ch, Hottingerstrasse 31) has a calm ambience and kitchen facilities. Singles/double rooms are Sfr110/150 with shower/WC or Sfr70/110 without; triples/quads are Sfr190/220 with, Sfr140/180 without. Prices are slightly lower in winter. Dorms are for women only and cost Sfr35. Telephone reservations are accepted.

Justinusheim (☎ 361 38 06, fax 362 29 82, Freudenbergstrasse 146) is a student home. Most beds are available during the student holidays (particularly from mid-July to mid-October), though it often has a few vacancies in term time too. Singles/doubles are Sfr60/100 with shower or Sfr50/80 without. Triples are Sfr120/140 with/without. It's just a few paces away from the woods of Zürichberg, and has a terrace with good views of Zürich and the lake. Take tram No 10 from the main train station to Rigiplatz, then the frequent Seilbahn to the top (city network tickets are valid).

In the old town, *Hotel Splendid* (☎ 252 58 50, fax 261 25 59, Rosengasse 5) has 43 beds.

SWITZERLAND

Singles/doubles/triples for Sfr56/93/123 are with hall showers. The optional breakfast is Sfr9.50 and there's live piano music nightly in the bar downstairs (open till 2 am).

Hotel Rothaus (☎ 241 24 51, fax 291 09 95, *uhk@swissonline.ch, Sihlhallenstrasse 1*) is in a seedy part of town west of the station, but has good-value rooms with shower/WC and TV. Prices start as low as Sfr60/98, depending on room size, season and length of stay.

Hotel St Georges (☎ 241 11 44, fax 241 11 42, *st-georges@bluewin.ch, Weberstrasse 11*) on the west bank of the Sihl River is quiet and comfortable and has a lift. Its singles/doubles are Sfr102/132 with shower or Sfr76/98 without.

In the old town is the *Zic-Zac Rock-Hotel* (☎ 261 21 81, fax 261 21 75, *rockhotel .ch@bluewin.ch, Marktgasse 17*). This theme hotel has varying rooms with rock pics and gold discs. Singles/doubles are around Sfr88/135 with shower or Sfr68/116 without, and breakfast is Sfr4.50. There's the lively Rock-Garden cafe downstairs.

Mid-Range In the city centre, *Hotel Limmathof* (☎ 261 42 20, fax 262 02 17, *Limmatquai 142*) has modern fittings but is in a noisy location. Singles/doubles with bath or shower and toilet are about Sfr110/155, and triples are Sfr198. The nearby *Alexander Guesthouse* (☎ 251 82 03, fax 252 74 25, *info@hotel-alexander.ch, Niederdorfstrasse 40*) charges from Sfr95/140 for a similar standard, though it also has more-expensive rooms.

Goldenes Schwert (☎ 266 18 18, fax 266 18 88, *hotel@rainbow.ch, Marktgasse 14*) has creatively decorated rooms from Sfr110/140 with private bath and toilet. It's a gay-friendly hotel and one floor has elaborate gay-themed rooms. Breakfast (Sfr9.50) is via room service. There's a disco downstairs. The three-star *Hotel Scheuble* (☎ 251 87 95, fax 251 76 78, *Mühlegasse 17*), also in the old town, has rooms with standard amenities including TV. Prices start from Sfr150 for one or two people in a queen-sized bed.

Places to Eat

Zürich has hundreds of restaurants serving all types of local and international cuisine. The Zürich speciality, *Geschnetzeltes Kalbsfleisch*

(thinly sliced veal in a cream sauce), generally costs more than Sfr20.

Budget There are various affordable places in and around the main train station, especially in the underground Shopville, which has a *Migros* supermarket open till 8 pm daily. Above ground by the station, the large *Coop* has a takeaway section serving hot food. Niederdorfstrasse in the old town is also a good street to explore, with takeaway places offering Bratwurst and bread for about Sfr6, or kebabs and Oriental food.

The large and busy *Mensa Polyterrace* (*Leonhardstrasse 34*) is next to the Seilbahn (funicular) top station. It has good meals for Sfr10.50 (Sfr8.10 for ISIC holders), including vegetarian options. It's open 11.15 am to 1.30 pm and 5.30 to 7.15 pm Monday to Friday, and 11.30 am to 1 pm every second Saturday. From mid-July to around mid-October it's open for lunch only. There is a cafe upstairs which is also popular (open 6.45 am to 7.45 pm weekdays). Just along the road, there is another *mensa* (*Rämistrasse 71*) in the university building, open weekdays and on alternate Saturdays to the Polyterrace.

The *EPA* department store at Bellevueplatz has a cheap restaurant, similar to the *Migros Restaurant* in the Migros City shopping centre. The Manor department store on Bahnhofstrasse has a good *Manora* buffet-style restaurant, open until 8 pm weekdays and 4 pm on Saturday.

EAM (*Schipfe 16*) is a busy little place with outside tables overlooking the Limmat River. *Menus* with soup start from about Sfr11 and it is open daytime, Monday to Friday.

Zürich has numerous cafes where you can linger over a coffee. Try the *Cafeteria zur Münz* (*Münzplatz 3*) where Jean Tinguely mobiles hang from the ceiling. It is open 6.30 am to 7 pm Monday to Friday (until 8 pm on Thursday) and 8 am to 5 pm Saturday.

Bernerhof (*Zeughausstrasse 1*) is a typical, simple restaurant with satisfying, filling food. Several daily *menus* from Sfr12 (including soup) are available at midday and evening. It's open until midnight daily (6 pm Saturday, closed Sunday). In the evening, locals come to drink, and play cards and board games.

Rheinfelder Bierhalle (*Niederdorfstrasse 76*) is a little rough and ready, but also typical.

It serves economical food all day and the beer's cheap, too (Sfr4.70 for 0.5L). Opening hours are 9 am to midnight daily.

Café Zähringer on Spitalgasse serves mostly organic food (from Sfr14), and it's a good place to linger for a game of chess, or for live music most Wednesdays (closed Monday till 6 pm). *Café Schlauch (Münstergasse 20)* is another good possibility for vegetarians (closed Monday and Tuesday).

Gran Café (Limmatquai 66) does look fairly grand, but usually has a bargain meal on offer, such as all-you-can-eat spaghetti for Sfr9.50. For a range of Rösti, try *Rösti Bar* in the main hall of the main train station.

Mid-Range All these places are open daily. Vegetarians will have a field day in the meat-free environment of *Hiltl Vegi (☎ 227 70 00, Sihlstrasse 28)* on two floors. Varied meals cost from Sfr16.50 and the salad buffet is both extensive and expensive. Nightly from 5 pm there's also an Indian buffet which costs Sfr4.60 per 100g or Sfr38 for all you can eat.

Mère Catherine (☎ 250 59 40, Nägelhof 3) is a popular French restaurant in a small courtyard. Main courses are about Sfr19.50 to Sfr38, though weekday lunch *menus* are Sfr15.50 and Sfr17.50.

Crazy Cow (Leonhardstrasse 1) is a popular, quirky place serving Swiss food from about Sfr16. Here you will find two things that many people believe don't exist: a written form of Swiss-German (on the menus), and examples of Swiss humour (bread is served in a slipper, chicken wings in a toy supermarket trolley).

Bodega Española (☎ 251 23 10) is on the 1st floor at Münstergasse 15. Enjoy quality Spanish food (Sfr18 to Sfr45) and Spanish wine (from Sfr33.50 a bottle) in an evocative, wood-panelled room, where hanging from the ceiling are strings of onions and garlic. Next door, *Gitano Mexikano* provides a fun environment for enjoying Mexican food.

Restaurant JOSEF (☎ 271 65 95, Gasometerstrasse 24) greets mainly youngish, trendy diners in elegant, candle-lit surroundings (reservations advised). There are creative and varied dishes for Sfr25 to Sfr40, and a bar. Beware – there's only a tiny sign and the entrance is on Josef Strasse. It's closed at weekend lunchtimes (and Sunday evening in winter).

Entertainment

Pick up the free events magazine *Züritipp* from the tourist office. Tickets for many events can be obtained from Billettzentrale (BIZZ; ☎ 221 22 83, Bahnhofstrasse 9). It's open 10 am to 6.30 pm Monday to Friday and until 2 pm on Saturday. Also check the ticket corner in large branches of the UBS bank. Cinema prices are reduced every Monday to Sfr11, from their normal price of around Sfr15. Films are usually in the original language. The *Comedy Club* performs plays in English – check venues in the events magazines, or the free newspapers by tram stops.

Many late-night pubs, clubs and discos are on Niederdorfstrasse and adjoining streets in the old town. This area is also a red-light district. *Älplibar (Ankengasse 5)* is a rustic bar, with taped Swiss folklore music and fondue for Sfr23.50 (not during summer). It's open nightly from 5 pm. English speakers gravitate towards *Oliver Twist*, which is an Irish pub on Rindermarkt.

Rote Fabrik (☎ 481 91 21 for concert information, ☎ 482 42 12 for theatre, Seestrasse 395) is a centre for alternative arts. Take Bus No 161 or 165 from Bürkliplatz. It's all closed Monday; otherwise there are concerts most nights, ranging from rock and jazz to avant-garde (Sfr10 to Sfr30) as well as original-language films, theatre, dance and a bar/restaurant. Check the Web site at www .rotefabrik.ch.

Getting There & Away

Air Kloten airport is 10km north of the city centre and has several daily flights to/from all major destinations. Swissair and Austrian Airlines share an office in the main train station, which is open on weekdays and Saturday morning.

Bus Various buses head east, to Budapest, Prague, Zagreb and elsewhere. The Eurolines office behind the train station is open 5.30 or 6 pm to 7.30 pm daily. For information, call ☎ 272 40 42.

Train The busy main train station has direct trains to Stuttgart (Sfr62, three hours), Munich (Sfr97, 4½ hours), Innsbruck (Sfr69, four hours), Milan (Sfr75, four hours) and many other international destinations. There are also at least hourly departures to most Swiss towns including Lucerne (Sfr22, 50 minutes), Bern (Sfr48, 70 minutes) and Basel (Sfr31, 65 minutes).

Car & Motorcycle The N3 approaches Zürich from the south along the shore of Lake Zürich. The N1 is the fastest route from Bern and Basel and the main entry point from the west. The N1 also services routes to the north and east of Zürich.

Getting Around
To/From the Airport Taxis cost around Sfr45, so take the train for Sfr5.40 – there's five an hour and the journey only takes 10 minutes.

Public Transport There is a comprehensive and unified bus, tram and S-Bahn service in the city, including boats on the Limmat River. All tickets must be bought in advance from dispensers at stops. There are English instructions, and a confusingly wide variety of tickets and zones available. Short *Kurzstrecke* trips of about five stops are Sfr2.10. For the city of Zürich, a one-hour pass costs Sfr3.60 and a 24-hour pass is Sfr7.20. Getting to the airport involves travel in an extra zone (Sfr10.80 for a 24-hour pass). A pass valid for unlimited travel within the canton of Zürich, including extended tours of the lake, costs Sfr28.40 for 24 hours or Sfr20 for a day pass after 9 am (the *9-Uhr-Pass*).

Lake steamers depart from Bürkliplatz, leaving every 30 to 60 minutes from early April to late October (Swiss Pass and Eurail valid, Inter-Rail 50% discount). For boat information, phone ☎ 487 13 33, or visit the Web site at www.zsg.ch.

Other Transport Taxis in Zürich are expensive, even by Swiss standards, at Sfr6 plus Sfr3.20 per kilometre. There's bicycle rental via SBB in the main train station, but use of city bikes is *free of charge* from Velogate on platform 18, year-round from 7.30 am to 9.30 pm. Bring photo ID and Sfr20 deposit. Free bikes are also available in summer only from a few other (less convenient) depots. The tourist office has a list of car-parking garages near the central pedestrian zone. A

Sfr10 pass from a police station allows all-day street parking in blue zones.

Central Switzerland

This is the region which many visitors think of as the 'true' Switzerland. Not only is it rich in typical Swiss features – mountains, lakes, tinkling cowbells, alpine villages and ski resorts – but it is also where Switzerland began as a nation 700 years ago. The original pact of 1291, signed by the communities of Uri, Schwyz and Nidwalden, can be viewed in the Bundesbriefarchiv hall in Schwyz town centre.

LUCERNE
☎ 041 • pop 61,000
Ideally situated in the historic and scenic heart of Switzerland, Lucerne (Luzern in German) is an excellent base for a variety of excursions. It also has a great deal of charm in its own right, particularly the medieval town centre.

Orientation & Information
The old town centre is on the northern bank of the Reuss River. The train station is nearby on the southern bank; extensive station facilities below ground level include bike rental (from 7 am to 7.45 pm) and money exchange. By platform three is the tourist office (☎ 227 17 17, fax 227 17 18, ✉ luzern@luzern.org), Zentralstrasse 5, which is open until 7.30 pm daily. From 1 November to 31 March closing time is 6 pm (1 pm on Sunday).

In front of the train station is the boat landing stage and close by is the main post office (Hauptpost, Luzern 1, 6000). The cheapest Internet access (Sfr2 for 30 minutes) is in the library (Stadtbibliothek), Löwenplatz 10, which has late opening till 9 pm on Thursday (closed Sunday).

American Express (☎ 410 00 77), Schweizerhofquai 4, is open on weekdays and (except in winter) Saturday morning.

A Visitor's Card (from your accommodation) can earn useful discounts.

Things to See
The picturesque old centre offers you 15th-century buildings with painted facades, and the towers of the city walls. Some towers can be

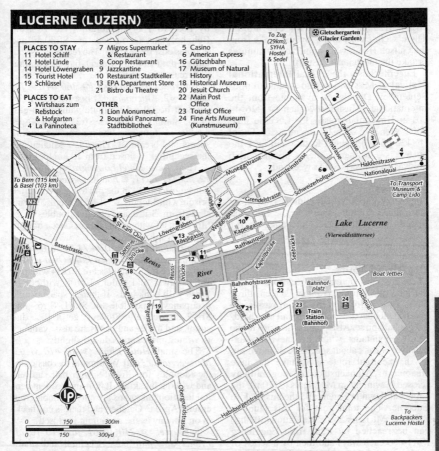

LUCERNE (LUZERN)

PLACES TO STAY
11 Hotel Schiff
12 Hotel Linde
14 Hotel Löwengraben
15 Tourist Hotel
19 Schlüssel

PLACES TO EAT
3 Wirtshaus zum Rebstock & Hofgarten
4 La Paninoteca

7 Migros Supermarket & Restaurant
8 Coop Restaurant
9 Jazzkantine
10 Restaurant Stadtkeller
13 EPA Department Store
21 Bistro du Theatre

OTHER
1 Lion Monument
2 Bourbaki Panorama; Stadtbibliothek

5 Casino
6 American Express
16 Gütschbahn
17 Museum of Natural History
18 Historical Museum
20 Jesuit Church
22 Main Post Office
23 Tourist Office
24 Fine Arts Museum (Kunstmuseum)

SWITZERLAND

climbed for extensive views. Be sure to walk along the two covered bridges, **Kapellbrücke**, with its water tower that appears in just about every photograph of Lucerne, and **Spreuerbrücke**. Both have a series of pictorial panels under their roof. Kapellbrücke dates from 1333 and was rebuilt in 1993 after suffering fire damage.

The poignant **Lion Monument**, carved out of natural rock in 1820, is dedicated to the Swiss soldiers who died in the French Revolution. Next to it is the fascinating **Gletschergarten** (Glacier Garden), Denkmalstrasse 4, where giant glacial potholes prove that 20

million years ago Lucerne was a subtropical palm beach. The potholes can be perused daily (except Monday in winter) and admission costs Sfr8 (students Sfr6). Also worth a look is the nearby **Bourbaki Panorama**, Löwenstrasse 18, an 1100 sq metre circular painting of the Franco-Prussian War (Sfr6, students Sfr5).

The large and widely acclaimed **Transport Museum** (Verkehrshaus), Lidostrasse 5, contains trains, planes and automobiles. It's east of the city centre, open daily, and charges Sfr18 (railpass/student reductions). It's more fun than it sounds; get there on bus No 2 from Bahnhofplatz. A Lucerne museums pass costs Sfr25 and is valid for one month. There's a fine **view** of the town and lake from the Gütsch Hotel; walk uphill for 20 minutes or take the Gütschbahn (Sfr3).

Lucerne hosts the annual **International Festival of Music** from mid-August to mid-September. Details are available from the Internationale Musikfestwochen (☎ 226 44 00) at Hirschmattstrasse 13, Lucerne CH-6002. Web site: www.lucernemusic.ch. **Sedel** (☎ 420 63 10), behind Rotsee and near the hostel, is a former women's prison which holds rock concerts at the weekend.

Activities
For bungy-jumping, paragliding, canyoning and other adventure sports in the Lucerne/Engelberg region, contact Outventure (☎ 611 14 41, fax 611 14 42). Its Web site is at www .outventure.ch.

Organised Tours
There are many options for scenic cruises on the lake; the farthest point is Flüelen, three hours away (Sfr42 return). Eurail passes are valid on all boat trips and Inter-Rail pass holders get half-price. Also popular are trips to the nearby mountains, which are inevitably expensive, but ask about special deals in winter.

An excellent route is to take the lake steamer to Alpnachstad, the cog railway (closed in winter) up Mt Pilatus (2120m), the cable car down to Kriens and the bus back to Lucerne. The total cost for this jaunt is Sfr77.60. Mt Titlis' top cable station (3020m) can be reached by train from Engelberg (Sfr14.80 each way) and then by a series of cable cars (Sfr73 return), but the tourist office's all-inclusive guided bus tour (Sfr85 from Lucerne) is cheaper. A combination steamer, cog railway and cable-car excursion up Mt Rigi (1797m) costs Sfr86. Rail pass holders get reductions on these prices.

Places to Stay
Camp Lido (☎ 370 21 46, Lidostrasse 8) on the northern shore and east of the town is open from 15 March to 31 October. It charges Sfr7.70 per adult, from Sfr3 per tent, Sfr5 per car, and Sfr13 for a bunk in a cabin.

The modern SYHA *hostel* (☎ 420 88 00, fax 420 56 16, Sedelstrasse 12) is a 15-minute

walk north of the city walls. You can get there by bus No 1 or (preferably) No 18 from Bahnhofplatz. Dorm beds are Sfr30.50 and doubles cost from Sfr75. The reception is shut until 2 pm (4 pm in winter), but the communal areas stay open.

Backpackers Lucerne (☎ 360 04 20, fax 360 04 42, Alpenquai 42) is a friendly independent hostel a 12-minute walk south-east of the station. It charges Sfr21.50/26.50 per person in four/two-bed rooms, excluding sheets and breakfast. There is a kitchen and the reception is closed from 10 am to 4 pm.

There's also *Hotel Löwengraben* (☎ 417 12 12, fax 417 12 11, ✉ hotel@loewengraben.ch, Löwengraben 18) in the old town, a converted prison with literally 'cell-like' rooms. Dorms start from Sfr20 and singles/doubles from Sfr75/90, all without breakfast. Check in from 3 pm onwards.

Tourist Hotel (☎ 410 24 74, fax 410 84 14, ✉ info@touristhotel.ch, St Karli Quai 12) has dorms for Sfr33. Doubles are Sfr134 with private shower and toilet, Sfr108 without or Sfr98 with bunk beds. If there's space, single occupancy is possible for Sfr81, Sfr69 and Sfr62 respectively. Students get a 10% discount, and triples and quads are also available. In winter, prices are reduced slightly.

The small *Hotel Linde* (☎/fax 410 31 93, Metzgerrainle 3) off Weinmarkt has basic singles/doubles for Sfr44/88 with hall showers and without breakfast. It is in an excellent central location but rooms are only available from around April to October, and there's no check-in on Sunday as the restaurant is closed.

Schlüssel (☎ 210 10 61, fax 210 10 21, Franziskanerplatz 12), is central and small-scale. It has singles/doubles for around Sfr80/120 with shower or Sfr55/90 without. Phone ahead on Sunday in winter.

Overlooking the river is the comfortable *Hotel Schiff* (☎ 418 52 52, fax 418 52 55, ✉ contact@hotel-schiff-luzern.ch, Unter der Egg 8). It has decent-sized singles/doubles with shower, toilet and TV from Sfr130/180 (less in winter), and some rooms using hall shower for Sfr80/120.

Places to Eat
Look out for the local speciality, *Kügeli-pastetli*, a vol-au-vent stuffed with meat and mushrooms and served with a rich sauce.

SWITZERLAND

Coop and *Migros* have restaurants close together on Hertensteinstrasse. *EPA* department store on Mühlenplatz has an excellent self-service restaurant with very competitive prices: meals from Sfr8.80, soup from Sfr2, salad buffet at Sfr2.10 per 100g, and tea or coffee for Sfr2. They're all open till 9 pm on Thursday and Friday. *Hotel Löwengraben* has cheap self-service Asian food, or for reduced pizza deals after 10 pm (from Sfr6), head to *La Paninoteca (Haldenstrasse 9)*.

Bistro du Theatre (Theaterstrasse 5) is popular among mainly young people for fairly inexpensive eating and drinking (closed Sunday). *Jazzkantine (Grabengasse 8)* is a bar-restaurant with a Tagesteller for Sfr12.50 and various vegetarian meals. There are usually free jazz concerts on Wednesday and Thursday night, except during school holidays (closed Sunday lunch).

If you really want to yodel along to a Swiss folklore show, go to *Restaurant Stadtkeller (☎ 410 47 33, Sternenplatz 3)*. Allow Sfr55 for the food and show, but note there are cheaper places in Geneva.

Wirtshaus zum Rebstock (☎ 410 35 81, St Leodegar Strasse 3) has meals from Sfr16 to Sfr38. It has several eating areas providing variety in style and cuisine, including the linked *Hofgarten* vegetarian restaurant beyond the garden. *Hotel-Restaurant Schiff* (see Places to Stay) has lunch specials with soup from Sfr15, but it's also a good place to shed some francs and gain some pounds on quality evening dining. Cuisines from different nationalities are featured regularly in winter.

Getting There & Away
Hourly trains connect Lucerne to Zürich (Sfr22, 50 minutes), Interlaken (Sfr27, two hours), Bern (Sfr32, 1½ hours), Lugano (Sfr58, 2½ hours) and Geneva (Sfr65, 3¼ hours, via Olten or Langnau). The N2/E9 motorway connecting Basel and Lugano passes by Lucerne, and the N14 provides the road link to Zürich.

INTERLAKEN
☎ 033 • pop 15,000
Interlaken is flanked by Lake Thun and Lake Brienz and within striking distance of the mighty peaks of the Jungfrau, Mönch and Eiger. Though Interlaken is a great base for exploring the delights of the Bernese Oberland, the Jungfrau Region also has good accommodation options, and that's where the scenic wonders of Switzerland really come into their own.

Orientation & Information
Most of Interlaken is coupled between its two train stations, Interlaken Ost and West. Each station offers bike rental and daily money-exchange facilities and behind each is a landing for boat lake services. The main shopping street, Höheweg, runs between the stations. You can walk from one to the other in 20 minutes.

The core of town is nearer Interlaken West, and that includes the tourist office (☎ 822 21 21, fax 822 52 21, ✉ mail@Interla kenTourism.ch), Höheweg 37. It's open 8 am to noon and 1.30 to 6 pm Monday to Friday and 8 am to noon Saturday. From mid-June to mid-October, it operates daily and for longer hours. Staff will book rooms (no commission), or you can use the hotel board and free phones outside and at both train stations. The main post office (3800, Postplatz) is nearby. Internet access is at The Wave, Rosenstrasse 13, open daily.

Things to See & Do
Numerous **hiking trails** dot the area surrounding Interlaken, all with signposts giving average walking times. The funicular up to **Harder Kulm** (Sfr21 return) yields an excellent panorama and further signposted paths.

Boats go to several towns and villages around the lakes (Eurail valid, Inter-Rail 50% off). On **Lake Thun**, Spiez (Sfr10.60 each way by steamer, Sfr8.40 by train) and Thun (Sfr15.60 by steamer, Sfr13.20 by train) both have a castle. Another fine castle is **Schloss Oberhofen** – boats stop right outside. Other resorts offer water sports. A short boat ride (Sfr5.80) from Interlaken are the **St Beatus Höhlen** (caves), with some impressive stalagmite formations, a small museum, and a feeble reconstruction of a prehistoric settlement. Combined entry is Sfr14 (students Sfr12). The caves can also be reached from Interlaken by bus or a 90-minute walk, and are open 9.30 am to 5 pm daily from Palm Sunday to late October.

SWITZERLAND

Lake Brienz has a more rugged shoreline and fewer resorts than its neighbour. Brienz (Sfr12.40 by steamer, Sfr6 by train) is the centre of the Swiss woodcarving industry and close to the **Freilichtmuseum Ballenberg**, a huge open-air park displaying typical Swiss crafts and houses. The park is open daily from mid-April to 1 November (Sfr14, students Sfr12).

Places to Stay
The Guest Card (available from accommodation places) gets useful discounts. Private rooms are good value – **Walter** (☎ 822 76 88, *Oelestrasse 35*) has four doubles (hall shower) from Sfr20 per person; the huge breakfast is Sfr7.

There are a dozen camping grounds in and around Interlaken. Behind Interlaken Ost train station is **Sackgut** (☎ 822 44 34) on Brienzstrasse, which costs Sfr7.10 per adult and from Sfr6 for a tent. It's open from April to October.

The lakeside SYHA **hostel** (☎ 822 43 53, *fax 823 20 58, Aareweg 21, am See, Bönigen*) is a 20-minute walk round Lake Brienz from Interlaken Ost, or take bus No 1. It has swimming facilities and a kitchen. Beds in large dorms are Sfr26.60 and check-in is from 4 pm. The hostel is closed from mid-November to late January.

Balmer's Herberge (☎ 822 19 61, fax 823 32 61, @ *balmers@tcnet.ch, Hauptstrasse 23*) is a 15-minute walk (signposted) from either station. It has excellent facilities (eg, leisure/games rooms, kitchen, cellar bar and restaurant) though some people find it noisy and too much like an American summer camp. Beds cost Sfr24 in dorms; singles/doubles are Sfr40/64 and triples/quads are Sfr90/120. Sign for a bed during the day (facilities are open) and check in at 5 pm. Nearby, behind the Mattenhof Hotel on Hauptstrasse, there's the **Funny Farm** (mobile/cellphone ☎ 079-652 61 27, @ *James@funny-farm.ch*). This free-and-easy place has an Australasian ambience, party atmosphere, swimming pool and bar. Accommodation can be basic (dorms from Sfr25) though there are some good budget rooms in the Mattenhof Hotel, and there are big plans for improvements.

Nearer Höheweg is **Backpackers Villa Sonnenhof** (☎ 826 71 71, fax 826 71 72, @ *backpackers@villa.ch, Alpenstrasse 16*). This well-run, renovated villa has a kitchen and dorms/doubles for Sfr29/37 per person. Reception is closed from 11 am to 4 pm. Also convenient is **Happy Inn Lodge** (☎ 822 32 25, fax 822 32 68, @ *happyinn@tcnet.ch, Rosenstrasse 17*). Simple dorms are Sfr19 and singles/doubles are Sfr35/70. There's a restaurant/bar with affordable food (breakfast Sfr7) and check-in is from 3 pm.

By Interlaken West train station is **Touriste Garni** (☎ 822 28 31, fax 822 28 28), with a few parking spaces. Variable singles/doubles are Sfr55/120 with shower or Sfr48/95 without. Not far away, **Hotel Alphorn** (☎ 822 30 51, fax 823 30 69, @ *accommodation@ Hotel-Alphorn.ch, Rugenaustrasse 8*), also known as Pilgerruhe, offers modern or old-style rooms for Sfr95/140 with shower and WC (Sfr70/110 in winter). There's ample free parking.

Hotel Splendid (☎ 822 76 12, fax 822 76 79, Höheweg 33) offers three-star comfort and a central location. Well-presented singles and doubles are Sfr130/196 with private shower/toilet or Sfr90/120 without; all rooms have a TV and telephone.

Places to Eat
Get cheap meals at the self-service restaurants at the supermarkets: **Migros**, opposite Interlaken West (late opening on Friday), and **Coop** on Bahnhofstrasse and opposite Interlaken Ost (both are open on Sunday). A good, inexpensive place for Italian food is **Pizzeria Mercato**, Postgasse, off Höheweg, open daily until midnight.

Anker Restaurant (Marktgasse 57) has tasty Swiss and vegetarian food (Sfr12 to Sfr38). Try the ostrich here. There is a games area at the back and occasional live music in winter (closed Thursday). The restaurant at **Hotel Splendid** is a good place for fondue from Sfr19.50; it's open at 6 pm daily in summer (only Friday to Sunday in winter).

For Mexican food from Sfr15 and free live music on Friday/Saturday nights, go to **El Azteca** (Jungfraustrasse 30). It's closed on Wednesday in the off season. **Gasthof Hirschen** on the corner of Hauptstrasse and Parkstrasse serves up Swiss food (mostly above Sfr20) in a rustic chalet; it's closed Tuesday and (in winter) Wednesday. **Hotel Metropole**, by the tourist office, has a *panoramic cafe* on the 18th floor. The food is affordable and it's worth going up to admire the view and walk round the balcony. The hotel's 1st-floor restaurant serves pricey Italian food.

Entertainment

Evening entertainment in Interlaken encompasses the casino with its folklore show, and several discos. *Buddy's Pub (Höheweg 33)* is a good place for a drink, though local youths head to *Café-Bar Hüsi (Postgasse 3)*.

Getting There & Away

Trains to Lucerne (Sfr27, two hours) depart hourly from Interlaken Ost. Trains to Brig and Montreux (via Bern or Zweisimmen) depart from Interlaken West or Ost. Main roads head east to Lucerne and west to Bern, but the only way south for vehicles, without a major detour around the mountains, is to take the car-carrying train from Kandersteg, south of Spiez.

JUNGFRAU REGION

☎ 033

The views keep getting better the farther south you go from Interlaken, and it's an ideal playground for hiking and skiing. Don't miss this region. You'll probably end up staying here longer than you planned.

There's a burgeoning adventure sports industry here, which has barely been dented by the canyoning disaster in 1999 in which 21 people lost their lives. Local operators such as Alpin Raft (☎ 823 41 00) and Alpin Center (☎ 823 55 23) offer bungy-jumping, paragliding, rafting and much else. Check the respective Web sites at www.alpinraft.ch and www.alpincenter.ch.

Grindelwald

Only 40 minutes by train from Interlaken Ost (Sfr9.40 each way) is Grindelwald, a busy resort under the north face of the Eiger. In the First region there are 90km of hiking trails above 1200m. Of these, 48km stay open year-round. In winter, the First is also the main skiing area, with a variety of runs stretching from Oberjoch at 2486m, right down to the village at 1050m. The cable car from Grindelwald-Grund to Männlichen, where there are more good views and hikes, is the

longest in Europe (Sfr28 up, Sfr46 return; nonskier reductions in winter). Grindelwald can be reached by road.

The tourist office (☎ 854 12 12, fax 854 12 10, ℮ touristcenter@grindelwald.ch) is in the centre at the Sportzentrum, 200m up from the train station. It's open daily in season, but closed on Sunday at other times.

Places to Stay & Eat Grindelwald has several *camping grounds*. The SYHA *hostel* (☎ 853 10 09, fax 853 50 29) is at Terrassenweg (great views), a 20-minute climb from the train station. Dorm beds are Sfr30.60 and doubles cost from Sfr71.20. Check-in is from 3 pm (5 pm on Sunday). Close by is the *Naturfreundehaus (☎ 853 13 33, fax 853 43 33)*, which has a kitchen, and dorms from Sfr30 without breakfast. Both hostels are closed between seasons. Other dorms are listed in the tourist office leaflet.

In the village centre, just off the main street (signposted), is *Lehmann's Herberge (☎ 853 31 41)*, with good-value rooms for one to six people costing Sfr40 or Sfr45 per person. Close by on the main street is *Hotel Tschuggen (☎ 853 17 81, fax 853 26 90)*, with attractive, renovated singles/doubles for Sfr90/144 with private shower and toilet or Sfr65/118 without.

For mid-priced food and accommodation, try *Fiescherblick (☎ 853 44 53, fax 853 44 57)* on the eastern side of the village. Nearby are a couple of bargains for food – Swiss food at *Älpli* in the Hotel Sunstar, and pizzas from just Sfr8.50 at *Onkel Tom's Hütte*, which is closed Tuesday lunch and Monday. A *Coop* supermarket is opposite the tourist office.

Lauterbrunnen Valley

This valley is the other fork branching out from Interlaken into the mountains. The first village reached by car or rail is **Lauterbrunnen**, known mainly for the trickling Staubbach Falls and the impressively powerful Trümmelbach Falls, which are 4km farther south (Sfr10; open April to October). Find out more from the tourist office (☎ 855 19 55, fax 855 10 32, ℮ info@lauterbrunnen.touris mus.ch) on the main street.

Above the village (via funicular) is Grütschalp, where you switch to the train to **Mürren** (Sfr9.40 total), a skiing and hiking

SWITZERLAND

resort. The ride yields tremendous unfolding views across the valley to the Jungfrau, Mönch and Eiger peaks. Mürren's efficient tourist office (☎ 856 86 86, fax 856 86 96, @ info@muerren.ch) is in the sports centre. A 40-minute walk down the hill from Mürren is tiny **Gimmelwald**, relatively undisturbed by tourists, and a steep 1½ hour hike from the valley floor.

Gimmelwald and Mürren can also be reached from the valley floor by the expensive Stechelberg cable car, which runs up to **Schilthorn** (2971m). From the top there's a fantastic panorama, and film shows will remind you that James Bond performed his stunts here in *On Her Majesty's Secret Service*. The return cable fare is a wallet-withering Sfr89, but ask about low season or first/last ascent of the day discounts.

Places to Stay & Eat Gimmelwald and Lauterbrunnen are cheaper for accommodation than Mürren. Another suitable base is Wengen, a hiking and skiing centre clinging to the eastern side of the valley. It has several hotels with dorms, as well as a backpacker hostel, *Hot Chili Peppers* (☎ 855 50 20, @ chilis@wengen.com).

Lauterbrunnen Both *Camping Schützenbach* (☎ 855 12 68) and *Camping Jungfrau* (☎ 856 20 10) have cheap dorms and bungalows in addition to camping. *Matratzenlager Stocki* (☎ 855 17 54) has a sociable atmosphere, and dorm beds for Sfr13. *Valley Hostel* (☎/fax 855 20 08, @ valleyhostel@bluewin.ch) charges Sfr21/25 per person in dorms/doubles. *Chalet im Rohr* (☎ 855 21 82) is a creaky wood chalet with singles/doubles for Sfr26 per person. All the above places have free kitchens but no breakfast.

Eating on the cheap is less easy. Stock up in the *Coop*, or try one of the hotel restaurants. *Crystalstübli*, opposite the tourist office, has meals from Sfr12 (closes around 8 pm).

Gimmelwald The *Mountain Hostel* (☎ 855 17 04, fax 855 26 88, @ mountainhostel@ tcnet.ch), close to the cable-car station and with a great view, has dorms without breakfast for Sfr16, and kitchen facilities (bring your own food – the hostel sells basic provisions but the village has no shop). There's

daytime access but check-in is from 5.30 pm. Next door is *Restaurant-Pension Gimmelwald* (☎/fax 855 17 30) with affordable accommodation and hot meals from Sfr15. Five minutes up the hill is *Mittaghorn* (☎ 855 16 58), sometimes known as Walter's. There's dorms (Sfr25) and doubles (Sfr60), but something of a shower shortage. Beer in the small cafe costs Sfr4 for 0.5L, though meals are only for guests, who must preorder.

Mürren By the train station is *Eiger Guesthouse* (☎ 855 35 35, fax 855 35 31, @ eigerguesthouse@muerren.ch), which charges Sfr39 in dorms and Sfr130/100 for doubles with/without shower and WC. The three-star *Hotel Edelweiss* (☎ 855 13 12, fax 855 42 02, @ edelweiss@muerren.ch) provides singles/doubles for Sfr90/160. Both places have a cheap restaurant with a terrace. The small *Staegerstübli*, next to the *Coop* supermarket, is another affordable place for food.

Jungfraujoch

The trip to Jungfraujoch by train (the highest in Europe) is excellent. Unfortunately, the price is as steep as the track and is hardly worth it unless you have very good weather (call ☎ 855 10 22 for taped forecasts or check cable TV). From Interlaken Ost, trains go via Grindelwald or Lauterbrunnen to Kleine Scheidegg. From here, the line is less than 10km long but took 16 years to build. Opened in 1912, the track powers through both the Eiger and the Mönch with majestic views from two windows blasted in the mountainside, before terminating at 3454m at Jungfraujoch.

On the summit, there is free entry to the **ice palace** (exhibition rooms cut within the glacier), and free use of plastic disks for sliding down glacial slopes. From the terrace of the Sphinx Research Institute (a weather station) the panorama of peaks and valleys is unforgettable, including the Aletsch Glacier to the south, and mountains as distant as the Jura and the Black Forest. Take warm clothing and sunglasses (for glacier walking). There's a self-service restaurant in the complex.

From Interlaken Ost, the journey is 2½ hours each way (Sfr162 return). Allow at least three hours at the site. There's a cheaper (or, more accurately, less exorbitant) 'good morning ticket' of Sfr125 if you take the first train (6.35 am from Interlaken) and leave the summit by noon. From 1 November to 30 April the reduction is valid for the 6.35 and 7.35 am trains, and the noon restriction does not apply. Reductions are no longer given with Inter-Rail within this region, though Eurail gets 25% off. It is not possible to walk up to Jungfraujoch.

Other Destinations

Marvellous views and hikes compete for attention from various other vantage points in the Jungfrau region, such as **Schynige Platte**, **Männlichen** and **Kleine Scheidegg**.

Skiing is a major activity in the winter months, with a good variety of intermediate runs plus the demanding run down the Schilthorn. Resort ski passes cost Sfr52 for a day, or Sfr105 (discount if you're over 62 or under 20) for a minimum of two days in the whole Jungfrau region.

Northern Switzerland

This part of the country is important for industry and commerce, yet is by no means lacking in tourist attractions. Take time to explore Lake Constance (Bodensee), the Rhine and the picturesque town centres of the region.

BASEL
☎ 061 • pop 177,000
Basel (Bâle in French) joined the Swiss Confederation in 1501. Although an industrial city, it retains an attractive old town and offers many interesting museums. The famous Renaissance humanist, Erasmus of Rotterdam, was associated with the city and his tomb rests in the cathedral.

Orientation & Information

Basel's strategic position on the Rhine at the dual border with France and Germany has been instrumental in its development as a commercial and cultural centre. On the northern bank of the Rhine is Kleinbasel (Little Basel), surrounded by German territory. The pedestrian-only old town and most of the sights are on the south bank in Grossbasel (Greater Basel).

The main tourist office (☎ 268 68 68, fax 268 68 70, ✆ office@baseltourismus.ch), by the Mittlere Brücke at Schifflände is open 8.30 am to 6 pm Monday to Friday and 10 am to 4 pm Saturday. Less than 2km south is the main SBB train station (Bahnhof) which has bike rental, money exchange (6 am to 9 pm daily), a Migros supermarket (daily until 10 pm) and another tourist office (☎ 271 36 84). This office is open 8.30 am to 6 pm Monday to Friday and 8.30 am to noon Saturday. Between 1 June and 30 September, it's also open until 7 pm weekdays, 1.30 to 6 pm Saturday and 10 am to 2 pm Sunday.

The main post office (4001 Basel 1, Freie Strasse) is in the city centre, though the office by the train station has a daily emergency counter (surcharge payable). Internet access costs Sfr5/8 for 30/60 minutes at Datacomm, Steinentor Strasse 11 (closed Sunday morning).

Things to See & Do

The tourist office has leaflets on walks through the old town that take in cobbled streets, colourful fountains and 16th-century buildings. The impressive rust-coloured **town hall** (Rathaus) has a frescoed courtyard. The 12th-century **cathedral** (Münster), restored in 1998, is another highlight with its Gothic spires and Romanesque St Gallus doorway.

There are many excellent museums – the BaselCard, costing Sfr25/33/45 for one/two/three days, gets free entry to them all. The **Museum of Fine Arts** (Kunstmuseum), St Albangraben 16, has a good selection of religious, Swiss and modern art, including a palette of Picassos. It is open 10 am to 5 pm Tuesday to Sunday (Sfr7, students Sfr5, free first Sunday of the month).

Basel's **zoo** is one of the best in Switzerland (open daily; Sfr12, students Sfr10). Be sure to take a look at the **fountain** on Theaterplatz. It's a typical display by the Swiss sculptor Jean Tinguely, with madcap machinery playing water games with hoses – art with a juvenile heart. The **Tinguely Museum** is at Grenzacherstrasse 210, east of the city centre (Sfr7; closed Monday and Tuesday).

Basel is also a carnival town. On the Monday after Ash Wednesday, Fasnacht begins. It's a three-day spectacle of parades, masks, music and costumes, all starting at 4 am!

SWITZERLAND

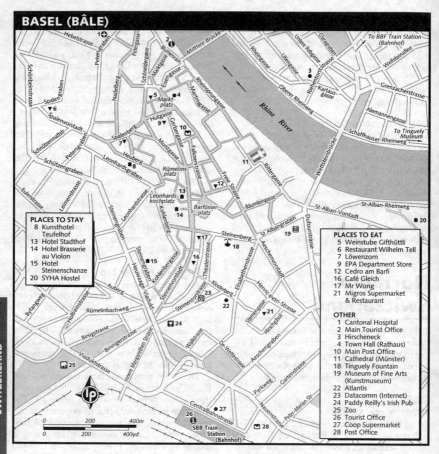

BASEL (BÂLE)

PLACES TO STAY
8 Kunsthotel Teufelhof
13 Hotel Stadthof
14 Hotel Brasserie au Violon
15 Hotel Steinenschanze
20 SYHA Hostel

PLACES TO EAT
5 Weinstube Gifthüttli
6 Restaurant Wilhelm Tell
7 Löwenzorn
9 EPA Department Store
12 Cedro am Barfi
16 Café Gleich
17 Mr Wong
21 Migros Supermarket & Restaurant

OTHER
1 Cantonal Hospital
2 Main Tourist Office
3 Hirscheneck
4 Town Hall (Rathaus)
10 Main Post Office
11 Cathedral (Münster)
18 Tinguely Fountain
19 Museum of Fine Arts (Kunstmuseum)
22 Atlantis
23 Datacomm (Internet)
24 Paddy Reilly's Irish Pub
25 Zoo
26 Tourist Office
27 Coop Supermarket
28 Post Office

Places to Stay

Hotels are expensive and liable to be full during numerous trade fairs and conventions, so book ahead. Unusually, July and August aren't too bad in Basel. Ask your accommodation for the free Mobility Card, good for free local transport. The tourist office in the SBB Bahnhof reserves rooms for Sfr10 commission, compared to Sfr5 in the main tourist office. Check the tourist office hotel list for cheaper, out-of-town accommodation.

Six kilometres south of the train station is *Camp Waldhort* (☎ 711 64 29, Heideweg 16, Reinach).

The SYHA *hostel* (☎ 272 05 72, fax 272 08 33) is fairly central at St Alban Kirchrain 10. Dorm beds are Sfr29 and double rooms are Sfr98. The reception is shut from 10 am to 2 pm, but the doors stay open.

In the old town, *Hotel Stadthof* (☎ 261 87 11, fax 261 25 84, Gerbergasse 84) has standard singles/doubles for Sfr70/120, using hall shower and without breakfast. Near the pedestrian zone is *Hotel Steinenschanze* (☎ 272 53 53, fax 272 45 73, *e* Steinenschanze@datacomm.ch, Steinengraben 69) which has singles/doubles with private shower and toilet for Sfr110/160.

The price for students under 25 is reduced to Sfr60 per person for the first three nights.

Take the stairs uphill to *Hotel Brasserie au Violon* (☎ 269 87 11, fax 269 87 12, ✉ auviolon@prolink.ch, Im Lohnhof 4), a former prison. Tiny doorways lead into reasonably sized rooms (two cells knocked through) with shower/WC. Singles/doubles are Sfr80/120, breakfast is Sfr10.

If you can afford to splash out on accommodation, the *Kunsthotel Teufelhof* (☎ 261 10 10, fax 261 10 04, ✉ info@teufelhof.com, Leonhardsgraben 47) is a unique option. Each of the rooms is 'environmental art' created by a different artist. They stay intact for about two years before being redesigned. The shock of waking up in a piece of art is quite something. Singles/doubles with shower and toilet start at Sfr250/277, or Sfr175/265 in the Galeriehotel annexe (with rooms created by designers rather than artists). Some rooms are more elaborately kitted out than others, but all are a welcome respite from standard hotel fixtures. It also has a good-quality restaurant.

Places to Eat
There are cheap self-service restaurants in the *EPA* department store *(Gerbergasse 4)*, with late opening till 9 pm on Thursday, and *Migros* supermarket *(Sternengasse 17)*.

The pedestrian-only Steinenvorstadt has lots of affordable restaurants, including *Mr Wong* at No 1a for self-service Asian food, and *Café Gleich* at No 23 for vegetarian food (closed weekends). *Cedro am Barfi*, a large place at Streitgasse 20, has pizzas from Sfr12 and set lunches for Sfr16. *Restaurant Wilhelm Tell (Spalenvorstadt 38)* by the Spalentor city gate, sticks to traditional Swiss food (from Sfr14; closed Sunday).

For Basel specialities in a typical ambience, try *Weinstube Gifthüttli* (☎ 261 16 56, Schneidergasse 11). Meals start at Sfr14.50 – check the menus written in bizarre local dialect. *Löwenzorn* (☎ 261 42 13, Gemsberg 2) is similar, if slightly more expensive. Both places are closed Sunday.

Entertainment
Basel has a lively student-led nightlife. Places with live music or DJs include *Atlantis* (☎ 228 96 98, Klosterbergstrasse 13) and the more alternative *Hirscheneck* (☎ 692

73 33, Lindenberg 23). *Paddy Reilly's Irish Pub (Steinentorstrasse 45)* is also popular.

Getting There & Away
Basel is a major European rail hub. On most international trains you pass the border controls in the station, so allow extra time. All trains to France leave from the SNCF section of SBB station; there are five or six daily to Paris (Sfr70, five hours). Trains to Germany stop at Badischer Bahnhof (BBF) on the northern bank; local trains to the Black Forest stop only at BBF, though fast EC services stop at SBB too. Main destinations along this route are Amsterdam (Sfr179, eight hours), Frankfurt (Sfr80, four hours), Hamburg (6½ hours) and Cologne (three hours). Services within Switzerland go from SBB: there are two fast trains hourly to both Geneva (Sfr67, three hours; via Bern or Biel/Bienne) and Zürich (Sfr30, 70 minutes). By motorway, the E25/E60 heads down from Strasbourg and passes by the EuroAirport, and the E35/A5 hugs the German side of the Rhine.

Getting Around
The yellow postbus outside the Swissair office at SBB station goes to/from the airport every 20 minutes (Sfr2.80). City buses and trams run every six to 10 minutes (Sfr1.80 for four or fewer stops, Sfr2.80 for the central zone, Sfr7.80 for a day pass). By SBB station is a hut offering *free* bike loans in summer.

SOLOTHURN
This town is a possible stop-off between Basel and Bern. It has an Italianate cathedral, a baroque Jesuit church, historic fountains and a good fine art museum (housing Hodler's classic painting of William Tell).

SCHAFFHAUSEN
Schaffhausen is on the northern bank of the Rhine, surrounded by Germany. The attractive old town is bursting with oriel windows, painted facades and ornamental fountains. The best streets are Vordergasse and Vorstadt; they intersect at Fronwagplatz, where you'll find the tourist office (☎ 625 51 41, fax 625 51 43, ✉ tourist@swissworld.com). Get an overview of the town from the **Munot** fortress on the hill (open daily; free). The **Allerheiligen Museum**, by the cathedral on Klosterplatz,

encompasses ancient bones and modern art (closed Monday; free).

The **Rhine Falls** (Rheinfall) can be reached by a 40-minute stroll westward along the river, or by bus No 1, 6 or 9 to Neuhausen. The largest waterfall in Europe drops 23m and makes a tremendous racket as 600 cubic metres of water crashes down every second. The 45km of the Rhine from Schaffhausen to Constance is one of the river's most beautiful stretches, passing by meadows, castles and ancient villages, including picturesque **Stein am Rhein**, 20km to the east, where you could easily wear out your camera in Rathausplatz.

Places to Stay & Eat
Schaffhausen can be visited on a day trip, but there are a few options if you want to stay overnight, including a SYHA *hostel (☎ 625 88 00, fax 624 59 54, Randenstrasse 65)* which is closed December to February.

There's cheap eating in the centre at *Migros* supermarket and restaurant at Vorstadt 39, *China Town Take Away (Vorstadt 36)*, *EPA* department store restaurant at Vordergasse 69, or at *Manora* in the Manor department store by the tourist office.

Getting There & Away
Hourly trains run to Zürich (Sfr16.40). Constance and Basel can be reached by either Swiss or (cheaper) German trains. Steamers travel to Constance several times daily in summer, and the trip takes four hours; they depart from Freier Platz (call ☎ 625 42 82 for information). Schaffhausen has good roads in all directions.

ST GALLEN
☎ 071 • pop 70,300
In AD 612, an itinerant Irish monk called Gallus fell into a briar. An irritating mishap, most people would think, but Gallus interpreted this clumsy act as a sign from God and decided to stay put and build a hermitage. From this inauspicious beginning the town of St Gallen evolved and developed into an important medieval cultural centre.

Orientation & Information
The main post office (Bahnhofplatz, 9001) is opposite the train station. Two minutes away

is the tourist office (☎ 227 37 37, fax 227 37 67, 📧 info@stgallen-bodensee.ch), Bahnhofplatz 1a, open 9 am to noon and 1 to 6 pm Monday to Friday, and 9 am to noon Saturday. It has a free hotel booking service. A few minutes to the east is the pedestrian-only old town. Internet access is at the Media Lounge, Katerinengasse 10, and at Quanta on Bohl.

Things to See
St Gallen has an interesting old-city centre. Several buildings have distinctive oriel windows – the best are on Gallusplatz, Spisergasse and Kugelgasse. The twin-tower **cathedral** cannot and should not be missed. Completed in 1766, it's immensely impressive and impressively immense. The ceiling frescoes were by Josef Wannenmacher; look out also for the pulpit, arches, statue groups and woodcarvings around the confessionals.

Adjoining the church is the **Stiftsbibliothek** (Abbey Library), containing some beautifully etched manuscripts from the Middle Ages and a splendidly opulent rococo interior. There's even an Egyptian mummy, dating from 700 BC and as well preserved as the average grandparent. Entry is Sfr7, students Sfr5, and it's closed for three weeks in November, and on Sunday from 1 December to 31 March.

The **Grabenhalle** (☎ 222 82 11, Blumenbergplatz) is a major venue for concerts and other arts events.

Places to Stay
The SYHA *hostel (☎ 245 47 77, fax 245 49 83, Jüchstrasse 25)* is a signposted but tiring 15-minute walk east of the old town, so take the Trogenerbahn from outside the station to 'Schülerhaus' (Sfr2.40). Beds are Sfr24 in a dorm or Sfr33 in a double room. The reception is closed from 10 am to 5 pm but there's usually daytime access to communal areas. The hostel closes mid-December to early March.

Weisses Kreuz (☎/fax 223 28 43, Engelgasse 9) is central and good value. Singles/doubles with shower and toilet are Sfr60/100, though extensive renovations may mean higher prices. The reception is in the bar downstairs (closed 2 to 5 pm weekdays). Nearby, *Elite Garni (☎ 222 12 36, fax 222 21 77, Metzgergasse 9-11)* offers a choice of rooms. It has singles/doubles with shower for Sfr78/125.

Hotel Vadian Garni (☎ 223 60 80, fax 222 47 48, Gallusstrasse 36) has attractive modern-looking rooms with TV from Sfr65/95, or Sfr84/128 with own shower and WC.

Places to Eat

Eating can be pretty good in St Gallen. At the basic level, look out for various fast-food stalls selling St Gallen sausage and bread for around Sfr5. The university *Hochschule Mensa*, west of the rail tracks on Dufourstrasse, offers cheap weekday lunches.

On St Leonhardstrasse is *Migros* supermarket and restaurant. Equally economical is the *EPA* department store's restaurant at Bohl, in the city centre. Both have late closing on Thursday to 9 pm. Next door to EPA is *Markthalle*, with a range of meals either in the bar or the smarter brasserie (closed Sunday). Close by is *Hörni*, straddling Marktplatz and Neugasse. It serves food from Sfr13.80 and, equally importantly, a dozen draught beers from Europe (from Sfr3.80 for 0.3L). It's open daily, including from 8.30 am Friday to 4 am Sunday without a break!

A good mid-range place is *Wirtschaft Zur Alten Post (☎ 222 66 01, Gallusstrasse 4)*. The food is typically Swiss, with meat and fish dishes above Sfr25, though lunches and vegie dishes start at Sfr17. Small and cosy, this restaurant fills quickly so reserve ahead (closed Sunday and Monday).

Getting There & Away

St Gallen is a short train ride from Lake Constance (Bodensee), upon which boats sail to Bregenz in Austria, and to Constance and Lindau in Germany (not in winter). There are also regular trains to Bregenz (Sfr16, one hour), Constance (Sfr16.40, one hour), Chur (Sfr34, 90 minutes) and Zürich (Sfr29, 70 minutes).

APPENZELL

Parochial Appenzellers, inherently resistant to change, are often the butt of Swiss jokes. Appenzell village reflects this conservatism and has an old-fashioned ambience that attracts plenty of tourists. It's a delight to wander around, with traditional old houses, painted facades and lush surrounding countryside. The streets are bedecked with flags and flowers on the last Sunday in April, when the locals vote on cantonal issues by a show of hands in the open-air parliament (Landsgemeinde). Everyone wears traditional dress for the occasion and many men carry swords or daggers as proof of citizenship.

Getting There & Away

There are hourly connections from St Gallen by narrow-gauge train (Swiss Pass and Eurail valid; Inter-Rail gets half-price) which meanders along, mostly following the course of the road (40 minutes). There are two routes so you can make it a circular trip.

Appendix I – Climate Charts

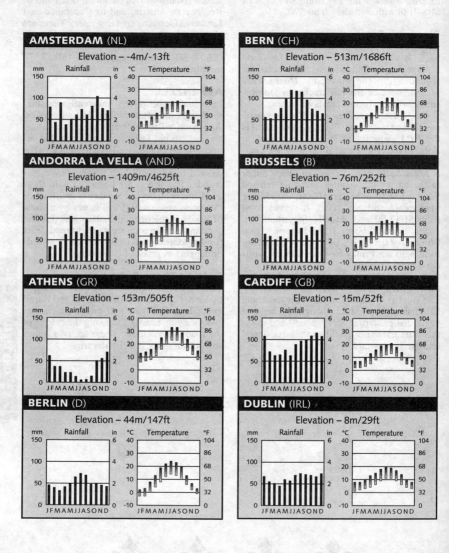

AMSTERDAM (NL)
Elevation – -4m/-13ft

ANDORRA LA VELLA (AND)
Elevation – 1409m/4625ft

ATHENS (GR)
Elevation – 153m/505ft

BERLIN (D)
Elevation – 44m/147ft

BERN (CH)
Elevation – 513m/1686ft

BRUSSELS (B)
Elevation – 76m/252ft

CARDIFF (GB)
Elevation – 15m/52ft

DUBLIN (IRL)
Elevation – 8m/29ft

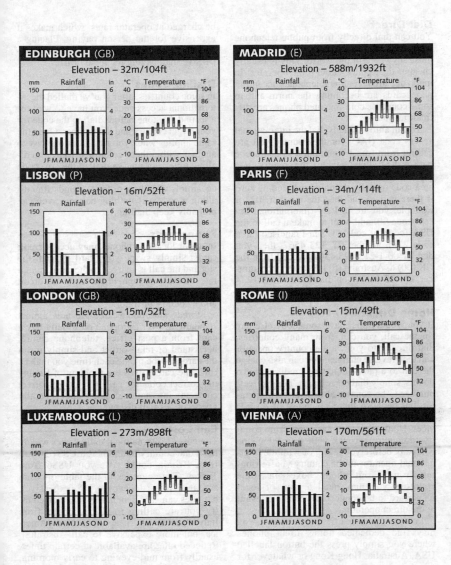

Appendix II – Telephones

Dial Direct

You can dial directly from public telephone boxes from almost anywhere in Europe to almost anywhere in the world. This is usually cheaper than going through the operator. In much of Europe, public telephones accepting phonecards are becoming the norm and in some countries coin-operated phones are difficult to find.

To call abroad simply dial the international access code (IAC) for the country you are calling from (most commonly 00 in Europe but see the following table), the country code (CC) for the country you are calling, the local area code (usually dropping the leading zero if there is one) and then the number. If, for example, you are in Italy (international access code 00) and want to make a call to the USA (country code 1), San Francisco (area code 212), number ☎ 123 4567, then you dial ☎ 00-1-212-123 4567. To call from the UK (00) to Australia (61), Sydney (02), number ☎ 123 4567, you dial ☎ 00-61-2-1234 5678.

Home Direct

If you would rather have somebody else pay for the call, you can, from many countries, dial directly to your home country operator and then reverse charges; you can also charge the call to a phone company credit card. To do this, simply dial the relevant 'home direct' number to be connected to your own operator. For the USA there's a choice of AT&T, MCI or Sprint Global One home direct services. Home direct numbers vary from country to country – check with your telephone company before you leave, or with the international operator in the country you're ringing from. From phone boxes in some countries you may need a coin or local phonecard to be connected with the relevant home direct number.

In some places (particularly airports), you may find dedicated home direct phones where you simply press the button labelled USA, Australia, Hong Kong or whatever for direct connection to the operator. Note that the home direct service does not operate to and from all countries, and that the call could be charged at operator rates, which makes it expensive for the person paying. Placing a call on your phone credit card is more expensive than paying the local tariff.

Dialling Tones

In some countries, after you've dialled the international access code, you have to wait for a second dial tone before dialing the code for your target country and the number. Often the same applies when you ring from one city to another within these countries: wait for a dialling tone after you've dialled the area code for your target city. If you're not sure what to do, simply wait three or four seconds after dialling a code – if nothing happens, you can probably keep dialling.

Phonecards

In major locations phones may accept credit cards: simply swipe your card through the slot and the call is charged to the card, though rates can be very high. Phone-company credit cards can be used to charge calls via your home country operator.

Stored-value phonecards are now almost standard all over Europe. You usually buy a card from a post office, telephone centre, newsstand or retail outlet and simply insert the card into the phone each time you make a call. The card solves the problem of finding the correct coins for calls (or lots of correct coins for international calls) and generally gives you a small discount.

Call Costs

The cost of international calls varies widely from one country to another: a call that costs US$1.20 from Britain could cost you US$6 from Turkey. The countries in the table opposite are rated from * (cheap) to *** (expensive), but rates can vary depending on which country you are calling to (for example, from Italy it's relatively cheap to call North America, but more expensive to call Australia). Reduced rates are available at certain times, usually from mid-evening to early morning, though it varies from country to country – check the local phone book or ask the operator. Calling from hotel rooms can be very

Telephone Codes & Costs

	CC	cost (see text)	IAC	IO
Albania	355	***		
Andorra	376	**	00	821111
Austria	43	*	00	09
Belgium	32	**	00	1224 (private phone)
				1223 (public phone)
Bosnia	387	**	00	901
Bulgaria	359	***	00	
Croatia	385	**	00	901
Cyprus	357	***	00	
Cyprus (Turkish)	90+392		00	
Czech Republic	420	***	00	0149
Denmark	45	**	00	141
Estonia	372	***	00	165
Finland	358	**	00, 990, 994, 999	020222
France	33	*	00(w)	12
Germany	49	*	00	11834
Gibraltar	350	***	00	100
Greece	30	*	00	161
Hungary	36	*	00(w)	199
Iceland	354	***	00	5335010
Ireland	353	*	00	114
Northern Ireland	44+28	*	00	155
Italy	39	**	00	15
Latvia	371	***	1 (w) 00	1 (w) 115
Liechtenstein	423	***	00	114
Lithuania	370	***	8(w)10	194/195
Luxembourg	352	**	00	0010
Macedonia	389	***	99	
Malta	356	**	00	194
Morocco	212	***	00(w)	12
Netherlands	31	**	00	0800-0410
Norway	47	**	00	181
Poland	48	**	0(w)0	901
Portugal	351	*	00	099
Romania	40	***	00	071
Russia	7	***	8(w)10	
Slovakia	421	**	00	0149/0139
Slovenia	386	**	00	901
Spain	34	**	00(w)	025
Sweden	46	**	00	0018
Switzerland	41	**	00	114
Tunisia	216	**	00	
Turkey	90	***	00	115
UK	44	*	00	155
Yugoslavia	381	***	99	901

CC – Country Code (to call into that country)
IAC – International Access Code (to call abroad from that country)
IO – International Operator (to make enquiries)
(w) – wait for dialling tone

Other country codes include: Australia 61, Canada 1, Hong Kong 852, India 91, Indonesia 62, Israel 972, Japan 81, Macau 853, Malaysia 60, New Zealand 64, Singapore 65, South Africa 27, Thailand 66, USA 1

Appendix III – European Organisations

Membership of Political & Economic Organisations

	Council of Europe	EU	EFTA	NATO	Nordic Council	OECD
Albania	✓	–	–	–	–	–
Andorra	✓	–	–	–	–	–
Austria	✓	✓	–	–	–	✓
Belgium	✓	✓	–	✓	–	✓
Bosnia-Hercegovina	✦	–	–	–	–	–
Bulgaria	✓	–	–	–	–	–
Croatia	✓	–	–	–	–	–
Cyprus	✓	–	–	–	–	–
Czech Republic	✓	–	–	✓	–	✓
Denmark	✓	✓	–	✓	✓	✓
Estonia	✓	–	–	–	–	–
Finland	✓	✓	–	–	✓	✓
France	✓	✓	–	✓	–	✓
Georgia	✓	–	–	–	–	–
Germany	✓	✓	–	✓	–	✓
Greece	✓	✓	–	✓	–	✓
Hungary	✓	–	–	✓	–	✓
Iceland	✓	–	✓	✓	✓	✓
Ireland	✓	✓	–	–	–	✓
Italy	✓	✓	–	✓	–	✓
Latvia	✓	–	–	–	–	–
Liechtenstein	✓	–	✓	–	–	–
Lithuania	✓	–	–	–	–	–
Luxembourg	✓	✓	–	✓	–	✓
Macedonia	✓	–	–	–	–	–
Malta	✓	–	–	–	–	–
Netherlands	✓	✓	–	✓	–	✓
Norway	✓	–	✓	✓	✓	✓
Poland	✓	–	–	✓	–	✓
Portugal	✓	✓	–	✓	–	✓
Romania	✓	–	–	–	–	–
Russian Federation	✓	–	–	–	–	–
Slovakia	✓	–	–	–	–	–
Slovenia	✓	–	–	–	–	–
Spain	✓	✓	–	✓	–	✓
Sweden	✓	✓	–	–	✓	✓
Switzerland	✓	–	✓	–	–	✓
Turkey	✓	–	–	✓	–	✓
UK	✓	✓	–	✓	–	✓
Ukraine	✓	–	–	–	–	–
Yugoslavia	–	–	–	–	–	–

✓ full member   ✦ special guest status

Council of Europe

Established in 1949, the Council of Europe is the oldest of Europe's political institutions. It aims to promote European unity, protect human rights and assist in the cultural, social and economic development of its member states, but its powers are purely advisory. Founding states were Belgium, Denmark, France, Ireland, Italy, Luxembourg, the Netherlands, Norway, Sweden and the UK. It now counts 41 members. Its headquarters are in Strasbourg.

European Union (EU)

Founded by the Treaty of Rome in 1957, the European Economic Community, or Common Market as it was once known, broadened its scope far beyond economic measures as it developed into the European Community (1967) and finally the European Union (1993). Its original aims were to develop and expand the economies of its member states by abolishing customs tariffs, coordinating transportation systems and general economic policies, establishing a common economic policy towards nonmember states, and promoting the free movement of labour and capital within its borders. Further measures included the abolition of border controls and the linking of currency exchange rates. Since the 1991 Maastricht treaty, the EU is committed to establishing a common foreign and security policy and close cooperation in home affairs and the judiciary. A single European currency called the euro came into effect in January 1999.

The EEC's founding states were Belgium, France, West Germany, Italy, Luxembourg and the Netherlands – the Treaty of Rome was an extension of the European Coal and Steel Community (ECSC) founded by these six states in 1952. Denmark, Ireland and the UK joined in 1973, Greece in 1981, Spain and Portugal in 1986 and Austria, Finland and Sweden in 1995. In 1998, membership negotiations opened with Cyprus, Czech Republic, Estonia, Hungary, Poland and Slovenia, with full membership expected to be granted in 2002. Bulgaria, Latvia, Lithuania, Malta, Romania and Slovakia joined accession talks in 2000. The main EU organisations are the European Parliament (elected by direct universal suffrage, with growing powers), the European Commission (the daily government), the Council of Ministers (ministers of member states who make the important decisions) and the Court of Justice. The European Parliament meets in Strasbourg; Luxembourg is home to the Court of Justice. Other EU organisations are based in Brussels.

European Free Trade Association (EFTA)

Established in 1960 in direct response to the creation of the European Economic Community, EFTA aims to eliminate trade tariffs on industrial products between member states, though each member retains the right to its own commercial policy towards nonmembers. Its four members (Iceland, Liechtenstein, Norway and Switzerland) cooperate with the EU through the European Economic Area agreement. Denmark and the UK left EFTA to join the EU in 1973 and others have since followed suit, leaving EFTA's future in doubt. Its headquarters are in Geneva.

North Atlantic Treaty Organisation (NATO)

The document creating this defence alliance was signed in 1949 by the USA, Canada and 10 European countries to safeguard their common political, social and economic systems against external threats (read: against the powerful Soviet military presence in Europe after WWII). An attack against any member state would be considered an attack against them all. Greece and Turkey joined in 1952, West Germany in 1955, and Spain in 1982; France withdrew from NATO's integrated military command in 1966 and Greece did likewise in 1974, though both remain members. NATO's Soviet counterpart, the Warsaw Pact founded in 1955, collapsed with the democratic revolutions of 1989 and the subsequent disintegration of the Soviet Union; most of its former members are now NATO associates. NATO's headquarters are in Brussels.

Nordic Council

Established in Copenhagen in 1952, the Nordic Council aims to promote economic, social and cultural cooperation among its member states (Denmark, Finland, Iceland, Norway and Sweden). Since 1971, the Council has acted as an advisory body to the Nordic Council of Ministers, a meeting of ministers from the member states responsible for the subject under discussion. Decisions taken by the Council of Ministers are usually binding, though member states retain full sovereignty. Environmental, tariff, labour and immigration policies are often coordinated.

Organisation for Economic Cooperation & Development (OECD)

The OECD was set up in 1961 to supersede the Organisation for European Economic Cooperation, which allocated US aid under the Marshall Plan and coordinated the reconstruction of postwar Europe. Sometimes seen as the club of the world's rich countries, the OECD aims to encourage economic growth and world trade. Its member states include most of Europe, as well as Australia, Canada, Japan, Mexico, New Zealand and the USA. Its headquarters are in Paris.

Appendix IV – Alternative Place Names

The following abbreviations are used:

(B) Basque
(C) Catalan
(D) Dutch/Flemish
(E) English
(F) French
(Fl) Flemish/Dutch
(G) German
(Gr) Greek
(Ir) Irish
(I) Italian
(L) Luxembourgian
(I) Italian
(P) Portuguese
(Rh) Romansch
(S) Spanish

AUSTRIA
Österreich
Carinthia (E) – Kärnten (G)
Danube (E) – Donau (G)
East Tirol (E) – Osttirol (G)
Lake Constance (E) – Bodensee (G)
Lower Austria (E) – Niederösterreich (G)
Upper Austria (E) – Oberösterreich (G)
Styria (E) – Steiermark (G)
Tirol (E, G) – Tyrol (E)
Vienna (E) – Wien (G)
Vienna Woods (E) – Wienerwald (G)

BELGIUM
België (Fl), Belgique (F)
Antwerp (E) – Antwerpen (Fl), Anvers (F)
Bruges (E, F) – Brugge (Fl)
Brussels (E) – Brussel (Fl), Bruxelles (F)
Courtrai (E, F) – Kortrijk (Fl)
Ghent (E) – Gent (Fl), Gand (F)
Liège (E, F) – Luik (Fl), Lüttich (G)
Louvain (E, F) – Leuven (Fl)
Mechlin (E) – Mechelen (Fl), Malines (F)
Meuse (River) (E, F) – Maas (Fl)
Mons (E, F) – Bergen (Fl)
Namur (E, F) – Namen (Fl)
Ostende (E) – Oostende (Fl), Ostende (F)
Scheldt (River) (E) – Schelde (Fl),Escaut (F)
Tournai (E, F) – Doornik (Fl)
Ypres (E, F) – Ieper (Fl)

FRANCE
Bayonne (F, E) – Baiona (B)
Basque Country (E) – Euskadi (B), Pays Basque (F)
Burgundy (E) – Bourgogne (F)
Brittany (E) – Bretagne (F)
Corsica (E) – Corse (F)
French Riviera (E) – Côte d'Azur (F)
Dunkirk (E) – Dunkerque (F)
Channel Islands (E) – Îles Anglo-Normandes (F)
English Channel (E) – La Manche (F)
Lake Geneva (E) – Lac Léman (F)
Lyons (E) – Lyon (F)
Marseilles (E) – Marseille (F)
Normandy (E) – Normandie (F)
Rheims (E) – Reims (F)
Rhine (River) (E) – Rhin (F), Rhein (G)
Saint Jean de Luz (F) – Donibane Lohizune (B)
Saint Jean Pied de Port (F) – Donibane Garazi (F)
Sark (Channel Islands) (E) – Sercq (F)

GERMANY
Deutschland
Aachen (E, G) – Aix-la-Chapelle (F)
Baltic Sea (E) – Ostsee (G)
Bavaria (E) – Bayern (G)
Bavarian Alps (E) – Bayerische Alpen (G)
Bavarian Forest (E) – Bayerischer Wald (G)
Black Forest (E) – Schwarzwald (G)
Cologne (E) – Köln (G)
Constance (E) – Konstanz (G)
Danube (E) – Donau (G)
East Friesland (E) – Ostfriesland (G)
Federal Republic of Germany (E) – Bundesrepublik Deutschland (abbrev BRD) (G)
Franconia (E) – Franken (G)
Hamelin (E) – Hameln (G)
Hanover (E) – Hannover (G)
Harz Mountains (E) – Harzgebirge (G)
Hesse (E) – Hessen (G)
Lake Constance (E) – Bodensee (G)
Lower Saxony (E) – Niedersachsen (G)
Lüneburg Heath (E) – Lüneburger Heide (G)
Mecklenburg-Pomerania (E) – Mecklenburg-Vorpommern (G)

1159

Munich (E) – München (G)
North Friesland (E) – Nordfriesland (G)
North Rhine-Westphalia (E) –
 Nordrhein-Westfalen (G)
Nuremberg (E) – Nürnberg (G)
Pomerania (E) – Pommern (G)
Prussia (E) – Preussen (G)
Rhine (E) – Rhein (G)
Rhineland-Palatinate (E) – Rheinland-Pfalz (G)
Romantic Road (E) – Romantische Strasse (G)
Saarbrücken (E, G) – Sarrebruck (F)
Saxon Switzerland (E) – Sachsische
 Schweiz (G)
Saxony (E) – Sachsen (G)
Swabia (E) – Schwaben (G)
Thuringia (E) – Thüringen (G)
Thuringian Forest (E) – Thüringer Wald (G)

GREECE
Hellas (or Ellas)
Athens (E) – Athina (Gr)
Corfu (E) – Kerkyra (Gr)
Crete (E) – Kriti (Gr)
Patras (E) – Patra (Gr)
Rhodes (E) – Rodos (Gr)
Salonica (E) – Thessaloniki (Gr)
Samothrace (E) – Samothraki (Gr)
Santorini (E, I) – Thira (Gr)

IRELAND
Eire
Aran Islands (E) – Oileáin Árainn (Ir)
Athlone (E) – Baile Átha Luain (Ir)
Bantry (E) – Beanntraí (Ir)
Belfast (E) – Beál Feirste (Ir)
Cork (E) – Corcaigh (Ir)
Derry/Londonderry (E) – Doire (Ir)
Dingle (E) – An Daingean (Ir)
Donegal (E) – Dún na nGall (Ir)
Dublin (E) – Baile Átha Cliath (Ir)
Galway (E) – Gaillimh (Ir)
Kilkenny (E) – Cill Chainnigh (Ir)
Killarney (E) – Cill Áirne (Ir)
Kilronan (E) – Cill Ronáin (Ir)
Limerick (E) – Luimneach (Ir)
Shannon (E) – Sionann (Ir)
Waterford (E) – Port Láirge (Ir)
Wexford (E) – Loch Garman (Ir)

ITALY
Italia
Aeolian Islands (E) – Isole Eolie (I)
Apulia (E) – Puglia (I)

Florence (E) – Firenze (I)
Genoa (E) – Genova (I)
Herculaneum (E) – Ercolano (I)
Lombardy (E) – Lombardia (I)
Mantua (E) – Mantova (I)
Milan (E) – Milano (I)
Naples (E) – Napoli (I)
Padua (E) – Padova (I)
Rome (E) – Roma (I)
Sicily (E) – Sicilia (I)
Sardinia (E) – Sardegna (I)
Syracuse (E) – Siracusa (I)
Tiber (River) (E) – Tevere (I)
Venice (E) – Venezia (I)

LUXEMBOURG
Letzeburg (L), Luxemburg (G)

THE NETHERLANDS
Nederland
Den Bosch (E, D) – 's-Hertogenbosch (D)
Flushing (E) – Vlissingen (D)
Hook of Holland (E) – Hoek van Holland (D)
Meuse (River) (E, F) – Maas (D)
Rhine (River) (E) – Rijn (D)
The Hague (E) – Den Haag (or
 's-Gravenhage) (D)

PORTUGAL
Cape St Vincent (E) – Cabo de São Vicente (P)
Lisbon (E) – Lisboa (P)
Oporto (E) – Porto (P)

SPAIN
España
Andalusia (E) – Andalucía (S)
Balearic Islands (E) – Islas Baleares (S)
Basque Country (E) – Euskadi (B), País
 Vasco (S)
Catalonia (E) – Catalunya (C), Cataluña (S)
Cordova (E) – Córdoba (S)
Corunna (E) – La Coruña (S)
Majorca (E) – Mallorca (S)
Minorca (E) – Menorca (S)
Navarre (E) – Navarra (S)
San Sebastián (E, S) – Donostia (B)
Saragossa (E) – Zaragoza (S)
Seville (E) – Sevilla (S)

SWITZERLAND
*Schweiz (G), Suisse (F), Svizzera (I),
 Svizzra (Rh)*
Basel (E, G) – Basle (E), Bâle (F), Basilea (I)

Bern (E, G) – Berne (E, F), Berna (I)
Fribourg (E, F) – Freiburg (G), Friburgo (I)
Geneva (E) – Genève (F), Genf (G), Ginevra (I)
Graubünden (E, G) – Grisons (F), Grigioni (I), Grishun – (Rh)
Lake Constance (E) – Bodensee (G)

Lake Geneva (E) – Lac Léman (F)
Lake Maggiore (E) – Lago Maggiore (I)
Lucerne (E, F) – Luzern (G), Lucerna (I)
Neuchâtel (E, F) – Neuenburg (G)
Ticino (E, I) – Tessin (G, F)
Valais (E, F) – Wallis (G)
Zürich (G) – Zurich (F), Zurigo (I)

Appendix V – International Country Abbreviations

The following is a list of official abbreviations that you may encounter on motor vehicles in Europe. Other abbreviations are likely to be unofficial ones, often referring to a particular region, province or even city. A vehicle entering a foreign country must carry a sticker identifying its country of registration, though this rule is not always enforced.

A	–	Austria
AL	–	Albania
AND	–	Andorra
B	–	Belgium
BG	–	Bulgaria
BIH	–	Bosnia-Hercegovina
BY	–	Belarus
CDN	–	Canada
CH	–	Switzerland
CY	–	Cyprus
CZ	–	Czech Republic
D	–	Germany
DK	–	Denmark
DZ	–	Algeria
E	–	Spain
EST	–	Estonia
ET	–	Egypt
F	–	France
FIN	–	Finland
FL	–	Liechtenstein
FR	–	Faroe Islands
GB	–	Great Britain
GE	–	Georgia
GR	–	Greece
H	–	Hungary
HKJ	–	Jordan
HR	–	Croatia
I	–	Italy
IL	–	Israel
IRL	–	Ireland
IS	–	Iceland
L	–	Luxembourg
LAR	–	Libya
LT	–	Lithuania
LV	–	Latvia
M	–	Malta
MA	–	Morocco
MC	–	Monaco
MD	–	Moldavia
MK	–	Macedonia
N	–	Norway
NGR	–	Nigeria
NL	–	Netherlands
NZ	–	New Zealand
P	–	Portugal
PL	–	Poland
RL	–	Lebanon
RO	–	Romania
RSM	–	San Marino
RUS	–	Russia
S	–	Sweden
SK	–	Slovakia
SLO	–	Slovenia
SYR	–	Syria
TN	–	Tunisia
TR	–	Turkey
UA	–	Ukraine
USA	–	United States of America
V	–	Vatican City
YU	–	Yugoslavia
ZA	–	South Africa

OTHER

CC	–	Consular Corps
CD	–	Diplomatic Corps
GBA	–	Alderney
GBG	–	Guernsey
GBJ	–	Jersey
GBM	–	Isle of Man
GBZ	–	Gibraltar

Language

This Language Guide contains pronunciation guidelines and basic vocabulary to help you get around Western Europe. For background information on each language see the individual country chapters. For more extensive coverage of the languages included here, get a copy of Lonely Planet's *Western Europe* or *Mediterranean Europe* phrasebooks.

Dutch

Pronunciation
Vowels

a	short, as the 'u' in 'cut'
a, aa	long, as the 'a' in 'father'
au, ou	pronounced somewhere between the 'ow' in 'how' and the 'ow' in 'glow'
e	short, as in 'bet', or as the 'er' in 'fern' (without pronouncing the 'r')
e, ee	long, as the 'ay' in 'day'
ei	as the 'ey' in 'they'
eu	a tricky one; try saying 'eh' with rounded lips and the tongue forward, then slide the tongue back and down to make an 'oo' sound; it's similar to the 'eu' in French *couleur*
i	short, as in 'it'
i, ie	long, as the 'ee' in 'meet'
ij	as the 'ey' in 'they'
o	short, as in 'pot'
o, oo	long, as in 'note'
oe	as the 'oo' in 'zoo'
u	short, similar to the 'u' in 'urn'
u, uu	long, as the 'u' in 'flute'
ui	a very tricky one; pronounced somewhere between **au/ou** and **eu**; it's similar to the 'eui' in French *fauteuil*, without the slide to the 'i'

Consonants

ch & g	in the north, a hard 'kh' sound as in the Scottish *loch*; in the south, a softer, lisping sound
j	as the 'y' in 'yes'; also as the 'j' or 'zh' sound in 'jam' or 'pleasure'
r	in the south, a trilled sound; in the north it varies, often guttural
s	as in 'safe'; sometimes as the 's' in 'pleasure'
w	at the beginning of a word, a clipped sound almost like a 'v'; at the end of a word as the English 'w'

Basics

Hello.	*Dag/Hallo.*
Goodbye.	*Dag.*
Yes.	*Ja.*
No.	*Nee.*
Please.	*Alstublieft/Alsjeblieft.*
Thank you.	*Dank U/je (wel).*
You're welcome.	*Geen dank.*
Excuse me.	*Pardon.*
Sorry.	*Sorry.*
Do you speak English?	*Spreekt U/spreek je Engels?*
How much is it?	*Hoeveel kost het?*
What's your name?	*Hoe heet U/je?*
My name is ...	*Ik heet ...*

Getting Around

What time does the ... leave/arrive?	*Hoe laat vertrekt/ arriveert de ...?*
(next)	*(volgende)*
boat	*boot*
bus/tram	*bus/tram*
train	*trein*
I'd like to hire a car/bicycle.	*Ik wil graag een auto/fiets huren.*
I'd like a one-way/ return ticket.	*Ik wil graag een enkele reis/een retour.*
1st/2nd class	*eerste/tweede klas*

Signs – Dutch

Ingang	Entrance
Uitgang	Exit
Kamers Vrij	Rooms Available
Vol	Full/No Vacancies
Informatie/ Inlichtingen	Information
Open/Gesloten	Open/Closed
Politiebureau	Police Station
Verboden	Prohibited
WC/Toiletten	Toilets
Heren	Men
Dames	Women

LANGUAGE

Emergencies – Dutch

Help!	Help!
Call a doctor!	Haal een dokter!
Call the police!	Haal de politie!
Go away!	Ga weg!
I'm lost.	Ik ben de weg kwijt.

left luggage locker	bagagekluis
bus/tram stop	bushalte/tramhalte
train station/	treinstation/
ferry terminal	veerhaven

Where is the ...?	Waar is de ...?
Go straight ahead.	Ga rechtdoor.
Turn left/right.	Ga linksaf/rechtsaf.
far/near	ver/dichtbij

Around Town

a bank	een bank
the ... embassy	de ... ambassade
my hotel	mijn hotel
the post office	het postkantoor
the market	de markt
the pharmacy	de drogist
the newsagents/	de krantenwinkel/
stationers	kantoorboekhandel
the telephone centre	de telefooncentrale
the tourist office	de VVV/het
	toeristenbureau

What time does it	Hoe laat opent/
open/close?	sluit het?

Accommodation

hotel	hotel
guesthouse	pension
youth hostel	jeugdherberg
camping ground	camping

Do you have any	Heeft U kamers vrij?
rooms available?	

single/double room	eenpersoons/twee-
	persoons kamer
one/two nights	één nacht/twee nachten

How much is it	Hoeveel is het
per night/	per nacht/
per person?	per persoon?
Does it include	Zit er ontbijt bij
breakfast?	inbegrepen?

Time, Days & Numbers

What time is it?	Hoe laat is het?
today	vandaag
tomorrow	morgen
in the morning	's-morgens
in the afternoon	's-middags

Monday	maandag
Tuesday	dinsdag
Wednesday	woensdag
Thursday	donderdag
Friday	vrijdag
Saturday	zaterdag
Sunday	zondag

0	nul
1	één
2	twee
3	drie
4	vier
5	vijf
6	zes
7	zeven
8	acht
9	negen
10	tien
11	elf
100	honderd
1000	duizend

one million	één miljoen

French

Pronunciation

A few tricky French sounds include:

- The distinction between the 'u' sound (as in *tu*) and 'oo' sound (as in *tout*). For both sounds, the lips are rounded and projected forward, but for the 'u' the tongue is towards the front of the mouth, its tip against the lower front teeth, whereas for the 'oo' the tongue is towards the back of the mouth, its tip behind the gums of the lower front teeth.

- The nasal vowels. During the production of nasal vowels the breath escapes partly through the nose and partly through the mouth. There are no nasal vowels in English; in French there are three, as in *bon vin blanc* (good white wine). These sounds occur where a syllable ends in a single 'n' or 'm'; the 'n' or 'm' is silent but indicates the nasalisation of the preceding vowel.

- The 'r'. The standard 'r' of Parisian French is produced by moving the bulk of the tongue backwards to constrict the air flow in the pharynx while the tip of the tongue rests behind the lower front teeth. It's similar to the noise made by some people before spitting, but with much less friction.

Basics

Hello.	*Bonjour.*
Goodbye.	*Au revoir.*
Yes.	*Oui.*
No.	*Non.*
Please.	*S'il vous plaît.*
Thank you.	*Merci.*
That's fine, you're welcome.	*Je vous en prie.*
Excuse me. (attention)	*Excusez-moi*
Sorry. (apology)	*Pardon*
Do you speak English?	*Parlez-vous anglais?*
How much is it?	*C'est combien?*
What's your name?	*Comment vous appelez-vous?*
My name is ...	*Je m'appelle ...*

Getting Around

When does the next ... leave/arrive?	*À quelle heure part/ arrive le prochain ...?*
boat	*bateau*
bus (city)	*bus*
bus (intercity)	*car*
tram	*tramway*
train	*train*
left luggage (office)	*consigne*
timetable	*horaire*
bus/tram stop	*arrêt d'autobus/ de tramway*
train station/ ferry terminal	*gare/gare maritime*
I'd like a ... ticket.	*Je voudrais un billet ...*
one-way	*aller simple*
return	*aller retour*
1st class	*première classe*
2nd class	*deuxième classe*
I'd like to hire a car/bicycle.	*Je voudrais louer une voiture/un vélo.*
Where is ...?	*Où est ...?*

Go straight ahead.	*Continuez tout droit.*
Turn left.	*Tournez à gauche.*
Turn right.	*Tournez à droite.*
far/near	*loin/proche*

Around Town

a bank	*une banque*
the ... embassy	*l'ambassade de ...*
my hotel	*mon hôtel*
post office	*le bureau de poste*
market	*le marché*
chemist/pharmacy	*la pharmacie*
newsagents/ stationers	*l'agence de presse/ la papeterie*
a public telephone	*une cabine téléphonique*
the tourist office	*l'office de tourisme/ le syndicat d'initiative*
What time does it open/close?	*Quelle est l' heure de ouverture/fermeture?*

Accommodation

the hotel	*l'hôtel*
the youth hostel	*l'auberge de jeunesse*
the camping ground	*le camping*
Do you have any rooms available?	*Est-ce que vous avez des chambres libres?*
for one person	*pour une personne*
for two people	*deux personnes*
How much is it per night/ per person?	*Quel est le prix par nuit/ par personne?*
Is breakfast included?	*Est-ce que le petit dé- jeuner est compris?*

LANGUAGE

Emergencies – French

Help!	*Au secours!*
Call a doctor!	*Appelez un médecin!*
Call the police!	*Appelez la police!*
Leave me alone!	*Fichez-moi la paix!*
I'm lost.	*Je me suis égaré/e.*

Time, Days & Numbers

What time is it?	*Quelle heure est-il?*
today	*aujourd'hui*
tomorrow	*demain*
yesterday	*hier*
morning	*matin*
afternoon	*après-midi*

Monday	*lundi*
Tuesday	*mardi*
Wednesday	*mercredi*
Thursday	*jeudi*
Friday	*vendredi*
Saturday	*samedi*
Sunday	*dimanche*

1	*un*
2	*deux*
3	*trois*
4	*quatre*
5	*cinq*
6	*six*
7	*sept*
8	*huit*
9	*neuf*
10	*dix*
100	*cent*
1000	*mille*

one million	*un million*

German

Pronunciation

Unlike English or French, German has no real silent letters: you pronounce the k at the start of the word *Knie*, 'knee', the p at the start of *Psychologie*, 'psychology', and the e at the end of *ich habe*, 'I have'.

Vowels As in English, vowels can be pronounced long, as the 'o' in 'pope', or short, as in 'pop'. As a rule, German vowels are long before one consonant and short before two consonants, eg, the o is long in the word *Dom*, 'cathedral', but short in the word *doch*, 'after all'.

a	short, as the 'u' in 'cut' or long, as in 'father'
au	as the 'ow' in 'vow'
ä	short, as in 'cat' or long, as in 'care'
äu	as the 'oy' in 'boy'
e	short, as in 'bet' or long, as in 'obey'
ei	as the 'ai' in 'aisle'
eu	as the 'oy' in 'boy'
i	short, as in 'it' or long, as in 'marine'
ie	as the 'brief'
o	short, as in 'not' or long, as in 'note'
ö	as the 'er' in 'fern'
u	as in 'pull'
ü	similar to the 'u' in 'pull' but with lips stretched back

Consonants Most German consonants sound similar to their English counterparts. One important difference is that b, d and g sound like 'p', 't' and 'k', respectively when word-final.

b	as in 'be'; as 'p' when word-final
ch	as in Scottish 'loch'
d	as in 'do'; as 't' when word-final
g	as in 'go'; as 'k' when word-final (except after i, when it's as 'ch' in Scottish *loch*)
j	as the 'y' in 'yet'
qu	as 'k' plus 'v'
r	can be trilled or guttural, depending on the region
s	as in 'sun'; as the 'z' in 'zoo' when followed by a vowel
sch	as the 'sh' in 'ship'.
sp, st	as 'shp' and 'sht' when word-initial
tion	the 't' is pronounced as the 'ts' in 'its'
v	as the 'f' in 'fan'
w	as the 'v' in 'van'
z	as the 'ts' in 'its'

Basics

Good day.	*Guten Tag.*
Hello. (in Bavaria and Austria)	*Grüss Gott.*
Goodbye.	*Auf Wiedersehen.*
Bye. (informal)	*Tschüss.*
Yes.	*Ja.*
No.	*Nein.*
Please.	*Bitte.*

Signs – German

Eingang	**Entrance**
Ausgang	**Exit**
Zimmer Frei	**Rooms Available**
Voll/Besetzt	**Full/No Vacancies**
Auskunft	**Information**
Offen	**Open**
Geschlossen	**Closed**
Polizeiwache	**Police Station**
Toiletten (WC)	**Toilets**
Herren	**Men**
Damen	**Women**

Thank you.	*Danke.*
You're welcome.	*Bitte sehr.*
Sorry. (excuse me, forgive me)	*Entschuldigung.*
Do you speak English?	*Sprechen Sie Englisch?*
How much is it?	*Wieviel kostet es?*
What's your name?	*Wie heissen Sie?*
My name is ...	*Ich heisse ...*

Getting Around

What time does ... leave/arrive?	*Wann (fährt ... ab/ kommt ... an)?*
the boat	*das Boot*
the bus (city)	*der Bus*
the bus (intercity)	*der (überland) Bus*
the tram	*die Strassenbahn*
the train	*der Zug*
What time is the next boat?	*Wann fährt das nächste Boot?*
I'd like to hire a car/bicycle.	*Ich möchte ein Auto/ Fahrrad mieten.*
I'd like a one-way/ return ticket.	*Ich möchte eine Einzel- karte/Rückfahrkarte.*

1st/2nd class	*erste/zweite Klasse*
left luggage lockers	*Schliessfächer*
timetable	*Fahrplan*
bus stop	*Bushaltestelle*
tram stop	*Strassenbahnhaltestelle*
train station	*Bahnhof (Bf)*
ferry terminal	*Fährhafen*

Where is the ...?	*Wo ist die ...?*
Go straight ahead.	*Gehen Sie geradeaus.*
Turn left.	*Biegen Sie links ab.*
Turn right.	*Biegen Sie rechts ab.*
near/far	*nahe/weit*

Around Town

a bank	*eine Bank*
the ... embassy	*die ... Botschaft*
my hotel	*mein Hotel*
the post office	*das Postamt*
the market	*der Markt*
the pharmacy	*die Apotheke*
the newsagents	*der Zeitungshändler*
the stationers	*der Schreibwaren- geschäft*
the telephone centre	*die Telefonzentrale*
the tourist office	*das Verkehrsamt*
What time does it open/close?	*Um wieviel Uhr macht es auf/zu?*

Accommodation

hotel	*Hotel*
guesthouse	*Pension, Gästehaus*
youth hostel	*Jugendherberge*
camping ground	*Campingplatz*

Do you have any rooms available?	*Haben Sie noch freie Zimmer?*
a single room	*ein Einzelzimmer*
a double room	*ein Doppelzimmer*
How much is it per night/person?	*Wieviel kostet es pro Nacht/Person?*
Is breakfast included?	*Ist Frühstück inbe griffen?*

Time, Days & Numbers

What time is it?	*Wie spät ist es?*
today	*heute*
tomorrow	*morgen*
yesterday	*gestern*
in the morning	*morgens*
in the afternoon	*nachmittags*

Monday	*Montag*
Tuesday	*Dienstag*
Wednesday	*Mittwoch*
Thursday	*Donnerstag*
Friday	*Freitag*
Saturday	*Samstag, Sonnabend*
Sunday	*Sonntag*

Emergencies – German

Help!	*Hilfe!*
Call a doctor!	*Holen Sie einen Arzt!*
Call the police!	*Rufen Sie die Polizei!*
I'm lost.	*Ich habe mich verirrt.*

0	*null*
1	*eins*
2	*zwei/zwo*
3	*drei*
4	*vier*
5	*fünf*
6	*sechs*
7	*sieben*
8	*acht*
9	*neun*
10	*zehn*
11	*elf*
12	*zwölf*
13	*dreizehn*
100	*hundert*
1000	*tausend*

one million   *eine Million*

Greek

Alphabet & Pronunciation

Pronunciation of Greek letters is shown using the closest-sounding English letter.

Greek	English	Pronunciation
Α α	a	as in 'father'
Β β	v	as the 'v' in 'vine'
Γ γ	gh, y	like a rough 'g', or as the 'y' in 'yes'
Δ δ	dh	as the 'th' in 'then'
Ε ε	e	as in 'egg'
Ζ ζ	z	as in 'zoo'
Η η	i	as the 'ee' in 'feet'
Θ θ	th	as the 'th' in 'throw'
Ι ι	i	as the 'ee' in 'feet'
Κ κ	k	as in 'kite'
Λ λ	l	as in 'leg'
Μ μ	m	as in 'man'
Ν ν	n	as in 'net'
Ξ ξ	x	as the 'ks' in 'looks'
Ο ο	o	as in 'hot'
Π π	p	as in 'pup'
Ρ ρ	r	slightly trilled 'r'
Σ σ	s	as in 'sand' ('ς' at the end of a word)
Τ τ	t	as in 'to'
Υ υ	i	as the 'ee' in 'feet'
Φ φ	f	as in 'fee'
Χ χ	kh, h	as the 'ch' in Scottish *loch*, or as a rough 'h'
Ψ ψ	ps	as the 'ps' in 'lapse'
Ω ω	o	as in 'lot'

Letter Combinations

ει, οι	i	as the 'ee' in 'feet'
αι	e	as in 'bet'
ου	u	as the 'oo' in 'mood'
μπ	b	as in 'be'
	mb	as in 'amber' (or as the 'mp' in 'ample')
ντ	d	as in 'do'
	nd	as in 'bend' (or as the 'nt' in 'sent')
γκ	g	as in 'go'
γγ	ng	as the 'ng' in 'angle'
γξ	ks	as in 'yaks'
τζ	dz	as the 'ds' in 'suds'

Some pairs of vowels are pronounced separately if the first has an acute accent (eg, ά), or the second has a dieresis (eg, ï).

All Greek words of two or more syllables have an acute accent which indicates where the stress falls. The suffix of some Greek words depends on the gender of the speaker, eg, *asthmatikos* (m) and *asthmatikya* (f), or *epileptikos* (m) and *epileptikya* (f).

Basics

Hello.	*yasu* (informal)
	yasas (polite/plural)
Goodbye.	*andio*
Yes.	*ne*
No.	*okhi*
Please.	*sas parakalo*
Thank you.	*sas efharisto*
That's fine/ You're welcome.	*ine endaksi/parakalo*
Excuse me. (forgive me)	*signomi*
Do you speak English?	*milate anglika?*

Signs – Greek

ΕΙΣΟΔΟΣ	Entrance
ΕΞΟΔΟΣ	Exit
ΠΛΗΡΟΦΟΡΙΕΣ	Information
ΑΝΟΙΚΤΟ	Open
ΚΛΕΙΣΤΟ	Closed
ΑΣΤΥΝΟΜΙΚΟΣ ΣΤΑΘΜΟΣ	Police Station
ΑΠΑΓΟΡΕΥΕΤΑΙ	Prohibited
ΤΟΥΑΛΕΤΕΣ	Toilets
ΑΝΔΡΩΝ	Men
ΓΥΝΑΙΚΩΝ	Women

Emergencies – Greek

Help!	voithia!
Call a doctor!	fona kste ena yatro!
Call the police!	tilefoniste stin astinomia!
Go away!	fighe/dhromo!
I'm lost.	eho hathi

How much is it? *poso kani?*
What's your name? *pos sas lene/ pos legeste?*
My name is ... *me lene ...*

Getting Around

What time does the ... leave/arrive? *ti ora fevyi/apo horito ...?*
boat *to plio*
bus (city) *to leoforio (ya tin boli)*
bus (intercity) *to leoforio (ya ta proastia)*
tram *to tram*
train *to treno*

I'd like a ... ticket. *tha ithela isitirio ...*
one-way *horis epistrofi*
return *met epistrois*
1st class *proti thesi*
2nd class *dhefteri thesi*

left luggage *horos aspokevon*
timetable *dhromologhio*
bus stop *i stasi tu leoforiu*

Go straight ahead. *pighenete efthia*
Turn left. *stripste aristera*
Turn right. *stripste dheksya*

Around Town

a bank *mia trapeza*
the ... embassy *i ... presvia*
the hotel *to ksenodho khio*
the post office *to takhidhromio*
the market *i aghora*
pharmacy *farmakio*
newsagents *efimeridhon*
the telephone centre *to tilefoniko kentro*
the tourist office *to ghrafio turistikon pliroforion*

What time does it open/close? *ti ora aniyi/klini?*

Accommodation

a hotel *ena xenothohio*
a youth hostel *enas xenonas neoitos*
a camp site *ena kamping*

I'd like a ... room. *thelo ena dhomatio ...*
single *ya ena atomo*
double *ya dhio atoma*

How much is it ...? *poso kostizi ...?*
per night *ya ena vradhi*
per person *ya ena atomo*

Time, Days & Numbers

What time is it? *ti ora ine?*
today *simera*
tomorrow *avrio*
yesterday *hthes*
in the morning *to proi*
in the afternoon *to apoyevma*

Monday *dheftera*
Tuesday *triti*
Wednesday *tetarti*
Thursday *pempti*
Friday *paraskevi*
Saturday *savato*
Sunday *kiryaki*

1	ena
2	dhio
3	tria
4	tesera
5	pende
6	eksi
7	epta
8	okhto
9	enea
10	dheka
100	ekato
1000	khilya

one million *ena ekatomirio*

Italian

Pronunciation
Vowels

a	as the second 'a' in 'camera'
e	as the 'ay' in 'day', but without the 'i' sound
i	as the 'ee' in 'see'
o	as in 'dot'
u	as the 'oo' in 'too'

Consonants

c	as 'k' before **a**, **o** and **u**; as the 'ch' in 'choose' before **e** and **i**
ch	a hard 'k' sound
g	as in 'get' before **a** and **o**
gh	as in 'get'
gli	as the 'lli' in 'million'
gn	as the 'ny' in 'canyon'
h	always silent
r	a rolled 'rrr' sound
sc	as the 'sh' in 'sheep' before **e** and **i**; a hard sound as in 'school' before **h**, **a**, **o** and **u**
z	as the 'ts' in 'lights' or as the 'ds' in 'beds'

Note that the **i** in 'ci', 'gi' and 'sci' isn't pronounced when followed by **a**, **o** or **u**, unless it's accented. Thus the name 'Giovanni' is pronounced 'joh-VAHN-nee' – the 'i' sound after the 'G' is not pronounced.

Stress Double consonants are pronounced as a longer, often more forceful sound than a single consonant.

Stress often falls on the next to last syllable, as in 'spa*ghe*tti'. When a word has an accent, the stress is on that syllable, as in *città* (city).

Basics

Hello.	*Buongiorno.* (polite)
	Ciao. (informal)
Goodbye.	*Arrivederci.* (polite)
	Ciao. (informal)
Yes.	*Sì.*
No.	*No.*
Please.	*Per favore/Per piacere.*

Signs – Italian

Ingresso/Entrata	**Entrance**
Uscita	**Exit**
Camere Libere	**Rooms Available**
Completo	**Full/No Vacancies**
Informazione	**Information**
Aperto	**Open**
Chiuso	**Closed**
Polizia/Carabinieri	**Police**
Questura	**Police Station**
Proibito/Vietato	**Prohibited**
Gabinetti/Bagni	**Toilets**
Uomini	**Men**
Donne	**Women**

Thank you.	*Grazie.*
That's fine/ You're welcome.	*Prego.*
Excuse me.	*Mi scusi.*
Sorry. (excuse me/ forgive me)	*Mi scusi/Mi perdoni.*
Do you speak English?	*Parla inglese?*
How much is it?	*Quanto costa?*
What's your name?	*Come si chiama?*
My name is ...	*Mi chiamo ...*

Getting Around

When does the ... leave/arrive?	*A che ora parte/ arriva ...?*
boat	*la barca*
ferry	*il traghetto*
bus	*l'autobus*
tram	*il tram*
train	*il treno*

bus stop	*fermata dell'autobus*
train station	*stazione*
ferry terminal	*stazione marittima*
1st class	*prima classe*
2nd class	*seconda classe*
left luggage	*deposito bagagli*
timetable	*orario*

I'd like a one-way/ return ticket.	*Vorrei un biglietto di solo andata/ di andata e ritorno.*
I'd like to hire a car/bicycle.	*Vorrei noleggiare una macchina/bicicletta.*

Where is ...?	*Dov'è ...?*
Go straight ahead.	*Si va sempre diritto.*
Turn left.	*Giri a sinistra.*
Turn right.	*Giri a destra.*
far/near	*lontano/vicino*

Around Town

a bank	*una banca*
the ... embassy	*l'ambasciata di ...*
my hotel	*il mio albergo*
post office	*la posta*
market	*il mercato*
chemist/pharmacy	*la farmacia*
newsagents	*l'edicola*
stationers	*il cartolaio*
telephone centre	*il centro telefonico*
the tourist office	*l'ufficio di turismo*
What time does it open/close?	*A che ora (si) apre/chiude?*

Emergencies – Italian

Help!	*Aiuto!*
Call a doctor!	*Chiama un dottore/ un medico!*
Call the police!	*Chiama la polizia!*
Go away!	*Vai via!*
I'm lost.	*Mi sono persoa.* (m/f)

Accommodation

hotel	*albergo*
guesthouse	*pensione*
youth hostel	*ostello per la gioventù*
camping ground	*campeggio*
Do you have any rooms available?	*Ha delle camere libere/ C'è una camera libera?*
How much is it per night/per person?	*Quanto costa per la notte/ciascuno?*
Is breakfast included?	*È compresa la colazione?*
a single room	*una camera singola*
a twin room	*una camera doppia*
a double room	*una camera matri- moniale*
for one night	*per una notte*
for two nights	*per due notti*

Time & Days

What time is it?	*Che ora è?/ Che ore sono?*
today	*oggi*
tomorrow	*domani*
yesterday	*ieri*
morning	*mattina*
afternoon	*pomeriggio*
Monday	*lunedì*
Tuesday	*martedì*
Wednesday	*mercoledì*
Thursday	*giovedì*
Friday	*venerdì*
Saturday	*sabato*
Sunday	*domenica*

Numbers

1	*uno*
2	*due*
3	*tre*
4	*quattro*
5	*cinque*
6	*sei*
7	*sette*
8	*otto*
9	*nove*
10	*dieci*
100	*cento*
1000	*mille*
one million	*un milione*

Portuguese

Portuguese pronunciation can be tricky for the uninitiated; like English, vowels and consonants have more than one possible sound depending on position and stress. Moreover, there are nasal vowels and diphthongs in Portuguese with no English equivalents.

Vowels

a	short, as the 'u' in 'cut' or long, as the 'ur' in 'hurt'
e	short, as in 'bet' or longer, as in 'heir'; silent at the end of a word and in un-stressed syllables
é	short, as in 'bet'
ê	long, as the 'a' in 'gate'
i	short, as in 'ring' or long, as the 'ee' in 'see'
o	short, as in 'pot'; long as in 'note'; as the 'oo' in 'good'
ô	long, as in 'note'
u	as the 'oo' in 'good'

Nasal Vowels Nasalisation is represented by an 'n' or an 'm' after the vowel, or by a tilde over it, eg, **ã**. The nasal 'i' exists in English as the 'ing' in 'sing'. For other vowels, try to pronounce a long 'a', 'ah', or 'e', 'eh', holding your nose, as if you have a cold.

Diphthongs Vowel combinations are relatively straightforward:

au	as the 'ow' in 'now'
ai	as the 'ie' in 'pie'
ei	as the 'ay' in 'day'
eu	as 'e' followed by 'w'
oi	similar to the 'oy' in 'boy'

Nasal Diphthongs Try the same technique as for nasal vowels. To say *não*, pronounce 'now' through your nose.

ão	nasal 'ow' (owng)
ãe	nasal 'ay' (eing)
õe	nasal 'oy' (oing)
ui	similar to the 'uing' in 'ensuing'

Consonants

c	as in 'cat' before **a**, **o** or **u**; as the 's' in 'sin' before **e** or **i**
ç	as the 'c' in 'celery'
g	as in 'go' before **a**, **o** or **u**; as the 's' in 'treasure' before **e** or **i**
gu	as in 'guest' before **e** or **i**
h	never pronounced when word-initial
nh	as the 'ni' in 'onion'
lh	as the 'lli' in 'million'
j	as the 's' in 'treasure'
m	not pronounced when word-final – it simply nasalises the previous vowel, eg, *um* (oong), *bom* (bõ)
qu	as the 'k' in 'key' before **e** or **i**; elsewhere as in 'queen'
r	when word-initial, or when doubled (**rr**) within a word it's a harsh, guttural sound similar to the 'ch' in Scottish *loch*; in the middle or at the end of a word it's a rolled 'r' sound. In some areas of Portugal it's always strongly rolled.
s	as in 'so' when word-initial and when doubled (**ss**) within a word; as the 'z' in 'zeal' when between vowels; as 'sh' when it precedes a consonant, or at the end of a word
x	as the 'sh' in 'ship', as the 'z' in 'zeal', or as the 'x' in 'taxi'
z	as the 's' in 'treasure' before a consonant or at the end of a word

Word Stress Word stress is important in Portuguese, as it can affect meaning. In words with a written accent, the stress always falls on the accented syllable.

Note that Portugese uses masculine and feminine word endings, usually '-o' and '-a' respectively – to say 'thank you', a man will therefore use *obrigado*, a woman, *obrigada*.

Basics

Hello/Goodbye.	*Bom dia/Adeus.*
Yes.	*Sim.*
No.	*Não.*
Please.	*Se faz favor.*
Thank you.	*Obrigado/a.* (m/f)
You're welcome.	*De nada.*
Excuse me.	*Com licença.*
Sorry. (forgive me)	*Desculpe.*
Do you speak English?	*Fala Inglês?*
How much is it?	*Quanto custa?*
What's your name?	*Como se chama?*
My name is ...	*Chamo-me ...*

Getting Around

What time does the ... leave/arrive?	*A que horas parte/ chega ...?*
boat	*o barco*
bus (city)	*o autocarro*
bus (intercity)	*a camioneta*
tram	*o eléctrico*
train	*o comboió*

bus stop	*paragem de autocarro*
train station	*estação ferroviária*
timetable	*horário*

I'd like a ... ticket.	*Queria um bilhete ...*
one-way	*simples/de ida*
return ticket	*de ida e volta*
1st class	*primeira classe*
2nd class	*segunda classe*

I'd like to hire ...	*Queria alugar ...*
a car	*um carro*
a bicycle	*uma bicicleta*

Where is ...?	*Onde é ...?*
Go straight ahead.	*Siga sempre a direito/ Siga sempre em frente.*
Turn left.	*Vire à esquerda.*
Turn right.	*Vire à direita.*

Signs – Portuguese

Entrada	**Entrance**
Saída	**Exit**
Quartos Livres	**Rooms Available**
Informações	**Information**
Aberto	**Open**
Fechado	**Closed**
Posto Da Polícia	**Police Station**
Proíbido	**Prohibited**
Empurre/Puxe	**Push/Pull**
Lavabos/WC	**Toilets**
Homens (h)	**Men**
Senhoras (s)	**Women**

Emergencies – Portuguese

Help!	*Socorro!*
Call a doctor!	*Chame um médico!*
Call the police!	*Chame a polícia!*
Go away!	*Deixe-me em paz!/*
	Vai-te embora! (inf)
I'm lost.	*Estou perdido/a.* (m/f)

near	*perto*
far	*longe*

Around Town

a bank	*um banco*
the ... embassy	*a embaixada de ...*
my hotel	*o meu hotel*
the post office	*os correios*
the market	*o mercado*
the chemist/	*a farmácia*
pharmacy	
the newsagents	*a papelaria*
the stationers	*a tabacaria*
the telephone centre	*a central de telefones*
the tourist office	*o (posto de) turismo*

What time does it	*A que horas abre/*
open/close?	*fecha?*

Accommodation

hotel	*hotel*
guesthouse	*pensão*
youth hostel	*pousada da juventude*
camping ground	*parque de campismo*
Do you have any	*Tem quartos livres?*
rooms available?	
How much is it per	*Quanto é por noite/*
night/per person?	*por pessoa?*
Is breakfast	*O pequeno almoço*
included?	*está incluído?*

a single room	*um quarto individual*
a twin room	*um quarto duplo*
a double bed room	*um quarto de casal*
for one/two night/s	*para uma/duas noite/s*

Time, Days & Numbers

What time is it?	*Que horas são?*
today	*hoje*
tomorrow	*amanhã*
yesterday	*ontem*
morning	*manhã*
afternoon	*tarde*

Monday	*segunda-feira*
Tuesday	*terça-feira*
Wednesday	*quarta-feira*
Thursday	*quinta-feira*
Friday	*sexta-feira*
Saturday	*sábado*
Sunday	*domingo*

1	*um/uma*
2	*dois/duas*
3	*três*
4	*quatro*
5	*cinco*
6	*seis*
7	*sete*
8	*oito*
9	*nove*
10	*dez*
11	*onze*
100	*cem*
1000	*mil*

one million	*um milhão*

Spanish

Pronunciation

Vowels Unlike English, each of the vowels in Spanish has a uniform pronunciation which doesn't vary. For example, the Spanish 'a' has one pronunciation rather than the numerous pronunciations we find in English, such as 'cat', 'cake', 'cart', 'care', 'call'. An acute accent (as in *días*) generally indicates a stressed syllable and doesn't change the sound of the vowel. Vowels are pronounced clearly even if they are in unstressed positions or at the end of a word.

a	as the 'u' in 'nut', or a shorter sound than the 'a' in 'art'
e	as in 'met'
i	somewhere between the 'i' in 'marine' and the 'i' in 'flip'
o	similar to the 'o' in 'hot'
u	as the 'oo' in 'hoof'

Consonants Some Spanish consonants are pronounced as per their English counterparts. The pronunciation of others is dependent on following vowels and also on which part of

Spain you happen to be in. The Spanish alphabet also contains three consonants that aren't found in the English alphabet: **ch**, **ll** and **ñ**.

Signs – Spanish	
Entrada	Entrance
Salida	Exit
Habtaciones Libres	Rooms Available
Completo	Full/No Vacancies
Información	Information
Abierto	Open
Cerrado	Closed
Comisaría	Police Station
Prohibido	Prohibited
Servicios/Aseos	Toilets
Hombres	Men
Mujeres	Women

b   as in 'but' when word-initial or preceded by a nasal; elsewhere it's almost a cross between English 'b' and 'v'

c   a hard 'c' as in 'cat' when followed by **a**, **o**, **u** or a consonant; as the 'th' in 'thin' before **e** and **i**

ch   as in 'church'

d   as in 'do' when word-initial; elsewhere as the 'th' in 'then'

g   as in 'get' when word-initial and before **a**, **o** and **u**; elsewhere much softer. Before **e** or **i** it's a harsh, breathy sound, similar to the 'h' in 'hit'

h   silent

j   a harsh, guttural sound similar to the 'ch' in Scottish *loch*

ll   as the 'lli' in 'million'; some pronounce it rather like the 'y' in 'yellow'

ñ   a nasal sound, as the 'ni' in 'onion'

q   as the 'k' in 'kick'; **q** is always followed by a silent **u** and is combined only with the vowels **e** (as in *que*) and **i** (as in *qui*)

r   a rolled 'r' sound; longer and stronger when initial or doubled

s   as in 'see'

v   the same sound as **b**

x   as the 'ks' sound in 'taxi' when between vowels; as the 's' in 'see' when it precedes a consonant

z   as the 'th' in 'thin'

Semiconsonant Spanish also has the semiconsonant **y**. When at the end of a word or when standing alone as a conjunction it's pronounced like the Spanish **i**. As a consonant, it's somewhere between the 'y' in 'yonder' and the 'g' in 'beige', depending on the region.

Basics

Hello/Goodbye.	*¡Hola!/¡Adiós!*
Yes.	*Sí.*
No.	*No.*
Please.	*Por favor.*
Thank you.	*Gracias.*
You're welcome.	*De nada.*
I'm sorry. (forgive me)	*Lo siento/Discúlpeme.*

Excuse me.	*Perdón/Perdoneme.*
Do you speak English?	*¿Habla inglés?*
How much is it?	*¿Cuánto cuesta?/ ¿Cuánto vale?*
What's your name?	*¿Cómo se llama?*
My name is ...	*Me llamo ...*

Getting Around

What time does the next ... leave/arrive?	*¿A qué hora sale/ llega el próximo ...?*
boat	*barco*
bus (city)	*autobús, bus*
bus (intercity)	*autocar*
train	*tranvía*

I'd like a ... ticket.	*Quisiera un billete ...*
one-way	*sencillo/de sólo ida*
return	*de ida y vuelta*
1st class	*primera clase*
2nd class	*segunda clase*

left luggage	*consigna*
timetable	*horario*
bus stop	*parada de autobus*
train station	*estación de ferrocarril*

I'd like to hire ...	*Quisiera alquilar ...*
a car	*un coche*
a bicycle	*una bicicleta*

Where is ...?	*¿Dónde está ...?*
Go straight ahead.	*Siga/Vaya todo derecho.*
Turn left.	*Gire a la izquierda.*
Turn right.	*Gire a la derecha/recto.*
near/far	*cerca/lejos*

Around Town

a bank	un banco
the ... embassy	la embajada ...
my hotel	mi hotel
the post office	los correos
the market	el mercado
chemist/pharmacy	la farmacia
newsagents/ stationers	papelería
the telephone centre	el locutorio
the tourist office	la oficina de turismo

What time does it open/close?	¿A qué hora abren/ cierran?

Accommodation

hotel	hotel
guesthouse	pensión/casa de huéspedes
youth hostel	albergue juvenil
camping ground	camping

Do you have any rooms available?	¿Tiene habitaciones libres?

a single room	una habitación individual
a double room	una habitación doble
a room with a double bed	una habitación con cama de matrimonio
for one night	para una noche
for two nights	para dos noches

How much is it per night/per person?	¿Cuánto cuesta por noche/por persona?
Is breakfast included?	¿Incluye el desayuno?

Time, Days & Numbers

What time is it?	¿Qué hora es?
today	hoy
tomorrow	mañana

yesterday	ayer
morning	mañana
afternoon	tarde

Monday	lunes
Tuesday	martes
Wednesday	miércoles
Thursday	jueves
Friday	viernes
Saturday	sábado
Sunday	domingo

1	uno, una
2	dos
3	tres
4	cuatro
5	cinco
6	seis
7	siete
8	ocho
9	nueve
10	diez
11	once
12	doce
13	trece
14	catorce
15	quince
16	dieciéis
100	cien/ciento
1000	mil

one million	un millón

Acknowledgements

THANKS FROM THE AUTHORS

Janet Austin Thanks to the extremely helpful staff at the various tourist information offices I visited, and to Giancarlo and Christina in Liguria. Special thanks go to Alice in Rome, Alex in La Spezia, Maria in Melbourne, Riddle and George, Beck and Moby, and last but not least to Dave who came along for the slog.

Carolyn Bain Firstly, thanks to those at LP who got me involved in this project, to David Willett, co-author of this Greece chapter, Ian Madanis for the (attempted) Greek lessons, and Dierdre Roberts for invaluable insights into all things Cretan.

A heartfelt *efharisto* to the many locals who helped me out in Greece. Special mention goes to Evangelos for playing impromptu tour guide in Mykonos; Francesco for demonstrating the calmer side of Ios; Petros and his family in Fira for letting me share in an authentic Greek Easter; Alexis and his family in Kos for treating me as one of their own; and Alex of Chios for helping me discover the best grilled octopus in the country. Cheers also to the expats and travellers I met, including Theo in Mykonos, Sara and the crew from Kafe Besara in Rhodes, and especially Rosa Fernandez and Lars Hedegaard.

Boundless gratitude to my sister Jules and her partner John for allowing me free run of their home in London, to my parents for their support, and to my friends for following my adventures with just the right amount of interest, encouragement and envy!

Neal Bedford Thanks firstly goes to Ryan Ver Berkmoes and Steve Fallon for setting me off on the right track and Damien Simonis and John Noble for their invaluable advice on Spain. A special thanks goes to the whole London LP office for the support I received, in particular for their extra special effort (which you had no choice in giving!) – Paul Bloomfield, Katrina Browning, Imogen Franks, Tom Hall, Howard Ralley, Tim Ryder, Sam Trafford, Angie Watts and Dave Wenk. And also to the ex LPers – Tom Bevan, Nicky Robinson and Anna Sutton. My gratitude and sympathy goes out to those who had

to put up with me on the road, the Bevans, John Richards, Robert Box, Claire Delamey, Nik Pickard and Rachel Parker. And a big bussi to Christina Tlustos for all the support and guidance.

Lou Callan Special thanks to Tony Cleaver, my husband and travel companion; to Sarah Biggs and Nigel Biggs in the UK, always so generous and helpful; and to Danny Foster in the UK, thanks for the beers and the info.

Fionn Davenport For the Italian section, my deepest thanks to Sandra, Giorgia and Luigi Sabarini for their hospitality and help. I couldn't have done it without you. Thanks also to the various tourist offices, particularly Rome, Naples and Cagliari, who went beyond the call of duty to facilitate my research. For the Britain section, I would like to express my gratitude to all in Cambridge for pointing me in the right direction.

Paul Dawson Thanks to Peter Dawson for his support and company on the road, Penelope Cottrill for teaching me the fine art of the Dublin pub crawl, and Jane Thompson for guidance and gentle rib-tickling and chin-lifting throughout the ordeal. There's also a thanks for Craig MacKenzie who made me realise that editors, generally, are not to be feared.

Jeremy Gray The utterly lovely, charitable staff in the French tourist offices I visited deserve my boundless gratitude. Isabelle at Le Conquet (Brittany) deserves a very special mention – I never would have found those secret treasures without her. Thanks, too, to Jen Wabisabi for getting lost with me at all those confusing roundabouts, and to Jacques and Gi Veit for being the consummate hosts (I'll never forget the truffle-scented eggs). Fellow authors Steve Fallon, Paul Hellander, Daniel Robinson, Miles Roddis and Nicola Williams all earn a *palme d'or* for being sooo professional and for infusing the France chapter with so much character.

Anthony Haywood I'd like to thank the helpful and friendly tourist office staff who kindly assisted in researching this new edition by providing valuable information and knowledge of their towns and regions. Special thanks go to Frau Klein in Erfurt and Frau Vorhagen in Aachen who provided particularly valuable advice, as did staff in Cologne, Hamburg, Weimar, Magdeburg and Naumburg. Last but no least, heartfelt thanks again to friends and family for their support and encouragement.

Paul Hellander Certain people and organisations who contributed to my work in one way or another deserve a mention. Thanks to the very co-operative *Offices de Tourisme* that plied me with excellent data and to SNCM for transport to and from Corsica. Thanks to my wife Stella for her assistance for her excellent photography. Special mention also to the following individuals: Louiza Maragozidis; Nicola Williams and Matthias Lüftkens; Stéphanie 4; Michel, Stella & Véronique le Petit; Iain & Liz Purce; Jean-Marie & Irène Casta and Deborah Palmer. To sons Byron and Marcus in Greece – another title bites the dust for you.

Mark Honan As usual, many thanks are due to staff in the press/media section of Switzerland Tourism and the Austrian National Tourist Office. Much credit to those who answered my diverse inquiries (most notably Charles Page in Rail Europe, Kathrin Rohrbach in the Bern tourist office and my fellow authors on these Europe guidebooks); much discredit to those who didn't (the AA – I'm still waiting). Thanks also to Sue in Geneva and Irmgard in Vienna.

Leanne Logan & Geert Cole Our deepest *bedankt* goes to Roos and Bert Cole for keeping the cellar well stocked...and for much, much more. To Katrin and Erik Cole, and Peter Van Roey – we appreciate your tips and advice. To Jan and Trudi Brandt, thanks for your hospitality. To Lyndall Lee and Sandy Thompson, without you both the grass and the girls would have been out of control!

Thanks also to the various tourism offices in the Benelux for their help, in particular to Toerisme Vlaanderen, the OPT (Office de Promotion du Tourisme Wallonie-Bruxelles), the TIB (Brussels), Vera Verschooren (Antwerp), Anne de Meerleer (Bruges), Eta Woutenberg (Nederlands Bureau voor Toerisme), Els Wamsteeker (Amsterdam), Marianne van der Zalm (The Hague), Helen Senior (Delft), Patricia van Caubergh (Rotterdam),

Jelle Ummels (Maastricht), Jean-Claude Conter (Luxembourg National Tourist Office) and Martine Voss (Luxembourg City Tourist Office).

Oda O'Carol Thanks to all the helpful staff at Cardiff TIC, the witty Nova at Porthmadog TIC, Eoin and Etain for their scintillating company on the road (and fixing my seat), Jim & Curley (happy surfing!), Gareth & Eva Evans for the Indian and gossip, Melvyn Williams and Ynyr Williams for all their useful information, Margaret Bamford in Dolgellau and Kathryn Maguire (who almost made it).

Nick Ray Many thanks to many people, most of all my loving girlfriend Kulikar for enriching my life, to my wonderful parents for their enduring support and to my fantastic friends who must be the finest on this planet. Thanks also to the many good folk of England who helped me out in many ways and proved that, but for a few idiots, the English are generally a pretty decent bunch.

Daniel Robinson My work in Strasbourg would not have been anywhere near as much fun were it not for my parents, Bernie and Yetta Robinson, who came to visit; and Corrine and Rachel of Radio Judaica, who helped me track down Salim Halali's unique Arabic version of the Yiddish classic *Œma Yiddische Mama'*. In Dijon, warmth and hominess were contributed by Professor Bob Wiener, Albert and Myrna Huberfel, and the Tenenbaum family: Françoise, Denis, Charles, Annabelle and Nathalie. Paris' relentness urbanness was softened by the staff of Lonely Planet's Paris bureau, including Arnot, Benjamin, Caroline, Didier, Rob and Zahia; Rabbis Pauline Bebe and Tom Cohen; Diane Holt and Michael Feldman, who are always up for a weekend away from Naples; David Saliamonis, whom life's journey has taken all the way from Glen Ellyn, Illinois to Paris; my almost-cousin Miel de Botton; Eliane Bebe; Antoine Bebe; and Kamal, Karim, Madame Sadou and the inimitable staff of the Hôtel Rivoli.

Miles Roddis To Ingrid for sharing it all, both the excitement and the tedium.

Andrea Schulte-Peevers People throughout my area of coverage were generous in answering questions and patient in putting up with my rusty Spanish. Those who stand out for going beyond the call of duty are: Jasone Aretxabaleta of the Dirección General de Turismo del País Vasco; Visi Urtiaga in Bilbao; Diana Draper in San Sebastián; Jason Kykendall and Mar Martín Alonso in Salamanca; Belén Cubo Allas in Segovia; Mónica Garcia Hernando in Valladolid; and Alberto Abad Pérez, Margarita and her parents in Soria.

The biggest round of applause, though, belongs to my husband David Peevers for keeping me company – and sane – on the road. Thanks for your good humor and patience in checking out Castilia's countless churches, castles and shower curtains.

Tom Smallman I'm deeply grateful to Sue Graefe for her patience and tolerant support. My thanks also to Hugh MacKenzie Gore for his encyclopaedic knowledge and his family's hospitality; to Alistair, Elspeth and family in Kelso; to Margaret and George in Dumfries; to all the people in the travel industry who patiently answered my questions; and to those readers who wrote in with comments on the previous edition.

Rebecca Turner *Vielen Dank* to all the tourist offices in Berlin, Brandenburg, Saxony, Bavaria and Baden-Württemberg, especially those in Baden-Baden, Berchtesgaden, Freiburg and Leipzig. The help of Natascha Kompatzki and Dr Heinz Buri of Berlin Tourismus Marketing was invaluable, as were the recommendations and comments of those readers who wrote in. Thanks also to Andrew McCathie in Berlin for his insights and tips. LP authors Anthony Haywood, Andrea Schulte-Peevers and Ryan ver Berkmoes were invaluable sources of help and guidance. Big thanks to my family for their endless support and most of all to Andrew Burrell for making me get my act together that dismal day in Berlin and for everything else.

Julia Wilkinson & John King Special thanks go to the following dedicated tourist officers: Miguel Gonzaga (Turismo de Lisboa), Anabela Pereira (Bragança), Maria do Rosário Graça (Vila Real) and Carla Basílio (Covilhã), along with long-suffering turismo staff at Beja, Braga, Portalegre and Sintra. Thanks also to Clara and Dionisio Vitorino, Michael Collins (Portuguese Arts Trust), Miranda Jessop (KTA International), Geraldine Ahearn (TAP Air Portugal), Anabela Esteves (ADERE), John Fisher (Connex South Eastern) and Peter Mills (Rail Europe). John Noble provided frequent, detailed help with Spain information.

David Willett My thanks go first to my partner, Rowan, and our son, Tom, for holding the fort at home during another extended stay away. Athens feels almost like home these days. I look forward to catching up with my friends (and guides) Yiannis and Katerina, Maria, Anna, Jarek and Tolis.

Nicola Williams *Un grand merci* in no particular order to Catherine Moulé at Saumur's École Nationale d'Équitation, Laurent de Froberville at Château de Cheverny, Christa Lüfkens, Monsieur and Madame Gaultier, and the myriad friends and acquaintances in Lyon for the feast of restaurant recommendations over the years. Oh, and to husband Matthias for being that perfect dining partner.

Ryan Ver Berkmoes Big thanks to Steve Fallon for laying some good ground-work for London and also to the many plums and peaches in the LP London office. Thanks as well to all the folks I pestered for info in Yorkshire. And deep thanks to my wife Sara who's responsible for me living in this lovely fog-drenched place in the first place, it reminds me of home.

THANKS

Many thanks to the travellers who used the last edition and wrote to us with helpful hints, useful advice and interesting anecdotes:

A Blums, Aaron & Natalie McKeown, Ad Tummers, Adam Portelli, Adam Weintraub, Alicia Wanek, Alister Miller, Allison Azzopardi, Amy Duckworth, Amy Wessels, Andris Blums, Anita Coia, Ann Price Chalem, Ann Sy, Anthony Andrews, Arnis Siksna, Ashley Cadogan-Cowper, Astrid Hofmann, Audrey Bosboom, August Rusli Lie, Bas Jan Peters, Belinda Watson, Bernadette Wood, Beth Little, Bettina Buesselmann, Bev & Michael Guinto, Bill & Annette Chessum, Brad Jessup, Brandy Tuzon, Brett Niver, Brian Lema, Brian Park, Brian Payne, Brooke McIntosh, Bruno Geoffrion, Buck & Nancy Pruetz, C Harris, Cameron Fincher, Caroline Althouse, Caroline Cloutier, Casper Kemp, Catherine Brew, Charles Kelland, Chris & Taria Russo, Chris Cariffe, Chris Colaidis, Chris Kramar, Chris Robinson, Chris Sorflaten, Chris Young, Christena Geenty, Christy Liu, Claire Imrie, Clare Person, Clare Sprosen, Claudia Williams, Cornelia Nauck, Cynthia Caughey, Daniel Meijer, Daryl Sproule, David Rogers, David Thornton, Denise Fletcher, Devin van Tongeren, Donna Barber, Dr Janak Desai, Elisabeth Tritscher, Emily MacWilliams, Eric Brouwer, Fiona Frayne, Frank Higginson, Frank Moschella, Gary Martin, Georgina Alaban, Gernot

Hedrich, Gerry Smith, Giulia Brandimarti, Graham Ferrreira, Grant Hornsby, Greg O'Beirne, Gunhild Abigt, Hendrik McDermott, Henry Skupek, Hollis Gardner, Ian Moseley, Jaci Thomas, Jack Shaw, James Manders, Jan Scott, Jeannot Van Melle Kensinger, Jeff Major, Jim Murcott, Joanne Smethurst, John H Smith, Jon Reinberg, Joyce Chia, Julie Parkes, Julieta & Vince Raschilla, Kang Rong, Karen Chung, Katy Appleton, Kerrie Warburton, Kevin Dowkes, Kevin Slater, Kevin van Damme, Kim Wilson, Kirsty Keter, Laura MacDonald, Lauren Welgus, Leigh Cantero, Leonie & Jim Murcott, Lisa Coulton, Lisa Zumbo, Lori Olsen, Lou Palumbo, Louise & Bryan Kelly, Lucy Sharp, Lynette Leo, M C J Fletcher, Malcolm O'Sullivan, Margaret Marszal, Maria & Lou Palumbo, Marion Phillips, Marius Jones, Mark & Marnie Hewitt, Mark Horner, Mark Walsh, Marleen Nederlof, Melanie Koppes, Melissa A'Vard, Melissa Casley, Merv Baker, Michael De La Vega, Michael Guinto, Michael J Pastroff, Michelle Chan, Mo Strucker, N P Padalino, Natalie McKeown, Neil Tempest, Nichola Coster, Noelle Zeilemaker, Pat & Margaret Nankivell, Patrick Ch Awart, Patrick Plummer, Paul Fraser, Paul Gaylard, Paul Harmsen, Paul Munnerley, Pauliina Hattunen, Pete & Misuk Nuland, Phil Torcasio, Rebecca Morarhy, Revathi Padmakumar, Richard Hilger, Richard Skilton, Rob Fowler, Rob Glas, Robert Harsanyi, Ros Holcombe, Ruben Escalona, Samantha Ipsa, Sander Meijer, Sandro Hansen, Sarah Goldstone, Sarah Joyce, Sarah Neumann, Sharon Sadler, Shaun Feruglio, Sherin Omran, Simone Hanks, Sofjan Sukman, Stephanie Johnson, Stephanie Leah Gill, Stephen Wahl, Sue Donovan, Sue Taylor, Suman Mohanka, Sunitha Kadrivel, Tang Huihong, Tara Ondra, Taria Russo, Ted Gibbens, Thng Hui Hong, Tim Topham, Timothy Watson, Tina Zoiti, Tom Sawyer, Tony Weston, Trevor Embury, Vanessa Hammond, Veronica W Rogers

LONELY PLANET

ON THE ROAD

Travel Guides explore cities, regions and countries, and supply information on transport, restaurants and accommodation, covering all budgets. They come with reliable, easy-to-use maps, practical advice, cultural and historical facts and a rundown on attractions both on and off the beaten track. There are over 200 titles in this classic series, covering nearly every country in the world.

 Lonely Planet Upgrades extend the shelf life of existing travel guides by detailing any changes that may affect travel in a region since a book has been published. Upgrades can be downloaded for free from **www.lonelyplanet.com/upgrades**

For travellers with more time than money, **Shoestring** guides offer dependable, first-hand information with hundreds of detailed maps, plus insider tips for stretching money as far as possible. Covering entire continents in most cases, the six-volume shoestring guides are known around the world as 'backpackers bibles'.

For the discerning short-term visitor, **Condensed** guides highlight the best a destination has to offer in a full-colour, pocket-sized format designed for quick access. They include everything from top sights and walking tours to opinionated reviews of where to eat, stay, shop and have fun.

CitySync lets travellers use their Palm™ or Visor™ hand-held computers to guide them through a city with handy tips on transport, history, cultural life, major sights, and shopping and entertainment options. It can also quickly search and sort hundreds of reviews of hotels, restaurants and attractions, and pinpoint their location on scrollable street maps. CitySync can be downloaded from **www.citysync.com**

MAPS & ATLASES

Lonely Planet's **City Maps** feature downtown and metropolitan maps, as well as transit routes and walking tours. The maps come complete with an index of streets, a listing of sights and a plastic coat for extra durability.

Road Atlases are an essential navigation tool for serious travellers. Cross-referenced with the guidebooks, they also feature distance and climate charts and a complete site index.

LONELY PLANET

ESSENTIALS

Read This First books help new travellers to hit the road with confidence. These invaluable predeparture guides give step-by-step advice on preparing for a trip, budgeting, arranging a visa, planning an itinerary and staying safe while still getting off the beaten track.

Healthy Travel pocket guides offer a regional rundown on disease hot spots and practical advice on predeparture health measures, staying well on the road and what to do in emergencies. The guides come with a user-friendly design and helpful diagrams and tables.

Lonely Planet's **Phrasebooks** cover the essential words and phrases travellers need when they're strangers in a strange land. They come in a pocket-sized format with colour tabs for quick reference, extensive vocabulary lists, easy-to-follow pronunciation keys and two-way dictionaries.

Miffed by blurry photos of the Taj Mahal? Tired of the classic 'top of the head cut off' shot? **Travel Photography: A Guide to Taking Better Pictures** will help you turn ordinary holiday snaps into striking images and give you the know-how to capture every scene, from frenetic festivals to peaceful beach sunrises.

Lonely Planet's **Travel Journal** is a lightweight but sturdy travel diary for jotting down all those on-the-road observations and significant travel moments. It comes with a handy time-zone wheel, world maps and useful travel information.

Lonely Planet's eKno is an all-in-one communication service developed especially for travellers. It offers low-cost international calls and free email and voicemail so that you can keep in touch while on the road. Check it out on **www.ekno.lonelyplanet.com**

FOOD & RESTAURANT GUIDES

Lonely Planet's **Out to Eat** guides recommend the brightest and best places to eat and drink in top international cities. These gourmet companions are arranged by neighbourhood, packed with dependable maps, garnished with scene-setting photos and served with quirky features.

For people who live to eat, drink and travel, **World Food** guides explore the culinary culture of each country. Entertaining and adventurous, each guide is packed with detail on staples and specialities, regional cuisine and local markets, as well as sumptuous recipes, comprehensive culinary dictionaries and lavish photos good enough to eat.

OUTDOOR GUIDES

For those who believe the best way to see the world is on foot, Lonely Planet's **Walking Guides** detail everything from family strolls to difficult treks, with 'when to go and how to do it' advice supplemented by reliable maps and essential travel information.

Cycling Guides map a destination's best bike tours, long and short, in day-by-day detail. They contain all the information a cyclist needs, including advice on bike maintenance, places to eat and stay, innovative maps with detailed cues to the rides, and elevation charts.

The **Watching Wildlife** series is perfect for travellers who want authoritative information but don't want to tote a heavy field guide. Packed with advice on where, when and how to view a region's wildlife, each title features photos of over 300 species and contains engaging comments on the local flora and fauna.

With underwater colour photos throughout, **Pisces Books** explore the world's best diving and snorkelling areas. Each book contains listings of diving services and dive resorts, detailed information on depth, visibility and difficulty of dives, and a roundup of the marine life you're likely to see through your mask.

LONELY PLANET

OFF THE ROAD

Journeys, the travel literature series written by renowned travel authors, capture the spirit of a place or illuminate a culture with a journalist's attention to detail and a novelist's flair for words. These are tales to soak up while you're actually on the road or dip into as an at-home armchair indulgence.

The new range of lavishly illustrated **Pictorial** books is just the ticket for both travellers and dreamers. Off-beat tales and vivid photographs bring the adventure of travel to your doorstep long before the journey begins and long after it is over.

Lonely Planet **Videos** encourage the same independent, tough-minded approach as the guidebooks. Currently airing throughout the world, this award-winning series features innovative footage and an original soundtrack.

Yes, we know, work is tough, so do a little bit of deskside dreaming with the spiral-bound Lonely Planet **Diary**, the tearaway page-a-day **Day-to-Day Calendar** or a Lonely Planet **Wall Calendar**, filled with great photos from around the world.

TRAVELLERS NETWORK

Lonely Planet Online. Lonely Planet's award-winning Web site has insider information on hundreds of destinations, from Amsterdam to Zimbabwe, complete with interactive maps and relevant links. The site also offers the latest travel news, recent reports from travellers on the road, guidebook upgrades, a travel links site, an online book-buying option and a lively traveller's bulletin board. It can be viewed at **www.lonelyplanet.com** or AOL keyword: lp.

Planet Talk is a quarterly print newsletter, full of gossip, advice, anecdotes and author articles. It provides an antidote to the being-at-home blues and lets you plan and dream for the next trip. Contact the nearest Lonely Planet office for your free copy.

Comet, the free Lonely Planet newsletter, comes via email once a month. It's loaded with travel news, advice, dispatches from authors, travel competitions and letters from readers. To subscribe, click on the Comet subscription link on the front page of the Web site.

LONELY PLANET

Guides by Region

Lonely Planet is known worldwide for publishing practical, reliable and no-nonsense travel information in our guides and on our Web site. The Lonely Planet list covers just about every accessible part of the world. Currently there are 16 series: Travel guides, Shoestring guides, Condensed guides, Phrasebooks, Read This First, Healthy Travel, Walking guides, Cycling guides, Watching Wildlife guides, Pisces Diving & Snorkeling guides, City Maps, Road Atlases, Out to Eat, World Food, Journeys travel literature and Pictorials.

AFRICA Africa on a shoestring • Cairo • Cape Town • Cape Town City Map • East Africa • Egypt • Egyptian Arabic phrasebook • Ethiopia, Eritrea & Djibouti • Ethiopian (Amharic) phrasebook • The Gambia & Senegal • Healthy Travel Africa • Kenya • Malawi • Morocco • Moroccan Arabic phrasebook • Mozambique • Read This First: Africa • South Africa, Lesotho & Swaziland • Southern Africa • Southern Africa Road Atlas • Swahili phrasebook • Tanzania, Zanzibar & Pemba • Trekking in East Africa • Tunisia • Watching Wildlife East Africa • Watching Wildlife Southern Africa • West Africa • World Food Morocco • Zimbabwe, Botswana & Namibia
Travel Literature: Mali Blues: Traveling to an African Beat • The Rainbird: A Central African Journey • Songs to an African Sunset: A Zimbabwean Story

AUSTRALIA & THE PACIFIC Auckland • Australia • Australian phrasebook • Australia Road Atlas • Bush-walking in Australia •Cycling New Zealand • Fiji • Fijian phrasebook • Healthy Travel Australia, NZ and the Pacific • Islands of Australia's Great Barrier Reef • Melbourne • Melbourne City Map • Micronesia • New Cale-donia • New South Wales & the ACT • New Zealand • Northern Territory • Outback Australia • Out to Eat – Melbourne • Out to Eat – Sydney • Papua New Guinea • Pidgin phrasebook • Queensland • Rarotonga & the Cook Islands • Samoa • Solomon Islands • South Australia • South Pacific • South Pacific phrasebook • Sydney • Sydney City Map • Sydney Condensed • Tahiti & French Polynesia • Tasmania • Tonga • Tramping in New Zealand • Vanuatu • Victoria • Watching Wildlife Australia • Western Australia
Travel Literature: Islands in the Clouds: Travels in the Highlands of New Guinea • Kiwi Tracks: A New Zealand Journey • Sean & David's Long Drive

CENTRAL AMERICA & THE CARIBBEAN Bahamas, Turks & Caicos • Baja California • Bermuda • Central America on a shoestring • Costa Rica • Costa Rica Spanish phrasebook • Cuba • Dominican Republic & Haiti • Eastern Caribbean • Guatemala • Guatemala, Belize & Yucatán: La Ruta Maya • Healthy Travel Central & South America • Jamaica • Mexico • Mexico City • Panama • Puerto Rico • Read This First: Central & South America • World Food Mexico • Yucatán
Travel Literature: Green Dreams: Travels in Central America

EUROPE Amsterdam • Amsterdam City Map • Amsterdam Condensed • Andalucía • Austria • Baltic States phrasebook • Barcelona • Barcelona City Map • Berlin • Berlin City Map • Britain • British phrasebook • Brus-sels, Bruges & Antwerp • Budapest • Budapest City Map • Canary Islands • Central Europe • Central Europe phrasebook • Corfu & the Ionians • Corsica • Crete • Crete Condensed • Croatia • Cycling Britain • Cycling France • Cyprus • Czech & Slovak Republics • Denmark • Dublin • Dublin City Map • Eastern Europe • Eastern Europe phrasebook • Edinburgh • Estonia, Latvia & Lithuania • Europe on a shoestring • Finland • Florence • France • Frankfurt Condensed • French phrasebook • Georgia, Armenia & Azerbaijan • Germany • German phrasebook • Greece • Greek Islands • Greek phrasebook • Hungary • Iceland, Greenland & the Faroe Islands • Ireland • Istanbul • Italian phrasebook • Italy • Krakow • Lisbon • The Loire • London • London City Map • London Condensed • Madrid • Malta • Mediterranean Europe • Mediterranean Europe phrasebook • Moscow • Munich • Norway • Out to Eat – London • Paris • Paris City Map • Paris Condensed • Poland • Portugal • Portuguese phrasebook • Prague • Prague City Map • Provence & the Côte d'Azur • Read This First: Europe • Romania & Moldova • Rome • Russia, Ukraine & Belarus • Russian phrasebook • Scandinavian & Baltic Europe • Scandinavian Europe phrasebook • Scotland • Sicily • Slovenia • South-West France • Spain • Spanish phrase-book • St Petersburg • St Petersburg City Map • Sweden • Switzerland • Trekking in Spain • Tuscany • Ukrainian phrasebook • Venice • Vienna • Walking in Britain • Walking in France • Walking in Ireland • Walking in Italy • Walking in Spain • Walking in Switzerland • Western Europe • Western Europe phrasebook • World Food France • World Food Ireland • World Food Italy • World Food Spain
Travel Literature: Love and War in the Apennines • The Olive Grove: Travels in Greece • On the Shores of the Mediterranean • Round Ireland in Low Gear • A Small Place in Italy

INDIAN SUBCONTINENT Bangladesh • Bengali phrasebook • Bhutan • Delhi • Goa • Healthy Travel Asia & India • Hindi & Urdu phrasebook • India • Indian Himalaya • Karakoram Highway • Kerala • Mumbai

LONELY PLANET

Mail Order

Lonely Planet products are distributed worldwide. They are also available by mail order from Lonely Planet, so if you have difficulty finding a title please write to us. North and South American residents should write to 150 Linden St, Oakland, CA 94607, USA; European and African residents should write to 10a Spring Place, London NW5 3BH, UK; and residents of other countries to Locked Bag 1, Footscray, Victoria 3011, Australia.

(Bombay) • Nepal • Nepali phrasebook • Pakistan • Rajasthan • Read This First: Asia & India • South India • Sri Lanka • Sri Lanka phrasebook • Tibet • Tibetan phrasebook • Trekking in the Indian Himalaya • Trekking in the Karakoram & Hindukush • Trekking in the Nepal Himalaya
Travel Literature: The Age of Kali: Indian Travels and Encounters • Hello Goodnight: A Life of Goa • In Rajasthan • A Season in Heaven: True Tales from the Road to Kathmandu • Shopping for Buddhas • A Short Walk in the Hindu Kush • Slowly Down the Ganges

ISLANDS OF THE INDIAN OCEAN Madagascar & Comoros • Maldives • Mauritius, Réunion & Seychelles

MIDDLE EAST & CENTRAL ASIA Bahrain, Kuwait & Qatar • Central Asia • Central Asia phrasebook • Dubai • Hebrew phrasebook • Iran • Israel & the Palestinian Territories • Istanbul • Istanbul City Map • Istanbul to Cairo on a shoestring • Jerusalem • Jerusalem City Map • Jordan • Lebanon • Middle East • Oman & the United Arab Emirates • Syria • Turkey • Turkish phrasebook • World Food Turkey • Yemen
Travel Literature: Black on Black: Iran Revisited • The Gates of Damascus • Kingdom of the Film Stars: Journey into Jordan

NORTH AMERICA Alaska • Boston • Boston City Map • California & Nevada • California Condensed • Canada • Chicago • Chicago City Map • Deep South • Florida • Hawaii • Hiking in Alaska • Hiking in the USA • Honolulu • Las Vegas • Los Angeles • Miami • Miami City Map • New England • New Orleans • New York City • New York City City Map • New York City Condensed • New York, New Jersey & Pennsylvania • Oahu • Out to Eat – San Francisco • Pacific Northwest • Puerto Rico • Rocky Mountains • San Francisco • San Francisco City Map • Seattle • Southwest • Texas • USA • USA phrasebook • Vancouver • Virginia & the Capital Region • Washington, DC City Map • World Food Deep South, USA
Travel Literature: Caught Inside: A Surfer's Year on the California Coast • Drive Thru America

NORTH-EAST ASIA Beijing • Cantonese phrasebook • China • Hiking in Japan • Hong Kong • Hong Kong City Map • Hong Kong Condensed • Hong Kong, Macau & Guangzhou • Japan • Japanese phrasebook • Korea • Korean phrasebook • Kyoto • Mandarin phrasebook • Mongolia • Mongolian phrasebook • Seoul • South-West China • Taiwan • Tokyo
Travel Literature: In Xanadu: A Quest • Lost Japan

SOUTH AMERICA Argentina, Uruguay & Paraguay • Bolivia • Brazil • Brazilian phrasebook • Buenos Aires • Chile & Easter Island • Colombia • Ecuador & the Galapagos Islands • Healthy Travel Central & South America • Latin American Spanish phrasebook • Peru • Quechua phrasebook • Read This First: Central & South America • Rio de Janeiro • Rio de Janeiro City Map • Santiago • South America on a shoestring • Trekking In the Patagonian Andes • Venezuela
Travel Literature: Full Circle: A South American Journey

SOUTH-EAST ASIA Bali & Lombok • Bangkok • Bangkok City Map • Burmese phrasebook • Cambodia • Hanoi • Healthy Travel Asia & India • Hill Tribes phrasebook • Ho Chi Minh City • Indonesia • Indonesian phrasebook • Indonesia's Eastern Islands • Jakarta • Java • Lao phrasebook • Laos • Malay phrasebook • Malaysia, Singapore & Brunei • Myanmar (Burma) • Philippines • Pilipino (Tagalog) phrasebook • Read This First: Asia & India • Singapore • Singapore City Map • South-East Asia on a shoestring • South-East Asia phrasebook • Thailand • Thailand's Islands & Beaches • Thailand, Vietnam, Laos & Cambodia Road Atlas • Thai phrasebook • Vietnam • Vietnamese phrasebook • World Food Thailand • World Food Vietnam

ALSO AVAILABLE: Antarctica • The Arctic • The Blue Man: Tales of Travel, Love and Coffee • Brief Encounters: Stories of Love, Sex & Travel • Chasing Rickshaws • The Last Grain Race • Lonely Planet Unpacked • Not the Only Planet: Science Fiction Travel Stories • On the Edge: Extreme Travel • Sacred India • Travel with Children • Travel Photography: A Guide to Taking Better Pictures

LONELY PLANET

You already know that Lonely Planet produces more than this one guidebook, but you might not be aware of the other products we have on this region. Here is a selection of titles that you may want to check out as well:

Read this First: Europe
Europe on a shoestring
Europe phrasebook
CitySync: Amsterdam
        London
        Paris
        Edinburgh
        Frankfurt
        Rome
Condensed Guides:
        Amstedam
        Crete
        Frankfurt
        London
        Paris
Walking Guides:
        Britain
        France
        Ireland
        Italy
        Spain
        Switzerland
City Maps: Amsterdam
        Barcelona
        Berlin
        Brussels
        Dublin
        London
        Paris
        Rome
World Food: France
        Ireland
        Italy
        Spain
Cycling Guides:
        France
        Britain
Out to Eat London
Portugal Travel Atlas
Diving & Snorkeling Scotland

Available wherever books
are sold

Index

Abbreviations

AND – Andorra
A – Austria
B – Belgium
CH – Switzerland
D – Germany

E – Spain
F – France
FL – Liechtenstein
GB – Britain
GR – Greece

I – Italy
IRL – Ireland
L – Luxembourg
NL – Netherlands
P – Portugal

Text

A

Aachen (D) 601-4
Aalsmeer (NL) 927
Aberdeen (GB) 303-4
Aberystwyth (GB) 317
accommodation 44-8
Adrigole (IRL) 748-9
Aegina (GR) 675
Aeolian Islands (I) 873-4
Afsluitdijk (NL) 939
Agrigento (I) 876-7
air travel
    to/from Western Europe 50-5
    within Western Europe 57
Aix-en-Provence (F) 432-3
Ajaccio (F) 452-5, **454**
Alcobaça (P) 974
Alexandroupolis (GR) 675
Algarve, The (P) 967-71, **968**
Algeciras (E) 1073
Alghero (I) 880-1
Alhambra (E) 1070
Alicante (E) 1057-60, **1058**
Alkmaar (NL) 927
Allihies (IRL) 748-9
Almería (E) 1071-2
Alonnisos (GR) 705-6
Alsace (F) 363-70
Althorp (GB) 254
Amalfi (I) 866-7
Amalfi Coast (I) 866-7
Amboise (F) 395-6
Ameland (NL) 940
Amrum (D) 624-5
Amsterdam (NL) 917-27, **918**
    accommodation 922-3

attractions 920-1
entertainment 924-5
food 923-4
shopping 925
tourist offices 917-20
travel to/from 925
travel within 926
Ancona (I) 858
Andalucía (E) 1061-74
Andorra 67-74, **68**
    accommodation 69
    embassies 67
    money 67
    post & communications 67-9
    travel to/from 69-70
    travel within 70
    visas & documents 67
Andorra la Vella (AND) 70-2, **70**
Anne Frankhuis (NL) 921
Annecy (F) 423-5, **424**
Antiparos (GR) 680, **679**
Antwerp (B) 150-4, **152**
Appenzell (CH) 1151
Apulia (I) 868-70
Aragón (E) 1085-93
Áran Islands (IRL) 757-9
Arcachon (F) 402
Ardennes, The (B) 165-8
Ardennes, The (L) 900-2
Arinsal (AND) 74
Arlberg (A) 131-2
Arles (F) 436-7
Arnhem (NL) 937
Arromanches (F) 379
Assisi (I) 857-8
Astorga (E) 1026
Asturias (E) 1080-5
Athens (GR) 647-58, **650**, **654**
    accommodation 653-5

attractions 651-3
entertainment 656-7
food 655-6
shopping 657
tourist offices 648
travel to/from 657-8
travel within 658
Augsburg (D) 551
Austria 75-132, **77**
    accommodation 84-5
    email 82-3
    embassies 80-1
    festivals 83-4
    history 75-8
    holidays 83-4
    Internet resources 82-3
    language 79
    money 81-2
    post & communications 82
    safe travel 83
    tourist offices 80
    tours 88
    travel to/from 86
    travel within 86-8
    visas & documents 80
Avebury (GB) 237
Aviemore (GB) 302-303
Avignon (F) 433-6, **434**
Ávila (E) 1020-1

B

Bad Ischl (A) 118-19
Baden-Baden (D) 568-9
Baden-Württemberg (D)
    562-78
Balearic Islands (E) 1046-53
Ballycastle (IRL) 767
Balmoral (GB) 303
Balmoral Castle (GB) 303

Bold indicates maps.

MAP LEGEND

CITY ROUTES

Freeway	Freeway
Highway	Primary Road
Road	Secondary Road
Street	Street
Lane	Lane
On/Off Ramp

| ==== | Unsealed Road |
| One Way Street |
| Pedestrian Street |
| Stepped Street |
| Tunnel |
| Footbridge |

REGIONAL ROUTES

Tollway, Freeway
Primary Road
Secondary Road
Minor Road

BOUNDARIES

International
State
Disputed
Fortified Wall

HYDROGRAPHY

River, Creek
Canal
Lake

Dry Lake; Salt Lake
Spring; Rapids
Waterfalls

TRANSPORT ROUTES & STATIONS

Train
Underground Train
Metro
Tramway
Cable Car, Chairlift

Ferry
Walking Trail
Walking Tour
Path
Pier or Jetty

AREA FEATURES

Building
Park, Gardens

Market
Sports Ground

Forest
Cemetery

Campus
Plaza

POPULATION SYMBOLS

✪ CAPITAL	National Capital
◉ CAPITAL	State Capital
● CITY	City
● Town	Town
● Village	Village
	Urban Area

MAP SYMBOLS

■	Place to Stay
▼	Place to Eat
●	Point of Interest

✈	Airport
⑨	Bank
⊟	Bus Terminal
⊟	Cable Car, Funicular
⊡	Castle, Château
✝	Church
⊞	Cinema

⊡	Embassy, Consulate
♨	Fountain
⊕	Hospital
⊡	Internet Cafe
☀	Lookout
⚲	Monument
⊞	Museum

⊡	National Park
⊡	Parking
)(	Pass
✚	Police Station
⊡	Post Office
⊡	Pub or Bar
⊠	Shopping Centre

⊡	Swimming Pool
⊡	Synagogue
⊡	Telephone
⊡	Theatre
❶	Tourist Information
⊡	Winery
⊡	Zoo

Note: not all symbols displayed above appear in this book

LONELY PLANET OFFICES

Australia
Locked Bag 1, Footscray, Victoria 3011
☎ 03 9689 4666 fax 03 9689 6833
email: talk2us@lonelyplanet.com.au

USA
150 Linden St, Oakland, CA 94607
☎ 8555 TOLL FREE: 800 275 8555
572
planet.com

UK
10a Spring Place, London NW5 3BH
☎ 020 7428 4800 fax 020 7428 4828
email: go@lonelyplanet.co.uk

France
1 rue du Dahomey, 75011 Paris
☎ 01 55 25 33 00 fax 01 55 25 33 01
email: bip@lonelyplanet.fr
www.lonelyplanet.fr

Wide Web: www.lonelyplanet.com *or* AOL keyword: lp
nely Planet Images: lpi@lonelyplanet.com.au